D0895650

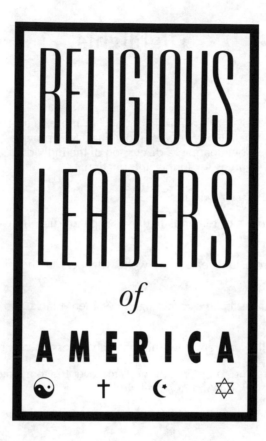

RELIGIOUS LEADERS of AMERICA

Highlights

Religious Leaders of America (RLA) is a biographical guide to more than 1000 men and women who have shaped American religious life since 1865. For each individual, *RLA* provides birth date and place; death date and place (if applicable); affiliation/occupation; a discussion of the individual's education, training, beliefs, and influence; and a bibliography of sources for further information.

Unprecedented Broad Coverage

Unlike other biographical directories of religious figures, which are usually weighted toward one mainstream, established denomination or another, *RLA:*

Profiles Roman Catholic and Protestant leaders as well as leaders of the non-Christian traditions, including newer and smaller religious groups.

Covers often-overlooked contributors to American religion: women, Black, and Native American leaders, among others.

Includes historical figures as well as current newsmakers such as Jesse Jackson and Elizabeth Clare Prophet.

RLA also goes beyond the leaders and founders of groups to cover the televangelists, songwriters, artists, poets, and writers who have left their mark on American religion.

Easy-to-Use Research Aids

RLA's unique features allow the user to:

Easily determine if a specific individual is profiled by consulting the **List of Profiled Leaders.**

Quickly identify all profiled leaders from a given religious tradition through the **Religious Affiliations Appendix.**

Readily locate individuals, publications, organizations, and other items of interest by checking the **Master Alphabetical and Keyword Index.**

ISSN 1057-2961

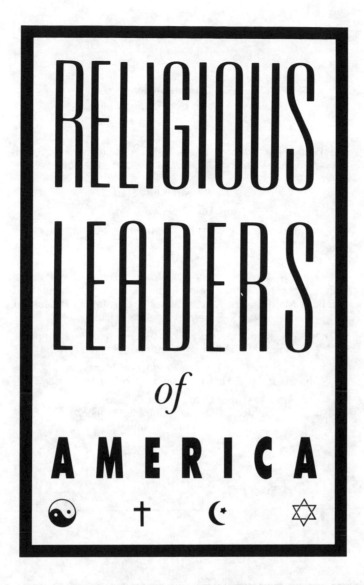

RELIGIOUS LEADERS of AMERICA

A Biographical Guide to Founders and Leaders of
Religious Bodies, Churches, and Spiritual
Groups in North America

J. GORDON MELTON

 Gale Research Inc. • DETROIT • LONDON

J. Gordon Melton
Gary L. Ward, *Contributing Author*

Aided by:

Michalene Fixico, Johnny Flynn, Aidan A. Kelly, James R. Lewis,
Christel Manning, Timothy Miller, and Matt Roberts

Gale Research Inc. Staff

Amy Lucas, *Senior Editor*

Peg Bessette and Kevin Hillstrom, *Project Coordinators*

Aided by:

Don Akers, Kimberly Burton, Kathleen J. Edgar, Gary P. Iott,
Michelle E. Janoschka, Terri Kessler, Ruth E. Littmann, Kathleen M. Lopez,
Archana Maheshwari, Annette Novallo, Christopher P. Scanlon,
Nan S. Soper, and Joanna Zakalik

Theresa A. Rocklin, *Supervisor of Systems and Programming*
Donald G. Dillaman, *Consulting Programmer*

Mary Beth Trimper, *Production Manager*
Shanna Philpott Heilveil, *External Production Assistant*

Arthur Chartow, *Art Director*
Kathleen Mouzakis, *Graphic Designer*
C.J. Jonik, *Keyliner*

The paper used in the publication meets the minimum requirements of American National Standard for Information Sciences—Permanence Paper for Printed Library Materials, ANZI Z39.48-1984.

ISBN 0-8103-4921-3
ISSN 1057-2961

Printed in the United States of America

Published simultaneously in the United Kingdom
by Gale Research International Limited
(An affiliated company of Gale Research Inc.)

Contents

Preface

Religious Leaders of America (RLA) has grown directly out of the two decades of work that previously led to the production of three editions of the *Encyclopedia of American Religions (EAR)*, also published by Gale Research Inc. During the production of the last edition of *EAR*, it became evident that there was no comprehensive biographical guide to American religion, especially for the period following the Civil War to the present. Since 1865, not only has America's population doubled several times over, but in the interval the great majority of all of the currently functioning religious organizations, both Christian and otherwise, have been founded. It was out of this recognition that *RLA* was born.

RLA Breaks New Ground

By providing biographical profiles on more than 1000 American and Canadian religious figures whose impact on the religious community has occurred since 1865, *RLA* breaks significantly new ground. Previous biographical volumes on American religion have as a whole been limited to Christian leaders, and rarely were these comprehensive in their coverage of the Christian community. Most were authored by Protestant authors and rarely covered Roman Catholicism more than superficially. In like measure, the several Roman Catholic volumes did not include Protestants. Neither covered individuals from other religious traditions.

RLA's broad coverage follows the lead set by two earlier reference works. Henry Bowden's *Dictionary of American Religious Biography* (1977) was the first biographical work to deal with America's growing pluralistic religious setting. Moving beyond the Reformation churches, it covered not only leaders from Roman Catholic and Protestant sectarian groups, but also included a modest number of profiles of individuals from non-Christian religious traditions. My own *Biographical Dictionary of American Cult and Sect Leaders* (1986) attempted to supplement Bowden by sketching some 200 founders and leaders from outside America's religious mainstream.

Religious Leaders of America goes beyond both of these earlier pioneering volumes in that it includes more than 1000 biographical profiles, more than twice the number in Bowden and five times the number in my own work. *RLA* further outdistances these volumes in its inclusion of a large number of living figures; previous volumes were limited to those who were deceased. In any coverage of recent religious leaders, the inclusion of contemporary figures who have contributed to the significant shifts in popular religion in recent decades seems necessary. The length of human lives today means that many people whose impact began half a century ago are still actively influencing the religious arena today.

Identifying the Religious Leaders

Virtually anyone making a survey of North American religious leaders of the last 150 years could quickly agree upon a core of figures to be included, from evangelist Dwight L. Moody to Cardinal James Gibbons to Norman Vincent Peale. However, in compiling *RLA* we have gone far beyond the obvious. Leaders of the major established religious bodies were the first to be added to our core list; these were the individuals who had created and guided the development of the Roman Catholic Church, the major Protestant traditions (Baptists, Methodists, Presbyterians, Lutherans, Episcopalians, Congregationalists, etc.), and the Jewish community in North America.

Next to be considered were the leaders of the ecumenical bodies, especially the National Council of Churches and its predecessor, the Federal Council of Churches. The list was then expanded by the addition of the founders/ leaders from newer and smaller religious traditions, beginning with the Holiness and Pentecostal churches and moving to the more recent arrivals: the Islamic, Eastern, and Metaphysical religious groups. Not to be forgotten were the self-proclaimed non-religious—the Humanists, Agnostics, and Atheists.

As each of the recognizable religious traditions of North America was surveyed, an initial list of leaders was compiled, including both those who primarily are remembered for their leadership of their own church or religious community and those who attempted to offer leadership within the larger religious setting. The individuals finally chosen represent a broad range of accomplishment, from intellectual leadership (scholars, theologians, social ethicists, historians) to administrators (denominational leaders) to ministers and evangelists.

Emphasis is on Those Who Influenced America

Specifically excluded from this volume were missionaries and others deemed to have made their major contribution outside of North America. However, two exceptions to this general exclusion will be found:

Some **home missionaries** have been profiled. These were missionaries who established ministries in the west coast and Alaska in the last half of the nineteenth century and who developed new missions to the cities and ethnic groups in the twentieth century.

Some **contemporary foreign religious leaders** also have been included, primarily Buddhist and Hindu teachers who are directing efforts to establish their religions in North America. Many of the religious teachers who have attracted popular support among North Americans, from Maharishi Mehesh Yogi to Swami Sivananda Saraswati, never resided in America; some never even visited. But their role in developing the contemporary religious community ranks them among the important leaders to whom Americans turn for inspiration and direction.

In future editions *RLA*'s scope may be expanded to include the many Americans and Canadians who contributed to the diffusion of North American religions around the world.

RLA Profiles the Forgotten: Women, Blacks, and American Indians

In choosing the leaders to be included in this volume, two considerations were of prime importance. Previous biographical volumes on American religion have tended to neglect and downplay the important contributions of women and Blacks. Every effort has been made here to begin to correct that injustice. Thus in surveying the religious community, we paid specific attention to the work of women in the development of women's organizations (from Roman Catholic orders to Protestant missionary societies), the movement of women into previously all-male realms of church administration and pastoral leadership, the role of women as founders of new religions, and the intellectual contributions of women.

In like measure, we have actively sought to identify the contributions of Blacks to American religions. Black ministers have built some of the largest American denominations (from the National Baptist Convention to the African Methodist Episcopal Church), although those who have built some of the less conventional religious groups are often better known (Father Divine, Daddy Grace, etc.). In addition, most of the larger denominations have significant black memberships out of which have emerged prominent denominational leaders. During the last century Blacks have served in virtually every position of power and influence in the major religious bodies of America.

While the contributions of Blacks and women were downplayed, the religious leadership of American Indians has been completely ignored. Throughout American history, including the period covered by this volume (1865 to the present), American Indians have played a significant role in the religious life of the United States and Canada. Some, like Sitting Bull, have made it into the history books (although his role as a religious leader is almost never mentioned), but not to the extent warranted by their contributions. Most American Indians included in this edition are unknown outside of the community of Native Americans and the few historians of their culture. While *RLA* barely begins to address the neglect given to traditional Indian religion in textbooks and reference sources, it is hoped that the inclusion of the Native Americans profiled here will initiate a process of integrating Native American religion into the story of American religious life.

Leaders of Popular Religious Life

The attention paid to the contributions of women, Blacks, and Native Americans also suggested the need to move beyond the leadership provided through denominations (although almost all religious leaders have a denominational affiliation) to consider the contributions of popular religious leaders. American religious life would be vastly different without those people who, apart from any particular official denominational status, have developed a large popular following by presenting their religious vision directly to the public. Through the media, individuals have become significant voices in American religious life quite apart from the opinions of their denominations' leaders. The evangelists who have directed their ministry through the mass media, newspaper columnists, radio preachers, and televangelists immediately come to mind. For a few, media audiences have become the source of initial recruits for new denominations.

Artists have also been included. The religious community would be much the poorer without its musicians, poets, and song writers. Similarly, it would miss its religious writers and novelists.

Finally, what would the religious scene be without the outcasts: the characters, the heretics, the losers, and those who fell from grace? America has had its share of people who, though well known, had little or no following, those remembered only as losers in a controversy, those who tested the boundaries of believability and went beyond. And not to be forgotten are the people who at one time possessed a position of influence and who lost it through a betrayal of the trust that had been placed in them.

Winnowing the List: Those Not Included

While in any publication of this nature there would be a general consensus on the first several hundred chosen for inclusion and majority agreement on many more, the choice becomes more difficult as the list grows. To assist with the difficult choices, a set of guidelines was developed early in the selection process.

First, all of the larger religious bodies (those with more than a million members) were to be liberally represented. Since it was impossible to have even a single individual from each of the 1500+ religious groups now functioning in North America, a representative selection of people from the smaller groups was selected. I then reviewed this list to ensure that people whose contributions varied widely were included.

Once the initial list was compiled a process of exclusion began. People whose contributions to the religious community were made largely before 1865 were the first to be excluded. Those who operated largely outside of North America were the next to be omitted. These criteria were among the toughest to apply, especially when it came to people such as John R. Mott and Robert Speer who made significant contributions both at home and abroad.

Equally difficult to apply was the exclusion of people who were known to be devoutly religious, but whose major contribution was judged to have been in the secular realm. For example, Sunday school teacher and former President Jimmy Carter could have been included but was not. Certainly his openness about his faith and his actions since leaving office qualified him for some consideration. On the other hand, former newspaperman and politician William Jennings Bryan was included. In spite of his secular career, the time and attention he gave to the fundamentalist cause made him a must.

The hardest decisions were in those many areas in which representative leaders had to be chosen from a list which included other equally qualified candidates. Which gurus, which televangelists, which hymn writers, or which metaphysicians go in? While I am sure that every one chosen to be included in this volume deserves to be in, there are certainly others who also could have been included. Future editions of RLA will undoubtedly include many individuals who did not make the final "cut" for this edition.

Lastly, as the deadline for completing this volume arrived, some individuals who would have otherwise been included had to be dropped because I was unable to locate sufficient information about them to compile a biographical sketch.

I am most aware that no single individual is qualified, even with all the advice I received during the course of preparing this volume, to decide who are and who are not the 1000 most significant religious leaders in America. However, in the end the choice was mine and I accept responsibility for the choice. I invite recommendations from those who would like to suggest individuals for inclusion in subsequent editions or supplements.

J. Gordon Melton
June 1991

Introduction

Religion is inexorably interwoven into the fabric of American life. It permeates every aspect of American culture, including politics, education, and social issues. Therefore, any attempt to understand the American experience is incomplete without an appreciation for, and understanding of, the men and women who have played key roles in the development and spread of religious beliefs throughout North America.

Religious Leaders of America (RLA) is the authoritative guide to information on more than 1000 individuals who have played leading roles in developing and expanding religious diversity in North America. Its detailed biographical profiles provide a comprehensive and convenient overview of these key religious figures. Leaders from a wide range of religious groups, from Adventists to Zen Buddhists, are profiled in *RLA*, including:

▶ The well-known (Jimmy Swaggert, Billy Graham, Cardinal John O'Connor) and the more obscure (James Luther Adams, Maggie Newton Van Cott, Menachem Mendel Schneerson).

▶ The current (Pat Robertson, Jane Roberts, Jesse Jackson) and the historical (Father Flanagan, Daniel Payne, William Jennings Bryan).

▶ Christian (Jerry Falwell, Cardinal Edmund Szoka, Dorothy Day) and non-Christian (Selena Fox, Anton LaVey, Sri Aurobindo).

▶ Men (Jim Jones, Solomon Goldman, Jack van Impe) and women (Aimee Semple McPherson, Corrie ten Boom, Tammy Faye Bakker).

▶ Black (Malcolm X, Martin Luther King, Jr., Mary McLeod Bethune), American Indian (Geronimo, Wovoka, Black Elk), and other cultural and ethnic groups.

RLA explores the impact each of these leaders and hundreds more have had on American society.

Covers Broad Range of Religious Leaders

RLA profiles scholars, theologians, social ethicists, historians, administrators, artists, ministers, evangelists, and other individuals—both living and dead—who have had a significant impact on American religious life since 1865. Emphasis has been placed on leaders of a single church or religious community as well as those who attempted to offer leadership within the larger religious setting. Specifically, *RLA* profiles:

▶ leaders of the major older religious bodies of America—the Roman Catholic Church, the major Protestant traditions, and the Jewish community

▶ leaders of ecumenical bodies

▶ founders/leaders of the newer and smaller religious traditions

▶ those who are self-proclaimed nonreligious—the Humanists, Agnostics, and Atheists

Special emphasis has also been placed on identifying and profiling women, Blacks, and American Indians who made a significant contribution to the religious life and tradition of North America.

In addition, *RLA* profiles a few home missionaries who extended religion to the west coast and Alaska in the last half of the nineteenth century, and contemporary foreign religious leaders—particularly Buddhist and Hindu teachers—who are attempting to export their beliefs to America and to whom many Americans turn for inspiration and direction.

Excluded from coverage are missionaries and others whose major contributions have been made outside North America and those individuals who, although devoutly religious, made their contributions in the secular realm. Those individuals for whom biographical information was unobtainable have also been excluded.

Content and Arrangement

Religious Leaders of America consists of biographical profiles, an appendix, and an index.

The *Profiles of Religious Leaders* provide basic biographical data; the leader's institutional or denominational affiliation or occupation; a discussion of the leader's role and impact on American religion; and lists of sources by and about the leader.

The *List of Profiled Leaders*, immediately following the "User's Guide," allows for a quick overview of the individuals profiled.

The *Religious Affiliations Appendix* classifies the profiled leaders into one of the 38 religious traditions with which they are associated. These traditions are derived from the religious families classification scheme developed for the *Encyclopedia of American Religions*.

The *Key to Religious Affiliations* immediately precedes the appendix and provides an alphabetical list of the religious families followed by a listing of the specific religious groups or denominations associated with each.

The *Master Alphabetical and Keyword Index* lists all individuals, organizations, publications, and other significant details covered within the biographical profiles, providing a single, convenient access point to the wealth of information included in *RLA*.

For more information on the content, arrangement, and indexing of *RLA*, consult the "User's Guide" which follows this introduction.

Compilation Methods

The profiles in *RLA* were compiled from the resources of the Institute for the Study of American Religion as well as from, in some cases, direct contact with the biographees. In 1985, that collection became the American Religions Collection at the University of California—Santa Barbara. The collection contains a variety of both primary and secondary materials on the religious tradition and leaders of North America.

Acknowledgments

I wish to acknowledge my gratitude to the following individuals for their contributions to this publication: Gary L. Ward, research director of the Institute for the Study of American Religion, Timothy Miller of the University of Kansas, James R. Lewis of the Santa Barbara Centre for Humanistic Studies, Johnny Flynn, Christel Manning, Matt Roberts, and Michalene Fixico.

Comments and Suggestions Welcome

Questions and comments regarding *Religious Leaders of America* are welcome, as are suggestions for individuals to be profiled in the next edition. Please contact:

Institute for the Study of American Religion
Box 90709
Santa Barbara, CA 93190-0709

J. Gordon Melton

User's Guide

Religious Leaders of America (RLA) consists of three main sections:

- Profiles of Religious Leaders

- Religious Affiliations Appendix

- Master Alphabetical and Keyword Index

The "List of Profiled Leaders" and "Key to Religious Affiliations" provide additional access points to the information presented in the main sections.

List of Profiled Leaders

The List of Profiled Leaders immediately following this guide provides, in a single alphabetic sequence, the names of all of the profiled leaders. Consult this list to obtain a quick overview of the contents of the "Profiles of Religious Leaders" section, and to quickly determine if a particular leader is included in this edition.

Profiles of Religious Leaders

RLA contains more than 1000 biographical profiles, arranged alphabetically by surname. An *RLA* entry typically provides the following information:

Entry number. Entries are numbered sequentially; these numbers are used to refer to entries in the Master Alphabetical and Keyword Index.

Biographee name. Generally the name by which the individual is best known. Birth, married, and other alternate names are provided in the text portion of the entry.

Birth date and place.

Death date and place (if applicable).

Affiliation/Occupation. A listing of the individual's occupation or institutional or denominational affiliation. Two affiliations or occupations are listed for some individuals.

Biography. A detailed discussion of the individual's life and beliefs, including:

- the leader's training and background

- the people, places, and events that helped shape the leader's beliefs

- any spiritual crises experienced by the leader

- the leader's contributions to his/her church's or group's establishment, development, and doctrine

Bibliographic citations. Complete citations are provided to publications by or about the leader, including monographs and periodical literature. Entries for a few of the profiled leaders do not include bibliographic citations. These individuals are not covered in standard printed reference sources nor have they authored any publications.

Attribution. The majority of the sketches have been written by the author; these are unsigned. All remaining entries are attributed to the individual writer responsible for a particular entry.

In some cases, a single entry may profile more than one leader. These entries cover individuals whose careers and influence on American religion are so intertwined that they cannot be easily separated. Examples of leaders profiled in this manner include the Fox Sisters, the Berrigan Brothers, and Jim and Tammy Faye Bakker. Birth and, if appropriate, death dates and places for each individual are provided parenthetically within the text portion of the entry.

The profiles also contain *see also* references designed to alert the reader to the presence of a separate profile for an individual mentioned within the text of a given entry. *See also* references are rendered in **boldface** type.

Religious Affiliations Appendix

The Religious Affiliations Appendix classifies each of the leaders profiled in this volume into one of 38 general religious traditions or families, which are listed alphabetically. These traditions are derived from the religious families classification scheme developed for the author's *Encyclopedia of American Religions*, also published by Gale.

Following each religious tradition in the appendix is an alphabetical list of the religious leaders profiled in *RLA* that are relevant to the history and growth of that tradition. Information on their denominational affiliations and/ or occupations is also included. For example, a user looking under "Adventism" is referred to 12 leaders profiled in this volume with a significant affiliation or link to the growth and development of Adventism.

Key to Religious Affiliations

The appendix is preceded by the Key to Religious Affiliations. The key lists, in a single alphabetical sequence, the 38 primary religious traditions used to classify the profiled leaders in the Religious Affiliations Appendix as well as references to more than 60 specific religious groups. References to specific groups include *see* references to the appropriate religious tradition. For example, a user looking under the heading "Jehovah's Witnesses" for information on profiled leaders of that group is referred to the heading "Adventism" in the appendix.

Master Alphabetical and Keyword Index

The Master Alphabetical and Keyword Index provides complete and convenient access in a single alphabetic sequence to:

- all individuals, including their birth, alternate, and married names

- organizations

- publications mentioned within the profiles' text

- other significant details mentioned in the text.

Citations to keywords appearing in organization and publication names are also provided.

The leading articles "A," "An," and "The" are disregarded for filing purposes within the index. Thus, "The Prayer of Peace" will be found filed under "P" and not "T."

Numbers appearing after a citation refer to entries in the main section, not to page numbers. A **boldface** number following an individual's name identifies the principal listing for that individual.

List of Profiled Leaders

The following is an alphabetical listing of the individuals profiled in this edition of Religious Leaders of America.

A

Francis Ellingwood Abbot
Lyman Abbott
Abdu'l-Baha
William Aberhart
Ralph David Abernathy
Swami Abhedananda
James Luther Adams
Theodore Floyd Adams
Walter Hollis Adams
George Adamski
Felix Adler
Margot Adler
Jaramogi Abebe Agyeman, Jr.
Mirza Ghulam Hazrat Ahmad
Peter Ainslie III
Asa Alonzo Allen
Charles Livingston Allen
John Maury Allin
Rulon Clark Allred
Mother Mary Amadeus of the Heart
   of Jesus
Edward Scribner Ames
Mataji Amritanandamayi
Shrii Shrii Anandamurti
Metropolitan Anastassy
Charles Palmerston Anderson
Victor H. Anderson
Brother Andre
Michael G. Andreades
Lynn V. Andrews
Ernest Angley
Michael A. Aquino
Annie Walker Armstrong
Garner Ted Armstrong
Herbert W. Armstrong
Benjamin William Arnett, Jr.
Eberhard Arnold
Bishop Arseny
Andras Corban Arthen
Deirdre Pulgram Arthen
Robert Archibald Ashworth
Patriarch Athenagoras
William Walker Atkinson
Sri Aurobindo
Martha Gallison Moore Avery
Anne Ayres

B

Baha'u'llah
Alice LaTrobe Bateman Bailey

Anne Penny Lee Bailey
James Chamberlain Baker
Jim Bakker
Tammy Faye Bakker
Edna Anne Wheeler Ballard
Guy Warren Ballard
Donald Grey Barnhouse
Amelia Edith Huddleston Barr
Harrison D. Barrett
Kate Harwood Waller Barrett
Bruce Barton
Donald Wilson Basham
Anthony Bashir
Josephine Abiah Penfield Cushman
   Bateham
William Wakefield Baum
Louis Sylvester Bauman
William John Ernest Baxter
Joseph A. Beebe
Henry Ward Beecher
Louis Nazaire Begin
Jacob Beilhart
Eudorus N. Bell
Daniel Henry Bender
Harold S. Bender
Elbert Benjamine
Belle Harris Bennett
DeRobigne Mortimer Bennett
John Coleman Bennett
Mary Katherine Jones Bennett
Ezra Taft Benson
Louis Berkhof
Pierre Arnold Bernard
Joseph Louis Bernardin
Daniel J. Berrigan
Philip Berrigan
Annie Wood Besant
Mary McLeod Bethune
Anthony J. Bevilacqua
William Edward Biederwolf
Theodore Bilbo
Nicolas Bjerring
Black Elk
Annie Walker Blackwell
Antoinette Brown Blackwell
Charles Edward Blake
Eugene Carson Blake
Charles Albert Blanchard
Jonathan Blanchard
Paul Beecher Blanshard
Helena Petrovna Blavatsky
Philip Paul Bliss
William Dwight Porter Bliss
Anton Theophilus Boisen

William Carpenter Bompas
William Bennett Bond
Philip Emmons Isaac Bonewits
Mary Lucinda Bonney
Ballington Booth
Evangeline Cory Booth
Maud Ballington Booth
William Booth
Margaret McDonald Bottome
Joseph Thomas Bowers
Walter Russell Bowie
Eva del Vakia Bowles
Borden Parker Bowne
Henry Allen Boyd
Malcolm Boyd
Richard Henry Boyd
Preston Bradley
George Freeman Bragg, Jr.
William Marrion Branham
Edward M. Brawley
Samuel Logan Brengle
Francis Brennan
Phineas Bresee
Charles Augustus Briggs
William Briggs
William Rohl Bright
Edgar Sheffield Brightman
Howard Haines Brinton
Emma Hardinge Britten
Charles William Britton
John Albert Broadus
Nona Lovell Brooks
Phillips Brooks
William Henry Francis Brothers
Luke Dennis Broughton
Egbert Ethelred Brown
Harrison D. Brown
Henry Harrison Brown
Olympia Brown
William Adams Brown
William Montgomery Brown
Edmond Lee Browning
William Jennings Bryan
Frank Nathan Daniel Buchman
Raymond Buckland
James Monroe Buckley
Zsusanna E. Budapest
Buffalo Bird Woman
Thomas H. Burgoyne
George Edwin Burnell
Marie Joseph Butler
Eric Butterworth
George Arthur Buttrick

C

Laurie Cabot
Frances Xavier Cabrini
Henry Joel Cadbury
Peter Caddy
Samuel Parkes Cadman
Harriet Emilie Cady
Shirley Caesar
Panos Demetrios Callimachos
Will Davis Campbell
Warren Akin Candler
Abraham Hoagland Cannon
Franklin Jenne Cannon
George Quayle Cannon
Aurelia Caouette
John Joseph Carberry
Carmel Henry Carfora
Shlomo Carlebach
Albert Carman
Edward John Carnell
Beverly Carradine
Benajah Harvey Carroll
Gerald Emmett Carter
Paul Carus
Shirley Jackson Case
Gaston Barnabas Cashwell
Samuel McCrea Cavert
Charles Thomas Cayce
Edgar Cayce
Hugh Lynn Cayce
Morris Cerullo
Lewis Sperry Chafer
James Blaine Chapman
John Wilbur Chapman
Hilda Charlton
Thornton Chase
Haridas Chaudhuri
Charles Edward Cheney
Mantak Chia
Herbert Walfred Chilstrom
Charles Paschal Telesphore Chiniquy
Swami Chinmayananda
Sri Chinmoy
Orestes Chornock
Matthew Wesley Clair, Sr.
Elmer Talmage Clark
Francis Edward Clark
Glenn Clark
Gordon Haddon Clark
James Freeman Clarke
William Newton Clarke
Anthony Forbes Moreton Clavier
John Boswell Cobb, Jr.
John Patrick Cody
George Albert Coe
Henry Sloane Coffin, Sr.
John Samuel Coffman
Leopold Cohn
Johnnie Coleman
William W. Colley
Michel Collin
Wilberforce Juvenal Colville
James Hal Cone
Charles William Conn
Russell Herman Conwell
Terence J. Cooke

Irving Steiger Cooper
Kenneth Copeland
Fanny Muriel Jackson Coppin
Levi Jenkins Coppin
Louis Craig Cornish
Charles Edward Coughlin
Harvey Gallagher Cox, Jr.
Malinda Elliott Cramer
Algernon Sidney Crapsey
Mabel Cratty
Florence Louise Crawford
Benjamin Creme
Edward Cridge
Wallie Amos Criswell
Fanny Crosby
Austin Crouch
William Saunders Crowdy
Aleister Edward Crowley
Alexander Crummell
Ambrose Blackman Crumpler
William Culbertson
Charles Cullis
Edward Cummings
George David Cummins
Charles Edward Curran
Harriette Augusta Curtiss
Richard James Cushing
Vera Charlotte Scott Cushman

D

Edwin Theodore Dahlberg
Father Damien of Molokai
Herbert Daniel Daughtry
Andrew Jackson Davis
Roy Eugene Davis
Joseph Martin Dawson
Dorothy Day
Richard De Baptiste
Gommar Albert De Pauw
John Francis Dearden
Martin Ralph DeHaan
James DeKoven
Harry Denman
Collins Denny
Amrit Desai
Sister Devamata
Gayatri Devi
Lakshmy Devi
Peter Deyneka, Sr.
Anagarika Dharmapala
Abby Morton Diaz
John Hassler Dietrich
Ralph Eugene Diffendorfer
Edwin John Dingle
Bishop Dionisije
Father Major Jealous Divine
Amzi Clarence Dixon
Dennis Dougherty
Lloyd Cassel Douglas
John Alexander Dowie
Horatio Willis Dresser
Timothy Drew
Katherine Mary Drexel
David Johannes Du Plessis
William Porcher DuBose
Ivy Oneita Duce

William H. Durham

E

Eknath Easwaran
Solomon Eby
Mary Baker Glover Eddy
James Arthur Edgerton
Henry Egly
Frederick J. Eikerenkoetter II
Isaac Errett
Warren Felt Evans
Archbishop Evdokim
Frank J. Ewart

F

Jerry Falwell
John Murphy Farley
Louis Farrakhan
Elizabeth Fedde
Nels Fredrik Solomon Ferre
Otto Fetting
Charles Sherlock Fillmore
Myrtle Fillmore
John Fire
George Park Fisher
Henry Lee Fisher
Mark Miles Fisher
George Bernard Flahiff
Edward Joseph Flanagan
Arthur Sherwood Fleming
Amanda Cameron Flower
Joseph James Roswell Flower
Arnold Josiah Ford
Arthur Augustus Ford
Harry Emerson Fosdick
George Burman Foster
Randolph Sinks Foster
Ann Fox
Emmet Fox
Kate Fox
Margaret Fox
Matthew Timothy Fox
Selena Fox
Arvy Glenn Freed
Donald Hudson Frew III
Stanley Frodsham
Gavin Frost
James Marion Frost
Yvonne Frost
Octavius Brooks Frothingham
Franklin Clark Fry
Rachmiel Frydland
Charles Edward Fuller
Thomas Oscar Fuller
John Fretz Funk

G

Arno C. Gaebelein
Wesley John Gaines
Bill Gaither
Gloria Gaither

Helen Hamilton Gardener
Gerald Brousseau Gardner
Susa Amelia Young Gates
Anne Nicol Gaylor
Joseph H. Gelberman
Emanuel Vogel Gerhart
Geronimo
Ursula Newell Gestefeld
Maha Ghosananda
James Gibbons
Jonathan C. Gibbs
Frederick Carnes Gilbert
Washington Gladden
John Joseph Glennon
William Samuel Godbe
Dwight Goddard
Morris Ellis Golder
Solomon Goldman
Joel Sol Goldsmith
Charles Leroy Goodell
Benjamin Cordell Goodpasture
Edgar Johnson Goodspeed
Adoniram Judson Gordon
Charles William Gordon
George Angier Gordon
Anagarika Govinda
Sweet Daddy Grace
August Lawrence Graebner
Billy Graham
Frederick William Grant
Heber Jeddy Grant
James Robinson Graves
James Martin Gray
Paul Gregoire
Louis George Gregory
Albert Catton Grier
Sutton Elbert Griggs
Samuel Joshua Grimes
Leon Grochowski
Darwin Gross
Roy Bergen Guild
Frank Wakeley Gunsaulus
Georgei Ivanovitch Gurdjieff

H

Kenneth Erwin Hagin, Sr.
Isaac Massey Haldeman
Emanuel Haldeman-Julius
Edward Everett Hale
Homer Richard Hall
Manly Palmer Hall
Phebe Ann Coffin Hanaford
Samuel Nathan Hancock
Billy James Hargis
Baba Hari Dass
Georgia Elma Harkness
Alison Harlow
Nolan Bailey Harmon, Jr.
Barbara Clementine Harris
Thomas Lake Harris
Judith S. Harrow
Gilbert Haven, Jr.
Raphael Hawaweeny
Patrick Joseph Hayes
Atticus Greene Haygood
Garfield Thomas Haywood

Eliza Healy
James Augustine Healy
Patrick Francis Healy
Isaac Thomas Hecker
Max Heindel
Eugene Russell Hendrix
Carl Ferdinand Howard Henry
George Went Hensley
George Davis Herron
Theodore Martin Hesburgh
Abraham Joshua Heschel
James Aloysius Hickey
Newell Dwight Hillis
John Elbridge Hines
Benny Hinn
Herschel Hobbs
Francis Hodur
Emil Hoffman
Wilson Thomas Hogue
John Holdeman
Horace Hotchkiss Holley
Ernest Shurtleff Holmes
John Haynes Holmes
Lucius H. Holsey
Henry Ritz Holsinger
Ivan Lee Holt
James Walker Hood
Emma Curtis Hopkins
John Horsch
Douglas Horton
William Henry Houghton
Herman Arthur Hoyt
Hsuan Hua
L. Ron Hubbard
Edwin Holt Hughes
Moses Hull
Rex Humbard
Ernest Hunt
William Reed Huntington
Jesse Lyman Hurlbut
George Willie Hurley

I

Archbishop Iakovos
Oscar Ichazo
Daisaku Ikeda
Yemyo Imamura
Robert Green Ingersoll
John Ireland
Metropolitan Ireney
Harry Ironside
Benjamin Hardin Irwin
Michael Francis Augustine Itkin
Anthony Woodward Ivins

J

Jesse Jackson
Joseph Harrison Jackson
Mahalia Jackson
Samuel Macauley Jackson
Sheldon Jackson
Henry Eyster Jacobs
Swami Rajasi Janakananda
Charles Edward Jefferson

Harley Bradley Jeffery
Leroy Jenkins
C. B. Jernigan
Bishop John
James Hervey Johnson
Sherrod C. Johnson
Charles Price Jones
Edgar DeWitt Jones
Franklin Jones
Jim Jones
Ozro Thurston Jones, Sr.
Prophet Jones
Robert Elijah Jones
Robert Jones, Sr.
Rufus Matthew Jones
Samuel Porter Jones
Clarence Jordan
Lars Jorgensen
William Quan Judge
Edward Judson
Swami Amar Jyoti
Swami Jyotir Maya Nanda

K

Henry Enoch Kagan
Meir Kahane
Khyyab Je Kalu Rinpoche
Mordecai Menahem Kaplan
Philip Kapleau
Daniel Kauffman
John Joseph Keane
Marshall Keeble
Catherine Bishop Kelley
Thomas Raymond Kelly
Samuel Kelsey
Gerald Hamilton Kennedy
Jiyu Kennett
Grady R. Kent
Essek William Kenyon
Sant Keshavadas
Benjamin Elias Kesler
Robert Thomas Ketcham
Hazrat Inayat Khan
Vilayat Inayat Khan
Ibrahim George Kheiralla
Frank Russell Killingsworth
Spencer Wooley Kimball
Coretta Scott King
Henry Churchill King
Joseph Hillery King
Martin Luther King, Jr.
Martin Luther King, Sr.
Willis Jefferson King
Martin Wells Knapp
J. Z. Knight
Adolph Ernst Knoch
George William Knox
Frederick Herman Knubel
Albert Cornelius Knudson
Kaufmann Kohler
Alexander Kohut
Ulrik Vilhelm Koren
Charles Porterfield Krauth
Gopi Krishna
Jiddu Krishnamurti
John Joseph Krol

Kathryn Kuhlman
Michio Kushi

L

John Graham Lake
Corliss Lamont
George Mamishisho Lamsa
Prince Rudolph Francis Edward de
    Landas Berghes
Brown Landone
Isaac Lane
Moses Lard
Kenneth Scott Latourette
Anton LaVey
John Benjamin Lawrence
Bernard Francis Law
Curtis Lee Laws
Alfred William Lawson
Robert Clarence Lawson
Henry Charles Lea
Charles Webster Leadbeater
Ervil Morrell LeBaron
Joel Franklin LeBaron
Gloria Lee
Harold Bingham Lee
Robert Greene Lee
Paul Emile Leger
Metropolitan Leonty
Edwin Lewis
Harvey Spencer Lewis
Joseph Lewis
Ralph M. Lewis
Samuel Leonard Lewis
Arthur Carl Lichtenberger
Joshua Loth Liebman
Gordon J. Lindsey
David Lipscomb
Frederic Ebenezer John Lloyd
John Norton Loughborough
Cummings Samuel Lovett
Joseph E. Lowery
Edith Elizabeth Lowry
Knut Olafson Lundeberg
Mary Reddington Ely Lyman

M

Clarence Edward Noble Macartney
Charles Steadman Macfarland
John Gresham Machen
Robert Machray
John Alexander Mackay
Shirley MacLaine
Hakuyu Taizan Maezumi
Judah Leon Magnes
Guru Maharaj Ji
Maharishi Mahesh Yogi
Roger Michael Mahony
Walter Arthur Maier
Malcolm X
Kathleen Moore Mallory
Basil Manly, Jr.
Timothy Manning
Bishop Mardary
Eugene A. Marino

Peter Marshall
Sarah Catherine Wood Marshall
Leo Louis Martello
William Clyde Martin
Martin Emil Marty
Enoch Mather Marvin
Charles Harrison Mason
Jasper Cortenus Massee
George Mastrantonis
Daya Mata
Samuel Liddell Mathers
Samuel Pritchard Matheson
Arnold Harris Mathew
Shailer Mathews
Wentworth Arthur Matthew
James Kenneth Matthews
Marjorie Swank Matthews
John Maximovich
William Sutherland Maxwell
Benjamin Elijah Mays
Robert Edward McAlister
William H. McAlpine
Charles Cardwell McCabe
William McCarrell
Alva J. McClain
John McCloskey
Walter McCollough
Francis John McConnell
Robert James McCracken
William Fraser McDowell
John William McGarvey
Austin McGary
Lewis A. McGee
Arthur Cushman McGiffert
James Charles McGuigan
George Alexander McGuire
Carl McIntire
Martha E. McIntosh
James Francis Aloysius McIntyre
David Oman McKay
Aimee Semple McPherson
Robert Crawford McQuilkin, Jr.
Holland Nimmons McTyeire
John Levin Meares
Henrietta Cornelia Mears
Humberto Sousa Medeiros
Meher Baba
Henry Pereira Mendes
Thomas James Merton
Meletios Metaxakis
Michael J. Metelica
Albert Gregory Meyer
Lucy Rider Meyer
Archbishop Michael
Lightfoot Solomon Michaux
William Henry Miles
Annie Rix Militz
D. D. Miller
Daniel Long Miller
John Allen Miller
Joseph Quinter Miller
Benjamin Fay Mills
Ramamurti S. Mishra
Mary Moise
Eugene Crosby Monroe
Carrie Judd Montgomery
Helen Barrett Montgomery
Dwight Lyman Ryther Moody

Sun Myung Moon
Edward Francis Mooney
Arthur James Moore
Joanna Patterson Moore
Henry Lyman Morehouse
Henry Victor Morgan
Elias C. Morris
Charles Clayton Morrison
Henry Clay Morrison
Virginia E. Moss
John R. Mott
Mountain Wolf Woman
Reuben Herbert Mueller
Aloisius Muench
Elijah Muhammad
Paramahansa Muktananda
Edgar Young Mullins
Bernard C. Mumford
George William Mundelein
Joseph Murphy
John Courtney Murray
John Gardner Murray
Dan T. Muse
Joseph White Musser
Abraham Johannes Muste
David Saville Muzzey

N

Swami Narayanananda
Louis H. Narcisse
Watchman Nee
Bishop Nestor
Albert Henry Newman
Joseph Fort Newton
Francis David Nichol
Bishop Nicholas
L. T. Nichols
Helmut Richard Niebuhr
Reinhold Niebuhr
Theophan S. Noli
John Franklyn Norris
Frank Mason North

O

John H. Oberholtzer
Patrick Aloysius O'Boyle
Harold John Ockenga
William O'Connell
John Joseph O'Connor
Abdullah Ofiesh
Madalyn Mays Murray O'Hair
John Francis O'Hara
Francisco Olazabal
Stephen Ortynsky
Charles Fulton Ousler, Sr.
Albert Cook Outler
Derwyn Trevor Owen
Ashton Oxenden
Garfield Bromley Oxnam

P

Sophia B. Packard
Ross Perry Paddock

Charles Fox Parham
Quanah Parker
William Alfred Passavant
Peter Pathfinder
James Oglethorpe Patterson, Sr.
Francis Landley Patton
Earl Pearly Paulk, Jr.
Diana L. Paxson
Daniel Alexander Payne
Lucy Whitehead McGill Waterbury
    Peabody
Norman Vincent Peale
James Martin Peebles
Jaroslav Jan Pelikan, Jr.
William Dudley Pelley
Francis Nathan Peloubet
Edith Mae Pennington
Romania Pratt Penrose
George Frederick Pentecost
John Dwight Pentecost
Harold Waldwin Percival
John M. Perkins
James De Wolf Perry, Jr.
Troy Deroy Perry
Macaki Peshewa
Isaak Peters
William Leroy Pettingill
Metropolitan Philaret
Charles Henry Phillips
Lesley Rebecca Phillips
Piapot
George Campbell Pidgeon
Franz August Otto Pieper
Robert (Bob) Willard Pierce
Arthur Tappan Pierson
James Albert Pike, Jr.
Metropolitan Platon
Plenty Coups
Daniel Alfred Poling
Catherine Ponder
Charles Francis Potter
Adam Clayton Powell, Jr.
Adam Clayton Powell, Sr.
Abhay Charan De Bhaktivedanta
    Swami Prabhupada
Jacob Aall Ottesen Preus
Eugenia Price
Peter Derek Prince
Elizabeth Clare Prophet
Marcus L. Prophet
Karl Hugo Reiling Pruter
James Morgan Pryse, Jr.
Jach Pursel
Hobart Lorentz Gottfried de
    Purucker

R

Paul Daniel Rader
Bhagwan Shree Rajneesh
Harris Franklin Rall
Baba Ram Dass
Swami Rama
Zen Master Rama
Sri Ramakrishna
Sri Ramana Maharshi
Joseph Eicher Ramseyer

Paschal Beverly Randolph
Reverdy Cassius Ransom
Walter Rauschenbusch
Cindy Ravensong
John H. Reble
Seth Cook Rees
Curtis Williford Reese
Agnes Gertrude Regan
Francis Israel Regardie
Charles Mason Remey
Johann Michael Reu
Bernard Revel
Fleming Hewitt Revell, Jr.
Hiram Rhoades Revels
John Richard Rice
Cora Lodencia Veronica Scott
    Richmond
Louis David Riel
William Bell Riley
Harry Rimmer
Joseph Elmer Ritter
Lizzie Roberson
Benjamin Titus Roberts
Brigham Henry Roberts
Jane Roberts
Oral Roberts
Ann Eliza Worcester Robertson
Archibald Thomas Robertson
James Robertson
Pat Robertson
Frank B. Robinson
Nicolas Konstantinovitch Roerich
Aurelia Spencer Rogers
Hubert Augustus Rogers
George Frederick Root
Hieromonk Seraphim Rose
Moishe Rosen
Maurice Roy
Swami Rudrananda
Charles Taze Russell
Joseph Franklin Rutherford
John Augustine Ryan
Adolphus Egerton Ryerson

S

Archimandrite Sabastian
Sai Baba (of Shirdi)
Sathya Sai Baba
Sanapia
Frank Weston Sandford
Elias Benjamin Sanford
Ira D. Sankey
Kyozan Joshu Sasaki
Ruth Fuller Everett Sasaki
Shigetsu Sasaki
Swami Satchidananda
James Wilbur Savage
Lee Rutland Scarborough
Lucille Marie Sherrod Scates
Zalman Schachter-Shalomi
Francis August Schaeffer
Philip Schaff
Robert W. Schambach
Solomon Schechter
Theodore Emanuel Schmauk
Alexander Schmemann

Friedrich August Schmidt
Menachem Mendel Schneerson
Robert Harold Schuller
Donna Cole Schultz
Charles John Seghers
Theodore Lorenzo Seip
Joseph Augustus Seiss
Nyogen Senzaki
Elisha G. Sewell
William Joseph Seymour
Demos Shakarian
Soyen Shaku
Anna Howard Shaw
Fulton John Sheen
Lawrence Joseph Shehan
Charles Monroe Sheldon
Andrew B. Shelly
S. McDowell Shelton
Henry Knox Sherrill
Lewis Joseph Sherrill
Thomas Todhunter Shields, Jr.
Shri Shivabalayogi Maharaj
Samuel Moor Shoemaker, Jr.
Shoghi Effendi Rabboni
Robert Pierce Shuler
Abba Hillel Silver
Eliezer Silver
William J. Simmons
Charan Singh
Darshan Singh
Kirpal Singh
Sant Thakar Singh
Sawan Singh
Sitting Bull
Swami Sivananda Saraswati
Tom Skinner
Harold Paul Sloan
John Slocum
Amanda Smith
Angie Frank Smith
Charles Lee Smith
Frederick Madison Smith
George Albert Smith
Gerald Lyman Kenneth Smith
Gipsy Smith
Hannah Whitall Smith
Israel Alexander Smith
Joseph Fielding Smith, Jr.
Joseph Fielding Smith, Sr.
Joseph Smith, III
Oswald Jeffery Smith
Uriah Smith
Wallace Bunnell Smith
Wilbur Moorehead Smith
William Wallace Smith
Smohalla
Reed Smoot
Eliza Roxey Snow
Lorenzo Snow
Ralph Washington Sockman
Maria Solares
David Spangler
Robert Elliott Speer
Francis Edward Spellman
Hubert J. Spencer
William Ambrose Spicer
W. Herbert Spraugh
Richard G. Spurling, Jr.

Sripad Bhakti Raksaka Sridhara
  Maharaja
George Augustus Stallings, Jr.
Virgil Oliver Stamps
Starhawk
Eliza Allen Starr
Rudolf Steiner
Bishop Stephen
Joseph Ross Stevenson
Lyman Stewart
John Roach Straton
James Henry Straughn
Samuel Alphonsus Stritch
Augustus Hopkins Strong
James Woodward Strong
Josiah Strong
Hans Gerhard Stub
Hudson Stuck
John Henry Wilbrandt Stuckenberg
Sivaya Subramuniyaswami
Muhammad Subuh
Thomas Osmond Summers
Lester Frank Sumrall
Sun Bear
Billy Sunday
Jabez Thomas Sunderland
Samu Sunin
Daisetz Teitaro Suzuki
Shunryu Suzuki
Jimmy Lee Swaggart
Arthur Sweatman
David Swing
Harold Vinson Synan
Joseph Alexander Synan
Edmund Casimir Szoka
Henrietta Szold

T

Alexandre Antonin Tache
Ethelbert Talbot
Louis Thompson Talbot
James Edward Talmage
Thomas DeWitt Talmage
Masaharu Taniguchi
Jefferson Davis Tant
Elzear Alexandre Taschereau
Mary Magdalena Lewis Tate
John Taylor
Luisah Teish
Corrie ten Boom
Milton Spencer Terry
Metropolitan Theodosius
Metropolitan Theophilus
Robert Bunger Thieme, Jr.
Charles Lemuel Thompson
Michael Thorn

Howard Thurman
Isaac Taylor Tichenor
Archbishop Tikhon
Paul Johannes Oskar Tillich
Charles Albert Tindley
Worth Marion Tippy
Joseph William Tkach
Augustine Tolton
Ambrose Jessup Tomlinson
Homer Aubrey Tomlinson
Penny Torres
Reuben Archer Torrey
Elizabeth Lois Jones Towne
Crawford Howell Toy
Aiden Wilson Tozer
Archbishop Valerian Trifa
Ralph Waldo Trine
George Washington Truett
Henry Clay Trumbull
Chogyam Trungpa Rinpoche
Henry St. George Tucker
Henry McNeal Turner
Joseph Marcel Turpin
Daniel Sylvester Tuttle
John Paul Twitchell

U

Benjamin Franklin Underwood

V

Louis-Albert Vachon
Milton Valentine
Margaret Newton Van Cott
Henry Pitney Van Dusen
Jack Leo Van Impe
Cornelius Van Til
Henry Clay Vedder
Krishna Venta
George Beauchamp Vick
Joseph Rene Vilatte
John Heyl Vincent
Swami Vishnu Devananda
Swami Vivekananda
Archbishop Vladimir
Valerie Voigt

W

Walking Buffalo
Aaron Wall
Foy Esco Wallace, Jr.
William Jacob Walls

Alexander Walters
Donald Walters
Harry Frederick Ward
Benjamin Breckinridge Warfield
William Fairfield Warren
George Douglas Watson
Alan Wilson Watts
Alexander Walker Wayman
Muhammad Alexander Russell
  Webb
Cynthia Clark Wedel
Gustave Weigel
Sidney A. Weltmer
Amos Daniel Wenger
Abdel Ross Wentz
Alma Birdwell White
Anna White
Ellen Gould Harmon White
James White
William Heth Whitsitt
Henry Nelson Wieman
Victor Paul Wierwille
Ella Wheeler Wilcox
David Ray Wilkerson
Frances Elizabeth Willard
George M. Williams
John Williams
Lacey Kirk Williams
Ernest C. Wilson
Gerald Burton Winrod
Isaac Mayer Wise
Stephen Samuel Wise
Jacob Wisler
Annie Turner Wittenmyer
Henry Wood
Victoria Claflin Woodhull
Wilford Woodruff
James Woodsworth
Maria Beulah Woodworth-Etter
Elwood Worcester
Clarendon Lamb Worrell
Wovoka
John Joseph Wright
Richard Robert Wright, Jr.

Y

Swami Paramahansa Yogananda
Ma Yogashakti Saraswati

Z

Morning Glory Zell
Otter Zell
Thaddeus F. Zielinski
Thomas Fletcher Zimmerman
John Roel Zook

Key to Abbreviations

Shown below are the abbreviations used throughout Religious Leaders of America's biographical profiles. Most abbreviations listed are academic or religious in nature.

A.B. - Bachelor of Arts
Abp. - Archbishop
A.M. - Master of Arts
b. - born
B.A. - Bachelor of Arts
B.D. - Bachelor of Divinity
B.L. - Bachelor of Laws; Bachelor of Literature; Bachelor of Letters
Bp. - Bishop
B.S. - Bachelor of Science
B.Theo. - Bachelor of Theology
ca. - circa
Card. - Cardinal
d. - died
D.D. - Doctor of Divinity
Dr. - Doctor
D.Th. - Doctor of Theology
Fr. - Father
J.C.B. - Bachelor of Canon Law; Bachelor of Civil Law
J.C.D. - Doctor of Canon Law; Doctor of Civil Law
J.D. - Doctor of Jurisprudence; Doctor of Law
J.U.D. - Doctor of Both Laws (i.e. Canon and Civil)
LL.B. - Bachelor of Laws
L.Th. - Licentiate in Theology
M.A. - Master of Arts
M.Div. - Master of Divinity
M.Re. - Master of Religion
M.R.E. - Master of Religious Education
M.S. - Master of Science
M.Th. - Master of Theology
Mus.B. - Bachelor of Music
Mus.D. - Doctor of Music
Ph.B. - Bachelor of Philosophy
Ph.D. - Doctor of Philosophy
Rev. - Reverend
S.S.L. - Licentiate of Sacred Scripture
St. - Saint
S.T.B. - Bachelor of Sacred Theology
S.T.D. - Doctor of the Science of Theology; Doctor of Sacred Theology
S.T.L. - Reader in Sacred Theology; Licentiate in Sacred Theology
S.T.M. - Master of Arts in Theology
Th.B. - Bachelor of Theology
Th.D. - Doctor of Theology
Th.M. - Master of Theology
Ven. - Venerable

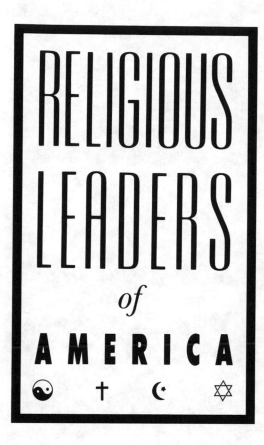

RELIGIOUS LEADERS of AMERICA

Religious Leaders of America

★1★
ABBOT, Francis Ellingwood
Cofounder, Free Religious Association
b. Nov. 6, 1836, Boston, Massachusetts
d. Oct. 23, 1903, Beverly, Massachusetts

Francis Ellingwood Abbot, who left Unitarianism to found the Free Religious Association, was the son of Fanny Ellingwood and Joseph Hale Abbot. Raised in Boston, he was given an excellent education at the Boston Latin School and then Harvard University, from which he graduated in 1859. He married Katherine Fearing Loring and continued his studies at Harvard Divinity School, a Unitarian seminary, for a year. In 1860 he left Massachusetts and became head of a girls school in Meadville, Pennsylvania. His job allowed him time to attend Meadville Theological School, also associated with the American Unitarian Association (AUA). He graduated in 1863. In 1864 he became pastor of a Unitarian church in Dover, New Hampshire, but from the beginning found even the relatively liberal spirit of Unitarianism too binding.

The crisis for Abbot came in the founding of a national organization for Unitarians in 1865. A statement was adopted that called for allegiance to "The Lord Jesus Christ." He rejected this statement as he had already begun to develop a humanistic religion which centered upon God's action in humanity. In 1867 he led in the founding of the Free Religious Association. He resigned his pastorate in 1868 and in 1869 moved to Toledo, Ohio, as the head of a formerly Unitarian congregation which had changed its name to the Independent Church. He began to issue a weekly periodical, the *Index*, which he continued for many years.

In 1873 Abbot moved to Cambridge, Massachusetts, and devoted himself full time to editing the *Index* and other writing. He was also able to finish a Ph.D. at Harvard in 1881. That same year he founded a boys school in Cambridge. He headed the school until 1892 when he received an inheritance that allowed him the freedom to write full time. His later thought had led to a more favorable assessment of world religions. He argued that the Free Religious Association should take a position avowing independence from all historical religions. Its refusal to follow his lead caused him to resign from the organization he had founded.

Abbot's most important writings were his *Scientific Theism* (1885) and *The Way Out of Agnosticism; or, The Philosophy of Free Religion* (1890), both written during his tenure as head of the boys school. He attacked German idealistic philosophy and argued for a real objective universe which must be intelligent and self-conscious. Abbot's second book was strongly attacked by his former professor, Josiah Royce. Abbot accused Royce of libeling him,

but was unable to obtain any redress. He then devoted his remaining years to producing a final synthesis of his thought, *The Syllogistic Philosophy*. He did not live to see his work published, however, as he died in 1903, possibly by suicide. His *Philosophy* was published in 1906, but was not well received. More recent observers have suggested that it was ahead of its time and would have had a better reception if published a generation later.

Sources:

Abbot, Francis Ellingwood. *Scientific Theism*. Boston: Little, Brown & Co., 1885. 219 pp.
———. *The Syllogistic Philosophy*. 2 vols. Boston: Little, Brown & Co., 1906.
———. *The Way Out of Agnosticism; or, The Philosophy of Free Religion*. Boston: Little, Brown & Co., 1890. 83 pp.
Dictionary of American Biography. 20 vols. and 7 supps. New York: Charles Scribner's Sons, 1928-1936, 1944-1981.
Persons, Stow. *Free Religion*. New Haven, CT: Yale University Press, 1947. 162 pp.
Robinson, David. *The Unitarians and the Universalists*. Westport, CT: Greenwood Press, 1985. 368 pp.

★2★
ABBOTT, Lyman
Minister, Congregational Church
b. Dec. 18, 1835, Roxbury, Massachusetts
d. Oct. 22, 1922, New York City, New York

Lyman Abbott, a leading modernist minister/journalist at the end of the nineteenth century, was the son of Jacob and Harriet Vaughn Abbott. When Lyman was three years old, the family moved to Farmington, Maine, where they lived until 1843, when his widowed father moved to New York City. He was only 14 years old when he entered New York University. When he graduated four years later, he practiced law with his brothers. In 1857 he married Abby Francis Hamlin. He had never really been happy with law, in spite of his relative success. Having had earlier thoughts about the ministry, in 1859 he decided to follow that calling. He prepared himself through a disciplined year of reading and in 1860 was ordained and moved to Terre Haute, Indiana, as pastor of the Congregational Church.

Abbott emerged as a supporter of Abraham Lincoln and his reconciling post-war policies and utilized the relative freedom of the pulpit granted by his congregation to espouse his views. At the beginning of 1865 he moved back to New York as the corresponding secretary of the American Union Commission, an organization created to assist the reconstruction of the South after the war. In 1866 he also became the pastor of the New England Congregational Church in Manhattan.

Back in New York, Abbott's literary talents came to the fore. His first book, *The Results of Emancipation in the United States*, was published in 1867, and two years later his book *Jesus of Nazareth* appeared. He also became book editor for *Harper's Magazine*, which brought him into contact with Harper & Brothers publishing firm. He slowly began to rely upon his writing as a means of support. In 1870 he became the editor of *The Illustrated Christian Weekly*, the periodical of the American Tract Society. In 1876 he began a long-term association with **Henry Ward Beecher** as the editor of Beecher's *Christian Union*. During the 1870s Abbott authored a number of books, primarily commentaries on various books of the Bible. In 1881 Abbott succeeded Beecher as editor-in-chief.

During the 1880s, Abbott began to espouse the new modernist theology that was calling for an accommodation with the new scientific findings, especially Darwinism. Beecher died in 1887 and Abbott was invited to take over his pulpit at Plymouth Congregational Church. After a period as a supply pastor he was formally installed in 1890. Even before pastoring at Plymouth, he made his mentor the subject of his writing and authored his first book on Beecher in 1883. Beecher's edited papers were published in two volumes in 1886, and Abbott's biography appeared in 1903.

Abbott served Beecher's congregation for a decade with great success. He continued to write other books, possibly the most important being *Theology of an Evolutionist*, a Christian defense of Darwinism aimed at a popular audience. He resigned the pastorate in 1899 to devote his full time to the *Christian Union*, (whose name had been changed to *Outlook* in 1893). Freed from pastoral duties, the next decade became a time of intense literary output. His *The Life and Literature of the Ancient Hebrews* (1901) was a defense of the new critical scholarship from Germany, again aimed at a popular audience. He also authored *The Other Room* (1903); *The Great Companion* (1904); and *The Spirit of Democracy* (1910).

The *Outlook* remained a significant voice in American Protestantism through the early decades of the twentieth century, due in no small part to the aging Abbott's selection of gifted assistants in the editorial department. Abbott supported the rising Progressive Party and Theodore Roosevelt and became one of the first religious leaders to advocate America's entrance into World War I. Among his last books were *Reminiscences* (1915), which was published in a revised and expanded edition after his death (1923), and his summary statement of faith, *What Christianity Means to Me* (1921).

Sources:

Abbott, Lyman. *The Great Companion*. New York: Grosset & Dunlap, [1904]. 160 pp.

———. *The Life and Literature of the Ancient Hebrews*. Boston: Houghton, Mifflin & Co., 1901. 408 pp.

———. *The Other Room*. New York: Macmillan Company, 1903. 120 pp.

———. *Reminiscences*. Boston: Houghton, Mifflin & Co., 1915. 509 pp.

———. *The Spirit of Democracy*. Boston: Houghton, Mifflin & Co., 1910. 215 pp.

———. *Theology of an Evolutionist*. Boston: Houghton, Mifflin & Co., 1897. 191 pp.

———. *What Christianity Means to Me*. New York: Macmillan Company, 1921. 194 pp.

Dictionary of American Biography. 20 vols. and 7 supps. New York: Charles Scribner's Sons, 1928-1936, 1944-1981.

★3★
ABDU'L-BAHA
Baha'i Faith
b. May 23, 1844, Persia
d. Nov. 28, 1921, Haifa Palestine

Abdu'l-Baha is, chronologically, the third major figure in Baha'i Faith history. Although he never resided in the United States, he did have a major impact on American Baha'i development. Born Abbas Effendi, he was the eldest son of Mirza Husayn Ali, later known as **Baha'u'llah** (Glory of God). Abbas Effendi's father in turn was a follower of Mirza Ali Muhammed, who had proclaimed himself the Bab, or Gate, through whom persons would come to know the promised successor to Muhammed.

The Bab was assassinated in 1850, but his followers maintained their activities, often in conflict with the government of Persia (today's Iran), leading to arrest and persecution. During a period in jail, Abbas Effendi's father realized that he was the predicted Holy One that the Bab had proclaimed, and he declared this openly in 1866. Abbas Effendi was his father's devoted follower from the outset, assisting in his father's work as they traveled in exile and writing the first history of the Baha'i movement in 1886.

Following Baha'u'llah's wishes, Abbas Effendi succeeded his father as head of the movement in 1892, though not without opposition from his half-brother, Mirza Mohammad Ali, and other relatives. Abbas Effendi's titles as leader included Abdu'l-Baha (Slave of Baha), Interpreter of Baha'u'llah, and Center of the Covenant. His writings are among those considered sacred scripture by the Baha'is, and are included in the major books of the faith, *Baha'i Scriptures* and *Baha'i World Faith*.

As leader of the Baha'i faith, Abdu'l-Baha promoted the universalism of Baha'i, emphasizing the unity of all the world's great faiths and Baha'i's place as the culmination of those faiths. He summarized the Baha'i teachings into ten principles: (1) the independent search for truth; (2) the unity of humanity; (3) the harmony of science and religion; (4) equality of the sexes; (5) compulsory education; (6) adoption of a universal language; (7) a world court; (8) working together of all people in love and harmony; (9) condemnation of prejudice; and (10) abolition of extremes of wealth and poverty.

Abdu'l-Baha received American visitors to his center in Acre, Palestine, sent missionaries to America in 1912, and the following year came to the United States as part of a larger tour, dedicating the grounds of the first Baha'i temple in North America, in Wilmette, Illinois. Upon his return home he settled in Haifa. After the conclusion of World War I, the British knighted Abdu'l-Baha for his work on behalf of peace in Palestine.

Sources:

Abdu'l-Baha [Abbas Effendi]. *Foundations of World Unity*. Wilmette, IL: Baha'i Publishing Trust, 1945. 112 pp.

———. *Memorials of the Faithful*. Translated by Marzieh Gail. Wilmette, IL: Baha'i Publishing Trust, 1971. 208 pp.

———. *Paris Talks*. 11th ed., London: Baha'i Publishing Trust, 1912, 1969. 184 pp.

———. The Promulgation of Universal Peace. Wilmette, IL: Baha'i Publishing Committee, 1943. 467 pp.

———. *The Secret of Divine Civilization*. Wilmette, IL: 1918.

———. *Some Answered Questions*. Translated by Laura Clifford Barney. Wilmette, IL: Baha'i Publishing Committee, 1930. 350 pp.

Balyuzi, H. M. *Abdu'l-Baha*. London: George Ronald, 1971. 560 pp.

Bowden, Henry Warner. *Dictionary of American Religious Biography*. Westport, CT: Greenwood Press, 1977. 572 pp.

Miller, William McElwee. *The Baha'i Faith: Its History and Teachings*. South Pasadena, CA: The William Carey Library, 1974. 443 pp.

Phelps, Myron H. *Abbas Effendi: His Life and Teachings*. New York: Putnam, 1903. 259 pp.

—*Gary L. Ward*

★4★
ABERHART, William
Independent Fundamentalist Bible Teacher
b. Dec. 30, 1878, Hibbard Township Canada
d. May 23, 1943, Vancouver Canada

William Aberhart, an independent fundamentalist teacher who became an important political leader in western Canada in the 1930s, grew up in rural Ontario with a Presbyterian background and eventually graduated from Queen's College in Kingston, Ontario, through a correspondence course. In the meantime, he had been making his living as a school teacher. Deeply religious, he had been offended by the study of higher biblical criticism, but around 1900 he encountered a correspondence course edited by fundamentalist Bible teacher, Cyrus I. Scofield. Aberhart found in the course the answer to his questions about the Bible, and he accepted Scofield's dispensational approach to scripture. Dispensationalism divides human history, as told in the Bible, into a number of periods, or, dispensations. In each dispensation God sets different rules for humans to follow and acts toward humanity somewhat differently. Dispensationalism solves a major problem for Bible students in that it assigns seemingly contradictory passages of scriptures to different dispensations, hence accounting for the Bible's changes in its teachings.

In 1902 Aberhart married and quickly became the father of two children. He was turned down for assistance to attend seminary by the Presbyterian Church in Canada because the church could not afford to support married students. He turned to teaching to make his money and pastored on the weekend at various small congregations of different denominations. By World War I he was in Calgary, Alberta, preaching at Westbourne Baptist Church. Each Sunday afternoon he taught a Bible class which, as it grew, became known as the Calgary Prophetic Bible Conference. During the 1920s he had to move to a local theater to accommodate the crowds. In 1924 he began the *Prophetic Voice*, a periodical, and the following year opened a more formal school, the Calgary Prophetic Bible Institute. The school opened at the height of the fundamentalist-modernist controversy in North America and in the same year the union of several liberal Protestant churches formed the United Church of Canada. By 1926 Aberhart was on the air with the Radio Sunday School through which he offered a correspondence course. With these various structures in place, over the next decade his work simply grew year by year. He was also able to find time to author a few books, *God's Great Prophecies* (1922); *Ecclesiastes: The Wisdom under the Sun* (1924); and *An Introduction to the Study of Revelation* (1924).

During the 1920s Aberhart emerged as a leading fundamentalist, but also became somewhat isolated from other fundamentalists by the introduction of some doctrinal peculiarities into his thought. He defended the inerrancy not only of the Bible, but of the King James version. Further, Aberhart began to introduce some emphases from Apostolic Pentecostalism on the baptism of the Holy Spirit, the exercise of spiritual gifts (I Corinthians 12), and water baptism in the name of Jesus only, rather than the traditional baptism in the name of the Father, the Son, and the Holy Spirit. Aberhart accentuated the difference with his denunciations of other denominations and demands that followers choose between them and his work. While his separatist views cost him many of his early supporters, he retained a large following into the depression era of the 1930s.

As the effects of the depression spread, Aberhart began to advocate the Social Credits plan through the *Prophetic Voice* and his radio show. He also authored two books, *The Douglas System of Economics* (1933) and *Social Credit Manual* (1935). Essentially the idea was to rearrange the credit system throughout the country and give each person $25 per month to prime the economic pump. Refused an audience by the reigning powers in the province, he formed the Social Credit Party. In 1935 he garnered 54 percent of the vote and 57 of 63 seats in the province's legislature. Aberhart became premier as the leader of the economic movement of God. He remained the premier for the rest of his life, he and his party winning again in 1940. Though unable to get his social credit proposals by the Canadian Supreme Court, he was able to assist the recovery of the farmers, and his party dominated Albertan politics for the next generation.

Sources:

Aberhart, William. *The Douglas System of Economics*. N.p., 1933.
_____. *Ecclesiastes: The Wisdom Under the Sun*. Calgary, Canada: Calgary Prophetic Bible Institute, 1924.
_____. *God's Great Prophecies*. Calgary, Canada: Calgary Prophetic Bible Institute, 1922.
_____. *An Introduction to the Study of Revelation*. Calgary, Canada: Calgary Prophetic Bible Conference, 1924.
_____. *Social Credit Manual*. Calgary, Canada: Western Printing and Litho, 1935. 64 pp.
Boudreau, Joseph Amedee. *Alberta, Aberhart, and Social Credit*. Toronto: Holt, Rinehart and Winston of Canada, 1975.
Clark, S. D. *Church and Sect in Canada*. Toronto: University of Toronto Press, 1948.
Johnson, L. P. N. and Ola MacNutt. *Aberhart of Alberta*. Edmonton, Canada: Institute of Applied Art, 1970.
Lippy, Charles H. *Twentieth-Century Shapers of American Popular Religion*. New York: Greenwood Press, 1989. 494 pp.
Mann, William E. *Sect, Cult, and Church in Alberta*. Toronto: University of Toronto Press, 1955. 166 pp.

★5★
ABERNATHY, Ralph David
Minister, American Baptist Churches in the U.S.A.
Civil Rights Leader
b. Mar. 11, 1926, Linden, Alabama
d. Apr. 17, 1990, Atlanta, Georgia

Ralph David Abernathy, Baptist minister and co-founder with **Martin Luther King, Jr.**, of the Southern Christian Leadership Conference (SCLC), grew up in rural Alabama. He attended Alabama State College, from which he received his B.S. in 1950. While at college, in 1948 he was ordained as a Baptist minister. He later did post-graduate work at Atlanta University. In 1951 he became pastor of the First Baptist Church in Montgomery, Alabama. In 1952 he married Juanita Odessa Jones.

In the mid-1950s in Montgomery, Abernathy met Martin Luther King, Jr. Abernathy helped organize the Montgomery Bus Boycott, and persuaded King to lead the Civil Rights Movement which grew out of it. He was one of the founders of the Southern Christian Leadership Conference, the primary organization to give focus to the movement. During the 1960s he served as SCLC's treasurer and then vice-president. Throughout this time he remained King's close confidant and lieutenant, and went to jail more than 20 times as a result of his efforts for civil rights. His civil rights activism cost him more than jail time; both his home and church were bombed. Abernathy was in Memphis when King was shot, and he held King's body as he died. Following King's assassination, in 1969 Abernathy, who had become pastor of Hunter Street Baptist Church in Atlanta in 1962, became president of the Southern Christian Leadership Conference.

As president of SCLC, Abernathy intervened in the hospital workers' strike in Charleston, South Carolina, and led a mule team march to Washington, D.C., but slowly lost the support of his colleagues. Among the first to depart was **Jesse L. Jackson**, who formed a rival organization in Chicago, Operation PUSH (People United to Save Humanity). After nine years as president of SCLC, Abernathy was replaced by **Joseph E. Lowery**. In the years that followed he became further estranged from the former leaders of the movement he had helped found.

Abernathy developed a running feud with **Coretta Scott King**, Martin Luther King's widow. He complained that she was taking money that should go to further SCLC and the continuing needs of civil rights in order to build the King Center in Atlanta, a monument to her late husband. Abernathy was not invited to participate in the 1986 ceremonies to commemorate the first national Martin Luther King national holiday.

In 1980 Abernathy alienated himself further from his former colleagues by supporting Ronald Reagan for president. That action was remembered in spite of his support for Jesse Jackson in 1984 and 1988. He also became involved with the Rev. Sun Myung Moon and the Unification Church and during the mid-1980s spoke at its conferences on a number of occasions.

Abernathy's final words came in 1989 when he published his autobiography, *And the Walls Come Tumbling Down*. The volume continued his feud with Coretta Scott King by relating accounts of Martin Luther King's extramarital affairs. When asked to retract the statements, he refused.

Sources:

Abernathy, Ralph. *And the Walls Came Tumbling Down*. New York: Harper & Row, 1989. 640 pp.
"King Aide Abernathy Dies at 64." *Houston Chronicle* (April 18, 1990).
May, Lee. "Ralph Abernathy, Aid to Dr. King, Dies." *Los Angeles Times* (April 18, 1990).

★ 6 ★
Swami ABHEDANANDA
Swami, Vedanta Society
b. Jan. 2, 1866, Calcutta India
d. Sep. 8, 1939, Calcutta India

Swami Abhedananda, one of the founders of Hinduism in North America, was the son of Rasiklal Chandra, an English teacher at the Oriental Seminary in Calcutta, and Nayantara Devi. He was originally named Kali Prasad Chandra (the product of the grace of the Divine Mother). He was a studious youth, mastering Sanskrit and becoming attracted to Hindu holy books. While at school, a classmate suggested that he visit **Sri Ramakrishna**, who was at the time residing nearby at Dakshineswar. During his first meeting with Ramakrishna, Chandra felt transformed and began to practice his meditative disciplines under Ramakrishna's guidance. He became known as one of the most studious of the group of youths that gathered around the teacher.

In January 1886 Kali participated with ten colleagues in a ceremony during which Ramakrishna gave them an ochre robe and a rosary and initiated them into the order of *sannyasa*, the renounced life. The group was organized informally with Narendra (**Swami Vivekananda**) as its leader. Ramakrishna died in August of 1886. On December 25, the disciples took a second sannyasa vow and soon afterward, Kali attached himself to the monastery at Barangore, and for a third time formally took the sannyasa vow and changed his family name. From that time on, Kali was known as Swami Abhedananda. The group banded together as an informal fraternity of monks. Within a few years, however, Abhedananda took up the itinerant life, wandering around India in contemplation.

Meanwhile, Vivekananda had made his triumphal trip to the World's Parliament of Religions in Chicago in 1893 and had organized the Vedanta Society in New York. In September 1894 Abhedananda organized a meeting in the town hall of Calcutta for the Hindu community to celebrate Vivekananda's activity. Vivekananda inspired in Abhedananda the goal of spreading the message of Vedantic Hinduism in the West.

In 1896 Abhedananda went to London to assist Vivekananda and delivered his first lecture at the Theosophical Society there. He was quickly recognized as a talented preacher. After a year in Lon-

don, he migrated to the United States, concentrating his efforts in New York and the East Coast. Through his speaking and travels he organized and spread the movement, and through his writings and university lectures he became one of the early forces in effectively introducing Hinduism to Americans.

In 1909 and 1910, Swami Abhedananda experienced a set of problems with the board of the New York Vedanta Society, which had run into financial difficulties. With money realized from the sale of his books, he purchased a center in Berkshire, Connecticut, that formerly belonged to the society. Unable to reconcile his differences with the society, he broke with the New York group and moved to Connecticut, where he worked as a teacher independent of the society in America. From his new headquarters, he continued to travel widely, extending his influence to California and to Europe.

In 1921, Abhedananda returned to India to spend the last years of his life. After settling in Belur, where the Indian branch of the Vedanta Society had its headquarters and monastery, he traveled to Tibet to study Buddhism. While at Bemis, he discovered a Tibetan record on the life of Jesus. He believed it to be the same material previously discovered by Nicolas Notovich. He had the manuscript translated into Bengali and published in his book, *Kashmir O Tibbate*. Upon his return to Belur he soon broke with the society and in 1923 reestablished himself in Calcutta. He established independent centers in Calcutta and Darjeeling. He worked for another decade, moving between the two centers. In one of his last public appearances, he chaired the Parliament of Religions celebration in 1937 of the centennial of Ramakrishna's birth.

In America, Abhedananda's organization eventually dissolved, and today he is most remembered for the many books he wrote. In India his work continues at the Ramakrishna Vedanta Math monastery in Calcutta.

Sources:

Abhedananda, Swami. *Complete Works*. Calcutta, India: Ramakrishna Vedanta Math, 1967. 10 vols.
Aiyer, P. Skeshadri, trans. *Spiritual Teachings of Swami Abhedananda*. Calcutta, India: Ramakrishna Vedanta Math, 1962. 55 pp.
Ghosh, Ashutosh. *Swami Abhedananda, The Patriot-Saint*. Calcutta, India: Ramakrishna Vedanta Math, 1967. 51 pp.
Shivani, Sister. [Mary LePage]. *An Apostle of Monism*. Calcutta, India: Ramakrishna Vedanta Math, 1947. 314 pp.

★ 7 ★
ADAMS, James Luther
Educator, American Unitarian Association
b. Nov. 12, 1901, Ritzille, Washington

James Luther Adams, Unitarian theologian and ethicist, is the son of Lella May Barnett and James Carey Adams. His father was a conservative Baptist minister. In college at the University of Minnesota, Adams rebelled against his religious upbringing and found an initial religious home in the humanistic teachings of Unitarian minister **John H. Dietrich**. After his graduation in 1924, Adams entered Harvard Divinity School (S.T.B., 1927). The year of his graduation he married, was ordained to the ministry by the American Unitarian Association (AUA), and became pastor of the Second Church (Unitarian) of Salem, Massachusetts. During his several years at Salem, he was able to pursue post-graduate studies at Harvard University (M.A., 1930). During his last year at Salem, he edited the Unitarian periodical *Christian Register*. In 1934 he moved to the congregation at Wellesley Hills, Massachusetts. During his early years in the ministry Adams became a critic of the overly individualistic nature of the liberal theology he had absorbed primarily from Dietrich and Irving Babbit, his teacher at Harvard. He rejected what he termed nonhistorical "universal" religion and argued for the social engagement of Unitarians with the present culture.

In 1935 Adams left the pastorate to study in Europe and returned after a year to become an instructor in psychology and philosophy of religion at Meadville Theological Seminary. In 1936 he assumed the editorship of the *Journal of Liberal Religion*, a position he retained until 1943 when he joined the Federated Theological Faculties at the University of Chicago as a professor of theology. During his years with the journal he authored two books, *Irving Babbitt, Man and Teacher* (1941) and *The Changing Reputation of Human Nature* (1943).

In Chicago, Adams' career blossomed. In 1946 he became one of the founders of the Society for the Scientific Study of Religion. In 1957 he became the Edward Mallinckrodt, Jr., Professor of Divinity at Harvard Divinity School. He stayed at Harvard nine years before becoming Distinguished Professor of Social Ethics at Andover Newton Theological Seminary in 1968. During these years Adams remained active in Unitarian affairs. In 1965 he assumed some national leadership with the association's department of social responsibility. He authored and edited numerous works, including *Taking Time Seriously* (1956) and *On Being Human Religiously* (1976). His doctoral studies had concentrated on the thought of **Paul Tillich**, and he authored several works on Tillich, including *The Theology of Paul Tillich* (1952) and *Paul Tillich's Philosophy of Culture, Science, and Religion*, a reprinting of his thesis (1945, 1965). He has continued an active writing and editing career since his formal retirement in 1972. A collection of many of his essays appeared in 1986 as *The Prophethood of All Believers*.

Sources:

Adams, James Luther. *The Changing Reputation of Human Nature*. Chicago: N.p., [1944]. 48 pp.
_____. *Paul Tillich's Philosophy of Culture, Science, and Religion*. Chicago: Thesis, University of Chicago, 1945. 313 pp.
_____. *Taking Time Seriously*. Glencoe, IL: Free Press, 1957. 74 pp.
_____, Wilhelm Pauck, and Roger Lincoln, eds. *The Thought of Paul Tillich*. San Francisco, CA: Harper & Row, 1985. 404 pp.
Beach, George K., ed. *The Prophethood of All Believers*. Boston: Beacon Press, 1986. 324 pp.
Robinson, David. *The Unitarians and the Universalists*. Westport, CT: Greenwood Press, 1985. 368 pp.
Stackhouse, Max L., ed. *On Being Human Religiously*. Boston: Beacon Press, 1976. 257 pp.

★8★
ADAMS, Theodore Floyd
President, Baptist World Alliance
Minister, Southern Baptist Convention
b. Sep. 26, 1898, Palmyra, New York
d. Sep. 26, 1980, Richmond, Virginia

Theodore Floyd Adams, a minister in the Southern Baptist Convention and president of the Baptist World Alliance, was the son of Evelyn Parkes and Floyd Holden Adams. He grew up in a devout Baptist home, where his father was a Baptist minister. He attended Denison University where he had an outstanding academic career and from which he earned his B.A. in 1921. He then pursued his theological studies at Colgate Rochester Divinity School. Following his graduation in 1924, he was ordained as a minister in affiliation with the Northern Baptist Convention and became pastor of a Baptist church in Cleveland. In 1925 he married Esther Josephine Jillson.

Adams stayed in Cleveland three years before moving to Toledo, Ohio, and then in 1936 he became pastor of First Baptist Church in Richmond, Virginia, a leading congregation of the Southern Baptist Convention, which became his base of operations for the rest of his active ministry. Adams' most outstanding contribution beyond his parish was his work with the Baptist World Alliance, the national and international fellowship of Baptist churches. He joined the executive committee of the alliance in 1934 while still at Tole-

do, and remained on it for the rest of his life. During that time he served as vice-president for three years (1947-1950) and president for five (1955-1960). His ecumenical spirit made him one of the leading Baptist voices in the creation of the World Council of Churches even though the Southern Baptist Convention withdrew support for the council due to what it saw as an overemphasis on the role of sacraments.

Within his denomination, Adams emerged as a leading proponent of building a strong missionary program and served two lengthy terms on the Foreign Missionary Board (1940-1950, 1961-1967). He also served on the board of a number of denominational institutions.

As pastor of a leading Baptist church, Adams initiated a radio ministry which lasted for 22 years, and during the last years of his ministry regularly appeared on television. He authored his first book, *Making your Marriage Succeed*, in 1953. It was followed by *Making the Most of What Life Brings* (1957) and *Tell Me How* (1964). His last book grew out of his work with the Baptist World Alliance, *Baptists Around the World* (1967). Upon his retirement in 1986, Adams was named pastor emeritus and became visiting professor of preaching at Southeastern Baptist Theological Seminary.

Sources:

Adams, Theodore F. *Baptists Around the World*. Nashville, TN: Broadman Press, 1967. 128 pp.
_____. *Making the Most of What Life Brings*. New York: Harper, 1957. 145 pp.
_____. *Making your Marriage Succeed*. New York: Harper, 1953. 156 pp.
Encyclopedia of Southern Baptists. 3 vols. Nashville, TN: Broadman Press, 1958, 1971.
Hill, Samuel S., ed. *Encyclopedia of Religion in the South*. Macon, GA: Mercer University Press, 1984. 878 pp.

★9★
ADAMS, Walter Hollis
Bishop, Anglican Episcopal Church of North America
b. Apr. 19, 1907, Liverpool England

Walter Hollis Adams, founder and archbishop of the Anglican Episcopal Church of North America, was raised in England and spent the greater part of his adult life in a secular career. During his early adult life, he worked in stocks and bonds, and in 1939, as World War II was beginning, he joined the British Diplomatic Service. In 1969 he moved to the United States to serve in the British Consul in Miami, Florida. While he had been an active churchman, only after his retirement in 1967 did he begin an ecclesiastical career. His efforts in religious leadership occurred as the Episcopal Church was experiencing intense internal tension over complaints by more conservative priests and laypeople about the ordination of women and homosexuals and what was seen as a general drift from moral standards.

Adams was initially ordained to the priesthood in 1971 by Frederick Littler Pyman, the founder and bishop of a small independent denomination, the Evangelical Orthodox (Catholic) Church in America (Non-Papal Catholic). In 1972 Adams founded the Anglican Episcopal Church of North America. On October 22, 1972, he was consecrated as the bishop for the new body by William Eliot Littlewood, an archbishop of the Free Protestant Episcopal Church, assisted by Pyman and Larry Lee Shaver, then a bishop in Pyman's jurisdiction. Adams went through a second consecration ceremony the next day under the hands of Herman Adrian Spruit, archbishop and patriarch of the Church of Antioch. Adams was consecrated a third time, by Pyman assisted by Shaver, on June 15, 1973.

As Adams began to build his jurisdiction, he encountered others who had left the Episcopal Church to form independent churches.

In 1975 he organized the Anglican Episcopal Council that included three other groups which were composed predominantly of former Episcopalians—the Anglican Church in America, the United Episcopal Church, and the Episcopal Church (Evangelical). The council was seen as a stage toward merger, which occurred within a few years. Meanwhile, a much larger schism of Episcopalians occurred in 1976, and Anglican orders for the bishops of the new Anglican Catholic Church (ACC) were provided in part by Francisco Pagtakhan, a bishop of the Philippine Independent Church, a full member of the Worldwide Anglican Communion. Unfortunately, the ACC began to splinter into warring factions soon after it was formed.

Adams continued to work for the union of the Anglicans, as the dissident Episcopalians had come to be designated. In 1981 he was reconsecrated by Pagtakhan and two other Philippine bishops, Sergio Mondala and Lope Rosete, and he brought his church into negotiations which were aimed at uniting four of the Anglican factions. As a result of the talks, a majority of the Anglican Episcopal Church merged into the American Episcopal Church (AEC). However Adams and the remainder of the church stayed out of the merger. Instead the remnant reorganized and was accepted into the ACC as the nongeographical Diocese of St. Paul. This arrangement did not prove a happy one, and in 1986, Adams led 11 priests and nine churches out and reconstituted the Anglican Episcopal Church in North America.

Adams retired in 1989 and named Robert H. Voight, whom he had consecrated, as his episcopal successor.

Sources:

The Apostolic Succession of the Anglican Episcopal Council of Churches. Atlanta: Anglican Episcopal Council of Churches, [1975]. 17 pp.

Ward, Gary, comp. *Independent Bishops: An International Directory.* Santa Barbara: Santa Barbara Centre, 1990. 450 pp.

★ 10 ★
ADAMSKI, George
Flying Saucer Contactee
b. Apr. 17, 1891, Poland
d. Apr. 23, 1965, Takoma Park, Maryland

George Adamski was an early leader in flying saucer interest and promotion. Little information about his parents or early life is known, except that he was brought to the United States from Poland at the age of two. He and his wife Mary settled in southern California. His interests became known when he founded the Royal Order of Tibet in 1936. This organization served as a format for teaching his ideas for the mastery of life.

Adamski's interest in flying saucers began a few years thereafter, as he worked in a cafe near Mt. Palomar, in southern California. His first claim to visual contact with a UFO was on October 9, 1946, well before the topic of UFOs became widely discussed. He wrote a novel, *Pioneers of Space* (1949), to encourage public interest in flying saucers, and was soon giving lecture tours, which included pictures of UFOs from his own observations.

Adamski gained far-reaching attention as a result of an article about him in *Fate* magazine and the success of his next book, *Flying Saucers Have Landed* (1953). In this book, he disclosed an important experience of purported telepathic contact with a Venusian on November 20, 1952, followed the next month by a second contact, which included a hieroglyphic message. His next book, *Inside the Space Ships,* further described such encounters, as well as extraterrestrial information, including the claim that our solar system actually has 12 planets and that the moon has a fertile far side.

Adamski's career gained new heights as a result of a worldwide tour in 1959. He began a monthly *Science Publications Newsletter* in 1962 (run by an associate, C. A. Honey). He also conducted seminars on *Cosmic Philosophy,* his last book. Though his projects

met with much success, they also met with a great deal of criticism. In 1957 UFO researcher James Moseley claimed that Adamski faked his photographs and used his close friends as "witnesses." The hieroglyphics were found to have been taken from a little-known scholarly work, and the Venusian encounter stories were said to have originally been written in the early 1940s as science fiction. C. A. Honey broke from Adamski in 1963 when he discovered that Adamski had rewritten the original Royal Order of Tibet materials to appear as messages from the space brothers.

Adamski's work did not end with his death in 1965, but has been carried on, despite the detractors, by former secretary Charlotte Blob's UFO Education Center in Valley Center, California, and Alice Wells' George Adamski Foundation in Vista, California.

Sources:

Adamski, George. *Behind the Flying Saucer Mystery.* New York: Paperback Library, 1967. 159 pp. Previously published as *Flying Saucers Farewell,* 1961.

_____. *Cosmic Philosophy.* Freeman, SD: Pine Hill Press, 1961. Reprint, 1972. 87 pp.

_____. *Inside the Flying Saucers.* New York: Paperback Library, 1967. 192 pp. Previously published as *Inside the Space Ships,* 1955.

_____. *Pioneers of Space: A Trip to the Moon, Mars and Venus.* Los Angeles: Leonard-Freefield Co., 1949. 260 pp.

_____. *Questions and Answers by the Royal Order of Tibet.* N.p.: Royal Order of Tibet, 1936. 67 pp.

Barker, Gray. *Book of Adamski.* Clarksburg, WV: Saucerian Publications, n.d. 78 pp.

Buckle, Eileen. *The Scoriton Mystery: Did Adamski Return?* London: Neville Spearman Ltd., 1967. 303 pp.

Cramp, Leonard G. *Space, Gravity and the Flying Saucer.* New York: British Book Centre, 1955. 182 pp.

Leslie, Desmond, and George Adamski. *Flying Saucers Have Landed.* New York: British Book Centre, 1953. 232 pp.

Shepard, Leslie. *Encyclopedia of Occultism & Parapsychology.* 3 vols., 2nd. ed. Detroit: Gale Research Co., 1984-1985.

Zinnstag, Lou. *George Adamski, Their Man on Earth.* Tucson, AZ: UFO Photo Archives, 1990. 208 pp.

_____ and Timothy Good. *George Adamski: The Untold Story.* Kent, England: Ceti Publications, 1983. 208 pp.

—Gary L. Ward

★ 11 ★
ADLER, Felix
American Ethical Union
b. Aug. 13, 1851, Alzey Germany
d. Apr. 24, 1933, New York, New York

Felix Adler, the founder of the American Ethical Union, was a pioneering leader in nontheistic ethical philosophy as a way of life. Born in Germany, Adler came to the United States at the age of six, when his father, a rabbi, accepted a post at Temple Emmanuel in New York City. Adler's situation and interests seemed destined to lead him into the rabbinate as well, but when he went to Germany for graduate work at Berlin University and Heidelberg University, his faith was shaken by his encounter with the new schools of higher criticism of the Bible and German philosophy. He eventually returned to New York a confirmed disbeliever in God and traditional religious systems, but steadfastly committed to the power of ethical philosophy.

Adler assumed his first teaching position at Cornell University in the areas of Hebrew and Oriental literature. At the same time he worked on his own message of the ethical life. His ideas were adopted by enough interested people that he was able to leave his post to found and head the Ethical Culture Society in New York City on May 15, 1876.

Under Adler's leadership, the society became well known for its intellectual acumen and its activism in social reform movements. Intensely interested in education, Adler founded a kindergarten using the ideas of German educator Friedrich Froebel, who emphasized working cooperation. The school, which became the Ethical Culture School, introduced the "workshop" into a grade school curriculum, a concept adapted over time by the public school system. The society was equally successful in other programs. In 1881 Adler developed a visiting nurse program for the city's poor, which the city embraced and enlarged. In 1894 Adler was named chair of the National Child Labor Committee, which worked to reduce and control the extent of child labor and strengthen the educational system. Adler held the post for 17 years. In 1902 he founded the Manhattan Trade School for Girls, and for many years he was a key spokesperson and sometime negotiator on behalf of the garment workers of New York City.

Adler's work gained such a following that Ethical Culture Societies were founded across the United States and abroad. In 1891 Adler formed the American Ethical Union as an umbrella group, followed in 1896 by the International Union of Ethical Societies. In addition to his organizational work, Adler wrote several books, including such works as *The Moral Instruction of Children* (1895), *The Religion of Duty* (1905), and *An Ethical Philosophy of Life* (1918).

Sources:

Adler, Felix. *Creed and Deed: A Series of Discourses*. New York: Putnam, 1877.
_____. *An Ethical Philosophy of Life*. New York: Appleton, 1918.
_____. *Life and Destiny*. New York: American Ethical Union, 1903. Reprint. 1944. 71 pp.
_____. *Our Part in This World*. Edited by Horace L. Friess. New York: King's Crown Press, 1946. 93 pp.
_____. *The Reconstruction of the Spiritual Ideal*. New York: Appleton, 1924.
_____. *The Religion of Duty*. New York: McClure, Phillips, 1905.
Bowden, Henry Warner. *Dictionary of American Religious Biography*. Westport, CT: Greenwood Press, 1977. 572 pp.
The Fiftieth Anniversary of the Ethical Movement, 1876-1926. New York and London: D. Appleton and Co., 1926. 276 pp.
Friess, Horace L. *Felix Adler and Ethical Culture*. New York: Columbia University Press, 1981. 272 pp.
Jacobs, Leo. *Three Types of Practical Ethical Movements of the Past Half Century*. New York: Macmillan, 1922. 184 pp.
Kraut, Benny. *From Reform Judaism to Ethical Culture: The Religious Evolution of Felix Adler*. Cincinnati, OH: Hebrew Union College Press, 1979. 285 pp.
Who Was Who in America. Chicago: Marquis Who's Who, Inc.

—Gary L. Ward

★12★
ADLER, Margot
Neo-Paganism Author
Gardnerian Wicca Priestess
b. Apr. 16, 1946, Little Rock, Arkansas

Margot Adler, a major public figure in the Neo-Pagan movement, achieved prominence with the publication of *Drawing Down the Moon* (1979), an overview of Neo-Paganism. Raised in a nonreligious household, her father was a psychiatrist, as was her grandfather, the world-renowned Alfred Adler. She holds degrees from the University of California at Berkeley (B.A. in political science, 1968) and the Columbia University Graduate School of Journalism (M.S., 1970), and has been a Nieman Fellow at Harvard University (1981-1982). Pursuing a career in broadcast journalism, she worked for WBAI-FM for almost a decade (1968-1977) and for National Public Radio from 1978 to the present.

Adler entered the Craft in 1972, originally through a study group in Brooklyn run by the traditionalist New York Coven of Welsh Traditional Witches. She became a Gardnerian in 1973, and co-ran the Manhattan Pagan Way through much of the mid-seventies. She was the priestess of Iargalon, a Gardnerian coven, from 1976 to 1981, a particularly fertile coven from which many other covens have been formed. Adler lectures and holds workshops throughout the country on Pagan spirituality, Goddess spirituality, and the polytheistic perspective on the modern world.

Adler married her long-time companion John Gliedman in a handfasting ceremony officiated by **Selena Fox**, priestess of Circle Wicca, in 1988. It was the first Wiccan handfasting to be written up in the society pages of the *New York Times*. Since 1982 Adler has practiced as a solitary (apart from a coven), but has become one of the most sought-after leaders for Pagan events nationally. She has become known for emphasizing the movement's creativity and diversity, and has advocated the movement's alignment with the women's spirituality movement.

Sources:

Adler, Margot. *Drawing Down the Moon*. New York: Viking Press, 1979. Rev. ed. Boston, MA: Beacon Press, 1986.
Guiley, Rosemary E. *Encyclopedia of Witchcraft & Witches*. New York: Facts on File, 1989. 400 pp.

★13★
AGYEMAN, Jaramogi Abebe
Founder, Pan African Orthodox Christian Church
b. Jun. 13, 1911, Indianapolis, Indiana

Albert Buford Cleage, Jr., the founder of the Shrine of the Black Madonna and the Pan African Orthodox Christian Church, is now generally known as Jaramogi Abebe Agyeman, the African name he has used through the 1980s. He is the son of Albert Buford Cleage, Sr., and Pearl Reed. He attended Wayne State University in Detroit, Michigan (A.B., 1937) and following his graduation worked for a year with Detroit's Department of Public Welfare. He decided to enter into the ministry and attended Oberlin Graduate School of Theology, where he earned his B.D. He later did graduate work at the University of Southern California and Wayne State. He married Doris Graham.

As a minister with the Congregational and Christian Churches (later the United Church of Christ), Cleage served a succession of parishes, including the Candler Memorial Congregational Church in Lexington, Kentucky (1942-1943); Church for the Fellowship of All People in San Francisco, California (1943-1944); and St. John's Congregational Church in Springfield, Massachusetts (1946-1951). In 1951 he moved back to Detroit as pastor of St. Mark's Community (Presbyterian) Church.

As a Black in mid-twentieth century America, Cleage began to deal theologically with the concept of race consciousness and white-dominated Christianity. The rise of the Nation of Islam and the civil rights movement, which had been sparked by the 1954 Supreme Court decision which spurred the desegregation of public schools and initiated a new phase in the struggle of Blacks, challenged Cleage's Christianity. Out of the ferment Cleage began the construction of a Christianity for the black community. Drawing upon insights from Marcus Garvey, he began to absorb themes from the religion of black nationalists earlier in the century. He argued that religions come from the black peoples of the world and that Jesus was a black Messiah, born of a black Madonna, who came to a black nation. Jesus did not build a church, but created a movement. Today the church must join that movement. As the civil rights movement blossomed, and especially as the black power phase emerged, Cleage came to the fore as a black Christian leader who saw his work as one that created structures that transferred power to the black community.

In 1953 Cleage took 300 members of St. Mark's out of the Presbyterian Church and formed Central Congregational Church. Cleage led the congregation in joining the fight to save a black congressional district in Detroit from gerrymandering in 1957. Through the 1960s Cleage reflected upon the civil rights struggle until one

Sunday in 1967, when he preached a sermon calling for a new black nationalist theology. That Sunday an 18-foot painting of a black madonna and child was unveiled and the Black Christian Nationalist Movement launched. Cleage quickly became a national voice in the black community as a religious leader willing to defend the concept of "black power" (which many black clergymen saw as tantamount to a rejection of the work of **Martin Luther King, Jr.**). Cleage detailed his perspective in two books, *The Black Messiah* (1968) and *Black Christian Nationalism* (1972). The development of Cleage's Black nationalism gradually led to a break with the United Church of Christ, the proliferation of Shrines of the Black Madonna as local congregations, and the formation of the Pan African Orthodox Christian Church as a new denomination. Through the 1970s the church developed centers in the South and expanded its services to the black community. Though no longer an object of media attention, Cleage and the shrine have persisted and continue to grow.

Sources:

Cleage, Albert B., Jr. *Black Christian Nationalism*. New York: William Morrow, 1972. 312 pp.
———. *The Black Messiah*. New York: Sheed and Ward, 1968. 278 pp.
Ward, Hiley H. *Prophet of the Black Nation*. Philadelphia: Pilgrim Press, 1969. 22 pp.

★ 14 ★
AHMAD, Mirza Ghulam Hazrat
Founder, Ahmadiyya Movement in Islam
b. Feb. 13, 1835, Qadian Pakistan
d. May 26, 1908, Lahore Pakistan

Although he never visited the United States, Mirza Ghulam Hazrat Ahmad has had a significant impact on black religious experience in America as the founder of the Ahmadiyya Movement in Islam. Born into a landed family in what is now Pakistan, he married a cousin (as was customary) in 1852, with whom he had two children. In 1865, at the age of 30, he entered government work, but left three years later to oversee the family holdings.

Ahmad was a very pious Muslim and became very concerned with what he perceived to be the declining state of Islam in the world. In 1880 he published a large book called *Barahin-i-Ahmadiyah*, in which he fulfilled his perceived calling to promote and defend Islam, especially against Christianity's claims. In 1891 Ahmad declared that he was not simply an apologist for Islam, but the Messiah and the Mahdi, the promised reformer of Islam. Ahmad believed the Christian expectation of the Messiah was mistaken. He acknowledged that Jesus was a great teacher and prophet, but claimed that he was not divine. Ahmad insisted that Jesus did not actually die on the cross, but rather fainted, and was able to escape later to Kashmir, in India, where he died of old age. The Messiah of the Second Coming was not to be the resurrected Jesus, but someone embodying his spirit and power, and Ahmad claimed to be that person.

In 1901, Ahmad took a further step away from orthodox Islam, asserting that he was a prophet, i.e. on equal footing with Muhammad. This action, coupled with his declaration of an end to *jihad*, or holy war, placed the Ahmadiyya Movement outside mainstream Islam, which rejected and persecuted it. Ahmad's following, however, did not die out, but continued to increase, and has been guided, since the creation of Pakistan, from its headquarters in Rabwah, Pakistan.

The Ahmadiyya Movement first appeared in the United States in 1921, well after Ahmad's death in 1908, though his influence was still vital. In the United States, though not the original intention, it became primarily a black religion. In the last 25 years or so, significant numbers of immigrants from the Middle East and Asia have also joined. The United States also has a branch of the Ahmadiyya Anjuman Ishaat Islam movement, which has attempted to re-enter

mainstream Islam by rejecting Ahmad's claim to prophethood, regarding it as an allegorical, not a literal, title.

Sources:

Ahmad, Mirza Ghulam Hazrat. *The Four Questions Answered*. Lahore, Pakistan: Nigar Press, 1947. 83 pp.
———. *Jesus in India*. London: Ahmadiyya Muslim Foreign Missions Department, 1978. 107 pp.
———. *Our Teaching*. Rabwah, West Pakistan: Ahmadiyya Muslim Foreign Missions Office, 1962. 68 pp.
———. *The Teachings of Islam*. Rabwah, West Pakistan: Ahmadiyya Muslim Foreign Missions Office, 1966. 175 pp.
Dard, A. R. *Life of Ahmad*. Lahore, Pakistan: Tabshire, 1948. 622 pp.
Khan, Muhammad Zafrulla. *Ahmadiyyat: The Renaissance of Islam*. London: Tabshire, 1978. 360 pp.
Nadwi, Abul Hasan Ali. *Qadianism: A Critical Study*. Lucknow, India: Academy of Islamic Research and Publications, 1974. 167 pp.

—*Gary L. Ward*

★ 15 ★
AINSLIE III, Peter
Minister, Christian Church (Disciples of Christ)
b. Jun. 3, 1867, Dunnsville, Virginia
d. Feb. 23, 1934, Baltimore, Maryland

Peter Ainslie III, a minister with the Christian Church (Disciples of Christ), was the son of Rebecca Etta Sizer and Peter Ainslie. Both his father and grandfather (also named Peter) had been ministers with their roots in the independent evangelical work led by the Haldane brothers and centered in late-nineteenth century Edinburgh, Scotland. The elder Ainslie came to America in 1811. He became a Baptist preacher but ran into trouble for his Haldane-influenced views. Leaving the Baptists, he joined the Christian Church (Disciples of Christ). The second Peter Ainslie also became a Disciples' minister and the younger Ainslie followed in their footsteps.

Ainslie decided early in life to enter the ministry and to that end he attended Translyvania College. Poor health prevented him from finishing the course of study and he left the school in 1889 after completing three years of work. He preached as a supply pastor for the next year and in 1891 was able to accept a full-time pastorate at Calhoun Street Christian Church (later the Christian Temple) of Baltimore, Maryland. He would make the church his home for the rest of his life.

Ainslie rose in prominence as a leading Disciples minister. He authored a number of books, including *Religion in Daily Doings* (1903); *Studies in the Old Testament* (1907); *God and Me* (1908); and *My Brother and I* (1911). In 1910 he served as president of the International Convention of Christian Churches. Over the years he had emerged as a strong supporter of the Disciples plan to unite all Christians through what he perceived as the New Testament plan. He opened the 1910 convention with a forceful plea for Disciples to pay more attention to developing a program to work toward Christian unity. To that end he called for an extra session, at which he proposed the formation of the Council of Christian Union of the Disciples of Christ. He was named as president.

The Council on Christian Union (later the Association for the Promotion of Christian Unity and the Council on Christian Unity) had as its purpose the distribution of literature and the holding of conferences on uniting of Christians of all denominations. In 1911 Ainslie and R. A. Long founded the *Christian Union Quarterly*, which Ainslie edited for the rest of his life. He also authored a number of books on the council's themes such as *The Message of the Disciples for the Union of the Church* (1913); *If not a United Church—What?* (1920); and *The Scandal of Christianity* (1929) with H. C. Armstrong. He organized a number of conferences which he hoped would become the prelude to formal merger negotiations among the larger Protestant denominations. To show his own commitment to the union efforts, he led his own congregation

to begin the practice of open communion (the reception of the Lord's supper, traditionally limited to church members in Disciples' churches).

Ainslie did not limit his work for Christian unity to America. Beginning in 1914 he made a number of trips to Europe to attend conferences of Christian unity and in 1927 became an early member of the Christian Unity League for Equality and Brotherhood. Ainslie was also active in the early twentieth century peace movement. He opposed the appointment of chaplains during World War I and became a trustee of the Church Peace Union.

Ainslie married relatively late in life (1925) to Mary Elizabeth Weisel.

Sources:

Ainslie, Peter. *God and Me*. Baltimore: Temple Seminary Press, 1908. 47 pp.

_____. *If not a United Church—What?* New York: Fleming H. Revell Company, 1920. 132 pp.

_____. *The Message of the Disciples for the Union of the Church*. New York: Fleming H. Revell Comnpany, 1913. 212 pp.

_____. *Working with God*. St. Louis, MO: Christian Board of Publication, 1917. 383 pp.

_____, and H. C. Armstrong. *The Scandal of Christianity*. Chicago: Willett, Clark and Colby, 1929. 212 pp.

Dictionary of American Biography. 20 vols. and 7 supps. New York: Charles Scribner's Sons, 1928-1936, 1944-1981.

McAllister, Lester G., and William E. Tucker. *Journey in Faith*. St. Louis, MO: Bethany Press, 1975. 506 pp.

★16★
ALLEN, Asa Alonzo
Pentecostal Evangelist
b. Mar. 27, 1911, Sulfur Rock, Arkansas
d. Jun. 11, 1970, San Francisco, California

Asa Alonzo Allen made his mark as a Pentecostal healing evangelist, establishing the organization known today as Miracle Life Fellowship International. Born into a poor Arkansas family, Allen struggled with an alcoholic father, his own alcoholism, and brushes with the law. In 1934 he attended a Methodist revival meeting led by Nina DePriestes, was converted, and shortly thereafter married his wife, Lexia.

Allen soon left the Methodist Church, however, and in 1936 he was licensed to preach by the Assemblies of God (AOG). After a brief church pastorate, he began work as a traveling evangelist. This proved unsatisfying and did not result in marked success. In 1947 he again attempted pastoring a local church, this time in Corpus Christi, Texas. At about this time, he was seeking a healing ministry, and during a momentous personal prayer time, realized what he called the 13 requirements for such a ministry. He became convinced that if he truly believed in the Bible promises, he could do all that Jesus did and more.

Allen re-entered the traveling ministry about 1950, associating himself with **William Marrion Branham**'s "The Voice of Healing" ministry. In 1951 he bought a tent and began his crusade, appealing successfully to those who identified with his unsophisticated approach. His healings were often spectacular, and he soon had a following of sufficient strength to establish the A. A. Allen Revivals, headquartered in Dallas, Texas. His stature was further enhanced by the introduction of the Allen Revival Hour radio ministry.

Allen was arrested in 1955 for driving under the influence, which seemed to confirm rumors that he never had been able to escape alcoholism. The incident caused "The Voice of Healing" administrators to drop him and take back their ministerial credentials. Allen quickly regrouped, began *Miracle Magazine*, and in 1956 formed the Miracle Revival Fellowship, an association of several hundred independent ministers and congregations. In 1958 he was given 1,250 acres near Tombstone, Arizona, where he created a spiritual community called Miracle Valley, which became the location of the new headquarters. It included a Bible college, publishing house, radio and television studios, and a healing pool.

At this time Allen became a vocal critic of segregationism, and as early as 1960 held completely integrated revivals in both the South and the North. This stance, as well as a new emphasis on prosperity, increased his popularity with the black population, and Blacks were added to his evangelistic team. His large following forgave his 1967 divorce from Lexia.

Allen died in 1970, alone in a San Francisco hotel room. The media reported the cause of death as cirrhosis of the liver. An associate, Don Stewart, succeeded his leadership, renamed A. A. Allen Revivals the Don Stewart Association, renamed the Miracle Revival Fellowship the Miracle Life Fellowship International, and left Miracle Valley to establish new headquarters in Phoenix.

Sources:

Allen, Asa Alonzo. *Born to Lose, Bound to Win*. Garden City, NY: Doubleday & Co., 1970. 202 pp.

_____. *My Cross*. Miracle Valley, AZ: A. A. Allen Revivals, n.d. 95 pp.

_____. *Power to Get Wealth: How You Can Have It!* Miracle Valley, AZ: A. A. Allen Revivals, 1963. 63 pp.

_____. *The Price of God's Miracle Working Power*. Lamar, CO: A. A. Allen, 1950. 122 pp.

_____. *The Riches of the Gentiles Are Yours*. Miracle Valley, AZ: A. A. Allen Revivals, 1965. 43 pp.

_____. *Witchcraft, Wizards, and Witches*. Miracle Valley, Arizona: A. A. Allen Revivals, 1968. 92 pp.

Harrell, David Edwin, Jr. *All Things Are Possible*. Bloomington, IN: Indiana University Press, 1975. 304 pp.

Hedgepath, William. "He Feels, He Heals, and He Turns You On to God." *Look* 33 (October 7, 1969): 23-31.

Randi, James. *The Faith Healers*. New York: Prometheus Books, 1987. 314 pp.

Stewart, Don. *Man from Miracle Valley*. Long Beach, CA: Great Horizons Company, 1971. 236 pp.

—*Gary L. Ward*

★17★
ALLEN, Charles Livingston
Minister, United Methodist Church
b. Jun. 24, 1913, Newborn, Georgia

Charles Livingston Allen, a minister in the United Methodist Church who has become well known as the author of numerous popular religious books, is the son of John Robert and Lulu Frank Allen. He attended Young Harris Junior College (1930-1932) and Wofford College from which he received his A.B. in 1934. While there in 1933 he was received on trial in the North Georgia Conference of the Methodist Episcopal Church, South. In 1934 he married Leila Jane Haynes. He entered Emory University, from which he received his B.D. in 1937. While at Emory, in 1935, he was received in full connection with the North Georgia Conference and following graduation in 1937 was ordained an elder in the church. He had served several student charges through the years, but was assigned to Acworth, Georgia, as his first full-time pastoral charge. While he was at Acworth, the Methodist Episcopal Church, South, merged with the Methodist Episcopal Church to produce the Methodist Church (1939-1968).

Allen distinguished himself as a preacher at his next charges, Douglasville (1940-1944) and Thomas (1944-1948). While at Thomas he founded *Pulpit Preaching*, a homiletical magazine. In 1948 he was appointed to Grace Methodist Church, a prominent pulpit in Atlanta, Georgia. There, in the early 1950s, he became nationally known. He was heard on radio broadcasts soon after moving to Atlanta. In 1949 he was able to convince a local

to put his Sunday worship service on the air. That same year he began a column for *The Atlanta Journal* (later *The Atlanta Constitution*). The column and his sermons led to a series of popular books, most notably *Roads to Radiant Living* (1951); *God's Psychiatry* (1953); and *The Touch of the Master's Hand* (1956).

The ministry in Atlanta blossomed, and in 1960 Allen was called to First Methodist Church in Houston, Texas, the largest congregation in American Methodism. He continued his radio ministry and his writings through the next 23 years. Among his most memorable books during his years in Houston were *The Twenty-third Psalm: An Interpretation* (1961); *Healing Words* (1961); *The Lord's Prayer: An Interpretation* (1963); *Life More Abundant* (1968); and *The Secret of Abundant Living* (1968). He also issued an autobiographical volume, *What I Have Lived By: An Autobiography*, in 1976. In 1981 he was named the minister of the year by the Religious Heritage Association.

Allen remained at Houston until his retirement in 1983. He has continued to write and to do a weekly television show. Three times a year he travels to Israel to lecture.

Sources:

Allen, Charles L. *The Charles L. Allen Treasury*. Charles L. Wallis, ed. Old Tappan, NJ: Fleming H. Revell Company, 1970. 191 pp.

———. *God's Psychiatry*. Old Tappan, NJ: Fleming H. Revell Company, 1953. 159 pp.

———. *Healing Words*. Old Tappan, NJ: Fleming H. Revell Company, 1961. 159 pp.

———. *Prayer Changes Things*. Old Tappan, NJ: Fleming H. Revell Company, 1964. 128 pp.

———. *Roads to Radiant Living*. New York: Fleming H. Revell Company, 1951. 157 pp.

———. *The Secret of Abundant Living*. Old Tappan, NJ: Fleming H. Revell Company, 1980. 157 pp.

———. *What I Have Lived By: An Autobiography*. Old Tappan, NJ: Fleming H. Revell Company, 1976. 159 pp.

Howell, Clinton H., ed. *Prominent Personalities in Methodism*. Birmingham, AL: Lowrey Press, 1945. 512 pp.

Who's Who in the Methodist Church. Nashville, TN: Abingdon Press, 1966.

★ 18 ★
ALLIN, John Maury
Presiding Bishop, Episcopal Church
b. Apr. 22, 1921, Helena, Arkansas

John Maury Allin, a former presiding bishop of the Episcopal Church, is the son of Richard and Dora Harper Allin. He grew up in Helena and in his late teens entered the University of the South at Sewanee, Tennessee, from which he received both his B.A. (1943) and B.D. (1945) degrees. He was ordained a deacon in 1944 and a priest in 1945. His first assignment was as a priest at St. Peter's Episcopal Church in Conway, Arkansas. While there, in 1949 he married Frances Ann Kelly.

In 1950 Allin became the curate of St. Andrew's Church in New Orleans and also served as the Episcopal chaplain at Tulane University and at the other colleges in the area. In 1952 he became rector of Grace Church in Monroe, Louisiana, where he stayed for six years. In 1958 he moved to Vicksburg, Mississippi, as president of All Saints Episcopal Junior College. He was still at that post in 1961 when he was elected bishop coadjutor of the Diocese of Mississippi. He was consecrated at St. James Church in Jackson, Mississippi.

As a bishop in the 1960s in Mississippi, Allin emerged as a national figure, offering a tempered voice amid events that threatened to completely polarize the church and the citizens of the state. He became bishop of Mississippi in 1966 and led in the founding of the Committee of Concern, an interracial group dedicated to the rebuilding of black churches bombed or burned during the period of intense racial conflict. At the same time he served nationally as a member of the Commission on Ecumenical relations of the Episcopal Church.

Allin was elected the presiding bishop of the Episcopal Church in 1973 and took office in June 1974. He was immediately faced with the most divisive issue to hit the church in the twentieth century, the ordination of women. In July 1974, 11 women were ordained by four bishops operating without approval or authority from the general church. Allin had asked the bishops not to act in this irregular fashion, but his request was not heeded. After the ordination Allin stated that the bishops had exceeded their authority and that the women would not be allowed to function as priests. In 1975 four more women were ordained. Presiding over his first convention, Allin oversaw the convention's approval of the ordination and its agreement to officially allow female priests in the church.

Allin, still opposed to the ordination of women but accepting of the church's action, suffered through a split when several thousand conservatives met in St. Louis, Missouri, and began establishing a new church which followed traditional patterns barring women from the priesthood. At the same time the Polish National Catholic Church (PNCC) withdrew communion with the Episcopal Church. Allin led the church as calmly as possible through the troubled times, and became a rallying point for those who disagreed with the direction the church was going but refused to leave it. One problem he was unable to solve was that of the continuing declining membership, the church having lost several hundred thousand members during his tenure in office. He served as presiding bishop for 12 years and then moved into retirement. He was succeeded by **Edmond Lee Browning** in 1986.

Sources:

Buursma, Bruce. "Election is Episcopals' Crossroads." *Chicago Tribune* (September 9, 1985).

Hill, Samuel S., ed. *Encyclopedia of Religion in the South*. Macon, GA: Mercer University Press, 1984. 878 pp.

Plowman, Edward E. "The Episcopal Church: Women Are Winners." *Christianity Today* (October 8, 1976): 48-52.

★ 19 ★
ALLRED, Rulon Clark
Apostolic United Brethren
b. Mar. 29, 1906, Chihuahua Mexico
d. May 10, 1977, Murray, Utah

Rulon Clark Allred was the organizer and leader of a major polygamy-practicing, fundamentalist Mormon group in the mid-1950s. Allred was no stranger to life on the outskirts of society, as his father, Byron Harvey Allred, a former Speaker of the House for the state of Idaho, fled to Mexico in 1903 in order to maintain a polygamous lifestyle. Allred's father eventually became associated with Lorin Woolley, who founded the polygamist United Order Effort in 1929. It was in Mexico that Rulon was born—the second of ten children. Despite the fierce devotion of his father to polygamic practices, Allred grew up content to be a member of the Church of Jesus Christ of Latter-day Saints, which had long since given up polygamy. He moved to Los Angeles, got married, and attended a naturopathic medical college. It was not until 1933, when his father wrote a book in defense of polygamy and Allred took up the pen to refute his father's ideas, that he was ironically himself converted at the age of 27. This led to radical changes in his life, ranging from separation from his wife and his church to a drastic reduction of his chiropractic business.

Four years later the elder Allred died, and Rulon Allred moved to Salt Lake City, Utah, joining the United Order Effort group there, which was headed by John Barlow. Allred soon had a thriving medical practice, a large family, a number of wives, and a large home for religious meetings. On March 7, 1944, however, a crack-

down on polygamists resulted in Allred's arrest and conviction. After seven months in jail, Allred was released on parole, but realized he could not maintain monogamy. In 1947 he, like his father before him, fled to Mexico, this time to the sympathetic LeBaron family ranch. He returned to Utah in 1948, served a few weeks in prison for violating parole, and resumed participation in the United Order Effort.

In 1951 Barlow died, leaving the leadership to **Joseph White Musser,** who was not a popular choice, and dissension filled the ranks. Musser named Allred, a firm supporter, as one of the new ruling assistants, and when Musser died in 1954, Allred was his designated successor. The group, however, was in a shambles at this point, and Allred reorganized those who would follow him into the Apostolic United Order. This order included a group in Mexico led by Margarito Bautista.

Under Allred's leadership the group grew several-fold, gaining an established colony in Pinesdale, Montana. It incorporated in 1975 as "The Corporation of the Presiding Elder of the Apostolic United Brethren," usually known simply as the Apostolic United Brethren. Members saw themselves as the legitimate successors to the work of the Mormon founder **Joseph Smith, Jr.,** and not a party to the worldly concessions made by the Church of Jesus Christ of Latter-day Saints.

Divisive forces among the Mormon fundamentalists brought Allred's career to an untimely end. Brothers Joel and **Ervil LeBaron** had both begun their own fundamentalist groups, and Ervil yearned to have all other fundamentalists under his control. To that end, he killed **Joel LeBaron** in 1972. In 1977, after repeated threats, two women walked into Allred's chiropractor's office and shot him. Ervil was convicted of Allred's murder, and Allred was succeeded in his work by his brother Owen Allred.

Sources:
Allred, Rulon Clark. *Treasures of Knowledge.* 2 vols. Hamilton, MT: Bitterroot Publishing Company, 1981.
Anderson, J. Max. *The Polygamy Story: Fiction and Fact.* Salt Lake City, UT: Publishers Press, 1979. 166 pp.
Bradlee, Ben, Jr., and Dale Van Atta. *Prophet of Blood.* New York: Putnam, 1981. 350 pp.
LeBaron, Verlan M. *The LeBaron Story.* Lubbock, TX: The author, 1981. 316 pp.
The Most Holy Principle. 4 vols. Murray, UT: Gems Publishing Company, 1970-1975.
Van Wagoner, Richard S. *Mormon Polygamy.* Salt Lake City, UT: Signature Books, 1986. 307 pp.

—*Gary L. Ward*

★20★
Mother Mary AMADEUS OF THE HEART OF JESUS
Nun, Roman Catholic Church
b. Jul. 2, 1846, Akron, Ohio
d. 1920, Seattle, Washington

Mother Mary Amadeus of the Heart of Jesus, a nun of the Roman Catholic Church who pioneered the establishment of church institutions in the northwestern United States, was born Sarah Theresa Dunne. Early in life she entered a parochial school run by the Ursuline Order and in 1862 at the age of 16 received her habit. She lived among the sisters in Toledo, Ohio, and in 1874, though the youngest member of the community, was chosen to become the superior. Five years later Bishop Brondell, the first bishop of the new diocese of Helena (Montana), issued a call for assistance on the frontier. With the blessing of the bishop of Toledo, Mother Mary headed west and began work in the Yellowstone Valley, where a mission and chapel were established. She soon won the respect of the Indians among whom she worked because of the austere life she led.

Her work in Montana of two decades became a matter of conversation in Rome in 1900 when a conference called by Pope Leo XIII reorganized the far-flung Ursuline work. Mother Mary was named superior of the Montana mission and provincial. On her way back to her work from Rome, she was injured in an accident which left her permanently crippled. Her leadership was still needed by her order, however, and a few years later she was named the provincial of the North of the United States, with headquarters established in Middletown, New York. Among her first acts was to open a novitiate for the training of new order members.

In 1905 Mother Mary first sent members of the order to Alaska, and five years later, as the work grew, she was appointed provincial there. She moved to Alaska and over the next two years founded St. Ursula's-by-the-Sea mission, a convent, and St. Mary's mission. She also developed ministries to the Eskimos. She settled in Seattle in 1912 and opened a novitiate for the Alaska mission. The rest of her life was spent moving between Seattle and Alaska. She died in 1920 and was buried in Montana.

Sources:
Delaney, John J. *Dictionary of American Catholic Biography.* Garden City, NY: Doubleday & Company, 1988. 621 pp.

★21★
AMES, Edward Scribner
Philosopher, Christian Church (Disciples of Christ)
b. Apr. 21, 1870, Eau Claire, Wisconsin
d. Jun. 29, 1958, Chicago, Illinois

Edward Scribner Ames, religious philosopher and minister in the Christian Church (Disciples of Christ), was the son of Lucius Bowles and Adeline Scribner Ames. During young Edward's childhood, his father, a Disciples minister, held parishes in Iowa and Illinois, where Edward grew up. Contrary to the anti-intellectual bias in much of the church's life, Ames was given a love for education and in 1886 he entered Drake University. After completing both his B.A. (1889) and his M.A. (1891) he attended Yale Divinity School. He received his B.D. in 1892. He remained at Yale for two additional years of graduate work in philosophy, during which time he married Mabel Van Meter, whom he had met in college. Ames finished his formal education at the University of Chicago, where in 1895 he received the first Ph.D. granted by that institution in the field of philosophy.

Following his graduation, Ames took a post in philosophy for three years (1897-1900) at Butler College. He then returned to Chicago where he would spend the rest of his life in a joint role as educator and minister. First, he joined the faculty of the University of Chicago and soon emerged as one of the nation's outstanding philosophers of religion. His two major works during his 35-year tenure were *The Psychology of Religious Experience* (1910) and *Religion* (1929). He retired in 1935 as chairman of the philosophy department.

In 1900 he also became minister of the small University Church of the Disciples of Christ. He spent his weekends for the next four decades building the church into a substantial congregation and establishing its pulpit as a leading center in liberal Protestantism in the nation. Ames' active career spanned the decades of the fundamentalist-modernist controversy, and he was a major force in leading his denomination firmly into the modernist camp. He associated with the Campbell Institute, an association of modernist ministers, and for almost half a century (1903-1951) edited its periodical, *The Scroll.*

Ames' theological/philosophical speculations led him to view religion as a natural phenomena which emerged out of human experience (rather than being revealed directly by supernatural forces) and as such could be seen as progressing (evolving) from more primitive to more sophisticated forms. Christianity, of course, represented its highest expression, and Jesus is the embodiment of all of the best in religious life. Religion, in its highest form, is present-minded, with its emphasis not on the next life but on the very real demands of moral activity in the creation of a more just society. That moral life is undergirded by the sense of awe encountered in the infinite mystery of God.

Though it is difficult to separate his roles as minister and philosopher, during his very ministerial years he authored additional books (some collections of sermons and essays) more reflective of his pastoral work, including *The Divinity of Christ* (1911); *The Higher Individualism* (1915); *The New Orthodoxy* (1918); and *Letters to God and the Devil* (1933).

He retired from the University of Chicago in 1935, but not from his active life. In 1937 he began eight years as dean of the Disciples Divinity House, a seminary located near the university campus. Following his second retirement in 1945, he worked on his autobiography, *Beyond Theology*, which was published posthumously in 1959.

Sources:
Ames, Edward Scribner. *Beyond Theology*. Ed. by Van Meter Ames. Chicago: University of Chicago Press, 1959. 223 pp.
———. *The Divinity of Christ*. Chicago: The New Christian Century Co., 1911. 123 pp.
———. *The Higher Individualism*. Boston: Houghton Mifflin Co., 1915. 161 pp.
———. *Letters to God and the Devil*. New York: Harper & Row, 1933. 113 pp.
———. *The New Orthodoxy*. Chicago: University of Chicago Press, 1918. 127 pp.
———. *The Psychology of Religious Experience*. Boston: Houghton Mifflin Co., 1910. 427 pp.
———. *Religion*. New York: Henry Holt and Co., 1929. 324 pp.
Dictionary of American Biography. 20 vols. and 7 supps. New York: Charles Scribner's Sons, 1928-1936, 1944-1981.
Garrison, Winifred F. *Faith of the Free*. Chicago: Willett, Clark & Co., 1940.

★ 22 ★
Mataji AMRITANANDAMAYI
Founder, Mata Amritanandamayi Center
b. Sep. 27, 1953, India

Mataji Amritanandamayi is the founder of the Mata Amritanandamayi Center, and a spiritual teacher in the Hindu tradition. Born into a humble fisherman's family, she was named Sudhamani (pure jewel) by her parents. She was a devout worshiper of Krishna even as a young girl, often singing praises to the Lord at her family's shrine. Like many other Hindu religious figures, her search for illumination was a difficult one. While still a young girl she happened to overhear a group of devotees conversing about the *Bhagavad Gita*, the story of Krishna's conversation with Arjuna. She immediately went into a trance and "became" the Lord. A similar sort of transformation occurred later when she "became" Devi, the Divine Mother.

Until the late 1970s, Mataji was regarded as merely a trance medium (or a "channel"). Such mediums are a familiar part of the religious landscape in south India. Gradually, however, some people came to see her as a realized soul, and began to take her as their guru. Her father, who originally thought his daughter to be insane, eventually came to accept her spiritual status and gave her the family land as the basis for an *ashram* (a spiritual center and community). As of mid-1987, there were over 30 *brahmacharis* and *brahmacharinis* (renunciates) living at the ashram. The devotees adhere to a strict program of *sadhana* (spiritual practices), study, and service.

Devotion, particularly as it is expressed in the singing of *bhajans* (devotional songs), is the centerpiece of Mataji's teachings. When Amritanandamayi was younger, she would become lost in devo-

tional bliss, and people sometimes found her unconscious at the seaside. In 1987, she undertook a world tour, including a three-month journey through the United States, with stops in France and Switzerland. A Mata Amritanandamayi Center has been established in San Francisco.

Sources:
Amritanandamayi, Mata. *For My Children: Spiritual Teachings of Mata Amritanandamayi*. Kerala, India: Mata Amritanandamayi Mission, 1986. 139 pp.
Chaitayna, Bramacharya Amritatma. *Mata Amritanandamayi: Life and Experiences of Devotees*. Kerala, India: Mata Amritanandamayi Mission Trust, 1988. 308 pp.
"Holy Woman Brings the Mother Spirit to the West: Mataji, 35, of Kerala Inspires Thousands with Devotion and Vedantic Truths During USA Tour." *Hinduism Today* 9, 4 (July 1987): 1, 15.

—James R. Lewis

★ 23 ★
Shrii Shrii ANANDAMURTI
Founder, Ananda Marga Yoga Society
b. 1923, Jamalpur India

Shrii Shrii Anandamurti, born Prabhat Rainjan Sarkar, is the founder of the Ananda Marga Yoga Society, an organization that, like certain other modernist Hindu groups, represents a cross between a traditional Hindu contemplative order and a social action/social reform movement. Little data are available on his early life beyond the information that he was the eldest son of a railway accounts clerk, and that he had to cut short his formal education to go to work for the railway when his father died. His writings, however, reflect a broad fluency in vedanta philosophy as well as modern social and economic theory. In the tradition of Indian hagiography (idealizing or idolizing biography), his followers recount miraculous stories about his childhood, such as incidents in which he rode a tiger, spouted long scriptural passages, and knew details of distant events.

In 1955 Sarkar announced to his fellow railway workers that he had achieved enlightenment, and that he was forsaking his clerk's job in order to form a new spiritual movement. He founded Ananda ("bliss") Marga ("path"), and took the title/name Shrii Shrii Anandamurti. The new movement expanded rapidly, so that by the mid-1960s Anandamurti was addressing large rallies and gaining many followers. Margis, as adherents are called, practice a form of tantric yoga and engage in social work. The group sees itself as a fully integrated "social-spiritual organization." Until it began to be persecuted by the Indian government, Ananda Marga membership was estimated to be in the millions, and the group's social outreach had established over 400 schools and 250 children's homes.

In 1958, under his given name, Prabhat Rainjan Sarkar, Anandamurti founded Renaissance Universal, an organization devoted to the propagation of his social ideas, which he systematized as the Progressive Utilization Theory (Prout). Prout philosophy was seen as an alternative to both communism and the reigning Indian government. Over the years he has produced books advocating his social program even as he taught his yoga philosophy as a spiritual revitalization movement. Critics saw little difference between the two phases of his activity.

Stimulated by the extreme corruption of the Indian government, the group's social action program began to find expression in the political sphere, and candidates were run in the 1967 and 1969 elections. Ananda Marga's focus on political corruption evoked repression from the central government. A number of violent clashes occurred, including an incident in 1967 in which five margis were killed. In 1969 the government issued a ban on membership in Ananda Marga by any government employee, although this was eventually overturned in a court action.

The persecution of the movement peaked in 1971 when Anandamurti was arrested on the charge of ordering the murder of former adherents, a charge almost certainly fabricated by the Indian government. He was still in jail when Emergency Rule was declared in 1975. Ananda Marga was one of 26 organizations that were banned at that time. Many of its members were subsequently imprisoned, and all of its assets were seized. Following the end of Emergency Rule and the loss of office by Indira Gandhi, Anandamurti was released and the Indian branch of Ananda Marga reestablished.

Sources:

Anandamurti, Shrii Shrii. *Ananda Marga (Elementary Philosophy)*. Wichita, KS: Ananda Marga Yoga Society, 1967. 210 pp.

———. *Baba's Grace*. Los Altos Hills, CA: Ananda Marga Publications, 1973. 197 pp.

———. *The Great Universe*. Los Altos Hills, CA: Ananda Marga Publications, 1973. 271 pp.

———. *The Spiritual Philosophy of Shrii Shrii Anandamurti*. Denver, CO: Ananda Marga Publications, 1981. 261 pp.

Melton, J. Gordon. *The Encyclopedia of American Religions*. Detroit: Gale Research, 1989. 1100 pp.

Sarkar, P. R. *Idea and Ideology*. Calcutta, India: Ananda Marga Pracaraka Samgha, 1967. 112 pp.

Tadblavananda Avadhuta, Acharya. *Glimpses of PROUT Philosophy*. Copenhagen, Denmark: Central Proutists Publications, 1981. 204 pp.

—*James R. Lewis*

★ 24 ★
Metropolitan ANASTASSY
First Hierarch, Russian Orthodox Church Outside of Russia
b. Aug. 6, 1873, Russia
d. May 9, 1965, New York, New York

Metropolitan Anastassy, first hierarch of the Russian Orthodox Church Outside of Russia, was the son of Fr. Alexis Gribbanovsky, a Russian Orthodox priest. He attended the church's seminary at Tombov, Russia, and then studied at the Moscow Theological Academy. Following his graduation he was ordained. Deciding not to marry, he was tonsured as a monk, at which time he took the name Anastassy. In 1898 he was elevated to the rank of hierodeacon and then hieromonk. He became an assistant inspector at the Moscow Academy and was shortly thereafter raised to the rank of archimandrite. In 1901 he became rector of the Moscow Theological Academy.

Anastassy was selected to the office of bishop in 1906 and consecrated as bishop of Serpukhov and vicar of the metropolitan of Moscow. In 1914 he was appointed bishop of Holmsk and Lublyan and the following year bishop of Kishinev and Hotin. In the sobor (a gathering of church leaders) of 1917-1918 he was considered for the office of patriarch, which was reinstituted at that time. Assigned as head of the church's mission in Constantinople, he was not in Russia in the 1920s when Russian church leaders outside of the Soviet Union organized provisionally in the face of what they saw as control of their church by an atheist government. From 1924 to 1935, Anastassy served as head of the church in Jerusalem.

In 1935 Metropolitan Anthony retired, and Anastassy was elected as the new First Hierarch of the Russian Orthodox Church Outside of Russia. He consequently moved to the church's headquarters in Yugoslavia. At the end of World War II, Metropolitan Anastassy decided to move the headquarters of the church farther away from territory controlled by the Soviet Army. Headquarters were moved first to Vienna, Austria; then Munich, Germany; and finally in 1950 to the United States.

During his years of leadership, Anastassy was primarily concerned with stabilizing the worldwide church over which he had jurisdiction. In the United States, the Russian Church was undergoing new upheavals as it adjusted to postwar changes in the Soviet Union. Anastassy led all-church sobors in 1952, 1953, 1956, 1959, 1962, and 1964. Each of these strove to preserve the traditional pattern of Russian Orthodox church life while specifically opposing the movements of both the Russian Orthodox Greek Catholic Church in America (the largest of the several Russian Orthodox factions, now known as the Orthodox Church in America) and the smaller body of parishes which had placed themselves directly under the patriarch of Moscow in 1950.

Following Anastassy's death in 1965, he was succeeded by **Metropolitan Philaret**.

Sources:

Who Was Who in America. Chicago: Marquis Who's Who, Inc.

★ 25 ★
ANDERSON, Charles Palmerston
Presiding Bishop, Episcopal Church
b. Sep. 8, 1864, Kemptville Canada
d. Jan. 30, 1930, Chicago, Illinois

Charles Palmerston Anderson, the seventeenth presiding bishop of the Episcopal Church, was the son of Henry and Maria S. Anderson. Raised in Canada, he attended Trinity College School in Port Huron, Ontario. He was ordained a deacon in the Church of England in Canada in 1887 and a priest in 1888. He was assigned to the Anglican church at Beachburg, Canada. While there he married Janet Glass in 1889. In 1891 Anderson moved to the United States and transferred into the Episcopal Church. He was named pastor of Grace Episcopal Church in Oak Park, Illinois.

Grace Church became Anderson's last parish as in 1900 he was elected suffragan bishop of Chicago. He became bishop of Chicago a few years later. Anderson had an immediate impact upon his diocese and the church throughout the Midwest through his attention to Western Theological Seminary in Chicago (now Seabury-Western Theological Seminary in Evanston, Illinois). The school had suffocated under the previous bishop who had allowed it to dwindle and finally close in 1904. Anderson moved to reopen the school immediately and began to build its faculty with capable scholars. By the end of the decade it was a flourishing institution.

Anderson's most lasting contribution as a leader was within the emerging ecumenical movement. In 1910, as a direct result of the impact of the World Missionary Conference held in Edinburgh, Scotland, a resolution was introduced into the general convention of the Episcopal Church to establish a joint commission to plan a conference of all Christian churches on questions of faith and order (beliefs and polity). Anderson was named as chairman of the commission. With the support of a number of American denominations secured, in 1912 he headed an American delegation to meet with the leaders of the Church of England, the Episcopal Church of Scotland, and the Church of Ireland to secure their support. The progress toward creating the proposed conference was stymied by the beginning of World War I, but in the midst of the war Anderson chaired a gathering of the American representatives at Garden City, New York, which first began work on the decisive questions that Faith and Order conferences would later have to tackle. In 1919, as soon as the war ended, Anderson led a delegation to Europe that centered its attention upon the Roman Catholic and Eastern Orthodox churches. By 1920, under Anderson's leadership, the movement toward a continuing dialogue on Faith and Order had been given both a broad ecumenical and international base.

Anderson's career in the church climaxed in 1929 with his election as presiding bishop of the Episcopal Church following the death of John Gardner Murray on November 3. Unfortunately, Anderson had no time to enjoy his new position as he died less than four months later.

Sources:

Anderson, Charles P. *Letters to Laymen*. Milwaukee, WI: Young Church-man Co., 1913. 120 pp.

_____. *Religion and Morality*. Milwaukee, WI: Morehouse Pub. Co., 1924. 50 pp.

_____. *The Religion of Our Lord*. N.p., n.d., 1923.

Cavert, Samuel McCrea. *The American Churches in the Ecumenical Movement, 1900-1968*. New York: Association Press, 1968. 288 pp.

DeMille, George E. *The Episcopal Church Since 1900*. New York: More-house-Gorham Company, 1955. 223 pp.

Rouse, Ruth and Stephen Charles Neill, eds. *A History of the Ecumenical Movement, 1517-1948*. Philadelphia: Westminster Press, 1954. 822 pp.

★ 26 ★
ANDERSON, Victor H.
Cofounder, Faery Wicca Tradition
b. 1917, New Mexico

Victor H. Anderson is co-founder (with his wife, Cora Anderson) of the Faery Wicca Tradition, an important disseminator of witch-craft on the West Coast of the United States. Shortly after his birth, his family moved to Oregon, where he claims that at the age of nine he encountered and was initiated into witchcraft by a group of witches who called themselves faeries. This coven, which consist-ed of people from the American South, existed before witchcraft and Paganism became a popular movement. The group empha-sized harmony with nature, magic, celebration, music, and danc-ing.

In 1950 Anderson married Cora, an Alabamian whose family practiced folk magic. They settled in the Bay Area of California. In 1960 Anderson published a book of Pagan poems, *Thorns of the Blood Rose*, which brought him to the attention of the emerging Neo-Pagan Movement. Among his first initiates was Thomas De-Long, who as a Pagan priest became well known as Gwydion Pendderwen. He had been a friend of the Anderson's son, and to-gether they assembled the materials which constituted the Faery Tradition. Through Pendderwen, materials from the Alexandrian Wicca Tradition (the tradition started by Alexander Sanders) were incorporated into the Faery Tradition.

Over the years Anderson has worked quietly and has never gained a large following. He has, however, trained a number of people who have moved on to take important leadership roles in the larger Neo-Pagan movement, including **Alison Harlow**, Vale-rie Voigt, Aidan A. Kelly, **Michael Thorn**, and **Starhawk**. Starhawk presented many of the teachings she received from Anderson in her best-selling book, *The Spiral Dance* (1979).

Sources:

Anderson, Victor H. *Thorns of the Blood Rose*. Privately published, 1960. Rpt. Redwood Valley, CA: Nemeton, 1970. 106 pp.

Guiley, Rosemary E. *Encyclopedia of Witchcraft & Witches*. New York: Facts on File, 1989. 400 pp.

Starhawk. *The Spiral Dance*. San Francisco: Harper & Row, 1979. 218 pp.

★ 27 ★
Brother ANDRE
Mystic and Healer, Roman Catholic Church
b. Aug. 9, 1845, St. Gregoire d'Iberville, Quebec, Canada
d. Jan. 6, 1937, Montreal, Quebec, Canada

Brother Andre, known for the many miracles which occurred at the shrine to St. Joseph that he erected in Montreal, was born Al-fred Bessette, to Clothilde Foisy and Isaac Bessette, a French Cath-olic couple. Bessette was raised in a pious environment, and even as a youth was known to spend much of his free time at the local church in prayer. The elder Bessette, a poor carpenter, died when Andre was five years old, and his mother followed seven years later. He went to live with his uncle, who apprenticed him to a cob-bler and then a baker. Bessette grew up without learning to read or write, and when his uncle left for California in 1860, Bessette

went to work as a farmhand. He spent three years during the Amer-ican Civil War in New England.

Returning to Canada, Bessette settled at Saint Cesaire and ap-plied for admission to the Congregation of the Holy Cross. He as-sumed the habit in 1870. He was sent to the Hotel Bellvue, a center for Holy Cross brothers in Montreal. In 1871 he moved to Saint Laurent. In 1872 he was at first denied the privilege to take his tem-porary vows because of his poor health, but with the intercession of Bp. Ignace Bourget, he was allowed to assume his vows in Au-gust of that year. He made his final profession two years later. In 1881 he moved to the new College of Notre-Dame-du-Sacre-Coeur (Our Lady of the Sacred Heart) in Montreal. He became the porter and was assigned a small cell in which to live. There he re-sided and worked for the next 40 years as an obscure member of the order. He became noticed by the other brothers for his great piety and devotion to St. Joseph, to whom the order was dedicat-ed.

In 1896 the order acquired land on Mount Royal near the col-lege. Brother Andre had already dreamed of erecting a shrine to St. Joseph on the sight and within a few weeks had carried a statue to the crest of the hill. The next year a first building was erected, and over the following years regular improvements were added. In 1904 he received permission to build a small shrine with $200 that had been collected, and a small chapel was erected. Within a short time cures were reported in association with Brother Andre and the shrine. In 1909 the Confraternity of St. Joseph at the Orato-ry was formed to assist in the development of the shrine. An official inquiry began in 1910 and reported favorably the following year. In 1912 a periodical was begun, and a nave built to the chapel. Brother Andre had a room under the belfry. The shrine increasingly became a site for pilgrimage, and it is estimated that over the re-maining years of Brother Andre's life over three million pilgrims vis-ited the place. Most importantly, many were healed of their physi-cal ailments due to, according to Brother Andre, the power of God working through St. Joseph.

Following his death in 1937, Brother Andre's body lay in state for five days, and an estimated half million people visited the shrine during this period. Today the shrine remains an important site for pilgrimage for members of the Roman Catholic Church and others and has retained its reputation as a Canadian Lourdes.

Sources:

Burton, Katherine. *Brother Andre of Mount Royal*. Notre Dame, IN: Ave Maria Press, 1943. 310 pp.

Hatch, Alden. *The Miracle of the Mountain*. New York: Hawthorn Books, 1959. 223 pp.

Wallace, W. Stewart. *The Macmillan Dictionary of Canadian Biography*. 4th ed., rev. Edited by W. A. McKay. Toronto: Macmillan of Canada, 1978.

★ 28 ★
ANDREADES, Michael G.
Priest, Russian Orthodox Church
b. Aug. 21, 1874, Constantinople Turkey
d. 1959, New Jersey

Michael G. Andreades, a Russian Orthodox priest who served outstandingly in the American mission, was also a pioneer priest in the development of Greek Orthodoxy in the early twentieth cen-tury. Born in Constantinople, the resident community of the Ortho-dox Church's leader, the Ecumenical Patriarch, Andreades grew up in a Greek family but received Russian training. As a teenager he was sent to a seminary school in the Crimea in Russia; he returned for further schooling in Constantinople in 1890. In 1895 he began five years of advanced theological work at the academy in St. Pe-tersburg. In 1901 he was ordained as a deacon and served as the deacon and instructor at the Greek parish of St. John the Forerunner in Kerch, Crimea. He then served two years at a Greek-Russian School in the Crimea.

In 1905 Andreades moved to San Francisco to serve the church in America. **Archbishop Tikhon** ordained him and after a brief stay in Scranton, Pennsylvania, Andreades began a decade of work in Seattle and Wilkeson, Washington. He also served briefly in Simpson, Pennsylvania, and Galveston, Texas. During this time he held administrative positions in the Russian Archdiocese as dean of the Russian-Serbian parishes on the West Coast (1909-1912), dean of the parishes in Alaska (1912-1916), and dean of the parishes in the Southern United States (1916-1918). Most of the parishes under Andreades supervision included people from a variety of national and ethnic backgrounds.

The Russian Revolution changed many facets of Andreades' life. The Revolution stopped the financial support that the church received from Russia, and resulted in most of the predominantly Greek-American parishes breaking off to form a Greek diocesan structure. In 1918 Andreades petitioned to be released to the newly created Greek Diocese of America. He came under the jurisdiction of Metropolitan Meletios Metaxakis. Just three years earlier he had completed an extensive report on the situation of the Greek parishes for the head of the Russian Orthodox Church in America.

Andreades thus began a second outstanding career as a Greek priest, serving parishes in Houston, Texas (1918-1919); Charleston, South Carolina (1919-1920); Savannah, Georgia (1920-1923); Lowell, Massachusetts (1924); Atlanta, Georgia (1924-1925); New York, New York (1925-1928); Newark, New Jersey (1929); Orange, New Jersey (1929-1932); Baltimore, Maryland (1932-1935); and Jamaica, New York (1935-1949). During the 1920s, when the church was experiencing schisms, he championed the cause of church unity in the parishes in the southern United States. He retired to New Jersey in 1949 at the age of 77.

Sources:

Tarasar, Constance J. *Orthodox America, 1794-1976: Development of the Orthodox Church in America.* Syosset, NY: The Orthodox Church in America, Department of History and Archives, 1975. 352 pp.

★ 29 ★
ANDREWS, Lynn V.
New Age Author and Teacher
b. 1945

Lynn V. Andrews is an author, teacher, and medicine woman who is a popular figure in New Age circles. In spite of the publication of many autobiographical accounts, few details of her early life are available for public scrutiny. Like Carlos Casteneda, whose writings have been one of the principal sources of inspiration for her productions, Andrews has left much of her personal background obscure.

By her own account, Andrews was a collector of Indian art who, in 1978, began a quest for personal spirit guides. In the course of a search for a mysterious Cree Indian marriage basket, she met two women, Agnes Whistling Elk and Ruby Plenty Chiefs, who became her teachers and guides. Across the course of several best-selling books, Andrews underwent a series of fantastic adventures until she was initiated into the Sisterhood of the Shields, an ancient, secret organization which commissioned her to reveal the sisterhood's teachings to the outside world. (In the past, the sisterhood was limited to Native Americans but, according to Andrews, because of certain planetary "energy changes," it became necessary to initiate women of other races.) In addition to her books, she has been holding seminars in which this knowledge is shared. Her teachings represent a syncretistic blend of elements drawn from several Native American tribes, as well as a certain interpretive framework which has its roots in the tradition of Angloamerican ro-

manticizing about American Indian spirituality (a tradition that has been revived and revitalized within the New Age subculture).

In recent years, Andrews' claim that the events related in her books represent a true story has become controversial. Not only scholars and Native Americans, but people within the New Age community have challenged the authenticity of her claim. Allegations of fabricated characters, ghost-written texts, and misrepresentations of traditional cultures have been the most persistent criticisms leveled against Andrews—allegations reminiscent of similar criticisms leveled against the earlier work of Carlos Casteneda. Her many writings include *Medicine Woman* (1981); *Flight of the Seventh Moon* (1984); *Jaguar Woman* (1985); *Star Woman* (1986); and *Teachings Around the Sacred Wheel* (1990).

Sources:

Andrews, Lynn. *Crystal Woman.* New York: Warner Books, 1987. 269 pp.
_____. *Flight of the Seventh Moon.* San Francisco: Harper & Row, 1984. 203 pp.
_____. *Jaguar Woman.* San Francisco: Harper & Row, 1985. 194 pp.
_____. *Medicine Woman.* New York: Harper & Row, 1981. 204 pp.
_____. *Star Woman.* New York: Warner Books, 1986. 246 pp.
_____. *Windhorse Woman.* New York: Warner Books, 1989. 210 pp.
Jonathan, Adolph and Richard Smoley, "Beverly Hills Shaman," *New Age Journal* (March/April 1989).
Melton, J. Gordon. *New Age Encyclopedia.* Detroit: Gale Research Inc., 1990. 586 pp.

—*James R. Lewis*

★ 30 ★
ANGLEY, Ernest
Independent Television Evangelist
b. 1921, Gastonia, North Carolina

Ernest Angley, popular television evangelist and founder of Grace Cathedral in Akron, Ohio, is the son of a devout Baptist textile worker. Although Angley attended church regularly as a child, he did not have a deep religious experience until his conversion at the age of 18. He then deserted the Baptist faith and became a Pentecostal. In response to a call to preach, he left North Carolina in 1941 for Cleveland, Tennessee, to study at the Church of God Bible Training School (now Lee College). He and his wife, Esther Lee "Angel" Sykes, preached as evangelists with the Church of God (Cleveland, Tennessee) throughout the South. At some point during the next decade, however, they became independent. Angley centered his message increasingly around healing after he was told by God to exercise the gift.

In 1952 Angley formed the Healing Stripes Evangelistic Association (a name based upon Isaiah 53:5, seen as a prophetic reference to Jesus, ". . .by his stripes we are healed"). Two years later he moved to Akron, Ohio, where he pursued his ministry while working in the city's expanding rubber industry. He attracted many to his preaching during the next few years, and in 1957 he was able to build a large tabernacle. In 1958 he integrated all of his now independent work under the church's new name, Grace Cathedral. About this same time he began a magazine, *The Power of the Holy Ghost*. Angley stayed in Akron most of the time until his wife's death in 1970. Since then he has actively toured the country conducting revival campaigns, using Akron as his base of operations.

As his evangelical work grew on a national level, Angley formed Ernest Angley Ministries as a network of supporters. He also developed a weekly television show centered around his revival meetings.

Angley has claimed special supernatural powers for his ministry; he teaches, as the title of one of his books proclaims, that *Faith in God Can Heal the Sick*. His promotion of a healing ministry has led to trouble on two occasions, when individuals died in his services. The first episode occurred in North Carolina, the second in

Germany in 1984. The latter incident led to a brief imprisonment, and became the subject of Angley's book, *Cell 15*. While many have expressed their lack of appreciation for Angley's distinctive speech patterns (which have frequently been parodied by comedians), he has attracted little serious controversy. Even James Randi, the self-proclaimed nemesis of clergymen with healing ministries, has pronounced Angley to be sincere and has not leveled any complaints concerning Angley's financial affairs.

Sources:

Angley, Ernest W. *Cell 15*. Akron, OH: Winston Press, 1984. 109 pp.
———. *Faith in God Heals the Sick*. Akron, OH: Winston Press, 1983. 78 pp.
———. *Miracles Are Real—I Got One!* Greensburg, PA: Manna Christian Outreach, 1975. 96 pp.
———. *Raptured*. Old Tappan, NJ: Fleming H. Revell, 1950. 247 pp.
Burgess, Stanley M., Gary B. McGee, and Patrick H. Alexander, eds. *Dictionary of Pentecostal and Charismatic Movements*. Grand Rapids, MI: Regency Reference Library, Zondervan Publishing House, 1988. 914 pp.
Simms, Patsy. *Can Somebody Shout Amen!* New York: St. Martin's Press, 1988. 234 pp.

★31★
AQUINO, Michael A.
Founder, Temple of Set
b. Oct. 16, 1946, San Francisco, California

Michael A. Aquino, founder of the Temple of Set, is currently a lieutenant colonel in the U.S. Army. A precocious youth, he became national commander of the Eagle Scouts Honor Society. Following his earning a B.A. (1968) in political science at the University of California—Santa Barbara, he became an Army officer specializing in psychological warfare. In 1969 he met **Anton S. LaVey** and joined the Church of Satan. Soon afterwards, he did a tour of duty in Vietnam. In 1971 he returned to the United States and was stationed in Kentucky. He was ordained as a Satanic priest and organized a grotto in his home. He quickly rose to prominence in the church and frequently contributed to its magazine, *The Cloven Hoof*.

However, Aquino had become dissatisfied with both the organizational control wielded by LaVey and his atheistic brand of Satanism (which actually denied the existence of Satan). In 1972 Aquino resigned and was soon joined by Lilith Sinclair and a number of others. In 1975 Aquino sought a new mandate to carry on the work of the Church of Satan by invoking His Infernal Majesty. Satan reportedly responded by appearing in the form of Set, the ancient Egyptian diety; giving to Aquino a document, *The Book of Coming Forth by Night*; and authorizing Aquino to found the Temple of Set to supercede the Church of Satan.

Aquino set the goal of the Temple of Set as awakening the divine power of the individual through the deliberate exercise of will and intelligence. The process by which the conscious evolution is accomplished is referred to as Xeper. For the most part, "Setians" work individually on their personal evolution, although they can form groups (pylons) and occasionally attend larger gatherings (conclaves). Teaching is carried out primarily by means of correspondence.

Meanwhile, Aquino returned to school and received his M.A. (1976) and Ph.D. (1980) degrees, also from the University of California—Santa Barbara, and has subsequently continued in his Army career. He also married Lilith Sinclair.

In the wake of the public hysteria over Satanism during the 1980s, it was perhaps natural that Aquino and the temple would become targets of less-than-reflective criticism. Sensationalistic, and almost invariably fabricated tales of abuse in Satanic cults led to the Temple of Set being tarred with the same brush. The one specific allegation to be made against Aquino was that he had been molesting children at the child care center in the San Francisco Pre-

sidio. This ungrounded criticism has been widely repeated while the actual facts of the case, that after a careful investigation the incident was traced to another Army officer and Aquino was completely exonerated, have received comparatively little attention.

Sources:

Aquino, Michael A. *The Church of Satan*. N.p.: The Author, 1989. 802 pp.
Lyons, Arthur. *Satan Wants You*. New York: The Mysterious Press, 1988. 192 pp.

★32★
ARMSTRONG, Annie Walker
Corresponding Secretary, Woman's Missionary Union, Southern Baptist Convention
b. Jul. 11, 1850, Baltimore, Maryland
d. Dec. 20, 1938, Baltimore, Maryland

Annie Walker Armstrong, cofounder and first corresponding secretary of the Woman's Missionary Union (WMU) of the Southern Baptist Convention, was the daughter of James Dunn, who died when she was two, and Mary Walker Armstrong. The family was well off, their money having been made in tobacco. While her mother was a strong churchwoman, Annie did not become a Christian until she was 20. Her mother was an original member of the Woman's Mission to Woman, the early Southern Baptist women's missionary group, in the 1870s. It was not until Annie saw the need for an increased effort to aid a school for American Indians that she got involved.

Once involved, however, Armstrong gave the effort her full attention. In 1886 a group of Maryland Baptist pastors decided to publish some literature to inform the convention of the missionary programs and opportunities. They asked the women to help. Armstrong became secretary and editor-in-chief of the Maryland Baptist Mission Rooms. She quickly built it into a major publisher of missionary material. In 1887 she met with the women who attended the 1887 Southern Baptist Convention and chaired the 1888 meeting, at which the Woman's Missionary Union was organized. **Martha E. McIntosh**, whose interest lay primarily in foreign missions, was elected president, while Armstrong, whose primary interest was in home missions, became corresponding secretary. She offered her office in Baltimore as union headquarters. She also recruited her sister Alice, to assist her as a writer. Since she was independently wealthy, she was able to do her work without salary.

During the next few years, Armstrong accomplished a number of tasks that aided not only the missionary cause, but also the development of the whole convention. She compiled the first mailing list of convention pastors and churches. She supplied the Sunday school board with a list of Sunday school superintendents and launched it on its statistic-gathering program. Through her correspondence with missionaries and frontier pastors she became one of the most well informed persons on the state of the church in both the home and foreign field. She also started a number of missionary efforts, especially among ethnic minorities, that were later taken over by the convention.

Armstrong did not like to travel, but she did when the need arose. She made several trips to Oklahoma to meet with and preach to the Indians, though she always refused to speak to mixed audiences, appearing only before women's groups. She used her experience to assist organizational efforts by the missionaries, who were in constant need of supplies.

Armstrong had an ideal of womanhood and propriety that led her into conflict with other women leaders. She strongly opposed the establishment of a women's training school by the Woman's Missionary Union, and in the face of intense criticism resigned in 1905. She remained at her post for one more year until the women found a replacement for her. In 1906, however, she closed the Maryland office and turned the work over to a group of volunteers.

She remained active in missionary work locally, but only occasionally appeared at national gatherings. The convention remembered her valued years of service, which did so much for their early missionary endeavors, and in 1934 they named the annual home mission's offering after her.

In her later years, Armstrong's health failed and she became confined to her apartment. She was bedridden during her last two years. She died shortly after the union she had helped found celebrated its 50th anniversary.

Sources:

Allen, Catherine. *Laborers Together with God*. Birmingham, AL: Women's Missionary Union, 1987. 246 pp.

Encyclopedia of Southern Baptists. 3 vols. Nashville, TN: Broadman Press, 1958, 1971.

★ 33 ★
ARMSTRONG, Garner Ted
Founder, Church of God International
b. Feb. 9, 1930, Portland, Oregon

Garner Ted Armstrong, the founder of the Church of God International, is the son of Loma Dillon and **Herbert W. Armstrong**. He was only four years old when his father founded the Radio Church of God (after 1968, the Worldwide Church of God). He grew up in Eugene, Oregon, where the church was headquartered. Shortly after his graduation from high school, his family moved to Pasadena, California, where the headquarters was being relocated. In 1948 he enlisted in the Navy in which he served four years. Slow to accept his father's unique teachings which included a belief in sabbatarianism (Saturday worship), the keeping of the annual Jewish feasts, and his father's apostleship, he nevertheless enrolled in the church's school, Ambassador College. In 1953 he married Shirley Hammer. During his college days he had a religious conversion and was finally baptized in the church.

Armstrong was ordained as a minister in 1955. He began writing articles for *The Plain Truth* (many of which later became booklets published by the church), the church's magazine, and speaking on the radio show, "The World Tomorrow." In 1958 he was named vice-president of the college and the church. Increasingly he became the public spokesperson for the church and, after 1906, the public image on television.

In 1971 Armstrong was accused of sexual misconduct and his marriage was in danger of coming apart. He was relieved of duties, reinstated, and again relieved of duties. The ongoing relationship led to considerable turmoil in the church until 1978 when a final break occurred. Armstrong left Pasadena and settled in Tyler, Texas. He founded the Church of God International and the Garner Ted Armstrong Evangelistic Association. Within a few months he was back on the radio and began forming congregations around a contingent of former Worldwide Church of God members who left with him.

Armstrong continued the main teaching of the Worldwide Church of God but developed a looser organizational structure and was somewhat more open on financial matters. He has devoted a considerable amount of time to rebuilding his support through his radio program and regularly travels to speak to congregations around the country. He has continued to write and has authored a number of books and booklets on behalf of the Church of God International. His most substantial book was *The Real Jesus* (1977), which was originally released through a commercial publishing house, but has been reprinted by the church. He has also written a new book on the church's most distinctive teaching, *Europe and America in Prophecy*, a discussion of the idea that the modern Anglo-Saxon peoples are the literal descendants of the ancient Israelites. Armstrong has continued the policy established by his father

of giving away his booklets and tapes of his talks to all who request them.

Sources:

Armstrong, Garner Ted. *The Answer to Unanswered Prayer*. Tyler, TX: Church of God International, 1989. 158 pp.

———. *Europe and America in Prophecy*. [Tyler, TX]: Church of God International, n.d. 165 pp.

———. *Facts You Should Know about Christmas!*. Tyler, TX: Church of God International, 1981. 24 pp.

———. *The Real Jesus*. Mission, KS: Sheed Andrews & McMeel, 1977. Rept.: New York: Avon, 1979. 310 pp.

———. *The Ten Commandments*. Tyler, TX: Church of God International, 1981. 85 pp.

★ 34 ★
ARMSTRONG, Herbert W.
Founder and Apostle, Worldwide Church of God
b. Jul. 31, 1892, Des Moines, Iowa
d. Jan. 16, 1986, Pasadena, California

Herbert W. Armstrong, the founder of the Worldwide Church of God, was the son of Horace and Eva Armstrong. He was given no middle name, but later added the "W." to his name. From an old Quaker family, he was raised in the Society of Friends. He dropped out of high school at the end of his sophomore year and went to work in advertising at the local newspaper. He held a number of jobs over the next few years until 1915 when he moved to Chicago and opened an advertising business. In 1917 he married Loma Dillon. His business failed in the early 1920s, and in 1924 he moved to Oregon. In Salem, his wife met Ira Runcorn, a Bible student who convinced her that the Sabbath (Saturday) is the correct day for worship. His wife's new opinions led Armstrong to consider not only sabbatarianism (worship on Saturday) but other religious issues such as evolution and baptism. As a result, he became a member, and then in 1931 was ordained as a minister, of the Oregon Conference of the Church of God. He also became a believer in British-Israelism, the idea that the modern Anglo-Saxon peoples are the literal descendants of the ten lost tribes of ancient Israel. Finally, he came to accept the necessity of observing the Jewish feasts as described in the Old Testament.

In 1934 Armstrong began an independent ministry, the Radio Church of God. He was able to secure time on a radio station in Eugene, Oregon, and began a periodical, *The Plain Truth*. The work grew slowly until several key events pushed him into prominence. Following World War II, he moved his headquarters to Pasadena, California, where in 1947 he opened Ambassador College. The rate of growth increased and work began in England in 1953. In 1960 a television ministry was added, and during the decade the circulation of *The Plain Truth* reached over a million. The church developed a following across North America, the Caribbean, Europe, Australia, New Zealand, and South Africa. In the midst of the growth, Loma Armstrong died in 1967.

In 1968, Armstrong changed the church's name to Worldwide Church of God. The spectacular growth, which continued into the 1970s, was halted in the mid-1970s due to a scandal that led to the removal of Armstrong's son **Garner Ted Armstrong** as the public spokesperson for the church and his founding a rival organization, the Church of God International, in 1978. His leaving was followed by a major lawsuit which tied up church resources for several years, and the defection of leading members, several of whom, such as Marion J. McNair and David Robinson, wrote expose type books attacking Armstrong and the church. Meanwhile, In 1977 Armstrong married Ramona Martin. They were divorced in 1984. By the time of his death in 1986, most of the controversy had died, though strong opposition to the church remained. He was succeeded by **Joseph W. Tkach**, the present pastor general of the church.

Over the years Armstrong authored several books and booklets, many beginning as articles in *The Plain Truth* and going through multiple editions as new material was added or changes made in the text. His key doctrinal book was entitled *The United States and Britain in Prophecy*. The most substantial was his *Autobiography* which, in its more recent editions, reached over 1300 pages. Part of the key to the church's success was Armstrong's policy of giving away all its publications, including its magazine, books, and correspondence course, to any who asked for them.

Sources:

Armstrong, Herbert W. *Autobiography*. 2 vols. Pasadena, CA: Worldwide Church of God, 1986-1987.

_____. *The Missing Dimension in Sex*. Pasadena, CA: Worldwide Church of God, 1981. 214 pp.

_____. *Mystery of the Ages*. Pasadena, CA: Worldwide Church of God, 1985. 315 pp.

_____. *Tomorrow. . .What Will It Be Like?* New York: Everest House, 1979. 110 pp.

_____. *The United States and Britain in Prophecy*. Pasadena, CA: Worldwide Church of God, 1980. 192 pp.

Hopkins, Joseph. *The Armstrong Empire: A Look at the Worldwide Church of God*. Grand Rapids, MI: William B. Eerdmans Publishing Company, 1974. 304 pp.

McNair, Marion J. *Armstrongism: Religion. . .or Rip-off*. Orlando, FL: Pacific Charters—Publishing Division, 1977. 339 pp.

Robinson, David. *Herbert Armstrong's Tangled Web*. Tulsa, OK: John Hadden Publishers, 1980. 268 pp.

★ 35 ★
ARNETT JR., Benjamin William
Bishop, African Methodist Episcopal Church
b. Mar. 6, 1838, Brownsville, Pennsylvania
d. Oct. 9, 1906, Wilberforce, Ohio

Benjamin William Arnett, Jr., the 17th bishop of the African Methodist Episcopal Church, was the son of Benjamin William Arnett, Sr., an active layman in the African Methodist Episcopal Church in Ohio. Arnett joined the African Methodist Episcopal Church as a teenager, a few weeks before his 18th birthday. The month he turned 20, he was forced to have his leg amputated because of a tumor. Later that year he married Mary Louisa Gordon. Though he did not attend college, he educated himself. In 1863 he was granted a teacher's certificate and became the only black school teacher in Fayette County, Pennsylvania. In 1864 he moved to Washington, D.C. While there he decided to go into the ministry and was licensed to preach by the Baltimore Conference in 1865. His first appointment came two years later when he transferred to the Ohio Conference and became pastor of the congregation at Walnut Hills (Cincinnati), Ohio. He was ordained a deacon in 1868 and an elder in 1870. Following his ordination he served parishes in Toledo, Cincinnati, Urbana, and Columbus, Ohio.

The decade of the Civil War proved determinative for Arnett. He became active in Republican Party politics and joined the National Equal Rights League headed by Frederick Douglass. He also joined the Faith and Hope League of Equal Rights and in 1864 organized league centers in six locations across Pennsylvania.

In 1872 Arnett attended his first general conference as a delegate from Ohio. In 1876 he was elected general secretary of the conference, and in 1880 he became both general secretary and financial secretary of the general conference. From his office as financial secretary he issued his most noteworthy literary production, *The Budget* of the African Methodist Episcopal Church (issued annually 1881-1904), in which he included not only matters of financial information about the church, but a vast collection of data about Methodism in general and other relevant cultural concerns. By the late 1880s the issues had grown to more than 500 pages in length. In 1886 Arnett was elected to the Ohio legislature and during his one term helped write the laws which abolished Ohio's "black" laws.

In 1888 Arnett was elected to the bishopric of the church and assigned to the Seventh Episcopal District (South Carolina). While in South Carolina Arnett became the subject of a biography, written in the then popular Horatio Alger style, entitled *Poor Ben: A Real Life Story* (1890). After a quadrennium in the South, he served successively the Fourth Episcopal District (Midwest and Northwest); the Third District (Pittsburgh area, Ohio, and California); and the First District (Philadelphia). As a young congressman, Arnett had met William McKinley, with whom he became friends. He presented McKinley with the Bible upon which he took his oath of office as president of the United States. Arnett was reputed to be the most influential black in the country at the White House during McKinley's administration. During the Spanish-American War Arnett served as a chaplain.

Arnett passed away suddenly in 1906 as a result of uremic poisoning. He possessed a large library of rare books, some of which later fell into the hands of W. E. B. DuBois.

Sources:

Harmon, Nolan B. *The Encyclopedia of World Methodism*. 2 vols. Nashville: United Methodist Publishing House, 1974.

Leete, Frederick D. *Methodist Bishops*. Nashville, TN: Privately printed, 1948.

Wright, Richard R., Jr., *The Bishops of the African Methodist Episcopal Church*. Nashville, TN: A. M. E. Sunday School Union, 1963. 389 pp.

★ 36 ★
ARNOLD, Eberhard
Founder, Hutterian Brethren of New York
b. Jul. 26, 1883, Konigsberg Germany
d. Nov. 22, 1935, Darmstadt Germany

Eberhard Arnold was the founder of the Christian communal group originally known as the Bruderhof or Society of Brothers, and more recently known as the Hutterian Brethren of New York. Arnold's father was a professor of church history at the University of Breslau, and Arnold received an active Christian faith from his parents, one that taught him to consider the needs of the downcast. In 1899, at the age of 16, he had a powerful religious experience that caused him to question accepted class differences and led him into work among the poor with groups such as the Salvation Army.

Arnold's parents pressured him to continue his schooling, and he completed his doctorate while continuing to work with radical Christian student groups. In 1909, two years after receiving his degree, he married Emmy von Hollander, and became well known as a travelling speaker. In 1913 he and his wife moved to the Tyrolean Alps for his health. Arnold began writing, utilizing the secretarial help of Emmy's sister Else. There he wrote *Innenland* and became engrossed in the history of the radical Reformation.

In 1914 Arnold was drafted into the Army, but his poor health made the term of service brief. In 1915 he and Emmy moved to Berlin, where he became literary director of Furche-Verlag. In 1919 he led a momentous Student Christian Movement meeting at Marburg, where he was struck anew by Jesus' stringent ethical demands in the Sermon on the Mount. He began gathering people to discuss his rapidly forming ideas about pacifism and the evils of private property. In 1920 he began a small commune in a three-bedroom apartment. The commune grew to include as many as 50 people before the 1922 German financial crisis drove most away.

In 1926 Arnold began a longer-lasting commune at the Sparhof, a farm near Rhon. The community, initially called the Rhonhof, eventually came to be known as the Bruderhof. With Arnold as the community's leader and writer, they lived simply, holding all things in common and running their own school for the children. In 1929 Arnold heard of the continued existence of the Hutterites in the

United States and Canada, and by 1930 he united the Bruderhof with them, though there were some differences between the two groups (which led to a break in 1956). In the early 1930s the rise of the Nazis to power led to increasing pressure on the community, and the children were removed to Lichtenstein, where a second hof and school were developed. This community gained some international attention after Arnold's lecture tour of 1935. In November of that year, Arnold had leg surgery. He died unexpectedly two days later, at the age of 52.

After Arnold's death a collective leadership emerged. When the Nazis forced the pacifist group to leave Germany, they moved first to England (1936), then Paraguay (1940), and then to a 100-acre site in New York (1954). They have since become known as the Hutterian Brethren of New York.

Sources:
Arnold, Eberhard. *The Early Christians.* Rifton, NY: Plough Publishing House, 1970.
_____. *Foundation and Orders, 1920-1929.* Rifton, NY: Plough Publishing House, 1976.
_____. *Love and Marriage in the Spirit.* Rifton, NY: Plough Publishing House, 1965.
_____. *Why We Live in Community.* Rifton, NY: Plough Publishing House, 1967.
_____, Emmy Arnold, and Heini Arnold. *The Heavens Are Opened.* Rifton, NY: Plough Publishing House, 1974. 180 pp.
Arnold, Heini, and Annemarie Arnold, eds. *Seeking for the Kingdom of God: Origins of the Bruderhof Communities.* Rifton, NY: Plough Publishing House, 1974. 284 pp.
Arnold, Emmy. *Torches Together.* 2nd ed. Rifton, NY: Plough Publishing House, 1971. 231 pp.
Hutterian Society of Brothers and John Howard Yoder, eds. *God's Revolution: The Witness of Eberhard Arnold.* NY: Paulist Press, 1984. 224 pp.
Zablocki, Benjamin. *The Joyful Community.* Baltimore, MD: Penguin, 1972. 362 pp.

★37★
Bishop ARSENY
Bishop, Russian Orthodox Church
b. Mar. 10, 1866, Russia
d. Oct. 4, 1945, New Canaan, Pennsylvania

Bishop Arseny of the Russian Orthodox Church in America was born Andrew Lyovich Chavrsov in rural Russia. He graduated from the Kharkov Theological Seminary in 1887 and was subsequently ordained to the diaconate and priesthood. He served as a priest until the turn of the century when in 1900 he was appointed Igumen of the Kuriansk Monastery. At this time he received tonsure and took the name Arseny.

In 1902 Arseny was transferred to the United States, where he served various parishes but carried with him the dream of founding a monastery for North America. In 1904 he was assigned to the parish at Mayfield, Pennsylvania, and began a campaign to build a monastery. His efforts caused the parish to support the project, and his suggestion found favor at the 1905 convention of the Russian church. Arseny oversaw the building of a monastery at nearby New Canaan, which was named in honor of St. Tikhon of Zadonsk, the patron saint of the Archbishop of the American work. Arseny was named abbot of the new monastic community in 1906.

Father Arseny was to enjoy life at his new community for only a brief period. He was assigned to the new parish church recently dedicated in Winnipeg and named dean and administrator of all the Canadian Orthodox parishes. Soon after assuming his duties, he returned to Russia for what was to be a brief visit but could not leave until after the Russian Revolution, when he was evacuated to Yugoslavia. In 1926 he was elected Bishop of Winnipeg by the bishops of the American Church and consecrated in Belgrade, Yugoslavia. During his years in Canada he did much to revitalize the church, which had suffered the loss of its Ukrainian members im-

mediately after the Russian Revolution. Among other accomplishments, he established a seminary for training priests at the cathedral at Winnipeg.

Arseny served as bishop until his retirement in 1937. At that time, he returned to the monastery he had founded. He established the Pastoral School at St. Tikhon's. In 1939 his lifetime of work was acknowledged by his elevation to the rank of archbishop.

Sources:
Tarasar, Constance J. *Orthodox America, 1874-1976: Development of the Orthodox Church in America.* Syosset, NY: Orthodox Church in America, Department of History and Archives, 1975. 352 pp.

★38★
ARTHEN, Andras Corban
Cofounder, EarthSpirit Community
b. Nov. 20, 1949, Spain

Andras Corban Arthen is the religious name of a leading Wiccan/Neo-Pagan leader in New England who has introduced several thousand people to witchcraft. Corban was educated at Curry College (B.A. in English and Education, 1972) and Harvard University, where he did post-graduate work in education. He first became involved in witchcraft and Neo-Paganism in 1969, when he was initiated into the practices of a Scottish family of witches. In 1975 he developed the Glainn Sidhr Order as a way to explore what he considered to be the shamanistic elements found in traditional witchcraft. Later, in 1979, he founded the Athanor Fellowship, a family of covens centered around the teachings of Glainn Sidhr Witchcraft and edited *Crossroads*, the fellowship's periodical.

Corban was a founding member of the Massachusetts Pagan Federation (MPF), an association of several dozen pagan groups formed in 1977. The MPF was the first such council to be formed in New England. In 1979, he organized the first Rites of Spring Pagan Celebration, a festival which has continued as an annual event ever since and has become the largest pagan gathering in the United States. With his wife, **Deirdre Pulgram Arthen**, Corban founded the EarthSpirit Community in 1980 as a vehicle for developing a viable and cohesive pagan community in the greater Boston area. EarthSpirit was the first legally incorporated pagan church in Massachusetts, and has evolved into one of the largest and most active pagan networks in the country. Corban is also one of the publishers of *FireHeart* magazine, a high quality journal devoted to magic and transformation.

Corban has been a public spokesperson on behalf of the Neo-Pagan movement since the mid-1970s. He has lectured widely throughout New England and served on the faculty of the Cambridge Center for Adult Education and the Center for Transpersonal Integration. He has also become a liaison between the New England Neo-Pagan community and other religions, and has worked as a consultant for law enforcement organizations investigating occult-related crime. As part of his outreach work, he has served as National Public Information Officer of the Covenant of the Goddess (COG) (the national association of Wiccan groups). Corban is the author of *Between the Worlds: Witchcraft, Shamanism and the Magical Reality*, which explores the relationship between European Witchcraft and the universal shamanic tradition.

★39★
ARTHEN, Deirdre Pulgram
Cofounder, EarthSpirit Community
b. Nov. 5, 1956, Atlanta, Georgia

Deirdre Pulgram Arthen is the co-founder of the EarthSpirit Community and an important Neo-Pagan leader in the New England. She holds degrees from Tufts University (B.A. in history and drama, 1978) and Wellesley College (M.A. in counseling psychology,

1986). She became involved in the Neo-Pagan movement in early 1980, and in June of that same year was initiated as a witch in the Glainn Sidhr Order, founded by her future husband, **Andras Corban Arthen**. Soon afterwards, she and her husband created the EarthSpirit Community in an attempt to provide an outlet for and access to Paganism in the greater Boston area. From its modest beginnings, EarthSpirit now includes several thousand witches and Pagans, mostly concentrated in the Northeast. Her work as director includes coordinating such programs as open seasonal celebrations, Pagans in Recovery meetings, and the training group of the Glainn Sidhr Order.

Pulgram Arthen also is a spiritual counselor. She creates and performs public rituals and publishes a monthly newsletter, as well as EarthSpirit's journal, *FireHeart*. One major focus of her work has been the development of four seasonal Pagan conferences, ranging in size from 100 to 700 participants from all parts of the country. These conferences—Rites of Spring, Suntide Celebration, Twilight Covening, and Hearthfire Gathering—each designed around a theme appropriate to the season, provide an opportunity for Pagans to network and learn from each other, and in the process to develop stronger community ties. Rites of Spring has become the largest such gathering in the country and rivals the slightly older Midwest Pagan festival as one of the longest standing, having been first held in 1979.

Pulgram Arthen has developed a counseling approach which incorporates not only traditional and holistic methods, but also includes spiritual practices derived from her experience in the Glainn Sidhr Order. She has developed techniques of assisting clients to create personal rituals with the goal of facilitating personal empowerment and transformation, a theme also evident in public classes and workshops. Both Pulgram Arthen and her husband have become major spokespersons for Wicca and neo-Paganism in New England and speak widely in public forums on its behalf.

★ 40 ★
ASHWORTH, Robert Archibald
Minister, Northern Baptist Convention
b. Jul. 26, 1871, Glasgow Scotland
d. Mar. 8, 1959

Robert Archibald Ashworth, a minister in the Northern Baptist Convention known for his many years of work in ecumenical and interfaith endeavors, was the son of Emma Gregson and John W. Ashworth. As a youth he moved to America where he attended Columbia University (A.M., 1892; A.M., 1894) and Union Theological Seminary (B.D., 1896). Ordained to the Baptist ministry that year, he became pastor of the Baptist church in Minerva, New York, for two years, after which he served at Bridgeton, New Jersey (1898-1900), and First Baptist Church in Meriden, Connecticut (1900-1911). In 1902, while at Meriden he married Mabelle Edgerton.

Ashworth moved to First Baptist Church in Milwaukee, Wisconsin, in 1911. In the meantime he had become an enthusiastic supporter of the ecumenical trends which had led to the formation of the Federal Council of Churches in 1908. In 1912 he was elected president of the Milwaukee Federation of Churches. Three years later the ecumenical spirit provided the inspiration for his first book, *The Union of Christian Forces in America*. While in Milwaukee, Ashworth also began his long official association with the Federal Council of Churches. He served on a variety of committees for it and for many years chaired its committee on publications. In 1921 he became pastor of the Church of the Redeemer in Yonkers, New York. While at Yonkers he also served as the editor of *The Baptist* from 1921 to 1930.

Ashworth's involvement in religious leadership expanded considerably in the 1930s. In 1931 he became a contributing editor for *The Christian Century* and assumed duties as a lecturer in Bap-

tist principles and polity at Union Theological Seminary. In 1928, in response to the dramatic growth of the Jewish population in the United States during the previous decades, he joined with a group of interested Jewish and Christian leaders to form the National Conference of Christians and Jews. In 1933 he left the parish and became the editorial secretary of the conference, a position he would keep for almost 20 years.

Ashworth also exercised leadership on an international level in the 1930s. In 1927 he was elected as a delegate to the Conference on Faith and Order held at Lausanne, Switzerland, and was returned to the 1937 conference in Edinburgh, Scotland. At Edinburgh he headed the committee which drafted the "Affirmation of Unity in Allegiance to Our Lord Jesus Christ" statement which called for a structure to give visible manifestation to the attending churches' unity. The next year he was present for the Utrecht Conference on the World Council of Churches and became a member of the American Committee for the World Council of Churches.

Ashworth retired in 1952 and settled in Yonkers, New York.

Sources:
Ashworth, Robert A. *Being a Christian*. Philadelphia: Judson Press, 1924. 102 pp.
_____. *The Union of Christian Forces in America*. Philadelphia: American Sunday-School Union, 1915. 266 pp.
Cavert, Samuel McCrea. *The American Churches in the Ecumenical Movement, 1900-1968*. New York: Association Press, 1968. 288 pp.

★ 41 ★
Patriarch ATHENAGORAS
Ecumenical Patriarch, Greek Orthodox Church
b. Mar. 25, 1886, Vassilikon (Tsarapalna) Greece
d. Jul. 6, 1972, Constantinople Turkey

Patriarch Athenagoras, for over two decades the acknowledged leader of the Eastern Orthodox world, served as an archbishop of the Greek Orthodox Archdiocese of North and South America. He was born Aristokles Spyrou, the son of Matthaois and Eleni Makarou Spyrou. He received his early education in Ioannina, the capital city of the Greek province of Epirus. Metropolitan Vassilias of Konitsa sponsored him as a student of the Ecumenical Patriarch's seminary on the island of Halki. He was ordained a deacon in 1910 and assigned to work in the schools at Monasteri, then in Turkish territory (now part of Yugoslavia). In 1918 he moved to Mt. Athos, and after a year of meditation and study, he became the Chief Secretary to the Holy Synod of the Church of Greece.

In 1922 Athenagoras was consecrated as a bishop and appointed as Metropolitan of Crofu and Paxoi. He had served at Crofu for eight years when in 1930 he was elected as the new archbishop for North and South America. He arrived in New York to assume control of a severely divided archdiocese. It had split in the 1920s into two factions, reflective of the political division in Greece between the supporters and opponents of the king of Greece. Athenagoras had the support of both factions, however, and he was able to unite the church by disbanding the several dioceses into which the church had been organized and reassigning the several bishops as administrative assistants to his office. He founded Holy Cross Orthodox Theological Seminary in Pomfret, Connecticut (more recently relocated to Brookline, Massachusetts), and organized the women of the church into the Ladies Philoptochos Sisterhood. He empowered both the laity and priesthood by expanding the work of the clergy-laity congresses. He also became one of the most popular figures in the archdiocese, as he frequently traveled to parishes in all parts of the continent.

In 1954 Athenagoras was selected to be the new ecumenical patriarch (officially the patriarch of Constantinople, but recognized as the symbolic leader of Eastern Orthodoxy and its autonomous national jurisdictions). He assumed as his first task as patriarch the reestablishment of Orthodox unity, which had been severely tested by the changes of two world wars. A fruit of his efforts was the Pan-Orthodox Conference held at Rhoades, Greece, in 1961. At the second Pan-Orthodox Conference, in 1963, he led in establishing a plan for dialogue with the Roman Catholic Church and in 1964 he had a historic meeting with Pope Paul VI, the first of several such meetings, in Jerusalem.

Athenagoras thus set the direction for the modern Greek Orthodox Church in North America, and provided a new and open setting for it to relate to the Roman Church in a global context.

Sources:

"Death of the Patriarch." *America* 127, 2 (July 22, 1972): 23-24.
Litsas, Fotios K., ed. *A Companion to the Greek Orthodox Church*. New York: Department of Communication, Greek Orthodox Archdiocese of North and South America, 1984. 324 pp.

★ 42 ★
ATKINSON, William Walker
New Thought Writer
Hindu Yogi
b. Dec. 5, 1862, Baltimore, Maryland
d. Nov. 22, 1932, Los Angeles, California

William Walker Atkinson was the first major popularizer of Hinduism in America, though he also made earlier achievements in the New Thought arena. He began his career as a lawyer and was admitted to the Pennsylvania bar in 1894 at the age of 32. The stress of the profession, however, took its toll, and after some years he experienced a nervous breakdown. After a time of searching, he found healing with New Thought, moved to Chicago (a major center of New Thought), and became an active promoter of that movement.

In 1899 Atkinson married Margaret Foster Black. In 1900 he became editor of *Suggestion*, a New Thought journal, and met Sydney Flowers, the famous New Thought publisher and businessman. Meanwhile, he was distributing his first pamphlet, "The Secret of the I AM," which became quite well known. In 1901 he teamed up with Flowers, editing his *New Thought* magazine from 1901 to 1905. He also founded the Psychic Club and the Atkinson School of Mental Science, both located in the same building as Flowers' Psychic Research Company and New Thought Publishing Company.

Atkinson also began writing books, publishing about ten books on New Thought subjects over the years, including *Nuggets of New Thought* (1902) and *Thought Vibrations* (1906). These books proved both popular and influential among New Thought practitioners such as Fenwicke Holmes, brother of **Ernest Holmes** and founder of the United Church of Religious Science.

Atkinson, however, was also interested in Hinduism, and in 1903 (the same year he was admitted to the Illinois bar, thus maintaining that part of his life) he assumed the pseudonym of Swami Ramacharacka and began to write on Hinduism. He wrote approximately 13 books under this identity, and they have overwhelmed his New Thought works in popularity. Published by the Yogi Publication Society in Chicago, the Hindu books included *Fourteen Lessons in Yoga Philosophy and Oriental Occultism* (1903) and *Spirit of the Upanishads* (1907). All remain in print.

In Atkinson's later years his New Thought books were published by **Elizabeth Towne**. He wrote articles for her magazine, *The Nautilus*, as well. From 1916 to 1919 he edited the journal *Advanced Thought*. Atkinson died in 1932 at the age of 70.

Sources:

Atkinson, William Walker [Yogi Ramacharacka]. *Advanced Course in Yogi Philosophy and Oriental Occultism*. Chicago: Yogi Publication Society, 1904. 337 pp.

———. *Dynamic Thought*. Los Angeles: Segnogram Publishing Co., 1906. 231 pp.
———. *Hatha Yoga*. Chicago: Yogi Publication Society, 1932. 243 pp.
———. *The Law of the New Thought*. Chicago: Psychic Research Co., 1902. 93 pp.
———. *Reincarnation and the Law of Karma*. Chicago: Yogi Publication Society, 1908. 249 pp.
———. *The Secret of Mental Magic*. Chicago: William Walker Atkinson, 1907. 380 pp.
———. *Self Healing by Thought Force*. Chicago: Library Shelf, 1907.
———. *Subconscious and Superconscious Planes of Mind*. New York: R.F. Fenno & Co., 1909. 200 pp.
———. *Your Mind and How to Use It*. Holyoke, MA: N.p., 1911.
The New Thought Annual. Chicago, 1902.
Shepard, Leslie. *Encyclopedia of Occultism & Parapsychology*. 3 vols., 2nd. ed. Detroit: Gale Research Co., 1984-1985.
Who Was Who in America. Chicago: Marquis Who's Who, Inc.

—*Gary L. Ward*

★ 43 ★
Sri AUROBINDO
Hindu Spiritual Leader
b. Aug. 15, 1872, Calcutta India
d. Dec. 5, 1950, Pondicherry India

Arvinda Ackroyd Ghose, later known as Sri Aurobindo was a major figure in bringing Hindu spirituality into the West. Born into a family enamored of the West, he was educated as a westerner, first in an Indian school run by Irish nuns, then, from the age of seven, in England. He attended college at Cambridge.

Despite his Western schooling, Aurobindo felt close bonds to India, and he began working for its independence from England. In 1893 he returned to India to serve the Maharaja of Baroda, becoming a professor and administrator of Baroda University. While there he finally had an opportunity to absorb the languages and culture of India, putting all of his learning to work in the independence movement. In 1906, at the age of 34, he became the principal of the Bengal National College in Calcutta, where he co-founded and edited *Bande Mataram*, the journal of the Bengal National Party. Soon he was the leader of the party itself, which led to his arrest in 1908 for inciting rebellion against the British. He was kept in prison for a year but was never convicted of the charges.

While in jail, Aurobindo concentrated his attention both on the yoga practice he had discovered a few years before and on reading the major Hindu scriptures, the *Bhagavad Gita* and the *Upanishads*. Utilizing the instruction of the yogi Vishnu Bhasakr Lele, whom he had met only a few months before going to jail, he reported the ability to silence his mind and encounter *Brahman* (the Divine). After his release from prison Aurobindo continued his periodical editing and his work with liberation groups. He continued to clarify his new focus and discuss it with others.

In 1910 Aurobindo received a spiritual direction to go to Pondicherry in French-controlled India. He subsequently developed an ashram there. He believed that India was on the inevitable road to independence and that his role needed to be of a more spiritual nature. He was visited in 1914 by Mira Richard (1878-1973), a French woman who had seen the Hindu god Krishna in a vision. She found, however, that her vision was of Aurobindo, not Krishna. She stayed and became Aurobindo's close partner, known to followers as the Mother.

On November 24, 1926, Aurobindo experienced "The Day of Siddhi," the descent of the divine consciousness into the physical. This was confirmation of his integral yoga approach, which did not seek to escape matter, but unite it with the spiritual and thus transform it. This evolutionary philosophy has been compared to that of Teilhard de Chardin. After this momentous event he retreated from direct contact with even his disciples, and communicated only through the Mother and his writings. Three years before his death, on August 15, 1947, he celebrated both his birthday and the declaration of India's independence. After his death, the Mother continued his work, supporting the rise in the West of a number of centers for his followers.

Sources:

Aurobindo, Sri. *Essays on the Gita*. New York: Sri Aurobindo Library, 1950. 579 pp.

_____. *Sri Aurobindo Birth Centenary Library*. 30 vols. Pondicherry, India: Sri Aurobindo Ashram, 1970-72.

Bharati, Shuddhananda. *Sri Aurobindo, The Divine Master*. 2d ed. Pondicherry, India: Pudu Yuga Nilayam, 1948. 104 pp.

Chaudhuri, Haridas. *Sri Aurobindo: The Prophet of Life Divine*. Pondicherry, India: Sri Aurobindo Ashram Press, 1951. 265 pp.

Diwakar, R.R. *Mahayogi: Life, Sadhana and Teachings of Sri Aurobindo*. Bombay, India: Bharatiya Vidya Bhavan, 1976. 292 pp.

Donnelly, Morwenna. *Founding the Life Divine*. London: Ryder and Co., 1955. Reprint. Lower Lake, CA: The Dawn Horse Press, 1976. 176 pp.

Kaul, H. K. *Sri Aurobindo: A Descriptive Bibliography*. New Delhi, India: Munshiram Manoharlal, 1972. 222 pp.

McDermott, Robert, ed. *The Essential Aurobindo*. New York: Schocken Books, 1973. 258 pp.

_____, ed. *Six Pillars: Introductions to the Major Works of Sri Aurobindo*. Chambersburg, PA: Wilson Books, 1974. 198 pp.

Minor, Robert Neil. *Sri Aurobindo: The Perfect and the Good*. Columbia, MO: South Asia Books, 1978. 191 pp.

Mitra, Sisirkumar. *The Liberator*. Bombay, India: Jaico Publishing House, 1970. 307 pp.

Pandit, M.P. *Sri Aurobindo: A Survey*. Pondicherry, India: Dipti Publications, 1972.

Sastry, T.V. Kapali. *Sri Aurobindo: Lights on the Teachings*. Madras, India: Amudasurabi Press, 1948. 186 pp.

Shepard, Leslie. *Encyclopedia of Occultism & Parapsychology*. 3 vols., 2nd. ed. Detroit: Gale Research Co., 1984-1985.

—*Gary L. Ward*

★ 44 ★
AVERY, Martha Gallison Moore
Lay Apostle, Roman Catholic Church
b. Apr. 6, 1851, Steuben, Maine
d. Aug. 8, 1929, Medford, Massachusetts

Martha Gallison Moore Avery, a Socialist and prominent Roman Catholic laywoman, was one of eight children of Albion King Paris Moore and Katherine Leighton Moore. Following her mother's death when she was 13, she lived with her grandfather, Samuel Moore, a member of the state senate in Maine. She created a millinery business in her early adult years in Ellsworth, Maine. She also began her religious quest in Ellsworth with her affiliation to the Unitarian church. In 1880 she married a member of the church, Millard Fillmore Avery (d. 1890). A short time later she moved to Boston.

In Boston, Avery encountered a wide variety of new religious and social currents. She studied metaphysics with Dr. Charles D. Sherman, an astrologer and student of Eastern religion. She joined the Nationalist Club, promoting the ideas of utopian author Edward Bellamy. By 1891 she had joined the Socialist Labor Party; over the years she became a leader in Socialist political movements. In 1896 she founded the Karl Marx Class, later renamed the Boston School of Political Economy.

Through her Socialist activities, Avery met and became friends with David Goldstein, an English-born Jew. Together they came to reject the anti-religious and anti-moral implications of their socialist ideals. This conflict culminated in 1902 with their introduction of a motion at the Massachusetts Socialist convention to repudiate all Socialists who attacked religion or advocated either violence or free love. When the motion was defeated, they withdrew and became active anti-Socialists. In 1903 they coauthored *Socialism: The Nation of Fatherless Children*.

Avery's alienation from Socialism paralleled a growing interest in the Roman Catholic Church. Impressed with the results of convent education, Avery sent her daughter to a parochial school. The daughter became a Catholic and eventually a nun. On May 1, 1904 (a traditional Marxist holiday), Avery herself was baptized as a Roman Catholic.

While rejecting Socialism, Avery continued her work for social reform; however, she now took Pope Leo III's encyclical of 1891, "Rerum Novarum," as her starting point. She became an advocate of trade unions and collective bargaining and, working through her school, she emerged as one of the early architects of the Catholic social justice movement. In 1922 she was elected president of the Common Cause Society, a Catholic labor organization, and remained its president for the rest of her life.

Avery's political activism was accompanied by a desire to evangelize for the Roman Catholic Church. In 1916 she and Goldstein founded, with the blessing of Card. **William O'Connell**, the Catholic Truth Guild. The guild centered its work on the streets of Boston, but extended its mission across the United States. It became the most extensive lay apostolate in the history of the Roman Catholic Church in America.

Avery continued her twin activities of social and labor reform and evangelism until the last days of her life. She died of arteriosclerosis in 1929.

Sources:

Carrigan, D. Owen. "Martha Moore Avery: Crusader for Social Justice." *Catholic Historical Review* (April 1968).

_____. "A Forgotten Yankee Marxist." *New England Quarterly* (March 1969).

Goldstein, David. *Autobiography of a Campaigner for Christ*. Boston, MA: Catholic Campaigners for Christ, 1936. 416 pp.

_____, and Martha Moore Avery. *Campaigning for Christ*. Boston, MA: Pilot Publishing Co., 1924. 463 pp.

★ 45 ★
AYRES, Anne
Founder, Sisterhood of the Holy Communion, Episcopal Church, U.S.A.
b. Jan. 3, 1816, London England
d. Feb. 9, 1896, New York City, New York

Anne Ayres, a pioneer in the establishment of sisterhoods within the Episcopal Church, U.S.A., was the daughter of Robert and Anne Ayres. She accompanied them to New York City and settled into a job of teaching the daughters of well-to-do parents. Through her students she came to know Rev. William Augustus Muhlenberg, the head of a church college on Long Island. In 1845 she responded to one of Muhlenberg's sermons with a commitment to a life of service to Christ. Without any thought of creating a sisterhood, Muhlenberg consecrated Ayres as Sister Anne.

It is likely that the idea of a sisterhood emerged out of Muhlenberg's knowledge of the Protestant deaconess movement that had been initiated in Germany, as no sisterhoods existed in either the Episcopal Church or the Church of England at that time. Muhlenberg had planned to build a new church in Manhattan, the Church of the Holy Communion, and through it provide a number of social services to the community along with his normal sacramental and pastoral duties. A deaconess-like organization could greatly expand his work. Thus in 1952 the Sisterhood of the Holy Communion was organized and attached to Muhlenberg's church. Ayres was appointed "First Sister."

The sisterhood was organized differently from both the traditional orders of nuns and the deaconess movement. The women who joined took no lifetime vows. Rather, they simply pledged three years of service, renewable as they saw fit. They also agreed not to marry during their time of service and to serve under the direction of the First Sister. They had a uniform-like dress that was contemporary in design and appearance.

During the next quarter century, Ayres and Muhlenberg worked closely together. Among their first projects was the establishment of a hospital. It began in 1853 as an infirmary and five years later emerged as St. Luke's Hospital. The hospital became the major focus of the sisterhood's work during its first decade. Immediately after the Civil War, Muhlenberg began a new project, St. Johnland on Long Island. He conceived of this new venture as a Christian industrial community, with special emphasis on services and accomodations for the poor, the handicapped, the aged, and orphans. Ayres placed the energies of the sisterhood behind the project, and a short time later it became known as the Sisterhood of St. Luke and St. John.

Ayres' abilities were recognized by the leadership of both the hospital and the community, and in 1876 the trustees voted her "Sister Superintendent," with administrative powers equal to Muhlenberg's. Muhlenberg died the next year. Ayres withdrew from the work at St. Luke's at that time and devoted her time to St. Johnland. She had already begun the process of editing his essays and speeches, which were published from 1975 to 1977. She then proceeded to write a biography of Muhlenberg. Following his instructions, she then destroyed his personal papers and, following his example, destroyed her own papers shortly before her death.

Though the sisterhood she created never grew very large and died out in 1940, Ayres is remembered as a pioneer in the modern revival of the monastic life in the Episcopal Church in America. She also brought Harriet Starr Cannon into the ordered life. Cannon left the sisterhood in the winter of 1962-1963 to found the Episcopal Community of St. Mary.

Sources:
Anson, Peter. *The Call of the Cloister*. London: S.P.C.K., 1958. 643 pp.
Ayres, Anne. *The Life and Work of William Augustus Muhlenberg*. New York: Harper & Brothers, 1880. 524 pp.
James, Edward T., ed. *Notable American Women, 1607-1950: A Biographical Dictionary*. 3 vols. Cambridge, MA: Harvard University Press, Belknap Press, 1971.
Muhlenberg, William Augusts. *Two Letters on Protestant Sisterhoods*. New York: R. Craighead, 1856.

★ 46 ★
BAHA'U'LLAH
Baha'i Faith
b. Nov. 12, 1817, Tehran Iran
d. May 29, 1892, Acre Palestine

Mirza Husayn-Ali, later known as Baha'u'llah, the founder of the Baha'i Faith, was born into an influential family in Tehran, Iran (then known as Persia). His father, Mirza Buzurg, held a number of powerful government posts. Baha'u'llah's childhood was typical of others around him; he received no formal education, since he was not in the family of a religious leader. In early adulthood he followed another typical cultural pattern and married three wives.

In 1844 the prophet Siyyid Ali Muhammad, called the Bab (Gate), revealed that he was the Gate, the announcer through whom the Promised One of Islamic and other religious prophecies would be known. Baha'u'llah became one of his chief spokespersons. The Bab was imprisoned in 1847 and executed in 1850. This led to retaliations on the part of his followers and continued savage persecution on the part of the shah's regime. Baha'u'llah was imprisoned in 1852. During this time he received a revelation that he was the Promised One of whom the Bab spoke.

In 1853, at the age of 36, Baha'u'llah was banished to Baghdad, Iraq, where over the next ten years he and his half-brother Mirza Yahya led the remnants of the movement. In 1863 Baha'u'llah left for Constantinople with a few followers, to whom he revealed his identity as the Promised One. After a few months in Constantinople he was again forced to move, this time to Adrianople (today's Edirne, in Turkey). He openly proclaimed his identity at that time in a series of tablets sent to world leaders. His basic teaching was that he constituted the final chapter in a series of progressive revelations by God through such figures as Krishna, Moses, and Jesus. He also proclaimed that Baha'i was finally able to proclaim and focus effectively on human equality, religious unity, education, and economic and social justice.

In 1868 Baha'u'llah was exiled to a penal colony at Akka, Palestine (now Acre, Israel). In about 1871 he was allowed to move his quarters out of barracks to a house. There he wrote the *Kitab-i-Aqdas* (the Most Holy Book) of laws, as well as dozens more volumes of material, most of which have yet to be translated out of Arabic or Persian. Baha'u'llah remained at Acre about 24 years, until his death in 1892 at the age of 75. His movement did not spread to the United States until several years later, but eventually found a substantial following.

Sources:
Baha'u'llah. *Epistle to the Son of the Wolf*. Wilmette, IL: Baha'i Publishing Trust, 1969. 193 pp.
_____. *Gleanings from the Writings of Baha'u'llah*. Translated by Shoghi Effendi. Wilmette, IL: Baha'i Publishing Committee, 1939. 360 pp.
_____. *Prayers and Meditations*. New York: Baha'i Publishing Committee, 1938. 347 pp.
_____. *The Proclamation of Baha'u'llah*. Haifa: Baha'i World Center, 1967. 127 pp.
_____. *The Seven Valleys and the Four Valleys*. Wilmette, IL: Baha'i Publishing Trust, 1945. 62 pp.
Balyuzi, H. M. *Baha'u'llah: The King of Glory*. Oxford: George Ronald, 1980. 539 pp.
_____. *Edward Granville Browne and the Baha'i Faith*. Oxford: George Ronald, 1970. 142 pp.
Miller, William McElwee. *The Baha'i Faith: Its History and Teachings*. South Pasadena, CA: William Carey Library, 1974. 443 pp.
Sears, William. *The Prisoner and the Kings*. Toronto, ON: General Publishing, 1971. 240 pp.

—Gary L. Ward

★ 47 ★
BAILEY, Alice LaTrobe Bateman
Founder, Arcane School
b. Jun. 16, 1880, Manchester England
d. Dec. 15, 1949, New York, New York

Alice LaTrobe Bateman Bailey was a well-known Theosophist before she became an independent spiritual leader and founder of several groups, including the Arcane School. Raised in a wealthy family in England, she was unhappy and reportedly attempted to commit suicide several times. She was a loyal member and church school teacher of the Church of England, but often felt the tension of a distinct mystical bent.

One Sunday, when Bailey was 15 years old, she was surprised to see a tall man wearing a turban enter her home and tell her that she was destined to participate in an important work. She interpreted the event as a visitation from Christ. Upon finishing school she began work for the YWCA, which took her to many places around the world, including India, where she met Walter Evans. They married in 1907 and moved to Ohio, where Evans studied for the Episcopal priesthood. They moved to California after his graduation. The relationship foundered, however, apparently due to Evans' temper. They were separated in 1915 and divorced by 1919.

In 1915, the year of Bailey's separation, Bailey was introduced by two friends to Theosophy via the society in Pacific Groves, California. Visiting the society's quarters, she was suprised to see a picture on the wall of the very man who had visited her at age 15. He was identified as Koot Hoomi, one of the spiritual masters who had communicated with **Helena Petrovna Blavatsky**, co-founder of the Theosophical Society. This incident revitalized her, and she soon was not only an active member, but editor of the society's magazine, *The Messenger*. In 1919 she was contacted by another spiritual entity, Master Djwhal Khul (or Djual Khool)—now popularly known as D. K. or the Tibetan. Djwhal Khul wished to produce, through her as a channel, writings to share with the world. Over the next 30 years they wrote 19 books under this arrangement.

The first book, *Initiation: Human and Solar*, was well received by the Theosophical Movement, but soon it was apparent that **Annie Besant**, the national leader at the time, was in conflict with both Bailey and her new romantic interest, Foster Bailey, the society's national secretary. Alice Bailey claimed that Besant wanted to control all spiritual communications. Bailey and Foster were eventually ousted from their positions.

They married in 1921, and by 1923 they had created a new organization—the Arcane School. They also established a magazine—*The Beacon*—and the Lucis Trust for publishing purposes. In addition, they completed three books, one of which was written by Bailey alone. Her teachings were similar to Theosophy, emphasizing a divine plan for the world, karma, reincarnation, the evolution of humanity to higher levels, and a spiritual hierarchy whose teachings and energy could be tapped, especially with ceremonies during auspicious times such as periods of the full moon.

In 1932 the Tibetan urged the creation of the New Group of World Servers as goodwill ambassadors of the coming new age. This group's mandate was similar to the work begun in 1937 by the Triangles, which encouraged spiritual service in groups of three. In 1937 Bailey released her most widespread work, "The Great Invocation," a paragraph-length prayer for the realization of God's great plan on earth. Several of her works predict a future world religion that will unite the East and West. After her death in 1949 her husband continued the work, though the Arcane School has experienced several schisms.

Sources:

Bailey, Alice Ann. *Discipleship in the New Age*. Vol. I. Philadelphia: George S. Ferguson Co., 1944. 790 pp.
_____. *The Reappearance of the Christ*. Philadelphia: George S. Ferguson Co., 1948. 189 pp.
_____. *A Treatise on Cosmic Fire*. 3d ed. New York: Lucis Publishing Co., 1925, 1944. 1316 pp.
_____. *A Treatise on White Magic*. New York: Lucis Publishing Co., 1934. 640 pp.
_____. *The Unfinished Autobiography*. New York: Lucis Publishing Co., 1951. 303 pp.
Judah, J. Stillson. *The History and Philosophy of the Metaphysical Movements in America*. Philadelphia: Westminister Press, 1967. 317 pp.
Shepard, Leslie. *Encyclopedia of Occultism & Parapsychology*. 3 vols., 2nd. ed. Detroit: Gale Research Co., 1984-1985.
Sinclair, Sir John R. *The Alice Bailey Inheritance*. Wellingborough, England: Turnstone Press, 1984. 208 pp.

★ 48 ★
BAILEY, Anne Penny Lee
Executive, Church of God in Christ
b. Sep. 22, 1894, Temple, Texas
d. Dec. 18, 1975, Detroit, Michigan

Mother Anne Bailey, an evangelist and supervisor of women's work for the Church of God in Christ, was the daughter of Reverend and Mrs. Felix Garrett. Her father was a Baptist minister, and at the age of 12 she had an experience of conversion and joined the Baptist church. In 1915 she accepted the Pentecostal ideas concerning sanctification (a belief in the total cleansing available to the believer) and the baptism of the Holy Spirit (an experience of the indwelling of the Holy Spirit initially evidenced by speaking in tongues), and joined the Church of God in Christ. She became

a pioneer in spreading the message among Blacks in Arkansas, Kansas, Missouri, and Illinois. She was an accomplished musician, a talent which greatly aided her evangelistic message.

After World War I, Mother Bailey's work took her to the northeast, and she concentrated her evangelical endeavors in Buffalo, New York City, and the surrounding states of New Jersey, Connecticut, and Massachusetts. She attended the first convocation for leaders in the church in New Jersey called by Elder J. F. Bryant and Mother Lula Cox in 1921. As a result of her work, in 1927 she was named state supervisor of women's work for Maryland. In 1928 responsibilities were added for Delaware and Washington, D.C. In 1943 she succeeded Lula Cox as supervisor for New Jersey. That same year she married John S. Bailey, a bishop in the church residing in Detroit, Michigan. In 1964 Bailey was appointed international supervisor of women's work for the Church of God in Christ, a position she retained for the rest of her life.

Sources:

Dupree, Sherry Sherrod. *Biographical Dictionary of African-American, Holiness-Pentecostals, 1880-1990*. Washington, DC: Middle Atlantic Regional Press, 1990. 386 pp.

—*Gary L. Ward*

★ 49 ★
BAKER, James Chamberlain
Bishop, Methodist Episcopal Church
b. Jun. 2, 1879, Sheldon, Illinois
d. Sep. 26, 1969, Claremont, California

James Chamberlain Baker, who helped develop the campus ministry program of the Methodist Episcopal Church (now the United Methodist Church), was born in rural Illinois, the son of Benjamin Webb Baker and Martha Frances Henry Baker. He graduated from Illinois Wesleyan University in 1898 and accepted a position teaching Greek at Missouri Wesleyan University. During his three years at the university, he was accepted on trial in the Illinois Conference of the Methodist Episcopal Church (1901), married Lena Sarah Benson (1901), and was ordained a deacon (1902). He left his teaching post to attend Boston University, from which he received an S.T.B degree in 1905. He was ordained an elder in the church following graduation. After serving two years at McLean, Illinois, he was assigned to Trinity Methodist Episcopal Church in Urbana, Illinois, adjacent to the University of Illinois campus.

Once at Urbana, Baker turned his attention to campus ministry and founded the first Wesley Foundation (the name attached to Methodist campus ministries today). He stayed in Urbana for over twenty years until his election to the bishopric in 1928. In subsequent years, the work begun in Illinois spread to almost every campus in the United States, and Baker helped guide the ministry for the rest of his active life. The campus work also brought him into contact with the YMCA, and he chaired the Geneva Big Ten Student Conference for a decade.

As Bishop, Baker was given a very different first assignment—supervision of the church's missions in Japan, Manchuria, and Korea (1928-1932). His work in Asia would continue in later years. Soon after his return to the United States, a colleague's illness forced him to assume duties over the Shanghai (China) Area (1933-1934). In 1941 he traveled to Japan with **Ralph Diffendorfer**, and it became their job to call the missionaries home before the United States was brought into the war in the Pacific. From 1941 to 1947, Baker served as chairman of the International Missionary Council (I.M.C.). In that capacity he joined the delegation of Protestant church leaders to Japan after the war.

In 1932 Baker was assigned to the San Francisco area, where he remained for 16 years. While there he participated in both the initial conference and the continuing committee, whose work led to the formation of the World Council of Churches. He was a member of the council's central committee from 1948 to 1954. He was a consultant at the organization of the United Nations in San Francisco following World War II. His stay in San Francisco carried him through the merger of the Methodist Episcopal Church, one of three churches that united to become the Methodist Church (1939-1968). His final assignment was to the Los Angeles area (1948-1952). His first year in Los Angeles, he also served as president of the church's Council of Bishops.

Following his retirement in 1952, Baker spent four years as a visiting professor at the University of Southern California. He then quietly lived the last years of his life in suburban Claremont, California.

Sources:

Baker, James Chamberlain. "The Church and the State University." *Methodist Review* (October-December 1914).

———. *The Church in a World in Ferment.* Los Angeles: The Author, 1947. 38 pp.

———. *The First Wesley Foundation.* N.p.: The Author, 1960. 117 pp.

———, and Ralph E. Diffendorfer. *Church and Mission in Japan in January 1941.* New York: Board of Missions and Church Extension, the Methodist Church, 1941. 79 pp.

Harmon, Nolan B. *The Encyclopedia of World Methodism.* 2 vols. Nashville, TN: United Methodist Publishing House, 1974.

Who's Who in the Methodist Church. Nashville, TN: Abingdon Press, 1966.

★50★
BAKKER, Jim and Tammy Faye
Independent Pentecostal Televangelists
The PTL (Praise the Lord) Club

Jim Bakker (b. Jan. 2, 1941 Muskegon, Michigan) and Tammy Faye LaValley (b. March 7, 1942 International Falls, Minnesota), who for a number of years headlined "The PTL [Praise the Lord] Club," a daily religious television show, and who were brought down by a major scandal in the late 1980s, began life in Assembly of God households in separate states. Jim Bakker was the son of Ralaigh and Furnia Bakker, both of Dutch background, who had left the Reformed Church for Pentecostalism. Shy in public situations as a child, he overcame his problem and became a disc jockey for dances in high school. His life was changed in 1958 when he ran over a little boy with a car. Fortunately the boy was not killed, but the accident launched a spiritual search that led Bakker to respond to a call to preach. The following year he entered North Central College, the Assemblies of God school in Minneapolis, Minnesota.

When Tammy was quite young, her mother divorced and she was raised by her mother and a new stepfather in a family with eight children. After high school, with the intention of becoming a missionary, she went to North Central College. There she met Jim Bakker. By the beginning of 1961, they had decided to marry, which was against school policy. Thus, in April they dropped out and began life together as itinerant evangelists. Jim Bakker was licensed by the Assemblies of God.

In 1965 they moved to Portsmouth, Virginia, with **Pat Robertson**, who had recently founded the Christian Broadcasting Network (CBN). Robertson soon recognized Jim Bakker as possessing a captivating personality which seemed especially suitable for television. Bakker's first program as a Christian talk show host was November 28, 1966. He stayed at CBN until 1973 when he claimed that God had told him to resign and move on. That same year, with Paul Crouch, the former assistant pastor of his home church, he founded Trinity Broadcasting Systems headquartered in Santa Ana, California. The association lasted only a few months however, and following a dispute he left Trinity in Crouch's hands and moved to North Carolina.

In November 1974 Bakker began his rise when he became the host of a pre-existing talk show on WRET-TV, which he renamed "The PTL Club." It became the start of a new Christian television network, the PTL or Inspirational Network. He moved into a former furniture showroom which he redecorated as a studio. Tammy Faye joined the program and worked with Jim. She co-hosted the show and often, when her husband was away, hosted it alone. There was no doubt, however, that Jim Bakker was ultimately in charge. In July 1976 he purchased 25 acres on Park Road in Charlotte which became the first Heritage Village, a sort of religious retreat center that later evolved into a massive Christian recreational-vacation center modeled somewhat on Disneyland and the other popular theme parks that have emerged around the country. That same year he finished writing *Move That Mountain*, an autobiographical work. Two years later he purchased land and broke ground for a new Heritage Village (later called Heritage U.S.A.) near Fort Mill, South Carolina, just over the state line from Charlotte. He raised money through the television show and developed a program for PTL partners who purchased lifetime shares that would allow them to stay at Heritage U.S.A. for a specified number of days each year.

Outwardly successful during the 1980s, the television show was one of the highest rated on religious television; three problems conspired to ultimately bring down the ministry. First, the Bakkers began to live in an opulent style that, while obviously acceptable to many in their listening audience, alienated them from colleagues in the ministry and administrators within their denomination. Second, and most substantively, as money poured into PTL, significant sums were diverted to the Bakkers and other staff members, and large sums were used for purposes other than those for which they had been raised. Jim Bakker regularly created new and larger building projects and, through the decade, the ministry moved into greater and greater debt. In the end, the financial mismanagement became the substantive problem which led the government to move against PTL and the Bakkers. Third, in 1980, Jim Bakker had a sexual encounter with Jessica Hahn. Further, Hahn was paid a large sum to keep quiet about the incident. But, bit by bit, the story became public, and along with it came the story of other sexual encounters including some of a homosexual nature.

As the scandal built and disaster seemed imminent, Bakker turned the corporation over to fellow televangelist **Jerry Falwell**. The Assemblies of God, acting upon the evidence of sexual misconduct, defrocked Bakker. The story of his sexual adventures became the subject of expose articles in popular periodicals from the *National Enquirer* to *Penthouse*. The corporation, heavily in debt, was placed in the hands of a new board and a series of efforts was made to salvage Heritage U.S.A. Eventually it was sold for debts.

In the meantime, with the continuing support of a small number of supporters, the Bakkers attempted to reestablish a new ministry. In November 1987, Jim Bakker was provided ministerial credentials from Faith Christian Fellowship International, a small organization that issues credentials to independent Pentecostal ministers. Those credentials were not renewed, and in 1988 he received credentials from the New Covenant Christian Church of Cranesville, Pennsylvania. Early in 1989 the Bakkers launched a new show, the "Jim and Tammy" show from Charlotte, but within a few months moved to Orlando, Florida, where they began the New Covenant Church of Orlando. However, before their new effort could get off the ground, Bakker was placed on trial on a number of a charges derived from the financial manipulation at PTL. Convicted, he began to serve a lengthy sentence in a federal prison. The decade of the 1980s ended with the Bakker story high on the list of important stories of the decade. The Bakkers have vowed to file an appeal, and it is not evident what course Tammy Faye Bakker might follow, in or out of religious work, in the future.

Sources:

Bakker, Jim. *Eight Keys to Success*. Charlotte, NC: PTL Television Network, 1980. 85 pp.

_____. *God Answers Prayer*. Charlotte, NC: PTL Television Network, 1979. 267 pp.

. _____. *You Can Make It!*. Charlotte, NC: PTL Enterprises, Inc., 1983. 126 pp.

_____, with Robert Paul Lamb. *Move That Mountain*. Plainfield, NJ: Logos International, 1976. 183 pp.

Bakker, Tammy with Cliff Dudley. *I Gotta Be Me*. Charlotte, NC: PTL Club, 1978. 138 pp.

_____, with Cliff Dudley. *Run to the Roar*. Harrison, AR: New Leaf Press, 1980. 139 pp.

Barnhart, Joe E. *Jim and Tammy: Charismatic Intrigue Inside PTL*. Buffalo, NY: Prometheus Books, 1988. 266 pp.

Lippy, Charles H. *Twentieth-Century Shapers of American Popular Religion*. New York: Greenwood Press, 1989. 494 pp.

Shepard, Charles E. *Forgiven*. New York: Atlantic Monthly Press, 1989. 635 pp.

Stewart, John. *Holy War*. Enid, OK: Fireside Publishing & Communications, 1987. 210 pp.

We Win. Charlotte, NC: PTL Club, 1978. 128 pp.

★51★
BALLARD, Edna Anne Wheeler
Cofounder, I AM Religious Activity
b. Jun. 25, 1886, Burlington, Iowa
d. Feb. 10, 1971, Chicago, Illinois

Edna Anne Wheeler Ballard, along with her husband, Guy W. Ballard, was an integral founder and leader of the "I AM" Religious Activity and Saint Germain Foundation. Raised in Iowa, she developed a keen interest in music, and in 1912, at the age of 26, she became a concert harpist. Four years later she married **Guy Warren Ballard**, with whom she shared another interest—the occult.

During the 1920s Edna Ballard worked in Chicago in the Philosopher's Nook bookstore and edited a magazine, *The American Occultist*. Her husband was often out of town on business, and while in California in 1930, he had his first encounters with the Ascended Master, the Comte de Saint Germain on Mt. Shasta. In letters home he explained to his wife what was happening, and when he returned to Chicago they founded the "I AM" Religious Activity, with its organizational carrier, the Saint Germain Foundation. The focus of their teaching involved cooperation with the Ascended Masters, the handful of humans who have so attuned themselves to their "I AM Presence" (God's presence in each individual) that they have ascended into the light to work spiritually on behalf of humanity. Both Ballards taught as Accredited Messengers of the Ascended Masters until Guy Ballard's death in 1939, when Edna assumed full leadership.

At about that time, several ex-members of the movement, including key staff members, accused the Ballards (including their son Donald) of fraud and of using the mail to solicit funds for a belief system they knew to be fictional. Court proceedings continued throughout the 1940s and beyond. Ballard and her group were denied use of the postal service for most of this time. In a landmark Supreme Court case (United States vs Ballard, April 24, 1944), the Ballards were acquitted as the court ruled that persons cannot be made to prove the validity or authenticity of their beliefs, even if the beliefs seem incomprehensible or false to others. Despite this victory, the turmoil continued. It was not until 1954 that Ballard managed to regain use of the mail. Their religious tax-exempt status was not returned until 1957.

Considering these public relations difficulties, Edna Ballard kept the reduced but still intact organization in a low profile, with no media access. As a result, new information on the group has been difficult to obtain. In 1951 a pilgrimage and conference site near Mt. Shasta was purchased. The 1950s also marked the expansion of the "I AM" textbooks and the introduction of a radio program,

which continues today. Since Edna Ballard's death in 1971 and Donald's death in 1973, the "I AM" Religious Activity has been controlled by the board of directors.

Sources:

Braden, Charles S. *These Also Believe*. New York: Macmillan, 1949. 491 pp.

Stupple, David W. *A Functional Approach to Social Movements with an Analysis of the I AM Religious Sect and the Congress of Racial Equality*. Kansas City, MO: Master's thesis, University of Missouri, 1965. 170 pp.

—Gary L. Ward

★52★
BALLARD, Guy Warren
Cofounder, I AM Religious Activity
b. Jul. 28, 1878, Newton, Kansas
d. Dec. 29, 1939, Los Angeles, California

Guy Warren Ballard was the founder and leader, with his wife Edna W. Ballard, of the "I AM" Religious Activity and its organizational support, the Saint Germain Foundation. Guy Ballard was raised in Kansas, attended business college, and supervised his uncle's lead and silver mine in Tucson, Arizona, for several years. In 1916 he married Edna, with whom he shared interests in occult religion. They soon settled in Chicago, though his business duties often kept him out of town.

In 1930, business took him to northern California, where he was anxious to visit Mt. Shasta, a place he knew from theosophical writings to be a special contact point for the mystic masters. In September, while hiking on the mountain, Ballard met another hiker who revealed himself to be Comte de Saint Germain, a European nobleman from the eighteenth century who was now looking to give mystic teachings to appropriate messengers to help usher in a new age on earth. Saint Germain appointed Ballard and his wife, who soon founded the "I AM" Religious Activity and Saint Germain Foundation and published the revelations in a number of books, beginning with *Unveiled Mysteries* in 1934. These books were often published under the pseudonym Godfre Ray King. The teaching is basically related to communication and cooperation with the Ascended Masters, those who have discovered the "I AM Presence" as the God within each person, and have so allied themselves with this presence that they have, upon physical death, ascended into the light and now work to uplift humanity. Forceful statements, called "decrees," are often used to activate this power.

By 1939 the movement reached successfully across the United States and encountered such powerful media response—most of it negative—that Ballard closed the introductory ten-day classes to the public. Ballard died in that year and did not live to see the Supreme Court battle in 1944 over the status of the "I AM" Religious Activity, the continuing presence of his group worldwide into the 1990s, or the large array of other groups that have since also proclaimed the Ascended Master message.

Sources:

Ballard, Guy W. [Godfre Ray King]. *The "I AM" Discourses*. 4th ed. Chicago: St. Germain Press, 1935, 1982. 361 pp.

_____. *The Magic Presence*. 5th ed. Chicago: St. Germain Press, 1935, 1982. 399 pp.

_____. *Unveiled Mysteries*. 4th ed. Chicago: St. Germain Press, Inc., 1934, 1982. 260 pp.

Braden, Charles S. *These Also Believe*. New York: Macmillan, 1949. 491 pp.

Bryan, Gerald B. *Psychic Dictatorship in America*. Burbank, CA: The New Era Press, 1940. 255 pp.

Stupple, David W. *A Functional Approach to Social Movements with an Analysis of the I AM Sect and the Congress of Racial Equality*. Kansas City, MO: University of Missouri, Master's thesis, 1965. 170 pp.

—Gary L. Ward

★53★
BARNHOUSE, Donald Grey
Minister, United Presbyterian Church in the U.S.A.
b. Mar. 28, 1895, Watsonville, California
d. Nov. 5, 1960, Philadelphia, Pennsylvania

Donald Grey Barnhouse, a fundamentalist Presbyterian minister and editor, was the son of Jane Ann Carmichael and Theodore Barnhouse, a pious Methodist couple living in northern California. As a youth Barnhouse attended the local meetings of the Christian Endeavor Society, a national Christian youth fellowship. During his high school years Barnhouse met Tom Haney, the Christian Endeavor field secretary for the area, who led him into a "born again" experience (in which he realized his sinful condition and accepted Christ as his Savior) which altered his life completely. After high school he followed Haney's lead and attended the Bible Institute of Los Angeles, where he studied under **Reuben A. Torrey**. Besides grounding him in Christian fundamentalism, it also led him away from the Methodist to the Presbyterian Church. After two years in Los Angeles, Barnhouse transferred to Princeton Theological Seminary, but his education was interrupted after two years when he went into the army (1917-1918). Immediately after his discharge, he was ordained as a Presbyterian minister and sailed for Brussels, Belgium, as a missionary with the Belgian Gospel Mission.

Barnhouse spent two years in Belgium and then resigned to become pastor of a French Reformed church in Fessinieres. During his two year pastorate he married Ruth Tiffany. In 1923 he moved to Mure d'Isere and while there became a graduate student at the University of Grenoble. Upon his return to the United States, he became pastor of Grace Presbyterian Church in Philadelphia and pursued graduate studies at the University of Pennsylvania and Eastern Baptist Theological Seminary, the latter school granting him a Th.M. in 1927. That year he became pastor of Tenth Avenue Presbyterian Church in Philadelphia, where he would stay for the rest of his life.

Barnhouse excelled as a pastor. The attendance at the church steadily increased, but it soon became obvious that he had a larger ministry as well. In 1928 he became the first Presbyterian minister to use a national radio network for a regular weekly show. In 1931 he launched *Revelation*, an independent evangelical magazine (later retitled *Eternity*). In 1933 he finished the first of his many books, *His Own Received Him Not But*. Beginning in 1940 the congregation released him for six months of each year for his work throughout the country and around the world. In 1949 he founded the Evangelical Foundation as an organizational focus for his ministries.

Barnhouse's early years in Philadelphia coincided with the disruption at Princeton that caused the more conservative faculty and students to leave and establish Westminster Theological Seminary in Philadelphia and eventually the Orthodox Presbyterian Church. Though sympathetic to their cause, Barnhouse refused to leave the Presbyterian Church and join his beleaguered colleagues. His willingness to stay in the church and work with the dominant liberal faction which controlled it created many differences between him and the independent fundamentalists in later years.

In 1952 Barnhouse experienced a major spiritual change in his life, which he articulated as a new realization of love and a desire to be more loving. He expressed a willingness to leave behind some of the lesser polemics of the past and to center his ministry upon more loving relationships in the present, especially with fellow Christians. Those around him testified to the genuine maturation that followed this change.

In 1954 Barnhouse, whose first wife died in 1944, married Margaret Nuckols. The following year, in what seemed to many evangelicals an extreme betrayal, Barnhouse appeared as a speaker on a program for the liberal National Council of Churches. While always following an independent course, much to the consternation of other evangelical leaders, even his detractors never seriously accused him of compromising the fundamentals of the faith he espoused.

Sources:

Barnhouse, Donald Grey. *God's Methods for Holy Living*. London: Pickering & Inglis, n.d. 93 pp.
_____. *Guaranteed Deposits*. Philadelphia: Revelation Publications, 1949. 160 pp.
_____. *His Own Received Him Not But*. New York: Fleming H. Revell Company, 1933. 185 pp.
_____. *Life by the Son*. Philadelphia: Revelation Publications, 1939. 127 pp.
_____. *Teaching the Word of Truth*. Philadelphia: Revelation Book Service, 140 pp.
Barnhouse, Margaret N. *That Man Barnhouse*. Wheaton, IL: Tyndale House Publishers, 1985. 415 pp.
Hopkins, Paul A. "What Made the Man?" *Eternity* 12, 3 (March 1961): 14-18, 35-41.
Reid, Daniel G., Robert D. Linder, Bruce L. Shelley, and Harry S. Stout. *Dictionary of Christianity in America*. Downers Grove, IL: InterVarsity Press, 1990. 1305 pp.

★54★
BARR, Amelia Edith Huddleston
Christian Writer and Novelist
b. Mar. 29, 1831, Ulverston United Kingdom
d. Mar. 10, 1919, Richmond Hill, Long Island, New York

Amelia Edith Huddleston Barr, a popular religious writer and novelist, was the daughter of a British Methodist minister. The family moved frequently, as was common to Methodists, but Barr spent most of her youthful years in northern England. She received a private school education as her father had income apart from his parish work. A family financial crisis led Amelia to begin a teaching career at the age of 16. She taught first at a school in Norfolk for a year and then in a school started by her mother and two sisters. She then worked for the Wesleyan Board of Education while attending the Normal School in Glasgow, Scotland. The Methodists hoped that she would eventually work in their schools for the poor. Her course of study in Glasgow was cut short by her marriage to Robert Barr, a businessman in Glasgow. During these years, she had a brief encounter with the American Congregationalist minister, Henry Ward Beecher, who was to re-enter her life in later years.

In 1851 Robert Barr went bankrupt. Two years later Amelia, her husband, and their two children immigrated to the United States. They moved to Chicago, Memphis, and Galveston before settling in Austin, Texas. She opened a school in Austin and became the mother of a large family. In 1866 her husband died of yellow fever, and she moved on to Galveston and later to Ridgewood, New Jersey. Her employer in Ridgewood became her first literary agent, helping her sell some writing. Thus in 1870 she moved to New York City and began a new career as an author.

In New York, Barr renewed her acquaintance with **Henry Ward Beecher**, then at the height of his career as pastor of Pilgrim Congregationalist Church in Brooklyn, New York, and editor of the *Christian Union*. He invited her to write for the *Union*, and during the 1870s she penned more than a thousand items for it, the *Christian Herald*, and the *New York Ledger*. In another periodical, the weekly *Working Church*, she serialized a novel, entitled "Eunice Leslie." Her first book, *Romances and Realities: Tales of Truth and Fancy*, was published in 1875. She eventually authored 81 books—mostly popular novels—and hundreds of articles, short stories, and poems. Her writings were characterized by a strong undercurrent of "interdenominational" Christianity and a sentimental, folksy approach to life. She drew upon her broad experience of life in both Scotland and Civil War Texas.

Among her most prominent novels were *Cluny MacPherson* (1883); *Jan Vedder's Wife* (1885); *The Bow of Orange Ribbon* (1886), *A Daughter of Fife* (1886); and *Remember the Alamo* (1888). In her eighties, she penned her autobiography, *All the Days of My Life* (1913); five years later she released her last book, *The Paper Cap*.

Her last days were spent in relative luxury. In 1885 she forsook New York City for Cornwall-on-Hudson and later Long Island, and she frequently traveled to Europe for the summer.

Sources:

Barr, Amelia Edith Huddleston. *All the Days of My Life*. New York: D. Appleton & Company, 1913. 527 pp.

_____. *The Bow of Orange Ribbon*. New York: P. F. Collier & Son, 1886. 345 pp.

_____. *Cluny MacPherson*. New York: Dodd, Mead & Co., 1898. 311 pp.

_____. *The Paper Cap*. New York: D. Appleton & Co., 1918. 154 pp.

_____. *Remember the Alamo*. New York: Dodd, Mead & Co., 1888. 431 pp.

James, Edward T., ed. *Notable American Women, 1607-1950: A Biographical Dictionary*. 3 vols. Cambridge, MA: Harvard University Press, Belknap Press, 1971.

★ 55 ★
BARRETT, Harrison D.
President, National Spiritualist Association
b. Apr. 25, 1863, Canaan, Maine
d. Jan. 12, 1911, Canaan, Maine

Harrison D. Barrett was the first president of the National Spiritualist Association, which is now the National Spiritualist Association of Churches, the oldest of the presently existing national Spiritualist organizations. Growing up in rural Maine, he was frequently ill and his education was sporadic. His grandfather had been a Spiritualist, and Barrett developed an interest in spirit contact as a youth following the death of his 12-year-old sister in 1880. Grieving over her death, one night in bed he heard some rappings, knocking sounds believed by Spiritualists to be caused by spirits of the dead wishing to communicate with the living. He began to ask it questions and concluded it was his sister and that she still lived in the spirit realm.

As a young man he traveled west and taught school in Minnesota and Wyoming. He affiliated with the American Unitarian Association (AUA) and in his early twenties moved back east to further his schooling. He completed the course of study at the Unitarian Theological Seminary, then located at Meadville, Pennsylvania, in 1889.

The prospect of a career in the Unitarian ministry led to a spiritual crisis, and Barrett was unable to resolve the conflict between the Unitarian beliefs and his Spiritualism. He left the Unitarians and soon became one of the more capable Spiritualist lecturers and mediums.

While Spiritualism had been in existence for over 40 years, and several state associations had formed, it had not created a stable national structure. The occasion for such an organization seems to have been the World's Parliament of Religions which met in Chicago in the summer of 1893. Spiritualism was not officially represented there. However, in September 1893, while the congress was still in session, a delegated convention of Spiritualists convened in Chicago and formed the National Spiritualist Association. Barrett was elected its first president and was reelected annually for the rest of his life. The inception of the association led to the modern reorientation of Spiritualism toward the establishment of Spiritualist churches and congregations.

As president, Barrett was influential in the writing and adoption in 1899 of the then six-part statement of Spiritualist beliefs, the "Declaration of Principles" of the National Spiritualist Association. He is also remembered for having defended a medium accused of witchcraft in court. Her acquittal is looked upon as a major step in the legal establishment of Spiritualism. Barrett also served as the editor of a prominent Spiritualist periodical, the *Banner of Light*, from 1897 to 1904. He authored several books, most importantly, *Life Work of Mrs. Cora L. V. Richmond*, a work on the prominent medium who served as the first vice-president of the association. He compiled and edited *Cassadaga, Its History and Its Teachings* (1891), a volume about the Spiritualist camp in Florida, with A.W. McCoy.

Barrett was only 48 years old when he passed away in 1911.

Sources:

Awtry, Marilyn, and Paul M. Vogt. *Who's Who in Spiritualism of Yesteryear*. Vol. I. N.p.: SAM Inc., 1981. 34 pp.

Barrett, Harrison D. *Life Work of Mrs. Cora L. V. Richmond*. Chicago: Hack & Anderson, 1895. 759 pp.

_____. *Pantheistic Idealism*. Portland, OR: Glass & Prudhomme Company, 1910. 54 pp.

_____, and A. W. McCoy, comps. *Cassadaga, Its History and Its Teachings*. Meadville, PA: The Gazette Printing Co., 1891. 247 pp.

Centennial Book of Modern Spiritualism in America. Chicago: The National Spiritualist Association of the United States of America, 1948. 253 pp.

★ 56 ★
BARRETT, Kate Harwood Waller
Cofounder, National Florence Crittenton Mission
Protestant Episcopal Church Laywoman
b. Jan. 24, 1857, Falmouth, Virginia
d. Feb. 23, 1925, Alexandria, Virginia

Kate Harwood Waller Barrett, cofounder of the National Florence Crittenton Mission, a pioneer ministry for unwed mothers and prostitutes, was the eldest child of ten born to Ann Eliza Stribbing and Withers Waller. Her father had been a colonel in the Confederate Army. She was educated primarily at home, though she spent two years at the Arlington Institute for Girls in Alexandria, Virginia. In 1876 she married a minister in the Episcopal Church, Robert South Barrett, rector of a church in the poorer section of Richmond, Virginia. The arrival of an unwed mother and her baby at her door changed Barrett's life. Barrett identified with her plight. She dedicated her life to help her sisters, those commonly called "fallen women."

Barrett's husband moved on to more prominent parishes. In 1880 he began a six-year stay in Henderson, Kentucky, and she initiated pastoral work among the local prostitutes. In 1886 he became dean of St. Luke's Cathedral in Atlanta, and she, now thoroughly committed to her avocation, enrolled at the Women's College of Georgia, from which she received her medical degree in 1892. The following year she opened a home for unwed mothers which, after countering the attacks of a hostile public, received the approval of the local ministerial association and the city council.

At about the time of her graduation from medical school, Barrett learned of Charles L. Crittenton. A decade earlier he had given up the business that had made him a millionaire and opened a mission, named for his daughter Florence, which targeted "fallen women." There were four such missions in New York and California. Barrett contacted him, and in 1893 he gave a substantial gift to Barrett's home in Atlanta, which became the fifth Florence Crittenton Mission.

Rev. Barrett moved to Washington, D.C., in 1894 as the general missioner of the Protestant Episcopal Church. He died two years later. In the meantime, however, in 1895, Crittenton and Barrett formed the National Florence Crittenton Mission. He served as president and she as vice-president and general superintendent. By the time the Mission was chartered in 1888, there were over 50 local centers, which Barrett superintended. She organized the annual conferences that began in 1897, edited the *Florence Crittenton Magazine*, and traveled widely throughout the work.

Barrett spelled out her perspective on mission work in *Some Practical Suggestions on the Conduct of a Rescue Mission*, published in 1903. She was a traditional evangelical, advocating an emphasis on conversion from sin. She advised mission leaders to refrain from giving much attention to the women's life stories and to concentrate on leading them to forsake their past life.

Under her guidance the mission placed more and more emphasis on working with unwed mothers, as opposed to the evangelical and pastoral attention to prostitutes. Barrett was among the first to argue for unwed mothers keeping their children, though her ancestry in a prominent Virginia family was apparent in her arguments. She urged that after the birth of the child, the mother move to a place where she would not bring shame upon the rest of her family.

In 1909 Crittenton died, and Barrett became president of the mission, a position she held for the rest of her life. During the early decades of the new century, the work of the mission was generally accepted and Barrett became a prominent spokesperson on women's issues and in women's organizations. In 1911 she was elected president of the National Council of Women and for two decades was active in the International Council of Women. She served 11 years as the vice-president of the Virginia Equal Suffrage League (1909-1920). She became president of the National Women's Auxiliary of the American Legion (1922- 1923).

After her death, Barrett's son, Robert South Barrett, began a 34-year tenure as president of the mission. In 1927 a hall at William and Mary College was named in her honor.

Sources:

Barrett, Kate Waller. *Some Practical Suggestions on the Conduct of a Rescue Home*. Washington, DC: National Florence Crittenton Mission, 1903. 115 pp.
Fourteen Years Work Among "Erring Girls" as Conducted by the National Florence Crittenton Mission. Privately Printed, 1897.
James, Edward T., ed. *Notable American Women, 1607-1950: A Biographical Dictionary*. 3 vols. Cambridge, Massachusetts: Harvard University Press, Belknap Press, 1971.
Wilson, Otto, with Robert South Barrett. *Fifty Years' Work with Girls, 1883-1933*. Alexandria, VA: The National Florence Crittenton Mission, 1933. 513 pp.

★57★
BARTON, Bruce
Popular Religious Writer, Congregational Church
b. Aug. 5, 1886, Robbins, Tennessee
d. Jul. 5, 1967, New York, New York

Bruce Barton, one of the most popular religious writers of the 1920s and 1930s, was the son of William E. Barton, a Congregationalist minister, and Esther Treat Bushnell Barton. His father served churches in Tennessee, Ohio, and finally Boston, where Barton attended high school. He developed an early bent toward writing and became editor of his high school newspaper. He attended Berea College in Ohio, his father's alma mater, for one year but then finished at Amherst College in Massachusetts where he distinguished himself academically and became president of the student council. His graduation in 1907 became the occasion for a personal crisis. Doubt-ridden, he moved to Montana and took a job with the railroad.

Resolving his doubts while in Montana, Barton concluded that he was not called to the ministry. Rather he would choose a secular occupation in which he could employ his religious values. He returned to Chicago and secured a job with a magazine, *Home Herald*. Within a short time he became its managing editor. In 1909

he moved to New York to work for *The Continent*, a Presbyterian magazine. He moved onto *The Housekeeper* and finally to *Collier's Weekly*. While working for Collier's he had his first marked business success with an advertising campaign he planned for the Harvard Classics and wrote his first book, *The Resurrection of the Soul* (1912). In 1913 he married Esther Randall.

In 1914 he authored the first of the several books which were to bring a generation's fame upon him. *A Young Man's Jesus* portrayed Jesus in a manner to appeal to the idealistic youth of the day. Barton's Jesus had lost his meekness and mild mannered ways in favor of physical strength, courage, and spiritual power. The book also stressed the emphasis that Barton would increasingly place upon personal striving and success, especially in business, as one ideal form of Christian life. These values became even more focused in the editorials he wrote for *Every Week*, a popular magazine he edited for five years (1914-1918).

In 1918, when *Every Week* failed, Barton began an advertising company with two friends. Here he finally found the financial success he had sought. Barton, Durstine, and Osborn (after 1927 Batten, Barton, Durstine & Osborn) became the third largest advertising company in the United States by the time Barton died.

Occupationally stable, Barton turned his attention to reconciling business and Christian values. He valued success, but saw the possibility of it without giving in to overriding concern with accumulation, ambition, and arrogance. Christian businessmen could emphasize service, humility, and goodness. Jesus could be the businessman's ideal. Barton's mature vision was developed and shared in a series of books, beginning with *It's a Good Old World* (1917) and *Better Days* (1924), both compilations of editorials from *Every Week*. They were followed by the three best selling volumes for which Barton is remembered: *The Man Nobody Knows* (1925), his biography of Jesus; *The Book Nobody Knows* (1926); and *What Can a Man Believe* (1927). Published at the height of the fundamentalist-modernist controversy, they were decidedly modernist. They were attacked by critics as superficial, but found a large audience of readers among the general public.

Briefly shaken in his faith by the Great Depression, he recovered to write one more book, *He Upset the World* (1932), but then left the world of popular religious writing for serious business pursuits. He first placed his immense talent and energies into developing advertising as a tool to rebuild the post-depression image of big business. On the heels of a number of successful ad campaigns, he entered politics. He became a New York State representative for four years (1937-1941) and ran an unsuccessful campaign in 1940 for U. S. senator. He retired from political life during World War II, a dedicated Republican noninterventionist, and until slowed by a stroke in 1957, remained an active corporate executive, and a power in the national business community.

Sources:

Barton, Bruce. *Better Days*. New York: Century Company, 1924. 116 pp.
———. *The Book Nobody Knows*. Indianapolis, IN: Bobbs-Merrill, 1926. 305 pp.
———. *He Upset the World*. Indianapolis, IN: Bobbs-Merrill, 1931. 186 pp.
———. *The Man Nobody Knows*. Indianapolis, IN: Bobbs-Merrill, 1925. 219 pp.
———. *What Can a Man Believe*. Indianapolis, IN: Bobbs-Merrill, 1927. 252 pp.
Ferreira, James M. "Only Yesterday and the Two Christs of the Twenties." *South Atlantic Quarterly* 80 (1981): 77-83. Lippy, Charles H. *Twentieth-Century Shapers of American Popular Religion*. New York: Greenwood Press, 1989. 494 pp.

★ 58 ★
BASHAM, Donald Wilson
Minister, Christian Church (Disciples of Christ)
b. Sep. 17, 1926, Texas
d. Mar. 27, 1989, California

Donald Wilson Basham, a minister with the Christian Church (Disciples of Christ) who became known for his work with the Charismatic Movement, was the son of Hal J. and Eileen Hicks Basham. Basham was raised a Baptist and began his adult life as a commercial artist. In the 1940s he met Alice Roling, and while they were dating he joined the Disciples of Christ, of which she was a member. In 1949 they married, and the following year he entered Phillips University with the intention of becoming a minister. While at Phillips, he and his wife both experienced the Pentecostal baptism of the Holy Spirit (as evidenced by their speaking in tongues) and associated with a Pentecostal prayer meeting where the experience was accepted and promoted. He continued his schooling receiving his B.A. in 1954 and his B.D. in 1957. He had been ordained in 1956, and after his graduation he became the pastor of a church in Washington, D.C. He later pastored in Toronto (1961-1964) and in Sharon, Pennsylvania (1964-1967).

Basham's pastoral years coincided with the emergence of a fledgling Charismatic Movement, a movement made up of members of mainline Christian churches who had experienced the baptism of the Holy Spirit, an experience usually confined to the Pentecostal churches. Having become active in the movement and wishing to spend all of his energies in a charismatic ministry, in 1967 Basham resigned his pastorate and moved to Ft. Lauderdale, Florida, as editor of *New Wine*, a charismatic agazine. That same year he released his first book, *Face Up with a Miracle*, the story of his pilgrimage.

In Ft. Lauderdale, Basham associated with Christian Growth Ministries. Along with colleagues **Bob Mumford**, Derek Prince, Charles Simpson, and **Ern Baxter**, Basham became a leading exponent of what was termed "shepherding," a form of organization designed to bring some order to the independent charismatic churches. Basham and his colleagues advocated the establishment of "shepherds" who would guide believers in becoming committed disciples. The abuse of the shepherding system and the criticism of shepherds meddling in the private lives of individuals led to the break-up of the ministry in Florida in the mid-1980s. Basham also championed the notion that Christians can be demon-possessed and in need of a deliverance ministry.

During his years in Ft. Lauderdale, Basham authored a number of books, including *Handbook on the Holy Spirit* (1968); *Can a Christian Have a Demon* (1970); *Deliver Us from Evil* (1973); *Beyond Blessing to Obedience* (1976); and *Lead Us Not into Temptation* (1987). In 1987, after *New Wine* ceased publication, Basham moved to Ohio and began publishing *Don Basham's Insights*. His health soon failed him, however, and after a year and a half of illness, he passed away from a heart attack.

Sources:
Basham, Don. *Face Up with a Miracle*. Northridge, CA: Voice Christian Publications, 1967. 169 pp.

———. *A Handbook on the Holy Spirit*. Monroeville, PA: Whitaker Books, 1969. 118 pp.

———. *A Handbook on Tongues, Interpretation, and Prophecy*. Monroeville, PA: Whitaker Books, 1971. 123 pp.

———. *Ministering the Baptism in the Holy Spirit*. Monroeville, PA: Whitaker Books, 1971. 68 pp.

———. *The Miracle of Tongues*. Old Tappan, NJ: Fleming H. Revell, 1973. 127 pp.

———. *True and False Prophets*. Greensburg, PA: Manna Books, 1973. 130 pp.

"Don Basham Remembered." *Charisma & Christian Life* 14, 10 (May 1989): 29.

★ 59 ★
BASHIR, Anthony
Metropolitan Archbishop, Antiochean Orthodox Christian Archdiocese of North America
b. Mar. 15, 1898, Douma Lebanon
d. Feb. 15, 1966, Boston, Massachusetts

Anthony Bashir, archbishop of the Antiochean Orthodox Christian Archdiocese of North America, was born in the mountain country of rural Lebanon. Raised in a devout Orthodox family, he attended Balamand Theological Seminary near Tripoli. He was ordained a deacon in 1916 and then continued his studies at the American University in Beirut and the School of Law in Baabda. He became a teacher at American University and secretary to the Archbishop of Lebanon. Among his scholarly accomplishments was his oversight of a new Arabic translation of the Christian New Testament.

In 1925 the Patriarch of Antioch sent Father Anthony to the United States. The following year he was made an archimandrite. As a special representative of the patriarch, Father Anthony traveled widely and used his bilingual talents to translate Arabic works into English. Included among his translations were many of the writings of Khalil Gibran, the Lebanese poet.

In 1935, following the death of Archbishop Victor Abou Assaley, Father Anthony was elected to fill the post of archbishop for the North American church. Patriarch Theodosios traveled to New York to perform the consecration service in February 1936. The new archbishop was faced with an immediate problem when Fr. Samuel David, who ran second in the vote for the archbishopric, turned for support to some bishops of the Russian Orthodox Church, who consecrated him as archbishop of a rival Antiochean body on the same day that Anthony was consecrated. Tension led Archbishop Anthony to briefly excommunicate Archbishop Samuel in 1937. (This schism was not healed until 1975.)

In spite of the schism, Archbishop Anthony enthusiastically worked to build his jurisdiction by traveling throughout Canada, the United States, and Mexico. He published numerous Orthodox books and founded *The Word*, the archdiocese's periodical. He encouraged the education of future priests and, unable to support a seminary, developed close ties between the archdiocese and St. Vladimir's Orthodox Seminary, the school of the Russian Orthodox Church.

Archbishop Anthony is remembered as one of the earliest and strongest voices of a united and Americanized Orthodoxy. He encouraged the formation of the Orthodox Federation (later superseded by the Standing Conference of Orthodox Bishops) and served for a number of years as its vice-president. He also encouraged the use of the vernacular in the liturgy and was among the first to introduce an English liturgy.

Archbishop Anthony died unexpectedly in 1966 and was succeeded by Archbishop Philip Saliba, whom he had ordained in 1959.

Sources:
Who's Who in America. Wilmette, IL: Marquis Who's Who, Inc.

★ 60 ★
BATEHAM, Josephine Abiah Penfield Cushman
Social Activist
Laywoman, Congregationalist Church
b. Nov. 1, 1829, Alden, New York
d. Mar. 15, 1901, Oberlin, Ohio

Josephine Abiah Penfield Cushman Bateham, a prominent social reformer, was one of six children born to Anson and Minerva Dayton Penfield. When Josephine was five years old, she moved to Oberlin, Ohio, with her family. Her father, a mechanic, was killed in an accident in 1839. In 1844 her mother married the Rev. Henry Cowles, a widower and professor at Oberlin Collegiate Institute (later Oberlin College). Cowles served as a trustee of the college and edited the *Oberlin Evangelist* while his new wife served on the Female Board of Managers, which governed the female department of the college. The family worshiped at the Congregational Church.

After graduating from Oberlin in 1847, Josephine taught school for a year. She married in 1848 and moved with her husband, Rev. Richard Cushman, to Haiti. Her husband died after only 11 months on the tropical mission field, and in 1849 Josephine returned to Oberlin as a widow. She married Michael Boyd Bateham, editor/publisher of the *Ohio Cultivator* and a prominent figure in the development of Ohio agriculture. Josephine Bateham became the women's editor for the magazine and, influenced by the liberal views of the college and community, used it to advocate a variety of social reforms, from women's rights to education to women's dress. She continued to write for the *Cultivator* for many years, even after her husband sold it.

In the decade before the Civil War, the Batehams became active in both the peace movement and the temperance movement. In 1853, Josephine Bateham became president of the State Temperance Society of the Women of Ohio.

After the Civil War, the Batehams moved to Painesville, Ohio, and settled into a domestic life. They managed a fruit farm and raised seven children. In 1874, however, the national temperance crusade swept through Ohio. Ms. Bateham took charge of the work in Painesville. She participated in the formation of the state's Woman's Christian Temperance Union (W.C.T.U.), and after her husband's death in 1880 became increasingly involved in the national organization. This was the period in which, under the leadership of national president **Frances Willard**, the W.C.T.U. developed a greatly diversified program. Bateham, who had become interested in the observance of the Christian sabbath, superintended the W.C.T.U.'s Department for the Suppression of Sabbath Desecration. (Given the general abandonment of laws respecting any religious group's holy days, it is often forgotten that, in the nineteenth century, sabbath reform was a vital part of the entire liberal social program.)

Bateham continued her leadership of the department for 12 years. She authored the *Sabbath Observance Manual* in 1892 and traveled widely to lecture on behalf of the cause. Her most intense work came following the introduction of a Sunday rest bill into the United States Senate in 1888. She testified for the measure which would have prohibited work on the sabbath, and organized a petition drive through the W.C.T.U. on its behalf. The bill was defeated in committee.

During the last decade of her life, Bateham moved frequently, first to Ashville, North Carolina, in 1890, then to Williamsburg, Kentucky, in 1892, and to Norwalk, Ohio, in 1897. She also left the Congregational Church and became a Presbyterian in these latter years.

Sources:

Bateham, Josephine Penfield. *The Invalid Singer*. Boston, MA: J. H. Earle, 1895.

James, Edward T., ed. *Notable American Women, 1607-1950: A Biographical Dictionary*. 3 vols. Cambridge, MA: Harvard University Press, Belknap Press, 1971.

★61★
BAUM, William Wakefield
Cardinal, Roman Catholic Church
b. Nov. 21, 1926, Dallas, Texas

William Wakefield Baum, a cardinal in the Roman Catholic Church, was the son of Mary Leona Hayes and Harry E. Baum. He

was raised in Kansas City, Missouri, where his family moved when he was a child. He entered a minor seminary at the age of 13 and then attended Kendrick Seminary in St. Louis, Missouri, from 1947 to 1951. He was ordained in 1951 and assigned as assistant pastor of Saint Aloysius Catholic Church, in Kansas City. He later became an instructor of theology and church history at the College of Saint Theresa. In 1956 he began a two-year period in Rome, during which time he earned an S.T.L. degree at the University of St. Thomas Aquinas.

Upon his return to Kansas City, Baum served in a variety of pastoral positions. In 1962 he became a peritus (expert) at Vatican II and in 1964 was named executive secretary of the American bishops' Committee on Ecumenical and Interreligious Affairs. In 1967 he was named chancellor of the diocese of Kansas City-Saint Joseph. In 1970 he was consecrated as bishop for Springfield-Cape Girardeau (Missouri).

In 1973 Baum was moved to Washington, D.C., as the successor of Abp. **Patrick O'Boyle**. O'Boyle, a staunch conservative, had angered many in the archdiocese, especially the more liberal elements in the church following the decrees of the Second Vatican Council. O'Boyle's conflict with the priests had been intensified by what was seen as harsh treatment given to priests who openly disagreed with him.

In 1976 Baum was elevated to cardinal and assigned duties with the Congregation for Catholic Education. Baum stayed in Washington a relatively short time. In 1980 he was called to Rome as prefect of the Congregation for Catholic Education. He has remained in Rome in the years since.

Sources:

MacEoin, Gary and the Committee for the Responsible Election of the Pope. *The Inner Elite*. Kansas City, MO: Sheed Andrews and McMeel, 1978. 301 pp.

★62★
BAUMAN, Louis Sylvester
Minister, Fellowship of Grace Brethren Churches
b. Nov. 13, 1875, Nora Springs, Iowa
d. Nov. 8, 1950, Washington, District of Columbia

Louis Sylvester Bauman, one of the founders of the Fellowship of Grace Brethren Churches, was the son of William J. H. and Amelia Leckington Bauman. His father was a Brethren minister who had originally been trained as a Roman Catholic priest. Bauman joined the local congregation of the Brethren Church (Ashland, Ohio) as a youth and began to preach when he was 17. He finished high school but did not go to college. He was ordained in 1894, and soon emerged as one of the church's most skilled evangelists. In 1898 he married Mary Melissa Wakeman. He became pastor of the First Brethren Church of Philadelphia in 1900.

While in Philadelphia Bauman developed two interests which were to become prime areas of concern for the rest of his life. In 1896 a speaker at the Brethren Church general conference first attracted his attention to foreign missions. In 1900 he became a charter member of the Foreign Missionary Society and in 1904 a member of its board of trustees. In 1906 he began a four decade job as the board's secretary. For a whole generation he became the person most known for missionary enthusiasm in Brethren Church circles.

Also while at Philadelphia Bauman began to assume theological emphases from the influence of independent fundamentalist teachers and evangelists, especially a particular concern for eschatology (the study of the final events of the world). He also moved from the more common nineteenth-century Brethren perspective of postmillennialism (the belief that the millennium, the thousand year earthly reign of Christ, will precede his coming back to earth) to the popular fundamentalist perspective called premillennialism (the belief that Christ's second coming is imminent and that the millennium will be established by him after he appears). The influence of fundamentalism is clear in Bauman's most important text, written in 1908 and frequently reprinted, *The Faith Once for All Delivered to the Saints*.

In 1909 Bauman's wife died. In 1911 he led an evangelist meeting in Los Angeles, California, where he met Retta Virginia Stover. Bauman married her the next year. In 1912 he conducted revival meetings in Long Beach, California, which led to the formation of a Brethren congregation in Long Beach. It soon became the largest congregation in the Brethren Church. He served the congregation for 35 years. During these years he moved in the conservative theological circles associated with the Bible School of Los Angeles.

During the 1930s Bauman served as a trustee of Ashland College, the denominational school of the Brethren Church. Through the early years of the decade he joined in the criticism of liberalism at the school. In 1935, following the firing of several of the college's prominent critics, including the president and a teacher of the associated Ashland Theological Seminary, he became one of the founders of the independent Grace Theological Seminary. Two years later, following the discussion of the new seminary at the Brethren Church conference, Bauman was one of those who walked out to found the National Fellowship of Brethren Churches (now known as the Fellowship of Grace Brethren Churches). He took his Long Beach congregation into the Grace Fellowship.

In 1940 Bauman finished his most important eschatological text, *Light from Bible Prophecy*. In 1948 he moved to Washington, D.C., as pastor of the Grace Brethren congregation which he pastored for the rest of his life.

Sources:

Bauman, Louis S. *The Faith Once for All Delivered to the Saints*. Winona Lake, IN: Brethren Missionary Herald Co., 1909, 1947. 122 pp.
———. *Light from Bible Prophecy*. New York: Fleming H. Revell Company, 1940. 169 pp.
———. *The Tongues Movement*. Winona Lake, IN: Brethren Missionary Herald Co., 1963. 47 pp.

★ 63 ★
BAXTER, William John Ernest
Independent Pentecostal Minister
b. 1914, Saskatoon, Saskatchewan, Canada

William John Ernest Baxter, generally known simply as Ern Baxter, was raised in the Presbyterian Church in Canada by his parents, W. E. and Annie Mae Baxter. His parents became Pentecostals when he was a teenager, but Ern initially rejected the change. Only gradually did he accept the new association. In 1932, while traveling with a friend who was conducting evangelistic meetings, he received the baptism of the Holy Spirit and spoke in tongues, an experience that is considered normative for Pentecostal believers.

During the 1930s Baxter began to pastor a Pentecostal Assemblies of Canada congregation, but left it over doctrinal differences. He became pastor of the Evangelistic Tabernacle, an independent congregation in Vancouver. In 1947 the independent healing evangelist **William Marrion Branham** came to Vancouver, and Branham asked Baxter to join his ministry. Baxter accepted and toured with Branham for the next five years. Attending those same Branham services in Vancouver were a group of people from a bible school in Saskatchewan who eventually returned to begin what became known as the Latter-Rain revival. Baxter was initially impressed with the new emphases of the revival, which stressed the gift of prophecy and the laying on of hands for reception of the Holy Spirit. After several years of working with Branham and helping to spread the revival's message, however, he found unaccept-

able aspects in both, and in 1953 he returned to the tabernacle, where he remained for many years.

During the 1960s Baxter met Dennis Bennett, the charismatic Episcopal priest who headed St. Luke's Episcopal Church in Seattle. Bennett persuaded Baxter to become involved in the Charismatic Movement, a new pentecostal movement growing within mainline denominations. He became deeply involved in the new movement, and developed a ministry of Bible teachings and Christian nurturing that led to his starting a magazine, *New Covenant Times*. In 1974 he attended a conference at Montreat, North Carolina. He met **Bob Mumford**, Charles Simpson, and others involved with Christian Growth Ministries. They were the major exponents of the concept of shepherding, a means of ordering the many new congregations that were appearing around the country in the wake of the charismatic revival. Shepherding involved the acceptance of the authority of more mature Christians by those newer in the faith. Baxter accepted the idea and joined the Ministries at its headquarters in Ft. Lauderdale, Florida, just as a major controversy over shepherding was emerging. Many saw the possibilities for abuse by the shepherds of their immature but trusting followers.

Baxter worked with the group for a decade and was a frequent contributor to *New Wine Magazine*. He moved with the ministry to Mobile, Alabama, in 1978, where Christian Growth Ministries became Integrity Communications. In the mid-1980s, consistent with their decision to decentralize their ministries, the leaders of the movement spread around the United States. Baxter moved to El Cajon, California, where he continues to minister to those who look to him for guidance.

Sources:

Baxter, Ern. *Thy Kingdom Come*. Ft. Lauderdale, FL: CGM Publishers, 1977. 62 pp.
Burgess, Stanley M., Gary B. McGee, and Patrick H. Alexander, eds. *Dictionary of Pentecostal and Charismatic Movements*. Grand Rapids, MI: Regency Reference Library, Zondervan Publishing House, 1988. 914 pp.
Riss, Richard M. *A Survey of 20th Century Revival Movements in North America*. Peabody, MA: Hendrickson Publishers, 1988. 202 pp.
Vintage Years. Mobile, AL: New Wine Magazine, 1980. 221 pp.

★ 64 ★
BEEBE, Joseph A.
Bishop, Christian Methodist Episcopal Church
b. Jun. 25, 1832, Fayetteville, North Carolina
d. Jun. 6, 1903

Joseph A. Beebe, a bishop of the Colored Methodist Episcopal Church (now the Christian Methodist Episcopal Church), was born into slavery, though both his father and grandfather had been Methodist local preachers of some renown. His family consisted of some 17 children, and several of his brothers became preachers. He was converted in 1851 and joined the Methodist Episcopal Church, South. Even though teaching Blacks to read was outlawed after the Nat Turner Rebellion, he learned to read from his master's wife, a pious white woman. Having been taught the shoemaker's trade, he read while he worked and thus became a relatively learned man for his time. In 1858 he married Cornelia Bockrum.

After the Civil War the Methodist Episcopal Church issued Beebe a license to preach, and he was ordained in 1866. At its general conference of 1866, the Methodist Episcopal Church, South gave consideration to the fate of its many black members who were now free men. Rejecting one plan to have them absorbed by the African Methodist Episcopal Church, they moved to set them apart in what became known as the Colored Methodist Church. The new church was established in 1870-1871. Beebe was appointed as presiding elder of the Washington District. In 1873 he was elected as a delegate to the general conference held at Augusta, Georgia, and while there was elected as one of three new bishops for the church and consecrated in the same service with **Lucius H. Holsey** and **Isaac Lane**.

Beebe was assigned as bishop of the Second Episcopal District, which covered the states of Georgia, South Carolina, North Carolina, and Virginia. Beebe served as bishop until 1892 when **William Henry Miles** died. He succeeded Miles as senior bishop, a post he held until his death in 1903.

Sources:

Harmon, Nolan B. *The Encyclopedia of World Methodism.* 2 vols. Nashville: United Methodist Publishing House, 1974.
Harris, Eula Wallace, and Maxie Harris Craig. *Christian Methodist Episcopal Church through the Years.* Jackson, TN: Christian Methodist Episcopal Church Publishing House, 1965. 121 pp.

★ 65 ★
BEECHER, Henry Ward
Minister, Congregational Church
b. Jun. 24, 1813, Litchfield, Connecticut
d. Mar. 8, 1887, Brooklyn, New York

Henry Ward Beecher, one of the best known of the "public clergymen" of the nineteenth century, was the son of Roxana Foote and Lyman Beecher. Beecher was descended from the New England Puritans of the seventeenth century, and his father, Lyman, was a well-known minister, vigorously engaged in the debates of his day. Henry was a sensitive child inclined toward a gentler theology than that of his Puritan forebears. He was also interested in the full range of human life, and more interested in addressing practical moral issues than in purely theological issues.

Beecher graduated from Amherst College in 1830, and trained for the ministry at Lane Theological Seminary in Cincinnati, which his father headed. In 1837 he was licensed to preach by the Cincinnati Presbytery and accepted a position at a small church in Lawrenceburg, Indiana. On August 3 of that year he married Eunice White Bullard, to whom he had become engaged while a student at Amherst. They would have a total of 10 children. In 1838 he was ordained as a Presbyterian minister by the New School Presbytery of Cincinnati. The next year he moved to Indianapolis and pastored a New School congregation for the next eight years.

Beecher was a talented speaker, and his sermons were exceptionally well received. His reputation as a gifted speaker was a major factor influencing the Plymouth Congregational Church of Brooklyn, New York, to offer him its pastorate. He began this ministry in 1847, and the congregation grew until he was addressing about 2,500 people every Sunday. Beecher became a New York landmark, attracting people who came to visit the city. His sermons were printed each week and widely circulated as pamphlets. He became a regular contributor to the *Independent*, and his link with this paper helped significantly to expand its readership. He was also editor of the *Christian Union* (1861-1864 and 1870-1881). Both in terms of instant name recognition and the number of people who heard or read him, Beecher was the most well-known and influential minister of his time.

In addition to his fame as a preacher, Henry Ward Beecher is most remembered for the scandal surrounding his connection with Theodore Tilton and Tilton's wife. The Tiltons were members of Beecher's church, and Beecher had influenced the *Independent* to take on Tilton as an assistant editor. Tilton had unconventional views on marriage and religion, and soon rumors of scandalous conduct began to circulate. Beecher eventually advised Mrs. Tilton to separate from her husband. Rumors also began circulating about Beecher's relationship with Mrs. Tilton. The matter was kept quiet for several years until Spiritualist writer **Victoria Woodhull**, who shared many of Tilton's radical notions on sexual behavior, published an account in 1872 in her newspaper, *Woodhull and Claflin's Weekly*. Beecher denied Woodhull's accusations, and an in-

vestigating committee from his church found nothing improper in his conduct. Then Tilton charged Beecher with adultery and took him to court. The trial, which lasted six months, received national coverage. Although Beecher was not convicted, the remainder of his career was overshadowed by the scandal.

In addition to his newspaper articles, pamphlets, publications of his sermons, and a volume on gardening, Beecher wrote *Life of Jesus Christ* (the first volume of which was published in 1871, and was completed by his sons) and a novel, *Norwood, or Village Life in New England* (1867). Beecher held controversial views, such as his disbelief in a literal hell and his belief in evolution. Against the members' protest, he withdrew from the Association of Congregational Ministers so that his fellow ministers would not have to be burdened with the responsibility of tolerating his views. His *Evolution and Religion* (1885) appeared shortly before his death in 1887.

Sources:

Beecher, Henry Ward. *Evolution and Religion.* Boston: Pilgrim Press, 1885. 440 pp.
_____. *Life of Jesus Christ.* New York: J. B. Ford & Co., 1871. 510 pp.
_____. *Norwood, or Village Life in New England.* 3 vols. London: Sampson Low, Son and Marston, 1867.
_____. *Sermons.* London: S. Low, 1870. 672 pp.
Clark, Clifford E., Jr. *Henry Ward Beecher.* Urbana, IL: University of Illinois Press, 1978. 288 pp.
Dictionary of American Biography. 20 vols. and 7 supps. New York: Charles Scribner's Sons, 1928-1936, 1944-1981.
Hibben, Paxton. *Henry Ward Beecher: An American Portrait.* New York: Charles H. Doran Company, 1927. 361 pp.
Walker, Altina L. *Reverend Beecher and Mrs. Tilton.* Amherst, MA: The University of Massachusetts Press, 1982. 177 pp.

★ 66 ★
BEGIN, Louis Nazaire
Cardinal, Roman Catholic Church
b. Jan. 10, 1840, Levis, Quebec, Canada
d. Jul. 18, 1925, Quebec, Quebec, Canada

Louis Nazaire Begin, archbishop of Quebec and cardinal of the Roman Catholic Church, was the son of Charles and Luce Paradis Begin, a French-Canadian couple. He was educated at the Catholic seminary in Quebec, and then studied at the Gregorian University in Rome and at the University of Innsbruck in Austria. He was ordained in Rome in 1865. That same year he received his doctorate in theology and returned to Canada. In 1868 he joined the faculty of Laval University, which had grown out of the seminary, and in 1884 became principal of the Normal School at the university. During his years at the university he had several papers published which not only brought him to the attention of his superiors but in 1882 earned him membership in the Royal Society of Canada.

In 1888 Begin became the second bishop of Chicoutini, but was only there for three years before being called back to Quebec as coadjutor to Archbishop **Elzear A. Taschereau**. He became administrator of the archdiocese in 1894 and succeeded Taschereau in 1898. During his reign he founded some 70 parishes and was instrumental in several new religious orders moving into Quebec. He presided over the first Plenary Council of Canada in 1909. He was named a cardinal in 1914.

Sources:

New Catholic Encyclopedia. 17 vols. New York: McGraw-Hill, 1967.
Wallace, W. Stewart. *The Macmillan Dictionary of Canadian Biography.* 4th ed., rev. Edited by W. A. McKay. Toronto: Macmillan of Canada, 1978.

★ 67 ★
BEILHART, Jacob
Founder, Spirit Fruit Society
b. Mar. 4, 1867, Fairfield, Ohio
d. Nov. 24, 1908, Ingleside, Illinois

Jacob Beilhart, founder of the communal Spirit Fruit Society, was born on an Ohio farm shortly after the Civil War to John Beilhartz, a first-generation German immigrant, and Barbara Schlotter Beilhartz. He was one of ten children, all of whom were raised as Lutherans. Jacob later rejected the emphasis on "hellfire and damnation" he heard as a youth. Armed with only a minimum of formal schooling, he left home in 1884 to seek employment. The following year he moved to Kansas, where he encountered a Seventh-day Adventist who hired him to work on his farm. Beilhart converted and became a colporteur, a literature evangelist. In 1887 he married and moved to Healdsburg, California, to attend Healdsburg College, the recently opened Seventh-day Adventist institution. He did not finish the school year, however, and he moved back to Kansas, where he was licensed to preach and conduct some evangelistic services.

In 1890 Beilhart became attracted to the work of Adventist Dr. John Harvey Kellogg. Beilhart moved to Battle Creek, Michigan, to work at Kellogg's sanitarium. While in Battle Creek he became interested in the possibilities of faith healing and Christian Science. Leaving Kellogg, he opened a small medical boarding house with C. W. Post, an independent Christian Scientist. By the end of the decade, however, Beilhart was developing his own outlook, which he would come to call "Universal Life." This new philosophy was a mixture of all he had previously encountered, including some theosophy which he had picked up through his reading.

Beilhart had come to feel that the Universal Spirit, God, is an impersonal force that pervades everything. Humans are its highest external expression and will, when perfected, be a complete expression of Spirit. Jesus is a representative human who has reached perfection. Beilhart also saw humans who are on the path to perfection as having a common need to unite with others who have reached the same level.

Thus in 1899 Beilhart moved to the little community of Lisbon (now New Lisbon), Ohio, near his birthplace, began a magazine, *Spirit Fruit*, and began to expound his ideas in lectures in the Midwest. As people were attracted to his low-key approach, he founded the Spirit Fruit Society, incorporated in 1901 with ten members. The membership was somewhat informal and no demands were placed upon those who came to reside on the farm outside of town where the group lived. The group was managed democratically, and a considerable amount of freedom (including sexual freedom) was allowed within the bounds of the demands of managing the farm and surviving financially.

In 1904 the group moved to Chicago and then in 1905 to a farm near Ingleside, Illinois, in Lake County. Here the group stabilized and began to develop a following. Just as the colony reached some level of prosperity, however, Beilhart unexpectedly died of peritonitis following an appendix operation. The society he founded survived Beilhart's death for many years. In 1914 members moved to a farm in Santa Clara County, California, called "Freedom Hill," where it existed until 1930. During the last years of the society, Beilhart's writings were reprinted and circulated by a former member, Leroy "Freedom Hill" Henry. His writings were being republished as late as the 1960s.

Sources:

Beilhart, Jacob. *Love Letters from Spirit to You*. Roscoe, CA: Freedom Hill Henry, 1929. 222 pp. Reprint. Los Angeles, CA: New Age Publishing Co., 1960. 93 pp.

_____. *My Life and Teachings*. Geneva, Switzerland: Quo Vadia?, 1932. 482 pp.

Grant, H. Roger. *Spirit Fruit, A Gentle Utopia*. DeKalb, IL: Northern Illinois University Press, 1988. 203 pp.

Henry, Leroy Freedom Hill, comp. *Jacob Beilhart: Life and Teachings*. Burbank, CA: Freedom Hill Pressery, 1925. 170 pp.

★ 68 ★
BELL, Eudorus N.
Assemblies of God
b. Jun. 27, 1866, Lake Butler, Florida
d. Jun. 15, 1923, Springfield, Missouri

Eudorus N. Bell was born into poverty but went on to become an educated leader and one of the founders of the Assemblies of God. His father died in 1868, when Eudorus and his twin brother, Endorus, were only two, placing the family in financial hardship. From early on, however, Eudorus felt called to the ministry. He persevered through college and graduate school at the University of Chicago, where he graduated in 1903, to become a pastor with the Southern Baptist Convention in Texas.

In 1907 Bell travelled to Chicago to attend several meetings. While there he witnessed the new pentecostal services of **William H. Durham**. Bell returned to Texas having himself received the Baptism of the Holy Spirit, though this meant leaving the Baptist ministry and moving to a small Pentecostal congregation in Malvern, Arkansas. He associated with a group of Pentecostals who, in contrast to the beliefs of Pentecostal leader **Charles Fox Parham**, believed that the Baptism of the Holy Spirit may come to any believer, and not just to one previously sanctified. They also believed in the need for some extra-congregational organization. They soon received permission from **Charles Harrison Mason** to share the use of the name of his largely black denomination, the Church of God in Christ. Bell became editor of their new periodical, *Word and Witness*, and in 1909 he married Katie Kimbrough.

In the December 20, 1913, issue of *Word and Witness*, Bell called for a national organization of Pentecostals and for a meeting to create such an organization. Bell chaired this meeting in Hot Springs, Arkansas, in 1914, marking the beginning of the General Council of the Assemblies of God. *The Word and Witness* became an Assemblies journal, and Bell, began teaching at the Gospel School in Findlay, Ohio. In 1915 a number of Californian Pentecostals began promoting a "Jesus Only" theology, which eliminated the Trinity and prescribed rebaptism in the name of Jesus only. Bell initially resisted this movement, but he was converted by L. V. Roberts. As a result, Bell lost his positions in the Assemblies of God. He then led a small church in Galena, Kansas.

The "Jesus Only" movement did not disappear, however, and soon the Assemblies of God asked Bell to serve on a committee to create a statement of faith. While working on that task, Bell reassessed his position and returned to Trinitarianism. This was reflected in the faith statement, which was supported by the convention in 1916, and the remaining "Jesus Only" believers left the church. Bell returned to leadership positions, and in 1918 was made editor of the *Evangel*, the church's renamed journal. He was made General Secretary of the Church in 1919, and served as chairman from 1920 until his death in Springfield, Missouri, in 1923.

Sources:

Bell, Eudorus N. *Questions and Answers*. Springfield, MO: 1923.

Bowden, Henry Warner. *Dictionary of American Religious Biography*. Westport, CT: Greenwood Press, 1977. 572 pp.

Brumback, Carl. *Suddenly From Heaven*. Springfield, MO: Gospel Publishing House, 1961. 380 pp.

Foster, Fred J. *Their Story: Twentieth Century Pentecostals*. St. Louis, MO: World Aflame Press, 1981. 187 pp.

Menzies, William W. *Annointed to Serve*. Springfield, MO: Gospel Publishing House, 1971. 436 pp.

Synan, Vinson. *Aspects of Pentecostal-Charismatic Origins*. Plainfield, NJ: Logos, 1975. 252 pp.

—Gary L. Ward

★69★
BENDER, Daniel Henry
Bishop, Mennonite Church
b. 1866, Grantsville, Maryland
d. 1945, Albany, Oregon

Daniel Henry Bender, a bishop who contributed to the organization of church-wide activities in the Mennonite Church, grew up in an Amish family. His father had moved to the United States in 1851 to escape compulsory military service in Germany. Bender attended the Preparatory and Normal School at Myerstown, Pennsylvania, and after graduation (while still in his teens) began two decades of teaching school at Grantsville.

In 1887 Bender was ordained to the ministry at Springs, Pennsylvania. As his double duties as teacher and minister allowed, he began to conduct Bible conferences and evangelistic meetings throughout the church. His growing work led him to see the need for various forms of cooperative activities and organizations for the Mennonite Church, which was basically organized around district conferences. He promoted the organization of a general conference for the entire church and helped in the initiation of cooperative endeavor in missions, education and publication.

After many years in Pennsylvania, Bender moved to Hesston, Kansas, where he was ordained as a bishop. Here he began important publishing activity. Much of the printing for the church had previously been done by **John Fretz Funk** in Elkhart, Indiana. Funk, however, was encountering difficulties which during the first decade of the new century would all but destroy his publishing efforts. In 1903, Bender began writing the *Advanced Sunday School Lesson Quarterly*, a pioneer Sunday school periodical for Mennonites. In 1904 he became editor for two years of the *Herald of Truth*, the church periodical published by Funk in Elkhart, and *Words of Cheer*, a children's magazine. In 1905 he began the *Primary Sunday School Quarterly*.

In 1906 Bender moved to the church's headquarters in Scottsdale, Pennsylvania, bringing the several Sunday school periodicals with him. He became editor of the *Gospel Witness*, which in 1908 merged with Funk's *Herald of Truth* to become the *Gospel Herald*. Bender edited the *Gospel Herald* for one year; in 1909 he moved back to Hesston, Kansas, to become principal of the recently opened Hesston Academy and Bible School and then president of Hesston College and Bible School when the college department was added. He continued in this position until his retirement in 1930.

During his years in Hesston, Bender became active in the cause of colonization, the movement of Mennonites from one community or country to another. For many years he was president of the Mennonite Board of Colonization, an interdenominational organization that assisted migrating Mennonites in finding new homes. Following his retirement, he resided during his last years in Albany, Oregon.

Sources:

Bender, Daniel Henry. *A Brief Sketch of My Life*. Privately printed.
The Mennonite Encyclopedia. 4 vols. Scottdale, PA: The Mennonite Publishing House, 1955.

★70★
BENDER, Harold S.
Educator and Peace Advocate, General Conference Mennonite Church
b. Jul. 19, 1897, Elkhart, Indiana
d. Sep. 21, 1962, Chicago, Illinois

Harold S. Bender, an outstanding educator of the Mennonite Church, was the son of a school teacher and devout Mennonite. Because of his father's work with the mission board of his church, young Harold often considered becoming a missionary, but during his years at Goshen College he developed a love for history. After his graduation in 1918 he moved to Kansas to teach at Hesston College. He then did graduate work at Princeton University and Princeton Theological Seminary. During these years he renewed his acquaintance with former classmate Elizabeth Horsch, the daughter of church historian John Horsch, and in 1923 they were married. After a year in Germany where Harold received his Th.D. at the University of Heidelburg, they settled in Elkhart, where both taught at the college and frequently worked together on historical research.

Bender had a long and outstanding career as a church historian. In 1927 he led in the formation of the Mennonite Historical Society and for many years was its president. That same year he became editor of the *Mennonite Quarterly Review*, a post he retained for many years. He regularly contributed articles to the *Review*. He also authored a number of books. Crowning his historical work was his editorship of the "Studies in Anabaptist and Mennonite History" series, to which he contributed two volumes, and *The Mennonite Encyclopedia*, for which he also authored many articles. He became dean of Goshen College in 1931, a post he held until becoming dean of Goshen College Biblical Seminary in 1944. That same year he was ordained as minister of the college congregation. Bender's scholarship was acknowledged beyond the Mennonite community with his election to the presidency of the American Society of Church History during World War II. Many would date the modern attention to the radical phase of the sixteenth century Reformation in Europe to his moving yet scholarly presidential address.

During the 1920s a growing conviction that war was sin had become focused in Bender's thinking. In 1930 he became a member of the Mennonite Central Committee. He also became secretary of the Peace Problems Committee of the Mennonite Church. Through his work on the committees, he saw the strong possibility of war and worked to keep Mennonites from participating in the war or profiting from it, and to provide means of alternate service.

Bender became a leader in the cause of Mennonite cooperation, a concern he had expressed as early as 1920 as chairman of an international Mennonite Young People's Conference. He was a major force in the organization of the Mennonite World Conference. In 1952 he was elected its president, a post he held for the rest of his life. He died shortly after presiding at the seventh conference in Kitchner, Ontario.

Sources:

Bender, Harold S. "The Anabaptist Vision." *Church History* 13 (1944): 3-14.
_____. *Conrad Grebel, Founder of the Swiss Brethren*. Scottsdale, PA: Herald Press.
_____, and Henry C. Smith, eds. *The Mennonite Encyclopedia*. 4 vols. Scottsdale, PA: Herald Press, 1965-1969.
_____. *These Are My People: The Nature of the Church and Discipleship According to the New Testament*. Scottsdale, PA: Herald Press, 1962.
_____. *Two Centuries of American Mennonite Literature, 1727-1928*. Scottsdale, PA: Herald Press.
Dyck, Cornelius J. *Twelve Becoming*. Newton, KS: Faith and Life Press, 1973. 126 pp.
Wenger, John Christian. *The Mennonites in Indiana and Michigan*. Scottsdale, PA: Herald Press, 1961. 470 pp.

★71★
BENJAMINE, Elbert
Church of Light
b. Dec. 12, 1882, Iowa
d. Nov. 18, 1951

Elbert Benjamine, the founder of the Church of Light, was one of America's most famous astrologers. A student of the occult as early as age 16, at age 18 Benjamine discovered the Brotherhood of Light and its more public teaching agency, the Hermetic Brotherhood of Luxor. He began studying with astrologer Minnie Higgins, a leader of the latter group, while supporting himself with odd jobs. On December 8, 1907, in Lake Charles, Louisiana, he received assurance from the invisible spiritual hierarchy that he was destined for an important role.

In 1907 Higgins died and Benjamine was called to the order's headquarters in Denver to take her position as one of the order's three leaders, along with the head seer and head scribe. The other two leaders implored him to write a series of lessons for use in increasing their outreach to the public, but he did not agree to do so until 1908, when he began studying for that task. In 1914 Benjamine began writing the first of 21 course lessons, corresponding to the 21 branches of occult science. The decision was made, however, to close down the Hermetic Brotherhood.

In May 1915 Benjamine moved to Los Angeles and began holding small, private classes, using copies of early drafts of his courses written under the pen name of C.C. Zain. On Armistice Day 1918, he opened the classes to the public. Among his new students was Elizabeth Dorris, whom he married in 1919. In 1932 the Brotherhood of Light was succeeded by Benjamine's incorporation of the Church of Light, which emphasizes teaching knowledge necessary for one's individual evolution within a tradition claiming to date back through the Brotherhood of Light to 2440 B.C. Egypt.

Benjamine finally completed all 21 courses in 1934. Under his own name, he published his personal statements on astrology in books such as *Astrological Lore of All Ages* (1945). Benjamine governed the Church of Light until his death in 1951, by which time the church's teachings had spread across the United States and abroad.

Sources:
Benjamine, Elbert. *Astrological Lore of All Ages*. Chicago: Aries Press, 1945.
_____. *Beginner's Horoscope Maker*. Chicago: Aries Press, 1943.
_____. [C. C. Zain]. *Brotherhood of Light Lessons*. 21 vols. Los Angeles: Church of Light, 1922-1932.
_____. *Church of Light Astrological and Reference Cyclopedia*. 2 vols. Los Angeles: Church of Light, 1972.
_____. *How to Use Modern Ephemerides*. Chicago: Aries Press, 1940.
_____. *The Influence of the Planet Pluto*. Chicago: Aries Press, 1939. 24 pp.
"The Founders of the Church of Light." *The Church of Light Quarterly* 45, 1 (February, 1970): 1-2.
"A Great Soul Marches On." *The Church of Light Quarterly* 26, 1 (July 1951-January 1952): 1-2.

—Gary L. Ward

★72★
BENNETT, Belle Harris
Founder, Scarritt Bible and Training School
Laywoman, Methodist Episcopal Church, South
b. Dec. 3, 1852, Whitehall, Kentucky
d. Jul. 20, 1922, Richmond, Kentucky

Belle Harris Bennett, one of the most prominent laywomen in Southern Methodism, was christened Isabel by her parents, Elizabeth Chenault and Samuel Bennett. Her father was a successful plantation owner in rural Kentucky. Her home atmosphere was imbued with both piety and education, the latter of which most attracted her. After attending the local schools, Bennett finished her education at Nazareth School in Bardstown, Kentucky, and then at College Hill, Ohio. Religion did not strongly affect her until she was 23, when, under the ministry of a passing evangelist, she had her first notable religious experience and joined the local congregation of the Methodist Episcopal Church, South. Shortly afterward she and her sister started a Sunday school for the county's poor children.

In 1884, at a revival among the Methodists, Bennett was sanctified, a second religious experience professed by many Methodists in which they believe that the Holy Spirit perfects them in love. In 1887 she became concerned with the inadequacy of the training for women going into the foreign mission field and learned of the educational efforts of **Lucy Rider Meyer**, who had organized the Chicago Training School for Women in the Methodist Episcopal Church. In 1888 she met Meyer at the Chautauqua assembly and returned committed to found a school. She attended the next meeting of her church's Woman's Board of Foreign Missions, and the members appointed her as the board's agent to collect the money to open the school.

Bennett began to travel and speak and was soon recognized as a talented orator. Within a few months she had obtained a grant of $25,000 and land in Kansas City, Missouri. Both the money and the land were donated by Dr. Nathan Scarritt. The church was hesitant, however, to establish a school in Kansas City, a city at the extreme northwestern edge of its prime membership territory. Moreover, the church initially refused to extend the format of the school to include the training of home missionaries as well as foreign workers. With Scarritt's help, however, Bennett was able to overcome these obstacles.

Scarritt Bible and Training School (now Scarritt College) opened in 1892 in Kansas City. Turning down the principalship of the school, Bennett worked for three more years to secure the additional funds needed to put it on secure footing. She also turned her considerable talent to the pioneering of home missions in the Methodist Episcopal Church, South. In 1892 she accepted a seat on the central committee of the Woman's Home Missionary Society. She adopted a plan proposed by her recently deceased sister and started a school in the mountain country of London, Kentucky.

In 1896 Bennett became president of the society and in 1898 was named president of its new governing body, the Women's Board of Home Missions. She turned her attention to informing the church of the needs of urban missions. Following her trip in 1901 to view the work developing in London, England, she proposed a plan to establish settlement houses across the south. These became known as Wesley Community Houses and Bethlehem Houses (the latter designating work among Blacks). Again taking her lead from Lucy Rider Meyer, Bennett in 1902 proposed the development of a deaconess program to meet the growing need of female recruits to staff the expanding projects.

The urban work quickly involved her in ministry to the black community, and she emerged as a Southern leader against racial prejudice. In 1901 she persuaded the board to establish a department for girls at the Paine Institute for Negroes in Augusta, Georgia. She recruited women to work on the Council for Interracial Cooperation. In Richmond, Kentucky, where she resided, she taught a Bible study class for black church leaders and organized a chautauqua for Blacks.

In 1906 the church made the first move to consolidate its mission work, which was at the time scattered among four organizations, into one Board of Missions. Bennett used the occasion to launch a drive to open the church conferences and boards to women. In 1910 the Methodist Episcopal Church, South consolidated its mission work and the Women's Missionary Council was created as a department of the Board of Missions. Thus the women's missionary work lost its previous autonomy, but Bennett was chosen president of the council, an office she held until her death, and she continued her drive for representation. It was finally granted in 1918, and in 1921 Bennett was the first woman elected as a delegate to the church's general conference.

During her years with the council, Bennett assumed duties over the women's foreign mission work, which increasingly claimed her attention. She led in the opening of mission fields in Japan and the Belgian Congo (now Zaire) and in the establishment of a college (now named for her) in Brazil and a medical college in Shanghai, China. By the time she was elected as a delegate to general conference, Bennett had developed cancer and was unable to attend. She died soon afterward. In 1924 Scarritt College for Christian Workers relocated in Nashville, Tennessee. A central group of buildings have been designated as a memorial to its founder.

Sources:

Harmon, Nolan B. *The Encyclopedia of World Methodism.* 2 vols. Nashville: United Methodist Publishing House, 1974.

Hill, Samuel S., ed. *Encyclopedia of Religion in the South.* Macon, GA: Mercer University Press, 1984. 878 pp.

James, Edward T., ed. *Notable American Women, 1607-1950: A Biographical Dictionary.* 3 vols. Cambridge, MA: Harvard University Press, Belknap Press, 1971.

MacDonell, Mrs. R. W. *Belle Harris Bennett, Her Life Work.* Nashville, TN: Board of Missions, Methodist Episcopal Church, South. 1928.

★73★
BENNETT, DeRobigne Mortimer
Freethought Editor and Author
b. Dec. 28, 1818, Springfield, New York
d. Dec. 9, 1882, Brooklyn, New York

DeRobigne Mortimer Bennett, nineteenth-century freethought editor and author, was raised in rural New York. His formal education ended when he was 12 years old and he became a printer's apprentice in Cooperstown, New York. When he was 14 years old his parents separated, and he happened upon a Shaker colony (a center of the United Society of Believers founded by Mother Ann Lee), at New Lebanon, New York. He was given further schooling and stayed at the colony for the next 14 years. He left in 1846 with several other young people (including his future wife, Mary Wicks), dissatisfied with the celibacy practiced among the Shakers. They settled in Louisville, Kentucky, where Bennett worked in a drugstore. He stayed in Louisville through the Civil War and, drawing on his Shaker training, eventually developed a business selling herbs and roots for medicines. When he was 54 he sold his business and moved to Paris, Illinois.

In Paris, in 1873, he got into an argument with two clergymen over the efficacy of prayer. When the local newspaper refused to carry his side of the argument, Bennett began his own periodical which his wife named *The Truth Seeker*. 12,000 copies of the first issue were distributed. Three more issues followed, and based upon the prospect of a successful venture he moved to New York City and became a full-time editor and writer. As *The Truth Seeker* increased in size and frequency, Bennett reprinted articles as pamphlets and became a distributor of freethought literature. He printed the first copy of many of the lectures of **Robert Green Ingersoll**, the popular freethought speaker.

In 1878 Bennett incurred the wrath of postal inspector and anti-obscenity crusader Anthony Comstock. Comstock induced Bennett to send him some pamphlets and then had Bennett charged for sending obscene materials through the mail. Through Ingersoll's intervention the charges were dismissed. However, Comstock moved again and ordered a copy of *Cupid's Yoke* by Ezra Heywood, a birth-control book. He was arrested and sentenced to 13 months in jail. While imprisoned he authored two books, *Letters from the Albany Penitentiary* and *The Gods and Religions of An-*

cient and Modern Times. Released in 1880, he returned to a heroes welcome at a freethought gathering in New York City and was selected as the delegate to the Freethought Congress to be held in Brussels, Belgium, the next year. His trip to Europe became the occasion for a series of letters later turned into a book. A short time after his return he became ill and died.

The Truth Seeker continues to be published as the oldest American freethought periodical. In the twentieth century it was taken over by **Charles Lee Smith** and became the organ of the American Association for the Advancement of Atheism. In the late 1980s it became the subject of a lawsuit following the death of editor **James Hervey Johnson** and is currently published by The Truth Seeker, Inc., in San Diego, California.

Sources:

Bennett, D. M. *The Gods and Religions of Ancient and Modern Times.* 2 vols. New York: D. M. Bennett, Liberal and Scientific Pub. House, 1880.

———. *Letters from the Albany Penitentiary.* New York: D. M. Bennett, [1880]. 40 pp.

———. *Thirty Discussions, Bible Stories, Essays and Lectures.* New York: The Author, 1879. 661 pp.

———. *A Truth Seeker Around the World.* 4 vols. New York: Truth Seeker Co., 1882.

———. *World's Sages, Infidels and Thinkers.* New York: D. M. Bennett, 1880. 1075 pp.

"Roots of Atheism: D. M. Bennett." Parts 1-3. *American Atheist* 20, 10-12 (October, November, December 1978).

Stein, Gordon. *The Encyclopedia of Unbelief.* 2 vols. Buffalo, NY: Prometheus Books, 1985.

★74★
BENNETT, John Coleman
Theologian, United Church of Christ
b. Jul. 22, 1902, Kingston, Ontario, Canada

John Coleman Bennett, a theologian, educator, and ecumenical leader with the United Church of Christ, is the son of Charlotte Rhoda Coleman and William Russell Bennett, a Presbyterian minister. Though born in Canada, his parents were American citizens, and he grew up in Morristown, New Jersey. He attended Williams College and received a B.A. degree in 1924. He then pursued theological studies at Mansfield College, Oxford University, and received a second B.A. in 1926 and his M.A. in 1930. In between the two degrees he earned his B.D. (1926) and S.T.M. (1927) at Union Theological Seminary. In 1930 he became assistant professor of Christian theology at Auburn Theological Seminary in New York. In 1931 he married Anna Louisa McGrew.

As a theologian Bennett considered himself a liberal Protestant who had learned from the anti-liberal reaction of Neo-Orthodoxy. But while a theologian by trade, Bennett's primary concern seems to have been the relation of church and the immediate social context. This theme dominated his first two books written at Auburn, *Social Salvation: A Religious Approach to the Problems of Social Change* (1935) and *Christianity—And Our World* (1936), and regularly reappeared in his later books and articles. In 1938 Bennett moved to the Pacific School of Religion. A year later he was ordained as a minister in the Congregational and Christian Churches.

In 1943 Bennett returned to Union Theological Seminary. Through his long career he distinguished himself both as a teacher and administrator. In 1957 he was named William E. Dodge Professor of Applied Christianity and three years later **Reinhold Niebuhr** Professor of Social Ethics. Meanwhile, in 1955 he had become dean of the school and in 1963 moved to the president's office. He retired from both teaching and the presidency in 1970.

During his years at Union, along with his continued stream of books and articles, Bennett became a leader in the international ecumenical movement. In 1937, prior to World War II, he had attended the Oxford Conference on Church, Community and State.

In 1948 he became a delegate to the founding gathering of the World Council of Churches and became a central figure in the deliberations on church and society at subsequent gatherings in 1954 (Evanston, Illinois), 1961 (New Delhi), and 1966 (Geneva).

Bennett has had an active retirement. In 1960 he became chairman of the editorial board of *Christianity and Crisis*. Following his retirement he became senior contributing editor. Having moved to southern California, he became a visiting professor at both Claremont School of Theology (1975) and the University of Southern California (1976). Among his writings were: *The Radical Imperative* (1975) and *U. S. Foreign Policy and Christian Ethics* (with Harvey Seifert, 1977).

Sources:

Bennett, John C. *Christian Faith and Political Choice*. Toronto: Ryerson Press, 1963. 60 pp.

_____. *Christian Realism*. New York: Charles Scribner's Sons, 1941. 198 pp.

_____. *Christianity—And Our World*. New York: Association Press, 1936. 65 pp.

_____. *Christians and the State*. New York: Charles Scribner's Sons, 1958. 302 pp.

_____. *The Radical Imperative*. Philadelphia: Westminster Press, 1975. 208 pp.

_____. *Social Salvation: A Religious Approach to the Problems of Social Change*. New York: Charles Scribner's Sons, 1935. 222 pp.

Lee, Robert. *The Promise of Bennett*. Philadelphia: J. P. Lippencott, 1969. 111 pp.

Smith, David. *The Achievement of John C. Bennett*. New York: Herder and Herder, 1970. 204 pp.

★ 75 ★
BENNETT, Mary Katherine Jones
Laywoman, Presbyterian Church
b. Nov. 28, 1864, Englewood, New Jersey
d. Apr. 11, 1950, Englewood, New Jersey

Mary Katherine Jones Bennett, prominent Presbyterian laywoman, was the younger daughter of Henry Jones and Winifred Davies Jones, two first-generation immigrants from North Wales. She received a good education through the Dwight School in Englewood and the Bordentown Academy. In 1881 she entered Elmira College and had an outstanding record during her four years there. After receiving her A.B. degree, she taught school for a number of years. During the 1890s, church work began to interest her, and in 1894 she became the national secretary of the young people's work for the Woman's Board of Home Missions of the Presbyterian Church in the U.S.A., the major Presbyterian body in the northern United States. She also became involved in the settlement house movement and joined the governing board of the College Settlements Association.

In 1896 she resigned her church job to marry Fred Smith Bennett, a prosperous businessman. They had no children and he fully supported her church career. Thus she soon returned as a member of the Woman's Board of Home Missions. She used her personal resources to travel widely speaking on behalf of the board's work.

During the first decade of the new century, Bennett expanded her activities into secular women's work as well as the Christian ecumenical movement. In 1901 she became the first president of the Englewood Civic Federation (1901-1911) and president of the Woman's Club (1902-1906). She represented the Presbyterians at the formation of the interdenominational Council of Women for Home Missions in 1908 and later became its second president (1916-1924).

Bennett's varied church work continued for another three decades. In 1909 she became president of the Woman's Board of Home Missions, and served until the Presbyterians placed the women's work under the Presbyterian Board of Home Missions in

1923. She was vice-president of the board until her retirement in 1941. Ecumenically, she worked with the Federal Council of Churches where, among other tasks, she served on the Commission on the Steel Strike of 1919. That committee's report is credited with reforming the steel industry, especially with the elimination of the 12-hour work day. She was a Presbyterian delegate to the Life and Work Conference in Edinburgh in 1937, one of the primary conferences moving toward the establishment of the World Council of Churches. Still active as World War II approached, she concentrated her last working years on the problems of American Indians and migrant workers.

Sources:

James, Edward T., ed. *Notable American Women, 1607-1950: A Biographical Dictionary*. 3 vols. Cambridge, MA: Harvard University Press, Belknap Press, 1971.

Who's Who in America. Wilmette, IL: Marquis Who's Who, Inc.

★ 76 ★
BENSON, Ezra Taft
President, Church of Jesus Christ of Latter-day Saints
b. Aug. 4, 1899, Whitney, Idaho

Ezra Taft Benson, the thirteenth president of the Church of Jesus Christ of Latter-day Saints, is the son of Sarah S. Dunkley and George Taft. He was raised on the family farm. He entered Utah State Agricultural College at Logan in 1918 and stayed there until 1921 when he left for the church's required period of missionary work. His two years were spent in Europe. Benson returned to the farm but was able to complete his B.S. degree at Brigham Young University in 1926. Later that year he married Flora Smith Amussen. In 1929 Benson began work with the University of Idaho, first as county agricultural agent in Preston and then in 1930 as head of a new department of agricultural economics and marketing. He also helped organize the Idaho Cooperative Council, in part as a response to the Depression, and in 1933 became its secretary. Through this time Benson remained an active Latter-day Saint and served a stint as president of the Boise stake (congregation).

Benson represented the council in Washington, D.C., for a number of years and as a result in 1939 was invited to become the executive secretary of the National Council of Farmer Cooperatives. Shortly after the beginning of World War II, he was asked by President Franklin D. Roosevelt to serve on the National Agricultural Advisory Commission. He emerged, however, as a major critic of the Roosevelt policy of farm subsidies and control. In Washington Benson also served as president of the Washington stake of his church.

In 1943 Benson was selected as a member of the Quorum of the Twelve Apostles which head the administration of the Church of Jesus Christ of Latter-day Saints. He retired from public life and moved to Salt Lake City to take up his duties there. He served as president of the European mission and assumed the task of coordinating relief work after the end of the war. Through the 1940s, however, he kept his hand in farm issues and remained a constant critic of what he considered the government's paternalistic intervention in the farming business. In 1952 President Dwight D. Eisenhower selected Benson as the new U.S. Secretary of Agriculture. He was granted a leave of absence from the church to assume his new duties in Washington. He served in that position through all eight years of the Eisenhower administration.

In 1960 Benson returned to his church duties. In the midst of the turmoil of that decade he became an outspoken conservative voice (often to the embarrassment of other leaders). He attacked the civil rights movement, closer relations with Russia, and women's rights. He flirted with (but did not join) the ultra-conservative John Birch Society. In 1973 he was elected president of the Quorum of Twelve and in 1985 he succeeded **Spencer W. Kimball** as president of the church. He became president in the midst of a generation of rapid expansion of the church; it has grown to over four million members in the United States, with two million additional members abroad. As an overseer of some of the church's missionary enterprises, he had much to do with the foreign expansion even before he took office as president. Since he has been in office the church has continued both its rapid growth and expansive building program. In 1989 Benson celebrated his 90th birthday.

Sources:
Arrington, Leonard J., ed. *The Presidents of the Church*. Salt Lake City, UT: Deseret Book Co., 1986. 460 pp.
Biography Index. New York: The H. W. Wilson Co.
Current Biography Yearbook. New York: H. W. Wilson Co.
People in History. Santa Barbara, CA: ABC-Clio, Inc.
Who's Who in Religion. 2d ed. Chicago: Marquis Who's Who, Inc., 1977.

★77★
BERKHOF, Louis
Theologian, Christian Reformed Church
b. 1873, Netherlands
d. May 18, 1957, Grand Rapids, Michigan

Louis Berkhof, a theologian of the Christian Reformed Church, was the son of Geesje ter Pooten and Jan Berkhof, both members of the Christelijke Gereformeerde Kerk (the body which had broken with the state-supported Reformed Church in the Netherlands and was related to the Christian Reformed Church in America). The family migrated to the United States when he was eight and settled in Grand Rapids, Michigan. He attended the Theological Schools of the Christian Reformed Church, later Calvin College and Calvin Theological Seminary. After his graduation in 1900, he was ordained as a minister and became the pastor of the church in Allendale, Michigan. In 1902 he entered Princeton Theological Seminary and having earned his B.D., returned to Grand Rapids as pastor of the Oakdale Park Church.

In 1906 Berkhof was chosen to fill a vacancy at the Theological Seminary, where he remained until his retirement in 1944. He served successively as a professor of Biblical theology (1906-1914), professor of New Testament (1914-1926), and professor of systematic theology (1926-1944). In 1931 he also assumed duties as president of the seminary. His career can be somewhat divided into segments. During his early years he established himself as an opponent of two attractive tendencies which had appeared within Reformed theology—a liberal modernism which accepted German critical biblical study and dispensational premillennialism. The former seemed to destroy the authority of the Bible. The latter was a perspective which viewed the Bible as divided into a number of periods in which God governed humanity in distinctly different ways, all leading to the imminent return of Christ to establish a thousand-year reign of peace (the millennium). This seemed an equally modern innovation. Berkhof is credited with driving both tendencies out of the Christian Reformed Church.

Constructively, Berkhof built a traditional Reformed theology, but one especially marked with anti-Modernist safeguards. His thought emphasized Reformed essentials of the sovereignty of God and the need for an obedient response from humanity. The Bible served as the infallible authority for his reflections. The major presentations of his conclusions are to be found in *Reformed Dogmatics* (1932, later retitled *Systematic Theology*) and the *Introductory Volume to Reformed Dogmatics* (1933). He also authored *The Vicarious Atonement through Christ* (1936); *History of Christian Doctrine* (1937); and *Recent Trends in Theology* (1944). Berkhof did not see himself as a creative theologian so much as the spokesperson for tradition followed by the Christian Reformed Church, a church struggling to deal with the modern world. His theology found an unexpected response by antidispensational evangelicals in a number of denominations.

By the time of his retirement, Berkhof had placed his stamp upon a generation of the Christian Reformed Church. He had trained almost all of its ministers during his 38 years of teaching. His *Systematic Theology* was used around the world and has been translated into five languages, including Chinese and Japanese. In 1946 he was named the president of the first assembly of the Reformed Ecumenical Synod. He continued to write during his retirement years and produced *Aspects of Liberalism* (1951); *The Kingdom of God* (1951); and *The Second Coming of Christ* (1953).

Sources:
Berkhof, Louis. *Aspects of Liberalism*. Grand Rapids, MI: William B. Eerdmans Publishing Company, 1951. 163 pp.
_____. *History of Christian Doctrines*. Grand Rapids, MI: William B. Eerdmans Publishing Company, 1937. 293 pp.
_____. *The Kingdom of God*. Grand Rapids, MI: William B. Eerdmans Publishing Company, 1951. 177 pp.
_____. *Reformed Dogmatics*. Grand Rapids, MI: William B. Eerdmans Publishing Company, 1932, 1941. 759 pp.
_____. *Systematic Theology*. Grand Rapids, MI: William B. Eerdmans Publishing Company, 1941. 759 pp.
Reid, Daniel G., Robert D. Linder, Bruce L. Shelley, and Harry S. Stout. *Dictionary of Christianity in America*. Downers Grove, IL: InterVarsity Press, 1990. 1305 pp.
Zwaanstra, Henry. "Louis Berkhof." In David F. Wells, ed. *Reformed Theology in America*. Grand Rapids, MI: William B. Eerdmans Publishing Company, 1985. 317 pp.

★78★
BERNARD, Pierre Arnold
Tantrik Order in America
b. 1875, Leon, Iowa
d. Sep. 27, 1955, New York, New York

Pierre Bernard, an intriguing and colorful leader, created the Tantrik Order in America, perhaps the first Hindu group in the United Stated founded by a Western student. His birth name was Peter Coons, and as a young man he moved from Iowa to California, where he worked at picking lemons and other odd jobs. In 1905, at the age of 30, he met Mortimer K. Hargis, with whom he teamed to form the Bacchante Academy to teach hypnotism and "soul charming," a phrase referring to sexual beliefs and practices. The 1906 San Francisco earthquake leveled the academy, and the partnership dissolved.

By 1909 Bernard (Coons) had made his way to New York City and at that time founded the Tantrik Order in America, giving himself the title Oom the Omnipotent. He taught yoga and Tantric Hinduism, a branch of Hinduism that is concerned with sexual energies and consciousness. In 1910, two women in the group went to the police to complain that Bernard (oom) was conducting orgies and keeping them against their will. Bernard was arrested, but the charges were dripped when the women left town, and he continued to expand his projects. The police allowed him to operate, though they kept an eye on him, suspecting that his motives were not entirely honorable. Bernard was also now serving as the guardian of his half-sister, Ora Ray Baker, who was later to become famous as the wife of **Hazrat Inayat Khan**, founder of the Sufi Order.

Soon Bernard opened the New York Sanskrit College and a physiological institute and took the name Dr. Pierre Arnold Bernard. About 1918 he met and marrie Blanche DeVries, a woman from upper class society, though she performed as an oriental belly dancer. By this marriage, Bernard became the cousin of **Mary Baker Eddy**, the founder of the Church of Christ, Scientist, and gained another famous relative. Blanche changed his life by introducing him to high society, and Ann Vanderbilt, among others, became a disciple.

In 1924 the now well-to-do Bernard moved to Nyack, New York and established a center and major oriental-occult library at his 78-acre estate, which became an attraction for gurus and other personalities and dignitaries. Bernard himself became a model citizen, building a community zoo, organizing parades, and running a local bank. During World War II his estate briefly closed in order to offer its services to refugees from Nazi Germany. Bernard's nephew, Theos Bernard, after spending some time at the Nyack colony, went on to attend Columbia University and write a thesis later published as *Hatha Yoga: The Report of a Personal Experience* (1944), now a classic text.

Bernard died in 1955 at the age of 80, leaving a legacy surrounded by controversy. It has been difficult for commentators to balance apropriately both his contributions to Hindu growth and knowledge and his doubtful claims to "doctor" status or to training in India, frequent name changes, and other questionable practices.

Sources:
Bernard, Pierre. *In Re Fifth Veda*. International Journal of the Tantrik Order. New York: Tantrik Order in America, n.d. [1909].
Boswell, Charles. "The Great Fume and Fuss Over the Omnipotent Oom." *True* (January, 1965): 31-33, 86-91.
Sann, Paul. *Fads, Follies, and Delusions of the American People*. New York: Bonanza Books, 1967.
Shepard, Leslie. *Encyclopedia of Occultism & Parapsychology*. 3 vols., 2nd. ed. Detroit: Gale Research Co., 1984-1985.

—*Gary L. Ward*

★79★
BERNARDIN, Joseph Louis
Cardinal, Roman Catholic Church
b. Apr. 2, 1928, Columbia, South Carolina

Joseph Louis Bernardin, the archbishop of Chicago and a cardinal in the Roman Catholic Church, is the son of Maria M. Simion and Joseph Bernardin. He attended a parochial elementary school and public high school in Columbia. He then entered the University of South Carolina as a premedical student, but during his second year he transferred to St. Mary's College in Kentucky after deciding to enter the priesthood. He received his B.A. in 1948 and entered Catholic University in Washington, D.C., from which he received an M.A. in 1952. He was ordained a priest that same year.

Following two years as an assistant parish priest, Bernardin became vice-chancellor of the Charleston, South Carolina, diocese. His movement upward was swift. He became chancellor in 1956, vicar general and diocesan consultor in 1962, and executive assistant to the bishop in 1964. In 1966 he was consecrated and assigned as auxiliary bishop of New Orleans, Louisiana. He stayed in New Orleans only two years before moving to Washington, D.C., as secretary to the National Conference of Catholic Bishops and the United States Catholic Conference.

In 1972 Bernardin was appointed archbishop of Cincinnati, Ohio. He emerged as a strong leader in his new post, but also as one who consulted both priests and laity before acting. He developed a strong program to bring the church's ministry and services to the poor. He often visited the prisons and migrant worker camps. He did away with many of the elegant trappings long associated with the office and worked long hours on both local and national issues. In 1974 he was elected president of the National Conference of Catholic Bishops and thus emerged as a spokesperson for the church in America. He voiced a liberal social policy, though he was quite conservative on the issues of abortion and women's ordination to the priesthood. In 1977, his term completed, he became chairman of the bishop's committee on war and peace.

In 1982 Bernardin was named to succeed the late Cardinal **John Cody** as archbishop of Chicago. He was named a cardinal in 1983. Bernardin has continued as one of the leading voices within the American church and has maintained the emphases of his earlier years. Inheriting an archdiocese troubled by financial scandal surrounding his predecessor, Bernardin moved to make the financial

records of the archdiocese public in one of his first major actions. He also confronted the issues of both homosexuality and AIDS. He took the lead in asserting the church's stance for the civil rights of AIDS victims and ordered Catholic service agencies to go out of their way to care for AIDS patients. At the same time he has moved against Dignity, the homosexual caucus within the Roman Catholic Church.

Sources:
The American Catholic Who's Who. Washington, D.C.: National Catholic News Service, 1979.
Biography Index. New York: The H. W. Wilson Co.
The Blue Book. New York: St. Martin's Press, 1976.
Current Biography Yearbook. New York: H. W. Wilson Co.
The New York Times Biographical Service. Ann Arbor, MI: University Microfilms International.
Who's Who in America. Wilmette, IL: Marquis Who's Who, Inc.

★80★
BERRIGAN BROTHERS
Activist Priests, Roman Catholic Church

Daniel J. (b. May 9, 1921 Virginia, Minnesota) and Philip (b. October 5, 1923 Virginia, Minnesota) Berrigan, two Roman Catholic priests who became known for their civil rights and anti-war activism, were the sons of Thomas and Freida Fromhart Berrigan. They were the youngest of six sons, one other of whom also went into the priesthood. They inherited their political activism in part from their father, who was a socialist. Because of his ties to socialism, when the brothers were but children, their father lost his railroad job. He moved the family to a farm near Syracuse, New York, where he founded the Electrical Workers Union and started a Catholic Interracial Council. The farm functioned as a hospitality center during the Great Depression. *The Catholic Worker*, **Dorothy Day**'s periodical, was standard reading material in their home.

Philip left home to affiliate himself with the Jesuits and attend Woodstock College in 1939 and, after graduation, the Jesuit school of theology at Weston, Massachusetts. He pursued a course that would see him ordained in 1952.

Meanwhile in 1941 Daniel entered St. Michael's College in Toronto, Canada, but in 1943 was drafted. He was deeply affected during his boot camp training in the South, where he first witnessed the oppression of Blacks. After the war he attended Holy Cross Seminary and graduated in 1950. He then became affiliated with the Society of St. Joseph, a predominantly black religious order which his older brother Jerry had already joined, and attended their seminary in Newburgh, New York. The brothers met often on the weekends in the late 1940s. The Catholics who had joined the Nazi resistance and who were promoting a theology of worldly involvement became their role models. This model became more firmly implanted in Daniel in 1953 when he was sent to work in Lyon, France, and was able to actually meet the worker-priests he had previously only read about. He returned from France to begin three years work in the preparatory school the Jesuits managed in Brooklyn, New York, and spent his free time in community organization. In 1957 he began a six year assignment to teach theology at LeMoyne College. While there in the early 1960s he founded the Catholic Peace Fellowship. In 1963, in part because of his outspoken opinions on government policy of using Blacks to fight in Vietnam, he was transferred to a poor parish in Baltimore, Maryland. Daniel's growing radicalism during these years was manifest in his writings: *Time Without Number* (1957); *The Bride: Essays in the Church* (1959); *The Bow in the Clouds: Man's Covenant with God* (1961); and *The World for Wedding Ring, Poems* (1962).

Meanwhile Philip was ordained a Josephite priest in 1955. He was assigned first to a ghetto parish in Washington, D.C., and then in 1975 to a black high school in New Orleans. He became active in the Urban League and the Congress for Racial Equality (CORE). He joined some of the early freedom rides in the South before being transferred in 1962 to the Josephite seminary. Firmly committed to social activism by now, he organized the seminarians to document building code violations in the poorer neighborhoods of town.

1964 culminated a process of theological transformation for both Philip and Daniel. They gave up their remaining hope for institutional reform and decided on a course of radical protest. Their decision was catalyzed both by the Selma (Alabama) Civil Rights March and the escalating war in Vietnam. Daniel's activities in helping form Clergy Concerned About Vietnam and the activities that followed, such as when a former student of Daniel's became among the first to burn his draft card, brought him to the attention of New York Cardinal **Francis Spellman**. Spellman, the most powerful leader in the Roman Catholic Church in America and a backer of government policy, pressured to have Berrigan reassigned outside the country. In response, thousands of priests, nuns, and seminarians signed a protest and forced Spellman to back away. From the brothers, this period produced *They Call Us Dead Men: Reflections on Life and Conscience* (1966) and *Consequences: Truth and. . .* (1967) from Daniel and *No More Strangers* (1965), Philip's first book.

Daniel became editor of *Jesuit Missions*, and then in 1967 became the director of religious work for the United Religious Work at Cornell University. The two most intense years for the two brothers were to follow. Before the year was out, Daniel had organized a group of pacifists and was arrested in a protest in front of the Pentagon. On October 27, 1967, Philip was one of four people who walked into a Baltimore draft board office and poured blood over the files. Early in 1968 Daniel traveled to North Vietnam to negotiate the release of prisoners of war. On May 17, 1968, both brothers were among the nine people who invaded a draft board in Catonsville, Maryland, and burned files with napalm, the fiery weapon that was being used in Vietnam. The event, filmed by television cameras as it occurred, led to the brothers' trial and conviction and became the focus for a new series of war protests. Philip was sentenced to six years and served three; Daniel served less than two. The period in prison and immediately following became a time of intense literary production by both. Philip wrote *Prison Journals of a Priest Revolutionary* (1970) and *Widen the Prison Gates: Writings from Jails, April 1970-December 1972* (1973). Daniel authored *No Bars to Manhood* (1970); *The Trial of the Catonsville Nine* (1970); *The Dark Night of Resistance* (1971), which won the National Book Award; and *Lights on in the House of the Dead: A Prison Diary* (1974).

After their release from prison, and more so since the end of the Vietnam War, the brothers have settled into less controversial activities. Philip left the priesthood in 1973 to marry Elizabeth McAlister. They established Jonah House, a commune in Baltimore. In 1979 a collection of his essays was published as *Of Beasts and Beastly Images: Essays Under the Bomb*. Daniel Berrigan remained a Jesuit and became a professor at Woodstock College. During the 1980s, though both have continued their work on social issues from feminism to nuclear proliferation and the exploration of the theology of the church on both theoretical and practical levels, their new activities have not produced the dramatic effects of their earlier protests.

Sources:

Berrigan, Daniel. *The Bride: Essays in the Church*. New York: Macmillan Company, 1959. 142 pp.
_____. *Consequences: Truth and. . ..* New York: Macmillan Company, 1967. 123 pp.
_____. *The Dark Night of Resistance*. Garden City, NY: Doubleday & Company, 1971. 181 pp.
_____. *Lights on in the House of the Dead: A Prison Diary*. Garden City, NY: Doubleday & Company, 1974. 309 pp.
_____. *No Bars to Manhood*. Garden City, NY: Doubleday Company, 1970. 215 pp.
_____. *The Trial of the Catonsville Nine*. Boston, MA: Beacon Press, 1970. 122 pp.
Berrigan, Philip. *Of Beasts and Beastly Images: Essays Under the Bomb*. Portland, OR: Sunburst Press, 1979. 90 pp.
_____. *Prison Journals of a Priest Revolutionary*. New York: Holt, Rinehart and Winston, 1970. 198 pp.
_____. *Widen the Prison Gates: Writings from Jails, April 1970-December 1972*. New York: Simon & Schuster, 1973. 268 pp.
Casey, William Van Etten and Philip Noble, eds. *The Berrigans*. New York: Avon Books, 1971. 253 pp.
Gray, Francine du Plessix. *Divine Disobedience: Profiles in Radical Catholicism*. New York: Alfred A. Knopf, 1970.
Klejment, Anne. *The Berrigans: A Bibliography of Published Works*. New York: Garland Publishing Company, 1979.
Lippy, Charles H. *Twentieth-Century Shapers of American Popular Religion*. New York: Greenwood Press, 1989. 494 pp.

★81★
BESANT, Annie Wood
Theosophical Society
b. Oct. 1, 1847, London England
d. Sep. 21, 1933, Adyar India

Annie Wood Besant was the leader of the Theosophical Society during its key period of worldwide expansion after the turn of the twentieth century. Besant's father died when she was five years old and her mother raised her in a devout Christian manner in London, England. In 1866, at the age of 19, she met Frank Besant, a minister and school teacher, whom she married. They had two children. Annie Besant's increasing religious skepticism and general independence, however, eventually led to a divorce.

Long interested in writing, Besant took to writing essays concerning her religious skepticism, which led her to the well-known atheist Charles Bradlaugh in 1874. She joined the National Secular Society, began to write for Bradlaugh's periodical, *National Reformer*, and began lecturing on topics such as women's rights. She developed a personal relationship with Bradlaugh such that in 1876 the two of them formed the Freethought Publishing Company, and Besant became co-editor of the *National Reformer*. One of their first published works contained advice on birth control, which landed Besant and Bradlaugh in court for publishing obscenity and corrupting morals.

Over the next decade, Besant and Bradlaugh grew apart, as she met George Bernard Shaw, joined the Fabian Society, and generally became a supporter of socialism. Yet another turn came in 1888, when she reviewed *The Secret Doctrine* by **Helena Petrovna Blavatsky**, co-founder of the Theosophical Society. Almost immediately, Besant became enamored of both Theosophy and Blavatsky, sensing that she had at last found her philosophical home. Blavatsky quickly made use of Besant's abilities, and soon Besant was a traveling representative and co-editor of the magazine, *Lucifer*. Blavatsky's death in 1891 elevated Besant to head of the Theosophical Society's Esoteric Section in Europe and India, a position of leadership second only to that of Col. Henry S. Olcott, the president. In 1892 she wrote two major books, the *Seven Principles of Man* and *Karma*, and in 1893 she made a spectacular tour of the United States, in which she gave famous addresses to huge crowds at the World Parliament of Religions at the Chicago World's Fair. Soon afterwards she moved to the Theosophical Society's headquarters in Adyar, India, established by Blavatsky and Olcott in 1879.

In 1894, **William Q. Judge**, an early associate of Blavatsky and Olcott who remained in New York, challenged Besant for leadership. The society split, with most of the American membership siding with Judge. Besant gradually rebuilt the American movement and oversaw a strong organization when she succeeded Olcott as president in 1907. Her position was momentarily shaken in 1906, when **Charles Leadbeater**, an Anglican priest who had become a high level Theosophist in India and a close friend of Besant, was charged with giving a group of boys in his care instruction in masturbation. Both Besant and Leadbetter survived the scandal, but the stigma lingered.

In 1909 Besant declared her belief that a new avatar or world teacher would soon appear to lead the world to a new stage of being, and she organized the Order of the Star of the East to promote that idea. Besant and others became convinced that **Jiddu Krishnamurti**, one of the children under the Society's care in Adyar, was this new teacher, and in 1912 they published a new magazine, *Herald of the Star*, to announce it. This pronouncement, however, became a major thorn in the society's side. Krishnamurti's father soon attempted to regain custody of his son, and Krishnamurti disassociate himself from his assigned role in 1929.

Besant continued to lead the Society until her death in 1933, continuing also to exercise her social activism. She worked for an independent India, serving as president of the Indian Nationalist Congress in 1917. She also established many of India's first schools for women.

Sources:

Besant, Annie Wood. *The Ancient Wisdom*. Wheaton, IL: Theosophical Press, 1928. 345 pp.

_____. *Autobiographical Sketches*. London: Freethought Publishing Company, 1885. 169 pp.

_____. *Esoteric Christianity*. Adyar, India: Theosophical Publishing House, 1913. 404 pp.

_____. *Shall India Live or Die?* N.p.: National Home Rule League, New India Bookshop, 1925. 184 pp.

_____. *The Spiritual Life*. Chicago: Theosophical Press, 1923. 282 pp.

Besterman, Theodore. *A Bibliography of Annie Besant*. London: Theosophical Society in England, 1924. 114 pp.

Bowden, Henry Warner. *Dictionary of American Religious Biography*. Westport, CT: Greenwood Press, 1977. 572 pp.

Bright, Esther. *Old Memories and Letters of Annie Besant*. London: Theosophical Publishing House, 1936.

Legg, L. G. Wickham, ed. *The Dictionary of National Biography, 1931-1940*. London: Oxford University Press, 1949.

Nethercot, Arthur H. *The First Five Lives of Annie Besant*. Chicago: University of Chicago Press, 1960.

_____. *The Last Four Lives of Annie Besant*. Chicago: University of Chicago Press, 1963.

Shepard, Leslie. *Encyclopedia of Occultism & Parapsychology*. 3 vols., 2nd. ed. Detroit: Gale Research Co., 1984-1985.

—*Gary L. Ward*

★ 82 ★
BETHUNE, Mary McLeod

Educator, Methodist Church
Founder, Bethune-Cookman College
b. Jul. 10, 1875, Mayesville, South Carolina
d. May 18, 1955, Daytona Beach, Florida

Mary McLeod Bethune, founder of Bethune-Cookman College, was born to former slaves Samuel and Patsy McLeod. Recognizing Mary's intellectual abilities, they sent her to the Mayesville Presbyterian Mission for Negroes. After completing her course at the age of 11, she was granted a scholarship to attend Scotia Seminary for Negro Girls in Concord, North Carolina. In 1894 she graduated at the head of her class and departed for Chicago, where she enrolled at Moody Bible Institute. She received her certificate the following year.

Unable to fulfill her early dream of being a missionary in Africa when the Presbyterians turned down her application, she joined the staff of the Haines Institute in Augusta, Georgia. She decided to remain in the South and work for the rise of Blacks. She moved

to Sumter, South Carolina, in 1895 and, while working at the Kindell Institute, met and married Albertus Bethune. They eventually moved to Florida; after three years, during which Mary worked at a Palatka Presbyterian grade school, they settled in Daytona Beach.

In Daytona Beach, Bethune opened the Daytona Literary and Industrial School for Negro Girls in 1904. It began with five students and grew into a large and stable academy. In 1923 the academy merged with the Cookman Institute, a Methodist school with a declining enrollment, to become the Bethune-Cookman Collegiate Institute. At that time Bethune became a member of the Methodist Episcopal Church.

The Methodist Episcopal Church had re-established itself in the South following the Civil War, but had quickly divided with separate conferences serving Blacks and Whites. Bethune quickly rose to prominence in the predominantly black Florida Conference (and was elected a delegate to the general conference of the Methodist Episcopal Church each quadrennium from 1928 through 1944). She became an important voice in the debates concerning merger with the Methodist Episcopal Church, South. While approving of the idea of union, she opposed the eventual plan of union because of its continued segregation of black church members into a separate jurisdiction.

While being in the minority on the union debates, Bethune-Cookman Collegiate Institute grew with Methodist support into an accredited junior college (1939) and then into a senior college (1941). As founder of what is known today as Bethune-Cookman College, Mary Bethune became the first black woman to have founded and headed such an institution in the United States. She retired in 1942.

During these same years, beyond the church, she became a national figure in the cause of Blacks in general. She was active in the antilynching campaign after World War I and worked for interracial harmony. Soon after Franklin Roosevelt took office, she became director of the Negro Division of the National Youth Administration. She organized the National Council of Negro Women in 1936 and became a staunch supporter of both the National Association for the Advancement of Colored People and the Southern Conference for Human Welfare.

During the last years of her life, Mary Bethune was widely honored for her life of accomplishments. She was appointed to the Charter Conference of the United Nations in 1945. In 1949 she received an honorary degree from Rollins College, becoming perhaps the first Black to receive such an honor from a southern white school.

Sources:

Harmon, Nolan B. *The Encyclopedia of World Methodism*. 2 vols. Nashville: United Methodist Publishing House, 1974.

Hill, Samuel S., ed. *Encyclopedia of Religion in the South*. Macon, GA: Mercer University Press, 1984. 878 pp.

Peare, Mary McLeod Bethune. New York: Vanguard Press, 1951.

★ 83 ★
BEVILACQUA, Anthony J.

Cardinal, Roman Catholic Church
b. Jun. 17, 1923, Brooklyn, New York

Anthony J. Bevilacqua, a cardinal and the archbishop of Philadelphia for the Roman Catholic Church, is the son of Maria Codella and Louis Bevilacqua. He studied at Cathedral College in Brooklyn (1941-1945) and then entered the Seminary of the Immaculate Conception in Huntington, New York, from which he graduated in 1949. Ordained a priest following his graduation, he served as an assistant pastor in Brooklyn and a professor of history at the Cathedral Preparatory Seminary for a year. He continued his education at the Gregorian University in Rome and received his doctorate in canon law in 1956. He later received an M.A. in political science from Columbia University (1962).

In 1968 Bevilacqua became the professor of canon law at the Seminary of the Immaculate Conception. While teaching he also pursued his studies in law. He completed his law degree at St. John's University School of Law in 1975 and in 1976 was admitted to the bar. That same year he took on additional duties as an adjunct professor of law at St. John's.

Meanwhile, in addition to his professorial responsibilities, Bevilacqua had assumed a role with the diocese of Brooklyn. In 1965 he had been named assistant chancellor of the diocese and during the 1970s he rose to become vice chancellor and then chancellor. His duties included the directorship of the Migration and Refugee Office of the diocese. In 1980 he was named titular bishop of Aquaealba and auxiliary bishop of Brooklyn. Bevilacqua was assigned episcopal duties as the chairman of the U.S. Bishops Committee on Canonical Affairs and a member of the Committee on Migration and Tourism. His continuing interest in the problems of migrants, undocumented workers, and immigrants was further reflected in his appointment to the Pontifical Committee on Migrants and Itinerants in 1984.

In 1983 Bevilacqua left Brooklyn to become the bishop of Pittsburgh. He served in Pittsburgh for five years before being named archbishop of Philadelphia in 1988 following the retirement of Cardinal **John Krol**. He was named a cardinal by Pope John Paul II in 1991.

Sources:
Who's Who in America. Wilmette, IL: Marquis Who's Who, Inc.

★84★
BIEDERWOLF, William Edward
Evangelist, Presbyterian Church
b. Sep. 29, 1867, Montecello, Indiana
d. Sep. 10, 1939, Palm Beach, Florida

William Edward Biederwolf, an evangelist in the tradition of J. Wilbur Chapman and **William A. "Billy" Sunday**, was the son of Abbie Schnitzer and Michael Biederwolf. As a teenager he had an experience of conversion to Christianity through the Presbyterian minister in his hometown, Frank N. Palmer. He studied at Wabash College for a year but transferred to Princeton University where he finished his B.A. in 1892. He stayed to finish an M.A. two years later, and in 1895 received his theological degree from Princeton Theological Seminary. He then left for Europe for two years of study at the Universities of Berlin and Erlangen in Germany. In 1896 he married Ida Casad.

Upon his return to the United States in 1897 Biederwolf was ordained a minister in the Presbyterian Church and became the pastor of the Broadway Presbyterian Church in Logansport, Indiana. His pastorate was interrupted in 1899 by a brief period of service as a chaplain in Cuba during the Spanish-American War. In 1900, however, he left the pastorate and became a full-time evangelist. For the first six years he was the assistant to J. Wilbur Chapman. During these years he wrote the first of his many books: *A Help to the Study of the Holy Spirit* (1903) and *The Growing Christian* (1903).

In 1906 Biederwolf left Chapman and for the next 18 years traveled the country as an itinerant evangelist. His messages combined the call to conversion with demands for reform and support for American life and values (especially during World War I). Throughout the twentieth century, Winona Lake, Indiana, has been a center for evangelistic activity and conferences for fundamentalist Christians, and Biederwolf has developed an association with the camp meeting grounds there during his days of traveling. In the years immediately after World War I, the work suffered, and beginning in

1922 Biederwolf, operating out of his family home in Montecello, Indiana, was able to assist in rebuilding. He became director of the Winona Lake Bible Conference, whose financial support had declined. Bringing it back to life, in 1923 he added duties as the director of the Winona Lake Bible School of Theology. He became president of the school in 1933. Biederwolf later founded the Winona Lake Publishing Company, which operated out of nearby Chicago. In 1929 he added duties as the pastor of the Royal Poincianna Chapel in West Palm Beach, Florida, a highly affluent congregation.

During his years of traveling Biederwolf wrote very little, but once he settled at Winona Lake, he began to author numerous books. Among the more important titles are *The Millennium Bible* (1924); *The Great Tribulation* (1929); *The Adventure of the Hereafter* (1930); *Whipping-Post Theology* (1930); and *The New Paganism* (1934). He was a premillennialist, and many of his books looked to the impending return of Christ to establish his literal millennial reign on the earth.

Sources:
Biederwolf, William Edward. *The Adventure of the Hereafter.* New York: R. R. Smith, 1930. 176 pp.
———. *The Growing Christian.* Chicago: Winona Lake Publishing Co., 1903. 121 pp.
———. *The Millennium Bible.* Chicago: W. P. Blessing Co., 1924. 728 pp.
———. *The New Paganism.* Grand Rapids, MI: William B. Eerdmans Publishing Company, 1934. 159 pp.
———. *Whipping-Post Theology.* Grand Rapids, MI: William B. Eerdmans Publishing Company, 1933. 395 pp.
Garrett, R. E. *William Edward Biederwolf: A Biography.* Grand Rapids, MI: Zondervan Publishing House, 1948. 116 pp.

★85★
BILBO, Theodore
Lay Baptist Preacher
Governor and Senator of Mississippi
b. Oct. 13, 1877, Juniper Grove, Mississippi
d. Aug. 21, 1947, New Orleans, Louisiana

Theodore Bilbo was a well known white supremacist and politician in the early twentieth century. Raised in poverty, he managed to work his way through school at the University of Nashville from 1897 to 1900. He married in 1898, but his wife died in 1900. At some point in the course of the next five years he received a preacher's license from the Bobolochitto Baptist Association. He remarried in 1903 and in 1905 began studying law at Vanderbilt. While still at Vanderbilt, he ran for State Senate in Mississippi and won. He was elected lieutenant governor in 1912, and governor in 1916. As governor, he embarked on an ambitious program that earned him the sobriquet "Bilbo the Builder." After being defeated in his bid for a Congressional seat in 1920, he retired to his farm and to a private law practice.

Reentering politics, Bilbo was again elected governor in 1928 and served one term, although this time his tenure in office was less constructive. Two years later he was elected Senator from Mississippi in a campaign noted for its energy and invective. He was a powerful speaker who mixed Biblical allusions with vigorous denunciations. For the most part he was quiet during his first few years in the Senate. Although conservative on many issues, he was a supporter of the New Deal. At the same time he was overtly racist, and opposed the Gavagan anti-lynching bill. He was also a prominent supporter of the idea of colonizing Blacks in Africa, and on June 6, 1938, he proposed the deportation of 12 million black Americans to Liberia as an amendment to the work-relief bill. In his four-hour speech, he praised the race consciousness evident in Italy and Germany. He later withdrew his amendment, but in the following year reintroduced his proposal in the form of a regular bill. At the same time he displayed a petition with the names of two and a half million Blacks who asserted that they would rather live in Africa than in the United States.

Bilbo based his support of colonization on the theory (which was very prominent in the pre-war era) that miscegenation would undermine civilization. In his *Take Your Choice: Separation or Mongrelization* (1947) he interpreted scripture so as to find support for this theory in Christianity, and condemned ministers who argued against segregation. Toward the end of his life, he was investigated by Senate committees on the charges that he had accepted gratuities from war contractors, and carried out an anti-black campaign during the 1946 primaries. As a result of these investigations, he was prevented from taking his seat in 1947. He died of cancer later the same year.

Sources:

Dictionary of American Biography. 20 vols. and 7 supps. New York: Charles Scribner's Sons, 1928-1936, 1944-1981.

Green, A. Wigfall. *The Man Bilbo*. Baton Rouge, LA: Louisiana State University Press, 1963. 150 pp.

Roy, Ralph Lord. *Apostles of Discord: A Study of Organized Bigotry and Disruption of the Fringes of Protestantism*. Boston: Beacon Press, 1953. 437 pp.

Swing, Raymond Gram. *Forerunners of American Fascism*. New York: Julian Messner, 1935. 168 pp.

★ 86 ★
BJERRING, Nicolas
Priest, Russian Orthodox Church
b. 1831, Denmark

Nicolas Bjerring, the founder of the first Orthodox church in the eastern United States, was born into a Roman Catholic family in Denmark. His father was a high official in the city of Vejle. After finishing his education in his hometown, he studied philosophy and theology at the University of Breslau. He taught in several schools in Europe and served in the mission in Lapland before being appointed in 1868 to St. Mary's Seminary in Baltimore, Maryland. He was in Baltimore when the first Vatican Council (1869-1870) met and promulgated the dogma of papal infallibility.

For a number of years prior to that council, Bjerring had been studying Orthodoxy. He had also been influenced by *L'Union Chretienne*, a French publication put out by a former Jesuit. The work of Vatican I provided the occasion for him to leave the Roman Catholic Church and identify with the Orthodox Church. In an open letter dated January 1870, he denounced Roman Catholic errors, especially papal infallibility. The letter was translated into several languages and widely circulated. He then requested to be received into the Russian Orthodox Church and traveled to St. Petersburg, where he was received into the church on April 25, 1870. The following month he was ordained to the diaconate and the priesthood. He was directed to return to America and establish a church in New York.

Bjerring arrived in New York in the summer of 1870. He quickly organized a parish. He converted the parlor of his home into a chapel and on November 24, Bishop Paul of Alaska served the first liturgy and dedicated the chapel as the home of the Holy Trinity parish. The parish remained small, but Bjerring made a most significant contribution to the growth of Orthodoxy in North America through his translations and publishing efforts.

Sources:

Tarasar, Constance J. *Orthodox America, 1794-1976: Development of the OrthodoxChurch in America*. NY: Orthodox Church in America, Department of History and Archives, 1975. 352 pp.

★ 87 ★
BLACK ELK
Medicine Man and Visionary, Lakota (Oglala Sioux)
b. 1863, Little Powder River, Wyoming
d. Aug. 17, 1950, Manderson, South Dakota

Black Elk, a medicine man of the Lakota Nation (Oglala Sioux) known for his collaboration on a famous text *Black Elk Speaks; the Life Story of a Holy Man of the Oglala Sioux*, was the son of Black Elk and Sees the White Crow. He experienced his first prophetic visions at the age of nine. His visions, about which he told no one, took on a prophetic cast, and he finally revealed what had been happening to him to his father. He was 13 in 1876, when he witnessed the Battle of the Little Big Horn at which the Indians soundly defeated General George Custer. His family joined then with Chief Crazy Horse and later fled to Canada to join **Sitting Bull**. They finally returned to the United States, by which time the young Black Elk had gained a wide reputation as a seer and visionary. He was believed to have prophetic powers which prevented disasters among the Lakota. Along the way, Black Elk married twice, to Kate Bissonette and to Angelina Bissonette.

In 1886-1889, Black Elk traveled with Buffalo Bill Cody's Wild West Show. His travels took him to England, where in 1887 he appeared before Queen Victoria as part of her Diamond Jubilee celebrations. He returned to encounter the phenomenon of the Ghost Dance, a new religion spread by **Wovoka**, a Puiute visionary, which offered reclamation of the Indian lands and protection from the white man's guns. Wovoka spread the practice of wearing brightly colored shirts which he said gave his followers invulnerability from bullets. Skeptical at first, Black Elk finally became a follower. Wovoka's confident followers were massacred, however, at Wounded Knee in 1890. Black Elk was not present but deeply felt the tragedy, which led him to a strong belief in the need for harmony among all peoples.

Black Elk lived quietly through the first decades of the twentieth century and would probably have retreated into complete obscurity had it not been for his meeting and working with writer John G. Neihardt. They produced Black Elk's autobiography, one of the single most important chronicles of American Indian life. He later worked with anthropologist Joseph E. Brown to produce what would later be published as *The Sacred Pipe* (1953).

Sources:

Brown, Joseph E. *The Sacred Pipe: Black Elk's Account of the Seven Rites of the Oglala Sioux*. Norman, OK: University of Oklahoma Press, 1953.

Neihardt, John G. *Black Elk Speaks; Being the Life of a Holy Man of the Oglala Sioux*. Reprint. Lincoln, NE: University of Nebraska Press, 1961. 280 pp.

Waldman, Carl. *Who Was Who in Native American History: Indians and Non-Indians from Early Contacts through 1900*. New York: Facts on File, 1990. 410 pp.

—*Michelene E. Fixico*

★ 88 ★
BLACKWELL, Annie Walker
Missionary Executive, African Methodist Episcopal Zion Church
b. Aug. 21, 1862, Chester, South Carolina
d. Dec. 7, 1922, Philadelphia, Pennsylvania

Annie Walker Blackwell, a prominent leader in the missionary endeavors of the African Methodist Episcopal Zion Church, was the daughter of Reverend C. I. Walker. Following the Civil War, Reverend Walker affiliated with the African Methodist Episcopal Zion Church and was a charter member of the South Carolina Conference established in 1867. In 1872 Walker was one of the first class of presiding elders in the South Carolina Conference and assisted in its rapid spread across the state. Thus Blackwell's formative years were spent in an African Methodist Episcopal Zion Church parsonage. She attended Scotia Seminary and in 1887 married the Reverend George Lincoln Blackwell, who had been ordained in the church two years earlier. Like his wife, Reverend Blackwell was missionary minded. He is credited with establishing the foundations for the church's missionary department.

The Woman's Home and Foreign Missionary Society of the African Methodist Episcopal Zion Church was established in 1880. It had a slow beginning through the first decades, but in 1901 held its first missionary convention. At the second convention the executive board was organized, and Annie Blackwell was named the assistant corresponding secretary and editor of the women's column in the *Star of Zion*, the denominational newspaper. During her first two years she began to work on molding the society into an effective organization throughout the church. Two years later she grabbed the attention of the board of bishops with a report lamenting the lack of missionary societies in many of the local churches. Blackwell urged that several immediate steps be taken to change the situation. First, the society was to be placed under the total control of the women, and second, that it was to be seen as the women's auxiliary of the Mission Board of the church.

At the 1904 general conference, Blackwell's position was considerably strengthened by the election of her husband to the office of bishop and his appointment as missionary secretary of the church. At that same conference, she was elected as corresponding secretary of the society. In 1905, the general conference having separated the work and given it totally to the women, the society held its first meeting under the new rules. In its first year it achieved a remarkable growth and new enthusiasm. Over her 18 years in office Blackwell became the organizational focal point of the society and is generally credited with turning it into a strong and vital part of the African Methodist Episcopal Zion Church's missionary life. She revived the idea of life memberships and the naming of Life Matrons, the first of which was enrolled in 1906. She was made a Life Member through the gifts of friends in 1908. She worked with Victoria Richardson in organizing the Young Woman's Society, a missionary organization for the youth.

Blackwell would serve in her post for the rest of her life. She died suddenly on the day of her 35th wedding anniversary, which she spent at home attending her ailing husband.

Sources:

Walls, William J. *The African Methodist Episcopal Zion Church.* Charlotte, NC: A.M.E. Zion Publishing House, 1974. 669 pp.

★89★
BLACKWELL, Antoinette Brown
First Female Minister, Congregational Church
b. May 20, 1825, Henrietta, New York
d. Nov. 5, 1921, Elizabeth, New Jersey

Antoinette Brown Blackwell was a women's rights activist and the first woman to be ordained in the Congregational Church. Born in a log cabin, the seventh child in a family of 10, she was raised in the hard-working atmosphere of a frontier farm. She joined the Congregational Church at nine, and at a young age became determined to get an education and become a minister. She paid her way through Oberlin, the only college then open to women. She graduated in 1847 and went on to study at the theological school, completing the course of study in 1850. She and another female student were not allowed to graduate, although Oberlin belatedly granted her M.A. in 1878, and an honorary D.D. in 1908.

During her years at Oberlin Blackwell became a feminist and an abolitionist, partly through her acquaintance with Lucy Stone, who would become a lifelong friend. For several years following her schooling, she pursued a career as a lecturer, speaking on slavery, temperance, and women's rights. On September 15, 1853, she was ordained as minister of the First Congregational Church in Butler and Savannah, Wayne County, New York. However, her more

liberal theological views diverged from this denomination, and on July 20, 1854, she was dismissed at her own request from the pulpit. Her views led her toward the American Unitarian Association (AUA), which had been founded by liberal ministers such as herself, and in later life she helped found All Souls' Unitarian Church in Elizabeth, New Jersey.

Blackwell spent 1855 as a volunteer in New York City slums and prisons, recording her observations in a series of articles for the *New York Tribune* that were afterwards collected into *Shadows of Our Social System* (1856). On January 24, 1856, she married Samuel Blackwell, a man who supported her feminist inclinations and social concerns; theirs was a happy marriage. She bore seven daughters, two of whom died in infancy.

Blackwell read avidly in philosophy, becoming particularly interested in the implications of evolution. She also continued to be active as a preacher and lecturer, particularly for women's rights. She authored many books, including *Studies in General Science* (1869); *The Sexes Throughout Nature* (1875); *The Physical Basis of Immortality* (1876); *The Philosophy of Individuality* (1893); *The Making of the Universe* (1914); and *The Social Side of Mind and Action* (1915).

Sources:

Blackwell, Antoinette Brown. *The Making of the Universe.* Boston: Gorham Press, 1914. 198 pp.
_____. *The Philosophy of Individual Action.* New York: Putnam, 1892. 519 pp.
_____. *The Physical Basis of Immortality.* New York: G. Putnam's Sons, 1876. 324 pp.
_____. *The Sexes Throughout Nature.* New York: G. P. Putnam's Sons, 1875. 240 pp.
_____. *The Social Side of Mind and Action.* New York: Neale Pub. Co., 1915. 140 pp.
James, Edward T., ed. *Notable American Women, 1607-1950: A Biographical Dictionary.* 3 vols. Cambridge, MA: Harvard University Press, Belknap Press, 1971.

★90★
BLAKE, Charles Edward
Bishop, Church of God in Christ
b. Aug. 5, 1940, Little Rock, Alaska

Charles Edward Blake, a bishop in the Church of God in Christ, was the son of Rev. J. A. Blake, Sr., also a bishop in the church, and Lula Champion Blake. As a teenager he had a Christian saving experience and preached his first sermon in 1957. That same year he was licensed to preach. He attended California Western University and following his graduation in 1962 was ordained to the ministry. He married Mae Lawrence Blake and moved to Georgia to attend the Interdenominational Theological Center. During his last year of seminary he served as the minister of the Marietta, Georgia, Church of God in Christ. He received his B.D. In 1965 Blake became co-pastor of the Greater Jackson (Mississippi) Church of God in Christ, but moved to California in 1969 to become pastor of the congregation in West Los Angeles, one of the largest in the Church of God in Christ. His tenure had been marked by his outstanding oratorical work, which earned him recognition from *Ebony Magazine* as one of "America's Fifteen Greatest Black Preachers."

At the denominational level, Blake served as editor of *Y.P.W.W. Topics* and vice-president of the church's publishing board. He was the founding chairman of the board of the C. H. Mason Theological Seminary. He was named an administrative assistant for the First Jurisdiction of Southern California and in 1985 was appointed bishop of that jurisdiction. He continues to serve as pastor of the West Los Angeles Church.

Interdenominationally Blake has served as a member of the black advisory committee at Fuller Theological Seminary (where he did some post-graduate study) and as a member of the board of his alma mater, the Interdenominational Theological Center. He was elected president of the Interdenominational Minister's Alliance in Los Angeles.

Sources:

Dupree, Sherry Sherrod. *Biographical Dictionary of African-American, Holiness-Pentecostals, 1880-1990*. Washington, DC: Middle Atlantic Regional Press, 1990. 386 pp.

★91★
BLAKE, Eugene Carson
Ecumenist and Minister, United Presbyterian Church in the U.S.A.
b. Nov. 7, 1906, St. Louis, Missouri
d. Jul. 31, 1985, Stamford, Connecticut

Eugene Carson Blake was a president of the World Council of Churches and a minister in the United Presbyterian Church in the U.S.A., which is now part of the Presbyterian Church in the U.S.A.. He was the son of Lulu Carson and Orville P. Blake. He attended Princeton University where he majored in philosophy (A.B., 1928). Following graduation he spent a year in Lahore, India, now Pakistan, as a teacher at Forman Christian College, before entering New College in Edinburgh. After a year in Scotland he returned to finish his ministerial degree at Princeton Theological Seminary (Th.B., 1932). In 1929 he married Valina Gillespie. He served St. Nicholas Collegiate Church in New York City (1932-1935), First Presbyterian Church in Albany, New York (1935-1940), and Pasadena Presbyterian Church (1940-1951). The church in Pasadena had its own radio station, and Blake began regular broadcasts while there.

In 1948 Blake was a delegate to the first assembly of the World Council of Churches in Amsterdam. The gathering launched his career as an international ecumenical figure. Two years later he preached the closing service for the constituting convention of the National Council of Churches. In 1951 he was elected the stated clerk of the general assembly of the United Presbyterian Church. In 1954 he became president of the National Council of Churches. His term as stated clerk was completed in 1958 but he continued to work for the general assembly through 1966, when he was elected general secretary of the World Council of Churches in Geneva, Switzerland.

Although Blake served the Protestant community as one of its major spokespersons, he is remembered primarily for the plan he introduced in 1960 at Grace Cathedral in San Francisco (the cathedral of the Episcopal diocese then headed by Bishop **James A. Pike**). As an official of the United Presbyterian Church, Blake invited the Episcopal Church, the Methodist Church (1939-1968), the United Church of Christ, and others to join in discussion aimed at the creation of a united Protestant Church. Out of this plan developed what was known as the Consultation on Church Union (COCU) which began to meet in 1962. Beginning in great hope, COCU on several occasions put forth plans for the formation of what was termed the Church of Christ Uniting, but was consistently turned down by the participating denominations.

Blake's ecumenical activity earned him the enmity of many conservative Presbyterians, some of whom, like fundamentalist **Carl McIntire**, attacked him as a Communist supporter and doctrinal heretic. The harshest attacks came after the reestablishment of contact with the Russian Orthodox Church in the late 1960s.

Following his retirement from the World Council in 1972, he lived in Stamford, Connecticut.

Sources:

Blake, Eugene Carson. *Christian Faith, Bulwark of Freedom*. Houston, TX: Elsevier Press, 1956. 57 pp.
_____. *The Church in the Next Decade*. New York: Macmillan Company, 1966. 152 pp.
_____. *He Is Lord of All*. Phladelphia: Westminster Press, 1958. 61 pp.
McIntire, Carl. *Eugene Carson Blake: The Chief Church Spokesman for Leftist Cause*. Collingswood, NJ: 20th Century Reformation Hour, [1963]. 71 pp.
Reid, Daniel G., Robert D. Linder, Bruce L. Shelley, and Harry S. Stout. *Dictionary of Christianity in America*. Downers Grove, IL: InterVarsity Press, 1990. 1305 pp.

★92★
BLANCHARD, Charles Albert
College President and Minister, Congregational Church
b. Nov. 8, 1848, Galesburg, Illinois
d. Dec. 20, 1925, Wheaton, Illinois

Charles Albert Blanchard, a minister in the Congregational Church and for over 40 years the president of Wheaton College, was the son of Mary Avery Bent and **Jonathan Blanchard**. At the time of his birth, his father, a Presbyterian minister, was the president of Knox College. In 1860 the family moved to Wheaton, Illinois, when his father became the first president of Wheaton College. Blanchard graduated from Wheaton College in 1870. Having been endowed with the anti-Freemasonry sentiments of his father he went to work with the National Christian Association as an anti-Masonry lecturer. In 1872 he began his long professional association with Wheaton College as principal of its preparatory school. In 1873 he married Ella Milligan.

In 1878 Blanchard became professor of English language and literature. Four years later he was ordained as a minister in the Congregational Church. Subsequently he became both the pastor of the College Church of Christ in Wheaton and vice-president of the college. In 1882 he succeeded his father as president of Wheaton, a post he retained for the rest of his life. He continued to preach at the college church for another year and then for two years preached at the Chicago Avenue Church founded by Dwight L. Moody in Chicago, known as the Moody Church.

Under Blanchard's leadership the college was increasingly identified with the most conservative elements within the Congregational Church and with the larger fundamentalist movement. In 1924 he participated in the founding of the Conservative Protestant Colleges of America (later the Association of Conservative Evangelical Colleges) to oppose what was seen as anti-Christian trends, especially the teaching of evolution, in modern education. He instituted a strict policy of allowing only men who signed an orthodox theological statement to be trustees of the college.

Blanchard continued strong support for the National Christian Association and the anti-secret societies crusade. In 1882 he had been the principal speaker at the dedication of the memorial to William Morgan, believed by association members to have been killed by Masons because of his expose of Masonic secrets. The height of his participation came in 1903 when he was elected president of the association. That year he also completed his major book on the subject, *Modern Secret Societies*. The book summarized the dangers he saw in a growing Freemasonry and the proliferation of similar types of secret orders and publicized the support of prominent conservative Protestant leaders in the fight.

Sources:

Blanchard, Charles A. *Educational Papers*. New York: Fleming H. Revell Company, 1883. 86 pp.
_____. *Getting Things from God*. Chicago: Bible Institute Colportage Association, 1915. 270 pp.
_____. *Light on the Last Days*. Chicago: Bible Institute Colportage Association, 1913. 149 pp.
_____. *Modern Secret Societies*. Chicago: National Christian Association, 1903. 310 pp.
_____. *Visions and Voices*. New York: Christian Allaince Publishing Company, 1916. 184 pp.
Blanchard, F. C. *The Life of Charles Albert Blanchard*. New York: Fleming H. Revell Company, 1932.

Cerza, Alphonse. *Anti-Masonry*. St. Louis, MO: Missouri Lodge of Research, 1962. 383 pp.

Reid, Daniel G., Robert D. Linder, Bruce L. Shelley, and Harry S. Stout. *Dictionary of Christianity in America*. Downers Grove, IL: InterVarsity Press, 1990. 1305 pp.

★93★
BLANCHARD, Jonathan
Minister and College President, Presbyterian Church
b. Jan. 19, 1811, Rockingham, Vermont
d. May 14, 1892, Wheaton, Illinois

Jonathan Blanchard, the first president of Whiten College, was the son of Jonathan and Mary Lovel Blanchard. An intelligent child, he became a school teacher at the age of 14. In 1828 he entered Middlebury College and graduated four years later. He then taught at Plattsburg Academy for two years before obtaining his seminary education, first at Andover Theological Seminary and then finishing at Lane Theological Seminary. In 1838 he married Mary Avery Bent, was ordained as a minister in the Presbyterian Church, and became pastor at Sixth Avenue Presbyterian Church in Cincinnati, Ohio. While there he founded and edited the *Herald and Presbyter*.

Blanchard had been an idealistic youth and in his early maturity enthusiastically participated in the great social crusades of the era. He was a strong supporter of temperance and at Lane, a center of anti-slavery sentiment, became an ardent abolitionist. In 1843 he became the president of the World's Anti-Slavery Society. In like measure he supported the crusade against Freemasonry. Only 15 when the murder of William Morgan, who had written an expose of Masonry, set off a wave of anti-Masonic actions, the anti-Masonic crusade began to strongly dominate Blanchard's later career.

In 1845 Blanchard was elected president of Knox College at Galesburg, Illinois. During his 12 years in that post he saw the financial situation of the college stabilize and the student body double. He also founded a new periodical, the *Christian Era*, which he continued to edit in the years after his resignation in 1857. In 1860 he became the first president of Wheaton College, then affiliated with the Congregational Church. He enjoyed a very successful 22 years in the presidency and was eventually succeeded by his son, **Charles Albert Blanchard**, who was president for over 40 years.

Blanchard probably would have been remembered most for his work at Wheaton had it not been for his continuance in anti-Masonic endeavors. In 1867 he hosted a gathering of ministers that sparked a new anti-Masonic movement. In 1868 he founded the *Christian Cynosure* and the National Christian Association to support the new crusade. Six years later, along with his son-in-law, Ezra A. Cook, he incorporated the National Christian Association, dedicated to the destruction of all secret societies, especially Freemasonry. He led the campaign to raise a memorial to Morgan which was dedicated at Batavia, New York, in 1882. As his son succeeded him in the presidency of the college, so he also continued his leadership of anti-Masonry forces among conservative Protestant Christians.

In 1882 Blanchard retired and was named president emeritus by Wheaton College. He died a decade later. Both the college and the National Christian Association remain as continuations of Blanchard's life work. In 1960 a biography of Blanchard was completed as part of Wheaton College's centennial celebration.

Sources:
Cerza, Alphonse. *Anti-Masonry*. St. Louis, MO: Missouri Lodge of Research, 1962. 383 pp.
Dictionary of American Biography. 20 vols. and 7 supps. New York: Charles Scribner's Sons, 1928-1936, 1944-1981.
Kilby, Clyde S. *A Minority of One*. Grand Rapids, MI: William B. Eerdmans Publishing Company, 1960. 252 pp.

★94★
BLANSHARD, Paul Beecher
Atheist Writer
b. Aug. 27, 1892, Fredericksburg, Ohio
d. Jan. 27, 1980, St. Petersburg, Florida

Paul Beecher Blanshard, an atheist writer most remembered for his controversial books attacking the Roman Catholic Church, was the son of Emily C. and Francis George Blanshard. His father was a Congregational Church minister and his twin brother was Brand Blanshard, the philosopher. His parents died while he was a child and he was raised by his grandmother. During his high school days he moved to Detroit, Michigan, and later attended the University of Michigan. After his graduation he moved to Massachusetts to attend Harvard Divinity School. While there he joined the Socialist Party and served as interim pastor of Maverick Congregational Church. In 1915 he married Julia Anderson.

In 1916 Blanshard moved to Tampa, Florida, as pastor of the First Congregational Church. He was subsequently ordained as a Congregational minister. As a pacifist and a socialist, Blanshard had a rough time in Tampa, and he left the ministry in 1917. He later attended Union Theological Seminary for a short while, but did not receive his degree. Instead he left religion altogether and became a union organizer and active Socialist Party member. He worked in Rochester, New York, for the Amalgamated Clothing Workers and then with the League for Industrial Democracy. His first books came out of this period: *An Outline of the British Labour Movement* (19—) and *What's the Matter with New York* (1932), co-authored with Norman Thomas.

In 1933 Blanshard quit the Socialist Party to work for the election of Fiorello LaGuardia as mayor of New York. As LaGuardia's Commissioner of Investigations and Accounts, Blanshard headed investigations which led to the expulsion of a number of city officials. In 1934 his wife died, and the following year he married Mary W. Hillyer. Working nights, in 1937 he completed his law degree at the Brooklyn Law School. He worked as a lawyer until the beginning of World War II and then served with the State Department through the war.

After the war Blanshard moved to rural Vermont. He had become interested in the question of Roman Catholic beliefs and power, and in 1947 he began to write articles for the *Nation* attacking the church. These articles grew into *American Freedom and Catholic Power* (1949), which, though banned in the New York schools, became a bestseller. He followed with *Communism, Democracy and Catholic Power* (1951) and *The Irish and Catholic Power—An American Interpretation* (1953). These books brought him to the attention of a number of Protestant leaders who were engaged in blocking efforts of the Roman Catholic Church to obtain public tax money to help support parochial schools. Blanshard soon became closely associated with Protestants and Others United for Separation of Church and State.

During the next 25 years Blanshard wrote a series of books attacking the Catholic Church, which he viewed as wielding undue influence and power in ways contrary to democratic goals and principles. He centered his attacks on issues of birth control, parochial schools, the church's hierarchical organization, and censorship. His later books included *The Right to Read—The Battle Against Censorship* (1955); *Freedom and Catholic Power in Spain and Portugal* (1962); and *Religion and the Schools: The Great Controversy* (1963).

In 1965 his second wife died, and he married Beatrice Enselman Mayer that same year. Blanshard's autobiography, *Personal and Controversial*, appeared in 1973. His last book was an anthology of the writings of free thinkers.

Sources:

Blanshard, Paul. *American Freedom and Catholic Power*. Boston: Beacon Press, 1949. 350 pp.
———. *Communism, Democracy and Catholic Power*. Boston: Beacon Press, 1951. 340 pp.
———. *The Irish and Catholic Power*. Boston: Beacon Press, 1953. 375 pp.
———. *Personal and Controversial*. Boston: Beacon Press, 1973. 308 pp.
———. *Religion and the Schools: The Great Controversy*. Boston: Beacon Press, 1963. 265 pp.

★ 95 ★
BLAVATSKY, Helena Petrovna
Founder, Theosophical Society
b. Jul. 30, 1831, Ekaterinoslav United Arab Emirates
d. May 8, 1891, London England

Madame Helena Petrovna Hahn Blavatsky (often referred to as H.P.B.), was the flamboyant co-founder of the Theosophical Society, and one of the most influential writers in the occult world. Born in Russia to a well-to-do family that was acquainted with the occult, she lived with her grandfather after her mother's death. In 1848, as she turned 17, she married General Nikifor Blavatsky, but after only a few months she left him and journeyed to Constantinople.

For the next 25 years or so, Blavatsky travelled around the world, exploring the occult. She claimed contact with the mahatmas, beings so evolved that they now actively participated in the divine plan of history. In France she met the medium Daniel D. Home, and in Egypt she created a Spiritualist society that was short-lived due to exposure of the society's fraudulent activity in the area of psychic phenomena. In 1874 she held seances in Vermont with the Eddy brothers. She then combined with Henry Steel Olcott to arrange spiritualist gatherings in New York City. In 1875, joined by the lawyer **William Q. Judge**, they formed the Theosophical Society, and by 1877 Blavatsky had written its major text, *Isis Unveiled*. The stated objectives of the Theosophical Society were to promote Universal Brotherhood, investigate laws of nature and latent human powers, and study comparative religion, philosophy, and science.

In 1879, with the Society struggling in New York, Blavatsky and Olcott left for India to found a new headquarters. The work in India prospered, and in 1882 they moved onto a large parcel of land in Madras. Blavatsky became better acquainted with Buddhism and Hinduism and slowly altered her philosophical views. She saw Theosophy as a move away from Spiritualism toward recognition of the evolutionary process away from mere matter, and she began to emphasize the contact with the spiritual Masters, or mahatmas, from whom letters began to arrive at the Madras home. In 1884, while both Olcott and Blavatsky were in London, a close associate back in India, Mrs. Emma Coulomb, accused Blavatsky of fraud. The Society of Psychical Research in London sent an investigator, who found that the letters from the Masters, which often appeared in a cabinet, actually arrived there through a secret opening from Blavatsky's bedroom. This discovery severely hurt the movement, and Blavatsky soon left India and settled in London permanently.

In 1887 Annie Besant met Blavatsky in London. She was immediately drawn to Theosophy. Utilizing Besant's abilities, Blavatsky was able to see the Society recover and grow before her death in 1891.

Sources:

Blavatsky, Helena P. *Collected Writings*. 16 vols. Wheaton, IL: Theosophical Publishing House, 1950-1987.
———. *Isis Unveiled*. 2 vols. New York: J. W. Bouton, 1877.
———. *The Key to Theosophy*. Pasadena, CA: Theosophical University Press, 1972. 373 pp.
———. *The Secret Doctrine*. 2 vols. London: Theosophical Publishing House, 1928.
Bowden, Henry Warner. *Dictionary of American Religious Biography*. Westport, CT: Greenwood Press, 1977. 572 pp.
Dictionary of American Biography. 20 vols. and 7 supps. New York: Charles Scribner's Sons, 1928-1936, 1944-1981.
Harris, Iverson L. *Mme. Blavatsky Defended*. San Diego, CA: Point Loma Publication, 1971. 174 pp.
James, Edward T., ed. *Notable American Women, 1607-1950: A Biographical Dictionary*. 3 vols. Cambridge, MA: Harvard University Press, Belknap Press, 1971.
Meade, Marion. *Madame Blavatsky*. New York: G. P. Putnam's Sons, 1980. 528 pp.
Murphet, Howard. *When Daylight Comes*. Wheaton, IL: Theosophical Publishing House, 1975. 277 pp.
Ryan, Charles J. *H. P. Blavatsky and the Theosophical Movement*. Pasadena, CA: Theosophical University Press, 1937. 358 pp.
Shepard, Leslie. *Encyclopedia of Occultism & Parapsychology*. 3 vols., 2nd. ed. Detroit: Gale Research Co., 1984-1985.
Who Was Who in America. Chicago: Marquis Who's Who, Inc.
Williams, Gertrude Marvin. *Priestess of the Occult*. New York: Alfred A. Knopf, 1946. 345 pp.

—*Gary L. Ward*

★ 96 ★
BLISS, Philip Paul
Evangelist and Hymn Writer, Congregational Church
b. Jul. 9, 1838, Clearfield County, Pennsylvania
d. Dec. 29, 1876, Astabula, Ohio

Philip Paul Bliss, one of the most popular song writers of the nineteenth century, was the son of Lydia Doolittle and Isaac Bliss. He grew up on a farm and worked for a while in a logging camp. He received very little formal schooling but was able to acquire sufficient education to himself teach school as a young man. He later attended music schools in Towanda, Pennsylvania, and Geneseo, New York, but picked up his musical abilities informally. In 1858 he married Lucy J. Young, a woman from a family of professional singers. During the Civil War he taught music in Bradford County, Pennsylvania.

In 1865 Bliss met **George F. Root** and went to work for Root & Cady, Root's publishing firm in Chicago. He began to write for Root, give musical concerts, and travel the country conducting musical conventions. He became the director of music and later the Sunday school superintendent for First Congregational Church in Chicago. In 1871 he produced his first songbook, *The Charm*, which made him popular in the new Sunday school movement as a composer. He quickly produced three more books—*The Song Tree* (1872); *The Sunshine* (1873); and *The Joy* (1873).

At this point **Dwight L. Moody**, the prominent evangelist who was headquartered in Chicago, stepped into Bliss' life and convinced him to travel with an evangelistic team. For several years Bliss traveled with Major D. W. Whittle in the southern and western states. In 1874 and 1875 he produced his most famous work, the two-volume *Gospel Songs*, in collaboration with Moody's song leader, **Ira D. Sankey**. This book contained his most popular and enduring hymns, such as "It Is Well with My Soul," "Let the Lower Lights Be Burning," "Hold the Fort," and "Almost Persuaded."

Bliss died suddenly in December 1876. He had been in a revival meeting with Major Whittle in Peoria, Illinois. He went to Rome, Pennsylvania, to spend the Christmas holidays with his family and was to return to Chicago to close the year in a meeting with Moody. On his way back to Illinois, he became a victim of a famous train wreck in Astabula, Ohio. Though he initially survived the wreck himself, once freed, he returned to attempt to save his wife. Both were burned to death.

Bliss joined a cadre of nineteenth-century musicians who created the style of gospel music which remains popular in Protestant and free churches. No style of religious music since has gained such popularity or been so influential to life of American Christianity.

Sources:
Bliss, Philip P. *The Charm*. Chicago: Root & Cady, 1871. 154 pp.
_____. *Gospel Songs*. Chicago: Fleming H. Revell Company, 1874. 128 pp.
_____. *The Joy*. Cincinnati, OH: J. Church & Co., 1873. 191 pp.
_____. *The Songs of P. P. Bliss*. Cleveland, OH: S. Brainard's Sons, 1877. 80 pp.
_____. *Sunshine for Sunday Schools*. Cincinnati, OH: J. Church & Co., 1873. 160 pp.
_____, and Ira David Sankey. *Gospel Hymns and Sacred Songs*. 3 vols. New York: Bigelow & Main, 1875-1878.
Dictionary of American Biography. 20 vols. and 7 supps. New York: Charles Scribner's Sons, 1928-1936, 1944-1981.
Stebbins, George C. *Reminiscences and Gospel Hymn Stories*. New York: George H. Doran Company, 1924. 327 pp.
Whittle, D. W. *Memoirs of Philip P. Bliss*. New York: A. S. Barnes, 1877. 367 pp.

★97★
BLISS, William Dwight Porter
Founder, Christian Socialist Society
b. Aug. 20, 1856, Constantinople Turkey
d. Oct. 8, 1926, New York, New York

William Dwight Bliss, a priest in the Episcopal Church, was the son of Edwin Lissha and Isabella Holmes Porter Bliss, both missionaries for the Congregational Church. He was raised in Turkey and attended Robert College in Constantinople. He came to the United States and continued his education at Phillips Academy, Amherst College, and Hartford Theological Seminary, from which he graduated in 1882. He became a pastor in Denver, Colorado, and in 1884 married Mary Pangalo, whom he had met in Constantinople. He became pastor of the Congregational church in South Natick, Massachusetts, which he served until 1886 when he left the Congregational Church and became a priest in the Protestant Episcopal Church. In 1887 he became the rector of Grace Episcopal Church in South Boston, Massachusetts.

Bliss' movement into the Episcopal Church coincided with his absorption of the writings of Frederick Denison Maurice and Charles Kingsley, two prominent Church of England advocates of Christian socialism. Bliss would become a leading American advocate of Christian socialism for the next 30 years. In 1887 he became the Labor Party candidate for lieutenant-governor of Massachusetts. In 1889 he organized the first Christian Socialist Society and launched a new periodical, *The Dawn*, on its behalf. In 1890 he left Grace Church and founded the Church of the Carpenter in Boston, Massachusetts, and served as its rector. While there, in 1891, he compiled and published two volumes of the social writings of John Ruskin and John Stuart Mill, and saw to the publication of Thorold Rogers' *Six Centuries of Work and Wages*. In 1894 he resigned his pastorate and became a national lecturer for the Christian Socialist Union. While with the union, he produced the *Handbook of Socialism* (1895) and the *Encyclopedia of Social Reform* (1897), but more importantly he emerged as a major American propagandist for Christian socialism, about which he spoke passionately and frequently.

Bliss returned to the pastorate in 1898 in San Gabriel, California, but in 1899 he became president of the National Social Reform Union. In 1902 he moved to Amityville, on Long Island, as pastor of the Episcopal parish. While there he joined with W. H. Tolman to produce the third volume of *Social Progress; A Year Book* (1906). That work appeared about the time that Bliss left the parish again to become an investigator for the United States Department of Labor, with whom he was employed for two years, from 1907 to 1909. While with the Labor Department he produced a new edition of his *Encyclopedia of Social Reform* (1908). In 1909 he went

to work for the American Institute for Social Service, which had been founded by **Josiah Strong**. With Strong he co-authored *Studies in the Gospel of the Kingdom*.

Bliss continued to work with the institute, but in 1919 he also was named pastor of the Episcopal church in West Orange, New Jersey. Both jobs came to an end in 1914 when, following the outbreak of World War I, he journeyed to Switzerland to work with interned soldiers. He returned to the United States after the war to become pastor of St. Martha's Church in New York City, where he would remain for the rest of his life. Bliss' career spanned the period in which socialism had its greatest success in the United States. Suppressed during World War I, it would never regain the popular support it had previously enjoyed.

Sources:
Bliss, William D. P. *A Handbook of Socialism*. New York: Charles Scribner's Sons, 1895. 291 pp.
_____. *The New Encyclopedia of Social Reform*. Rev. Ed. New York: Funk & Wagnalls Co., 1908. 1321 pp.
_____. *Social Progress: A Year Book and Encyclopedia of Economic, Industrial, Social and Religious Statistics*. 3 vols. New York: Baker & Taylor Co., 1904-1906.
Dictionary of American Biography. 20 vols. and 7 supps. New York: Charles Scribner's Sons, 1928-1936, 1944-1981.

★98★
BOISEN, Anton Theophilus
Pastoral Counselor, Presbyterian Church
b. Oct. 29, 1876, Bloomington, Indiana
d. Oct. 1, 1965, Elgin, Illinois

Anton Theophilus Boisen was the founder of the movement for clinical pastoral education, which during the 1970s became a standard element in the professional education of ministers. He followed one of the more distinct pilgrimages in religious leadership of any in the twentieth century. During his life he suffered a number of psychological crises, including at least six periods in which he was disabled by psychotic episodes, any one of which might have wrecked the religious career he was pursuing. However, he made those episodes the substance of religious reflection, and he devoted much of his life to exploration of the psychological factors in religious experience.

Boisen was the son of Herman Baltazar Boisen, an eccentric professor of modern languages and botany at Indiana University, and Louise Wylie, one of the first women to enroll at Indiana University. He lost the use of his left eye when he was seven, which increased his sense of insecurity and shyness. Following his graduation from Indiana in 1897, at a time when psychology was still very much in its infancy, he entered graduate work in modern languages. During these years he had his initial overwhelming bout with depression, which subsided but led to his changing fields from languages to forestry. He left Indiana for Yale University to study for his new career.

Three years after entering Yale, he again changed his career plans and decided to enter the ministry. In 1908 he entered Union Theological Seminary in New York City, and there encountered **George Albert Coe**, one of the pioneer psychologists of religion. Coe's influence shaped much of Boisen's remaining life. After graduation in 1911, he was ordained by the Presbyterian Church. He served two years in rural work in Tennessee and Missouri, five years in the pastorate, two years with the YMCA in France, and a year in rural North Dakota.

Then in October 1920, to all outward appearances destined to a life as an obscure minister in a large denomination, Boisen suffered a severe psychological breakdown and spent 15 months in a mental-care ward in the Massachusetts State Hospital at Westboro. By the time of his release he had become convinced of the intimate relation of religion and psychological health. He began an intense period of study of theology and psychology, including studying for a time under Richard C. Cabot and William McDougall at Harvard. In July 1924 he became chaplain at the State Hospital at Worcester, Massachusetts, and the following year offered the first summer program in pastoral clinical education, sharing his evolving ideas on the relationship of mental disorders and religious experience. That same year he also began to spend part of each year in the Midwest as an instructor at Chicago Theological Seminary. In 1926 he published his first major book, *Lift Up Your Hearts*, and two years later he released the account of his own mental struggles as *My Own Case Record*.

In 1930 the fruit of Boisen's work began to manifest nationally with the incorporation of the Worcester work as the Council for the Clinical Training of Theological Students. Unfortunately, just as the program was expanding, Boisen had another disabling psychotic episode that took him out of leadership. Upon his recovery, he transferred his work to the State Hospital at Elgin, Illinois. A final psychotic episode in 1935 again temporarily disabled him, but again he recovered, this time to begin his mature active intellectual period. He authored *Exploration of the Inner World* in 1936, which was followed by numerous articles exploring the role of religion in times of personal crisis. He retired in 1945 but continued writing, including two books: *Problems in Religions and Life* (1946) and *Religion in Crisis and Custom* (1955).

Boisen is remembered for providing some more positive directions for psychology, generally hostile to religion, to consider the religious life. He is known for his concept of religious experience as "regression in service of the ego." He suggested that intense religious experience, which might appear to be psychologically regressive upon first examination (and hence a negative phenomenon) actually served a healing function for the individual allowing him/her to make greater progress in the future.

Sources:

Boisen, Anton T. *Exploration of the Inner World.* Chicago; Willett, Clark & Co., 1936. 822 pp.

———. *Lift Up Your Hearts.* Boston: Pilgrim Press, 1926. 96 pp.

———. *Problems in Religion and Life.* New York: Abingdon-Cokesbury Press, 1946. 159 pp.

———. *Religion in Crises and Custom.* New York: Harper, 1955. 271 pp.

★ 99 ★
BOMPAS, William Carpenter
Missionary Bishop, Church of England in Canada
b. Jan. 20, 1834, London United Kingdom
d. Jun. 9, 1906, Cariboo Crossing, Yukon Territory, Canada

William Bompas, a bishop of the Church of England assigned to Canada, was the son of a London lawyer. He was converted as a youth among the Baptists but was later attracted to an evangelical Anglican group. He was confirmed in the Church of England and became a worker for the Church (of England) Missionary Society (C.M.S.). Bompas was a deacon working in the C.M.S. office in the 1860s when he became inspired to go to the Yukon Territory. A spot had reportedly opened up due to the failed health of Archdeacon Robert McDonald. Bompas became the first person to be ordained a priest by **Robert Machray**, who happened to be in London to be consecrated as a bishop for Canada. Bompas left England on June 30, 1865. He arrived at Fort Simpson, in the Yukon, on Christmas Day. Unfortunately for Bompas, McDonald had recovered his health and resumed his duties. Bompas was sent on to Fort Norman, near the Arctic Circle. From Fort Norman he began a series of journeys among the Indians and Eskimos, often accompanied by his wife. These journeys soon made him a legendary figure in the territory and among his fellow missionaries. A skilled linguist, he soon picked up the various Indian languages.

In 1874 the new diocese of Athabasca was carved out of the territory where Bompas was roaming, and he was selected as its first bishop. His diocese stretched from Aklavik in the Arctic Circle to Edmonton, Alberta. He fixed his headquarters at Fort Simpson on the MacKenzie River, and presided over the first diocesan synod in 1876. He had four priests, an archdeacon, and a catechist. Bompas divided the diocese into four districts. The area which included Fort Simpson he traveled with the assistance of the catechist. By 1883, the work had grown to the point that allowed the diocese to be divided. The northern part became the Diocese of the MacKenzie River, and Bompas remained in charge of it. During these years he authored one book about his work, *History of the Diocese of MacKenzie River* (1888).

In 1891 the Diocese of MacKenzie River was again divided with its northern and Western half (next to Alaska) set off as the Diocese of Selkirk. Bompas became the first bishop of Selkirk. By all accounts Bompas had become entirely devoted to his missionary work. Never one who liked meetings, he now stayed away from synods and sent representatives to speak for him. He spent all of his time either with the Eskimo converts or his language studies, especially Hebrew and Syriac. He was stirred from his studies in 1897 by the influx of people drawn by the gold strike on the Klondike River. He moved his diocesan headquarters to Forty Mile on the Yukon River and then in 1903 to Cariboo Crossing. Bompas retired in 1905 and died the following year.

Sources:

Bompas, William C. *History of the Diocese of MacKenzie River.* London: SPCK, 1888. 108 pp.

Cody, H. A. *An Apostle of the North.* Toronto: Seeley & Co., 1908. 385 pp.

Heeney, W. B. *Leaders of the Canadian Church.* Toronto: The Musson Book Co., 1902. 319 pp.

Mockridge, C. H. *The Bishops of the Church of England in Canada.* Toronto: F. N. W. Brown, 1896. 380 pp.

Wallace, W. Stewart. *The Macmillan Dictionary of Canadian Biography.* 4th ed., rev. Edited by W. A. McKay. Toronto: Macmillan of Canada, 1978.

★ 100 ★
BOND, William Bennett
Primate, Anglican Church of Canada
b. Sep. 15, 1815, Turo England
d. Oct. 9, 1906, Montreal, Quebec, Canada

William Bennett Bond, the primate of all Canada for the Church of England, immigrated to Canada as a teenager and went into business. He settled first in Newfoundland, where he was deeply influenced by John West, a lay preacher and Bible class leader at St. John's. Around 1840 Bond moved to Montreal. He was ordained as a priest in 1841 and began his ministry as a traveling missionary in the Eastern Townships of what today is known as Quebec. He became the organizer for the diocese of Montreal, and as rector of St. George's Church in Montreal (appointed in 1862) he was one of the diocese's strongest leaders. He was a strong proponent of missionary dioceses building self-supporting church centers. In 1872 he was also named dean of St. George's church. Bond represented the low church, or evangelical section of the church in Canada, and his appointment (which coincided with the problems created by **Edward Cridge**, another evangelical priest, in British Columbia) was evidence of the strong support that the low church faction possessed in eastern Canada.

In 1878 Bond was elected bishop of Montreal and was consecrated by Bishop John Medley. He was consecrated at St. George's but enthroned at Christ Church Cathedral. He held all three appointments for a year or two but finally found replacements for him as dean and rector of St. George's. He served as bishop of Montreal during the crucial period of the consolidation of the Church of England's work in Canada and the emergence of the Anglican Church of Canada in 1893. Following the merger, the formerly autonomous provinces of the Church of England were incorporated as administrative units under the new organization. In 1901 Bond became the metropolitan and archbishop of the province of Canada (which included all of Canada east of Manitoba in its territory). Three years later, he succeeded **Robert Machray** and became the second primate of the Anglican Church of Canada. His primacy lasted only two years, however, as he passed away in 1906.

Sources:

Carrington, Philip. *The Anglican Church in Canada*. Toronto: Collins, 1963. 320 pp.

Wallace, W. Stewart. *The Macmillan Dictionary of Canadian Biography*. 4th ed., rev. Edited by W. A. McKay. Toronto: Macmillan of Canada, 1978.

★101★
BONEWITS, Philip Emmons Isaac
Druid Priest and Founder of Ar nDraiocht Fein
b. Oct. 1, 1949, Royal Oak, Michigan

Philip Emmons Isaac Bonewits is the founder of Arn Draiocht Fein (ADF), a contemporary Druid group, and is an important figure in the larger Neo-Pagan movement. Raised in a Roman Catholic household, he entered a Catholic high school seminary in the ninth grade, but soon realized that he did not want to be a Catholic priest. He entered the University of California at Berkeley in 1966 and enrolled in their interdisciplinary studies program. He became the subject of widespread media coverage in 1970 when it became known that he had finished his degree program and that the university was awarding him a degree in magic.

While in college, Bonewits had roomed with Robert Larson, an alumnus of Carleton College. Carleton had been the place where a Neo-Druidic faith had been created by some students, originally as a protest of compulsory chapel attendance. They formed the Reformed Druids of North America and groves (organizations of three or more covens) were established across the country as student members from Carleton graduated. Bonewits and Larson established a Druid grove, and in 1969 Bonewits was ordained as a Druid priest. The grove was oriented to the Gardnerian Paganism of the Neo-Pagan groups in the Bay area and thus organized as the New Reformed Druids of North America to distinguish them from their midwestern parent body.

In 1973 Bonewits moved to Minneapolis and became editor of *Gnostica*, a Pagan-magical periodical published by Llewellyn Publications. Bonewits married soon after the move. He also established two other organizations: a new Druid group, which he called the Schismatic Druids of North America, and the Aquarian Anti-Defamation League, a short-lived Pagan defense organization. During this period he compiled, edited, and published *The Druid Chronicles (Evolved)* which included all of the holy writings of the several branches of the Reformed Druids.

In 1976 Bonewits was divorced and he returned to Berkeley. He rejoined the New Reformed Druids, and in 1978 established *The Druid Chronicles* (later *Pentalpha Journal*). In 1979 Bonewits married a second time, a relationship that was to last but three years. He also left the New Reformed Druids. In 1983 he married Sally Eaton. He was initiated as a third degree priest into the New Orthodox Order of the Golden Dawn, the old Neo-Pagan organization in the Bay Area, and moved to New York City.

In New York he met Shenain Bell, another Neo-Pagan, and the two decided to form yet another Druid group, Ar nDraiocht Fein (Irish Gaelic for "Our Own Druid Faith"), over which Bonewits was named Archdruid. He divorced his wife and in 1988 married Deborah Lipp. Currently, in addition to his role as Archdruid of the ADF, he assists his wife, a third degree Gardnerian priestess, in running a Pagan Way group.

Sources:

Bonewits, P. E. I. *Authentic Thaumaturgy*. Albany, CA: The CHAOSium, 1978. 98 pp.

_____. *Druid Chronicles (Evolved)*. Berkeley, CA: Berkeley Drunemetom Press, 1976.

_____. *Real Magic*. New York: Coward, McCann & Geohegan, 1971. 236 pp.

Guiley, Rosemary E. *Encyclopedia of Witchcraft & Witches*. New York: Facts on File, 1989. 400 pp.

★102★
BONNEY, Mary Lucinda
Indian Rights Advocate
Baptist Laywoman
b. Jun. 8, 1816, Hamilton, New York
d. Jul. 24, 1900, Hamilton, New York

Mary Lucinda Bonney, whose work led to the first popular reform movement on behalf of American Indians, was the daughter of Benjamin and Lucinda Wilder Bonney. Her father was a farmer and her mother a former school teacher. Bonney received a good education, and after finishing at the local Hamilton Academy, she attended the Troy, New York, Female Academy headed by Emma Willard, from which she graduated in 1835. She taught in Jersey City, New Jersey, and in New York City before returning to her alma mater in the 1840s.

In 1842 Bonney moved to South Carolina, where she taught at Beaufort and Robertville. While in the south, she met a Baptist minister, Thomas Rambaut, and under his ministry left the Episcopal Church in which she had been raised, and became a Baptist. After six years in the south she returned north to Providence, Rhode Island. She then moved to Philadelphia, where in 1850 she opened the Chestnut Street Female Seminary, a successful venture at which she was employed as senior principal until 1888. (In 1883 the school moved to Ogontz, Pennsylvania.) She also joined the First Baptist Church of Philadelphia.

Once in Philadelphia, Bonney affiliated with the local branch of the interdenominational Woman's Union Missionary Society of America for Heathen Lands and regularly donated funds, especially for women missionaries trained to reach the secluded women of the Orient. Her attention, however, was being increasingly drawn to the plight of Native Americans. Her concern gained real force following the accounts of the movement of Whites into Oklahoma in 1879, for proposals had been introduced into Congress that would allow settlers to take possession of land assigned to Indian tribes by treaty. Outraged, Bonney began to give voice to her concern at her church.

Bonney financed a campaign to circulate a petition calling for the honoring of all treaties with the Indians. It was presented to the President and to Congress in February 1880. She then circulated a second petition to protect all Indian lands. To give structure to what was becoming a long-term project, she organized the Central Indian Committee (later renamed the Indian Treaty Keeping and Protective Association). After completing and presenting the second petition, the organization circulated a third petition calling for the giving of tribal lands to individual Indians. This petition stood against the legislation then being worked on by Massachusetts senator Henry L. Dawes, which was drafted specifically to prevent individual ownership of land by Indians. Dawes. The 1887 Dawes Act set tribal authority in place for another half century.

Renamed the Women's National Indian Association in 1883, Bonney's group continued to advocate Indian concerns, though with the Dawes Act in place it refocused its activity. The group launched a missionary and education program aimed at "elevating" Indian women through a variety of efforts from training in child care to instruction in English.

In 1884 Bonney resigned as president of the association, but remained on the executive board and missionary committee. Her generous financial contributions had kept the organization solvent, and she contributed annually for the rest of her life. She continued to teach for four more years and then retired.

At about the same time as her retirement, Bonney traveled to London to attend the Centenary Conference on the Protestant Missions of the World. There she again met Thomas Rambaut, the Baptist minister whom she had encountered in South Carolina. He was now a widower and a retired college president, and she had never married. They were married in London and returned to live in Hamilton, New York. He died in 1890. She lived another decade, residing with her brother in the small town where she was born.

Sources:

James, Edward T., ed. *Notable American Women, 1607-1950: A Biographical Dictionary*. 3 vols. Cambridge, MA: Harvard University Press, Belknap Press, 1971.

★ 103 ★
BOOTH, Ballington
Cofounder, Volunteers of America
b. Jul. 28, 1857, Brighouse England
d. Oct. 5, 1940, Blue Point, New York

Ballington Booth, the founder of the Volunteers of America, was the son of Catherine Mumford and **William Booth**, the founder of the Salvation Army. He was only eight years old when the Salvation Army was founded, and he grew up in the context of its growth. Booth attended a preparatory school before entering the Institute for Theological and Missionary Training (now Paton Congregational College) in Nottingham. He became a Salvation Army officer at the age of 17 and, as the general's son, rose quickly in the ranks.

In 1883, with the rank of marshal, Booth moved to Australia as the co-commander of the Salvation Army. His two years there were deemed quite successful and he returned to England. The Australian tour became the subject of his first book, *The Salvation War. . .Or How We Marched in 1884 through Australasia* (1885). In 1886 he married Maud Elizabeth Charlesworth, who as **Maud Ballington Booth** would be his partner in all of his important endeavors in the future. In 1887 they left for America to assume the leadership of the fledgling Salvation Army corps which had been established in the United States. Early in his tenure he authored a second book, *From Ocean to Ocean* (1891). They adapted well to their new position and in 1895 became citizens of the United States.

At the time their citizenship was granted, they were in the early stages of an intense internal conflict that involved not only the organization but the large Booth family. In the end they resigned from the Salvation Army and in March 1896 founded the Volunteers of America, an organization very much modeled on the Salvation Army, but more democratic in structure. In September 1896 he accepted an ordination by Bishop Samuel Fallows of the Reformed Episcopal Church as a "presbyter in the Church of God in General," the intent being to emphasize his role as a nondenominational "general" evangelist to society. Booth and his talented wife put their skills to work in building and directing their new endeavor. He was an outstanding orator and an accomplished musician who played several instruments and wrote a number of hymns. They consciously avoided establishing centers in areas where they would compete with the Salvation Army.

Booth led the Volunteers of America for four decades. It developed a wide variety of humanitarian social services, including shelters for the homeless and facilities for unwed mothers. Possible its most oustanding contribution was in the prison and parole work

established by the Booths and largely supervised by Booth's wife. Before his death, over 70 posts had been established.

Sources:

Booth, Ballington. *From Ocean to Ocean*. New York: J.S. Olgivie, 1891. 186 pp.

—. *The Prayer that Prevails*. New York: Volunteers of America, 1920. 94 pp.

—. *The Salvation War. . .Or How We Marched in 1884 through Australasia*. 3 vols. London: International Headquarters, 1885.

Dictionary of American Biography. 20 vols. and 7 supps. New York: Charles Scribner's Sons, 1928-1936, 1944-1981.

Welty, Susan F. *Look Up and Hope! The Life of Maud Ballington Booth*. New York: Thomas Nelson & Sons, 1961. 284 pp.

Wisbey, Herbert A., Jr. *Soldiers Without Swords: A History of the Salvation Army in the U.S.* New York: Macmillan Company, 1955. 242 pp.

★ 104 ★
BOOTH, Evangeline Cory
General, Salvation Army
b. Dec. 25, 1865, London England
d. Jul. 17, 1950, Hartsdale, New York

Evangeline Cory Booth, the fourth general of the Salvation Army, was one of eight children of General **William Booth** and Catherine Mumford Booth, founders of the Salvation Army. She was named after Little Eva, a character in *Uncle Tom's Cabin*. Evangeline was educated at home by private tutors in the atmosphere of the Salvation Army, which had been created the year of her birth. She put on the uniform of the army at the age of 15 and began to sell the group's magazine, *War Cry*. After working on the streets for several years, she was placed in charge of the International Training College at Clapton and made commander of the Salvation Army in London.

Booth became known as an effective troubleshooter for the organization and was sent to America to serve in that capacity in 1896. Her brother, **Ballington Booth**, and his wife, **Maud Ballington Booth**, had split with William Booth and founded the rival Volunteers of America. Evangeline Booth took control through the crisis until her sister Emma took command of the American work. At that time, Evangeline moved to Canada to lead the work there. In 1903 Emma was killed in a tragic accident, and Evangeline returned to the United States.

Evangeline Booth headed the work in the United States for the next 30 years. Emma had just begun to implement the broad program of social service for which the Salvation Army has become so famous. The new commander expanded the services for unwed mothers, food and shelter centers, and work with prisoners and ex-prisoners. In 1906, in response to the San Francisco earthquake, the Army developed its emergency disaster service. Booth was honored by the government for the Army's canteen program for the servicemen during World War I.

Booth expanded the organization within a short time to the point that it became necessary to divide it into four districts and issue separate editions of *War Cry*. She accomplished this expansion in part by her ability to develop a large financial base among people not otherwise associated with the Army. Following the war she conducted the first national fundraising drive.

During the 1920s, with the Salvation Army's work in America growing at a steady pace, Evangeline was forced to deal with an international crisis within the Army. Her brother, Bramwell Booth, had been appointed the new general, or international leader, of the Army at the time of William Booth's death in 1912. The Army's leadership and members, however, rejected much of what they felt to be his arbitrary authority. In 1922 he tried to remove Evangeline from her American post. Faced with hostile public opinion, he backed down. The following year Evangeline became an American citizen. She also became the focus of a movement to change the

Army's organization. In 1929 the leadership met in London, deposed Bramwell (who was quite ill at the time), and adopted a policy of electing future generals.

In 1934 Evangeline was elected the fourth general of the Salvation Army. She moved to London and headed the work for five years before retiring. She then moved back to the United States and lived out her retirement years at her home in Hartsdale, New York. She died at the age of 85 of arteriosclerosis.

Sources:

Booth, Evangeline Cory. *Desperation*. New York: Salvation Army, 1904.
———. *Love Is All*. New York: Press of Reliance Trading Co., 1908. 112 pp.
———. *Songs of the Evangel*. New York: Salvation Army, 1927. 51 pp.
———. *Toward a Better World*. Garden City, NJ: Doubleday, Doran & Co., 1928. 244 pp.
———. *Woman*. New York: Fleming H. Revell, 1930. 40 pp.
———, and Grace Livingston Hill. *The War Romance of the Salvation Army*. Philadelphia: J. B. Lippencott Co., 1919. 356 pp.
James, Edward T., ed. *Notable American Women, 1607-1950: A Biographical Dictionary*. 3 vols. Cambridge, MA: Harvard University Press, Belknap Press, 1971.
Wilson, Philip Whitwell. *General Evangeline Booth of the Salvation Army*. New York: Fleming H. Revell, 1935. 127 pp.

★105★
BOOTH, Maud Ballington
Cofounder, Volunteers of America
b. Sep. 13, 1865, Limpsfield United Kingdom
d. Aug. 26, 1948, Great Neck, Long Island, New York

Maud Ballington Booth, cofounder of the Volunteers of America, was the daughter of Rev. Samuel Beddome Charlesworth, an Anglican clergyman, and Maria Beddome Charlesworth. She was christened Maud Elizabeth Charlesworth. When she was three, her father moved the family to London, where he served a parish in one of the poorest sections of the city. Thus Maud, though protected from the worst, grew up knowing the slums. In her mid-teens, she was sent to a school in Suffolk. In 1881 a series of events altered her life permanently. In March, her older sister married. Responding to Maud's loneliness, her mother took her to a Salvation Army meeting at which Ballington Booth, the son of Salvation Army founder General **William Booth**, spoke. In November her mother died.

Impressed with the Salvation Army's program, Maud signed up a year after her mother's death, and joined Catherine Booth in starting the Army's work in France and Switzerland. She returned to London to work in the training center for women and helped initiate the "slum sisters" program. Slum sisters lived in the poorer sections, carrying out various social services. In spite of her father's disapproval, she became engaged to Ballington Booth, whom she married in 1886. She adopted both of his names as her own.

As a couple, the newlyweds were placed in charge of the Salvation Army's recently inaugurated work in the United States. They took command in 1887. Their work progressed for nine years. Maud built a ministry in the New York City slum area modeled on the English "slum sister" efforts. In 1895 they both became United States citizens. Some friction, however, had been developing with Ballington's father, who, the following year, ordered them to return to London. Rejecting William Booth's authority, they resigned from the Army.

Having found much support in the previous nine years, they drew upon it to start a new movement. The Volunteers of America resembled the Salvation Army, but had an elected, rather than appointed, general. Ballington held the post for the rest of his life. Maud gave her initial attention to prison work through a subsidiary organization, the Volunteer Prison League. She began in the spring of 1896 at Sing Sing Prison. The program allowed her a new area

of service that did not directly compete with the Salvation Army's work in the slums. As her work developed, Booth emphasized prisoner self-rehabilitation and further worked to assist the families of prisoners and to secure employment for convicts after their release. She established halfway houses, "Hope Halls"—first in Flushing, New York, then in Chicago, and then in other cities. The high rate of rehabilitation among convicts in the program led to numerous endorsements by surprised prison officials, and the program spread accordingly. Her work and its ideological basis were documented in several books: *Branded* (1897); *Did the Pardon Come Too Late?*; and *After Prison—What?* (1903).

Booth's ministry led her to become a public advocate of prison reform. She conceived of prisons as centers for rehabilitation rather than punishment, and she became an active member of the American Prison Association. The gradual acceptance of many of her insights can be seen in the development of the prison parole system, which in turn largely replaced the work of the Volunteer Prison League, which gradually died out.

In 1940, after Ballington's death, Booth was elected to succeed him as general of the Volunteers of America. Though 75 years old, she did not accept the post as only an honorary desk job, but actively traveled across the United States to oversee the work and speak on behalf of the organization. She continued her active schedule for seven years, until just before her death at the age of 82.

Sources:

Booth, Maud Ballington. *After Prison—What?* New York: Fleming H. Revell, 1903. 290pp.
———. *Beneath Two Flags*. New York: Funk & Wagnalls, 1889. 288 pp.
———. *Branded*. New York: A. D. F. Randolph Company, 1897. 49 pp.
———. *Did the Pardon Come Too Late?* New York: Fleming H. Revell, 1897. 45 pp.
———. *Twilight Fairy Tales*. New York: G. P. Putnam's Sons, 1906. 278 pp.
James, Edward T., ed. *Notable American Women, 1607-1950: A Biographical Dictionary*. 3 vols. Cambridge, MA: Harvard University Press, Belknap Press, 1971.
Welty, Susan F. *Look Up and Hope!* New York: T. Nelson, 1961. 284 pp.

★106★
BOOTH, William
Founder, Salvation Army
b. Apr. 10, 1829, Nottingham England
d. Aug. 20, 1912, London England

William Booth was the charismatic British founder of the Salvation Army, one of the most successful of the nineteenth-century holiness movements. The failure of his father's entrepreneurial efforts forced William to leave school and apprentice to a pawnbroker in 1842, at the age of 13. When his father died a few years later, William found comfort in religion, became a Methodist, and even began preaching on his own.

Booth moved to London in 1849, where he began work as a pawnbroker and was an active member of the Reformers, a schismatic group with roots in Methodism. Three years later he became a full-time preacher for them, though he soon decided that the New Connection, another Methodist splinter group, was where he really wanted to be. After studying for their ordination, he was admitted probationally in 1854 and appointed to the staff of a church in London, where he spent much of his time in evangelism. In 1855, the same year he married Catherine Mumford from the Reformers Church, he was appointed to evangelism full-time. He was immensely successful, with more than 3,000 people converted during his first year alone.

In 1858 Booth became pastor of the Gateshead church, a dying enterprise that he revived in three years. This fueled his desire to return to full-time evangelism. The church would not allow it, however, so he turned independent. His wife Catherine, meanwhile, had discovered her own preaching talents, and in 1865 she tried them out in the slums of London. Booth joined her, and together they created the East London Christian Mission and its magazine, *East London Evangelist*. Like all of his previous work, this project became very successful, sprouting many branch centers across London and beyond.

Around 1878 the idea of a "Salvation Army" was born, as a way of forming a more disciplined corps of workers to accomplish all the tasks before them. Over a period of time, the name was changed, uniforms were adopted, Booth's title of general superintendent was shortened to just general, and the magazine became the *Salvationist*. The success of the group continued, and in 1888, at the age of 59, Booth discovered a new arena of work. He realized the extent of the physical needs of the poverty-stricken persons with whom he worked and began to address these needs, opening an overnight shelter. He became so concerned about the topic that he wrote his most famous book, *In Darkest England, and the Way Out*, a thorough investigation of poverty in England combined with plans for eliminating it. Soon the Salvation Army was known at least as much for its social relief efforts as for its other activities.

After Catherine died in 1890, Booth began to travel, preaching his message wherever he went. He was given honors by the president of the United States and the king of England. Oxford University gave him an honorary doctorate and the city of London gave him its highest honor, the "Freedom of the City" award. Before his death in 1912 at the age of 83, he witnessed the spread of the Army into 58 countries.

Sources:

Begbie, Harold. *The Life of General William Booth.* 2 vols. New York: Macmillan, 1920.
Bishop, Edward. *Blood and Fire!* Chicago: Moody Press, 1965. 114 pp.
Booth, William. *Holy Living.* London: Salvation Army Publications Departments, 1890. 31 pp.
_____. *In Darkest England, and the Way Out.* London: International Headquarters of the Salvation Army, 1890. 285pp.
_____. *Purity of Heart.* London: Salvation Army Book Room, 1902. 118 pp.
_____. *Salvation Soldiery.* London: International Headquarters, 1890. 156 pp.
Collier, Richard. *The General Next to God.* New York: E. P. Dutton, 1965. 320 pp.
Coutts, Frederick. *Bread for My Neighbor.* London: Hodder and Stoughton, 1978. 192 pp.
Dictionary of American Biography. 20 vols. and 7 supps. New York: Charles Scribner's Sons, 1928-1936, 1944-1981.
Irvine, St. John. *God's Soldier: General William Booth.* 2 vols. London: William Heineman, 1934.
Nelson, William Hamilton. *Blood and Fire: General William Booth.* New York: Century Co., 1929. 269 pp.

—*Gary L. Ward*

★ 107 ★
BOTTOME, Margaret McDonald
President, International Order of the King's Daughters and Sons
b. Dec. 29, 1827, New York, New York
d. Nov. 14, 1906, New York, New York

Margaret McDonald Bottome, writer and religious reformer, was the daughter of William and Mary Willis McDonald. She received her education at Prof. Greenleaf's school in Brooklyn Heights. In 1850 she married a minister in the Methodist Episcopal Church, the Rev. Frank Bottome, and became progressively more interested in religious pursuits. She was named associate editor of the *Ladies' Home Journal*. For many years she gave informal talks on Biblical subjects.

On January 13, 1886, she and nine other women organized themselves into a Bible study and self-improvement group which they called the King's Daughters. The organization expanded by having each of the original members organize other groups of ten women, who in turn would go on to found yet other groups of ten. In 1887 the King's Daughters expanded to include men and became the King's Daughters and Sons. The organization was incorporated in 1889, and in 1891 the word "International" was added to the group's name, and the group became the International Order of the King's Daughters and Sons. By 1907, the membership was estimated to be half a million in 26 states and Canada.

For 16 years, Bottome wrote a column called "Mrs. Bottome's Heart to Heart Talks with the King's Daughters" for the *Ladies Home Journal*. Bottome's group met monthly to read and pray. The International Order of the King's Daughters and Sons was nonsectarian, and concentrated on Christian service and the development of character. Members undertook such service as work for foreign missions, aid to the aged and seamen, and the establishment of such institutions as the Day Nursery of Los Angeles, the Frank Bottome Memorial Settlement in New York, and the Gordon Rest for working women and girls in New England.

The Order began publishing a monthly magazine, *Silver Cross*, in October 1888. Bottome wrote constantly for the *Silver Cross*. She also published a number of small works, mostly with a devotional slant. Her writings include *Crumbs from the King's Table* (1888); *A Sunshine Trip: Glimpses of the Orient* (1897); *Our Lord's Seven Questions after Easter* (1889); and *Death and Life* (1897). In 1896 the Medical Missionary Society elected her as president.

Sources:

Bottome, Margaret McDonald. *Crumbs from the King's Table.* New York: W. McDonald & Co., 1888. 366 pp.
_____. *Death and Life.* Philadelphia: Christian Standard Co., 1897. 54 pp.
_____. *Our Lord's Seven Questions after Easter.* New York: E. Scott, 1889. 30 pp.
_____. *A Sunshine Trip: Glimpses of the Orient.* New York: E. Arnold, 1897. 215 pp.
Dictionary of American Biography. 20 vols. and 7 supps. New York: Charles Scribner's Sons, 1928-1936, 1944-1981.

★ 108 ★
BOWERS, Joseph Thomas
Bishop and President, United Holy Church of America
b. Apr. 14, 1918, Wilson, North Carolina

Joseph Thomas Bowers, the bishop and general president of the United Holy Church of America, is the son of Sallie Stevens and Horace Bowers. His father was an active minister in the church and pastored three churches in and around Wilson, North Carolina. Following high school, Bowers attended Temple University and the New Era Theological Seminary. He later did post-graduate work at the University of Maryland. He had had an initial experience of faith in his teens and acknowledged a call to the ministry in 1939. He preached his first sermon in 1940, was ordained in 1941, and was named assistant pastor of the Mt. Pisgah United Holy Church in Philadelphia, Pennsylvania (thus facilitating his attendance at Temple University). He married Clara Washington in October 1942 and a month later began a two year period of service in the army.

After his discharge from the army in 1944, Bowers returned to Mt. Pisgah and Philadelphia. In 1950 he became pastor of Faith Tabernacle in Washington, D.C., a position he has retained in addition to his general church responsibilities. His broader leadership was initially demonstrated both in his evangelistic endeavors, being one of the best orators in the church, and his missionary endeavors. From 1951 to 1961 he served as the church's representative of foreign affairs. He traveled widely developing the church in Africa, Barbados, Trinidad, Haiti, and the Philippines. In 1961 he was named a bishop of the church. In 1962 he was named vice-president of the Northern District.

In 1972 Bowers became second vice-general president of the church. He continued his missionary endeavors and devoted particular attention to the spread of the church in Africa. He was in Africa in 1980 when called to the general presidency.

As general president of the United Holy Church he immediately let it be known that he planned an extensive outreach by the church into the surrounding culture. His vision for the United Holy Church had two main thrusts: a self-conscious effort to plant churches in places where no United Holy Church congregations presently existed and the development of community service outreach programs by presently existing congregations. He led in the movement of the church into Alaska and the development of a headquarters complex in Greensboro, North Carolina. He has conducted an extensive building program for the church in Liberia, a project especially close to his heart. Finally, he has articulated plans for the development of a church-owned apartment complex and education system.

Sources:

Gregory, Chester W. *The History of the United Holy Church of America, Inc., 1886-1986*. Baltimore, MD: Gateway Press, 1986.

★ 109 ★
BOWIE, Walter Russell
Educator, Protestant Episcopal Church
b. Oct. 8, 1882, Richmond, Virginia
d. Apr. 23, 1969, Alexandria, Virginia

Walter Russell Bowie, a priest in the Protestant Episcopal Church, was the son of Walter Russell and Elizabeth H. Branch Bowie. He attended Harvard University where he earned both his B.A. (1904) and M.A. (1905) degrees. He returned to Virginia for his theological work at the Protestant Episcopal Theological Seminary. He graduated in 1908, and later that same year he was ordained a deacon and a priest and became the rector of Emmanuel Church in Greenwood, Virginia. After three years in Greenwood, he moved to Richmond as pastor of the prestigious St. Paul's Episcopal Church. It was while he was the rector of St. Paul's that he emerged as a leading spokesperson for the social gospel and modernist theology within the Episcopal Church. He endorsed the League of Nations and openly opposed the Ku Klux Klan. During this period he also authored his first books, *The Master of the Hill* (1917) and *The Road to the Star* (1922).

In 1923 Bowie became rector of Grace Episcopal Church in New York City. During his years at Grace he authored a number of popular books on a wide variety of subjects, including *Some Open Ways to God* (1922); *The Inescapable Christ* (1925); *On Being Alive* (1931); and *When Christ Passes* (1932). He also delivered the Lyman Beecher Lectures at Yale (published as *The Renewing Gospel* in 1935) and wrote several religious books for children. During the years at Grace he began the long-term work that was to become his most significant and lasting contribution to the larger American religious community—his efforts on behalf of the American Standard Bible Committee. The committee worked through the 1930s. In 1946 the committee issued the Revised Standard Version of the New Testament and in 1952 produced a similar Old Testament text.

In 1939, in the midst of his work on the committee, Bowie was invited to join the faculty at Union Theological Seminary as a professor of practical theology. He became dean of students in 1945. He continued to produce new books while at Union, among his most popular being *Lift Up Your Hearts* (1939); *Sunrise in the South* (1942); and *Which Way Ahead?* (1943).

In 1950 Bowie left Union and returned to the seminary in Virginia as a professor of homiletics. Growing out of his work on the Revised Standard Version of the Bible, Bowie became an associate editor for *The Interpreter's Bible* (1955), the most popular biblical helps used by the Protestant clergy in the decades since its appearance. *The Interpreter's Bible* included the commonly accepted King James Version of the Bible in a parallel column with the new Revised Standard Version.

Bowie retired in 1955 but remained a visiting lecturer at the seminary for the rest of his life. His last book, finished shortly before his death, was an autobiography, *Learning to Live* (1969).

Sources:

Bowie, Walter Russell. *The Inescapable Christ*. New York: Charles Scribner's Sons, 1925. 206 pp.
———. *Learning to Live*. Nashville, TN: Abingdon, 1969. 288 pp.
———. *Lift Up Your Hearts*. New York: Macmillan Company, 1939. 118 pp.
———. *On Being Alive*. New York: Charles Scribner's Sons, 1931. 252 pp.
———. *The Renewing Gospel*. New York: Charles Scribner's Sons, 1935. 296 pp.
Hill, Samuel S., ed. *Encyclopedia of Religion in the South*. Macon, GA: Mercer University Press, 1984. 878 pp.
Jones, Edgar DeWitt. *Royalty of the Pulpit*. New York: Harper, 1951.

★ 110 ★
BOWLES, Eva del Vakia
Episcopal Laywoman
Executive, Young Women's Christian Association (YWCA)
b. Jan. 24, 1875, Albany, Ohio
d. Jun. 14, 1943, Richmond, Virginia

Eva del Vakia Bowles, a prominent leader with the Young Women's Christian Association (YWCA), was born into a relatively well-to-do black family in Ohio. Her father was the first black man employed as a postal clerk. In 1883 the family moved to Columbus, where Eva grew up. She attended a business school and did some work at Ohio State University. After finishing her schooling, she began a teaching career with the American Missionary Association in Lexington, Kentucky. She then served schools in St. Augustine, Florida; Raleigh, North Carolina; and Lawrenceville, Virginia.

In 1905 Bowles was appointed secretary of the Harlem branch of the New York YWCA, the largest branch for black members in the nation. YWCA work among Blacks was just 15 years old and was still managed on a segregationist and subordinationist model. Bowles stayed in Harlem for three years and then took a job with the Associated Charities of Columbus, Ohio, as a case worker. In 1913 she returned to New York, this time to join the national staff of the YWCA. She became the first secretary of the subcommittee on "colored work." Her new position required great tact as she nurtured the slowly growing work among Blacks while at the same time rejecting any trend toward the permanent establishment of a "colored department."

World War I provided Bowles with an important opportunity for service. Given leadership over the black concerns of the YWCA's War Work Council, she had the task of creating facilities for approximately two million black women who entered industry during the war. The immediate problem was creating entertainment centers, but the more important underlying problem became race relations and understanding.

As soon as the war ended, the immigration of Blacks into northern urban centers placed sharp pressure on those YWCAs that served Blacks. Bowles gave increased leadership as her job as a committee leader grew into leadership of the Bureau of Colored Work (1920) and the Council on Colored Work (1922). As general coordinator of the black work, Bowles worked to stop separatist tendencies among the younger black leadership while advocating greater change in the national YWCA. She won a major victory when the Council on Colored Work was discontinued in 1931, an action that reflected a degree of integration of the YWCA's work, at least on the national level.

While Bowles was an Episcopalian, her major work was with the YWCA, through which her years of Christian service were channeled. Bowles retired in 1932.

Sources:

James, Edward T., ed. *Notable American Women, 1607-1950: A Biographical Dictionary.* 3 vols. Cambridge, MA: Harvard University Press, Belknap Press, 1971.

★ 111 ★
BOWNE, Borden Parker
Philosopher, Methodist Episcopal Church
b. Jan. 14, 1847, Leonardville, New Jersey
d. Apr. 1, 1910, Boston, Massachusetts

Borden Parker Bowne, whose personalistic philosophy came to dominate the thinking of twentieth-century Methodism, was the son of Margaret Parker and Joseph Bowne. Raised in a pious environment he attended Pennington Seminary to prepare to begin college at the University of the City of New York. Graduating valedictorian in 1871, he taught school and then became a pastor in the Methodist Episcopal Church for a year. In 1873, he left for two years study in Germany at the Universities of Halle and Goettingen. While he was away, his first book, *The Philosophy of Herbert Spencer*, was published. Upon his return in 1875 he became an assistant professor in modern languages at his alma mater. In 1876, Boston University, in the midst of a period of significant growth, asked him to head the department of philosophy. He would remain in that position for the next 35 years.

Bowne's first book after moving to Boston set the tone for the work of his career, the development of a philosophical system known as Personalism. As the name might imply, his perspective gave central importance to the reality of personality in the universe which he saw dominated by a personal deity and infused with a radical freedom for individuals. His emphasis upon human freedom placed him in opposition to much of the deterministic thinking of his philosophical contemporaries. He spelled out the system in a series of texts beginning with *Studies in Theism* (1879); and continuing through *Metaphysics* (1982); *The Theory of Thought and Knowledge* (1897); *Principles of Ethics* (1892); *The Immanence of God* (1905); and *Personalism* (1908).

Early in the new century, having articulated his philosophical system, Bowne began to shift his attention to theology, which many thought to be his real interest. He was known to have a deep piety and faith, two of the factors in his staying at Boston, a church school with an associated seminary, when he received a number of offers to move to other schools. His philosophical system had also posited religion as a central, not a peripheral, component of life. He authored a number of theological texts including: *The Christian Revelation* (1896); *The Christian Life* (1899); *The Atonement* (1900); and *Studies in Christianity* (1909). His sermons, collected by his wife under the title *The Essence of Religion* (1910) were published posthumously.

Bowne's philosophy, which gave expression to Methodist emphases on free will was transmitted to a generation of Methodists not only through his own writings and teaching but that of two of his students, **Edgar Sheffield Brightman** and **Francis J. McConnell**, the former a professor at Boston and the latter a bishop in the Methodist Episcopal Church.

Sources:

Bowne, Borden Parker. *The Christian Revelation.* Cincinnati: Jennings & Pye, 1896. 107 pp.
———. *Metaphysics: A Study in First Principles.* New York: Harper & Bros., 1882. 534 pp.
———. *Personalism.* Boston: Houghton, Mifflin Company, 1908. 326 pp.
———. *Studies in Christianity.* Boston: Houghton, Mifflin Company, 1909. 399 pp.
———. *Studies in Theism.* New York: Phillips & Hunt, 1879. 444 pp.
Dictionary of American Biography. 20 vols. and 7 supps. New York: Charles Scribner's Sons, 1928-1936, 1944-1981.
Harmon, Nolan B. *The Encyclopedia of World Methodism.* 2 vols. Nashville: United Methodist Publishing House, 1974.

★ 112 ★
BOYD, Henry Allen
Publisher, National Baptist Convention of America
b. Apr. 15, 1876, Grimes County, Texas
d. May 28, 1959, Nashville, Tennessee

Henry Allen Boyd, for over 35 years the secretary-treasurer of the National Baptist Publication Board, was the son of Hattie Moore and **Richard Henry Boyd**. He grew up in San Antonio, Texas, where his father was an outstanding, black Baptist minister. He absorbed his father's concern for the improvement of the situation of Blacks in the United States, and as a young man became the first Black hired as a postal clerk in San Antonio's post office. In 1896, the year after the founding of the National Baptist Convention, his father moved to Nashville, Tennessee, to found the National Baptist Publication Board. Boyd and his family moved soon afterward and joined the work at the board.

Boyd had a keen entrepreneurial sense and organized a number of businesses and educational ventures in Nashville's black community during his first decade in Tennessee. In 1904 he was ordained as a Baptist minister and integrated his religious and business interests within a comprehensive ideal of upliftment of his black brothers and sisters.

In 1915 relations between the convention and the Boyds reached a crisis. The convention incorporated and attempted to assert control over the publishing board and the Boyds. The board, however, existed as a business that the elder Boyd had founded and financed, and thus owned. The Boyds took the board out of the convention and promoted the establishment of a second convention, the National Baptist Convention of America, with which the board began to operate. They also successfully defended their operation against attempts by the convention to win control in court. By this time it had become evident to all that the elder Boyd had groomed his son to take over the board as his heir.

In 1922 R. H. Boyd died and Henry Allen Boyd became the secretary-treasurer of the board, the formal name of the position of leadership. Even before, Boyd had taken over as manager of the board and the several other enterprises founded by his father, two of which were located in the board's building: the National Baptist Church Supply Company and the National Negro Doll Company. Beginning in 1905 Boyd had also managed the *Nashville Globe*, the city's first black newspaper. In this capacity Boyd became the organizer and corresponding secretary of the National Negro Press Association. Among his major cultural activities was the successful lobbying for the founding of the Tennessee Agricultural and Industrial State Normal School (now Tennessee State University) and the placement of the school in Nashville.

Boyd became owner as well as manager of all of his father's enterprises in 1922 when his father died. They included the presidency of Citizens Savings Bank (which he guided successfully through the Great Depression of the early 1930s) and directorship of the Supreme Liberty Life Insurance Company. He expanded the business empire far beyond Nashville. Following his death in 1959, he was succeeded by his brother Theophilus Batholomew Boyd.

Sources:

Lamon, Lester C. *Black Tennesseans, 1900-1930*. Knoxville, TN: University of Tennessee Press, 1977. 320 pp.

Logan, Rayford W., and Michael R. Winston, eds. *Dictionary of American Negro Biography*. New York: W. W. Norton & Co. 1982. 680 pp.

★113★
BOYD, Malcolm
Priest, Episcopal Church
b. Jun. 8, 1923, New York, New York

Malcolm Boyd, social activist Episcopal priest and author, is the son of Melville and Beatrice Lowrie Boyd. He attended the University of Arizona (B.A., 1944) where he majored in English. He became a writer/director in Hollywood, and in 1949 with Mary Pickford and Buddy Rogers formed Pickford, Rogers & Boyd, Inc., a programming agency for radio and television. That same year he was elected the first president of the Television Producers Association of America. Two years later, however, he gave up his career and entered the Divinity School of the Pacific to prepare for the priesthood. After receiving his B.D. in 1954, he studied a year at Oxford. He was ordained in 1955 and continued his studies with **Reinhold Niebuhr** at Union Theological Seminary (S.T.M., 1956). His first book, *Crisis in Communications*, appeared in 1957.

Boyd's first parish experience (1957-1959), at St. George's Episcopal Church in Indianapolis, Indiana, came to an end due to the congregation's reaction to his exchanging pulpits with a black minister. While there he did finish his second book, *Christ and Celebrity Gods* (1958). He was then assigned as chaplain to Colorado State University in Fort Collins, where he received his first ecclesiastical rebuke for centering his ministry in an off-campus coffeehouse. In 1961 he moved to a joint appointment at Wayne State University and Grace Episcopal Church in Detroit, Michigan. In 1964 he became assistant pastor of the Church of the Atonement in Washington, D.C.

While in Washington, Boyd became a national celebrity with the popularity of a book, *Are You Running with Me Jesus?* (1965), a volume of unconventional prayers which became a best seller. In 1965 he was granted a leave as a chaplain-at-large to American universities and campuses, the first three years being spent as the national field representative of the Episcopal Society for Cultural and Racial Unity. In 1966 he went to San Francisco for a month-long engagement at a popular night spot, where he read from his book. By this time he had become a staunch supporter of the civil rights movement, to which he contributed all of the salary he earned at the San Francisco club. As chaplain-at-large, Boyd involved himself in a variety of short-term projects and continued his writing.

During the 1970s Boyd's struggle on the racial front gave way to a struggle with his sexuality. In 1978 he finished *Take Off the Masks*, the book through which he publicly announced his homosexuality. In 1981 he was appointed chaplain to Integrity, the Episcopal gay caucus. He has since authored several books on homosexuality and his experience of it, *Look Back in Joy: Celebration of Gay Lovers* (1981); *Half Laughing/Half Crying* (1986); and *Gay Priest: An Inner Journey* (1984). His formal position allows Boyd to continue with his writing and to work in the media on what he sees as significant shows built around moral and religious questions. He has authored over 25 books.

Sources:

Boyd, Malcolm. *Are You Running With Me, Jesus?* New York: H. Holt, 1965.

_____. *As I Live and Breathe: Stages of an Autobiography*. New York: Random House, 1970.

_____. *Free to Live, Free to Die*. New York: Holt, Rinehart & Winston, 1967. 114 pp.

_____. *Gay Priest: An Inner Journey*. New York: St. Martin's Press, 1984. 163 pp.

_____. *Half Laughing/Half Crying*. New York: St. Martin's Press, 1986. 277 pp.

_____. *Look Back in Joy: A Celebration of Gay Lovers*. San Francisco: Gay Sunshine, 1981.

_____. *Take Off the Masks*. Garden City, NY: Doubleday, 1978.

★114★
BOYD, Richard Henry
Publisher, National Baptist Convention of America
b. Mar. 15, 1843, Nexubee County, Mississippi
d. Aug. 19, 1922, Nashville, Tennessee

Richard Henry Boyd, the founder of the National Baptist Publication Board, was born as Dick Gray, a slave on a Mississippi plantation. In 1849 the owners of the plantation relocated to Washington County, Texas, and took their slaves with them. As Dick Gray, Boyd accompanied his master to the battles during the Civil War. The master was killed at Chattanooga, and after the war the family made Boyd the manager of the plantation. He later left the plantation and held several jobs. In 1867 he changed his name to Richard Henry Boyd and began the process of securing an education. He was able to learn enough on his own so that in 1869 he could enter Bishop College. That year he also married Hattie Moore and became a Baptist preacher. He dropped out of college before graduation and became a full-time minister.

In 1870 Boyd organized the first black Baptist association in Texas; it included six churches. Over the next 26 years he organized six other churches in various parts of the state. In 1876 he was chosen to represent Texas Baptist at the Centennial Exposition, and generally rose to a position of prominence among black Baptists as the National Baptist Convention worked toward its formal organization in 1895. In 1896 Boyd moved to Nashville and became the secretary of the home missions board and founded the National Baptist Publishing Board. He formally held the position of secretary-treasurer of the board, but, as the owner, he controlled the board completely. Over the next two decades the work of the board and the convention grew. The board issued over two million dollars worth of literature, including a number of books Boyd wrote, edited, and compiled. The property was valued at approximately $350,000.

During his years in Nashville, Boyd also became a prominent businessman and financier. He helped organize the Citizens Savings Bank and was its president in 1904. In 1906 he became the president of a secular publishing concern, the Nashville Globe Publishing Company. In 1911 he founded the National Negro Doll Company, among the first to create dolls with black flesh tones.

In 1915 Boyd became the center of a major controversy as the National Baptists moved to incorporate the National Baptist Convention. Boyd opposed incorporation, and in the meantime it was discovered that the publishing house was built on property owned by Boyd, and that all of the literature had been copyrighted in his name personally. As it incorporated, the convention moved to assert its equity in the publishing house and its authority over the board. Boyd took both entities out of the convention and made them the center of a new National Baptist Convention of America. Boyd pointed out that he had built and developed the publishing house with his own funds, without the assistance of the convention. He spent the last period of his life fighting off legal attempts to take over the publishing operation.

Sources:

Boyd, Richard Henry. *Ancient and Modern Sunday-School Methods*. Nashville, TN: National Baptist Publishing Board, 1909. 80 pp.

_____. *The National Baptist Hymn Book*. Nashville, TN: National Baptist Publishing Board, 1906. 542 pp.

_____. *The National Baptist Pastor's Guide and Parliamentary Rules.* Nashville, TN: National Baptist Publishing Board, 1900. rev. ed. 1983. 62 pp.

_____. *The Separate or "Jim Crow" Car Laws or Legislative Enactments of Fourteen Southern States.* Nashville, TN: National Baptist Publishing Board, 1909. 67 pp.

_____. *A Story of the National Baptist Publishing Board.* Nashville, TN: National Baptist Publishing Board, 1915. 145 pp.

Logan, Rayford W., and Michael R. Winston, eds. *Dictionary of American Negro Biography.* New York: W. W. Norton & Co. 1982. 680 pp.

★ 115 ★
BRADLEY, Preston
Minister, Unitarian Universalist Association
b. Aug. 18, 1888, Linden, Michigan
d. Jun. 1, 1983, Morrisville, Vermont

Preston Bradley, for many years the pastor of the Peoples Church, a Unitarian congregation in Chicago, was the son of Anna Elizabeth Warren and Robert McFarlan Bradley. As a young man, he attended Alma College for a year (1905-1906) but left to study law. In 1907 he became a part-time pastor of a Congregational church at Grand Blanc, Michigan. He returned to college in 1909 for a year at the University of Michigan. In 1911 he moved to Chicago and for a period served as pastor of Church of Providence, a Presbyterian congregation. Withdrawing from the Presbyterian Church because of his liberal views, in 1912, with 62 members of his former congregation, he founded the Peoples Progressive Church. He was soon approached by member of the Peoples Church, an independent church which had been founded by Hiram H. Thomas, a liberal Methodist minister in the 1880s. He merged his congregation into the older one and became its pastor. The new Peoples Church began meeting in rented facilities on Chicago's north side. In 1915 Bradley married Grace Wilkins Thayer.

The Peoples Church soon grew into a congregation numbering in the thousands. In 1922 Bradley began his regular radio broadcasts. As his popularity grew he was speaking twice daily and his Sunday sermons were also carried nationally. At their height, the broadcasts had an audience of five million, and when Bradley retired it was the oldest continuing religious broadcast on radio. In 1922 the church affiliated with the Unitarians and was granted full membership the next year. The still unordained Bradley remained as pastor. In 1926 the church finished construction on a building which could house its approximately 4,000 members.

Bradley issued the first of his several books, most collections of his talks, as *Courage for Today* in 1934. Others soon followed: *Mastering Fear* (1935); *Power from Right Thinking* (1936); *Life and You* (1940); *New Wealth for You* (1941); *Meditations* (1941); *Daily Strength* (1943); *Happiness through Creative Living* (1955); and *Along the Way* (1962). As the titles might indicate, Bradley matured as he absorbed some of the positive thinking attitudes of New Thought metaphysics.

As an independent-minded Unitarian minister, Bradley manifested a liberal spirit toward his own denomination. In 1933 he joined with several independent Catholics in the founding of the Order of Antioch. In 1942 he was quietly consecrated as a bishop by Frank Dyer, a Congregational minister who was also a bishop of the Holy Orthodox Church in America, a small independent denomination. He later received two other consecrations, one from Howard E. Mather of the Order of Antioch (1942) and the other from **Carmel Henry Carfora** of the North American Old Roman Catholic Church (N.A.O.R.C.C.) (1943).

In 1950, his first wife having died, Bradley married June Haslet. As his career peaked he turned down several offers to leave the ministry and go into politics. He retired in 1976 after half a century at Peoples Church. America's most well-known Unitarian minister died seven years later at his summer home in Vermont.

Sources:

Bradley, Preston. *Along the Way: An Autobiography.* New York: McKay, 1962. 280 pp.

_____. *Happiness Through Creative Living.* Garden City, NY: Hanover House, 1955. 256 pp.

_____. *Mastering Fear.* Indianapolis, IN: Bobbs-Merrill Co., 1935. 223 pp.

_____. *New Wealth for You.* New York: Frederick A. Stokes Co., 1941. 164 pp.

_____. *Power from Right Thinking.* Indianapolis, IN: Bobbs Merrill Co., 1936. 251 pp.

"Preston Bradley, Radio Theologian, Dies at 94." *Chicago Sun-Times* (June 2, 1983).

★ 116 ★
BRAGG JR., George Freeman
Priest, Episcopal Church
b. Jan. 25, 1863, Warrenton, North Carolina
d. Mar. 12, 1940, Baltimore, Maryland

George Freeman Bragg, Jr., a priest in the Episcopal Church, was born to George and Mary Bragg during the Civil War. In 1865 the family moved to Petersburg, Virginia, where his father's mother lived. She had been the slave of an Episcopal minister and during the last two years of her life she led in the founding of St. Stephen's Church for Negroes in Petersburg. Bragg grew up in that church and attended the parochial school attached to it. In 1879 he entered the Theological School for Negroes in Petersburg, which was a branch of Virginia Theological Seminary in Alexandria, Virginia. In 1870, however, he was suspended from the seminary because the rector did not find him sufficiently humble. For four years, beginning in 1882, he published *The Lancet*, one of the first weeklies serving the black community in Virginia. In 1885 he was able to reenter the seminary, as the rector had been replaced by that time. In 1886 *The Lancet* was superseded by the *Afro-American Churchman* (later the *Church Advocate*).

Bragg was ordained a deacon in 1887 and later that year married Nellie Hill. In 1888 he was ordained a priest in Norfolk where he was assigned. During his several years there he built up the congregation, built a new sanctuary, and founded the Industrial School for Colored Girls. In 1891 he was sent to Baltimore to take over St. James Church, which had fallen on bad times. Within a few years he had developed a self-sustaining parish and built a new sanctuary, which would become the center of his ministry for the next five decades.

Both within and outside of the church Bragg became a leader in black affairs. His work in Norfolk laid the foundation for a long-term commitment to educational opportunities for Blacks. During his early years at Baltimore he worked with Booker T. Washington, though later in life he saw Washington's philosophy as too conservative and ultimately detrimental to black progress. He led the fight to hire black teachers in predominantly black schools in Maryland. He also founded the Maryland Home for Friendless Colored Children, and did pioneering work in child welfare. In Baltimore, Bragg also continued his publishing work. He founded the *Ledger* (later the *Afro-American*) and for a while was active in the National Colored Press Association.

Bragg became a vocal critic of racist patterns within the church. He denounced the exclusion of Blacks from church synods and promoted the creation of a missionary district for black members headed by a black bishop. There was some talk that Bragg might succeed James Holly as bishop for Haiti, but a white man was chosen. He was also passed over for the position of Bishop Suffragan of Arkansas; Edward Thomas Demby was chosen, although Bragg was the popular choice.

During his Baltimore years Bragg also found time to write a number of books, including a number of pioneering efforts to tell the story of Blacks within the Episcopal Church. Among his titles are: *The Colored Harvest of the Old Virginia Diocese* (1901); *A Bond-*

Slave of Christ: Entering the Ministry Under Great Difficulties (1912); *The History of the Afro-American Group of the Episcopal Church* (1922); and *The Story of the First Blacks, The Pathfinder, Absalom Jones, 1746-1818* (1929).

Sources:

Bragg, George Freeman, Jr., *A Bond-Slave of Christ: Entering the Ministry Under Great Difficulties*. [192-?].

―――. *The Colored Harvest of the Old Virginia Diocese*. 1901.

―――. *The First Negro Priest on Southern Soil*. Baltimore, MD: Church Advocate Print, 1909. 72 pp.

―――. *The History of the Afro-American Group in the Episcopal Church*. Baltimore, MD: Church Ad. Press, 1922. 319 pp.

―――. *A Race with a History and a Country*. Baltimore, MD: C. M. Dorsey & Sons Printers, n.d. [193-?]. 40 pp.

―――. *The Story of the First Blacks, The Pathfinder, Absalom Jones, 1746-1818*. 1929.

Logan, Rayford W., and Michael R. Winston, eds. *Dictionary of American Negro Biography*. New York: W. W. Norton & Co. 1982. 680 pp.

★117★
BRANHAM, William Marrion
Independent Pentecostal
b. Apr. 6, 1909, Burkesville, Kentucky
d. Dec. 24, 1965, Amarillo, Texas

William Marrion Branham, an independent healing evangelist whose work directly influenced later leaders such as **Oral Roberts**, began his life in Kentucky in poverty. His father, a part-time logger, was an alcoholic. From very early on, however, Branham knew he was destined for something special. At the age of seven, while living in Jeffersonville, Indiana, he was visited by a voice that said, "Never drink, smoke, or defile your body in any way, for I have a work for you to do when you get older."

Some years later Branham joined the Pentecostal Church, where he experienced a healing and a call to preach. In 1933, at the age of 24, he began an independent Baptist tent ministry. It quickly became a success, gaining a more permanent structure—the Branham Tabernacle. The following year he married Hope Brumbech. Branham avoided his earlier association with Pentecostals because of their low social status, and his continuing visitations and visions made him unwelcome among the Baptists. He did, however, establish an association with the non-Trinitarian "Oneness" Pentecostals, for whom there is no "Father, Son and Holy Spirit," only Jesus.

After the promising start, Branham's life took a turn for the worse. The ministry did not increase enough to be self-supporting, so Branham was forced to secure another job as well. In 1937 his wife and child were killed in the Ohio River flood. He was patient, however, and in 1946 he received the message he was anticipating. An angel promised him healing power and foreknowledge, quickly tested when he was called to pray for the sick daughter of a fellow pastor. She recovered, setting off a series of events for Branham that brought him Rev. Jack Moore as his manager. **Gordon Lindsey**, an Assemblies of God minister, joined Branham as well.

In 1948, with the beginning of *The Voice of Healing* magazine, Branham's healing career flourished. A 1950 photograph showing Branham with a halo around his head magnified his healing reputation, and he toured Europe and Africa in the early 1950s. This healing revival brought other healing preachers into association with him, including **Morris Cerullo**, **Asa Alonzo Allen**, and Oral Roberts. In 1955, however, the Internal Revenue Service brought suit against Branham for tax evasion. Although the case was settled out of court, the organization was hurt, and money questions continued to plague him.

Around 1960 Branham began to isolate himself from many of his followers and fellow healers by highlighting doctrines he had long kept silent, such as non-Trinitarianism, the evils of denominationalism, and the coming destruction of the United States. He also reduced his flamboyant emphasis on miracle healings. In 1963 he began to imply that he might be the messenger of the end times spoken of in Malachi 4:5. This further reduced his support, but also encouraged many followers to be sure that his messages were preserved through The Voice of God Recordings and Spoken Word Publications. Branham died in a car accident in 1965 at the age of 56. He left behind not only the many healers influenced by his work, but also the Branham Tabernacle and Related Assemblies (now headed by Rev. Billy Paul Branham) and the continuing Spoken Word Publications.

Sources:

Branham, William Marrion. *Conduct, Order, Doctrine of the Church*. 2 vols. Jeffersonville, IN: Spoken Word Publications, 1974.

―――. *An Exposition of the Seven Church Ages*. Jeffersonville, IN: Branham Campaigns, n.d. 381 pp.

―――. *Footprints on the Sands of Time*. Jeffersonville, IN: Spoken Word Publications, n.d. 703 pp.

―――. *The Revelation of the Seven Seals*. Tucson, AZ: Spoken Word Publications, 1967. 579 pp.

In Memory of William Branham. Queenstown, Singapore: Prophetic Revelation, 1966. 41 pp.

Lindsey, Gordon. *William Branham: A Man Sent from God*. Jeffersonville, IN: William M. Branham, 1950. 216 pp.

―――. "William Branham As I Knew Him." *The Voice of Healing* 18 (February 1966): 3, 11, 14.

Pement, Eric. *An Annotated Bibliography of Material By and About William Marrion Branham*. Chicago: Cornerstone Magazine, 1986. 7 pp.

Sproule, Terry. *A Prophet to the Gentiles*. Blaine, WA: n.p., n.d. 39 pp.

Weaver, C. Douglas. *The Healer-Prophet, William Marrion Branham*. Macon, GA: Mercer University Press, 1987. 186 pp.

—*Gary L. Ward*

★118★
BRAWLEY, Edward M.
Minister and Educator, National Baptist Convention, U.S.A., Inc.
b. 1851, Charleston, South Carolina
d. 1923, United States

Edward M. Brawley, a leading minister in the creation of the National Baptist Convention, U.S.A., Inc., was born to James M. and Ann L. Brawley, free Blacks in Charleston, South Carolina, in the decade prior to the Civil War. His parents placed him into a private school, and he continued his schooling until after the incident at Harper's Ferry, which led to the closing of many schools in the South. As the war began, he was sent to Philadelphia for further schooling. He attended the Institute for Colored Youth from 1864 to 1866. He then returned to Charleston and was apprenticed to a shoemaker.

After learning his trade, Brawley settled in Philadelphia and joined the Baptist Church located there. He experienced a calling to preach and in 1870 entered Howard University in Washington, D.C. He stayed there only a few months before transferring to Lewisburg (now Bucknell) University at Lewisburg, Pennsylvania. In 1872 he was licensed to preach by the local Baptist church, and in 1875 he graduated and was ordained.

After graduation Brawley was given a position with the predominantly white American Baptist Publication Society as a missionary in South Carolina. At that time, the American Baptists spurred the writing and publication of most of the material used by black Baptist churches. In addition to his activities as a literature agent, Brawley became active in organizing the scattered churches into a state convention. He resigned that post in 1883 to accept the presidency of Alabama Normal and Theological School (now Selma University). Over the next two years, he completely overhauled the curriculum and brought it up to college status. In 1885, due to health problems in his family, he resigned and returned to South Carolina. While back home, he edited the *Baptist Pioneer*.

In the late 1880s Brawley again affiliated himself with the American Baptist Publication Society, serving for several years as the district secretary for the Atlantic Coast District. In that capacity he became the editor of *The Negro Baptist Pulpit*, the first collection of black theological and denominational writing ever published. He soon resigned, however, to become pastor of the Harrison Street Baptist Church in Petersburg, Virginia.

During the years of Brawley's most active missional and pastoral work, the black Baptists were undergoing significant changes. They faced the challenge of publishing their own material and educating their ministers. Brawley became a voice championing both causes. In 1886 he was a major leader in the formation of the American National Baptist Convention. In 1891, following the death of its founder, he served a year as its president. Following his year in office, he gave up control of the convention and, though he remained an active worker, slowly faded from leadership positions.

Sources:

Jackson, J. H. *A Story of Christian Activism: The History of the National Baptist Convention, U.S.A., Inc.* Nashville, TN: Townsend Press, 1980. 790 pp.

Pegues, A. W. *Our Baptist Ministers and Schools.* Springfield, MA: Wiley & Co., 1892. New York: Johnson Reprint Corp., 1970.

★ 119 ★
BRENGLE, Samuel Logan
Evangelist, Salvation Army
b. Jun. 1, 1860, Fredericksburg, Indiana
d. May 19, 1939, Scarsdale, New York

Samuel Logan Brengle, a leading figure in the second generation of the Salvation Army, was the son of Rebecca Ann Horner and William Nelson Brengle. He never really knew his father, who was killed in the Battle of Vicksburg during the Civil War. After the war his mother remarried, and in 1868 the family moved to Shoals, Indiana. There Brengle became active in church and in 1872 had a conversion experience during a prayer meeting at the local Methodist Episcopal Church. In 1877 he entered the Methodist sponsored Asbury University (now DePauw University) where he majored in speech. Having experienced a call to the ministry in 1882, he was persuaded to serve the Brookston/Chambers circuit as a minister in the Northwest Indiana Methodist Conference following his 1884 graduation.

After a year in the parish, Brengle left Indiana to attend Boston School of Theology, where he studied with holiness theologian Daniel Steele. Brengle was impressed with the holiness perspective that offered believers the possibility of sanctification, or perfection in love, as a second immediate act of the Holy Spirit. Brengle experienced sanctification and dropped out of seminary to become an evangelist. Soon afterwards he met and fell in love with Elizabeth Swift, a woman affiliated with the Salvation Army, which had just begun work in America. They were married in 1887 and immediately after their wedding Brengle left for England to attend the army's training school.

By the end of 1887 Brengle was back in the United States and assigned to Taunton, Massachusetts. A year later he moved to Boston. While working in the city, however, he was hit in the head with a brick and spent the next two years recovering. Upon his return to health, he became the district officer of the Salvation Army for Maine and New Hampshire. In 1895 he was promoted to staff captain and named district officer for Western Massachusetts and Rhode Island.

In 1896 the Salvation Army faced a major crisis when Ballington Booth, the son of the founder, withdrew. In the midst of the controversy, Brengle emerged as a staunch supporter of the army. He was raised in rank to major and appointed general secretary of the Central Chief Division. A year later he was assigned to California with the Pacific Coast Division.

Throughout his career, Brengle had become known as both a capable administrator and one of its most appealing preachers. A short time after his move to California, he received an appointment as a "spiritual special," the Army's equivalent of an "evangelist." In this role Brengle was at his best and was his happiest. For the next twenty years he spoke widely around the country and did much to counter the public's early negative images of the army. Also during this period he began to author the eight books which were to remain behind as his literary legacy.

Brengle served as an evangelist until 1915 when he was called to New York as the principal of the army's training school. He retired in 1931 and lived quietly for the last years of his life.

Sources:

Brengle, Samuel Logan. *At the Center of the Circle.* Ed. by John D. Waldron. Kansas City, MO: Beacon Hill Press of Kansas City, 1976. 88 pp.
_____. *Helps to Holiness.* London: Salvationist Publishing and Supplies, 1896, 1952. 145 pp.
_____. *The Way of Holiness.* London: Salvationist Publishing and Supplies, 1902, 1951. 55 pp.
_____. *When the Holy Ghost is Come.* London: Salvationist Publishing and Supplies, 1902, 1951. 55 pp.
Hall, Clarence W. *Samuel Logan Brengle: Portrait of a Prophet.* Chicago: The Salvation Army Supply and Purchasing Department, 1933. 254 pp.

★ 120 ★
BRENNAN, Francis
Cardinal, Roman Catholic Church
b. May 7, 1895, Shenandoah, Pennsylvania
d. Jul. 2, 1968, Philadelphia, Pennsylvania

Francis Brennan, a cardinal in the Roman Catholic Church, was raised in Pennsylvania. He attended St. Charles Borromeo Seminary in Overbrook, Pennsylvania. He continued his studies at the Pontifical Roman Seminary. He was ordained to the priesthood in 1920 in Rome. He stayed in Rome to complete his J.U.D. degree in 1924 at the Apollinaire. Upon his return to the United States, he settled in West Philadelphia as an assistant pastor at St. Charles Borromeo Church and a teacher of Latin at the West Philadelphia High School for Boys.

In 1928 Brennan was invited to the faculty of St. Charles Borromeo, Seminary where he taught theology and canon law for the next 21 years. In 1949 he was summoned to Rome, where he was assigned to be an auditor at the Roman Rota, the church's court of appeals; he was the first American to serve there. He became dean in 1959. While in Rome he participated in several of the preparatory commissions for the Second Vatican Council. In 1967 he was consecrated as titular bishop of Tubane and Mauratania, and the next day he was made a cardinal by Pope Paul VI. As a bishop he never served over a diocese in the United States, but remained in Rome in the church's administrative offices.

Brennan was one of the few Americans to serve in the Roman Catholic Church's administration at the Vatican, and in 1968 he became the first American to become prefect of the Congregation for the Discipline of the Sacraments. He was also assigned to serve in the Congregation for the Propagation of the Faith and the Congregation of Sacred Rites. For a time he also sat as president of the Vatican Court of Appeals.

Sources:

Delaney, John J. *Dictionary of American Catholic Biography.* Garden City, NY: Doubleday & Company, 1988. 621 pp.
Dictionary of American Biography. 20 vols. and 7 supps. New York: Charles Scribner's Sons, 1928-1936, 1944-1981.

★121★
BRESEE, Phineas
Church of the Nazarene
b. Dec. 31, 1838, Franklin Township, New York
d. Nov. 13, 1915, Los Angeles, California

Phineas Bresee, considered the founding father of the Church of the Nazarene, was born in rural New York to a farming family. At the age of 17 he was converted in a Methodist class meeting and not long after that was licensed to exhort. The next year, in 1856, the family moved to Iowa, and Bresee began preaching regularly. He adopted the name Franklin as a middle name, after the township in which he was born. In 1858 he became a full-time Methodist minister, and two years later he married Maria E. Hibbard of New York, whom he knew only through the mail.

For more than twenty years Bresee labored faithfully in Iowa Methodism. In 1883 he transferred to California to lead the First Methodist Church in Los Angeles. There he began to act and preach on the holiness movement of which he had felt a part since he experienced the gift of sanctification in 1866. The holiness perspective teaches that Christians should seek a second act of grace after that of conversion, thus enabling the Holy Spirit to make one perfect in love. Over the ensuing years Bresee held a number of important posts in the Methodist Episcopal Church of that area, including that of Los Angeles District Superintendent. He also encouraged holiness events for church people during this time.

In 1894 Bresee requested a special appointment to lead the Peniel Mission, a Los Angeles interdenominational holiness center. Other Methodist leaders, who had long been uncomfortable with his leanings, denied his request. Bresee left his 36-year Methodist career and went to the mission anyway. Within a year, however, that position proved problematic, and in October 1895 he and several followers moved down the street and opened a new church, the Church of the Nazarene.

The Church of the Nazarene was so successful that in 1897 they opened a branch in Berkeley, and by 1905 Bresee was general superintendent of many churches, which were organized in three districts and spread as far east as Chicago. In 1907 they merged with the Association of Pentecostal Churches on the East Coast, and became the Pentecostal Church of the Nazarene. The official beginning of the Church of the Nazarene, however, is considered to be the union in 1908 with the Holiness Church of Christ, whose strength was in the South. In 1919 the Pentecostal Church of the Nazarene became simply Church of the Nazarene, to avoid confusion with the more charismatic groups. Bresee continued to oversee the church's work from his Los Angeles church until his death in 1915, at the age of 77.

Sources:
Bresee, Phineas Franklin. *The Certainties of Faith*. Kansas City, MO, 1958.
_____. *Emmanuel*. Kansas City, MO: Nazarene Publishing House, 1927.
_____. *Sayings of Our Founder*. Houston, TX: Chandler & Roach Publishers, 1948.
_____. *Sermons*. Kansas City, MO: Nazarene Publishing House, 1903.
_____. *Sermons on Isaiah*. Kansas City, MO: Nazarene Publishing House. 1926.
Brickley, Donald Paul. *Man of the Morning*. Kansas City, MO: Nazarene Publishing House, 1960. 279 pp.
Brown, Harrison D. *Personal Memories of the Early Ministry of Dr. Phineas F. Bresee*. Seattle, WA: The author, 1930.
Girvin, Ernest Alexander. *Phineas F. Bresee: A Prince in Israel*. Kansas City, MO: Pentecostal Nazarene Publishing House, 1916. 463 pp.
Harmon, Nolan B. *The Encyclopedia of World Methodism*. 2 vols. Nashville: United Methodist Publishing House, 1974.

★122★
BRIGGS, Charles Augustus
Theologian and Biblical Scholar, Presbyterian Church, Episcopal Church
b. Jan. 15, 1841, New York, New York
d. Jun. 8, 1913, New York, New York

Charles Augustus Briggs, Presbyterian biblical scholar and theologian who became the subject of a famous heresy trial in the 1890s, was the son of Alanson Briggs, a successful businessman, and Sarah Mead Berrian. Soon after his completing his college work at the University of Virginia, where he was converted to Christianity, he fought with the Union Army for a few months in the Civil War. He left the army, however, to attend Union Theological Seminary. Due to his father's illness, he could not complete his seminary work and he dropped out to spend the rest of the war in business. In 1865 he married Julia Valentine Dobbs, and the following year they began a three year stay in Europe wherein Briggs completed his doctoral work at the University of Berlin.

In Berlin, Briggs gave up the conservative approach to Scripture and adopted the new German historical-critical approach, though he remained relatively conservative in his theology. He returned to New York in 1869. The following year, he was ordained a minister in the Presbyterian Church and became pastor of the congregation in Roselle, New York. He served the church until 1874 when he began his four decade career at Union Theological Seminary. Under their new professor of Hebrew, the seminary quickly emerged as a major center of Old Testament studies. Through his first two decades he authored a number of articles and several important books, *Biblical Study: Its Principles, Methods and History* (1883); *American Presbyterianism: Its Origin and Early History* (1885); and *Messianic Prophecy* (1886).

In 1890 a new chair in Biblical theology was created at Union. Briggs was selected for the position, but in his inaugural address on the authority of the Bible, he offended many of the more conservative Presbyterians. The church's general assembly, its highest lawmaking body, blocked the appointment. Further, in 1892 he was put on trial for heresy. The Presbytery of New York, which conducted the trial, acquitted Briggs, but in an appeal to the general assembly, he was condemned and stripped of his ministerial credentials. The affair led the seminary to sever its official relationship with the assembly. While still considered primarily a Presbyterian seminary, the Briggs Union began its move to its present position as an outstanding graduate school serving all liberal Protestants.

Briggs continued to teach at the seminary throughout the 1890s and produced three important books during the decade: *The Messiah in the Gospels* (1894); *The Messiah of the Apostles* (1895); and *General Introduction to the Study of Holy Scripture* (1899). In 1899 he was granted ministerial credentials in the Episcopal Church and remained related to that church for the rest of his life. The next years were spent in producing his most important biblical work, a two-volume *Critical and Exegetical Commentary on the Book of Psalms* (1906-1907).

In 1904 Briggs resigned his chair in Biblical theology and spent the rest of his life concentrating on more formal systematic theology. During this very productive time, he wrote *Church Unity* (1909); *Theological Symbolics* (1914); and *History of the Study of Theology* (1916). He died of pneumonia in his home adjacent to the seminary.

Sources:
Briggs, Charles A. *American Presbyterianism: Its Origin and Early History*. New York: Charles Scribner's Sons, 1885. 373 pp.
_____. *The Authority of Holy Scripture: An Inaugural Address*. New York: Charles Scribner's Sons, 1891. 111 pp.
_____. *Biblical Study: Its Principles, Methods and History*. New York: Charles Scribner's Sons, 1883. 506 pp.

_____. *Critical and Exegetical Commentary on the Book of Psalms*. 2 vols. New York: Charles Scribner's Sons, 1906-1907.

_____. *General Introduction to the Study of Holy Scripture*. 2 vols. New York: Charles Scribner's Sons, 1916.

_____. *History of the Study of Theology*. 2 vols. New York: Charles Scribner's Sons, 1916.

_____. *Theological Symbolics*. New York: Charles Scribner's Sons, 1914. 429 pp.

Dictionary of American Biography. 20 vols. and 7 supps. New York: Charles Scribner's Sons, 1928-1936, 1944-1981.

Shriver, George H. *American Religious Heretics*. Nashville, TN: Abingdon Press, 1966. 240 pp.

Smith, Henry Preserved. "Charles Augustus Briggs." *American Journal of Theology* 17 (October 1913).

★ 123 ★
BRIGGS, William
Publisher and Minister, Methodist Church, Canada
b. Sep. 19, 1836, Banbridge Ireland
d. Nov. 5, 1922, Toronto, Ontario, Canada

William Briggs, outstanding preacher and publisher of Canadian Methodist literature, was born in Ireland but moved to England as a young man and was educated at Liverpool. Around the middle of the century, he migrated to Canada, where in 1858 he was received on trial by the Wesleyan Methodist Church in Canada, one of several branches into which Canadian Methodism was then split. He served a number of parishes in the provinces of Quebec and Ontario for the next 20 years, completing his pastoral work at the Metropolitan Church in Toronto. In 1874 the Wesleyan Methodist Church in Canada merged with two other Methodist groups to become the Methodist Church in Canada. In 1878, Briggs was appointed book steward for the new church.

Under Briggs' thirty-year tenure, the Methodist publishing venture was transformed from a rather primitive effort into a varied and successful concern. He oversaw the construction of the Methodist Book Room, a new publishing facility in Toronto, which was able to print the church newspaper, books, Sunday school literature, and general religious items. The Methodist Book Room became one of the most successful publishing houses in the country. As book agent his name appeared on almost all of the publications.

Briggs also participated in the process of Canadian Methodist union. He helped initiate the union process that led to the 1874 merger. He was a delegate to all of the succeeding general conferences until 1918, and he worked for the merger of 1884, in which his own Methodist Church in Canada united with the remaining independent branches of Methodism to form the Methodist Church, Canada. He worked for the merger of the Methodists into the United Church of Canada, although he did not live to see it completed. As an active member of the conference, Briggs also served on the Mission Board that developed the largest foreign mission enterprise—the one that eventually would be taken into the new United Church. As a member of the board of regents of Victoria College, he helped work out the plan of merger with the University of Toronto in 1890.

Briggs retired in 1918 after 60 years in the ministry. He died a few years later.

Sources:

Harmon, Nolan B. *The Encyclopedia of World Methodism*. 2 vols. Nashville: United Methodist Publishing House, 1974.

★ 124 ★
BRIGHT, William Rohl
Founder, Campus Crusade for Christ
b. Oct. 19, 1921, Coweta, Oklahoma

William Rohl "Bill" Bright, the founder of Campus Crusade for Christ, though raised in a pious Methodist environment, left it for the business world. After finishing college, he established Bright's California Confections and was on his way to a successful business career when he began attending various activities at Hollywood Presbyterian Church. At that time the church was in the midst of a growth phase that would make it one of the largest and most influential congregations in conservative Evangelical Christianity in North America. Under the influence of **Henrietta C. Mears**, who developed the church's Sunday school program, it would become the focus of a host of new programs which would affect Protestantism nationally.

In 1946 Bright entered Princeton Theological Seminary but the following year returned to southern California to finish his course at Fuller Theological Seminary in Pasadena. In 1948 he married Vonette Zachary. He never finished seminary. During his last year he experienced a call to preach. He quit the seminary, sold his business, and began evangelical work out of a house near the University of California at Los Angeles. The immediate success of this effort, the beginning of Campus Crusade, can in large part be attributed to Bright's development of a simple presentation of the Christian gospel as four "spiritual" laws, which he wrote down in a small booklet, *Have You Heard of the Four Spiritual Laws?*, copies of which now run into the millions. The four laws, which he taught his developing leadership to share simply and without elaboration, stated: (1) God loves you and has a plan for your life; (2) sin separates us from God; (3) Jesus is the only provision for man's sin; and (4) we must individually receive Christ as Savior. The booklet added instructions on receiving Christ with a simple prayer.

With Bright's directions for using the booklet, Campus Crusade workers began to target campuses one by one with a saturation evangelism. By 1960 the crusade had become a national movement, in part assisted by **William Frank (Billy) Graham** lending his support. In 1961 Bright purchased a new headquarters, Arrowhead Springs, an old resort hotel, which became the sight for numerous national staff gatherings and conventions. As the program developed he was able to gain the help of a number of popular entertainers who were also outspoken Christians, such as Dale Evans and Johnny Cash.

As Campus Crusade has grown Bright has used it as a base for far-reaching evangelical activities. He has begun to sponsor large rallies, "Expos," primarily aimed at enlisting Christian young people in evangelical endeavors using his simple technique. He has expanded Campus Crusade overseas, the first foreign Expo being in Korea in 1974. Among his most ambitious campaigns was Key 73, an attempt to enlist Evangelical Christians across the United States in a saturation campaign that would reach every household in the country. The effort of the campaign, noted for the slogan "I Found It" (it being the new life of the converted Christian), was blunted by criticism by Jews, who saw the campaign as singling out Jews for conversion. In addition, church leaders saw the effort as superficial, hence producing few new church members for all of its time and work.

Along the way, Bright has taken the time to write a number of books, most brief and all easy to read. Many, such as *Revolution Now* (1969) and *Come Help Change Our World* (1979) aimed at recruiting the reader into Campus Crusade's overall program work. Others such as *Ten Basic Steps Toward Christian Maturity* (1968) and *Handbook of Concepts for Living* (1981) explored the Evangelical Christian lifestyle.

In spite of the Crusade's ups and downs, it has continued to grow, with a chapter on most college campuses in North America and having spread its activity around the globe. Bright's 1990 goal was to train five million in the use of his simple witnessing technique.

Sources:

Bright, Bill. *Believing God for the Impossible*. San Bernadino, CA: Campus Crusade, 1979.

_____. *Come Help Change Our World*. San Bernadino, CA: Campus Crusade, 1979. 223 pp.

_____. *Come Help Change the World*. Old Tappan, NJ: Fleming H. Revell Company, 1985. 276 pp.

_____. *Handbook for Christian Maturity*. San Bernadino, CA: Campus Crusade, 1981. 371 pp.

_____. *Handbook of Concepts for Living*. San Bernadino, CA: Campus Crusade, 1981.

_____. *Ten Steps Toward Christian Maturity*. 10 vols. San Bernadino, CA: Campus Crusade, 1986.

Lippy, Charles H. *Twentieth-Century Shapers of American Popular Religion*. New York: Greenwood Press, 1989. 494 pp.

Quebedeaux, Richard. *I Found It! The Story of Bill Bright and Campus Crusade*. San Francisco: Harper and Row, 1977.

★125★
BRIGHTMAN, Edgar Sheffield
Theologian, Methodist Episcopal Church
b. Sep. 20, 1884, Holbrook, Massachusetts
d. Feb. 25, 1953, Newton Center, Massachusetts

Edgar Sheffield Brightman, one of the most influential American philosopher/theologians of the twentieth century, was the son of George Edgar and Mary Charlotte Sheffield Brightman. He attended Brown University from which he received both his A.B. (1906) and A.M. (1908) degrees. He then attended Boston University, where he earned his S.T.B. (1910) and studied with philosopher **Borden Parker Bowne**. He continued his studies in Berlin and Marburg (1910-1911), returning to Boston for his Ph.D. in Philosophy in 1912. While pursuing his education, Brightman also engaged in the process of entering the ministry of the Methodist Episcopal Church. In 1910 he was ordained a deacon and admitted on trial in the New England Southern Conference. He was later ordained an elder and admitted into full connection. He married Charlotte Hulsen in 1912. After her death in 1915, he married Irma Fall in 1918.

Following completion of his doctoral studies, Brightman became professor of philosophy and religion at Nebraska Wesleyan College. After three years he returned to New England as a professor of ethics and religion at Wesleyan University in Middletown, Connecticut. At that time he transferred his ministerial credentials to the New England Conference. In 1919 he accepted the Borden Parker Bowne chair in the Graduate School at Boston University, a post he retained for the rest of his life.

As a philosopher and theologian Brightman developed and expanded what became identified as a typical "Methodist" theological perspective originally developed by Bowne. "Personalism," as this perspective is known, emphasized the importance of the person as the basic unit of philosophical thought and of God as the highest expression of the personal. As an exponent of this view, Brightman brought Bowne's thought to a new generation of students (including many prominent church leaders) and trained a generation of philosophers and theologians who occupied seminary teaching positions for another generation. Through students such as Gordon W. Allport, his thought significantly affected contemporary psychological studies. He authored 15 books, including: *Religious Values* (1924); *The Problem of God* (1930); *Personality and Religion* (1934); and *The Spiritual Life* (1942). His *A Philosophy of Religion* (1940) was a popular textbook.

Brightman was most important for his development of personalism's discussion of the problem of evil. In trying to reconcile the goodness of an omnipotent God with the existence of radical evil, Brightman posed the concept of a self-limited deity. The solution retained an emphasis upon God's goodness and allowed for human freewill (a characteristic position of Methodists as opposed to the Calvinist Presbyterian emphasis upon the sovereignty of God

and predestination). Brightman became the center of a lifelong controversy over the concept, which eventually attained a dominant position among Methodists with the assistance of such popularizers as Bishop **Francis J. McConnell**.

Brightman remained an active teacher right up until the time of his death at the age of 69.

Sources:

Brightman, Edgar Sheffield. *Personality and Religion*. New York: Abingdon Press, 1934. 160 pp.

_____. *A Philosophy of Religion*. Englewood Cliffs, NJ: Prentice-Hall, Inc., 1940. 539 pp.

_____. *The Problem of God*. New York: Abingdon Press, 1930. 209 pp.

_____. *Religious Values*. New York: Abingdon Press, 1924. 285 pp.

_____. *The Spiritual Life*. New York: Abingdon-Cokesbury Press, 1942. 218 pp.

Flewelling, Ralph Tyler. "Brightman: Ex Umbras in Lucem." *The Personalist* 34, 4 (Autumn 1953) 341-46.

Harmon, Nolan B. *The Encyclopedia of World Methodism*. 2 vols. Nashville: United Methodist Publishing House, 1974.

Howell, Clinton H., ed. *Prominent Personalities in Methodism*. Birmingham, AL: Lowrey Press, 1945. 512 pp.

McConnell, Francis. *Is God Limited?* New York: Abingdon Press, 1924. 297 pp.

★126★
BRINTON, Howard Haines
Director, Pendle Hill Community
Cofounder of the Pacific Yearly Meeting of the Religious Society of Friends
b. Jul. 24, 1884, West Chester, Pennsylvania
d. Apr. 9, 1973, Wallingford, Pennsylvania

Howard Baines Brinton, for many years director of the Pendle Hill Community, was the son of Ruthanna Haines Brown and Edward Brinton. Raised in an old Society of Friends (Quaker) family, Brinton attended the Friends School in West Chester, Pennsylvania, and the local high school. He then attended Haverford College where he studied with Quaker mystic **Rufus M. Jones**. He stayed at Haverford for both a B.A. (1904) and an M.A. (1905) and later attained a second M.A. from Harvard University (1909). Interrupting his education, in 1907 he began teaching at the Friends select school in Philadelphia and in 1907 moved to Barnesville, Ohio, to teach at the Olney Boarding School. He then moved to North Carolina as head of the mathematics department at Guilford College and for one year filled in as acting president (1917-1918).

Immediately after World War I Brinton became publicity secretary of the American Friends Service Committee and worked on the rebuilding of post-war Europe. Upon his return to the United States, he settled in California to pursue a Ph.D. In 1921 he married Ann Shipley Cox, then a professor of Latin at Mills College in Oakland, California, whom he had met in Europe. Both their family and professional lives were intertwined during the next three decades. In 1925 he completed a Ph.D. in philosophy and physics at the University of California (Berkeley), but in the meantime had become head of the physics department at Earlham College, the Quaker school in Richmond, Indiana. The Brintons returned to California in 1928, where he became a professor of religion and she a professor of archeology. Brinton finished his first book, a study of the mystic Jacob Boehme, while at Mills.

In Oakland, Brinton became active in the Friends Church in Berkeley and soon became aware of the scattered congregations in the larger Bay Area. In 1931 he called representatives of these congregations together and during a two day gathering organized the Pacific Coast Association of Friends. In 1947 within the Pacific Coast Association, the Pacific Yearly Meeting of the Religious Society of Friends was organized and now consists of over 40 monthly meetings (congregations).

In 1936 the Brintons moved to Pendle Hill, a unique Quaker community/study center in Wallingford, Pennsylvania. Brinton was named director of studies and his wife became associate director. Pendle Hill had been founded in 1929, but its founding director, Henry T. Hodgkin, had died just three years later. Pendle Hill became the Brintons' life work. The center had a small staff of permanent residents and annually accepted a new group of people who lived, worshipped, and studied together communally for a year.

During the next decades, the Brintons shaped Pendle Hill into a model of Quaker life and devotion. Among other activities, they created the Pendle Hill series of pamphlets, authoring a few and editing over 100 titles. After retiring from their posts, she in 1949 and he in 1954, and after spending a brief time in Japan, they returned to Pendle Hill where he continued to write and teach. Besides becoming the major teacher at the community, Brinton served the larger Quaker community through his authoring of a number books on Quaker life, thought, and history. Brinton's wife died in 1969, and in 1971 he married Yuki Takahashi.

Sources:

Barbour, Hugh, and J. William Frost. *The Quakers.* New York: Greenwood Press, 1988. 407 pp.

Brinton, Howard H. *Byways in Quaker History.* Wallingford, PA: N.p., 1944.

_____. *Children of Light.* New York: Macmillan Company, 1938.

_____. *Creative Worship.* London: Allen & Unwin, 1931. 94 pp.

_____. *Guide to Quaker Practice.* Wallingford, PA: Pendle Hill Publications, 1955. 64 pp.

Faith and Practice. San Francisco: Pacific Yearly Meeting of the Religious Society of Friends, 1973. 75 pp.

★ 127 ★
BRITTEN, Emma Hardinge
Independent Occultist
Spiritualist
b. 1823, London England
d. Oct. 2, 1899, Manchester England

Emma Hardinge Britten played a leading role as a speaker and writer in the occult awakenings of the late nineteenth century. She was born Emma Floyd, daughter of a sea captain who died while she was still a child. Her mother encouraged her two main interests—music and the occult. At the age of 11 she was performing as a singer and pianist, and in a secret occult society she developed as a medium and clairvoyant. She took the name Hardinge after someone in the society by that name claimed to have married her while she was in a trance. She never conceded that she was married, but took his name anyway in revenge.

In 1855, at the age of 32, Hardinge's musical abilities and fame landed her an invitation to perform at the Broadway Theater and elsewhere in New York City. She stayed in the United States for ten years, becoming a key leader in American Spiritualism and making a living as director of music at the Dodsworth House. In 1865 she returned to England, but came back to New York in 1869 to meet with the publishers of her forthcoming book. On this trip she met William Britten, whom she married in 1870. They moved to Boston and began an occult magazine, *The Western Star*, but a devastating fire ended that effort. After the publication of her book, *Modern American Spiritualism*, she moved to New York with her husband.

By 1875, her Spiritualist interests had been altered by a deepening interest in Theosophy, and she attended the meeting in September 1875 at which the idea of forming the Theosophical Society was introduced. Britten published three more books in 1876—*Ghostland*, *Art Magic* and *The Faith, Facts and Frauds of Religious History*. The first two reflected her Theosophical views, and so garnered poor reviews from Spiritualist circles. The third book was a sympathetic introduction to non-Christian religions and a refutation of Christianity's exclusive claims.

Britten and her husband continued to travel, lecture and write, without either founding a new group or completely attaching themselves to any existing group. Theosophy looks to Emma Britten as an early leader, as does the Church of Light, which makes much of her *Art Magic* account of the teachings of the Brotherhood of Light. Since her death in 1899 at the age of 76, her writings have remained important in spiritualist and occult fields of study.

Sources:

Britten, Emma Hardinge. *Ghostland.* Chicago: Progressive Thinker Publishing House, 1897.

_____. *Modern American Spiritualism.* New York, 1870. Reprint. New Hyde Park, NY: University Books, 1970. 565 pp.

_____. *Nineteenth Century Miracles.* New York: William Britten, 1884. 556 pp.

_____, Alfred Kitson, and H. A. Kersey. *The Lyceum Manual.* Rochdale, UK: Trustees for the British Spiritualists Lyceum Union, 1924.

The Church of Light Quarterly 50, 2 & 3 (Spring-Summer 1975): ii-vi.

Shepard, Leslie. *Encyclopedia of Occultism & Parapsychology.* 3 vols., 2nd. ed. Detroit: Gale Research Co., 1984-1985.

—*Gary L. Ward*

★ 128 ★
BRITTON, Charles William
Minister/Evangelist, Pentecostal Latter-Rain Movement
b. 1918, Willow Springs, Missouri
d. Jul. 16, 1985, Long Beach, California

Charles William "Bill" Britton, an early leader in the Pentecostal Latter-Rain Movement of the mid-twentieth century, was the son of George and Nora Britton. His parents divorced when he was three and he grew up in his mother's care in Springfield, Missouri. He attended the Baptist church and was baptized at the age of twelve. In the 1930s he lived across the street from a pentecostal church and there, in 1934, initially attracted by the noise, he had his first experience of God. He began to attend the neighboring church and became an active member, though it was not until 1941 that he had the experience of being baptized with the Holy Spirit (the definitive Pentecostal experience which is confirmed by the believer speaking in an unknown tongue).

In December 1941 Britton moved to St. Louis, Missouri, but spent most of World War II as a Marine paratrooper. Discharged in 1946, he married his wife Nadine and returned to Springfield. He attended Drury College and Central Bible Institute (the school of the Assemblies of God). In 1948 he became the pastor of Peace Chapel Assembly of God. He was ordained as an Assemblies minister in 1949.

Soon after his ordination Britton moved to Florida and became pastor of a small church at Highland View. About the same time he began to hear of the Latter-Rain Movement that was spreading from its beginning place in Saskatchewan, Canada. The movement was centered upon the traditional spiritual gifts of pentecostalism but placed special emphasis upon prophecy, the laying on of hands to receive the Holy Spirit, and a five-fold organization of the church. Britton's attraction to the movement led to his break with the Assembly of God, which disapproved of some of the revival's excesses. While at Faith Temple, a center of the movement in Memphis, Britton received a prophecy that he was to be a prophet.

During the 1950s Britton had to be content with a part-time ministry that included evangelical work, preaching in small churches, and a radio show, while he largely supported his family by selling insurance. In 1962, however, he moved back to Springfield and began a literature ministry built around tracts which were mailed out to people he had met during his evangelistic travels. Beginning with a number of shorter works, Britton went on to author several substantive books. The ministry became a success, and over the years he found himself both the leader of a small but growing congregation in Springfield and an acknowledged prophet for a network of Latter Rain congregations around the United States.

The work in Springfield, the Overcomer Ministry, expanded to include a church (the House of Prayer) on a nine-acre plot of land used for regular national and regional conventions, a publishing office, a school for children, and a school for training ministers. Britton also initiated foreign missionary work. His last years were spent in writing, leading the growing work in Springfield, and traveling around the world on evangelistic tours. During the last years of his life, Britton wrote his autobiography, which was originally published in a series of booklets and sent out to people on his mailing list.

Sources:

Britton, Bill. *Hebrews: The Book of Better Things*. Springfield, MO: The Author, 1977. 159 pp.
_____. *Jesus the Pattern Son*. Springfield, MO: The Author, 1966. 77 pp.
_____. *Light Out of Shadows*. Springfield, MO: The Author, n.d. 84 pp.
_____. *Prophet on Wheels: The Life Story of Bill Britton*. Shippensburg, PA: Destiny Image Publishers, 1987. 244 pp.
_____. *Reach for the Stars*. Springfield, MO; The Author, 1970. 109 pp.
_____. *To God Be the Glory*. Springfield, MO: The Author, 1983. 111 pp.

★129★
BROADUS, John Albert
Educator, Southern Baptist Convention
b. Jan. 24, 1827, Culpepper, Virginia
d. Mar. 16, 1895, Louisville, Kentucky

John Albert Broadus, for 36 years professor of homiletics and New Testament at Southern Baptist Theological Seminary in Louisville, Kentucky, began life in the Blue Ridge Mountains of Virginia, the son of Edmund Broadus, an active Baptist and a member of the Virginia legislature, and Nancy Sims. He was converted at the age of 16 and decided to enter the ministry. In 1846 he entered the University of Virginia, there being no seminary serving the Southern Baptist Convention, which had formed the year before. He received his M.A. degree in 1850 and before the year was out accepted a job at a small school at Fluvanna, Virginia, was ordained, and married Maria Harrison.

He moved back to Charlottesville to accept a post at the university as a tutor in Latin and Greek and become pastor of the Baptist church in town. He resigned from the university after one year to devote himself full-time to the growing pastoral effort.

During the mid-1850s, Broadus worked toward the development of the convention's first theological school. When the plans were approved in 1858, he was offered a position as a faculty member. He initially turned down the offer, but finally relented. When the school opened at Greenville, South Carolina, in the fall of 1859, he was one of the original four faculty members. The school was closed during the Civil War, and Broadus returned to the pastorate and served a term as chaplain in the Confederate Army. Also in 1859, his wife having died two years previously, he married Charlotte Eleanor Sinclair.

The seminary reopened after the war, and the next years were among the most intense of Broadus' life. He was a major force in keeping the struggling school open. In 1870 he published *On the Preparation and Delivery of Sermons*, a classical homiletic text used far beyond his own church's boundaries. That same year he left for a year in Europe to recover his health, impaired under the strain of his work for the school. His book had made him a celebrity, and he turned down a number of offers to move from the seminary. He stayed with the still unstable seminary and helped build it into a strong institution.

His mature career brought a reputation for scholarship to both Broadus and the school he represented. During the 1870s he authored one important homiletic text, *Lectures on the History of Preaching* (1876). He joined the International Sunday School Lesson Committee in 1878 and continued on it until his death. During the 1880s he authored a *Commentary on the Gospel of Matthew* (1886) and published his *Sermons and Addresses* (1887). In 1889 he delivered the Lyman Beecher lectures on preaching at Yale. All the while he was a frequent writer for denominational periodicals and active in denominational affairs. He became the second president of the seminary in 1889. During his years as president he published two major works, *Jesus of Nazareth* (1890) and *Harmony of the Gospels* (1893).

Sources:

Broadus, John A. *Commentary on the Gospel of Matthew*. Philadelphia: American Baptist Publication Society, 1886.
_____. *Harmony of the Gospels*. New York: George H. Doran Co., 1922.
_____. *Jesus of Nazareth*. New York: A. C. Armstrong & Son, 1890. 105 pp.
_____. *Lectures on the History of Preaching*. New York: Sheldon & Co., 1876. 241 pp.
_____. *On the Preparation and Delivery of Sermons*. New York: Harper & Bros., 1944. 392 pp.
_____. *Sermons and Addresses*. Baltimore: H. M. Wharton & Co., 1886. 445 pp.

★130★
BROOKS, Nona Lovell
Divine Science
New Thought Movement
b. Mar. 22, 1861, Louisville, Kentucky
d. Mar. 14, 1945, Denver, Colorado

Nona Lovell Brooks was the founder of the Divine Science Church and a prominent leader in the early New Thought movement. Born in Kentucky, she grew up near Charleston, West Virginia, in a staunch Presbyterian family. As a child she had the experience of being engulfed in a supernatural light as she was alone in the garden. The memory of this made her determined to be closer to God.

As a teenager, Brooks' life became more difficult. Her father's prosperous salt mine faltered when salt deposits were found in New York, and the family was forced to move to Pueblo, Colorado, for her mother's health. In addition, Brooks' boyfriend found another love while away at seminary. Finally, her father died in 1880, when she was nineteen. In 1887 Brooks' sister, Althea Small, encouraged her to attend some classes taught by Mrs. Kate Bingham. Bingham was a friend of Small who had gone to Chicago to seek help for an illness and had been cured by Mabel MacCoy, a student of **Emma Curtis Hopkins**, from whom Bingham went on to take classes. Bingham subsequently began teaching New Thought classes herself in Pueblo. While Brooks and Small were attending, Brooks found herself healed of a persistent throat infection and was able to eat normally for the first time in months.

Thus began a new career for Brooks, though she did not know it yet herself. Both she and Small found that they could heal others. The Presbyterian Church looked askance at this strange work, however, and would not allow Brooks to teach Sunday School anymore. In 1890, at the age of 29, Brooks decided she needed to prepare to make a long-term living, so she went first to Pueblo Normal School and then to Wellesley College for a year to become a teacher. Meanwhile, Brooks' other sister, Fannie James, was in Denver teaching metaphysical classes similar in scope to **Malinda Cramer**'s "Divine Science" teaching in San Francisco. Brooks began working with James full-time, and they were soon joined by Small as well.

In 1898 Brooks received her ordination from Cramer, and the Denver Divine Science College was opened, followed in 1899 by the first Divine Science Church. The sisters went on to build a thriving organization based upon the affirmation of God as pure Spirit, equally present everywhere and at all times. In 1902 Brooks began the periodical *Fulfillment*, and in 1915 she began *Daily Studies in Divine Science*, now known as *Daily Studies*, the oldest of the New Thought daily studies.

The 1906 San Francisco earthquake killed Cramer and destroyed the organization there, but the Denver work kept the movement alive. After James' death during World War I, Brooks succeeded her as head of the college. In 1922 she brought Divine Science into the International New Thought Alliance (INTA), in which she figured prominently. She became a well-known and respected citizen of Denver, serving in many agencies and even becoming part of the Ministerial Alliance in 1926.

In the late 1920s Brooks resigned her work and traveled extensively for a decade, opening two centers in Australia. In 1938 she returned to Denver to preside again over the college until 1943, two years before her death at the age of 84.

Sources:

Beebe, Tom. *Who's Who in New Thought*. Lakemont, GA: CSA Press, 1977. 318 pp.
Braden, Charles S. *Spirits in Rebellion*. Dallas: Southern Methodist University Press, 1963. 571 pp.
Brooks, Louise McNamara. *Early History of Divine Science*. Denver, CO: First Divine Science Church, 1963. 571 pp.
Brooks, Nona L. *Mysteries*. Denver, CO: The author, 1924. 133 pp.
———. *The Prayer That Never Fails*. Denver, CO: Divine Science Church and College, 1935. 61 pp.
———. *Short Lessons in Divine Science*. Denver, Co: The Author, 1928. 92 pp.
———. *Studies in Health*. Denver, CO: Divine Science Federation International, 1979. 50 pp.
Neale, Hazel. *Powerful Is the Light*. Denver, CO: Divine Science College, 1945. 206 pp.

—Gary L. Ward

★131★
BROOKS, Phillips
Bishop, Episcopal Church
b. Dec. 13, 1835, Boston, Massachusetts
d. Jan. 23, 1893, Boston, Massachusetts

Phillips Brooks, the outstanding preacher and bishop in the Episcopal Church, was shaped by the community of his birth and in turn, during his mature years, helped shape it. He was the product of two families which had come to Massachusetts in the seventeenth century, the son of William Gray Brooks and Mary Ann Phillips. Though as an infant he was baptized in First (Congregational) Church in Boston, when he was four, the family joined St. Paul's Episcopal Church and young Phillips was raised as an Episcopalian. He entered Harvard at the age of 16. He excelled in languages and after graduation he took a position in the Boston Latin School he had attended prior to college. He was not suited to handling a class of teenagers, however, and he resigned after six months.

The sense of failure at his first job precipitated a change of career plans, and he entered the seminary at Alexandria, Virginia, to prepare for the ministry. He was ordained a deacon in 1859 and was assigned to the Church of the Advent in Philadelphia. His immediate success as a preacher led to his assignment to Holy Trinity Church at the beginning of 1862. He became known for his loyalty to the Union during the war, and in 1865 was called upon to preach while the body of Lincoln lay in state at Independence Hall in Philadelphia. During his years at Trinity he produced what is possibly the single most remembered item of his long career, the Christmas carol "O Little Town of Bethlehem," a poem he wrote for his Sunday school and introduced on Christmas in 1868.

On Halloween 1869, Brooks returned to his home town as pastor of Trinity Church in Boston. This period was a triumphal time during which he regularly commanded a large audience with his eloquent addresses. He turned what might have been a significant disaster, the burning of the church building in 1872, into a catalyst to erect an even more impressive building in Copley Square, dedicated in 1877. Meanwhile, he was preaching to two packed audiences every week at Huntington Hall. During this period he preached what many saw as a message of easy religion to a comfortable, affluent audience. He stayed clear of both the intellectualism of the Unitarians and the dogmatism of the Congregationalists. He saw religion as the natural life of humans as they gradually became ever more godlike.

The years immediately following his ascending the pulpit of the new church were the most productive literary years of his life. He published in succession his *Yale Lectures on Preaching* (1877); *Sermons* (1878); *The Influence of Jesus* (1879); *The Candle of the Lord* (1981); *Sermons Preached in English Churches* (1883); *Twenty Sermons* (1886); and *The Light of the World* (1890). In 1880 he became the first American invited to preach before the Queen of England at the Royal Chapel at Windsor.

During most of his ministry Brooks had expressed an almost irreverent attitude toward the Episcopal hierarchy and had expressed doubts about the validity of the concept of apostolic success (the belief that the church's bishops have their authority from a lineage of consecrations that go back to Jesus' apostles in the first century). He also disliked the dryness of church administration. Then in 1891 he was elected to the bishopric as the successor to the bishop of Boston. Though his election was delayed while the House of Bishops considered accusations of doctrinal deviation, it was finally confirmed and he was consecrated on October 14, 1891. He was able to serve only a short time, however, as he succumbed to a brief illness and died at the beginning of 1893. He was but 57 years old.

Sources:

Brooks, Phillips. *The Candle of the Lord*. London: Macmillan, 1881. 370 pp.
———. *Essays and Addresses*. New York: E. P. Dutton, 1894. 529 pp.
———. *The Influence of Jesus*. New York: E. P. Dutton, 1879. 274 pp.
———. *The Light of the World*. New York: E. P. Dutton, 1890. 373 pp.
———. *Sermons*. 10 vols. New York: E. P. Dutton, 1879-1904.
Clarke, William Newton. *Huxley and Phillips Brooks*. Boston: Houghton Mifflin & Co., 1903. 51 pp.
Lawrence, William. *Life of Phillips Brooks*. New York: Harper & Bros., 1930. 151 pp.
———. *Phillips Brooks*. Boston: Houghton Mifflin & Co., 1903. 51 pp.

★132★
BROTHERS, William Henry Francis
Old Catholic Church in America
b. Apr. 7, 1887, Nottingham England
d. Jul. 21, 1979, Woodstock, New York

William Henry Francis (who added his mother's maiden name, Brothers, later in life) founded the Old Catholic Church in America. His childhood was spent first in England and then in Waukegan, Illinois, where his father built the first mechanized lace-making factory in the United States. Brothers felt the call to spiritual disciplines at an early age, and in 1908, at the age of 21, he joined a small monastic community founded by Dom Augustine de Angelis Harding.

In 1909 the group moved to Fond du Lac, Wisconsin. It took new leadership from Protestant Episcopal Bishop Charles C. Grafton, became the resident group at St. Dunstan's Abbey, and was renamed the American Congregation of the Order of St. Benedict. Grafton appointed Brothers as prior of the abbey and introduced him to the independent Old Catholic circles in which Grafton was then moving. In 1910, Brothers was ordained to the priesthood by **Joseph Rene Vilatte**, but this alliance did not last long. In 1911 Grafton shifted the congregation into the care of Bishop J. F. Tichy of the Polish Old Catholic Church. By 1914 Grafton had died, Tichy was in poor health, and most of the membership had transferred to the Polish National Catholic Church (PNCC). Brothers assumed leadership of the group, which was facing severe difficulties.

Brothers moved the group back to Waukegan and in 1916 was consecrated as a bishop at the hands of the Duc de Landas Berghes, of the line of **Arnold Harris Mathew**, an Old Catholic bishop in London. This alliance was short-lived. Brothers broke with them in 1917 and claimed the titles of archbishop and metropolitan of the Old Catholic Church in America (one Polish congregation in Chicago at the time).

Brothers then set about the difficult task of rejuvenating his church. He ordained Antonio Rodriguez to work among the Portuguese in New England and brought Bishop Stanislaus Mickiewicz of the Lithuanian National Catholic Church and independent Polish Bishop Joseph Zielonko into the church. Brothers managed also to attract the influential **William Montgomery Brown**, the former Episcopal bishop of Arkansas. In 1927 Brothers was given oversight of the Polish Mariavites in the United States. By 1936 the Old Catholic Church in America listed 24 parishes and 5,470 members.

The church's fortunes declined steadily in the 1950s, however, with defections of leaders and the Americanization of the ethnic laity. In 1962 Brothers decided to move the whole church into the Russian Orthodox Church and take the title of mitred archpriest. In 1967, however, he changed his mind and recreated the Old Catholic Church in America, consecrating Joseph MacCormack as his successor. By the time of Brothers' death in 1979 at the age of 92, his resurrected church had grown to several hundred members.

Sources:

Anson, Peter F. *Bishops at Large.* London: Faber & Faber, 1964. 593 pp.
Brothers, William Henry Francis. *Concerning the Old Catholic Church in America.* New York: Old Catholic Church in America, 1925. 15 pp.
_____. *The Old Catholic Church in America and Anglican Orders.* New York: Old Catholic Church in America, 1925. 15 pp.
Febronius, J. *What is Old Catholicism?* New York: Old Catholic Church in America, 1939. 15 pp.
LoBue, John. "An Appreciation: Archbishop William Henry Francis Brothers, 1887-1979." *The Good Shepherd* 12 (1980): 5-6, 16.
Piepkorn, Arthur C. *Profiles in Belief.* 3 vols. New York: Harper & Row, 1977.
Pruter, Karl, & J. Gordon Melton. *Old Catholic Sourcebook.* New York: Garland Publishing Co., 1983. 254 pp.

—*Gary L. Ward*

★133★
BROUGHTON, Luke Dennis
Independent Astrologer
b. Apr. 20, 1828, Leeds, Yorkshire England
d. 1898, New York, New York

Luke Dennis Broughton was a key figure in the nineteenth-century revival of astrology. One of six children, Broughton was the product of two generations of physicians who were also astrologers, and he continued this tradition. He was particularly influenced by his father, who had accurately predicted his early speech impediments. He also had Mark, an elder brother, to look up to as an astrologer. Mark Broughton was a leader and author in astrology circles, both in England and in the United States.

Luke Broughton studied astrology and weaving, married at the age of 24, and came to Philadelphia, Pennsylvania, two years later, in 1854. While working as a weaver he attended the Eclectic Medi-

cal College and restored a journal his brother had let die, renaming it *Broughton's Monthly Planet Reader and Astrological Journal* (1860-1869). In 1863, he opened a medical office, specializing in herbs and astrology. Unlike his ancestors, however, Broughton utilized showmanship and entrepreneurial skills to bring astrology to a wider public. In 1866 he rented a hall and began to give public lectures, which became very popular. He became the country's foremost distributor of astrological literature and the inspiration for a new generation of astrologers.

Due in large part to Broughton's work, astrology became a nationwide phenomenon. He became the debating champion on behalf of astrology, taking on scientific debunkers such as astronomer Richard Proctor. He was quick to debunk other astrologers he thought to be charlatans. He denounced Eleanor Kirk's books as pseudo-astrology and attacked the author of the first astrology book published in America, C. W. Roback, as a fraud. Broughton also wrote several books on astrology that became standards in their field, such as *Planetary Influence* (1893) and *The Elements of Astrology* (1898). Broughton died in 1898 at the age of 70, leaving behind a legacy of a new generation of astrologers who continued the family tradition.

Sources:

Broughton, Luke Dennis. *The Elements of Astrology.* New York: The author, 1898.
_____. *Planetary Influence.* New York: The author, 1898.
_____. *Remarks on Astrology and Astro-Medical Botany.* New York: The author, 1880.

—*Gary L. Ward*

★134★
BROWN, Egbert Ethelred
Black Unitarian Minister
b. Jul. 11, 1875, Falmouth Jamaica
d. Feb. 17, 1956, New York, New York

Egbert Ethelred Brown, founder of the first Unitarian church in Harlem, was the son of James and Florence Brown. His father was an auctioneer, but did not earn enough to provide for Ethelred's higher education, even though he had shown himself skilled in oratory and a likely candidate for the pulpit or bar. Instead, he entered the civil service at the age of 19 and in 1899 was promoted to first clerk of the treasury. He married, and he and his wife Ella had four children. In 1907 he was dismissed from his job. Reexamining his life, he decided to enter the ministry.

While in the Anglican Church, Brown had already accepted Unitarian ideas that centered upon his rejection of the Trinity, the idea of the one God in three aspects taught in orthodox Christianity. There were no Unitarians in Jamaica, however, so he affiliated with the Wesleyan Methodists. He finally made contact with the Unitarians in America and worked out plans to attend Meadville Theological Seminary. Overcoming several obstacles, he finally made it to Meadville in 1910. He graduated in 1912 and returned to Montego Bay to start a mission. He was able to gather a small group, but faced the racial attitudes of the American Unitarian Association, which had doubts about the value of attempting to build Unitarianism among Blacks. Heavily in debt, and having lost any financial support from the United States, Brown left Jamaica for New York in 1920.

Brown settled in Harlem just as it was burgeoning with the black migration following World War I. He took a job and started the Harlem Community Church without denominational backing. He soon had a small congregation of about 30 people, which met in rented facilities on alternate Sunday evenings. By the mid-1920s, the congregation had grown to about 85 members, but the denomination, while retaining him as a member, offered no financial assistance. Brown's own personal situation worsened as well. One son became an alcoholic and another committed suicide. His wife was ill, and he was often broke.

The situation for Brown did not change until 1937, when the association finally recognized him and began to supply financial support. The church then came under the aegis of the Department of Unitarian Extension and Church Maintenance. In 1940 membership was at 54. It dropped suddenly the next year, possibly because some of the men joined the armed services.

Brown continued to minister until his death in 1956. He had affiliated with numerous causes in Harlem and had become well-known within the community despite his personal setbacks. His pioneering church work, however, proved in the long run unsuccessful and was eventually superseded by the efforts of the older and larger Community Church of New York, which in 1948 hired a black minister of education and attracted many Harlem residents. Brown's ministry could possibly have been more successful if he had been accepted more quickly by the Unitarian Association. He is remembered today only as a pioneer in a community in which Unitarians have yet to find strong support.

Sources:

Morrison-Reed, Mark D. *Black Pioneer in a White Denomination*. Boston, MA: Beacon Press, 1984. 217 pp.

★ 135 ★
BROWN, Harrison D.
Minister, Church of the Nazarene
b. Nov. 1, 1846, Burlington, Iowa
d. Feb. 13, 1940, Seattle, Washington

Harrison D. Brown, who established the Church of the Nazarene in the Pacific Northwest, was born in rural Iowa. As a youth, he was converted in a Methodist revival and joined the Methodist Episcopal Church. He entered the ministry and became a leading minister in the developing Methodism of the plains states. While serving as presiding elder in the Dakotas, he had the experience of entire sanctification, a second blessing believed by holiness people to cleanse the heart of the believer by the power of the Holy Spirit and make him or her perfect in love. He began to preach the holiness doctrine just at the time when Methodism was rejecting it.

In the 1890s Brown was assigned to the Battery Street Methodist Church in Seattle. While there, in 1896, he organized the Washington State Children's Home Society. During his pastorate he also led in the organization of the interdenominational Western Washington Holiness Association. In 1901 former Methodist **Phineas (Franklin) Bresee** came to Seattle and Brown attended his services, where he learned of the Church of the Nazarene, the new holiness denomination founded by Bresee in Los Angeles. Brown left his pulpit that year but did not join Bresee. Rather, he worked full-time for the children's society he had formed. In 1904 he helped Bresee organize the Northwest District of the Church of the Nazarene. Bresee appointed Brown as district superintendent (the first to hold such an office in the church) with responsibility to organize Nazarene congregations in the four states of Washington, Oregon, Idaho, and Montana. As a new executive in the church, among his first tasks was to work on the merger of the Nazarenes with the Holiness Church of Christ, which was consummated in 1908.

During his first years with the Church of the Nazarene, Brown stayed with the children's society but began to hold meetings in his home. This group became the First Church of the Nazarene of Seattle in 1906, which Brown continued to serve for many years. During his five years in that office, the work spread to Oregon and along the Snake River Valley in Idaho. He ventured as far east as the Dakotas in work which eventually led to the formation of new congregations.

In 1911 Brown went to Canada to survey possibilities of the church expanding into Alberta, where independent holiness work had already begun. After a Church was begun in Calgary following a revival meeting in August, Brown became the first district superintendent in Canada.

During his last years Brown slowed but did not stop. In 1927 he began holding meetings in his home that resulted in the formation of the Central Church of the Nazarene, a second congregation in burgeoning Seattle. Following his retirement he stayed in Seattle, where he died at age 93.

Sources:

Seals, B. V., "Pen Sketch of H. D. Brown, the Northwest's Great Pioneer." *The Preacher's Magazine* 33, 6 (June 1958): 8-11.
Smith, Timothy L. *Called Unto Holiness*. Kansas City, MO: Beacon Hill Press, 1963. 413 pp.

★ 136 ★
BROWN, Henry Harrison
Founder, Now Folk
b. Jun. 26, 1840, Uxbridge, Massachusetts
d. May 8, 1918, San Francisco, California

Henry Harrison Brown, a teacher and Unitarian minister, was the founder of the "Now" Folk, an early New Thought metaphysical group in San Francisco, California. Brown was born in Massachusetts to Pemberton Brown and his wife, Paulina Whitman Brown. Little is known of his early life. He attended Nichols Academy in Dudley, Massachusetts, and became a teacher in 1857, while still in his teens. He served in the Civil War, first in the 18th Connecticut Volunteers and then as a lieutenant for the 29th Connecticut Volunteers, a black regiment. He married Fannie M. Hancox in 1873, though they were later divorced.

Brown gave up his teaching work in 1880 and for five years lectured on various topics, including spiritualism, social reform and ethical concerns. In 1885 he entered the Unitarian Divinity School at Meadville, Pennsylvania; after graduation he served Unitarian parishes at Petersham, Massachusetts (1887-1888), and Salem, Oregon (1890-1892). In 1893 he returned to the lecture trail, having become a student of metaphysical healing. In about 1900 he settled in San Francisco.

In San Francisco Brown organized the "Now" Folk, described as a small body of men and women voluntarily associated together in a "Common Spirit with a Common Purpose," that purpose being to teach people to know themselves as manifestations of the one infinite energy. Operating through the "Now" Folk Soul Culture Institute, Brown began a monthly magazine, *Now*, remained a popular lecturer, and taught numerous classes. He authored several lesson series which were compiled into correspondence courses offered to students around the country. Among the most popular of these courses were the *Art of Living* (1902); *Suggestion* (1906); *Dollars Want Me: A New Road to Opulence* (1903); and *Psychometry* (1906). Besides the common New Thought emphasis upon mental healing, Brown also offered classes and gave demonstrations of a number of psychic phenomena such as telepathy, clairvoyance, automatic writings, and the diagnosing of disease through psychic power.

Brown was unique among New Thought exponents, known for their strong individualism, in his emphasis upon community. Soon after founding the "Now" Folk, he gathered them into a common residence, the "Now" Home. In 1906 he established a cooperative community at nearby Glenwood, California, which continued until his death in 1918.

Following Harrison's death, his work was carried on by Sam E. Foulds, who became the editor and publisher of *Now* and continued to circulate Brown's booklets and courses for many years.

Sources:
Brown, Henry Harrison. *Art of Living.* San Francisco: "Now" Company, 1902. 25 vols.
———. *Psychometry.* San Francisco: "Now" Folk, 1906. 12 vols.
———. *The Six Steps in Mental Mastery.* San Francisco, CA: "Now" Co., 1918. 108 pp.
———. *Suggestion.* San Francisco: Now Folk, 1906. 25 vols.
Third Annual Announcement. San Francisco: "Now" Folk, 1903.
Who Was Who in America. Chicago: Marquis Who's Who, Inc.

★ 137 ★
BROWN, Olympia
Universalist Minister
b. Jan. 5, 1835, Prairie Ronde, Michigan
d. Oct. 23, 1926, Baltimore, Maryland

Olympia Brown, one of the first formally ordained woman ministers in the United States, was the daughter of Asa B. and Lephia Olympia Brown. Her parents were Universalists who had moved from Vermont to farm in what was then frontier country. She was encouraged by her parents to pursue her education. In 1854 she returned to New England to attend the Mount Holyoke Female Seminary in Massachusetts, but left after a year, unable to accept the strict orthodox Christianity that pervaded the campus. The next year she enrolled at Antioch College in Yellow Springs, Ohio, from which she graduated in 1860.

During her years at Antioch, Brown had the opportunity to hear **Antoinette Brown Blackwell**, the Congregationalist minister, and she soon decided to enter the ministry as well. She began a two-year course of study at the theological school at St. Lawrence University in 1861. Shortly after her graduation, she was ordained by the Northern Universalist Association, the first church body to so ordain a woman. (Blackwell had been ordained by a local church.) In 1864 she accepted her first parish, at Weymouth, Massachusetts.

Brown's long-standing interest in social reform was given new life in 1866 when she accepted an invitation to attend a suffrage meeting in New York City. She became a charter member of the American Equal Rights Association, which brought her frequently into the company of Susan B. Anthony and Lucy Stone. She spent four months in 1867 traveling in Kansas on a campaign to pass a suffrage amendment to the state's constitution. The next year she organized the New England Woman Suffrage Association and sat on its executive board. She tried to refrain from taking sides when the suffrage movement split in 1869, but worked most closely with the National Woman Suffrage Association. In 1870 she moved to Bridgeport, Connecticut, to pastor the Universalist church. During her tenure, in 1873, she met and married John Henry Willis and bore two children. Brown continued to use her maiden name. She served the Bridgeport church until 1876, when her daughter was born.

In 1878 the family moved to Racine, Wisconsin, where Brown returned to the pastorate and her husband became part owner of the *Racine Times*. After settling into her job, she intensified her suffrage activity. In 1884 she became president of the state Woman Suffrage Association, a post she held for 28 years. That same year she became vice-president of the National Woman Suffrage Association. In 1887 she resigned her pastorate to work full-time for the suffrage cause. That year she had been presented a opportunity she could not resist. Two years previously, Wisconsin had passed a law giving women the right to vote in any election pertaining to school matters. Brown was able to locate a school issue in almost any election, and she advised women to claim the ballot aggressively. In 1887, however, she was refused a ballot in an election, and she filed suit.

Although she argued clearly and forcefully, Brown lost the suit and in the process placed the suffrage association heavily in debt.

She had to devote many hours in future years simply to keeping the organization in existence. She also retained her role in the national suffrage movement. In 1890 the two major branches merged to form the National American Woman Suffrage Association. Increasingly, however, Brown, as head of the Wisconsin association, found herself at odds with the new national body. She believed that suffrage must come through enfranchisement on the national level, while the NAWSA concentrated on state action. Thus in 1892 Brown called a convention in Chicago and formed the Federal Suffrage Association. She was elected vice-president and in 1903 president. The group survived until after the passage of the suffrage amendment to the United States constitution, but is generally considered of minor importance to the suffrage cause. Although Brown remained president of the association, she did her most important work in the years just prior to the granting of suffrage through the Congressional Union (also known as the National Woman's Party).

Brown's daughter lived in Baltimore thus facilitating her travel across the country to campaign, demonstrate, and speak in Washington, D.C. During her last year she regularly visited her daughter for months at a time. On one such visit, at the age of 91, she died of heart disease.

Sources:
Brown, Olympia. *Acquaintances, Old and New, Among Reformers.* Milwaukee, WI: S. E. Tate Printing Co., 1911. 115 pp.
———. *Democratic Ideals.* N. p.: Federal Suffrage Association, 1917. 116 pp.
———. *Woman's Suffrage.* Racine, WI: Wisconsin Woman's Suffrage Association, 1907. 33 pp.

★ 138 ★
BROWN, William Adams
Theologian, Presbyterian Church
b. Dec. 29, 1865, New York, New York
d. Dec. 15, 1943, New York, New York

William Adams Brown, a leading liberal ecumenical Presbyterian theologian, was the son of John Crosby Brown and Mary Elizabeth Adams. He was raised in affluent Presbyterian families, his maternal grandfather having been pastor of Madison Avenue Presbyterian Church and both families having strong ties to Union Theological Seminary. He did his undergraduate work at Yale in economics and the classics. He received his B.A. in 1886 and continued another year for a masters degree in economics. In 1887 he entered Union where he studied under **Charles Augustus Briggs**, who was at that time involved in a controversy that would lead to his trial for heresy in 1892. After Brown graduated from Union in 1890, he received a two-year fellowship for work at the University of Berlin, where he studied with Aldolph Harnack, champion of the idea of discovering the "essence of Christianity," its important core of eternal ideas. He returned in 1892 to join the staff at Union just as his former professor was at the height of his ordeal. That same year he married Helen Gillian Noyes. In 1898 he was named professor of systematic theology at Union.

In January 1893, Brown was ordained as a minister of the Presbyterian Church in the U.S.A. He received his Ph.D. in 1901 from Yale. His doctoral dissertation, based in part upon Harnack's theological focus, was published as *The Essence of Christianity* (1902).

From the beginning his career as minister and professor had an activist and moral center. He entered into his professional career just as the "social gospel" was capturing the imagination of many young Protestant ministers. In 1895 he helped found the Union Settlement House in New York City. He fought the Tammany Hall government corruption and joined the anti-vice crusades. In 1909 he was named chairman of the Home Missions Committee of the New York Presbytery and a year later he was elected to the Board of Home Missions of his denomination.

Brown was also active in the causes of church unity through the Federal Council of Churches in the U.S.A. During World War I he served as executive secretary of the General War-Time Commission of the Churches and after the war became chairman of the Council's Department of Research and Education.

His theological work led to the authoring of some 15 books, including *Christian Theology in Outline* (1906); *Is Christianity Practicable?* (1916); *Beliefs That Matter* (1928); and *The Church: Catholic and Protestant* (1935). He was a co-founder and the first president of the American Theological Society. He helped conduct the first major survey of theological education and wrote the final volume of the four-volume report, *The Education of American Ministers* (1934).

His last years at Union were spent as research professor in applied Christianity (1930-1936). During his retirement year he authored his autobiography, *A Teacher and His Times* (1940).

Sources:

Brown, William Adams. *Beliefs That Matter*. New York: Charles Scribner's Sons, 1928. 333 pp.

_____. *Christian Theology in Outline*. New York: Charles Scribner's sons, 1906. 468 pp.

_____. *The Church: Catholic and Protestant*. New York: Charles Scribner's Sons, 1935. 421 pp.

_____. *The Essence of Christianity*. New York: Charles Scribner's Sons, 1902. 332 pp.

_____. *Is Christianity Practicable?* New York: Charles Scribner's Sons, 1916. 246 pp.

_____. *A Teacher and His Times*. New York: Charles Scribner's Sons, 1904. 391 pp.

Cavert, Samuel McCrea, and Henry P. Van Dusen, eds. *The Church through Half a Century: Essays in Honor of William Adams Brown*. New York: Charles Scribner's Sons, 1936.

★ 139 ★
BROWN, William Montgomery
Bishop, Old Catholic Church in America
Bishop, Protestant Episcopal Church
b. Sep. 4, 1855, Orrville, Ohio
d. Oct. 31, 1937, Galion, Ohio

William Montgomery Brown is remembered as one of the more radical and independent bishops in the Protestant Episcopal Church and later the small Old Catholic Church in America. Brown was born in rural Ohio shortly before the Civil War. After his father was killed in the war, Brown was indentured to a Dunkard (German Baptist Brethren) farmer who overworked and underfed him. Eventually he was rescued and placed in the care of Jacob Gardner, a Methodist. Brown thus joined the Methodist Episcopal Church. Given a stake when he turned 21, he went to Nebraska to work and prepare himself for college. Five years later he returned to Ohio and met Mrs. Mary Scranton Bradford, a wealthy member of the Protestant Episcopal Church. She steered him into the Episcopal ministry and financed him through Seabury Divinity School. In 1883 he was ordained to the diaconate, and two years later he married Ella Bradford, the cousin and adopted daughter of his benefactor. Eventually he inherited the family fortune.

Brown's first pastorate was Grace Church, at Galion, Ohio. So successful was he that he was made a general missionary and in 1890 was appointed the Archdeacon of the Diocese of Ohio. He was also appointed as a special lecturer at Bexley Hall, the theological school at Kenyon College in Gambier, Ohio. During this time he wrote *The Church for Americans* (1894), a popular introduction to the Episcopal Church.

In 1898 Brown was elected Bishop Coadjutor of Arkansas; a year later he became Bishop of Arkansas. He then entered his most controversial phase. He became disturbed by the church's inability to attract black members. Out of his concern, he proposed a plan that would establish an independent Episcopal Church led by Blacks and for Blacks. He was attacked by some for proposing to segregate black members and by traditionalists who were horrified by a proposal that would place two legitimate bishops in the same city over the same geographical territory.

Turning his attention next to ecumenism, Brown authored *The Level Plan for Church Union* (1910), in which he proposed a plan of church operation which would in essence ignore the peculiarities of the Episcopal Church. Again he was severely criticized by his colleagues, especially the more traditional ones. Given a leave of absence in 1911, he resigned his bishopric in 1912. Meanwhile, while living quietly, he read Karl Marx's *Capital*. Brown became convinced that Marxism was the answer to the problems of the world. He issued a series of books that advocated his developing communist perspective and attempted to interpret Christianity in this light. Among the first was *Communism and Christianism* (1921), which advocated an abandonment of traditional supernatural religion in favor of Marxism.

The reaction to Brown's writing was slow, but eventually, in 1924, three bishops pressed charges. At the trial Brown argued that he accepted all of the teachings of the church, but interpreted them symbolically. He was found guilty of heresy and in October 1925 was deposed from the ministry. Meanwhile, Brown had turned for support to William Francis Brothers, Archbishop of the independent Old Catholic Church in America, and was secretly reconsecrated in a service in the library of his home in Galion.

As the Old Catholic Church was small and Brown financially established, there was little activity for him as bishop. The church drew strength from its association with Brown and his unquestioned episcopal lineage. On at least two occasions Brown exercised his episcopal office. On January 2, 1927, he consecrated Wallace D. de Ortega Maxey, and two years later he consecrated *sub-conditione* Arthur Wolfort Brooks, an independent Episcopal clergyman in Queens, New York. de Ortega Maxey and Brooks would later be associated in the Apostolic Episcopal Church.

Brown spent his last years quietly in Galion. He formed a publishing company through which he continued to write, and he authored a number of books, including several defending his Marxist position. Though he described himself as a communist, he regularly attended the church he once pastored and received communion as a layman. His wife died in 1935, two years before his own death in 1937. His library was eventually given to Kenyon College.

Sources:

Brown, William Montgomery. *The Bishop Brown Case*. Galion, OH: 1925.

_____. *The Catholic Church and the Color Line*. New York: Thomas Whittaker, 1910. 50 pp.

_____. *The Church for Americans*. New York: Thomas Whittaker, 1896. 501 pp.

_____. *Communism and Christianism*. Galion, OH: Bradford-Brown Educational Co., 1921. 223 pp.

_____. *Communism: The New Faith for a New World*. Galion, OH: Bradford-Brown Educational Co., 1935.

_____. *The Crucial Race Question* Little Rock, AR: The Arkansas Churchman's Publishing Co., 1907. 323 pp.

_____. *My Heresy*. New York: John Day Company, 1926. 273 pp.

_____. *Why I am a Communist*. Galion, OH: Bradford-Brown Educational Co., 1932. 48 pp.

Pruter, Karl, and J. Gordon Melton. *The Old Catholic Sourcebook*. New York: Garland Publishing Company, 1983. 254 pp.

Seitz, William Clinton. "Bishop Brown of Galion." *The Bulletin of Bexley Hall* 5, 4 (December 1961): 1-2.

★140★
BROWNING, Edmond Lee
Presiding Bishop, Episcopal Church
b. Mar. 11, 1930, Corpus Christi, Texas

Edmond Lee Browning, the presiding bishop of the Episcopal Church, is the son of Cora Mae Lee and Edmond Lucian Browning. He attended the University of the South from which he received a B.A. in 1952 and a B.D. in 1954. In 1953, while pursuing his theological studies, he was married to Patricia Sparks. He was ordained a priest in 1954, and returning to Texas, was named curate of the Church of the Good Shepherd in Corpus Christi. Two years later he became rector of the Church of the Redeemer in Eagle Pass, Texas.

In 1959 Browning transferred to the missionary district of Honolulu which included Okinawa, where he became rector of All Soul's Church. In 1965 he moved to St. Matthews Church as well as becoming archdeacon for the Okinawa Episcopal Church. In 1968 he was designated the first missionary bishop of Okinawa. Through the 1970s and 1980s, unlike most bishops, Browning served a variety of different posts in his episcopal role. In 1971 he became the bishop of the Convocation of American Churches in Europe. In 1971 he moved to New York having been designated the executive of the National and World Mission Executive Council of the Episcopal Church. Then in 1976 he became the bishop of Hawaii. Among his actions as bishop of Hawaii he joined with 20 of his episcopal colleagues in signing a statement in opposition to the church's stance which denied ordination of homosexuals.

Browning was the bishop of Hawaii in 1985 when he was elected as the new presiding bishop of the Episcopal Church. Browning was seen as a liberal. His diocese had the largest percentage of female ministers of any other church, approximately ten percent. He had spoken out against the nuclear arms race and had a commitment to ecumenical goals especially toward the Roman Catholic Church.

Sources:
Cornell, George W. "Elected Episcopal Bishop Supports Peace, Gay Rights." *Santa Barbara (CA) News Press* (September 11, 1985).

★141★
BRYAN, William Jennings
Politician and Fundamentalist, Presbyterian Church
b. Mar. 19, 1860, Salem, Illinois
d. Jul. 26, 1925, Dayton, Tennessee

William Jennings Bryan, secretary of state under Woodrow Wilson and thrice a candidate for president of the United States, has a secure place in secular history, but also is remembered for his fundamentalist religious convictions which molded his political career and dominated his public life after he left public service. Bryan was the son of Silas Lillard and Mariah Elizabeth Jennings Bryan, and was raised in the Presbyterian Church, an affiliation he kept throughout his life. His father placed great importance on education, and Bryan was sent to Jacksonville, Illinois, to study first at the Academy and then Illinois College. He graduated in 1881 and moved to Chicago to attend the Union College of Law. Finishing in 1883, he returned to Jacksonville where he practiced law. The next year he married Mary Baird.

In 1887 Bryan moved to Nebraska and became affiliated with the Democratic Party. He was elected to Congress for the first time in 1890 from a normally Republican district. After two terms in Congress he made an unsuccessful bid for a Senate seat, and then turned to journalism. He became editor-in-chief of the Omaha World-Herald. He also became one of the most popular lecturers on the Chautauqua circuit. At the 1896 Democratic Convention Bryan aligned himself with the element calling for the free coinage of silver. On behalf of the silver interests he made possibly the most

famous oration of his life, generally referred to as the "Cross of Gold" speech. Though only 36 years old, he was nominated for the presidency. In spite of his tireless campaigning and his magnificent speaking ability, he narrowly lost to William McKinley. In 1900 he was nominated and lost again to McKinley.

Following the 1900 defeat, Bryan let his deeply felt but outwardly suppressed religious life become more visible. He became an elder in the Presbyterian Church in Lincoln, Nebraska. He began to speak on specifically religious topics and identified himself with the emerging fundamentalist Protestant coalition. In his talks and writings, he strongly defended the literal interpretation of Scripture and opposed the theory of evolution.

In 1901 Bryan began *The Commoner*, a newspaper, in which he wished to crusade against the influence of wealth in politics, the issue to which the silver question had led him. The paper also became a sounding board for his views on peace and arbitration, to which he had a deep commitment. He remained active in party affairs, especially the setting of platform positions, but did not run for the presidency in 1904. In 1908 he was nominated again and for the third time went down to defeat. In 1912, he supported Woodrow Wilson and, when Wilson was elected, Bryan was appointed secretary of state. He served from March 4, 1913, to June 9, 1915. Bryan resigned following the sinking of the *Lusitania*, refusing to follow Wilson's policy regarding the arbitration treaties Bryan had set in place with Germany. Bryan had also become somewhat of a pacifist and could see that America was heading toward war. He supported Wilson through the war, but his heart was not in it. His peace stance led to a slippage of his political power, though he stayed active in party concerns for the rest of his life.

In 1921 he moved to Florida and found some support for his candidacy for office. He also began to write his memoirs, which were published in 1925. He was planning to run for the Senate when the Scopes trial appeared on the horizon. John Scopes, a teacher in Dayton, Tennessee, had been charged with violating the Tennessee law forbidding the teaching of evolution in the public schools. The case was a test case with Clarence Darrow defending Scopes and evolution. Bryan offered his services as the prosecutor. In the end he won the case, but suffered a humiliating public defeat in the press when called as a witness and cross examined by Darrow, who destroyed his simple biblical literalism. Bryan died in his sleep five days later.

Sources:
Anderson, David D. *William Jennings Bryan*. Boston, MA: Twayne Publishers, 1981.
Bryan, William Jennings. *The Bible and Its Enemies*. Chicago: Bible Institute Colportage Association, 1921. 38 pp.
———. *The First Commandment*. New York: Fleming H. Revell Company, 1917. 38 pp.
———. *Heart to Heart Appeals*. New York: Fleming H. Revell Company, 1917. 189 pp.
———. *In His Image*. New York: Fleming H. Revell Company, 1922. 266 pp.
———. *Is the Bible True?*. Chicago: Bible Institute Colportage Association of Chicago, 1924. 28 pp.
———. *The Memoirs of William Jennings Bryan*. Philadelphia, PA: John C. Winston, 1925. 560 pp.
———. *The Prince of Peace*. Chicago: Reilly and Britton, 1909. 32 pp.
Dictionary of American Biography. 20 vols. and 7 supps. New York: Charles Scribner's Sons, 1928-1936, 1944-1981.
Hill, Samuel S., ed. *Encyclopedia of Religion in the South*. Macon, GA: Mercer University Press, 1984. 878 pp.
Levine, Lawrence W. *Defender of the Faith: William Jennings Bryan, The Last Decade, 1915-1925*. New York: Oxford University Press, 1965.
Lippy, Charles H. *Twentieth-Century Shapers of American Popular Religion*. New York: Greenwood Press, 1989. 494 pp.
Smith, Willard H. *The Social and Religious Thought of William Jennings Bryan*. Lawrence, KS: University Press of Kansas, 1975.

★ 142 ★
BUCHMAN, Frank Nathan Daniel
Moral Re-Armament
b. Jun. 4, 1878, Pennsburg, Pennsylvania
d. Aug. 7, 1961, Freudenstadt Germany

Frank N. D. Buchman was the founder of Moral ReArmament (MRA), which has had a profound effect on the religious perspectives of many, especially those of the World War II generation. Born in Pennsylvania into a pious Lutheran family, Buchman attended the Lutheran Theological Seminary from 1899 to 1902 and became a pastor in Overbrook, Pennsylvania. As pastor he created a home for poor young men which was quite successful, but in 1908 a fight with the trustees caused Buchman to leave his position. This break left him exhausted and in a spiritual crisis. He took a tour around England that brought him to Keswick Chapel, where he experienced a cleansing away of resentment and a profound sense of renewal.

Buchman returned to the United States and served as the YMCA secretary at Pennsylvania State College, switching in 1916 to a position as extension lecturer at Hartford Theological Seminary in Connecticut. Both positions allowed him to address groups internationally, and he slowly developed a style of evangelization that incorporated what he had learned in Keswick Chapel. In 1918 he organized the first "house party" on a trip to China. In the setting of a private home, persons were encouraged to reveal themselves and their shortcomings and allow God to transform their lives. This kind of personal, powerful encounter became Buchman's trademark, and led in 1921 to the creation in England of the First Century Christian Fellowship.

In the 1930s the movement was international in scope and was popularly known as the "Oxford Group," so dubbed by a South African reporter because many of its participants were from Cambridge or Oxford University. Along with its successful message of reconciliation and recreation through confession and rejection of moral compromise, the movement also faced increasing criticism. The group was attacked for what were seen as lurid or sensationalistic "sharing" encouraged at the house parties. Buchman was criticized for his easy relationships with the rich and famous, and for his endorsement of Hitler because of his anti-communist stance. The accusations of pro-Nazism, however, have never been proven. Buchman's main detractor, journalist Tom Driberg, has since been revealed to be a Soviet agent, and Nazism has never been demonstrated in the MRA's programs and policies.

In 1938, as World War II drew nearer, Buchman introduced Moral Re-Armament (MRA) as the successor movement, out to change the world through the moral absolutes of honesty, purity, unselfishness, and love. The MRA hoped to avoid war by seeking God's guidance through quiet prayer. At the same time, however, MRA was utilized by the military in America to create the program "You Can Defend America." Other countries had similar morale-boosting, patriotic uses for the group. After the war, Buchman oversaw the establishment in Caux, Switzerland, of a program for offering reconciliation opportunities for war-time participants. Buchman directed the organization until his death in 1961 at the age of 83. The MRA continues in many countries today, although its peak was during Buchman's leadership.

Sources:

Austin, H. W. "Bunny". *Frank Buchman as I Knew Him*. London: Grosvenor Books, 1975. 197 pp.
Bowden, Henry Warner. *Dictionary of American Religious Biography*. Westport, CT: Greenwood Press, 1977. 572 pp.
Buchman, Frank. *Remaking the World*. London: Blandford Press, 1961. 396 pp.
Driberg, Tom. *The Mystery of Moral Re-Armament*. New York: Alfred A. Knopf, 1965. 317 pp.
Eister, Allan W. *Drawing-Room Conversion*. Durham, North Carolina: Duke University Press, 1950. 236 pp.
Frank Buchman—Eighty, By His Friends. London: Blandford Press, 1958. 214 pp.
Lean, Garth. *Frank Buchman: A Life*. London: Constable & Co., 1985. 590 pp.
Who Was Who in America. Chicago: Marquis Who's Who, Inc.

—Gary L. Ward

★ 143 ★
BUCKLAND, Raymond
Pioneer American Wiccan Priest
Founder, Seax-Wica Tradition
b. Aug. 31, 1934, London England

Raymond Buckland is the founder of the Seax-Wica Tradition, and was an early pioneer in initiating the witchcraft movement in North America. His father was a Gypsy, but Buckland was raised in the Church of England. He attended King's College, London, and served for two years in the Royal Air Force. Buckland's metaphysical interests began at the age of 12 when an uncle lent him a book on Spiritualism. A voracious reader from an early age, he quickly read his uncle's other books and then moved on to the public library. In the late 1950s he read Margaret Murray's *God of the Witches* (1933). A few years later he came across **Gerald B. Gardner**'s *Witchcraft Today* (1954). Together these two works changed the direction of his life. He immediately wrote to Gardner, who had created the Neo-Wiccan Faith in the 1940s, and soon established a friendship with both him and his high priestess, the Lady Olwen (Monique Wilson). He was eventually initiated by Lady Olwen a few months prior to Gardner's death. Buckland's wife, Rosemary Buckland (Lady Rowan), was soon also initiated by Wilson.

The Bucklands established the first Gardnerian Wicca coven in the United States, and any inquiries directed to Gardner from North America were forwarded to Buckland. They also established America's first Museum of Witchcraft and Magic (modeled on the museum Gardner operated on the Isle of Man) in New York in 1966. (The museum was later moved to New Hampshire.) Partly as a result of the museum and partly as a result of their availability to the media, the Bucklands were instrumental in stimulating the Wiccan movement in this country. Raymond Buckland was particularly concerned with correcting public misconceptions. He quickly became a spokesman for the movement.

With Gardner's books out of print, Buckland recognized a need for occult material from a Wiccan perspective. Buckland wrote several books, including *A Pocket Guide to the Supernatural* (1969); his first book on Wicca, *Witchcraft Ancient and Modern* (1970); *Candle Spells and Rituals* (1970); and *Witchcraft from the Inside* (1971). He also authored a humorous spoof on the Lemurian books of James Churchward which he called *Mu Revealed* (1969) under the pseudonym of Tony Earll, an anagram for "not really." In the early 1970s, Buckland's marriage dissolved, and he began to realize that he was not comfortable with certain aspects of the Gardnerian tradition. Thus in 1973 he turned the leadership of the tradition over to a couple he had initiated, Lady Theos and Phoenix, and he founded a more democratic tradition of the Craft which he called Seax Wica. He wrote a book on this uniquely non-secret tradition titled *The Tree—The Complete Book of Saxon Witchcraft* (1974). He also married Joan Helen Tayler, who became his new high priestess. This new tradition is now practiced around the globe. More recently, Buckland, who now resides in Southern California, has assembled what he considers his most authoritative statements on the Craft in his book *Buckland's Complete Book of Witchcraft*, and in a 60-minute video, *Witchcraft: Yesterday and Today*.

Sources:

Buckland, Raymond. *Ancient and Modern Witchcraft*. New York: H C Publishers, 1970. 192 pp.

———. *Buckland's Complete Book of Witchcraft*. St. Paul, MN: Llewellyn Publications, 1986. 251 pp.

———. *Candle Spells & Rituals*. N.p.: Acrowley Publications, 1970. 62 pp.

———. *A Pocket Guide to the Supernatural*. New York: Ace Publishing Company, 1969. 189 pp.

———. *Practical Color Magick*. St. Paul, MN: Llewellyn

★ 144 ★
BUCKLEY, James Monroe
Editor, Methodist Episcopal Church
b. Dec. 16, 1836, Rahway, New Jersey
d. Feb. 8, 1920, Morristown, New Jersey

James Monroe Buckley, for over 30 years the editor of the *New York Christian Advocate*, was raised in New Jersey and attended Wesleyan University in Middletown, Connecticut. In 1858 he was received into the New Hampshire Conference of the Methodist Episcopal Church, and served churches successively in Exeter, Dover, and Manchester. Following the Civil War, from 1866 to 1869, he studied medicine. In the 1870s he transferred to the Detroit Conference and served in Detroit, Michigan. Later in the decade he transferred to the New York East Conference and pastored at Brooklyn, New York, and Stamford, Connecticut. In 1872 he was elected for the first time as a delegate to the quadrennial general conference, an honor accorded him every four years for the rest of his active life. He was also a delegate to the international Ecumenical Methodist Conference of 1881, 1891, and 1901.

During the early 1870s Buckley began to make a name for himself with his writings for the several Methodist periodicals. He issued a number of short polemical works including an early booklet against "modern miracles." He received very favorable comment for his contribution to the new revised hymnal of 1876. He also became an influential member of the committee which prepared the judicial code for the acceptance of the 1880 general conference.

In 1880 Buckley became editor of the *New York Christian Advocate*, the largest circulating periodical in American Methodism at the time. Buckley soon became one of the most powerful voices in the church and his editorials among the most read features of the *Advocate*. His public influence, combined with a vast knowledge of the political process within the church, gave him virtual veto power at the general conferences. In 1888, for example, he was able to organize resistance to the conference's seating the several women delegates who had been elected. In addition, on several occasions he was able effectively to block the election of men to the episcopacy.

Besides his editorial work on the *Advocate*, Buckley wrote a number of books. His most popular was a travelogue, *Travels to Three Continents* (1894). He authored several books on Methodist history, including: *A History of Methodism in the United States* (1898) and his authoritative *Constitutional and Parliamentary History of the Methodist Episcopal Church* (1912). He attacked both Roman Catholicism and Mormonism in the *Advocate*, but had a life-long interest in miracles and spiritual healing which led to his book against Christian Science and the other contemporary healing movements, issued in 1906 as *Faith Healing, Christian Science and Kindred Phenomena*.

Buckley retired in 1912 and lived the last years of his life in Morristown, New Jersey.

Sources:

Buckley, James M. *Constitutional and Parliamentary History of the Methodist Episcopal Church*. New York: Jennings & Graham, 1912. 414 pp.

———. *Faith Healing, Christian Science and Kindred Phenomena*. New York: The Century Co., 1887, 1906. 308 pp.

———. *A History of Methodism in the United States*. New York: Harper & Brothers, 1898. 714 pp.

———. *Travels on Three Continents*. New York: Hunt & Eaton, 1895. 614 pp.

Harmon, Nolan B. *The Encyclopedia of World Methodism*. 2 vols. Nashville: United Methodist Publishing House, 1974.

Mains, George Preston. *James Monroe Buckley*. New York: Methodist Book Concern, 1917.

★ 145 ★
BUDAPEST, Zsuzsanna E.
Priestess, Dianic Wicca
b. Jan. 30, 1940, Budapest Hungary

Zsuzsanna E. Budapest, better known as Z. Budapest, is the founder of the main branch of Dianic (feminist) Wicca as well as one of the major organizations which has given Dianic Wicca its public expression, the Women's Spirituality Forum. Dianic Wicca places more stress on the centrality of the Goddess than do the other Wiccan traditions (for whom the Goddess is also central, but who usually place Her on par with the male God). Through the Forum, Budapest has worked to bring Goddess consciousness into the mainstream of the feminist movement. Her female-centered theology celebrates Mother Earth, postulates Goddess worship as humanity's earliest religion, and sees the earlier Goddess eras as periods of peace that were destroyed by the rise of men and patriarchal deities (a kind of feminist Fall story). Budapest is viewed as the "Initiator of the Women's Spirituality Movement," and is the teacher of such feminist Wiccans as **Starhawk**.

Born Zsuzsanna Mokcsay, Budapest was raised in Hungary but left soon after the suppression of the Hungarian revolt of 1956. She settled in Austria for a short period before coming to the United States, where she had been offered a scholarship to study at the University of Chicago. She married, had two children, and in 1970, following the dissolution of her marriage, she moved to California. In California she became involved in the women's movement as well as witchcraft. She began to develop a form of witchcraft which would embody her feminist ideas. Thus, in 1971 the Susan B. Anthony Coven was formed by Budapest and six other women. She also opened a bookstore in Venice, California. The coven began a newsletter, *Themis* (now *Thesmorphoria*), and in 1979 moved its center to Oakland, California, where Budapest continues to reside.

Her first book, *The Feminist Book of Lights and Shadows* (1976), became a basic text of Dianic Wicca. It was later enlarged and reprinted as *The Holy Book of Women's Mysteries* (1979). Later books include *The Rise of the Fates* (1976), a play; *Selene, The Most Famous Bull-leaper on Earth* (1976), a children's book, and *The Grandmother of Time* (1989).

Budapest teaches classes and trains priestesses for Goddess ministries in the San Francisco Bay Area. She also has her own Cable TV show called "13th Heaven" that is syndicated in the Bay Area.

Sources:

Budapest, Z. *The Feminist Book of Lights and Shadows*. Venice, CA: Luna Publications, 1976. 127 pp.

———. *The Grandmother of Time*. San Francisco: Harper & Row, 1989. 262 pp.

———. *The Holy Book of Women's Mysteries*. 2 vols. Los Angeles: Susan B. Anthony Coven Number One, 1979-1980.

———. *The Rise of the Fates*. Los Angeles: Susan B. Anthony Coven Number One, 1976. 91 pp.

———. *Selene, The Most Famous Bull-leaper on Earth*. Baltimore, MD: Diana Press, 1976. 51 pp.

Guiley, Rosemary E. *Encyclopedia of Witchcraft & Witches*. New York: Facts on File, 1989. 400 pp.

★ 146 ★
BUFFALO BIRD WOMAN
Medicine Woman, Hidatsa Indians
b. 1839, Sakakawea, North Dakota
d. 1929, Fort Berthold, North Dakota

Buffalo Bird Woman, whose Indian name was Maxidiwiac, was a traditional medicine woman among the Hidatsa Indians. She was born in the Hidatsa Indian village of Sakakawea, along the Knife River in what is now central North Dakota. Her mother was Weahtee ("Wants to be a woman"), and, by virtue of Hidatsa matrilineal clan inheritance, Buffalo Bird Woman became a "sister" (somewhat equivalent to a member) of the Prairie Chicken clan. Small Ankle, her father, kept the religious function of sacred bundle holder of the Midipadi clan of the Hidatsa and chief of one of the major Hidatsa groups, who were finally relocated near Independence, North Dakota, on the present-day Fort Berthold Indian Reservation.

When Buffalo Bird Woman was born, the Hidatsa were on the verge of major changes. Pressure from the Lakota (Sioux) Indians to the south and west, and the Americans from the east, forced the Hidatsa to move in 1845 to the village of Like-a-Fishhook. In her own words, Buffalo Bird Woman said that she was born three years after the smallpox winter of 1835-36, which devastated Indian tribes on the upper Missouri River. She was the descendant of chiefs on both sides of her family, so at an early age was educated in the ancient ways and beliefs of her people. Because the Hidatsa inheritance was matrilineal, she received ownership of the fields and gardens of her mother's clan, as well as the responsibilities for production of their fruits.

Producing food for the Hidatsa, whether by hunting or agriculture, was a sacred task and was undertaken using knowledge accumulated over millennia and contained in a vast body of songs and oral literature. Buffalo Bird Woman learned the songs and stories and became known among her people as an industrious and pious supporter of the old ways of life. When the United States government enforced the policies of allotment after the passage of the Daves Act in 1887, the Hidatsa were forced out of the village of Like-a-Fishhook. After the Hidatsa moved forty miles north to Independence, on the Fort Berthold Indian Reservation, the Indian agent for the tribe ordered the village of Like-a-Fishhook destroyed. Buffalo Bird Woman's family was lucky; they were allotted lands at the new site that were near to each other, and they were able to continue some semblance of their old ways of life.

Buffalo Bird Woman was married for the first time at the age of 18 to a man named Magpie, but their decade-long marriage produced no children. Magpie died of tuberculosis around 1867 and, after a traditional year of mourning, Buffalo Bird Woman married Son of Star, a Mandan Indian of some stature. In the autumn of 1869 their only child, Goodbird, was born. He was raised in the traditional manner of the Hidatsa and at puberty was sent on a vision quest seeking his personal spirit helper. Goodbird, later known as Edward Goodbird, became a Christian missionary among his people later in his life, but Buffalo Bird Woman remained committed to the old Hidatsa ways and refused to speak and learn English. Edward Goodbird serving as interpreter, Buffalo Bird Woman, and her brother, Wolf Chief, worked with anthropologist Gilbert L. Wilson to record the beliefs and lifeways of the Hidatsa people. Goodbird and Buffalo Bird Woman each dictated biographies to Wilson, which were published in the early part of the twentieth century. Buffalo Bird Woman died in 1929 and is buried on the Fort Berthold Indian Reservation.

Sources:
Gilman, Carolyn, and Mary Jane Schneider. *The Way to Independence: Memories of a Hidatsa Indian Family*. St. Paul, MN: Minnesota Historical Society Press, 1987.

Goodbird, Edward, as told to Gilbert L. Wilson. *Goodbird the Indian: His Story*. St. Paul, MN: Webb Publishing Company, 1921.
Maxidiwiac [Buffalo Bird Woman], as told to Gilbert L. Wilson. *Waheenee: An Indian Girl's Story*. St. Paul, MN: Webb Publishing Company, 1921.
Maxidiwiac [Buffalo Bird Woman], as told to Gilbert L. Wilson. *Buffalo Bird Woman's Garden*. St Paul, MN: Minnesota Historical Society Press, 1987.

—*Johnny Flynn*

★ 147 ★
BURGOYNE, Thomas H.
Hermetic Brotherhood of Luxor/Church of Light
b. Apr. 14, 1855, Scotland
d. Mar. 1894, Humboldt County, California

Thomas H. Burgoyne was one of the founders of the Hermetic Brotherhood of Luxor, the public teaching branch of the Brotherhood of Light, today continued as the Church of Light. Born in Scotland, he was an amateur naturalist and seer, reportedly able even as a child to see the spiritual entities known to occultists as the Brotherhood of Light. As an adult he met M. Theon, the earthly keeper of that tradition, who taught Burgoyne about the Brotherhood. In 1880 Burgoyne came to America and joined with Captain Norman Astley, a retired British Army officer.

Burgoyne first stayed in New York, where Astley had met his wife, Genevieve Stebbins, herself already a member of the Brotherhood there. Burgoyne wrote several articles on the tarot that were published in *The Platonist* in 1887 and 1888. Burgoyne then moved to Carmel, California, where he stayed at Astley's home and wrote a basic set of lessons called *The Light of Egypt*, published in 1889. With the help of interested followers such as Dr. Henry Wagner and his wife, Belle, the Hermetic Brotherhood of Luxor was formed. This order was designed to bring the teachings of the Brotherhood of Light to a wider audience further disseminating the message of an occult order understood to have existed since 2440 B.C.E. in Egypt. This teaching involved astrology and the concept of correspondences between the macrocosm (the larger creation) and the microcosm (the individual). Burgoyne did not accept the more eastern occult ideas of rebirth and karma.

Burgoyne led the Hermetic Brotherhood as its scribe until his death in 1894 at the young age of 39. Some of his works, such as volume two of *The Light of Egypt* (1900) and *Celestial Dynamics* (1896), were not published until after his death. The Hermetic Brotherhood was closed in 1913, and **Elbert Benjamine**, functioning at that time as the astrologer for the group, took over its mission and eventually incorporated it as the Church of Light.

Some aspects of Burgoyne's identity and history are still a matter of controversy. Researcher Arthur Edward Waite has suggested that Burgoyne was none other than Thomas Henry Dalton, a convicted fraud, who left England with Peter Davidson (also known as M. Theon and Norman Astley) under a cloud of scandal. In any case, Burgoyne's legacy as a major force in the nineteenth century occult revival remains intact.

Sources:
Burgoyne, Thomas H. *Celestial Dynamics*. Denver, CO: Astro-Philosophical Publishing Co., 1896. 107 pp.
———. *The Language of the Stars*. Denver, CO: Astro-Philosophical Publishing Co., 1892. 100 pp.
———. *The Light of Egypt*. 2 vols. San Francisco: Religio-Philosophical Publishing House, 1889.
"Founders of the Church of Light." *The Church of Light Quarterly* 45 (February 1970): 1-3.

—*Gary L. Ward*

★148★
BURNELL, George Edwin
Founder, Burnell Foundation
b. Jul. 9, 1863, Hartford, Connecticut
d. Oct. 24, 1948, Arcadia, California

George Edwin Burnell, New Thought writer and founder of the Burnell Foundation, was the son of Edwin and Mary Malloy Burnell. When he was four years old his family moved to Minneapolis, where he attended school, eventually graduating from the University of Minnesota. He entered the Morgan Park Theological Seminary in Chicago, graduating in 1887, with the intention of entering the Baptist ministry. He left the Baptist Church for the Congregational Church and studied briefly at the Union Theological Seminary, also in Chicago.

Burnell's dissatisfaction with Protestant Christianity led him to Christian Science and to a new school, the Christian Science Theological Seminary, just established by independent teacher **Emma Curtis Hopkins**, the founder of what has become known as New Thought. He became her student and then a teacher at the seminary. While at the school, he met Mary Irene Lamoreaux (1871-1949). They married in 1891. They worked at the school and frequently traveled with Hopkins. Burnell also entered the real estate business and participated in the development of the opening of the Auburn Park section of Chicago, from which he became a wealthy man.

Hopkins closed her school in 1895 and moved to New York. Shortly after Hopkins left Chicago, the Burnells moved to California, where he again established himself in the real estate business and became an officer in several corporations, including the California Irrigated Farms Company, the San Joaquin Farms Company, and the Rich Groves Land Company. Within a few years he became independently wealthy. He moved to Arcadia, California, where he located his headquarters.

Once established in the business, Burnell and his wife continued their New Thought ministry, first simply as independent teachers and then in the early twentieth century through the incorporation of the Burnell Foundation. In the next decades, Burnell authored a number of booklets, the most important being *Axioms: The Book of Health and the Science of Truth* (1902). He gave weekly talks for many years and these were later collected and published as a series of mimeographed stenographic reports. His talks covered not only the wide range of metaphysical topics but broad reflections on religion in general. They remain as a massive documentation of his work.

Burnell taught that faith and reason are united in the search for truth. He listed the basic assumptions about truth in a series of axioms which underlie his teachings. Truth was equated with spirit, universality, unity, God, eternity. Truth as individuality is perceived in humanity.

The Burnells gathered a small following of students but disseminated their teaching throughout the New Thought community through their numerous publications. Following their deaths shortly after World War II, their work was carried on by their daughter, Genevieve Burnell, who headed the foundation and created the Burnell Library of Religious Research, through which she continued to publish her parents' lectures and booklets.

Sources:

Burch, H. A. *George Edwin Burnell and Man and Teacher*. Arcadia, CA: Burnell Library of Religious Research, n.d.
Burnell, George. *Axioms; A Book of Health and Science of Truth*. Los Angeles: The Author, 1902. 80 pp.
———. *Doctrine of the Lord*. Arcadia, CA: Burnell Foundation, 1913.
———. *List of Stenographic Reports*. Arcadia, CA: Burnell Foundation, 1964. 37 pp.

★149★
BUTLER, Marie Joseph
Mother General, Congregation of the Sacred Heart of Mary, Roman Catholic Church
b. Jul. 22, 1860, Ballynunnery Ireland
d. Apr. 23, 1940, Tarrytown, New York

Mother Marie Joseph Butler, who became the first American to head an order of the Roman Catholic Church based in a foreign land, was born Johanna Butler, the daughter of John and Ellen Forrestal Butler. She was raised on the family estate and as a teenager became interested in the religious life. In 1876 she entered the convent at Beziers, France, of the Congregation of the Sacred Heart of Mary, an order founded in the 1840s with a mission of educating the female children of the upper classes. Later in the year, when she took her veil, she became known as Sister Marie Joseph. In 1879 she was sent to Portugal to teach in the order's school at Oporto. While there in 1880 she took her first vows. In 1881 she moved to Braga, Portugal, as head of the English and French departments. Her leadership, manifest both in her popularity among the students and her ability to deal with local officials, led to her appointment as superior of the school in 1893.

In 1903 Sister Marie Joseph was sent to the United States with the job of heading the order's school at Sag Harbor, New York, and expanding the work of the order in the United States. In 1907, with property given to her by her family, she began to fulfill an original intention of the order, and founded a college. She opened Marymount School at Tarrytown, New York, in 1907, and pursued the task of raising the money which would allow it to evolve into a liberal arts college for women. That task was completed by 1918 and she then turned to founding branches of the college in other locations. Marymount College of Los Angeles opened in 1921-1922. In 1923 the French branch opened in Paris.

The curriculum at Marymount anticipated changes in the role of Catholic women both in the church and in the world. Butler trained each student in apologetics so they could become articulate defenders of the faith. She initiated a retreat movement which would later spread to other orders and involve millions of Catholic laywomen. She motivated them in charitable work and founded a number of Mother Butler Mission Guilds in local congregations. In addition she expanded the curriculum to provide preparation for non-domestic occupational pursuits by her students.

Butler's international leadership led to her being elected Mother General of her order in 1926. The following year she became an American citizen. While making New York her home, she traveled extensively, overseeing and building the order on an international scale. Her work included the opening of new branches of Marymount in Rome, Italy (1930), and Santa Barbara, California (1938). In Rome in the summer of 1939 she became ill, but returned to Tarrytown to celebrate the fiftieth anniversary of her profession before her death in 1940.

Sources:

Burton, Katherine. *Mother Butler of Marymount*. New York: Longmans, Green & Co., 1944. 290 pp.
Delaney, John J. *Dictionary of American Catholic Biography*. Garden City, NY: Doubleday & Company, 1988. 621 pp.
James, Edward T., ed. *Notable American Women, 1607-1950: A Biographical Dictionary*. 3 vols. Cambridge, MA: Harvard University Press, Belknap Press, 1971.
Leahy, J. Kenneth. *As the Eagle: the Spiritual Writings of Mother Butler*. New York: P. J. Kenedy, 1954. 206 pp.
New Catholic Encyclopedia. 17 vols. New York: McGraw-Hill, 1967.

★150★
BUTTERWORTH, Eric
Minister, Association of Unity Churches
b. 1916, Canada

Eric Butterworth is a minister with the Association of Unity Churches, the fellowship of ministers and churches affiliated with the Unity School of Christianity, which is, in turn, the largest of the American New Thought denominations. He was born in Canada but raised in California. His mother was a Unity minister, and he was raised in New Thought metaphysics. By the age of 16 he was teaching in the local Unity center. He became active in Youth of Unity and in 1942 became its national president. He attended Fresno State College in California and Capital University in Columbus, Ohio.

As a young man, Butterworth began to work at the Unity School's headquarters in Kansas City. For three years he was active at Silent Unity, the 24-hour prayer ministry, and attended the ministerial school. He became assistant minister at Unity Temple in Kansas City (1945-1947). He became pastor of the congregation in Rockford, Illinois, in 1947 for a year. In 1948 he was formally ordained to the Unity ministry and became pastor of the church in Pittsburgh, Pennsylvania. In 1949 he began a very successful 12 years in Detroit, Michigan. While there he built a new sanctuary which welcomed some 2,500 attendees each Sunday.

In 1961, Butterworth became the minister of the Unity Church in New York City. There his ministry blossomed far beyond the congregation as he developed a daily radio show which lasted more than three decades, and began to author a number of popular books beginning with *Unity: A Quest for Truth* in 1965. It was followed by *Life Is for Living* (1965); *Discover the Power within You* (1968); *Unity of All Life* (1969); *Life Is for Loving* (1973); and *In the Flow of Life* (1975). During his years in New York, Butterworth became involved in the professionalization of the Unity ministry which had begun with the formation of the Unity Minister's Association in 1946 (with which he served a term as president) and led eventually to the organization of the Association of Unity Churches. The association, as a fellowship of ministers and churches, assumed the responsibility for training Unity ministers and chartering Unity churches. In 1965 he was placed in charge of the Unity Minister's Conference Ordination Research Committee and was a charter member of the Association of Unity Churches. Over the years he has frequently taught and lectured in the ministerial school and served as chairman of the association's executive committee.

Butterworth continues to teach and write. He is assisted by his wife, Olga Butterworth, also a Unity minister. Among his recent books are *Spiritual Economics: The Prosperity Process* (1983) and *Celebrate Yourself* (1984).

Sources:

Beebe, Tom. *Who's Who in New Thought.* Lakemont, GA: CSA Press, 1977. 318 pp.

Butterworth, Eric. *Discover the Power Within You.* New York: Harper & Row, 1968. 239 pp.

_____. *Life Is for Loving.* New York: Harper & Row, 1973. 99 pp.

_____. *Spiritual Economics: The Prosperity Process.* Unity Village, MO: Unity School of Christianity, 1983. 212 pp.

_____. *Unity: A Quest for Truth.* Unity Village, MO: Unity Books, 1965, 1985. 102 pp.

_____. *Unity of All Life.* New York: Harper & Row, 1969. 209 pp.

★151★
BUTTRICK, George Arthur
Minister, Presbyterian Church
b. Mar. 23, 1892, Seaham Harbour United Kingdom
d. Jan. 23, 1980, Louisville, Kentucky

George Arthur Buttrick, one of the outstanding preachers of twentieth-century America, was the son of Tom and Jessie Lambert Buttrick. He grew up in England and attended Victoria University in Manchester and the Lancaster Independent Theological Seminary. He completed his degrees from both institutions in 1915. That same year he was ordained as a Congregational minister and became the pastor of the church in Quincy, Illinois. In 1916 he married Agnes Gardner. After three years in Illinois, he became the pastor of congregations in Rutland, Vermont (1919-1921), and then Buffalo, New York (1921-1927), before becoming pastor of Madison Avenue Presbyterian Church in New York City, where he would remain for the next quarter century as an acknowledged master craftsman of the homiletic arts.

At Madison Avenue Buttrick's literary skills emerged alongside his oratorical presence. His first book, *The Parables of Jesus*, appeared in 1928. It was the first of a number of books which emerged out of his sermons. Buttrick became a major popularizer of liberal Protestant Christianity and attempted to speak to a literate audience. Among his major books are: *The Christian Fact and Modern Doubt: A Preface to a Restatement of Christian Faith* (1934); *Prayer* (1942); and *Christ and Man's Dilemma* (1946). In 1939 he began a two-year term as president of the Federal Council of Churches.

Over the years of his ministry Buttrick had worked with Abingdon-Cokesbury Press (the publishing concern of the Methodist Church), and following World War II was chosen as the general editor of *The Interpreter's Bible*, a twelve-volume set of commentaries on the books of the Bible. *The Interpreter's Bible* helped introduce the new Revised Standard Version of the Bible to many ministers and congregations and became the most popular Bible study help among liberal Protestants during the last half of the twentieth century. Upon publication of *The Interpreter's Bible*, to which he contributed several articles himself, Buttrick became general editor of *The Interpreter's Dictionary of the Bible*, a four-volume companion set.

Following his retirement from Madison Avenue in 1954, Buttrick remained active in teaching and writing. He moved to Harvard University as a campus preacher and professor of Christian morals. His years at Harvard culminated in two books: *Sermons Preached in a University Church* (1959) and *Biblical Thought and the Secular University* (1960). In 1960 he became professor emeritus and moved back to New York for a year at Union Theological Seminary. In 1961 he began nine years at Northwestern University and Garrett Theological Seminary. While at Garrett he authored two of his most significant books: *Christ and History* (1963) and *God, Pain, and Evil* (1966). Following his retirement from Garrett and Northwestern, he made his home in Louisville, Kentucky, and he continued as a popular lecturer and preacher through the 1970s.

Sources:

Buttrick, George A. *Christ and History.* New York: Abingdon Press, 1963. 176 pp.

_____. *The Christian Fact and Modern Doubt: A Preface to a Restatement of Christian Faith.* New York: Charles Scribner's Sons, 1934. 311 pp.

_____. *God, Pain, and Evil.* Nashville, TN: Abingdon Press, 1966. 272 pp.

_____, general editor. *The Interpreter's Bible.* 12 vols. Nashville, TN: Abingdon-Cokesbury Press, 1951-1957.

_____, general editor. *The Interpreter's Dictionary of the Bible.* 4 vols. Nashville, TN: Abingdon-Cokesbury Press, 1962.

_____, general editor. *The Interpreter's Bible.* 12 vols. Nashville, TN: Abingdon-Cokesbury Press, 1951-1957.

_____, general editor. *The Interpreter's Dictionary of the Bible.* 4 vols. Nashville, TN: Abingdon-Cokesbury Press, 1962.

★152★
CABOT, Laurie
Founder, Witches' League for Public Awareness
b. Mar. 3, 1933, Wewoka, Oklahoma

After being named the official Witch of Salem by Massachusetts Governor Michael Dukakis in 1977, Laurie Cabot emerged as a major spokesperson for witchcraft in the Northeast. Amid the media coverage which she received in the intervening years, her serious pursuit of witchcraft as a religious faith was often lost. However, she has made a serious study of magic and witchcraft since her teenage years.

According to Cabot, at age 16 she was taught Druid/Celtic witchcraft and was initiated as high priestess by three Druid/Celtic priestesses of that tradition. She subsequently attended Fullerton Junior College and Massachusetts College of Art before being awarded a full scholarship to attend Rhode Island School of Design. All through her collegiate education, she continued her studies with Druid/Celtic witchcraft, working both with her teachers and independently. Through her private study and consultation with her professors and elders, she began to connect witchcraft to psychic science. Her practice of Druid/Celtic witchcraft extended to include Hermetic science, laws, and magic.

Cabot developed the teaching of "Witchcraft As A Science" privately during the 1960s and gave her first public classes during 1971 at the Wellesley Adult Education program at Wellesley High School. She also taught for seven years during the 1970s at the Cambridge Center for Adult Education and at Salem State College. She was asked by the then-president of Salem State to present a 16-week curriculum in "Witchcraft As A Science" to be incorporated into the regular curriculum of the school as an accredited course, but this suggestion was never accepted by the school's board of directors.

Cabot founded the Temple of Isis in Salem, Massachusetts, and the grove of the Council of Isis Community. (A grove is an organization of three or more covens.) She ended her public classes in the late 1970s, but has continued to teach and provide psychic consultation and healing to both private parties and organizations such as the police nationwide. In April of 1977 she was awarded the Paul Revere Patriots Award for her work with special needs children, an honor bestowed by Governor Dukakis, who used the occasion to give her the informal designation of "The Official Witch of Salem." During the 1980s, Cabot put much of her time into the defense of witchcraft from the media and the mainline religious community. She founded the Witches' League for Public Awareness and mobilized the Neo-Pagan community to support an activist stance against anti-Pagan attacks. In 1989 she completed her first book, *Power of The Witch: The Earth, The Moon, and The Magical Path To Enlightenment.*

Sources:

Cabot, Laurie. *Power of the Witch: The Earth, The Moon, and The Magical Path to Enlightenment.* New York: Delacorte Press, 1989. 311 pp.

★153★
CABRINI, Frances Xavier
Founder, Institute of the Missionary Sisters of the Sacred Heart, Roman Catholic Church
b. Jul. 15, 1850, Lodigiano Italy
d. Dec. 22, 1917, Chicago, Illinois

Mother Frances Xavier Cabrini, the first American canonized by the Roman Catholic Church, was born Maria Francesca Cabrini, the daughter of Augustino and Stella Oldini Cabrini. She was raised in a pious atmosphere, first taking a vow of chastity at the age of 12. She was trained as a teacher and received her normal school diploma in 1870. In 1872 she came down with smallpox which necessitated a lengthy recuperation. Denied entrance into the Daughters of the Sacred Heart because of her questionable physical condition, she became the supervisor of an orphanage. She took formal vows in 1877. Subsequently, she recruited and trained a few young women in the religious life, and in 1880 founded her own order, the Institute of the Missionary Sisters of the Sacred Heart.

The institute acquired an abandoned convent as headquarters, and the order soon expanded to several Italian centers where orphanages were opened. In 1888 the rules of the order were formally approved. The previous year Mother Cabrini had vowed to go to China, but Pope Leo XIII directed her to the United States to work among Italian immigrants. With six of her sisters, she arrived in New York in 1889 ready to work among children and to spread the veneration of the Sacred Heart, a form of Catholic piety which directs contemplation upon Jesus' compassion for the world. From a beginning in a basement apartment she soon established a day school, orphanage, and a novitiate.

The order grew in spite of some episcopal resistance. Persistent and assertive, Cabrini led in the establishment of centers across the country as far west as Denver, Colorado, and Seattle, Washington. The first of several modern hospitals opened in New York in 1892. The American centers became the launching pad for foreign outreach, first to Panama, Peru, and Brazil in 1895, and subsequently to Spain and England. In 1909 she became an American citizen and in 1910 was named mother-general of the order for life. By the time of her death in 1917 she had recruited some 4,000 women to the religious life and founded approximately 70 institutions.

In 1928 Cardinal **George W. Mundelein** of Chicago initiated the hearings which would lead to Mother Cabrini's canonization. Pope Pius XII introduced her cause in 1931 and two years later she was pronounced venerable. She was beatified in 1937 and canonized in 1946. In 1950 Pope Pius XII designated her the patroness of immigrants. The Roman Catholic Church celebrates her feast day on November 13.

Sources:

Delaney, John J. *Dictionary of American Catholic Biography.* Garden City, NY: Doubleday & Company, 1988. 621 pp.
Dictionary of American Biography. 20 vols. and 7 supps. New York: Charles Scribner's Sons, 1928-1936, 1944-1981.
James, Edward T., ed. *Notable American Women, 1607-1950: A Biographical Dictionary.* 3 vols. Cambridge, MA: Harvard University Press, Belknap Press, 1971.
New Catholic Encyclopedia. 17 vols. New York: McGraw-Hill, 1967.

★154★
CADBURY, Henry Joel
Biblical Scholar, Five Years Meeting, Religious Society of Friends
b. Dec. 1, 1883, Philadelphia, Pennsylvania
d. Oct. 7, 1974, Bryn Mawr, Pennsylvania

Henry Joel Cadbury, a biblical scholar credited with introducing important aspects of modern German biblical criticism to American audiences, was born into an old Quaker family. He was the son of Anna Kaighn Lowry and Joel Cadbury. He attended the William Penn Charter School and upon graduation entered Haverford College. His B.A. at Haverford (1903) prepared him for Harvard College, from which he received his M.A. in 1904. He then taught at the University Latin School in Chicago (1904-1905) and Westtown School (1905-1908) before returning to Harvard to finish his Ph.D., which was awarded in 1914. In 1910 he joined the faculty at Haverford College.

While at Haverford, he worked with the Young Friends Movement and became deeply involved in the peace movement as World War I loomed closer. In 1915 he organized a peace conference at Winona Lake, Indiana. The meeting led to the formation of the National Peace Committee, later renamed the American Friends Service Committee. He remained active with the committee for the rest of his life. In 1916, amid the growing activity of his life, he married Lydia Caroline Brown.

In 1919 Cadbury accepted a position at Andover Theological Seminary. The following year Harvard University Press published his doctoral dissertation, *The Style and Literary Method of Luke*. As a New Testament scholar Cadbury had been studying the new critical methods for appraising the various gospels and in 1923 he introduced what was called form criticism, a method of studying elements of the gospels as differing story forms—parable, miracle story, paradox, etc., to American audiences. He expanded upon his initial paper on the topic in his book, *The Making of Luke-Acts* (1927).

In 1926 Cadbury moved to Bryn Mawr College. While there he joined the committee that produced the Revised Standard Version of the Bible. He kept a seat on the committee for over 20 years, and worked with the group for the rest of his life. In 1934 he returned to Harvard College as the Hollis Professor of Divinity. While at Harvard he wrote what many have considered his major work, *The Perils of Modernizing Jesus* (1937), a contribution to the ongoing debates about our knowledge of the historical Jesus. In both this book and a sequel, *Jesus, What Manner of Man* (1947), he argued that Jesus must be first understood as a first-century Jew and that it was vital to avoid a too-easy twisting of his teaching by the imposition of modern misconceptions. At Harvard he also became active in the Cambridge Monthly Meeting (congregation) and led it in affiliating with the two large national Friends' organizations, the Five Years Meeting and the Friends General Conference. Still active in the American Friends Service Committee, he traveled to Oslo in 1947 to receive the Nobel Peace Prize on behalf of the organization.

Cadbury retired in 1954 and returned to Haverford College to lecture and teach at Pendle Hill, the nearby Quaker study community. He became even more active in the peace movement. His last years were filled with honors for a lifetime of achievement. In 1959 he was elected president of the Society of New Testament Studies (he had already served a term as president of the Society of Biblical Literature). The American Friends Service Committee issued a volume in his honor, *Then and Now*, in 1960. He was also able to turn some time to Quaker history and had three books he edited in that area published in 1972: *Friendly Heritage*; *The Narrative Papers of George Fox*; and *John Woolman in England*. He lived to enjoy his 90th birthday celebration hosted by Bryn Mawr College.

Sources:

Barbour, Hugh, and J. William Frost. *The Quakers*. New York: Greenwood Press, 1988. 407 pp.

Cadbury, Henry J. *The Books of Acts in History*. New York: Harper, 1955. 170 pp.

———. *Jesus, What Manner of Man*. New York: Macmillan Company, 1947. 123 pp.

———. *The Making of Luke—Acts*. New York: Macmillan Company, 1927. 385 pp.

———. *The Perils of Modernizing Jesus*. New York: Macmillan Company, 1937. 216 pp.

Reid, Daniel G., Robert D. Linder, Bruce L. Shelley, and Harry S. Stout. *Dictionary of Christianity in America*. Downers Grove, IL: InterVarsity Press, 1990. 1305 pp.

Kenworthy, Leonard S. *Living in the Light: Some Quaker Pioneers of the 20th Century*. Kennet Square, PA: Friends General Conference and Quaker Publications, n.d.

★ 155 ★
CADDY, Peter
Leader, New Age Movement
b. 1917, England

Peter Caddy, co-founder of the Findhorn Community in Scotland and one of the architects of the contemporary New Age Movement, is the son of Frederick Caddy. His father, a sufferer of arthritis, introduced his son to the occult/metaphysical world through visits to spiritual healers and Spiritualist mediums. Caddy was 10 years old when, in a session with medium Lucille Rutterby, he asked the spirit speaking through the medium a question. He remembers the spirit's answer as his first direct confrontation with spiritual reality.

At the age of 17 Caddy began to learn the hotel and catering business. He spent his free time studying and experiencing metaphysical and occult realities. During World War II he was sent to Burma with the Royal Air Force and had several opportunities to travel and meet spiritual teachers. Among them was Ram Sareek Singh, under whose guidance Caddy decided to become a self-realized person. Self-realization, a state of enlightenment and knowledge of one's true spiritual nature, is the goal of many Eastern religions.

Caddy remained in the RAF after the war. Back in England he married Sheena Govan, a mystic who also became his spiritual teacher. In 1953, while stationed in Iraq, he met Eileen Combe, the wife of an RAF wing commander. They had an affair and upon their return to England both were divorced from their spouses and began to live together. In 1956 the Caddys moved to Scotland, where Peter managed a hotel. They were joined by Dorothy McClean, another of Govan's students. Caddy was fired from his job in 1962. The three settled in Findhorn Caravan Park, near Inverness. The trio began to live according to the spiritual guidance received by Eileen Caddy and they slowly began to prosper. In 1967 a little booklet of material by Eileen was published as *God Spoke to Me*. People began to seek out the Caddys and what would become the Findhorn community developed around them. Essential to the Caddys' guidance and subsequent lifestyle was an attempt to attune their activities, especially gardening, to the nature spirits believed to inhabit the area.

Peter Caddy began to network with similarly-minded groups throughout England. Many of these groups shared the hope of a coming new age of peace and spiritual enlightenment; they became the nucleus of the modern New Age Movement. In the 1970s the Caddys made their first trips to America, where they found a lively response to their work. In the late 1970s the Caddys separated. Peter Caddy subsequently moved to the United States. In 1982 the Caddys were divorced, and Peter remarried. He moved to Mt. Shasta, California, with his new wife, Paula. There they founded The Gathering of the Ways, a New Age Community modeled somewhat on Findhorn.

Sources:

Caddy, Eileen. *Flight into Freedom*. Longmead, Dorset: Element Books, 1988. 227 pp.

Hawken, Paul. *The Magic of Findhorn*. New York: Harper & Row, 1985. 216 pp.

★ 156 ★
CADMAN, Samuel Parkes
Minister, Congregational Church
b. Dec. 18, 1864, Wellington, Salop England
d. Jul. 12, 1936, Plattsburg, New York

Samuel Parkes Cadman, a prominent Congregational minister, was raised in a coal mining region in England, the son of Betsy Parkes and Samuel Cadman. His pious family passed along a knowledge of the Bible and the works of John Bunyan and when he was 16 Cadman had a religious conversion experience. He affiliated with the Wesleyan Methodist Connection and in 1884 was licensed as a lay preacher. He attended Wesleyan College in Richmond, Surrey, from which he graduated in 1889. That same year he married Lillian Esther Wooding. He migrated to the United States and after serving several small churches in Millbrook and Yonkers, New York, became the pastor of Metropolitan Tabernacle in New York City in 1895.

In the United States Cadman identified with the Congregational Church from whom he received his ordination. In 1901 he became pastor of Central Congregational Church in Brooklyn, New York. Under his leadership it became one of the most prominent congregations in America, and he remained there for the rest of his life. Settled in Brooklyn, Cadman became one of the leading spokespersons for the new liberal theology that was attempting to be ecumenical, open to new findings in science and biblical scholarship, and socially relevant, without losing the emphasis upon the unique centrality of Jesus. His personal appropriation of these themes was expressed in several books, including: *Charles Darwin and Other English Thinkers* (1911); *Christianity and the State* (1924); *Imagination and Religion* (1926); and *The Christ of God* (1929); *The Parables of Jesus* (1931); and *The Prophets of Israel* (1933).

From his days at the Metropolitan Tabernacle and his participation in the Open and Institutional Church League, Cadman emerged as a leader in the ecumenical movement. He was active in the Federal Council of Churches (founded in 1908) and in 1924 began a four-year term as its president. During his tenure he also headed the American section of the Stockholm Conference on Life and Work (one of the conferences that prepared the way for the formation of the World Council of Churches following World War II). In 1928 he became the speaker for the Federal Council of Churches radio show on NBC. During the eight years he hosted the show, he emerged as one of the most well-known preachers in the United States. In 1931 his own denomination merged with the Christian Church, and in 1934 the National Council of Congregational and Christian Churches elected him as its moderator, the highest elected office in the denomination.

Sources:

Cadman, S. Parkes. *Charles Darwin and Other English Thinkers*. Boston: Pilgrim Press, 1911. 284 pp.

_____. *The Christ of God*. New York: Macmillan Publications, 1929. 180 pp.

_____. *Christianity and the State*. New York: Macmillan Company, 1924. 370 pp.

_____. *The Parables of Jesus*. Philadelphia: David McKay Company, 1931. 163 pp.

_____. *The Prophets of Israel*. New York: Macmillan Company, 1933. 197 pp.

Dictionary of American Biography. 20 vols. and 7 supps. New York: Charles Scribner's Sons, 1928-1936, 1944-1981.

Leiper, H. S., and E. D. Staples. *S. Parkes Cadman: A Great Churchman and Christian*. Boston: N.p., 1967. 65 pp.

Peel, Albert. *The Congregational Two Hundred*. London: Independent Press, Ltd, 1948. 288 pp.

★ 157 ★
CADY, Harriet Emilie
Author, Unity School of Christianity
b. 1848, Dryden, New York
d. Jan. 3, 1941, New York, New York

Harriet Emilie Cady, one of the first woman physicians in America, was the author of *Lessons in Truth*, the first textbook of the Unity School of Christianity. She became and remains one of the most popular authors of the New Thought movement of the late-nineteenth century. Cady was born in Dryden, New York, the daughter of Oliver and Cornelia Cady. Little is known of her early life.

In the late nineteenth century, following her graduation from the Homeopathic College in New York City, Cady established a medical practice in the city. Early in her career, she became intrigued with the ministry of Albert Benjamin Simpson, the founder of the Christian and Missionary Alliance (CMA) and one of the first proponents of a faith healing ministry. She attended many of his services, but while intrigued by his healing and the necessity of a bridge between medicine and religion, she did not accept his theology or revivalistic practices. She also read the books of metaphysical healer Warren Felt Evans during this time.

In November 1887, Cady attended a Christian Science class given by independent teacher **Emma Curtis Hopkins**, who was finally able to reconcile Cady's several divergent concerns. Shortly after attending the class, Cady authored a booklet, "Finding the Christ in Ourself." This booklet fell into the hands of **Charles Fillmore**, also a former Hopkins student and then editor of *Unity Magazine*. Through Hopkins, Fillmore contacted Cady and invited her to write for the magazine. The first article, "Neither Do I Condemn Thee," appeared in January 1892. Two years later, Fillmore invited Cady to write a set of lessons that would systematically present Unity's perspective. These appeared in 12 installments and were later printed as a book, *Lessons in Truth*, which remains one of the standard introductory Unity texts.

Cady's thought emphasized the identification of God as Spirit, the intangible but very real something humans call Life, the Source of Being. People have access to God through the central "I" of our being which Cady identified with God. Following Hopkins' lead, Cady stressed a method of spiritual advancement and course of healing which emphasized the use of formal denials of the condition of the visible mortal self and affirmations of the reality of the true inner godly self.

Through her single book, Cady became second only to Fillmore in shaping Unity's life and thought. She wrote a second popular book, *God, A Present Help*, and a number of her articles were later collected into a book, *Miscellaneous Writings* (later retitled *How I Used Truth*). In spite of her popularity, Cady never became a public personality, choosing to live quietly in New York and conduct her medical practice. She never married. She died in 1941 after a six-month illness.

Sources:

Cady, H. Emilie. *God, A Present Help*. New York: R. F. Fenno & Company, 1912. 117 pp.

_____. *Lessons in Truth*. Kansas City, MO: Unity School of Christianity, 1919. 174 pp.

_____. *Miscellaneous Writings*. Rev. ed. as, *How I Used Truth*. Lees' Summit, MO: Unity School of Christianity, 1934.

Pomeroy, Ella, "From Medicine to Metaphysics." *The New Thought Bulletin* 29, 1-2 (Winter-Spring 1946): 3-5.

Wilson, Ernest C. "Dr. H. Emilie Cady, Author with Authority." *Unity* 159, 6 (June 1979): 4-9.

★ 158 ★
CAESAR, Shirley
Evangelist and Gospel Singer, Mt. Calvary Holy Church
b. Oct. 13, 1938, Durham, North Carolina

Shirley Caesar, outstanding gospel singer and minister/evangelist with the Mt. Calvary Holy Church, is the daughter of the Reverend Jim and Haille Caesar. Her father, who was a gospel quartet singer with a group known as Just Come Four, died when she was a child, and she was raised by her mother. She attended North Carolina Central College for a while and later completed her business degree at Shaw University, but from childhood seemed destined to find her career in music. Caesar made her first appearance at the age of eight and within two years was singing in the Caesar Sisters, a quartet which included her sisters Anne and Joyce and a cousin Esther. She later sang with the Charity Singers, and interrupted her college work in 1958 to join the Caravans. In 1961 she became an evangelist.

In 1966 Caesar left the Caravans and put together her own music group which featured her as soloist. She was an immediate success, and in 1972 she became the first black female gospel singer to win a Grammy award for her recording of "Put Your Hand in the Hand of the Man from Galilee." In 1982 she won a Dove Award from the Gospel Music Association.

Caesar married Harold Ivoy Williams, a minister (now bishop) with the Mt. Calvary Holiness Church. The wedding became a event within gospel music circles, with over 2,500 in attendance. In 1983, after her marriage, she and her husband became co-pastors of the Mt. Calvary Baptist Holy Church in Winston-Salem, North Carolina.

Sources:

Dupree, Sherry Sherrod. *Biographical Dictionary of African-American, Holiness-Pentecostals, 1880-1990*. Washington, DC: Middle Atlantic Regional Press, 1990. 386 pp.

Lawson, Steven. "Shirley Caesar Remembers Her Mom," *Charisma* 15, 10 (May 1990): 52.

★ 159 ★
CALLIMACHOS, Panos Demetrios
Priest Greek Orthodox Archdiocese of North and South America
Activist, Hellenism
b. Dec. 4, 1879, Madytos, Dardanelles Turkey
d. Oct. 13, 1963, New York, New York

Panos Demetrios Callimachos, a leading priest of the Greek Orthodox Archdiocese of North and South America, was born Demetrios Paximadas, the son of Panagiotis and Grammatiki Paximadas. He attended college in Constantinople and Smyrna, and did his divinity work at the University of Athens, from which he received a D.D. degree in 1902. He grew to manhood in some of the darker days of Greek history, Greece having suffered a humiliating defeat in a war with Turkey in 1898. Callimachos became a strong proponent of Hellenism, the advocacy of the advancement of the Greek people, especially with regard to the recovery of the territory lost in the war. This was his main endeavor in the years after his graduation.

In 1906 Callimachos became secretary to the Patriarchate of Alexandria. Two years later he married Olga Andres. He served briefly as a chaplain during the Balkan War (1912-1913) but stayed with the patriarch until 1914 when he migrated to America. Callimachos' purpose in migrating to the United States was to revitalize the Panhellenic Union as an instrument to foster the Hellenic spirit among Greek Americans. He became editor of the *National Herald*, a daily newspaper in Greek. He argued for a more democratic government in Greece and supported Greece joining the Allies in World War I as a means of regaining her lost territory. In 1918 he briefly left the *Herald* to become a priest at St. Constantine's Church in Brooklyn, but returned in 1922.

During the 1920s, Callimachos emerged as a champion, opposing the Americanization of the Greek community and church. He argued effectively for the perpetuation of the Greek language and traditions, and authored a number of books, all in Greek. As the editor of the *Herald* he became one of the major leaders in the church throughout its upheavals in the 1930s, its continued growth, and the eventual establishment of the archdiocese. His opinions helped mold the life of the church for several decades.

In 1944 he again resigned from the *Herald*, this time over disagreements with its new owner. He then became editor of *Eleutheros (Free Press)*. During the last phase of World War II and the year immediately after the war, he became a bitter enemy of the Communists within the Greek community and lessened his attacks upon the royalists, a king being preferable in his vision to a Communist.

In 1947 Callimachos returned to the *Herald* as editor emeritus. He devoted his last years to work within the larger Greek-American community, and was increasingly recognized and honored for his lifetime of work on its behalf. He continued to promote Hellenism, although his particular perspective bequeathed to him in childhood was seen as an obsolete position by his younger contemporaries in light of the political changes produced by World War II.

Sources:

Dictionary of American Biography. 20 vols. and 7 supps. New York: Charles Scribner's Sons, 1928-1936, 1944-1981.

★ 160 ★
CAMPBELL, Will Davis
Minister, Southern Baptist Convention
b. Jul. 18, 1924, Amite County, Mississippi

Will D. Campbell, a Southern Baptist Convention minister best known for his work for civil rights in the 1960s and 1970s, was born into a Baptist family in southern Mississippi. His father had at one time aspired to the ministry, but became a farmer instead. At the age of seven Campbell was converted in a Baptist church and quite early in life decided to be a preacher. He began to preach during his teen years and was ordained by his church at the age of 17. He enrolled in Louisiana College but dropped out after a year and joined the Army during World War II.

Campbell served as a medic in the South Pacific, and while there he began to meditate upon the plight of southern Blacks. The reading of Howard Fast's *Freedom Road* had a marked effect upon him and led to his decision to spend his life dealing with what he termed the "tragedy of the South." He finished his military service and returned to marry Brenda Fisher, a Louisiana College girlfriend, and complete his bachelor's degree at Wake Forest College from which he graduated in 1948. He then earned a master's degree in English literature from Tulane and a B.D. from Yale Divinity School in 1952. He began his professional career at Taylor Baptist Church in northern Louisiana. In 1954 he moved to the University of Mississippi as the school's director of religious life. While at the university, his commitment to civil rights raised one issue after another, culminating in the university's canceling of a speaker scheduled for a religious emphasis week. The cancelled speaker was an Episcopal priest who had supported the NAACP. Campbell retaliated by staging an hour for reflection before the empty stage.

In 1956 Campbell moved to Nashville, Tennessee, to work with the National Council of Churches Department of Racial and Cultural Relations. As one of the few Southern, white religious leaders publicly working for civil rights in the South, he found himself in some unique and historic situations. He was the only white person present for the formation of **Martin Luther King, Jr.**'s Southern Christian Leadership Conference. Campbell was there when the first black children enrolled in the white public schools of Little Rock, Arkansas. He frequently found himself in the middle of civil rights negotiations as the movement grew and shifted across the South.

Campbell worked with the Council of Churches for seven years, simultaneously writing his first book, *Race and Renewal in the Church* (1962). About the time the book appeared, he was asked in an informal theological discussion to summarize the gospel in a brief sentence. He replied, "We are all bastards but God loves us anyway." He was then challenged to apply that gospel to white southerners, in particular a sheriff who had recently shot a student registering black voters. The challenge made him realize that, in a most unchristian manner, he had been taking sides. He was now forced to see the problems of, and even sympathize with, his fellow Whites whom he also saw as oppressed, as victims of the system. Some statements in this regard angered his superiors, and eventually he resigned rather than submit to their censorship of his public statements, which touched on his sympathies toward Whites.

His break with the council led to the formation of the Committee of Southern Churchmen, an informal gathering of people who shared Campbell's radical perspective. Through its journal, *Katallagete*, Campbell and the committee speculated on a variety of problems, and they touched a broad spectrum of people from poor Blacks to the exploited, poor, white lower class. The work of the committee led Campbell to emerge as a prophet who targeted institutions of all types as the victimizers of the poor, the outcast, and the dispossessed. His message became paradoxical. While seeing institutions as the embodiment of evil, he was aware of the necessity of participating in them to some extent, especially if one wanted to effectively correct injustice.

As the work of the committee ended and its constituents moved on, Campbell settled in Mt. Juliet on a farm. He is now established as a minister to those who come to visit, especially those alienated from the institutional church, an institution believed no less evil than secular ones. He again was in the news in the 1980s for ministering to Ku Klux Klansmen. During this time he has partially supported himself through writing books, including: *Brother to a Dragonfly* (1977); *The Glad River* (1982); *Cecelia's Sin* (1983); and *God on Earth: The Lord's Prayer for Our Time* (1983). He has also written two autobiographical volumes: *An Oral History with Will Davis Campbell, Christian Preacher* (1980) and *Forty Acres and a Goat: A Memoir* (1986).

Sources:
Campbell, Will D. *Brother to a Dragonfly*. New York: Seabury Press, 1977.
_____. *Cecelia's Sin*. Macon, GA: Mercer University Press, 1983.
_____. *Forty Acres and a Goat: A Memoir*. Atlanta, GA: Peachtree, 1986.
_____. *The Glad River*. New York: Holt, Rinehart and Winston, 1982.
_____. *Race and the Renewal of the Church*. Philadelphia: Westminister Press, 1962.
_____, with Bonnie Campbell and Will McBride. *God on Earth: The Lord's Prayer for Our Time*. New York: Crossroad, 1983.
Connelly, Thomas L. *Will Campbell and the Soul of the South*. New York: Continuum, 1982.
Lippy, Charles H. *Twentieth-Century Shapers of American Popular Religion*. New York: Greenwood Press, 1989. 494 pp.

★ 161 ★
CANDLER, Warren Akin
Bishop, Methodist Episcopal Church, South
b. Aug. 23, 1857, Villa Rica, Georgia
d. Sep. 25, 1941, Atlanta, Georgia

Warren Akin Candler, a bishop in the Methodist Episcopal Church, South, was the son of Samuel Charles and Martha Beale Candler, and grew up in Georgia in the Reconstruction era following the Civil War. He attended Emory College, from which he graduated in 1857, a time when few southern Methodist ministers attended college, and fewer still attended seminary. At the time of his graduation, he joined the North Georgia Conference of the Methodist Episcopal Church, South. Two years later he married Nettie Cartwright. He rose rapidly to a place of prominence in the conference and after serving pastorates for 11 years, became the assistant editor of the church's periodical, *Christian Advocate*, then being issued from Nashville, Tennessee. In 1886 he also was elected as a delegate to the church's general conference.

In 1888 Candler became the president of the college he had graduated from a decade before. During his 10 years as a college president he was again elected to return to general conference in 1890 and to be a delegate to the Ecumenical Methodist Conference of 1891. Then in 1898 he was elected bishop.

As a bishop, beyond his normal administrative duties, he was an active author. He wrote, among other titles: *Christus Auctor* (1900); *Great Revivals and the Great Republic* (1904); *Wesley and His Work* (1912); *Life of Thomas Coke* (1923); *The Christ and the Creed* (1927); and *Bishop Charles Butts Galloway, A Prince of Preachers and a Christian Statesman* (1927). He also served as co-chairman on the joint commission (with the Methodist Episcopal Church) to produce a new hymnal for the two churches (1930-1934).

In 1914 the Methodist Episcopal Church, South severed its connection to Vanderbilt University, and Candler headed a church committee to deal with the loss. It decided to support two universities, one on either side of the Mississippi River. Southern Methodist University was the chosen school for the west, while Emory College was moved from Oxford, Georgia, to become Emory University in Atlanta. Bishop Candler's brother gave an initial gift of one million dollars to the project. Candler became its chancellor from 1914 until 1921. Almost immediately a school of theology (later renamed after Candler) was opened, and during Candler's tenure, the Lamar School of Law (1916), a School of Business Administration (1919), and a Graduate School of Arts and Sciences (1919) were added.

Candler is perhaps most remembered as a strong opponent of the Methodist union of 1939 which merged the Methodist Episcopal Church, South, the Methodist Episcopal Church and the Methodist Protestant Church into the Methodist Church (1939-1968). A staunch conservative in racial and political matters, he was one of the leaders in defeating the merger proposal of 1922. However, once union was accepted in 1938, he spoke against those who left the church over the merger.

After his retirement he lived his few remaining years in Atlanta and was buried at Oxford, Georgia. He was but one member of his family who became prominent in the life of the Methodist Episcopal Church, South and southern life in general during the twentieth century.

Sources:
Candler, Warren Akin. *The Christ and the Creed*. Nashville, TN: Cokesbury Press, 1927. 134 pp.
_____. *Christus Auctor*. Nashville, TN: Barbie and Smith, 1900. 255 pp.
_____. *Current Comments on Timely Topics*. Nashville, TN: Cokesbury Press, 1926. 280 pp.
_____. *Easter Meditations*. Nashville, TN: Cokesbury Press, 1930. 116 pp.
_____. *Great Revivals and the Great Republic*. Nashville, TN: Publishing House of the Methodist Episcopal Church, South, 1904. 344 pp.
_____. *The History of Sunday Schools*. New York: Phillips and Hunt, 1880. 149 pp.
_____. *The Life of Thomas Coke*. Nashville, TN: Publishing House of the Methodist Episcopal Church, South, 1923. 408 pp.
_____. *Wesley and His Work*. Nashville, TN: Publishing House of the Methodist Episcopal Church, South, 1912. 223 pp.
Dempsey, Elam Franklin, ed., *Wit and Wisdom of Warren Akin Candler*. Nashville, TN: Cokesbury Press, 1922. 285 pp.
Harmon, Nolan B. *The Encyclopedia of World Methodism*. 2 vols. Nashville: United Methodist Publishing House, 1974.
Pierce, Alfred Mann. *Giant Against the Sky, the Life of Warren Akin Candler*. New York: Abingdon-Cokesbury, 1948. 270 pp.

★ 162 ★
CANNON, Abraham Hoagland
Mormon Leader
b. Mar. 12, 1859, Salt Lake City, Utah
d. Jul. 19, 1896, Salt Lake City, Utah

Abraham Hoagland Cannon, a prominent Mormon leader who continued the practice of polygamy after the 1890 manifesto abolishing its practice in the Church of Jesus Christ of Latter-day Saints, was the son of **George Quayle Cannon**, a prominent church leader, and his first wife, Elizabeth Hoagland. He was raised in a polygamous family; his father married two plural wives. As a youth, Abraham worked at the *Deseret News*, was apprenticed as a carpenter and architect during the building of the temple in Salt Lake City, and eventually graduated from the University of Deseret.

Cannon was married for the first time in 1878, to Sarah A. Jenkins. The following year he married Wilhelmina M. Cannon, a cousin. He entered plural marriage just as the intense effort by the United States government to abolish its practice was growing. About this same time he also began a three-year mission in Europe. Upon his return in 1882, he entered into the printing business with his father and brother and helped develop George Q. Cannon & Sons Publishing Company into a major publishing house. Through the decades of work with his father, he diversified his business interests, which included railroads, mining, banking, and furniture. He also owned a stationery and book store in Ogden, Utah. In 1892 Cannon & Sons, which he and his brother headed, took control of the *Deseret News*, Salt Lake City's leading newspaper. Cannon's success in business paralleled his rise in the church. In 1882 he was invited to became a church official as a member of the First Council of the Seventy, and by the end of the decade he was a member of the Quorum of the Twelve Apostles.

Cannon, like his father, was committed to the principle and practice of plural marriage. In 1886 he openly confessed his status and was convicted of "unlawful cohabitation." He was fined $300 and spent six months in the Utah penitentiary. Cannon's commitment to plural marriage continued through the period immediately after the passing of a manifesto that ended polygamy. During the 1890s, in a number of instances, plural marriages were conducted outside of the United States with the approval of church authorities. In 1896 Cannon contracted such an additional plural marriage, to Lillian Hamblin. They were married off the coast of California. Several weeks after the marriage, however, Cannon contracted meningitis following surgery for a chronic mastoid infection and died. The child of his last marriage, Marba Cannon, was born eight months later.

Sources:

Jensen, Andrew. *Latter Day Saints Biographical Encyclopedia* 4 vols. Salt Lake City, UT: Andrew Jensen History Co., 1901.
Van Wagner, Richard S., and Steven C. Walker. *A Book of Mormons*. Salt Lake City, UT: Signature Books, 1982. 454 pp.

★163★
CANNON, Franklin Jenne
Mormon Leader
b. Jan. 25, 1859, Salt Lake City, Utah
d. Jul. 25, 1933, Denver, Colorado

Franklin Jenne Cannon, the dissenting member of the prominent Cannon family in the Church of Jesus Christ of Latter-day Saints, was born to **George Quayle Cannon** and his second wife, Jane Jenne. In 1882, four years after his marriage to Martha Brown, Cannon faced his first problem with the church after fathering an illegitimate child. He publicly confessed and was not excommunicated. However, for many years afterward, he was periodically drunk and in attendance at the local brothel in Salt Lake City.

In 1886 Cannon was convicted of assaulting the district attorney who was actively pursuing evidence against Cannon's father. He served a brief prison term. Apparently, about this same time, he was busy writing a book, the *Life of Joseph Smith the Prophet*. The published book was quite acceptable to its Mormon audience. Because of Cannon's reputation, however, the publisher cited Cannon's father as the author.

As the intensity of the anti-polygamy crusade in Utah reached its climax, Cannon became active in politics and was among the organizers of the Republican Party in Utah. In 1890, at his father's request, he went to Washington to lobby against the Cullom-

Strubble Bill, which sought to disenfranchise all Mormons. Cannon later claimed that his negotiations between church leaders and leaders in Congress led directly to the issuance of the church's anti-polygamy manifesto in September 1890.

Cannon continued to be active in politics through the 1890s. In 1892 and 1896 he was a delegate to the Republican national convention, and he served as Utah's territorial delegate to Congress in 1895-1896. Following the proclamation of Utah's statehood, Cannon overcame the church's early support of his father to become the first senator elected from the new state.

The brevity of his career as a senator seems to have been determined by silver and sugar. In 1896 he strongly supported the re-monitization of silver, a position that the Republican Party did not accept. Cannon was among those "Silver Republicans" who that year supported Democrat **William Jennings Bryan**. Then in 1898 he became the only Republican to vote against the Dingley Tariff, which the extensive sugar interests in Utah wanted. He lost the election in 1898 and in 1900 joined the Democratic Party. He continued to show his concern for the issues growing out of the silver controversy and served as chairman of the International Silver Commission and as president of the Bimetalical Association in Denver, Colorado.

In 1903 Cannon became editor of the *Utah State Journal*, aligned to the Democratic Party, and when that paper failed he became editor of the *Salt Lake Journal*. As an editor, he launched a campaign against the church's control of the state's political machinery. He attacked **Joseph Fielding Smith, Sr.**, the church president, for re-establishing an absolute control of church members that extended to all areas of life, especially the political. When he refused suggestions that he voluntarily withdraw, he was excommunicated in 1905. He summarized his attack in an autobiographical book, *Under the Prophet in Utah* (1911). He followed it with a second book, *Brigham Young and His Mormon Empire* (1913).

Cannon died in 1933 of an infection following surgery.

Sources:

Cannon, Frank J. *Brigham Young and His Mormon Empire*. New York: Fleming H. Revell, 1913. 398 pp.
_____, and Harvey J. O'Higgins. *Under the Prophet in Utah*. Boston, MA: C. M. Clark Publishing Co., 1911. 402 pp.
Van Wagoner, Richard S., and Steven C. Walker. *A Book of Mormons*. Salt Lake City, UT: Signature Books, 1982. 454 pp.

★164★
CANNON, George Quayle
Writer, Editor, Church of Jesus Christ of Latter-day Saints
b. Jan. 11, 1827, Liverpool United Kingdom
d. May 12, 1901, Monterey, California

George Quayle Cannon, a key leader in the Church of Jesus Christ of Latter-day Saints at the height of the polygamy controversy, was the son of George Cannon and Ann Quayle Cannon. His family was converted to Mormonism by **John Taylor**, who had met and married Cannon's aunt in Canada. Taylor had been sent to England on a mission in 1842. The family immigrated to Nauvoo, Illinois, where the church had established headquarters. Cannon's mother died at sea, however, and his father died soon after their arrival in their new home. George was subsequently adopted by John Taylor.

Following the death of **Joseph Smith, Jr.**, the prophet and founder of the Church of Jesus Christ of Latter-day Saints, Cannon moved to Salt Lake City with the Taylors. He went on his first mission to California in 1849 and in 1850 accompanied a group to Hawaii. They initiated what became a fruitful mission among native Hawaiians. While there, Cannon began to translate the Book of Mormon into Hawaiian. He returned to Salt Lake City in 1854 to marry his first wife, Elizabeth Hoagland, whom he took to San Francisco, California, where the Hawaiian Book of Mormon was printed. He stayed on to edit the *Western Standard*, the church's paper, and in 1856 succeeded Parley Pratt as head of the mission.

Following his work in California, Cannon was sent to head the Eastern States Mission in 1958 and two years later to England to preside over the European Mission. Prior to his leaving for England, Brigham Young, then the president of the church, ordained him an apostle. He remained in England for four years except for a brief and unsuccessful mission in Washington as a delegate from the "State of Deseret." It was his job to lobby for statehood, but the petition was denied, and in its place the first federal anti-polygamy laws were passed. Upon his return to Utah in 1864 Cannon became the personal secretary of Brigham Young. During his three years with Young he became concerned about the relative lack of attention being paid to the children growing up in Utah. In 1866 he launched the *Juvenile Instructor*, a periodical for youth, and the following year he became the general superintendent of the newly founded Sunday School Union, a post he held for the rest of his life.

In 1872 Cannon was named Utah's territorial delegate to Congress, a post he held for nine years until his expulsion because of his polygamy. Over the years he married four additional wives: Jane Jenne, Eliza Lamercia Tenny, Martha Telle, and Caroline Young Croxall, Brigham Young's daughter. During this time he also developed his business interests in cooperation with his sons. He soon had considerable wealth derived from mining, publishing, banking, sugar, and the railroads. He was also a prolific writer. His books included *My First Mission*, *The Life of Nephi*, *The Latter-day Prophet: Young People's History of Joseph Smith*, and the *Life of Joseph Smith the Prophet*. This latter volume, though issued in Cannon's name, seems to have been written primarily by his son, **Frank J. Cannon**. In 1873 he was appointed as special counselor to the First Presidency of the church and served under three presidents until his death in 1901.

As the anti-polygamy campaign intensified in the mid-1880s, Cannon became a fugitive. He was arrested in 1886 but released on bond. Forfeiting the bond, he returned to an underground existence. In a deal arranged by his son, Frank J. Cannon, Cannon surrendered himself in 1888, pleaded guilty to two charges of unlawful cohabitation, and served 175 days in prison. Following his release from prison and the issuance of the church's manifesto against polygamy, Cannon lived a relatively quiet last decade, managing his business interests and traveling for the church. Among the highlights of his travel was his trip to Hawaii for the mission's jubilee celebration in 1900. He died of the grippe a few months later.

Sources:

Cannon, George Quayle. *The Latter-day Prophet: Young People's History of Joseph Smith*. Salt Lake City, UT: Deseret Book Company, 1914. 192 pp.

_____. *Life of Joseph Smith the Prophet*. Salt Lake City, UT: Juvenile Instructor Office, 1888. 512 pp.

_____. *The Life of Nephi*. Salt Lake City, UT: Juvenile Instructor Office, 1883. 108 pp.

_____. *My First Mission*. Salt Lake City, UT: Juvenile Instructor Office, 1879. 66 pp.

Cannon, M. Hamlin. "Prison Diary of a Mormon Apostle." *Pacific Historical Review* 16 (November 1947): 395-409.

Evans, Beatrice Cannon, and Janath Russell Cannon, eds. *Cannon Family Historical Treasury*. Salt Lake City, UT: G. Q. Cannon Family Association, 1967.

Jensen, Andrew. *Latter Day Saints Biographical Encyclopedia* 4 vols. Salt Lake City, UT: Andrew Jensen History Co., 1901.

Van Wagoner, Richard S., and Steven C. Walker. *A Book of Mormons*. Salt Lake City, UT: Signature Books, 1982. 454 pp.

★165★
CAOUETTE, Aurelia
Founder, Sisters and Adorers of the Precious Blood, Roman Catholic Church
b. Jul. 11, 1833, St. Hyacinth, Quebec, Canada
d. Jul. 6, 1905, St. Hyacinth, Quebec, Canada

Aurelia Caouette, the founder of the Sisters and Adorers of the Precious Blood, an order of nuns within the Roman Catholic Church, was the daughter of Joseph and Marguerite Olivier Caouette. She entered the boarding school of the Sisters of the Congregation of Notre Dame. When she finished her five years of schooling and returned home, she became increasingly ill and in 1851 was sent to a hospital to recover. At the hospital she encountered people who accepted her explanation that her sufferings were of supernatural origin, and who understood the visions she had seen and voices she had heard. She was convinced that she would be united with Jesus through his sufferings. Recovering in 1852, she took a vow of virginity and took the name Catherine, for Saint Catherine of Alexandria. Her visions and periods of ecstasy increased. She wished to enter a contemplative order, but none existed at that time in Quebec.

In 1854, following a vision of St. Dominic, Catherine entered the third order of the Dominicans. Over the next few years, the extraordinary experiences in her life and in those who were around her continued. In 1858 she began to experience the stigmata, bleeding from her forehead and the palms of her hands, as Christ is pictured bleeding while on the cross.

In 1859, while on retreat in Montreal, Bishop Ignace Bourget of Montreal suggested that Sister Catherine consider the founding of a new contemplative order, the Sisters and Adorers of the Precious Blood. His suggestion was confirmed in a vision of Jesus, and two years later, Bishop Joseph LaRocque, the recently appointed bishop of St. Hyacinth, authorized the first community of sisters. Sister Catherine was named superior of the group.

During the rest of her life, Sister Catherine lived primarily at St. Hyacinth, but was periodically called away on duties as the new order expanded. In 1869 she journeyed with a group of sisters to inaugurate the foundation of a monastery in Montreal which opened in 1874. In 1882, reacting to complaints about the lack of austerity at the monastery at St. Hyacinth, the bishop appointed a vice-superior who assumed administrative duties. Finding little substance to the complaints, he soon turned the control of the order back to Sister Catherine.

The next few years were times of rapid expansion of the order with centers opened in Ottawa (1887), Three Rivers (1889), Sherbrooke (1895), and Nicolet (1896). The work expanded to the United States with houses in Brooklyn, New York (1890); Portland, Oregon (1892); and Manchester, Massachusetts. Sister Catherine was unable to attend the inauguration of an eleventh center in 1902 in Havana, Cuba.

In 1893 Pope Leo XIII named Sister Catherine superior general of the order for life and sent definitive approval of the order's rules and constitution. During the last years of her life, her health began to fail her. She died in 1905 at the monastery at St. Hyacinth.

Sources:

Maric, Raymond. *Aurelia Caouette, A Soul Afire With Love for God*. Torino, Italy: Stige-Torino Fotogravure Sele Offset, 1986. 30 pp.

★166★
CARBERRY, John Joseph
Cardinal, Roman Catholic Church
b. Jul. 31, 1904, Brooklyn, New York

John Joseph Carberry, a cardinal in the Roman Catholic Church, was raised in an Irish Catholic family in Brooklyn, New York. He is a product of Catholic parochial education and finished his high school years at the diocesan preparatory seminary. He then went to Rome and studied at the North American College. He was ordained in Rome in 1929. He finished his education at Catholic University in Washington, D.C., where he concentrated on canon law and earned three degrees—the S.T.D., Ph.D., and J.C.D. After completing his studies, he served as curate at Glen Cove, New York, and at Huntington, New York. In 1935 he moved to Trenton, New Jersey, as secretary to the bishop and assistant chancellor of the diocese. In 1941 he returned to Brooklyn as an instructor in the diocesan seminary and in 1945 was named *officialis* (marriage judge).

Carberry was consecrated assistant bishop of Lafayette (Indiana) in 1956. The following year he succeeded to the post of bishop upon the death of Bishop John George Bennett. He stayed in Lafayette for nine years and as bishop of Lafayette attended the sessions of the Second Vatican Council, where he emerged as a conservative voice who opposed many of the changes brought about by council action. In 1965 he became bishop of Columbus (Ohio). He stayed in Columbus only three years, for in 1968 he was named archbishop of St. Louis (Missouri). In 1969 he was made a cardinal. He serves on the curial Congregation for the Evangelization of Peoples.

As a cardinal, Carberry has emerged as one of the most conservative leaders in contemporary American Catholicism. He has shown the least reaction to the changes heralded by Vatican II and in the intervening years has give little support to changes not specifically mandated by pope and council.

Sources:

MacEoin, Gary, and the Committee for the Responsible Election of the Pope. *The Inner Elite*. Kansas City, MO: Sheed Andrews and McMeel, 1979. 301 pp.

★ 167 ★
CARFORA, Carmel Henry
Archbishop and Primate, North American Old Roman Catholic Church
b. Aug. 27, 1878, Naples Italy
d. Jan. 11, 1958, Chicago, Illinois

Carmel Henry Carfora, who was raised as a Roman Catholic in Naples, Italy, was a cofounder and leader of the North American Old Roman Catholic Church (N.A.O.R.C.C.). In 1895 he entered the Order of Friars Minor. He became a priest in 1901, at the age of 23, at which time he was sent to the United States. His assigned task was to serve as a missionary to Italian immigrants in New York. He later (1906) served in West Virginia. In 1908, however, he ran into conflict with the Apostolic Delegate and decided to break with Rome.

Carfora formed mission bodies from sympathetic followers, and in June of 1912 he incorporated his work as the National Catholic Diocese in North America. Meanwhile he formed a relationship with Bishop Paolo Miraglia-Gulotti, leader of the Italian National Episcopal Church, who may have given Carfora his second ordination. In any case, it is certain that in 1916 Carfora received an ordination to the episcopacy at the hands of the Duc de Landas Berghes, a bishop of Arnold Harris Mathew's Old Roman Catholic Church. In 1917 Landas Berghes and Carfora united their jurisdictions under a new name, North American Old Roman Catholic Diocese, centered in Chicago. When Landas Berghes returned to the Roman Church in 1919, Carfora assumed complete control of the group and renamed it the North American Old Roman Catholic Church.

Over the next several decades, Carfora built a following of as many as 50,000. He solidified his own position as papal in scope and authority, declaring in 1923 his title as "Most Illustrious Lord,

the Supreme Primate." His creed was based on acceptance of pre-Vatican I Roman Catholic theology and practice, with the exception of allowing a married priesthood. His strategy for growth was to build congregations of first generation immigrants, consecrating at least thirty bishops to serve Polish, Lithuanian, Portuguese, Ukranian, Mexican, and most successfully, West Indian constituents.

This coalition gradually eroded in the 1950s with most of his bishops leaving for other jurisdictions. After looking into the possibility of merging with the Ukrainian Orthodox Church, Carfora decided against it. Thirty parishes decided to make that move anyway in 1952.

In his older years Carfora suffered from asthma and heart trouble, which slowed him down. During a stay in a Roman Catholic hospital in Texas in 1953, he was pressured by Roman Catholics to renounce his work, and his episcopal ring was stolen. Shortly thereafter he retired and was leader only in title until his death in 1958 at the age of 80. Although his church remains today as a small cluster of mostly West Indian parishes, Carfora's enduring, though largely unintended, legacy is rather the establishment, through his numerous episcopal consecrations, of many independent Catholic churches in the United States.

Sources:

Anson, Peter. *Bishops at Large*. London: Faber and Faber, 1964. 593 pp.
Carfora, Carmel Henry. *Historical and Doctrinal Sketch of the Old Roman Catholic Church*. Chicago, IL: The Author, 1950. 23 pp.
Melton, J. Gordon. *Biographical Dictionary of American Cult and Sect Leaders*. Garland Reference Library of Social Science, vol. 212. New York: Garland Publishing, 1986. Pruter, Karl, and J. Gordon Melton. *The Old Catholic Sourcebook*. New York: Garland Publishing Company, 1983.
Trela, Jonathan. *A History of the North American Old Roman Church*. Scranton, PA: The Author, 1979. 124 pp.

—Gary L. Ward

★ 168 ★
CARLEBACH, Shlomo
Neo-Hassidic Rabbi
b. 1926, Berlin Germany

Shlomo Carlebach, the popular Neo-Hassidic rabbi and singer, is the son of Rabbi Nephtali Hartwig and Paula Cohn Carlebach. He is the descendent of a family of rabbis, most of whom had aligned themselves with Hassidism, the mystical form of Judaism which emerged in central and eastern Europe in the eighteenth century. Carlebach was but 13 when in 1939 his family left Germany to escape the ever-increasing Nazi persecution of Jews. They emigrated to America, and on the West Side of Manhattan his father founded a synagogue, Kehillath Yaakov. Meanwhile Carlebach began his training at the Lakewood Yeshiva (academy) and Columbia University. As he pursued his rabbinical training, Carlebach began to assist his father with the services at Kehillath Yaakov.

Carlebach's real talent began to manifest itself in other directions, however, when he emerged as a talented singer and guitarist. His modernized Hassidic songs, which he performed accompanying himself on the guitar, struck a responsive cord among contemporary Jewish young people during the 1960s. He began to develop a unique combination of traditional Hassidic mysticism and orthodox Jewish practice that seemed to many to resonate with basic themes in the youthful, "hippie" counter-culture. His form of Judaism included a place for health foods, communalism, and the search for self-fulfillment.

Among the most committed of the respondents to his music and message, in 1969 Carlebach organized the House of Love and Prayer, a *havurot* or commune, in San Francisco. (Havurots had emerged among Jewish youth earlier in the 1960s. Possibly the most famous commune was the Havurot Shalom in Boston.) During the 1970s as many as 40 people lived with the group. Through them Carlebach was responsible for initiating two periodicals—*Holy Beggers' Gazette* and *Tree Journal*. A similar community, Or Chadash, emerged among his followers in Los Angeles.

Since the early 1970s Carlebach has spent a significant part of the years traveling both across America and to Jewish communities abroad. He developed a following in Israel and it was there that a third communal group, Mishav Meot Midin, a communal farm, was formed. Its founding occurred about the same time the House of Love and Prayer disbanded in San Francisco, and several former members of the house moved to Israel.

Through the 1980s, the synagogue, the community, and Israel gave organizational focus to Carlebach's roving ministry. He has adapted his message to the New Age Movement, and feels a new age is coming as humanity recognizes the limitations of scientific knowledge. As a new higher heavenly knowledge spreads among people, Carlebach feels that Jews will have a special role to play, reminding the world that there is only one God. To further his work, he had recorded approximately 20 albums and several songbooks.

Sources:

American Jewish Biographies. New York: Facts on File, 1982. 493 pp.
Jacobs, Susan. "A New Age Jew Revisits Her Roots." *Yoga Journal* (March/April, 1985), 32-34, 59.
"Of God & Blintzes." *The New Sun* 1, 2 (January 1977), 18-22. Shir, Leo. "Shlomo Carlebach and the House of Love and Prayer." *Midstream* (February 1970), 27-42. Weintraub, Michael, and Michele Weintraub. "Rabbi Shlomo Carlebach: Half a Story, Half a Prayer." *New Directions* 27 (1977), 9-15.

★ 169 ★
CARMAN, Albert
Superintendent, Methodist Episcopal Church of Canada
b. Jun. 27, 1833, Matilda Township Canada
d. Nov. 2, 1917, Toronto Canada

Albert Carman, prominent Canadian Methodist educator and leader, was born in what is today Ontario into a family that had left New York after the American Revolution. He attended Dundas High School and Victoria College. While at college, he was converted. Two years after his graduation, he was accepted on trial by the Methodist Episcopal Church in Canada. In 1857 he became professor of mathematics at Belleville Seminary, a new church college, and the following year became its principal. As principal he pioneered a number of innovative measures to strengthen enrollment and ensure financial stability. His efforts resulted in the seminary being chartered as Albert University in 1866. In 1864 he was ordained as an elder in the church.

In 1874 Carmen was elected bishop of the Methodist Episcopal Church in Canada at a time when the western half of the nation was being opened by the railroad. As bishop he emphasized the need for a spiritual life, a disciplined church, an educated ministry, a missionary emphasis (especially in the western provinces), and for cooperation among the various branches of Canadian Methodism. In promotion of these endeavors he became one of the founders of Alma College, a liberal arts school for women at St. Thomas, Ontario.

In 1881 Carman attended the first Methodist Ecumenical Conference in London. He used the occasion to open informal talks with leaders of the other Canadian Methodist groups. As a result, in 1882 he was appointed chairman of the committee which met to work out a plan of union between three Canadian Methodist churches. The union was completed in 1884 by the creation of the Methodist Church in Canada. Carman was one of two superintendents named to head the church, which, following the model of British Methodism, did away with the office of bishop. Carman

served in that role until 1914, when he became general superintendent emeritus.

During his years as superintendent, Carmen took the lead in numerous endeavors at home and abroad. He helped found the Methodist Church of Japan. He led in the formation of the joint committee on union with the Congregational and Presbyterian churches in Canada that eventually led to the formation of the United Church of Canada in 1925. He was also a strong campaigner against what he saw as the evils of society. But while Carman was socially active and a leader in ecumenical concerns, he was theologically a staunch conservative dedicated to the perpetuation of Methodist standards. His theological ideas found expression in one book, *The Guiding Eye or the Holy Spirit's Guidance of the Believer*, but took a more controversial expression in his conflict with leaders of the Methodist theological colleges over the acceptance of modern Biblical criticism, which he rejected.

Under Carman's generation of leadership, Methodism prospered. His work is continued by the United Church of Canada.

Sources:

Harmon, Nolan B. *The Encyclopedia of World Methodism*. 2 vols. Nashville: United Methodist Publishing House, 1974.
Wallace, W. Stewart. *The Macmillan Dictionary of Canadian Biography*. 4th ed., rev. Edited by W. A. McKay. Toronto: Macmillan of Canada, 1978.

★ 170 ★
CARNELL, Edward John
Baptist Theologian
b. Jun. 28, 1919, Antigo, Wisconsin
d. Apr. 25, 1967, Oakland, California

Edward John Carnell, the theologian largely responsible for articulating the contemporary Protestant Neo-Evangelical theological position, was raised in a fundamentalist Baptist home. His early development was heavily influenced by the conflict he observed within fundamentalism between the positive defense of historical Christianity, which he admired, and the often hostile and unloving attitudes displayed by fundamentalist leaders. He attended Wheaton College where he was influenced by **Gordon Clark**, a conservative theologian who had a major interest in apologetics, the intellectual defense of the faith. From Wheaton he moved to Philadelphia, Pennsylvania, to study with **Cornelius Van Til**, the Orthodox Presbyterian theologian at Westminister Theological Seminary. After completing his Th.B. and Th.M. at Westminister, he entered the doctoral program at Harvard in theology. Upon completion he then secured a Ph.D. in philosophy under **Edgar S. Brightman** at Boston University.

In 1945, while pursuing his graduate studies at Harvard, Carnell became pastor of the Baptist church at Marblehead, Massachusetts, and at the same time served as professor of philosophy and religion at Gordon College and Divinity School. During these years he completed his first book, *An Introduction to Christian Apologetics* (1948), which soon became a standard textbook in Evangelical Christian colleges and seminaries. That same year Carnell joined the faculty of the newly created Fuller Theological Seminary in Pasadena, California. Fuller's president, **Harold J. Ockenga**, had the year before coined the term Neo-Evangelicalism to describe a new phase of Christian fundamentalism which, without betraying any of the doctrinal concerns of the older fundamentalism, emphasized academic excellence, concern for social questions, a warmhearted faith, and strong evangelism.

At Fuller, Carnell centered his theological endeavors on apologetics, and over the 20 years he remained in Pasadena he published a significant number of texts which defined the task of Neo-Evangelicalism. Shortly after his arrival his Harvard dissertation was published as *The Theology of Reinhold Niebuhr* (1950). It was followed by *A Philosophy of the Christian Religion* (1952), a companion to his *Apologetics*, and *Christian Commitment* (1957). In 1954 he began a five-year tenure as president of the seminary. During that time he was selected by Westminster Press to represent traditional Protestantism as the author of *The Case for Orthodoxy* (1959), one volume in a series on contemporary theological viewpoints. Carnell emerged as a defender of what is termed propositional revelation, the belief that God's revelation has cognitive content as opposed to it being limited to a sense of His unitive presence.

Carnell died suddenly while attending a conference at the still youthful age of 47. He was remembered by liberal Protestants as an important link between the liberal and conservative movements, as he had moved away from the separatism which characterized classic fundamentalism. A collection of his essays, *The Case for Biblical Christianity* (1969), was published posthumously.

Sources:

Carnell, Edward John. *The Case for Biblical Christianity*. Grand Rapids, MI: William B. Eerdmans Publishing Co., 1969.

_____. *The Case for Orthodox Theology*. Philadelphia: Westminister Press, 1959.

_____. *An Introduction to Christian Apologetics*. Grand Rapids, MI: William B. Eerdmans Publishing Co., 1948.

_____. *A Philosophy of the Christian Religion*. Grand Rapids, MI: William B. Eerdmans Publishing Co., 1952.

_____. *The Theology of Reinhold Niebuhr*. Grand Rapids, MI: William B. Eerdmans Publishing Co., 1950.

Haines, Aubrey B. "Edward John Carnell: An Evaluation." *Christian Century1* (June 7, 1967): 571 pp.

Nelson, Rudolph. *The Making and Unmaking of an Evangelical Mind*. Cambridge: Cambridge University Press, 1987. 252 pp.

Sims, John A. *Edward John Carnell: Defender of the Faith*. Washington, DC: University Press of America, 1979. 175 pp.

★171★
CARRADINE, Beverly
Holiness Minister, Methodist Episcopal Church, South
b. Apr. 4, 1848, Yazoo County, Mississippi
d. 1919

Beverly Carradine, an outstanding holiness evangelist and pastor for the Methodist Episcopal Church, South, had a notable adult career which began and ended in some obscurity. Little is known of his life prior to his conversion to Christianity in 1874. He attended the University of Mississippi for two years (1865-1867) at the close of the Civil War. Soon after his conversion he was called to preach, and before the year was out he joined the Mississippi Conference of the Methodist Episcopal Church, South, was licensed to preach, and was stationed at Vicksburg. In 1876 he was ordained a deacon; he became an elder two years later. He served in Vernon, Madison, Brandon, and Crystal Springs, Mississippi, before transferring to the Louisiana Conference in 1882. He served the St. Charles and Carondelet congregations in New Orleans, and became locally known for his leadership in the fight against the state lottery. In 1889, while at Carondelet, he claimed to have experienced the instantaneous baptism of the Holy Spirit, which is believed by holiness people to confer sanctification or perfection in love.

Soon after his sanctification experience, Carradine transferred to the St. Louis Conference. He served both Centenary and First Church in St. Louis with distinction. In 1890 he issued his first book, *Sanctification*, a classic statement of the holiness position. He also became deeply involved in the so-called "come-out" controversy, in which many Methodists who had received the baptism of the Holy Spirit had grown restless with the Methodist Episcopal Church, South's growing hostility to both the holiness position and the presence of independent holiness associations. Carradine clearly stated the case for those who proposed that Methodists not

leave for independent churches. However, by the time of his second book, *The Second Blessing in Symbol* (1893) Carradine had become convinced that Methodism had become cold to the gospel. In 1893 he resigned his position with the conference and became a local minister. He spent at least part of his next years as an itinerant evangelist and author. For a brief period he pastored the Oliver Gospel Mission in Columbia, South Carolina. Among his many literary productions from this period were *The Old Man* (1896); *The Sanctified Life* (1897); *The Better Way* (1898); *Heart Talks* (1899); and *Graphic Scenes* (1911).

For many years Carradine, a fiery orator, had a successful career as an evangelist and an author, speaking across the United States. Eventually, however, because of his lack of official ministerial relations to the Methodist Church and his refusal to join the independents, he suffered some financial hardship. He found partial relief from the assistance of some ministerial colleagues who learned of his plight. He died in 1919 and was buried in Vicksburg, Mississippi.

Sources:

Carradine, Beverly. *The Better Way*. Cincinnati, OH: M. W. Knapp, 1898. 193 pp.

_____. *Bible Characters*. Chicago: Christian Witness Company, 1907. 250 pp.

_____. *The Old Man*. Noblesville, IN: Newby Book Room, 1965. 270 pp.

_____. *Sanctification*. Syracuse, NY: A. W. Hall, Publisher, 1895. 222 pp.

_____. *The Sanctified Life*. Cincinnati, OH: The Revivalist, 1897. 286 pp.

_____. *The Second Blessing in Symbol*. Louiss

★172★
CARROLL, Benajah Harvey
Educator, Southern Baptist Convention
b. Dec. 27, 1843, Carrolton, Mississippi
d. Nov. 11, 1914, Fort Worth, Texas

Benajah Harvey Carroll, founder of Southwestern Baptist Theological Seminary, was the son of Benajah and Mary Eliza Mallard Carroll. His father was a farmer-preacher, first in Mississippi, then in Arkansas (1848) and Texas (1858). A year after moving to Texas, Carroll entered Baylor University, but before finishing his course of study, he left to join the Texas Rangers and guard the border during the Civil War. In 1862 he transferred to the Confederate Army, where he served for the next three years. Baylor University granted him his A.B. degree even though he never returned to finish his classes.

In 1865 Carroll experienced a Christian conversion and joined a Baptist church at Caldwell, Texas. During the war he had engaged in an intense struggle with skepticism (which would later become the subject of a famous sermon he preached, "My Infidelity and What Became of It"). The following year he was both ordained to the ministry in the Southern Baptist Convention and married to Ellen Virginia Bell. During the rest of the decade he served Providence Baptist Church in Burleson County, Texas, and New Hope Baptist Church in McLennan County, where he also taught school. He developed a reputation for both his preaching ability and his intellect, and in 1870 he was called to Waco, Texas, where Baylor University was located, as pastor of First Baptist Church.

Carroll experienced four productive decades at Waco. In 1872 he joined the university faculty as an instructor in Bible and theology. He authored more than 20 books, including: *The Bible Doctrine of Repentance* (1897); *The Genesis of American Anti-Missionism* (1902); *Baptists and Their Doctrines* (1913); and *Evangelistic Sermons* (1913). The majority of his titles were published posthumously.

Carroll also served in a number of denominational positions in the Texas Baptist Convention and gave freely of his time to promote his favorite causes: evangelism, prohibition, home missions, and Christian education.

As the Baptist work in Texas grew, the need for a separate ministerial training program became evident, and in 1905 Carroll organized the Baylor Theological Seminary, which was then superseded by Southwestern Baptist Theological Seminary (charter granted in 1908). Carroll was named president of Southwestern and moved with it to Fort Worth in 1910. He remained president of the school until his death in 1914, and had a hand in choosing his successor, **Lee R. Scarborough.**

Sources:
Carroll, Benajah Harvey. *Baptists and Their Doctrines*. New York: Fleming H. Revell Co., 1913. 208 pp.
_____. *The Bible Doctrine of Repentance*. Louisville, KY: Baptist Book Concern, 1897. 132 pp.
_____. *The Genesis of American Anti-Missionism*. Louisville, KY: Baptist Book Concern, 1902. 229 pp.
_____. *Inspiration of the Bible*. New York: Fleming H. Revell, 1930. 122 pp.
_____. *Sermons and Life Sketch of B. H. Carroll*. Comp. by J. B. Cranfill. Philadelphia: American Baptist Publication Society, 1895. 466 pp.
Encyclopedia of Southern Baptists. 3 vols. Nashville, TN: Broadman Press, 1958, 1971.

★ 173 ★
CARTER, Gerald Emmett
Cardinal, Roman Catholic Church, Canada
b. Mar. 1, 1912, Montreal, Quebec, Canada

Gerald Emmett Carter, a cardinal and archbishop of Toronto for the Roman Catholic Church, is the son of Thomas Joseph and Mary Kelty Carter. Raised in Montreal, he attended Montreal College and Montreal University, from which he received his B.A. (1933), Th.B. (1936), M.A. (1940), and Ph.D. (1947). He was ordained in 1937 and assigned as supervisor of the Montreal Catholic School Commission. He also founded St. Joseph's Teacher's College, which he headed for a number of years. In 1945 he became a co-founder of the Thomas More Institute for adult education. In 1948 he became rector of St. Lawrence College in Quebec, a post he retained until 1961. While at St. Lawrence, Carter authored three books reflecting upon his experience as an educator: *Catholic Public Schools of Quebec* (1957); *Psychology and the Cross* (1959); and *The Modern Challenge to Religious Education* (1961).

In 1961 Carter was named auxiliary bishop of London, Ontario. He became bishop of London in 1964. In his new office, Carter played a key role in the ongoing liturgical reforms of the era. He was appointed by Pope Paul VI as Canadian representative to the 1966 Consilium for Liturgy which convened in Rome. He also became chairman of the Canadian Liturgical Commission (English Sector) and president of the Office of Liturgy (English Sector) of the Canadian Conference of Catholic Bishops. In 1970 he was made a member of the Sacred Congregation for Divine Worship in Rome, and in 1971 he was named chairman of the International Committee for English in the Liturgy. During his tenure in London, his leadership was recognized by his fellow bishops who elected him vice-president (1971-1973) and president (1975-1977) of the Canadian Conference of Catholic Bishops. In 1978 he was selected as the new archbishop of Toronto, generally recognized as the seat of power for English-speaking Catholics in Canada. He was named a cardinal the following year.

Sources:
Carter, Gerald Emmett. *Catholic Public Schools of Quebec*. Toronto: W. J. Gage, 1957. 128 pp.
_____. *The Modern Challenge to Religious Education*. New York: W. H. Sadler, 1961. 422 pp.
_____. *Psychology and the Cross*. Milwaukee, WI: Bruce Publishing Company, 1959. 135 pp.

★ 174 ★
CARUS, Paul
Philosopher, Author of works on Buddhism
b. Jul. 18, 1852, Ilsenburg Germany
d. Feb. 11, 1919, La Salle, Illinois

Philosopher Paul Carus, although not himself a Buddhist, contributed greatly to the growth of Buddhism in the United States. Born in Germany, his father was First Superintendent of the Protestant state church of Prussia. Following the family emphasis on education, Carus was an excellent scholar; he received a doctorate at Tubingen in 1876, and took a teaching post at the military academy of Dresden. His religious views were considered too liberal, however, and he was forced to resign before very long. He moved to England in 1881, but moved again in 1884, at the age of 32, to America.

In Chicago, in 1887, Carus became editor of *Open Court*, a new journal begun by zinc manufacturer Edward G. Hegler. The journal sought out new ideas in a variety of fields, and Carus contributed many articles himself, particularly in the area of the reformation of religion by science. Carus developed his own monistic philosophy, based on a belief that God is not the traditional transcendent spirit, but rather a way of talking about the logical processes by which the universe functions. People do not have souls that survive their death, but have only the immortality of their influence in the world. This approach made Carus very appreciative of Buddhism's nonsupernaturalism and practical spirit, and he studied it a great deal, though he never claimed to have converted to it.

In 1888 Carus married Hegler's daughter, Mary. The success of *Open Court* led to the founding in 1890 of the *Monist*, a magazine which he also edited, dedicated to more technical philosophical works. In 1893 a major turning point in his life came when he attended the World Parliament of Religions in Chicago and met the Buddhist delegates, **Anagarika Dharmapala** and the Zen monk **Soyen Shaku.** Carus agreed to help introduce Americans to Buddhism by leading Dharmapala's Maha Bodhi Society in the United States, and by arranging Dharmapala's 1896 national tour. Shaku arranged for **Daisetz Teitaro Suzuki** to come to America in 1897, where he stayed with Carus until 1909. Suzuki and Carus worked together translating several works, including the *Tao Te Ching*.

Carus became most well known as the first major American spokesperson for Buddhism. His book, *The Gospel of Buddhism* (1894), was lauded by Buddhists and westerners alike, and was translated into several languages. It was the most successful of the more than 50 books he wrote. His written work was voluminous and wide ranging in scope, including mathematics and poetry. Some of his poems have been set to music and are today included among the hymns of the Buddhist Churches of America. When he died in 1919 at the age of 67, he left behind a legacy which he would appreciate as his appropriate form of immortality.

Sources:
Bowden, Henry Warner. *Dictionary of American Religious Biography*. Westport, CT: Greenwood Press, 1977. 572 pp.
Carus, Paul. *The Canon of Reason and Virtue*. Chicago: Open Court Publishing Co., 1913. 209 pp.
_____. *The Dawn of a New Religious Era*. Chicago: Open Court Publishing Co., 1916. 131 pp.
_____. *The Dharma*. Chicago: Open Court Publishing Co., 1906. 169 pp.
_____. *The Gospel of Buddha*. Chicago: Open Court Publishing Co., 1894. 311 pp.
_____. *Karma, A Story of Buddhist Ethics*. Chicago: Open Court Publishing Co., 1894. 46 pp.
Fields, Rick. *How the Swans Came to the Lake*. Boulder, CO: Shambhala, 1986. 445 pp.
Melton, J. Gordon. *Biographical Dictionary of American Cult and Sect Leaders*. Garland Reference Library of Social Science, vol. 212. New York: Garland Publishing, 1986.

|

Peiris, William. *The Western Contribution to Buddhism*. Delhi, India: Motilal Banarsidas, 1973. 287 pp.
Who Was Who in America. Chicago: Marquis Who's Who, Inc.

—*Gary L. Ward*

★ 175 ★
CASE, Shirley Jackson
Church Historian, Free Baptist Church
b. Sep. 28, 1872, Hatfield Point Canada
d. Dec. 5, 1947, Lakeland, Florida

Shirley Jackson Case, an outstanding Christian church historian, was the son of George F. and Maria Jackson Case, both members of the very liberal Free Baptist Church. He attended Acadia University, from which he received his B.A. (1893) and M.A. (1896). He taught mathematics for a year before moving to the United States to teach Greek at the New Hampshire Literary Institute. He also served as the pastor for the local community church. In 1899 he married Evelyn Hill.

In 1901 Case began work on a divinity degree at Yale University Divinity School. He specialized in early Christianity, and following the reception of his B.D. in 1904 he began the doctoral program, which he completed in 1906. As in New Hampshire, Case pastored nearby churches while pursuing his studies. Immediately after receiving his Ph.D. he began his teaching career at Bates College in the history and philosophy of religion. In 1908 he began a distinguished career as a scholar at the University of Chicago Divinity School. Beginning as an assistant professor of New Testament, he became a professor of church history in 1917 and chairman of the church history department in 1923.

Case authored his first book, *The Historicity of Jesus*, in 1912. It launched his reputation as the foremost exponent of his generation of the sociohistorical method in the study of the early church. The method involved not only a careful attention to factual details and original materials, but a broad understanding of historical events through the environment within which they occurred. Thus, ancient documents were reviewed in the light of the whole cultural context in which they appeared.

Using this rather exacting method, Case delivered a stream of books reviewing the early church beginning with the life of Jesus. His major books were *The Evolution of Early Christianity: A Genetic Study of First Century Christianity in Relation to its Religious Environment* (1914); *The Book of Revelation* (1918); *The Millennial Hope: A Phase of Wartime Thinking* (1918); *The Social Origins of Christianity* (1923); *Jesus: A New Biography* (1927); *Jesus through the Centuries* (1932); *The Social Triumph of the Ancient Church* (1933); *The Christian Philosophy of History* (1943); and *The Origins of Christian Supernaturalism* (1946).

Case is also remembered for his role as department chair in bringing together a singularly outstanding faculty. It included John T. McNeill, Wilhelm Pauck, Matthew Spinka, Charles Lyttle, W. E. Garrison, and William Warren Sweet, each of whom made their own contribution to the development of church history. In 1924 Case became president of the American Society of Church History. The largely moribund organization was brought back to life during his period of leadership, and its periodical, *Church History*, began its regular publication. In 1925 he was elected president of the Chicago Society of Biblical Research and the following year was named president of the Society of Biblical Literature and Exegesis. In 1927 he became editor of the *Journal of Religion*, the divinity school's quarterly.

In 1933 Case became dean of the divinity school, which had come to rival Harvard as the leading center of religious research and higher education in the United States. He retired in 1938. He spent the next year as a special Lecturer as Bexley Hall, the Episcopalian seminary in Ohio, and in 1940 became professor of religion at Florida Southern College and dean of the Florida School of Religion, two posts he held for the rest of his life.

Sources:
Case, Shirley Jackson. *The Book of Revelation*. Chicago: University of Chicago Press, 1918. 38 pp.
_____. *The Christian Philosophy of History*. Chicago: University of Chicago Press, 1943. 221 pp.
_____. *The Evolution of Early Christianity: A Genetic Study of First Century Christianity in Relation to Its Religious Environment*. Chicago: University of Chicago Press, 1914. 385 pp.
_____. *The Historicity of Jesus*. Chicago: University of Chicago Press, 1912. 352 pp.
_____. *Jesus: A New Biography*. Chicago: University of Chicago Press, 1927. 452 pp.
_____. *Jesus through the Centuries*. Chicago: University of Chicago Press, 1932. 381 pp.
_____. *The Millennial Hope: A Phase of Wartime Thinking*. Chicago: University of Chicago Press, 1918. 253 pp.
_____. *The Origins of Christian Supernaturalism*. Chicago: University of Chicago Press, 1946. 239 pp.
_____. *The Social Origins of Christianity*. Chicago: University of Chicago Press, 1923. 263 pp.
_____. *The Social Triumph of the Ancient Church*. New York: Harper & Brothers, 1933. 250 pp.
Dictionary of American Biography. 20 vols. and 7 supps. New York: Charles Scribner's Sons, 1928-1936, 1944-1981.
Jennings, Louis B. *The Bibliography and Biography of Shirley Jackson Case*. Chicago: University of Chicago Press, 1949.
_____. *Shirley Jackson Case: A Study in Methodology*. Chicago: University of Chicago, doctoral dissertation, 1964.

★ 176 ★
CASHWELL, Gaston Barnabas
Pioneer Pentecostal Minister
b. 1860, Sampson County, North Carolina
d. 1916

Gaston Barnabas Cashwell, who introduced Pentecostal Christianity into the Southern United States, was born in rural North Carolina, near the town of Dunn, just as the Civil War began. As a young man Cashwell joined the North Carolina Conference of the Methodist Episcopal Church, South. Around the turn of the century he came under the influence of holiness preacher **Ambrose Blackman Crumpler**. In 1903 he left the Methodists to join the Holiness Church of North Carolina, which had been founded that year by Crumpler.

Cashwell had pastored in the new denomination for several years when he read of a revival in Los Angeles at a mission on Azusa Street, at which the baptism of the Holy Spirit was being poured out. Enthusiastic about the report, he traveled to Los Angeles, where he received the baptism and spoke in tongues (believed by Pentecostal Christians to be the initial evidence of having received the baptism). Cashwell returned to North Carolina just after Christmas in 1906, and on New Year's Eve he introduced the idea of the Pentecostal baptism to his congregation at Dunn. He then sent letters to his fellow holiness ministers, asking them to attend meetings at Dunn during January. At these meetings, most of the ministers of the Holiness Church of North Carolina were baptized in the Spirit. Other Holiness ministers who attended would later be part of the Pentecostal Holiness Church, the Pentecostal Fire-Baptized Holiness Church, and the Pentecostal Free-Will Baptist Church.

During the next months, Cashwell took the new message throughout the South. Cashwell began a periodical, the *Bridegroom's Messenger*, to promote his work. The number of conversions under his ministry in 1907 led to the establishment of the Church of God (Cleveland, Tennessee), the Assemblies of God, and much of Pentecostalism in the South. He was also supported, at least in his early revivals, by Crumpler, who covered his meetings in the *Holiness Advocate*, the periodical of the Holiness Church of North Carolina. By the end of 1907, however, Crumpler had begun to oppose Cashwell's teachings, specifically rejecting the idea that speaking in tongues was the only initial evidence of the baptism of the Holy Spirit. The issue reached its crisis in 1908 at the annual conference of the Holiness Church. The ministers backed Cashwell, though they reelected Crumpler as their church president. Crumpler did not agree with their direction, and the next day he resigned from the church. Cashwell led in rewriting the church's articles of faith to include the new emphasis on pentecostal baptism.

The following year, for reasons not fully understood, Cashwell also left the church and became an independent evangelist. He is most remembered for his contributions to the spread of Pentecostalism in 1907 in the South. Its penetration of southern religious life completely altered the religious character of that region during the twentieth century.

Sources:

Burgess, Stanley M., Gary B. McGee, and Patrick H. Alexander, eds. *Dictionary of Pentecostal and Charismatic Movements.* Grand Rapids, MI: Regency Reference Library, Zondervan Publishing House, 1988. 914 pp.

Hill, Samuel S., ed. *Encyclopedia of Religion in the South.* Macon, GA: Mercer University Press, 1984. 878 pp.

Synan, Vinson. *The Old-Time Power: A History of the Pentecostal Holiness Church.* Franklin Springs, GA: Advocate Press, 1973. 296 pp.

★177★
CAVERT, Samuel McCrea
Ecumenist, United Presbyterian Church in the U. S. A.
b. Sep. 19, 1888, Charlton, New York
d. Dec. 21, 1976, Bronxville, New York

Samuel McCrea Cavert, a major architect of the modern ecumenical movement, grew up in upstate New York. During his years at Union College, he became active in the Young Men's Christian Association (YMCA) and following his graduation in 1910 worked as the director of the student YMCA at Union. He pursued graduate work at Columbia University and Union Theological Seminary, earning his M.A. in philosophy in 1914 and his B.D. in 1915. In 1915 he was ordained as a minister in the Presbyterian Church in the U.S.A. Rather than go into the pastorate, however, he stayed at Union as a assistant to William Adams Brown. He spent a year in India and the Far East before the United States entered World War I and in 1917 he returned to America to begin work with the War-Time Commission of the Churches. In 1918 he married Ruth Miller and about the same time joined the Army as a chaplain. Unfortunately, his marriage was cut short in 1920 by the death of his wife following the birth of their daughter.

In 1921 Cavert began his long association with the Federal Council of Churches as its secretary of the Committee on the War and the Religious Outlook. In 1920 he became the associate secretary of the Federal Council and in 1921 he was appointed general secretary, a position he would hold for the remaining years of the Federal Council. For the first few years he shared the title of general secretary with **Charles S. Macfarland**, but in 1930 the job became his alone. For the next 20 years he epitomized the council's commitment to the ideal of Protestant church unity and the undergirding liberal Protestant theological consensus upon which the ecumenical venture proceeded. In 1927 he married Ruth Twila Lytton.

During the 1930s he became involved with the growing international ecumenical organizations. In 1937 he was one of the leading figures at the meeting of the Committee of Thirty-Five which included his former professor William Adams Brown and Archbishop William Temple. This meeting put together the proposal to form what became the World Council of Churches, a name suggested by Cavert. The following year he became a member of the provision committee of the World Council of Churches and worked to-

ward the successful formation of the council in 1948 in Amsterdam. In the meantime he had also become active in planning for the post-World War II reconstruction of Europe.

In 1950 the Federal Council of Churches merged with several other national organizations to become the National Council of Churches. Cavert became the first executive secretary of the new organization. Four years later he attended the World Council assembly in Evanston, Illinois, and retired from his job with the National Council. During his retirement years he authored two important histories of the ecumenical movement: *The American Churches in the Ecumenical Movement, 1900-1968* (1968) and *Church Cooperation and Unity in America, 1900-1970* (1970).

Sources:

Cavert, Samuel McCrea. *The Adventure of the Church.* New York: Council of Women for Home Missions and Missionary Education Movement, 1927.
_____. *The American Church in the Ecumenical Movement, 1900-1968.* New York: Association Press, 1968. 288 pp.
_____. *Church Cooperation and Unity in America, 1900-1970.* New York: Association Press, 1970. 400 pp.
_____. *On the Road to Christian Unity.* New York: Harper & Brothers, 1961. 192 pp.
_____, and Henry P. Van Dusen. *The Church Through Half a Century.* New York: Charles Scribner's Sons, 1936.
Schmidt, William J. *Architect of Unity: A Biography of Samuel McCrea Cavert.* New York: Friendship Press, 1978. 330 pp.

★178★
CAYCE, Charles Thomas
President, Association for Research and Enlightenment (A.R.E.)
b. Oct. 7, 1942, Virginia Beach, Virginia

Charles Thomas Cayce, the president of the Association for Research and Enlightenment (A.R.E.), is the son of Sally Taylor and **Hugh Lynn Cayce**, and the grandson of psychic **Edgar Cayce**. He was born and raised in Virginia Beach, Virginia, where the Cayce family had moved in 1925 to establish the headquarters for Edgar Cayce's work through the Association for Research and Enlightenment, the Edgar Cayce Foundation, and several related structures. Charles Thomas received his name through a trance reading given by his grandfather immediately after his birth.

Charles Thomas worked at his father's office during his teen years, but after high school left to attend Hampden-Sydney College. His initial plans to become a physician were gradually altered, and he majored in psychology. He knew he did not want to work in Virginia Beach. He continued in post-graduate studies at the University of California in Berkeley and at the University of Maryland, from which he received a Ph.D. in child psychology in 1968. He taught at the University of Maryland for several years and then joined the staff of the U.S. Department of State as an educational consultant.

It was not until 1972 that Charles Thomas returned to Virginia Beach to become the youth director for A.R.E. Over the years he had grown closer to the association's teachings as he found them both personally valuable and useful in his professional life. In 1976 his father suffered a heart attack and retired from his major responsibilities as president of the association. He tapped his son to be his successor. That same year Charles Thomas married Leslie Goodman.

Charles Thomas has brought a somewhat different leadership to A.R.E. He has developed the organization administratively and initiated a research program, while choosing to leave the majority of speaking and public appearances to other staff persons.

Sources:

Smith, A. Robert. *Hugh Lynn Cayce: About My Father's Business.* Norfolk, VA: The Donning Company, 1988. 316 pp.

Zuromski, Paul. "A Conversation with Charles Thomas Cayce." *Psychic Guide* (September/October/November 1984): 14-19.

★ 179 ★
CAYCE, Edgar
Founder, Association for Research and Enlightenment (A.R.E.)
b. Mar. 18, 1877, Hopkinsville, Kentucky
d. Jan. 3, 1945, Virginia Beach, Virginia

Edgar Cayce, one of the most famous psychics of the twentieth century, was the founder of the Association for Research and Enlightenment. The son of a businessman in rural Kentucky, Cayce achieved only a grammar school education. His family belonged to the local Christian Church (Disciples of Christ). In 1898, at the age of 21, Cayce's life was changed when he cured himself of a long-standing laryngitis condition by diagnosing it while in a trance induced by a hypnotist friend. When news of this spread, neighbors began to ask Cayce to do "readings" for them.

In 1903 Cayce moved to Bowling Green, Kentucky, to establish himself as a photographer. Indebtedness from a fire ruined that venture, and in 1909 he moved to Alabama to try photography there. Just before that move, however, he diagnosed and cured Dr. Wesley Ketchum, a homeopathic practitioner in Hopkinsville, Kentucky. Ketchum was very impressed and for a brief time in 1910 he brought Cayce back from Alabama to team up for daily readings for the sick. Cayce was not dependent upon a hypnotist; he could put himself into a trance state. This ability was not unlike that of a number of other psychics who practiced what was called in the nineteenth century "traveling clairvoyance." From 1911 to 1923, Cayce occasionally involved himself in psychic activities, but spent most of his time as a photographer.

In 1923 Cayce was brought to Dayton, Ohio, by Theosophist Arthur Lammers to give metaphysical readings. Under Lammers' coaxing, Cayce found himself able to see the past lives of people, in addition to recognizing their health disorders. This shift in emphasis proved enticing enough to both Cayce and his followers that Cayce was able to close his photography shop and move first to Dayton and then, in 1925, to Virginia Beach, Virginia. There, with the financial backing of businessman Morton Blumenthal, Cayce opened Cayce Hospital (1928) and Atlantic University (1930). His readings and teachings now closely resembled Theosophy, with an emphasis on karma and reincarnation. Unfortunately, his new enterprises were not yet self-supporting when Blumenthal's business failed, and Cayce was forced to start from scratch again.

In 1932 he and a few friends began the Association for Research and Enlightenment, producing a newsletter and keeping records of all Cayce's readings, which he began to give out of his home. These extensive records make the study of Cayce unique; the Association's large library of Cayce's trance statements has provided the basis for its ongoing work and continued attraction.

Cayce collapsed from exhaustion in 1944 and died in early 1945 at the age of 68.

Sources:

Cayce, Edgar. *The Edgar Cayce Reader.* 2 vols. New York: Paperback Library, 1969.
Cayce, Hugh Lynn. *Venture Inward.* New York: Paperback Library, 1966. 207 pp.
Leary, David M. *Edgar Cayce's Photographic Legacy.* Garden City, NY: Doubleday & Company, 1978. 233 pp.
Melton, J. Gordon. *Biographical Dictionary of American Cult and Sect Leaders.* Garland Reference Library of Social Science, vol. 212. New York: Garland Publishing, 1986.
Millard, Joseph. *Edgar Cayce.* Greenwich, CT: Fawcett, 1967. 224 pp.
Neimark, Anne E. *With This Gift.* New York: William Morrow and Company, 1978. 192 pp.
Puryear, Herbert. *The Edgar Cayce Primer.* New York: Bantam Books, 1982. 247 pp.
Shepard, Leslie. *Encyclopedia of Occultism & Parapsychology.* 3 vols., 2nd. ed. Detroit: Gale Research Co., 1984-1985.
Stern, Jess. *A Prophet in His Own Country.* New York: William Morrow and Company, 1974. 301 pp.
Who Was Who in America. Chicago: Marquis Who's Who, Inc.

—*Gary L. Ward*

★ 180 ★
CAYCE, Hugh Lynn
President, Association for Research and Enlightenment (A.R.E.)
b. Mar. 16, 1907, Bowling Green, Kentucky
d. Jul. 4, 1982, Virginia Beach, Virginia

Hugh Lynn Cayce, president of the Association for Research and Enlightenment (A.R.E.) and the related Edgar Cayce Foundation, was the son of Gertrude Evans and **Edgar Cayce**, the famous psychic. During the years of his childhood, his father worked as a photographer, his psychic abilities evident but not yet well known. Hugh Cayce's childhood was punctuated by a dramatic accident in which his eyes were severely burned. Overriding the advice of doctors who wished to remove one eye, Cayce's father went into a trance and prescribed treatments. The eye was saved.

In 1925 the family moved to Virginia Beach, where Edgar Cayce's career as a psychic blossomed. Hugh Lynn attended Norfolk Business College and in 1926 entered Washington and Lee University. At college he met Thomas Segrue, who would later write a biography of Hugh Lynn's father, *There Is a River: The Story of Edgar Cayce.* In 1929 they began to publish a periodical for A.R.E., *The New Tomorrow.* By the time he finished college, Hugh Lynn had developed a new appreciation of his father's work and of the concept of reincarnation, so central to Cayce's teachings. In 1930 he went to work for the association.

Through the 1930s Hugh Cayce helped build the association. In 1941 he married Sally Taylor and two weeks later began a period in the army which lasted through World War II. While he was stationed in Europe at the end of the war, both his parents died. By the time he returned to Virginia Beach, the A.R.E. was almost defunct.

Cayce set about reviving the work without the presence of his father giving regular readings. He reoriented the thrust of the association around research into the many records of Cayce's readings. Two decades of effort began to bear fruit after the publication in 1966 of Cayce's book, *Venture Inward*, and a biography of Cayce's father by Jess Stern, *The Sleeping Prophet* (1967). Their success led to a series of books on Cayce published by Paperback Library. Included in the series was a two-volume compilation of selected Cayce material, *The Edgar Cayce Reader I & II* (1969).

Hugh Lynn led A.R.E. until 1976, when a heart attack forced him to reconsider his position. He called his son, **Charles Thomas Cayce**, to be the new president of A.R.E., and Hugh Lynn became chairman of the board. The slower pace of responsibility allowed him to concentrate on some special topics of interest, and he authored two books in his semi-retired years: *Faces of Fear* (1980) and *Earth Changes Update* (1980). A collection of his speeches on Jesus was published posthumously as *The Jesus I Knew* (1984).

Sources:

Cayce, Hugh Lynn. *Earth Changes Update.* Virginia Beach, VA: A.R.E. Press, 1980. 130 pp.
———. *The Edgar Cayce Reader I & II.* New York: Paperback Library, 1969.
———. *Faces of Fear.* New York: Berkley Books, 1980. 198 pp.
———. *The Jesus I Knew.* Virginia Beach, VA: A.R.E. Press, 1984. 81 pp.
———. *Venture Inward.* New York: Paperback Library, 1966. 207 pp.
Smith, A. Robert. *Hugh Lynn Cayce: About My Father's Business.* Norfolk, VA: The Donning Company, 1988. 316 pp.

★181★
CERULLO, Morris
Healing Evangelist, Assemblies of God
b. Oct. 2, 1931, Passaic, New Jersey

Morris Cerullo, prominent healing evangelist and founder of World Evangelism, was the youngest child of Joseph Cerullo, an Italian, and a Jewish mother. His father was an alcoholic, and his mother died when Morris was two years old. He and his brothers and sisters were placed in a foster home. At the age of eight, he was placed in the Daughters of Miriam Orphanage in Clifton, New Jersey, which was managed by strict orthodox Jews. He studied in the synagogue and learned Hebrew. When he was 14, Helen Kerr came to work at the orphanage. She shared a copy of the Christian New Testament and some literature from the Assemblies of God, with which she was associated, with him. When her actions were discovered, Kerr was dismissed from her position. A short time later, Cerullo ran away from the orphanage and went to live with Kerr's brother in Patterson, New Jersey.

The Sunday after moving into his new home, Cerullo attended the local Assemblies of God church, received the baptism of the Holy Spirit, and began to speak in tongues. He also prophesied that God was calling him to a special work. He began to speak in churches in the surrounding area in New Jersey. About six months later, he had a vision that convinced him of a calling into the ministry with a worldwide emphasis. He also felt a calling to present the Christian message to every Jew on earth before Christ's return.

Cerullo attended Northeastern Bible College. In 1951 he married Theresa Le Pari, and the following year he was ordained by the Assemblies of God as a minister. He pastored an Assemblies of God church in New Hampshire (1952-1953), but then entered full-time evangelism. He later briefly pastored a church in South Bend, Indiana (1959), but then in 1961 founded World Evangelism as an evangelical organization with headquarters in San Diego. In the early years of his ministry, he associated with various evangelists, such as **William Marrion Branham**, who emphasized healing in their evangelical work. This became an emphasis in Cerullo's work as well.

Following the founding of World Evangelism, some 80 percent of Cerullo's ministry was directed toward foreign countries. His first foreign crusade was in Athens, Greece, in 1955. Cerullo came to believe that the only way to accomplish his evangelical task would be through indigenous church leaders, and he began to add schools of ministry to his evangelical efforts. In 1970 he began a new emphasis on North American evangelism. He announced a "new anointing" of God's Spirit that would allow spiritual breakthroughs comparable to those being experienced in science and medicine. By the end of the decade he had conducted services in over 60 cities.

As part of both the foreign and domestic evangelism efforts, Cerullo developed a mission to reach every Jew in the world with the Christian message. He began to broadcast from a station in Cyprus whose signal reached Israel. He developed a Messianic Bible Correspondence Course and claimed during the 1970s to have enrolled 25,000 Israeli Jews. In 1977 he distributed a book, *Two Men from Eden*, to over three million Jewish homes in North America and began translating it into every language spoken by a significant Jewish population.

Over the years Cerullo has authored more than 30 books and maintained a demanding schedule of preaching, teaching through numerous schools of ministry, and administrative duties. Since 1972 he has annually conducted a "World Conference" for ministry supporters.

Sources:

Cerullo, Morris. *The Backside of Satan*. Carol Stream, IL: Creation House, 1973. 224 pp.

———. *A Guide to Total Health and Prosperity*. San Diego, CA: World Evangelism, 1977. 157 pp.

———. *The Miracle Book*. San Diego, CA: World Evangelism, 1984. 169 pp.

———. *My Story*. San Diego, CA: World Evangelism, 1965. 87 pp. Reprinted as *From Judaism to Christianity*. San Diego, CA: World Evangelism, 1976.

———. *Revelation Healing Power*. San Diego, CA: World Evangelism. 1979. 104 pp.

———. *Victory Miracle Living, It's Harvest Time*. San Diego, CA: World Evangelism, 1982. 95 pp.

★182★
CHAFER, Lewis Sperry
Theologian, Presbyterian Church in the U.S. and Founder, Dallas Theological Seminary
b. Feb. 27, 1871, Rock Creek, Ohio
d. Aug. 22, 1952, Dallas, Texas

Lewis Sperry Chafer, a leading theologian of modern fundamentalist Christianity, was the son of Losi Lomita Sperry and Thomas Franklin Chafer. His father was a minister in the Congregational Church and died when Chafer was 11 years old. His mother sent him to New Lyme Academy and then to Oberlin College (1889-1892). While at Oberlin he improved his baritone voice during three semesters at the conservatory of music. He then studied theology privately with Rev. Frank E. Fitch. In 1896 he married Ella Loraine Case.

Chafer worked with evangelist Arthur T. Reed through the early 1890s, but following his marriage became assistant pastor at the Painesville Congregational Church. He moved to First Congregational Church in Buffalo, New York, where he was ordained in 1900 as a Congregationalist minister. In 1901 he moved to Northfield, Massachusetts, where the evangelist **Dwight L. Moody** had previously developed a complex of schools and summer activities. There he met Cyrus I. Scofield, who introduced him to dispensationalism, a way of studying the Bible by dividing its story into a number of periods or dispensations in which God deals with humanity in different ways. For the next decade he farmed, taught in the Northfield schools, and assisted at the summer conferences. In 1907 he transferred his ministerial credentials to the Presbyterian Church in the U.S.A. While at Northfield he authored his first books, which included: *Satan: His Motive and Methods* (1909); *True Evangelism* (1911); and *The Kingdom in History and Prophesy* (1915).

In 1915 Chafer moved to New York as an extension teacher for Scofield's Bible correspondence school. He traveled widely and spoke at Bible conferences in this capacity, and gradually formulated an idea to create a school that would combine the experience of the Bible conferences with a seminary education. In the early 1920s he settled in Dallas, Texas, as the pastor of the Scofield Memorial Church and director of the Central American Mission. Among the books produced during this period of his life were *Salvation* (1917); *He That Is Spiritual* (1918); and *Grace* (1922).

In 1924 Chafer opened Evangelical Theological College. He was appointed president and professor of systematic Theology, two posts he retained for the rest of his life. As the school, renamed Dallas Theological Seminary in 1936, prospered and took its place as a leading training center for fundamentalist ministers, Chafer emerged as a major spokesperson for the dispensational premillennial theology his mentor Scofield had largely introduced to evangelical Protestant audiences. Amid his teaching and administrative duties, Chafer worked for many years on his primary literary product, the multi-volume *Systematic Theology* (1948), published a few years before his death.

Sources:

Chafer, Lewis Sperry. *Grace*. Philadelphia: Sunday School Times Company, 1922. 378 pp.

_____. *The Kingdom in History and Prophecy*. New York: Fleming H. Revell Company, 1915. 159 pp.

_____. *Salvation*. Findley, OH: Dunham, 1917. 149 pp.

_____. *Satan: His Motive and Methods*. New York: Gospel Publishing House, 1909. 162 pp.

_____. *Systematic Theology*. 8 vols. Dallas, TX: Dallas Theological Seminary, 1947-1948.

_____. *True Evangelism*. New York: Gospel Publishing House, 1911. 159 pp.

Reid, Daniel G., Robert D. Linder, Bruce L. Shelley, and Harry S. Stout. *Dictionary of Christianity in America*. Downers Grove, IL: InterVarsity Press, 1990. 1305 pp.

★ 183 ★
CHAPMAN, James Blaine

General Superintendent, Church of the Nazarene
b. Aug. 30, 1884, Yale, Illinois
d. Feb. 30, 1947, Indian Lake, Michigan

James Blaine Chapman, a general superintendent of the Church of the Nazarene, was born in Southern Illinois, but when he was 14 his family moved to a farm near Oklahoma City, Oklahoma. His family did not attend church, but during his teen years he began to attend holiness meetings held near his home. At the age of 15 he was saved and sanctified. (In holiness teachings, sanctification begins with the action of the Holy Spirit upon the believer, cleansing him/her from outward sin and making the newly sanctified person perfect in love.) Chapman became the leader of a small prayer meeting and soon felt a call to preach. He began preaching regularly the next year and delivered over 200 sermons his first year. The holiness movement was at the time still in the process of forming stable organizations. Chapman associated with the World's Faith Missionary Association and the Texas Holiness Association for a brief period. After meeting **C. B. Jernigan**, however, he became a minister with the Independent Holiness Church. He formed a local congregation near his home and traveled widely in evangelistic endeavors. In 1883, at the age of 19, he was ordained as an Independent Holiness minister. At the same meeting he was ordained, he married Maud Frederick. He continued in evangelistic endeavors for several years, but in December 1905 he organized a holiness church in Durant, Oklahoma, and settled there as its pastor.

Soon recognized as one of the holiness movement's most capable preachers, Chapman also emerged as a forceful leader in the attempts to bring the scattered independent holiness groups together into one organization. He backed the merger of the Independent Holiness Church with the New Testament Church of Christ and was appointed as one of the delegates to complete the negotiations that led to the creation of the Holiness Church of Christ in 1905. As president of the Texas-Oklahoma Council of the Holiness Church of Christ in 1907, he promoted its merger with the Pentecostal Church of the Nazarene. That 1908 merger is considered the birth date of the Church of the Nazarene.

In 1908 Chapman moved to Vilonia, Arkansas, as pastor of the holiness church. While there he was able to gain the education previously unavailable to him by attending the Arkansas Holiness College. He finished the two-year course in 1910 and was asked to remain as president of the school. In 1911 he moved to Peniel, Texas, as a student at Texas Holiness University. He completed his A.B. in 1912 and taught during the 1912-1913 school year while completing his B.D. Finishing in 1913, again he was asked to remain as president of the school, now renamed Peniel University. He left the school in 1918 to return to a pastorate in Bethany, Oklahoma, and evangelistic work.

In 1921 Chapman was named associate editor of the *Herald of Holiness*, the Church of the Nazarene's principal periodical. He be-

came the journal's editor the next year and devoted much of his energy through the 1920s to overcoming the continual sectional feelings still evident in the church, which had been created by the merger of a number of small regional holiness bodies. In 1926 he started the *Preacher's Magazine* as a professional periodical for the church's ministers. In 1928 he was elected as a general superintendent, a post to which he was regularly re-elected until he retired in 1946. Two years after his first wife died in 1940, he married Louise Robinson. Among his major accomplishments as general superintendent was the encouragement he gave to the founding of the Nazarene Theological Seminary.

Sources:

Chapman, James B. *Christian Men in a Modern World*. Kansas City, MO: Nazarene Publishing House, 1942. 137 pp.

_____. *A Day in the Lord's Court*. Kansas City, MO: Beacon Hill Press, 1948. 144 pp.

_____. *A History of the Church of the the Nazarene*. Kansas City, MO: Nazarene Publishing House, 1926. 160 pp.

_____. *Religion and Everyday Life*. Kansas City, MO: Beacon Hill Press, 1945. 141 pp.

_____. *Some Estimates of Life*. Kansas City, MO: Nazarene Publishing House, [1920?]. 114 pp.

Wiseman, Neil B., ed. *Two Men of Destiny: Second Generation Leaders in the Nazarene Movement*. Kansas City, MO: Beacon Hill Press of Kansas City, 1983. 211 pp.

★ 184 ★
CHAPMAN, John Wilbur

Evangelist, Presbyterian Church
b. Jun. 17, 1859, Richmond, Indiana
d. Dec. 25, 1918, New York, New York

John Wilbur Chapman, a Presbyterian evangelist, was the son of Lorinda McWhinney and Alexander Hamilton Chapman. Chapman joined the Presbyterian Church at the age of 16. He attended Oberlin College for a year but completed his B.A. at Lake Forest University in 1879. He finished his theological work at Lane Theological Seminary in 1882. That same year he married Irene E. Steddom and was ordained as a Presbyterian minister. He pastored two churches in Indiana for the first year before moving to Schuylerville, New York, to serve as pastor of the Old Saratoga Dutch Reformed Church. He subsequently served the Dutch Reformed Church of Albany, New York (1885-1890); the Bethany Presbyterian Church of Philadelphia, Pennsylvania (1890-1893, 1896-1899), and the Fourth Presbyterian Church in New York City. In 1888, his first wife having died, he married Agnes Pruyn Strain.

Chapman became increasingly concerned about the evangelism of the unchurched public and began to assist in evangelistic campaigns in 1892. In 1893 he assisted **Dwight L. Moody** in his Chicago campaign. In 1901 the Presbyterian Church's general assembly selected him to head its committee on evangelism. In 1903 he decided to become a full-time evangelist. Chapman was able to gain the services of Charles M. Alexander as a music leader and the two conducted campaigns together for the next fifteen years. The Boston (1909) and Chicago (1910) campaigns are generally viewed as the most successful held by the pair. A gifted orator, Chapman set an exhausting pace for himself. Health problems interrupted his career no less than thirteen times.

Chapman contributed one significant innovation to the urban evangelism of the day—the organization of the simultaneous campaign. In addition to the main services at which Chapman preached during the weeks of his activity in a city, Chapman organized numerous smaller meetings around the city which served to attract people to the main meetings and associated classes.

Chapman authored and edited over 30 books, among the most important being *The Secret of a Happy Day* (1899); *The Surrendered Life* (1899); *The Life and Work of D. L. Moody* (1900); *Re-*

vivals and Missions (1900); *S. H. Hadley of Water Street* (1906); *Revival Sermons* (1911); and *When Home is Heaven* (1917). He also compiled several hymn books. He was married for the last time in 1910 to Mabel Cornelia Multon. In 1917 he was elected moderator of the general assembly of the Presbyterian Church.

Sources:

Bowden, Henry Warner. *Dictionary of American Religious Biography.* Westport, CT: Greenwood Press, 1977. 572 pp.

Chapman, J. Wilbur. *The Life and Work of D. L. Moody.* Chicago: Int'l Printing, 1900. 555 pp.

_____. *Revivals and Missions.* New York: Lentilhan & Co., 1900. 220 pp.

_____. *S. H. Hadley of Water Street.* New York: Fleming H. Revell Company, 1906. 289 pp.

_____. *The Secret of a Happy Day.* Boston: United Society of Christian Endeavor, 1899. 103 pp.

_____. *When Home Is Heaven.* New York: Fleming H. Revell Company, 1917. 296 pp.

Dictionary of American Biography. 20 vols. and 7 supps. New York: Charles Scribner's Sons, 1928-1936, 1944-1981.

Ottman, Ford C. *J. Wilbur Chapman: A Biography.* Garden City, NY: Doubleday, 1920. 326 pp.

Reid, Daniel G., Robert D. Linder, Bruce L. Shelley, and Harry S. Stout. *Dictionary of Christianity in America.* Downers Grove, IL: InterVarsity Press, 1990. 1305 pp.

Soden, D. E. "Anatomy of a Presbyterian Urban Revival: J. W. Chapman in the Pacific Northwest." *American Presbyterians* 64 (1986): 49-57.

★ 185 ★
CHARLTON, Hilda
Independent Eastern Metaphysical Teacher
b. 1910, London United Kingdom
d. Jan. 29, 1988, New York, New York

Hilda Charlton was an influential teacher of Eastern metaphysics in the late-twentieth century. Much of the information on her early life, including her birthdate around 1910, is lost in obscurity. She was born in London and moved to the United States with her parents when she was four. She grew up in Salt Lake City, Utah, and Los Angeles. As a teenager she studied dance and began dancing in public when she was 18. She settled in San Francisco and worked as a dancer and dance teacher in the years between the two world wars. In 1947 she went to India to dance and stayed for three years. While there an interest in Hinduism flowered and she stayed to study under several gurus who were open to Western seekers: Swami Nityananda, the guru of **Swami Paramahansa Muktananda**; Sri Mahadevananda; and, most importantly, Sri Sathya Sai Baba.

Charlton returned to the United States in 1965, just as the wave of immigration from India brought a number of Eastern teachers to America. Interest in Hinduism, meditation, and Eastern and theosophical metaphysics took a dramatic upward turn. Beginning with just two students, within a few years Charlton had hundreds who heard about her as the new spiritual communities were developing across America. Among those who found her council valuable was Baba Ram Dass (Richard Alpert). Through Charlton he met Joyce Green, now known as Ma Bharata. Their much publicized relationship and break had the side effect of bringing Charlton to the attention of the larger community of Hindu and metaphysical seekers in America. By 1976 her audiences had grown to the point that she moved her meetings to the Cathedral Church of St. John the Divine in New York City. She also began to write a column for *The New Sun*, an early New Age movement magazine.

Charlton did not build a movement in the manner of many spiritual teachers, but left behind many people who were affected by her teachings. Following her death some of her close students gathered her writings and have begun to publish them under the imprint of Golden Quest.

Sources:

Charlton, Hilda. *The New Sun.* Woodstock, NY: Golden Quest, 1989. 142 pp.

_____. *Saints Alive.* Woodstock, NY: Golden Quest, 1989. 288 pp.

★ 186 ★
CHASE, Thornton
Leader, Baha'i Faith
b. Feb. 22, 1847, Springfield, Massachusetts
d. Sep. 13, 1912, Los Angeles, California

Thornton Chase, the first convert to the Baha'i Faith in the United States, grew up in a staunch Baptist family, his father being a deacon. He served in the Union Army during the Civil War, though he was only a teenager at the time, and then attended Brown University. He also went into the insurance business, at which he became quite successful. Following a mystical experience in 1874, he became a religious seeker and was affiliated briefly with the Church of the New Jerusalem, which advocated the teachings of Emanuel Swedenborg, the eighteenth-century Swedish seer.

By the summer of 1894 Chase had somewhat despaired of finding a satisfactory personal religion when he learned of the presence of **Ibrahim Kheiralla**, a Baha'i teacher, in Chicago. He had already heard of the Baha'i Faith, and had begun to investigate the claims being made about **Baha'u'llah** and his son **Abdu'l-Baha** through reading the modest amount of literature on the topic then available in English. He was among the first four people to accept the teachings and the only one to remain with them throughout his life. In 1899 Kheiralla challenged Abdu'l-Baha and broke with the faith. Of the earliest converts, all but Chase were lost in the ensuing controversy. Chase was helped through these trying times by the arrival in 1900 of two Baha'i teachers from the Middle East, Mirza Asadu'llah and Mirza Hasan-i-Khurasani.

In 1907 Chase made a pilgrimage to Akka, in Palestine, where Abdu'l-Baha resided. Chase noted that many of the misconceptions about the faith which he had absorbed from Kheiralla were corrected during his visits with Abdu'l-Baha.

Shortly after his return to the United States, Chase's company transferred him to California. He continued to travel in his work and spread the faith as he went. In 1909 he published *The Baha'i Revelation*, one of the first comprehensive English-language books on the history and beliefs of the Baha'i Faith. It became an important tool in the spread of the Baha'i faith in the early decades of this century.

In 1912 Chase was among the group of Baha'is who invited Abdu'l-Baha to visit the United States. Unfortunately, Chase did not live to participate in the festivities; he died the month before Abdu'l Baha's arrival. Abdu'l-Baha did, however, alter his itinerary in order to visit Chase's grave in Inglewood, California.

Sources:

Chase, Thornton. *The Bahai Revelation.* New York: Bahai Publishing Committee, [1909].

_____. "A Brief History of the American Development of the Bahai Movement." *Star of the West* 5 (January 5, 1915).

_____. *In Galilee.* Chicago: Baha'i Publishing Society, 1908.

Scheffler, Carl. "Thornton Chase: First American Baha'i." *World Order* 11, 5.

Stockman, Robert H. *The Baha'i Faith in America.* Wilmette, IL: Baha'i Publishing Trust, 1985. 277 pp.

Whitehead, O. Z. *Some Early Baha'is of the West.* Oxford, UK: George Ronald, 1976. 227 pp.

★ 187 ★
CHAUDHURI, Haridas
Founder, California Institute of Integral Studies
b. May 24, 1913, Calcutta India
d. 1975

Haridas Chaudhuri, the founder of the California Institute of Integral Studies, was the son of Sailendra Mohan and Saila Bala Devi Chaudhuri. He was orphaned at an early age, but did not allow this liability to prevent him from achieving distinction in the academic arena. Chaudhuri won the Ramtanu Gold Medal in Bengali literature when he graduated from high school in 1929, and received his B.A. and M.A. degrees with honors from Vidyasagar College in Calcutta. He was also awarded the Gold Medal for highest scholastic achievement, as well as the Silver Medal from his department. He received his Ph.D. degree from the University of Calcutta in 1949, and went on to become a member of the educational service of the government of West Bengal and chairman of the department of philosophy at Krishnager College.

Chaudhuri was a follower of the great Indian seer **Sri Aurobindo**, and it was through his link with Aurobindo that Chaudhuri came to America. While engaged in research in India, Dr. Frederic Spiegelberg, then Professor of Indic and Slavic Studies at Stanford University, had received darshan from Sri Aurobindo, with whom he had been most favorably impressed. Later, after Spiegelberg became director of the American Academy of Asian Studies, Aurobindo recommended Chaudhuri for an appointment in the Academy, and he moved to the United States in 1951. Chaudhuri and his wife established an organization, the Cultural Integration Fellowship, and it was out of the Fellowship that the Institute evolved. Over the next two decades he authored a number of books.

The California Institute of Asian Studies began as the educational branch of the Fellowship in 1968, and was incorporated separately as a private, non-sectarian graduate school in 1974. M.A. and Ph.D. degrees were offered in unusual subject areas, such as integral counseling psychology. In 1980 the name was changed to the California Institute of Integral Studies (CIIS) to better reflect the institution's holistic approach to knowledge, as well as its roots in Aurobindo's integral yoga. The Institute was awarded full accreditation by the Western Association of Schools and Colleges in 1981. Unlike many other private schools struggling in the "educational economy" of the 1980s, CIIS continued to grow, partially because of the attraction of attending an academically demanding school in which personal spiritual growth is also encouraged.

Sources:

Chaudhuri, Haridas. *Being Evolution and Immortality*. Wheaton, IL: Theosophical Publishing House, 1974. 204 pp.
_____. *The Evolution of Integral Consciousness*. Wheaton, IL: Theosophical Publishing House, 1977. 140 pp.
_____. *Integral Yoga*. London: George Allen & Unwin, 1965. 160 pp.
_____. *Mastering the Problems of Living*. Wheaton, IL: Theosophical Publishing House, 1968, 1975. 222 pp.
_____. *Modern Man's Religion*. Santa Barbara, CA: J. R. Rowny Press, 1966. 87 pp.
_____. *The Philosophy of Integralism*. 1954 Rev. ed. Pondicherry, India: Sri Aurobindo Ashram, 1967. 186 pp.
_____. *Philosophy of Meditation*. New York: Philosophical Library, 1965. 55 pp.

★ 188 ★
CHENEY, Charles Edward
Bishop, Reformed Episcopal Church
b. Feb. 12, 1836, Canandaigua, New York
d. Nov. 15, 1916, Chicago, Illinois

Charles Edward Cheney, the second bishop of the Reformed Episcopal Church, was the son of Altie Chipman and Ephraim Warren Cheney. He decided to enter the ministry of the Protestant Episcopal Church and to that end attended Hobart College. Following his graduation in 1857 he moved on to the Virginia Theological Seminary. Leaving the seminary after only a year, he became the assistant rector of St. Luke's Church in Rochester, New York. In 1858 he was also ordained as a deacon. In 1860 he was ordained to the priesthood. A month later he married Clara E. Griswold, and they moved to Chicago where he became rector of Christ Episcopal Church, a position he was to hold for the rest of his life.

Cheney's career coincided with the emergence of a major controversy within the Episcopal Church between high church ritualists and low church evangelicals. Cheney, a strong supporter of the low church position, soon came into conflict with the Episcopal bishop of Chicago, Henry J. Waterhouse, a leading advocate of the high church position. In 1869 Cheney signed the "Chicago Protest," a document that accused the high church leaders of introducing un-Protestant tendencies into the church. Thus Cheney was singled out by his bishop as a target. Waterhouse discovered that it was Cheney's practice to alter the liturgy of the church's baptismal service (so as to eliminate any understanding of the service as being a regenerating act in itself). In the early 1870s Waterhouse filed charges and had Cheney brought to trial by the church. Cheney was found guilty and deposed from the ministry.

Cheney protested the judgment and continued to officiate at his church. The diocese filed suit to have him removed, but the local court decided that the property belonged to the congregation. The court also found that a technical aspect of the church's efforts to remove Cheney had not been in accordance with church law. Hence Cheney was allowed to stay at the church, and the court declared that he had been deposed illegally.

As Cheney's case was being adjudicated (1873-1874), the high church-low church controversy emerged elsewhere when Bishop **George D. Cummins** joined non-Episcopalians in a communion service. Cheney found common cause with Cummins and in December 1873 became one of the priests who assisted him in organizing the Reformed Episcopal Church. The congregation in Chicago also affiliated with the new church. On December 14, 1873, Cheney was consecrated as missionary bishop of Chicago for the Reformed Episcopal Church. Among his successes as missionary bishop was the extension of the church into Canada, where in 1878 he consecrated Edward Cridge as bishop for British Columbia.

Cheney was named bishop of the Synod of Chicago in 1878. He provided administrative leadership for the growing church for almost 40 years. During that time he authored a number of books, the most important being two collections of his sermons and a doctrinal text, *What Reformed Episcopalians Believe* (1888).

Sources:

Cheney, Charles E. *The Barefoot Maid at the Fountain Inn*. Chicago: Chicago Literary Club, 1912. 40 pp.
_____. *A King of France Unnamed in History*. Chicago: Chicago Literary Club, 1902. 86 pp.
_____. *A Neglected Power and Other Sermons*. New York: Fleming H. Revell Co., 1916. 222 pp.
_____. *Sermons*. Chicago: Cushing, Thomas & Co., 1880. 375 pp.
_____. *What Reformed Episcopalians Believe*. Philadelphia: Reformed Episcopal Pub. Society, 1888. 193 pp.
Dictionary of American Biography. 20 vols. and 7 supps. New York: Charles Scribner's Sons, 1928-1936, 1944-1981.
Price, Annie D. *History of the Formation and Growth of the Reformed Episcopal Church*. Philadelphia: J. M. Armstrong, 1902. 308 pp.

★189★
CHIA, Mantak
Founder and Director, Healing Tao Center
b. Apr. 4, 1944, Thailand

Master Mantak Chia is the founder of the Healing Tao Center, originally, the Taoist Esoteric Yoga Center. Although born into a family of Chinese Christians, he became interested in the Buddhism of his Thai homeland and learned meditation from Buddhist monks while still a young child. In grammar school he studied Thai boxing and Tai Chi Chuan with Master Lu, and also became acquainted with yoga and aikido. While a student in Hong Kong, he was introduced to esoteric Taoism by Cheng Sue-Sue who presented him to Master Yi Eng. With these two adepts he studied the Taoist way of life and such practices as how to pass the life force out of his hands. In his early twenties, he worked with Master Meugi in Singapore, from whom he learned kundalini yoga and the Buddhist Palm, the latter a practice for eliminating energy blockages, both in one's own body and the bodies of others.

In his late twenties, Chia studied with Master Pan Yu, whose system synthesized certain Taoist and Buddhist teachings. From Yu he learned about the exchange of yin and yang energies between males and females, as well as a technique that prevents the body from decaying. He also studied with Master Cheng Yao-Lun who taught him secret practices for generating internal power and for cleansing and regenerating the body. To better understand the teachings he had been imparted and to relate them to contemporary science, Chia undertook a study of Western medicine and anatomy. During these studies, he worked as a manager for Gestetner Company, a manufacturer of office equipment.

After studying with diverse masters, Chia began to perfect a unified system that would bring these teachings together. He eventually developed the Healing Tao system and began teaching it to others. He established the Natural Healing Center in Thailand and five years later decided to take his teachings to the West. A Healing Tao Center was opened in New York in 1979. Centers have since been established in many other cities, including Los Angeles, Boston, San Francisco, London, and Bonn. Chia has been putting his great learning into print, by 1986 publishing a half-dozen Healing Tao books, including *Awaken Healing Energy through the Tao* (1983); *Taoist Secrets of Love* (1984); and *Taoist Ways to Transform Stress into Vitality* (1985).

Sources:
Chia, Mantak. *Awaken Healing Energy through the Tao*. New York: Aurora Press, 1983. 193 pp.
_____. *Taoist Ways to Transform Stress into Vitality*. Huntington, NY: The Healing Tao Press, 1985. 146 pp.
_____, and Maneewan Chia. *Healing Love through the Tao: Cultivating Female Sexual Energy*. Huntington, New York: Healing Tao Books, 1986. 328 pp.
_____, and Michael Winn. *Taoist Secrets of Love: Cultivating the Male Sexual Energy*. New York: Aurora Press, 1984. 285 pp.
Esoteric Taoist Yoga. Chinatown, NY: Taoist Esoteric Yoga Center and Foundation, n.d. 31 pp.
Webster, Sam. "Mantak Chia Interview: Taoist Master Teaches Natural Flow of Energy." *Whole Life Monthly* 67 (October 1987): 28-29.

★190★
CHILSTROM, Herbert Walfred
Presiding Bishop, Evangelical Lutheran Church in America (1988)
b. Oct. 18, 1931, Litchfield, Minnesota

Herbert Walfred Chilstrom, the presiding bishop of the Evangelical Lutheran Church in America, the fifth largest Christian denomination in the United States, is the son of Ruth Lindell and Walfred Emmanuel Chilstrom. He attended Augsburg College from which he graduated in 1954. That same year he married Corinne Hansen and entered Augustana Theological Seminary. He received his B.D.

in 1958, was ordained to the ministry of the Lutheran Church in America, and called to pastor Faith Lutheran Church at Pelican Rapids, Minnesota. He stayed in Minnesota for four years before becoming academic dean at Luther College in Teaneck, New Jersey. While in New Jersey he was able to work on a Th.M. at Princeton Theological Seminary, which was granted in 1966.

In 1970 Chilstrom returned to the pastorate as the senior minister of First Lutheran Church, St. Peter, Minnesota. It was to be his last pastorate, since in 1976 he was elected bishop of the Minnesota Synod of the Lutheran Church in America.

Shortly after Chilstrom took office, his denomination began to seriously consider a merger with two other Lutheran bodies, the American Lutheran Church and the Association of Evangelical Lutheran Churches. He had a record of participation in ecumenical concerns and in 1982 had been named to the Faith and Order Commission of the National Council of Churches. That same year he was selected as a member of the Commission for a New Lutheran Church. Through the 1980s, Chilstrom authored three books, *Hebrews, A New and Better Way* (1984); *When We Reach for the Sun* (1986); and *Foundation in the Future* (1987).

The work of the commission for a New Lutheran Church culminated in April 1986, in time for the summer conventions of the three churches, all of which voted to accept the merger proposal. The constituting convention met the following year. On the fifth ballot Chilstrom edged out Bishop David Preus of the American Lutheran Church to become the first presiding bishop of the Evangelical Lutheran Church in America. This officially came into being on January 1, 1988. In the wake of his election as head of the new Lutheran church, he was elected vice-president of the Lutheran World Federation in 1990.

Among the first issues confronting Chilstrom has been the ordination of homosexuals. In January 1990 two churches in San Francisco ordained homosexual pastors. They were supported by Krister Stendal, a retired bishop of the Church of Sweden (Lutheran). Chilstrom not only chided Stendal publicly, but moved to support the church's position against ordaining practicing homosexuals, while noting that celibate homosexuals who otherwise qualified could be ordained.

Sources:
Almen, Lowell G. and Herbert W. Chilstrom, eds. *The Many Faces of Pastoral Ministry: Perspective by Bishops of the Evangelical Lutheran Church in America*. Minneapolis, MN: Augsburg Fortress Press, 1989. 128 pp.
Chilstrom, Herbert W. *Foundation in the Future*. 1987.
_____. *Hebrews, A New and Better Way*. Philadelphia: Fortress Press, 1984.
_____. *When We Reach for the Sun*. 1986.

★191★
CHINIQUY, Charles Paschal Telespore
Minister, Presbyterian Church in Canada
b. Jul. 30, 1809, Kamouraska, Quebec, Canada
d. Jan. 16, 1899, Montreal, Quebec, Canada

Charles Paschal Telespore Chiniquy, a former priest in the Roman Catholic Church who became a Presbyterian minister and anti-Catholic polemicist, was the son of Charles Chiniquy and Rheine Perrqult. He grew up in Murray Bay, Quebec, and was taught to read and write by his mother, there being no school in the town. In 1819 he was sent to school in St. Thomas and in 1822 he moved to the College of Nicolet. After graduation in 1829 he attended the seminary in Quebec and was ordained as a Roman Catholic priest in 1833. His first assignment was a position as vicar at St. Charles parish. He later served at Charlesborough; St. Roch's Church in Quebec City; and Kamouraska.

While serving as chaplain of Quebec Marine Hospital in the 1830s Chiniquy became impressed with the dangers of alcohol and emerged in the 1840s as a leading temperance advocate throughout the diocese of Montreal. In this cause he authored his first book, *Manual ou Reglement de la Societe de Temprance* (1844).

In 1851 Chiniquy moved to Illinois to begin missionary work among new Roman Catholic settlers. He helped found the settlement that later became the town of St. Anne. A group of French-speaking settlers gathered quickly at the site. Through the remaining years of the decade, however, Chiniquy developed a number of problems with the church and in 1858 he led a revolt within his parish that caused both he and a number of members to leave. The schismatic group called themselves Christian Catholics and was soon courted by a number of Protestant denominations. In 1863 Chiniquy affiliated with the Presbyterian Church in Canada.

The rest of Chiniquy's career was spent in missionary work among Roman Catholics and in attacking his former church in both lectures and writings. In 1870 he authored his first anti-Catholic book, *L'Eglise de Rome*. In 1875 he was assigned to Craig Street Presbyterian Church in Montreal, but two months after his arrival an outraged mob drove him from the premises. (He was soon installed at Cote Street Presbyterian Church, where he stayed for a number of years.) Much of the hostility he encountered from the Roman Catholics stemmed from his 1875 book, *Le Petre, la femme, et le confessional*.

In 1886 Chiniquy finished his most famous book, still kept in print, *Fifty Years in the Church of Rome*. This autobiography was marked by lengthy harsh polemics against his former church and colleagues. Over the years he traveled widely as an anti-Roman lecturer, and back in Illinois in the 1890s he participated in the new national wave of anti-Catholic feelings with a book that accused the Society of Jesus (the Jesuits) of the murder of Abraham Lincoln. He spent his last years in Montreal, where he authored *Forty Years in the Church of Christ* (1899), a sequel to his earlier autobiographical volume.

Sources:

Chiniquy, Charles. *Fifty Years in the Church of Rome*. London: Protestant Literature Depository, 1886. 597 pp.
_____. *Forty Years in the Church of Christ*. Chicago: Fleming H. Revell, 1900. 498 pp.
_____. *L'Eglise de Rome*. Montreal: impr. de l'Aurore, 1870. 16 pp.
_____. *The Murder of Abraham Lincoln Planned and Executed by Jesuit Priests*. Indianapolis: The Ironclad Age, 1893. 11 pp.
Moir, John S. *Enduring Witness: A History of the Presbyterian Church in Canada*. Centennial Committee, Presbyterian Church in Canada, 1975. 311 pp.
Wallace, W. Stewart. *The Macmillan Dictionary of Canadian Biography*. 4th ed., rev. Edited by W. A. McKay. Toronto: Macmillan of Canada, 1978.

★192★
Swami CHINMAYANANDA
Founder, Chinmaya Mission West
b. May 1916, India

Swami Chinmayananda, formerly known as Sri Balakrishna Menon (Swami is a title; Chinmayananda is a monastic name), is the founder of the Chinmaya Mission West (Chinmaya is short for Chinmayananda). His father was a prominent society figure who held important positions in the judiciary of Cochin. He graduated from Madras University in 1939, and then went to Lucknow for a post-graduate degree in literature and law. Not finding law suitable to his temperament, he moved to Delhi and worked as a journalist. His participation in the Indian independence movement earned him a prison term. While serving his term, he became seriously ill and was transferred to a hospital where he happened to read some material authored by Swami Sivananda Saraswati, one of contem-

porary India's most famous modernist swamis. After his release he sought out Sivananda at Rishikish, eventually decided to take up the renounced life, and in 1943 took *sannyas* and became Swami Chinmayananda.

While studying with Sivananda, who taught an integrated path of several different yogas, Chinmayananda became attracted to the path of jnana yoga. With Sivananda's encouragement, he placed himself under the instruction of Swami Tapovanam of Uttar Kasi, India, an authority on the traditional Hindu scriptures. Chinmayananda studied with Tapovanam for eight years, under austere conditions and strict discipline. While meditating on the banks of the sacred Ganges river, Chinmayananda felt a call to begin a public teaching ministry. Tapovanam discouraged his student from following this calling and instead sent him on a long pilgrimage to India's holy places. Upon his return Chinmayananda's call was still strong, and this time Tapovanam sent his student out with his blessings.

Chinmayananda's teaching mission began with his first public lecture, held in Poona, in 1951. Writing commentaries on the scriptures, and lecturing throughout India, Chinmayananda's mission grew until he was able to found two institutions, the Sandeepany Sadhanalaya (Academy of Knowledge) in Bombay, and the Tapovan Kuti, a center for meditation and spiritual training in the Himalayas. The mission also supported such activities as hospitals and nursery schools. Chinmayananda became an international teacher in 1965, and has lectured at many major universities in the United States. The Chinmaya Mission West was officially incorporated in 1975, and the American parallel to the Academy of Knowledge, Sandeepany West, was established in northern California. The Mission grew rapidly, but suffered setbacks following Chinmayananda's heart attack in 1980 and the defection of Chinmayananda's spiritual heir-apparent, Swami Dayananda, who left the Mission in 1982.

Sources:

Chinmayananda, Swami. *The Art of Man-Making*. Calcutta, India: Central Chinmaya Mission Trust, 1975. 538 pp.
_____. *Discourses on Mandukya Upanishad with Gaudapada's Karika*. Madras, India: Chinmaya Publication Trust, n.d. 431 pp.
_____. *The Holy Geeta*. Bombay, India: Central Chinmaya Mission Trust, n.d. 1133 pp.
_____. *Kindle Life*. Madras, India: Central Chinmaya Publications Trust, n.d. 193 pp.
Mangalwadi, Vishal. *The World of Gurus*. New Delhi, India: Nivedit Good Books Distributors, 1987. 298 pp.
Melton, J. Gordon *The Encyclopedia of American Religions*. 3d ed. Detroit: Gale Research Inc.,1988. 1102 pp.
"Swami Dayananda Renounces Chinmaya Mission West: Changes and Challenges Ahead." *The New Saivite World* 5, 4 (Fall, 1983): 2.

★193★
Sri CHINMOY
Founder, Sri Chinmoy Meditation Centres
b. Aug. 27, 1931, Chittagong India

Sri Chinmoy, born Chinmoy Kumar Ghose (Sri is an honorific rather than a name), is a popular teacher of meditation and founder of Sri Chinmoy Meditation Centres. He had profound mystical experiences in his childhood, achieving *nirvikalpa samadhi*, an experience of self-realization, while still a youth. After the death of his parents, he moved to the **Sri Aurobindo** Ashram at Pondicherry to live with relatives. He remained at Pondicherry for 20 years engaged in the practice of spiritual disciplines. At the inner prompting of the Supreme (God), he left in 1964 to come to the West and teach.

Chinmoy arrived in New York in April 1964, and soon afterwards opened the AUM Centre in Manhattan and began the publication of *AUM Magazine*. By 1968 he had opened centers in New

York, Puerto Rico, and Florida. In 1970 he began conducting twice-weekly meditations for peace at the United Nations. From this point, the movement expanded rapidly.

During the 1980s Chinmoy became a well-known figure through his music, his art, his sponsorship of athletic events, and a few celebrity disciples. He has performed at a number of peace concerts programmed by his centers across the world. He often sponsors and runs in races and marathons, an example of what he refers to as the meditation of action. Chinmoy has also written and published several hundred books and booklets, most of which are transcripts of his talks, collections of his poetry, or selections of spiritual aphorisms.

Sources:

Chinmoy, Sri. *Arise! Awake! Thoughts of a Yogi.* New York: Frederick Fell, 1972.
_____. *Meditation: Man-Perfection in God-Satisfaction.* Jamaica, NY: Agni Press, 1978. 304 pp.
_____. *My Flute.* Jamaica, NY: Agni Press, 1975. 94 pp.
_____. *Sri Chinmoy Primer.* Forest Hills, NY: Vishma Press, 1974. 122 pp.
The Expanding Light: Sri Chinmoy's Manifestation as Reflected in the World Press, November 1967—July 1974. Jamaica, NY: Agni Press, 1974. 370 pp.
Madhuri [Nancy Elizabeth Sands]. *The Life of Sri Chinmoy.* 2 vols. Jamaica, NY: Agni Press, 1972, 1984.

★ 194 ★
CHORNOCK, Orestes
Metropolitan, American Carpatho-Russian Orthodox Greek Church
b. 1883, Russia
d. Feb. 17, 1977, Stratford, Connecticut

Little is known of the early years of Orestes Chornock, the founder and first bishop of the American Carpatho-Russian Orthodox Greek Church. He was born in the Carpathian Mountains region in the southwestern part of the Ukraine, now part of the Soviet Union. He was raised in the Roman Catholic Church and came to America as a priest. He emerged out of obscurity in 1930 as a priest of a Ruthenian Roman Catholic parish in Bridgeport, Connecticut. (Ruthenia is a Roman Catholic designation of the area in Eastern Europe from the southern border of Lithuania to the Carpathian Mountains.) Earlier in the century the Ruthenian Catholics in the United States were set off in a separate nongeographical diocese, and in 1924 the Ukrainian Catholics were set off from the Carpatho-Russians and Hungarians. It was the common practice among Eastern Rite (or Uniate) Catholics, of which the Ruthenians were one example, for priests to complete their education, then marry prior to ordination (the practice shared in common with the Eastern Orthodox Church). However, in the United States, the dominant Latin rite bishops had requested that only celibate priests function in North America. Chornock was among the relatively few married priests in America.

The marriage issue culminated in a major controversy in 1930 when three American candidates for the priesthood, who had completed their studies in Europe and had married, were refused ordination by Bp. Basil Tukach, the Eastern Rite bishop for the Carpatho-Russians in America. In December 1930 Tukach published a decree mandating that only celibate priests come to the United States to work. Chornock became the center of a group of dissidents who protested the decree as a denial of their ethnic traditions. He was joined by activists from the Greek Catholic Union. As a result of his outspoken protest, he was suspended from the priesthood and then excommunicated. Chornock and several other priests refused to stop their priestly activity or to surrender the property of the parish they served.

After several years of polemics, Chornock called a group together to organize a separate church body. In 1937 a church council

was formed, independence from Rome asserted, and a return to Eastern Orthodoxy declared. Not wishing to align with the Russian Orthodox Church, Chornock turned to the Greek Orthodox and through its American leader, Archbishop Athenagoras, was placed in contact with the Ecumenical Patriarch in Constantinople. As Chornock's wife had died in 1936, he was eligible for the episcopate. Thus in 1938 he traveled to Constantinople and was consecrated. He established diocesan headquarters in Bridgeport. In 1940 he established a seminary.

During the 1940s Chornock was beset with legal problems as law suits were filed by the Roman Catholic bishop to recover parish properties. In 1948 the Bridgeport church had to be abandoned as a result of these legal battles. Chornock relocated his diocesan headquarters to Johnstown, Pennsylvania, where a new cathedral was completed in 1954. After the move the church began to stabilize. In 1965 Chornock was elevated to the rank of metropolitan and he appointed a successor, John Martin.

Sources:

Magocsi, Paul Robert. *Our People: Carpatho-Russians and Their Descendants in North America.* Toronto: Multicultural History Society of Ontario, 1984. 160 pp.
Roman, Jaroslav. "The Establishment of the American Carpatho-Russian Orthodox Greek Catholic Diocese in 1938: A Major Carpatho-Russian Uniate Return to Orthodoxy." *St. Vladimir's Theological Quarterly* 20, 3 (1976): 132-160.

★ 195 ★
CLAIR SR., Matthew Wesley
Bishop, Methodist Episcopal Church
b. Oct. 21, 1865, Union, West Virginia
d. Jun. 28, 1943, Covington, Kentucky

Matthew Wesley Clair, Sr., one of the first two black men elected to the episcopacy in the predominantly white Methodist Episcopal Church, was the son of Anthony and Ollie Green Clair. The family moved to Charleston, West Virginia, while he was a youth, and when he was 15 years old, he experienced salvation as a member of Simpson Methodist Episcopal Church. Licensed to preach, he attended Morgan College, from which he graduated in 1889. Shortly after graduation he married Fannie Walker. That same year he was admitted on a trial basis into the Washington Conference of the Methodist Episcopal Church (an administrative district serving black members in the Baltimore-Washington, D.C., area).

Clair served churches in West Virginia and Washington, D.C., and was appointed as a district superintendent on two occasions (1896-1897 and 1919-1920). During his long pastorate at Asbury Church in Washington, he edited the conference paper, the *Banner*, and led in the construction of an 1800-seat sanctuary. On three different occasions he was elected as a delegate to the church's general conference. In 1920, culminating a process that had required many years of work, he and **Robert E. Jones** were elected as the church's first black bishops.

Though there were about 19 black conferences in the Methodist Episcopal Church which needed episcopal supervision, Clair was not immediately assigned to oversee work in America. He was sent to Liberia, where the church had a flourishing mission, and there he developed an outstanding record during an eight-year tenure in Africa. He returned to America in 1924 to attend the general conference and was invited to offer the prayer when President Calvin Coolidge dedicated a statue to Methodist Bishop Francis Asbury in Washington, D.C. In Liberia, the country's president appointed him to serve on the nation's board of education, and he was a member of the American Advisory Commission on the Booker Washington Agricultural and Industrial Institute of Liberia. In 1925 Clair's wife died and the following year he married Eva F. Wilson.

In 1928 Clair returned to America and was assigned as bishop of the Covington, Kentucky, Episcopal Area, which included black conferences in the Midwest. He served for eight years and then retired and lived quietly until his death in 1943. He is noteworthy within Methodism as the only bishop to have a son who also became a bishop.

Sources:

Ballard, Margaret B. *Bishop Matthew W. Clair, Sr.: A Biography.* Buchanan, WV: Commission on Archives and History, West Virginia Conference, United Methodist Church, 1973. 34 pp.

Harmon, Nolan B. *The Encyclopedia of World Methodism.* 2 vols. Nashville: United Methodist Publishing House, 1974.

Howell, Clinton H., ed. *Prominent Personalities in Methodism.* Birmingham, AL: Lowrey Press, 1945. 512 pp.

★196★
CLARK, Elmer Talmage
Historian and Church Executive, Methodist Episcopal Church, South
b. Sep. 9, 1886, Randolph County, Arkansas
d. Aug. 30, 1966, Birmingham, Alabama

Elmer Talmage Clark, a missionary executive and Methodist historian, was the son of Henry A. and Ellen A. Kirkpatrick Clark. When he was nine his parents moved to Thayer, Missouri, where he grew to manhood. Clark attended Hendrix College and in 1908 accepted an appointment as a Methodist minister with the St. Louis Conference of the Methodist Episcopal Church, South. He was accepted on a trial basis the following year and served several charges around the state. He was also able to finish another year of school at Vanderbilt University. During World War I he served as a foreign correspondent for several St. Louis newspapers. His articles were collected in a volume which became his first book, *Social Studies of the War* (1919). After the war he served on two major campaigns of the Methodist Episcopal Church, South, the Missionary Centenary and the Christian Education campaigns, which raised about $75,000 for church endeavors. Following the campaigns, he was named editorial secretary for the church's board of missions (headquartered in Nashville, Tennessee) and editor of *World Outlook*, the board's magazine. He wrote almost a book a year during the 1920s to inform members and to promote the church's missionary enterprises. He continued with the mission board through the 1939 merger of the Methodist Episcopal Church, Methodist Episcopal Church, South, and Methodist Protestant Church. Following the merger, he moved to New York where the board's headquarters had been relocated. In 1923 he married Mary Alva Yarbrough.

While assuming ever more responsible tasks for the church, Clark continued his education in a most unorthodox fashion. He received his S.T.D. (Doctorate of the Science of Theology) from Temple University in 1925. He then received his B.A. from Birmingham-Southern College in 1926. He also completed his work at Peabody College for his doctorate to be awarded in 1927. However, his dissertation had been accepted by Macmillan Publishing Company, which wanted to rush it into print. Peabody College refused to give a doctorate on a previously published book and granted Clark an M.A. instead. The book became a classic text in the psychology of religion, *The Psychology of Religious Awakening* (1927).

All through his life Clark had been interested in the many small religious groups which had emerged in the twentieth century in the South. He collected materials on these and other unique religious groups which culminated in a classic text, *The Small Sects in America* (1937), his single most popular book, which remains in print.

The other great interest of Clark's life was Methodist history. In 1948 he was elected the executive secretary of the Association of Methodist Historical Societies. Three years later he was elected

secretary for the Western Hemisphere of the World Methodist Council. He founded and edited *World Parish*, a magazine serving both organizations. In 1952 he resigned his job with the board of missions and moved to Lake Junaluska, North Carolina, a Methodist center that became the nucleus of Methodist historical work. He also oversaw the erection of a building to house the World Methodist Council. During these "retirement" years he wrote extensively on Methodist history. His most prominent titles included *An Album of Methodist History* (1952) and *Methodism in Western North Carolina* (1966). He edited the three volumes of *The Journal and Letters of Francis Asbury*, personal documents of the first American Methodist bishop. Through the 1950s he began the compilation and writing of what would become the *World Methodist Encyclopedia*, but several years before his death, he turned responsibility for the completion of the project over to **Nolan B. Harmon**.

Clark compiled a vast personal library during his life. Some of it remains in the World Methodist Council building at Lake Junaluska, and some has been transferred to the United Methodist Archives in Madison, New Jersey. The material used to write *The Small Sects in America* was donated by his widow to the Institute for the Study of American Religion, and is now located in the American Religious Collection at the University of California-Santa Barbara.

Sources:

Clark, Elmer T. *An Album of Methodist History.* New York: Abingdon-Cokesbury Press, 1952. 336 pp.

_____. *Methodism in Western North Carolina.* N.p.: Western North Carolina Conference, The Methodist Church, 1966. 197 pp.

_____. *The Psychology of Religious Awakenings.* New York: Macmillan Company, 1929. 170 pp.

_____. *The Small Sects in America.* New York: Abingdon-Cokesbury, 1937, rev. ed. 1949. 256 pp.

_____. *Social Studies of the War.* New York: George H. Doran Co., 1919. 283 pp.

Harmon, Nolan B. *The Encyclopedia of World Methodism.* 2 vols. Nashville: United Methodist Publishing House, 1974.

Howell, Clinton H., ed. *Prominent Personalities in Methodism.* Birmingham, AL: Lowrey Press, 1945. 512 pp.

Vernon, Walter N., ed. "Elmer T. Clark: World Methodist." *Methodist History* (1971).

★197★
CLARK, Francis Edward
Founder, Young People's Society of Christian Endeavor
b. Sep. 12, 1851, Aylmer Canada
d. May 26, 1927, Newton, Massachusetts

Francis Edward Clark, a minister in the Congregational Church best known for his work with youth and the founding of the Young People's Society of Christian Endeavor, was the son of Charles Carey Symmes and Lydia Clark Symmes. All of his immediate family died in his early years, and at the age of eight he was adopted by his uncle, the Reverend Edward W. Clark, a Congregationalist pastor at Auburndale, Massachusetts. At the time of his adoption he assumed his uncle's (and his mother's maiden) name. He attended Dartmouth College and Andover Theological Seminary, from which he graduated in 1873 and 1876, respectively. Soon after he graduated from Andover, he married Harriet E. Abbott.

Clark's first pastorate was the Williston Congregational Church in Portland, Maine. His work with the youth became an important part of the church's growth, and early in 1881 he organized the Williston Young People's Society of Christian Endeavor. This fellowship was designed to lead the youth into a dedicated Christian adulthood. Members pledged to "endeavor" to live a Christian life, to pray and read the Bible daily, and to participate in the variety of local congregational meetings scheduled both for worship and business. The response was immediate and intense. In response to requests for information from colleagues who had heard of the society's success, Clark authored an article for the *Congregationalist* in August 1881 and the next year produced first a pamphlet and then a book, *The Children and the Church*. In 1883 he moved to South Boston to pastor the Phillips Congregational Church, but the work of a growing Christian Endeavor movement took an increasing amount of his time. The United Society of Christian Endeavor was incorporated in 1885. In 1886 a periodical, *The Golden Rule*, was purchased, and Clark began to edit it as the official organ of the society. In 1887 Clark resigned his pastorate to give his full attention to the society. He was elected president of the United Society and held the office for the next 38 years. During this time, he earned his income as an author and as editor of *The Golden Rule*, which was owned by a private corporation, and was thus able to donate much of his time to the promotion of the United Society without charge.

The Christian Endeavor movement spread throughout the Protestant world during the next generation. In 1888 Clark traveled to England at the invitation of the British Sunday School Association to initiate the work in Great Britain. Several years later he embarked on a round-the-world tour that became the subject of his next books, *Our Journey Around the World* (1894) and *World-wide Endeavor* (1895). In 1895 he helped to organize the World's Christian Endeavor Union and served as its first president.

During the more than two decades that Clark directed the Christian Endeavor movement, he continued to edit the society's periodical (renamed *Christian Endeavor World* in 1897). Clark also authored a number of books, including: *A New Way Around an Old World* (1900); *Christian Endeavor in All Lands* (1906); *The Continent of Opportunity* (1907); *The Holy Land of Asia Minor* (1914); and *In Christ's Own Country* (1914). As indicated by the subjects of his books, he traveled widely as part of his duties.

Clark retired as editor of *Christian Endeavor World* in 1919, but was named honorary editor. In his retirement years he wrote an autobiographical volume, *Memories of Many Men in Many Lands* (1922). As his last duty, in 1926 he presided at the World's Christian Endeavor Union convention in London. The Christian Endeavor movement remained a strong force in Protestant circles for several generations, but began to wane after World War II.

Sources:

Clark, Francis Edward. *The Children and the Church*. Boston: Congregational Sunday School and Publication Society, 1882. 108 pp.

———. *Christian Endeavor in All Lands*. Philadelphia: The Author, 1906. 633 pp.

———. *In Christ's Own Country*. New York: Christian Herald, 1914. 128 pp.

———. *Memories of Many Men in Many Lands*. Boston: United Society of Christian Endeavor, 1922. 704 pp.

———. *A New Way Around the World*. New York: Harper & Brothers, 1900. 212 pp.

———. *World-wide Endeavor*. Philadelphia: Gillespie, Metzgar & Kelley, 1895. 644 pp.

Dictionary of American Biography. 20 vols. and 7 supps. New York: Charles Scribner's Sons, 1928-1936, 1944-1981.

★198★
CLARK, Glenn
Founder, Camp Farthest Out
b. Mar. 13, 1882, Des Moines, Iowa
d. Aug. 16, 1956, Minneapolis, Minnesota

Glenn Clark, founder of a devotional-prayer movement called Camp Farthest Out (CFO), was the son of Fannie Page and James S. Clark, members of the Congregational Church. During his high school days Clark began his serious pursuit of a writing career. He attended Grinell College and following his graduation in 1905 returned to his home town as principal of Oak Park High School. In 1907 he married Louise Miles, a Presbyterian, and he joined the local Presbyterian church. In 1908 he moved to Aledo, Illinois, to

teach at William and Vashti College, and then to St. Paul, Minnesota, in 1912 to Macalester College. He gained some minor recognition in his academic field in 1921 with the publication of *The Manual of Short Story Art*, which became a popular textbook.

Clark seemed destined to lead the life of an obscure scholar when his father's death led him into a period of spiritual turmoil. He turned to prayer. Clark experienced a spiritual renewal and in 1924 wrote an article for the *Atlantic Monthly* in which he described what he had learned about prayer. "The Soul's Sincere Desire" garnered tremendous reader response, leading him to extend the article into a book with the same name. He was soon labeled an authority on the subject of prayer.

Clark began to teach a Bible class at the local Plymouth Congregational Church. This class became an experimental group for Clark as he developed ideas on prayer and gained a real expertise in the spiritual life. From his background coaching high school athletes, he spoke of "spiritual athletes," an idea that suggested the need of a training camp in the spiritual life. In 1930 the first Camp Farthest Out was held. It attracted Christians of a wide spectrum of backgrounds, some Jews, and even a few of the self-styled nonreligious. Even as he grew in his own perceptions, Clark nurtured the leadership that emerged at the camps and became the mentor of a new generation of spiritual leaders such as Agnes Sanford, Starr Daily, and Rufus Moseley, whose writings found popular acclaim, especially among liberal Protestants.

As Camp Farthest Out grew Clark founded Macalester Park Publishing Company, which would publish the majority of the more than fifty books he authored over the rest of his life. In 1940, with his sister Helen Clark, he began a magazine, *Clear Horizons*. In 1944 he retired from Macalester College. The rest of his life was one of expanding concerns and responsibilities. In the early 1950s he was given two magazines which had been started by a V. P. Randall; he integrated *The Fellowship Messenger* and the *Manual of Prayer* into the CFO program.

Clark left a legacy of spirituality that reached across denominational lines and has given him a continuing influence in the years since his death. CFO, still headquartered in St. Paul, has become international in scope.

Sources:

Clark, Glenn. *How to Find Health through Prayer*. New York: Harper & Brothers, 1940. 154 pp.

———. *A Man's Reach*. New York: Harper & Brothers, 1949. 314 pp.

———. *The Soul's Sincere Desire*. Boston: Little, Brown and Company, 1926. 114 pp.

———. *The Way, the Truth and the Life*. New York: Harper & Brothers, 1946. 179 pp.

———. *What Would Jesus Do?* St. Paul, MN: Macalester Park Publishing Company, 1950. 286 pp.

Clark, Miles. *Glenn Clark: His life and Writings*. Nashville, TN: Abingdon Press, 1975. 160 pp.

★199★
CLARK, Gordon Haddon
Philosopher/Theologian, Reformed Presbyterian Church
b. Aug. 31, 1902, Philadelphia, Pennsylvania
d. Apr. 9, 1985, Colorado

Gordon Haddon Clark, a philosopher and theologian of the Reformed Presbyterian Church, was the son of Elizabeth Yates Haddon and David Scott Clark. He attended the University of Pennsylvania, where he earned his B.A. in 1924. He stayed there as an instructor in philosophy while working on a Ph.D., which was completed in 1929. That year he married Ruth Schmidt. Also while in Philadelphia, Clark, a conservative Presbyterian, followed closely the problems at Princeton which led to the ouster and later defrocking of **J. Gresham Machen**, the leading voice for conservative theology in the Presbyterian Church. Clark sided with Machen and as a lay person helped establish the Orthodox Presbyterian Church in 1936. Having picked up a year at the Sorbonne (1931) in the meantime, in 1936 he left the University of Pennsylvania for a post at Wheaton College as a professor of philosophy.

Clark's first books appeared during his Wheaton years: *Readings in Ethics* (1931); *Selections from Hellenistic Philosophy* (1941); and *A History of Philosophy*. However, Clark was quite traditional as a theologian, and he continually clashed with the dominant theology at Wheaton, which had absorbed a considerable amount of Arminianism. (Arminianism is a form of Reformed theology which emphasizes elements of human free will as opposed to the more traditional Reformed-Presbyterian emphasis upon predestination.) As a result, he left Wheaton in 1943. He taught briefly at the Reformed Episcopal Theological Seminary in Philadelphia before joining the faculty at Butler University in 1945, where he spent the bulk of his career.

In 1945 Clark passed the examination and received ordination from the Orthodox Presbyterian Church. His ordination, however, was challenged by students of **Cornelius Van Til**, then the leading philosopher theologian in the denomination and a professor at Westminster Theological Seminary. The resulting controversy, which centered upon some of the philosophical presuppositions which undergirded Clark's theology, led Clark to withdraw and join the Reformed Presbyterian Church.

During the next decades Clark found a comfortable home at Butler, and was appointed chairman of the department of philosophy in 1946, a post he retained until his retirement. He authored a number of books which found a following among conservative Presbyterians, including: *A Christian Philosophy of Education* (1946); *A Christian View of Men and Things* (1952); *What Presbyterians Believe* (1956); *Religion, Reason and Revelation* (1961); and *Historiography: Secular and Religious* (1971). The vast literature he created has been seen as a philosophical alternative to the more popular Van Til, and Clark's philosophical views have developed strong support during the 1980s.

In 1974 Clark retired and was named professor emeritus. He used his retirement years to continue his writing and for a decade served as a visiting lecturer at Covenant College, his denomination's school at Lookout Mountain, Georgia. Near the end of his life he moved to Colorado and became a visiting professor at Sangre de Cristo Seminary in Colorado. Among the important titles produced during his retirement years are *Language and Theology* (1980); *Behaviorism and Christianity* (1982); and *God's Hammer: The Bible and Its Critics* (1982). He left one book to be published after his death. An answer to many of his critics, it was published as *Clark Speaks from the Grave* (1986). In recent years Clark's thought has been promoted by the Trinity Foundation of Jefferson, Maryland. Its president, John Robbins, is Clark's intellectual successor.

Sources:

Clark, Gordon H. *Behaviorism and Christianity*. Jefferson, MD: Trinity Foundation, 1982. 106 pp.

_____. *Clark Speaks from the Grave*. Jefferson, MD: Trinity Foundation, 1986. 83 pp.

_____. *God's Hammer: The Bible and Its Critics*. Jefferson, MD: Trinity Foundation, 1982. 190 pp.

_____. *In Defense of Theology*. Milford, MI: Mott Media, 1984. 119 pp.

_____. *What Do Presbyterians Believe?* Phillipsburg: Presbyterian and Reformed Publishing Company, 1956, 1965. 284 pp.

Robbins, John. "America's Augustine: Gordon Haddon Clark." *The Trinity Review*, (1985): 1-2.

★ 200 ★
CLARKE, James Freeman
Minister, American Unitarian Association
b. Apr. 4, 1810, Hanover, New Hampshire
d. Jun. 8, 1888, Boston, Massachusetts

James Freeman Clarke, a leading nineteenth-century minister in the American Unitarian Association (AUA), was the son of Samuel and Rebecca Parker Hull Clarke. His father, a poor handyman, moved to Newton, Massachusetts, when James was a child, and he was brought up primarily by his grandfather, Dr. James Freeman, the former minister of King's Chapel in Boston. Clarke was sent to the Boston Latin School in 1821 to prepare him for college. He attended Harvard College. After his graduation in 1829, he went on to Harvard Divinity School, from which he graduated in 1833. He was ordained in Boston and left to become the Unitarian pastor in Louisville, Kentucky. While there, from 1836 to 1839, he edited the *Western Messenger*, a midwestern Unitarian periodical. He returned to Boston in 1840.

In 1841 Clarke accepted the pastorate of the Church of the Disciples, which had caused considerable stir in religious circles because of the unusual (for the time) amount of power placed in the hands of the laity. He served the church into 1850 when his health failed; he was forced to take a leave for several years. The church survived his rather lengthy illness and welcomed him back to the pulpit in 1854. During his time of recovery, he authored his first two books, *The Christian Doctrine of Forgiveness of Sins* (1852) and *The Christian Doctrine of Prayer* (1854).

Once back in Boston and at his pulpit, Clarke was ready to begin the mature phase of his career. He became deeply involved in the community and in social issues. He was named to the state Board of Education (1863-1869) and served several terms as a member of the board of overseers of Harvard College. He publicly supported the temperance and women's suffrage causes.

Though primarily functioning as a pastor, Clarke wrote some of the more famous theological texts of the day, representative of the best of Unitarian thinking. He is still remembered for his pioneering two-volume work on comparative religion, *Ten Great Religions* (1871, 1883), and his development of a new, more accepting approach to non-Christian religions. While arguing for Christianity's superiority, his approach suggested that there was much good in all of the major religious traditions. His work on other religions also led to a search for the essential nature of the religious life and to two other books: *Common Sense in Religion* (1874), and *Essentials and Non-Essentials in Religion* (1878). Other works he authored in what came to be known as the Liberal Christocentric theological tradition were: *Orthodoxy: Its Truths and Errors* (1866); *Self-Culture* (1882); *Anti-Slavery Days* (1884); and *The Problem of the Fourth Gospel* (1886).

Clarke served as a professor at Harvard Divinity School (1867-1871) and as a lecturer on ethnic religion following the publication of *Ten Great Religions*. He remained pastor of the Church of the Disciples until his death at the age of 68.

Sources:

Clarke, James Freeman. *The Christian Doctrine of Forgiveness of Sins*. Boston: Crosby & Nichols, 1852. 172 pp.

_____. *The Christian Doctrine of Prayer*. Boston: Crosby & Nichols, 1854. 224 pp.

_____. *Common Sense in Religion*. Boston: J. R. Osgood, 1874. 443 pp.

_____. *Essentials and Non-Essentials in Religion*. Boston: American Unitarian Association, 1878. 443 pp.

_____. *Self-Culture*. Boston: J. R. Osgood, 1882. 446 pp.

_____. *Ten Great Religions*. 2 vols. Boston: Houghton, Mifflin & Co., 1871, 1883.

Dictionary of American Biography. 20 vols. and 7 supps. New York: Charles Scribner's Sons, 1928-1936, 1944-1981.

Hale, Edward Everett, ed. *James Freeman Clarke. Autobiography; Diary and Correspondence.* Boston: Houghton, Mifflin & Co., 1891.

★201★
CLARKE, William Newton
Theologian, Northern Baptist Convention
b. Dec. 2, 1841, Cazenovia, New York
d. Jan. 14, 1912, Deland, Florida

William Newton Clarke, a modernist theologian of the Northern Baptist Convention, was the son of a Baptist clergyman, William Clarke, and Urania Miner Clarke, both descendants of old colonial families. Except for two years when his father pastored at Whitesboro, New York, Clarke grew up in the parsonage at Cazenovia. After graduating from the local school, Cazenovia Seminary, in 1858, he attended Madison University (B.A., 1861) and Colgate Seminary (B.D., 1863). He was ordained in 1856; his first pastorate was in Keene, New Hampshire. In May 1869 he was called to the First Baptist Church at Newton Center, Massachusetts. Five months later he married Emily A. Smith.

The move to Newton Center proved most providential, as many members of the faculty and student body of the nearby Newton Theological Institution attended his services. They provided an atmosphere for Clarke's theological development. During his 11 years at the church he began to move away from traditional theological affirmations and toward a reinterpretation of Christian faith in modern terms. The process began with an examination of the doctrine of the atonement, that is, the nature of the saving work of Christ. His sermons began to manifest his dropping of the more traditional static view of the atonement in favor of a more dynamic language.

Sensing some opposition from the old church members at Newton Center, in 1880 Clarke moved to Olivet Baptist Church in Montreal, Quebec. He remained in Montreal for three years, during which time he wrote his first book, *Commentary on Mark* (1881). He moved on to Toronto in 1883 and accepted a call to teach New Testament at the Baptist Theological School. In 1887 he returned to the pastorate in Hamilton, New York, where he attended college. Shortly after the move, Ebenezer Dodge, the president of Colgate Seminary, died, and Clarke assumed some of his load in theological instruction. In 1890 he was elected to the J. J. Joslin Professorship of Christian Theology.

Clarke entered the most productive phase of his career just as the modernist-fundamentalist debate was heating up, and he became a champion of the modernists. During the 1890s he prepared a number of manuscripts which were circulated to the student body and used as textbooks. As the decade closed he began to publish them. His most important text, also his first, was *An Outline of Christian Theology* (1898), noted as one of the first systematic presentations of the modernist position, which accepted both the historical criticism of the Bible and the new scientific-evolutionary worldview. It was followed quickly by *Can I Believe in God the Father?* (1899); *What Shall We Think of Christianity?* (1899); *A Study of Christian Missions* (1900); and *The Use of the Scriptures in Theology* (1905).

The immense importance of Clarke's work is best understood when seen in conjunction with the work of his colleague **Walter Rauschenbusch**, a professor at nearby Rochester (N.Y.) Theological Seminary. Rauschenbusch's monumental effort on the social interpretation of Christian theology matured as Clarke was publishing his more significant volumes, and Rauschenbusch's key books began to appear in 1907. Together, Clarke and Rauschenbusch moved the majority of the Northern Baptist Convention into the modernist camp and set the stage for the most intense phase of the battles over fundamentalism in the 1920s.

Clarke retired in 1908, but stayed on at Colgate as a lecturer in Christian ethics. He published three more books in his remaining years: *The Christian Doctrine of God* (1909); *Sixty Years with the Bible* (1909); and *The Ideal of Jesus* (1911). His health began to fail, however, and he died in Florida where he and his wife had wintered for a number of years.

Sources:

Clarke, Emily. *Wm. Newton Clarke; a Biography, with Additional Sketches by His Friends and Colleagues.* 1916.
Clarke, William Newton. *Can I Believe in God the Father?* New York: Charles Scribner's, 1899. 215 pp.
_____. *The Christian Doctrine of God.* New York: Charles Scribner's, 1909. 477 pp.
_____. *The Ideal of Jesus.* New York: Charles Scribner's, 1911. 329 pp.
_____. *An Outline of Christian Theology.* New York: Charles Scribner's, 1898. 458 pp.
_____. *The Use of the Scriptures in Theology.* New York: Charles Scribner's, 1905. 170 pp.
Dictionary of American Biography. 20 vols. and 7 supps. New York: Charles Scribner's Sons, 1928-1936, 1944-1981.

★202★
CLAVIER, Anthony Forbes Moreton
Archbishop, American Episcopal Church (AEC)
b. Apr. 19, 1940, Yorkshire England

Anthony Forbes Moreton Clavier has emerged out of the world of independent Catholicism in England to become the leader of one of the most substantive of the several churches that have been established in recent decades as a conservative alternative to the Episcopal Church. Raised in England, in 1958 Clavier entered the Bernard Gilpin Society, Sands House, a pre-theological college in Durham. He left after a year to take a job as a teacher. In 1961 he was ordained as a minister in the Countess of Huntington's Connection, a conservative Calvinist church which had emerged in the eighteenth century.

In 1962 Clavier began a pilgrimage through the world of independent Episcopal churches. He was ordained a priest that year by Francis Everden Glenn of the Catholic Episcopal Church. In April 1963 he was reordained by Archbishop Charles Dennis Boltwood, head of the Free Protestant Episcopal Church. A month later, he was ordained again by Charles Leslie Saul of the English Episcopal Church. Then in 1964 he returned to the Catholic Episcopal Church. During this time he had his first writings published—*Why a New Church?* (1964); *False Motives* (1964); and *English Old Catholicism* (1965). In 1965 Clavier briefly affiliated with the Old Roman Catholic Church and its Archbishop Gerard George Shelley, but in 1966 was reordained by Hugh George de Willmott Newman of the Catholic Apostolic Church. He remained in Newman's jurisdiction until his move to the United States in 1967. In America, he associated with the Anglican Orthodox Church (AOC), one of the first of the several recent churches to break from the Episcopal Church. He stayed with the AOC for only a short time, as in 1968 he returned to England and the Catholic Episcopal Church.

In 1969 Clavier moved to the United States a second time and finally found what was to become his permanent church home. He associated himself as a priest under James Hardin George, who had founded the American Episcopal Church (AEC). On February 11, 1970, George consecrated Clavier and appointed him as his suffragan. Later that year, George resigned in Clavier's favor and Clavier served as primate for the next six years. Except for a brief period (1976-1981) when Harold L. Trott was primate, Clavier has headed the steadily growing jurisdiction.

In 1976 several thousand conservative Episcopalians left the church in protest of the trend to ordain women and homosexuals as priests and a perceived general moral drift. The early organization of this group, the Anglican Catholic Church (ACC), was given a high degree of legitimacy in part by the participation of Francisco Pagtakhan, a bishop of the Philippine Independent Church, in consecrating its bishops. Over the next few years the ACC split into several factions. Pagtakhan set himself the task of bringing some unity to the situation. As part of that effort, in the midst of merger negotiations among several of the churches, including the American Episcopal Church, Pagtakhan consecrated and thus passed his lines of apostolic succession to Clavier. The movement of former Episcopalians remains splintered, but the AEC and the ACC have emerged as its two largest and most stable national bodies. Clavier has also overseen the development of AEC foreign missions in several countries.

Sources:

Clavier, Anthony. *The American Episcopal Church.* Valley Forge, PA: Brotherhood of the Servants of the Lord, 1975. 21 pp. Rev. ed. as: *The American Episcopal Church: An Introduction.* Greenville, SC: The American Episcopal Church, n.d. 31 pp.

———. "Disunity Among Traditionalists." *The Living Church* (December 12, 1976): 15.

———. *English Old Catholicism.* London: Catholic Episcopal Church, 1965. 34 pp.

———. *False Motives.* London: Church of the servants of Christ, 1964. 5 pp.

———. *Why a New Church?* London: Church of the Servants of Christ, 1964. 5 pp.

Molineaux, Louis. "The Rise of Anthony Clavier; A Chapter in Parentheses in the History of the Continuing Church Movement in North America." *The Glastonbury Bulletin* 66 (June 1983): 177-86.

★ 203 ★
COBB JR., John Boswell
Theologian, United Methodist Church
b. Feb. 9, 1925, Kobe Japan

John Boswell Cobb, Jr., a theologian in the United Methodist Church, is the son of Theodora Atkinson and John Boswell, Sr., missionaries with the Methodist Episcopal Church, South. His early life in Japan was to have a continuing influence in his career and eventually set his own Christian theological efforts in dialogue with Japanese Buddhism. Cobb came to the United States prior to World War II and attended Emory University (1941-1943) and the University of Michigan (1944). In 1947 he married Jean O. Loftin. He completed his graduate studies at the University of Chicago, where he received both his M.A. (1949) and his Ph.D. (1952). Meanwhile, he had affiliated with the North Georgia Conference of the Methodist Church (1939-1968), and was received on trial in 1950. He pastored a church in Towns County, Georgia (1950-1951), during the first year of his teachings at Young Harris College. He was ordained a deacon in 1952. In 1953 he began teaching at Emory University and in 1955 was ordained an elder in the Methodist Church.

In 1958 Cobb moved to Claremont, California, and began his long relationship with the School of Theology, the Methodist seminary for the United Methodist Church's western jurisdiction. His first books appeared soon afterwards: *Varieties of Protestantism* (1960) and *Living Options in Protestant Thought* (1962). In 1964 he was named Ingraham Professor of Systematic Theology at Claremont. During his more than three decades at Claremont, Cobb became best known as the major American exponent of process theology, a theology built upon the philosophical insight of Alfred North Whitehead and Charles Hartshorne, with whom Cobb had studied at the University of Chicago. He announced his effort to build a process theology most clearly in the issuance of *A Christian Natural Theology* in 1965. Over the years he argued for his perspective in numerous articles and an impressive set of books. The most important of his books included *The Structure of Christian Existence* (1967); *God and the World* (1969); *Process Theology: An Introductory Exposition*, written with David Griffin; and

Theology and Pastoral Care (1977). The work in process theology bore fruit in the formation of the Center for Process Theology, for which he was the first director.

Cobb's long-time interest in Buddhism came to the fore in the 1970s. His Armstrong Lectures (1976) at Kalamazoo College and Rall Lectures (1979) at Garrett-Evangelical Theological Seminary led to his first book centered upon the Buddhist-Christian encounter, *Beyond Dialogue* (1982). More recently he released *The Emptying God: A Buddhist Christian Conversation* (1990) with Christopher Ives.

Cobb retired in 1990, but is continuing pursuit of his theological agenda, which includes not only process thought and Buddhism, but parapsychology.

Sources:

Buse, Paul Custodio. *Ethics in John Cobb's Process Theology.* Atlanta: Scholar's Press, 1988. 184 pp.

Cobb, John B. *Beyond Dialogue: Toward a Mutual Transformation of Christianity and Buddhism.* Philadelphia: Fortress Press, 1982. 156 pp.

———. *A Christian Natural Theology.* Philadelphia: Westminster Press, 1965.

———. *God and the World.* Philadelphia: Westminster Press, 1969.

———. *The Structure of Christianity.* Philadelphia: Westminster Press, 1967.

———, and David Griffin. *Process Theology: An Introductory Exposition.* Philadelphia: Westminster Press, 1976.

Griffin, David Ray, and Thomas J. J. Altizer, eds. *John Cobb's Theology in Process.* Philadelphia: Westminster Press, 1977. 201 pp.

★ 204 ★
CODY, John Patrick
Cardinal, Roman Catholic Church
b. Dec. 4, 1907, St. Louis, Missouri
d. Apr. 25, 1982, Chicago, Illinois

John Patrick Cody, a cardinal and archbishop of Chicago in the Roman Catholic Church, was the son of Irish immigrant parents. He began his move to the priesthood in the St. Louis Preparatory Seminary, which he entered at the age of 12. He continued his studies at the North American College and the Appolonaris in Rome, where he received his advanced degrees of Ph.D. (1928), S.T.D. (1932) and J.C.D. (1938). He was ordained in Rome in 1931. Following his ordination, while pursuing further studies, he became the assistant to the rector at the North American College for a year and then joined the staff of the Vatican Secretary of State.

Upon his return to the United States, Cody became secretary to Archbishop **John Joseph Glennon** in St. Louis. He also served as chaplain at St. Mary's Home for Girls. He became chancellor of the archdiocese in 1940. As chancellor, he accompanied Glennon to Rome when the latter was named a cardinal and was thus with him three weeks later in Ireland when Glennon died. Cody officiated at the requiem mass for Glennon.

Cody became auxiliary bishop of St. Louis and titular bishop of Apollonia in 1947. He became coadjutor bishop of Kansas City-St. Joseph, Missouri, in 1956 and succeeded to leadership of the diocese when the former bishop resigned later that same year. In successive steps in 1961, 1962, and 1964, he became coadjutor, apostolic administrator, and archbishop of New Orleans. As archbishop of New Orleans, Cody stepped into the national spotlight after following through on his predecessor's efforts to desegregate the Catholic schools of the city.

After a year in New Orleans, Cody moved to Chicago as its new archbishop. In Chicago he became involved in one major controversy after another. The first was internal, as clergy protested his traditional authoritative (and some charged, arbitrary) leadership. Rome saw the situation differently and in 1967 made Cody a cardinal. The next year Cody offended many white Catholics by initiating a plan to bus minority children from the inner city to less crowded suburban schools. In the 1970s he was praised by black leaders for his support of inner-city schools—which were predominantly black, but nonCatholic in enrollment—but denounced by other groups for closing several inner city schools that were increasing debt-ridden.

The last years of Cody's life were filled with allegations that he used church funds for personal purposes. He died while the matter was in the hands of a grand jury. After his death, the jury refused to return an indictment, and the issue was allowed to die.

Sources:

Delaney, John J. *Dictionary of American Catholic Biography*. Garden City, NY: Doubleday & Company, 1988. 621 pp.

★ 205 ★
COE, George Albert
Liberal Protestant Religious Educator
Psychologist
b. Mar. 26, 1862, Mendon, New York
d. Nov. 9, 1951, Claremont, California

George Albert Coe, an influential theorist in modern approaches to the psychology of religion and religious education, was the son of Harriet Van Voorhis and George W. Coe, a minister in the Methodist Episcopal Church. The pietistic environment in which he was raised became a problem for him as a teenager, as he had no experience of conversion (among pietists conversion is a confirmation of a personal relationship with God). During his college years his faith was integrated into a worldview that included evolution (and hence saw little need for a disjunctive conversion experience), and he became committed to the scientific method. After finishing his A.B. degree at the University of Rochester, he entered the School of Theology at Boston University. He abandoned his plans to enter the parish ministry and shifted his emphasis to philosophy. He received his S.T.B. degree in 1887 and the following year completed an M.A. in philosophy. Later that year he married Sadie E. Knowland and began teaching at the University of Southern California. He finished the requirements of his Ph.D. in 1891 and was named a professor of philosophy at USC. In 1893 he was named John Evans Professor of Philosophy of Religion at Northwestern University.

Coe's teaching career began at a time when psychology was struggling into existence as a separate discipline. Coe, as a student of the new science, began to search for psychological insights into the nature of religious experience. He had earlier come to believe that religious experience was the basis of the religious life. In his first books, *The Spiritual Life: Studies in the Science of Religion* (1902) and *The Religion of a Mature Mind* (1902), he argued for the legitimacy of both science and religion in the quest for truth and that the religious quest began with human experience rather than metaphysical speculation.

By the beginning of the twentieth century, the Sunday school movement had given birth to religious education as a separate discipline concerned with the development of young Christians. In 1903 Coe became one of the founders of the Religious Education Association and guided it in its commitment to use contemporary knowledge in the development of religious education programs and curricula. This was the subject of his next book, *Education in Religion and Morals* (1904).

In 1909 Coe's pioneering efforts were recognized. He was named a professor of religious education and psychology of religion at Union Theological Seminary in New York City and was elected president of the Religious Education Association. While at Union he wrote his most important books, *The Psychology of Religion* (1916) and *A Social Theory of Religious Education* (1917).

The former work placed him with such theorists as William James and Edwin Starbuck as proponents of psychological insights in understanding religious dynamics. The latter became possibly the most influential work on the development of religious education for the next generation.

In 1922 Coe moved to Teachers College at Columbia University and authored two more books, *Law and Freedom in the School* (1923) and *What Ails Our Youth* (1924), before his retirement in 1927. He lived his retirement years in Claremont, California. He lived for many years after his move to California and authored several additional books, including *What Is Christian Education?* (1929) and *What Is Religious Education Doing to Our Conscience?* (1943).

During the last years of his life Coe emerged as a defender of liberal Protestantism in the face of the new Neo-Orthodox theology coming to America from Europe. He became an exponent of a Marxist social perspective and found himself a target for the Committee on Un-American Activities of the U.S. Congress.

Sources:

Archibald, Helen A. *George Albert Coe: Theorist for Religious Education in the Twentieth Century*. Urbana, IL: University of Illinois, Ph.D. dissertation, 1975.
Coe, George Albert. *Education in Religion and Morals*. Chicago: Fleming H. Revell Co., 1904. 434 pp.
———. *The Psychology of Religion*. Chicago: University of Chicago Press, 1916. 365 pp.
———. *The Religion of a Mature Mind*. Chicago: Fleming H. Revell Co., 1902. 442 pp.
———. *A Social Theory of Religious Education*. New York: Charles Scribner's Sons, 1917. 361 pp.
———. *The Spiritual Life: Studies in the Science of Religion*. New York: Eaton & Mains, 1900. 279 pp.
———. *What Is Christian Education?* New York: Charles Scribner's Sons, 1929. 300 pp.
Dupree, Sherry Sherrod. *Biographical Dictionary of African-American, Holiness-Pentecostals, 1880-1990*. Washington, DC: Middle Atlantic Regional Press, 1990. 386 pp.
Westerhoff, John Henry, III. "George Albert Coe: Revaluer of Values." *Religion in Life* (Winter 1952-1953).

★ 206 ★
COFFIN SR., Henry Sloane
Minister and Educator, Presbyterian Church
b. Jan. 5, 1877, New York, New York
d. Nov. 25, 1954, Lakeville, Connecticut

Henry Sloane Coffin, Sr., a leading liberal Presbyterian minister, who for many years served as president of Union Theological Seminary in New York City, was the son of Edmund and Euphemia Sloane Coffin. The staunch Presbyterianism of his mother had a decided influence on him, and he had decided to enter the ministry even before he began his college education at Yale University in 1893. After his graduation in 1897, he attended New College, the theological school of the Free Church of Scotland (Presbyterian) in Edinburgh for two years. After the summer session of 1899 at the University of Marburg, Germany, he returned to complete his last year at Union Theological Seminary, from which he received his B.D. in 1900. He was ordained that same year by the Presbytery of New York.

Coffin's first parish was Bedford Park Presbyterian Church in the Bronx, New York. The church's growth under his leadership led to his call to Madison Avenue Presbyterian Church, a traditionally important Manhattan pulpit, but at the time a congregation which had suffered some reverses in the fast-changing urban environment. During Coffin's 21 years as its pastor, it became one of the leading centers of New York's religious life. Shortly after moving to Madison Avenue, he married Dorothy Prentice Eels.

Coffin's early years in Manhattan coincided with the development of the social gospel, the theological perspective articulated by Baptist theologian **Walter Rauschenbusch** which emphasized the application of Christian teaching for the reform of society as a whole. Beyond his pastoral work, which began in 1904, Coffin became an early exponent of the social gospel, which he integrated into the classes he taught in practical theology at Union Seminary. It was also reflected in a hymnbook he published in 1910, *Hymns of the Kingdom*, and in his first books, such as *In a Day of Social Rebuilding: Lectures on the Ministry of the Church* (1918) and *More Christian Industrial Order* (1920). As the fundamentalist-modernist controversy heated up after World War I, he became an influential liberal leader in the Presbyterian Church.

Coffin served the Madison Avenue congregation until 1926, when he accepted the post as president of Union Theological Seminary. He served as president for 19 years, during which time the seminary emerged as one of the most important theological schools in North American Protestantism. This was due in no small part to the faculty Coffin helped to assemble; members included **Reinhold Niebuhr** and **Paul J. Tillich**. Coffin had trouble accepting the new theology of his leading professors, however, and remained a typical early twentieth-century liberal. He summarized his mature thought in a volume published in 1940, *Religion Yesterday and Today*. In 1943 he was honored by his church, which elected him as moderator, its highest office. He retired from the presidency of the seminary in 1945.

Coffin had become active in the ecumenical movement during his last decade at Union and beginning in 1937 devoted many hours to the committee which developed a plan of union between the Presbyterian and Episcopal churches. In one of the few major setbacks in his distinguished career, that plan was rejected in 1946.

Coffin remained active in his retirement years, always in demand as a speaker. His most important lectures during these years were the George Craig Stewart Lectures on Preaching at Seabury-Western Theological Seminary in Evanston, Illinois, later published as *Communion through Preaching* (1952). Shortly after his death in 1954, an anthology of his prayers and sermons was published under the title *Joy in Believing*.

Sources:

Coffin, Henry Sloane. *Communion through Preaching*. New York: Charles Scribner's, 1952. 124 pp.
_____. *In a Day of Social Rebuilding: Lectures on the Ministry of the Church*. New Haven, CN: Yale University Press, 1918. 176 pp.
_____. *More Christian Industrial Order*. New York: Macmillan Company, 1920. 86 pp.
_____. *Religion Yesterday and Today*. Nashville, TN: Cokesbury, 1940. 183 pp.
Dictionary of American Biography. 20 vols. and 7 supps. New York: Charles Scribner's Sons, 1928-1936, 1944-1981.
Noyes, Morgan Phelps. *Henry Sloane Coffin: The Man and His Ministry*. New York: Charles Scribner's, 1964. 274 pp.

★ 207 ★
COFFMAN, John Samuel
Evangelist, Mennonite Church
b. Oct. 16, 1848, Rockingham County, Virginia
d. Jul. 22, 1899, Elkhart, Indiana

John Samuel Coffman, a pioneer evangelist in the Mennonite Church, was the son of Samuel and Frances Weaver Coffman. He grew up on his father's farm. He was baptized and joined the Mennonite Church at the age of 16 but soon had to flee the territory to avoid the draft into the Confederate Army in the last month of the Civil War. He married Elizabeth Rhodes Heatrole in 1869. He received little education, but through self-study was able to obtain a teacher's certificate. In 1874 he began teaching school. He attended the Bridgewater Normal School for a term in 1875.

In 1875 Coffman was chosen by lot as a minister in the Mennonite Church and was ordained at Bank Church near Rushville, Virginia. He preached widely in the area and did much to bring music into the worship service. In 1879 **John F. Funk** invited Coffman to join his publishing enterprise in Elkhart, Indiana. Coffman became assistant editor of the *Herald of Truth* and soon became involved in the production of Sunday school literature. During the rest of the century Coffman led two lives, one as the writer of educational materials for the church and the other as an evangelist. His evangelical efforts eventually changed the life of the church as a whole.

Coffman preached his first set of evangelistic services in Kent County, Michigan, in 1881. The initial success led to further invitations, and slowly the church began to accept evangelism into its life. Coffman was gifted with a forceful speaking voice and a tactful, winsome personality that won over the strong opposition to protracted meetings. He was also able to use the meetings as a tool in promoting church schools and other gatherings for youth. His evangelistic endeavors had in part begun out of his concern for the inability of weaker churches to compete with larger congregations of other denominations in attracting their youth.

During the 1890s Coffman began to exert national leadership. In 1889 he was named both president and tract editor of the Mennonite Book and Tract Society, positions he retained for many years. He served on the committee to compile a new hymnal, which appeared in 1890 as Hymns and Tunes. In 1891 he published several books with Funk, including: *The Minister's Manual*; *Confession of Faith*; and *Fundamental Bible References*. His work on church school material expanded to weekly lesson sheets for the periodical *Worlds of Cheer*, and a new series of lesson helps which began in 1890.

Coffman also advocated liberal education for the church's young people. He encouraged church support of the Elkhart Institute Association's business and normal school, which eventually grew into Goshen College.

Coffman's career was cut short at a relatively young age, when he developed stomach cancer.

Sources:

Coffman, Barbara F. *His Name Was John*. Scottdale, PA: Herald House, 1964. 352 pp.
Hostetler, Beulah Stauffer. *American Mennonites and Protestant Movements*. Scottdale, PA: Herald Press, 1987. 366 pp.
The Mennonite Encyclopedia. 4 vols. Scottdale, PA: The Mennonite Publishing House, 1955.

★ 208 ★
COHN, Leopold
Founder, American Board of Missions to the Jews
b. 1862, Berezna Hungary
d. Dec. 19, 1937

Leopold Cohn, pioneer Christian missionary to the Jews and founder of the American Board of Missions to the Jews, was born in a small town in Hungary into an Orthodox Jewish family. Both his parents died when he was seven. At the age of 13, he decided to study for the rabbinate and by the age of 18 had mastered Hebrew and was an accomplished student of the Talmud. Through S. L. Teitelbaum, Cohn's rabbi and a leader among the Hassidim in Sziget, he came to know his future wife, Rose Hoffman. They were married in 1880 and resided near Sziget where Cohn studied under Teitelbaum. His studies raised doubts as he attempted to reconcile passages from the Talmud, the volumes of Jewish wisdom, with the Jewish Bible (or Christian Old Testament), especially on the issue of the coming of the Messiah.

In the early 1890s Cohn was advised to go to America, and in 1892 he migrated to New York where, for the first time, he encountered Hebrew Christians and was given a copy of the New Testament written in Hebrew. He soon accepted Jesus as the Messiah, an action that led to his rejection by the Jewish community. Subsequently, he moved to Scotland, where he was baptized as a Christian, and in the meantime lost contact with his wife, who had heard of his conversion. In Edinburgh he attended the New College of the Free (Presbyterian) Church. He was eventually able to contact his wife and arrange for her to join him in Scotland, and soon she too was converted to Christianity. In 1893 they returned to New York, and with the support of his Scottish acquaintances he opened a mission in the Brownsville section of Brooklyn.

In 1896 Cohn gained the support of the American Baptists, and he opened the Williamsburg Mission to the Jews. Two years later he began a magazine, *The Chosen People*. The work prospered. Cohn's son, Joseph Hoffman Cohn, graduated from Moody Bible Institute in 1906 and joined the staff. In 1909 Cohn opened another mission in Brooklyn which was named Beth Bar Shalom.

Only one incident marred the progress of the mission. In 1913, several people claiming to be relatives and friends of Itzak Leib Joszovics, a convicted felon whose life seemed to closely parallel Cohn's, swore in a New York court that Joszovics and Cohn were the same person. Cohn denied the accusations and the court refused to act upon the charge.

In 1920 Cohn began the bilingual (Yiddish/English) *Shepherd of Israel*. Four years later the name of the organization was changed from Williamsburg Mission to the American Board of Missions to the Jews, by which it is still known today. It became the most successful of the evangelical Christian missionary organizations dedicated to the conversion of Jews. Cohn was succeeded as the head of the board by his son.

Sources:

Cohn, Joseph Hoffman. *I Have Fought a Good Fight*. New York: American Board of Missions to the Jews, 1953. 316 pp.

Cohn, Leopold. *A Modern Missionary to an Ancient People*. New York: American Board of Missions to the Jews, 1911. 59 pp.

Eichhorn, David Max. *Evangelizing the American Jew*. Middle Village, NY: Jonathan David Publishers, 1978. 210 pp.

★209★
COLEMAN, Johnnie
Founder, Universal Foundation for Better Living
b. 1920?, Mississippi

Johnnie Coleman, founder of the Universal Foundation for Better Living, a New Thought metaphysical denomination serving a predominantly black constituency, is the daughter of John Haley and Lula Haley Parker. She grew up in Mississippi in the 1920s as a member of the Methodist Church and graduated from Union Academy in Columbus, Mississippi. She then attended Wiley College, a Methodist school in Marshall, Texas, from which she received a B.A. She taught school in Canton, Mississippi, for six years and then moved to Chicago, where she worked as a price analyst in the Chicago Market Center.

In 1953 Coleman was told by a doctor that she had a terminal illness. He gave her six months to live. It was at this time she was introduced to the teachings of the Unity School of Christianity by her mother, who had been reading its literature for many years. She moved to Kansas City and enrolled as a full-time student at the school. Within six months all signs of her disease had vanished; however, she now had to face racial barriers at the school. She was not permitted to live on campus at Unity Village, some 15 miles from Kansas City, and was not allowed to eat in the school cafeteria. For over three years she commuted daily and brought a sack lunch. During her last year, however, she threatened to quit, and within a short time accommodations were made for her to live and dine on campus. Ordained in 1956, she returned to Chicago and

organized Christ Unity Temple, the first predominantly black Unity congregation.

By 1963 Christ Unity Temple, with some 20 members, moved into its own building. The church continued to grow and in the early 1970s Coleman was elected as the first black president of the Association of Unity Churches. In 1974, her first husband having died, she married Don Nedd, founder of the Brooklyn Truth Center for Better Living. That same year, complaining of the organization's continuing racism, she broke with the school and association and formed the independent Christ Universal Temple for Better Living. She also opened a metaphysical school, the Johnnie Coleman Institute, to train New Thought ministers. As other ministers were trained and, following her example, went out to form their own congregations, the Universal Foundation for Better Living was incorporated as a New Thought denomination. By the late 1980s there were 23 member congregations.

By 1978 Coleman was speaking at three services each Sunday to an audience in excess of 1,000 people. She began to plan for a larger church. In 1981 she began her television show, "Better Living with Johnnie Coleman." Her increasing duties heightened the need to consolidate her work under one roof. In 1985, on land acquired on Chicago's far south side, she opened a new Christ Universal Temple, which includes a 3,500-seat auditorium, the school, and television facilities. While the temple was under construction both her husband and mother died.

During the 1980s Coleman emerged as one of Chicago's most prominent black ministers and has served in a variety of positions in the city.

Sources:

Coleman, Johnnie. *From the Founder's Desk*. Chicago: Universal Foundation for Better Living, 1987. 67 pp.

———. *"It Works If You Work It."* 2 vols. Chicago: Universal Foundation for Better Living, n.d.

Poinsett, Alex. "Rev. Johnnie Coleman's Dream Church." *Ebony* 40, 12 (December 1985): 74-80.

★210★
COLLEY, William W.
Corresponding Secretary, Foreign Mission Convention of the United States of America (National Baptist)
b. Feb. 12, 1847, Prince Edward County, Virginia
d. Dec. 24, 1909, Winston-Salem, North Carolina

William C. Colley was the organizer of the National Baptist Foreign Mission Convention of the United States of America, which would later merge to become a constituent part of the National Baptist Convention, U.S.A., Inc., the largest religious organization among blacks in the United States. Colley was believed by many to be black , and he allowed the misperception to go uncorrected throughout his adult life. Only after his death was it learned that, in fact, his father was Scottish and his mother was an American Indian. Little is known of his life prior to the age of 23, when he was baptized and joined the Gravel Hill Baptist Church. He entered Richmond Institute in 1870 and spent his summers preaching. He was ordained in 1873 as a minister affiliated with the Southern Baptist Convention.

Shortly after his graduation in 1874, Colley was appointed as a missionary to the Yoruba people in West Africa (the area now known as Nigeria). He left for Africa in January 1875 and by the fall had settled in Lagos. A church was organized in 1876. Colley stayed in Africa until 1879 when ill health forced him to return to the United States. His return also became the occasion for his break with the Southern Baptist Convention, the reasons for which are not altogether clear. However, following his resignation from the board in November 1879, he to revived the previous efforts of black Baptists to organize missionary work. He turned to the most active Baptist organization of the time, the Colored Baptist Convention of Virginia which hired him to organize a new missionary convention. He sent out a call to his colleagues to meet November 24, 1880, in Montgomery, Alabama.

The more than 150 delegates at Montgomery turned to Colley as the first president of the new National Baptist Foreign Mission Convention of the United States of America. He declined the offer, and **William H. McAlpine** was chosen. Colley accepted the position of corresponding secretary. It appears that, during his years as secretary he also married, for in 1883 when the board accumulated enough money to send out its first missionaries, Colley and his wife were appointed to return to Africa. He and the other missionaries established a station in Bendoo, Liberia, the mother church of National Baptist work on the continent.

Colley remained active in the work of the convention and was in its employ for a time. However, given his accomplishment in organizing the convention, he moved into relative obscurity in his last years. It is believed that he lived past the turn of the century and eventually died in 1909.

Sources:

Boone, Theodore S. *Negro Baptists in Pictures and History.* Detroit: The Voice of Destiny, 1964. 54 pp.
Garrett, Chan C. and William T. Moore. *Speaking to the Mountain.* N.p., n.d.
Jackson, J. H. *A Story of Christian Activism: The History of the National Baptist Convention, U.S.A., Inc.* Nashville, TN: Townsend Press, 1980. 790 pp.

★ 211 ★
COLLIN, Michel
Independent Catholic Bishop
b. 1905, Beachy France
d. Jun. 23, 1974, Nancy France

Michel Collin, a traditionalist French priest who claimed to be the true Catholic pope, had a revelation at the age of seven that he would be a priest, then a bishop, and finally the pope. His childhood was filled with such visions, including discussions with Jesus and Mary. He did indeed become a priest in 1933, and created two new missionary orders in France, the Apostles of Infinite Love and the White Phalanx.

Rome began to realize that Collin was an unusual man when, in the 1940s, he sent the Vatican more than 300 pages of accounts of his visions, which included his claim that he had been mystically consecrated a bishop by Jesus on April 28, 1935, at Vaux-le-Metz. On October 7, 1950, Collin further alarmed the church hierarchy by proclaiming that God had made him the true pope, and that his appointment was part of what the Virgin Mary had revealed in the 1917 miracle at Fatima, Portugal. The Vatican quickly condemned him and took away his orders.

Collin kept a low profile for a while but in 1961 he declared that Jesus had ordered him to begin functioning as Pope Clement XV, regardless of who had the title of pope in Rome. Collin promptly moved to Clemery in Lorraine to set up his headquarters. A farmhouse in the area became Le Petit Vatican de Marie Coredemptrice. A newsletter, *La Verite*, was begun, as was a hotel for pilgrims in the nearby village of Pont-a-Mousson.

Clement (Collin) taught that the secret of Fatima predicted that after 1960 the pope would not be chosen in the traditional way, and that each pope would choose his own successor. Clement claimed that he was the successor that Pope John XXIII had secretly chosen. Clement considered the Virgin Mary part of the Trinity, allowed priests to marry, and allowed women to be bishops (but not cardinals).

Clement's main strength was always in France, Switzerland, Germany, Belgium, Luxembourg, and The Netherlands, but his influence has certainly been felt in North America. In 1965 he was ordained by Archbishop Cyprian Camge, an independent Catholic in the lineage of **Joseph Rene Vilatte**. Clement in turn ordained Father Jean de la Trinite, leader of a Canadian-based traditionalist group, who brought his Canadian group under Clement's authority. In 1968, however, Father Jean broke away and declared himself Pope Gregory XVII. A second group influenced by Clement began when John Higgins, an American priest, was ordained by Clement in 1969 and became the priest of the independent Parish of St. Joseph in Cicero, Illinois. By the time of Clement's death in 1974, he had put together an international following of about 8,000 people.

Sources:

Hart, Denis. "Revelations in a French Farmhouse," *The Critic.* XXXII (July-September, 1974): 26-33.
"Self-Styled 'Pope' Dies in France," *The Chicago Tribune* (June 24, 1974).
Melton, J. Gordon. *Biographical Dictionary of American Cult and Sect Leaders.* Garland Reference Library of Social Science, vol. 212. New York: Garland Publishing, 1986.

—Gary L. Ward

★ 212 ★
COLVILLE, Wilberforce Juvenal
Spiritualist Writer and Lecturer
b. Sep. 5, 1859?
d. Jan. 15, 1917

Little is known of the early life of Wilberforce Juvenal Colville, the prominent late-nineteenth century spokesperson for Spiritualism. Sources disagree on his birth date, varying from 1856 to 1862. A biographical sketch in an early Colville text, however, indicates that he was born in 1859. He grew up in England. His mother died when he was still an infant and his father died when he was eight years old. He was raised by a guardian as a member of the Church of England. As a child he saw spirit beings, most notably a beautiful woman who claimed to be his mother, an experience which later made him quite receptive to Spiritualism. In 1874 he heard Cora H. V. Richmond, the outstanding American medium, deliver a trance message in London. Later that evening he, for the first time, went into trance and an entity spoke through him.

Two years later Colville began public platform work and at the age of 18 made his first tour of the United States. His common approach to public work was to go into trance and speak on any subject suggested by the audience. He also frequently composed impromptu poems at the audience's request. He spent the rest of the 1880s touring in England and the United States. He became an early exponent of spiritual healing outside of the orthodox Christian tradition, and several of his most important books— *Inspirational Discourses* (1886); *The Spiritual Science of Health and Healing* (1887); and *Studies in Theosophy* (1889)—appeared at the end of this period.

During the 1890s Colville extended his travels to include Australia, where he stayed for two years. Upon his return, he made the United States his home, and took only occasional trips out of the country.

Colville became a student of the entire field of occultism from astrology to chromotherapy, but was especially interested in alternative forms of healing. During his mature years, numerous books came from his pen. They included *Spiritual Therapeutics; or, Divine Science* (1894); *Our Places in the Universal Zodiac* (1895); *Old and New Psychology* (1897); *Law of Correspondences Applied to Healing* (1898); *Life and Power from Within* (1900); *People's Handbook on Spiritual Science* (1902); *Universal Spiritualism* (1906); *Light and Color* (1914); and *Students' Questions Answered* (1914).

Sources:

Colville, W. J. *Light and Color*. New York: McCoy Publishing and Masonic
Supplies, 1914. 169 pp.

_____. *The Spiritual Science of Health and Healing*. Chicago: Garden
City Publishing Company, 1888. 270 pp.

_____. *Spiritual Therapeutics; or, Divine Science*. Chicago: Educator Pub-
lishing Company, 1894. 332 pp.

_____. *Studies in Theosophy*. Boston: Colby & Rich, 1890. 503 pp.

_____. *Universal Spiritualism*. New York: R. F. Fenno & Company, 1906.
352 pp.

★ 213 ★
CONE, James Hal
Theologian, African Methodist Episcopal Church
b. Aug. 8, 1938, Fordyce, Arkansas

James Hal Cone, a theologian of the African Methodist Episcopal
Church, is the son of Lucille and Charlie M. Cone. He attended
Shorter College for two years (1954-1956) but transferred to Philander Smith College to finish his A.B. in 1958. He received his
seminary education at Garrett Theological Seminary (B.D. 1961)
and remained in Evanston, Illinois to receive a Ph.D. at Northwestern University in 1965. He married Rose Hampton. In 1964 he
began teaching at Philander Smith College. Two years later he
moved to Adrian College in Adrian, Michigan. In 1969 he became
an assistant professor at Union Theological Seminary, and in 1977
he was named Charles A. Briggs Professor of Systematic Theology,
a position he continues to hold.

Cone burst upon the theological scene in 1969 with the publication of *Black Theology and Black Power*, which was quickly followed by *A Black Theology of Liberation* (1970). These books, issued in the context of the Civil Rights Movement of the 1960s and
the articulation of the goal of black power in one wing of that
movement, called for a theology particularized to the conditions
and needs of the American black community. They objected to the
goals of integration of the black community into white society with
a call for the complete emancipation of Blacks from white oppression by whatever means necessary. Liberation both socially and religiously became the central theme of Cone's presentation. Cone
argued that Jesus' work was primarily a liberating work and hence
directed toward the oppressed. Commitment to the oppressed
from the first century would lead to a commitment to blackness in
the twentieth century.

Beginning with Cone's call for black liberation, responses came
from others also seeking liberation for a special constituency, most
notably women and the poor of Latin America. As Cone has entered into dialogue with these other liberation theologians, he has
broadened his concerns, though he still speaks self-consciously out
of the context of black America.

Cone has continued to develop his theology through a series of
books, including *The Spirituals and the Blues* (1972); *God of the
Oppressed* (1975); and *My Soul Looks Back* (1982). In examining
the black spirituals Cone found a vivid illustration of the contemporary struggles of the black community. Cone argued that debates
over the originality of black music, a popular academic topic, miss
the heart of the spirituals, which can only be grasped in sharing the
spirit and faith of the people who created them.

Sources:

Cone, James H. *Black Theology and Black Power*. New York: Seabury
Press, 1969. 165 pp.

_____. *A Black Theology of Liberation*. Philadelphia: Lippencott, 1970.
254 pp.

_____. *God of the Oppressed*. New York: Seabury Press, 1975. 280 pp.

_____. *Martin and Malcolm and America*. Maryknoll, NY: Orbis Books,
1991. 358 pp.

_____. *My Soul Looks Back*. Nashville, TN: Abingdon, 1982. 144 pp.

_____. *The Spirituals and the Blues*. New York: Seabury Press, 1972. 152
pp.

★ 214 ★
CONN, Charles William
Executive, Church of God (Cleveland, Tennessee)
b. Jan. 20, 1902, Atlanta, Georgia

Charles William Conn, an executive and former general overseer
of the Church of God (Cleveland, Tennessee), one of the larger
Pentecostal denominations, is the son of Albert C. and Rosa Bell
Brimer Conn. Active in the church as a teenager, Conn became
Sunday school and youth director for the Church of God in 1940.
In 1941 he married Edna Louise Minor. He was ordained to the
ministry of the Church of God in 1946. In 1948 he was named the
national director of the Sunday school and youth literature.

Conn's major impact upon the Church of God began in the
1950s. In 1952 he became a member of the church's executive
council and editor-in-chief of its publications. His duties included
the editorship of both *Church of God Evangel* and *Lighted Pathway*, two of the church's periodicals. During the decade while he
served as the church's editor, he also authored his first book, *Like
a Mighty Army* (1955), a history of the Church of God (Cleveland,
Tennessee). It was followed by *Pillars of Pentecost* (1956), a doctrinal survey; *The Evangel Reader* (1958), a selection of articles
from the church periodical; *Where the Saints Have Trod* (1959);
The Rudder and the Rock (1960); and *The Bible: Book of Books*
(1961).

In 1962 Conn was elected assistant general overseer of the
Church of God, and four years later he was promoted to general
overseer. Following a quadrennium as general overseer, in 1970
he became president of Lee College, the denominational school.
Under his leadership the school continued its upward climb toward
becoming a first-rate liberal arts college. He continued to write and
produced a number of books, many on Biblical themes: *A Guide
to the Pentateuch* (1963); *Christ and the Gospels* (1964); *Acts of
the Gospels* (1965); *A Certain Journey* (1965); *Why Men Go Back*
(1967); and *A Survey of the Epistles* (1969). While at Lee college
he wrote *The Pointed Pen* (1973); *Highlights of Hebrew History*
(1975); and *A Balanced Church* (1975). In 1981 he published
three more books: *The Anatomy of Evil*; *Poets and Prophets of Israel*, and *Cradle of Pentecost*.

In 1980 Conn left Lee College and became the superintendent
of Virginia for the Church of God. He has also been active as a lecturer for the church, on whose behalf he travels extensively.

Sources:

Conn, Charles W. *The Anatomy of Evil*. New York: Revell, 1981.

_____. *The Evangel Reader*. Cleveland, TN: Pathway Press, 1958. 251 pp.

_____. *Like a Mighty Army*. Cleveland, TN: Pathway Press, 1955. 380 pp.

_____. *Pillars of Pentecost*. Cleveland, TN: Pathway Press, 1956. 141 pp.

_____. *The Pointed Pen*. Cleveland, TN: Lee College Alumni Association,
1973. 113 pp.

★ 215 ★
CONWELL, Russell Herman
Minister, Baptist Church
b. Feb. 15, 1843, South Worthington, Massachusetts
d. Dec. 6, 1925, Philadelphia, Pennsylvania

Russell Herman Conwell, a minister in the Baptist Church, is remembered primarily as the author of a single lecture, *Acres of Diamonds*, which he delivered over 6,000 times and which was reprinted in numerous editions during and after his life. He was the
son of Martin Conwell and Miranda Wickham Conwell. His abolitionist father turned their family farm into a stop on the underground railroad in the years prior to the Civil War, and possibly
passed to his son a desire to live his life by his own standards. As
a young man, Conwell ran away from home and went to Europe.
He returned to attend Wilbraham Academy and to begin a life as
a teacher after his graduation in 1859.

After a year of teaching, Conwell entered Yale, where he studied law. During this period he became an avowed atheist. His schooling was interrupted by the Civil War, and in the fall of 1862 he raised a company of Massachusetts volunteers over which he became the captain. After a term of service in North Carolina and Virginia, he returned to Massachusetts and raised a second company. He was then made a lieutenant-colonel under General McPherson. He saw action in east Tennessee, but his military career ended after he was wounded at Kenesaw Mountain. The injury also turned his attention to religion.

Conwell returned to school and was admitted to the bar in 1865. That same year he married Jennie Hayden. As a lawyer, he worked first in Minneapolis, Minnesota, where he also founded a newspaper, *The Daily Chronicle*, and then in Massachusetts, where he founded the *Somerville Journal*. His wife died in 1872, and his renewed interest in religion became more intense. He began to assist in a small Baptist church in Lexington, Massachusetts, and built it into a strong congregation. He married again in 1874, to Sarah Sanborn. He was finally ordained into the ministry in 1879.

During the 1870s Conwell began to obtain some fame as a popular writer. He authored a number of books on the life of famous men, including presidents Grant, Hayes, and Garfield, and clergymen Charles Spurgeon, Bayard Taylor, and John Wannamaker. Other books included *How and Why* (1871); *History of the Great Fire in Boston* (1873); and *Woman and the Law* (1875).

In 1880 Conwell was called to pastor Grace Baptist Church in Philadelphia. He quickly brought the congregation out of debt and turned it into one of the most important churches in the city. In 1891 he dedicated the new 3,000-seat church sanctuary, which became known as Baptist Temple. The temple became the center for a number of important philanthropic endeavors. He began what is today Temple University in the basement of the building. It was originally intended as a college for working people, and he donated the proceeds of his famous "Acres of Diamonds" lecture to assist students. He also led in the foundation of three hospitals for the city.

Conwell remained active as pastor of the Baptist Temple for over four decades. He continued to lecture and write, authoring a popular book, *Why Lincoln Laughed* (1922), as he was approaching his eightieth year.

Sources:

Burr, Agnes Rush. *Russell H. Conwell and His Work*. Philadelphia: John C. Winston Company, 1917. 438 pp.

. Conwell, Russell H. *History of the Great Fire in Boston*. Boston: B. B. Russell, 1873. 312 pp.

_____. *How and Why*. Boston: Lee & Shepherd, 1871. 283 pp.

_____. *Why Lincoln Laughed*. New York: Harper & Brothers, 1922. 147 pp.

_____. *Woman and the Law*. Boston: H. L. Shepherd, 1875. 22 pp.

Dictionary of American Biography. 20 vols. and 7 supps. New York: Charles Scribner's Sons, 1928-1936, 1944-1981.

★ 216 ★
COOKE, Terence J.
Cardinal, Roman Catholic Church
b. Mar. 1, 1921, New York, New York
d. Oct. 6, 1983, New York, New York

Terence J. Cooke, a cardinal and archbishop of New York in the Roman Catholic Church, was the son of Michael Cooke and Margaret Cooke, both first-generation Irish immigrants. His father was a construction worker. His mother died when Terence was nine, and he went to live with his aunt. He received his education at Cathedral College in New York City and St. Joseph's Seminary in Yonkers, New York. He thus became the first archbishop of New York to be educated locally and one of the few cardinals without educational experience in Rome. He was ordained in 1945.

Cooke began his pastoral career at St. Athanasius Church in the Bronx (1946-1947) and as chaplain at St. Agatha's Home in Nanuet, New York. He received his Ph.D. at Catholic University and pursued further post-graduate studies at the University of Chicago. Returning to New York in 1949, he became assistant director of the Catholic Youth Organization (1949-1954), assisted at St. Jude's Parish (1949-1954) and taught in the School of Social Service at Fordham University (1949-1956). In 1954 he became procurator at St. Joseph's Seminary (1954-1957).

In 1957 Cardinal **Francis Spellman** named Cooke as his new secretary, the first step in Cooke's steady climb to the top of the Roman hierarchy in America. In 1958 Cooke became vice-chancellor of the archdiocese of New York. In 1961 he was named a domestic prelate with the title of monsignor and became chancellor of the archdiocese. In 1965 he was ordained as auxiliary bishop of New York and titular bishop of Summa. In 1966 the archdiocese was divided into six vicariates and he was named one of the episcopal vicars, with responsibility for Manhattan and the Bronx. Following Spellman's death in December 1967, Cooke succeeded him as archbishop of New York in early 1968. As archbishop, Cooke also became the head (military vicar) of the Roman Catholic chaplains in the armed services.

Cooke received his cardinal's hat in 1969. During his 14 years as cardinal-archbishop, he gained fame for his attempts to adopt the principles of Vatican II in managing the archdiocese, especially by involving more people in decision-making processes and by decentralizing authority. He did, however, use his office to deal with social issues facing the church. He opposed abortion and for ten years headed the Committee on Pro-Life Activities of the National Conference of Catholic Bishops. He also attacked racism and terrorism. He followed up on a program begun by his predecessor to give special attention to the growing Hispanic membership of his archdiocese, and strengthened the program to recruit and train Spanish-speaking priests. He also instituted a program to move financial support from wealthier sections of his diocese to poorer sections, especially in support of intercity parochial schools.

At the time he became archbishop, Cooke had already been diagnosed as suffering from leukemia. He finally died of the disease in 1983.

Sources:

Delaney, John J. *Dictionary of American Catholic Biography*. Garden City, NY: Doubleday & Company, 1988. 621 pp.

★ 217 ★
COOPER, Irving Steiger
Regionary Bishop, Liberal Catholic Church in the United States
b. Mar. 16, 1882, Santa Barbara, California
d. Jan. 17, 1935, Hollywood, California

Irving Steiger Cooper was the first Regionary Bishop of the Liberal Catholic Church in the United States, and was a leading force in the development of that group's organization and liturgy. Raised in California, he attended the University of California. Shortly after graduation he was introduced to Theosophy. Within a few years he was a national lecturer for the Theosophical cause, and in 1911 he ventured to the headquarters in Adyar, India, for the annual meeting. He remained in India for a number of years, gaining a position as secretary for international officer **Charles Webster Leadbeater**.

While in India, Cooper wrote a number of books on Theosophy, the first of which was *Methods of Psychic Development* (1912). In 1917 he moved to Australia as a lecturer, following Leadbeater, who had moved to Sydney in 1914. Leadbeater had become involved with Bishop James Ingall Wedgwood, who was helping to create the Liberal Catholic Church from followers of the Old Catholic Bishop **Arnold Harris Mathew**, who wanted to combine that independent Catholic tradition with Theosophy. Leadbeater became the Australian leader of the Liberal Catholic Church, and Cooper soon was involved as well. Cooper was ordained a priest in that church in 1918. He helped Wedgwood and Leadbeater put together *The Liturgy of the Mass* (1917) and its revision, *The Liturgy of the Holy Eucharist* (1918).

Wedgwood brought Cooper to the United States in 1919 as its first regionary bishop. Cooper set up office at the Krotona location in Hollywood, California, where he built St. Alban's Cathedral. For many years he promoted both the Liberal Catholic Church and Theosophy. In 1926 he toured with **Annie Besant** and **Jiddu Krishnamurti** in an effort to show Krishnamurti as the new World Teacher. The following year he married Susan L. Warfield. In 1928 Cooper presided over the church's first Provincial Convocation and incorporation. In the early 1930s his workload decreased due to a prolonged illness, but he still managed to publish his masterwork, *Ceremonies of the Liberal Catholic Rite* (1934), a thorough rewrite of the church's liturgy which has since become the standard for the church. He passed away within a year of its completion.

Sources:

Cooper, Irving S. *Ceremonies of the Liberal Catholic Rite*. Los Angeles, CA: St. Alban Press. 1934. Rev. ed., 1964. 380 pp.
_____. *Reincarnation, A Hope of the World*. Wheaton, IL: Theosophical Publishing House, 1979. 106 pp.
_____. *The Secret of Happiness*. Wheaton, IL: Theosophical Publishing House, 1976. 75 pp.
_____. *Theosophy Simplified*. Wheaton, IL: Theosophical Publishing House, 1979. 89 pp.
_____. *Ways to Perfect Health*. Chicago: Theosophical Press, 1923. 119 pp.
"Irving S. Cooper." *Ubique* 4 (March, 1935).

—Gary L. Ward

★218★
COPELAND, Kenneth
Pentecostal Television Evangelist
b. 1937

Kenneth Copeland, popular television evangelist and founder of Kenneth Copeland Ministries, Inc., grew up in west Texas. In 1962 both he and his wife, Gloria Copeland, were converted to Christianity. In 1967 they moved from Fort Worth, Texas, to Tulsa, Oklahoma, where he entered Oral Roberts University to train for the ministry. He was hired by Roberts as a pilot for his crusade flights across the United States. While working for Roberts' crusades, he had his first opportunity to see and participate in a ministry of prayer for the sick.

Although Copeland was enthusiastic about **Oral Roberts'** ministry, he was even more deeply impressed by independent Pentecostal teacher **Kenneth Hagin**, and he began to attend his seminars. Copeland adopted much of Hagin's message and decided to enter the ministry full-time. Dropping out of the university the following year, he returned to Fort Worth to found the evangelistic association that bears his name. The Copelands began holding meetings in homes in Fort Worth and their work spread rapidly. Copeland's effective preaching style was augmented by his abilities as a singer of gospel hymns.

In 1973 the Copelands, who have worked closely together in the growing ministry, began a periodical, *Believer's Voice of Victory*. In 1976, in response to God's command given in prayer, they began a radio ministry; they began a television ministry in 1979. During the 1980s, with the use of satellite hook-ups, their broadcasts have become global in scope.

Copeland's ministry reflects the strong influence of both Hagin and **Essek William Kenyon**, and emphasizes the need of Christians to live by and confess their faith. It is God's will for the Christian to be healthy and prosperous, and both health and prosperity can be the inheritance of believers who pray for and positively claim God's promises for their lives. What some fellow Pentecostals see as an overemphasis upon these themes has made the Copelands, along with Hagin and Frederick K. C. Price—Hagin's student in Los Angeles—subjects of intense controversy.

Copeland has attempted to answer his critics primarily with his record of success. His meetings (he conducts approximately 15 revival campaigns annually) are noted for their reported healings. Instances of recovery from cancer and AIDS have been claimed.

By the mid-1980s, there were approximately 700,000 people receiving the *Believers' Voice of Victory*. The Copelands have written a few books and have produced and circulated numerous tapes of their meetings, teaching sessions, and music.

Sources:

Barron, Bruce. *The Health and Wealth Gospel*. Downers Grove, IL: InterVarsity Press, 1987. 204 pp.
Burgess, Stanley M., Gary B. McGee, and Patrick H. Alexander, eds. *Dictionary of Pentecostal and Charismatic Movements*. Grand Rapids, MI: Regency Reference Library, Zondervan Publishing House, 1988. 914 pp.
Copeland, Gloria. *God's Will for You*. Fort Worth, TX: Kenneth Copeland Publications, 1972. 107 pp.
_____. *God's Will Is Prosperity*. Fort Worth, TX: Kenneth Copeland Publications, 1978. 128 pp.
Copeland, Kenneth. *The Laws of Prosperity*. Fort Worth, TX: Kenneth Copeland Publications, 1974. 121 pp.
_____. *Walking in the Realm of the Miraculous*. Fort Worth, TX: Kenneth Copeland Publications, 1979. 112 pp.

★219★
COPPIN, Fanny Muriel Jackson
Teacher and Executive, African Methodist Episcopal Church
President, Women's Home and Foreign Missionary Society
b. 1837, Washington, District of Columbia
d. Jan. 21, 1913, Philadelphia, Pennsylvania

Fanny Muriel Jackson Coppin, the wife of African Methodist Episcopal Church Bishop **Levi Jenkins Coppin**, was an educator and church executive whose accomplishments equaled those of her husband in an era when women were still fighting for basic access to education and leadership positions. She was born into slavery as Fanny Jackson, but her maternal aunt Sarah Clark bought her freedom. She lived with several free aunts in Bedford, Massachusetts, and Newport, Rhode Island. As a teenager she went to work and found schooling. She was able to attend the Rhode Island State Normal School and after finishing in 1869 enrolled at Oberlin College. During her junior year she was one of the first black female students and the first black student to be chosen as a pupil-teacher. She was elected class poet and gave one of the school's graduation lectures in French.

Upon graduation in 1865, Jackson received a job offer from the Institute for Colored Youth, a Quaker school in Philadelphia, Pennsylvania. She began to transform the institute into a normal school to train the teachers who were so in demand around the country. She also initiated a trade school and used her oratorical skills to speak and travel around the area to raise money for it. She became a symbol of the benefits of education, and emerged as a champion for industrial training for Blacks in the Northeast.

In 1879 Jackson offered her services to assist in the fundraising program to save the *Christian Recorder*, the periodical of the African Methodist Episcopal Church and currently the oldest continuously published black periodical in the United States. In the process of the very successful campaign, she met Rev. Levi J. Coppin, pastor of a local African Methodist Episcopal Church congregation. They were married in 1881 and moved to Baltimore, where Reverend Coppin had been transferred. She continued her work for industrial education, and the Coppins rented a dwelling next to their parsonage to house the students looking for work.

Without dropping her educational concerns, Coppin added church work, especially the administrative and fundraising tasks associated with the African Methodist Episcopal Church's foreign missions program to her duties. She soon became president of the Women's Home and Foreign Missionary Society and on its behalf attended the Centenary of Missions gathering in London in 1888. The meeting, which was marked by a speech by one male minister who warned females against assuming ministerial functions, aroused her sense of feminist justice.

In 1900 Reverend Coppin was elected a bishop of the church and assigned to South Africa. Mrs. Coppin closed out her educational responsibilities and joined him at Bethel Institute, his mission station in Cape Town, in 1902. She then threw herself into organizing temperance and missionary societies and worked among the women across the territory assigned to her husband. Upon their return to Philadelphia in 1904 her health failed, and for the rest of her life she was confined to her home. Shortly before her death, her book *Reminiscences of School Life, and Hints on Teaching* (1913), which contained an autobiographical sketch, was published.

Sources:

Coppin, Fanny J. *Reminiscences of School Life, and Hints on Teaching.* Philadelphia: A. M. E. Book Concern, 1913. 191 pp. Reprint. New York: Garland Publishing, 1987. 191 pp.

Coppin, Levi Jenkins *Unwritten History.* Philadelphia: A.M.E. Book Concern, 1919. 375 pp.

Harmon, Nolan B. *The Encyclopedia of World Methodism.* 2 vols. Nashville: United Methodist Publishing House, 1974.

Logan, Rayford W., and Michael R. Winston, eds. *Dictionary of American Negro Biography.* New York: W. W. Norton & Co. 1982. 680 pp.

Perkins, Linda M. *Fanny Jackson Coppin and the Institute for Colored Youth, 1865-1902.* New York: Garland Publishing, 1987. 347 pp.

Wright, Richard R., Jr., comp. *Encyclopedia of African Methodism.* Philadelphia: Book Concern of the AME Church, 1947. 688 pp.

★ 220 ★
COPPIN, Levi Jenkins
Bishop, African Methodist Episcopal Church
b. Dec. 24, 1848, Frederickstown, Maryland
d. Jun. 25, 1924, United States

Levi Jenkins Coppin, a bishop of the African Methodist Episcopal Church, was one of eight children born to Jane Lilly and John Coppin, a free black family residing in Maryland in the decades before the Civil War. His mother taught him to read and write, and at the close of the Civil War he began to teach in a local church school. The church affiliated itself with the African Methodist Episcopal Church. At about the same time he had a conversion experience to Christianity. He furthered his own education locally, but strove toward a goal of becoming a fully educated man. He moved to Wilmington, Delaware, where he went into business and became active in Bethel African Methodist Episcopal Church. In 1875 he married Martha Grinnage, who died after she gave birth to their son, only 18 months after the marriage.

It was around this time that Coppin decided to go into the ministry and was licensed to preach in 1876 by Rev. John F. Thomas; the following year he joined the Philadelphia Conference. Coppin was assigned to the City Mission in Philadelphia, and was ordained a deacon in 1879 and sent to Bethel Church in Philadelphia. In 1880 he was ordained and for the first time elected as a delegate to the general conference. The following year he was transferred to the Bethel Church in Baltimore, Maryland, and married Fanny Muriel Jackson Coppin.

In 1884 Coppin became a member of the church's board of the Sunday School Union, serving this post for four years. He also requested a transfer back to Philadelphia's Allan Chapel, a small church which gave him time to pursue his theological education at the Protestant Episcopal Divinity School, from which he graduated in 1887. He later attended Wilberforce University. In 1888 Coppin was elected successor to B. T. Tanner as editor of the *A. M. E. Review,* a position he held for eight years. He gave up the editorship in 1896 to become pastor of Bethel Church in Philadelphia, the original church from which the denomination developed. During these years in the pastorate he authored several books, including *The Sunday School, Its Work and How to Do It* and *The Key to Scriptural Interpretation* (1895).

In 1900 Coppin was elected to the African Methodist Episcopal Church bishopric and assigned to South Africa. After overcoming initial suspicions of the local government, he was able to found a number of churches among the Bantu and other black Africans. He returned to America in 1904 to begin his four-year leadership over the Seventh Episcopal District (South Carolina) and then in 1908 began a long tenure over the Second Episcopal District (Baltimore, Virginia, North Carolina). He lived in Washington, D.C., where he emerged as one of the most powerful black leaders in the city. Fanny Coppin died in 1913, and in 1914 he married M. Evelyn Thompson. In 1916 he was assigned to the Fourth Episcopal District, which included the Midwest and the city of Winnipeg, Manitoba. He lived in Philadelphia where he passed his last years, and where he wrote his autobiography, *Unwritten History* (1919).

Sources:

Coppin, Levi J. *Fifty-two Suggestive Sermon Syllabi.* Philadelphia: A. M. E. Book Concern, 1910. 268 pp.

———. *The Key to Scriptural Interpretation.* Philadelphia: Publishing House of the A. M. E. Church, 1895. 207 pp.

———. *Observation of Persons and Things in South Africa, 1900-1904.* Philadelphia: A. M. E. Book Concern, n.d. 205 pp.

———. *The Relation of Baptized Children to the Church.* Philadelphia: A. M. E. Publication Department, 1890. 106 pp.

———. *The Sunday School, Its Work, and How to Do It.*

———. *Unwritten History.* Philadelphia: A.M.E. Book Concern, 1919. 375 pp.

Harmon, Nolan B. *The Encyclopedia of World Methodism.* 2 vols. Nashville: United Methodist Publishing House, 1974.

Logan, Rayford W., and Michael R. Winston, eds. *Dictionary of American Negro Biography.* New York: W. W. Norton & Co. 1982. 680 pp.

Wright, Richard R., Jr., comp. *Encyclopedia of African Methodism.* Philadelphia: Book Concern of the AME Church, 1947. 688 pp.

★ 221 ★
CORNISH, Louis Craig
President, American Unitarian Association
b. Apr. 18, 1870, New Bedford, Massachusetts
d. Jan. 6, 1950, Orlando, Florida

Louis Craig Cornish, a president of the American Unitarian Association, was the son of Frances W. Hawkins and Aaron Cornish. He entered Harvard in 1889 and completed his B.A. in 1893. In 1894 he became the secretary to William Lawrence, the bishop of the Episcopal Church in Massachusetts. In 1898 he returned to Harvard and completed his M.A. (1899). After his graduation he was ordained as a Unitarian minister. He took his first and only parish in 1900, but spent 15 fruitful years at the Unitarian church in Hingham, Massachusetts. In 1915 he joined the national staff of the American Unitarian Association as its secretary-at-large.

As an association staff person Cornish distinguished himself in the area of international affairs, particularly with Unitarians in Europe. In the early 1920s he led an investigation into the problems faced by Unitarians in Transylvania, Romania, which resulted in the publication of two books: *Transylvania in 1922* (1923) and *The Religious Minorities in Transylvania* (1925). The problems faced by religious minorities, especially Unitarians, in Romania became a life-long concern. A large percentage of his time was also spent traveling to develop networks among Unitarians around the world.

In 1927 Samuel A. Eliot ended his three decades as president of the association, and Cornish was selected to succeed him. The future looked bright. However, the Depression had a disastrous effect upon the association and upon Cornish's plans. Cornish had hoped that his leadership would be a time of association prosperity during which an enlarged, visible, international Unitarian brotherhood would become evident. His plans were dashed against the international tension that finally resulted in World War II. Neither his interests nor his abilities were capable of meeting the immediate needs of the association, which was suffering both financial and membership losses. The problems led to the appointment of a Committee of Appraisal which reported in 1936. One of the results of its recommendations was that Cornish left his post as president of the association the following year. He summarized his vision of his presidency in *Work and Dreams and the Wide Horizon* (1937).

Following his years in the association presidency, Cornish remained active in the task of international networking. He authored two additional books out of his experience, *The Philippines Calling* (1942) and *Transylvania: The Land Beyond the Forest* (1947).

Sources:

Cornish, Louis Craig. *The Philippines Calling.* Philadelphia: Dorrance and Co. 1942. 313 pp.
_____. *The Religious Minorities in Transylvania.* Boston: Beacon Press, 1925. 174 pp.
_____. *Transylvania in 1922.* Boston: Beacon Press, 1923. 169 pp.
_____. *Transylvania: The Land Beyond the Forest.* Philadelphia: Dorrance & Co., 1947. 258 pp.
_____. *Work and Dreams and the Wide Horizon.* Boston: Beacon Press, 1937. 403 pp.
Robinson, David. *The Unitarians and the Universalists.* Westport, CT: Greenwood Press, 1985. 368 pp.

★ 222 ★
COUGHLIN, Charles Edward
Priest and Radio Minister, Roman Catholic Church
b. Oct. 25, 1891, Hamilton, Ontario, Canada
d. Oct. 27, 1979, Birmingham, Michigan

Charles Edward Coughlin was a priest in the Roman Catholic Church and a populist leader who achieved fame through his radio broadcasts, and notoriety for his anti-Semitic, pro-Nazi stance in the years leading up to World War II. The son of a Great Lakes seaman, Coughlin was educated at St. Michael's College, University of Toronto, and ordained in 1916. He taught for several years at Assumption College in Sandwich, Ontario. Serving the church in various capacities in the Detroit area, he was sent to found a parish at Royal Oak, Michigan, in 1926. There he built and served as pastor of the Shrine of the Little Flower until he retired in 1966. The shrine was the first to be dedicated to Therese Martin, popularly known as the Little Flower, who had just been canonized and to whom Coughlin had a great personal devotion.

Following an incident in which the Ku Klux Klan burned a cross in his churchyard, Coughlin was given a chance to explain Catholicism on radio station WJR. He followed this up with a series of talks, talks that did not attract much attention until he turned to social and political issues. His audience then grew rapidly until it was estimated that about 40 million people listened to him every Sunday afternoon. His early radio talks, sponsored by the Radio League of the Little Flower, were published under the title *By the Sweat of Thy Brow* (1931). Initially focusing his attack on Communism, Coughlin gradually drifted into anti-Semitism and pro-Nazism. He supported Franklin D. Roosevelt in 1932, but turned against him soon after the election and became an ardent anti-New Dealer. He also adopted a strong anti-union, isolationist stance.

In 1934 Coughlin organized the National Union for Social Justice, and two years later founded the magazine *Social Justice* to promote the Union's program, a program that involved such radical measures as abolishing private banking, nationalizing certain key resources, and establishing a central bank to control prices. The Union Party was organized in 1936 to challenge Roosevelt, and ran William Lemke for president. Through his radio speeches and books, Coughlin continued to promote anti-Semitism, and ardently opposed the entry of the United States into the war, even after the attack on Pearl Harbor. Church authorities eventually pressured him to go off the air, and the government stopped the mailing of *Social Justice* in 1942 because it violated the Espionage Act. Coughlin lived quietly during the later years of his life, although he did continue to write anti-Communist tracts as well as tracts denouncing Vatican II.

Sources:

Brinkley, Alan. *Voices of Protest.* New York: Vintage Books, 1983. 348 pp.
Coughlin, Charles E. *Bishops versus Pope.* Bloomfield Hills, MI: Helmet and Sword, 1969. 220 pp.
_____. *By the Sweat of Thy Brow.* Detroit, MI: The Radio League of the Little Flower, 1931. 191 pp.
_____. *Eight Lectures on Labor, Capital, and Justice.* Royal Oak, MI: Radio League of the Little Flower, 1934. 132 pp.
_____. *Money! Questions and Answers.* Royal Oak, MI: National League for Social Justice, 1936. 118 pp.
_____. *The New Deal in Money.* Royal Oak, MI: Radio League of the Little Flower, 1933. 128 pp.
_____. *Why Leave Our Own.* Royal Oak, MI: The Author, 1939. 176 pp.
Hutting, A. M. *Shrine of the Little Flower Souvenir Book.* Royal Oak, MI: Radio League of the Little Flower, 1936. 110 pp.
Mugglebee, Ruth. *Father Coughlin of the Shrine of the Little Flower.* Boston, MA: L. C. Page & Company, 1933. 321 pp.
Roy, Ralph Lord. *Apostles of Discord: A Study of Organized Bigotry and Disruption on the Fringes of Protestantism.* Boston: Beacon Press, 1953. 437 pp.
Ward, Louis B. *Father Charles E. Coughlin: An Authorized Biography.* Detroit, MI: Tower Publications, 1933. 352 pp.

★ 223 ★
COX JR., Harvey Gallagher
Theologian, American Baptist Churches in the U.S.
b. May 19, 1929, Phoenixville, Pennsylvania

Harvey Gallagher Cox, Jr., a Baptist theologian who emerged suddenly in 1965 as the voice of a generation of restless young Christians, is the son of Dorothea Dunwoody and Harvey Gallagher Cox, Sr. He grew up in Pennsylvania and attended the University of Pennsylvania (A.B., 1951). He received his B.D. from Yale in 1955, following which he became the director of religious activities at Oberlin College. While there, in 1957 he married Nancy Nieburger. In 1958 he joined the staff of the American Baptist Home Missionary Society as a program associate. He also worked on a doctorate at Harvard Divinity School, which was awarded in 1963. In 1962 he moved to East Germany for a year of work with the Gossner Mission. In 1963 he was named assistant professor of theology at Andover Newton Theological Seminary.

In 1964 Cox began to prepare a small volume for use as a study guide by the National Student Christian Federation. Its intent was to address the issues of secularization and urbanization in a positive way in light of biblical and theological insights. Soon after the book appeared, Cox suddenly jumped from being an obscure theologian to the most talked about theological author of the year. *The Secular City* became a best seller, and the controversy it raised prompted both a volume of responses, *The Secular City Debate* and a second edition the following year. In the wake of the book's appearance, Cox moved back to Harvard Divinity School, where he continues to teach.

The spectacular success of *The Secular City* has overshadowed much of Cox's later work, and hindered an assessment of his long-term contribution. He has undoubtedly been at his best when commenting upon the world's changing scene (including his own maturing pilgrimage) from a Christian theological (liberal Protestant) perspective. He has also been one of the few theologians to take the new Eastern and Neo-Pagan religions seriously and attempt to enter into some kind of a meaningful dialogue with them. During his Harvard years Cox has written several other books, including: *God's Revolution and Man's Responsibility* (1965); *The Feast of Fools* (1969); *The Seduction of the Spirit* (1973); *Turning East: The Promise and Perils of the New Orientalism* (1977); *Just As I Am* (1983); *The Silencing of Leonardo Boff: The Vatican and the Future of World Christianity* (1988); and *Many Mansions: A Christian's Encounter with Other Faiths* (1988).

Sources:

Callahan, Daniel, ed. *The Secular City Debate.* New York: Macmillan Company, 1966. 218 pp.

Cox, Harvey. *The Feast of Fools.* Cambridge, MA: Harvard University Press, 1969. 204 pp.

———. *God's Revolution and Man's Responsibility.* New York: Macmillan Company, 1965.

———. *Many Mansions: A Christian's Encounter with Other Faiths.* Boston: Beacon Press, 1988. 216 pp.

———. *The Secular City.* New York: Macmillan Company, 1965. 276 pp.

———. *Turning East: The Promise and Perils of the New Orientalism.* New York: Simon and Schuster, 1977. 192 pp.

★224★
CRAMER, Malinda Elliott
Founder, Divine Science Federation International
b. Feb. 12, 1844, Greensboro, Indiana
d. Aug. 2, 1906, San Francisco, California

Malinda Elliott Cramer, founder of Divine Science, was the daughter of Obediah and Mary Henshaw Elliott, Quakers originally from North Carolina. Little is known of her childhood. In 1870 she moved to San Francisco. She had been ill for ten years and hoped that the climate change would help her physical condition. In 1872 she married Charles Lake Cramer, also a Quaker, who ran a photography studio. The climate did little to help her physically, and by the mid-1880s she had become somewhat of an invalid.

During the mid-1880s, however, the Christian Science movement had begun to manifest in San Francisco, and in 1885, possibly through the ministrations of independent Christian Scientist Miranda Rice, Cramer received a healing experience. By 1886 a group of independent metaphysical healers, primarily women, had organized in the city, and in April 1887, Cramer joined many of them to study under **Emma Curtis Hopkins**, the founder of what today is called New Thought.

Cramer responded positively to Hopkins' lectures and quickly emerged as a teacher. In May 1888, she formally incorporated Home College and began to offer courses for future practitioners. Later that year, with her husband's help, she began publishing *Harmony*, one of the most influential of the late-nineteenth century metaphysical magazines. She also began to term her teachings Divine Science, to distinguish her work from Christian Science, though it was a term which had been previously utilized by **Mary Baker Eddy** as a synonym for Christian Science. Possibly Cramer picked it up from Wilberforce Juvenal Colville, who had published a book using the term in the title in 1888.

During the next few years Cramer made several trips through the Western half of the United States. An 1891 trip took her to teach at the centers established by Hopkins in Chicago and by **Charles S. Fillmore** in Kansas City. In 1890 she published her first book, *Lessons in the Science of Infinite Spirit*, the substance of which were the basic metaphysical lessons previous published in her magazine. These lessons would be completely rewritten and published in 1902 as *Divine Science and Healing.*

Cramer gradually conceived of a network to encompass the numerous independent metaphysical centers that had emerged around the country, and in 1892 she founded the International Divine Science Association as such an umbrella organization. Meetings of the association were held annually beginning in 1894; they continued through the decade. The Association was the first of several attempts to create an ecumenical organization for New Thought. After the association ceased, the Metaphysical League, headquartered in Boston, met for several years. Finally, in 1916, a more stable International New Thought Alliance (INTA) was created.

In 1893 Cramer opened the second Home College in Oakland. In Denver she developed a following centered around three sisters, Fannie James, **Nona Lovell Brooks**, and Althea Small, all of whom had previously studied with Hopkins' students. James had originally opened a small center, and by 1898 decided to begin Sunday services. Nona Brooks traveled to San Francicso to study with and—on December 1, 1898—be ordained by Cramer. The sisters incorporated the Colorado College of Divine Science College in Denver and began public services on New Years Day 1899.

Cramer's growing movement suffered a severe setback in 1906, when the work in San Francisco was destroyed by the earthquake. Cramer suffered injuries from the quake and died several months later. Thus the thrust of her movement shifted to the new leadership in Denver, through whom it survived and became a major New Thought perspective.

Sources:

Cramer, Malinda Elliott. *Divine Science and Healing.* San Francisco, CA: C. L. Cramer, 1907. 293 pp.

———. *Lessons in the Science of Infinite Spirit.* San Francisco, CA: The author, 1890. 258 pp.

★225★
CRAPSEY, Algernon Sidney
Priest, Episcopal Church
b. Jun. 28, 1847, Fairmount, Ohio
d. Dec. 31, 1927, Rochester, New York

Algernon Sidney Crapsey, a priest of the Episcopal Church best known for his trial for heresy in 1906, was the son of Jacob Tomkins and Rachel Morris Crapsey. The decline of his father's law practice forced the 11-year-old Crapsey to seek work. For four months he served as an infantryman in the Union Army during the Civil War, but he was sent home as an invalid with what was diagnosed as a hypertrophied heart. He settled in New York City and became a bookkeeper. He joined the Episcopal Church and after a short while felt a call to the ministry. He attended St. Stephens College, from which he graduated in 1869, and then began three years at General Theological Seminary in New York City. In 1872, following his graduation, he was ordained deacon, and the following year was ordained as a priest. He joined the staff of Trinity Episcopal Church in Manhattan and was assigned the care of St. Paul's Chapel. In 1875 he married Adelaide Trowbridge.

In 1879 Crapsey was presented with the opportunity of assuming leadership of a parish. He resigned from St. Paul's to move to Rochester, New York, as rector of St. Andrew's Episcopal Church. A small parish, St. Andrew's grew into a large and influential congregation under their new soft-spoken priest. They were known within the church for their well-developed community social program. An eloquent and personable man, over the next 25 years Crapsey became a popular speaker and retreat leader within the larger denomination. He spoke widely around the region. He also authored a number of books, including: *Meditations on the Five Joyful Mysteries* (1888); *The Greater Love* (1902); and *Religion and Politics* (1905).

Crapsey also became known for his liberal theological views. In a lecture in the middle of the first decade of the new century, he made the remarks that were to call his career into question. As would be noted in his trial, he had offered as his opinion that, "in the light of scientific research the founder of Christianity, Jesus the son of Joseph, no longer stands apart from the common destiny of man in life and death, but He is in all things physical like as we are, born as we are born, dying as we die, and both in life and death in the keeping of that same divine Power, that heavenly Fatherhood, which delivers us from the womb and carries us down to the grave" (*Arguments*, 1906). In an era in which the fundamentalist-modernist controversy was moving into all of the major denominations, Crapsey's remarks questioned several of what were considered fundamental Christian affirmations on the virgin birth and resurrection of Jesus. He was tried in Batavia, New York, in April 1906, before the court of the Diocese of Western New York. He was convicted of holding heretical views. When called before his bishop and asked to recant, he declined. He was subsequently deposed from the ministry of the church.

Following his removal from the ministry, Crapsey stayed in Rochester, writing and lecturing to his supporters, and remained an influential community leader. During the last two decades of his life he would author a number of books: *The Rebirth of Religion* (1907); *The Rise of the Working Class* (1914); *International Republicanism* (1918); *The Ways of the Gods* (1920); *Lewis Henry Morgan* (1923); and an autobiography, *The Last of the Heretics* (1924). He was a delegate to the International Peace Conference at the Hague in 1907. In 1914 he was named a New York state parole officer.

Sources:

Arguments for Presenters and Defense of Reverend A. S. Crapsey Before the Court of Review of the P. E. Church Upon His Appeal from the Judgment of the Court of the Diocese of Western N. Y. New York: T. Whittaker, 1906. 221 pp.

Crapsey, Algernon Sidney. *The Last of the Heretics.* New York: A. A. Knopf, 1924. 297 pp.

_____. *The Rebirth of Religion.* New York: John Lane Co., 1907. 323 pp.

_____. *Religion and Politics.* New York: T. Whitaker, 1905. 326 pp.

_____. *The Rise of the Working Class.* New York: The Century Company, 1914. 382 pp.

Dictionary of American Biography. 20 vols. and 7 supps. New York: Charles Scribner's Sons, 1928-1936, 1944-1981.

★ 226 ★

CRATTY, Mabel

Executive, Young Women's Christian Association (YWCA)
b. Jun. 30, 1868, Bellaire, Ohio
d. Feb. 27, 1928, New York, New York

Mabel Cratty, a social worker who was active in the Young Women's Christian Association (YWCA), was the daughter of Charles Campbell and Mary (Thoburn) Cratty. Her uncle was the missionary bishop of the Methodist Episcopal Church in India, Bishop James M. Thoburn, and her aunt was Isabella Thoburn, the first unmarried American female foreign missionary. After attending public school in Bellaire, Ohio, she was educated at Eire Seminary and Ohio Wesleyan University (B.L. degree, 1890). She served as a teacher at the Wheeling Female Seminary in West Virginia, at high schools in Kent and Delaware, Ohio, and as the principal of the Delaware high school during the years 1900-1904.

Mabel Cratty also became involved with the YWCA, serving on the Ohio state committee (1902), as associate general secretary of the American Committee of the YWCA (1904), and, after the unification of the YWCA, as general secretary of the National Board (1906). She held the last position until her death. She was also active in the Institute of Pacific Relations, National Social Work Council, Camp Fire Girls of America, National Committee on the Cause and Cure of War, and the National Council of Churches committee to study relations between the YMCA and the Council of Churches. She attended many meetings of the World's Committee of the YWCA, and visited YWCA headquarters in many European countries, as well as YWCA headquarters in Honolulu, China, and Japan. She was named a delegate to the Institute of Pacific Relations at Honolulu in July of 1927. After a brief bout of pneumonia, she passed away seven months later in the Rockefeller Institute Hospital.

Cratty was sometimes referred to as the "statesman" of the Young Women's Christian Association. She worked diligently to secure social justice, world peace, and the improvement of conditions for working women. She was a highly successful organizer, although she preferred to do her work out of the limelight. She deserves a major part of the credit for the success of the YWCA, which in 1928 enjoyed a membership of around 600,000 with more than 1,300 local associations.

Sources:

Dictionary of American Biography. 20 vols. and 7 supps. New York: Charles Scribner's Sons, 1928-1936, 1944-1981.

★ 227 ★

CRAWFORD, Florence Louise

Founder, Apostolic Faith Church (Mission)
b. Sep. 1, 1872, Coos County, Oregon
d. Jun. 20, 1936, Portland, Oregon

Florence Louise Crawford was the founder of an international Pentecostal group originally called the Apostolic Faith Church of Portland, Oregon. Growing up, she attended freethought meetings with her parents, who often hosted atheist speakers passing through Oregon. She was curious about the Christian faith, however, and was introduced to it one day when she and a friend visited a church without her parents' knowledge.

After her marriage to Frank M. Crawford, Florence Crawford was converted while at a dance party. She heard a voice say, "Daughter, give me thine heart." She left the dance to reflect on what she took to be God's voice, and soon accepted God's claim on her life. She affiliated with a Methodist church and threw herself wholeheartedly into active Christian work. She became president of the California Woman's Christian Temperance Union (W.C.T.U.). She also acted as a slum worker and reformer. She believed, based on John Wesley's writings, that the Holy Spirit can effect a work of sanctification in a believer.

In 1906 Crawford heard about the now-famous Asuza Street church, which was bringing the Pentecostal revival to Los Angeles. She visited the church on several occasions, and experienced sanctification on one night and the baptism of the Holy Spirit (speaking in tongues) on another night. These events not only wrought a change in her spiritual life, but also in her physical life; she was healed of her various bodily afflictions, which included spinal meningitis and lung trouble. The church's pastor, Rev. **William J. Seymour**, appointed her State Director, enabling her to travel up and down California as an itinerant home missionary.

In December 1906 Crawford traveled to Salem, Oregon, to expand the ministry into that state. People from Portland who heard her speak were so impressed that they invited her to take over their little mission church, which she did. She thus broke with Seymour and named her ministry Apostolic Faith, first used by Rev. **Charles Fox Parham**, the initiator of the modern Pentecostal movement and the source of Seymour's conversion. She discontinued the practice of taking offerings at meetings, and relied solely on tithes and voluntary gifts. She firmly preached the holiness doctrine of a strict moral code that included footwashing as a third ordinance with baptism and the Lord's Supper.

Crawford continued to do a lot of traveling. The local ministry was eventually assisted by her son, Raymond Robert, who became ordained to work with her. In 1908 she began putting out *The Apostolic Faith*, a magazine which was soon available in Norwegian and German editions. In 1911 a missionary established a church in Sweden; another started in Norway in 1912. Crawford became increasingly convinced that her call was to a worldwide ministry. In 1913 she began evangelizing the sailors at Portland's harbor, who in turn began taking the Apostolic Faith all over the world. In 1919 an airplane was used to distribute church literature in the Northwest. When Crawford died in 1936 at the age of 64, she headed a solid Pentecostal ministry with its base in the northwestern United States and Canada and with mission reaches in Scandinavia and elsewhere.

Sources:

An Historical Account of the Apostolic Faith. Portland, OR: Apostolic Faith Mission, 1965. 315 pp.

The Life That Brought Triumph. Portland, OR: Apostolic Faith Publishing House, 1955. 33 pp.

Melton, J. Gordon. *Biographical Dictionary of American Cult and Sect Leaders*. Garland Reference Library of Social Science, vol. 212. New York: Garland Publishing, 1986.

Saved to Serve. Portland, OR: Apostolic Faith Publishing House, 1967. 96 pp.

—*Gary L. Ward*

★ 228 ★
CREME, Benjamin
Founder, Share International Foundation
b. 1922, Glasgow Scotland

Benjamin Creme is a professional artist who paints images of an inner reality perceived through meditation. He attracted considerable public attention in the early 1980s when he announced the impending arrival of Maitreya, the coming world teacher whose imminent appearance is hoped for by many in the theosophical tradition. Maitreya, a figure in Buddhist thought, has been identified with Christ by some theosophists. Many people associated with Creme in both North America and Europe after his pronouncement and he received broad coverage by the news media. When Maitreya failed to appear in 1982 as predicted, Creme passed out of the limelight, although his work continues with his followers through the Share International Foundation, headquartered in Amsterdam, Holland. In North America the work is coordinated through the Tara Center in North Hollywood, California.

Creme began painting at the age of 14, and left school two years later to devote more time to painting. For a short time he attended the Glasgow School of Art, but dropped out when his "modernist" approach developed in other directions. He studied with Jankel Adler in the early 1940s, developing a style, mediated to him by Adler, that showed the influence of the later work of Picasso.

Creme also read widely in theosophy and the occult. He studied the works of Wilhelm Reich, **Helena P. Blavatsky**, **Charles W. Leadbeater**, **Swami Vivekananda**, Sivananda Saraswati, and Ramana Maharshi, but was most influenced by the writings of **Alice LaTrobe Bailey Bateman**. Particularly important for understanding Creme's later development is *The Reappearance of the Christ* (1948), in which Bailey announced that a new world teacher would appear by the end of the century. He also read some of UFO contactee **George Adamski**'s works in which he described his encounters with space beings, and eventually became involved with George King's Aetherius Society, a religious group built around communications with extraterrestrials.

In the late 1950s Creme began to receive messages from the Great White Brotherhood, the hierarchy of spiritual masters which Theosophical literature describes as guiding the spiritual evolution of the planet. Creme was informed that he would have a role in proclaiming the coming of Maitreya, the head of the Brotherhood. In the 1970s he began to form an organization, publish, and speak in public on the topic of the "Reappearance of the Christ." He traveled throughout Europe and North America, and published *The Reappearance of the Christ and the Masters of Wisdom* in 1979. By 1981 a magazine, *Share International*, had been founded to promote the work. In 1982 he began an intensive period of traveling to announce Christ's (Maitreya's) imminent return. On April 25 he took out full-page ads in 17 major newspapers announcing "The Christ is Now Here" and that Maitreya's identity would be known within two months. When Christ failed to appear as predicted, many deserted Creme. Although he no longer attracts significant public attention, Creme continues to travel and promote the idea of Christ's presence and imminent manifestation.

Creme appealed primarily to members of the amorphous spiritual subculture that has come to be referred to as the New Age Movement, although many people associated with the movement disowned his message. The embarrassment felt when Maitreya failed to appear caused movement participants to back away from the millenarian dimension of New Age thinking.

Creme's activity also contributed to the conservative Christian community's

Sources:

Creme, Benjamin. *Maitreya's Mission*. Amsterdam, The Netherlands: Share International, 1986. 384 pp.

———. *The Reappearance of the Christ and the Masters of Wisdom*. London: Tara Press, 1980. 255 pp.

———. *Transmission: A Meditation for the New Age*. North Hollywood, CA: Tara Center, 1983. 144 pp.

Cumby, Constance. *Hidden Dangers of the Rainbow*. Shreveport, LA: Huntington House, 1983.

A Master Speaks. Amsterdam, The Netherlands: Share International Foundation, 1985. 96 pp.

Messages from Maitreya the Christ. 2 vols. London: Tara Press, 1980, 1982.

Melton, J. Gordon. *New Age Encyclopedia*. Detroit: Gale Research Inc., 1990. 586 pp.

Nelson, Rudolph. *The Making and Unmaking of and Evangelical Mind*. Cambridge, United Kingdom: Cambridge University Press, 1987. 252 pp.

Shepard, Leslie. *Encyclopedia of Occultism & Parapsychology*. 3 vols., 2nd. ed. Detroit: Gale Research Co., 1984-1985.

★ 229 ★
CRIDGE, Edward
Bishop, Reformed Episcopal Church (Canada)
b. Dec. 17, 1817, Bratton-Heming England
d. May 6, 1913, Victoria, British Columbia, Canada

Edward Cridge, the first Canadian bishop of the Reformed Episcopal Church, was the son of John Cridge and was raised within the Church of England. He attended St. Peter's College, Cambridge, from which he received his B.A. in 1848. That same year he was ordained a deacon and in 1849 was named a priest of the Church of England. He became curate of Christ Church, Stratford, in London. In 1854 he was accepted as chaplain for the Hudson's Bay Company on Vancouver Island in British Columbia. He had just married, and with his new wife, Mary Winnell, he sailed for Canada, arriving at Victoria in April 1855. His parish church, named Christ Church, opened in August 1856.

In 1860 Bishop George Hills arrived to take charge of the work in the area. Cridge's church became one of the more prosperous churches in the new diocese and quickly moved to become self-supporting. His wife started a parochial school adjacent to the church. In 1865 Hills selected Victoria as the seat of his diocese and Christ Church as the cathedral church. He appointed Cridge, the senior minister in the diocese, as dean of Christ Church Cathedral.

The proximity of Hills and Cridge set the stage for the controversy that would drive the latter from the church. Cridge was a strong evangelical in both belief and practice. Hills, on the other hand, favored the revival of ritual and ceremony which was under way throughout the Church of England and its sister churches, such as the Protestant Episcopal Church in America. The level of tension between the two erupted into open warfare in 1872 following the dedication sermon for the new cathedral. In the sermon, Archdeacon William Reece suggested that church ceremony led to increased devotion by church members. In his closing remarks following the sermon, Cridge rebuked Reece for his views.

Cridge's refusal to back down and apologize for his breach of etiquette toward Reece led to a lengthy dispute which resulted in 1874 in his being tried, convicted, and suspended from the ministry by the diocese. He then moved to organize support in the church he had pastored for 16 years. Cridge refused to vacate the pulpit, and the case moved to the civil court. When he lost the case, Cridge and his supporters (the large majority of the congregation) established a second church and aligned themselves with the Reformed Episcopal Church, which had grown out of a similar controversy in the United States. In 1875 Bishop **Charles Edward Cheney** came to Victoria to consecrate Cridge and formally organize the Reformed Episcopal Church in Canada. Cridge's diocese included all of Canada and the United States west of the Rocky Mountains. The new headquarters church, the Church of Our Lord, opened in January 1876.

Cridge administered the diocese, vast in territory but small in membership, for the rest of his life.

Sources:
Cridge, Edward. *As It Was in the Beginning.* Chicago: Fleming H. Revell Co., 1890. 121 pp.
Peake, Frank A. *The Anglican Church in British Columbia.* Vancouver, BC: Mutual Press, 1959. 208 pp.
Pethick, Derek. *Men of British Columbia.* Saanichton, BC: Hancock House Publishers, 1975. 223 pp.
Wallace, W. Stewart. *The Macmillan Dictionary of Canadian Biography.* 4th ed., rev. Edited by W. A. McKay. Toronto: Macmillan of Canada, 1978.

★ 230 ★
CRISWELL, Wallie Amos
President, Southern Baptist Convention
b. Dec. 19, 1909, Eldorado, Oklahoma

Wallie Amos Criswell, the pastor of First Baptist Church in Dallas, one of the largest congregations in the United States, grew up with just the initials "W. A.," by which he is still popularly known. He took the name Wallie Amos at the prompting of government officials who insisted he needed a conventional name. He grew up in Texline, Texas, a small town near the New Mexico border that offered little in the way of entertainment beyond the activities of the local Baptist church. Consequently, Criswell became an avid reader. He experienced a Christian conversion at the age of 10 and two years later accepted a call to the ministry. He attended Baylor University, from which he graduated magna cum laude in 1931. During his college years, his mother moved away from the rest of the family in Texline to Waco to support him through his college work.

Following his graduation, Criswell entered Southern Baptist Theological Seminary in Louisville, Kentucky. During his next six years he earned his Th.M. (1934) and his Ph.D. (1937). He also married Betty Mae Harris on February 14, 1935, Valentine's Day. During his years in the seminary he had preached frequently, in part as a pastor on the weekends, to support himself while attending school. His oratorical abilities had become well-known in the school and beyond. Thus upon graduation he was offered a substantial position as pastor of First Baptist Church, Chickasha, Oklahoma. The church prospered and in 1941 he was called to First Baptist Church, Muskogee, Oklahoma. While in Muskogee he perfected the biblical expository style of preaching for which he has become recognized.

In 1944 Criswell was called to succeed the recently deceased **George Washington Truett**, who for 47 years had been pastor of the 7,000 member First Baptist Church of Dallas. Criswell was an immediate success. In 1946 he announced a most ambitious new sermon series. He would preach through the entire Bible, which would take him 17 years. His emphasis was continually on evangelism, and the already large congregation continued to grow. Shortly after the move to Dallas Criswell authored his first book, an unassuming volume, *The Church Library Reinforcing the Work of the Denomination*. However in 1953, with the publication of *These Issues We Must Face*, he began to write approximately a book a year. Many volumes are collections of his sermons; others are expositions of books of the Bible. Still others are polemic, such as *Did Man Just Happen?* (1957); *In Defense of the Faith* (1967); and *Why I Preach the Bible Is Literally True* (1969), his single most famous book. In the 1950s he led a coalition of Protestant clergy who fought the nomination and election of John F. Kennedy because he was a Roman Catholic.

As Criswell's church grew, its membership began to include a few of the rich and famous, including millionaire oilman H. L. Hunt, evangelist **William Frank (Billy) Graham**, and radio news analyst Paul Harvey (the 20,001st member). The church developed an annual budget in excess of 10 million dollars and gave millions to the Southern Baptist Convention. In 1968 he was elected president of the Southern Baptist Convention. He has been a leader of the conservative faction in the convention, and his concern over the teachings permitted at the Baptist schools led him to found the Criswell Center for Biblical Studies, which includes the Criswell Bible College and the Graduate School of the Bible. Beginning in 1970 he broadcast the Sunday morning service, which by the mid-1980s was heard throughout the southwest. In 1989 the church's 100,000 watt radio station received its license to begin broadcasting. After four decades of leadership, Criswell remains firmly at the head of the leadership of the congregation, which is itself larger than many of America's denominations. In 1985, he completed his most substantial writing, a five-volume set on the *Great Doctrines of the Bible*.

Criswell truly emerged into national prominence in the 1960s as the conservative faction began to dominate the Southern Baptist Convention. His election as convention president in 1968, the publication of *Why I Preach the Bible Is Literally True* (1969), and the opening of the Bible school (1970) were major signals alerting the convention to what was to come in the subsequent decades in which conservatives would dominate all aspects of the convention. However, Criswell has consistently refused to join with his more conservative colleagues in purging the convention of ideological moderates.

Sources:
Criswell, W. A. *Did Man Just Happen?* Grand Rapids, MI: Zondervan Publishing House, 1957. 121 pp.
_____. *Great Doctrines of the Bible.* 5 vols. Grand Rapids, MI: Zondervan Publishing House, 1982-1985.
_____. *In Defense of the Faith.* Grand Rapids, MI: Zondervan Publishing House, 1967. 88 pp.
_____. *Why I Preach the Bible Is Literally True.* Nashville, TN: Broadman Press, 1969. 160 pp.
Hill, Samuel S., ed. *Encyclopedia of Religion in the South.* Macon, GA: Mercer University Press, 1984. 878 pp.
Keith, Billy. *W. A. Criswell: The Authorized Biography.* Old Tappan, NJ: Fleming H. Revell Company, 1973. 224 pp.

Lippy, Charles H. *Twentieth-Century Shapers of American Popular Religion.* New York: Greenwood Press, 1989. 494 pp.

Russell, C. Allyn. "W. A. Criswell: A Case Study in Fundamentalism." *Review and Expositor* Winter 1981: 107-131.

★ 231 ★
CROSBY, Fanny
Hymn Writer, Methodist Episcopal Church
b. Mar. 24, 1820, Southeast, New York
d. Feb. 12, 1915, Bridgeport, Connecticut

Frances Jane Crosby, known popularly as Fanny Crosby, the most popular hymn writer of the American church, was the daughter of John and Mercy Crosby. The victim of an incompetent doctor, she was blinded when she was but six weeks old. Her father died before the year was out. A short time later her mother moved to North Salem, New York, and in 1828 to Ridgefield, Connecticut, where Fanny grew up. In 1835 she became one of the fortunate youth able to attend the New York Institution for the Blind in New York City. During her student years there she met a phenologist visiting from Scotland who learned of her habit of writing simple verses. He convinced her she was a poet and encouraged her to put some effort into her writing.

The school responded to Crosby's efforts and featured her work with that of a troupe of students who made public appearances on the school's behalf. Among her first published poems was a eulogy to William Henry Harrison published in 1841. In 1843 she graduated from the school and joined its faculty as a teacher of English and history. In 1844 she appeared before a joint session of Congress showcasing abilities of the blind, and later that year her first book of poems, *The Blind Girl and Other Poems*, was published. Her second book, *Monterey and Other Poems*, appeared in 1851.

In the early 1850s Crosby began serious work with **George F. Root**, the music director at the school, who became one of the great hymn writers of the century. They collaborated on a cantata and on some secular songs, a few of which became popular songs of the day. In 1858 she resigned from the school and married Alexander Van Alstyne, who was also blind and a teacher at the school. That year her third volume of poetry appeared, *A Wreath of Columbia's Flowers*.

In the late 1850s Crosby was affected by the religious revival which swept New York City. She began to attend different churches, including St. John's Methodist Episcopal Church and the Plymouth Congregational Church pastored by **Henry Ward Beecher**. In 1864 she was introduced to William Bradbury, the most prolific hymn writer of the period, who was looking for someone who could produce words for his music. W. B. Bradbury & Co. was the first of several companies for whom she would work and produce poems on demand. Over the remaining decades of her life she would write many thousands of poems for hymns and collaborate with the likes of **Ira Sankey**, who was **Dwight L. Moody**'s song leader, and Howard Doane, who set more than a thousand of her poems to music. The exact number of hymns she wrote is unknown, as many of her poems were published under a pseudonym.

Crosby's poems became commercial successes and developed a continuing popularity, especially among the Methodists. Among her most enduring hymns are "Blessed Assurance," "Pass Me Not, O Gentle Savior," "Jesus, Keep Me Near the Cross," "Rescue the Perishing," "I Am Thine, O Lord," and "Savior, More Than Life to Me."

Crosby lived into her 90s. Her last years were spent in her home in Ridgefield, Connecticut. Among her last literary productions were two autobiographical volumes: *Fanny Crosby's Life-Story* (1903) and *Memories of Eighty Years* (1906).

Sources:

Barrett, Ethel. *Fanny Crosby.* Ventura, CA: Regal Books, 1984. 144 pp.

Crosby, Frances J. *The Blind Girl and Other Poems.* New York: Wiley & Putnam, 1844. 159 pp.

_____. *Fanny Crosby's Life-Story, by Herself.* New York: Everywhere Publishing Co., 1903. 160 pp.

_____. *Memories of Eighty Years.* Boston: James H. Earle, 1906. 253 pp.

_____. *Monterey and Other Poems.* New York: R. Craighead, 1851. 203 pp.

_____. *A Wreath of Columbia's Flowers.* New York: H. Dayton, 1858. 138 pp.

Jackson, Samuel Trevena. *Fanny Crosby's Story of Ninety-four Years.* New York: Fleming H. Revell, 1915.

Ruffin, Bernard. *Fanny Crosby.* New York: Pilgrim Press, 1976. 257 pp.

★ 232 ★
CROUCH, Austin
Executive, Southern Baptist Convention
b. Jul. 13, 1870, Carrolton, Missouri
d. Aug. 28, 1957, Nashville, Tennessee

Austin Crouch, credited with developing the Southern Baptist Convention during the crucial years between the World War I and World War II as the executive secretary-treasurer of the convention's executive committee, was the son of Adelaide Newell and Elbert Hildebrand Crouch. He was ordained as a Baptist minister in 1893 and later attended Baylor University (A. B., 1898) and Southern Baptist Theological Seminary (1898-1900). In 1900 he married Arianna Hill. He earned his master's degree from Howard College (now Stanford University) in 1906. During the first decades of the twentieth century, Crouch was a pastor serving churches in Texas, Mississippi, Alabama, Arkansas, and Tennessee. He also served a brief stint as the superintendent of church extension for the Home Mission Board of the Southern Baptist Convention. He authored his first book, *The Plan of Salvation* in 1924.

Crouch emerged out of obscurity in 1925 when he called for a Business Efficiency Committee to address the problems of the financially and organizationally troubled convention. At that same meeting, the convention adopted a program to encourage the participation of local churches in offering a greater level of financial support and cooperation to the convention. Called to the task of executive secretary-treasurer of the executive committee in 1927, Crouch was assigned the task of making the Cooperative Program (organized to encourage cooperation between the churches of the convention and its national offices) work. Meeting the opposition from many pastors and church leaders who complained that the program was creating a super-denomination, Crouch is credited with overcoming the opposition and bringing the great majority of the churches into participation. His efforts allowed the convention to overcome the severe financial problems encountered during, and following, the Great Depression.

Crouch retired in 1946, in part due to failing eyesight. However, having become a widower, that same year he married Myrtle Oldham. Though almost blind, he spent much of his retirement years preaching and writing. While one of his books, *How Southern Baptists Do Their Work* (1951), reflected his intimate knowledge of the workings of the Southern Baptist Convention, the majority of them grew out of his own theological and pastoral convictions: *The Progress of the Christian Life* (1949); *The Bright Side of Death* (1951) and *Is Baptism Essential to Salvation?* (1953). Much of Crouch's success as an administrator was due to his combining effective practical leadership with his own personal piety.

Crouch died suddenly in 1957 as the victim of a car accident.

Sources:

Crouch, Austin. *The Bright Side of Death.* Nashville, TN: Broadman Press, 1951. 32 pp.

_____. *How Southern Baptists Do Their Work.* Nashville, TN: Broadman Press, 1951. 99 pp.

_____. *The Plan of Salvation*. Nashville, TN: N.p., 1924.
_____. *The Progress of the Christian Life*. Nashville, TN: Sunday School Board of the Southern Baptist Convention, 1949. 98 pp.
Encyclopedia of Southern Baptists. 3 vols. Nashville, TN: Broadman Press, 1958, 1971.

★ 233 ★
CROWDY, William Saunders
Founder, Church of God and Saints of Christ
b. 1847, Charlotte Hall, Maryland
d. Aug. 4, 1908, Washington, District of Columbia

William Saunders Crowdy, founder of the Church of God and Saints of Christ, one of the first black Jewish groups, was born into slavery, the son of Basle and Sarah Ann Crowdy. In 1863 he joined the Union Army. After the war he moved to Guthrie, Oklahoma, and purchased a 100-acre farm. He joined the local Baptist church. He stayed in Guthrie for many years, but in the 1890s moved to Kansas City, Missouri, and became a hotel cook. He met and married Lovey Yates Higgins. He soon returned to the Guthrie farm, where he had a vision that became the basis of a new church movement.

Crowdy's vision, which occurred in 1893, began with a group of tables covered with filth. Each table was labeled with the name of a different church. Then a white table, the Church of God and Saints of Christ, appeared. Subsequently, Crowdy was given the rules and guidelines, the "7 Keys," which he interpreted as instructions for founding a new movement, the true church.

On November 8, 1896, Crowdy formed the Church of God and Saints of Christ. Within two years there were 29 congregations in Kansas and surrounding states. He moved to Chicago to launch the church in Illinois and slowly worked his way east.

During these years he delivered a number of sermons which were published and which have set the beliefs and practices of the group. Crowdy attempted to synthesize Judaism and Christianity. He adopted the practice of observing passover and other Jewish holidays and worshipping on the Sabbath. He taught that Blacks were the ten lost tribes of Israel. He retained the practice of foot washing from his Baptist heritage.

In 1900 Crowdy moved to Philadelphia, where over a period of several years he built a congregation of 1,500 members. The passover, which has become an annual event, was first observed in Philadelphia. He established a printing press and began a periodical, the *Weekly Prophet*. He also married again, to Saint Hallie Brown, the assistant grand secretary. He later came to denounce the practice of remarriage and subsequently left his second wife and returned to his first one. In 1903 a smallpox epidemic broke out in Philadelphia. Crowdy moved to Washington, D.C., at the urging of his followers.

During his Washington years, Crowdy appointed his nephew Joseph Wesley Crowdy, as well as Calvin S. Skinner and William Henry Plummer, as his successors. In 1907, while in Newark, New Jersey, Crowdy suffered a stroke. He never recovered his health and died the following year.

In the years since his death, the church that Crowdy established has moved toward the further incorporation of Jewish beliefs and practices as originally advocated by Crowdy.

Sources:

Crowdy, William Saunders. *The Bible Gospel Told: The Revelation of God Revealed*. Washington, DC: Church of God and Saints of Christ, 1902.
_____. *The Bible Story Revealed*. Belleville, VA: Church of God and Saints of Christ, 1902.
Walker, Beersheba Crowdy. *The Life and Works of William Saunders Crowdy*. Philadelphia: Elfreth Walker, 1955. 62 pp.

Wynia-Trey, Elly. "The Church of God and Saints of Christ: A Black Judeo-Christian Movement Founded in Lawrence, Kansas, in 1896." Lawrence, KS: University of Kansas, A. B. Honors thesis, 1988. 150 pp.

★ 234 ★
CROWLEY, Aleister Edward
Outer Head of the Order, Ordo Templi Orientis
b. Oct. 12, 1875, Leamington, Warwickshire England
d. Dec. 1, 1947, Hastings England

Aleister Edward Crowley was the most famous religious practitioner of magic in the twentieth century. His birth name was Edward Alexander Crowley, and his father was a preacher in the Exclusive Plymouth Brethren, a fundamentalist Christian group. Crowley grew up so rebellious of the household's strict rules that even his mother called him "The Beast 666" (from Revelation 13:18). His father died in 1887, and Crowley's public school experience after that was erratic. In 1894 he entered King's College. He studied at Trinity College, Cambridge, from 1894 to 1897, but did not obtain a degree. Crowley was more interested in poetry, magic and the occult, and sex than his studies.

In 1898 Crowley began his occult journey with his initiation into the Hermetic Order of the Golden Dawn. He married Rose Edith Kelly in 1903. He climbed through the ranks of the Golden Dawn's membership. Before long, however, he became embroiled in a larger dispute between the Order's British members and their leader in Paris, and decided it would be better to head elsewhere. He went briefly to the United States, but his important experience took place in Cairo, Egypt. There, his wife pressed him to sit for three days (April 9-11, 1904) for communication from Aiwass, a spirit entity. The result of Aiwass's dictation was *The Book of the Law*, the substance of his brand of magic, which he called "Thelema," from the Greek word for "will." The main tenet of this system was "Do what thou will shall be the whole of the law," meaning that the magician is to find his or her true destiny and follow it.

In 1907 Crowley founded his own order, the Argenteum Astrum (Silver Star). In 1909 he began publishing his semiannual *Equinox*, which brought much of the magical material to public attention. That same year he divorced his wife. Crowley shifted his focus in 1912 after meeting Theodore Ruess, head of the Ordo Templi Orientis (O.T.O.), a German-based occult fraternity. Crowley soon became an active part of its highest levels. The O.T.O. taught rituals of autoerotic and heterosexual sex magic, and Crowley added new rituals which included homosexual magic.

Crowley spent 1914 to 1919 in America, where he continued his training and declared his attainment of the status of "magus," the second highest magician level. 1919 to 1923 was spent in Italy, where he attained "ipsissimus," the highest magical level. After Mussolini forced his exit, Crowley went to Tunis and France before settling again in England. In 1929 he married again, this time to Maria Theresa Ferrari de Miramar. The remainder of his life was spent in England, where he fought his addiction to heroin and oversaw the activities of the O.T.O.

At the time of Crowley's death in 1947, the O.T.O. had as yet shown little vitality. Limited to one functioning center, it almost went out of existence entirely during the 1960s. It re-emerged in the 1970s, however, and in the 1980s spread internationally with a surprising and unprecedented vigor. In spite of the performance of the Ordo Templi Orientis during his lifetime, Crowley left a powerful reputation. His impact, especially through his writings, has been felt since his death throughout all branches of magic and the occult.

Sources:

Cammell, C.R. *Aleister Crowley*. London: New English Library, 1969. 109 pp.

Crowley, Aleister Edward. *Confessions*. New York: Hill and Wang, 1969. 960 pp.
_____. *Crowley on Christ*. Edited by Francis King. London: C. W. Daniel Company, 1974. 232 pp.
_____. *The Holy Books of Thelema*. York Beach, ME: Samuel Weiser, 1983.
_____. *Magical Record of the Beast 666*. Montreal: Next Step Publications, 1972.
_____. *Magick in Theory and Practice*. New York: Samuel Weiser, 1974. 511 pp.
_____. *Magick Without Tears*. St. Paul, MN: Llewellyn Publications, 1973.
King, Francis. *The Magical World of Aleister Crowley*. New York: Coward, McCann & Goeghegan, 1978. 210 pp.
Melton, J. Gordon. *Biographical Dictionary of American Cult and Sect Leaders*. Garland Reference Library of Social Science, vol. 212. New York: Garland Publishing, 1986.
Parfitt, Will, and A. Drylie. *A Crowley Cross-Index*. New York, 1976.
Roberts, Susan. *The Magician of the Golden Dawn*. Chicago, 1978.
Shepard, Leslie. *Encyclopedia of Occultism & Parapsychology*. 3 vols., 2nd. ed. Detroit: Gale Research Co., 1984-1985.
Suster, Gerald. *The Legacy of the Beast: The Life, Work and Influence of Aleister Crowley*. York Beach, ME: Samuel Wizer, 1989. 229 pp.

—*Gary L. Ward*

★ 235 ★
CRUMMELL, Alexander
Priest, Protestant Episcopal Church
Founder, St. Luke's Episcopal Church
b. 1819, New York, New York
d. Sep. 10, 1898, Red Bank, New Jersey

Alexander Crummell, a priest in the Protestant Episcopal Church, was the son of a free black woman and Boston Crummell, an African immigrant. As a youth he attended the African Free School in Manhattan, and in 1835 entered the Noyes Academy in Canna, New Hampshire. Unfortunately, a few months after moving to New Hampshire, neighbors who were angry at the presence of Blacks at the school forced Crummell and his black classmate to leave. The next year he entered Oneida Institute in upstate New York, from which he graduated in 1839. Having decided to become an Episcopal priest, he was frustrated by General Theological Seminary's refusal to admit him because he was black. He pursued his theological studies on his own and in 1844 was finally ordained in Philadelphia. During these years he also became an outspoken advocate concerning abolition of slavery and the removal of all legal restrictions which inhibited the full participation of Blacks in society. Refused admission to the Diocese of Pennsylvania, he returned to New York, where he tried unsuccessfully to raise funds to start a congregation among poor Blacks. It was then suggested that he go to England and raise financial support there.

In 1848 Crummell went to England. He spent three years raising money and then entered Cambridge University, from which he graduated in 1853. He then moved to Liberia, where he became a citizen and a voice for Liberian nationalism. While there he organized several churches and served as master of Mount Vaughn High School at Cape Palmas. In 1861 he received an appointment as a professor at Liberia College, recently established in Monrovia. That same year he finished his first book, *The Relations and Duties of Free Colored Men in America to Africa*. The next year he followed it with a second, *The Future of Africa*.

In 1872 Crummell left Liberia and returned to the United States. He settled in Washington, D.C., where he founded and pastored St. Luke's Episcopal Church. Several years after the death of his first wife, in 1880 he married Jennie M. Simpson. He soon emerged as the senior black priest in the predominantly white denomination and a spokesperson for Blacks looking for greater recognition and leadership positions in the church. The crucial issue before the church was the extension of the episcopacy to Blacks. In 1883 he called a meeting of his fellow black priests and supportive laity to protest the refusal of the church to consecrate a black bishop. The Conference of Church Workers among Colored People emerged from this meeting. This post-Reconstruction era, one in which segregated structures were becoming entrenched in society, kept Crummell busy speaking and lecturing against racism. A consistent theme he developed was the necessity of the black community to produce an educated leadership to lead in the redemption of the race.

During his years at St. Luke's, Crummell authored several books, *The Greatness of Christ* (1882); *Africa and America* (1891); and his autobiography, *Alexander Crummell, 1844-1894: The Shades and Light of Fifty Years Ministry* (1894). Following his retirement, he taught at Howard University for two years (1895-1897). Among his last accomplishments, in 1879 he organized the American Negro Academy to encourage excellence among black intellectuals. Among its 40 members were W. E. B. Du Bois and Paul Laurence Dunbar.

Sources:
Crummell, Alexander. *Africa and America*. Springfield, MA: Wiley & Co., 1891. 466 pp.
_____. *The Future of Africa*. New York: Charles Scribner, 1862. 354 pp.
_____. *The Greatness of Christ*. New York: Thomas Whittaker, 1882. 352 pp.
_____. *The Relations and Duties of Free Colored Men in America to Africa*. Hartford, CT: Lockwood & Co., 1861. 54 pp.
Du Bois, W. E. B. *The Souls of Black Folks*. Chicago: A. C. McClurg & Co., 1903. 264 pp.
Logan, Rayford W., and Michael R. Winston, eds. *Dictionary of American Negro Biography*. New York: W. W. Norton & Co. 1982. 680 pp.
Scruggs, Otey M. *We the Children of Africa in This Land: Alexander Crummell*. Washington, DC: Department of History, Howard University, 1972. 25 pp.

★ 236 ★
CRUMPLER, Ambrose Blackman
Founder, Holiness Church of North Carolina
b. 1863, Clinton, North Carolina
d. 1952, Clinton, North Carolina

Ambrose Blackman Crumpler, a prominent holiness minister at the beginning of the twentieth century, was born in rural North Carolina. Little is known of his early life, but as a young man he moved to Missouri and entered the ministry. He was licensed to preach by the Methodist Episcopal Church, South. He followed the ministry of **Beverly Carradine**, a prominent Southern Methodist minister who preached holiness doctrine, a belief that individuals can receive a second blessing from God through the agency of the Holy Spirit and thus become perfect in love. Crumpler became convinced of the truth of this idea and became active in the National Camp Meeting Association for the Promotion of Holiness. This was just at the time that the "come-out" movement (a movement aimed at forming holiness churches independent from Methodism) had begun in response to Methodist leaders who were not in affinity with the holiness thinking.

In about 1896, Crumpler returned to the area of his birth in North Carolina with a goal of establishing holiness in his home state. He traveled through eastern North Carolina holding evangelistic meetings, sometimes in Methodist churches, and at other times in tents. Crumpler became somewhat controversial in that he claimed not only to have been made perfect in love, but to have become perfect—that is, without sin—since his sanctification experience in 1890. In May 1897 he gained enough support to form a state association in affiliation with the National Holiness Association. He was elected president, and with his new base of support continued his evangelistic work.

In the summer of 1898 the Methodist Episcopal Church, South forbade evangelists from holding meetings in the immediate vicinity of other Methodist work without the permission of the pastor.

Crumpler ignored this rule and held a meeting at Elizabeth City, North Carolina. Facing the criticism of his colleagues, in November 1898 he withdrew and formed a congregation at Goldsboro, North Carolina, which he called the Pentecostal Holiness Church. He then rejoined the Methodist Episcopal Church, South, hoping to overturn the troublesome rule. Instead, after some meetings in Stedman, North Carolina, Crumpler was tried for again violating the rule. Though acquitted, he left the church again.

In 1900 Crumpler led in the formation of the Pentecostal Holiness Church, which was modeled on the Methodist organization, and began to edit a periodical, the *Holiness Advocate*. Approximately a dozen churches affiliated with the movement. Crumpler pastored the church in Goldsboro. In 1903 the group became known as the Holiness Church of North Carolina.

The new denomination was almost immediately torn apart by controversy. **Gaston Barnabas Cashwell**, a ministerial member of the group, had gone to the revival that had begun in Los Angeles in 1906, at which the baptism of the Holy Spirit as evidenced by speaking in tongues was being preached. Cashwell had the experience and returned to share it with Crumpler and his colleagues. At a gathering in Dunn, North Carolina, in 1907, nearly all of the ministers received the baptism. Crumpler did not receive the baptism, but he did not oppose the practice, and he continued to support Cashwell's evangelistic endeavors in the state. By 1908, however, Crumpler had become vocally antagonistic to the idea that tongues was the "only" initial evidence of the baptism.

In 1908, at the church's meeting in Dunn, Crumpler and his supporters were defeated on the issue of tongues, although he was still elected president of the church. The following day, however, he left the church and returned to the Methodist Episcopal Church, South. He preached for a few years, but eventually returned to the status of local preacher and practiced law in Clinton. He lived quietly for many more years, occasionally preaching but no longer championing the holiness perspective. He did support prohibition and its abstinence ideals.

Sources:

Burgess, Stanley M., Gary B. McGee, and Patrick H. Alexander, eds. *Dictionary of Pentecostal and Charismatic Movements*. Grand Rapids, MI: Regency Reference Library, Zondervan Publishing House, 1988. 914 pp.

Campbell, Joseph E. *The Pentecostal Holiness Church, 1898-1948*. Franklin Springs, GA: Pentecostal Holiness Church, 1951. 573 pp.

Hill, Samuel S., ed. *Encyclopedia of Religion in the South*. Macon, GA: Mercer University Press, 1984. 878 pp.

Synan, Vinson. *The Old Time Power: A History of the Pentecostal Holiness Church*. Franklin Springs, GA: Advocate Press, 1973. 296 pp.

★ 237 ★
CULLBERTSON, William
Bishop, Reformed Episcopal Church
b. Nov. 18, 1905, Philadelphia, Pennsylvania
d. Nov. 16, 1971, Chicago, Illinois

William Culbertson, a bishop of the Reformed Episcopal Church best known for his leadership of the Moody Bible Institute, grew up in Philadelphia. Following high school he entered the Reformed Episcopal Theological Seminary. In 1927 he graduated, was ordained a deacon, and became the pastor of Grace Reformed Episcopal Church in Collingdale, Pennsylvania. In 1929 he began teaching at the seminary and at the nearby Philadelphia School of the Bible. In 1929 he married Catherine Gantz. In 1930 he became pastor of St. John's-by-the-Sea Reformed Episcopal Church at Ventnor, New Jersey. He stayed in New Jersey for three years before returning to Philadelphia as pastor of the Church of the Atonement. Back in Philadelphia he was able to complete his college work at Temple University, from which he graduated in 1939. While studying at Temple, in 1937 he was named bishop of New York and Philadelphia by the church.

In 1942 Culbertson began his long career at Moody Bible Institute as the dean of education. In 1947 **Will H. Houghton**, the president of the institute, died. Culbertson was appointed as acting president and early in 1948 he was named the new president. He remained in that post for the next 22 years. He proved ideal for the task. He was an able administrator who worked to transform Moody from a basically lay training school into a professional school that produced pastors, missionaries, and other church workers. Through his speaking and writing (primarily sermons and brief articles for Christian magazines), he built broad support for the school.

In improving the quality of instruction at Moody, Culbertson was also a staunch supporter of orthodox premillennial dispensational fundamentalism. He opposed any accommodation to the liberal trends then coming to the fore in most of the major denominational bodies, and continued the institute's affirmation of the soon return of Christ and a view of the Bible that understood its account of humanity as following a series of divisions (dispensations) in which God progressively worked out his plan for the salvation of humanity. Culbertson was also dedicated to the cause of Jewish missions, an enterprise which found a renewed response from conservative evangelical Christians in the 1950s after the establishment of the state of Israel. Many evangelicals saw Israel as a sign that Christ would soon appear. Not only did Culbertson support and help strengthen the Jewish evangelism program at Moody, but in 1948 became the chairman of the advisory board of the American Association for Jewish Evangelism, one of the older of the Jewish evangelism groups also headquartered in Chicago.

His career at Moody was recognized in 1970 with the dedication of a new men's dormitory, Culbertson Hall. In 1970 he retired from the president's office and was named chancellor.

Sources:

Reid, Daniel G., Robert D. Linder, Bruce L. Shelley, and Harry S. Stout. *Dictionary of Christianity in America*. Downers Grove, IL: InterVarsity Press, 1990. 1305 pp.

Wiesbe, Warren E. *William Culbertson: A Man of God*. Chicago: Moody Press, 1974.

★ 238 ★
CULLIS, Charles
Healer, Episcopal Church
b. Mar. 7, 1833, Boston, Massachusetts
d. Jun. 18, 1892

Charles Cullis, an Episcopal Church layperson remembered for his pioneering work in the revival of modern spiritual healing, was the son of John Cullis. A sickly child and a survivor of a period of serious illness as a young man, Cullis turned toward medicine. He did his preliminary reading during his recovery and eventually graduated from the University of Vermont's medical department. He settled in Boston as a homeopathic physician.

Cullis' illness also heightened his religious life, and he was baptized in his family church, the same church from which he had earlier fallen away. He was most impressed by the stories of prominent European Christians such as Herman Franke, George Mueller, and Dorothea Trudel. Trudel's life and faith-healing work so stirred him that he later would write a popular biography of her. Somewhat recovered, he married, but his wife soon died. In reaction, and as an expression of his new faith, he vowed to devote his life and income to the works of charity and religion.

In 1865, Cullis opened a home for victims of tuberculosis, then an incurable disease. The home soon outgrew its facilities, and he purchased 11 acres in suburban Grove Hall, Massachusetts. He not only moved the original facility, but constructed a series of charitable institutions to serve the ill, orphans, and deaconesses on this site. With a combination of his own money and contributions, he expanded his work to include various missions around the country, two churches in Boston, and two missions in India. He launched tract depositories which published and distributed religious literature, including the Willard Tract Depository in Boston. In 1885, the twentieth anniversary of the beginning of his ministry, W. H. Daniels authored a book describing *Dr. Cullis and His Work* in its many aspects.

Each summer Cullis held revival meetings at both Intervale, New Hampshire, and Old Orchard, Maine. To Old Orchard came William Boardman, a leader of the holiness movement in England, and Albert Benjamin Simpson, founder of the Christian and Missionary Alliance (CMA), the first modern denomination to emphasize spiritual healing as an integral part of its ministry. Both Boardman and Simpson were healed under Cullis' ministry. His belief in and practice of religious healing stimulated and inspired the growing religious healing movement in the Boston area, which included Christian Science, the Emmanuel Movement (founded by Episcopal minister **Elwood Worcester**), and New Thought.

In 1873 he opened a training school and a bookstore adjacent to one of the Boston churches. Also, he established the "Faith Cure House" near the church for those who came to services from so far away that they had to stay overnight. During the 1880s, the height of his ministry, Cullis authored a number of books which grew out of his healing experiences.

If there was one flaw in the vast charitable network of organizations largely sustained by Cullis' charisma and managerial ability, it was that he made no provisions for their continuation after his death. He had always lived as if God would meet all needs. During Cullis' lifetime the work prospered. However, most of Cullis' charitable network died by the end of the century.

Sources:

Boardman, William. *Faith Work Under Dr. Cullis in Boston*. Boston: Willard Tract Depository, 1876. 296 pp.
Cullis, Charles. *Dorothea Trudel, or the Prayer of Faith*. Boston: Willard Tract Depository, 1872.
_____. *Faith Cures; Or, Answers to Prayer in the Healing of the Sick*. Boston: Willard Tract Depository, 1879. 109 pp.
_____. *Other Faith Cures*. Boston: Willard Tract Depository, 1885. 160 pp.
_____. *Songs of Victory*. Boston: Willard Tract Depository, 1889. 159 pp.
_____. *A Work of Faith*. Boston: J. E. Farwell & Co., 1867. 88 pp.
Daniels, W. H. *Dr. Cullis and His Work*. Boston: Willard Tract Depository, 1885. 364 pp.
Dictionary of American Biography. 20 vols. and 7 supps. New York: Charles Scribner's Sons, 1928-1936, 1944-1981.

★ 239 ★
CUMMINGS, Edward
Minister, American Unitarian Association (AUA)
b. Apr. 2, 1861, Colebrook, New Hampshire
d. Nov. 2, 1926, Boston, Massachusetts

Edward Cummings, Unitarian minister and social activist, was the son of Edward N. and Lucretia F. Merrill Cummings. Raised in Massachusetts, he attended Harvard College, from which he graduated magna cum laude in 1883. He remained at Harvard for his M.A. (1885) and then entered the Harvard Divinity School, where he studied with Reverend Francis G. Peabody, a pioneer teacher in the then new field of social ethics. While attending the divinity school he was a lecturer at Harvard in English, political economy, and sociology. He also received the first Robert Taft Paine fellowship for the study of social science abroad.

In 1893 Cummings became an assistant professor in sociology at Harvard, a post he held for eight years. During this time he served as an editor of the *Quarterly Journal of Economics*. A number of his articles dealt with the cooperative movement, and he twice served as president of the Harvard Cooperative Society.

Cummings' real career, however, lay in his mixing of religious leadership with the social theory he had mastered. In 1900 he was ordained in the Unitarian ministry at South Congregational Society, Unitarian, where he became the associate pastor under **Edward Everett Hale**. Upon Hale's retirement in 1909, Cummings became senior minister. He described himself as an applied sociologist, and most of his work was in the public sphere. He became president of the Benevolent Fraternity of Unitarian Churches and the Massachusetts Civic League. He took the lead in prison reform, and became director of the Massachusetts Prison Association. He also directed the work at Hale House, a pioneering social settlement.

Among the most important concerns of Cummings' life was peace. He joined the World Peace Federation, was elected to its board in 1910, and became its general secretary in 1916. In the years ahead the federation claimed at least half of his working hours. In 1921 he traveled to Europe to survey the damage resulting from World War I and became very interested in relief work, especially directed toward Europe and the Near East. When the United States voted to stay out of the League of Nations, his federation office became the official center for the United States for the dissemination of information from the League and the Permanent Court of International Justice.

Cummings retired from the pastorate in 1925, at which time his congregation merged with First Church, Boston. He was succeeded in the pulpit by Charles Park and became pastor emeritus. Unfortunately, the following year he was killed in an accident at a railroad crossing during a snowstorm.

Sources:

Dictionary of American Biography. 20 vols. and 7 supps. New York: Charles Scribner's Sons, 1928-1936, 1944-1981.

★ 240 ★
CUMMINS, George David
Bishop, Reformed Episcopal Church
b. Dec. 11, 1822, Smyrna, Delaware
d. Jun. 26, 1876, Lutherville, Maryland

George David Cummins was the founder and first bishop of the Reformed Episcopal Church, an evangelical schism from the Protestant Episcopal Church. In 1836, at the age of 14, Cummins went to Dickinson College with the intention of pursuing a law degree. When he was 17, however, there was a revival at the college. He was converted and decided to devote his life to the ministry. Methodism was his denomination of choice, and in 1842 he was ordained into the Baltimore Conference of the Methodist Episcopal Church.

In July of 1845, Cummins shifted over to the Protestant Episcopal Church and began a distinguished ministry. In 1846 he was named the assistant minister of Christ Church in Baltimore, and in 1847 he was ordained as a priest and moved to his own parish at Christ Church in Norfolk, Virginia. On June 24, 1847, he married Alexandrine Balch. After six years in Norfolk, he went on to serve St. James in Richmond, Trinity Church in Washington, D.C., St. Peter's Church in Baltimore, and Trinity Church in Chicago. In June, 1866, he was elected Assistant Bishop for Kentucky, and was ordained to that office in November.

Cummins still identified with the evangelical style of his earlier Methodism, and he became known as a leader of the Low Church movement, which emphasized conversion and opposed the High Church emphasis on liturgy. This clash in perspective came to a head in 1873, when Cummins spoke before the Evangelical Alliance meeting in New York City and then took part in an interdenominational communion service. His fellow bishops attacked this action, and the following month, on November 10, 1873, he resigned. Cummins believed that the Anglo-Catholic High Church movement in the church had overrun the Protestant character of the Episcopal doctrine, and he called upon others to join him in creating a new church.

This new body was formed on December 2, 1873, as the Reformed Episcopal Church, with Cummins as its first bishop. It maintained what it saw as its heritage of the episcopacy, Anglican liturgy, Reformed doctrine, and evangelical fellowship, with some slight variations. The office of bishop was no longer a separate order of ministry, and the House of Bishops was eliminated. Full authority was given to the general council, over which a bishop presided. Cummins lived only three years after the establishment of the new church, but it grew rapidly, and he saw its influence stretch across the nation. He died at home at the age of 54.

Sources:

Carter, Paul A. "The Reformed Episcopal Schism of 1873: An Ecumenical Perspective," *Historical Magazine of the Protestant Episcopal Church* 33 (September, 1964): 225-238.

Melton, J. Gordon. *Biographical Dictionary of American Cult and Sect Leaders.* Garland Reference Library of Social Science, vol. 212. New York: Garland Publishing, 1986.

Price, Anne Darling. *A History of the Formation and Growth of the Reformed Episcopal Church, 1873-1902.* Philadelphia: J. M. Armstrong, 1902. 308 pp.

—Gary L. Ward

★241★
CURRAN, Charles Edward
Theologian, Roman Catholic Church
b. Mar. 30, 1934, Rochester, New York

Charles Edward Curran is the best-known Catholic moral theologian in the United States. He achieved prominence in 1986 when, at the instigation of the Vatican, he was dismissed from the faculty of the Catholic University of America for his comparatively liberal views in the areas of sexual and medical ethics. He was the first American ever to be so disciplined by Rome. The son of a devout mother of German descent and a Democratic father of Irish descent, he began thinking of the priesthood at the age of 12, and entered St. Andrew's Minor Seminary in Rochester at the age of 13. He then went on to complete a B.A. at St. Bernard's Seminary. Sent to Rome by his supervisors, he earned two doctorates there in 1961, one from the Lateran University and the other from the Gregorian University.

Returning to the United States, Curran taught moral theology at St. Bernard's Seminary in Rochester and, beginning in 1965, at the Catholic University of America in Washington, D.C. The board of trustees of the university voted not to renew his contract following the publication of his *Christian Morality Today* (1966), due to some of the controversial material covered in the book, but a faculty-student protest in the wake of his dismissal influenced the board to reinstate him.

While Curran has taken controversial positions on many subjects, from divorce to homosexuality, he did not begin to attract the wrath of the Holy See until he led American Catholic resistance to Pope Paul VI's encyclical of 1968 condemning all methods of contraception. His stance on this and related issues, in combination with the increasing conservatism of the church, caused him to be accused of deviating from orthodoxy by the Congregation for the Defense of the Faith in the early 1980s. Curran refused to recant, insisting on his right to dissent on matters of faith and morals on which Rome had not spoken *ex cathedra*. The controversy came to a head on August 18, 1986, when the Vatican formally announced that Curran could no longer teach theology at the Catholic University.

Curran is the author of over a dozen books, most produced during his prolonged period of controversy with the Vatican, including: *Catholic Moral Theology in Dialogue* (1972); *Politics, Medi-*

cine and Christian Ethics: A Dialogue with Paul Ramsey (1973); *Ongoing Revision: Studies in Moral Theology* (1975); *Issues in Sexual and Medical Ethics* (1978); *Transition and Tradition in Moral Theology* (1979); *American Catholic Social Ethics: Twentieth Century Approaches* (1982); *Critical Concerns in Moral Theology* (1984); and *Directions in Catholic Social Ethics* (1985).

Sources:

Curran, Charles E. *American Catholic Social Ethics: Twentieth Century Approaches.* Notre Dame, IN: University of Notre Dame Press, 1982. 353 pp.

———. *Catholic Moral Theology in Dialogue1.* Notre Dame, IN: Fides Press, 1972. 270 pp.

———. *Critical Concerns in Moral Theology.* Notre Dame, IN: University of Notre Dame Press, 1984. 264 pp.

———. *Directions in Catholic Social Ethics.* Notre Dame, IN: University of Notre Dame Press, 1985. 287 pp.

———. *Issues in Sexual and Medical Ethics.* Notre Dame, IN: University of Notre Dame Press, 1978. 233 pp.

—Tim Miller

★242★
CURTISS, Harriette Augusta
Cofounder, Universal Religious Foundation
Cofounder, Order of Christian Mystics
b. 1856, Philadelphia, Pennsylvania
d. Sep. 22, 1932, Washington, District of Columbia

Born into a literary family, Harriette Augusta Curtiss founded the Order of Christian Mystics (1908) and then the Universal Religious Foundation (1929), an important theosophical-occult organization in the early twentieth century. Her husband F. Homer Curtiss, played a key role in co-founding the institutions. She was the daughter of Emma Brightly Brown and John Horace Brown, organizer of the Pennsylvania State Teachers' Association. She had a cultured education and became a proficient musician and actress. After starring in a number of amateur theatre productions in Philadelphia, she turned down an offer to become a professional at her mother's request. For many years she authored a column for the *Philadelphia Inquirer* under the pen name "The Bachelor Girl."

Harriette also emerged as a gifted clairvoyant. In this function she eventually found her life's work. In 1907, already in mid-life, she married F. Homer Curtiss, and they began a collaborative effort as occult teachers and writers. In 1907 they founded the Order of the 15 and Harriette began to issue monthly lessons for students, a practice she continued for the rest of her life. Within the order she was known as Rahmea.

The purpose of the Order was to correlate theosophical teachings with orthodox Christian teachings. Accordingly, the Order of the 15 soon assumed the more descriptive title of Order of Christian Mystics. Curtiss assumed the role of teacher for the order while her husband acted as its secretary. Together they prepared material for publication, though Harriette was the prime author. The first volume was edited from written responses to questions posed to Harriette and was entitled *Letters from the Teacher* (1909). The early lessons were gathered into what became the basic introductory text for the order, *The Voice of Isis* (1912). A more advanced text, *The Message of Aquaria*, was issued in 1921.

During World War I, the Curtisses authored several books dealing with war implications, two of which are *The War Crisis* (1914) and *Realms of the Living Dead?* (1917). During the war the Curtisses also formed the Church of the Wisdom Religion, a more open group than the esoteric order. The church was later incorporated as the Universal Religious Foundation after the Curtisses moved to Washington, D.C.

Throughout their lives the Curtisses continued to travel, teach, and write. Among the many additional books they authored are:

The Key to the Universe (1915); *The Key of Destiny* (1919); *Coming World Changes*; and *Inner Radiance*.

Sources:
Curtiss, Harriette Augusta and F. Homer Curtiss. *The Key of Destiny*. New York: E. P. Dutton, 1919. 328 pp.
_____. *Letters from the Teacher*. 2 vols. Hollywood: Curtiss Philosophic Book Co., 1918.
_____. *The Message of Aquaria*. San Francisco: The Curtiss Philosophic Book Co., 1921. 487 pp.
_____. *theatre Philosophy of War*. Washington, D.C.: Curtiss Philosophic Book Co., 1939. 168 pp.
_____. *The Voice of Isis*. Washington, D.C.: Curtiss Philosophic Book Co., 1935. 426 pp.
Lawrence, Alberta, ed. *Who Was Who Among North American Authors*. 2 vols. Detroit: Gale Research Co., 1976.

★ 243 ★
CUSHING, Richard James
Cardinal, Roman Catholic Church
b. Aug. 24, 1895, Boston, Massachusetts
d. Nov. 2, 1970, Boston, Massachusetts

Richard James Cushing, a cardinal in the Roman Catholic Church, was the son of Irish immigrants Patrick and Mary Dahill Cushing. After finishing his work in the public schools, he entered Boston College, where he made a commitment to the priesthood. After his sophomore year, he transferred to St. John's Seminary in Brighton, Massachusetts. He received his D.D. and LL.D. degrees and was ordained in 1921. He served only one year in the parish, as curate of St. Patrick's Church in the Roxbury district and then St. Benedict's Church in East Somerville.

In 1922 Cushing became assistant to the archdiocesan director of the Society for the Propagation of the Faith. He went on to become director of the society in 1928, and developed it into one of the most effective missionary offices of any diocese in the United States. He championed the cause of establishing seminaries to train future priests for what are presently mission fields.

In 1939 Pope Pius XII made Cushing a domestic prelate with the title right reverend monsignor. Two months later he was named titular bishop of Mela and auxiliary bishop of Boston, succeeding **Francis Spellman** who had become archbishop of New York. Cushing became archbishop of Boston following the death of **William O'Connell** in 1944.

Boston was growing in the years following World War II, and Cushing inherited a growing church. During the quarter century of his reign, he saw to the building of 80 churches, the chartering of three colleges, and the development of the Pope John XXIII Seminary, a school for men entering the priesthood late in life. He established six new hospitals and opened homes for children and the aged. Never losing his zeal for missions, he embarked on a unique adventure in forming the Missionary Society of St. James the Apostle which he founded in 1958. The Missionary Society helped to facilitate diocesan priests spending several years on the mission field as part of their priestly career. He also established the first diocesan radio and television center.

In 1954, on the tenth anniversary of Cushing's reign, Pope Pius XII appointed him Assistant at the Pontifical Throne, a prelude to his being named a cardinal in 1958.

In the 1960s Cushing attained some additional fame as a friend of the family of President John F. Kennedy. He offered the invocation at Kennedy's inauguration and presided at his funeral. He was active at the Second Vatican Council, especially in the area of liturgical reform.

Sources:
Delaney, John J. *Dictionary of American Catholic Biography*. Garden City, NY: Doubleday & Company, 1988. 621 pp.
Fenton, John H. *Salt of the Earth: An Informal Portrait of Richard Cardinal Cushing*. New York: Coward-McCann, Inc., 1965. 242 pp.
Thornton, Francis Beauchesne. *Our American Princes*. New York: G. P. Putnam's Sons, 1963. 319 pp.

★ 244 ★
CUSHMAN, Vera Charlotte Scott
Executive, Young Women's Christian Association (YWCA)
b. Sep. 19, 1876, Ottawa, Illinois
d. Feb. 1, 1946, Savannah, Georgia

Vera Charlotte Scott Cushman was a leader and organizer in the Young Women's Christian Association (YWCA). She was the second child and the only daughter of Samuel Swann and Anna Margaret Tressler Scott. Her father was an emigrant from Northern Ireland who, along with his brothers, founded a dry goods business in Illinois which grew to become Carson, Pirie, Scott and Company. Her mother, a Pennsylvania native descended from German and French families, was devoted to community and church work. The family lived in the Chicago area, except for a dozen years when Samuel Scott was the president of a bank in Salina, Kansas. They were devoutly religious. The youngest child, Rev. George T. Scott, became the assistant director, and eventually the executive secretary, of the Presbyterian Board of Foreign Missions.

Vera Scott attended Ferry Hall in Lake Forest, Illinois, and graduated from Smith College in 1898. While at Smith, she became involved in the YWCA and served as president of the student YWCA. She continued to be active in that organization after leaving Smith, and in 1905 was appointed to the Joint Committee which, by the next year, was able to bring together the two existing YWCA organizations to form the YWCA of the U.S.A. She was a member of the National Board for the next three decades, and served as vice-president of the national YWCA between 1906 and 1936.

On October 15, 1901, Vera Scott married James Stewart Cushman, who was involved with paper manufacturing and real estate in New York City. They never had children. Vera Cushman became a well-known hostess, famous for her skill at bringing together people with common interests. She continued to be active in the YWCA, helping to coordinate the various YWCA activities in the city, and serving as the first president of the YWCA of New York City. She was also one of the leaders of the YWCA campaign that in 14 days raised four million dollars.

Cushman served as chairman of the War Work Council, created by the government as one of seven war service organizations. Under her direction, over 100 Hostess Houses were built near training camps, naval stations, and hospital camps in Europe and the United States. These Houses provided recreational facilities and housing for signal corps workers, nurses, and other females involved in the military and in defense industries. As a result of her service during the first world war, Cushman was one of six women to be awarded the Distinguished Service Medal in the summer of 1919, and was chosen to christen one of seven ships that were named in tribute to war service organizations, The Blue Triangle. After the war, Cushman worked for the World Council of the YWCA as vice-president during the years 1924-1938, served on the executive committee of the Presbyterian Women's Board of Foreign Missions during the years 1920-1921, served as vice-president of the League of Nations Non-Partisan Association in 1923, was a delegate to the International Suffrage Convention in Geneva in 1920, and was associated with the boards of the China Christian Colleges.

Sources:
Dictionary of American Biography. 20 vols. and 7 supps. New York: Charles Scribner's Sons, 1928-1936, 1944-1981.

Marion O. Robinson. *Eight Women of the YWCA.* New York: National Board of the Young Women's Christian Association of the U.S.A., 1966. 118 pp.

★ 245 ★
DAHLBERG, Edwin Theodore
Baptist Minister
President, National Council of Churches
b. Dec. 27, 1892, Fergus Falls, Minnesota
d. Sep. 6, 1986, Phoenix, Arizona

Edwin Theodore Dahlberg, a Baptist minister and social activist, was the son of Christine Ring and Elof Dahlberg. During Dahlberg's high school days, the family moved to Minneapolis. Dahlberg was baptized and joined the Olivet Baptist Church in Minneapolis. The church's minister was a major influence on Dahlberg's decision to enter the ministry. He attended the University of Minnesota (B.A., 1914) and Rochester Theological Seminary (B.D., 1917). While at the university he was a leader in the local branch of the Christian Endeavor Union. While at Rochester, he earned some of his livelihood as the secretary to **Walter Rauschenbusch**, the theological architect of the social gospel.

Ordained as a minister with the Northern Baptist Convention (later the American Baptist Convention and American Baptist Churches in the U.S.A.) in 1918, Dahlberg was called to First Baptist Church in Potsdam, New York. He would then serve in succession Maple Street Baptist Church in Buffalo, New York (1921-1931); First Baptist Church in St. Paul, Minnesota (1931-1939); and First Baptist Church in Syracuse, New York (1939-1950). During his years in St. Paul, he authored his first book, *Youth and the Homes of Tomorrow* (1934). While at Syracuse, Dahlberg was elected president of the American Baptist Convention (1946-1948). His increasing involvement in national Baptist affairs led him into national and international ecumenical endeavors. In 1948 he traveled to Amsterdam as a delegate to the first gathering of the World Council of Churches, and was elected a member of the central committee of the council. He was also a delegate to the 1954 council assembly in Evanston, Illinois.

In 1950 Dahlberg moved to St. Louis as pastor of the Delmar Baptist Church, a congregation which had dual alignments to the American Baptist Convention and the Southern Baptist Convention. That same year Dahlberg participated in the founding of the National Council of Churches. In 1957 he was elected president of the National Council (1957-1960). During his presidency of the council, Dahlberg spoke out forcefully against the buildup of arms he saw around the world and also led the council to move in support of integration of black and white society. In response to complaints that the council was becoming too politically involved, Dahlberg tied evangelism and salvation to issues of social justice. Dahlberg retired from his St. Louis parish in 1962.

During his retirement years, Dahlberg became an even more vocal advocate for social causes in the turbulence of the 1960s. He used his relatively free position to crusade against the Vietnam War and work for interracial harmony. The American Baptist Convention named its peace prize after Dahlberg.

Sources:

Current Biography Yearbook. New York: H. W. Wilson Company, 1958.
Dahlberg, Edwin T. *Herald of the Evangel; 60 Years of American Christianity.* St. Louis, MO: Bethany Press, 1965. 221 pp.
_____. *This Is the Rim of East Asia.* New York: Friendship Press, 1962. 32 pp.
_____. *Youth and the Homes of Tomorrow.* Philadelphia: Judson Press, 1934. 160 pp.

★ 246 ★
Father DAMIEN OF MOLOKAI
Priest, Roman Catholic Church
b. Jan. 3, 1840, Tremeloo Belgium
d. Apr. 15, 1889, Molokai, Hawaii

Father Damien, a priest of the Roman Catholic Church who cared for lepers at the colony on Molokai, one of the Hawaiian Islands, was born Joseph de Veuster in a small town in Belgium. His parents, Francis and Anne Catherine de Veuster, were prosperous, hardworking, and pious. Two of Joseph's sisters became nuns and one brother a priest. At the age of 19 Joseph entered the Society of the Sacred Hearts of Jesus and Mary and of Perpetual Adoration of the Most Blessed Sacrament of the Altar. He pursued his studies with diligence and entered the seminary at Louvain. His priest brother Pamphile had been scheduled to go to Hawaii as a missionary. He developed typhoid, however, and could not go. Joseph went in his brother's stead. He arrived in Honolulu in March 1864. He was ordained a priest a few months later.

Damien became very popular with the native population as he traveled around the big island building churches, schools, and houses. In the mid-1860s leprosy arrived in Hawaii and spread among the population. In 1865 the government began to isolate the ill and established a colony on a remote peninsula of Molokai. Damien was the first of four priests assigned in 1873 to rotate from Honolulu every three months. Damien quickly concluded that it was important for one priest to stay permanently at the colony. Molokai became his home for the rest of his life.

The first need of the colony was for shelters. Within five years Damien had supervised the building of more than 300 houses and a church at Kalaupapa, and four chapels, a school, and a rectory at Topside. He lived intimately with his parishioners. He ate with them, tended their wounds, and eventually developed their disease. In the process he taught them how to improve the conditions under which they lived to the point that life was at least bearable.

In the later years of his work on Molokai, Damien came under attack. He was accused of illicit sexual relations with some of his colonists. Shortly before his death, however, an investigation exonerated him. In 1890 Robert Louis Stevenson wrote an impassioned defense of Damien in response to an attack by a Protestant minister in Honolulu.

Damien died in 1889. He was buried next to St. Philomena Catholic Church at Kalawao. In 1931 the state of Hawaii had a statue of Damien placed in Washington, D.C. In 1936 the Belgian government was given permission to exhume the body and take it home, where it was buried in a place of honor at St. Joseph's Chapel in Louvain.

In 1977 Pope Paul VI beatified Damien, declaring him a fit person to venerate, an important step toward declaring him a saint. Efforts toward his canonization by the Roman Catholic Church continue.

Sources:

Delaney, John J. *Dictionary of American Catholic Biography.* Garden City, NY: Doubleday & Company, 1988. 621 pp.
Hutchinson, Robert J. "Father Damien, Saint or Sinner?" *30 Days in the Church and the World* 2, 5 (May 1989): 61-67.
Prindiville, Raymond J. *Damien, Martyr of Molokai.* New York: Paulist Press, 1937. 24 pp.

★ 247 ★
DAUGHTRY, Herbert Daniel
National Presiding Minister, House of the Lord Churches
b. Jan. 13, 1931, Savannah, Georgia

Herbert Daniel Daughtry, the national presiding minister of the House of the Lord Churches, a predominantly black Pentecostal denomination, is the son of Alonzo Austin Daughtry, who in 1903 had left the ministry of the United House of Prayer for All People (led by Charles Emmanuel Grace) to found the House of the Lord Churches. Daughtry's childhood was spent in Georgia, but in 1942 the family moved to New York where congregations were begun in Harlem and in Brooklyn. He married Karen Smith. In 1952 the elder Daughtry died, and following eight years when the church was led by Mother Inez Conroy, Daughtry assumed the position of national presiding minister.

As the church's leader, Daughtry immediately became involved in community affairs. During the 1960s he worked with the Congress of Racial Equality (CORE) and Operation Breadbasket in the struggle for community control of schools. In 1969 he became the chairman of Ministers Against Narcotics. In 1977 he helped create the Coalition of Concerned Leaders and Citizens to Save Our Youth and founded the Commission on African Solidarity.

Daughtry has been a leader among Pentecostals on the international level. As early as 1969 he participated in the U.S. Conference of the World Council of Churches (held at Bush Hill Falls, Pennsylvania) and began three years work with the council's commission on World Mission and Evangelism on the quadrennial theme of "Salvation Today."

During the 1980s he continued to be active internationally. In 1980 he helped form the National Black United Front. He participated in the International Conference on Sanctions Against South Africa. His travels took him to a number of key tension spots around the globe, including Northern Ireland, Cuba, and East Germany. In the meantime he has overseen the growth of the House of the Lord Churches, which has become a national denomination.

Sources:

Daughtry, Herbert. *The House of the Lord Pentecostal Church: Official Orientation Material.* Brooklyn, NY: House of the Lord, n.d.

Dupree, Sherry Sherrod. *Biographical Dictionary of African-American, Holiness-Pentecostals, 1880-1990.* Washington, DC: Middle Atlantic Regional Press, 1990. 386 pp.

★ 248 ★
DAVIS, Andrew Jackson
Spiritualist Medium
b. Aug. 11, 1826, Blooming Grove, New York
d. Jan. 13, 1910, Watertown, Massachusetts

Andrew Jackson Davis is the person with whom modern Spiritualism may be said to have begun. His father was an occasional farmer, weaver, and shoemaker who moved the family regularly in his search for work. In Poughkeepsie, New York, in 1841, Davis was apprenticed to a shoemaker at the age of 15. In 1843 a phrenologist and mesmerist named Grimes came through town; a local tailor, William Levingston, learned mesmerism from him and began to practice on Davis. Davis not only proved able to go into a deep hypnotic trance, but showed clairvoyant capabilities as well. The discovery changed his life.

The first major experience which set the course of his future career occurred on March 6, 1844, when Davis wandered out into the countryside without having completely exited from a trance. While there he had visionary meetings with Galen, the physician of ancient Greece, and Emanuel Swedenborg, the famous medium of the 1700s. Davis claimed that these figures gave him the ability to diagnose and heal, talk to spirits, and channel cosmic knowledge. He and Levingston opened a clairvoyance clinic. All of the clinic's trance sessions were devoted to healing.

Davis left Levingston in 1845 to work in New York with Dr. S. S. Lyon and Rev. William Fishbough. In a period of a little over a year, they met regularly to receive spiritual information. This information was produced as a book, *The Principals of Nature* (1847).

By 1847, aided by a clinic opened with Lyon, Davis began to attract followers. He started a periodical, *The Univercoelum* (1847-1849), and discovered that he did not need the help of a magnetizer or anyone else to enter a trance; he could do so at will and even remember its events afterward. In 1848 he married Della E. ("Katie").

Davis' relationships with women proved problematic for his early career. He supported the idea that men and women should seek out their soul-mates, who rarely turned out to be their husband or wife. Davis' counterpart was a married woman, Mary Robinson Love, who had underwritten the publication of *The Principles of Nature*. Their relationship resulted in the loss of some support. In particular, Rev. **Thomas Lake Harris** of the New York Swedenborgian Church and S. B. Brittan, editor of *The Univercoelum*, withdrew their connection to Davis.

After the loss of his own periodical, Davis lent his name to the *Spirit Messenger*, published in Springfield, Massachusetts, and in 1860 to the *Herald of Progress*. He wrote many books, the most important of which was *The Great Harmonia*, published in five volumes from 1850-1855. In 1855 he married his spiritual partner, Mary Love.

Davis' ideas strongly influenced the early spiritualist movement. Davis believed that God was the active moving principle in nature, and supported the idea of Summer Land, a place of eternal abundance and sunshine where highly evolved souls go after death. Davis also claimed that the soul connects at the time of death with the sphere most appropriate to that soul's immediate condition, and is able then to progress upwards through many other conditions toward the Summer Land spheres and God.

Davis earned his living through lectures and writing. In 1886 he earned a medical degree from the United States Medical College in New York, and so added the practice of medicine and herbology. He also opened a bookstore in Boston. He retired on his 83rd birthday in 1909 and died in January of the following year.

Sources:

Bowden, Henry Warner. *Dictionary of American Religious Biography.* Westport, CT: Greenwood Press, 1977. 572 pp.

Brown, Slater. *The Heyday of Spiritualism.* New York: Pocket Books, 1970. 296 pp.

Davis, Andrew Jackson. *Beyond the Valley.* Boston, MA: Colby and Rich, 1885. 402 pp.

_____. *Events in the Life of a Seer.* Boston, MA: Banner of Light Publishing Co., 1867.

_____. *The Great Harmonia.* Vol. 1. 13th ed. Boston, MA: Banner of Light Publishing Co., 1859. 466 pp.

_____. *The Harmonial Philosophy.* Milwaukee, WI: National Spiritualist Association of Churches, n.d. 428 pp.

_____. *The Magic Staff.* Rochester, 1910.

_____. *The Penetralia.* Boston, MA: Bella Marsh, 1858.

Dictionary of American Biography. 20 vols. and 7 supps. New York: Charles Scribner's Sons, 1928-1936, 1944-1981.

Melton, J. Gordon. *Biographical Dictionary of American Cult and Sect Leaders.* Garland Reference Library of Social Science, vol. 212. New York: Garland Publishing, 1986.

Podmore, Frank. *Mediums of the 19th Century.* 2 vols. New Hyde Park, NY: University Books, 1963.

Shepard, Leslie. *Encyclopedia of Occultism & Parapsychology.* 3 vols., 2nd. ed. Detroit: Gale Research Co., 1984-1985.

—*Gary L. Ward*

★ 249 ★
DAVIS, Roy Eugene
Director, Church of the Christian Spriritual Alliance (CSA)
Founder, New Life Worldwide
b. Mar. 9, 1931, Leavittsburg, Ohio

Roy Eugene Davis is a spiritual teacher in the lineage of **Swami Paramahansa Yogananda** and director of the Church of the Christian Spiritual Alliance (CSA), previously known as Church of the Center for Spiritual Awareness (CSA) in Lakemont, Georgia. He was raised on a farm in northeast Ohio, and attended a congregation of the Church of the United Brethren. Davis was an avid reader, and became interested in yoga practices through reading about yogis. He ordered a copy of Yogananda's *Autobiography of a Yogi*, and began taking the mail-order yoga lessons offered by the Self-Realization Fellowship (SRF). In 1949, he graduated from high school and eventually made his way to the Fellowship's headquarters in Los Angeles. For almost four years he was an SRF monk and then became leader of the SRF center in Phoenix, Arizona.

In 1953, Davis withdrew from the organization and, after a tour of duty in the U.S. Army, began to work as an independent spiritual teacher. He formed New Life Worldwide headquartered in St. Petersburg, Florida. While Davis' move from SRF to New Life Worldwide seemed amicable, over the years Davis was criticized by some who claimed that he had not been authorized to initiate people into *kriya yoga* (the "secret" technique taught by Yogananda and his lineage). He defended his authorization in his recent autobiography, *God Has Given Us Every Good Thing* (1986).

During the early 1960s Davis also became associated with H. Edwin O'Neal and the Christian Spiritual Alliance in Lakemont, Georgia. He worked with O'Neal for a number of years, traveling and speaking on the organization's behalf. During this time he authored a number of books which CSA published: *God's Revealing Word* (1968); *Studies in Truth* (1969); *Health, Healing & Total Living* (1976); and *Yoga Darsana, The Philosophy and Light of Yoga* (1976).

Davis's teaching ministry expanded through CSA. He made many contacts with New Thought churches and joined the New Thought Alliance (INTA); International. Through an association with **Masaharu Taniguchi**, founder of the Japanese New Thought movement Seicho-No-Ie, Davis toured and taught in Japan. He later authored a biography of Taniguchi, *Miracle Man of Japan* (1970). He also developed links with other teachers in the Hindu tradition, such as **Swami Rama**, Swami Paramahansa Muktananda, and Sathya Sai Baba. Davis moved to Lakemont from Florida in 1973. In 1977 O'Neal resigned as chairman of the board and head of the publishing concern, and Davis assumed both posts. Over the next few years, O'Neal's largely psychic New Age concerns were totally replaced with the teachings of Davis, who in the meantime has continued his heavy schedule of lecturing and writing.

Sources:

Davis, Roy Eugene. *God Has Given Us Every Good Thing*. Lakemont, GA: CSA Press, 1986. 223 pp.

———. *Miracle Man of Japan*. Lakemont, GA: CSA Press, 1970. 159 pp.

———. *The Teachings of the Masters of Perfection*. Lakemont, GA: CSA Press, 1979. 314 pp.

———. *This Is Reality*. Lakemont, GA: CSA Press, 1962. 211 pp.

———. *The Way of the Initiate*. St. Petersburg, FL: New-Life World-wide, Inc., 1968. 144 pp.

———. *With God We Can!*. Lakemont, GA: CSA Press, 1978. 248 pp.

———. *Yoga Darsana, The Philosophy and Light of Yoga*. Lakemont, GA: CSA Press, 1976. 202 pp.

★250★
DAWSON, Joseph Martin
Minister, Southern Baptist Convention
b. Jun. 21, 1879, Ellis County, Texas
d. Jul. 6, 1973, Corsicana, Texas

Joseph Martin Dawson, the leading southern baptist voice on issues of separation of church and state during the mid-twentieth century, was the son of Laura Underwood and Martin Judy Dawson, Jr. Raised among Texas Baptists, he was ordained in the First Baptist Church, Waco, Texas, in 1900, and later attended Baylor University (B.A., 1904). Following his graduation he served as an

assistant secretary of the Texas Baptist Education Commission (1904-1905) and editor of *The Baptist Standard* (1907-1908). In 1908 he married Willie Turner and that same year began his pastoral career at First Baptist Church, Hillsboro, Texas. After three years at First Baptist Church in Temple, Texas (1912-1915), he became pastor of First Baptist Church of Waco, Texas.

During Dawson's long pastorate at Waco, he emerged as a voice of conscience among southern baptists. He was one of the few prominent leaders in the church who regularly spoke on the application of Christianity to the modern world. While the cause of religious liberty was his primary concern, his leadership also manifested a deep conviction on issues of social justice, civil rights, and world peace. In 1944 he became the chairman of the Southern Baptist Convention Committee on World Peace. Also while at Waco, he authored three books: *The Light that Grows* (1924); *The Spiritual Conquest of the Southwest* (1926); and *Christ and Social Change* (1937); he also served as a correspondent for *The Christian Century* (1924-1946).

In 1939 the Southern Baptist Convention began to cooperate with the Northern Baptist Convention on matters of public relations. Over the years of World War II, the duties of the committee expanded to include a broad range of public affairs issues to which Baptists wished to speak. In 1946 Dawson left the parish to become the first executive secretary of what emerged in 1950 as the Baptist Joint Committee on Public Affairs, the organization that has given focus to the Baptist perspective on social issues. He founded and edited, until his retirement in 1953, the committee's periodical, *Report from the Capital*. Dawson's primary interest in matters of church and state led him to assist in the founding of Protestants and Others United for Separation of Church and State in 1947 and he took on additional duties as that organization's executive secretary for the first year. He led the Baptist delegation to the founding ceremonies of the United Nations and carried a petition calling for the inclusion of a declaration of religious freedom in the United Nations charter. He featured the church-state issues in two of his books from this period, *Separate Church and State Now* (1948) and *America's Way in Church, State, and Society* (1953).

In 1957 Baylor established the J. M. Dawson Studies in Church and State and now sponsors the J. M. Dawson Church State Research Center and the annual J. M. Dawson Lectures in Church and State. Dawson was active at the center for many years as a member of the editorial council of the *Journal of Church and State* (1959-1973). He completed his autobiography *A Thousand Months to Remember: An Autobiography* in 1964.

Sources:

Dawson, Joseph M. *America's Way in Church, State, and Society*. New York: Macmillan Company, 1953. 189 pp.

———. *Baptists and the American Republic*. Nashville, TN: Broadman Press, 1956. 228 pp.

———. *Christ and Social Change*. Philadelphia: Judson Press, 1937. 22 pp.

———. *Separate Church and State Now*. New York: R. R. Smith, 1948. 220 pp.

———. *A Thousand Months to Remember: An Autobiography*. Waco, TX: Baylor University Press, 1964. 280 pp.

Encyclopedia of Southern Baptists. 3 vols. Nashville, TN: Broadman Press, 1958, 1971.

Wood, James, Jr. "The Legacy of Joseph Martin Dawson: 1879-1973." Journal of Church and State (1979).

★251★
DAY, Dorothy
Founder, Catholic Worker Movement, Roman Catholic Church
b. Nov. 8, 1897, Brooklyn, New York
d. Nov. 29, 1980, New York, New York

Dorothy Day, founder of the Catholic Worker movement, one of the most significant social reform efforts in the twentieth century, was the daughter of journalist John I. Day and Grace Satterlee Day. The family moved to Oakland, California, when Dorothy was six, but left for Chicago after the San Francisco earthquake of 1906. She attended the University of Illinois for two years, during which time her enthusiasm for Socialist ideas grew.

In 1915, when her father took a job with the *New York Morning Telegram*, Day took a job with *The Call*, a socialist paper, and then with *Masses*, a Communist paper that was suppressed in 1917. As a Communist and radical she was arrested in November 1917 during a woman's suffrage demonstration. She became a vocal pacifist during World War I and after the war adopted a free bohemian lifestyle. In 1919 she married another radical, Forster Batterman.

During the 1920s Day began to seriously investigate Catholicism. Following the birth of her daughter, Tamar Therese, Day had her baptized a Catholic. She left her husband and formally joined the church the following year.

In 1932 Day met Peter Maurin, an event that was to change her life. They began to publish *The Catholic Worker*, a newspaper that channeled Day's concern for social justice with the teaching of the church especially as manifest in the papal encyclicals. The first copies were released on May Day 1933. The major concerns of *The Catholic Worker* were pacifism and poverty. Day turned from all ideas of bloodshed and war, even the acceptable just war of traditional Christian teachings. She also identified with the poor. She had little use for wealthy Roman Catholic orders, which effectively undercut vows of poverty, and she led a simple lifestyle.

In 1935 Day established a house of hospitality in New York City that became a center for assisting the needy and downtrodden. Soon similar houses were established in other cities; some 40 were in existence by the time the United States entered World War II. For those associated with Day, protest of the war took the form of refusal to pay income taxes and to participate in air raid drills.

In the years after the war, Day became involved in a series of social causes, especially that of Ceasar Chavez and the grape workers in California. She suffered a heart attack in 1975 which slowed her considerably, and died in 1980.

Sources:

Coles, Robert. *Dorothy Day: A Radical Devotion*. Reading, MA: Addison-Wesley Publishing Corp., 1987. 182 pp.

Day, Dorothy. *By Little and by Little: the Selected Writings of Dorothy Day*. New York: Alfred E. Knopf, 1938. 371 pp.

———. *Loaves and Fishes*. New York: Harper & Row. 1963. 215 pp.

———. *The Long Loneliness*. New York: Curtis Books, 1952. 288 pp.

Delaney, John J. *Dictionary of American Catholic Biography*. Garden City, NY: Doubleday & Company, 1988. 621 pp.

Miller, William D. *Dorothy Day: A Biography*. San Francisco: Harper & Row, 1982. 527 pp.

Reilly, Bob. "The Catholic Worker Turns 50: The Legacy of Dorothy Day Lives On." *St. Anthony Messenger* 90, 12 (May 1983): 10-17.

★ 252 ★
DE BAPTISTE, Richard
President, Consolidated American Baptist Convention
b. Nov. 11, 1831, Fredericksburg, Virginia
d. Apr. 21, 1901, Chicago, Illinois

Richard De Baptiste, a Baptist minister who emerged as one of the most prominent organizers of black Baptists in the decades following the Civil War, was born a free man in Virginia, the son of Eliza and William De Baptiste. His grandfather, an immigrant from France, was a Revolutionary War veteran. His father, the owner of a construction company, saw to his education. In 1840 the family moved to Detroit, where they attended Second Baptist Church. The pastor, Rev. Samuel Davis, continued De Baptiste's education. In 1855 he married Georgianna Brische. Three years later, the church gave De Baptiste a license to preach. He was ordained in

1860 at Mount Pleasant, Ohio, where he had moved to pastor the Negro Baptist Church and teach school. In 1863 he moved to Chicago as pastor of the Olivet Baptist Church.

At the time De Baptiste moved to Chicago, the Olivet Church had approximately 100 members. Under his leadership it developed a school and soon became the church home of an increasing number of immigrants from the South. There were almost 500 members by 1868 when he oversaw the building of a new 800-seat sanctuary. When the church was destroyed by fire in 1874, he built a three-story structure as its replacement. As the pastor of Chicago's largest black church, De Baptiste's voice reverberated through the black Baptist community. He emerged during the war years as an advocate of black separation and the formation of all-black associations (the basic unit of organization above the congregational level for Baptists). He led Olivet into the Woods Creek Baptist Association, the oldest all-black association in Illinois. As the war came to a close he moved swiftly to bring the churches of the South and Midwest into a single organization and in 1864 organized the Southern and Northwest [Baptist] Convention. Then in 1866 he led it to unite with the American Missionary Convention (centered in New England) to form the Consolidated American Baptist Convention. This convention, the first truly national black Baptist organization, was a forerunner of the present National Baptist Convention in the U.S.A. As its president from 1867 to 1873, he promoted its fledgling missionary program in the West and in Haiti and was a corresponding editor for the convention's *National Observer*.

De Baptiste's career peaked in the late 1860s and early 1870s. Beginning with the death of his wife in 1872, he experienced a number of setbacks. In the late 1870s, the membership of Olivet declined and the organization of the Consolidated Convention was in disarray. In 1878 he became the editor of the *Conservator*, Chicago's first black newspaper. However, by 1881, his children's health was failing, and the membership of Olivet declined to the point that he had to resign as pastor. During the 1880s he continued a double career as the pastor of several small Baptist churches and as a journalist. For a while he was a corresponding editor for the *St. Louis Monitor* and the *Baptist Herald* of Keokuk, Iowa. In 1884 he founded the *Western Herald*, but it did not survive for very long. He also edited the *Baptist Observer*, in Chicago for a while. He died in Chicago, having been left behind by the movement he had done so much to build.

Sources:

Fisher, Mark Miles. *The History of Olivet Baptist Church of Chicago*. Chicago: M.A. Thesis, University of Chicago, 1922.

Logan, Rayford W., and Michael R. Winston, eds. *Dictionary of American Negro Biography*. New York: W. W. Norton & Co. 1982. 680 pp.

★ 253 ★
DE PAUW, Gommar Albert
Founder, Catholic Traditionalist Movement
b. Oct. 11, 1918, Stekene Belgium

Gommar Albert De Pauw, founder of the Catholic Traditionalist Movement, was born in Belgium, the son of colonial American parents. His father, Desire De Pauw, was the co-founder of the Christian Labor Movement and the Roman Catholic school system in Belgium. Gommar received a fine education. In 1936 he graduated magna cum laude from the College of St. Nicolas in East Flanders, Belgium. His studies at the diocesan seminary at Ghent, Belgium, were interrupted by World War II. He served in the Belgian Army, was captured by the Germans, escaped, returned to Ghent, and in 1942 was ordained to the priesthood. During the liberation of Belgium, De Pauw served as a chaplain for the Belgian Underground Army and the First Free Polish Armored Division, from whom he received the Medal of Honor.

After the war, De Pauw completed three years of postgraduate study at the University of Louvain, receiving both the bachelors and licentiate degrees in canon law. In 1949 De Pauw joined his family in the United States. He served a parish in New York City and continued his studies at Catholic University of America, which granted him a Ph.D. in canon law in 1953. The previous year he had joined the faculty of Mount St. Mary's College, Emmetsville, Maryland, as a professor of theology and canon law.

From 1962 to 1965 De Pauw served as a consultant to his former professor, Bishop Charles J. Calawaert at the Vatican Council. Calawaert officially presented the 1962 Constitution on Liturgy, later accepted by the Council. Though he approved the document as presented, by 1964 De Pauw had become a critic of the interpretation and application of the document, which he saw as leading to chaotic liturgical experiments. On December 31, 1964, he sent a letter to Pope John XXIII, all the cardinals of the Curia (the Roman Catholic Church offices in the Vatican), all the American bishops, and others. That letter, made public on March 15, 1965, would later be known as the Traditionalist Catholic Manifesto. It included 12 tenets that asked that the Latin Mass be given the same privileges as the new vernacular masses in the continuing worship of the church and called for a renewed emphasis upon the devotion to the Virgin Mary, loyalty to the pope, celibacy in the clergy, and traditional attire for priests and nuns.

The issuance of the Manifesto brought the wrath of Cardinal **Lawrence Shehan**, De Pauw's immediate superior. He removed De Pauw from his teaching post and assigned him to parish work. Meanwhile, De Pauw traveled to Rome to attend the last session of the council. While there, he was introduced to Luigi Favari, Bishop of Trivoli, Italy, who accepted De Pauw into his diocese. De Pauw then moved to New York and incorporated the Catholic Traditionalist Movement. He began a periodical, *Sounds of Truth and Tradition*. He also received the public support of Most Rev. Blase Kurz (1894-1973), titular bishop of Terenuti and exiled prefect apostolic of Yungchow, China, who declared De Pauw to be under his supervision while some technical problems with his transfer to the Diocese of Trivoli were being completed. Kurz also became the Bishop-Moderator of the Catholic Traditionalist Movement.

Thwarted in his attempts to work within the church, De Pauw and the movement purchased a church building on Long Island, New York, later renamed Ave Maria Chapel, which became their headquarters. From the chapel, De Pauw has carried on his campaign to have the Latin Mass again recognized and to have new emphasis placed upon traditional Roman Catholic moral values. In 1970 he began the "World-wide Radio Mass," through which those opposed to the new vernacular mass have been able to hear the worship with which they grew up. It is heard in approximately 80 countries. He also has begun a second periodical, *Quote . . . Unquote.*

While championing "traditionalist" causes within the Roman Catholic Church, De Pauw also has attacked Archbishop Marcel Lefebvre as a danger to the traditionalist cause. According to De Pauw, Lefebvre was operating his seminary in defiance of both Papal authority and canon law and was not, in spite of public image to the contrary, defending the traditional Latin mass. More recently, the Lefebvre movement has moved into open schism with the Roman Catholic Church.

Sources:

Current Biography Yearbook. New York: H. W. Wilson Co., 1974.
De Pauw, Gommar. *The Challenge of Peace through Strength*. New York: CTM Publications, 1989. 197 pp.
_____. *The Rebel Priest*. New York: Catholic Traditionalist Movement, 1976. 16 pp.
_____. *Weighed and Found Wanting: The American Catholic Bishops and Their Pastoral Letter on War and Peace*. New York: Catholic Traditionalist Movement, 1983. 88 pp.

"Mass Movement." *Newsweek* (February 4, 1973): 56.
Who's Who in America. Wilmette, IL: Marquis Who's Who, Inc. 1974.

★254★
DEARDEN, John Francis
Cardinal, Roman Catholic Church
b. Oct. 15, 1907, Valley Falls, Rhode Island
d. Aug. 1, 1988, Southfield, Michigan

John Francis Dearden, a cardinal of the Roman Catholic Church, was the son of Agnes C. Gregory and John S. Dearden. He attended St. Mary's Seminary in Cleveland, Ohio, and following his graduation (S.T.D., 1929), he began five years in Rome at the North American College. He was ordained in Rome in 1932 and received his LL.D. in 1934. He returned to Ohio and was assigned as a parish priest in Painesville. In 1937 he transferred to his alma mater as a professor of philosophy and in 1944 was named rector of the school. It was from this position in 1948 that he was named bishop coadjutor of Pittsburgh. He was consecrated on May 18, 1948, and two years later, upon the death of Bishop Hugh O'Boyle, became the bishop of Pittsburgh.

In 1957 Dearden was named an assistant at the Pontifical Throne, an honorary title within the church. A year later he was named archbishop of Detroit; he was installed in 1959. Dearden attended the sessions of the Second Vatican Council, where he had a significant floor fight with Cardinal Ottavani over the wording of the council's document on marriage. It is believed that this encounter had some effect in delaying Dearden from being named a cardinal until 1969.

As a church leader Dearden emerged as a liberal in many respects, especially on issues concerning the church's relation to the world. He became a prominent spokesperson, especially during his years as head of the National Conference of Catholic Bishops (1966-1971), against antisemitism and racism and in favor of married clergy, female priests, and greater authority for national hierarchies (as opposed to the authority of Rome).

In 1976 Dearden organized one of the more significant religious commemorations of the United States Bicentennial, the "Call to Action." Beginning as a two-year consultation, the "Call to Action" culminated in a three-day gathering of 1,300 Catholics (including 110 bishops) from some 92 organizations who made final decisions on a set of seven substantive documents outlining a program of social action for the church in the years ahead. The final documents, developed in part from over 800,000 responses from discussion groups operating at the parish level, produced a picture of the church's opinion. The documents, among other things, called for women's ordination, full accounting of church finances, and a local voice in the election of bishops. While many found the exercise of producing the documents an exhilarating experience, the documents offended many church leaders, including many of the bishops who attended the conference.

In 1977 Dearden suffered a heart attack and his poor health hobbled him for the rest of his active career. He retired in 1980 and lived quietly in Detroit until his death in 1988.

Sources:

MacEoin, Gary, and the Committee for the Responsible Election of the Pope. *The Inner Elite*. Kansas City, MO: Sheed Andrews and McMeel, 1979. 301 pp.
Untener, Kenneth E. "Cardinal Dearden: A Gentleman of the Church." *America* 159, 16 (November 26, 1988): 434-436.

★ 255 ★
DEHAAN, Martin Ralph
Founder, Radio Bible Class
b. Mar. 23, 1891, Zeeland, Michigan
d. Dec. 13, 1965, Grand Rapids, Michigan

Martin Ralph DeHaan, a pioneer radio minister and founder of the still popular Radio Bible Class, was the son of Reitze DeHaan, a cobbler and first-generation immigrant from Holland, and Johanna Rozema, both residents of the large Dutch-American community of western Michigan. When Martin was ten, his younger brother died in an accident. The lack of pastoral concern expressed by their pastor led his parents to leave the Christian Reformed Church, in which they had been strong members, and join the Reformed Church in America. In 1909 Martin began a year at the Reformed Church's Hope College in Holland, Michigan.

Following his year at Hope, DeHaan moved to Chicago to attend the College of Medicine of the University of Illinois and prepare for a career as a doctor. During his years there, he met Priscilla Venhuizen, whom he eventually married. In 1914 DeHaan graduated as class valedictorian, was licensed to practice medicine, and was married, all within a matter of months. He established a practice in Byron's Corner, 14 miles east of his hometown. He settled down to become a much-loved but obscure country doctor.

Seven years later, the church-going doctor faced a crisis following an almost fatal reaction to some medicine he had been given. He reexamined his life while in the hospital and had a born-again experience. The following year he sold his practice and entered Western Theological Seminary to prepare for the ministry. He also gave up the use of alcohol, which he had been known to abuse occasionally. During the summers of his seminary years he had his first experience as a pastor. Following graduation in 1925, he became the pastor of Calvin Reformed Church in Grand Rapids.

While at seminary, DeHaan had begun to absorb the teaching known as premillennialism, a belief that Christ's return is imminent and that it will be followed by his millennial reign on earth. He also became friends with ministers such as **William McCarrell**, founder of the premillennialist Independent Fundamental Churches of America (IFCA). He used the *Scofield Reference Bible*, which contained premillennialist notes. In the process of his Bible study he also became convinced that there was no biblical justification for infant baptism. His acceptance of premillennialism and denial of infant baptism put him at odds with the Reformed Church, which was amillennialist and practiced infant baptism.

In 1929 DeHaan withdrew from the Reformed Church in America and founded the Calvary Undenominational Church, an independent fundamentalist congregation. He pastored the church for nine years, but resigned in 1938 after suffering a heart attack and facing some strong disagreements among his church members. He began informally to teach Bible classes in the evenings, and at McCarrell's suggestion started a radio show on a Detroit radio station. The program was a success, and in 1941 it became the Radio Bible Class. DeHaan established the new ministry's headquarters in Grand Rapids.

The radio ministry grew steadily into a national program through which DeHaan offered Bible lessons and through which he distributed numerous sermon booklets (edited transcripts of his talks). The progress of the show was marked in 1946 when DeHaan had a heart attack while conducting a live broadcast. He finished the show, and his son took over during his recovery. During his more than 25 years on the air, DeHaan authored a number of substantive books, some bible expositions and many works of a doctrinal nature. He frequently wrote and spoke of the popular theme of the second coming of Christ.

In 1964 he celebrated his golden wedding anniversary. The following year he was in an automobile accident; he died several months later as a result of injuries. His son, Richard W. DeHaan, succeeded him as head of the ministry.

Sources:

Adair, James R. *M. R. DeHaan, The Man and His Ministry*. Grand Rapids, MI: Zondervan Publishing House, 1969. 160 pp.
DeHaan, M. R. *Daniel the Prophet*. Grand Rapids, MI: Zondervan Publishing House, 1947. 330 pp.
_____. *Dear Doctor: I Have a Problem*. Grand Rapids, MI: Radio Bible Class, 1961. 278 pp.
_____. *508 Answers to Bible Questions*. Grand Rapids, MI: Zondervan Publishing House, 1952. 254 pp.

★ 256 ★
DEKOVEN, James
Minister, Protestant Episcopal Church
b. Sep. 19, 1831, Middletown, Connecticut
d. Mar. 19, 1879, Racine, Wisconsin

James DeKoven, the leader of the high church "ritualistic" faction within the Protestant Episcopal Church in the years after the Civil War, was the son of Henry Louis and Margaret Sebor DeKoven. He decided upon the priesthood at an early age and with that intent attended Columbia College and General Theological Seminary (1851-1854). He was ordained as a deacon soon after graduating from seminary, and he moved to the diocese of Wisconsin as the professor of ecclesiastical history at Nashotah Seminary and vicar at St. Bartholomew's Mission. He soon founded St. John's Hall, a preparatory school (now St. John's Military Academy). In 1955 he was ordained as a priest.

DeKoven built a reputation as a scholar and in 1859 was invited to become warden at Racine College, at the time the most important Episcopal school west of the Alleghany Mountains. During the 1860s he emerged as the most able defender of the high church "Anglo-Catholic" perspective with the Episcopal Church. In 1868 he was elected for the first time to represent the diocese at the church's general convention, an honor accorded him regularly for the rest of his life. In the early 1870s DeKoven opposed the low church element in the church that was pushing for the adoption of a uniform "low church" practice in the church's liturgy. He effectively answered the attack of his low church critics that the Anglo-Catholic movement was "Romanism." His most outstanding defense came in a paper prepared for the diocesan convocation of 1874, but he regularly contributed articles to the church's periodicals advocating the ritualist position.

DeKoven's defense of high church liturgical practices probably contributed decisively to his failure to become a bishop, in spite of his reputation as a pious and accomplished leader. He was nominated on several occasions. In 1873 he missed election by a single vote. He lost again the following year amid charges about his Romanist practices. In 1875 he was elected bishop of Illinois, but the standing committee of the general convention refused to confirm him and he withdrew.

He remained at Racine for the last years of his life. Shortly before his death a collection of his papers was published as *Tracts of Dr. DeKoven and Others*, and a posthumous collection of his sermons was published in 1880 as *Sermons Preached on Various Occasions*. In 1886 the general convention meeting in Chicago honored DeKoven by adjourning their session and making a pilgrimage to his grave site.

Sources:

DeKoven, James. *Sermons Preached on Various Occasions*. New York: D. Appleton & Co., 1880. 364 pp.

Dibbert, R. B. *In Grateful Memory: A Collection of Literature on the Life and Work of the Reverend Doctor James DeKoven.* Akron, OH: The Author, 1986. 48 pp.

Dictionary of American Biography. 20 vols. and 7 supps. New York: Charles Scribner's Sons, 1928-1936, 1944-1981.

Pope, William C. *Life of James DeKoven.* New York: James Pott & Co. 1899. 102 pp.

★257★
DENMAN, Harry
Denominational Executive, United Methodist Church
b. Sep. 23, 1893, Birmingham, Alabama
d. Nov. 8, 1976, Birmingham, Alabama

Harry Denman, for many years the executive secretary of the Board of Evangelism of the United Methodist Church, was the son of William Henry and Hattie Leonard Denman. He received both his B.A. and M.A. degrees from Birmingham-Southern College in 1921 and 1930, respectively. In 1915 he became secretary of the Birmingham, Alabama, Sunday School Association, a position he retained until he became the church manager for First Methodist Church in Birmingham. During the 1920s and 1930s, Denman established a reputation throughout the Methodist Episcopal Church, South as a strong lay leader with a vital evangelistic concern. He was elected as a delegate to the general conferences of the Methodist Episcopal Church, South in 1934 and 1938 and to the uniting conference of 1939.

In 1939 the Methodist Episcopal Church, South united with the Methodist Episcopal Church and the Methodist Protestant Church to form the Methodist Church, which existed from 1939 to 1968. Denman was offered the post of general secretary of the Commission (later Board) of Evangelism of the new church. He held that position until his retirement in 1965. Concurrently with his position on the board, he served as chairman of the Committee on Evangelism of the World Methodist Council.

Denman also became famous—especially in the southern church—for his evangelistic fervor. Unmarried, he traveled extensively throughout the country. His simple lifestyle became a model for many Methodists, and his evangelistic activity brought many members into the church.

In his honor, a prayer room was named for him at the Methodist Camp at Lake Junaluska, North Carolina, where the World Methodist Council has its headquarters.

Sources:

Harmon, Nolan B. *The Encyclopedia of World Methodism.* 2 vols. Nashville: United Methodist Publishing House, 1974.

Howell, Clinton H., ed. *Prominent Personalities in Methodism.* Birmingham, AL: Lowrey Press, 1945. 512 pp.

Rogers, Harold. *Harry Denman: A Biography.* Nashville, TN: The Upper Room, 1977. 142 pp.

Who's Who in the Methodist Church. Nashville, TN: Abingdon Press, 1966.

★258★
DENNY, Collins
Bishop, Methodist Episcopal Church, South
b. May 24, 1854, Winchester, Virginia
d. May 12, 1943, Richmond, Virginia

Collins Denny, a bishop in the Methodist Episcopal Church, South, was the son of William R. Denny and Margaret A. Collins Denny. He studied at Princeton University (B.A., 1876; M.A., 1879) and the University of Virginia (LL.B., 1877). He married Lucy C. Chapman and they had six children.

Denny began his law practice in Baltimore in 1877 but in 1880 entered the ministry through the Baltimore Conference of the Methodist Episcopal Church, South. He served several parishes before being appointed to visit the missions in Asia from 1886 to

1888. He was chaplain at the University of Virginia (1889-1891) and professor of mental and moral philosophy at Vanderbilt University (1891-1910). During this time he also served as secretary of the general conference of 1894, chairman of the church's book committee (1898-1910), and elected delegate to the church's general conferences in 1894, 1898, 1902, 1906, and 1910.

In 1910 Denny was elected bishop. During his tenure as bishop he became best known for his foundational work toward the unification of American Methodism and his subsequent staunch opposition to the plan that was finally adopted and implemented in 1939. Denny served as a fraternal delegate from the Southern Methodists to the Methodist Episcopal Church in 1908, and served on several unification committees. He supported the unification plan of 1914, which was defeated. He retired from the ministry in 1934 before the 1939 plan came to a vote by the church, but his opposition to that unification plan, which created the Methodist Church, was so strong that he continued to call himself a retired bishop of the Methodist Episcopal Church, South and refused to accept a pension from the new united church. The Methodist Church continued until 1968, when it joined the United Methodist Church.

During his years as bishop, Denny developed a reputation as one of the best minds of the church. In particular, he put his legal skills in the service of the church. He edited six editions of the *Discipline*, the church's book of church law, and revised Bishop **Holland McTyeire**'s companion volume, *The Manual of the Discipline*.

Denny also was known for his knowledge of secular history, especially that of the South. He assisted Douglas Freeman by reading and checking his monumental biography of Robert E. Lee. He was also a frequent contributor to *The Methodist Quarterly Review* and other church periodicals.

Sources:

Harmon, Nolan B. *The Encyclopedia of World Methodism.* 2 vols. Nashville: United Methodist Publishing House, 1974.

Who's Who in the Methodist Church. Nashville, TN: Abingdon Press, 1966.

★259★
DESAI, Amrit
Founder, Kripalu Yoga Fellowship
b. Oct. 16, 1932, Halol India

Yogi Amrit Desai is a popular yoga teacher and founder of the Kripalu Yoga Fellowship. He was the second son of the Indian merchant Bhuriben Desai and his wife, Chimanlal. From an early age he showed signs of being a spiritual seeker. He met his guru, Swami Kripalvananda (after whom the fellowship and Desai's distinctive variation on hatha yoga were named), at age 15. His brother Shanti Desai also became a disciple of Kripalvananda and is the head of the Shanti Yoga Institute in New Jersey.

Desai's initial education was in engineering (a popular Indian profession for the upwardly mobile), but he didn't enjoy it. He subsequently served in the Indian Air Force, and then returned to Halol to teach high school. He was married on January 29, 1955. After his marriage, he attended the Sheth C. N. School of Art and studied Hindi literature at Gujarat College. In 1960 he traveled to the United States to study at the Philadelphia School of Art. He also began to teach hatha yoga. By the time Desai was ready to embark on a professional art career, he had become a highly successful yoga teacher. Purchasing some land outside of Philadelphia for a retreat in 1970, he continued to attract students until he had the nucleus of an ashram by early 1972.

In 1970, while doing his daily practice of hatha yoga, Desai began to experience a spontaneous flow of yoga *asanas* (postures)

in which the innate and autonomous intelligence of his body performed the postures without conscious or willful direction from his mind. Desai repeated the experience on subsequent occasions and from his observations began to develop a technique by which anyone could also experience the same spontaneous flow. The technique, named after his guru, became known as kripalu yoga.

At about this time, Desai also received *shaktipat diksha* from his guru, and began to initiate his own disciples. (Shaktipat diksha is an experience of the guru's power which is supposed to awaken the kundalini power in each individual. The kundalini is pictured as a latent force residing at the base of the spine. When awakened it travels upward along the spinal column to the top of the head.) After this point the Kripalu community began to expand rapidly, and has twice moved to larger facilities. The current headquarters are in Lenox, Massachusetts. The fellowship has received favorable publicity from the New Age press as a result of its holistic health program.

Sources:

Desai, Amrit. *Guru and Disciple*. Sumneytown, PA: Kripalu Yoga Ashram, 1975. 60 pp.

———. *Happiness Is Now*. Summit Station, PA: Kripalu Publications, 1982. 57 pp.

———. *Kripalu Yoga: Meditation in Motion*. Summit Station, PA: Kripalu Publications, 1981. 41 pp.

———. *Shaktipat Kundalini Yoga, Frequently Asked Questions*. Sumneytown, PA: Kripalu Yoga Ashram, 1975. 40 pp.

———. *Working Miracles of Love*. Lenox, MA: Kripalu Publications, 1985. 184 pp.

Warren, Sukanya. *Gurudev: The Life of Yogi Amrit Desai*. With Frances Mellen and Peter Mellen. Summit Station, PA: Kripalu Publications, 1982. 117 pp.

★ 260 ★
Sister DEVAMATA
Leader, Ananda Ashrama
b. 1867, Cincinnati, Ohio
d. 1942

Sister Devamata, Swami Paramananda's first American disciple and an early leader of the Ananda Ashrama, was born Laura Franklin Glenn into a prominent, cultured family descended from Benjamin Franklin on her mother's side. A graduate of Vassar, she lived in Europe for 10 years, studying at the Sorbonne and other European universities. Her religious temperament led her to try a period as a lay sister in an Episcopal convent. She heard **Swami Vivekananda**, founder of the Vedanta Society, speak in New York in 1896, and regularly attended his lectures while he was in the area. In 1902 she joined the New York Vedanta Society, then under the direction of **Swami Abhedananda**, and was placed in charge of the society's publishing ventures.

On December 23, 1906, following a trip to India, Abhedananda returned to the United States with a new assistant, Swami Paramananda. Paramananda was more devotionally inclined than the highly intellectual Abhedananda, and a number of Vedanta Society members with similar religious temperaments attached themselves to Paramananda. Laura Glenn was initiated by the new swami on March 19, 1907, and was given the name Devamata, meaning Mother of the Gods. She was Paramananda's first disciple. In order to more fully imbibe the spirit of vedanta, Devamata soon afterwards journeyed to India, and studied and worked in Madras with Paramananda's long time associate, Swami Ramakrishnananda. An accomplished stenographer, she had previously transcribed Paramananda's lectures for his second and third books. She now accomplished the same task for Ramakrishnananda, and through her work his first book was published. Devamata also spent time in Calcutta serving Sri Sarada Devi, **Sri Ramakrishna**'s wife (Ramakrishna, who had been Vivekananda's guru, had passed away several decades earlier).

Due to the growth of the work in New York and the frequent travels of Abhedananda, Paramananda was named acting head of the New York Center in September of 1907. In late 1908, however, he moved to Boston, and early the next year started a vedanta center in that city. Paramananda's first book, *The Path of Devotion*, which was written while he was still in New York, consisted of extracts from letters which he had penned to Devamata. She became deeply involved in his work, serving as Paramananda's platform assistant as well as leader of the center during his absence. After he had become established, Paramananda began his own publishing enterprise, which published Devamata's compositions as well as his own. She suffered a collapse of health in 1922 from which she never fully recovered, and devoted much of the rest of her life to literary work. Her many books include *Days in an Indian Monastery* (1927); *Swami Paramananda and His Work* (1926, 1941), a two-volume work; and *Sri Ramakrishna and His Disciples* (1928). She died in 1942, within a few years of her master's passing.

Sources:

Devamata, Sister [Laura Franklin Glenn]. *Days in an Indian Monastery*. 3d ed. Cohasset, MA: Vedanta Centre Publishers, 1975.

———. *Development of the Will*. Boston: Ananda Ashrama, 1918. 13 pp.

———. *The Indian Mind and Indian Culture*. Boston: The Vedanta Centre, 1912. 14 pp.

———. *Sri Ramakrishna and His Disciples*. La Crescenta, CA: Ananda Ashrama, 1928. 201 pp.

———. *Swami Paramananda and His Work*. 2 vols. La Crescenta, CA: Ananda Ashrama, 1926, 1941.

Levinsky, Sara Ann. *A Bridge of Dreams*. West Stockbridge, MA: Lindisfarne, 1984. 590 pp.

Melton, J. Gordon. *Biographical Dictionary of American Cult and Sect Leaders*. Garland Reference Library of Social Science, vol. 212. New York: Garland Publishing, 1986.

★ 261 ★
Gayatri DEVI
Leader, Ananda Ashrama
b. 1906, Dacca India

Srimata Gayatri Devi, the leader of Ananda Ashrama, the organization founded by her uncle, Swami Paramananda, was born in India in a part now included in the new country of Bangladesh. She was the second eldest daughter of Paramananda's brother, Bibhu Charan. An intelligent, talented woman, she wrote to her uncle expressing interest in helping with his work when she was 15 years old. The swami was delighted with the request but never answered her letter, perhaps because he desired to wait until she was a little older. The next year he discovered that she was going to be married. Paramananda attempted to stop the marriage, but failed. While Paramanada was visiting India several years later, however, Gayatri's husband died of meningitis, and Paramanada was able to persuade his niece to accompany him back to the United States.

Sailing for America in May of 1926, the swami almost immediately began training Gayatri for public work, and in 1927 he ordained her. She became one of a small group of talented women (which included Sister Devamata) who gathered around Paramananda as a monastic sisterhood. Paramananda took Gayatri with him wherever he went. When people would invite him to speak before their group, he would ask that they also request his niece to speak. Part of the reason for his focus on Gayatri was his championing of the rights of women, particularly Indian women, and consequently he wished to have a living exemplar of women's potential. Paramananda's critics, including fellow swamis within the Vedanta Society, censured him. They asserted that no monk should travel about in the company of an attractive young woman. The swami, however, never backed down.

The conflict over the women's rights issue culminated when Paramananda passed away in 1940. The leadership of the Vedanta Society, the parent organization of Ananda Ashrama, refused to recognize Gayatri Devi's leadership. Ananda Ashrama subsequently established itself as a completely independent organization. Gayatri Devi has been the spiritual guide of the organization since that time. She oversaw the abandonment of the Ananda Ashrama's Boston center in the early 1950s. Since that time the organization has consisted of two American ashrams, one in Cohasset, Massachusetts, and one in La Crescenta, California, as well as other centers in India. Although smaller than its parent organization, the group has kept most of Paramananda's and Devamata's writing in print and for many years published a periodical, *The Message of the East*. In keeping up her far-flung responsibilities, Gayatri Devi is constantly traveling across the United States (several times annually) and to India every other year.

Sources:

Devi, Srimata Gayatri. *One Life's Pilgrimage*. Cohasset, MA: Vedanta Centre, 1977. 342 pp.

Levinsky, Sara Ann. *A Bridge of Dreams*. West Stockbridge, MA: Lindisfarne, 1984. 590 pp.

Melton, J. Gordon *The Encyclopedia of American Religions*. 3d ed. Detroit: Gale Research Inc.,1988. 1102 pp.

★262★
Lakshmy DEVI
*Founder, Sri Rajarajeshwari Peetham of the Holy
  Shankaracharya Order*
d. Jul. 19, 1981

Lakshmy Devi, whose full name and title was Her Holiness Divine Mother Mahamandaleshwari Swami Lakshmy Devyashram, was the founder of an ashram that became the Sri Rajarajeshwari Peetham of the Holy Shankaracharya Order U.S.A.. An American of Jewish heritage, she married at a young age and had three children. In the 1960s she became involved in Hindu spirituality in New York through hatha yoga classes taught by **Swami Vishnu Devananda**, one of **Swami Sivananda Saraswati**'s disciples. In 1968 she purchased a 35-acre farm in the Poconos and established a yoga ashram. She took *sannyas* (a renounced life) and received the name Lakshmy Devi not long afterwards. In 1970 the ashram was incorporated as the Sivananda Yoga Camp-Retreat-Poconos.

The swami journeyed to India in 1972, saw what she described as a "Living Temple" in Khajuraho, and decided to build a "Living Temple" on the ashram grounds. In 1974, after establishing a relationship with one of the Indian Shankaracharyas (one of the four recognized religious authorities of Hinduism), the Sivananda Yoga Ashram became the Holy Shankaracharya Order, U.S.A., and Lakshmy Devi was appointed as Mahamandaleshwari by Sringeri Jagadguru Shankaracharya. In the same year property was purchased for the construction of an ashram/temple complex in Virginia.

The year 1978 was a particularly busy one for Devi. Swami Lakshmy received a mandate from Jagadguru Shankaracharya Abhinava Vidyateertha Maharaj, whose seat of authority is at Sri Sharada Peetham, Sringeri, to establish a Shakti Peetham in the United States. Formal temple worship of Lord Ganesha and Sri Rajarajeshwari was initiated in April. The publication of the ashram's journal, *Punarnava*, was begun in the same year, and the first of the ashram's successful Hindu Heritage Summer Camps was held. In 1981 Swami Lakshmy Devi was elected the first Mahamandaleshwari of the Holy Shankaracharya Order, U.S.A. She died later that year and was succeeded by Swami Saraswati Devi, one of her American disciples. The various activities initiated by Lakshmy Devi were well-established enough to continue to grow after she passed away.

Sources:

Melton, J. Gordon. *The Encyclopedia of American Religions*. Detroit: Gale Research Co., 1989. 1100 pp.

"A Portrait of Divine Grace: Her Holiness Divine Mother Mahamandaleshwari." *Punarnava* 1, 1 (September/October 1978): 16-18.

★263★
DEYNEKA SR., Peter
Founder, Slavic Gospel Association
b. 1898, Storlolemya Russia
d. Jul. 26, 1987, Chicago, Illinois

Peter Deyneka, Sr., evangelist to Russian-American immigrants and the founder of the Slavic Gospel Association, was raised in Chomsk, a small town in White Russia. He was the son of Nahum and Anastasia Deyneka, both members of the Russian Orthodox Church. In 1941 his family sent Deyneka to the United States to make his fortune, and he settled with relatives in Chicago, Illinois. He got a job and eventually joined the International Workers of the World, the radical union organization. He also encountered some fundamentalist Christians and began to attend Moody Bible Church. In 1920 he had an experience of salvation after which he became an active participant at Moody and soon decided to enter full-time Christian service.

In 1922 Deyneka enrolled at St. Paul Bible School in Minneapolis, Minnesota. He spent his summers in evangelistic work among Russian-American immigrants in the Dakotas. It was at the end of the summer in 1925 that he felt a call to return to his homeland as an evangelist. Before the year was out he arranged a trip back to his hometown which, as a result of changing boundaries following World War I, had become a part of Poland. In Chomsk he not only built a small congregation but met Vera Demidovich, whom he married in 1926 before returning to the United States. He then became an evangelist for the All Russian Evangelical Christian Union and worked to raise money for Bibles and hymnbooks. in 1930, just prior to the government's institution of new anti-religion measures, he was able to make a trip to evangelize the people.

In 1931 Deyneka joined the Chicago Gospel Tabernacle, then pastored by **Paul Rader**, the outstanding minister of the Christian and Missionary Alliance (CMA). Deyneka became head of the work among Russian-Americans. In 1934 he organized the Russian Gospel Association (now the Slavic Gospel Association), an independent fundamentalist missionary agency to evangelize among Russian immigrants in America and around the world. From his headquarters in Chicago, he spent the rest of his life organizing religious work.

Among Deyneka's successes was the opening of a mission in 1938 in Alaska, where the association still supports churches. In 1943 he worked with **Oswald J. Smith**, pastor of the Peoples Church in Toronto, Ontario, in the founding of a Bible institute for Russian evangelists, at which he taught part-time. Seven years later the school moved to Argentina, where it has continued as the only Bible school for Russians in the West. After World War II he helped organize relief for Eastern Europe.

Deyneka remained as general director of the association until his retirement in 1975 at which time his son, Peter Deyneka, Jr., succeeded him.

Sources:

Deyneka, Peter. *The Life and Sufferings of Christians in Solovki and Siberia Russia*. Grand Rapids, MI: Zondervan Publishing House, 1940. 58 pp.

———, and Anita Deyneka. *Christians in the Shadow of the Kremlin*. Elgin, IL: D. C. Cook Publishing Co., 1974. 96 pp.

———. *A Song in Siberia*. Elgin, IL: D. C. Cook Publishing Co., 1977. 235 pp.

Rohrer, Norman B., and Peter Deyneka, Jr. *Peter Dynamite: Twice Born Russian*. Grand Rapids, MI: Baker Book House, 1975. 192 pp.

★ 264 ★
DHARMAPALA, Anagarika
Buddhist Lecturer
Founder of the Maha Bodhi Society
b. Sep. 17, 1864, Columbo Sri Lanka
d. Apr. 29, 1933, Sarnath India

Anagarika Dharmapala was one of the key figures in introducing to the United States and Europe. He was born to a Sinhalese family and given the name David Hewivitarne. His family was devoted to Ceylonese Buddhism, and he regularly attended the Kotahena Temple nearby. David was educated at a time of high nationalist sentiment, as the British tried to convert their colony of Ceylon (today's Sri Lanka) to Christianity. David's parents sought to give him the best education possible, sending him to St. Benedict's Anglican School and then St. Thomas' Collegiate School, where church attendance and religious indoctrination were compulsory. His personal allegiance to Buddhism never wavered, however, and he saw typical Christian behavior as highly hypocritical. In 1883, at the age of 19, he witnessed a riot caused by Christians attacking a Buddhist procession. He decided to leave the school and study on his own in the library.

David soon joined the Theosophical Society, which had entered Ceylon with strong Buddhist connections. He went to India to visit the founder, Madame **Helena P. Blavatsky**, and began a study of Pali, the original language of the Buddhist scriptures. In 1884 Colonel Henry S. Olcott, president of the Theosophical Society, persuaded the British Secretary of the Colonies to make several policy changes; Ceylon marriages could be performed in places other than Christian churches, and Buddha's birthday (Wesak) was designated a holiday. These changes significantly strengthened the hand of Theosophy in Ceylon and David spent a number of years working with Olcott, organizing Buddhist schools and uniting Buddhist groups. At this time he took the name, Anagarika Dharmapala, meaning "homeless protector of the Dharma."

Dharmapala's larger influence came during his international travels, which began with a trip to Japan with Olcott in 1888. In 1891 he visited Buddhist holy sites such as Bodh Gaya, where the Buddha attained Enlightenment, and was distressed to find the places in such poor condition. He quickly organized the Maha Bodhi Society to raise funds for their restoration and upkeep, and in 1892 he began the *Maha Bodhi Journal*. In 1893 he made his famous trip to Chicago to address the World Parliament of Religions. On that trip he spoke persuasively on behalf of Buddhism and convinced **Paul Carus** to begin and head the American chapter of the Maha Bodhi Society. Dharmapala also initiated the Swiss Theosophical visitor, C. T. Strauss into Buddhism—the first Westerner to make that formal conversion in the West.

Dharmapala was to make several more trips to the United States, partly courtesy of Mary E. Foster, a wealthy Hawaiian who became his patron. On the 1896-1897 tour he celebrated the first Wesak festival in the United States. On a 1925-1926 trip to England he established the Maha Bodhi Society there, as well as the periodical, *British Buddhist*. He would lead the first Wesak there on a special trip in 1927. On January 13, 1933, he was honored by a group of Sinhalese monks who ordained him as a *bhikkhu*, or monk. This took place at Sarnath, India, and was the first such ordination on Indian (primarily Hindu) soil in over seven centuries. Dharmapala died that same year, at the age of 69, having given the western world a Buddhist organization and a bridge between East and West.

Sources:

Dharmapala, Anagarika. "The World's Debt to Buddha," and "Buddhism and Christianity," in J.W. Hanson, ed., *The World's Congress of Religions*, Chicago: Monarch Book Company, 1894. pp. 377-87, 413-16.
Fields, Rick. *How the Swans Came to the Lake*. Boston, MA: Shambhala, 1986. 445 pp.
Melton, J. Gordon. *Biographical Dictionary of American Cult and Sect Leaders*. Garland Reference Library of Social Science, vol. 212. New York: Garland Publishing, 1986.
Sangharakshita, Maha Sthavira. *Flame in Darkness: The Life and Sayings of Anagarika Dharmapala*. Yerawada, Pune, Maharastra, India: Triratna Grantha Mala, 1980. 143 pp.

—*Gary L. Ward*

★ 265 ★
DIAZ, Abby Morton
Feminist, Author, New Thought Lecturer
b. 1821, Plymouth, Massachusetts
d. Apr. 1, 1904, Belmont, Massachusetts

Abby Morton Diaz, a feminist leader, educator, and New Thought lecturer, was the only daughter of Patty Weston and Ichabod Morton. Her father's life had been changed by a vision of supernatural light and of a world governed by the principles of universal brotherhood. He began to work toward the realization of that ideal first in the temperance crusades and then as an abolitionist. As a young girl, Abby became the secretary of a juvenile abolitionist society. As his vision of society matured, Ichabod became a part of the Brook Farm communal experiment, and Abby went to live there in 1842. While there she became acquainted with the idealism of Ralph Waldo Emerson and adopted much of his perspective.

She continued at Brook Farm as a teacher of children even after the rest of her family left in 1843. The community was short-lived, however, and eventually she married Emanuel Diaz and settled into domestic life. They had two children before separating. She then taught school in Plymouth. In May 1861 her writing pastime produced results when the *Atlantic Monthly* published her autobiographical short story "Pink and Blue." With her success, she decided to become a full-time writer. She turned out numerous magazine articles and over a book a year for the rest of her life. Her storybooks for children were her most popular works.

Leaving Plymouth after her children were grown, Diaz settled in Belmont, Massachusetts, a Boston suburb. There she became a member of the New England Women's Club and active in education for women. Morton emerged as an active feminist and, beginning with *Domestic Problems* (1884), wrote four books for that cause. She founded the Boston Women's Educational and Industrial Union and served as its president for 12 years and then as vice-president during her retiring years. She also became president of the Moral Education Association. She devoted two afternoons a week to the free reading room for boys and girls in Cambridge, Massachusetts.

The first generation of the New Thought Movement was heavily influenced by and associated with the women's movement, and Diaz was drawn to it as an arena which integrated her Emersonian idealism and women's rights issues. She became a founding member of the Metaphysical Club, the early New Thought philosophical association in the city, and frequently included it on her lecture schedule around the Northeast. She published the most important statement of her metaphysical beliefs as four articles on the "Science of Human Beings" in the *Metaphysical Magazine*, December 1901 through September 1902, and in a series for *Mind* (New York) entitled "Hindrances to World Betterment."

Sources:

Diaz, Abby Morton. *Domestic Problems*. Boston: D. Lothrop & Co., 1884. 236 pp.
_____. *Neighborhood Talks*. New Vienna, OH: Peace Association of Friends in America, 1876. 102 pp.
_____. *Only a Flock of Women*. Boston: D. Lothrop & Co., 1893. 224 pp.
Dictionary of American Biography. 20 vols. and 7 supps. New York: Charles Scribner's Sons, 1928-1936, 1944-1981.

Patterson, Charles Brodie. "Abby Morton Diaz: A Biographical Sketch." *Mind* (1901): 167-72.

★ 266 ★
DIETRICH, John Hassler
Minister, American Unitarian Association
b. Jan. 14, 1878, Chambersburg, Pennsylvania
d. Jul. 22, 1957, Berkeley, California

John Hassler Dietrich, an early spokesperson for Humanism within the American Unitarian Association (AUA), was the son of Sarah Ann Sarbaugh and Jerome Dietrich. He attended Franklin and Marshall College from which he received both B.A. (1900) and M.A. (1902) degrees. He had been raised in the Reformed Church and, having decided to enter the ministry, he enrolled in Eastern Theological Seminary in Lancaster, Pennsylvania. Upon his graduation in 1905, he was ordained as a minister in the Reformed Church in the United States and became pastor of the St. Mark's Reformed Church in Pittsburgh, Pennsylvania.

Throughout the years of his pastorate in Pittsburgh, Dietrich found himself in constant conflict with both the Reformed Church's creedal statement and the sanctions imposed against ministers who came into disagreement with it. Eventually he was charged with heresy and in 1911 defrocked. Dietrich then joined the Unitarian Church and became pastor of the First Unitarian Society in Spokane, Washington. He quickly emerged as a major architect of a form of religious humanism and found himself in contact with others of a similar vein around the continent, most notably **Charles F. Potter** and **Curtis W. Reese**. In 1916 he moved to Minneapolis, Minnesota, as head of the First Unitarian Society and during the rest of his active life stood with one foot in the American Unitarian Association and the other in the larger Humanist movement which was just emerging.

By 1927 Dietrich had largely developed his mature philosophy. That year he authored two books: *The Fathers of Evolution and Other Addresses* and *The Significance of the Unitarian Movement*, and began the publication of *The Humanist Pulpit*. *Pulpit* would prove his most lasting literary contribution. In 1933 Dietrich joined with 33 colleagues in signing and issuing "The Humanist Manifesto," a brief document which summarized their perspective. In 1938 the Unitarians published his brief summary of the nature of *Humanism*.

"The Humanist Manifesto" describes the world as self-existing, not created, and humans as a result of evolution. The end of religion is to assist persons to find fulfillment in this life. While the manifesto would lead to the founding of the American Humanist Association, Dietrich chose to remain organizationally with the Unitarians and thus become a force in moving them toward their present stance which is so accepting of the Humanist perspective.

Dietrich retired in 1938 and was named minister emeritus of the First Unitarian Society of Minneapolis.

Sources:
Dietrich, John H. *The Father of Evolution and Other Addresses*. Minneapolis, MN: First Unitarian Society, 1927. 276 pp.
_____. *Humanism*. Boston: American Unitarian Association, 1938. 25 pp.
_____. *The Significance of the Unitarian Movement*. Boston: American Unitarian Association, 1927. 22 pp.
Robinson, David. *The Unitarians and the Universalists*. Westport, CT: Greenwood Press, 1985. 368 pp.

★ 267 ★
DIFFENDORFER, Ralph Eugene
Missionary Executive, Methodist Episcopal Church
b. Aug. 15, 1879, Hayesville, Ohio
d. Jan. 31, 1951, Madison, New Jersey

Ralph Eugene Diffendorfer, an executive with the board of missions of the Methodist Episcopal Church, was the son of Frank and Addie L. Arnold Diffendorfer. He attended Ohio Wesleyan University, from which he received his B.A. degree in 1902. He did his seminary work at Drew University in Madison, New Jersey, and completed his B.D. in 1907. In 1903 he married Edna Saylor. He later did postgraduate work at Union Theological Seminary. Though seminary trained, he did not go into the pastoral ministry, but chose to work in the missionary field. In 1904 he accepted a position as the secretary of the Missionary Educational Movement. He also worked part time at the Washington Square Methodist Episcopal Church in New York.

In 1916 Diffendorfer went to work for the church's Board of Missions and Home Extension, which would remain his employer for the rest of his life, except for a brief year (1919-1920) with the Interchurch World Movement. He served first as the education secretary and then assistant secretary for the Centenary Commission. In 1924 he became the corresponding secretary for the board of missions, a position he retained until the merger of the Methodist Episcopal Church, the Methodist Protestant Church, and the Methodist Episcopal Church, South in 1939. Diffendorfer brought great personal enthusiasm and creativity to his new position, and he soon became the single most influential person in directing the mission program of the Methodist Episcopal Church. Active in the ecumenical scene, he also influenced policy for the Federal Council of Churches.

Following the merger of the branches of Methodism in 1939, he was appointed executive secretary of the Board of Foreign Missions of the new Methodist Church (1939-1968). He again emerged as a dominant force in spite of the presence of outstanding missionary leaders such as **Elmer Talmage Clark** and Bishop **Arthur James Moore** from the southern church. His immediate task was to take charge of the massive foreign missions enterprise in the new wartime situation. He developed wire communications with the most threatened mission stations and provided day-by-day instructions, especially directions leading mission personnel away from ever-shifting frontlines. After the war, he gave direction to the post-war recovery. During his decades with the board of missions, Diffendorfer authored a number of books, most either explanatory of the church's mission program or educational texts for young readers.

After ten years he retired and settled in Madison, New Jersey. During his retirement years, he became active in the effort to found an international Christian university in Japan.

Sources:
Diffendorfer, Ralph E. *China and Japan?* New York: Methodist Book Concern, 1938. 59 pp.
_____. *The Church and the Community*. New York: Council of Women for Home Missions and Interchruch World Movement of North America, 1920. 177 pp.
_____. *Missionary Education in Home and School*. New York: Abingdon Press, 1917. 407 pp.
_____. *Thy Kingdom Come*. Missionary Education Movement of the United States and Canada, 1914. 62 pp.
Harmon, Nolan B. *The Encyclopedia of World Methodism*. 2 vols. Nashville: United Methodist Publishing House, 1974.
Howell, Clinton H., ed. *Prominent Personalities in Methodism*. Birmingham, AL: Lowrey Press, 1945. 512 pp.

★ 268 ★
DINGLE, Edwin John
Founder, Institute of Mentalphysics
b. Apr. 6, 1881, Paignton, Devonshire England
d. Jan. 27, 1972, Yucca Valley, California

Edwin John Dingle, founder of the Institute of Mentalphysics, was raised in Cornwall, England. His birth on April 6, 1881 was later said to match the death date of a lama, signalling that he was the lama's reincarnation. After his father's death, he and his brother lived with his grandparents. Following in his father's footsteps, he learned the newspaper trade and became a journalist. In 1900 he went to Singapore to cover the Orient. While there he met a guru with whom he studied meditation and yoga. At a certain point in the teachings, his master required him to make a pilgrimage. Fortunately, this coincided with a newspaper assignment to journey into central China and report on its geography.

On February 22, 1909, at the age of 28, Dingle left Singapore for a year-long expedition and pilgrimage. Dingle survived the anti-West Chao-t'ong Rebellion but caught malaria, and was forced into a period of recuperation in Burma. While still in a fevered state, his guru appeared to him to say that teachers were awaiting him in Tibet. As soon as he was able, Dingle made his way there and spent nine months in a monastery. The masters there reportedly trained him in remembering his past lives, breathing properly (so as to extract *prana*, the energy of life, from the air), and other disciplines.

After Tibet, Dingle returned to England, where he wrote *Across China on Foot* (1911) and *China's Revolution, 1911-1912*. Some years later he returned to China to establish the Far East Geographical Establishment, which published his bilingual "New Map of China" (1914), *Dingle's New Atlas and Commercial Gazetteer of China* and a weekly periodical, *China and the Far East Finance and Commerce*. These publications were so influential that the Royal Geographical Society made him a fellow.

In 1921 Dingle retired to Oakland, California. In 1927 he gave a lecture in New York, where he was asked to lead a special class on what he had learned from his masters. This was the unofficial beginning of the Institute of Mentalphysics, which was not actually incorporated until 1934. In addition to meditation, *pranayama* (breathing exercises), and yoga, Dingle emphasized vegetarianism, the belief in an Omnipotent Creator, the oneness of Life, and the Holy Trinity of Body, Mind and Spirit. He taught that the Tibetans were the preservers of the wisdom of the Arayans, the people who founded the Indian, Mediterranean, and Anglo-Saxon cultures.

A center was developed in Los Angeles, the International Church of the Holy Trinity. Dingle taught classes at the center, which served also as the base for a correspondence course which attracted students internationally. He adopted a religious name of Ding Le Mei. In 1941 a retreat center in Yucca Valley, California, was purchased, and this became the institute's headquarters. Dingle died in 1972, having built a significant organization and following; he was succeeded in leadership by Donald L. Waldrop.

Sources:
"Ding Le Mei Memorial Issue," *The Mansion Builder* (September, 1972).
Dingle, Edwin John. *Borderlands of Eternity*. Los Angeles: Institute of Mentalphysics, 1939. 560 pp.
———. *Breathing Your Way to Youth*. Los Angeles: Institute of Mentalphysics, n.d. 104 pp.
———. *Key to the Mysteries of Life*. Yucca Valley, CA: Institute of Mentalphysics, n.d. 15 pp.
———. *The Voice of the Logos*. Los Angeles: Econolith Press, 1951. 242 pp.
Melton, J. Gordon. *Biographical Dictionary of American Cult and Sect Leaders*. Garland Reference Library of Social Science, vol. 212. New York: Garland Publishing, 1986.

Shepard, Leslie. *Encyclopedia of Occultism & Parapsychology*. 3 vols., 2nd. ed. Detroit: Gale Research Co., 1984-1985.

—*Gary L. Ward*

★ 269 ★
Bishop DIONISIJE
Bishop, Serbian Eastern Orthodox Church in North America
b. Jul. 26, 1898, Rabrovac Serbia
d. May 15, 1979, Libertyville, Illinois

Bishop Dionisije Milivojevich, for almost four decades the leader of the Serbian Eastern Orthodox Church in North America, was the son of Stamenija and Zivota Milivojevich. He grew up in rural Serbia (now Yugoslavia) and after high school entered the University of Belgrade to study law. After finishing his law degree, he attended the theological college for four years and became a teacher at his high school in Kragujevac. In 1925 and 1926 he also taught in the local teaching college. In 1924 he had married, but his wife died after only six months. In 1926 he resigned from his teaching post, journeyed to Mt. Athos in Greece, and became a monk, taking the name Dionisije at that time.

Upon his return to his homeland, he was assigned as an instructor at the monastery at Dracha for two years and was then transferred as a professor to the monastery at Rakovitsa (where the Serbian bishop in America at the time, **Bishop Mardary**, had worked). In 1931 he pursued further studies at the Halka of Constantinople and upon completion of his work became a professor at the Seminary of Sremski Karlovci. While there Dionisije finished his work and in 1933 received his master's degree from the University of Belgrade. He was then appointed director of the monastic school in Visoki Dechani.

In 1933 Dionisije was consecrated as a bishop and served as vicar to the patriarch of Belgrade, the head of the Serbian church. In 1940 Bishop Dionisije became the new bishop for North America, assuming the responsibility of the caretaker administrators who ran the church in America following Bishop Mandary's death in 1935.

After World War II, Bishop Dionisije emerged as a vocal opponent of Marshal Tito, the Marxist ruler of postwar Yugoslavia, who asked the church to remove Dionisije. However, Dionisije remained in place until 1963 when the Yugoslavian bishops suspended him. They then moved to disband the diocese and replace it with three new dioceses. In 1964 the church defrocked Dionisije. Bishop Firmilian was appointed as administrator of one of the new dioceses which covered the midwestern United States and the headquarters of the church at St. Sava Monastery in Libertyville, Illinois. The arrival of the new administrator-bishops led to a split in the church between those clergy and parishes who were aligned to Bishop Dionisije and those aligned to the patriarch in Belgrade. A series of law suits were filed as each side tried to claim church properties and assets. During the lengthy period of adjudication, Dionisije continued to pursue his episcopal duties in those parishes loyal to him.

A 1976 Supreme Court ruling became the decisive event in the bitterly contested fight. The property at Libertyville, where Dionisije resided, was awarded to the Belgrade faction. While various legal maneuvers postponed the actual transfer of the property, Dionisije passed away just a few days before his 81st birthday. A short time later, his successor, Bishop Irinije, abandoned the Libertyville property. As leader of the church, now renamed the Serbian Orthodox Free Diocese of the United States and Canada, Irinije built a new headquarters in Third Lake, Illinois.

Sources:
"Bishop Milivojevic, Serbian Leader, Dies." *American Review of Eastern Orthodoxy* 25, 5 (September/October 1979): 2-8.

Frisbie, Tom. "Bishops Weigh High-Court Ruling." *Chicago Daily News, Suburban Week* (June 30 & July 1, 1976).

★270★
DIVINE, Father Major Jealous
Founder, Peace Mission Movement
b. 1877?, Savannah
d. Sep. 10, 1965, Philadelphia, Pennsylvania

Father Major Jealous Divine is one of the more interesting and mysterious of American twentieth century religious leaders. By his own choosing, his life prior to 1919 is unknown. Followers claim that he married his first wife, Mother Penniah Divine, on June 6, 1882, and that he was subject to lynch mob activity in the South during Grover Cleveland's administration (1893-1897). This would make him extremely old at the time of his death in 1965. Alternative chronologies, however, such as one by John Hickerson which claims that Divine was born in 1880 as George Baker, are not very reliable.

What is clear is that just before 1919 Divine was active in a ministry in Brooklyn, New York, with a small group of followers and other preachers, including Samuel Morris (Father Jehovah) and John Hickerson (Bishop St. John the Divine). In 1919 Divine moved to the small village of Sayville, New York, to a home bought by his first wife, known as Penniah or Sister Penny. His ability to heal illness and provide free food, jobs, and other abundance in the face of seeming poverty drew increasing numbers of needy black followers. During the 1920s the idea that he was God incarnate began to take hold. In 1926 Whites from the holiness and metaphysical churches began to join his congregation.

Complaints from the townspeople about the size of his following led to a 1931 conviction of Divine for disturbing the peace. The judge sentenced him to one year in jail, a tougher sentence than the jury recommended. Two days later, on June 7, the judge unexpectedly died of a heart attack, and Divine was reported to have said, "I hated to do it!" This incident made him a nationally known figure, and his followers ever since have celebrated the anniversary of the judge's demise. Divine's conviction was overturned shortly thereafter, and he decided to expand his ministry by moving to Harlem.

In the midst of the Depression, and particularly in hard-hit Harlem, Divine managed to offer shelter, an employment service, and lavish banquets, either free or for a nominal fee. Followers were told to work hard, expect a fair wage, pay off their debts, return stolen items, and pay their own way. After a while, several hotels were taken over and turned into "heavens," where people could make a new start. In 1941 and 1942 the church was incorporated as the Peace Mission Movement. Followers began businesses which employed other followers. Congregational beliefs included Father Divine as the Second Coming of Christ, heaven as a state of consciousness, though being materialized in America, the birthplace of the Kingdom of God on earth. Although his popularity in Harlem was immense, authorities were not so pleased, and Divine moved his work to Philadelphia in 1942.

On April 29, 1946, Divine married Edna Rose Ritchings, Sister Penny having died about 1940. Ritchings has since been known as Mother Divine, and their wedding date has become an official holiday of the church, as has September 10-12, the anniversary of the dedication of the suburban Philadelphia Woodmont Estate, which was given to the church in 1954. The Peace Mission Movement gained a great deal of respect because of its emphasis on brotherhood, equality, justice, self-respect, and dedication to the poor. Mother Divine took over leadership of the movement following her husband's death in 1965.

Sources:

Bowden, Henry Warner. *Dictionary of American Religious Biography.* Westport, CT: Greenwood Press, 1977. 572 pp.
Burnham, Kenneth E. *God Comes to America.* Boston: Lambeth Press, 1979. 167 pp.
Divine, Mother. *The Peace Mission Movement.* Philadelphia: Imperial Press, 1982. 191 pp.
Harris, Sara. *Father Divine.* New York: Collier Books, 1971. 377 pp.
Hoshor, John. *God in a Rolls Royce.* New York: Hillman, Curl, 1936. 272 pp.
Melton, J. Gordon. *Biographical Dictionary of American Cult and Sect Leaders.* Garland Reference Library of Social Science, vol. 212. New York: Garland Publishing, 1986.
Weisbrot, Robert. *Father Divine and the Struggle for Racial Equality.* Urbana, IL: University of Illinois, 1983. 241 pp.

—*Gary L. Ward*

★271★
DIXON, Amzi Clarence
Fundamentalist Baptist Evangelist
b. Jul. 6, 1854, Shelby, North Carolina
d. Jun. 14, 1925, Baltimore, Maryland

Amzi Clarence Dixon, one of the most outspoken of the Christian fundamentalist ministers in the early twentieth century, was the son of Thomas and Amanda Dixon. His father was an evangelist, and at the age of 12 Amzi was one of 98 youths who were baptized after responding to revival messages preached by his father. He attended Shelby Academy and then Wake Forest University, where he graduated in 1874. He was committed to the ministry by this time and was soon ordained. In 1875 he entered the Southern Baptist Theological Seminary at Greenville, South Carolina. After completing his studies, he became the pastor of the Baptist church at Chapel Hill, North Carolina, and directed his evangelistic efforts toward the adjacent university campus.

In 1880 Dixon moved to Asheville, North Carolina, as pastor and shortly thereafter married Susan Mary Faison. In 1882 he turned down an offer to become president of Wake Forest College to accept the pastorate of Immanuel Baptist Church in Baltimore. He was there for eight years before leaving the South to become pastor of Hanson Place Baptist Church in Brooklyn, New York.

During the 11 years he spent in Brooklyn, Dixon began to attract national attention. He had always had an evangelistic fervor, but he added to it an involvement in public issues, especially temperance, a crusade which was moving toward the prohibition era. He also became known as a staunch and capable opponent of the "liberal" trends which were appearing in the Protestant church in general and the Baptist Church in particular. One manifestation of the new liberalism, which included a tolerance of non-Christian religion, was the World's Parliament of Religions, which met in Chicago in 1893. Dixon took a month off to join evangelist **Dwight L. Moody** that summer preaching in Chicago against the parliament.

Dixon went on to pastor several prominent fundamentalist pulpits, including Ruggles Street Baptist Church in Boston, Massachusetts (1901-1906), and Moody Church in Chicago (1906-1911). During his tenure at Moody, he traveled to Los Angeles to preach at a conference. **Lyman Stewart**, the wealthy Presbyterian oil man, was in the audience. As a result of their meeting, Stewart gave Dixon the money to assemble the famous set of ten booklets, *The Fundamentals: A Testimony to the Truth* (1910-1915). These booklets were distributed widely to ministers across the country in an attempt to counter the spread of modernism and remain an early definitive statement of the fundamentalist perspective.

In 1911 Dixon moved to England to become pastor of the Metropolitan Tabernacle, a church famous for the many years it was served by Charles H. Spurgeon, one of the most famous nineteenth-century Baptist preachers. He stayed in London through World War I and returned to the United States in 1919.

During the last years of his life, Dixon threw himself into the fundamentalist-modernist controversy which was dividing American Protestants. He conducted Bible conferences, held evangelistic meetings, and wrote frequently on behalf of fundamentalism. In 1922 he settled in Baltimore as pastor of the University Baptist Church and anchored the remaining years of his ministry there. His first wife having died in 1922, in 1924 he married Helen C. Alexander, who would author a biography of Dixon several years after his death.

Sources:

Dixon, A. C. *Back to the Bible.* London: S. W. Partridge, n.d. 239 pp.

_____. *The Christian Science Delusion.* Philadelphia: Presbyterian Board of Publication & Sabbath School Work, 1903. 42 pp.

_____. *Evangelism Old and New.* New York: American Tract Society, 1905. 209 pp.

_____. *The Glories of the Cross.* London: S. W. Partridge, n.d. 253 pp.

_____. *Lights and Shadows of American Life.* Boston: H. H. Smith, 1903. 197 pp.

_____. *The Person and Work of the Holy Spirit.* Baltimore, MD: Wharton, Barron & Co., 1890. 187 pp.

Dixon, Helen. *A. C. Dixon—A Romance of Preaching.* New York: G. P. Putnam's, 1931. 324 pp.

The Fundamentals: A Testimony to the Truth. 10 vols. N.p. 1910-1915.

Southern Baptist Encyclopedia . 4 vols. Nashville: Broadman Press.

★ 272 ★
DOUGHERTY, Dennis
Cardinal, Roman Catholic Church
b. Aug. 16, 1865, Homesville, Pennsylvania
d. May 31, 1951, Philadelphia, Pennsylvania

Dennis Dougherty, a cardinal of the Roman Catholic Church, was born in 1865 to Patrick and Bridget Dougherty, both recent immigrants to America from Ireland. After attending public school in a nearby town, Dougherty was sent to St. Mary's College, a Jesuit school in Montreal. In 1885 he was sent by Archbishop Patrick John Ryan to the North American College in Rome, then under the leadership of William O'Connell, its rector. In 1890, in the course of just a few weeks, he was both ordained to the priesthood and granted his doctor of divinity degree.

Dougherty was appointed to teach at St. Charles Seminary at Overbrook, Pennsylvania. His tenure at the seminary came to an end after the Spanish-American War. American annexation of the Philippines required the appointment of American bishops to halt the disruption of the church, now in a land ruled by Protestants. Dougherty was chosen bishop of Nueva Segovia with headquarters at Vigan, about 30 miles from Manila. After a trip to Rome for consecration, he returned to Pennsylvania and recruited five priests to return to Vigan with him to assist in rebuilding a seminary ruined in the war. Over the next few years he staffed the 110 parishes in the diocese, reopened the girls' academy, and repaired the damaged buildings.

In addition to dealing with the damage caused by the war, Dougherty had to face the major schism led by Father Gregory Aglipay, which had led to the founding of the Philippine Independent Church. Their independents had taken over a large percentage of the church's property, and he had to enter lengthy litigation to have it returned.

In 1908, in recognition of his accomplishments, Dougherty was asked to take over the larger diocese of Jaro, which had not fared well after the war. Half of its parishes were still without priests. During the next years he accomplished a rebuilding similar to that in Nueva Segovia, including the reopening of a leper colony and the building of a hospital. Shortly after the silver jubilee of his priest-

hood, he was appointed Bishop of Buffalo, New York, and he returned to the United States.

Dougherty's new diocese was heavily in debt. He established a parish tax to retire the debt, reorganized the schools and charities, and established 15 new parishes, all within three years. By the time of his elevation to Archbishop of Philadelphia, he had retired the diocese's debt of over a million dollars.

Dougherty's new assignment began in crisis due to the flu epidemic of 1918. As he became aware of the seriousness of the epidemic, he opened the Catholic facilities as infirmaries and placed his personnel at the disposal of the health authorities. Only after the epidemic passed did he resume his task of reorganizing the archdiocese. He had been at his post only three years when word reached him of his appointment to the College of Cardinals. He traveled to Rome and received the signs of his office on March 10, 1921. He took charge of his titular parish in the diocese of Rome, the church of Saints Nereus and Achilles, on Palm Sunday, March 20.

His years as Archbishop of Philadelphia were marked by many substantive achievements. He established 106 new parishes, expanded the social services (including new orphanages and homes for the aged), and supported missionary work among Blacks and American Indians. Several long memoranda sent by Dougherty to the pope are credited with opening the practice of medicine to American nuns.

Dougherty's piety was most visible in his support for the sainthood of Therese of Lisieux, popularly known as the "Little Flower." He was an early advocate of her cause, which he discussed with several popes, and he publicized her life by his visits to her shrine. He dedicated the basilica in 1937 following her canonization.

The later years of Dougherty's life were highlighted by the golden jubilee of his priesthood in 1951. He lived a quiet last decade and died the day after celebrating the sixtieth anniversary of his ordination.

Sources:

Finn, Brendan A. *Twenty-Four American Cardinals.* Boston: Bruce Humphries, 1947. 475 pp.

Thornton, Francis Beauchesne. *Our American Princes.* New York: G. P. Putnam's Sons, 1963. 319 pp.

Walsh, James Joseph. *Our American Cardinals.* New York: D. Appleton and Co., 1926. 352 pp.

★ 273 ★
DOUGLAS, Lloyd Cassel
Minister, Congregational Church
b. Aug. 27, 1877, Columbia City, Indiana
d. Feb. 13, 1951, Los Angeles, California

Lloyd Cassel Douglas, a minister of the Congregational Church, is remembered primarily as the author of a series of religious novels which were turned into popular movies, the most famous being *The Robe.* He was the son of Alexander Jackson and Sarah Douglas. He was raised as a Lutheran in a pious family, his father having once considered going into the ministry rather than the law. Douglas attended Wittenburg College and Hamma Divinity School, schools affiliated with the General Synod of the Lutheran Church and now with the Evangelical Lutheran Church in America (1988), from which he graduated in 1903. He pastored churches in North Manchester, Indiana; Lancaster, Indiana; and Washington, D.C. While at North Manchester in 1904 he married Besse Io Porch. While at Lancaster his first novel, *More Than a Prophet* (1905) was published. The book held out little promise for future success, and it would be 15 years before he tried again.

In spite of conservative Lutheran training, Douglas had never been theologically attentive. He emphasized the practical side of

Christianity and saw the power to transform people and society in Christianity's ideals, rather than a program of social gospel activism. His obvious speaking ability and his message, which largely ignored conservative-liberal theological differences, led to his early call to a prestigious pulpit in Washington in 1909. However, his position also led to his doubting the value of Lutheranism in the modern world. Thus, in 1911 when offered a position as director of religious work for the YMCA at the University of Illinois, he took the opportunity to resign from the Lutheran Church and become a minister in the Congregational Church.

After three years in Illinois, he became pastor of the Congregational church in Ann Arbor, Michigan. Believing it would lead to the reconstruction of society, he threw himself into the war effort. Immediately after the war he led a campaign for the Interchurch World Movement effort to raise several billion dollars to complete the task of Christianizing the world. The campaign failed, and out of the failure Douglas wrote his next book, *Wanted: A Congregation* (1920). The book noted the problem of the churches in holding the next generation and offered a solution in what was termed "pulpit power," the imaginative use of advertising, promotion, and an appealing religious message.

The next decade proved the low point in Douglas' ministry. He moved from Ann Arbor in 1921 to Akron, Ohio, and from there to Los Angeles. He stayed out of the fundamentalist-modernist debate, again attempting to emphasize practical religion, though a modernist perspective undergirded his work. He authored two books, *The Minister's Everyday Life* (1924) and *Those Disturbing Miracles* (1927), neither of which brought much response. In 1928 he moved from Los Angeles to St. James United Church in Montreal, Canada, which would be his last parish. At the time of the move he decided to try writing another novel.

In 1929, while the world watched the stock market crash, he saw *Magnificent Obsession* published. It had steady sales through the worst of the depression, and in 1931 went through eight printings. The success continued through the next year. It sold 6,000 copies a month at the end of 1932. That year *Forgive Us Our Trespasses* was published and it too became a best seller. In the wake of his success, claiming that he could reach more people with his novels, he resigned his parish. He settled in Wellesley, Massachusetts, and turned out two more popular novels, *Green Light* (1935) and *White Banners* (1936).

Magnificent Obsession was filmed for the first time in 1935, and the following year he moved to Beverly Hills, California. There he authored *Disputed Passage* (1939); *Doctor Hudson's Secret Journal* (1939); *Invitation to Live* (1940); *The Robe* (1942); and *The Big Fisherman* (1948). Through the novels run threads of optimism and the power of Christianity to transform the inner life. Douglas' novels were dismissed by literary critics, but had an intense mass appeal with their simple religiosity. *The Robe* became the best selling of them all.

In his last years he worked on an autobiography, *Time to Remember* (1951), which was published posthumously.

Sources:

Bode, Carl. "Lloyd Douglas: Loud Voice in the Wilderness." *American Quarterly* 2 (1950): 340-358.
Douglas, Lloyd C. *The Big Fisherman*. Boston: Houghton Mifflin Company, 1948. 551 pp.
———. *Disputed Passage*. Boston: Houghton Mifflin Company, 1939. 432 pp.
———. *Doctor Hudson's Secret Journal*. Boston: Houghton Mifflin Company, 1939. 295 pp.
———. *Magnificent Obsession*. Chicago: Willett, Clark and Colby, 1929. 330 pp.
———. *The Minister's Everyday Life*. New York: Charles Scribner's Sons, 1924. 220 pp.
———. *The Robe*. Boston: Houghton Mifflin Company, 1942. 695 pp.
———. *Time to Remember*. Boston: Houghton Mifflin Company, 1951. 238 pp.
Lippy, Charles H. *Twentieth-Century Shapers of American Popular Religion*. New York: Greenwood Press, 1989. 494 pp.

★274★
DOWIE, John Alexander
Founder, Christian Catholic Church
b. May 25, 1847, Edinburgh Scotland
d. Mar. 9, 1907, Zion, Illinois

John Alexander Dowie, the famous healer and founder of the Christian Catholic Church, was born to a poor family in Scotland. He was a sickly child who only occasionally made it to school. Religiously devout, Dowie read the entire Bible when he was only six, and took a vow of temperance at the age of seven. As a teenager he moved with his family to Australia, where his chronic dispepsia was healed. He eventually pursued a ministerial education back in Edinburgh and served as a minister in the Australian Congregational Church.

During the plague in Australia in 1876, Dowie discovered the divine healing power that would change the course of his ministry. That same year he married his cousin, Jeanne Dowie, and formed an independent congregation in Sydney. He emphasized both divine healing and the sins of liquor, theaters, newspapers, physicians and other churches. He was so strident in his condemnation of the latter that his office was bombed. In 1882 he founded the International Divine Healing Association.

In 1888 Dowie began a new chapter in his ministry by resigning from his church position in order to travel worldwide and spread the gospel of healing. He spent a number of years preaching in the United States, and in 1893 made Chicago his headquarters by building a tabernacle near the entrance to the World's Fair. His repudiation of regular medical practice earned him both praise and scorn. He was arrested several times for practicing medicine without a license, and the Post Office balked at mailing his magazine, *The Leaves of Healing*. Nevertheless, he persisted, and formally incorporated the Christian Catholic Church in 1896.

In 1901 the congregation purchased 6600 acres on the shores of Lake Michigan, and headquarters were moved there, where the city of Zion was built. Zion was patterned somewhat after Salt Lake City, Utah, and was conceived as a holy city without liquor, tobacco, pork, or drugstores. Dowie proclaimed himself the fulfillment of certain Old Testament prophecies, such as Elijah the Restorer (Malachi 4), and he envisioned cities like Zion all over the world. By 1906, however, Zion was in financial difficulties unacknowledged by Dowie, who was partially paralyzed by a stroke. When he went to Mexico to begin another city, his second-in-command, Wilbur Glenn Volivia, led the followers to remove Dowie from his position, electing Volivia in his place. Dowie died less than a year later at the age of 60. His church has endured in several countries, although Zion now has a number of different religions within its boundaries.

Sources:

Cook, Philip L. *Zion City, Illinois, John Alexander Dowie's Theocracy*. Zion, IL: Zion Historical Society, 1970.
———. "Zion City, Illinois—The Kingdom of Heaven and Race." *Illinois Quarterly* 38 (Winter, 1975): 50-62.
Dowie, John Alexander. *Zion's Conflict with Methodist Apostasy*. Chicago: Zion Publishing House, 1900. 204 pp.
Lindsay, Gordon, ed. *Champion of the Faith: The Sermons of John Alexander Dowie*. Dallas, TX: Christ for the Nations, 1979. 125 pp.
———. *John Alexander Dowie*. Dallas, TX: Christ for the Nations, 1980.

—*Gary L. Ward*

★ 275 ★
DRESSER, Horatio Willis
New Thought Writer/Lecturer
b. Jan. 15, 1866, Yarmouth, Maine
d. Mar. 30, 1954, Boston, Massachusetts

Horatio Willis Dresser, an early New Thought writer and lecturer, was the son of Julius and Annetta Seabury Dresser, both of whom had been introduced to metaphysical thought through their study with Phineas Parkhurst Quimby, the mental healer from Portland, Maine. Dresser was born just a few months before Quimby's death, after which his parents moved west, where his father worked as a newspaper editor in Denver, Colorado, and later Oakland, California. At the age of 13 Dresser left school to go to work. In 1882 the family moved to Boston, Massachusetts, where his father became deeply involved in a controversy with **Mary Baker Eddy**. Eddy had also been a student of Quimby's, and the elder Dresser accused her of stealing Quimby's ideas and using them to build Christian Science. Dresser appeared as an expert witness in a suit Eddy leveled against one of her students, Edward J. Arens, for plagiarizing from her writings. Eddy won the suit, but Julius Dresser claimed that she was victorious only because Quimby's sons refused to release the Quimby manuscripts as evidence in the case. Horatio Dresser grew up amid the controversy.

During the 1880s Dresser was able to educate himself enough to be admitted to Harvard in 1891. In 1893 his father died and he was forced to drop out of school and begin his career as a writer and lecturer. He had by this time become associated with the fledgling New Thought movement and in 1895 became one of the founders of one of the more important New Thought groups, the Metaphysical Club of Boston. That same year he published his first book, *The Power of Silence*. In 1896 he founded the Philosophical Publishing Company and the *Journal of Practical Metaphysics*, which he edited until 1898 when it was absorbed into *The Arena*. He became associate editor of *The Arena*. In 1898 he married Alice Mae Reed.

In 1899 Dresser began a second New Thought magazine, *The Higher Law*. Along with editing it, he authored a correspondence course in New Thought and shared the leadership of the Institute of Metaphysics with Warren A. Rodman. In 1903 he returned to Harvard to work on his doctorate. He became an assistant in philosophy in 1903 and completed his Ph.D. in 1907.

Except for several years teaching at Ursinius College in Philadelphia (1911-1913), Dresser spent the rest of his life writing and lecturing. From 1917 through 1922 he was especially active in New Thought. He authored a number of significant New Thought texts beginning with *The Handbook of New Thought* and *The Spirit of New Thought* in 1917 which together served to revive the Quimby controversy again. In 1919 he wrote *A History of New Thought* which championed the case for Quimby as the founder of New Thought. Also in the years after World War I, the Quimby materials, which had been deposited at the Library of Congress, became available. In 1921 Dresser finished his compilation of Quimby's writings, released as *The Quimby Manuscripts*. Dresser's notes included an argument for his father's charges against Mary Baker Eddy.

Meanwhile, Dresser joined and in 1919 was ordained as a minister in the General Convention of the New Jerusalem, one of the churches built around the teachings of eighteenth-century seer Emanuel Swedenborg. He briefly served as the minister of a small Swedenborgian church in Portland, Maine, but primarily continued his career as an author. His last major works were a series of texts produced for Thomas Y. Crowell Company on psychology and philosophy. During the last years of his life he became interested in applied psychology and in 1931 began to work in a clinic in Boston which combined religious and medical approaches. He withdrew briefly from the ministry in 1929 so as not to embarrass the church in his then controversial work, but was reinstated in 1942.

Sources:

Anderson, C. Alan. *Horatio W. Dresser and the Philosophy of New Thought*. Boston: University of Boston, Ph. D. dissertation, 1963. 356 pp.

Dresser, Horatio W. *Handbook of New Thought*. New York: G. P. Putnam's Sons, [1917]. 263 pp.

_____. *History of the New Thought Movement*. New York: Thomas Y. Crowell, 1919. 352 pp.

_____. *The Power of Silence*. Boston: Geo. H. Ellis, 1895. 219 pp.

_____, ed. *The Quimby Manuscripts*. New York: Thomas Y. Crowell, [1921]. 442 pp.

_____, ed. *The Spirit of New Thought*. New York: Thomas Y. Crowell Company, 1917. 297 pp.

★ 276 ★
DREW, Timothy
Founder, Moorish Science Temple of America
b. Jan. 8, 1886, North Carolina
d. Jul. 20, 1929, Chicago, Illinois

Timothy Drew founded the Moorish Science Temple of America and was instrumental in establishing among many Blacks in the United States an affinity for the religion of Islam. He was born in rural North Carolina, but managed, prior to World War I, to travel extensively around the world, where he was particularly impressed by the racial acceptance in the Middle East. He said that Sultan Asis Abn Saud gave him the title "Ali" during a visit to Mecca.

Drew's travels and readings led him to some remarkable ideas about the identity and history of Blacks in America, who he said were not of Ethiopian origin (as some early Black nationalists were suggesting). Drew instead claimed that they were Moors, descendants of the Moabites of Canaan, with the homeland of Morocco. Prior to the American Revolution Blacks were free and flew their bright red Moorish flag. It was this flag that George Washington cut down (not a cherry tree). The Continental Congress robbed them of their nationality and assigned them to slavery. Over time, the slaves forgot their true religion of Islam and turned to Christianity. Drew saw his mission as a prophet of Allah as one of preaching liberation from their accepted status and recognition of a new Moorish identity. He first dramatized this search for identity by asking President Woodrow Wilson to return the Moorish flag, which Drew believed had been kept in a safe in Independence Hall since 1776.

Drew opened his first Moorish Temple in Newark, New Jersey, in 1913, and became known as Noble Drew Ali. He soon instituted centers in several cities, establishing a headquarters in Chicago in 1925. In 1926 the organization was incorporated as the Moorish Temple of Science, which was changed in 1928 to the Moorish Science Temple of America. In 1927 he published *The Holy Koran*, (not to be confused with the *Koran* of orthodox Islamic faith). Ali's *Koran* was a 60-page compilation of Moorish Science beliefs. It drew on a variety of sources, including *The Aquarian Gospel of Jesus Christ* by Spiritualist Levi Dowling.

Ali believed that Christianity was opposed to the interests of God's Blacks, and that Jesus was a Black man who had tried to redeem the Black Moabites, only to be executed by the white Romans. He thought that only Islam could unite Blacks, but he did not live to see such unification. His Chicago work became strife ridden when several Temple leaders were accused of exploiting members by selling products such as Old Moorish Healing Oil and Moorish Purifier Bath Compound. Ali tried to oust these leaders, and a period of struggle ensued. When Ali was out of town, his business manager was killed. Ali was arrested on his return. He died of unknown causes before the trial began. He left behind a movement that became the source for many groups combining black activism and Islamic beliefs, such as the *Nation of Islam.*

Sources:

Calverly, Edwin E. "Negro Muslims in Hartford," *Moslem World* 55 (October, 1965): 340-345.

Essien-Udom, E. U. *Black Nationalism: A Search for an Identity in America.* New York: Dell Publishing, 1964.

Fauset, Arthur Huff. *Black Gods of the Metropolis.* Philadephia, PA: University of Pennsylvania Press, 1944. 126 pp.

Melton, J. Gordon. *Biographical Dictionary of American Cult and Sect Leaders.* Garland Reference Library of Social Science, vol. 212. New York: Garland Publishing, 1986.

Simpson, Frank T. "The Moorish Science Temple and Its Koran" *Moslem World* 37 (January, 1947): 56-61.

—*Gary L. Ward*

★ 277 ★
DREXEL, Katherine Mary
Founder, Sisters of the Blessed Sacrament for Indians and Colored People
b. Nov. 26, 1858, Philadelphia, Pennsylvania
d. Mar. 3, 1955, Cornwall Heights, Pennsylvania

Katherine Mary Drexel, founder of the Sisters of the Blessed Sacrament for Indians and Colored People, a religious community within the Roman Catholic Church, was the daughter of Francis Drexel, a banker-philanthropist, and Hannah Jane Langstroth. Her mother died when Katherine was a baby, and she was educated at home by governesses. In 1883 her stepmother died and her father passed away two years later, leaving her with a large fortune. She continued her father's philanthropic endeavors, but wanted to do more. In 1887 she had a private audience with Pope Leo XIII, who advised her to devote her life, not just her fortune, to the work her money was establishing.

In 1889 Drexel entered the Sisters of Mercy as a novice. She took her final vows two years later, at which time she departed to found a new order, the Sisters of the Blessed Sacrament for Indians and Colored People, over which she became superior general. Initially headquartered in her family's summer estate at Torresdale, Pennsylvania, the order moved in 1892 to St. Elizabeth's Convent in Cornwall Heights, Pennsylvania.

Drexel launched a broad program of missions, especially schools, among American Indians and within the black community. The first was St. Catherine's Boarding School for Pueblo Indians, in Santa Fe, New Mexico. Other centers were located across the United States. In 1913 the pope gave final approval of the order. The sisters responded two years later with their most challenging effort, the founding of Xavier University in New Orleans, the first Roman Catholic university in the United States for Blacks (dedicated in 1932). It also became a major training center for teachers to staff the more than 60 schools Drexel was to lead in founding.

Drexel headed the continually growing work of the order for 46 years. In 1934 she was hobbled by a stroke. In 1937 she relinquished her position and was appointed vicar-general. Her golden jubilee of ordered service was celebrated in 1941. She continued to participate in the affairs of the order, but her health deteriorated, and in her last years she was confined to a wheelchair.

By the time of her death, the order had 500 members. The money Drexel originally put at its disposal had created 49 elementary schools, 12 high schools, and one university. In 1988 Mother Drexel was beatified by Pope John Paul II. Beatification means she is considered a "blessed" one of the Roman Catholic Church and a proper object for veneration. Beatification is a significant step toward being named a saint and was confirmed after the Vatican's offices concluded that a verified healing had occurred following prayers asking for Mother Drexel's intercession.

Sources:

Delaney, John J. *Dictionary of American Catholic Biography.* Garden City, NY: Doubleday & Company, 1988. 621 pp.

James, Edward T., ed. *Notable American Women, 1607-1950: A Biographical Dictionary.* 3 vols. Cambridge, MA: Harvard University Press, Belknap Press, 1971.

★ 278 ★
DU PLESSIS, David Johannes
Evangelist, Assemblies of God
b. Feb. 5, 1905, Twenty-four Rivers Republic of South Africa
d. Jan. 1987, Pasadena, California

David Johannes Du Plessis, the most influential spokesperson for Pentecostalism in the larger ecumenical world of Christianity, was the son of Anna C. and David J. Du Plessis. Born in a small town in South Africa, Du Plessis was raised in a Pentecostal household. In 1916 the family moved to Basutoland (now Lesotho), where his carpenter father worked to construct a mission compound. Du Plessis had a conversion experience shortly after the move. He was baptized and joined the Apostolic Faith Mission the following year. Two years later he experienced the baptism of the Holy Spirit and spoke in tongues for the first time. (Such a baptism with its accompanying evidence of speaking in tongues is the definitive Pentecostal experience.)

Du Plessis attended Grey University in Bloemfontein. In 1927 he married Anna Cornelia Jacobs. He was ordained in the Apostolic Faith Mission. He became editor of the *Comforter/Trooster,* the denominational magazine. In 1936 he was elected general secretary, a post he retained until 1947. He introduced American-style revivals to the denomination, led in the founding of an orphanage, and set up a pension system for ministers.

The first meeting of the Pentecostal World Conference (PWC) in 1947 was marked by Du Plessis' resignation as general secretary of his denomination. He moved to Basel, Switzerland, and served as organizational secretary of the PWC through 1958. Moving his base to the United States in 1948, he helped initiate the Pentecostal Fellowship of North America, though he missed that organization's first meeting due to an automobile accident. Having affiliated with the Church of God (Cleveland, Tennessee) in 1949, Du Plessis joined the faculty of Lee College in Cleveland. In 1952 he moved to Stamford, Connecticut, as pastor of the Stamford Gospel Tabernacle, and on to Dallas in 1956 to work with **Gordon Lindsey** as secretary of the Voice of Healing Fellowship.

Through the 1950s Du Plessis inserted himself into the emerging world ecumenical movement and took every opportunity afforded him to meet with mainline church leaders to present the case for Pentecostalism. He attended the assembly of the World Council of Churches in 1954 in Evanston, Illinois, and each succeeding one for the rest of his life. While rejected by some Pentecostals for his ecumenism (the Assemblies asked him to surrender his credentials in 1962), he was able to pave the way for the acceptance of the many mainline Christians who were attracted to pentecostalism and who created the Charismatic Movement in the 1960s.

During the 1970s Du Plessis was at his peak as an ambassador of Pentecostalism within the Christian world. He was invited to help establish a Roman Catholic-Pentecostal dialogue and chaired the first ten sessions. The dialogue led to his meetings with several popes, and in 1983 Pope John Paul II gave him the Good Merit Medal, the first non-Catholic so honored. In recognition of his accomplishments, the Assemblies of God returned his credentials in 1980.

Du Plessis accepted an invitation to deposit his papers at Fuller Theological Seminary, which created the David J. Du Plessis Center for Christian Spirituality in 1985. Du Plessis moved to Pasadena,

California, and worked at the seminary as the resident consultant for ecumenical affairs.

Sources:

Burgess, Stanley M., Gary B. McGee, and Patrick H. Alexander, eds. *Dictionary of Pentecostal and Charismatic Movements*. Grand Rapids, MI: Regency Reference Library, Zondervan Publishing House, 1988. 914 pp.

Du Plessis, David J. *Simple and Profound*. Pentwater, MI: Paraclete Press, 1986. 207 pp.

_____. *The Spirit Bade Me Go*. Oakland, CA: The Author, 1961, Rev. ed. Plainfield, NJ: Logos International, 1977.

_____, and Bob Slosser. *The Man Called Mr. Pentecost*. Plainfield, NJ: Logos International, 1977.

Reid, Daniel G., Robert D. Linder, Bruce L. Shelley, and Harry S. Stout. *Dictionary of Christianity in America*. Downers Grove, IL: InterVarsity Press, 1990. 1305 pp.

Robinson, Martin. *To the Ends of the Earth: The Pilgrimage of an Ecumenical Pentecostal, David J. Du Plessis (1905-1987)*. Birmingham, United Kingdom: University of Birmingham, Ph.D. Dissertation, 1987.

★ 279 ★
DUBOSE, William Porcher
Theologian, Protestant Episcopal Church
b. Apr. 11, 1836, Winnsboro, South Carolina
d. Aug. 18, 1918, Sewanee, Tennessee

William Porcher DuBose, a theologian for the Protestant Episcopal Church, was the son of Theodore Marion and Jane Porcher DuBose, both of French Huguenot descent. He grew up on his father's plantation. He was educated at Mt. Sion Institute in Winnsboro and at the Citadel, from which he graduated with honors in 1855. He earned his M.A. at the University of Virginia and then attended the Episcopal Church's theological seminary at Camden, South Carolina. His education was interrupted by the Civil War, and in 1861 he joined the Confederate Army as the adjutant for the Holcombe Legion, a unit commanded by the former commandant of the Citadel. He was captured at one point and, after participating in a prisoner exchange, served the remainder of the war as a chaplain. In 1863 he married Ann Barnwell Peroneau.

After the war, DuBose was ordained as a priest and began his ministerial career in 1865 at his home town parish. He then served at Abbeville, South Carolina, until 1871, when he moved to Sewanee, Tennessee, where he served as chaplain and professor of ethics and Christian apologetics for the University of the South. He remained at Sewanee for the rest of his life. In 1873 his first wife died, and in 1878 he married Louisa Yeager.

During his active years at the school DuBose led in the founding of the theological department of the university and in 1894 was elected its dean. He also taught New Testament exegesis in the new department. During his early years on the faculty, apart from his essays published in *Constructive Quarterly*, he did very little writing; he published his first book in 1892. The series of six books he eventually wrote, however, beginning with *The Soteriology of the New Testament*, earned him a permanent place in Anglican theological thought. His first book dealt with the philosophy of salvation. He followed it with *The Ecumenical Councils* (1896), a philosophical interpretation of Christian doctrine as espoused in the ancient church councils; *The Gospel in the Gospels* (1906), the most systematic presentation of his theology; *The Gospel According to St. Paul* (1907), his study of the Pauline documents; and *High Priesthood and Sacrifice* (1908).

DuBose retired from active teaching in 1908 and spent his retirement years writing his last book, *The Reason of Life*, which was published in 1911. His work attempted to interpret the Christian position in modern terms, and while it can be said that he dominated the theological life of the university, his work was not as well received through the denomination. In spite of the recognition of his intellectual prowess, he found more appreciation in Great Britain than in America.

Sources:

Dictionary of American Biography. 20 vols. and 7 supps. New York: Charles Scribner's Sons, 1928-1936, 1944-1981.

DuBose, William Porcher. *The Ecumenical Councils*. New York: Christian Literature Company, 1896. 350 pp.

_____. *The Gospel According to St. Paul*. New York: Longmans, Green and Co., 1907. 303 pp.

_____. *The Gospel in the Gospels*. New York: Longmans, Green and Co., 1906 289 pp.

_____. *High Priesthood and Sacrifice*. New York: Longmans, Green and Co., 1908. 248 pp.

_____. *The Reason of Life*. New York: Longmans, Green and Co., 1911. 274 pp.

_____. *The Soteriology of the New Testament*. New York: Macmillan Company, 1892. 391 pp.

_____. *William Porcher DuBose: Selected Writings*. Ed. by Jon Alexander. Mahwah, NJ: Paulist Press, 1988. 336 pp.

Hill, Samuel S., ed. *Encyclopedia of Religion in the South*. Macon, GA: Mercer University Press, 1984. 878 pp.

★ 280 ★
DUCE, Ivy Oneita
Leader, Sufism Reoriented
b. Feb. 25, 1895, Jersey City, New Jersey

Murshida Ivy Oneita Duce is the leader of Sufism Reoriented, a Sufi Order which accepts **Meher Baba** as the Qutb, the hub of the Sufi universe. An unusually strong-willed individual, she was trained as a lawyer at a time when few women went into such "male" professions. She was also an operatic singer for a short period of time. She attended an Episcopalian Sunday school, and belonged to the Episcopal Church for 40 years. During World War I she served as a Red Cross secretary in France, an experience that caused her to question the traditional assertion that "God is Love." After the war she worked as a bank secretary and met James Terry Duce, a geologist with Texaco, while she was traveling in South America on bank business. Three years later, when she was working for *Century Magazine*, they were married. They had one daughter, Charmian.

In 1940 the Duces met an astrologer, and the subsequent accuracy of her predictions was important in prompting Ivy Duce to study metaphysical religion. It was through an astrology class that she met Murshida Rabia Martin. Martin was the woman whom **Hazrat Inayat Khan**, the founder of the Sufi Order in the West, had appointed as his successor (an appointment that had not been recognized by European members of the order). Martin had heard about Meher Baba, an Indian spiritual teacher. She began to correspond with him and came to accept him as the Qutb. In 1947, the year of Martin's death, the Murshida appointed Duce as her successor. When Terry Duce had to travel to the Near East on a business trip in 1948, his wife and daughter took the opportunity to visit Meher Baba. During this visit, Ivy and Charmian both came to accept him as a true spiritual master. While Ivy Duce would have preferred simply to have become his disciple, Meher Baba confirmed her status as Murshida and directed her to carry on the Sufi work. This directive placed her in a somewhat awkward position. While other Sufi groups did not particularly care for Duce's interest in Meher Baba as the new *avatar* (the ancient One who has come age after age in forms such as Krishna, Buddha, Jesus, and Muhammad, to renew Divine Love in the world), many followers of Meher Baba felt that a Sufi structure was superfluous to devotion to Baba. In 1952 Baba composed a new charter for the group entitled "Chartered Guidance from Meher Baba for the Reorientation of Sufism as the Highway to the Ultimate Universalized." In this document he dropped certain traditional practices and certain other aspects of Sufism. Since that time the Order has become known as Sufism Reoriented. The group is best known as a publisher of books by and about Meher Baba, including *Discourses, How a Master Works, Life at Its Best*, and others.

Sources:
All about Sufism Reoriented. Walnut Creek, CA: Sufism Reoriented, 1977. 44 pp.
Duce, Ivy Oneita. *How a Master Works.* Walnut Creek, CA: Sufism Reoriented, 1975. 768 pp.
———. *What Am I Doing Here?* San Francisco: Sufism Reoriented, 1966. 59 pp.
———. *Gurus and Psychotherapists: Spiritual versus Psychological Learning.* Lafayette, CA: Searchlight Publications, 1981. 108 pp.
———, and James Mackie. *Conversations with a Western Guru.* Lafayette, CA: Searchlight Publications, 1981. 73 pp.
Meher Baba and the Sufis. San Francisco: Sufism Reoriented, n.d. 30 pp.
Meher Baba. *Chartered Guidance from Meher Baba for the Reorientation of Sufism as the Highway to the Ultimate Universalized.* San Francisco: Sufism Reoriented, n.d. 11 pp.

★ 281 ★
DURHAM, William H.
Independent Pentecostal Minister
b. 1873, Kentucky
d. Jul. 7, 1912, Los Angeles, California

William H. Durham was the pastor of the first Pentecostal church in Chicago and the developer of the "Finished Work of Calvary" perspective on Pentecostalism. Raised in rural Kentucky, he joined the Baptist Church when he was 18, but did not have a conversion experience until 1898, at the age of 25. Two years later he had a sanctification experience, and he joined the Holiness movement, which advocated sanctification (the eradication of the inherited sinful nature by a second work of grace, subsequent to conversion). He became a minister and took a small Holiness church in Chicago.

In 1906 Durham heard about the Azusa Street Pentecostal revival in Los Angeles, where Rev. **William J. Seymour** was preaching that after sanctification one could receive the baptism of the Holy Spirit, evidenced by speaking in tongues. Although initially skeptical, Durham became convinced of the truth of that message, and in 1907 he took a leave of absence from his church to visit Los Angeles and seek the baptism, which came on March 2. He returned to Chicago preaching Pentecostalism, and the North Avenue Mission grew rapidly, adding ten satellite missions. In 1908 Durham began the periodical *Pentecostal Testimony.*

Durham was, however, struggling with Pentecostal/Holiness theology. He decided that salvation and sanctification were both accomplished by Christ on the cross and were available to everyone through faith; therefore no need existed for a second work of grace. Durham returned to Los Angeles in 1911 to test his ideas. He was rejected by the Upper Room Mission of mostly white Pentecostalists, but accepted by the mostly black Azusa Street Mission, whose pulpit he assumed while Seymour was out of town. When Seymour heard of Durham's innovations, he returned and locked him out of the church. Durham, however, had gained enough followers by that time to open his own successful mission in Los Angeles.

In February of 1912 Durham went to Chicago to bolster his original work back there, but caught a cold and died of resulting complications at the age of 39. His "Finished Work" message constituted the first major theological break in Pentecostalism and was eventually accepted by a wide range of Pentecostalists, including, in 1914, the General Council of the Assemblies of God.

Sources:
Bartleman, Frank. *Another Wave Rolls In!.* Northridge, CA: Voice Publications, 1962. 128 pp.
Blumhofer, Edith. "The Finished Work of Calvary." *Assemblies of God Heritage* 3 (Fall 1983): 9-11.

Melton, J. Gordon. *Biographical Dictionary of American Cult and Sect Leaders.* Garland Reference Library of Social Science, vol. 212. New York: Garland Publishing, 1986.

—Gary L. Ward

★ 282 ★
EASWARAN, Eknath
Founder, Blue Mountain Center of Meditation
b. Kerala India

Eknath Easwaran is a teacher of meditation and founder of the Blue Mountain Center of Meditation. He was born into an ancient, aristocratic family in Kerala, South India, that maintained a highly orthodox tradition. A large section of Kerala's population is matrilineal, and Easwaran's family name, Eknath, came to him through his mother's side. His given name, Easwaran, refers to God ("He who rules from within"), and was a gift from his grandmother. He considers her to have been his spiritual teacher and the biggest influence on his life.

At the age of 16 Easwaran went to study at a small Catholic college 50 miles away from his village. Easwaran's major interest was English literature, and he became an English instructor after earning advanced degrees in English and law. He also published fiction and eventually became chairperson of the English department of an Indian university. It was during these years that he began having deep spiritual experiences in his meditations, and at one point he was meditating up to four hours a day.

Easwaran first came to the United States on a Fulbright fellowship in 1959. In Berkeley, he began giving talks on the Upanishads (Hindu scriptures) and teaching meditation. In 1961 he and his American wife, Christine Easwaran, founded the Blue Mountain Center of Meditation. The terms of his fellowship, however, required that he return to India. In December of 1965 he returned to Berkeley, and was soon offering regular talks at his home and, eventually, on the University of California campus. He would not advertise or charge money for his talks. Within a few years, the Blue Mountain Center of Meditation became a thriving center for people desiring to build their lives around meditation practice. In 1970 he and his wife moved to rural property in Marin County that had in the past been a dairy ranch and a small Catholic seminary. It was there that he first established his spiritual center. In 1986 he began to offer overnight meditation retreats at the Santa Sabina Center run by Dominican sisters.

Easwaran considers himself to be what he calls a "practical idealist." This means, among other things, that genuine mystical experiences should change the way one lives and the way one sees the world. He has authored over a dozen books, including *Gandhi the Man* (1972); *The Mantram Handbook: Formulas for Transformation* (1977); *Meditation* (1978); and *Dialogue with Death* (1981). The Blue Mountain Center of Meditation also publishes a quarterly, *The Little Lamp*, in which Easwaran writes articles.

Sources:
Easwaran, Eknath. *The Bhagavad Gita for Daily Living.* 2 vols. Vol. I. Berkeley, CA: Blue Mountain Center for Meditation, 1975. 433 pp. Vol. II. Petaluma, CA: Nigiri Press, 1979. 455 pp.
———. *Dialogue with Death.* Petaluma, CA: Nigiri Press, 1981. 276 pp.
———. *The Mantram Handbook: Formulas for Transformation.* Petaluma, CA: Nigiri Press, 1977. 260 pp. Reprinted as *Formulas for Transformation.* Petaluma CA: Nigiri Press, 1985. 260 pp.
———. *Meditation.* Petaluma, CA: Nigiri Press, 1978. 237 pp.
Flinders, Tim, and Carol Flinders. "Eknath Easwaran Climbs High in Meditation Mountains." *Hinduism Today* 12, 3 (March 1990): 1, 7.
———. *The Making of a Teacher: Conversations with Eknath Easwaran.* Petaluma, CA: Nigiri Press, 1989. 191 pp.

—James R. Lewis

★ 283 ★
EBY, Solomon
Founder, Mennonite Brethren in Christ Church
b. May 15, 1834, Waterloo County, Ontario, Canada
d. 1931

Solomon Eby, the founder of the Mennonite Brethren in Christ Church (now an integral part of the Missionary Church), was the son of Benjamin and Elizabeth Cressman Eby. He was born and raised on a farm in rural Ontario. In 1855 he married Catherine Shantz and soon afterwards settled in Port Elgin, Ontario, and affiliated with the local Mennonite congregation. In 1858 he was chosen by lot as a minister and was ordained to that office in the Mennonite Church. Eby took his task seriously and began to exhort his fellow Mennonites to a new level of commitment. Under his leadership a church building was erected, and services were held every Sunday rather than the current norm of biweekly gatherings. More importantly, Eby, in part under the influence of preaching by the Evangelical Association (German-speaking Methodists), began to question his own religious experience. This led him to a religious crisis and a conversion experience in 1869. He soon adopted an evangelical Wesleyan holiness theological stance.

In the enthusiasm of his newfound faith, Eby began to travel and share the experience. He also began to insist that such a conversion experience was necessary for salvation. His preaching, including his advocacy of an emphasis on holiness, brought him into conflict with more traditional church leaders, and in 1874 he was expelled from the Mennonite Church. In the meantime he had met and become friends with Daniel Brenneman, an American Mennonite who had had a similar conversion experience and had also been expelled. The two organized the Reformed Mennonites with initial support in Indiana and Ontario.

Once organized, Eby and Brenneman learned of other, similar groups with a Mennonite background that had been influenced by Methodist preaching. In the Niagara area a small group called the New Mennonites had emerged. Eby led the merger of the two groups into the United Mennonites. In 1879 a group calling itself the Evangelical Mennonites joined with the United Mennonites to form the United Evangelical Mennonites. In 1883 a group of River Brethren from Pennsylvania, the Brethren in Christ, merged with the United Mennonite Church to form the Mennonite Brethren in Christ.

During the next 23 years Eby was a leader among the Mennonite Brethren in Christ. He chaired the first general conference in 1885 and attended the next five. He served most years as a presiding elder in the Ontario Conference. He held pastorates in Breslau, Elmwood, New Dundee, Markham, and Kitchner, Ontario. In 1906, at the age of 72, he retired from active ministry.

Though he retired from leadership, the Eby story did not end. In 1912 he encountered Pentecostalism, with its emphasis upon speaking in tongues. Converted to this new perspective, he resigned from the church he founded and for the remaining 29 years of his life was a Pentecostal. The church he founded later changed its name to the United Missionary Church.

Sources:
Lageer, Eileen. *Merging Streams*. Elkhart, IN: Bethel Publishing Company, 1979. 374 pp.
The Mennonite Encyclopedia. 4 vols. Scottdale, PA: The Mennonite Publishing House, 1955.

★ 284 ★
EDDY, Mary Baker Glover
Founder, Church of Christ, Scientist
b. Jul. 16, 1821, Bow, New Hampshire
d. Dec. 3, 1910, Brookline, Massachusetts

Mary Baker Glover Eddy established the Church of Christ, Scientist, the first and most successful of the institutionally organized "metaphysical" religious groups. Eddy was raised in New Hampshire by pious Congregationalist parents. She had chronic health problems and often took refuge in writing poetry. In 1843, at the age of 22, she married George W. Glover, by whom she had one child; Glover died prematurely in 1844. In the next several years she was forced to cope with single parenthood, a fiance who also died prematurely, and the death of her mother in 1849.

In 1853 Mary married Daniel Patterson, and her life improved briefly. He was away much of the time, however, and she had continuing problems with her health. Patterson served with the Union Army in the Civil War, but eventually returned safely. While he was gone, Eddy entered a water-cure sanitorium, where she heard about Phineas Parkhurst Quimby, a mental healer in Maine. She went to visit him in 1862, received great relief, and stayed to become his devoted student. Over time, she realized she had some differences with him, and occasionally her symptoms would return. On February 1, 1866, two weeks after Quimby's death, she fell on some ice and for three days was practically immobile. Then, according to her account, while reading the Bible the healing truth came to her, and she was healed immediately. From that point she claimed to have left Quimby's approach and developed her own.

In 1867 Mary healed her niece, Ellen Pilsbury, and began writing *The Science of Man*, which she used as a textbook with her students, beginning in 1870. In 1872 she began writing *Science and Health*. She finished it in 1875, during which time she also was granted a divorce from her husband. In 1876 she organized her students into the Christian Science Association, married Asa Gilbert Eddy in 1877, and in 1879 formed the Church of Christ, Scientist. The organization picked up speed with the chartering of the Massachusetts Metaphysical College in 1881 and the beginning of the *Journal of Christian Science* in 1883. In 1889 Eddy rethought the organizational structure and dissolved the Christian Science Association, the college, and the church. In 1892 the reorganization was completed, and the association met for the last time in 1893 at the World's Parliament of Religions at the World's Fair in Chicago.

In the 1890s Julius and Annetta Dresser sued Eddy for presenting Quimby's teachings as her own. The suit was settled in her favor, although some key pieces of information, such as the Quimby manuscripts, were not available for consultation. The controversy has continued to this day. Certainly Eddy shared some ideas with Quimby. She differed with him in some key areas, however, such as specific healing techniques. Moreover, she did not share Quimby's hostility toward the Bible and Christianity. When she died in 1910, at the age of 89, she left behind a church that had achieved an international scope. It also spawned numerous other groups to populate this new metaphysical, or "New Thought," part of the American religious landscape.

Sources:
Beasley, Norman. *The Cross and the Crown*. Boston: Little, Brown and Co., 1952. 664 pp.
Braden, Charles S. *Christian Science Today*. Dallas, TX: Southern Methodist University Press, 1958.
Dictionary of American Biography. 20 vols. and 7 supps. New York: Charles Scribner's Sons, 1928-1936, 1944-1981.
Eddy, Mary Baker. *Church Manual*. Boston: Christian Science Board of Directors, 1895. 138 pp.
_____. *Poetical Works*. Boston, MA: Trustees Under the Will of Mary Baker Eddy, 1936. 79 pp.

_____. *Prose Works*. Boston: Trustees under the Will of Mary Baker G. Eddy, 1925. 366 pp.

_____. *Science and Health with Key to the Scriptures*. Boston: Trustees under the Will of Mary Baker G. Eddy, 1906. 700 pp.

Gottschalk, Stephen. *The Emergence of Christian Science in American Religious Life*. Berkeley, CA: University of California Press, 1973. 305 pp.

James, Edward T., ed. *Notable American Women, 1607-1950: A Biographical Dictionary*. 3 vols. Cambridge, MA: Harvard University Press, Belknap Press, 1971.

Melton, J. Gordon. *Biographical Dictionary of American Cult and Sect Leaders*. Garland Reference Library of Social Science, vol. 212. New York: Garland Publishing, 1986.

Peel, Robert. *Mary Baker Eddy: The Years of Authority*. New York: Holt Rinehart and Winston, 1977. 528 pp.

_____. *Mary Baker Eddy: The Years of Discovery*. New York: Holt, Rinehart and Winston, 1966. 372 pp.

_____. *Mary Baker Eddy: The Years of Trial*. New York: Holt, Rinehart and Winston, 1971. 391 pp.

Shepard, Leslie. *Encyclopedia of Occultism & Parapsychology*. 3 vols., 2nd. ed. Detroit: Gale Research Co., 1984-1985.

Studdert Kennedy, Hugh A. *Mrs. Eddy*. San Francisco: Farallon Press, 1947. 507 pp.

Who Was Who in America. Chicago: Marquis Who's Who, Inc.

Wilbur, Sibyl. *The Life of Mary Baker Eddy*. Boston, MA: Christian Science Publishing Society, 1913. 423 pp.

—*Gary L. Ward*

★285★
EDGERTON, James Arthur

President, International New Thought Alliance
b. Jan. 30, 1869, Plantsville, Ohio
d. Dec. 3, 1938, Alexandria, Virginia

James Arthur Edgerton, the first president of the New Thought Alliance (INTA); International, was the son of Tamar Vernon and Richard Edgerton. He attended Lebanon Normal College (B.A., 1887) and Marietta College (M.A., 1895). In 1895 he married Blanche Edgerton, a second cousin. An interest in politics led to his becoming chairman of the Populist State Committee in Nebraska in 1895 and secretary of the Populist National Committee in 1896. He retained this latter post until 1904. In 1897 he was nominated for clerk of the House of Representatives. Occupationally, he worked as a newspaper reporter on several small newspapers, but in 1899 moved to Colorado and took a position with the *Denver Post*. In 1904 he moved to New York and took a post with the *New York American* for a year before joining the staff of the American Press Association in 1907.

During Edgerton's years in Denver, it was pointed out to him that his editorials sounded like what was being called "New Thought" metaphysics. Upon reading some New Thought literature he became a vocal advocate of the movement and authored two important early New Thought texts: *Glimpses of the Real* (1904) and *In the Gardens of God* (1904). He also joined with Eugene Del Mar in founding the Church of the Living Christ, a New Thought center in Denver. After his move to New York, he was asked to speak at the 1906 convention of the International Metaphysical alliance, which had begun among New Thought organizations in the northeast United States. In 1909 he was elected vice-president of the alliance and in 1910 became its president.

In 1913 he left the American Press Association and became a purchasing agent for the United States Post Office. In 1914 the National New Thought Alliance held its first meeting in London and began a transformation into the International New Thought Alliance, with Edgerton continuing in his role as president, a position to which he was elected annually through 1923 (when he resigned). In 1916 he was among several New Thought leaders to submit proposed texts for what would become the organization's "Declaration." His text was accepted in 1917 and, as amended in 1918, was used by the alliance for many years.

Edgerton had become interested in the prohibition movement and in 1920 became the federal prohibition director for New Jersey. The height of his involvement in prohibitionist politics came in 1928 when he ran as the national vice-presidential candidate on the Prohibitionist Party ticket. Following his unsuccessful campaign he again became active in New Thought circles. He authored two more books, *The Philosophy of Jesus* (1928) and *Invading the Invisible* (1930). In 1934 he was again elected president of the International New Thought Alliance, a position he retained until his death in 1938.

Sources:

Braden, Charles S. *Spirits in Rebellion*. Dallas, TX: Southern Methodist University Press, 1963. 571 pp.

Edgerton, James. *Glimpses of the Real*. Denver, CO: Reed Publishing Co., 1903. 202 pp.

_____. *In the Gardens of God*. New York: The Essene, 1904. 30 pp.

_____. *Invading the Invisible*. Washington, DC: New Age Press, 1931. 361 pp.

_____. *The Philosophy of Jesus: The Basis of a New Reformation*. Boston: Christopher Publishing House, 1928.

★286★
EGLY, Henry

Founder, Defenseless Mennonite Church of North America
b. 1824, Baden Germany
d. Jun. 23, 1890, Geneva, Indiana

Henry Egly, the founder of the Defenseless Mennonite Church of North America, was the son of Abraham and Magdalena Reber Egly. As a teenager, in 1839, Egly left Germany accompanied by his father; he settled in Butler County, Ohio. He joined the local Amish Mennonite congregation and at the age of 17 was baptized. In 1849 he married Katherine Goldsmith, the daughter of the Amish bishop in Lee County, Iowa. In 1850 he was ordained a deacon. In 1851 he moved to Adams County, Indiana, where he lived for the remainder of his life.

In 1854 Egly was ordained as a minister. His ordination had been preceded by a lengthy illness during which he had undergone a life-changing spiritual experience to which he attributed his recovery. As a minister he began to stress the necessity of a conversion experience and the need of the church to be more careful of allowing the unregenerate into membership. A series of conversations with church members on living "closer to the Lord" resulted in Egly developing even more extreme views of unregenerate church members. In 1858 three Amish were sent to investigate him, but they concluded their examination by laying their hands on him and consecrating him as an elder (bishop) for his church. He continued to preach the necessity of an experience of grace and of a regenerate membership. While winning many to his position, he alienated others.

The issues raised by Egly came to a focus in his opinion that a person baptized without a prior repentance of sin had in fact never been baptized. He offered to rebaptize any (especially those baptized originally as a youth) who had experienced a subsequent regeneration experience. Because of the difference of opinion on this matter, the congregation found it difficult to hold communion services (generally held twice annually). In the fall of 1865, Egly held a separate communion service for those who followed his teachings. In 1866 he resigned, and with his supporters he founded an independent congregation.

In succeeding years Egly's ideas spread among the Amish, and small groups of followers began to emerge in Amish communities in America and Canada. He continued the major distinctive practices associated with the Amish, and practiced a strict discipline in matters of dress. He was a pioneer in use of church buildings rather than homes for Sunday worship. He organized these groups into congregations and formed the Defenseless Mennonite Church of

North America as a separate Amish denomination. Egly made his living as a farmer. The spread of his church coincided with the maturing of his many children, who were able to take over the farm chores, thus allowing him to travel widely as an evangelist. He died at his home of typhoid fever.

Sources:

Egly, Henry. *Autobiography.* Trans. by Emma Steury. Berne, IN: Evangelical Mennonite Church of Berne, Indiana, 1975.

The Mennonite Encyclopedia. 4 vols. Scottdale, PA: The Mennonite Publishing House, 1955.

★ 287 ★
EIKERENKOETTER II, Frederick J.
Founder, United Church and Science of Living Institute
b. Jun. 1, 1935, Ridgeland, South Carolina

Frederick J. Eikerenkoetter II, the flamboyant minister better known as Reverend Ike, is the son of a fundamentalist Baptist minister. It was his early intention to follow in his father's footsteps, and at the age of 14 he became the assistant pastor for his father's congregation, the Bible Way Church in Ridgeland, South Carolina. After completing high school, he attended the American Bible College in Chicago, from which he received a B.Th. degree in 1956. He spent two years in the Air Force chaplain's corps, after which he returned to South Carolina to found the United Church of Jesus Christ for All People. In 1964 he moved to Boston, Massachusetts, and opened the Miracle Temple. In 1966 he moved to New York City. In 1969 he purchased an abandoned theatre that became the headquarters for the United Church and Science of Living Institute and the United Christian Evangelistic Association.

During the 1960s Eikerenkoetter began to deviate from his Baptist teachings, especially with regard to its emphasis upon otherworldly rewards. In looking for a way to assist parishioners in the present, he came under the influence of New Thought, and absorbed both its emphasis on mental healing and especially its teachings on prosperity consciousness. During his early years in New York he developed his own version of New Thought, which he termed the Science of Living. He quickly emerged (along with **Johnnie Coleman** in Chicago) as one of the first New Thought leaders in the black community. The institute awarded him Ph.D. (1969) and D.Sci. (1971) degrees.

Among Eikerenkoetter's first actions to assist church members to experience the possibilities of living prosperously was the "Blessing Plan," a simplified version of previous prosperity programs which emphasized believing in one's own bountiful conditions, giving of one's worldly goods, and manifesting prosperity. Reverend Ike became known for his blunt acceptance of the goodness and power of money and his advocacy of a reorganized self-image as the essential precondition for becoming wealthy.

Eikerenkoetter began a radio ministry and within a few years was on over 80 stations nationwide. In this way he quickly gained a national following which included many Whites. He began a magazine, *Action!*, which reached an audience of over one million by the mid-1970s. He spoke to overflowing crowds as he toured the country. His message of the individual's responsibility to strive for success tended to alienate him from both his fellow ministers, who saw him deviating from Christianity, and the black civil rights leadership, as he saw the hope of the black community in their individually changing their consciousness rather than in social reform.

In the context of the 1970s, Reverend Ike was a controversial phenomenon and the object of significant media attention. In the 1980s, while continuing his popular ministry in the higher profile of New Thought, he was seen more as part of the religious landscape. He has brought his ministry within the fellowship of the International New Thought Alliance (INTA), for which he is a popular speaker.

Sources:

Dupree, Sherry Sherrod. *Biographical Dictionary of African-American, Holiness-Pentecostals, 1880-1990.* Washington, DC: Middle Atlantic Regional Press, 1990. 386 pp.

Eikerenkoetter, Frederick. *Reverend Ike's Secrets for Health, Happiness and Prosperity-For You.* New York: Reverend Ike Prayer Tower, n.d. 280 pp.

Martin, William C. "This Man Says He's the Divine Sweetheart of the Universe." *Esquire* (June 1974): 76-78, 140-143.

Morris, James. *The Preachers.* New York: St. Martin's Press, 1973. 418 pp.

★ 288 ★
ERRETT, Isaac
Editor, Christian Churches and Churches of Christ
b. Feb. 2, 1820, New York, New York
d. Dec. 19, 1888, Cincinnati, Ohio

Isaac Errett, founder of the *Christian Standard*, one of the most influential periodicals of what is today termed the Christian Churches and Churches of Christ, was born in New York City into a Scotch Presbyterian family. His father, Henry Errett, died when Isaac was five years old. His mother, Sophia Kemmish Errett, subsequently opened a boarding house. When she remarried, the family moved to a farm in New Jersey. In 1832 Errett's stepfather opened a lumber mill in Pittsburgh and the family moved again. Young Errett, while very religious, developed a dislike of what he considered the stern legalistic faith of Presbyterianism. In 1833 he was baptized into the Christian Church.

Errett apprenticed himself to a printer for several years and in 1839 began to teach school. About the same time he began to speak periodically to the congregation. He was "set apart," or designated, as an evangelist in 1840. Shortly afterward, a new Christian Church congregation was opened in Pittsburgh, and Errett resigned his teaching post to become its preacher. The following year, he married Harriet Reeder.

After four years with the Pittsburgh congregation, Errett moved to New Lisbon, Ohio. In 1849 he moved to North Bloomfield, Ohio, and in 1856 he relocated to Lyon, Michigan. During the 1850s he became more widely involved with the larger Christian Church community. He conducted evangelistic meetings and a few debates. He also became a supporter of the American Christian Missionary Society, an organization to raise funds to support foreign missionaries, whose very existence was a matter of great contention in the fellowship. He served as corresponding secretary of the society from 1857 to 1860. In 1861 he became coeditor of the *Millennial Harbinger*, the movement's original periodical, founded by Alexander Campbell. He also became an agent for securing funds for Bethany College, the fellowship's major school. During the Civil War, Errett emerged as a staunch partisan whose patriotic speeches often ran counter to the dominant pacifist sentiment in the church.

In 1862, he took the pastorate of a new congregation in Detroit. Shortly after his move, he authored and had published a brief document called "A Synopsis of The Faith and Practice of The Church of Christ," consisting of 10 statements of belief and a set of bylaws. The document created an immediate controversy among the noncreedal leaders of the Christian Churches, who saw it as a creed.

As the Civil War came to a close, there were two prominent periodicals serving the Christian Churches, the *Gospel Advocate* issued from Nashville, Tennessee, and the *American Christian Review*. Both had opposed the war and been cold to the idea of missionary societies. Thus, as the war moved to a close, Errett decided to publish a new periodical representing the more "liberal" element in the church. The first issue of the *Christian Standard* appeared April 1, 1866. Errett moved to Cleveland as the editor. After an initial period of financial instability, the magazine proved a success and became the dominant voice among Christian churches in the North. It championed the cause of the churches' missionary society, but opposed the introduction of instrumental (organ) music into the meeting houses. Errett also advocated the development of a settled salaried ministry. Before the war, he had been one of the first ministers to serve a church large enough to fully support him.

Errett edited the magazine for the next 20 years. He is considered one of the major forces in the creation of what is today known as the Disciples of Christ (Christian Church). In the mid-1880s his health began to fail. He took an extended tour of Europe, North Africa, and the Holyland in 1887 in hopes of recouping, but it did little to help; six months after his return he passed away. The magazine, however, continued, and around it Errett's successors built a large independent publishing house that issued books and church school material for Christian churches. The publishing house opposed the schism of 1906, which separated most of the Southerners into the Churches of Christ. In recent decades it has been identified with the more independent and loosely organized faction which separated from the Disciples of Christ (Christian Church) and whose members refer to themselves as the Christian Churches and Churches of Christ.

Sources:

McAllister, Lester G., and William E. Tucker. *Journey in Faith*. St. Louis, MO: The Bethany Press, 1975. 506 pp.
Memoirs of Isaac Errett. 2 vols. Cincinnati, OH: Christian Standard Publishing Co., 1893.

★289★
EVANS, Warren Felt
Independent New Thought Writer
b. Dec. 23, 1817, Rockingham, Vermont
d. Sep. 4, 1889, Salisbury, Massachusetts

Warren Felt Evans was an influential New Thought author. Raised in a farming family, he left college in his junior year to become a Methodist minister and marry Charlotte Tinker (1840). He served 11 charges between 1844 and 1864, but during that time began reading Emanuel Swedenborg. He was eventually converted and joined the Church of the New Jerusalem in 1863. Bothered at the time by chronic ill health, Evans learned of Phineas Parkhurst Quimby, the mental healer in Maine, and went to investigate. Evans was not only healed, but converted anew to Quimby's ideas. He moved to Claremont, New Hampshire, and established his own healing practice.

Evans, like Quimby, never attempted to organize a group of followers. Unlike Quimby, however, Evans wrote books for publication. *The Mental Cure*, which came out in 1869, holds the honor of being the first book in America on New Thought. (The first edition of **Mary Baker Eddy**'s *Science and Health* did not appear until 1875.) Evans was a prolific writer, and has at least seven books to his name, including his most popular work, *Primitive Mind Cure* (1885). His ideas stemmed from the theories of both Quimby and Swedenborg. He agreed with Quimby that disease is a work of the mind. He also concurred with Swedenborg, who argued that the material and spiritual worlds have a relationship of correspondence (as in one, so in the other). Unlike Quimby, however, Evans emphasized diagnosis of the disease, and often approached diagnosis through what we might today call psychosomatic medicine.

Evans felt that mind cure was the recovery of primitive Christianity, which had been lost over the centuries. He called his approach "Christian pantheism," meaning that creation is constantly being drawn from an omnipresent God, who is both lovingly personal and an impersonal principle, sometimes called the Christ or Logos. Evans' many writings were instrumental in spreading New Thought ideas among the general public, both before and far after his death in 1889 at the age of 72.

Sources:

Beebe, Tom. *Who's Who in New Thought*. Lakemont, GA: CSA Press, 1977. 318 pp.
Bowden, Henry Warner. *Dictionary of American Religious Biography*. Westport, CT: Greenwood Press, 1977. 572 pp.
Braden, Charles S. *Spirits in Rebellion*. Dallas, TX: Southern Methodist University Press, 1963. 571 pp.
Dictionary of American Biography. 20 vols. and 7 supps. New York: Charles Scribner's Sons, 1928-1936, 1944-1981.
Evans, Warren Felt. *The Divine Law of Cure*. Boston: H. H. Carter & Co., 1884. 302 pp.
_____. *Esoteric Christianity and Mental Therapeutics*. Boston: H. H. Carter & Karrick, 1886. 174 pp.
_____. *The Mental Cure*. Glasgow: James M'Geachy, 1870. 301 pp.
_____. *Mental Medicine*. Boston, MA: H. H. Carter & Karrick, 1872. 216 pp.
_____. *Primitive Mind Cure*. Boston: H. H. Carter & Karrick, 1885. 215 pp.
_____. *Soul and Body*. Boston: H. H. Carter & Co., 1876. 147 pp.
Judah, J. Stillson. *History and Philosophy of the Metaphysical Press*, 1967. 317 pp.
Melton, J. Gordon. *Biographical Dictionary of American Cult and Sect Leaders*. Garland Reference Library of Social Science, vol. 212. New York: Garland Publishing, 1986.

—*Gary L. Ward*

★290★
Archbishop EVDOKIM
Archbishop, Russian Orthodox Church
b. Apr. 1, 1869, Vladimir Russia
d. 1935, Moscow Union of Soviet Socialist Republics

Archbishop Evdokim, the second archbishop of the Russian Orthodox Church in North America, was born Basil Mikhailovich Mischersky, the son of a lay reader in the Russian church. He attended the Moscow Theological Academy, from which he graduated in 1894. That same year he was tonsured as a monk and ordained as a deacon and priest. He was appointed inspector at the seminary at Novgorod, but decided also to continue his own studies at the academy. He soon earned a master's degree in theology. He was named an archimandrite in 1898, and in 1903 he was named director of Novgorod seminary and soon afterward dean of the Moscow academy. In December 1904 he was consecrated as a vicar bishop for the diocese of Moscow.

Evdokim found intellectual stimulus in what has been termed the Russian religious renaissance, a movement that sought revival of the church as it interacted meaningfully with secular culture. In 1906 he began to publish a journal, *The Christian*, which aimed at the Christianization of society.

In 1909 Evdokim became bishop of Kashir and held that position until 1914, when he was called to replace Metropolitan Platon as the head of the Diocese of the Aleutian Islands and North America. He settled in America in 1915. During his brief stay in America, he tried to carry out the policies of his predecessors, establishing an overall goal of building ethnic Orthodox communities (from Lebanese to Greeks) that could find their common union in the single Russian Orthodox Church.

Evdokim returned to Russia in the midst of revolution after less than three years in America. In 1919 he became Archbishop of Nizhegorod, and a few years later associated himself with the "Living Church" faction of the Russian church, that faction most aligned to the new Soviet government. He became the Living Church's Metropolitan of Odessa.

Sources:

Tarasar, Constance J. *Orthodox America 1897-1974*. Syosset, NY: Department of History and Archives, Orthodox Church in America, 1975. 361 pp.

★ 291 ★
EWART, Frank J.
Minister and Evangelist, United Pentecostal Church
b. 1876, Bendigo Australia
d. 1947, California

Frank J. Ewart, one of the first Pentecostal leaders to accept and preach the non-Trinitarian Oneness doctrine of God, was raised in rural Australia. Shortly after his graduation from high school, he had a vision of Jesus on the cross and became a Baptist missionary in the bush country. In 1903, his health failed, and he migrated to Canada in hopes that a change of climate would help him. He applied for and received an assignment as pastor to a small Baptist church. His health improved slowly and he soon met and married a young woman.

In 1907 Ewart traveled to Portland, Oregon, to attend a camp meeting, one of the first Pentecostal camp meetings in the Northwest. While there he was not only healed of the need to wear glasses, but received the baptism of the Holy Spirit (the definitive religious experience of Pentecostals signified by the believer speaking in tongues). His preaching the new truth led to a break with the Baptists. In 1911 he moved to Los Angeles where he became the pastor of the church which had been founded by **William H. Durham**, another pioneer Pentecostal minister.

In 1913 Ewart was present at a camp meeting in which Canadian minister **R. E. McAlister** preached a famous sermon on baptism in the name of Jesus. Basing his message on Acts 2:38, McAleister argued for baptism simply in the name of Jesus rather than in the traditional Trinitarian formula of Father, Son, and Holy Ghost. This practice had direct implications for the understanding of the Godhead. Ewart came to believe that God's name was, in fact, Jesus, and hence Jesus was the Father, the Son, and the Holy Spirit, not just to be identified, as tradition dictated, as the Son. As a result of his acceptance of the new perspective, he left Durham's church and began evangelistic meetings on Main Street in Los Angeles in cooperation with McAleister and Glenn A. Cook.

The meetings in Los Angeles were eventually moved to Belvedere, California, where Ewart established a congregation which he pastored for the rest of his long life, except for a brief period in 1917-1918 when he pastored a church in Portland, Oregon. He had begun a periodical, *Meat in Due Season*, which became the popular organ for spreading the Oneness message. Ewart had associated with those ministers who formed the General Council of the Assemblies of God, though he and his church remained independent. However, in 1916, the council passed a strong Trinitarian statement which effectively disfellowshipped the believers in the Oneness message. Most of the Oneness people associated with the Pentecostal Assemblies of the World (PAW), an older organization which had accepted the Oneness message and which had standing with the government, the disfellowshipping having occurred during World War I. This proved an unhappy arrangement as the assemblies were integrated and hence could not meet in the South. Through a series of schisms and mergers, the majority of white members left and eventually came together in 1945 as the United Pentecostal Church. Ewart received credentials from the new body shortly before his death. Among his last accomplishments was a biographical history of the emergence of the Oneness movement, *The Phenomenon of Pentecost* (1947).

Sources:

Burgess, Stanley M., Gary B. McGee, and Patrick H. Alexander, eds. *Dictionary of Pentecostal and Charismatic Movements*. Grand Rapids, MI: Regency Reference Library, Zondervan Publishing House, 1988. 914 pp.
Ewart, Frank J. *Jesus, the Man and Mystery*. Nashville, TN: Baird-Ward Press, 1941. 165 pp.
————. *The Name and the Book*. Chicago: Ryerson, 1936. 174 pp.
————. *The Phenomenon of Pentecost*. Houston, TX: Herald Publishing House, 1947. 207 pp.

Fisher, Fred J. *Think It Not Strange*. St. Louis, MO: Pentecostal Publishing House, 1965. 109 pp.

★ 292 ★
FALWELL, Jerry
Minister and Founder, Liberty Baptist Fellowship
b. Aug. 11, 1933, Lynchburg, Virginia

Jerry Falwell, popular television preacher and founder of the Liberty Baptist Fellowship, is the son of Helen and Carey H. Falwell. He grew up in Lynchburg, Virginia, and in 1950 entered Lynchburg College. His mother's faith had not been passed on and it was not until 1952, as a result of listening to a broadcast of **Charles Fuller**'s Old Fashioned Gospel Hour that he was led to a born again experience. He began to attend the Park Avenue Baptist Church and decided to enter the ministry. In 1953 he entered the Baptist Bible College, the school of the Baptist Bible Fellowship in Springfield, Missouri. He attended a year, returned to Lynchburg for a year, and finished his second year in 1955-1956.

In 1956 Falwell settled in Lynchburg where he was asked by a dissenting group from the Park Avenue Church to become their pastor. He agreed and began to build the Thomas Road Baptist Church. The move led to his break with the Baptist Bible Fellowship, and the congregation went on its own. Following Fuller's lead, before the year was out Falwell was on the radio and on one television station. Under Falwell's leadership, the church grew steadily and established a set of auxiliary ministries beginning in 1959 with the Elim Home for Alcoholics (Falwell's father had been an alcoholic). That same year a second television station picked up the church's broadcast, which had been named the "Old-Time Gospel Hour." In 1964 a new sanctuary which seated 1,000 people was dedicated.

Through the 1970s the ministries associated with Thomas Road Church continued to expand. In 1970 a 3,200 seat sanctuary was dedicated. In 1971 a most ambitious project, Liberty University, was begun. Its success would depend upon the support of people who watched the "Old-Time Gospel Hour" which now appeared on 300 stations. Thomas Road Bible Institute was added in 1972 and the Lynchburg Baptist Theological Seminary opened in 1973. With the opening of the seminary, the church had all of the machinery necessary to educate ministers who could in turn go out from the school and found other churches on the Thomas Road pattern. The early graduates of the seminary would in the 1980s come together to form the Liberty Baptist Fellowship, a new Baptist denomination.

In the late 1970s Falwell became one of the important organizers of the Moral Majority Foundation and Moral Majority, Inc., two national organizations dedicated to reestablishing moral values in the national consciousness. Keystones of the movement's platform included opposition to the Equal Rights Amendment, the return of prayer to public schools, support for Israel, and a strong military. The movement which grew around the two organizations worked to elect Ronald Reagan president, though observers disagree on its actual contribution to his campaign.

In the late 1980s Falwell became involved in the scandal that destroyed the ministry of fellow television evangelist **Jim Bakker**. He took over Bakker's PTL Club for a while and tried to save it. In the end the problems proved insurmountable. The Bakker affair damaged all of the television-based ministries, and Falwell returned to Lynchburg to concentrate on the organizations he headed. In 1989 he announced the disbanding of the national Moral Majority movement, which he said had accomplished its task. Others noted that the movement had also suffered greatly from the Bakker scandal.

Over the years Falwell has written a number of books, among the most recent his autobiography, *Strength for the Journey* (1987).

Sources:

D'Souza, Dinesh. *Falwell Before the Millennium: A Critical Biography.* Chicago: Regnery Gateway, 1984. 205 pp.

Falwell, Jerry, ed. *How You Can Clean Up America.* Lynchburg, VA: The Author, 1981. 118 pp.

_____. *If I Should Die Before I Wake. . .* Nashville, TN: Thomas Nelson Publishers, 1986. 219 pp.

_____. *Listen America!* Garden City, NY: Doubleday & Company, 1980.

_____. *Strength for the Journey: An Autobiography of Jerry Falwell.* New York: Simon and Schuster, 1987. 456 pp.

_____, with Harold Willmington. *When It Hurts Too Much to Cry.* Wheaton, IL: Tyndale House Publishers, 1985. 123 pp.

Strober, Gerald, and Ruth Tomczak. *Jerry Falwell: Aflame for God.* Nashville, TN: Thomas Nelson Publishers, 1979. 188 pp.

★293★
FARLEY, John Murphy
Cardinal, Roman Catholic Church
b. Apr. 20, 1842, Newton Hamilton Ireland
d. Sep. 17, 1918, New York, New York

John Murphy Farley, a cardinal in the Roman Catholic Church, was born in rural Ireland in a section of land dominated by Protestants. He was orphaned at an early age. In spite of his later fame and position, little is known of his life prior to his immigration to America in 1864. He had studied at St. McCarten's College in Monaghan, Ireland. Once in America he finished his college work with a year at Fordham University and then entered the seminary at Troy, New York. After a year he was selected to attend the North American College in Rome from 1866 to 1867. Returning to America, he graduated from seminary in time to go to Rome as an observer at the First Vatican Council. He was ordained there in 1870.

Farley's pastoral career began at New Brighton on Staten Island, New York. In 1872 he became secretary to Bishop **John McCloskey**, the future cardinal. He traveled to Rome with McCloskey to receive his cardinal's hat in 1878. Farley was made a papal chamberlain with the title of monsignor in 1884 and was assigned to St. Gabriel's Church in Manhattan, which he was to serve for 17 years. He turned the parish into a model church, paying off its debts, refurbishing its building, and improving its parochial school. In 1891 he was appointed vicar-general of the archdiocese, a post that carried with it the chairmanship of the Catholic school board. He quickly distinguished himself by improving both the quality and public image of the school system.

In 1893 he was named prothonotary apostolic and shortly afterwards named Auxiliary Bishop of New York. He became Archbishop of New York in 1902. As archbishop, Farley took the lead in projecting a new image of Catholicism, which was to that point still viewed with suspicion by most Americans. He authored *The History of St. Patrick's Cathedral* (1908), now America's most famous Catholic parish, and *The Life of Cardinal McCloskey* (1918), America's first cardinal and Farley's mentor. More substantively, he initiated the production of and wrote many articles for the monumental *Catholic Encyclopedia* (1907-1922). In 1911 Farley traveled to Rome to receive his cardinal's hat (Cardinal Gibbons, America's only other cardinal at the time, was in his seventies). Two other Americans, Archbishop William O'Connell and former Apostolic Delegate Falconia, were elevated on the same day, November 29. Following the reception of the signs of his new office, he assumed control of his titular Roman parish, Santa Maria Sopra Minerva, the same one formally assigned to Cardinal McCloskey.

Back in New York, war clouds gathered as Farley saw to the appointment of **Patrick Joseph Hayes** as Auxiliary Bishop of New York. Once the United States entered World War I, he assigned Hayes to the war effort, and Hayes recruited some 1,500 priests as chaplains. Farley also created the New York Catholic War Council, which was responsible for the creation of canteens for the armed forces and the establishment of a hospital for victims of shell shock. He participated in many war bond campaigns. After putting so much into the war effort, Farley did not live to see the end of conflict, dying shortly before the armistice was signed in 1918.

Sources:

Farley, John Murphy. *The Catholic Church, the Teacher of Mankind.* 3 vols. New York: 1905.

_____. *History of St. Patrick's Cathedral.* New York: Society for the Propagation of the Faith, Archdiocese of New York, 1908. 262 pp.

_____. *The Life of John, Cardinal McCloskey.* New York: Longmans, Green & Company, 1918. 401 pp.

Hayes, Patrick Joseph. "John Cardinal Farley." *Historical Records and Studies* 6, 2 (1912): 5-68.

★294★
FARRAKHAN, Louis
Founder, Nation of Islam
b. May 11, 1933, New York, New York

Louis Farrakhan, leader of the most prominent of the several organizations known as the Nation of Islam, was born Louis Eugene Farrakhan. He grew up in the Roxbury district of Boston. He was active in the Episcopal Church and was an honor student and track star at Boston English High School. He attended Winston Salem Teachers College in North Carolina for two years before dropping out of school to begin a career as a singer/musician. He married Betsy Wolcott. In 1955, while playing an engagement in a nightclub, he was invited to hear **Elijah Muhammad**, the leader of the Nation of Islam. Subsequently, he had a dream in which he was faced with a choice between the world of show business and an unknown future. He chose the unknown.

After joining the Nation of Islam, or Black Muslims, as they are popularly known, he quickly assumed a leadership role. As was common practice, he changed his name to Louis X, the X taking the place of an unknown Muslim name. He returned to Boston and became chief of the local Fruit of Islam, the organization's male fraternity which acted as a security force, and then head of the temple. He was second only to **Malcolm X** as a spokesperson for the Nation, and after Malcolm X's defection in 1963, Louis X became the leader of the New York temple and the major voice against his former colleague.

Thought of as the best qualified successor to Elijah Muhammad, he was passed over for Wallace Deem Muhammad, the leader's son. Even as he was changing the hostile attitude of the Nation of Islam toward Whites, Muhammad transferred Louis X, now known as Louis Farrakhan, to Chicago as the movement's national ambassador. Muhammad also changed the name of the organization, first to World Community of Islam in the West and then to American Muslim Mission. Unable to accept Wallace Muhammad's changes, Farrakhan became one of several leaders who broke away and attempted to reform the Nation of Islam as it had existed before Elijah Muhammad's death.

The stabilization of the new Nation of Islam coincided with the emergence of **Jesse Louis Jackson** and Operation PUSH (People United to Save Humanity) into the national spotlight. Farrakhan, becoming a strong supporter of Jackson, was soon thrust into the spotlight as he moved around the country and made several controversial remarks. During the 1984 presidential campaign he became embroiled in Jackson's difficulties with the Jewish community. During a radio speech in March he called Hitler a "great man" and was vilified in the press as an anti-Semite. The Anti-Defamation League published a monograph attacking him. Jackson tried to distance himself from Farrakhan's remarks but refused to separate himself from the Muslim leader.

In more recent years Farrakhan has continued to travel around the United States and internationally to predominantly Muslim and black countries, building his organization and developing a program of economic and political power for Blacks. He continues to be one of the most controversial figures in American religion, and his presence is usually seen as a crisis for local black politicians who are called upon to support his programs for the improvement of the black community, some of which they find quite attractive.

Sources:

Farrakhan, Louis. *The Meaning of F.O.I.* Chicago: The Honorable Elijah Muhammad Educational Foundation, 1983. 20 pp.
———. *Warning to the Government of America.* Chicago: Hon. Elijah Muhammad Educational Foundation, 1983. 55 pp.
The Honorable Louis Farrakhan: A Minister for Progress. New York: Practice Press, 1987. 54 pp.
Page, Clarence. "Deciphering Farrakhan." *Chicago* (August 1984): 130-134.
Schwartz, Alan M. "Louis Farrakhan." *ADL Facts* 29, 1 (Spring 1984): 1-23.

★ 295 ★
FEDDE, Elizabeth
Pioneer Lutheran Deaconess
b. Dec. 25, 1850, Feda Norway
d. Feb. 25, 1921, Egersund Norway

Elizabeth Fedde, a pioneer Lutheran deaconess in America, was the daughter of Andreas Villunsen Feda and Anne Marie Olsdatter. She was brought up in the atmosphere of the pietistic Haugean movement within the Lutheran Church. At the age of 19 Fedde went to work in Stavanger in a private home. Four years later, in 1873, she entered the motherhouse of the new deaconess movement in Oslo. She disliked the black robes and bonnets, but put her personal taste aside while accepting the discipline and the training in nursing skills. After finishing her training in 1878, Fedde was sent to Tromso, in northern Norway, where she worked for four years.

In 1882 Fedde received a letter from her brother-in-law, informing her of the needs of Norwegian immigrants in New York. Most faced considerable problems adjusting to a new land where Norwegian was a foreign language. With the help of the pastor of the Norwegian Seaman's Mission, he had received support for a social worker from the Norwegian consul. Even though the deaconess leaders in Norway disowned her, Fedde immigrated to America and enlisted the initial support of the Norwegian Lutheran pastors in New York.

In April 1883, less than two weeks after her arrival, Fedde organized the Voluntary Relief Society for the Sick and Poor. Unable to gain support from the deaconesses in Norway, she began to train assistants. In 1885 she opened a small hospital in Brooklyn. The Voluntary Relief Society became the Norwegian Relief Society and in 1889 built a larger hospital. The society reincorporated in 1892 as the Norwegian Lutheran Deaconesses' Home and Hospital, and is today known as the Lutheran Medical Center.

In 1888 the work in Brooklyn was stable enough that Fedde felt able to accept an invitation to begin a deaconess home in Minneapolis. She devoted two years to that project before returning to her Brooklyn center. She stayed in New York long enough to oversee the first steps in its Americanization as it began to serve people of all religious and national backgrounds. After 13 years of work, she had organized the first effective nursing system within the Scandinavian-American community; the two hospitals she started have grown into major medical facilities.

In 1896 Fedde returned to Norway to marry Ola A. P. Slettebo, who had waited for her during her 13 years in the United States. They settled on a farm near Egersund, Norway, where she lived for many years.

Sources:

Folkedahl, Beulah. "Elizabeth Fedde's Diary, 1883-88." *Norwegian-American Studies and Records* 20 (1959).

James, Edward T., ed. *Notable American Women, 1607-1950: A Biographical Dictionary.* 3 vols. Cambridge, MA: Harvard University Press, Belknap Press, 1971.

★ 296 ★
FERRE, Nels Fredrik Solomon
Theologian, Congregational Christian Churches
b. Jun. 8, 1908, Luleaa Sweden
d. Feb. 6, 1971

Nels Fredrik Solomon Ferre, a prominent liberal Protestant theologian of the mid-twentieth century, was the son of Maria Wickman and Frans August Ferre, a Swedish clergyman. As a young man he immigrated to the United States and attended Boston University (A.B., 1931). He continued his graduate studies at Andover Newton Theological Seminary (B.D., 1934) and while there in 1932 he married Katherine Louise Pond. Following his graduation he was ordained as a minister with the Congregational Christian Churches. He then entered Harvard University, from which he received his M.A. (1936) and Ph.D. (1938).

In 1937 Ferre became an instructor at Andover Newton, where he steadily moved up the academic ladder; he was named Abbot Professor of Christian Theology in 1940. While at Andover Newton he authored the first of the many books he was to produce over his lifetime, *Swedish Contributions to Modern Theology* (1939). He followed it quickly with theological texts of his own which began to establish him as a prominent liberal spokesperson: *The Christian Fellowship* (1940); *The Christian Faith* (1942); *Return to Christianity* (1942); and *Faith and Reason* (1946).

In 1950 Ferre moved to the Divinity School at Vanderbilt University. The following year he produced his most popular book, *Strengthening the Spiritual Life*, which appeared almost simultaneously with one of his more substantive volumes, *The Christian Understanding of God*. In 1952 he was cited by John Wesley Soper as one of the *Major Voices in American Theology*. In 1957 he returned to Andover Newton where he resumed his post as abbot professor and taught until 1965. During his last years at Andover Newton, he authored *Christ and the Christian* (1958); *Know Your Faith* (1959); *Searchlights on Contemporary Theology* (1961); *The Finality of Faith* (1963); *Reason in Religion* (1963); and *A Theology of Christian Prayer* (1963). He retired in 1965 after producing over 25 books on theology and popular religious thought. He remained active, however, in teaching and writing for many more years.

In 1965 Ferre moved to Iowa as a scholar-in-residence at Parsons College. In 1968 he became Ferris Professor of Philosophy at the College of Wooster in Wooster, Massachusetts, a post he held at the time of his death. During his retirement years he finished *The Living God of Nowhere and Nothing* (1966); *A Theology of Christian Education* (1967); and *The Universal Word* (1969).

Sources:

Ferre, Nels F. S. *The Christian Understanding of God.* New York: Harper, 1951. 277 pp.
———. *The Living God of Nowhere and Nothing.* London: Epworth, 1966. 237 pp.
———. *Searchlights on Contemporary Theology.* New York: Harper, 1961. 241 pp.
———. *Strengthening the Spiritual Life.* New York: Harper, 1951. 63 pp.
———. *Swedish Contributions to Modern Theology.* New York: Harper, 1939. 250 pp.
———. *A Theology of Christian Prayer.* Nashville, TN: Tidings, 1963. 71 pp.
Soper, David Wesley. *Major Voices in American Theology.* 2 vols. Philadelphia: Westminster Press, 1953, 1955.

★297★
FETTING, Otto
Church of Christ (Fettingite)
b. Nov. 20, 1871, St. Clair, Michigan
d. Jan. 30, 1933, Port Huron, Michigan

Otto Fetting led in the creation of the Church of Christ (Fettingite), one of a number of Mormon branches using the Church of Christ title. Fetting was raised in the Reorganized Church of Jesus Christ of Latter Day Saints, becoming a priest in 1899, at the age of 28. He served in that capacity for many years, until he decided to shift his allegiance to the Church of Christ (Temple Lot) in 1925. This was a group that had broken away from the Reorganized Church in the mid-nineteenth century, and owned the land in Independence, Missouri, that **Joseph Fielding Smith, Jr.** the Mormon founder, had originally designated as the temple site. Fetting immediately became a leader in that group, and in 1926 was ordained one of their 12 apostles.

In February of 1927, Fetting received the first of many revelations from an angelic being identified as John the Baptist. This first message indicated that it was time to rebuild the temple, and was received warmly by the church. The next several messages concerned the timing of the building plans, and in accordance with one of these, ground was broken in 1929. During the excavation, the original foundation markers placed by Smith were uncovered. On July 18, 1929, the 12th message caused a great schism in the church. It was interpreted to mean that all members who had transferred from the Reorganized Church (most members) would have to be rebaptized. This "new doctrine" was rejected, and both Fetting and another apostle, Walter F. Gates, were cut off from the church.

Fetting did not retreat, but organized a new church in April 1929, and called it the Church of Christ. About one-third of the membership (1,400) of the Church of Christ (Temple Lot) followed Fetting in this new endeavor. In 1936, three years after Fetting's death, the Temple Lot Church officially rejected all of his revelations, including the first ones about the temple, which they had initially accepted. In 1937 the continuing Church of Christ (Fettingite) was split by the claim of an elder, W. A. Draves, to have received messages from the same John the Baptist visitor.

Sources:

Arbaugh, George Bartholomew. *Revelation in Mormonism.* Chicago, IL: University of Chicago Press, 1932. 252 pp.
Denominations That Base Their Beliefs on the Teachings of Joseph Smith. Salt Lake City, UT: Daughters of Utah Pioneers, 1969. 68 pp.
Fetting, Otto. *The Midnight Message.* Independence, MO: Church of Christ (Temple Lot), 1927. 36 pp.
_____. *The Word of the Lord.* Independence, MO: Church of Christ, 1975. 93 pp.
Flint, B. C. *An Outline History of the Church of Christ (Temple Lot).* Independence, MO: Board of Publication, Church of Christ (Temple Lot), 1953. 160 pp.
Melton, J. Gordon. *Biographical Dictionary of American Cult and Sect Leaders.* Garland Reference Library of Social Science, vol. 212. New York: Garland Publishing, 1986.
Rich, Russell R. *Little Known Schisms of the Restoration.* Provo, UT: Brigham Young University, 1967. 76 pp.
Smith, Willard J. *Fetting and His Messenger's Messages.* Port Huron, MI: The Author, n.d. 45 pp.

—*Gary L. Ward*

★298★
FILLMORE, Charles Sherlock
Unity School of Christianity
b. Aug. 22, 1854, St. Cloud, Minnesota
d. Jul. 5, 1948, Kansas City, Missouri

Charles Sherlock Fillmore, with his wife, **Mary Caroline "Myrtle" Fillmore**, co-founded the Unity School of Christianity, which became the largest of the New Thought metaphysical groups. Fillmore was raised in rural Minnesota by a father who was a roaming Indian trader and a mother who was an Episcopalian seamstress. He had little formal schooling but liked to read.

In the mid-1870s Fillmore moved to Denison, Texas, and became a railroad clerk. There he met schoolteacher Mary Caroline "Myrtle" Page, whom he eventually married. First, however, he lost his job at the railroad in 1879 by sticking up for a friend. He moved to Gunnison, Colorado, where he tried his hand at mining and real estate. Meanwhile, Myrtle had returned to Clinton, Missouri, where Fillmore went to marry her in 1881. He returned with her to Pueblo, Colorado, where he had set up a real estate business with the brother-in-law of **Nona Lovell Brooks**, who was later to found the Divine Science Church.

In 1884 they moved to Kansas City, Missouri, where Myrtle attended some lectures on Christian Science in 1886. The affirmations she learned cured her of tuberculosis over a period of months. Charles was more skeptical, but continued exposure to the ideas convinced him, and in 1889 he left real estate to create a magazine, *Modern Thought.* In 1890 they both attended **Emma Curtis Hopkins'** Christian Science Theological Seminary in Chicago and were ordained by her in 1891. In 1890 Myrtle formed the Society of Silent Help, a prayer group for those who could not attend classes in person. That same year they changed the name of the magazine to *Christian Science Thought,* though it soon was changed to *Thought,* due to **Mary Baker Eddy**'s objections to use of the term "Christian Science." In 1891 Charles came up with the name "Unity," which soon became their identifying logo, along with the winged sphere symbol.

In 1903 the Unity School of Practical Christianity was incorporated (changed in 1914 to the Unity School of Christianity), and in 1909 another magazine, *Weekly Unity,* was added, along with Charles' first book, *Christian Healing.* The 1920s saw the opening of a vegetarian restaurant in Kansas City called Unity Inn; radio broadcasts on the venerable station WOQ beginning in 1922; the publication in 1924 of *Unity Daily Word,* a monthly magazine of daily meditations which became their biggest seller; and the purchase of station WOQ the same year. In 1925 the Unity Annual Conference was formed as a means of maintaining a degree of control over the ministers and teachers associated with Unity and the content of their teaching.

Myrtle died in 1931, the year of publication of the *Metaphysical Bible Dictionary,* a guide to an allegorical style of New Thought Bible interpretation. In 1933, Charles married Cora G. Dedrick and retired from the pulpit to a time of travel and lecturing. He was active until just before his death in 1948 at the age of 93.

Sources:

Bowden, Henry Warner. *Dictionary of American Religious Biography.* Westport, CT: Greenwood Press, 1977. 572 pp.
Braden, Charles S. *Spirits in Rebellion.* Dallas, TX: Southern Methodist University Press, 1963. 571 pp.
D'Andrade, Hugh. *Charles Fillmore.* New York: Harper & Row, 1974.
Fillmore, Charles Sherlock. *Christian Healing.* Kansas City, MO: Unity School of Christianity, 1909. 255 pp.
_____. *Jesus Christ Heals.* Kansas City, MO: Unity School of Christianity, 1940. 205 pp.
_____. *Metaphysical Bible Dictionary.* Kansas City, MO: Unity School of Christianity, 1931. 706 pp.
_____. *The Twelve Powers of Man.* Lee's Summit, MO: Unity School of Christianity, 1955. 188 pp.
Freeman, James Dillet. *The Story of Unity.* Unity Village, MO: Unity Books, 1978. 269 pp.
Melton, J. Gordon. *Biographical Dictionary of American Cult and Sect Leaders.* Garland Reference Library of Social Science, vol. 212. New York: Garland Publishing, 1986.

Who Was Who in America. Chicago: Marquis Who's Who, Inc.

—*Gary L. Ward*

★ 299 ★
FILLMORE, Myrtle
Unity School of Christianity
b. Aug. 6, 1845, Pagetown, Ohio
d. Oct. 6, 1931, Kansas City, Missouri

Mary Caroline Page Fillmore, known as "Myrtle" since childhood, was the co-founder of Unity School of Christianity with her husband, Charles, and creator of the oldest children's magazine in the United States. She was raised in an influential family of strict Methodists in Ohio, and entered Oberlin College in 1867 at the age of 22, taking the "Literary Course for Ladies." At graduation she moved to Clinton, Missouri, where her brother David taught school. When she was about 30 she found a teaching job in Denison, Texas, where she met Charles Fillmore. Their romance was interrupted for a time, when Charles went to Colorado and she returned to Clinton, but they finally married in 1881. They went first to Colorado for a few years, and then in 1884 moved to Kansas City, Missouri.

In Kansas City, Myrtle was diagnosed as having tuberculosis, and her prospects were dim. In 1886, however, she and Charles attended some lectures by Eugene B. Weeks, a prominent New Thought healer, and she began to carry with her a thought he offered: "I am a child of God and therefore I do not inherit sickness." Over a period of months, her mental outlook and her physical condition completely changed, and she was healed. Charles was far more skeptical at first, but he eventually was convinced of this new metaphysical approach. In 1889 he left his real estate business to share these ideas in the magazine *Modern Thought*.

In 1890 Myrtle pioneered the Society of Silent Help (now known as Silent Unity) as a healing prayer group for those who could not come to classes in person. That same year, she and Charles went to Chicago to attend Emma Curtis Hopkins' Christian Science Theological Seminary, and the next year Hopkins ordained them. They tried to rename their magazine *Christian Science Thought*. Heeding Mary Baker Eddy's objections, however, they changed the name to *Thought*. It was in 1891 that Charles came up with their eventual trade name, Unity. In 1903 they incorporated the Unity School of Practical Christianity (renamed Unity School of Christianity in 1914), followed by another magazine, *Weekly Unity*, in 1909. Although Myrtle shared generally in the leadership of Unity, her special area of interest, other than the Society of Silent Help, was children. As a wife, mother, and career woman, she was concerned to maintain attention to the needs of children. Her answer was to start *Wee Wisdom* in 1893, the oldest children's magazine in America, which she edited for 30 years. She was also in charge of the Sunday School at the Kansas City center, and wrote dozens of articles for several periodicals. She died in 1931, at the age of 86, shortly after celebrating her fiftieth wedding anniversary.

Sources:

Bowden, Henry Warner. *Dictionary of American Religious Biography*. Westport, CT: Greenwood Press, 1977. 572 pp.

Braden, Charles S. *Spirits in Rebellion*. Dallas, TX: Southern Methodist University Press, 1963. 571 pp.

Fillmore, Myrtle S. *How to Let God Help You*. Unity Village, MO: Unity Books, 1956. 186 pp.

———. *The Letters of Myrtle Fillmore*. Kansas City, MO: Unity School of Christianity, 1936. 172 pp. Reprint as *Myrtle Fillmore's Healing Letters*. Unity Village, MO: Unity Books, n.d. 188 pp.

Melton, J. Gordon. *Biographical Dictionary of American Cult and Sect Leaders*. Garland Reference Library of Social Science, vol. 212. New York: Garland Publishing, 1986.

Wee Wisdom's Way. Kansas City, MO: Unity School of Christianity, 1920.

Witherspoon, Thomas E. *Myrtle Fillmore, Mother of Unity*. Unity Village, MO: Unity Books, 1977. 306 pp.

—*Gary L. Ward*

★ 300 ★
FIRE, John
Ceremonial Leader, Lakota Indians
b. Mar. 17, 1895, Rosebud Sioux Indian Reservation, South Dakota
d. Dec. 15, 1976, Rosebud Sioux Indian Reservation, South Dakota

John Fire, whose Lakota name was Tahka Ushte (or Lame Deer), was a ceremonial leader and advocate for traditional religion among the Lakota Indians. He was one of 12 children of Silas Fire and Sally Red Blanket. The Lame Deer name can be traced to John Fire's paternal great-grandfather, Tahka Ushte, who was an important leader of the Mniconjou band of Lakota Indians in the mid/late decades of the nineteenth century. Both of John Fire's parents' families were noted political and religious leaders of the Lakota, and he was educated in these areas from birth. Raised by his grandparents among the traditionalists of the early reservation period, Fire witnessed many of the religious ceremonies which the Lakota were forced to continue in relative secrecy due to a United States government ban on their ancient religious practice.

Fire's native language and religion were Lakota, and he was given the name Tahka Ushte during his *hanbleciyapi*, or "cry for a vision ceremony." As a young man, John Fire learned the songs and ritual prayers of the seven sacred rites of the Lakota. After an early life on the reservation, he traveled the rodeo circuit as a rider and rodeo clown, and also served in the United States military during World War II. Throughout his life, Lame Deer maintained contact with the religious leaders of the Lakota nation, periodically renewing his own vows and commitments to the ancient religious ceremonies.

As he grew older, Lame Deer's advice and participation in religious matters were sought by the Lakota, as well as traditional leaders from other native groups. Lame Deer learned to conduct the *yuwipi*, *inipi*, *hanbleciyapi*, *lowanpi*, and *wotuhan* ceremonies (the significant rituals of the Lakota religious life), and was taught the philosophy and rites of the pipe, sundance, and peyote ways of the Lakota. When he was in his sixties, Lame Deer took an active interest in the national Indian movement and served as a spiritual advisor to leaders of the American Indian Movement(AIM), although he requested no public acknowledgment of his role.

From 1966 through 1970, Lame Deer collaborated with author Richard Erdoes in producing an autobiography titled *Lame Deer: Seeker of Visions*, published in 1972. Written in the first person as a series of stories about Lame Deer and his Lakota people, the work details the transition period from the old ways of life to the reservation existence. Lame Deer laments the loss of language and knowledge of the ancient Lakota traditions, which he viewed as plainspoken but profound in their ability to chronicle the human religious experience. After publication of the book, Lame Deer traveled extensively throughout the United States and Europe, accompanied in later years by his son, Archie Fire. Both John and Archie Fire are recognized as leaders and founders of the pan-Indian religious movements which use the Lakota ways of the sweat lodge, pipe, and sundance ceremony. After a short illness, John Fire died in 1976. Honoring his wishes, his body was cremated and the ashes scattered over Lakota Indian country. Archie Fire carries on the name of Tahka Ushte, and lives in Sturgis, South Dakota.

Sources:

Fire, John [Lame Deer], and Richard Erdoes. *Lame Deer: Seeker of Visions*. New York: Simon and Schuster, 1972.

Mattiessen, Peter. *In the Spirit of Crazy Horse.* New York: Viking Press, 1983.

—*Johnny Flynn*

★301★
FISHER, George Park
Church Historian, Congregational Church
b. Aug. 10, 1827, Wrentham, Massachusetts
d. Dec. 20, 1909, Litchfield, Connecticut

George Park Fisher, for four decades a professor of ecclesiastical history at Yale Divinity School, was the son of Louis Whiting Fisher and Nancy Fisher. He grew up in Massachusetts, but received his college training at Brown University. Following his graduation in 1847, he spent a year each at Yale Divinity School, Auburn Theological Seminary, and Andover Theological Seminary, from which he graduated in 1851. He decided to continue his study abroad, and in 1852 began two years of post-graduate work in Germany.

Upon his return from Europe in 1854, Fisher was named to the Livingston Professorship in Divinity at Yale College. His duties included the pastoring of the Congregational church adjacent to the college, and his acceptance of the post became the occasion for his ordination to the ministry. During his seven years at Yale College, he authored his first book, *History of the Church in Yale College* (1858), and married Adeline Louisa Forbes (1860). He left the church and college in 1861 to begin his highly productive career at the Divinity School.

Fisher's mature career is marked primarily by the numerous books he authored. Among his most noteworthy were *The Reformation* (1873); *Outlines of Universal History* (1885); *The Colonial Era* (1892); *History of the Christian Church* (1887); and *History of Christian Doctrine* (1896). Not as well known today but possibly of more lasting historical importance were the several books he wrote in opposition to what is known as the Tuebingen school of historical criticism. While in Europe, Fisher had become aware of the rationalist approach to historical scholarship (especially as regards the New Testament period) espoused by Ferdinand Christian Baur and his colleagues at the University of Tuebingen. Baur, an important figure in the development of modern historical critical methodology, approached history using the categories developed by German philosophers, especially George W. F. Hegel. Conservative thinkers such as Fisher opposed the subversion of their historical work to foreign philosophical categories and the implied loss of the supernatural element in a totally rationalist approach to religious history. Thus a number of Fisher's books dealt directly with Christian apologetics in opposition to Tuebingen thought: *Essays on the Supernatural Origin of Christianity* (1865); *Faith and Rationalism* (1879); *Discussions in History and Theology* (1880); *The Christian Religion* (1882); *The Grounds of Theistic and Christian Belief* (1883); and *The Manual of Christian Evidences* (1890). While the Tuebingen theories are no longer espoused by contemporary historians, the conflict they produced played a significant role in the emergence of modern scholarship. Fisher's leadership in the debate was acknowledged by his election on several occasions to the presidency of the American Society of Church History.

In 1895 Fisher was named dean of the Divinity School, a post he retained until his retirement in 1901. He continued to reside in New Haven, Connecticut, as a professor emeritus until his death in 1909.

Sources:

Dictionary of American Biography. 20 vols. and 7 supps. New York: Charles Scribner's Sons, 1928-1936, 1944-1981.
Fisher, George Park. *The Christian Religion.* New York: Charles Scribner's, 1882. 66 pp.
———. *Faith and Rationalism.* New York: Charles Scribner's, 1879. 188 pp.
———. *History of the Christian Church.* 1887.
———. *History of Christian Doctrine.* New York: Charles Scribner's Sons, 1896. 583 pp.
———. *Manual of Christian Evidences.* New York: Charles Scribner's, 1890. 123 pp.
———. *The Reformation.* New York: Scribner's, Armstrong & Co., 1873. 620 pp.

★302★
FISHER, Henry Lee
Bishop and President, United Holy Church of America
b. 1874, Salisbury, North Carolina
d. 1947, Henderson, North Carolina

Henry Lee Fisher was for almost three decades a bishop and president of the United Holy Church of America, a predominantly black holiness church founded in the late nineteenth century. He was raised in North Carolina and first came into contact with holiness teaching when he was 18 years old in Wilmington. Holiness theology advocates the attainment of a state of holiness of the heart (sanctification as a second action of the Holy Spirit). The sanctified believer is thought to have been made perfect in love. He joined the United Holy Church and became an effective minister/evangelist to whom the establishment of many of the early congregations is credited. In 1904 he was invited to Durham, North Carolina, to dedicate a new tabernacle and to conduct a set of revival services during the following month. These services had such success that Fisher stayed in Durham as pastor of the Durham Tabernacle, later renamed the Gospel Tabernacle. He remained as pastor for the next 40 years, using it as a base of operation for his general church work.

Fisher's missionary endeavors soon brought him to the attention of the larger church, and his organizational abilities were clearly demonstrated in his authoring of the 1910 edition of the church's *Manual.* Thus in 1916 he was named bishop and president of the church, then known as the United Holy Church of North Carolina and Virginia. It quickly became evident to church members that as their president he would impress his priorities for expansion and organization upon the church.

Within his first years as the church's president, he oversaw its transformation from a small regional holiness church to a national body. In 1918 he led in the formal incorporation of the church as a nonprofit organization. By that time, he had organized the Missionary Department. This effort followed on the heels of his promotion of the annual women's Home and Foreign Missionary Convention. In 1920, as members followed the post-World War I migration north, he organized the Northern District and later the Western and Pacific Coast District and the New England District. In 1920 he negotiated the reception of a gift from the Christian and Missionary Alliance (CMA) for Boynton Institute, a school in Boynton, Virginia, for use by the church as a training institute. He showed the church his concern for their support of mission endeavors by his trips to the West Coast, Bermuda, and Barbados. During the 1924-1928 quadrennium, he traveled over 40,000 miles.

Fisher saw the church through the years of World War II, during which time he became deeply concerned with what he saw as a general moral breakdown in both society and the church. His last messages to the church's leaders called upon the now international membership to maintain the high standards as preached since its founding.

Sources:

Dupree, Sherry Sherrod. *Biographical Dictionary of African-American, Holiness-Pentecostals, 1880-1990.* Washington, DC: Middle Atlantic Regional Press, 1990. 386 pp.
Gregory, Chester W. *The History of the United Holy Church of America, Inc., 1886-1986.* Baltimore, MD: Gateway Press, 1986.

★ 303 ★
FISHER, Mark Miles
Historian and Minister, National Baptist Convention, U.S.A., Inc.
b. Oct. 29, 1899, Atlanta, Georgia
d. Dec. 14, 1970, Richmond, Virginia

Mark Miles Fisher, Baptist minister and church historian, was the son of Florida Neely and Elijah John Fisher. He attended Morehouse College in Atlanta, Georgia, from which he received his B.A. in 1918. Moving to Chicago, he attended Northern Baptist Theological Seminary and the University of Chicago. During his seminary days he wrote his first book, a short biography of *Lott Carey*, the pioneer black Baptist missionary. In 1922 he was awarded a B.D. from the seminary and an M.A. from the university. That same year he completed his first book, a tribute to his father, *The Master's Slave—Elijah John Fisher*. He married Ada Virginia Foster and was ordained as a Baptist minister.

Fisher next turned his attention to the study of black history and work on his Ph.D. The first product of his efforts was a history of *Virginia Union University and Some of Her Achievements* (1924). In 1933 he finished his *A Short History of the Baptist Denomination*, an early history of the National Baptists. That same year he became the pastor of White Rock Baptist Church in Durham, North Carolina, a position he was to hold for the rest of his active life. He also began teaching church history at the national Baptist Shaw University in Raleigh, North Carolina.

Shaw completed the requirements at the University of Chicago for his Ph.D. in 1948 with a dissertation on slave songs. Published in 1953 as *Negro Slave Songs in the United States*, the dissertation won the American Historical Association's prize as the outstanding historical volume of the year. In the volume he began the reinterpretation of the black response to the slave experience by arguing that the slave songs had a double meaning. Religiously they talked of the biblical Exodus experience which, to the slaves, became a code for expressing hopes of freedom and escape north to Canada. Fisher helped set the direction for future studies of slave culture.

In 1965 Fisher retired from both Shaw University and his pastorate. His pastoral career had been marked by his being named one of America's ten top ministers in 1954. The church named him minister emeritus.

Sources:
Fisher, Miles Mark. *Lott Carey*. Philadelphia: Foreign Mission Board, N.B.C. Publishers, 1921. 51 pp.
_____. *The Master's Slave—Elijah John Fisher*. Philadelphia: Judson Press, 1922. 194 pp.
_____. *Negro Slave Songs in the United States*. Ithaca, NY: Cornell University Press, 1953. 223 pp.
_____. *A Short History of the Baptist Denomination*. Nashville, TN: Sunday School Publication Board, 1933. 188 pp.
_____. *Virginia Union University and Some of Her Achievements*. Richmond, VA: Brown Print Shop, 1924. 110 pp.
Hill, Samuel S., ed. *Encyclopedia of Religion in the South*. Macon, GA: Mercer University Press, 1984. 878 pp.
Page, James A. *Selected Black American Authors: An Illustrated Bio-Bibliography*. Boston: G. K. Hall & Co., 1977. 398 pp.

★ 304 ★
FLAHIFF, George Bernard
Cardinal, Roman Catholic Church
b. Oct. 26, 1905, Paris, Ontario, Canada

George Bernard Flahiff, the former archbishop of Winnipeg and a cardinal in the Roman Catholic Church, is the son of Eleanor Fleming and John James Flahiff. He attended the College of St. Michael at the University of Toronto from which he received his B.A. in 1926. He then entered St. Basil's Seminary and joined the Basilian Fathers, a religious order. He was ordained in 1903 after completing his seminary studies. His studies next took him to the University of Strausbourg where he worked for a year before beginning four years at the Ecole des Chartes and Ecole des Haute Etudes in Paris. He received his doctorate in medieval studies in 1935.

Following the completion of his education, Flahiff returned to Canada as a professor of history at the Pontifical Institute of Medieval Studies at the University of Toronto. He stayed at the university for almost two decades until he was elected the superior general of the Basilian Fathers. During his term he was also elected president of the national assembly of Major Superiors in Canada in 1958. In 1960 he was reelected superior general, but did not finish his term as in 1961 he was named archbishop of Winnipeg.

Flahiff emerged as a liberal voice of reform at Vatican II, and in the 1967 Synod of Bishops in Rome he openly protested the slow implementation of the liturgical reforms ordered by the council. He also showed particular attention to the rights and role of women in the church, though he was careful not to commit himself publicly on the issue of women's ordination to the priesthood.

In 1967 Flahiff was named a member of the Sacred College for Religious at the Vatican, and two years later was named a cardinal. After 21 years in Winnipeg, Flahiff retired in 1982 and settled in Toronto.

Sources:
The American Catholic Who's Who. Washington, D.C.: National Catholic News Service, 1979.
Biography Index. New York: The H. W. Wilson Co.
The Blue Book. New York: St. Martin's Press, 1976.
Who's Who in America. Wilmette, IL: Marquis Who's Who, Inc.

★ 305 ★
FLANAGAN, Edward Joseph
Priest, Roman Catholic Church
Founder, Boys Town
b. Jul. 13, 1886, Roscommon Ireland
d. May 15, 1948, Berlin Germany

Edward Joseph Flanagan, the founder of Boys Town, one of the most famous facilities for the rehabilitation of youth, was raised a devout Roman Catholic in his native Ireland. He attended Summer Hill College in Sligo, Ireland, and graduated with high honors. His older brother, already a priest, had been assigned to mission work in rural Nebraska, and his sister resided in New York, so young Edward decided to finish his education in the United States. At the direction of Archbishop James A. Farley of New York City, Flanagan first attended Mount St. Mary's College, Emmetsburg, Maryland, from which he received an A.B. degree in 1906. He then studied at St. Joseph's Seminary, Dunwoodie, New York, and at the Gregorian University in Rome, but problems with his lungs continually hampered his progress. Finally, he was able to complete his studies through the University of Innbruck, Austria, and was ordained in 1912 in the Archdiocese of Omaha, Nebraska.

Flanagan was assigned to O'Neill, in rural Nebraska, but after a short stay was reassigned to St. Patrick's Church in Omaha. In 1913 a number of homeless men, products of a drought, began to filter into Omaha, and Flanagan began to organize food and shelter services to assist them. In 1914 he founded the Workingmen's Hotel, which became a major social agency for the city, serving food to as many as 500 men a day.

While reflecting upon his inability to change substantially the men with whom he was working, Flanagan began to encounter homeless boys. He reasoned that if he redirected his efforts toward youth, he could help them before they reached the stages of hopelessness so apparent in the older men. He began to study juvenile delinquency and some of the attempts to deal with the situation in non-court related structures such as the Commonwealth for Boys in Albion, Michigan.

Released by his archbishop to proceed, Flanagan gave up his work at the hotel and started a home for boys in rented facilities in Omaha. In 1922 the present site of Boys Town—formerly Over-brook Farm, ten miles west of Omaha—was purchased. He spent the next 20 years building his work.

Boys Town embodied the basic insights developed by Flanagan in his years of work with the homeless and juveniles. He was con-vinced that rehabilitation of individuals had to be started at an early age. More importantly, he asserted that rehabilitation was possible because problems are not a matter of birth but of environment. He also emphasized religion's role in the rehabilitation process, and though a Roman Catholic priest, always worked from an interfaith basis. From this ideological base, Boys Town grew into a large and established institution, and Flanagan became a recognized authori-ty on juvenile delinquency. Flanagan's personality and program brought him friends and support from both the Protestant and Jew-ish religious communities and the secular world. He became a major factor in the changing attitude of the non-Catholic public to-ward the Roman Catholic Church in twentieth-century America.

After World War II, at the invitation of General Douglas MacAr-thur, Flanagan went to Japan and Korea to consult on their youth problems. He followed that trip with a similar tour of Central Eu-rope, where a heart condition flared up, and he died in Berlin in 1948.

Sources:
New Catholic Encyclopedia. 17 vols. New York: McGraw-Hill, 1967.
Ousler, Fulton, and Will Ousler. *Father Flanagan of Boys Town.* Garden City, NY: Doubleday & Company, 1948. 302 pp.

★306★
FLEMING, Arthur Sherwood
Lay Leader, United Methodist Church
b. Jun. 12, 1905, Kingston, New York

Arthur Sherwood Fleming, a Methodist ecumenical leader, is the son of Harriet Sherwood and Harry H. Fleming. He attended Ohio Wesleyan University, from which he received an A.B. in 1927. Fol-lowing his graduation he joined the staff at American University as an instructor in government while completing his masters degree, which he received in 1928. In 1930 he became an editorial writer for *U.S. News and World Report.* Meanwhile, he attended George Washington University, which awarded him an LL.B. degree in 1932. That same year he assumed additional duties as the editor for *Uncle Sam's Diary,* a high school current events weekly. In 1934 he married Bernice Virginia Moler.

In 1939 Fleming became a member of the U.S. Civil Service Commission. He retained that position until 1948 when he became president of Ohio Wesleyan University. For many years an active layman in the Methodist Church, Fleming was chosen vice-president of the newly created National Council of Churches in 1950. He remained at Wesleyan until 1953 when he was called by President Dwight D. Eisenhower to serve as director of the Of-fice of Defense Mobilization and a member of the National Securi-ty Council. In 1957, when Fleming left office to return to Ohio Wesleyan, Eisenhower awarded him the Medal of Freedom. A year later he returned to Washington as Secretary of Health, Education and Welfare for the remainder of Eisenhower's administration.

In 1961 Fleming became the president of Oregon University. While there, his leadership in the ecumenical movement blos-somed. In 1964 he became president of the Oregon Council of Churches and again became the vice-president of the National Council of Churches. Two years later he began a four-year tenure as president of the Council, one of the few laymen to hold that po-sition. In 1969 he left Oregon and moved to Minnesota as presi-dent of Macalester College. He retired from Macalester in 1971, but has remained active as a participant in various capacities, espe-

cially in the areas of aging and civil rights. He served as chairman of the Commission on Civil Rights for seven years (1975-1982). Over his long and varied career, Fleming became an exemplar of the active lay Christian for many Protestants.

Sources:
Harmon, Nolan B. *The Encyclopedia of World Methodism.* 2 vols. Nash-ville: United Methodist Publishing House, 1974.
Howell, Clinton H., ed. *Prominent Personalities in Methodism.* Birming-ham, AL: Lowrey Press, 1945. 512 pp.

★307★
FLOWER, Amanda Cameron
Founder, Independent Spiritualist Association of the United States of America
b. Oct. 15, 1863, Owen Sound Canada
d. Nov. 20, 1940

Amanda Cameron Flower, founder of the Independent Spiritual-ist Association of the United States of America, was one of four children born to Abraham and Margaret Day Cameron. Little is known of her early life, but at the age of 27 she moved from Cana-da to the United States, eventually settling in Michigan. She mar-ried a Mr. Coffman, with whom she had one son, but following his death, she married Frank Flower.

Amanda Flower was attracted to Spiritualism in her early adult life and served her first pastorate in Owosso, Michigan. Shortly after the turn of the century, she used money from her first hus-band's insurance to purchase a church building, which she opened as the Church of Truth in Grand Rapids, Michigan. She pastored the church for thirty-five years (1904-1939). In 1908 she incorpo-rated the Spiritualist Temple Society (Church of Truth) in Grand Rapids. Flower associated with the Michigan State Spiritualist Asso-ciation, a unit of the National Spiritualist Association of Churches (N.S.A.C.).

During her years with the N.S.A.C., Flower was active in the for-mation of Spiritualist congregations throughout the Midwest. In the 1920s, however, she began to reject some of the regulations gov-erning N.S.A.C churches and ministers. She especially disagreed with the restriction against ministers working outside the associa-tion's own churches. In 1924 she had a vision for a new association that would correct the problems by emphasizing the role of inde-pendent associations controlled only by their unity. She withdrew from the N.S.A.C. and incorporated the Independent Spiritualist Association of the United States of America.

Under Flower's vigorous leadership, the association grew rapid-ly, though it was geographically limited to several midwestern states. She began and also edited (until 1935) the association's newsletter. In 1931 she was elected president of the association for life. As part of her duties, she regularly traveled among the associa-tion churches. In 1933 she was a speaker at the World's Fair in Chi-cago.

Sources:
Corey, Kathleen. *Rev. Amanda C. Flower.* Holly, MI: The author, n.d. 13 pp.
Judah, J. Stillson. *The History and Philosophy of the Metaphysical Move-ments in America.* Philadelphia, PA: Westminister Press, 1967. 317 pp.

★308★
FLOWER, Joseph James Roswell
Assemblies of God
b. Jun. 17, 1888, Belleville, Ontario, Canada
d. Jul. 23, 1970, Springfield, Missouri

Joseph James Roswell Flower was a founder of the Assemblies of God, one of the largest of the Pentecostal denominations in North America. He was born in Canada to a Methodist household. When he was young, his parents were impressed by the Christian

Catholic Church and founder John Alexander Dowie's healing of a crippled man. They moved to Dowie's religious community of Zion, Illinois, in 1902. Once there, however, they became disenchanted with the discord and other conditions, and moved to Indianapolis, where Flower's father worked for the Indiana Seed Company. The family joined the Christian and Missionary Alliance (CMA) Church in Indianapolis.

In 1907, when Flower was 19, a minister named Glenn A. Cook, who had received the Pentecostal baptism of the Holy Spirit under **William J. Seymour**'s ministry in Los Angeles, came to town and preached at the Alliance church. Flower's parents received the baptism (speaking in tongues). A year later, Flower received the baptism as well. Instead of his proposed law career, he went into the ministry. He began to travel with gospel bands and work at meetings. He founded and edited a periodical, *The Pentecost* (later called *Grace and Glory*). In 1911 he married Alice Marie Reynolds, and they did missionary work in Indiana for about a year before helping D. Wesley Myland begin Gileah Bible School in Plainfield, Indiana. Flower was ordained by Myland's World's Faith Missionary Association, and created the periodical *The Christian Evangel* (later called *Pentecostal Evangel*).

When **Eudorus N. Bell** and others saw the need for more stable organization among Pentecostal churches, Flower was very supportive and became a major leader at the exploratory convention in 1914, at which was born the General Council of the Assemblies of God. In 1915 Flower moved to St. Louis, Missouri, and *The Word and Witness*, Bell's periodical, was merged with the *Christian Evangel*. Over the next year, the Assemblies doctrinal positions were hammered out, focusing on the "Jesus Only" movement, in which Bell and others were re-baptized in the name of Jesus only, no longer believing in the Trinity. Flower fought for the more orthodox position, and for the position that sanctification is not a separate act of grace. Both of these positions were upheld in a 1916 vote.

Flower was secretary of the General Council from 1914 to 1917, at which point he moved to Springfield, Missouri, to oversee the publishing house. He was foreign missions secretary from 1919 to 1925, when his backing of an unpopular constitutional proposal cost him his post. He moved to Scranton, Pennsylvania, to pastor a congregation, and slowly worked his way back up the church ladder. In 1929 he became superintendent of the eastern district, and in 1931 he returned to a national position as assistant general secretary, followed by a stint as general secretary and treasurer beginning in 1935. He retired from national office in 1959 after a distinguished career in building up a significant church organization. He died in 1970 at the age of 82.

Sources:

Boucher, Mark T. *J. Roswell Flower*. Springfield, MO: The Author, 1983.

Brumback, Carl. *Suddenly From Heaven*. Springfield, MO: Gospel Publishing House, 1961. 380 pp.

Burgess, Stanley M., Gary B. McGee, and Patrick H. Alexander, eds. *Dictionary of Pentecostal and Charismatic Movements*. Grand Rapids, MI: Regency Reference Library, Zondervan Publishing House, 1988. 914 pp.

Melton, J. Gordon. *Biographical Dictionary of American Cult and Sect Leaders*. Garland Reference Library of Social Science, vol. 212. New York: Garland Publishing, 1986.

Menzies, William W. *Annotated to Serve*. Springfield, MO: Gospel Publishing House, 1971. 436 pp.

Who Was Who in America. Chicago: Marquis Who's Who, Inc.

—*Gary L. Ward*

★ 309 ★
FORD, Arnold Josiah
Black Jewish Leader and Founder, Beth B'nai Abraham Congregation
b. 1890?, Barbados
d. 1935?, Addis Ababa Ethiopia

Arnold Josiah Ford was one of the early leaders of black Judaism in America and the founder of the Beth B'nai Abraham Congregation in New York City. Little is known about his early years, other than that he was born in Barbados, probably in the 1890s, the son of an evangelist. He spent time as a clerk and in the British navy as a music teacher before coming to the United States in 1912. From 1912 to 1920, he was the bandmaster for the New Amsterdam Musical Association in New York.

In 1917 he met Marcus Garvey, the West Indian black nationalist who founded the Universal Negro Improvement Association (U.N.I.A.). Ford became the choirmaster and band leader for the U.N.I.A., and co-wrote its anthem, "Ethiopia, Land of Our Fathers." He worked on and wrote many of the pieces in *The Universal Ethiopian Hymnal*. Ford meanwhile had converted to Judaism, believing that God would lead the Blacks back to their homeland in Ethiopia. Although Garvey did not share Ford's Judaism, their relationship remained intact.

In 1924 Ford founded Beth B'nai Abraham as a black Jewish synagogue, learning Hebrew and introducing orthodox Jewish practices. There were some other Black Jewish groups existing in New York at the time which benefited from Ford's knowledge of Judaism. Meanwhile, news of the discovery of the Falashas, the Jewish Ethiopian tribe, had become common knowledge, and speculation was made that they represent the true identity of all Blacks and Jews, that the biblical Jews were all black, and that this knowledge was later lost, especially as a result of slavery. Ford felt a powerful need to visit Ethiopia, and when his congregation foundered financially in 1930, he turned it all over to **Wentworth A. Matthew**, head of a similar group called the Commandment Keepers, and left for Africa.

Ford settled in Addis Ababa, Ethiopia, not with the Falashas, but with a small group of American Blacks. Not much is known about his activities there except that he was well known for his music, and that he survived long enough to see Haile Selassie's coronation in 1935. In the 1940s his wife founded the Princess Zannaba Warq School. The Commandment Keepers are still active in the United States today.

Sources:

Burkett, Randall K. *Garveyism as a Religious Movement*. Metuchen, NJ: Scarecrow Press, 1978.

Ehrman, Albert. "Black Judaism in New York," *Journal of Ecumenical Studies*: 8 (Winter, 1971), 103-113.

Ford, Arnold Josiah. *The Universal Ethiopian Hymnal*. New York: 1920s.

King, Kenneth J., "Some Notes on Arnold J. Ford and New World Black Attitudes to Ethiopia," in Randall K. Burkett and Richard Newman, *Black Apostles*. Boston: G. K. Hall & Co., 1978.

Melton, J. Gordon. *Biographical Dictionary of American Cult and Sect Leaders*. Garland Reference Library of Social Science, vol. 212. New York: Garland Publishing, 1986.

—*Gary L. Ward*

★ 310 ★
FORD, Arthur Augustus
Spiritualist Medium, International General Assembly of Spiritualists
b. Jan. 8, 1897, Titusville, Florida
d. Jan. 2, 1971, Miami, Florida

Arthur Augustus Ford was the most famous Spiritualist medium of the twentieth century and the founder of the International General Assembly of Spiritualists. His father made sure that he was baptized Episcopalian, but his mother made sure that he was raised Baptist. In his early teen years a conversion experience led him to be rebaptized as a Baptist, but at age 16 he was dismissed from the church because of his acceptance of Unitarian views. He then joined the Christian Church (Disciples of Christ), and in 1917 went to Transylvania College in Lexington, Kentucky, to prepare for the ministry.

In 1918-1919, his college studies were interrupted by World War I service, where he began to notice unusual psychic phenomena for the first time. He heard voices giving names, which soon appeared on casualty lists. When he became pastor of the Christian Church in Barbourville, Kentucky, in 1920, he began investigating psychic phenomena on his own, going to New York to visit the American Society for Psychical Research and Spiritualism. In 1922 he married Sallie Stewart, and his oratorical abilities landed him a position as lecturer with the Swarthmore Chautauqua Association of Pennsylvania. During this time he met **Swami Yogananda**, who entered the country in 1924. Ford also discovered his ability to go into a trance, and became acquainted with Fletcher, the life-long spirit guide who would control his future trances.

Ford developed a following which enabled him to found the First Spiritualist Church of New York City. His independent spirit, in addition to his Yogananda-inspired belief in reincarnation, made him subject to obstructions from the National Spiritualist Association, though he remained a member. In 1936 he formed the International General Assembly of Spiritualists, and was either its formal or informal leader for many years. In 1937 he married Valerie McKeown, having divorced his first wife in 1927. Also in 1937 he moved to Hollywood and became a full-time spokesperson for Spiritualism.

After World War II he founded and led the Church of Metaphysical Science in Miami, Florida. Although that experience was short-lived, he continued to make Florida his home base as he made connections with mainstream religious leaders around the country. His work led to the creation in 1956 of the Spiritual Frontiers Fellowship, a national church-related organization for the exploration of psychic and religious phenomena, a group to which Ford devoted much time. In 1965 he gave a reading for **Sun Myung Moon**, the leader of the Unification Church, which was positive, even laudatory, in tone. The Unification Church, of course, was pleased and used this for their public relations, but the Spiritual Frontiers Fellowship's reputation suffered.

The last major event of his career was a televised seance with Episcopal Bishop **James A. Pike**, whose beliefs and actions were significantly affected by this event. After Ford's death in 1971, however, it was discovered that the seance was faked, and charges of other such incidents began to emerge from a few associates. While most followers continued to believe in his real abilities, this evidence has caused some reevaluation of his remarkable career. In the wake of his death, several mediums, most importantly Ruth Montgomery, published books in which they claimed contact with the spirit of Ford.

Sources:

Ford, Arthur. *The Life Beyond Death*. New York: G. P. Putnam's Sons, 1971. 249 pp.
_____. *Nothing So Strange*. New York: Harper & Row, 1958. 250 pp.
_____. *Unknown but Known*. New York: Harper & Row, 1968.
_____. *Why We Survive*. Cooksburg, NY: The Gutenberg Press, 1952. 105 pp.
Melton, J. Gordon. *Biographical Dictionary of American Cult and Sect Leaders*. Garland Reference Library of Social Science, vol. 212. New York: Garland Publishing, 1986.
Montgomery, Ruth. *A World Beyond*. New York: Coward, McCann & Geoghegan, 1971. 210 pp.
Shepard, Leslie. *Encyclopedia of Occultism & Parapsychology*. 3 vols., 2nd. ed. Detroit: Gale Research Co., 1984-1985.
Spraggett, Allen, and William V. Rauscher. *Arthur Ford: The Man Who Talked with the Dead*. New York: New American Library, 1973. 301 pp.

—*Gary L. Ward*

★311★
FOSDICK, Harry Emerson
Minister, Northern Baptist Convention
b. May 24, 1878, Buffalo, New York
d. Oct. 5, 1969, Bronxville, New York

Harry Emerson Fosdick, the most prominent ministerial spokesperson for modernism during the fundamentalist-modernist controversy of the 1920s, was the son of Frank Sheldon and Annie Inez Weaver Fosdick. He was raised in a devout but liberal Baptist family. He attended Colgate University from which he received his B.A. degree in 1900. His college days included a period of intense religious doubt but, having resolved it by the time he graduated, he decided to enter the ministry. He attended Hamilton Theological Seminary but after a year transferred to Union Theological Seminary, the independent Presbyterian school in New York City. A few months after his graduation in 1904 he married Florence Allen Whitney.

Fosdick became pastor of the First Baptist Church of Montclair, New Jersey. His oratorical ability earned him a part-time teaching post in homiletics in 1908 at Union. He began to travel and speak and had the first of his many books published in 1908, The Second Mile. His sermons and books, many of which were compilations of his sermons, began to emphasize the rationality of faith and to attempt restatements of Christianity in a manner Fosdick felt was intellectually acceptable in the dawning scientific era. He argued that faith worked on a practical level and provided resources for facing life. Among his important books written before he left Montclair were The Manhood of the Master (1913) and The Meaning of Prayer (1915).

In 1915 Fosdick accepted a full-time teaching post at Union, but kept it only three years. In 1918 he was offered the pulpit at the prestigious Madison Avenue Presbyterian Church. He enjoyed relative peace for several years and in 1922 began a radio show, "National Vespers" that ran for several decades. He also authored a string of books including: The Meaning of Faith (1917); The Assurance of Immortality (1918); The Meaning of Service (1920); Christianity and Progress (1922); Twelve Tests of Character (1924); and The Modern Use of the Bible (1924), one of the clearest statements of the modernist approach to scripture. Fosdick's books clearly identified him with the modernist camp as the fundamentalist-modernist controversy entered a new phase following World War I. Then in 1922 Fosdick moved into the center of the controversy with his famous sermon, "Shall the Fundamentalists Win?" in which he argued for stripping the faith of unbelievable affirmations such as biblical inerrancy, the virgin birth, the bodily resurrection, and the second coming. Instead, he suggested the church must center its teaching on the inner core of the love of God and the possibility of spiritual help for an ethical life. The conservative Presbyterians attacked him, finding a vulnerable spot. Fosdick was a Baptist in a Presbyterian pulpit. They demanded his resignation. The General Assembly partially agreed, but said that Fosdick could remain if he became a Presbyterian and professed belief in the doctrine of the Westminster Confession of Faith. These requirements were unacceptable to Fosdick and he resigned from the pulpit. He was immediately hired by the Park Avenue Baptist Church which, with John D. Rockefeller's backing, agreed to erect a new interdenominational sanctuary to accommodate the thousands who regularly came to hear Fosdick.

Riverside Church was dedicated in 1931, and Fosdick preached there until his retirement in 1946. Soon after settling in at his new position on Riverside Drive, two of his more memorable books were released: As I See Religion (1932) and The Hope of the World

(1933). These works represented the mature statement of his modernist faith. In 1935 he preached his second most famous sermon, "Beyond Modernism." As the fundamentalist controversy died, he reflected on the extremes it had produced and saw weak points in modernism, such as an overemphasis on intellectualism, a naive optimism, and a dangerous moral accommodation that solved moral dilemmas without invoking moral absolutes. However, while becoming aware of the depth and continuing power of sin and evil, Fosdick never abandoned the essential positions of modernism.

Before his retirement from Riverside in 1946, Fosdick authored some of his most popular books, including A Guide to Understanding the Bible (1938); On Being a Real Person (1943); A Great Time to Be Alive (1944); and On Being Fit to Live With (1946). As World War II progressed, he became a vocal pacifist. During his retirement years he spent time writing his autobiography, The Living of These Days (1956), and remained active until he developed severe arthritis during the 1960s.

Sources:

Bowden, Henry Warner. *Dictionary of American Religious Biography*. Westport, CT: Greenwood Press, 1977. 572 pp.
Dictionary of American Biography. 20 vols. and 7 supps. New York: Charles Scribner's Sons, 1928-1936, 1944-1981.
Fosdick, Harry Emerson. *As I See Religion*. New York: Harper & Brothers, 1932. 201 pp.
_____. *A Guide to Understanding the Bible*. New York: Harper & Brothers, 1938. 348 pp.
_____. *The Living of These Days*. New York: Harper and Row, 1956. 324 pp.
_____. *The Meaning of Faith*. New York: Association Press, 1917. 318 pp.
_____. *On Being a Real Person*. New York: Harper and Brothers, 1943. 295 pp.
_____. *Twelve Tests of Character*. New York: Association Press, 1923. 213 pp.
Lippy, Charles H. *Twentieth-Century Shapers of American Popular Religion*. New York: Greenwood Press, 1989. 494 pp.
Miller, Robert Moats. *Harry Emerson Fosdick: Preacher, Pastor, Prophet*. New York: Oxford University Press, 1985.

★ 312 ★
FOSTER, George Burman
Theologian, Northern Baptist Convention
b. Apr. 2, 1858, Anderson, West Virginia
d. Dec. 22, 1918, Chicago, Illinois

George Burman Foster, a theologian with the Northern Baptist Convention, was the son of Oliver Harrison Foster and Helen Louise Skaggs Foster. He grew up in West Virginia, where he received his undergraduate education at Shelton College (1876-1879) and West Virginia University, from which he received his B.A. in 1883. In 1879 he had been ordained to the ministry in the Baptist church, and following graduation he became pastor of the congregation at Morgantown, West Virginia, for a year. In 1884 he married Mary Lyon. That same year he entered Rochester Theological Seminary, from which he graduated in 1887.

Following completion of his seminary work, Foster again became a pastor, and for four years resided in Saratoga Springs, New York. In 1891 he left the congregation to begin a year of further studies at the universities of Goettingen and Berlin in Germany. He returned to finish his Ph.D. at Dennison University. In 1892 he became professor of philosophy at McMaster University in Toronto. In 1895 he moved to the University of Chicago where he would remain for the rest of his life as a professor of systematic philosophy (1895-1905) and then philosophy of religion (1905-1918).

Through his books and teaching, Foster became a potent force in the modernist theological movement of the early twentieth century. His major books include: *The Finality of the Christian Reli-*

gion (1905); *The Function of Religion in Man's Struggle for Existence* (1909); *The Function of Death in Human Experience* (1905); and *Christianity in Its Modern Expression* (published posthumously in 1921). As the modernist-fundamentalist controversy heated up, Foster became an active participant in debating fundamentalists. The most famous of these encounters occurred in 1909 with Rev. Johnson Myers, pastor of the Immanuel Baptist Church in Chicago.

Foster also debated freethinker Clarence Darrow on the issue of free will. Darrow was a champion of social determinism, a philosophy he used to great effect in legal arguments for the lenient treatment of accused murderers. Foster was a philosophical defender of human free will. Foster's approach to theology and philosophy was anti-authoritarian, opposed to both tradition and a harsh rationalism. He defended religion as a part of human experience, of the essence of human nature. To Foster, religion found its highest expression in the life (and legend) of Jesus.

Sources:

Dictionary of American Biography. 20 vols. and 7 supps. New York: Charles Scribner's Sons, 1928-1936, 1944-1981.
Foster, George B. *Christianity in Its Modern Expression*. New York: Macmillan Company, 1921. 294 pp.
_____. *The Finality of the Christian Religion*. Chicago: University of Chicago Press, 1906. 518 pp.
_____. *The Function of Death in Human Experience*. Chicago: University of Chicago Press, 1915. 218 pp.
_____. *The Function of Religion in Man's Struggle for Existence*. Chicago: University of Chicago Press, 1909. 293 pp.

★ 313 ★
FOSTER, Randolph Sinks
Bishop, Methodist Episcopal Church
b. Feb. 22, 1820, Williamsburg, Ohio
d. May 1, 1903, Newton Center, Massachusetts

Randolph Sinks Foster, a bishop of the Methodist Episcopal Church, was the son of Israel and Polly Kain Foster. As a youth, Randolph moved with his family to Kentucky. He later attended Augusta College in Augusta, Kentucky. At school he showed himself a capable preacher and friends advised him to quit school and begin preaching immediately. He joined the Ohio Conference of the Methodist Episcopal Church in 1837 and was appointed to the Charleston, West Virginia, circuit. He was ordained as a deacon two years later. In 1840 he married Sarah A. Miley. He was ordained as an elder in 1841. He served a series of pastorates in Ohio during the rest of the decade, ending at Wesley Chapel in Cincinnati. While at Cincinnati, he carried on a controversial debate with a Presbyterian minister on Calvinist predestination versus the Methodist position of free will. This controversy led to his first book, *Objections to Calvinism* (1849).

Foster transferred to the New York Conference in 1950 and remained a member for the next 18 years, serving pastorates throughout the state. In 1857 he took a special appointment for three years as president of Northwestern University in Evanston, Illinois. In Chicago Foster became an integral part of the new movement to emphasize the teachings of Christian holiness first articulated by Methodism's founder, John Wesley. According to Wesley, it was possible for the believer to become sanctified or perfect in love by an act of the Holy Spirit. This was an experience Foster advocated, and in 1851 he authored a book, *The Nature and Blessedness of Christian Purity*, which became a holiness classic.

Foster's steady rise within the church was evidenced by his election as a delegate to general conference in 1864, 1868, and 1872. In 1870 he left the pastorate permanently to become professor of systematic theology at Drew Theological Seminary. The job did not last long, as the church, in the midst of a holiness revival, elected Foster a bishop in 1872.

Though Foster was a holiness advocate elected as the holiness wave was growing in intensity, in his 24 years as a bishop he watched the church largely turn on the holiness movement; many of the movement's leaders left the church to found independent work. In spite of the reluctance he expressed in taking the job, Foster proved to be one of the church's most active and hardworking bishops. He traveled widely, visiting all of the missions of the Methodist Episcopal Church in Europe, Asia, and South America.

During the last years of his episcopacy Foster returned to writing and produced the *Philosophy of Christian Experience* (1890) and his magnum opus, the six volume *Studies in Theology* (1889-1899).

Sources:

Dictionary of American Biography. 20 vols. and 7 supps. New York: Charles Scribner's Sons, 1928-1936, 1944-1981.

Foster, Randolph S. *Centenary Thoughts for the Pew and Pulpit of Methodism.* New York: Phillips & Hunt, 1884. 186 pp.

———. *Evidences of Christianity.* New York: Hunt & Eaton, 1889. 430 pp.

———. *The Nature and Blessedness of Christian Purity.* New York: Carlton & Porter, 1851. 226 pp. Revised ed. as *Christian Purity, or the Heritage of Faith.* New York: Nelson & Phillips, 1869. 364 pp.

———. *Philosophy of Christian Experience.* New York: Hunt & Eaton, 1890. 188 pp.

———. *Studies in Theology.* 6 vols. Cincinnati, OH: Cranston & Stowe, 1889.

Harmon, Nolan B. *The Encyclopedia of World Methodism.* 2 vols. Nashville: United Methodist Publishing House, 1974.

Leete, Frederick D. *Methodist Bishops.* Nashville, TN: Privately printed, 1948.

★314★
FOX, Emmet
Minister, Church of the Healing Christ
b. Jul. 30, 1886, Ireland
d. Aug. 13, 1951, Paris France

Emmet Fox, for many years the pastor of the Church of the Healing Christ in New York City, reputed to be the largest congregation in the United States during the 1940s, was born of Irish parents. His parents had previously immigrated to America, but during his mother's pregnancy they returned to Ireland, where he was born and raised. His early training was as a Roman Catholic, and during his teen years he attended Stamford Hill Jesuit College in London. While there he had a profound mystical experience which led him to the study of mystical literature. He left the college without completing his course and began to study engineering, at which he was employed for many years. Back in Ireland he met J. Dimsdale Stocker, an early New Thought teacher, who introduced him to its idealistic philosophy of the omnipresence of God. He also became acquainted with Judge Thomas Troward, the author of an important set of New Thought books in the early twentieth century.

Through Troward, Fox became aware of the New Thought Alliance, which in 1914 expanded its scope to Europe with a meeting in London and became the New Thought Alliance (INTA); International. Fox attended the London gathering. After World War I he became active in the alliance in England. In 1928 he gave his first New Thought lecture in Mortimer Hall in London. His work was well received, and soon afterward he conducted a lecture tour of England and Scotland. He gradually gave up his engineering career.

In 1931 Fox visited New York as the first stop on a lecture tour. In his audience was Herman Wolhorn, a lay leader at the Church of the Healing Christ, a congregation affiliated with the Divine Science Federation. He accepted Wolhorn's offer to become the minister of the church. W. John Murray, the founder of the congregation, had built a church of over 1,000 members, but in the several

years since his death it had dwindled considerably. As the congregation revived under Fox's leadership, Sunday services were held at the Astor Hotel, and several midweek meetings were held at various other locations. In 1937 Fox moved his headquarters to the Hippodrome and in 1938 to Carnegie Hall, where he would conduct services for the rest of his active life.

In 1934 Fox published first book, a metaphysical commentary on *The Sermon on the Mount*. This was but the first of a series of volumes, most of which remain in print to this day. They include: *Power Through Constructive Thinking* (1940); *Sparks of Truth* (1941); *Make Your Life Worthwhile* (1946); and *Alter Your Life* (1950). He also authored a number of pamphlets, including an important one detailing a belief in reincarnation. Several volumes appeared posthumously, including *Stake Your Claim* (1952); *Around the Year with Emmet Fox* (1952); *The Ten Commandments* (1953); and *Diagrams for Living* (1968). He was succeeded by Herman Wolhorn.

Sources:

Fox, Emmet. *Alter Your Life.* New York: Harper & Brothers, 1950. 238 pp.

———. *Power Through Constructive Thinking.* New York: Harper & Brothers, 1940. 281 pp.

———. *The Sermon on the Mount.* New York: Harper & Brothers, 1934. 199 pp.

———. *Sparks of Truth.* New York: Grosset & Dunlap, 1941. 245 pp.

———. *The Ten Commandments.* New York: Harper & Row, 1953. 158 pp.

Gaze, Harry. *Emmet Fox: The Man and His Work.* New York: Harper & Brothers, 1952. 150 pp.

Wolhorn, Herman. *Emmet Fox's Golden Keys to Successful Living.* New York: Harper & Row, 1977. 229 pp.

★315★
FOX, Matthew Timothy
Theologian, Roman Catholic Church
b. Dec. 21, 1940, Madison, Wisconsin

Matthew Timothy Fox, O.P., a controversial theologian in the Roman Catholic Church, is the son of Beatrice Sill and Thomas Fox. As a teenager he decided to enter the priesthood, and following his high school years he entered Aquinas Institute of Philosophy and the Dominican College of St. Rose of Lima at River Forest, Illinois, from which he received his M.A. in 1964. Meanwhile, in 1960 he had joined the Ordo Pradicatorum (literally, the Order of Preachers, the Roman Catholic order popularly referred to as the Dominicans). Fox took his theological training at the Aquinas Institute of Philosophy and Theology at Dubuque, Iowa, and following his graduation in 1967 he was ordained as a Roman Catholic priest. He received his S.T.D. from the Institut Catholique de Paris in 1970 and became an assistant professor of theology at the Aquinas Institute. During the next few years he held several teaching posts before settling at Barat College in Lake Forest, Illinois, as professor and chairman for the department of religious studies.

While engaged in his doctoral studies, Fox had been introduced to creation-oriented theology by M. C. Chenu, the prominent church historian. He also began to listen to the stories told by female students, especially at Barat College, and slowly adopted a feminist perspective. These ideas were present but not yet the significant theme in his early books—*Religion USA: An Inquiry into Religion and Culture by Way of Time Magazine* (1971) and *On Becoming a Musical, Mystical Bear: Spirituality American Style* (1972). However, beginning with his third book, *Whee! We, Wee, All the Way Home: A Guide to the New Sensual Spirituality* (1976), they were to become predominant elements.

In 1977 Fox founded the Institute in Culture and Christian Spirituality, the purpose of which is to celebrate creation as a blessing and to cherish the sacred quality of nature, the environment, and God's creative energy. Creation spirituality seeks to empower individuals by drawing forth their mystical aspect. Fox elaborated on his thinking in his subsequent books, especially, *A Spirituality Named Compassion and the Healing of the Global Village, Humpty Dumpty and Us* (1979); *Original Blessing* (1983); and *The Coming of the Cosmic Christ* (1988). In 1983 he moved the institute to Oakland, California, where he had been named a professor at Holy Names College. Once in California, the faculty of the institute expanded to include the members of a variety of religious traditions, but the addition of Neo-Pagan priestess **Starhawk**, an outspoken Wiccan leader, became a matter of intense controversy.

In 1984 conservative Roman Catholics began to complain of Fox's teachings and of his association with Starhawk. Before the year was out, Cardinal Joseph Ratzinger ordered the Dominican Order to examine Fox's activities and teachings. After a year of review, the committee appointed to read Fox's books stated that they could find no heresy. Ratzinger questioned the report and, following a period of dialogue with Fox's defenders, he moved to silence Fox. Fox accepted the silencing, but just before the period began, in August 1988 he issued a paper, "Is the Catholic Church Today a Dysfunctional Family?" in which he charged that he was being silenced for political reasons rather than any valid criticism of his thought or work.

Fox has since ended his year of silence, but the issue between himself and Cardinal Ratzinger is still unresolved. Further controversy seems inevitable.

Sources:

Fox, Matthew. *The Coming of the Cosmic Christ.* New York: Harper & Row, 1988. 278 pp.
_____. "Is the Catholic Church Today a Dysfunctional Family?" *Creation* 4, 5 (November-December 1988): 23-37.
_____. *On Becoming a Musical, Mystical Bear: Spirituality American Style.* New York: Harper & Row, 1972. 156 pp.
_____. *Original Blessing: A Primer in Creation Spirituality.* Santa Fe, NM: Bear & Co., 1983. 348 pp.
_____. *A Spirituality Named Compassion and the Healing of the Global Village, Humpty Dumpty and Us.* Minneapolis, MN: Winston Press, 1979. 285 pp.
_____. *Whee! We, Wee All the Way Home: A Guide to the New Sensual Spirituality.* Wilmington, NC: Consortium, 1976. 226 pp.

★ 316 ★
FOX, Selena
Founder and Priestess, Circle Sanctuary
b. Oct. 20, 1949, Arlington, Virginia

Selena Fox, one of America's best known Wiccan priestesses, is the founder of Circle Sanctuary, a legally recognized Wiccan church headquartered on a 200-acre nature preserve in southwestern Wisconsin. She graduated with honors from the College of William and Mary (B.S. in psychology, 1971), and pursued additional studies in clinical and social psychology at such institutions as Rutgers University, the University of Wisconsin, and the Mendota Mental Health Institute.

In addition to academic and professional training in psychology, Fox has studied many spiritual disciplines, including alchemy, yoga, ceremonial magic, Druidism, Taoism, Neo-Pagan witchcraft, Christian spiritualism, Buddhism, and Native American shamanism. She has participated in and led a variety of rituals, meditations, vision quests, and other ceremonial experiences as part of her work in these areas.

In 1974 Fox founded the Church of Circle Wicca (now known as Circle Sanctuary), generally referred to as simply Circle, one of the first Wiccan churches in the United States to be officially recognized as a church by state and federal governments. At the time she was working with Jim Alan, Circle's high priest, and a small group of Neo-Pagans in the Madison, Wisconsin, area. Fox and Alan quickly made an impact upon the national Neo-Pagan community with their networking activity, ritual leadership, and the popular Pagan music created by Alan. In 1977 Fox founded Circle Network, a networking ministry serving nature religions practitioners worldwide. In 1978 she incorporated the church and began a newsletter, *Circle Network News*, which quickly became and remains the largest circulating Neo-Pagan periodical in North America.

Partially in response to the formation of the Covenant of the Goddess (COG), a national fellowship of Neo-Pagan witches, Fox organized the Pagan Spirit Alliance, a national fellowship for Pagans which included those who did not describe themselves as witches. The following year she organized the first Pagan Spirit Gathering, an event held annually since then.

In 1983 the church purchased 200 acres in rural Wisconsin which became the home base for the church, soon renamed Circle Sanctuary. The land became home to Fox and became the site of a variety of activities, including regular Pagan gatherings. Such activities were especially prevalent in the summer. At the sanctuary, Fox founded the School for Priestesses, the first contemporary ecumenical ministerial program of its type for women involved in goddess-oriented forms of spirituality. Fox practices a form of Wiccan Shamanism, an eclectic form of Neo-Pagan Goddess worship, that is reflective of her broad training in world religions. In 1984 Fox and Alan ended their relationship, and in 1986 Fox married Dennis Carpenter, who now functions as high priest for Circle.

In the mid 1980s, word of the existence of Circle Sanctuary and the magical activities being held there circulated through the county in which it is located, and an intense battle followed. Local residents, offended by the presence of witches, used a number of strategies to dislodge and/or limit the operation of the church. In response, Fox mobilized support from the Pagan community (as the Pagan Strength Web) and with the assistance of civil rights activists fought to save the sanctuary. In 1988 the local government recognized the church's right to exist and use the land. In the process hundreds of Pagans were sensitized to broader religious rights issues facing the Pagan community, and a national agenda developed for the web.

Sources:

Eklund, Christopher. "Witches Jim Alan and Selena Fox Let Their Cauldron Bubble with Minimal Toil and Trouble." *People* (Nov. 5, 1979) 47, 50, 55, 58.
Elson, Mary. "Witches Clean Up Their Old Evil Image." *Chicago Tribune* (April 13, 1980).
"Selena Fox: Building Bridges of Understanding; An Interview." *Fireheart* (Spring/Summer 1989): 10-17.

★ 317 ★
FOX SISTERS
Pioneer Spiritualist Mediums

Modern Spiritualism, at least insofar as general public recognition and support are concerned, originated with the three Fox sisters—Leah (also known as Anne; b. circa 1814 Rockland County, New York; d. Nov. 1, 1890 New York, New York), Catherine (often called Kate; b. Bath, Consccon, Ontario; d. July 2, 1892 New York, New York), and Margaret (b. Bath, Consccon, Ontario; d. March 8, 1893 Brooklyn, New York). Leah was married long enough to have a child before her husband left her; they divorced in the 1830s, and she lived in Rochester with her daughter, working as a music teacher. In 1847 John Fox became the blacksmith of Hydesville in Wayne County, New York, and the family moved into a vacant cottage.

In March of 1848 they began to hear strange rapping noises in the house, and Margaret and Kate discovered that the noise was an intelligent phenomenon with which they could communicate. Word of this spread, and neighbors flocked to hear for themselves.

Life became so hectic that Kate and Margaret went to live out of town for a while. The rappings continued, however, and some, like Eliab W. Capron, began to believe that they were communicating with the dead. He organized a citizen's committee to investigate the matter, and both this and a second committee could find no logical way of accounting for the rapping. In 1850 Capron took the sisters to New York, where they gave demonstrations and gained the support of Horace Greeley, editor of the *New York Tribune*.

Suddenly it seemed the whole world knew of the story, and many groups formed to try to contact the dead. The Fox sisters toured the country on a regular basis, and a Spiritualist movement led by people such as **Andrew Jackson Davis** and **Thomas Lake Harris** gained momentum. The personal lives of the sisters, however, did not fare very well. Margaret had met the famous arctic explorer Elisha Kent Kane at a lecture. After his death in 1857, she claimed that in 1856 they had made love vows to each other, and that she was thus due an annuity he had left her as a common-law wife. She eventually published a book about their relationship. Meanwhile, Leah ended a second marriage as a widow in 1853. She married a third time, this time to Daniel Underhill, in 1858. Underhill helped her drop into a semi-retired domestic life.

Kate remained the most active sister, speaking on behalf of the Society for the Diffusion of Spiritual Knowledge, created by a patron, Horace H. Day. Kate's stumbling block, was alcoholism, a sickness also evident in her sister Margaret. Her husband, Henry D. Jencken, whom she married in 1872, was a great help, but no progress seemed more than temporary. After he died in 1881, the problem got worse, and her two children were removed from her in 1888. This incident prompted Margaret to rise to her defense, claiming that Kate had been under great emotional strain in keeping up their Spiritualist hoax. She claimed Leah was the one who forced them early on to continue the charade.

The Spiritualist community was shocked and dismayed by these revelations, which were not the only accusations of fraud in the movement. In 1889, however, Margaret retracted her confession, saying she had been tricked into saying those things. She engaged in a public tour to reaffirm her belief in Spiritualism, but the public did not respond, and the sisters spent the rest of their lives out of the spotlight. Kate and Margaret ended their lives in the despair of poverty and alcohol. Despite the unfortunate ending of their careers, Spiritualists still acknowledge the Fox sisters as the first of the popular modern mediums.

Sources:

Brown, Slater. *The Heyday of Spiritualism*. New York: Pocket Books, 1970. 296 pp
Fornell, Earl L. *The Unhappy Medium: Spiritualism and the Life of Margaret Fox*. Austin, TX: University of Texas Press, 1964. 204 pp.
Kane, Margaretta Fox. *The Love-Life of Dr. Kane*. New York: Carlton, 1865.
Melton, J. Gordon. *Biographical Dictionary of American Cult and Sect Leaders*. Garland Reference Library of Social Science, vol. 212. New York: Garland Publishing, 1986.
Pond, Miriam Buckner. *Time Is Kind*. New York: North River Press, 1947. 334 pp.
Taylor, William G.L. *Katie Fox*. New York: G. P. Putnam's Sons, 1933.
Underhill, Ann Leah. *The Missing Link in Modern Spiritualism*. New York: Thomas R. Knox & Co., 1885. 477 pp.

—*Gary L. Ward*

★318★
FREED, Arvy Glenn
Educator, Churches of Christ
b. 1863, Sattillo, Indiana
d. Nov. 11, 1931, Nashville, Tennessee

Prominent among the second generation of leadership of what would become the Churches of Christ after 1906 was Arvy Glenn

Freed. Born in Indiana, he attended Valparaiso University. As a young man he joined the Christian Church and became a minister. In 1889 he moved to Essary Springs, Tennessee, and opened a school in response to an item in the *Gospel Advocate*, the Churches of Christ periodical published in Nashville, Tennessee. At the time the Church supported the West Tennessee Christian College located at Henderson, Tennessee. In 1893 the president of the school resigned and Freed succeeded him. The school prospered under Freed's care, and in 1897 the school was renamed the Georgia Robertson Christian College in honor of the daughter of a donor.

Shortly after the turn of the century, the school became a local focus of the controversy over the use of instrumental music (primarily in the form of church organs) in the church. Though Freed and most of the faculty opposed their introduction, at least one professor and many church members in the Henderson congregation favored it. In 1902 Freed debated J. N. Hall, a Kentucky minister on the issue.

In 1906 the split within the Christian Church Movement, one symbol of which was the use of musical instruments in worship, was formally recognized. In 1908 the more liberal party now known as the Christian Church (Disciples of Christ), gained control of the school. Freed left and founded the National Teachers' Normal and Business College in Henderson, with one of the professors, Nicholas Brodie Hardeman.

Freed stayed at Henderson until 1923, at which time he moved to Nashville to take a position at David Lipscomb College. He served in several different positions there over the remainder of his life. He was not a writer of books, but was in great demand as a speaker throughout the Churches of Christ. Several collections of his talks appeared under various titles.

After the deaths of Freed and Hardeman, the school they founded was renamed Freed-Hardeman College in their honor.

Sources:

Hill, Samuel S., ed. *Encyclopedia of Religion in the South*. Macon, GA: Mercer University Press, 1984. 878 pp.
Srygley, F. B. "A Great Man Has Fallen This Day." *Gospel Advocate*. December 1931, reprinted in Foy E. Wallace, Jr., *The Present Truth*. Ft. Worth, TX: Foy Wallace Publications, 1977.

★319★
FREW III, Donald Hudson
Public Information Officer and First Officer of Covenant of the Goddess
b. May 11, 1960, Long Beach, California

Donald Hudson Frew III is a Neo-Pagan leader best known for his work as the Public Information Officer of the Covenant of the Goddess (COG), a national association of Wiccan covens. A member of a non-religious family, Frew was relatively free to pursue his interests in the mysterious and the occult, and by his early teens was involved with a local witch coven. He was educated at the University of California at Berkeley, where he majored first in anthropology and then in religious studies. During his college years he joined the Rosicrucians (AMORC), studied with **Anton LaVey** of the Church of Satan, sought and received training in the Gardnerian Wicca tradition, and studied the New Reformed Order of the Golden Dawn (NROOGD) tradition of Wicca with Coven Firestar (in which **Philip Emmons Isaac Bonewits** was an elder). In 1988 Frew "hived" from Firestar to become high priest of Black Oak Coven.

In 1985 Frew was elected Public Information Officer of the Covenant of the Goddess. Feeling that it was time for COG to enter the "mainstream," Frew sought out and made contact with groups which had attacked the craft. For example, in the wake of some crimes associated with the Neo-Pagan community, he made contact with the San Francisco Police Department. He eventually became a consultant on occultism and ritual crime for police departments around the country. Frew also was designated COG's representative to the Berkeley Area Interfaith Council (BAIC) in 1985. In 1986 he was elected to the executive committee of the council. In 1987 he was elected the BAIC's executive secretary, a position he continued to hold as of 1989.

In 1986 Frew opened communications with the Spiritual Counterfeits Project, an Evangelical Christian counter-cult organization, with whom he participated in a day of dialogue. That same year, he also lectured at meetings of the Committee for Scientific Investigation of Claims of the Paranormal, an organization of humanists/ skeptics who attempt to debunk and expose occult claims. This led to him becoming a special consultant on the occult for the related Committee for Scientific Examination of Religion, with whom he worked on a study of Satanism in America.

In 1988 Frew and **Diana L. Paxson** were elected COG's First Officers, and in 1989 they became members-at-large of COG's National Board. At present, Frew functions as high priest for two covens, Black Oak and Tobar, while continuing his work with law enforcement and interfaith groups.

Sources:

Rufus, Anneli. "Among the Believers: A Berkeley Witch Goes to a Christian Convention and Lives". *California Magazine*. June (1990): pp 18.

★ 320 ★
FRODSHAM, Stanley
Independent Pentecostal Writer and Editor
b. Mar. 1, 1882, Bournemouth England
d. Dec. 8, 1969, Springfield, Missouri

Stanley Frodsham, a pioneer Pentecostal leader, was the son of Marianne Ensworth and Henry Frodsham. His parents were both devout Christians and Frodsham was raised in the Congregational Church. He left school at the age of 14 and went to work in London. While there he attended a meeting of the YMCA where he had a conversion experience. He eventually found himself back in Bournemouth in a family business operating concessions at the popular tourist center. In the winter of 1906-1907 he traveled to Canada and there heard of the Pentecostal revival which had broken out at the Azuza Street mission in Los Angeles. His continued interest led to his receiving the baptism of the Holy Spirit in 1908. The baptism of the Holy Spirit, evidenced by the believer speaking in tongues, is the definitive religious experience of the Pentecostal movement.

Frodsham soon came to know Smith Wigglesworth, one of the pioneer Pentecostal leaders in England, and at his urging began to publish tracts. There being a dearth of Pentecostal literature in England, Frodsham began *Victory*, the first Pentecostal periodical in England. He also became the leader of an independent Pentecostal fellowship in Bournemouth. During a 1909 return visit to Canada, he was introduced to Alice Rowlands. Two years later Wigglesworth married them. They resided in England until 1916 when Frodsham ceased the publication of *Victory* and moved to the United States.

Frodsham affiliated with the General Council of the Assemblies of God and was chosen general secretary and associate editor for the Assemblies. He lived in St. Louis for two years but moved to Springfield, Missouri, in 1918 when the Gospel Publishing House was established there. Following a brief period in Chicago in 1920, he became editor of *The Pentecostal Evangel*, the main church periodical, as well as *Our Pentecostal Boys and Girls*, a children's magazine. In 1921 he was named general church editor. Among his accomplishments during the 1920s was the authoring of a history of the Pentecostal movement, *With Signs Following*. Frodsham

resigned his editorial position in 1928 to take a less taxing position with the Church Worker's Union in Framingham, Massachusetts. He returned to Springfield in 1929, where he remained as a writer and editor for the next 20 years. He also taught Pentecostal history at the Central Bible College.

The final phase of Frodsham's career began in 1949 when he heard of the Latter Rain revival which had been brought by Assemblies minister Myrtle Beall to her church in Detroit. The revival included a reemphasis upon the gifts of the spirit, especially healing and prophecy, and a new organizational pattern. Frodsham became an enthusiastic supporter of the revival, which led to his break with the Assemblies. He was the most outstanding Assemblies leader to follow the Latter Rain, and for the next 13 years became an active itinerant speaker on its behalf. During the last years of his life he moved back to Springfield and associated briefly with Charles William Britton, another independent Latter Rain advocate. As a result his accomplishments as a pentecostal pioneer were largely ignored until his biography was published by the Assemblies in 1974.

Sources:

Campbell, Faith. *Stanley Frodsham: Prophet with a Pen*. Springfield, MO: Gospel Publishing House, 1974. 146 pp.

Frodsham. Stanley. *The Coming Crises and the Coming Christ*. Springfield, MO: Gospel Publishing House, 1936. 64 pp.

_____. *Jesus Is Victor*. Springfield, MO: Gospel Publishing House, 1930. 127 pp.

_____. *Smith Wigglesworth, Apostle of Faith*. Springfield, MO: Gospel Publishing House, 1948. 153 pp.

_____. *With Signs Following*. Springfield, MO: Gospel Publishing House, 1926. 254 pp.

★ 321 ★
FROST, Gavin
Cofounder, Church and School of Wicca
b. Nov. 20, 1930, Staffordshire England

Gavin Frost is a co-founder of the Church and School of Wicca (1968), the oldest incorporated church of witchcraft in the United States. Together with his wife, **Yvonne Frost**, he is one of the more controversial figures within the larger Neo-Pagan movement. He holds a bachelors degree in mathematics and a doctorate in physics and math from London University, and a Doctor of Divinity degree from the School of Wicca. His early career was in the aerospace industry. His job led him to settle in California in the early 1960s. There he met Yvonne Wilson, a spiritualist, whom he married in 1970.

From a Welsh background, Frost was interested in witchcraft at an early age. While working on the Salisbury Plain he became interested in Stonehenge, and it was the exploration of this interest that eventually led him to the Craft. In the mid-1960s, he and Yvonne moved to St. Louis, where they met a Wiccan priest and were initiated into the Craft. Together, in 1965, they started the School of Wicca, which they incorporated as a religious body. (It received its federal tax exemption status as a religious body in 1972.) They began to advertise for pupils for the course in witchcraft they wrote through such periodicals as *Fate* magazine and began to author books about the Craft. Their first major book, *The Witch's Bible* (1972), created a controversy within the movement because of such points as the assertion that the Ultimate Deity was not definable, an assertion that runs against the Goddess emphasis found in most other Wiccan traditions. While the Frosts have not been disfellowshipped from the larger Wiccan community, their very real disagreements with the main body of Goddess-worshipping Wiccans have kept their church somewhat separated.

Through the years the Frosts have devoted most of their time to nurturing the church, which has members and covens across the United States, and to writing a number of books, including: *Magic*

Power of Witchcraft (1976), the *A Witch's Guide to Life* (1978), and *Power Secrets from a Sorcerer's Private Magnum Arcanum* (1980).

Sources:

Frost, Gavin, and Yvonne Frost. *The Magic Power of Witchcraft.* West Nyack, NY: Parker Publishing Company, 1976. 203 pp.

_____. *Meta-Psychometry: Key to Power and Abundance.* West Nyack, NY: Parker Publishing Company, 1978. 239 pp.

_____. *Power Secrets from a Sorcerer's Private Magnum Arcanum.* West Nyack, NY: Parker Publishing Company, 1980. 217 pp.

_____. *The Witch's Bible.* Los Angeles: Nash Publishing Company, 1972.

_____. *A Witch's Guide to Life.* Cottonwood, AZ: Esoteric Publications, 1978. 136 pp.

★322★
FROST, James Marion
Founder, Sunday School Board, Southern Baptist Convention
b. Feb. 10, 1848, Georgetown, Kentucky
d. Oct. 30, 1916, Nashville, Tennessee

James Marion Frost, who pioneered Sunday school work among Southern Baptists, was raised in Georgetown and attended Georgetown College. He married Nanney Riley. During the 1870s and 1880s he served successively First Baptist Church, Maysville, Kentucky; Upper Street Baptist Church, Lexington, Kentucky; First Baptist Church, Staunton, Virginia; First Baptist Church, Selma, Alabama; and Leigh Street Baptist Church, Richmond, Virginia. Over the years he had become attentive of the growing Sunday school movement and felt that Sunday schools should be promoted throughout the convention. The Southern Baptist Convention placed a great emphasis upon the authority and role of the local church, and expressed a certain reluctance to proliferate structures which seemed to take any authority away from the local church (such as dictating what literature to use in educational programs).

While at Richmond, however, Frost began to move on the issue and introduced legislation to establish a Sunday school board. With the help of **John A. Broadus**, the legislation passed in 1891. Frost moved to Nashville to serve as the board's first secretary. He experienced some loneliness, as many Baptists did not understand his work. He had only limited financial support and personally desired to return to the pastorate. Thus, at the end of 1892, he accepted the offer to become pastor of First Baptist Church in Nashville, and relinquished his role with the board. He stayed at the church four years, but in 1896 again assumed the secretaryship of the board, a position he retained for the following two decades.

Frost became a strong leader for the board. He imposed upon it the task of developing and publishing its own Baptist curriculum, not merely serving as a printing establishment for literature. He created both a graded lesson series and a teacher-training program. He developed standards for measuring the program's success. Possibly most importantly, he emphasized the integral relationship between the Sunday schools and the local churches (there being no inherent connection) and the relationship of both to the convention. Frost also created the Baptist Young People's Union.

Over the years of Frost's leadership, the board became the primary supplier of Sunday school material to Southern Baptist churches, began to publish more general church-related materials, and developed as a publisher of books. Shortly before World War I, Frost oversaw the erection of the board's new offices, a five-story structure in downtown Nashville.

Once the board was somewhat stable, Frost found time to write. He produced a series of books: *Moral Dignity of Baptism* (1905); *The Memorial Supper* (1908); *An Experience of Grace* (1908); *Our Church Life* (1909); *The School and the Church* (1911); and *Sunday School Board History and Work* (1914). In 1916, while on a trip, he became sick and died a short time later.

Sources:

Encyclopedia of Southern Baptists. 3 vols. Nashville, TN: Broadman Press, 1958, 1971.

Frost, James M. *An Experience of Grace.* Nashville, TN: Sunday School Board, Southern Baptist Convention, 1908.

_____. *The Memorial Supper.* Nashville, TN: Sunday School Board, Southern Baptist Convention, 1908. 282 pp.

_____. *Moral Dignity of Baptism.* Nashville, TN: Sunday School Board, Southern Baptist Convention, 1905. 282 pp.

_____. *The School and the Church.* New York: Fleming H. Revell Co., 1911. 193 pp.

_____. *Sunday School Board History and Work.* Nashville, TN: Sunday School Board, Southern Baptist Convention, 1914. 96 pp.

★323★
FROST, Yvonne
Cofounder, Church and School of Wicca
b. 1931, Los Angeles, California

Yvonne Frost is a co-founder of the Church and School of Wicca (1968), the oldest incorporated "church" of witchcraft in the United States. Together with her husband, Gavin, she is one of the more controversial figures within the larger Neo-Pagan movement. She was born Yvonne Wilson into a conservative Baptist family. Dissatisfied with her inherited Baptist beliefs, she began to study world religions in order to find a more personally satisfying faith. She married in 1950, but the marriage ended ten years later and she returned to school. She attended Fullerton, California Junior College, from which she received an associate of arts degree in 1962. She also became involved in the study of psychic development and spiritualism.

Shortly after her graduation she met her future husband, **Gavin Frost**, an employee in the aeronautics industry. They discovered their mutual interest in the occult and began to pursue the study of witchcraft together. They were initiated in the Celtic tradition of Wicca in the mid-1960s, and in 1965 they formed the Church and School of Wicca. They began to reach people through a correspondence course that they advertised in occult periodicals. The school soon developed an extensive following. It enrolled many thousands, although only a minority have finished the course, and only several hundred have been accepted by the Frosts for initiation.

Yvonne serves as bishop of the church. Much of her time is consumed by the administrative duties of nurturing the church and its members across the United States. Yvonne has authored a number of books with her husband. The first, *The Witch's Bible* (1972), was the most controversial. It was rejected by many Neo-Pagans as not representative of the beliefs of witchcraft, as its teachings are not centered on the Goddess, the prime deity for most Neo-Pagans. Other books include: *The Magic Power of Witchcraft* (1976), *A Witch's Guide to Life* (1978), *Meta-Psychometry: Key to Power and Abundance* (1978), and *Power Secrets from a Sorcerer's Magnum Arcanum* (1980).

Sources:

Frost, Gavin and Yvonne Frost. *The Magic Power of Witchcraft.* West Nyack, NY: Parker Publishing Company, 1976. 203 pp.

_____. *Meta-Psychometry: Key to Power and Abundance.* West Nyack, NY: Parker Publishing Company, 1978. 239 pp.

_____. *Power Secrets from a Sorcerer's Private Magnum Arcanum.* West Nyack, NY: Parker Publishing Company, 1980. 217 pp.

_____. *The Witch's Bible.* Los Angeles: Nash Publishing Company, 1972.

_____. *A Witch's Guide to Life.* Cottonwood, AZ: Esoteric Publications, 1978. 136 pp.

Guiley, Rosemary E. *Encyclopedia of Witchcraft & Witches.* New York: Facts on File, 1989. 400 pp.

★324★
FROTHINGHAM, Octavius Brooks
President, Free Religious Association
b. Nov. 26, 1822, Boston, Massachusetts
d. Nov. 27, 1895, Boston, Massachusetts

Octavius Brooks Frothingham, author and liberal clergyman, was the second of five children of Ann Gorham Brooks and Nathaniel Langdon Frothingham. He graduated from Harvard in 1843. He then attended Harvard Divinity School, where he graduated in 1846. He was ordained as pastor of the North Church of Salem (affiliated with the Congregational Church) on March 10, 1847, and two weeks later married Caroline E. Curtis. He eventually broke with his congregation over his activism against slavery, and in 1855 moved to Jersey City, New Jersey, as minister of a new Unitarian society.

Frothingham was a popular spiritual leader, and in 1859 the Third Congregational Unitarian Society (later called the Independent Liberal Church) was organized by his admirers in New York City. He was at the peak of his powers during the 20 years of this pastorate, and was regarded as the intellectual heir of Theodore Parker, the New England free religious thinker. His sermons were circulated as pamphlets and in newspapers and aroused widespread discussion. To the far left of even liberal Unitarianism, he eventually left the Unitarian fold to become one of the founders of the Free Religious Association in Boston on May 30, 1867. He served as the association's first president until 1878.

Frothingham's health broke down in 1879 and he was forced to give up active work. His congregation disbanded and, after a year of rest in Europe, he lived in semi-retirement in Boston for the balance of his life. During this period he continued to write and produced a number of books, including: *The Religion of Humanity* (1872); *The Safest Creed* (1874); *Transcendentalism in New England: A History* (1876); *Gerrit Smith: A Biography* (1877); *Boston Unitarianism, 1820-1850: A Study of the Life and Work of Nathaniel Langdon Frothingham* (1890), and *Recollections and Impressions* (1891). At his request, his body was cremated upon his death in Boston.

Sources:

Dictionary of American Biography. 20 vols. and 7 supps. New York: Charles Scribner's Sons, 1928-1936, 1944-1981.

Frothingham, Octavius Brooks. *Gerrit Smith: A Biography.* New York: Putnam, 1877. 381 pp.

_____. *Recollections and Impressions.* New York: G. P. Putnam's Sons, 1891. 305 pp.

_____. *The Religion of Humanity.* New York: D. G. Francis, 1872. 338 pp.

_____. *The Safest Creed.* New York: A. K. Butts & Co., 1874. 238 pp.

_____. *Transcendentalism in New England: A History.* New York: G. P. Putnam's Sons, 1876. 395 pp.

★325★
FRY, Franklin Clark
President, Lutheran Church in America
b. Aug. 30, 1900, Bethlehem, Pennsylvania
d. Jun. 6, 1968, New Rochelle, New York

Franklin Clark Fry, the first president of the Lutheran Church in America, was the son of Minnie Clark McKeown and Franklin Foster Fry. He grew up in Rochester, New York, where his father was the pastor of Reformation Lutheran Church. He made an early decision to go into the ministry and as a youth also developed an interest in classical literature. He studied Greek during his high school years and majored in classics at Hamilton College. Following his graduation in 1921 he was able to spend a year abroad at the American School for Classical Studies in Athens. He took his theological work at the Lutheran Theological Seminary in Philadelphia, and upon graduation in 1925 was ordained in the United Lu-

theran Church in America (ULCA) and became the pastor of the Lutheran Church of the Redeemer in Yonkers, New York. In 1927, while in Yonkers, he married Hilda A. Drewes.

In 1929 Fry moved to Trinity Lutheran Church in Akron, Ohio. While there he began to serve on national boards and committees for his denomination and gain a reputation as a preacher, administrator, and parliamentarian. In 1934 he was named a member of the executive board of the ULCA. In 1936 he was a member of the national preaching mission of the Federal Council of Churches. In 1944 he became the president of the ULCA, a full-time position which took him out of the parish. From that point on he assumed an ever more prominent position in Lutheran affairs, both nationally and internationally.

As ULCA president, Fry was immediately confronted with the post-war situation in Germany. In 1946 he helped organize Lutheran World Relief and the following year led in the formation of the Lutheran World Federation, of which he was named treasurer in 1948. He was honored by both Germany and Austria for his relief work. While both organizations were focused upon post-war Europe, both have subsequently broadened their concerns and programs. Fry's international involvement placed him in the position to contribute to the 1948 formation of the World Council of Churches (especially in the writing of its constitution and by-laws). He was named vice-chairman of the council's central committee. He was able to assist in a similar vein in the formation of the National Council of Churches and chaired the opening session of the council's constituting meeting in 1950.

Through the 1950s Fry's leadership roles increased. In 1952 he became the vice-president of the Lutheran World Federation and was named president in 1957. In 1954 he became the chairman of both the central committee and the executive committee of the World Council. During this period, while also remaining president of the ULCA, he also worked for the reunion of American Lutheranism. A major step toward such a reunion was taken in 1962 with the merger of the ULCA and several other churches to form the Lutheran Church in America (now a constituent part of the Evangelical Lutheran Church in America). Fry was elected as the first president of the new church. Illness overtook him in 1968 and he resigned his presidency shortly before his death. At the time he was one of the most well-known church leaders in the world.

Sources:

Fischer, Robert H. *Franklin Clark Fry: A Palette for a Portrait.* Springfield, OH: The Lutheran Quarterly, 1972. 369 pp.

★326★
FRYDLAND, Rachmiel
Hebrew Christian Minister
Founder, Messianic Literature Outreach
b. Mar. 15, 1919, Chelm Poland
d. Jan. 12, 1985, Cincinnati, Ohio

Rachmiel Frydland, for over 40 years a Christian missionary to Jews, was born in rural Poland, the son of Abraham and Charma Frydland. The family were followers of a Hassidic rebbe who resided at the town of Reywitz. Rachmiel went to a Jewish school in a nearby town, Ruta-Huta, and at the yeshiva in Chelm, and as a teenager he traveled to Warsaw to study in a yeshiva there. In 1936 he left the yeshiva and went into the retail clothing business. After hearing about a meeting to be held by "missionaries," Frydland attended a gathering led by Paul Rosenberg, a Hebrew Christian. He obtained a New Testament and after reading it became convinced that Jesus (Yeshua) was the Jewish Messiah.

After becoming a Christian, Frydland began to attend a mission in Warsaw sponsored by the Mildmay Mission to the Jews, a British organization. It offered free English lessons. In November, he began to work at the mission and was baptized at the German Baptist Church. After the Nazi invasion of Poland, he fled to the countryside. Arrested and sent to a slave labor camp, he escaped and managed to survive until the Russians drove the Nazis out. Reconnecting with the Mildmay Mission after the war, he immigrated to London in 1947 and pursued his studies at the All Nations Bible College. He went on to the University of London and earned a B.D. and an M.A. in Hebrew.

In 1952 Fryland immigrated to America and went to work at Hermon House, a Hebrew Christian center in Manhattan, while pursuing a Ph.D. at New York University. He discontinued the program before he completed his work, though he did receive a M.A. In 1961 he moved to Israel as a representative of the International Hebrew Christian Alliance. While there he married. He returned to the United States in 1965 with his wife and their first two children and began a brief pastorate at New Covenant Messengers, a congregation in Newark, New Jersey. He then assumed a position at Tennessee Temple University in Chattanooga as professor of Jewish Studies. While in Chattanooga, he authored his autobiography, *Joy Cometh in the Morning* (1972). He also became associated with Jacob Gartenhaus, founder of the American Board of Jewish Missions. In 1973 he moved to Toronto as a missionary with the board. After two years in Toronto, he moved to Cincinnati as pastor of Beth Messiah Congregation and then in 1976 became pastor of Kehilat Meshiach, another Hebrew Christian Messianic congregation in Cincinnati. In 1975 he began to edit the *Messianic Jewish Quarterly*, a task he continued until 1979.

In addition to all of these various activities, he founded the Messianic Literature Outreach and its quarterly magazine, *The Messianic Outreach*. By this time Frydland had become identified with the new aggressive movement among young Jewish converts to Christianity called Messianic Judaism.

In 1979 Fryland developed a relationship with the Hineni Ministries, Inc., or Jews for Jesus. He began a year of intensive training in Jewish Studies with the Jews for Jesus staff and then began to work with their missionary center in New York. From 1979 to 1984 he alternated two month periods at home with two month periods in San Francisco and/or New York. In 1984 cancer began to overtake him, and he died the following year.

Sources:

Frydland, Rachmiel. *Joy Cometh in the Morning*. Chattanooga, TN: Messianic Fellowship, Tennessee Temple Schools, 1972. 52 pp. Rev. ed. as *When Being Jewish Was a Crime*. Nashville, TN: Thomas Nelson, 1978. 166 pp.
"Rachmiel Frydland Memorial Issue." *The Messianic Outreach* 4, 4 (June-August 1985).

★ 327 ★
FULLER, Charles Edward
Independent Fundamentalist Radio Minister
Founder, Fuller Theological Seminary
b. Apr. 25, 1887, Los Angeles, California
d. Mar. 18, 1968

Charles Edward Fuller, whose "Old Fashioned Revival Hour" was one of the most popular and longest running religious radio shows in the mid-twentieth century, grew up in a devout Methodist home on his parents' orange grove near Redlands, California. His successful father was a strong supporter of world missions. Fuller attended Pomona College from which he graduated cum laude in chemistry in 1901. In 1911 he married Grace Payton, whom he had dated since high school, and settled down to work for his father. In 1913 the family moved to Placentia, California, and became active in the Placentia Presbyterian Church.

In 1916 Fuller had a life changing experience listening to **Paul Rader**, who was then visiting southern California from his pulpit at Moody Church in Chicago. As a result he began teaching a Sun-

day school class. Then, in 1919 he returned to school and pursued a degree at the Bible Institute of Los Angeles (BIOLA), the independent school funded by fundamentalist oil man **Lyman Stewart**. He graduated in 1921. Meanwhile, his Sunday school class continued to grow. By 1925 his intense fundamentalist perspective had created a rift in the congregation, and Fuller and his supporters left the church and founded the independent Calvary Church. He was ordained by representatives of the Baptist Bible Union, a fundamentalist association, and he became the church's pastor.

Fuller extended his ministry through evangelistic meetings up and down the California coast. In 1930 he made his most significant step by initiating a radio ministry. His congregation did not share his enthusiasm for the new medium, and in 1933 he resigned and founded the Gospel Broadcasting Company. He had begun by simply broadcasting his church's Bible study and worship services. After trying several formats and names for the show, he decided to adopt the format of a Sunday evening worship service and to call the program the "Old Fashioned Revival Hour."

At first his program was carried along the west coast and then throughout the western United States to the Mississippi River. Then, in 1937 he reached an agreement with the Mutual Broadcasting Network. Starting with 14 stations in 1937, by 1942 he aired on 456 stations and hosted one of the most popular shows in the nation. His rapid expansion was undergirded with an aggressive repertoire of personal appearances at revival services around the country. He was able to broadcast the services from the different points served by the network. He also sought and won endorsements from other fundamentalist leaders.

During World War II the "Old Fashioned Revival Hour" reached its largest audience, being broadcast around the world, but faced a crisis that almost proved fatal in 1944. Mutual, following the lead of other networks, dropped all paid religious broadcasts. Fuller responded by aggressively developing a network of independent stations to air the show. He had an estimated audience of 20 million when ABC finally picked up the show in 1949.

During the war Fuller also began to put money aside to found a school. He convinced **Harold John Ockenga** to gather a faculty, and the school opened in Pasadena in 1947 as the Fuller Theological Seminary.

From his peak in the 1940s, Fuller began to decline in popularity and influence. His first problem came from his inability to make the transition from radio to television. Through the 1950s he lost his hour show, cut to a half hour in 1958, and ABC dropped it altogether in 1963. He had to return to a network of independent stations. Meanwhile he came into open conflict with the seminary. Fuller, an unreconstructed fundamentalist, discovered that Ockenga was committed to Neo-Evangelicalism, a new movement which intended to drop the separatist tendencies of fundamentalism and present an intellectually sound defense of traditional Protestantism. In spite of his problems with the school's direction he continued to support it, in part because of the urgings of his son Dan Fuller, who had studied under theologian Karl Barth in Switzerland. Charles Edward Fuller continued preaching on independent stations until his death in 1968.

Sources:

Armstrong, Ben. *The Electronic Church*. Nashville, TN: Thomas Nelson, 1979. 192 pp.
Fuller, Daniel P. *Give the Winds a Mighty Voice: The Story of Charles E. Fuller*. Waco, TX: Word Publishing, 1972.
Marsden, George M. *Reforming Fundamentalism: Fuller Seminary and the New Evangelicalism*. Grand Rapids, MI: William B. Eerdmans Publishing Company, 1987.
Siedell, Barry. *Gospel Radio*. Lincoln, NB: Back to the Bible Broadcast, 1971. 158 pp.

Smith, Wilbur M. *A Voice for God: The Life of Charles E. Fuller, Originator of the Old Fashioned Revival Hour.* Boston: W. A. Wilde, 1949.

★ 328 ★
FULLER, Thomas Oscar
Minister and Executive, National Baptist Convention in the U.S.A.
b. Oct. 25, 1867, Franklinton, North Carolina
d. 1942, United States

Thomas Oscar Fuller, an executive with the National Baptist Convention in the U.S.A., was the son of Mary Eliza and J. Henderson Fuller. His father, a carpenter, had been able to buy his freedom from slavery and after the Civil War had become a land owner. He had also learned to read and write and had passed along the ideal of education to his children. Fuller began his schooling in Franklinton, North Carolina, received his B.A. from Shaw University in 1890, and finished his M.A. three years later. In April 1893 he was ordained as a Baptist minister.

The 1890s were still relatively open in North Carolina, and during these years Fuller mixed his religious life with some political aspirations. He pastored several different churches, but made his living teaching in the public schools. He organized the Girl's Training School in Franklin, and in 1895 he became the principal of Shiloh Institute in Warrenton, North Carolina. Then in 1898 he ran successfully for a seat as a senator in the North Carolina legislature. The only black legislator when the session opened in 1899, he was seated last and not assigned to any committee. During his time in office, which followed a famous race riot in Wilmington, North Carolina, the state passed an amendment to the constitution which effectively disenfranchised Blacks and ended Fuller's brief political career.

In 1900 Fuller became pastor of First Baptist Church of Memphis, Tennessee, and principal of Howe Institute, a position he held for the next 30 years. He also became active within the National Baptist Convention and served as a secretary of the convention for over 25 years. He became the director of publicity for the convention and for a number of years was its representative on the executive board of the Baptist World Alliance.

Over the years of his life in Memphis, Fuller authored a number of books, including: *Twenty Years of Public Life: 1890-1910*, an autobiographical volume (1910); *Banks and Banking* (1920); *Flashes and Gems of Thought and Eloquence* (1920); *Pictorial History of the American Negro* (1933); *History of the Negro Baptists of Tennessee* (1936); and *"Bridging the Racial Chasms": A Brief Survey of Interracial Attitudes and Relations* (1936). Fuller looked for and worked for the gradual acceptance of Blacks in society and saw such organizations as the Commission on Interracial Co-operation and the Federal Council of Churches as among the most effective organizations bringing about interracial harmony. He also aligned himself with Booker T. Washington's more conservative philosophy at a time when it was being increasingly criticized within the black community.

Sources:
Fuller, Thomas Oscar. *Banks and Banking.* Memphis, TN: Pilcher Printing Co., 1920. 41 pp.
_____. *"Bridging the Racial Chasm": A Brief Survey of Interracial Attitudes and Relations.* Memphis, TN: The Author, 1937. 73 pp.
_____. *History of the Negro Baptists of Tennessee.* Memphis, TN: Haskins Printing, 1936. 346 pp.
_____. *Pictorial History of the American Negro.* Memphis, TN: Pictorial History, 1933. 375 pp.
_____. *Twenty Years in Public Life: 1890-1910.* Nashville, TN: National Baptist Publishing Board, 1910. 279 pp.
Logan, Rayford W., and Michael R. Winston, eds. *Dictionary of American Negro Biography.* New York: W. W. Norton & Co.   1982. 680 pp.

★ 329 ★
FUNK, John Fretz
Editor, Publisher, Bishop, Mennonite Church
b. Apr. 6, 1835, Hilltown Township, Pennsylvania
d. Jan. 8, 1930, Elkhart, Indiana

John Fretz Funk, influential editor and publisher for the Mennonite Church during the late nineteenth century, was born in rural southeastern Pennsylvania to a Mennonite couple, Jacob and Sara Fretz Funk. He lived on the family homestead for 22 years. He served two terms at Freeland Seminary (later known as Ursinius College) and taught school briefly before going into the lumber business in Chicago in 1857. The pace of his life quickened the following year after he was converted to Christianity at a Presbyterian revival. In 1859 he returned home to be baptized. The next year he met and began to work with fundamentalist evangelist **Dwight L. Moody** in his city missions. In January 1864 he married Salome Kratz and later that year established a printing/publishing business. Among the first items off of the press was the *Herald of Truth* (*Herold der Wahrheit*). During the late nineteenth century, this periodical became the unofficial voice of the scattered Mennonite Church. In 1865 Funk had a call to the ministry and was ordained as a Mennonite minister for the Cullom, Illinois, congregation. In 1867 he moved his printing concern to Elkhart, Indiana, where he was to reside for the rest of his life. In 1871 he founded the Prairie Street Mennonite Church, which he pastored for many years.

In Indiana, Funk established himself as a champion of a solid middle-of-the-road Mennonite position. He combined strong conservative positions with the advocacy of measured progressivism, and he wrote against any deviations toward which he saw Mennonites moving. His one book, *The Mennonite Church and Her Accusers*, answered attacks on the church by the Reformed Mennonites. He also brought around him a number of men who later became outstanding leaders in their own right: **John Horsch, J.S. Coffman**, G. L. Bender, and H. A. Mumaw. He became the catalyst in turning Elkhart into one of the major centers of American Mennonites.

Funk's most measurable contribution to the Mennonite Church was through his publishing concern, the Mennonite Publishing Co. (prior to 1875 known as John F. Funk and Brother). He published *Menno Simon's Complete Works* and the *Martyr's Mirror* in both English (1871) and German (1876) editions, as well as numerous books by historian John Horsch. He also published many editions of prayer books, hymnals, and commonly used confessional and catechetical materials. He wrote and published the first church school magazine and teaching aids.

In 1873 Funk became knowledgeable of and interested in the plight of the Russian Mennonites through his publishing work, and he contributed greatly to their resettlement in North America. His strongest ties were to those who came to reside in Manitoba, and he became their publisher as well. While keeping Mennonites attuned to their tradition, he pioneered Sunday school and youth work, helped establish foreign mission work, helped found the Mennonite Aid Plan and the first relief agency of the church, and conducted the first evangelistic services in the Mennonite Church. He was made a bishop in 1892.

After four decades of significant contributions to the Mennonite Church, Funk saw his career largely end during the first decade of the new century. In 1900 his congregation in Elkhart split. In 1902, strained relations with the congregations under his oversight led to the withdrawal of his position as bishop. The following year a bank failure cost him $40,000, and a fire in 1906 sent his publishing company into bankruptcy.

Though he lived for two more decades, Funk's active role in the church was over. The Mennonite Church stepped into the vacuum caused by the loss of his publishing concern and through its new

Publication Board established the Mennonite Publishing House. Goshen College, which Funk had supported in its early years, became a major educational center for the church. In spite of the problems at the end of his career, Funk was undoubtedly one of the most influential persons in shaping the present course of the Mennonite Church.

Sources:

Kolb, A.C. "John Fretz Funk, 1835-1930: An Appreciation." *Mennonite Quarterly Review* 4 (1932): 44-55, 250-63.
The Mennonite Encyclopedia. 4 vols. Scottdale, PA: The Mennonite Publishing House, 1955.
Wenger, John Christian. *The Mennonites in Indiana and Michigan.* Scottsdale, PA: Herald Press, 1961. 470 pp.

★330★
GAEBELEIN, Arno C.
Independent Fundamentalist Writer/Editor
b. Aug. 27, 1861, Thuringia Germany
d. Dec. 25, 1945, Mount Vernon, New York

Arno C. Gaebelein, for many years the editor of *Our Hope*, a Christian fundamentalist magazine, was raised in Germany and emigrated to the United States in 1879, in part to avoid military conscription. He settled in Lawrence, Massachusetts, where he encountered some fellow Germans who invited him to their small Methodist church. He joined the Methodist Episcopal Church in 1880 and the following year became the assistant to Rev. Augustus Wallon, a Methodist minister in New York City, who tutored Gaebelein in theology and church history. In the fall of 1881 he became a supply pastor for a church in Bridgeport, Connecticut, and the following year moved to a church in Baltimore, Maryland. He was ordained a deacon in the East German Conference of the Methodist Episcopal Church in 1884 and assigned to a church in Harlem, New York. While there, in 1885, he married Emma Grimm. The following year he was ordained an elder in the Methodist Episcopal Church.

In 1887 Gaebelein moved to the church at Hoboken, New Jersey, where he met Samuel Goldstein, a Hebrew-Christian, who encouraged Gaebelein to begin a ministry to the growing Jewish community in New York City. His work at a Jewish mission spurred his acceptance of a premillennialist theology. Premillennialism is a belief that Jesus Christ will soon return to establish a literal reign of a thousand years on earth. In 1881 Gaebelein was appointed as a full-time missionary to the Jews. His work grew into the Hope of Israel Mission in the early 1890s. In 1893 he began a magazine in Hebrew, *Tiqweth Israel—The Hope of Israel Monthly*. About this same time he met Ernst F. Stroeter who joined him the next year and together they began *Our Hope*, a monthly written in English. Over the next months branches of the mission opened in Baltimore, Maryland; Philadelphia and Pittsburgh, Pennsylvania; and St. Louis, Missouri.

Our Hope was the pivot around which Gaebelein's life would swing. Both he and the magazine quickly became a part of the emerging fundamentalist movement, and Gaebelein played a significant role in placing prophecy at the center of the movement's agenda, and emphasizing the role of the Jewish people in Christian prophecy. Gaebelein emerged as one of the very few Methodists associated with fundamentalism, basically a Baptist and Presbyterian concern. He welcomed the founding of the Zionist movement, which he saw as a possible tool in the creation of a Jewish state in Palestine, an event he believed was predicted in the Bible.

In 1897 Gaebelein separated the mission from the New York City Church Extension and Missionary Society of the Methodist Episcopal Church. Increasingly aligned to the fundamentalist movement, in 1899 he resigned from the Methodist Episcopal Church. He spent the rest of his life writing, speaking, and editing *Our Hope*. Many of his approximately 50 books were commen-

taries on the Bible. Other important volumes were on Biblical prophecy. In his own opinion, his most important work was a nine-volume *Annotated Bible*.

Sources:

Gaebelein, Arno C. *Annotated Bible*. 9 vols. New York: Publication Office of *Our Hope*, 1913-1924.
_____. *Half a Century: The Autobiography of a Servant*. New York: Publication Office of *Our Hope*, 1930. 261 pp.
_____. *The Healing Question*. New York: Publication Office of *Our Hope*, 1925. 132 pp.
_____. *The Jewish Question*. New York: Publication Office of *Our Hope*, 1912. 137 pp.
Rausch, David A. *Arno C. Gaebelein, 1861-1954: Irenic Fundamentalist and Scholar*. New York: Edwin Mellen Press, 1983. 297 pp.

★331★
GAINES, Wesley John
Bishop, African Methodist Episcopal Church
b. Oct. 4, 1840, Wilkes County, Georgia
d. Jan. 12, 1912, Atlanta, Georgia

Wesley John Gaines, a bishop in the African Methodist Episcopal Church, was the son of Louisa and William Gaines, slaves on the plantation of Gabriel Toombs. A somewhat sickly child, and hence exempt from work, he taught himself to read. He was raised a Methodist, his father being a member of the Methodist Episcopal Church, South. In 1849 he was converted to Christianity. In 1856 he was sent to a plantation in Muscogee County, Georgia. While there he met and in 1863 married Julia A. Camper. After the Civil War he was able to actualize his desire to be a minister. Encouraged by Toombs, his former owner, he was licensed to preach in the Methodist Episcopal Church, South in 1865. However, his older brother, William Gaines, had become a minister in the African Methodist Episcopal Church and brought Gaines into that church. He was assigned the task of organizing churches in Muscogee and Chattahoochee Counties. In 1866 he was admitted to the South Carolina Conference (whose territory covered all of the Southeast) and ordained a deacon. That same year the Georgia Conference was organized and he transferred into it. In 1867 he was ordained an elder.

Gaines served pastorates in Georgia for the next 20 years. His churches were located in Atlanta, Athens, Macon, and Columbus. Along the way he took the opportunity to further his education. While in Athens in 1870 he studied theology with the local Episcopal minister. From 1875 to 1878, he studied with Joseph S. Key, later a bishop in the Methodist Episcopal Church, South. He took the lead in 1881 in initiating the program that led to the founding of Morris Brown College in Atlanta four years later. Also while in Atlanta, he built Bethel African Methodist Episcopal Church, at the time the largest black church in the South.

In 1885 Gaines was elected a bishop of the African Methodist Episcopal Church. He was assigned the Second District, which covered Maryland, Virginia, the District of Columbia, and North Carolina. During his tenure as bishop, Gaines authored several books, including *African Methodism in the South* (1890) and *The Negro and the White Man* (1897). He was the founder of several African Methodist Episcopal Church conferences. In 1891 Payne Theological Seminary was founded, and Gaines served as vice-president. He died suddenly of a heart attack in 1912.

Sources:

Dictionary of American Biography. 20 vols. and 7 supps. New York: Charles Scribner's Sons, 1928-1936, 1944-1981.
Gaines, Wesley John. *African Methodism in the South*. Atlanta, GA: Franklin Publishing House, 1890. 305 pp.
_____. *The Negro and the White Man*. Philadelphia: A. M. E. Publishing House, 1897. 218 pp.
Harmon, Nolan B. *The Encyclopedia of World Methodism*. 2 vols. Nashville: United Methodist Publishing House, 1974.

★332★
GAITHER, Bill and Gloria
Musicians, Church of God (Anderson, Indiana)

Bill (b. March 28, 1936 Alexandria, Indiana) and Gloria Gaither (b. March 4, 1942 Michigan), who have emerged as dominant forces in popular contemporary gospel music, date their involvement with gospel music from their childhood days when it was an integral part of their church and home life. After high school, Bill attended Anderson College, sponsored by the Church of God (Anderson, Indiana). After his graduation in 1959 he entered Ball State University, where he earned a master's degree in guidance. While there his first song, "I've Been to Calvary," was published. At Anderson he met Gloria, his future wife, the daughter of a minister from Michigan. When Gaither finished his college work in 1961, he secured a job as an English teacher, but spent most of his spare time mastering gospel music. He married Gloria Gaither in 1962, and she joined her husband and his brother Danny as the Bill Gaither Trio. In 1963 Gloria received her bachelor's degree. That same year, "He Touched Me" became the trio's first hit. (The song would later be recorded by a number of singers ranging from Elvis Presley to Kate Smith.) This initial success was followed through the 1960s by a string of popular new contemporary-style gospel songs, and they began to travel the country in concert.

During the 1970s the dominance of Gaither in the gospel music field was signaled by his being named songwriter of the year for 1969-1970 and 1972-1977. In addition, he was given a special award of merit for his contribution to the field. "Because He Lives" (song) was named gospel song of the year in 1974. Anderson College gave Gaither an honorary doctor of music degree in 1973.

Gloria Gaither emerged as an author with her first book in 1971, *Make Warm Noises*, which was followed by *Rainbows Live at Easter* (1974) and *Because He Lives* (1977), which drew its title from one of their more popular songs. Three more titles appeared in the 1980s.

The 1980s was a period of continued success. Both the quality of their music and their popularity enabled them to overcome criticism concerning the introduction of elements of contemporary popular music into their gospel recordings. In 1981 Gaither formed the New Gaither Vocal Band which has been able to expand the range of musical styles offered in their performances. Continued success also brought additional honors. In 1982 Gaither was inducted into the Gospel Music Hall of Fame.

Meanwhile, Gloria received the Dove award from the Gospel Music Association on two occasions, in 1985 as the lyricist for the song of the year and in 1986 as songwriter of the year.

While new music continued to be produced, the earlier songs began to find their way into the hymn books being used in a wide variety of Protestant churches. Bill Gaither emerged as the president of the Gaither Music Company, his publishing concern, and Alexandria House, a distribution company. The trio has produced some four million albums under 35 titles. Their standing in the world of gospel music is unquestioned.

Sources:
Banas, Casey. "Bill and Gloria Gaither: They Sing the Way You Feel." *Christian Life* 40 (August 1978): 34-35, 51-52.

Gaither, Gloria. *Because He Lives*. Old Tappan, NJ: Fleming H. Revell Company, 1977. 202 pp.

_____. *Decisions: A Christian's Approach to Making Right Choices*. Waco, TX: Word Publishing, 1982. 184 pp.

_____. *Fully Alive*. Nashville, TN: Thomas Nelson Publishers, 1984. 175 pp.

_____. *Make Warm Noises*. Nashville, TN: Impact Books, 1971. 79 pp.

_____. *Rainbows Live at Easter*. Nashville, TN: Impact Books, 1974.

_____, and Shirley Dobson. *Let's Make a Memory*. Waco, TX: Word Publishing, 1983. 223 pp.

★333★
GARDENER, Helen Hamilton
Freethought Writer and Activist
b. Jan. 21, 1853, Winchester, Virginia
d. Jul. 26, 1925, Washington, District of Columbia

Helen Hamilton Gardener, feminist activist and Freethinker, was born Alice Chenoweth, the daughter of Katherine A. Peel Chenoweth and Alfred Griffith Chenoweth, a Methodist circuit rider. The year Alice was born, Chenoweth freed his several slaves and moved the family first to Washington, D.C., and then to Greencastle, Indiana. Alice grew up in Indiana, but attended high school in Cincinnati, Ohio. She graduated from Cincinnati Normal School in 1873 and began teaching school. In 1875 she married Charles Selden Smart. They moved to New York City in 1880. Alice studied at Columbia, taught at the Brooklyn Institute of Arts and Sciences, and published her first pieces of professional writings in the local newspapers.

While in New York, she met and discovered the similarity of her thought with that of **Robert Green Ingersoll**, the famous Freethought lecturer. On his advice, she began to deliver Freethought lectures around 1884. These lectures were published in 1885 as her first book, *Men, Women, and Gods and other Lectures*. She published the book under the name Helen Hamilton Gardener and continued to use that name both publicly and privately from that time on.

Feminism was possibly the major theme in Gardener's Freethought writings. She condemned Christianity for its subordination of women and expressed her outrage in two novels: *Is This Your Son, My Lord?* (1890) and *Pray You, Sir, Whose Daughter?* (1892). The former dealt with prostitution and the latter with the inferior lot of married women. She wrote a number of articles for popular journals and produced three more volumes: *A Thoughtless Yes* (1890), *Pushed by Unseen Hands* (1892), and *Facts and Fictions of Life* (1893). The last volume contained a famous essay she had written, "Sex in Brain," which refuted the notion that women are inferior because of a general lack of brain size. The essay attracted the attention of Elizabeth Cady Stanton, who invited Gardener to help in the production of the *Woman's Bible* (1895).

In 1901, Gardener's husband died, and she married Selden Allen Day the following year. They left the country for a tour of the world that lasted for six years. Settling in Washington, D.C., upon their return, she for a while left her reforming opinions behind her. By the end of the decade, however, she had emerged as a feminist lobbyist for the cause of woman's suffrage. In 1913 the militant wing of the Nation American Woman's Suffrage Association resigned from their Congregational Committee, and Gardener stepped into the vacuum to reorganize the group and serve as its vice-chairperson. In 1917 she became vice-president of the association, just at the time she was becoming a confidant of President Woodrow Wilson. In her many meetings with him she offered suggestions which he incorporated into his pro-suffrage speeches.

In 1920, Wilson appointed Gardener to the United States Civil Service Commission, at the time the highest federal position held by a woman. She served for five years, until her death in 1925. Following her Freethought commitment, no religious observances were held at her funeral. She willed her brain to research, and it was removed before burial.

Sources:
Gardener, Helen Hamilton. *Facts and Fictions of Life*. Chicago: C. H. Kerr & Co., 1893. 269 pp.

_____. *Is This Your Son, My Lord?* Boston, MA: Arena Publishing Company, 1890. 257 pp.

_____. *Men, Women, and Gods and Other Lectures*. New York: Bedford, Clarke & Co., 1885. 172 pp.

_____. *Pray You, Sir, Whose Daughter?* Boston, MA: Arena Publishing Company, 1892. 183 pp.
_____. *Pushed by Unseen Hands*. Boston, MA: Arena Publishing Company, 1892. 303 pp.
_____. *A Thoughtless Yes*. New York: Bedford, 1890. 231 pp.
James, Edward T., ed. *Notable American Women, 1607-1950: A Biographical Dictionary*. 3 vols. Cambridge, MA: Harvard University Press, Belknap Press, 1971.
Stein, Gordon. *The Encyclopedia of Unbelief*. 2 vols. Buffalo, NY: Prometheus Books, 1985.

★ 334 ★
GARDNER, Gerald Brousseau
Witch
b. Jun. 13, 1884, Blundellsands England
d. Feb. 12, 1964

Gerald Brousseau Gardner was the founder of the modern religion of Wicca or Witchcraft. Born in 1884 into a Scottish family, Gardner suffered from asthma as a child and gained most of his education through reading on his own. At the age of 16 he moved to Ceylon (now called Sri Lanka) and worked on a plantation until becoming a civil servant in 1923. His various government and private jobs allowed him the flexibility to travel widely throughout Asia, where he absorbed as much of the various cultures as he was able. In 1927 he married a woman named Donna.

Gardner's lack of formal education did not prevent him from becoming a devoted amateur anthropologist, and he even wrote the standard book on the *kris*, the Malaysian ceremonial weapon, called *Kris and Other Malay Weapons* (1936). He was highly interested in magical practices. He spoke to many religious leaders about them, and briefly joined a Masonic lodge in Ceylon. At one point, recovering from a leg injury, he discovered the value of sunbathing and nudism, elements he would later incorporate into witchcraft.

Just before World War II, Gardner retired and returned to England, where he joined an occult group, the Corona Fellowship of Rosicrucians. Through this group he reportedly met practicing witches and their priestess, Dorothy Clutterbuck. She initiated him into the craft, though he was not allowed to tell anyone what he learned until after her death. In 1949, in his novel *High Magic's Aid*, written under the pseudonym Scire, Gardner revealed much about the beliefs and practices of witches. In 1951 the last of England's laws prohibiting witchcraft were abolished, and Gardner wrote his influential book, *Witchcraft Today* (1954), in which he regretfully described Wicca as a dying religion. His writings, however, were instrumental in creating a new generation of witches who turned to him for initiation.

Although Gardner never visited the United States, his work came here via **Raymond Buckland** and his wife, Rosemary Buckland, whom he initiated in 1963. Alexander Sanders, another initiate, brought his own variations to the United States in the late 1960s.

After Gardner's death on an ocean voyage in 1964, his papers and artifacts from his Isle of Man Witchcraft Museum were sold to *Ripley's Believe It or Not*. Examination of those papers has revealed a much different account of the origins of his Wicca rituals than those Gardner had presented during his life. Rather than having been initiated into a pre-existing Wiccan tradition, he created his rituals from various texts such as the medieval *Greater Key of Solomon*, the writings of the Freemasons and **Aleister Crowley**, and a smattering of Asian practices and beliefs, such as ritual scourging, karma, and reincarnation. He developed the *athame*, the witch's ritual knife, from the Malaysian *kris*, and from the eight ancient pagan agricultural festivals he produced the major holy days (sabbats), adding the biweekly gatherings (esbats). Although Gardner's creation may not have the long tradition he claimed for it, it has had tremendous influence, and has obviously struck a re-

sponding chord among the vast majority of Wicca practitioners, whose activities today can, in one way or another, be traced to the work of Gardner.

Sources:
Bracelin, J.L. *Gerald Gardner: Witch*. London: Octagon Press, 1960. 224 pp.
Gardner, Gerald B. *A Goddess Arrives*. London: A. W. Stockwell, 1948. 382 pp.
_____. *High Magic's Aid*. New York: Samuel Weiser, 1975. 352 pp.
_____. *Kris and Other Malay Weapons*. Singapore: N.p. 1936.
_____. *Meaning of Witchcraft*. London: Aquarian Press 1959. 283 pp.
_____. *Witchcraft Today*. London: Jerrolds, 1954. 192 pp.
Melton, J. Gordon. *Biographical Dictionary of American Cult and Sect Leaders*. Garland Reference Library of Social Science, vol. 212. New York: Garland Publishing, 1986.
Shepard, Leslie. *Encyclopedia of Occultism & Parapsychology*. 3 vols., 2nd. ed. Detroit: Gale Research Co., 1984-1985.
Valiente, Doreen. *An ABC of Witchcraft, Past and Present*. New York: St. Martin's Press, 1973. 416 pp.

—*Gary L. Ward*

★ 335 ★
GATES, Susa Amelia Young
Women's Leader, Church of Jesus Christ of Latter-day Saints
b. Feb. 18, 1856, Salt Lake City, Utah
d. May 27, 1933, Salt Lake City, Utah

Susa Amelia Young Gates, a leader of women's work in the Church of Jesus Christ of Latter-day Saints, was the forty-first child of Brigham Young, the president of the church. Her mother was Lucy Bigelow, one of Young's more than 50 wives. Gates entered the University of Deseret at the age of 13, but was forced to withdraw due to her father's displeasure at her role in the elopement of her sister Dora. He sent her to St. George, Utah, where in 1877 she had the distinction of being the first person to be baptized for the dead in the new St. George Temple. In 1862, at the age of 16, she married. Her husband, George Dunford, a dentist, was an alcoholic. In 1877 she divorced him and moved back to Salt Lake City. In 1880 she married Jacob F. Gates, to whom she bore 11 children. Of the 11, seven died in childhood.

After her second marriage, Gates began to write articles for various church periodicals, though her work commonly appeared under a pseudonym, "Homespun." In 1885 she accompanied her husband on a four-year mission to Hawaii. Upon her return she founded the *Young Woman's Journal*, and became well-known as a public speaker and editor of the *Relief Society Magazine*.

Over the remaining decades of her life, Gates developed two arenas of action. In Utah she became possibly the most powerful woman in the church. She joined the board of the Young Ladies Mutual Improvement Association (Y.L.M.I.A.) in 1899 and two decades later became the corresponding secretary of the General Board of the Relief Society. She was the only woman given an office in the Church Office Building, and her position was informally acknowledged by people referring to her as the "thirteenth apostle."

On a national level, Gates became involved with the National Council of Women in the United States and represented the Y.L.M.I.A. seven times at their meetings. The Council appointed her as one of the speakers at the International Council meeting in London in 1899 and in Copenhagen in 1901.

Gates was one of the founders of the geneological work for which the Church of Jesus Christ of Latter-day Saints has become so renowned in recent decades. As president of the Daughters of the Utah Pioneers, she founded their Hall of Relics. In 1923 she became head of the Geneological Society of Utah's Library and Research Department.

In addition to all of her other endeavors, Gates wrote a number of books, including *Lydia Knight's History*, *John Steven's Courtship*, *History of the Young Ladies Mutual Improvement Association*, *The Prince of Ur*, and the *Surname Book and Racial History*. With her daughter Leah Dunford Widtsoe, she wrote *The Life Story of Brigham Young*.

Sources:

Burgess-Olson, Vicky, ed. *Sister Saints*. Provo, UT: Brigham Young University Press, 1978. 494 pp.

Bushman, Claudia, ed. *Mormon Sisters*. Cambridge, MA: Emmeline Press, 1976.

Cracroft, R. Paul. *Susa Young Gates: Her Life and Her Work*. Salt Lake City, UT: University of Utah, Master's thesis, 1959.

Gates, Susa Young, and Leah Dunford Widtsoe. *The Life Story of Brigham Young*. New York: Macmillan, 1930.

Jensen, Andrew. *Latter Day Saints Biographical Encyclopedia* 4 vols. Salt Lake City, UT: Andrew Jensen History Co., 1901.

Van Wagoner, Richard S., and Steven C. Walker. *A Book of Mormons*. Salt Lake City, UT: Signature Books, 1982. 454 pp.

★ 336 ★
GAYLOR, Anne Nicol
Founder and Director, Freedom from Religion Foundation
b. Nov. 25, 1926, Tomah, Wisconsin

Anne Gaylor, the founder of the Freedom from Religion Foundation, a national atheist organization, was raised in a home of freethinkers who considered people who believed in the Bible to be less than true intellectuals. Her father was a farmer and her mother a school teacher. She attended the University of Wisconsin from which she graduated in 1949. She married Paul Gaylor. In the late 1960s, they bought the *Middleton Times*, a newspaper serving a Madison, Wisconsin, suburb.

In the 1970s Gaylor became active in both atheist and feminist causes. She joined and assumed a leadership role in the Wisconsin chapter of American Atheists, Inc., the organization founded by **Madalyn Murray O'Hair**. She came to see religion as a major force in the oppression of women and the elimination of religion as a step toward their liberation. In the mid-1970s, however, she became involved with a group within American Atheists who complained of O'Hair's autocratic management of the organization. In 1976 Gaylor was expelled, and with her supporters she formed the Freedom from Religion Foundation, which quickly emerged as a rival national atheist organization. She also led in the formation of the Freethinkers Anti-Defamation League, to protect the rights and reputations of atheists, agnostics, secular humanists, and *Freethought Today*, the Freedom from Religion Foundation's periodical. In 1983, a collection of Gaylor's writings, many from *Freethought Today*, were published as *Lead Us Not into Penn Station*.

Her feminist concerns led Gaylor to found the Women's Medical Fund to assist women in paying for abortions. She became an officer in Protect Abortion Rights, Inc., and in 1975 published a book on abortion rights.

While sharing many opinions with O'Hair, Gaylor has been less flamboyant in her approach to the atheists' major concern with separation of church and state, interpreted as stopping all religious influence on government policy and action. During the 1980s Gaylor filed a variety of separationist lawsuits including one in 1982 to stop Ronald Reagan from naming 1983 the Year of the Bible. In 1987 she fought the establishment of a monolith with the text of the Ten Commandments being erected in LaCrosse, Wisconsin. In 1988 she protested the use of church buildings as voting sites, and initiated a campaign to have hotels and motels remove Bibles from guest rooms.

Sources:

Gaylor, Anne Nicol. *Abortion Is a Blessing*. New York: Psychological Dimensions, 1975.

_____. *Lead Us Not into Penn Station*. Madison, WI: Freedom from Religion Foundation, 1983. 60 pp.

★ 337 ★
GELBERMAN, Joseph H.
Rabbi and Founder, Little Synagogue
b. Jan. 27, 1912, Nagyesced Hungary

Joseph H. Gelberman is a New Age, neo-Hassidic rabbi and founder of the Little Synagogue in Manhattan. Although raised in a pious Hassidic family, he was ordained as an Orthodox (non-Hassidic) rabbi after attending a yeshiva. He married and had a daughter. Fearing the long range consequences of Hitler's rise to power, he traveled to the United States to find a job as a rabbi and a safe haven for him and his family. After being hired by Zichron Efraim in New York, he filled out the papers to have his family join him. Unfortunately, they did not make it out of Europe, and died in a concentration camp.

After the war, Gelberman accepted a call from the Israel Center of Hillcrest Manor in Flushing on Long Island. He also went back to school, graduating from both City College of New York and Yeshiva University. He helped form the United Hungarian Jews of America and became a member of the Rabbinical Assembly of America, the Orthodox rabbinical association. In 1952 he accepted a call from Milford, Connecticut, and later, in 1959, to Princeton, New Jersey.

During his Princeton years, Gelberman began a spiritual search that led him back to his Hassidic roots, and he eventually separated from his synagogue. He took a position as a part-time rabbi, and picked up his earlier training in therapy to provide himself with stable financial support. He opened the Little Synagogue in New York, a synagogue with a very non-traditional slant. He felt a particular mission to reach disaffiliated Jews, but was also open to people from other religious backgrounds. Other structures grew out of the synagogue, such as the Mid-Way Counseling Center, the Wisdom Academy, the Metaphysical Circle, the New Seminary, the Foundation for Spiritual Living, and the Kabbalah Center.

Gelberman, who had already studied the Kabbalah, read widely in New Thought metaphysics, and began to develop an approach to Kabbalah based on New Thought teachings. He started a journal, *Kabbalah for Today*, in 1974 and authored a number of books and booklets. In the 1970s, he emerged as a popular speaker in the New Age community. He also became a teacher and advocate of yoga.

Sources:

Gelberman, Joseph H. *Psychology and Metaphysics for Every Day*. New York: The Little Synagogue Press, n.d. 49 pp.

_____. *The Quest & Other Essays*. Boulder Creek, CA: Circle Press, 1976. 62 pp.

_____. *The Quest for Love*. Farmingdale, NY: Coleman Publishing, 1985. 185 pp.

_____. *To Be. . .Fully Alive*. Farmingdale, NY: Coleman Publishing, 1983. 89 pp.

_____, and Dorothy Kobak. *Wisdom Therapy*. New York: The Little Synagogue Press, n.d. 19 pp.

★ 338 ★
GERHART, Emanuel Vogel
Theologian, German Reformed Church
b. Jun. 13, 1817, Freeburg, Pennsylvania
d. May 6, 1904, Lancaster, Pennsylvania

Emanuel Vogel Gerhart was a theologian and college president for the German Reformed Church, which, through a series of mergers in the twentieth century, continues as an integral part of the

United Church of Christ. He was the son of Sarah Vogel and Isaac Gerhart. His father, his first teacher, sent his 16 year old son to the Classical Institute of the Reformed Church at York, Pennsylvania. While Gerhart was at the institute, it moved to Mercersburg, Pennsylvania, to become Marshall College. He graduated in 1838 and entered Mercersburg Theological Seminary. He was licensed to preach in 1841 and ordained in 1842. In 1843 he became the pastor of four small churches in and near Gettysburg, Pennsylvania. That same year he married Eliza Rikenbaugh.

In 1850 Gerhart was sent as a missionary to Cincinnati, Ohio, to build a congregation. He also traveled through the adjoining states as far west as Wisconsin. In 1851 he was invited to become the president and professor of theology at the new theological seminary created in connection with Heidelberg College in Tiffin, Ohio. While he was there, Marshall College merged with Franklin College to form Franklin and Marshall College in Lancaster, Pennsylvania. The denomination tried to persuade one of their leading scholars, John Williamson Nevin or **Philip Schaff**, to become president of the new college. They both refused the offer. Thus Gerhart was approached and he accepted.

Gerhart found the college bereft of both students and finances, and he began a campaign to build up the school. He saw it through the depression of 1857 and the Civil War into a somewhat stable condition, only to have the board of trustees give his job to Nevin. Gerhart was named vice-president. At about this same time his wife died (1864) and he married Mary M. Hunter (1865), who died in 1866. In 1868 some amends were made when he was named president and professor of systematic theology at Mercersburg Theological Seminary. The seminary moved to Lancaster in 1871, and Gerhart resided there for the rest of his life. Over the next three decades he emerged as the most prominent theological voice of the German Reformed Church in the U.S. Also an active churchman, Gerhart at various times was asked to serve as president of both the Eastern and Ohio synods and of the General Synod of the church.

Above and beyond his many articles, Gerhart produced three main literary works, *An Introduction to the Study of Philosophy* (1858); *Prolegomena to Christian Dogmatics* (1891); and the two-volume *Institutes of the Christian Religion* (1891, 1894). In 1875 he married for the third time, to Lucia Cobb, with whom he lived the rest of his life. He taught classes right up until a week before his death.

Sources:

Dictionary of American Biography. 20 vols. and 7 supps. New York: Charles Scribner's Sons, 1928-1936, 1944-1981.

Gerhart, Emanuel V. *Institutes of the Christian Religion*. New York: C. A. Armstrong & Son, 1891, 1894. 754 pp.

———. *An Introduction to the Study of Philosophy*. Philadelphia: Lindsay & Blakiston, 1858. 359 pp.

———. *Prolegomena to Christian Dogmatics*. Lancaster, PA: Lecture Printing Society of the Theological Seminary of the Reformed Church, 1891. 136 pp.

Reid, Daniel G., Robert D. Linder, Bruce L. Shelley, and Harry S. Stout. *Dictionary of Christianity in America*. Downers Grove, IL: InterVarsity Press, 1990. 1305 pp.

★339★
GERONIMO
Indian Medicine Man and Patriot, Bedonkohe Apache Indians
b. Jun. 1829, Fort Tulerosa, Arizona
d. Feb. 17, 1909, Fort Sill, Oklahoma

Geronimo, a Bedonkohe Apache Indian medicine man and patriot, was born in the early summer of 1829 along the headwaters of the Gila River in what is now eastern Arizona. Very few Indian leaders survived the conquering wars of the United States government, and of those who did, none achieved the notoriety of Geronimo. His given name was Goyahkla and has been translated as both "one who yawns," and "shrewd or clever." Although his mother was full-blood Apache, she carried the name of Juana, due possibly to an early childhood captivity among the Mexicans. Geronimo's father, Taklishim (The Gray One), was the son of Chief Mahko of the Bedonkohe division of Apaches.

The mountainous region of the Bedonkohe territory allowed them to live in relative isolation both from other Indian groups and for a while, the mounting pressure from the United States to the east. But in 1838 some Mimbreno Apaches, close relatives of the Bedonkohes, were attacked by a group from the town of Santa Rita. Steady but intermittent warfare broke out between Mexican settlers and the various bands of Apache, including the Bedonkohe. In 1850 a group of Bedonkohe Apaches were attacked near Janos, Chihuahua, by a mixed group of Mexican troops and settlers, and Geronimo's mother, wife, and three children were killed. Until he surrendered for the last time in 1886, Geronimo conducted a personal war of revenge against settlers in northern Mexico, killing more than he could count.

Among many Indian tribes of North America, leadership in the conduct of war was within the realm of responsibility of the medicine men. Such was the case with Geronimo. Geronimo was known by both enemies and friends as a strong and powerful fighter skilled in the use of guns, bows, and other weapons of war. Although he suffered some early failures in leading war parties into battle, he was consistently successful throughout his free-riding career as a patriot-fighter for the Apache homeland. He received his powers as a young man when, after the deaths of his family, he sat alone in the mountains weeping for his loss. Four times his name was called, after which he was told that he could never be killed by a bullet and that the spirits would always guide his arrows.

There are two versions, both plausible and not exclusive, as to the origin of his name Geronimo. One version is so popular his own people use it; it further accounts for the introduction of Geronimo's name into the American language as a battle cry. Both stories stem from the first fight Geronimo conducted after the spirits spoke to him. Troops involved in the Janos massacre were stationed at the small town of Arispe, Sonora, Mexico, and they met the Apache war party outside of town. Because of his great family loss, Goyahkla was given command of the fighting. The fight lasted two hours, and when it was finished, the Apaches were in command of the field. Goyahkla's bravery caused the Mexicans to cry out, "Cuidado (Watch out), Geronimo." Geronimo, the name, is said to originate from a Mexican pronunciation of Goyahkla. Others speculate that the troops that day might have named the Apache war leader for Saint Jerome, the fiery fourth century saint depicted in Christian art as a lion.

At first Geronimo was friendly to the Americans who crossed the southwest. But as the trickle across became a flood, Geronimo was increasingly restive, escaping the reservation imposed on his people several times. Mexico was usually the target of his early raids, but as more American treachery took Apache lives through violence or starvation, Geronimo turned his attention to American towns and shipping. In the fall of 1886 Geronimo surrendered for the last time and was shipped first to a Florida prison, and then, in the winter of 1894, to Fort Sill, Oklahoma, where Geronimo lived his remaining years. Geronimo was part of an Indian exhibition at the Louisiana Purchase Exhibition in St. Louis in 1904, and rode in Theodore Roosevelt's inaugural parade in Washington the following spring. Wherever he traveled his conduct was genteel and polite, in direct contrast to his portrayal in the popular press of the time. During his Fort Sill years, Geronimo took up Christianity, but he was still known as a gifted healer in the native tradition. Geronimo died February 17, 1909, true to his powers, from a natural, not violent, cause. He was buried in the Fort Sill Cemetery near Lawton, Oklahoma.

Sources:

—Johnny Flynn

★ 340 ★
GESTEFELD, Ursula Newell
New Thought
b. Apr. 22, 1845, Augusta, Maine
d. Oct. 22, 1921, Chicago, Illinois

Ursula Newell Gestefeld was a prominent Christian Science and New Thought leader. Born in Maine in 1845, she was a frail child who was not expected to live very long. She grew to adulthood, however, and married newspaperman Theodore Gestefeld in the 1860s, moved to Chicago in the 1870s, and raised four children. Her husband was an editor for the German-language newspaper *Staats-Zeitung* and reported for the *Chicago Tribune*.

In 1884, at the age of 39, Gestefeld was introduced to **Mary Baker Eddy**'s *Science and Health with Key to the Scriptures*, and joined Eddy's first Chicago class. Gestefeld's native abilities came to the fore, and Eddy soon made her a leader in the Church of Christ, Scientist. In 1887, Gestefeld published *What Is Mental*, the first of at least a dozen books. Her second and third books, *Ursula N. Gestefeld's Statement of Christian Science* (1888) and *The Science of the Christ* (1889), caused a rift with Eddy, since they mentioned her only in passing. In addition, the books did not refer to *Science and Health*, a book that Gestefeld felt was hard to understand, as the authoritative text. Eddy, who was trying to cope with other rivals, reacted harshly, condemning Gestefeld as a distorter of Christian Science and dismissing her from the church. Gestefeld responded to the initial accusations with the book *Jesuitism in Christian Science* (1888).

Gestefeld's husband died in about 1891 and for a few years thereafter she lived in New York City. For the most part, however, she made Chicago her permanent home and developed her own version of Christian Science, called "Science of Being," which had fewer Christian overtones than Eddy's organization. She made a living writing books, lecturing, and from the organizations she founded, which included a Science of Being center in England and the Exodus Club in Chicago, which in 1904 became the Church of New Thought. She edited a monthly New Thought periodical, *The Exodus*, from 1896 to 1904, and was a leader in the growing international New Thought movement. In 1899 she addressed the first convention of the International New Thought League, and in 1903 became its vice-president.

Gestefeld created the Gestefeld Publishing Company, which published most of her books, including *The Woman Who Dares* (1892), a feminist novel about women coping with the unreasonable sexual demands of husbands. Her most important work was *The Builder and the Plan* (1910), which was the mature presentation of her Science of Being. She died in 1921 at the age of 76, and although her Church of New Thought did not long survive, her influence and popularity remained strong for many years through her writings.

Sources:

Braden, Charles S. *Christian Science Today*. Dallas, TX: Southern Methodist University Press, 1958. 571 pp.
Gestefeld, Ursula N. *The Builder and the Plan*. Chicago: Exodus Publishing Co., 1910. 273 pp.
_____. *How to Control Circumstances*. Chicago: Exodus Publishing Company, 1901. 100 pp.
_____. *Jesuitism in Christian Science*. Chicago: The Author, 1888.
_____. *The Science of the Christ*. Chicago: The Author, 1889. 463 pp.
_____. *A Statement of Christian Science*. Chicago: The Author, 1888. 259 pp.
Melton, J. Gordon. *Biographical Dictionary of American Cult and Sect Leaders*. Garland Reference Library of Social Science, vol. 212. New York: Garland Publishing, 1986.
Who Was Who in America. Chicago: Marquis Who's Who, Inc.

—Gary L. Ward

★ 341 ★
Maha GHOSANANDA
Monk and Leader, Cambodian Buddhism
b. 1924

The Venerable Maha Ghosananda is a senior Buddhist monk and leader of Cambodian Buddhists in the United States. Born Va Yav, he began serving as a temple boy at a village *wat* (temple) in Takeo, Cambodia, at the age of eight. He was a disciple of the former head of the Cambodian Buddhist Sangha (community of monks), Samdech Prah Sangh Raja Chuon Noth. He is a graduate of the Buddhist University in Phnom Penh, and studied at another Buddhist University in Battambang. Maha Ghosananda is one of the few Khmer monks to do academic work in India, studying at Nalanda University in Bihar for 15 years. He received a master's degree in Buddhism from Nalanda and completed research for a Ph.D. He was also a student of the Japanese monk Nichidatsu Fujii, founder of the Nihonazn Mayohaji sect, who was said to have been close to Mahatma Gandhi (many Cambodians refer to Ghosananda as the Gandhi of Cambodia). At the age of 40 Ghosananda began to pursue the life of a forest monk (a meditation monk or *thudong*) in southern Thailand. There he stayed under the tutelage of meditation master Buddha Dasa for more than 10 years.

In 1975, under the terror of the Khmer Rouge, Buddhist temples were systematically destroyed and 99 percent of Cambodia's monks were killed. Ghosananda escaped only because he was in Thailand at the time. In 1978 he left his mountain retreat to work among the refugee camps that had formed on the Thai border. For the next three years he was one of only a few Buddhist monks serving several hundred thousand refugees, and as a consequence traveled among all six refugee camps. He was able to remain politically neutral while simultaneously becoming active in the negotiations among the warring groups in Cambodia. Working closely with some Christian missionaries, he established the Inter-Religious Mission for Peace in Cambodia in 1980. In the same year he was invited to the United Nations as a representative for the Khmer Program of the World Conference on Religion and Peace.

In 1981 Maha Ghosananda accepted a request from the Khmer community in Providence, Rhode Island, to come to the United States for the purpose of establishing the New England Buddhist Society. A temple, the *Dharmmakarama* (garden of the dharma), was established and became the base for establishing more temples for Cambodian refugees across the world. By 1983 he was also actively recruiting refugee Khmer Buddhist monks for his work in America. By late 1986 there were 80 such monks in the United States, 60 of whom had been recruited by Ghosananda. He had also established 30 additional temples in North America by that year.

Sources:

"The Venerable Maha Ghosananda." From *Remaining Buddhist or Becoming Christian*. Providence, RI: Khmer Buddhist Society Report, 1988. 15 pp.

★ 342 ★
GIBBONS, James
Cardinal, Roman Catholic Church
b. Jul. 23, 1834, Baltimore, Maryland
d. Mar. 24, 1921, Baltimore, Maryland

James Gibbons, the first American-born cardinal in the Roman Catholic Church, was the son of Thomas and Bridget Walsh Gibbons, Irish farmers who had migrated to America in the 1820s. Soon after James' birth, the family returned to Ireland, where he grew up in a devout Catholic atmosphere. His father died in the great potato famine. In 1853 his mother brought the family back to America and settled in New Orleans. Soon after their arrival, yellow fever struck the city and Gibbons was taken ill. The crisis of the sickness led Gibbons to a decision to enter the priesthood. In 1855 he journeyed to Maryland and entered St. Charles College at Ellicott City. He graduated in 1857 and immediately entered St. Mary's Seminary in Baltimore. He graduated in 1861 and was ordained a priest.

After a brief assignment in Baltimore, Gibbons was assigned the two parishes of St. Bridget's in Canton, Maryland, and St. Lawrence, about a mile outside the town across the river. He also became a chaplain for nearby Fort McHenry and Fort Marshall. After the war he became secretary to the Archbishop of Baltimore, and was given responsibility for much of the organization of the 1866 plenary council (Gibbons later led the plenary council of 1878). At the 1866 council, a new vicariate was created in North Carolina, and for that assignment Gibbons was consecrated bishop in 1868; he was only 33 years old. He had been at his task of building the Catholic work in the state for a year when he was summoned to Rome for the First Vatican Council, the council at which the infallibility of the Pope was declared. Gibbons voted with the council majority.

Upon his return to North Carolina, Gibbons followed up on a suggestion that he write a book summarizing Roman Catholic beliefs. *Faith of Our Fathers* became the most important American Catholic book of the generation. Millions of copies were sold and thousands of converts came to the church after reading it. In 1852 Gibbons assumed additional duties, first as administrator of the vacant diocese of Richmond, Virginia, and then as assistant to the ill Archbishop Bayley of Baltimore. Recognizing Gibbons' talents, Bayley requested that he be named Coadjutor Bishop of Baltimore with right of succession. He had barely finished the paperwork when he died. Gibbons became Archbishop of Baltimore in 1877, and threw his immense skill and energy into the development of an American Catholic church. Among his early actions was the commending of the celebration of Thanksgiving Day, considered by most a Protestant holiday, to Roman Catholics.

In 1886, following the death of Cardinal **John McCloskey**, Gibbons was made a cardinal. He was given his biretta on June 30, 1886. Traveling to Rome the next year, he received his cardinal's hat on March 17, 1887, and a week later took charge of his titular parish in the diocese of Rome, Santa Maria, in Tratevere. While in Rome, Gibbons took the opportunity to intervene with the pope and obtain a reversal of a decision condemning the Knights of Labor, the workingman's organization in the United States.

Returning home to America, Gibbons was confronted with ethnic divisions of the growing American church and with leaders determined to keep ethnic boundaries intact. Gibbons offered able leadership in the gradual anglicization of the church. Among the hottest issues was the acceptance of public schools. While parochial schools were most desirable, many Catholic children could not attend. Gibbons became a dominant force in gaining an official toleration of the public school system by the hierarchy of the church.

The quelling of the school controversy, however, set the stage for the climax of a growing polarization between liberal and conservative American bishops. In the midst of what became known as the "Americanism" controversy, Gibbons refused to publish a decree against several secret societies and was censured by the recently appointed apostolic delegate. He went to Rome just as a book praising the "Americanist" position, which included the advocacy of watering down church doctrine to attract converts, was published in France. He attacked the book as a distortion of the position of the more progressive wing of the American church. In light of Gibbons' letter, the pope acted in an encyclical in 1898 by condemning the errors of the French book but refusing to accuse any Americans of committing such errors. Gibbons signaled the end of the controversy by authoring a letter stating that the condemned opinions had never existed. The end of the controversy had the desired effect of rehabilitating some people identified with the Americanist position. It eventually led, however, to a more conservative separatist Catholicism in America in the first half of the twentieth century.

Gibbons continued to serve the church for another two decades but spent most of those years writing, building the Catholic University of America, in which he had taken a special interest, and administering what had become the largest religious body in the United States. His last years were marked by his trip to Rome to participate in the election of Pope Pius X, and the fiftieth anniversary of his priesthood, celebrated in 1911.

Building upon the organizational strides of his predecessors, Gibbons emerged in the late nineteenth century as the most important figure in the development of a public image of the Roman Catholic Church in America as an American institution with an important role to play in American public life. He mediated the more radical opinions of his colleagues while rejecting efforts that he believed would turn the church into a set of ethnically-isolated enclaves hostile to the main thrusts of American society.

Sources:

Ellis, John Tracy. *The Life of Cardinal James Gibbons, Archbishop of Baltimore, 1834-1921.* 2 vols. Milwaukee, WI: Bruce Publishing Company, 1952.
Gibbons, James. *Beacon Lights.* Baltimore, MD: John Murphy Company, 1911. 192 pp.
———. *Discoveries and Sermons for Every Sunday and the Principal Festivals of the Year.* Baltimore, MD: John Murphy Company, 1908. 531 pp.
———. *Faith of Our Fathers.* Baltimore, MD: John Murphy Company, 1877. 438 pp.
———. *Our Heritage.* Baltimore, MD: John Murphy Company, 1895. 523 pp.
———. *A Retrospect of Fifty Years.* 2 vols. Baltimore, MD: John Murphy Company, 1916.
Thornton, Francis Beauchesne. *Our American Princes.* New York: Putnam's Sons, 1963. 319 pp.
Will, Allen Sinclair. *Life of Cardinal Gibbons.* 2 vols. New York: E. P. Dutton & Co., 1922.

★ 343 ★
GIBBS, Jonathan C.
Minister, Presbyterian Church
b. 1827, Philadelphia, Pennsylvania
d. Aug. 14, 1874

Jonathan C. Gibbs, who led in the process of organizing southern Blacks for the Presbyterian Church in the decade after the Civil War, was the son of Jonathan C. and Maria Gibbs. His father was a Wesleyan Methodist minister who died while Gibbs was still a child. He was apprenticed at an early age to a carpenter. As a youth he converted to Presbyterianism and was finally able to get enough schooling to prepare him for Dartmouth College. He entered in 1848 as one of two black students, and graduated in 1852. He went to Princeton University and studied under A. A. Hodge and Archibald Alexander. In 1854 he was ordained as a Presbyterian minister.

Gibbs began his ministerial career with a black congregation in Troy, New York. Nathan Lord, the president of Dartmouth, came to Troy to preach the installation service. He moved to Philadelphia in the late 1850s. During the Civil War he became deeply involved with obtaining various rights for Blacks and participated in the meeting in 1864 in Syracuse, New York, from which the National Equal Rights League emerged.

As the Civil War came to a close, the Presbyterian Church sent him into those areas of the Carolinas already pacified and under the control of Union troops to organize congregations and schools. He worked with the former slaves into 1867, when he moved to Florida. His arrival in Florida coincided with Reconstructionist legislation which enfranchised the black voters. He decided to enter the political realm in addition to his ongoing church work. He was elected to the Constitutional Convention of 1868 and subsequently became Florida's secretary of state (1868-1873) and superintendent of public instruction (1873-1874).

In 1874 he began to run for Congress as a Republican, but died in the midst of the campaign. The official cause of death was given as apoplexy. However, there has been considerable speculation that he was poisoned by members of the Ku Klux Klan, who had opposed his political career, and the race for Congress had created enemies within the Republican Party. The actual cause of death is lost to history.

Sources:

Logan, Rayford W., and Michael R. Winston, eds. *Dictionary of American Negro Biography*. New York: W. W. Norton & Co.   1982. 680 pp.
Richardson, Joe M. "Jonathan C. Gibbs: Florida's Only Negro Cabinet Member." *Florida Historical Quarterly* (April 1964): 363-68.

★344★
GILBERT, Frederick Carnes
Jewish Missionary, Seventh-day Adventist Church
b. Sep. 30, 1867, London England
d. 1946

Frederick Garnes Gilbert, a missionary to Jews with the Seventh-day Adventist Church, was born into a pious Jewish family in mid-nineteenth century London. He attended a Jewish school from ages five to 13, and went through the traditional bar mitzvah ceremony. During his teen years he was frequently sick. He dropped out of school and went to work, apprenticed to a tinsmith. During his years of work, he had a severe accident from a fall. His injuries were further complicated because he initally refused to allow anyone to help him. The effects of the accident—several ribs that refused to mend properly—stayed with him for many years.

As Gilbert approached adulthood, tuberculosis developed and he was sent to a hospital. Though he did not convert to Christianity at the time, he had his first contact with Christian ministers as a patient. Regaining some of his health, he sailed for America in the mid-1880s, hoping in part that the voyage would have further curative affects. He settled first in Manhattan, where he worked in a clothing factory, but soon moved on to Massachusetts. He roomed with a family that belonged to the Seventh-day Adventist Church. Gilbert was impressed with these sabbatarian Christians, who had a great respect for the Jewish Bible (the Old Testament) and its commandments, and who were so kind to him, especially during a time he suffered from scarlet fever. In 1889 he converted to the Seventh-day Adventist Church.

A short time after his conversion, Gilbert quit his job and became a colporteur, selling adventist literature door-to-door. He attended South Lancaster Academy, an adventist school in Massachusetts, and was ordained following his graduation in 1894. He began a missionary effort in Boston but was soon assigned as a general missionary in western Massachusetts. In 1896 he married Ella M. Graham.

After a decade in western Massachusetts Gilbert was able to begin the work that was really his prime concern. He returned to Boston and founded a Seventh-day Adventist Church mission to the Jews. About this same time he authored his first book, *Practical Lessons From the Experience of Israel for the Church of To-day* (1902). He also began a magazine, *The Good Tidings of the Messiah*.

As the mission grew, Gilbert developed a special program for children. He also purchased Good Tidings Home, a farm near Concord, Massachusetts, which became a second center for his work. In 1911 he joined the staff of the church's North American Division, which supervises work in North America. In 1918 he became secretary of the Jewish department of the general conference, and in 1922 was appointed a field secretary. His increased evangelistic duties eventually took him around the world. He died in 1946.

Sources:

Gilbert, F. C. *Divine Predictions of Ellen G. White Fulfilled*. South Lancaster, MA: Good Tidings Press, 1922. 456 pp.
_____. *From Judaism to Christianity*. Concord, MA: Good Tidings, 1911. 384 pp.
_____. *The Jewish Problem*. Takoma Park, MD: Review and Herald Publishing Association, 1940. 188 pp.
_____. *Judaism and Christianity*. Takoma Park, MD: Review and Herald Publishing Association, 1942. 191 pp.
_____. *Messiah in His Sanctuary*. Takoma Park, MD; Review and Herald Publishing Association, 1937. 248 pp.
_____. *Practical Lessons from the Experience of Israel for the Church of To-day*. South Lancaster, MA: South Lancaster Printing Company, 1902. 390 pp.
Seventh-Day Adventist Encyclopedia. Washington, DC: Review and Herald Publishing Association, 1966. 1454 pp.

★345★
GLADDEN, Washington
Minister, Congregational Church
b. Feb. 11, 1836, Pottsgrove, Pennsylvania
d. Jul. 2, 1918, Columbus, Ohio

Washington Gladden, a Congregational minister best known as an early proponent of the social gospel, was the son of Solomon Gladden and Amanda Daniels Gladden. His father died when he was six years old and he was raised by his uncle, Ebenezer Daniels, a farmer near Owego, New York. At the age of 16 he began work on the local newspaper. Three years later he enrolled at Owego Academy and in 1856 was able to transfer to Williams College. He paid his way through school by teaching part-time and working on the *Springfield (MA) Republican*. He returned to Owego after graduation in 1859 and began to teach school.

Soon after his return to Owego, Gladden began a new career as a minister. He was licensed by the Susquehanna Association of Congregational Ministers. The following year he became pastor of the First Congregational Methodist Church in Brooklyn, New York, where he was ordained in November 1860. A month later he married Jennie O. Cohoon. He stayed only a year in Brooklyn before moving to Morrisania, New York, where he pastored during the war years. This period was a time for theological reflection, and the writings of Horace Bushnell and Frederick W. Robertson introduced him to the new liberal theology that was emerging among Congregationalists. At his next pastorate, North Adams, Massachusetts, he began to write, initially some articles defending Bushnell and then his first book, *Plain Thoughts on the Art of Living* (1868).

Gladden left the parish in 1871 to join the staff of the New York *Independent*, however he returned to pastoral work in 1875 at the North Congregational Church in Springfield, Massachusetts. While at Springfield, he wrote the first of the books which would thrust him into the leadership of a movement to apply Christian principles to social problems. The movement also strove to find solutions to social problems by adjusting social structures in conformity with

Christian values, rather than attempting to evangelize the world. He laid out the basics of the social gospel in *Being a Christian* (1871); *Working People and Their Employers* (1876); and *The Christian Way* (1877).

At the end of 1882 Gladden accepted the call to First Congregational Church in Columbus, Ohio, where he would remain for the rest of his life. Here he would emerge as a national spokesperson for a number of the newer theological trends that were taking center stage in Protestant theological debates in North America. Besides further books on the social gospel, he would argue for the new modernist theology and support ecumenism and church cooperation. His first book at his new post, describing the *Church League of Connecticut* (1883), became a handbook fostering church federation around the country. He followed it with one of his most articulate statements of the social gospel, *Applied Christianity* (1886) and his first major work on modernist theological issues, *Burning Questions* (1890).

The 1890s were equally prolific for Gladden. He authored *Who Wrote the Bible?* (1891); *The Cosmopolis City Club* (1893); *Tools and the Man: Property and Industry under the Christian Law* (1893); and *How Much Is Left of the Old Doctrines?* (1899). He became famous for his opposition to his own church's mission board, the American Board of Commissioners for Foreign Missions, in soliciting a $100,000 gift from Standard Oil, the very image of social evil in the eyes of social gospel advocates. He was also recognized for his opposition to the wave of anti-Catholicism which swept the country in the middle of the decade.

Gladden entered the new century as one of the leading ministers in his denomination, and in 1904 he began a three year term as the moderator of the National Council of the Congregational Churches. He continued to write; among his titles were: *Social Salvation* (1902); *Where Does the Sky Begin* (1904); *The New Idolatry* (1905); *The Church and Modern Life* (1908); *Recollections* (1909), his autobiography; and *Present Day Theology* (1913). His pietistic side was revealed in a volume of poems, *Ultima Veritas and Other Verses* (1912), and he is today remembered as much for a single hymn, ''O Master Let Me Walk with Thee'' as for any of his writings.

Gladden is best appreciated as a pioneer in Protestant Christian social conscience even though in retrospect his thought appears naive. He advocated the change of society by a process of calling people to the ideals of love, social justice, and service, and he was quickly superseded in the next century by more sophisticated analysis of the social situation and calls for alterations of unjust, entrenched social structures. Modern social gospel advocates, however, do honor Gladden as a pioneer cutting a unique path in unchartered lands.

Sources:

Dictionary of American Biography. 20 vols. and 7 supps. New York: Charles Scribner's Sons, 1928-1936, 1944-1981.

Gladden, Washington. *Applied Christianity*. Boston: Houghton, Mifflin and Company, 1886. 320 pp.

_____. *The Church and Modern Life*. Boston: Houghton, Mifflin and Company, 1908. 221 pp.

_____. *How Much Is Left of the Old Doctrines?*. Boston: Houghton, Mifflin and Company, 1899. 321 pp.

_____. *Present Day Theology*. Columbus, OH: McClelland & Company, 1913. 220 pp.

_____. *Recollections*. Boston: Houghton, Mifflin and Company, 1909. 445 pp.

_____. *Social Salvation*. Boston: Houghton, Mifflin and Company, 1902. 290 pp.

_____. *Who Wrote the Bible?*. Boston: Houghton, Mifflin and Company, 1891. 381 pp.

★346★
GLENNON, John Joseph
Cardinal, Roman Catholic Church
b. Jun. 14, 1862, Kinnegad Ireland
d. Mar. 9, 1946, Dublin Ireland

John Joseph Glennon, a cardinal in the Roman Catholic Church, was the son of Matthew and Catherine Glennon, residents of rural Ireland. He attended St. Finian's College, where he distinguished himself in the study of the classics. He continued his outstanding record at All Hallows College, Dublin, where he completed his theological studies at the age of 22. Just as he finished his education, Bishop John Hogan of the newly created Diocese of Kansas City, Missouri, was recruiting priests. Responding to Hogan's stated needs, Glennon immigrated to the United States in 1883 and the following year was ordained. He was assigned to St. Patrick's Church in Kansas City.

After several years in Kansas City, Glennon went to Germany for further education. Upon his return, he joined the bishop's staff at the cathedral in Kansas City and rose quickly in the hierarchy. In 1892 he was named vicar general of the diocese, and in 1894 he was named administrator. In 1896 he was appointed titular bishop of Pinara and coadjutor of the diocese of Kansas City. In 1903 he was transferred to St. Louis as coadjutor of the archdiocese with right of succession. Before the year was out, the archbishop died and Glennon became archbishop of St. Louis. He remained in that post for the rest of his life, over four decades.

Glennon's first task as archbishop was to build a new cathedral, which was dedicated in 1914. Concurrently, he organized and built Kenrick Seminary for the training of priests. Construction of the seminary was completed in 1915. Over 400 additional positions were created and filled during his reign. He later built the St. Louis Preparatory Seminary (1930-1931). He also built up the archdiocese in an impressive manner. Over the next several decades, he created 43 new parishes and greatly expanded the parochial school system, especially at the high school level.

During Glennon's years as archbishop, St. Louis received many new immigrants from Europe. Glennon developed programs to integrate them into church life and into their new home. He encouraged the development of colonies in rural Missouri and worked with the Catholic Rural Life Council. As the United States entered World War I, Glennon became one of the founders of the National Catholic War Council, now the National Catholic Welfare Conference.

Papal recognition of Glennon's work came in two prominent actions. In 1941 Glennon was named an assistant at the Pontifical Throne, and in February 1946, after the war ended in Europe, he traveled to Rome to be named a cardinal. He was 84 at the time, still vigorous and active. He decided to return home by way of his native Ireland. Soon after his landing in Ireland on March 4, 1946 it was discovered that he had developed uremic poisoning. He died a few days later.

Sources:

Delaney, John J. *Dictionary of American Catholic Biography*. Garden City, NY: Doubleday & Company, 1988. 621 pp.

Thornton, Francis Beauchesne. *Our American Princes*. New York: G. P. Putnam's Sons, 1963. 319 pp.

★347★
GODBE, William Samuel
Founder, Church of Zion
b. Jun. 26, 1833, Middlesex United Kingdom
d. Aug. 1, 1902, Brighton, Utah

William Samuel Godbe, founder of the Church of Zion, a splinter group from the Church of Jesus Christ of Latter-day Saints, was raised in England, where he became a sailor in his youth. In 1849, at the age of 16, he was converted to the church and made his way to Utah, sailing around the Atlantic to the Great Lakes and then traveling by land to Salt Lake City. Starting as a store clerk, he established himself in retailing and became one of the wealthiest men in the territory. In 1855 he married for the first time to Annie Thompson. He subsequently married Mary Hampton, Rosina Cilborn, and Charlotte Ives Cobb, daughter of one of Brigham Young's wives.

Godbe began to rise in the church and served as counselor to Bishop Edwin D. Woolley in Salt Lake City. However, during the 1860s he became increasingly concerned with the church's (i.e., Brigham Young's) control over the political and economic spheres of Utah life. He also noticed an accompanying reduction of spirituality. To bring his concerns before the public, he founded, with E.L.T. Harrison, the *Utah Magazine*. He later founded the *Mormon Tribune* (forerunner of the *Salt Lake Tribune*). Godbe and Harrison argued for the privilege of freely discussing issues of importance, especially those upon which they were called by the church to act. Unwilling to soften their position, they were excommunicated in 1869.

Though excommunicated, Godbe traveled to Washington, D.C., in 1870 to lobby against the Cullom Bill, the latest in a series of pieces of anti-Mormon legislation. He was granted interviews with both Vice President Schuyler Colfax and President Ulysses S. Grant, and appears to have been a major factor in ultimately killing the bill.

That same year, while on a trip to New York, Godbe and Harrison claimed to have received a revelation from the angels. Mormonism, the revelation claimed, was founded to gather a people who were open to continuing revelation and thus could be altered by new revelation. Acting upon this understanding, Godbe led in the founding of the Church of Zion.

In the wake of the founding of the new church, the Mormon church's general conference declared a boycott against those who had been cut off from the church (apostates). The church established Zion's Cooperative Mercantile Institution as a part of the boycott strategy, and within two years Godbe was broke and heavily in debt. He turned to mining and eventually, with backing from English financiers, was able to recoup his losses in the process of opening the mining industry in Utah, Wyoming, and Nevada.

Sources:

Van Wagoner, Richard S., and Steven C. Walker. *A Book of Mormons.* Salt Lake City, UT: Signature Books, 1982. 454 pp.

★ 348 ★
GODDARD, Dwight
Fellowship Following Buddha
b. Jul. 5, 1861, Worcester, Massachusetts
d. Jul. 5, 1939, Randolph, Vermont

Dwight Goddard founded the Fellowship Following Buddha and was one of the first non-Asian Buddhists in the United States. He grew up in Massachusetts and received an engineering degree from Worcester Polytechnical Institute in about 1881. After 10 years as a mechanical engineer, he decided to become a Christian missionary and enrolled at Hartford Theological Seminary. After graduating in 1894 he went to China as a Baptist missionary, where he met and married his first wife, a medical missionary.

After 20 years in the mission field, Goddard grew discouraged with the church's progress and decided that a program of dialogue toward some kind of combination of Buddhism and Christianity was in order. In 1924 he proposed the formation of a Christian and Buddhist Fellowship, though this did not become a reality. Instead, he went to Japan to study with Roshi Taiko Tamazaki at the Shokoku (Zen) monastery. This study led to the publication in 1927

of his first book, *Was Jesus Influenced by Buddhism?*. Gradually, however, Goddard came to feel that the goal of mixing the two religions was a mistake, and that what he really wanted to do was promote Buddhism, particularly the Zen Buddhism that he felt was closest to the teachings of Buddha.

After divorcing his first wife, then divorcing a second wife, Goddard built a home and temple near Union Village, Vermont, which also served as headquarters for the magazine, *Zen*. In 1934 he created the Fellowship Following Buddha as an organization to spread Buddhism among non-Asian Americans. He envisioned two community homes of monks, one in Vermont and one in California, where inquirers could visit and study and which would serve as bases of a traveling outreach ministry. In 1938 he published his most important book, *A Buddhist Bible*, a collection of key Buddhist writings, many translated for the first time into English from Indian, Chinese, Japanese, and Tibetan schools. Goddard died in 1939 at the age of 78, and although his community homes were never realized and the Fellowship Following Buddha did not survive his death, his writings, which were reprinted in the 1970s, helped create a new, popular Buddhism movement in the United States.

Sources:

Fields, Rick. *How the Swans Came to the Lake.* Boulder, CO: Shambhala, 1986. 445 pp.

Goddard, Dwight. *Buddha, Truth and Brotherhood.* Santa Barbara, CA: The Author, 1934. 166 pp.

_____. *A Buddhist Bible.* Thetford, VT: The Author, 1938. 677 pp.

_____. *Buddhist Practice of Concentration.* Santa Barbara, CA: The Author, 1934. 59 pp.

_____. *A Nature Mystic's Clue.* Thetford, VT: The Author, 1925. 282 pp.

_____. *Self-Realization of Noble Wisdom.* Thetford, VT: The Author, 1932. 152 pp.

_____. *Was Jesus Influenced by Buddhism?* Thetford, VT: The Author, 1927. 249 pp.

Melton, J. Gordon. *Biographical Dictionary of American Cult and Sect Leaders.* Garland Reference Library of Social Science, vol. 212. New York: Garland Publishing, 1986.

Starry, David. "Dwight Goddard—the Yankee Buddhist," *Zen Notes* XXVII (July, 1980): 1-3.

—*Gary L. Ward*

★ 349 ★
GOLDER, Morris Ellis
Bishop, Pentecostal Assemblies of the World
b. 1913, Indianapolis, Indiana

Morris Ellis Golder, a bishop for the Pentecostal Assemblies of the World (PAW), was raised in Indianapolis, Indiana, during the early years of the Pentecostal movement. He experienced salvation under the ministry of **Garfield T. Haywood**, the presiding bishop of the Assemblies and pastor of Christ Temple. His father, Earl Golder, was a deacon at the temple, and his grandfather, Francis Golder, had been an early member. In 1930, though still a teenager, Golder was called into the ministry. After his graduation from high school, he also attended Butler University, from which he earned his B.A. and M.A. degrees, and then finished his B.D. at Christian Theological Seminary. In 1934, at the first denominational National Youth Convention, Golder was elected the historian of the group.

Around 1934, Golder began his pastoral career at Bethesda Temple in St. Louis, Missouri, where he stayed for 13 years. In 1947 he returned to Indianapolis to become pastor of Christ Temple, considered by many the mother church of the denomination. During his six years at the church, he initiated a radio ministry and purchased a farm which produced food for the parishioners. From 1949 to 1953, he also served as editor of the *Christian Outlook*, the denomination's magazine. In 1953 he became the pastor of

Grace Apostolic Church in Indianapolis, a congregation he organized, and where he has remained until the present.

While having an outstanding pastoral career, Golder is known for his work at the denominational level. He has emerged as the denomination's prime historian and has authored and published three important books: *History of the Pentecostal Assemblies of the World* (1973); *The Life and Works of Bishop Garfield Thomas Haywood* (1977); and *The Bishops of the Pentecostal Assemblies of the World* (1980). He has also served as the denomination's treasurer, a member of its board of directors, and vice-chairman of the board of Aenon Bible School. In 1972 he was elected to the bishopric and assigned duties over Episcopal District 11, which includes the states of Kentucky and Tennessee.

Sources:

Christ Temple Church Souvenir Booklet. Indianapolis, IN: Christ Temple Church, 1974. 72 pp.

Dupree, Sherry Sherrod. *Biographical Dictionary of African-American, Holiness-Pentecostals, 1880-1990*. Washington, DC: Middle Atlantic Regional Press, 1990. 386 pp.

Golder, Morris E. *The Bishops of the Pentecostal Assemblies of the World*. Indianapolis, IN: The Author, 1980. 69 pp.

———. *Grace Gleanings*. Indianapolis, IN: The Author, 1977. 125 pp.

———. *History of the Pentecostal Assemblies of the World*. Indianapolis, IN: The Author, 1973. 195 pp.

———. *The Life and Works of Bishop Garfield Thomas Haywood*. Indianapolis, IN: The Author, 1977. 71 pp.

★350★
GOLDMAN, Solomon
Conservative Jewish Rabbi
b. Aug. 19, 1893, Kozin Poland
d. May 14, 1953

Solomon Goldman, Zionist leader and one of the major twentieth-century architects of Conservative Judaism, was the son of Jeanette Grossman and Abraham Abba Goldman. When he was a child the family moved to Brooklyn, New York, where he grew up. He attended Isaac Elchanan Yeshiva and in 1912 entered the Jewish Theological Seminary. Following his graduation in 1918, he married Alice Lipkowitz and accepted a call to Cleveland, Ohio, as rabbi of B'nai Jeshuran. The beginning of his career coincided with the ending of a period of massive migration of Eastern European Jewry to America and Goldman tackled the problem of integrating the new emigrants into American life.

In 1922 Goldman moved to the Cleveland Jewish Center, a synagogue formed by the merger of two traditionalist synagogues. Through the 1920s he built it into the largest Jewish congregation in the country. He also devoted a major amount of time to the problem of providing effective Jewish education to the younger generation and worked with A. H. Friedland to develop a a Hebrew school system.

In 1929 Goldman resigned from his Cleveland post to become the rabbi for Anshe Emet Synagogue in Chicago. The congregation was quite small compared to the one in Cleveland but, in spite of the Depression, he soon built it back into a nationally influential center. In the process he emerged as a leader offering direction to the larger Conservative movement within Judaism by providing practical guidelines to move between the overt modernizing of Reform and what he saw as the adhesion to outmoded traditions of Orthodoxy. His perspective matured as he attended to the needed reforms of the Jewish Theological Seminary, the leading Conservative school.

Goldman also became an effective spokesperson for Zionism at a time when the Zionist cause still did not have the clear majority support in the American Jewish community it currently enjoys. His own study of Jewish history had convinced him that Jewish nationhood was at the heart of Jewish self-identity, and he carried that

argument into his first books, *A Rabbi Takes Stock* (1931); *The Jew and the Universe* (1936); and *Crisis and Decision* (1938). In 1938 he became the president of the Zionist Organization of America and presided at the World Zionist Congress in 1939 in Switzerland. His work for the Zionist cause also made him a strong critic of the older Zionist leadership, who controlled the Zionist organizations. He began a program to recruit younger supporters to the cause and to develop the financial backing of the Jewish community as a whole for Zionism.

When not working for Zionist efforts, Goldman dedicated much of the last decade of his life to the writing of a projected 13-volume commentary on the Jewish Bible (the Christian Old Testament). Part of his concern was to present a refutation of modern German biblical criticism which he saw as permeated with anti-Semitic premises. He was able to complete only two volumes of *The Book of Destiny*: an introductory volume, *The Book of Books* (1948) and *In the Beginning* (1949), which concerned the book of Genesis. The third book, a volume on Exodus, *From Slavery to Freedom* (1958), was completed by Harry Olinsky and released posthumously.

Sources:

Goldman, Alex J. *Giants of Faith: Great American Rabbis*. New York: Citadel Press, 1964. 349 pp.

Goldman, Solomon. *The Book of Books*. Philadelphia: Jewish Publication Society of America, 1948. 459 pp.

———. *Crisis and Decision*. New York: Harper & Brothers, 1938. 206 pp.

———. *From Slavery to Freedom*. Philadelphia: Jewish Publication Society of America, 1958. 751 pp.

———. *In the Beginning*. Philadelphia: Jewish Publication Society in America, 1949. 892 pp.

———. *The Jew and the Universe*. New York: Harper & Brothers, 1936. 184 pp.

———. *A Rabbi Takes Stock*. New York: Harper & Brothers, 1931. 247 pp.

Weinstein, Jacob J. *Solomon Goldman: A Rabbi's Rabbi*. New York: KTAV Publishing House, 1973. 295 pp.

★351★
GOLDSMITH, Joel Sol
Founder, Infinite Way
b. Mar. 10, 1892, New York, New York
d. Jun. 17, 1964, London England

Joel Sol Goldsmith was a spiritual healer and teacher, and founder of the Infinite Way. His parents were non-practicing Jews, and his bar mitzvah training was minimal. He did not finish high school, choosing instead to work full-time in his father's importing business. Goldsmith's life was changed when his father became critically ill while on a business trip to England in 1915. Doctors could do nothing for him, but Goldsmith's girlfriend, who was a Christian Science practitioner, offered to treat him. When his father completely recovered, Goldsmith decided to investigate Christian Science.

World War I intervened, and after serving in the Marines, Goldsmith went back to his father's business, which did poorly. Finally, he was forced to take a different job as a salesman. He developed tuberculosis, and was given three months to live. Having an active interest in Christian Science, he went to a practitioner, was healed, and was able to start rebuilding his career. Later, in 1928, Goldsmith was brought to a new level of commitment to Christian Science when a practitioner cured him of a cold and, as an unexpected side benefit, also relieved him of the desire for tobacco, alcohol, and gambling. To his additional surprise, Goldsmith found that he had gained the ability to heal people who turned to him for healing prayer. He finally joined the church and began his new business as a healing practitioner.

Goldsmith's business slowly grew to be a remarkable success, and he married Rose Robb. In 1933 he moved his office to Boston, and was eventually situated across the street from the Mother Church of the Church of Christ, Scientist. He became First Reader at Third Church in Boston. In 1943 his wife died, and Goldsmith moved to Santa Monica, California, where he married a long-time friend, Nadea Allen, in 1945. For reasons not entirely clear, he then decided to sever most of his social and organizational ties, leaving the church in 1946. He turned to a semi-retired life of reading, writing, and healing the few who came to him. He also experienced in this time what he described as a mystical initiation into spiritual truth, as explained in his book, *The Infinite Way* (1947). He began accepting lecture invitations, including one in Hawaii (1950) which he enjoyed so much that he moved to Honolulu. His marriage experienced a break-up about this time, and he was finally divorced in 1956. He married one of his students, Emma Lindsey, the following year.

The rest of Goldsmith's life was spent very productively in Hawaii, writing books, teaching classes, and touring as a lecturer. His message was that through meditation we can come to realize the God within. When that connection is made, we then have access to the fulfillment of all that we need. He refused to organize his students into another bureaucratic religious group, but they did gather informally to study and distribute his teachings. They continue to do so today, under the rubric Infinite Way, which designates not so much an organized group as Goldsmith's teachings and those everywhere who follow them. He died on a trip to London, England, in 1964, at the age of 72.

Sources:

Goldsmith, Joel S. *The Contemplative Life*. New York: Julian Press, 1961. 209 pp.

———. *The Heart of Spiritual Healing*. New York: Harper & Bros., 1959. 190 pp.

———. *The Infinite Way*. San Gabriel, CA: Willing Publishing Co., 1947. 199 pp.

———. *Living the Infinite Way*. New York: Harper & Bros., 1961. 128 pp.

Melton, J. Gordon. *Biographical Dictionary of American Cult and Sect Leaders*. Garland Reference Library of Social Science, vol. 212. New York: Garland Publishing, 1986.

Muhl, Barbara Mary. *The Royal Road to Reality*. Newhall, CA: Christus Publishing, 1982. 327 pp.

Sinkler, Lorraine. *The Alchemy of Awareness*. New York: Harper & Row, 1977. 149 pp.

———. *The Spiritual Journey of Joel S. Goldsmith*. New York: Harper & Row, 1973. 194 pp.

—*Gary L. Ward*

★ 352 ★

GOODELL, Charles Leroy
Minister, Methodist Episcopal Church
b. Jul. 31, 1854, Dudley, Massachusetts
d. Apr. 26, 1937, New York, New York

Charles Leroy Goodell, noted evangelist in the Methodist Episcopal Church, was the son of Warren and Clarinda Healy Goodell. Raised in Massachusetts, he attended Boston University (A.B., 1877). He was admitted to membership in the Providence Conference of the Methodist Episcopal Church in 1879 and served the congregation at Acushnet, Massachusetts, as his first assignment. As Methodists regularly move pastors from church to church every few years, he followed his year at Acushnet with assignments at Broadway in Providence, Rhode Island (1880-1883); Chestnut Street, Providence (1883-1886); Trinity, Providence (1886-1889); Winthrop Street, Boston (1889-1894); and First Methodist Episcopal Church, Boston (1894-1897). While at First Church, Boston, in 1896 he married Mary F. Blair.

In 1897 Goodell transferred to the New York Conference, and served Hanson Place, Brooklyn (1897-1904); Calvary, New York City (1904-1913); and St. Paul's, New York City (1913-1918). During his years in New York Goodell's oratorical abilities and his

evangelistic endeavors, which produced growing parishes wherever he pastored, pushed him into the national spotlight. He also authored several books on evangelism, including: *The Drill Master of Methodism* (1902); *The Price of Winning Souls* (1906); and *Pastoral and Personal Evangelism* (1907). For reasons not entirely understood, he developed some conflict with **James M. Buckley**, the influential editor of the *New York Christian Advocate*. In 1908, as a delegate to the Methodist general conference, Goodell emerged as a strong contender to be elected bishop until Buckley organized opposition to him, and in the end he fell short.

In 1918 Goodell left the pastorate for an executive position with the Federal Council of Churches as executive secretary of its Commission on Evangelism. As a pastor, he had developed a reputation for church growth in the various congregations he served. At Calvary Church he overcame initial opposition to evangelistic services and added over 400 members the first year, and more than doubled the congregation during his tenure. His position with the Federal Council gave him a national audience, and he traveled widely, preaching and promoting evangelism throughout mainline Protestantism. He stayed with the Federal Council until 1934.

In 1928 Goodell developed a radio show, "Sabbath Reveries," which continued through 1936. At its height, over 4,000 copies of his sermons were being mailed out to listeners. He continued to write through the 1920s. Among his titles were *Motives and Methods of Modern Evangelism* (1926) and *Twilight Reveries* (1929). Following his retirement in 1934 Goodell lived in New York City.

Sources:

Goodell, Charles L. *The Drill Master of Methodism*. New York: Eaton & Mains, 1902. 248 pp.

———. *Motives and Methods of Modern Evangelism*. New York: Fleming H. Revell Company, 1926. 185 pp.

———. *Pastoral and Personal Evangelism*. New York: Fleming H. Revell Company, 1907. 221 pp.

———. *The Price of Winning Souls*. New York: Fleming H. Revell Company, 1906. 32 pp.

———. *Twilight Reveries*. New York: Fleming H. Revell Company, 1929. 168 pp.

★ 353 ★

GOODPASTURE, Benjamin Cordell
Editor, Churches of Christ
b. Apr. 9, 1895, Livingston, Tennessee
d. 1977

Benjamin Cordell Goodpasture, an elder and editor with the Churches of Christ, was the son of Lora Thompson and John Jefferson Goodpasture. He was named for two Tennessee politicians, one of whom (Cordell Hull) went on to hold national office. He was raised in a family which attended the Christian Church and was baptized at the age of 14, shortly after the church had in 1906 split into the Churches of Christ and the Christian Church (Disciples of Christ). Most of the congregations in Tennessee adhered to the Churches of Christ.

Goodpasture began to preach when he was 17, about the same time he was ordained in 1912. He attended Dixie College in Cookesville, Tennessee, and finished his schooling at Nashville Bible College (now David Lipscomb College) with an A.B. in 1918. That same year he married Emily Cleveland Client.

Following graduation, Goodpasture became the minister of a congregation in Shelbyville, Tennessee. He then worked in Alabama before settling in Atlanta, where he would remain for almost two decades. During his Georgia years he was a very popular preacher for protracted meetings. In 1939 he became the president of the Gospel Advocate Company, a major publishing concern which issued books, church school literature, and evangelistic tracts. The main publication of the company was the *Gospel Advocate*, the most prominent of several periodicals serving the Churches of Christ. It had been founded by Tolbert Fanning in 1855 as the voice of the Christian Church in the deep South. Goodpasture served as editor of the *Advocate* for the rest of his life. At the same time he became the minister at the Hillsboro Church of Christ in Nashville, Tennessee, which he served until his retirement in 1951.

During his years in Tennessee Goodpasture became the voice of consensus within the Churches of Christ. He was generally known to take a middle position in major controversies (as contrasted with the often fiery polemics of former *Gospel Advocate* editor **Foy E. Wallace, Jr.**), and is credited with being a stabilizing influence among the loosely organized congregations. He authored several books including *Biographies and Sermons of Pioneer Preachers* (1954) and *Sermons and Lectures* (1964). He served as editor of many more publications such as the *Gospel Advocate Centennial Volume* (1956). He also became a friend and admirer of **Marshall Keeble**, the most notable of the black ministers in the Church of Christ, and promoted and encouraged his career through the pages of the *Advocate*.

Sources:

Choate, J. E. *The Anchor That Holds: A Biography of B. C. Goodpasture.* 1971.
Goodpasture, B. C., ed. *Biography and Sermons of Marshall Keeble, Evangelist.* Nashville, TN: Gospel Advocate, 1964. 102 pp.
_____. *Sermons and Lectures.* Nashville, TN: Gospel Advocate Company, 1964. 159 pp.
_____, and William Thomas More, eds. *Biographies and Sermons of Pioneer Preachers.* Nashville, TN: B. C. Goodpasture, 1954.
_____, comp. *The Gospel Advocate Centennial Volume.* Nashville, TN: Gospel Advocate Company, 1956.
_____, comp. *The Sermon Outlines of M. C. Kurfees.* Atlanta, GA: B. C. Goodpasture, 1936.
Hill, Samuel S., ed. *Encyclopedia of Religion in the South.* Macon, GA: Mercer University Press, 1984. 878 pp.
Reid, Daniel G., Robert D. Linder, Bruce L. Shelley, and Harry S. Stout. *Dictionary of Christianity in America.* Downers Grove, IL: InterVarsity Press, 1990. 1305 pp.

★354★
GOODSPEED, Edgar Johnson
Bible Scholar, Baptist Church
b. Oct. 23, 1871, Quincy, Illinois
d. Jan. 13, 1962, Chicago, Illinois

Edgar Johnson Goodspeed, one of the most prominent Biblical scholars of the first half of the twentieth century, was the son of a Baptist minister, Thomas Wakefield Goodspeed, and his wife, Mary Ellen Broeke Goodspeed. When Edgar was five, the family moved to Chicago, where his father became a teacher at the Baptist Union Theological Seminary. Edgar's youth was thus pervaded with both piety and education, and he began early in life to master Latin and then Greek. In 1886 he entered Denison University, majoring in classics. After graduating in 1890, he attended Yale University.

During his years in college, Goodspeed's father was working to reestablish the University of Chicago. He was able to secure a large donation from John D. Rockefeller for the project. When the school opened in 1892, Goodspeed entered to complete his doctorate; his former professor from Yale, William Rainey Harper, became the school's first president. Goodspeed received his Ph.D. in New Testament in 1898. He spent the next two years in Germany, during which time he studied with Aldolf Harnack. He also visited the Holyland before returning to take a post at the University of Chicago. In 1901 he married Elfleda Bond.

Goodspeed began teaching at the University of Chicago in 1902 and by 1915 had become a full professor. His scholarly output was spectacular, both during the 35 years of his active teaching career at the university and in the 20 years following his formal retirement in 1937. His first works were technical papers drawn from his study

abroad, but he began to reach a wider audience with his *The Epistle to the Hebrews* (1908) and especially *The Story of the New Testament* (1916). During his years of teaching he became concerned with public ignorance of the Bible, and he devoted an important segment of his time to writing popular, scholarly sound books for a general audience.

In 1923 Goodspeed published one of his major works, *The New Testament: An American Translation*, which became one of the best selling titles of the University of Chicago Press. That same year he was named chairman of the New Testament department. In 1930 he was named to the Revised Standard Bible Committee and helped produce the *Revised Standard Version of the New Testament* (1946). In 1933 he was designated the Ernest Dewitt Burton Distinguished Professor of the University of Chicago. That same year, working with J. M. Powis Smith, he brought out *The Bible: An American Translation*, and an abridged version, *The Short Bible: An American Translation*, which appeared two years later. Among his more interesting works of this period was *Strange New Gospels* (1931), later reissued as *Modern Apocrypha*, which gave accounts of a number of nineteenth and twentieth century spurious texts purporting to be ancient Christian gospels.

Following his retirement in 1937, Goodspeed began a translation of *The Apocypha* which appeared the following year. He spent four years at the University of California at Los Angeles (1938-1942). He then turned back to writing and produced the series of books for which he is most remembered: *A History of Early Christian Literature* (1942); *How to Read the Bible* (1946); *Paul* (1947); *A Life of Jesus* (1950), *The Twelve: The Story of Christ's Apostles* (1957) and *Matthew, Apostle and Evangelist* (1959). He also authored an autobiography, *As I Remember* (1953).

Sources:

Cobb, J. I., and L. B. Jennings. *A Biography and Bibliography of Edgar Johnson Goodspeed.* Chicago: University of Chicago Press, 1948.
Cook, James I. *Edgar Johnson Goodspeed, Articulate Scholar.* Chico, CA: Scholars Press, 1980. 88 pp.
Goodspeed, Edgar J. *As I Remember.* New York: Harper & Bros., 1953.
_____. *How to Read the Bible.* Philadelphia: John C. Winston Co., 1946.
_____. *A Life of Jesus.* New York: Harper & Bros., 1950.
_____. *The New Testament: An American Translation.* Chicago: University of Chicago Press, 1923.
_____. *Strange New Gospels.* Chicago: University of Chicago Press, 1931.

★355★
GORDON, Adoniram Judson
Minister, Baptist Church
b. Apr. 19, 1836, Dana, New Hampshire
d. Feb. 2, 1895, Boston, Massachusetts

Adoniram Judson Gordon, the outstanding fundamentalist Baptist minister, was the son of John Calvin Gordon, a staunch Calvinist Baptist who named his son after the famous Baptist missionary. As a youth, Adoniram worked in his father's woolen mill. At the age of 15 he had a conversion experience and a few months later, around his 16th birthday, he decided to go into the ministry. He attended school in nearby New London, New Hampshire, and in 1856 entered Brown University in Providence, Rhode Island. He was an average student, and showed little promise of future greatness. After finishing his courses in 1860, he moved on to Newton Theological Seminary. After graduating, he was ordained as pastor of Jamaica Plain Baptist Church in West Roxbury, Massachusetts, in 1863. He married and had three children.

In 1869 Gordon moved to Clarendon Street Baptist Church in Boston, where he was to remain for the rest of his active life. He had earlier absorbed some of the newer ideas about congregational life and worship and began to introduce them into the church. The most controversial of these was congregational singing. To assist his parishioners he wrote one of his first books, *Congregational*

Worship (1872), and edited a new hymn book (1874). He also wrote *In Christ*, which was both a study of the presence of Christ in the heart of the believer and a study guide to aid in living the Christian life. It was during this period of his life that Gordon began reading significant amounts of the literature circulated by the Plymouth Brethren, a British group from which fundamentalism largely originated. He also began to follow the career of evangelist **Dwight L. Moody**, who was also heavily influenced by the Brethren. In 1877 Moody came to Boston and pitched his tent next door to Gordon's church. Among those who were converted were a number of alcoholics; as a result, the church discontinued the use of wine in their communion services. Gordon's connection with Moody lasted the rest of his life, and he regularly taught at Moody's summer headquarters in Northfield, Massachusetts.

During his quarter century at Clarendon, Gordon built a large congregation and used his position to influence the course of a number of special causes. In the 1880s he joined the Prohibition Party, which in 1884 drew enough votes from the Republicans to oust the latter party from key political offices. In the face of growing Catholic power in Boston and city harassment of Protestant evangelistic efforts, Gordon allowed himself to be arrested on Boston Commons for preaching to a YMCA open air meeting without a city permit. He attacked the new religion of Christian Science, answering it with a book on *The Ministry of Healing* (1882).

Among Gordon's most persistent activities was work in support of missions. He demonstrated his concern by spending much of his summer vacations working in the small churches of rural New Hampshire. He served for many years on the executive committee of the American Baptist Missionary Union and became chairman of the union in 1888. He used the occasion to attend the London International Missionary Conference that year and tour Scotland as an evangelist-missionary. During the 1890s, he supported a Jewish mission and a Chinese mission in Boston and traveled to Chicago in 1893 to assist Moody in his evangelistic effort to counter the World's Parliament of Religions and its promotion of non-Christian faiths.

Gordon was the author of a number of books, among them *The Two-Fold Life* (1884); *The Ministry of the Spirit* (1894); and *How Christ Came to Church* (1895), an autobiographical reflection. He died just a few months after celebrating his 25th anniversary as Clarendon's pastor.

Sources:

Gordon, Adoniram Judson. *Congregational Worship*. Boston, MA: Young & Bartlett, 1874. 120 pp.

———. *How Christ Came to Church, A Spiritual Autobiography*. New York: American Baptist Publication Society, 1985. 123 pp.

———. *In Christ*. Boston, MA: Garnett, 1883. 209 pp.

———. *The Ministry of the Spirit*. New York: Fleming H. Revell, 1894. 229 pp.

———. *The Vestry Hymn and Tune Book*. New York: H. A. Young & Co., 1872. 297 pp.

Gordon, Ernest B. *Adoniram Gordon Judson, A Biography*. New York: Fleming H. Revell, 1896. 386 pp.

Lambert, D. W. *Heralds of Holiness*. Burslem, Stoke-on-Trent, UK: 1975. 80 pp.

★ 356 ★
GORDON, Charles William
Moderator, Presbyterian Church in Canada
Novelist
b. Sep. 19, 1860, Glengarry County, Ontario, Canada
d. Oct. 31, 1937, Winnipeg, Manitoba, Canada

Charles William Gordon was both a prominent Canadian Presbyterian minister and, under his pen name, Ralph Connor, the most successful Canadian novelist of the early twentieth century. Gordon was the son of Mary Robertson and David Gordon, a Presbyterian minister. He attended the University of Toronto and graduated from Knox College in 1887. He pursued further theological studies for a year in Edinburgh, Scotland. In 1890 he was ordained in the Presbyterian Church in Canada. As his first ministerial assignment, he was sent by **James Robertson** (whose biography he would later write) as a missionary to Banff, Alberta, to work among the miners and lumberjacks. After three years in the West he spent a year in Scotland raising funds, and then in 1894 he accepted a call to the St. Stephen's Presbyterian Church in Winnipeg, Manitoba, where he remained for the rest of his life. In 1899 he married Helen Skinner King.

Settled in his pastorate, Gordon began to write stories drawing upon his experience on the frontier. These were published in *The Westminster*, a Presbyterian magazine. They were collected into what became his first book in 1898. Their success led to more stories which would generally appear initially as a series in *The Westminster*, and then as a book. The fictional stories, written under the Ralph Connor pen name, have been described as fast-paced novels centered upon the conflict of good and evil. They were set on the Canadian frontier and included a minister as one of the main characters. The early titles were the most popular and gave him an audience that allowed him to continue writing through the rest of his life.

In the meantime, as a minister, Gordon had become involved in the temperance crusades and was president of the Social Service Council of Manitoba. During World War I he took a leave from his congregation to become the chaplain of the 43rd Highlanders, many of whom had been recruited out of his parish. He soon became the senior Protestant chaplain to the Canadian armed forces and in 1917 was sent on tour to the United States to lecture on the Allied view of the war. After the war, in 1920, he became chairperson of the Manitoba Council of Industry, and devoted much of the next four years of his life to mediating strike disputes. In the midst of his other work, in 1921 he was elected moderator of the Presbyterian Church in Canada. In that capacity he became a major worker in the negotiations union which produced the United Church of Canada in 1925. He remained as a parish minister in the new church.

In his mature years Gordon branched out considerably from the frontier adventure novels which were his stock and trade. He authored a few historical novels, several books reflecting on the life of Christ, and several which grew out of his involvement with labor. His autobiography, *Postscript to Adventure*, was published in 1938, shortly after Gordon's death.

Sources:

Gordon, Charles William [Ralph Connor]. *Black Rock: A Tale of the Selkirks*. Toronto: Westminster, 1898. 327 pp.

———. *The Life of James Robertson: Missionary Superintendent in Western Canada*. New York: Fleming H. Revell Company, 1908. 403 pp.

———. *The Man from Glengarry*. Chicago: Fleming H. Revell Company, 1901. 473 pp.

———. *Postscript to Adventure*. London: Hodder & Stoughton, 1938. 381 pp.

———. *The Sky Pilot: A Tale of the Foothills*. Chicago: Fleming H. Revell Company, 1899. 300 pp.

Moir, J. S. *Enduring Witness: A History of the Presbyterian Church in Canada*. N.p.: Centennial Committee, Presbyterian Church in Canada, 1975. 311 pp.

Toye, William, ed. *The Oxford Companion to Canadian Literature*. Toronto: Oxford University Press, 1983. 843 pp.

★ 357 ★
GORDON, George Angier
Minister, Congregational Church
b. Jan. 2, 1853, Oyne, Aberdeenshire Scotland
d. Oct. 25, 1929, Boston, Massachusetts

George Angier Gordon, a leading modernist minister in the Congregational Church, was the son of George and Catherine Hutcheon Gordon. He grew up on the farm on which his father was the overseer. In his late teens, in 1871, he immigrated to Boston, Massachusetts. He found work as a laborer and joined the local Presbyterian church. He was befriended by the pastor, Luther H. Angier, who encouraged him to seek a career in ministry. (Eventually he would adopt Angier as a middle name in honor of his mentor.) In 1874, though without a college degree, Gordon was able to enter the Congregational Church's theological seminary in Bangor, Maine. He graduated in 1877 and was ordained to the ministry at Temple, Maine, where he had been pastoring a small congregation. Angier then secured Gordon's enrollment at Harvard College as a special student. Having demonstrated his ability Gordon was admitted to the senior class in 1880 and in 1881 graduated with an A.B. degree, with honors in philosophy.

In April 1881 Gordon became pastor of Second Congregational Church in Greenwich, Connecticut. He served for three years and then moved to Boston as pastor of Old South Church, one of the more prominent parishes in the denomination. In 1890 he married Susan Huntington.

Gordon was to remain in the Old South pulpit for 43 years. During the 1890s he emerged as a champion for modernist theology, in part a reflection of the Unitarian leanings of his Harvard teachers. Apart from the well-publicized sermons he preached at his church, he had a significant effect as a liberal voice before the American Board of Commissioners for Foreign Missions, the missionary arm of the Congregational Church. He took pains to separate himself from Unitarianism with his strong defense of the Trinity, and he distanced himself from the universalists by his advocacy of a human free will so strong it could in the end hold out against God's grace. The major idea for which he argued was the ephemeral nature of Christian theology. In the context of the missionary enterprise, the concern of the American Board, Gordon argued against the imposition of traditional Western Christian teachings (which he saw as so much excess baggage) on foreign cultures. Rather, the missionaries should merely present Christ and allow the various peoples of the world to respond to Him.

Gordon's perspective was presented in a series of books beginning with *The Witness to Immortality in Literature, Philosophy and Life* (1893). He elaborated upon his Christology in *The Christ of To-day* (1895), which was followed by a second book on life after death, *Immortality and the New Theodicy* (1897). His other books included: *The New Epoch for Faith* (1903); *Through Man to God* (1906); *Religion and Miracle* (1909); *Revelation and the Ideal* (1913); *Aspects of the Infinite Mystery* (1916); *Humanism in New England Theology* (1920); and *Unto Victory* (1927). In 1925 he authored an autobiographical volume: *My Education and Religion: An Autobiography.*

Sources:

Buckham, J. W. *Progressive Religious Thought in America.* Boston: Houghton Mifflin & Co., 1919. 352 pp.
Dictionary of American Biography. 20 vols. and 7 supps. New York: Charles Scribner's Sons, 1928-1936, 1944-1981.
Gordon, George A. *The Christ of To-day.* New York: Houghton Mifflin & Co., 1895. 322 pp.
_____. *My Education and Religion: An Autobiography.* Boston: Houghton Mifflin & Co., 1925. 352 pp.
_____. *The New Epoch for Faith.* Boston: Houghton Mifflin & Co., 1901. 412 pp.
_____. *Religion and Miracle.* Boston: Houghton Mifflin & Co., 1909. 244 pp.
_____. *Through Man to God.* Boston: Houghton Mifflin & Co., 1906. 395 pp.
Hutchison, William R. *The Modernist Impulse in American Protestantism.* Cambridge, MA: Harvard University Press, 1976. 347 pp.

★358★
GOVINDA, Anagarika
Founder, Arya Maitreya Mandala
Buddhist Author
b. May 17, 1898, Waldheim Germany
d. Jan. 14, 1985, Mill Valley, California

Lama Anagarika Govinda, born Ernst Lothar Hoffmann, was the founder of the Arya Maitreya Mandala and was an internationally known Buddhist author. He studied at the University of Freiburg, the University of Naples, the University of Cagliari, and at Buddhist monasteries in Sri Lanka. He grew up speaking three languages and at the age of 18 wrote his first book, *The Fundamental Ideas of Buddhism and Their Relation to the Concept of God*. He achieved recognition as one of the foremost Buddhists in Europe after the publication of a booklet on Satipathana meditation in 1922. In Sri Lanka in 1928 he became a buddhist lama under the guidance of the Venerable. Mahathera Nyanatiloka, Brahmacari Govinda. He first met his guru, Tomo Geshe Rinpoche (Lama Ngawang Kolsang), at the All India Buddhist Conference in Darjeeling. Thereafter he remained in India, earning a living as a university lecturer.

After an expedition to western Tibet in 1933, Lama Govinda founded the Arya Maitreya Mandala, an order with the professed ideal of establishing a Buddhist society that would be vitally related to the times. A few years later he also founded the International Buddhist University Association to sponsor a Buddhist University at Sarnath, the spot in India at which Gautama, the founder of Buddhism, became enlightened (i.e. the Buddha). Govinda was also an accomplished artist who during this period held many exhibitions in India. Because of his acquaintance with independence leaders such as Jawaharlal Nehru, he was detained for a total of five years. He became an Indian national after India achieved independence in 1947. In the same year he married an art student, Li Gotami.

During the next several decades Lama Govinda wrote his most famous works, including *The Foundations of Tibetan Mysticism* (1959) and *The Way of the White Clouds* (1966). He and his wife also traveled extensively throughout Asia and the rest of the world. The Govindas first visited the United States in 1968, lecturing to university audiences and to such groups as the Theosophical Society, the Zen Center of San Francisco, the Nyingma Institute, and the Esalen Institute. From 1976 onwards, their activities were centered in North America. During his lecturing in the San Francisco area, Lama Govinda worked out the meditative and spiritual practice of his group, Arya Maitreya Mandala. He died peacefully and unexpectedly at his California home.

Sources:

Contemporary Authors. Detroit, MI: Gale Research Inc.
Gottmann, Karl-Heinz. "The Way of the White Clouds: In Memory of Lama Anagarika Govinda." *Vajradhatu Sun* (March 1985).
Govinda, Lama Anagarika. *Creative Meditation and Multi- Dimensional Consciousness.* Wheaton, IL: Theosophical Publishing House, 1976. 294 pp.
_____. *Foundations of Tibetan Mysticism.* London: Rider, 1959. 311 pp.
_____. *The Psychological Attitude of Early Buddhist Philosophy.* London: Rider, 1961.
_____. "Special Meditation Issue." *Human Dimensions* 1, 4 (1972).
_____. *The Way of the White Clouds: A Buddhist Pilgrim in Tibet.* Berkeley, CA: Shambhala, 1966. 305 pp.

★359★
GRACE, Sweet Daddy
Founder, United House of Prayer for All People
b. Jan. 25, 1881, Brava Cape Verde
d. Jan. 12, 1960, Los Angeles, California

Charles Manuel Grace, better known to his followers and the public as "Sweet Daddy" Grace, was one of a small number of unique charismatic religious leaders who functioned in the American black community during the twentieth century. He was born Marcelino Manoel de Graca, a name that was anglicized after he moved to Bedford, Massachusetts, in 1908. He worked at various odd jobs until 1920 when he made a visit to the Holy Land. Upon his return he began to preach in Bedford and nearby Wareham. He preached up and down the east coast of America, and in 1926 founded the United House of Prayer for All People in Charlotte, North Carolina.

Unlike several other black religious figures of the era, Grace did not claim to be God, merely the point of mediation between God and humanity. He often spoke in a manner that played upon his name and God's grace, and was reported to have said that if one sinned against God, Grace could save the individual, but if one sinned against Grace, even God's power could not help. Grace used his authority to impose a traditional holiness-Pentecostal belief and practice.

Grace built an elaborate organization around himself. He developed a flamboyant appearance. His fingernails were painted red, white, and blue. His hair was long, and jewels bedecked his fingers. He favored green suits with a cutaway coat. He began to establish houses of prayer throughout the eastern half of the nation and before the end pushed to the West Coast. He ruled the church with autocratic authority.

Grace's movement was characterized by its emotional, expressive worship in which members were encouraged to dance and feel the presence of Grace. Worship services were held daily. Most churches had facilities to sell a variety of products bearing Grace's name, including coffee, eggs, and various toiletries. Some of these products came from the church-owned coffee plantation in Brazil and the egg hatchery in Cuba.

Grace traveled constantly, spending an estimated 300 days a year on the road. He opened 11 houses of prayer in his lifetime, and acquired a number of homes in different parts of the United States. His Los Angeles mansion had 85 rooms and 21 baths. Among his other properties were a Manhattan apartment building, a castle in Connecticut, and the Detroit mansion that had belonged to **James Francis Marion "Prophet" Jones** in the 1950s.

Grace was plagued for many years by the Internal Revenue Service. He was taken to court in 1934, but the case was thrown out. He finally died of a heart attack and stroke while visiting his followers in Los Angeles. He was succeeded by **Walter McCollough**.

Sources:

Bowden, Henry Warner. *Dictionary of American Religious Biography*. Westport, CT: Greenwood Press, 1977. 572 pp.

Dupree, Sherry Sherrod. *Biographical Dictionary of African-American, Holiness-Pentecostals, 1880-1990*. Washington, DC: Middle Atlantic Regional Press, 1990. 386 pp.

Fauset, Arthur Huff. *Black Gods of the Metropolis*. Philadelphia: University of Pennsylvania Press, 1971. 128 pp.

Lincoln, C. Eric. *The Black Religious Experience*. Garden City, NY: Doubleday, 1974. 369 pp.

★ 360 ★
GRAEBNER, August Lawrence
Theologian, Lutheran Church-Missouri Synod
b. Jul. 10, 1849, Frankentrost, Michigan
d. Dec. 7, 1904, St. Louis, Missouri

August Lawrence Graebner, a prominent church historian and theologian of the Lutheran Church-Missouri Synod at the close of the nineteenth century, was the son of Jacobine Denninger and Johann Heinrich Philip Graebner, a minister in the Missouri Synod. The elder Graebner sent his son to Concordia College in Fort Wayne, Indiana, in 1865. Graebner was unable to complete his degree program due to illness. Nevertheless, in 1870 he entered Concordia Theological Seminary (the Missouri Synod's seminary) in St.

Louis. During his years there he became known for his knowledge of the classics and the writings of Martin Luther. He also was strongly influenced by his study with Carl Ferdinand Wilhelm Walther, the founder of the Missouri Synod. But again he was forced by illness to withdraw before completing his course of study.

In 1872 Graebner began teaching at the Lutheran high school in St. Louis. The following year he married Anna Schaller, the daughter of one of his former professors at the seminary. In 1875 he moved to Watertown, Wisconsin, as a professor at Northwestern College, and three years later joined the faculty of the new seminary in Milwaukee, Wisconsin, founded by the Wisconsin Synod (which was, like Missouri, a very conservative synod). Shortly after the move, he was ordained as a minister and became editor of the synod's periodical, *Gemeinde-blatt*. While in Milwaukee he authored his first books, *Dr. Martin Luther: Lebensbild des Reformators* (1883) and *Johann Sebastian Bach* (1886).

In 1887 Graebner succeeded his father-in-law as professor of church history at Concordia Theological Seminary, at which time he returned to St. Louis. Following the death of C. H. R. Lange, he also assumed duties as a lecturer in dogmatic theology. His most important scholarly work from his Concordia years is *Geschichte der Lutherischen Kirke in America, Erster Theil* (1892), which covers Lutheran history in America to 1820. He also authored a history of the Missouri Synod, *Half a Century of Sound Lutheranism in America* (1893). The last years of Graebner's life were concentrated on theology. In 1897 he issued the first copies of the *Theological Quarterly*, which he not only edited, but for which he wrote most of the articles. He continued his editorial efforts for the rest of his life. In 1898 he finished his major theological work, *Outlines of Doctrinal Theology*. He is remembered for his unabashed orthodoxy and the often harsh treatment he gave to those in whom he found doctrinal aberrations. At the same time he was known for his learning, which included a mastery of 13 languages. His health failed in 1903 and he died after a rather pain-filled year.

Sources:

Dictionary of American Biography. 20 vols. and 7 supps. New York: Charles Scribner's Sons, 1928-1936, 1944-1981.

Graebner, August L. *Dr. Martin Luther: Lebensbild des Reformators*. Milwaukee, WI: G. Brunder, 1883. 543 pp.

———. *Geschichte der Lutherischen Kirke in America, Erster Theil*. St. Louis, MO: Concordia Pub. House, 1892. 726 pp.

———. *Half a Century of Sound Lutheranism in America*. St. Louis, MO: Concordia Pub. House, 1893. 30 pp.

———. *Johann Sebastian Bach*. Milwaukee, WI: G. Brunder, 1886. 160 pp.

———. *Outlines of Doctrinal Theology*. St. Louis, MO: Concordia Pub. House, 1898. 288 pp.

★ 361 ★
GRAHAM, Billy
Evangelist, Southern Baptist Convention
b. Nov. 7, 1918, Charlotte, North Carolina

William Franklin "Billy" Graham, America's best known evangelist, was born into a strict Presbyterian family in North Carolina. Converted under the preaching of evangelist Mordecai F. Ham in 1934, he attended Bob Jones College and then Florida Bible Institute. While in Florida, Graham joined the Southern Baptist Convention. Following graduation he attended Wheaton College where he met his future wife, Ruth McCue Bell. They were married in 1943 a few months after each had graduated. He became the pastor of a small church in Chicago.

In Chicago Graham was introduced to broadcast evangelism when the congregation began to sponsor a radio show, "Songs in the Night." He also joined the staff of Youth for Christ and in 1947 issued his first book, *Calling Youth to Christ*. That same year, **William Bell Riley** called Graham to the presidency of the Northwestern Schools he had founded in Minnesota. Reluctantly he accepted and moved to Minneapolis, which has remained his headquarters over the years. During his presidency he became nationally famous because of an evangelistic campaign in Los Angeles in the summer of 1949. The scheduled two weeks of revival services became two months, and he had numerous calls for further engagements. As his evangelistic career blossomed, he instituted practices to give his efforts a high degree of integrity and financial accountability.

In 1950, following the death of popular Lutheran radio minister **Walter A. Maier**, he founded the Billy Graham Evangelistic Association and launched his own radio show, "The Hour of Decision." In 1951 he resigned from the Northwestern Schools and became a full-time evangelist. In 1952 he began his daily "My Answer" newspaper column, which was syndicated nationally, and in 1953 issued *Peace with God*, the first of several best-selling books.

Graham had become identified with Neo-Evangelicalism, the conservative Protestant movement which grew up in the 1940s around such men as **Harold J. Ockenga**, **Carl. F. H. Henry**, and **Edward John Carnell**. Graham emerged as the popular spokesperson of the new movement and with the other leaders helped launch *Christianity Today*, the movement's popular journal. His leadership among the Neo-Evangelicals also led to intense criticism from the fundamentalists who saw the new movement as a betrayal of orthodox Christianity.

In 1957 Graham's ministry took another step forward with the televising of his crusade (a term he popularized for his evangelistic meetings) in New York City, which lasted for four months. As his work expanded, he emerged as America's foremost evangelist, and he began to assume a leadership role in the evangelical efforts around the world. He launched *Decision*, a magazine which carried regular articles he wrote and news of his growing number of endeavors. In 1960 he convened a conference on world evangelism in Montreaux, Switzerland, the first of a series held over the next three decades. The most recent of these was the 1986 International Conference of Itinerant Evangelists in Amsterdam, Holland. In 1967 he began the Billy Graham School of Evangelism to train pastors and other church workers to be more effective evangelists.

Graham's fame also allowed him access to powerful American political figures, beginning with Strom Thurmond in the 1950s. During the Nixon administration he was often a guest at White House gatherings. Following the Watergate scandal, however, he came to the unpleasant realization that Nixon had merely used him as a pious smokescreen to hide the administration's crooked dealings. Embarrassed, Graham withdrew from the political arena. His bad experience with the Nixon administration kept him from associating with the New Religious Right when it emerged in the 1980s. Among the national evangelistic ministries, he suffered the least in the wake of the scandals which plagued the ministries of **Jim Bakker** and **Jimmy Swaggart**.

Sources:

Barnhart, Joe E. *The Billy Graham Religion*. Philadelphia: United Church Press, 1972.

Frady, Marshall. *Billy Graham: A Parable in American Righteousness*. Boston: Little, Brown, 1979.

Graham, Billy. *Angels: God's Secret Agents*. Garden City, NY: Doubleday & Company, 1975.

———. *Approaching Hoofbeats: The Fourhorsemen of the Apocalypse*. Waco, TX: Word Books, 1983.

———. *My Answer*. Garden City, NY: Doubleday & Company, 1960.

———. *Peace with God*. Waco, TX: Word Books, 1953. Rev. ed. Minneapolis, MN: World Wide Publications, 1984. 221 pp.

———. *World Aflame*. Garden City, NY: Doubleday & Company, 1965.

Hill, Samuel S., ed. *Encyclopedia of Religion in the South*. Macon, GA: Mercer University Press, 1984. 878 pp.

Lippy, Charles H. *Twentieth-Century Shapers of American Popular Religion*. New York: Greenwood Press, 1989. 494 pp.

Pollock, John. *Billy Graham: The Authorized Biography*. New York: McGraw-Hill, 1966.

★362★
GRANT, Frederick William
Leader, Plymouth Brethren
b. Jul. 25, 1834, London England
d. Jul. 25, 1902, Plainfield, New Jersey

Frederick William Grant, founder of an influential branch of the Plymouth Brethren in the late 1800s, was raised in England. He moved to Canada in 1855 at the age of 21. There, due to the shortage of priests, he was ordained by the Church of England in Canada, despite his lack of seminary education. Before long, however, he was converted to the Plymouth Brethren position by their literature. He moved away, finally settling in Plainfield, New Jersey, where he made a living by lecturing and writing books, including *Life and Immortality* (1871) and the *Numerical Structure of Scripture* (1877).

Grant sided with the Exclusive Brethren, those who did not fellowship with non-Brethren groups. He began to realize, however, that he had some differences with the aging John Nelson Darby, the founder of the Plymouth Brethren. After Darby died in 1883, Grant voiced these differences in *Life and the Spirit* (later called *Life in Christ and Sealing with the Spirit*). Grant taught that God saved people through Christ in all dispensations (meaning, for example, that the Old Testament saints received eternal life in Christ), that the Christian may be justified and not know it, and that saving faith is not in the atonement (work) of Christ, but in the risen and glorified Christ.

Grant's teachings caused much discussion among the Plymouth Brethren, and on November 27, 1884, the Brethren in Montreal asked him to withdraw his book. Soon thereafter they dismissed him from the church. Grant immediately gathered his supporters together, including his home congregation in Plainfield, and formed a new group. Among his allies were Paul Loizeaux and his brother Timothe Ophir Loizeaux, who had established the major Brethren publishing company in North America. They published his writings in the coming years.

Various segments of the Grant Brethren began to advocate limited fellowship with the Open Brethren in the 1890s, despite Grant's adamant exclusivist stance. This led to a split in the group, but the movement toward openness was not yet complete. Grant published the various volumes of his single most famous book, *The Numerical Bible*, between 1892 and 1903. Long a student of the Psalms, he believed he had found a five-fold internal arrangement in them that was replicated throughout the Bible.

After Grant's death in 1902, the Grant Brethren merged with another branch of the Plymouth Brethren in 1920. Over the next decade many of the congregations continued the earlier "open" leaning and gradually affiliated with some of the remaining Plymouth Brethren (Open or Christian Brethren). Congregations were absorbed into the several fellowships of Exclusive brethren. Grant's writings continue to influence those in the Brethren tradition.

Sources:

Grant, Frederick William. *Atonement in Type, Prophecy and Accomplishment*. New York: Loizeaux Brothers, Bible Truth Depot, n.d. 218 pp.

———. *A Divine Movement*. New York: Loizeaux Brothers, Bible Truth Depot, n.d. 106 pp.

———. *Genesis in the Light of the New Testament*. New York: Loizeaux Brothers, 1945.

———. *Lessons of the Ages*. New York: Loizeaux Brothers, Publishers, n.d. 126 pp.

———. *The Numerical Bible*. New York: Loizeaux Brothers, 1892-1903.

———. *The Numerical Structure of Scripture*. New York: Loizeaux Brothers, Bible Truth Depot. 1887. 155 pp.

_____. *The Prophetic History of the Church*. New York: Loizeaux Brothers, 1902. 183 pp.

Ironside, H. A. *A Historical Sketch of the Brethren Movement*. Grand Rapids, MI: Zondervan Publishing House, 1942. 219 pp.

Melton, J. Gordon. *Biographical Dictionary of American Cult and Sect Leaders*. Garland Reference Library of Social Science, vol. 212. New York: Garland Publishing, 1986.

Noel, Napoleon. *The History of the Brethren*. 2 vols. Denver, CO: W. F. Knapp, 1936.

Pickering, Hy. *Chief Men Among the Brethren*. London: Pickering & Inglis, 1918. 223 pp.

—*Gary L. Ward*

★ 363 ★
GRANT, Heber Jeddy
President, Church of Jesus Christ of Latter-day Saints
b. Mar. 22, 1856, Salt Lake City, Utah
d. May 14, 1945, Salt Lake City, Utah

Heber Jeddy Grant, the seventh president of the Church of Jesus Christ of Latter-day Saints, was raised in the church, the son of Apostle Jedediah M. Grant and Rachael Ridgeway Ivins. His father died eight days after Heber's birth. As a child, Heber suffered from astigmatism and from severe headaches that resulted from that condition. His physical condition interfered with his education and caused other children to consider him a sissy, an image he worked diligently to overcome.

Grant secured a job as an office boy when he was 15 years old, but he soon began to sell insurance on the side. By 1880 he was able to form a syndicate which purchased $350,000 worth of stock in Zion's Cooperative Mercantile Institution. His business career led him to the presidency of the State Bank of Utah, Home Fire Insurance Company, and the Heber J. Grant Insurance Company, among others.

Grant married Lucy Stringham in 1877. As his economic condition improved he married Hulda Augusta Winters and Emily J. Harris Wells, both in 1884. During the 1880s his position in the church continued to rise. He became a stake president in 1880, an Apostle in 1882. He went to Arizona on a mission to the Moquis Indians in 1883-1884, to Japan as mission president from 1901 to 1903, and to England as president of the British and European Mission from 1903 to 1906. In 1916 Grant became president of the Quorum of the Twelve Apostles, and in 1918, upon the death of **Joseph Fielding Smith, Sr.,** he became the seventh president of the church.

Grant's quarter of a century tenure as president of the church was second in length only to that of Brigham Young. Although his term continued through the depression that began in 1929, the period was generally an era of prosperity for the church. The dramatic spread of the church followed the expansion of the mission program, although Grant was forced to close the Japan mission, which had shown little growth. Overall membership almost doubled and new temples were dedicated in Hawaii, Alberta, and Arizona. In response to the depression, Grant inaugurated the Church Welfare Program which has contributed prominently in building an image of the church as one that kept its members off of government welfare programs.

During the majority of his last five years of life, Grant was a semi-invalid. He was unable to attend many public functions or meetings of the church leadership. He died of cardiac arrest in 1945.

Sources:

Gibbons, Francis M. *Heber J. Grant: Man of Steel, Prophet of God*. Salt Lake City, UT: Deseret Book Company, 1979.

Nibley, Preston. *The Presidents of the Church*. Salt Lake City, UT: Deseret Book Company, 1941. 477 pp.

Van Wagoner, Richard S., and Steven C. Walker. *A Book of Mormons*. Salt Lake City, UT: Signature Books, 1982. 454 pp.

★ 364 ★
GRAVES, James Robinson
Baptist Minister
Founder, Landmark Movement
b. Apr. 10, 1820, Chester, Vermont
d. Jun. 26, 1893, Memphis, Tennessee

James Robinson Graves was a prominent nineteenth-century Baptist pastor who is remembered for his work in promoting the Landmark Movement, a conservative Baptist movement that emerged within the Southern Baptist Convention. His father died soon after his birth, and he was raised in an impoverished household. Deprived of educational opportunities, he worked hard at educating himself, eventually teaching school in Kentucky and Ohio. In 1843 he married Florence Spencer. Not long after moving to Nashville, Tennessee, in 1845 as a teacher, he accepted the pastorate of the Second Baptist Church. Within a few years (1848), he also became senior editor of *The Baptist*. This experience led him to become involved in the publishing business, so that by the next decade he was a successful publisher with a large Baptist leadership.

By the time the Civil War broke out, *The Baptist*, which had been renamed *The Tennessee Baptist*, had become the most popular Baptist periodical in the Southwest and mid-South regions. Graves himself had also become one of the best-known Baptist personalities as a result of his publishing activities. After the war finally ended, he reactivated his paper, once again calling it *The Baptist*, and around 1870 he accepted the pastorate of the First Baptist Church in Memphis and moved his publishing effort there.

Graves is best remembered as the initiator and leader of what he called "Old Landmarkism." The movement began in the early 1850s, in large part as a response to the formation of the Southern Baptist Convention and the perceived centralization of missions in the convention's hands. Graves opposed any assumption of powers by associations beyond the local church. Landmarkism also asserted that the Baptist Church was the only true church. Graves argued against "alien" or non-Baptist baptisms, especially baptism of babies and baptism by means other than immersion. Graves also argued that the true church (the Baptists) has been in continuous existence since the time of Jesus, and cited as proof the existence of the various pre-Protestant heretical groups that have periodically surfaced throughout Christian history. Graves promoted his doctrines through his paper, his personal leadership, and his many books, which include *The Trilemma* (1861), an anti-Roman Catholic tract; *The First Baptist Church in America*; *Old Landmarkism—What Is It?* (1880); and *Intercommunion: Unscriptural, Inconsistent, and Productive of Evil Only* (1881). He attacked the Methodist Episcopal Church, South, the other large church in the South, in his *Great Iron Wheel or Republicanism Backwards and Christianity Reversed* (1855). This touched off a major controversy between the two churches. It was answered by W. G. Brownlow in *The Great Iron Wheel Examined, or Its False Spokes Extracted and an Exhibition of Elder Graves, Its Builder* (1856). Toward the end of his life he authored a systematic theology, *The Work of Christ in the Covenant of Redemption; Developed in Seven Dispensations* (1883).

After the death of his first wife, Graves married Lou Snider, and following her death he married his second wife's sister, Georgie Snider. At the time of Graves' death Old Landmarkism was still a minority opinion within the Southern Baptist Convention. In 1899 Graves' followers separated themselves and formed the American Baptist Association, the primary organizational expression of the Old Landmark perspective.

Sources:

Brownlow, W. G. *The Great Iron Wheel Examined, or Its False Spokes Extracted and an Exhibition of Elder Graves, Its Builder.* Nashville: Graves and Marks, 1856.

Graves, James R. *The First Baptist Church in America.*

_____. *Intercommunion: Unscriptural, Inconsistent, and Productive of Evil Only.* Texarkana, AK: Baptist Sunday School Committee, [1928]. 272 pp.

_____. *Old Landmarkism: What Is It?.* Texarkana, AK: Baptist Sunday School Committee, [1928]. 529 pp.

_____. *The Trilemma.* Nashville: South-Western Publishing House, 1861. 156 pp.

_____. *The Work of Christ on the Covenant of Redemption; Developed in Seven Dispensations.* Memphis, TN: Baptist Book House, [1883]. 569 pp.

Hill, Samuel S., ed. *Encyclopedia of Religion in the South.* Macon, GA: Mercer University Press, 1984. 878 pp.

Nevins, William Manlius. *Alien Baptism and the Baptists.* Ashland, KY: Press of Economy Printers, 1962. 118 pp.

★365★
GRAY, James Martin
Minister, Reformed Episcopal Church and President, Moody Bible Ins titute
b. 1851, New York, New York
d. Sep. 21, 1935, Chicago, Illinois

Little is known of the early life of James Martin Gray, who rose from obscurity to become one of the most prominent leaders in the fundamentalist movement of the 1920s. Probably raised in a low church tradition within the Protestant Episcopal Church, he was ordained in 1877 in the Reformed Episcopal Church. It had been recently formed by Episcopalians who opposed an over emphasis on ritualism and adhered to a conservative evangelical Protestantism. He became pastor of the Church of the Redemption in Greenpoint, New York, in 1878 and then of the Church of the Cornerstone in Newburgh, New York, the following year. In 1880 he became pastor of the First Reformed Episcopal Church in Boston, Massachusetts, where he would serve for the next 12 years. While in Boston he came into fellowship with Baptist minister **Adoniram J. Gordon**. Gordon introduced him to the larger circle of evangelicalism associated with popular evangelist **Dwight L. Moody**, and Gray taught part-time at the missionary school founded by Gordon. In 1892 he moved to Philadelphia to assume a lectureship at the Reformed Episcopal Theological Seminary.

In 1893 Gray began to preach at the summer conferences held annually by Moody at Northfield, Massachusetts. He was soon spending his time as an independent evangelist. The relationships he developed over the next decade led to an invitation to become the first dean of Moody Bible Institute in 1904. The position pushed Gray into the forefront of the developing fundamentalist movement. He worked with Cyrus I. Scofield as one of the editors for the first edition of the *Scofield Reference Bible* (1910) and contributed the article on ''The Inspiration of the Bible'' to volume three of *The Fundamentals* (1910-1915). The modern fundamentalist movement is frequently seen as beginning with the publication of *The Fundamentals*.

During his several decades at Moody, Gray gave a shape and stability to what became the leading institution of the fundamentalist movement. He authored numerous books, among the most important being *Christian Workers' Commentary on the Old and New Testaments* (1915). He frequently served as the supply preacher at Moody Memorial Church located a few blocks from the institute. In 1925 he was named president of the institute, a position he held until his death.

Gray is remembered for charting a middle road for Moody. While a staunch opponent of liberalism, he refused to take the school into an intellectual isolationism and equally shunned the informal evangelism of **William A. ''Billy'' Sunday** and similar others.

Sources:

Getz, G. A. *MBI: The Story of Moody Bible Institute.* Chicago: Moody Press, 1969. 393 pp.

Gray, James M. *Christian Workers' Commentary on the Old and New Testaments.* New York: Fleming H. Revell Company, 1915. 447 pp.

_____. *Primers of the Faith.* New York: Fleming H. Revell Company, 1906. 296 pp.

_____. *Satan and the Saint.* Chicago: Bible Institute Colportage Association, 1909. 125 pp.

_____. *Synthetic Bible Studies.* Cleveland, OH: F. M. Burton, 1900. 217 pp.

Reid, Daniel G., Robert D. Linder, Bruce L. Shelley, and Harry S. Stout. *Dictionary of Christianity in America.* Downers Grove, IL: InterVarsity Press, 1990. 1305 pp.

Runyan, William M., Jr. *Dr. Gray at Moody Bible Institute.* New York: Oxford University Press, 1935. 186 pp.

★366★
GREGOIRE, Paul
Cardinal, Roman Catholic Church
b. Oct. 24, 1911, Verdun, Quebec, Canada

Paul Gregoire, the archbishop of Quebec and a cardinal in the Roman Catholic Church, is the son of Marie Lavoie and Albert Gregoire. He attended l'Ecole Superieure Richard in his hometown, the Seminaire de Ste. Therese in Quebec, and the Grand Seminary of Montreal. He was ordained to the priesthood in 1937. He became the director of the Seminaire de Ste. Therese and was later a professor of the philosophy of education at l'Ecole Normale Secondaire and l'Institut Pedagogique. In 1950 he became the students' chaplain at the University of Montreal.

In 1961 Gregoire was named auxiliary bishop of Montreal and additionally designated vicar general and director of the office of the clergy for the archdiocese. He was also appointed president of the French section of the Episcopal Commission on Ecumenism. In 1967 he became the Apostolic Administrator of the archdiocese and in 1968 was named archbishop of Montreal.

During his two decades in office, Cardinal Gregoire has served on the board of the Canadian Conference of Catholic Bishops and presided over the Episcopal Assembly of the Bishops of the Montreal Region. He was a member of the Canadian delegation to the 1971 Synod of Bishops in Rome. In 1978 he was named by Pope John Paul II to the Sacred Congregation for the Clergy and in 1983 to the Sacred Congregation for Catholic Education (The sacred congregations are departments of the Roman Catholic Church's international administration headquartered in the Vatican.)

Sources:

Simpson, Kieran, ed. *Canadian Who's Who.* Toronto: University of Toronto Press, 1987.

★367★
GREGORY, Louis George
Leader, Baha'i Faith
b. Jun. 6, 1874, Charleston, South Carolina
d. Jul. 30, 1951, Eliot, Maine

Louis George Gregory, the first Black to serve on the national administrative body of the Baha'i Faith in the United States, and for many years a teacher of the faith across the United States, was the son of a slave, Ebenezer George. His father died when he was five years old, and his mother married George Gregory. He took his stepfather's name out of love and respect for him. His stepfather was educated and somewhat prosperous. Young Louis attended a private high school and then spent four years at Fisk University, where he earned an A.B. degree in 1896. He returned to Charleston to teach. He stayed only a short time, however, before moving to Washington, D.C., to study for a law degree from Howard University. He received his LL.B. in 1902.

Gregory practiced law in Washington until 1906, when he took a job with the Treasury Department. While working for the government, he learned of the Baha'i Faith, which he joined in 1909. Shortly afterward, he received a Tablet (letter) from **Abdu'l-Baha**, the son of the founder, calling him to become an instrument in racial harmony. In 1911 he was elected to a position on Washington's working committee, which oversaw Baha'i activities in the area. That same year Gregory traveled to Egypt to meet Abdu'l-Baha, and in 1912 Abdu'l-Baha gave Gregory the place of honor at the banquet held during his visit to Washington. Abdu'l-Baha also introduced Gregory to Louisa Mathew, a white woman, and at his suggestion they were married. A third momentous event of 1912 was Gregory's election to national office as a member of the Executive Board of Baha'i Temple Unity, the national committee formed to build the temple in Wilmette, Illinois.

In 1914 Abdu'l-Baha asked Agnes Parsons to hold a Conference for Amity and Unity between the white and black races. Gregory spoke at the conference, emerging as the major Baha'i spokesperson for racial harmony. He served as a member and/or chairman of the Baha'i National Committee for Race Unity for most of the next 35 years. He not only spoke regularly around the country on behalf of race relations, but was the most effective Baha'i voice in introducing Blacks to the faith. When the National Spiritual Assembly, the national governing body for Baha'is in America, was formed, he was elected to its membership, through he was specifically told by Shoghi Effendi, the Guardian of the Faith, to continue his speaking and not let administrative details destroy his effective work. He served on the assembly a total of 14 years until health problems curtailed his work in 1946.

During the last five years of his life Gregory was forced to cease his travels, which had taken him across the United States and to many foreign countries. He lived quietly at his home in Eliot, Maine, where he died in 1951. In 1972 the Louis B. Gregory Baha'i Institute at Hemingway, South Carolina, was dedicated in his honor.

Sources:

"Louis G. Gregory." *Baha'i World* 12 (1956): 666-70.
Morrison, Gayle. *To Move the World*. Wilmette, IL: Baha'i Publishing Trust, 1982. 399 pp.

★ 368 ★
GRIER, Albert Catton
Founder, Churches of the Truth
b. Feb. 27, 1864, Bay City, Michigan
d. Oct. 31, 1941, Laguna Beach, California

Little is known of the early life of Albert Catton Grier, founder of the Churches of the Truth, prior to his ordination in the 1890s as a minister in the American Universalist Association. He served several parishes before becoming pastor of the Universalist church in Spokane, Washington, shortly after the turn of the century. In 1910 Grier read an article by Clara Stocker in a New Thought magazine. The article, later reprinted as a booklet, *Realization through Concentrated Attention*, removed a cloud of despondency which had settled over Grier and led him into New Thought. Stocker had been one of the students of **Emma Curtis Hopkins**, the founder of New Thought.

By 1912 Grier had become a vocal advocate of New Thought, and he began *The Truth*, a monthly New Thought magazine. The following year he resigned from the Universalist ministry and with the majority of the congregation formed the Church of the Truth. A new church building was constructed and dedicated. In 1914 he extended his work through the Northwest and, with the assistance of H. Edward Mills, whom he ordained, established a second con-

gregation in Couer d'Alene, Idaho. During these years he become acquainted with the larger New Thought movement, especially **Ernest S. Holmes**, later the founder of the Church of Religious Science, and **Nona Brooks**, leader of the Divine Science movement. In 1918 he joined with Brooks in co-founding the Truth Association, an ecumenical New Thought association, formed in protest of the lack of clear Christian emphases in the International New Thought Alliance (INTA), which had just adopted a new "Declaration of Principles." They were soon joined by Holmes. By 1921 the differences with the Alliance were worked out and the Truth Association merged into it. Grier became an honorary president of the Alliance.

In 1922 Grier became a field lecturer for INTA and spent almost six months on an East Coast tour. He increasingly spent time away from Spokane and in 1924 was granted a formal leave of absence. During that time he organized the Church of the Truth in Pasadena, California, and traveled to Boston to ordain **Elizabeth Towne**, editor of the *Nautilus Magazine*. In 1925 he moved to New York City to succeed W. John Murray as pastor of the Church of the Healing Christ. This did not prove a happy move and in 1926 he broke with the congregation and formed a new Church of the Truth in the city. He pastored the church through the 1920s but gradually turned over the duties to his daughter, Gladys C. Grier. He retired to Laguna Beach, California. The Churches of the Truth had become a national organization of loosely affiliated congregations and ministries, and Grier turned much of the national leadership over to Alice Wells, pastor of the Couer d'Alene church. He would live in retirement in Laguna Beach, California, to see Wells serve three years as president of INTA. The Church of the Truth, reorganized in the 1980s as the International Alliance of the Churches of the Truth, continues as a New Thought denomination with congregations in the United States and Canada.

Sources:

Brooks, Louise McNamarra. *Early History of Divine Science*. Denver, CO: First Divine Science Church, 1963. 127 pp.
Grier, Albert C. *The Spirit of the Truth*. Thomas Gaus' Sons, 1930. 190 pp.
_____. *The Truth Way*. New York: Thomas Gaus' Sons, 1928. 232 pp.
_____. *Truth's Cosmology and Other Discourses*. Spokane, WA: Church of the Truth, n.d. 117 pp.
_____. and Agnes M. Lawson. *Truth and Life*. New York: E. P. Dutton, 1921. 256 pp.

★ 369 ★
GRIGGS, Sutton Elbert
Minister, National Baptist Convention of America
b. 1872, Chatfield, Texas
d. 1933, Houston, Texas

Sutton Elbert Griggs, a minister affiliated with the National Baptist Convention of America, was the son of a Baptist minister, Allen R. Griggs. He grew up in Dallas, Texas, and attended Bishop College in Marshall, Texas. Following his graduation from college, in 1890 Griggs entered Richmond Theological Seminary (now Virginia Theological Seminary) and graduated in 1893. He served his first church in Beckley, Virginia, but in 1895 moved to Tennessee to begin his lengthy pastorate at First Baptist Church in East Nashville. In 1897 he married Emma J. Williams.

The East Nashville years proved to be the most important and fruitful of his career. The move to legislate, and hence institutionalize, segregation across the South peaked, and a wave of racist books disparaging Blacks were being published. Sutton took it upon himself to respond to the situation with a series of novels and several non-fiction books. Beginning with *Imperium in Imperio* in 1899, he wrote five novels: *Overshadowed* (1901); *Unfettered* (1902); *The Hindered Hand* (1905); and *Pointing the Way* (1909). He published all of these books himself and marketed them within the black community. Through their sentimental stories they moralized on the necessity of placing ethical concerns before expedient personal or political goals. Among his more significant works of social/ political comment was *Wisdom's Call* (1909).

Griggs' perspective held several ideas in a polar tension. He longed for a racially harmonious society, and saw the South as the place where such a society could emerge. At the same time he opposed the assimilation of the race within the dominant white culture.

After a decade in Nashville, Griggs moved to Memphis, Tennessee, as the pastor of Tabernacle Baptist Church. By this time he had emerged as a popular leader in the National Baptist Convention of America and served for many years in its education department. In 1925-1926 he served for a year as president of the American Baptist Theological Seminary. During the Memphis years, he continued to write. His publications included: *Life's Demands, or According to the Law* (1916); *Guide to Racial Greatness* (1923); *Kingdom Builders Manual* (1924); and numerous smaller works. These did not enjoy the same success that his earlier works had, and the printing costs exhausted him financially. Abandoning plans to enlarge his church building, he resigned in 1930, and moved back to Texas. He became pastor of Hopewell Baptist Church in Denison, where his father had at one time pastored. He was not able to reestablish himself in Texas, as he died shortly after the move.

Sources:
Fleming, Robert E. "Sutton E. Griggs: Militant Black Novelist." *Phylon* (March 1973): 73-77.

Gloster, Hugh M. "Sutton E. Griggs: Novelist of the New Negro." *Phylon* (Fourth Quarter, 1943): 335-345.

Griggs, Sutton E. *The Hindered Hand*. Nashville, TN: Orion Publishing Co., 1905. 303 pp.

———. *Imperium in Imperio*. Cincinnati, OH: The Editor Publishing Co., 1899. 265 pp.

———. *Light on Racial Issues*. Memphis, TN: National Public Welfare League, 1921. 62 pp.

———. *Overshadowed*. Nashville, TN: Orion Publishing Co., 1901.

———. *Pointing the Way*. Nashville, TN: Orion Publishing Co., 1908. 233 pp.

———. *Unfettered*. Nashville, TN: Orion Publishing Co., 1902. 276 pp.

———. *Wisdom's Call*. Nashville, TN: Orion Publishing Co., 1909. 193 pp.

Logan, Rayford W., and Michael R. Winston, eds. *Dictionary of American Negro Biography*. New York: W. W. Norton & Co. 1982. 680 pp.

★ 370 ★
GRIMES, Samuel Joshua
Presiding Bishop, Pentecostal Assemblies of the World
b. Jan. 3, 1884, Barbados West Indies
d. Jun. 13, 1967, New York, New York

Little is known of the early life of Samuel Joshua Grimes, for over three decades the presiding bishop of the Pentecostal Assemblies of the World (PAW). During his youth he experienced salvation under the ministry of an elder, W. W. Rue. As a young man he moved to Indianapolis and was greatly influenced by the ministry of **Garfield T. Haywood**, the presiding bishop of the Pentecostal Assemblies of the World, and was among the earliest members of the new denomination. He attended the National Bible College in Philadelphia and the Philadelphia College of the Bible. Grimes and his wife, Carolyn, were also among the first to receive the missionary call and travel to Liberia as ministers.

Returning from Liberia in 1923, Grimes became active in the Assemblies during the last years of Haywood's leadership. He settled in New York City and there founded and led the Eastern District Council. In 1930, at the last convention Haywood attended, Grimes was elected editor of the *Christian Outlook*, the denomination's magazine. He served as editor for 19 years. Following Haywood's death, the church was faced with the vacuum left by the absence of a strong leader to assume his duties and was ravaged by an unsuccessful merger attempt with the predominantly white Apostolic Churches of Jesus Christ. The negotiations cost the previously interracial Assemblies much of its white membership. In 1932, as the church began its reorganization, Grimes was elected as the new presiding bishop.

Among his first duties as bishop, Grimes oversaw the formation of the Women's Federation and the National Pentecostal Young People's Union, both of which were begun in 1933. More importantly, Grimes resisted the move to have the Assemblies become an all-black organization and led the attempt by the Assemblies to keep a racial balance. In the wake of this decision, the Assemblies have remained the only predominantly black Pentecostal organization to retain a small but measurable white membership and Whites in leadership positions. Grimes also promoted the development of the episcopacy as a means of building the church's organization. This process was often misused, and men were elected to the office as an honor apart from organizational needs.

Among the major accomplishments during Grimes' lengthy period of leadership, above and beyond the spread of the organization, were the founding and development of Aenon Bible School (1940), over which he served as director for many years, and the emergence of a home missions board (1948). He also encouraged the education of Ellen M. M. Hopkins as a nurse and sent her and her husband, Bp. Easter Richard Hopkins, to Liberia, where they founded the Samuel Grimes Maternity and Welfare Center. Grimes also opened mission fields in the British West Indies and the Leeward Islands.

In 1952 Grimes faced the only challenge to his leadership when Bp. **Samuel N. Hancock**, who had been elected to the bishopric five years before Grimes, challenged Grimes in the election. Hancock argued that he had been prevented from becoming presiding bishop in 1931 by a resolution to keep the office vacant for a year out of respect for Haywood. In the meantime, forces organized around Grimes and against Hancock. Grimes won in a close vote. In 1957 Hancock left the Assemblies and formed the Apostolic Faith Church of God. Grimes continued in his leadership until his death in 1967. He was succeeded by **Ross Paddock**, a white man who served as the assistant presiding bishop under Grimes.

Sources:
Dupree, Sherry Sherrod. *Biographical Dictionary of African-American, Holiness-Pentecostals, 1880-1990*. Washington, DC: Middle Atlantic Regional Press, 1990. 386 pp.

Golder, Morris E. *The Bishops of the Pentecostal Assemblies of the World*. Indianapolis, IN: The Author, 1980. 69 pp.

———. *History of the Pentecostal Assemblies of the World*. Indianapolis, IN: The Author, 1973. 195 pp.

Richardson, James C., Jr. *With Water and Spirit*. Washington, DC: Spirit Press, 1980. 151 pp.

★ 371 ★
GROCHOWSKI, Leon
Prime Bishop, Polish National Catholic Church
b. Oct. 11, 1886, Skupie Poland
d. Jul. 19, 1969, Poland

Leon Grochowski, the second Prime Bishop of the Polish National Catholic Church (PNCC), was born in rural Poland. In danger of arrest during the anti-Czarist uprisings, he left Poland and came to America. He became involved in the Polish National Catholic Church during its formative years and was among the first to enter its Savonarola Theological Seminary. He was ordained to the priesthood by Bishop **Francis Hodur**, founder of the Polish National Catholic Church, in 1910, just four years after the creation of the church. He served successively as parish priest at All Saints Church, Chicago; Saints Peter and Paul Church, Passaic, New Jersey; and St. Asalbert's Church, Sickson, Pennsylvania. He was also seen as a rising star in the church. He was invited to accompany Hodur to Poland in 1920, and was named secretary of the Great

Church Council. He also assumed duties as editor of the church's newspaper.

In 1924 Grochowski was elected bishop and placed in charge of the newly created Western Diocese. He made his headquarters in Chicago and began to move among the largely Roman Catholic Polish-American population which had increased greatly in the previous two decades. A vigorous worker, he began a weekly publication, *Przebudzenie* (*Awakening*). He established "Schools of Christian Living," lay academies soon copied throughout the church, and began a radio ministry.

Grochowski remained in Chicago for over three decades. During that time his diocese grew from 20 parishes to 50. In 1949 he was elected to succeed Hodur as Prime Bishop of the church. He assumed office in 1953, at the time of Hodur's death, but did not move his residence until 1955.

Among his important duties as Prime Bishop was to reestablish formal relations with the National Church in Poland, which had gone through many changes through the century. In August 1957 Grochowski participated in a ceremony marking the sisterly affiliation of the two churches. He also led in the establishment of the Missionary Diocese of Canada.

In 1969 Grochowski traveled to Poland to take part in jubilee celebrations. During the conference, following a talk he had given on the Polish National Catholic Church, he had a heart attack and died. He was 83 years old.

Sources:
Wlodarski, Stephen. *The Origin and Growth of the Polish National Catholic Church*. Scranton, PA: Polish National Catholic Church, 1974. 239 pp.

★ 372 ★
GROSS, Darwin
Spiritual Leader, Sounds of Soul
b. Jan. 3, 1918, Denhoff, North Dakota

As the 972nd Living ECK Master, Sri Darwin Gross took over the spiritual leadership of ECKANKAR following the death of **John Paul Twitchell** in 1971. He served in this role for 10 years, until he passed the "Rod of Power" (a sign of leadership) to Harold Klemp in 1981. The third of five children and a native of North Dakota, his parents moved to Portland, Oregon, when he was in his early teens. He attended Portland State College for a short period of time. After serving in the military, he studied music and electronics, and at various times worked as a musician as well as an electrical engineer.

According to Gross, from an early age he was aware of superior beings watching over him from another plane of existence. He recalls that as a child he had adverse feelings toward his paternal grandfather, a stern minister of the Mennonite Brethren Church, and as a youth rejected his religious upbringing. His spiritual quest led him to explore other churches and, eventually, to an interest in "alternative" spiritualities. He experienced astral projection (the experience of having one's consciousness separated from one's body) and studied in Eastern religions. In 1966 he was returning home from working late at an electronics plant when his car was suddenly surrounded by bright light. A soft voice with a Southern accent began to speak to him from the light (he later identified it as Paul Twitchell's voice), and from that point on the manifestation would return periodically to offer him instruction. In 1969 he became active in ECKANKAR.

While ECKists conceive of their path as being very ancient, the ECKANKAR organization, as outsiders know it, was founded by Paul Twitchell in 1965. Twitchell was a student of **Kirpal Singh**, among others, and the spiritual teachings of ECKANKAR are clearly related to Singh's Sant Mat lineage. Soon after Twitchell's unex-

pected death in 1971, the Rod of Power was passed to Gross. Partially because of Gross' comparative "beginner" status in ECKANKAR a number of high-ranking ECKists left the organization in the wake of his assumption of leadership. A year later, on October 27, 1972, Darwin Gross and Gail Atkinson Twitchell (Paul's widow) were married. While serving as the ECK Master, Gross wrote a number of books. Some, such as *Leadership in ECK* were limited to circulation within the organization, but others, such as *Your Right to Know* (1979) and *Gems of Soul* (1980) aimed for a more general audience.

Gross' marriage to Gail Atkinson ended in a divorce on December 31, 1977. The next years brought a period of intense internal discord to ECKANKAR. Then in October of 1981, with little prior warning, Harold Klemp was named the 973rd Living ECK Master. To ease the transition, Gross was retained in an advisory capacity, but soon all ties between Gross and ECKANKAR ended. He was given the copyrights to most of his written material and eventually founded a new organization called Sounds of Soul, through which he is now continuing his teaching work and circulating his writings.

Sources:
Gross, Sri Darwin. *Consciousness Is Life*. Oak Grove, OR: SOS Publishing, 1986. 202 pp.
_____. *From Heaven to the Prairie: The Story of the 972nd Living ECK Master*. Menlo Park, CA: IWP Publishing, 1980. 289 pp.
_____. *Gems of Soul*. Menlo Park, CA: IWP Publishing, 1980. 165 pp.
_____. *Leadership in ECK*. Menlo Park, CA: ECKANKAR, 1982. 146 pp.
_____. *My Letter to You: Discourses*. Oak Grove, OR: The Author, 1987. 151 pp.
_____. *You Can't Turn Back*. Oak Grove, OR: The Author, 1985. 98 pp.
_____. *Your Right to Know*. Menlo Park, CA: IWP Publishing, 1979. 163 pp.
Lane, David Christopher. *The Making of a Spiritual Movement: The Untold Story of Paul Twitchell and ECKANKAR*. Del Mar, CA: Del Mar Press, 1983. 154 pp.
_____. "When God Gets Dethroned: The Downfall of Darwin Gross." *Understanding Cults and Spiritual Movements* 2 (1978): 1-13.

★ 373 ★
GUILD, Roy Bergen
Minister, Congregational Church
b. Dec. 1, 1871, Galva, Illinois
d. Jan. 13, 1945

Roy Bergen Guild, a Congregational minister best known for his work in the ecumenical movement, was the son of Sarah Fidelia Bergen and Rufus Bernard Guild. He entered Washburn College in 1891 but transferred after only a year to Knox College, where he earned his A. B. in 1894. He obtained his theological training at Chicago Theological Seminary and received his B.D. in 1897, the same year he completed the requirement for his M.A. from Knox and was ordained by the Congregational Church. His first pastorate was at Woodstock, Illinois. In 1898 he married Winifred A. Everhard.

Over the next 15 years Guild served in a variety of congregational and noncongregational positions. In 1900 he moved to Chicago to serve as pastor of Leavitt Street Congregational Church. Six years later he left the pastorate for a two-year period as secretary of the Illinois Home Missionary Society. In 1908 he moved to Boston to work with the Congregational Church Building Society. In 1911 he became the executive secretary of the Men and Religion Forward Movement, which had as a major goal the stabilization of the Federal Council of Churches (founded in 1908) through the creation of a number of councils of churches in the major urban complexes of the United States. After the Forward Movement campaign stopped, Guild became pastor of the Central Congregational Church in Topeka, Kansas, a congregation made famous by its previous pastor, **Charles M. Sheldon**. After three years in Kansas, he picked up the thrust of the Forward Movement as the new executive secretary of the Federal Council's Commission on Councils of Churches. He remained at his post for ten years, during which time he authored *The Manual of Interchurch Work* (1917), the standard guide to interchurch cooperation for his generation, and *Practicing Christian Unity* (1919).

In 1925 Guild left the council to become pastor of the Trinitarian Congregational Church in New Bedford, Massachusetts. He stayed in the pastorate for four years before returning to New York as the associate general secretary of the Federal Council of Churches. Guild retired in 1939 and was named secretary emeritus of the council. He lived out his retirement years in Winter Park, Florida.

Sources:

Cavert, Samuel McCrea. *The American Churches in the Ecumenical Movement, 1900-1968.* New York: Association Press, 1968. 288 pp.

Guild, Roy B. *The Manual of Interchurch Work.* New York: Inter-church Federations of the Federal Council of the Churches of Christ in America, 1915.

———. *Practicing Christian Unity.* New York: Association Press, 1919. 85 pp.

★ 374 ★
GUNSAULUS, Frank Wakeley
Minister, Congregational Church
b. Jan. 1, 1856, Chesterville, Ohio
d. Mar. 17, 1921, Chicago, Illinois

Frank Wakeley Gunsaulus, for many years pastor of the independent Central Church in Chicago, Illinois, was the son of Joseph and Mary Hawley Gunsaulus. His Methodist mother had a deep influence upon him, and Gunsaulus attended Ohio Wesleyan University on his pilgrimage to the Methodist ministry. After receiving his A.B. degree in 1875, he was ordained as a minister in the Methodist Episcopal Church and began serving a circuit of churches centered in Harrisburg, Ohio. In 1876 he married Georgiana Long. That year he was assigned to Worthington, Ohio, and in 1878 he was reassigned to Chillicothe. In 1879 he left the Methodists and affiliated with the Congregational Church.

Gunsaulus' first Congregationalist pastorate was at Eastwood Church in Columbus, Ohio, but before the year was out he had settled at High Street Church in the same city. He successively served First Congregational Church, Newtonville, Massachusetts (1881-1885), and Brown Memorial Presbyterian Church, Baltimore Maryland (1885-1887), before moving to Chicago in 1887. In Chicago Gunsaulus would emerge as one of the most prominent preachers in the United States. He served first at Plymouth Congregational Church, the congregation in Brooklyn, New York, made famous by **Henry Ward Beecher**. During his lengthy pastorate he issued his first book, *The Transfiguration of Christ* (1886), and several volumes of popular poetry: *Loose Leaves of Song* (1888); *Phidias and Other Poems* (1891); and *Songs of Night and Day* (1896). These works were followed by additional titles: *Monk and Knight* (1891); *William Ewart Gladstone* (1898); and *The Man of Galilee* (1899).

Among Gunsaulus' significant sermons preached while at the Plymouth Church was one on the theme, "What I would do if I had a million dollars." He suggested the establishment of a technical institute at which the poorest would have the opportunity for training. Following the sermon, a wealthy member, Philip Danforth Armour, put up the money, and in 1893 the Armour Institute of Technology was founded with Gunsaulus as president. He served in that office for the rest of his life.

In 1899 Gunsaulus was invited to become pastor of Central Church as the successor of **Newell Dwight Hillis**. Since its founding in the 1870s in response to difficulties that its first pastor, **David Swing**, had experienced with the Presbyterian Church, Central Church had become one of the country's most well-known theo-

logically liberal pulpits. During his years there Gunsaulus' oratorical and literary skills flowered. He authored a number of books, including: *Paths to Power* (1905); *Paths to the City of God* (1906); *The Higher Ministries of Recent English Poetry* (1907); *The Minister and the Spiritual Life* (1911); and *Martin Luther and the Morning Hour in Europe* (1917). Frequently invited to lecture around the country, in 1911 he was invited to give the Lyman Beecher Lectures at Yale Divinity School. In 1912 he became a lecturer at the University of Chicago Divinity School.

From his various activities, Gunsaulus prospered financially, and in the mature years of his life he became an art collector of note. Among his important donations were the Gunsaulus collections of Wedgewood and near-Eastern pottery to the Art Institute of Chicago. He also gave the Gunsaulus Collection of Incunabula to the University of Chicago library. In 1919 Gunsaulus resigned from his pulpit to devote all his time to the Armour Institute.

Sources:

Bancroft, Edgar. *Dr. Gunsaulus, the Citizen.* [Chicago]: The Author, 1921. 15 pp.

Dictionary of American Biography. 20 vols. and 7 supps. New York: Charles Scribner's Sons, 1928-1936, 1944-1981.

Gunsaulus, Frank W. *The Man of Galilee.* Chicago: Monarch Book Co., 1899. 682 pp.

———. *Paths to Power.* New York: Fleming H. Revell Co., 1905. 362 pp.

———. *Paths to the City of God.* New York: Fleming H. Revell Co., 1906. 311 pp.

———. *Songs of Night and Day.* Chicago: A. C. McClurg & Co., 1896. 267 pp.

———. *Transfiguration of Christ.* Boston: Houghton, Mifflin & Co., 1886. 267 pp.

★ 375 ★
GURDJIEFF, Georgei Ivanovitch
Sufi-influenced Spiritual Teacher
b. 1866?, Alexandropol Armenia
d. Oct. 29, 1949, Paris France

Georgei Ivanovitch Gurdjieff was one of the most mysterious and influential spiritual teachers of the twentieth century. Various dates have been suggested for his birth, including November 28, 1877, from his passport; January 13, 1872, from his followers; and other dates from biographers. His presumed birth place, Alexandropol, near the Turkish-Armenian border, was later renamed Leninakan. His family was Greek, and as a boy he spent some time studying with the dean of a Russian Orthodox Cathedral. He was very curious about science and the phenomena such as miracles that science was at a loss to explain.

In 1896, at about the age of 20, Gurdjieff left home and began wandering; he later claimed to have been part of a legendary band called the Seekers of the Truth, a group dedicated to the search for esoteric wisdom. For many years he traveled from Ethiopia to Tibet, making a living at different trades and studying with different teachers, the most significant influence perhaps coming from Turkish Sufi orders. In 1912 he appeared in Moscow; he married the Countess Ostrowsky in about 1914. He gathered a number of groups between St. Petersburg and Moscow that he taught. From one of these groups came Pyotr Demianovitch Ouspensky, his greatest disciple.

In 1917 Gurdjieff, Ouspensky, and others fled the spreading Russian Revolution and eventually settled in Paris. In 1922, at a chateau near Fontainebleau, he founded the famous Institute for the Harmonious Development of Man, gathering students such as novelist Katherine Mansfield, A. R. Orage, and Maurice Nicoll. Gurdjieff taught that humans are psychically, emotionally, and spiritually asleep, and until they "wake up," they will have no control over the forces that direct their lives. He developed a number of techniques to assist the awakening process, including the Gurdjieff movements, a series of dance-like exercises. He also developed ways of placing the student under severe conflict and pressure in order to break open the self-conscious conscious awareness—a procedure that created some controversy. His system has been called the Fourth Way, a spiritual method of engaging ordinary life, as opposed to the spiritual paths of the yogi, monk, or fakir. This system is symbolized in the Enneagram, a nine-pointed symbol in a circle.

Gurdjieff made his first visit to America in 1924. Ouspensky's book, *Tertium Organum* (1920) had already made his name known in some circles. After he returned to France, he was involved in an automobile accident which required hospitalization. After his recovery he put more of his energies into writing books such as the semi-autobiographical *Meetings with Remarkable Men*, and *The Herald of Coming Good*, which was the only book published before his death. In 1933 Gurdjieff closed the Institute and spent the rest of his days traveling and working with his students in Paris and New York. He died in 1949 at the age 77; only after his death, with the publication of his books and through the activities of his students, did his name become widely known. His secretary, Jeanne de Salzmann, founded the Gurdjieff Foundation in Paris in 1950, and since then similar foundations have been created around the world.

Sources:

Driscoll, J. Walter and the Gurdjieff Foundation of California. *Gurdjieff: An Annotated Bibliography*. New York: Garland Publishing Company, 1985. 363 pp.

Gurdjieff, George I. *All and Everything*. 3 vols. London: Routledge & Kegan, 1974.

_____. *The Herald of Coming Good*. New York: Samuel Weiser, 1969. 87 pp.

_____. *Life Is Real Only Then, When "I Am"*. New York: E. P. Dutton, 1975. 170 pp.

Melton, J. Gordon. *Biographical Dictionary of American Cult and Sect Leaders*. Garland Reference Library of Social Science, vol. 212. New York: Garland Publishing, 1986.

Shepard, Leslie. *Encyclopedia of Occultism & Parapsychology*. Second edition. Detroit: Gale Research Co., 1984-1985.

Speeth, Kathleen Riordan. *The Gurdjieff Work*. Berkeley, CA: And/Or Press, 1976. 114 pp.

_____, and Ira Friedlander. *Gurdjieff, Seeker of Truth*. New York: Harper & Row, 1980. 175 pp.

Webb, James. *The Harmonious Circle*. New York: G.P. Putnam's Sons, 1980. 608 pp.

—*Gary L. Ward*

★376★
HAGIN SR., Kenneth Erwin
Pentecostal Television Evangelist
b. Aug. 20, 1917, McKinney, Texas

Kenneth Erwin Hagin emerged in the 1980s as one of the most influential television evangelists. He was born in rural Texas with several serious health problems. He was a premature baby, weighing only two pounds at birth, and possessed a congenital heart defect. As a result of his sickly childhood, he received only a limited formal education. A few months, before his sixteenth birthday, his illness worsened, and he was completely bedridden. On his first day of confinement to bed, in April 1933, he became a Christian. During the next months he read the Bible and developed a determination to escape his situation. His healing came as he pondered and then acted upon Mark 11:24, "What things soever ye desire, when ye pray, believe that ye receive them, and ye shall have them." In August 1934 he was healed after 16 months in bed.

Shortly after his healing he began his ministry in the Baptist church in which he had been raised. He soon found fellowship, however, among the Pentecostals, who readily accepted his healing. In August 1937 he received the gift of the Holy Spirit and spoke in tongues. He became a pastor in the Assemblies of God, a position he held for the next 10 years. In 1943 he experienced a special anointing by God to teach. In 1947 he gave up his pastorate and became a traveling evangelist.

Hagin had been a visionary since his teenage years. His first vision, which had been a trip to hell, had occurred on the very day of his becoming bedridden. One important vision occurred in 1950 when Jesus appeared to him and gave him a special anointing to minister to the sick. Jesus told him that when he prayed for the sick, at times the spiritual fire would jump from one of his hands to the other; that would be a sign that the person was possessed of a demon that needed exorcising. Two years later he received an anointing to the prophetic office. (Within Pentecostal circles, a prophet is one who is used by God to speak to the congregation.)

In 1962 Hagin formed the Kenneth E. Hagin Evangelistic Association, now known as Kenneth Hagin Ministries Inc. and subsequently dropped his affiliation with the Assemblies of God. Four years later he moved to Tulsa, Oklahoma, where his colleague in the healing ministry, Oral Roberts, had already established headquarters. Hagin went on the radio with the "Faith Seminar of the Air," began *The Word of Faith* magazine (1968), and launched the Rhema Correspondence Bible School. By 1979 over 5,000 students had enrolled in the school. In 1974 he founded the Rhema Bible Training Center, now located in Broken Arrow, a Tulsa suburb. Approximately 6,000 students have graduated from the school, including a number of prominent independent Pentecostal ministers such as Fred Price and **Kenneth Copeland**, who look upon Hagin as their father in the faith. The Rhema Bible Church, a local congregation which Hagin pastored, was stationed adjacent to the training center.

In the late 1970s controversy began to whirl around Hagin and some distinctive doctrines that he preached. From his healing experience and his subsequent readings, especially of the works of **Essek William Kenyon**, Hagin developed what has come to be known as "faith" teaching. The teaching centers upon the idea that if Christians will, when praying for something, believe in their heart that they will receive it, and will confess the same with their mouth, God will give it to them. It popularly has been reduced to a phrase, "Name it, claim it," and Hagin and his colleagues frequently have been referred to as the Positive Confession Movement. In 1980, the Assembly of God passed an official statement denouncing the movement.

In the wake of the controversy, Hagin has continued his successful ministry. In 1979 he and a group of ministers led by his son-in-law, Doyle "Buddy" Harrison, many of whom were Rhema graduates, formed the loosely affiliated International Convention of Faith Churches and Ministers. In 1985 Hagin led in the formation of the Rhema Ministerial Association International, a tightly knit organization of ministers dedicated to the evangelization of the world. In the 1970s the work of Kenneth Hagin Ministries had reached beyond the borders of the United States, and by the late 1980s it circled the globe. During the 1980s Hagin continued to travel and preach, developed a national television ministry, and led in the development of Faith Library Publications, which publishes his many books and booklets. He now shares leadership in Kenneth Hagin Ministries Inc. with his son, Kenneth Hagin, Jr.

Sources:

Hagin, Kenneth. *The Art of Intercession*. Tulsa, OK: Faith Library Publications, 1981. 145 pp.

_____. *I Believe in Visions*. Old Tappan, NJ: Fleming H. Revell Company, 1972. 126 pp.

_____. *The Ministry of a Prophet*. Tulsa, OK: The Author, n.d. 30 pp.

_____. *The Present Day Ministry of Jesus Christ*. Tulsa, OK: The Author, n.d. 32 pp.

_____. *The Real Faith*. Tulsa, OK: The Author, n.d. 29 pp.

_____. *Seven Things You Should Know About Divine Healing*. Tulsa, OK: Faith Library Publications, 1979. 71 pp.

Hagin, Jr., Kenneth. *Kenneth Hagin's Fifty Years in the Ministry, 1934-1984*. Tulsa, OK: Faith Library, 1984.

McConnell, D. R. *A Different Gospel*. Peabody, MA: Hendrickson Publishers, 1988. 195 pp.

★377★
HALDEMAN, Isaac Massey
Minister, Northern Baptist Convention
b. Feb. 13, 1845, Concordville, Pennsylvania
d. Sep. 27, 1933, New York, New York

Isaac Massey Haldeman, the fundamentalist pastor of First Baptist Church in New York City for almost half a century, was the son of Rachel Ann Massey and Reuben Johnson Haldeman. He grew up in Pennsylvania and attended West Chester Academy. He was ordained as a minister in the Northern Baptist Convention in 1870 and the following year became pastor of the church at Chadds Ford, Pennsylvania. He moved to Wilmington, Delaware, in 1875. While there in 1883 he married Edda Bell Quinby. In 1884 he was called to the First Baptist Church in New York City, where he would remain for the rest of his life. During his lengthy pastorate he issued numerous books and pamphlets, many of a polemic nature and most derived from talks and sermons he gave.

In his new pulpit Haldeman's oratorical skills soon established him as one of the leading preachers in the country, regularly preaching to a standing room only worship service. He also joined with the conservative elements in the Northern Baptist Convention, one of the strongholds of the new modernist liberal theology. In the first decade of the twentieth century, he became a leading spokesperson for dispensational premillennialism, his 1910 volume *The Signs of the Times* being the most complete presentation of that perspective to an American audience at that time. Dispensationalism is a method of understanding the Bible by dividing its story of Israel's history into various periods or dispensations in which God established different relationships with humanity in his attempt to save them. According to the theory, humans are now living in the era of grace, which will soon end, and will be followed by a thousand-year reign of peace, the millennium. Premillennialists believe that Christ will soon return to establish that millennial period.

Dispensationalism had been brought to America by the followers of John Nelson Darby, the British originator of the idea, and popularized by evangelist **Dwight L. Moody**. Haldeman was a thorough-going premillennialist who believed that the world was degenerating at a rapid rate and that Jesus would return soon. In the meantime, he argued, attempts at social reform were a waste of time. He opposed worldliness, but just as strongly opposed the social gospel or even moral crusades, such as prohibition, on the grounds that such crusades were wasted activity which could not solve the problem of the human condition.

Within the Northern Baptist Convention Haldeman contended with liberal voices such as **Walter Rauschenbusch**, a major advocate of the social gospel, and **Harry Emerson Fosdick**. Unlike some of his colleagues, however, he never carried his fundamentalist stance to the point of seriously considering a break with the Northern Baptist Convention. He died before the formal break by fundamentalists who had lost any hope of driving the liberals from the convention occurred in the 1940s.

Sources:

Haldeman, I. M. *Can the Dead Communicate with the Living?* New York: Fleming H. Revell Company, 1920.

_____. *Christian Science in the Light of Holy Scripture*. New York: Fleming H. Revell Company, [1909].

_____. *The Coming of Christ, Both Pre-Millennial and Imminent*. New York: C. C. Cook, [1906].

_____. *The Signs of the Times*. New York: C. C. Cook, 1910. 455 pp.

_____. *Why I Preach the Second Coming*. New York: Fleming H. Revell Company, 1919. 160 pp.

Marsden, George M. *Fundamentalism and American Culture: The Shaping of Twentieth Century Evangelicalism, 1870-1925*. New York: Oxford University Press, 1980. 307 pp.

Reid, Daniel G., Robert D. Linder, Bruce L. Shelley, and Harry S. Stout. *Dictionary of Christianity in America*. Downers Grove, IL: InterVarsity Press, 1990. 1305 pp.

★378★
HALDEMAN-JULIUS, Emanuel
Publisher of Freethought Literature
b. Jul. 20, 1889, Philadelphia, Pennsylvania
d. Jul. 31, 1951, Girard, Kansas

Emanuel Haldeman-Julius, one of the most prolific publishers of popular freethought and atheist literature, was born Emanuel Julius, the son of first generation Russian Jewish immigrants, who were part of the massive wave of Jews who left Russia in the wake of the persecutions of the 1880s. Attending school only to the seventh grade, Julius worked at various jobs, during which time he became attracted to socialism. He became widely read in both its economic and anti-religious literature. In 1906, alienated from his family, he went to New York to pursue a newspaper career. While working in Tarrytown, New York, he was introduced to Mark Twain. The notes of their conversation became the basis of his first published article, "Mark Twain: Radical" published in 1910 in the *International Socialist Journal*.

In 1911 Julius was hired by the *New York Evening Call*, the first of a series of jobs with Socialist newspapers. He also began to write for the *Coming Nation*, a Socialist magazine published in Girard, Kansas. Julius was also a fiction writer, and he published numerous short stories. After a few months, he moved from New York to Wisconsin to work on the *Milwaukee Leader*, and in 1912 to Chicago to work on the *Chicago Evening World*. By the end of the year he had moved to Los Angeles to write for two California newspapers, and the following year he founded the short-lived *Western Comrade*, a Socialist magazine. Disdainful of the moderate socialist colony of Llano del Rio located on the edge of California's Mojave Desert, he refused to join. He sold them the *Western Comrade*, and returned to New York to work on the *Call* again.

In New York, Julius became infatuated with Anna Marcet Haldeman, an actress, who in 1915 was forced to move to Girard, Kansas, her hometown, to take care of her family's business. Julius relocated in Girard and became associated with the *Appeal to Reason*, the weekly started by J. A. Wayland. In 1916 he married the wealthy Haldeman, at that time the president of the State Bank of Girard. Influenced by Jane Addams (of Chicago's Hull House), who was Haldeman's aunt, Julius joined their last names. In 1918, with his wife's money, Haldeman-Julius bought the *Appeal to Reason* and its publishing plant, and began his own publishing career. Anna Haldeman-Julius also shared her husband's literary interest, and together they wrote several novels.

In 1919 Haldeman-Julius launched the People's Pocket Series, designed as a mass education effort utilizing inexpensive pocket-size paperback books. The series was largely inspired by the Pocket Series of the sixteenth century Aldine Press of Italy. The People's Pocket Series featured socialist and atheist anti-religious titles. Following the suggestion of John W. Quinn, Haldeman-Julius renamed the series the Little Blue Books (the covers were printed on blue card stock), by which name they became widely known. Haldeman-Julius also published several magazines (most were short-lived) during the 1920s, and added a more substantial paperback series of Big Blue Books.

The successful publishing concern became the basis for a series of controversies into which Haldeman-Julius entered. In the late

1920s he issued widely circulated broadsides against Herbert Hoover, ran for governor on the Socialist Party ticket, and attempted to take over the Socialist Party in Kansas. Although unsuccessful in these efforts, he attracted the attention of the F.B.I., which launched a 20-year investigation of his company. He added to his tension with the government by publishing a booklet that linked the Roman Catholic Church with the Axis during World War II, and in 1948 he published an expose of the F.B.I. He was eventually charged with income tax evasion and convicted in April 1951. A few months later, the conviction under appeal, he accidentally drowned in his swimming pool at home.

Sources:

Horsch, John. *Infant Baptism, Its Origin among Protestants.* Scottdale, PA: The author, 1917. 157 pp.

_____. *Menno Simons.* Scottsdale, PA: Mennonite Publishing House, 1916. 324 pp.

_____. *Mennonites in Europe.* Scottsdale, PA: Mennonite Publishing House, 1942. 427 pp.

_____. *Modern Religious Liberalism.* Scottsdale, PA: Fundamental Truth Depot, 1920. 331 pp.

_____. *The Principle of Nonresistance, as Held by the Mennonite Church: An Historical Survey.* Scottsdale, PA: Mennonite Publishing House, 60 pp.

Hostetler, Beulah Stauffer. *American Mennonites and Protestant Movements.* Scottsdale, PA: Herald Press, 1987. 366 pp.

John Horsch Memorial Papers. Scottsdale, PA: Mennonite Publishing House, 1947.

The Mennonite Encyclopedia. 4 vols. Scottsdale, PA: The Mennonite Publishing House, 1955.

★ 379 ★
HALE, Edward Everett
Minister, American Unitarian Association
b. Apr. 3, 1822, Boston, Massachusetts
d. Jun. 10, 1909, Boston, Massachusetts

Edward Everett Hale, a minister in the American Unitarian Association (AUA), was the son of Nathan and Sarah Preston Everett Hale. His father was the owner/editor of the *Boston Daily Advertiser.* He attended the Boston Latin School and at the age of 13 entered Harvard College. He graduated in 1839. He was second in his class, the class poet, and a member of Phi Beta Kappa. He became a teacher at the Boston Latin School while privately preparing himself for the Unitarian ministry. In 1842 he began to preach and in 1846 was ordained. For a decade he pastored the Church of the Unity in Worcester, Massachusetts. While at Worcester, in 1852, he married Emily Baldwin Perkins. In 1856 he became the pastor of South Congregational Church in Boston, where he would remain for the rest of his active ministry.

Hale had a prosperous ministry at South Church, but attained national fame through his writings. He produced approximately 150 books and pamphlets during his lifetime. His first influential piece, and still his most famous contribution to American literature, was a short story, "The Man Without a Country" (originally appearing in the *Atlantic Monthly,* December 1863). It was credited for producing a marked rise in patriotic fervor in the United States, which was then in the midst of the Civil War. After the war, a number of his stories were collected into his first book, *If, Yes, and Perhaps. Four Possibilities and Six Exaggerations, with Some Bits of Fact* (1868). His second book, *The Ingram Papers* (1869), appeared the next year. In 1870 he became the editor of *Old and New,* a literary journal which lasted for five years. During this period two more collections of his stories were published as *Ten Times One Is Ten* (1871) and *In His Name* (1873).

Hale's stories and other writings after the Civil War had a common theme of renovating society through the influence of liberal Christianity. He was an advocate of what would later be known as the social gospel, the altering of the structures of society in ac-

cordance with Christian ideals. An ardent Unitarian, he nevertheless looked for common cause with the liberalizing forces and people across the Protestant spectrum.

During the later years of his life, Hale produced three important autobiographical/historical books: *A New England Boyhood* (1893); *James Russell Lowell and His Friends* (1899); and *Memories of a Hundred Years* (1902). He also had two honors bestowed upon him. In the final hours of the nineteenth century, he was chosen to read the 90th Psalm from the balcony of the Massachusetts State House to the assembled crowd. In 1903 he was designated as chaplain for the United States Senate. He used his position in Washington to urge the country's leaders to give their energy to the cause of peace.

Sources:

Dictionary of American Biography. 20 vols. and 7 supps. New York: Charles Scribner's Sons, 1928-1936, 1944-1981.

Eliot, Samuel Atkins, ed. *Heralds of a Liberal Faith.* Boston: Beacon Press, 1952. 273 pp.

Hale, Edward Everett. *If, Yes and Perhaps. Four Possibilities and Six Exaggerations, with Some Bits of Fact.* Boston: Ticknor & Fields, 1868. 296 pp.

_____. *In His Name.* Boston: Roberts Brothers, 1873. 268 pp.

_____. *The Ingram Papers.* Boston: Fields, Osgood & Co., 1869. 266 pp.

_____. *James Russell Lowell and His Friends.* Boston: Houghton, Mifflin & Co., 1899. 303 pp.

_____. *Memories of a Hundred Years.* 2 vols. New York: Macmillan Company, 1902.

_____. *A New England Boyhood.* New York: Cassell Publishing Co., 1893. 267 pp.

_____. *Ten Times One Is Ten.* Boston: Little, Brown & Co., 1917. 110 pp.

Hale, Edward Everett, Jr. *The Life and Letters of Edward Everett Hale.* 2 vols. Boston: Little, Brown & Company, 1917.

★ 380 ★
HALL, Homer Richard
Founder, United Christian Church and Ministerial Association

Homer Richard Hall, the founder of the United Christian Church and Ministerial Association, was raised in western North Carolina. His mother, who had been raised a Baptist, was among the first in that area in the early twentieth century to respond to the new Pentecostalism and receive the baptism of the Holy Spirit (the definitive experience of Pentecostals, which is evidenced by speaking in tongues). Already widowed by this time, his mother became a minister with the Church of God in Cleveland, Tennessee. His mother had also had a dream of a son born with a caul over his face who would grow up to be a minister. Richard was that son.

At age 13 Hull had a vision of a light coming into his room. He related his vision to his mother, who explained her earlier vision of the plan of his life. Several months later he received the baptism of the Holy Spirit. At age 14 he began preaching on street corners. After graduating from high School, he attended the Church of God of Prophecy Bible Training School. He also studied at the Atlanta Institute of Speech and Expression with the goal of becoming a lawyer, but he developed tuberculosis and had to drop out of school. Three months later, following another vision, he got out of bed and began preaching again. He was ordained at the age of 24.

Hull became the state overseer for the Church of God of Prophecy in Colorado, Utah, and western Texas. In 1952, as the healing revival that had grown around **William Marrion Branham** was emerging, Hall heard a voice urging him to preach deliverance. He left the Church of God of Prophecy and began life as an itinerant evangelist, working primarily in small towns. In 1956 he founded the United Christian Ministerial Association to organize independent healing evangelists, ministers, and churches, and launched a periodical, *The Healing Broadcast* (now *The Shield of Faith*). He also began a radio ministry that was heard on some 30 stations in the South.

During the 1960s Hull began a ministry among the street people and hippies and was able to integrate them effectively into his fellowship of conservative old-line Pentecostals. In 1972 he founded a congregation in Cleveland, Tennessee, across town from the headquarters of his former denomination, and the name of the organization was changed to the United Christian Church and Ministerial Association. He also developed a ministerial training center, the United Christian Academy.

Sources:

Burgess, Stanley M., Gary B. McGee, and Patrick H. Alexander, eds. *Dictionary of Pentecostal and Charismatic Movements.* Grand Rapids, MI: Regency Reference Library, Zondervan Publishing House, 1988. 914 pp.

Harrell, David Edwin, Jr. *All Things Are Possible.* Bloomington, IN: Indiana University Press, 1975. 304 pp.

Sims, Patty. *Can Somebody Shout Amen!* New York: St. Martin's Press, 1988. 234 pp.

★381★
HALL, Manly Palmer
Founder, Philosophical Research Society
b. Mar. 18, 1901, Peterborough Canada

Manly Palmer Hall, one of the most sophisticated of modern occult writers and lecturers, came from a Massachusetts family with Scottish Presbyterian roots. Hall was born in Canada at the turn of the century to William S. and Louise Palmer Hall. He moved with his family to the United States in 1904. Part of his youth was spent in Sioux Falls, South Dakota, but the family moved frequently. Hall has carried particularly fond memories of his paternal grandmother, who first brought him to California and about whom he later wrote a book.

During his youth, Hall developed an interest in occult matters and joined, among other organizations, the Theosophical Society, the Freemasons, the Societas Rosecruciana in Civitatibus Folderatis (a Rosicrucian fellowship whose membership is limited to Masons), and the American Federation of Astrologers. Ordained to the ministry in 1923, he became the leader of the Church of the People, an occult/metaphysical congregation in Los Angeles. The church, located in the Trinity Auditorium building, became the center of his publishing concern, The Hall Publishing Company, and a magazine, *The All Seeing Eye*, begun in 1923. (In 1942, *The All Seeing Eye* was superseded by *Horizon*, now called the *PRS Journal*.) During this period Hall authored his first important occult texts, including *The Initiates of the Flame* (1922), *Shadow Forms* (1925), *Man, the Grand Symbol of the Mysteries* (1932), and *The Story of Astrology* (1933). His writing, especially the publication of his comprehensive *An Encyclopedic Outline of Masonic, Hermetic, Qabbalistic, and Rosicrucian Symbolical Philosophy* (1928), quickly established him as a major apologist of occult thought.

In 1934 Hall realized a personal dream by establishing a philosophical/religious institution modeled on the ancient school of Pythagoras. This school, the Philosophical Research Society, would become an instrument for disseminating the ancient wisdom throughout the West. Ground was broken for the first building in the headquarters complex in 1935, with major additions in 1950 and 1959. Hall had also begun to accumulate a large library on mysticism, the occult, Eastern religion, parapsychology, and related topics. He donated this library, now composed of more than 50,000 volumes, including many rare texts, to the society.

As leader of the society, Hall devoted most of his waking hours to lecturing and writing. In addition to more than 50 major books, he authored hundreds of shorter works, including the published transcripts of his lectures. His most influential titles include *Reincarnation: The Cycle of Necessity* (1939), *First Principles of Philosophy* (1942), *Self-Unfoldment by Disciplines of Realization* (1942), *Very Sincerely Yours* (1948), *The Mystical Christ* (1951), *The Secret Destiny of America* (1958), and, most recently, *The*

Rosicrucians and Magister Christoph Schlegel: Hermetic Roots of America (1986). Hall's extensive body of work covers the entire scope of occult, metaphysical and religious thinking. Hall also enlarged his audience by developing correspondence courses on the "Wisdom of the Ages," "Studies in Consciousness," "Survey Course in Philosophy," and "Lectures on Ancient Philosophy."

Besides his weekly lectures in Los Angeles, Hall lectured periodically around the United States during most of his life. By 1940, it was claimed that he had delivered over 7,000 lectures. He currently lives in semi-retirement, with most of the teaching work at the society having been assumed by colleagues and former students.

Sources:

Blight, Reynold E. and Maud Fletcher Galigher. *Hymnal of the Church of the People.* [Los Angeles] Glass Book Binding Co., n.d.

Contemporary Authors. Detroit, MI: Gale Research Inc.

Hall, Manley. *Growing Up with Grandmother.* Los Angeles: Philosophical Research Soceiety, 1985. 116 pp.

_____. *The Little World of PRS.* Los Angeles: Philosophical Research Society, 1982. 80 pp.

_____. *The Mystical Christ.* Los Angeles: Philosophical Research Society, 1951. 248 pp.

_____. *Reincarnation: The Cycle of Necessity.* Los Angeles: Philosophical Research Society. 1942. 210 pp.

_____. *The Rosicrucians and Magister Christoph Schlegel: Hermetic Roots of America.* Los Angeles: Philosophical Research Society, 1986. 250 pp.

_____. *The Secret Destiny of America.* Los Angeles: Philosophical Research Society, 1958. 200 pp.

_____. *Self-Unfoldment by Disciplines of Realization.* Los Angeles: Philosophical Research Society, 1946. 221 pp.

The Philosophy of Purposeful Living. Los Angeles: Philosophical Research Society, 1945. 32 pp.

Shepard, Leslie. *Encyclopedia of Occultism & Parapsychology.* 3 vols., 2nd. ed. Detroit: Gale Research Co., 1984-1985.

★382★
HANAFORD, Phebe Ann Coffin
Minister, American Universalist Association
b. May 6, 1829, Nantucket Island, Rhode Island
d. Jun. 2, 1921, Rochester, New York

Phebe Ann Coffin Hanaford, the first female New Englander to be ordained to the ministry, was the daughter of George and Phoebe Ann Bernard Coffin, both descendants of an old New England family. Well educated, she began writing for the local newspapers at age 13, and by the time she was 16, she was teaching school. In 1849 she married Joseph H. Hanaford. Reared a Quaker, she became a Baptist after her marriage and in her early adulthood placed her literary talents in the service of evangelism, temperance, and abolition of slavery. She became the chaplain of the Daughters of Temperance and wrote poems and hymns for their use in public gatherings. Her first book, *My Brother*, a collection of prose and poetry, was published in 1852. It was followed by *Lucretia, the Quakeress* (1853), an antislavery volume, and *The Best of Books and Its History* (1860), her lectures on the Bible. During the last year of the Civil War, she published three books, *The Young Captain*, *Frank Nelson; or the Runaway Boy*, and *Abraham Lincoln: His Life of Public Service*, possibly her single most successful title.

During the 1860s, Hanaford became a Universalist. In 1865 she preached her first sermon, and in 1866 she substituted in the pulpit for Olympia Brown, then the pastor of the Universalist Church at South Canton, Massachusetts. She also assumed duties as editor of the *Ladies Repository*, a Universalist magazine, and the *Myrtle*, a second magazine also published in Boston. At Brown's suggestion she developed aspirations for the ministry, and in 1867 became the preacher for the Universalist church in Hingham, Massachusetts. The following year she was ordained as a minister with the American Universalist Association and formally installed as the pastor of the Hingham congregation. In 1870 she moved to New Haven,

Connecticut, and while there was invited to officiate as chaplain for the state legislature, the first woman so honored by a state legislative body in the United States.

Hanaford's entrance into the ministry coincided with her increasing public activity in the cause of women's rights. In 1869 she helped organize the American Woman Suffrage Association. She remained active in the suffrage movement throughout her life. She would later assist in the funeral services of both Elizabeth Cady Stanton and Susan B. Anthony.

In 1872 Hanaford moved to New Jersey as pastor of the Church of the Good Shepherd in Jersey City. In 1874, however, the congregation split over the issue of the inclusion of women in the ministry. With her supporters, she formed a new congregation, which met in a public hall. Her last book, *Daughters of America; or, Women of the Century* (1882), appeared during this phase of her life. In 1884 she returned to New Haven as pastor of Second Church (Universalist), and she lectured frequently around New England. She retired in 1891 and lived in New York City.

Sources:
Dictionary of American Biography. 20 vols. and 7 supps. New York: Charles Scribner's Sons, 1928-1936, 1944-1981.
Hanaford, Phebe A. C. *Abraham Lincoln; His Life and Public Service.* Boston: B. B. Russell, 1865. 216 pp.
_____. *The Best of Books and Its History.* Philadelphia: American Baptist Pub. Soc., 1860. 238 pp.
_____. *Daughters of America; or, Women of the Century.* Augusta, ME: True & Co., 1882. 750 pp.
_____. *Lucretia, the Quakeress.* Boston: J. Buffum, 1853. 172 pp.
_____. *My Brother.* Cambridge, MA: John Fod & E. Robbins, 1852. 128 pp.
_____. *The Young Captain.* Boston: Degen, Estes & Co., 1865. 226 pp.
James, Edward T., ed. *Notable American Women, 1607-1950: A Biographical Dictionary.* 3 vols. Cambridge, MA: Harvard University Press, Belknap Press, 1971.

★ 383 ★
HANCOCK, Samuel Nathan
Founder, Apostolic Faith Church of God
b. Nov. 9, 1883, Adair County, Kentucky
d. 1963, Detroit, Michigan

Samuel Nathan Hancock, for many years a bishop in the Pentecostal Assemblies of the World (PAW) before becoming the founder of the Apostolic Faith Church of God, was the son of John Wyatt and Lottie Winston Wheat Hancock. The family had six children and was poor. Hancock was raised in rural Kentucky and after 1888 in Norwood, Indiana. His father disappeared when he was 13, and he had to get a job to help support the family. At the age of 17 he was converted to Christianity and soon afterward began attending the church in Indianapolis, Indiana, pastored by **Garfield T. Haywood**, the head of the Pentecostal Assemblies of the World. In 1908 he married Bertha Valentine.

The Pentecostal Assemblies of the World was an Apostolic Pentecostal church. It preached the possibility of believers receiving the baptism of the Holy Spirit, which was initially evidenced by the person speaking in tongues. It also rejected the doctrine of the Trinity and believed that Jesus was the One God. It offered water baptism to members in the name of Jesus Only. Hancock was baptized in 1914, and soon afterward received the baptism of the Holy Spirit and began preaching on the streets of Indianapolis. He became the assistant pastor of the Apostolic Faith Assembly in Indianapolis for a period before moving to Detroit. In Detroit he served a small mission, which grew into the Greater Bethlehem Temple, and founded a home for unwed mothers in Detroit.

In 1927 he was made a bishop and named to the original board of bishops of the Pentecostal Assemblies of the World. His diocese consisted of Illinois, Iowa, Nebraska, and Wyoming, though he

continued to serve the temple in Detroit which grew to 3,000 members. In 1932, following Haywood's death, **Samuel Grimes**, was elected as the new presiding bishop. He held the post until 1967, his lengthy tenure preventing others of the original bishops from serving in that capacity. Hancock, on at least one occasion, in 1952, challenged Grimes for the position and lost in a close election.

In 1957 Hancock left the Assemblies and formed an independent denomination built around the Detroit congregation.

Sources:
Dupree, Sherry Sherrod. *Biographical Dictionary of African-American, Holiness-Pentecostals, 1880-1990.* Washington, DC: Middle Atlantic Regional Press, 1990. 386 pp.
Golder, Morris E. *The Bishops of the Pentecostal Assemblies of the World.* Indianapolis: The Author, 1980. 69 pp.
Richardson, James C., Jr. *With Water and Spirit.* Martinsville, VA: The Author, n.d. 151 pp.

★ 384 ★
HARGIS, Billy James
Founder, Church of the Christian Crusade
b. Aug. 3, 1925, Texarkana, Texas

Billy James Hargis, founder and pastor of the Church of the Christian Crusade, grew up in the Great Depression. While his education beyond high school was limited to a year and a half at the Ozark Bible College, he was ordained at the Rose Hill Christian Church (Disciples of Christ) in 1943 and went on to serve a series of pastorates in Arkansas, Missouri, and Oklahoma. However, in the years immediately following World War II, he became concerned about the threat to American society and Christianity posed by worldwide Communism, especially as manifest in liberal leaders and radical social movements. He left the parish and founded Christian Echos National Ministry, headquartered in Tulsa, Oklahoma. As its special task, the ministry assumed the mobilization of Christian America against godless Communism.

Hargis was lifted out of the mass of anti-Communist voices of the early 1950s (otherwise remembered as the McCarthy Era) by his attempt in 1953 to airlift portions of the Bible into Eastern Europe using balloons. The effort earned him an honorary degree from the Defender Seminary in Puerto Rico (a school founded by Gerald B. Winrod). As his crusade continued, Bob Jones University awarded him an honorary degree in 1960. He also received B.A. and B.Theo. (1958) degrees from Burton College and Seminary, a ''degree mill'' that flourished for several years in Colorado. His popular anti-Communist text, *Communist America—Must It Be?* (1960) was widely circulated.

Hargis' ministry burgeoned throughout the South during the 1960s as the Civil Rights movement angered Whites and as many churches refused to align themselves against the movement. Hargis regularly organized and spoke at anti-Communist rallies and identified himself with military and political leaders, most notably retired U. S. Army General Edward Walker, who often appeared on the platform with Hargis. In 1962 Hargis held his First National Anti-Communist Leadership School. He was direct in attacking the Kennedy brothers, **Martin Luther King, Jr.**, and Lyndon Johnson by name. His political activities led to his ministry losing its tax-exempt status for several years.

Throughout this period Hargis wrote a series of books describing and denouncing Communists, liberals, and radicals, including *Communism, The Total Lie* (1961); *Facts About Communism and the Churches* (1962); *The Real Extremists—The Far Left* (1964); *Distortion by Design* (1965); and *Why I Fight for a Christian America* (1974).

In 1966 Hargis withdrew from the Disciples of Christ and organized the Church of the Christian Crusade, the primary congregation being in Tulsa. His expanded ministry included David Livingston Missionary Foundation, which conducted missionary and humanitarian work overseas. In 1970, in the shadow of Oral Roberts University, he founded the American Christian Crusade College, and appeared to be on his way to building an enterprise to rival the ever-expanding empire of **Oral Roberts** which was located just across town. The growth of Hargis' ministries, however, came to an abrupt end in 1974. Several students, of both sexes, accused Hargis of having engaged in sexual relations with them. The leaders at the college stood by the students and forced Hargis into retirement.

Hargis returned a year later and regained control of the church and the David Livingston Missionary Foundation. However, he could not regain control of the college. Unable to raise money once it became independent from Hargis, the college closed in 1977. Hargis then founded the Billy James Hargis Evangelistic Association and the Good Samaritan Children's Foundation. In 1981 he was granted a license to operate a television station. Through the 1980s he continued to operate his several ministries, but has not been able to regain anything approaching his pre-1974 following. In 1986 he released an autobiographical work which discussed his rise, fall, and return, *My Great Mistake*.

Sources:

Dudman, Richard. *Men of the Far Right.* New York: Pyramid Books, 1962. 192 pp.
Hargis, Billy James. *Christ and His Gospel.* Tulsa, OK: Christian Crusade Publications, 1996. 175 pp.
_____. *Communism: The Total Lie.* Tulsa, OK: Christian Crusade, 1961. 88 pp.
_____. *Communist America—Must It Be?* Tulsa, OK: Christian Crusade, 1960. 176 pp.
_____. *Distortion by Design.* Tulsa, OK: Christian Crusade, 1965. 318 pp.
_____. *Facts About Communism and the Churches.* Tulsa, OK: Christian Crusade, 1962.
_____. *The Far Left.* Tulsa, OK: Christian Crusade, 1964. 288 pp.
_____. *My Great Mistake.* Tulsa, OK: Christian Crusade, 1986. 149 pp.
_____. *Why I Fight for a Christian America.* Tulsa, OK: Christian Crusade, 1974.
Lippy, Charles H. *Twentieth-Century Shapers of American Popular Religion.* New York: Greenwood Press, 1989. 494 pp.
Morris, James. *The Preachers.* New York: S. Martin's Press, 1973. 418 pp.
Redekop, John Harold. *The American Far Right: A Case Study of Billy James Hargis and Christian Crusade.* Grand Rapids, MI: William B. Eerdmans Publishing Company, 1968.

★385★
Baba HARI DASS
Founder, Sri Rama Foundation
b. 1921?, India

Baba Hari Dass is a Hindu spiritual teacher in the tradition of Patanjali, and founder of the Sri Rama Foundation. Little information is available about his early life, except that he left home at the age of eight to join a renunciate sect in the jungle. At some point he became a *mouni sadhu*, a holy man who has taken vows of silence. While in India he managed a number of ashrams, designed and engineered the construction of temples and associated buildings, and developed a system for teaching ashtanga yoga (the "eight-limbed" yoga described in Patanjali's classic *Yoga Sutras*).

Babaji remembers seeing Westerners pursuing traditional yoga practices in the Himalayas when he was 14 years old. He was impressed, feeling that they were true seekers. In the late 1960s, while working in tandem with the great Hindu saint Neem Karoli Baba, he oversaw the training of a Westerner who would have a major impact on counter-culture spirituality, Richard Alpert. Alpert, a former spokesman for the psychedelic movement, returned to the United States as **Baba Ram Dass**, and become a spokesman for the emerging spiritual culture that provided the starting point for the New Age Movement. Progressively larger numbers of

Americans were drawn to India to work under Neem Karoli Baba. Some of these individuals were able to persuade Baba Hari Dass to move to the United States, which he did in 1971.

Hari Dass began to hold regular satsangs (spiritual gatherings) in Santa Cruz, California, and eventually gathered a group of disciples around him. In 1974, he asked some devotees living in Vancouver, Canada, to publish a series of books and journals that would serve as practical guides to spiritual development. This was the origin of the Dharma Sara Series that included such titles as *The Essence of One's Duty*; *Between Pleasure and Pain: The Way of Conscious Living*; and *Living Oneness*. The principal center for Babaji's students is Mount Madonna Center for the Creative Arts and Sciences in Watsonville, California (not far from Santa Cruz). Mount Madonna is a combination community, learning institution, and retreat center.

Baba Hari Dass long had a dream of founding an orphanage in India that would treat children as part of a family rather than as orphans. Land outside of Haridwar was acquired for such an orphanage in 1984, and the institution was ready to operate by 1987. While continuing to solicit charitable donations for the Sri Rama Orphanage, Mount Madonna, as well as the community's store in Santa Cruz, were severely damaged by the San Francisco earthquake of 1989, and have had to seek donations to stay afloat and to rebuild.

Sources:

Dass, Baba Hari. *Ashtanga Yoga Primer.* Santa Cruz, CA: Sri Rama Publishing, 1981.
_____. *Between Pleasure and Pain, The Way of Conscious Living.* Sumas, WA: Dharma Sara Publications, 1976.
_____. *Hariakhan Baba, Known, Unknown.* Davis, CA: Sri Rama Foundation, 1975. 93 pp.
_____. *Silence Speaks: From the Chalkboard of Baba Hari Dass.* Santa Cruz, CA: Sri Rama Foundation, 1977. 213 pp.
_____. *Sweeper to Saint.* Santa Cruz, CA: Sri Rama Publishing, 1980.
Shri Ram Orphanage. Santa Cruz, CA: Sri Rama Foundation, n.d. 16 pp.
Melton, J. Gordon *The Encyclopedia of American Religions.* 3d ed. Detroit: Gale Research Inc.,1988. 1102 pp.

★386★
HARKNESS, Georgia Elma
Theologian, Methodist Church (1939-1968)
b. Apr. 21, 1891, Harkness, New York
d. Aug. 21, 1974, Claremont, California

Georgia Harkness, a Methodist theologian, was the daughter of Lillie Merrill and J. Warren Harkness. She grew up on the family farm near the town in Western New York which had been named for her grandfather. She had her first personal religious experience at the age of nine and five years later joined the local congregation of the Methodist Episcopal Church. She attended Cornell University where, under the impact of the Student Volunteer Movement, she committed her life to foreign missions. Following her graduation in 1912, she taught school. In 1918 she entered Boston University where she earned two master's degrees (M.R.E. and M.A.) in religious education and stayed to complete her Ph.D. in 1923.

During her last year in graduate school Harkness also taught religious education at Elmira College, and joined its philosophy faculty in 1923. She was ordained as a local deacon in 1926 (a position which did not carry any relationship to her annual conference) and a local elder in 1938. In 1929 she published her first book, *Conflicts in Religious Thought*. She had emerged from Boston as a supporter of theological and philosophical personalism as advocated by Bound and Brightman. This was the dominant perspective for which the Boston religious community had become known. During the 1930s she slowly shifted her interest to theology. In 1937 she left Elmira College to teach religion at Mount Holyoke College, and then moved on to Garrett Biblical Institute (now Garrett-

Evangelical Theological Seminary) where she taught applied theology.

First at Garrett and after 1950 at the Pacific School of Religion, Harkness developed a concern to make theology applicable to lay people. Her intellectual work in this endeavor led to a series of very readable texts in theological disciplines: *Prayer and the Common Life* (1948); *Toward Understanding the Bible* (1954); and *Christian Ethics* (1957). Possibly her two most important books were written during her years at Garrett: *The Dark Night of the Soul* (1945), a discussion of suffering and faith; and *Understanding the Christian Faith* (1947), which appeared on the course of study for Methodist ministers for many years.

Her own religious commitments led Harkness into church leadership beyond her academic accomplishments. In 1937 she was named a delegate to the Oxford Conference on Faith and Life, her first leadership position in international ecumenical endeavors. Later she served as a delegate to the first gathering of the World Council of Churches in 1948 in Amsterdam and attended Council meetings in 1952 in Lund, Sweden, and in 1956 in Evanston, Illinois. Her work on the national level within Methodism began in 1944 with her election to the Board of World Peace (she had been a pacifist for most of her life). She was a delegate to the general conference in 1948, 1952, and 1956.

Harkness retired in 1961 and settled in Claremont, California. She continued to write (eventually producing close to 50 books) and speak around the country. She finished her career as the most well-known female theologian in America. More recently, Garrett named a chair in Applied Theology in her honor.

Sources:
Harkness, Georgia. *Christian Ethics.* New York: Abingdon Press, 1957. 240 pp.
_____. *The Dark Night of the Soul.* New York: Abingdon-Cokesbury Press, 1945. 192 pp.
_____. *Prayer and the Common Life.* New York: Abingdon-Cokesbury, 1948. 224 pp.
_____. *Toward Understanding the Bible.* Cincinnati, OH: Woman's Division of Christian Service, Board of Missions and Church Extension, Methodist Church, 1952. 134 pp.
_____. *Understanding Christian Faith.* New York: Abingdon-Cokesbury Press, 1947. 187 pp.
James, Edward T., ed. *Notable American Women, 1607-1950: A Biographical Dictionary.* 3 vols. Cambridge, MA: Harvard University Press, Belknap Press, 1971.
Johnson, Helen. "She Made Theology Understandable." *United Methodists Today* (October 1974).

★ 387 ★
HARLOW, Alison
Cofounder, Covenant of the Goddess
Cofounder, Nemeton
b. Aug. 29, 1934, New York, New York

Alison Harlow is a co-founder of the Covenant of the Goddess (COG), a national fellowship of witchcraft covens, as well as a co-founder of Nemeton, a Neo-Pagan association that is now a publishing group associated with the Neo-Pagan Church of All Worlds. Harlow was educated in New York, received a degree in mathematics from Columbia University (M.A., 1962), and took up a career in the field of computers.

Raised in an agnostic household, Harlow had a religious experience with the Goddess in 1966. In 1970 she began to study with **Victor H. Anderson**, a pioneer of modern Neo-Paganism in the San Francisco Bay area and co-founder of the Faerie Tradition, and was initiated into the Old Religion, as adherents frequently term Neo-Paganism. Harlow assisted Gwydion Pendderwen in the founding of the Nemeton Fellowship and helped to publish the *Nemeton Journal.* In 1975 she started the Wings of Vanthi, a

coven that combines the Faerie Tradition with some Gardnerian elements. Vanthi is considered to be a Goddess related to the Dark (New) Moon, who appears with black iridescent wings shot with moonlight.

One of Harlow's primary concerns from the very beginning of her Craft activity has been networking and communication among diverse traditions and groups within the Old Religion. It was thus natural that she should have been a co-founder, with Gwydion Pendderwen and Aidan A. Kelly, of the Covenant of the Goddess. She helped to initiate the initial meetings and was its founding First Officer. Over the years she has also promoted the development of Pagan music and on that behalf has led in the publication of several Pagan songbooks.

Sources:
Songs for the Old Religion. Oakland, CA: Nemeton, 1972. 16 pp.
Songs of Love and Pleasure. N.p.: Vanthi, 1977. 12 pp.

★ 388 ★
HARMON JR., Nolan Bailey
Bishop, United Methodist Church
b. Jul. 14, 1892, Meridian, Mississippi

Nolan Bailey Harmon, Jr., a prominent author/editor and bishop in the United Methodist Church, is the son of Nolan Bailey and Juliet Howe Harmon. He attended Millsaps College and received his A.B. in 1914, just as World War I began. He served a time in the Army as a chaplain, for which he was ordained in 1918. He was received on trial into the Baltimore Conference of the Methodist Episcopal Church, South in 1919. After his war service he attended Princeton University (M.A., 1920), and upon graduation was appointed as pastor of the church at Rockville, Maryland. He was received into full connection with the Baltimore Conference in 1921.

In 1925 Harmon moved from Rockville to Royal Front, Virginia, for three years. While at Royal Front he completed his first important book, *The Rites and Rituals of Episcopal Methodism* (1926), and two years later completed what has become his most enduring and practical book, *Ministerial Ethics and Etiquette* (1928), its revised editions still standard reading for most young ministers. In 1928 he assumed his first editorial job as editor of *Baltimore Southern Methodist.* In 1933 he returned to the pastorate at Greene Memorial Methodist Episcopal Church, South, Roanoke, Virginia. In 1939 the Methodist Episcopal Church, South, the Methodist Episcopal Church, and the Methodist Protestant Church merged to become the Methodist Church (1939-1968). Following the merger, Harmon became the book editor of the new church. His duties included the editing of the church's intellectual quarterly, *Religion in Life*, and its quadrennial editions of *The Book of Discipline.* Among his last editorial tasks was serving as general editor for the monumental Biblical volumes, *The Interpreter's Bible* (1955). During these years he also wrote two additional books of significance, *The Organization of the Methodist Church* (1948) and *Understanding the Methodist Church* (1955), both of which have been revised by new editors in light of the formation of the United Methodist Church in 1968.

Toward what appeared to be the end of a long and fruitful career, in 1956 Harmon was elected bishop and assigned to the Charlotte, North Carolina area. In 1960, at the beginning of what was to be his last four years, he was assigned to Kentucky. However, a few months after the quadrennium began, the bishop of the Birmingham, Alabama area died, and Harmon was assigned additional duties in North Alabama. He thus had the unenviable task of leading a divided Alabama Methodism through the most explosive years of the Civil Rights demonstrations of **Martin Luther King, Jr.**

Following his retirement in 1964, Harmon became a visiting professor at Candler School of Theology, Emory University, and picked up the task of completing the *Encyclopedia of World Methodism* (1974) from **Elmer T. Clark**. As of this writing (1991), Harmon remains an active retiree, frequently preaching and speaking, primarily in the South.

Sources:

Harmon, Nolan B. *The Encyclopedia of World Methodism*. 2 vols. Nashville: United Methodist Publishing House, 1974.
_____. *Ministerial Ethics and Etiquette*. Nashville, TN: Cokesbury Press, 1928. 180 pp.
_____. *The Organization of the Methodist Church*. Nashville, TN: Abingdon-Cokesbury Press, 1948. 281 pp.
_____. *The Rites and Rituals of Episcopal Methodism*. Nashville, TN: Publishing House of the Methodist Episcopal Church, South, 1926. 417 pp.
_____. *Understanding the Methodist Church*. Nashville, TN: Methodist Publishing House, 1955. 191 pp.

★ 389 ★
HARRIS, Barbara Clementine
Bishop, Episcopal Church
b. Jun. 12, 1930, Philadelphia, Pennsylvania

Barbara Clementine Harris, the first female bishop of the Episcopal Church, is the daughter of Walter and Beatrice Waneidah Price Harris, a black couple in Philadelphia. She did not go to college, but entered the business world and became a public relations executive for Joseph Baker Associates and then the Sun Oil Company. She married Raymond Rollins in 1960 but was divorced in 1963. She was active in St. Barnabas Episcopal Church in Philadelphia from her childhood years and became a social activist in the 1960s. She marched in Selma, Alabama, with **Martin Luther King, Jr.**, spoke out against apartheid in South Africa, and worked with Paul Washington at the Church of the Advocate. In 1974 she cut a business trip short to lead the processional at the Church of the Advocate when the first women priests were ordained in the Episcopal Church. She has expressed support for the ordination of homosexuals.

Harris became interested in the priesthood in the mid-1970s. She attended Villanova University for two years (1977-1979) and in 1979 was ordained a deacon in the Episcopal Church. She did her seminary work via correspondence with the Urban Training Unit in Sheffield, England. She finished her S.T.D. in 1981. She had previously been ordained as a priest in October 1980.

In 1984 she became the director of the Episcopal Church Publishing Co., a socially liberal corporation which publishes *The Witness*, considered by most as the most liberal periodical serving the Episcopal Church community. Her editorials on various social issues built her reputation in the church. During the 1980s she also served as interim rector at the Church of the Advocate.

Harris was elected to the episcopacy at a diocesan convention in September 1988 and confirmed by vote of the other diocese over the next few months. The possibility of her election had been the subject of the 1988 Lambeth Conference of the Worldwide Anglican Communion, consisting of those churches which derive directly from the Church of England and remain in communion with it. Following a lengthy debate, the conference voted to allow any national church to consecrate a female bishop if they so choose. She was consecrated in Boston as suffragan bishop for the Massachusetts Diocese. The consecration was embroiled in controversy. Most of the criticism surrounded the fact that she was a woman. However, critics also complained of her being the first divorced person ever to have been consecrated and cited her poor theological education as making her unfit for the office. Supporters have seen her elevation as a general boost for women, especially in other liturgical churches which have been reluctant to welcome women into the priesthood.

Sources:

Cuniberti, Betty. "The Bishop of Controversy." *Los Angeles Times* (February 15, 1989).
Schmidt, Richard D. "It's Bishop Harris Now!" *The Episcopalian* 154, 3 (March 1990): 1, 5-6.
Walker, Richard. "Episcopalians Test Lambeth Ruling." *Christianity Today* (October 21, 1988): 47, 49.

★ 390 ★
HARRIS, Thomas Lake
Spiritualist Leader
Brotherhood of the New Life
b. May 15, 1823, Fenny Stratford, Buckinghamshire England
d. Mar. 23, 1906, New York, New York

Thomas Lake Harris was the founder of the Brotherhood of the New Life and of an influential style of Spiritualism. He was born in England to a strict Calvinist family that moved to New York when he was five. His mother died soon afterward, and when a stepmother entered the family, Harris decided, at the young age of nine, to leave home. Somehow he made his way in the outside world, eventually becoming a Universalist minister in the New York City area. He married Mary Van Arnum in 1845.

As a Universalist minister Harris became acquainted with the ideas of visionary Emanuel Swedenborg and was converted. In 1847 he became pastor of the Swedenborgian First Independent Church Society of New York. He was briefly associated with Spiritualist **Andrew Jackson Davis**, until Davis created a scandal because of his relationship with a "spiritual mate" who was not his wife. Harris' own wife died in 1850. In 1851 he became associated with J. D. Scott, a trance medium who formed the Mountain Cove Community in Fayette County, Virginia. When a split developed in the group, Harris was brought in. He ran the community for a year. He then returned to New York to pastor the Swedenborgian church on Washington Square and work as a trance lecturer, where he developed his distinctive Spiritualism. He married Emily Isabella Waters in 1855.

In 1859 Harris went to Scotland and England to seek followers. He found several, including the wealthy Laurence Oliphant, and in 1861 founded his Brotherhood of the New Life near Wassaic, New York. In 1863 he moved to new land near Amenia, New York, and in 1867 he moved yet again, to Brocton, New York. The latter move was made possible by the arrival of the wealthy Oliphant. In 1875 Harris and a few others founded the Fountain Grove community in Santa Rosa, California, in order to escape the New York winters and to be in better contact with fairies, the spiritual beings who prefer warm weather. In 1881 Harris closed Brocton altogether and the community members moved to California.

The style of Spiritualism espoused by Harris was subject to much misinterpretation. Similar in content to the beliefs of Andrew Jackson Davis, and in conjunction with Swedenborg's idea of conjugal love, followers were to seek out their spiritual counterpart, who was always someone of the opposite sex and rarely the existing spouse. This new relationship was to replace the married relationship, and outsiders typically thought that the result was rampant sexuality, especially given Harris's sensual poetry and belief in a male/female deity. Contrary to expectations, however, Harris was celibate and counseled the same for all his followers, saying that only in that context could a true spiritual relationship form.

In 1885 Harris's second wife died and in 1891 he married longtime follower Jane Lee Waring. The next year they moved out of the community and back to New York, where they remained. The community suffered under this blow, and by 1900 there were only five remaining members, to whom Harris finally sold his share of the land. Harris died in 1906, at the age of 83; the last surviving member of the Brotherhood of the New Life died in 1934.

Sources:

Cuthbert, Arthur A. *The Life Worldwork of Thomas Lake Harris, Written from Direct Personal Knowledge*. Glasgow, Scotland, 1909.

Dictionary of American Biography. 20 vols. and 7 supps. New York: Charles Scribner's Sons, 1928-1936, 1944-1981.

Harris, Thomas Lake. *Brotherhood of the New Life: Its Fact, Law, Method and Purpose*. Fountain Grove, CA: Fountain Grove Press, 1891. 15 pp.

_____. *An Epic of the Starry Heaven*. New York: Partridge and Britten, 1854. 210 pp.

_____. *God's Breath in Man and in Humane Society*. Santa Rosa, CA: The Author, 1891. 314 pp.

_____. *A Lyric of the Golden Age*. New York: Partridge and Britten, 1856. 381 pp.

_____. *The Marriage of Heaven and Earth*. Glasgow, Scotland: C. W. Pearce & Co., 1903. 287 pp.

_____. *The New Republic*. Santa Rosa, CA: Fountaingrove Press, 1891.

Hine, Robert V. *California's Utopian Colonies*. New Haven, CT: Yale University Press, 1966. 209 pp.

Kagan, Paul. *New World Utopias*. Baltimore, MD: Penguin, 1975. 191 pp.

Melton, J. Gordon. *Biographical Dictionary of American Cult and Sect Leaders*. Garland Reference Library of Social Science, vol. 212. New York: Garland Publishing, 1986.

Schneider, Herbert W., and George Lawton. *A Prophet and a Pilgrim*. New York: Columbia University Press, 1942.

Shepard, Leslie. *Encyclopedia of Occultism & Parapsychology*. 3 vols., 2nd. ed. Detroit: Gale Research Co., 1984-1985.

Swainson, William P. *Thomas Lake Harris and His Occult Teaching*. London: William Rider & Son, 1922. 68 pp.

—Gary L. Ward

★391★
HARROW, Judith S.
Priestess, Gardnerian Witchcraft
b. Mar. 3, 1945, Bronx, New York

Judith Harrow is a priestess and national leader in the Gardnerian Wicca movement, the original Neo-Witchcraft tradition begun by **Gerald B. Gardner** in England in the 1940s. She is a graduate of the Western College for Women (B.A., 1966) and the Graduate School of Education of the City College of New York (M.S. in counseling, 1979). She began to study Witchcraft in 1976, was initiated as a priestess in September of 1977, and founded Inwood Study Group in June of 1980. After receiving the Third Degree (Gardnerian) in November of 1980, the Inwood group became Coteus Coven and affiliated almost immediately with the Covenant of the Goddess (COG), a national fellowship of witchcraft covens. Harrow served as convening First Office of the Northeast Local Council of COG in 1983, National First Officer of COG in 1984, Co-chair of COG Grand Council in 1985, and various other positions on the COG National and Local Boards of Directors. In 1985, following a five-year effort that required the assistance of the New York Civil Liberties Union, she became the first COG member to be legally registered as clergy in New York City.

Harrow also founded the Pagan Pastoral Counseling Network, and served as the first editor of the network's publication. She also founded the New York Area Coven Leaders' Peer Support Group, and served as Program Coordinator for the first Mid-Atlantic Pan Pagan Conference and Festival and for seven other Pagan gatherings. Harrow produced "Reconnections," a weekly feature on the activities of religious progressives of all faiths for WBAI radio in New York. Her writings have appeared in the newsletter of the Association for Humanistic Psychology and *Counseling and Values* (the journal of the Association for Religious and Value Issues in Counseling), as well as in Pagan publications such as *Hidden Path*, *Harvest*, and the Covenant of the Goddess *Newsletter*.

★392★
HAVEN JR., Gilbert
Bishop, Methodist Episcopal Church
b. Sep. 19, 1821, Malden, Massachusetts
d. Jan. 3, 1880, Malden, Massachusetts

Gilbert Haven, Jr., a bishop in the Methodist Episcopal Church, was the son of Squire Gilbert Haven and Hannah Burrill. Squire Haven had organized the Methodist Sunday school in Malden, Massachusetts, and superintended it for many years. In 1939 young Gilbert left home to attend the Wesleyan Academy at Wilbraham, in western Massachusetts. While there he had a religious experience which made his Christianity a personal relation to God, and he began to develop the abolitionist views that were to come to dominate his life. In 1842 he entered Wesleyan University from which he graduated in 1846.

Following his graduation, Haven took a position as professor of Greek and German at a seminary in Amenia, New York. In 1851 he married Mary Ingraham. That same year he left his teaching position to join the New England Conference of the Methodist Episcopal Church and during the rest of the decade served pastorates in various parts of Massachusetts. During these years he became an outspoken abolitionist.

In 1860, his wife having died, Haven signed up as a chaplain in the Union Army. He served a year and spent much of the rest of the war attempting to clarify the issues concerning slavery which underlay the fighting. He made several trips to Europe to speak about the conflict. In 1865, having just returned from Europe, he was assigned to the North Russell Street Church in Boston.

Though having a significant career before the war, Haven's role was to grow in importance afterward. In 1867 he was elected editor of the influential *Zion's Herald*, the most liberal of Methodism's several newspapers. He was elected as a delegate to the general conferences of 1868 and 1872 and at the latter was elected bishop. As bishop he was assigned to Atlanta, Georgia. Following the Civil War, the Methodist Episcopal Church had moved into the South to establish conferences among both black and white members. Haven not only brought his abolitionist reputation, but in his associating with black Methodists as equals, angered many white Methodists, even those who had chosen to join the Methodist Episcopal Church.

As part of his episcopal duties, he also traveled to Mexico to begin Methodist work there in 1873. In 1876 he went to Liberia. While there he contracted malaria from which he never fully recovered, and which eventually took his life.

Sources:

Daniels, William Haven. *Memorials of Gilbert Haven*. Boston, MA: B. B. Russell & Co., 1880.

Gravely, William B. *Gilbert Haven, Methodist Abolitionist*. Nashville, TN: Abingdon Press, 1973. 272 pp.

Harmon, Nolan B. *The Encyclopedia of World Methodism*. 2 vols. Nashville: United Methodist Publishing House, 1974.

Prentice, G. *The Life of Gilbert Haven*. New York: Phillips & Hunt, 1883.

★393★
HAWAWEENY, Raphael
Bishop, Russian Orthodox Church
b. Nov. 1, 1860, Damascus Syrian Arab Republic
d. Feb. 27, 1915

Raphael Hawaweeny, a bishop of the Russian Orthodox Church who worked among Syrian Orthodox believers in the United States, was the first Orthodox bishop consecrated in the United States. After completing his early theological training at the Ecumenical Patriarchate's Theological School in the Princes Islands, he was ordained a deacon. He finished his education at the Kiev Theological Academy in Russia, and in 1894 the Holy Synod of the

Russian Orthodox Church appointed him professor of Arabic Language and Literature at Kazan Theological Academy.

Hawaweeny might have spent the rest of his life as a professor had events in the United States not intervened. During the 1890s, the Syrian-American community grew to the point that Syrian Orthodox Christians desired some recognition apart from the larger Orthodox community, which was dominated by the Russian church. In 1892 the Russian Orthodox Church organized a Syrian Mission. In the wake of Hawaweeny's theological appointment at Kazan, Dr. Ibrahim Arbeely, president of the Syrian Orthodox Benevolent Society, contacted Hawaweeny. After conferring with his ecclesiastical superiors, Hawaweeny agreed to come to the New World. He was duly ordained to the priesthood and elevated to the rank of archimandrite, and in 1895, he arrived in the United States with two colleagues, John Shamie and Constantine Abou Adal.

The major accomplishment of Hawaweeny's twenty years of service was his gathering and organizing of the American Syrian Orthodox community, which numbered approximately 25,000 at the time of his death. He began his work in New York City, where he organized St. Nicholas parish in Brooklyn. He traveled widely and within a few years had established Syrian-Arab parishes across the United States. In 1898 he published an *Arabic Service Book* for their use.

Hawaweeny's success did not go unheralded in Syria. Twice in 1901 the Antiochean Orthodox Church elected him bishop, but he declined the offer, which would have meant abandoning his American work to return home. Two years later, Bishop Tikhon, who headed the Russian Church in North America, traveled to Russia to seek approval to have Hawaweeny consecrated as one of his vicar-bishops in the American diocese. On March 11, 1904, **Bishop Tikhon** and Bishop Innocent consecrated Archimandrite Raphael as bishop of Brooklyn.

Although he concentrated his work on his Syrian flock, Bishop Raphael remained a bishop of the Russian Church. In 1905, in the absence of Bishop Tikhon, he presided over the Orthodox clergy conference and later consecrated the grounds of St. Tikhon's Monastery and Orphanage. Most important, however, was his work with the Syrians to prepare them to become an autonomous body within the context of the Russian Church. During the last year of his life, Metropolitan Germanos came to the United States and began to organize Syrian parishes separately from Russian jurisdiction. For a decade following Bishop Raphael's death, his mission and that of Germanos competed. They finally united in 1925, becoming what is today known as the Antiochean Orthodox Christian Archdiocese of North America.

Sources:

Tarasar, Constance J. *Orthodox America, 1794-1976: Development of the Orthodox Church in America.* Syosset, NY: Orthodox Church in America, Department of Archives and History, 1975. 352 pp.

★ 394 ★
HAYES, Patrick Joseph
Cardinal, Roman Catholic Church
b. Nov. 20, 1867, New York, New York
d. Sep. 4, 1938, Monticello, New York

Patrick Joseph Hayes, a cardinal of the Roman Catholic Church, was born in Manhattan in a tenement, the son of Irish immigrants. After his mother's death when he was three years old, he lived increasingly with his mother's sister. The living arrangements became a full-time one after the death of his father, Daniel Hayes, when he was about nine. His aunt sent him to parochial school and in 1883 to the De La Salle Institute, run by the Christian Brothers, where future cardinal **George William Mundelein** was among Hayes' fellow students. He finished in two years and went on to Manhattan College and then to St. Joseph's Seminary in Troy, New

York. Having come to the attention of Archbishop Corrigan, who ordained him in 1892, he was given the chance to study either in Rome or at the new Catholic University in Washington, D.C. He chose the latter.

After two years of graduate study, Hayes was assigned to St. Gabriel's Church in Manhattan, where future cardinal **John Farley** was the rector. The following year Farley became auxiliary bishop of New York and took Hayes with him as his new secretary. Farley became archbishop in 1902 and again named Hayes as his secretary. The following year Hayes was named chancellor of the archdiocese and he set about the task of organizing the Cathedral College. In recognition of his work, he was granted a doctor of divinity degree from Rome. In 1907 he was appointed a domestic prelate with the title of monsignor. In 1914, on a trip to Rome with Cardinal Farley, Hayes was named auxiliary bishop of New York. During these years, Hayes made many scholarly contributions, in addition to his administrative work. The most important of these contributions were the articles he wrote for the *Catholic Encyclopedia*, a major project initiated by Cardinal Farley.

With the outbreak of World War I, Farley appointed Hayes as bishop ordinary for the Armed Forces of the United States. Hayes eventually supervised approximately 900 chaplains in the Army and Navy. In 1918, just as the war was ending, Farley died, and Hayes was chosen the new Archbishop of New York. He was installed on March 19, 1919.

Among his first efforts as Archbishop was the reorganization of Catholic charities both to cut out overlapping efforts and to plan for new demands. He then moved to consolidate them under the umbrella of the Catholic Charities of the Archdiocese of New York. The result was a more efficient gathering and distribution of funds and a broadening of services throughout the archdiocese. Hayes also gave his blessing to the organization of the Parish Visitors of Mary Immaculate, a new religious community formed by Julia Terese Tallon dedicated to social work in the homes of the poor.

In the spring of 1924 Hayes traveled to Rome and, along with Archbishop George Mundelein of Chicago, received his cardinal's hat. He was assigned Santa Maria in Via as his titular parish in the diocese of Rome. Among his last actions was the organization of the Cardinal Hayes Literature Committee, composed of writers and editors. It published a monthly, *The Book Survey*, which recommended the better books for Catholics to read amid the flood of writing being produced daily.

Hayes died of a heart attack in 1938 while saying his evening prayers.

Sources:

Delaney, John J. *Dictionary of American Catholic Biography.* Garden City, NY: Doubleday & Company, 1988. 621 pp.
Finn, Brendan A. *Twenty-Four American Cardinals.* Boston: Bruce Humphreys, 1947. 475 pp.
Thornton, Francis Beauchesne. *Our American Princes.* New York: G. P. Putnam's Sons, 1963. 319 pp.
Walsh, James Joseph. *Our American Cardinals.* New York: D. Appleton & Company, 1926. 352 pp.

★ 395 ★
HAYGOOD, Atticus Greene
Bishop, Methodist Episcopal Church, South
b. Nov. 19, 1839, Watkinsville, Georgia
d. Jan. 18, 1896, Oxford, Georgia

Atticus Greene Haygood, a bishop of the Methodist Episcopal Church, South best known for his efforts on the behalf of black people in the South in the decades following the Civil War, was the son of Greene B. Haygood, a prominent lawyer. Raised in a comfortable environment, Atticus received most of his early education from his mother. In 1852 the family moved to Atlanta. In 1858 Atticus left home to attend Emory College in Oxford, Georgia. While there he was licensed as an exhorter in the Methodist Episcopal Church, South in May 1858 and licensed to preach four months later. In 1859 he graduated, married Mary Fletcher Yarbrough, joined the Georgia Conference of the Methodist Episcopal Church, South on trial, and began preaching as the junior preacher on the Oxford Circuit, working with future bishop Lovick Pierce.

Haygood remained in the pastorate through most of the Civil War, though he did serve two brief periods as a chaplain, including a year as chaplain with General Longstreet's Corps in Tennessee in 1863-1864. In 1870 the general conference of the rebuilding Methodist Episcopal Church, South elected him Sunday school secretary and its first editor of Sunday school publications. He moved to Nashville, Tennessee, where he pioneered the publication of attractive church school literature. In 1873 he became the associate secretary of the board of missions and editor of its magazine, *Our Mission*. In 1874 his wife's health forced him to resign his duties in Nashville and return to Georgia.

In 1876 Haygood became president of his alma mater. He is credited with saving Emory through the introduction of a new vocational curriculum that included courses in telegraphy, bookkeeping, and manual arts. While at Emory, in 1878 he assumed additional duties as editor of *The Wesleyan Christian Advocate*, the periodical for Georgia and Florida Methodists.

During the 1870s Haygood's concern for the situation of Blacks emerged into prominence. In 1881 he published *Our Brother in Black*, one of the most progressive books on race relations in America of the era. Risking his popularity in the church he attacked many of the cruel practices directed against Blacks such as the convict lease system and lynching. In 1882 he was elected bishop, but declined the honor. He stayed at Emory and threw his time and energy behind his most significant project, the founding of Paine Institute (now Paine College) as a cooperative endeavor between the Methodist Episcopal Church, South and the Christian Methodist Episcopal Church, the predominantly black denomination established by the Methodist Episcopal Church, South after the war. Paine was opened in 1883. He also became part-time agent for the Slater Fund whose purpose was to aid the education of Blacks. In 1884 he resigned his presidency and worked full time for the Slater Fund.

In 1890 Haygood was again elected to the episcopacy, and this time he accepted. He was assigned to California. After three years on the West Coast, Haygood returned to Georgia in ill health and lived the last years of his life as a semi-invalid with **Warren A. Candler**, his successor, as president of Emory at Oxford. During these years he authored a novel, *The Monk and the Prince* (1895). He died there in 1896.

Sources:

Dempsey, Elem F. *Atticus Green Haygood*. Nashville, TN: Parthenon Press, 1940. 720 pp.

Dictionary of American Biography. 20 vols. and 7 supps. New York: Charles Scribner's Sons, 1928-1936, 1944-1981.

Harmon, Nolan B. *The Encyclopedia of World Methodism*. 2 vols. Nashville: United Methodist Publishing House, 1974.

Haygood, Atticus G. *Jack-knife and Brambles*. Nashville, TN: Southern Methodist Publishing House, 1881. 252 pp.

_____. *The Man of Galilee*. Baltimore, MD: J. E. Wilson & Co., 1889. 156 pp.

_____. *The Monk and the Prince*. Nashville, TN: Publishing House of the M. E. Church, South, 1895. 371 pp.

_____. *Our Brother in Black*. Nashville, TN: Southern Methodist Publishing House, 1881. 252 pp.

_____. *Pleas for Progress*. Nashville, TN: Publishing House of the Methodist Episcopal Church, South, 1889. 320 pp.

Hill, Samuel S., ed. *Encyclopedia of Religion in the South*. Macon, GA: Mercer University Press, 1984. 878 pp.

Mann, Harold W. *Atticus Greene Haygood: Methodist Bishop, Editor, and Educator*. Athens, GA: University of Georgia Press, 1965. 254 pp.

★ 396 ★
HAYWOOD, Garfield Thomas
Presiding Bishop, Pentecostal Assemblies of the World
b. Jul. 15, 1880, Greencastle, Indiana
d. Apr. 12, 1931, Indianapolis, Indiana

Garfield Thomas Haywood was the first presiding bishop of the Pentecostal Assemblies of the World (PAW). He was born in the Indiana countryside but grew up in Indianapolis, the son of a foundry worker and a schoolteacher. He was active in both the Methodist Episcopal Church and the Baptist church. His mother encouraged him to be an avid reader, but he finished only two years of high school, whereupon he used his artistic skills as a cartoonist for two weeklies that served the black community. He married Ida Howard in 1902.

In 1907 several people from the Pentecostal revival on Asuza Street in Los Angeles came to Indianapolis to tell their story, and a small interracial Pentecostal church, the Apostolic Faith Assembly, arose as a result. Haywood joined in 1908 and soon became a leader, succeeding Elder Henry Prentiss as pastor in 1909. Under Haywood's leadership the church was very successful. It began to publish its own periodical, *The Voice in the Wilderness*, in 1910 using the print shop Haywood set up in his home. Haywood also printed many booklets and a hymnal, *The Bridegroom Cometh*. He led the congregation into an association with the Pentecostal Assemblies of the World, which in 1913 had its annual convention in the new building of the Apostolic Faith Assembly.

In 1914 the Pentecostal movement was divided by a new "Jesus Only" teaching, which identified Jesus as Jehovah of the Old Testament and denied the existence of the Trinity. Haywood accepted this message and was rebaptized in the name of Jesus only, and the rest of the Pentecostal Assemblies of the World soon followed suit. A general increase in membership resulted, and in 1918 the Assemblies merged with the other major Jesus Only group, the General Assembly of the Apostolic Assemblies, keeping the Pentecostal Assemblies of the World name. Haywood was elected the secretary-treasurer of the new body, in addition to pastoring what had become one of the largest Pentecostal congregations in the world. He also continued to write poems and hymns and edit the Pentecostal Assemblies of the World periodical, the *Christian Outlook*.

In 1924 the Apostolic Faith Assembly was renamed Christ Temple as it relocated to a 1200-seat building. That same year the Pentecostal Assemblies of the World experienced racial conflict, and many of the white members left to form the United Pentecostal Church. This left Haywood the clearly dominant leader of the now mostly black Pentecostal Assemblies of the World, which completely reorganized, creating the office of bishop and electing Haywood to that office. Haywood served both as bishop and as pastor of Christ Temple until his death in 1931 at the age of 51.

Sources:

Dugas, Paul D., ed. *The Life and Writings of Elder G. T. Haywood*. Portland, OR: Apostolic Book Publishers, 1968.

Foster, Fred J. *Their Story: 20th Century Pentecostals*. St. Louis, MO: World Aflame Press, 1983. 192 pp.

Golder, Morris E. *The Bishops of the Pentecostal Assemblies of the World*. Indianapolis, IN: The Author, 1980. 69 pp.

_____. *History of the Pentecostal Assemblies of the World*. Indianapolis, IN: The Author, 1973. 195 pp.

_____. *The Life and Works of Bishop Garfield Thomas Haywood*. Indianapolis, IN: The Author, 1977. 71 pp.

Haywood, Garfield Thomas. *The Birth of the Spirit in the Days of the Apostles*. Indianapolis, IN: Christ Temple Book Store, n.d. 40 pp.

_____. *Feed My Sheep*. Indianapolis, IN: Christ Temple Book Store, n.d. 62 pp.

_____. *The Finest of the Wheat*. Portland, OR: Apostolic Book Publishers, n.d. 90 pp.

_____. *The Victim of the Flaming Sword*. Indianapolis, IN: Christ Temple Book Store, n.d. 71 pp.

Melton, J. Gordon. *Biographical Dictionary of American Cult and Sect Leaders*. Garland Reference Library of Social Science, vol. 212. New York: Garland Publishing, 1986.

Tyson, James L. *Before I Sleep*. Indianapolis, IN: Pentecostal Publications, 1976. 108 pp.

—Gary L. Ward

★ 397 ★
HEALY, Eliza
Convent Superior, Congregation of Notre Dame, Roman Catholic Church
b. Dec. 23, 1846, Macon, Georgia
d. 1918, Staten Island, New York

Eliza Healy, who as Sister Mary Magdalen became the first black to rise to a position of leadership in a religious order in North America, was the daughter of Michael Morris Healy, an Irish immigrant plantation owner, and his slave and common-law wife, Eliza Smith. Healy's brothers, **James Augustine Healy** and **Patrick Francis Healy**, would in like measure pioneer paths for Blacks in the Roman Catholic Church in America. It was her father's plan to sell the plantation and move north, since that was the only way, under Georgia law, that he could free his family from slavery. Before he could do that, both he and his wife died in 1850. Fortunately, the executors of the estate sent Healy and her even younger siblings to New York to live with an older brother.

In 1851 they were given into the care of the Notre Dame sisters in Quebec. Healy finished her elementary schooling with the nuns at St. Johns, Quebec, and then attended school at Villa Maria in Montreal. After graduation she settled in Boston with her brother Eugene and sister Amanda Josephine. In 1864 they settled in a home in West Newton, Massachusetts, purchased for them by their brother and bishop-to-be, James, whose career in the diocese of Boston was blossoming.

In 1874 Eliza decided to enter the Congregation of Notre Dame and returned to Montreal to become a novitiate. She made her profession in 1876 (final vows in 1882). Sister Mary Magdalen (the name by which Healy would be henceforth known) was assigned as a teacher at St. Patrick's School in Montreal and over the next two years taught at various locations in Ontario and Quebec. In 1895 she was assigned to a financially faltering school at Huntington, Quebec, and also appointed superior of the community of French sisters. She restored it to financial solvency and in 1898 moved on to the congregation's Mother House in Montreal as directress of English studies. Two years later she was assigned to the congregation's normal school, also in Montreal.

In 1903 Sister Mary Magdalen became superior of Villa Barloe at St. Alban's, Vermont, a finishing school with an associated convent. As headmistress of the school, she had the task of returning it to a sound financial state, which she accomplished with some of the skills she had learned from her late brother. She also won the support of the sisters in the convent, who admired her devotional life, hard work, and willingness to follow the same discipline which she imposed upon them.

Sister Mary Magdalen's last assignment was to Staten Island, New York, as superior to the College of Notre Dame. She died there following an injury and infection.

Sources:

Logan, Rayford W., and Michael R. Winston, eds. *Dictionary of American Negro Biography*. New York: W. W. Norton & Co.   1982. 680 pp.

★ 398 ★
HEALY, James Augustine
Bishop, Roman Catholic Church
b. Apr. 6, 1830, Jones County, Georgia
d. Aug. 5, 1900, Portland, Maine

James Augustine Healy was the first black person ordained as a priest by the Roman Catholic Church in the United States and later the first black person to be consecrated a bishop in the Roman Catholic Church. He was the son of an Irish immigrant farmer, Michael Morris Healy, and his slave and common-law wife, Eliza Smith. He was the first child of the union and like his sister **Eliza Healy** and his brother **Patrick Francis Healy**, had an outstanding career in the Roman Catholic Church. According to Georgia law, Healy was born a slave and could not be emancipated while living within the state. Thus in 1837 the elder Healy took his son to Long Island and enrolled him in a Quaker school. Seven years later, along with several of his brothers, he enrolled at the College of the Holy Cross, the Jesuit school at Worcester, Massachusetts. He received his B.A. in 1849. He decided to become a Catholic priest and moved to Montreal to attend the Grand seminary. He received his M.A. two years later. He then moved to Paris where in 1852 he began work at the Sulpician Seminary. He was ordained in Paris in 1854.

Upon his return to the United States, Healy was welcomed by John Fitzpatrick, the bishop of Boston, and served as Fitzpatrick's secretary and diocesan chancellor. During the Civil War he was assigned as pastor of the Cathedral of the Holy Cross. His acceptance and fame grew as people became aware of his oratorical skills and his personable manner. At the end of the war he became pastor of St. James, the largest Catholic congregation in Boston, and during his nine years there led in the building of a new basilica. The same leadership qualities which led to his appointment to St. James (in spite of the racial obstacles) led to his appointment as the bishop's deputy for social action. He oversaw the establishment of the Home for Destitute Catholic Children and promoted St. Ann's Foundling Home. He joined with union organizers in the formation of the first Catholic labor union in the city. His efforts with public officials led in 1875 to the first Roman Catholic religious services offered to inmates of correctional institutions.

In 1875 Healy was named bishop of Portland, Maine, by Pope Pius IX. He remained head of the diocese for the rest of his life. During this time he oversaw the building of over 60 churches, 18 schools, and a number of convents and monastic centers. He became well known for his efforts to care for those widowed and orphaned by the war and for his crusade against child labor. He won over the masses of Catholics by his friendliness and willingness to constantly be moving about his diocese personally assisting the poor, the immigrants, and the sick. He was often seen riding through town on his horse with saddle bags full of provisions he was distributing.

Healy was also a national figure within the church. He served on the commission that founded Catholic University of America. He was a permanent member of the Commission on Negro and Indian Missions established by the Third Plenary Council of the American Church. Pope Leo XIII, whom he knew personally, appointed him an assistant at the papal throne (the highest office in the church below a cardinal). While the church honored him and his New England parishioners loved him, he was the constant recipient of racial slurs, especially when he attended meetings in Southern cities. He bore them with as little regard as possible and did not allow them to distract from his work.

Sources:

Foley, Albert S. *Bishop Healy: Beloved Outcaste*. New York: Farrar, Strauss, and Young, 1954. 243 pp.

Logan, Rayford W., and Michael R. Winston, eds. *Dictionary of American Negro Biography.* New York: W. W. Norton & Co. 1982. 680 pp.
Lucey, William L. *The Catholic Church in Maine.* Francestown, NH: M. Jones Co., 1957. 372 pp.

★399★
HEALY, Patrick Francis
Priest, Roman Catholic Church
b. Feb. 27, 1834, Jones County, South Carolina
d. Jan. 10, 1910, Washington, District of Columbia

Patrick Francis Healy was the first Black accepted into the Society of Jesus (the Jesuits) in North America, the first awarded a doctorate in the United States, and the first to be named the president of a Catholic college. Healy was the son of an Irish immigrant plantation owner, Michael Morris Healy, and his slave and common-law wife, Eliza Smith. The family of 10 children produced several Roman Catholic leaders of note, including **Eliza Healy** and Bishop **James Augustine Healy**. Healy was born a slave and it was against the law in Georgia for him to be freed. While still a child he was sent to live with an older brother who was attending school in Flushing, Long Island, New York. In 1844 he joined several of his brothers who were enrolled at Holy Cross College in Worcester, Massachusetts. He received his B.A. in 1850. The summer following graduation, he decided to become a Jesuit and began his two years training as a novitiate at Frederick, Maryland. In 1852 he began six years of teaching, first at St. Joseph's College in Philadelphia and then at Holy Cross.

In 1858 Healy was sent to study in Rome but in 1859 transferred to Louvain, Belgium, where he finished his theological courses. He was ordained in Belgium in 1864. Continuing at Louvain, he finished his doctoral studies in 1865 and immediately began a year of retreat at Lyon, France.

In 1866 Healy returned to the United States and became professor of philosophy at Georgetown University. In 1867 he made his final profession of vows as a Jesuit. His career at Georgetown was one of steady advancement. In 1868 he became dean of the college and the following year vice president of the university. In 1873 he became vice rector of the school and served as acting president. Upon being officially confirmed by Rome, he became president of the university in 1874. He served as president of the school for eight years, until he resigned in 1882 for reasons of health. As president of Georgetown he began a remodeling of the school along gothic lines reminiscent of Louvain. He also made substantial changes in an effort to modernize the curriculum. He became a person of note in Washington society, a friend of three presidents, and, especially on tasks related to his position with the Catholic Commission on Indian Affairs, worked with government officials on a wide variety of issues.

After a period of recovery, he became associate pastor of St. Joseph's Church in Providence, Rhode Island, in 1891 and then pastor of St. Lawrence Church in New York City in 1895. His final assignment was as spiritual director at St. Joseph's College in Philadelphia (1906-1908). His health having failed him, in 1908 he returned to Georgetown and spent the last two years of his life at the infirmary.

Sources:

Foley, Albert S. *God's Men of Color.* New York: Farrar, Strauss, and Young, 1955. 243 pp.
Logan, Rayford W., and Michael R. Winston, eds. *Dictionary of American Negro Biography.* New York: W. W. Norton & Co. 1982. 680 pp.

★400★
HECKER, Isaac Thomas
Founder, Congregation of the Missionary Priests of St. Paul the Apostle (Paulist Fathers)
b. Dec. 18, 1819, New York, New York
d. Dec. 22, 1888, New York, New York

Isaac Thomas Hecker, founder of the Paulist Fathers of the Roman Catholic Church, was the son of John and Susan Caroline Friend Hecker, who were German immigrants. Shortly after her marriage, his mother had left the Lutheran Church and joined the Methodist Episcopal Church. Hecker had only a few years of formal education; he left school to work for the Methodist newspaper and eventually joined his brothers in a bakery company. He worked with his brothers all through his teen years. In 1841 he met Orestes Brownson, who introduced him to the German philosophers and became the catalyst for an intense spiritual crisis. Hecker had several dreams/visions in which he renounced his past and, among other things, decided never to marry. In 1842 he began a brief stay at Brook Farm, the communal experiment headed by Transcendentalist George Ripley. After eight months, however, he returned to New York City. By 1944 he had decided that the church was the only permanent solution to his religious quest, and in August of that year he was received into the Roman Catholic Church.

In 1845 Hecker joined the Redemptorist Order and traveled to St. Troud College in Belgium to study for the priesthood. He was ordained in 1849 and spent a year in a parish in England. In 1852 he joined a small group of converts and returned to America as a missionary, working primarily among German-speaking immigrants. As a Redemptorist, Hecker authored his first two books, *Questions of the Soul* (1855) and *Aspirations of Nature* (1857). His work convinced him of the need for a mission to English-speaking non-Catholic Americans. Since he had not obtained permission for such work from his superiors in the order, he was expelled from the Redemptorists. In 1857, encouraged by Bishop John Hughes of New York, he traveled to Rome. The pope gave him a dispensation from his vows and encouraged him to found a new order. In 1858 he returned to America and, with three other former redemptorists, founded the Congregation of the Missionary Priests of St. Paul the Apostle, commonly called the Paulist Fathers. Hecker was elected superior of the order. Headquarters were established in New York City.

Though the mission was slowed somewhat by the war, visible progress was swift as soon as peace returned. In 1865 Hecker founded *The Catholic World* and edited it for the next several decades. In 1866 he addressed the plenary council meeting in Baltimore and received its blessing to establish a Catholic Publication Society. In 1870 he founded a youth magazine, *The Young Catholic.* This vigorous activity took its toll on his health, and in 1873 Hecker traveled to Europe to recover. He returned in 1875. He then published his important pamphlet, *An Exposition of the Church in View of Recent Difficulties and Controversies and the Present Needs of the Age.* This pamphlet became the first chapter in his major publication, *The Church and the Age* (1887). Hecker emerged as the major theoretician of a view of the church adapted to the modern world, centered in the free individual, directed by the Holy Spirit, and guided by the church. Hecker was himself unable to make the most of his new approach as his health remained a problem. He became, for all practical purposes, an invalid for the last five years of his life. After his death in 1888, however, the Paulists quickly became integral to the growing Roman Catholic Church in America.

Hecker did not live to see one controversial ramification of his work. Shortly after his death, a memorial volume by Walter Elliott was translated into French and became the basis for an accusation that Hecker and his associates were preaching a set of "false" ideas, which came to be known as "Americanism." These ideas were officially condemned in a papal encyclical in 1899, though, due to the quick intercession of Hecker's associates, no one was accused of actually holding the ideas.

Sources:

Delaney, John J. *Dictionary of American Catholic Biography*. Garden City, NY: Doubleday & Company, 1988. 621 pp.
Elliott, Walter. *The Life of Father Hecker*. New York: Columbus Press, 1898. 428 pp.
McSorley, Joseph. *Isaac Hecker and His Friends*. New York: Paulist Press, 1962. 304 pp.
The Pulpit, the Press, and the Paulists. New York: The Paulists Fathers, 1957. 48 pp.

★401★
HEINDEL, Max
Founder, Rosicrucian Fellowship
b. Jul. 23, 1865, Germany
d. Jan. 6, 1919, Oceanside, California

Max Heindel, founder of the Rosicrucian Fellowship, was born Carl Louis von Grasshof, the eldest son in an aristocratic German family. At the age of 16 he went to Glasgow, Scotland, to study maritime engineering; he eventually became chief engineer on one of the Cunard oceanliners. In 1895, at the age of 30, he moved to New York City as a consulting engineer and married his first wife. Eight years later he moved to Los Angeles, where he was introduced to the occult. He joined the Theosophical Society in America, led by Katherine Tingley, and was vice-president of the Los Angeles branch in 1904 and 1905. He became interested enough in astrology to begin lecturing on it at various places along the west coast, though continuing heart trouble prevented his schedule from becoming too hectic.

In 1907 Heindel traveled to Germany, where a spiritual being, later identified as an Elder Brother of the Rosicrucian Order, appeared in his room and told him he had passed a test. Heindel was then led to the Temple of the Rosy Cross near the Germany-Bohemia border, where he remained for a month. There, he was given the information contained in his first book, *The Rosicrucian Cosmo-Conception*. While he was still editing this material, he returned to the United States, and in 1908, in Columbus, Ohio, he established the first center of what would become the Rosicrucian Fellowship.

Heindel's teachings are heavily theosophic, but differ in their greater emphasis on astrology, Christianity, Christian symbols, and a Rosicrucian heritage. His teachings also show the influence of **Rudolf Steiner**, with whom he may also have studied in Germany. Members must abstain from meat, tobacco, and alcohol. After the Ohio center was begun, Heindel quickly started other centers in Seattle, Washington; North Yakima, Washington; Portland, Oregon; and Los Angeles, California. In March, 1910, his heart trouble put him into a hospital, where an out-of-body experience showed him plans for future Rosicrucian work. In August 1910 he married Augusta Foss, a woman he had known since before his first wife's death in 1905. In 1911 part of his hospital vision was fulfilled when headquarters were established at Mt. Ecclesia near Oceanside, California, complete with a sanctuary, offices, a women's dormitory, cottages, and a vegetarian cafeteria.

Heindel's last years were very productive. He wrote several books and produced a regular column in his monthly magazine, *Rays from the Rosy Cross*. The Fellowship became a major force in the spread of astrology, and many astrologers not otherwise connected with the group make use of the annual *Ephemeris* (daily chart of planetary positions) and *Table of Houses*, both published at Oceanside. After Heindel's death in 1919, at the age of 54, his wife carried on the leadership duties of the Fellowship.

Sources:

Heindel, Max. *The Message of the Stars*. Oceanside, CA: Rosicrucian Fellowship, 1963. 723 pp.
_____. *The Rosicrucian Christianity Lectures*. Oceanside, CA: The Rosicrucian Fellowship, 1955. 374 pp.
_____. *The Rosicrucian Cosmo-Conception*. Seattle, WA: Rosicrucian Fellowship, 1909. 540 pp.
_____. *The Rosicrucian Mysteries*. Oceanside, CA: The Rosicrucian Fellowship, 1911. 198 pp.
_____. *The Rosicrucian Philosophy, Questions and Answers*. Oceanside, CA: Rosicrucian Fellowship, 1922. 418 pp.
_____. *Simplified Scientific Astrology*. Oceanside, CA: The Rosicrucian Fellowship, 1928. 198 pp.
McIntosh, Christopher. *The Rosy Cross Unveiled*. Wellingborough, UK: Aquarian Press, 1980. 160 pp.

—Gary L. Ward

★402★
HENDRIX, Eugene Russell
Bishop, Methodist Episcopal Church, South
b. May 17, 1847, Fayette, Missouri
d. Nov. 11, 1927, Kansas City, Missouri

Eugene Russell Hendrix, a bishop of the Methodist Episcopal Church, South, was the son of Isabel Jane Murray and Adam Hendrix. His parents sent him north to school as the Civil War was ending, and in 1867 he received his A.B. degree from Wesleyan University in Middletown, Connecticut. He obtained some seminary training at Union Theological Seminary in New York City but returned home in 1869 to join the St. Louis Conference of the Methodist Episcopal Church, South. His first appointment was to Leavenworth, Kansas. After a year he served at Macon, Missouri (1870-1871); Francis Street Methodist Episcopal Church, South in St. Louis (1872-1876); and Glascow, Missouri (1877-1878). His pastoral years were marked by his marriage to Annie E. Scarrett in 1872 and his accompanying Bishop Enoch Marvin on a round-the-world tour in 1876.

In 1878 Hendrix became president of Central College, a Methodist school at Fayette, Missouri. Eight years later he was elected bishop. During his 32 years in the active episcopacy, Hendrix became known for his work for church union. In 1908 he was named the first president of the newly formed Federal Council of Churches. He put in many hours in the effort to unite the Methodist Episcopal Church, South and the Methodist Episcopal Church. One of the main efforts in that regard was launched by a speech he gave as fraternal delegate to the 1916 general conference of the Methodist Episcopal Church. The negotiations carried on by the Commissions on Union in the 1920s were turned down but had the effect of highlighting the problems which the next set of negotiations would have to solve. The two churches were finally united in 1939.

As a bishop Hendrix was active throughout Southern Methodism. He worked for the development of the church in Mexico, South America, and the Orient. He authored a number of books including: *Skilled Labor for the Master* (1900); *The Religion of the Incarnation* (1903); *The Personality of the Holy Spirit* (1904); *Christ's Table Talk* (1908); and *If I Had Not Come* (1916). Hendrix continued to preside over annual conferences of the church into the 1920s.

In 1889 the Methodist Episcopal Church, South renamed the Central Collegiate Institute in Altus, Arkansas, to Hendrix College. In 1950 when the Federal Council of Churches was superseded by the National Council of Churches, the Hendrix family donated the gavel used by Bishop Hendrix in 1908 to the new council for use in its initial sessions.

Sources:

Harmon, Nolan B. *The Encyclopedia of World Methodism*. 2 vols. Nashville: United Methodist Publishing House, 1974.

Hendrix, Eugene R. *Christ's Table Talk*. Nashville, TN: Publishing House of the M. E. Church, South, 1908. 212 pp.
_____. *If I Had Not Come*. New York: Methodist Book Concern, 1916. 209 pp.
_____. *The Personality of the Holy Spirit*. Nashville, TN: Publishing House of the M. E. Church, South, 1904. 219 pp.
_____. *The Religion of the Incarnation*. Nashville, TN: Publishing House of the M. E. Church, South, 1903. 271 pp.
_____. *Skilled Labor for the Master*. Nashville, TN: Publishing House of the M. E. Church, South, 1900. 326 pp.
Holt, Ivan Lee. *Eugene Russell Hendrix*. Nashville, TN: Parthenon Press, 1950. 221 pp.

★ 403 ★
HENRY, Carl Ferdinand Howard
Theologian, American Baptist Churches in the U.S.A.
b. Jan. 22, 1913, New York, New York

Carl Ferdinand Howard Henry, a Baptist theologian who helped create the conservative Protestant theological position termed Neo-Evangelicalism, is the son of Johanna Vaethroeder and Karl F. E. Henry. He attended Wheaton College from which he received a B.A. (1938) and M.A. (1940). In 1940 he married Helga Bender and the following year finished his seminary work at Northern Baptist Theological Seminary. He was also ordained as a minister in what was then the Northern Baptist Convention (now the American Baptist Churches in the U.S.A.) in 1941.

In 1940 Henry became an assistant professor at Northern Baptist Theological Seminary and in that capacity saw his first book, *A Doorway to Heaven*, published in 1941. In 1942 he was named chairman of the department of philosophy of religion. During the years of World War II Henry participated with colleagues such as **Harold J. Ockenga** in the articulation of a new position for fundamentalism, which had become isolated from the major intellectual streams in American culture. In 1947 he moved to Pasadena, California, as a professor of theology and Christian philosophy at the newly opened Fuller Theological Seminary, over which Ockenga presided. In 1948 he published his first major book, *The Uneasy Conscience of Modern Fundamentalism*, in which he called conservative Protestants to re-enter the mainstream.

During his nine years at Fuller, Henry authored a number of books, many of which dealt with his opinion that Western culture was drifting into a non-Christian philosophical base and that fundamental Christianity was needed to address the social context. His volumes included *The Protestant Dilemma* (1949); *The Drift of Western Thought* (1951); and *Glimpses of a Sacred Land* (1953).

In 1956 Henry left Fuller to become the first editor of *Christianity Today*, a popular journal and the major periodical of Neo-Evangelicalism. Besides giving his editorial leadership to that journal over the next 12 years, Henry continued to write substantive books offering direction to the larger Christian community: *Evangelical Responsibility in Contemporary Theology* (1957); *Frontiers in Modern Theology* (1966); and *Evangelicals at the Brink of Crisis* (1967). He retired in 1968 but retained the title of editor-at-large.

During his retirement years Henry has remained active lecturing and writing. His most important product was a six-volume theological text, *God, Revelation and Authority: God Who Speaks and Shows* (1976-1983). Since 1974 he had been associated with World Vision as a lecturer-at-large. Continuing his interest in cultural drift, in the 1980s he authored *The Christian Mindset in a Secular Society* (1984) and *Christian Countermoves in a Decadent Culture* (1986). Most recently he has penned his autobiography, *Confessions of a Theologian: An Autobiography* (1986).

Sources:
Henry, Carl F. H. *Christian Countermoves in a Decadent Culture*. Portland, OR: Multimah, 1986. 149 pp.

_____. *Confessions of a Theologian: An Autobiography*. Waco, TX: Word Books, 1986. 416 pp.
_____. *Evangelicals at the Brink of Crisis*. Waco, TX: Word Books, 1967. 120 pp.
_____. *Frontiers in Modern Theology*. Chicago: Moody Press, 1966. 160 pp.
_____. *God, Revelation and Authority: God Who Speaks and Shows*. 6 vols. Waco, TX: Word Books, 1976-1983.
_____. *The Uneasy Conscience of Modern Fundamentalism*. Grand Rapids, MI: Eerdmans, 1948. 89 pp.

★ 404 ★
HENSLEY, George Went
Snake Handler and Founder, Church of God with Signs Following
d. Jul. 25, 1955, Lester's Shed, Florida

George Went Hensley introduced the practice of snake handling into Pentecostalism and became the leader of religious snake handling in the Appalachian region of the United States. Little is known about his early life, other than that he was probably born in the 1870s. He was converted and joined a Holiness church in 1908 at about the time when the modern Pentecostal movement (e.g. speaking in tongues) was spreading across the country. He began preaching in Owl Holler, near Cleveland, Tennessee, on the subject of Mark 16:17-18 and the signs marking believers. Some hecklers turned a box of poisonous snakes loose in front of him while he was preaching, but he surprised everyone by picking up some of the snakes and continuing to preach.

This incident began Hensley's career. **A. J. Tomlinson**, a leader of the Church of God (Cleveland, Tennessee), was very impressed with this display of faith. He brought Hensley to Cleveland to introduce the practice throughout the church. About 1914 Hensley founded a church near Sale Creek in Grasshopper Valley and almost 10 years went by without any problem with the snakes. Finally, however, a member, Garland Defries, was bitten and remained in serious condition for several weeks before recovering. Enthusiasm for Hensley's ministry declined, and he moved to Pine Mountain, Kentucky, where he led the East Pineville Church of God. The ministry was further restricted in 1928 when the Church of God General Assembly, dealing with both theological and public relations issues, denounced the practice of snake handling.

Hensley continued in his snake handling ministry, which was hurt by the Church of God pronouncement, but which was still carried on by a number of independent churches from West Virginia to Florida. In the 1940s Hensley moved to pastor a church in Brightsville, Tennessee. In 1945 he was arrested and fined $50 for handling snakes in front of a member's home and disturbing the peace. In 1948 Hensley became the assistant pastor of a new church, the South Chattanooga Church of God, a position which allowed him time to concentrate on his traveling ministry, supporting the various snake handling churches. He claimed to have been bitten several hundred times during his career. On July 24, 1955, Hensley was bitten by a diamond-head rattlesnake, in a service at Lester's Shed, near Altha, Florida. He died the following day.

Sources:
Collins, J. B. *Tennessee Snake Handlers*. Chattanooga, TN: The Author, [1946]. 36 pp.
La Barre, Weston. *They Shall Take Up Serpents*. Minneapolis, MN: University of Minnesota Press, 1962. 208 pp.
Melton, J. Gordon. *Biographical Dictionary of American Cult and Sect Leaders*. Garland Reference Library of Social Science, vol. 212. New York: Garland Publishing, 1986.
Tomlinson, A. J. *Diary of A. J. Tomlinson, Volume I*. Queens Village, NY: Church of God, World Headquarters, 1949. 267 pp.

—*Gary L. Ward*

★405★
HERRON, George Davis
Socialist and Minister, Congregational Church
b. Jan. 21, 1862, Montezuma, Indiana
d. Oct. 9, 1925, Munich Germany

George Davis Herron, a social gospel advocate who eventually left the ministry for socialism, was the son of William and Isabella Davis Herron. He grew up with a strong conviction concerning a coming kingdom of God, a belief which dominated his ministry and in a secularized form his later years as a socialist. His formal education was limited to three years at Ripon College in Wisconsin (1879-1882). In 1883 he married Mary Everhard and became a minister in the Congregational Church.

Herron served several parishes in the Midwest, but first became known in 1891 as the result of a talk given before the annual meeting of the Minneapolis State Association of Congregational Ministers. Herron, then pastor of First Congregational Church in Lake City, Minnesota, spoke on Christian business ethics under the title "The Message of Jesus to Men of Wealth." The presentation led to his call to the pastorate of First Congregational Church in Burlington, Iowa. That year he also authored his first book, *The Larger Christ*, to be followed by *The Call of the Cross* and *A Plea for the Gospel* in 1892. In 1893 Mrs. E. D. Rand, a member of the church, gave money to Iowa College (now Grinell College) to fund a chair in applied Christianity which was offered to Herron. He stayed at Iowa for six years and became the center of controversy for his increasingly radical statements. While there he wrote three more books, *The Christian State* (1895); *Social Meanings of Religious Experience* (1896); and *Between Caesar and Jesus* (1899).

He left the school in 1899 and moved his work to the Socialist Party, in which he placed great hope, as described in his next book, *Why I Am a Socialist* (1900). He attempted to organize a social crusade within it. As his work proceeded, his wife divorced him, and he married Carrie Rand, the daughter of his financial backer. As a result of the events surrounding the divorce, he was deposed from the ministry. He increasingly became alienated from Christianity, which he had come to feel was not adequate for the far-reaching social changes he believed were needed. In 1914 his wife died and he soon married Friede B. Schoeberle.

As was the case with many socialists, Herron was forced to make significant ideological adjustments during World War I. As the war proceeded, Herron became both anti-German and anti-Marxist, and developed an image of the United States as a unique nation which had gone to war for humanitarian purposes, a view which dominated his 1918 volume, *Germanism and the American Crusade*. In spite of his anti-German feelings, he had hoped President Wilson would be able to keep the allies from punishing Germany after the war. He took part in some of the peace negotiations, but lost face when the harsh terms of the peace were made known.

With all of his previous hopes for a new just social order dashed, in the 1920s he turned to Italy, and became one of a handful of English-speaking leaders to place their hope in the Italian future. He saw it as having the possibility of building the most Christ-like society the world had ever seen. He died before the worst of the Mussolini era became evident.

Sources:
Dictionary of American Biography. 20 vols. and 7 supps. New York: Charles Scribner's Sons, 1928-1936, 1944-1981.
Herron, George Davis. *Between Ceasar and Jesus.* New York: T. Y. Crowell & Co., 1899. 278 pp.
_____. *The Christian State.* New York: T. Y. Crowell, 1895. 216 pp.
_____. *The Larger Christ.* New York: Fleming H. Revell, 1891. 122 pp.
_____. *A Plea for the Gospel.* New York: T. Y. Crowell & Co., 1892. 237 pp.
_____. *Social Meanings of Religious Experience.* New York; T. Y. Crowell & Co., 1896. 237 pp.
_____. *Why I Am a Socialist.* Chicago: C. H. Kerr, 1900. 32 pp.

★406★
HESBURGH, Theodore Martin
Roman Catholic Priest
President, University of Notre Dame
b. May 25, 1917, Syracuse, New York

Theodore Martin Hesburgh, as president of the University of Notre Dame, became a national figure because of his work with the federal government, ecumenicism, and philanthropy. Over the course of his presidency, the University of Notre Dame became one of the country's top universities.

The son of Theodore Bernard Hesburgh and Anne Marie Murphy Hesburgh, he is of German and Irish descent. He was educated in Catholic schools in Syracuse, New York, and at the Holy Cross minor seminary at Notre Dame. He took his monastic vows with the Congregation of the Holy Cross. He then attended the Gregorian University in Rome (B.A. 1937) and studied theology for two years at the Holy Cross Seminary in Washington, D.C., before being ordained a priest on June 24, 1943. He received his doctorate in theology in 1945 from the Catholic University of America in Washington, D.C.

Hesburgh was assigned by his order to Notre Dame as a chaplain and religion teacher. He became head of the department of religion in 1948, executive vice-president of the university in 1949, and president in 1952. An active and innovative administrator, he eliminated the majority of rules which attempted to regulate the personal lives of students, and began vigorously to build Notre Dame into a major university. In 1967 the university was reorganized so that control passed from exclusively clerical hands to a predominantly lay board of trustees. Hesburgh came to national attention in 1969 when he issued an ultimatum to student protesters that anyone substituting force for rational persuasion would be dismissed from the university. Following this confrontation, Hesburgh manifested a growing opposition to the Vietnam War, and, using his position as president of Notre Dame, spoke increasingly against the federal administration's pursuit of the war.

Hesburgh extended his influence through his work with a number of prominent organizations. He has, for example, been a member of the National Science Foundation; chairman of the board of trustees of the Rockefeller Foundation; a member of the Carnegie Commission on the Future of Higher Education; a trustee of the Carnegie Foundation for the Advancement of Teaching, the Woodrow Wilson National Fellowship Foundation, the Institute of International Education, the Nutrition Foundation, and the United Negro College Fund; and a director of the American Council on Education, the Freedoms Foundation, the Valley Forge Foundation, and the Adlai Stevenson Institute for International Affairs. He also has served on the United States Commission on Civil Rights, as chairman of the Overseas Development Council, and as chairman of the Select Commission on Immigration and Refugee Policy. His publications include *Patterns for Educational Growth* (1958); *Thoughts for Our Times* (1962); *The Humane Imperative* (1974); and *U.S. Self-Interest and International Moral Imperatives* (1974).

Sources:
Hesburgh, Theodore M. *The Humane Imperative.* New Haven, CT: Yale University Press, 1974. 115 pp.
_____. *Patterns for Educational Growth.* Notre Dame, IN: University of Notre Dame Press, 1958. 71 pp.
_____. *Theodore M. Hesburgh: A Bio-Biography.* Compiled by Charlotte A. Ames. Westport, CT: Greenwood Press, 1989. 280 pp.
_____. *The Theology of Catholic Action.* Notre Dame, IN: Ave Maria Press, 1946. 199 pp.

_____. *Thoughts for Our Times.* Notre Dame, IN: University of Notre Dame Press, 1962. 58 pp.
_____. *U.S. Self-Interest and International Moral Imperatives.* Santa Barbara, CA: Center for the Study of Democratic Institutions, 1974. Phonograph record.

★ 407 ★
HESCHEL, Abraham Joshua
Jewish Theologian
Founder, Institute of Jewish Learning in London
b. 1907, Warsaw Poland
d. Dec. 23, 1972, New York, New York

Abraham Joshua Heschel, a Jewish theologian, was the son of Reisel Perlow and Moshe Mordecai Hershel. He received his Ph.D. from the University of Berlin in 1933 and continued his studies at the Hichschule fuer die Wissenschaft des Judentums, from which he graduated in 1934. In 1937 he became a lecturer at the Mittelstelle fuer Juedische Erwachsen-enbildung in Frankfurt, Germany, and the next year joined the faculty at the Institute for Jewish Studies in Warsaw. His career on the continent came to an end with the beginning of World War II, and he escaped to England where in 1940 he founded the Institute of Jewish Learning in London. However, before the year was out he migrated to America where he became an instructor in Hebrew Union College in Cincinnati, Ohio, the primary institution of Reform Judaism.

In 1943 Heschel found a more compatible home at the Jewish Theological Seminary of America in New York City, the school most closely associated with Conservative Judaism. Beginning as a professor of Jewish philosophy and rabbinics, in 1945 he was named professor of Jewish ethics and mysticism, a position he retained for the rest of his life. That same year he married Sylvia Straus.

While Heschel had written several books during the years of his teaching career, he began to make a significant impact with the publication of *The Earth Is the Lord's: The Inner World of the Jew in Eastern Europe* (1950). It was followed by *Man's Quest for God: Studies in Prayer and Symbolism* (1954); *God in Search of Man: A Philosophy of Judaism* (1955); *Sacred Images of Man* (1958); and *Between God and Man: An Interpretation of Judaism* (1959). The work of this decade established him as one of the most important Jewish thinkers of the century. Not readily classified, his perspective mixed his own Hassidic heritage from Eastern Europe with modern scholarship and philosophy. He was called by some a Neo-hassidic.

During the 1960s Heschel's literary output continued with *Who Is Man?* (1965); *The Insecurity of Freedom* (1966); and *Israel: An Echo of Eternity* (1969), among other titles. His last book, *A Passion for Truth* appeared in 1973. A selection from his writings, *The Wisdom of Heschel,* was published posthumously in 1975, and a number of his volumes have been translated into other languages.

At the height of his career (1965-1966), Heschel was invited to spend a year at Union Theological Seminary as the Harry Emerson Fosdick Visiting Professor. He was the first Jewish scholar to receive a faculty appointment from Union.

Sources:
Heschel, Abraham Joshua. *Between God and Man: An Interpretation of Judaism.* New York: Harper, 1959.
_____. *God's Search for Man: A Philosophy of Judaism.* New York: Farrar, Straus, 1955.
_____. *Man's Quest for God: Studies in Prayer and Symbolism.* New York: Charles Scribner's Sons, 1954.
_____. *The Wisdom of Heschel.* New York: Farrar, Straus, 1975.
_____. *Who Is Man?* Palo Alto, CA: Stanford University Press, 1965.

★ 408 ★
HICKEY, James Aloysius
Cardinal, Roman Catholic Church
b. Oct. 11, 1920, Midland, Michigan

James Aloysius Hickey, archbishop of Washington, D.C., and a cardinal in the Roman Catholic Church, is the son of Agnes Ryan and James Hickey. Raised in Michigan, he attended Sacred Heart Seminary in Detroit. He graduated in 1942 (B.A.) and moved on to Catholic University of America in Washington, D.C., where he completed his S.T.L. in 1946. That same year he was ordained as a priest and began work in Saginaw, Michigan, where he established an apostolate among Mexican immigrants. He then continued his post-graduate studies in Rome at the Lateran University, from which he earned a doctorate in canon law (J.C.D.) in 1950. He completed a second doctorate in sacred theology (S.T.D.) the following year at Angelicum University.

Hickey returned to Michigan in 1951 and became secretary to Bishop Woznicki of the Diocese of Saginaw. In 1957 he was assigned the task of organizing St. Paul, the diocesan seminary; when it opened three years later, he was named rector. In 1962 his skills in canon law and theology were used at the Vatican Council, where he served as peritus. In 1963 he was named a domestic prelate with the title monsignor.

In 1967 Hickey was named auxiliary bishop of Saginaw and titular bishop of Tarqua. Two years later he was transferred to Rome as rector of the North American College, at which post he served with distinction for five years. He returned to the United States in 1974 as the new bishop of Cleveland (Ohio). During his tenure in Cleveland he was named by the National Conference of Catholic Bishops as chair of their committee on Pastoral Research and Practice. He was in Cleveland for only six years when he was named archbishop of Washington, D.C., and chancellor of Catholic University of America. He succeeded William Baum, who had been called to Rome.

Since his move to Washington, Hickey has served as chairman of the board of trustees of the National Shrine of the Immaculate Conception (1980-present) and chairman of the Bishop's Committee on Human Values (1984-1987). He was elevated to the rank of cardinal in 1988. That same year he assumed duties as chairman of the Bishop's Committee on the North American College and chairman of the North American College Board of Directors.

Sources:
The American Catholic Who's Who. Washington, D.C.: National Catholic News Service, (1979).
Biography Index. New York: The H. W. Wilson Co.
Who's Who in America. Wilmette, IL: Marquis Who's Who, Inc.
Who's Who in the Midwest. Wilmette, IL: Marquis Who's Who, Inc.

★ 409 ★
HILLIS, Newell Dwight
Minister, Congregational Church
b. Sep. 2, 1858, Magnolia, Iowa
d. Feb. 25, 1929, Bronxville, New York

Newell Dwight Hillis, a minister in the Congregational Church, was the son of Margaret Hester and Samuel Ewing Hillis. He was raised on a farm in Nebraska. His meager education was supplemented by reading, and at the age of 17 he accepted a position with the American Sunday School Union, organizing Sunday schools and churches in the West. He is credited with establishing the first Sunday school in the state of Wyoming. It met in a saloon. As a young man he was finally able to enter Lake Forest College, Lake Forest, Illinois, and after his graduation in 1884 attended McCormick Theological Seminary in Chicago. Upon completion of his theological degree in 1887, he married Annie Louise Patrick, was ordained by the Presbyterian Church, and accepted the call to the pastorate of First Presbyterian Church in Peoria, Illinois.

Hillis' career blossomed and in 1890 he became pastor of the First Presbyterian Church in Evanston, Illinois. He was there for only five years before he accepted the invitation to succeed **David Swing** as the minister at Central Church, the independent congregation established by Swing's followers when he left the Presbyterian Church rather than face further charges of heresy. Hillis gained a national reputation as a speaker while at Central Church and in 1896 issued his first book, *A Man's Value to Society*. It was quickly followed by *The Investment of Influence* (1898) and *Great Books as Life-Teachers* (1899).

That Hillis had emerged as one of the most influential liberal Protestant ministers in America was amply demonstrated in 1899 by his call to Plymouth Congregational Church in Brooklyn, New York, the pulpit formerly held by **Henry Ward Beecher** and **Lyman Abbott**. The congregation had experienced some bad times in an aging section of the city, and Hillis brought it back to life. He was an eloquent speaker, and his sermons were reprinted each week in the *Brooklyn Eagle*. He led in the renovation of the building, which included the placement of a set of stained-glass windows depicting events in the history of freedom. These became the center of a city beautification campaign. During his early years at Plymouth, he also authored three more books: *The Influence of Christ in Modern Life* (1901); *Building a Working Faith* (1903); and *The Quest of John Chapman* (1904).

During World War I he emerged as one of the strongest voices backing America's early participation in the Allied cause. He backed the Liberty Loan program, and his tours raised hundreds of millions of dollars for the war effort.

Hillis was forced to retire in 1924 after suffering a cerebral hemorrhage. He survived the event and, after some months of recuperation, was again able to preach occasionally and to complete a book on the life of Christ. He published more than 25 books that were widely read in the early twentieth century, but are today remembered more as artifacts of the era than for any lasting contribution to religious life.

Sources:
Dictionary of American Biography. 20 vols. and 7 supps. New York: Charles Scribner's Sons, 1928-1936, 1944-1981.
Hillis, Newell Dwight. *Great Books as Life-Teachers*. Chicago: Fleming H. Revell, 1899, 1906. 339 pp.
_____. *Great Men as Prophets of a New Era*. New York: Fleming H. Revell Company, 1922. 221 pp.
_____. *The Influence of Christ in Modern Life*. New York: Macmillan Company, 1901. 416 pp.
_____. *The Investment of Influence*. New York: Fleming H. Revell Company, 1899. 299 pp.
_____. *Studies in the Great War*. New York: Fleming H. Revell Company, 1915. 272 pp.

★410★
HINES, John Elbridge
Presiding Bishop, Episcopal Church
b. Oct. 3, 1910, Seneca, South Carolina

John Elbridge Hines, a former presiding bishop of the Episcopal Church, was the son of Edgar Alphonso and Mary Woodbury Moore Hines. His father, a rural physician, was a Presbyterian, but his mother was a devout Episcopalian. There were nine children, of which five became Episcopalians and four Presbyterians. Intending to be a doctor, Hines enrolled in the pre-medical course at the University of the South in Sewanee, Tennessee. He graduated in 1930 but instead of going to medical school decided to go into the ministry and entered the Protestant Episcopal Seminary in Alexandria, Virginia. In 1933, while still a seminarian, he was ordained a deacon. He graduated in 1934.

There being no job openings in South Carolina, he moved to St. Louis to become a curate at Sts. Michael and George Episcopal Church. He was ordained a priest in the Diocese of Missouri. In 1935 he married Helen Louise Orwig. He later served successively as rector of Trinity Church in Hannibal, Missouri, (1935-1937); St. Paul's Church in Augusta, Georgia, (1937-1941); and Christ Church in Houston, Texas (1941-1945). It was from his position as rector at Christ Church that in 1945 he was elected bishop coadjutor. In 1955 he became bishop of Texas.

In 1964 Presiding Bishop Arthur Litchtenberger retired early (his tenure was to last to 1970) due to ill health. The triennial convention of the church meeting in St. Louis elected Hines as his successor. He came into the office in the midst of the racial turmoil in the southern United States where the church had a significant proportion of its members. He responded to his election by citing race relations as the crucial issue facing the church at that moment in time. He saw the church through the remaining years of intense racial turmoil only to begin work on two other crucial issues—revision of the prayer book, the major Episcopal liturgical document, and the ordination of women, the more explosive of the two issues. Hines was not a radical on either issue, but promoted both issues.

Hines submitted his decision to retire to the church's convention in 1973, six years short of the mandatory end of his term in office. He was succeeded by **John Maury Allin** who took office in 1974.

Sources:
McCahill, Dolores. "Episcopal Church Elects Texan as Presiding Bishop." *Chicago Sun-Times* (October 18, 1964).

★411★
HINN, Benny
Televangelist and Pastor, Orlando Christian Center
b. Dec. 3, 1952, Jaffa Israel

Benedictus (Benny) Hinn, popular Pentecostal healing evangelist and pastor of the independent Orlando Christian Center in Orlando, Florida, was born in Israel. His Greek father, Constandi Hinn was for a number of years the mayor of Jaffa. His mother, Clemence Hinn, was an Armenian Christian who named him after Patriarch Benedictus of the Greek Orthodox Church who christened him as a baby. As a child Hinn attended a Roman Catholic school in Jaffa.

Hinn's first significant religious experience was as a youth of 11 when Jesus appeared to him in a vision. This occurred just a short time before the family moved to Toronto, Ontario, where Hinn had a relatively normal youth and public school education. Then, a series of events which began in 1972, with a second vision of Jesus in a dream and a born again experience which included a feeling of being cleansed from sin led him into the ministry. Hinn connected with a group of Pentecostal students and began to attend charismatic services at a local Anglican church. In 1973 he attended a healing service led by healer **Kathryn Kuhlman** in Pittsburgh, Pennsylvania. During the service he felt the presence of the Holy Spirit. He had also felt a call to the ministry but had resisted because of a stuttering problem. In 1974 he was healed of the stuttering and the following year, in spite of the opposition of his parents, began to preach regularly in Toronto.

As was characteristic of the Kuhlman's meetings, spontaneous healings began to occur in Hinn's meetings. These events brought him some media coverage and led to a weekly television show that was broadcast on Sunday evenings. He also began to travel across the continent holding healing and evangelistic services. He met his wife, Suzanne Harthern, the daughter of an Assemblies of God minister in 1978, and they were married the following year.

Hinn made Toronto his headquarters until 1983 when he moved to Orlando, Florida, and founded the Orlando Christian Center, an independent Pentecostal congregation. As the center grew, he developed a new weekly television show and soon became one of the best known of the contemporary healing evangelists. His services follow the pattern which people had come to know from the Kuhlman's meetings. Rather than laying hands upon people and praying for their healing, Hinn waits for people who feel that they have been healed during the services he leads and invites them forward to testify of their newly found health. He will then bless them frequently, and they will fall backward under the influence of the Holy Spirit, an experience termed "slaying in the Spirit" within Pentecostal circles. Besides his work in the large congregation in Orlando, Hinn continues to travel widely with his healing message.

Sources:

Hinn, Benny. *God's Anointing for You.*
_____. *Good Morning Holy Spirit.* Nashville, TN: Thomas Nelson, 1990. 177 pp.
_____. *War in the Heavenlies.*

★412★
HOBBS, Herschel
Minister, Southern Baptist Convention
President, Southern Baptist Convention
b. Oct. 24, 1907, Talladega Springs, Alabama

Herschel Hobbs, a leading minister and former president of the Southern Baptist Convention, is the son of a farmer who passed away when Hobbs was only two years old. Much of his youth was spent working on the family farm or at various jobs in Talladega Springs. He experienced a conversion to Christianity at the age of 12 and was baptized in the Baptist church at Montevallo, Alabama. When he was 13, the family moved to Birmingham, Alabama. He was more inclined to earning a wage than obtaining an education, and only under the persistent urging of his mother did Hobbs finish high school. He settled down with a job at a car dealership and married Frances Jackson. Though active in a local church, he found his life pulled between some rather worldly friends and his Christian commitment, which his wife shared. Gradually he became more and more active in the church and finally decided to go into the ministry. He was ordained in 1929 at Ensley Baptist Church in Birmingham.

Hobbs entered Howard College (now Sanford University) in Birmingham and finished the course of study in two and a half years. In 1932 he entered Southern Baptist Theological Seminary and earned both a Th.M. and Ph.D. (1938) with a concentration in New Testament studies. He then became pastor of Calvary Heights Baptist Church in Fountain Heights, Alabama (1938-1939), the first of several pastorates he served in Alabama and Louisiana over the next few years. He was at Dauphin Way Baptist Church in Mobile, Alabama, in 1949 when he was called to First Baptist Church in Oklahoma City, Oklahoma. He would stay in Oklahoma City for the next 24 years.

While at Oklahoma City, Hobbs, an excellent orator, became known both for his learning and for his folksy, winsome pulpit style. He was invited to serve on a number of the church's boards and agencies and was elected president of the General Convention of Oklahoma. In 1961 he was elected president of the Southern Baptist Convention, a position he served for two years. It was during his presidency that the task for which he is most remembered, his contributions to the "Baptist Faith and Message", was thrust upon him.

In 1962 the Southern Baptist Convention was upset by the publication of Ralph Elliott's *The Message of Genesis* by the convention's own Broadman Press. Elliott, a professor at Midwestern Theological Seminary, had questioned the literal truth of some of the account in the biblical book of Genesis and was eventually forced to resign. The controversy erupted as the convention was considering the wording of a revised text of the "Baptist Faith and

Message," a doctrinal statement first issued in 1925. In the controversy Hobbs emerged as the important voice on the committee. He suggested a number of changes in words and phrases and wrote most of the introduction to the new statement. He championed the position that Baptists held a doctrinal position based solidly upon their reading of the Bible, but that any given statement should not be turned into a creed that could be used to test whether any individual was a true Baptist.

During his long career Hobbs authored over 100 books, many expositions of New Testament books, and has continued to be active in convention affairs in the several decades since his retirement in 1973.

Sources:

Garrison, Greg. "Herschel Hobbs: Baptist Ship Won't Capsize, he says." *Birmingham News* (June 16, 1989).
Hobbs, Herschel. *Fundamentals of Our Faith.* Nashville, TN: Broadman Press, 1960.
_____. *Messages on the Resurrection.* Grand Rapids, MI: Baker Book House, 1959.
_____. *New Testament Evangelism.* Nashville, TN: Convention Press, 1961.
_____. *What Baptists Believe.* Nashville, TN: Broadman Press, 1964.
_____. *You Are Chosen: The Priesthood of All Believers.* San Francisco: Harper and Row, 1990.

★413★
HODUR, Francis
Prime Bishop, Polish National Catholic Church
b. Apr. 1, 1866, Zarki Poland
d. Feb. 16, 1953, Scranton, Pennsylvania

Francis Hodur, the founder and first Prime Bishop of the Polish National Catholic Church (PNCC), was born the son of a Polish farmer. After attending grade school locally, he went to high school in Cracow. Graduating in 1889, he studied at the Roman Catholic seminary at Cracow. He did not finish his studies; he was expelled in 1893 because the ruling Austrian government viewed his nationalist-Polish political activities, which were inspired by radical priest Stanislaus Stojalowski, with disfavor. He immigrated to the United States, where he was befriended by Father Dean Benvenuto Gramlewicz, who assisted his entrance into St. Vincent Seminary in Beatty, Pennsylvania. Hodur passed his examinations after a few months of intensive study and was ordained before the end of the year. He was assigned first to Sacred Heart of Jesus Church in South Scranton, Pennsylvania, and then to the Slovak Roman Catholic Church in Scranton. He was eventually assigned to the Holy Trinity parish in Nanticoke, Pennsylvania.

During his years at Nanticoke, Hodur became known as a supporter of Polish enterprises in America, and he began to counsel and support the parishioners of the new St. Stanislaus parish in Scranton, who were struggling with a young and hostile Irish bishop. In March 1897, the parishioners asked Hodur to be their pastor. He accepted their offer, and the next day was suspended from the exercise of his priestly functions by the bishop. In response, the church organized and adopted a constitution. Hodur started a weekly periodical, *Straz* (The Guard) in April and consecrated the church in July. In so doing he was enunciating his belief that Polish parishes in America should belong to the Polish immigrants, not to foreign-born bishops.

The movement in the St. Stanislaus parish set off a chain reaction and soon other Polish communities were forming independent parishes. At the beginning of 1898, Hodur left for Rome to present the case before Pope Leo XIII. Leaving his petition in Rome, he returned to America, where he was excommunicated in September. For several years he hoped and worked for a solution to the problems. Finding no support in Rome, however, he made a final break with the Roman Catholic Church in December 1900. The move to form an independent Polish National Catholic Church had begun. At the Christmas Eve mass, Hodur introduced a liturgy in Polish, which gave an even more distinctive flavor to the new church and its sister congregations. Hodur also denied the infallibility of the Pope.

In 1904 Hodur called the first synod of the Polish National Catholic Church, at which he was elected bishop. He was not consecrated, however, until September 29, 1907, when he was able to get the support of the Old Catholic bishops in Holland. The work of Bishop Hodur's life was that of building the American church. He immediately founded the Savonarola Theological Seminary to train future priests. In 1908 a major step was taken with the founding of the Polish National Union of America, a church-wide insurance company which quickly began to serve social and humanitarian needs in general. He also edited the church periodical, *Rola Boza* (God's Field) for many years.

Hodur also turned his attention to his homeland, visiting it in 1907, 1911, and 1914. Following World War I, when the church formally decided to extend its work to Poland, Hodur visited Poland again and initiated activity to establish the church there. A church was formed, though it was not recognized by the government. In 1928 he traveled to Poland for the first general synod of the missionary diocese. The church was decimated by World War II, but revived quickly and was legalized in 1946.

During the 1940s, Hodur's health began to fail. He went blind in 1945. In 1949, at the age of 83, he began the process of retirement, and the church chose Bishop **Leon Grochowski** to succeed him.

Sources:

The Growth of a Church. Scranton, PA: Straz Printery, 1965. 130 pp.
The Origin and Growth of the Polish National Catholic Church. Scranton, PA: Polish National Catholic Church, 1974. 239 pp.

★414★
HOFFMAN, Emil
President, Canada Synod, General Council of the Lutheran Church in America
b. Mar. 1, 1866, Oebisfelde Germany
d. Apr. 11, 1926, Waterloo, Ontario, Canada

Emil Hoffman, for 17 years the president of the Evangelical Lutheran Synod of Canada, was raised in Saxony and attended the University at Halle and the Ebenezer Theological Seminary at Kropp, a school established in 1882 in Schleswig-Holstein especially for preparing German-speaking pastors for North America. He graduated in 1886 and migrated to Ontario, where he became the minister of the North Easthope-Wellesley-St. Paul's parish. In 1888 he moved to St. Paul's Lutheran Church in Hamilton, Ontario, where he was to have a long and fruitful pastorate. While there, in 1896, Hoffman was first elected to the presidency of the predominantly German-speaking Evangelical Lutheran Synod. During his initial term in office, the synod saw fit to acknowledge the growth of English-speaking work and in 1896 formed the English district of the synod.

Hoffman's first tenure as president lasted for three years. In 1902 he was again elected to the presidency and served in that office for the next five years. During the term he moved to Kitchener to become pastor of St. Matthew's Lutheran Church. Meanwhile the English work continued to progress and in 1908 was finally set apart from the German-speaking work. After a two year rest (1907-1908), Hoffman began a third term in 1909 as president of the synod. This term was marked by the founding of the Waterloo Seminary. Originally proposed by the English-speaking brethren, in 1910 the two Canadian synods began a process for locating a site and building the proposed school. Hoffman led the delegation of the synod for this project. The seminary was dedicated in 1911.

In 1912 Hoffman became pastor of First Lutheran Church in Toronto. He continued active oversight of the new seminary and of the new high school (called Waterloo College) founded in 1914. That same year he was named president of the schools' board of governors. The beginning of World War I placed tremendous pressure on German-speaking people in North America to hasten their transition to the use of English. Assisting this process was the proposed merger of several branches of American Lutheranism, including the General Council (with which the two Canada Synods were affiliated) to form the United Lutheran Church in America in 1918. Hoffman worked for the larger union among the Canadian churches.

In 1920 Hoffman was called as president of both the Waterloo schools, a position he held for the rest of his life. While a capable administrator and teacher, his last years are best remembered for his efforts on behalf of the union of the two Canadian synods, which was finally accomplished in 1925. That same year he was appointed to represent his Canadian colleagues as a delegate to the World Lutheran Conference which met in Eisanach, Germany.

Sources:

Cronmiller, Carl R. *A History of the Lutheran Church in Canada.* N.p.: Canadian Lutheran Synod of Canada, 1961. 288 pp.

★415★
HOGUE, Wilson Thomas
Bishop, Free Methodist Church
b. Mar. 6, 1852, Lyndon, New York
d. Feb. 13, 1920, Springfield, Illinois

Wilson Thomas Hogue, a bishop in the Free Methodist Church, was the son of Thomas Hogg (later changed to Hogue), a first-generation immigrant from Scotland, and Sarah Carpenter Hogue. Both parents had converted to Methodism and joined the Methodist Episcopal Church, but ran into church conflicts when they attended a camp meeting sponsored by the Free Methodists, a group which broke with the Methodist Episcopal Church at the time of the Civil War. Leaving the Methodist Episcopal Church, they became staunch Free Methodists. Young Wilson had an initial saving experience of God when he was nine years old. Two years later he experienced a call to preach but would not accept it until he was 16. He was licensed to preach when 19 and soon afterward experienced the sanctifying experience which Free Methodists, in common with other holiness Christians, believe makes one perfect in love. Hogue joined the Genesee Conference in 1873, was ordained a deacon in 1875 and an elder in 1877. Beginning in 1873, he served a succession of pastorates in the Genesee Conference and as presiding elder on the Genesee and Buffalo districts. In 1874 he married Emma L. Jones.

During his years in the pastorate, Hogue had developed a dream of a Free Methodist college, and eventually, such a college was made possible by the gift of a Methodist in Illinois. In 1892 Hogue was called to be president of the new school, Greenville College at Greenville, Illinois. Hogue had developed the ideal of teaching culture based upon reverence for God and the biblical principles of righteousness. He presided over the growing school for 12 years, resigning only after his election as bishop in 1903. During his time as president he also had served as an interim bishop (1893-1894) and from 1894 as editor of the *Free Methodist*. For several years he took yet another task of editing the Sunday school material. His first book was written in 1887. *Hogue's Homiletics and Pastoral Theology* became a necessary volume for the young ministers. While serving in these capacities, Hogue, with no formal education when assuming leadership of the college, went back to school and proceeded through the program at Illinois Wesleyan University and successively received his Ph.B. (1897), A.M. (1899), and Ph.D. (1902)

As bishop, Hogue's greatest accomplishment was the expansion of the publishing program of the church. He began a missionary supplement in the *Free Methodist* which was taken over by the Women's Missionary Society and became *The Missionary Tidings*. He lobbied for a central publishing house which was finally established in Chicago in 1907. He wrote several books including a biography of C. Harry Agnew, a missionary in Africa, and a study of church hymns, *Hymns That Are Immortal* (1906). Unfortunately, just as the publishing venture seemed to be established, in 1908 Hogue had a stroke which forced him to retire from the work for two years. His illness also led to the ceasing of *The Earnest Christian*, a periodical originally started and edited by church founder, **Benjamin T. Roberts**. Hogue had become the editor after Roberts' death.

Never fully recovering, he struggled to complete the next goal he had set, the writing of the *History of the Free Methodist Church*. This two volume work was finally completed in 1918. In September 1918 he collapsed while on his way to the Kentucky and Tennessee Conference meeting, and his health failed from that time until his death from pneumonia at his home in 1920.

Sources:

Blews, Richard R. *Master Workmen*. Winona Lake, IN: Light and Life Press, 1960. 303 pp.

Harmon, Nolan B. *The Encyclopedia of World Methodism*. 2 vols. Nashville: United Methodist Publishing House, 1974.

Hogue, Wilson Thomas. *G. Harry Agnew, Pioneer Missionary*. Chicago: Free Methodist Publishing House, 1905. 317 pp.

_____. *A Handbook of Homiletics and Pastoral Theology*. Chicago: T. B. Arnold, 1887. 399 pp.

_____. *History of the Free Methodist Church of North America*. Chicago: The Free Methodist Publishing House, 1918. 2 vols.

_____. *The Holy Spirit: A Study*. Chicago: W. B. Rose, 1916. 408 pp.

_____. *Hymns That Are Immortal*. Chicago: S. K. J. Chesbro, 1906. 326 pp.

★416★
HOLDEMAN, John
Founder, Church of God in Christ, Mennonite
b. Jan. 31, 1832, New Pittsburg, Ohio
d. Mar. 10, 1900, Galva, Kansas

John Holdeman was the founder of the Church of God in Christ, Mennonite. He grew up among Mennonites in rural Ohio. He was initially converted at age twelve, but that did not prevent rather untamed youthful years. He was married to Elizabeth Ritter in 1852, at age 20, with their first child born five months after the ceremony. The scandal surrounding this event caused him to re-evaluate his years of "wicked sinfulness," and in 1853 he experienced divine forgiveness and a call to the ministry. He was baptized and retreated into a six-year period of studying the Bible, Mennonite history, and languages.

In 1859 Holdeman began to travel and preach, with a message that the church was allowing too many unconverted members, was not sufficiently ostracizing the excommunicated, and was generally too worldly. While his views were not unpopular, few outside of his own family decided to join him in this reformation. He wrote several books to spread his views during this time, such as *The Old Ground and Foundation* (1863), *Taken from the Word of God* (German edition, 1862; English edition, 1863), and *Eine Vertheidigung gegen die Verfaelscher unserer Schriften* (1865). His first big success came in McPherson County, Kansas, where he converted many of the Russian General Conference Mennonites. He had similar success in Manitoba, Canada, where he converted the bishop and about half the membership of the Kleine Gemeinde, another Russian Mennonite group.

Holdeman was the first to introduce revivalism into the Mennonite community, which accounted for the rapid growth of the group among immigrant communities. His Church of God in Christ, Mennonite, followed the Anabaptist-Mennonite tradition of believer's baptism, separation from the world, nonresistance, plain dress, beards for men, and modest covering for the women. In 1882 Holdeman's mother died, and he decided to sell the family farm. He moved to Jasper County, Missouri, followed by many church members, where he centered his pastoring and writing until 1897. At that time he moved to McPherson County, Kansas, where he worked until his death in 1900, at the age of 68. He left behind a solid church organization which in the late 1980s reported over 13,000 members worldwide.

Sources:

Durnbaugh, Donald F., ed. *The Brethren Encyclopedia*. 3 vols. Philadelphia: The Brethren Encyclopedia, Inc., 1983.

Hiebert, Clarence. *The Holdeman People*. South Pasadena, CA: William Carey Library, 1973. 663 pp.

Holdeman, John. *A History of the Church of God as It Existed from the Beginning Whereby It May Be Known, and How It Was Propagated until the Present Time*. Lancaster, PA: John Baer's Sons, 1876.

_____. *A Mirror of Truth*. Hesston, KS: Church of God in Christ, Mennonite Publication Board, 1956.

_____. *The Old Ground and Foundation, Taken from the Word of God*. Lancaster, PA: John Bear's Sons, 1863.

_____. *A Treatise on Magistracy and War*. Carthage, MO: Press Book and Job Printing House, 1891.

The Mennonite Encyclopedia. 4 vols. Scottdale, PA: The Mennonite Publishing House, 1955.

Unruh, Inez, "Portrait of a Prophet," *Mennonite Life* (July, 1959): 123-4.

—*Gary L. Ward*

★417★
HOLLEY, Horace Hotchkiss
Hand of the Cause, Baha'i Faith
b. Apr. 7, 1887, Torrington, Connecticut
d. Jul. 12, 1960, Haifa Israel

Horace Hotchkiss Holley, a national and international leader of the Baha'i Faith, was born into an old New England family. He attended Williams College (1906-1909) in Williamstown, Massachusetts. After finishing college he traveled to Europe. On the voyage across the Atlantic he met Bertha Herbert, whom he later married. It was she who gave him a book about **Abdu'l-Baha**, the leader of the Baha'i Faith. He was immediately impressed with Abdu'l-Baha. After his marriage, however, he settled with his wife, an artist, in Europe. He wrote and published several volumes of poems and did little to explore the Baha'i Faith for several years.

In 1911 Holley was given the opportunity to meet Abdu'l-Baha, who had stopped in Europe on the trip that would eventually take him to the United States. Deeply impressed with his spirituality, Holly began to write a book on his new-found faith. It appeared in 1913 as *Baha'ism—The Modern Social Religion*. Abdu'l-Baha praised the book highly. As World War I began Holley returned to the United States, where he moved within the artistic community of New York City. He began work on his second book on the Baha'i Faith, *The Social Principle* (1916) and before the war was over published two more books, *Divination and Creation* and *Read-Aloud Plays*, both in 1917.

In 1918 Holley started work in an advertising company. His first marriage ended in divorce, and he married Doris Pascal, another Baha'i. In 1921 he authored *Baha'i-The Spirit of the Age* and, possibly more importantly, edited a collection of the writings of Baha-u-llah and Abdu'l-Baha called *Baha'i Scriptures* (1923). This latter volume (revised and reissued in 1943 as *Baha'i World Faith*) was a central text for American Baha'is for many years. In 1922 the first American National Spiritual Assembly was organized and Horace began a 36-year tenure on it in 1923.

Abdu'l-Baha died in 1921 and was succeeded by Shoghi Effendi, his nephew, as guardian of the faith. Holley developed a close relationship with Effendi. In 1925 Holley relinquished his advertising job to become National Secretary of the American Baha'i Spiritual Assembly. Among his first suggestions was that a publication to reflect the worldwide growth of the movement be established. Thus did Baha'i World, a periodic book-length summary of Baha'i activity around the globe, emerge. Horace edited the "International Survey of Baha'i Activities" for each issue during his lifetime. He also started the impetus that led to the issuance of Baha'i News.

In 1939 the movement's national office moved to Wilmette, Illinois, where the Baha'i Temple was located. Holley made the move as well.

In 1951 Effendi appointed Holley a Hand of the Cause. In 1957, following the death of Effendi, Holley traveled to Haifa, the world headquarters of the faith, and participated in the writing of the first proclamation of the hands of the Cause as a group who had assumed authority in the interim after the death of the guardian. He was asked to become one of the Hands serving in the Holy Land, so he returned home to conclude his business and return to Haifa in December 1959. He lived only a few months, dying there the following summer.

Sources:

Bjorling, Joel. The Baha'i Faith: An Historical Bibliography. New York: Garland Publishing Company, 1986.
Holley, Horace H. Baha'i—The Spirit of the Age. New York: Brentano's, 1921. 212 pp.
———. Baha'ism—The Modern Social Religion. New York: Mitchell Kennerly, 1913.
———. Religion for Mankind. London: George Ronald, 1956. 248 pp.
Ruhiyyih. "Horace Hotchkiss Holley." Baha'i World 13 (1970): 849-58.

★418★
HOLMES, Ernest Shurtleff
Founder, United Church of Religious Science
b. Jan. 21, 1887, Lincoln, Maine
d. Apr. 7, 1960, Los Angeles, California

Ernest Shurtleff Holmes, the founder of Religious Science, was born to a poor family in Maine. He attended public school up to age 15, at which point he left home and found odd jobs in Boston. In 1908, at the age of 21, he decided to improve himself by taking a two-year course in public speaking at the Leland Powers School of Expression. While working at that, several others at the school introduced Holmes to Christian Science and its main book, *Science and Health with Key to the Scriptures*. This influence was added to his own reading of Ralph Waldo Emerson and other Transcendentalists.

In 1912 Holmes moved to Venice, California, where his brother, Fenwicke Holmes, was a Congregationalist minister. Holmes got a job with the city. He and his brother enjoyed reading discussions of New Thought, including the works of Judge Thomas Troward and **William Walker Atkinson**. Holmes took a correspondence course from Christian Larsen, a New Thought writer and teacher. A local engineer took an interest in New Thought and invited Holmes to speak to an informal gathering at his house. This event led in turn to a speaking engagement in 1916 at the Metaphysical Library, where he first spoke about Troward.

In 1917 Holmes and Fenwicke founded the Metaphysical Institute and the periodical *Uplift*, began lecturing in Los Angeles and Long Beach, and opened a Metaphysical Sanitarium in the latter. With initial success, they expanded their lecture tours nationwide, and in 1919 they came out with their first books, *Creative Mind* by Holmes and *The Law of Mind In Action* by Fenwicke. This partnership lasted until 1925, when Holmes decided to stop touring and settle in Los Angeles. For a brief time in 1924, Holmes was the

last student of **Emma Curtis Hopkins**, a seminal New Thought pioneer who gave his thought its mystical aspects. In 1926 he published his major work, *The Science of Mind*, which he understood as the study of the Mind or Spirit manifest in each person through Law and expressed as Love.

In 1927 Holmes married Hazel Durkee Foster and began the organization through which his following could grow, the Institute of Religious Science and School of Philosophy. He also began the *The Science of Mind* magazine. The movement grew in stature, with affiliate centers scattered around the country. In 1935 it was reincorporated as the Institute of Religious Science and Philosophy and moved to its permanent headquarters on Wilshire Boulevard in Los Angeles. By this time Holmes had a regular Sunday audience of almost 3,000. In 1949 he began a radio show called, "This Thing Called Life," and in 1953 he finally changed his Institute's name to the Church of Religious Science. He designated the affiliate centers as churches and realigned their relationship with the church headquarters. This led to some opposition and the creation of Religious Science International and various independent Science of Mind churches. In 1967 Holmes' church added "United" in front of its name.

Holmes died in 1960 at the age of 73. He left behind a church which in the late 1980s numbered over 100,000 members, as well as the various other churches which originated in his work. His teaching was distinctive in combining the general New Thought affirmation of the unity and power of Mind or Spirit with the recognition of the difference between the objective mind (waking consciousness) and subjective mind (subconscious).

Sources:

Armor, Reginald C. Ernest Holmes, The Man. Los Angeles: Science of Mind Publications, 1977. 111 pp.
Awbrey, Scott. Path of Discovery. Los Angeles: United Church of Religious Science, 1987. 31 pp.
Beebe, Tom. Who's Who in New Thought. Lakemont, GA: CSA Press, 1977. 318 pp.
Bowden, Henry Warner. Dictionary of American Religious Biography. Westport, CT: Greenwood Press, 1977. 572 pp.
Braden, Charles C. Spirits in Rebellion. Dallas, TX: Southern Methodist University Press, 1963. 571 pp.
Holmes, Ernest S. Creative Mind. New York: Robert M. McBride Company, 1923. 78 pp.
———. How To Use the Science of Mind. New York: Dodd, Mead & Company, 1948. 150 pp.
———. The Science of Mind. New York: Robert M. McBride and Company, 1938. 667 pp.
———. This Thing Called Life. New York: Dodd, Mead & Company, 1943. 153 pp.
———. What Religious Science Teaches. Los Angeles, CA, 1944.
Holmes, Fenwicke L. Ernest Holmes: His Life and Times. New York, 1970.
Hornaday, William H. D., and Harlan Ware. The Inner Light. New York: Dodd, Mead & Company, 1964. 275 pp.

—*Gary L. Ward*

★419★
HOLMES, John Haynes
Minister, American Unitarian Association
b. Nov. 29, 1879, Philadelphia, Pennsylvania
d. Apr. 3, 1964, New York, New York

John Haynes Holmes, a Unitarian minister and social activist, was the son of Alice Fanny and Marcus Morton Holmes. The family moved to New England in 1884 and Holmes grew up in Malden, Massachusetts. He attended Harvard University (1898-1902) and then entered the Harvard Divinity School. While at the Divinity School he was especially impressed by ethicist Francis Greenwood Peabody from whom he absorbed a priority of applying his theology to social issues. Following his graduation in 1904, he was ordained as a minister by the American Unitarian Association (AUA), was called as pastor by the church in Dorchester, Massachusetts, and married Madeline Hosmer Baker.

During his years at Dorchester, Holmes continued to educate himself reading a variety of contemporary social theorists. In 1907 he was called to the Church of the Messiah in New York City. He would stay there until his retirement in 1949. In New York he launched a social ministry that would be considered radical, even for Unitarians. It began in 1908 with the formation of the Unitarian Fellowship for Social Justice. From his readings of such people as **Walter Rauschenbusch**, George Bellemy, and Henry George, he had come to equate socialism with the social program of Christianity.

Holmes was one of the founders of the National Association for the Advancement of Colored People (NAACP) in 1909 and served as that organization's national vice-president for over 50 years. He made his first statement of a social vision in 1912 with the publication of *The Revolutionary Function of the Modern Church*. One result was a direct involvement in politics, first in the Progressive Party, organized around Theodore Roosevelt, and later in the 1930s in the Socialist Party.

When World War I began, Holmes was in the forefront of pacifist activists. He joined the Fellowship of Reconciliation (FOR) and the American Union Against Militarism and helped organize the American Civil Liberties Union (A.C.L.U.) to support dissenters from the war who had been arrested. His views were published in his book *New Wars for Old* (1916). In 1919, alienated from most Unitarians due to his pacifism, he left the association, and the congregation changed its name to the Community Church. In 1921 he began to edit a magazine, *Unity*, not to be confused with the still-popular inspirational magazine of the same title issued by the Unity School of Christianity.

After the war, he became a prohibitionist, a friend of labor, and a supporter of Clarence Darrow's efforts to prevent the execution of convicted murders Nicola Sacco and Gaetano Vanzetti. He toured the Holy Land with his friend Rabbi **Stephen S. Wise** and emerged a supporter of Zionism, as reflected in his 1929 book *Palestine Today and Tomorrow*.

Holmes' pacifist tendencies were reinforced in 1931 when he met Mohandas Gandhi, and he quickly absorbed the nonviolent philosophy Gandhi had developed. His pacifism carried him in a rejection of Hitler and Stalin, and further alienation from friends as World War II began.

Holmes retired in 1949. He developed symptoms of Parkinson's disease in 1950 but was able to finish his book on Gandhi, which was published in 1953, and led a somewhat active life for another decade. He angrily attacked the House Committee on Un-American Activities allegations that he had assisted a Communist infiltration of the American churches. Among his last accomplishments was his completion of his autobiography, *I Speak for Myself*. In 1960 he reaffiliated with the Unitarians, who had in the intervening decades adopted much of Holmes' social stance, and had become more tolerant of such radical moral positioning.

Sources:

Dictionary of American Biography. 20 vols. and 7 supps. New York: Charles Scribner's Sons, 1928-1936, 1944-1981.

Holmes, John Haynes. *I Speak for Myself.* New York: Harper, 1959. 315 pp.

———. *My Gandhi.* New York: Harper & Row, 1953. 186 pp.

———. *New Wars for Old.* New York: Dodd, Mead and Co., 1916. 369 pp.

———. *Rethinking Religion.* New York: Macmillan Company, 1938. 249 pp.

———. *The Revolutionary Function of the Modern Church.* New York: G. P. Putnam's Sons, 1912. 264 pp.

Lavan, Spencer. *Unitarians and India: A Study in Encounter and Response.* Boston: Skinner House, 1977. 217 pp.

Voss, Carl H. *Rabbi and Minister: The Friendship of Stephen S. Wise and John Haynes Holmes.* Cleveland, OH: World Publishing Co., 1964. 383 pp.

★ 420 ★
HOLSEY, Lucius H.
Bishop, Colored Methodist Episcopal Church
b. Jul. 3, 1842, Columbus, Georgia
d. Aug. 3, 1920

Lucius H. Holsey, the fourth bishop of the Colored (now Christian) Methodist Episcopal Church, was born into slavery. For several years prior to the Civil War, he was owned by Richard Malcolm Johnston, a professor at the University of Georgia. In spite of the law of Georgia, which prohibited Blacks from learning to read and write, Holsey mastered these skills. During the war he resided in Sparta, Georgia, where he met and married a servant who lived in the home of George Foster Pierce, a bishop of the Methodist Episcopal Church, South. The bishop performed the wedding ceremony.

After the war Bishop Pierce assisted Holsey in his quest to become a Methodist minister. Holsey was licensed in 1868 and served the Hancock (Georgia) Circuit before moving to Savannah in 1869. It was during this period that southern Methodists decided to establish their former slave members in a separate, autonomous church. Holsey attended the first general conference of the new church held in 1870. In 1871 he was appointed to the Augusta Colored Methodist Episcopal Church and moved to Augusta. He was still the pastor when the second general conference met at his church in 1873. At that conference, Holsey was one of three men elected to the bishopric.

As bishop, Holsey rendered almost a half century of service to the Colored Methodist Episcopal Church. He continued to live in Augusta and became an acquaintance of **Atticus Greene Haygood**, the leading voice in Southern Methodism advocating the mission of the church in providing for the education of Blacks. In 1880 both the Southern Methodists under Haygood's inspiration and the Colored Methodist Episcopals led by Holsey began work on a black college that was to be a joint venture between the two denominations. Holsey was the first vice-president of the board of trustees of the school named Paine College. Not content with the establishment of Paine, Holsey also founded Holsey Industrial Institute, a secondary school, at Cordele, Georgia; it has since become defunct.

Holsey also distinguished himself in service to the church. He was responsible for revising the *Book of Discipline* (the church law) and its companion, *Manual of Discipline*. He worked with F. M. Hamilton in the preparation of a hymnal, *Songs of Love and Mercy*, published in 1904. Holsey contributed one of his own hymns, "O Raptuous Scenes," to the new hymnal.

As one of the more educated members of the Church in the late nineteenth century, Holsey authored several books, most prominently his biography of Bishop Vanderhorst and his own *Autobiography*. He also edited a periodical, the *Gospel Trumpet*, for a number of years. He was elected as a delegate to the first Ecumenical Methodist Conference, held in London in 1881.

Sources:

Cade, J.B. *Holsey—The Incomparable.* New York: N.p., 1963.

Holsey, Lucius H., *Autobiography, Sermons, Addresses, and Essays.* Atlanta, GA: Franklin Printing and Publishing Co., 1898. 288 pp.

———. *Life of Bishop Vanderhorst.* Jackson, TN: CME Publishing House, 1929. 15 pp.

———. *Little Gems.* Atlanta, GA: Franklin Printing and Publishing Co., 1905. 55 pp.

★421★
HOLSINGER, Henry Ritz
Founder, Brethren Church (Ashland, Ohio)
b. May 26, 1833, Morrisons Cove, Pennsylvania
d. 1905, Johnstown, Pennsylvania

Henry Ritz Holsinger, who following his expulsion from the German Baptist Brethren (the Church of the Brethren) founded the Brethren Church (Ashland, Ohio), was the son of Daniel Mack Holsinger, a Brethren minister. He received little education, and worked as a farmer, carpenter, and teacher in his early life. He was baptized in 1855. In 1856 he became an apprentice for a year to Henry Kurtz, who published the *Monthly Gospel Visitor*. The work changed the course of his life, and he decided to find his life's calling in the arena of church publishing. In 1864 he married Susanna Shoup.

In 1863 he purchased *The Tyrone (PA) Herald*, a secular newspaper with a Republican Party orientation. In 1865 he began publishing a religious periodical, the *Christian Family Companion*. The following year he was ordained as a minister among the Brethren. He proceeded to become the leading spokesperson for what is generally referred to as the Progressive Brethren. He used his paper to argue for a number of reforms, including: salaries for ministers, options in dress styles, heightened interest in education, and Sunday schools. He found considerable support for reform among the Brethren, but the voicing of his opinions led to opposition among the more conservative elements still in control. Heated arguments with the church leadership became a regular event at the annual meetings.

In 1873 Holsinger sold the *Companion* to James Quinter and the next year he moved to Berlin, Pennsylvania, where he began to raise money for a high school. The school never materialized and in 1878, with the assistance of J. W. Beer, he began *The Progressive Christian*. In one of his early articles for the new periodical, he compared the Standing Committee of the Brethren to a secret society (an organization most disapproved among the Brethren). In 1881 the annual meeting received charges against Holsinger and a committee was established to visit Holsinger. Their report recommended he be disfellowshipped. The report was acted upon in 1882. Following the expulsion, Holsinger moved to Ashland, Ohio, and merged his paper with *The Gospel Preacher*. It continued as *The Brethren Evangelist*. In 1883 Holsinger and his supporters formed the Brethren Church.

Holsinger continued *The Brethren Evangelist* for several years and spent two years raising money for Ashland College, a school which became aligned with the Progressive Brethren after the schism. In 1886 Holsinger sold *The Brethren Evangelist* and became a pastor in Berne, Indiana, for a year before moving to Lathrop, California. In 1888 he began publishing *The Brethren Evangelist* again, but in 1892 he sold it to the Brethren Church.

As a last adventure in publishing, Holsinger decided to write a history of the Brethren. He was forced by his failing health to dictate much of it, but by 1901 he had completed and published it. Unfortunately, *The History of the Tunkers and the Brethren Church* was not well received and became a financial disaster. Disappointed, Holsinger retired from public life and lived his last years with his daughter.

Sources:
Durnbaugh, Donald F. "H. R. Holsinger." *Brethren Life and Thought* 24 (1979): 142-146.
_____., ed. *The Brethren Encyclopedia*. 3 vols. Philadelphia: The Brethren Encyclopedia, Inc., 1983.
Holsinger, Henry R. *The History of the Tunkers and the Brethren Church*. Lathrop, CA: Pacific Press Pub. Co., 1901. 826 pp.

★422★
HOLT, Ivan Lee
Bishop, Methodist Church (1939-1968)
b. Jan. 9, 1886, DeWitt, Alaska
d. Jan. 12, 1967, Atlanta, Georgia

Ivan Lee Holt, a bishop of the Methodist Church (1939-1968), was the son of Ella Thomas and Robert Paine Holt. He attended Vanderbilt University (A.B., 1904), and after graduation he taught at the Stuttgart Training School in Arkansas. In 1906 he married Leland Burks. In 1907 he moved to Illinois to finish a Ph.D. at the University of Chicago. He received his degree in 1909 and moved to St. Louis as the pastor of University Methodist Episcopal Church, South. In 1909 he published his first book, *Babylonian Contract Tablets*, a scholarly study growing out of his doctoral work. Two years later he became pastor of Centenary Church in Cape Girardeau, Missouri. In 1915 he went to Southern Methodist University as chaplain of the university, chairman of the theological faculty, and professor of Old Testament literature. Then in 1918 he returned to St. Louis as pastor of St. John's Methodist Church, where he remained for the next 20 years.

His later years at St. John's were quite busy ones. He authored two books, *The Return of Spring to Man's Soul* (1934) and *The Search for a New Strategy in Protestantism* (1936). In 1935 Holt was elected president of the Federal Council of Churches. Then in 1938 he was among the last group of men elected to the bishopric of the Methodist Episcopal Church, South prior to its merger with the Methodist Episcopal Church and Methodist Protestant Church to form the Methodist Church (1939-1968). During the preceding quadrennium he had worked on the Joint Commission on Unification and prepared the communion ritual later adopted by the united church. As bishop he served in the Texas-New Mexico Area (1939), Dallas Area (1940-1944) and the Missouri Area (1944-1956). Among his first duties as a bishop was to attend the All-European Methodist Conference in 1939.

As a bishop Holt emerged as one of the church's primary ecumenical statesmen. In 1948 he attended the first gathering of the World Council of Churches in Amsterdam. He would later lead the communion service at the 1954 council gathering in Evanston, Illinois. He helped draft the charter for the National Council of Churches, which was inaugurated in 1950. In 1951 he was elected president of the newly formed World Methodist Council. Following his retirement he was named president emeritus. He served one term as president of the Council of Bishops of the Methodist Church and as president of the Board of Pensions. He retired in 1956.

Sources:
Harmon, Nolan B. *The Encyclopedia of World Methodism*. 2 vols. Nashville: United Methodist Publishing House, 1974.
Holt, Ivan Lee. *Eugene Russell Hendrix, Servant of the Kingdom*. Nashville, TN: Parthenon Press, 1950. 221 pp.
_____. *The Methodists of the World*. New York: Division of Education and Cultivation, Board of Missions and Church Expansion, Methodist Church, 1950. 126 pp.
_____. *The Missouri Bishops*. Nashville, TN: Parthenon Press, 1953. 96 pp.
_____. *The Return of Spring to Man's Soul*. New York: Harper & Bros., 1934. 119 pp.
_____. *The Search for a New Strategy in Protestantism*. Nashville, TN: Cokesbury Press, 1936. 190 pp.

★423★
HOOD, James Walker
Bishop, African Methodist Episcopal Zion Church
b. May 30, 1831, Kennett Township, Pennsylvania
d. Oct. 30, 1918, Fayetteville, North Carolina

James Walker Hood, later to become a bishop of the African Methodist Episcopal Zion Church, began life in poverty as the son of a tenant farmer. Though he would later receive honorary degrees from both Lincoln University and Livingstone College, he had only a few months of formal schooling; his grandmother taught him to read and write and interested him in speaking. His father was a local Methodist preacher as well as a farmer, and as a child James was nurtured in the faith.

Walker delivered his first public talk as a youth, an abolitionist speech in reaction to the Dred Scott decision. Hood predicted the emancipation of Blacks in the near future. During the next few years he experienced a period of religious doubt that was finally resolved into a strong Christian commitment at about the age of 18. He married Hannah L. Ralph in 1852; she died in 1855. He then married Sophia J. Nugent. In 1856 Hood felt a call to preach and began to prepare himself. In 1859 he was accepted on trial by the New England Conference of the African Methodist Episcopal Zion Church and the following year he was ordained and sent to Nova Scotia as a missionary.

In 1864 Hood was sent to North Carolina to work among the emancipated slaves in territory occupied by the Union Army. He was to reside in North Carolina for the rest of his life. In the decade after the war ended, he served as a delegate to write the new state constitution and as assistant superintendent of public instruction.

In 1872 the African Methodist Episcopal Zion Church elected Hood to the bishopric. He made his headquarters in Fayetteville. Shortly after his election, his second wife died. He married Katie P. McCoy two years later.

Among his many accomplishments as bishop in North Carolina, Hood oversaw the establishment of the denomination's first collegiate institution, Zion Wesley Institute (now Livingstone College), in 1877. He served as chairman of the board for 36 years. In 1884 he authored the first collection of sermons written by a black man; a second volume was issued in 1908. He also authored two volumes of denominational history. He spoke at the first two Ecumenical Methodist Conferences in London (1881) and in Washington, D.C. (1891). He also served as a consultant to Teddy Roosevelt, advising the president on questions concerning the black people.

Hood served the African Methodist Episcopal Zion Church for 44 years, retiring in 1916, the oldest bishop in the church. A few years before his retirement, the church honored its longtime bishop by naming its new theological seminary, located on the Livingstone College campus, after him.

Sources:

Harmon, Nolan B. *The Encyclopedia of World Methodism.* 2 vols. Nashville: United Methodist Publishing House, 1974.

Hood, James Walker. *The Negro in the Christian Pulpit: Twenty-one Practical Sermons.* Raleigh, NC: Edward & Broughton Co., 1884. 336 pp.

———. *One Hundred Years of the A. M. E. Zion Church.* New York: A. M. E. Zion Book Concern, 1895. 625 pp.

———. *The Plan of the Apocalypse.* York, PA: Anstadt & Sons, 1900. 192 pp.

———. *Sermons.* York, PA: Anstadt & Sons, 1908. 154 pp.

———. *Sketch of the Early History of the African Methodist Episcopal Zion Church.* Vol. II. N.p.: The Author, 1914. 125 pp.

Walls, William J. *The African Methodist Episcopal Zion Church.* Charlotte, NC: A. M. E. Zion Publishing House, 1974. 669 pp.

Who Was Who in America. Chicago: Marquis Who's Who, Inc.

★424★
HOPKINS, Emma Curtis
Founder, New Thought Movement
b. Sep. 2, 1849, Killingly, Connecticut
d. Apr. 8, 1925, Killingly, Connecticut

Emma Curtis Hopkins, the founder of what is today known as the New Thought Movement, was the daughter of Lydia Phillips and Rufus Curtis. Well educated, she married an English teacher,

George Irving Hopkins, on July 19, 1874. In 1881 she had a healing experience through Christian Science, and in December 1883 she moved to Boston to take the primary class at the Massachusetts Metaphysical College from **Mary Baker Eddy**. She was subsequently listed as a Christian Science practitioner. Eddy immediately recognized her as a student of ability and named her as the editor of the *Christian Science Journal* in September 1884. The following year, however, Hopkins split with Eddy and moved with her husband to Chicago. In the spring of 1886 she established an office as an independent Christian Science practitioner.

Urged by her associate, Mary Plunkett, Hopkins founded the Emma Hopkins College of Christian Science, from which she taught her own classes beginning in the summer of 1886. Her students soon organized the Hopkins Metaphysical Association. In the remaining years of the century, the work initiated by Hopkins slowly evolved from a single independent center for teaching Christian Science in Chicago into the national and even international New Thought Movement. By the end of 1887, schools and branch associations had been founded in 17 cities. By December 1, 1887, Hopkins dedicated a permanent headquarters building. In 1888 she initiated a complete reorganization of the work along ecclesiastical lines. Convinced that independent Christian Science had been shaped too much by an emphasis upon its business aspects, she transformed her school into the Christian Science Theological Seminary and revamped the curriculum to train Christian Science ministers.

The seminary's first class graduated in January 1889. On January 10 of that year, Hopkins became the first woman in modern times to assume the role of a Christian bishop and ordain others—the majority of whom were also women—to the ministry. During the next four years, 111 students completed the course of study and were ordained by Hopkins.

During her years in Chicago, Hopkins departed from Eddy's teachings on a number of points, especially in the development of a strong feminist orientation. She taught that, through history, God had manifested in three aspects: Father (during the period of the patriarchs); the Son (during which the lower classes had begun their rise from servitude); and the Mother-Spirit (signified by the rise of women beginning in the nineteenth century). Hopkins thus became the first modern thinker to tie the idea of a feminine deity to elevation of the status and role of women.

Just as suddenly as she emerged in the mid-1880s, Hopkins retired in 1895 from her work in Chicago and moved to New York. While she taught a few more classes, she soon limited her teaching to select students whom she taught weekly on an individual basis. During her early years in New York she wrote her most famous book, *High Mysticism*. The epitome of her mature thought, this book became the basis of her later teachings. She continued to take individual students for 30 years, her last being **Ernest Holmes**, the founder of Religious Science.

Every major contemporary New Thought organization can be directly traced to Hopkins' teaching work. During her 40-year career, Hopkins taught almost all of those people who formed the first generation of leadership for the New Thought Movement: **Malinda Cramer** (founder of Divine Science); **Charles Fillmore** and **Mary Caroline Fillmore** (co-founders of the Unity School of Christianity); Nellie Van Anderson (founder of the Church of Higher Life); Annie Rix Militz (founder of the Homes of Truth); **Ella Wheeler Wilcox**; and **H. Emilie Cady**. Hopkins' students taught Albert Grier (founder of the Church of the Truth); **Nona Brooks**, Althea Small, and Fannie James (founders of the Divine Science movement in Denver, Colorado); and **Elizabeth Towne**, the prominent New Thought editor.

Sources:

Anderson, Ferne. *Emma Curtis Hopkins—Springboard to New Thought.* Denver, CO: Master's Thesis, University of Denver, 1981. 75 pp.

Cushing, Margaret. "Emma Curtis Hopkins, The Teacher of Teachers." *New Thought Bulletin* 28, 2 (Spring 1945): 5-7.

Hopkins, Emma Curtis. *Class Lessons 1888.* Edited by Elizabeth C. Bogart. Marina del Rey, CA: DeVorss & Co., 1977. 282 pp.

_____. *Gospel Series in Spiritual Science.* Alhambra, CA: Sanctuary of Truth, n.d. 184 pp.

_____. *High Mysticism.* Santa Monica, CA: DeVorss & Co., 1874. 368 pp.

_____. *Resume.* Marina del Rey, CA: DeVorss & Co., n.d. 117 pp.

_____. *Scientific Christian Mental Practice.* Marina del Rey, CA: DeVorss & Co., n.d. 279 pp.

James, Edward T., ed. *Notable American Women, 1607-1950: A Biographical Dictionary.* 3 vols. Cambridge, MA: Harvard University Press, Belknap Press, 1971.

Melton, J. Gordon. *Biographical Dictionary of American Cult and Sect Leaders.* Garland Reference Library of Social Science, vol. 212. New York: Garland Publishing, 1986.

_____. "New Thought's Hidden History: Emma Curtis Hopkins, Forgotten Founder." *META* 1, 1 (1989).

★425★
HORSCH, John
Historian, Editor, Mennonite Church
b. Dec. 18, 1867, Giebelstadt Germany
d. Oct. 7, 1942, Scottsdale, Pennsylvania

John Horsch, a leading historian, writer, and editor in the Mennonite Church, was born in rural Germany and seemed destined to become a farmer. As a young man he attended the Bavarian State Agricultural School in Wurzburg and graduated in 1886. During this period he also became interested in Mennonite history, in large part out of his acquaintance with the archivist/historian Ludwig Keller. Shortly after graduation, however, he came to accept nonresistance to violence and war as a personal position and migrated to America to escape the military draft.

Arriving in New York in January 1887, he moved to Halsted, Kansas, and attended the Indian Missionary School to learn English. He then moved to Elkhart, Indiana, to work at the Mennonite Publishing House under **John F. Funk.** The next seven years were spent between his work in Elkhart and his absences to attend colleges. He studied at Evangelical Theological Seminary, Naperville, Illinois; Valparaiso University, Valparaiso, Indiana; Baldwin-Wallace College, Berea, Ohio; and the University of Wisconsin, Madison, Wisconsin. He began his own short-lived periodical, *Farm and Haus* (1898-1900), before moving to work at the Light Hope Publishing Co. Finally, in 1908, he moved to Scottsdale, Pennsylvania, to become the German editor for the Mennonite Publishing House, a position he held for the rest of his life.

Horsch's writing career was undergirded by a desire to revive the Mennonite Church by holding aloft the early Mennonite standards, hence his interest in history. While he had authored several books prior to his move to Scottsdale, including *The Mennonites, Their History, Faith, and Practice* (1893), not until he moved to Scottsdale and had access to the valuable resources in the American Mennonite heartland did his efforts bear memorable fruit in his several books and numerous articles. In 1916 he published his first major book, *Menno Simons*, a biography of the founder of the Mennonites. A decade later he published two detailed studies which clearly illustrated his interest in Mennonite distinctiveness: *Infant Baptism, Its Origin among Protestants* (1917) and *The Principle of Nonresistance as Held by the Mennonite Church, An Historical Survey* (1927).

Horsch is remembered among historians primarily for his discovery of the modern Hutterite colonies and their collection of historical documents. Through his articles in the *Mennonite Quarterly Review* and his book, *The Hutterian Brethren: A Story of Martyrdom and Loyalty, 1528-1931* (1931), he introduced the Hutterites

to the modern scholarly community at a period when they had fled the United States for Canada to avoid military conscription during World War I.

Also, during the 1920s, Horsch was drawn into the modernist-fundamenatalist controversy that had entered the Mennonite Church. He attacked the modernist cause in one popular book, *Modern Religious Liberalism* (1920), which went through three editions, and in three influential pamphlets: *The Higher Criticism and the New Theology* (1917); *The Mennonite Church and Modernism* (1924); and *Is the Mennonite Church of America Free of Modernism?* (1926).

During the 1930s he devoted himself to the most memorable accomplishment of his life, a new history of Mennonites in Europe. The manuscript was completed in 1939, but the book was not published until 1942, some months after illness had claimed its author.

Sources:

Horsch, John. *Infant Baptism, Its Origins Among Protestants.* Scottsdale, PA: The Author, 1917. 157 pp.

_____. *Menno Simons.* Scottsdale, PA: Mennonite Publishing House, 1916. 324 pp.

_____. *Mennonites in Europe.* Scottsdale, PA: Mennonite Publishing House, 1942. 427 pp.

_____. *Modern Religious Liberalism.* Scottsdale, PA: Fundamental Truth Depot, 1920. 331 pp.

_____. *The Principle of Nonresistance, as Held by the Mennonite Church, An Historical Survey.* Scottsdale, PA: Mennonite Publishing House, 1927. 60 pp.

Hostetler, Beulah Stauffer. *American Mennonites and Protestant Movements.* Scottsdale, PA: Herald Press, 1987. 366 pp.

John Horsch Memorial Papers. Scottsdale, PA: Mennonite Publishing House, 1947.

The Mennonite Encyclopedia. 4 vols. Scottdale, PA: The Mennonite Publishing House, 1955.

★426★
HORTON, Douglas
Minister, Congregational and Christian Churches
b. Jul. 27, 1891, Brooklyn, New York
d. Aug. 21, 1968, Berlin Germany

Douglas Horton, a Congregational leader whose efforts greatly contributed to the 1957 merger which created the United Church of Christ, was the son of Elizabeth Swaim Douglas and Byron Horton. He received his B.A. degree from Princeton University in 1912. After a year of study in Scotland and England, he attended Hartford Theological Seminary and received his B.D. in 1915. He was ordained to the ministry and became assistant minister of the First Church of Christ in Middletown, Connecticut. The next year he married Carol Scudder Williams and became the minister of the church in Middletown.

In 1925 he moved to Brookline, Massachusetts, and became pastor of Leyden Congregational Church. While at Leyden he authored his first books: *Out into Life* (1925) and *A Legend of the Grail* (1926). More importantly, he translated one of the first books of German theologian Karl Barth into English, *The Word of God and the Word of Man* (1928). This book is justly credited with being one of the important introductions of Neo-Orthodox theology to English-speaking audiences. His third and last parish was the United Church of Hyde Park, located adjacent to the University of Chicago (1931-1938). During most of these years he also served as a lecturer in practical theology at the Chicago Theological Seminary. While in Chicago he authored *Taking a City* (1934) and *The Art of Living Today* (1935).

In 1938 Horton was selected to replace the retiring Charles E. Burton as general secretary of the General Council of the Congregational and Christian Churches. At the time the duties of the secretary were enlarged to include general leadership of the religious life for the churches and council agencies. Over the years Horton represented the denomination at many levels but especially in its contact with other churches. During the 1940s Horton initiated a number of the contacts between his denomination and the Evangelical and Reformed Church that eventuated in their merger into the United Church of Christ in 1957. From 1943 to 1955 he also found time to lecture regularly at Union Theological Seminary.

In 1955 Horton left the staff of the council and became dean of Harvard Divinity School. He retired in 1959. His retirement years were among his most productive. He served on the General Committee for the World Council of Churches (1957-1963). He authored several books, including a study of the new denomination, *The United Church of Christ* (1962). He then served as an official Protestant observer at the Second Vatican Council, the subject of a series of books, *Vatican Diary* (1963, 1964, 1965, 1966). His last book summarized his own ecumenical vision, *The Undivided Church* (1967).

Sources:

Gunnemann, Louis H. *The Shaping of the United Church of Christ.* New York: Pilgrim Press, 1977. 257 pp.

Horton, Douglas. *The Art of Living Today.* Chicago: United Church of Hyde Park, 1935. 112 pp.

———. *Out into Life.* New York: Abingdon Press, 1925. 284 pp.

———. *Taking a City.* New York: Harper & Row, 1934. 116 pp.

———. *The Undivided Church.* New York: Assocation Press, 1967. 96 pp.

———. *The United Church of Christ.* New York: Thomas Nelson & Sons, 1962. 287 pp.

★427★
HOUGHTON, William Henry
President, Moody Bible Institute
b. 1887, South Boston, Massachusetts
d. Jun. 14, 1947, Los Angeles, California

William Henry Houghton, a Baptist minister who for twelve years served as president of Moody Bible Institute in Chicago, was the son of Carrie Maude Grant and John William Houghton. During the 1890s his father died and the family moved to Lynn, Massachusetts. In 1901 Houghton had an experience of conversion to Christianity, and in 1902 he joined the Cliftondale Pentecostal Church, a holiness congregation affiliated with what is now known as the Church of the Nazarene. Houghton decided to become an entertainer and eventually found his way into vaudeville. In 1909 he attended a Nazarene church in Brooklyn, New York, and had a spiritual renewing experience. He decided to leave the stage and enter Eastern Nazarene College at North Scituate, Rhode Island.

Houghton soon dropped out of school to enter evangelistic work as the singer for evangelist John Quincy Adams Henry, through whom he met and initiated a long-term friendship with **Reuben A. Torrey** of Moody Bible Institute. In 1914 he married Adelaide Franks. In 1915 he was called as pastor of the Baptist church in Canton, Pennsylvania, and ordained as a pastor in the Northern Baptist Convention. While at Canton his first wife died. In 1918 he moved to New Bethlehem, Pennsylvania, and while pastoring the church there married Elizabeth Andrews.

During his years at New Bethlehem, Houghton emerged as a fundamentalist leader. He authored a number of tracts which were frequently reprinted and widely disseminated. He also began a magazine which attacked modernism. Though *The Baptist Believer* only lasted for three issues in 1920, Houghton had been noticed. Before the year was out he had been offered a pastorate of the First Baptist Church in Norristown, Pennsylvania. Four years in Norristown was followed by six fruitful years at the Baptist Tabernacle in Atlanta, Georgia. In 1930 Houghton was selected to succeed fundamentalist minister **John Roach Straton** at Calvary Baptist Church in New York City.

In 1934 Houghton's highly successful career was capped with his selection to follow **James Martin Gray** as president of Moody Bible Institute. In addition to his presidential duties, he also assumed the editorship of the *Moody Monthly* (1934-1936). Active through the rest of the 1930s, Houghton has been credited with building Moody's faculty, extending its influence through a system of conferences across the nation, and increasing the circulation of the *Moody Monthly*. In 1938 he began a radio show which became the basis for his book, *Let's Go Back to the Bible*. Among Houghton's his most lasting contributions was his promotion of a professional society which could serve as a meeting ground for scientists who were also Christians. Out of his early efforts in this regard came the American Scientific Affiliation.

Houghton was quite ill during the last years of his life. He died in California, where he had gone to seek some relief and possibly recover his health.

Sources:

Houghton, William H. *Let's Go Back to the Bible.* New York: Fleming H. Revell Company, 1939. 156 pp.

Moyer, Elgin S., ed. *Who Was Who in Church History.* Chicago: Moody Press, 1968.

Smith, Wilbur M. *A Watchman on the Walls: Life Story of Will H. Houghton.* Grand Rapids, MI: William B. Eerdmans Publishing Company, 1951. 191 pp.

★428★
HOYT, Herman Arthur
Minister and Educator, Fellowship of Grace Brethren Churches
b. Mar. 12, 1909, Greenfield, Iowa

Herman Arthur Hoyt, a founder of the National Fellowship of Brethren Churches (since 1976 known as the Fellowship of Grace Brethren Churches), was the son of Anna Leona Dorsey and Clarence Lyman Hoyt. As a child Hoyt was raised in the local congregation of the Brethren Church (Ashland, Ohio). He attended Ashland College from which he received his B.A. in 1932. He continued through Ashland Theological Seminary and was granted a B.D., summa cum laude, in 1935. He joined the faculty of Ashland Seminary as a professor of New Testament and Greek. During the 1930s, the Brethren Church experienced a major schism along liberal-conservative lines. Hoyt and **Alva J. McClain**, conservative leaders, were dismissed from the faculty in 1937. Within a few weeks, McClain founded Grace Theological Seminary as an alternative ministerial training school within the denomination. Hoyt joined the faculty. He also took the opportunity to further his own education and attended the University of Michigan for a short period. In 1939 he was awarded his M.Th. from Grace Seminary. That same year he married Harriet L. Fitz.

At the 1939 general conference of the Brethren Church, the confrontation over the new seminary led its supporters to walk out and form a new denomination, the Fellowship of Grace Brethren Churches. Hoyt served a number of important posts denominationally as president of the National Brethren Bible Conference (1940-1941) and the Grace Brethren National Conference (1943). In 1940 he became the first president of the board of directors of the Brethren Missionary Herald Company and served as chairman of the first committee on publications. During these years he also continued his education and expanded the range of courses he taught. In 1945 he received his Th.D from Grace.

As the fellowship passed through its initial organizational phase into a somewhat settled existence, Hoyt emerged as one of its major theoreticians. He authored three important studies of Brethren beliefs and practice: *Do This in Remembrance of Me* (1947); *All Things Whatsoever I Have Commanded* (1948); and *Then Would My Servants Fight* (1956).

During the 1950s he became known as a Bible teacher and spoke at conferences across the United States. He specialized in the area of eschatology (the doctrine of the end times) and Bible prophecy. His most important studies of the topic are *Studies in Revelation* (1953) and *The End Times* (1969). The study of prophecy also led him to consideration of the role assigned in Biblical teachings to the Jewish nation. In 1962 he joined the board of the American Association for Jewish Evangelism for, upon which he has served ever since.

Sources:

Durnbaugh, Donald F., ed. *The Brethren Encyclopedia.* 3 vols. Philadelphia: The Brethren Encyclopedia, Inc., 1983.

Hoyt, Herman A. *All Things Whatsoever I Have Commanded.* 1948.

_____. *The End Times.* Chicago: Moody Press, 1969. 256 pp.

_____. *The First Christian Theology.* Grand Rapids, MI: Baker Book House, 1977. 127 pp.

_____. *Studies in Revelation.* Winona Lake, ON: BMH Books, 1953, 1977. 148 pp.

_____. *Then Would My Servants Fight.* Winona Lake, IN: Brethren Missionary Herald Company, 1956. 115 pp.

_____. *Do This in Remembrance of Me.* 1947.

★429★
HUA, Hsuan
Leader, Dharma Realm Buddhist Association
b. May 5, 1908, Manchuria People's Republic of China

Tripitaka Master Hsuan Hua is a Chinese Ch'an (Zen Buddhist) master and the leader of the Dharma Realm Buddhist Association (founded as the Sino-American Buddhist Association). He was the son of Pai Fu-hai and his wife, Hu. When he was 11, he happened to stumble across a child's corpse while crossing a field near his village in northeast China. He had never before encountered death and, upon asking his devoutly Buddhist mother what it meant, was informed that everyone must die eventually. He asked further if there was any way to avoid death, and a visiting stranger explained that the "only way to escape is to practice the Tao so as to enlighten one's mind and understand one's inner self." Hua then resolved to become a monk. After his parents passed away, he took the vows of a novice. In 1947 he journeyed across China to visit the Venerable Abbot Hsu Yun, at that time 109 years of age. Hsu Yun recognized Hsuan Hua's enlightenment, and transmitted the mindseal of the Wang Yei lineage to him.

Hua fled to Hong Kong in 1949 following the Communist takeover, and engaged himself in raising funds to provide for elderly Chinese monks. Master Hua also taught the dharma, built lecture halls and temples, and reprinted sutras. He left Hong Kong in 1959, first traveling to Australia, where he taught Chinese. In 1962 he moved to San Francisco, where some of his disciples had founded the San Francisco Buddhist Lecture Hall in 1958. Word gradually spread that an enlightened Ch'an master was living in San Francisco, and Americans began to find their way to him. In the summer of 1968 he held his first 96-day-long dharma assembly on the *Shurangama Sutra.* The next year five of the Americans who had attended the assembly accompanied him to Taiwan, where they received novice ordinations.

In 1972 the Gold Mountain Monastery was founded in the Mission District of San Francisco. All five schools of Chinese Buddhism are taught and practiced, with a base in Ch'an. Westerners are often surprised at the union of the Ch'an and Pure Land schools, which are quite separate in Japanese Buddhism. In the Chinese Buddhist tradition, however, they are viewed as complementary rather than as contradictory traditions. In 1976 Hua's group was able to purchase the 237-acre Mendocino State Hospital for the Criminally Insane near Ukiah, California, which they renamed the City of Ten Thousand Buddhas. This became the site of a monastery and a convent, as well as the site of the Dharma Realm University. The monks and nuns of Gold Mountain have been active in translation activity, and the Buddhist Text Translation Society has published a number of exemplary translations. The goal of the society is to publish the entire Tripitaka (Buddhist holy writings) in English and other European languages. The society also publishes transcripts of the talks and other writings of Master Hua.

Sources:

Fields, Rick. *How the Swans Came to the Lake: A Narrative History of Buddhism in America.* 1981. Rev. ed. Boston, MA: Shambhala, 1986. 445 pp.

Hua, Hsuan. *Buddha Root Farm.* San Francisco: Buddhist Text Translation Society, 1976. 70 pp.

_____. *Herein Lies the Treasure Trove.* Talmage, CA: Dharma Realm Buddhist University, 1983. 153 pp.

_____. *The Ten Dharma-Realms Are Not Beyond a Single Thought.* San Francisco: Buddhist Text Translation Society, 1976. 70 pp.

Melton, J. Gordon *The Encyclopedia of American Religions.* 3d ed. Detroit: Gale Research Inc.,1988. 1102 pp.

The Shurangama Sutra. Commentary by Hsuan Hua. 4 vols. San Francisco: Buddhist Text Translation Society, 1979-1980.

Yin, Heng. *Records of the Life of the Venerable Master Hsuan Hua.* 2 vols. San Francisco: Committee for the Publication of the Biography of the Venerable Master Hsuan Hua, 1973, 1975.

★430★
HUBBARD, L. Ron
Founder, Church of Scientology International
b. Mar. 13, 1911, Tilden, Nebraska
d. Jan. 24, 1986, Creston, California

Lafayette Ronald Hubbard, the founder of the Church of Scientology International, was the son of Dora Mae Waterbury de Wolfe and Harry Ross Hubbard, an officer in the United States Navy. Much of his childhood was spent in Montana on his grandfather's ranch. His father's occupation provided him with occasions for travel as a teenager in the Pacific and Orient. Returning to the United States he attended the Swavely Preparatory School in Virginia and in 1930 entered George Washington University, where he studied for the next two years. In 1933 he married Margaret Louise Grubb. During the rest of the decade he divided his time between expeditions as an explorer and writing. He published over 150 articles and short stories which ranged from adventure to science fiction. His first book, *Buckskin Brigades*, appeared in 1937. In 1940 he was elected a member of the Explorers Club in New York.

Hubbard served in the U. S. Navy through World War II. After the dissolution of his first marriage, in 1946 he married Sara Northrup. Following the war he returned to his writing career and began to synthesize a new philosophy of human nature. The first publication of his new approach came in the May 1950 issue of *Astounding Science Fiction*, a magazine for which Hubbard had previously written. It was followed a few weeks later by a book, *Dianetics: The Modern Science of Mental Health*. In the book Hubbard described his technique for ridding individuals of the causes of aberrant behavior patterns and leading them to a state of "clear." The response to the book prompted the founding of the Hubbard Dianetic Research Foundation. Hubbard expanded on his theories in several books and also wrote the course material for dianetic students and teachers.

During the early 1950s Dianetics was expanded into a complete philosophical-religious system, which Hubbard called Scientology, and in 1954 the first Church of Scientology was opened in Los Angeles. Dianetics had already become an international phenomenon and Scientology soon followed suit. Meanwhile, his second marriage having ended in divorce, in 1952 Hubbard married Mary Sue Whipp. The rest of his life was spent in the development of Scientology and the provision of guidelines for the organization of the church. In 1966 he resigned from any official position in the church, but continued to write extensively as he elaborated on his basic concepts in a wide variety of areas. He eventually dropped out of public sight, and stayed in contact with only a few close colleagues from the church and some of his family members.

During the last years of his life Hubbard returned to fiction writing and issued one major novel, *Battlefield Earth*, and a ten-volume science fiction series, *Mission Earth*. Hubbard left behind a huge body of writings, including both his many works of fiction and a mass of Scientology materials. He also left behind continuing controversy, both for the church he founded and for those seeking to do his biography. Church members consider him the creator of an approach to life which is the future hope for humanity. Undeniably, many have found Scientology a meaningful path. Others have been just as staunchly condemnatory. Since Hubbard's death several biographical studies have appeared which call significant details of Hubbard's own autobiographical claims into question. In turn officials of the church have attacked both the accuracy of these works and the motivations of the authors.

Sources:

Atack, Jon. *A Piece of Blue Sky: Scientology, Dianetics and L. Ron Hubbard Exposed.* New York: Lyle Stuart, 1990. 428 pp.

Hubbard, L. Ron. *Battlefield Earth.* New York: St. Martin's Press, 1982. 819 pp.

_____. *Dianetics: The Modern Science of Mental Health.* New York Hermitage House, 1905. 452 pp.

_____. *Mission Earth.* 10 vols. Los Angeles: Bridge Publications, 1985-1987.

_____. *Science of Survival.* Los Angeles: Publications Organization, United States, 1951. 324 pp.

_____. *Scientology: A New Slant on Life.* Los Angeles: Publications Organization, United States, 1965. 158 pp.

_____. *Scientology: The Fundamentals of Thought.* Los Angeles: Publications Organization, United States, 1956. 128 pp.

L. Ron Hubbard: The Man and His Work. Los Angeles: North Star Publishing. 1986. 19 pp.

Miller, Russell. *Bare-Faced Messiah: The True Story of L. Ron Hubbard.* New York: Henry Holt and Company, 1987. 390 pp.

★431★
HUGHES, Edwin Holt
Bishop, Methodist Episcopal Church
b. Dec. 7, 1866, Moundsville, West Virginia
d. Feb. 12, 1950, Washington, District of Columbia

Edwin Holt Hughes, a bishop of the Methodist Episcopal Church and later of the Methodist Church, was the son of a Methodist minister, T. B. Hughes of the West Virginia Conference of the Methodist Episcopal Church, and Louisa Holt Hughes. His family had split loyalties at the time of the Civil War and the conflicting emotions continued with Hughes into his mature career. Hughes attended West Virginia University and Grinnell College in Iowa, but completed his college work at Ohio Wesleyan (A.B., 1889). He completed his seminary work at Boston University in 1892. While at Iowa Hughes had joined the Iowa Conference. Following graduation he transferred to the New England Conference and was assigned to Newton Center, Massachusetts, as his first charge. He also married Isabel Ebbert that same year.

Hughes rose quickly in the church. He spent four years at Newton Center and then was appointed to Center Church at Malden, Massachusetts, then the strongest Methodist congregation in the conference. After seven years at Malden, he became president of DePauw University at Greencastle, Indiana. Hughes has been given credit for saving DePauw from financial disaster and placing it on a firm financial footing. After only five years in Indiana, however, in 1908 Hughes, then but 41 years old, was elected to the episcopacy. During the next 32 years he would be the resident bishop successively in San Francisco, Chicago, Boston, and Washington, D.C.

Hughes brought to the episcopacy both outstanding oratorical talents and administrative skills. As a master of the homiletic art,

he was known to carefully prepare and then memorize his text. Hughes placed his skills in the service of what became his major contribution to Methodism, his work for the union of northern and southern Methodist churches in the 1930s. He had felt the schism of Methodism in the 1840s personally, through his own family in West Virginia. In 1922 he was appointed to the Methodist Episcopal Church's Commission on Unification and, with the exception of a brief period of time, remained on it during his active episcopacy. He toured the South during the 1930s using his passion for union and his pulpit abilities to win Southern Methodists to the cause. In 1938 on the eve of unification, Bishop **William F. McDowell**, the chairman of the commission, died, and Hughes was appointed to succeed him.

In 1939 at the united conference, Hughes delivered what is possibly his most remembered speech, "The Methodists Are One People," before an audience of 14,000. It became the occasion for a photograph of Hughes clasping hands with Bishop John M. Moore of the Methodist Episcopal Church, South and Bishop **James H. Straughn** of the Methodist Protestant Church which was widely distributed and became a symbol of the merger of the three churches to form the Methodist Church (1939-1968).

Along the way, Hughes wrote over ten books, including his autobiography, *I Was Made a Minister* (1943), published shortly after his retirement in 1940. Hughes was buried on the campus of DePauw University.

Sources:

Harmon, Nolan B. *The Encyclopedia of World Methodism.* 2 vols. Nashville: United Methodist Publishing House, 1974.

Howell, Clinton H., ed. *Prominent Personalities in Methodism.* Birmingham, AL: Lowrey Press, 1945. 512 pp.

Hughes, Edwin Holt. *The Bible and Life.* New York: Methodist Book Concern, 1915. 239 pp.

_____. *Christianity and Success.* Nashville, TN: Abingdon-Cokesbury, 1943. 328 pp.

_____. *Evangelism and Change.* New York: Methodist Book Concern, 1938. 180 pp.

_____. *The Teaching of Citizenship.* Boston: W. A. Wilde Company, 1909. 240 pp.

_____. *I Was Made a Minister.* New York: Abingdon-Cokesbury, 1943. 328 pp.

★432★
HULL, Moses
Spiritualist Writer/Apologist
b. 1835, Delaware County, Ohio
d. Jan. 10, 1907, San Jose, California

Moses Hull, who emerged in the late nineteenth century as a leading Spiritualist writer and apologist, came from an old New England colonial family that was traditionally Baptist. Hull's father, a physician, completed his studies a few years after Moses's birth and moved his family to Missouri. The family affiliated with members of several churches, finally joining the Church of the United Brethren, a German Methodist group. Moses joined after his conversion in a revival meeting in 1851. He soon began a trek, however, that led him quickly through several new religious groups.

Within months of joining the United Brethren, Hull became acquainted with Adventists, followers of the teachings of William Miller, who believed that the world would soon end with Christ's second coming or advent. They accepted the doctrine of soul sleep, the idea that the souls of the dead remain in a state of unconsciousness until the final resurrection. Hull's acceptance of this doctrine led to his excommunication from the Brethren. He began to preach for the Adventists, and his travels brought him into contact with the Seventh-day Adventist Church, whose teachings he accepted while attending some tent meetings in Greenvale, Illinois, in July 1857. He commenced to preach for the Seventh-day Adventist Church and was ordained the following year. He soon became one of their most prominent evangelists and apologists, producing a book, *The Bible from Heaven*, and one of the first booklets against Spiritualism and in defense of the idea of soul sleep. (Soul sleep was directly contradicted by the Spiritualist claim to talk to the so-called dead through mediums.)

During the early 1860s, Hull began to investigate Spiritualism in great depth. He attended seances and became friends with Spiritualist leaders. In the process, he began to doubt his earlier convictions, and after losing a debate with a Spiritualist, withdrew from the Adventists in 1865. After a brief period as a trunkmaker, he entered into active work as a Spiritualist writer. He began a periodical, *The Progressive Age*, which was later moved to Chicago. Under its new name, *The Religio-Philosophical Journal*, it became a leading Spiritualist publication.

Hull's major contribution to Spiritualism was his introduction of the Bible to the movement, which heretofore had accepted the Freethought attack upon the Bible. In his writings, Hull argued that the Bible testifies to the experience of ancient divines and shows that the experiences upon which they based their beliefs were remarkably like those of modern Spiritualists.

Hull's book, *The Question Settled* (1869), was the first of more than 20. Following the sale of *The Progressive Age* in 1868, he launched *Spiritual Rostrum*. This periodical briefly merged into *Hull's Crucible*, but published again under its original name from 1873 to 1877, while Hull resided in Baltimore, Maryland. In 1880 Moses began *The Commoner* with his brother Daniel Hull. It was published for several years from Boston, Massachusetts. His final publishing effort was *The New Thought*, begun in 1884 after Hull had moved to Maquoketa, Iowa. *The New Thought* was eventually sold to an early Spiritualist colony at Summerland, California.

In the mid-1870s Hull became involved in a significant controversy over divorce and marriage. He and his first wife, Elvira, decided to dissolve their marriage, and she married Hull's friend Dr. D. W. Allen. Hull's friendship with both Elvira and Dr. Allen remained strong, and he eventually preached Allen's funeral. Hull in turn found a new partner in Mattie Sawyer, with whom he united by the expediency of a mutual contract rather than a marriage ceremony. As all of these events were publicly announced, Hull became the object of significant criticism.

Hull spent the remainder of his life editing his several periodicals, traveling widely as a lecturer for Spiritualism, and debating. His most famous debate was in 1898 with W. R. Covert of the Anti-Spiritualist Society of America. He participated in the formation of the National Spiritualist Association of Churches, and held a license from them. He also began a training school for Spiritualist ministers. After several faltering starts and the gift of a building in Whitewater, Wisconsin, in 1902, the school emerged as the still-existing Morris Pratt Institute. He served as president for its first five years.

Hull died while on a speaking tour in the West in 1907. His widow preached his funeral service.

Sources:

Hull, Daniel. *Moses Hull*. Wellesley, MA: Maugus Printing Company, 1907. 106 pp.

Hull, Moses. *Bible from Heaven*. Battle Creek, MI: Seventh-day Adventists Publishing Association, 1863. 182 pp.

_____. *A Debate on Spiritualism between Moses Hull and Eld. W. R. Covert*. Chicago: Progressive Thinker Publishing House, 1899. 106 pp.

_____. *Encyclopedia of Biblical Spiritualism*. Chicago: The author, 1895. 385 pp.

_____. *Jesus and the Mediums*. Chicago: The author, 1890. 47 pp.

_____. *The Question Settled*. Boston, MA: William White and Company, 1869. 236 pp.

_____. *The Spiritual Alps and How to Ascend Them*. Chicago: The author, 1893. 106 pp.

★433★
HUMBARD, Rex
Television Evangelist
Founder, Rex Humbard World Outreach Ministry
b. Aug. 13, 1919, Little Rock, Arkansas

Television evangelist Alpha Rex Emmanuel Humbard is the son of Martha Bell Childers and Alpha E. Humbard, both Pentecostal evangelists. Humbard was the oldest of six children and was converted in a gospel meeting as a child. His father was pastoring the Gospel Temple, an independent church in Little Rock, Arkansas, when he was born, and as the children grew up he encouraged their musical training. They first performed as a group on a station in Little Rock. In 1939 the family moved to Dallas to sing on the radio with Virgil O. Stamps and work at Bethel Temple. Here Humbard met Maude Aimee Jones who, though only 15 years old, had been singing on the radio for a decade and whom he eventually married in 1942. As a couple they worked and sang with the Humbard family, then traveled as a gospel team.

Soon after his marriage, Humbard decided to enter the ministry and was ordained in 1953 at the Gospel Tabernacle in Greenville, South Carolina. He received credentials from the International Ministerial Federation, an organization of independent Pentecostal ministers. After a decade on the road, a 1952 meeting in Akron, Ohio, proved to be a turning point. The tremendous response of those who attended their services led Rex and Maude Aimee, and Rex's brother-in-law Wayne Jones, to leave the team and settle in Akron. At first they leased the Copley Road Theater. In 1953 they incorporated their work as Calvary Temple and purchased another old theater in which they could hold services. In 1956 Humbard began construction of a new facility with seating for 5,000 which was dedicated in 1958 as the Cathedral of Tomorrow. As early as 1953 he put the Sunday services on television. In 1968 the show became national in scope, and by 1971 the show was on over 300 stations. By 1979 the program covered a wider geographic coverage than any religious program in the world. The number of stations doubled over the next decade and began to be heard overseas in Japan, Australia, the Philippines, and parts of Africa and South America.

In 1983 Humbard resigned as pastor of the Cathedral of Tomorrow but continued control of the Rex Humbard World Outreach Ministry to carry on the growing television work. Wayne Jones succeeded as pastor of the cathedral and Humbard was named pastor emeritus. Through the televangelistic ups and downs of the 1980s, the Humbard program has retained a significant share of the religious television audience and has developed a professional format that features music by the members of the large Humbard family and preaching by Humbard. Humbard has written a number of books including an autobiography that has gone through several editions under different titles.

Sources:

Humbard, A. E. *My Life Story (Just a Little Bit Different): From the Plowhandle to the Pulpit*. The Author, 1945. 254 pp.

Humbard, Maude Aimee. *Maude Aimee. . .I Look to the Hills*. Akron, OH: Rex Humbard Ministry, 1976.

Humbard, Rex. *How to Stay on Top When the Botton Falls Out*. Akron, OH: Rex Humbard Foundation, 1981. 211 pp.

_____. *Put God on Main Street*. Akron, OH: Cathedral of Tomorrow, 1970. 162 pp. Rev. ed. as *Miracles in My Life: Rex Humbard's Own Story*. Old Tappan, NJ: Fleming H. Revell Company, 1971.

_____. *The Third Dimension*. Old Tappan, NJ: Fleming H. Revell Company, 1972. 154 pp.

_____. *Where Are the Dead?* Akron, OH: Rex Humbard World Outreach Ministry, 1977. 128 pp.

_____. *Why I Believe Jesus Is Coming Soon*. Pasadena, CA: Compass Press, 1972. 133 pp.

_____. *Your Key to God's Bank*. Akron, OH: Rex Humbard Foundation, 1977. 138 pp.

Lloyd, Mark. *Pioneers of Prime Time Religion*. Dubuque, IA: Kendall/Hunt Publishing Co., 1988. 221 pp.

★434★
HUNT, Ernest
Founder, Western Buddhist Order of the Honpa Hongwanji of Hawaii
b. Aug. 16, 1878, Hoddesdon, Hertfordshire England
d. Feb. 7, 1967, Honolulu, Hawaii

Ernest Hunt was a leading priest of the Honpa Hongwanji Buddhists in Hawaii, and became well-known as the founder of the Western Buddhist Order and a leader of the Hawaiian branch of the International Buddhist Institute. He was born in England and as a seaman traveled much of the world, including India, where he was introduced to Buddhism. Once back in England he studied at Eastbourne College and trained to be an Anglican priest. On the very eve of his ordination, however, he converted to Buddhism.

In 1915, at the age of 37, he and his wife, Dorothy, moved to one of the Hawaiian islands to work on a plantation. In the early 1920s they moved to the island of Hawaii and opened Buddhist Sunday schools for the English-speaking children of Japanese plantation workers. In 1924 Bishop **Yemyo Imamura** of the Honpa Hongwanji Buddhists (known on the mainland as the Buddhist Churches of America) ordained both Hunt and his wife. Hunt took the new name of Shinkaku, meaning "true light-bearer," on this occasion. In 1926 he became head of the Hongwanji English Department in Honolulu, a division created to reach the non-Japanese-speaking youth of the Hawaiian Buddhist families. He wrote the *Vade Mecum*, a book of Buddhist ceremonies in English, and his wife wrote many hymns for the services.

As a well-read Anglo with a non-sectarian approach to Buddhism, Shinkaku attracted many Western students. In 1928, about 60 of those students were initiated into Buddhism. They founded the Western Buddhist Order as a nonsectarian branch of the Honpa Hongwanji Mission, with the express purpose of spreading Buddhism to more Westerners. Shinkaku became involved in breaking down other barriers when he became the first vice-president in 1929 of the new Hawaiian branch of the International Buddhist Institute, a group designed to promote dialogue and reduce tension along sectarian lines within Buddhism.

Shinkaku believed that Nirvana became available through *metta*, or active goodwill. Through his position with the Institute, he organized many programs of social aid, including prison visits, care for the sick, library construction, and a Sunday school for the deaf and blind. He also produced many published works, such as a booklet, *An Outline of Buddhism: The Religion of Wisdom and Compassion*, for which the Burmese Theravada Buddhists granted him (and his wife) ordination and the honorary degree Doctor of the Dharma. He edited the Institute's magazine, *Navayana*, and edited four volumes of the *Hawaiian Buddhist Annual*.

This productive and distinguished career was suddenly rerouted when his mentor and leader, Bishop Imamura, died in late 1932. Imamura was succeeded in 1935 (after a brief stay by Bishop Ashikaga) by Bishop Gikyo Kuchiba, who was a strong Japanese nationalist and dedicated Shin Buddhist. He opposed Shinkaku's nonsectarian approach, fired him, and disbanded the Institute's English department. Shinkaku moved over to the Soto Temple under Bishop Komagata, who ordained him a Soto Zen priest in 1953. In 1963 Shinkaku became the only Caucasian priest in the West to receive the Soto rank of Osho. He continued to write and publish, and also spent much time in the temple speaking to tourists about Buddhism. He died in 1967 at the age of 89.

Sources:
Hunt, Ernest. *Essentials and Symbols of the Buddhist Faith*. Honolulu, HI: The Author, 1955. 53 pp.

_____. *Gleanings from Soto-Zen*. Honolulu, HI: The Author, 1953. 58 pp.
_____. *An Outline of Buddhism*. Honolulu, HI: Hongwanji Buddhist Temple, 1929. 43 pp.
_____. *Short Talks on Buddhism*. 2 vols. Honolulu, HI: Soto Zen Temple, n.d.
Hunter, Louise H. *Buddhism in Hawaii*. Honolulu, HI: University of Hawaii Press, 1971.
Melton, J. Gordon. *Biographical Dictionary of American Cult and Sect Leaders*. Garland Reference Library of Social Science, vol. 212. New York: Garland Publishing, 1986.
Peiris, William. *The Western Contribution to Buddhism*. Delhi, India: Motilal Banarsidass, 1973. 287 pp.

—*Gary L. Ward*

★435★
HUNTINGTON, William Reed
Minister, Episcopal Church
b. Sep. 20, 1838, Lowell, Massachusetts
d. Jul. 26, 1909, New York, New York

William Reed Huntington, for two decades pastor of Grace Episcopal Church in New York City, was the son of Elisha Huntington and Hannah Hinckley Huntington. William was given a good education and attended Norwich University (1853-1855) and Harvard University, from which he received his bachelor's degree in 1859. Deciding to enter the ministry, he was tutored privately by Rev. Frederic Dan Huntington, all the while serving as an assistant at Emmanuel Church in Boston. He was ordained in 1862 and began 21 years as pastor of All Saints Episcopal Church in Worcester, Massachusetts. The following year he married Theresa Reynolds.

Huntington's years in Worcester were prosperous ones. He authored his first book, *The Church-Idea* (1870), in which he began to develop the ideas for which he is most remembered. He had become concerned about the disunity of the church, and began to develop a plan for church union that would reach out to both free churches and Catholicism. He saw in the Episcopal Church, which had always had both low church (more evangelical) and high church (more sacramental) members, as an ideal institution to embody an ecumenical program. He proposed as a basis of church union four principles: (1) the Holy Scriptures as the Word of God, (2) the primitive creeds as the rule of faith, (3) the two sacraments mentioned in the Bible as having been instituted by Christ (Baptism and the Lord's Supper), and (4) the episcopacy as the central focus of organizational unity.

These principles gained a quick and broad acceptance within the Episcopal Church and the larger Anglican Communion (which includes the Church of England and other Anglican churches around the world). In 1889, the Lambeth Conference of the Anglican leaders accepted these principles as guiding principles in their pursuit of union, and they have since become known as the Lambeth Quadrilateral.

In 1883, after two decades in Massachusetts, Huntington left All Saints to become pastor of Grace Church in Manhattan. He summarized his Massachusetts years with his first autobiographical book, *Twenty Years of a Massachusetts Rectorship* (1883). He soon emerged as one of the leading pastors in the church.

During his New York years, Huntington became well known for his advocacy of the reform of the prayer book, the central liturgical volume used by Episcopalians. In 1880 he had been appointed to the joint committee on the *Book of Common Prayer*. His study, *The Book Annexed to the Report of the Joint Committee* (1883), was an important factor in the eventual revision accepted in 1892. A year later he authored *A Short History of the Book of Common Prayer* (1893). Also during his New York years Huntington promoted the building of the Cathedral of Saint John the Divine, a gothic reconstruction. A chapel named in Huntington's memory is now located in the cathedral.

As pastor of Grace Church, Huntington authored many books including *The Causes of the Soul* (1891); *A National Church* (1898); *Popular Misconceptions of the Episcopal Church* (1891); *Psyche* (1899); *Theology's Eminent Domain* (1902); and *Briefs on Religions* (1902). His last book was a second autobiographical volume, *Twenty Years of a New York Rectorship* (1903).

Sources:

Dictionary of American Biography. 20 vols. and 7 supps. New York: Charles Scribner's Sons, 1928-1936, 1944-1981.

Huntington, William Reed. *The Causes of the Soul.* New York: E. P. Dutton & Co, 1891. 390 pp.

_____. *The Church-Idea.* New York: E. P. Dutton & Co., 1870. 235 pp.

_____. *Popular Misconceptions of the Episcopal Church.* New York: J. Pott & Co., 1891. 87 pp.

_____. *A Short History of the Book of Common Prayer.* New York: T. Whittaker, 1893. 74 pp.

_____. *Twenty Years of a Massachusetts Rectorship.* Worcester, MA: Press of C. Hamilton, 1883. 39 pp.

_____. *Twenty Years of a New York Rectorship.* New York: The De Vinne Press, 1903. 31 pp.

★ 436 ★
HURLBUT, Jesse Lyman
Minister/Educator, Methodist Episcopal Church
Popular Writer
b. Feb. 15, 1843, New York City, New York
d. Aug. 2, 1930, Newark, New Jersey

Jesse Lyman Hurlbut, minister, educator, and writer of popular Christian literature, was the son of Samuel and Evelina Proal Hurlbut. As a child, Jesse moved with his family to New Jersey, where he grew up. He graduated from Wesleyan University in Connecticut in 1864. After a year of teaching, he joined the Newark Conference of the Methodist Episcopal Church. He served successively churches in Newark (1865-1867), Montclair (1867-1869), Paterson (1869-1872), Staten Island (1872-1874), Plainfield (1874-1877) and Hoboken, New Jersey (1877-1879). In 1867 he married Mary M. Chase. They had seven children.

During his early years as a minister, Hurlbut became interested in Sunday school work, and under his leadership the schools in the conference were transformed into efficient Bible training schools. His work led to his contact with **John H. Vincent**, the church's executive secretary of the Sunday school department. In 1875 Hurlbut traveled to Chautauqua, New York, where Vincent had organized the Sunday School Assembly. Hurlbut returned to Chautauqua each summer for 50 years and became one of the founding participants in the Chautauqua Movement, possibly his major contribution to American culture. In 1882 he graduated from the first Chautauqua Literary and Scientific Circle class and was its president. He is remembered with a bronze statue in the Hall of Fame at Chautauqua, New York.

In 1879 Hurlbut became a field agent under Vincent for the Sunday School Union and Tract Society and in 1884 became the group's assistant secretary and editor. In 1888, when Vincent was elected bishop, Hurlbut assumed his post as head of the Sunday School Union. While working for the Sunday School Union he became a strong advocate of graded Sunday school lessons (lessons written for each age group), a standard practice in all contemporary churches. In 1890 he led in the organization of the Epworth League, a national organization to mobilize Methodist Youth, now known as the United Methodist Youth Fellowship. His efforts toward giving new depth and direction to the Sunday school were a lasting contribution to the development of the church.

In spite of his important work as an organizer of the Chautauqua Movement and with the Sunday school and the youth of Methodism, Hurlbut's greatest fame was achieved as a writer of popular religious books. Of his more than 30 titles, his most popular (still in print 80 years later) is *Hurlbut's Story of the Bible* (1901). He

also wrote *Sunday Half Hours with the Great Preachers* (1905); *Hurlbut's Handy Bible Encyclopedia* (1908); *Traveling in the Holy Land through the Stereoscope* (1913); *Hurlbut's Story of Jesus* (1915); and *Hurlbut's Story of the Christian Church* (1918). Along the way he produced a number of instructional books for sunday school leaders and his last book, *The Story of Chautauqua* (1921).

In 1901 Hurlbut again became a pastor serving churches in Morristown, (1901-04), Orange (1904-06), and Bloomfield (1906—9). He became a district superintendent (1909-1914) and ended his professional career as a teacher of the Bible at Centenary Collegiate Institute.

Sources:

Adams, Oscar Fay. *A Dictionary of American Authors.* 5th ed., rev. New York: Houghton Mifflin Co., 1904. Reprint. Detroit: Gale Research Co., 1969.

Dictionary of American Biography. 20 vols. and 7 supps. New York: Charles Scribner's Sons, 1928-1936, 1944-1981.

Harmon, Nolan B. *The Encyclopedia of World Methodism.* 2 vols. Nashville: United Methodist Publishing House, 1974.

Hurlbut, Jesse Lyman. *Hurlbut's Handy Bible Encyclopedia.* Philadelphia: J. C. Winston Company, 1908. 390 pp. _____. *Hurlbut's Story of Jesus.* Philadelphia: J. C. Winston Company, 1915. 496 pp.

_____. *Hurlbut's Story of the Bible.* Chicago: J. C. Winston Company, 1932. 731 pp.

_____. *Hurlbut's Story of the Christian Church.* Rev. ed. Grand Rapids, MI: Zondervan, 1986.

_____. *The Story of Chautauqua.* New York: G. P. Putnam's Sons, 1921. 429 pp.

Kirk, John Foster. *A Supplement to Allibone's Critical Dictionary of English Literature and British and American Authors.* 2 vols. Philadelphia: J.B. Lippincott & Co., 1891. Reprint. Detroit: Gale Research Co., 1965.

The National Cyclopaedia of American Biography 61 vols. New York and Clifton, NJ: James T. White & Co., 1892-1982.

Johnson, Rossiter, ed. *The Twentieth Century Biographical Dictionary of Notable Americans.* 10 vols. Boston: The Biographical Society, 1904. Reprint. Detroit: Gale Research Co., 1968.

Kunitz, J., and Howard Haycraft, eds. *Twentieth Century Authors: A Biographical Dictionary of Modern Literature.* New York: H.W. Wilson Co., 1942.

Wallace, W. Stewart, comp. *A Dictionary of North American Authors Deceased before 1950.* Toronto: Ryerson Press, 1951. Reprint. Detroit: Gale Research Co., 1968.

Who Was Who in America. Chicago: Marquis Who's Who, Inc.

★ 437 ★
HURLEY, George Willie
Founder, Universal Hagar's Spiritual Church
b. Feb. 17, 1884, Reynolds, Georgia
d. Jun. 23, 1943, Detroit, Michigan

George Willie Hurley was the charismatic founder and leader of the Universal Hagar's Spiritual Church, a predominantly black spiritualist denomination. He was raised in rural Georgia as a Baptist, and became first a Baptist, then a Methodist minister. He and his wife, Cassie Bell Martin, moved to Detroit in 1919, where Hurley joined and became a minister of a holiness church called Triumph Church and Kingdom of God in Christ that taught both sanctification (by an instantaneous work of grace) and fire baptism (an experience of the power of the Holy Spirit). Hurley rose in the church to become its Presiding Prince of Michigan.

Hurley's religious path, however, was altered by two incidents. The first of these incidents occurred when he was invited to a spiritualist church and was converted. He left the holiness church and was soon a minister in the International Spiritual Church. (What the white community calls a "spiritualist" church the black community usually calls a "spiritual" church.) The second step came soon after this, when, in 1923, he had a vision of a "brown-skinned damsel" who was transformed into an eagle. He interpreted the eagle as representing the church he was to found, and on September 23, 1923, he began the Universal Hagar's Spiritual Church. In 1924 he added the School of Mediumship and Psychology, in order to train members in psychic phenomena.

In his church, Hurley was able to exercise his creative spirituality and leadership. He made use of a variety of sources, including the Ethiopianism popular among American Blacks after World War II and Levi Dowling's classic spiritualist book, the *The Aquarian Gospel of Jesus Christ*. Hurley taught that Blacks (Ethiopians) were God's original Hebrew people and that the pale skin of Whites is a mark of the curse of Cain, from whom they are descended. Hurley began to claim for himself something of a divine stature, proclaiming that he was God's Spirit on earth in the Aquarian Age, just as Jesus was for the Piscean Age, and so on for Moses and Adam. Hurley taught that the Aquarian Age began after the Armistice was signed ending World War I, would last 7,000 years, and would see the end of Protestantism, segregation, and injustice. Hurley died in 1943 at the age of 59, and his widow led his group of nearly 40 congregations until her death in 1960.

Sources:

Baer, Hans A. *The Black Spiritual Movement: A Religion's Response to Racism*. Knoxville, TN: University of Tennessee Press, 1984. 221 pp.

Melton, J. Gordon. *Biographical Dictionary of American Cult and Sect Leaders*. Garland Reference Library of Social Science, vol. 212. New York: Garland Publishing, 1986.

—*Gary L. Ward*

★438★
Archbishop IAKOVOS
Metropolitan, Greek Orthodox Archdiocese of North and South America
b. Jul. 29, 1911, St. Theodore Turkey

Archbishop Iakovos, the leader of Greek Orthodox Christians in the Western Hemisphere, was born Demetrios A. Coucouzes on Imbros Island, a Greek island in the Aegean Sea. He was the son of Athanasios and Maria Coucouzes. In 1923 Turkey took possession of the island, and it has remained a part of their territory ever since. As a young man, Demetrios wanted to teach, and he was able to obtain a scholarship to Haiki Theological Seminary, the school of the Ecumenical Patriarchate. The scholarship was paid for by **Bishop Iakovos Papapaisiou**, the bishop whose diocese included Imbros.

Young Demetrios left for school in Constantinople in 1927. He returned to Imbros in 1934 as a preacher and teacher and founded a catechetical school. On November 11, 1934, he had a dream that he interpreted as a call from God. On November 25, 1934, he was ordained a deacon in the Greek Orthodox Church. He was assigned to the Metropolitate of Derkion and also served as secretary in the army hospital in Constantinople. He remained in Constantinople until just prior to World War II.

In 1939 Coucouzes immigrated to the United States. He was assigned to Holy Cross Seminary, then located in Pomfret, Connecticut. He also pastored St. George's Greek Orthodox Church at Hartford, Connecticut. He was ordained a priest in 1940. During the next few years he served churches in New York City, St. Louis, and Boston. While serving as dean of the cathedral church in Boston, he studied at Harvard, from which he received a S.T.M. in 1945. In 1947 Holy Cross was moved to Brookline, Massachusetts, and he became dean of the seminary.

Coucouzes remained at the seminary until 1954, when he was named bishop of Melita. It was at this time that he assumed the name of the bishop who had been his mentor many years before. He was consecrated the following year and assigned as the representative of the Ecumenical Patriarch to the World Council of Churches in Geneva. During his years in Geneva, he served as president of the council on two occasions. In 1959 he made an of-ficial visit to Pope John XXIII, the first such contact between the papacy and the Ecumenical Patriarch since 1054.

In 1959 Bishop Iakovos was elevated to the archbishopric as the new leader of the church in the Americas. As archbishop he has taken the lead in moving what had essentially been an immigrant-ethnic church into a church solidly established within middle America. He became widely known outside of Orthodox circles when he joined **Martin Luther King, Jr.** in the civil rights marches in the 1960s. Within the Orthodox community in America he has been a leader in the Americanization process, though he has at times differed sharply on particulars with the Russian and Antiochean leadership. He was a founder of the Standing Conference of Canonical Orthodox Bishops, through which Eastern Orthodoxy speaks with a united voice in North America.

In 1965 Iakovos led in the founding of LOGOS, the League of Greek Orthodox Stewards, a prime lay stewardship organization for the archdiocese within the Greek communion. In 1969 he founded Ionian Village, a camp for Greek-American children in Greece. In 1971 he established the *Orthodox Observer*, a periodical for the archdiocese. In 1979 Iakovos was awarded the Medal of Freedom by President Carter.

Sources:

Poulos, George. *A Breath of God*. Brookline, MA: Holy Cross Seminary Press, 1984. 177 pp.

Who's Who in Religion. 2d ed. Chicago: Marquis Who's Who, Inc., 1977.

★439★
ICHAZO, Oscar
Founder, Arica Institute
b. 1931, Robore Bolivia

Oscar Ichazo is the founder of the Arica Institute, a "mystery school" that eclectically combines a number of different strands of thought and practice from the traditions of Sufism and the teachings of **George I. Gurdjieff**. Ichazo's parents were nominal Catholics, and he was educated in a Jesuit school. His father was a prominent Bolivian politician. His spiritual quest was prompted by periodic cataleptic attacks that he began having in late 1937 at the age of six. The attacks, which would occur when he was between waking and sleeping, consisted of great pain, fear of death, and then the experience of leaving his body. The attacks continued for many years and led him to become interested in techniques for controlling his own consciousness.

When he was nine years old, Ichazo's search for a cure led him to study martial arts. He also became friends with some *curanderos* (Indian medicine men) who introduced him to mind-altering drugs. As was the case with a number of the participants in the 1960s counter-culture, these drug experiences stimulated him to undertake a mystical quest. While still in Bolivia, he investigated Zen meditation, hypnosis, yoga, eastern martial arts, spiritualism, theosophy, and Hindu philosophy.

Ichazo earned his living as a writer and journalist. At 19, he was director of Bolivia's Library of Congress. In the early 1950s he was invited to Buenos Aires, where he became involved with a mystical group that had been influenced by the teachings of Gurdjieff. In the late 1950s, he started a number of study groups in Santiago, Chile, and during the same period made a number of trips to the East. His travels took him to Hong Kong, India, and Tibet. Particularly important for the development of Arica was the time he spent with Sufis in Iran and Afghanistan. In 1964 he went to his father's house in Bolivia, where he spent a year in solitude. During this period, he had an experience which he subsequently referred to as a "divine coma." He came back from this enlightening experience with the feeling that he should now begin to teach what he had learned, and he quickly established a training center in Arica, Chile.

On July 1, 1970, between 50 and 60 North Americans, many of them from the Esalen Institute, came to Arica to undertake 10 months of intensive training. Claudio Naranjo, John and Kathy Bleibtreu, and John Lilly had visited Arica the year before and brought back highly favorable reports. The training at Arica combined metaphysical teachings, calisthenics, and such spiritual practices as *zhikr* (a Sufi technique involving the repetition of divine names). The attention given to the training by the human potentials movement, and the positive publicity contained in Lilly's *Center of the Cyclone*, encouraged Ichazo to begin to establish branches of his school in North America. He began teaching in the United States in 1971, and the Arica Institute was founded in New York. The training enjoyed a brief surge of widespread popularity, and then Arica settled down to occupy a relatively humble place on America's religious landscape.

Ichazo has spent the intervening years leading Arica training and further refining his teachings. He lectures frequently on Arica, and many of the lectures have been transcribed and published.

Sources:

De Christopher, Dorothy. "I Am the Root of a New Tradition." *The Movement Newspaper* 6, 5 (1981). 8 pp.
Hill, Ann, ed. *A Visual Encyclopedia of Unconventional Medicine: A Health Manual for the Whole Person.* New York: Crown, 1978. 240 pp.
Ichazo, Oscar. *Arica Psychocalisthenics.* New York; Simon and Schuster, 1976. 107 pp.
_____. *Between Metaphysics and Protoanalysis.* New York: Arica Institute, 1982. 119 pp.
_____. *Five Lectures to Advanced Trainings of the Arica Institute.* New York: Arica Institute, 1975. 159 pp.
_____. *Interviews with Oscar Ichazo.* New York: Arica Institute Press, 1982. 190 pp.
_____. *Kinerhythm Meditation.* New York: Arica Institute, 1972. 53 pp.
_____. *The Temple Ritual.* New York: Arica Institute, 1976. 25 pp.
_____. *Three Lectures.* New York: Arica Institute, 1975.
Keen, Sam. "'We Have No Desire to Strengthen the Ego or Make It Happy': A Conversation about Ego Destruction with Oscar Ichazo." *Psychology Today* (July 1971).

★440★
IKEDA, Daisaku
President, Soka Gakkai International
b. Feb. 2, 1928, Tokyo Japan

Daisaku Ikeda, the honorary president of the worldwide Buddhist organization known as Soka Gakkai International, which is represented in the United States by Nichiren Shoshu of America (NSH), was born Taisaku (meaning burly builder) Ikeda to Nenokicki and Ichi Ikeda. His father processed laver, a form of seaweed, a prosperous business enterprise in early twentieth-century Japan. An earthquake in 1923, however, destroyed many of the seaweed beds around Tokyo Bay and thus his business was in decline as Taisaku was growing up. He attended public school from 1934 to 1940 and then entered a two-year higher elementary school just as some of his older brothers were departing for war. During much of the war he worked at the Niigata Iron Works and continued his schooling in the evening as he was able.

Ikeda was devastated by Japan's defeat in 1945. Two years later, Ikeda met Josei Toda, who was able to answer the questions about life that had dominated Ikeda's thoughts as he grew to manhood in postwar Japan. On August 24, 1947, he was received into Nichiren Shoshu, one branch of the faith established by Nichiren, the eighth-century Buddhist reformer, and began to work with Toda, a leader in the Soka Gakkai, the Nichiren Shoshu lay organization. During the next few years, Nichiren Shoshu and Soka Gakkai suffered some misfortunes. The publication of the magazine *Boy's Adventures* (later *Boy's Japan*), which Ikeda edited, was suspended within a year of its appearance (1949). But Ikeda was able during these difficult months to continue with his schooling. He fin-

ished at Tokyo School of Commerce and then attended Taisei Institute. In 1952 he married.

In about 1951 the misfortunes that had plagued the Soka Gakkai lessened. Toda became its second president, and Ikeda worked full time as head of the young men's corps. During 1952 he began to travel widely throughout Japan and helped organize the Komei Party, a political affiliate of Soka Gakkai. It is during this time that Ikeda started using the name Daisaku.

In 1958 Toda died. Ikeda was appointed executive director and in 1960 was elected the third president of Soka Gakkai. His decades of leadership were times of tremendous growth for the organization, which by 1962 had members in over three million Japanese families. In that year Ikeda established the Institute of Oriental Philosophy, a research facility dedicated to the study of Asian culture. Over the next 15 years he established a number of additional educational facilities: the Soka junior and senior high schools for boys (1968); Soka University (1971); the Soka girls schools (1973); Soka kindergarten (1976); and Soka elementary school (1978). In 1964 Ikeda announced plans to build the Sho Hondo as a worldwide center for Nichiren faith. It was completed in 1970.

In 1974 Ikeda resigned as president of Soka Gakkai. The following year he was named president of Soka Gakkai International, with duties to oversee the international development of the organization's work, which had established a presence in over 100 countries. He resigned that post in 1979 and was named honorary president.

During the years of Ikeda's leadership, members of Nichiren Shoshu had immigrated to America. In 1960 he made his first trip to the United States to organize the work formally. This became but one of the countries to which the movement spread. He returned in 1975 and on a number of occasions in the 1980s. In the mid-1980s, he inaugurated a branch of Soka University in Calabasas, California.

Over the years, Ikeda has been a prolific speaker and writer. Many of his speeches have been compiled into books and many of his writings translated into English. Among his more important writings are *Guidance Memo* (1966); *The Human Revolution* (1972-74); *Buddhism: The First Millennium* (1977); and *Daily Guidance* (1983). A volume of poetry was published as *Songs of My Heart* (1978), and an autobiography, *My Recollections*, appeared in 1980. During the early 1970s, Ikeda had an extended series of conversations with historian Arnold Toynbee, which were published as *Choose Life: A Dialogue* in 1976.

Sources:

Ikeda, Daisaku. *Buddhism: The First Millennium.* Tokyo: Kodansha International, 1977. 172 pp.
_____. *Daily Guidance.* Los Angeles: World Tribune Press, 1983. 400 pp.
_____. *Guidance Memo.* Tokyo: The Seikyo Press, 1966. 297 pp.
_____. *The Human Revolution.* 2 vols. New York: Weatherhill, 1972-1974.
_____. *My Recollections.* Los Angeles: World Tribune Press, 1980. 145 pp.
_____. *Songs of My Heart.* New York: Weatherhill, 1978. 111 pp.
_____, and Arnold Toynbee. *Choose Life: A Dialogue.* London: Oxford University Press, 1976. 348 pp.
Soka Gakkai. Tokyo: Soka Gakkai, 1983. 127 pp.

★441★
IMAMURA, Yemyo
Bishop, Honpa Hongwanji Mission of Hawaii
b. 1867, Japan
d. Dec. 22, 1932, Honolulu, Hawaii

Little information is available on the early life of Yemyo Imamura, for over 30 years the director of the Honpa Hongwanji Buddhist Mission in the Hawaiian Islands. Prior to his arrival in Hawaii, he had attended Keio Gijuku (Keio University) where he had studied literature and later became a school teacher. As a priest of the Honpa Hongwanji Buddhists, he arrived in Honolulu in 1899 accompanied by Hoji Satomi, the first bishop of the newly created Hawaii "diocese." Satomi stayed only a short time and left the work in the hands of Imamura. His first task was the completion of the new temple in Honolulu. He oversaw the dedication of the new structure in November of 1900.

Imamura's immediate task was the organization of the many Japanese Buddhists in the islands. He began in 1900 with the formation of the Young Men's Buddhist Association. He next moved to the rural areas and led in the construction of temples on all the major plantations. The amiable Imamura was able to gain the cooperation of the plantation owners who had a record of generally acting in favor of Christian missions. His reputation with the plantation owners, however, was solidified in 1904 when he helped calm a riotous strike at Waipahu plantation on Oahu. Imamura's efforts were noted in Japan in 1906 by the elevation of the work in Honolulu to the status of *betsuin*, or detached temple and branch headquarters. Imamura then applied for and received a charter as a religious organization. The temples in the islands were then formally attached to the betsuin in Honolulu. In 1908 Imamura presided over the first inter-island conference to strategize for the future of Buddhism in Hawaii. That same year he became the first American Buddhist to obtain a license to officiate at weddings.

Imamura worked many hours to make a place for the Japanese in American culture and argued that Buddhism was compatible with American democracy and not an instrument fostering Japanese nationalism. In this endeavor he authored a booklet, *Democracy According to the Buddhist Viewpoint* (1918). Imamura's perspective would later undergird the participation of Japanese-Americans in the U.S. Army during World War II.

The seriousness of Imamura's program to integrate Buddhism into American culture was embodied in the 1918 creation of an English department to spread Buddhist teachings among non-Japanese. He soon gathered a number of able converts led by M. T. Kirby, George Wright, and **Ernest Hunt**. Imamura also worked for the promotion of pan-Buddhism in the West, and in that regard, with Hunt's assistance, in 1929 he founded the Hawaii branch of the International Buddhist Institute. He was elected president for life. The institute sponsored a number of activities to help change the negative image of Buddhism held by many Hawaiians. It published a magazine, *Navayana*, issued a yearbook, and held lectures for English-speaking audiences.

Some of Imamura's work was carried on by Hunt, but a great deal of the good will he had built with the caucasian community was lost during the tenure of Gikyo Kuchiba who became bishop in 1935. Kuchiba opposed Imamura's Americanizing program and dismantled as much as he could in the years leading to the disruption of World War II. After the war, however, Imamura's three decades of work provided the more enduring base from which the Japanese-Hawaiians could build a positive future. A statue of Bishop Imamura now resides in the main temple in Honolulu.

Sources:

Hunter, Louise H. *Buddhism in Hawaii*. Honolulu, HI: University of Hawaii Press, 1971. 266 pp.

Imamura, Y. *Democracy According to the Buddhist Viewpoint*. Honolulu, HI: Honpa Hongwangi Mission, 1918.

_____. *A Short History of the Hongwanji Buddhist Mission in Hawaii*. Honolulu, HI: The Mission, 1927.

Yamamoto, George Y. *Origin of Buddhism in Hawaii*. Honolulu, HI: YBA of Honolulu, [1955]. 32 pp.

★ 442 ★
INGERSOLL, Robert Green
Freethought Orator
b. Aug. 11, 1833, Dresden, New York
d. Jul. 21, 1899, Dobbs Ferry, New York

Robert Green Ingersoll, the most persuasive exponent of Freethought in nineteenth-century America, was the son of John Ingersoll, a Congregationalist minister and abolitionist, and his wife, Mary. Robert's mother died when he was three, and his father moved to the Midwest, where he served several congregations. Because of the frequent changes of residence, Robert's education was sporadic, but he possessed both a native intelligence and a photographic memory. In 1854 he settled in Peoria, Illinois, and opened a law office with his brother. He also married Eva Parker, the daughter of an atheist.

Ingersoll joined the Union Army during the Civil War. He was given a commission as a colonel and given command over the 11th Illinois Cavalry. Early in the fighting Ingersoll and the unit were captured, imprisoned, and released, after promising that they would not reenlist. Prior to the war he had left the Democratic Party and become a Republican over the slavery issue. After the war he was appointed attorney general of Illinois, but he did not pursue his political opportunities beyond that single office because of his religious views.

Ingersoll's career as a public orator really began in 1876 when he was invited to give the nominating speech at the Republican convention for presidential hopeful James G. Blaine. After the convention he moved to Washington, D.C., and for the rest of his life divided his worktime between the practice of law and traveling on the lecture circuit. He developed a set of lectures which he repeated in different towns through the years. His most famous lecture, frequently spoken and reprinted, was entitled "Some Mistakes of Moses," in which he recounted his problems with the Bible in its literal reading. His personal credo was summarized best in another lecture, "Why I Am an Agnostic," in which he articulated a practical atheism. While leaving the question of the existence of God and the reality of human immortality open, he specifically denied the existence of any supernatural reality that can or does answer prayer.

Ingersoll's career spanned a quarter of a century. Though blocked from holding elected office due to his opinions, his great following in towns small and large and his continued use by Republicans in political settings indicated not only his great oratorical skills but significant popular support for his skeptical ideals, a support frequently unacknowledged by religious historians of the era. In his mature life he influenced a generation of social reformers and thinkers from Elizabeth Cady Stanton to Andrew Carnegie. He gave his early support to the women's cause and spoke in favor of women's suffrage, artificial birth control, and equal pay for equal work for females.

Ingersoll died suddenly in 1899.

Sources:

Cramer, Clarence H. *Royal Bob*. Indianapolis, IN: Bobbs-Merrill, 1952. 314 pp.

Encyclopedia of Southern Baptists. 3 vols. Nashville, TN: Broadman Press, 1958, 1971.

Greeley, Roger E. *Ingersoll: Immortal Infidel*. Buffalo, NY: Prometheus Books, 1977.

Ingersoll, Robert G. *The Works of Robert G. Ingersoll*. 12 vols. New York: C. P. Farrell, 1900.

Stein, Gordon. *Robert G. Ingersoll, A Checklist*. Kent, OH: Kent State University Press, 1969. 128 pp.

Wakefield, Eva Ingersoll. *Letters of Robert G. Ingersoll*. New York: Philosophical Library, 1951. 747 pp.

★ 443 ★
IRELAND, John
Archbishop, Roman Catholic Church
b. Sep. 11, 1838, Burnchurch Ireland
d. Sep. 25, 1918, St. Paul, Minnesota

John Ireland, an archbishop in the Roman Catholic Church, was the son of Judith Naughton and Richard Ireland, who migrated to the United States in 1849. They lived for a while in Burlington, Vermont, but soon moved westward. They finally settled in St. Paul, Minnesota. Singled out by the bishop at St. Paul, Ireland was sent to study for the priesthood in France, first at the Seminaire de Meximieux, and then Scolasticat a Montbel, both near Toulousse. He returned to St. Paul to be ordained in 1861. He served for a year (1862-1863) as a chaplain in the Union Army, but was forced to resign because of illness. He was assigned to the cathedral church and became its pastor in 1867.

During the years after the war, Ireland gained some fame because of his oratorical skills, which he turned upon what he perceived to be political corruption in St. Paul. Seeing much of the corruption associated with the liquor interests, he began a temperance crusade which carried from Minnesota into the national arena and provoked the positive response of Protestants.

His rise in the church began in 1870 when he journeyed to Rome as a representative at the First Vatican Council. In 1875 he was named vicar apostolic for Nebraska, but his own bishop intervened and had him named coadjutor bishop of St. Paul. He became bishop in 1884, and quickly emerged as the leading liberal voice in the American hierarchy. He signaled his position soon after taking office in an address on "The Catholic Church and Civil Society" to the Plenary Council which met in Baltimore just weeks after he assumed his office. His position, which advocated a strong American patriotism and a positive attitude toward American culture, was later to be termed "Americanism." In 1888 Ireland was named the first archbishop of St. Paul.

Ireland put his ideas into action on many fronts. He organized the St. Paul Catholic Colonization Society which facilitated the movement of over 4,000 people from overcrowded slums to western farmland. As a result he became the founder of a number of towns in Minnesota and Nebraska. Over the years he opposed efforts to segregate the American church into ethnic factions and demanded the use of English-language texts in all Catholic schools. He supported the efforts of labor to organize and helped persuade Pope Leo not to condemn the Knights of Labor.

Throughout his life he worked for Catholic scholarship. He established St. Thomas Seminary in his own diocese in 1885. He supported the establishment of Catholic University in Washington, D.C., in 1887. He established St. Paul Seminary in St. Paul in 1894 and nurtured St. Catherine College, founded in 1905.

In 1892 he traveled to France where he spoke freely on the church in the United States and the positive effects of separation of church and state. His ideas were taken up and developed in Europe and gave rise to an 1899 encyclical by the pope condemning a series of ideas which he called "Americanism." The encyclical was taken by many as a slap at Ireland and other liberal bishops, but Ireland joined colleagues **John J. Keane** and James Gibbons in denying that any of the condemned ideas were advocated by church leaders.

Through his involvement in numerous controversies within the church and his attempts to bring the church into the mainstream of American life, he became one of the most notable American Catholics of all time. He ended almost a quarter century of leadership of Minnesota Catholics in 1918.

Sources:
Delaney, John J. *Dictionary of American Catholic Biography.* Garden City, NY: Doubleday & Company, 1988. 621 pp.
Dictionary of American Biography. 20 vols. and 7 supps. New York: Charles Scribner's Sons, 1928-1936, 1944-1981.
Monnihan, James H. *The Life of Archbishop John Ireland.* New York: Harper, 1953. 441 pp.
O'Connell, Marvin R. *John Ireland and the American Catholic Church.* St. Paul, MN: Minnesota Historical Society Press, 1988. 610 pp.
Shannon, James P. *Catholic Colonization on the Western Frontier.* New Haven, CT: Yale University Press, 1957. 302 pp.

★ 444 ★
Metropolitan IRENEY
Archbishop, Orthodox Church in America
b. Oct. 2, 1892, Mezhirech Russia
d. Mar. 18, 1981, Staten Island, New York

Metropolitan Ireney, the head of the Orthodox Church in America, the oldest of the several Eastern Orthodox churches in North America, was born John Bekisk in southwestern Russia. He attended Kholm Theological Seminary from which he graduated in 1914. He served as a lay reader for several years and was married. He was ordained in 1916. Following his ordination he was appointed assistant rector of the cathedral in Lublin, Poland. In the years after World War I and the Russian Revolution, he served in a variety of positions in the church. He became a member of the consistory of the diocese of Pinsk (Russia) and was chairman of its missionary committee. He then served parishes in Sarna and Kamen-Kashursk (also in Russia), and eventually was appointed dean of the two deaneries.

World War II became the disruptive force in Bekisk's life. He became a refugee and found himself in Belgium as a parish priest at Charleroi. In 1952 he moved to the United States and became a priest at McAdoo, Pennsylvania, with the Russian Orthodox Greek Catholic Church in America, the largest of the several Russian Orthodox bodies then functioning in the country. His wife having died, in 1953 he was elected bishop of Tokyo, was tonsured (became a monk), and was given the name Ireney. He provided strong leadership for the small church in Japan, his most noticeable accomplishment being the opening of the theological seminary in 1954.

In 1960 he returned to the United States and was appointed bishop of Boston (Massachusetts) and New England and assistant to **Metropolitan Leonty**, who was in poor health. Following Leonty's death in 1965 Ireney was elected to succeed him.

During Ireney's tenure as metropolitan, the major issues between the American church and the patriarchate of Russia were resolved, and in 1970 His Holiness Alexis, the patriarch of Moscow, formally granted the Russian Orthodox Greek Catholic Church of America autonomous status. At that time the church assumed its present name, Orthodox Church in America. The church bestowed the title "Beatitude" on Ireney at that time. Unfortunately, this new status and new name for Russian Orthodoxy in North America did not find acceptance with other Orthodox jurisdictions. Ireney, in spite of numerous attempts, was unable to persuade the other major jurisdictions (especially the numerically larger Greek Orthodox Archdiocese of North and South America) to come into the new church or even approve the Russian's action. Several months after the high point of obtaining autonomy, Ireney traveled to Alaska to preside over services to canonize St. Herman of Alaska (1756-1837), the first Orthodox saint in America so designated.

In 1977 Ireney retired and was succeeded by **Metropolitan Theodosius**, formerly bishop of Pittsburgh and West Virginia. Ireney's final years were lived on Staten Island, New York.

Sources:

Tarasar, Constance J. *Orthodox America, 1794-1974*. Syosset, NY: Department of History and Archives, Orthodox Church in America, 1975. 361 pp.

★ 445 ★
IRONSIDE, Harry

Pastor, Moody Memorial Church
b. Oct. 14, 1876, Toronto, Ontario, Canada
d. Jan. 15, 1951, Cambridge New Zealand

Henry Allen Ironside, usually called "Harry," was an evangelist with the Plymouth Brethren who served for a number of years as pastor of the independent fundamentalist Moody Memorial Church in Chicago. He was the son of John Williams and Sophia Stafford Ironside, who had immigrated to Canada from Great Britain shortly before his birth. The elder Ironside joined the Brethren in Toronto and became active as a street preacher. He died when Harry was three years old. In 1886 Harry's mother moved the family to Los Angeles, where two years later Harry attended the revival meetings of **Dwight L. Moody**.

Though Ironside had decided that he wanted to preach like Moody, it was not until 1890 that Ironside had a personal born-again experience with God that established him within the evangelical community. Shortly after the experience he associated himself with the Salvation Army and began to preach for them. He dropped out of school and took a job with a photographer. At the age of 16 he was commissioned by the army and during the next few years worked at San Bernadino and other California communities. He also experienced what the Salvation Army calls the second blessing or sanctification. Like other holiness groups, the army taught that it was possible, by an act of the Holy Spirit, to be made perfect in love. Several years after professing the experience, however, Ironside became doubtful of it, and later resigned his commission when he could no longer in good conscience believe in it.

By 1896 Ironside had returned to the Brethren, joining the branch known as the Grant Brethren (after **Frederick Grant**, a popular Brethren teacher). He relocated to San Francisco, where he began to preach and teach the Bible. In 1898 he married Helen Schofield. In 1900 they moved to Oakland, where they led a meager existence for a number of years off of the offerings from Ironside's preaching. He also began to author a series of Bible studies. The first volumes included *Notes on Esther* (1900); *Notes on Jeremiah* (1902); *Notes on the Minor Prophets* (1904); and *Notes on Proverbs* (1906). In 1912 he also penned a booklet refuting the Salvation Army teachings, *Holiness: the False and the True*.

In 1914 Ironside opened the Western Book and Tract Company, which became his headquarters for many years and from which he published and distributed his many books, as well as those of other Brethren authors. He traveled constantly, spending time each summer with the American Indian tribes in the Southwest. In the years after World War I, he continued to write books at a significant rate. Besides additional Bible commentaries, he authored *Adders' Eggs and Spiders' Webs* (1924); *The Mass vs. the Lord's Supper* (1926); *Lectures to a Roman Catholic Priest* (1926); and *The Midnight Cry* (1928).

In 1930, in spite of his not being ordained (a practice frowned upon in Brethren circles), Ironside was invited to become pastor of Moody Memorial Church. His duties as leader of this prominent congregation included the preaching of the funeral sermon for evangelist **William "Billy" Sunday** in 1935. In 1937, having stepped into the shoes of his teenage hero, he traveled to England to celebrate the Moody centennial, the first of three trips Ironside made to preach in the British Isles. During the years of his pastorate, his literary production continued and included *The Unchanging Christ* (1934); *Except Ye Repent* (1937); *Random Reminis-*

cences (1939); and *A Historical Sketch of the Brethren Movement* (1942).

After 18 years at Moody, Ironside retired, although he continued to preach frequently. He died in 1951 while on a preaching tour in New Zealand. He was also buried there.

Sources:

English, E. Schuyler. *H. A. Ironside, Ordained of the Lord*. Oakland, CA: Western Book and Tract Co., 1956. 276 pp.

Ironside, H. A. *The Continual Burnt Offering*. New York: Loizeaux Brothers, 1941.

_____. *Except Ye Repent*. New York: Loizeaux Bros., 1937. 191 pp.

_____. *A Historical Sketch of the Brethren Movement*. Grand Rapids, MI: Zondervam Publishing House, 1942. 219 pp.

_____. *Holiness: the False and the True*. New York: Loizeaux Brothers, 1948. 142 pp.

_____. *The Lamp of Prophecy*. Grand Rapids, MI: Zondervan Publishing House, 1951. 159 pp.

_____. *Wrongly Dividing the Word of Truth*. Neptune, NJ: Loizeaux Brothers, Inc. Bible Truth Depot, n.d. 66 pp.

★ 446 ★
IRWIN, Benjamin Hardin

Founder, Fire-Baptized Holiness Association
b. 1854, Mercer, Missouri

Benjamin Hardin Irwin, founder of the Fire-Baptized Holiness Association, an 1890s precursor to the Pentecostal movement, was raised in rural Iowa. We know little of his youthful years and nothing of his last days. His father was arrested during the Civil War (possibly for being a southern sympathizer) and the family moved from Iowa to Nebraska in 1863. His mother died in 1865. He was raised in the Baptist church but never joined. As a young man, Irwin moved from the family farm to the nearby town of Tecumseh, Nebraska. He married and became a lawyer. During these years, he saw himself as a wicked man, prone to lying, cheating, and when drunk, abusing his wife and children. In 1879, however, he was converted to Christianity. He joined the local Baptist church and made restitution for his past life. He eventually became pastor of the congregation.

Shortly after assuming his pastoral duties, Irwin encountered members of the Iowa Holiness Association, who traveled to Tecumseh preaching their message of a second work of grace which brought sanctification, a heart of perfect love, to the believer. Irwin desired this deeper experience of God and received it in a highly emotional event in 1891. Irwin believed that his sinful nature had been eradicated by the Holy Spirit. As a result of his experience he resigned from the Baptist church and eventually joined the Wesleyan Methodist Church, which believed in the holiness doctrine.

Irwin began to read voraciously in Methodist literature. In the writings of John Fletcher, an early British Methodist, he came upon discussion of still another experience that awaited the sanctified believer, "the baptism of burning love."

Irwin became an itinerant evangelist through Iowa, Nebraska, Illinois, and adjacent states. In 1895, while in Oklahoma, he experienced the baptism of fire, described as being surrounded by a fiery presence which leads to an intensification of faith, love, courage, and hope. It raised the believer to a higher level of spirituality. Irwin published an account of his experience in a pamphlet. Before the year was out he had alienated many holiness people. He began to form local fire-baptized holiness associations, which were affiliated into the Iowa Fire-Baptized Holiness Association. By the end of 1896 Irwin had left the Wesleyan Methodist Church. One independent holiness periodical, *The Way of Faith*, supported him. By 1897 he had also experienced a healing and began to add a message of divine healing to his sermons.

During the next few years, Irwin's message spread across the south and southwest, and north into Ohio, Pennsylvania, and even Canada. Associations appeared in nine states, and in 1898 he organized a national Fire-Baptized Holiness Association at Anderson, South Carolina. Irwin led the new association through his formal, almost dictatorial, association position, his articulate speaking talents, and his writing ability. In 1899 Irwin began a periodical, *Live Coals of Fire*, which he edited.

Just as the association was growing, its future was placed in jeopardy when Irwin was discovered walking the street of Omaha, Nebraska, drunk and smoking a cigar. He later confessed to having led a double life for some years. His work was turned over to **Joseph Hillery King**, his associate. Irwin disappeared, never to be heard from again. Within a few years, his association encountered the new Pentecostal movement, and under King's leadership was almost entirely swept into it, becoming part of what is today known as the International Pentecostal Holiness Church. The Pentecostal message suggested that what Irwin was trying to articulate in his evangelistic efforts was the baptism of the Holy Spirit as evidenced in speaking in tongues. Blacks who had become a part of the movement formed an independent church. It kept Irwin's original name—the Fire-Baptized Holiness Church of God of the Americas—though it operated with a Pentecostal doctrine.

Sources:

Campbell, Joseph E. *The Pentecostal Holiness Church, 1898-1948.* Franklin Springs, GA: Pentecostal Holiness Church, 1951. 573 pp.

Schrag, Martin. "The Spiritual Pilgrimage of the Reverend Benjamin Hardin Irwin," *Brethren in Christ History and Life* 4, 1 (June 1981): 3-29.

★447★
ITKIN, Michael Francis Augustine
Founder, Community of the Love of Christ (Evangelical Catholic)
b. Feb. 7, 1936
d. Aug. 1, 1989, San Francisco, California

Michael Francis Augustine Itkin, one of the first openly homosexual religious activists in America and founder of the Community of the Love of Christ (Evangelical Catholic), began his religious career as a teenager in the South. He was ordained in 1952 by Rev. Claude Williams, leader of the People's Institute of Applied Religion. In 1946, a young minister, George Augustine Hyde, founded the first homosexual congregation, the Eucharistic Catholic Church, in Atlanta, Georgia. The congregation operated quietly until 1954 when Hyde placed an announcement in the magazine *One*, published by the Mattachine Society. Among the people attracted by the announcement was Michael Itkin. Itkin was licensed by the church in 1955. Hyde became a bishop in 1957 and on May 6 of that year ordained Itkin to the priesthood.

Itkin worked with Hyde for two years, but, claiming that Hyde had departed from an openly gay ministry, split away in 1959. On November 12, 1960, he was consecrated by independent Bp. Christopher Carl Jerome Stanley of the United Old Catholic Patriarchate of the World. He founded a new Old Catholic jurisdiction, originally called the Primitive Catholic Church (Evangelical Catholic). The church experienced several name changes before Itkin heard of the work of Ulric Herford (1886-1938) and the Evangelical Catholic Communion in England. Through Herford's successors in Great Britain, he was given permission to reformulate and continue the communion's tradition in North America.

During the 1960s Itkin developed a version of a theology of revolution which revolved around pacifism, liberation from oppression, and civil rights. Integral to his perspective were gay liberation and an ultimate goal of moving toward a universal androgynous community. He formed an order within the communion called the Brotherhood of the Love of Christ (later changed to Community of the Love of Christ). In 1965 he participated in three episcopal con-

secration services presided over by various independent bishops. He was initially consecrated on May 16 by Robert William Zimmer of the North American Old Roman Catholic Church (N.A.O.R.C.C.). Two days later he was consecrated sub conditione by Mark I. Miller of the American Orthodox Catholic Church. Finally on August 31, he was consecrated by Lawrence Francois Pierre of the American Orthodox Catholic Church.

As a demonstration of his new theology, in 1968 Itkin began to ordain women, an action which split his jurisdiction. The dissidents continued as the Evangelical Catholic Communion, and he reorganized as the Community of the Love of Christ (Evangelical Catholic). In the early 1970s he moved his headquarters to Los Angeles, renounced his episcopal orders and adopted a Mennonite theology (minus its emphasis on the heterosexual nuclear family). His flirtation with Mennonite theology was short-lived, however, and in 1984 he again resumed his episcopal office. He underwent another consecration, this time from Ronald Powell (also known as Richard Duc de Palatine) of the Pre-Nicene Gnostic Church. He moved to San Francisco and operated his church from within the homosexual community there for the rest of his life.

In 1980 he underwent two further consecrations (the practice of multiple consecrations having become common among independent Catholic and Orthodox bishops). The first was received from George Michael Zaharakis of MeBasrim Fellowship and the second from Joseph Vredenburgh of the Federation of St. Thomas Christians. While Itkin became well-known as an activist within the gay community, he was never able to build a substantial following. In the mid-1980s it became known that he had an AIDS-related disorder, from which he died in 1989. He was succeeded by his coadjutor, Marcia Alice Mari Herndon.

Sources:

Itkin, Michael F. A. *The Hymn of Jesus.* New York: Pax Christi Press, 1963. 11 pp.

_____. *The Radical Jesus and Gay Liberation.* Long Beach, CA: Communiversity West, 1972. 64 pp.

_____. *The Spiritual Heritage of Port-Royal.* New York: Pax Christi Press, 1966. 49 pp.

_____. *Statement . . . Hearings on "Hallucinogenic Drugs".* Washington, DC: Pax Christi Institute Press, 1966. 13 pp.

_____. *Towards Christian Revolution.* New York: Pax Christi Press, 1966. 6 pp.

★448★
IVINS, Anthony Woodward
Member of the First Presidency, Church of Jesus Christ of Latter-day Saints
b. Sep. 16, 1852, Toms River, New Jersey
d. Sep. 23, 1934, Salt Lake City, Utah

Anthony Woodward Ivins, a Mormon leader best known for his officiation at plural marriages in the decades following the 1890 manifesto abolishing polygamy in the Church of Jesus Christ of Latter-day Saints, was the first cousin of Heber Jeddy Grant, the seventh president of the church. The Ivins family moved to Utah in 1853 and were among the original settlers of St. George, Utah, in 1861. Ivins was ordained as an elder at age 13. Two years later he became constable of St. George, and the following year he married Elizabeth Ashby Snow. Though he remained monogamous, he was destined to have an important role in the continuance of polygamy in the Church of Jesus Christ of Latter-day Saints.

In 1875, at the age of 23, Ivins went on a mission to Arizona and New Mexico to locate possible sites for new colonies. He returned to New Mexico in 1877-1878. He became a successful rancher in St. George and eventually became owner of the Mojave Land and Cattle Company, the first of several prosperous enterprises which led him into banking. (In later years he served as president of the Utah Savings and Trust Company.) He also taught himself law, and in 1882 was elected prosecuting attorney for Washington County, Utah. That same year, however, he was sent to Mexico City to preside over the Mexican Mission. Upon his return from Mexico he plunged again into ranching and also became politically active. He helped organize the Sagebrush Democrats in an attempt to align the rather parochial Utah politics with the national parties. In 1890 he became mayor of St. George and later served two terms in the Utah legislature. On the eve of Utah's obtaining statehood, he was considered to be a candidate for governor or Congress, but at that point he was called by the church to return to Mexico.

In 1895 Ivins was appointed presiding officer of eight Mormon settlements in Sonora and Chihuahua, Mexico, which had become havens for Mormon families facing persecution for polygamy in the United States. As stake president and vice president of the Mexican Colonization and Agricultural Company, his word was law. And during the next nine years Ivins attained his permanent place in Mormon history.

The church had publicly abandoned plural marriages in 1890 in conformity to the law of the United States. Through Ivins, however, the First Presidency of the church quietly authorized a number of such ceremonies until they were completely abandoned by the action of President **Joseph Fielding Smith, Sr.** in 1904. Ivins' papers contain records of over 40 plural marriages he performed. Inadvertently, Ivins became a bridge from the period in which the church advocated polygamy to the period after World War I, when a number of polygamous splinter groups arose.

In 1907 Ivins was ordained as an Apostle. One of his most important assignments was overseeing the evacuation of the Mexican colonies during the Revolution in 1912. In 1921 he was named a counselor to President Grant. He became first counselor in 1925. He rose to a high position in a church largely identified with the Republican Party, and used his position to moderate the partisan policies. He died at age 82 of a heart attack.

Sources:

Dictionary of American Biography. 20 vols. and 7 supps. New York: Charles Scribner's Sons, 1928-1936, 1944-1981.

Wallace, W. Stewart, comp. *A Dictionary of North American Authors Deceased before 1950.* Toronto: Ryerson Press, 1951. Reprint. Detroit: Gale Research Co., 1968.

Who Was Who in America. Chicago: Marquis Who's Who, Inc.

★449★
JACKSON, Jesse
Minister, Baptist Church
Political Activist
b. Oct. 8, 1941, Greenville, South Carolina

Jesse Louis Jackson, best known for his political career which has seen him twice run for president of the United States, is a Baptist minister who has successfully integrated his faith and public life. Born out of wedlock, he was the son of Helen Burns and Noah Louis Robinson. His mother later married Charles Henry Jackson, who adopted Jackson in 1957. As a youth Jackson was a football star who led his high school to a state championship. He went to the University of Illinois on a football scholarship, but left after a year, having discovered that Blacks were not allowed to play quarterback, the position he had played in high school. He transferred to North Carolina Agricultural and Technical State College in Greensboro where he had an outstanding college career in both athletics and scholarship.

Jackson's college career coincided with the years of the civil rights movement in the South. He joined the movement locally and helped integrate Greensboro. After graduation in 1964, he attended Chicago Theological Seminary. He left before graduation, however, to work with îMartin Luther Kingï, Jr., and the Southern Christian Leadership Conference (SCLC). King then appointed Jack-

son to head the Chicago branch of Operation Breadbasket, SCLC's effort to deal with the business community in promoting jobs for Blacks. The next year, 1967, he appointed Jackson the national director of Operation Breadbasket. Six months later, in April 1968, King was assassinated.

Jackson was with King at the time of the assassination, as was **Ralph David Abernathy**. But it was Abernathy who succeeded King. Jackson remained with SCLC amid rumors of tension with Abernathy. In 1971 he left SCLC and founded Operation PUSH (People United to Save Humanity), taking much of Chicago's former SCLC support with him. PUSH's program to build self-esteem and deal with the major problems of black youth won Jackson national attention and support.

Jackson began to enter the international arena during the days of the Carter administration. He embarked on trips to South Africa and the Middle East and began to speak out on apartheid and Arab-Israeli tensions. At the end of 1983 he entered the presidential campaign and announced the formation of a Rainbow Coalition of people from different racial and ethnic backgrounds to oppose what he saw as the elitist policies of the Reagan administration. He made a strong run, but was unable to defeat Walter Mondale for the Democratic nomination. His campaign was marked by controversy with both the Jewish community and **Louis Farrakhan** of the Nation of Islam.

In 1986 Jackson formally resigned his post with Operation PUSH (he had taken a leave of absence to run for office) and established the National Rainbow Coalition, an organization of his supporters within the Democratic Party. He again ran unsuccessfully for the Democratic Party nomination in 1988, but continues as a force in national politics.

Sources:

Brackney, William Henry. *The Baptist.* New York: Greenwood Press, 1988. 327 pp.

★450★
JACKSON, Joseph Harrison
President, National Baptist Convention, U.S.A.
b. Sep. 11, 1900, Jenestown, Mississippi

Joseph Harrison Jackson, for 29 years the president of the National Baptist Convention, U.S.A., the fourth largest denomination in America, was the son of Henry and Emily Johnson Jackson. He was raised in Mississippi and ordained to the Baptist ministry in 1922. He attended Jackson College, from which he received his B.A. degree in 1926. While a student in college, in 1925, he became pastor of First Baptist Church in Macomb, Mississippi. In 1926 he married Maude Thelma Alexander. In 1927 he moved to Omaha, Nebraska, as pastor of Bethel Baptist Church. He continued his education at Colgate Rochester Divinity School (B.D., 1932) and Creighton University (M.A., 1933). In 1934 he began a seven-year ministry at Monumental Baptist Church in Philadelphia and in 1941 moved to Olivet Baptist Church in Chicago, where he would remain for the rest of his active ministry.

The same year he moved to Monumental, Jackson became secretary of the National Baptist Convention's Foreign Missions Board. He also authored his first book, *A Voyage to West Africa and Some Reflections on Modern Missions* (1936). A second book, *Stars in the Night* (1950), appeared after the move to Chicago. In 1953, Jackson was elected president of the National Baptist Convention.

Shortly before Jackson was elected, the Baptists had amended their constitution to limit the president's tenure in office to four one-year terms. In 1957 Jackson mustered support and won a fifth term after he declared the amendment unconstitutional. Jackson, now firmly in control of the convention, would run it for almost three decades. He faced two serious challenges in 1960 and 1961. In 1960, those opposed to Jackson united to support Gardner Taylor, a minister from Brooklyn, New York, but he was defeated. A more serious challenge came in 1961, when the supporters of **Martin Luther King, Jr.** sought both Jackson's and the convention's support for the Civil Rights Movement. When they obtained neither, they broke away and formed the Progressive National Baptist Convention. Jackson then emerged as one of the most conservative black leaders in the United States with a significant following. He did not oppose civil rights for Blacks, but did oppose the practice of civil disobedience, the tactic at the heart of the Civil Rights Movement. As an alternative, in light of the successes in the past, he suggested that Blacks should use the courts to obtain their goals. His statements were often used by conservative white leaders in attempts to divide the black community against King. In 1969, We the People!, a right-wing political group, named Jackson "Patriot of the Year." In spite of his conservative stand, he retained the support of the majority of black Baptists. During his term in office, the denomination was estimated to have grown from some four to five million members to between seven and nine million.

In 1980 Jackson authored the 790-page centennial history of the National Baptist Convention, A Story of Christian Activism. Two years later he was finally beaten in the presidential race by Theodore Judson Jemison, pastor of Mount Zion Baptist Church in Baton Rouge, Louisiana. Jackson remains as minister of Olivet Baptist Church.

Sources:

Jackson, Joseph H. Stars in the Night. Philadelphia: Christian Education Press, 1950. 72 pp.

————. A Story of Christian Activism. Nashville, TN: Townsend Press, 1980. 790 pp.

————. A Voyage to West Africa and Some Reflections on Modern Missions. 1936.

★451★
JACKSON, Mahalia
Gospel Singer, National Baptist Convention
b. Oct. 26, 1911, New Orleans, Louisiana
d. Jan. 27, 1972, Evergreen Park, Illinois

Mahalia Jackson, possibly the most famous gospel singer of the twentieth century, was the daughter of Charity Clark and John Jackson. She was raised in a pious Baptist environment by her aunt, with whom she lived after her mother's death around 1916. Jackson had little formal education as she had to leave school in her early teens to go to work. She did have a varied musical experience in the rich New Orleans atmosphere. In 1928 she left the South for Chicago. While earning her living as a maid, she became an active member of the Greater Salem Baptist Church. She started her own musical career as a church choir member, but was soon chosen as a soloist. In 1936 she married Isaac Hockenhull.

In 1930 Jackson formed a gospel group, the Johnson Gospel Singers. Within a few years they were traveling the country and helping to create the new black gospel music which would soon become the dominant form of music in most Baptist churches. She introduced an energy and enthusiasm which soon won her national appeal. Her first recording, "God Gonna Separate the Wheat from the Tares" became a popular gospel hit. After World War II she became an important recording artist with her first major hit recording, "Move On Up a Little Higher." In 1950 she began to appear at annual concerts of gospel music at Carnegie Hall. She was invited to appear on television and made several widely acclaimed tours of Europe and Asia. She had eight songs which sold a million records, including "I Believe" and "He's Got the Whole World in His Hands." In 1961 she sang at the inauguration of John F. Kennedy as President. In the midst of her growing success she was divorced from Hockenhull.

Jackson became active in the civil rights movement beside her fellow Baptist **Martin Luther King, Jr.**, and sang as a prelude to his famous speech at the Lincoln Memorial which culminated the 1963 March on Washington.

Much energy during Jackson's years of success was given to the issue of secular music. She complained that her first husband did not appreciate her commitment to gospel music and wanted her to exploit her talents in the secular music field. She consistently turned down lucrative offers for her to leave gospel music. In 1964 she married Sigmund Galloway, but the marriage only lasted three years. She was hampered during her last years by ill health and eventually died of a heart attack.

Sources:

Anderson, Robert, and Gail North. Gospel Music Encyclopedia. New York: Sterling Publishing Co., 1979. 320 pp.

Jackson, Mahalia. Movin' On Up. New York: Hawthorn Books, 1966. 219 pp.

James, Edward T., ed. Notable American Women, 1607-1950: A Biographical Dictionary. 3 vols. Cambridge, MA: Harvard University Press, Belknap Press, 1971.

★452★
JACKSON, Samuel Macauley
Minister, Presbyterian Church
b. Jun. 19, 1851, New York, New York
d. Aug. 2, 1912, New York, New York

Samuel Macauley Jackson, Presbyterian scholar and minister, was the son of George T. Jackson, an Irish immigrant, and Letitia Jane Aiken Macauley. He grew up in New York City and attended the City College of New York. After graduating with his A.B. in 1870, he attended Princeton Theological Seminary (1870-1871) and Union Theological Seminary (1871-1873) to prepare for the ministry. At Union he studied under **Philip Schaff**, who awakened an interest in church history, and after finishing his seminary studies, Jackson left for two years of study abroad at Leipzig and Berlin. Upon his return he finished a master's degree at City College of New York (1876) and that same year was ordained and became the minister of the Presbyterian Church in Norwood, New Jersey.

Jackson's career in the pastoral ministry proved difficult as he was uncomfortable in many public situations, and he resigned from his church in 1880. Able to obtain private financial support, he devoted his life to twin careers in social service and religious history. The social service aspect of his life began in 1885 when he became associated with the Charity Organization Society. During the 1890s he also worked for the Prison Association of the State of New York and taught in the Amity School for Christian Workers. In 1903 he became the vice president of the Charity Organization Society, a position he retained for the rest of his life.

Jackson is primarily remembered for his scholarly work, especially his collaboration with Philip Schaff in the production of a number of reference books. His first contributions were additions to the Dictionary of the Bible (1880). He became an associate editor for Schaff's A Religious Dictionary: or Dictionary of Biblical, Historical, Doctrinal, and Practical Theology (1882-1884), popularly known as the Schaff-Herzog Encyclopedia. Pulling together the material for a biographical dictionary of leading clergymen, Jackson and Schaff produced the Encyclopedia of Living Divines and Christian Workers (1886) which was incorporated into later editions of the Encyclopedia. Jackson moved on independently to edit a Concise Dictionary of Religious Knowledge (1891) and to develop the religious material for two secular encyclopedias—Johnson's Universal Cyclopedia (1893-1895) and the New International Encyclopedia (1902-1905). He also worked on the Standard Dictionary (1895) and New International Dictionary (1900). In the midst of these projects he began writing up his own research on Huldreich Zwingli, the Swiss leader of the Reformation, which appeared in 1901 as *Huldreich Zwingli, The Reformer of German Switzerland*. He also promoted a multi-volume English-language edition of Zwingli's writings (apart from the biblical commentaries). He oversaw the publication of an initial *Selected Works on Huldreich Zwingli* in 1901, and saw the release of the first volume of the series in 1912, *The Latin Works and the Correspondence of Huldreich Zwingli*. The other volumes appeared after his death.

Shortly after the turn of the century he developed his earlier work with Schaff (d. 1893) and became editor-in-chief of a 13-volume edition of an expanded *New Schaff-Herzog Encyclopedia of Religious Knowledge* (1904-1908). Jackson's life of work was acknowledged in 1911 by his election as president of the American Society of Church History, but he died before he was able to deliver his presidential address, a paper on a ninth century figure, Servatus Lupus.

Sources:

Dictionary of American Biography. 20 vols. and 7 supps. New York: Charles Scribner's Sons, 1928-1936, 1944-1981.

★ 453 ★
JACKSON, Sheldon
Home Missionary, Presbyterian Church
b. May 18, 1834, Minaville, New York
d. May 2, 1909, Ashville, North Carolina

Sheldon Jackson, a missionary for the Presbyterian Church in the western United States, was the son of Samuel Clinton Jackson and Delia Sheldon Jackson. He was raised in a cultured and pious home, and his parents encouraged a missionary career from his childhood years. He attended several private academies before entering Union College (Schenectady, New York) from which he graduated in 1855. He graduated from Princeton Theological Seminary three years later and was ordained to the ministry. He married Mary Voorhees and began his career in the Oklahoma Indian territory at a school at Spencer for Choctaw (Indian) boys.

After a year in Oklahoma, he began a five-year stay in Minnesota interrupted in the summer of 1863 for several months of duty with the United States Christian Commission. In 1864 he took a pastorate in Rochester, Minnesota, but resumed his missionary work in 1870 when he was appointed superintendent for the board of missions for those six Rocky Mountain states dominated by the Church of Jesus Christ of Latter-day Saints. He pioneered Protestant church building in the predominantly white communities and oversaw the development of Presbyterian Indian missions. In 1872 he began the *Rocky Mountain Presbyterian* which he edited for a decade.

In 1882 Jackson moved to New York as the business manager of the Presbyterian Home Missions Board and watched his periodical grow to become the *Presbyterian Home Missionary*. Then in 1884 he left New York for Alaska. He had first visited Alaska in 1877, but now found in his new home the career for which he had been prepared. He spent his first year in Alaska surveying the territory and establishing schools. The government appointed him the first superintendent of public instruction for the territory, a job he retained until his retirement.

Among Jackson's most ambitious projects in Alaska was a plan to improve the life of the Eskimos, whose natural food sources had been depleted by developing reindeer herds. The first were imported in 1892 and by 1928, over 600,000 were to be found in the several domesticated herds.

Jackson authored several books on behalf of his developing mission. In 1880, *Alaska, and Missions of the North Pacific Coast* appeared, and was followed by *The Presbyterian Church in Alaska, An Official Sketch of Its Rise and Progress, 1877-1884* (1886) and *Introduction of Reindeer into Alaska* (1890). In 1897 his work was

acknowledged by the church in his election as moderator of the general assembly of the church.

Even in his last years he continued to put his energy behind the work he had developed. At the age of 74 he delivered an address about the Alaska mission just days before an operation from which he never recovered.

Sources:

Dictionary of American Biography. 20 vols. and 7 supps. New York: Charles Scribner's Sons, 1928-1936, 1944-1981.
Jackson, Sheldon. *Alaska, and Missions on the North Pacific Coast.* New York: Dodd, Mead, 1880. 400 pp.
_____. *Introduction of Reindeer into Alaska.* Washington, DC: Government Printing Office, 1891.
_____. *The Presbyterian Church in Alaska, An Official Sketch of Its Rise and Progress, 1877-1884.* Washington, DC: Press of T. McGill & Co., 1886.
Stewart, R. L. *Sheldon Jackson.* New York: Fleming H. Revell Company, 1908. 488 pp.

★ 454 ★
JACOBS, Henry Eyster
Church Historian and Theologian, United Lutheran Church of America
b. Nov. 10, 1844, Gettysburg, Pennsylvania
d. Jul. 7, 1932, Philadelphia, Pennsylvania

Henry Eyster Jacobs, the outstanding Lutheran theologian and church historian, was the son of a Lutheran clergyman and scientist, Michael Jacobs, and his wife, Julianna M. Eyster Jacobs. Young Henry was raised in a pious and intellectual atmosphere. He entered Pennsylvania College from which he graduated in 1862 and immediately continued his studies at Gettysburg Seminary. He was a seminarian when the Civil War was brought to his home, and a few months later he was in the audience for Lincoln's Gettysburg Address.

Following his graduation from seminary he joined the staff as a tutor and in 1867 began a year as a home missionary in Pittsburgh. Finally in 1868, he began his 64-year teaching career with his appointment as instructor at Thiel Hall (now Thiel College). After two years, he returned to Pennsylvania College in 1870 to teach classical languages and history. He married Laura H. Downing in 1872. Then in 1883 he moved to the Lutheran Theological Seminary in Philadelphia where he was to experience his most productive years as a scholar and a church leader.

Jacobs authored nine books during his long career, the most important being *Lutheran Movement in England during the Reigns of Henry VIII and Edward VI and Its Literary Monuments* (1890); *A History of the Evangelical Lutheran Church in the United States* (1893); and a *Summary of the Christian Faith* (1905). The second of these has been credited with giving American Lutherans, then scattered in a number of separate synods, a renewed sense of history and unity. In 1907 he was elected president of the American Society of Church History. Conservative in theology, he championed Lutheran unity and liturgical development, two efforts that marked his church activities.

Jacobs worked for many years on the common service committee of his church and helped develop the liturgy which was adopted by the new United Lutheran Church of America in 1918. He served as the president of the board of foreign missions of the Lutheran General Council. He presided over the three general ecumenical conferences of Lutherans which met in 1899, 1902, and 1904.

In 1894, after 14 years as a professor of systematic theology, Jacobs was named dean of the seminary, and succeeded to the presidency in 1920. He retired from the presidency in 1927, but continued to teach until shortly before his death.

Sources:

Dictionary of American Biography. 20 vols. and 7 supps. New York: Charles Scribner's Sons, 1928-1936, 1944-1981.

Jacobs, Henry Eyster. *A History of the Evangelical Lutheran Church in the United States.* New York: The Christian Literature Company, 1893. 539 pp.

———. *Lutheran Movement in England during the Reigns of Henry VIII and Edward VI and Its Literary Monuments.* Philadelphia: G. W. Frederick, 1890. 376 pp.

———. *Summary of the Christian Faith.* Philadelphia: General Council Publishing House, 1905. 637 pp.

★455★
Swami Rajasi JANAKANANDA
President, Self-Realization Fellowship
b. May 5, 1892, Archibald, Louisiana
d. Feb. 20, 1955, Borrego Springs, California

Swami Rajasi Janakananda, born James J. Lynn, was the second president of the Self-Realization Fellowship, the organization founded by **Swami Paramahansa Yogananda**. Lynn was raised in a hard-working farm family. The fourth of six children, he was recognized as being something of a child prodigy, but his family's relative poverty influenced him to enter the workforce as soon as he graduated from grammar school. He worked for the railway and, after a move to Kansas City, went back to school in the evenings. After seven years he had not only completed high school and law school, but had studied accounting and passed the C.P.A. exam with the highest grade on record. It was toward the end of this period of intensive education that he met Freda Josephine Prill. They were married in October of 1913.

After doing some valuable accounting work for the U. S. Epperson Underwriting Company, Lynn accepted an offer to become general manager of that company at the young age of 24. In 1921 Epperson became ill and decided to sell his business. Lynn was able to obtain a large loan and purchase U. S. Epperson Underwriting. Within a few years he turned a large profit and moved into other fields, including the oil business. Within a relatively short period of time, Lynn became a self made millionaire.

While Lynn had always been interested in religion, he had never accepted any particular church. He was introduced to Hindu thought through an English translation of the *Bhagavad Gita*, but he was too caught up in worldly affairs to pursue his spiritual interests. According to his own account, his life was business and the business world. He was in a mentally and physically disturbed state when he met Yogananda in February of 1932. Afflicted with nervousness, he was impressed with the feelings of peace that he experienced in Yogananda's presence. The two men quickly became close friends, and Lynn's worldly wealth enabled him to assist Yogananda in expanding his organization. Applying the same concentration to yoga that he had applied to his businesses, Lynn made rapid spiritual progress. After five years of daily meditation, he achieved illumination. When his spiritual master passed away in 1952, he succeeded Yogananda as president of Self-Realization Fellowship. He lived only three years after assuming control of the organization.

Sources:

Rajasi Janakananda (James J. Lynn): A Great Western Yogi. Los Angeles: Self-Realization Fellowship, 1959. 110 pp.

—*James R. Lewis*

★456★
JEFFERSON, Charles Edward
Modernist Pastor, Congregational Church
b. Jul. 29, 1860, Cambridge, Ohio
d. Sep. 12, 1937, Fitzwilliam, New Hampshire

Charles Edward Jefferson, a leading modernist minister within the Congregational Church of the 1920s, was the son of Dr. Milton Jefferson and Ella Saechett Jefferson. He attended Ohio Wesleyan University from which he received both a B.S. degree (1882) and a B.A. (1886). He entered Boston University to begin his studies for a law career, but was diverted by Episcopal minister **Phillips Brooks**. Jefferson pursued his studies in the school of theology and received his S.T.B. in 1887. He was ordained to the ministry, married Belle Patterson, and became pastor of Central Congregational Church in Chelsea, Massachusetts.

He served in Chelsea for 11 years. In 1898 he was called to the Broadway Tabernacle Church in Manhattan, where for the next three decades he had a successful career as a popular preacher and popularizer of liberal Protestant theological ideas. His first books, *Quiet Talks to Growing Preachers in My Study* (1901) and *Things Fundamental* (1903) soon appeared, but his ministry was interrupted by a fire that destroyed the tabernacle. He responded by leading the congregation in building the "skyscraper" church at 56th and Broadway.

From his new pulpit Jefferson championed the liberal modernist cause which heated to a climax in the creation-evolution debate of the 1920s. His ideas were recorded in a series of books including *The Minister as Prophet* (1905); *The Character of Jesus* (1908); *The Building of the Church* (1910); *The Minister as Shepherd* (1912); *Christianity and International Peace* (1915); *What the War Has Taught Us* (1919); *Cardinal Ideas of Isiah* (1925); and *Christianizing a Nation* (1929). His ideas permeated liberal Protestantism through the several books authored for his colleagues also in the ministry. He was especially effective because, even though a liberal, he emphasized the deity of Jesus and the authority of the Bible.

At the time of his retirement in 1930, he had regularly filled the large tabernacle sanctuary twice each Sunday for many years. He had been active in denominational affairs and attained a national fame for his preaching. His autobiography, *Thirty Years on Broadway* (1930), appeared just as he finished his pastoral career. He lived quietly during his retirement years, finishing one book, *Like a Trumpet* (1934), a few years before his death.

Sources:

Dictionary of American Biography. 20 vols. and 7 supps. New York: Charles Scribner's Sons, 1928-1936, 1944-1981.

Jefferson, Charles E. *The Building of the Church.* New York: Macmillan Company, 1910. 306 pp.

———. *The Character of Jesus.* New York: T. Y. Crowell & Co., 1908. 353 pp.

———. *Christianizing a Nation.* Garden City, NY: Doubleday, Doran & Co., 1929. 200 pp.

———. *Like a Trumpet.* New York: Harper & Bros., 1934. 125 pp.

———. *Things Fundamental.* New York: The Author, [1903].

★457★
JEFFERY, Harley Bradley
Pioneer New Thought Writer/Teacher
b. Jan. 26, 1872, Syracuse, New York
d. Jan. 19, 1954, Santa Monica, California

Harley Bradley Jeffery, a popular writer and teacher of New Thought in the first half of the twentieth century, was the son of George Adams Jeffery, a printer employed by the *Syracuse Herald*, and Ellen Clapp Jeffery. He and his two brothers were raised as members of the Christian Church (Disciples of Christ). After completing high school, Jeffery went to work for an architectural firm in Syracuse and later entered the construction business. In about 1903, he met Charles Brodie Patterson, an independent metaphysical teacher from England who convinced Jeffery to join him in his endeavors in lecturing and mental healing in New York City. Patterson returned to England several years later, and Jeffery took over the work, which he expanded by opening an office in Philadelphia. He supplemented his learning by taking classes at Harvard University and Columbia University.

In 1905 Jeffery met **Emma Curtis Hopkins**, the founder of New Thought, who was residing in New York City and accepting private students. He worked with her to produce her classic volume, *High Mysticism*. In 1911 he toured England and continental Europe, lecturing upon what he had learned from Hopkins. In England, he met Judge Thomas Troward and worked with him during his most productive years as a metaphysical writer.

Upon his return to the United States, Jeffery began his mature career as an author and lecturer. He authored eight books, including *Christianity* (1938); *The Spirit of Prayer* (1938); *The Principles of Healing* (1939); *Three Treatments* (1939); *The Fruit of the Spirit* (1940); and *Coordination of Spirit, Soul, and Body* (1948).

In 1939, with Jeffery's blessing, Alden Truesdell and his wife, Nell Truesdell, founded the Christ Truth League in Fort Worth, Texas. Christ Truth League is an independent New Thought ministry that has perpetuated the teachings of Jeffery and kept many of his writings in print.

Sources:

Jeffery, Harley Bradley. *Christianity*. Cambridge, MA: Ruth Laighton, 1938. 50 pp.
_____. *Coordination of Spirit, Soul, and Body*. Cambridge, MA: Ruth Laighton, 1948. 164 pp.
_____. *The Fruit of the Spirit*. Cambridge, MA: Ruth Laighton, 1940. 103 pp.
_____. *The Spirit of Prayer*. Cambridge, MA: Ruth Laighton, 1938. 190 pp.

★ 458 ★
JENKINS, Leroy
Independent Pentecostal Evangelist
b. 1935, Fort Mill, South Carolina

Leroy Jenkins, a controversial Pentecostal healing evangelist, grew up in Greenwood, South Carolina, where his parents had moved when he was three. His father was an alcoholic. Jenkins claimed that as a young child, he heard God speak to him, and that he had seen visions. God called him into the ministry. He did not respond, however, and when, at the age of 17, he married Ruby Garrett; neither was a church member. They settled in Atlanta where he joined the Presbyterian Church.

A crisis in Jenkins' life occurred on Mother's Day, 1960. His arm was almost completely cut off in an accident. He refused to let the doctors amputate it. Several days later he attended a meeting conducted by **Asa Alonzo Allen**. During the service he had a vision of God, during which his arm was completely healed. He began to preach and pray for others. A man gave him a small tent and, like Allen, Jenkins began to speak before integrated audiences, even amid attacks by the Ku Klux Klan.

In 1963 Jenkins conducted his first crusade outside of the United States, in Nassau in the Bahamas. His work took him regularly around the United States. His headquarters were established in Delaware, Ohio, where he founded the Church of What's Happening Now. A boost was given to his career when he was able to obtain the ten thousand-seat tent formerly owned by healer-evangelist Jack Coe. In 1977 he moved back to Greenville, South Carolina, and founded a new congregation, the Spirit of Truth Church.

Jenkins' career was interrupted in 1979 when he was arrested on two counts of arson. He was convicted and began serving his term in Ohio. He was granted a work release in 1982 and began to revive his ministry prior to being paroled in 1985. He reestablished headquarters in Anderson, South Carolina, and has resumed his healing ministry.

Sources:

Burgess, Stanley M., Gary B. McGee, and Patrick H. Alexander, eds. *Dictionary of Pentecostal and Charismatic Movements*. Grand Rapids, MI: Regency Reference Library, Zondervan Publishing House, 1988. 914 pp.
Jenkins, Leroy. *God Gave Me a Miracle Arm*. Delaware, OH: Leroy Jenkins Evangelistic Association, 1963. 28 pp.
_____. *How I Met the Master*. Delaware, OH: Leroy Jenkins Evangelistic Association, [1970]. 61 pp.
_____. *How You Can Receive Your Healing*. Delaware, OH: Leroy Jenkins Evangelistic Association, 1966. 88 pp.
_____. *Man Shall Not Live by Bread Alone*. N.p.: The Author, 1974. 119 pp.
Randi, James. *The Faith Healers*. Buffalo, NY: Prometheus Press, 1987. 314 pp.

★ 459 ★
JERNIGAN, C. B.
Minister, Church of the Nazarene
b. Sep. 4, 1863, Mississippi
d. Jun. 21, 1930

C. B. Jernigan, a leading figure in the development of holiness churches in Texas and Oklahoma, was the son of a doctor and plantation owner in southern Mississippi. Ruined by the destruction of the Civil War, the Jernigan family moved to a farm in Hunt County, Texas, on the Red River. The 11 children were educated at the school at Hog Eye, a nearby village. The family also attended the annual camp meeting at Harrell's campgrounds. C. B. was converted at the age of nine. A few years later he heard a woman testify to the experience of sanctification, a second work of God which is believed to make one perfect in love. He sought and received that experience a few days later.

Now sanctified, Jernigan followed a dual path as a preacher-songleader and medical student. He married and joined the Methodist Episcopal Church, South, in Greenville, Texas. In 1894 E. C. DeJernett, a Methodist evangelist, established a community called Peniel, near Greenville. He attracted many holiness people (i.e., those such as Jernigan who had been sanctified). Jernigan cooperated with the people at Peniel in organizing a Holiness Association of Texas, a broad ecumenical group. Meanwhile, Jernigan had become a full time holiness preacher and was having trouble with the Methodist Episcopal Church, South, which was becoming increasingly hostile to the holiness movement. In 1901 he formed an independent congregation at Van Alstyne, Texas. While pastoring it, he led in the formation of some 20 similar congregations in Texas and Oklahoma. These banded together as the Independent Holiness Church. Jernigan broke with the Peniel community, projecting a similar community of his own, which he called Bethany. Such a community began to develop at Pilot Point, Texas, where an orphanage, school, and home for unwed mothers were opened.

Jernigan saw the Independent Holiness Church as merely a step to the eventual unification of the independent holiness people, and he pursued mergers with other groups. In 1905 he led his church into union with the New Testament Church of Christ, thus forming the Holiness Church of Christ. Three years later, the Holiness Church merged into the Pentecostal Church of the Nazarene, which soon dropped the word Pentecostal from its name.

After leading his people into the Church of the Nazarene, Jernigan was appointed district superintendent for Oklahoma and Kansas. Unfortunately, there was no salary with the appointment, and only six churches in the territory. Jernigan earned money during the day as a photographer and preached in the evenings. As his district was organized, he began to preach in neighboring states. He organized over 130 Nazarene churches during his active years. He also founded Oklahoma Holiness College (now Southern Nazarene University) in Bethany, Oklahoma.

While serving as district superintendent, Jernigan also sat on the church's general board. He edited one periodical, the *Holiness Evangel*, and founded a second, *Highway and Hedges*. He wrote several books the most famous being his autobiographical *Pioneer Days of the Holiness Movement in the Southwest* (1919). Over 100,000 copies of his pamphlet, *Entire Sanctification* have been circulated. He died quite suddenly in 1930, while still actively engaged in his life's work.

Sources:

Jernigan, C. B. *Entire Sanctification*. Kansas City, MO: Nazarene Publishing House, n.d. 32 pp.

————. *Pioneer Days of the Holiness Movement in the Southwest*. Kansas City, MO: Pentecostal Nazarene Publishing House, 1919. 157 pp.

★460★
Bishop JOHN
Bishop, Russian Orthodox Church
b. 1836, Kaluga District Russia
d. May 3, 1914, Astrakhan District Russia

In 1867 the United States purchased Alaska from Russia. Three years later the Russian Orthodox Church consecrated the first bishop for what was to be a new autonomous diocese of the Aleutian Islands and Alaska. Their candidate for the new position was Father Stephen Mitropolsky, remembered today under his ecclesiastical name, Bishop John. Mitropolsky was born in rural Russia and as a young man attended the Moscow Theological Academy, from which he graduated in 1862. While in school he had been tonsured as a monk (meaning he had decided to remain unmarried as a priest). He learned English, and at the relatively young age of 34 was consecrated as bishop for Alaska. It was a small diocese, having lost many of its priests and laity who returned to Russia after the sale of Alaska. He would be assisted by the newly formed Russian Imperial Missionary Society.

It was Bishop John's desire to not only head the diocese but to enlarge it by preaching to the "heterodox" (i.e., Christians, primarily Protestants, who had not accepted the fullness of the Orthodox faith). To this end he wrote a five-volume work: *From the History of Religious Sects in America*, which reviewed the doctrinal position of a number of groups, including the Congregationalists, Methodists, Episcopalians, and Presbyterians. Pursuing his evangelistic goals, he became quite adept in using the American press to present the church's claims. His major accomplishment during his brief reign, however, was the movement of the seat of episcopal authority from Sitka, Alaska, to San Francisco, California, a symbol of the church's commitment to grow in America and not limit itself to Russian or other Orthodox immigrants.

In 1876 Bishop John was recalled to Russia and reassigned. He was succeeded in California by Bishop Nestor. He eventually retired to Protection Monastery where he died in 1914.

Sources:

Afonsky, Bishop Gregory. *A History of the Orthodox Church in Alaska (1794-1917)*. Kodiak, AK: St. Herman's Theological Seminary, 1977. 105 pp.

Tarasar, Constance J. *Orthodox America, 1794-1974*. Syosset, NY: Department of History and Archives, The Orthodox Church in America, 1975. 351 pp.

★461★
JOHNSON, James Hervey
President, American Association for the Advancement of Atheism
b. Aug. 2, 1901, Portland, Oregon
d. Aug. 6, 1988, San Diego, California

James Hervey Johnson, for over a quarter of a century the eccentric leader of the American Association for the Advancement of Atheism, was born in Oregon but as a child moved to southern California. Little is known of his early life, but as a young man in the 1930s he was elected tax assessor for San Diego County. He offended many by advocating the taxing of church property and was eventually removed from office when he was convicted on a charge of misusing public funds. The court concluded that he had overstepped his bounds in refunding tax money.

Over the years Johnson became not only an atheist but a health food devotee and was known for taking periodic fasts and following a vegetarian diet. He refused all drug treatments. Over the years he also amassed a fortune in stocks.

In 1949 Johnson published his atheistic conclusions in a book, *Superior Men*. In the years following he became active in organized atheism. He joined the Freethinkers Society of San Diego, a group organized in the late 1940s. When the society was formally incorporated in 1960, Johnson was one of the original directors. In 1964 Johnson purchased *The Truth Seeker*, America's oldest freethought journal, and then paid for its editor and former owner, **Charles Lee Smith** to move to San Diego and continue in his work. He shared with Smith not only his atheist sentiments but also strong racist anti-black opinions.

Smith was also the head of the American Association for the Advancement of Atheism, an organization he founded in 1925. When Smith died a few months after moving to San Diego, Johnson became the new head of the association and editor of *The Truth Seeker*. In 1967, when he was elected the president of the Freethinkers Society of San Diego, Johnson became the focus of organized atheism in the city and leader of one of the country's most important national atheist organizations.

Johnson continued the inclusion of racist material in *The Truth Seeker* and distributed anti-lack material through the association. That activity cost him the support of the greater portion of the atheist community, and the organizations he led dwindled to but a few members. *The Truth Seeker* eventually ceased publication. Johnson died at the age of 87 of a heart attack, alone in his small, austerely furnished apartment. His estate was valued in excess of 16 million dollars.

Johnson's death led to a major court battle instigated by **Madalyn Murray O'Hair** and members of the American Atheists, Inc., which had sought control of *The Truth Seeker* for a number of years. O'Hair was unsuccessful in her efforts to overturn the dictates of Johnson's will, which left control of *The Truth Seeker* to Bonnie Lange, a Mormon, and the estate in the control of its executor, Lawrence Y. True, an Episcopalian.

Sources:

Acune, Armando. "Unbelievers Crusading for Control of Atheist's Fortune." *Los Angeles Times* (April 30, 1989).

Johnson, James Hervey. *Superior Men*. San Diego: The Author, 1949. 192 pp.

★462★
JOHNSON, Sherrod C.
Founder, Church of The Lord Jesus Christ of the Apostolic Faith
b. Nov. 24, 1899, Pine Tree Quarter, Edgecomb County, North Carolina
d. Feb. 22, 1961, Kingston Jamaica

Little is known of the early life of Sherrod C. Johnson, founder of the Church of The Lord Jesus Christ of the Apostolic Faith, one of several prominent Pentecostal denominations serving predominantly black members. In the 1920s he became a pastor of the Church of *Our* Lord Jesus Christ of the Apostolic Faith, which was founded in 1919 by Bishop **R. C. Lawson**. Lawson, known to be very strict on the issues of divorce and remarriage, was nevertheless somewhat liberal (for Pentecostals) in allowing women to wear brightly colored clothes and some makeup. Johnson rejected that liberal stance, which led him to leave Lawson and establish an independent organization in Philadelphia. He merely changed "Our" to "The" in the church name when incorporating his new church. He became known as the apostle and overseer of the new church.

From his church Johnson began a radio ministry and issued a number of tracts explaining his unique perspective. He demanded that women members of his church wear opaque cotton stockings and long plainly colored dresses, and of course, the use of makeup was forbidden. Johnson also came to feel that Christmas, Lent, Palm Sunday, and Easter were basically pagan festivals and should not be celebrated.

In 1958 the church in Philadelphia was destroyed. Johnson led in the building of a new church and denominational headquarters which was dedicated in 1960. The church building became the center of what in 1972 became known as Apostolic Square, which now includes a number of buildings for church offices and housing for many members.

Johnson eventually completed his Ph.D. at Rutgers University. He was succeeded by Bishop **S. McDowell Shelton** as apostle and universal overseer.

Sources:

Dupree, Sherry Sherrod. *Biographical Dictionary of African-American, Holiness-Pentecostals, 1880-1990.* Washington, DC: Middle Atlantic Regional Press, 1990. 386 pp.

Johnson, S. C. "The Christmas Spirit Is a False Spirit." Undated tract.

_____. "False Lent and Pagan Festivals." Undated tract.

_____. "Jehovah God of the Old Testament Is Jesus Christ of the New Testament." Undated tract.

_____. "Sermon." *The Whole Truth* 25, 2 (February 1972): 16-18.

★463★
JONES, Charles Price
Founder, Church of Christ (Holiness) U.S.A.
b. Dec. 9, 1865, Texas Valley, Georgia
d. Jan. 19, 1949, Los Angeles, California

Charles Price Jones was the founder of the Church of Christ (Holiness) U.S.A. in the early 1900s. Raised as a Baptist in Georgia, he left home after his mother died, settled in Crittendon County, Arkansas, and joined the Locust Grove Baptist Church in 1885. In 1887 he was licensed to preach, and after graduating from Arkansas Baptist College in 1891, he became the pastor of Bethlehem Baptist Church in Searcy, Arkansas. He had previously gained pastoring experience at Pope Creek Baptist Church and St. Paul Baptist Church in Little Rock. In 1892 he moved to the Tabernacle Baptist Church in Selma, Alabama.

In Selma, Jones encountered the holiness movement, which taught about the experience of sanctification, a second work of grace after conversion or salvation, which made one holy. Jones had this experience in 1894 and in 1895 began preaching holiness to his new congregation at Mt. Helm Baptist Church in Jackson, Mississippi. This sort of teaching was not a part of the Baptist heritage, and he met much opposition. In 1896 he published a booklet to spread the word, *The Work of the Holy Spirit in the Churches*, and began a holiness magazine, *The Truth*. In 1897 he gathered a group of like-minded black holiness Baptist clergy, and they decided that the future probably held schisms. In 1900 he withdrew from the Jackson Missionary Baptist Association and other connections with the National Baptist Convention, and tried to remove the name "Baptist" from the Mt. Helm church. He was prevented from this and in 1902 was forced to leave. He and his followers then formed the Christ Temple Church as part of a new confederation of churches founded by **Charles Harrison Mason** and called themselves the Church of God.

In 1907 the confederation split when C. H. Mason encountered the Pentecostal movement in Los Angeles and tried to convince the Church of God to work toward speaking in tongues and other Spirit manifestations. After some court litigation that ended in 1909, Mason took most of the members and Jones led the rest. Jones reorganized the latter group into the Church of Christ (Holiness) U.S.A. In 1915 an independent Church of Christ (Holiness) U.S.A. was developed in Los Angeles by William Washington, who invited Jones to hold a series of revival services. Jones liked the area so much that he organized the Christ Temple Church of Los Angeles in 1917 and pastored that church for the rest of his life. Jones not only continued to lead the related churches (in 1927 he switched his leadership title from "president" to "senior bishop" and gained four assistant bishops), he also was well known as a poet. He wrote more than 1,000 songs, many published in the church's hymn book, the *Jesus Only Standard Hymnal.* Jones died in 1949 at the age of 84.

Sources:

Cobbins, Otho B. *History of the Church of Christ (Holiness) U.S.A., 1895-1965.* New York, 1966.

Jones, Charles Price. *His Fullness.* Jackson, MS: 1913.

_____. *The History of My Songs.* Los Angeles: n.d.

_____. *Jesus Only, Songs and Hymns.* Jackson, MS: 1901.

—Gary L. Ward

★464★
JONES, Edgar DeWitt
Minister, Christian Church (Disciples of Christ)
b. Dec. 5, 1876, Hearne, Texas
d. Mar. 26, 1956

Edgar DeWitt Jones, a minister of the Christian Church (Disciples of Christ) and president of the Federal Council of Churches, was the son of Mary Virginia Rumble and DeWitt Clinton Jones. He attended the University of Missouri for a year (1894-1895) and later Kentucky (now Transylvania) University for two years (1898-1900) with the aim of becoming a lawyer. However, he abandoned his legal career for the ministry and in 1901 was ordained a minister for the Disciples of Christ. As was common among Disciples he served a number of smaller churches through the next few years. In 1902 he married Frances G. Willis.

In 1906 Jones began a long pastorate as the minister of the First Christian Church at Bloomington, Illinois. He soon emerged as one of the leading Disciples ministers. In 1910 he went to Edinburgh, Scotland, as a delegate to the World Missionary Conference. In 1914 he was elected president of the International Convention of the Disciples of Christ. He was elected again in 1917 and 1918. While at Bloomington he began what became a prodigious literary output that saw him author over 20 books during the period of his active ministry. His first book, *The Inner Circle*, appeared in 1914.

In 1920 Jones moved to Detroit where he would spend the rest of his active life. He settled in at Central Christian Church (after 1927 Central Woodward Christian Church) where he remained for over a quarter of the century. During the 1920s Jones developed what was almost a second career as a journalist. In 1922 he joined the staff of *The Detroit News*. In 1926 he became a member of the staff of *The Christian* and in 1927 of *The Christian Century*.

During the 1930s the issue of ecumenism began to dominate Jones' public life. He became the president of the Association for the Promotion of Christian Unity (1931-1941), the organization founded by Disciples minister **Peter Ainslie, III** to promote Christian unity. Then in 1937 he was elected president of the Federal Council of Churches. Through this period he continued to write and among the titles from the 1930s are *Blundering into Paradise* (1932); *American Preachers of Today* (1933); *The Pulpit Stairs* (1934); and *This Great Business of Being Christian* (1938).

Jones had always had a love of history, and as his retirement approached he gave an increasing amount of time to that interest. He had been a member of the Illinois Historical Society for many years and eventually authored three books on Abraham Lincoln: *The Greatening of Abraham Lincoln* (1946); *Lincoln and the Preachers* (1948); and *The Influence of Henry Clay on Abraham Lincoln* (1952). He retired in 1947 and settled in Pleasant Hill, Michigan.

Sources:

Jones, Edgar DeWitt. *American Preachers of Today*. Indianapolis, IN: Bobbs-Merrill Co., 1933. 317 pp.

———. *The Inner Circle*. New York: Fleming H. Revell Company, 1914. 232 pp.

———. *A Man Stood Up to Preach*. St. Louis, MO: Bethany Press, 1943. 224 pp.

———. *The Pulpit Stairs*. St. Louis, MO: Bethany Press, 1934. 192 pp.

———. *This Great Business of Being a Christian*. New York: Harper & Bros., 1936. 113 pp.

★465★
JONES, Franklin
Founder, Free Daist Communion
b. Nov. 3, 1939, Jamaica, New York

Franklin Jones is a teacher of *advaita vedanta*, a type of Indian thought which emphasizes the unity and identity of the human self and the Brahman, the soul of all things. As his work has developed over the years, he has assumed a number of different religious names—Bubba Free John, Da Free John, and most recently, Heart-Master Da Love Ananda. He is also the founder of a spiritual community whose name, as of 1990, the Free Daist Communion, has also fluctuated. According to his own account, although enlightened in infancy, he was forced by the circumstances of his early environment to relinquish his illumined state as he grew up. A graduate of Columbia University (B.A., 1961), he also did graduate work in English literature at Stanford University (1961-1962) and spent a year in the Lutheran Theological Seminary in Philadelphia (1966-1967). His spiritual search, which began at a young age, was further stimulated by his participation in certain drug experiments that were conducted at the Veterans Administration Hospital in Mountain View, California, in 1962.

These experiences and others led Jones to seek a spiritual teacher. In 1964 he began working under Albert Rudolph (**Swami Rudrananda** or "Rudi"), an eclectic teacher who had studied under Swami Nityananda and **Swami Paramahansa Muktananda**, and had studied the work of Georgei Ivanovitch Gurdjieff and the Subud movement. Feeling a need for deeper spiritual experience, Jones eventually left Rudrananda and in 1968 journeyed to India and stayed for more than a year with Swami Muktananda. Once back in the United States, Jones felt that he achieved "Permanent Re-Awakening" while meditating at the Vedanta Society temple in Hollywood, California, in the summer of 1970. Soon afterward he founded the Dawn Horse Fellowship, later called the Free Daist Communion. Feeling that he should now become a spiritual teacher in his own right, he began his public ministry on April 25, 1972, after the publication of his first book, *The Knee of Listening*. Gatherings were held in Hollywood at the spiritual center which he initially called the Shree Hridayam Ashram. During a trip to India in 1973, he severed his connection with Muktananda and began calling himself Bubba Free John. That same year he published his second and last book under his given name, *The Method of the Siddhas*.

As Bubba Free John, Jones worked closely with a small group of devotees forcing them into intense encounters with money, sexuality, and psychic experiences. Many of his talks from this period were transcribed and, in published form, became some of his most popular books, including: *The Paradox of Instruction* (1977); *The Enlightenment of the Whole Body* (1978); *Love of the Two-Armed Form* (1978); and *The Eating Gorilla Comes in Peace* (1979). In 1979 he withdrew from active teaching and assumed the name Da (giver) Free John. As Da Free John, he saw his work as primarily that of transmitting the "transcendental condition" to his students. He did continue to write and lecture, and a number of books appeared in this period, including: *The Bodily Location of Happiness* (1982); *Crazy Da Must Sing, Inclined to His Weaker Side* (1982); and *The Transmission of Doubt* (1984). During this time he withdrew from his followers almost completely and began living with a few disciples on a South Pacific island. In the late 1980s, another transition in name was made and Jones emerged as Heart-Master Da Love Ananda (bliss). His most important recent volume appeared at the time of the change, *The Dawn Horse Testament* (1985). It was followed by *The Holy Jumping Off Place* (1986); *Everything Must Change* (1988); and *The Basket of Tolerance* (1989).

Just as the last change was occurring, Jones became the center of a major controversy when several disgruntled former community members filed a lawsuit (a case that was eventually settled out of court). During the 1980s, observers also charged that a gap existed between his message of non-egotism and an extreme egotism manifest in his preaching activity. With respect to this latter issue, detractors perceive Jones as a megalomaniac, while defenders point out that his egotism is far too exaggerated to be taken seriously. In other words, they claim Jones is (according to the second interpretation) acting out a caricature of an egocentric guru in order to force his students to discover the truth beyond mere guru worship.

Sources:

Jones, Franklin. [Heart-Master Da Love Ananda]. *The Basket of Tolerance*. Clearlake, CA: Free Daist Communion, 1989. 301 pp.

———. [Da Free John]. *The Bodily Location of Happiness*. Clearlake, CA: Dawn Horse Press, 1982. 258 pp.

———. *Crazy Da Must Sing, Inclined to His Weaker Side*. Clearlake, CA: Dawn Horse Press, 1982. 123 pp.

———. [Heart-Master Da Free John]. *The Dawn Horse Testament*. San Rafael, CA: Dawn Horse Press, 1985. 801 pp.

———. [Bubba Free John]. *The Eating Gorilla Comes in Peace*. Middletown, CA: Dawn Horse Press, 1979. 565 pp.

———. *The Enlightenment of the Whole Body*. Middletown, CA: Dawn Horse Press, 1978. 600 pp.

———. *The Holy Jumping-Off Place*. San Rafael, CA: Dawn Horse Press, 1986. 198 pp.

———. *The Knee of Listening*. Los Angeles: Dawn Horse Press, 1972. 271 pp.

———. *Love of the Two-Armed Form*. Middletown, CA: Dawn Horse Press, 1978. 462 pp.

———. *The Method of the Siddhas*. Los Angeles: Dawn Horse Press, 1973. 364 pp.

———. *The Transmission of Doubt*. Clearlake, CA: Dawn Horse Press, 1984. 484 pp.

Lane, David Christopher. "The Paradox of Da Free John: Distinguishing the Message from the Medium." *Understanding Cults and Spiritual Movements* 1, 2 (1985).

Shepard, Leslie. *Encyclopedia of Occultism & Parapsychology*. 3 vols., 2nd. ed. Detroit: Gale Research Co., 1984-1985.

Shepard, Leslie. *Encyclopedia of Occultism & Parapsychology*. 3 vols., 2nd. ed. Detroit: Gale Research Co., 1984-1985.

★466★
JONES, Jim
Founder, Peoples Temple
Pastor, Christian Church (Disciples of Christ)
b. May 13, 1931, Lynn, Indiana
d. Nov. 18, 1978, Jonestown Guyana

James Warren Jones was the leader of the Peoples Temple and gained particular infamy as the organizer of the tragic mass suicide/murders in Guyana which ended his following. Jones was the son of an alcoholic road construction worker in Indiana. He became interested in religious matters at a relatively young age, and inquired into a wide variety of religious groups. He married Marceline Baldwin in 1949, then attended Indiana University briefly. He received sufficient church training to become minister of the Somerset Methodist Church in Indianapolis. Before becoming fully ordained as an elder, he left Methodism to create an independent church nearby, which he called Community Unity.

Community Unity combined Jones' two main interests in Pentecostal-flavored worship and a socially active vision of racial harmony. In 1956 he moved into a larger building and renamed the group Wings of Deliverance. It was soon renamed the Peoples Temple. Around this time he met Father Major J. Divine and began to model the Peoples Temple after the Peace Mission. He also began to emulate the exalted position Father Divine had relative to his congregation. In 1960 the Peoples Temple affiliated with the Christian Church (Disciples of Christ). In 1961 Jones finished his B.S. degree at Butler University in Indianapolis and, due to negative reactions to his controversial ministry of interracial social activism, decided to diffuse the situation by taking a two-year leave, during which he visited Hawaii, Texas, and Brazil.

Shortly after his return, in 1964, Jones was ordained as a Christian Church (Disciples of Christ) minister. At about the same time, he had a vision of a nuclear holocaust and the following year moved the congregation to Ukiah, California, a "safer" location. In California, Jones held increasingly autocratic authority in his church, and worked hard to become a leading political citizen. He led the Mendocino County grand jury, was appointed to the San Francisco Housing Authority, and moved with the wealthy and influential. In 1971 congregations were begun among poor Blacks and Whites in both Los Angeles and San Francisco. Jones subsequently received humanitarian awards, and his church was praised in the journals of several major denominations as a model of Christian social concern and action.

Jones' ministry, despite the honors, continued to prompt concern among many people, who urged investigation into the church's beliefs and practices. Of concern to some was the church's unconventional worship service, which included dashes of Pentecostalism, Spiritualism, and miracle healing. Another concern was that Jones reportedly exercised excessive control over the lives of individuals—rearranging marriages, physically punishing children, and engaging in sexual relationships with both men and women in the congregation.

In 1973 Jones founded an agricultural colony in Guyana, South America, to which Jones and many members moved in 1977, under the threat of an expose article by *New West* magazine. Over the next year the population of what was called "Jonestown" grew to more than 900 people. The community, however, still had to deal with the threat of court actions and the increasing loss of disil-

lusioned members. Jones became increasingly paranoid. Drills to prepare for group suicide were occasionally carried out, and the tense situation exploded in November of 1978 when Congressman Leo Ryan came to Guyana with a group to investigate Jonestown. He and many in his party were shot to death, and almost all the residents of Jonestown either willingly or forcibly ended their lives via poison or bullets. Jones himself died from a gunshot wound which may or may not have been self-inflicted.

In the wake of this infamous tragedy, the Peoples Temple in the United States was disbanded and its assets sold. "Jonestown" became a rallying cry for those proclaiming the dangers of "cults," and numerous books have been written exploring Jones, his movement, and its ultimate demise.

Sources:

Krause, Charles. *Guyana Massacre*. New York: Berkley Books, 1978. 210 pp.

Melton, J. Gordon, ed. *The Peoples Temple and Jim Jones*. New York: Garland Publishing Company, 1990. 452 pp.

Moore, Rebecca, and Fielding M. McGehee, ed. *The Need for a Second Look at Jonestown*. Lewiston, NY: Edwin Mellen Press, 1989. 244 pp.

———. *New Religious Movements, Mass Suicide, and Peoples Temple*. Lewiston, NY: Edwin Mellen Press, 1989. 251 pp.

Reiterman, Tim. *Raven*. New York: E. P. Dutton, 1982. 622 pp.

—*Gary L. Ward*

★467★
JONES SR., Ozro Thurston
Presiding Bishop, Church of God in Christ
b. Mar. 26, 1891, Fort Smith, Arkansas
d. Sep. 23, 1972, Philadelphia, Pennsylvania

Ozro Thurston Jones, Sr., the former presiding bishop of the Church of God in Christ, the largest Pentecostal denomination in the United States, was the son of Merion and Mary Jones. He was raised as a Baptist. As a young man, in 1912, he experienced salvation, was baptized with the Holy Spirit (the definitive religious experience of Pentecostals), and had a call to the ministry, all under the spiritual guidance of Elder Justice Bowe, then an evangelist for the Church of God in Christ. Soon afterwards, he, his older sister, and a brother became an evangelist team in northwest Arkansas and the surrounding states. Over the next few years 18 congregations were established as a direct result of their evangelistic endeavors. In 1914 Jones organized the youth department of the Church of God in Christ and served as its first president. Two years later he founded and edited the *Y. P. W. W. Quarterly Topics*, an education-oriented journal. In 1920 he was appointed assistant to the state overseer in Oklahoma.

In 1925 Jones' career took a decisive turn when he became pastor of a small congregation of Pentecostal believers in Philadelphia. He moved to Philadelphia, where he would reside for the rest of his life. The congregation grew into Holy Temple Church of God in Christ. In 1926 he became state overseer for Pennsylvania. Not forgetting his work with youth, in 1928 he founded the International Youth Congress of the Church of God in Christ.

In 1933 **Charles Harrison Mason**, the founder of the Church of God in Christ, selected Jones as one of five men to be consecrated as the denomination's first bishops. Jones was later selected to serve on the executive commission created by Mason to assist him during his last years in office. Following Mason's death in 1961, the commission administered the affairs of the church for a year, and then the board of bishops moved to select a new senior bishop. They chose Jones and placed his name before the church's general assembly which approved the motion. He resigned his work with the Y.P.W.W. and his parish to devote full time to the new office.

Events moved smoothly for several years, but opposition began to appear in 1965. Voices rose, demanding regular elections for the office of presiding bishop. The situation threatened to split the denomination, and a lawsuit was filed. The courts finally ordered an election, and in 1968 a constitutional convention held its first session on January 30. The convention established clear guidelines for the election of leaders, and in the fall the elections were held. **James Oglethorpe Patterson, Sr.** became the new presiding bishop. Jones moved into retirement and died a few years later.

Sources:

Cornelius, Lucille J. *The Pioneer History of the Church of God in Christ.* N.p.: The Author, 1975. 102 pp.

Dupree, Sherry Sherrod. *Biographical Dictionary of African-American, Holiness-Pentecostals, 1880-1990.* Washington, DC: Middle Atlantic Regional Press, 1990. 386 pp.

★468★
JONES, Prophet
Founder, Church of the Universal Triumph/the Dominion of God
b. 1908, Birmingham, Alabama
d. Aug. 12, 1971, Detroit, Michigan

James Francis Marion Jones, better known as "Prophet Jones," was one of the better-known religious figures in the black community in the mid-twentieth century. Born in poverty in Alabama, he was the son of a railroad brakeman and a school teacher. Little is known of his life prior to 1938 when he arrived in Detroit. He had quit school when he was 11 years old to preach for a holiness-Pentecostal church, Triumph the Church and Kingdom of God in Christ, which had been founded in Birmingham in 1904 by Elias Dempsey Smith. In 1938 he was sent to Detroit by the church, but in the mid-1940s he developed a conflict over the church's claiming ownership of gifts given him by members of his congregation. He left and founded his own denomination, the Church of the Universal Triumph/the Dominion of God. He soon had followers across the United States, 10 percent of which were estimated to be whites.

The essence of Jones' rather spectacular success during the next decade was derived from his claims to be God's prophet and even God Himself. Within the church, he operated as a person of kingly rights and privileges. He organized the church as a kingdom and installed a throne which he claimed to be a replica of King Solomon's and upon which he sat during public services. Members were designated as citizens of the dominion. Speaking in the 1950s, Jones proclaimed that all persons living in the year 2000 A.D. would become immortal.

In order to stay alive until the end of the twentieth century, members were to follow the decrees issued by Jones. The 50 decrees, derived from common holiness admonitions, established a strict code of morality. It banned illicit sexual relations, tobacco, alcohol, coffee, and tea. Citizens were not to fraternize with noncitizens. Women were to wear girdles. Christmas was celebrated in November.

The most controversial aspect of the dominion, however, concerned money. Jones called for complete support from members of the dominion and expected substantial contributions. In return he allowed members personal access to his prophet powers each Thursday. People who felt he had personally intervened in their life for good often gave very generous gifts. Jones adopted a flamboyant lifestyle that included a mansion, several limousines, and expensive clothing, especially an infamous white mink coat he was given in 1953.

Jones' career suffered a severe setback in 1956 when he was arrested in Detroit for making an indecent proposition to a policeman. Though acquitted in court, many of his supporters deserted him. His limousines and home were seized by creditors. The house was eventually bought by Charles Emmanuel "Sweet Daddy" Grace. Jones moved to Chicago and commuted to Detroit.

Jones was quite ill during his last year of life and lived with Claude Haley, a follower in Detroit who had been appointed by the court as his guardian.

When Jones died, an elaborate funeral was attended by 2,000 people. Jones' casket cost $10,000. He was succeeded after the 60 days of prescribed mourning by James Schaffer, one of his assistants. A year and a half after his death, his bank boxes were opened and found to be stuffed with cash.

Sources:

Dupree, Sherry Sherrod. *Biographical Dictionary of African-American, Holiness-Pentecostals, 1880-1990.* Washington, DC: Middle Atlantic Regional Press, 1990. 386 pp.

Gill, John. "Death Ends Lavish Career of Prophet Jones." *The Detroit News* (August 13, 1971).

Kobler, John. "Prophet Jones: Messiah in Mink." *Saturday Evening Post* (March 5, 1955): 21, 74, 76.

★469★
JONES SR., Robert
Fundamentalist Evangelist
Founder, Bob Jones University
b. Oct. 30, 1883, Skipperville, Alabama
d. Jan. 16, 1968, Greenville, South Carolina

Robert "Bob" Jones, Sr., who emerged as a voice of the most strict form of Protestant fundamentalism in the South in the early twentieth century, was the 11th child of William Alexander Jones, a poor farmer, and his wife, Georgia Creel Jones. His parents recognized his talents and assisted him in developing as a public speaker. Also as a child, he had a conversion experience at the local congregation of the Methodist Episcopal Church, South, which his parents attended. At the age of 12, he preached his first revival and was speaking to a congregation he had raised by the next year. He was licensed to preach at age 15 and was given a circuit appointment the following year by the Alabama Conference of the Methodist Episcopal Church, South. (It has been the common practice in Methodism to assign a minister to a circuit, that is, several churches grouped together, none of which could support a full-time minister by itself.) About this time, both of his parents died.

Having struggled through his teen years to get some education, Jones entered Southern University (now Birmingham-Southern College) in 1901. Shortly after graduation, he married Bernice Sheffield in 1905. Unfortunately she died 10 months later of tuberculosis (then an incurable disease). Jones launched a career as a full-time evangelist, one of the most effective in the church, second in appeal and results only to **William "Billy" Sunday**. In 1908 he married Mary Gaston Stollenwerck. They settled in Birmingham, Alabama.

In the years following World War I, as the fundamentalist-modernist controversy was building, Jones became concerned with the problem of secularization of higher education. Simply put, children of church members were going to college, only to become atheists during their school years. His solution was to establish Bob Jones College which opened in 1926 in St. Andrews, Florida. It moved to Cleveland, Tennessee, in 1933 and emerged in 1947 in Greenville, South Carolina, as Bob Jones University.

As fundamentalism grew and changed, and especially with the emergence of neo-evangelicalism in the 1940s, Jones and his school became a center for the most conservative form of fundamentalism, which emphasized a complete separatism from any church or individuals who were tainted with heretical belief, and even further, disassociation from other fundamentalists who did not so separate themselves. **William Frank (Billy) Graham**, for example, a former student of the college, came under attack for his associations with liberal ministers. As pressure came upon the school to integrate, Jones also defended racial separation on religious grounds.

The school prospered, however. From a beginning of less than 100 students, it had more than 4,000 students by the time of Jones' death. He had turned the administration of the school over to his son, Bob Jones, Jr., soon after its founding, and the elder Jones used it as a center from which to move around the country on his evangelistic trips. Jones did not write any books, but a number of volumes of his sermons have been published over the years.

Sources:

Dictionary of American Biography. 20 vols. and 7 supps. New York: Charles Scribner's Sons, 1928-1936, 1944-1981.

Hill, Samuel S., ed. *Encyclopedia of Religion in the South.* Macon, GA: Mercer University Press, 1984. 878 pp.

Johnson, R. K. *Builder of Bridges.* Murfreesboro, TN: Sword of the Lord, 1969.

Jones, Sr., Robert. *Bob Jones' Revival Sermons.* Wheaton, IL: Sword of the Lord, 1948.

_____. *Bob Jones' Sermons.* Montgomery, AL: Paragon Press, 1911.

_____. *Heritage of Faith.* Greenville, SC: Bob Jones University Press, 1973.

_____. *My Friends.* Greenville, SC: Bob Jones University Press, 1983.

_____. *Things I Have Learned.* Chapel Talks at Bob Jones College. New York: L. B. Printing Co., 1944.

Lippy, Charles H. *Twentieth-Century Shapers of American Popular Religion.* New York: Greenwood Press, 1989. 494 pp.

Tice, Margaret Beall. *Bob Jones University.* Greenville, SC: Bob Jones University Press, 1976.

★ 470 ★
JONES, Robert Elijah
Bishop, Methodist Episcopal Church
b. Feb. 19, 1872, Greensboro, North Carolina
d. 1960

Robert Elijah Jones, one of the first two black men elected as bishops of the predominantly white Methodist Episcopal Church, was the son of Sidney Dallas and Mary Jane Holley Jones. He experienced salvation at the age of 16 and three years later joined the all-black North Carolina Conference. He attended Bennett College where he earned an A.B. in 1895. He moved to Atlanta, Georgia, to attend Gammon Theological Seminary and earned his B.D. in 1897. That year he assumed duties as the assistant editor of the *Southwestern Christian Advocate*, a denominational newspaper serving the black conferences. Returning to Bennett, he earned an M.A. in 1898. In 1901 he married Velana C. MacArthur.

Jones served as pastor of Methodist churches in Leaksville, Lexington, Thomasville, and Reidsville, North Carolina. In 1904 he became the editor of the *Southwestern Christian Advocate*. Beginning that year he was regularly returned as a delegate to general conference. During this period the church debated the feasibility of electing a black bishop. The process of deliberation culminated in 1920 with the election of Jones and Matthew Wesley Clair, Sr., to that position. At the time there were 19 all-black conferences and, since Clair was selected to head the missionary work in Liberia, Jones itinerated among the several American conferences. He shared his duties with several of his white episcopal colleagues. The same year he was elected to the episcopacy. His wife having died, he married H. Elizabeth Brown.

Jones is remembered for two contributions to the church. First, he promoted the establishment of the Gulfside Assembly, Waveland, Mississippi, which functioned as a summer gathering spot and important network center for black Methodists. But he is more importantly remembered for his work on the Joint Commission on Unification which led to the merger of the Methodist Episcopal Church, Methodist Episcopal Church, South, and Methodist Protestant Church in 1939.

The reunion of Episcopal Methodism dominated the thoughts of many white leaders of the Methodist Episcopal Church and Methodist Episcopal Church, South during the first decades of the twentieth century. Black members, almost all in the Methodist Episcopal Church, felt they had a special concern as the early proposals for union seemed to leave black members even more segregated, if not completely separated. Finally in the mid-1930s a plan was devised to create five geographical jurisdictions for the united church along with a non-geographical "Central Jurisdiction" which would include all of the black conferences of the Methodist Episcopal Church. Jones was one of the major voices opposing the plan, as it would not only approve a de facto segregation, but make racial segregation a matter of the church's legal structure. In the end he saw that it had met with the approval of the great majority of the church members.

Jones was attacked, as a member of the Joint Commission on Unification, by people who opposed the plan, though he had voted against it. At the general conference where it was presented, all the black delegates either voted against it or abstained from voting. Jones remained in the church for four years as an active bishop in the central jurisdiction. He retired in 1944.

Sources:

Harmon, Nolan B. *The Encyclopedia of World Methodism.* 2 vols. Nashville: United Methodist Publishing House, 1974.

Howell, Clinton H., ed. *Prominent Personalities in Methodism.* Birmingham, AL: Lowrey Press, 1945. 512 pp.

Richardson, Harry V. *Dark Salvation.* New York: Doubleday & Company, 1976. 324 pp.

★ 471 ★
JONES, Rufus Matthew
Mystic and Scholar, Society of Friends
b. Jan. 25, 1863, South China, Maine
d. Jun. 16, 1948, Haverford, Pennsylvania

Rufus Matthew Jones, a Quaker scholar who gained fame for his historical writing, his mystical faith, and his activism in the cause of peace, was the son of Edwin and Mary Jones, farmers in rural Maine. He had an early bent toward the educated life and traveled first to the Friends School in Providence, Rhode Island, and then to Haverford College to pursue his studies. After graduation, he moved back to Poughkeepsie, New York, and in 1885 began teaching at the Oakwood seminary. Two years later he returned to Providence to teach at the Friends School. In 1888 he married Sallie Coutant. The following year he began a four-year tenure at Oak Grove Seminary in Vassalboro, Maine.

In 1893 Jones began his 41-year relationship with Haverford College as an instructor. He also became editor of *The Friends Review* (merged the next year to become *The American Friend*). In 1897 Jones made one of the more important proposals of his life, urging the organic union of the various American yearly meetings of the Friends. This proposal was acted upon during the next years and in 1902 Jones attended the first sessions of the Five Years Meeting. He was named to the business committee. He served on the committee for the rest of his life and was its chairman from 1912 until his death. In the meantime, his personal life had undergone important changes. His first wife died in 1899. He attended Harvard for a year and received his M.A. in 1901. In 1902 he married Elizabeth Cadbury.

In 1905, following the death of his friend John Wilhelm Rowntree, Jones initiated plans for a series of books on Quaker history using the material Rowntree had collected. Eventually six volumes were produced, two authored by William C. Braithwaite and four by Jones. Jones' titles were *Studies in Mystical Religion* (1909); *The Quakers in the American Colonies* (1911); *Spiritual Reformers of the 16th and 17th Centuries* (1914); and *The Later Periods of Quakerism* (1921).

In 1915, Jones helped organize the Fellowship of Reconciliation (FOR), an ecumenical pacifist organization, in reaction to the outbreak of World War I. Not content to merely oppose the war, in 1917 Jones became one of the founders of the American Friends Service Committee, which dealt with the needs of relief and other services following the war. Jones chaired the committee in the years after the war. The committee has subsequently grown into an important service agency as well as a meeting ground for Friends.

Many who did not know of Jones' historical work responded to his many books on mysticism, prayer, and the religious life. Among his many titles are *Spiritual Energies in Daily Life* (1922); *Finding the Trail of Life* (1926); *New Studies in Mystical Religion* (1928); *New Eyes for Invisibles* (1943); *The Luminous Trail* (1947); and *A Call to What Is Vital* (1949). Baptist minister **Harry Emerson Fosdick** edited an anthology of his works in 1951.

The years after his retirement from Haverford in 1934 remained full. In addition to his continued literary output, in 1935 he became presiding clerk of the Five Year Meeting. In 1937 he chaired the meeting of Friends that led to the formation of the Friends World Committee. One of the few Americans who understood the threat faced by the Jews, in 1938 he traveled to Germany in an attempt to intercede on their behalf. His continuing concern for the Jews came to the fore again when, just months before his death, he made an equally valiant, if unsuccessful, effort to mediate the Palestinian crisis.

Sources:

Fosdick, Harry Emerson, ed. *Rufus Jones Speaks to Our Time.* New York: Macmillan Company, 1951. 289 pp.
Jones, Rufus M. *A Call to What Is Vital.* New York: Macmillan Company, 1949. 143 pp.
_____. *New Eyes for Invisibles.* New York: Macmillan Company, 1943. 185 pp.
_____. *The Quakers in the American Colonies.* New York: W. W. Norton, 1966. 605 pp.
_____. *Spiritual Energies in Daily Life.* New York: Macmillan Company, 1922. 179 pp.
_____. *Spiritual Reformers in the 16th and 17th Centuries.* Boston, MA: Beacon Press, 1959. 362 pp.
Moore, J. Floyd. "Rufus Jones: Quaker Prophet." *The Christian Century* 80, 4 (January 23, 1963): 107-09.
Moyer, Elgin S., ed. *Who Was Who in Church History.* Chicago: Moody Press, 1968.
Rufus Jones Centennial 1863-1963. Richmond, IN: Board of Publication of the Five Years Meeting of Friends, 1963.

★472★
JONES, Samuel Porter
Evangelist, Methodist Episcopal Church, South
b. Oct. 16, 1847, Chambers County, Alabama
d. Oct. 15, 1906, Perry, Alaska

Samuel Porter Jones, one of the popular evangelists of the late nineteenth century, was the son of John J. and Nancy Porter Jones and was raised in a Methodist family. His mother died when he was nine years old. His father remarried and in 1859 moved the family to Cartersville, Georgia. His father served in the Civil War, and Jones, left on his own, turned to drinking. After the war he began to read law and in 1869 was admitted to the bar. A month after becoming a lawyer, he married Laura McElwain. He moved about during the next few years and sunk into poverty and drunkenness.

In 1872, as his father was dying, he made a promise to him to reform. In the process of deciding what to do with his life, he was told by several ministers that he had a gift for speaking and a calling to be a preacher. He began to preach as opportunity was presented, and several months later was accepted on trial in the North Georgia Conference of the Methodist Episcopal Church, South as

a preacher. His first appointment was the Van Wert Circuit, in Polk County, Georgia. Through the remainder of the decade he succeeded in remaining sober and became a popular preacher in North Georgia. He moved after three years at Van Wert to the de Soto Circuit in Floyd County, then to the Newberne Circuit in Newton County, and finally the Montecello Circuit in Jasper County.

In 1879 he began regularly to hold revival meetings around the state of Georgia, as time could be allowed away from his circuit. In 1881 he accepted the task of raising funds for the Methodist North Georgia Orphans' Home, which allowed him to travel widely and spend more time in evangelistic work.

The next measurable step in Jones' career came in 1883 when he was invited to Memphis to lead a series of revival services which were widely covered by the newspapers. His great success led to an invitation from **T. DeWitt Talmage**, the famous Presbyterian pastor in Brooklyn, New York, for Jones to speak at his church in January 1885. He followed his visit north with a memorable stay in Nashville, Tennessee. By that time, his career was launched, and for the rest of the century he was fully engaged as an evangelist, regularly moving from one city to another and speaking to packed houses. He was acknowledged as one of the preeminent orators of his day, though his sermons were attacked by many as crude and sentimental. A major theme, the hypocrisy of nominal Christians, had a massive appeal to the large percentage of his audiences.

The last six years of his life he tended to stay close to home, and he preached almost exclusively in the South. He died at a relatively early age, and his funeral was officially acknowledged by the Georgia State legislature.

Sources:

Dictionary of American Biography. 20 vols. and 7 supps. New York: Charles Scribner's Sons, 1928-1936, 1944-1981.
Jones, Laura, ed. *The Life and Sayings of Sam P. Jones.* Atlanta: Franklin-Turner Co., 1907. 464 pp.
Jones, Sam. *Sam Jones' Own Book.* Cincinnati, OH: Cranston & Stowe, 1886. 539 pp.
_____. *Sam Jones' Sermons.* 2 vols. Chicago: Rhodes & McClure Publishing Co., 1886.

★473★
JORDAN, Clarence
Founder, Koinonia Community
b. Jul. 29, 1912, Talbotton, Georgia
d. Oct. 29, 1969, Americus, Georgia

During the height of the Civil Rights Movement of the 1960s, Clarence Jordan attained fame as the founder of Koinonia, a radical Christian communal experiment in Georgia, and was also well known as the originator of the folksy "Cotton Patch" interpretation of the Christian New Testament. Jordan was raised as a Baptist in Georgia and attended the Georgia State College of Agriculture from 1929 to 1933. After graduation he was offered a military commission based on his R.O.T.C. training, but turned it down after reflection on how military service clashed with his deepening religious convictions.

Jordan entered the Southern Baptist Theological Seminary in 1933, received his Th.M. in 1936, and went on for his Ph.D., which he received in 1939. At the same time, he pastored various churches part-time and taught briefly at Simmons University, a predominantly black school. During this time he became increasingly convinced that the Bible did not condone the kind of racial segregation and discrimination typical in the country in general and also in the Southern Baptist Convention. When he finished his schooling, he became director of the Sunshine Center in the black community of Louisville, Kentucky. He soon was promoted to superintendent of missions for the Long Run Baptist Association, where he had a greater chance to spread his ideas on racial interaction.

One of the seminarians who worked with Jordan at this time began a campus Christian group named *Koinonia*, a Greek word used in the Bible to describe the close community among Christians. Jordan's work with this group, and also with the pacifist group Fellowship of Reconciliation (FOR), helped him develop his increasing beliefs in pacifism, racial equality, and communal sharing of property. In 1941 he and a missionary, Martin English, devised a communal farm arrangement to put their beliefs into practice, and in 1942 the Koinonia Farm was founded on 400 acres near Americus, Georgia. They gained some initial financial support through egg production and other agricultural products, and as Jordan spoke around the nation, other families joined Koinonia.

The farm enjoyed working relationships with the outside community until 1948, when Koinonia openly opposed the post-war draft. In 1950 the Rehobeth Baptist Church revoked the memberships of Jordan and others on the farm, who thereafter did not relate to a specific denomination. In 1956 further friction was caused when Jordan attempted to help two black students integrate a college. This caused a general boycott of Koinonia's goods and various acts of violence and harassment by the White Citizens Council and others. Koinonia managed to keep economically afloat by marketing its shelled pecans across the country, thus bypassing the local area. The violence caused Jordan to work on a new translation of the New Testament, which would place the Gospel message geographically in the South in contemporary situations and use vernacular language. The result was the Cotton Patch Gospel, which found expression in various publications.

Koinonia suffered hardships throughout the 1960s, and in 1968 Jordan reorganized the farm as Koinonia Partners. Its program focused on communication of the Cotton Patch vision, especially with visitors, a Fund for Humanity to give the poor capital to help themselves economically, and the idea of life lived in partnership with God. Jordan died in 1969 at the age of 57.

Sources:

Jordan, Clarence. *A Letter to the Christians in Atlanta or First Corinthians*. Americus, GA: Koinonia Farm, 1968. 289 pp.

_____. *A Second Letter to the Christians in Atlanta or Second Corinthians*. Americus, GA: Koinonia Farm, 1968. 19 pp.

_____. *The Substance of Faith and Other Cotton Patch Sermons*. Dallas Lee, ed. New York: Association Press, 1972. 160 pp.

_____. *To God's People in Washington or Romans*. Americus, GA: Koinonia Farm, 1968. 24 pp.

_____, and Bill Lane Doulos. *Cotton Patch Parables of Liberation*. Scottdale, PA: Herald Press, 1976. 160 pp.

Lee, Dallas. *The Cotton Patch Evidence*. New York: Harper & Row, 1971. 240 pp.

Encyclopedia of Southern Baptists. 3 vols. Nashville, TN: Broadman Press, 1958, 1971.

—*Gary L. Ward*

★ 474 ★
JORGENSEN, Lars
Pioneer Danish Baptist Minister
b. Apr. 27, 1837, Hauge Denmark
d. Feb. 27, 1927, Pierre, South Dakota

Lars Jorgensen, the first Danish Baptist minister in America, was the son of a woman who had become one of the first converts to the Baptist church in Denmark. Lars was converted at the age of 19 and began preaching his newfound faith soon after joining the church. In 1858 he immigrated to America and settled at Raymond, Wisconsin, where, two years prior to his arrival, a group of Baptist laypeople who had immigrated from Denmark had organized the first Danish Baptist church in North America under the auspices of the American Baptists. Soren Larsen preached at the

church for a time, but he soon left over a dispute concerning the role of women in the congregation. Jorgensen assumed preaching duties in the pastorless church and in 1859 was ordained to the ministry by the congregation.

Under Jorgensen's leadership, a Sunday school was opened and new work was begun at Waushara and New Denmark. Jorgensen left Raymond in 1862. In 1863 he organized the church at Clarks Grove, Wisconsin. In 1864 he traveled to Chicago and, finding a group of Danish Baptists residing there, organized them at the First Danish "Baptizing" Church of Chicago. Some Swedish Baptists were among the church members, but they withdrew in 1866. Jorgensen remained in Chicago as the church's pastor, but resigned in 1867.

While pastoring in Chicago, Jorgensen began to campaign for a Danish Baptist press. He began a short-lived periodical, *Missionsbladet*, in 1866 and the following year published the *Psalmer og Aandelige Sange* (Psalms and Spiritual Songs). In 1878 he tried again to begin a periodical, but the *Nordstjernen* (the North Star) lasted for only one issue.

In 1869 Jorgensen's successor at the First Danish Baptist Church of Chicago left the congregation and the members voted to recall Jorgensen. That vote led to a split, and a group of members withdrew. Under Jorgensen's leadership, the congregation requested to be admitted to the membership of Second Baptist Church, an American Baptist congregation, and be reorganized as a Danish mission. They continued in that capacity until 1873, when they again organized as the Scandinavian Baptist Union Church. After many years working to build the pioneer Danish Baptist churches in the Midwest, Jorgensen became interested in work among the American Indians and spent the last years of his life as a missionary in South Dakota, where he died in 1927, just before his 90th birthday.

Sources:

Seventy-Five Years of Danish Baptist Missionary Work in America. Philadelphia: Danish Baptist General Conference of America, 1931. 304 pp.

★ 475 ★
JUDGE, William Quan
Founder, Theosophical Society
b. Apr. 13, 1851, Dublin Ireland
d. Mar. 21, 1896, New York, New York

William Quan Judge was one of the cofounders of the Theosophical Society and the leader of a branch that broke off from it, the Theosophical Society in America. Born to a Methodist family in Ireland, he was a sickly child, a weakness that followed him into adulthood. In 1864 Judge's family moved to the United States, and in 1872 Judge became a citizen and was admitted to the bar as a lawyer, specializing in commercial law. In 1874, at the age of 23, he married Ella M. Smith.

The same year of his marriage, Judge's career was changed when he heard about Henry Steel Olcott and **Helena Petrovna Blavatsky**'s Spiritualist adventures; he sought them out in New York City. In 1875 the three founded the Theosophical Society, one of the first formal occult organizations in the United States, with Judge acting as legal counsel. When Blavatsky and Olcott left for India in 1878, the organization in America faltered, in part due to resentment at being controlled from far off India. Judge was not in a good position to lead it, due to lack of occult knowledge, frequent illnesses, and business trips abroad. In 1884 he made a trip to India which seemed to restore his enthusiasm. By 1886 an official American section was formed and Judge was elected general secretary.

At this point events went quite well for Judge, who led the American section into prosperity and produced a number of major Theosophical writings. These included translations of key Hindu scriptures, the *Yoga Aphorisms of Patanjali* (1889); the *Bhagavad Gita* (1890); and the classic Theosophical work, *The Ocean of Theosophy* (1893). He also created two new journals, *The Path* (1886) and *The Theosophical Forum* (1889). (His articles from these periodicals were collected and published in the 1970s as *Echoes of the Orient*). In 1888, at a meeting in London, Judge became a leader in the new Esoteric Section, a group for the most dedicated Theosophists, and wrote *The Book of Rules* for it.

When Blavatsky died in 1891, there was some jockeying for position between her heir apparent, Annie Besant, and Judge, who hoped to become international president. Judge proposed to Besant that he lead the Esoteric Section in America while she lead it in Europe and India. This was confirmed by a later message from one of the spiritual Masters (Morya) saying, "Judge's plan is right."

In 1893 Judge had to call upon all of his physical and organizational abilities in order to put together and manage the appearances of **Annie Besant**, **Anagarika Dharmapala**, and G. N. Chakravarti at the World's Parliament of Religions at the Chicago World's Fair. After that event, Judge had to deal with the increasing tensions within Theosophy. It was charged that his continuing messages from the Masters were really from himself. He initially cleared himself at a London trial in 1894, but the media eventually found out about the messages and charges and exposed him. Judge responded by saying that Annie Besant no longer had authority and was under the control of dark forces. In April of 1895, at the American Theosophists' Convention in Boston, Judge declared the Americans independent of the British and Indian Sections, and so formed the Theosophical Society in America, taking the majority of the American branches with him. Judge was elected president of the new group, but was not to enjoy it for long. He died in early 1896, at the young age of 45.

Sources:

Eek, Sven, and Boris de Zirkoff. *William Quan Judge, 1851-1896*. Wheaton, IL: Theosophical Publishing House, 1969. 96 pp.

Judge, William Q. *Echoes from the Orient*. New York: The Path, 1890. 68 pp.

———. *Echoes of the Orient*. 2 vols. San Diego: Point Loma Publications, 1975, 1980.

———. *Isis and the Mahatmas*. London: 1895. 30 pp.

———. *Letters That Have Helped Me*. New York: The Path, 1891.

———. *The Ocean of Theosophy*. Pasadena, CA: Theosophical University Press, 1893, 1973. 173 pp.

Shepard, Leslie. *Encyclopedia of Occultism & Parapsychology*. 3 vols., 2nd. ed. Detroit: Gale Research Co., 1984-1985.

—*Gary L. Ward*

★ 476 ★
JUDSON, Edward
Minister, Baptist Church
b. Dec. 27, 1844, Moulmein Myanmar
d. Oct. 23, 1914, New York, New York

Edward Judson, generally credited with initiating the institutional church movement in American Protestantism, was the son of Adoniram Judson, the pioneer Baptist missionary in Burma, and Sara Judson. His mother died shortly after he was born, and his father remarried, but soon afterward died himself. In 1851, with his stepmother, Emily Judson, he left Burma to come to America for the first time. Emily Judson died in 1854 and young Edward, now an orphan, went to live with Dr. Ebenezer Dodge, a professor at Madison University in Hamilton, New York. At the age of 12, he entered the university's preparatory school. After graduating he moved to Plymouth, Rhode Island, and attended Brown University, from which he graduated in 1865. His father had been the valedictorian in 1807, and Edward was chosen to deliver the classical oration.

Judson's first job was principal of the Leland and Gray Seminary in Townsend, Vermont. In 1867 he entered Madison University as a student in the theology department. However, within a few weeks he joined the faculty as a professor of Latin and modern languages. He married Antoinette Barsow, and began to preach in nearby churches. Then in 1873 he resigned his teaching post, was ordained a Baptist minister, and departed with his wife for a year in Italy as pastor of the American Union Church in Rome.

Judson returned to America in 1873 to become pastor of the Baptist Church of North Orange, New Jersey, one of the more prominent parishes in the Northern Baptist Convention, and under his care it flourished. His career seemed firmly in place. Then in 1881, to everyone's suprise, he resigned his pastorate and became the pastor of a small church in the lower east side of Manhattan. Under his leadership the Berean Baptist Church took in almost 100 members a year for the next seven years. More importantly, Judson quickly became sensitive to the overcrowding and poverty of his new home. In an effort to conquer these injustices, he established the Kinmuth Memorial Home in 1882. Here he could send city people for a two weeks' vacation in the summer. In 1885 he established the first kindergarten within a church in America. As new ministries were established, he developed the vision of a large institutional church which would meet a variety of social service needs for its immediate community. Over the years the services he initiated included a facility for homeless men, a coal yard, and a free reading room. Some were incorporated into the church, others were turned over to other public agencies.

As Judson's success in New York became known, the offers from other prominent pulpits came and were refused. He stayed in New York to build what he saw as a monument to his father. He had written his first book, *Adoniram Judson*, published in 1894, soon after moving to New York. He now turned to building Judson Memorial Church, which was completed in 1892 and became a model of the institutional church as the center of a community's social philanthropy.

In 1897 Judson accepted a teaching post at Colgate Theological Seminary with the understanding that he would not have to give up his pulpit. During his next years he wrote a book describing the accomplishments and vision of *The Institutional Church* (1899), others of which were appearing around the United States.

In 1903 Judson was given a year's leave of absence from his church and moved to Chicago to teach homiletics at the University of Chicago. While enjoying the work, he nevertheless felt an obligation to continue in New York, to which he returned in 1904. His church now became a training ground for ministerial students who were sent there as part of their seminary training. He pastored the church for another decade, until his death in 1914.

Sources:

Judson, Edward. *Adoniram Judson*. Philadelphia: American Baptist Publication Society, 1894. 176 pp.

———. *The Institutional Church*. New York: Lentolhon & Company, 1899. 211 pp.

Sears, C. H. *Edward Judson, Interpreter of God*. Philadelphia: Griffith & Rowland Press, 1917.

Stewart, Walter Sinclair. *Later Baptist Missionaries and Pioneers*. Philadelphia: The Judson Press, 1928. 268 pp.

★ 477 ★
Swami Amar JYOTI
Founder, Truth Consciousness
b. May 6, 1928, Larkana India

Swami Amar Jyoti, the founder of Truth Consciousness (United States) and Ananda Niketan Trust (India), is a religious teacher in the Hindu tradition. He was born in a part of India which is now located in Pakistan. As a youth he was a promising student of both the sciences and the arts. However, much to the surprise of his family and friends, he renounced the world a few months prior to his college graduation to seek spiritual enlightenment. In 1960, after 10 years of solitude and meditation, Amar Jyoti emerged from the high ranges of the Himalayas as a liberated soul. He embarked on a pilgrimage through India, eventually establishing an ashram in Poona.

In 1961, at the request of a disciple, Amar Jyoti journeyed to the United States. In Albuquerque, he attracted his first American students. For the next 12 years, however, the swami focused his energies in India, and did not return until 1973. In 1974 he began establishing his American ashrams, the first being in Boulder, Colorado. Henceforth Amar Jyoti was on the road, lecturing in colleges and religious centers, and, in the next five years, founding ashrams in Arizona, Michigan, and California. Yet other centers developed in the Los Angeles and Chicago areas. A more intensive community, Truth Consciousness Community, was established in Tucson, Arizona.

This busy schedule did not cause Amar Jyoti to abandon his Indian work, and in 1978, he established Rishi Ashram in the Himalayan region on a slope above the Kulu Valley. Journals, newsletters, and pamphlets are issued by both his American and his Indian organizations. An extensive series of the swami's discourses, recorded live at his satsangs, as well as tapes of devotional music, are also distributed by Truth Consciousness. He is the author of three books: *Spirit of Himalaya: The Story of a Truth Seeker* (1979); *Retreat into Eternity* (1981); and *In the Light of Wisdom* (1983).

Sources:
Frey, Kessler. *Satsang Notes of Swami Amar Jyoti*. Boulder, CO: Truth Consciousness, 1977. 102 pp.
Jyoti, Swami Amar. *In the Light of Wisdom*. Boulder, CO: Truth Consciousness, 1983. 73 pp.
———. *Retreat into Eternity*. Boulder, CO: Truth Consciousness, 1981. 128 pp.
———. *Spirit of Himalaya: The Story of a Truth Seeker*. Boulder, CO: Truth Consciousness, 1979, 1985. 123 pp.

★478★
Swami JYOTIR MAYA NANDA
Founder, Yoga Research Foundation
b. Feb. 3, 1931, Dumari Buzurg, District Saran, Bihar India

Swami Jyotir Maya Nanda was born into a pious Hindu family in his native India. After completing his studies at the Science College of Patna University, he embarked on a spiritual quest. At the age of 22 he received *sannyas* (entered the renounced life) at Swami Sivananda Saraswati's ashram in Rishikish, in northern India, and served the Divine Light Mission (Sivananda's organization) in various capacities for the next nine years. He was, for instance, a professor of religion at Sivananda's Yoga Vedanta Forest Academy and the editor of the *Yoga Vedanta* journal. He was particularly adept at explaining yoga and vedanta philosophy to foreign students. He was also frequently invited to lecture at the All India Vedanta Conferences in Delhi, Amritsar, Ludhiana, and other parts of India.

Jyotir Maya Nanda decided to travel to the West in 1962, and on June 11 founded the Temple of the Eternal Religion of India in Puerto Rico. For the next six years, he taught yoga in Puerto Rico. He held regular classes, gave two radio lectures every week (in Spanish and English), and published a magazine. In 1969 he moved to Miami, where he established the International School of Yoga and Vedanta Philosophy. For many years he has given weekly classes in yoga and meditation at his ashram. He has traveled widely to disseminate the teachings of yoga, touring Europe and the Americas on a number of occasions. He has also lectured at various universities around the country, and has spoken at the Men-

ninger State Hospital. Jyotir Maya Nanda is recognized as an exceptionally gifted teacher/scholar in a lineage that has produced many noteworthy teachers. He has devoted much of the time away from the classroom to writing books and translating sacred Hindu texts, which the foundation has published.

Sources:
Jyotir Maya Nanda, Swami. *Raja Yoga Sutras*. Miami: Yoga Research Foundation, 1978. 264 pp.
———. *The Way of Liberation*. Miami: Swami Lalitananda, 1976. 239 pp.
———. *Yoga Can Change Your Life*. Miami: Swami Lalitananda, 1975. 239 pp.
———. *Yoga Essays for Self-Improvement*. Miami: Yoga Research Foundation, 1981. 248 pp.
———. *The Yoga of Divine Love*. Miami: Yoga Research Foundation, 1982. 240 pp.
———. *Yoga Vasistha*. 3 vols. Miami: Yoga Research Foundation, 1977, 1980, 1986.

★479★
KAGAN, Henry Enoch
Reform Jewish Rabbi
b. Nov. 28, 1906, Sharpsburg, Pennsylvania
d. Aug. 16, 1969, Pittsburgh, Pennsylvania

Henry Enoch Kagan, a rabbi of Reform Judaism who led in the introduction of contemporary psychotherapy into Judaism and also played an important role in the relations of Jews and Christians in the 1960s, was the son of Alexander Benjamin and Sarah Rivlin Ginsburg Kagan. On his mother's side of the family, he was the descendent of an unbroken line of rabbis that went back over four centuries. He grew up in Washington, Pennsylvania, but the family moved to Cincinnati, Ohio, while he was in high school. He attended the University of Cincinnati, from which he received a B.A. degree in 1928. He studied theology for a year at Hebrew Union and was ordained in 1929. He then spent a year as rabbi at Temple Beth Zion in Johnstown, Pennsylvania. In 1930 he became the rabbi at Temple Israel in Uniontown, Pennsylvania. During the four years at Uniontown, he also directed the Hillel Foundation at West Virginia University and earned an M.A. in political science. He next spent three years at Temple Rodef Shalom in Pittsburgh, Pennsylvania, before accepting in 1957 the call of Sinai Temple in Mount Vernon, New York, where he would remain for the next three decades. In 1939 he married Esther Ruth Miller.

By the time he moved to his suburban synagogue, Kagan had become convinced that psychology was an important tool for the contemporary rabbi. He entered graduate school at Columbia University, finally earning his doctorate in 1949. He began a campaign to promote the integration of psychological insights and practices into the rabbinical ministry. He became the first practicing rabbi to deliver a paper before the American Psychological Association and he served on the association's committee on relations between psychology and religion. Kagan became the first rabbi to gain official certification as a psychologist in the state of New York. He also founded the Committee on Psychiatry and Religion of the Central Conference of American Rabbis, the Reform Jewish rabbinical association, and the Counseling Center of the New York Federation of Reformed Synagogues.

Kagan's other great passion in life was the reduction of anti-Semitism, and he used the psychological insights he had gained in that endeavor. His doctoral dissertation focused upon work with youth in dealing with anti-Jewish feelings. Published in 1952 as *Changing the Attitudes of Christian toward Jew: A Psychological Approach Through Religion*, it remained his most influential book, though other important titles would appear: *Judaism and Psychiatry* (1956); *Six Who Changed the World* (1963), and *Rabbi as Counselor* (1964).

Kagan's work led to an invitation from Roman Catholic authorities to teach pastoral psychology at St. John's Abbey in Minnesota and at Iona College in New York. In 1963 he presented a paper in Milan, Italy, relating the New Testament account of the crucifixion of Jesus to anti-Semitism. As a result he was invited to offer advice on the document of the Second Vatican Council which redefined the Roman Catholic Church's relation to the Jews. Kagan served as a consultant to Augustin Cardinal Bea in that endeavor, which eventuated in a formal statement by the council that declared that the Jews were not responsible for the death of Christ.

Sources:

Dictionary of American Biography. 20 vols. and 7 supps. New York: Charles Scribner's Sons, 1928-1936, 1944-1981.

Kagan, Henry Enoch. *Changing the Attitude of Christian toward Jew: A Psychological Approach Through Religion.* New York: Columbia University Press, 1952. 155 pp.

———. *Six Who Changed the World.* New York: T. Yoseloff, 1963. 278 pp.

★480★
KAHANE, Meir
Orthodox Jewish Rabbi and Founder, Jewish Defense League (JDL)
b. Aug. 1, 1932, Brooklyn, New York
d. Nov. 5, 1990, New York, New York

Rabbi Meir Kahane, the founder of the activist Jewish Defense League (JDL), was born Martin David Kahane, the son of Charles and Sonia Kahane. His father, the rabbi of Sha'arei Tef'ilah Congregation in Brooklyn, was a Palestinian and active Zionist. Kahane grew up in Brooklyn. His early life seems to have been deeply affected by the death of four of his family in Palestine in an attack by Palestinian Arabs in 1938 and by the Holocaust of World War II. In the years immediately after World War II, he joined Betar, a more militant wing of the Zionist movement, and in 1947 was arrested for tossing vegetables at British minister Ernest Bevin.

During the 1950s Kahane attended school. He received his B.A. from Brooklyn College in 1954. In 1956 he married Libby Blum. In 1957 he finished both a law degree from the New York Law School and an M.A. from New York University. That same year he was ordained a rabbi at which time he changed his name to Meir. In 1958 he became the rabbi at the Howard Beach Jewish Center in Queens, New York. Fired for being too Orthodox, he began to write for the *Brooklyn Daily* (later called *The Jewish Post*). Through the 1960s he also worked for the United States government investigating extremist groups and building Jewish support for Vietnam. In that regard he authored *The Jewish Stake in Vietnam* (1968).

In 1968 Kahane founded the Jewish Defense League, one of the most controversial Jewish activist groups of this generation. The JDL attacked black groups who made anti-Semitic statements, agitated for Soviet Jews, and engaged in anti-PLO activity. By 1971 there were an estimated 10,000 members. Over the years the group was responsible for a number of acts of violence, including the bombing of perceived enemies of the Jewish community. During the 1970s, Kahane directed much of his attention to building the JDL in Israel. In 1973 he ran for the Knesset on a platform that called for the expulsion of all Arabs from Israel. He was defeated. He ran again in subsequent elections and was defeated twice more before finally being elected in 1984, though his Kach Party received only one seat. All during this period he was moving back and forth to America directing JDL activities and staving off attempts by the American leadership to wrest control of the organization from him.

After his election, the Knesset moved to block his activity. He was banned from Arab villages, Israeli high schools, and radio and television. In 1988 the U. S. government stripped Kahane of his passport. He appealed the action in court, claiming he had never

taken the required oath of office for a Knesset member. In winning the court case, he lost in Israel, as the Knesset stripped him of his parliamentary privileges. In 1988 the Knesset banned the Kach Party on the grounds that it was racist and anti-democratic. Thus Kahane was driven out of the Israeli government. However, he continued his career of agitation in both Israel and America until unexpectedly assassinated on the streets of New York in November 1990.

The JDL continues as an organization, but shows little sign that it will be a factor in either the Israeli or American Jewish community in the near future.

Sources:

Friedman, Robert I. *The False Prophet: Rabbi Meir Kahane from FBI Informant to Knesset Member.* Brooklyn, NY: Lawrence Hill Books, 1990. 282 pp.

Kahane, Meir. *Never Again!* Los Angeles: Nash Publishing Co., 1971. 287 pp.

———. *Our Challenge: The Chosen Land.* Radner, PA: Chilton Book Company, 1974. 181 pp.

———. *The Story of the Jewish Defense League.* Radnor, PA: Chilton Book Company, 1973. 338 pp.

★481★
KALU RINPOCHE, Khyyab Je
Tibetan Lama and Founder, Kagyu Dharma
b. 1905, Hor Treshu Tibet
d. May 10, 1989, Sonada India

His Eminence Khenpo Kalu Rinpoche was a highly respected Tibetan Buddhist lama who initiated a number of different centers under the collective name Kagyu Dharma. (Rinpoche, literally "precious one," is a title given to senior abbots and those considered to be incarnate lamas.) He was born into the Ratak family in Hor Treshu, Tibet. His father, the Ratak Tulku, named Pema Norbu, was a disciple of both Jamyang Khyentse and Jamgon Kongrul the Great. Even as a child Kalu Rinpoche was disinterested in worldly attractions, and was said to have exhibited the excellent virtues of selflessness, compassion, and devotion. As a teenager he went to Pepung Monastery, the seat of the Kagyu sect (one of the four principal schools of Tibetan Vajrayana Buddhism), where he was ordained by the Situ Rinpoche, Pema Wangchuk Gyalpo. After completing an extensive course of study and the traditional three-year retreat, he went back to his homeland to teach at Bengen Monastery.

Kalu Rinpoche undertook a 12-year mountain retreat at the age of 25. After the end of this period he became director of Jamgon Kontrul's retreat center. At the request of Situ Rinpoche, he returned to Pepung, where he became Vajra Master. Kalu Rinpoche was a masterful teacher who trained many accomplished disciples during his stay in Pepung. Entering a new cycle of activity, he went on a pilgrimage to Central Tibet that included a stay in Lhasa. During this cycle he rebuilt the meditation hall of Jamgon Kongrul at Pepung.

Shortly before the Chinese invasion of Tibet in 1959, Kalu Rinpoche established meditation halls in both Bhutan and India in preparation for a Tibetan community-in-exile. At Sonada, his home monastery near Darjeeling, India, Kalu Rinpoche taught three successive three-year retreats.

Kalu Rinpoche made his first trip to the West in 1971. During this journey he visited several European countries and made a trip to the Vatican, where he had an audience with the Pope. He then visited North America, where he taught at various centers for nine months and, in the spring of 1972, established his first Western center, Kagyu Kunchab Chuling, in Vancouver. In 1974-1975, during his second Western trip, he founded centers in Europe and in North America. During his third trip in 1976 he initiated the first three-year retreat for Westerners in France. Afterwards he visited North America and made his first trip to the Far East. Kalu Rinpoche authored many books, one of which, *The Gem Ornament of Manifold Oral Instructions Which Benefits Each and Everyone Appropriately*, is available in English. Recently, an American disciple, Kenneth McLeod, has compiled a selection of his shorter works in *Writings of Kalu Rinpoche*.

Sources:

Badiner, Allan. "Two Venerable Masters." *Vajradhatu Sun* (August/September 1987).

The Chariot for Traveling the Path to Freedom: The Life Story of Kalu Rinpoche. Trans. by Kenneth McLeod. San Francisco: Kagyu Dharma, 1985. 101 pp.

Fields, Rick. *How the Swans Came to the Lake: A Narrative History of Buddhism in America*. 1981. Rev. ed. Boston: Shambhala, 1986. 445 pp.

Kalu Rinpoche. *The Gem Ornament of Manifold Oral Instructions which Benefits Each and Everyone Appropriately*. 206 pp.

_____. *Writings of Kalu Rinpoche*. Trans. by Kenneth McLeod. Vancouver, BC: Kagyu Kunchab Chuling, 1976. 71 pp.

"Open Letter to Disciples and Friends of Khyan Je Kalu Rinpoche." *Snow Lion Newsletter and Catalogue* 4, 2 (Fall 1989): 3.

★482★
KAPLAN, Mordecai Menahem
Founder, Jewish Reconstructionist Foundation
b. Jun. 11, 1881, Swenziany Lithuania
d. Nov. 8, 1983, New York, New York

Mordecai Menahem Kaplan, the founder of Reconstructionist Judaism, was born into an Orthodox Jewish family and spent his early childhood years in his home country of Lithuania. When he was nine his parents migrated to the United States. He was first trained by his father, a Talmudic scholar, and then attended the City College of New York (A.B, 1900) and Columbia University (M.A., 1902). He took his theological training at Jewish Theological Seminary of America while completing his degree at Columbia. He was ordained in 1902 and became rabbi of Kehillah Jeshurun, an orthodox synagogue in New York.

Increasingly, as Kaplan pursued his studies, he felt forced to abandon Orthodoxy and began to adopt the more liberal Conservative Jewish perspective. In 1909 he was appointed dean of the Teacher's Institute at Jewish Theological Seminary. The following year he added duties as a teacher at the seminary in homiletics. During his early years as a professor, he began to develop his unique theological perspective. In brief, Kaplan centered his thinking upon the reality of the Jewish people and defined Judaism as an evolving religious civilization. From this starting point, Kaplan concluded that the meaning of God and Torah were to be understood primarily in relation to the Jewish people. He also emphasized the current situation of the Jewish people as a counter balance to the authority of ancient texts. His thinking also led him to become an ardent Zionist.

A systematic presentation of Kaplan's ideas was published in 1934 in his most important text, *Judaism as a Civilization*. The next year he founded a periodical *The Reconstructionist* and the Jewish Reconstructionist Foundation. Synagogues soon followed. Kaplan emphasized the role of the synagogue as a center for all of Jewish life, including the secular aspects. The secular elements of Jewish culture, he emphasized, were crucial to Jewish spirituality. His ideas were expanded in *Judaism in Transition* (1936).

Reconstructionism grew as a perspective within Conservative Judaism and only gradually over the decades separated as a distinct branch of American Judaism. Kaplan introduced several issues surrounding the introduction of women in many Jewish rituals, heretofore a separate male domain. For example, Kaplan developed the Bat Mitzvah, the female equivalent of the Bar Mitzvah, the coming of age ceremony through which male Jews are inducted as adults

into the community. He published a *Sabbath Prayer Book* in 1945 which denied the nature of the Jews as a chosen people and the divine inspiration of the Torah. It was soundly condemned by the Union of Orthodox Rabbis, who took the further symbolic step of excommunicating him.

Throughout the storms of his career, he continued to teach at the Jewish Theological Seminary. In 1947 he became professor of philosophies of religion. He continued to author books, among his most important being *The Future of the American Jew* (1949); *A New Zionism* (1955); *Judaism without Supernaturalism* (1958); and *The Meaning of God in Modern Judaism* (1962). At the end of the 1950s, after five decades as a professor, he retired.

Sources:

Kaplan, Mordecai M. *The Future of the American Jew*. New York: Macmillan Company, 1949. 571 pp.

_____. *Judaism as a Civilization*. New York: Theodor Herzl Foundation. 1955. 173 pp.

_____. *Judaism in Transition*. New York: Bloch, 1936. 312 pp.

_____. *Judaism without Supernaturalism*. New York: Reconstructionist Press, 1958. 254 pp.

_____. *The Meaning of God in Modern Judaism*. New York: Reconstructionist Press, 1962. 381 pp.

_____. *A New Judaism*. New York: Theodor Herzl Foundation, 1955. 172 pp.

★483★
KAPLEAU, Philip
Zen Master and Founder, Zen Meditation Center of Rochester
b. 1909

Philip Kapleau Roshi is the founder of the Zen Meditation Center of Rochester and the author of *The Three Pillars of Zen*, one of the first detailed and most popular books ever published on the topic of Zen Buddhism. Kapleau became acquainted with Zen when he was in Tokyo in 1946 as a court reporter in the war crimes trials. After returning to the United States, he began attending **Daisetz Teitaro Suzuki**'s lectures on Zen philosophy at Columbia University in 1951. However, dissatisfied with simply intellectualizing about Zen, he decided to return to Japan to explore the experiential dimension by undertaking a traditional course of training in *zazen* (Zen meditation). He arrived there in the fall of 1953. At the time he was 44, persistently ill, and deeply dissatisfied with life.

Kapleau's first efforts to locate an appropriate teacher were frustrating, because at the time Zen masters were reluctant to take on students who did not speak Japanese. He eventually met Soen Nakagawa Roshi, who agreed to assume guidance over his training, and Kapleau began his tenure at the Ryutakuji Monastery. After six months, he went to the Soto Zen Monastery of Hosshin-ji, and practiced as a lay monk under Harada Roshi for the next three years. Then, in November of 1956, he began studying under Yasutani Roshi. It was under this last master's guidance that he experienced *kensho* (a high level of realization, though not yet full enlightenment) in the summer of 1958. In the East for a total of 13 years, Kapleau also toured other parts of the Buddhist world, studying and practicing Theravada Buddhist meditation. He continued sitting with Yasutani, and acted as his interpreter for Westerners as he could now speak fluent Japanese. Yasutani eventually ordained him as a Zen monk, and, just before Kapleau returned to America, sanctioned him as a teacher of Zen.

Yasutani had granted him permission to transcribe *dokusans* (private interviews between meditators and their teacher), and some of these transcriptions came to constitute the living core of *The Three Pillars of Zen* (1965). This book was highly significant at the time it appeared because it stressed the importance of meditation practice. Until its publication, English-language works on Zen had emphasized Zen philosophy. Originally published in Japan in 1965, the book was read by Chester Carlson, the founder of Xerox Corporation, and his wife, Doris. They were impressed enough to buy thousands of copies for distribution to libraries, and to invite Kapleau to visit Rochester. It was this association that led to the creation of the Rochester Zen Center.

The center has prospered, many serious students being attracted through *Three Pillars* and Kapleau's other writings, such as *The Wheel of Death* (1972) and *To Cherish All Life* (1981). Several branch centers have been established in the United States and Canada.

Sources:

Buckley, Tim. "History of the Zen Meditation Center of Rochester." *Wind Bell* 8, 1-2 (Fall 1969): 51-53.
Fields, Rick. *How the Swans Came to the Lake: A Narrative History of Buddhism in America*. Boulder, CO: Shambhala, 1981. 433 pp. Rev. ed.: Boston: Shambhala, 1986. 445 pp.
Kapleau Roshi, Philip. *The Three Pillars of Zen*. Boston: Beacon Press, 1965. 363 pp. Rev. ed. Garden City, NY: Doubleday & Company, 1980 400 pp.
_____. *To Cherish All Life*. Rochester, NY; Zen Center, 1981. 106 pp.
_____. *Wheel of Death*. London, England: George Allen & Unwin, 1972. 110 pp.

★484★
KAUFFMAN, Daniel
Bishop, Mennonite Church
b. Jun. 20, 1865, Juniata, Pennsylvania
d. Jan. 6, 1944, Parnell, Iowa

Daniel Kauffman, the most prominent leader in the Mennonite Church during the early twentieth century, was the son of Bishop David D. and Elizabeth Winey Kauffman. The family moved to Missouri in 1869 and Kauffman grew up there. He attended Missouri State University, earned a degree of Principal of Pedagogics, and in 1883 began to teach school. Four years later he married Ota J. Bowlin. During the 1890s he became an active leader among the Mennonites. He was then converted and joined the Mennonite Church (1890). He was ordained a minister (1892) and became a bishop (1896). In 1897 he founded a private business college which he managed for several years. After the death of his first wife, he married Mary C. Shank in 1902.

Around the turn of the century Kauffman emerged as a major Mennonite leader through a combination of speaking ability, editorship, and organizational skills. He published the first of his many books in 1898, *A Manual of Bible Doctrines*. He followed it with *One Hundred Lessons in Bible Study* (1899) and *A Talk with Church Members* (1900). In 1905 he began his 39-year career as an editor with the *Gospel Witness* (after 1908 the *Gospel Herald*). Through his writings he guided the life of the church and was recognized as its major spokesperson.

Organizationally, Kauffman helped create the national organization which continues in the Mennonite Church. In the 1890s he helped set up the Mennonite General Conference, and though only 33, was selected as its first moderator; he is the only person to serve as moderator four times. At one time or another he chaired all the major committees of the church, and at one point he was a member of 22 committees and boards. Before moving from Missouri in 1909 he served as moderator of the Missouri Iowa Conference. After he moved to Scottdale, Pennsylvania, he served as moderator of the Southwestern Pennsylvania Conference. He was respected as a mediator and conciliator of the various factions within the church.

During his years in Pennsylvania, his books covered a wide range of subjects. Among his titles were: *The Conservative Viewpoint* (1918); *The Mennonite Church and Conservative Issues* (1923); *The Way of Salvation* (1923) and *The Devotional Side of Life* (1942). He authored one historical work, *Mennonite History* (1927) and an autobiographical account of *Fifty Years in the Men-*

nonite Church (1941). He retired as editor of the *Gospel Herald* in 1943.

Sources:

Kauffman, Alice. *The Life and Times of Daniel Kauffman*. Scottdale, PA: Herald Press, 1954. 160 pp.
Kauffman, Daniel. *Bible Doctrine*. Scottdale, PA: Mennonite Publishing House, 1914.
_____. *A Manual of Bible Doctrines*. Elkhart, IN: Mennonite Publishing Company, 1898. 272 pp.
_____. *The Mennonite Church and Current Issues*. Scottdale, PA: Mennonite Publishing House, 1923. 136 pp.
_____. *Mennonite Cyclopedic Dictionary*. Scottdale, PA: Mennonite Publishing House, 1937. 443 pp.
_____. *Mennonite History*. Scottdale, PA: Mennonite Publishing House, 1927. 147 pp.
_____. *One Hundred Lessons in Bible Study*. Spring Grove, PA: Mennonite Book and Tract Society, 1899. 228 pp.
_____. *A Talk with Church Members*. Dakota, IL: J. S. Shoemaker, 1900. 142 pp.
The Mennonite Encyclopedia. 4 vols. Scottdale, PA: The Mennonite Publishing House, 1955.

★485★
KEANE, John Joseph
Archbishop, Roman Catholic Church
b. Sep. 12, 1839, Ballyshannon Ireland
d. Jun. 22, 1918, Dubuque, Iowa

John Joseph Keane, an archbishop in the Roman Catholic Church, was the son of Hugh and Fannie Keane, who had migrated to Canada in 1846 and eventually settled in Baltimore, Maryland, in 1848. Keane was educated by the Christian Brothers, and at the age of 20 enrolled at St. Charles College in Elliott City, Maryland. In 1862 he entered St. Mary's Seminary in Baltimore, and following his graduation in 1866 he was ordained as a priest. He was appointed curate at St. Patrick's Church in Washington, D.C., where he remained until called to the bishopric in 1878. He was consecrated as bishop of Richmond (Virginia).

Among his first accomplishments was the establishment of Catholic University in Washington, on whose behalf he spoke at the Plenary Council of the church held in 1884. He joined Bishop **John Ireland** in persuading the pope to approve the new school. After the school opened in 1889, he was named its rector as titular bishop of Jasso. While there he emerged as one of the liberal voices in the hierarchy supporting the movement of the Catholic Church into the mainstream of American life. In 1893 he was a spokesperson for the church at the World's Parliament of Religions held in Chicago.

Keane's appointment as rector at the university was for an indefinite period, but in 1896 a policy to limit the term of the rector was introduced. Keane was offered a post in Rome with the Congregation of Propaganda and the Congregation of Studies. He was named archbishop of Damascus. He settled in Rome just as the "Americanist" controversy began. In 1899 the pope would issue an encyclical refuting a number of ideas which he termed "Americanist." Keane was seen by many as a target of the encyclical, but he quickly moved to assure the pope that in wanting to see the American church active in American life, no one in the hierarchy in America espoused the condemned ideas.

Keane returned to the United States in 1899 and, after spending a year raising funds for Catholic University, in 1900 became archbishop of Dubuque (Iowa). While in office, a volume of his sermons and addresses was published under the title *Onward and Upward* (1902). He remained as archbishop until 1911 when he retired because of health problems. He was appointed titular bishop of Cios and served as vicar general for the archdiocese under his successor, James John Keane (no relation). During his last years a second compilation of his sermons was issued as *Emmanuel* (1915).

Sources:
Delaney, John J. *Dictionary of American Catholic Biography.* Garden City, NY: Doubleday & Company, 1988. 621 pp.
Dictionary of American Biography. 20 vols. and 7 supps. New York: Charles Scribner's Sons, 1928-1936, 1944-1981.
Keane, John J. *Emmanuel.* Philadelphia: J. J. McVey, 1915. 221 pp.
_____. *Onward and Upward.* Baltimore: John Murphy Co., 1902. 387 pp.

★486★
KEEBLE, Marshall
Evangelist, Churches of Christ (Non-Instrumental)
b. Dec. 7, 1878, Rutherford County, Tennessee
d. 1968, Nashville, Tennessee

Marshall Keeble, an evangelist who brought many Blacks into the Churches of Christ (Non-Instrumental), was the son of former slaves, Robert and Minnie Keeble. When he was four years old his family moved from the farm to Nashville, Tennessee, where his father obtained work with the city. The family joined a congregation of the Christian Church (Disciples of Christ) during the years when the issues which were to split the Disciples were coming to the fore. Keeble was baptized at the age of 14 but soon afterward joined with a group under the leadership of Preston Taylor. Taylor formed a separate congregation which would eventually identify with the Church of Christ (Non-Instrumental) after the split became formalized in 1906.

Finishing what little formal school he was able to obtain, Keeble went to work in a soap factory. At the age of 18 he married Winnie Womack, the daughter of Christian minister S. W. Womack. Together they opened a grocery which Winnie tended while Keeble sold produce door-to-door. Around the turn of the century Keeble began to preach occasionally and showed himself to be a capable orator. By 1890 he was preaching regularly at a mission on Dozier Street. His fame spread, and he was invited to preach at various locations around the state. In 1914 he became a full-time evangelist and began to travel the country and speak. Saturdays would usually find him on the streets in a town where blacks had gathered for their weekly shopping. As was a common practice by ministers of the Churches of Christ, he also periodically engaged in public religious debates.

In 1918 Keeble had his first great success at Oak Creek, Tennessee, where following a three-week revival a church was organized. Other similar successes followed. In 1924 he made his first trip to the West Coast to speak at Oakland, California. The next decades of evangelistic activity were marked by the publication of the *Biography and Sermons of Marshall Keeble, Evangelist* (1931) edited by **B. C. Goodpasture**, owner of the Gospel Advocate Company, the leading Churches of Christ publishing center. The next year Minnie Keeble died and in 1934 Keeble married Laura Catherine Johnson.

The need for education for blacks, a continuing problem, led Keeble to participate in the reopening of the Nashville Christian Institute in 1940. Keeble sat on the board of trustees and led in the effort to have the school accredited as an elementary and high school, which was accomplished in 1942. He worked on behalf of the school for the next 25 years and served as its president from 1942 to 1958.

Keeble remained active through the 1950s and became the only black to participate in the development of the Churches of Christ on a national level. In the 1960s he was afflicted with cataracts, but was able to make his first overseas trip to the Holyland and to Nigeria in 1962. In 1964 he culminated a long career with a round-the-world tour.

Sources:
Choate, J. E. *Roll Jordan Roll: A Biography of Marshall Keeble.* Nashville, TN: Gospel Advocate Company, 1986. 143 pp.
Goodpasture, B. C., ed. *Biography and Sermons of Marshall Keeble, Evangelist.* Nashville, TN: Gospel Advocate Company, 1931.
Hill, Samuel S., ed. *Encyclopedia of Religion in the South.* Macon, GA: Mercer University Press, 1984. 878 pp.
Rhodes, F. N. *A Study of the Sources of Marshall Keeble's Effectiveness as a Preacher.* Southern Illinois University, Ph.D. dissertation, 1970.

★487★
KELLEY, Catherine Bishop
President, Daughters of Zion, Reorganized Church of Jesus Christ of Latter Day Saints
b. Nov. 9, 1853, Albia, Iowa
d. Nov. 21, 1944, Independence, Missouri

Catherine Bishop Kelley, the first president of the Daughters of Zion and a leader in women's work with the Reorganized Church of Jesus Christ of Latter Day Saints, grew up in rural Iowa and became a school teacher. In 1874 it became necessary for her to go to Glenwood, Iowa, to renew her teaching certificate. While there she met Edmund L. Kelley. They were married three years later. They settled in Glenwood, but after only a few months they moved to Kirkland, Ohio. Kirkland had been the former headquarters of the Mormons, but few members remained there in the 1880s. In 1880 her husband, a lawyer, secured clear title for the abandoned Kirkland Temple for the Reorganized Church. He also taught his wife about the Reorganized Church of Jesus Christ of Latter Day Saints, and convinced her that it was the true church. She joined in 1882 and together they organized a branch of the Reorganized Church of Jesus Christ of Latter Day Saints. Catherine became a dedicated worker in her new faith.

After a number of years in Kirkland, the Kelleys moved to Lamoni, Iowa, at that time the major center of the Reorganized Church. In 1893, at the general conference, the women organized the Daughters of Zion and elected Kelley as president. She saw 23 local groups formed the first year. She became the first editor of a column for the church's women's department that appeared in the youth magazine, *Autumn Leaves.* Her work during her four years as president did much to lay the foundation for the women's department.

During her last years in Lamoni, Kelley took special interest in Graceland College, the church's school. She organized the Patroness Society to help college students make the transition to life away from home and to raise funds for Patroness Hall. She also assisted in the establishment of the Saints' Home for the elderly.

In 1905 she moved to Independence, Missouri, where the church headquarters had been transferred. She remained active in church affairs in spite of being mother to eight children. Among her first major projects in Independence was the organization of a Patroness Society for the benefit of the church's hospital and sanitarium, which had run into financial difficulty. She organized women to do a variety of tasks, from mending sheets to cooking.

During her later years, Kelley retired from church work and took up painting as a hobby. Her husband died in 1930 and she lived another 14 years. She is remembered as a woman who, in a day when women's involvement in church life was narrowly confined, demonstrated the organizational and administrative ability of female members, thus paving the way for a more varied participation in the next century.

Sources:
Phillips, Emma M. *33 Women of the Restoration.* Independence, MO: Herald House, 1960. 197 pp.

★ 488 ★
KELLY, Thomas Raymond
Philosopher, Society of Friends (Quakers)
b. Jun. 4, 1893, Chillicothe, Ohio
d. Jan. 17, 1941, Haverford, Pennsylvania

Thomas Raymond Kelly, a Quaker philosopher best remembered for his mystical devotional writings, was the son of Madora Elizabeth Kersey and Carlton Weden Kelly, both devout members of the Society of Friends (Quakers). His father died when he was four. When he was 10 his mother moved to Wilmington, Ohio, where Kelly would have the opportunity of Quaker schooling. He eventually attended Wilmington College, from which he graduated in 1913. He then studied a year at Haverford College, where he worked with **Rufus M. Jones**, though Kelly was a chemistry major. He taught at Pickering College in Canada for two years (1914-1961), after which he entered Hartford Theological Seminary to prepare for missionary work in Japan. He graduated from Hartford in 1919. The day after graduation he married Lael Macy, and the couple moved back to Wilmington, Ohio, where Kelly had accepted a job as a teacher of the Bible.

Kelly stayed in Wilmington two years before returning to Hartford to work on a Ph.D. in philosophy. He still hoped to go to Japan as a teacher. He received his Ph.D. in 1924. He did not go to Japan, however, but to Germany as the leader of a Quaker center in Berlin. After a year in Germany he became professor of philosophy at Earlham College, the Quaker institution in Richmond, Indiana. He stayed only two years, however, before moving to Cambridge, Massachusetts, for a year at Harvard. A temporary appointment at Wellesley College allowed him to stay for a second year. He returned to Earlham in 1932 where he worked diligently on a study of the philosophy of Emile Myerson. In 1935, having finished the Myerson book, he moved to the University of Hawaii for a year before taking a post at Haverford College, the leading Quaker institution, where he replaced D. Elton Trueblood. In 1937 *Explanation and Reality in the Philosophy of Emile Myerson* was published.

At about this time, Kelly underwent a profound mystical change. He emerged in 1938 with a new sense of a Presence in his life, and by all accounts his lectures and writing were permeated with the new reality he had discovered. He gathered a group of students around him to read devotional classics and sit in the silence. He began to write regularly in *The Friend*, a Quaker journal. His essays produced a great response within the Quaker community, and it was with some regret that the Society of Friends learned of Kelly's sudden death in 1941. Five of his essays were gathered and published posthumously as *A Testament of Devotion*, now a classic in Quaker literature.

Sources:

Kelly, Richard M. *Thomas Kelly: A Biography.* New York: Harper & Row, 1966. 125 pp.
Kelly, Thomas R. *A Testament of Devotion.* New York: Harper & Brothers, 1941. 124 pp.

★ 489 ★
KELSEY, Samuel
Bishop, Church of God in Christ
b. 1906, Sandville, Georgia

Samuel Kelsey, a bishop in the Church of God in Christ, is the son of Samuel and Ella Kelsey. In 1915, as a nine year old boy in rural Georgia, Kelsey attended services led by a Pentecostal minister. The services were being held in the Pentecostal Firstborn Church, a house church which met in a home of a nearby black farmer. On May 16, 1915, Kelsey experienced sanctification (or cleansing from sin) and the baptism of the Holy Spirit (evidenced by his speaking in tongues). In 1920 Kelsey worked his way north to Philadelphia, Pennsylvania. In Philadelphia, Kelsey met Henry

McCrary, who had also been a member of the Firstborn Church in Georgia, but who had discovered the Church of God in Christ in Detroit. Under McCrary's influence Kelsey affiliated with the Church of God in Christ, as did most of the members of the Firstborn churches in Georgia. Also, shortly after his arrival in Philadelphia, Kelsey met Jeanette Cooper, whom he married in December of that year.

Kelsey settled in Philadelphia and became an active member and preacher for the local Church of God in Christ congregation. Then in 1923 he was invited by W. C. Thompson, an overseer in the church, to accompany him to Washington, D.C., and assist in a tent revival. This revival resulted in the organization of a local congregation over which Kelsey presided. As winter approached, the group moved out of the tent into a storefront. In 1923 Kelsey also founded the Temple Church of God in Christ, a second congregation in Washington, D.C. The work in the area expanded through the 1930s, and in 1940 he was appointed overseer for Delaware and Washington, D.C.

In 1941 Kelsey began a radio show which included both his music and sermons. The broadcasts continued into the 1980s. They also led to the production of records. Two men who had heard him on the radio became his distributors. Later, when he had the opportunity to travel to Europe, he discovered that his music had preceded him. In 1949 his first wife died and in 1950 he married Annie Ruth.

In 1950 Kelsey was named a bishop in the church and was invited to sit on the board of bishops for the church. He continued as pastor of Temple Church, which grew to over 1,000 members, and during the next decades oversaw the development of the Church of God in Christ in his area, which had 23 congregations in the 1980s. In 1972 the Samuel Kelsey Housing Complex was dedicated. For many years, in addition to his pastoral duties, he served as a parole officer working with delinquent youth.

In recent years, Kelsey, as one of the senior ministers in Washington, D.C., has been frequently honored for his lifetime of service to the community. In 1976 the U.S. Congress published a "Salute" to him. In 1977 the Committee of 100 Ministers cited him for his leadership.

In 1988 failing health forced Kelsey to retire and he was succeeded as bishop by George W. Crudup.

Sources:

Dupree, Sherry Sherrod. *Biographical Dictionary of African-American, Holiness-Pentecostals, 1880-1990.* Washington, DC: Middle Atlantic Regional Press, 1990. 386 pp.

★ 490 ★
KENNEDY, Gerald Hamilton
Bishop, United Methodist Church
b. Aug. 7, 1907, Bensonia, Michigan
d. Feb. 17, 1980, Laguna Hills, California

Gerald Hamilton Kennedy, the youngest man ever elected to the episcopacy in American Methodism, was the son of Herbert Grant Kennedy, a Methodist lay preacher, and Marian Phelps Kennedy. Kennedy preached his first sermon while still in high school, and was licensed to preach by the Methodist Episcopal Church at the age of 15. He traveled to the West Coast for his college training, receiving an A.B. from the University of the Pacific in 1929 and an M.A. and B.D. from the Pacific School of Religion in 1931 and 1932, respectively. He was admitted on trial and ordained a deacon in the California-Nevada Conference of the Methodist Episcopal Church in 1931 and ordained an elder in 1932. In 1928, while in college, he married Mary Leeper. They moved to Hartford, Connecticut, where Kennedy pursued advanced work at Hartford Theological Seminary, from which he received both the S.T.M. and

Ph.D. in 1934. While in graduate school he pastored the First Congregational Church at Collinsville, Connecticut (1932-1936).

Returning to California in 1936, Kennedy was assigned to Calvary Methodist Episcopal Church in San Jose. Already making a name for himself as a master of the sermon, in 1938 he began teaching homiletics part-time at the Pacific School of Religion, a position that continued through his next pastorate at Palo Alto (1940-1942). In 1942 he moved to Nebraska to become pastor of First Methodist Church in Lincoln (adjacent to the University of Nebraska). During these years he authored his first books, *His Word through Preaching* (1947) and *Have This Mind* (1948). He remained in Nebraska until his election as bishop in 1948 at the age of 40.

He was assigned the Portland, Oregon area, which he served for four years before moving to Los Angeles, where he remained throughout the years of his active episcopacy. During his years as bishop he developed a reputation among his fellow ministers for disciplined study and avid reading. He also gained a national reputation beyond Methodism for his preaching and writing. He was in constant demand as a guest preacher and authored over 20 books, including: *With Singleness of Heart* (1951), *Who Speaks for God?* (1954), *The Methodist Way of Life* (1958), *The Parables* (1960), *While I'm On My Feet* (1963), and *Fresh Every Morning* (1966). He also authored a popular book review column for the denominational magazine, *Together*.

During his years as bishop of the Los Angeles Area, Kennedy assumed a leadership role in the area of evangelism. He served as president of the denomination's board of evangelism (1964-1968). In his area, which included churches in Arizona, Nevada, California, and Hawaii, over one hundred new congregations were started and church membership reached over a quarter of a million. He also spoke out on racial issues in the church, and demonstrated his commitment to end segregated structures in 1964 by appointing a black minister to head a predominantly white congregation. His dedication to the ecumenical movement led to his appointment as a member of the general board of the National Council of Churches of Christ in the U.S.A. in 1957, a position he retained throughout the 1960s. He stood out as an ecumenical leader because of his effective vocal opposition to the Consultation on Church Union (COCU), a plan to unite a number of Protestant denominations. He also served as president of the council of bishops of the Methodist Church in 1960-1961.

In 1968, feeling the need to preach more regularly, Kennedy appointed himself preaching minister at First Methodist Church in Pasadena, California, a large, prominent pulpit. This proved to be one of the most controversial actions of his episcopacy. No other bishop in Methodism had ever tried to assume such a dual role, and it led to significant negative criticism from ministers in Southern California and denominational leaders across the country.

Kennedy retired in 1972. In his honor, a chair in homiletics was created at the Methodist-supported School of Theology in Claremont, California.

Sources:

Harmon, Nolan B. *The Encyclopedia of World Methodism.* 2 vols. Nashville: United Methodist Publishing House, 1974.

Kennedy, Gerald H. *Fresh Every Morning.* New York: Harper & Row, 1966. 194 pp.

_____. *The Methodist Way of Life.* Englewood Cliffs, NJ: Prentice-Hall, 1958. 216 pp.

_____. *The Seven Worlds of the Minister.* New York: Harper & Row, 1968. 173 pp.

_____. *With Singleness of Heart.* New York Harper & Row, 1951. 157 pp.

Who's Who in the Methodist Church. Nashville, TN: Abingdon Press, 1966.

★491★
KENNETT, Jiyu
Zen Master and Founder, Order of Buddhist Contemplatives
b. Jan. 1, 1924, St. Leonards-on-Sea, Sussex England

The Reverend Roshi Jiyu-Kennett, Zen Buddhist master and founder of the Order of Buddhist Contemplatives, was born Peggy Teresa Nancy Kennett into a very conventional British family. She was introduced to Buddhism through a statue of the Buddha at her boarding school, and attributes her becoming a Buddhist to her calling to the priesthood (a calling that she was blocked from pursuing in the Church of England). She was educated at the Trinity College of Music and at the University of Durham. Her first career was in music, and she performed and taught in England from 1943 until 1961. Her early association with Buddhism was through the London Buddhist Society, and she identified herself as a Theravadin Buddhist. She later began to study Zen under **Daisetz Teitaro Suzuki**.

She was ordained in 1962 in the Chinese Rinzai Zen Buddhist tradition in Malaysia, and then embarked on a study of Soto Zen in Japan under the Very Reverend Chisan Koho Zenji, chief abbot of Dai Hon Zan Soji-ji Temple. She received the Dharma transmission from this abbot in 1963, and later held several positions of responsibility, including head of the temple's Foreign Guest Department, and abbess of a temple in Mie Prefecture. While in Japan she was granted a Sei Degree (a priesthood degree, roughly equivalent to a Doctor of Divinity).

Jiyu-Kennett left Japan for the United States with two Western disciples in 1969, and founded the Shasta Abbey at the foot of Mount Shasta in 1970. She had received a commission to train and ordain priests, and this has been the primary thrust of her Order. A complete course of study is offered in Theravadin and Soto Zen Buddhism. The Order lays great stress upon its Buddhist heritage. Pupils live full-time at the monastery. For priest trainees, offerings include practical instruction in such skills as temple management.

Over her years of leadership at Shasta Abbey, besides her teaching and administrative duties, Jiyu-Kennett has authored a number of books, including *Selling Water by the River* (1972); *How to Grow a Lotus Blossom* (1977), and the *The Wild White Goose* (Vol. I, 1977; Vol. II, 1978). These books, in combination with her lecture tours and the availability of trained clergy, stimulated the growth of a number of affiliated centers. Priories have been established in Santa Barbara and Albany, California; Portland, Oregon; and locations in Canada and the United Kingdom. There are also numerous study-meditation groups along the West Coast of North America and in England.

Sources:

Boucher, Sandy. *Turning the Wheel: American Women Creating the New Buddhism.* New York: Harper & Row, 1988. 401 pp.

Fields, Rick. *How the Swans Came to the Lake: A Narrative History of Buddhism in America.* Boulder, CO: Shambhala, 1981. 433 pp. Rev. ed.: Boston: Shambhala, 1986. 445 pp.

Friedman, Lenore. *Meetings with Remarkable Women: Buddhist Teachers in America.* Boston: Shambhala, 1987. 288 pp.

Kennett, Jiyu. *How to Grow a Lotus Blossom.* Mount Shasta, CA: Shasta Abbey, 1977. 283 pp.

_____. *Selling Water by the River.* New York: Vintage Books, 1972. 317 pp. Rev. ed.: *Zen Is Eternal Life.* Emeryville, CA: Dharma Publishing, 1976. 447 pp.

_____. *The Wild White Goose.* 2 vols. Mount Shasta, CA: Shasta Abbey, 1977-78.

Melton, J. Gordon *The Encyclopedia of American Religions.* 3d ed. Detroit: Gale Research Inc.,1988. 1102 pp.

★492★
KENT, Grady R.
Founder, Church of God (Jerusalem Acres)
b. Apr. 26, 1909, Rosebud, Georgia
d. Mar. 31, 1964

Grady R. Kent was the founder of the Church of God (Jerusalem Acres). Born in rural Georgia, he had only a third-grade education, and was converted at age 21 to the Congregational Holiness Church. Within a year, however, he moved to Pentecostalism via the Church of God (Cleveland, Tennessee). He wanted to preach, but did not want to go to Bible school, which was the requisite for ordination. He took to traveling and ministering in various Church of God locations in the mountains, presenting himself as someone with the proper credentials, until the church administration caught up with him and excommunicated him.

Kent next turned to a rival group, the Church of God of Prophecy, to which he was ordained in 1932 and appointed evangelist for Georgia. He then held similar positions in Minnesota and Nebraska before returning to Georgia in 1938 as pastor of a Church of God of Prophecy congregation. His preaching there angered the Ku Klux Klan, and on one particular occassion he almost died at their hands. He later told the story of this problem in the book, *Sixty Lashes at Midnight* (1963). Kent then moved to the Wildwood Avenue Church of God of Prophecy in Cleveland, Tennessee, where he also led the Church of God Marker Association, a group that marked significant sites in the history of the church. Kent came up with the idea for the Field of the Woods, a 160-acre site in North Carolina to mark where **Ambrose Jessup Tomlinson**, founder of the Church of God of Prophecy, originally joined the Church of God (Cleveland, Tennessee) in 1903.

Kent's view was that the true church was lost in the Middle Ages and later restored, beginning with Tomlinson's joining that church in 1903, and especially when Tomlinson broke away to found the Church of God of Prophecy. Tomlinson died in 1944, and his son Milton succeeded him as leader of the church and began proposing more democratic structures. Kent opposed these moves and desired a more rigid adherence to structures he thought were mandated in the Bible. He also began to foretell about the end times, saying that someone with the spirit of John the Revelator would arise to summon the church to its last duties.

In February of 1957 he resigned from the church. He and his followers purchased some land called Jerusalem Acres in Cleveland, Tennessee, and founded the Church of God (Jerusalem Acres). The next three and a half years, symbolizing the time of Jesus' earthly ministry, were designated as the time of reformation. Kent led the church in setting its distinctive practices, such as banning events like Christmas and Easter as pagan festivals and substituting Old Testament feasts. The birth of Christ celebration was moved to October. Kent died in 1964 at the age of 55, and was considered by his followers to be the one with the spirit of John the Revelator.

Sources:

Kent, Grady R. *The Church of God Manual of Apostle Doctrine and Business Procedure.* Cleveland, TN: Church Publishing Company and Press, n.d.
———. *Sixty Lashes at Midnight.* Cleveland, TN, 1963.
———. *Treatise of the 1957 Reformation Stand.* Cleveland, TN: Church Publishing Company, 1964. 20 pp.
Murphy, Lynn. "Grady R. Kent: St. John II" (unpublished paper in the files of Lee College, Cleveland, TN).

—*Gary L. Ward*

★493★
KENYON, Essek William
Independent Evangelist
Founder, Bethel Bible Institute
b. Apr. 24, 1867, Saratoga County, New York
d. Mar. 19, 1948, Seattle, Washington

Essek William Kenyon, independent evangelist and educator, was the son of a logger and a school teacher. Though he never received a degree for completion of an educational program, his mother instilled within him a drive to learn. Kenyon was converted to Christianity in his mid-teens, and at the age of 19 he preached his first sermon in a Methodist church at Amsterdam, New York.

Kenyon attended several schools in New York but in 1892 moved to Boston, where he enrolled in Emerson College. While the college specialized in oratory, much attention has been given to the New Thought metaphysical perspective professed by its president and major teacher, Charles Wesley Emerson, and by faculty member **Ralph Waldo Trine**. It is likely that during his brief stay at Emerson, Kenyon was introduced to New Thought, which later colored his presentation of Christianity. About this time Kenyon left the Methodist Church and became a nonaligned Baptist. By the end of the decade he was engaged in an independent itinerant ministry of evangelism throughout New England. Kenyon married during this period, but his wife died within a few years.

In about 1900 John and Susan Marble donated a farm to Kenyon, upon which Kenyon opened Bethel Bible Institute. He helped support the school, which was partially modeled on the hospices of Episcopalian physician and spiritual healer **Charles Cullis**, with his expanded evangelical activities, which became national in scope. Activities of the school were highlighted in a magazine, *Realities*. In 1914 Kenyon married Alice Whitney. He also authored his first major book while at Bethel, *The Father and His Family* (1917).

The Bethel Institute suffered reverses during World War I, when the number of students dropped sharply. In 1923 Kenyon resigned as superintendent and severed his connection with the school, and moved to Dudley, Massachusetts, where the school merged with Nichols Academy. Kenyon moved to California and concentrated his evangelical work on the West Coast. He accepted the pastorate of a Baptist congregation in Pasadena in 1926 but soon left to found an independent church in Los Angeles.

In 1931 Kenyon moved to Seattle and founded the New Covenant Baptist Church. Possibly inspired by his friend Aimee Semple McPherson, he started a radio show, "Kenyon's Church of the Air." The radio show became the focus of his ministry for the remaining years of his life. Many of his talks were transcribed and published by the Kenyon Gospel Publishing Society. His many books include *Jesus the Healer*, his most popular book; *The Wonderful Name of Jesus* (1927); *The Two Kinds of Life* (1943); *In His Presence* (1944); *New Creation Realities: A Revelation of Redemption* (1945); and *What Happened from the Cross to the Throne* (1945). He developed correspondence courses for his radio audience on "Personal Evangelism" and the systematic study of the Bible, later published as *The Bible in the Light of Our Redemption*. He also began *Kenyon's Herald of Life*, which at the time of his death in 1948 had a circulation of 20,000. Kenyon's daughter continued her father's ministry through the *Herald* and the Kenyon Gospel Publishing Society and published two of his books that had been in manuscript form at the time of his death. Kenyon was not well known nationally during his lifetime, though the Oneness Pentecostals widely used his book, *The Wonderful Name of Jesus*. Only in the 1980s did he gain wide notoriety through his influence on a number of popular independent Pentecostal ministers such as **Kenneth E. Hagin**, **Kenneth Copeland**, Frederick K. C. Price, and Charles Capps, together known as the Positive Confession Movement. Critics of this movement have accused Kenyon of gnostic tendencies. While there are some themes

Kenyon shared with New Thought Christianity, however, he always affirmed the essential teachings of evangelical Christianity in his writings. This is especially apparent in the more systematic presentation of his theology in *The Bible in the Light of Our Redemption*.

Sources:

Kenyon, Essek William. *The Bible in the Light of Our Redemption*. Old Tappen, NJ: F. H. Revell, 1969. 303 pp.
_____. *Christ the Healer*. Seattle, WA: Kenyon Gospel Publishing Society, 1968. 104 pp.
_____. *The Father and His Family*. Spencer, NY; Reality Press, 1916. 272 pp.
_____. *In His Presence*. Seattle, WA: Kenyon's Gospel Publishing Society, 1944. 186 pp.
_____. *What Happened from the Cross to the Throne*. Seattle, WA: Kenyon Gospel Publishing Society, 1945. 205 pp.
Matta, Judith A. *The Born Again Jesus of the Word-Faith Teaching*. Fullerton, CA: Spirit of Truth Ministry, 1987. 160 pp.
McConnell, D. R. *A Different Gospel*. Peabody, MA: Hendrickson Publishers, 1988. 195 pp.

★ 494 ★
Sant KESHAVADAS
Founder, Temple of Cosmic Wisdom
b. Jul. 22, 1934, Bhadragiri India

Sadguru Sant Keshavadas, founder of the Temple of Cosmic Wisdom, was born Keshava Pai into a poor but pious Brahmin family. His mother, as well as his village school teacher, would direct his mind toward the divine by telling him stories about the gods and the saints. At the age of 11 when he was tending some cows, he happened to go into a run-down temple of Lord Panduranga Vittala (Vishnu). A beautiful light being materialized near the lord's image, touched the astounded boy, and told him, "Sing My Name." The lord's touch was a blessing that inspired him to compose and sing songs of god from that time onwards. Keshava quickly became well-known for his kirtans (devotional songs), and was soon invited by surrounding villages to sing. Through the donations received from these performances he was able to finance his education, and eventually received his B.A. and LL.B. degrees.

While still a boy, he was initiated by H. H. Shri Sudhindra Tirtha who gave him the title "Bala Haridas" (boy servant of the immortal lord). Keshava was married at age 19 to Rama Bai, and together they had three children. For a year and a half he worked as a lawyer at the high court in Bangalore, while lecturing in various temple halls in the evenings. He eventually renounced his law practice in order to devote himself full-time to preaching and to spiritual singing. The path of seeking the lord by singing his names is a venerable Indian tradition. The core of Keshava's teaching is simple and quite similar to that of the traditional Bhakta (devotional) saints: Life is short and precious, and should be used to seek god and directly experience him through love.

Keshavadas is a great musician who can play the flute, the harmonium, and the tabla. Many of the 2500 songs he has composed are quite popular and are sung in homes throughout India. He is also a dramatist who writes pieces for which he frequently plays the part of the saint. In 1959 he began thinking about opening a spiritual training center, and in 1960 opened Dasashram in Bangalore. At the center, people are instructed in how to teach spirituality through kirtan, and research work is done on the lives and the teachings of the saints. In 1966 he began teaching to the larger world, and in 1967 began establishing centers in the United States. During his second world tour, Keshavadas taught at the California Institute of Asian Studies for four months.

Sources:

Keshavadas, Sant. *Cosmic Shakti Kundalini (The Universal Mother); A Devotional Approach*. Washington, D. C.: Temple of Cosmic Religion, 1976. 112 pp.
_____. *Healing Techniques of the Holy East*. Oakland, CA: Viswa Dharma Publications, 1980. 116 pp.
_____. *Lord Panduranga & Mystic Ministrels of India (Saints of India)*. Rajamudry, India: Saraswati Power Press, 1975. 168 pp.
_____. *The Purpose of Life*. New York: Vantage Press, 1978. 112 pp.
_____. *Sadguru Speaks: Spiritual Disciplines and Spiritual Teachings*. Washington, D. C.: Temple of Cosmic Wisdom, 1975. 96 pp.
_____. *Stories and Parables*. New York: Vantage Press, 1979. 100 pp.
_____. *This Is Wisdom*. N.p.: The Author, 1975. 96 pp.
Life and Teachings of Sadguru Sant Keshavadas: A Commemoration. Southfield, MI: Temple of Cosmic Religion, 1977. 150 pp.
Mukundadas (Michael Allan Makowsky). *Minstrel of Love: A Biography of Satguru Sant Keshavadas*. Nevada City, CA: Hansa Publications, 1980. 334 pp.

—*James R. Lewis*

★ 495 ★
KESLER, Benjamin Elias
Minister, Dunkard Brethren Church
b. Mar. 6, 1861, Franklin County, Virginia
d. Aug. 1, 1952, Goshen, Indiana

Benjamin Elias Kesler, one of the founders of the Dunkard Brethren Church, one of several groups which trace their origin to the Church of the Brethren, was the son of Stephen and Sophiah Sink Kesler. When he was 17 he joined the German Baptist Brethren. As a young man he attended Halesford Classical and Mathematical School in Halesville, Virginia, and in 1879 returned to Franklin County as a school teacher. In 1884 he married Mattie Lorrea Hunt. That same year he was ordained as a Brethren minister. He was advanced to the second degree of ministry around 1894 and ordained an elder in 1898.

Beginning in the 1890s Kesler served a variety of congregations. He moved to Illinois and became the pastor of several mission congregations in the Southern Illinois District. He worked for a series of years for the German Baptist General Mission Board and served congregations in Arkansas, Tennessee, Missouri, Kansas, and Colorado through the World War I era. During these years he participated in a number of debates with ministers of other denominations, the most memorable one being with a minister from the Christian Church (Disciples of Christ) in Arkansas.

In the early twentieth century, pressures for reform among the Brethren began to appear, especially in matters of dress, higher education, and general accommodation to the larger social environment. Kesler emerged as one of the leading conservative voices in this period. In 1910 he was a member of the "dress committee" which prescribed a standard for simple dress. In the years after World War I, fashionable clothes which deviated from the plain dress of former years had begun to appear. More youth were heading for college, and in general signs of accommodation to the world abounded. In 1922 Kesler, then pastoring in Missouri, began to issue a periodical, *The Bible Monitor*, advocating the retention of conservative standards.

The publication of the *Monitor* set off a chain of events which led to a new schism among the Brethren. In 1923 Kesler was denied a seat at the annual conference of the Brethren. Later that year a meeting of supporters of the *Monitor* met in Denton, Maryland. Similar meetings were held in 1924, 1925, and 1926. At the last meeting the gathering declared that it had no recourse but to form a new denomination. It advocated a conservative dress, used the King James Bible, and affirmed the Bible as the only creed. The first general conference met in 1927, and Kesler was elected moderator. He served as an officer in most subsequent general conferences.

In the 1930s Kesler moved to Goshen, Indiana, and served a Dunkard Brethren Church there. The fellowship has remained small, with little more than 1,000 members in less than 30 congregations.

Sources:

Durnbaugh, Donald F., ed. *The Brethren Encyclopedia*. 3 vols. Philadelphia: The Brethren Encyclopedia, Inc., 1983.

★ 496 ★
KETCHAM, Robert Thomas
Founder, General Association of Regular Baptist Churches
b. Jul. 22, 1889, Nelson, Pennsylvania
d. Aug. 21, 1978, Chicago, Illinois

Robert Thomas Ketcham was a leading fundamentalist and a founder of the General Association of Regular Baptist Churches. Ketcham's mother died when he was seven. When his father remarried, the previously Methodist household changed to accommodate the new stepmother's Baptist beliefs. Ketcham left his rural Pennsylvania home when he was 16, never finishing high school. When he was 20, he experienced a conversion and call to ministry, and in 1912 became the pastor of the First Baptist Church in Roulette, Pennsylvania. While there, he tried to further his education by taking a correspondence course from Crozer Theological Seminary, but found some of the material too liberal for him and dropped it. He also began to deal with a serious eye impairment called keratocoma that would plague him the rest of his life.

Ketcham had good success in the church, was ordained in 1915, and moved on to pastor churches in Brookville and Butler. Meanwhile, he firmly identified with the fundamentalists who resisted any compromise with what they saw as essential Christian doctrines about the virgin birth of Jesus, the divinity of Christ, etc. He became particularly concerned about liberal encroachments on the Northern Baptist Convention when it launched the New World Movement in 1919, a program he saw as liberal in content and authoritarian in implementation. He wrote a pamphlet called *A Statement of the First Baptist Church Butler, Pennsylvania, with Reference to The New World Movement and the $100,000,000 Drive* (1919), which was widely distributed and made his name prominent among fundamentalists. His first wife, Clara, died in 1920.

In 1923, a year after he married Mary Smart, Ketcham helped form the Bible Baptist Union to unify fundamentalist Baptists, though its program never got far off the ground. By this time he had moved to Ohio, first to a church at Niles, then Elyria (1926). In 1928 he helped found the Ohio Association of Independent Baptist Churches, and in 1932 the Bible Baptist Union was replaced by the General Association of Regular Baptist Churches. Although Ketcham did not attend the first meeting in 1932, he was present at key meetings in 1933 and 1934, at which he was elected vice president and president, respectively. He successfully campaigned to have the association separate itself completely from the Northern Baptist Convention as a different fellowship of congregations.

For the next 30 years he shaped the General Association of Regular Baptist Churches, though he abolished the president's office in 1938 in favor of a collective council of 14. He was the national representative of the association from 1946 to 1960 and national consultant from 1960 to 1966. He edited *The Baptist Bulletin* from 1938 to 1945, and at the same time pastored the largest Baptist church in Iowa—the Walnut Street Church in Waterloo—from 1939 to 1946. He then began to work full time for the association outside the pastorate and again edited *The Baptist Bulletin* from 1946 to 1955. He had a major heart attack in 1960, and his health and eyesight continually deteriorated, though he remained as active as possible. His last sermons were delivered from a stool. He died in 1978 at the age of 89.

Sources:

Dollar, George W. *A History of Fundamentalism in America*. Greenville, SC: Bob Jones University Press, 1963. 411 pp.
Hull, Merle R. *What a Fellowship!* Schaumburg, IL: Regular Baptist Press, 1981. 78 pp.
Ketcham, Robert Thomas. *The Answer*. Chicago: General Association of Regular Baptists, 1956. Rev. ed. 1965. 74 pp.
_____. *I Shall Not Want*. Chicago: Moody Press, 1953, 1972. 128 pp.
_____. *A Statement of the First Baptist Church Butler, Pennsylvania, with Reference to The New World Movement and the $100,000,000 Drive*. Butler, PA: 1919.
Murdoch, J. Murray. *Portrait of Obedience*. Schaumburg, IL: Regular Baptist Press, 1979. 328 pp.

—Gary L. Ward

★ 497 ★
KHAN, Hazrat Inayat
Founder, Sufi Order in the West
b. Jul. 5, 1882, Baroda, Gujerat India
d. Feb. 2, 1927, Delhi India

Hazrat Inayat Khan was the founder of the Sufi Order in the West, the first Sufi organization in both Europe and North America. He was born in India to a musical family, and at the age of 12 he left home to pursue a life of contemplation and music. He eventually succeeded in becoming a court musician for the Nizam of Hyderabad. While there, he began a spiritual search among the Sufis and was initiated by a sheikh of the Nizami branch of the Chishti (Sufi) Order (one of the main Sufi orders of India), Murshid Khwaja Abu Hashim Madani. After some time, Khan received the mantle of succession from his murshid (roughly equivalent to the ordination of a minister), whereupon he toured India on pilgrimage. While in Calcutta, he founded a music school, as had his grandfather. On September 13, 1910, he left for New York, where he would carry out his mission to take Sufism to the West. It was hoped that by bringing East and West together, the foundation of religious unity would be laid.

Khan obtained a job at Columbia University lecturing in music and Sufism, and also began to lecture around the country. In Berkeley, California, he met his first initiate, Mrs. Ada Martin, who was then given the name Rabia. In Nyack, New York, he met Ora Ray Baker, who was to become his wife. Baker was not only the cousin of Christian Science Founder **Mary Baker Eddy**, but was at the time under the guardianship of her half-brother, **Pierre Arnold Bernard**, founder of the Tantrik Order in America. Bernard prevented the relationship of Baker and Khan temporarily from advancing, though they eventually reunited in England and were married there on March 20, 1913.

Khan and his new wife stayed in London, and Khan founded the Sufi Order there in 1916. A strong base was built, and a quarterly magazine, *Sufism*, was begun. After World War I, he moved the order's headquarters to Suresnes in France. Khan continued to nurture his students in the United States, including lecture tours in 1923 and 1925, and Rabia Martin was made a murshid. In 1926 he built the Universal Temple at Suresnes for all religions as an expression of his belief in their essential unity. He then left for India, where he died in 1927, at the young age of 44.

Khan's unexpected death caused turmoil for the order. Murshid Martin claimed the right of succession, and most of the American members went with her. Her successor, **Ivy Oneita Duce**, became a disciple of **Meher Baba** and altered the group to become Sufism Reoriented. The European members who did not accept Martin's leadership turned to Khan's surviving family members and eventually to Khan's son, **Pir Vilayat Inayat Khan**, who reintroduced the Sufi Order to the United States in the 1960s and has led it ever since. Pir Vilayat has also collected his father's writings into a 12-volume set, *The Sufi Message of Hazrat Inayat Khan*.

Sources:

Biography of Pir-O-Murshid Inayat Khan. The Hague, Netherlands: East West Publications, 1979. 628 pp.

deJong-Keesing, Elisabeth. *Inayat Khan.* The Hague, Netherlands: East West Publications Fonds B.V., 1974. 302 pp.

Fuller, Jean Overton. *Noor-un-nisa Inayat Khan.* Rotterdam, Holland 1952, 1971. 271 pp.

Khan, Musharaff Moulamia. *Pages in the Life of a Sufi.* London, England: Sufi Publishing Company, 1971. 155 pp.

Khan, Vilayat Inayat. *The Message in Our Time.* New York: Harper & Row, 1978. 442 pp.

———, ed. *The Sufi Message of Hazrat Inayat Khan.* 12 vols. London, England: Barrie & Jenkins, 1960-69.

Stams, Kismet Dorothea. *Rays.* The Hague, Netherlands: East West Publications Fonds B. V., n. d. 148 pp.

Stolk, Sirkar Van, and Daphne Dunlop. *Memories of a Sufi Sage, Hazrat Inayat Khan.* The Hague, Netheralnds: East-West Publications Fonds B. V., 1967, 1975. 205 pp.

—Gary L. Ward

★ 498 ★
KHAN, Vilayat Inayat
Leader, Sufi Order in the West
b. Jun. 19, 1916, London United Kingdom

Pir Vilayat Inayat Khan, the present leader of the Sufi Order in the West and one of the more respected teachers of meditation in North America, is the son of Pir **Hazrat Inayat Khan** and Ora Baker. Pir Vilayat's father had come to the West early in this century and founded the Sufi Order, the first of its kind in Europe or North America. He had met his wife in America. She ran away to London to marry him, despite the attempts of her relatives to prevent their union. Pir Vilayat was their eldest child. He grew up in England and France as the order spread across post-war Europe. When Vilayat was 10 years old, his father named him as his successor. The next year his father died. The family took control of the order while Vilayat pursued his education.

Khan attended Paris University, receiving a B.A. in philosophy, and later did postgraduate work at Oxford in comparative religion. He also studied music (his father had been a professional musician for a time) at the Normale de Musique de Paris. His spiritual training was accomplished in India and the Middle East, where he studied with a variety of Sufi masters until he had matured to the point where he could assume leadership of the order. He was recognized as Pir-o-Murshid by the Sufi leaders in Amjer, India, where the international center of the Chishti Order of Sufis, to which the Sufi Order in the West is associated, is located.

The work of the order in Europe survived in spite of World War II, but the order in North America was lost completely because of the family's refusal to recognize the person, a female, Rabia Martin, who Hazrat Inayat Khan had left in charge. She eventually led the American followers into an association with Indian teacher **Meher Baba**. Pir Vilayat reintroduced the order to America in the 1960s, and serves as its main teacher.

A significant aspect of the leadership which Khan has given to the order has been in his collection and publication of the writings of his father. Besides reprinting many individual volumes, he oversaw the compilation of a 12-volume set of his complete works, *The Sufi Message of Hazrat Inayat Khan* (1960-1967). In 1978 he completed a biography of Pir Hazrat, *The Message in Our Time.* Other writings include *Toward the One* (1974); *Sufi Masters,* and *Physics and the Alchemy of Consciousness.*

Pir Vilayat also expanded the work of the order. In 1977 he founded the Omega Institute for Holistic Studies, which exists both as a community of Sufi initiates and a center for conferences and programs representative of the broad approach of holistic health. He has also nurtured the spread of the Universal Worship of the Chuurch of All, a worship approach that assumes the essential unity of the major religions of the world. Under Pir Vilayat Khan's leadership the order has revived and spread across Europe and North America.

Sources:

Khan, Pir Vilayat Inayat. *The Message in Our Time.* San Francisco, CA: Harper & Row, 1978. 442 pp.

———. *Toward the One.* New York: Harper & Row, 1974.

"Sufi Order." *The Message* 2, 11 (November 1976).

★ 499 ★
KHEIRALLA, Ibrahim George
Founder, National Organization of the Universal Religion
b. Nov. 11, 1849, Bhamdoun Syrian Arab Republic
d. Mar. 8, 1929

Ibrahim George Kheiralla (also spelled "Khayrullah"), who first brought the message of the Baha'i Faith to America but who soon left the faith to found his own separate group, was born in Syria. Little is known of his childhood other than that he was raised in an Orthodox Christian family. He attended the National School of Butrus Bustani, a college preparatory school, and in 1866 enrolled in the Syrian Protestant College (now American University). Following his graduation in 1870, Kheiralla moved to Cairo and went into business. He married, but after bearing three children, his first wife soon died. He married a second time, but that marriage ended in divorce. He had married a third time when in 1892 he left for the West. During this time in Egypt, he also developed an interest in occult matters, especially psychic healing.

Around 1888, in the diverse religious atmosphere that had emerged in Cairo, he first encountered the teachings of **Baha'u'llah**, the founder of the Baha'i Faith, as delivered to him orally through some Baha'is who had settled in Cairo. He became enthused about the new faith and in 1890 became a Baha'i.

In 1892, within weeks of the death of Baha'u'llah and the emergence of **Abdu'l-Baha**, his son, as the new leader of the faith, Kheiralla immigrated to the United States, where he was to introduce the teachings and facilitate the first conversions. At this time, Kheiralla possessed copies of only a few Baha'i writings coupled with a distorted understanding of many of the teachings he had picked up in Egypt. He had also never met the founder or his son, and he had to fill in the gaps of his knowledge with personal speculations.

Within two years, Kheiralla had begun to gather the first serious students. The first of these became Baha'is the following year. He married one of the students, Marrion Miller (after divorcing his third wife when she refused to join him in America). Of this first group, only **Thornton Chase** would remain a Baha'i through his life, and he, not Kheiralla, is generally regarded as the first Baha'i convert in America.

In 1896 Kheiralla issued the first of several books, *Za-ti-et Al-lah, The Identity and Personality of God,* followed in 1897 by *Bab-ed-Din.* Both books introduced Baha'i teachings and advertised private lessons on the faith. In 1898 he traveled to Akka, Palestine, and met Abdu'l-Baha. The trip merely highlighted a number of differences between what Baha'u'llah had taught and what Kheiralla had been teaching. During 1899-1900, these differences with Abdu'l-Baha, which Kheiralla refused to discard, and Abdu'l-Baha's refusal to recognize him as the American Baha'i leader, led to a disruption within the American Baha'i movement and Kheiralla's disassociation from it. He re-established himself as an independent teacher. Just as the disruption was reaching its critical point, he published his next book, entitled *Baha'u'llah.* It put into print the substance of his classes, and highlighted his distinct perspective.

Through the rest of his life Kheiralla continued to lead his group and to author a number of books. The group reorganized in 1914 as the National Organization of the Universal Religion. Kheiralla served as president of the group. He had little contact with his followers, however, and spent most of his remaining life in the homes of his relatives, most of whom were not believers in his faith. He wrote a few more shorter works, but left the organization to William E. Dreyer, a follower who eventually succeeded him as head of the group. Dreyer was reprinting Kheiralla's works as late as the 1940s.

Sources:

Kheiralla, Ibrahim. *Bab-ed-Din; The Door of True Religion.* Chicago: Charles H. Kerr, 1897. 84 pp.
———. *Baha'U'llah.* Chicago: I. G. Kheiralla, 1900. 545 pp.
———. *An Epistle of Peace.* N.p., 1918.
———. *Facts for Behaists.* Chicago: The Author, 1901.
———. *Za-ti-et Al-lah, The Identity and Personality of God.* N.p., 1896.

★500★
KILLINGSWORTH, Frank Russell
Founder, Kodesh Church of Immanuel
b. Nov. 28, 1873, Winsboro, South Carolina
d. Apr. 20, 1976

Frank Russell Killingsworth, the founder of the Kodesh Church of Immanuel, a holiness denomination with a predominantly black membership, was the son of Frank and Sarah R. Killingsworth, both former slaves. His father was a minister for many years in the African Methodist Episcopal Zion Church. Killingsworth professed to have experienced salvation as a youth and some time later to have experienced sanctification (through which, holiness people believe, one is made perfect in love). He attended Livingston College, the AME Zion school, and received his A.B. in 1899. He later did graduate work at State College in York, South Carolina, from which he received a D.D. in 1907. In 1908 he married Laura A. Penn. He became principal of Jefferson Graded School in York, South Carolina. In 1911 he became a teacher and administrator of the Manassas, Virginia, Industrial Institute, where he remained until 1915. He then became a pastor in the AME Zion Church. During his eight years in Arlington, Virginia, he oversaw the building of their church edifice.

In 1929 Killingsworth left the AME Zion Church and founded the Kodesh Church of Immanuel. It differed from its parent body in that Killingsworth did not include bishops in the organization. He believed that adequate congregational supervision could be exercised without autocracy or financial oppression. The new church also emphasized the doctrine of entire sanctification. The name of the church was derived from a Hebrew word, *behadrath*, meaning holiness, and can be roughly translated "Holy Church of Jesus."

Killingsworth established churches in Washington, D.C. (where the headquarters were), and throughout Pennsylvania. In 1934 he accepted the Christian Tabernacle Union, a holiness body headquartered in Philadelphia, Pennsylvania, into the church. Shortly after World War II, the church was granted 300 acres in Liberia and the Killingsworth Mission was begun there.

Killingsworth labored for many years in the Washington, D.C., area. He turned 100 in 1973. Annually thereafter, *The Star of Zion*, the newspaper of the AME Church, with whom Killingsworth had remained on relations, printed articles as he grew another year older.

Sources:

"Dr. Killingsworth, Marvelous Man." *The Star of Zion* (February 6, 1975): 4.
Dupree, Sherry Sherrod. *Biographical Dictionary of African-American, Holiness-Pentecostals, 1880-1990.* Washington, DC: Middle Atlantic Regional Press, 1990. 386 pp.
Killingsworth, Frank R. "The Kodesh Church of Immanuel." *The Star of Zion* (February 6, 1975):, 1-2.

★501★
KIMBALL, Spencer Wooley
President, Church of Jesus Christ of Latter-day Saints
b. Mar. 28, 1895, Salt Lake City, Utah
d. Nov. 9, 1985, Salt Lake City, Utah

Spencer Wooley Kimball, the twelfth president of the Church of Jesus Christ of Latter-day Saints, was the son of Olive Wooley and Andrew Kimball. Though born in Salt Lake City, Kimball grew up on a farm in Thatcher, Arizona, where his father was a bishop in the church. He attended Gila Academy (1910-1914) and afterwards spent two years in Missouri doing the missionary work required of young males by his church. In 1917 he married Camilla Eyring. He went into business, first at a bank, and then in 1927 he opened a real estate/insurance agency.

An active churchman since his return for his mission, in 1938 he was named president of the Mount Graham Ward district. Five years later he was named to the Council of Twelve Apostles. At that time he moved to Salt Lake City. Once normal activities returned with the end of World War II, he was placed in charge of the church's very active work among American Indians. He developed a placement program for Indian students who would live in Mormon homes during the school year.

His years as a member of the Council of Twelve Apostles was highlighted by his tour of Europe in 1955 during which time he dedicated the new Mormon temple in Switzerland where Latter-day Saints hold weddings and other special ceremonies. In 1965 the church was divided into twelve administrative districts and Kimball was assigned supervision over the work in South America for the first four years and then reassigned to oversee Europe. He also authored his two books: *The Miracle of Forgiveness* (1969) and *Faith Precedes the Miracle* (1972).

In 1974 Kimball was selected to succeed **Harold B. Lee** as the president of the Church of Jesus Christ of Latter-day Saints. During his first year he saw the completion of the Mormon temple in Washington, D.C. As president, Kimball continued some reformist trends previously set in motion, his most significant action being the opening of the priesthood to black males. At the same time he was a staunch supporter of conservative Mormon values concerning the centrality of family life. For this reason he resolutely spoke out against birth control, women's rights, and sexual intimacy apart from marriage. He also reinforced church prohibitions against the use of tobacco, alcohol, and drugs.

In the early 1980s Kimball's health began to fail him and he pushed much of his administrative duties over to his counselor Gordon B. Hinckley. He rarely left his living quarters during the last four years of his life. At his death he was succeeded by **Ezra Taft Benson**.

Sources:

Kimball, Edward L. and Andrew E. Kimball, Jr., *Spencer W. Kimball: Twelfth President of the Church of Jesus Christ of Latter-day Saints.* Salt Lake City, UT: Bookcraft, Inc. 1977. 438 pp.
Kimball, Spencer W. *Faith Precedes the Miracle.* Salt Lake City, UT: Deseret Book Co., 1972. 364 pp.
———. *The Miracle of Forgiveness.* Salt Lake City, UT: Bookcraft, 1969. 376 pp.
Presidents of the Church. Institutes of Religion of the Church Educational System, Church of Jesus Christ of Latter-day Saints, 1979. 377 pp.

★502★
KING, Coretta Scott
Baptist Laywoman
Civil Rights Activist
b. Apr. 27, 1927, Marion, Alabama

Coretta Scott King will always be remembered first as the wife of **Martin Luther King, Jr.**, but she made her own important contributions to the civil rights movement and to other social justice causes. Although her family was not as poor as others in the area, her childhood was one of hard work and few luxuries. With help from her determined parents she was able to leave the rural South to attend the newly integrated Antioch College in Ohio. There she joined the National Association for the Advancement of Colored People (NAACP) and other civil rights groups. At Antioch she also began to study music seriously; upon graduation in 1951 she pursued further musical study at the New England Conservatory, earning Mus.B. (1954) and Mus.D. (1971) degrees. In Boston she met her future husband, who was in graduate school at Boston University at the time. They were married in 1953. After another year in Boston, during which they both finished school, the Kings moved to Montgomery, Alabama, where Martin had accepted the pastorate of the Dexter Avenue Baptist Church.

The Kings' life was changed forever when, in 1955, Rosa Parks refused to give her seat on a Montgomery city bus to a white man, and with the subsequent bus boycott the civil rights movement was under way. Although Coretta had just given birth to the Kings' first child, she served the freedom movement vigorously. She was active in organizing and planning components of the bus boycott, and she participated in marches and demonstrations in Montgomery. In later years she gave concerts to raise funds for the Southern Christian Leadership Conference, the civil rights organization which emerged from the bus boycott, and she delivered many speeches, often filling in for her busy husband. In the meantime she raised a family of two sons and two daughters.

After the assassination of her husband in April 1968, Coretta King realized that her presence would lend continuity to the civil rights movement. Immediately after the funeral she traveled back to Memphis, where Martin Luther King had been shot, and led a protest march he had been organizing at the time of his death. Two months later she provided leadership and spoke at the Poor People's Campaign in Washington, D.C., which her husband had also been deeply involved in planning. She also maintained her long interest in world peace, an involvement which had led her to participate in a disarmament conference in Geneva in 1961 as a representative of the American group Women Strike for Peace. During the 1970s she supported legislation designed to ensure full employment; she was also active in seeking equal rights and economic justice for women.

Sources:

King, Coretta Scott. *My Life with Martin Luther King, Jr.* New York: Holt, Rinehart and Winston, 1969.

Vivian, Octavia. *Coretta: The Story of Mrs. Martin Luther King, Jr.* Philadelphia: Fortress Press, 1970.

—Timothy Miller

★ 503 ★
KING, Henry Churchill
Theologian, Congregational Church
b. Sep. 18, 1858, Hillsdale, Michigan
d. Feb. 27, 1934, Oberlin, Ohio

Henry Churchill King, a liberal Congregational Church theologian, was the son of Sarah Lee and Henry Jarvis King. He grew up in Hillsdale, Michigan, and began his college work at Hillsdale College, where his father was secretary-treasurer. However, in his sophomore year he transferred to Oberlin College. He graduated in 1879 and stayed to attend the Oberlin Theological Seminary. Following his graduation in 1882, he married Julia M. Coates. He pursued post-graduate philosophy studies at Harvard and returned to Oberlin in 1884 as an associate professor of mathematics. He moved to philosophy in 1890 and became a full professor in 1891. In 1893-1894 he went to Germany to study at the University of Berlin. He returned deeply influenced by the philosophy of Herman Rudolf Lotze, and the liberal theology of Albrecht Ritschl. In

1897 he became a professor of theology at Oberlin Theological Seminary, and soon became widely known as a leading liberal Protestant voice. His first major books were published soon after the turn of the century: *Reconstruction in Theology* (1901) and *Social Consciousness* (1902).

In 1902 King became president of Oberlin, and to his theological endeavors he added a career in educational innovation. In addition to his attempts to improve Oberlin's intellectual offerings, he emphasized the development of character and of the whole person. His concerns led to the marked improvement of Oberlin's curriculum in music, morals, fine arts, and religion. His contributions were recognized by his election to head such organizations as the Religious Education Association and the Association of American Colleges.

Though busy with presidential duties, King did not let his own intellectual life slacken and authored a number of books, including *Rational Living* (1904); *The Laws of Friendship* (1909): and *The Moral and Religious Challenge of Our Times* (1911). There were two additional theological treatises, *The Ethics of Jesus* (1910) and *Fundamental Questions* (1917).

All the while King retained an active relationship with the Congregational Church. At various times he headed the Congregational Commission on Missions and the Congregational Foundation for Education, and for two years he served as moderator of the General Council of Congregational Churches (1919-1921).

In 1919 King was appointed to the Inter-Allied Commission on Mandates in Turkey. Along with colleague Charles R. Crane, he spent months of investigation only to see his report ignored by the Peace Conference following World War I. The effort to prepare the report and the disappointment over its treatment undermined his health, which began a slow deterioration. He retired from the presidency of Oberlin in 1927 and died a few years later.

Sources:

Dictionary of American Biography. 20 vols. and 7 supps. New York: Charles Scribner's Sons, 1928-1936, 1944-1981.

King, Henry Churchill. *The Ethics of Jesus.* New York: Macmillan Company, 1910. 293 pp.

_____. *Fundamental Questions.* New York: Macmillan Company, 1917. 256 pp.

_____. *Rational Living.* New York: Macmillan Company, 1905. 271 pp.

_____. *Reconstruction in Theology.* Chicago: N.p., 1901. 323 pp.

_____. *Theology and the Social Consciousness.* New York: Macmillan Company, 1902. 252 pp.

★ 504 ★
KING, Joseph Hillery
General Superintendent, Pentecostal Holiness Church
b. Aug. 11, 1869, Anderson County, South Carolina
d. Apr. 23, 1946, Anderson, South Carolina

Joseph Hillery King was a leader in the developments that led to the formation of the Pentecostal Holiness Church, since 1975 the International Pentecostal Holiness Church. King was one of 11 children born to a poor tenant farmer in South Carolina, and he received very little formal education. At the age of 16 he was converted at a Methodist holiness camp meeting. Within a few months he experienced not only a call to ministry, but also sanctification, defined in holiness groups as a second work of grace by which the inward nature is cleansed and perfected. King received his exhorter's license from the Methodists on his second attempt, in 1887.

After a tour with the Army, King married Willie Irene King in 1890, although she proved so opposed to his religious career that they soon divorced. By 1892 he was assigned his first charge as the assistant pastor for the Rock Spring-Walton circuit in the Georgia Conference of the Methodist Episcopal Church (which had been reestablished in the South after the Civil War). After other assignments, he went to the Lookout Mountain circuit in 1895, which allowed him to attend the School of Theology at U. S. Grant University in Chattanooga, Tennessee. During this time, he increasingly felt that Methodism was not fully accepting of his brand of holiness. He joined a radical holiness group led by **Benjamin H. Irwin**, the Fire-Baptized Holiness Association, which advocated a "third work of grace," after sanctification, called "fire-baptism." Upon graduation from the School of Theology in 1897, King left Methodism and became a full-time evangelist for the association.

Between 1898 and 1900 King evangelized around Toronto, Canada, then went to Iowa to assist Irwin in leadership and in editing their periodical, *Live Coals of Fire*. Soon thereafter a scandal toppled Irwin from power, and King was elected general superintendent as well as editor. He instituted a Methodist-like itinerancy throughout the church, moved the headquarters to Georgia, and in 1902 changed the name to Fire-Baptized Holiness Church of God of the Americas. In 1907 King encountered the new Pentecostal message through a revival led by **G. B. Cashwell**, and after much struggle accepted it. Soon the whole church accepted it as the fullness of what they had earlier called fire-baptism. The insistence on the Pentecostal gift as only coming after justification and sanctification continues to distinguish the church (Pentecostal Holiness) from other Pentecostal bodies.

In 1909 King founded the Falcon Publishing House for the church's publishing needs, including the periodical, now called the *Apostolic Evangel*. Both the publishing house and a new orphanage were established in Falcon, North Carolina. In 1911 he left on a two-year-long world foreign mission tour, during which he still managed to guide the church into a merger with the Pentecostal Holiness Church, whose name they took, with King then becoming assistant general superintendent and president of the General Mission Board. In 1917 he was elected general superintendent of the Pentecostal Holiness Church, a position he held for the rest of his life. In 1920 he married his second wife, Blanche Leon Moore. When he died in 1946 at the age of 77, the church was already a major force within the larger Pentecostal community.

Sources:

Beacham, A.D., Jr. *A Brief History of the Pentecostal Holiness Church*. Franklin Springs, GA: Advocate Press, 1983. 123 pp.

Campbell, Joseph E. *The Pentecostal Holiness Church, 1898-1948*. Franklin Springs, GA: Publishing House of the Pentecostal Holiness Church, 1951. 573 pp.

King, Joseph H. *From Passover to Pentecost*. Franklin Springs, GA: Advocate Press, 1976. 208 pp.

———. *Yet Speaketh*. Franklin Springs, GA: Publishing House of the Pentecostal Holiness Church, 1940. 387 pp.

Melton, J. Gordon. *Biographical Dictionary of American Cult and Sect Leaders*. Garland Reference Library of Social Science, vol. 212. New York: Garland Publishing, 1986.

—Gary L. Ward

★505★
KING JR., Martin Luther
Minister, Progressive National Baptist Convention
Civil Rights Leader
b. Jan. 15, 1929, Atlanta, Georgia
d. Apr. 4, 1968, Memphis, Tennessee

Martin Luther King, Jr., civil rights advocate, Baptist preacher, and winner of the Nobel Peace Prize, was the son of Martin Luther King, Sr., and Alberta Williams King. His father was assistant pastor and later pastor, of Ebenezer Baptist Church in Atlanta, Georgia. King grew up in a relatively stable and comfortable environment, although well aware of the racial injustice which surrounded Blacks in America. An excellent student, he completed high school early and enrolled at Morehouse College in 1944 at age 15. After graduation he entered Crozer Theological Seminary in Chester, Pennsyl-

vania, where he earned a divinity degree in 1951 and where he was introduced to the thought of **Walter Rauschenbusch**, Gandhi, and other social reformers. He went on to the advanced study of ethics at Boston University, where he received a Ph.D. in 1955.

In Boston, King met Coretta Scott, a music student at the New England Conservatory; they were married in 1953. The following year King accepted a call to the pastorate of the Dexter Avenue Baptist Church in Montgomery, Alabama. On December 1, 1955, when Rosa Parks refused to give her seat on a bus to a white man, the black community of Montgomery rose up to protest the injustice of segregation. To his surprise, King was quickly elected to head the Montgomery Improvement Association, formed to supervise a boycott of the local bus system. The boycott continued for slightly over a year, accompanied by great strife in Montgomery. King's home was bombed and his life was threatened repeatedly. Victory came, however, when the U.S. Supreme Court ruled that Alabama laws requiring segregation on buses were unconstitutional. King was thereafter a nationally-known hero of racial justice.

Although the first battle had been won, the towering edifice of segregation remained. In 1957 King and other black leaders formed the Southern Christian Leadership Conference (SCLC) to coordinate civil rights activity. King assumed the organization's presidency and devoted himself to a daunting schedule of meetings and speeches. He also authored the first of several books to detail his approach to social change, *Stride Toward Freedom* (1958). In 1960 he resigned from the Dexter Avenue Church to devote all of his energies to the work of the SCLC, headquartered in Atlanta.

King thereafter provided personal leadership in major civil rights confrontations. Early in 1963 he arrived in Birmingham, Alabama, to lead ongoing protests against segregation in public facilities. Police Commissioner "Bull" Conner, an avowed segregationist, ordered his forces to attack the demonstrators with police dogs and high-pressure firehoses; later that year a black church was bombed and four Sunday school students killed. National sympathy for the black cause increased as the violence continued. Incarcerated for refusing to obey a court order to cease leading demonstrations, King wrote his "Letter from Birmingham Jail" to a group of white ministers, perhaps his most powerful statement of the evils of racial discrimination.

In 1964 King was awarded the Nobel Peace Prize; at 35, he was the youngest recipient to receive the honor. In 1965 he plunged into another major action, a campaign for voting rights centered in Selma, Alabama. Police violence again gave the cause nationwide publicity, and at King's call, hundreds of members of the clergy from around the country came to join a march to Montgomery, the state capital. The Selma protests led directly to the national voting-rights act which ensured equal access to the ballot.

King thereafter expanded his targets, working against racial injustice and poverty in the North. Victories as in Montgomery and Selma were, however, harder to come by in the North. In August 1965 he began spirited denunciations of the American role in the war in Vietnam, which cost him some of his support. Trying to break the stagnation of the movement late in 1967, King announced the Poor People's Campaign, a program of mass civil disobedience to take place the following spring in Washington, D.C. In the meantime, he was persuaded to travel to Memphis to make one of his innumerable personal appearances for social justice, this time to support a strike by local sanitation workers. There, on April 4, 1968, he was killed by an assassin's bullet. After funeral services in Atlanta he was carried to his grave in a crude farm cart pulled by two mules, a final expression of his solidarity with the poor. Since his death, **Coretta Scott King** has carried on his work through the King Center in Atlanta, Georgia.

Sources:

Cone, James H. *Martin and Malcolm and America*. Maryknoll, NY: Orbis Books, 1991. 358 pp.

Garrow, David J. *Bearing the Cross: Martin Luther King, Jr., and the Southern Christian Leadership Conference*. New York: Morrow, 1986.

King, Martin Luther, Jr. *A Martin Luther King Treasury*. New York: W. Lads, [1964]. 352 pp.

_____. *Strength to Live*. New York: Harper & Row, 1963. 146 pp.

_____. *Stride Toward Freedom*. New York: Harper & Row, 1958.

_____. *Where Do We Go from Here: Chaos or Community?* Boston: Beacon Press, 1968. 209 pp.

Lewis, David Levering. *King: A Biography*. Urbana, IL: University of Illinois Press, 1978.

Miller, William Robert. *Martin Luther King, Jr.: His Life, Martyrdom and Meaning for the World*. New York: Weybright and Talley, 1968.

Oates, Stephen B. *Let the Trumpet Sound: The Life of Martin Luther King, Jr.* New York: Harper and Row, 1982.

—*Timothy Miller*

★506★
KING SR., Martin Luther
Minister, Progressive National Baptist Convention
b. Dec. 19, 1899, Stockbridge, Georgia
d. Nov. 11, 1984, Atlanta, Georgia

Martin Luther King, Sr., best known as the father of civil rights leader **Martin Luther King, Jr.**, was also a strong advocate of racial equality in his own right. Born in rural Georgia, he was raised in the poverty typical of the era. At the age of 16 he walked 20 miles to Atlanta, where he worked at various manual jobs, including shoveling coal on locomotives, and went to school at night, eventually completing high school in 1925. He then enrolled at Morehouse College, where he received a bachelor's degree in theology in 1931. While in college he pastored two small churches in Atlanta. In 1926 he married Alberta Williams, daughter of A. D. Williams, pastor of Ebenezer Baptist Church; he assumed the Ebenezer pastorate after Williams died in 1931. He led the church for 44 years, greatly expanding its program and membership, before retiring in 1975.

Tragic death came to three members of King's immediate family. Martin Luther King, Jr., was assassinated in 1968; another son, A. D. King, was drowned in a swimming pool in 1969; and Alberta King was shot and killed by a gunman while playing the organ at Ebenezer in 1974.

King was an advocate of social change and racial equality as well as a preacher. He became an active member of the Social Action Committee of the National Association for the Advancement of Colored People (NAACP), helping to win equal salaries for black and white teachers in Atlanta. He challenged poll tax and literacy text requirements, whose main purpose and effect was to keep Blacks from voting, and in 1936 he led a march of several hundred on city hall to demonstrate for voting rights. For years thereafter he worked, primarily at the negotiating table, to improve the lot of Blacks in Atlanta.

In 1960 Martin Luther King, Jr. left his own pastorate in Montgomery, Alabama, to join his father at Ebenezer and opened an office for the Southern Christian Leadership Conference (SCLC) nearby. After the assassination of his son in 1968, "Daddy" King, as he was by now generally known, made many public appearances, especially at events where the memory of his son was honored. The themes he articulated in his speeches were much like those of his son: concern for the poor, nonviolent opposition to oppression, faith in God.

In 1976 King supported Jimmy Carter for the U.S. presidency and played an important role in delivering black votes for Carter's successful candidacy. He delivered benedictions at both the 1976 and 1980 Democratic National Conventions. After a long bout with heart disease he died on November 11, 1984.

Sources:

Colins, David R. *Not Only Dreamers: The Story of Martin Luther King, Sr. and Martin Luther King, Jr.* Elgin, IL: Brethren Press, 1986.

King, Martin Luther, Sr., and Clayton Riley. *Daddy King: An Autobiography*. New York: Morrow, 1980.

—*Timothy Miller*

★507★
KING, Willis Jefferson
Bishop, Methodist Episcopal Church
b. Oct. 1, 1886, Rosehill, Texas

Willis Jefferson King, a bishop in the Methodist Episcopal Church, was the son of Anderson W. and Emma Blackshear King. He was admitted on trial and ordained as a deacon in the Texas Conference of the Methodist Episcopal Church in 1908 while attending Wiley College, from which he received his A.B. in 1910. He attended Boston University, which awarded him an S.T.B. in 1913. That same year he married Parmella J. Kelly, was ordained an elder, and was admitted into full connection with the Texas Conference. He remained in Boston as pastor of Fourth Methodist Episcopal Church while engaged in graduate work in Old Testament.

He returned to Texas in 1915 and served St. Paul Methodist Episcopal Church in Galveston (1915-1917) and Trinity Church in Houston (1917-1918). In 1918 he became a professor of Old Testament literature at Gammon Theological Seminary in Atlanta, Georgia. While there he completed the requirements for his Ph.D., which was awarded by Boston University in 1921, and he authored his first book, *The Negro in American Life* (1926). In 1930 he became president of Samuel Houston College in Austin, Texas, but returned to Atlanta as the president of Gammon in 1932.

King emerged as a leader among black members of the Methodist Episcopal Church at a crucial moment, as the church was negotiating a merger with the two other main branches of Methodism, the Methodist Episcopal Church, South and the Methodist Protestant Church. Possibly the major stumbling block to the negotiation was a resolution of the role of the black members of the Methodist Episcopal Church, most of whom lived in the South. The Methodist Episcopal Church, South wanted assurance that they would not be integrated into the all-white conferences of the Methodist Episcopal Church, South. King had become a member of the Texas Conference in the last stages of the battle to have black bishops elected. In the 1930s he sat on the commission which developed the plan of union of the three churches. In the end the commission developed the idea of a nongeographic "Central Jurisdiction" in which the predominantly black conferences would be organized. King fought the plan, looking instead for a less segregated solution, but in the end acquiesced to it.

King continued to serve at Gammon through the 1939 merger of American Methodism which produced the Methodist Church (1939-1968). In 1943 he co-authored *Personalism in Theology*, a reflection of his Boston University background, and authored the *Christian Basis of World Order*. Then in 1944 he was elected as a bishop by the Central Jurisdiction. He served for 16 years before his retirement in 1960.

Sources:

Harmon, Nolan B. *The Encyclopedia of World Methodism*. 2 vols. Nashville: United Methodist Publishing House, 1974.

King, Willis Jefferson. *The Negro in American Life*. New York: The Methodist Book Concern, 1926. 154 pp.

Richardson, Harry V. *Dark Salvation*. Garden City, NY: Doubleday & Company, 1976. 324 pp.

_____. *History of Methodist Mission in Liberia*. N.p.: 1945. 77 pp.

_____. "The Negro Membership of the (Former) Methodist Church in the (New) United Methodist Church." *Methodist History* 7, 3 (April 1969): 32-43.

★508★
KNAPP, Martin Wells
Founder, International Holiness Union and Prayer League
b. Mar. 27, 1853, Clarendon, Michigan
d. Dec. 7, 1901, Cincinnati, Ohio

Martin Wells Knapp was the founder of the International Holiness Union and Prayer League, which through a series of mergers is now a constituent part of the Wesleyan Church. Knapp's father was a farmer in Michigan and a class leader in the Methodist Episcopal Church. But the younger Knapp did not take well to the church. He attended Albion College sporadically from 1870 to 1876, but never finished his degree due to the demands of farm work and his father's ill health. At college, however, he met Lucy Glenn, whom he married in 1877. She was a strong Methodist, and her encouragement led to a conversion experience for Knapp, followed by a call to preach.

Knapp joined the Michigan Conference of the Methodist Episcopal Church and served various charges between 1877 and 1887. In the early 1880s, Knapp experienced sanctification, the second act of grace taught by the holiness movement, which cleanses one's inner self of sin and frees one for perfect love. From this point on he became increasingly involved in the holiness movement, and wrote the first of his holiness books in 1886, *Christ Crowned Within*. In 1887, at his request, the conference removed him from itinerancy to enable him to try evangelistic work without the burden of caring for a congregation. In 1888 he began a holiness periodical, *The Revivalist*, but his work was continually troubled by finances and the health problems which led to the early death of his wife in 1890.

In 1892 Knapp regrouped by moving to Cincinnati, marrying Minnie C. Ferle, and beginning his publishing and other work anew. In 1894 he bought land near Flat Rock, Kentucky, where he built Beulah Heights School and a nearby tabernacle, where he held annual camp meetings. In 1897 he began a mission in Cincinnati and helped form the International Holiness Union and Prayer League, which was intended to be an inspirational association but not a separate church. Nevertheless, his activities began to draw unfavorable attention within the Methodist Episcopal Church, which was moving further and further away from a holiness stance. In 1898 the Michigan conference censured him for holding an unauthorized revival meeting, though this blot was removed when he took an early retirement in 1899.

By 1900 Knapp felt completely divorced from Methodism. Now free from that obstacle, he proceeded with his plans to build God's Bible School in Cincinnati. This proved to be his last major act, however, as he died of typhoid in 1901 at the young age of 48. *The Revivalist* and God's Bible School lived on under independent boards related to the International Holiness Union and Prayer League, which grew into being its own denomination, forming churches. Through a number of mergers it became the Pilgrim Holiness Church in 1922, and then part of the Wesleyan Church in 1968.

Sources:
Hills, A.M. *A Hero of Faith and Prayer.* Cincinnati, OH, 1902.
Knapp, Martin Wells. *Christ Crowned Within.* Albion, MI: Revivalist Publishing Co., 1886.
_____. *Holiness Triumphant.* Cincinnati, OH: God's Bible School Book Room, 1900. 253 pp.
_____. *Impressions.* Cincinnati, OH: God's Revivalist Office, 1892. 144 pp.
_____. *Out of Egypt into Canaan.* Albion, MI: Revivalist Publishing Co., 1887. 196 pp.
Melton, J. Gordon. *Biographical Dictionary of American Cult and Sect Leaders.* Garland Reference Library of Social Science, vol. 212. New York: Garland Publishing, 1986.

—Gary L. Ward

★509★
KNIGHT, J.Z.
New Age Channel
b. Mar. 16, 1946, Dexter, New Mexico

J. Z. Knight, who serves as the medium for the disembodied spirit Ramtha, is perhaps the best-known of contemporary New Age channelers. She was born Judith Darlene Hampton into a family of impoverished farm laborers, the daughter of Charles and Helen Printes Hart Hampton. Judith grew up to be a popular majorette and rodeo queen at Artesia High School in Artesia, New Mexico. Her religious training was as a fundamentalist Baptist. She rejected this training early in her life, but did not reject her belief in God. She recalls having seen a UFO during an eighth-grade slumber party, but otherwise her early life was not remarkably unusual.

She married young and had two sons by her first husband, Otis Henley. At the time of her first encounter with Ramtha, she had divorced Henley and married Jeremy Burnett, a dentist from Tacoma, Washington. In her autobiography, *A State of Mind: My Story* (1987), she says that in 1977 she and her husband were making pyramids (having heard about their wonderful, unusual properties, such as preserving food) when she had a vision of Ramtha. Ramtha responded to her question, "Who are you?" with the statement, "I am Ramtha the Enlightened One, and I have come to help you over the ditch" (the "ditch" of limited thought). After initial confusion and fear that Ramtha might be the devil, she was guided by a spiritualist, Lorraine Graham, to interpret her vision as a contact with a spiritual entity.

According to many occultists, Ramtha describes himself as having been a warrior on Lemuria, the ancient lost continent in the Pacific, some 35,000 years ago. Ramtha began to teach her, and Knight developed into a trance channeler. She held her first public channeling on December 17, 1978, and by the early 1980s was making appearances across the United States. Ramtha's message is typical of New Age teachings, stressing the divinity within and the power of the mind/imagination to create its own reality.

During the years after Ramtha's appearance, Knight and Burnett were divorced, and in 1983 she married Jeffery Knight. Her career was subsequently boosted by the endorsements of such celebrities as **Shirley MacLaine** and appearances on popular programs like the "Merv Griffin Show." Knight's success as a public medium in combination with her husband's successful horse breeding business allowed them to live a comfortable lifestyle and to build an expensive home.

After Ramtha became a national media figure in 1986-1987, the anti-cult movement began to portray Knight as a typically manipulative "cult" leader, and at least one adherent was deprogrammed. Also, the press focused on the price of Knight's workshops and on her accumulated wealth, implying that her channeling work was merely a money-making scam. Unable to discover financial improprieties, however, the latter controversy experienced a quick demise.

Sources:
Knight, J. Z. *Ramtha.* Edited by Steven Lee Weinberg. Eastsound, WA: Sovereignty, Inc., 1986. 217 pp.
_____. *A State of Mind: My Story.* New York: Warner, 1987. 447 pp.
Vrazo, Fawn. "Indeed!" *Albuquerque (NM) Journal Magazine* (May 31, 1983).

—James R. Lewis

★510★
KNOCH, Adolph Ernst
Founder, Concordant Publishing Concern
b. Dec. 12, 1874, St. Louis, Missouri
d. Mar. 28, 1965, Los Angeles, California

Adolph Ernst Knoch is known for his Concordant version of the Bible and as founder of the periodical, *Unsearchable Riches*. Born to German-American parents in St. Louis, Missouri, he moved to Los Angeles at age 10. As a young man he was converted by reading the Bible and became active in the Plymouth Brethren (Open), a group based on the work of John Nelson Darby, which divided the history recounted in the Bible into dispensations—periods defined according to the different ways God related to humanity. Knoch married Olive Elizabeth Hyde and earned a living as a printer.

Knoch's continuing study of the Bible led him into some disagreements with the Brethren, who excommunicated him around the year 1900. In 1906 Knoch sent an article to the Anglican Bible student Ethelbert A. Bullinger in England. Bullinger produced the magazine *Things To Come*, a well-known periodical which advocated some variations on Darby's teachings. Bullinger published the article and converted to its premise, which was that the spirit baptism of Ephesians 4:5 superseded water baptism. Vladimir Galesnoff, a reader who was impressed by the article, began to share ideas with Knoch. In 1909 they founded the Concordant Publishing Concern and began a magazine for Bible students, *Unsearchable Riches*. This magazine led to the formation of many groups of Bible students who gathered to read the Bible through Knoch's eyes. In addition to dispensationalism, these students learned universal salvation, the impersonality of the Holy Spirit, and Saturday worship—doctrines which set Knoch apart from others in the Darby tradition.

Knoch also began work on his plans to make a new translation of the Bible, one where each Greek or Hebrew word would be given a standard English equivalent word. This came to be called the Concordant (meaning agreeable or corresponding) version of the Bible, and the first installment appeared in 1919 as *The Unveiling of Jesus Christ* (that is, the Book of Revelation). The complete New Testament was done by 1926, the same year his wife died. Knoch took various trips abroad, to places such as Germany and the Holy Land, gathering material to begin work on the Old Testament. In Germany, he met Countess Sigrid von Kanitz, who was producing a magazine similar to *Unsearchable Riches*. They married in 1932, and Knoch stayed in Germany to write a German version of the Concordant New Testament. They left for Los Angeles in 1939 as the Second World War began, and Knoch resumed his work in the United States. The German edition was published in 1944, and although he finished his Old Testament work, only parts of Genesis and Isaiah were published before his death in 1965.

Sources:
Adolph Ernst Knoch, 1874-1965. Saugus, CA: Unsearchable Riches, 1965. 48 pp.
The Concordant Version in the Critics Den. Los Angeles: Concordant Publishing Concern, n.d. 96 pp.
Knoch, Adolph Ernst. *Concordant Literal New Testament*. Saugus, CA: Concordant Publishing Concern, 1966. 639 pp.
_____. *Concordant Studies in the Book of Daniel*. Saugus, CA: Concordant Publishing Concern, 1968. 464 pp.
_____. *The Problem of Evil and the Judgments of God*. Canyon Country, CA: Concordant Publishing Concern, 1976. 351 pp.
_____. *Spirit, Spirits and Spirituality*. Canyon Country, CA: Concordant Publishing Concern, 1977. 157 pp.
_____. *The Unveiling of Jesus Christ*. Los Angeles: Concordant Publishing Concern, 1932. 591 pp.
Melton, J. Gordon. *Biographical Dictionary of American Cult and Sect Leaders*. Garland Reference Library of Social Science, vol. 212. New York: Garland Publishing, 1986.
Sloan, Raymond E. Jr. "A History of the Concordant Version," *The Bible Collector* 8 (October-December, 1966): 3-5.
The Story of the Concordant Version. Saugus, CA, N.p. n.d.

—Gary L. Ward

★511★
KNOX, George William
Theologian, Presbyterian Church
b. Aug. 11, 1853, Rome, New York
d. Apr. 25, 1912, Seoul Republic of Korea

George William Knox, a Presbyterian theologian, was the son of a Presbyterian minister, William Eaton Knox, and Alice Woodward Jenckes Knox. He attended Hamilton College, from which he graduated in 1874. He did his seminary work at Union Theological Seminary in New York City, where he specialized in missionary studies. Following his graduation in 1877, he successively married Caroline Holmes, was ordained by the Chemung Presbytery, and sailed for Japan to begin the first phase of his career.

In Japan he applied himself to learning Japanese, and after he finished his language school course, decided not to enter evangelistic work but to teach at Union Theological Seminary in Tokyo. During his 12 years at the seminary he authored a set of texts on various theological topics in Japanese, but showed greater enthusiasm for an analysis and understanding of Japanese religion. He authored three books in English detailing his findings: *Japanese Systems of Ethics* (1886); *The Mystery of Life* (1890); and *A Japanese Philosopher* (1891). Recognizing his outstanding work on Confucianism, the Asiatic Society of Japan elected him vice president (1891-1892) of the organization.

In 1893 Knox returned to the United States and pastored in Rye, New York, for three years before he received an appointment to his alma mater in New York City. He lectured in apologetics for three years before becoming a full professor of philosophy and the history of religions. While at Union he wrote several theological volumes—*The Direct and Fundamental Proofs of the Christian Religion* (1903), the William Taylor Lectures at Yale Divinity School; and *The Gospel of Jesus* (1909)—and was selected to author the entries on Christianity for the 11th edition of the *Encyclopedia Britanica*. However, Knox's major interest continued to be informing his colleagues and the church at large about Japan. His concerns manifested in four additional books: *Japanese Life in Town and Country* (1904); *Imperial Japan: The Country and Its People* (1905); *The Spirit of the Orient* (1906); and *The Development of Religion in Japan* (1907).

In 1911 Knox was commissioned by the seminary to conduct a lecture tour on its behalf in the Orient. He was scheduled to speak in China, Japan, India, and Korea, but he was unable to finish his assignment. While in Korea he became ill and died.

Sources:
Dictionary of American Biography. 20 vols. and 7 supps. New York: Charles Scribner's Sons, 1928-1936, 1944-1981.
Knox, George William. *The Development of Religion in Japan*. New York: G. P. Putnam's Sons, 1907. 204 pp.
_____. *The Direct and Fundamental Proofs of the Christian Religion*. New York: Charles Scribner's Sons, 1903. 196 pp.
_____. *The Gospel of Jesus*. Boston, MA: Houghton, Mifflin and Co., 118 pp.
_____. *The Spirit of the Orient*. New York: T. Y. Crowell, 1906. 311 pp.

★512★
KNUBEL, Frederick Herman
President, United Lutheran Church in America
b. May 22, 1870, New York, New York
d. Oct. 16, 1945, New Rochelle, New York

Lutheran minister Frederick H. Knubel graduated from the Gettysburg Lutheran Seminary in Gettysburg, Pennsylvania, in 1895 and did his graduate work at the University of Leipzig in Germany in the years 1895-1896. He was ordained in 1896 and founded and pastored the Church of the Atonement in New York City from 1896 to 1923. He was the first president of the newly formed United Lutheran Church in America from 1918 to 1936. He was also active in the work of the American Bible Society and the American Tract Society, and was the author and editor of numerous publications.

Beyond his work as president of the ULCA, Knubel is best remembered for his work in the ecumenical movement. He was introduced to formal interdenominational work when he was chosen to head the National Lutheran Commission for Soldiers' and Sailors' Welfare, formed in response to the first world war. Through this organization, 13 Lutheran bodies cooperated to provide a ministry to servicemen. From this activity, he went on to become one of the founders of the National Lutheran Council, which was organized on September 6, 1918, and of the Lutheran World Convention (LWC) meeting in Eisenach, Germany, in 1923. He was vice-president of the latter organization for some years.

When the National Lutheran Council was organized, one of the areas of anticipated cooperation was in establishing a home missions program. There was, however, some apprehension voiced that the program might constitute a form of unionism which would not be acceptable to member churches. After a meeting of a special joint committee, a modified version of a paper presented by Knubel was accepted as the council's official declaration on such cooperative endeavors. The "Washington Declaration" affirmed that the church is one because Christ is one, and that, in spite of differences in their understanding of the Gospel, different church bodies can enter into cooperative programs and organizations, particularly in works of serving love. At the same time, doctrinal differences must be acknowledged and respected. These understandings and other principles of cooperation (such as the stipulation that only *official* representatives of member churches would be recognized), hammered out in inter-Lutheran dialogue, were incorporated into the working principles of the World Council of Churches.

Sources:

Bodensieck, J. *The Encyclopedia of the Lutheran Church*. Vol. 2. Minneapolis, MN: Augsburg Publishing House, 1965.
Flesner, Dorris A. "Frederick H. Knubel: Advocate of Sound Ecumenical Principles." *The Lutheran Historical Conference*. Lutheran Historical Conference, 1968.

★513★
KNUDSON, Albert Cornelius
Theologian and Biblical Scholar, Methodist Episcopal Church
b. Jan. 23, 1873, Grand Meadows, Minnesota
d. Aug. 28, 1953, Cambridge, Massachusetts

Albert Cornelius Knudson, a theologian and biblical scholar in the Methodist Episcopal Church, was born into a Norwegian family, the son of Rev. Asle and Susan Fosse Knudsen. His father was a pioneer in the Norwegian-Danish Conference of the Methodist Episcopal Church. Knudson, who adopted this spelling of his name, attended the University of Minnesota (A.B., 1893) and the School of Theology at Boston University (S.T.B., 1896; Ph.D., 1900). At Boston, he became a close philosophical disciple of **Borden Parker Bowne** and absorbed his personalistic perspective. Between his ministerial program and his doctoral work, he studied in Germany at the universities of Jena (1897) and Berlin (1897-1898).

Upon his return from Germany, while still finishing his doctoral work, Knudson assumed a teaching post at Iliff School of Theology in Denver, Colorado. There he married Mathilda Johnson, a minister's daughter. He moved to Baker University in Baldwin, Kansas, in 1900 and began four years at Allegheny College in Meadville, Pennsylvania, in 1902. He was ordained in 1901.

In 1906 he returned to Boston University as a professor of Hebrew and Old Testament exegesis. He began his duties there just as the battles over the use of higher criticism as a proper means of studying the Bible were at their most intense within Methodism. His major contributions to the debates were *The Old Testament Problem* (1908) and *The Religious Teachings of the Old Testament* (1918). He staunchly defended the use of the higher criticism.

While he achieved a significant position as a biblical scholar, Knudson's real interest, from his days with Bowne, were with the philosophical and theological implications of the Christian faith. Thus, when the opportunity was offered, he changed positions and assumed a professorship in systematic theology. In this capacity he became one of the significant voices in making Bowne's personalism the dominant position in Methodist theology throughout most of the twentieth century. Among his books from this era are *Present Tendencies in Religious Thought* (1924), *The Philosophy of Personalism* (1927), *The Doctrine of God* (1930), *The Doctrine of Redemption* (1933), and *The Validity of Religious Experience* (1937). In 1926 he also became dean of the School of Theology, a post he retained for 12 years.

Knudson was also an active churchman. He transferred into the New England Conference after returning to Boston. He was elected as a delegate to the 1932 and 1936 general conferences and to the uniting conference in 1939 at which the Methodist Episcopal Church merged with the Methodist Episcopal Church, South and the Methodist Protestant Church to form the Methodist Church (1939-1968).

Sources:

Harmon, Nolan B. *The Encyclopedia of World Methodism*. 2 vols. Nashville: United Methodist Publishing House, 1974.
Howell, Clinton H., ed. *Prominent Personalities in Methodism*. Birmingham, AL: Lowrey Press, 1945. 512 pp.
Knudson, Albert C. *Basic Issues in Christian Thought*. New York: Abingdon-Cokesbury Press, 1950. 220 pp.
_____. *The Beacon Lights of Prophecy*. New York: Methodist Book Concern, 1914. 281 pp.
_____. *The Doctrine of Redemption*. New York: Abingdon Press, 1933. 512 pp.
_____. *The Religious Teaching of the Old Testament*. New York: Abingdon Press, 1918. 416 pp.

★514★
KOHLER, Kaufmann
Reform Jewish Rabbi and Educator
b. May 10, 1843, Fuerth Germany
d. Jan. 28, 1926, New York, New York

Kaufmann Kohler, a Reform Jewish rabbi, was the son of Moritz and Babette Loewenmayer Kohler, who raised him in a strict Orthodox Jewish tradition. He developed an early intention to become a rabbi and studied under Samson Raphael Hirsh, a noted Orthodox leader. In 1864 he entered the University of Munich for a year and continued his education at Berlin and Erlangen, from which he received his Ph.D. in 1867. During his university years, however, he had come to believe that Judaism was historically conditioned and that some parts of it were more valuable than others. His doctoral dissertation was a call for the modernization of the Jewish religion in particular, and of all religion in general. He continued his post-graduate work at the University of Leipzig, but unable to secure a rabbinical position in Germany due to his reformist views, in 1867 he accepted a call from Beth-El Congregation in Detroit, Michigan, and moved to the United States, where Reform Judaism had become strong. A year later he married Johanna Einhorn, the sister of another prominent Reform rabbi, David Einhorn.

After two years in Detroit, Kohler was called to Sinai Temple in Chicago, where he began to introduce reform in earnest. In 1874 he instituted Sunday services in addition to the traditional Sabbath worship, the most controversial of his innovations. In 1879 he succeeded David Einhorn, who had recently died, as rabbi of Temple Beth-El in New York. Here he began to introduce further reforms, continuing the program he had begun in Chicago. He met strong opposition, however, from the new immigrants who began to arrive from Eastern Europe. His most decisive opponent was **Alexander Kohut**, whose traditionalist approach would lead to what is today known as Conservative Judaism.

Horrified at the departure from tradition evident in the Reform centers in New York, Kohut issued an attack in a book called *The Ethics of the Fathers* (1885). Kohler saw a need to respond and denounced Kohut's position in *Backwards or Forwards* (1885). He also called a meeting of his rabbinical colleagues, who gathered in November 1885 and issued what has become known as the Pittsburgh Platform, one of the definitive statements of the Reform position. The Platform is somewhat of an embarrassment to twentieth-century Jews for its rejection of Zionism.

Kohler remained in New York for two more decades. He edited the *Jewish Reformer*, beginning in 1886, and worked on the first edition of the *Jewish Encyclopedia*. He was one of the founders and for many years the president of the New York Board of Jewish Ministers, the title of the organization denoting the extent of accommodation Kohler advocated. In 1906 he succeeded **Isaac Mayer Wise** as president of Hebrew Union College in Cincinnati. His presidency was noted for his work in raising the academic standards of the institution. He also authored his most famous book, *Jewish Theology Systematically and Historically Considered* (1910) during his time as president.

Kohler retired in 1921 and moved back to New York, where he lived his last years in the acclaim of an appreciative Reform community. He authored two books during these last years, *Heaven and Hell in Comparative Religion* (1923) and *The Origins of the Synagogue and Church* (1929). A collection of his papers were published posthumously as *Studies, Address, and Personal Papers* (1931), which included a brief autobiographical item.

Sources:

Dictionary of American Biography. 20 vols. and 7 supps. New York: Charles Scribner's Sons, 1928-1936, 1944-1981.
Goldman, Alex J. *Giants of Faith*. New York: Citadel Press, 1964. 349 pp.
Kohler, Kaufmann. *Dr. Kaufmann: Reminiscences of My Early Life*. Cincinnati: The Author, 1918. 12 pp.
_____. *Heaven and Hell in Comparative Religion*. New York: Macmillan Comnpany, 1923. 158 pp.
_____. *Jewish Theology Systematically and Historically Considered*. New York: Macmillan Company, 1918. 505 pp.
_____. *The Origins of the Synagogue and the Church*. New York: Macmillan Company, 1929. 294 pp.
_____. *Studies, Addresses, and Personal Papers*. New York: Alumni Association of Hebrew Union College, 1931. 600 pp.
Landman, Isaac, ed. *Universal Jewish Encyclopedia*. 10 vols. New York: The Universal Jewish Encyclopedia, 1940.
Marx, Robert J. *Kaufmann Kohler as Reformer*. Cincinnati: n.p., 1951. 145 pp.
Oko, Aldolph S. *Bibliography of Rev. Kaufman Kohler, 1867-1913*. Berlin: G. Reimer, 1913. 37 pp.
Singer, Isidore, ed. *The Jewish Encyclopedia*. New York: KTAV Publishing House, 1964.

★515★

KOHUT, Alexander

Conservative Jewish Rabbi and Scholar
b. Apr. 22, 1842, Felegyhaza Hungary
d. May 25, 1894, New York, New York

Alexander Kohut, one of the founders of Conservative Judaism, was the son of Jacob and Cecelia Hoffman Kohut. He was raised in relative poverty in Hungary, and could neither read nor write until around the age of 10 because his parents could not afford a teacher. Once his family moved to Ketskemet, Hungary, however, his education proceeded and he proved an apt pupil. He attended high school in Budapest and attended the University of Leipzig, from which he received his doctorate in languages in 1865. He continued his education at the Jewish Theological Seminary in Breslau, from which he received his rabbinical diploma in 1867, after which he was ordained a rabbi.

Kohut began a career as a rabbi at Stuhlweissenburg (Szekesfehervar), Hungary, but in 1872 he moved to Fuenfkirchen and in 1880 to Groswardein. He became known for his oratorical abilities, and in 1884 he was elected to the Hungarian parliament. The 1880s were a time of massive migration of Eastern Europeans (including Hungarians) to the United States, and before Kohut took his seat in parliament, he was called to New York to become the rabbi of a group of Hungarian Jews, Congregation Ahabath Chesed.

In New York Kohut was almost immediately repulsed by what he saw as the deviation from tradition practiced by the Reform Jewish Movement. He began a series of lectures that became classic statements of the Conservative position which, while allowing for some reform of European Orthodox Jewish practice, did not proceed in the radical direction of the American Reform Movement. The lectures were published as *The Ethics of the Fathers* (1885). The book not only became a significant document defining Conservatism, but forced the Reform advocates to reply, most notably in a volume by Rabbi **Kaufmann Kohler**, and further define their position.

Kohut then joined with Sabato Morais and other traditionalists in 1887 to form the Jewish Theological Seminary. He became the professor of Talmud. Though a better than average speaker, Kohut did not seek the limelight; he settled into a quiet life as a scholar. In 1886 his first wife, Julia Weissbrunn, died and in 1887 he married Rebekah Bettelheim, who would later emerge as a leader among Jewish women. Kohut's life work, however, having already made his mark as a defender of the tradition, was in the production of the *Srukh ha-Shalem*, an eight-volume lexicon of talmudic terms. Four volumes had been published in Hungary prior to his arrival in the United States. He finished the last volume just a few years before his death.

As he approached his fiftieth year, Kohut's health began to fail and he was forced on many occasions to teach from his sick bed. In March 1894 he learned of the death of his friend, Hungarian patriot Louis Kossuth. Against doctor's orders he got out of bed and went to the synagogue and preached a sermon on Kossuth and Judaism. At the end of the sermon he collapsed and was taken home. He lived only a few more weeks.

His family memorialized him through the founding of the Kohut Foundation, which has made major donations to Yale University for its program in Semitic studies.

Sources:

Dictionary of American Biography. 20 vols. and 7 supps. New York: Charles Scribner's Sons, 1928-1936, 1944-1981.
Kohut, Alexander. *The Ethics of the Fathers*. New York: "The American Hebrew," 1885. 188 pp.
Kohut, G. A. *Concerning Alexander Kohut: a Tentative Bibliography*. Budapest: The Author, 1927. 6 pp.
Kohut, Rebekah. *My Portion*. New York: T. Seltzer, 1925. 301 pp.
Landman, Isaac, ed. *Universal Jewish Encyclopedia*. 10 vols. New York: The Universal Jewish Encyclopedia, 1940.
Singer, Isidore, ed. *The Jewish Encyclopedia*. New York: KTAV Publishing House, 1964.

★516★
KOREN, Ulrik Vilhelm
Minister, Norwegian Synod (Lutheran Church)
b. Dec. 22, 1826, Bergen Norway
d. Dec. 20, 1910

Ulrik Vilhelm Koren, one of the most influential Norwegian-American Lutheran ministers in the late nineteenth century, was the son of Paul Schonvig Koren, a sea captain frequently away from home, and Henriette Christine Rulffs Koren. His mother saw to a good education, and in 1844 Ulrik entered the University of Christiania (now Oslo). By the time he finished in 1852, he had received his bachelor's, master's, and theological degrees. He married Else Elisabeth Hysing and taught school for a year, but in 1853 left for America.

Koren arrived in Washington Prairie, a small community in northeast Iowa, on Christmas Eve, 1853, and preached his first sermon the next day. He affiliated with the newly organized Norwegian (Lutheran) Synod, one of eight pastors who together served some 28 congregations. He soon rose to a leading position in the growing synod and was elected its secretary in 1855. The annual meeting of the synod gathered at his church in 1857, and he became most influential in the discussion over the founding of Luther College. He selected the sight at nearby Decorah, Iowa, and nurtured its erection. It opened in 1861.

Koren is remembered as the most eloquent preacher in the Norwegian Synod, his oratorical skills accounting for much of his influence. His pastoral ministry took him over a large part of northeast Iowa, which was just beginning to receive large waves of European immigrants. He developed and served congregations until they could call a pastor. Over 20 separate congregations emerged out of his work. He continued to serve the Washington Prairie congregation for 57 years, marking his work with his annual Christmas sermon which, he never missed.

Within the synod, he held ever more important offices as he matured. In 1871 he became vice president of the synod. After five years he became president of the Iowa district (the synod now reaching across several states). During his time in that office, the college burned to the ground. He exerted his considerable influence to see that it was rebuilt in Decorah rather than being moved to any of the several alternative locations that had been suggested. In 1894 he became president of the synod, a position he retained for the rest of his life.

Koren's active life covered the first generation in which Norwegian Lutherans were establishing their institutional presence in America. The Norwegian Synod was but one of several to emerge in this period. Koren did not live to see these Norwegian bodies consolidate their common work, which occurred in 1917. Today his church, which experienced a series of denominational mergers, is a constituent part of the Evangelical Lutheran Church in America. Koren's sermons and papers were collected and published by his son Paul Koren in a four-volume set, *Samlede Skrifter*, in 1912.

Sources:
Dictionary of American Biography. 20 vols. and 7 supps. New York: Charles Scribner's Sons, 1928-1936, 1944-1981.
Koren, Paul, ed. *Samlede Skrifter*. 4 vols. Decorah, IA: Lutheran Publishing House Drytrykkeri, 1912.
Tolo, Harold M. *U. V. Koren*. Minneapolis: M.A. thesis, University of Minnesota.

★517★
KRAUTH, Charles Porterfield
Theologian, General Council, Lutheran Church in America
b. Mar. 17, 1823, Martinsburg, Virginia
d. Jan. 2, 1883, Philadelphia, Pennsylvania

Charles Porterfield Krauth, the outstanding Lutheran theologian, was the son of one of the most prominent early nineteenth-century Lutheran educators, Charles Philip Krauth (1799-1867), and his wife, Catherine Susan Heiskell. Growing up in the shadow of his father, Krauth received a good education. In 1839 he graduated at the age of 16 from Gettysburg (Pennsylvania) College (of which his father was president) and completed his work at Gettysburg Theological Seminary two years later. He was ordained to the Lutheran ministry and went on to serve a number of small parishes in Maryland and Virginia. In 1844 he married Susan Reynolds. In 1848 he moved to Winchester, Virginia, to begin a seven-year pastorate. While there his wife died, and in 1855 he married Virginia Baker.

At Gettysburg Krauth had studied under Samuel S. Schmucker, the most prominent Lutheran teacher in America in the first half of the nineteenth century. Schmucker was the exponent of a more liberal approach to Lutheranism which emphasized piety and had a rather loose attachment to the Augsburg Confession and the other classical Lutheran doctrinal statements. In his early pastoral years Krauth defended Schmucker's position, but he later began to favor a return to the standards of the Lutheran doctrine and practice outlined in the confessions. This new stance came in part from the influence of his father who urged him to study the works of older European founders of the faith.

Krauth left Winchester, Virginia, for pastorates in Pittsburgh and Philadelphia. These were the years that he came into prominence as the major opponent of his former professor. He contributed a number of articles to the *Evangelical Review*, which came to represent the confessional position. In 1861 he became editor of the *Lutheran and Missionary*, through which he gained an even larger following. In the 1860s the issues between Schmucker and Krauth came to a climax when the Philadelphia Ministerium pulled out of the General Synod and led in the formation of the conservative and German-dominated General Council in 1867. Along the way, the Ministerium lost a fight to control the seminary at Gettysburg and have Krauth installed as the successor of Schmucker. The Lutheran Theological Seminary at Philadelphia, a school attuned to the council's position, was formed and Krauth became its first professor of theology. He held that position for the rest of his life.

Through his writings, most of them brief article-length works, Krauth built a dominance over the thinking of a large segment of Lutheranism that extended well into the twentieth century. His most important book was a compilation of his writings published in 1871, *The Conservative Reformation and Its Theology*. In 1882 he founded and edited the *Lutheran Church Review*, the theological journal most reflective of the confessional theology which he by that time most embodied.

Sources:
Dictionary of American Biography. 20 vols. and 7 supps. New York: Charles Scribner's Sons, 1928-1936, 1944-1981.
Krauth, Charles Porterfield. *The Conservative Reformation and Its Theology*. Philadelphia: J. B. Lippencott & Co., 1871. 840 pp.
Spaeth, Adolph. *Charles Porterfield Krauth*. 2 vols. New York: Christian Literature Company, 1898.

★518★
KRISHNA, Gopi
Founder, Kundalini Research Foundation
b. Jun. 3, 1903, Gairoo India
d. Jul. 31, 1984, Srinigar India

Pandit Gopi Krishna Shivpuri, founder of the Kundalini Research Foundation, was the son of deeply religious Hindu parents. Following an ancient custom, his father renounced the world and became a religious recluse. Partially as a consequence of his father's resolve, Gopi Krishna and his siblings were raised in poverty. He read widely in high school, and reacted against his religious upbringing by becoming an ardent rationalist. When he failed his college exam in 1920, however, he was forced to review his life, and this led him to begin studying yoga and meditation disciplines. From 1923 until 1950 he worked for the government, initially as a clerk in the Irrigation Division, and later in the Education Department. He married at the age of 23, and had three children.

Gopi Krishna meditated every morning from the age of 17 to 34. On Christmas morning of 1934, he experienced a superconscious state that he interpreted as the awakening of kundalini. According to the tradition of Hindu yoga, the kundalini is a dormant energy that is normally "asleep" at the base of the spine. Through special yoga practices, the energy can be "awakened," drawn up the spine (actually, up a channel in the subtle body corresponding with the spine), and directed into the centers of higher awareness (the chakras) in the head. In Gopi Krishna's case, unfortunately, the kundalini rose up a side channel (the pingala) rather than up the main central channel (the sushumna), and as a consequence he began to experience severe health problems.

Going from one yogi to another, he was unable to find anyone who could help relieve his condition. Gopi Krishna was eventually able to harmonize this strange force, but not before concluding that true knowledge about the nature of kundalini had been forgotten long ago. He therefore resolved to devote the rest of his life to the investigation of the kundalini energy, and founded the Kundalini Research Foundation to further this research. He asserted that "This mechanism, known as kundalini, is the real cause of all genuine spiritual and psychic phenomenon; the biological basis of evolution and development of personality; the secret origin of all esoteric and occult doctrines; the master key to the unsolved mystery of creation; the inexhaustible source of philosophy, art and science; and the fountainhead of all religious faiths, past, present and future" (Introduction to *The Inner World*). Gopi Krishna believed that the physical aspects of an aroused kundalini could be studied scientifically, and cooperated with scientists for this purpose. He was not interested in establishing a religious group with himself at the head. He lived simply, and seldom made public appearances beyond his contact with scientists and co-workers. Gopi Krishna was also socially active with the Samaj Sundhar Samiti organization, which aimed at such reforms as the abolition of the dowry system. He wrote extensively, both on the kundalini as well as on his visions of forthcoming world disasters. His titles include, *The Biological Basis of Religion and Genius* (1971), *The Secret of Yoga* (1972), *The Awakening of Kundalini* (1975), and *The Shape of Events to Come* (1979).

Sources:
Shepard, Leslie. "About Gopi Krishna and His Work." N.p., n.d. 5 pp.
Krishna, Gopi. *The Awakening of Kundalini*. New York: E. P. Dutton & Co., 1975. 129 pp.
_____. *The Biological Basis of Religion and Genius*. New York: Harper & Row, 1972. 118 pp.
_____. *The Inner World*. Toronto, Ontario: Kundalini Research Institute of Canada, n.d. 12 pp.
_____. *The Riddle of Consciousness*. New York: Kundalini Research Foundation, 1976. 156 pp.
_____. *The Secret of Yoga*. New York: Harper & Row, 1972. 207 pp.
_____. *The Shape of Events to Come*. New Delhi, India: Kundalini Research and Publication Trust, 1979. 201 pp.
_____. *The Wonder of the Brain*. Noroton Heights, CT: Kundalini Research Foundation, 1987. 116 pp.

—James R. Lewis

★519★
KRISHNAMURTI, Jiddu
Teacher, Krishnamurti Foundation
b. May 11, 1895, Madanapalle India
d. Feb. 17, 1986, Ojai, California

Jiddu Krishnamurti was an independent spiritual teacher and the inspiration behind the Krishnamurti Foundation. He was the eighth child of a family of Telugu-speaking Brahmins. His great-grandfather had been a Sanskrit scholar who had held a position in the East India Company; his grandfather had been a civil servant; and his father worked as an official in the Revenue Department in the British administration. Both parents were interested in Theosophy, his father having been a member of the society since 1882. Krishnamurti's mother, Sanjeevamma, died in 1905. His father, Narianiah, retired at the end of 1907, and subsequently arranged to work full-time for the Theosophical Society in exchange for free accommodation for himself and his four sons.

Annie Besant, the leader of the society at the time, had predicted the coming in the flesh of a new world teacher. One of Besant's close associates, **Charles Webster Leadbeater**, was living in Adyar and became interested in Krishnamurti's potential as a spiritual teacher. Leadbetter convinced Besant that Krishnamurti was the vehicle for the Avatar (divine incarnation), and Besant established an organization, the Order of the Star of the East, to promote him. This project encountered a number of difficulties, the last of which proved fatal to the Order. Krishnamurti's father began to demand the return of his son. The German lodges under the leadership of **Rudolf Steiner** defected from the Society over the issue of Besant's promotion of Krishnamurti as the new Christ. In 1927 Krishnamurti rejected the messiah role in which he had been cast. The last action alienated Krishnamurti from most Theosophists, and he was subsequently on his own.

Krishnamurti soon established himself as an independent teacher, writing and lecturing to promote his viewpoint. Though somewhat difficult to summarize, in many ways, Krishnamurti's thought is close to the spirit of Zen, in the sense that he emphasizes that "truth" or "reality" is experienced through a wordless awareness of the present moment. Freedom lies in being open to the now, unburdened by the weight of our prior conditioning. While these understandings are universal in the world's mystical traditions, most other teachings include such metaphysical elements as detailed descriptions of how the larger cosmos works. (Theosophy is particularly rich in this type of metaphysical development.) Krishnamurti's teaching, by way of contrast, dispenses entirely with this kind of high-flying metaphysics, and concentrates on immediate experience. A series of foundations were established around the world to support Krishnamurti's teaching activities, and many of his lectures have been transcribed and published. His mature life was spent in constant movement among his students in Asia, North America, and Europe.

Sources:
Fouere, Rene. *Krishnamurti: The Man and His Teaching*. Bombay, India: Chetana, 1950. 7th ed., 1973. 86 pp.
Jayakar, Pupul. *Krishnamurti: A Biography*. San Francisco: Harper & Row, 1986. 516 pp.
Krishnamurti, Jiddu. *Commentaries on Living*. 3 vols. Wheaton, IL: Theosophical Publishing House, 1956-1960.
_____. *Education and the Significance of Life*. New York: Harper & Row, 1953. 125 pp.
_____. *The First and Last Freedom*. Wheaton, IL: Theosophical Publishing House, 1954. 288 pp.

_____. *Life Ahead.* London, England: Victor Gollancz, 1963. 191 pp.
_____. *Life in Freedom.* New York: Horace Liveright, 1928. 96 pp.
_____. *Talks with American Students.* Berkeley, CA: Shambhala Publications, 1970. 182 pp.
Lutyens, Lady Emily. *Candles in the Sun.* Philadelphia: J. B. Lippincott, 1957. 196 pp.
Lutyens, Mary. *Krishnamurti: The Years of Awakening.* New York: Farrar, Straus and Giroux, 1975. 326 pp.

—*James R. Lewis*

★520★
KROL, John Joseph
Cardinal, Roman Catholic Church
b. Oct. 26, 1910, Cleveland, Ohio

John Joseph Krol, a cardinal of the Roman Catholic Church, was the son of Anna Pietruszka and John Krol. He attended St. Mary's College in Orchard Lake, Michigan, and St. Mary's Seminary in Cleveland, Ohio, where he majored in canon law. He was ordained in 1937 and in 1938 he began two years of study at Gregorian University in Rome. He finished with a doctorate from Catholic University in Washington, D.C., in 1942. He taught canon law at St. Mary's Seminary for a year and then in 1943 became vice-chancellor of the diocese of Cleveland. During his tenure he also served a term as president of the Canon Law Society of the United States. In 1951 he was named chancellor of the diocese of Cleveland.

In 1953 Krol became auxiliary bishop of Cleveland. He served in that position until 1961 when to the surprise of most he was named archbishop of Philadelphia. He was named an undersecretary for the Second Vatican Council and worked closely with the conservative Archbishop Pericle Felici. At the council he leaned in a conservative direction on most issues but was a staunch supporter of the document which proclaimed the Jews innocent of killing Christ. From his work as a canon lawyer, he took a strong position on keeping the rules concerning marriage, especially those related to marriage between Roman Catholic and non-Roman Catholic Christians. He was named a cardinal in 1967.

During the 1970s he emerged as a conservative voice against that of fellow cardinal **John Francis Dearden**. In 1976 Dearden had organized a massive conference of Roman Catholics to prepare a set of documents to be given to the church as a "Call to Action." The documents called for female priests, public accounting of church finances, and a local voice in the choosing of bishops. Krol found the proposals offensive and was a major force in stalling any response on the part of the American hierarchy to the documents.

Krol's lengthy leadership of the Philadelphia archdiocese has provided a firm base of support for his conservative opinions. He became known for his strong support of both Pope Paul VI and Pope John Paul II. He did join with the American bishops in their opposition to capital punishment and gave strong support to the papal encyclical *Humanae Vitae* and his opposition to abortion.

Sources:
The American Catholic Who's Who. Washington, DC: National Catholic News Service, 1979.
Biography Index. New York: The H. W. Wilson Co.
The Blue Book. New York: St. Martin's Press, 1976.
Current Biography Yearbook. New York: H. W. Wilson Co.
Who's Who in America. Wilmette, IL: Marquis Who's Who, Inc.

★521★
KUHLMAN, Kathryn
Founder, Kathryn Kuhlman Foundation
b. May 7, 1907, Concordia, Missouri
d. Feb. 20, 1976, Tulsa, Oklahoma

Kathryn Kuhlman was one of the best known spiritual healers of the twentieth century and founder of the Kathryn Kuhlman Foundation. She was born in Concordia, Missouri, where her father was mayor. She attended both her father's Methodist church and her mother's Baptist church. At the age of 14 she experienced conversion while sitting in the Methodist worship and became increasingly interested in religion. After her sophomore year of high school, she dropped out and went westward, soon preaching primarily to Baptist groups around Idaho, as the Methodists did not yet allow women to preach.

She eventually did some preaching in Denver, Colorado, and became well known enough to be asked to be the pastor of the independent Denver Revival Tabernacle. She agreed and was ordained by the Evangelical Church Alliance. In 1938, when Kuhlman invited evangelist Burroughs Waltrip to preach at the tabernacle, he became so enamored of her that he divorced his wife and married her. Unfortunately, their divorce several years later destroyed the congregation. At that point, Kuhlman moved to pastor a small church in Franklin, Pennsylvania. On her third night there, a woman reported that the previous evening she had felt God move through her, and that she had been healed of a tumor. Several months later a man was similarly healed of blindness. Kuhlman shifted her ministry to include this healing aspect, and her following began to grow rapidly.

In 1947, Kuhlman moved her services to Pittsburgh and rented the Carnegie Auditorium from the city. Soon she was also holding weekly services in Youngstown, Ohio, and monthly services in Los Angeles, California. She was a widely sought-after speaker and healer across the country, connecting with such groups as the International Full Gospel Businessmen's Fellowship. A radio ministry was begun, and expanded across North America. In 1962 she published a book recounting the healings in her ministry, *I Believe in Miracles*, which became a best-seller and brought her nationwide recognition. This popular acquaintance was significantly bolstered by a weekly television show she began in the mid-1960s, which continued until her death. She also started the Kathryn Kuhlman Foundation, which organized foreign missions, two overseas radio stations, food assistance, and ministries such as Teen Challenge, led by Pentecostal minister **David Wilkerson**.

Kuhlman was known for her flamboyant style, energetic presence, and speaking ability. Unlike most Pentecostal healing services, she did not have the sick come forth for healings, but only allowed the already healed to come forward. She died in 1976, at the age of 68, after a long struggle with heart disease. Her foundation did not long survive her, but her work is being perpetuated by Florida Pentecostal minister, **Benny Hinn**.

Sources:
Casdorph, H. Richard. *The Miracles.* Plainfield, NJ: Logos International, 1976. 173 pp.
Hosier, Helen Kooiman. *Kathryn Kuhlman.* Old Tappan, NJ: Fleming H. Revell, 1976.
Kuhlman, Kathryn. *God Can Do It Again.* Englewood Cliffs, NJ: Prentice-Hall, 1969.
_____. *I Believe in Miracles.* Englewood Cliffs, NJ: Prentice-Hall, 1962.
_____. *Nothing Is Impossible with God.* Englewood Cliffs, NJ: Prentice-Hall, 1974.
_____. *10,000 Miles for a Miracle.* Minneapolis, MN: Dimension Books, 1974. 91 pp.
_____. *Twilight and Dawn.* Minneapolis, MN: Dimension Books, 1976. 94 pp.

Melton, J. Gordon. *Biographical Dictionary of American Cult and Sect Leaders*. Garland Reference Library of Social Science, vol. 212. New York: Garland Publishing, 1986.

Nolen, William A. *Healing: A Doctor in Search of a Miracle*. New York: Random House, 1974. 308 pp.

Spraggett, Allen. *Kathryn Kuhlman, the Woman Who Believes in Miracles*. New York: 1970.

—Gary L. Ward

★ 522 ★
KUSHI, Michio
Founder, East West Foundation
b. 1926, Wakayama Province Japan

Michio Kushi, teacher of macrobiotics and the founder of the East West Foundation, is the son of a university professor who provided his son with a good education. Too young for the draft, Kushi was able to spend much of World War II at Tokyo University. Soon after the war he encountered the two movements which were to help structure the rest of his life. He became involved with the World Federalist Movement, a utopian movement for world peace. He also met George Ohsawa, the creator of the philosophy of macrobiotics, an ideology which advocates a vegetarian diet and a spiritual world view based upon ancient oriental beliefs and practices as refined in the nineteenth and twentieth centuries. After studying with Ohsawa, in 1949 Kushi was able to arrange a trip to America through the efforts of the World Federalist Movement. He became a student at Columbia and began to organize a small macrobiotics movement. He was joined by another of Ohsawa's students, Tomoko Yokohama. They were eventually married and she today goes by the name Aveline Kushi.

Through the 1950s and into the mid-1960s the Kushis worked with Herman Aihara and his wife Cornelia to build the Ohsawa Foundation. Then in 1965, a woman following the most strict form of the macrobiotic diet died. A scandal followed and in the wake of the tragedy many withdrew their support from Kushi's endeavor. Aihara moved the foundation to California. Kushi decided to start afresh in Boston, Massachusetts.

In their new home, Aveline Kushi founded Erewhon Trading Company to provide macrobiotic foods and supplies while Kushi opened the East West Foundation and an educational organization to teach macrobiotics, and as part of the educational program launched a magazine, *The Order of the Universe*. In 1968 a macrobiotic restaurant was opened. A second periodical, of more general interest, *East West Journal*, began in 1970. From these small beginnings Kushi has emerged as the most creative and popular successor to Ohsawa.

In 1975 Kushi began summer resident courses for his more advanced students. Two years later he founded the Kushi Institute, primarily to train macrobiotic teachers. That same year he authored *The Book of Macrobiotics*, a survey of his thought which has become a primary textbook of the movement. In 1979 he led the first North American Macrobiotics Conference. During the 1980s, the movement has continued to prosper. The peace theme reemerged as an important visible aspect of the work when, in 1986, Kushi began the One Peaceful World campaign. Kushi has argued that peace really begins with individuals and local communities rather than politicians and governments. As individuals adopt a more natural peaceful lifestyle, peace will emerge.

Sources:
Kotsch, Ronald E. *Macrobiotics Yesterday and Today*. Tokyo: Japan Publications, 1985. 292 pp.

Kushi, Michio. *The Book of Macrobiotics*. Tokyo: Japan Publications, 1977. 182 pp. Rev. ed.: 1987. 371 pp.

———. *The Macrobiotic Way*. Wayne, NJ: Avery Publishing Group., 1985. 251 pp.

———. *Natural Healing through Macrobiotics*. Tokyo: Japan Publications, 1978. 204 pp.

———. *Oriental Diagnosis*. London: Red Moon Publications, 1976. 80 pp.

———. *The Origin and Destiny of Man*. Boston: East West Foundation, 1971. 140 pp.

★ 523 ★
LAKE, John Graham
Pentecostal Healer and Founder of several Apostolic churches
b. Mar. 18, 1870, St. Mary's, Ontario, Canada
d. Sep. 16, 1935, Spokane, Washington

John Graham Lake was an early Pentecostal healer and the founder of a number of Apostolic churches on the West Coast. He was the sixteenth child of a Methodist family in Canada. The family moved to Michigan in 1886. Four years later, at the age of 20, Lake moved to Chicago. The following year he became a minister with the Methodist Episcopal Church. Instead of taking a church position, however, he started a newspaper and dabbled in the insurance business. He married Jenny Stevens in 1898, and about that time he became interested in the tabernacle and healing home built in Chicago by **John Alexander Dowie**, the healer and moralist who founded the Christian Catholic Church. Lake became a devoted believer when his invalid brother, cancer-stricken sister, and new wife with tuberculosis and heart trouble were all cured.

These experiences ordered his life for the next several years. He moved to Zion, Illinois, where Dowie built his model community, and worked as the manager of the building department. He also maintained his insurance business on the side. In 1904, as Zion slid into financial ruin, Lake moved back to Chicago, expanded his business enterprises, and gained a seat on the Chicago Board of Trade. He also worked as a lay healing evangelist at **W. H. Durham**'s North Avenue Mission. When Durham received the gift of speaking in tongues in 1907—a gift spreading rapidly from its beginning at the Azusa Street revival in Los Angeles in 1906—Lake received it shortly thereafter.

This new combination of being both a healer and a Pentecostalist rejuvenated Lake's religious enthusiasm, and he gave away all his money to go to Africa as a missionary with other Pentecostals in 1908. In South Africa he helped establish the Apostolic Faith Mission in 1910 and became the pastor of the Apostolic Tabernacle in Johannesburg. In 1912 his wife died while he was on an expedition into the Kalahari Desert, and he decided to return to the United States. There he married Florence Switzer in 1913, and in 1914 founded the Apostolic Church in Spokane, Washington. This church served as headquarters for his various evangelistic efforts, which resulted in an Apostolic Church in Portland, Oregon, in 1920 and another later in San Diego, California. Among the converts in Portland was **Gordon Lindsey**, who became a major figure in Pentecostal healing in the 1950s. Lake died in 1935 at the age of 65.

Sources:
Hollenweger, Walter J. *The Pentecostals*. Minneapolis, MN: Augsberg Press, 1972.

Lake, John Graham. *Adventures in God*. Tulsa, OK: Harrison House, 1981. 131 pp.

———. *The John G. Lake Sermons on Dominion Over Demons, Disease and Death*. Gordon Lindsey, ed. Dallas: Voice of Healing Publishing Co., 1949. 144 pp.

———. *The New John G. Lake Sermons*. Gordon Lindsey, ed. Dallas: Christ for the Nations, n.d. 61 pp.

———. *Spiritual Hunger, The God-Men, and Other Sermons*. Gordon Lindsey, ed. Dallas: Christ for the Nations, 1976. 103 pp.

Lindsey, Gordon. *The Gordon Lindsey Story*. Dallas: Voice of Healing Publishing Co., n.d. [1970].

Melton, J. Gordon. *Biographical Dictionary of American Cult and Sect Leaders*. Garland Reference Library of Social Science, vol. 212. New York: Garland Publishing, 1986.

—*Gary L. Ward*

★524★
LAMONT, Corliss
Humanist Leader
b. Mar. 28, 1902, Englewood, New Jersey

Corliss Lamont, a Humanist spokesperson possibly best known for his efforts in defense of civil liberties, was the son of Florence Corliss and Thomas W. Lamont. His father was a successful banker who rose to become the chairman of the board of J. P. Morgan & Co. Lamont's childhood was spent in Englewood, New Jersey, a Manhattan suburb, though the family moved to Manhattan when he was 13 years old. Wealth and his own abilities opened educational doors to Lamont, who attended Phillips Exeter Academy (1916-1920) and Harvard College (1920-1924). Following his graduation *magne cum laude*, he spent a year at new College Oxford during which time he roomed at the home of Julian Huxley, a prominent British humanist. In 1925 he returned to the United States and attended Columbia to work on his Ph.D.

In 1928, having finished his class work, Lamont became an instructor in philosophy at Columbia and that same year married Margaret Hayes Irish. In 1932 he completed his Ph.D. with a dissertation on the question of immortality. That same year he resigned his post at Columbia. Given a legacy by his father, he was able to devote the majority of his time to his intellectual pursuits and several causes near to his heart. He became a member of the board of the American Civil Liberties Union (A.C.L.U.). His maturing thought was focused in humanism and socialism, neither of which were popular perspectives in America, and he was frequently accused of being a communist.

Lamont's philosophical speculation led him to the conclusion that this life is all there is. This opinion was firmly stated in his first major book, *The Illusion of Immortality* (1935). He had not signed the original "Humanist Manifesto" issued in 1933, though he agreed with most of its statements, but he did become a charter member of the American Humanist Association, founded in 1941, and wrote frequently for the *American Humanist*, the association's magazine.

Through the 1940s and 1950s, Lamont was publicly identified with the American Civil Liberties Union. He was also identified with the National Council of Soviet-American Friendship and authored several books on post-Revolutionary Russia. Thus in 1946 it was no surprise when he came into open conflict with the House Committee on Un-American Activities. This conflict led to a direct confrontation with Senator Joseph McCarthy. The battle ended in the courts with Lamont the victor. As the fight was culminating, Lamont was completing possibly his most important statement of humanist belief, *Humanism as a Philosophy* (1952).

In 1962 Lamont divorced his wife and a short time later married Helen Boyden Lamb. In 1973 he was one of more than 200 individuals who signed "Humanist Manifesto II," an updated revision of the 1933 document. The following year he was named honorary president of the American Humanist Association and in 1977 was named Humanist of the Year. Among his last writings was an autobiography, *Yes to Life* (1981).

Sources:

Lamont, Corliss. *Humanism as a Philosophy*. New York: Philosophical Library, 1952. rev. ed. as *The Philosophy of Humanism*. New York; Frederick Ungar Publishing Co., 1965.
_____. *The Illusion of Immortality*. New York: G. P. Putnam's Sons, 1935.
_____. *The Independent Mind*. New York: Horizon Press, 1951.

_____. *The Peoples of the Soviet Union*. New York: Harcourt Brace & Co., 1946.
_____. *Yes to Life*. New York: Horizon Press, 1981. 220 pp.
Wittenberg, Philip, ed. *The Lamont Case: History of a Congressional Investigation*. New York: Horizon Press, 1957.

★525★
LAMSA, George Mamishisho
Independent Bible Scholar
b. Aug. 5, 1890, Kurdistan Turkey
d. Sep. 22, 1975

George Mamishisho Lamsa, an independent Bible scholar best known for his translation of the Assyrian text of the Bible (the Peshitta) into English, was the son of Jando Pesah and Sarah Pesah Yokhanan Lamsa, members of a nomadic shepherding tribe. His exact birth date is unknown, there being no calendars among his people. He attended a Presbyterian grammar school and later entered the Archbishop of Canterbury's College, a Church of England institution in Urmiah, Persia (now Reza'iyeh, Iran), from which he graduated in 1907. He attained his doctorate in 1908 from the Archbishop of Canterbury's College in Van, Turkey. When World War I began, he left Turkey for South America. In 1917 he immigrated to New York. Going through customs he adopted an Anglicized name in part from a man named George he met at Ellis Island and the name of his tribe, Masisho.

After the war ended in 1918, Lamsa asked the Episcopal bishop in New York for assistance in furthering his education. Thus he obtained a scholarship to attend the Virginia Theological Seminary and earned extra money working as a translator. He graduated in 1921 and went to work as a lecturer. His first book, *The Secret of the Near East*, appeared in 1923. In 1925 he became the field secretary of the Archbishop of Canterbury's Assyrian Mission in the United States, which involved him in raising money to rebuild schools and colleges in post-War Turkey and Iran.

During his early years in America Lamsa became the advocate of the idea that the New Testament was originally written in Aramaic, the language Jesus and his 12 disciples actually spoke, rather than Greek, as is commonly believed. He argued that much of the New Testament cannot be understood except in relation to the metaphors of the Aramaic tongue. He developed his arguments in this matter in a series of books, beginning with *The Oldest Christian People* (1926) and *The Origin of the Gospel* (1927). His writing effort had been underwritten by businessman William Wood. He also began to work on a translation of the Aramaic (Peshitta) text, one of the oldest manuscripts of the Bible (though not as old as some of the Greek texts). The translation of *The Four Gospels* appeared in 1933 and the complete Bible in 1957.

In 1943 Lamsa founded the Aramaic Bible Society through which he worked to complete his translation and to produce his many books. As a whole, his ideas were never accepted by Bible scholars. Lamsa never joined a particular church, in spite of his close association with the Episcopal Church for many years. In his mature years as a controversial Bible scholar, he did influence a number of leaders of diverse religious movements, from **Victor Paul Wierwille** of The Way International to the leaders of the Unity School of Christianity. Through one of his students, Rocco Errico, an independent metaphysical minister, his translation has become popular in both Unity and Religious Science churches. Unity published one of his last books, *The Kingdom on Earth* (1966).

Sources:

Lamsa, George M. *Gospel Light*. Philadelphia: A. J. Holman, 1926. 408 pp.
_____. *The Holy Bible from the Peshitta*. Philadelphia: A. J. Holman, 1957.
_____. *The Kingdom on Earth*. Lee's Summit, MO: Unity Books, 1966. 192 pp.

_____. *The Life of George M. Lamsa, Translator*. Tom Aleya, ed. St. Petersburg, FL: Aramaic Bible Society,   1975   24 pp.

_____. *My Neighbor Jesus*. Philadelphia: Aramaic Research, 1932. 148 pp.

_____. *The Oldest Christian People*. New York: Macmillan Publishers, 1926.

_____. *The Origin of the Gospel*. New York: Winston, 1927.

★526★
LANDAS BERGHES, Prince Rudolph Francis Edward de
Cofounder, North American Old Roman Catholic Church (N.A.O.R.C.C.)
b. Nov. 1, 1873, Naples Italy
d. Nov. 17, 1920, Philadelphia, Pennsylvania

Prince Rudolph Francis Edward de Landas Berghes, co-founder of the North American Old Roman Catholic Church (N.A.O.R.C.C.), was born to Austrian nobility. He was educated at the Universities of Paris and Cambridge, and received a Ph.D. from the University of Brussels. He served with the British Army, and was on Lord H. H. Kitchener's staff in the Sudan around 1911. He retired in England with the rank of lieutenant colonel, and then sought ordination at the hands of Old Catholic Bishop Arnold Harris Mathew, who adhered to pre-Vatican I (1870) Roman Catholicism. Vatican I was the Council that declared the pope's infallibility when speaking ex cathedra. De Landas Berghes, Matthew and others were against such actions by the Council as they considered them to be unwarranted innovations. These alienated feelings were exacerbated by actions that the Roman Catholic Church took in Austria to prevent the growth and continuity of the Old Catholic movement.

De Landas Berghes was ordained a priest by Matthew in 1912, attained the level of bishop in 1913, and was assigned to develop believers in Scotland. Before that work could begin, however, England went to war with Austria and needed to deal with the presence of such a prominent Austrian as de Landas Berghes. They decided to send him to America rather than put him in prison, and he arrived in New York on November 7, 1914. He immediately went to the Old Catholic Abbey in Waukegan, Illinois, and visited its leader, William H. F. Brothers. He also communicated with another Old Catholic priest, **Carmel Henry Carfora**, and related well with the Episcopal Church, even helping consecrate H. R. Hulse, the new Episcopal bishop of Cuba, in 1915.

De Landas Berghes planned to create an American branch of Matthew's church, and to that end ordained Brothers and Carfora in October 1916, as bishops to work with him. Brothers broke away in a matter of weeks, and in 1917 de Landas Berghes and Carfora joined their jurisdictions (largely on paper) as the North American Old Roman Catholic Diocese. After two more years of unsuccessful work and another failed partnership (with Stanislaus Mickiewicz, who briefly replaced Brothers), de Landas Berghes became too frustrated to continue. On December 22, 1919 he resigned from the church and resubmitted himself to the Roman Catholic Church at St. Patrick's Cathedral in New York City.

Part of the agreement de Landas Berghes made with the Roman Catholic Church was that he would retire and join an order, but would still be recognized as a bishop. In 1920 he became a novice with the Order of Saint Augustine and was appointed to teach French at Villanova University near Philadelphia. Meanwhile, Carfora was in charge of the other work, now called the North American Old Roman Catholic Church. However, no acknowledgment of de Landas Berghes' status as bishop was forthcoming from Rome, and he felt betrayed. He informed Carfora of his intention to return to the N.A.O.R.C.C., but died on November 17, 1920, at the age of 47, before the two could meet. His legacy as the man, who along with **J. R. Vilatte** pioneered the introduction of Old Catholicism into the United States, remains.

Sources:

Anson, Peter F. *Bishops At Large*. London, England: Faber and Faber, 1964. 593 pp.

Melton, J. Gordon. *Biographical Dictionary of American Cult and Sect Leaders*. Garland Reference Library of Social Science, vol. 212. New York: Garland Publishing, 1986.

Pruter, Karl and J. Gordon Melton. *The Old Catholic Sourcebook*. New York: Garland Publishing Company, 1983. 254 pp.

Trela, Jonathan. *A History of the North American Old Roman Catholic Church*. Scranton, PA: The Author, 1979. 124 pp.

—Gary L. Ward

★527★
LANDONE, Brown
New Thought Metaphysical Teacher
Founder, Landone Foundation
b. Mar. 6, 1847
d. Oct. 10, 1945, Winter Park, Florida

Brown Landone, popular independent New Thought writer and lecturer, was born to British parents (of French descent) while they were on an ocean voyage. He grew up in England and studied for the priesthood in the Church of England. Shortly after completing his divinity studies, however, he decided to study medicine. He left the ministry, finished his medical degree, and became a doctor, specializing in neurology (or what today would be termed psychiatry). Landone married and had four sons, all of whom were killed in war. As a result he developed a passion for peace and worked on a plan for a United States of Europe, a plan abandoned when World War I began.

Landone spent the years just prior to World War I in France, and he became the president of the International Institute of the Science of the Arts in Paris. One year he lectured in the Sorbonne (1913-1914). After the war started he was appointed as a special ambassador to the United States by the president of France.

Landone remained in the United States after the war. Professionally, he served as a consultant to several corporations. In 1930 he moved to Hollywood. He began to write metaphysical books and to associate with the New Thought Alliance (INTA); International. Among his first books were *How to Turn Your Desires and Ideals into Realities* (1922); *The Methods of Truth Which I Use* (1924); and *The Success Principle* (1927). All of these titles were expositions of what is generally termed "prosperity consciousness" and grew out of questions concerning business success. A number of his early books were printed by Milton H. Smith, owner of the American Book Co. in Louisville, Kentucky.

In 1938 Landone moved to Winter Park, Florida, where he resided for the rest of his life. In his 90s he founded the Landone Foundation, through which he published and distributed a large number of books, booklets, and lessons in metaphysical subjects, many of which presented a unique perspective in combining his medical and anatomical knowledge with New Thought. Among his titles from these retiring years are *Prophecies of Melchi-zedek in the Seven Temples* (1940); *What to Do With Truth Now* (1944); and *Your Path Direct to the Goal You Desire* (n.d.). He also never lost his interest in the cause of peace; among his final publications was a booklet, *The Golden Continent Rising Out of the Seas of War* (n.d.).

Landone was succeeded by his long-time colleague Clark Maxwell, who put several of Londone's books (compiled from his correspondence lessons) into print posthumously.

Sources:

Landone, Brown. *The Golden Continent Rising Out of the Seas of War*. Orlando, FL: Landone Foundation, n.d. 31 pp.

_____. *How to Turn Your Desires and Ideals into Realities*. Brookline, MA: Elizabeth Towne Co., 1924. 157 pp.

_____. *The Methods of Truth Which I Use*. Holyoke, MA: Elizabeth Towne Co., 1928. 102 pp.

_____. *Prophecies of Melchi-zedek in the Seven Temples*. Orlando, FL: Landone Foundation, 1940. 202 pp.

_____. *The Success Process*. 1927. Albuquerque, NM: Sun Books, 1981. 233 pp.

_____. *Transformation of Your Life in Twenty-four Hours*. Louisville, KY: American Book Society, 1947. 40 pp.

★528★
LANE, Isaac
Bishop, Christian Methodist Episcopal Church
b. Mar. 3, 1834, Jackson, Tennessee
d. Dec. 5, 1937, Jackson, Tennessee

Isaac Lane, for over half a century a bishop of the Christian Methodist Episcopal Church (at the time known as the Colored Methodist Episcopal Church), was born in slavery. His mother, Rachel, was married to another slave, Josh. However, Lane's father was a white man, Cullen Lane, who owned Rachel. As a youth, Isaac adopted the name of his white father, and grew up on the Lane farm near Jackson, Tennessee. As a young man, he stole a book and taught himself to read. In 1854 he married Francis Anne Boyce, a slave at a neighboring farm. Soon afterward he had his first Christian experience and he joined the Methodist Episcopal Church, South. He was licensed to exhort in 1856, but no further action was taken until after the war when the Methodist Episcopal Church, South began to establish all-black conferences as it considered the future of its black members.

In 1866 he was ordained deacon and elder in the newly formed Tennessee/North Alabama/North Mississippi Conference and at the close of the conference session was appointed presiding elder of the Jackson District, which covered western Tennessee. By 1870 a decision had been made to form the Colored Methodist Episcopal Church, and Lane became a delegate to the first general conference. He was appointed to Liberty Christian Methodist Episcopal Church Church in Jackson which he served as pastor for the next three years. In 1872, Bishop R. H. Vanderhorst died, and at a special session of the general conference in 1873 Lane was elected bishop. He was assigned as a missionary bishop to organize the work in Texas, Oklahoma, and Louisiana, and as his duties in Tennessee allowed, during the year he traveled westward to form conferences and start churches.

With the general conference of 1874 Lane began to work for the formation of a school to train ministers and educate lay people. He initiated the process of raising money for the school and gaining the support of the leaders of the Methodist Episcopal Church, South. Finally, in 1882 the school opened as the Christian Methodist Episcopal Church High School in Jackson with Lane sitting on the board of trustees. In 1885 it was renamed Lane Institute. In 1888 he oversaw the addition of a theological school to the institute. Through the years Lane was its main fund raiser, and he made the school a matter of constant concern during his episcopal travels. In 1896 it was renamed Lane College. By the early years of the new century, he believed he had given the school a sound financial basis and could return to missionary activity and organizing new congregations. However, in 1904, much of the school was destroyed in a fire, and he had to return to fund-raising to rebuild.

In 1896 his first wife died. The following year he married Mary Elizabeth Long Smith. In 1914 he formally retired from active ministry, but used his retirement years to do some of the missionary work so dear to his heart. He organized churches throughout Ohio, Missouri, and Illinois, which would in later decades become the base for the national spread of the church.

Lane lived to be 103 years old. He died of a stroke in his home in Jackson.

Sources:

Lakey, Othal Hawthorne. *The History of the Christian Methodist Episcopal Church Church*. Memphis, TN: The Christian Methodist Episcopal Church Publishing House, 1985.

Lane, Isaac. *Autobiography*. Nashville, TN: Methodist Publishing House, 1916. 192 pp.

Savage, Horace C. *Life and Times of Bishop Isaac Lane*. Nashville, TN: National Publication Company, 1958. 240 pp.

★529★
LARD, Moses
Minister and Editor, Churches of Christ
b. Jan. 29, 1818, Shelbyville, Tennessee
d. Jun. 17, 1880, Lexington, Kentucky

Moses Lard was one of the most important figures in the second generation of the Christian Church (Disciples of Christ) Restoration Movement begun by Barton Stone and Alexander Campbell. He was the son of Leaven Lard, who died when Moses was nine years old. After his father's death, he was forced to leave home and make his own way in the world. He thus had almost no schooling, and as a teenager he taught himself how to write. He married and had several children and became a tailor. Through reading the *Gospel Restored* by Walter Scott, an early Disciples of Christ minister he was converted. Through the kindness of General Alexander Donipahn, in 1845 Lard was sent to Bethany College, the school in Kentucky established by Alexander Campbell. He finished with honors in 1848, and became a minister in the Disciples of Christ, and during the 1850s served churches in Missouri.

Lard's first venture into writing came in 1857 when he wrote *Review of Rev. J. E. Jeter's Book Entitled "Campbellism Examined"*, a reply to an attack on Campbell. In 1859 Lard decided to publish a periodical but he was unable to secure enough subscriptions. In 1863 he began publishing *Lard's Quarterly*, to advocate the cause of apostolic Christianity. Though the magazine never paid for itself, he continued to publish it until 1868.

In 1869 Lard joined with four other Disciples ministers in the issuance of the *Apostolic Times*. The *Times* became his vehicle for reaching the membership of the churches. He developed a policy of opposing instrumental music, creedal statements, open communion, and the assumption of preachers of pastoral functions. He thus became identified as a leader opposing the liberalizing tendencies of **Isaac Errett** and the *Christian Standard*, which he published. These issues would all later be identified with the conservative branch within the Disciples that would formally separate in 1906 to form the Churches of Christ as distinct from the Christian Church (Disciples of Christ). Through his editorial work, Lard did much to strengthen the bond between the less affluent members of the Campbellite movement in the South and the more middle class members in the North.

During the last years of his life, Lard wrote a pamphlet in which he endeavored to demonstrate that the word usually translated into English as "everlasting" did not always carry that connotation. The thrust of his argument suggested the possibility that eternal punishment in Hell is not a biblical teaching. The pamphlet raised a somewhat bitter controversy. Some of his colleagues suggested that he was becoming a Universalist (advocating that everyone would be saved) and wanted him cast out of the fellowship. He was able to weather the storm, however, and died with the respect of his colleagues.

Sources:

Dictionary of American Biography. 20 vols. and 7 supps. New York: Charles Scribner's Sons, 1928-1936, 1944-1981.

West Earl Irvin. *The Search for the Ancient Order: A History of the Restoration Movement, 1849-1906*. 2 vols. Nashville, TN: Gospel Advocate Company, 1963-1964.

★530★
LATOURETTE, Kenneth Scott
Historian, Baptist Church
b. Aug. 9, 1884, Oregon City, Oregon
d. Dec. 26, 1968, New Haven, Connecticut

Kenneth Scott Latourette, the outstanding historian of world Christianity, was born into a prominent Oregon family. His father, Dewitt Clinton Latourette, and his mother, Rhoda Ellen Scott, were college teachers, and his uncle was a bank president. His parents were also devout Christians. He was a member of the Baptist Church, and attended public school in what was then still a relatively small town. In 1901 he entered McMinnville College and graduated three years later with a B.S. in chemistry. After a year at home, he enrolled at Yale University in 1905, the beginning of a lifelong affiliation with the university. He received a B.A. in history in 1906, his M.A. in 1907, and his Ph.D. in 1909.

The year after his graduation from Yale, Latourette worked as a traveling secretary for the Student Volunteer Movement, but left the country in 1910 to become a faculty member of Yale-in-China, an outpost of the University in Changsha, China. Amoebic dysentary forced him home after a year, and he suffered its effects for several years. In 1914 he began lecturing at Reed College and wrote his first book (apart from his doctoral dissertation), *The Development of China* (1917), which began to establish him as one of the few scholars on the Far East then at work in the United States. In 1916 he joined the history faculty at Dennison University and while there published *The Development of Japan* (1918) and *The Christian Basis of World Democracy* (1919). In 1918 he was ordained in the Baptist Church at Oregon City.

In 1921 Latourette was named D. Willis James Professor of Missions at Yale. During his early years he also served as a trustee of Yale-in-China, an American correspondant to the International Review of Missions, and a member of the board of managers of the American Baptist Foreign Missionary Society. He worked with **John R. Mott** in the World Student Christian Federation. During these years, Latourette grappled with religious doubts and questions of faith. These issues were only cleared up over a period of years. In the 1920s he became a pacifist, a position he had rejected during World War I, and joined the Fellowship of Reconciliation (FOR).

In 1927 Latourette became professor of missions and oriental history, emphasizing his continued work on the Orient. He wrote two of his more important books, *History of Christian Missions in China* (1929) and *The Chinese: Their History and Culture* (1934), soon afterward. Underlying all of his work from this period on, as he recovered his convictions, was a belief that Christianity was for all people. In 1938 he became chairman of the department of religion at Yale. During this time he also commenced work on one of his two major writings, a seven-volume *History of the Expansion of Christianity* (1937-1948).

During the 1930s, Latourette became deeply involved in the ecumenical movement. He served on the American Committee for Faith and Order and in 1938 went to Utrecht, the Netherlands, for the preliminary meeting that led to the formation of the World Council of Churches after World War II. He spoke at the 1948 Amsterdam meeting at which the World Council was formed. He believed the ecumenical movement, a movement to unite the various branches of the Christian church, was a new phenomenon in history, as he could find no time when the church was ever united.

In the decades after World War II, his accomplishments as both a scholar and a churchman were honored. In 1946 he became director of graduate studies in religion at Yale. In 1947 he was elected president of the American Historical Association. In 1949 he was named Sterling Professor of Missions and Oriental History at the Yale Divinity School. In 1951 he was elected president of the

American Baptist Convention. In 1953 he retired and was named professor emeritus. During his last years as a teacher, he also authored the *Short History of the Far East* (1946), *The American Record in the Far East, 1945-1951* (1952), and *A History of Christianity* (1953).

During the years after his retirement Latourette spent much of his time on what is possibly his most important and lasting contribution, the five-volume history of the Christian church in the nineteenth century, *Christianity in a Revolutionary Age*, completed in 1963. His last work was an autobiography completed in 1967.

Sources:
Latourette, Kenneth Scott. *Beyond the Ranges*. Grand Rapids, MI: William B. Eerdmans Publishing Company, 1967. 161 pp.
_____. *Christian World Mission Today*. New York: Harper & Row, 1954. 192 pp.
_____. *Christianity in a Revolutionary Age*. 5 vols. New York: Harper & Row, 1958-1962.
_____. *The Development of China*. Boston, MA: Houghton Mifflin Company, 1917. 273 pp.
_____. *History of Christian Missions in China*. New York: Macmillan Company, 1929. 930 pp.
_____. *History of Christianity*. New York: Harper & Row, 1953. 1,516 pp.
_____. *The History of the Expansion of Christianity*. 7 vols. New York: Harper & Row, 1937-1948.

★531★
LAVEY, Anton
Founder, Church of Satan
b. Apr. 11, 1930, Chicago, Illinois

Howard Anton Szandor LaVey, founder and high priest of the Church of Satan, was the son of a traveling salesman. The family moved to San Francisco shortly after LaVey's birth, and by the time he reached adolescence, he had become interested in the occult and the supernatural. He also studied music, Judo, hypnotism, and the works of such occultists as **Aleister Crowley**. He joined the Clyde Beatey Circus after dropping out of high school, and worked both as a calliope player and a trainer of big cats. Later he worked in carnivals, where he learned stage magic.

LaVey married in 1950 and fathered a daughter in 1952. During this period he took a job as a police photographer, but in 1955 returned to his earlier profession as an organ player. He became involved with a young woman, Diane Hegarty, and divorced his wife in 1960. Diane LaVey was to become his right hand in the Church of Satan. In the early 1960s, LaVey began to hold "midnight magic seminars," and it was from the regular seminar participants that he drew the core group for the Church of Satan. The church was founded on the night of April 30, 1966. LaVey shaved his head and announced the year 1 S.A. (anno Satanas). He had a flair for attracting public attention, and the church received a great deal of publicity in its early years. In 1967, for example, LaVey performed the first Satanic wedding as well as the first Satanic funeral, both of which attracted significant media attention. He also became the occult advisor on films such as *Rosemary's Baby*, and played a bit part as the devil in the aforementioned film.

LaVey, while obviously playing on the traditional Christian image of Satan worshippers, redefined Satanism in several important ways. First, the organization was strictly opposed to any illegal activity—ritual murder and the desecration of graves were definitely not part of his modern Satanic revival. Second, Satanism was redefined so as to represent both the life urges and the selfish virtues repressed by Christianity—the natural drives which mainstream religion has identified as "evil." These views were expressed in LaVey's first book, *The Satanic Bible*, and in his two later volumes, *The Compleat Witch* (1970) and *The Satanic Rituals* (1972).

The church began to splinter around 1972, and by 1975 much of its membership disappeared in a series of organizational disruptions. In the wake of the disturbances, LaVey reorganized the church as a secret society and eliminated the grottos, the local organizations. Of the several splinters, the major one to survive as a viable organization has been the Temple of Set, established by former Church of Satan leaders **Michael A. Aquino** and Lilith Sinclair in 1975. The church has enjoyed some popularity in the 1980s and has begun to spread in Europe, especially Holland.

Although the Church of Satan never developed a significantly large following (2000 was probably its maximum membership), it is important for the attention it attracted and the reaction it created. Many conservative Christian writers, for example, took the Church seriously, and pointed to it as significant evidence that the "Great Deceiver" is alive and well on planet earth. During the 1980s, more secular anti-Satanists have pointed to the existence of the church as support for their attempts to mobilize society to fight what they see as a rising tide of Satanic violence.

Sources:

Harrington, Walt. "The Devil in Anton LaVey." *The Washington Post Magazine* (February 23, 1986): 6-9, 12-17.

LaVey, Anton. *The Compleat Witch*. New York: Lancer Books, 1971. 274 pp.

———. *The Satanic Bible*. New York: Avon Books, 1969. 272 pp.

———. *The Satanic Rituals*. Secaucus, NJ: University Books, 1972. 220 pp.

Lyons, Arthur. *Satan Wants You*. New York: The Mysterious Press, 1988. 192 pp.

Wolfe, Burton H. *The Devil's Avenger*. New York: Avon Books, 1974. 222 pp.

★532★
LAW, Bernard Francis
Archbishop and Cardinal, Roman Catholic Church
b. Nov. 4, 1931, Torreon Mexico

Bernard Francis Law, the archbishop of Boston and a cardinal in the Roman Catholic Church, is the son of Helen A. Stubblefield and Bernard A. Law. He attended Harvard University, from which he received his B.A. in 1953. His post-graduate work was pursued at St. Joseph Seminary in St. Benedict, Louisiana, and at Pontifical Josephinum in Worthington, Ohio. He was ordained as a priest in the Natchez-Jackson, Mississippi, diocese in 1961. In 1963 he became the editor of the diocese's newspaper, serving through the period of the height of the racial turmoil in the state. He left Mississippi and journalism in 1969 to become the executive director of the U.S. Bishops Committee on Ecumenical and Interracial Affairs.

Law returned to Mississippi in 1971 when he was named vicar general of the diocese of Natchez-Jackson. He stayed only two years, however, as in 1973 he was designated a bishop and assigned to the diocese of Springfield-Cape Girardeau, Missouri. In 1975 he assumed the chairmanship of the U.S. Bishops Committee on Ecumenical and Interracial Affairs for which he had previously worked, and the following years was added to the Vatican Commission on Religious Relations with Jews. From 1980 to 1982 he was an ecclesiastical delegate for matters pertaining to former Episcopal priests, who had joined the Roman Catholic Church. He remained in Missouri until 1984 when he was named archbishop of Boston, Massachusetts. The following year he was designated a cardinal.

Sources:

The American Catholic Who's Who. Washington, DC: National Catholic News Service, 1979.

Biography Index. New York: The H. W. Wilson Co.

The New York Times Biographical Service. Ann Arbor, MI: University Microfilms International.

Who's Who in America. Wilmette, IL: Marquis Who's Who, Inc.

★533★
LAWRENCE, John Benjamin
Executive, Southern Baptist Convention
b. Jul. 10, 1871, Florence, Mississippi
d. Sep. 5, 1968, Atlanta, Georgia

John Benjamin Lawrence, for almost a quarter a century the executive secretary-treasurer of the Home Mission Board of the Southern Baptist Convention, grew up in Mississippi. He attended Mississippi College from which he received a B.A. in 1899. In 1900 he was ordained as a Baptist minister, became pastor of the church at Greenwood, Mississippi, and married Helen Alford. While at Greenwood he completed his M.A. at Mississippi College (1902). He moved on in 1903 to serve the churches at Brownsville and Humbolt, Tennessee (1903-1907). In 1907 he moved to New Orleans where he first pastored at Coliseum Place Baptist Church before moving to First Baptist Church, one of the convention's leading congregations. During his New Orleans years he authored the first of his more than 20 books: *Power for Service* (1909). While in New Orleans, Lawrence began to emerge as a significant denominational leader. In 1913 he moved to Mississippi to become editor of the *Baptist Record* and corresponding secretary of the Mississippi Baptist Convention. His tenure, which carried through the years of World War I, is credited with stabilizing the still maturing convention. He moved from Mississippi in 1922 to take the presidency of Oklahoma Baptist University. Again he was credited with putting the school on a stable footing and in 1926 moved to Missouri as executive secretary of the Missouri Baptist Convention.

In 1929 Lawrence was called to the convention's headquarters in Nashville as executive secretary-treasurer of the Home Mission Board, a post he would retain for the next 24 years. The board was but a step away from dissolution. It was $2,500,000 in debt, having just sustained a major loss from the former treasurer having embezzled $900,000 of its funds. In the midst of the Great Depression Lawrence was consumed with the task of paying off the board's indebtedness and reestablishing its reputation. He was able to accomplish both goals by 1943. He had also assumed the editorship of *Home Missions*, the board's periodical, and authored a host of books, including: *The Bible: A Missionary Book* (1935); *Taking Christ Seriously* (1935); *Missions and the Divine Plan for Support* (1936); and *Home Missions in the New World* (1943).

As the financial situation of the board eased, he was able to develop what became one of the most impressive home missionary programs of any American church. The board came to support a multi-dimensional agenda which emphasized schools of missions, the military chaplaincy, cooperative work with Blacks, and church extension, especially outside of the South. Lawrence provided the base upon which the Southern Baptist Convention would build in the next generation as it grew in a spectacular fashion and transformed itself from a regional church body into the second largest denomination in America, with congregations in every state of the Union.

Lawrence retired in 1954. During his last years he would finish *A History of the Home Mission Board* (1958) and a final volume, *A New Heaven and a New Earth* (1960).

Sources:

Encyclopedia of Southern Baptists. 3 vols. Nashville, TN: Broadman Press, 1958, 1971.

Lawrence, John B. *The Bible a Missionary Book*. Atlanta, GA: Home Mission Board of the Southern Baptist Convention, 1935. 140 pp.

———. *A History of the Home Mission Board*. Nashville, TN: Broadman Press, 1958. 170 pp.

———. *A New Heaven and a New Earth*. New York: American Press, 1906. 165 pp.

———. *Power for Service*. New Orleans, LA: C. O. Chambes, 1909. 261 pp.

_____. *Taking Christ Seriously*. Atlanta, GA: Home Mission Board of the Southern Baptist Convention, 1935. 126 pp.

★534★
LAWS, Curtis Lee
Editor, Northern Baptist Convention
b. Jul. 14, 1868, Aldie, Virginia
d. Jul. 7, 1946, New York, New York

Curtis Lee Laws, the fundamentalist Baptist editor of the *Watchman-Examiner*, was the son of Laura J. Nixon and John T. Laws. He grew up in Virginia and attended Richmond College (A.B., 1890). He went north for his seminary work at Crozer Theological Seminary in Chester, Pennsylvania. He graduated in 1893 just as Crozer was beginning its realignment with current modernist theological and scholarly perspectives, a change that Laws deplored. He associated with the Northern Baptist Convention and accepted a pastorate at First Baptist Church in Baltimore, Maryland. In 1894 he married Grace Burnett. Following 15 years in Baltimore, he moved to Brooklyn, New York, as pastor of Greene Avenue Baptist Church.

In 1913 Laws left the pastorate to become editor of the *Watchman-Examiner*, a Baptist periodical published in New York City. By this time Laws had become closely identified with the conservative forces in the convention who stood in opposition to its increasing movement into the modernist theological camp. Early in his new duties, he announced that he would not be neutral in his defense of the fundamentals of the faith. In 1920 he joined with **J. Frank Norris** and **William Bell Riley** in a major conference of conservative leaders. That year, in an article in the *Watchman-Examiner* connected with the gathering, Laws coined the term "fundamentalist" to describe the increasingly-organized voice of dissent in the convention. He is credited with first using the term as a label for those people who defended what they saw as the "fundamentals" of the faith and were willing to fight on their behalf. At the 1920 convention he worked to convince his fellow fundamentalists to cease boycotting the convention meetings but attend as advocates for their program. His perspective largely laid the groundwork for the fundamentalist-modernist controversy of the 1920s and the subsequent splitting of the convention in the 1930s.

As the splits began to occur, Laws chose to remain within the convention and make his periodical the focus of the fundamentalist wing of the church. He also was not able to accept the premillennial perspective of the majority who left to form new Baptist associations. (Premillennialism is a belief in the imminent return of Christ to establish a literal earthly kingdom of a thousand years.) Laws supported the founding of Eastern Baptist Theological Seminary and the Association of Baptists for World Evangelism as fundamentalist-controlled institutions for the training of ministers and commissioning of missionaries. Laws retired in 1938 and moved back to Baltimore.

Sources:

Brackney, William Henry. *The Baptist*. New York: Greenwood Press, 1988. 327 pp.
Laws, Curtis Lee. *Baptist, Why and Why Not*. Nashville: 1904.
_____. *The Fiery Furnace: Present Struggles of the NonConformists in England for Religious Liberty*. Baltimore, MD: First Baptist Church, 1904. 31 pp.
_____. *Who and What Are the Christian Scientists*. Baltimore, MD: The Author, 1899. 20 pp.
Lewis, Frank Grant, and Rittenhouse Neisser, comp. *Alphabetic Biographical Catalog, Crozer Theological Seminary, 1855-1933*. Chester, PA: Crozer Theological Seminary, 1933. 244 pp.

★535★
LAWSON, Alfred William
Founder, Humanity Benefactor Foundation
b. Mar. 24, 1869, London England
d. Nov. 29, 1954, Des Moines ?, Iowa

Alfred W. Lawson was a pioneer aviator, unorthodox economist, and founder of the religion of Lawsonomy, whose beliefs are perpetuated today by the Humanity Benefactor Foundation. He was the son of Robert Henry and Mary Anderson Lawson. Three weeks after his birth, the family settled in Windsor, Ontario, Canada, and a few years later moved across the river to Detroit, Michigan, where Lawson grew up. He dropped out of school at age 12, though he did complete an industrial training course. Then at the age of 18 he discovered baseball. He began his career as a pitcher for a team in Frankfort, Indiana. While he played only one year in the majors, he stayed in baseball as a player and a manager for two decades. In 1890 he organized an exhibition team which he took to Cuba. He also pioneered night baseball. In addition, during his baseball years he gave a hint of things to come by writing an uninspired utopian novel, *Born Again* (1904). But in 1908 he left baseball, having discovered an even more captivating pursuit—aviation.

In 1908 Lawson began one of the earliest aviation periodicals, *Fly, the National Aeronautic Magazine*, published in Pittsburgh, Pennsylvania. Two years later he started a second magazine, *Aircraft*, the recognized voice of pioneer aviation in the United States. He continued *Aircraft* until the beginning of World War I, at which time he was able to locate financial backing for a company to manufacture military craft. The Lawson Aircraft Company opened in Green Bay, Wisconsin, in 1914. Before they could fill any order, the war ended and the company dissolved. Lawson found more backing and reorganized to manufacture passenger airplanes. The prototype of the modern passenger liner appeared in 1919. A new company, Lawson Airline Transportation Company, came into being to exploit the passenger market. The company had high hopes but floundered through the 1920s from lack of capital and bad business decisions. It finally died in the Depression of 1929.

The Great Depression provided Lawson with another arena for his creativity and vast storehouse of energy. Like a number of people adversely affected by the financial problems of the decade, Lawson championed a plan for economic recovery and stability built around the concept of direct credits, in which the government offered free credit to its industrious citizens. To emphasize his commitment, he divested himself of all his property and money in 1931. As the founder/leader of the Direct Credits Society, he mobilized hundreds of thousands of people behind his economic ideas, though they were never adopted by any legislative body and hence never put into action.

Concurrently, and not easily distinguished from his economic program, Lawson began to articulate a new religion he called Lawsonomy, built around his understanding of God as humankind's benefactor. Lawsonomy provided the metaphysical underpinning for his social program. Religion, according to Lawson, centers upon the fact of the immortality of the soul. Lawson's religion represented a new evolvement of religion based upon God's laws as they manifest in the physical, mental, moral, and spiritual realms of life. He organized the Humanity Benefactor Association, and in 1934 began a periodical, *The Benefactor*, through which his religious ideas were first spread. In 1943 he opened the University of Lawsonomy in Wichita, Kansas. In 1948 his religious ideas had developed to the point that he could formally announce the formation of the Lawsonian religion, which he predicted would be accepted worldwide by the year 2000 C.E. He presented his formative ideas in a book, *Lawsonian Religion* (1949).

By the time of Lawson's death, his mass following had collapsed (in the demands and financial prosperity of World War II), and was reduced to a core of believers in his social and religious program. That small group has survived, and its members continue to circulate Lawson's books from the University of Lawsonomy, which has been relocated to Sturtevant, Wisconsin.

Sources:

Henry, Lyell D., Jr. "Alfred W. Lawson, the Forgotten 'Columbus of the Air.'" *Journal of American Culture* 7, 1, & 2, (Spring/Summer, 1984): 93-99.

Lawson, Alfred W. *The Almighty* . Detroit: Humanity Publishing Company, 1939. 222 pp.

_____. *Born Again*. Detroit: Humanity Publishing Company, 1904. 239 pp.

_____. *Creation*. Detroit: Humanity Publishing Company, 1931. 224 pp.

_____. *General Order/ Direct Credits Society*. Detroit: Humanity Publishing Company, [1941]. 96 pp.

_____. *Lawsonian Religion*. Detroit: Humanity Benefactor Association, 1949. 256 pp.

_____. *Manlife*. Detroit: Humanity Publishing Company, 1923. 220 pp.

★536★
LAWSON, Robert Clarence
Founder, Church of Our Lord Jesus Christ of the Apostolic Faith
b. May 5, 1883, New Iberia, Louisiana
d. Jul. 1961, New York, New York

Robert Clarence Lawson was the founder of the Church of Our Lord Jesus Christ of the Apostolic Faith, one of the largest of the predominantly black Pentecostal denominations. He was raised by his aunt, Peggy Frazier, following the death of his parents when he was still a child. He left home to work as a teenager and began a promising career as a singer in the nightclubs in Louisiana. Then around 1913 he became sick with tuberculosis, still an incurable disease at the time. He was visited by a woman, a "mother" in an Apostolic Faith congregation. Apostolic Pentecostals reject the traditional doctrine of the Trinity and baptize people in the name of "Jesus Only."

Converted, he was taken to Indianapolis to attend the church of **Garfield T. Haywood**, one of the early prominent Apostolic advocates, and under his ministry was healed and received the baptism of the Holy Spirit (as evidenced by speaking in tongues). Lawson became a worker in the Pentecostal Assemblies of the World (PAW), which Haywood led, establishing congregations in St. Louis, Missouri, and San Antonio, Texas. On an evangelistic trip to Leavenworth, Kansas, he met his future bride, Carrie Fields. He eventually became a pastor in Columbus, Ohio.

In 1919 Lawson had a disagreement with Haywood over the issue of divorce. Lawson was adamantly opposed to divorce, while Haywood was somewhat more lenient, especially with people who had been divorced before becoming a Christian. As a result of their differences, Lawson left the Pentecostal Assemblies and moved to New York City, where in July he began services on the street. He was soon invited into a home which became his temporary headquarters. Before the year was out he had organized the Refuge Church of Our Lord, the mother church of what was soon to become the Church of Our Lord Jesus Christ of the Apostolic Faith (adopted in 1923).

Lawson expanded his ministry in 1923 with the addition of a radio program and the opening of the R. C. Lawson Institute in Southern Pines, North Carolina. He founded funeral homes, a day care center, a book store, a record store, a grocery, and a small publishing company which published the church's magazine, *Contender for the Faith*. In 1926 he founded the Church of Christ Bible Institute. Beginning in 1935, Lawson led in the expansion of the church into the Caribbean, establishing missions in the Virgin Islands, Antigua, Jamaica, and Trinidad. Toward the end of World

War II the congregation purchased an abandoned theater and in August 1945 moved into their new sanctuary. During these years he visited Ethiopia and was granted an audience with the Emperor Haile Selassie. Shortly thereafter, when Selassie visited New York, he presented Lawson with the Star of Ethiopia. In 1946 his first wife died. He married Evelyn Burke in 1951.

The last decade of his life was spent building his church into an international denomination. These final years were marred by a major schism when several leaders of the church, complaining of Lawson's authoritarianism, left in 1957 to found the Bible Way Church of the Lord Jesus Christ World Wide. Lawson was succeeded by **Hubert Spencer**.

Sources:

Dupree, Sherry Sherrod. *Biographical Dictionary of African-American, Holiness-Pentecostals, 1880-1990*. Washington, DC: Middle Atlantic Regional Press, 1990. 386 pp.

Lawson, R. C. *For the Defense of the Gospels.*

★537★
LEA, Henry Charles
Historian, Publisher, and Publicist
b. Sep. 19, 1825, Philadelphia, Pennsylvania
d. Oct. 24, 1909, Philadelphia, Pennsylvania

Henry Charles Lea, publisher and historian, was the son of Isaac and Frances Anne (Carey) Lea. He was a precocious child, and at the age of 15 contributed a paper on fossilized shells to the *American Journal of Science and Arts*. He never attended college, though he received a considerable amount of private tutoring. In 1843 he began working in his father's publishing house, while continuing to write articles on science and literature. During the anti-Catholic riots in 1844 in Philadelphia, he helped defend a nearby Roman Catholic church. He married Anna Caroline Jaudon, his first cousin, on May 27, 1850.

Lea experienced a health breakdown at the age of 22, and during his recovery became interested in history. His early interest was in the history of jurisprudence, and in 1866 he published *Superstition and Force*. His study of the history of legal institutions led him to become interested in the medieval Roman Catholic Church, and during the next few years he authored *An Historical Sketch of Sacerdotal Celibacy* (1867) and *Studies in Church History* (1869). This literary output was impressive, considering his simultaneous activity running a publishing business. Lea was also active in politics, especially as a campaigner against political corruption.

In 1880, Lea retired from the publishing business with the formation of Lea's Son & Company. His retirement, undertaken partially for reasons of poor health, allowed him to turn his full attention to study and writing. His many works include *A History of the Inquisition of the Middle Ages* (3 vols., 1887), *A History of Auricular Confession and Indulgences* (3 vols., 1896), and *A History of the Inquisition of Spain* (4 vols., 1906-1907). At the time of his death he was working on a history of witchcraft. *A History of the Inquisition of the Middle Ages* and other works were translated into French by liberals seeking to influence public opinion with respect to the church/state struggle.

Though lacking a formal education, Lea and his work were recognized by his scholarly colleagues. Lea received honorary degrees from Pennsylvania, Harvard, Princeton, and the University of Giessen. He also served a term as president of the American Historical Association, was made a fellow of the Imperial University of Moscow, and was an honorary member of learned societies in Italy, Germany, and Great Britain. Finally, Lea was a philanthropist who was responsible for, among other things, the Institute of Hygiene of the University of Pennsylvania, an epileptic farm, a new wing for the Library Company building in Philadelphia, and an increase in salaries at the University of Pennsylvania.

Sources:

Bradley, Edward S. *Henry C. Lea*. Philadelphia: University of Pennsylvania Press, 1931. 391 pp.

Dictionary of American Biography. 20 vols. and 7 supps. New York: Charles Scribner's Sons, 1928-1936, 1944-1981.

Lea, Henry Charles. *An Historical Sketch of Sacerdotal Celibacy in the Christian Church*. Philadelphia: J. P. Lippencott & Co., 1867. 601 pp.

———. *A History of Auricular Confession and Indulgences*. 3 vols. Philadelphia: Lea Brothers & Co., 1896.

———. *A History of the Inquisition in the Middle Ages*. 3 vols. New York: Harper & Brothers, 1887.

———. *A History of the Inquisition of Spain*. 4 vols. New York: Macmillan Company, 1906-1907.

———. *Studies in Church History*. Philadelphia: H. C. Lea, S. Low, Son & Marston, 1869. 515 pp.

★538★
LEADBEATER, Charles Webster
Bishop, Liberal Catholic Church
b. Feb. 16, 1854, Stockport, Cheshire England
d. Mar. 1, 1934, Perth Australia

Charles Webster Leadbeater was an early theosophical leader and the second bishop of the Liberal Catholic Church. The only son of a railroad worker, he was not financially able to attend college. This would normally have prevented the fulfillment of his wish to become an Anglican priest, but his uncle, W. W. Capes, a reader in ancient history at Queen's College in Oxford, helped him through the proper channels. He was ordained deacon in 1878, became a curate at his uncle's church at Bramshott in Hampshire, and became a priest in 1879.

Not long after this, Leadbeater's interest in psychical research led him to Madame **Helena Petrovna Blavatsky** and her Theosophical Society. He joined the society in November 1883, and early in 1884, received two letters from one of the cosmic spiritual masters spoken of in theosophy, Koot Hoomi, which advised him to follow Blavatsky to India. He followed this advice, even though it meant cutting off his budding career as a priest. On his way to India, he stopped at Ceylon (now Sri Lanka) and met with Henry S. Olcott, president of the society. Olcott was involved with helping the spread of Buddhism, and Leadbeater decided to show solidarity for the cause by taking vows as a Buddhist and joining Olcott on a trip to Burma.

Upon arrival in Adyar, India, where Blavatsky had established a center, Leadbeater became editor of the magazine, *The Theosophist*, and recording secretary of the society. He quickly became popular as a writer and lecturer. When **Annie Besant** came to India to live in the early 1890s, they became good friends. Over the years, he co-authored many books and toured as a lecturer with her. Leadbeater became the focus of controversy in 1906, when he was charged with improper sexual behavior with a group of boys under his charge. Leadbeater resigned his positions, but was able to remain active in the society, thanks to Annie Besant's defense of him. Meanwhile, Besant declared that a new avatar, or world teacher, would be coming soon to lead the world into a new stage of evolution. In 1909, a society member asked the group to care for his two motherless boys, one being **Jiddu Krishnamurti**. Leadbeater became immediately convinced that Krishnamurti was the next great spiritual leader, and Besant asked Leadbeater to come back to a position in the society in order to work with Krishnamurti.

Leadbeater instructed Krishnamurti in occult matters for the next two years, and the result was a famous book, *At the Feet of the Master*. Besant also became convinced of Krishnamurti's future role and began a magazine, *Herald of the Star*, to announce his presence. His father, however, did not appreciate all of this, and began to ask for his son's return. He also revived sexual impropriety charges against Leadbeater, and sued the society in court. The society won the case, but Leadbeater's position had so deteriorat-

ed that he had to leave. In 1914 he moved to Sydney, Australia, where he soon became associated with J. I. Wedgwood, the first bishop of the Liberal Catholic Church, a splinter from the Old Catholic Church which combined Old Catholic and theosophical traditions.

On July 22, 1916, Wedgwood consecrated Leadbeater as regionary bishop of Australia, and he began a new chapter in his varied career. He wrote the two main theological works for the Liberal Catholic Church, *The Science of the Sacraments* (1920) and *The Hidden Side of the Christian Festivals* (1920). His involvement with the church gave rise to much controversy in theosophy, especially among those in America who fought Besant's leadership, who charged that she was condoning a sell-out to Catholicism. In 1919 Leadbeater and Wedgwood together consecrated **Irving Steiger Cooper** as the first bishop for the United States. In 1923 Leadbeater succeeded Wedgwood as the presiding bishop of the church. Leadbeater died in 1934 at the age of 80.

Sources:

Leadbeater, Charles Webster. *The Christian Creed*. London, England: Theosophical Publishing House, 1920. 172 pp.

———. *The Hidden Side of Christian Festivals*. Los Angeles, CA: St. Alban Press, 1920. 508 pp.

———. *An Outline of Theosophy*. Chicago: Theosophical Book Concern, 1903.

———. *The Science of the Sacraments*. Los Angeles: St. Alban Press, 1920. 560 pp.

Melton, J. Gordon. *Biographical Dictionary of American Cult and Sect Leaders*. Garland Reference Library of Social Science, vol. 212. New York: Garland Publishing, 1986.

Nethercot, Arthur H. *The Last Four Lives of Annie Besant*. Chicago: University of Chicago Press, 1963.

Shearman, Hugh. *Charles Webster Leadbeater, A Biography*. Sydney, Australia: St. Alban Press, 1982. 39 pp.

Shepard, Leslie. *Encyclopedia of Occultism & Parapsychology*. 3 vols., 2nd. ed. Detroit: Gale Research Co., 1984-1985.

Tillett, Gregory. *The Elder Brother: A Biography of Charles Webster Leadbeater*. London, England: Routledge & Kegan Paul, 1982. 337 pp.

Wedgwood, James Ingall, "The Beginnings of the Liberal Catholic Church," *Ubique* (February, 1966).

—*Gary L. Ward*

★539★
LEBARON, Ervil Morrell
Founder, Church of the Lamb of God
b. Feb. 22, 1925, Colonia Juarez, Chihuahua Mexico
d. Aug. 16, 1981, Utah State Prison, Point of the Mountain, Utah

Ervil Morrell LeBaron was a leader among polygamy-practicing Mormons, and founded the Church of the Lamb of God. He was born in Mexico to Alma Dayar LeBaron, also a polygamy-practicing Mormon. After finishing high school, Ervil and his brother **Joel Franklin LeBaron** went on a mission among the Mexican Indians, but this act of piety did not prevent the whole LeBaron family from being excommunicated from the Church of Jesus Christ of Latter-day Saints, possibly for continued rejection of the 1890 Manifesto abolishing polygamy.

In 1944, the year of their excommunication, the LeBarons created their own religious community, which they called Colonia LeBaron, near Galeana. Over time they became acquainted with two other polygamy leaders, Margarito Bautista and **Rulon Clark Allred**, through whose influence the family associated itself with **Joseph Musser**'s Apostolic United Brethren in Utah. Bautista baptized Ervil and his brother Joel in 1951. In 1954, Allred took over Musser's group, but the LeBaron family would not remain long in that camp, as Joel LeBaron had a revelation in 1955 that he was the "One Mighty and Strong" prophesied by Mormon Founder **Joseph Smith, Jr.**, who would set things straight. Joel founded the

Church of the First Born of the Fulness of Times and named Ervil president of the (Mexican) missions. In 1961, Joel appointed Ervil patriarch, the second highest office in the church.

All during the 1960s, Ervil was controversial within the church and in the public outside. He began to exercise authority over the private lives of church members—even telling member Anna Mae Morton to divorce her husband and marry him—while advocating civil coercive enforcement of church attendance. In 1969 Joel removed him from the patriarchal office, and in 1971 excommunicated him for threatening violence. In 1972, Ervil issued an open letter to the Covenant People suggesting that interference with himself as ambassador of the kingdom deserved the death penalty. On August 20, 1972, Joel was shot to death in Ensenada, Mexico, by Ervil's followers. Three months later, Ervil was captured by authorities and sentenced to 12 years for homicide. After serving only one year, however, a higher court reversed the ruling and released him. Within a matter of days, his followers burned much of Los Molinos, a town in Baja, California, where many members of Joel's church lived, two of whom were killed. In 1975, Dean Vest, an associate of Joel's, was killed. In 1976 Ervil was again arrested and convicted, but served only eight months.

By this time, Ervil had decided to establish a rival church, which he called the Church of the Lamb of God, but his feud with the others continued. On May 10, 1977, Ervil ordered followers to shoot Rulon Allred, who now was the leader of the Apostolic United Brethren. Two years later authorities captured Ervil and again convicted him for murder, and sentenced him to life in prison. On August 16, 1981, after serving a little more than a year of his sentence, he died of a seizure at the age of 56. On the same day, a brother Verlan LeBaron, who had sided with Joel and whom Ervil had earlier plotted to kill, died in an auto accident in Mexico City. Ervil's church moved into unknown status with his death, but Joel's church and those of other polygamy-practicing Mormons have continued, both in the United States and Mexico.

Sources:

Bradlee, Ben, Jr. and Dale Van Atta. *Prophet of Blood*. New York: G. P. Putnam's Sons, 1981. 350 pp.

Fessier, Michael, Jr., "Ervil LeBaron, the Man Who Would Be God." *New West* (January, 1981), 80-84, 112-117.

LeBaron, Ervil. *An Open Letter to a Former Presiding Bishop*. San Diego, CA: The Author, 1972.

———. *Priesthood Expounded*. Cuidad Juarez, Mexico: Church of the First Born, 1956. 56 pp.

LeBaron, Verlan M. *The LeBaron Story*. Lubbock, TX: The Author, 1981. 316 pp.

Melton, J. Gordon. *Biographical Dictionary of American Cult and Sect Leaders*. Garland Reference Library of Social Science, vol. 212. New York: Garland Publishing, 1986.

—*Gary L. Ward*

★540★
LEBARON, Joel Franklin
Founder, Church of the First Born of the Fulness of Times
b. Jul. 9, 1923, Laverkin, Utah
d. Aug. 20, 1972, Chapaltepec Mexico

Joel Franklin LeBaron was a polygamy-practicing Mormon leader and founder of the Church of the First Born of the Fulness of Times. Joel was the seventh son of Alma Dayar LeBaron, a polygamist whose grandfather was a follower and friend of **Joseph Smith, Jr.**, the founder of Mormonism. It was about the time of Joel's birth that his father formally began practicing polygamy, which necessitated a move outside the United States to a Mormon polygamous settlement in Colonia Juarez, Mexico.

In 1944 the LeBaron family was excommunicated from the Church of Jesus Christ of Latter-day Saints, possibly due to their continued rejection of the 1890 Manifesto against polygamy, and

they moved to start a new settlement near Galeana, Mexico, that they called Colonia LeBaron. The LeBarons also became acquainted with Margarito Bautista and **Rulon Clark Allred**, polygamist leaders who led the family into association with the Apostolic United Brethren. Bautista baptised Joel and his brother **Ervil Morrell Lebaron** in 1951, the same year Joel married Magdelena Soto. In 1955, at the age of 32, Joel ventured to Utah—a trip that was marked by a revelation in which angels told him he was the "One Mighty and Strong," prophesied by Joseph Smith, who would set the church on the right path. Joel proceeded to found the Church of the First Born in the Fulness of Times in Salt Lake City, Utah, and appointed his brother Ervil as head of the Mexican mission (the only mission).

Joel had two particular doctrinal emphases, one being that God's intention was that the Ten Commandments be the basis of political order and that Christ would return only when a community of people obeyed them. The other emphasis was on the lineage of priestly authority. He believed that Joseph Smith founded the office of the First Grand Head, had passed that on to Benjamin Johnson, Joel's great-grandfather, and so on down to Joel. Under this office is that of the patriarch, which Joel believed had been passed to Bautista, and when Bautista died in 1961, Joel gave it to brother Ervil. In the 1960s Joel worked to build an interfaith group of people who believed in civil life lived by the Ten Commandments. This led in 1966 to the founding of the Alliance for Pastors and Christian Teachers, later called the Christian Judaic Evangelical Brotherhood.

Meanwhile Ervil was becoming increasingly controversial and troublesome, calling for coercion of church attendance and taking dubious authority in the private lives of church members. In November of 1969, Joel finally relieved Ervil of the patriarchal office, and in 1971 excommunicated him for threatening violence. On August 20, 1972, followers of Ervil, carried out his order to kill Joel. Ervil was then imprisoned for the deed, but served less than one year before he was released by a higher-court ruling. Ervil continued to commit other violent acts against rival polygamist groups, and finally died in jail in 1981. Another of Joel's brothers, Verlan LeBaron, succeeded Joel as leader of the Church of the First Born of the Fulness of Times. The church continues today in parts of Mexico, California and Utah.

Sources:

LeBaron, Verlan M. *The LeBaron Story*. Lubbock, TX: The Author, 1981. 316 pp.

Melton, J. Gordon. *Biographical Dictionary of American Cult and Sect Leaders*. Garland Reference Library of Social Science, vol. 212. New York: Garland Publishing, 1986.

Richards, Henry W. *A Reply to "The Church of the Firstborn of the Fulness of Times"*. Salt Lake City, UT: The Author, 1965. 159 pp.

Wright, Lyle O. *Origins and Development of the Church of the Firstborn of the Fulness of Times*. Provo, UT: Brigham Young University thesis, 1963.

—*Gary L. Ward*

★541★
LEE, Gloria
Founder, Cosmon Research Foundation
b. Mar. 22, 1926, Los Angeles, California
d. Dec. 2, 1962, Washington, District of Columbia

Gloria Lee gained fame as a flying saucer contactee and as the founder of the Cosmon Research Foundation. She grew up in Los Angeles and was a Hollywood child actress for a while. As an adult, she became an airline stewardess, and after her marriage to William Byrd in 1952, she switched to the role of ground hostess at Los Angeles International Airport. It was in 1952 that **George Adamski** became the first person to gain prominence by professing contact with extraterrestrials. In September 1953, Lee herself became a contactee by way of automatic writing done at the airport.

After this initial contact, Lee joined several different groups in the psychic and theosophical areas in an attempt to learn more about the experience. She regularly received messages, at first in automatic writing and later by telepathy, from an entity described as an inhabitant of Jupiter named J.W. He identified Lee herself as a reincarnated Venusian. Various psychics claimed to see J.W. around Lee, and J.W. reportedly clued Lee into a UFO appearance that was later verified independently by people across the city. These experiences caused her to establish the Cosmon Research Foundation in 1959 and publish her first book, *Why We Are Here!* (1959), which transforms the theosophical spiritual hierarchy into an interstellar command.

The book and the foundation made her a well-known leader in the contactee community. In 1960 she visited the newly organized contactee group, the Mark-Age Meta Center in Florida, and discovered that she and Mark (the public name of Charles Boyd Gentzel), one of the founders, were twin souls. She also later discovered through the other founder, psychic Yolanda (public name of Pauline Sharpe), that J.W. had been incarnated in the person of Jim Speed, whom Lee met at the center. In 1962 Lee published her second book, *The Changing Conditions of Your World*, and then in September of that year, traveled to Washington, D.C. to talk to government officials. J.W. had telepathically given her plans for a spaceship, and had instructed her to present the plans to scientists in the government. Following J.W.'s directions, Lee and partner Hedy Hood checked into the Hotel Claridge, and Lee began a fruit juice fast, awaiting the officials who would visit. No one ever came, and she finally died of her fast on December 2.

When Yolanda heard of Lee's death, she received a message that future communications would occur, and on December 12, Lee contacted Yolanda. Their conversations resulted in the booklet, *Gloria Lee Lives!* (1963), and other works, which significantly aided the growth of the Mark-Age Meta Center. Verity, a medium with the Heralds of the New Age in New Zealand, also claimed contact with Lee, beginning January 21, 1963. Verity produced a book of Lee's dictations, which claimed that Lee had joined the Ashtar Command, "an Etheric Band of Beings whose Commander-in-Chief is Jesus of Nazareth." Lee was remembered for many years as a martyr of the early contactee movement.

Sources:

Gloria Lee Lives!. Miami, FL: Mark-Age Meta Center, 1963. 40 pp.

Lee, Gloria. *The Changing Conditions of Your World*. Palos Verdes Estates, CA: Cosmon Research Foundation, 1962. 213 pp.

_____. *Why We Are Here!* Palos Verdes Estates, CA: Cosmon Research Foundation, 1959. 183 pp.

Melton, J. Gordon. *Biographical Dictionary of American Cult and Sect Leaders*. Garland Reference Library of Social Science, vol. 212. New York: Garland Publishing, 1986.

Steiger, Brad. *The Aquarian Revelations*. New York: Dell, 1971. 158 pp.

Verity. *The Going and the Glory*. Auckland, New Zealand: Heralds of the New Age, 1966. 73 pp.

—*Gary L. Ward*

★542★
LEE, Harold Bingham
President, Church of Jesus Christ of Latter-day Saints
b. Mar. 28, 1899, Clifton, Idaho
d. Dec. 26, 1973, Salt Lake City, Utah

Harold Bingham Lee, eleventh president of the Church of Jesus Christ of Latter-day Saints, was raised in Idaho, where he became a school teacher and, at the age of 18, principal of a four-room school in Oxford, Idaho. Following his period of service as a lay missionary in Denver, Colorado, he settled in Salt Lake City in 1920 as a school principal. He married Fern Lucinda Tanner in 1923. In 1929 he became the youngest stake president in the church when he accepted the position as head of Salt Lake City's Pioneer Stake.

As stake president, Lee was immediately called to exercise extraordinary skill when the depression put half of his members on the unemployment line. He instituted programs to provide emergency relief and jobs, many in the employ of the church. His programs became the model and motivation for a churchwide welfare program. In 1935 he began to serve on the Church Security (Welfare) Committee and became its managing director in 1937.

Lee's work in church welfare and his singular organizational skills launched his steady ascendancy in the church's leadership. In 1941 he was called to the Quorum of Twelve Apostles. In 1961 he became chairman of the church correlation committee charged with coordinating the many diverse programs which had been spawned by various departments of the church over the years. This committee also oversaw the planning and production of a coordinated church curriculum. That same year his wife died. In 1962 he married Freda Joan Jensen.

In 1970 Lee became president of the Quorum of the Twelve Apostles and was named as the first counselor to church president **Joseph Fielding Smith, Jr.** Two years later, upon Smith's death, Lee succeeded him as president of the church. His brief administration, the shortest of all the church's presidents, was marked by significant internal reorganization of the church. He restructured the auxiliary general boards and, possibly most important for the church's long-term future, created internal and external communications committees to handle church public relations. Presiding over a church that places great emphasis on family life, he also developed new programs for single young adults.

Lee died after only 17 months in office of a heart ailment.

Sources:

Lee, Harold Bingham. *Decision for Successful Living*. Salt Lake City, UT: Deseret Book Company, 1973. 265 pp.

_____. *From the Valley of Despair to the Mountain Peaks of Hope*. Salt Lake City, UT: Deseret Book Company, 1971.

_____. *Stand Ye in Holy Places*. Salt Lake City, UT: Deseret Book Company, 1974. 398 pp.

_____. *Ye Are the Light of the World*. Salt Lake City, UT: Deseret Book Company, 1974. 364 pp.

_____. *Youth and the Church*. Salt Lake City, UT: Deseret Book Company, 1970. 261 pp.

Van Wagoner, Richard S., and Steven C. Walker. *A Book of Mormons*. Salt Lake City, UT: Signature Books, 1982. 454 pp.

★543★
LEE, Robert Greene
Minister, Southern Baptist Convention
b. Nov. 11, 1886, York County, South Carolina

Robert Greene Lee, one of the most famous preachers in the Southern Baptist Convention, was the son of sharecroppers Sarah Elizabeth Bennett and David Ayers Lee. Lee was born in a log cabin in rural South Carolina. When Robert was a child the Lees lived in Charlotte, North Carolina, for a short time, but the family moved back to South Carolina when he was eight years old and purchased a farm. A member of a devout Baptist family, as a youth Lee had a salvation experience during a meeting in July 1898. The next month he was baptized and decided to become a minister. He stayed on the farm, however, assisting his father, until he was 21. He studied the dictionary during this time to improve his vocabulary. In 1907 he went to Panama to work on the canal as a means of raising money to attend college.

In 1908 Lee entered Furman University. He was ordained in 1910 and served a variety of student pastorates. In 1913 he graduated *magna cum laude* and married Bula Gentry. He continued to pastor several rural congregations until 1917 when he moved to Saluda, South Carolina, as the full-time pastor of the Red Bank Baptist Church. While there he also taught Latin at Furman. In 1918 he moved to New Orleans to attend Tulane University with the idea of possibly making a career as a college instructor. He turned away from that idea, however, and in 1818 returned to South Carolina as pastor of First Baptist Church at Edgefield. He continued his studies and in 1919 was awarded a Ph.D. from the Chicago Law School. While at Edgefield he first preached the sermon which he was to preach on numerous occasions and with which he was to become popularly identified, ''Pay Day-Some Day.'' Based upon the biblical story of Ahab and Jezebel, the sermon emphasized Lee's belief that individuals cannot get away with evil-doing in the long run.

In 1922 Lee, by now becoming well-known in Baptist circles, moved to First Baptist Church in New Orleans. Three years later he returned to South Carolina as pastor of Citadel Square Baptist Church in Charleston. While at Citadel, he saw the publication of the first of his more than 30 books, a collection of sermons, *From Feet to Fathoms* (1925). In 1927 he moved to Memphis, Tennessee, as pastor of Bellvue Baptist Church, where he was to remain for the rest of his life. The church began to grow soon after his arrival, and even the Depression did not prevent the congregation from completing a new educational wing in 1930. In 1932 he was elected to the first of three consecutive terms as president of the Tennessee Baptist Convention. In 1948 he was elected president of the Southern Baptist Convention and served for three years (in a post that is normally held only for two years). His most memorable action as president was to oppose and help defeat the Aldridge amendment which would have barred ministers and churches in the Southern Baptist Convention who cooperated with the Federal Council of Churches from holding offices in the convention. Lee argued effectively that such legislation would turn the convention into a legislative rather than advisory body.

In 1953 Bellvue moved into a new and larger facility which made it one of the largest churches in the convention. During the 1950s the church developed a television studio and became a pioneer in televising Sunday services. In 1960, after 50 years in the ministry, Lee retired from Bellvue. His congregation had grown to 9,000 members under his leadership. His retirement years were spent in constant travel and speaking around the country.

Sources:

English, E. Schuler. *A Chosen Vessel*. Grand Rapids, MI: Zondervan Publishing House, 1949.
Huss, John E. *Robert G. Lee: The Authorized Biography*. Grand Rapids, MI: Zondervan Publishing House, 1967. 252 pp.
Lee, Robert G. *From Feet to Fathoms*. Nashville, TN: Sunday School Board of the Southern Baptist Convention, 1926.
_____. *The Must of the Second Birth*. New York: Fleming H. Revell, 1959.
_____. *Robert G. Lee's Sourcebook of 500 Illustrations*. Grand Rapids, MI: Zondervan Publishing House, 1964.
_____. *This Critical Hour*. Grand Rapids, MI: Zondervan Publishing House, 1942.
_____. *The Wonderful Savior*. Grand Rapids, MI: Zondervan Publishing House, 1965.

★544★
LEGER, Paul Emile
Cardinal, Roman Catholic Church (Canada)
b. Apr. 26, 1904, Valley Field, Quebec, Canada

Paul Emile Leger, as of 1990 the oldest living cardinal in the Roman Catholic Church, was raised in a French Canadian family and attended parochial schools. He entered the seminary at Quebec and upon completion of his studies was ordained a priest in 1929. He joined the Sulpician Order, a society of priests who live together, but do not take traditional monastic vows. In 1929 he traveled to France to spend a period at the Sulpician retreat house at Issyles-Moulineaux. He also attended the Catholic Institute of Paris, where the next year he earned a degree in canon law. In 1931 he began to teach canon law at the Catholic seminary in Paris and at the same time served as novice master.

In 1933 Leger was sent to Japan where he established and headed a seminary through most of the years leading up to World War II. But in 1939, just as the war was beginning, he returned to Canada and became an instructor in social sciences at the Montreal seminary. The following year he also became the vicar general of the archdiocese and pastor of the cathedral parish. After the war, in 1947 he moved to Rome as head of the Canadian College, the position from which he was appointed archbishop of Montreal in 1950.

In 1953 Leger was named a cardinal and later assumed posts in the curial Congregation for the Evangelism of Peoples, the Commission for the Reform of Canon Law, and the Commission of Pastoral Concern for Migrants and Tourists. In the early 1960s he became a leading liberal voice at the Second Vatican Council. Early in the council proceedings he called for a spirit of collegiality to pervade the discussions and denounced what he saw as the antiquated mentality of the church's administrative center in the curia. His most important liberal stance was his insistence on a full discussion of birth control (after the pope had asked that the council not make a statement upon the subject) coupled with his insistence that the creation of a community of love was a true goal of a marriage, aside from the goal of procreation.

In 1968 Leger resigned as archbishop of Montreal and took up what became a second career. He went to Africa as a missionary to work among lepers. He returned in 1974 as a parish priest, but in 1975 resigned and in 1976 left for three more years in Africa. He formally retired in 1979 and settled in Montreal. He remained active, however, and over the next few years assisted in the resettlement of Cambodian and Laotian refugees. In 1981 he founded the Jules and Paul-Emile Leger Foundation and in 1982 opened a hospital for lepers in India. In 1985 he constructed a hospital in Haiti for lepers. Still alive in his 90s, in his retirement years he has exemplified the ideals which he preached as the leader of the French Canadian church.

Sources:

MacEoin, Gary. *The Inner Elite: Dossiers of Papal Candidates*. Kansas City, KS: S. Andrews and McMeel, 1978. 300 pp.

★545★
Metropolitan LEONTY
Archbishop, Russian Orthodox Greek Catholic Church of America
b. Aug. 8, 1876, Kremenetz Russia
d. May 14, 1965, Syoset, New York

Metropolitan Leonty, born Leonid Turkevich, was an archbishop of the Russian Orthodox Greek Catholic Church in America (now known as the Orthodox Church in America). His father was a Russian Orthodox priest in Western Russia. He attended the Kiev Theological Seminary, receiving his doctorate in theology. After graduating in 1900, he assumed a teaching post in an ecclesiastical school. As a layman he taught at Kursk, in central Russia, and at Ekaterinoslav, Ukraine. He married Anna Chervinsky in 1905 and was soon afterward ordained. He became parish priest in Kremenetz, succeeding his father.

The young priest had been at his first post only about a year when Leonty was selected by **Bishop Tikhon**, head of what was then the American mission, to be the rector of a new seminary being established in Minneapolis. He moved to America in the fall of 1906 and spent the next six years at the school and as pastor of St. Mary's Church in Minneapolis. In 1912 he moved with the school to Tenefly, New Jersey. In 1914, Father Leonid became editor of the Russian-American *Orthodox Messenger* and emerged as the church's main theological voice. He was appointed dean of St. Nicolas Cathedral in New York City and became an advisor to the bishops as a member of the Consistory. In 1917 he traveled to Russia to represent the American mission at the Great Sobor in Moscow, held in the shadow of the Revolution.

At the time of Father Leonid's return from Moscow, the American church entered into its most tumultuous period as rival factions argued over the church's relationship to the Moscow patriarch now under the rule of a Communist government. Leonty led what became the majority party that in 1924 declared itself autonomous from Moscow. Leonty's wife died in 1925. In 1933 he was consecrated Bishop of Chicago.

Bishop Leonty's selection as an episcopal leader put a certain stamp of authority upon an ideal for which he had become the leading spokesperson. As early as 1916, he had argued for the development of a universal American Orthodoxy that, while acknowledging Russian heritage, would be transnational in practice. He thus began the process that eventually led to the formation of the Orthodox Church in America. As a proponent of Orthodox unity, Metropolitan Leonty also led in the formation of the Standing Conference of Orthodox Canonical Bishops in America in 1960.

Bishop Leonty was elected to be archbishop and metropolitan of the church in 1950, following the death of **Metropolitan Theophilus**. Among the most important contributions during his tenure in office was his oversight of a new set of regulatory statutes for the American church, and the complete restructuring of the central administration of the church. The new structure not only clarified differing roles and responsibilities within the church but also provided for some democratic participation.

During the mid-1960s, as the new statutes were being adopted, Metropolitan Leonty entered a period of poor health which led to his death in 1965. He was succeeded by Archbishop Ireney.

Sources:

Tarasar, Constance J. *Orthodox America, 1794-1976: Development of the Orthodox Church in America*. Syoset, NY: Orthodox Church in America, Department of History and Archives, 1975. 352 pp.

★546★
LEWIS, Edwin
Theologian, Methodist Episcopal Church
b. Apr. 18, 1881, Newbury United Kingdom
d. Nov. 29, 1959, Madison, New Jersey

Edwin Lewis, a theologian in the Methodist Episcopal Church, was the son of Joseph and Sarah Newman Lewis. Lewis crossed the Atlantic at the age of 19 with Sir Wilfred Grenfell, who was doing missionary work in Labrador. He joined the Methodist Church in Canada in Newfoundland in 1900 and served the church as a minister for three years while attending Sackville College. In 1904 he married Louise Newhook Frost and shortly thereafter moved to the United States, where he served for a year in the North Dakota Conference of the Methodist Episcopal Church. He finished his education at Middlebury College in Vermont, the United Free Church College in Glasgow, Scotland, and Drew Theological Seminary, from which he received his B.D. in 1908. In 1910 he transferred to the Troy (New York) Conference and served at North Chatham and Rensselaer. In 1916 he joined the faculty at Drew as an instructor in Greek and theology and completed his Th.D., which was granted in 1918. He became a professor of theology after his graduation and stayed at Drew until his retirement in the 1950s.

During the 1920s Lewis became a prominent liberal theological voice within the Methodist Church. He authored a number of books, including *Jesus Christ and the Human Quest* (1924), *A Manual of Christian Beliefs* (1927), and *God and Ourselves* (1931). He also co-authored the *Abingdon Bible Commentary* (1929). In the 1930s, however, he underwent a profound theological change analogous to the Neo-Orthodox movement that was occurring among liberal theologians in Germany. His theology took

a decided conservative turn, and he became critical of his own earlier liberalism. He authored several books from this new perspective, including *A Christian Manifesto* (1934), *The Faith We Declare* (1938), *A Philosophy of Christian Revelation* (1930), and *A New Heaven and a New Earth* (1941).

In one of his later and more controversial books, *The Creator and the Adversary* (1948), he attacked the idea that the world was basically good, which he referred to as "a benevolent monism," and made a case that a real spirit of evil, the Devil, actually existed.

Following his retirement from Drew, Lewis taught for a time at Temple University in nearby Philadelphia, but continued to reside in Madison, New Jersey. He died in 1959.

Sources:

Harmon, Nolan B. *The Encyclopedia of World Methodism*. 2 vols. Nashville: United Methodist Publishing House, 1974.

Howell, Clinton H., ed. *Prominent Personalities in Methodism*. Birmingham, AL: Lowrey Press, 1945. 512 pp.

Lewis, Edwin. *A Christian Manifesto*. New York: Abingdon Press, 1934. 245 pp.

_____. *The Faith We Declare*. Nashville, TN: Cokesbury Press, 1939. 236 pp.

_____. *God and Ourselves*. New York: Abingdon-Cokesbury Press, 1931. 311 pp.

_____. *Great Christian Teachings*. New York: The Methodist Book Concern, 1933. 121 pp.

_____. *A Manual of Christian Beliefs*. New York: Charles Scribner's Sons, 1927. 152 pp.

★547★
LEWIS, Harvey Spencer
Founder, Ancient and Mystical Order of the Rosae Crucis (AMORC)
b. Nov. 25, 1883, Frenchtown, New Jersey
d. Aug. 2, 1939, San Jose, California

Harvey Spencer Lewis was the founder of the Ancient and Mystical Order of the Rosae Crucis (A.M.O.R.C.), the largest Rosicrucian organization in the world. Lewis grew up in New York City as a Methodist, and at one point was an artist and columnist*New York Herald*. In 1904, at the age of 21, he established the New York Institute for Psychical Research, which was primarily Rosicrucian in orientation. In 1908 a British Rosicrucian, Mrs. May Banks-Stacey, who was Legate of the Order in India, put Lewis in touch with Rosicrucians internationally, and in 1909 he went to Toulouse, France, to be initiated by members of the International Rosicrucian Council. When he returned, he had authority to begin a new order in America.

The new Rosicrucian order met for a number of years before it formally announced itself with the publication of *The Great Manifesto of the Order* (1915), and the beginning of a periodical, *The American Rosae Crucis*. By 1917 the group was successful enough to hold a national convention in Pittsburgh, which fatefully approved the idea of a correspondence course. Written by Lewis, this became the means for the group to expand worldwide into places no similar group had reached. Unfortunately, this willingness to be so public also meant facing some persecution. On June 17, 1918, police in New York arrested Lewis and charged him with selling fraudulent bonds and collecting money under false pretenses. Although the charges were subsequently dropped, Lewis felt compelled to move the group to San Francisco later that same year.

Lewis spent about seven years in San Francisco, during which he established relations with various occult groups in Europe, and met **Aleister Crowley**, head of the Ordo Templi Orientis (O.T.O.). In 1921 Lewis received a charter from the O.T.O. in Germany, which had split from Crowley. In 1925 Lewis moved the headquarters to Tampa, Florida, where the order built and managed radio station WJBB over a period of two years. In 1927 Lewis moved to a piece of land in San Jose, California, where major components of the order's headquarters were built during the next dozen years. Lewis also served as bishop of an affiliated church called the Pristine Church of the Rose Cross, an effort that ended after a few years as the order began to emphasize its nature as a nonreligious fraternal group.

Lewis was an extremely prolific writer, especially after the move to San Jose, and it is through his books that he has become known to a public beyond the Rosicrucian order. His best-known works include *Rosicrucian Questions and Answers* (1929) and *Mansions of the Soul* (1930). Another famous book, *Lemuria, The Lost Continent of the Pacific* (1931), was written by Lewis under the pseudonym W. S. Cerve. In *The Mystical Life of Jesus* (1929), Lewis very generously borrowed from *The Aquarian Gospel of Jesus the Christ* by Levi Dowling. Lewis' teachings generally center on mastering the ability to create material reality through one's mental imaging, using techniques understood to have been passed down from as long ago as Amenhotep IV in ancient Egypt. Lewis died in 1939, at the age of 56, and his son, **Ralph M. Lewis**, took over the leadership of the order.

Sources:

Clymer, R. Swinburne. *The Rosicrucian Fraternity in America*. Quakertown, PA: The Rosicrucian Foundation, 1935. 2 vols.

Lewis, Harvey Spencer. *Mansions of the Soul*. San Jose, CA: Rosicrucian Press, 1930. 334 pp.

———. *Rosicrucian Principles for the Home and Business*. San Jose, CA: Supreme Grand Lodge of AMORC, 1929. 241 pp.

———. *Rosicrucian Questions and Answers with Complete History*. San Jose, CA: Supreme Lodge of AMORC, 1929. 9th edition, 1969. 343 pp.

———. *Self Mastery and Fate with the Cycles of Life*. San Jose, CA: Rosicrucian Press, 1929. 255 pp.

McIntosh, Christopher. *The Rosy Cross Unveiled*. Wellingborough, Northhamptonshire, United Kingdom: Aquarian Press, 1980. 160 pp.

Melton, J. Gordon. *Biographical Dictionary of American Cult and Sect Leaders*. Garland Reference Library of Social Science, vol. 212. New York: Garland Publishing, 1986.

The Rosicrucian Manual. San Jose, CA: Rosicrucian Press, 1952. 200 pp.

Shepard, Leslie. *Encyclopedia of Occultism & Parapsychology*. 3 vols., 2nd. ed. Detroit: Gale Research Co., 1984-1985.

—*Gary L. Ward*

★548★
LEWIS, Joseph
Founder, Freethinkers of America
b. Jun. 11, 1889, Montgomery, Alabama
d. Nov. 4, 1968, New York, New York

Joseph Lewis, founder of the Freethinkers of America, was one of the most well-known spokespersons for atheism in twentieth-century America. He was born to a poor family in Alabama, and was forced to stop his schooling at the age of nine in order to earn money. He had a great desire to learn, however, and read on his own, gravitating to the works of Thomas Paine and **Robert Green Ingersoll**. These freethinkers of the eighteenth and nineteenth centuries became his life-long heroes, and he abandoned the Jewish faith of his family.

About 1920, at the age of 31, Lewis moved to New York City and became very successful in the dollar shirt business. He discovered a small, informal group of freethinkers, joined them, and became their leader. In 1925 he formalized the group by incorporating it, and was its first president—a position he held for the next 43 years. Lewis also became an active author on behalf of atheism, starting in the 1920s with such books as *The Tyranny of God* and *The Bible Unmasked*. To assist in publishing this material, he founded his own publishing company, the Freethought Press Association. In the early 1930s he also started the Eugenics Publishing Company to issue sex education and birth control information—

the kind of information that was difficult to obtain in those days. He married Ruth Stoller Grubman in 1952.

Lewis' work, like that of atheist literature in general, was often emotionally charged, as in *An Atheist Manifesto* (1954), boldy published at the height of the Cold War. He tried to emphasize that one could be an atheist and a good American, and pointed out the unorthodox beliefs of leaders like Paine, Benjamin Franklin, and Thomas Jefferson. He even mustered some evidence to show that Paine was the real author of the Declaration of Independence, not Jefferson, though historians did not agree that the evidence was conclusive. Lewis extolled the memory of Paine and Ingersoll, his two main heroes, in as many ways as possible—through various publications, including articles in the society's magazine, *The Age of Reason*; through erecting statues to them in the United States and abroad; and through finally convincing the Post Office to issue a Thomas Paine stamp.

Lewis was able to publicize atheism in the media, especially by appearing as a guest on a number of radio and television shows. He died of a heart attack in 1968, at the age of 79. Without his particular charismatic leadership, the Freethinkers of America did not long continue.

Sources:

Brown, Marshall G. and Gordon Stein. *Freethought in the United States*. Westport, CT: Greenwood Press, 1978. 146 pp.

Howland, Arthur H. *Joseph Lewis: Enemy of God*. Boston, MA: Stratford, 1932.

Lewis, Joseph. *Atheism and Other Addresses*. New York: Freethought Press Association, 1941.

———. *An Atheist Manifesto*. New York: Freethought Press Association, 1954. 64 pp.

———. *The Bible Unmasked*. New York: Freethought Press Association, 1926. 235 pp.

———. *Ingersoll the Magnificent*. New York: Freethought Press Association, 1957. 569 pp.

———. *The Ten Commandments*. New York: Freethought Press Association, 1946. 244 pp.

Melton, J. Gordon. *Biographical Dictionary of American Cult and Sect Leaders*. Garland Reference Library of Social Science, vol. 212. New York: Garland Publishing, 1986.

Stein, Gordon, ed. *The Encyclopedia of Unbelief*. 2 vols. Buffalo, NY: Prometheus Books, 1985.

—*Gary L. Ward*

★549★
LEWIS, Ralph M.
Imperator, Ancient and Mystical Order of the Rosae Crucis (A.M.O.R.C.)
b. Feb. 14, 1904, New York, New York
d. Jan. 12, 1987, San Jose, California

Ralph M. Lewis was for 48 years the imperator of the largest Rosicrucian organization in North America, the Ancient and Mystical Order of the Rosae Crucis (A.M.O.R.C.). Lewis was the son of **Harvey Spencer Lewis**, the founder of the order, and Mollie Goldsmith Lewis. Most of his education was received at a military academy in New Jersey. By the time of Ralph's graduation, his father had founded the Rosicrucian order (1915) and had moved its headquarters to California. In 1918 Ralph joined his parents and studied law and accounting in San Francisco. In 1923 he married Gladys Natishna Hammer.

Lewis formally became a member of the order in 1921. He progressed through the program of teachings and in 1924 became the supreme secretary. He moved to Tampa, Florida, where the order was headquartered briefly before its permanent establishment in San Jose, California, in 1927. Through the 1930s, Lewis traveled and spoke on the order's behalf both in North America and Europe. He is most credited with the centralization of the order's activities and a resultant expansion of membership in North America.

In 1939, following the death of his father, he was elected the new imperator and the following year became president of the International Supreme Council of the Order Rosae Crucis, the order's international structure, and director of the museum and planetarium which the order had built in San Jose.

As leader of the Rosicrucians, Lewis was involved in the administration of the increasingly worldwide organization, beginning with the reconstruction of its organization in Europe after World War II. He traveled extensively to conclaves around the world. He oversaw the development of Rosicrucian Park in San Jose into one of the leading tourist attractions in the state. An avid amatuer egyptologist and archeologist, he conducted film expeditions to Egypt and Asia on several occasions in the 15 years after the war and produced several documentary movies.

Lewis added greatly to the Rosicrucian literature as the author of a number of articles for the *Rosicrucian Digest* and the *Rosicrucian Forum*, the order's two major periodicals. He also wrote several books, including: *Behold the Sign* (1944), *The Sanctuary of the Self* (1948), *The Conscious Interlude* (1957), and *Yesterday Much to Tell* (1973).

Sources:

Lewis, Ralph M. *Behold the Sign*. San Jose, CA: Supreme Grand Lodge of the AMORC, 1944. 99 pp.

_____. *The Conscious Interlude*. San Jose, CA: Supreme Lodge of the AMORC, 1957. 363 pp.

_____. *The Sanctuary of the Self*. San Jose, CA: Supreme Lodge of the AMORC, 1948. 351 pp.

_____. *Yesterday Has Much to Tell*. San Jose, CA: Supreme Lodge of the AMORC, 1973. 435 pp.

"Special Ralph M. Lewis Memorial Issue." *Rosicrucian Digest* (1987).

★550★
LEWIS, Samuel Leonard
Spiritual Teacher, Sufi Order
b. Oct. 18, 1896, San Francisco, California
d. Jan. 15, 1971, San Francisco, California

Samuel Leonard Lewis was a spiritually wide-ranging teacher who most identified as a Sufi Murshid (a clergy-type designation), but was also ordained as a Zen master, and had significant acquaintance with several other religious traditions. Born in San Francisco to Jewish parents and raised in that tradition, Lewis, as a young man, showed an inclination to explore beyond that faith. In 1915, at the age of 19, he visited the World's Fair in San Francisco. There he discovered Theosophy and studied that for some time. In 1919 he found Sufism and began to study with American Sufi Murshid Rabia Martin, a disciple of Pir **Hazrat Inayat Khan**, founder of the Sufi Order. In 1923 Khan himself formally initiated Lewis as a Sufi.

In 1920 Lewis met **Nyogen Senzaki**, an early Zen teacher in California, and worked with him in establishing his zendos in San Francisco (1928) and Los Angeles (1929). In 1930, when Sokei-an Sasaki Roshi (also known as **Shigetsu Sasaki Roshi**) founded the First Zen Institute of America in New York, Lewis went to sit with him. Sokei-an gave him dharma transmission, thus recognizing him as a revered Zen teacher. Zen Buddhism has a nondualistic philosophy compatible with Hinduism's Advaita Vedanta tradition, and in the 1930s Lewis (through Paul Brunton) was initiated into the yoga practices of **Ramana Maharshi** (1879-1950), a sage of that tradition who lived in South India.

Meanwhile, Lewis maintained his primary Sufi orientation. In 1925 Pir Hazrat Inayat Khan pronounced Lewis "Protector of the Message," and from 1927 to 1942 he assisted Rabia Martin, Khan's first American initiate and successor, with the work in Fairfax, California. From 1942 to 1945 he served in the U.S. Army Intelligence, during which time Martin reoriented the group toward **Meher Baba**. Lewis did not like the changes and dropped out finally in 1949, existing for several years as an independent Sufi, despite the honors earlier given him by Khan.

In 1953 Lewis was initiated by Hindu Swami Ram Dass of Kanhangad, India, and in 1956 he was initiated into Shingon Buddhism by Zen masters of Japan. That same year found him in Pakistan, where he was initiated into the Naqshbandi order of Sufis, and then in India, where he was ordained by the Nizami (Chishti) order, Khan's original group. In 1960 Lewis returned to Asia for two years, during which time he was initiated into the Rifai and Shadhili Sufi orders in Egypt, and the Khalandar and Khidri-Chishti-Kadri orders of Pakistan. The combined Chishti, Kadiri, and Sabri orders ordained him as a murshid.

In 1966 Lewis founded a Sufic group in San Francisco, naming his first center the Mentorgarten, after Senzaki's earlier zendo. He also helped found the Holy Order of MANS, an esoteric Christian order in San Francisco, and in 1967 was ordained a Zen master by Korean master Kyung-Bo Seo. About this time he discovered that Hazrat Inayat Khan's son, **Pir Vilayat Inayat Khan**, had come to the United States to reintroduce his father's Sufi Order, after the earlier group had been subsumed under Meher Baba's leadership. Lewis merged his group into the new Sufi Order in 1968. He spent the last years of his life actively traveling and teaching, and died in 1971 at the age of 74. He is most remembered in these last years for his introduction of spiritual dances and walks, often in combination with breath control and mantra repetition, that were designed to lead to ecstasy and devotion to Allah. In 1977 some of his students had disagreements with the Sufi Order and formed the Sufi Islamia Ruhaniat Society.

Sources:

Lewis, Samuel L. *In the Garden*. New York, 1975.

_____. *The Jerusalem Trilogy*. Novato, CA: Prophecy Pressworks, 1975. 335 pp.

_____. *Sufi Vision and Initiation*. San Francisco: Sufi Islamia/Prophecy Publications, 1986. 379 pp.

_____. *This Is the New Age, in Person*. Tucson, AZ: Omen Press, 1972. 158 pp.

_____. *Toward Spiritual Brotherhood*. Tucson, AZ: Omen Press, 1972. 101 pp.

Melton, J. Gordon. *Biographical Dictionary of American Cult and Sect Leaders*. Garland Reference Library of Social Science, vol. 212. New York: Garland Publishing, 1986.

—*Gary L. Ward*

★551★
LICHTENBERGER, Arthur Carl
Presiding Bishop, Episcopal Church
b. Jan. 8, 1900, Oshkosh, Wisconsin

Arthur Carl Lichtenberger, the twenty-first presiding bishop of the Episcopal Church, was the son of Theresa Heitz and Adam Lichtenberger. He attended Kenyon College and the Episcopal Theological School in Cambridge, Massachusetts, from which he received his B.D. in 1925. In 1924, while in seminary, he married Florence Elizabeth Tate. That same year he was ordained a deacon and left the United States to become a professor of New Testament at St. Paul's Divinity School in Wuchang, China. He was ordained as a priest in 1926.

Upon his return to the United States in 1927, Lichtenberger became the rector of Grace Episcopal Church in Cincinnati, Ohio, and later moved to St. Paul's Episcopal Church in Brookline, Massachusetts. In 1938 he returned to the classroom as a lecturer in pastoral care at the Episcopal Theological School. In 1941 he became dean of Trinity Cathedral in Newark, New Jersey, and in 1948 became professor of pastoral theology at General Theological Seminary in New York City.

In 1950 Lichtenberger was elected bishop coadjutor for the diocese of Missouri and was consecrated the following year in St. Louis. In 1952 he succeeded William Scarlett as bishop of Missouri. Among other notable activities while bishop of Missouri, he chaired the 1956 delegation of Episcopal leaders who traveled to India to study the Church of South India, a unique ecumenical church body.

In 1958 Lichtenberger was elected Presiding bishop of the Episcopal Church to succeed **Henry Knox Sherrill**. The beginning of his term coincided with the emergence of the Civil Rights Movement, and Lichtenberger gave it his full support. He led in the formation of the Commission of Religion and Race of the National Council of Churches and was named its first chairman. Two months after the commission's establishment, Lichtenberger gave his support to the March on Washington at which **Martin Luther King, Jr.**, gave his famous "I Have a Dream" speech. He then became a leading force in the churches' move to gain congressional support for the civil rights bill.

Lichtenberger's work as presiding bishop and his role in setting the direction for the churches' involvement in the Civil Rights Movement was, unfortunately, cut short in 1964 when he was forced to retire because of health problems. He lived in Cambridge, Massachusetts, during his retirement years and was succeeded by **John Elbridge Hines**.

Sources:

Cavert, Samuel McCrea. *The American Churches in the Ecumenical Movement, 1900-1968.* New York: Association Press, 1968. 288 pp.
The Episcopal Church Annual. New York: Morehouse-Gorham, Co., 1959. 548 pp.

★552★
LIEBMAN, Joshua Loth
Rabbi, Reform Judaism
b. Apr. 7, 1907, Hamilton, Ohio
d. Jun. 9, 1948, Boston, Massachusetts

Joshua Loth Liebman, a rabbi of Reform Judaism, was the son of Simon Liebman and Sabina Loth Liebman. Somewhat of a prodigy, the young Joshua entered high school at the age of 10 and graduated from the University of Cincinnati (B.A., 1926) at the age of 19 when most of his contemporaries were just finishing high school. He attended Hebrew Union College and finished his rabbinical training and was ordained in 1930. While attending Hebrew Union, he held a position as lecturer in Greek at the university. Upon finishing his training, he married Fannie Loth, his first cousin, and they spent the next year moving from Harvard to Columbia to the Hebrew University in Jerusalem on Liebman's traveling fellowship. Upon their return, Liebman assumed a post as an instructor in Bible and medieval exegesis at Hebrew Union.

In 1934 Liebman became rabbi of Kelilath Anshe Maarab Temple in Chicago. In 1939 he received his doctorate from Hebrew Union and that same year accepted the position as rabbi of Temple Israel in Boston. Already a large congregation with over 500 families, it grew to 1,400 families within its first decade under Liebman's leadership. Liebman's abilities led to his becoming a member of the faculty of Andover Newton Theological Seminary, the first Christian school to appoint a rabbi to a regular faculty position. He also began a radio show on which he preached each Sunday morning.

During his years in Boston, Liebman began to focus on the problems of relating psychology and religion, a concern becoming prominent in the theological agenda as psychology gained in importance. In 1946, Liebman authored *Peace of Mind*, a popular book which attempted to integrate psychological and religious themes and which became an instant best seller. Within weeks of its release it was selling over 5,000 copies per week. It went through more than 40 printings and was translated into several foreign languages.

Liebman assumed that religion and psychology shared a common goal: to promote individual maturity and inner security. Religion provided guidance in the moral realm. Psychology provided an overall perspective. Liebman had absorbed the optimism of liberal Protestant thought as well as New Thought metaphysical themes. He saw God as Infinite Mind, the "Power" of the higher ideals of humankind—righteousness, artistic values, and intangible spiritual qualities.

Liebman stayed at Temple Israel for the remainder of his active life. He published one sequel to *Peace of Mind, Hope for Man* (1964) which, though popular, never attained the success of his first book.

Sources:

Dictionary of American Biography. 20 vols. and 7 supps. New York: Charles Scribner's Sons, 1928-1936, 1944-1981.
Liebman, Joshua. *Hope for Man.* New York: Simon & Schuster, 1964. 250 pp.
———. *Peace of Mind.* New York: Simon & Schuster, 1946. 203 pp.

★553★
LINDSEY, Gordon J.
Founder, Christ for the Nations
b. Jun. 18, 1906, Zion, Illinois
d. Apr. 1, 1973, Dallas, Texas

Gordon J. Lindsey was born at Zion, Illinois, the commune founded by healing evangelist **John Alexander Dowie**. He became the founder of Christ for the Nations, a prominent Pentecostal missionary agency, and of the Full Gospel Fellowship of Ministers and Churches, an association of independent Pentecostal ministers and congregations. When he was still a child, however, the community went through a severe internal struggle and financial crisis. The Lindsey family left and moved to Idaho, and then Oregon, before settling in rural, southern California at the Pisgah Grande commune in the Santa Susanna Mountains. However, the Pisgah Grande community soon collapsed, and the family relocated in Portland, Oregon, where Lindsey had his most stable childhood years.

At the age of 14, Lindsey discovered John D. Lake, one of the leading independent Pentecostal ministers, who then pastored a church in Portland. On his first visit to Lake's church, Pentecostal founder **Charles Fox Parham** was preaching. Parham's sermon became the instrument of Lindsey's conversion. Several days later he first spoke in tongues. (Speaking in tongues, which is seen as evidence of the believer having received the baptism of the Holy Spirit, is the definitive pentecostal experience.) He soon felt a call to preach and began a street ministry. In 1924 he moved to southern California, and in San Diego again encountered John D. Lake, who gave him a large tent. Lindsey was now equipped to become a full-time evangelist.

In 1932 back in Portland, Lindsey met Freda Schimpf, a young woman who had been saved in one of his meetings. She was a member of the International Church of the Foursquare Gospel (founded by **Aimee Semple McPherson**). Later Lindsey became pastor of the Foursquare church in the San Fernando Valley, California. He married Freda in 1937. The next years were spent pastoring churches in Tacoma, Washington, and Billings, Montana, and on evangelistic work. In 1944 Lindsey moved to Ashland, Oregon, as pastor of an Assemblies of God congregation.

Lindsey was still at Ashland when he met **William Marrion Branham**, the healing evangelist in 1947. Leaving Freda in charge of the church, he became Branham's manager and started the *Voice of Healing*, a magazine that publicized and supported the revivals conducted by Branham and his colleagues. In 1948 he established headquarters in Shreveport, Louisiana, and the following year he organized a Voice of Healing Fellowship and held the first annual Voice of Healing convention.

After he moved the headquarters of the Voice of Healing to Dallas in 1952, Lindsey's work grew steadily. Publishing expanded, a correspondence course initiated, and a Native Church Crusade launched to plant churches overseas. In 1962, the Voice of Healing Fellowship was superseded by the Full Gospel Fellowship of Ministers and Churches. As the work grew, a Christian center was purchased in 1966 and in the next years the transformation of the work was completed as the Voice of Healing, name under which much of the work had been conducted, was replaced by Christ for the Nations. In 1970 the first Bible school opened. Since Lindsey's death, his wife has continued to lead the still-expanding worldwide endeavor.

Lindsey was a prolific writer. He authored more than 250 books and pamphlets between 1940 and the time of his death. Through these and his magazine he left an important chronicle of modern Pentecostalism, especially the healing movements of the mid-twentieth century. Besides his own autobiography, he authored biographies of William Branham and John Alexander Dowie, and reprinted many of the sermons of John D. Lake.

Sources:

Harrell, David Edwin, Jr. *All Things Are Possible*. Bloomington, IN: Indiana University Press, 1975.
Lindsey, Freda. *My Dairy Secrets*. Dallas, TX: Christ for the Nations, 1976. 289 pp.
Lindsey, Gordon. *The Baptism of the Holy Spirit*. Dallas, TX: Christ for the Nations, 1971. 92 pp.
_____. *Bible Days Are Here Again*. Shreveport, LA: The Author, 1949. 290 pp.
_____. *False Christs, False Prophets*. Dallas, TX: Christ for the Nations, 1983. 79 pp.
_____. *The Gordon Lindsey Story*. Dallas, TX: The Author, n.d.
_____. *John Alexander Dowie: A Life Story of Trials, Tragedies and Triumphs*. Dallas, TX: Christ for the Nations, 1980. 275 pp.
_____. *William Branham: A Man Sent from God*. Jeffersonville, IN: William Branham, 1905. 216 pp.

★554★
LIPSCOMB, David
Minister, Churches of Christ
Editor, Gospel Advocate
b. Jan. 21, 1831, Franklin County, Tennessee
d. Nov. 11, 1917, Nashville, Tennessee

David Lipscomb was, for 47 years, the editor of the *Gospel Advocate*, the nineteenth century focal point for what became the Churches of Christ. He was born in rural Tennessee, the son of Granville Lipscomb, a member of the anti-mission Primitive Baptist Church. In 1835, Granville Lipscomb, convinced that slavery was wrong, moved to Illinois for a year and freed his slaves. However, within a year, his wife and three children and the remaining family returned to Tennessee.

In 1845, at the age of 14, young David encountered Tolbert Fanning, an early Churches of Christ minister who had just founded Franklin College in Nashville, Tennessee. Fanning baptized Lipscomb, and the following year Lipscomb entered Franklin College. During his years there he firmly adhered to Fanning's opinions against Christian participation in war, missionary societies, and centralized church government. Lipscomb graduated in 1849 and was chosen valedictorian. He returned to farming and was quite successful. Though active in the church, he only began to preach in the late 1850s. He actively spoke out against the Civil War, which made him unpopular with both warring factions.

After the war, Lipscomb decided to make an effort to revive the church, which had been so hurt by the war. With the help of Fanning, Lipscomb began to reissue the *Gospel Advocate*, which Fanning had founded before the war. The paper became a self-consciously Southern periodical, devoid of the offensive political references that seemed integral to other periodicals issued in the church. It soon became the leading Christian church organ in the South, with little circulation in the rest of the country. Fanning gradually withdrew, and the paper became exclusively Lipscomb's work, and he personally carried it through several financial crises in the first few years.

During his years as editor, Lipscomb emphasized a strict literal Biblical faith, generally stated as speaking where the Bible speaks and keeping silent where it keeps silent. He became most identified with the cause of opposing the innovative introduction of instrumental music and missionary societies into the churches. Over the decades of his editorship, he led most of the congregations in the South to accept his views. Gradually, these churches began to refer to themselves as the Churches of Christ. Those churches in the North who accepted instrumental music (the installation of organs in church buildings) and the organization of centralized missionary societies to collect money and support missionaries gradually became known as the Christian Church (Disciples of Christ).

A split gradually developed between the Churches of Christ and the Disciples, though their decentralized state prevented a formal schism. The split is generally dated from 1906, when the Churches of Christ were listed separately from the Disciples in the *Religious Census*.

In addition to his editing chores at the *Gospel Advocate*, Lipscomb penned several books, including a biography of colleague Jesse Sewell, a volume on civil government, and several bible commentaries. In his later years, Lipscomb's interest in education came to the fore. In 1884 he helped organize the Fanning Orphan School and in 1891 the Nashville Bible School (now David Lipscomb College). He served as chairman of the board of trustees for both institutions. He died in 1917.

Sources:

Hill, Samuel S., ed. *Encyclopedia of Religion in the South*. Macon, GA: Mercer University Press, 1984. 878 pp.
Lipscomb, David. *Biography and Sermons of Jesse Sewell*. Nashville, TN: Gospel Advocate Company, 1891.
_____. *Civil Government*. Nashville, TN: McQuiddy Printing Co., 1913. 158 pp.
_____. *Queries and Answers*. Nashville, TN: McQuiddy Printing Co., 1910. 458 pp.
_____. *Salvation from Sin*. Nashville, TN: McQuiddy Printing Co., 1913. 440 pp.
West, Earl Irwin. *The Search for the Ancient Order*. 2 vols. Nashville, TN: Gospel Advocate Company, 1964.
_____. *Times of David Lipscomb*. Henderson, TN: Religious Book Service, 1954. 288 pp.

★555★
LLOYD, Frederick Ebenezer John
Archbishop, American Catholic Church
b. Jun. 5, 1859, Milford Haven Wales
d. Sep. 11, 1933, Chicago, Illinois

Frederick Ebenezer John Lloyd, the second primate of the American Catholic Church, was born in South Wales and raised in England. He attended the Dorchester Missionary College and, following his graduation in 1882, was ordained as a deacon in the Church of England. Shortly thereafter he left for Labrador and Newfoundland where Wilfred T. Grenfell had established his famous mission. Rather than returning to England after his three years in the field, Lloyd decided to remain in Canada and was ordained a priest by the bishop of Quebec of the Church of England in Canada. Lloyd became rector at Levis, Quebec, remaining in Canada until 1894 when he moved to the United States and transferred to the Episcopal Church. He served in Bloomington, Illinois, as pastor of St. Matthew's Episcopal Church for a few months before settling in Hamilton, Ohio, as rector of Trinity Episcopal Church. He later pastored at St. Mark's in Cleveland, Ohio (1898-1903) and St. Peter's Church in Uniontown, Pennsylvania. During most of these years he edited the *American Church Directory* (also called *Lloyd's Clerical Directory*) an annual directory of Episcopal Church personnel and affairs. In 1903 he also founded he Society of St. Philip the Apostle to train missionary priests.

The first decade of the new century proved tumultuous for Lloyd. In 1905 he was elected bishop coadjutor of Oregon. However, after objections to his election were raised by a group in Oregon, he withdrew. In 1907 he withdrew from the Episcopal Church and joined the Roman Catholic Church, but returned to the Episcopalians at the end of the decade. In 1911 he became pastor of the Grace Episcopal Church in Oak Park, Illinois.

Finally in 1914 Lloyd left the Episcopal Church permanently, and in 1915 affiliated with the American Catholic Church headed by Abp. **Joseph Rene Vilatte**. Vilatte consecrated Lloyd a bishop on December 29, 1915. In 1917, Lloyd, a widower, married Philena R. Peabody, the widow of millionaire Hiram P. Peabody.

In 1920 Vilatte retired and turned the leadership of the church over to Lloyd who became archbishop and primate. He was able to recruit several former Episcopal priests and developed an impressive hierarchy, though the small size of the membership did not warrant such a multiplication of bishops. After 12 years of leading the church, Lloyd retired in 1932, and was succeeded by D. C. Hinton whom he had consecrated in 1927. Following Lloyd's death in 1933, Hinton began to lead the church toward the Liberal Catholic position by accepting theosophical teachings.

Sources:

Anson, Peter F. *Bishops at Large*. London: Faber and Faber, 1954. 593 pp.
Lloyd, Frederic E. J. *Two Years in the Region of Icebergs and What I Saw There*. London: Society for Promoting Christian Knowledge, 1944. 127 pp.
Ward, Gary L. *Independent Bishops: An International Directory*. Detroit: Apogee Books, 1990. 524 pp.

★ 556 ★
LOUGHBOROUGH, John Norton
Minister, Seventh-day Adventist Church
b. Jan. 26, 1832, United States
d. 1924

John Loughborough's path to the ministry began when, as a young man, he became attracted to the adventist message of the soon return of Christ and began to preach for the adventist cause around 1849. In 1852 he met Seventh-day Adventist Church preacher J. N. Andrew and converted to sabbatarianism. By the end of the year he had become a full-time Seventh-day Adventist minister. He was ordained in 1854 and for over a decade served as an evangelist in the East and Midwest. By 1865 he had settled in Michigan and was elected president of the Michigan Conference (1865-1868). Victimized by health problems that had developed in the early 1860s, Loughborough became deeply interested in the church's natural health leanings and wrote his first book out of his exploration, *Hand Book of Health: or a Brief Treatise on Physiology and Health* (1868).

In 1868 Loughborough traveled to California with D. T. Bourdeau to open the adventist work on the West coast. Beginning with the congregation in Petaluma, Loughborough oversaw the growth of the movement. The first church building was erected in Santa Rosa. Five congregations had been organized by 1871, and the first gathering of leaders occurred in 1872. In 1873 a conference was formed, and Loughborough was elected its first president. He served for five years, during which time he pushed into Nevada. When the Nevada Association was formed in 1878, he was elected its president.

In 1878 Loughborough was directed to England to develop the fledgling work already begun there. While in England he developed the church at Southhampton. Returning to America in 1883 he was sent as a missionary to the Pacific Northwest. He served as president of the Upper Columbia Conference (Eastern Washington and Idaho) for two years (1884-1885). Returning to California, he became conference president a second time in 1887 and held the post for three years. Concurrently he remained as editor of the *Pacific Health Journal* (now *Life and Health*).

After his last tenure as conference president, Loughborough stayed in California and authored the church's first denominational history, *The Rise and Progress of the Seventh-day Adventists* (1892, revised as *The Great Second Advent Movement* in 1905). He also authored *The Church, Its Organization, Order, and Discipline* (1907), which was used as the denominational organizational manual for many years. In 1908 he made a world tour, after which he retired.

Sources:

Loughborough, John N. *The Church, Its Organization, Order, and Discipline*. Washington, DC: Review & Herald Publishing Assn., 1907. 184 pp.
_____. *Handbook of Health; or, a Brief treatise on Physiology and Health*. Battle Creek, MI: Steam Press of the Seventh-day Adventist Publishing Association, 1868. 227 pp.
_____. *The Rise and Progress of the Seventh-day Adventists*. Battle Creek, MI: General Conference Association of Seventh-Day Adventists, 1892. Rev. ed. as: *The Great Second Advent Movement*. Nashville, TN: Southern Publishing Association, 1905. 480 pp.

★ 557 ★
LOVETT, Cummings Samuel
Founder, Personal Christianity Chapel
b. Jan. 26, 1917, Tulare, California

Cummings Samuel "C. S." Lovett, a Baptist minister and founder of Personal Christianity, a literature ministry based at Personal Christianity Chapel in Baldwin Park, California, is the son of Clyde A. and Agnes Nicewonger Lovett. While Lovett was still a small child, his parents separated and he was raised by his mother's parents. During his teen years his mother remarried, and at the age of 15 he moved to Los Angeles with her. He attended Santa Monica Junior College. At the age of 21 he met his father for the first time and went into business with him constructing motels and apartments. An interest in flying led him into the Civilian Pilot Training Program in 1941 and the following year, after Pearl Harbor, into the the Army Air Force. In 1942 he married Marjorie Seyring. After the war, which included some time spent stationed in India, Lovett returned to his business life in southern California and began attending Beverly Hills Presbyterian Church.

Not a particularly religious man, Lovett unwillingly attended a minister's conference in 1947 at which an informal conversation he overheard became the catalyst for a conversion experience. That experience in turn led to his joining La Cienega Baptist Church, a congregation affiliated with the Conservative Baptist Association. A call to the ministry soon followed, and in 1951 he entered the California Baptist Theological Seminary. He also participated in the founding of the Baldwin Park Baptist Church. His work at the seminary, which included preaching on the streets, led him to seek and devise a simple way to communicate the Christian message to people quickly. Through trial and error he developed a step-by-step approach to introducing people to what he termed personal Christianity. He discussed the method in a booklet, *Soul Winning Made Easy* (1952). It was soon followed by a second volume, *Dynamic Truths for the Spirit-filled Life* (1957), to help train the new believer in the Christian life.

Lovett graduated from the seminary and was ordained as a Conservative Baptist minister. He developed a vision of a congregation that would be the basis of a national, and even worldwide, evangelistic effort through the production and distribution of literature. The Baldwin Park congregation rejected his proposal, however, and he left to found Personal Christianity Chapel, which has remained the base of his ministry.

Through the 1950s the basic volume, *Soul Winning Made Easy*, became a popular text and went through many editions. Lovett has authored a variety of additional books, including commentaries on the books of the Bible and books on practical topics for individuals such as dieting, exercise, and parenting. In 1976 the idea that the ministry was preparing people for the return of Jesus Christ led him to the concept of the "Maranatha Man." The concept of "maranatha" (a Greek word literally translated as "come quickly"), which strives for Jesus' prompt second coming, has dominated the work of Personal Christianity in recent years. In 1978 Lovett authored his autobiography, *C. S. Lovett: Maranatha Man*.

Sources:

Lovett, C. S. *C. S. Lovett: Maranatha Man*. Baldwin Park, CA: Personal Christianity, 1978. 232 pp.

———. *Dynamic Truths for the Spirit-filled Life*. Baldwin Park, CA: Personal Christianity, 1957, 1973. 221 pp.

———. *Help Lord—The Devil Wants Me Fat*. Baldwin Park, CA: Personal Christianity, 1977. 240 pp.

———. *Soul-Winning Made Easy*. Baldwin Park, CA: Personal Christianity, 1959, 1978. 144 pp.

———. *What's a Parent to Do?* Baldwin Park, CA: Personal Christianity, 1971. 268 pp.

★558★
LOWERY, Joseph E.
President, Southern Christian Leadership Conference
b. 1925, Alabama

For one so prominent, little information on the early years of Methodist minister and civil rights activist Joseph E. Lowery has become part of the public record. He was born in Alabama in 1925 and raised in Huntsville, where his father managed a pool hall and store. At various times he attended Knoxville College in Tennessee, Alabama A & M College, and Paine College, and he took his seminary work at Paine Theological Seminary. He earned both a B.A. and B.D. He later did postgraduate work at Garrett Theological Seminary and in 1950 was admitted to the predominantly-black Central Alabama Conference of the Methodist Church (1939-1968). He married Evelyn Gibson.

In 1952 Lowery was appointed to the Warren Street Methodist Church in Mobile, Alabama. While there he joined with **Martin Luther King, Jr.**, in 1957 in the formation of the Southern Christian Leadership Conference (SCLC), the primary organization to guide the civil rights movement. He was named vice-president of SCLC. He stayed in Mobile until 1961 when he moved to Nashville, Tennessee, as administrative assistant to Bp. Charles F. Golden. In Nashville he became active in the move to desegregate hotels and restaurants. In 1964 he returned to Alabama as pastor of St. Paul's Methodist Church in Birmingham. Lowery's early years at St. Paul's coincided with the final efforts of the Methodist Church to merge with the Evangelical United Brethren to form the United Methodist Church. He led a demonstration of black delegates at the 1966 Methodist general conference and became the major voice in convincing the new church to drop the continuing segregated structures at the national, jurisdictional, and conference level.

In 1967 Lowery became chairman of the board of SCLC. The next year, the year of the formation of the United Methodist Church, Lowery moved to Atlanta, Georgia, where he became the

pastor of the Central United Methodist Church. SCLC spent the next decade in internal turmoil and in 1977 **Ralph David Abernathy** was forced out of office as president. Lowery succeeded Abernathy and has remained as president during the intervening years.

Lowery's first task was to rebuild SCLC, then $10,000 in debt and suffering from a dwindling membership. He redirected the overall program into backing efforts to give Blacks social, economic, and political access to the predominantly white society. He also became directly involved in international issues, opposing trade with South Africa and supporting the Palestinian cause. The Palestinian question was raised after the dismissal of Andrew Young in 1979 as the United States ambassador to the United Nations. Young's favorable remarks about Palestine triggered Lowery's curiosity. His work on subsequent Middle Eastern issues has placed him at odds with American Jewish leadership. More recently he became a supporter of Korean minister **Sun Myung Moon** during the latter's losing court battle over tax issues.

Sources:

Biography Index. New York: The H. W. Wilson Co.
Current Biography Yearbook. New York: H. W. Wilson Co.
The Negro Almanac. Detroit: Gale Research Inc.
Who's Who in America. Wilmette, IL: Marquis Who's Who, Inc.
Who's Who in Religion. 2d ed. Chicago: Marquis Who's Who, Inc., 1977.

★559★
LOWRY, Edith Elizabeth
Executive, National Council of Churches
b. Mar. 23, 1897, Plainfield, New Jersey
d. Mar. 11, 1970, Claremont, New Hampshire

Edith Elizabeth Lowry, who for several decades directed an interdenominational ministry to migrant workers, was the daughter of Elizabeth Darling and Robert Hanson Lowry, a banker. She joined her parents' church, First-Park Baptist Church of Plainfield, New Jersey. She attended Wellsley College, from which she received her A.B. in 1920. In 1922 she joined the staff of the Department of Education and Publicity of the Board of Missions of the Presbyterian Church in the U.S.A., and in 1926 became executive secretary of the Council of Women for Home Missions, one of the early national America ecumenical agencies.

With the Council of Women, Lowry was assigned particular responsibility for work among migrant workers and in 1929 became director of the migrant ministries program. She was in place in the 1930s when post-Depression America became most aware of the problems of migrants. She developed and directed a growing staff of professionals to work among the migrants, including social workers, nurses, and school teachers. She was an effective speaker and writer and was frequently called upon to describe her experiences in the ministry as she traveled the country.

In 1936 Lowry was named executive secretary of the Council of Women. She authored two books during these years of council leadership, *They Starve that We Might Eat* (1938), a widely circulated booklet on the migrants, and *Tales of Americans on Trek* (1940). In 1939 she became the first woman invited to speak on the National Radio Pulpit. During her brief tenure as president, she led the Council of Women to merge into another similar agency, the Home Missions Council of North America. She was named co-executive secretary of the Home Missions Council.

In her elevated position Lowry did not forget the migrants. She pioneered new services among them in the 1940s. Her major accomplishment during this time was the institution of day care centers for the working parents. In 1950 the Home Missions Council merged with several other agencies, including the Federal Council of Churches, to form the National Council of Churches. Lowry became the first secretary of the Council's board of Home Missions. In her new position she was able to bring the considerable resources and prestige of the council to bear on the migrant's plight. She organized a program to reach people in the more remote migrant camps, and secured the use of several station wagons to carry recreational, health, and religious supplies to the workers.

Following her retirement in 1962, Lowry consulted for two years with the National Council on Agricultural Life and Labor in Washington, D.C. She then retired to a farm in Vermont where she quietly lived out the rest of her life.

Sources:

Lowry, Edith E. *Migrants of the Crops: They Starve that We Might Eat.* New York: Council of Women for Home Missions and Missionary Education Movement, 1938. 72 pp.

_____. *Tales of Americans on Trek.* New York: Friendship Press, 1940. 95 pp.

James, Edward T., ed. *Notable American Women, 1607-1950: A Biographical Dictionary.* 3 vols. Cambridge, MA: Harvard University Press, Belknap Press, 1971.

★560★
LUNDEBERG, Knut Olafson
Founder, Church of the Lutheran Brethren
b. Jan. 23, 1859, Telemarke Norway
d. Jun. 6, 1942?

Knut Olafson Lundeberg, the founder and first president of the Church of the Lutheran Brethren, was the son of Olav and Aslang Stormyr. As a child he lived with his half sister and her husband whose last name, Lundeberg, he adopted as his own. He grew up in an environment strongly affected by the revival which swept through Norwegian Lutheranism led by Hans Neilsen Hauge. He attended the Teacher Training School and in 1879, shortly after his graduation, migrated to the United States. He continued his schooling as he could, and in 1886 entered the Lutherske Presterkole, a school at St. Olaf's College in Northfield, Minnesota. It had been established by Norwegian pastors opposed to some of the emphases in the Lutheran Church-Missouri Synod, with which they had formerly been associated. He studied under **Frederich A. Schmidt** and Markus O. Borkman. Lundeberg graduated in 1889 at the head of his class, was called to pastor two small churches at Kenyon, Minnesota, and was ordained to the Lutheran ministry. In 1890 the anti-Missouri group joined with several other Norwegian Lutheran groups to form the United Norwegian Lutheran Church.

At Kenyon, Lundeberg ran into trouble among the more conservative and staid church members as he preached the need of a personal religion. As a result he was forced out of one parish and eventually, with former members, formed a parish independent of the United Evangelical Lutheran Church, Bethany Lutheran Church. In 1899 he began a periodical, *Broderbaandet.* Over the next year other similar free congregations appeared, and in December 1900, Lundeberg traveled to Milwaukee to a conference of delegates from several of them. At that meeting the Church of the Lutheran Brethren was formed, and Lundeberg was elected its first president. Among the first issues to confront the new church was the establishment of a Bible school. Lundeberg was one of two teachers elected to the faculty of the school, which began to meet in Zion Lutheran Church in Wahpeton, North Dakota.

In 1910 Lundeberg suddenly announced his resignation from the Church of the Lutheran Brethren. He had come to disagree with its most important concept of the church consisting of independent free congregations of believers only. He published his views in a pamphlet, *Svar paa Sporsmaal on Hvorfor jeg forlot Brodersamfundet of gik ind i Den forenede Kirke* (*Why I Left the Lutheran Brethren and Joined the United Lutheran Church*). The break was as free of hostility as such an important parting could be. After a period of shock and sorrow, Lundeberg occasionally contributed

articles to the church's periodical and from 1932 to 1934 was invited again to teach at the Bible school.

Sources:

Levang, Joseph H. *The Church of the Lutheran Brethren, 1900-1975.* Fergus Falls, MN: Lutheran Brethren Publishing Company, 1980. 396 pp.

★561★
LYMAN, Mary Reddington Ely
Theologian, Congregational Church
b. Nov. 24, 1887, St. Johnsbury, Vermont
d. Jan. 9, 1975, Claremont, California

Mary Reddington Ely Lyman, one of the first woman theologians in American Protestantism, was the daughter of Adelaide Newell and Henry Guy Ely, a businessman. She grew up in the Congregational Church and was active in the Society of Christian Endeavor. She attended Mount Holyoke College, from which she graduated in 1911. She taught school for two years and then served as general secretary of the YWCA at Mount Holyoke. In 1916 she took the opportunity to attend Union Theological Seminary in New York. She was the only woman in her class and was not allowed to sit with the class when she graduated, even though she was the top scholar in the class. She followed her three years in seminary with two at Cambridge, only to discover that the school refused to issue her a theological degree or a transcript. She returned to America to teach at Vassar College and work on her Ph.D. at the University of Chicago (granted in 1924). Her dissertation was published in 1925 as *The Knowledge of God in Johannine Thought*.

In 1926 she married Eugene W. Lyman, a professor at Union Theological Seminary. After several years away from her career, she took a position at Bernard College in 1929 and also taught part time at Union. As a Bible teacher and theologian, Mary Lyman became concerned with making the findings of Biblical criticism available to lay people. This concern undergirds her major works of the 1930s, *The Fourth Gospel and the Life of Today* (1931); *The Christian Epic* (1936), and *Jesus* (1937). In 1940 her husband retired from teaching. They moved to Virginia and she took a post at Sweet Briar College. Her husband died in 1948 and she returned to her alma mater in New York as Professor of the English Bible and dean of students, the first woman to hold a full faculty position at Union. That same year he was named to the Commission on Life and Work of the World Council of Churches. In 1949 she was ordained as a minister in the Congregational Church. Recognizing her unusual role, she became an advocate for women in the higher echelons of the church.

Lyman retired from Union in 1955. She continued to be active, especially as a bible teacher. She worked on two books, both of which were published in 1960, *Death and the Christian Answer* and *In Him Was Life: A Study Guide on the Gospel of John.* In 1961 she moved to Claremont, California, where she lived her last years.

Sources:

Lyman, Mary E. *The Christian Epic.* London: Ivor Nicholson and Watson, 1936. 275 pp.

_____. *Death and the Christian Answer.* Wallingford, PA: Pendle Hill, 1960. 16 pp.

_____. *The Fourth Gospel and the Life of Today.* New York: Macmillan Company, 1931. 156 pp.

_____. *Into All the World.* New York: Union Theological Seminary, 1956. 71 pp.

_____. *Knowledge of God in Johannine Thought.* New York: Macmillan Company, 1925. 151 pp.

James, Edward T., ed. *Notable American Women, 1607-1950: A Biographical Dictionary.* 3 vols. Cambridge, MA: Harvard University Press, Belknap Press, 1971.

★562★
MACARTNEY, Clarence Edward Noble
Minister, Presbyterian Church in the U.S.A.
b. Sep. 18, 1879, Northwood, Ohio
d. Feb. 19, 1957

Clarence Edward Noble Macartney, a minister in the Presbyterian Church in the U.S.A., was the son of Catherine Robertson and J. L. Macartney. He did his college work at the University of Wisconsin and, following his graduation (B.A., 1901), attended Princeton University (M.A., 1904) and Princeton Theological Seminary. Following the completion of his theological studies, in 1905 he was ordained and called to First Presbyterian Church in Paterson, New Jersey. He moved to Arch Street Presbyterian Church in Philadelphia, Pennsylvania, in 1914.

During the 1920s Macartney gained some fame as a spokesperson for the fundamentalist wing of the denomination. On May 21, 1922, liberal Baptist minister **Harry Emerson Fosdick**, serving as pastor of First Presbyterian Church in New York City, preached his now famous sermon, "Shall the Fundamentalists Win?" Macartney responded with a sermon, "Shall Unbelief Win?" and sounded the battle cry against Fosdick. He led the Philadelphia Presbytery to petition the General Assembly to condemn the opinions expressed by Fosdick and to instruct the New York Presbytery to prevent any further sermons such as the one Fosdick delivered to be preached in New York. Successful at the 1923 assembly, Macartney saw the surge of support carry him into office as moderator of the general assembly in 1924, and the same surge forced Fosdick out of his New York pulpit. 1924 marked the high point of fundamentalist strength in the Presbyterian Church.

Princeton professor **J. Gresham Machen** had assisted Macartney in his battle with Fosdick, and Macartney attempted to help Machen when the reorganization of Princeton Theological Seminary occurred in 1929. Unable to prevent the influx of liberal professors, Macartney supported the formation of the independent Westminster Theological Seminary in Philadelphia. He refused to leave the church, however, in the mid-1930s when Machen and others formed the Orthodox Presbyterian Church. In 1927 he had moved to First Presbyterian Church in Pittsburgh where he was to enjoy a 26-year pastorate.

Over the years Macartney authored over 50 books on a broad range of religious and historical subjects. He had an abiding interest in the Civil War, and at the height of his participation in the fundamentalist-modernist battles, he saw his volume on the *Highways and By-Ways of the Civil War* (1926) published. Among his earliest books was a popular title on *The Parables of the Old Testament* (1916) which appeared soon after he moved to Philadelphia. In 1952 he issued a closing statement of his continuing conservative belief, *The Faith Once Delivered*. He retired in 1957 and authored an autobiography, *The Making of a Minister*.

Sources:

Macartney, Clarence E. *The Faith Once Delivered*. New York: Abingdon-Cokesbury, 1952. 175 pp.
_____. *Highways and By-Ways of the Civil War*. Philadelphia: Dorrance & Company, 1926. 274 pp.
_____. *The Making of a Minister*. Great Neck, NY: Channel Press, 1961. 224 pp.
_____. *The Parables of the Old Testament*. New York: Fleming H. Revell Company, 1916. 122 pp.
Marsden, George M. *Fundamentalism and American Culture*. Oxford: Oxford University Press, 1980. 307 pp.
Reid, Daniel G., Robert D. Linder, Bruce L. Shelley, and Harry S. Stout. *Dictionary of Christianity in America*. Downers Grove, IL: InterVarsity Press, 1990. 1305 pp.

★563★
MACFARLAND, Charles Steadman
Minister, Congregational Church
b. Dec. 12, 1866, Boston, Massachusetts
d. Oct. 26, 1956, Towaco, New Jersey

Charles Steadman Macfarland, a minister of the Congregational Church and for many years an executive with the Federal Council of Churches, was the son of Sarah Abigail Crafts and Daniel Macfarland. He began his adult life as a businessman with T. O. Gardner & Co., a manufacturing firm, but in 1892 became the general secretary of the YMCA in Melrose, Massachusetts, and pastored the Maverick Congregational Church in East Boston for a year before entering Yale University in 1894. He completed a B.D. in 1897 and a Ph.D. in 1899. MacFarland was ordained to the ministry in 1897 and in 1900 became pastor of the Maplewood Congregational Church. While there he married Mary Perley Merrill in 1904. He moved to South Norwalk, Connecticut, in 1906, as pastor of the Congregational church.

While MacFarland was at South Norwalk, the Federal Council of Churches was formed amid a flurry of excitement. By 1911 there were doubts of its survival. Macfarland risked his career to become the first secretary of the council's Committee on the Church and Social Service. In 1912 he was named a secretary, later general secretary, for the council. He came on the scene just as **Elias B. Sanford**, whose ecumenical vision had largely been realized in the council, was developing some health problems and nearing retirement. More organizationally oriented, Macfarland aggressively assumed the central role in stabilizing the council's finances and building its support structures. He remained with the council until his retirement in 1931.

Through the years Macfarland authored a number of books, the largest number of which concerned either the church's role in social service or Christian unity. He used his retirement years to write, and among the numerous books he penned were *The New Church and the New Germany* (1934); *Trends of Christian Thinking* (1937); *Steps toward the World Council* (1938); *I Was in Prison* (1939); and *Christian Unity in the Making* (1949). His autobiography, *Across the Years*, appeared in 1936.

Sources:

Macfarland, Charles S. *Across the Years*. New York: Macmillan Company, 1936. 367 pp.
_____. *Christian Unity in the Making*. New York: Federal Council of Church of Christ in America, 1949. 376 pp.
_____. *I Was in Prison*. New York: Fleming H. Revell Company, 1939. 112 pp.
_____. *The New Church and the New Germany*. New York: Macmillan Company, 1934. 209 pp.
_____. *Trends of Christian Thinking*. New York: Fleming H. Revell Company, 1937. 207 pp.

★564★
MACHEN, John Gresham
Founder, Orthodox Presbyterian Church
b. Jul. 28, 1881, Baltimore, Maryland
d. Jan. 1, 1937, Bismarck, North Dakota

John Gresham Machen is still remembered primarily as one of the more prominent conservative Presbyterian theologians of the early twentieth century, but equally important was his role as the principal founder of the Orthodox Presbyterian Church. Born into a highly cultured household, Machen began attending Johns Hopkins University when he was 17, and graduated three years later as valedictorian. Subsequently he attended Princeton Theological Seminary, earning both his master's degree and a B.D. Prior to accepting a post at the seminary as a theology instructor, Machen also spent a year studying in Germany. He eventually became an eminent religious scholar who authored such works as *The Origin* of Paul's Religion (1921), Christianity and Liberalism (1923), The Virgin Birth of Christ (1930), The Christian Faith in the Modern World (1936), and The Christian View of Man (1937).

Brought up in a religiously conservative family, Machen experienced a crisis of faith as a result of his sojourn in Europe. These inner struggles caused him to delay his ordination until after he had resolved his conflict in 1914. Leaving his doubts behind, he went on to become a major scholarly spokesperson for traditional, evangelical Protestant Christianity.

While the Presbyterian Church had experienced dissension between its conservative and liberal wings for quite some time, matters did not ignite until the missions controversy in the early 1930s. The year 1932 saw the publication of W. E. Hocking's Re-Thinking Missions, a work that seemed, particularly from the perspective of traditionalists, to stress the medical and social aspects of missionary enterprise at the expense of its primary goal—saving souls. Machen and other Presbyterians of like mind charged that the foreign missions board supported missionaries who did not preach Christ as the exclusive path to salvation, and formed an Independent Board of Presbyterian Foreign Missions. In the wake of these actions, Machen's presbytery tried and convicted Machen of being schismatic. Machen and his supporters in turn left the church and formed the Orthodox Presbyterian Church. Machen passed away shortly after the formation of the new denomination.

Sources:

Coray, Henry W. J. Gresham Machen, A Silhouette. Grand Rapids, MI: Kregel Publications, 1981. 128 pp.

Machen, J. Gresham. Christian Faith in the Modern World. Grand Rapids, MI: W. B. Eerdmans Pubishing Co., 1936.

_____. Christianity and Liberalism. Grand Rapids, MI: W. B. Eerdmans Publishing Co., 1923.

_____. Contemporary American Theology. New York: Round Table Press, 1933.

_____. Education, Christianity and the State. Ed. by John W. Robbins. Jefferson, MD: Trinity Foundation, 1987. 179 pp.

_____. The Origin of Paul's Religion. New York: Macmillan Co., 1921.

_____. The Virgin Birth of Christ. New York: Harper & Row, 1930.

★565★
MACHRAY, Robert
Primate, Anglican Church of Canada
b. May 17, 1831, Aberdeen Scotland
d. Mar. 9, 1904, Winnipeg, Manitoba, Canada

Robert Machray, the first primate of the Church of England in Canada (now the Anglican Church of Canada), was the son of Christian Macallum and Robert Machray. Machray grew up as a Presbyterian in Scotland and attended King's College, Aberdeen, from which he received his M.A. degree in 1851. He then entered Sidney Sussex College, Cambridge, from which he received his B.A. in 1855. That same year he received a fellowship and stayed to complete his M.A. in 1858. While at Cambridge he decided to join the Church of England and become a priest. He was ordained in 1856. In 1862 he became vicar of Madingley (a town near Cambridge). During these years he became strongly involved with the Church Missionary Society (C.M.S.), the Church of England's foreign missionary arm. In 1865 he was called up to become the new bishop of Rupert's Land (now Manitoba) in Canada, the former bishop, David Anderson, having resigned.

Consecrated at Lambeth Palace, Machray began his duties almost immediately by ordaining a young C.M.S. deacon, **William Carpenter Bompas**, as a missionary for the Yukon territory. Machray arrived in Winnipeg in 1866. He quickly moved to reorganize the diocese, reopen St. John's College (which his predecessor had founded but which had ceased to function), and tour the land under his jurisdiction. His survey convinced him that Manitoba would soon become a church province, and he made plans to

divide the territory into several dioceses. Manitoba became a Canadian province in 1870. In 1872 the diocese of Moosonee (James Bay area) was set off from Rupert's Land. In 1873 the Algoma missionary diocese was created east of Winnipeg, and a year later the diocese of Saskatchewan was formed.

In 1875 Machray called the first Provincial Synod and organized the Province of Rupert's Land over which he became the metropolitan. The progress in the previous nine years was due in no small part to his ability to work with the C.M.S. and recruit priest-missionaries for the West. Machray oversaw the development of the church in the West. Through the 1880s there was a move to unite the several autonomous Church of England jurisdictions in Canada. At a first general synod meeting in Toronto in 1893 a consolidated church, uniting the separate provinces of Eastern Canada, Rupert's Land, and British Columbia, was created. Machray was elected the first primate and named an archbishop. In creating the general synod, the church in effect moved from its former jurisdiction under the archbishop of Canterbury and became a separate Anglican Church of Canada, and part of the worldwide Anglican communion. Machray oversaw the work of the Canadian church for 11 years, during which time it passed through its critical adjustment period to the new realities of a geographically united Canada.

Sources:

Carrington, Philip. The Anglican Church in Canada. Toronto: Collins, 1963. 320 pp.

★566★
MACKAY, John Alexander
Educator, Presbyterian Church of the U.S.A.
b. May 17, 1889, Inverness Scotland
d. Jun. 9, 1983, Heightstown, New Jersey

John Alexander Mackay, for over 20 years the president of Princeton Theological Seminary, was the son of Isabella Macdonald and Duncan Mackay. He attended the University of Aberdeen, but after attaining his A.B. in 1912 he came to the United States and completed his ministerial training at Princeton Theological Seminary (B.D., 1915). Returning to Scotland, in 1916 he was ordained in the Free Church of Scotland and married Jane Logan Wells. They left for Peru where he founded and was principal of the Anglo-Peruvian College in Lima. In 1925 he was employed by the YMCA as a writer/lecturer/evangelist in South America. He moved to Montevideo, Uruguay, and later to Mexico City.

In 1932 Mackay returned to the United States as president of the Board of Missions of the Presbyterian Church in the U.S.A. In 1933 he finished his first important book, The Other Spanish Christ, a religious history of Spain and South America, originally issued in Spanish and later translated into English. It reflected his strong Protestant biases and contained a number of strong anti-Roman Catholic statements, opinions he would later modify. In 1936 Mackay became president of Princeton Theological Seminary, where he would remain through the rest of his active career. While there he founded and edited (1944-1951) Theology Today.

At Princeton Mackay began to emerge as a leader in the ecumenical movement. His leadership took form in both organizational activity and intellectual endeavor. In 1941 Mackay began the process toward the ecumenical theology he would later construct. The intellectual development began with A Preface to Christian Theology (1941), a survey of those immediate aspects of the culture which theology should address. In Heritage and Destiny Mackay established a dialogue between the future and the past. One moves into the future best, he argued, after appropriating the knowledge of the past. History thus provided for Mackay a clue to God's activity in the present and the direction he is leading. In Christianity at the Frontier, a collection of miscellaneous essays, he affirmed the need for reformation in the church and called for

Christian unity based upon an evangelical catholicism, that is, a unity of all who pledge loyalty to Jesus and manifest the fruits of the Spirit (love, joy, peace, patience, etc.).

Christianity at the Frontier appeared just after the first meeting of the World Council of Churches in Amsterdam in 1948. Mackay had been a central figure in the council's founding and for the first quadrennium served as chairman of the Joint Committee for the World Council of Churches. Thus, in *Christianity at the Frontier* he offered a direction toward which the World Council could proceed in its search for unity. He then expanded his approach to church unity in his last two books, *God's Orders* (1953) and his most complete and systematic statement, *Ecumenics: The Science of the Church Universal* (1964). During the time he was working on these books he was also elected the moderator of the general assembly of the Presbyterian Church (1953) and president of the Presbyterian World Alliance (1954-1959).

Sources:

Mackay, John A. *Ecumenics: The Science of the Church Universal.* Englewood Cliffs, NJ: Prentice-Hall, 1964. 294 pp.

_____. *God's Orders.* New York: Macmillan Company, 1953. 214 pp.

_____. *Heritage and Destiny.* New York: Macmillan Company, 1943. 109 pp.

_____. *The Other Spanish Christ.* London: Student Christian Movement Press, 1933. 288 pp.

_____. *A Preface to Christian Theology.* New York: Macmillan Company, 1941. 187 pp.

Reid, Daniel G., Robert D. Linder, Bruce L. Shelley, and Harry S. Stout. *Dictionary of Christianity in America.* Downers Grove, IL: InterVarsity Press, 1990. 1305 pp.

Soper, David Wesley. *Men Who Shape Belief.* Vol. II. Philadelphia: Westminster Press, 1955. 124 pp.

★567★
MACLAINE, Shirley
New Age Spokesperson
b. Apr. 24, 1934, Richmond, Virginia

Shirley MacLaine, best known as an actress and film star, emerged in the 1980s as a major spokesperson for the New Age movement, the somewhat nebulous occult metaphysical movement which appeared in North America in the 1970s. Born Shirley MacLean Beatty, she was raised in a Southern Baptist environment. Dance lessons began in her pre-school years and by high school she was dancing professionally. She moved to New York after finishing high school and in 1954 married Steve Parker. That same year she got her first big break when she took over the lead from Carol Haney on Broadway in *The Pajama Game*. She went on to star in a continuing series of Hollywood films.

During the 1960s she was one of a number of Hollywood personalities who became politically active. She became a delegate to the 1968 and 1972 Democratic Party conventions, and her statements against United States involvement in Vietnam, for protection of the environment, and supporting civil rights, were widely quoted in the press.

As her political career was peaking, MacLaine made her appearance as an author with her first two books, *Don't Fall Off of the Mountain* (1970) and *You Can Get There from Here* (1975). At the same time, her marriage was coming to an end, and in a reluctant manner, she was becoming attracted to, and convinced of, the reality of the occult spiritual world. Her experiences included the visits to a number of Spiritualist mediums, or channels as they have come to be referred to within the New Age movement. Swedish medium Sture Johanssen and San Francisco medium Kevin Ryerson were among the channels who particularly affected her. An anonymous figure, named "David" in her book, a composite of several people, is generally believed to mainly refer to Charles A. Silva. The story of her psychic adventures were recounted in her 1983 book,

Out on a Limb. The New Age Movement immediately adopted her as one of their own.

MacLaine's explorations continued through the 1980s. She had some sessions with **J. Z. Knight**, the channel for an entity named Ramtha, the experience of which she discussed in her 1985 book *Dancing in the Light*, which also recounted further sessions with Ryerson. MacLaine's real leadership in the movement came about as a result of the television adaptation of *Out on a Limb* which aired in 1987. Acting in response to the public reaction to her story, she began to give lectures and workshops teaching what she had learned in her 15 years of experience. The first Higher Life seminar was held in 1987, and through them she has raised money to open New Age centers, the first of which, Ariel Village, is located in Crestone, Colorado. Subsequently, without abandoning her movie career, she has written a book on meditation, *Going With: A Guide for Inner Transformation* (1989) along with a popular home video, Shirley MacLaine's *Inner Workout* (1989).

Sources:

MacLaine, Shirley. *Dancing in the Light.* New York: Bantam Books, 1985. 405 pp.

_____. *Going Within: A Guide for Inner Transformation.* New York: Bantam Books, 1989. 263 pp.

_____. *It's All in the Playing.* New York: Bantam Books, 1987. 338 pp.

_____. *Out On a Limb.* New York: Bantam Books, 1983. 372 pp.

_____. *You Can Get There from Here.* New York: W. W. Norton & Co., 1975.

Shepard, Leslie. *Encyclopedia of Occultism & Parapsychology.* 3 vols., 2nd. ed. Detroit: Gale Research Co., 1984-1985.

Zuromski, Paul. "A Conversation with Shirley MacLaine." *Psychic Guide* 2, 3 (December 1983): 11-15.

★568★
MAEZUMI, Hakuyu Taizan
Founder, Zen Center of Los Angeles
b. 1931, Japan

Hakuyu Taizan Maezumi Roshi is the founder and director of the Zen Center of Los Angeles, one of the largest Zen centers in the United States. Born in his father's temple in Japan, he was ordained as a Soto Zen monk at the tender age of 11. After completing degrees at Komazawa University in Oriental philosophy and literature, he studied Zen at Sojiji, one of the principal Soto monasteries in Japan. Also, at age 16, he began to train under Koryu Osaka Roshi, a lay Rinzai master. In 1955 he received dharma transmission from his father, Hakujun Kuroda Roshi, in the Soto lineage.

He came to the United States in 1956 to study English at San Francisco State and at Pasadena City College. After his studies, he took up duties as a priest at the Zenshuji Soto Mission in Los Angeles, while continuing to practice *zazen* (Zen meditation). He broadened his exploration of Zen by becoming friends with **Nyogen Senzaki** and studying Zen Master Eihei Dogen's *Shobogenzo* with Soto's American bishop, Reirin Yamada Roshi. He also began to hold weekly zazen meetings at Zenshuji. Yasutani Roshi came to the United States in 1962, and persuaded Maezumi to return to Japan to round out his Zen training.

By 1967, Maezumi's zazen group had moved out of Zenshuji and began to rent an independent house to serve as a Zen center, and Yasutani began to hold *sesshins* (meditation intensives) there. They incorporated in 1968, originally with the name Los Angeles Zendo (later renamed Zen Center of Los Angeles). In time, the Zendo was officially registered as a Soto temple. Maezumi traveled to Japan to practice under Yasutani in 1970, and received *inka* (approval as a teacher) from him. This gave Maezumi the unusual distinction of having received dharma transmission from both the Soto and the Rinzai tradition.

In the 1970s, the center began to develop a vigorous publishing outreach, and Maezumi developed a nationwide following. Affiliated groups sprang up in Arizona, Oregon, New York, and Utah. Rural centers were established at Mountain Center, California, and at Mt. Tremper, New York. Groups also emerged in England, Mexico, and Holland. In Los Angeles the center expanded from a single house to an entire block, with many students living in the surrounding neighborhood. The Institute for Transcultural Studies was founded in 1976 as the group's educational outreach.

In 1978 Maezumi-Roshi named the first of the four dharma heirs he has trained, Bernard Tetsugen Glassman. The others are Dennis Genpo Mersel, Jan Chozen Soule, and Charlotte Joko Beck. In the early 1980s it became public knowledge that Maezumi-Roshi was suffering from acute alcoholism. He entered a rehabilitation treatment program and was eventually able to resume active leadership of his center, which now includes leadership of branches in Europe. During the crisis of leadership a number of members left, including dharma heir Beck, who now heads the independent San Diego Zen Center.

Sources:

Fields, Rick. *How the Swans Came to the Lake: A Narrative History of Buddhism in America.* Boulder, CO: Shambhala, 1981. 433 pp. Rev. ed.: Boston, MA: Shambhala, 1986. 445 pp.

Maezumi, Hakuyu Taizan. *The Way of Everyday Life.* Los Angeles: Center Publications, 1978. 136 pp.

_____. *On Zen Practice.* 2 vols. Los Angeles: Zen Center of Los Angeles, 1976.

_____, and Bernard Tetsugen Glassman, eds. *The Hazy Moon of Enlightenment.* Los Angeles: Center Publications, 1977. 191 pp.

Melton, J. Gordon *The Encyclopedia of American Religions.* 3d ed. Detroit: Gale Research Inc.,1988. 1102 pp.

★569★
MAGNES, Judah Leon
Reform Jewish Rabbi
President, Hebrew University
b. Jul. 5, 1877, San Francisco, California
d. Oct. 27, 1948, New York, New York

Judah Leon Magnes, a prominent Reform Jewish rabbi and the first president of Hebrew University in Jerusalem, was the son of David and Sophie Abrahamson Magnes. His father was from a family of first generation Polish immigrants and his mother from a German family; Magnes inherited both traditions. He grew up in Oakland, California, where his father was in the dry goods business. The family Americanized and after finishing high school Magnes enrolled in Hebrew Union College, the reform school in Cincinnati, Ohio. He concurrently pursued a degree at the University of Cincinnati, from which he received a B.A. in 1898. He was ordained as a rabbi in 1900. Following his ordination he did postgraduate work at Berlin and then Heidelberg, from which he received his Ph.D. in 1902. While in Europe he became an ardent Zionist.

In 1902 Magnes returned to Ohio and served as a librarian at Hebrew Union College for two years before being called to Temple Israel in Brooklyn and in 1906 to Temple Emanu-EL in Manhattan as an associate rabbi. In 1908 he married Beatrice Lowenstein. In New York Magnes emerged as a Jewish activist. In 1905 he organized demonstrations to protest the pogroms (massive persecutions) in Russia. He became Secretary of the Federation of American Zionists. In 1906 he served on the original executive board of the American Jewish Committee. In 1908 he helped establish the Kehillah of New York City, a comprehensive structure for coordinating Jewish community affairs, and provided it with its strongest leadership. Through Kehillah he involved himself in a number of social reform activities, from labor arbitration to anti-crime campaigns. In 1910 he came into open conflict with Temple Emanu-EL over his demand that it introduce a more traditional ritual. As a result, his contract was not renewed and he left the active rabbinate.

During World War I Magnes became interested in relief work and helped found the American-Jewish Joint Distribution Committee. He also became a pacifist and spoke at several anti-war rallies in 1917. His radical political position, which led him to criticize President Woodrow Wilson's policies toward Russia, led to criticism of his activities by fellow Jewish leaders. Magnes and the Kehillah also came under strong criticism from people who accused Magnes and the organization's other leaders of using the Kehillah to promote the interests of the wealthier "uptown" Jews (as represented by Temple Emanu-EL) and to control the first generation immigrant Jews located across town. The Kehillah ceased to exist in 1922.

After the disbanding of the Kehillah, Magnes and his family moved to Palestine for what was to be a year or two. While he was there, however, Hebrew University opened in Jerusalem. In 1925 he was asked to become its chancellor. He held that position for ten years and then became the president of the school. His efforts to build the school into the major academic center it became, frequently brought Magnes back to the United States to raise money and support. In 1929, following a series of anti-Jewish riots, he began to work for an accommodation between the Jews and Palestinians. His plan to voluntarily limit Jewish immigration to Palestine as a means of making peace with the larger Arab community lost Magnes the support of most of the Jewish community. His continued efforts to bridge the gap between the Jewish and Arab community in Palestine moved against the currents of history and the post-World War II drive to create a Jewish state. In 1948 he came to New York with a plan for a joint Jewish and Palestinian policy in Palestine. He was in New York when the State of Israel was declared. He died in New York a few months later. He was buried in Brooklyn, but his body was moved to Israel in 1955.

Sources:

Bentwich, Norman. *For Zion's Sake: A Biography of Judah L. Magnes.* Philadelphia: Jewish Publication Society of America, 1954. 329 pp. *Dictionary of American Biography.* 20 vols. and 7 supps. New York: Charles Scribner's Sons, 1928-1936, 1944-1981.

Landman, Isaac, ed. *Universal Jewish Encyclopedia.* 10 vols. New York: The Universal Jewish Encyclopedia, 1940.

Magnes, Judah Leon. *In the Perplexity of the Times.* Jerusalem: Hebrew University, 1946. 165 pp.

_____. *Like All Nations?* Jerusalem: Weiss Press, 1930. 77 pp.

_____. *War-Time Addresses.* New York: T. Seltzer, 1923. 114 pp.

_____, and Martin Buber. *Arab-Jewish Unity: Testimony Before the Anglo-American Committee.* London: V. Gollancz, 1947. 96 pp.

Singer, Isidore, ed. *The Jewish Encyclopedia.* New York: KTAV Publishing House, 1964.

Szajkowski, Zosa. "The Pacifism of Judah Magnes." *Conservative Judaism* 22 (1968): 36-55.

★570★
Guru MAHARAJ JI
Spiritual Teacher, Elan Vital
b. Dec. 10, 1957, Hardwar India

Guru Maharaj Ji, more recently known as Maharaj, is the spiritual leader of Elan Vital. (Guru Maharaj Ji is a title rather than a name; Maharaj Ji was born Prem Pal Singh Rawat.) The Elan Vital organization has superseded the former Divine Light Mission in the West. Maharaj Ji originally inherited his position from his father, Shri Hans Maharaj Ji, who was a spiritual teacher in the Sant Mat tradition and founder of the mission. Shri Hans had been a follower of **Sawan Singh**, a prominent Sant Mat leader who was the direct or indirect source of a number of different spiritual groups on the American scene. Shri Hans established independent work in Delhi in 1930. The work was formally organized as Divya Sandesh Parishad, or Divine Light Mission, in 1960. At his death in 1966 he was succeeded by his youngest son, only eight then, who assumed the title Guru Maharaj Ji.

Encouraged by young Westerners who had traveled to India and became premies (initiates), Maharaj Ji journeyed to the United States in 1971 and addressed a large crowd at a gathering in Colorado. The people initiated at this meeting became the core of the movement, and headquarters were established in Denver. The mission grew rapidly, so that by late 1973 hundreds of centers had been established and tens of thousands of premies had been initiated. In addition, social service facilities were established and periodicals began to be published.

The movement's early growth phase began to spiral down in November 1973 with "Millennium 73," a gathering at the Houston Astrodome that failed to attract enough people to pay the Astrodome's rental fee. The fiasco also attracted attacks against Maharaj Ji's followers by the anti-cult movement. The last series of events to set back the organization began in 1974 when Maharaj Ji, then 16 years old, married his 24-year-old secretary, Marolyn Johnson. He announced that she was an incarnation of the Hindu goddess Durga. The marriage ruptured the already strained relations between Maharaj Ji and his family. His mother declared her youngest son fallen, and further declared his oldest brother the new guru. The conflict ended in a court battle in which Maharaj Ji assumed control of the mission outside India, while his brother and mother were awarded the organization inside India.

In the early 1980s, Maharaj Ji began a process of disbanding the mission and its local ashrams. He dropped the remaining Indian cultural trappings, began to call himself simply Maharaj, and, adopting an extremely low profile, chose to relate to his followers on a one-to-one basis. He created the North American Sponsorship Program to raise financial support for his home in Malibu and his many travels.

Over the years, many of Maharaj Ji's talks were transcribed for publication in the various mission periodicals. Others were circulated on cassette tapes. Only a few were collected and published as books or booklets.

Sources:

Cameron, Charles. *Who is Guru Maharaj Ji?*. New York: Bantam, 1973. 303 pp.

Maharaj Ji, Guru. *The Living Master*. Denver, CO: Divine light Mission, 1978. 109 pp.

★ 571 ★
MAHARISHI MAHESH YOGI
Founder, World Plan Executive Council

Little is known concerning Maharishi Mahesh Yogi, the Indian teacher of Transcendental Meditation, prior to his establishment of the Spiritual Regeneration Movement in 1957. It is a common practice among those who have entered the religious life to not speak again of their previous secular existence. According to one source he was born in 1911, the son of an income tax official. Another asserts that he was born in 1918, the son of a forest ranger. What is affirmed is that he graduated from Allahabad University around 1940 with a major in physics. He then spent 13 years with Guru Brahamananda Saraswati, affectionately known as Guru Dev, from whom he learned meditation. In 1953, in part occasioned by the death of Guru Dev, he retired into the mountains at Uttar Kashi, in the Himalayas. Two years later he emerged and traveled south to Karala, where he began to teach and where, in 1956, a Spiritual Development Movement was organized. He then traveled around India until the last days of 1957, when a conference was held at Madras. On January 1, 1958, Maharishi announced the formation of a worldwide Spiritual Regeneration Movement to spread the teachings of Transcendental Meditation, thus leading to the spiritual regeneration of humankind.

Several months after the conference Maharishi left for a round-the-world tour which led him to Burma, Malaysia, and Hong Kong

prior to his arrival in the United States at Honolulu, Hawaii, as the year was ending. He spent most of 1959 in the United States, where he put together a three-year plan to introduce Transcendental Meditation to all of the countries of the world. He left for Europe at the end of the year and spent 1960 there. He returned to India in 1961. A second world tour began before the year was out and a third was made in 1962. In 1963 he finished his first major book, *The Science of Being and Art of Living*, the most complete and systematic presentation of his thought. In 1965 he completed his commentary on the *Bhagavad-Gita*.

With the Spiritual Regeneration Movement established around the world, Maharishi has spent the last 25 years developing the work of the foundation laid by his early travels and writings. A key event occurred in 1972 with the announcement of the World Plan, his design for reorganizing society in such a way as to solve the basic problems of humankind. This announcement was followed by the establishment of the World Plan Executive Council as the umbrella of all of his varied activities. His movement was given a boost in 1974 with the announcement by several scientists of research results that supported Transcendental Meditation's claims to improve life.

While one can trace the growth of Maharishi's movement decade by decade on the international scene, it has by no means enjoyed a course of steady progress. In 1975 Maharishi European University opened in Switzerland. In 1977 the university announced a new siddhi program which would teach meditators a number of extraordinary skills, including the ability to levitate. The claims became the source of considerable skepticism, ridicule, and lawsuits (by ex-siddha students). The movement has weathered the storms thus far, however, and Maharishi has succeeded in building a stable worldwide organization to continue to spread his ideas after his death.

Sources:

Ebon, Martin, ed. *Maharishi the Guru*. New York: New American Library, 1968. 144 pp.

His Holiness Maharishi Mahesh Yogi, Thirty Years Around the World, Dawn of the Age of Enlightenment. Vol. I. The Netherlands: MVU Press, 1986. 600 pp.

Jefferson, William. *The Story of Maharishi*. New York: Pocket Books, 1976. 128 pp.

Maharishi Mahesh Yogi. *Bhagavad-Gita: A New Translation and Commentary*. N.p., International SRM Publications, 1967.

———. *The Divine Plan*. Los Angeles: The S.R.M. Foundation, 1962. 18 pp.

———. *Love and God*. N.p.: International SRM Publications, 1964. 54 pp.

———. *Meditation*. Honolulu: International Meditation Center, 1958. 95 pp.

———. *Science of Being and Art of Living*. London: International SRM Publications, 1963. Rev. ed. 1967. 334 pp.

———. *The Treasury and the Market*. London: The Spiritual Regeneration Movement Foundation for Great Britain, 1961. 24 pp.

★ 572 ★
MAHONY, Roger Michael
Cardinal, Roman Catholic Church
Archbishop, Roman Catholic Church
b. Feb. 27, 1926, Hollywood, California

Roger Michael Mahony is a cardinal in the Roman Catholic Church and serves as the Archbishop of Los Angeles. He was raised in North Hollywood, California. He entered a minor seminary at the age of 14 and graduated from St. John's Seminary in Camarillo, California (A.B., 1958; S.T.B., 1962). While at St. John's, he perfected his Spanish and began to work in the farm labor camps in the area. Ordained in 1962, he was sent to Catholic University in Washington, D.C., where he earned a master's degree in social work in 1964, and then became director of Catholic Charities in Fresno. In 1965 he was thrust in the middle of the labor problems created by the attempts to organize the workers in the grape fields. Most of the workers and the owners were Catholics. In 1975 he was asked by the governor of California to serve on the state's new Agricultural Labor Relations Board.

Mahony's social involvement and his positive, reconciling efforts led to his being named bishop of Stockton in 1980. Though not in the center of church activity, Mahony used his position as a platform to speak out with a combination of theological conservativism and social liberalism. He called the church to stand with the poor and opposed nuclear proliferation.

In 1985 Mahony accepted an invitation to succeed **Timothy Manning** as archbishop of Los Angeles, the largest Roman Catholic Church diocese in North America. Since that time, issues have tended to shift and Mahony has allowed his conservative side to come to the forefront. He has become a leader in the church in fighting abortion, married priests, and homosexuality. At the same time he has led in the church's response to the AIDS crisis, mandating the creation of residential care facilities and joining fellow bishops in issuing the most liberal document on the subject by church leaders. He has also provided shelters for the homeless and come to the aid of illegal immigrants (most of whom, like the farm workers, are Roman Catholic).

As its administrative leader, he moved to introduce modern business techniques and organization into the burgeoning archdiocese. His major problem has been the limited supply of priests that has been unable to keep up with the membership.

Mahoney was named cardinal in May 1991.

Sources:

Ciotti, Paul. "The Plugged-In Archbishop." *Los Angeles Times Magazine* 5, 51 (December 17, 1989): 15-22, 52-55.

★573★
MAIER, Walter Arthur
Biblical Scholar and Radio Minister, Lutheran Church-Missouri Synod
b. Oct. 4, 1893, Boston, Massachusetts
d. Jan. 11, 1950, St. Louis, Missouri

Walter Arthur Maier, known to millions in the 1930s and 1940s as the voice of "The Lutheran Hour," was the son of William and Anna Katherine Schad Maier, both first generation immigrants from Germany. Maier was raised in the Lutheran Church-Missouri Synod, one of the most conservative Lutheran bodies; however, as a youth, he did not attend one of the synod's parochial schools. He did attend Concordia Collegiate Institute, but switched for his final year at Boston University, where he completed his B.A. degree in 1913. He then attended Concordia Theological Seminary from which he graduated in 1916. He began graduate work at Harvard Divinity School that same year and was ordained in 1917.

In 1918 Maier moved from the Divinity School to Harvard Graduate School of Arts and Sciences. He finished his M.A. in 1920 and began a Ph.D. dissertation. However, some trouble over his conservative views and the distraction of his new job as executive secretary of the Walther League (the synod's youth program) and editor of its periodical, the *Messenger*, pushed his quest for a doctorate aside.

In 1922 Maier was asked to become professor of Old Testament interpretation and history at Concordia Theological Seminary. He resigned his post with the league to take it, though he continued to edit the *Messenger*. From his position in the seminary, he began to urge the synod to shift its emphasis on evangelism among German immigrants and look more to the general English-speaking public. Along the way, in 1924 he married Hulda Augusta Eickhoff, and in 1929 finally finished his Ph.D. Then in 1930 he was invited to give the first series of talks on "The Lutheran Hour," then just a radio experiment for the synod. The program had a brief run and

was suspended due to the general shortage of funds during the depression. It was revived in 1935 with Maier as the speaker. It has continued since that time, Maier being the speaker for 17 years.

Maier offered a solidly Lutheran perspective in a very winsome manner and gained an audience far beyond the Missouri Synod, even beyond Lutheranism. He attacked many aspects of modern culture, especially the modernist theology which had come to dominate most large Protestant denominations. It is estimated that by 1950 his message was being heard in 55 countries by an audience of 20 million. Beginning with *Christ for the Nation*, in 1936 he turned out an average of a book a year into the 1950s, 20 of which were developed from his radio talks. Meanwhile, he authored over 800 periodical articles.

In 1944 Maier was given a leave of absence from the seminary to concentrate on the show and its related activities, especially the Lutheran Hour Rallies he held around the country. In 1945 he relinquished the editorship of the *Messenger*. In 1949, "The Lutheran Hour" went on television for the first time. Maier had one season before his death from heart failure in 1950.

Sources:

Dictionary of American Biography. 20 vols. and 7 supps. New York: Charles Scribner's Sons, 1928-1936, 1944-1981.
Lippy, Charles H. *Twentieth-Century Shapers of American Popular Religion*. New York: Greenwood Press, 1989. 494 pp.
Maier, Paul L. *A Man Spoke, A World Listened: The Story of Walter Maier and the Lutheran Hour*. New York: McGraw-Hill, 1963. 411 pp.
Maier, Walter W. *The Airwaves Proclaim Christ*. St. Louis, MO: Concordia Publishing House, 1948. 297 pp.
———. *Christ for Every Crisis*. St. Louis, MO: Concordia Publishing House, 1931. 174 pp.
———. *The Lutheran Hour*. St. Louis, MO: Concordia Publishing House, 1931. 324 pp.
———. *One Thousand Radio Voices for Christ*. St. Louis, MO: Concordia Publishing House, 1950. 454 pp.

★574★
MALCOLM X
Founder, Muslim Mosque, Inc.
b. May 19, 1925, Omaha, Nebraska
d. Feb. 21, 1965, New York, New York

Malcolm X, a leader of the Nation of Islam ("Black Muslims"), was born Malcolm Little, the son of Baptist minister Earl Little and Louise Little. During his childhood, his family suffered severe persecution from the Ku Klux Klan because his father, a Baptist preacher who espoused the black separatism of Marcus Garvey, was vigorous in denouncing the oppression of Blacks. While Malcolm was still very young the family moved to Lansing, Michigan, where his father's outspoken ways led to the burning of the family's home by white racists. When he was six his father was apparently murdered for his independent thoughts.

The family lived on welfare for a time, but Malcolm's mother became mentally ill and the children were placed in the care of others. Malcolm was sent to a home for boys. Dropping out of school at 15, he moved to Boston to live with a sister; he soon became active in the underworld in Boston and Harlem, in the areas of drugs, prostitution, and gambling.

In 1946 Malcolm Little was sentenced to ten years in prison for burglary. While incarcerated he was converted to the Nation of Islam and became a disciplined adherent of that strict black separatist movement. He also developed an obsession for learning and read voraciously in the prison library. Upon his release in 1952 he moved to Detroit and soon was appointed assistant minister of the local mosque. By now he was known as Malcolm X, following the standard Black Muslim practice of giving up one's "slave" name for the initial X. After other assignments he was dispatched to Harlem in 1954 to lead the important mosque there. Soon he was the most prominent spokesman of the Nation of Islam. During an era when the civil rights movement was promoting integration, he was a powerful advocate of racial separation and black independence, urging American Blacks to renounce nonviolence, Christianity, and the goal of racial integration.

By the early 1960s Malcolm X had enemies within the Muslim movement. Some thought he was too powerful; some were jealous of his prominence. When, shortly after the assassination of Pres. John F. Kennedy in 1963, Malcolm commented that the killing was a case of "the chickens coming home to roost," he was suspended from the movement. The following March he announced that he was founding two new organizations, the Muslim Mosque, Inc., and the Organization of Afro-American Unity. Traveling to Mecca on a Muslim pilgrimage in 1964, he was startled to see genuine friendship among Muslims of various races. He soon concluded that all Whites were not evil after all, and he moved toward a more orthodox understanding of Islam than that preached by **Elijah Muhammad**. He began reaching out to other black organizations and cooperating in the struggle for civil rights.

Malcolm X's new course was cut short, however, when he was shot and killed on February 21, 1965. Three members of the Nation of Islam were subsequently convicted of the murder, which was presumed to be an official act of vengeance by that organization.

Sources:

Breitman, George. *The Last Year of Malcolm X: The Evolution of a Revolutionary*. New York: Pathfinder Press, 1967. 169 pp.

Clarke, John Henrik, ed. *Malcolm X: The Man and His Times*. New York: Collier Books, 1969. 360 pp.

Cone, James H. *Martin and Malcolm and America*. Maryknoll, NY: Orbis Books, 1991. 358 pp.

Johnson, Timothy V. *Malcolm X: A Comprehensive Annotated Bibliography*. New York: Garland, 1980. 192 pp.

Malcolm X. *By Any Means Necessary: Speeches, Interviews and a Letter by Malcolm X*. Edited by George Breitman. New York: Pathfinder Press, 1970.

———. *Malcolm X on Afro-American History*. New York: Pathfinder Press, 1970. 74 pp.

———. *Malcolm X Speaks: Selected Speeches and Statements*. Edited by George Breitman. New York: Merit Publishers, 1965. 226 pp.

Malcolm X, with Alex Haley. *The Autobiography of Malcolm X*. New York: Grove Press, 1965. 460 pp.

—*Timothy Miller*

★575★
MALLORY, Kathleen Moore
Executive Secretary, Woman's Missionary Union, Southern Baptist Convention
b. Jan. 24, 1879, Summerfield, Alabama
d. Jun. 17, 1954, Selma, Alabama

Kathleen Moore Mallory, the executive secretary of the Woman's Missionary Union (WMU) of the Southern Baptist Convention from 1912 to 1948, held the distinction of remaining in her office longer than any executive in the history of the convention. During the 36 years of her leadership, the WMU grew at a spectacular rate, surpassing even the expectations of the organization's founders.

Mallory was the daughter of the mayor of Selma, Alabama, who was a prominent attorney from an equally prominent family, which was all Baptist for several generations. Kathleen had made a profession of faith at age ten. A good student, she later attended the Woman's College of Baltimore (now Goucher College), graduating in 1902. She was engaged to be married, but her fiance died of tuberculosis in 1907. After her fiance's death, she threw herself into church work and soon agreed to lead the Woman's Missionary Union for the Baptist association in her area. At the Alabama State

Baptist Convention in 1908, however, missions came alive for her, and in 1909 she became the secretary of the state WMU organization.

During Mallory's years as the Alabama WMU secretary, she caught the eye of national WMU leaders. In 1912, when the office of national corresponding secretary was vacated by Edith C. Crane who took a position with the Baptist World Alliance, Mallory was elected to assume the post. She moved to Baltimore and began the austere regimen that was to characterize her life henceforth. She rented a one-room apartment and devoted her existence to the WMU. She lived an organized life, and became known for the systematic manner in which she carried out her duties. Except for two extended stays on the mission field (1923-1924 in the Orient and the summer of 1930 in South America), she stayed close to her office, though making a number of trips through the South to various WMU functions.

From the first year in office, Mallory edited and wrote most of the annual *WMU Yearbook*. She used this as a tool to standardize the union work throughout the convention. In 1917 she wrote her only book, the *Manual of WMU Methods*. Three years later she became the editor of *Royal Service*. The following year she oversaw the transfer of the headquarters of the union to Birmingham, Alabama, closer to the center of convention strength.

During her many years in office, Mallory was known for carrying out the numerous administrative tasks assigned her. However, she attained heightened notoriety as she welded the loosely organized WMU into an efficient fund-raising instrument for the convention and its missionary programs. During the darkest days of the depression, WMU offerings kept it financially solvent. She is generally credited with making the union the potent force it is within the convention today. As prosperity returned, the offerings increased. In 1946, the Lottie Moon Christmas Offering for WMU missions surpassed the one million dollar mark.

Mallory retired in 1948 and, after several years in Birmingham, returned to Selma for her last years. The WMU memorialized her career in a variety of buildings that bear her name. The Alabama WMU named its state missions offering after her. Black Baptists remember her for the effort to drop traditional southern racial attitudes in order to work effectively, while Selma University, a black Baptist school, gave her an honorary doctorate.

Sources:

Allen, Catherine. *Laborers Together with God*. Birmingham, AL: Woman's Missionary Union, 1987. 246 pp.

Mallory, Kathleen. *Manual of WMU Methods*. Nashville: Broadman Press, 1917. Rev. ed. 1949

Ussery, Anne Wright. *Kathleen Mallory*. Nashville, TN: Broadman Press, 1956.

★576★
MANLY JR., Basil
Minister and Theologian, Southern Baptist Convention
b. Dec. 19, 1825, Edgefield County, South Carolina
d. Jan. 31, 1892, Louisville, Kentucky

Basil Manly, Jr., a professor at the Southern Baptist Theological Seminary in the late nineteenth century, was the son of Basil Manly, Sr., one of the founders of the Southern Baptist Convention, and Sarah Murray Rudolph Manly. As a child, young Basil accompanied his family to Tuscaloosa, Alabama, where his father had become the president of the University of Alabama. He attended the University and in 1840 graduated at the head of his class. He joined the local Baptist church and in 1844, as he was preparing to leave for the seminary, was licensed to preach.

Manly went north for his theological education (there being no Baptist theological school in the South at that time). He attended the Newton Theological Institution in Newton Centre, Massachusetts, but in 1845, the Southern Baptists split with the Northern Baptists, so Manly withdrew from Newton. He finished his theological work at Princeton and graduated in 1847.

Manly returned to Tuscaloosa long enough to be ordained. Then he moved on to pastor Providence Baptist Church in Sumter County, Alabama. At the same time he supplied for two other congregations. By the end of the year, however, his health failed him and he temporarily retired from the ministry. During this time he compiled hymns which he and his father published as the *Baptist Psalmody* (1850). It included nine written by Manly. In 1850 he accepted a call to First Baptist Church, Richmond, Virginia, the largest white church in the convention, and one of the most influential. While there he helped start the Richmond Female Institution, and in 1854 gave up the pulpit to become the school's president. While there he made his second compilation of hymns, published in 1859 as *Baptist Chorals*.

In 1859 the Southern Baptist Theological Seminary was opened. Manly was named to the faculty and was asked to draw up the articles of belief which would be signed by each faculty member. The school was successful for a short while, but was forced to close by the Civil War. In 1865 the school reopened but struggled through its next years. Manly left in 1869, evidently discouraged by the instability of the institution, and became president of Georgetown College in Kentucky. In 1877, then on more secure footing, the seminary moved to Louisville, Kentucky. Manly returned as the professor of Old Testament.

During his years of tenure at the seminary, Manly worked on a number of denominational projects, possibly the most significant being the convention's Sunday School Board. He led in the formation of the board and served as its first president.

Among the controversies which swirled around the seminary during Manly's years, the Toy controversy on biblical inspiration was probably the most intense. German-trained **Crawford Howell Toy** had brought biblical criticism to the classroom and was eventually forced out of the school. The controversy led to the writing of Manly's only major theological work, *The Bible Doctrine of Inspiration* (1888).

Manly's last literary effort was a third compilation of hymns, *Manly's Choice*, published in 1891, the year before his death. Manly is remembered for the many and varied projects for the seminary and the convention he pursued, often in the absence of anyone else to initiate and carry them through. As a result, he did not particularly excel in any one area. Both the school and the church would have looked quite different, however, had he not been there to carry out the numerous tasks. Manly was memorialized in 1909 by the seminary's establishment of the Basil Manly Chair of Religious Education and Church Administration.

Sources:

Encyclopedia of Southern Baptists. 3 vols. Nashville, TN: Broadman Press, 1958, 1971.
Manly, Basil. *The Bible Doctrine of Inspiration.* New York: A. C. Armstrong, 1888. 266 pp.

★577★
MANNING, Timothy
Cardinal, Roman Catholic Church
b. Nov. 15, 1909, Ballingreary Ireland
d. Jun. 23, 1989, Los Angeles, California

Timothy Manning, archbishop of Los Angeles and a cardinal in the Roman Catholic Church, was raised in Ireland. He began his studies for the priesthood in his native Ireland at the Jesuit school in Mungret, Limerick, but came to America in 1928 in answer to an appeal for priests in the growing Los Angeles diocese. He attended St. Patrick's Seminary in Menlo Park, California, and follow-

ing his graduation in 1934 spent four years studying canon law in Rome and the Pontifical Gregorian Institute. He returned in 1938 to become secretary to John Cantwell, the first archbishop of Los Angeles. He became a United States citizen in 1944.

In 1946 Manning became the auxiliary bishop for Los Angeles, and in 1948 assumed additional duties as chancellor and vicar general. In 1967 he moved to Fresno, California, and became the first bishop of that diocese. He returned to Los Angeles two years later as coadjutor and succeeded Archbishop **James Francis McIntyre** in 1970. Stepping into the conservative McIntyre's shoes, he dealt with the more liberal elements in the archdiocese by allowing the formation of a priests' senate and the Interparochial Council of East Los Angeles (as a forum for Mexican-American parishes). He also began to institute the other changes mandated by Vatican II to which McIntyre had been resistant. Manning was made a cardinal in 1973.

As archbishop, Manning centered his work in quiet administrative activities of his ever growing archdiocese. His primary public activities were in interfaith work (his first major address as archbishop was in the Wilshire Boulevard Temple [Jewish]), opposing abortion and pornography, and nurturing the growing Mexican-American parishes. He worked to protect the rights of unregistered aliens. In 1978 Manning was appointed a member of the Vatican's Sacred Congregation for the Evangelization of Peoples and in 1983 was named one of the three co-presidents of the 1983 World Synod of Bishops, which met in Rome.

Manning resigned his office in 1984 but stayed on until a successor was named in 1985. He retired to Holy Family Parish in South Pasadena, California, and served as a parish priest. In 1989 cancer appeared in his spine, and he died after a short period in the hospital. Manning's reign is remembered as a transition between the archconservative leadership of McIntyre and the very active social role of his successor, Archbishop **Roger M. Mahony**.

Sources:

Dart, John. "Cardinal Manning Dies; Led Archdiocese for 15 Years." *Los Angeles Times* (June 24, 1989).
MacEoin, Gary, and the Committee for the Responsible Election of the Pope. *The Inner Elite.* Kansas City, MO: Sheed Andrews and McMeel, 1979. 301 pp.

★578★
Bishop MARDARY
Bishop, Serbian Orthodox Diocese in America
b. 1889, Titograd Yugoslavia
d. Dec. 12, 1935

Bishop Mardary, who organized the Serbian Orthodox Diocese in America, was born Ivan Uskokovich in Podgoritsa (now Titograd, Yugoslavia). In 1907 he became a monk at the Studenitsa monastery in his native country and took the name Mardary. He soon went to Russia to study at the St. Petersburg Theological Academy, a school of the Russian Orthodox Church. He was ordained as a Russian Orthodox priest upon his graduation. He volunteered for the Alaskan mission and as the Russian mission grew he settled in the United States. Along the way he was elevated to the rank of archimandrite. At the beginning of the twentieth century, the relatively few Serbian Christians were members of the Russian Orthodox Church. By the end of World War II, a small number of Serbian priests and predominantly Serbian parishes had emerged as a visible presence in the Russian church.

In 1919 Archimandrite Mardary was selected as a candidate for bishop of a Serbian diocese, but due to the unsettled conditions in Russia, the American bishops could not get clearance to consecrate him. Thus he was sent to Belgrade for consecration. Upon his arrival in Serbia, however, he was assigned to head a monastery at Rakovitsa. Meanwhile the American Serbians requested some episcopal oversight and Bishop Nicholai Velimirovich was dispatched to the United States. He gave leadership to the Serbians for several years, during which time Mardary returned as his administrative assistant. When he returned from Serbia, Mardary remained as diocesan administrator and parish priest in Chicago. Using some of his own funds, Mardary purchased the land in Libertyville, Illinois, upon which St. Sava Monastery would be built.

Finally in 1926 Mardary was called to Belgrade and consecrated as bishop for America. He returned to the United States in May 1927 and immediately called the first Serbian Church Assembly. Work was begun on the organization of an independent Serbian diocese, a process slowed by dissent in the ranks of the priests and by Mardary's health. He had developed a case of tuberculosis, at the time an incurable disease, and he died in 1935.

Mardary is remembered for his forebearance and patience in handling the transition from Russian to Serbian authority in the new diocese. He is given credit for unifying and organizing the diocese at a time when it was receiving many new members who were emigrating to America. The diocese also extended into Canada. Mandary was eventually succeeded by Bishop Dionisije Milivojevich who was sent to the United States in 1940.

Sources:
Tarasar, Constance J. *Orthodox America, 1794-1974*. Syosset, NY: Department of History and Archives, Orthodox Church in America, 1975. 361 pp.

★579★
MARINO, Eugene A.
Archbishop, Roman Catholic Church
b. May 29, 1934, Biloxi, Mississippi

Eugene A. Marino, the first black priest named as an archbishop by the Roman Catholic Church in the United States, was the son of Jesus Maria and Lottie Irene Bradford Marino, immigrants to southern Mississippi from Puerto Rico. His father helped build the church serving black Catholics in Biloxi, Our Mother of Sorrows. Marino began his seminary work in 1952 and was ordained in 1962 as a priest in the Society of St. Joseph of the Sacred Heart, popularly called the Josephites, an order founded in the nineteenth-century to serve the black Catholic community. He was assigned as a professor of science and religion at the Josephite Seminary in Newburgh, New York.

His rise within the church came quickly. In 1972 Marino was named vicar general of the Josephites, the first Black to hold a similar position in the order. In 1974 he was consecrated as titular bishop of Walla Walla and named auxiliary bishop of Washington (D.C.). A theological conservative, he emerged in Washington as a staunch advocate of the poor and oppressed. He also nurtured and gave leadership to the growing visibility of black Catholics and furthered their attempts to build a new place in the church's life and worship. With his encouragement, familiar black cultural forms invaded the mass of black churches.

In 1984 Marino joined other black bishops in the preparation of the lengthy pastoral "We Have Seen and We Have Heard" which addressed the situation of black Roman Catholics. Among other issues, it called for the support of parochial schools, an authentically black liturgy, and the black family. In 1985 Marino became the first black bishop named as secretary of the National Conference of Catholic Bishops. In 1987 he hosted and served as liturgist for the National Black Catholic Congress which met in Washington, D.C., the first such gathering since 1894.

In 1990 Marino was named archbishop of Atlanta (Georgia), the first American Black so honored. He began his work with an installation address signaling his intention to be the bishop of the whole archdiocese, less than ten percent of whose members are black.

He further signaled his willingness to be a strong leader by making the first item in his agenda the investigation of child molestation by a priest, a scandal which had broken out before he took charge of the diocese. Unfortunately, Marino's reign as archbishop came to an abrupt end in the summer of 1990 when it became public knowledge that he had been having an affair with a young woman in violation of his vows of celibacy.

Sources:
Treadwell, David. "Black Archbishop in Pioneer Roll Again." *Los Angeles Times* (July 9, 1988).

★580★
MARSHALL, Peter
Minister, Presbyterian Church
b. May 27, 1902, Coatbridge Scotland
d. Jan. 25, 1949

Peter Marshall, a prominent pastor in the Presbyterian Church who served as chaplain to the U. S. Senate, grew up in Scotland. As a teenager working in a tube mill and going to school in the evening, he was greatly influenced by the example of Eric Liddell, the missionary who became an olympic runner. His early faith was catalyzed by an event in which he was saved, by what he believed was God's intervention, from what could have been a fatal accident. He decided to enter full-time Christian service. Following the suggestion of a cousin, he left Scotland in 1929 to make his way in America.

Marshall's days in America were drudgery until a chance meeting with an old friend who had previously migrated to the United States. The meeting led to Marshall's being offered a job with the Birmingham News in Alabama. He moved to Birmingham and soon was an active member at First Presbyterian Church. Some of the congregation recognized his potential and underwrote his study at Columbia Seminary in Decatur, Georgia. After graduation and ordination, in 1930 he became the pastor of the Presbyterian church in Covington, Georgia. In 1933 he was called to Westminster Presbyterian Church in Atlanta. The dying congregation was brought back to life, and Marshall was soon preaching to a standing-room-only crowd each Sunday. He was not only a gifted speaker in his own right, but possessed the added asset of a winsome Scottish brogue.

Among those attracted to the church in Atlanta was Sarah Catherine Wood, whom Marshall married in 1936. A year later they moved to Washington, D.C., where he became pastor of the New York Avenue Presbyterian Church. His ministry was as successful here as it had been in Georgia, but was also hampered by illness; **Sarah Catherine Wood Marshall** had a two-year bout with tuberculosis (1943-1945) and he suffered a heart attack in 1946. In January 1947 he was asked to become the chaplain for the U. S. Senate. He held this post for two years until his death in 1949 from a second heart attack.

While Marshall was an outstanding pastor, he would have soon been forgotten had it not been for his widow's accepting an invitation to edit a collection of his sermons. *Mr. Jones, Meet the Master* became a best seller. Catherine then wrote a biography, *A Man Called Peter*, which was even more successful and eventually was turned into a movie starring Richard Todd as Marshall. In the decade after his death, Marshall thus touched more lives and became more famous than he had in life. He emerged as a symbol of a fulfilled, practical existence lived in the experience of God and the resulting piety such an experience produces.

Sources:
Lippy, Charles H. *Twentieth-Century Shapers of American Popular Religion*. New York: Greenwood Press, 1989. 494 pp.
Marshall, Catherine. *A Man Called Peter*. New York: McGraw-Hill, 1951. 354 pp.

Marshall, Peter. *The Exile Heart.* Washington, D.C.: Scottish Memorial Committee, 1949. 157 pp.

———. *Mr. Jones, Meet the Master: Sermons and Prayers. . . .* Edited by Catherine Marshall. New York: Fleming H. Revell Company, 1949. 192 pp.

———. *The Prayers of Peter Marshall.* Edited by Catherine Marshall. New York: McGraw-Hill, 1954. 243 pp.

★ 581 ★
MARSHALL, Sarah Catherine Wood
Writer, Presbyterian Church
b. Sep. 27, 1914, Johnson City, Tennessee
d. Mar. 18, 1983

Sarah Catherine Wood Marshall, the widow of Presbyterian minister **Peter Marshall**, who emerged in her own right as a bestselling writer of religious books in the 1950s, was the daughter of a Presbyterian minister. Born in Tennessee, she grew up in Mississippi and West Virginia where her father pastored congregations. While religious, she professed a lack of any real personal experience of faith as she matured into womanhood. Following high school, she moved to Atlanta, Georgia, to attend Agnes Scott College in suburban Decatur. She heard of Peter Marshall, the new minister at Westminster Presbyterian Church, and began to attend his services. Sarah Catherine Wood and the winsome preacher with the Scottish accent were married in 1936. The following year they moved to Washington, D.C., where he pastored the New York Avenue Presbyterian Church.

In March 1943 Sarah contracted tuberculosis. Despite the recent discovery of penicillin, tuberculosis was still a serious disease, causing her to remain in bed for two years. The illness was the crisis that led to a birth of faith for her. One evening, having surrendered her condition to God, she felt a sense of Christ's healing presence. At that point she began a steady recuperation. She recovered, however, only to face her husband's first heart attack (1947), followed by his career's triumph in being named chaplain for the U. S. Senate (1947), and death in 1949 from a second heart attack. Having been dependent on her father and then her husband, she was forced, at age 35, to make an independent life.

An immediate opening came when the Fleming H. Revell Company suggested she prepare an edited edition of her husband's sermons. *Mr. Jones, Meet the Master*, which appeared before the year was out, became a best seller. She followed it in 1951 with a biography, *A Man Called Peter*, which was even more successful. In 1953 she was named "Woman of the Year" by the Women's National Press Club. She continued to edit her husband's material for several years, though attention became focused on the movie version of the biography, which was released in 1955. In the process of writing about her husband, Catherine Marshall also became a public figure herself. Her second solely authored book, an autobiography entitled *To Live Again*, was also well received. In 1959 she married Leonard LeSourd, the executive editor of *Guideposts*, a step she opened herself to only after she concluded that she was not betraying her first husband and that she needed a family to fulfill her own life.

Though now functioning as a mother again, Sarah continued her literary career. Her successful books included *Beyond Ourselves* (1961); *Christy* (1967), a novel; *Something More: In Search of a Deeper Faith* (1974); and *Adventures in Prayer* (1975). In the mid 1970s the LeSourds joined with popular writers Elizabeth and John Sherrill to found Chosen Books, a publishing imprint which has made its way in the very competitive religious book publishing industry. *Adventures in Prayer* (1975) was her first contribution to the new publishing venture. She later published *The Helper* (1978); *Meeting God at Every Turn* (1980); and *Catherine Marshall's Story Bible* (1983) through the new company.

Ultimately, the lung problem from her days with tuberculosis reasserted itself, and Sarah died in 1983. Her last literary products were a final editing of some of Peter Marshall's writings, a co-authored book on prayer with LeSourd, and a second novel, *Julie* (1984), published posthumously. She left her diaries to her husband, and he edited some selections which were published in 1986 as *A Closer Walk: Spiritual Discoveries from Her Journals*.

Marshall's writing has been largely ignored by the world of religious scholarship and literature, but as a writer of popular inspirational literature, she built a mass audience and emerged as a significant representative of late twentieth-century Protestant piety.

Sources:

Goin, Mary Elisabeth. "Catherine Marshall: Three Decades of Popular Religion." *Journal of Presbyterian History* 56 (Fall 1978): 219-235.

LeSourd, Leonard, ed. *A Closer Walk: Spiritual Discoveries from Her Journals.* Old Tappan, NJ: Chosen-Revell, 1986. 251 pp.

Lippy, Charles H. *Twentieth-Century Shapers of American Popular Religion.* New York: Greenwood Press, 1989. 494 pp.

Marshall, Catherine. *Adventures in Prayer.* Chappaqua, NY: Chosen Books, 1975. 134 pp.

———. *Beyond Our Selves.* New York: McGraw-Hill, 1961. 266 pp.

———. *Christy.* New York: McGraw-Hill, 1967. 496 pp.

———. *Julie.* New York: McGraw-Hill, 1984. 363 pp.

———. *A Man Called Peter.* New York: McGraw-Hill, 1951. 354 pp.

———. *Meeting God at Every Turn.* Lincoln, VA: Chosen Books, 1980. 254 pp.

———. *To Live Again.* New York: McGraw-Hill, 1957. 335 pp.

★ 582 ★
MARTELLO, Leo Louis
Founder, Witches International Craft Associates
Founder, Witches Anti-Defamation League
b. Sep. 26, 1931, Dudley, Massachusetts

Dr. Leo Louis Martello is a prolific occult author who took the lead in the 1970s in demanding religious rights for Neo-Pagans and Witches through the founding of the Witches Liberation Movement and the Witches Anti-Defamation League (WADL). He was educated at Assumption College and Hunter College, and received a Doctor of Divinity degree from the National Council of Spiritual Consultants (a spiritualist church/seminary in which he was also ordained). In the 1960s, as a Spiritualist minister and medium, he founded the Temple of Spiritual Guidance and the Spiritual Independents Movement. He also worked as a professional graphologist and hypnotist. He became for a period the staff graphologist for the *Psychic Observer*, a popular Spiritualist periodical. He authored his first books during his Spiritualist years, including *Your Pen Personality* (1961) and *It's In the Cards* (1964).

Martello claims that he was initiated into a Sicilian family Stregerma (traditional Sicilian Witches) on September 26, 1949, though he did not become a "public Witch" until 1969. The following year he formed the Witches International Craft Associates (WICA).

Once Martello publicly announced his membership in the Witchcraft community, he quickly emerged as a well known figure in the larger Wiccan/Neo-Pagan movement in the wake of the publicity surrounding the first Halloween Witch-In in New York's Central Park in 1970, an event sponsored by Martello. At first refused a permit by the parks department, he took his case to the American Civil Liberties Union (A.C.L.U.) and threatened to file suit for discrimination against a minority religion. The city backed down, and Martello received the permit, which constituted the first civil rights victory for Wiccans in recent history. The Witch-In, attended by about 1,000 people, was filmed and became a documentary.

Martello's many books include *How to Prevent Psychic Blackmail* (1966); *Witches Liberation* (1971); *What it Means to Be a Witch* (1972); and *Witchcraft: The Old Religion* (1973). He has also published some 300 articles in periodicals as diverse as the *Psychic Observer* and the *Negro Digest*. Martello himself published *Witchcraft Digest* and *WICA Newsletter* until 1975, and is currently contributing editor and writer for *Rosegate Journal*. He has also appeared on many radio and television shows and has often lectured at colleges. Early on in his public career he advocated legal Wiccan Churches, tax-exempt status for such churches, paid holidays for witches, legal witch weddings, and other privileges usually assumed by religious groups. He lives in New York City and distributes his books through Hero Press, which he founded and heads.

Sources:

Guiley, Rosemary E. *Encyclopedia of Witchcraft & Witches*. New York: Facts on File, 1989. 400 pp.

Martello, Leo Louis. *Curses in Verses*. New York: Hero Press, 1971. 32pp.

_____. *Hidden World of Hypnotism*. New York: HC Publishers, 1969. 224 pp.

_____. *How to Prevent Psychic Blackmail*. New York: Samuel Weiser, 1975. 192 pp.

_____. *It's In the Cards*. New York: Key Publishing Co., 1964. 95 pp.

_____. *Weird Ways of Witchcraft*. New York: HC Publishers, 1969. 224 pp.

_____. *What It Means to Be a Witch*. New York: The Author, [1975]. 28 pp.

_____. *Witchcraft, The Old Religion*. Secaucus, NJ: University Books, 1973. 287 pp.

_____. *Your Pen Personality*. New York: Hero Press, 1961.

★583★
MARTIN, William Clyde
Bishop, Methodist Church (1939-1968)
b. Jul. 28, 1893, Randolph, Tennessee

William Clyde Martin, a bishop of the Methodist Church (1939-1968), is the son of Leila Ballard and John Harmon Martin. He attended the University of Arkansas for a year (1913-1914) but later transferred to Hendrix College, from which he received his A.B. degree in 1918. Shortly after his graduation he married Sally Katherine Beene. He began his seminary education with a year at the Free Church College in Aberdeen, Scotland, but returned to the United States for his last two years at Southern Methodist University, which granted him a B.D. in 1921. That same year he was ordained as a minister in the Texas Conference of the Methodist Episcopal Church, South and appointed to Grace Methodist Church in Houston, Texas.

A talented minister and speaker, Martin quickly rose in the ranks and served First Methodist Church, Port Arthur, Texas (1925-1928); First Methodist Church, Little Rock, Arkansas (1928-1931); and First Methodist Church, Dallas, Texas (1931-1938), one of the largest and most prominent congregations in Methodism. In 1938 Martin became the fourth pastor of that church to be elected to the episcopacy. He was assigned to the Pacific Coast Area.

Martin's election came just as the Methodist Episcopal Church, South was about to merge with the Methodist Episcopal Church and Methodist Protestant Church to create the Methodist Church (1939-1968), and most of his episcopal activity occurred in the new church. In 1940 he was assigned to the Kansas-Nebraska Area, but in 1948 he moved to the Dallas-Fort Worth Area where he stayed until his retirement in 1964. During his first four years in the new church, he began long tenures on the Board of Missions and Church Extension and the Board of Education. He served one term as chairman of the church's Rural Life Commission (1944-1948). In 1949 he completed his first book, *To Fulfill This Ministry*, a basic text on the meaning of ministry which appeared on the church's ministerial course of study and was read by almost all Methodist ministers for a generation. In 1953 he was elected to a term as president of the Council of Bishops of the Methodist Church.

During his Dallas years Martin increased his ecumenical activity and was prominent in the founding of the National Council of Churches in 1950. In 1952 he was elected president of the Council. Upon completion of his term in 1956 he began six years as a member of the central committee of the World Council of Churches. Following his retirement in 1964 he became a lecturer in church administration at Perkins School of Theology in Dallas, where he had frequently spoken over the years of his administration.

Sources:

Harmon, Nolan B. *The Encyclopedia of World Methodism*. 2 vols. Nashville: United Methodist Publishing House, 1974.

Howell, Clinton H., ed. *Prominent Personalities in Methodism*. Birmingham, AL: Lowrey Press, 1945. 512 pp.

Martin, William C. *Those Were God's People: A Bible History*. Nashville, TN: South-Western Co., 1966.

_____. *To Fulfill This Ministry*. New York: Abingdon-Cokesbury Press, 1949. 142 pp.

Who's Who in the Methodist Church. Nashville, TN: Abingdon Press, 1966.

★584★
MARTY, Martin Emil
Church Historian, Evangelical Lutheran Church in America
b. Feb. 5, 1928, West Point, Nebraska

Martin Emil Marty, a church historian and possibly the most influential interpreter of religion to contemporary secular society, is the son of Anne Louise Wuerdemann and Emil A. Marty. He was raised in a conservative German-American environment within the Lutheran Church—Missouri Synod. After graduating from high school he left home to attend Concordia Junior College in Milwaukee, Wisconsin. He developed an early interest in art and partially paid his way through college working as an artist. During his college days, however, he noticed a significant shift in his primary interest from art, to art history and history. At the same time he felt a call to the ministry. Finishing his A.B. in 1949 at Washington University in St. Louis, Missouri, he entered Concordia Theological Seminary, across town. Completing his M.Div. in 1952 and enthused with the study of religion, he moved to the Lutheran School of Theology in Chicago (S.T.M., 1945) and the University of Chicago (Ph.D., 1956).

After graduate school, Marty turned down a position at the University to become pastor of the Church of the Holy Spirit in Elk Grove Village, a suburb of Chicago. While there, he joined the editorial staff of the *The Christian Century*, the leading liberal Protestant journal for pastors and laypeople, a position he has retained over the years. In 1963 he returned to the University of Chicago where he has remained since. In 1978 he was named the Fairfax M. Cone Distinguished Service Professor. He was elected president of the American Society of Church History in 1971 and of the American Academy of Religion in 1987. His work across the wide spectrum of American religious history was signaled in 1981 with his election as president of the American Catholic Historical Society.

Marty's influence as the leading interpreter of American religion has been focused in his teaching activity at the University of Chicago (from which a number of his students have taken college and university teaching posts); his accessiblity to the media, in which he is frequently quoted; and, most importantly, his many books. Between 1959 and 1987 he authored 50 books, co-authored seven more, and edited 21 additional titles. He has also authored numerous articles, contributed to over 130 other books, and since 1969 has edited a personal bi-weekly newsletter, *Context*. Among his many literary products, his most enduring will possibly be *The New Shape of American Religion* (1960); *Righteous Empire: The Protestant Experience in America* (1970); *A Nation of Behavers* (1976); *Pilgrims in their Own Land: Five Hundred Years of Religion in America* (1984); *Modern American Religion* (1986); and the ten volumes he edited under the collective title, *New Theology* (1966-1973).

During the 1970s, the Missouri Synod was split along conservative-liberal lines. Marty was among the liberals who left the church and formed the Association of Evangelical Lutheran Churches. That church merged with the American Lutheran Church and the Lutheran Church in America to become the Evangelical Lutheran Church in America.

Sources:

Marty, Martin E. *Modern American Religion.* Chicago: University of Chicago Press, 1986.

_____. *The New Shape of American Religion.* New York: Harper, 1959.

_____. *Pilgrims in Their Own Land: Five Hundred Years of Religion in America.* Boston: Little, Brown, 1984.

_____. *Righteous Empire: The Protestant Experience in America.* New York: Dial, 1970.

_____. *A Short History of Christianity.* New York: Meridian, 1959.

_____, ed. *New Theology.* 10 vols. New York: Macmillan Company, 1964-1973.

Quebedeaux, Richard. "Who Is Martin Marty?" *The World and I* (September 1987): 466-471.

★585★
MARVIN, Enoch Mather
Bishop, Methodist Episcopal Church, South
b. Jun. 12, 1823, Wright City, Missouri
d. Nov. 26, 1877, St. Louis, Missouri

Enoch Mather Marvin, a bishop in the Methodist Episcopal Church, South, was the son of Wells and Mary Davis Marvin. Raised in a nonreligious home, he began to attend Methodist services on his own and was converted in 1840. He felt a call to the ministry and in 1941 joined the Missouri Conference of the Methodist Episcopal Church. In spite of his lack of formal education, he showed promise as a pulpit orator, and was ordained a deacon in 1843. A significant year for him was 1845. The Methodist Episcopal Church had split in 1844, and when forced to decide, in 1845, he sided with the southern jurisdiction. Later that year he was ordained an elder and he married Harriet Brotherton Clark.

Marvin served churches across the state through the 1840s and 1850s. In 1852 he became a presiding elder of the St. Charles District. He was elected a delegate to the general conference in 1852 and 1858. In 1857 he began a period in St. Louis first at Centenary Methodist Episcopal Church, South (1855-1857), then at First Church (1857-1858), and back at Centenary (1859-1861). The Roman Catholic atmosphere of St. Louis provided him with the occasion of his first book, *Errors on Transubstantiation and Other Errors of the Papacy* (1860).

Unable to take the oath of allegiance after the Civil War started, Marvin headed south and served as a chaplain in the Confederate Army. He ended the war in Greenwood, Louisiana, and moved to Marshall, Texas, in 1865. He was not a delegate to the 1866 general conference, but was elected as a bishop on the first ballot. Assigned to the Indian Mission (Oklahoma), he brought the work out of its post war doldrums.

Marvin, along with fellow bishop **Holland Nimmons McTyeire**, is given a significant amount of credit for reviving the Methodist Episcopal Church, South in the years after the war. He turned his oratorical abilities to defending the church and its rights to expand geographically. He settled in St. Louis and put his energies into raising the money necessary to establish St. John's Church and to endow Central College. He also authored his second book, *The Work of Christ* (1867). Toward the end of the decade, he began a 17-month stay on the Pacific Coast developing the work in the far west. His third book was *The Life of William Goff Caples* (1870).

In 1874, Marvin was chosen as the bishop to visit the mission fields in the Orient. He staged the event so as to dramatize the missionary cause throughout the church. His 10-month journey began from San Francisco, California, in November 1876. He died very soon after his return and his account of the trip, *To the East by Way of the West*, which became a popular success, was published posthumously (as was his last book, *The Doctrinal Integrity of Methodism*, in 1878).

Sources:

Finney, Thomas M. *Life and Labors of Enoch Mather Marvin.* St. Louis, MO: James H. Chambers, 1880.

Godbold, Albea. "Bishop Enoch Mather Marvin." *Methodist History* 2, 3 (April 1964): 1-22.

Harmon, Nolan B. *The Encyclopedia of World Methodism.* 2 vols. Nashville: United Methodist Publishing House, 1974.

Marvin, Enoch M. *The Doctrinal Integrity of Methodism.* St. Louis, MO: Advocate Publishing House, 1878. 132 pp.

_____. *The Life of William Goff Caples.* St. Louis, MO: Southwestern Book & Publishing Co., 1870. 440 pp.

_____. *Sermons.* Nashville, TN: Publishing House of the Methodist Episcopal Church, South, 1876. 552 pp.

_____. *To the East by Way of the West.* St. Louis, MO: Bryan, Brand & Co., 1877. 606 pp.

_____. *The Work of Christ.* St. Louis, MO: P. M. Pinkard, 1867.

McAnally, D. R. *Life and Labors of E. M. Marvin.* St. Louis, MO: Advocate Publishing House, 1878.

★586★
MASON, Charles Harrison
Founder, Church of God in Christ
b. Sep. 8, 1866, Bartlett, Tennessee
d. Nov. 17, 1961, Memphis, Tennessee

Charles Harrison Mason, the founder of the Church of God in Christ, the largest Pentecostal denomination in North America, was the son of Jerry and Eliza Mason. He grew up on a farm in rural Tennessee. In 1878 he had a conversion experience and was baptized in the Baptist Church (black Baptists at the time were in the process of forming the National Baptist Convention). In 1893 Mason was licensed to preach and began his religious career as a Baptist preacher later that year. Successful as a speaker at revivals, Mason entered Arkansas Bible College to prepare himself for the ministry, but left after three months when he concluded that the education he was receiving there was not helping him to become a better preacher. As a result of his adherence to Holiness doctrine, the belief that the believer can be perfected in love through an experience of the Holy Spirit, and his declaration that he had had such an experience, he was eventually forced out of the Baptist Church. Subsequently, he and another baptist preacher, **Charles P. Jones**, founded the Church of God in Christ in 1894. Having been divorced from his first wife, Alice Saxton, in 1903 Mason married Lelia Washington.

The new church prospered, but Mason's continued quest for a deeper spiritual life led him to undertake a journey to Los Angeles in 1907 in order to experience the Pentecostal awakening that was occurring in that city. After receiving the baptism of the Holy Spirit, the definitive experience shared by Pentecostals and evidenced by the individual speaking in tongues, he returned to share the new teaching with his church. As a result the church split, with Jones leading the non-Pentecostal members to found the Church of Christ (Holiness) U.S.A., and the original church reforming under Mason. D. J. Young, who had gone to Azusa Street in Los Angeles with Mason, became editor of the church's periodical, *The Whole Truth.* Under Mason, who lived into his nineties, the church grew to become the largest Pentecostal denomination in America.

Mason's wife died in 1936, and in 1943 he married Elsie Washington. During the last years of his life he ruled the church in an arbitrary manner, but he allowed significant room for creativity and the space for ministers to develop their work around the country. At first named general overseer, the church later designated him senior bishop and chief apostle.

Sources:
Cornelius, Lucille J. *The Pioneer History of the Church of God in Christ.* The Author, 1975. 102 pp.
Mason, Mary Esther. *The History and Life Work of Elder C. H. Mason and His Co-Laborers.* The Author, n.d. 93 pp.
Patterson, J. O., German R. Ross, and Julia Mason Atkins. *History and Formative Years of the Church of God in Christ with Excerpts from the Life and Works of Its Founder—Bishop C. H. Mason.* Memphis, TN: Church of God in Christ Publishing House, 1966. 143 pp.

★587★
MASSEE, Jasper Cortenus
Fundamentalist Minister, Baptist Church
b. Nov. 22, 1871, Marshallville, Georgia
d. Feb. 25, 1965, Atlanta, Georgia

Jasper Cortenus Massee, outstanding Baptist spokesperson for fundamentalism, was the youngest of 13 children born to Drewry Washington Massee and Susan Elizabeth Bryan Massee. His father was a physician in the small Georgia community of Marshallville. The family was Southern Baptist, and Massee joined the local congregation in his youth. He entered nearby Mercer University in 1888. Four years later, after distinguishing himself on the debating team, he graduated and decided to enter the ministry. However, he first spent a year teaching school. In December 1893 he married, was ordained, and began serving the Baptist church in Kissammee, Florida. In 1896, after his first wife died, he remarried and with his new bride moved to Louisville, Kentucky, where he entered Southern Baptist Theological Seminary.

Massee stayed at the seminary for only a year and then accepted a call to a church in Orlando, Florida. After two years in Orlando, Massee served a string of Baptist churches in Lancaster, Kentucky (1899-1901); Mansfield, Ohio (1901-1903); Raleigh, North Carolina (1903-1908); Chattanooga, Tennessee (1908-1913); and Dayton, Ohio (1913-1919). He accepted a call to a church in Brooklyn, New York, just as the fundamentalist-modernist controversy was entering its most intense phase.

Soon after his arrival in Brooklyn, Massee joined with other conservative forces in the Northern Baptist Convention to hold a conference on the "Fundamentals of Our Baptist Faith" at Buffalo, New York, prior to the 1920 convention meeting. Massee presided at the gathering and was elected president of the Fundamentalist Federation that was formed. The federation forced an investigation of liberalism in the Baptist schools, but in the process Massee began to feel alienated by the spirit of some of his more aggressive fundamentalist colleagues, such as **John Roach Straton**. He continued to support them, however, in their quest for the convention to adopt a statement of faith as a standard for Baptists.

In 1922 Massee accepted a call from the Tremont Baptist Temple in Boston. In 1923, soon after the beginning of Massee's prominent seven-year pastorate at the temple, radical fundamentalists in the church formed the Baptist Bible Union. Massee remained in charge of the more moderate federation. He soon found himself attacked by his former colleagues for cooperating with the liberals, while the liberals had little use for his theology. Meanwhile, he was building Tremont Temple into the largest congregation associated with the convention.

In 1925, Massee resigned his leadership of the Fundamentalist Federation. He resigned for several reasons. The work of the temple consumed his time, his wife had become an invalid, and he wished to rid himself of the waves of bitterness toward his colleagues that had resulted from involvement in convention politics. He focused upon work for reconciliation of the moderate funda-

mentalists and the evangelical liberals. He had a prime opportunity presented when he spoke at the 1926 convention and called for a moratorium on the fight and a denomination-wide evangelical program. His suggestion was accepted, and his voice is generally credited with returning some level of relative calm to the convention's future meetings, and with ensuring a continuing voice for conservatives within convention life.

In 1929, following his successful years at Tremont, Massee began nine years on the road as an evangelist and Bible conference speaker. He concluded his professional life as a homiletics professor at the Eastern Baptist Theological Seminary in Philadelphia from 1838 to 1941. He then retired to Atlanta, where he lived the last years of his life. A number of his sermons, especially those delivered during his Tremont years, were compiled into books.

Sources:
Dollar, George W. *A History of Fundamentalism in America.* Greenville, SC: Bob Jones University Press, 1973. 411 pp.
Massee, Jasper Cortenus. *The Gospel in the Ten Commandments.* New York: Fleming H. Revell, 1923. 159 pp.
_____. *Revival Sermons.* New York: Fleming H. Revell, 1928. 156 pp.
_____. *The Second Coming.* Philadelphia: Philadelphia School of the Bible, 1919. 251 pp.
_____. *The Ten Greatest Christian Doctrines.* New York: George H. Doran Company, 1925. 188 pp.
Russell, C. Allyn. *Voices of American Fundamentalism.* Philadelphia, PA: Westminister Press, 1976. 304 pp.

★588★
MASTRANTONIS, George
Founder, OLOGOS (Orthodox Lore of the Gospel of Our Savior)
b. Mar. 10, 1906, Karystos Greece
d. Aug. 14, 1988, St. Louis, Missouri

George Mastrantonis, a priest of the the Greek Orthodox Archdiocese of North and South America and a major apologist for the Orthodox faith, was born in Greece and educated at the University of Athens. In 1936, shortly after finishing his schooling, he married Presvytera Parakevi and was ordained in the Greek Orthodox Church. He became chancellor to the Bishop of Corinth. In 1939, just as World War II was beginning, he went to Leipzig to begin work on a doctorate. The following year he immigrated to the United States. He was assigned to St. Spyrion Greek Orthodox Church in Chicago. Over the next few years he pursued further studies at the University of Chicago, Yale Divinity School, and Concordia Theological Seminary in St. Louis, Missouri. Though he did not complete his doctorate, he was awarded the M.S.T. from Concordia in 1969.

Mastrantonis followed his work at St. Spyrion with pastoral leadership at St. Andrew and The Church of the Assumption, both Greek congregations in Chicago.

In 1950, while still in Chicago, Mastrantonis was the major force in the founding of the Hellenic Foundation, a welfare agency created to attend to the needs of recent Greek immigrants and the elderly. In 1951 he founded the Plato Grammar School. That same year he organized the Federation of Eastern Orthodox Churches in Greater Chicago, one of the early cooperative agencies working within the wider Orthodox community. In 1953 Mastrantonis was assigned as pastor of St. Nicholas Church in St. Louis, Missouri. He remained in that post, during which time he oversaw the expansion of the church and parish, until 1959, when he was forced to retire because of Parkinson's disease. He was named pastor emeritus, and for the next several years he continued to assist in the worship until his health prevented it.

In spite of his measurable contributions to Greek Orthodoxy, Mastrantonis is most remembered for his founding of OLOGOS, an evangelistic and missionary organization that published a wide variety of inexpensive booklets and tracts on the Orthodox faith. These numerous, relatively small pamphlets explained Orthodoxy to the the larger Christian community, strengthened the faithful in their belief, and led to the conversion of others to the faith. In the process of disseminating the literature, Mastrantonis became one of the most well-known priests of the Archdiocese.

Though unable to carry on his role in the active pastorate during the 1960s, Mastrantonis continued to make substantial contributions through his scholarly work. In 1966 he translated the Divine Liturgy of St. John Chrysostom, the common liturgy of most Orthodox Churches, into English. He also translated for publication the important correspondence between Patriarch Jeremiah of Constantinople and the Lutheran theologians of Tubingen (Germany) University, which occurred from 1573 to 1581, just as the gains of the Reformation were being consolidated. Among his several books was a catechetical text, *A New Style Catechism on the Eastern Orthodox Faith for Adults*, completed in 1969.

Mastrantonis died in St. Louis in 1988. His funeral was conducted by **Archbishop Iakovos**.

Sources:

"A Golden Pen Falls Silent." *Orthodoxia* 1, 1 (January 1989): 9-11.
Mastrantonis, George. *A New Style Catechism on the Eastern Orthodox Faith for Adults.* St Louis, MO: OLOGOS Mission, 1969. 276 pp.

★589★
Daya MATA
Leader, Self-Realization Fellowship
b. Jan. 31, 1914, Salt Lake City, Utah

Sri Daya Mata, born Faye Wright, is the third president of the organization founded by **Swami Paramahansa Yogananda**, the Self-Realization Fellowship (SRF). She is the daughter of Clarence Aaron and Rachel Terry Wright. While a young girl of eight, she was introduced to India at school, and felt mysteriously drawn to the country. When she returned home, she declared to her mother, "When I grow up I will never marry; I will go to India." At the age of 15, she was given a copy of one of contemporary Hinduism's most important scriptures, the *Bhagavad Gita*, and was deeply affected by its spiritual message. She resolved to devote herself to the task of seeking God. After going from one religious authority to another, she remained dissatisfied because no one she met seemed to really have direct knowledge of God.

In 1931, at the age of 17, Wright attended a public lecture in Salt Lake City at which she saw Yogananda (well-known author of *The Autobiography of a Yogi*). Yogananda immediately impressed her as someone with deep, experiential knowledge of the Divine, and she formed an immediate resolve to follow him as someone who could lead her to God. She had left school because of a severe blood disorder, and the bandages covering her swollen face attracted Yogananda's attention when she attended the classes he offered. When he asserted to the audience that the young woman would be healed within a week, Wright felt emboldened by the teacher's attention and requested that she be permitted to enter his ashram to seek God. Yogananda replied that her desire would eventually be granted, although she had to overcome her family's strong opposition. Within two weeks she was allowed to join the ashram in Los Angeles.

Daya Mata was one of Yogananda's closest followers, and he worked on transforming her into an exemplary disciple. As the great master approached the end of his life, he began giving more and more responsibility to his students. Before his death, Daya Mata was the administrator in charge of the Mount Washington headquarters. When Yogananda died in 1952, he left his organization in charge of **Swami Rajasi Janakananda** (James J. Lynn). Janakananda outlived his master by only three more years, and Daya Mata became the third president of the Self-Realization Fel-

lowship. Her many years of leadership have included, besides her administrative duties, frequent speaking (with many of her lectures now available on cassette tape), and one book, *"Only Love"* (1976).

Sources:

Mata, Sri Daya. *Qualities of the Devotee.* Los Angeles: Self-Realization Fellowship, 1971. Rev. ed. as: *"Only Love"*. 1976. 279 pp.

★590★
MATHERS, Samuel Liddell
Founder, Hermetic Order of the Golden Dawn
b. Jan. 8, 1854, London England
d. Nov. 20, 1918, Paris France

Samuel Liddell Mathers was an important literary figure in the magical revival in the late nineteenth century. He was also one of the founders of the Hermetic Order of the Golden Dawn, and later emerged as its leader. Although he never traveled to America, his literary influence in combination with his chartering of three temples in this country make him one of the most important sources of the twentieth century magical revival in the United States.

Born into a Scottish family living in London, Mathers later asserted his ancestry by adding MacGregor to his name. He received a good classical education, although he never attended college. His father died while he was young, and his mother moved to Bournemouth. Mathers eventually took a job as a clerk in that city, where he lived with his mother until he was 31. During this period he joined the Masons, and somewhat later, the Rosicrucian Society In Anglia. Beyond his involvement in occultism, Mathers also developed an interest in military matters.

Mathers moved to London in 1885, where he soon became involved in Theosophy. As a result of his own research on the Kabbalah, he produced an edited edition, *The Kabbalah Unveiled*, in 1887. In 1888 he published *Fortune-Telling Cards, the Tarot, Its Occult Significance and Methods of Play*. During the same year, Mathers also helped to found, in conjunction with William Woodman and Wynn Wescott, the Hermetic Order of the Golden Dawn (OGD). Mathers had the particular responsibility of editing a manuscript on ritual that would become the basis of the rites of the OGD. In 1888 Mathers also met Henri Bergson's sister, Mina Bergson, whom he renamed Moina and, two years later, married. Stimulated by new information on a more advanced level of rituals, Mathers moved to Paris in 1891 where he established the Ahathoor Temple of the OGD.

The practices and the view of the world that resulted from the OGD synthesis would be copied, with variations, by later magical groups. The basis of the OGD worldview was the microcosm-macrocosm relationship, which entails a correspondence between the principles that make up the human being and the universe. The links that are established via these correspondences allow the individual to tap the power of the macrocosm through magical operations.

For the future of ritual magic in the United States, one of the most significant acts of Mathers' career was his admission of **Aleister Crowley** into the higher grades of the order. Crowley later split with Mathers, but he kept and eventually published many of the secret materials of the OGD. These publications as well as Crowley's several visits to the United States were important for stimulating interest in the magical movement in this country.

After Mathers' death, Moina returned to England where she established and led a temple. Mathers books have been frequently reprinted, and most remain in print today.

Sources:

Coloquhoun, Ithell. *Sword of Wisdom: MacGregor Mathers and the Golden Dawn.* New York: G. P. Putnam's Sons, 1975. 307 pp.

Mathers, S. L. MacGregor. *The Book of the Sacred Magic of Abra-Melin.* New York: Causeway Books, 1974. 268 pp.

_____. *The Greater Key of Solomon.* Chicago: The de Laurence Company, 1914. 130 pp.

_____. *The Kabbalah Unveiled.* London: Routledge & Kegan Paul, 1951. 360 pp.

_____, and others. *Astral Projection, Ritual Magic, and Alchemy.* Comp. by Francis King. Rochester, VT: Destiny Books, 1987. 288 pp.

★591★
MATHESON, Samuel Pritchard
Primate, Anglican Church of Canada
b. Sep. 20, 1852, Klidonan, Manitoba, Canada
d. May 19, 1942, Winnipeg Canada

Samuel Pritchard Matheson, the fourth primate of the Anglican Church of Canada, was the first primate born in Canada. He was the nephew of Samuel Pritchard, who had been chosen by Bishop John Machray as tutor at the revived St. John's College in Winnipeg, Manitoba. Matheson was one of the first pupils of the new school. He received his B.A. degree in 1880. While a student, in 1876, he was ordained a priest in the Church of England. He became one of the leading priests of the diocese of Rupert's Land (now Manitoba). He was named a canon in the church and placed in charge of St. John's College School and lectured at St. John's College. In 1883 he became secretary of the Rupert's Land provincial synod. In that capacity he participated in all of the negotiations concerning the consolidation of the several separate provinces of the Church of England in Canada into the one Anglican Church of Canada, the process of consolidation culminating in 1893.

In 1903 he was named bishop coadjutor with right of succession for the diocese of Rupert's Land. He was consecrated by Archbishop **Robert Machray**, who had headed the diocese for almost 40 years. Machray died in 1904 and Matheson became bishop of Rupert's Land. The following year he became archbishop in charge of the province of Rupert's Land, and oversaw several provinces in central and western Canada.

In 1909, following the very short tenures of the previous two primates of the church, Matheson was named the fourth primate of the Anglican Church of Canada. During his reign a new Prayer Book, which the church would use for the next 40 years, was edited and adopted (1918). During his first decade in office he oversaw the completion of the church's organization and its movement into an entirely self-sustaining position financially. The Church Missionary Society (the foreign mission arm of the Church of England) withdrew the last remnants of its financial support in 1902. Possibly as important as any problem he faced, Matheson attempted negotiations with the Canadian Methodists, Presbyterians, and Congregationalists who were in the process of forming the United Church of Canada. No agreement was reached on the inclusion of the Anglicans in the merger, in spite of Matheson's attempt to find common ground between his church and the other Protestant bodies.

In 1930 Matheson, then in his late 70s and having been primate for 21 years, resigned. He was succeeded by Bishop Isaac Stringer as archbishop of Rupert's Land, and by Archbishop **Clarendon L. Worrell** as primate. Matheson lived another 12 years in retirement.

Sources:

Carrington, Philip. *The Anglican Church of Canada.* Toronto: Collins, 1963. 230 pp.

Wallace, W. Stewart. *The Macmillan Dictionary of Canadian Biography.* 4th ed., rev. Edited by W. A. McKay. Toronto: Macmillan of Canada, 1978.

★592★
MATHEW, Arnold Harris
Founder, Old Catholic Church in England
Bishop, Old Catholic Church in England
b. Aug. 6, 1852, Montpellier France
d. Dec. 20, 1919, South Mymms England

Arnold Harris Mathew, the founder of the Old Catholic Church in England, was the son of Henry Octerlony Mathew. Originally baptized a Roman Catholic, he was later rebaptized as an Anglican because of his mother's adherence to the Church of England. As a young man, he decided to become a priest and initially chose the Roman Catholic Church. He attended the College of the Holy Spirit (1874-1875) and St. Peter's seminary in Glasgow, Scotland, from which he received his D. D. in 1877. Ordained a priest in the Roman Catholic Church, he served parishes for the next 12 years, except for a period in a Dominican novitiate (1878-1879). Suddenly in 1889 he left the church and professed to having become a Unitarian.

After a year among the Unitarians Mathew reclaimed his orthodox faith and applied for admission to the Church of England. He served several parishes, but was never licensed because he refused to sign a statement renouncing the unique Roman Catholic doctrines. In 1892 he married Margaret Duncan, an action which permanently cut him off from returning to the Roman Catholic Church as a priest.

Shortly after the turn of the century, unable to find acceptance as an Anglican and having left the Roman Catholics behind, he initiated correspondence with the Old Catholic Church on the Continent concerning the possibility of his establishing Old Catholicism in England. The Old Catholic Church had come into existence as a traditionalist movement which rejected the changes in the Roman Catholic Church made at the First Vatican Council. Most importantly the Old Catholics rejected the idea of the infallibility of the Pope. The church also allowed priests to marry.

Mathew was consecrated a bishop in 1908 in Holland by Archbishop Gerard Gul. However, he returned to England only to discover that promised support did not exist, and that he would have to build the church from nothing. In 1910 he broke his agreement with the Dutch bishops by consecrating two of his priests to the episcopacy. By this action he completely isolated himself, but he also passed the episcopal authority necessary to create an apostolic church. He later consecrated other bishops in what proved to be an unsuccessful attempt to build a church from the top downward.

Mathew never attempted to create an American branch, but nevertheless became responsible for the Old Catholic movement coming to North America. He consecrated Austrian nobleman Rudolf, the Duc de Landas Berghes, who spent World War I in the United States. Through him Mathew's orders where passed on to several American clergymen who, in turn, freed them upon the independent catholic community. More than 50 jurisdictions and literally hundreds of independent bishops now trace their apostolic authority through Mathew. In 1914 Mathew also consecrated Frederick Samuel Willoughby. A resulting controversy over Willoughby's adherence to theosophical teachings led to the formation of the Liberal Catholic Church. In 1916 Mathew consecrated Bernard Mary Williams, who eventually succeeded him as head of the Old Catholic Church in England.

Mathew had been a prolific writer and wrote a number of books for his church including a discussion of the validity of Anglican orders and a missal for use in worship.

Sources:

Anson, Peter. *Bishops at Large.* London: Faber & Faber, 1964. 593 pp.

Brandreth, H. R. T. *Episcopi Vagantes and the Anglican Church.* London: S.P.C.K., 1961. 140 pp.

Cockerham, A. W. *The Apostolic Succession in the Liberal Catholic Church*. London: The St. Alban Press, 1966, 1980. 47 pp.

Mathew, Arnold Harris. *The Catholic Scholar's Introduction to English Literature*. New York: Benziger, 1904. 419 pp.

_____. *An Episcopal Odyssey*. Kingsdown, Kent, UK: 1915.

_____. *The Old Catholic Missal and Ritual*. London: 1909; Rept. New York: AMS Press, 1969. 326 pp.

_____. *Woman Suffrage*. Edinburgh: T. C. & E. C. Clark, 1907. 119 pp.

Ward, Gary L. *Independent Bishops: An International Directory*. Detroit: Apogee Books, 1990. 524 pp.

★593★
MATHEWS, Shailer
Theologian, Northern Baptist Convention
b. May 26, 1863, Portland, Maine
d. Oct. 23, 1941, Chicago, Illinois

Shailer Mathews, a leading modernist Baptist theologian, was the son of Sophia Lucinda Shailer and Jonathan Bennett Mathews. He was raised in a Baptist family. His father, the son of a Baptist minister, was a flour and tea merchant. He attended Colby College in Waterville, Maine, which granted him the A.B. degree in 1884. Though not particularly interested in the ministry, he took seminary work at Newton Theological Institute in Massachusetts (B.D., 1897). Though licensed to preach, he did not seek ordination but went into teaching. He taught at Colby for three years. In 1890 before leaving for graduate study at the University of Berlin, he married May Philbrick Elden.

He returned to teach history at Colby in 1892 and produced the first result of his European trip, *Select Medieval Documents* (1892). In 1894 he was invited to join the faculty at the University of Chicago as an assistant professor in New Testament history and interpretation. He was made full professor in 1897 and dean of the Divinity School in 1908. He remained in that position until his retirement in 1933.

Among his first writings after arriving in Chicago, *The Social Teachings of Jesus* (1897) explored the sayings of Jesus in the light of modern sociological insight and was immediately acknowledged as a key expository text for the social gospel, the movement to make Christian ideas relevant to social problems. Mathews went on to become one of the leading architects and spokespersons for modernism, the early twentieth-century attempt to make traditional Christianity responsive to new insights from science and other academic disciplines. Mathews, with his background in history and helping to form what would become known as the "Chicago" school of theology, considered historical consciousness as an integral element in theological reconstruction. In his writings Mathews directed attention away from consideration of the church as the defender of an eternal teaching and toward a religious institution which was very much the product of its times and of the historical processes with which it has interacted over the centuries. His ideas then served as a basis for a reconsideration of the conditioned nature of Christian doctrine. His theological opponents saw his work as an attack upon the existence of an essential Christian orthodoxy which survived from generation to generation.

Mathews' ideas were expanded in a series of books which appeared at the height of the fundamentalist-modernist controversy: *The Faith of Modernism* (1924); *The Atonement and the Social Process* (1930); *The Growth of the Idea of God* (1931); and *Christianity and the Social Process* (1934). To Mathews, much of the vitality of Christianity came from its ability to undergo necessary restatements at various points in history.

While Mathews emerged as a leading modernist theologian and a target of fundamentalist attack, he was also an active churchman. He was a major architect of the reorganization of northern Baptists that resulted in the formation of the Northern Baptist Convention in 1907. He was elected president of the Federal Council of Churches in 1912. In the middle of his four year tenure, he was also elected president of the Northern Baptist Convention (1915). His lengthy leadership in interdenominational work in Chicago led to his election as president of the Chicago Church Federation in 1929. Shortly after his retirement he authored *New Faith for Old: An Autobiography*.

Sources:

Arnold, Charles H. *Near the Edge of the Battle*. 1966.

Bowden, Henry Warner. *Dictionary of American Religious Biography*. Westport, CT: Greenwood Press, 1977. 572 pp.

Dictionary of American Biography. 20 vols. and 7 supps. New York: Charles Scribner's Sons, 1928-1936, 1944-1981.

Mathews, Shailer. *The Atonement and the Social Process*. New York: Macmillan Company, 1930. 212 pp.

_____. *Christianity and the Social Process*. New York: Harper & Bros., 1934. 221 pp.

_____. *The Faith of Modernism*. New York: Macmillan Company, 1924. 182 pp.

_____. *The Growth of the Idea of God*. New York: Macmillan Company, 1931. 237 pp.

_____. *New Faith for Old: An Autobiography*. New York: Macmillan Company, 1936. 303 pp.

_____. *The Social Teachings of Jesus*. New York: Macmillan Company, 1897. 235 pp.

Reid, Daniel G., Robert D. Linder, Bruce L. Shelley, and Harry S. Stout. *Dictionary of Christianity in America*. Downers Grove, IL: InterVarsity Press, 1990. 1305 pp.

★594★
MATTHEW, Wentworth Arthur
Founder, Commandment Keepers Congregation of the Living God
b. Jun. 23, 1892, Lagos Nigeria
d. 1973, New York, New York

Wentworth Arthur Matthew was the founder of an important black Hebrew group, the Commandment Keepers Congregation of the Living God. Born in West Africa, Matthew was raised in the West Indies and moved to New York City when he was 21. Working at various jobs, he eventually became a minister for a small black Pentecostal church that had the unique distinction of being the only such group to officially endorse Marcus Garvey and the Universal Negro Improvement Association.

Matthew organized his own congregation in 1919 and, probably through his contact with fellow Garvey supporter **Arnold Josiah Ford**, began to integrate elements of Judaism into his church. Both men were interested in the Falashas, the black Jews of Ethiopia. Ford moved to Ethiopia in 1930, and left the care of his congregation in the hands of Matthew. After Ford's departure, Matthew dropped almost all connections with Christianity and, in line with his identification with the Falashas, transformed his church into a black Jewish congregation.

The Commandment Keepers believe that Blacks are Falashas who had their true identity stripped from them during the era of slavery. Similar to other black Jewish groups, they also believe that the Old Testament patriarchs were black. Christianity is denounced as the religion of white gentiles. In the area of religious practice, the Commandment Keepers adopted many of the rites and holidays of orthodox Judaism. Kosher food laws are kept, and a Jewish prayer book is used in the group's services. Matthew also founded the Ethiopian Hebrew Rabbinical College which trains leaders in Talmud, Jewish history, mishnah, Josephus, and legalism. A few elements of Christianity, such as foot washing and gospel hymns, have been retained, but the services are free of the emotionalism associated with Pentecostalism, the church out of which Matthew emerged.

Matthew also taught Kabbalistic Science, a practice which he saw as related to the folk art of conjuring. This practice is used in healing, one of the other important emphases that was carried over from Pentecostalism. Matthew was succeeded by Rabbi David M. Dore, his grandson, who in 1977 was the second Black to receive a bachelor's degree from Yeshiva University.

Sources:

Brotz, Howard M. *The Black Jews of Harlem.* New York: Schocken Books, 1970. 144 pp.

Ehrman, Albert. "The Commandment Keepers: A Negro Jewish Cult in America Today." *Judaism* 8, 3 (Summer 1959): 266-270.

★ 595 ★
MATTHEWS, James Kenneth
Bishop, United Methodist Church
b. Feb. 10, 1913, Breezewood, Pennsylvania

James Kenneth Matthews, a bishop of the United Methodist Church, is the son of James Davenport Matthews, a minister in the Methodist Episcopal Church, and Laura Mae Wilson Matthews. He grew up in Ohio and Texas, and later attended Lincoln Memorial University (A.B., 1934) and then the Biblical Seminary of New York (S.T.B., 1937). During the 1937-38 school year, while pursuing graduate work at Boston University, he answered a call for missionaries. He was commissioned by the church and assigned to the pastorate of the Bowen Memorial Church in Bombay, India. Having previously been ordained a deacon, he was ordained an elder in the church shortly after his arrival in India. In 1940 he married Eunice Treffry Jones, the daughter of E. Stanley Jones, the prominent Methodist missionary.

Matthews seemed destined for leadership in missions. In 1941 he became district superintendent of the Dhulia-Puntamba District. He then entered the military and served for four years during World War II. Upon leaving the army, he returned to New York City and in 1946 was elected secretary for Southern Asia of the Board of Missions of the Methodist Church. In 1952 he became the associate general secretary for world missions of the board with responsibility for work in 44 countries. During this time he wrote two of his popular books, *South of the Himalayas* (1955) and *To the Ends of the Earth* (1959).

Matthews' missionary work seemed to reach a culmination in 1956 with his election as bishop for the Southern Asia Central Conference. However, he refused the task, believing that it should go to an Asian. Then in 1960, the North Central Jurisdiction of the church elected him as bishop and assigned him to the Boston area. At this point Matthews began what was almost a second career as a leading spokesperson among American Methodists for the foreign missionary enterprise and the ecumenical movement.

During his 20 years as an active bishop, Matthews served the Methodist Church (and its successor body the United Methodist Church) as the chairman of the Department of College and University Life and an episcopal member of the General Boards of Evangelism, Education, Missions, and Ecumenical Affairs. He was chairman (1968-1970) of the Consultation on Church Union (COCU) (the ill-fated attempt to unite a number of mainline denominations), and the Methodist Committee on Overseas Relief.

Matthews was active in the World Council of Churches from the days of its beginning in 1948, and prior to that time in the International Missionary Council (I.M.C.). He served for a number of years as a member of the World Council's central committee and as chairman of its structure committee. He also became a vice-president of the National Council of Churches in the U.S.A. His talents at negotiation and developing creative solutions to difficult problems were widely heralded in his ecumenical endeavors.

Matthews retired from the episcopacy in 1980. However, in 1985, the council of bishops of the United Methodist Church called him out of retirement to deal with a situation in Zimbabwe where Bishop Abel T. Muzorewa had become deeply involved in the political turmoil of the nation. Matthews served until Muzorewa was able to resume his duties.

Sources:

Harmon, Nolan B. *The Encyclopedia of World Methodism.* 2 vols. Nashville: United Methodist Publishing House, 1974.

Matthews, James K. *Eternal Values in a World of Change.* Cincinnati, OH: Women's Division of Christian Service, Board of Missions of the Methodist Church, 1960. 46 pp.

_____. *A New Church for a New World.* 1968.

_____. *South of the Himalayas.* New York: Board of Missions of the Methodist Church, 1955. 155 pp.

_____. *To the Ends of the Earth.* Nashville, TN: National Methodist Student Movement, 1959. 131 pp.

Who's Who in the Methodist Church. Nashville, TN: Abingdon Press, 1966.

★ 596 ★
MATTHEWS, Marjorie Swank
Bishop, United Methodist Church
b. Jul. 11, 1916, Onaway, Michigan
d. Jul. 2, 1986, Grand Rapids, Michigan

Marjorie Swank Matthews, a bishop in the United Methodist Church and the first woman to be elected bishop of a major American denomination, grew up in Onaway and Alma, Michigan. During her childhood, she developed a desire to be a missionary teacher in the Orient, but was unable to pursue her education due to the Great Depression of the 1930s. She attended secretarial school instead of college. In 1938 at the age of 22, she married, later had a son, and moved about frequently, as her husband was in the military. In 1946 her marriage ended in divorce, and she was faced with the need to care for her son. She became the secretary to the president of a manufacturing company and treasurer of the company. During this time she began to serve small Methodist churches as a part-time supply pastor. She was ordained a deacon in 1963 and an elder in 1964. She later joined the West Michigan Annual Conference of the United Methodist Church.

After 17 years, Matthews went back to college. At the age of 51 she graduated summa cum laude from Central Michigan University. She then attended Colgate Rochester Divinity School from which she received a B.D. in 1970. She completed her education at Florida State University with an M.A. in 1971 and a Ph.D. in 1976. Upon the completion of her schooling, she was appointed district superintendent of the Grand Traverse District of her conference. That same year she was elected as a delegate to the church's general conference. Between the years 1976 and 1980, she had a bout with cancer, but was able to survive.

In 1980 Matthews was elected to head the delegation from West Michigan to the general conference. Several weeks later, at the North Central Jurisdictional Conference she was elected to the episcopacy and assigned to the Wisconsin Area. She was also assigned to work with the General Conference Commission to Study the Episcopacy and District Superintendency. By age 64 when elected, Matthews served only one term as an active bishop, before she was forced to retire by the rules of the church. She lived only two more years, dying of cancer in 1986.

Sources:

Lyles, Jean Caffey. "An Improbable Episcopal Choice." *Christian Century* (August 13-20, 1980): 779-80.

New York Times, July 2, 1986.

★597★
MAXIMOVICH, John
Bishop, Russian Orthodox Church Outside of Russia
b. Jun. 4, 1896, Kharkov District Russia
d. Jun. 19, 1966, Seattle, Washington

John Maximovich, a bishop of the Russian Orthodox Church Outside of Russia remembered most for his saintliness, was given the name Michael Maximovich at his baptism as an infant. His parents wished him to become a lawyer and to that end he entered the law school in Kharkov. However, he found himself most attracted to the lives of the saints, the volumes of which form an important aspect of the pious literature of the Russian Orthodox Church. At the time of the Russian Revolution, he accompanied his family to Belgrade, Serbia (now Yugoslavia). There he was able to enter the theological department of the university, from which he graduated in 1925. In 1926 he was tonsured as a monk and took the name John. Later that year he was ordained as a hieromonk and became an instructor at the Serbian Orthodox Seminary of St. John the Theologian at Bitol, Serbia. While he was at Bitol he first gained a reputation for saintliness and also became known for the ascetic rigor by which he lived.

When he was 38, Maximovich was consecrated as a bishop and assigned to Shanghai, China. His saintly habits became an important factor in bringing unity to the community suffering the first stages of the what would become World War II. He founded an orphanage and gathered the homeless children off of the street. The instances of several miraculous cures added to his reputation, and people began to think of him as a miracle worker.

Bishop John held the community of Russians together through the war, but after the Chinese Revolution he led their migration first to the Philippines and then to the United States in 1950. In 1951 he was sent to work in Western Europe where he stayed for eight years. In 1960 he was called to California to once again work among the immigrants from China who had become divided over the building of the new cathedral in San Francisco. He brought the community together and oversaw the completion of the edifice.

Bishop John, as is common among Orthodox Christians, had developed a measure of piety around holy pictures, or icons. In 1966 he was visiting San Francisco with a special icon, one of Mary the Mother of God, which was believed to have miracle-working powers. While in Seattle, he passed away. His body was flown back to San Francisco where the city's board of supervisors changed the law to allow his body to be buried in a chapel under the cathedral's altar.

Sources:
Maximovich, John. *The Orthodox Veneration of the Mother of God.* Platina, CA: Saint Herman of Alaska Brotherhood, 1978. 54 pp.
Savva of Edmonton, Bishop. *Blessed John.* Platina, CA: Saint Herman of Alaska Brotherhood, 1979. 156 pp.

★598★
MAXWELL, William Sutherland
Pioneer, Baha'i Faith, Canada
b. 1874, Montreal, Quebec, Canada
d. Mar. 25, 1952, Montreal, Quebec, Canada

William Sutherland Maxwell, the first follower of the Baha'i Faith in Canada, was born into a Scottish family which had migrated to Canada in the early nineteenth century. After high school, he moved to Boston and began to work in building design. In 1899 he attended the Ecole des Beaux Arts in Paris, France, and worked in an architectural business. There he met the brother of his future wife, who had previously become a Baha'i. He returned to Canada to become a partner in his brother's business, but traveled to London in 1902 to meet his soon-to-be-wife May Bolles, and they were married.

In moving to Canada, May Bolles Maxwell introduced the Baha'i faith into Canada. But her husband was not convinced until 1909, when he met **Abdu'l-Baha**, the leader of the faith then residing in exile in Akka. After the visit, the Maxwell home became the teaching center for the Baha'i Faith in Canada. In 1910 the Maxwells had a child, Mary Sutherland Maxwell.

As a professional architect and design artist, Maxwell and his brother designed many buildings which are now Canadian landmarks. Maxwell became a fellow of the Royal Institute of Architects, president of the Royal Architectural Institute of Canada, and vice-president of the Royal Canadian Academy. When the Montreal Spiritual Assembly of Baha'is was organized, he served on its board and was frequently its president for many years.

In 1926 Maxwell's daughter married Shoghi Effendi, the Guardian of the Faith, who had become the international leader of the Baha'i Faith following the death of Abdu'l-Baha. In 1940, May Maxwell died, and Shoghi Effendi invited Mr. Maxwell to move to Haifa, where he had made his headquarters. During the 12 years in Haifa he did a number of architectural tasks for the movement, including the final design for the Shrine of the Bab, the forerunner of the Baha'i Faith, to be built in Haifa. His health gave way in 1949 while the shrine was being built, and he returned to his home to recover. In 1951 he was named a Hand of the Cause. He died the following year.

Sources:
"William Sutherland Maxwell." *Baha'i World* 12 (1965), 657-662.

★599★
MAYS, Benjamin Elijah
Educator, National Baptist Convention, U.S.A., Inc.
b. Aug. 1, 1895, Ninety-Six, South Carolina
d. Mar. 28, 1984, Atlanta, Georgia

Benjamin Elijah Mays, a minister and educator with the National Baptist Convention, U.S.A., Inc., was the son of Louvenia Cater and Hezekiah Mays, both former slaves. He grew up in the days of increasing racial disenfranchisement of Blacks in the South. Following high school, he attended Bates College in Lewiston, Maine (B.A., 1920). He was ordained as a Baptist minister in 1921. During the next years he had a number of different positions as he sought to complete his graduate work. In between pastoring in Atlanta and teaching at Morehouse College and South Carolina State College, he earned an M.A. at the University of Chicago.

In 1903 he was commissioned by the Institute of Social and Religious Research to direct a comprehensive study of the black church. Published in 1933, *The Negro's Church* remains a frequently quoted classic in sociology of religion. In 1934 Mays became dean of the School of Religion at Howard University. The following year he completed his Ph.D. at the University of Chicago. In the late 1930s he first attracted widespread attention as the School of Religion radically improved its standards and received an excellent rating from the American Association of Theological Schools.

In 1940 Mays became president of Morehouse College, a Baptist school in Atlanta. During his 27 years there he dedicated himself and the school to turning out graduates who could compete in the white-dominated society as equals. From his presidential platform he began a steady call for reform of American society so that Blacks could be welcomed as equals under the law and fairly considered for jobs. Among the students who he influenced during his early years was **Martin Luther King, Jr.** The later years of his tenure at Morehouse coincided with the beginnings of the King-led Civil Rights Movement, and Mays emerged as a moderate black leader who eschewed the radical militant voices of the far left while constantly working for racial harmony.

Mays retired in 1967 as a senior statesman among black Baptists. While at Morehouse he had regularly served as the National Baptist representative at the meeting of the National Council of Churches and in 1954 was its delegate to the World Council of Churches assembly in Evanston, Illinois. Freed from administrative duties, he used his retirement years to work with groups such as the Baptist World Alliance, the National Council of Churches, and the World Council of Churches to sharpen their understanding of and commitment to Christian approaches in handling racial strife and promoting human dignity. Among the multitude of honors he received was the Spingarn Award, the highest honor given by the National Association for the Advancement of Colored People (NAACP).

Sources:

Hill, Samuel S., ed. *Encyclopedia of Religion in the South.* Macon, GA: Mercer University Press, 1984. 878 pp.

Mays, Benjamin Elijah. *Born to Rebel: An Autobiography.* New York: Charles Scribner's Sons, 1971. 380 pp.

Reid, Daniel G., Robert D. Linder, Bruce L. Shelley, and Harry S. Stout. *Dictionary of Christianity in America.* Downers Grove, IL: InterVarsity Press, 1990. 1305 pp.

Young, Henry J. *Major Black Religious Leaders Since 1940.* Nashville, TN: Abingdon Press, 1979. 160 pp.

★ 600 ★
MCALISTER, Robert Edward

Minister, Pentecostal Assemblies of Canada
b. 1800, Cobden, Ontario, Canada
d. 1953, Canada

Robert Edward McAlister, one of the architects of the non-Trinitarian Oneness theology within modern Pentecostalism, was raised in a Scottish immigrant family in Ontario. As a young man he became involved in the holiness movement, attended a holiness Bible college, and became a worker with the Holiness Movement Church, a Canadian holiness denomination. In 1906 he heard of the revival at Azusa Street in Los Angeles and traveled there to see what was occurring. He received the baptism of the Holy Spirit, as evidenced by his speaking in tongues, and he returned to Canada as one of its first Pentecostal preachers. In 1908 he worked in the Ottawa Valley where a significant revival spread Pentecostalism in the area.

In 1913 McAlister returned to Los Angeles to speak at a Pentecostal camp meeting. His sermon, rendered just prior to the baptizing of several new converts, spoke of the necessity of baptizing in a first-century biblical mode. He spoke forcefully against the traditional Trinitarian baptismal formula, "in the name of the Father, the Son, and the Holy Ghost." While his ideas were rejected by most in attendance, Frank J. Ewart began discussing with McAlister his idea of baptizing in the name of Jesus only, and the implications the practice would have for understanding the nature of God. They concluded that Jesus was God's name and that Jesus, the one God, operated as Father, Son, and Holy Spirit.

The conclusions reached by McAlister and Ewart led the two to initiate a series of meetings on Main Street in Los Angeles and further develop their ideas. After a short while Ewart settled in southern California, while McAlister returned to Canada. McAlister led many of the Canadian Pentecostal leaders into the "Jesus Only" movement. In 1919 McAlister became one of the founders of the Pentecostal Assemblies of Canada. The Assemblies, in their interaction with the Assemblies of God in the United States, repudiated the "Jesus Only" position in 1920. McAleister seemed to have changed his position in line with that of his colleagues. He served for many years as the denominational secretary-treasurer (1919-1932) and for 17 years as the editor of its periodical, *The Pentecostal Testimony.*

McAlister emerged toward the end of his life as a spokesperson for the Pentecostal Assemblies of Canada in opposition to the Latter-Day Revival which had begun among former Assemblies people in Saskatchewan. The movement, which advocated a new appreciation of prophecy and argued for a new form of church government, affected the Assemblies for several years.

Sources:

Burgess, Stanley M., Gary B. McGee, and Patrick H. Alexander, eds. *Dictionary of Pentecostal and Charismatic Movements.* Grand Rapids, MI: Regency Reference Library, Zondervan Publishing House, 1988. 914 pp.

Foster, Fred. *Their Story: 20th Century Pentecostals.* Hazelwood, MO: World Aflame Press, 1981. 187 pp.

★ 601 ★
MCALPINE, William H.

President, National Baptist Foreign Mission Convention of the United States of America
b. Jun. 1847, Buckingham County, Virginia

William M. McAlpine (or McAlpin), the first president of the National Baptist Foreign Mission Convention of the United States of America, was born into slavery near Farmersburg, Virginia. When he was three years old, he, his mother, and his brother were sold to Robert McAlpine, an Alabama Presbyterian minister. He was later inherited by the minister's son, whose wife saw to his education in spite of legal sanctions against teaching slaves to read and write. The minister's son also led McAlpine to convert to Christianity, and in 1864 he was baptized and accepted into the membership of a white Baptist church in Talladega, Alabama.

After the war, McAlpine became a school teacher at Mardisville, Alabama, and in 1868 began to work his way through Talladega College. Attending part time through 1874, he was six months from graduation when financially forced to curtail his formal education. Meanwhile, McAlpine became an active Baptist and participated in the organization of several early Baptist church associations, Russian Springs, Mount Pilgrim, and Snow Creek. In 1868 he was a leader in the formation of the Colored Baptist Missionary State Convention. A year later he was licensed as a Baptist preacher and was ordained in 1871.

In 1873, McAlpine attended the joint meeting of the Colored Baptist Missionary State Convention with its white counterpart. He presented a resolution calling upon his colleagues to establish a school for the black Baptists of Alabama. Even though the white Baptists opposed it, he convinced his black colleagues to go ahead. There being no money, the convention appointed him as the agent to accumulate the resources. By 1877 a site in Selma, Alabama, was purchased and the building of Selma University commenced through the labor of the first students. In 1881 McAlpine was named the first president. He resigned two years later in hopes the school would find someone with a full college education to lead it. As the school was being created, McAlpine threw his support behind William W. Colley's efforts to create a National Baptist Foreign Mission Convention, and attended the organizational meeting in 1880 in Montgomery, Alabama. When Colley refused the presidency, McAlpine was chosen. He served two terms as president.

McAlpine's last years are somewhat obscure. He was invited to serve on the board of Lincoln Normal University, the only non-White so designated. He stayed on the board for six years. He was also the first editor of the *Baptist Pioneer.*

Sources:

Boone, Theodore S. *Negro Baptists in Pictures and History.* Detroit: The Voice of Destiny, 1964. 54 pp.

Freeman, Edward A. *The Epoch of Negro Baptists and the Foreign Mission Board, National Baptist Convention, U.S.A., Inc.* Kansas City, KS: The Central Seminary Press, 1953.

Jackson, J. H. *A Story of Christian Activism: The History of the National Baptist Convention, U.S.A., Inc.* Nashville, TN: Townsend Press, 1980. 790 pp.

Pelt, Owen D. and Ralph Lee Smith. *The Story of the National Baptists.* New York: Vantage Press, 1960. 272 pp.

★ 602 ★
MCCABE, Charles Cardwell
Bishop, Methodist Episcopal Church
b. Oct. 11, 1836, Athens, Ohio
d. Dec. 19, 1906, New York, New York

Charles Cardwell McCabe, a bishop in the Methodist Episcopal Church who oversaw Methodism's extention in the West in the late nineteenth century, grew up in a Methodist family. His grandfather, a Methodist class leader, was an advisor to pioneer Indian missionary John Stewart. His father, Robert McCabe, was a class leader and exhorter, and his mother, Sarah Robinson McCabe, a frequent contributor to the *Ladies Repository.* In 1847 the McCabes moved to Chillicothe, Ohio, and three years later on to Burlington, Iowa. Here the young Charles McCabe experienced a conversion and formally joined the Methodist Episcopal Church in which he had been raised. By the age of 15 he was a class leader. In 1854 he began studies at Ohio Wesleyan University, where he was admittedly only an average student, as he tended to pay more attention to preaching in the surrounding towns than to class work.

After graduation in 1860, McCabe married Rebecca Peters, joined the Ohio Conference, was ordained a deacon, and was stationed at Putnam (now Zanesville), Ohio. After two years at Putnam, he joined the Ohio Volunteer Infantry as chaplain. His unit was captured in June 1863, and he spent four months in Libby Prison before an exchange of prisoners was arranged. He would later memorialize his experience in a lecture he gave many times during his life, ''The Bright Side of Libby Prison.''

In 1864 McCabe joined the United States Christian Commission, which had grown out of the Y.M.C.A. to serve the soldiers and sailors on active duty. He worked as a chaplain and as a fundraiser in Iowa, Wisconsin, and Illinois. Beyond preaching to the young men in the service, he was blessed with a fine singing voice and has been given much credit for popularizing the ''Battle Hymn of the Republic.''

In 1865 McCabe was assigned to Spencer Chapel in Portsmouth, Ohio, serving concurrently as the conference Centenary and Educational Agent (1866) and financial agent for his alma mater, Ohio Wesleyan. In 1868 the general conference elected him as financial agent (after 1872, assistant corresponding secretary) for the Church Extension Society. He moved to Philadelphia to assume the duties he was to have for the next 16 years. During this tenure he attained lasting fame within the church for his reply to freethinker **Robert Green Ingersoll**'s statement that the church was dying. As was later put into a song, McCabe's telegram to Ingersoll asserted, ''All hail the power of Jesus' name! We're building two [churches] a day.'' In 1870, while serving with the society, he transferred to the New York Conference.

Having successfully guided the church extension program, in 1884 McCabe was elected corresponding secretary of the church's missionary society. Almost immediately he set a goal of raising one million dollars for missions annually, and within a few years the church surpassed it. In 1896 his career was capped by his election to the episcopacy, a job that sent him all over America and to Mexico during the last decade of his life. He died after a brief illness and was buried in Rose Hill Cemetery in Chicago.

Sources:
Bristol, Frank Milton. *The Life of Chaplain McCabe.* Cincinnati, OH: Jennings and Graham, 1908. 416 pp.
Dictionary of American Biography. 20 vols. and 7 supps. New York: Charles Scribner's Sons, 1928-1936, 1944-1981.
Harmon, Nolan B. *The Encyclopedia of World Methodism.* 2 vols. Nashville: United Methodist Publishing House, 1974.

★ 603 ★
MCCARRELL, William
Founder, Independent Fundamental Churches of America
b. Feb. 8, 1886, Chicago, Illinois
d. Aug. 25, 1979

William McCarrell, the founder of the Independent Fundamental Churches of America (IFCA), was the son of first-generation Irish immigrants, Samuel and Sarah McCarrell, both staunch Presbyterians. When William was around five, the family moved to Harlem (now Forest Park), Illinois, where he grew up. In 1904 he had the experience of receiving Christ as his personal Savior and began a regular study of the Bible. In 1910 he enrolled at Moody Bible Institute. While there he met Minnie Mense, his future wife. He graduated in 1912 and became pastor of a small Congregational church in Cicero, Illinois, in 1913. Not wishing to be ordained by the Congregation Association, tainted by ministers who he felt denied the fundamentals of evangelical Christianity, he was ordained by a group of dissidents headed by **Charles Blanchard** of Wheaton College. The church prospered and in 1914 he and Minnie were married.

During the 1920s, now the pastor of a large congregation, McCarrell assumed a leading role in the growing fundamentalist movement. He hosted the first gathering of the Chicago Fundamentalist Ministers. His tenuous relation to the Congregational Church was severed in 1930 when he and his congregation left the association. The immediate cause of the break was a 1928 resolution by the Illinois Congregationalists favoring denominational union with the Universalists. He joined with other conservative Congregational ministers in sending a booklet to their colleagues warning of the dangers in the move toward universalism (the belief that all persons will be saved and live eternally with God). He changed the name of his church to the Cicero Bible Church and affiliated with the American Conference of Undenominated Churches.

In 1930 the American Conference of Undenominated Churches met at McCarrell's church and voted to become the Independent Fundamental Churches of America (IFCA), a loose fellowship of funadamentalist ministers and churches, determined to separate from all apostasy. McCarrell, a powerful speaker, was elected the first president of the new fellowship, and headquarters were established at his church. The next decade was one of growth for both the fellowship and of McCarrell's own congregation. He also began a radio ministry and taught pastoral care at Moody. He focused upon developing new congregations in neighboring communities without an independent fundamentalist church.

In 1942, as World War II was beginning, McCarrell led the IFCA into the American Council of Christian Churches (ACCC), an ecumenical agency of fundamentalist churches. ACCC, among other services, represented smaller fundamentalist churches to the chaplain's office in the armed services and facilitated the appointment of evangelical ministers to positions as chaplains. Within the ACCC McCarrell, always the diplomat, became known for his ability to make peace between the often strong-willed ACCC leaders.

During the 1940s, McCarrell was a leader in the ACCC, and he attended the 1948 meeting in Amsterdam when the International Council of Christian Churches was formed by evangelicals in response to the organization of the World Council of Churches. However, in 1953 he took the IFCA out of the ACCC when he saw the emphasis upon separation. Although McCarrell basically supported separation, he could not support what he determined to be an overly negative tone in the condemning of other Christians. In 1958 McCarrell retired from the pastorate. He founded a Christian work center and continued to travel and speak during most of his last years.

Sources:
Martin, Dorothy. *The Story of Billy McCarrell.* Chicago: Moody Press, 1983. 220 pp.

★ 604 ★
MCCLAIN, Alva J.
Founder, Fellowship of Grace Brethren Churches
b. Apr. 11, 1888, Aurelia, Iowa
d. Nov. 11, 1968, Waterloo, Iowa

Alva J. McClain, one of the founders of the National Fellowship of Brethren Churches (now the Fellowship of Grace Brethren Churches), was the son of Mary Ellen Gnagy and Walter Scott Mc-Clain, a minister in the Brethren Church (Ashland, Ohio). In 1911 McClain married Josephine Gingrich and formally became a member of the Brethren Church. As a student at the University of Washington, he attended a Bible Conference led by Louis S. Bauman. He had a conversion experience which caused him to transfer to the Bible Institute of Los Angeles, an independent fundamentalist school which had recently been opened under the leadership of **Reuben A. Torrey**. When he completed his work at the institute, he attended Xenia Theological Seminary, a Presbyterian school in Ohio; Antioch College; and Occidental College, from which he received his B.A. He was ordained as a minister in 1917.

In 1918 McClain became pastor of First Brethren Church of Philadelphia and also taught at the Philadelphia School of the Bible (1919-1923). While there he became one of a group of conservative Brethren ministers who had been influenced by fundamentalism and who drew up what became known as the "Message of the Brethren Ministry." It was adopted by the National Ministerial Association, though with an acknowledgment that it was not to be considered a creedal statement.

In 1925 McClain moved to Ashland, Ohio, to teach at Ashland College, and returned to teach at the Bible Institute of Los Angeles in 1927. In 1903 he was asked to reorganize Ashland Theological Seminary as a graduate school of theology. He served as associate dean and professor of theology and apologetics. He became dean in 1932. During the 1930s, the tension between conservatives and liberals within the denomination resurfaced more intensely. McClain was finally fired from his position at the seminary. He immediately founded Grace Theological Seminary at Winona Lake, Indiana, as a focus of conservative discontent. He served as president and professor of theology at the seminary. The issue of the independent school came to a head at the 1939 general conference of the Brethren Church. McClain and his supporters walked out and formed the National Fellowship of Brethren Churches.

McClain's major contribution to the new denomination was as a leader at its schools. In 1948 he took the lead in founding Grace College and served as its first president. During the 1950s he authored two of his more important books, *Law and the Christian Believer in Relation to the Doctrine of Grace* (1954) and *The Greatness of the Kingdom* (1959). He also served on the *Schofield Reference Bible* revision committee, and on the board of directors of both the Winona Lake Christian Assembly and the American Association for Jewish Evangelism. McClain retired in 1962 and was named professor emeritus of the college.

Sources:
Durnbaugh, Donald F., ed. *The Brethren Encyclopedia.* 3 vols. Philadelphia: The Brethren Encyclopedia, Inc., 1983.
McClain, Alva J. *Bible Truths.* Ashland, OH: The Author, 1935. 75 pp.
_____. *Daniel's Prophecy of the Seventy Weeks.* Grand Rapids, MI: Zondervan Publications, 1940. 62 pp.
_____. *The Greatness of the Kingdom.* Grand Rapids, MI: Zondervan Publishing House, 1959. 556 pp.
_____. *Law and the Christian Believer in Relation to the Doctrine of Grace.* 1954.

_____. *Romans: The Gospel of God's Grace.* Chicago: Moody Press, 1937. 253 pp.

★ 605 ★
MCCLOSKEY, John
Cardinal, Roman Catholic Church
b. Mar. 20, 1810, Brooklyn, New York
d. Oct. 10, 1885, New York, New York

John McCloskey, the first American to be named a cardinal in the Roman Catholic Church, was born in 1810 to Patrick and Elizabeth Herron McCloskey, who had recently immigrated to the United States from Ireland. His father had a position with the H. B. Pierrepont Company, and as a child John was sent to Mrs. Milmoth's Brooklyn school, a private school used by the more prominent families. When John was seven the family moved to Manhattan, where he attended the Latin school headed by Thomas Brady. At the age of 11 he was ready for preparatory school and was sent to Mount St. Mary's in Emmetsburg, Maryland, where he finished both his prep courses and his college education. During the winter of 1826-1827, McCloskey suffered an accident from which he never fully recovered and which prompted him to join the priesthood. He graduated in 1828.

After a year at his mother's farm, McCloskey returned to Emmetsburg to pursue his seminary work. He was ordained a priest in 1934 in St. Patrick's Cathedral in Manhattan, and it became his first parish assignment. He had been there only a few months when he became vice-president and professor of philosophy at the diocese's new seminary in Nyack, New York. Unfortunately, the seminary burned to the ground a few months later. McCloskey took the opportunity to further his studies in Rome. He stayed for two years, but left before completing his doctoral work to tour Europe, especially Ireland, for a year.

Upon his return to the United States, McCloskey was assigned as parish priest to St. John's Church in Manhattan, one of several parishes involved in trustee struggles. During his first months he had to contend with the action of lay trustees who were fighting with the bishop for more local control. McClosky eventually won the support of most of the parishes. He stayed at St. John's until 1840, when Bishop John Hughes called him to become president of the new diocesan seminary, the College of St. John. His health, however, forced him to return to his parish in 1842. In 1844, on his 34th birthday, he was consecrated Coadjutor Bishop of New York (then the largest diocese in America). His consecration came during the height of Bishop Hughes' controversy over state aid for the parochial schools.

During McCloskey's tenure as bishop coadjutor, the diocese grew tremendously through immigration, especially in its northern and western regions. Buffalo and Albany were set off as separate dioceses in 1847, and McCloskey became Bishop of Albany. As the diocese's first bishop, it was his task to build it institutionally, which he accomplished during the 17 years of his leadership. He left the diocese in 1864 to become Archbishop of New York. Reconciliation became a theme of his reign and he spent many hours working to integrate new immigrants, the differing religious orders, and various political factions within the church's life.

In 1866 McCloskey gave the opening address at the plenary council gathered in Baltimore. Just prior to its delivery, however, he received news that the cathedral in New York had burned. He attended the First Vatican Council in 1869-1870. It was here that the infallibility of the Pope—when he spoke *ex cathedra* on matters of faith and morals—was declared dogma. McCloskey did not think that the time was right for the declaration of the new dogma, but in the end he voted for it.

In 1875, after more than a decade of rumors concerning the possible naming of an American to the College of Cardinals, McCloskey was tapped for the honor. The ceremony of the bestowal of the biretta was held on April 27 in St. Patrick's Cathedral. Later that year, McCloskey traveled to Rome to take possession of his titular church, Santa Maria Sopra Minerva (all cardinals, whatever their official titles, also have a position assigned to them in the diocese of Rome). Because of the illness of Pope Pius IX, however, he did not actually receive his cardinal's hat until March 1878, when it was conferred by Pope Leo XIII.

McCloskey's years in the cardinate were not the happiest of his life. His health declined noticeably, and his leadership was marked by only a few triumphs, such as the dedication of the new St. Patrick's Cathedral in 1879 and his priesthood jubilee in 1884. He died in 1885 and was buried under the high altar of the cathedral.

Sources:

Farley, Cardinal John. *The Life of Cardinal McCloskey*. New York: Longmans, Green & Company, 1918. 401 pp.

Thornton, Francis Beauchesne. *Our American Princes*. New York: G.P. Putnam's Sons, 1963. 319 pp.

★606★
MCCOLLOUGH, Walter
Bishop, United House of Prayer for All People
b. May 22, 1915, Great Falls, South Carolina

Walter McCollough, the bishop of the United House of Prayer for All People, was the successor in office to Charles Emmanuel Grace, one of the most flamboyant and charismatic figures in the American religious community of the mid-twentieth century. Though overshadowed by Grace as he began his era of leadership, McCollough has emerged as an important leader in the black religious community in his own right. Little is known of his early life, but he became an early follower of Grace and rose to a position of leadership through the 1950s, succeeding Grace in 1960 as the absolute leader of the denomination and its several hundred congregations. He married Clara Bell Price.

McCollough has worked to bring the House of Prayer for All People into the mainstream of black Christianity. He had used the wealth acquired by his predecessor to fund a number of needy projects. In the early 1970s, for example, he developed a 90-unit housing project for inner-city Washington, D.C. This was followed by similar projects in New Haven, Connecticut, and Charlotte, North Carolina. The church has also been generous in supplying scholarships to needy teenagers.

In 1985, McCollough was given the annual award by the National Urban Coalition for his life of achievement.

Sources:

Dupree, Sherry Sherrod. *Biographical Dictionary of African-American, Holiness-Pentecostals, 1880-1990*. Washington, DC: Middle Atlantic Regional Press, 1990. 386 pp.

Feaver, Douglas. "Hymns and Speeches Launch an Unusual Inner-City Project." *Washington Post* (August 25, 1974).

Marshall, Steve. "Bishop Deals in Answers to Needs of Poor." *USA Today* (September 10, 1985).

★607★
MCCONNELL, Francis John
Bishop, Methodist Episcopal Church
b. Aug. 18, 1871, Trinway, Ohio
d. Aug. 18, 1953, Lucasville, Ohio

Francis John McConnell, a bishop of the Methodist Episcopal Church, and a significant popularizer of what became known as the Boston theology, was the son of the Reverend I. H. and Nancy J. Chalfant McConnell. Raised in a Methodist parsonage, he attended Ohio Wesleyan University (A.B., 1894) and Boston University (S.T.B., 1897; Ph.D., 1899). In 1894 McConnell joined the New England Conference of the Methodist Episcopal Church and was

assigned to West Chelmsford, Massachusetts, while attending school. In 1897 he married Eva Thomas. Following his graduation, McConnell served the church in Ipswich, Massachusetts; Harvard Street Methodist Episcopal Church in Cambridge, Massachusetts; and New York Avenue Church in Brooklyn, New York, before assuming the duties as president of DePauw University in 1909. In 1906, while at New York Avenue Church, he authored his first book, *The Diviner Immanence*. In 1912 he was elected as bishop, a position he held until his retirement in 1944.

During his years as a bishop, McConnell wrote regularly for *The Church School Journal*, and authored 24 books. Possibly his most famous book, *Is God Limited?* (1924), dealt with a major theological problem, theodicy, the justification of God's love in the face of the reality of evil. Bostonian theology was known for its suggestion that God limited Himself and allowed evil to exist in the universe for the greater good of allowing human freedom. This idea is generally seen as derived from the work of two of McConnell's teachers, philosophers **Borden Parker Bowne** (the subject of another of McConnell's books) and **Edgar S. Brightman**. Other titles by McConnell included: *The Christlike God* (1927); *The Prophetic Ministry* (1930); *John Wesley* (1939); and his autobiography, *By the Way* (1952).

McConnell took an active role in ecumenical and public affairs. He became president of the Religious Education Association in 1916 and of the Federal Council of Churches in 1929. He participated in the activist Methodist Federation for Social Action in 1912 and remained a leader and supporter through its controversial history in the 1920s and 1930s. In 1919 he was one of several church leaders who became involved in the investigation of the Pittsburgh steel strike for the Interchurch World Movement. The final report championed the rights of the workers and became a significant factor in reducing their 12-hour work day. His work on the report, and his firmness in the face of intense pressure seeking his repudiation of it, first brought him to national prominence as an American church leader.

McConnell was also known for his sermons, though he was known more for his appeal to an intellectual audience rather than moving people's hearts. In 1930 he was invited to deliver the Lyman Beecher Lectures at Yale. He became the Barrows lecturer in India (a lectureship which grew out of the World's Parliament of Religions in 1893). He served as a visiting professor at Columbia University in 1932-1933 and at both Drew Theological Seminary and Garrett Biblical Institute in 1934. McConnell retired in 1944. He died on his 82nd birthday.

Sources:

Harmon, Nolan B. *The Encyclopedia of World Methodism*. 2 vols. Nashville: United Methodist Publishing House, 1974.

McConnell, Francis J. *Borden Parker Bowne: His Life and Philosophy*. New York: Abingdon Press, 1929. 291 pp.

_____. *By the Way*. New York: Abingdon-Cokesbury Press, 1952. 286 pp.

_____. *The Christlike God*. New York: Abingdon Press, 1927. 275 pp.

_____. *The Diviner Immanence*. New York: Eaton & Mains, 1906. 159 pp.

_____. *Is God Limited?*. London: Williams & Norgate, 1924. 297 pp.

_____. *John Wesley*. Chicago: Abingdon Press, 1939. 355 pp.

_____. *The Prophetic Ministry*. New York: Abingdon Press, 1930. 308 pp.

★608★
MCCRACKEN, Robert James
Minister, Baptist Church
b. Mar. 28, 1904, Motherwell Scotland
d. 1973

Robert James McCracken, for many years pastor of Riverside Church in New York City, was the son of Sarah Carson and Joseph McCracken. He prepared himself for the ministry through his studies at the University of Glasgow from which he received a

M.A. in 1925 and a B.D. in 1928. He was ordained as a Scottish Baptist minister in 1928 and began serving Marshall Street Baptist Church in Edinburgh. While in Edinburgh, in 1929 he married Maud Orr Ibbotson. He moved back to Glasgow in 1932 as the pastor of Dennistown Baptist Church. He also taught systematic theology at the Baptist Theological Seminary in Glasgow. In 1937 he was a Baptist delegate to the Faith and Order Conference, one of the meetings leading up to the formation of the World Council of Churches.

In 1938 McCracken moved to Canada as a professor of Christian theology and philosophy of religion at McMaster University, the school in Hamilton, Ontario, associated with the Canadian Baptist Federation. In 1944 he became head of the department of theology and philosophy of religion. In 1945 he was elected president of the Baptist Convention of Ontario and Quebec. In 1946 **Harry Emerson Fosdick** retired from Riverside Church, previously known as Park Avenue Baptist Church, where Fosdick had begun preaching after being forced out of First Presbyterian Church in Manhattan. McCracken was invited to succeed Fosdick at Riverside.

McCracken, whose Scottish brogue appealed to American audiences, soon made his own place at Riverside as one of America's outstanding preachers. In 1949 he was invited to join the staff at Union Theological Seminary as a part-time lecturer in practical theology. During his Riverside years he authored four books: *Questions People Ask* (1951); *The Meaning of the Sermon* (1956); *Putting Faith to Work* (1960); and *What Is Sin? What Is Virtue?* (1966). McCracken is remembered for his ability to speak out of his accomplished theological training without losing his mastery in communicating with people.

McCracken retired in 1967 from both Riverside and Union and was named pastor emeritus.

Sources:

Fant, C. and W. Pinson, Jr., eds. *20 Centuries of Great Preaching*. 13 vols. Waco, TX: Word Books, 1971.

McCracken, Robert J. *The Making of the Sermon*. New York: Harper & Row, 1956. 104 pp.

_____. *Putting Faith to Work*. New York: Harper & Row, 1960. 179 pp.

_____. *Questions People Ask*. New York: Harper & Row, 1951. 188 pp.

_____. *What Is Sin? What Is Virtue?* New York: Harper & Row, 1966. 94 pp.

Reid, Daniel G., Robert D. Linder, Bruce L. Shelley, and Harry S. Stout. *Dictionary of Christianity in America*. Downers Grove, IL: InterVarsity Press, 1990. 1305 pp.

★609★
MCDOWELL, William Fraser
Bishop, Methodist Episcopal Church
b. Feb. 4, 1858, Millersburg, Ohio
d. Apr. 26, 1937, Washington, District of Columbia

William Fraser McDowell, a bishop in the Methodist Episcopal Church, was the son of David A. and Rebecca Fraser McDowell. His father had been an active layperson in the Methodist Church and was chosen as a delegate to the church's general conference in 1904. McDowell attended Ohio Wesleyan University (A.B., 1879) and completed his seminary work at Boston University (S.T.B., 1882). He married Clotilde Lyon shortly after his graduation from seminary. He joined the North Ohio Conference and was appointed to the church at Lodi. McDowell was ordained a deacon in 1883 and an elder in 1886. After serving churches at Oberlin and Tiffin, he left Ohio to become the chancellor at the University of Denver. During his nine years there he completed the requirements for a Ph.D., which Ohio Wesleyan awarded him in 1893.

In 1899 McDowell became the corresponding secretary of the Board of Education of the Methodist Episcopal Church. Over the years he gained a reputation as a great orator/preacher, and in 1900 and 1904 he was elected as a delegate to the general confer-

ence. At the 1904 conference he was elected to the bishopric. During his years as a bishop in the church, he was invited to give a number of the academic lectures on homiletics beginning with the Cole Lectures at Vanderbilt University in 1910. Among the more outstanding invitations was Yale's for the Lyman Beecher Lectures in 1917.

His preaching and his lectures on preaching became the major source for McDowell's eight books which appeared between 1910 and 1934. They were *In the School of Christ* (1910); *A Man's Religion* (1913); *Good Ministers of Jesus Christ* (1917); *This Mind* (1922); *Making a Personal Faith* (1924); *That I Might Save Some* (1928); *Them He Also Called* (1929); and *Creative Men: Our Fathers and Brethren* (1934).

In the years after World War I, McDowell took up the cause of the reunion of American Methodism. In 1916 he was appointed to the Methodist Episcopal Church's commission on church union, and remained on the commission for the rest of his life. In 1932 he succeeded Bishop Earl Cranston as its chairperson. He spent long hours working on solutions to the more crucial problems of the union, especially the racial question. He helped formulate the idea of creating a segregated central jurisdiction for the black church members, and after concluding that it was the best possible, he was the one who presented the Plan of Union to the 1936 general conference. He saw his church accept the plan, but died before the union was effected in 1939.

McDowell remained active to the very end of his life. Two weeks prior to his death he delivered a set of lectures at Boston University, published posthumously as *In All His Offices* The day before his death he preached at Morganton, North Carolina, and traveled back to his home in Washington, D.C.

Sources:

Harmon, Nolan B. *The Encyclopedia of World Methodism*. 2 vols. Nashville: United Methodist Publishing House, 1974.

McDowell, John Thomas. *Creative Men: Our Fathers and Brethren*. New York: Abingdon Press, 1934. 246 pp.

_____. *Good Ministers of Jesus Christ*. New York: Abingdon Press, 1917. 307 pp.

_____. *In the School of Christ*. New York: Fleming H. Revell Company, 1910. 303 pp.

_____. *Making a Personal Faith*. New York: Abingdon Press, 1924. 155 pp.

_____. *A Man's Religion*. New York: Eaton & Mains, 1913. 225 pp.

_____. *That I Might Save Some*. New York: Abingdon Press, 1928. 180 pp.

_____. *Them He Also Called*. New York: Abingdon Press, 1929. 234 pp.

_____. *This Mind*. New York: Methodist Book Concern, 1922. 183 pp.

★610★
MCGARVEY, John William
Minister and Editor, Churches of Christ
b. Mar. 1, 1829, Hopkinsville, Kentucky
d. Nov. 6, 1911, Lexington, Kentucky

John William McGarvey, a leading minister in the second generation of the Christian Church (Disciples of Christ) Restoration Movement begun by Barton Stone and Alexander Campbell, was the son of Sallie Ann Thompson and John McGarvey. McGarvey's father died when he was still a child; his mother subsequently married Dr. G. F. Saltonstall. He moved to Illinois with his new stepfather in 1839. He finished high school and entered Bethany College, the Kentucky school founded by Alexander Campbell, in 1847. After graduation in 1850 he moved to Fayette, Missouri, where he opened a boys' school. In 1851 he was ordained as a minister and preached in Fayette and surrounding towns. Early in 1853 he moved to Dover, Missouri, and later that year married Ottie F. Hix.

McGarvey both preached and taught school in Dover. As was common at the time, he frequently engaged in debate with ministers from other churches. As the Civil War began he assumed an unpopular, though traditional position within the Movement by signing a pacifist statement, "Concerning the Duties of Christians in this Conflict." His parishioners also criticized him for the time he spent teaching a group of Blacks to read. Thus in 1862, when the call came to become the preacher at the Main Street Christian Church in Lexington, Kentucky, he moved. In 1865 Kentucky University moved to Lexington, and McGarvey helped plan the course of study for an associated College of the Bible. He became a teacher at the school.

In 1873 McGarvey came into conflict with the president of the university over funding for the college, and McGarvey was dismissed from his teaching post. He was reinstated in 1875 and assisted in the College's efforts to become an autonomous institution. He also became associated with **Moses Lard** during this time and in 1868 helped establish the *Apostolic Times* as a conservative voice against the liberalism within the Disciples Movement exemplified by **Isaac Errett** and the *Christian Standard*. Among McGarvey's major contributions to the *Times*, he wrote extensively against the use of the higher (historical) criticism of the Bible. Many of his arguments were gathered in the two-volume *Evidences of Christianity* (1886, 1891). In 1895 he was named president of the College of the Bible, a post he retained the rest of his life.

During his mature years, McGarvey authored a number of books that provided a perspective on Biblical teachings for the conservative wing of the Disciples Movement: *Jesus and Jonah* (1896); *The Authorship of the Book of Deuteronomy* (1902); and the four-volume *Standard Bible Commentary* (1905-1908). He lived to see the split between the liberals and conservatives in the movement and is seen as a major figure in the history of the Churches of Christ (the name taken in 1906 by the conservatives at the time the split was formally acknowledged).

Sources:

Dictionary of American Biography. 20 vols. and 7 supps. New York: Charles Scribner's Sons, 1928-1936, 1944-1981.
Hill, Samuel S., ed. *Encyclopedia of Religion in the South*. Macon, GA: Mercer University Press, 1984. 878 pp.
McGarvey, John W. *The Authorship of the Book of Deuteronomy*. 1902.
———. *Jesus and Jonah*. 1896.
———. *Sermons Delivered in Louisville, Kentucky, June-September 1893*. 1894.
———. *Short Essays in Biblical Criticism*. 1910.
———. *The Standard Bible Commentary*. 4 vols. 1905-1908.
West, Earl Irvin. *The Search for the Ancient Order: A History of the Restoration Movement, 1849-1906*. 2 vols. Nashville, TN: Gospel Advocate Company, 1905-1906.

★611★
MCGARY, Austin
Minister and Editor, Churches of Christ
b. Mar. 6, 1846, Huntsville, Texas
d. Feb. 6, 1928, Houston, Texas

Austin McGary, a leading spokesperson in the Churches of Christ in Texas, was the son of Isaac McGary, an obscure soldier in Sam Houston's army whose moment of fame came when he was assigned to guard the captured General Santa Ana after the battle at San Jacinto. Austin grew up in the small town of Huntville, and at the age of 16 enlisted in the Confederate Army, serving along the coast of Texas. After the war he married Narcissus Jenkins. She died in 1872, about the time he entered politics. He was elected sheriff and served two terms. In 1875 he married Lucie Kitrell. In 1878 he left his work as sheriff and went to work at the state penitentiary.

In 1880 McGary left the penitentiary and began to think about religion. He concluded that he was an infidel, but decided to make a study of the subject. He was attracted by the preaching of a min-

ister in the Christian Church and at the end of 1881 was baptized in the church. Soon he was preaching at every opportunity. In 1883 he moved to Austin, Texas, which would remain his home for the rest of his life.

At the time McGary settled in Austin, the church was being rent with controversy over the formation of missionary societies and the introduction of instrumental music in worship. McGary opposed both, and in defense of the more conservative position, began the periodical *Firm Foundation* in 1884. After a slow beginning the magazine became quite successful and emerged as the central voice of what would become the Churches of Christ in Texas. The formal split between the Churches of Christ and the more liberal faction, now known as the Christian Church (Disciples of Christ), came in 1906. Texas was one of the strongholds of the Churches of Christ, for which McGary received much of the credit. *Firm Foundation* remains a leading Churches of Christ periodical.

Above and beyond his defense of Church of Christ distinctives, McGary took a radical position on the question of the rebaptism of new Church of Christ members who came from other churches. In general, the church practiced baptism by immersion, and it was common practice to rebaptize those who had never been immersed. McGary argued that all new members, even former Baptists who had been immersed, must be rebaptized. For many years he carried on a running debate on this issue with **David Lipscomb**, the editor of the *Gospel Advocate*, the leading Churches of Christ journal from Nashville, Tennessee, who opposed McGary's extreme position.

In 1897 McGary's second wife died. In 1898 he married Lillian Otey. He stayed as editor of *Firm Foundation* until 1903 when he moved to Los Angeles, California. There he began a short-lived paper, *The Outlook*, but before the year was out, he moved to Oregon. He returned to Texas in 1904. After a short time in Arkansas he settled in Houston, where he lived his last years.

Sources:

Hill, Samuel S., ed. *Encyclopedia of Religion in the South*. Macon, GA: Mercer University Press, 1984. 878 pp.
West Earl Irvin. *The Search for the Ancient Order; A History of the Restoration Movement*. 2 vols. Indianapolis, IN: Earl West Religious Book Service, 1906.

★612★
MCGEE, Lewis A.
Founder, Free Religious Association
b. Nov. 11, 1893, Scranton, Pennsylvania
d. Oct. 10, 1979, Pullman, Washington

Lewis A. McGee, founder of the Free Religious Association, the first permanent, predominately black Unitarian congregation in America, was the son of a minister in the African Methodist Episcopal Church. He received a good education, first at the University of Pittsburgh and then at Payne Theological Seminary of Wilberforce University (B.D.). He was ordained as an African Methodist Episcopal Church minister in 1917. In 1918 he became a chaplain in the army. He served several small churches after the war. One day he chanced upon a copy of a Unitarian magazine and found himself favorably disposed to the theological liberalism he found. In 1927 he met Humanist minister **Curtis Reese** and began to identify himself as a Humanist-Unitarian. He left the pulpit and returned to school in Chicago. In 1936 he received his B.A. in social work, and then returned to the pulpit for several years serving churches in Iowa, Illinois, and Indiana. In 1941 he assumed a position on the board of the American Humanist Association, while still pastoring "orthodox" churches.

McGee again enlisted in the Army during World War II. After the war he enrolled at Meadville Theological School (1946-1947) and at the end of his year formally joined the American Unitarian Association (AUA). He also occasionally attended the Chicago Humanist Association meetings. A conversation there one Sunday led to the formation of a liberal religious congregation for Blacks on the south side of Chicago. Beginning with a small group meeting in a home, the Free Religious Association held its first meeting in October 1947, and the following year was formally received into the Unitarian Association with approximately 50 members. While predominantly black in membership, it was officially interracial in design. McGee found a greater degree of acceptance from the association, which had shown little support for work in the black community previously. There was only one other black congregation in the association at the time, a weak church in Harlem headed by **Egbert Ethelred Brown** which was struggling to exist and would soon die.

In 1953 McGee turned the congregation over to a successor and moved to Springfield, Ohio, to become field secretary for the American Humanist Association. Five years later he moved to Los Angeles as the associate minister at the First Unitarian Church. In 1961 he became the pastor of the Unitarian Fellowship in Chico, California, the first black minister to pastor a white Unitarian church. He ended his career with pastorates in Anaheim (1962-1963); Pasadena (1963-1964); and Humbolt (1964-1966), California. He was named minister emeritus of the Humbolt Unitarian Fellowship in 1966. He lived his last years in quiet retirement.

Sources:

Morrison-Reed, Mark D. *Black Pioneers in a White Denomination.* Boston: Beacon Press, 1984. 217 pp.

★613★
MCGIFFERT, Arthur Cushman
Church Historian, Congregational Church
b. Mar. 4, 1851, Sauquoit, New York
d. Feb. 25, 1933, Dobbs Ferry, New York

Arthur Cushman McGiffert, a church historian first with the Presbyterian Church and later the Congregational Church, was the son of the Rev. Joseph Nelson and Harriet Whiting Cushman McGiffert. He attended Western Reserve University (A.B., 1882) and completed his divinity degree at Union Theological Seminary (B.D., 1885) in New York City. In June 1885 he married Eliza Isabelle King. He did his doctoral work in Germany, first at Berlin, and finally graduated with a Ph.D. from Marburg in 1888. At Marburg he became a student of Aldolf Harnack, from whom he absorbed a modernist approach to Protestant thought.

In 1888 McGiffert returned to the United States and was ordained as a Presbyterian minister. He affiliated with the Presbytery of Cleveland and joined the faculty of Lane Theological Seminary. His first wife had died in 1887, and in 1891 he married Gertrude Huntington Boyce. During his years at Lane he translated the "Church History" of Eusebius, the early church historian, which was included in *A Select History of the Nicene and Post Nicene Fathers* being edited by **Philip Schaff**. In 1893 he moved back to New York as the professor of church history at Union where he was to remain for the next 34 years.

The years at Union were productive but not without controversy. Among McGiffert's his first works after joining the Union staff was *A History of Christianity in the Apostolic Age.* In one footnote for the book, McGiffert suggested that the Lord's Supper had been instituted by Jesus as a perpetual ritual to be performed by the Christian church. This remark brought the condemnation of ministerial colleagues who raised the issue before the General Assembly of the Presbyterian Church in 1898. The Assembly voted its disapproval, though it did not charge McGiffert with heresy. His critics persisted in appealing the case, and in 1899 McGiffert quietly withdrew from the Presbyterian Church and joined the Congregational Church.

The controversy quelled, he returned to his scholarly pursuits and produced a number of books. The first was *The Apostles' Creed: Its Origin, Its Purpose, and Its Historical Interpretation* (1902). He followed with *Protestant Thought Before Kant* (1911); *Martin Luther, the Man and His Work* (1911); *The Rise of Modern Religious Ideas* (1915); *The God of the Early Christians* (1914); and his magnum opus, *A History of Christian Thought* (1932-33), a two-volume historical survey of theology.

In 1917 McGiffert became president of Union. He inherited a school in debt and proceeded to raise the necessary funds to pay all of the bills and provide for the school through the new decade. He also introduced a number of educational innovations and developed the still-existing cordial relationship with the school's new neighbor (since 1910), Columbia University.

McGiffert gave up the presidency in 1926 and retired from teaching in 1927. Following his death, his son gathered a collection of his personal religious talks and writings which were published as *Christianity as History and Faith* (1934).

Sources:

Dictionary of American Biography. 20 vols. and 7 supps. New York: Charles Scribner's Sons, 1928-1936, 1944-1981.
McGiffert, Arthur Cushman. *The Apostles' Creed: Its Origin, Its Purpose, and Its Historical Interpretation.* Edinburgh, Scotland: T. & T. Clark, 1902. 206 pp.
_____. *Christianity as History and Faith.* New York: Charles Scribner's Sons, 1934. 322 pp.
_____. *The God of the Early Christians.* Edinburgh, Scotland: T. & T. Clark, 1924. 200 pp.
_____. *A History of Christian Thought.* 2 vols. New York: Charles Scribner's Sons, 1932-33.
_____. *Martin Luther, The Man and His Work.* London, England: T. F. Unwin, 1911. 397 pp.
_____. *Protestant Thought before Kant.* New York: Charles Scribner's Sons, 1911. 261 pp.
_____. *The Rise of Modern Religious Ideas.* New York: Macmillan Company, 1915. 315 pp.
McGiffert, Arthur Cushman, Jr. "A Son Looks at His Father's Faith," *Chicago Theological Seminary Register* (January 1935).

★614★
MCGUIGAN, James Charles
Archbishop and Cardinal, Roman Catholic Church
b. Nov. 26, 1894, Hunter River, Prince Edward Island, Canada
d. Apr. 8, 1974, Toronto, Ontario, Canada

James Charles McGuigan, the archbishop of Toronto and a cardinal in the Roman Catholic Church, was the son of Anne Monoghan and George Hugh McGuigan. He was educated at Wales College in Charlottetown, Prince Edward Island (1908-1911). He then attended St. Dunstan's University and Laval University from which he received his B.A. in 1914. He took his theological course at the Grand Seminary of Quebec and received his doctorate in 1918. That same year he was ordained to the priesthood. He taught at St. Dunstan's for a year before becoming the secretary of Archbishop O'Leary of Charlottetown. When O'Leary became Archbishop of Edmonton, Alberta, McGuigan moved west with him.

In Edmonton, McGuigan held a number of posts. He became chancellor of the archdiocese in 1922 and vicar general in 1923. He added duties as rector of St. Joseph's Cathedral in 1925. In 1927 he became rector of St. Joseph's Seminary. In the midst of his work he found time for post-graduate work in canon law at Catholic University of America.

In 1930 McGuigan was named archbishop of Regina, Saskatchewan. He was there only four years before being called east as the new archbishop of Toronto. The position carried with it the unofficial leadership of non-French Roman Catholics in Canada. By the time McGuigan assumed his chair, Roman Catholics had emerged to a position of some importance in the province of Ontario and he served through a period of rapid expansion, especially in the years immediately after World War II. To handle the growing archdiocese, McGuigan was called upon to establish a variety of new educational and service facilities and enlarge all that previously existed.

McGuigan's accomplishments were recognized by his being named a papal aide and Roman count in 1943 and a cardinal in 1946. He retired from active administrative duties in 1961 and turned his responsibilities over to his coadjutor, Archbishop Philip Francis Pocock. At the time there were half a million church members in the archdiocese.

Sources:

Barnett, Herbert E. and Hugh Fraser, assoc. eds. *Who's Who in Canada.* Toronto: International Press Limited, 1969.

Fisher, Claude Laing. *James Cardinal McGuigan, Archbishop.* Toronto: McCleeland & Steward, 1948. 133 pp.

★615★
MCGUIRE, George Alexander
Founder, African Orthodox Church
b. Mar. 26, 1866, Sweets West Indies
d. Nov. 10, 1934, New York, New York

George Alexander McGuire was the founder of the African Orthodox Church. A native of the West Indies, McGuire was baptized into the Anglican faith, the church of his father, but his religious interests were also shaped by the Moravian faith of his mother. After graduating from Nisky Theological Seminary of St. Thomas, he pastored a Moravian congregation at St. Croix in the Virgin Islands for some half-dozen years. In 1892 he married Ada Eliza Roberts.

McGuire emigrated to the United States in 1894, joined the Protestant Episcopal Church, and became a priest in that denomination by 1897. From 1905 to 1908 he worked as archdeacon for the Commission for Work among the Colored People under the church's Board of Missions. He served in a variety of positions within the church, becoming pastor of St. Bartholomew's Church in Cambridge in 1909. In 1911 he became the field secretary of the American Church Institute for Negroes in New York. Frustration with the Episcopal Church's failure to promote Blacks to higher positions of leadership eventually prompted him to return to Antigua where he pastored St. Paul's Church in Sweets.

While in the West Indies McGuire joined black nationalist Marcus Garvey's Universal Negro Improvement Association (U.N.I.A.), and in 1919 returned to the United States in order to be an active member of that organization. He became U.N.I.A.'s chaplain-general and, at the same time, joined the Reformed Episcopal Church. He eventually established himself as the leader of an independent church and, in this role, as well as by virtue of his position in the Garvey organization, authored *Universal Negro Ritual* and *Universal Negro Catechism*. McGuire's long-term goal seems to have been the establishment of a black church of worldwide scope, utilizing U.N.I.A. as his organizational base.

In 1921, however, McGuire broke with Garvey and transformed his independent church into the African Orthodox Church. Less than a month after the formation of the new church, McGuire was consecrated by Old Catholic Archbishop **Joseph Rene Vilatte**. He became an archbishop three years later, and devoted himself to building up his church. To this end, McGuire organized a small seminary for training African Orthodox priests, and the church grew steadily, though slowly, for the balance of his life.

Sources:

Garveyism as a Religious Movement. Metuchen, NJ: Scarecrow Press, 1978. 216 pp.

McGuire, George Alexander, comp. *The Universal Negro Catechism.* [New York]: Universal Negro Improvement Association: 1921. 35 pp.

———. *The Universal Negro Ritual.* [New York]: Universal Negro Improvement Association, 1921. 138 pp.

Newman, Richard. "The Origins of the African Church." *The Negro Churchman.* Millwood, NY: Kraus Reprint Co., 1977.

Terry-Thompson, Arthur C. *History of the African Orthodox Church.* New York: The Author, 1956. 139 pp.

White, Gavin. "Patriarch McGuire and the Episcopal Church." *Historical Magazine of the Protestant Episcopal Church* 38, 2 (June 1969): 109-141.

★616★
MCINTIRE, Carl
Founder, Bible Presbyterian Church
b. May 17, 1906, Ypsilanti, Michigan

Carl McIntire, fundamentalist Presbyterian minister and founder of the Bible Presbyterian Church, is the son of Charles Curtis McIntire, also a Presbyterian minister. He grew up in Oklahoma. He entered Southeastern State College, Durant, Oklahoma, intent upon becoming a lawyer. He transferred to Park College, Parkville, Maryland, for his senior year, during which time he decided to enter the ministry. He entered Princeton Theological Seminary to complete his ministerial studies just as the school became involved in the reorganization mandated by the Presbyterian Church. As a result of the changes, **J. Gresham Machen**, the conservative theology professor, left the school in 1929 and founded Westminster Theological Seminary. McIntire followed Machen and completed his seminary education at Westminster. Following his graduation in 1931, McIntire married Fairy Davis, was ordained a minister in the Presbyterian Church, and moved to Atlantic City, New Jersey, as pastor of the Chelsea Presbyterian Church.

McIntire stayed at Chelsea for two years before being invited to become pastor at Collinswood, New Jersey, where he would remain as pastor the rest of his life. Soon after his arrival he began radio broadcasts of the Sunday services which continue to the present. Once in Collinswood, McIntire also became deeply involved in the continuing problems in the Presbyterian Church. To counter liberal teaching on the mission field, Machen had organized the Independent Board of Foreign Missions. In 1934 McIntire joined the board. In 1936 the Presbyterian Church moved against the board and demanded the resignation of all of its members. In the midst of the controversy, McIntire was put on trial. The Collinswood church voted to leave the denomination, and McIntire submitted his resignation to the Presbytery. He and the church then affiliated with the Machen-led Presbyterian Church in the U.S.A., now called the Orthodox Presbyterian Church.

Soon after the formation of the Presbyterian Church of America, a number of issues arose which set McIntire against Machen. The most important one concerned premillennialism, the belief that Christ will return soon, prior to establishing a thousand-year reign of peace on earth. Machen was postmillennial in his view, as was Presbyterianism traditionally. McIntire broke with Machen and founded the Bible Presbyterian Church and Faith Theological Seminary. The Presbytery moved to claim the property in Collinswood from the dissident congregation. In 1938 a judge awarded the property to the Presbytery, and the congregation was forced to seek other facilities. In the midst of the controversy, in 1936, McIntire released the first issue of the *Christian Beacon*. Two years later, he published the first of his 12 books, *A Cloud of Witnesses*.

McIntire began to organize the beleaguered fundamentalist forces which were leaving the older denominations and reorganizing. In 1941 he led in the formation of the American Council of Christian Churches (ACCC), which worked against the liberal Protestant Federal Council of Churches. McIntire soon came to feel that liberal Protestantism not only had departed from the faith but had been infiltrated by Marxist ideology. In 1947 he issued the call that led to the formation of the International Council of Christian Churches.

McIntire faced two significant challenges to his leadership. First, in 1956 the Bible Presbyterian Church split, and the larger faction rejected McIntire and reorganized. He continued on with the support of congregations in New Jersey, California, Kentucky, and Tennessee. Then in 1969 McIntire was removed from the board of the American Council of Christian Churches. He took his supporters and formed the American Christian Action Council.

McIntire has continued his ministry. While increasingly working from a smaller base of support in the United States, through the International Council of Christian Churches he has found continued support for his anti-Communist fundamentalist Christianity worldwide.

Sources:

Carl McIntire's 50 years, 1933-1983, as Pastor of the Congregation of the Bible Presbyterian Church of Collinswood, N.J. Collinswood, NJ: Bible Presbyterian Church, 1983. 48 pp.
Harden, Margaret G. A Brief History of the Bible Presbyterian Church and Its Agencies. Collinswood, NJ: Bible Presbyterian Church, n.d. 162 pp.
McIntire, Carl. Author of Liberty. Collinswood, NJ: Christian Beacon Press, 1946. 233 pp.
———. Modern Tower of Babel. Collinswood, NJ: Christian Beacon Press.

★617★
MCINTOSH, Martha E.
President, Women's Missionary Union, Southern Baptist Convention
b. Sep. 29, 1848, Society Hill, South Carolina
d. Oct. 14, 1922, Ridgecrest, North Carolina

Martha McIntosh (Bell), the founding president of the Woman's Missionary Union (WMU) of the Southern Baptist Convention, was the daughter of James H. McIntosh, a wealthy planter in pre-Civil War South Carolina. She was named for her mother, Martha Gregg McIntosh, but was called Mattie. The family attended the Welsh Neck Baptist Church. She attended St. David's Academy and later a boarding school in Charleston, South Carolina. Though the family plantation was ransacked during the Civil War, the family was able to survive with much of their fortune intact. While the several sons became prominent in their professions, Mattie and her sister Louisa developed an interest in foreign missions.

McIntosh's attention to missions was perked in 1872 by Ellen C. Edwards, a member of the Welsh Run Church who had affiliated with Woman's Mission to Woman, an early Baptist missionary organization. In 1874 a local woman's missionary society was organized, and the McIntosh sisters joined. Hearing of the work at Welsh Run, J. A. Chambliss of the Convention's Foreign Mission Board invited the women to create a central committee for the promotion of women's missionary societies in other churches in South Carolina. Martha became the secretary of this new committee.

As secretary of the committee, McIntosh felt a middle name was needed, and she added an ''E.'' to her signature. Over the next few years, the women of South Carolina led all states in giving to foreign missions. During the 1880s, she also attended the annual meetings of the Southern Baptist Convention with her pastor, John Stout, and his wife Fanny, where informal meetings of women interested in the missionary work were conducted. In 1887 McIntosh and **Annie Walker Armstrong** of Maryland emerged as the leaders among the women, who had decided to organize the next year. McIntosh was placed in charge of planning the 1888 meeting. At that session she was elected the first president of the new Woman's Missionary Union (WMU). She placed her fortune in service to the organizational needs of the still fragile organization. The fact that her brother was a lawyer in Baltimore facilitated contact with Armstrong, the union's new secretary. Among McIntosh's first actions

was having the union back an annual Christmas offering for foreign missions that had been suggested by pioneer missionary Lottie Moon.

McIntosh served four years as president and declined reelection. She then served as vice-president from South Carolina, but declined to serve beyond 1895. That year she married T. B. Bell, head of the convention's Sunday school board. They moved to Nashville for a year and then moved to Atlanta where Bell owned the *The Christian Index*, a Baptist newspaper. In Atlanta, McIntosh worked on the *Index* and sat on the executive board of the Women's Missionary Union of Georgia.

In 1914 McIntosh's daughter Ada went to China as a missionary. The next year, in poor health, Bell sold the *Index* and moved to the Ridgecrest Baptist Assembly grounds in North Carolina. After Bell died in 1916, Ada invited her mother to join her in China. Thus in 1918 at the age of 70, McIntosh journeyed around the world to Tengchow, North China, Lottie Moon's former base of operations. Three years later McIntosh and Ada returned to Ridgecrest, where McIntosh lived quietly, sharing her experience with the many visitors to the grounds until her unexpected death in 1922. The union which McIntosh helped found went on to become a major force in the development of the Southern Baptist Convention worldwide.

Sources:

Allen, Catherine. Laborers Together with God. Birmingham, AL: Women's Missionary Union, 1987. 246 pp.

★618★
MCINTYRE, James Francis Aloysius
Cardinal, Roman Catholic Church
b. Jun. 25, 1886, New York, New York
d. May 27, 1979, Chicago, Illinois

James Francis Aloysius McIntyre, a cardinal in the Roman Catholic Church, was the son of an Irish-American policeman, James Francis McIntyre, and Mary Pelley McIntyre. He followed an unusual course for a future cardinal. Unable to get into the overcrowded parochial school, he attended public school. At the age of 13, he dropped out of school to pursue a career in business, and to care for his now invalid father. He got a job as an errand boy for a stock broker. He soon returned to school, in the evenings, studying at Columbia University and New York City College. By 1914 his advancement had proceeded to the point that he was offered a junior partnership in the company. However, his father had recently died, and he was now free to follow his growing desire to enter the priesthood.

McIntyre entered the Cathedral College, through which he quickly passed and moved on to St. Joseph's Seminary, the major seminary for the diocese. He graduated in 1921 and, after ordination, was assigned to St. Gabriel's parish as the assistant pastor. The parish had been previously served by Archbishop **John J. Farley** as well as the then archbishop, **Patrick Joseph Hayes**. In 1923 Hayes invited McIntyre to become one of the assistant chancellors of the archdiocese. The chancery office was to be his home for the next 25 years.

In 1934 McIntyre became chancellor and was made a papal chamberlain with the title of monsignor. In 1936 he was made a domestic prelate. When **Francis Spellman** became archbishop of the now debt-ridden archdiocese of New York, McIntyre was one of the few reappointed to his chancery office. The war was in its opening stages in Europe, and Spellman's national and international roles as military vicar were expanding. Spellman saw to McIntyre's appointment as titular bishop of Ctrene and auxiliary of New York. After the war, McIntyre was named vicar-general and in 1946 coadjutor archbishop of New York. Since the beginning of the war, he had largely managed the administration of the archdiocese.

In 1948 McIntyre was named archbishop of Los Angeles. His task was enormous, as the archdiocese had expanded rapidly during the war, and its facilities were no match for the demands being made upon it. He reorganized the diocesan structure. McIntyre began a drive to build new parochial schools with emphasis upon the poorer sections of the archdiocese. During his reign 21 new high schools were opened and the student body quadrupled.

In the midst of his development of the archdiocese, in 1952 he was named to the college of cardinals. The recognition, if anything, merely quickened his pace. By 1962 over 200 new priests were at work, women at work in religious orders had doubled, and the number of priests in preparation had almost doubled. He also built a new junior seminary, Our Lady Queen of the Angels in San Fernando.

As a public figure, McIntyre was successful in having a state tax on church schools removed and in opposing a liberal abortion law. He also supported federal aid to parochial schools. He was frequently criticized for his lack of leadership in the Civil Rights Movement. During Vatican II, McIntyre emerged as a conservative, especially opposing the introduction of mass in the vernacular and the modernizing of nuns' dress and routine. He retired in 1970 and was ill during much of the last years of his life.

Sources:
Delaney, John J. *Dictionary of American Catholic Biography.* Garden City, NY: Doubleday & Company, 1988. 621 pp.
Thornton, Francis Beauchesne. *Our American Princes.* New York: G. P. Putnam's Sons, 1963. 319 pp.

★ 619 ★
MCKAY, David Oman
President, Church of Jesus Christ of Latter-day Saints
b. Sep. 8, 1873, Huntsville, Utah
d. Jan. 18, 1970, Salt Lake City, Utah

David Oman McKay, the ninth president of the Church of Jesus Christ of Latter-day Saints, was born in a small town in rural Utah. At the age of 20 he became the principal of the local schools, but soon left to attend the University of Utah. He graduated in 1897 and was designated class valedictorian. In 1899 he began teaching at the Weber Academy in Ogden, Utah, but two years later was called to become the Weber Stake Sunday School superintendent. As superintendent, his innovations in developing materials and new styles of meetings caught the attention of church authorities and were eventually adopted throughout the church. His innovations also led to his being called to membership as a general church officer. In 1906 he was ordained as a member of the Quorum of the Twelve Apostles.

During his years on the Quorum, McKay served as superintendent to the Sunday school program and was for ten years the church's commissioner of education. He left that position in 1922 to serve for two years as head of the European Mission. He was subsequently selected to be the second counselor to presidents **Heber Jeddy Grant** (1934-1945) and **George Albert Smith** (1945-1951). In 1950 he became president of the Quorum of the Twelve.

In 1951 McKay succeeded George Albert Smith as president of the church. The Church of Jesus Christ of Latter-day Saints was at that time still largely concentrated in the western United States, although it had operated a foreign mission for over a hundred years. McKay instilled a new missionary spirit in the church, and during the 19 years of his presidency the number of missionaries increased from 2,000 to 13,000, the number of missions doubled, and overall membership in the church increased from one million to almost three million. As the number of stakes increased from 184 to 500, he instituted building programs. Over 3,700 buildings were erected. They included five new temples in Los Angeles and Oakland, California, as well as temples in Switzerland; London, England; and New Zealand. In his efforts, McKay traveled more than two million miles on church business.

McKay also moved to reoganize the church's business operations. As president, he became chairman of the board for each church-owned business enterprise. He appointed full-time president-managers and moved to build the church's legal, accounting, and communication departments.

McKay possessed a winsome, nondoctrinaire style and a willingness to state his feelings on social issues. He supported civil rights and emerged as a foe of communism. He was a vigorous speaker and his sermons were regularly compiled into books. He also authored several autobiographical volumes. He died of heart failure at the age of 96.

Sources:
Dictionary of American Biography. 20 vols. and 7 supps. New York: Charles Scribner's Sons, 1928-1936, 1944-1981.
Gibbons, Francis M. *David O. McKay.* Salt Lake City, UT: Deseret Book Co., 1986 443 pp.
McKay, David Oman. *Ancient Apostles.* Salt Lake City, UT Sunday School Union, 1918. 277 pp.
———. *Cherished Experiences from the Writing of President David O. McKay.* Comp. by Clare Middlemiss. Salt Lake City: Deseret Book Co., 1955. 209 pp.
———. *Gospel Ideals.* Salt Lake City, UT: The Improvement Era, 1953. 598 pp.
———. *Stepping Stones to an Abundant Life.* Salt Lake City, UT: Deseret Book Company, 1971. 445 pp.
———. *Treasures of Life.* Salt Lake City, UT: Deseret Book Co., 1963. 562 pp.
———. *True to the Faith.* Salt Lake City, UT: Bookcraft, 1966. 445 pp.
McKay, Llewellyn R., comp. *Home Memories of David O. McKay.* Salt Lake City: Deseret Book Company, 1956. 280 pp.
Morrell, Jeanette McKay. *Highlights in the Life of President David O. McKay.* Salt Lake City, UT: Deseret Book Co., 1966. 318 pp.
Nibley, Preston. *The Presidents of the Church.* Salt Lake City, UT: Deseret Book Company, 1971. 477 pp.

★ 620 ★
MCPHERSON, Aimee Semple
Founder, International Church of the Foursquare Gospel
b. Oct. 9, 1890, Ingersoll, Ontario, Canada
d. Sep. 27, 1944, Oakland, California

Aimee Semple McPherson was the founder of the International Church of the Foursquare Gospel, and one of the more publicized and controversial figures of the Pentecostal Movement. Her early religious training was in the Holiness Movement under her mother, who was a member of the Salvation Army. As a teenager, she experienced her conversion and baptism with the Holy Spirit at a Pentecostal meeting in 1907. Events moved quickly over the next several years. In 1908 she married Robert Semple, the minister who had converted her. The next year, Aimee herself became a preacher. Then in 1910 the couple moved to China in the capacity of missionaries, but shortly after their arrival, when Aimee was eight months pregnant, Robert Semple died of malaria. She returned to the United States, where she married Rolf Kennedy McPherson in 1912. The marriage was an unhappy one, and they separated within a few years.

In 1915 Aimee Semple McPherson conducted a series of revival meetings near her birthplace in Ontario that were to become the turning point in her life. It was during this period that she felt called to become an itinerant evangelist, and she pursued this occupation for the next several years. She established her headquarters in Los Angeles in 1918, though she continued to tour the country for some time afterwards. During this period she also began the publication of her ministry's periodical, *Bridal Call.*

In the 1920s McPherson became more settled in the Los Angeles area, a setting down of roots represented most concretely by the construction of the Angelus Temple. This building was opened in 1923, and remained at the center of her ministry for the balance of her career. She opened her own radio station in 1924, and was one of the pioneers of religious broadcasting. A few years later, she also opened the Lighthouse of International Evangelism, a Bible college for training the workers needed for her increasingly expanding ministry. McPherson's institution building culminated in the formation of the International Church of the Foursquare Gospel as an independent denomination.

Aimee Semple McPherson is best known for her healing ministry and for the highly dramatic style that she brought to preaching. Although doctrinally orthodox with respect to the Pentecostal mainstream, her flamboyance in combination with the prejudice against women ministers made her a center of controversy. The single greatest controversy in her career, however, developed as a result of something quite different from either of these two issues. In 1926 she disappeared for a month and, upon returning, claimed to have been kidnapped. Critics asserted that instead of being kidnapped, McPherson had intentionally run away. She was indicted, but charges were eventually dropped due to lack of evidence. By the time of her death, the International Church of the Foursquare Gospel had become a major Pentecostal church.

In 1931 McPherson married David L. Hutton. McPherson left a vast record of her activities, both writings and recordings. She authored several autobiographical accounts of her life and has been the subject of a number of books, both friendly and hostile in depicting her life.

Sources:
Bahr, Robert. *Least of All the Saints*. Englewood Cliffs, NJ: Prentice-Hall, 1979. 308 pp.
Cox, Raymond L. *The Verdict Is In*. Los Angeles: Research Publishers, 1983. 247 pp.
McPherson, Aimee Semple. *The Foursquare Gospel*. Comp. by Raymond L. Cox. Los Angeles: Foursquare Publications, 1969. 296 pp.
———. *In the Service of the King*. New York: Boni and Liveright, 1927.
———. *The Second Coming of Christ*. Los Angeles: The Author, 1921. 120 pp.
———. *The Story of My Life*. Los Angeles: Echo Park Evangelistic Association, 1951. 246 pp.
———. *This Is That*. Los Angeles: Bridal Call Publishing, 1919. Rev. ed., Los Angeles: Echo Park Evangelistic Association, 1923. 791 pp.
Thomas, Lately. *The Vanishing Evangelist*. New York: Viking Press, 1959. 334 pp.

★621★
MCQUILKIN JR., Robert Crawford
Educator, Fellowship of Independent Evangelical Churches
b. Feb. 16, 1886, Philadelphia, Pennsylvania
d. Jul. 15, 1952, Asheville, North Carolina

Robert Crawford McQuilkin, Jr., for almost thirty years the president of Columbia Bible School, was the son of Lucy Kirkpatrick and Robert Crawford McQuilkin. As a young man McQuilkin had a conversion experience and joined the United Presbyterian Church of North America. After finishing high school in 1902 he entered the business world as an employee of William Steele and Sons in Philadelphia. However, in 1911 at a missionary conference he had an experience that revived and renewed his spiritual life out of which he developed an association with Charles G. Trumbull. In 1912 he became the associate editor of Trumbull's *Sunday School Times*. That same year he married Marguerite Lambie. While working at the *Times* he decided to return to school and in 1917 graduated from the University of Pennsylvania.

McQuilkin and Trumbull had both been deeply affected by the Keswick Movement, a branch of the nineteenth century holiness movement which emphasized victorious living through the attain-

ment of freedom over the power of sin by the action of the Holy Spirit. For the next decade McQuilkin spoke out of this perspective as a popular Bible conference teacher. In 1913 he also initiated a series of Victorious Life conferences, which he led annually through 1923. In 1918 he authored his first book, *Victorious Life Studies*.

McQuilkin had developed strong aspirations to become a missionary but was unable to travel to Africa because of World War I. Instead, he led the Victorious Life conferences to support mission work. He also became a director of the Latin American Mission and the Mexican Indian Mission.

The annual conferences were superseded in 1923 when McQuilkin joined with other victorious life supporters in the formation of Columbia Bible College in Columbia, South Carolina. The school remains centered upon the victorious life doctrine. During his years as a college president, he led in the founding of Ben Lippen Bible Conference Center in Asheville, North Carolina, in 1928, and the Ben Lippen School in 1940. He wrote several additional books, including: *Studying Our Lord's Parables* (1925); *The Baptism of the Spirit: Shall We Seek It?* (1935); *The Lord Is My Shepherd* (1938); *Victory in Christ* (1939); *The Message of Romans: An Exposition* (1947) and *Law and Grace* (1958). Having become a member of the Presbyterian Church in the U.S.A. while in the South, he withdrew in 1951, a year before his death, and joined with the more conservative Fellowship of Independent Evangelical Churches.

McQuilkin was concerned with the quality of education of the independent Bible schools and in 1931 helped to found the Evangelical Teacher Training Association over which he presided for its first decade. He remained president of Columbia until he died in 1952.

Sources:
McQuilkin, Robert C. *The Baptism of the Spirit: Should We Seek It?* Columbia, SC: N.p, 1935. 36 pp.
———. *The Lord Is My Shepherd*. Columbia, SC: N.p., 1938. 37 pp.
———. *The Message of Romans: An Exposition*. Grand Rapids, MI: Zondervan publishing Company, 1947. 178 pp.
———. *Studying Our Lord's Parables*. Grand Rapids, MI: Zondervan Publishing Company, 1925. 168 pp.
———. *Victorious Life Studies*. Philadelphia: Christian Life Literature Fund, 1918. 128 pp.
Reid, Daniel G., Robert D. Linder, Bruce L. Shelley, and Harry S. Stout. *Dictionary of Christianity in America*. Downers Grove, IL: InterVarsity Press, 1990. 1305 pp.

★622★
MCTYEIRE, Holland Nimmons
Bishop, Methodist Episcopal Church, South
b. Jul. 28, 1824, Barnwell County, South Carolina
d. Feb. 15, 1889, Nashville, Tennessee

Holland Nimmons McTyeire, the bishop most responsible for the revival of the Methodist Episcopal Church, South in the years immediately after the Civil War, grew up in rural South Carolina and attended Cokesbury School in Greenwood County, South Carolina. He finished his college at Randolph-Macon College. He was admitted on trial in the Virginia Conference of the new Methodist Episcopal Church, South, which had just been formed by a division of the Methodist Episcopal Church. He immediately rose to prominence in the church. After two years at his first charge in Williamsburg, Virginia, he moved to Mobile, Alabama, and served the St. Francis Street church for two years (1847-1849). Then he moved to New Orleans and in 1851 he founded the *New Orleans Christian Advocate*. While in New Orleans he married Amelia Townsend. He remained in New Orleans until 1858 when he was invited to move to Nashville, Tennessee, to become the editor of the denominational paper, the *Christian Advocate*.

McTyeire remained in Nashville as a strong supporter of the Southern cause until 1862, when the Union Army occupied Nashville and took over the building that housed the Methodists' publishing concern. McTyeire became a refugee and spent much of the rest of the war in south Alabama. He eventually became pastor of a church in Montgomery, Alabama, where he served until 1866. At the general conference he emerged as the leader of the church's reconstruction. He silenced those who favored the immediate reunion with the Methodist Episcopal Church. He negotiated the establishment of the black members in an autonomous body, now known as the Christian Methodist Episcopal Church. To assist in the quick recovery of the war-ravaged denomination he argued for lay representation in the conferences and the extension of the term of ministers at local chuches from two to four years. (Methodist ministers are appointed on a year-to-year basis to their pastoral assignment.)

The general conference accepted his suggestions and also elected him bishop. He would serve in that capacity for 23 years. Among his major contributions was the establishment of Vanderbilt University. He secured the original gift of $500,000 from Cornelius Vanderbilt (who later added an additional $500,000) and other gifts from various members of the Vanderbilt family. He overcame resistance from many Methodists who saw no need for the university. He was appointed president of the school's board of trustees, over which he was given full veto powers.

McTyeire was the author of several books, including *A History of Methodism* (1884) and *Duties of Masters to Servants* (1851). He was a recognized authority on ecclesiastical law and was responsible for both *A Manual of the Discipline of the Methodist Episcopal Church* (the Methodist book of church law) (1890) and *A Catechism on Church Government* (1878), both of which were revised and republished on a number of occasions. He resided at the university, and there he died in 1889.

Sources:

Harmon, Nolan B. *The Encyclopedia of World Methodism*. 2 vols. Nashville: United Methodist Publishing House, 1974.

Hill, Samuel S., ed. *Encyclopedia of Religion in the South*. Macon, GA: Mercer University Press, 1984. 878 pp.

McTyeire, Holland N. *A Catechism of Bible History*. Louisville, KY: W. P. Churchill, 1874. 160 pp.

_____. *A Catechism on Church Government*. Nashville, TN: Publishing House of the Methodist Episcopal Church, South, 1878. 128 pp.

_____. *Duties of Masters to Servants*. Charleston, SC: Southern Baptist Publication Society, 1851: Rev. as: *Duties of Christian Masters*. Nashville, TN: Southern Methodist Publishing House, 1859. 287 pp.

_____. *A History of Methodism*. Nashville, TN: Southern Methodist Publishing House, 1884. 692 pp.

_____. *A Manual of the Discipline of the Methodist Episcopal Church, South*. Nashville, TN: Southern Methodist Publishing House, 1870. 264 pp.

_____. *Passing Through the Gates, and Other Sermons*. Edited by John J. Tigert. Nashville, TN: Publishing House of the Methodist Episcopal Church, South, 1890. 319 pp.

Tigert, J. J. *Bishop Holland Nimmons McTyeire*. Nashville, TN: Vanderbilt University Press, 1955. 279 pp.

★623★
MEARES, John Levin
Founder, Evangel Temple
b. 1920, Largo, Florida

John Meares is a bishop in the International Evangelical Church and Missionary Association and founder of Evangel Temple, a large independent Pentecostal congregation in Washington, D.C. He is the son of Sylvia Sherman and Richie Meares. His father had helped found the congregation of the Church of God (Cleveland, Tennessee), at Largo and served as one of its deacons. After finishing high school in 1938, he entered Lee College in Cleveland, Tennessee, for a year. While there he experienced the baptism of the Holy Spirit (the definitive Pentecostal experience signified by the believer speaking in tongues). He returned to Florida but soon accepted a call to the ministry and went back to Lee in 1941. In 1944 he married Mary Lee Bell, and began to travel around the country as an evangelist. In 1945 he entered the University of Tennessee at Knoxville, and became pastor of a small church at John Sevier, Tennessee.

In 1947, following his university graduation Meares moved to Athens, Tennessee, and then on to Memphis in 1950. Finally in 1955 he resigned from the church in Memphis and moved to Washington, D.C., initially to assist Jack Coe in revival services, after which he stayed to build a church. He also went on the radio with the "Miracle Time" show. The church he raised, orginally called Washington Revival Center, was predominantly black in membership. The leadership of the Church of God did not approve of his actions and forced him out of the denomination. Meanwhile his congregation moved several times but in 1957 finally located in an abandoned theater and became known as the National Evangelistic Center. The work prospered as a center of miracles and healings.

The late 1960s were a time of crises. Meares changed the emphasis of his worship from miracles to a teaching ministry. At about the same time, several evangelists tried to split the congregation. By 1971 the church had dwindled to just a few hundred members. Though now comparatively small, the congregation decided to build its own center at a cost of three million dollars. The new Evangel Temple opened in 1975. As the church expanded, the pastoral leadership of the church expanded, and a missionary and outreach program developed through the International Evangelical Church and Missionary Association, a fellowship of some 400 Pentecostal churches.

As Evangel Temple and the outreach program blossomed, Meares became closely associated with **Earl P. Paulk** of the Gospel Harvester Church in Georgia, **Robert McAlister** of the New Life Pentecostal Church in Rio de Janeiro, and the other bishops of the international ecumenical association the International Communion of Charismatic Churches. In 1982, Paulk and McAlister consecrated Meares as a bishop in the International Communion. More important to the larger Pentecostal community, Meares has become known for his ability to work as a white man within the black community where Pentecostalism has some of its major strength. Beginning in 1984 Evangel Temple has hosted an annual Inner-City Pastor's Conference which draws ministers from across the country.

Sources:

Evangel Temple's 30th Anniversary Historical Journal. Washington, DC: Evangel Temple, 1985. 61 pp.

Meares, John. *Bind Us Together*. Old Tappan, NJ: Fleming H. Revell, 1987. 159 pp.

_____. *Faith Cometh. . .by the Word*. Washington, DC: National Evangelistic Press, 1956.

_____. *The Inheritance of Christ in the Saints*. Washington, DC: Evangel Temple, 1984. 109 pp.

★624★
MEARS, Henrietta Cornelia
Founder, Gospel Light Publishers
b. Oct. 23, 1890, Fargo, North Dakota
d. Mar. 18, 1963, Los Angeles, California

Henrietta Cornelia Mears, for many years the director of Christian education at the First Presbyterian Church in Hollywood, California, emerged as a Christian leader of national renown in the Sunday school movement. In doing so, she founded one of the largest publishers of Christian education literature. When she was quite young, her father, a banker, moved the family to Minneapolis, Minnesota, where they became members of First Baptist Church, pastored by **William Bell Riley**, one of America's leading fundamentalist pastors. She had a natural talent for teaching and began to teach Sunday school at the age of 12.

Mears attended the University of Minnesota and after graduation began a career as a school teacher. She held her first teaching positions successively at Beardsley and North Branch, Minnesota, and then moved back to Minneapolis to teach at Central High School and to work again in the Sunday school at First Baptist. In the mid-1920s she met the pastor of First Presbyterian Church in Hollywood, who, impressed with the way she had helped build the program in Minneapolis, offered her a position at his church. She accepted, and by 1930 the Sunday school had grown from 1,450 pupils to over 4,000.

In 1929, with growing concern with the inadequacies of the literature being used in the then fast growing Sunday school program at the church, Mears made a thorough survey of available church school literature. Finding it all inadequate—either doctrinally suspect, inadequately graded, or unattractively presented—she began to write her own. Soon afterward she met Marion Falconer, who encouraged her to publish the material. In 1933, she founded Gospel Light Press and put 12 courses into print. By the end of the year, 13 different Sunday schools were using them. The following year sales tripled. In 1938 Mears added a Christian Education Training Course in Los Angeles. Mears led in the founding of the National Sunday School Association and is given a large percentage of the credit for reviving the Sunday school concept. By 1940, Gospel Light Press (since 1956 Gospel Light Publishers) had become the fourth largest independent publisher of Sunday school literature in the country.

During the 1930s, Mears also developed a college-level program that included, among other features, opportunities for summer service overseas. In 1937 she purchased the Forest Home Camp Grounds near San Bernadino, California, which became a retreat center, especially for the college-age youth. During a trip to Europe after World War II, she developed a vision to reach out to campus populations across the United States. This vision was shared with several young people in the congregation, and they formed the Fellowship of the Burning Heart to pursue the vision. Out of the 1947 meeting, one of the men, William Bright, developed Campus Crusade for Christ. Also emerging from the Fellowship was the Hollywood Christian Group, a gathering including many famous people whose spiritual life suffered from their inability to attend church as ordinary worshippers.

In 1951, Mears' sister died. She moved into a house with William and Yvonne Bright, where she lived the rest of her life. She died peacefully in her sleep in 1963. Among her last accomplishments was the founding of Gospel Literature in National Tongues (GLINT) to provide Sunday school literature in a variety of foreign languages.

Sources:
Baldwin, Ethel May and David V. Benson. *Henrietta Mears and How She Did It*. Glendale, CA: G/L Publications, 1966. 343 pp.
Mears, Henrietta. *What the Bible Is All About*. Glendale, CA: G/L Publications, 1966. 675 pp.
Moyer, Elgin S., ed. *Who Was Who in Church History*. Chicago: Moody Press, 1968.
Powers, Barbara Hudson. *The Henrietta Mears Story*. Westwood, NJ: Fleming H. Revell Company, 1957.

★ 625 ★
MEDEIROS, Humberto Sousa
Cardinal, Roman Catholic Church
b. Oct. 6, 1915, Arrifes Portugal
d. Sep. 17, 1983, Boston, Massachusetts

Humberto Sousa Medeiros, a cardinal in the Roman Catholic Church, was the son of Antonio Sousa and Maria de Jesus Sousa Massa Medeiros. Born on Sao Miguel, an island of the Azores, he moved to the United States in 1931 and became a naturalized citizen in 1940. He attended the Catholic University in Washington, D.C., from which he received his M.A. in 1942 and his S.T.L. in 1946. In 1946 he was ordained as a priest for the Diocese of Fall River (Massachusetts), and served successively St. John of God Church, Somerset; St. Michael's, Fall River; Our Lady of Health, Fall River; St. Vincent de Paul, Health Camp; and Mt. Carmel, New Bedford. In 1949 he studied for a year at the North American College in Rome, but returned in 1950 to serve at Holy Name Church in Fall River. In 1951 he was named chancellor of the diocese. He completed his doctoral studies at Catholic University in 1952.

In 1953 Medeiros was named a domestic prelate with the title of monsignor. He remained within the Fall River diocese until 1956 when he was named bishop of Brownsville (Texas). Formally he was the second bishop of the diocese, but since his predecessor had died on his way to take up his post, he was in fact the first. In Brownsville, he gained the reputation as a friend of migrant workers and an early advocate of their unionization.

In 1970 Medeiros was named archbishop of Boston, Massachusetts, a move interpreted as an attempt by the church to become more inclusive and end the traditional dominance of the American church by the Irish. He quickly asserted his authority by moving several priests whom he viewed as having become entrenched in their parishes. He was named a cardinal in 1973 and appointed to positions in the Congregation for the Bishops and the Congregation for Catholic Education.

Sources:
The American Catholic Who's Who. Washington, D.C.: National Catholic News Service, 1979.
Biography Index. New York: The H. W. Wilson Co.
Current Biography Yearbook. New York: H. W. Wilson Co.
Delaney, John J. *Dictionary of American Catholic Biography*. Garden City, NY: Doubleday & Company, 1988. 621 pp.
The New York Times Biographical Service. Ann Arbor, MI: University Microfilms International.
Who's Who in America. Wilmette, IL: Marquis Who's Who, Inc.

★ 626 ★
MEHER BABA
Spiritual Teacher
b. Feb. 25, 1894, Poona India
d. Jan. 31, 1969, Poona India

Meher Baba, born Merwan Sheriar Irani, was the child of an Indian Parsi (Zoroastrian) family. While at Deccan College he encountered Hazrat Babajan, a female mystic and spiritual teacher in the Islamic tradition. He became her student and soon experienced self-realization under her guidance. He also traveled around the country and met other spiritual teachers who confirmed his status as avatar, the incarnation of God for the present age.

In 1922 Meher Baba established an ashram near Bombay. It was during this period that his disciples began calling him Meher Baba, meaning compassionate father. In 1924 he and his followers reestablished themselves near Ahmednager, at a site that would become Meherabad. Over and above the ashram, the spiritual center at Meherabad included a poorhouse, a hospital, and a free school.

With little prior warning, Baba became silent in 1925, a not uncommon practice for holy men on the Indian subcontinent. He remained silent for the rest of his life, communicating with an alphabet board through which he dictated his many speeches and several books, including *God Speaks*; *Discourses*; *The Everything and Nothing*; *The Path of Love*; and *Life at Its Best*. He later abandoned this method of communication for hand signs. According to Baba, one of the reasons for his silence was that enough words had been said; it was now time to live the ideals about which prior spiritual teachers had spoken. In line with this ideal, he did not found a new religion. "Baba Lovers," as his followers refer to themselves, adhere to no set beliefs or practices, and there is no Meher Baba church or organization that Baba Lovers are required to join.

In 1931 Baba began making trips to the West, where he acquired numerous disciples. A spiritual center was established at Myrtle Beach, South Carolina, which Baba visited for the first time in 1952. In this same year he accepted a Sufi group that had been initiated in the United States by **Hazrat Inayat Khan**, a group which was renamed Sufism Reoriented. Sufism Reoriented is one of several autonomous organizations that promote Baba's teachings within the loosely structured Meher Baba movement.

Baba asserted that he was the avatar in the most literal sense of the term, claiming to be an embodiment of the same ancient one who had incarnated as Christ, Krishna, Buddha, and so forth. With respect to religious practices, his teaching was very simple; one should love God and humanity. This practice of love embraces both the more concrete goal of service to humanity as well as the goal of mystical union with God in a state of Divine Love.

Sources:

Adriel, Jean. *Avatar*. Santa Barbara, CA: J. F. Rowny Press, 1947. 284 pp.

Anzar, Naosherwan. *The Beloved: The Life and Work of Meher Baba*. North Myrtle Beach, SC: Sheriar Press, 1974. 146 pp.

Meher Baba. *Discourses*. 3 vols. San Francisco, CA: Sufism Reoriented, 1967.

———. *The Everything and the Nothing*. Sydney, Australia: Meher House, 1963. 111 pp.

———. *God to Man and Man to God*. North Myrtle Beach, SC: Sheriar Press, 1975. 287 pp.

———. *Life at Its Best*. New York: Harper & Row. 1972. 106 pp.

———. *Mastery of Consciousness*. New York: Harper & Row, 1977. 202 pp.

———. *The Path of Love*. New York: Samuel Weiser, 1976. 102 pp.

Purdom, C. B. *The God-Man*. London: George Allen & Unwin, 1964. 463 pp.

★ 627 ★
MENDES, Henry Pereira
President, Union of Orthodox Jewish Congregations of the United Sta tes and Canada
b. Apr. 13, 1852, Birmingham England
d. Oct. 20, 1937, Mt. Vernon, New York

Henry Pereira Mendes, one of the founders of the Union of Orthodox Jewish Congregations in the United States and Canada, began his education at Northwick College, a school founded by his father, Rabbi Abraham Pereira, descendent of an old Sephardic Jewish family. He attended University College, London (1870-1872) and in 1875 became the rabbi of a Sephardic congregation in Manchester. He left England in 1877 to assume the post of rabbi at Shearith Israel Congregation in New York City, the oldest congregation in America. While there he continued his studies at New York University, from which he graduated in 1884.

In New York Mendes quickly distinguished himself as a man of boundless energy and a leader of the Jewish community which was just beginning to experience the massive growth from Eastern European immigration. In 1882 he helped found the New York Board of Jewish Ministers and for the next 25 years served as its secretary. In 1885 he founded a branch of the Alliance Israelite Universalle, an organization to unite the Jewish community and assist Jews suffering persecution and distress. During the 1890s he emerged as one of the country's first Zionists. He helped to organize the Federation of American Zionists and served as its vice-president. He was also active in the World Zionist Organization and attended the meetings in Vienna (1898) and Basel (1899).

Mendes championed what would later be called an enlightened Orthodoxy. As one of his first projects in America, he involved

himself in the founding of the Jewish Theological Seminary of America (later associated with the Conservative Jewish movement). The seminary formally opened in Shearith, Israel, in 1887. Mendes served as president of the seminary's advisory board for many years and taught Jewish history. His volume on *The Jewish Religion Ethically Presented* grew out of his teachings and was circulated in a privately printed form before its formal publication in 1889. It subsequently went through numerous editions. He served as president of the seminary for five years (1897-1902).

In 1898, with the assistance of his cousin Meldola de Sola, he organized the Union of Orthodox Jewish Congregations of the United States and Canada. For the first fifteen years he served as its president. He retired from Shearith Israel in 1923.

All during his life Mendes was also a prolific writer. As early as 1884 he published *The Position of Women in Jewish Law and Custom*. Other writings include: *The Sphere of Congregational Work* (1885); *The Lifting of the Veil* (1888); and *England and America, The Dream of Peace* (1897). In his mature years he produced several important liturgical works: *The Burial Service as Used in the Congregation Shearith Israel* (1910) and *Mekor Hayim, the Mourner's Handbook* (1915).

Sources:

Landman, Isaac, ed. *Universal Jewish Encyclopedia*. 10 vols. New York: The Universal Jewish Encyclopedia, 1940.

Mendes, Henry P. *Bar-mitzvah for Boyhood, Youth and Manhood*. New York: Union of Orthodox Jewish Congregations of America, 1938. 89 pp.

———. *The Jewish Religion Ethically Presented*. New York: The Author, 1905. 188 pp.

———. *The Lifting of the Veil*. New York: Cowan, 1888. 18 pp.

———. *Looking Ahead*. London: F. T. Neely, 1899. 381 pp.

———. *The Sphere of Congregational Work*. New York: Cowan, 1885. 25 pp.

★ 628 ★
MERTON, Thomas James
Trappist Monk, Roman Catholic Church
b. Jan. 31, 1915, Prades France
d. Dec. 10, 1968, Bangkok Thailand

Thomas James Merton, a monk and contemporary writer of mystical literature who is credited with introducing Roman Catholics to the spirituality of Zen Buddhist meditation, was the son of Owen Heathcote and Ruth Jenkins Merton. He was raised in the Anglican tradition. Following his mother's death when he was six, he moved frequently until his father settled in England in 1928. Three years later his father died, leaving Merton to make his way in the world. He made his way through the British educational system to Clare College at Cambridge, and in 1936 transferred to Columbia University in New York.

In New York Merton fell in with a small group of what became close friends. He also began to consider the Roman Catholic faith, leading to his conversion to Roman Catholicism. He graduated from Columbia in 1938 and continued for his master's degree. A course in scholastic theology became an important step in this process. In 1938 he was baptized and took his first communion. In 1939 he received his master's degree in English. A short time later he considered becoming a priest, but eventually decided instead to enter the Third (or lay) Order of Franciscans, which he accomplished in 1941. But upon visiting the Gethsemani Trappist monastery in Kentucky, he discovered the ideal life for himself. He would adopt the simple way of life followed by the Cistercians of the Strict Observance (as the Trappists are officially known).

Merton moved to Kentucky in December 1941, and two months later became a novice. His progress in the order was marked by his simple vows, made in 1944, and his solemn vows in 1947. The quiet life at Gethsemani allowed him to write, and in 1944 his first volume, *Thirty Poems*, appeared. His autobiographical *The Seven*

Storey Mountain (1948) became a popular seller and brought Merton some degree of fame. Merton was ordained as a priest in 1949 and was known among his brothers as Father M. Louis Merton. In 1951 he was naturalized as a U. S. citizen.

Merton's major activity for the rest of his life was writing, though he served the monastery as the master of scholastics (students aspiring to the priesthood) from 1951-1955 and master of novices from 1955-1965. Finishing two or three books a year, he began to author a series of devotional titles as well as volumes on the mystical contemplative life. His books were immensely popular and widely read, especially by both lay and religious Roman Catholics. Then in 1967 he issued *Mystics and Zen Masters*. The book revealed his interest in interreligious dialogue, the underlying unity of religious experience and Eastern mysticism and meditation practices. It became a sanctioning volume for many Roman Catholic religious who, in the relatively free and experimental atmosphere following the Second Vatican Council, began to explore non-Christian forms of spiritual practice. Zen meditation was a most popular spiritual discipline compared to that traditionally offered in Roman Catholic orders. He followed with *Zen and the Birds of Appetite* (1968).

In 1968 Merton traveled to Bangkok, Thailand, to attend a conference of Benedictine and Cistercian monastic leaders. While there he held three well publicized sessions with the Dalai Lama. Merton died suddenly in Bangkok, where it is believed he was accidentally electrocuted in the conference center due to a defective wire on a fan.

Posthumously three large volumes of his writings were published: *The Collected Poems of Thomas Merton* (1977); *The Secular Journal of Thomas Merton* (1977); and *The Literary Essays of Thomas Merton* (1981). A Thomas Merton Studies Center has been established at Bellermine College in Louisville, Kentucky, which publishes a quarterly journal, *Merton Seasonal*.

Sources:

Baker, James Thomas. *Thomas Merton, Social Critic*. Lexington, KY: University of Kentucky Press, 1971.

Dictionary of American Biography. 20 vols. and 7 supps. New York: Charles Scribner's Sons, 1928-1936, 1944-1981.

Grayston, Donald and Michael W. Higgins, eds. *Thomas Merton*. Toronto: Griffin Gouse, 1983.

Lippy, Charles H. *Twentieth-Century Shapers of American Popular Religion*. New York: Greenwood Press, 1989. 494 pp.

Merton, Thomas. *The Collected Poems of Thomas Merton*. New York: New Directions, 1977.

_____. *The Literary Essays of Thomas Merton*. Edited by Father Patrick Hart. New York: Farrar, Straus and Giroux, 1977.

_____. *Mystics and Zen Masters*. New York: Farrar, Straus and Giroux, 1967.

_____. *The Secular Journal of Thomas Merton*. Edited by Brother Patrick Hart. New York: New Directions, 1981.

_____. *Seeds of Contemplation*. Norfolk, CT: New Directions, 1949. 201 pp.

_____. *The Seven Storey Mountain*. New York: Harcourt Brace, 1948. Rept. New York: New American Library, 1948. 412 pp.

_____. *The Waters of Siloe*. New York: Harcourt, Brace and Company, 1949. 377 pp.

_____. *Zen and the Birds of Appetite*. New York: New Directions, 1968.

Nouwen, Henri J. *Thomas Merton, Contemplative Critic*. San Francisco, CA: Harper & Row, 1981.

Shannon, William H. *Thomas Merton's Dark Path*. New York: Farrar, Straus, Giroux, 1981. 245 pp.

★629★
METAXAKIS, Meletios
Archbishop, Greek Orthodox Archdiocese of North and South America
b. Sep. 21, 1871, Parsa Greece
d. Jul. 27, 1935

Archbishop Meletios Metaxakis, who formally organized the Greek Orthodox Archdiocese of North and South America, was raised on the island of Crete. He entered the priesthood of the Greek Orthodox Church and was serving as a bishop in 1917 when the Greek Revolution drove King Constantine from the throne. Metropolitan Theokleitos, Archbishop of Athens, anathematized Venizelos, the leader of the revolution, and the members of his revolutionary government. The church's ecclesiastical tribunal, however, found that Theokleitos acted against canon law and deposed him. Bishop Meletios was elected to become the new Metropolitan of Athens and All Greece.

In 1918, under Meletios' leadership, the church's synod voted to organize the church in America. At that time all Orthodox Christians in America were under the jurisdiction of the Russian Orthodox Church (the first Orthodox Church body to establish work in the country). In light of the growing numbers of Greek-Americans, however, Archbishop Meletios traveled to the United States to survey the situation. He began to organize the Greek parishes and appointed Alexander, the titular bishop of Rodostolou, as the synod legate to administer the work.

In 1920 elections were held in Greece. The royalists won and Venizelos was thrown out of office. Very quickly Meletios was also deposed. Still claiming his position as head of the Church of Greece, he came to America and took control of the work in the United States. He held the first clergy-laity conference in September 1921, which led to the formal establishment of the Archdiocese on September 17 of that year. This act not only separated the American Greek Orthodox from the Russian Church, but also from the Greek Church as well. He then established Saint Athanasios Greek Orthodox Seminary for the training of priests.

In November 1921, after only three months in America, Meletios was elected ecumenical patriarch, the unofficial head of all of the Eastern Orthodox Church. He moved quickly to reverse the Act of 1908 by which the Church of Greece claimed authority for Greek Americans. He thus placed the American church under the authority of the Ecumenical Patriarchate. In 1922 the Greek Orthodox Archdiocese was officially recognized, and Meletios devised a unique governing system whereby the American church would be led by three bishops under the archbishop.

The remaining years of the decade were ones of intense strife as Meletios' supporters in America had to contend with royalist Bishop Germanos Troianos, who came to America to organize a rival diocesan structure. The split was not healed until 1931 with the arrival of Archbishop Athenagoras following an agreement worked out by Meletios and the new Metropolitan of Athens.

Sources:

Efthimiou, Miltiades B., and George A. Christopoulos, eds. *History of the Greek Orthodox Church in America*. New York: Greek Orthodox Archdiocese of North and South America, 1984.

Litsas, Fotios K. *A Companion to the Greek Orthodox Church*. New York: Department of Communication, Greek Orthodox Archdiocese of North and South America, 1984. 324 pp.

★630★
METELICA, Michael J.
Founder, Renaissance Church of Beauty
b. Jul. 27, 1950, Turner Falls, Massachusetts

Michael J. Metelica is the founder of the Renaissance Church of Beauty, a church as well as an intentional community that was a large and influential movement in upstate Massachusetts in the mid-1970s. His family had immigrated to America from Russia early in the century. He was raised in the Episcopal Church and had a noticeable bent toward spirituality and piety even as a youth. Dropping out of school in 1967, Metelica traveled across the country in an attempt to find "true brotherhood." He also became involved in the drug culture. Returning to Massachusetts, he resolved to stop using drugs and to devote his energies to renewing the social order.

Metelica took up residence in a treehouse adjacent to his family property, and the nucleus of a fellowship began to gather around him. As the community developed, they moved several times and rules evolved, such as no drugs, violence, or promiscuity. They also experienced a good deal of antagonism from the societal mainstream. Initially a counter-cultural commune, Renaissance eventually developed a spiritual dimension that we might now identify as "New Age" (e.g., an emphasis on love, the belief in reincarnation, and so forth).

They were finally able to establish themselves in a stable location and initiated a number of business enterprises. Several of them were quite successful, such as Renaissance Greeting Cards and Michaelworks Productions. As with a number of other communal groups, the very success of the community was its undoing. They became so large that an intimate sense of community was difficult, and their economic success led them to conform more to the social mainstream. As a result of these changes, members began leaving in large numbers in 1977 and 1978, although enough people remained for the community to continue to the present, though on a much reduced scale.

Sources:
Borowski, Karol. *Attempting an Alternative Society: A Sociological Study of a Selected Communal-Revitalization Movement in the United States.* Volume II of the Communal Societies and Utopian Studies Book Series. Norwood, PA: Norwood Editions, 1984. 281 pp.

★631★
MEYER, Albert Gregory
Cardinal, Roman Catholic Church
b. Mar. 9, 1903, Milwaukee, Wisconsin
d. Apr. 9, 1965, Chicago, Illinois

Albert Gregory Meyer, a cardinal in the Roman Catholic Church, was the son of Peter and Matilda Thelen Meyer. His father was a businessman. Meyer attended the local parochial school at St. Mary's Church, which was run by the School Sisters of Notre Dame. During his teen years, he lived in the German-American community in a tense atmosphere created by America's entry into World War I. Albert finished his studies at St. Mary's, did a year at Marquette Academy, and entered St. Joseph's Seminary. Finishing in 1921, he departed for Rome to complete his education at the North American College. He was ordained in 1926 and received his S.T.D the following year. Staying in Rome, he received his S.S.L. degree from the Pontifical Institute in 1929.

After his return to the United States, Meyer was assigned as curate to St. Joseph's Parish in Waukesha, Wisconsin. Then in 1931 he began teaching at St. Joseph's Seminary. He became the seminary's rector in 1937 and the following year became a papal chamberlain with the title of monsignor.

In 1946 Meyer was named the bishop of Superior, Wisconsin. He immediately inaugurated a diocesan expansion program, called a diocesan synod, and established the diocesan Council of Catholic Women. He also created a diocesan edition of the archdiocese of Milwaukee's paper, the *Herald Citizen*. Then in 1953, he was appointed archbishop of Milwaukee. He brought his programs from Superior with him and soon inaugurated an expansion program in the archdiocese. Over the decade new churches and schools were

built, old ones renovated and enlarged, and colleges expanded. Meyer encouraged the growth of lay organizations and lay participation in church life.

However, in 1958, just as the Milwaukee program was securely in place, Meyer was called to Chicago as its new archbishop. In 1959 he was named a cardinal. He arrived in Chicago just as the Civil Rights Movement was beginning. He vigorously supported the movement and carried out his predecessor's efforts to desegregate all Catholic institutions. As in Superior and Milwaukee, he instituted an expansion program which led to the creation of 30 new parishes and the construction of 73 churches, 69 elementary schools, 15 high schools, and a number of social service facilities.

Meyer was recognized as an intellectual leader within the church. In 1959 he was appointed to the Congregation of the Propagation of the Faith, in 1962 to the Pontifical Commission on Biblical Studies, in 1963 to the commission to revise the canon law, and in 1964 to the Supreme Congregation of the Holy Office.

Meyer emerged as one of the leaders of the American delegation at the Second Vatican Council and was one of its 12 presidents. He made a bold if unsuccessful attempt to place the declaration on religious freedom before the third session of the council even as conservative voices pushed to the fourth session.

Meyer's vigorous efforts at the third session are partially credited with his health failing following that session. Upon his return to Chicago he entered Mercy Hospital and underwent brain surgery from which he did not recover.

Sources:
Delaney, John J. *Dictionary of American Catholic Biography.* Garden City, NY: Doubleday & Company, 1988. 621 pp.
Thornton, Francis Beauchesne. *Our American Princes.* New York: G. P. Putnam's Sons, 1963. 319 pp.

★632★
MEYER, Lucy Rider
Deaconess, Methodist Episcopal Church
b. Sep. 1, 1849, New Haven, Vermont
d. Mar. 16, 1922, Chicago, Illinois

Lucy Rider Meyer, the founder of the deaconess movement within American Methodism, was the daughter of Richard D. and Jane Child Rider. Raised a Baptist, she was converted to Methodism as a teenager in a revival meeting. Urged by her mother to get an education, she attended Oberlin College (A.B., 1872) and then spent some time at the Philadelphia Medical School. In the mid-1870s she met **John Heyl Vincent**, a Methodist bishop-to-be and one of the leaders in the Sunday school movement. At his urging she began to write Sunday school literature. She also worked as a science teacher, and her first book, *The Fairy Land of Chemistry* (187-), grew out of these scientific interests. In 1879 she became a professor of chemistry at McKendree College in Lebanon, Illinois. The following year she was awarded her M.A. from Oberlin.

1880 became a turning point in her life. She was a delegate to the World Sunday School Convention in London and upon her return took a job as field secretary for the Illinois Sunday School Association. Her first popular book grew out of her Sunday school work, *Children's Meetings and How to Conduct Them* (1884). Her four years with the association convinced her of the need for a training school for women who desired to enter Christian work. Overcoming established opposition to the rise of women, she opened the Chicago Training School (now an integral part of Garrett-Evangelical Theological Seminary) in 1885. That same year she married Dr. Josiah S. Meyer. While leading the school, she decided to finish her medical education and received her M.D. from the Women's Medical College at Northwestern University in 1887.

Following the first graduation in 1887, some of the women decided to stay in Chicago and work in the city under the direction of Meyer. Taking her lead from the Lutherans and the German Methodists, Meyer proposed the creation of an order of deaconesses, which was approved by the 1888 general conference of the Methodist Episcopal Church. Once the deaconesses were in place and growing with each class from the school, the work expanded steadily. One by one as needs were spotted, Meyer presented them to the Rock River Conference of the Methodist Episcopal Church for funding. Over the next years she created Wesley Hospital, a children's home, a senior citizens home, a retired deaconess' home, and several boarding schools. At the end of her life, she had created every benevolent institution supported by the Rock River Conference with the exception of its university and seminary. On behalf of the deaconesses she also wrote several books: *Deaconesses: Biblical, Early Church, European, American* (1890); *Deaconess Stories* (1900); and *Mary North*, a novel (1903).

The last years of her life were spent defending herself and the movement she had created. Every general conference of the Methodist Episcopal Church attempted to take control of the deaconess movement out of her hands and place it under the control of the Women's Home Missionary Society. She fought off the assault successfully and the issue was resolved in 1924 (two years after Meyer's death) with the creation of a Board of Hospitals, Homes, and Deaconess Work which assured the continued autonomy of the deaconess effort.

Her work was acknowledged in 1904 by her election to general conference. Previously, in 1888, women had been elected but the conference refused to seat them. Thus Meyer was among the first group of women seated at a Methodist general conference.

Sources:

Harmon, Nolan B. *The Encyclopedia of World Methodism*. 2 vols. Nashville: United Methodist Publishing House, 1974.

Horton, Isabelle. *High Adventure, Life of Lucy Rider Meyer*. Cincinnati, OH: Methodist Book Concern, 1928. 359 pp.

Meyer, Lucy Rider. *Deaconess Stories*. Chicago: Hope Publishing Co., 1900. 253 pp.

———. *Deaconesses: Biblical, Early Church, European, American*. Chicago: The Message Publishing Company, 1889. 158 pp.

———. *Mary North*. New York: Fleming H. Revell, 1903. 339 pp.

Rider, Lucy J. and Nellie M. Carman. *Children's Meetings and How to Conduct Them*. New York: Fleming H. Revell Company, 1884. 207 pp.

★633★
Archbishop MICHAEL
Archbishop, Greek Orthodox Archdiocese of North and South America
b. May 27, 1892, Marinia Greece
d. Jul. 13, 1958, New York, New York

Archbishop Michael, for nine years the head of the Greek Orthodox Archdiocese of North and South America, was raised in Greece and attended the Ecumenical Patriarch's theological school at Halki. After graduation he spent four years (1915-1919) in Russia studying at the theological schools in Kiev and St. Petersburg. At the time of the Russian Revolution he moved to Constantinople and in 1919 was ordained deacon and priest. He served in a variety of pastoral and administrative positions in both Greece and Turkey during the next decade, but in 1927 was appointed dean of St. Sophia Greek Orthodox Cathedral in London, England. During the next 12 years he developed as an ecumenical leader and frequently was called upon to represent the Patriarchate in ecumenical gatherings. In 1939 he was named Metropolitan of Corinth and consecrated as a bishop.

After a decade in Corinth, Metropolitan Michael was chosen to succeed Archbishop Athenagoras as head of the church in America. (Athenagoras was chosen as the church's new ecumenical pa-

triarch.) The new archbishop inherited a united church that under Athengoras' guidance had successfully passed through its first generation. As it matured, however, it faced a new set of concerns. Archbishop Michael turned first to the problem of loss of identity by the youth growing up in a foreign land. He created the Greek Orthodox Youth of America, which enrolled over 30,000 members during the 1950s. He also initiated the founding of the first Greek-American high school. To put the archdiocese on a sound financial footing he created the Dekadollarion plan, which mobilized lay support for the archdiocese's programs. He also founded the first home for the aged to serve Greek-Americans.

Within the archdiocese, many have seen Archbishop Michael's greatest accomplishment in the securing of official government recognition of the Orthodox community. During his years in office, 26 states passed resolutions recognizing the presence of Orthodoxy as a significant religious community in America. Michael led the church into full participation in both the National Council of Churches (founded in 1950) and the World Council of Churches (founded in 1948). He served a term as president of the World Council of Churches. He died in 1958 and was succeeded by **Archbishop Iakovos**.

Sources:

"Death Comes to the Archbishop." *Orthodox Observer* (August 1958).

Efthimiou, Miltiades B., and George A. Christopoulos, eds. *History of the Greek Orthodox Church in America*. New York: Greek Orthodox Archdiocese of North and South America, 1984.

Papaioannau, George. *Patriarch Athenagoras I and the Greek Orthodox Church of North and South America*. Boston: Boston University School of Theology, 1976. 283 pp.

★634★
MICHAUX, Lightfoot Solomon
Founder, Gospel Spreading Church
b. Nov. 7, 1884, Newport News, Virginia
d. Oct. 20, 1968, Washington, District of Columbia

Elder Lightfoot Solomon Michaux was the son of a successful merchant and became a merchant himself at an early age. Although brought up in the Baptist church, Michaux became interested in the Holiness Movement, and eventually joined a church affiliated with the Church of God (Holiness). He was a committed member, becoming the congregation's secretary-treasurer. Michaux was eventually ordained as a minister. In 1906 he married Mary Eliza Pauline.

After World War I, Michaux formed the Gospel Spreading Tabernacle Building Association to support his ministry. In 1921 Michaux split with **Charles P. Jones**, founder of the Church of God (Holiness), and formed an independent church. In 1928 Elder Michaux moved to Washington, D.C. He had developed a sense of the potential of radio broadcasting while still in Virginia, and the year after his arrival in the nation's capital he initiated a highly successful radio ministry at WJSV. When the station was purchased by CBS, he was able to expand his outreach until his message was being broadcast on 50 stations that touched the lives of an estimated 25 million listeners. His program was also carried by shortwave so that he was able to reach an international audience. He was the first black minister to receive such broad exposure. His sermons blended Holiness teachings with "positive thinking" themes. Michaux's ministry published a magazine, the title of which, *Happy News*, reflected this blend.

Other congregations of Michaux's church were formed in response to his radio program, although this aspect of his ministry began to decline in importance by the mid-1930s. Partially as a result of his widespread popularity, he was able to gain friends in the Washington establishment, and received support from both Eleanor Roosevelt and Mamie Eisenhower (President Eisenhower became an honorary member of his church). Elder Michaux was particularly active in community work, developing programs to assist orphans, the aged, and the unemployed. He also initiated a black housing project, Mayfair Mansions. Michaux reorganized his church under the new corporate name Gospel Spreading Church shortly before his death in 1968.

Sources:

Lark, Pauline, ed. *Sparks from the Anvil of Elder Michaux*. New York: Vantage Press, 1950. 139 pp.
Webb, Lilian Ashcraft. *About My Father's Business: The Life of Elder Michaux*. Westport, CT: Greenwood Press, 1981. 210 pp.

★ 635 ★
MILES, William Henry
Bishop, Christian Methodist Episcopal Church
b. Dec. 26, 1828, Springfield, Kentucky
d. Nov. 14, 1892, Louisville, Kentucky

William Henry Miles, the first bishop of the Christian Methodist Episcopal Church, was born in slavery. In 1854 his owner, Mary Miles, died and granted him freedom as a clause in her will. However, due to various legal problems, including laws against manumission, he did not formally receive his freedom until 1864. In the meantime, in 1855, he converted to Christianity and joined the Methodist Episcopal Church, South. He was licensed to preach in 1857 and was ordained a deacon by Bishop James Osgood Andrew in 1859. Following the Civil War, Miles, who had by this time married, moved with his family to Ohio, but returned to Kentucky in 1867. There he joined the African Methodist Episcopal Zion Church and almost immediately became one of their leading preachers. He was appointed as pastor of the Center Street African Methodist Episcopal Zion Church in Louisville and was elected as a delegate to the 1868 general conference.

Just as quickly as Miles had risen to a position of prominence in the African Methodist Episcopal Zion Church, he experienced some difficulty (of an unknown nature). In 1868 he rejected his appointment as a general missionary, joined the newly formed Kentucky Colored Conference of the Methodist Episcopal Church, South, and became pastor of the church in Lexington, Kentucky. The predominantly white Southern Methodists were at the time organizing the black former members into what would become a new black denomination. In 1869 Miles became the pastor of the church at Mt. Sterling and presiding elder of the Mt. Sterling district. In 1870 he was also elected as a reserve delegate to the organizational session of the new church. At the conference, he assumed a leadership role in the various debates which attended the formation process and, though only a reserve delegate, he was the first person elected to the bishopric. It is noted that Miles' election was aided by his previously having been a member of the African Methodist Episcopal Zion Church and the need for leadership to counter the movement of it and the African Methodist Episcopal Church among southern Blacks. Miles was consecrated as a bishop by Bishops Robert Paine and **Holland N. McTyeire** of the Methodist Episcopal Church, South.

Miles was called to lead a church of poor people in a land ravaged by war. Miles turned his energy to the organization of the new church. Among his early tasks was calling for a special general conference following the unexpected death of Bishop R. H. Vanderhorst in 1873. However, by the time the regular session of the general conference gathered in 1874, he had been able to solidify the financial support of the Methodist Episcopal Church, South who donated both money and property to the new church. A publishing house, which would take a number of years to become self-supporting, and a periodical, *The Christian Index*, had also been established. Fifteen annual conferences serving approximately 75,000 members were in existence by 1874. That year Miles proposed the establishment of a school for the training of ministerial

leadership, and though the plan failed, in later years a school would be founded in Birmingham, Alabama, and named for him.

Miles is best remembered during the 22 years of his leadership for his ability to interpret the position of the church, which refused to repudiate the white church out of which it was organized, and to handle the attacks of the African Methodists who condemned the church as merely a continuation of the institution of slavery.

Sources:

Harris, Eula Wallace and Maxie Harris Craig. *Christian Methodist Episcopal Church through the Years*. Revised by Eula Wallace Harris and Naomi Ruth Patterson. Jackson, TN: Christian Methodist Episcopal Church Publishing House, 1965. 121 pp.
Lakey, Othal Hawthorne. *The History of the Christian Methodist Episcopal Church*. Memphis, TN: The Christian Methodist Episcopal Church Publishing House, 1985.

★ 636 ★
MILITZ, Annie Rix
Founder, Homes of Truth
b. Mar. 1856, California
d. Jun. 22, 1924, Los Angeles, California

Annie Rix Militz, founder of the Homes of Truth, one of the earliest New Thought denominations, was the first child of Hale and Annie P. Rix. She was born in the gold rush days of early California. Little is known of the first two decades of her life. She emerged as a school teacher at about the age of 20 in San Francisco, where, in April 1887, **Emma Curtis Hopkins**, the founder of the New Thought movement, had journeyed to teach a class in what was then still called "Christian Science." Both Annie and her sister, Harriet Hale Rix attended the class, during which Annie was healed both of a migraine headache that had periodically plagued her and deafness in one ear. On her way home from the class she announced to Harriet, "I have found my lifes work."

Before the end of the year Annie, Harriet, and Sadie Gorie founded the Christian Science Home, soon to be renamed the Home of Truth. In 1890 Annie left San Francisco to pursue advanced studies with Emma Curtis Hopkins at her Christian Science Theological Seminary in Chicago. She graduated and was ordained by Hopkins on June 1, 1981, the same time that Charles and **Mary Caroline Fillmore**, founders of the Unity School of Christianity, were also ordained. Annie joined the seminary staff as "Professor of Scripture Revelation," and during the winter of 1892, married Paul Militz, whom she had met at the school. In 1893 Militz and her husband moved back to California, and, finding the work in the Bay area thriving (a second Home of Truth had been formed in Alameda that year), established themselves in Los Angeles in 1894.

During her years at the seminary, Militz began to write for Charles and Myrtle Fillmore, founders of the Unity movement. In 1893 she initiated a regular column in their magazine, *Unity*, a commentary on the popular International Sunday School lessons. In these columns she gave voice to what were to become increasingly popular Unity teachings. For example, she introduced the idea of Jesus' twelve apostles representing 12 powers inherent in humans. After she left the seminary, her relationship to the Fillmores continued to strengthen. They publicized the Home of Truth and she wrote lessons and articles for *Unity*. In 1898, at **Charles Fillmore**'s request, Militz began a series of 12 lessons presenting a systematic outline of her basic teachings. Published the next year as *Primary Lessons in Christian Living and Healing*, her first book served for a decade as a Unity textbook and for many decades as the basic text for the Homes of Truth. Two other books written by Militz in the first decades of the twentieth century also began as *Unity* articles: *Spiritual Housekeeping* (1910) and *Prosperity through Knowledge and Power of the Mind* (1913).

By 1911 Militz's work with the Homes of Truth, which had spread along the West Coast and eastward to Chicago, led her to found her own magazine, *Master Mind*, and her own publishing enterprise, the Master Mind Publishing Company, from which a stream of books and pamphlets began to appear. During the next 13 years, Homes of Truth were established northward into Canada and eastward to Boston. These were years of triumph for Militz, who became a world traveler and spokesperson for the New Thought movement. In 1914 and 1915 she made her second world tour, which included the 1914 meeting of the International New Thought Alliance (INTA) in London and culminated in the 1915 Alliance meetings (in connection with the Panama-Pacific Exposition) in San Francisco. Following the success of the tour and exposition, in 1916 Militz founded the University of Christ in Los Angeles to train New Thought leaders.

During her years of affiliation with the Fillmores, Militz departed from their teaching of reincarnation in favor of a doctrine of ascension. Thus when she died, her immediate followers refused to bury her, waiting instead for her body to come back to life. When, several days later, this had not occurred, the body was cremated.

Militz, while not well-known today, built one of the early New Thought congregational associations. By the mid-1980s only one center, in Alameda, California, remained. Through her popular writings, however, she became an important source for the teachings of other metaphysical groups, including the "I AM" Religious Activity, which later adopted her central teachings concerning the "I AM" (or God-self) and ascension, and the practice of saying decrees, a form of positive prayer.

Sources:

Deering, Mary. "Annie Rix Militz." *The New Thought Bulletin* 28, 3 (Summer 1945): 5-8.
Militz, Annie Rix. *Primary Lessons in Christian Living and Healing.* New York: Absolute Press, 1904. 181 pp.
———. *Prosperity through Knowledge and Power of the Mind.* Los Angeles: Master Mind Publishing Co., 1913. Rev. ed as *Both Riches and Honor.* Kansas City, MO: Unity, 1959. 131 pp.
———. *Spiritual Housekeeping.* New York: Absolute Press, 1910. 90 pp.
Simmons, John Kent. *The Ascension of Annie Rix Militz and the Home(s) of Truth: Perfection Meets Paradise in Early 19th Century Los Angeles.* Ph.D. diss. Santa Barbara, CA: University of California—Santa Barbara, 1987. 285 pp.

★ 637 ★
MILLER, D. D.
Bishop, Mennonite Church
b. Dec. 10, 1864, Lagrange County, Indiana
d. 1944, Indiana

D. D. Miller, a prominent minister-evangelist among the Amish and Mennonite people, was the son of Daniel P. and Anna Hershberger Miller. Growing up in Indiana, he first prepared himself to teach school. In the 1880s he moved to Cass County, Missouri, to pursue his profession. While there he joined the Amish Mennonite Church. A few years later he returned to his home community in Indiana and there affiliated with the Forks Amish Mennonite Church. In 1889 he married Nettie Hostetler, and all of their 11 children who reached maturity also served as school teachers for at least part of their adult life.

In 1890 Miller was selected as deacon for his local congregation, and the following year was chosen as minister. In 1906 he was made a bishop and the next year adopted the plain clothes which were common but not demanded by the Amish Mennonite Church at this time. As a bishop, he traveled widely as a speaker and Bible teacher among both the Amish Mennonites and the members of the Mennonite Church. He frequently contributed articles to the *Gospel Herald*, the magazine of the Mennonite Church. He served

in a variety of leadership capacities with the Indiana-Michigan Amish Mennonite Conference.

During his first decade as bishop, Miller supported and worked for a merger between the Amish Mennonite Church and the Mennonite Church, a merger which took place in 1916. Following the merger he was the first moderator of the united Indiana-Michigan Conference of the Mennonite Church, a position to which he was elected a number of times. Nationally he was active with the Mennonite General Conference, the Mennonite Board of Education, and the Mennonite Board of Missions and Charities. He served as president of the latter for fifteen years (1920-1935). He continued as an active member of the church until his health failed him suddenly in his 80th year.

Sources:

The Mennonite Encyclopedia. 4 vols. Scottdale, PA: The Mennonite Publishing House, 1955.

★ 638 ★
MILLER, Daniel Long
Editor and Publisher, Church of the Brethren
b. Oct. 5, 1841, Hagerstown, Maryland
d. Jun. 8, 1921, Huntington, Pennsylvania

Daniel Long Miller, a minister with the Church of the Brethren, was best known for his many writings. He was the son of Abram and Catherine Long Miller, and grew up working at his father's mill. Miller had little formal schooling; he supplemented his education by reading numerous books. In 1860 he moved to Ogle County, Illinois, where he worked with his brother. In 1868 he married Elizabeth Talley and soon afterward became a prosperous grocer. In 1879 he became part owner and served as secretary and business manager of Mt. Morris College, a school of the German Baptist Brethren (that is, the Church of the Brethren). Though formally uneducated, he served as president of the school for two years (1881-1883).

In 1882 Miller, while still president of Mt. Morris, went into business with Joseph Amick and founded the Brethren Publishing Company. They published *Brethren at Work*, an independent Brethren periodical, and numerous tracts, pamphlets, and other pieces of Brethren literature. In 1883 *Brethren at Work* merged with *The Primitive Christian*, another independent periodical, to become *The Gospel Messenger*. The *Messenger* became Miller's life work. He became managing editor in 1885 and editor in chief in 1891, a position he held for the rest of his life. He became a Brethren minister in 1887 and was ordained an elder in 1891. During his many years as editor Miller emerged as one of the most powerful voices in the church. He was seen as a stable voice amid controversy and a strong advocate of the official church programs, Sunday schools, higher education, and missions.

For a number of years as the Brethren Publishing Company prospered, Miller had argued that the church as a whole should own it, but action on his suggestion was slow. Finally in 1897 Miller turned the Brethren Publishing Company over to the Church of the Brethren, at which time it became the Brethren Press. Over the years Miller also authored a number of popular books, the first being a travelogue of his journeys in Europe and the Holy Land which originally appeared as articles in the *Messenger*: *Letters from Europe and Bible Lands* (1884). He later authored *Eternal Verities* (1902) and *Some Who Led* (1912), a biographical volume of Brethren leaders.

Miller moved to Pennsylvania toward the end of his life and lived his last days with his sister Anna Martha Miller.

Sources:

Durnbaugh, Donald F., ed. *The Brethren Encyclopedia.* 3 vols. Philadelphia: The Brethren Encyclopedia, Inc., 1983.

Bates, Bess Royer. *The Life of D. L. Miller.* Elgin, IL: Brethren Publishing Co., 1924. 340 pp.

Miller, D. L. *Eternal Verities.* Elgin, IL: Brethren Publishing House, 1902. 370 pp.

———. *Letters from Europe and Bible Lands.* Mt. Morris, IL: Brethren Publishing Co., 1884. 438 pp.

———. *Some Who Led.* Elgin, IL: Brethren Publishing House, 1912. 273 pp.

★639★
MILLER, John Allen
Educator, Brethren Church
b. Aug. 2, 1866, Rossville, Indiana
d. Mar. 27, 1935, Ashland, Ohio

John Allen Miller, college president and church executive for the Brethren Church, was the son of William Miller, a school teacher. Miller took up his father's profession as the age of 17. A year later he joined the Brethren Church at Edan Mills, Indiana. He was baptized and a few months later called to the ministry. He began preaching a week later. In 1887 he entered Ashland College. During the early 1880s the Church of the Brethren had experienced a split, and the more liberal faction had formed the Brethren Church and gained control of Ashland College. After receiving his B.A. in 1890, Miller became pastor of Glenford, Ohio, and continued his studies at Hillsdale College. In 1892 he began a two-year pastorate at Elkhart, Indiana. In 1894 he moved to Ashland, Ohio, as president of Ashland College. In 1896 the college closed due to insufficient income, and Miller used the occasion to finish his schooling at Hiram College, from which he received his B.D. and M.A. in 1898.

In 1898 Miller married Clara Worst and, with the encouragement of the church leaders, reopened Ashland College. He served as president for the next eight years. In 1906 he became dean of the Bible department, which served as the seminary for the Brethren Church, and continued in that post until 1930 when the Ashland Theological Seminary was formally constituted and he became dean of the seminary. He also served as pastor of Ashland First Brethren Church during most of these years.

By the time the college was reopened, Miller had emerged as one of the most powerful national leaders within the Brethren Church and he served on almost every important committee of the church established during the next 40 years. He was elected moderator of the general conference in 1907 and 1924. As a leader of the church he became deeply involved in the doctrinal controversy which shook the church in the early twentieth century. He was appointed to serve on the committee which considered the church's position on the infallibility of the Bible and later on the committee that formulated the "Message of the Brethren Ministry," a conservative theological document which represented the unofficial consensus of Brethren Church belief. The church is non-creedal and accepted the Bible as its standard of faith and teachings.

Miller was especially interested in foreign missions. He became a member of the Missionary Committee of the Brethren Church and served on its executive committee from the time of its founding in 1900. In 1903 he began a 32-year tenure as the committee's president. In 1901 he became the first president of the board of directors of the Brethren Home located in Flora, Indiana.

At the time of Miller's retirement from the college in 1933, the church was involved in a dispute between liberals and conservatives which would soon split it. Miller did not live to see the formal schism, but is remembered as possessing a winsome spirit which made him a friend to both parties in the dispute.

Sources:

Durnbaugh, Donald F., ed. *The Brethren Encyclopedia.* 3 vols. Philadelphia: The Brethren Encyclopedia, Inc., 1983.

★640★
MILLER, Joseph Quinter
Minister and Ecumenist, Church of the Brethren
b. 1899, Mt. Sidney, Virginia
d. 1983

Joseph Quinter Miller, for over a quarter of a century an executive with the Federal Council of Churches, and the continuing National Council of Churches, was the son of Minnie Cline and Samuel Daniel Miller. He grew up in Virginia and attended Bridgewater College (B.A., 1921). He was ordained as a minister with the Church of the Brethren and continued his education at Boston University (M.R.E., 1923). After graduation he became the city superintendent of religious education for the Cleveland, Ohio, Church Federation. In 1924 he married Mae Hooker.

After four years in Cleveland, Miller returned to Boston University as an instructor in religious education. In 1929 he moved to Connecticut as the executive secretary of the New Haven Council of Religious Education. While there he was able to begin work on a Ph.D. at Yale. In 1930 he became executive secretary of both the Connecticut Council of Religious Education and the Connecticut Council of Churches. In 1931 he completed his Ph.D. at Yale.

At the time Miller moved to Connecticut, the larger ecumenical movement in the United States was recognizing a major problem. Ecumenical organizations, especially at the state level, had emerged around specific issues. In many states a council for religious education competed with the council of churches for a limited amount of funds which hindered each from operating effectively. Miller was the first state executive able to effect a merger between two such councils. It became a model for the rest of the country. He remained as state executive for the merged Council of Churches and Religious Education through the 1930s. While there he wrote his first book: *Community Organization in Religious Education* (1932).

In 1938 Miller assumed additional duties as executive secretary for the field department of the Federal Council of Churches. In 1948 he left Connecticut to associate general secretary of the Federal Council. He retained a similar executive position with the National Council of Churches which superseded the Federal Council in 1950. In that position he helped form almost a thousand local and state councils of churches. He also authored several additional books summarizing his administrative knowledge: *Foundation Principles in the Philosophy of a Council of Churches* (1954) and *Christian Unity: Its Relevance to a Community* (1957). Miller retired from the National Council in 1966. In 1963 he had become president of the Church Executive Development Board, and remained in that office until 1970.

Sources:

Durnbaugh, Donald F., ed. *The Brethren Encyclopedia.* 3 vols. Philadelphia: The Brethren Encyclopedia, Inc., 1983.

Miller, J. Quinter. *Christian Unity: Its Relevance to the Community.* Shenandoah Publishing House, 1957. 122 pp.

———. *Community Organization in Religious Education.* New Haven, CT: Yale University Press, 1932.

★641★
MILLS, Benjamin Fay
Liberal Presbyterian Minister
b. Jun. 4, 1857, Rahway, New Jersey
d. May 1, 1916, Grand Rapids, Michigan

Benjamin Fay Mills led two lives, first as a prominent evangelist and then as a liberal social gospel advocate. He was the son of Thornton A. and Anna Cook Mills. His mother was once a missionary in India and his grandfather had been elected the moderator of the Presbyterian Church in the U.S.A.. Mills attended Lake Forest University from which he graduated in 1879. While a student he had been ordained to the ministry in 1878. After graduation he married Mary Russell Hill and served several brief pastorates in New England. In 1884 he was called as minister of the Congregational Church at West Rutland, Vermont.

Soon after Mills' arrival at West Rutland, a series of events altered the course of his pastoral career. He had great success in preaching, and a revival spread among his parishoners. As a result he was asked to conduct a series of special services at Middlebury, Vermont. The church and the students at Middlebury College responded with more than 300 conversions. Mills felt led into revival work and in 1886 resigned to become a full-time evangelist. For the next decade he was one of the most sought-after preachers in the cities of America. He authored several books, including *Power from On High* (1890); *A Message to Mothers* (1892); *Victory through Surrender* (1892); and *God's World and Other Sermons* (1894).

While traveling the sawdust trail, Mills became acquainted with George D. Herron, a professor at Grinnell College. Herron began to present Mills with the social claims of liberal Protestantism. Mills responded by beginning to question the value of his evangelistic successes. Invited to address the World's Parliament of Religions, the pioneering international interfaith gathering at Chicago in 1893, he used the occasion to question publicly the course of his life. In 1895 he accepted a pastorate at Albany, New York, and used the time to reevaluate his commitments. By 1897 he had left his evangelist work behind and was traveling regularly to Boston to speak on social reform and religious ideals. He also lost his belief in the exclusivity of biblical revelation and began to associate himself with the American Unitarian Association (AUA). In 1899 he became minister of the First Unitarian Church in Oakland, California. One element of his evangelistic days remained, however, and he continued to travel widely preaching, but now on social gospel themes. In 1904 he broke with the Unitarians and founded the Los Angeles Fellowship, an independent liberal congregation which he led. In 1911 he left Los Angeles and founded a second similar congregation, the Chicago Fellowship. During his liberal phase, Mills authored two important statements of his perspective, *Twentieth Century Religion* (1898) and *The Divine Adventure* (1905).

In 1915 Mills experienced what was described as a reconversion to Christianity. He was admitted back into the Presbyterian ministry through the Chicago Presbytery, and he returned to his evangelistic endeavors during the last year of his life. Shortly before his death he authored three articles for *The Advance*, a Presbyterian periodical, attempting to explain his recent change of mind and heart.

Sources:

Dictionary of American Biography. 20 vols. and 7 supps. New York: Charles Scribner's Sons, 1928-1936, 1944-1981.

Mills, Benjamin F. *The Divine Adventure.* Los Angeles: Fellowship Publishing Company, 1905. 244 pp.

_____. *God's World, and Other Sermons.* New York: Fleming H. Revell, 1894. 322 pp.

_____. *A Message to Mothers.* New York: Fleming H. Revell, 1892. 32 pp.

_____. *Power from On High.* New York: Fleming H. Revell, 1890. 32 pp.

_____. *Victory through Surrender.* New York: Fleming H. Revell, 1892. 82 pp.

★ 642 ★

MISHRA, Ramamurti S.

Founder, Intercosmic Center of Spiritual Awareness (I.C.S.A.)
b. Benares India

Dr. Ramamurti S. Mishra, more recently known as Swami Brahmananda Saraswati, is the founder of the Intercosmic Center of Spiritual Awareness (I.C.S.A.), formerly the International Center for Self-Analysis. He was born near Benares, into a Brahmin family

with a long tradition of interest in yoga. His mother, a Sanskrit scholar and a spiritual teacher with many disciples, served as his first guru. His father was a justice in the Supreme Court of India and also had a deep knowledge of astrology. Mishra had many renowned teachers, including the past president of India, Dr. S. S. Radhakrishnan, and the famous saint Sri **Ramana Maharshi**.

Dr. Mishra's first college degree was in Sanskrit studies at Benares Hindu University. He also studied medicine, eventually becoming chief of service in internal medicine and surgery at Podar Medical College and Hospital. He traveled to the West for advanced study in medicine, first to England and later to Canada's McGill Neurological Institute at Montreal, joining the staff at Queen Mary Veterans Hospital in their Department of Neurology and Psychiatry. He came to the United States in 1956 to continue his research on Western healing methods, where he was on the staff of New York University's Post-Graduate Medical College, Bellevue Hospital, Bird S. Coler Memorial Hospital, Metropolitan Hospital, and Rhode Island State Hospital. During this time Dr. Mishra also gave instruction on the philosophy and practice of yoga, inspiring the opening of such groups as the Yoga Society of New York in 1958.

Dr. Mishra gave up the practice of medicine in 1965 to devote himself to the teaching of yoga. He also became a serious student of acupuncture. When **Bhaktivedanta Swami Prabhupada**, the founder of the International Society for Krishna Consciousness (ISKCON), first came to New York, Mishra took him in, in spite of the philosophical differences between them. At his Ananda Ashrama in Monroe, New York, he briefly experimented with LSD during the early years of the drug culture. Dr. Mishra, now Swami Brahmananda Saraswati, took sannyas (that is, became a renunciate in the Hindu tradition) in the early 1980s. He was prompted to this action by the experience of a stroke in November of 1983 that left him partially paralyzed, an experience that he claims left him fully enlightened. A gifted writer, he has authored such works as *Fundamentals of Yoga* (1959); *Textbook of Yoga Psychology* (1963); and *Self Analysis and Self Knowledge* (1977).

Sources:

Albert, Mimi. "Shri Brahmananda Sarasvati." *Yoga Journal* 83 (November/December 1988): 27-32.

Biography of Dr. Ramamurti S. Mishra. Monroe, NY: Ananda Ashram, n.d. 4 pp.

Melton, J. Gordon *The Encyclopedia of American Religions.* 3d ed. Detroit: Gale Research Inc.,1988. 1102 pp.

Mishra, Rammurti. *Fundamentals of Yoga.* New York: Julian Press, 1959. Rept: New York: Lancer Books, 1969. 254 pp.

_____. *Self Analysis and Self Knowledge.* Lakemont, GA: CSA Press, 1977. 272 pp.

_____. *Textbook of Yoga Psychology.* New York: Julian Press, 1963. 538 pp.

"Turning Tragedy into Teaching Awareness: Stroke Victim Swami Brahmananda Tests a Yogi's Mind-Over-Brain." *Hinduism Today* 10, 7 (July 1988): 1, 5.

★ 643 ★

MOISE, Mary

Pentecostal Social Worker
Founder, Moise Faith Home
b. 1850, Richmond, Virginia
d. Sep. 12, 1930, St. Louis, Missouri

Mary Moise, founder of the Moise Faith Home in St. Louis, Missouri, was born Maria Christina Gill, the daughter of a prominent southern family. She was raised an Episcopalian. In the 1880s, she moved with her husband, Albert Welborne Moise, a Confederate Army veteran, to St. Louis, Missouri. At the encouragement of Bishop **Daniel S. Tuttle**, she began to volunteer her home as an Episcopal mission for women in trouble, either through prostitution, financial distress, or other unfortunate circumstances. While Moise became enthusiastic for her work, her husband developed a distinctly critical perspective. In 1905, their children grown, he arranged an amicable separation.

Around the turn of the century, Moise's work began to earn her a certain amount of fame. In 1904 she was honored at the St. Louis World's Fair for her efforts. In 1905 she founded the Door of Hope Rescue Mission and served as its director. Two years later Seeley Kinney established the first Pentecostal work in the city, and at some point in the next year or two, Moise became a Pentecostal.

In 1909 Moise moved into a large brick structure on Washington Street in St. Louis. She was soon joined by Leonore O. (Mother Mary) Barnes and her husband, Victor Barnes. Mother Mary Barnes was a skillful evangelist who shared Moise's social vision and used her abilities to serve the new Christian Faith Home.

Moise remained independent of any particular Pentecostal group and was a friend to all of them. She closely associated with Roswell Flowers, superintendent of the Assemblies of God, and with **Evangeline Booth** of the Salvation Army. In the 1920s, however, she accepted two beliefs that put her at odds with many Pentecostal leaders. First, she was among the early converts to the so-called "Oneness teaching," which denied the doctrine of the Trinity and called for "baptism in the name of Jesus Only." She became good friends with Iranian Pentecostal Oneness missionary Andrew Urshan, who was affiliated with what is today known as the United Pentecostal Church. Second, during the 1920s she came to believe that Christians need never die if they had faith to live until Jesus returned.

Moise lived to her 80th year. Her three decades of work befriending wayward women had made her a celebrity in St. Louis. She had the support of the community, which had given generously to her work. Even her ex-husband had assisted in raising funds and supplies for the mission. At various times, Moise had been able to open other missions around the city, but in the end only the first center remained. It closed in about 1940.

Sources:

Burgess, Stanley M., Gary B. McGee, and Patrick H. Alexander, eds. *Dictionary of Pentecostal and Charismatic Movements.* Grand Rapids, MI: Regency Reference Library, Zondervan Publishing House, 1988. 914 pp.

Warner, Wayne. "Mother Mary Moise of St. Louis." *Assemblies of God Heritage* 6, 1 (Spring 1966): 6-7, 13.

★ 644 ★
MONROE, Eugene Crosby
Founder, Shiloh Trust
b. May 30, 1880, Sherman, New York
d. Mar. 25, 1961, Sherman, New York

Eugene Crosby Monroe, the founder of Shiloh Trust, was the son of Anne Elizabeth Crosby and Edward William Monroe. He attended the schools of his community and completed his formal studies through the LaSalle Correspondence School. In 1902 he married Grace Marjorie Blanchard. In 1906 he began a career as a draftsman and engineer, working for several companies. By 1921 he had become a branch manager with the Van Dorn Iron Works. However, through his adult life Monroe had felt a call to the ministry. Thus, while working with the Van Dorn Iron Works in Philadelphia, Pennsylvania, he affiliated first with the Highway Mission and then in 1923 was ordained as a minister by the Apostolic Church, a British Pentecostal church which had recently begun work in the United States. He became a part-time pastor while making his living in a secular job.

In 1928 Van Dorn phased out the branch Monroe headed. To make a living, he then founded the Monroe Artcraft Shop which specialized in the restoration of old furniture. In 1942 medical problems forced him to retire from both his secular occupation and church work. He moved back to his hometown and purchased a farm. Unable to resume his preaching, he began to write. Over the next years, as his writings circulated, young adults began to arrive at his home to receive his ministry. As a small community developed, Shiloh Trust was created with the stated purpose of rehabilitating the mind, body and spirit of people. The group began to support itself with several cottage businesses, the first being a bakery. Monroe led daily spiritual meetings of the community. Soon a support network of nonresidents who lived across the United States and Canada developed.

In 1948 Monroe's wife died. The next year he married Frieda Weigand McFarland. He continued to lead the community until his death in 1961. In 1986 the community relocated to Sulfur Springs, Arkansas, where it continues to the present.

Sources:

Mathieu, Barbara. "The Shiloh Farms Community." In Jon Wagner, ed. *Sex Roles in Contemporary American Communes.* Bloomington, IN: Indiana University Press, 1982. 242 pp.

★ 645 ★
MONTGOMERY, Carrie Judd
Pentecostal Writer and Teacher, Assemblies of God
b. Apr. 8, 1858, Buffalo, New York
d. 1945, Oakland, California

Carrie Judd Montgomery, whose lengthy career as a writer, editor, and leader of faith homes spanning more than half a century, was born Carrie Judd to a pious Episcopal couple in Buffalo, New York. She was confirmed in the church, and attended Buffalo Normal School preparing for a life of teaching. However, at school one day she had an accident and became an invalid. She was healed through the ministrations of a black woman, Mrs. Edward Mix. Out of the experience she wrote a book, *The Prayer of Peace* (1880), which recounted her experience and advocated prayers for physical healing. The book was read by Albert Benjamin Simpson, a Presbyterian minister who would later found the Christian and Missionary Alliance (CMA) out of his own healing experience. He brought her into contact with the other pioneers who were promoting the healing ideal at the end of the nineteenth century.

In 1881 Judd began a public ministry by launching a periodical, *Triumphs of Faith*. She also started speaking at healing conventions, giving the story of her healing, but she did not limit herself to mere testimony. In 1885, when Simpson formally organized the Christian Missionary Alliance, Judd became recording secretary of the board. Judd also turned the room in which she had been healed into a prayer room and opened Faith Rest Cottage in Buffalo as a place to pray for and comfort the sick.

In 1890 Judd moved to Oakland, California. Soon after the move she married George S. Montgomery, a wealthy businessman. They organized a Christian and Missionary Alliance congregation in 1891, but soon developed an additional affiliation with the Salvation Army. They owned land in Oakland upon which Carrie established the Home of Peace in 1893, similar to Faith Rest Cottage, but destined to serve as a center for a variety of ministries. In 1894 they established Shalom Training School for missionaries. In 1905 they opened an orphanage which was given to the Salvation Army in 1908. They also gave land to the army to build a rescue home for girls.

When the Pentecostal revival broke out in Los Angeles in 1906, the Montgomerys were among the first to hear of it. Carrie began to pray for the baptism of the Holy Spirit and in 1908 had the experience of speaking in tongues, which Pentecostals consider the evidence of having received the baptism. Remarkably, even though the alliance was not Pentecostal, as Montgomery shifted her allegiance, she was able to remain on good relations with the alliance leadership and continued to speak at their meetings. In 1914, however, she became a charter member of the Assemblies of God, now one of the largest Pentecostal denominations in America.

Montgomery became a major force in spreading the Pentecostal revival. Evidence of the revival was featured in her magazine. She also authored several books, including *Secrets of Victory* (1921) and *Heart Melody* (1922). Her last book was her autobiography, *Under His Wings* (1936).

The Home of Peace continues to this day. Montgomery's magazine continued into the 1970s.

Sources:

Burgess, Stanley M., Gary B. McGee, and Patrick H. Alexander, eds. *Dictionary of Pentecostal and Charismatic Movements*. Grand Rapids, MI: Regency Reference Library, Zondervan Publishing House, 1988. 914 pp.

Montgomery, Carrie Judd. *Heart Melody*. Oakland, CA: Office of *Triumphs of Faith*, 1922. 102 pp.

———. *Heart Whisperings*. Mills College, CA: Office of *Triumphs of Faith*, 1897. 73 pp.

———. *The Life of Praise*.

———. *Lilies from the Veil of Thought*. Buffalo, NY: H. H. Otis, 1878. 109 pp.

———. *The Prayer of Faith*. Buffalo, NY: H. H. Otis, 1880. 163 pp.

———. *Secrets of Victory*. Oakland, CA: Office of Triumphs of Faith, 1921. 188 pp.

———. *Under His Wings*. Oakland, CA: Office of *Triumphs of Faith*, 1936. 256 pp.

★646★
MONTGOMERY, Helen Barrett

Bible Translator and President, Northern Baptist Convention
b. Jul. 31, 1861, Kingsville, Ohio
d. Oct. 19, 1934, Summit, New Jersey

Helen Barrett Montgomery, the first woman elected to head a major denomination in the United States, was born into a Baptist family, the daughter of Emily Barrows and Adoniram Judson Barrett. Her upbringing was thoroughly Baptist. Her father attended the University of Rochester in New York while Nellie, as she was called then, was still a pre-teen, and in 1870 he began to teach at the Collegiate Institute in Rochester. He graduated from Rochester Theological Seminary in 1876. He became pastor of the Lake Avenue Baptist Church in Rochester, which he served until his death in 1889. Helen attended Wellesley College from 1880 to 1884 and then taught at the Rochester Free Academy and Wellesley Preparatory School prior to her marriage to successful businessman William A. Montgomery in 1887.

Following her marriage, Montgomery settled into her father's church and organized a large women's bible class, which she continued to teach for many years. In 1892 she was licensed to preach by the congregation. In 1893 she became the first president of the Women's Educational and Industrial Union, through which she launched a number of campaigns for civic improvement. The union persuaded the local schools to introduce manual training and art classes into the curriculum. It made legal aid available to the poor, oversaw the development of the first public playground, and built a settlement house in the Italian neighborhood. The union backed movement in the city aimed at improving government and bureaucratic effectiveness in last years of the century. As a result, the school board was reorganized, with Montgomery as its first female member. Contemporaneously, she was working in a major campaign to raise money to support women students at the University of Rochester.

During the early years of the new century, Montgomery developed a strong interest in overseas missions. She authored two study books, *Christus Redemptor* (1906) and *Western Woman in Eastern Lands* (1919). In 1913 she toured the Orient to see the state of the missions firsthand. In 1914 her interest led to her appointment as president of the Woman's American Baptist Foreign Mis-

sion Society. During a part of her tenure (1917-1918) she also served as president of the ecumenical National Federation of Women's Boards of Foreign Missions. Without giving up her job at the mission board, she was elected president of the Northern Baptist Convention (now the American Baptist Churches)in 1921.

In addition to all of her other accomplishments, she also rendered one of the first translations of the New Testament into modern English. *The Centenary Translation of the New Testament* appeared in 1924.

Sources:

James, Edward T., ed. *Notable American Women, 1607-1950: A Biographical Dictionary*. 3 vols. Cambridge, MA: Harvard University Press, Belknap Press, 1971.

Montgomery, Helen Barrett. *The Bible and Missions*. West Medford, CT: Central Committee of the United Study of Foreign Missions, 1920. 240 pp.

———. *Centenary Translation of the New Testament*. Philadelphia: American Baptist Publication Society, 1924.

———. *Christus Redemptor*. New York: Macmillan, 1906. 282 pp.

———. *Following the Sunrise*. Philadelphia: American Baptist Publication Society, 1913. 291 pp.

———. *Helen Barrett Montgomery: From Campus to World Citizen*. New York: Fleming H. Revell, 1940. 140 pp.

———. *The Preaching Value of Missions*. Philadelphia: Judson Press, 1931. 196 pp.

———. *The Story of Jesus*. Philadelphia: Judson Press, 1927.

———. *Western Women in Eastern Lands*. New York: Macmillan, 1910. 286 pp.

★647★
MOODY, Dwight Lyman Ryther

Independent Christian Fundamentalist Evangelist
b. Feb. 5, 1837, East Northfield, Massachusetts
d. Dec. 22, 1899, East Northfield, Massachusetts

Dwight Lyman Ryther Moody, the greatest Protestant Christian evangelist of the late nineteenth century, was the sixth of seven children born to Edwin Moody and Betsy Holton Moody. His father was a mason and died when Moody was still a child. His mother was a devout Unitarian, and Moody was baptized in the Unitarian church. He had little formal schooling, and in 1854 he left home to find work in Boston. He lived with his uncle and became a shoe clerk. The next year he became a born again Christian under the guidance of his Sunday school teacher.

Moody joined the Plymouth Congregational Church and under their direction began to gather children to form a Sunday school class. He brought in enough for several classes and then developed a separate Sunday school which met on the city's north side. It eventually grew to about 1,500 in attendance.

In 1860 Moody quit his sales position and entered full-time work as an evangelist, although he was never ordained. His first love was work with youth, and he became a regular speaker at the Sunday school conventions. He supported the YMCA and became their national president in 1865. It was at a YMCA meeting in Indianapolis, Indiana, in 1870 that he was impressed by the singing of **Ira David Sankey** and persuaded Sankey to join him in evangelistic work.

In 1863 Moody erected a church on Chicago's north side. It burned in the great fire of 1871, and he rebuilt. In 1871 he both began a new phase of his evangelical career and launched the great era of urban evangelism in America with the first of his city-wide cooperative church evangelism campaigns. Then in 1873, he teamed with Sankey for the memorable two-year tour of England, Scotland, and Ireland. Relatively unknown when they left, both men returned to the United States as international celebrities. They toured the country together during the remaining years of their lives. Among the more famous campaigns was the Chicago meeting in 1893 in response to the pioneering interfaith gathering at the World's Parliament of Religions.

In the wake of his success, Moody was able to create and support a number of associated ministries. In 1879 he established Northfield Seminary for girls and two years later the Mount Herman School for boys. In 1886 he opened the Chicago Evangelization Society, one of the first Bible schools in America, and the forerunner of the Moody Bible Institute. In 1880 he began a series of summer conferences on the campus of the schools in Northfield, Massachusetts, out of which the Student Volunteer Movement emerged in 1886. In 1895 he founded the Colportage Association to publish inexpensive Christian literature. Through it all he was able to author a modest number of books, most developed from his sermons and Bible teaching classes.

Moody died while conducting his last campaign in Kansas City in 1899. Soon after his death, the work he created in Chicago found permanent form in the Moody Bible Institute, Moody Press, and the Moody Memorial Church. During his career, hundreds of thousands of people converted to Christianity. Much of his success lay in his ability to work ecumenically with all of the churches in an urban community. Much of that success was denied his successors, as churches separated under the impact of the fundamentalist-modernist controversy in the early twentieth century. Evangelists associated with Moody Bible Institute identified themselves as fundamentalist and refused to cooperate with mainline Protestant churches which had accepted modernist theological ideals.

Sources:

Curtis, Richard K. *They Called Him Mister Moody*. Garden City, NY: Doubleday & Company, 1962. 378 pp.

Day, Richard Ellsworth. *Bush Aglow*. Grand Rapids, MI: Baker Book House, 1977. 340 pp.

DeRemer, Bernard R. *Moody Bible Institute, A Pictorial History*. Chicago: Moody Press, 1960. 128 pp.

Hartzler, H. B. *Moody in Chicago*. Chicago: Bible Institute Colportage Association, 1894. 255 pp.

Moody, Dwight L. *Heaven*. Chicago: Moody Press, n.d. 127 pp.

———. *How to Study the Bible*. Philadelphia: Henry Altemus Company, 1897. 31 pp.

———. *Men of the Bible*. Chicago: Bible Institute Colportage Association, 1898. 126 pp.

———. *Notes from My Bible*. Chicago: Fleming H. Revell Company, 1895. 236 pp.

———. *Secret Power*. Chicago: F. H. Revell, 1881. 116 pp.

Moody, Paul D. and A. P. Fritt. *The Shorter Life of D. L. Moody*. Chicago: Bible Institute Colportage Association, 1900. 125 pp.

Moody, William R. *D. L. Moody*. New York: Macmillan Company, 1931. 556 pp.

Moyer, Elgin S., ed. *Who Was Who in Church History*. Chicago: Moody Press, 1968.

Powell, Emma Moody. *Heavenly Destiny*. Chicago: Moody Press, 1943. 343 pp.

★648★
MOON, Sun Myung
Founder, Holy Spirit Association for the Unification of World Christianity
b. Jan. 6, 1920, Cheong-ju, Pyeong-an Buk-do Republic of Korea

Sun Myung Moon, the founder of the Holy Spirit Association for the Unification of World Christianity, popularly referred to as the Unification Church, grew up in Korea. When he was ten years old his parents converted to Christianity and became active in the Presbyterian Church. According to later accounts, on Easter Day, 1936 he was visited by Jesus and told that God had chosen him to establish the kingdom of Heaven on earth. To all outward appearances his next years were normal. He attended high school in Seoul and in 1941, following his graduation, he enrolled in Waseka University, in Japan. He married. However, during these same years he was

continually receiving revelations from angels and the spirits of religious leaders such as the Buddha and Moses, and he engaged in a successful spiritual warfare with the forces of Satan.

After World War II Moon became a full-time preacher. In 1946, having received a revelation to move to Pyeong-yang in northern Korea, he founded the Kwang-ya Church but made little progress because of his arrest and imprisonment. Liberated in 1950 he migrated south to Pusan, lived in a shack on the side of a mountain, and again began to preach. In 1953 he moved to Seoul and the following year officially founded the Holy Spirit Association for the Unification of World Christianity. Some of his revelations were written down and published in 1957 as *The Divine Principle*. (*The Divine Principle* has gone through a number of revisions and its text is still in flux.)

The sanctity of marriage is an important part of Moon's teachings. Unfortunately, his first marriage was not in tune with his mission in life, and he and his wife separated. In 1960 he married Hak Ja Han. She has fulfilled her role as mother to Moon's children and symbolically to the Unification Church members. She also assists publicly in the ritual leadership of the church.

While Moon led the church in Korea, in 1959 he sent disciples to the United States to spread the movement. Moon made his first tour of the United States in 1965. During this initial visit, he spoke to the small group of church members, had a sitting with Spiritualist medium **Arthur A. Ford**, and had his picture taken with Dwight D. Eisenhower. In 1969 he made a world tour that included a wedding of thirteen couples in Washington, D.C. and his first visit to Europe. In 1971-1972, he made a second world tour which ended with a national speaking engagement and his settling in the United States. Here he began to build the Unification Church through a steady recruitment of members and the establishment of numerous organizations to gain the support of non-church members who, nevertheless, agreed with some of his ideals. The most successful of these organizations, the International Conference for the Unity of the Sciences, focused upon his call for a return to absolute values in the midst of a relativistic world. Some of the speeches Moon delivered during this period were compiled and published as his early books in English. Moon's speeches are preserved and issued individually in a series called *The Master Speaks*. Because of the controversial nature of some of his remarks, and the use by critics of the church of what church leaders feel are quotations taken out of context, this series has not been accessible to the general public.

As the church began to grow, it and Moon became the target of an intense attack supported primarily by the parents and families of people who had joined the Unification Church. He was accused of teaching his leaders to recruit using a high level of deceit and of brainwashing converts. Through the years since, Moon has been the center of intense controversy. Supporters praised him for his leadership. He founded many organizations and built numerous institutions. Critics denounced him as a false messiah and tried numerous ways to stop him. The most successful attack against him led to his conviction on tax evasion, in spite of the support of a wide variety of religious leaders from **Jerry Falwell** to **Joseph Lowrey**. Exhausting all appeals, he served 13 months (1984-1985) in prison, after which he again assumed his rigorous schedule. His response to his prison experience was a two volume book, *God's Warning to the World* (1985). While yet the target of frequent attacks, as the church has become a familiar part of the urban landscape, he has been able to see the tension with the surrounding Western culture gradually lessen.

Sources:

Barker, Eileen. *The Making of a Moonie*. Oxford: Basil Blackwell, 1984. 305 pp.

Mickler, Michael L. *The Unification Church in America: A Bibliography and Research Guide*. New York: Garland Publishing Company, 1987. 227 pp.

Moon, Sun Myung. *Christianity in Crisis: New Hope*. New York: HSA-UWC, 1974. 123 pp.

_____. *God's Warning to the World*. 2 vols. New York: HSA-UWC, 1985.

_____. *The New Future of Christianity*. Washington, DC: Unification Church International, 1974. 144 pp.

_____. *New Hope*. New York: Holy Spirit Association for the Unification of World Christianity, 1973. 103 pp.

_____. *A Prophet Speaks Today*. New York: HSA-UWC Publications, 1975. 159 pp.

Sontag, Frederick. *Sun Myung Moon and the Unification Church*. Nashville, TN: Abingdon Press, 1977. 224 pp.

★ 649 ★
MOONEY, Edward Francis
Cardinal, Roman Catholic Church
b. May 9, 1882, Mount Savage, Maryland
d. Oct. 25, 1958, Rome Italy

Edward Francis Mooney, a cardinal in the Roman Catholic Church, was the son of Thomas Mooney and Sarah Henegan Mooney, both Irish immigrants. When Mooney was but five, the family moved to Youngstown, Ohio, where his father worked in a steel tube plant. After his father's death during his teen years, Mooney worked in the bakery his mother established. Mooney decided to enter the priesthood and was sent to St. Charles College, Ellicott, Maryland (B.A., 1905), and St. Mary's Seminary, Baltimore (M.A., 1906). He then was able to attend the North American College in Rome where he received his Ph.D. in 1907 and his D.D. in 1909. He was ordained in Rome in 1909.

Upon his return to the United States, Mooney was assigned as a professor in dogmatic theology at St. Mary's Seminary in Cleveland, Ohio. After seven years, in 1916 he became headmaster of the Cathedral Latin School and in 1922 pastor of St. Patrick's Church in Youngstown. Less than a year after his assignment to Youngstown, he was called to Rome to become spiritual director of the North American College. He attracted the attention of the Curia, and in 1926, when a troubleshooter was needed in India, he was named apostolic delegate to India and consecrated as titular bishop of Irenopolis. In India he had to deal with the problem of Portuguese control over various conclaves of Indian Catholics. His work helped end missionary rule of three native dioceses. While there, he also brought two Indian Jacobite bishops, Mar Ivanios and Mar Theophilus, and their following into the Roman Catholic Church. He also opened 11 new missionary territories.

Following his successful years in India, Mooney was sent as apostolic delegate to Japan in 1931. His main accomplishment was resolving the conflict in which Catholics as Japanese citizens had been mandated to attend rites at Shinto shrines.

In 1933 Mooney was appointed archbishop of Rochester, New York, where he was to develop a whole new role as a spokesperson for Catholicism on social issues. He served on the administrative board of the National Catholic Welfare Conference. He chaired the Social Action Department (1933-1937) and presided over the administrative board for two terms (1935 and 1941-1945). During World War II, he became the first chairman of the Bishop's War Emergency and Relief Committee, the first president of the National Catholic Community Service, and the co-chairman of the Clergy Committee of the United Services Organization (USO).

When Detroit was elevated to an archdiocese, he became the first archbishop in 1937. His social commitments were immediately put to the test with the drive to organize the auto workers union. He backed the union efforts, and advised Catholic workers to join the union. He also faced an archdiocese heavily in debt. He brought it back into financial solvency and then oversaw its growth as the number of Catholics more than doubled in the burgeoning archdiocese. He also had to face the problem of the controversy growing around one of his most popular priests, Fr. **Charles E. Coughlin**, whose radio program and commentary on contemporary affairs had developed an anti-Semitic and pro-Nazi stance. While moving cautiously, Mooney applied pressure to Coughlin that eventually led to the discontinuance of the radio show.

After World War II, Mooney's work was recognized by Rome in his being made a cardinal in 1946, at the same service in which **John Joseph Glennon** was equally honored. Mooney died in Rome while attending the conclave of bishops that elected Pope John XXIII.

Sources:

Delaney, John J. *Dictionary of American Catholic Biography*. Garden City, NY: Doubleday & Company, 1988. 621 pp.

Thornton, Francis Beauchesne. *Our American Princes*. New York: G. P. Putnam's Sons, 1963. 319 pp.

★ 650 ★
MOORE, Arthur James
Bishop, Methodist Episcopal Church, South
b. Dec. 26, 1888, Argyle, Georgia
d. Jun. 30, 1974, Atlanta, Georgia

Arthur James Moore, a bishop of the Methodist Episcopal Church, South, was the son of John Spencer and Emma Victoria Moore. Not particularly religious as a youth, he was converted during his college days at Emory College, and began to preach a short time afterward. He never attended seminary, though he later received a number of honorary degrees as his accomplishments mounted. He married Mattie T. McDonald in 1906.

Moore joined the South Georgia Conference of the Methodist Episcopal Church, South in 1909 and was ordained a deacon in 1912. He had become known for his oratorical skills, and the same year he was ordained to the diaconate, he began an eight-year appointment as a general evangelist. He was ordained an elder in 1914. After his year in evangelical work, he became the pastor of Travis Park Methodist Church in San Antonio, Texas. After six years in Texas, he moved to First Methodist Church of Birmingham, Alabama, in 1926—traditionally one of the most influential pulpits in southern Methodism—where he remained until his election to the episcopacy in 1930.

The new bishop was assigned the Pacific Coast area for four years and then was placed in charge of the church's missionary activities that included work in China, Japan, Korea, the Belgian Congo, Belgium, Czechoslovakia, and Poland. He threw his abilities into the work and led a campaign to rekindle the missionary zeal that he saw waning in southern Methodism and to rid the mission board of a post-depression debt of $700,000. He remained with the missionary conferences through the merger of the Methodist Episcopal Church, South into the Methodist Church (1939-1968). In 1940 he was assigned to the Atlanta area (as bishop over the North Georgia and South Georgia conferences) and at the same time became president of the new church's board of missions. He retained both positions until his retirement in 1960.

Moore's interest in missions dominated his episcopal career. He was frequently sent by the council of bishops to represent their interests in world hot spots. He also served a number of other administrative positions, including a period as president of the council of bishops (1951-52). During his active career he also found time to write, penning a number of books, most on missionary topics. These included *The Sound of the Trumpets* (1934); *Central Certainties* (1943); *The Mighty Savior* (1952); and *Fight On! Fear Not!* (1962). His last book was an autobiography, *Bishop to All People*, published in 1973.

Following his retirement, he returned to active status as a churchwide evangelist. For a number of years, he remained a popular speaker until hobbled by age and failing health.

Sources:

Clark, Elmer T. *Arthur James Moore, World Evangelist.* New York: Board of Missions of the Methodist Church, 1960. 45 pp.

Harmon, Nolan B. *The Encyclopedia of World Methodism.* 2 vols. Nashville: United Methodist Publishing House, 1974.

Moore, Arthur J. *Bishop to All People.* Nashville, TN: Abingdon Press, 1973. 144 pp.

_____. *Central Certainties.* Nashville, TN: Abingdon-Cokesbury, 1943. 142 pp.

_____. *Christ After Chaos.* New York: Board of Missions and Church Extension, the Methodist Church, 1944. 127 pp.

_____. *Christ and Our Country.* New York: Board of Missions, the Methodist Church, 1945. 126 pp.

_____. *Fight On! Fear Not!* New York: Abingdon Press, 1962. 144 pp.

_____. *Immortal Tidings in Mortal Hands.* Nashville, TN: Abingdon-Cokesbury, 1953. 128 pp.

_____. *The Mighty Savior.* New York: Abingdon-Cokesbury, 1952. 154 pp.

_____. *The Sound of Trumpets.* Nashville, TN: General Commission on Benevolences, Methodist Episcopal Church, South, 1934. 77 pp.

★651★
MOORE, Joanna Patterson
Pioneer Baptist Home Missionary
b. Sep. 26, 1832, Clarion County, Pennsylvania
d. Apr. 15, 1916, Selma, Alabama

Joanna Patterson Moore, the first person commissioned by the Woman's American Baptist Home Missionary Society, was the daughter of Irish immigrants. Her father, an Episcopalian, raised her in that church, but her mother, a Presbyterian, also taught her the Westminister Catechism. At the age of 15, Moore began to teach in a private school. Joanna had experienced a conversion at the age of nine, but claimed that she had backslidden from her faith. Thus in 1852 she made a public dedication at a Baptist revival meeting and soon afterward joined the Baptist Church. Two years later she felt a call to the mission field, and she was urged to seek more education before pursuing her goal.

In 1858 the family moved to Illinois. She was able to pick up some schooling, but in 1862 she entered Rockford (Illinois) Seminary. In 1863, in the wake of the Emancipation Proclamation amid the Civil War, she found her calling as a missionary to former slaves. The American Baptist Home Missionary Society gave her a commission, but no salary. In November 1863, with support from her home church at Belvidere, Illinois, she began working on an island in the Mississippi River. In 1864 she moved to Helena, Arkansas, and worked at an orphanage just established by the Quakers. In 1868 she transferred to another Quaker orphanage at Lauderdale, Mississippi, arriving just prior to an outbreak of cholera. In 1869 she returned to Illinois for several years to be near her mother, who had become ill.

During the 1860s, the American Baptists, who had been reluctant to commission women, changed their policy and began actively to recruit them. Thus in the 1870s three regional women's missionary organizations were formed. Moore was close at hand when, in 1871, women in the Midwest formed the Woman's Foreign Mission Society of the West. She was commissioned by the society and in 1873 moved to Louisiana to resume her missionary work among the Blacks. Then in 1877 the Woman's American Baptist Home Missionary Society was formed, and she was the first person commissioned by the new society. They sent her four assistants, and she was able to extend the work through Louisiana and to neighboring states. She also started a home for elderly women in New Orleans.

After 10 years in New Orleans, she began to move her headquarters. In 1884, in Morgan City, Louisiana, she began the Bible Band to distribute Bibles in the black community. The following year, while living in Plaquemine, Louisiana, she began *Hope* magazine. She continued as editor for the next 26 years and wrote the Bible lessons for it until her death. In 1887 she began a training school for black women, but in 1890 was run out of town by the White League, a white supremacist group which opposed her work among Blacks.

Moore moved to Little Rock, Arkansas, in 1891, and began the Sunshine Bands, an effort to establish Sunday schools in people's homes to reach children not in church. The following year she began what is generally regarded as her greatest contribution to the evangelization of southern Blacks, the Fireside School. Using her magazine, she began to promote a time of daily prayer and study in the home of each family. The family reported monthly to their church which in turn reported to Moore. Beyond the material in the magazine, Moore compiled and wrote a three-year curriculum. This program was turned over to the Woman's Home Missionary Society in 1906 and continued for another generation.

In 1894 Moore moved to Nashville, Tennessee, where she resided for the next 22 years. Much of her time was spent in writing and editing. She penned the story of her work, *In Christ's Stead*, in 1903. She also traveled widely, encouraging the work and raising money. During such a trip in 1916, while in Selma, Alabama, she caught bronchitis and died at 84 years of age.

Sources:

Hull, Eleanor. *Women Who Carried the Good News.* Valley Forge, PA: Judson Press, 1975. 96 pp.

Moore, Joanna P. *In Christ's Stead.* Chicago: Woman's American Baptist Home Mission Society, 1903.

Stewart, Walter Sinclair. *Later Baptist Missionaries and Pioneers.* Philadelphia: The Judson Press, 1928. 268 pp.

★652★
MOREHOUSE, Henry Lyman
Home Missionary Secretary, American Baptists
b. Oct. 2, 1834, Stanfordville, New York
d. May 5, 1917, Brooklyn, New York

Henry Lyman Morehouse, the outstanding home missionary executive for the American Baptists at the end of the nineteenth century, was the son of Seth S. and Emma Bentley Morehouse. He was raised in western New York and attended the Genesee Wesleyan Seminary, which prepared him for the University of Rochester (B.A., 1858) and Rochester Theological Seminary. He finished his education as the Civil War was in its initial stages. He was ordained in 1864 after his call to East Saginaw, Michigan, where he served as pastor for nine years. In 1873 he returned to Rochester, New York, to serve six years at the East Avenue Baptist Church.

In 1879 Morehouse left the pastorate to begin his 38-year stay with the American Baptist Home Mission Society. He became corresponding secretary of the society, a post he retained until 1917, except for the period from 1893 to 1902 when he served as the society's field secretary. He made his task one of further extending the work of the society which had largely recovered from the effects of the war. During his tenure, he succeeded in increasing the work and the budget of the society ninefold, to almost one million dollars annually. He extended the work of the society across America, and publicized it in his first book, *Baptist Home Missions in America* (1883).

The only area in which Morehouse's efforts were blunted was in some parts of the South where the Southern Baptist Convention had begun to develop its mission program. Prior to the formation of the Southern Baptist Convention, and throughout its first generation as it faced the problems of organization and the devastation of the war, the American Baptists had continued to support home mission projects in the South. In the decades after the war they expanded them. However, during the tenure of its new secretary, **Isaac Taylor Tichenor** (1882-1899), the Southern Baptist Convention demanded and was largely given hegemony over work in the South. Morehouse had more than enough work left in the West.

As a second major contribution to the American Baptists, Morehouse promoted the organization of the American Baptist Education Society, which took the lead in the development of the program of higher education for the denomination. From 1893 to 1902 he served as the new society's corresponding secretary along with his duties at the Home Mission Society.

Morehouse was unsuccessful in his efforts to lessen the effects of the schism which had divided Northern and Southern Baptists in 1845 (resulting in the formation of the Southern Baptist Convention). He proposed the formation of a general convention of Baptists of North America, but the plan never found widespread support. More successful was his work for employment benefits for ministers and missionaries. He was instrumental in having the denomination, by that time renamed the Northern Baptist Convention, establish a Ministers and Missionaries Benefit Board, over which he served as president from 1911 until 1917.

Morehouse wrote a second book during his years with the missionary society, *History of Seventy-five Years of the First Baptist Church, Brooklyn* (1898). He also became a staunch supporter of American Baptist membership and Federal Council of Churches. He remained in office until he died in 1917. Morehouse never married.

Sources:

Crandall, Lathan Augustus. *Henry Lyman Morehouse: A Biography.* Philadelphia: American Baptist Publication Society, 1919. 240 pp.
Dictionary of American Biography. 20 vols. and 7 supps. New York: Charles Scribner's Sons, 1928-1936, 1944-1981.
McBeth, H. Leon. *The Baptist Heritage.* Nashville, TN: Broadman Press, 1987. 850 pp.
Morehouse, Henry L. *Baptist Home Missions in America.* Philadelphia: American Baptist Home Missionary Society, 1883.

★653★
MORGAN, Henry Victor
Metaphysical Poet, New Thought
b. Jul. 10, 1865, Napanee, Ontario, Canada
d. Mar. 2, 1952, Tacoma, Washington

Little has been written about the early life of Henry Victor Morgan, for forty years the minister of the independent Church of the Healing Christ in Tacoma, Washington. Morgan grew up in Canada and at some point migrated to the United States. He became a Universalist minister. Early in the twentieth century he married Adda Laine. He also became influenced by New Thought idealism and became an advocate of its philosophy.

Shortly before World War I, Morgan settled in Tacoma, Washington, and founded the Church of the Healing Christ, a Universalist congregation for a number of years prior to its becoming independent. Morgan associated with the New Thought leadership on the West Coast and was a frequent speaker at the various centers and at the annual International New Thought Alliance (INTA) meetings. He also was a frequent contributor to various New Thought periodicals. Morgan operated the Master Christian Healing Circle every morning at 10 A.M. and invited people to join them. Their periodical, *The Master Christian*, tied together their prayer partners and supporters around the country into the Master Christian Fellowship.

Morgan's major contribution to the movement was his poetry. As early as 1911 he authored *Songs of Victory*. Later, after settling in Tacoma, he published many of his poems in *The Master Chris-*

tian and then reprinted collections of them in a number of widely-circulated booklets. Some of his poems were put to music and became an integral part of New Thought's developing hymnology. Among his other poetry books are *Hymns of Health and Gladness: New Words to Old Tunes* (1913) and *The Singing Spirit and Other Poems* (1921).

Morgan was also a popular metaphysical teacher. His lessons in Tacoma were also compiled into a series of booklets. The most substantial of these included: *The Healing Christ: Studies in the Science of Jesus* (1917); *Soul Powers and Privileges* (1920); *The Pathway to Blessedness*; and *The Pathway of Prayer*.

Sources:

Beebe, Tom. *Who's Who in New Thought.* Lakemont, GA: CSA Press, 1977. 318 pp.
Morgan, Henry Victor. *Hymns of Health and Gladness: New Words to Old Tunes.* Tacoma, WA: Master Christian Publishing Co., 1913. 22 pp.
———. *The Pathway of Blessedness.* Chichester, England: Henry Thomas Hamblin, n.d. 48 pp.
———. *The Pathway of Prayer.* Tacoma, WA: Master Christian Publishing Co., n.d. 65 pp.
———. *The Singing Spirit and other Poems.* Tacoma, WA: Master Christian Publishing Co., 1921. 60 pp.
———. *Songs of Victory.* Chicago: The Library Shelf, 1911. n.d.
———. *Soul Powers and Privileges.* Tacoma, WA: Master Christian Publishing Co., n.d. 72 pp.

★654★
MORRIS, Elias C.
President, National Baptist Convention, U.S.A., Inc.
b. May 7, 1855, Springplace, Georgia
d. Sep. 2, 1922, Helena, Arkansas

Elias C. Morris was for almost thirty years the president of the National Baptist Convention. He was born in 1855, the son of former slaves James and Cora Morris. After the Civil War, he moved with his parents first to Chattanooga, Tennessee, and then to Stevenson, Alabama. His parents died by the time he was fourteen, and he subsequently went to live with Rev. Robert Caver. In 1874 he was converted to the Baptist faith. A year later he was called and licensed to preach, though he earned his living as a shoemaker. In 1877 he moved to Helena, Arkansas, where two years later he became the pastor of the Centennial Baptist Church, which he built into one of the largest churches in the state.

At the 1880 Baptist State Convention, Morris was elected secretary, and in 1882 he began a lengthy tenure as president. From this post he organized a company to publish the first black Baptist periodical in the state, *The Arkansas Times*, and he later became the editor of *The People's Friend*. In 1884 he launched the Arkansas Baptist College, served as its president for two years, and then sat on its board of trustees.

At the same time that Morris served as pastor of Centennial Baptist Church and was active in Arkansas state Baptist affairs, he participated in several attempts to establish a national Baptist organization. He worked with the Foreign Mission Convention (organized in 1880) and in the 1890s became president of the American National Baptist Convention, originally organized in 1886. In 1895 these two organizations merged with the National Baptist Educational Convention, which had been organized in 1893 and over which Morris had been elected to preside in 1894. This merger resulted in the formation of the National Baptist Convention. Morris was elected as the first president of the new convention, a post he held for the next 27 years. Morris was among the most vocal of black leaders, calling on his fellow church members to exercise control over their own institutions.

It was Morris' job to lead the convention through its early learning stages. He oversaw the organization of many of the convention's new structures, such as the Baptist Young People's Union and the Women's Auxiliary. He was immediately faced with a schism by members of the former foreign missions board, who set themselves up in competition to the convention. But perhaps the most significant long-term issue he confronted was that of publishing black religious literature.

Morris had been elected by convention delegates who knew of his strong opinions about black Baptists creating their own publications. He led the fight to quickly form a publication society that would publish material written by black authors. The National Baptist Publication Board was created in 1896. The new board, however, was created as an independent corporation whose ties to the unincorporated convention were never clarified. This issue reached a climax in 1915, at which time the convention had incorporated. The membership of the convention continued to support Morris. **Richard Henry Boyd**, the head of the publishing board, left with his supporters. A new publishing board was created.

Morris continued to run the convention until his death in 1922. He is credited with taking the new independent-minded National Baptists and turning them into a unified body.

Sources:

Jackson, J.H. *A Story of Christian Activism: The History of the National Baptist Convention, U.S.A., Inc.* Nashville, TN: Townsend Press, 1980. 790 pp.

Pegues, A.W. *Baptist Ministers and Schools.* Springfield, MA: John Wiley & Sons, 1892. 645 pp.

★ 655 ★
MORRISON, Charles Clayton
Minister, Christian Church (Disciples of Christ)
b. Dec. 4, 1874, Harrison, Ohio
d. Mar. 2, 1966, Chicago, Illinois

Charles Clayton Morrison, a minister in the Christian Church (Disciples of Christ) and the editor of *The Christian Century*, was the son of Anna MacDonald and Hugh T. Morrison. He was ordained as a minister in 1892 at the age of 18. He became the pastor of Clarinda Disciples congregation in Perry, Iowa. He attended Drake University from which he received a B.A. in 1898. He later became pastor of the Monroe Street congregation in Chicago and for two years studied philosophy at the University of Chicago (1902-1904). In 1906 he married Laurel Scott.

In 1908 Morrison purchased *The Christian Century*, a defunct periodical serving the Disciples of Christ, and began to turn it into a broad based liberal Protestant magazine. Morrison nurtured the magazine's appeal by his insistence upon well-written articles and an accompanying editorial concern which highlighted those areas in which religion interacted with culture. He made his impact felt very soon after taking over the magazine with his attacks upon popular evangelist **William A. "Billy" Sunday** whom he charged with religious superficiality. As each world war approached he edged close to pacifism and opposed the entrance of the United States into war. Peace became the subject of one of his early books, *The Outlawry of War: A Constructive Policy for World Peace* (1927). Through the 1930s he supported the implementation of the increasingly obsolete Kellogg-Briand Pact, a major factor in **Reinhold Niebuhr** and others forming *Christianity and Crisis* as a rival voice among liberal Protestants.

From his Disciples of Christ background, Morrison inherited a strong ecumenical vision, though he was critical of the approach of his own denomination, whose ultracongregational organization had proved ecumenically ineffective. Beginning with the World Missionary Conference of 1910, he used *The Century* to promote various alternatives which looked toward the union of the many Christian churches.

As *The Christian Century* prospered, Morrison developed two associated periodicals: *Pulpit*, which he edited from 1929 to 1956,

and *Christendom*, which he edited from 1935 to 1941. He retired from the editorship of *The Christian Century* in 1947 but continued to edit *Pulpit* for another nine years. While Morrison was anchored theologically in the liberal Protestantism of the early twentieth century, his position developed and matured over the decades of his editorship. By the 1940s, reacting to the popularization of Neo-Orthodox theology, he was calling for a "new liberalism." The statement of his mature liberal perspective can be found in his last books, *What Is Christianity?* (1940) and *The Unfinished Reformation* (1953).

Sources:

Bowden, Henry Warner. *Dictionary of American Religious Biography.* Westport, CT: Greenwood Press, 1977. 572 pp.

Morrison, Charles C. *Can Protestantism Win America?* New York: Harper, 1948.

_____. *The Outlawry of War: A Constructive Policy for World Peace.* Chicago: Willett, Clark & Colby, 1927.

_____. *The Social Gospel and the Christian Cultus.* New York: Harpe & Brothers, 1933.

_____. *The Unfinished Reformation.* New York: Freeport, NY: Books for Libraries Press, 1953, 1968.

_____. *What Is Christianity?* New York: Willett, Clark & Co., 1904.

★ 656 ★
MORRISON, Henry Clay
Methodist Minister and Founder, Asbury Theological Seminary
b. Mar. 10, 1857, Bedford, Kentucky
d. Mar. 24, 1942, Elizabeth, Tennessee

Henry Clay Morrison, a Methodist minister remembered for his defense of the doctrine of holiness and his leadership of two of the holiness movement's most important schools, was the son of James S. and Emily Durham Morrison. His Methodist mother had dedicated him to the ministry as an infant and though both his parents died in his early childhood, he eventually lived up to his mother's hope. He experienced a Christian conversion at the age of 13. He later attended Ewing Institute in Perryville, Kentucky, and spent one year at Vanderbilt. He was licensed to preach in 1878 and began serving a Methodist circuit (several churches each too small to afford a full-time minister) the following year. In 1881 he was admitted on trial in the Kentucky Conference of the Methodist Episcopal Church, South. He was ordained deacon in 1886 and elder in 1887. In 1888 he married Laura Bain.

Morrison served various churches in Kentucky, but requested location (withdrawal from full conference membership) in 1890 so he could pursue full-time evangelism. At this time, the holiness movement was peaking, and he had become its enthusiastic supporter. He founded the *Pentecostal Herald*, which he edited for the next 35 years, to serve both the movement and his evangelistic ministry. Holiness doctrine emphasized the possibility of the believer having a second encounter with the Holy Spirit which made him/her perfect in love. Morrison's two decades as an evangelist coincided with the decline within Episcopal Methodism of the holiness movement and its retreat from official favor. While most holiness people left the Methodist Episcopal Church and Methodist Episcopal Church, South, Morrison was among the leading voices who stayed in. At one point in 1904, his over-zealous behavior at his revival services led to his being tried for "contumacious conduct," though he was acquited.

Over the years of his active life, besides editing the *Pentecostal Herald*, Morrison authored approximately 25 books, all of a popular nature, many collections of sermons and articles from the *Herald*. Shortly before his death he finished an autobiographical account, *Some Chapters of My Life Story* (1941). In 1893 his first wife died, and in 1895 he married Geneva Pedlar.

In 1910 he became president of Asbury College, a small school founded in 1895 to serve the holiness movement. While there, in

1923 he established Asbury Theological Seminary and served as its president. He relinquished his duties as president of the college in 1925 (though he served a second term from 1933 to 1940). During his more than three decades at the school he dominated it with his powerful presence and oratory. During his first term as president of the college, in 1914, his second wife died. He married Bettie Whitehead in 1916.

For several generations after Morrison's death, Asbury remained independent, and many future Methodist ministers attended it. However, in the last half of the twentieth century, the Methodist Church (after 1986 the United Methodist Church) became increasingly hostile to its theological perspective, and many of its conferences refused to accept its graduates. In recent years it has been formally recognized by several of the holiness denominations.

Sources:

Harmon, Nolan B. *The Encyclopedia of World Methodism.* 2 vols. Nashville: United Methodist Publishing House, 1974.

Hill, Samuel S., ed. *Encyclopedia of Religion in the South.* Macon, GA: Mercer University Press, 1984. 878 pp.

Morrison, Henry Clay. *The Christ of the Gospels.* New York: Fleming H. Revell Company, 1926. 103 pp.

_____. *Is the World Growing Better; or Is the World Growing Worse?* Louisville, KY: Pentecostal Publishing Co., 1941. 269 pp.

_____. *Life Sketches and Sermons.* Louisville, KY: Pentecostal Publishing Co., 1903. 112 pp.

_____. *The Simple Gospel.* Louisville, KY: Pentecostal Publishing Co., 1919. 436 pp.

_____. *Some Chapters of My Life Story.* Louisville, KY: Pentecostal Publishing Co., 1941. 269 pp.

_____. *Two Lawyers: A Story of the Times.* Louisville, KY: Pentecostal Publishing Co., 1898. 240 pp.

Wesche, P. A. *Henry Clay Morrison, "Crusader Saint".* Nampa, ID: The Author, 1963.

Wimberly, C. F. *A Biographical Sketch of Henry Clay Morrison.* New York: Fleming H. Revell Company, 1922. 214 pp.

★ 657 ★
MOSS, Virginia E.
Pentecostal Educator
b. 1875, Susquehanna, Pennsylvania
d. 1919

Virginia E. Moss, founder of an early Pentecostal bible college, was born into a Methodist family. Her mother was an active worker in the Woman's Christian Temperance Union (W.C.T.U.). Young Virginia was a sickly child, and at age 13 she fell on some ice and suffered permanent spinal damage. However, her poor health did not prevent her from marrying, and in 1899 she moved with her husband to Newark, New Jersey. The next few years were ones of increased incapacitation, and by 1904 she was paralyzed from the waist down.

Later that year, possibly as a result of the ministry of the Christian Missionary Alliance, Moss was completely healed of her paralysis. She consecrated her life to Christian service only to discover that among those who did not receive her healing testimony with great enthusiasm was the local Methodist pastor. She began to meet with a small group who shared her interests, and in 1906 she opened the Door of Hope Mission with a double emphasis on evangelism and healing and on giving assistance to wayward women.

Soon after opening the mission, Moss read of a revival on Azusa Street in Los Angeles which had been characterized by the deeper work of the Holy Spirit. At Azusa, people were being baptized with the Holy Spirit, evidenced by their speaking in tongues. Thus in 1907 she and some of her associates traveled to Nyack, New York, where a group that had been to Azusa were holding meetings for the purpose, according to Moss, "of seeking God, and the baptism of the Holy Ghost and Fire, and speaking in tongues." At Nyack, one member of the group received the baptism of the Holy Spirit,

and subsequently Moss and others received it. In 1908 nightly services were held for any who desired to receive the baptism.

In 1909, feeling led to enlarge the ministry, Moss opened a rest home. In 1910 she purchased property and consolidated her work as the Beulah Heights Assembly in North Bergen, New Jersey. Soon after settling in North Bergen, Moss recalled an unfulfilled wish of her mother to go to India. Moss felt called to open a school to train workers to spread the Pentecostal message around the world. Though opposed by many Pentecostals, who looked upon formal schools as unnecessary, she followed her promptings and opened Beulah Heights Bible and Missionary Training School in 1912. It was one of the first schools to serve the movement.

During the remaining seven years of Moss' life, the school graduated many people who later assumed leadership positions in the quickly developing world Pentecostal ministry. Most became missionaries with the Assemblies of God after its formation in 1914. Eventually the school became associated with the Assemblies and was taken over by the New York-New Jersey District.

Sources:

McGee, Gary B. "Three Notable Women in Pentecostal Ministry." *Assemblies of God Heritage.* 6, 1 (Spring 1986). 3-5, 12, 16.

★ 658 ★
MOTT, John R.
Chairman, Student Volunteer Movement and President, World Council of Churches
President, World Young Men's Christian Association (YMCA)
b. May 25, 1865, Livingston Manor, New York
d. Jan. 31, 1955, Orlando, Florida

John R. Mott, the first president of the World Council of Churches, was the son of John Stitt and Elmira Dodge Mott. His parents gave him no middle name; he would later add the initial. Soon after his birth the family moved to Postville, Iowa, where Mott was raised in a pious Methodist home. He had a conversion experience while attending a revival meeting in February 1879. He joined the Methodist Episcopal Church (now a constituent part of the United Methodist Church) and remained a Methodist all of his life, though his primary Christian commitments would find expressions elsewhere.

Mott entered Upper Iowa University in 1881 for a year. In 1885 he moved to New York to attend Cornell University. At Cornell he encountered the YMCA in which he would remain involved for the rest of his life. In the summer of 1886 he attended the summer conference for young men held by evangelist **Dwight Lyman Ryther Moody** at Mt. Hermon, Massachusetts. He was one of a handful of students at the conference who became concerned with world missions. Through the several weeks of the conference, their concern led 100 attendees, later called the "Mt. Hermon 100," to dedicate their lives to the missionary enterprise. They organized the Student Volunteer Movement for Foreign Missions (S.V.M.) to recruit others for the same cause. Mott was named chairman, a position he held for the next 32 years. Their motto, with which Mott is intimately identified, was "The world for Christ in this generation."

Meanwhile, back at Cornell, Mott built the YMCA chapter into the largest in the country and attracted the attention of the national leadership. Following his graduation in 1888 he was offered a position as general secretary of the intercollegiate YMCA. In his job he was encouraged to integrate his work with the concerns of the S.V.M. A roving student evangelist, he began to emerge as one of the most important leaders, first nationally, then internationally, just as the early twentieth-century ecumenical world Protestant missionary push began.

In 1891 Mott married Leila Ada White and that same year made his first trip to England. The trip was an initial step leading to the organization of the World's Student Christian Federation (W.S.C.F.) in 1895. Mott was named its general secretary. He set out around the world and by 1897 had formed W.S.C.F. units in 10 countries. The trip became the subject of his first book, *Strategic Points in the World's Conquest* (1897). In 1901 he was named associate general secretary of the International Committee of the Y.M.C.A. and given responsibility for directing the organization's world expansion. His life became a constant routine of travel, speaking, writing, and organizing on behalf of the Y.M.C.A, the S.V.M., and the W.S.C.F. Among his books from this period were *Evangelization of the World in This Generation* (1900); *The Future Leadership of the Church* (1908); *The Present World Situation* (1914); and *Confronting Young Men with the Living Christ* (1924). His work challenged different Christian groups to cooperate in world missions and led to the World Missionary Conference in 1910, which Mott chaired. He was then named chairman of the conference's Continuation Committee.

Mott's missionary work undergirded the growing world ecumenical movement, and he was diverted from his organizing activity only long enough to respond to war relief needs after World War I. In 1921 the Continuation Committee gave way to the International Missionary Council (I.M.C.). Mott gave up his jobs with the S.V.M. and the W.S.C.F. to become chairman of the new council. He retained his post with the YMCA and became president of World YMCA in 1926. He led the meetings of the I.M.C. in Jerusalem in 1928 and Madras, India, in 1938. After 21 years, he resigned as chairman of the I.M.C. in 1942.

After World War II, in 1946, Mott was awarded the Nobel Peace Prize. That same year the first of the six-volume compilation of his *Addresses and Papers* (1946-1947) appeared. During the war, he had worked on the provisional committee that led to the foundation of the World Council of Churches in 1948. Mott, then in his eighties, was named its president. He died in 1955 after a half century of shaping the development of international Christianity; the effects of that leadership will be felt for centuries.

Sources:

Dictionary of American Biography. 20 vols. and 7 supps. New York: Charles Scribner's Sons, 1928-1936, 1944-1981.

Harmon, Nolan B. *The Encyclopedia of World Methodism.* 2 vols. Nashville: United Methodist Publishing House, 1974.

Lippy, Charles H. *Twentieth-Century Shapers of American Popular Religion.* New York: Greenwood Press, 1989. 494 pp.

Mott, John R. *Addresses and Papers.* 6 vols. New York: Association Press, 1946-1947.

_____. *Confronting Young Men with the Living Christ.* New York: Association Press, 1923. 203 pp.

_____. *The Decisive Hour of Christian Missions.* Edinburgh, Scotland: Foreign Missions Committee of the Church of Scotland, 1910. 294 pp.

_____. *The Evangelization of the World in This Generation.* New York: Student Volunteer Movement for Foreign Missions, 1900. 245 pp.

_____. *The Future Leadership of the Church.* New York: Student Department of the YMCA, 1908. 208 pp.

_____. *The Present World Situation.* New York: Student Volunteer Movement for Foreign Missions, 1914. 259 pp.

★659★
MOUNTAIN WOLF WOMAN
Healer and Peyotist, Winnebago
b. Apr. 1884, East Fork River, Wisconsin
d. Nov. 9, 1960, Black River Falls, Wisconsin

Mountain Wolf Woman, a Winnebago healer and peyotist who spent much of her life in Wisconsin, was born into the Thunder Clan. As a small child Mountain Wolf Woman became very sick, and her mother took her to an old woman to be healed. In the Winnebago traditional way of *Woengaire* (to give away), Mountain Wolf Woman's mother gave her away to the healer. This act of honoring the child meant Mountain Wolf Woman would continue to live with her parents, but that she could claim certain benefits

from the healer as well as have certain obligations to her. In return for this gift of the child, the old woman cured Mountain Wolf Woman by offering her own life and longevity to the child in addition to carrying out the usual healing with herbal medicines. By doing so the healer was carrying out the Winnebago belief that if she did not live an entire life span of 100 years, she could distribute the unused portion of good things from her remaining years, as well as share the force of her personal power before her death, with Mountain Wolf Woman. The old woman also bestowed the Wolf Clan name Xehaciwigga (Mountain Wolf Woman) on the child, which signified the protection of the clan spirit. The Winnebago consider clan names sacred, and the property of the clan. Presumably Mountain Wolf Woman had the blessings of two clans since she was a member of her father's clan, the Thunder Clan, and her name belonged to the Wolf Clan.

Mountain Wolf Woman learned about Indian medicine from a relative she called grandfather out of respect, and because she desired to learn sacred knowledge from him. He told Mountain Wolf Woman that from the time she was a little girl he knew that she was meant to learn about medicines. He recalled that she used to act as an interpreter whenever one woman would give medicines to Whites. The grandfather told Mountain Wolf Woman she would become a medicine woman and cure sickness. Mountain Wolf Woman not only learned Indian medicine, she was also a healer in many other ways. She was a midwife up through the 1930s, which is when Winnebago women routinely started going to hospitals to have their babies. Between 1944 and 1946 she also served as "health officer" at Black River Falls mission, where she informed the county public health nurse about people who were ill. Throughout her lifetime she cared for others. One winter she took care of an old woman with arthritis who had no one to care for her. In line with Winnebago custom she also took care of some of her grandchildren, including one child whom she raised from the age of two months until she was an adult.

Mountain Wolf Woman had her first experience with peyote in Nebraska at the time she was about to give birth to her third child. Her husband also took peyote that year, and from then on she and her family attended peyote meetings, whenever they were held. Her younger son became active in leading Half Moon meetings which is a branch of the peyote church, and her brother, Hagaga, was made a peyote leader by the people in Nebraska. Mountain Wolf Woman had a vision once while taking peyote and felt a sensation of great joyousness and content. She knew then that the peyote religion was holy and directed toward God. She also believed that peyote had great curative power, and she felt that peyote cures that were used as a last resort could be likened to miracles. After she and her husband moved back to Wisconsin, they held peyote meetings every Saturday. In 1958 Mountain Wolf Woman financed a peyote meeting in commemoration of the fiftieth anniversary of the introduction of peyote into Wisconsin.

Although Mountain Wolf Woman believed the peyote way was more effective than traditional ways, she did attend Winnebago ceremonies and dances. At times she and other peyotists would be the only Winnebago to carry out the singing or dancing properly according to tradition. Once, at the end of a victory dance, Mountain Wolf Woman had a dream or vision in which she saw the Winnebago obtaining the power which had belonged to a white soldier. Her nephew, Lone Man, told her she received this dream because she had respected the victory dance and had followed it through to the end properly. Mountain Wolf Woman also continued to follow traditional customs like gift giving and respect for proper social behaviors, although they had practically died out among the Winnebago.

Mountain Wolf Woman, through her own actions and efforts, has helped to preserve and exemplify the important roles of Winnebago women in healing, ceremonies, and customs. Her autobiography, compiled by Nancy O. Lurie, is an invaluable documentation on the lives of Winnebago women. Mountain Wolf Woman participated in three traditions at a time when religious diversification and confusion permeated Winnebago life. She was baptized and confirmed at a mission boarding school. Later she practiced the peyote way, and she participated in traditional ceremonies. Her influence among these three groups was perhaps best reflected after her death in 1960. Her traditionalist friends and relatives held a version of a Winnebago wake for her, the peyotists conducted a peyote meeting at her house the night before her burial, and she received a Christian burial at the mission church and was buried in the mission cemetery.

Sources:

Lurie, Nancy Oestreich, ed. *Mountain Wolf Woman: Sister of Crashing Thunder: The Autobiography of a Winnebago Indian.* Ann Arbor, MI: The University of Michigan Press, 1966. 142 pp.

—*Michelene E. Fixico*

★ 660 ★
MUELLER, Reuben Herbert
Bishop, Evangelical United Brethren and the United Methodist Church
b. Jun. 2, 1897, St. Paul, Minnesota
d. 1982, United States

Reuben Herbert Mueller, who as bishop of the Evangelical United Brethren assumed a leadership role in the merger that created the United Methodist Church, was the son of Reinhold M. and Emma Bunse Mueller. He was raised in Minnesota as a member of the Evangelical Church, a German Methodist denomination founded in the early nineteenth century. He moved to Illinois to attend the schools of the Evangelical Church in Naperville, and graduated from North Central College in 1919. Shortly after graduation he married Magdalene Stauffacher.

The Muellers moved to Minnesota where Reuben taught school and served as part-time pastor of the Oakland Avenue Evangelical Church. He was ordained as a deacon and elder and became the pastor of the church in South Bend, Indiana. The church was close enough to Naperville to allow him to finish his B.D. from the Evangelical Theological Seminary in 1926. In 1932 he moved from South Bend to become pastor of New York Street Evangelical Church in Indianapolis, Indiana. After a successful pastorate, he became a district superintendent in the Indiana Conference.

In 1946, the Evangelical Church and the United Brethren in Christ merged to become the Evangelical United Brethren. Mueller was appointed general secretary of Christian education and associate secretary of evangelism for the new denomination. In 1954 he was elected to the episcopacy and in 1959 became president of the Brethren's Board of Bishops. He served as bishop over the west central area which included the Indiana and Michigan conferences as well as work in Canada and Europe.

As the leading bishop in the Evangelical United Brethren, Mueller placed his office behind the drive to unite American Methodism, specifically to unite the Methodist Church (1939-1968) with his own denomination. As president of the Commission on Church Union, he worked diligently on the plan of union that led to the formation of the United Methodist Church in 1968. He was one of the first bishops chosen to serve as president of the council of bishops in the United Methodist Church (1969-1970). During the years of his episcopacy he also worked in the larger ecumenical movement and served as president of the National Council of Churches of Christ in the U.S.A. for three years (1963-1966). He also held leadership posts with the World Council of Churches and the Consultation on Church Union (COCU). Meuller retired in 1972.

Sources:

Harmon, Nolan B. *The Encyclopedia of World Methodism.* 2 vols. Nashville: United Methodist Publishing House, 1974.

★ 661 ★
MUENCH, Aloisius
Cardinal, Roman Catholic Church
b. Feb. 28, 1889, Milwaukee, Wisconsin
d. Jan. 25, 1962, Rome Italy

Aloisius Muench, a cardinal in the Roman Catholic Church, was the son of businessman Joseph Muench and grew up in the German-American community of turn-of-the-century Milwaukee. He entered St. Francis Seminary in 1904 and was ordained soon after he graduated. He was assigned first to St. Michael's Church in Milwaukee and then became assistant to the chaplain at the Newman Club at the University of Wisconsin in Madison in 1917. While there he was able to pursue further studies at the university and received his M.A. in 1919. With his archbishop's approval, Muench then traveled to Switzerland to work toward a doctorate at the University of Fribourg, which he received in 1921. Soon after his arrival on the continent, he met Eugenio Pacelli, later Pope Pius XII.

Muench continued his studies at several locations in Europe for another year but returned to the United States in 1922 to teach theology at St. Francis. From 1929 through 1935 he also served as the seminary rector. In 1934 he was made a domestic prelate with the title of monsignor. The following year he was consecrated as the bishop of Fargo, North Dakota.

Surveying his new territory, Bishop Muench saw the conditions produced by the annual weather cycle and the still recent national depression. Most of the churches were in debt, so he organized the Catholic Church Extension Fund, which over the next 11 years raised millions of dollars for local parishes. He then organized the Confraternity of Christian Doctrine, which developed an outreach and correspondence program to teach and catechize isolated families. He developed a scholarship fund to further assist candidates for the priesthood from poorer families. He founded the diocesan newspaper, *Catholic Action News*, and he called the first diocesan synod to discuss the problems before the priests.

In 1946 he was invited to go to Rome, where Archbishop Samuel Stritch was to receive the cardinal's hat. While there Pope Pius XII asked him to become the apostolic visitor to post-war Germany. Not only did he keep the Vatican informed on the situation in the chaos following the war, but he worked with the occupation forces on matters affecting Catholic life. The German people accepted him immediately because of his previous opposition to the so-called Morgenthau Plan, which advocated the reduction of Germany to a pastoral economy after the war.

The time spent away from his diocese grew into years. In 1949 Muench was named regent of the nunciate (occupied Germany). In 1950 he was named titular archbishop of Selembryia, an honorific title with no new responsibilities but a recognition of his work. In 1951 he was named papal nuncio to West Germany, a position he held until 1960. In 1959 he finally resigned as bishop of Fargo to become an officer in the Curia, the first American so appointed. He died in Rome several years later.

Sources:

Delaney, John J. *Dictionary of American Catholic Biography.* Garden City, NY: Doubleday & Company, 1988. 621 pp.
Thornton, Francis Beauchesne. *Our American Princes.* New York: G. P. Putnam's Sons, 1963. 319 pp.

★662★
MUHAMMAD, Elijah
Founder, Nation of Islam
b. Oct. 10, 1897, Sandersville, Georgia
d. Feb. 27, 1975, Chicago, Illinois

The Honorable Elijah Muhammad was the founder of the Nation of Islam, the most well-known "Black Muslim" group. Elijah Muhammad, born Elijah Poole, was the child of Georgia tenant farmers. He left home at an early age, moving first to Atlanta and later to Detroit. In 1919 he married Clara Evans. While in Detroit he became the follower of Wallace D. Fard, a man who claimed to be the reincarnation of **Timothy Drew** who was known publicly as Noble Drew Ali, founder of the Moorish Science Temple of America. Fard claimed that he had been sent from Mecca to secure freedom, justice, and equality for American Blacks. While some of his followers believed Fard to be a prophet, others believed him to be the simultaneous incarnation of Allah, the Madhi, and the second coming of Christ.

Elijah Poole, renamed Elijah Muhammad, became Fard's chief minister and emerged as the group's leader when Fard dropped from sight in 1935. Muhammad was arrested in 1934 for educating his children in the movement's school rather than in the public schools, and again in 1942 for encouraging his followers to resist the draft. He served four and a half years in prison as a result of this latter conviction. The Nation of Islam grew steadily in the following years, numbering 30 temples by the end of the 1950s.

Elijah Muhammad taught that humankind was originally all black, but that an evil scientist had created Whites. Because of the Blacks' disobedience to the will of God, Allah had permitted Whites to rule the earth for 6,000 years as punishment. The appearance of Fard indicated the end of this cycle of oppression and the reestablishment of black ascendancy. Elijah's teachings are contained in a number of books, including *Message to the Blackman* (1965); *The Fall of America* (1973); and *Our Savior Has Arrived* (1974).

Members of the Nation of Islam dropped their last names, which had been adopted from their white enslavers, and began using "X" for the surname they lost when kidnapped into slavery. Members also accepted a strict discipline that regulated food, dress, and behavior patterns. The group's rituals were modified forms of rites taken ultimately from Orthodox Islam. Parochial schools were established, and a University of Islam opened. The movement also preached a strong work ethic, and promoted black capitalism. As reflected in the name of the movement, Elijah Muhammad's long-range goal was the establishment of an independent black nation.

The growing presence of the Nation of Islam in combination with the Civil Rights Movement served to attract media attention, especially when the group's beliefs on race became widely known. It was as a result of media exposure that one of Elijah Muhammad's most articulate ministers, **Malcolm X**, emerged as a national figure. This exposure, combined with a vigorous program of proselytization, resulted in a spectacular rate of growth so that, by the time of Elijah Muhammad's death in 1975, the movement could count over one hundred thousand members in approximately 70 temples across the United States.

Elijah Muhammad was succeeded by his son Wallace, now known as Warith Deen Muhammad, who changed the name of the movement to the American Muslim Mission and led it into the Sunni mainstream. One of the by-products of this redirection was the formation of splinter groups adhering to Elijah Muhammad's original message, such as the splinter organization headed by **Louis Farrakhan**.

Sources:

Alexander, E. Curtis. *Elijah Muhammad on African American Education.* New York: ECA Associates, 1989. 120 pp.
Cushmeer, Bernard. *This Is the One: Messenger Elijah Muhammad.* Phoenix, AZ: Truth Publications, 1971. 160 pp.
Davis, Charles H., Jr. *Black Nationalism and the Nation of Islam.* 4 vols. Los Angeles: The John Henry and Mary Louisa Dunn Bryant Foundation, 1962.
Lincoln, C. Eric. *The Black Muslims in America.* Boston: Beacon Press, 1961. 276 pp.
Lomax, Louis. *When the Word Is Given.* Cleveland, OH: World Publishing Company, 1963. 223 pp.
Melton, J. Gordon. *Biographical Dictionary of American Cult and Sect Leaders.* Garland Reference Library of Social Science, vol. 212. New York: Garland Publishing, 1986.
Muhammad, Elijah. *The Fall of America.* Chicago: Muhammad's Temple of Islam No. 2, 1973. 265 pp.
———. *How to Eat to Live.* Chicago: Muhammad Mosque of Islam No. 2, 1967. 132 pp.
———. *The Supreme Wisdom.* 2 vols. Brooklyn: Temple of Islam, 1957.

—Timothy Miller

★663★
MUKTANANDA, Paramahansa
Founder, Siddha Yoga Dham
b. May 16, 1908, Dharmasthala India
d. Oct. 2, 1982, Ganeshpuri India

Swami Paramahansa Muktananda, founder of the Siddha Yoga Dham, was born into a high caste family in south India. He left home at the age of 15 and adopted the life of a wandering holy man. Muktananda studied at the feet of various spiritual masters until 1947 when he met Bhagawan Sri Nityananda, whom he accepted as his guru. Muktananda achieved complete enlightenment under Nityananda's direction, and moved to Ganeshpuri to be with him. When Nityananda died in 1961, Muktananda established the Shri Gurudev Ashram in honor of his master, and the ashram (a gathering place for Hindus) became the center of his own work.

Nityananda taught a spiritual discipline that he called *siddha yoga*. In common with many other forms of Indian yoga, siddha yoga sees the key to God-realization as being the *kundalini*, a powerful but normally latent energy that is often symbolized as a coiled serpent "asleep" at the base of the spine. By "awakening" the kundalini (also called *shakti*) and drawing it up the spine into the crown of the head, one activates the higher spiritual centers (*chakras*) and achieves enlightenment. In most yoga systems accepting this theory of liberation, the kundalini is awakened through the efforts of the individual disciple, acting under the guidance of a guru. Siddha yoga differs from many other forms of yoga by stressing the activity of the guru, who intervenes directly to activate the disciple's kundalini—to "impart shaktipat," in the language of siddha yoga.

In 1970, at the request of his Western devotees, Muktananda went out on a world tour that took him through Europe, North America, and Australia. Richard Alpert, a former associate of Timothy Leary (Alpert, under the name **Baba Ram Dass**, was himself a spiritual teacher), accompanied Muktananda during much of this first tour. The success of this initial "foray" outside of India enabled Muktananda to establish the Siddha Yoga Dham as an international movement. At the time of his death, there were over 100 siddha yoga centers in the United States. Muktananda's former translator, Swami Chidvilasananda, succeeded him as head of the movement.

Important in his own right, Muktananda is also significant for his impact on a number of American spiritual teachers. Beyond his association with Werner Erhart, who sponsored the Swami's visit to the West in 1974, Muktananda initiated two Americans who eventually broke with their master and became gurus themselves. Albert Rudolph became a disciple of Muktananda in India and, as **Swami Rudrananda**, established his own movement after he came back to the United States. **Franklin Jones**, a former student of Rudolph's, traveled to India to receive instruction under Muktananda but, like Rudolph, returned to this country to set up the Dawn Horse Communion (now the Johannine Daist Communion), an organization he led under the name Bubba Free John (now Da Love Ananda).

Sources:

Amma. *Swami Muktananda Paramahansa*. Ganeshpuri, India: Shree Gurudev Ashram, 1969. 89 pp.

Melton, J. Gordon. *Biographical Dictionary of American Cult and Sect Leaders*. Garland Reference Library of Social Science, vol. 212. New York: Garland Publishing, 1986.

Muktananda, Swami. *Guru*. New York: Harper & Row, 1971. 175 pp.

_____. *I Have Become Alive*. South Fallsburg, NY: SYDA Foundation, 1985. 227 pp.

_____. *The Perfect Relationship*. South Fallsburg, NY: SYDA Foundation, 1980. 208 pp.

_____. *Satsang With Baba*. 5 vols. Oakland, CA: SYDA Foundation, 1974-1978.

_____. *Where Are You Going?* South Fallsburg, NY: SYDA Foundation, 1981. 154 pp.

Prajnananda, Swami. *A Search for Self*. Ganeshpuri, India: Gurudev Siddha Peeth, 1979. 142 pp.

★664★
MULLINS, Edgar Young
Educator, Southern Baptist Convention
b. Jan. 5, 1860, Franklin County, Mississippi
d. Nov. 23, 1928, Louisville, Kentucky

Edgar Young Mullins, for many years the president of the Southern Baptist Theological Seminary, was the son of Seth Granberry and Cornelia Blair Tillman Mullins. After the Civil War the family moved to Cosicana, Texas, where his father, a Baptist minister, pastored a church and established a school. Mullins went to work as a youth to assist the family financial situation, but was able finally to get away and attend Texas A & M University, from which he graduated in 1879. It was his intention to become a lawyer and he began to prepare himself. In 1880, however, he was converted to his father's faith and decided to enter the ministry. He left home for Louisville, Kentucky, and the Southern Baptist Theological Seminary. He graduated in 1885.

Following the completion of his formal education, Mullins was ordained in the Southern Baptist Convention and became pastor of the church at Harrodsburg, Kentucky. While there, in 1886, he married Isla May Hawley. His pastoral career led him to Lee Street Baptist Church in Baltimore, Maryland, in 1888, and to Newton Centre, Massachusetts, in 1896. In 1899 he was offered the presidency of his alma mater, and he left New England for Louisville, Kentucky.

At Southern Baptist Theological Seminary Mullins served as president and professor of theology. As the school's president he was recognized as a most capable administrator. His work in theology became known throughout the convention through his many writings. He authored numerous tracts, pamphlets, and articles on religious themes. His books included: *Why Is Christianity True?* (1905); *The Axioms of Religion* (1908); *Baptist Beliefs* (1912); *Freedom and Authority in Religion* (1913); *The Life of Christ* (1917); *theatre Christian Religion in Its Doctrinal Expression* (1917); and *Christianity at the Cross Roads* (1924). He articulated a conservative evangelical perspective but stayed aloof from the more intense fundamentalism which grew in strength during the period of his teaching career.

Mullins remained active in convention affairs and promoted the cause of Baptist unity. In 1921 he began a three-year term as president of the Southern Baptist Convention. In 1923 he began a four-year term as president of the Baptist World Alliance. He remained president of the seminary until his death in 1928.

Sources:

Dictionary of American Biography. 20 vols. and 7 supps. New York: Charles Scribner's Sons, 1928-1936, 1944-1981.

Mullins, Edgar Y. *Baptist Beliefs*. Louisville, KY: Baptist World Pub. Co., 1912. 96 pp.

_____. *The Christian Religion in Its Doctrinal Expression*. Philadelphia: Judson Press, 1917. 514 pp.

_____. *Christianity at the Cross Roads*. New York: George H. Doran Co., 1924. 289 pp.

_____. *The Life of Christ*. New York: Fleming H. Revell Co., 1917. 239 pp.

_____. *Why Is Christianity True?* Chicago: Christian Culture Press, 1905. 450 pp.

Mullins, Isla May. *Edgar Young Mullins*. Nashville, TN: Sunday School Board of the Southern Baptist Convention, 1929. 216 pp.

★665★
MUMFORD, Bernard C.
Pentecostal Minister
Founder, Lifechangers, Inc.
b. 1930, Steubenville, Ohio

Bernard C. "Bob" Mumford, a popular independent Pentecostal minister and author, was not raised in church. He initially accepted Jesus when he was 12, but soon rejected his faith in the face of the criticism of his friends. Two years later he dropped out of school to assist his recently divorced mother. At the age of 20, he joined the Navy. In 1954, while on leave, he attended an Assemblies of God church and renewed his commitment. He was baptized a few weeks later at Glad Tidings Tabernacle in San Francisco and spoke in tongues for the first time during the service. Before leaving the Navy, he decided to become a minister. He obtained his high school equivalency certificate and enrolled in bible school. While in school he met and married Judy Huxoll.

After graduation in 1959, wanting to become a missionary, Mumford spent a year at the missionary medical training school in Toronto, Ontario, Canada. Unable to find a position, however, he became pastor of the Assemblies of God congregation in Kane, Pennsylvania. He then moved to Elim Bible College in Lima, New York, to teach about the New Testament and missions. While there he encountered the waves of the Latter Rain movement which had swept through the school a decade earlier. In 1966 he entered the Reformed Theological Seminary to obtain a M.Div. degree. He also was a pastor at a church in Wilmington, Delaware.

About the time of Mumford's graduation, a special relationship grew between him and three other pentecostal ministers—Charles V. Simpson, Derek Prince, and **Donald Basham**. Responding to the teaching ministry of the four, a group in Ft. Lauderdale, Florida, formed the Holy Spirit Teaching Mission, and began issuing *New Wine Magazine*, soon to become one of the most influential periodicals in the charismatic revival. Asked to intervene when the mission faced a crisis, the four moved to Florida in 1970 and assumed leadership over the mission and control of the magazine. They covenanted together to carry forth their ministry, which soon began to include oversight of independent charismatic congregations, many of which were led by inexperienced new ministers. Having found strength in their mutual covenant, they began to enter into similar relationships with leaders around the country in order to assist their maturing as shepherds of their congregations. Mumford and his colleagues taught that each person should have a personal pastor to whom they should submit their life of spiritual growth. By the mid 1970s, a pyramid of such relationships stretched across the United States. In 1974 the four were joined by **Ern Baxter**.

Quite apart from the work in Ft. Lauderdale, Mumford was emerging as one of the most popular speakers and writers in the charismatic revival. In 1972 he began *Plumbline*, a newsletter, and issued a recommended tape-of-the-month. His several books sold more than a quarter of a million copies. His popularity was disturbed in the mid-1970s by the so-called shepherding controversy.

Critics charged that the shepherding-submission relations had been widely abused and damaged many young Christians. In the face of the criticism, Mumford and the others moved to correct the abuses.

Along the way, the ministry's headquarters was moved to Mobile, Alabama, and Mumford moved there in 1981. In the mid-1980s, the covenant between the five began to disintegrate. Derek Prince disassociated himself in 1984, and in 1986 the four remaining men separated and moved to various parts of the country. Mumford settled in San Rafael, California, where he issues a new newsletter, *Life Changers*, and continues to speak frequently and write books. He also heads a personal ministry called Lifechangers, Inc. and issues a newsletter.

Sources:

Burgess, Stanley M., Gary B. McGee, and Patrick H. Alexander, eds. *Dictionary of Pentecostal and Charismatic Movements*. Grand Rapids, MI: Regency Reference Library, Zondervan Publishing House, 1988. 914 pp.

Ghezzi, Bert. "Bob Mumford, After Discipleship." *Charisma* 13, 1 (August 1987): 20-24.

Mumford, Bob. *Christ in Session*. Ft. Lauderdale, FL: The Author, 1973. 96 pp.

_____. *15 Steps Out*. Plainfield, NJ: Logos International, 1969. 90 pp.

_____. *The King and You*. Old Tappan, NJ: Fleming H. Revell Company, 1974. 25 pp.

_____. *Living Happily Ever After*. Ft. Lauderdale, FL: Life Changers, 1973. 64 pp.

_____. *The Problem of Doing Your Own Thing*. Ft. Lauderdale, FL: The Author, 1972. 118 pp.

_____. *Take Another Look at Guidance*. Plainfield, NJ: Logos International, 1971. 156 pp.

★666★
MUNDELEIN, George William
Cardinal, Roman Catholic Church
b. Jul. 2, 1872, New York, New York
d. Oct. 2, 1939, Chicago, Illinois

George William Mundelein, the first archbishop of Chicago to be granted a cardinal's hat in the Roman Catholic Church, was born in a tenement in the German section of Manhattan. His great-grandfather was the first Union soldier killed in the battle at Fort Sumter at the opening of the Civil War. Mundelein attended parochial school and as a youth turned down an appointment to Annapolis to study for the priesthood. He graduated from Manhattan College in 1889. He then attended St. Vincent's Archabbey for a time before being placed at the Urban College of Propaganda in Rome by Bishop McDonnell of Brooklyn. He lived at the North American College, and his stay overlapped that of future Cardinal **William O'Connell**, who was rector of the college.

Mundelein completed his course of study in 1895 but stayed in Rome another year, until he was twenty-four, the proper age of ordination. Shortly before his birthday, however, Bishop McDonnell visited Rome, and a special dispensation was granted that allowed McDonnell to ordain him several weeks early, in June 1896. Mundelein became McDonnell's secretary. He then briefly served the Lithuanian Chapel in Brooklyn and the diocese's cathedral chapel, before being appointed chancellor of the Brooklyn diocese in 1896. Noting his accomplishments, Rome conferred successive honors on him as censor of the Liturgical Academy (1903); domestic prelate in the pope's household with the title of monsignor (1906); and a member of the academy of Arcadia (1907). The last position came about as a direct result of a defense written by Mundelein of the papal encyclical on modernism. He increasingly assumed duties for the now aging Bishop McDonnell, and in 1909 was named Auxiliary Bishop of Brooklyn. At the same time, he became rector of the Cathedral College of the Immaculate Conception. Six years later he was named Archbishop of Chicago.

Upon his arrival in Chicago, the new archbishop was treated to a celebrative welcome and a civic dinner in which an anti-Catholic chef put arsenic in the soup. Fortunately, no one was killed.

As archbishop, Mundelein first attacked the problem of the Catholic schools. He reorganized the parochial system under a board of school supervisors. He initiated a new preparatory seminary and named it after his predecessor. He acted on social problems and promoted rehabilitation institutions for delinquent youth. He then moved to reorganize and centralize Catholic charities. He initiated the establishment of Misericordia Hospital. He promoted the opening of Rosary College in River Forest and Mundelein College in Chicago to give Catholic women better access to higher education. As World War I began, he joined his fellow bishops in the promotion of the Liberty Bond drives.

As the diamond jubilee of the archdiocese grew near, Mundelein began a drive to build a new senior seminary in suburban Libertyville on the shores of Lake Area. Eventually the town changed its name to Mundelein in recognition of the Archbishop's achievements.

Mundelein was given the cardinal's hat in the spring of 1924, in the same ceremony as **Patrick Joseph Hayes**. He was the first American of non-Irish ancestry to be so honored. He returned home to lay plans for a eucharistic congress in Chicago for the summer of 1926. It attracted over one million Roman Catholics and dignitaries from around the world, and was a festive success. He followed this by accepting a project to build a new Urban College in Rome. Upon its completion, the pope gave Mundelein his place at the Solemn Pontifical Mass for the dedication of the building and then further honored Mundelein by appearing at the ceremony to congratulate him publicly.

In 1928 Mundelein chose Father Bernard Sheil as his auxiliary bishop. As auxiliary bishop, Sheil created the first Catholic Youth Organization, a program that eventually was established throughout the church in the United States.

Mundelein had been a friend of Mother Cabrini, and after her death he promoted the cause of her sainthood. He officiated at her beatification ceremonies in 1938. His last year was as eventful as any in his life. He was appointed papal legate to the Eucharistic Congress in New Orleans in the fall of 1938. After the congress he was invited to the White House to speak with President Franklin Roosevelt on establishing more formal relations with the Vatican. As a result of that meeting, the United States later appointed an official observer at the papal court.

Mundelein died the next year of a heart attack, 12 days after the celebration of his thirtieth anniversary of his consecration as bishop.

Sources:

Finn, Brendan A. *Twenty-four American Cardinals*. Boston, MA: Bruce Humphreys, 1947. 475 pp.

Thornton, Francis Beauchesne. *Our American Princes*. New York: G.P. Putnam's Sons, 1963. 319 pp.

Walsh, James Joseph. *Our American Cardinals*. New York: D. Appleton and Company, 1926. 352 pp.

★667★
MURPHY, Joseph
Minister, Divine Science
b. 1898, Cork County Ireland
d. Dec. 1981

Joseph Murphy, for many years the pastor of the Divine Science Church in Los Angeles, was born into a Roman Catholic Church family in Ireland. His father was head of a private boy's school. Two of his sisters became nuns and he studied for the priesthood, eventually joining the Society of Jesus (the Jesuits). However, in the early 1920s he experienced a healing of a malignancy by prayer. This healing became the catalyst for a number of changes. He left the Jesuits and in 1922 moved to the United States. Equipped with a degree in chemistry, Murphy opened a pharmacy in the Algonquin Hotel in New York City.

Following the arrival of **Emmet Fox** in the country in 1931, Murphy began to attend the Church of the Healing Christ which Fox, a Divine Science minister, pastored. After World War II Murphy moved to Los Angeles, where he became associated with **Ernest S. Holmes**. In 1946 Holmes ordained Murphy, who began to teach at the Institute of Religious Science. Traveling around the country, he met Erwin Gregg, the president of the Divine Science Association at the time, and was reordained as a Divine Science minister. He became the minister of the Divine Science Church in Los Angeles in 1949, and remained there for the rest of his life. Like Emmet Fox before him, he built the congregation, which gathered weekly in the Wilshire Ebell Theatre, into one of the largest New thought congregations in the country. During the 1950s he married. He also continued his education, earning a Ph.D in psychology from the University of Southern California.

During the years of his active ministry, Murphy extended his influence through his numerous books and booklets, most of which were of a self-help nature. They include: *The Miracles of Your Mind* (1953); *Peace Within Yourself* (1956); *Prayer Is the Answer* (1965); *The Miracle of Mind Dynamics* (1964); *Your Infinite Power to Be Rich* (1966); *Psychic Perception: The Magic Of Extrasensory Perception* (1971); and *The Cosmic Energizer: Miracle Power of the Universe* (1974). In 1976, his first wife having died, he married Jean Whight, a Divine Science minister and his secretary for the previous 17 years. That year he also moved his weekly gatherings to the Saddleback Valley Theatre in Orange County, California. During his years there he continued to produce books regularly, including: *"These Truths Can Change Your Life"* (1979); *How to Use the Laws of Mind* (1980); and *Songs of God* (1982).

Murphy died in 1981. He requested that no funeral be held and that no obituary be written. His work was carried on by his wife for a number of years, but in 1989 services of the congregation were discontinued.

Sources:

Beebe, Tom. *Who's Who in New Thought*. Lakemont, GA: CSA Press, 1977. 318 pp.

Murphy, Joseph. *The Miracle of Mind Dynamics*. Englewood Cliffs, NJ: Prentice-Hall, 1964. 221 pp.

_____. *The Miracles of Your Mind*. San Gabriel, CA: Willing Publishing Company, 1953. 89 pp.

_____. *Peace within Yourself*. San Gabriel, CA: Willing Publishing Company, 1956. 300 pp.

_____. *Prayer Is the Answer*. Marina del Rey, CA: DeVorss & Co., 1956. 190 pp.

_____. *These Truths Can Change Your Life*. Marina del Rey, CA: DeVorss & Co., 1982. 274 pp.

_____. *Your Infinite Power to Be Rich*. West Nyack, NY: Parker Publishing Company, 1966. 206 pp.

★668★
MURRAY, John Courtney
Theologian, Society of Jesus, Roman Catholic Church
b. Sep. 12, 1904, New York, New York
d. Aug. 16, 1967, New York, New York

John Courtney Murray was a Jesuit priest and theologian. Considered to be an expert on the Trinity, he is best known for his writings on religious pluralism and was one of the principal authors of the Second Vatican Council's "Declaration on Religious Liberty." He was initially educated at Boston College where he received his B.A. (1926) and M.A. (1927) degrees. He was ordained in the Jesuit order in 1933. He received another degree from Woodstock College in 1934, and completed his doctoral study three years later

at the Gregorian University in Rome. For three years he taught English and Latin in the Philippines (1927-1930), and later taught theology at Woodstock College (1937-1967).

Murray is best remembered for his articulation of a new Roman Catholic perspective on church-state relations. Murray disagreed with the traditional Roman Catholic view that the church should administer both the spiritual and civic rights of states. Instead, he argued for a secular state in which church and political authorities could reach consensus through the common ground of rational purposes. Murray contended that religion has power in, but not over, the political order. Roman Catholics should work through state structures to see that moral and ethical principles are injected into the common life. The focus of his thinking was on articulating principles of ecclesiastical political theology that would be valid in whatever situations the church might find itself. Because his views departed so radically from tradition, he was for a period subjected to an order of silence, which he obeyed until Vatican II.

During his long career, Murray expounded his ideas in his many writings. For over a quarter century he edited *Theological Studies* (1941-1967) and additionally served briefly as associate editor for *America* (1945-1946); he also contributed to the journal *Thought*. Among his writings are *The Problem of God: Yesterday and Today* (1964); *We Hold These Truths: Catholic Reflections on the American Proposition* (1960); *Morality and Man* (1960); and *The Problem of Religious Freedom* (1965).

Sources:

Bowden, Henry Warner. *Dictionary of American Religious Biography*. Westport, CT: Greenwood Press, 1977. 572 pp.

Goerner, Edward A. *John Courtney Murray and the Problem of Church and State*. Chicago: University of Chicago, 1959. 255 pp.

Love, Thomas T. *John Courtney Murray: Contemporary Church-State Theory*. Garden City, NY: Doubleday & Company, 1965. 239 pp.

Murray, John Courtney. *Morality and Modern War*. New York: Council on Religion and International Affairs, 1959. 23 pp.

_____. *The Problem of God: Yesterday and Today*. New Haven, CT: Yale University Press, 1964. 121 pp.

_____. *The Problem of Religious Freedom*. London: Geoffrey Chapman, 1965. 112 pp.

_____. *We Hold These Truths: Catholic Reflections on the American Proposition*. New York: Sheed and Ward, 1960. 336 pp.

★669★
MURRAY, John Gardner
Presiding Bishop, Protestant Episcopal Church
b. Aug. 31, 1857, Lonaconing, Maryland
d. Oct. 3, 1929, Atlantic City, New Jersey

John Gardner Murray, the first person elected as presiding bishop of the Protestant Episcopal Church, was the son of James and Anne Kirkwood Murray. In 1876 he began a course of study at Wyoming Seminary in Wilkes Barre, Pennsylvania, but in 1877 moved to Kansas with his family. About this time he decided to enter the ministry, and in 1879 he moved to Madison, New Jersey, to attend Drew Theological Seminary, a school of the Methodist Episcopal Church. Unfortunately, his education was cut short by the death of his father as he had to withdraw from school and get a job to support his mother and sisters.

Murray obtained a job with the Carbon Coal Company and in 1882 was sent to Alabama where he became the secretary-treasurer of the related Brierfield Iron Company (just when the iron industry was beginning to grow in the state). He stayed in Alabama for a number of years. By 1886 he had left Methodism and was confirmed in the Episcopal Church. In 1889 he married Clara Ann Hunsicker and settled in Selma, Alabama, as a real estate dealer and wholesale grocer.

While quite successful in business, Murray still retained his love of the ministry. He was very active in the church through the 1880s and in 1891 was licensed as a lay reader. Slowly he began to move toward the ministry. In 1893 he was ordained a deacon and in 1894 a priest. He served as a diocesan missionary along the Alabama River for two years before being selected as rector for the Church of the Advent in Birmingham, the largest Episcopal parish in Alabama. He stayed at the church for seven years, during which time (1900) he was elected bishop of Alabama, but turned down the post.

In 1903 Murray moved to Baltimore as rector of the Church of St. Michael and All Angels, the largest parish in Maryland. During his very successful tenure at the church, he was elected bishop of Kentucky and of Mississippi, both of which he turned down. In 1909 he was elected coadjutor of the Diocese of Maryland, a post he accepted. He was consecrated bishop on September 19, 1909. He became bishop of Maryland in 1911. His 20 years of office were marked by his wise business policies and his personal popularity throughout the diocese—a diocese which enjoyed one of its most prosperous eras.

In 1925 Murray became the first bishop elected as the presiding bishop of the denomination. It came at a time when the church was in debt and decided to reorganize the office of presiding bishop and give it administrative duties in addition to the ceremonial functions. Previously, the office had been held by the senior bishop in the church. Although Murray only held the office for four years, he not only balanced the budget, but increased it considerably. He also expended energy, with his warmth and his oratorical ability, in leading the church in a general spiritual reawakening.

Murray died while presiding over a session of the House of Bishops. His death came just days before the stock market crash which wiped out many of Murray's accomplishments. Due in large part to Murray's previous efforts, however, the church was better able to sustain itself through the Depression.

Sources:

Dictionary of American Biography. 20 vols. and 7 supps. New York: Charles Scribner's Sons, 1928-1936, 1944-1981.

★670★
MUSE, Dan T.
Bishop, Pentecostal Holiness Church
b. Mar. 15, 1882, Booneville, Mississippi
d. Feb. 1950

Dan T. Muse, a bishop of the Pentecostal Holiness Church (now the International Pentecostal Holiness Church), was born in Mississippi but raised in Texas, where his family moved when he was three years old. When Muse was four years of age, his dying grandfather prayed that he would grow up to become a minister. As a young teenager he moved to the Oklahoma Indian Territory. He married and found work in a printer's office. There he met James A. Campbell. The Muses and Campbells became close friends but separated as both men took different jobs. In 1912 they found themselves employed by the same newspaper and were able to renew their friendship. Campbell had become a devout Christian, and in January 1913 he led Muse into an experience of Christ as personal Savior. Through Campbell he was also led to the Pentecostal Holiness Church, where he soon experienced sanctification (an experience in which the believer is cleansed from inward sin and made perfect in love through the Holy Spirit) and the baptism of the Holy Spirit as evidenced by speaking in tongues.

Muse offered his services as sexton to the pastor of the church. After a few months he felt the call to preach and began to hold services on the street and in the local jail. Through the years of World War I, he worked as a missionary establishing churches in Oklahoma. He was ordained in the Oklahoma Conference in 1918. He soon emerged as a leader in the conference, first as head of the Sunday school work and then as president of the camp meeting as-

sociation. In 1925 he became the secretary of the conference. During his long tenure in that position he began to gain a national reputation. He served on the church's general board beginning in 1929 and became active in missionary concerns as Secretary for Foreign Missions and editor of the missions column in *The Advocate*, the denominational magazine. In 1933 he was elected secretary of the church and the following year he became the superintendent of the Oklahoma Conference.

In 1937 Muse was elected general superintendent (bishop) of the church, succeeding **Joseph Hillery King**, who, as the church's first superintendent, had led the church for several decades. Muse represented a new generation of leadership for a growing church. Muse served as senior bishop from 1941 to 1945 to allow the aging King more time for speaking. King resumed his top position in 1945, but died the following year. Muse again resumed the senior bishop's role. He remained in that position until his own death in 1950. He was succeeded by **Joseph A. Synan**.

Sources:

Beacham, A. D., Jr. *A Brief History of the Pentecostal Holiness Church.* Franklin Springs, GA: Advocate Press, 1983. 123 pp.
Campbell, Joseph E. *The Pentecostal Holiness Church, 1898-1948.* Franklin Springs, GA: The Publishing House of the Pentecostal Holiness Church, 1951. 573 pp.

★671★
MUSSER, Joseph White
Founder, Apostolic United Brethren
b. Mar. 8, 1872, Salt Lake City, Utah
d. Mar. 19, 1954, Salt Lake City, Utah

Joseph White Musser, founder of the Apostolic United Brethren, one of the largest of the several fundamentalist, polygamy-practicing Mormon groups, was the son of Amos Milton Musser and Mary Elizabeth White. Musser's mother was the second wife of Musser's father. His childhood years coincided with the United States government's effort to stamp out polygamy as practiced by members of the Church of Jesus Christ of Latter-Day Saints. He was still in his teens when in 1890 the church issued a manifesto which formally abandoned the practice. Receiving little education, Musser went to work for the court as a stenographer. In 1892 he married Rose Selms Borquist, his first wife. In 1895 he began a three-year mission for the church as a missionary in the southern United States.

Musser's life changed dramatically after his return to Utah. According to his own account, he was told by **Lorenzo Snow**, the president of the church (1898-1901), that he had been selected to enter plural marriage. (It is now known that the church sanctioned a few plural marriages, primarily ones performed outside of the United States, in the years immediately following the manifesto.) His first wife was initially opposed, but in 1901 he finally married Mary Caroline Hill. By this time the church was actively opposing plural marriages and Musser affiliated with a group of fundamentalists at the Granite Stake near Forestdale, Utah. About this time he married his third wife, Ellis R. Shipp, and later entered a fourth marriage. In 1910 Musser was named, along with two hundred others, as a new polygamist, a person who was in open defiance of the manifesto and had contracted marriages against the church's present policy.

Through the 1920s Musser claimed authority to teach and practice polygamy. He first asserted that in 1915 one of the church's apostles had given him authority to seal plural marriages, a ceremony usually performed only at a Mormon temple. In 1929 he publicly claimed that he had been commissioned to see that no year passed without children being born from polygamous marriages. He then aligned himself with Lorien Woolley, who professed to have a similar commission as a leader in the United Effort. The group around Woolley founded the famous polygamous colony at Short Creek (now Colorado City), Arizona.

During the 1930s Musser emerged as the major apologist for the fundamentalist position. In 1934 he issued the *Supplement to the New and Everlasting Covenant of Marriage* and the next year began issuing *The Truth*, a magazine which he continued to publish until 1950. His later books, *The Laws of Plural Marriage* and *Celestial or Plural Marriage*, both issued in the 1940s, remain the most popular defense of the fundamentalist perspective.

Musser succeeded John Barlow as head of the United Effort in 1951, however many opposed his leadership as he was in poor health. The controversy created by his choosing a completely new set of leaders led to a schism, and the majority rejected Musser. He reorganized his following as the Apostolic United Brethren. He began a new periodical, *The Star of Truth* to defend his position. He died a few years later and was succeeded by **Rulon Clark Allred**.

Sources:

Joseph W. Musser, 1872-1954. N.p., n.d. 155 pp.
Musser, Joseph. *Celestial or Plural Marriage*. Salt Lake City, UT: Truth Publishing Co., 1944, 1970. 154 pp.
_____. *The Economic Order of Heaven*. Lehi, UT: The Books of the House of Israel Publishing House, n.d. 75 pp.
_____. *The Law of Plural Marriage*. Salt Lake City, UT: Truth Publishing Co., n.d. 9 pp.
_____. *Michael Our Father and Our God*. Salt Lake City, UT: Truth Publishing Co., 1963. 139 pp.
Rich, Russell R. *Those Who Would Be Leaders*. Provo, UT: Brigham Young University, 1967. 89 pp.
Van Wagoner, Richard S. *Morman Polygamy: A History*. Salt Lake City, UT: Signature Books, 1986. 307 pp.

★672★
MUSTE, Abraham Johannes
Independent Protestant Minister
Social Activist
b. Jan. 8, 1885, Zierikzee Netherlands
d. Feb. 11, 1967, New York, New York

Abraham Johannes Muste, a leading advocate of peace and nonviolent social protest, was the son of Martin and Adriana Jonker Muste. He was but six years old when his family moved from the Netherlands to the large Dutch-American community in Grand Rapids, Michigan. Muste was raised in the Dutch Reformed Church (now the Reformed Church in America). He attended Hope College, from which he graduated in 1905. He taught school for a year and then entered the New Brunswick Theological Seminary in New Jersey. Following his graduation in 1909 he married Anna Huizenga, was ordained, and became pastor of Fort Washington Collegiate Church in New York City.

In New York City Muste continued his studies at Union Theological Seminary (B.D., 1913). He also began to lose his belief in the conservative Calvinist doctrines espoused by his denomination, and as a result he resigned his parish in 1915 and became a Congregationalist and pastor of Central Congregational Church in Newtonville, Massachusetts. He continued to change theologically and, under the influence of writers such as Quaker **Rufus M. Jones**, soon emerged as a pacifist. He became a peace activist and soon left the Congregational Church. In 1918 he became a Quaker minister with the Providence (Rhode Island) Friends' Meeting.

By the end of 1918, however, Muste had become both a theological and social radical. He moved to Boston, Massachusetts, and affiliated with the Comradeship, a small group of pacifists. He joined a strike in Lawrence, Massachusetts, and in the successes achieved became nationally known as a labor leader. He became chairman of the faculty at Brookwood Labor College in Katonah, New York, and general secretary of the Amalgamated Textile

Workers Union. Within the larger labor movement, Brookwood College became a leading critic of the more conservative American Federation of Labor.

In 1929 Muste led in the formation of the Conference on Progressive Labor Action (CPLA), whose increasingly radical program developed in response to the depression. Among other goals, it advocated the entrance of labor into politics through a labor party. The situation in the 1930s led Muste increasingly away from Christianity and toward Marxism. In 1933 he quit Brookwood and turned the CPLA into the American Workers Party, which the next year merged with the American Trotskyite League of America to become the Workers Party.

Muste's Marxist career ended in 1936 as the result of a religious experience which led him back to Christian pacifism. He left the Labor Party and became an executive with the Fellowship for Reconciliation (FOR), a Christian pacifist organization. His perspective of Christian pacifism was set down in his first book, *Nonviolence in an Aggressive World* (1940). When World War II began, he became FOR's executive secretary. He represented the most radical segment of the antiwar movement and openly assisted those who refused to cooperate with the draft. In 1942 the Congress of Racial Equality (CORE) developed from FOR with special interest in the welfare of black Americans. Martin Luther King, Jr., credited Muste as a major source of the civil rights movement's commitment to a nonviolent philosophy.

Muste's commitment to pacifism and nonviolence gave the appearance of growing in the years after the war. He labored tirelessly at organizing people, especially social influentials. He authored a second book published in 1947, *Not by Might*. Active to the end, Muste was among the first to organize protests against the Vietnam War in the 1960s; the year before his death he traveled to Saigon and Hanoi on peace missions.

Sources:

Dictionary of American Biography. 20 vols. and 7 supps. New York: Charles Scribner's Sons, 1928-1936, 1944-1981.
Hentoff, Nat. *Peace Agitator*. New York: Macmillan Company, 1963. 269 pp.
Muste, Abraham J. *The Essays of A. J. Muste*. Ed. by Nat Hentoff. New York: Simon & Schuster, 1967. 515 pp.
_____. *Nonviolence in an Aggressive World*. New York: Harper & Bros., 1940. 211 pp.
_____. *Not by Might*. New York: Harper & Bros., 1947. 227 pp.
Robinson, Jo Ann. *Abraham Went Out*. Philadelphia: Temple University Press, 1981. 341 pp.

★673★
MUZZEY, David Saville
Leader, American Ethical Union
b. Oct. 9, 1870, Lexington, Massachusetts
d. Apr. 14, 1965, Yonkers, New York

David Saville Muzzey, for many years a professor of history at Columbia University and a leader in the Ethical Culture Movement begun by **Felix Adler**, was the son of David W. Muzzey and Annie W. Saville Muzzey. After finishing at Boston Latin School he attended Harvard University (1889-1893) and then took a position teaching mathematics at Robert College in Constantinople, Turkey, for a year. Upon his return to the United States, with the intention of becoming a minister, he spent three years at Union Theological Seminary from which he earned a B.D. in 1897. He furthered his studies at the University of Berlin (1897-1898) and the Sorbonne (1898-1899). The years in Europe were important in his personal transition from formal religion to his adoption of the humanist perspective of the Ethical Culture Movement. Ethical Culture had little use for traditional supernaturalism and piety and saw the religious life primarily embodied in the development and spread of moral values and ideals.

Following his return to the United States, in 1900 Muzzey took a position teaching Latin and Greek at the Ethical Culture School in New York City. Later that year he married Ina Jeanette Bullis. While at the school he wrote his first book, *Spiritual Heroes* (1902), an initial statement of the humanistic idealism in which he so fervently believed. In 1903 he became director of the school for two years. In 1905 he was invited to join the faculty at Columbia University. He taught at Bernard College while finishing his Ph.D., which he received in 1907. That year he also finished *The Spiritual Franciscans* (1907). Quite apart from his advocacy of Ethical Culture, Muzzey became a controversial author of high school textbooks in American History. In 1911 his *An American History* (which was to go through several editions and in 1939 be retitled *History of Our Country*) was published. It was one of the first books to begin to demythologize many of the accounts of the nation's past and speak frankly about some of the less laudatory aspects, such as graft and corruption in the government. While widely used, the text was heavily criticized as un-American, and Muzzey was attacked in the press as a destroyer of the country's foundations. He followed with another text, *The United States of America* (1924) and noteworthy biographies of *Thomas Jefferson* (1918) and *James G. Blaine: Political Idol of Other Days* (1934).

In 1934, Muzzey's wife died, and in 1937 he married J. Emilie Young. Muzzey had been named a member of the graduate faculty at Columbia in 1923. In 1938 he was named the first holder of the Gouveneur Morris chair in American History. He retired in 1940.

In retirement Muzzey was able to give more time to the Ethical Culture Movement and frequently lectured for it in New York and elsewhere. In 1951 his mature statement of his position, *Ethics as a Religion*, was issued. Then in his eighties, he declared his growing faith in the reasonableness, the timeliness, the adequacy, and the eventual triumph of the Religion of Ethics.

Sources:

Dictionary of American Biography. 20 vols. and 7 supps. New York: Charles Scribner's Sons, 1928-1936, 1944-1981.

Muzzey, David Saville. *An American History*. Boston: Ginn & Company, 1911. 662 pp.

_____. *Ethical Imperative*. New York: American Ethical Union, 1946. 63 pp.

_____. *Ethics as Religion*. New York: Simon and Schuster, 1951. 273 pp.

_____. *James G. Blaine: A Political Idol of Other Days*. New York: Dodd, Mead & Company, 1934. 514 pp.

_____. *Spiritual Heroes*. New York: Doubleday, Page & Company, 1902. 305 pp.

_____. *Thomas Jefferson*. New York: Charles Scribner's Sons, 1918. 319 pp.

★674★
Swami NARAYANANANDA

Founder, Narayanananda Universal Yoga Trust
b. Apr. 12, 1902, Kongana India

Sri Swami Narayanananda is the founder of the Narayanananda Universal Yoga Trust. He had a normal childhood and was a well-rounded student as a boy, proficient in both sports and academic studies. He did, however, regularly practice meditation in both the morning and the evening. On September 4, 1929, at the age of 27, he renounced the world and set out in search of a guru. At the main center of the Ramakrishna Mission in Calcutta, the Belur Math, he met Mahapurush Swami Shivananda, who he accepted as his teacher. As his spiritual life deepened, he felt the need for a more secluded environment. His guru directed him to travel to the Himalayas in order to intensify his *sadhana* (union with the Infinite). It was there, on the night of Shivaratri in February of 1933, that he achieved the superconscious state of Nirvikalpa Samadhi (complete enlightenment).

Following this experience, Swami Narayanananda continued to live a simple, secluded life. Rather than accept disciples and create a religious order, he engaged himself in the introspective study of the human mental processes, using his own consciousness as a laboratory. These observations were recorded in manuscripts which he stored away, making no effort to have them published. The spectacle of the violence associated with the partition of India influenced him to leave his seclusion and do what he could to aid suffering humanity. He began to accept disciples, who soon encouraged the Swami to publish his manuscripts. In 1955 Narayananda's followers began a printing press at Rishikish, India. In the course of time, the numbers of his disciples grew until a formal organization seemed to be in order, and in 1967 the Narayanananda Universal Yoga Trust (N.U. Yoga Trust) was established. This group is viewed as the foundation for the Universal Religion that Narayanananda wishes to see established.

For many years, young Danes visited Swami Narayanananda and brought his spiritual message back to Denmark. His books, which include *The Secrets of Mind Control, The Way to Peace, Power and Long Life, Revelation*, and *The Gist of Religions*, were translated into Danish. In addition, an old farm was purchased for the establishment of an ashram. To help establish the community, Narayananada journeyed to Denmark in 1971. From this visit, the work expanded to other places in Europe; the farm ashram in Gylling, Denmark, became the international headquarters of the group. Centers were also established in North America, and in 1978 a secluded ashram was begun outside of the town of Winter, Wisconsin. In June of 1980 Narayanananda traveled to the United States for his first visit, where he spent time at both a Chicago center and the Winter ashram.

Sources:

Melton, J. Gordon *The Encyclopedia of American Religions*. 3d ed. Detroit: Gale Research Inc.,1988. 1102 pp.

Narayanananda, Swami. *The Gist of Religions*. 4th ed. Gylling, Denmark: N. U. Yoga Trust & Ashrama. 1979. 131 pp.

_____. *The Mysteries of Man, Mind and Mind Functions*. 5th ed. Gylling, Denmark: N. U. Yoga Trust & Ashrama, 1979. 530 pp.

_____. *A Practical Guide to Samadhi (Spiritual Teachings)*. 2nd ed. Rishikish, U. P., India: Narayanananda Universal Yoga Trust, 1966. 228 pp.

_____. *Revelation*. 4th ed. Gylling, Denmark: N. U. Yoga Trust & Ashrama, 1979. 243 pp.

_____. *The Secrets of Mind Control*. 3rd ed. Rishikish, U. P., India: N.p. 1970. 280 pp.

Sri Swami Narayanananda: His Life, His Books, His Organization & His Guidance. Chicago: N. U. Yoga Center, 1982. 6 pp.

Works of Swami Narayanananda. Gylling, Denmark: N. U. Yoga Ashrama, 1976. 48 pp.

★675★
NARCISSE, Louis H.

Founder, Mt. Zion Spiritual Temple
b. 1921, Gretna, Louisiana
d. Feb. 3, 1989, Detroit, Michigan

Louis H. Narcisse, one of the more flamboyant of the independent black ministers in the last half of the twentieth century, grew up in Gretna, Louisiana. He was originally ordained by the Metropolitan Spiritual Churches, Inc., but in 1945 broke away to found the Mt. Zion Spiritual Temple in Oakland, California. He began the radio ministry "Moments of Meditation" and developed a national following with an estimated audience of 1.5 million. He became associated with his theme song title and oft repeated motto, "It's so nice to be nice." During the 1950s and 1960s he cut a number of records on which he both sang and played the piano.

In 1956 bishops from the Church of God in Christ and the Church of God crowned him as "king" of Oakland. In subsequent years he lived out the fantasy of his imperial realm. For example, aides traveling with him would at each stop unroll a red carpet so that his feet need never touch the ground. He was treated in a manner befitting royalty within the church community he led and was known to anoint the back of the hands of people during the taking of offerings. He saw himself as a symbol of black dignity.

Over the years he established affiliated churches in Sacramento, California; New Orleans and Baton Rouge, Louisiana; Orlando, Florida; and Houston, Texas. He integrated an emphasis on black pride into his messages. His Oakland center was always open to the homeless and his churches regularly fed the hungry.

In 1971 Narcisse came to Detroit to attend the funeral of **James Francis Jones**, popularly known as Prophet Jones. He had a revelation to stay, and he soon founded the local congregation of the Mt. Zion Spiritual Temple (later known as the King Narcisse Memorial Temple). He began local radio broadcasts but was hampered in fully developing his work by high blood pressure. However, his continued work with the hungry and homeless won him the Spirit of Detroit Award (1981), the acknowledgment of the Michigan state legislature (1983), and the Mayor Coleman Young Award (1987).

Sources:

Dupree, Sherry Sherrod. *Biographical Dictionary of African-American, Holiness-Pentecostals, 1880-1990*. Washington, DC: Middle Atlantic Regional Press, 1990. 386 pp.

Fears, Darryl. "King Narcisse is Dead at 67; A Flamboyant Religious Leader." *Detroit Free Press* (February 7, 1989).

★ 676 ★
NEE, Watchman
Founder, Local Church
b. Nov. 4, 1903, Swatow People's Republic of China
d. Jun. 1, 1972, People's Republic of China

Watchman Nee, born Ni Shu-tsu, was the founder of a decentralized Evangelical Christian movement that came to be known as the Local Church. Born into a Chinese Methodist family, he rejected all religion while in college, but was reconverted in 1920 under the ministry of a Methodist missionary, Dora Yu. He studied for a while at Yu's Bible school in Shanghai, and eventually returned to Fuchow to initiate his own ministry.

Nee began to use the name To-Sheng (Watchman), which had been suggested to him by his mother, and also began to rethink church structure in the light of what he perceived to have been the organization of Christian bodies during New Testament times. The basis of Nee's vision of church structure was the notion that there should be one church per city, a decentralized organization that resulted in his movement's informal designation as the "Local Church." These autonomous churches would be governed by elders, strongly evangelical, and unstructured in worship. He began to find other people who accepted these principles, and eventually emerged as the leader of an independent Christian group.

Through an independent missionary, Margaret Barber, Nee had been introduced to the writings of one of the founders of the Plymouth Brethren, John Nelson Darby. Soon after the Local Church came into being, he was contacted by the branch of the Plymouth Brethren headed by James Taylor, who established fellowship with Nee's movement. He traveled to England at their request, but while there broke bread with a non-Brethren group led by Theodore Austin-Sparks. This action, in combination with some comparatively minor divergences on points of belief and practice, caused Taylor to break off relations with Nee.

During World War II Nee took a job in a factory owned by his brother so as not to be a financial burden to his congregation. After the war he turned the factory over to the church, and other members followed his example. This church-business connection hurt the movement when the communists, who suppressed the move-

ment because of its capitalist activities, seized control. Nee was arrested in 1952 and spent the remaining 20 years of his life in prison.

The movement went underground on the mainland, and the Taiwan church, under the leadership of Witness Lee, became the new center of the movement. Lee moved to California in 1962 and established the Living Stream Ministry. The Local Church movement had been initiated in the United States some 10 years earlier, but its growth in the 1960s and 1970s provoked intense controversy because of its alleged deviations from Christian doctrine. This controversy resulted in a number of lawsuits, which the Local Church eventually won.

Sources:

Chen, James. *Meet Brother Nee*. Hong Kong: The Christian Publishers, 1976. 104 pp.

Kinnear, Angus I. *Against the Tide*. Fort Washington, PA: Christian Literature Crusade, 1973. 191 pp.

Nee, Watchman. *Do All to the Glory of God*. Manassas, VA: Christian Fellowship Publishers, 1974. 214 pp.

———. *The King and the Kingdom of Heaven*. Manassas, VA: Christian Fellowship Publishers, 1978. 386 pp.

———. *The Latent Power of the Soul*. Hollis, NY: Christian Fellowship Publishers, 1972. 86 pp.

———. *The Normal Christian Church Life*. Washington, DC: International Students Press, 1969. 127 pp.

———. *The Normal Christian Life*. Fort Washington, PA: Christian Literature Crusade, 1961. 192 pp.

———. *The Release of the Spirit*. Indianapolis, IN: Sure Foundation, 1965. 94 pp.

———. *Sit, Walk, Stand*. London: Witness and Testimony Publishers, 1958.

Roberts, Dana. *Understanding Watchman Nee*. Plainfield, NJ: Haven Books, 1980. 196 pp.

★ 677 ★
Bishop NESTOR
Bishop, Russian Orthodox Church
b. Dec. 20, 1825, Archangelsk Russia
d. Jun. 30, 1882, Alaska

Bishop Nestor, head of the American work of the Russian Orthodox Church, was born into a family of Russian gentry. He began his adult life in the Russian navy, and acquired fluency in German, French, and English. He spent a year in the United States during the period of the Civil War. After the war he decided to become a priest and educated himself in the theological disciplines. He was consecrated for the Alaskan work in 1879 and given a special assignment of reporting on the condition of the various parishes and Eskimo missions under the new government (the United States having purchased Alaska in 1867).

Upon his arrival in America, he settled in San Francisco but placed his attention on Alaska and the Aleutian Islands. He initiated a translation of the Bible into Eskimo. He made one extended trip to the mission stations in 1881 and in May 1882 left for a second such trip. Unfortunately, while returning to San Francisco, he was drowned in the Bering Sea. His body was found, and he was buried in Holy Ascension Cathedral in Unalaska, Alaska.

Sources:

Afonsky, Bishop Gregory. *A History of the Orthodox Church in Alaska (1794-1917)*. Kodiak, AK: St. Herman's Theological Seminary, 1977. 106 pp.

Tarasar, Constance J. *Orthodox America, 1794-1974*. Syosset, NY: Department of Archives and History, The Orthodox Church in America, 1975. 351 pp.

★ 678 ★
NEWMAN, Albert Henry
Church Historian, Baptist Church
b. Aug. 25, 1852, Edgefield, South Carolina
d. Jun. 4, 1933, Austin, Texas

Albert Henry Newman, the prominent Baptist Church historian, was the son of John Blackstone and Harriet Whitaker Newman. At the age of nine, during the early years of the Civil War, Albert's mother died, and his father soon moved to Thomson, Georgia. Newman was able to attend the private school in Thomson run by the Rev. E. A. Stead, the local Baptist pastor. He excelled in his studies and moved on in 1869 to Mercer University. He graduated in 1871 at the head of his class. He decided to attend seminary in the North, at Rochester Theological Seminary, in western New York. He attracted the attention of the school's president, **Augustus Hopkins Strong**, who became his mentor. During his seminary days, in 1873, he married Mary Augusta Ware.

Following his graduation from seminary in 1875, Newman gave up plans to study in Germany to accept an appointment at the new Southern Baptist Theological Seminary in Greenville, South Carolina. He stayed two years before returning to Rochester, where he taught church history and specialized in Semitic and Oriental languages, areas of study in which he had shown a marked ability.

In 1881 Newman was invited to become the first professor of church history at McMaster University in Toronto, a school created by the merger of Woodstock and Toronto Baptist Colleges. His move to Toronto marked the beginning of his most productive period, in which he became the author and/or editor of a number of significant works. Historian **Philip Schaff** invited Newman to assist in the compilation and editing of *A Select Library of the Nicene and Post Nicene Fathers of the Christian Church* (1887), an important collection of texts written by the early church leaders. He also authored *A History of the Baptist Churches in the United States* (1894) and *A History of Anti-Pedobaptism* (1897), and edited *A Century of Baptist Achievement* (1901). Possibly his most important work was the two-volume *A Manual of Church History* (1900-1903), which went through 16 editions.

In 1901 Newman was lured away from his Canadian post to teach at the new seminary at Baylor University. He stayed at Baylor for seven years, and in 1908 he moved to Fort Worth to the Southwestern Baptist Theological Seminary where he was dean from 1908 to 1913. He then returned to Baylor, where he taught until 1921, at which time he was elected to hold the chair of church history at the new seminary attached to Mercer University. He returned to Georgia and stayed until his retirement in 1929. He settled in Austin, Texas, to live out his final years but was killed in an automobile accident after only a few weeks.

Sources:

Dawson, J. M. "Our Greatest Baptist Historian." *Watchman-Examiner* (June 29, 1933).
Dictionary of American Biography. 20 vols. and 7 supps. New York: Charles Scribner's Sons, 1928-1936, 1944-1981.
Newman, Albert H. *A History of Anti-Pedobaptism.* Philadelphia: American Baptist Publication Society, 1897. 414 pp.
_____. *A History of the Baptist Churches in the United States.* New York: Christian Literature Company, 1894. 513 pp.
_____. *A Manual of Church History.* 2 vols. Philadelphia: American Baptist Publication Society, 1900-1903.

★ 679 ★
NEWTON, Joseph Fort
Minister, Protestant Episcopal Church
b. Jul. 21, 1876, Decatur, Texas
d. Jan. 24, 1950, Philadelphia, Pennsylvania

Joseph Fort Newton, a liberal minister and writer of the Protestant Episcopal Church, was the son of Sue Green Battle and Lee Newton. His father was a Baptist preacher, from whom he inherited his first religious affiliation, and his mother was a teacher, from whom he inherited a desire for learning. Newton was ordained as a minister in the Southern Baptist Convention in 1895 and called as pastor of the church at Rose Hill, Texas. Later that year he entered Southern Baptist Theological Seminary in Louisville, Kentucky. He used the opportunity to widen his horizons and found himself following liberal Protestant, mystical, and even skeptical authors. The mystical aspect of his life provided a spiritual point of unity that made him increasingly impatient with sectarian doctrinal divisions. He became involved briefly in the defense of his seminary teacher, **William Heth Whitsitt**, who had been attacked for denying the continuity of Baptist churches from the days of Christ. He left the seminary in 1897 and briefly served a church in Texas before leaving the Baptist fold altogether.

In 1900 Newton married Jennie Mai Deatherage and moved to St. Louis as a minister of the Christian Church (Disciples of Christ). Newton, however, could not find a home in the more liberal Disciples of Christ and began to search for a new church. In 1903 he moved to Dixon, Illinois, as pastor of an independent Peoples Church modeled somewhat on Central Church in Chicago, the independent congregation headed by **David Swing**, the liberal former-Presbyterian. While at Dixon, Newton authored his first book, a biography of Swing.

In 1908 Newton became pastor of a congregation affiliated with the American Universalist Association in Cedar Rapids, Iowa. His career, at least its literary aspect, seems to have blossomed in Iowa. A homiletic master, Newton saw his sermons regularly reprinted in the local newspaper, and each year he issued a volume of his collected addresses. He authored several books, including his popular presentation of Free Masonry, *The Builders: A Story and Study of Free Masonry* (1914). His writings earned him an invitation to pastor City Temple in London, England, one of the most famous independent liberal congregations in the world. He moved in 1915 and stayed until 1919 when he became pastor of Church of the Divine Paternity, a Universalist congregation in New York City.

In New York he became one of the most popular speakers, not only at his church but at numerous midweek functions. He continued to issue annual volumes of his sermons. His interest in Free Masonry remained strong and he not only edited *The Master Mason* (a monthly Free Masonry journal) for many years but authored a second popular book on the subject, *The Men's House* (1923). After leaving the Baptists, he had been an advocate of ecumenism and railed against the adherence to denominational peculiarities that meaninglessly divided religious people. In the midst of his whirlwind life, he found the suggestion of a home in the Episcopal Church appealing and in 1925 made his last denominational switch.

He assumed a role as lay reader of the Memorial Church of St. Paul in Overbrook, Pennsylvania, and was ordained a deacon and priest the following year. In 1930 he became the rector of St. James' Episcopal Church in Philadelphia. In 1935 he became involved in a plan to unite his congregation with two others and to that intent was assigned as special preacher to the Associated Churches. The attempt failed. In 1938 Newton became rector of Epiphany, one of the other churches where he remained for the next 12 years. While at Epiphany, he authored his autobiography, *River of Years* (1946). He died suddenly of a heart attack in 1950.

Sources:

Dictionary of American Biography. 20 vols. and 7 supps. New York: Charles Scribner's Sons, 1928-1936, 1944-1981.
Newton, Joseph Fort. *The Builders: A Story and Study of Freemasonry.* Cedar Rapids, IA: Torch Press, 1914. 317 pp.
_____. *The Men's House.* Washington, DC: The Masonic Service Association of the United States, 1923. 261 pp.

_____. *The New Preachings*. Nashville, TN: Cokesbury Press, 1930. 187 pp.

_____. *The One Great Church*. New York: Macmillan Company, 1948. 122 pp.

_____. *River of Years*. New York: J. B. Lippencott, 1946. 390 pp.

_____. *Some Living Masters of the Pulpit*. New York: George H. Doran, 1923. 261 pp.

_____. *Where Are We in Religion?* New York: Macmillan Company, 1945. 82 pp.

Reid, Daniel G., Robert D. Linder, Bruce L. Shelley, and Harry S. Stout. *Dictionary of Christianity in America*. Downers Grove, IL: InterVarsity Press, 1990. 1305 pp.

★ 680 ★
NICHOL, Francis David
Editor, Seventh-day Adventist Church
b. Feb. 14, 1897, Thirlmese Australia
d. Jun. 3, 1966, Takoma Park, Maryland

Francis David Nichol, an editor of Seventh-day Adventist periodicals for over 40 years, was born in Australia to parents who, as Irish immigrants, had converted to Adventism. John and Mary Nichol had converted from Presbyterianism and Catholicism respectively, and in their fervor raised their children as loyal members of their new faith. Nichol attended the Adventism school in nearby Walroonga prior to the family's move to California in 1905. He then attended school at Loma Linda. He later attended Isaacs Woodbury Business College and Pacific Union College (1918-1920). In 1919 he married Rose Macklin.

Following graduation from college, Nichol became assistant pastor of the congregation at Vallejo, California. During the year he attracted the attention of the managers of *Signs of the Times*, an Adventist periodical which was published in Mountain View, California. In 1921 he became assistant editor and moved to Mountain View. In 1923 he was ordained as an Adventist minister.

Nichol's years with *Signs of the Times*, coincided with the heightened debate over creationism and evolution, and he emerged as a major apologist for the Adventist creationist stance. He occasionally engaged in debates with evolutionists and authored two books on the subject: the *San Francisco Debates on Evolution by Maynard Shipley* (1925) and *Creation—Not Evolution* (1926). He was soon promoted to associate editor and in 1928 was lured away to become the associate editor for the *Review and Herald*, the official denominational periodical issued from the headquarters in Takoma Park, Maryland (a Washington, D.C., suburb).

Following the move to the East Coast, Nichol threw himself into a disciplined and varied career. In 1931 he helped organize a church in Hyattsville, Maryland, and became its evangelist and pastoral leader. In 1933 he added duties as editor of a second periodical, *Present Truth*, and the following year of a third, *Life and Health*. The latter magazine had almost died, but he was able to build its circulation into the hundreds of thousands and give it a solid future. Besides his editorial duties, Nichol authored several books during his early years in Takoma Park, including *Signs of Christ's Second Coming* (1931); *Answers to Objections* (1932); and *Behold, He Cometh* (1938). He also began research on the first of several important books on Adventist themes. *The Midnight Cry*, which appeared in 1944, was a landmark survey of Adventist history which, among its other contributions, laid to rest the anti-Adventist stories about their gathering in ascension robes to await the second coming of Christ in the 1840s.

The multiplication of Nichol's duties led him to resign his position as leader of the congregation in Hyattsville in 1942. In 1944 he became editor of the *Review and Herald* and soon had to drop his duties with *Life and Health*. He continued to author books and the years after World War II became his most prolific period. *The Midnight Cry* was followed by *Reasons for Our Faith* (1947); *Let's Live Our Beliefs* (1947); *Certainty of My Faith* (1948); and *Letters from Afar* (1948).

In 1950 Nichol became involved as the editor of the massive *Seventh-day Adventist Bible Commentary*. He had just finished what has remained his second most important book, *Ellen G. White and Her Critics* (1951), a detailed refutation of objections to the prophetic claims of the founder of the Seventh-day Adventist Church, especially those of Adventist apostate Elder Dudley Marvin Canright. In recognition of Nichol's work, in 1950 he became a trustee of the Ellen G. White Estate, which retains ownership of White's manuscripts and copyrights. In 1963 he became president of the board of trustees.

Nichol continued to work right to the end of his life, dying suddenly after a brief illness in 1966. Through his books and editorials for the church's periodicals, he emerged as one of the most vital exponents of the Seventh-day Adventist Church in the twentieth century.

Sources:

Nichol, Francis N. *Ellen G. White and Her Critics*. Takoma Park, MD: Review and Herald Publishing Association, 1951. 703 pp.

_____. *The Midnight Cry*. Takoma Park, MD: Review and Herald Publishing Association, 1944. 576 pp.

Wood, Miriam, and Kenneth Wood. *His Initials Were F.D.N.* Takoma Park, MD: Review and Herald Publishing Association, 1967. 236 pp.

★ 681 ★
Bishop NICHOLAS
Bishop, Russian Orthodox Church
b. May 21, 1851, Kherson District Russia
d. 1915, Petrograd Russia

Bishop Nicholas, head of the Russian Orthodox Church in the United States, was born Michael Zacharovich Ziorov. He attended the Moscow Theological Academy from which he graduated in 1878. He was not ordained immediately, but as a lay person he became inspector for the Vologda Seminary and later the Mogilev Seminary. He did not marry, but in 1887 was successively tonsured, ordained as a deacon, and ordained as a priest. He became rector at his former school, the Moscow Theological Seminary. From that post he was selected as the new bishop for the Aleutian Islands and Alaska.

Bishop Nicholas was consecrated in 1891 and upon his arrival in America organized the diocese in a manner to promote growth. He initiated an English-language weekly, the *Russian American Messenger*. He visited the parishes, by this time strung across the country and throughout Alaska. He organized new parishes, more than tripling the number outside of Alaska. He also became the first Orthodox bishop to visit Canada.

In 1898 he was recalled to Russia and became archbishop of Tver and Kashim and later archbishop of Warsaw. He died in 1915 in Petrograd (now Leningrad).

Sources:

Afonsky, Bishop Gregory. *A History of the Orthodox Church in Alaska (1794-1917)*. Kodiak, AK: St. Herman's Theological Seminary, 1977. 106 pp.

Tarasar, Constance J. *Orthodox America, 1794-1974*. Syosset, NY: Department of History and Archives, Orthodox Church in America, 1975. 361 pp.

★ 682 ★
NICHOLS, L. T.
Founder, Meggido Mission Church
b. Oct. 1, 1844, Elkhart, Indiana
d. Feb. 28, 1912, Battle Creek, Michigan

L. T. Nichols, the founder of the Meggido Mission Church, had no first name. His father merely passed along his initials to his son.

L. T. grew up in rural Wisconsin. He received little formal education as he had to work to help support the family. There being no church in his neighborhood, religious training was limited to the occasional visits of traveling preachers. However, Nichols became an avid Bible student, and as he grew to manhood took every opportunity to interact with the itinerant ministers who passed through his area. His study of the Bible convinced him that truth lay behind the man-made fables shared by the different churches available to him. He came to doubt a number of orthodox Christian beliefs: the trinity, the immortality of the soul, the fall of humankind, and the existence of hell.

As Nichols' perspective matured he began to preach in his neighborhood. Very early in his ministry, he decided not to affiliate with any denomination and not to accept money for his preaching. A small group began to be attracted to his teachings, and in 1874 he and his followers moved to Oregon. He attracted more followers through his writings and his participation in religious debates, a popular nineteenth-century activity.

In 1880 Nichols promulgated what was to become his most unique and definitive teaching. He had come to believe that perfection of character (i.e., the keeping of the whole of the law) was necessary for salvation. Sin was transgression of the law, and no one could be saved apart from knowing and keeping every commandment of God. The proclamation of this truth came to be seen as the true reformation of the church.

In 1883 Nichols settled in Dodge City, Minnesota, and entered the manufacturing business. Through the remainder of the century, he traveled and preached as he could, and congregations aligned to his teachings emerged around the Midwest. In 1901 he purchased a boat which he named the "Meggido," meaning God is in this place with a band of soldiers. He invited his followers to join him on the river and the group of some 30 families constituted the Meggido Mission. They worked the river for several years and then sold the boat and settled in Rochester, New York, still the home of the mission. There Nichols made his last discovery, that Christmas really occurred in the spring and should be celebrated on Abib 1 according to the Jewish calendar.

Nichols developed heart trouble during his last years, and leadership gradually transferred to Maude Hambree, his successor. He died in Battle Creek, Michigan, where he had traveled to stay at the Kellogg-founded sanitarium there.

Sources:

History of the Meggido Mission. Rochester, NY: Meggido Mission Church, 1967. 67 pp.
Nichols, L. T. *The Devil and Hell of the Bible.* Rochester, NY: Megiddo Mission Church, n.d. 64 pp.
_____. *A Treatise on the Trinity.* Rochester, NY: Meggido Mission Church, 1906. 76 pp.

★683★
NIEBUHR, Helmut Richard
Theologian, United Church of Christ
b. Sep. 3, 1894, Wright City, Missouri
d. Jul. 5, 1962, Greenfield, Massachusetts

Helmut Richard Niebuhr, one of the outstanding Protestant thinkers of the twentieth century, was the son of Gustav and Lydia Hosto Niebuhr. He was reared in a pious home, his father being a minister and his mother a minister's daughter. Education and culture were also emphasized. Niebuhr was one of three children who became professors. His brother **Reinhold Niebuhr** taught for many years at Union Theological Seminary, and his sister Hulda became a professor at McCormick Theological Seminary. Niebuhr was quite young when he decided to enter the ministry.

In 1908 Niebuhr entered Elmhurst College. Following his graduation (B.A., 1912) from Elmhurst he attended Eden Theological Seminary, from which he graduated in 1915. He was ordained in the Evangelical Synod in 1916 and served as pastor of the Walnut Park Evangelical Church in St. Louis, Missouri. At the same time he pursued an M.A. degree in history at Washington University, which was granted in 1917. In 1919 he became an instructor in theology and ethics and the following year married Florence Marie Mittendorff. Desiring further education, in 1922 he entered Yale Divinity School, where he earned his B.D. (1923) and Ph.D. (1924). Following his graduation he became president of Elmhurst College. His major accomplishment as president was assisting the school to attain its full accreditation.

In 1927 Niebuhr moved back to St. Louis to rejoin the faculty at Eden Seminary. While there he rewrote his dissertation, which appeared in 1929 as *The Social Sources of Denominationalism,* one of his most well-known books, still used as a college text. Combining the insights of history and sociology, he argued that social, not theological, factors accounted for much of the denominational divisions in American Protestantism. In 1930 Niebuhr studied for a year with Karl Barth and **Paul Tillich** in Germany. Upon his return he accepted a post at Yale teaching Christian ethics. Among his first accomplishments in his new position was to introduce Tillich to America by translating his first book into English, *The Religious Situation* (1932). Shortly after joining the Yale staff, Niebuhr's denomination merged with the Reformed Church in the United States to become the Evangelical and Reformed Church.

At Yale, Niebuhr had his most productive years. Over his first two decades he produced a series of significant texts, including *The Church Against the World* (1935), with Wilhelm Pauck and Francis P. Miller; *The Kingdom of God in America* (1937); *The Meaning of Revelation* (1941); and *Christ and Culture* (1951). The latter title attempted to present a broad survey of the different ways religious groups relate to culture and remains his most widely read piece.

During the 1950s, much of Niebuhr's time was consumed in a massive study of the Protestant ministry. The results appeared in three volumes he edited with Daniel Day Williams: *The Ministry in Historical Perspectives* (1956); *The Purpose of the Church and Its Ministry* (1956); and *The Advancement of Theological Education* (1957). His last publication, a collection of essays and papers entitled *Radical Monotheism and Western Culture,* appeared in 1960, though one significant volume, *The Responsible Self,* appeared posthumously (1963).

H. Richard Niebuhr has taken his place beside Paul Tillich, Karl Barth, Emil Brunner, Rudolf Bultmann, and his brother Reinhold as one of the leading figures in the Protestant Christian theological renaissance of the mid-twentieth century. The contributions for which he will be most remembered are the sociological and historical insights he brought to the theological task. He died just after the Evangelical and Reformed Church merged with the Congregational-Christian Churches to form the United Church of Christ.

Sources:

Dictionary of American Biography. 20 vols. and 7 supps. New York: Charles Scribner's Sons, 1928-1936, 1944-1981.
Godsey, John D. *The Promise of H. Richard Niebuhr.* Philadelphia: Lippencott, 1970.
Niebuhr, H. Richard. *Christ and Culture.* New York: Harper & Row, 1951. 259 pp.
_____. *The Kingdom of God in America.* New York: Harper & Brothers, 1937. 215 pp.
_____. *The Meaning of Revelation.* New York: Macmillan Company, 1941. 196 pp.
_____. *The Responsible Self.* New York: Harper & Row, 1963. 183 pp.
_____. *The Social Sources of Denominationalism.* Hamden, CT: Shoe String Press, 1954.
Ramsey, Paul. *Faith and Ethics: The Theology of H. Richard Niebuhr.* New York: Harper, 1957. 306 pp.

★ 684 ★
NIEBUHR, Reinhold
Theologian, United Church of Christ
b. Jun. 21, 1892, Wright City, Michigan
d. Jun. 1, 1971, Stockbridge, Massachusetts

Reinhold Niebuhr, arguably the most important American-born Protestant theologian of the twentieth century, was the son of Lydia and Rev. Gustav Niebuhr, and the brother of theologian-sociologist **H. Richard Niebuhr**. The son of a Reformed minister, he was educated at Elmhurst College, Eden Theological Seminary (B.D., 1914), and Yale (M.A., 1915). In 1915 he was ordained in the Evangelical Synod. The synod, a small German Lutheran body, merged with the Reformed Church in the United States in 1934 to form the Evangelical and Reformed Church, which in turn merged with the General Council of Congregational-Christian Churches to form the United Church of Christ in 1956. Niebuhr pastored the Bethel Evangelical Church in Detroit from 1915 to 1928. From 1928 until his retirement in 1960, he taught at the Union Theological Seminary in New York City. While a professor at Union, he met and in 1931 married Ursula Mary Keppel-Compton.

During his Detroit years, Niebuhr was a theological modernist whose focus of attention was directed to building the kingdom of God through addressing social and economic concerns. This orientation was reflected in his first book, *Does Civilization Need Religion?* (1927), but his years in the pastorate slowly stripped him of his optimism. While the direction that his later thought would take can be discerned in this initial work, Niebuhr's disenchantment with liberal Christianity would be more fully expressed in his transitional books, *Leaves from the Notebook of a Tamed Cynic* (1929) and his celebrated *Moral Man and Immoral Society* (1932). The latter book's antagonism toward the perceived unrealistic optimism of liberal Protestantism caused Niebuhr's contemporaries to classify him in the "Neo-Orthodox" camp, in spite of the clear differences between his position and the theology of Karl Barth, for whom the label was originally coined.

Niebuhr was primarily an ethicist, holding successively the position of associate professor of philosophy of religion (1928-1930), William E. Dodge Jr. Professor of Applied Christianity (1930-1955), and Charles A. Briggs Graduate Professor of Ethics and Theology (1955-1960) while at Union. In this capacity he authored a number of outstanding books: *An Interpretation of Christian Ethics* (1935); *Christianity and Power Politics* (1940); *The Children of Light and the Children of Darkness* (1944); *Christian Realism and Political Problems* (1953); and *Pious and Secular America* (1958). In addition he was the co-founder of both the Fellowship of Socialist Christians and Americans for Democratic Action. Niebuhr was a contributing editor for *The Christian Century*, *Nation*, and *New Leader*, and for a quarter century he edited *Christianity and Crisis* (1941-1966), the popular journal of Christian social ethics.

In 1939, as World War II was beginning, Niebuhr was invited to give the prestigious Gifford Lectures in Scotland, in which he developed the most systematic presentation of his theological views. Later published as *The Nature and Destiny of Man* (1941-1943), the lectures are one of the premier theological works of the twentieth century.

Niebuhr retired in 1960 and was named professor emeritus. During his final years he authored several books reflecting upon the conclusions of a lifetime of thought: *Man's Nature and His Communities* (1965) and *The Democratic Experience, Past and Prospects* (1969), written with Paul E. Sigmund.

Sources:

Harland, Gordon. *The Thought of Reinhold Niebuhr*. New York: Oxford University Press, 1960.
Niebuhr, Reinhold. *Christianity and Power Politics*. New York: Charles Scribner's Sons, 1940.

_____. *An Interpretation of Christian Ethics*. New York: Harper & Row, 1935.
_____. *Leaves from the Notebook of a Tamed Cynic*. New York: Willet Clark, 1929.
_____. *Moral Man and Immoral Society*. New York: Charles Scribner's Sons, 1932.
_____. *The Nature and Destiny of Man*. 2 vols. New York: Charles Scribner's Sons, 1941-43.
_____. *Pious and Secular America*. New York: Charles Scribner's Sons, 1958.
Robertson, D. B. *Reinhold Niebuhr's Works: A Bibliography*. Boston: Hall, 1979.
Scott, Nathan A., Jr. *Reinhold Niebuhr*. Long Prairies, MN: University of Minnesota, 1963. 48 pp.

★ 685 ★
NOLI, Theophan S.
Metropolitan, Albanian Orthodox Archdiocese of America
b. Jan. 6, 1882, Thrace Turkey
d. Mar. 13, 1965

Theophan (Fan) S. Noli, founder and archbishop of the Albanian Orthodox Archdiocese of America, was born in a small Albanian community in a northwestern Turkish town near the Greek border, and grew up in a large peasant family. His education was primarily Greek and he developed an early affinity for Byzantine music. As a young man he became the main cantor at the Greek Orthodox cathedral in Adrianople (now Edirne), Turkey. After high school, he traveled widely and visited Albanian colonies in Europe, Africa, and the United States.

By 1907 Noli had settled in Boston, Massachusetts, which was home to one of the largest Albanian communities in America. He arrived at a time when American Albanians, who brought with them the experience of centuries of denial of the use of the Albanian language in their schools and churches, were engulfed in an experience of liberation. Noli found himself in the midst of a dispute between the Albanians and the Greek priest who presided over their congregation. They asked Noli to become their priest, and he turned to the Russian Orthodox archbishop, who had jurisdiction over all the Orthodox membership in America at the time. Archbishop Platon ordained Noli in New York, and Noli returned to Boston to institute Albanian services. He also introduced the community to an Albanian translation of the Orthodox liturgy he had made earlier.

Noli became an activist in the revitalization of the Albanian community both in America and Europe, especially after the declaration of Albanian independence in 1914. He wrote widely for Albanian newspapers and promoted community organizations. He also developed close ties with the church leaders in Albania and led in the establishment of a number of Albanian Orthodox parishes. In 1918 he was appointed administrator of an Albanian Orthodox Mission in America (a unit within the Russian Orthodox Church in America). That same year he took monastic vows and was elevated to the rank of archimandrite.

In 1919 he was elected bishop of what was to become the Albanian Orthodox Church in America, but conditions in Albania, where the church was under the authority of the Ecumenical Patriarchate, prevented his immediate consecration. Meanwhile he became involved in the rapid changes in both church and state in Albania. In 1922 he was among the church leaders who proclaimed the autonomy of the Albanian Orthodox Church (from the Ecumenical Patriarchate), and in 1923 he was consecrated bishop and appointed to the diocese of Durres, Gora, and Shapta. Meanwhile he had become Albania's Minister of Foreign Affairs, and in 1924 he was elected Prime Minister. Among his accomplishments during this period was the further translation of liturgical services into Albanian. Rapid political changes in Albania forced Noli out of the country before the end of the year, and he spent the next eight years in Germany trying to get back into the United States. He finally obtained a visa in 1932.

In the United States he dropped all political activities and concentrated entirely on his duties as bishop of the Albanian Orthodox Church in America. He published the Albanian liturgical books and additionally translated eight texts into English (in recognition that many Albanian-Americans could only speak English). Under Noli's leadership, the American diocese remained tied to both the Russian Orthodox Greek Catholic Church in America and the Albanian Orthodox Church in Albania. Following World War II, however, a Communist government came into power in Albania, and Noli broke ties with the church and declared the American church's independence.

Noli's authority was challenged in 1949 when Mark I. Lipa came to the United States with authority to reorganize the Albanian Orthodox in America under the Ecumenical Patriarchate. In the ensuing controversy the church was divided. A majority adhered to Noli, who continued to lead what became known as the Albanian Orthodox Archdiocese in America until his death in 1965. In 1970 the archdiocese was received into the Orthodox Church in America where it was given administrative autonomy and continued ethnic identity.

Sources:
Tarasar, Constance J. *Orthodox America, 1794-1974*. Syosset, NY: Department of History and Archives, Orthodox Church in America, 1975. 361 pp.

★ 686 ★
NORRIS, John Franklyn
Founder, World Baptist Fellowship
b. Sep. 18, 1877, Dadeville, Alabama
d. Aug. 20, 1952, Keystone Heights, Florida

Fundamentalist minister J. Frank Norris, founder of the World Baptist Fellowship, was the child of poor sharecroppers. After a move to Texas, he was converted and received a call to preach at a young age. He was educated at Baylor University and the Southern Baptist Theological Seminary in Louisville, Kentucky, both institutions of the Southern Baptist Convention. He returned to Texas where in a few years time he had built a 1,000-member church out of what had begun as a minuscule congregation. Norris also became the editor of the official organ of the Southern Baptists in Texas, the *Baptist Standard*, a position that brought him into conflict with many of the denomination's leaders because of his ultra-fundamentalist views.

Norris left this post in 1909 to accept the pastorate of the First Baptist Church in Fort Worth. From a membership of 1,200, the charismatic Norris built the Fort Worth congregation into an imposing 28,000 members in less than 10 years. He also had a popular radio ministry, and initiated his own magazine, the *Fence-Rail* (later known as *The Fundamentalist*).

Norris was one of the most flamboyant and popular leaders of the Fundamentalist Movement. He was especially outspoken in his criticism of Catholicism, and waged a verbal campaign against the Catholic mayor of Fort Worth, H. C. Meacham. This antagonism led to an argument between Norris and a friend of Meacham's, D. E. Chipps, which ended with Norris shooting and killing this Fort Worth businessman. Although acquitted on grounds of self-defense, the incident served to deepen the rift that had already developed with his denomination as a result of the fundamentalist controversy.

Norris finally left the Southern Baptist Convention in 1931 and, with the aid of sympathetic pastors and congregations, founded the World Baptist Fellowship (originally the Premillennial, Fundamental, Missionary Fellowship). His ministry continued to expand in the

1930s. Norris became pastor of Detroit's Temple Baptist Church in 1935, and for over a decade ministered to both his Fort Worth and his Detroit congregations. In 1939 he organized the Bible Baptist Institute, which later became the Bible Baptist Seminary in Arlington, Texas.

In 1948 **G. Beauchamp Vick** took over the Detroit pastorate. A few years afterwards Vick and Norris had a falling out. Norris and other dissatisfied members separated to form an independent group, the Baptist Bible Fellowship. In 1952 Norris died of a heart attack while at a youth rally in Florida.

Sources:
Entzminger, Louis. *The J. Frank Norris I Have Known for Thirty-four Years*. N.p., n.d.
Norris, J. Frank. *The Gospel of Dynamite*. N.p., n.d.
_____. *Infidelity among Southern Baptists Endorsed by Highest Officials*. N.p., n.d.
_____. *Inside History of First Baptist Church*. N.p., n.d.
Russell, C. Allyn. *Voices of American Fundamentalism*. Philadelphia: Westminster Press, 1976. 304 pp.
Tatum, E. Roy. *Conquest of Failure? A Biography of J. Frank Norris*. Dallas: 1966.

★ 687 ★
NORTH, Frank Mason
Minister, Methodist Episcopal Church
b. Dec. 3, 1850, New York, New York
d. Dec. 27, 1935, Madison, New Jersey

Frank Mason North, a minister of the Methodist Episcopal Church, was the son of Elizabeth Mason and Charles Carter North. He attended Wesleyan University in Middletown, Connecticut, from which he received his A.B. degree in 1872. He was ordained in the New York Conference in 1873 and appointed to Amenia, New York. In 1874 he married Fannie L. Stewart. That year he was appointed to Cold Spring-on-Hudson, New York. While there he was able to complete his M.A. at Wesleyan in 1875. He then pastored in New York City (1876-1878); White Plains (1878-1881); and again in New York City at Calvary Methodist Episcopal Church (1881-1887). In 1887 he transferred to the New England Conference and served the church in Middletown, Connecticut (1887-1892).

In 1892 North moved back to New York City, where the Methodists put his knowledge of the city and proven administrative skills to work as the corresponding secretary of the New York City Church Extension and Missionary Society. This was a home missionary agency which supervised a complex of urban parishes, benevolent enterprises, and new congregations, many serving immigrant or minority groups. At the same time he became the director of the National City Union and editor of *The Christian City*. In 1901 North became a Methodist Episcopal Church delegate to the Ecumenical Methodist Conference (the first of four he would attend), and in 1908 he was elected as a delegate to the Methodist general conference (the first of five).

North had become a leader in the social application of the gospel, especially in the urban areas. His concerns led him to become a founder of the Methodist Federation for Social Service created by the general conference of 1908 to work for social justice. The conference also for the first time adopted a social creed which North had helped edit. Later that same year he participated in the founding of the Federal Council of Churches. He became the head of its Committee on the Church and Modern Industry and led in the adoption by the council of a slightly modified version of the Methodist Social Creed.

By 1912 North had emerged as a Protestant church statesman of the highest caliber. He was named the corresponding secretary of the Board of Foreign Missions by the Methodist general conference and elected chairperson of the Executive Committee of the

Federal Council. In 1916 he became president of the Federal Council and served through the important years in which the council responded to the post-war rebuilding of Europe. For his efforts he was decorated by both the French and Greek governments. In 1921 North participated in the founding of the International Missionary Council (I.M.C.).

In spite of North's outstanding career of church leadership, he is possibly best remembered today for his authorship of a poem which became a popular hymn, "Where Cross the Crowded Ways of Life." He also authored several other poems that were placed in the *Methodist Hymnal*, "O Master of the Waking World" and "The World's Astir!" He retired in 1928 and lived his last years in Madison, New Jersey.

Sources:

Harmon, Nolan B. *The Encyclopedia of World Methodism*. 2 vols. Nashville: United Methodist Publishing House, 1974.

Lacy, C. *Frank Mason North*. Nashville, TN: Abingdon Press, 1967. 300

★ 688 ★
OBERHOLTZER, John H.
Founder, General Conference Mennonite Church
b. Jan. 10, 1809, Clayton, Pennsylvania
d. Feb. 15, 1895, Quakertown, Pennsylvania

John H. Oberholtzer, one of the founders of the General Conference Mennonite Church, was the son of Abraham and Susanna Oberholtzer. Oberholtzer decided not to follow the farming career of his father and after obtaining some education, began work as a school teacher. Oberholtzer also became a locksmith, the occupation he followed most of his life. In the 1830s he married Mary Riehn, and they joined the Great Swamp Mennonite Church near Germantown, Pennsylvania, a congregation affiliated with the Franconia Conference of the Mennonite Church.

In 1842 Oberholtzer's life was altered by his being chosen by lot as a minister for the Big Swamp Church. Over the next few years he emerged as a leader of the younger members that were pressing for changes in traditional Mennonite practice. He refused to wear the standard Mennonite minister's straight-collar coat. He preached in non-Mennonite churches and on occasion accepted honorariums for his work. He accepted members into the church who had married outside the community. Oberholtzer organized Bible classes, *Kinderlehre*, for the children. These grew into the first Mennonite Sunday school in America. He imported a catechism from the European Mennonites as a text.

Oberholtzer introduced a constitution and written church order to the congregation, but in 1947 met stiff opposition when he first tried to have the general membership drawn into the decision making process and then asked that written minutes of the church meetings be kept. The debate over his innovations reached a fevered pitch and led to the withdrawal of his followers and the organization of an independent congregation. By 1852 he was able to purchase a printing press and to begin issuing a periodical, the *Religioser Botschafer (Religious Messenger)*. In 1860, hearing of three independent congregations in Iowa that seemed to share his opinions, he attended their conference and hammered out a merger of their work. The new organization, the General Conference Mennonite Church is now the second lagest Mennonite body in North America.

Oberholtzer served as the first chairman of both the General Conference and of its eastern conference. He initiated their first mission project, a society to evangelize the Indians, and served on its board. He retired in 1872 but continued to edit the periodical and work on various mission projects. He preached until a few months before his death in 1895.

Sources:

Kaufman, Edmund G. *General Conference Mennonite Pioneers*. North Newton, KS: Bethel College, 1973. 437 pp.

The Mennonite Encyclopedia. 4 vols. Scottdale, PA: The Mennonite Publishing House, 1955.

★ 689 ★
O'BOYLE, Patrick Aloysius
Cardinal, Roman Catholic Church
b. Jul. 18, 1896, Scranton, Pennsylvania
d. Aug. 10, 1987, Washington, District of Columbia

Patrick Aloysius O'Boyle, the archbishop of Washington, D.C., and a cardinal in the Roman Catholic Church, was the son of Mary Muldoon and Michael O'Boyle, both of Irish descent. He was 11 when his father died, and he worked through his teen years to help support the family. He attended St. Thomas College, now Scranton University, and after his graduation in 1917 entered St. Joseph's Seminary. He graduated and was ordained in 1921. He was assigned to St. Columbia's Church in New York City. Here he began blending his church career and social work. He moved on in 1926 to become the executive director of the Catholic Guardian Society. He also returned to school and completed his degree from the New York School of Work in 1931.

O'Boyle taught for a period at Fordham University, and served with both Catholic Charities and the Immaculate Heart Mission Station on Staten Island through the 1930s. In 1943 he was picked to head the church's War Relief Services. After the war Cardinal Francis Spellman chose O'Boyle as head of Catholic Charities for the archdiocese of New York and as consultant to the archbishop. He had worked for the archdiocese only a few weeks, however, when he was chosen as the first archbishop of the newly created archdiocese of Washington, D.C.

O'Boyle quickly emerged as a social liberal. He advocated a number of social reforms, including a liberalized immigration policy, calling new attention to the inner city, and government allowances to poor families. He also joined with several of his episcopal colleagues in initiating the integration of the parochial schools of the archdiocese. As his involvement in social issues continued, O'Boyle became controversial in the extreme as critics charged that his thinking was outdated. While interested in charity, he seemed opposed to systemic changes that would alleviate oppressive social conditions.

In 1965 the pope created the position of providence of Washington, D.C., and added the Virgin Islands to its territory. He elevated the leadership position to that of metropolitan. In 1967 he made O'Boyle a cardinal.

While O'Boyle would possibly like to be remembered for his social service, he gained his greatest publicity for his handling of a controversy following the 1968 encyclical *Humanae Vitae*, which banned all methods of artificial birth control. He ordered his priests to follow the precepts without exception. A group of professors issued a response which was picked up by the Association of Washington Priests. O'Boyle responded to his priests by threatening them with sanctions. Forty priests refused to be quiet, however, and he took action to silence them. The heated controversy continued until settled by a statement of the Congregation for the Clergy in Rome. The Congregation upheld O'Boyle's teaching authority, but also equally supported the role of conscience in making moral decisions. Both sides declared it an acceptable solution, and the silenced priests returned to their parishes.

O'Boyle announced his retirement in 1971 at the age of 75, and two years later it was accepted. He lived out his final years in Washington, D.C.

★ 690 ★
OCKENGA, Harold John
Minister, Presbyterian Church
b. Jul. 6, 1905, Chicago, Illinois
d. Feb. 8, 1985, Hamilton, Massachusetts

Harold John Ockenga was a minister of the Presbyterian Church best remembered for coining the term "Neo-Evangelicalism" to describe a new phase in conservative Reformed Protestant thinking in the decades immediately after World War II. He was the son of Herman and Angelina Tetzlaff Ockenga. He attended Taylor University (A.B., 1927) and was among the earliest students at Westminister Theological Seminary (Th.B., 1930), the independent school established by **J. Greshen Machen** and the fundamentalist leaders who left Princeton Theological Seminary. Following his graduation he became the assistant minister of First Presbyterian Church in Pittsburgh, Pennsylvania. In 1931 he was ordained and became pastor of the Breeze Point Presbyterian Church also in Pittsburgh.

In 1936 Ockenga began his pastorate at Park Street Church in Boston, which would last over three decades. While there he preached an average of four times a week and developed a popular radio ministry. Shortly after assuming the pulpit he began to gain some national attention with his early books: *These Religious Affections* (1937); *Our Protestant Heritage* (1938); *Have You Met These Women?* (1940); *Everyone That Believeth* (1942); and *The Comfort of God* (1944). In 1941 he became one of the founders of the National Association of Evangelicals, a fundamentalist alternative to the Federal Council of Churches, and served as the organization's first president (1942-1944).

After the war Ockenga emerged as a leader in calling for a new type of conservative Protestant faith to which he gave the name Neo-Evangelicalism. Neo-Evangelicalism grew out of fundamentalism but, while upholding conservative theological standards, attempted to present a warmer, less hostile face to the larger Christian community and the world. It was also characterized by intellectual rigor, an attempt to deal with social questions, and a willingness to cooperate with liberal Protestants on issues not compromising orthodox faith. He elaborated upon his position in several books, including: *Our Evangelical Faith* (1946); *The Spirit of the Living God* (1947); and *Faithful in Christ Jesus* (1948).

In 1947, without relinquishing his post at the church, Ockenga became one of the founders and the first president of Fuller Theological Seminary, a new school in Pasadena, California, begun with resources provided by radio evangelist **Charles E. Fuller**. The school became the showcase of Neo-Evangelical thought, and Ockenga gathered an outstanding faculty. He continued as president until 1954 and later served a second term (1959-1963). In 1956 he began a quarter century as chairman of the board of *Christianity Today*, viewed by many as the major periodical representative of Neo-Evangelicalism. In 1969 he retired from Park Street and became president of Gordon-Conwell Theological Seminary and Gordon College. He served at Gordon-Conwell until his retirement and was named president emeritus.

Sources:
Frame, Randy. "Modern Evangelicalism Mourns the Loss of One of Its Founding Fathers." *Christianity Today* 29, 5 (March 15, 1985): 34-36.
Ockenga, Harold J. *Faithful in Jesus Christ.* New York: Revell, 1948.
———. *Our Evangelical Faith.* New York: Revell, 1946.
———. *Our Protestant Heritage.* Grand Rapids, MI: Zondervan, 1938.
———. *The Spirit of the Living God.* New York: Revell, 1947.
———. *These Religious Affections.* Grand Rapids, MI: Zondervan, 1937.

★ 691 ★
O'CONNELL, William
Cardinal, Roman Catholic Church
b. Dec. 8, 1859, Lowell, Massachusetts
d. Apr. 22, 1944, Boston, Massachusetts

William O'Connell, a Cardinal in the Roman Catholic Church, was born the last child in the large family of John O'Connell and Bridget Farley O'Connell. The poverty of the family existence was intensified by the death of William's father when he was four, and his childhood was further marred by anti-Irish and anti-Catholic bigotry. In 1876 he left home to attend St. Charles College in Endicott City, Maryland, where he learned to play the piano, a talent which stayed with him for the rest of his life. Sickness forced him to return home at the end of his second year, and he finished his education at Boston College. He was selected to attend the North American College in Rome to begin his seminary work. He was ordained in Rome in 1884, at the beginning of his third year. Unfortunately, poor health again intervened, and during his fourth year he was forced to return home before he could finish his doctorate.

Back in the United States, O'Connell was assigned to a parish in Medford, Massachusetts. Two years later, in 1886, he joined the staff at St. Joseph's parish in Boston. He stayed until 1893, when unexpectedly he was appointed rector at the North American College in Rome. The former rector had been deeply involved in the controversies over "Americanism," i.e., the level of accommodation to American culture the church could make, and had been reassigned. O'Connell's success in revitalizing the school was marked two years later by his appointment as domestic prelate, a position that carried with it the title of monsignor. He stayed at the school until his consecration as Bishop of Portland, Maine, in 1901.

In 1904 the recently elected Pope Pius X, on the advice of Cardinal Sarto of Venice, appointed O'Connell as a papal envoy to Japan to deal with the problems of violence that had been experienced by missionaries in the wake of the Russo-Japanese War. The success of his mission was signaled by the establishment of a Catholic school in Tokyo two years later and by O'Connell's appointment as coadjutor archbishop of Boston. In 1907, after the death of Archbishop Williams, O'Connell became archbishop of Boston.

Inheriting a disorganized archdiocese, O'Connell decided upon reforming it completely. He consolidated charitable work under the Catholic Charitable Bureau. He strengthened Boston College and created new schools. He reorganized the chancery in agreement with canon law. His reforms became a model for his colleagues.

In 1911 O'Connell was called to Rome and received his cardinal's hat on November 29, the same day as the Archbishop of New York, **John Farley**. He returned to Rome again in 1914, but did not arrive in time to participate in the election of the new pope. Controversy arose when he protested the unrealistic amount of time allowed for cardinals in distant residences to make the journey.

Upon his return to Boston, O'Connell continued his reforms and improvements in the archdiocese. He organized a number of guilds for professional men. He purchased the Boston *Pilot* and turned it into a top-quality diocesan newspaper. He encouraged a young priest of his archdiocese to found a foreign missions society, which became the Maryknoll Fathers. The people of Boston remember his willingness to turn many Catholic institutions into infirmaries during the flu epidemic of 1918.

O'Connell's reign lasted almost 40 years. In 1934 he penned his autobiography, *Recollections of Seventy Years*. He finally passed away of pneumonia at the age of 85.

Sources:

Blunt, Hugh Francis. *Readings from Cardinal O'Connell*. New York: D. Appleton Company, 1934.

Delaney, John J. *Dictionary of American Catholic Biography*. Garden City, NY: Doubleday & Company, 1988. 621 pp.

O'Connell, William. *Recollections of Seventy Years*. Boston: Houghton Mifflin Company, 1934.

Sexton, John E. *Cardinal O'Connell: A Biographical Sketch*.

★ 692 ★
O'CONNOR, John Joseph
Cardinal, Roman Catholic Church
b. Jan. 15, 1920, Philadelphia, Pennsylvania

John Joseph O'Connor, archbishop of New York and a cardinal in the Roman Catholic Church, is the son of Dorothy M. Gomple and Thomas O'Connor. O'Connor attended both public and parochial schools as he was growing up. In 1936 he entered St. Charles Borromeo Seminary in Philadelphia and upon completion of his work in 1945 was ordained a priest. He was assigned to St. James High School in Chester, Pennsylvania, and served as curate at St. Gabriel's Roman Catholic Church in Norwood. Over the next few years he began to work with mentally handicapped children, a task which was interrupted by the Korean War. In 1952 he became a chaplain in the navy.

O'connor's initial two-year stint in the navy was extended year by year until he decided to make his position permanent. Among other tasks, he worked on problems in naval leadership, which became the subject of his first book, *Principles and Problems of Naval Leadership*. He served not only in Korea, but returned to Asia for service in Vietnam. In 1966 he was awarded the Legion of Merit with Gold Star for his service in the war. In 1968 he authored a book about his wartime experiences, *A Chaplain Looks at Vietnam*. In 1974 he authored *The Professional Officer and the Human Person* and the next year was named naval chief of chaplains. He retired from the navy in 1979 with the rank of rear admiral.

In May 1979 O'Connor was consecrated and assigned as auxiliary bishop in charge of military chaplains. He moved into the New York Archdiocese which traditionally had charge of the church's relations to the military. In his new post, articulation of issues of war and peace were a significant part of his task. He authored *In Defense of Life* in 1981. In 1983 he helped draft the American Bishops pastoral letter "The Challenge of Peace: God's Promise and Our Response."

In 1983 O'Connor was named bishop of Scranton, Pennsylvania. He stayed only a year before he was named archbishop of New York. The following year he was named a cardinal. O'Connor lost no time in making his presence known, emerging as a staunch foe of abortion and attacking the position of Geraldine Ferraro, the 1984 Democratic Party vice-presidential candidate, on that issue. In succeeding years he has emerged as one of the most powerful conservative voices in the American hierarchy. His conservative views on sexual behavior, especially the use of contraceptives, led to conflict with the liberal mayor of New York City at the time, Edward I. Koch. Their exchange of opinions became the substance of a 1989 book, *His Eminence and Hizzonor*.

Sources:

Hentoff, Nat. *John Cardinal O'Connor: At the Center of a Changing American Catholic Church*. New York: Scribner, 1988. 290 pp.

O'Connor, John J. *A Chaplain Looks at Vietnam*. Cleveland, OH: World Publishing Co., 1968. 256 pp.

———. *In Defense of Life*. Boston: St. Paul Editions, 1981. 140 pp.

———, and Edward I. Koch. *His Eminence and Hizzonor: A Candid Exchange*. New York: William Morrow, 1989. 356 pp.

★ 693 ★
OFIESH, Abdullah
Founder and Archbishop, American Orthodox Catholic Church
b. Oct. 22, 1880, Mohiedhthet Lebanon
d. 1971

Abdullah (Aftimios) Ofiesh, the founder and first archbishop of the American Orthodox Catholic Church, was the son of a priest of the Orthodox Church in Lebanon. He also decided to enter the priesthood, and eventually graduated as valedictorian of his class at the Middle Eastern Orthodox Ecclesiastical Seminary. At the time of his ordination he chose Aftimios as his religious name. In 1898 he became the assistant to the bishop of Lebanon. In 1900 he became the archdeacon at Latikia, Lebanon. He also became involved in a reform movement aimed at changing the administrative system of the church. He was almost excommunicated for his efforts, and in 1905 he requested a transfer to the United States.

In America Ofiesh came under the jurisdiction of Bishop Raphael Hawaweeny, bishop of Brooklyn, New York, who was in charge of Arab Christians within the Russian Orthodox Church. The Russian church, as the first Orthodox jurisdiction in the country, had charge of all Orthodox believers. After a year assisting Hawaweeny, he moved to Montreal, Quebec, as pastor of St. Nicolas Church.

In 1915 Ofiesh was selected to succeed the recently deceased Hawaweeny and was consecrated by Bishop Evdokim. Under his leadership the diocese greatly expanded and in 1923 he was elevated to the rank of archbishop. During the 1920s the Russian church entered into a period of turmoil as a result of the Russian Revolution. Pro- and Anti-Soviet factions fought for control and the ethnic groups became restless and demanded independent jurisdictions. In response, in 1926, Ofiesh proposed the formation of an independent American Orthodox Church. He suggested that all Orthodox bishops be released from any foreign attachments and that they reconstitute themselves as an independent American Orthodoxy. The Russian bishops responded favorably to the idea and in 1927 gave him permission to form the Holy Eastern Orthodox Catholic and Apostolic Church in America, generally called the American Orthodox Catholic Church.

The new church had problems. First, the patriarchs of Constantinople, Alexandria, Antioch, and Jerusalem refused to support it. That would not have been an insurmountable obstacle, but the Russian bishops had not counted upon the absolute opposition of the Episcopal Church. Episcopalians considered themselves the American Orthodox Church and at the time they were paying many of the bills of the Russian Church. Yielding to the pressure of the Episcopal Church, the Russians denounced the new church and Ofiesh was left abandoned. Utilizing his parishes as a power base, Ofiesh responded by asserting his position and claimed authority over the Orthodox community in North America.

The Russian Church moved to reclaim the property and cathedral in Brooklyn. The court awarded it to them in 1932. In the wake of the court's decision, Ofiesh was left with only six parishes. In the end he might have recovered and even built a significant following, but in 1933 he went against all Orthodox tradition and married. Bishop Joseph Zuk, who had stood by him in the court battle, assumed control of his church which slowly dissolved, though the apostolic orders were passed along to others through Bp. W. A. Nichols and became the basis of contemporary claims by a variety of independent bishops to be Ofiesh's successor.

Ofiesh retired to obscurity and, with him, the possibility of a united American Orthodoxy. He lived until 1971, but no longer functioned as a bishop.

Sources:
Morris, John W. "The Episcopate of Aftimios Ofeish." *The Word* 25 (February & March, 1981).
Ofeish, Aftimios. *Constitution of the Holy Eastern Orthodox Catholic and Apostolic Church in North America*. Brooklyn: Orthodox Catholic Review, 1927. 48 pp.
_____. *The Orthodox Situation in America: A Practical Survey and Program for Unity*. Brooklyn: Division of Publications, the Holy Synod of the Holy Eastern Orthodox Catholic and Apostolic Church in North America, 1931.
Tarasar, Constance J. *Orthodox America, 1994-1976: Development of the Orthodox Church in America*. Syosset, NY: The Orthodox Church in America, Department of Archives and History, 1975.

★694★
O'HAIR, Madalyn Mays Murray
Founder, American Atheists, Inc.
b. Apr. 14, 1919, Pittsburgh, Pennsylvania

Madalyn Mays Murray O'Hair, founder of American Atheists, Inc., is the daughter of Lena Scholle and John Irwin Mays. According to her report, she became an atheist when she was in the sixth grade after reading the Bible from cover to cover. However, she listed her life's goal at the time of her graduation from high school as serving God for the betterment of humanity. She attended the University of Toledo and the University of Pittsburgh, but in 1941 eloped with J. Roths. Two months later, after the U.S. entered World War II, he was shipped out to the Pacific front. She served in North Africa and Italy as a cryptographer. At the end of the war, back in the United States, she had an affair with William J. Murray, Jr., and conceived a child who bore his father's name. After the war the Roths were divorced, and she assumed the name of her son's father.

Murray returned to college and finally received her B.A. from Ashland College in 1948. Following her graduation she became a psychiatric social worker and worked in that capacity for various government agencies in Baltimore, Maryland. She pursued postgraduate study and eventually received a law degree from South Texas College of Law in 1953.

While in Baltimore, she filed a lawsuit claiming that her son, William J. Murray, III, was being discriminated against when he was being teased by other children after asking to be excused from the Bible reading and recitation of the Lord's Prayer which generally began public school classes each morning. Her suit asked that Bible reading and the recitation of the Lord's Prayer be banned from the public schools. The case was appealed through the court system. In 1962, after it had been joined with another similar case, the Supreme Court ruled in her favor.

Following the settlement of the case the family moved to Hawaii and then to Mexico. There she met Richard F. O'Hair. They settled in Austin, Texas, and in 1965 married. During the rest of the decade she began to create a national atheist movement. In 1968 she developed the American Atheist Radio Series and began *American Atheists Magazine*. In 1969 her book *What on Earth Is an Atheist?* which evolved out of the radio series, became the first book from the American Atheist Press. The next year she authored a book on the court case in Baltimore, formed the Society of Separationists (later renamed American Atheists, Inc.), and opened the Charles E. Stevens American Atheist Library and Archives. American Atheists, Inc., would develop into a national atheist organization.

During the two decades after the formation of the Society of Separationists, O'Hair became the most well-known public atheist in America. She used various shock techniques (such as filing suits to have the motto "In God We Trust" removed from U.S. currency) to attract media attention and debated clergymen, the most famous being Bob Harrington, on the existence of God. Within the larger atheism community she became equally controversial. In the mid-1970s members of her organization complained that she ran it in an undemocratic fashion and left to form the Freedom from Religion Foundation under the leadership of **Anne Nicol Gaylor**. In 1977 her son, William J. Murray III, withdrew from association with her, later converted to Christianity, and formed the Faith Foundation to counteract atheism.

In 1986 O'Hair resigned as president of American Atheists, Inc. in favor of Jon Murray, her second son. In 1990 O'Hair tried unsuccessfully to take over the American Association for the Advancement of Atheism whose leader, **James Hervey Johnson**, had died in 1988.

Sources:
Murray, William J. *My Life Without God*. Nashville, TN: Thomas Nelson, 1982. 252 pp.
O'Hair, Madalyn Murray. *Bill Murray, the Bible and the Baltimore Board of Education*. Austin, TX: American Atheist Press, 1970. 315 pp.
_____. *Freedom Under Siege*. Los Angeles: J. P. Tarcher, 1974. 278 pp.
_____. *What On Earth Is An Atheist?*. Austin, TX: American Atheist Press, 1970. 282 pp.
Stein, Gordon. *The Encyclopedia of Unbelief*. 2 vols. Buffalo, NY: Prometheus Books, 1985.

★695★
O'HARA, John Francis
Cardinal, Roman Catholic Church
b. May 1, 1888, Ann Arbor, Michigan
d. Aug. 28, 1960, Philadelphia, Pennsylvania

John Francis O'Hara, archbishop of Philadelphia and a cardinal in the Roman Catholic Church, was the son of Ella Thornton and John W. O'Hara. His father served for a time as the U.S. consul to Uruguay and O'Hara began his college education at Collegio del Sagrado Corazon, a Jesuit school in Montevideo, Uruguay. He later transferred to the University of Notre Dame, from which he received his Ph.B. in 1911. In 1912 he entered the Congregation of the Holy Cross, and for several years, beginning in 1913, he pursued graduate studies at Holy Cross College and Catholic University of America. He was ordained as a priest in 1916.

In 1917 O'Hara returned to Notre Dame as an instructor in religion and prefect of religion. During his teaching years he served a term (1920-1924) as dean of the College of Commerce. In 1933 he became the vice-president of the university, and in 1934 was named president of Notre Dame. His five years as university president were marked by a significant expansion of the school through a building program and an enlarged faculty. Once in the president's chair, O'Hara's previous South American experience came to the fore. He developed an exchange program with several South American schools. He also established a Latin-American news service for some 75 newspapers in Central and South America. The mixture of his training in economics and religion led President Roosevelt to appoint him as a delegate to the eighth Inter-American Congress in Lima, Peru, in 1938. As a result of his participation he was asked to head a social service commission for Venezuela.

The beginnings of World War II changed O'Hara's life. He was named a bishop and called to assist Archbishop **Francis Spellman** as the military vicar of the United States. Taking charge of the Roman Catholic chaplains, he reorganized the military ordinariate and supervised the chaplains throughout World War II. When the war ended, he was appointed bishop of Buffalo, New York.

While he had formally left the teaching field, O'Hara never lost his commitment to education, especially Catholic education. In Buffalo he devoted his energies to developing educational programs while creating new parishes and expanding the work of the diocese. In 1951 he was called to become archbishop of Philadelphia. During his 19 years in the archdiocese, he created one of the most impressive parochial school systems in the nation. He oversaw the opening of 55 new elementary schools and 14 new high schools. He also developed a program for educating the handicapped.

O'Hara's accomplishments were recognized in 1958 when he was appointed a cardinal.

Sources:
Delaney, John J. *Dictionary of American Catholic Biography*. Garden City, NY: Doubleday & Company, 1988. 621 pp.

★696★
OLAZABAL, Francisco
Founder, Latin American Council of Christian Churches
b. Oct. 12, 1886, El Verano Mexico
d. Jun. 9, 1937, Alice, Texas

Francisco Olazabal, one of the important figures in the introduction of Pentecostalism among Spanish-speaking Christians and the founder of the Latin-American Council of Christian Churches, was born and raised in rural Mexico. His father was the mayor of El Verano, his hometown. His mother, a Methodist, had become a lay missionary for the Methodist Episcopal Church, South. When he was 18 he rebelled against the faith of his parents and left Mexico for San Francisco, California. There he encountered **Carrie Judd Montgomery** and her husband, who were at that time ministers with the Christian and Missionary Alliance (CMA), and was converted to Christianity.

Olazabal returned to Mexico and entered Wesleyan College at San Luis, Poposi. After graduation in 1910 he became the pastor of a Spanish-speaking congregation in El Paso for a year, but in 1911 decided to return to school. He moved to Chicago to attend Moody Bible Institute. By the end of the year, however, he was back in California as a Methodist missionary, first in Compton (1911-1913) and then in Pasadena (1913-1916) and Sacramento/San Francisco. During his last pastorate he was ordained as an elder by the Methodist Episcopal Church, South.

In northern California, Olazabal renewed his relationship with the Montgomerys. In the intervening years, they had become Pentecostals and they introduced him to the experience of speaking in tongues (the definitive religious experience of Pentecostalism). He left the Methodists and became a minister with the Assemblies of God. Settling at El Paso, he created the first Assemblies Spanish-speaking congregation and promoted the development of like congregations in nearby communities.

Olazabal broke with the Assemblies over the issue of Mexican control of the Spanish-speaking work which had the American Henry Ball as its overseer. The issue came to a head in 1922 and Olazabal led the majority of the Spanish-speaking members out of the church. In 1923 they formed the Latin American Council of Christian Churches. Olazabal was named the first president and he retained the position for the rest of his life.

Olazabal directed the spread of the church in both the United States and Mexico, and in 1934 initiated work in Puerto Rico. In the mid-1930s he came into contact with **Ambrose J. Tomlinson** of the Church of God and began negotiations toward merging the council with it. Fraternal relations were formally established in 1936. However, before the merger could be completed Olazabal was killed in an automobile accident and his successors decided to remain independent. In subsequent decades the Pentecostal movement has enjoyed remarkable success in Mexico and among the Spanish-speaking populations of both North and South America.

Sources:
De Leon, Victor. *The Silent Pentecostals*. Taylor, SC: Faith Printing Company, 1979.
Tomlinson, Homer A. *Miracles of Healing in the Ministry of Rev. Francisco Olazabal*. Queens Village, NY: The Author, 1939. 27 pp.

★697★
ORTYNSKY, Stephen
Bishop, Roman Catholic Church
b. Jan. 29, 1866, Ortyntsi Russia
d. Mar. 24, 1916, Philadelphia, Pennsylvania

Stephen Ortynsky, a bishop of the Roman Catholic Church, was born in the Ukraine. During his late teens, in 1884, he joined the order of Saint Basil the Great. He attended Graz University (in Austria) where he earned a doctorate in theology. In 1891 he was ordained to the priesthood. During the next few years as he taught and did missionary work in the Ukraine, he became known as both an effective preacher and a Ukrainian patriot. In 1907 he was appointed the Roman Catholic bishop for the American immigrants from Ruthenia (a designation by the Roman Catholic Church for the territory south of Lithuania and north of the Carpathian Mountains). Ruthenia included the Ukraine, Byelorussia, and the eastern parts of Hungary and Austria, and for Roman Catholics was tied together by the use of a common Eastern liturgy (rather than the Latin one used in the Western church). The designation of a bishop for this group departed from the policy of the Roman Catholic Church in America, which had decided to ethnically integrate the church as much as possible. However, the Ruthenians were separated by both their liturgy and their allowance of a married priesthood, as is common in the Eastern Orthodox Church.

Ortynsky's first task was to form the diocese which ideally would consist of the more than 100 Ukrainian Catholic parishes already in existence. He established headquarters in Philadelphia and called an initial meeting of priests in New York City. The convention took steps to outline the territory of the diocese, grouping the parishes into nine deaneries, and provide for the support of the bishop. He faced opposition from both the Latin-rite bishops and the Ruthenians from Austrio-Hungary who saw Ortynsky as a Ukrainian nationalist.

By 1910 he had dedicated a new cathedral in Philadelphia and was able to host the visit of Ruthenian Metropolitan Sheptysky. In 1911 he opened St. Basil's Orphanage and brought members of the Sisters of St. Basil the Great to Philadelphia to take charge of it. By 1912 there were over 100 orphans living at St. Basil's, and the bishop founded a number of associated businesses—including a bookstore, a printing establishment, and a church supply house—to help fund the work. He also established a beneficial corporation for Ruthenian Catholics, the Province Association.

In 1913 Pope Pius X conferred full episcopal powers over the Ruthenian parishes and priests in America on Ortynsky, an act which freed them completely from control of the Latin-rite bishops. There were over 150 parishes at this time, of which over 100 were in Pennsylvania, with significant lesser concentrations in the surrounding states of New York, New Jersey, and Ohio.

Ortynsky's last years were divided between fighting the constant efforts of the Russian Orthodox Church in America to woo his parishes into the Orthodox camp and organizing the Ruthenians to support those in the Ukraine suffering the effects of World War I. He encouraged the North American Ukrainians to separate themselves both ecclesiastically and politically from Russian dominance. In the midst of these activities, Ortynsky died. He had, however, established a stable structure in which Ukrainian Catholics could perpetuate their unique traditions within Roman Catholicism.

Sources:
Procko, Bohdan P. *Ukrainian Catholics in America*. Washington, DC: University Press of America, 1982. 170 pp.

★698★
OUSLER SR., Charles Fulton
Inspirational Writer, Roman Catholic Church
b. Jan. 22, 1893, Baltimore, Maryland
d. May 24, 1952, New York, New York

Charles Fulton Ousler, Sr., was the author of the best selling work of religious nonfiction ever published in the United States, *The Greatest Story Ever Told*, a life account of Jesus Christ. Ousler was the son of William Clarence and Lillian Sappington Ousler. He grew up an only child, both of his sisters having died when they were quite young, in a somewhat isolated atmosphere. His isolation was accentuated both by his being a Baptist in an otherwise Roman Catholic neighborhood and his status as a poor member of a Baptist church of predominantly wealthy members. Poverty forced him out of school in the eighth grade, but two years later he landed a job as a reporter on the *Baltimore American*. He proved to be a talented writer and gradually received better assignments, supplementing his income by submitting articles to magazines. He was 18 when he married Rose Killian Karger.

In 1918 Ousler moved to New York City to join the staff of *Music Trades*. Three days after reporting for work, the editor entered officer-training school in the army, and Ousler was named as the new managing editor. He stayed with the magazine for four years, but in 1922 became the supervising editor for Macfadden Publications. Bernarr Macfadden was, in the era between the world wars, America's best-known natural health advocate, and Ousler remained on his staff for two decades. Beginning with magazines such as *Brain Power* and *Physical Culture*, the company diversified and produced a number of pulp magazines such as *True Story*; *Master Detective*; and *Liberty Magazine*. Ousler eventually supervised 13 different magazines. In 1924 he wrote a novel, *Behold the Dreamer!*, the first of several to appear over the next few years.

In 1925 Ousler divorced his first wife and married Grace Perkins, a Roman Catholic. Having dropped out of church some years before, he considered himself an agnostic. In the meantime his writing career blossomed. He began a series of popular detective novels under the pseudonym Anthony Abbot. In 1931 he became editor of *Liberty Magazine*. The next year, without giving up his position with Macfadden, he moved to Hollywood where three books from his pen and two from his wife's were quickly turned into movies. He returned east in 1934 and found a niche in radio broadcasting with two shows: "Stories That Should Be Told" and "Liberty's Forum of the Air".

In the mid-1930s, Ousler wrote *A Skeptic in the Holy Land* (1936) while on a trip to the Middle East and began to experience a reawakening of faith. His conviction in the world's need for Jesus' ethics led to a decision to write about the life of Christ. He studied the Bible and developed an interest in his wife's church. In 1941 he began to receive instruction in the Roman Catholic faith and in 1943 joined. He had left Macfadden Publications in 1942 to become the senior editor of *Reader's Digest*, a post he would retain for the rest of his life. His wife became the editor of *Guideposts*, the magazine begun by **Norman Vincent Peale** as a spiritual *Reader's Digest*.

The progress in Ousler's new faith became manifest in an initial popular inspiration book, *Three Things We Can Believe In* (1942), the first of 13 titles, including a volume on Father **Edward Joseph Flanagan** and Boys Town, he would write during this last decade of his life, though three would appear posthumously. Of the several books, he is remembered for three. *The Greatest Story Ever Told, a Life of Christ* (1949), became the best selling work on the life of Jesus ever written in the English language, and the best-selling religious nonfiction book in American publishing history. It had, in part, grown out of a successful radio show with the same title that had begun in 1947 on ABC. Two sequels, *The Greatest Book Ever*

Written (1951), about the Old Testament, and *The Greatest Faith Ever Known* (1953), a biography of St. Paul, also became bestsellers. In one decade, Ousler, known for his production of pulp fiction and his interest in mundane and superficial realities of crime, romance, and public personalities, became the decade's most heralded purveyor of popular religious piety. Following his death from a heart attack, Bishop **Fulton J. Sheen** spoke at his funeral. A decade after his death, his son edited and saw to the publication of Ousler's autobiography, which carried the same name as his early novel, *Behold the Dreamer!* (1964).

Sources:

Lippy, Charles H. *Twentieth-Century Shapers of American Popular Religion*. New York: Greenwood Press, 1989. 494 pp.
Ousler, Fulton. *Behold the Dreamer! An Autobiography of Fulton Ousler*. Edited by Fulton Ousler, Jr. Boston: Little, Brown and Company, 1964.
_____. *Father Flanagan of Boys Town*. Garden City, NY: Doubleday & Company, 1949. 302 pp.
_____. *The Greatest Book Ever Written: The Old Testament Story*. Garden City, NY: Doubleday & Company, 1951. 489 pp.
_____. *The Greatest Story Ever Told: A Tale of the Greatest Life Ever Lived*. Garden City, NY: Doubleday & Company, 1949. 299 pp.
_____. *A Skeptic in the Holy Land*. New York: Farrar and Rinehart, 1936. 250 pp.
_____, with April Armstrong Ousler. *The Greatest Faith Ever Known: The Story of the Men Who First Spread the Religion of Jesus and of the Momentous Times in Which They Lived*. Garden City, NY: Doubleday & Company, 1953. 383 pp.

★699★
OUTLER, Albert Cook
Theologian and Historian, United Methodist Church
b. Nov. 17, 1908, Thomasville, Georgia
d. Sep. 1, 1989, Bradenton, Florida

Albert Cook Outler, a theologian, ecumenist, and historian, is remembered most for his work in reviving interest in the life and thought of John Wesley among twentieth-century Methodists. He was the son of Gertrude Flint Dewberry and John Morgan Outler. He attended Wofford College (A.B., 1928), Emory University (B.D., 1933), and Yale University (Ph.D, 1938). In 1931 he married Carlotta Grace Smith. Ordained as a Methodist minister, he affiliated with the South Georgia Conference of the Methodist Episcopal Church, South and pastored churches in Baxley, Pineview, Gordon, and Macon, prior to accepting a position as instructor in theology at Duke University in 1938.

Outler taught at Duke for seven years before moving to New Haven, Connecticut, to accept a position in theology at his alma mater. In 1948 Yale named him Dwight Professor of Theology. While at Yale he completed his first books: *A Christian Context for Counseling* (1946) and *Colleges, Faculties and Religion* (1949). In 1951 he accepted a position as professor of theology at Perkins School of Theology, the Methodist seminary at Southern Methodist University. There he would remain for the rest of his career.

During the 1950s Outler emerged as one of the leading Methodist voices of the ecumenical movement in whose cause he authored one of his most significant books, *The Christian Tradition and the Unity that We Seek* (1957). He was a delegate to the Third World Council on Faith and Order (Lund, Sweden, 1952); the third assembly of the World Council of Churches (New Delhi, 1962); and served as vice chairman of the Fourth World Council on Faith and Order (Montreal, 1963). He was also a Protestant observer at the Second Vatican Council. Outler is given much credit for the formation of the Consultation on Church Union (COCU), an attempt to unite a number of liberal Protestant churches. Although the attempt ultimately failed, it provided a forum for significant dialogue and understanding between the participating denominations.

In many ways Outler's ecumenical concern contrasted sharply with his more memorable work on John Wesley, the founder of

Methodism. Largely ignored by his contemporaries, Outler spearheaded a revival of interest in Wesley. He wrote a volume, *John Wesley*, for the Library of Protestant Thought, and engaged in more than two decades of work on the Wesley Works Project, which brought together the best of the Wesley scholars to produce a new critical edition of Wesley's writings. Outler led the project with his four volumes on Wesley's Sermons. In 1963 he was elected president of the American Society of Church History.

As a Methodist theologian, Outler was asked to chair the Commission on Doctrine and Doctrinal Standards to resolve the problem of a doctrinal statement for the United Methodist Church created by the merger of the Methodist Church (1939-1968) and the Evangelical United Brethren. The report, adopted in 1972, is remembered for its discussion and acceptance of Methodism's theological pluralism.

Outler formally retired in 1974, but remained very active in pursuing his scholarly work until his death in 1989.

Sources:

Harmon, Nolan B. *The Encyclopedia of World Methodism*. 2 vols. Nashville: United Methodist Publishing House, 1974.
Outler, Albert C. *The Christian Tradition and the Unity We Seek*. New York: Oxford University Press, 1957. 165 pp.
_____. *A Methodist Observer at Vatican II*. Westminster, MD: Newman Press, 1967. 189 pp.
_____, ed. *John Wesley*. New York: Oxford University Press, 1964. 516 pp.
Who's Who in the Methodist Church. Nashville, TN: Abingdon Press, 1966.

★ 700 ★
OWEN, Derwyn Trevor
Bishop, Church of England in Canada
b. Jul. 29, 1876, Twickenham England
d. Apr. 14, 1947, Toronto, Ontario, Canada

Derwyn Trevor Owen, primate of the Church of England in Canada (now the Anglican Church in Canada), was the son of Florence Paynter and Trevor Randolph Owen. When he was still quite young, his family moved to Canada, where he grew up. He was ordained a deacon in 1900 and served as curate at St. John's Anglican Church in Toronto. In 1901 he was ordained a priest in the Church of England. After a year in England, he returned to Canada in 1902 to become curate at St. James Cathedral in Toronto. In 1904 he married Nora Grier Jellet. While at St. James he was able to attend Trinity College, Toronto, from which he received an L.Th. in 1907.

In 1908 Owen became assistant rector at Holy Trinity Church in Toronto. Beginning with his being named rector in 1910, his career began a steady climb. In 1914 he became rector of Christ's Church Cathedral in Hamilton, Ontario. The next year he added additional duties as dean of Niagara. He remained at these posts until 1925 when he was selected as the new bishop of Niagara. While at Niagara, Owen became involved with the Anglican National Commission which was established to review the state of the church nationally. By 1931, when the commission reported, Owen had become its chairman and, on its behalf, had traveled across the church. The adoption of part of the commission's report was a major step in establishing a strong and effective central structure in the church.

In 1932 Owen became the new Anglican bishop of Toronto. In 1934 he was the first primate chosen by the new process established by the commission report three years earlier. Owen continued the work of the commission in reorganizing the church with its new powers. The constitution and canons were revised and the various boards were turned into departments under the executive council of the general synod. In 1937 a new hymn book was approved and a board of finance instituted.

Owen has been described as an amiable man of great spirituality. His steady personality guided the church through the tumultuous years of World War II and the continuing organizational adjustments the emerging organization needed. He died in 1947 having completed a major task for the church.

Sources:

Carrington, Philip. *The Anglican Church in Canada*. Toronto: Collins, 1963. 320 pp.
Riley, Charles Edward. *Derwyn Trevor Owen: Primate of All Canada*. Toronto: Ryerson Press, 1966. 175 pp.

★ 701 ★
OXENDEN, Ashton
Bishop, Church of England in Canada
b. Sep. 20, 1808, Canterbury England
d. Feb. 22, 1892, Biarritz France

Ashton Oxenden, the bishop of Montreal for the Church of England in Canada (now the Anglican Church in Canada), was the son of Mary Graham and Sir Henry Oxenden, a baronet. He attended school at Ramsgate and Harrow and finished his college work at University College, Oxford. He received his B.A. in 1831 and was ordained a priest in the Church of England in 1833. He became curate at Barham, Kent, but was forced to resign in 1838 due to ill health. He was unable to resume his work until 1849 when he became rector at Pluckley in Kent.

As he regained his health in the 1840s, Oxenden began to write popular theological works, the first of which were collected in a six-volume work, *The Cottage Library* (1846-1851). Possibly the most popular work was *The Pathway of Safety* (1856). It was followed by *Family Prayers* (1858); *Fervent Prayer* (1860); *The Home Beyond* (1861); and *Words of Peace* (1863), among others. In 1864 he was made honorary canon of Canterbury Cathedral, and that same year married Sarah Bradshaw.

In 1869 Oxenden was elected bishop of Montreal. He stepped into the midst of the growing high church-low church controversy; Montreal was a center of that conflict. High church elements were focused in St. John the Evangelist Anglican Church, and in the school located at Lennoxville. In 1874 Oxenham founded a new college in Montreal, because, he said, Lennoxville was too far away. In fact, he was greatly influenced by the Catholic tendencies of the school and wanted a low church option. While in Montreal he continued his writings and penned an important chronicle of his early experiences in *My First Year in Canada* (1871). Other titles from his Canadian years include: *A Christian Life* (1870); *A Simple Explanation of the Psalms* (1872); *Counsel to the Confirmed* (1878); *Touchstones; of, Christian Graces and Characters Tested* (1884); and *Short Comments on the Gospels* (1885).

After almost two years as bishop and metropolitan of the Canadian church, in 1878 Oxenden resigned and returned to England. In 1897 he became a vicar of St. Stephen's, near Canterbury. Unfortunately, his last years were hampered by a return of poor health. His last book, *The History of My Life: An Autobiography*, appeared the year before his death.

Sources:

Oxenden, Ashton. *The Christian Life*. London: Hatchards, 1870. 271 pp.
_____. *Family Prayers*. New York: A. D. F. Randolph & Co., 1858. 236 pp.
_____. *The History of My Life: An Autobiography*. London: Longmans, Green & Co., 1891. 264 pp.
_____. *My First Year in Canada*. London: Hatchards, 1871. 128 pp.
_____. *The Pathway of Safety*. London: Wertheim, Macintosh, & Hunt, 1856. 294 pp.
Stephen, Leslie and Sidney Smith, eds. *The Dictionary of National Biography*. Oxford: Oxford University Press, 1917.

★702★
OXNAM, Garfield Bromley
Bishop, Methodist Church (1939-1968)
b. Aug. 14, 1891, Sonora, California
d. Mar. 12, 1963, White Plains, New York

Garfield Bromley Oxnam, one of the most outspoken and controversial Methodist ministers of the mid-twentieth century, was the son of Thomas Henry and Mary Ann Jobe Oxnam. Part of his childhood was spent in Nevada. He entered the University of Southern California in 1909 and while there was deeply influenced by his study of American labor history under Alexander Berkman and Eugene V. Debs. He received his B.A. in 1913 and was received on trial by the Southern California Conference of the Methodist Episcopal Church. He did his seminary work at Boston University where he studied under ethics professor and socialist **Harry F. Ward**. In 1914 he married Ruth Fisher. After receiving his S.T.B. in 1915, he was ordained a deacon and pursued post-graduate studies at Harvard and the Massachusetts Institute of Technology before returning to California.

Oxnam's first church was in Popular, California, but in 1919, the same year he was ordained, he was appointed to the Church of All Nations in Los Angeles. During his nine years there he also taught social ethics at the University of Southern California (1919-1923) and authored his first books, *The Mexican in Los Angeles* (1920); *The Social Principles of Jesus* (1923); *Russian Impressions* (1927); and *Youth and the New Americans*. Oxnam had become thoroughly identified with liberal Protestant theology and the social gospel. In 1924 he was for the first time elected as a delegate to the Methodist general conference. In 1927 he was invited to his other alma mater as a professor of practical theology and moved with his family back to Boston.

Oxnam stayed at Boston only one year before becoming the president of DePauw University in Greencastle, Indiana. While there he became the focus of major controversy by allowing the students to dance (a forbidden activity for most Methodists at the time) and advocating the abolition of compulsory military training. He identified himself with the radial Methodist Federation for Social Service (the brainchild of his former professor Harry Ward). He emerged as a leading spokesperson of the more liberal activist elements in the church while earning the strong denuciations of the more conservative voices.

In 1936 Oxnam was elected a bishop of the Methodist Episcopal Church just as the church was completing a merger with the Methodist Episcopal Church, South and the Methodist Protestant Church which would form the Methodist Church (1939-1968) just three years later. He served those three years in the Omaha area as bishop over Iowa and Nebraska. Following the merger, he was assigned to the Boston area. He served five years in Boston, and then had assignments in New York (1944-1952) and Washington, D.C. (1952-1960). During those years he authored a number of books, among the most important being *Preaching in a Revolutionary Age* (1944); *The Church and Contemporary Change* (1950); and *On This Rock* (1951). As part of his episcopal duties, he served as the secretary of the church's Council of Bishops and was given significant credit for transforming the occasional gatherings into strategic planning sessions. He also originated the plan to send all bishops to different foreign missionary fields to learn of the work firsthand.

Oxnam's energetic leadership was also recognized on the ecumenical level. He was president of the Federal Council of Churches (1944-1946), was the presiding officer at the organization of the National Council of Churches in 1950, and was one of the presidents of the World Council of Churches (1948-1954).

While one of the more competent bishops of the church administratively, Oxnam became known for his battles in the arena of human rights. Although not a pacifist, during the early years of his episcopacy he emerged as a champion of the rights of conscientious objectors. He pioneered Protestant-Catholic cooperation around the issue of anti-Semitism in the 1940s, but in 1948 earned the reproach of Catholic leaders for denouncing the denial of religious freedom in Spain, Colombia, and Argentina and leading in the founding of Protestants and Other Americans United for Separation of Church and State.

In Oxnam's final battle, he took on the infamous House Committee on Un-American Activities, which was threatening to investigate the churches for communist infiltration. When he moved to Washington, D.C., he charged the committee with releasing false information which accused him of being a communist. He demanded and got a hearing during which he refuted the accusations. He received favorable press coverage and later wrote a book about his experiences, *I Protest* (1954).

Affected with Parkinson's disease, Oxnam's health failed in the late 1950s and he retired in 1960. He died three years later.

Sources:

Dictionary of American Biography. 20 vols. and 7 supps. New York: Charles Scribner's Sons, 1928-1936, 1944-1981.
Harmon, Nolan B. *The Encyclopedia of World Methodism*. 2 vols. Nashville: United Methodist Publishing House, 1974.
Oxnam, G. Bromley. *The Church and Contemporary Change*. New York: MacMillan Company, 1950. 132 pp.
_____. *I Protest*. New York: Harper & Row, 1954. 186 pp.
_____. *On This Rock*. New York: Harper, 1951. 117 pp.
_____. *Preaching in a Revolutionary Age*. New York: Abingdon- Cokesbury Press, 1944. 207 pp.
_____. *Preaching in a Social Crisis*. New York: Abingdon Press, 1932. 234 pp.

★703★
PACKARD, Sophia B.
Baptist Laywoman
Founder, Spelman College
b. Jan. 3, 1824, New Salem, Massachusetts
d. Jun. 21, 1891, Washington, District of Columbia

Sophia B. Packard, founder of Spelman College in Atlanta, Georgia, was the daughter of Rachel Freeman and Winslow Packard, a farmer from an old New England family. She obtained a good education through sheer persistence, often alternating a year of teaching with a year of schooling. In 1850 she graduated from the Charlestown Female Seminary in Massachusetts. After teaching in Cape Cod, she took a position in 1855 at New Salem Academy, where she had previously been a student. Here she met Harriet E. Giles (1833-1909), and the two became lifelong friends and co-workers.

The position at New Salem Academy began a 12-year period of teaching that took Packard (and Giles) to Orange, Massachusetts; Fitchburg, Massachusetts; the Connecticut Literary Institution in Suffield (1859-1864); and Oread Collegiate Institute in Worcester, Massachusetts. They left Oread under somewhat unclear circumstances and moved to Boston. Packard worked in an insurance company until 1870, when she became the assistant to Rev. George C. Lorimer at Shawmut Avenue Baptist Church.

The work with Lorimer carried Packard, in spite of criticisms of her unwomanly duties, to Tremont Baptist Temple in Boston, where he became pastor in 1873. She continued her duties of conducting a women's prayer meeting, teaching in the Sunday school, and visiting the sick. While at Tremont she became interested in the problems facing former slaves still living in the South. She became the leader of a group of several hundred women with similar concerns, who in 1877 organized the Woman's American Baptist Home Mission Society, an auxiliary to the American Baptist Home Mission Society. Packard chaired the first meeting and was appointed treasurer. The following year she was appointed corresponding secretary. In 1880 she traveled to the South and in her report urged the establishment of a school for black women in Georgia.

In March 1881 the society gave their backing to the idea. Packard and Giles moved to Atlanta. With the blessing of Rev. Frank Quarles, they opened the Atlanta Baptist Female Seminary in April in the basement of the Friendship Baptist Church, which Quarles pastored. The school met a real need and grew rapidly, but in June the society withdrew its support, including financial backing. Packard persisted, however, and at the beginning of the next year, the society renewed its support and even sent a third teacher to assist with the 150 pupils.

At the end of the year, additional outside support came from the American Baptist Home Mission Society, which made the down payment on a parcel of land, and from John D. Rockefeller, who gave money to complete the purchase. The school moved into the already existing buildings on the land at the beginning of 1883, and in 1884 Packard named the new college after Rockefeller's wife and parents, who had a firm record of abolitionist advocacy.

The years following the movement into the new facilities were dominated by fundraising efforts. By the end of 1883 the school boasted 400 students and an expanded program. The school required additional buildings. A building that had burned down was rebuilt in 1888 and named Packard Hall. That same year the school was chartered as Spelman Seminary, and Packard, who had headed the fundraising drives, was named treasurer of the board of trustees. She already served as president and teacher.

In 1890 Packard vacationed in Egypt and the Holyland to recover from an illness. The next summer she traveled to New England. She became ill en route and died unexpectedly from a cerebral hemorrhage. Giles succeeded her as president. During the twentieth century, Spelman College (as it was renamed in 1924) grew into a prominent institution of higher learning, and in 1929 affiliated with Morehouse College and Atlanta University to become part of a major center of education within the southern black community.

Sources:

James, Edward T., ed. *Notable American Women, 1607-1950: A Biographical Dictionary*. 3 vols. Cambridge, MA: Harvard University Press, Belknap Press, 1971.

Read, Florence M. *The Story of Spelman College*. Atlanta: The Author, 1961. 399 pp.

★704★
PADDOCK, Ross Perry
Presiding Bishop, Pentecostal Assemblies of the World (PAW)
b. Mar. 9, 1907, South Haven, Michigan

Ross Perry Paddock, a former presiding bishop of the Pentecostal Assemblies of the World (PAW), was born and raised in Michigan. His wife, Francis, gave birth to 12 children. He experienced salvation under the ministry of Elder Glenn Boardwell and became associated with the Pentecostal Assemblies of the World. The PAW is one of the oldest of the presently existing Pentecostal bodies, having been formed in 1906 in Los Angeles. It was interracial in membership from the beginning, though following the failure of merger negotiations with an all-white denomination in the 1920s, many of the white members left and the church became predominantly black. Under the leadership of **Samuel Grimes**, the presiding bishop elected in 1932, the church articulated and has kept a commitment to retain its white members and to allocate positions of leadership at every level to them.

Paddock, though a white man, proved to be one of the most effective leaders in the PAW. Shortly after his salvation, he was called to the ministry, and he became the pastor of Christ Temple

in Kalamazoo, Michigan, a post he retained throughout his active career. Over the years he served in most of the general church offices, including a period as the denomination's treasurer and as the lay director.

In 1952 Paddock was elected to the bishopric and assigned leadership of Episcopal District 15 (which includes Arizona and New Mexico) and Episcopal District 5 (Michigan and Ontario). In the PAW, bishops are not required to reside in their episcopal district. During his last years in office, Grimes also tapped Paddock to serve in a new post as assistant presiding bishop. In 1967, following Grimes' death, Paddock began an eight-year tenure as the first White to head the church since its institution of episcopal leadership in 1925. He was noted for his calm sure guidance at the church's conventions.

Paddock retired in 1974 and has lived quietly in the intervening years.

Sources:

Dupree, Sherry Sherrod. *Biographical Dictionary of African-American, Holiness-Pentecostals, 1880-1990*. Washington, DC: Middle Atlantic Regional Press, 1990. 386 pp.

Golder, Morris E. *The Bishops of the Pentecostal Assemblies of the World*. Indianapolis, IN: The Author, 1980. 69 pp.

Richardson, James C., Jr. *With Water and Spirit*. Washington, DC: Spirit Press, 1980. 151 pp.

★705★
PARHAM, Charles Fox
Founder, Apostolic Faith Church
b. Jun. 4, 1873, Muscatine, Iowa
d. Jan. 29, 1929, Baxter Springs, Kansas

Charles Fox Parham, founder of the modern Pentecostal Movement and its first organizational expression, the Apostolic Faith Church, was the son of Ann Maria Eckel and William M. Parham. He grew up in a pioneer family in rural Kansas, where the family had moved when he was five. He was converted to Christianity at the age of 13 while attending a revival meeting at the community's schoolhouse. He soon became a Sunday school teacher and was licensed to preach by the Methodist Episcopal Church. When he was 16, he entered Southwestern Kansas College. While at college he became sick with what was diagnosed as rheumatic fever. Given up by the doctors, he was cured by prayer, an event that confirmed to him his call to the ministry. He left school and became the preacher for a Methodist circuit.

In 1894, after two years with the Methodists, Parham withdrew from that church and renounced "denominationalism." He launched a career as an independent evangelist. In 1896 he married Sarah Thislethwaite and in 1898 they opened Bethel, a healing home in Topeka, Kansas. Those who came to reside at Bethel were taught to rely upon God alone for their healing. Parham began a periodical, *The Apostolic Faith*, and slowly a following grew up around him. While away on an evangelistic trip in 1900, however, his ministry was taken over by others, and he had to begin again. He moved across town and opened a new center, where the events which were to change his life were to occur a few months later.

Over the holiday season of 1900, Parham left for Kansas City, Kansas. He gave his small band of loyal students a task to perform in his absence, to interpret the second chapter of Acts and other references to the baptism of the Holy Spirit. When he returned, they reported that they had reached a consensus that the coming of the Holy Spirit was always signified by the appearance of speaking in tongues. Then one student, Agnes Ozman, asked that Parham and the students pray for her to receive the Holy Spirit. As they prayed over her, she began to speak in what was understood to be Chinese and was unable to speak English for the next three days. She became the first person in modern history to ask for and receive the gift of speaking in tongues as an answer to prayer for the baptism of the Holy Spirit.

Parham took his students and the new message of baptism in the Holy Spirit as evidenced by speaking in tongues to Kansas City a few weeks later. Over the next five years he traveled through Kansas, Oklahoma, and Texas, and finally opened a Bible school in Houston in 1905. Among the students at the school was **William J. Seymour**, a holiness minister, who took Parham's teachings to Los Angeles, where a great revival broke out in the small mission he established.

While Seymour was leading the revival in Los Angeles, Parham was traveling again, first to Kansas, and then to Zion, Illinois, the community established by **John Alexander Dowie**. When news arrived of the revival which had begun in April 1906 in Los Angeles, Parham traveled to Seymour's mission. He was horrified at what he saw and denounced Seymour for involvement in Spiritualism and hypnotism. As Pentecostalism spread from Los Angeles, Parham abandoned any leadership role and opposed attempts to organize the Pentecostal churches which began to spring up around the country. In 1911 he settled in Baxter Springs, Kansas, and spent the rest of his life as an evangelist and Bible school teacher. The loose association of congregations which grew up around his ministry became known as the Apostolic Faith Church.

Sources:

Goff, James R., Jr. *Fields White Unto Harvest: Charles F. Parham and the Missionary Origins of Pentecostalism.* Fayetteville, AR: University of Arkansas Press, 1988. 263 pp.
Parham, Charles Fox. *A Voice Crying in the Wilderness.* Baxter Springs, KS: Apostolic Faith Bible College, 1910.
_____, and Parham, Sarah E. *Selected Sermons of the Late Charles Fox Parham and Sarah E. Parham.* Robert L. Parham, comp. Baxter Springs, KS: 1941.
Parham, Sarah E. *The Life of Charles F. Parham, Founder of the Apostolic Faith Movement.* Joplin, MO: Hunter Printing Company, 1930. 452 pp.

★706★
PARKER, Quanah
Founder, Native American Church
b. 1845, Texas
d. Feb. 23, 1911, Fort Sill, Oklahoma

The life of Quanah Parker, a principal founder of the Native American Church and early advocate of the peyote religions, has been the subject of dozens of fictional treatments in world literature and movies. A noted Indian leader, Parker was both white and Indian in ancestry and worldview. He was born around 1845 in west Texas buffalo country. Quanah's father was Peta Nocona, a Comanche Indian spiritual leader and chief, and his mother was Cynthia Anne Parker, a white woman who had been taken captive by the Comanches in 1835 when she was 12 years old. Cynthia Anne lived with the Comanches for 25 years, returning to her south Texas family in 1860. Peta Nocona died three years later, leaving Quanah a teenage orphan. His mixed ancestry put him at the edge of his Kwahadi band of Comanches. Early records indicate that Quanah distinguished himself as a good hunter and noted defender of Comanche hunting territory in west Texas.

After the Civil War, the United States directed its military attention towards efforts to subdue the Indian nations of the high plains country from Canada to Mexico. The Comanches in their turn were consigned to a reservation in Southwest Oklahoma, with the Kwahadi settling there in 1875. The year before, the Kwahadi had trapped a group of buffalo hunters in an abandoned adobe in west Texas. Eschiti, a noted spiritual leader, led the band in the fight. He apparently claimed that the medicine shirts worn by the Indian forces would turn away the bullets of the buffalo hunters. Instead, the Comanches were turned away by the hunters' newly acquired

Sharp's repeating rifles. In later years Quanah indicated that this fight at Adobe Walls discouraged his beliefs in the ancient ways of the Comanche and sent him on a search for a new religion. Sometime around 1880, the songs and prayers of the Peyote Road began to be heard among the Comanches and their neighbors, the Kiowa, Kiowa/Apache, Caddo, and Wichita.

Peyote, the cactus *Lophophora Williamsii*, was used by Native American medical practitioners throughout its growing zone in the American Southwest and Mexico. Indian groups in the southwest advocated its ingestion for medical reasons. Quanah Parker came into contact with the ceremonial use of the herb when he traveled to south Texas to visit his mother Cynthia's relatives. According to later accounts, Quanah was injured and suffered even under the care of competent doctors. A woman healer of unknown Indian origin was sent for, and she ministered him with peyote tea. Quanah dreamed of a ceremony where a woman brought peyote, and its attendant care through ritual songs and prayers, to the Comanches. By the end of the decade the peyote ceremony had spread throughout a number of tribes in Oklahoma. Many of the tribes' oral histories indicated that Quanah was an early advocate of its integration with Christian symbolism.

Quanah Parker proved to be an astute leader of the progressive faction of Comanches on the reservation, and he prospered as a cattle rancher and paid leader under the United States government title of Chief of the Comanches. Through diplomacy and tact, Parker was able to stall the earliest federal efforts to suppress the Native American use of peyote, and it prospered as an alternative religion to the messianic Ghost Dance of Wovoka. After the 1890 killings of Ghost Dancers at Wounded Knee, South Dakota, the Native American Church spread throughout Indian country; it is now one of the largest pan-Indian religions in North America.

Quanah Parker was a noted advocate of biculturalism for the Indians in western Oklahoma. To that end, he integrated Christianity into the peyote ceremony; encouraged Christian missionization, although he remained a polygamist; dressed in three piece suits, but wore his hair in braids; and agreed to suppress peyote as a reservation justice in the 1890s, while serving at the same time as its major advocate and importer. Quanah Parker was buried with a peyote feather fan in his hands near Cache, Oklahoma, on March 31, 1911. As the coffin was lowered into the grave, the nearly 1500 people in attendance joined in the song "Nearer My God to Thee."

Sources:

Hagan, William T. "Quanah Parker." in R. David Edmunds. *American Indian Leaders.* Lincoln, NE: University of Nebraska Press, 1980.
Jackson, C. L., and G. Jackson. *Quanah Parker: The Last Chief of the Comanches.* New York: Exposition Press, 1963.
Petrullo, Vincenzo. *The Diabolic Root.* Philadelphia: University of Pennsylvania Press, 1934.
Stewart, Omer C. *Peyote Religion: A History.* Norman, OK: University of Oklahoma Press, 1987.

—Johnny Flynn

★707★
PASSAVANT, William Alfred
Home Missionary, General Council of the Evangelical Lutheran Church in North America
b. Oct. 9, 1821, Zelienople, Pennsylvania
d. Jun. 3, 1894, Pittsburgh, Pennsylvania

William Alfred Passavant, Lutheran pastor, editor, and home missionary, was the son of Philip Louis and Zelie Basse Passavant. He was raised in relative comfort on an estate originally purchased by his grandfather. He attended Jefferson College in Canonsburg, Pennsylvania, and, after graduating in 1840, entered Gettysburg Theological Seminary. At Gettysburg he studied under Samuel S. Schmucker, one of the most prominent American Lutheran theologians of the period, and came to accept Schmucker's moderate pietist approach to Lutheran faith. He graduated in 1842 and was licensed by the Maryland Synod of the Lutheran Church. He became pastor of a church at Canton, Maryland. He was ordained in 1843 and moved to Pittsburgh as pastor of the English Lutheran Church. In 1845 he married Eliza Walter.

During his seminary days Passavant began the missionary and literary activities which were to so mark his mature career. He did missionary work in the hill country near Gettysburg. He compiled and published two editions of a *Lutheran Almanac* for 1842 and 1843. In 1842 he joined the staff of the *Lutheran Observer*, which was aligned to Schmucher's thought. In 1845 Passavant helped found the Pittsburgh Synod. The following year he traveled to Germany and visited the deaconess institute at Kaiserswerth founded by Theodor Fliedner.

In Pittsburgh, however, Passavant became friends with **Charles Porterfield Krauth**, a prominent American Lutheran theologian and champion of a conservative confessional Lutheran faith. Passavant gradually moved from Schmucher's to Krauth's perspective, a process completed by 1848, at which time he resigned from the *Lutheran Observer* and began the *Missionary*. The *Missionary* had a double task, to champion Krauth's confessional theology and to promote home missions, especially among English-speaking people. In 1849 Passavant opened a small hospital in Pittsburgh, the first Protestant hospital in America. Fliedner brought four deaconesses to Pittsburgh. The four remained at the hospital, thus introducing deaconess work to America (and inspiring similar work among Episcopalians and Methodists).

In 1855 Passavant resigned his parish, but continued as editor of the *Missionary* until 1861, when it was absorbed into the *Lutheran*, published in Philadelphia. He concentrated his efforts on the promotion of mission facilities. Through the Institution of Protestant Deaconesses, which he incorporated at Pittsburgh, he founded hospitals in Milwaukee, Wisconsin, and in Chicago and Jacksonville, Illinois. Orphanages were located in Mt. Vernon and Rochester, New York; Germantown and Zelienople, Pennsylvania; and West Roxbury, Massachusetts. He also founded the Lutheran Theological Seminary in Chicago and Thiel College in Greenville, Pennsylvania.

In 1867 Passavant became one of the founders of the General Council of the Evangelical Lutheran Church in North America, an alignment of the conservative confessional Lutheran synods (most of the other synods were a part of the General Synod dominated by Schmucher's perspectives). The General Council and General Synod merged in 1918 and through a series of further mergers became constituent parts of the Evangelical Lutheran Church in America formed in 1988. In 1881 he founded the *Workman*, a newspaper which he edited until his death in 1894. For half a century, Passavant was the dominant influence in the Pittsburgh Synod and one of the most influential leaders in the General Council.

Sources:

Dictionary of American Biography. 20 vols. and 7 supps. New York: Charles Scribner's Sons, 1928-1936, 1944-1981.

Gerberding, G. H. *Life and Letters of W. A. Passavant, D.D.* Greenville, PA: 1906. 615 pp.

Nelson, E. Clifford. *The Lutherans in North America.* Philadelphia: Fortress Press, 1980. 564 pp.

★708★
PATHFINDER, Peter
Founder, Aquarian Tabernacle Church
b. Mar. 22, 1937, Jersey City, New Jersey

Peter Pathfinder, also known as Pierre C. Davis, is the founder of the Aquarian Tabernacle Church in Washington state and is an assertive proponent of Neo-Paganism in the Northwest. He is a professional in the security industry, and has taken career-oriented

coursework at Rutgers University, Pacific Lutheran University, and the University of Oklahoma. Before moving to Washington, he served his town for over 14 years in various official capacities, from councilman to police commissioner and mayor. He was also state constable and court constable. After relocating in Seattle, he was a branch manager for the electronic security division of the William J. Burns International Detective Agency.

Functioning for many years as a self-identified Wiccan, Davis studied for the priesthood with a variety of different teachers, and formed the Aquarian Tabernacle Church in 1979. He also served as the first Public Information Officer of the Covenant of the Goddess (COG) (a national fellowship of witchcraft covens), and also the group's first official spokesperson, authoring and editing COG's first official "press packet." The focus of the tabernacle is to operate an open, fully recognized church where Pagans of various paths can worship together in a traditional outdoor circle of large standing stones. The church also operates a retreat house, the Center for Non-Traditional Religions, and sponsors large public worship gatherings and a number of open festivals each year.

The Aquarian Tabernacle has achieved both state and federal recognition as a tax-exempt church, and participates in the Washington State Interfaith Council, the Covenant of the Goddess, the Fellowship of Isis (an international fellowship of Pagans), and the Wiccan Information Network. Davis has been a consultant on the Old Religion, as its adherents frequently term Neo-Paganism, to the Attorney General of Washington and has served as an expert witness in federal district court. He also serves as the Wiccan advisor to the Washington State Department of Corrections Religious Program, and was responsible for gaining acceptance for this tradition within the state's institutions. He has assisted law enforcement agencies in the investigation of occult-related crimes.

Sources:

Melton, J. Gordon. *New Age Encyclopedia.* Detroit: Gale Research Inc., 1990. 586 pp.

★709★
PATTERSON SR., James Oglethorpe
Presiding Bishop, Church of God in Christ
b. Jul. 21, 1912, Derma, Mississippi
d. Dec. 29, 1989, Memphis, Tennessee

James Oglethorpe Patterson, Sr., the former presiding bishop of the Church of God in Christ, the largest Pentecostal church in the United States, was raised in rural Mississippi, the son of William and Mollie Patterson. He was raised as a member of the Church of God in Christ and had his initial experience of salvation through it. He attended the Howe School of Religion in Memphis. In 1934 he married Deborah Indiana Mason, the daughter of **Charles Harrison Mason**, the founder of the Church of God in Christ. He was ordained as a minister in the church in 1936. He served a congregation in Gates, Tennessee, and later pastored in New Jersey. He served as the pastor for many years of Pentecostal Temple Church of God in Christ in Memphis, Tennessee.

In 1952 Patterson became a member of the denomination's executive board, and the following year was consecrated by Mason as a bishop for the church. He served as the jurisdictional bishop for Tennessee and then as a member of the secretariat of the denomination. Mason died in 1961. He was succeeded by Ozro Thurston Jones, Sr.; however, a protest movement demanding elections for the office of presiding bishop arose and led to a bitter lawsuit. The protesters won the suit and forced an election in 1968. At that time Patterson was elected as Jones' successor. He held the position for the rest of his life while regularly submitting to quadrennial elections.

Patterson brought both organizational skill and a dedication to education to his new job. He reorganized the church and improved both its financial condition and membership. He founded the Chisca Hotel and Motel to provide revenue for the church. In 1970 he conducted the first census of church membership. Previously believed to be several hundred thousand strong, membership proved to be several million. It grew to over three million by 1989.

Patterson founded the Charles Harrison Mason Seminary in Atlanta, Georgia, which was followed by the C. H. Mason System of Bible Colleges, the J. O. Patterson Fine Arts Department, the Historical Museum and Fine Arts Center, and the Charles Harrison Mason Foundation. He led the denomination in opening the Church of God in Christ Bookstore and Church of God in Christ Publishing House. The Presiding Bishop's Benefit Fund, which he established, provides scholarships to needy students; the Good Shepherd Fund provides needed support to ministers.

During his last decade in office Patterson projected a vision of the All Saints Center to include a World Outreach Center and All Saints University, and a multilingual publishing house. These projects remain on the drawing board, but land for this purpose has been donated to the church.

In 1985 Deborah Patterson died. In 1989 Patterson married Mary Peat. He died eight months later, and was succeeded by Louis Henry Ford. Ford had run second to Patterson in 1968 and had served as his assistant presiding bishop through the years.

Sources:

"COGIC Leader Patterson Dies." *Charisma and Christian Life* 15, 8 (March 1990): 24.
Cornelius, Lucille J. *The Pioneer History of the Church of God in Christ.* N.p.: The Author, 1975. 102 pp.
Dupree, Sherry Sherrod. *Biographical Dictionary of African-American, Holiness-Pentecostals, 1880-1990.* Washington, DC: Middle Atlantic Regional Press, 1990. 386 pp.
Patterson, J. O., German R. Ross, and Julia Mason Atkins. *History and Formative Years of the Church of God in Christ.* Memphis, TN: Church of God Publishing House, 1969. 143 pp.

★710★
PATTON, Francis Landley
Theologian, Presbyterian Church
b. Jan. 22, 1843, Warwick Bermuda
d. Nov. 25, 1932, Warwick Bermuda

Between his boyhood and his death on the island of Bermuda, Francis Patton emerged as a leading conservative Presbyterian scholar in the late-nineteenth century. He was the son of George John Bascombe and Mary Jane Steele Patton. A precocious child, he began his mastery of Latin when he was but seven years of age. He completed his elementary education in Canada and then entered Knox College and the University of Toronto. He received his theological education at Princeton Theological Seminary, from which he graduated in 1865.

Shortly after graduation Patton was ordained to the ministry, married Rosa Antoinette, and became pastor of the Eighty-fourth Street Presbyterian Church in New York City. In 1867 he moved to Nyack, New York, where he wrote his first book, *The Inspiration of the Scriptures* (1869), and then in 1871 to Brooklyn, New York.

Chicago was still recovering from the effects of the great fire when Patton moved there in 1872 to become the Cyrus H. McCormick Professor of Didactic and Polemical Theology at the Presbyterian Theological Seminary of the Northwest (now McCormick Theological Seminary). In addition to his teaching duties he became editor of *The Interior*, a Presbyterian periodical, in 1873, and in 1874 was named pastor of the Jefferson Park Presbyterian Church. He emerged as one of the most powerful voices of the conservative wing of the church when in 1874 he moved against **David Swing**, the pastor of the Fourth Avenue Presbyterian Church and a representative of the most liberal wing of the church.

Following the publication of *Truths for Today*, a compilation of Swing's sermons, Patton filed charges against Swing for deviating from the church's official doctrine as contained in the Westminster Confession. After the Presbytery of Chicago, North, ruled in Swing's favor, Patton filed an appeal with the Illinois Synod. Before the appeal was heard, Swing withdrew and the issue died, but not before Patton had gained considerable notoriety.

In 1881 Robert L. Stuart founded a chair at Princeton, the Professorship of the Relations of Philosophy and Science to the Christian Religion, with Patton in mind. Patton moved back to his alma mater to assume the post. In addition, in 1883 he began to teach ethics at Princeton. He held both positions until 1888, when he became president of the college. He proved an able if eccentric, president employing no secretary and operating with the faculty in a very personal manner. He began to improve the quality of the faculty, broaden the subject offering, and open the curriculum. In 1896 the College of New Jersey became Princeton University. The name change merely spurred Patton to further improvements in the school, especially in its research facilities and graduate offerings. During the remaining years of Patton's administration the undergraduate student body more than doubled. He also found time to publish his second major book, *A Summary of Christian Doctrine* (1898).

In 1902 Patton, weary of his administrative tasks, resigned the presidency and assigned himself a teaching post in ethics and the philosophy of religion. He nominated Woodrow Wilson to succeed him. Patton was then named president of the theological seminary. He retired in 1913 and returned to Bermuda, though annually he made a trip to Princeton to lecture. He lived another two decades, during which time he produced his most memorable work, *Fundamental Christianity* (1926).

Sources:

Dictionary of American Biography. 20 vols. and 7 supps. New York: Charles Scribner's Sons, 1928-1936, 1944-1981.
Hutchinson, William R. *The Modernist Impulse in American Protestantism.* Cambridge, MA: Harvard University Press, 1976. 347 pp.
Patton, Francis L. *Fundamental Christianity.* New York: Macmillan Company, 1926. 334 pp.
———. *The Inspiration of the Scriptures.* Philadelphia: Presbyterian Board of Publication and Sabbath School Work, 1869. 139 pp.
———. *A Summary of Christian Doctrine.* Philadelphia: Westminster Press, 1898. 116 pp.

★711★
PAULK JR., Earl Pearly
Televangelist and Founder, Gospel Harvesters Church
b. 1927, Baxley, Georgia

Earl Pearly Paulk, Jr., Pentecostal bishop and founder of Gospel Harvester Church, is the son of Addie Mae Tomberlin and Earl P. Paulk, Sr. His father, a minister with the Church of God (Cleveland, Tennessee), rose to become assistant general overseer of that denomination. When Paulk was three, the family moved to Logan, West Virginia, the first of a number of moves during his childhood and youth as his father changed pastoral assignments. When he was 15, the family settled in Greenville, South Carolina. Paulk entered Furman University where he became a track star. Two years later he answered a call to the ministry and began preaching as opportunity allowed. In 1946 he married Norma Davis. He also accepted the position of state youth director for the church, the income of which allowed him to complete his work at Furman in 1947.

After his graduation Paulk taught at Lee College in Cleveland, Tennessee, for a year before enrolling at Candler School of Theology, a Methodist seminary in Atlanta, Georgia. Following his graduation in 1952 he became pastor of the Hemphill Church of God in Atlanta. While at Hemphill Paulk began to introduce innovations which deviated from the standard practice of the Church of God, including his approval of the wearing of wedding bands for women whose husbands were away fighting in the Korean War. He also began to appear frequently on television. He became identified with more liberally minded ministers during Atlanta's racial crisis in the 1950s. While at Hemphill he authored his first book, *Your Pentecostal Neighbor* (1958). Through his eight years at Hemphill, Paulk came into continued conflict with the policies of the Church of God. In 1960, he and his brother-in-law, Harry Mushegan, the cousin of **Demos Shakarian** and also a Church of God pastor, resigned from the Church of God and began an independent itinerant evangelistic work as the Harvesters, but soon settled in Atlanta to build a new church. Soon two congregations emerged. In 1973 Paulk's congregation moved to suburban Decatur and became known as the Chapel Hill Gospel Harvesters Church. The congregation has grown to include over 6,000 members and developed a multi-faceted social outreach in the community. In 1978 he returned to television with taped versions of the Sunday services that grew into the Harvester Hour.

During the early 1980s Paulk's growing ministry led him into contact with Archbishop Benson Idahosa of the Miracle Center in Benin City, Nigeria, and Bishop **Robert McAlister** of the New Life Pentecostal Church in Rio de Janeiro, Brazil. These men had formed the International Communion of Charismatic Churches. In 1982 McAleister consecrated Paulk as a bishop in the Communion. Before the year was out, Paulk would participate in the consecration of **John L. Meares**, his long-time friend and pastor of the Evangel Temple in Washington, D.C.

Sources:

Burgess, Stanley M., Gary B. McGee, and Patrick H. Alexander, eds. *Dictionary of Pentecostal and Charismatic Movements*. Grand Rapids, MI: Regency Reference Library, Zondervan Publishing House, 1988. 914 pp.

Paulk, Earl. *20/20 Vision: A Clear View of the Kingdom of God*. Atlanta, GA: Kingdom Publishers, 1988. 44 pp.

———. *Satan Unmasked*. Atlanta, GA: K Dimension Publishers, 1984. 316 pp.

———. *Ultimate Kingdom*. Atlanta, GA: K Dimension Publishers, 1984. 342 pp.

———. *Your Pentecostal Neighbor*. Cleveland, TN: Pathway Press, 1958.

Weeks, Tricia. *The Provoker*. Atlanta, GA: K Dimension Publishers, 1986. 382 pp.

★712★
PAXSON, Diana L.
Founder, Fellowship of the Spiral Path
b. Feb. 20, 1943, Detroit, Michigan

Diana L. Paxson is the founder of several Neo-Pagan groups in the San Francisco Bay area, most notably the Fellowship of the Spiral Path, and is a nationally known author of fiction containing Pagan themes. Raised in California, she is a graduate of Mills College (B.A., 1964) and the University of California (M.A., 1968). Her interest in mythology and ritual began in childhood, and while in graduate school she studied the archetypes of medieval and classical literature. She also trained as a teacher and worked for 10 years developing educational materials. Since 1978 she has published more than two dozen short stories and a dozen novels dealing with religious themes under the guise of fantasy, including several contemporary novels featuring the Pagan scene and the *Chronicles of Westria*, which deal with the spiritual ecology of California. Her best-known book to date is *The White Raven* (1989), which portrays Celtic culture at a moment when Paganism co-existed with Christianity.

During the 1970s, Paxson was initiated into the Aquarian Order of the Restoration, a group based on the teachings of British ritual magician Dion Fortune, and she began her study of Kabbalah and ritual. She wrote a women's rite of passage in 1979 which led to the formation of the Dark Moon Circle, a Women's Mystery (magi-

cal) tradition group. In 1980-1981 she wrote the "Liturgy of the Lady," which has been presented monthly in Berkeley since then. The following year she organized a clergy training program, and was ordained as a priestess. In 1985 Paxson led an intensive 13-month study of the Tree of Life, a study based upon Jewish mystical teachings around the Kabbalah, for a group of 30 students. In 1986 she founded Equinox circle, a co-ed coven, and in 1988 started Hrafnir, a group which works with the runes and Norse shamanism.

In 1986 the Center for Non-Traditional Religions, which had sheltered the Dark Moon and Equinox groups, was disbanded, and Paxson reestablished it as the Fellowship of the Spiral Path, a tradition of the Old Religion which draws its practices from Native European, tribal, and ceremonial sources. Spiral now includes around two dozen groups (circles, classes, and discussion groups, as well as the Clergy Collegium, an association for Neo-Pagan leaders) in Northern California. Public services include the Liturgy of the Lady and an on-going series of classes on the Old Religion (which she taught for the first two years of the fellowship's existence). She has written and directed many rituals for the larger Bay Area Pagan community.

From 1981 to 1986 Paxson served as chair and president of the Center for Non-Traditional Religions and more recently served as president of the Fellowship of the Spiral Path. In 1987 she was elected first officer of the Covenant of the Goddess (COG), an international association of Wiccan groups, and served a second term as co-first officer in 1988-89. She is active in writing, counseling, and conducting workshops. Future plans include working to forge links among the many traditions of the Old Religion.

Sources:

Paxson, Diana. *Brisingamen*. New York: Berkeley, 1986. 272 pp.

———. *The Earthstone*. New York: St. Martin's Press, 1987. 288 pp.

———. *The Paradise Tree*. New York: Ace Books, 1987. 256 pp.

———. *The Sea Star*. New York: St. Martin's Press, 1988. 384 pp.

———. *White Mare, Red Stallion*. New York: Berkeley, 1986. 240 pp.

———. *The White Raven*. New York: Avon, 1989. 40 pp.

★713★
PAYNE, Daniel Alexander
Bishop, African Methodist Episcopal Church
b. Feb. 24, 1811, Charleston, South Carolina
d. Nov. 2, 1893, Wilberforce, Ohio

Daniel Alexander Payne, the sixth bishop of the African Methodist Episcopal Church, was the son of Londo and Martha Payne, free Blacks living in antebellum South Carolina. His parents died when he was 12, but not before they passed to him their piety and their concern for education. He obtained two years of formal schooling at the Minor's Moralist Society School, but continued his education through extensive reading. A tutor taught him English, math, and several languages. In 1826 he joined the Methodist Episcopal Church and two years later began a school for Blacks. The school was a success until an 1834 law stopped the educating of Blacks in the state. In 1835, Payne left South Carolina and settled in Gettysburg, Pennsylvania, where he studied at the Lutheran Theological Seminary for two years. In 1837 he was licensed to preach and in 1839 was ordained in the Frankean Synod of the Lutheran Church.

In 1840 Payne opened a school in Philadelphia where he encountered, and in 1841 joined, the African Methodist Episcopal Church. He was received into the Philadelphia Conference and assigned to Israel Bethel Church in Washington, D.C. He moved on to Bethel Church in Baltimore, and then to Ebenezer Church in Baltimore. In 1847 he married Julia A. Ferris. Shortly after beginning his ministry at Ebenezer, he encountered stiff opposition. Church members rejected him as too genteel. He in turn sought the approval of the general conference in 1848 to allow him to write a history of the church. He traveled widely during the next four years, gathering the church's documents. In 1852 he was elected bishop. He spent the next 12 years traveling around the church, establishing schools, and generally advocating the education of Blacks. In 1853, his first wife having died, he married Eliza J. Clark.

In 1863 Payne purchased Wilberforce University in Xenia, Ohio, from the Methodist Episcopal Church. He became president of the institution and, during his 13 years as bishop, placed the school on a firm financial footing. At the same time he continued his episcopal duties. He returned to South Carolina in 1865 and personally founded the South Carolina Conference of the African Methodist Episcopal Church, which became a launching pad for building the church throughout the south. In 1866 his lengthy historical research bore fruit when he published his monumental *Semi-Centenary and the Retrospection of the African Methodist Episcopal Church Church in the United States of America.*

In 1876 Payne resigned as president of Wilberforce but stayed at the school as chancellor and dean of the theological school. The church relieved him of some of his episcopal duties so he could have time to write. During the 1880s he produced two important volumes, *Treatise on Domestic Education* (1885) and *Recollections of Seventy Years* (1888). His last major public appearance was at the World's Parliament of Religions in Chicago in 1893. He returned home to Xenia after the parliament and died a few weeks later.

Sources:

Coan, Josephus Roosevelt. *Daniel Alexander Payne, Christian Educator.* Philadelphia: A.M.E. Book Concern, 1935. 139 pp.
Dictionary of American Biography. 20 vols. and 7 supps. New York: Charles Scribner's Sons, 1928-1936, 1944-1981.
Payne, Daniel A. *Pleasures and Other Miscellaneous Poems.* Baltimore, MD: Sherwood, 1850. 43 pp.
_____. *Recollections of Seventy Years.* Nashville, TN: Pub. House of the A.M.E. Sunday School Union, 1888. 335 pp.
_____. *Semi-Centenary and the Retrospection of the AME Church in the United States of America.* Baltimore, MD: Sherwood, 1866. 189 pp.
_____. *Treatise on Domestic Education.* Cincinnati, OH: Cranston & Stowe, 1885. 184 pp.
Smith, C. S. *The Life of Daniel Alexander Payne.* Nashville, TN: Pub. House of the A.M.E. Sunday School Union, 1891. 57 pp.

★714★
PEABODY, Lucy Whitehead McGill Waterbury
Founder, Baptists for World Evangelism
b. Mar. 2, 1861, Belmont, Kansas
d. Feb. 26, 1949, Danvers, Massachusetts

Lucy Whitehead McGill Waterbury Peabody, founder of Baptists for World Evangelism, was the daughter of Sarah Jane Hart and John McGill, a merchant who emigrated to Belmont, Kansas, from Canada. Belmont was destroyed in the Civil War and the McGills moved to Pittsford, New York, and then to Rochester, New York, in 1873. In 1878 Lucy graduated from Rochester Academy, and for the next three years she taught in the local school for the deaf while attending classes at Rochester University. In 1881 she married Norman Mather Waterbury, a Baptist minister. They immediately sailed for India, where Rev. Waterbury began mission work among the Telegu people. He died in 1886, and Lucy Waterbury and her three children (one of whom died on the voyage home) returned to the United States.

In 1890 Waterbury moved to Boston to become secretary of the Woman's Baptist Foreign Missionary Society, a position she held until she resigned in 1906 and married Henry W. Peabody, a wealthy merchant. He died two years later, however, leaving Lucy an independently wealthy widow.

During the early twentieth century, Peabody emerged as spokesperson for two ideas that would come into direct conflict.

First, as early as the 1890s she began to argue for ecumenical and cooperative approaches by Protestants on the foreign mission field. She joined **Helen Barrett Montgomery** in advocating an annual interdenominational day of prayer for missions. That practice has since become institutionalized as the World Day of Prayer. In 1900 Peabody helped organize the Committee on the United Study of Foreign Missions. She was appointed chairperson in 1902. In that capacity she authored numerous study materials, organized conferences and summer schools, and represented America at international mission conferences, most importantly the 1910 conference in Edinburgh, Scotland. In 1906 she began *Everyland*, a children's mission magazine, which she edited for the next 12 years.

In 1913 the American Baptists merged several mission agencies to create the Woman's Baptist Foreign Mission Society. Montgomery became president and Peabody vice-president for the foreign department. Following a tour to the Orient with Montgomery in 1913-1914, Peabody made the establishment of women's colleges in India, China, and Japan her major programmatic goal. Working through the Federation of Women's Boards of Foreign Missions, other ecumenical agencies, various denominational mission boards, and with a gift from John D. Rockefeller, she raised money for seven women's colleges. The final amounts were secured in early 1923.

Just as Peabody's mission work was succeeding, she became involved in the fundamentalist-modernist controversy that was splitting the Northern Baptists. While committed to ecumenicity, she was also committed to fundamentalism and its assigned primacy of evangelism over education. She joined those calling for the withdrawal of support from all missionaries with modernist theological tendencies. For Peabody, the issue reached its crucial stage when the mission board restricted the evangelistic activities of her son, a long-time missionary in the Philippines. She took the issue to the floor, lost the vote, walked out, and resigned all of her denominational offices. Her son-in-law and several other supporters in the Philippines also withdrew.

Peabody subsequently organized the independent and fundamentalist Association of Baptists for Evangelism in the Orient, which began to develop new mission fields in the Philippines. Peabody started a magazine, the *Message*, to publicize the association's work. She served as president of the organization until 1935, when at the age of 74 she retired. The association began work in Brazil in 1939 and changed its name to the Association of Baptists for World Evangelism, by which it is known today. The association has adopted a doctrinal statement aligned with that of the General Association of Regular Baptist Churches and is one of several approved missionary agencies through which the General Association conducts its foreign missionary activities.

During her last active years, Peabody was an advocate of prohibition and in 1934 she wrote a book denouncing its repeal.

Sources:

James, Edward T., ed. *Notable American Women, 1607-1950: A Biographical Dictionary.* 3 vols. Cambridge, MA: Harvard University Press, Belknap Press, 1971.
Peabody, Lucy McGill. *Everyland Childrens.* Cambridge, MA: Central Committee on the United Study of Foreign Missions, 1926.
_____. *Henry Wayland Peabody, Merchant.* West Medford, MA: M. H. Levis, 1909. 234 pp.
_____. *Just Like You.* Boston: M. H. Levis, 1937. 186 pp.
_____. *Kidnapping the Constitution.* Marblehead, MA: N. A. Lindsey, 1934. 110 pp.
_____. *A Wider World for Women.* New York: Fleming H. Revell, 1936. 128 pp.

★715★
PEALE, Norman Vincent
Minister, Reformed Church in America
b. May 31, 1898, Bowersville, Ohio

Norman Vincent Peale, a minister in the Reformed Church in America best known for his advocacy of the "power of positive thinking," was the son of Charles Clifford and Anna Delaney Peale. His father was a physician who had become a Methodist minister, and Peale grew up in the several communities in Ohio in which his father pastored congregations. He attended Ohio Wesleyan University and, following his graduation in 1920, began a career in journalism. In 1921, however, he entered Boston Theological Seminary. Upon his graduation he transferred to the New York Conference of the Methodist Episcopal Church and was appointed to Kings Highway Church in Brooklyn.

In 1927 Peale was transferred to University Methodist Church in Syracuse, New York, and, as at Brooklyn, he soon created a thriving ministry which included a radio show. He met and in 1930 married Ruth Stafford. In 1932 he received two calls, one from First Methodist Church in Los Angeles and the other from Marble Collegiate Church in Manhattan. The former was a large congregation with several thousand in attendance each Sunday; the latter was one of the oldest congregations in the country with only a few hundred supporting it. He accepted the challenge of the New York job even though it meant changing his denominational affiliation.

During the early years at Marble Collegiate, Peale was deeply influenced by reading the literature of New Thought—the Unity School of Christianity and Religious Science as well as the writings of Glenn Clark. Its positive and practical approach to life became central to his message, though he always kept an acceptable orthodox theological base within which to cast his presentation. In New York he also continued his radio ministry. In 1933, under the auspices of the Federal Council of Churches (later superseded by the National Council of Churches), he began a show called "The Art of Living" that would run for 40 years and provide the substance and title of his first book. A short time later he began to broadcast his Sunday sermons. He developed two emphases which would become the hallmark of his ministry: he sought to empower individuals to achieve their goals in life and to provide them with tools for a confident, happy, and successful existence.

By 1940 Peale not only was preaching two services each Sunday, but had become a national figure. He began to publish his sermons and mail them from his home at Pawling, New York. The office in Pawling evolved into the Foundation for Christian Living, which became the publishing arm of his ministry. During World War II he began a small periodical, *Guideposts*, a spiritual digest, created in part as a religious *Reader's Digest*. *Guideposts* would eventually attain a circulation of over one million readers.

Peale authored several more books: *You Can Win* (1938); *Faith Is the Answer* (1940, with Smiley Blanton); *A Guide to Confident Living* (1948); and *The Art of Real Happiness* (1950), all of which enjoyed a moderate success. In 1952, however, Prentice-Hall released *The Power of Positive Thinking*. The book climbed onto the bestseller lists, where it remained for three years; the book continues in print to this day. This book, more than any other element of Peale's ministry, established him as a significant force in American popular religion. In 1953 *Life* magazine profiled him as one of America's 12 great preachers. His biography, written by Arthur Gordon, *Norman Vincent Peale: Minister to Millions*, appeared in 1958 and was turned into a Hollywood movie.

During the years since Peale's remarkable success in the 1950s, both the church and the foundation have extended their ministries. Peale developed a staff to assist him and to insure the continuance of the work when he could no longer be on the scene. He devoted his time to his radio show, his travel and lecturing around the coun-try, and his writing. He turned out a number of other popular books, including: *Stay Alive All Your Life* (1957); *Enthusiasm Makes the Difference* (1967); *You Can If You Think You Can* (1974); and most recently, the *Power of the Plus Factor* (1987).

In the wake of the success of *The Power of Positive Thinking*, Peale became the object of attacks by his colleagues who disapproved of the emphases of his ministry. He survived the attacks to win the eventual support and respect of his colleagues, who in 1969 elected him as president of the Reformed Church in America. The leadership had turned to him at a particularly tense moment in the church's life as a person who had stayed apart from the controversy that was dividing the denomination along liberal-conservative lines.

Sources:

Detrich, Richard Lewis. *Norman Vincent Peale*. Milwaukee, WI: Ideals Publishing Corporation, 1969. 80 pp.
Gordon, Arthur. *Norman Vincent Peale: Minister to Millions*. Englewood Cliffs, NJ: Prentice-Hall, 1958. 311 pp.
Lippy, Charles H. *Twentieth-Century Shapers of American Popular Religion*. New York: Greenwood Press, 1989. 494 pp.
Peale, Norman Vincent. *The Art of Living*. New York: Abingdon-Cokesbury, 1937. 144 pp.
_____. *Enthusiasm Makes the Difference*. Carmel, NY: Guidepost Associates, 1967. 252 pp.
_____. *A Guide to Confident Living*. New York: Macmillan Company, 1948. 248 pp.
_____. *The Power of Positive Thinking*. New York: Prentice-Hall, 1952. 237 pp.
_____. *The Power of the Plus Factor*. Old Tappan, NJ: Fleming H. Revell Company, 1987. 221 pp.
_____. *You Can If You Think You Can*. Greenwich, CT: Fawcett, 1974. 321 pp.
"Twelve Great American Preachers." *Life* 34 (April 6, 1953): 126.

★716★
PEEBLES, James Martin
Spiritualist Author and Lecturer
b. Mar. 23, 1822, Whittingham, Vermont
d. Feb. 15, 1922, Los Angeles, California

James Martin Peebles, a prominent and effective advocate of Spiritualism through the last half of the nineteenth century, was one of seven children born into a pious Scottish Presbyterian home. He graduated from Oxford Academy in upstate New York in 1841, before studying at Pennsylvania University. He left the Presbyterianism of his parents and became a minister in the Universalist Church. He was ordained in 1846 and later served churches at Kellogville, Elmira, and New York, New York, and in Baltimore, Maryland. He became deeply involved in the pre-Civil War social crusades, especially temperance and abolitionism. He was a friend of John Brown (of Harper's Ferry fame) and William Lloyd Garrison, who shared an interest in Spiritualism.

Peebles' interest in Spiritualism began while he was serving the church at Kellogville. He was invited by some parishioners to attend a demonstration of Spiritualist phenomena at nearby Auburn, New York. Here he first encountered spirit rapping, in which it was believed that spirit entities made knocking sounds in response to yes-or-no questions from the audience. On another occasion soon afterward he attended what was to be a trance lecture by a young uneducated man. Peebles was invited to name the subject. He chose "The Philosophical Influence of the Nations of Antiquity Upon the Civilization of Modern Europe and America." Peebles then watched as the entranced man delivered a learned discourse on the chosen subject lasting almost two hours. In reaction, he preached a sermon on "The Spiritual Gifts" (I Corinthians 12) which was very negatively received by his congregation. He resigned from his church and the ministry and took up the practice of medicine and the championing of Spiritualism.

In the years immediately after the Civil War Peebles settled in Cleveland, Ohio. He became the western editor for the *Banner of Light*, one of the older Spiritual periodicals published in Boston, Massachusetts. He then became editor-in-chief of the *Spiritual Universe* and later editor of *The American Spiritualist*, published in Cleveland. Beginning in the 1860s a veritable flood of books flowed from his pen; many were transcripts of his talks and a few accounts of his travels (he circled the globe on five different occasions). Among his early titles were *Seers of the Ages* (1869); *Jesus: Myth, Man, or God* (1870); *Spiritualism Defined and Defended* (1874); *Around the World: or, Travels in Polynesia, China, India, Arabia, Egypt, Syria* (1875); and one of the earliest American books on Buddhism, *Buddhism and Christianity, Face to Face; or, An Oral Discussion* (1878).

In his mature years Peebles was also an advocate of peace. In this regard he was sent in 1869 by President U. S. Grant as the United States Consul to Turkey and that same year appointed to the United States at the Arbitration League in Paris. He was a long-time member of the Universal Peace Union. During the late nineteenth century, he established the Peebles Institute of Health in Battle Creek, Michigan, which issued many of his books. Among his most substantive were *Reincarnation; or, The Doctrine of the Soul's Successive Embodiments* (1904); *The Demonism of the Ages, Spirit Obsessions So Common in Spiritism, Oriental and Occidental Occultism* (1904); *Spirit Mates Their Origin and Destiny, Sex-Life, Marriage, Divorce* (1909); and *Five Journeys Around the World; Travels in the Pacific Islands, New Zealand, Australia, Ceylon, India, Egypt, and other Oriental Countries* (1910). The aging but still active Peebles finally retired to Los Angeles, California, where he operated the Peebles Publishing Company. He died there just a few days short of his 100th birthday.

Sources:

Cutlip, Audra. *Pioneers of Modern Spiritualism.* vol. I. Milwaukee, WI: National Spiritualist Association of Churches, n.d. 40 pp.
Peebles, J. M. *The Demonism of the Ages, Spirit Obsession So Common in Spiritism, Oriental and Occidental Occultism.* Battle Creek, MI: Peebles Medical Institute, 1904. 382 pp.
————. *Jesus: Myth, Man, or God.* London: J. Burns, Progressive Library, 1870. 104 pp.
————. *Reincarnation: or the Doctrine of the "Soul's" Successive Embodiments.* Battle Creek, MI: Peebles Medical Institute, 1904. 100 pp.
————. *Seers of the Ages: Embracing Spiritualism Past and Present.* 1869. Rept. Chicago: Progressive Thinker Publishing House, 1903. 376 pp.

★717★
PELIKAN JR., Jaroslav Jan
Church Historian, Lutheran Church—Missouri Synod
b. Dec. 17, 1923, Akron, Ohio

Jaroslav Jan Pelikan, Jr., one of the most prominent Christian church historians of the late twentieth century, is the son of Jaroslav Jan Pelikan, Sr., a Lutheran minister, and Anna Buzek Pelikan. He attended Concordia Junior College and in 1946 graduated from both Concordia Theological Seminary (B.D.) and the University of Chicago Divinity School (Ph.D.). That same year he married Sylvia Burica, was ordained a minister in the Lutheran Church—Missouri Synod, and assumed a post as a professor at Valparaiso University in Indiana.

Pelikan stayed at Valparaiso for two years before moving to Concordia Seminary in 1949. While at Concordia he authored his first book, *From Luther to Kierkegaard* (1950). In 1953 he returned to the University of Chicago to teach for nine years, during which time he authored *Fools for Christ* (1955); *The Riddle of Roman Catholicism* (1959); and *Luther the Expositor* (1959). Then in 1962 he moved to Yale University as the Titus Street Professor of Ecclesiastical History. He has remained at Yale, and was named Sterling Professor of History and Religious Studies in 1972. From 1975 to 1978 he was also acting dean of the graduate school.

Pelikan's major contribution has come through his many books, the majority of which have concentrated either on the ancient church or the Reformation era. On the former he has produced such works as *The Shape of Life, Death, and Immortality in the Early Fathers* (1961); *The Light of the World: A Basic Image in Early Christian Thought* (1962); and more recently, *Mystery of Continuity*, a study in the thought of St. Augustine. In Reformation studies, he distinguished himself as the general editor of the first 30 volumes of the collected *Works of Martin Luther*, which began to appear in 1958. He also authored *Obedient Rebels: Catholic Substance and Protestant Principle in Luther's Reformation* (1964) and *Spirit versus Structure: Luther and the Institutions of the Church* (1968). As a mature scholar he has produced a variety of texts which provide perspectives on church history through the centuries. As early as 1971 he produced his *Historical Theology: Continuity and Change in Christian Doctrine* and the first volume of *The Christian Tradition: A History of the Development of Doctrine*. More recently he finished his highly acclaimed *Jesus through the Centuries* (1985). Pelikan's work has received numerous awards, and in 1965 he was elected president of the American Society of Church History.

Sources:

Pelikan, Jaroslav. *The Christian Tradition: A History of the Development of Doctrine.* 5 vols. Chicago: University of Chicago Press, 1971-1989.
————. *From Luther to Kierkegaard.* St. Louis, MO: Concordia Publishing House, 150. 171 pp.
————. *Jesus through the Centuries.* New Haven, CT: Yale University Press, 1985. 270 pp.
————. *Obedient Rebels: Catholic Substance and Protestant Principle in Luther's Reformation.* London: SCM Press, 1964. 212 pp.
————. *The Riddle of Roman Catholicism.* New York: Abingdon Press, 1959. 272 pp.

★718★
PELLEY, William Dudley
Author and Founder, Soulcraft, Inc.
b. Mar. 12, 1890, Lynn, Massachusetts
d. Jun. 1965, Indianapolis, Indiana

William Dudley Pelley was the founder of Soulcraft, Inc., a metaphysical "school" and publishing concern, although he is better remembered as the founder of the Silver Shirts, an ultra-rightist organization that was partially inspired by Adolf Hitler. He was the only son of William George Apsey Pelley, a minister of the Methodist Episcopal Church, and Grace Goodale Pelley. Pelley later attributed his grim disposition to the combined effects of his father's stern theology and the straitened circumstances of his childhood. He desired higher education, but his family's impoverishment forced him to begin working at the mills when he was 14. He compensated for his lack of formal education by reading voraciously. He also became something of a religious iconoclast, a tendency that was at least partially a protest against his upbringing. In *My Seven Minutes in Eternity* (a description of an out-of-body experience) he wrote that, "For ten years I was one of the worst agnostics that ever had books come to his post office box in plain wrappers from freak publishing houses."

Pelley's attraction to the written word led him into newspaper work. Difficulties with his business, an unsuccessful marriage, and such tragedies as the death of his first daughter did nothing to improve his disposition. In 1918 the Methodist Episcopal Church sent him to Asia to report on foreign missions. He was also commissioned by the Young Men's Christian Association (YMCA) to report on the Russian Revolution, and he went to Siberia with the Japanese forces. Back in the United States, he went to work writing scores for motion pictures. He also wrote fiction, and gained a national reputation as a magazine writer during the 1920s.

Pelley had been reading religious and metaphysical works during the years leading up to an out-of-body experience that he spontaneously experienced in 1927. He described this experience in an article published in the popular magazine *American Mercury*. He was transformed into a less bitter person, whose interests were now firmly directed toward occult and metaphysical topics, and he began to receive messages from spirit entities, messages which formed the groundwork for the Soulcraft philosophy. The basic ideas of this philosophy were that all human beings are part of the Godhead, and that people are here on earth to learn to become more aware of ourselves and of our relationship with both God and other human beings. The idea of a cosmic course of learning that was carried out through successive incarnations was also part of the philosophy. Pelley never tried to found a church, but rather focused on disseminating the Soulcraft philosophy in the form of his publications.

Most accounts of Pelley focus on his political views and activities rather than on his metaphysical speculations. In the 1930s he became known for his anti-New Deal views, and for his attacks on Communism and Jews. On January 31, 1933, the day after Hitler came to power in Germany, Pelley launched the Siver Shirts, an ultra-right organization modeled along the lines of the Nazi brown shirts. His social ideas were put forth in a book, *No More Hunger* (1933), and an autobiographical apology, *The Door to Revelation* (1936). Even after the bombing of Pearl Harbor he did not change his views, and this led to an arrest and trial on charges of sedition in 1942. Pelley was convicted, but the Supreme Court eventually threw his case out. After the war, he spent the remaining years of his life on his metaphysical work, the primary activity being the authoring of a number of books and the *Soulcraft Scripts*, 12 volumes of lessons which contain the essence of Pelley's teachings.

Sources:

Melton, J. Gordon *The Encyclopedia of American Religions*. 3d ed. Detroit: Gale Research Inc.,1988. 1102 pp.
Myers, Gustavus. *History of Bigotry in the United States*. New York: Capricorn, 1960. 474 pp.
Pelley, William Dudley. *The Door to Revelation*. Asheville, NC: The Foundation Fellowship, 1936. 312 pp.
_____. *The Golden Scripts*. Noblesville, IN: Soulcraft Chapels, 1951. 257 pp.
_____. *My Seven Minutes in Eternity*. Asheville, NC: Pelley Publishers, n.d. 16 pp.
_____. *Road to Sunrise*. Noblesville, IN: Soulcraft Press, 1950. 658 pp.
_____. *Undying Mind*. Noblesville, IN: Soulcraft Chapels, 1955. 318 pp.
Something about Soulcraft and Its Founder, William Dudley Pelley. Noblesville, IN: Fellowship Press, n.d. 14 pp.

★ 719 ★
PELOUBET, Francis Nathan
Minister, Congregational Church
b. Dec. 2, 1831, New York, New York
d. Mar. 27, 1920, Auburndale, Massachusetts

Francis Nathan Peloubet, a minister in the Congregational Church best known for his work promoting the Sunday school movement, was the son of Louis Michel Francois Chabrier and Harriet Hanks Peloubet. His grandfather had emigrated to America as an exile of the French Revolution. Though born in New York City, Peloubet grew up in Bloomfield, New Jersey. He attended Williams College, from which he graduated in 1853. After a year off he entered Bangor Theological Seminary, from which he graduated in 1857; he was ordained a few months later. During his seminary days, he had prepared himself for the mission field, but at the last minute he decided to stay in America in the pastorate.

As a minister Peloubet served successive pastorates in several Massachusetts communities, Incorporated Lanesville (1857-1860), Oakham (1860-1866), Attleboro (1866-1871), and Natick (1872-1883). In 1859, while at Lanesville, he married Mary Abby Thaxter. While at Oakham, he took leave on two occasions, to visit the war front on behalf of the Christian Commission.

Peloubet labored for a quarter of a century as a pastor, but he is most remembered for his work on behalf of the Sunday school movement. That work began at Attleboro. He prepared two question-discussion books for use in churches, but was unable to find a willing publisher. During his stay at Natick, the International Sunday School Lesson Plan was adopted by most Protestant church bodies, and in 1874 he prepared a set of question-discussion books built around the lessons. These became an immediate success. In 1875 he met a second need by preparing his first set of *Select Notes on the International Sabbath* (later titled *Sunday School Lessons*), a commentary on the International Lessons for teachers. These works achieved a similar, immediate, and positive response.

In 1883 Peloubet left the pastorate and settled in Auburndale, Massachusetts, to spend the rest of his life writing. He authored the *Select Notes* annually for almost 40 years (the last issue under his personal authorship was the 1921 edition). He also authored a number of books, including commentaries on the biblical books of Matthew, John, and Acts; *Select Songs for the Singing Service in the Prayer Meeting and Sunday School*; *Loom of Life and If Christ Were a Guest in Your Home* (1900); *The Front Line of the Sunday School Movement* (1904); *Studies in the Book of Job* (1906); *Treasury of Biblical Information* (1913); and *Oriental Light Illuminating Bible Tests and Bible Truth* (1914). In 1912 he finished a revision of the *International Bible Dictionary*, originally compiled by William Smith. More recent reprints have simply been called *Peloubet's Bible Dictionary*.

Sources:

Dictionary of American Biography. 20 vols. and 7 supps. New York: Charles Scribner's Sons, 1928-1936, 1944-1981.
Peloubet, Francis N. *The Front Line of the Sunday School Movement*. Boston, MA: W. A. Wilde Company, 1904. 287 pp.
_____. *Loom of Life and If Christ Were a Guest in Your Home*. Boston, MA: United Society of Christian Endeavor, 1900. 64 pp.
_____, ed. *Select Songs for the Singing Service in the Prayer Meeting and Sunday School*. 2 vols. New York: Bigelow & Maine, 1884. 224 pp.
_____. *Studies in the Book of Job*. New York: Charles Scribner's, 1906.

★ 720 ★
PENNINGTON, Edith Mae
Pentecostal Evangelist
b. Jun. 9, 1902, Pine Bluff, Arkansas
d. May 16, 1974, Shreveport, Louisiana

Edith Mae Pennington, Pentecostal evangelist and pastor, was born Edith Mae Patterson, the daughter of Arch and Julie Patterson. Her father was a foreman with the railroad. In 1920 she entered Rice Institute to prepare herself for a teaching career. But in 1921 Edith Mae's heretofore quiet life was changed irrevocably by the actions of her aunt, Mrs. W. J. Miller, who submitted a photograph of her niece to the newspaper for a contest to name the "Most Beautiful Girl in the U.S." Edith Mae won in November 1921. The prize was $2,500.

After winning, Edna Mae toured the country, developed a nightclub act, and was offered a Hollywood contract. She married J. B. Pennington and had a child, named Edith Lorraine. In 1925, however, feeling dissatisfied with her life, she went to a small Pentecostal church in Oklahoma City, where her life was dramatically changed for the second time. In the church she was converted, and later baptized in the Holy Spirit. Pennington also felt a call to the ministry. She returned to her hometown of Pine Bluff, Arkansas, and became the assistant pastor at the Assemblies of God church for the next two years. During this time she was divorced. She was ordained by the Assemblies of God in 1930.

After two years in Pine Bluff, Pennington began to travel and preach in Assemblies of God churches around the country. She consistently displayed marked oratorical skills that filled the churches and led to many conversions. She continued to travel for almost two decades. In 1937 she settled in Shreveport, Louisiana, to found the Full Gospel Temple (affiliated with the Assemblies of God).

After thirteen years as an Assemblies pastor, Pennington unexpectedly resigned from the denomination. In a letter to the general secretary she stated simply that God wanted her to separate from the Assemblies and had called her to an independent church, The Plant of Renown. There was some indication that she had become influenced by the Latter-Rain controversy that was at the time shaking the Assemblies, but she denied having any new "teachings, practices, or interpretations" such as those introduced by the Latter-Rain.

Following Pennington's death in 1950, her daughter became the pastor of the church.

Sources:

Burgess, Stanley M., Gary B. McGee, and Patrick H. Alexander, eds. *Dictionary of Pentecostal and Charismatic Movements*. Grand Rapids, MI: Regency Reference Library, Zondervan Publishing House, 1988. 914 pp.
Pennington, Edith Mae. *From the Floodlights to the Light of the Cross*. N.p.: The Author, n.d.
Warner, Wayne. "From the Flood Lights to the Light of the Cross: The Story of Evangelist Edith Mae Pennington." *Assemblies of God Heritage*. 7, 4 (Winter 1987) 6-9, 20.

★721★
PENROSE, Romania Pratt
Women's Advocate, Church of Jesus Christ of Latter-day Saints
b. Aug. 8, 1839, Indiana
d. Nov. 9, 1932, Salt Lake City, Utah

Romania Pratt Penrose, a pioneer female physician and woman's advocate within the Church of Jesus Christ of Latter-day Saints, was born Romania Brunnell on a farm in rural Indiana. When she was a young child, her family converted to Mormonism and she moved with them to Nauvoo, Illinois. They arrived just as Nauvoo's largely Mormon population abandoned the town to trek west to the Great Salt Lake in Utah. Unable to afford provisions to go west, the family returned to Indiana. Leaving Romania and her mother on the farm, her father then went to California during the Gold Rush. He died of typhoid in a mining camp.

As a youth, Romania was able, as were few of her contemporaries, to attend school. While attending the Female Seminary in Crawfordsville, Indiana, she developed a desire to learn medicine, the knowledge of which could possibly have saved the life of a friend.

In 1855 Romania and her mother made their way to Omaha, Nebraska, and joined a wagon train to Salt Lake City. Four years later Romania became the first wife of Parley Pratt, Jr., the son of an outstanding first generation Mormon family. They quickly had seven children, five of which survived infancy. She also helped her husband edit his father's papers, which were published as *The Autobiography of Parley Pratt*.

In 1873 Mormon president Brigham Young called on women to study medicine, primarily obstetrics and pediatrics, to care for women in childbirth and their babies. She sold her possessions, left her children with her mother, and departed for New York. Young helped support her education, and she graduated in 1877. She then spent two years in Philadelphia specializing in treating diseases of the eye and ear.

Upon her return to Salt Lake City, Romania was welcomed by the church leadership. In 1879 she established her practice, taught classes in basic anatomy and physiology, and authored a number of articles on hygiene and related topics for the church's women's magazines. She was also startled to learn that her husband had taken a second wife. As she had always accepted polygamy as a basic doctrine, she was not particularly upset. But over the next few years she decided, for other reasons, that the marriage was over. She divorced Pratt in 1881.

The divorce did not seem to slow her activities nor create any hostile reaction. In 1882 she traveled to New York to the Woman's Suffrage Convention and became an advocate of the cause. The following year she became a visiting professor at Deseret Hospital. In 1886 she married again, this time becoming the third wife of Charles Penrose, who was himself on his way to prominence. In 1904 he became an apostle and in 1907 he was assigned to leadership of the European Mission. Romania worked on the development of the church's relief societies. In 1908 Romania represented Utah and spoke at the Woman's International Suffrage Alliance meeting in Amsterdam. She became counselor to the church president in 1911.

In 1912 Romania Penrose retired after more than three decades as a physician. She devoted the remainder of her life to women's work in the church through the relief societies. Her husband died in 1925. She lived quietly until her death in 1932.

Sources:

Van Wagoner, Richard S., and Steven C. Walker. *A Book of Mormons*. Salt Lake City, UT: Signature Books, 1982. 454 pp.
Waters, Christine Craft. "Romania P. Penrose." In *Sister Saints*, edited by Vicky Burgess-Olson, pp. 343-360. Provo, UT: Brigham Young University Press, 1978.

★722★
PENTECOST, George Frederick
Minister, Baptist Church
b. Sep. 23, 1842, Albion, Illinois
d. Aug. 7, 1920, Philadelphia, Pennsylvania

George Frederick Pentecost, a popular minister in the Baptist Church at the beginning of the twentieth century, was the son of Hugh L. and Emma Flower Pentecost. In 1856 at the age of 14, Pentecost traveled to the Kansas Territory where he eventually became the secretary to the governor and clerk of the U. S. district court. In 1860 he entered Georgetown College in Kentucky. While there he was converted and in 1862 he left the school to enlist as a chaplain in the Union Army. During the war years, he married Ada Webber (1863). The next year he formally became a Baptist minister. His first congregation was in Greencastle, Indiana. He subsequently served congregations in Evansville, Indiana; Covington, Kentucky; Brooklyn, New York (Hanson Place, 1869-1872); and Boston, Massachusetts (Warren Avenue, 1872-1878). During the 1870s he published his first books, *The Angel in the Marble* (1875) and *In the Volume of the Book* (1879) and gained a national reputation as both an excellent pulpit orator and an author of popular religious books. He left Warren Avenue to spend two years with evangelist **Dwight L. Moody** in evangelistic work.

After his work with Moody, in 1880 he became pastor of Tomkins Avenue Congregational Church in Brooklyn, New York. While there he authored *Out of Egypt* (1884) and most of the volumes of his 12-volume set of *Bible Studies* (1880-1889), his most popular books. By the end of the decade he had begun a period of life abroad doing evangelistic work, first in Scotland (1887-1888), then in India (1888-1891), and finally in London (1891-1897). While in London he pastored the Marylebone Church. His last year there he published *The Birth and Boyhood of Jesus* and *Grace Abounding in the Forgiveness of Sins*.

Pentecost returned to the United States in 1897 and became pastor of First Presbyterian Church in Yonkers, New York. While there he published *Systematic Beneficence* (1898) and *Precious Truths* (1898). In 1902 he left the parish to make a mission tour in the Orient, after which he retired. He lived in retirement for 11 years, but was persuaded in 1914 to supply the pulpit at Bethany

Presbyterian Church. Two years later, the 74-year-old Baptist minister was named pastor of the church. He served with great vigor for four years. He was especially active in support of the war and in opposition to pacifism. He died suddenly in 1920.

Sources:

Dictionary of American Biography. 20 vols. and 7 supps. New York: Charles Scribner's Sons, 1928-1936, 1944-1981.

Headley, P. C. *George F. Pentecost: Life, Labors, and Bible Studies.* Boston: J. H. Earle, 1880. 456 pp.

Pentacost, George F. *The Birth and Boyhood of Jesus.* London: Hodder and Staughton, 1897. 399 pp.

_____. *Grace Abounding in the Forgiveness of Sins.* London: T.F. Downie, 1897. 174 pp.

_____. *In the Volume of the Book.* Philadelphia: Times Printing House, 1879. 102 pp.

_____. *Out of Egypt.* New York: Funk & Wagnalls, 1884. 214 pp.

_____. *Precious Truths.* New York: The Author, 1898.

_____. *Systematic Beneficence.* New York: A. D. F. Randolph Co., 1898. 60 pp.

★ 723 ★
PENTECOST, John Dwight
Fundamentalist Minister and Scholar
b. Apr. 15, 1915, State College, Pennsylvania

John Dwight Pentecost, for over three decades a professor at Dallas Theological Seminary, is the eldest son of John and Edna Pentecost. His father, an electrical engineer, moved the family first to Schenectady, New York, soon after Pentecost's birth, and later to Chester, Pennsylvania, where they joined the Third Presbyterian Church. During his high school years he decided to become a minister. He attended Hampden-Sydney College in Virginia, from which he graduated magna cum laude in 1937. He then entered Dallas Theological Seminary, an independent fundamentalist school strongly identified with premillennial theology. Such theology strongly emphasized the imminent second coming of Jesus Christ and his establishment of a thousand-year period of justice and peace on earth. While at Dallas he married Dorothy Harrison, whom he had met during his college days.

Following his graduation from seminary (Th.M., 1941), Pentecost returned to Pennsylvania where he was ordained in the Presbyterian Church and became pastor of the congregation at Cambridge Springs. A short time later he moved to Saint John's Presbyterian Church at Devon, Pennsylvania. While there he was called upon to teach at the Philadelphia School of the Bible. He remained at Devon until 1953 when he returned to Dallas to work on his doctorate. He concentrated much of his studies on eschatology (the doctrine of last things) and his 1956 Th.D. dissertation was published as *Things to Come* (1958). A popular study of eschatology, it has remained in print for over 30 years.

Following his graduation, Pentecost joined the Dallas faculty. He spent the rest of his professional life as a teacher. He served first in the department of systematic theology, later as a professor of New Testament exegesis, and in 1962 became chairman of the department of Bible Exposition. He retired from his chairmanship in 1980, though he remained a full-time professor. Along the way in the 1960s he also became the minister of Grace Bible Church in Dallas. He has authored numerous books, among the most popular being *The Divine Comforter* (1963) and *The Words and Work of Jesus Christ* (1970). In addition to his teaching and pastoring duties, Pentecost has traveled widely both nationally and internationally as a Bible conference speaker.

Sources:

Pentecost, J. Dwight. *The Divine Comforter.* Chicago: Moody Press, 1963. 256 pp.

_____. *Joy of Fellowship.* Grand Rapids, MI: Zondervan Publishing House, 1977.

_____. *Joy of Living.* Grand Rapids, MI: Zondervan Publishing House, 1990. 160 pp.

_____. *Things to Come.* Grand Rapids, MI: Zondervan Publishing House, 1958.

_____. *The Words and Work of Jesus Christ.* Grand Rapids, MI: Zondervan Publishing House, 1970.

Toussaint, Stanley D., and Charles H. Dyer, eds. *Essays in Honor of J. Dwight Pentecost.* Chicago: Moody Press, 1986. 238 pp.

★ 724 ★
PERCIVAL, Harold Waldwin
Founder, Word Foundation
Cofounder, Theosophical Society of New York
b. Apr. 15, 1868, Bridgetown Barbados
d. Mar. 6, 1953, New York, New York

Harold Waldwin Percival, one of the founders of the Theosophical Society of New York and the founder of the Word Foundation, was the son of a British couple, Elizabeth Ann Taylor and James Percival. Unsatisfied by his parents' Christianity, he began an alternative spiritual quest. Following the death of his father when he was ten years old, he moved with his mother to the United States, eventually settling in New York.

In 1892 Percival joined the American branch of the Theosophical Society then headed by **William Q. Judge**. After Judge died in 1896, the society began to split into factions. Percival joined with J. H. Salisbury, Donald Nicholson, and other New York theosophical members to form the independent Theosophical Society of New York. Percival also formed the associated Theosophical Publishing House, which published, among its many titles, Percival's first books: *The Zodiac* (1906); *Karma, the Law of Life* (1910); and *Hell and Heaven, on Earth and after Death* (1911). In 1904 he launched a periodical, *The Word*, which he edited for the next 13 years.

Over the years of his theosophical affiliation, Percival had begun to put together a personal vision of the world. He dated his own growth from a mystical experience he had in 1893 which he described as his having become "conscious of consciousness." Around 1912 he had outlined his new system and began to dictate a book to a colleague. Finally, in 1932 the results of his labors appeared as *The Law of Thought*. He went to work rewriting and revising it and in 1946 a new edition appeared as *Thinking and Destiny*. Percival asserted that in the state of being conscious of consciousness, one could know about any subject simply by thinking. He defined thinking as holding the "Conscious Light" within the subject of the thinking. To think, one must first select the subject, hold the conscious light on that subject, focus the light, and realize the knowledge of the subject.

Following his completion of *Thinking and Destiny*, Percival and several colleagues formed the Word Publishing Company to publish and distribute his book. In 1950 he founded the Word Foundation to perpetuate his insights. Subsequently he authored three additional books in which he elaborated upon his ideas: *Man and Woman and Child* (1951); *Masonry and Its Symbols* (1952); and *Democracy is Self-Government* (1953). Since his death, a small group of followers have continued to teach Percival's ideas and circulate his books.

Sources:

Percival, Harold Waldwin. *Democracy is Self-Government.* New York: Word Publishing Co., 1953. 237 pp.

_____. *Man and Woman and Child.* New York: Word Publishing Co., 1951. 232 pp.

_____. *Masonry and its Symbols.* New York: Word Publishing Co., 1952. 63 pp.

_____. *Thinking and Destiny.* New York: Word Publishing Co., 1946, 1950. 1014 pp.

Portanda, Alex. "The Legacy of Harold Percival." *Psychic Guide* 4, 3 (December 1985-January & February 1986): 26-29.

★725★
PERKINS, John M.
*Founder, John M. Perkins Foundation for Reconciliation and
Development*
b. 1930, New Hebron, Mississippi

John M. Perkins is an independent evangelical minister and
founder of the Harambee Christian Family Center and the John M.
Perkins Foundation for Reconciliation and Development. He is the
son of Jap and Maggie Perkins, black sharecroppers in rural Mississippi. His mother died a few months after his birth, and he was
raised by his grandmother. In 1947 his brother was killed in a fight
with the town marshal. Perkins left Mississippi soon afterwards and
settled in California. In 1951 he was drafted and a few days before
shipping out for Okinawa married Vera Mae Buckley. Released
from duty in 1953, he settled in California.

Not a particularly religious man, he became involved with Jehovah's Witnesses and later with other religious groups. He eventually was invited to a local Church of God (Holiness) congregation
and had his first positive experience with Christians. He joined the
adult Bible class and began to read and study the Bible. In November 1957 he had an experience of accepting Christ and his life
began to change dramatically. He began to testify in public meetings. He involved himself with Child Evangelism, a ministry to children. He visited prisoners and shared his story. In 1960 he decided
to move back to Mississippi.

In his home territory, Perkins began a ministry among the youth
and was welcomed into the schools. His work was supported by
Calvary Bible Church in Burbank, California, and he began to operate under the name Voice of Calvary, with headquarters in Mendenhall. In 1964 he founded the Berean Bible Church. His ministry
emerged in the midst of the growing Civil Rights Movement, and
he seized the opportunity as both a black leader and evangelical
Christian to work for the people among whom he had been ministering. He organized a voter registration drive (1966), a housing cooperative (1967), and a leadership training program (1968). His efforts led to his arrest in December 1969, which brought a response
by Blacks who boycotted the local stores and began civil rights
marches every Saturday. On February 7, 1970, he was again arrested in another county and subjected to a night of beatings and
torture. He survived to win some modest but very real victories in
court. Voice of Calvary survived as a model of an evangelistic ministry's involvement in social activism. Perkins' 1976 account of his
ministry, *Let Justice Roll Down*, boosted his role as a national
spokesperson for black ministers in the evangelical community.

In 1978, with the emergence of a mature local leadership in
Mendenhall, Perkins shifted his headquarters to Jackson. In 1981
the Mendenhall work incorporated as Mendenhall Ministries. That
same year Perkins returned to California and settled in a high crime
community in northwest Pasadena. Perkins defined the church as
a group of Christian people in a specific place who are committed
to sharing God with the people of their community. Harambee
Christian Family Center has developed a wide range of educational
and religious programs. The John M. Perkins Foundation for Reconciliation and Development has fostered the creation of similar centers in other communities.

Sources:
Aeschliman, Gordon D. *John Perkins: Land Where My Father Died.* Ventura, CA: GL Publications, 1987. 172 pp.
Perkins, John. *Let Justice Roll Down.* Ventura, CA: GL Publications, 1976.
223 pp.

★726★
PERRY JR., James De Wolf
Presiding Bishop, Episcopal Church
b. Oct. 3, 1871, Germantown, Pennsylvania
d. Mar. 20, 1947, Summerville, South Carolina

James De Wolf Perry, Jr., the eighteenth presiding bishop of the
Episcopal Church, was the son of Elisabeth Russell Tyson and
James De Wolf Perry, Sr., also an Episcopal minister. Perry grew
up in Pennsylvania and attended the Germantown Academy which
prepared him to enter the University of Pennsylvania in 1887. He
received his B.A. in 1891 and entered Harvard University, from
which he received a second degree in 1892. He attended the Episcopal Theological School in Cambridge, Massachusetts, and was
granted a B.D. in 1895. Shortly after graduation he was ordained
a deacon and assigned as assistant minister at Christ Episcopal
Church in Springfield, Massachusetts. He was ordained as a priest
in 1896.

In 1897 Perry became the rector of Christ Episcopal Church in
Fitchburg, Massachusetts. During his Fitchburg years he also
served as the chaplain of the Sixth Massachusetts Infantry, including the years of the Spanish-American War. In 1904 Perry moved
to Connecticut as rector of what was to prove to be his last parish,
St. Pauls's Episcopal Church in New Haven. While there, in 1908
he married Edith Dean Weir.

In 1910 Perry was elected bishop of Rhode Island and consecrated in January 1911. He had a lengthy and successful career in
his diocese until 1930. That year, **Charles Palmerston Anderson**
died after less than four months in office as the presiding bishop
of the Episcopal Church. Perry was selected to fill out Anderson's
term until the next general convention in 1931, when he was formally elected as the presiding bishop for a standard six-year term.
At the time the presiding bishop remained the bishop of his own
diocese in addition to his general church duties. This arrangement
had worked in the past. The pressures of an increased work load,
due in part to the Great Depression following the 1929 market
crash, and the demands of holding what amounted to two full time
positions proved too much for Perry, and he was unable to satisfac-
torily meet the expectations of the church's leadership. In 1937 he
was defeated for re-election. He returned to his diocese, where he
served until 1946.

Perry's predicament led the church to act, and at the 1937 convention the organization was changed to separate the office of presiding bishop for diocesan duties. Succeeding presiding bishops resigned their diocesan office and became a bishop for the general
church.

Sources:
DeMille, George E. *The Episcopal Church Since 1900: A Brief History.*
New York: Morehouse-Gorham Company, 1955. 223 pp.

★727★
PERRY, Troy Deroy
*Founder, Universal Fellowship of Metropolitan Community
Churches*
b. Jul. 27, 1940, Tallahassee, Florida

Troy Deroy Perry, the founder of the Universal Fellowship of
Metropolitan Community Churches, is the son of Edith Allen and
Troy Perry. His father died when Perry was a child, and his mother
remarried. Perry, faced with an abusive stepfather, ran away from
home and lived with relatives. He finally returned to his mother
when she separated from her second husband. Settled in Winter
Haven, Florida, Perry was licensed to preach by the local Baptist
church when he was 15, but he was more drawn to Pentecostalism
and the following year became an evangelist for the Church of God
(Cleveland, Tennessee). At the age of 18 he married Pearl Pinion,
the daughter of a Church of God minister. They moved to Illinois

where he attended Midwest Bible College and pastored a Church of God congregation in Joliet, Illinois. While at Joliet, a homosexual affair was discovered, and he was immediately dismissed from the Church of God. He continued his ministry with the Church of God of Prophecy, the leadership of which was unaware of his homosexual involvements.

Perry finished two years at Midwest Bible College and then went to Moody Bible Institute for a year (1960-1961). Following his year at Moody, he moved to Southern California as pastor of a church in Santa Ana. He soon encountered the homosexual community in California and developed a clearer understanding of his personal homosexual orientation. His acceptance of his own gayness led both to a dissolution of his marriage and a break with the Church of God of Prophecy.

In 1965 Perry went into the Army for two years. Upon his release in 1967 he settled in Los Angeles. The months after the stint in the Army became a time for reflection upon his own calling to the ministry and his relation to a Christianity which basically condemned his sexual life. In 1968, following up on the suggestion of a friend, he began a church for the homosexual community in Los Angeles, the Metropolitan Community Church. From a small beginning, the effort was marked with an immediate success, riding the wave of a developing openness within the homosexual community corresponding with the emergence of the gay rights movement. Within a few years Perry emerged as the leader of a new national Christian denomination and as a very visible national spokesperson for gay rights. The story of the founding of the church was told initially in Perry's first autobiographical work, *The Lord Is My Shepherd and He Knows I'm Gay* (1972). That same year Perry led in the expansion of the church into England and two years later into Australia.

Perry served as pastor of the initial congregation of the Metropolitan Community Church, but gave up the pulpit in 1974 when he was named the first moderator of what had become the Universal Fellowship of Metropolitan Community Churches. Since that time he has led the church's participation in battles for gay rights, and during the 1980s in the response to the AIDS epidemic. Most recently he has authored a new autobiographical volume, *Don't Be Afraid Anymore* (1990).

Sources:

Perry, Troy, with Thomas L. P. Swicegood. *Don't Be Afraid Anymore.* New York: St. Martin's Press, 1990. 355 pp.

Perry, Troy, with Charles L. Lucas. *The Lord Is My Shepherd and He Knows I'm Gay.* New York: Nash Publishing Corp., 1972.

★728★
PESHEWA, Macaki
Priest, Native American Church of the Southeast
b. May 23, 1941, Spartanburg, South Carolina

Macaki Peshewa, the leader of the Native American Church of the Southeast, is a Shawnee Indian. Raised in South Carolina, he attended Spartanburg Junior College, from which he received his associates degree in 1966. He completed his degree program at Wofford College with a B.A. in 1968. He pursued graduate studies at Furman University (1969), the University of South Carolina (1971-1972), and the University of Tennessee at Knoxville. He received his M.S. degree from the last institution in 1974. He continued his studies at Auburn University and Native Americas University, from which he received doctorates in 1975 and 1976. Settling in Knoxville, Peshewa became the chairman of the Systems Theories and Human Development Corporation.

In his adult life Peshewa has emerged as a major Native American leader in the Southeastern United States. He is the founder of the Native American Indians in Media, Inc. and chairman of the Indian Historical Society of the Americas. He is the southeastern

regional coordinator for the Native Americas University and serves on the board of regents of the Indian Voters League.

Religiously, Peshewa has for many years been involved with the Native American Church, an organization which emerged in stages during the early twentieth century as the organizational expression of a pan-Indian movement centered upon the use of the peyote cactus. Peyote has an intoxicating and psychedelic effect when ingested, and is the center of the rituals of the church. He founded and is the leader of the Native American Church of the Southeast. The associated interest in parapsychology and nonconventional states of consciousness led him to become the president of the Consciousness Expansion Movement of Native Americans.

Sources:

Klein, Barry T. *Reference Encyclopedia of the American Indian.* 2 vols. New York: Todd Publications, 1986.

★729★
PETERS, Isaak
Founder, Defenseless Mennonite Brethren of Christ in North America
b. Dec. 1, 1826, Pordenau Russia
d. 1911

Isaak Peters, the founder of the Defenseless Mennonite Brethren of Christ in North America (now known as the Fellowship of Evangelical Bible Churches), was born in Russia the son of Jacob and Sarah Toews Peters. Little is known of his early life, but in 1849 he married Anna Steingardt. Even as a young man, he is remembered as a strict Mennonite, especially about questions of separation from the world. He was also a man of great learning who advocated the values of reading in theology and history. He became an elder in the Pordenau congregation, but his strict leadership led to a split. He was expelled, and along with his supporters, formed a new congregation. In 1850 he settled at Furstenau as an elder.

In his new home, Peters emerged as an opponent of the concept of the millennium (and Mennonites have traditionally been disbelievers of the idea of a literal millennium, or thousand-year reign of Christ on earth), and of baptism by immersion. Mennonites generally baptize by pouring, and Peters defended that practice with reference to John 1:7 in which John the Baptist said, "I baptize you *with* water." Peters noted it did not say that he baptized *in* water.

In the 1870s, pressure on Mennonites, heretofore a protected community, to serve in the Russian Army increased, and many felt that the only recourse was to migrate. Peters was a staunch advocate of traditional nonresistance ideas and began to preach that emigration was the logical option. For his preaching the government expelled him from the country. He migrated to America with a small group of his Russian congregation and settled in Henderson, Nebraska, where he affiliated with the Bethesda Mennonite Church. The church soon chose him as an elder.

Peters began to impose the strict discipline he had always taught, which again precipitated a split, and in 1880 he was forced to withdraw. With his small cadre of followers, in 1882 he organized the Ebenezer Mennonite Church. This church soon found another congregation of similar order which had been founded by **Aaron Wall** in Minnesota, and in 1889 Peters and Wall led in the founding of the Conference of United Mennonite Brethren of North America. The name was soon changed to Defenseless Mennonite Brethren of Christ in North America. Peters remained a leader in the new church, but was forced to retire by ill health in 1892. In his retirement years he wrote several booklets, though the most important literary production was an 1893 translation into German of a Dutch book by George Hansen on the fundamentals of the Christian life.

In 1937 the Defenseless Mennonites became the Evangelical Mennonite Brethren Conference and in 1987 assumed its present name.

Sources:

Hansen, George. *Ein Fundamentbuch der Christlichen Lehre*. Translated by Issak Peters. Elkhart, IN: 1893.
The Mennonite Encyclopedia. 4 vols. Scottdale, PA: The Mennonite Publishing House, 1955.

★730★
PETTINGILL, William Leroy
Minister, Independent Fundamental Churches of America
b. Aug. 27, 1866, Central Square, New York
d. Sep. 15, 1905

William Leroy Pettingill, fundamentalist author and minister, was the son of Sarah Melissa Yertor and John Benjamin Pettingill. Little is recorded of his early life, but in 1890 he married Harriet Block Lockhart and in 1899 at the age of 33 he was ordained as a Baptist minister with the Northern Baptist Convention. In 1903 he became pastor of North Church in Wilmington, Delaware, a post he would retain for the next twenty years. He emerged as a champion of the fundamentalist cause as the modernist-fundamentalist controversy heated up in the first decades of the twentieth century. On behalf of fundamentalism he authored a number of popular books such as *Israel—Jehovah's Covenant People* (1905) and the first of many "simple studies" of books of the Bible: *Simple Studies in Daniel* (1909) and *Simple Studies in Matthew* (1910). Each of these went through a number of editions. He became one of the consulting editors of the *Scofield Reference Bible*, originally issued in 1909. In 1911 he founded a monthly magazine, *Serving-and-Waiting*.

In 1914 Pettingill joined with Cyrus I. Scofield in the founding of the Philadelphia School of the Bible. Scofield served as president of the school and Pettingill as dean. He remained in that position until his retirement in 1928. During these years his writings included: *Simple Studies in Romans* (1915); *Simple Studies in The Revelation* (1916) and *God's Prophecies for Plain People* (1925).

After his retirement he began another periodical, *Just a Word*, which superseded *Serving-and-Waiting*. When the Independent Fundamental Churches of America (IFCA) was founded in the 1930s, he affiliated with it, and served for a while as its vice-president. He continued his voluminous output of writing through his retirement years, including *Bible Questions Answered* (1935); *The Gospel of the Kingdom* (1935); *Simple Studies in Galatians* (1938) and *Nearing the End* (1948). In 1948, two years before his death, he became pastor of First Baptist Church in Manhattan.

Sources:

Pettingill, William L. *Bible Questions Answered*. Findley, OH: Fundamental Truth Publishers, 1935. 559 pp.
_____. *God's Prophecies for Plain People*. Philadelphia: Philadelphia School of the Bible. 1905. 240 pp.
_____. *Israel—Jehovah's Covenant People*. Harrisburg, PA: F. Kelker, 1905. 70 pp.
_____. *Nearing the End*. Chicago: Van Kampen Press, 1948. 93 pp.
_____. *Simple Studies in Daniel*. Philadelphia: Philadelphia School of the Bible, 1909, 1920. 117 pp.
_____. *Simple Studies in The Revelation*. Philadelphia: Philadelphia School of the Bible, 1916. 132 pp.
Reid, Daniel G., Robert D. Linder, Bruce L. Shelley, and Harry S. Stout. *Dictionary of Christianity in America*. Downers Grove, IL: InterVarsity Press, 1990. 1305 pp.

★731★
Metropolitan PHILARET
First Hierarch, Russian Orthodox Church Outside of Russia
b. Mar. 22, 1903, Kursk Russia
d. Nov. 24, 1985, New York, New York

Metropolitan Philaret, a first hierarch of the Russian Orthodox Church Outside of Russia, was born George Nikolaevich Voznesensky, the son of a Russian Orthodox priest. In the wake of the Russian Revolution, in 1920 the family moved to Harbin, China, where he attended and graduated from the Russian-Sino Polytechnical Institute in electrical engineering. Following the death of his mother, his father was tonsured as a monk and consecrated as Bishop Dimitri of Hailar (in Manchuria). Voznesensky received his theological training in Manchuria and in 1931 was ordained as a deacon and priest. Tonsured as a monk, he took the name Philaret. When Soviet forces overran Manchuria, Philaret decided to stay in Harbin, though his father returned to the Soviet Union. In 1934 he was elevated to the rank of hegumen and in 1937 he was named an archimadrite.

Philaret stayed in Manchuria through World War II and the Chinese Revolution. He became known for his persistent anti-Soviet, anti-Stalin stance. He worked to secure the transportation of the members of his congregation out of China to Australia. He also stayed in touch with the bishops of the Russian Orthodox Church Outside of Russia, the leaders of the staunchest anti-Communist faction of the Russian Orthodox Church. This branch had slowly coalesced as the realization of the permanence of the Russian Revolution and its continued hostility to the Orthodox Church became evident to all. During the 1950s the church attempted to obtain a travel visa for Philaret, but not until 1962 was he able to move to Hong Kong (British territory) and then Australia. Among former parishioners in Brisbane, Australia, Philaret was asked to become their bishop and was consecrated in 1963. The next year, following the retirement of Metropolitan Anastasy, he was elected the new first hierarch of the church. He took up residence in New York City where the international headquarters were established.

Philaret became known for his opposition to any cooperation with the leadership of the Russian Orthodox Church, which he felt to be under the control of the atheist government of the Soviet Union. He raised this issue on each occasion of the visitation in the West of Russian church leaders and the accommodation of other Russian-American Orthodox to the authority of the patriarch of Moscow. He also opposed the ecumenical endeavors of Orthodox leaders such as the Ecumenical Patriarch Athenagoras to build bridges of openness with both Protestants and Roman Catholics.

In a less polemical vein, Philaret had the opportunity in 1965 to preside at the glorification (naming of a saint) of Saint John of Kronstadt, the first service of canonization held in the United States. He subsequently celebrated the glorification of Saint Herman of Alaska in 1970. In 1978 he presided at a celebration for all the martyrs and confessors of the faith in the years since the Russian Revolution.

Bishop Philaret died on November 8, 1985, according to the common calendar. However, the Russian Orthodox Church Outside of Russia still follows the Julian Calendar, according to which he died on November 24.

Sources:

Philaret, Metropolitan. *Selective Writings*. Compiled by Demetrios Serfes. Moundsville, WV: A Father Demetrios Serfes Publication, n.d. 23 pp.
"A True Confessor of These Latter Times." Undated 7-page tract.

★732★
PHILLIPS, Charles Henry
Bishop, Christian Methodist Episcopal Church
b. Jan. 17, 1858, Milledgeville, Georgia
d. Apr. 12, 1951, Cleveland, Ohio

Charles Henry Phillips, the most important leader of the Christian Methodist Episcopal Church at the beginning of the twentieth century, was the son of George and Nancy Phillips. He grew up in rural Georgia and attended a freedman's school operated in the local Baptist church. In 1874 he was converted to Christianity and joined the local congregation of Christian Methodist Episcopal Church. In 1875 he began work at Atlanta University in the Junior Preparatory Class. In 1878 he was licensed to preach. That same year he transferred to Central Tennessee College in Nashville at the suggestion of **Isaac Lane**, a bishop in the Christian Methodist Episcopal Church. During his first year he was also the pastor of the Pilot Knob Circuit in the West Tennessee Conference. In 1879 he was ordained as a deacon. He finished his B.A. in 1880 and stayed to complete a medical degree at Meharry Medical College, then associated with Central Tennessee. He finished his medical degree in 1882 and was ordained as an elder in 1883.

Following his ordination, Phillips became the principal at Jackson High School in Jackson, Tennessee. He stayed at Jackson for two years and then briefly served at the school at Union City. By the end of 1885 he had begun a serious ministerial career at Collins Chapel Christian Methodist Episcopal Church in Memphis, Tennessee. He quickly rose to prominence and in 1886 was sent as a delegate to the general conference. He gained some notice from the delegates when he opposed **William Henry Miles**, the senior bishop, on a matter of substance and won the conference's vote.

In 1887 Phillips was assigned to Israel Memorial Church in Washington, D.C., and after four successful years moved to Center Street Church in Louisville, Kentucky. In Louisville he became a leading spokesperson for the black community, a position most clearly demonstrated in his successful opposition to the passing of a new Jim Crow law which would have segregated railroad coaches. In 1894 Phillips became the presiding elder of the Mt. Sterling (Kentucky) District and editor of *The Christian Index*. He remained as editor until elected to the bishopric in 1902.

As bishop, Phillips' territory included Ohio, Indiana, the Southwest, New Mexico, Arizona, and California... areas primarily outside of the Old South. He assumed his office just as many southern Blacks were migrating out of the South, and Phillips took the lead in establishing congregations to receive the migrants. Under Phillips' leadership the Christian Methodist Episcopal Church became a national church.

Although acknowledged for the extensive development of the church outside of the South, Phillips is best remembered as the person who most helped the Christian Methodist Episcopal Church assume an image of equality with the other Methodist churches serving a predominantly black membership. As a church founded by ex-slaves with the assistance of their former masters, the Christian Methodist Episcopal Church had been the object of scorn and ridicule by other black Methodists whose churches had been formed as a clear protest of white authority.

Sources:

Lakey, Othal Hawthorne. *The History of the Christian Methodist Episcopal Church Church.* Memphis, TN: The Christian Methodist Episcopal Church Publishing House, 1985.

★733★
PHILLIPS, Lesley Rebecca
Cofounder and Co-Chair, Covenant of Unitarian Universalist Pagans
b. Jul. 18, 1945, New York, New York

Lesley Rebecca Phillips, the co-founder of the Covenant of Unitarian Universalist Pagans (CUUPS), a Goddess-oriented fellowship within the Unitarian Universalist Association, originally prepared herself for a career in law. She attended the University of Pennsylvania, from which she received both her A.B. (1967) and J.D. (1971) degrees. She entered law and practiced for more than a decade. During the early 1980s, however, she experienced a spiritual crisis/awakening as she dealt with what she saw as the forces of oppression operating on various sexual, racial, and economic minorities. She concluded that liberal religion was one of the few remaining forces in Western society still capable of both effectively countering the forces of oppression while at the same time creating healing communities for those feeling the effects of contemporary social fragmentation. She affiliated with the Unitarian Universalists and felt a call to the ministry.

In the mid-1980s Phillips returned to school to study for the Unitarian Universalist ministry. By this time she had developed a theology and spirituality grounded in the larger women's movement and the worship of the Mother Goddess. She had also aligned herself with those Unitarian Universalists who had come to feel that the association should open itself to insights from pre-Christian spiritual traditions, especially Native American and Old European (Pagan/Wiccan) traditions. She had become a Pagan, a worshiper of the Goddess. Working in 1985 with Linda S. Pinti, also a Unitarian Pagan, Phillips called together a small group of like-minded individuals and formed the Covenant of Unitarian Universalist Pagans (CUUPS). She and Pinti have since served as co-chairs of the organization and co-editors of its newsletter.

While still in seminary at Harvard Divinity School, Phillips moved for the acceptance of CUUPS as an independent affiliate organization of the Unitarian Universalist Association. This status was granted in 1987. That same year Phillips was named chair of the Unitarian Universalist Common Vision Project and led in the establishment of the "Welcoming Congregation" Program which calls upon congregations to be truly open and welcoming to the outcasts of society, including gays, lesbians, people of color, the poor, people with AIDS, and other minorities.

Phillips graduated from Harvard and was ordained to the ministry. She became interim minister of First Parish (Unitarian Universalist) of Kingston, Massachusetts, in 1988, but has devoted most of her energies to the building of CUUPS, which has become one of the largest Pagan groups in North America. By 1990 it included several thousand members and over 25 chapters. Phillips sees CUUPS as one entry point for Pagans to openly operate within the mainstream of American culture.

Sources:

Renner, Gerald. "Unitarians Show Their Acceptance of Pagans." *The Hartford Courant* (June 27, 1989).

★734★
PIAPOT
Traditional Religious Leader, Cree Indian Tribe
b. 1816, Manitoba, Canada
d. 1908

Only a few details of the early life of Piapot (or Payepot) a leader chief and religious leader among the Crees, a tribe which originally lived on the Great Plains of western Canada, are available. He was originally named Kikikwawason (Flash in the Sky). When he was still a child his parents died in a smallpox epidemic (the major source of deaths among Indians after the arrival of the first Europeans). A short time later he and his grandmother were taken prisoner by the Sioux, but were freed 14 years later by a small band of Cree warriors. After he once again resumed life with his own people he became known as Piapot or "One Who Knows the Secrets of the Sioux." He used his knowledge to aid his people and became one of their most significant leaders.

As a young man Piapot became first a warrior and then a successful chief in the continuing conflicts with the Crees' traditional enemies, the Lakotas (Sioux) and Blackfoot. In 1870, however, a short time after Piapot's forces had scored a victory in a battle with the Blackfoot, the enemy regrouped and handed Piapot a major defeat that included the loss of half his warrior army. Consequent of the defeat, the Crees no longer enjoyed the relatively superior position they had long wielded in relation to the Blackfoot.

Piapot was then immediately faced with an even greater threat— the westward migration of whites into his land. In 1875 he was forced to sign a treaty ceding tribal lands in Manitoba. Rather than move onto the reservation, however, he led his people into Saskatchewan. To thwart white settlement efforts Piapot attacked the railroad and disrupted its laying of track, though he was careful to avoid armed conflict. He eventually settled his people near Regina, Saskatchewan.

Piapot functioned as both the secular and spiritual leader of his tribe. The Crees were among the tribes which had adopted the practice of the sun dance, an elaborate celebration that had spread through the Great Plains during the nineteenth century. Both the United States and Canada had outlawed the practice. Some years after settling near Regina, Piapot organized a giant sun dance celebration. The Canadian government responded by removing him as chief. The members of the tribe, however, ignored the action and continued to recognize him as their political and spiritual leader.

Sources:

Dockstader, Frederick J. *Great North American Indiana: Profiles in Life and Leadership*. New York: Van Norstrand Reinhold Company, 1977. 386 pp.

★735★
PIDGEON, George Campbell
Moderator, United Church of Canada
b. Mar. 2, 1872, Maria, Quebec, Canada
d. Jun. 15, 1971, Toronto, Ontario, Canada

George Campbell Pidgeon, the first moderator of the United Church of Canada, was the son of Mary Campbell and Archibald M. Pidgeon. He was born and raised in a Scottish community in predominantly Roman Catholic Quebec. He attended Morrin College in Quebec and McGill University (B.A., 1891) and received his theological training at the Presbyterian Theological College in Montreal (B.D., 1895). There, ten years later, he completed the work on his D.D. After serving a student parish in Montreal, in 1898 he became pastor of the Presbyterian church in Streetsville, Ontario. That same year he married Helen Jones.

Pidgeon, a most capable orator, soon became known through the church as both a preacher and a person deeply involved with social concerns. In 1903 he became pastor of Victoria Presbyterian Church in Toronto. While there, in 1907, he became the first convenor of the Presbyterian committee on Moral and Social Reform. In 1909 he moved across the country to assume the post of professor of practical theology at Westminster Hall in Vancouver. Soon after his arrival he became the president of the Social Service Council of British Columbia. In 1915 he was called to Bloor Street Presbyterian Church in Toronto, one of the most prominent Presbyterian churches in North America. He would remain there for over 40 years.

In Toronto, Pidgeon soon made his presence felt nationally. In 1917 he became the convenor of the Board of Home Missions for the Presbyterian Church. World War I having just begun, he began to work with the YMCA and in 1917 took a leave from his pulpit to spend time with the association in France and England. Upon his return he became the national president of the Social Service Council of Canada. He also picked up his duties with the Board of Home Missions. His work with the board, coupled with his own experience in the West, led him to see church union as a necessity for a strong Protestant presence in the Western provinces. In 1921 he became the convenor for the committee working to structure what would become the United Church of Canada. He championed the union within his own denomination and helped work out the compromise with a dissenting faction that did not wish to join the new church and instead wanted to continue as the Presbyterian Church in Canada. In the spring of 1925, the majority part elected him as the last moderator of the old Presbyterian Church in Canada, and in the summer at the time of the merger, he was elected the first moderator of the new united church. He served a one year term.

Pidgeon was a theological conservative who hoped that the merger would speak to a spiritual revival in the church. In 1930 he became chairman of the interchurch Committee on the Evangelization of Canada, a post he retained for the next twelve years. In 1938 he was elected president of the Western section of the Alliance of Reformed Churches.

Pidgeon retired in 1948 and was succeeded at Bloor Street by E. M. Howse.

Sources:

Grant, J. W. *George Pidgeon: A Biography*. Toronto: Ryerson Press, 1962. 158 pp.
Reid, Daniel G., Robert D. Linder, Bruce L. Shelley, and Harry S. Stout. *Dictionary of Christianity in America*. Downers Grove, IL: InterVarsity Press, 1990. 1305 pp.
Wallace, W. Stewart. *The Macmillan Dictionary of Canadian Biography*. 4th ed., rev. Edited by W. A. McKay. Toronto: Macmillan of Canada, 1978.

★736★
PIEPER, Franz August Otto
Theologian, Lutheran Church-Missouri Synod
b. Jun. 27, 1852, Carwitz Germany
d. Mar. 3, 1931, St. Louis, Missouri

Franz August Otto Pieper, a dominant figure in the Lutheran Church-Missouri Synod in the late nineteenth century, was the son of Augustus and Perta Lohff Pieper. His father was the mayor of Carwitz and sent both Pieper and his brother to junior college. However, he died while Pieper was a teenager, and in 1870 his mother brought the family to America. He continued his education at Northwestern University at Watertown, Wisconsin, (A.B., 1872), and Concordia Theological Seminary in St. Louis, Missouri, from which he graduated in 1875. That same year he was called to a church in Centerville, Wisconsin, and ordained as a Lutheran minister. In 1876 he moved to Manitowoc, Wisconsin. He married Minnie Koehn in 1877.

In 1878 Pieper was called back to Concordia Seminary to teach dogmatics and study with Carl F. W. Walther, the leader of the Missouri Synod. In 1880 a major controversy emerged between Walther and the Missouri Synod and other conservative Lutheran leaders and synods (especially Iowa, Ohio, and Buffalo) in the Midwest over predestination. Pieper emerged as Walther's strong ally. Like Walther, he became a strong critic of rationalism in theology.

Pieper's prodigious writings led to his becoming editor of *Lehre and Wehre*, the seminary's journal. He became president of the seminary in 1887, a post he would retain for the rest of his life. In

1899 he began a 12-year tenure as president of the Missouri Synod.

Pieper's influence began as he became the theological teacher of a generation of Missouri Synod pastors. During his tenure as president of Concordia Seminary, it became the largest seminary in America; its small student body grew to include over 500 students. In like measure, the synod grew to over a million members during his presidency. He also developed the church's work among Blacks.

During his many years at the seminary, Pieper authored a wide variety of articles on the several controversies affecting the synod's life. In 1913 he wrote a final summary article of the long, involved predestinarian controversy in which he called for peaceful coexistence between the participants—*Zur Einigung der Amerikanisch-lutherischen Kirke in der Lehre von der Bekehrung and Gnaden-wahl* (*Conversion and Election: a Plea for a United Lutheranism in America*). He culminated his intellectual career with the publication of a three-volume *Christliche Dogmatik* (1917-1924) which has been given additional life by its translation into English.

Sources:

Dictionary of American Biography. 20 vols. and 7 supps. New York: Charles Scribner's Sons, 1928-1936, 1944-1981.

Pieper, Franz A. O. *Christliche Dogmatik.* 3 vols. St. Louis, MO: Concordia Publishing House, 1917-1924.

———. *Conversion and Election: A Plea for a United Lutheranism in America.* St. Louis: Concordia Publishing House, 1913. 151 pp.

——— *What Is Christianity?.* Ed. and trans. by John T. Mueller. St. Louis: Concordia Publishing House, 1933. 290 pp.

★ 737 ★
PIERCE, Robert (Bob) Willard
Founder, World Vision, Inc.
b. Oct. 8, 1914, Fort Dodge, Iowa
d. Sep. 6, 1978, Los Angeles, California

Robert "Bob" Willard Pierce was the founder of World Vision, Inc., a multinational, evangelical, Christian humanitarian and missionary support agency. He was the son of Flora Belle Harlow Evison and Fred Asa Pierce. While still a child, Pierce moved with his family to Greeley, Colorado, and at the age of 12 to Redondo Beach, California. There he affiliated with the Church of the Nazarene, through which he had his first experience with God. He later attended Pasadena Nazarene College, but before finishing his degree he dropped out to marry Lorraine Johnson. In 1938 he became an evangelist, initially among the Nazarenes but later in a broader context. In 1940 he was ordained as a Baptist minister in a church in Wilmington, California, and became the assistant pastor of the Los Angeles Evangelistic Center, an independent ministry founded by his wife's parents. While there he had his first experience of radio ministry, and he met **Oswald J. Smith**, the pastor of the Peoples Church in Toronto, who impressed upon him the importance of foreign missions.

The 1940s proved a time of continuing crises in Pierce's life as he was developing a sense of personal mission. So intense were his inner struggles that he dropped out of church work altogether for a short interval. In 1944 he moved to Seattle to work for Youth for Christ, and in 1945 became their vice-president at large. In 1948 and 1949 he made two trips to China during which he was, for the first time, confronted with the extreme needs of the missionary fields in Asia. Out of these trips also came his first professional-quality films depicting the situation overseas. In 1950 he went to Korea, out of which came the significant film "The 38th Parallel" which vividly depicted the horrors of the Korean War. After that trip he formed World Vision, originally headquartered in Portland, Oregon. World Vision had as its initial task the aiding of missionaries in the Orient.

Through the 1950s World Vision grew immensely as new geographical areas came within its realm of concern, and a variety of projects were implemented. In 1956 Pierce went on the air with a weekly radio program. By 1963, however, his health began to fail, and in 1964 he was placed on medical leave. In 1967 he was forced to retire and turn over control of World Vision to the board of directors. Exhausted, he spent a year in the hospital (1968-1969) but was finally able to make something of a comeback. He was offered the leadership of a small organization, Food for the World, previously founded by World Literature Crusade. Using his many contacts, he began to rebuild it as the Samaritan's Purse, and was able, as his health allowed, to return to his worldwide mission. Meanwhile, the strain of his illness had taken its toll on his personal life, and in 1970 he and his wife separated. In 1973 he was diagnosed with leukemia, from which he died in 1978.

Sources:

Dunker, Marilee P. *Days of Glory, Seasons of Night.* Grand Rapids, MI: Zondervan Publishing House, 1984. 172 pp.

Graham, Franklin, and Jeannette Lockerbee. *Bob Pierce: This One Thing I Do.* Waco, TX: Word Books, 1983. 220 pp.

★ 738 ★
PIERSON, Arthur Tappan
Presbyterian Minister
Independent Evangelist
b. Mar. 6, 1837, New York, New York
d. Jun. 3, 1911, Brooklyn, New York

Arthur Tappan Pierson, a prominent Presbyterian clergyman who left the Presbyterian Church for life as an independent Baptist lay speaker, was the son of Stephen Haines and Sally Ann Wheeler Pierson. He was given the best education available, beginning with several college preparatory schools in upstate New York. He graduated from Hamilton College in 1857 and entered Union Theological Seminary, from which he graduated in 1860. Shortly after graduation he was ordained by the Presbyterian Church and married Sarah Frances Benedict.

Pierson began his pastoral career as a supply pastor in West Winsted, Connecticut, and served briefly in Binghamton, New York, and Waterford, New York, before moving to Fort Street Presbyterian Church in Detroit, Michigan. He spent 13 years in Detroit, followed by six years in Philadelphia. During these years he became a friend of evangelist **Dwight L. Moody**. He frequently attended and spoke at the Northfield (Massachusetts) Bible conference Moody organized, and through the 1880s developed a zeal for worldwide evangelism and missions.

Pierson's passion for missions became evident in his first book, *The Crisis in Missions* (1886). In 1888 he became an associate editor of the *Missionary Review*. The following year, he resigned his pastorate to enter evangelistic work. In 1890 he became the editor of the *Missionary Review*, a post he retained, in spite of his many travels and changes of residency, for the rest of his life. In 1891, for example, Pierson began a two-year stay in the pulpit of the Metropolitan Tabernacle in London after its pastor, Charles H. Spurgeon, became ill. In addition, he authored a series of mission-oriented volumes, including: *The Divine Enterprise of Missions* (1891); a four-volume survey of missionary activity called *The Miracle of Missions* (1891-1901); *The New Acts of the Apostles* (1894); *Forward Movements of the Last Half Century* (1900); and *The Modern Mission Century* (1901). Pierson's stint in the Metropolitan Tabernacle, a Baptist church, had a marked effect on him, as he became convinced that the Baptist position on baptism was correct. Baptists believe that baptism should be reserved for adults who profess a faith in Christ and should be by total immersion, as opposed to Presbyterians who practice infant baptism, usually by pouring. In 1896 Pierson was immersed and as a result separated from the Presbyterians. He never again held ministerial credentials in any church.

During his stay in England, Pierson also became associated with the Keswick Movement, a movement which stressed the reception of the power of the Holy Spirit to undergird a life of personal holiness. During the last two decades of his life, he would combine his continuing primary interest in missions with a public advocacy of Keswick holiness. In this regard he authored a series of books, including *Life Power; or, Character, Culture, and Conduct* (1895), *In Christ Jesus; or, The Sphere of the Believer's Life* (1898), and *The Keswick Movement in Precept and Practice* (1903). He also authored a number of other popular religious books.

In 1910 Pierson began a tour of mission work in the Orient but was forced to curtail the trip due to illness. He returned to his home in Brooklyn, where he died a short time later.

Sources:

Dictionary of American Biography. 20 vols. and 7 supps. New York: Charles Scribner's Sons, 1928-1936, 1944-1981.
McLean, J. K. *Dr. Pierson and His Message.* New York: Association Press, 1911.
Pierson, Arthur Tappan. *The Divine Enterprise of Missions.* New York: Baker and Taylor Co., 1891. 333 pp.
_____. *Forward Movements of the Last Half Century.* New York: Funk and Wagnalls, 1900. 428 pp.
_____. *In Christ Jesus; or, The Sphere of the Believer's Life.* New York: Funk and Wagnalls, 1819. 197 pp.
_____. *The Keswick Movement in Precept and Practice.* New York: Funk and Wagnalls, 1903. 124 pp.
_____. *Life Power; or, Character, Culture, and Conduct.* New York: Fleming H. Revell, 1895. 214 pp.
_____. *The Miracles of Missions.* 4 vols. New York: Funk and Wagnalls, 1891-1901.
_____. *The New Acts of the Apostles.* New York: Baker & Taylor, 1894. 451 pp.
Pierson, Delavan L. *Arthur T. Pierson.* London: J. Nisbet, 1912. 333 pp.

★739★
PIKE JR., James Albert
Bishop, Protestant Episcopal Church
b. Feb. 14, 1913, Oklahoma City, Oklahoma
d. Sep. 3, 1969?, Jaffa Israel

James Albert Pike, Jr., controversial bishop in the Protestant Episcopal Church during the 1960s, was the son of James Albert and Pearl Agatha Wimsatt Pike. His father died when Pike was two years old and he was raised by his mother in the Roman Catholic Church. In 1921 the family moved to Hollywood, California. After high school, Pike entered the University of Santa Clara to begin preparation for the priesthood. He developed severe doubts about the church and his faith, and dropped out during his sophomore year. In 1933 he entered the University of Southern California and earned a law degree. He was admitted to the bar in 1936, but left for Yale, where he obtained a doctorate in law. He had an outstanding career ahead of him. Moving to Washington, he was by 1904 certified to practice before the Supreme Court and a member of the faculty of the George Washington Law School. Having overcome his skepticism, he had joined the Episcopal Church. He had also experienced his first divorce.

He served in the Navy during World War II. In 1942 he married Esther Yanovsky and that year became a postulant for the Episcopal priesthood. He was ordained as a deacon in 1944, and while serving as curate at St. John's Episcopal Church in Washington, entered the Virginia Theological Seminary to study for the priesthood. His last year at Union Theological Seminary he studied under **Paul Tillich** and **Reinhold Niebuhr**. He was ordained in 1946 and became rector of Christ Episcopal Church in Poughkeepsie, New York. In 1949 he moved to Columbia University as chairman of the department of religion and chaplain. He is credited with building

the department into a first-rate program during the several years he was there. In 1952 he became the dean of the Cathedral of St. John the Divine, the largest Episcopal church in the United States, and was soon attracting large crowds with his sermons. He became a public personality with his books (the first two of which, *Beyond Anxiety* and *The Faith of the Church*, coauthored with Norman Pittenger, appeared in 1953), his television show, and his controversial public statements. Other important books included *If You Marry Outside of Your Faith* (1954), *Roadblocks to Faith* (1954), and *Doing the Truth* (1955).

In 1958 he was elected Bishop Coadjutor of California. Before the year was out, he became Bishop of California upon the death of his predecessor. While popular with the members of his diocese, Pike became the center of one controversy after another. A major theological storm began with an article in the *The Christian Century* of December 21, 1960, in which he expressed doubts about several central Christian doctrines—the Trinity, the virgin birth, and Christ as the only way to salvation. His fellow clergy complained of his heresies. On three occasions charges of heresy were filed against him—first in 1961 by some Georgia priests, then in 1965 by some Arizona priests, and finally in 1966 by a group under the leadership of fellow bishop Henry I. Loutit from Florida. Pike responded to the charges with three of his most important books: *A Time for Christian Candor* (1964); *What Is This Treasure?* (1966); and *If This Be Heresy* (1967).

In the midst of his theological troubles, personal tragedy emerged. In 1964 he admitted to a longstanding drinking problem, and joined Alcoholics Anonymous. He had an affair with a woman whom he supported with diocesan funds. In 1966 his son committed suicide. In 1967 his mistress committed suicide and his wife divorced him. His daughter also attempted suicide.

Pike raised new controversy when he claimed that he had made contact with his dead son through a medium and then had a public seance on Canadian television with Spiritualist medium **Arthur Ford**. Pike found the seance with Ford very convincing though it was later discovered that Ford had used notes and faked the event. Pike's adventures in the psychic realm were the subject of his last book, *The Other Side* (1968), written with Diane Kennedy, who became his third wife.

In 1968 he resigned as bishop of California and moved to Santa Barbara. He affiliated with the Center for the Study of Democratic Institutions on the campus of the University of California—Santa Barbara. He formed the Foundation of Religious Transition with an announced goal of ministering to former church members and others on the margin of church life.

In August 1969 he traveled to the Holy Land and decided to make a trip into the Judean wilderness. He got lost and died alone in the desert (the exact date is not known). After her return to the states, Pike's wife wrote a moving account of their trip to the desert and Pike's death, *Search: The Personal Story of a Wilderness Journey* (1970). She also changed the name of the foundation to the Bishop Pike Foundation. It survived for several years but was finally merged into the Love Project, an organization founded by Arlene Lorrance with whom Diane Pike had begun to work.

Sources:

Lippy, Charles H. *Twentieth-Century Shapers of American Popular Religion.* New York: Greenwood Press, 1989. 494 pp.
Pike, Diane Kennedy. *Search: The Personal Story of a Wilderness Journey.* Garden City, NY: Doubleday & Company, 1970. 198 pp.
Pike, James A. *Doing the Truth.* Garden City, NY: Doubleday & Company, 1955. 192 pp.
_____. *If This Be Heresy.* New York: Harper & Row, 1967. 205 pp.
_____. *If You Marry Outside of Your Faith.* New York: Harper & Row, 1954. 159 pp.

_____. *A Time for Christian Candor*. New York: Harper & Row, 1964. 160 pp.

_____. *What Is This Treasure?* New York: Harper & Row, 1966. 90 pp.

_____ and Diane Kennedy. *The Other Side*. New York: Doubleday & Company, 1968. 398 pp.

Stringfellow, William and Anthony Towne. *The Bishop Pike Affair*. New York: Harper & Row, 1967. 266 pp.

_____. *The Death and Life of Bishop Pike*. Garden City, NY: Doubleday & Company, 1976. 446 pp.

★ 740 ★
Metropolitan PLATON
Metropolitan, Russian Orthodox Church
b. Feb. 23, 1866, Kursk Eparchy Russia
d. Apr. 20, 1934, New York, New York

Metropolitan Platon, metropolitan of the American diocese of the Russian Orthodox Church in the years immediately after the Russian Revolution, was born Porphyry Theodorovich Rozhdeatvensky. His father was a parish priest in the Russian Orthodox Church, and the son decided to follow his father's calling. He attended Kursk Theological Seminary and, as is the custom in Eastern Orthodoxy, married before his ordination in 1887. His first assignment was to Lukashevky as a parish priest. After only a few years his wife died, and he entered Kiev Theological Academy with the intention of becoming a monk. He was tonsured in 1894, at which time he was given the name Platon. He graduated from the academy the following year, but stayed in Kiev to both continue his studies and teach. He received his master's degree in 1898. He became the inspector at the academy and elevated to the rank of archimandrite.

In 1902 Platon was consecrated as a bishop and began to serve both as rector for the seminary and a vicar for the diocese of Kiev. He worked within the Kiev diocese for five years, but in 1907 was transferred to the United States where he succeeded Archbishop Tikhon. He inherited a growing work in need of further organization. He established the Orthodox Women's Aid Society and the Russian Immigrant's Home to assist the large number of immigrants who would continue to flow into the United States until 1924. He developed a multi-ethnic leadership, as the Russian church had charge of Orthodox Americans from Greek, Lebanese, Syrian, Serbian, and Albanian backgrounds. Among his major accomplishments, he was able to woo a number of Unite (Roman Catholic) Carpatho-Russians back into Orthodoxy. He moved the seminary to Tenafly, New Jersey, nearer the center of Orthodox population strength.

In 1914 Platon was called back to Russia as the bishop of the diocese of Kishniece and Khotin. He served in that position for only a short time before being sent to Georgia as the exarch. He then became bishop of Kherson and Odessa. He was in Odessa when the Russian Revolution and the ensuing disruption of the church occurred. He fled the country and returned to the United States in 1922. At that time, Metropolitan Alexander resigned in Platon's favor, and Platon again became metropolitan of what had become a North American diocese. He inherited a diocese in an extreme financial crisis, made all the worse by loans and mortgages which his predecessor had taken out to meet some immediate bills. At the same time the diocese was in an organizational crisis due to the subordination of the church in Russia to the Soviet government. He had to reorganize the diocese in order to protect its property from Bishop John Kedrowsky, the representative of the Soviet-backed faction of the church.

In 1924 the diocese declared itself temporarily self-governing, although it still recognized its spiritual ties to the Patriarch in Moscow. Meanwhile, Kedrowsky moved to possess St. Nicholas Cathedral, the diocese headquarters in New York, and it was awarded to him in 1925. Platon was forced to conduct services at a nearby Episcopal church. Adding to his woes, the various ethnic groups which were functioning as sub-groupings in the Russian Orthodox Church were growing to the point that one by one they broke away to establish independent dioceses with direct links to their homelands. Platon guided the diocese through this significant transition period. The diocese under his leadership continued to grow and gain a new understanding of itself in its North American context.

Sources:

Tarasar, Constance J. *Orthodox America, 1794-1974*. Syosset, NY: Department of History and Archives, The Orthodox Church in America, 1975. 350 pp.

★ 741 ★
PLENTY COUPS
Chief and Dreamer, Absaroka (Crow) Indians
b. 1848, Billings, Montana
d. Mar. 4, 1932

Plenty Coups, known among the Crow Indians as Aleek-chea-ahoosh (literally, "Many Achievements"), served as both a chief and religious leader among his people. Of all the tribes of the western Great Plains, the Crow (or Absaroka) Indians have the most unique history in terms of their relationship with the United States government. The Crow became allies with the government at a time when the majority of the plains tribes, from Canada to Mexico, were fighting the invasion of the Whites onto their lands. Crow Indians served as scouts and auxiliary forces to the United States Army for many years, and were allies in a number of battles, including the Battle of Little Big Horn in 1876. Much of the credit for the Crow tribe's ability to hang onto their homes when so many tribes were losing vast tracts of land can be attributed to the dream of Aleek-chea-ahoosh.

Plenty Coups was born in the summer of 1848 in a Crow Indian village near the present site of Billings, Montana. His mother, Otter Woman, and his father, Medicine Bird, were both members of prominent families in the Crow nation. At one time the Crow lived a sedentary farming life with the Hidatsa along the upper Missouri River and its tributaries. Myths of the Crow say that the two groups split over political differences, which may date to about the same time the horse arrived in the northern plains, sometime in the eighteenth century. The Crows moved west, and by the time Plenty Coups was born, his people were seasoned horse Indians fighting for their hunting grounds against the Blackfeet, Lakota, Cheyenne, Arapaho, and others. Although a relatively small tribe in the midst of enemies, the Crow tribe held its own and developed a lifestyle that revered bravery and dedication to family, clan, and tribe. Plenty Coups would become a premier performer in the drama of Crow survival, and he attributed his success to his dreams.

Dreaming is an integral part of many Native American religions. Plenty Coups' name came about as a result of his grandfather's dream, in which he saw his grandson as a chief of the Crows and a person who would have many achievements. Plenty Coups felt obliged to live up to his name, and at an early age began to seek his own dreams. At the age of nine, when his brother was killed in a fight on the Powder River with some Lakota, Plenty Coups went into the hills to fast for a dream. He spent four days with no food or water, and used sweat baths to cleanse his mind and body. Plenty Coups traveled in his dream to the lodge of the Little People. The Little People gave no talisman to Plenty Coups, only advice. He would be a great chief if he learned to use the powers he already possessed. Plenty Coups' initial dream was followed by another, more important, dream in which he was given his spirit-helper and a vision of the future that would guide the Crow tribe into the twentieth century.

The Crows had camped near the Crazy Mountains, a popular place for seeking visions. Plenty Coups went into the mountains where he stayed for four days, naked, without food or water. On the fourth day, having no vision or dream, Plenty Coups cut the tip of one finger off and allowed the blood to flow. That night his dream came, and he acquired the power of the Chickadee, a bird that listens. He dreamed of the end of the buffalo, the beginning of white intrusion, and the policies the Crow nation should adopt in order to survive. When the dream was later interpreted by the tribal elders, they realized its significance, and when the Whites came, the Crow tribe became their allies as foretold in the dream of Plenty Coups. Plenty Coups lived to be an old man and was tribal leader for many years. When the tomb of the Unknown Soldier was dedicated at Arlington National Cemetery in 1921, Plenty Coups was chosen to lay the wreath on behalf of all Indian tribes.

Sources:

Linerman, Frank B. *Plenty Coups: Chief of the Crows.* Lincoln, NE: University of Nebraska Press, 1962.

Lowie, Robert H. *The Crow Indians.* New York: Holt Rinehart and Winston, 1935.

★742★
POLING, Daniel Alfred
Editor, Christian Herald
b. Nov. 30, 1884, Portland, Oregon
d. Feb. 7, 1968, Philadelphia, Pennsylvania

Daniel Alfred Poling, for many years editor of the interdenominational magazine *Christian Herald*, was the son of the Reverends Charles Cupp Poling and Savilla Ann Kring. Both parents were ministers in the United Evangelical Church (UEC); his mother was the first female ordained in that body. He was raised in Portland and Lafayette, Oregon, and attended Dalles College. He intended to enter law, but decided to become a minister toward the end of his college career. Following his graduation in 1904, he was licensed by the UEC. That same year his family moved to Pennsylvania and he accepted an assignment as assistant pastor of the congregation at Canton, Ohio. In 1906 he married Susan Jane Vandersall. That same year he was ordained a deacon in the UEC and became pastor of a congregation in Columbus, Ohio. While there he was able to pursue some post-graduate studies at Ohio State University.

Throughout the early years of his ministry Poling was active both in the International Society of Christian Endeavor, an interdenominational youth movement, and in work for prohibition. In 1908 he became the general secretary for Ohio of the Christian Endeavor Union, a step toward later national leadership. His concern for alcohol reform led him to become active in the Prohibition Party, under whose banner he ran for governor of Ohio in 1912. In 1915 Poling became the associate president (and in fact the head) of the International Society of Christian Endeavor, whose aging president, Francis E. Clark, could no longer carry the administrative burdens. During World War I he worked for the Allied cause through the YMCA and assisted in the organization of a chaplaincy corps in France. While near the front, he was caught in a gas attack, an event featured prominently in his first book, *Huts in Hell* (1918).

In 1918 Poling's wife died, and the following year he married Lillian Diebod Heingartner. He moved to New York City to become the associate general secretary of the Interchurch World Movement. In this capacity he investigated the American steel strike, his first direct encounter with the harsh corporate response to the labor movement and the inspiration for his 1925 novel, *The Furnace.* In 1920 he became the assistant minister at the Marble Collegiate Church, the oldest Christian congregation in America. As a result he changed denominations and became a minister in the Reformed Church in America, a denomination which would later elect him its president. In 1923 he became the senior pastor of the church. He expanded his ministry into radio with a national youth-oriented show. Having become acquainted with retailer J. C. Penny, Poling helped him found the J. C. Penny Foundation. Penny, in turn, convinced Poling to take the post as editor of the

Christian Herald. In addition to all of these activities, in 1927 he succeeded Clark as head of International Christian Endeavor.

In 1939 Poling resigned as minister of Marble Collegiate Church, and became the owner of the *Christian Herald.* With assistance from Penny, he reorganized the several ministries supported by the *Herald* under the Christian Herald Association. This work, which included the authoring of a number of books, would constitute his major activity until 1936 when, having previously given up strong denominational allegiances, he accepted the pastorate of the Baptist Temple in Philadelphia. He served the church for 12 years.

During World War II, Poling's son Clark Poling joined the Army Chaplain Corps. He became one of the four chaplains on the *U.S.S. Dorchester* who died after the ship was torpedoed. The four had all given up their life jackets. The story became the subject of Poling's most popular book, *Your Daddy Did Not Die* (1944).

During the post-war years, Poling emerged as a conservative anti-Communist who gave strong support to General Douglas MacArthur and Chaing Kai-shek. In 1951 he ran for mayor (and lost) as a Republican. Several years later he moved back to New York City where he continued as editor of the *Christian Herald* until his retirement in 1965. His autobiography, *Mine Eyes Have Seen the Glory,* appeared in 1959.

Sources:

Dictionary of American Biography. 20 vols. and 7 supps. New York: Charles Scribner's Sons, 1928-1936, 1944-1981.

Poling, Daniel A. *An Adventure in Evangelism.* New York: Fleming H. Revell, 1925.

———. *The Furnace.* New York: George H. Doran Co., 1925. 311 pp.

———. *Huts in Hell.* Boston: Christian Endeavor World, 1918. 214 pp.

———. *Mine Eyes Have Seen the Glory.* New York: McGraw-Hill, 1959. 297 pp.

———. *A Preacher Looks At War.* New York: Macmillan Company, 1943. 101 pp.

———. *What Men Need Most.* New York: George H. Doran Co., 1923. 232 pp.

———. *Your Daddy Did Not Die.* New York: Greenberg, 1944. 148 pp.

★743★
PONDER, Catherine
Minister, Association of Unity Churches
b. Feb. 14, 1927, Hartsville, South Carolina

Catherine Ponder, a minister with the Association of Unity Churches, is the daughter of Kathleen Parrish and Roy Charles Cook. She attended the University of North Carolina and Worth Business College (B.S., 1948). Deciding to enter the ministry, she attended the Unity School of Christianity Ministerial School from which she graduated in 1956. Following her graduation she moved to Alabama and became minister of the Unity church at Birmingham. She was formally licensed as a minister by Unity in 1957 and ordained in 1958 by Lowell Fillmore, the son of Unity founder **Charles S. Fillmore.** Five years later she moved to Austin, Texas, where she became the founder and minister of a new Unity congregation. While in Austin she authored the first of her many books, *The Dynamic Laws of Prosperity* (1962), which was quickly followed by *The Prosperity Secret of the Ages* (1964); *The Dynamic Laws of Healing* (1966); and *The Healing Secret of the Ages* (1967). Through these books she became well known throughout the metaphysical New Thought community and began to lecture around the United States. In 1968 she authored *Pray and Grow Rich,* a volume whose title echoed upon the earlier New Thought classic by Napoleon Hill, *Think and Grow Rich.* In 1969 she moved to the Unity Church in San Antonio, Texas. In 1970 she married chiropractor Robert Sterns.

Ponder moved to California in 1973 and founded Unity Church Worldwide at Palm Desert, which she built into one of the largest and most significant congregations in the Association of Unity

Churches. Once settled in California, she returned to writing and soon produced a string of books which helped establish her reputation as the premier contemporary exponent of what has become known as "Prosperity consciousness." Prosperity consciousness is based upon the Unity/New Thought perspective that God is the only reality and that God has created an abundant supply of resources for everyone. According to this understanding poverty is a product of wrong thinking. Prosperity can be received by changing one's basic attitudes toward the world. Ponder spelled out her understanding of prosperity consciousness in *Keys to Prosperity*, the monthly newsletter from her church, and her many books, including: *The Millionaires of Genesis* (1976); *The Millionaire Moses* (1977); *The Millionaire Joshua* (1978); *The Millionaire from Nazareth* (1979); *The Secret of Unlimited Prosperity* (1981); *Open Your Mind to Receive* (1983); *Dare to Prosper: The Prospering Power of Prayer* (1983); *The Prospering Power of Love* (1984); *Open Your Mind to Prosperity* (1985); and *The Dynamic Laws of Prayer* (1987).

Sources:

Beebe, Tom. *Who's Who in New Thought*. Lakemont, CA: CSA Press, 1977. 318 pp.

Ponder, Catherine. *The Dynamic Laws of Healing*. Los Angeles: Scrivener & Co., 1971. 224 pp.

_____. *The Dynamic Laws of Prosperity*. Englewood Cliffs, NJ: Prentice-Hall, 1962. 253 pp.

_____. *The Millionaire from Nazareth*. Marina del Rey, CA: DeVorss & Co., 1979. 292 pp.

_____. *Open Your Mind to Prosperity*. Unity Village, MO: Unity Books, 1971. 185 pp.

_____. *Pray and Grow Rich*. West Nyack, NY: Parker Publishing Company, 1968. 228 pp.

★744★
POTTER, Charles Francis
Humanist Leader
b. Oct. 28, 1885, Marlboro, Massachusetts
d. Oct. 4, 1962, New York, New York

Charles Francis Potter, the prominent Humanist spokesperson, was the son of Charles Henry Potter and Flora Ellen Lincoln. His parents were Baptist, and Potter was raised in a pious evangelical home. He decided to enter the ministry at a youthful age. He was licensed to preach at 17. In 1903 he entered Bucknell University, from which he received his B.A. in 1907. The following year he married Clara Adelaide Cook and was ordained. He went on to seminary at Newton Theological Seminary, where he received a B.D. in 1913 and an S.T.M. in 1916. In 1916 he also received an M.A. from Bucknell.

During his seminary years Potter had begun to depart from the orthodox faith of his parents and accept the modernist Christianity that had come to dominate the schools of the Northern Baptist Convention. By 1919 Potter had ideologically distanced himself from his Baptist faith, and he accepted a call from the West Side Unitarian Church in New York City. He assumed his new duties just as the fundamentalist-modernist controversy was growing in intensity, and he entered the situation decidedly on the modernist side. A series of radio debates with Baptist pastor **John Roach Straton** in 1924 brought Potter some national fame. The next year he consulted with Clarence Darrow on the issues raised by nineteenth century biblical scholars. Darrow used the information in his famous cross-examination of **William Jennings Bryan** at the Scopes monkey trial.

Potter eventually moved beyond Unitarian Christianity, which merely rejected several traditional Christian affirmations, and began to question the very nature of religion and the necessity of belief in God. In 1925 he resigned from the church and became a professor of comparative religion at Antioch College. He returned to the parish briefly in 1928 as the minister of Church of the Divine

Paternity, a Universalist congregation in Manhattan. He had moved to such a radical position, however, that the following year he left Universalism to found the First Humanist Society of New York. He enlisted the support of other prominent humanists such as John Dewey and Julian Huxley, who served on the society's advisory board.

In founding the Humanist Society, Potter also left the professional ministry behind and declared that the society would have neither creed, clergy, baptisms, nor prayers. It was his platform from which to speak, work for social reform, and write the 15 books he authored over the next several decades. Among the social issues to which he devoted his time were birth control, the abolition of capital punishment, and euthanasia. He founded the Euthanasia Society in 1938.

Potter's first book, *The Story of Religion*, appeared in 1929, the same year he founded the Humanist Society. It attempted to present a perspective on religion through biographical sketches of the founders of the major religions. Other books by Potter included: *Humanism, a New Religion* (1930); *Humanizing Religion* (1933); *Beyond the Senses* (1939); and *The Great Religious Leaders* (1958). Among his last books, and the one with the most enduring audience, was *The Lost Years of Jesus Revealed*, which built upon the discovery of the Dead Sea Scrolls. It made a case for Jesus having been a member of the Dead Sea sect.

The Humanist Movement has remained one of the smaller religious communities in North America, but one which has had influence far beyond its size due to its appeal to a highly educated elite. Potter will be remembered as one of its most capable early twentieth century leaders.

Sources:

Dictionary of American Biography. 20 vols. and 7 supps. New York: Charles Scribner's Sons, 1928-1936, 1944-1981.

Potter, Charles Francis. *Beyond the Senses*. New York: Doubleday, Doran & Co., 1939. 278 pp.

_____. *Humanism, a New Religion*. New York: Simon & Schuster, 1930. 132 pp.

_____. *Humanizing Religion*. New York: Harper & Brothers, 1933. 265 pp.

_____. *The Lost Years of Jesus Revealed*. Greenwich, CT: Fawcett Publications, 1958. 128 pp.

_____. *The Story of Religion*. Garden City, NY: Garden City Publishing Co., 1929. 627 pp.

★745★
POWELL JR., Adam Clayton
Minister, Baptist Church
b. Nov. 29, 1908, New Haven, Connecticut
d. Apr. 4, 1972, Miami, Florida

Adam Clayton Powell, Jr. inherited the leadership of the Abyssinian Baptist Church in New York City from his father, who had been its pastor for many years. He was born in Connecticut to **Adam Clayton Powell, Sr.** and Mattie Fletcher Powell, but moved to New York with his family almost immediately. He grew up in New York City and attended Colgate University. Following the completion of his B.A. in 1930 he became the manager and assistant pastor at his father's church. Back in New York, he attended Columbia University, from which he received his M.A. in 1932. In 1933 he married Isabel G. Washington.

In 1937 Powell became pastor of the Abyssinian Baptist Church at the time of his father's retirement. He had already absorbed the ideas for the improvement of the lives of Blacks from Marcus Garvey and through the 1930s emerged as an activist. Throughout the decade he organized demonstrations and boycotts promoting jobs for Blacks, the most successful in connection with the 1939-1940 World's Fair. To handle the problems of the Great Depression, he also extended the social service program of the church which had previously been initiated by his father. His activism soon led him into the political arena, and in 1941 he became the first black person elected to the New York City Council. For the rest of his career he would combine politics and religion in a unique fashion that would alter the course of the black community and anticipate the changes of the 1960s. Also during his council years, he was divorced from his first wife, and in 1943 he married Hazel Scott.

During his four years in the council, Powell developed a political organization centered on Harlem and in 1945 was elected to Congress. In Washington he became the leading spokesperson in the fight to end discrimination against Blacks, beginning with his use of nominally segregated facilities which could not turn away the service of a Congressman. Over the years he rose to a position of power in Congress, eventually becoming the chairman of the Committee on Education and Labor. The committee was responsible for over 40 pieces of major social legislation.

Powell's career took a major turn in 1960 when a Harlem woman won a libel case against him. Powell refused to recognize the case or the verdict, and refused to pay the money awarded by the court. Henceforth, he went to New York only on Sunday (when no legal action could be taken against him) to preach at the church. In 1966 he was convicted of criminal contempt, and consequently he moved to Bimini, an island in the Bahamas. As a result of his action the House of Representatives moved against him and in 1967 expelled him from the Congress, the first committee chairman so treated in the twentieth century. Later that year, in a special election, he was overwhelmingly supported by his Harlem constituency and returned to the House. The Supreme Court ruled that his unseating was an unconstitutional act. He was reseated in 1969 only after settling the libel case, paying a fine, and being stripped of his seniority.

In the 1969 election, Powell was defeated after it had become known that he had developed cancer, from which he died three years later. His death occurred on the fourth anniversary of the assassination of **Martin Luther King, Jr.** Before his death he was able to finish his autobiography, which appeared in 1971.

Sources:

Alexander, E. Curtis. *Adam Clayton Powell, Jr. and the Harlem Renaissance*. New York: ECA Associates, 1988. 45 pp.
Metzger, Linda. *Black Writers*. Detroit, MI: Gale Research Company, 1989. 619 pp.
Powell, Adam Clayton, Jr. *Adam by Adam: The Autobiography of Adam Clayton Powell, Jr.*. New York: Dial Press, 1971. 260 pp.
_____. *Keep the Faith, Baby!* New York: Trident, 1967. 293 pp.
_____. *Marching Blacks: An Interpretive History of the Rise of the Black Common Man*. New York: Dial Press, 1945. 219 pp.
_____. *The New Image in Education: A Prospectus for the Future by the Chairman of the Committee on Education and Labor*. Washington, DC: U.S. Government Printing Office, 1962. 12 pp.

★746★
POWELL SR., Adam Clayton
Minister, Baptist Church
b. May 5, 1865, Soak Creek, Virginia
d. Jun. 12, 1953, New York, New York

Adam Clayton Powell, Sr., for many years pastor of the Abyssinian Baptist Church in New York City, one of the oldest and largest predominantly black Baptist congregations in America, was the son of former slaves, Anthony and Sally Dunning Powell. One of a small minority of Blacks able to secure an education, he attended Rendville Academy in Perry, Ohio, and Wayland Seminary and College in Washington, D.C., from which he graduated in 1892. While at Wayland, in 1889, he married Mattie Fletcher Schaefer. After a brief pastorate at Ebenezer Baptist Church in Philadephia, in 1893 Powell became pastor of the Immanuel Baptist Church in New Haven, Connecticut. During his pastorate for a year (1895-

1896) he was able to pursue post-graduate studies at Yale University Divinity School.

In 1908 Powell became pastor of the Abyssinian Baptist Church. His first task was to clean up the neighborhood in which he was given an apartment to live. He went to work and saw that the houses of prostitution were soon closed. Following World War I, Powell discerned the development of a concentration of Blacks in Harlem, and he led the congregation to purchase land on 138th Street. Ground was broken for a new building in 1922, and the following year both a sanctuary and community house (the first in the area) were formally dedicated. Powell then began work on a home for the aged which was completed in 1926. During the Great Depression he mobilized the church to assist and feed the poor. He also worked on building the congregation which by the mid-1930s had over 14,000 members.

Powell emerged through the 1920s as one of the most important leaders in what was becoming one of the most important black communities in America. He was invited to lecture on his work and on the general topic of race relations at Colgate University, City College of New York, and Union Theological Seminary. He became an editorial writer for the *Christian Review* and at one point served as vice president of the NAACP.

Having built the church, in 1937 he retired and was succeeded by his son, **Adam Clayton Powell, Jr.** He was named pastor emeritus. During his retirement years he had time to write and authored several books: *Palestine and Saints in Caesar's Household* (1939); his autobiography, *Against the Tide* (1938); *Picketing Hell* (1942); and *Riots and Ruins* (1945).

Sources:

Logan, Rayford W., and Michael R. Winston, eds. *Dictionary of American Negro Biography*. New York: W. W. Norton & Co. 1982. 680 pp.
Powell, Adam Clayton. *Against the Tide*. New York: R. R. Smith, 1938. 327 pp.
_____. *Palestine and Saints in Caesar's Household*. New York: R. R. Smith, 1939. 217 pp.
_____. *Picketing Hell*. New York: W. Malliet and Co., 1942. 254 pp.
_____. *Riots and Ruins*. New York: R. R. Smith, 1945. 171 pp.
_____. *Upon This Rock*. New York: Abyssinian Baptist Church, 1949. 132 pp.

★747★
PRABHUPADA, Abhay Charan De Bhaktivedanta Swami
Founder, International Society for Krishna Consciousness (ISKCON)
b. Sep. 1, 1896, Calcutta India
d. Nov. 14, 1977, Vrindavan India

Abhay Charan De Bhaktivedanta Swami Prabhupada, the founder of the International Society for Krishna Consciousness (ISKCON), was born Abhay Charan De, the son of Rajani and Gour Mohan De, a cloth merchant. Though a householder (one who works at a secular occupation and has a family), De's father taught him Hindu temple deity worship from an early age, as there was a temple across the street from their home. In 1916 De entered the Scottish Churches College. While there, to obey his father, he married the 11-year-old Padharani Satta. It was not a happy marriage. Upon completion of his college work in 1920 he refused his degree, a means at the time of showing solidarity with Ghandi's call to boycott British goods. He went to work in a pharmaceutical company.

Soon after going to work, De met Sri Srimad Bhaktisiddhanta Saraswati Goswami, the head of the Guadiya Math, a Hindu organization which carried on the *bhakti* (devotional) tradition originally articulated by Sri Chaitayna, a Bengali saint of the sixteenth century. Bahktisiddhanta became De's guru (teacher). Over the next several decades De really led two lives, one as a businessman and husband, a life he increasingly disliked, and the other as that of a religious seeker. His religious life was punctuated by several important events. In 1932 he had a meeting with his guru at Vrindavan, the holy city associated with the deity Krishna, during which he was formally initiated and his name changed to Abhay Charanaravinda (one who fearlessly takes shelter at the feet of the Lord). Then in 1936, Bhaktisiddhanta told him to prepare himself to spread the worship of Krisha to the West. He put the suggestion aside, however, as he still had family responsibilities that demanded his attention.

Over the next few years De became an accomplished student of the scriptures and authored his first books: an *Introduction to the Geetopanishad* and the *Bhagavad-Gita As It Is*. The latter volume, a commentary on a Hindu holy book from a position which accepts Krishna as a personal deity, earned him the honorific title Bhaktivedanta from his colleagues at the Guadiya Math. His several efforts to organize a movement floundered due to the distractions of his family life. Finally in 1956 he took the vows of the renounced life and left his secular responsibilities behind. He emerged as A.C. Bhaktivedanta Swami Prabhupada.

In 1965 Prabhupada was able to travel to America and begin work on the lower east side of New York City. In 1966 he opened a storefront center and started an American edition of *Back to Godhead*, a magazine he had published sporadically in India. The movement spread rapidly and by 1967 had reached California. In 1972 he founded the Bhaktivedanta Book Trust to publish his books. The 12 years between his arrival in the United States and his death were spent teaching his disciples, traveling to the various centers, and writing, though the latter activity came to increasingly dominate his time. Over 60 volumes of his writings were published before he died and others have been published over the years since.

By the mid-1970s, the movement Prabhupada founded had become one of the most controversial of the new religions which appeared in the West in the 1960s. He had little time for the controversy, however, as he had to plan for the transition of authority and the training of leadership. Several years before his death he turned the society over to a set of designated initiating gurus and other leaders who together composed a governing council and currently administer the international movement which resulted from Prabhupada's effort. Following his death, one disciple authored a six-volume biography of Srila Prabhupada and a five-volume set of his letters was published. Annually a commemorative volume, *Sri Vyasa Puja*, is published on Prabhupada's birthday, and in 1988 the first volume of a projected 20-volume set of transcripts of Prabhupada's conversations and lectures appeared.

Sources:

Prabhupada, A. C. Bhaktivedanta Swami. *Bhagavad-Gita As It Is*. New York: Bhaktivedanta Book Trust, 1972. 981 pp.
———. *Conversations with Srila Prabhupada*. Vol. I. Los Angeles: Bhaktivedanta Book Trust, 1988. 392 pp.
———. *KRSNA, The Supreme Personality of Godhead*. 3 vols. New York: Bhaktivedanta Book Trust, 1970.
———. *Letters from Srila Prabhupada*. 5 vols. Culver City, CA: Vaishnava Institute, 1987.
———. *The Nectar of Devotion*. Los Angeles: Bhaktivedanta Book Trust. 1970, 439 pp.
———. *The Science of Self Realization*. Los Angeles: Bhaktivedanta Book Trust, 1977. 360 pp.
———. *Teachings of Lord Caitanya*. Los Angeles: Bhaktivedanta Book Trust, 1974. 440 pp.
Satsvarupa dasa Goswami. *Srila Prabhupada-iliamrta*. 6 vols. Los Angeles: Bhaktivedanta Book Trust, 1980-1984.

★748★
PREUS, Jacob Aall Ottesen
Educator and Executive, Lutheran Church—Missouri Synod
b. Jan. 8, 1920, St. Paul, Minnesota

Jacob Aall Ottesen Preus, the former president of the Lutheran Church—Missouri Synod, is the son of Idella Haugen and Jacob Aall Ottesen Preus, a Norwegian-American Lutheran couple. His father was the founder of the Lutheran Brotherhood. When Preus was six years old, his family moved to the Chicago area and settled in Highland Park, Illinois. Here he first became acquainted with the Missouri Synod, which had the only Lutheran congregation in town. The family, however, was primarily associated with the Evangelical Lutheran Church, a Norwegian Lutheran body formed in 1917 by the merger of several Norwegian synods. The Evangelical Lutheran Church is now a constituent part of the Evangelical Lutheran Church in America.

In 1937 Preus entered Luther College, the old school founded by Norwegian Lutherans in the mid-nineteenth century in Decorah, Iowa. He graduated *magne cum laude* in 1941 and entered Luther Theological Seminary. In 1943, while in seminary, he married Delpha Mae Holleque.

Preus had become increasingly unhappy with what he discerned as the "liberal" atmosphere at Luther Seminary and within the Evangelical Lutheran Church. Thus, following his graduation in 1945, he was ordained in the Evangelical Lutheran Synod, a smaller, more conservative Norwegian-Lutheran body which had not participated in the 1917 merger. He became the pastor of Trinity Lutheran Church in South St. Paul, Minnesota. While there he completed an M.A. at the University of Minnesota. In 1947 he was asked to join the faculty of the synod's school, Bethany Lutheran College, in Mankato, Minnesota. He stayed there for three years before returning to the pastorate in Leverne, Minnesota, during which time he was able to complete his Ph.D. at the University of Minnesota in 1951. He returned to the Bethany faculty in 1956.

In 1958 Preus made a significant move in leaving Bethany and the Evangelical Lutheran Synod to become a professor of New Testament at Concordia Theological Seminary in Springfield, Illinois, and a member of the Lutheran Church—Missouri Synod. From this position he rose to become the most powerful man in the synod. In 1962 he was named president of Concordia.

During the 1960s the Missouri Synod was troubled by what many saw as the influx of liberal theology and biblical criticism into the synod's schools, especially Concordia Theological Seminary in St. Louis. Preus emerged as a voice of the conservatives and in 1969 was elected president of the Missouri Synod. In 1970 he launched an inquiry into alleged doctrinal irregularities at Concordia. In 1972 he produced a substantive document, his *Report of the Synodical President to the Lutheran Church—Missouri Synod*, which included a position paper, *A Statement of Scriptural and Confessional Principles*, viewed by many as a standard by which the seminary would subsequently be judged. A study edition was released the next year.

In 1972 Preus accused seminary president John Tietjen and other professors of holding false doctrines. When the synod sustained Preus in 1973, Teitjen and others formed the Evangelical Lutherans in Mission. In 1974 Preus suspended Tietjen and 43 (of 47) Concordia faculty members and most of the student body went on strike in protest. They eventually left the campus to form a new seminary that would not be under the control of Preus or the synod. The formation of the Seminary-in-Exile further polarized the situation and in 1976 the dissenting element left the synod and established the Association of Evangelical Lutheran Churches, now a constituent part of the Evangelical Lutheran Church in America.

Preus remained as president of the synod until 1981, and since that time has returned to a more sedate life as a teacher at Concordia Seminary in St. Louis. His presidency, however, set the direction of the synod for at least the next generation.

Sources:

Adams, James E. *Preus of Missouri and the Great Lutheran Civil War*. New York: Harper & Row, 1977. 242 pp.

Preus, Jacob A. O. *Report of the Synodical President to the Lutheran Church—Missouri Synod*. St. Louis, MO: Lutheran Church—Missouri Synod, 1972. 160 pp.

———. *Study Edition of A Statement of Scriptural and Confessional Principles*. Ed. by Ralph A. Bohlmann. St. Louis, MO: Lutheran Church—Missouri Synod, 1972. 47 pp.

★749★
PRICE, Eugenia
Author of Christian Inspirational Books
b. Jun. 22, 1916, Charleston, West Virginia

Eugenia Price, a popular author of religious literature, is the daughter of Walter Wesley and Anna Davidson Price. She was raised a Methodist, but by the time she had graduated from high school in 1932 she had become alienated from religion. She attended Ohio University and while there became an atheist. In 1935 she entered Northwestern University dental school but dropped out in 1937 to enter the University of Chicago to study philosophy. However, she soon discovered literature and began to write. Over the next few years she became a successful writer of radio scripts, first with the National Broadcasting Company (1939-1942) and then with Proctor and Gamble. In 1945 she founded the very successful Eugenia Price Productions.

During the 1940s she was also engaged in an intense personal spiritual struggle. Her reconnection with an old friend who worked at Calvary House, the center attached to Calvary Episcopal Church and pastored by **Samuel Moor Shoemaker**, became a catalyst that led to a conversion experience in 1949. The new life led to a reorganization of her career. She became the mistress of ceremonies of a new show, "A Visit with Genie," which led to an offer to write for the Pacific Garden Mission's radio show, "Unshackled" (1950-1956).

Having settled in Chicago, in the early 1950s she began to write books, the first of which, *Discoveries Made from Living My New Life*, appeared in 1953. It was followed with a narrative of her conversion in *The Burden Is Light!: The Autobiography of a Transformed Pagan Who Took God at His Word* (1955). Over the next decade she authored eight additional inspirational titles.

Having established herself as a religious writer of ability, in 1965 Price released *The Beloved Invader*, a novel set in St. Simon's Island, Georgia, where she had moved. It was followed by *New Moon Rising* (1971) and *Lighthouse* (1971). This St. Simon trilogy established her as a popular Christian novelist. While occasionally writing additional nonfiction and autobiographical works, Price's career has centered upon her novels. By the mid-1980s, over 15 million copies of her books had been sold, and titles had been translated into 16 languages. During the 1980s her main books were the Savannah quartet: *Savannah* (1983); *To See Your Face Again* (1985); *Before the Darkness Falls* (1987); and *Stranger in Savannah* (1989). Price has not written Christian novels in the traditional sense, but historical novels in which the intervention of the Divine into the midst of normal lives is highlighted. It is a reality in which she intensely believes.

Sources:

Price, Eugenia. *At Home On St. Simon's*. Atlanta, GA: Peachtree Publishers, 1981. 90 pp.

———. *The Burden Is Light!: The Autobiography of a Transformed Pagan Who Took God at His Word*. Westwood, NJ: Fleming H. Revell, 1955. 221 pp.

———. *Discoveries Made from Living My New Life*. Grand Rapids, MI: Zondervan Publishing House, 1953. 119 pp.

———. *Early Will I Seek Thee: Journal of a Heart That Longed and Found*. New York: Dial Press, 1956. 138 pp.

———. *St. Simon's Memoir*. Philadelphia: J. P. Lippencott & Co., 1978. 224 pp.

———. *What Really Matters*. New York: Dial Press, 1983. 119 pp.

★750★
PRINCE, Peter Derek
Independent Pentecostal Writer
b. Aug. 14, 1915, Bangalore India

Peter Derek Prince, popular independent Pentecostal writer and teacher, is the son of Gwendolen Vaughn and Paul Ernest Prince. His father was an officer in the British Army stationed in India during the colonial period. Prince was educated at King's College, Cambridge, from which he received a B.A. (1937) and M.S. (1941). As a conscientious objector, he served in the British Royal Army Medical Corp during World War II. While in North Africa he became a Christian. Stationed in Palestine during the last months of the war, he met Lydia Christensen, who ran an orphanage. They were married in 1946, and he became the father of her eight adopted children. They spent the next two years in Jerusalem where Prince attended Hebrew University.

After the establishment of the state of Israel, Prince moved to London and became the pastor of a Pentecostal church. In 1957 he took a position in Kenya as principal of the Nyangori Teacher Training College. He returned to England in 1961 and in 1963 moved to the United States where he pastored churches in Minneapolis, Seattle, and Chicago. In America Prince associated with the emerging Charismatic Movement, a movement of ministers and lay people who had experienced the Pentecostal Baptism of the Holy Spirit (as evidenced by their speaking in tongues) but who were connected primarily with mainline Christian denominations rather than the older Pentecostal churches. He became a popular lecturer and writer within the Charismatic Movement and in 1968 founded Derek Prince Publications, through which he has issued a host of booklets on a variety of topics relevant to Christian teachings.

Prince's first writings were a series of basic books on entering and living the Christian life that he termed the Foundation series (1965-1966). In 1967 he moved to Ft. Lauderdale, associated with Christian Growth Ministries, and entered a covenantal relationship with Bob Mumford, Charles Simpson, and **Donald Basham**. Together they founded Good News Church in Ft. Lauderdale. Nationally, they attempted to bring some order out of the new Charismatic Movement through a process called shepherding, the designation of a group of elders in local assemblies who were tied to and responsible to each other in an ascending order of shepherds. The process of shepherding, the subject of Prince's volume *Discipleship, Shepherding, Commitment* (1976), became the most controversial element in the Ministries' work.

In 1975 Prince's wife died. In 1978 he married Ruth Hemmingson Baker over the initial objections of his associates. In 1979 he began "Today with Derek Prince," a 15-minute daily radio show. During the early 1980s, Prince, who had continued to operate his independent Derek Prince Ministries, initiated the Global Outreach program to make Christian literature available free in Third World countries. He also became the first of the Ft. Lauderdale leaders to disassociate himself from the covenant relationship and the teaching on shepherding. When Simpson relocated the Ministries to Mobile and renamed it Integrity Ministries, Prince remained in Ft. Lauderdale. He had already developed a second center in Jerusalem, the focus of the Global Outreach program, where he resides for approximately half of every year.

Sources:

Derek Prince: The Man and His Ministry. Ft. Lauderdale, FL: Derek Prince Ministries, 1984. 14 pp.

Howard, Linda. "A New Beginning." *Charisma* 9, 9 (April 1984): 38-43.

Prince, Derek. *Burial by Baptism*. Ft. Lauderdale, FL: Derek Prince Publications, 1970. 18 pp.

_____. *Chords from David's Harp*. Grand Rapids, MI: Zondervan, 1983.

_____. *Discipleship, Shepherding, Commitment*. Ft. Lauderdale, FL: Derek Prince Ministries, 1976.

_____. *From Jordan to Pentecost*. Ft. Lauderdale, FL: Derek Prince Publications, [1966]. 97 pp.

_____. *Last Word on the Middle East*. Lincoln, VA: Chosen Books, 1984. 157 pp.

_____. *The Marriage Covenant*. Ft. Lauderdale, FL: Derek Prince Publications, 1978.

_____. *Resurrection of the Dead*. Ft. Lauderdale, FL: Derek Prince Publications, [1966]. 88 pp.

★751★
PROPHET, Elizabeth Clare
Messenger, Church Universal and Triumphant
b. Apr. 8, 1940, Red Bank, New Jersey

Elizabeth Clare Prophet, born Elizabeth Clare Wulf, is the current leader of the Church Universal and Triumphant, a New Age group in the Theosophical tradition. Raised a Christian Scientist, she was a youthful spiritual seeker when she began reading material that had been produced by the "I AM" Movement, a Theosophical development begun in the 1930s by **Guy Warren Ballard**. She was a college student when she met **Mark L. Prophet** at Boston University on April 22, 1961. Mark had been active in groups inspired by the "I AM" Movement, specifically, the Bridge to Freedom and the Lighthouse of Freedom, and in 1958 formed his own "I AM"-type group, Summit Lighthouse, in Washington, D.C. There was an immediate personal affinity between them that was strongly reinforced by their common spiritual background, and the two were married within a year of their meeting. Together they received messages which later were published as separate books, such as *Prayer and Meditation* (1978) and *Corona Class Lessons* (1986), and together they authored the church's basic text, *Climb the Highest Mountain* (1972).

Summit Lighthouse has moved a number of times, first to Colorado Springs in 1966, then to Pasadena and Malibu, and most recently to Montana. When her husband died in 1973, Elizabeth Prophet took over control of the organization. She also took over her role as the messenger for the spiritual hierarchy of the Great White Brotherhood, which she believed he had joined. Under her leadership, the group has grown considerably and as it expanded and diversified, she gave it a new name, the Church Universal and Triumphant. The Summit Lighthouse remains as the church's educational arm. Shortly after Mark Prophet's death, she married Randall King.

Prophet, known affectionately to the church's members as Guru Ma, serves as spiritual leader of the church. Her primary task, above and beyond her role as teacher and liturgical leader, is being the messenger (some would say "channel," though she dislikes the term) of the ascended masters of the Great White Brotherhood, who are believed to guide human destiny. In that capacity she will, at regular intervals, publically bring messages. These are published in the church's periodical, the *Pearls of Wisdom*, which is bound into volumes annually. Other messages, especially those given on a special occasion, have become the subject of her many volumes. For example, a set of messages received at a gathering of church members at Mount Shasta, California, in 1975 provided the substance of Prophet's volume *The Great White Brotherhood in the Culture, History, and Destiny of America* (1976). Other channeled volumes include: *The Chela and the Path* (1976); *Quietly Comes the Buddha* (1977); and *Mysteries of the Holy Grail* (1984).

Both Prophet and her church have endured a steady stream of attacks from former church members and the anti-cult movement. She has been denounced as a charismatic leader who controls the life of church members. In the late 1980s she was criticized for her apocalyptic teachings concerning a possible holocaust which led the church to construct a number of bomb shelters on their Montana property. Among her most severe critics was Randall King, whom she had divorced. She later married Edward Francis, her present husband.

During the 1980s Prophet began to describe the church and herself as Gnostic Christians. She wrote three volumes on what she considered the lost aspects of Jesus' ministry: *The Lost Years of Jesus* (1984) and *The Lost Teachings of Jesus* (two volumes, 1986, 1988).

Sources:

Harris, Ron. "Offbeat Church Stirs Fear in Montana." *Los Angeles Times* (December 27, 1989).

Prophet, Elizabeth Clare. [El Morya] *The Chela and the Path*. Colorado Springs, CO: Summit University Press, 1976.

_____. *The Great White Brotherhood in the Culture, History and Religion of America*. Los Angeles: Summit University Press, 1976. 352 pp.

_____. [Gautama Buddha] *Quietly Comes the Buddha*. Colorado Springs, CO: Summit Lighthouse, 1972. 147 pp.

_____. *The Lost Teachings of Jesus*. 2 vols. Livingston, MT: Summit University Press, 1986, 1988.

_____. *The Lost Years of Jesus*. Livingston, MT: Summit University Press, 1984. 401 pp.

Prophet, Mark L. and Elizabeth Clare Prophet. *Climb the Highest Mountain*. Colorado Springs, CO: Summit Lighthouse, 1972. 516 pp.

Rubenstein, Sara. "Trouble in Paradise." *The Sunday Oregonian* (October 4, 1987).

★752★
PROPHET, Marcus L.
Founder, Summit Lighthouse (Church Universal and Triumphant)
b. Dec. 24, 1918, Chippewa Falls, Wisconsin
d. Feb. 26, 1973, Colorado Springs, Colorado

Marcus L. (Mark) Prophet, the founder of the Summit Lighthouse, an organization known today as the Church Universal and Triumphant, was the son of Thomas and Mabel Prophet. Little is known of his early life. During the 1930s he worked for the Soo Line Railroad and later served in the Air Force during World War II. After the war, for a short while he was a salesman. However, in the 1950s he became deeply involved with the teachings of the Ascended Masters, exulted beings who are believed to have finished their earthly work and have now become the teachers of humankind. Together the masters compose the Great White Brotherhood, which is believed to be ultimately guiding the human race toward its spiritual destiny.

A new phase of the Ascended Master teachings was initiated by **Guy Warren Ballard**, who founded the I AM Religious Activity in the 1930s. Following his death in 1939, his wife, **Edna Anne Wheeler Ballard**, continued his work as the Messenger of the Ascended Masters and head of the I AM Activity. In the 1950s, however, several other people arose who claimed to be messengers. One of these, Geraldine Innocente, became the messenger for a new group, the Bridge to Freedom (now the New Age Church of the Christ). Associated with Innocente was Francis K. Ekey, who led a group in Philadelphia. During the 1950s, Ekey's group became independent and assumed the name Lighthouse of Freedom. Mark Prophet became an associate of Ekey and founded an affiliated Lighthouse of Freedom group in Washington, D.C. In 1958 Prophet became independent of Ekey and his small group became known as the Summit Lighthouse. He began to publish a newsletter, *Ashram Notes*, and to travel around the East Coast lecturing on his convictions.

In early 1961 he met Elizabeth Clare Wulf Ytreberg (now known as **Elizabeth Clare Prophet**), then a student at Boston University. They felt an immediate affinity and during the year both obtained divorces. In October 1961 they married. They moved to Beacons Head, Virginia; their home, known as "Holy Tree House," doubled as their church and teaching center. In 1962 Prophet, on the instruction of the Masters, established the Keepers of the Flame Fraternity, an ordered group made up of those associated with the Summit Lighthouse especially dedicated to the Masters' plan—the establishment of the freedom and enlightenment of humanity. Mark Prophet's major tasks during these years included the activity of allowing the Ascended Masters to speak through him on a regular basis. These dictations from the Masters were published in the *Ashram Notes* and the more important ones collected into booklets. Among the earliest booklets were *Sacred Ritual of the Keepers of the Flame* and a booklet on decreeing, the basic form of prayer used in Ascended Master groups, called *The Overcoming of Fear through Decrees* (1965).

In 1966 the Prophets moved the headquarters of the Summit Lighthouse to Colorado Springs, Colorado. During the next years, the organization prospered. In 1971 Summit University was founded in Santa Barbara, California, to provide more intensive and personal instruction to members of the Keepers of the Flame Fraternity. In 1972 the Prophets published a volume of basic teachings of the Summit Lighthouse, *Climb the Highest Mountain*, the major literary production of Mark Prophet prior to his death in 1973. Posthumously, the messages channeled through him have been republished in a number of books, such as *Studies in Alchemy* (1974); *Intermediate Studies in Alchemy* (1975); and *Understanding Yourself: Doorway to the Superconsciousness* (1981). Much more of the material he dictated has been published in volumes that also contain chapters dictated through Elizabeth Clare Prophet and issued under their joint authorship. Some of Prophet's own writings were published as *The Souless One* (1981).

Following Prophet's death, his wife became head of the Summit Lighthouse and as a Messenger received dictations from her late husband under his name as an Ascended Master, Lanello. Under her leadership, what had been the Summit Lighthouse was transformed into the Church Universal and Triumphant, though the name Summit Lighthouse has been retained as one aspect of the new church.

Sources:

Germain, Saint [through Mark L. Prophet]. *Intermediate Studies in Alchemy.* Colorado Springs, CO: Summit University Press, 1975. 132 pp.

———. *Studies in Alchemy.* Colorado Springs, CO: Summit University Press, 1974. 91 pp.

Maitreya, Lord [through Mark L. Prophet]. *The Overcoming of Fear through Decrees.* Colorado Springs, CO: Summit Lighthouse, 1966. 50 pp.

Prophet, Mark L. *The Souless One: Cloning a Counterfeit Creation.* Los Angeles: Summit University Press, 1981. 214 pp.

———. *Understanding Yourself: Doorway to the Superconscious.* Los Angeles: Summit University Press, 1981. 144 pp.

★753★
PRUTER, Karl Hugo Reiling
Founder, Christ Catholic Church
b. Jul. 3, 1920, Poughkeepsie, New York

Karl Hugo Rehling Pruter, founder and bishop of Christ Catholic Church, one of the more substantial of the independent Old Catholic movements in North America, was raised as a Protestant. He attended Lutheran Theological Seminary in Philadelphia, Pennsylvania (B.D. 1945), and became a Congregationalist minister. During the 1940s he was a major participant in the Free Catholic Movement, a loose association of Congregationalist ministers (several of whom eventually received episcopal orders from independent Catholic bishops) who had concluded from their research in

church history that the early church was Christocentric and that worship had centered on the Blessed Sacrament (i.e., the Eucharist). During the 1950s, as pastor of the North Berwyn (Illinois) Congregational Church, he tried to build the Free Catholic Movement in the Midwest, but found little support. One of his first books, *The Theology of Congregationalism* (1957), emerged from this period.

For Pruter, the merger in the late 1960s of the Congregational-Christian Churches with the Evangelical and Reformed Church to form the United Church of Christ generated a crisis, and he despaired of the future of the Free Catholic Movement in the new church. He took his concern with him on a trip to Europe in 1965, during which he met with the Old Catholic leadership. Upon his return to America, he settled in Boston and began to search for a Free Catholic church with which to associate. He was unsuccessful on that quest, but he did locate Archbishop Peter A. Zhurawetsky, an independent Orthodox bishop who headed the Orthodox Catholic Patriarchate of America. Zhurawetsky ordained Pruter to the priesthood on November 7, 1965, and commissioned him to begin Christ Catholic Church as a parish in the Back Bay area of Boston. On the same day two years later at Wren Oak, New York, Zhurawetsky, assisted by Archbishop Uladyslau Ryzy-Ryski, the Byelorussian leader of the American World Patriarchs, consecrated Pruter as an independent Catholic bishop. The following year Pruter separated himself completely from Zhurawetsky and began to build Christ Catholic Church as an independent denomination.

Pruter founded St. Willibrord's Press, through which he services the independent Catholic and Orthodox community as a mail order house for books and supplies. As his movement slowly grew he moved first to New Hampshire and then Scottsdale, Arizona. He located in Chicago in 1975. Over the years of his episcopacy he has authored a number of booklets (including some centered upon his concern for world peace) and several books. He emerged as one of the historians of the Old Catholic movement writing *A History of the Old Catholic Movement* (1973) and co-authoring *The Old Catholic Sourcebook* (1983) with J. Gordon Melton. Possibly his major contribution to the movement has been his periodic production of the address directory for independent bishops, most recently titled *A Directory of Autocephalous Bishops.*

In 1983 he retired to Highlandsville, Missouri, in the Ozark Mountains. He pastors a small congregation which meets at Christ Cathedral, a building dubbed the smallest cathedral in the world. In 1988 he extended his jurisdiction into Canada with the consecration of Frederick P. Dunleavy as bishop of Christ Catholic Church of Canada and the acceptance of the former Ontario Old Roman Catholic Church into Christ Catholic Church.

Sources:

Pruter, Karl Hugo R. *A History of the Old Catholic Church.* Scottsdale, AZ: St. Willibrord's Press, 1973. 76 pp.

———. *Neo-Congregationalism.* Zuni, NM: St. Willibrord's Press, 1973. 90 pp.

———. *The Theology of Congregationalism.* Berwyn, IL: The Brownist Press, 1957. 100 pp.

———, and J. Gordon Melton. *The Old Catholic Sourcebook.* New York: Garland Publishing, 1983. 254 pp.

Ward, Gary L. *Independent Bishops; An International Directory.* Santa Barbara, CA: Apogee Books, 1990. 500 pp.

★754★
PRYSE JR., James Morgan
Theosophist and Founder, Gnostic Society
b. Nov. 14, 1859, New London, Ohio
d. Apr. 22, 1942, Los Angeles, California

James Morgan Pryse, Jr., a popular Theosophical writer and founder of the Gnostic Society, was the son of a Welsh Presbyterian minister, James Morgan Pryse, and Mary Morgan, also of Welsh extraction. Pryse grew up in parsonages in the Midwest, his father moving several times during his youth. Integral to the home environment were the legends of the ancient Druids. The Reverend Pryse was a member of the Welsh Order of Druid Bards. Pryse began to read law after finishing high school, but just as he was ready to be admitted to the bar, he decided not to pursue the field. He eventually became a newspaper editor in first Red Cloud and then Blue Springs, Nebraska.

Pryse's early adult years were marked by a certain restlessness, and he moved frequently. In 1885 he became associated with the ill-fated plans to build a railroad line to Topolobampo, Mexico, along with an associated cooperative colony. He organized and edited the Topolobampo Colony periodical while living in Hammonton, New Jersey. It was during this time he became acquainted with theosophy (the Theosophical Society having been formed in 1875). He joined the society in 1886 after moving to Los Angeles. He became very active in the society and settled in New York in 1889 to work for the Aryan Press. Before the year was out, he moved to London at the request of **Helena P. Blavatsky**, founder of the Theosophical Society, to work with her and establish the H.P.B. Press.

In 1894 Pryse moved to Ireland to work with the *Irish Theosophist*. Here he wrote his first book, *The Sermon on the Mount* (1896), published under the pseudonym Aretas. Like the others which were to follow, it was devoted to a theosophical interpretation of the Bible. In 1895 he moved to New York to work with theosophical leader **William Q. Judge**. He lived in New York for most of the next 15 years, during which time he authored some of his most important books, including *Reincarnation in the New Testament* (1900); *The Magical Message According to Ionnes* (1909); and *The Apocalypse Unsealed* (1910). In 1901 he married Jessie Mayer.

Around 1910 Pryse settled in Los Angeles and began writing his magnum opus, *The Restored New Testament*, a new translation of the New Testament, which was completed in 1914. In the meantime, Pryse remained a frequent contributor to theosophical publications. In 1925 Pryse organized the Gnostic Society as an informal group of six people who gathered weekly to discuss theosophy. The society was incorporated in the 1930s. It was never a large group, but its spirit has been continued in the Gnostic Society headed by Stephan A. Hoeller in Hollywood, California.

Sources:

de Zirkoff, Boris, comp. *H. P. Blavatsky: Collected Writings*. vol. 12. Wheaton, IL: Theosophical Publishing House, 1980.

Pryse, James Morgan. *The Apocalypse Unsealed*. Los Angeles: The Author, 1931. 222 pp.

———. *Reincarnation in the New Testament*. New York: Theosophical Publishing Co. of New York, 1900. 92 pp.

———. *The Restored New Testament*. Los Angeles: The Author, 1914. 819 pp.

———. *The Sermon on the Mount*. New York: Theosophical Society, 1904. 80 pp.

★ 755 ★
PURSEL, Jach
New Age Channel for Lazaris
Founder, Concept: Synergy
b. Lansing, Michigan

Jach Pursel, the channel for the disembodied entity Lazaris, is a popular New Age personality. Pursel attended the University of Michigan with the aim of eventually going to law school, but settled for a career with State Farm Insurance. In 1972 he learned to meditate. Two years later he began receiving communications from a spirit that called himself Lazaris. On October 3, 1974, during a meditation session with his wife, Peny, he went into a trance and Lazaris spoke through him for two hours. Lazaris informed Peny that he needed to practice with her husband for two weeks to allow

him to adjust to the process of speaking through Jach. Within a year, she and Lazaris were holding psychic development classes in the Pursel home.

In Spiritualist terms, Pursel is regarded as a "trance medium"—a medium who loses consciousness when the controlling spirit takes over. Where New Age channeling differs from Spiritualist mediumship is in the area of the message content. Spiritualist mediums usually deliver messages of comfort from a departed person to her or his loved ones, whereas New Age channels usually discourse on metaphysical matters. In addition, unlike the spirits channeled by Spiritualists, Lazaris claims that he is a non-physical entity who has never incarnated in a human body.

The Pursels' teaching activity, as well as Lazaris' counseling practice, expanded until Jach Pursel was able to quit his job in 1976. As channeling became a more significant focus of the New Age movement in the 1980s, Pursel's reputation grew. Lazaris' teachings circulated in the form of cassette tapes in the early years. By the mid-1980s video tapes began to be released. Books on Lazaris were published as well, including *A Spark of Love* (1986), *The Sacred Journey: You and Your Higher Self* (1987), and *Lazaris Interviews* (1988). By the late 1980s, Lazaris' fame was second only to that of Ramtha's in the New Age community. At present, Pursel regularly conducts workshops and other programs. His organization, Concept: Synergy, moved from the San Francisco Bay Area to Florida in 1988.

Sources:

Lazaris [Jach Pursel]. *Lazaris Interviews*. 2 vols. Palm Springs, FL: Synergy Publishing, 1988.

———. *The Sacred Journey: You and Your Higher Self*. Beverly Hills, CA: Synergy Publishing, 1987. 144 pp.

———. *A Spark of Love*. Beverly Hills, CA: Synergy Publishing, 1987.

★ 756 ★
PURUCKER, Hobart Lorentz Gottfried de
Leader, Theosophical Society
b. Jan. 15, 1874, Suffern, New York
d. Sep. 27, 1942

Hobart Lorentz Gottfried de Purucker, the theosophical leader and writer, was the son of Gustaf Adolf H. E. F. von Purucker, a German Reformed pastor, and Juliana Smyth. He grew up in parsonages in Texas, Missouri, and New York, before moving in 1888 to Geneva, Switzerland, where his father had become chaplain of the American Church. While de Purucker studied at the College de Geneve, his education largely depended on tutors. He left this environment at the age of 18 and returned to America. He roamed the country working at various jobs and finally settled in San Diego, California. He joined the Theosophical Society, a demonstration of his distance from his parents' perspectives.

Shortly before returning to Geneva, de Purucker met national theosophical leader **William Q. Judge**. Back in Geneva, in 1896, he met Judge's successor Katherine A. W. Tingley and was able to assist her in purchasing land on Point Loma, the peninsula west of San Diego, California, where she established the headquarters of the American Theosophical Society. De Purucker stayed in Europe during the early years of Point Loma, but following his father's death in 1902 he was free to return to the states. In 1903 he moved to the community that had gathered around Tingley.

De Purucker quickly became an intimate associate of Tingley as her personal secretary. In 1911 he became the first editor of *The Theosophical Path*. The society's work became his life. He never married. In 1929, following Tingley's death, he became the president of the society. Among his first actions was to begin a second periodical, *The Theosophical Forum*. He also assumed the major duties as a lecturer and teacher for the Point Loma community. His lectures became the basis for a number of books, including *Ques-*

tions We All Ask (1930-1931); *Theosophy and Modern Science* (1930); *Golden Precepts of Esotericism* (1931); *Fundamentals of Esoteric Philosophy* (1932); and *The Esoteric Tradition* (1935).

The beginning of World War II presented special problems to de Purucker. The society had faced some financial crises in the 1930s, but now had additional problems due to the very real possibility felt by many that Japan might try to invade the West Coast. Thus de Purucker oversaw the abandonment of the community, the sale of the property, and the establishment of new headquarters for the society at Covina, California, in the summer of 1942. He died suddenly, just weeks after the move was accomplished.

After his death, the society moved to publish a number of volumes of de Purucker's writings which had been left in manuscript form. Of these the most important were *Studies in Occult Philosophy* (1945) and *Dialogues of G. de Purucker* (1948). More recently an important set of booklets first issued in 1936 have been compiled and edited as *Fountain Source of Occultism* (1974).

Sources:

De Zirkoff, Boris, comp. *H. P. Blavatshy: Collected Writings*. vol. 12. Wheaton, Il: Theosophical Publishing House, 1980.

de Purucker, Gottfried. *The Dialogues of G. de Purucker*. 3 vols. Covina, CA: Theosophical University Press, 1948.

———. *The Esoteric Tradition*. 2 vols. Point Loma, CA: Theosophical University Press, 1935.

———. *Fountain-Source of Occultism*. Pasadena, CA: Theosophical University Press, 1974. 744 pp.

———. *Fundamentals of the Esoteric Philosophy*. London: Rider & Co., 1932. 555 pp.

———. *Questions We All Ask*. 4 vols. Covina, CA: Theosophical University Press, 1947-1948.

———. *Studies in Occult Philosophy*. Covina, CA: Theosophical University Press, 1945. 744 pp.

★757★
RADER, Paul Daniel
Evangelist, Christian and Missionary Alliance (CMA)
b. 1879, Denver, Colorado
d. Jul. 1938

Paul Daniel Rader, the pastor of the Moody Church in Chicago and a president of the Christian and Missionary Alliance (CMA), was the son of a Methodist minister/evangelist. He grew up in Denver, Colorado, and attended the University of Denver and the University of Colorado, where he played football and boxed. Later he attended the University of Puget Sound. Upon completion of his schooling he became the athletic director of Hamline University in St. Paul, Minnesota, but decided to enter the ministry. His first pastorate was a Congregational church in Boston, Massachusetts. In 1906 he moved to a similar parish in Portland, Oregon. However, by 1908 he became discouraged, left the ministry, and moved to New York City.

Back in the East Rader encountered E. D. "Daddy" Whiteside, the head of the Christian and Missionary Alliance work in Pittsburgh. Under his ministry, Rader experienced a renewal of his Christian life and in 1912 joined Whiteside at the Pittsburgh CMA Tabernacle as an assistant minister. His oratorical abilities and evangelistic emphases led to an invitation in 1915 to become the pastor of the Moody Church in Chicago. While serving the congregation, in 1919 he was elected vice-president of the CMA. Albert Benjamin Simpson, the founder, died later that same year, and Rader became the new president. For the next two years he moved between New York and Chicago trying to keep up both jobs, but in 1921 resigned from the Moody Church after trying unsuccessfully to have the CMA headquarters moved to Chicago. During his presidency he made a world tour of CMA mission stations that became the subject of an early book, *Round the World* (1922).

As CMA president, Rader came into contact with **Oswald J. Smith**, then an up-and-coming minister in the alliance. Together they tried to promote what became known as "tabernacalism," a move to build evangelistic tabernacles, temporary structures seating up to 3,000 people, which would become the scene of ongoing daily evangelistic services in the midst of an urban complex. Rader started the Chicago Gospel Tabernacle as an example. The alliance was not very supportive of the idea, and both Rader and Smith resigned in 1924. Rader and Smith then organized the Christian World Couriers, with Smith as the Canadian leader. Within a few years Smith left to develop his own independent ministry, and Rader continued his ministry based out of the Chicago Gospel Tabernacle. In 1925 he initiated the first radio ministry in Chicago, a daily show, the "Breakfast Brigade," each morning on station WHT. He also promoted other similar tabernacles around the country. In 1933 he turned the leadership of the Chicago Tabernacle over to Clarence Erickson and concentrated more upon evangelism around the country.

Sources:

Rader, Paul. *The Fight for Light and Other Sermons*. New York: The Book Stall, 1916. 62 pp.

———. *The Midnight Cry*. Chicago: Chicago Gospel Tabernacle, [1938]. 20 pp.

———. *Round the World*. New York: Fleming H. Revell Company, 1922. 248 pp.

Reid, Daniel G., Robert D. Linder, Bruce L. Shelley, and Harry S. Stout. *Dictionary of Christianity in America*. Downers Grove, IL: InterVarsity Press, 1990. 1305 pp.

Tucker, W. Leon. *Rader's Redemption*. New York: The Book Stall of the Wonderful World Pub. Co., 1918.

★758★
RAJNEESH, Bhagwan Shree
Indian Spiritual Leader
Founder, Rajneesh Foundation International (Oshu Commune International)
b. Dec. 11, 1931, Kuchwada India
d. Jan. 19, 1990, Poona India

Rajneesh Chandra Mohan was an Indian spiritual leader with a predominantly Western following. He was known by various names and titles over his career, most prominently Bhagwan Shree Rajneesh. Following a year of meditation and personal struggle, he announced that he had been enlightened on March 21, 1953. After finishing an M.A. degree in 1957 he became a college professor and soon was well known for his unorthodox ideas. Following his resignation from Jabalpur University in 1966 he became even more outspoken, challenging prevailing Indian thinking about Hinduism, the teachings of Gandhi, and proper sexual behavior. Soon he was advising his listeners that "sex is divine" and that sex held the potential of elevating one's consciousness greatly.

As early as 1964 Rajneesh had begun holding organized meditation camps, eventually teaching what was first called "Chaotic Meditation" and later "Dynamic Meditation." Drawing from such diverse traditions as Tibetan Buddhism, Sufism, and modern psychology, Rajneesh taught that meditation began with the body, not the mind; chaotic meditation involved, among other things, screaming and removing articles of clothing. In 1970 he founded a sannyas movement, or congregation of disciples, in Bombay. In 1971 Rajneesh assumed the title "Bhagwan," meaning God. He said that the new name would convey, symbolically, the fact that he wanted his teaching to be direct, from one soul to another, and not intellectual. Over the years he released many books, almost all of them transcripts of the daily talks he gave to his followers.

The growing congregation needed more room, so in 1974 it moved to a six-acre compound in Poona. Many Americans and Europeans joined the movement there, where disciples listened to Rajneesh's discourses, practiced Dynamic Meditation, and did assigned physical chores. Cultural and artistic endeavors were prominent in the ashram at Poona.

By the late 1970s the movement, now mostly populated by Westerners, had become decidedly unpopular among Indians who deemed Rajneesh's ways immoral. Opposition peaked with an attempt on Rajneesh's life in 1980. Soon thereafter the movement purchased a huge, 100 square mile cattle ranch in Oregon and began moving there in 1981. In 1981 Rajneesh took a vow of silence, announcing that he would have only heart-to-heart communication with his followers; he finally began speaking again in 1984.

Opposition to the movement turned out to be as vocal in Oregon as it had been in India. It centered on the attempts of Rajneesh and his disciples to build a communal city, called Rajneeshpuram, in an area zoned for agricultural use only. Local residents resented the exotic guru who had been presented with 93 Rolls-Royces by his disciples, and the disciples exhibited a fair amount of disdain for Oregonians. After increasingly heated confrontations, Rajneesh was charged with immigration fraud. He pled guilty and left the country, traveled the world for several months, and in 1987 settled again in Poona.

In Poona, Rajneesh began to rebuild his movement and in the process announced a change of name to Osho. His disciples also launched a campaign to rehabilitate his tarnished reputation. In April 1989 he announced the formation of a new 21-person Inner Circle which provided oversight for the ashram and movement worldwide. A short time later, he suddenly died.

Sources:

Bharti, Ma Satya. *Drunk on the Divine: An Account of Life in the Ashram of Bhagwan Shree Rajneesh*. New York: Grove Press, 1980. 220 pp.

Forman, Juliet. *Bhagwan: Twelve Days That Shook the World*. Cologne, Germany: Rebel Publishing House, 1989. 518 pp.

Gordon, James S. *The Golden Guru: The Strange Journey of Bhagwan Shree Rajneesh*. Lexington, MA: Stephen Greene Press, 1987. 248 pp.

Meredith, George. *Bhagwan: The Most Godless Yet the Most Godly Man*. Poona, India: Rebel Publishing House, 1987. 316 pp.

Rajneesh, Bhagwan Shree. *The Book of Secrets*. 2 vols. New York: Harper & Row. 1975.

———. *Meditation: The Art of Ecstasy*. New York: Harper and Row, 1976.

———. *The Mustard Seed*. San Francisco: Harper and Row, 1975. 508 pp.

———. *My Way: The Way of the White Clouds*. New York: Grove Press, 1978.

———. *The Rajneesh Bible*. 3 vols. Rajneeshpuram, OR: Rajneesh Foundation International, 1984-1985.

Thompson, Judith and Paul Heelas. *The Way of the Heart: The Rajneesh Movement*. Wellingsborough, Northhamptonshire, UK: Aquarian Press, 1986. 142 pp.

—James R. Lewis

★759★
RALL, Harris Franklin
Theologian, Methodist Episcopal Church
b. Feb. 23, 1870, Council Bluffs, Iowa
d. Oct. 13, 1964

Harris Franklin Rall, a major proponent of liberal theology in the Methodist Episcopal Church during the twentieth century, was raised in a parsonage of the Evangelical Association, a German Methodist group in which his father was a minister. He attended the University of Iowa and the Yale Divinity School, from which he graduated in 1897. He married Rose St. John and left to do his doctoral work in Germany, first at the University of Berlin and then at Halle-Wittenberg, from which he received his Ph.D. in 1899.

Rall returned to the United States and affiliated with the New England Southern Conference of the Methodist Episcopal Church and pastored at East Berlin, Connecticut. After several years he transferred to the Baltimore Conference and became pastor of First Church in Baltimore. During his pastoral years he authored his first

book, *New Testament History* (1904). In 1910 he became president of Iliff School of Theology in Denver, Colorado, where he stayed for five years before assuming the chair in systematic theology at Garrett Biblical Institute (now Garrett-Evangelical Theological Seminary). While at Iliff he authored *A Working Faith* (1914).

Soon after settling in at Garrett, Rall found himself in the midst of the Methodist Episcopal Church's brief battle over fundamentalism. During the previous generation the Methodist Episcopal Church had gradually moved into the modernist theological camp with a minimum of controversy. When controversy did arise, it was focused on what was termed the "Course of Study," a correspondence course available to ministerial candidates who for whatever reason were unable to attend seminary. In the early twentieth century there was still a measurable percentage of ministers who received their training in this manner.

In 1916 Rall became a member of the Commission on the Course of Study, the group which chose which books were to be included in the Course of Study curriculum. His first book, *New Testament History* had a prominent place in the course. As the fundamentalist controversy heated up in the Baptist and Presbyterian churches, a small fundamentalist organization, the Methodist League for Faith and Life, attacked the inclusion of modernist books in the Course of Study. Strong attacks were made on the Course of Study in 1920 and 1924. The issue came to a head at the 1928 general conference when the president of the League, Harold Paul Sloan, along with several colleagues on the commission, attacked Rall by name. The conference voted against Sloan, effectively ending the controversy.

Rall went on to write a number of texts, including *The Coming Kingdom* (1924) and *The Meaning of God* (1925). He was an active member of the socially liberal Methodist Federation for Social Action and served as its secretary for many years.

Rall taught at Garrett until his retirement in 1945. In 1949 the school created the Harris Franklin Rall Lectureship as an annual event in Rall's honor. Following his death in 1964, the *Garrett Tower* devoted an issue to reflection upon his career and contribution to Christian thought.

Sources:

Harmon, Nolan B. *The Encyclopedia of World Methodism*. 2 vols. Nashville: United Methodist Publishing House, 1974.

Rall, Harris Franklin. *The Coming Kingdom*. New York: Methodist Book Concern, 1924. 119 pp.

———. *The Meaning of God*. Nashville, TN: Cokesbury Press, 1925. 149 pp.

———. *New Testament History*. New York: Abingdon Press, 1904. 314 pp.

———. *A Working Faith*. New York: Abingdon Press, 1914. 263 pp.

★760★
RAM DASS, Baba
Teacher, New Age Movement
Founder, Hanuman Foundation
b. Apr. 6, 1931, Boston, Massachusetts

Baba Ram Dass, also known as Richard Alpert, is a popular New Age teacher working in the Hindu tradition, and founder of the Hanuman Foundation. He attended Tufts University (B.A., 1952), Wesleyan University (M.A., 1954), and Stanford University (Ph.D., 1957). Alpert was teaching psychology at Harvard University when he met Timothy Leary. Together with Leary he experimented with mind-altering drugs, to the extent that they were both kicked off of the faculty. For some years following this dismissal, Alpert was a major spokesperson for the psychedelic drug movement.

In 1967 Alpert went to India, met his guru, Neem Karoli Baba, and was given the spiritual name Ram Dass, ("God's servant"). After returning to the United States, he began to give lectures and to tell the story of his experiences. His highly popular book *Be Here Now* (1972) established him as a major figure in North America's spiritual counterculture. Although the language and some of the concerns of this work seem somewhat dated to contemporary readers (it is still in print), at the time of its first publication it spoke directly and very powerfully to seekers who had come to the spiritual quest out of psychedelic experience. The needs of coordinating Ram Dass' speaking schedule and disseminating his tapes and written material led to the formation of several organizations, which were eventually merged into the Hanuman Foundation. During this decade he authored a number of important, widely read texts that found an audience among academics, Americans predisposed to Indian spiritual wisdom, and members of the burgeoning New Age Movement. They included *The Only Dance There Is* (1976); *Grist for the Mill* (1977); and *Journey of Awakening* (1978).

In the mid-1970s he became associated with two spiritual teachers, Hilda Charlton and Joya Santayana (now known as Jaya Sati Bhavagati Ma) in New York City. He broke with Santayana two years later, an embarrassing incident for Ram Dass that he later wrote about in an article in *Yoga Journal* entitled "Egg on My Beard." After a period of withdrawal from public life, he resumed his routine as an independent writer and lecturer. He continues to be a popular workshop leader on the New Age lecture circuit.

Sources:

Leary, Timothy, Ralph Metzner, and Richard Alpert. *The Psychedelic Experience*. New Hyde Park, NY: University Books, 1964. 157 pp.

Ram Dass, Baba [Richard Alpert]. "Egg on My Beard." *Yoga Journal* 11 (November/December 1976): 6-11.

———. *Grist for the Mill*. Santa Cruz, CA: Unity Press, 1977. 173 pp.

———. *Journey to Awakening*. New York: Bantam Books, 1976. 395 pp.

———. *Miracle of Love*. New York: E. P. Dutton, 1979. 414 pp.

———. *The Only Dance There Is*. New York: Aronson, 1976. 180 pp.

★761★
Swami RAMA
Founder and Spiritual Director, Himalayan International Institute of Yoga Science and Philosophy
b. Oct. 26, 1925, Uttar Pradesh India

Swami Rama, founder and spiritual director of the Himalayan International Institute of Yoga Science and Philosophy, is perhaps best known for his contributions to the scientific study of yoga. (Swami is a title given to Indian renunciates rather than a name, and Rama is his monastic name.) Born into a learned Brahmin family in north India, he was orphaned at a young age and raised by his spiritual master, Sri Madhavananda Bharati. Rama was instructed in yoga and the Hindu tradition as a child, and he taught the Upanishads and Buddhist scriptures in various schools and monasteries while still a teenager. He studied psychology and philosophy in Varanasi and Prayag, India, and received a medical degree from Darbhanga Medical School in 1945.

In 1949 Swami Rama was asked to take on the duties of *Shankaracharya*, one of Hinduism's highest seats of spiritual authority, in south India. He accepted this position, but renounced it three years later. He then began to study Western philosophy and psychology, at the same time teaching yoga philosophy at European universities. In 1970, he became involved with a group investigating the voluntary control of involuntary bodily functions at the Menninger Clinic in the United States. He astounded researchers with such things as his ability to control his own brainwaves and his ability to temporarily stop the flow of blood through his heart. The research carried out on Swami Rama provided some of the foundational studies for the development of biofeedback therapy.

In 1971, Swami Rama established the Himalayan Institute in a Chicago suburb. The institute was initially an *ashram*, a monastic community and teaching center in the Hindu tradition. The institute

grew, and branch centers were established. After the headquarters moved to Honesdale, Pennsylvania, in 1978 it also became a school and research center, offering instruction in such things as stress management, and carrying out scientific research on breathing, pranayama, and other similar yoga-related subjects.

During the 1970s, Swami Rama authored and co-authored a number of books, such as *Lectures on Yoga* (1972); *Life Here and Hereafter* (1976); and *A Practical Guide to Holistic Health* (1978). He currently teaches at the Himalayan Institute. Since the mid 1970s the institute has been sponsoring a yoga congress every summer, a gathering that reaches out beyond the students of Swami Rama, and that has become a major annual event in the international yoga community. Among his other activities, the Swami has established a leper hospital in the Himalayan foothills, a school in New Delhi for the study and preservation of Indian culture, and a number of other centers and ashrams in Europe and South Asia.

Sources:

Ajaya, Swami. *Living with the Himalayan Masters: Spiritual Experiences of Swami Rama*. Honesdale, PA: Himalayan Institute, 1978. 490 pp.

Coon, Michael. "Swami Rama of the Himalayas." *Yoga Journal* (September-October, 1976): 8-11.

Green, Elmer. "Biofeedback for Mind-Body Self-Regulation: Healing and Creativity." *The Varieties of Healing Experience*. Los Alton, CA: The Academy of Parapsychology and Medicine, 1971.

Rama, Swami. *Freedom from Karma*. Prospect Heights, IL: Himalayan International Institute of Yoga Science and Philosophy of USA, 1973. 79 pp.

———. *Lectures on Yoga*. Arlington Heights, IL: Himalayan International Institute of Yoga Science and Philosophy, 1972. 126 pp.

———. *Life Here and Hereafter*. Glenview, IL: Himalayan International Institute of Yoga Science and Philosophy, 1976. 168 pp.

———. *A Practical Guide to Holistic Health*. Honesdale, PA: Himalayan International Institute of Yoga Science and Philosophy, 1978. 109 pp.

Webster, Katherine. "The Case Against Swami Rama of the Himalayas." *Yoga Journal* 95 (Nov.-Dec., 1990): 58-69, 92-94.

"Wisdom of the Himalayas Gains Western Popularity," *Hinduism Today* 11:10 (October, 1989): 1, 7.

★762★
Zen Master RAMA
Founder, Rama Seminars
b. Feb. 9, 1950, San Diego, California

Frederick Lenz, better known as Rama or as Zen Master Rama, is a New Age meditation teacher and founder of Rama Seminars. He was born in California, but when he was two, his parents moved to Connecticut where his father eventually became mayor of Stamford. He is a graduate of the University of Connecticut, and holds M.A. and Ph.D. (1979) degrees from the State University of New York. He became a disciple of **Sri Chinmoy**, a popular Indian teacher of meditation, and received the name Atmananda. While completing his graduate work, he taught at the New School for Social Research and wrote his first book, *Life Times, True Accounts of Reincarnation* (1979).

After completing his degree, Lenz moved to San Diego. In 1980, he opened a Chinmoy meditation center. However, he soon closed the center and established his own organization, named after the Hindu goddess Lakshmi, and set up headquarters in Los Angeles. He changed his name to Rama in 1983, closed Lakshmi, and in 1985 reestablished his group as Rama Seminars. The transformation of Lenz into Rama can be traced through the ads he placed in *Yoga Journal* and other New Age periodicals. In the earliest stage of his public activity, he listed his academic credentials and went by the name Frederick Lenz, Ph.D. In the middle stage, he dropped any mention of his scholarly achievements and replaced them with a list of his earlier incarnations as a Zen master and yoga teacher. He also used his religious name, Shri Atmananda. And in the final stage, he assumed the name Rama, and described himself as the ninth incarnation of Vishnu, a Hindu deity.

This transformation occurred within the short space of a few years. Rama's public activity involved the teaching of what he referred to as Tantric Zen, an approach to Zen that is more formless than Japanese Zen and that is in some ways related to Vajrayana (Tibetan) Buddhism (hence the appellation ''Tantric'').

Beginning in 1987, a number of former disciples publicly accused Rama of forcing sex and drugs upon them, and he became the subject of both negative media attention and of attacks by the anti-cult movement. Rama responded to these claims by asserting that they were simply fabricated by ex-lovers and disgruntled former followers. However by the end of the decade, the public activities of Rama Seminars had almost totally ceased.

Sources:

Lenz, Frederick. [Rama]. *The Last Incarnation: Experiences with Rama in California*. Malibu, CA: Lakshmi, 1983. 403 pp.
———. *Life-Times: True Accounts of Reincarnation*. Indianapolis, IN: The Bobbs-Merrill Company, 1979. 205 pp.
———. ''Statement to the Press.'' n.p. 1988. 7 pp.
Okerblon, Jim. ''Yuppie Guru.'' *The San Diego Union* (January 10, 1988).
Senders, Cherri, and Kathleen, Moloney. ''The Cosmic Seducer.'' *L. A. Weekly* (January 22-18, 1988): 17-24, 37.

★763★
Sri RAMAKRISHNA
Hindu Priest
b. Feb. 18, 1836, Kamarpukur India
d. Aug. 16, 1886, Calcutta India

Sri Ramakrishna never came to North America, nor was he a leader or member of any group which later established work there. Nevertheless, he was the inspiration for the movement of Hinduism to the United States and his work led directly to the formation of the first Hindu organization. Now known internationally as Sri Ramakrishna (an honorific title coupled with the name of two Hindu deities, Rama and Krishna) he was born Gadagkar Chattopadhyay, the son of Chandra Devi and Khudiram Chattopadhyay. His family was poor, and his hometown an obscure village. An unusual child, he was known to prefer meditation to study and often went into spontaneous altered states of consciousness. He was able to escape village life as a youth and moved to Calcutta, India to assist his brother who operated a Sanskrit school.

In 1955 Ramakrishna was offered the opportunity to become a priest in a temple dedicated to the goddess Kali. Not particularly eager to become a priest, he accepted since it would allow him time to meditate. Once installed in the temple, however, he developed a strong desire to experience union with Kali. A short time later he had a vision of her. His mystical experiences were viewed as odd by temple participants, and word reached his parents of their concern. They decided that a marriage would be the best cure, and arranged for him to marry Saradamani Devi, a five-year-old child.

In 1861 Ramakrishna resumed his priestly functions. In 1865 he began the quest for complete unity with God. At one point he remained in a trance for six months, at the end of which Kali appeared and told him, for the sake of humanity, to content himself with remaining on the threshold of relative consciousness, in a conscious waking state. He did as told but also began to explore the mystical aspects of Christianity and Islam which led him to conclude that there is a mystical harmony among all religions.

In 1872, now more mature, Ramakrishna's wife joined him at the temple and, despite their age difference, they had a satisfying, if platonic, relationship. By this time Ramakrishna had gained a reputation as a mystic. His behavior led some to consider him mentally ill, while others revered him as a god-intoxicated individual. Among the latter was a group of young men questing on the spiritual path, who gathered around him. Following Ramakrishna's death

in 1885 one of the men, Narendra Datta, later to become famous as **Swami Vivekananda** organized the others into a Ramakrishna Order of monks. This same Vivekananda would bring Hinduism to the West in 1893 and found the Vedanta Society to perpetuate the memory and teachings of Sri Ramakrishna.

Sources:

Gambhirananda, Swami. *History of the Ramakrishna Math and Mission*. Calcutta, India: Advaita Ashrama, 1957. 452 pp.
Isherwood, Christopher. *Ramakrishna and His Disciples*. New York: Simon and Schuster, 1965. 348 pp.
Nikhilananda, Swami. *Ramakrishna: Prophet of New India*. New York: Harper & Brothers, 1948. 304 pp.
Ramakrishna, Sri. *The Gospel of Ramakrishna*. Boston: Beacon Press, 1947. 436 pp.
Rolland, Romain. *The Life of Ramakrishna*. Calcutta, India: Advaita Ashrama, 1930.
Shepard, Leslie. *Encyclopedia of Occultism & Parapsychology*. 3 vols., 2nd. ed. Detroit: Gale Research Co., 1984-1985.

★764★
Sri RAMANA MAHARSHI
Indian Spiritual Teacher
b. Dec. 30, 1879, Tirucculi India
d. Apr. 14, 1950, Tiruvannamalai India

Sri Ramana Maharshi, one of the most noteworthy mystics of twentieth-century India, was the inspiration for Sri Ramanasramam (an ashram/center in Indian) and the various Sri Ramana Maharshi centers throughout the world. Ramana is a shortened form of his given name, Venkataraman (Sri and Maharshi are honorifics). He was the second son of a pleader in the local law court. While growing up, he was an indifferent student, more interested in athletics than academics. Young Ramana was also indifferent to spiritual matters. The first inkling of the future course of his life came at age 14 when a relative casually mentioned that he had just come from Arunchala, a hill regarded as a natural embodiment of God (a Shiva-Lingam). The name of the hill seemed to thrill him, but the magical effect of the name soon faded. Some time later, however, he happened to read the *Periapuranam*—a record of the lives of 63 famous Tamil Saints—and was deeply impressed.

The crucial incident in Ramana's transformation occurred in June of 1896 when he began to contemplate his own death. (His father had passed away when he was 12, and this may have helped incline him to reflect on his mortality.) He became convinced that the ''Self'' was the spirit rather than the body, and began to exhibit unusually intense religious behavior. He spent long hours worshiping in the local Meenakshi temple in Madurai, the city where his family had moved following the death of his father. Eventually he moved to Arunchala and became a *sadhu* (a renounced holy man). In the early years of his *tapas* (austerities), Ramana was an isolated sage, but his evident sanctity gradually began to attract seekers. Ganapathi Muni, a great scholar with disciples of his own, sought out guidance from Ramana Maharshi because the scholar's spiritual discipline was not producing marked results. After receiving a satisfying reply to his questioning, Ganapathi suggested to the devotees present that their teacher should be called Bhagavan Sri Ramana Maharshi, and henceforth he was addressed by that name. Ganapathi and his students became disciples of the saint (as considered by his followers), and Ganapathi Muni recorded the more important of Ramana's teachings in a work that was published as the *Sri Ramana Gita*. As Ramana wrote very little, most of his works are transcripts of talks or answers to questions put to him by disciples and inquirers.

As Ramana Maharshi became well-known, a large ashram grew up around him. His mother, who had at one time encouraged her son to return to worldly life, spent her last six years in the ashram as a simple devotee. After her death, Ramana had a temple of Sri

Matrubhuteswara (the Lord in the Form of the Mother) built over her grave.

In the latter decades of Ramana Maharshi's life, his fame was such that many foreigners would visit the ashram. Among the earliest accounts of the saint can be found in Paul Brunton's *Search in Secret India* (1934) and its sequel, *A Message from Arunchala* (1936). After the publication of Brunton's works, many other Westerners visited and wrote about Ramana Maharshi. Rider & Company, Brunton's publishers, released many titles about Ramana and published *The Collected Works of Ramana Maharshi*.

Sources:

Brunton, Paul. *A Message from Arunchala.* 1936. Reprint. New York: Samuel Weiser, 1971. 144 pp.
———. *Search in Secret India.* London Rider & Company, 1936.
Mahadevan, T. M. P. *Ramana Maharshi: The Sage of Arunchala.* London: George Allen & Unwin, 1977. 186 pp.
Osborne, Arthur. *Ramana Maharshi and the Path of Self-Knowledge.* New York: Samuel Weiser, 1970. 207 pp.
———., ed. *The Teachings of Ramana Maharshi.* 1962. Reprint. New York: Samuel Weiser, 1978. 200 pp.
Ramana Maharshi. *The Collected Works of Ramana Maharshi.* 20 vols. London: Rider & Company.
Sri Maharshi: A Short Life-Sketch. 5th ed. Tiruvannamalai, India: Sri Ramanasramam, 1973. 56 pp.

—James R. Lewis

★765★
RAMSEYER, Joseph Eicher
President, Missionary Church Association
b. Feb. 7, 1869, New Hamburg, Ontario, Canada
d. Jan. 25, 1944, Ft. Wayne, Indiana

Joseph Eicher Ramseyer, for over four decades the president of the Missionary Church Association (which merged in 1969 to become a part of the Missionary Church), was the son of Michael and Mary Ramseyer, both members of the Amish Mennonite Church. Following his father's death, the four-year-old Ramseyer moved in with his grandfather and grew up in rural Ontario. The family moved to Zurich, Ontario, in the 1880s, and it was there in 1885 that Ramseyer had a conversion experience to the Christian faith. He moved to Elkton, Michigan, in 1890, and soon afterward began to preach. He was ordained in 1892 by two ministers of the Defenseless Mennonites (now known as the Conference of the Evangelical Mennonite Church), an evangelistic movement founded in the 1860s among the Amish by **Henry Egly**.

Ramseyer served as pastor of the Defenseless Mennonite congregation in Elkton for several months but moved to Archbold, Ohio, as minister in 1893. He had a successful ministry at Archbold. However, he began to absorb holiness ideas from associates in the Christian and Missionary Alliance (CMA), especially the idea of a second work of grace (sanctification) which makes a believer perfect in love. In 1895 he became the first superintendent of the Bethany Bible Training Institute at Bluffton, Ohio. 1896 proved a watershed year for him. In August he was baptized by immersion (the Mennonites generally baptized by pouring) at a Christian and Missionary Alliance conference; in October he married Katherine Zeller; and in December he was excommunicated from the Defenseless Mennonites for the adoption of unacceptable holiness doctrines.

In 1898, with support of former members of both the Defenseless Mennonites and the Christian and Missionary Alliance, Ramseyer led in the formation of the Missionary Church Association. He was elected president and retained that post for the rest of his long life.

Ramseyer and his wife spent most of their time traveling, conducting evangelistic services, and establishing congregations. After his wife died in 1899 he continued to travel alone until 1902 when he married Mary Garth. In 1904 he led in the founding of the Fort Wayne Bible Institute to train Christian workers. In 1911 he became general superintendent of the school, and in 1912 president, a post he also carried until his death.

Ramseyer wrote little, but a number of his shorter works were compiled after his death into a volume, *Dwell Deep*.

Sources:

Lageer, Eileen. *Merging Streams.* Elkhart, IN: Bethel Publishing Company, 1979. 374 pp.
The Mennonite Encyclopedia. 4 vols. Scottdale, PA: The Mennonite Publishing House, 1955.
Ramseyer, Joseph E. *Dwell Deep.* Comp. by S. A. Witmer. Fort Wayne, IN: Fort Wayne Bible Institute, 1948.
Ramseyer, Mary Garth. *Joseph E. Ramseyer, "Yet Speaking".* Fort Wayne, IN: Fort Wayne Bible Institute, 1945. 295 pp.

★766★
RANDOLPH, Paschal Beverly
Founder, Fraternitas Rosae Crucis
b. Oct. 8, 1825, New York, New York
d. Jul. 29, 1875, Boston, Massachusetts

Paschal Beverly Randolph, founder of the occult Fraternitas Rosae Crucis (the Rosicrucian Fraternity, not to be confused with other Rosicrucian organizations), was the son of William Beverly Randolph and Flora Randolph. His father was from a prominent Virginia family, his mother a slave from Madagascar. Randolph, always embarrassed by his heritage, claimed that his mother was not a negro but a member of Madagascan royalty. When his mother died of small pox, Randolph was raised by one of her friends. At the age of 16 he ran away from home and went to sea. He sailed for five years until an injury prevented him from sailing again. He settled down to menial work until he finished his medical education. He would later make his living as a physician.

In 1850 Randolph traveled to Europe where he claimed he had been initiated in a Rosicrucian Fraternity while in Germany. On a second trip in 1854 he met occult magicians Eliphas Levi, Kenneth McKenzie, and Edward Bulwer-Lytton. Back in England in 1858 he was made the Supreme Grand Master of the Western World and a Knight of L'Ordre du Lis. Following this initial trip he founded the first modern Rosicrucian group in the United States.

As the Civil War approached, Randolph left the United States on a world tour. He returned to spend a year recruiting black soldiers for the Union Army. Then, after the fall of New Orleans, he moved there at the personal request of Abraham Lincoln to work among the freed slaves. During this time he wrote his first books, *Dealing with the Dead* (1861); *The Grand Secret, or Physical Love in Health and Disease* (1862); and *Ravalette, the Rosicrucian's Story* (1863). After the war, he was the only Black to join the train ride taking Lincoln's body back to Illinois for burial, but was put off the train by the offended Whites.

During the war, the fraternity had fallen upon bad times. Randolph moved to Boston and reorganized the work. New books appeared including *Seership* (1868) and *Love & the Master Passion* (1870). In 1872 he was arrested and tried on a charge of writing and circulating books on free love. The substance of the charges stemmed from the fact that he counseled patients on matters of marital bliss, and several of his books covered his beliefs on the subject. However, at the trial he was acquitted fully of all charges. Randolph did teach a form of sex magic as part of the instructions of the inner order of the Rosicrucian Fraternity, and his teachings would later be passed to sex magicians on the continent and return to the United States through the teachings of twentieth century magician **Aleister Crowley**.

In the end, Randolph shot and killed himself following his discovery of his wife's involvement in an adulterous relationship.

Sources:

Clymer, R. Swinburne. *Dr. Paschal Beverly Randolph and the Supreme Grand Dome of the Rosicrucians in France.* Quakertown, PA: Philosophical Publishing Company, 1929. 52 pp.

_____. *The Rose Cross Order.* Allentown, PA: Philosophical Publishing Co., 1916. 208 pp.

_____. *The Rosicrucian Fraternity in America.* 2 vols. Quakertown, PA: The Rosicrucian Foundation, 1935.

Randolph, Paschal Beverly. *Eulis: The History of Love.* Toledo, OH: Randolph Publishing Co., 1874. Rept. as: Eulis: Affectional Alchemy. Quakertown, PA: The Confederation of Initiates, 1903. 230 pp.

Ravalette: The Rosicrucian's Story. Quakertown, PA: Philosophical Publishing Company, 1863, 1939. 283 pp.

_____. *Seership: Guide to Soul Sight.* Quakertown, PA: Confederation of Initiates, 1868, 1930. 517 pp.

_____. *Soul! The World Soul.* Quakertown, PA: Confederation of Initiates, 1932. 246 pp.

★767★
RANSOM, Reverdy Cassius
Bishop, African Methodist Episcopal Church
b. Jan. 4, 1861, Flushing, Ohio
d. Apr. 22, 1959, Wilberforce, Ohio

Reverdy Cassius Ransom, the 48th bishop elected by the African Methodist Episcopal Church, was the son of Harriet Johnson and George Ransom. Though his ancestors had at one time been slaves, he was raised as a free man and experienced his first years of formal education in an elementary school run by the African Methodist Episcopal Church. In 1881 he entered Wilberforce University and transferred to Oberlin College in 1882. He stayed at Oberlin only a short time before returning to Wilberforce, where he completed his work and was awarded a B.D. in 1886. While in college, in 1883 he was licensed to preach by the Ohio Conference of the African Methodist Episcopal Church. He was ordained a deacon in 1886 and assigned to Altoona, Pennsylvania, as his first pastorate. His first wife having died, in 1886 he married Emma Sarah Connor. He became an elder in 1888 and moved to head the congregation at Alleghany, Pennsylvania. In 1890 he became pastor of North Street Church in Springfield, Ohio. His first book appeared at about this time, *School Days at Wilberforce* (1890).

While at his next pastorate in Cleveland, Ransom became deeply influenced by the deaconess movement which was growing among the women of the Lutheran and Methodist Episcopal Churches. In 1894 he organized the first board of deaconesses within African Methodism. In 1896 he moved to Chicago to pastor Bethel Church, one of the most prominent congregations in the denomination. He worked with Jane Addams and Hull House, and with her assistance purchased and opened the Institutional Church and Social Settlement. At one point during his pastorate, the new church center was bombed following Ransom's attack upon gambling in the community. He also used his influence to raise a regiment of black soldiers which fought in the Spanish-American War. From his Chicago pastorate, Ransom represented the African Methodist Episcopal Church at the Methodist Ecumenical Conference of 1901 in London.

In 1905 Ransom moved to Boston as pastor of Charles Street African Methodist Episcopal Church. While there his black militancy reached new levels. He joined the Niagara Movement founded by W. E. B. Du Bois and spoke out on the legitimacy of the black presence in America. He attacked Booker T. Washington's policies as ultimately undermining black progress. In 1907 he moved to New York City and in 1912 was elected editor of the *A.M.E. Review*, a symbol of the denomination's support of his militant stance. He served as the *Review*'s editor until 1924 when he was elected bishop, at the age of 63. He went on to serve the church as an active

bishop until 1952 and retired at the age of 91. During his years as bishop he authored several important books, including *The Negro: The Hope and Despair of Christianity* (1935) and his autobiography, *The Pilgrimage of Harriet Ransom's Son* [1949]. In the later 1940s he became the denominational historian and in that regard published *A Preface to the History of the A.M.E. Church* (1950). He retired to Wilberforce, Ohio, and died in his home.

Sources:

Harmon, Nolan B. *The Encyclopedia of World Methodism.* 2 vols. Nashville: United Methodist Publishing House, 1974.

Logan, Rayford W., and Michael R. Winston, eds. *Dictionary of American Negro Biography.* New York: W. W. Norton & Co.   1982. 680 pp.

Ransom, Reverdy C. *The Negro: The Hope and Despair of Christianity.* Boston: Ruth Hill, Publisher, 1935. 98 pp.

_____. *The Pilgrimage of Harriet Ransom's Son.* Nashville, TN: Sunday School Union, n.d. [1949]. 336 pp.

_____. *A Preface to the History of the A.M.E. Church.* Nashville, TN: A. M. E. Sunday School Union, 1950. 220 pp.

_____. *School Days at Wilberforce.* Springfield, OH: New Era, 1892. 66 pp.

★768★
RAUSCHENBUSCH, Walter
Church Historian and Social Gospel Theologian, North American Baptist Conference and Northern Baptist Convention
b. Oct. 4, 1861, Rochester, New York
d. Jul. 25, 1918, Rochester, New York

Walter Rauschenbusch, the leading exponent of what became known as the social gospel in the first decades of the twentieth century, was the son of Augustus and Caroline Rhomp Rauschenbusch. His parents had come to the United States in 1848 following the political upheavals that year in Germany, and his father became one of the founders of the North American Baptist Conference, a German-American Baptist fellowship. His father also became a professor at Rochester Theological Seminary, and Rauschenbusch was raised in a home that emphasized both piety and intellect. He attended a gymnasium in Germany for part of his college work, and following his graduation primus omnium in 1883, he returned to Rochester. In 1884 he received his A.B. degree from the University of Rochester and two years later finished his ministerial degree at the seminary. In 1886, following his graduation, he was ordained and accepted a call as pastor of the Second German Baptist Church in New York City.

During his 11 years in New York, Rauschenbusch worked with German-speaking immigrants. He also became acquainted with the new social thought of people such as Henry George, Edward Bellamy, Karl Marx, and Leo Tolstoi. In England in 1891 and 1892 he encountered Fabianism and the Salvation Army. The depression of 1893 served as a catalyst in forcing him to rethink his theological views in the light of immediate social crises. In 1897 he was called to succeed his father as professor of New Testament interpretation in the German department at the seminary in Rochester. He held the post until 1902, when he became professor of church history. However, it is neither as a New Testament interpreter nor church historian that he is best remembered.

At Rochester Rauschenbusch began to integrate all he had learned of social philosophy with the work of a fledgling movement to apply Christian teachings to the social context. The publication of Rauschenbusch's *Christianity and the Social Crisis* (1907) immediately thrust him into the limelight as the leading exponent of the social gospel, a perspective which set as the church's agenda the redemption of society as a whole through altering social structures in conformity with Christian ideals. His work took its lead from Jesus' concept of the kingdom of God. The first book was followed by *Prayers of the Social Awakening* (1910); *Christianizing the Social Order* (1912); *The Social Principles of Jesus* (1916); and

A Theology for the Social Gospel (1917). These volumes became so central to the developing social gospel movement that much of what had preceded them was simply forgotten. In 1892 he founded the Brotherhood of the Kingdom which gave some organizational focus to the movement.

While at Rochester, Rauschenbusch began a long-term association with the Northern Baptist Convention, the major organization serving Baptists outside of the South, and for many years served as the convention's secretary.

During World War I, Rauschenbusch felt the impact of anti-German sentiment in the United States. He continued his work for justice in the social order, however, and labored on behalf of peace. He died as the war was ending, but was unable to live to see the reconciliation of German-Americans with their fellow citizens.

Sources:

Dictionary of American Biography. 20 vols. and 7 supps. New York: Charles Scribner's Sons, 1928-1936, 1944-1981.
Rauschenbusch, Walter. *Christianity and the Social Crisis.* New York: Macmillan Company, 1907. 429 pp.
———. *Christianizing the Social Order.* Boston: Pilgrim Press, 1912. 493 pp.
———. *Prayers of the Social Awakening.* Boston: Pilgrim Press, 1910. 126 pp.
———. *The Social Principles of Jesus.* New York: Association Press, 1916. 198 pp.
———. *A Theology for the Social Gospel.* New York: Macmillan Company, 1917. 279 pp.

★769★
RAVENSONG, Cindy
Archpriestess, Aquarian Tabernacle Church
b. Aug. 30, 1953, Renton, Washington

Cindy Ravensong, also known as Cynthia Tibbetts Davis, is archpriestess of the Aquarian Tabernacle Church and a major force in developing that tradition. She was trained at Green River Community College in electro-mechanical drafting, a career she has since followed. She married Pierre C. Davis (also known as **Peter Pathfinder**), founder of the Aquarian Tabernacle Church, on April 30, 1988, and has since been responsible for formalizing the tradition's by-laws and liturgy (which had not been codified in spite of the Tabernacle's nine-year existence).

In addition to various positions of responsibility that accompany her role as archpriestess, Ravensong also teaches classes and helps manage cross-tradition events in the broader Seattle Pagan community. She is largely responsible for the conduct of the church's outreach activities, both in overseeing the open worship circles as well as the annual public festival gatherings. These gatherings include the Spring Mysteries Festival, a recreation of the Eleusinian Mysteries of ancient Greece held over the Spring Equinox; the Hecate's Sickle Gathering, a gathering focusing on introspection and self-evaluation held at Samhian (Halloween); and the Solitary convention, an exchange of information and knowledge between solitary Wiccan practitioners which is now being sponsored by the Aquarian Tabernacle Church each August at the church's retreat house.

The tradition's activities are centered at the church property in the mountains near Seattle where the tabernacle is based, although some festivals and worship gatherings are held at other locations more suitable to the large numbers of attendees. The archpriestess and archpriest reside on the church's property and operate the retreat house and other facilities, which are open to and supportive of the larger Pagan community in the Pacific Northwest.

★770★
REBLE, John H.
President, Evangelical Lutheran Synod of Canada
b. Dec. 14, 1887, Kropp-Schleswig Germany

John H. Reble, the first full-time president of the Evangelical Lutheran Synod of Canada, was raised in Germany. He obtained his college and seminary training at the Ebenezer Lutheran Theological Seminary at Kropp, Germany, which had been especially created to train pastors for work in North America. He graduated from the pro-seminary in 1903 and the seminary in 1906. He traveled to Canada a few years later and was ordained in 1909. His first parish was at Denbigh, Ontario. Reble was quickly seen as a leader by his colleagues. He worked on the founding of the synod's seminary at Waterloo (opened in 1911) and for many years sat on the board of the seminary and the associated college. In 1912 he moved to Linwood, and while there in 1923 was elected vice-president of the synod.

In 1925 Reble began a long pastorate at St. Paul's Lutheran Church in Hamilton, Ontario. That same year he was elected president of the synod, a post he would hold for over two decades. At the time of Reble's election, the Canada Synod was an integral part of the United Lutheran Church in America. In 1925 the Canadian work, which had previously been divided into an English-speaking and a German-speaking synod, was merged, this in part an effect of World War I which tended to hasten the decline of the use of the German language by church groups in North America. Among Reble's first tasks was the completion of the Anglicization process among Canadian Lutherans, and within a few years German was no longer spoken at sessions of the synod. At the same time there was a steady flow of immigrants from Germany who had to be integrated into the life of the church. That immigration also accounted for most of the steady growth experienced by the church during Reble's presidency. By 1945 the tasks as president of the synod required a full time person, and Reble resigned his parish to devote his energies to the increased demands of post-war leadership.

Reble cooperated in the formation of the Lutheran World Federation in 1947 and served as chairman for the national committee for Canada for the federation. In 1954 he retired from the presidency of the synod and moved to Germany to become the federation's chaplain to refugees. He returned to Canada in 1956 and spent his retirement years ministering at St. Peter's Lutheran Church in Kitchener as a pastor to new Canadians.

Sources:

Cronmiller, Carl R. *A History of the Lutheran Church in Canada.* Toronto: Evangelical Lutheran Synod of Canada, 1961. 288 pp.

★771★
REES, Seth Cook
Cofounder, Pilgrim Holiness Church
b. Aug. 6, 1854, Westfield, Indiana
d. May 22, 1933, Pasadena, California

Seth Cook Rees, one of the founders of the Pilgrim Holiness Church, was born into a Quaker family in Westfield, Indiana. Converted at the age of 19, he felt a call to the ministry and began to preach at local churches. His future wife recommitted herself to the faith under his preaching. Rees pastored a number of churches in the Midwest, and also served as a missionary to American Indians in Kansas for several years.

Rees experienced the "second work" of God's grace in 1883. The notion of this second work, called sanctification, is central to the Holiness movement. The theory postulates conversion as a "first work" which turns sinners toward God. Sanctification, the second step, purifies individuals of sin so that they can live perfected Christian lives. Following this experience, Rees became associated with the founder of the Christian and Missionary Alliance

(CMA), Albert Benjamin Simpson, preaching for Simpson at his summer camp and serving as president of the Michigan Auxiliary.

After pastoring a holiness congregation in Rhode Island for a few years, Rees became an evangelist when he met **Martin Wells Knapp** and joined Knapp to found the International Holiness Union and Prayer League. Rees led the union, both as its president and as its supervisor, and pushed for an international ministry. Knapp died in 1901 and some years later, following a disagreement over the use of donations solicited through the union's periodical, *The Revivalist*, Rees resigned and went back to evangelistic work.

While in Pasadena, California, serving as pastor of the University Church near Nazarene University, Rees became friends with the university's president, H. Orton Wiley. A conflict developed within the denomination connected with Wiley, however, and Rees and his congregation were excommunicated. As a result Rees founded the Pilgrim Church of California (originally called the Pentecostal Pilgrim Church) in 1917. Other disaffected Nazarenes joined the new body, and the church quickly became a denomination that was able to establish a Bible college, publish a periodical, and support foreign missionaries. The new denomination was further strengthened by its merger in 1922 with the Holiness Union that Rees had helped to found with Knapp. The merged body was named the Pilgrim Holiness Church. Some time later, in 1968, the denomination merged with the Wesleyan Methodist Church and took the name Wesleyan Church.

Sources:

Melton, J. Gordon. *Biographical Dictionary of American Cult and Sect Leaders*. Garland Reference Library of Social Science, vol. 212. New York: Garland Publishing, 1986.
Rees, Paul S. *Seth Cook Rees: The Warrior Saint*. Indianapolis, IN: 1934.
Rees, Seth C. *Back to the Bible: or, Pentecostal Training*. Cincinnati: 1902.
_____. *Burning Coals*. Cincinnati: M. W. Knapp, 1898. 84 pp.
_____. *Fire from Heaven*. Cincinnati: M. W. Knapp, 1899. 329 pp.
_____. *The Holy War*. Cincinnati: The Revivalist Office, 1904. 246 pp.
_____. *The Ideal Pentecostal Church*. Cincinnati: M. W. Knapp, 1897.
_____. *Miracles in the Slums*. Chicago: The Author, 1905. 301 pp.
_____. *Pentecostal Messengers*. Cincinnati: M. W. Knapp, 1898.
_____. *Wings in the Morning*. Greensboro, NC: W. R. Cox, 1926. 253 pp.
Thomas, Paul Westphal, and Paul William Thomas. *The Days of Our Pilgrimage*. Marion, IN: 1976.

★772★
REESE, Curtis Williford
Minister, American Unitarian Association
b. Sep. 3, 1887, Madison County, North Carolina
d. Jun. 5, 1961, Chicago, Illinois

Curtis Williford Reese, an early spokesperson for Humanism within the American Unitarian Association (AUA), was the son of Rachel Elizabeth Buckner and Patterson Reese. He attended Mars Hill College in his native North Carolina. He was raised a Southern Baptist and, following his decision to go into the ministry, attended the Southern Baptist Theological Seminary. He graduated in 1910. While at the seminary, he was ordained as a minister in the Southern Baptist Convention. After graduation he did a further year of post-graduate work at Ewing College in Illinois. In 1911 he became the pastor of the First Baptist Church in Tiffin, Ohio. While there, in 1913, he married Fay Rowlett Walker.

Beginning with his seminary days when the study of Biblical criticism began to erode his belief in an inerrant Bible, Reese nurtured doubts that led him step-by-step away from the Baptist faith of his youth. He absorbed the teachings of the social gospel, and became increasingly liberal in his thought. Finally, in 1913, he left the Baptists and converted to Unitarianism, becoming the pastor of the First Unitarian Church at Alton, Illinois. Two years later he moved to Des Moines, Iowa, and in 1919 he became the secretary of the Western Unitarian Conference, headquartered in Chicago. Enter-

ing a situation noted for its lack of growth, Reese was responsible for starting new congregations and claiming several important independent liberal congregations for the Unitarians. Possibly his greatest coup was the entrance of **Preston Bradley** into the Unitarian fold. While in Chicago he also briefly held two additional positions: editor of *Unity* (1925-1933) and president of Lombard College (1928-1929).

During the 1920s, Reese felt the freedom to articulate his form of what he termed a democratic humanism. He opposed the image of an autocratic God which he had left behind with the Baptists, and saw humanism as a liberating force both socially and intellectually. He presented this perspective in several books, *Humanism* (1926) and *Humanist Sermons* (1927). In 1930 he left his secretary's post and became the dean of the Abraham Lincoln Center, a facility known for its radical social reformist perspective. He remained at the center for 27 years. While there he became one of the 34 men who signed the *Humanist Manifesto* (1934) and during the rest of his life would be a leading spokesperson for the emerging Humanist movement and for the Humanist perspective as a valid option for Unitarians. His last book was a defense of the Humanist perspective, *The Meaning of Humanism* (1945). Though one of the founders of modern Humanism, Reese decided to stay with the Unitarians rather than align with any of the several Humanist organizations.

Sources:

Lyttle, Charles H. *Freedom Moves West*. Boston: Beacon Press, 1952. 198 pp.
Reese, Curtis W. *Humanism*. Chicago: Open Court Publishing Company, 1926. 85 pp.
_____. *The Meaning of Humanism*. Boston: Beacon Press, 1945. 53 pp.
_____, ed. *Humanist Sermons*. Chicago: Open Court Publishing Company, 1927. 262 pp.
Robinson, David. *The Unitarians and the Universalists*. Westport, CT: Greenwood Press, 1985. 368 pp.

★773★
REGAN, Agnes Gertrude
Writer and Educator, Roman Catholic Church
b. Mar. 26, 1869, San Francisco, California
d. Sep. 30, 1943, Washington, District of Columbia

Agnes Regan was a social reformer and Catholic educator. Born into a family of nine, she was the fourth child of Mary Ann Morrison Regan and James Regan (who changed his name from Santiago del Carmen O'Regan when he migrated to the United States). After a brief period in the gold fields, he was for 10 years the private secretary to Joseph S. Alemany, the first Catholic archbishop of San Francisco. Regan was later associated with the law firm of Tobin & Tobin through a brother-in-law, and was the director of the Hibernian Bank. He married Mary Ann Morrison, whose family had migrated from Ireland, in 1863.

Agnes Regan attended St. Rose Academy and the San Francisco Normal School, graduating from the latter in 1887. She then undertook a career in the public school system of San Francisco, beginning as an elementary school teacher from 1887 to 1900, then as a principal from 1900 to 1914, and then as a member of the board of education from 1914 to 1919. She also served on the city playground commission from 1912 to 1919 and worked to secure California's first pension act for teachers. In 1920 she represented the San Francisco diocese at the organizational meeting of the National Council of Catholic Women in the nation's capital, where she was elected a member of the board of directors and second vice-president. A few months later she moved to Washington after accepting an appointment as executive secretary.

The National Council of Catholic Women was a federation of women's organizations that reflected the increasing involvement of the Roman Catholic Church in social concerns. In its role as a coordinating organization, it supported research on social problems, disseminated information regarding impending social legislation, and worked for the representation of Catholic women on governmental agencies and committees that dealt with social issues. In her role as executive secretary of the National Council, Agnes Regan mobilized Catholics on such issues as urban housing, recreational facilities, religious education, immigration, child labor laws, birth control, and divorce. She also helped to organize training programs for immigrants, community centers, and welfare services. She proposed the Sheppard-Towner Act, which passed in 1921, providing maternity aid to indigent mothers.

Agnes Regan was also a key figure in the education of social workers. In 1921, the National Council assumed control of "Clifton," a school that had been established by the National Catholic War Council, and reorganized it as the National Catholic Service School for Women (later renamed the National Catholic School of Social Service). The earlier program was extended from six months to two years. People who successfully completed the program were awarded a certificate—or, for college graduates, a master's degree—from the Catholic University of America. Regan was appointed instructor in community organization at the school in 1922, and in 1925 she became assistant director. She held the latter position until her death. (She served for two years, from 1935 to 1937, as acting director). She also continued to work for the National Council, was a member of the White House Conference on Children in Democracy (1939-1940), served on the board of directors of the National Travelers' Aid Society, served on the advisory committee of the Federal Women's Bureau, and participated in the Catholic Association for International Peace. She received many honors, including the papal decoration Pro Ecclesia et Pontifice (1933).

Sources:
Dictionary of American Biography. 20 vols. and 7 supps. New York: Charles Scribner's Sons, 1928-1936, 1944-1981.
Lawler, L. R. *Full Circle: The Story of the National Catholic School of Social Service.* Washington: [D. A. Mohler], 1951. 200 pp.

★774★
REGARDIE, Francis Israel
Ritual Magician
b. Nov. 17, 1907, London United Kingdom
d. Mar. 10, 1985, Sedona, Arizona

Francis Israel Regardie, though not the leader of a group himself, emerged as the premier ceremonial magician and successor to **Aleister Crowley** during the late twentieth century. He was born Israel Regardie to orthodox Jewish parents. In 1921 the family moved to the United States and settled in Washington, D.C. There at the age of 15 Regardie first encountered the writings of Madame **Helena P. Blavatsky**, founder of the Theosophical Society, and began his long trek into and through the occult. Meanwhile he attended the Philadelphia School of Art. His reading led him to Hinduism and Buddhism and eventually to the writings of Aleister Crowley, who had written an early text on yoga. He met Karl Germer, Crowley's representative in America, and in 1928 sailed for Paris, where Crowley was then residing.

In Paris, Regardie assumed duties as Crowley's secretary. He worked with Crowley for several years, during which time they were expelled from France as undesirable aliens. After leaving Crowley Regardie began to write magical books himself, several of his earlier ones being classics in their own right, including *The Garden of Pomegranates* (1932) and *The Tree of Life: A Study in Magic* (1932). It was at this time he added Francis to his name. As a result of the books he met some members of the Stella Matutina, an offshoot of the Hermetic Order of the Golden Dawn, a ritual magic group. He joined. While enthused with the Golden Dawn rituals, he despaired of the corrupt nature of the order's leadership.

This led him to break his oath of secrecy and in two books reveal everything to the public. The first, *My Rosicrucian Adventure* (1935), described the inner workings of the order. He then returned to America in 1937 and there published the entire texts of the rituals in a four-volume set, *The Golden Dawn* (1938-1940).

Following his adventure into magic, Regardie turned to psychology. He took a degree at the Chiropractic College of New York (1941), studied with psychoanalyst Nandor Fordor, and joined the Army (1942-1945). After the war the earned a degree in psychology, moved to Los Angeles, and established an office as a chiropractor and psychoanalyst. He became enthusiastic with the ideas about healing energies of the radical psychoanalyst Wilhelm Reich.

Regardie did little with magic for the next two decades, but as new interest developed in the 1960s, he began to slowly emerge again. *The Tree of Life* was reprinted in 1969. *The Eye in the Triangle*, a description of his encounters with Crowley, came out the next year. Over the rest of his life he wrote a number of books and took a few students, though as the occult revived in the 1970s and 1980s, many sought his guidance. Some of his final students have started a new set of Golden Dawn oriented temples. His books have been kept in print by Llewellyn Publications and Falcon Press.

Sources:
Regardie, Israel. *The Eye in the Triangle.*London: Rider.
———. *The Garden of Pomegranates.* St. Paul, MN: Llewellyn Publications, 1932, 1970. 160 pp.
———. *My Rosicrucian Adventure.* Chicago: Aries Press, 1936. 144 pp.
———. *The Tree of Life.* New York: Samuel Weiser, 1932, 1969. 284 pp.
———. *What Every One Should Know About the Golden Dawn.* Phoenix, AZ: Falcon Press, 1983. 186 pp.
———, ed. *The Golden Dawn.* 4 vols. Chicago: Aries Press, 1938-1940.
Shepard, Leslie. *Encyclopedia of Occultism & Parapsychology.* 3 vols., 2nd. ed. Detroit: Gale Research Co., 1984-1985.
Suster, Gerald. *Crowley's Apprentice.* London: Rider, 1989. 182 pp.

★775★
REMEY, Charles Mason
Founder, Orthodox Abha World Faith
b. May 15, 1874, Burlington, Iowa
d. Feb. 4, 1974, Florence Italy

Charles Mason Remey, founder of the Orthodox Abha World Faith, was the eldest son of a distinguished Civil War veteran, Rear Admiral George Collier Remey. While pursuing a career in architecture in Paris, Charles Remey encountered a Baha'i group which he subsequently joined. In 1901 he met **Abdu'l-Baha**, son of **Baha'u'llah** and leader of the Baha'i Faith.

Returning to the United States, Remey taught at George Washington University for a few years before leaving to work as a commercial architect, a profession that gave him time to propagate his adopted faith. After touring Baha'i communities in the Middle East, he composed an account of his journey, *The Baha'i Movement* (1912), at Abdu'l-Baha's request. Remey was the source of many other English-language works at a time when Baha'i was an unfamiliar religion in Europe and America, works such as *Observations of a Baha'i Traveller* (1914); *Twelve Articles Introductory to the Study of the Baha'i Teachings* (1925); and *Universal Consciousness of the Baha'i Religion* (1925). Abdu'l-Baha also asked him to be the architect for the temple on Mount Carmel in Israel, and Remey later designed a number of other Baha'i temples.

Shoghi Effendi, remembered as the Guardian, assumed control of the Baha'i movement upon the death of his grandfather, Abdu'l-Baha. Under the new administration, Remey, already an important Western convert, became one of the principal leaders of the Baha'i faith. In 1951 Effendi established an administrative body, the International Baha'i Council, to which he appointed Remey as president. Effendi also transformed the Hands of the Cause, a group of leading Baha'is who had been singled out by Abdu'l-Baha into a formal ruling body that included Remey among its members.

At the time of Effendi's death in 1957, no successor had been designated, and there was no obvious family member to whom the leadership should pass. Remey was one of nine Baha'i leaders, members of the Hands of the Cause, who together assumed the role of Guardian until a new ruling body, the Universal House of Justice, was elected in 1963. In the interim, however, Remey came to hold the view that the role of Guardian had been intended by Abdu'l-Baha to be an ongoing position—a position for which he, Remey, was the obvious choice. The other members of the Hands of the Cause disagreed with him, and excommunicated Remey from the faith. Remey gathered his supporters and organized the Orthodox Abha World Faith, a body that itself splintered into three new groups after Remey's death in 1974.

Sources:

Melton, J. Gordon. *Biographical Dictionary of American Cult and Sect Leaders*. Garland Reference Library of Social Science, vol. 212. New York: Garland Publishing, 1986.

Remey, Charles Mason. *The Baha'i Movement*. Washington, DC: The Author, 1912. 115 pp.

_____. *Baha'i Reminiscences, Dairy, Letters and Other Documents*. Washington, DC: The Author, 1940.

_____. *Extracts from Daily Observation of the Baha'i Teachings*. New York: Joel Bray Marangella, [1960] 144 pp.

_____. *Observations of a Baha'i Traveler*. Washington, DC: The Author, 1914. 133 pp.

_____. *Twelve Articles Introductory to the Study of the Baha'i Teachings*. New York: Baha'i Publishing Committee, 1925. 184 pp.

_____. *Universal Consciousness of the Baha'i Religion*. Florence, Italy: Tipografia Sordomuti, 1912, 1925. 60 pp.

Spataro, Francis Cajetan. *Charles Mason Remey and the Baha'i Faith*. New York: Carleton Press, 1987. 40 pp.

_____. *The Lion of God*. Bellerose, NY: The Remey Society, 1981.

_____. *The Remeum*. Bellerose, NY: The Author, 1980.

★776★
REU, Johann Michael
Theologian, Evangelical Lutheran Synod of Iowa
b. Nov. 16, 1869, Diebach Germany
d. Oct. 14, 1943, Dubuque, Iowa

Johann Michael Reu, an American Lutheran theologian, grew up in Germany and was educated in the Latin School at Oettingen and the Mission Seminary at Neuendettelsau. The seminary was the product of a neo-Lutheran Revival in Germany in reaction to the forced merger of Lutheran and Reformed churches in Prussia. Leading the revival was Wilhelm Loehe (1808-1872) who stressed allegiance to the Lutheran Church and its confessions, which he saw as being in exact conformity to New Testament thought and practice. He also stressed the importance of the liturgy and the role of the ordained ministry.

Loehe had sent a number of his graduates to America, many of whom affiliated with the Lutheran Church-Missouri Synod. However, Loehe had come to disagree with the congregational polity of the synod. The Evangelical Lutheran Synod of Iowa was formed in 1853 by Loehe supporters. Reu, one of the last trainees sent to America by Loehe, aligned himself with his American supporters. Reu arrived in the United States in 1889 and was soon ordained as a minister. He served a church in Illinois for a year, but in 1889 was called as a professor to Wartburg Seminary, the school of the Iowa Synod located at Dubuque, Iowa. The school, founded in 1853, had just relocated to Dubuque.

During his lengthy tenure at Wartburg, Reu taught every subject in the curriculum but clearly excelled in systematic theology and Luther studies. He is particularly remembered for his scholarly contribution to the understanding of Luther's use of the Bible and his catechism. He authored an 11-volume study of Luther's Cate-

chism, for which he was finally awarded a Doctor of Theology degree from the Friedrich Alexander University at Erlangen, Germany. In 1904 he became editor of the seminary's journal, *Kirchliche Zeitschrift*, which he edited for 40 years.

While Reu's theological work (mostly written in German) remained largely relevant to the Lutheran scholarly community, his church work had a deep influence on the shape of Lutheran organizational life in America, especially the merger of the many independent Lutheran church groups in the first half of the twentieth century. By 1918, for example, the need for cooperative action by Lutherans became evident, and Lutherans of a variety of perspectives formed the National Lutheran Council while the more liberal synods merged to form from the United Lutheran Church. Reu emerged as a major conservative critic of the council, protesting that its activities implied recognition of doctrinally loose Lutheran synods. Following World War I, Iowa formed its own post-war relief program. During the next decade Reu worked in a variety of synodical committees leading to the merger of the Iowa Synod into the more conservative American Lutheran Church in 1930. (That church is now an integral part of the Evangelical Lutheran Church in America formed in 1988).

Reu also had an important role to play in the developing stand of the American Lutheran Conference, a cooperative Lutheran association which existed between the very conservative Missouri Synod and the more liberal United Lutheran Church. While questioning the orthodoxy of the United Lutheran Church, Reu was seen as a "liberal" voice opposing the attempt to have the conference adopt a statement supporting Biblical inerrancy on other than doctrinal issues.

Sources:

Nelson, E. Clifford, ed. *The Lutherans in North America*. Philadelphia: Fortress Press, 1975. 541 pp.

Reu, J. Michael. *The Augsburg Confession*. Chicago: Wartburg Press, 1930. 258 pp.

_____. *Christian Ethics*. Columbus, OH: Lutheran Book Concern, 1935. 482 pp.

_____. *Luther and the Scriptures*. Columbus, OH: Wartburg, OH: 1949. 211 pp.

_____. *Lutheran Dogmatics*. 2 vols. Dubuque, IA: Wartburg Seminary, 1941-1942.

_____. *Lutheran Faith and Life*. Columbus, OH: Lutheran Book Concern, 1935. 160 pp.

_____. *Thirty-five Years of Luther Research*. Chicago: Wartburg, 1917. 155 pp.

Weiblen, W. H. "J. Michael Reu—A Self-Made Theologian." *Currents in Theology and Mission* 16, 5 (October 1989): 341-347.

★777★
REVEL, Bernard
Orthodox Jewish Educator
b. Sep. 17, 1885, Oren Lithuania
d. Dec. 2, 1940, New York, New York

Bernard Revel, the president of Rabbi Isaac Elchanan Theological Seminary (now Yeshiva University) during the 1920s and 1930s, was the son of a Jewish rabbi, Nahum Sheraga Revel, and Leah Gitilevitz Revel. Showing an ability and interest in Talmudic studies, he was sent to the Yeshiva at Telsche, Lithuania. He migrated to the United States in 1906 and attended successively the University of Pennsylvania, New York University (M.A., 1909), and Dropsie College (Ph.D., 1911). In 1909 he married Sarah Travis. In 1912 he became a United States citizen.

After obtaining his doctorate, Revel moved to Tulsa, Oklahoma, and went into business refining natural gas. At the request of several of the leaders of Orthodox Judaism, however, he gave up his business to move to New York City to become president of the Rabbi Isaac Elchanan Theological Seminary, popularly called the Yeshiva. The school had been established by Orthodox Jews primarily of an eastern European background and had barely survived over the years. Revel set about the task of building it into a stable institution that could serve future generations. He soon responded to student suggestions that the curriculum be broadened to include secular subjects, most notably Jewish history and Hebrew literature. He then added several adjunct institutions, an academic high school and, in 1915, a Talmudic Academy. In 1928 Yeshiva College, a liberal arts institution, was chartered.

Revel believed that only a combination of traditional training and contemporary enlightened studies could produce the rabbinical and lay leadership necessary for the survival and progress of the Orthodox community in the American setting. Under the program the percentage of American-born students steadily increased. So did the debts. Thus in the early 1920s Revel took a leave of absence to return to business in Oklahoma with the hope of raising enough money to undergird the school. He was unsuccessful and the school faced lean years until revived by the prosperity of the late 1920s. Unfortunately, it was immediately threatened by the financial disaster of 1929. Revel was able to keep its doors open through the recovery of the 1930s.

In 1937 Revel led in the founding of a graduate school for Jewish and Semitic studies which offered a doctorate of Hebrew literature. This school was later renamed the Bernard Revel Graduate School. Revel died in 1940 and thus did not live to see the reorganization of what he had created as the Yeshiva University, still the academic center of North American Orthodoxy. Revel had served as the honorary president of the Union of Orthodox Rabbis, the Orthodox rabbinical association composed primarily of Eastern European Jews.

Sources:

Dictionary of American Biography. 20 vols. and 7 supps. New York: Charles Scribner's Sons, 1928-1936, 1944-1981.
Goldman, Alex J. *Giants of Faith.* New York: Citadel Press, 1964. 349 pp.
Hoenig, S. B. *Rabbinic and Research: the Scholarship of Dr. Bernard Revel.* New York: Yeshiva University, 1968. 167 pp.
Landman, Isaac, ed. *Universal Jewish Encyclopedia.* 10 vols. New York: The Universal Jewish Encyclopedia, 1940.
Revel, Bernard. *Karaite Halakah and Its Relation to Sadducean, Samaritan and Philonian Halakah.* Philadelphia: Pressof Cahan Printing, 1913. 88 pp.
Singer, Isidore, ed. *The Jewish Encyclopedia.* New York: KTAV Publishing House, 1964.

★778★
REVELL JR., Fleming Hewitt
Fundamentalist Christian Publisher
b. Dec. 11, 1849, Chicago, Illinois
d. Oct. 11, 1931, Yonkers, New York

Fleming Hewitt Revell, Jr., a Presbyterian layman and the founder of the Fleming H. Revell Publishing Company, was the son of Fleming Hewitt Revell, Sr., and Emma Manning Revell, first generation immigrants who had moved to America from London in the 1840s. Arriving in Chicago in 1849, the senior Revell worked as a boat builder on Lake Michigan. The family was poor, and young Fleming, the only male child, left school at the age of nine to go to work. Eventually, Revell's sister Emma would marry evangelist **Dwight L. Moody**. Revell was deeply influenced by Moody's sermons and advice.

As a result of listening to Moody, in 1869 Revell began a monthly periodical, *Everybody's Paper*, which became his first publishing venture. He traveled the Midwest selling subscriptions. The burgeoning business was wiped out by the Chicago fire of 1871, but with Moody's assistance he began anew. In 1872 he married Josephine Barbour. Over the next decade he began to specialize in the publication of books by Moody and his evangelical colleagues. He published more than 100 titles during the 1870s, and went on to

become one of the largest publishers of religious literature of the century. A branch was opened in New York in 1887, and branches opened in Toronto, London, and Edinburgh before the end of the century. Revell moved to New York in 1906 and soon moved the firm's headquarters there.

Revell developed a keen sense of the needs of the growing evangelical-fundamentalist churches and emerged as a master of marketing. He carried a wide range of books, pamphlets, and tracts, as well as related paraphernalia such as maps, banners, and picture cards. The company moved into the Sunday school arena and developed a complete collection of literature for youth. As a result of the growth of his business, Revell became quite wealthy. He contributed large sums to his main charities, which included Moody's schools at Northfield, Massachusetts, the American Mission to Lepers, and the educational and mission concerns of the Presbyterian Church. He retired in the 1920s and turned the business over to his son.

Sources:

Dictionary of American Biography. 20 vols. and 7 supps. New York: Charles Scribner's Sons, 1928-1936, 1944-1981.

★779★
REVELS, Hiram Rhoades
Politician, Educator, and Minister, African Methodist Episcopal Church
Politician, Educator, and Minister, Methodist Episcopal Church
b. Sep. 1, 1822, Fayetteville, North Carolina
d. Jan. 16, 1901, Aberdeen, Mississippi

Hiram Rhoades Revels, an educator, U.S. senator, and minister of the African Methodist Episcopal Church, was of mixed African and Croatian Indian descent and was born to free parents in Fayetteville, North Carolina. He studied at a Quaker seminary in Liberty, Indiana, and at Knox College in Galesburg, Illinois. Entering the ministry of the African Methodist Episcopal Church in 1845, he taught school, lectured, and preached in the Midwest for the next eight years. He eventually settled in Baltimore, Maryland, where he pastored a church and served as the principal of a school for Blacks.

After the outbreak of the Civil War, Revels helped to recruit Blacks for the Union Army in Missouri and Maryland. He became chaplain of a black Mississippi regiment in 1864 and, for a short time, served as provost marshal of Vicksburg. He organized several African Methodist Episcopal Church congregations in Jackson, and then settled at Natchez in 1866. He joined the Methodist Episcopal Church in 1868 and in the same year was elected alderman.

Revels entered politics reluctantly, concerned about the potential for racial friction and the possibility that his political activities might interfere with his religious activities. However, he was able to win the support of Whites and to keep his church work separate from politics. He was elected to the state Senate in 1869, and was elevated to the U.S. Senate by the legislature the next year. He served in the Senate until March 4, 1871.

After leaving the Senate, Revels was elected president of Alcorn University, a newly established black school. In the wake of the sudden death of James Lynch, he served a few months as interim secretary of state of Mississippi. He lost his Alcorn position as a result of his dissenting from the activities of the state's "carpetbag" (opportunistic) government, but was restored to that position in 1875 after elections changed the state's administration. He served at Alcorn until 1883.

Revels transferred into the Mississippi Conference of the Methodist Episcopal Church in 1875, and was appointed to Holly Springs. He served as a minister without giving up the presidency of Alcorn until 1880. After retiring from Alcorn, he was presiding elder in what became the Upper Mississippi Conference. He passed away while attending the session of the annual conference at Aberdeen.

Sources:

Dictionary of American Biography. 20 vols. and 7 supps. New York: Charles Scribner's Sons, 1928-1936, 1944-1981.
Harmon, Nolan B. *The Encyclopedia of World Methodism.* 2 vols. Nashville: United Methodist Publishing House, 1974.

★ 780 ★
RICE, John Richard
Independent Fundamentalist Baptist Evangelist and Author
b. Dec. 11, 1895, Cook County, Texas
d. Dec. 29, 1980, Murfreesboro, Tennessee

John Richard Rice, an independent Baptist evangelist best known as the founding editor of *The Sword of the Lord*, a weekly newspaper, was the son of Sallie Elizabeth LaPrade and William H. Rice. He grew up in rural Texas in a pious Southern Baptist family. He had his initial experience of salvation at the age of 12 and joined a nearby Baptist congregation. He was educated in the local schools and as a young man was able to obtain a teacher's certificate. He began to teach school, which in his part of the state only lasted four months of the year. In 1916 he entered Decatur Baptist College in Decatur, Texas, but in 1918 was drafted into the Army. Discharged in 1919 he went to Baylor University from which he graduated in 1920. In the spring of 1921 he was in attendance at the University of Chicago, intent upon pursuing a secular career when it became clear to him that he was destined for the ministry. He dropped out of school and returned to Texas. He married Lloys McClure Cooke and a short time later entered Southwestern Baptist Theological Seminary to prepare himself as a minister with the Southern Baptist Convention.

Eager to begin full-time ministry, Rice did not finish his seminary curriculum. In 1923 he became the assistant pastor at Plainview, Texas, and the following year the senior pastor at Shamrock, Texas. In college he had already distinguished himself as a speaker, and in 1926 he left the pastorate for the work of a full-time evangelist. He settled in Fort Worth, Texas, where he was brought into contact with **J. Frank Norris**, pastor of First Baptist Church, who was already having trouble with the convention. Rice started a radio show on Norris' station. His association with Norris coupled with his own criticisms of the convention led inevitably to his own break with the Southern Baptists in 1927.

In 1932 Rice organized the Fundamentalist Baptist Church of Oak Cliff (a section of Dallas), and in 1934 issued the first copies of *The Sword of the Lord*. About this time he broke with Norris, accusing him of dictatorial policies. In 1939 he moved *The Sword of the Lord* to Wheaton, Illinois, and returned to full-time evangelism. He had already expanded his literature ministry to include what would become over 100 books and booklets. His most popular publication was an early pamphlet, *What Must I Do to Be Saved*, over 40 million copies of which have been printed in more than 40 languages. Over 60 million copies of his books have been printed in some 37 languages. His most popular books were *Prayer—Asking and Receiving* (1942); *The Home: Courtship, Marriage and Children* (1945); *The Power of Pentecost* (1949); and *Bible Facts About Heaven* (1950).

Following World War II Rice began to organize national evangelism conferences, the first being held at Winona Lake, Indiana, at the old campgrounds associated with **William A. "Billy" Sunday**. As his work spread, Rice became the center of controversies with other evangelicals. For example, he attacked **Lewis Sperry Chafer**, the president of Dallas Theological Seminary. Chafer, in his book *True Evangelism*, had stated his objections to various mass evangelism methods, methods Rice used as a matter of course. The most serious controversy centered upon **Billy Graham**, whom

Rice condemned for cooperating with modernist ministers in the furtherance of his evangelistic campaigns. The Graham controversy cost Rice over two million of his five million subscribers. He spent over a decade rebuilding his paper's circulation.

In 1963 Rice moved his headquarters to Murfreesboro, Tennessee, and during the last years of his life (to within a few weeks of his death) continued his evangelism. His paper became a major factor in the promotion of independent Baptist churches.

Sources:

Barlow, Dr. Fred M. *John R. Rice: Giant of Evangelism.* Murfreesboro, TN: Sword of the Lord Publishers, 1983. 29 pp.
Rice, John R. *Eternal Retribution.* Wheaton, IL: Sword of the Lord Publishers, 1951. 128 pp.
_____. *Immanuel: "God With Us".* Wheaton, IL: Sword of the Lord Publications, 1950. 157 pp.
_____. *Prayer—Asking and Receiving.* Wheaton, IL: Sword of the Lord Publishers, 1942. 328 pp.
_____. *Revival Appeals.* Wheaton, IL: Sword of the Lord Publishers, 1945. 216 pp.
_____. *When Skeletons Come Out of the Closets!* Wheaton, IL: Sword of the Lord Publishers, 1943. 191 pp.
Sumner, Robert L. *Man Sent from God: A Biography of Dr. John R. Rice.* Murfreesboro, TN: Sword of the Lord Publishers, 1959. 323 pp.

★ 781 ★
RICHMOND, Cora Lodencia Veronica Scott
Medium, National Spiritualist Association
b. Apr. 21, 1840, Cuba, New York
d. Jan. 3, 1923, Chicago, Illinois

Cora Lodencia Veronica Scott Richmond, one of the most famous American Spiritualist mediums of the nineteenth century, was the daughter of Lodencia Veronica Butterfield and David W. Scott. She was born with a "veil," an occurrence which in popular lore is believed to portend a person with supernatural gifts, hence she was named Cora, a seeress. Her father also insisted upon naming her with her mother's names, which she disliked and acknowledged only as initials. In her adult life, she was generally referred to as Cora L. V. Richmond. During the 1840s, Richmond's Presbyterian parents developed an interest in Spiritualism. In 1851, the family moved first to Hopedale, Massachusetts, where Universalist minister Hosea Ballou had started a Spiritualist-influenced colony, and then on to Waterloo, Wisconsin, where a Midwestern branch had been formed.

At Waterloo, Cora's gifts as a medium began to materialize, and a mild interest in Spiritualism became a passion within the family. Cora's mother and several aunts also became mediums. Cora began platform work (demonstrating her mediumistic prowess before a public audience) when she was 11. In 1853 she moved to Buffalo, New York, as a medium for a small church. Two years later she moved to New York City. There she married a magnetist (a practitioner of hypnotism) named Hatch, but was soon granted a divorce because of his physically abusing her. At the age of 16 she moved to Baltimore where she stayed until 1873 when she moved to England. While in Baltimore she published a 250-page poem, *Hesperia*.

Richmond's tour of England stretched from six months to two years. She had large audiences impressed both by her speaking ability and her remarkable demonstrations of trance phenomenon. She met most of the leading lights of British Spiritualism including a young **Wilberforce J. Colville**, a medium with whom she was to appear when he visited America. In 1878 she married William Richmond, a businessman who became her publisher. They settled in Chicago where Cora pastored a church.

Richmond pastored in Chicago for the rest of her life. Her time there was punctuated by the formation of the National Spiritualist Association which she and **Harrison D. Barrett** had helped estab-

RELIGIOUS LEADERS OF AMERICA, First Edition

lish. At its first meeting she was elected vice-president, a post she held for five years. That same year she addressed the World's Parliament of Religions on behalf of the Spiritualist community. Richmond also wrote two books during her Chicago years: *The Soul in Human Embodiments* (1887) and *Psychosophy*, which appeared in two volumes (1888, 1915).

Sources:

Barrett, Harrison D. *Life Work of Cora L. V. Richmond*. Chicago: Hack & Anderson, 1895. 759 pp.
Cutlip, Audra. *Pioneers of Modern Spiritualism*. 4. vols. Milwaukee, WI: National Spiritualist Association of Churches, n.d.
Richmond, Cora L. V. *Psychosophy*. Chicago: The Author, 1888, 1915. 436 pp.
_____. *The Soul in Human Embodiments*. Chicago: The Spiritualist Publishing Co., 1887. 118 pp.

★782★
RIEL, Louis David
Prophet, Eglise Catholique Apostolique et Vitale des Montagnes Lumineuses
b. Oct. 22, 1844, Red River Settlement Canada
d. Nov. 16, 1885, Regina, Saskatchewan, Canada

Louis David Riel, a leader among the Metis (descendants of mixed marriages between the Canadian Indians and Whites) and founder of a new religion that grew out of their struggle for status in Canadian society, was the son of Louis Riel and Julie Lagimodiere. His family were devout Roman Catholics and Riel was confirmed by Bishop **Alexandre Antonin Tache**. Tache also arranged for Riel's education in Quebec beginning at St. Boniface College in 1858 and later theological studies at the College de Montreal. Riel did not finish his studies for the priesthood. He was dismissed from the school for repeated infractions of the rules shortly before his projected graduation in 1865. He studied law for a while before returning to his hometown in 1868.

Riel emerged from obscurity in 1869, just as Manitoba (then called Rupert's Land) was being transferred from the control of the Hudson Bay Company to Canada. The Metis, most members of the Roman Catholic Church, feared an influx of Protestants. The college educated Riel immediately became a leader of the Metis' protest and in 1869 was named president of a provisional government through which the Metis attempted to keep Manitoba independent. When the Metis were defeated by Canadian forces sent to quell the rebellion, Riel fled to North Dakota. In the agreements following the rebellion, the self-exiled Riel never received a pardon. Four years later he was elected to Parliament, but was never really able to function as an arrest warrant was issued for him.

In 1874 in Washington, D.C. Riel had a series of visionary mystical experiences which led him to assume the role of the "Prophet of the New World". It was at this time he added "David" to his name. Riel's self-proclaimed prophetic task was nothing less than the renovation the Roman Catholic Church. The vision called upon him to found a successor organization, the Eglise Catholique Apostolique et Vitale des Montagnes Lumineuses. His bizarre behavior following the visions led to his confinement to a mental institution for several years. He used the time to think out his new perspective, which included an understanding of the Indians as the descendants of the ancient Jews, whom he would convert to Christianity. Together the Metis (already Christians) and the newly converted Indians would establish an independent nation. Out of the hospital, Riel did not immediately act out his vision. Rather, he settled in Montana. In 1881 he married Marguerite Monet and two years later became an American citizen.

Only in 1884 did Riel return to Canada to assist the Metis in settling their claims from previous years. While there Riel again found himself leading a Metis revolt, during which time he actually tried to establish the new church which he had created in his mind.

Among initial followers, he instituted sabbatarianism (worship on Saturday) and organized a totally new ecclesiastical administration. The second rebellion collapsed even more quickly than the first. Riel was captured, tried, and executed several months later. Before his death he formally recanted the ideas of his new church, though his people seem to have continued to hold many of the ideas concerning his prophetic mission.

Sources:

Charlebois, P. *The Life of Louis Riel*. Toronto: New Canada Pubs, 1975. 254 pp.
Flanagan, Thomas. *Louis 'David' Riel: Prophet of the New World*. Toronto: University of Toronto Press, 1979.
_____. *Riel and the Rebellion: 1885 Reconsidered*. Saskatoon, Saskatchewan: Western Producer Prairie Books, 1983. 177 pp.
Stanley, George F. G. *Louis Riel*. Toronto: Ryerson Press, 1963. 433 pp.

★783★
RILEY, William Bell
Fundamentalist Baptist Minister and Educator
b. Mar. 22, 1861, Green County, Indiana
d. Dec. 5, 1947, Golden Valley, Minnesota

William Bell Riley, leading fundamentalist educator and minister, was born just as the Civil War began, the son of Branson Radish Riley and Ruth Ann Jackson Riley. His father's pro-slavery sentiments prompted him to move the family to Kentucky soon after young William was born. Riley grew up in Kentucky. He had a rather quiet Christian conversion experience at the age of 17. He originally developed plans for a law career but felt a persistent call to the ministry to which he finally surrendered. To raise money for school he worked as a tenant farmer for his father. He attended Valparaiso (Indiana) Normal School and Hanover College, a Presbyterian school in Indiana. He was granted his A. B. degree in 1885. He spent the next three years at Southern Baptist Theological Seminary, graduating in 1888.

Riley served successive Baptist pastorates in Illinois, Indiana and Kentucky. His early pastoral years were highlighted by his marriage to Methodist Lillian Howard and his baptism of her six weeks later. In 1893 he moved to Chicago and began a four year pastorate of Calvary Baptist Church, before moving to First Baptist Church in Minneapolis in 1897, where he was to remain for the rest of his life.

By the time Riley moved to Minnesota, he had become concerned about the neglect that small rural churches faced. Riley opened a school, the Northwestern Bible and Missionary Training School, primarily to prepare pastors to serve rural churches. He also became concerned about the growth of modernism in the Northern Baptist Convention. As the leader of a prominent and growing congregation, he was in a position to act on his concerns. He entered vigorously into the controversy that was to dominate early twentieth century Baptist life. He published two books, *The Crisis of the Church* (1914) and *The Menace of Modernism* (1919), with his views on the issue. In 1919 he played a leading role in the formation of the World's Christian Fundamentals Association. He gave the keynote address and led the organization through the 1920s. He frequently debated modernist spokespersons, especially on the issue of evolution.

In 1923 he joined **J. Frank Norris** and **T. T. Shields** in forming the Baptist Bible Union, the major fundamentalist organization among Northern Baptists. As the modernists and fundamentalists continued their fight, and as the latter scored few victories and numerous defeats, Riley saw dangers in the development of an un-Baptist centralized authority in the Northern Baptist Convention. He argued against centralization and encouraged Baptists to withhold financial gifts to convention programs run by liberal Baptists. He led the Minnesota State Baptist Convention to take an independent stance against the national organization. During this time he continued to pastor the church and teach in the college he had founded.

In 1938 Riley founded a second school, Northwestern Theological Seminary, which had a particularly urban emphasis. Riley retired from the pastorate in 1942. Two years after his retirement from the pastorate, he led in the founding of Northwestern College, a four-year liberal arts school. He devoted his last years to work with the schools he had created, and he left them in the care of a young evangelist, **William Frank (Billy) Graham**, shortly before his death.

Following Riley's passing, Graham served as interim president for three and a half years, eventually leaving the schools for full-time evangelism. The year following Riley's death, the Minnesota Baptist Convention voted to disassociate itself from the Northern Baptist Convention and became, in effect, an independent Baptist denomination.

Sources:

Dollar, George W. *A History of Fundamentalism in America*. Greenville, SC: Bob Jones University Press, 1973. 411 pp.

Riley, Marie Acomb. *The Dynamic of a Dream: The Life Story of Dr. William B. Riley*. Grand Rapids, MI: Wm. B. Eerdmans Publishing Company, 1938.

Riley, William Bell. *The Conflict of Christianity with Counterfeits*. Minneapolis, MN: Irene Woods, 1940. 147 pp.

———. *The Crisis in the Church*. New York: C. C. Cook, 1914. 197 pp.

———. *The Evolution of the Kingdom*. New York: C. C. Cook, 1913. 188 pp.

———. *Inspiration or Evolution*. Cleveland, OH: Union Gospel Press, 1926. 273 pp.

———. *The Menace of Modernism*. New York: Christian Alliance Publishing Co., 1917. 181 pp.

———. *Ten Sermons on the Greater Doctrines of Scripture*. N.p. Leader Publishing Company, 1891.

Russell, C. Allyn. *Voices of American Fundamentalism*. Philadelphia: Westminister Press, 1976. 304 pp.

Szasz, Ferenc M. "William B. Riley and the Fight Against Teaching of Evolution in Minnesota." *Minnesota History* (Spring 1969): 201-16.

★784★
RIMMER, Harry
Fundamentalist Minister
Founder, Research Science Bureau
b. Sep. 9, 1890, San Francisco, California
d. Mar. 19, 1955, Pacific Palisades, California

Harry Rimmer, fundamentalist Bible teacher most known for his attempts to reconcile science and Biblical teachings, was the son of William Henry and Katherine Dunkan Rimmer. He attended the Hahneman Medical College, a homeopathic school in San Francisco, but in 1912 was converted to Christianity and entered the Bible College of San Francisco, a small independent fundamentalist school. In 1914 he married Mignon Brandon and they moved to Los Angeles where in 1915 he was ordained in the Friends Church (Quakers) and entered Whittier College. He served the First Friends Church of Los Angeles for three years (1916-1919) and also spoke at the nearby army encampments.

In 1919 Rimmer left the Friends Church and joined the Presbytery of Los Angeles (the Presbyterian Church), a group with which he was more at home theologically. In 1920 he embarked upon the career for which he was to become nationally known as an evangelist and Bible lecturer, working primarily in the early years with the Young Men's Christian Association (YMCA) In 1920 he also founded the Research Science Bureau, and as he traveled around the country he frequently debated the issue of evolution. He was known for offering a $100 reward to anyone who could point out a scientific error in the Bible.

In 1934 Rimmer accepted the pastorate of the First Presbyterian Church in Deluth, Minnesota. While there he began to produce the

more than 20 books he was to author over his lifetime. He began work on a six-title set of apologetic writings, the first volume of which appeared in 1936 as *The Harmony of Science and Scripture*. Other volumes soon followed: *Modern Science and the Genesis Record* (1937); *Internal Evidences of Inspiration* (1938); *Dead Men Tell Tales* (1939); *Crying Stones* (1941); and *Christology: The Magnificence of Jesus* (1943).

As World War II approached Rimmer turned his attention to issues of Biblical prophecies and their possible relevance to the impending conflict. In 1939 he resigned his pastorate and returned to the lecture trail. Without abandoning his apologetic concerns he began to produce material on eschatological issues such as: *Palestine, the Coming Storm Center* (1940); *The Coming War and the Rise of Russia* (1940); *The Coming League and the Roman Dream* (1941); *Rethinking Prophecy* (1943); and *Christianity and Modern Crises* (1944). While these proved popular during the war years, interest faded as predictions Rimmer made about Europe proved ill-founded. Thus he is remembered today only for his contribution in apologetic writings.

In 1951 Rimmer was diagnosed with cancer, and he died the following year.

Sources:

Rimmer, Harry. *The Coming War and the Rise of Russia*. Grand Rapids, MI: Wm. B. Eerdmans Publishing Company 1940. 87 pp.

———. *Dead Men Tell Tales*. Berne, IN: The Berne Witness Company, 1939. 352 pp.

———. *The Harmony of Science and Scripture*. 25 vols. Glendale, CA: Glendale Pub., 1925-1934.

———. *Internal Evidences of Inspiration*. Grand Rapids, MI: Wm. B. Eerdmans Publishing Co., 1937. 370 pp.

———. *Modern Science and the Genesis Record*. Grand Rapids, MI: Wm. B. Eerdmans Publishing Co., 1937. 370 pp.

———. *The Shadow of Coming Events*. Grand Rapids, MI: Wm. B. Eerdmans Publishing Co., 1946. 19 pp.

Rimmer, Mignon Brandon. *Fire Inside: The Harry Rimmer Story*. Berne, IN: Publishers Printing House, 1968. 362 pp.

★785★
RITTER, Joseph Elmer
Cardinal, Roman Catholic Church
b. Jul. 20, 1892, New Albany, Indiana
d. Jun. 10, 1967, St. Louis, Missouri

Joseph Elmer Ritter, the archbishop of St. Louis (Missouri) and a cardinal in the Roman Catholic Church, was the son of Bertha Louette and Nicholas Ritter, both products of the German community that came into the Ohio Valley in the nineteenth century. Ritter attended a parochial school as a youth and entered St. Meinrad's Seminary, a Benedictine school. Following his graduation in 1917 he was ordained a priest. He was assigned as assistant priest at the Cathedral of Saints Peter and Paul in Indianapolis, Indiana, and in 1920 became the cathedral's rector. In 1930 he became a consultor to the bishop of Indianapolis.

The cathedral became Ritter's only pastoral charge, as he was elected to the bishopric from his post. He became the auxiliary to the bishop of Indianapolis in 1933, the youngest Roman Catholic bishop in the United States. He became bishop of Indianapolis the next year. In 1944 Indianapolis was elevated to an archdiocese and Ritter became its first archbishop. Ritter's reign in Indianapolis was marked by his reorganization of Catholic Charities, his quietly integrating the Catholic school system, and his organization of the Archdiocesan Council of Catholic Women.

In 1946 Archbishop **John Glennon** died and Ritter succeeded him as archbishop of St. Louis, Missouri. Among his first self-assignments was the integration of the Catholic school system. Unable to accomplish it quietly, as he had in Indiana, he mandated integration at the beginning of the 1947 school year. He dealt with angry opposition to his move with a threat of excommunication. Having quelled the opposition, he then integrated the other Catholic institutions.

With the racial issue behind him, Ritter turned to building the archdiocese. He fostered the development of chapters of the National Council of Catholic Men and the National Council of Catholic Women and used the councils to assist in fundraising and building programs. He led in the development of new hospitals, homes, and schools for the still growing archdiocese which covers a significant part of the state of Missouri. Ritter also initiated a mission in Bolivia, the first in South America under American Catholic sponsorship. In 1958 Ritter's work in liturgical reform led to his being named head of the Bishops' Commission on the Liturgical Apostalate. In 1964 the first official Mass in the vernacular was said in St. Louis under Ritter's authority.

Ritter was named a cardinal in 1960. He assumed a leadership role at Vatican II, especially in blocking attempts by conservative cardinals to water down the council's important statements on religious liberty, absolving the Jews of responsibility for the death of Christ, and confirming the authority of bishops beside the pope.

Sources:
Johnson, James. *Joseph Cardinal Ritter*. Notre Dame, IN: Notre Dame Press, 1964. 48 pp.

★786★
ROBERSON, Lizzie
Overseer of Women's Work, Church of God in Christ
b. Apr. 5, 1860, Philips County, Arkansas
d. 1945, Memphis, Tennessee

Lizzie Roberson, the founder and overseer of the women's work for the Church of God in Christ, the largest Pentecostal denomination in North America, was born a slave in rural Arkansas. Details of her early life as a freed woman are lost in obscurity. Her father died during the war, but her mother, who could neither read nor write, saw to the education of all her children. Roberson learned to read out of the Bible. In 1881 she married Henry Holt, but he died a short time later. She married William Woods several years after Holt's death. In 1892 she joined the Baptist church. It was not until 1901 that she had a saving experience of Christianity, which came as a result of reading a paper called "Hope" written by **Joanna Patterson Moore**, a pioneer home missionary with the American Baptist Home Missionary Society.

Moore arranged for the society to send Roberson to school for two years at the Baptist Academy in Dermott, Arkansas. While there she recounted the ministry of Elder D. W. Welk of the Church of God in Christ. In 1911 **Charles Harrison Mason**, the founder of the Church of God in Christ, preached at the Baptist Academy. Under his ministry Roberson received the baptism of the Holy Spirit (with the initial evidence of speaking in tongues), the definitive Pentecostal religious experience. She left the Baptists and joined the Church of God of Christ. She began to work with Elder R. L. Hart in Tennessee.

While traveling in Tennessee, Roberson met Lillian Brook, an evangelist who encouraged her to attend the national convocation in Memphis. While the organization of the women in the church had begun, it was progressing slowly. Mason convinced her to accept the post of overseer for the women's work. Drawing upon her experience with the Baptists, she began to organize prayer and Bible bands, sewing circles, and sunshine bands. In 1912 she was made the general supervisor of women's work in the church. She organized every state under a state mother. She is also remembered for giving Mason the money to open the first bank account for the church.

Her second husband having died, on her first missionary tour Roberson met and married an Elder Roberson with whom she traveled as an evangelist. Her teachings for the women were strict and out of the holiness tradition. Women were to dress modestly with skirts below the knees and shoes without open toes. She condemned jewelry and feathers as ornaments.

In her mature years she moved to Omaha, Nebraska, where she and Elder Roberson established a church. Elder Roberson settled down as the pastor, but she continued to travel on behalf of the women's work. She organized a campaign to support the building of the national headquarters, and she lived just long enough to see it completed and to walk through the hall named after her. She died shortly after the work of the convocation was completed. She was succeeded by Lillian Coffey.

Sources:
Cornelius, Lucille J. *The Pioneer History of the Church of God in Christ.* N.p.: The Author, 1975. 102 pp.
Dupree, Sherry Sherrod. *Biographical Dictionary of African-American, Holiness-Pentecostals, 1880-1990.* Washington, DC: Middle Atlantic Regional Press, 1990. 386 pp.

★787★
ROBERTS, Benjamin Titus
Founder, Free Methodist Church
b. Jul. 25, 1823, Cattaraugus, New York
d. Feb. 27, 1893, Cattaraugus, New York

Benjamin Titus Roberts, the founder of the Free Methodist Church, was the son of Sally Ellis and Titus Roberts. An intelligent youth, he was teaching school when he was 16. In 1842 he began studying law, but in 1844 he was converted in a revival meeting and dropped his ambitions in the legal profession for the ministry. He entered Lima Seminary in 1845 to finish preparation to attend Wesleyan University. He graduated in 1848 but not before he had absorbed Methodist holiness teachings and liberal opinions on slavery.

Following graduation he was admitted to the Genesee (western New York) Conference of the Methodist Episcopal Church. That same year he married Ellen L. Stowe. He served a number of charges around the conference over the next decade. While at Pike, New York, in 1849-1850, he experienced sanctification, an event, so holiness doctrine teaches, in which the believer is made perfect in love and cleansed from outward sin. The meeting was led by Phoebe Palmer. During the 1850s he emerged as a staunch foe of innovations within Methodism including renting out church pews, the wearing of gold and costly apparel, and the use of church organs, all signs of the growing affluence of Methodists.

In 1857 Roberts authored an article entitled "New School Methodism". Originally printed in the *Northern Independent*, it was later reprinted as a pamphlet. His bishop publicly censured him and the Genesee Conference tried him for conduct unbecoming a minister. In 1858 he was expelled from the conference. While awaiting an appeal to the church's general conference, which did not meet until 1860, he became a popular speaker. When the general conference refused to accept Robert's case, he led in the organization of the Free Methodist Church. He was elected general superintendent, a post he held for life. The name of the church refers to its refusal to rent pews, which in all Free Methodist congregations were open to everyone.

Roberts authored the basic documents for the new church, including a church *Discipline* and a hymnal. He began a periodical, the *Earnest Christian* and penned the first book, an apology for the new church, *Why Another Sect?* (1879). The rest of his life was spent in building the church, for whose cause he traveled widely. He purchased a farm in North Chili, New York, where a school was constructed, and he carried the mortgage for 20 years while the school got on its feet.

In 1910 the Genesee Conference of the Methodist Episcopal Church held its centennial celebration. It invited the Free Methodist Church to send a fraternal delegate. Roberts' son, Benson Howard Roberts was selected. In response to his speech, the conference acknowledged its error, voted to rescind its actions of 1858 and, returned his father's surrendered credentials to him.

Sources:

Dictionary of American Biography. 20 vols. and 7 supps. New York: Charles Scribner's Sons, 1928-1936, 1944-1981.

Harmon, Nolan B. *The Encyclopedia of World Methodism*. 2 vols. Nashville: United Methodist Publishing House, 1974.

Hogue, Wilson T. *History of the Free Methodist Church of North America*. 2 vols. Chicago: Free Methodist Publishing House, 1918.

Marston, Leslie R. *From Age to Age a Living Witness*. Winona Lake, IN: Life and Light Press, 1960. 608 pp.

Roberts, Benjamin Titus. *First Lessons in Money*. Rochester, NY: The Author, 1886.

_____. *Fishers of Men*. Rochester, NY: G. L. Roberts, 1878. Rept.: Chicago: W. B. Rose, 1918. 337 pp.

_____. *Holiness Teachings*. Ed. by Benson Howard Roberts. North Chili, NY: Earnest Christian Publishing House, 1893. 256 pp. Rept.: Salem, OH: H. E. Schmul, 1964. 256 pp.

_____. *Why Another Sect?* Rochester, NY: Earnest Christian Publishing House, 1879.

Roberts, Benson Howard. *Benjamin Titus Roberts: A Biography*. North Chili, NY: Earnest Christian Office, 1900.

★ 788 ★
ROBERTS, Brigham Henry
Historian and Theologian, Church of Jesus Christ of Latter-day Saints
b. Mar. 13, 1857, Warrington United Kingdom
d. Sep. 27, 1933, Salt Lake City, Utah

Brigham Henry Roberts, historian, theologian, church leader, missionary, and political leader, rose out of poverty and an unhappy childhood to become one of the most prominent men in early twentieth century Mormonism. When Roberts was five years old, his mother, who had converted to Mormonism, left his father and the family to migrate to Centerville, Utah. At nine years of age, accompanied by his sister Polly, Roberts immigrated to America soon after the conclusion of the Civil War. As a teenager he moved into the mining camps and tried prospecting. His lifestyle led to a brief period of excommunication. At the age of 17 he gave up mining for blacksmithing. Still relatively poor, in 1878 he married Sarah Louisa Smith and attended Deseret University.

After graduation Roberts spent several years as a missionary in Iowa, Nebraska, and Tennessee. He married Celia Ann Dibble in 1884, just as the government was pressuring the church to rid itself of plural marriages. In December 1886, while serving as associate editor of the *Salt Lake Herald*, he was arrested for unlawful cohabitation. Before the day was over, he jumped bail and left for England. He quietly returned in 1888 and was called to the First Council of the Seventy. Tiring of life as a fugitive, he surrendered to the authorities in the spring of 1889. He served his months in prison and then, as the manifesto against polygamy was being prepared by church president **Wilford Woodruff**, Roberts took his third wife, Dr. Margaret Curtis Shipp, in 1890. He fathered a total of fifteen children with his wives.

In 1891 Utah underwent a political transformation and the local People's Party disbanded in favor of the national parties. Roberts, generally acknowledged as one of the great orators in the church, became a Democrat and launched the first of three somewhat parallel careers. As a politician, he helped write Utah's constitution and emerged as a leader of those opposed to women's suffrage. He ran for a congressional seat in 1895 but was defeated due to

church opposition. Relenting to church authority, he ran again in 1898 and was elected. However, because he was a polygamist, Congress refused to seat him. He returned to Utah and became Democratic Party Chairman. As party chairman, he became heavily critical of Republican **Reed Smoot**, who was elected to the Senate in 1903. Throughout his life he advocated causes unpopular with the predominantly Republican church authorities.

As a churchman, Roberts came into additional criticism during his most politically active years. His alcoholism asserted itself and he was frequently drunk. Many saw him neglecting his church office. He recouped some of his standing, however, when he served as an Army chaplain in World War I, distinguishing himself during the flu epidemic. In 1921 he prepared two apologetic pieces on the Book of Mormon for the Quorum of Twelve Apostles, and became president of the Eastern States Mission from 1924 to 1927.

The ambiguous nature of Roberts' relation to the church is shown in his theological writings. On the one hand he emerges as a defender of the faith, especially of the authenticity of the Book of Mormon. He authored several important theological treatises such as volumes II and III of *New Witnesses for God in America* and *The Mormon Doctrine of Deity*. During the last decade of his life, however, he raised new controversy through his further theological writings. He championed the cause of the church's development of an intellectually sound theology, but numerous critics in the hierarchy of the church rejected many of his conclusions. He spent years working on a systematic theology only to have the church refuse to publish it. Church President **Joseph Fielding Smith** denied Roberts' teachings on such points as, for example, his contention that a race of humans existed prior to Adam.

Roberts' most lasting contribution to the church came neither in his role as politician or churchman/theologian. As an active amateur historian he left a massive set of writings behind, including biographies of church founder **Joseph Smith, Jr.** and church president **John Taylor**. He also authored both a general Christian church history and a history of the Church of Jesus Christ of Latter-day Saints, and edited an additional comprehensive history of the Church of Jesus Christ of Latter-day Saints.

The controversial Roberts died of diabetes at the age of 76. In more recent years his standing as a church leader has been more favorably evaluated.

Sources:

Jensen, Andrew. *Latter Day Saints Biographical Encyclopedia* 4 vols. Salt Lake City, UT: Andrew Jensen History Co., 1901.

Madsen, Truman G. *B. H. Roberts: Defender of the Faith*. Salt Lake City, UT: Bookcraft, 1980.

Malan, Robert H. *B. H. Roberts*. Salt Lake City, UT: Deseret Book Co., 1966.

Roberts, Brigham Henry. *A Comprehensive History of the LDS*. 6 vols. Salt Lake City, UT: Deseret News Press, 1930.

_____. *Discourses of B. H. Roberts*. Salt Lake City, UT: Deseret Book Co., 1948. 128 pp.

_____. *Life of John Taylor*. Salt Lake City, UT: George Q. Cannon & Sons, 1892. 408 pp.

_____. *New Witnesses for God*, II & III. Salt Lake City, UT: Deseret News, 1909.

_____. *Outline of Ecclesiastical History*. Salt Lake City, UT: George Q. Cannon and Sons, 1893. 467 pp.

_____. *Studies in the Book of Mormon*. Urbana, IL: University of Illinois Press, 1985. 375 pp.

★ 789 ★
ROBERTS, Jane
New Age Channel
b. May 8, 1929, Albany, New York
d. Sep. 5, 1984, Elmira, New York

Jane Roberts was the channel for Seth, a spirit entity that was described both as an "energy personality essence" and as a "dramatization of the unconscious.'' (Roberts rejected the idea of Seth as simply a discarnate former human being.) The Seth books, particularly *The Seth Material* (1970) and *Seth Speaks* (1972), have been viewed as one of the starting points, or at least as a transitional stage, for New Age channeling. Roberts was the first well-known American medium since **Edgar Cayce** to consistently channel metaphysical information rather than messages of comfort from departed individuals to their loved ones (which had been the emphasis of Spiritualist mediumship).

Roberts was the daughter of Delmar Hubbell and Marie Burdo Roberts. She attended Skidmore College from 1947 to 1950, and married Robert Butts in 1954. She worked at a variety of jobs, and wrote one novel. She and her husband began experimenting with a Ouija board in 1963. They soon began to receive messages from Seth. Not long afterwards, Seth began to speak through her while she was in a trance. The sessions in which Seth spoke were recorded and later transcribed for publication in book form. The popularity of the first publications inspired other works, so that eventually Roberts was producing books at the rate of almost two per year.

In spite of the growing popularity of the Seth material, Roberts herself continued to lead a quiet life. She rarely spoke in public, and refused to organize Seth's following into a formal movement. She became ill in 1983 and died the following year. In part because of her refusal to assume a public role, other individuals felt free to begin tapping into Seth's popularity. For example, during Roberts' lifetime other people began to claim that they were also channeling Seth—claims that Roberts denied. Similarly independent of Roberts, the Austin Seth Center was formed to perpetuate the ideas of the Seth material. Seth societies subsequently emerged in a number of locales. At one time there were at least three Seth magazines/bulletins.

Sources:

Roberts, Jane. *The Coming of Seth*. New York: Frederick Fell Publishers, 1966.
_____. *Seth: Dreams and Projection of Consciousness*. Walpole, NH: Stillpoint Publishing, 1987. 385 pp.
_____. *The Seth Material*. Englewood Cliffs, NJ: Prentice-Hall, 1970. 304 pp.
_____. *Seth Speaks*. Englewood Cliffs, NJ: Prentice-Hall, 1972.
_____. *The Unknown Reality*. 2 vols. Englewood Cliffs, NJ: Prentice-Hall, 1977, 1979. Melton, J. Gordon. *New Age Encyclopedia*. Detroit: Gale Research Inc., 1990. 586 pp.
Watkins, Susan M. *Conversations with Seth*. 2 vols. Englewood Cliffs, NJ: Prentice-Hall, 1981.

★790★
ROBERTS, Oral
Television Healing Evangelist, United Methodist Church
b. Jan. 24, 1918, Pontotoc County, Oklahoma

Granville Oral Roberts, the pioneer televangelist, was the son of Ellia M. and Claudius Irwin Roberts. His father was an independent Pentecostal evangelist. Roberts grew up in poverty, and stuttered as a child. At the age of 15, he left home to attend school in another town, but was stricken with tuberculosis and in 1935 returned home. Several months later he attended a revival meeting led by George Moncey. He was healed when Moncey prayed for him. He delivered his first sermon that evening. Through his father he was brought into the ministry of the Pentecostal Holiness Church and wrote for the *Pentecostal Holiness Advocate*. In 1938 he married Evelyn Lutman and finished his first book, *Salvation by the Blood*.

Roberts became a Pentecostal Holiness evangelist traveling the continent. In 1941, his second book, *The Drama of the End Time*, appeared and he accepted a call to become pastor of an independent congregation in Fuquay Springs, North Carolina. Unable to convince the church to affiliate with the Pentecostal Holiness

Church, he resigned in 1942. He successively served churches in Shawnee, Oklahoma; Toccoa, Georgia; and Enid, Oklahoma. While at Enid, a series of events occurred which changed his life's course. He had been attending Phillips University, and in class one day he heard the voice of God command him to bring healing to the people. He responded by adding a Sunday afternoon healing service to his weekly schedule. The success led him to renting a hall in Enid. Again successful, he left the pastorate, moved to Tulsa, Oklahoma, and became a full-time healing evangelist. Before the year was out, he had started his own magazine, *Healing Waters*, and written one of his most widely read books, *If You Need Healing—Do These Things*.

In 1948 Roberts purchased a tent. His growing successes made him the center of controversy. In 1954 he went on television, and the following year began to film the revival crusade services under the tent. He experienced increasing support throughout the 1950s. He also authored a number of books, including the first of several autobiographical volumes, *Oral Roberts' Life Story* (1952). During the 1960s his ministry changed radically. He began the decade with the announcement of the beginning of a new university. Oral Roberts University was dedicated in 1967. The time Roberts spent in crusades began to diminish and they were discontinued in 1968. That same year he left the Pentecostal Holiness Church and joined the United Methodist Church. He pursued their course of study and was ordained to the ministry (as a local elder) in the church.

During the 1970s and 1980s Roberts reigned as the head of a significant Pentecostal ministry centered on the school and medical complex, which includes a medical college and hospital, the City of Faith. His television show, while not at the top of the ratings, has remained among the most popular as others have risen and fallen. In 1970 Roberts had signaled a new direction in his ministry with the issuance of *The Miracle of Seed Faith*. The book highlighted a message that not only healing but prosperity was part of God's plan for the faithful. While costing him many older followers, his total support continued to increase.

At the same time, Roberts has continued to be the subject of attack both by those opposed to his healing ministry and people formerly close to him who have written exposes. He also faced some bitter tragedies, including the death of a daughter (1977) and a son (1982), and the divorce of his son and heir-apparent Richard Roberts in 1979. Richard's former wife, Patti, authored one of the expose volumes, *Ashes to Gold*, in 1985. Roberts himself generated much of the controversy that surrounded his ministry with incidents such as his report in 1980 of an encounter with a 900-foot-tall Jesus and more recently a claim that he would die if a required amount of money was not raised for the City of Faith.

Now in his senior years, Roberts moves with patriarchal authority among his Pentecostal colleagues, and the structures he established ensure the continued impact of his life for decades to come.

Sources:

Harrell, David E. *Oral Roberts: An American Life*. Bloomington, IN: Indiana University Press, 1985.
Hutchinson, Warner. *The Oral Roberts Scrapbook*. New York: Grosset & Dunlap, 1978. 128p.
Lippy, Charles H. *Twentieth-Century Shapers of American Popular Religion*. New York: Greenwood Press, 1989. 494 pp.
Roberts, Evelyn. *His Darling Wife, Evelyn*. New York: Dell Publishing Co., 1976. 256 pp.
Roberts, Oral. *The Call*. New York: Doubleday & Company, 1972. 216 pp.
_____. *If You Need Healing—Do These Things*. Tulsa, OK: Standard Printing Co., 1947. 130 pp.
_____. *The Miracle of Seed Faith*. Charlotte, NC: Commission Press, 1970. 167 pp.
_____. *My Twenty Years of Miracle Ministry*. Tulsa, OK: The Author, 1967. 96 pp.
_____. *Oral Roberts' Life Story*. Tulsa, OK: The Author, 1952. 160 pp.

_____. *Salvation by the Blood*. Franklin Springs, GA: Pentecostal Holiness Publishing House, 1938.

Roberts, Patti, with Sherry Andrews. *Ashes to Gold*. New York: Jove Publications, 1985. 171 pp.

Robinson, Wayne A. *Oral; The Warm Intimate Unauthorized Portrait of a Man of God*. Los Angeles: Acton House, 1976. 154 pp.

★791★
ROBERTSON, Ann Eliza Worcester
Bible Translator
Missionary to the American Indian
b. Nov. 7, 1826, Brainerd Mission, Tennessee
d. Nov. 19, 1905, Muskogee, Oklahoma

Ann Eliza Worcester Robertson, who gained fame as a missionary to the Creek Indian Nation, was the daughter of an equally famous Indian missionary, Samuel Austin Worcester, and his wife, Ann Orr Worcester. Shortly after his ordination as a Congregationalist minister in 1825, Worcester moved to the Brainerd Mission in Tennessee. In 1831 he refused to recognize the authority of the government over the Cherokee land and was sent to prison. He appealed to the Supreme Court and won a famous decision for the Indian, *Worcester vs. Georgia*. However, Andrew Jackson ignored the court and removed the Cherokees to Oklahoma. Ann Eliza was born at the Brainerd Mission, but her family soon moved to New Echota, Georgia, the capital of the Cherokee Nation. She went with her parents to Oklahoma, where they established the Park Hill Mission in 1836. In 1843 she went to the St. Johnsbury (Vermont) Academy and during her years there excelled in her studies of the Latin and Greek languages. She graduated in 1847.

Immediately after graduation, Ann Eliza returned to Park Hill, her basic desire to assist her parents. In 1849, however, she was asked to go to the Tullahasse Manual Labor Boarding School, which was jointly run by the Creek Nation and the Presbyterians. The school opened in January 1850, and a few months later she married its principal, Presbyterian minister William Schenck Robertson. She became a Presbyterian at that time. At the new school she had to become a multifaceted person. She bore four children, supervised housekeeping at the school, taught classes, and worked with her husband in producing texts in the Creek language.

The mission was disrupted by the Civil War. The Creeks made a treaty with the new confederate government and expelled the missionaries. The Robertsons moved to the Midwest, and Reverend Robertson continued his missionary work in Kansas. At the end of 1866 the Creeks requested their return. It took a year to rebuild the boarding school, but it opened in 1868. During the next 12 years, the Robertsons continued their missionary, teaching, translating, and publishing work. They produced a hymnal, much literature, and translated portions of the Bible into the Creek language. In 1880 the school burned. Reverend Robertson died a few months later.

After her husband's death, Robertson went to live with her daughter Alice (destined to become the second woman ever elected to the United States Congress) in Muskogee, Oklahoma. She devoted her remaining years to her translating work and in 1887 completed the Creek New Testament. She spent the rest of her life revising the New Testament, translating Genesis and the Psalms, and producing a new hymnal. She was given an honorary doctorate for her accomplishments in 1892 by the University of Wooster.

Sources:

Forman, Carolyn Thomas. *Park Hill*. Privately printed, 1948.

Holway, Hope. "Ann Eliza Worcester Robertson as a Linguist." *Chronicles of Oklahoma* (Spring 1959).

★792★
ROBERTSON, Archibald Thomas
Biblical Scholar, Southern Baptist Convention
b. Nov. 6, 1863, Chatham, Virginia
d. Sep. 24, 1934, Louisville, Kentucky

Archibald Thomas Robertson, who as a professor of New Testament at Southern Baptist Theological Seminary shaped the thought of the Southern Baptist Convention for over half a century, was the son of Ella Martin and John Robertson. He was raised on a farm in Virginia. When he was 12 years old, the family moved to North Carolina, where at the age of 13 he had a conversion experience. At the age of 16 he was licensed as a Southern Baptist preacher. He attended Wake Forest College from which he graduated in 1885, and then pursued seminary work at the Southern Baptist Theological Seminary (Th.M., 1888). Following graduation he was ordained and became the pastor of the New Castle (Kentucky) Baptist Church but had to resign due to health within a few months. He became an assistant instructor at the seminary and was promoted to professor in 1892. In 1894 **John A. Broadus**, the professor of New Testament interpretation at the seminary, died. A few months previously, Robertson had married Ella Thomas Broadus, his daughter, and in 1895 he was elected to succeed Broadus.

During his long career, Robertson specialized in the study of New Testament Greek, which led to the publication of 45 books. His most popular volume was *Harmony of the Gospels* (1922), a project he had begun as a revision of a similar book compiled by Broadus. Robertson broke with previous tradition by not building on the feasts Jesus is reported to have attended as the measurable turning points in his life. On the other hand, he stressed the historical nature of the Gospel of John at a time when many of his colleagues were calling it into question. As a scholar, his most important contribution was *A Grammar of the Greek New Testament in the Light of Historical Research* (1914), whose 1,454 pages consumed over 26 years in its preparation.

Robertson is also remembered for suggesting the possibility of Baptists worldwide meeting for fellowship and discussion of global issues. First mentioned in an article in the *Baptist Argus* in 1904, his suggestion was picked up and an initial Baptist World Conference was held in 1905, at which Robertson helped write the constitution for the Baptist World Alliance.

Throughout his career Robertson wrote for the laity as well as his fellow scholars. His interest in spreading a popular knowledge and appreciation for the Bible is seen in such books as his *Commentary on Matthew in Bible for Home and School* (1910); *John the Loyal, or Studies in the Ministry of the Baptist* (1911); *Paul's Joy in Christ* (1917); and *New Testament History (Airplane View)* (1923).

Sources:

Brackney, William Henry. *The Baptist*. New York: Greenwood Press, 1988. 327 pp.

Gill, Everett. *A. T. Robertson: A Biography*. New York: Macmilla Company, 1943. 250 pp.

Robertson, A. T. *A Grammar of the Greek New Testament in the Light of Historical Research*. London: Hodde and Stoughton, 1914. 1340 pp.

_____. *Harmony of the Gospels for Students of the Life of Christ*. 1922.

_____. *John the Loyal, or Studies in the Ministry of the Baptist*. New York: Charles Scribner's Sons, 1911. 315 pp.

_____. *Syllabus of New Testament Greek Syntax*. Louisville, KY: The Author, 1900. 99 pp.

_____. *Word Pictures in the New Testament*. 6 vols. New York: R. R. Smith, 1933.

★793★
ROBERTSON, James
Home Missionary Executive, Presbyterian Church in Canada
b. Apr. 24, 1839, Dull Scotland
d. Jan. 4, 1902, Toronto, Ontario, Canada

James Robertson, who led in the building of the Presbyterian Church in Canada in the western Canadian provinces, grew up in Scotland, but migrated with his family to Oxford County, Ontario, as a teenager in 1855. He was the son of Christina McCallum and James Robertson. He attended the University of Toronto and took his seminary work in the United States at Princeton and Union Theological Seminaries. He was ordained as a Presbyterian minister in 1869 and was called to Norwich, Ontario. Robertson stayed at Norwich until 1874 when he moved to Winnipeg as pastor of the congregation of the Presbyterian Free Church, one of several factions into which the Canadian Presbyterians were split at the time. Upon his arrival, he found a minister of the Church of Scotland at the church who refused to allow Robertson to take over. Rather than fight, Robertson took several months and toured the remote regions around Winnipeg.

As a result of his tours, by the time Robertson finally settled in the parish at Winnipeg, he had become enthusiastic over the promise of the lands to the west, and he regularly took further missionary trips into the frontier. In 1875 the major mergers of the several Presbyterian churches were accomplished, and the new Presbyterian Church in Canada began to see the potential as the western lands were settled. In 1881 it appointed Robertson as the superintendent of western missions. At the time there were but two Presbyterian congregations, though there were some 161 preaching points visited occasionally by the 28 ministers. Robertson spent the major part of the next year in visiting his newly-assigned territory, starting new congregations, and overseeing the ones in existence. The rest of the year he spent in the east raising money and recruiting missionaries. He recruited young men, fresh out of school, showing some ability to manage a horse and usually not yet married, and he modeled their ministry somewhat on the pattern of Methodist circuit riders. His leadership style and real authority in the mission soon earned him the unofficial designation as the "Presbyterian bishop" of western Canada. In 1890 British Columbia was added to his territory. By 1892, primarily due to his efforts, he could boast that 141 ministers served 73 congregations and 667 preaching points. The work had been organized in two synods and 10 presbyteries.

Over the next decade the population of western Canada grew threefold. In spite of the large numbers of non-English speaking settlers of Roman Catholic and eastern Orthodox backgrounds, Robertson was able to keep a growing operation. By the time of his death the work had expanded to two synods, 18 presbyteries, and 258 congregations. He was succeeded by two men who divided his work load between them. In recognition of his abilities and accomplishments, in 1895 Robertson was elected moderator of the Presbyterian Church in Canada.

Sources:
Gordon Charles William. *The Life of James Robertson*. London: Hodder, 1908. 427 pp.
McFadden, I. *He Belonged to the West: James Robertson*. New York: Friendship Press, 1958.
Moir, John S. *Enduring Witness: A History of the Presbyterian Church in Canada*. N.p., Centennial Committee, Presbyterian Church in Canada, 1975. 311 pp.
Reid, Daniel G., Robert D. Linder, Bruce L. Shelley, and Harry S. Stout. *Dictionary of Christianity in America*. Downers Grove, IL: InterVarsity Press, 1990. 1305 pp.

★794★
ROBERTSON, Pat
Founder, Christian Broadcasting Network (CBN)
b. Mar. 22, 1930, Lexington, Virginia

Marion Gordon Robertson, Baptist minister and founder of the Christian Broadcasting Network (CBN), was the son of A. Willis Robertson, congressman (1933-1947) and senator from the state of Virginia, and Gladys Churchill Willis Robertson. He attended the McCallie School, a prep school in Chattanooga, Tennessee. He then entered Washington and Lee University, from which he graduated magna cum laude in 1950. He did post-graduate work in economics at the University of London and served in the Marine Corps for two years during the Korean War. After his period of service, he attended Yale Law School and while there in 1954 married Adelia Elme. He graduated with a J.D. degree in 1955. In the process, however, he became disillusioned with law and failed his bar exam. He chose instead to enter business.

About this time his life was interrupted by a meeting (arranged by his mother) with Baptist minister Cornelius Vanderbeggen. Vanderbeggen led him into a "born again" experience. In 1956 he entered New York Theological Seminary and was invited to become an associate minister at the First Reformed Church in Mount Vernon, New York. The church's minister, Harald Bredesen, had become a Pentecostal and he introduced Robertson to the gifts of the Holy Spirit, especially speaking in tongues. Following his graduation in 1959, he purchased a defunct television station in Portsmouth, Virginia, the birthplace of CBN.

In 1961 Robertson was ordained to the ministry of the Southern Baptist Convention. In October of that year the first CBN broadcast was made. The effort grew slowly but steadily over the years. He added **Jim Bakker** and his wife, **Tammy Faye Bakker**, to the staff in 1965. In 1966 he began the "700 Club," a talk show which anchored the network programs and transformed Robertson into a public personality in the evangelical Christian world. The "700 Club" also became the basis for a variety of new ministries. In 1972 the "700 Club" became nationally syndicated. That same year he issued his biographical volume *Shout It from the Housetops*.

Three years later, Robertson laid the foundation for the most impressive extension of his ministry, CBN University, with the purchase of land in Virginia Beach, Virginia. The school included a number of professional departments in such areas as business, communications, and public policy, and in 1986 added a law school. In 1979 he founded CBN Continental Broadcasting Network, a for-profit corporation to work beside the non-profit CBN. A decade later, CBN Continental Broadcasting Network was grossing over $200 million annually.

Through the 1980s Robertson built a perspective on America's problems, which he spelled out in several books, most importantly, *America's Date with Destiny* (1986). He felt that the situation had a religious base and that the rise of secular humanism had turned America from its Judeo-Christian heritage. In 1987 he resigned from the ministry and announced his candidacy for the office of President of the United States. Though he turned in a surprising showing in several primaries, he eventually faded behind George Bush, and after the election returned to CBN and the "700 Club."

Sources:
Harrell, David Edwin, Jr. *Pat Robertson: A Personal, Religious, and Political Portrait*. San Francisco: Harper & Row, 1987. 246 pp.
Lippy, Charles H. *Twentieth-Century Shapers of American Popular Religion*. New York: Greenwood Press, 1989. 494 pp.
Morken, Hubert. *Pat Robertson: Religion and Politics in Simple Terms*. Old Tappan, NJ: Fleming H. Revell Company, 1987.
Robertson, Pat. *America's Date with Destiny*. Nashville, TN: Thomas Nelson, 1986. 322 pp.

_____. *Answers to 200 of Life's Most Probing Questions*. Nashville, TN: Thomas Nelson, 1984. 290 pp.

_____. *Beyond Reason*. New York; William Morrow and Co., 1984. 178 pp.

_____. *My Prayer for You*. Old Tappan, NJ: Fleming H. Revell Company, 1977. 127 pp.

_____. *The Secret Kingdom*. Nashville, TN: Thomas Nelson, 1983. 223 pp.

_____. *Shout It from the Housetops*. South Plainfield, NJ: Logos International, 1972. 255 pp.

★ 795 ★
ROBINSON, Frank B.
Founder, Psychiana
b. Jul. 5, 1886, New York, New York
d. Oct. 19, 1948, Moscow, Idaho

Frank B. Robinson, founder of Psychiana, one of the earliest mail-order religions, was the son of a Baptist minister. His early life is difficult to reconstruct with any degree of certainty. Records are scarce and the accounts differ somewhat in the two autobiographical works Robinson penned. We do know that he was an ordained Baptist minister (like his father) who attended the Baptist Bible Training School in Toronto. Robinson was also, at different times, a member of the Salvation Army, a Mountie, and a pharmacy worker.

Robinson claims that he had many unpleasant experiences with traditional Christianity which caused him to embark on a spiritual search that eventually led him to New Thought, and he attended an early New Thought school, the College of Divine Metaphysics. After becoming the manager of a pharmacy in Moscow, Idaho, in 1928, he settled into a career as an independent metaphysical teacher. He composed a series of lessons and gave New Thought-inspired lectures in Moscow. In 1929 he began to develop Psychiana as a mail-order religion and metaphysical school. It quickly expanded to become one of the most successful of New Thought groups. Robinson founded a periodical, the *Psychiana Quarterly*, and assumed the title of archbishop. By the last years of his life, he had appointed four bishops to assist him with the work of the Psychiana Brotherhood. His son carried on his work for a few years after his death, but the movement eventually collapsed.

A prolific writer, Robinson authored such works as *The God Nobody Knows* (1930); *Crucified Gods Galore* (1933); *Life Story of Frank B. Robinson* (1934); *What God Really Is* (1935); *God and Mr. Bannister* (1941); and *The Pathway to God* (1943). His second attempt at autobiography appeared in 1949 as *The Strange Autobiography of Frank B. Robinson*.

Robinson identified God as the impersonal, spiritual Law (the God-Law), which, for practical purposes, was the power behind the visible cosmos. Matter is a condensation of this power. The Psychiana lessons, authored by Robinson, taught how, through an understanding of the Law, one could acquire wealth and health.

Sources:

Bach, Marcus. *He Talked with God*. Portland, OR: Metropolitan Press, 1951. 95 pp.

Braden, Charles S. *These Also Believe*. New York: Macmillan Company. 1949. 491 pp.

Melton, J. Gordon. *Biographical Dictionary of American Cult and Sect Leaders*. Garland Reference Library of Social Science, vol. 212. New York: Garland Publishing, 1986.

Robinson, Frank B. *Gems of Spiritual Truth*. Moscow, ID: Psychiana, 1947. 341 pp.

_____. *The God Nobody Knows*. Moscow, ID: Psychiana, 1941. 205 pp.

_____. *Life Story of Frank B. Robinson*. Moscow, ID: Psychiana, 1934. 239 pp.

_____. *The Pathway to God*. Moscow, ID: Psychiana, 1943. 185 pp.

_____. *The Strange Autobiography of Frank B. Robinson*. Moscow, ID: Psychiana, 1949. 274 pp.

★ 796 ★
ROERICH, Nicolas Konstantinovitch
Cofounder, Agni Yoga Society
b. Oct. 9, 1874, St. Petersburg Russia
d. Dec. 13, 1947, Punjab India

Nicolas Konstantinovitch Roerich, co-founder with his wife, Helena Ivanovna Roerich, of the theosophically-inspired Agni Yoga Society, was the son of a Russian lawyer. Although trained in law at his father's insistence, Roerich's real calling was in the arts. Interested in archaeology and writing, he became an internationally known artist. He held positions in the Society for the Encouragement of the Fine Arts in Russia, and was elected to the Russian Imperial Academy of the Fine Arts in 1909.

Leaving Russia at the time of the revolution, Roerich was in Europe for a few years before accepting an invitation to visit the United States in 1920. After a national tour, he settled in New York and founded the Master Institute of the United Arts. Roerich and his wife joined the Theosophical Society and explored Theosophical break-off groups, such as **Alice LaTrobe Bailey Bateman**'s Arcane School. Theosophy gradually came to dominate the Roerichs' lives, with Helena translating *The Secret Doctrine*, a work by Theosophy's founder **Helena P. Blavatsky**, into Russian. Both Blavatsky and Bailey claimed to have received their teachings from a hidden hierarchy of spiritual masters, and Helena eventually claimed to have the same kind of link with one of the Theosophical masters, Master Morya. Helena recorded Morya's teachings in a series of books, the first being *Leaves of M's Garden*, volume one (1924). The Agni Yoga Society was formed to study the Morya material.

At around the same time that M's teachings were beginning to be published, Roerich started touring Asia, eventually settling in India in 1929. He founded the Himalayan Research Institute in the Punjab to carry out archaeological research and similar projects.

Second only to his devotion to art was Roerich's concern for peace. As a manifestation of his aspirations in this direction, he created the idea of what was termed the Roerich Pact and Banner of Peace, a plan whereby the nations of the earth would agree to keep sites of educational and cultural significance inviolate during time of war. He authored one major book promoting this idea, *The Banner of Peace* (1933), which was accepted by several governments, including that of the United States, during the mid-1930s.

The Agni Yoga Society continues to publish Morya's teachings and to promote study groups organized around them.

Sources:

Conlan, Barnett D. *Nicolas Roerich: A Master of the Mountains*. Liberty, IN: FLAMMA, Association for Advancement of Culture, 1938. 108 pp.

Fosdick, Sina. *Nicolas Roerich*. New York: Nicolas Roerich Museum, 1964. 15 pp.

Melton, J. Gordon. *Biographical Dictionary of American Cult and Sect Leaders*. Garland Reference Library of Social Science, vol. 212. New York: Garland Publishing, 1986.

Nicolas Roerich, 1874-1947. New York: Nicolas Roerich Museum, 1974. 30 pp.

Paelian, Garabed. *Nicolas Roerich*. Agoura, CA: Aquarian Educational Group, 1974. 96 pp.

Roerich, Nicolas. *Adamant*. New York: Corona Mundi, 1922. 139 pp.

_____. *The Banner of Peace*. Colombo, Ceylon: The Buddhist, 1933.

_____. *The Flame in the Chalice*. New York: Nicolas Roerich Museum, 1929.

_____. *Heart of Asia*. New York: Alatas Publishing Company, 1929.

_____. *The Invincible*. New York: Nicolas Roerich Museum, 1974. 379 pp.

_____. *Realm of Light*. New York: Nicolas Roerich Museum, 1931. 333 pp.

—*James R. Lewis*

★797★
ROGERS, Aurelia Spencer
Children's Worker, Church of Jesus Christ of Latter-day Saints
b. Oct. 4, 1834, Deep River, Connecticut
d. Aug. 19, 1922, Farmington, Utah

Aurelia Spencer Rogers, founder of the Primary Association of the Church of Jesus Christ of Latter-day Saints, was born Aurelia Read Spencer, the daughter of Catherine Curtis Spencer and Orson Spencer, a prominent early Mormon. Her family moved to Nauvoo when she was seven. Her mother died in the mid-1840s at the same time that Nauvoo was being abandoned and the Mormons were beginning the trek to Utah. With her father on a mission in England, she and her older sister Ellen cared for the four younger children. She was 17 when she married Thomas Rogers and settled in Farmington, Utah. She had a large family, which she saw grow to maturity.

In the spring of 1878, some 27 years after her settlement in Farmington, Rogers had a conversation with **Eliza Snow**, who was one of the plural wives of the late Mormon president Brigham Young and the president of the Relief Society. She expressed some concern about the number of young boys who were growing up in an undisciplined manner and suggested the formation of an organization to train them in manhood. With Snow's backing, the church's president, **John Taylor**, authorized the new organization for the ward and appointed Rogers as its first president. She organized the first Primary Association and taught her pupils the value of obedience, faith in God, prayer, punctuality, and good manners. The idea of the Primary Association soon spread throughout the Church of Jesus Christ of Latter-day Saints.

In 1893 Rogers was called to the Primary General Board, leading what had become a church-wide effort. By this time she had broadened her concerns to include the status and role of women. That same year she was Utah's delegate to the Woman's Suffrage Convention in Atlanta. In 1895 she was the delegate to the National Council of Women meeting in Washington, D.C.

Rogers lived to be almost 90 years old. She died quietly in her home.

Sources:

Ritchie, Elizabeth Kohler. "Aurelia S. Rogers." In *Sister Saints*, edited by Vicky Burgess-Olson. Provo, UT: Brigham Young University Press, 1978.
Van Wagoner, Richard S., and Steven C. Walker. *A Book of Mormons*. Salt Lake City, UT: Signature Books, 1982. 454 pp.

★798★
ROGERS, Hubert Augustus
Primate, North American Old Roman Catholic Church
b. Mar. 9, 1887, St. Eustatius, Wisconsin
d. Aug. 25, 1976, St. Maarten's Island, Wisconsin

Hubert Augustus Rogers, the second primate of the North American Old Roman Catholic Church (N.A.O.R.C.C.), was raised as a Methodist in the West Indies. In 1916 he migrated to the United States where he joined and served as a lay-reader for the Harlem Christian Church in Manhattan. In New York, he was caught up in the Universal Negro Improvement Association (U.N.I.A.) and its black nationalist ambitions. He also became a leader in the Independent Episcopal Church (soon renamed the African Orthodox Church), one of the major religious structures to arise out of the U.N.I.A. He had a stormy career with the African Church which saw him leave it for several years, but by 1925 he had returned and was ordained to the priesthood by Archbishop George Alexander McGuire.

Rogers became canon at Holy Cross Cathedral under Archbishop McGuire, and after several years became pastor of the Chapel of the Messiah, also in New York. On November 7, 1937, he was consecrated to the episcopacy by William Ernest James Robertson

and sent to St. Leonard's African Orthodox Church in Brooklyn. (Most of the African Orthodox bishops have also pastored churches.) Rogers stayed with the African Orthodox Church only three more years. In 1940 he left, taking both the Chapel of the Messiah and St. Leonard's with him. At the prompting of Bishop Richard A. Marchenna, he brought the churches into the North American Old Roman Catholic Church, which had developed as a multi-ethnic and multi-racial organization. On July 30, 1942, Rogers was consecrated sub conditione by Archbishop Carmel Henry Carfora, the church's primate. Four years later, he elevated Rogers to the position of archbishop, and assigned him the task of bringing another segment of the African Orthodox Church into Carfora's jurisdiction.

In 1952 Carfora appointed Rogers first to the post of Dean of the Consistory and the following year as his coadjutor, with right of succession. He increasingly took control of administrative matters over the next five years, but in 1957, after a lengthy argument, Carfora removed Rogers and replaced him with Cyrus A. Starkey. Carfora died a short time later, in January 1958. However, at the synod of the church a few months later, Rogers was elected as primate, and Starkey stepped aside. Rogers was immediately beset with racial problems, as some white members resented his being black and many black members resented his being a West Indian. Over the next few years the majority of parishes left the organization and Rogers was left with only five in his jurisdiction.

Rogers attempted to revive the church. He initiated a mission among the Hispanics of New York and soon added three new parishes, but these were lost in 1969. That same year he consecrated three new bishops, but two left by 1971. In 1971 the synod voted to limit the term of the primate to a decade. Rogers' decade was up. Given the downward trend of the church, he saw the synod's action as a slap in the face. On April 30, 1972, he resigned as primate and three months later, on the 30th anniversary of his consecration, angry and hurt, he resigned from the church. He returned to his homeland and became the pastor of Trinity Methodist Church on St. Maarten's Island. He died there several years later.

Sources:

Trela, Jonathan. *A History of the North American Old Roman Catholic Church*. Scranton, PA: The Author, 1981. 124 pp.
Ward, Gary L. *Independent Bishops: An International Directory*. Santa Barbara, CA: Apogee Books, 1990. 500 pp.

★799★
ROOT, George Frederick
Musician, Presbyterian Church
b. Aug. 30, 1820, Sheffield, Massachusetts
d. Aug. 6, 1895, Bailey Island, Maine

George Frederick Root, a musician and businessman who played an important role in the development of gospel music in the nineteenth century, was the son of Frederick Ferdinand and Sarah Flint Root. He grew up in Reading, Massachusetts, but in 1828 moved to Boston to study with choirmaster A. N. Johnson. While in Boston he met church musician Lowell Mason and worked for him at the Boston Academy of Music. In 1844 he moved to New York, and in 1845 he married Mary Olive Woodman.

In New York Root taught at several different schools, including Union Theological Seminary and the New York State Institution for the Blind. At the latter he met, and for a while collaborated with, future hymn writer **Fanny Crosby**, though most of the music they produced together was of a secular nature. His first original musical score, "The Flower Queen" was composed with poetry which Crosby had written. In 1853, with William Bradbury, he founded the New York Normal Institute to train music teachers. Under Bradbury's influence, Root began to write gospel music especially designed for Sunday school use, and composed his first successful piece of sacred music, "The Shining Shore". As the school became successful, he began to hold music conventions around the country, a major structure for spreading new developments in both secular and sacred music through the culture.

In 1859 Root moved to Chicago as a partner in Root & Cady, a music publishing firm and retail store originally founded by his brother, E. T. Root. The war brought Root some fame as several of his songs, such as "The Battle Cry of Freedom" and "Tramp, Tramp, Tramp, the Boys Are Marching" became national hits. The firm prospered until 1871, when it was destroyed in the Chicago Fire. Its major assets, including the plates and the copyrights, were then sold to the John Church Company in Cincinnati. Root formed a new company, George F. Root & Sons, which operated as the agent in Chicago for the Church company. He concentrated upon teaching and composing for the rest of his life.

By the end of his life, Root's published songs numbered over 200, and he was responsible for the compilation and publication of more than 70 song books. Among his most enduring hymns were "I've Found a Friend" and "Ring the Bells of Heaven".

Sources:

Dictionary of American Biography. 20 vols. and 7 supps. New York: Charles Scribner's Sons, 1928-1936, 1944-1981.
Root, George F. *The Story of a Musical Life.* Cincinnati, OH: J. Church & Co., 1891. 256 pp.
Stebbins, George C. *Reminiscences and Gospel Hymn Stories.* New York: Charles H. Doran Company, 1924. 327 pp.

★ 800 ★
ROSE, Hieromonk Seraphim
Monk, Russian Orthodox Church Outside of Russia
b. 1934, California
d. Sep. 2, 1982, Platina, California

Hieromonk Seraphim Rose, founder of the St. Herman of Alaska Brotherhood, a monastic order in the Russian Orthodox Church Outside of Russia, was born Eugene Rose. He attended Pomona College and did graduate work at the University of California at Berkeley where he earned his master's degree in Chinese. In 1961 he attended a lecture by a Russian Orthodox monk, Abbot Herman (Gleb Podmoshensky). He soon joined the church, was tonsured as a monk (taking the name Seraphim), and ordained as a priest. By 1963 he had decided to form a new order which would have as its primary purpose the conversion of English-speaking peoples to Orthodoxy. He opened an icon and book store in a building in San Francisco adjacent to the new cathedral on Geary Street. In 1965, with a hand-operated press, Father Seraphim launched *The Orthodox Word*, an English-language periodical.

In 1967 Father Seraphim began the search for a site for a monastery, and land near Platina, California, was located and purchased. The move to the site, some 250 miles north of San Francisco, was accomplished in 1969. Meanwhile he had worked for the glorification (canonization) of Saint Herman of Alaska, an event which was finally celebrated by Metropolitan Philaret in 1970.

In Platina, Seraphim settled into the life of a monk. He spent many hours in prayer and became the author of a number of articles for *The Orthodox Word*. He supervised the growth of the monastic community into an important focus of the church's life and St. Herman of Alaska Press into a significant publisher of English-language Orthodox literature. Father Seraphim wrote several books on a variety of topics, and translated a number of items from Russian into English.

In 1977 he was elevated to the rank of hierodeacon and then hieromonk. He died at the relatively young age of 48.

Sources:

"Father Seraphim the Philosopher." *The Orthodox Word* 23, 5 (September-October 1987): 291-299.

Little Russian Philokalia. Tran. by Father Seraphim Rose. 2 vols. Platina, CA: Saint Herman of Alaska Monastery Press, 1983.
Rose, Seraphim. *Orthodoxy and the Religion of the Future.* Platina, CA: Saint Herman of Alaska Brotherhood, 1983. 242 pp.

★ 801 ★
ROSEN, Moishe
Founder, Jews for Jesus
b. Apr. 12, 1932, Kansas City, Missouri

Martin Meyer Rosen, better known under his public name, Moishe Rosen, the founder of Jews for Jesus, is the son of Rose Baker and Ben Rosen. He was raised in a nominal Reform Jewish home in Denver, Colorado, where his family had moved when he was two years old. As he grew older, he observed Jewish traditions, but had come to doubt any religious truths. In 1947 he enrolled at Colorado University, but dropped out in 1951 before completing his degree. During his college days, in 1950, he married Ceil Starr. A chance meeting with Orville Freeman, an Evangelical Christian, prompted a spiritual search for both Rosen and his wife. Both converted to Christianity in 1953.

Rosen decided to become a Jewish missionary. He moved to New York City and associated with the American Board of Missions to the Jews. He attended Northeastern Bible College, received his diploma, and was ordained as a Baptist minister in 1957. He had already become a missionary for the American Board. In 1957 he moved to Los Angeles as a minister of several Hebrew-Christian fellowships. He returned to New York in 1967 as the director of recruitment and training for the board. While in New York he authored his first books, *How to Witness Simply and Effectively* (1968) and *Revolutionary for Our Time* (1969).

Impressed by the phenomenon of the street people, the "hippies," Rosen moved to San Francisco, California, and began to minister to Jews who had become a part of the street culture. His basic message was that Jews can accept Jesus without giving up their Jewishness. Traditionally, Jews have cut off individuals who converted from the Jewish community, and Christians have sought to assimilate converts into Gentile culture. With the affirmation that recognition of Jesus as Lord and Jewish culture were compatible, Rosen founded the Jews for Jesus movement and its corporate structure Hineni Ministries, Inc. Rosen recounted the story of his early life and the founding of his unique ministry in his next book, *Jews for Jesus* (1974). Jews for Jesus became an integral part of the street ministries which created the Jesus People Revival of the early 1970s and soon spread to Jewish communities around the United States. Rosen became involved in the massive Key '73 national evangelism campaign initiated by William Rohl Bright and Campus Crusade for Christ.

Through the 1980s Rosen's ministry grew and has become, for the Jewish community, synonymous with all Jewish missionary efforts. It is frequently confused with the Messianic Jewish movement which has established separate Jewish-Christian synagogues. One prominent counter organization took the name Jews for Judaism. As part of his work of overseeing the large organization which Hineni Ministries has become, Rosen has written several additional books, including two co-authored by his wife.

Sources:

Rosen, Ceil, and Moishe Rosen. *Christ in the Passover.* Chicago: Moody Press, 1978. 1122 pp.
———. *Share the New Life with a Jew.* Chicago: Moody Press, 1976. 80 pp.
Rosen, Moishe, with William Proctor. *Jews for Jesus.* Old Tappan, NJ: Fleming H. Revell Company, 1974. 126 pp.
———. *The Sayings of Chairman Moishe.* Carol Stream, IL: Creation House, 1974. 106 pp.
———. *Y'shua: The Jewish Way to Say Jesus.* Chicago: Moody Press, 1982. 149 pp.

Rosen, Ruth. *Jesus for Jews*. San Francisco, CA: A Messianic Jewish Perspective, 1987. 320 pp.

★ 802 ★
ROY, Maurice
Cardinal, Roman Catholic Church, Canada
b. Jan. 25, 1905, Quebec, Ontario, Canada
d. Oct. 24, 1985, Montreal, Quebec, Canada

Maurice Roy, a cardinal of the Roman Catholic Church and the first bishop named primate of the church for Canada, was the son of Mariette Legendre and Ferdinand Roy. His father was a judge and dean of the faculty at Laval University, the Catholic school in Quebec. In 1915 he entered the Petit Seminaire at Quebec. He finished high school and college (B.A., 1923) there and then decided to enter the priesthood. He entered the Grand Seminaire at Laval and in 1927 was awarded his doctorate in theology and ordained to the priesthood. He then journeyed to Rome to begin two years of study in philosophy at the Institutum Angelicum from which he received a second doctorate in 1929. He completed his education by spending a year at the Sorbonne.

Upon his return to Canada in 1930, Roy joined the faculty of the Grand Seminaire as a professor of theology. He held his teaching position through World War II, though he was on leave as a chaplain in Europe beginning in 1939. In England for several years, he accompanied the Canadian troops in Italy (1943) and subsequently in Northern Europe. In 1944 he was named head of Canadian chaplains in the armed forces. In 1945 he returned to his teaching duties in Canada.

Roy's return to teaching was very brief, as he was named bishop of the diocese of Trois Rivieres at the beginning of 1946. In the summer of 1947 he was named archbishop of Quebec. In 1956 the See of Quebec was named the Primatial See and Roy thus became the primate of Canada. He was made a cardinal in 1967 and at the same time placed in charge of two new offices in the Curia, the Council for Laity and the Justice and Peace Commission. Among his first duties was to attend the Congress on the Lay Apostolate in which he advocated the freedom of lay expression in the church. His wartime experiences had made him an enemy of armed conflict and a supporter of conscientious objectors. He also helped develop the argument in the pope's letter on the eightieth anniversary of *Rerun Novarum*, the late-nineteenth century encyclical that set the direction for the church's more recent social policies.

Roy remained as head of the two commissions until 1976. By that time he had also become a member of the Sacred Congregation for the Clergy, the Congregation for Catholic Education, and the Commission for the Revision of the Code of Canon Law upon which he continued to serve. He retired in 1981.

★ 803 ★
Swami RUDRANANDA
Founder, Rudrananda Foundation
b. 1928, New York, New York
d. Feb. 21, 1973, New York

Swami Rudrananda, better known as Rudi, was the founder of the Rudrananda Foundation. He was born Albert Rudolph into a poor Jewish family, and was raised in Brooklyn under the strained circumstances brought on by the depression. He quit school and joined the army at 18, but attended night school after his discharge in order to obtain a high school diploma. After completing night school, he entered North Carolina State College, from which he eventually earned a degree in textile engineering. After returning to New York, he opened a small Oriental art store.

Rudi had a profound interest in spirituality from an early age. His first formal teachers were Tibetan Buddhists. He was also deeply

involved with the work that grew out of the teachings of **George Ivanovitch Gurdjieff** and Subud. He was, however, most deeply involved with Hindu teachers, and he spent a great deal of time with Hindus such as Sri Shankaracharya of Puri, Bhagwan Nityananda, and **Swami Paramahansa Muktananda**. For over 20 years, he went back and forth between North America and India in his quest for spiritual knowledge. He acquired his name from Muktananda, who initiated him as a swami in 1966. Rudi was the individual principally responsible for Muktananda's first trip to the West. He broke his ties with Swami Muktananda in 1971, however, and spent the remaining years of his life developing his own organization. For a short period of time after his death in 1973 his group was run by a core of eight disciples, but it eventually splintered into several independent groups, the most substantial of which formed the Nityananda Institute, led by Swami Chetanananda.

Rudi was an eclectic teacher. Muktananda's siddha yoga, which emphasized the disciple's awakening as a result of the direct spiritual activity of the guru, was at the core of his teachings. He also relied on tactics derived from the Gurdjieff work, and was something of an iconoclast with respect to the expectations of his students. He required that disciples support themselves through regular work, and Rudi himself worked hard at his art business for several decades. He died in a plane crash in the Catskills at the comparatively young age of 45. Rudi's one book, *Spiritual Cannibalism* (1973), was published shortly after his death.

Sources:

Jones, Franklin. *The Knee of Listening*. Los Angeles: Dawn Horse Press, 1973. 271 pp.
Mann, John. *Rudi: Fourteen Years with My Teacher*. Cambridge, MA: Rudra Press, 1987. 343 pp.
Rudi [Swami Rudrananda]. *Spiritual Cannibalism*. Woodstock, NY: Overlook Press, 1973, 1978. 196 pp.

★ 804 ★
RUSSELL, Charles Taze
Founder, Watch Tower Bible and Tract Society
b. Feb. 16, 1852, Pittsburgh, Pennsylvania
d. Oct. 31, 1916, Pampa, Texas

Charles Taze Russell, founder of the Watch Tower Bible and Tract Society, the official corporate name of what is popularly termed the Jehovah's Witnesses, was born into a family of Scotch-Irish Presbyterians. In his youth, Russell rejected religion and became a partner in his father's retail clothing business. He was taken out of this career through contact with Jonas Wendall, an Adventist teacher who predicted that the end of the world and the return of Christ would take place in 1874. Russell began his own group to study the Bible in light of Wendall's predictions.

American Adventism has its origins in the activity of a Baptist layman, William Miller. After studying the Bible for several years, Miller became convinced both that the end of the world was near and that he should broadcast the news. He preached this message for a dozen years before his following, which had grown to 50,000, pressured him into setting a specific date for Christ's return. When both the first and then a second, revised date (1844) passed uneventfully, some followers defected and Miller gradually faded into retirement, but new leaders, such as Wendall, arose to set new dates.

In the course of his study of the Bible and the writings of other Adventists, Russell began to develop doctrinal views that departed from traditional interpretations, such as the idea that unrepentant sinners would be annihilated rather than eternally tormented. He also rejected the doctrine of the Trinity, deeming it non-biblical. He parted from Wendall after finding that the more literal meaning of the Greek word *parousia* (the term usually translated as ''return'') was ''presence,'' and came to believe that Christ's second presence had actually arrived in 1874. Finally, in line with his rejection of the idea of eternal torment, he came to a somewhat different understanding of the atonement of Christ.

Russell initiated the publication of *The Watch Tower and Herald of Christ's Presence* in 1879 and began to put out a number of tracts. *Food for Thinking Christians*, an exposition of, among other things, his unique doctrinal position, was published in 1880. The movement grew steadily, both in the United States and Europe. Its growth attracted controversy, and Russell engaged in a number of public debates with mainstream ministers, debates which further stimulated the growth of the movement.

In 1886 Russell issued the first volume of the *Millennial Dawn* series, the most comprehensive presentation of his mature thought. Six volumes appeared during his lifetime. A seventh volume (not generally accepted by his followers) appeared soon after his death. The series was renamed *Studies in the Scriptures*, under which name it is presently kept in print.

For many years Russell had predicted that the millennium, which had dawned in 1874, would climax with the establishment of God's rule on earth in 1914. The advent of World War I seemed to confirm his prediction, but God's continued reluctance to intervene after that year caused Russell to change the date to 1918. He died in 1916, and it would be left to **Joseph F. Rutherford** to reorganize the movement in the 1920s into the Jehovah's Witnesses.

Sources:

Horowitz, David. *Pastor Charles Taze Russell*. New York: Philosophical Library, 1986. 159 pp.

Melton, J. Gordon. *Biographical Dictionary of American Cult and Sect Leaders*. Garland Reference Library of Social Science, vol. 212. New York: Garland Publishing, 1986.

Russell, Charles Taze.*Millennial Dawn*. 6 vols. Alleghany, PA: Watch Tower Bible and Tract Society, 1886-1899.

_____. *Our Most Holy Faith*. East Rutherford, NJ: Dawn Bible Students Association, 1958. 719 pp.

_____. *Pastor Russell's Sermons*. Brooklyn: Peoples Pulpit Association, 1917. 803 pp.

_____. *What Pastor Russell Said*. Chicago: Leslie W. Jones, 1917. 776 pp.

_____. *What Pastor Russell Taught*. Chicago: Leslie W. Jones, 1919. 392 pp.

White, Timothy. *A People for His Name*. New York: Vantage Press, 1967. 418 pp.

★ 805 ★
RUTHERFORD, Joseph Franklin
Leader, Jehovah's Witnesses
b. Nov. 8, 1869, Morgan County, Missouri
d. Jan. 8, 1942, San Diego, California

Joseph Franklin Rutherford, the "second founder" of the Jehovah's Witnesses, was born into a farming family in Missouri. Deciding to take up a career as a lawyer at a young age, he worked his way through law school and in 1892 was admitted to the Missouri bar. He came into contact with **Charles Taze Russell**'s movement in 1894, was baptized into the faith in 1906, and became the group's lawyer in 1907. A prolific writer, his *Man's Salvation from a Lawyer's Viewpoint* (1906) was published during his first year as a member of the Watch Tower Bible and Tract Society, the corporation started by Russell.

Rutherford was elected to the presidency of the society in 1916, a short time after Russell passed away. Predictably, a succession struggle commenced in the wake of the founder's death, and Rutherford won out only after a prolonged battle that resulted in the loss of a large number of members. As soon as that crisis had ended, new troubles emerged in 1918 in the form of Canada's banning the society, and the arrest of Rutherford and other leaders for discouraging military service during the war. Sentenced to 80 years, they

served less than a year before being released on bail, and the sentence was eventually reversed.

In a few short years the movement had suffered a number of hard blows, from the failure of Russell's prediction for 1914 (the year God's millennial rule was to have begun) through the succession struggle to government persecution. Between 1919 and his death in 1942, Rutherford reorganized and rebuilt the society into the strong, successful movement that we now know as the Jehovah's Witnesses (the name Rutherford gave the society in 1931). A new periodical, *Awake* (originally *The Golden Age*), was initiated and the literature reorganized, with Rutherford himself authoring much of it. Literature distribution campaigns involving a mobilization of the membership also were started. Because of its pacifist stance, the movement suffered another wave of persecution during World War II, but it was not as serious a crisis as that experienced by the society in World War I.

Sources:

Bergman, Jerry, ed. *Jehovah's Witnesses I: The Early Writings of J. F. Rutherford*. New York: Garland Publishing, 1990.

Curran, Edward. *Judge "for Four Days" Rutherford*. Brooklyn, NY: 1940.

Melton, J. Gordon. *Biographical Dictionary of American Cult and Sect Leaders*. Garland Reference Library of Social Science, vol. 212. New York: Garland Publishing, 1986.

Rutherford, Joseph F. *Can the Living Talk with the Dead?*. Brooklyn: International Bible Students Association, 1920. 126 pp.

_____. *Children*. Brooklyn: Watch Tower Bible and Tract Society, 1941.

_____. *Deliverance*. Brooklyn: International Bible Students Association, 1906. 379 pp.

_____. *A Great Battle in the Ecclesiastical Heavens, As Seen By a Lawyer*. New York: The Author, 1915. 64 pp.

_____. *The Harp of God*. Brooklyn: International Bible Students Association, 1921. 375 pp.

_____. *Millions Now Living Will Never Die*. Brooklyn: International Bible Students Association, 1920. 124 pp.

★ 806 ★
RYAN, John Augustine
Priest and Social Ethics Scholar, Roman Catholic Church
b. May 25, 1869, Vermillion, Minnesota
d. Sep. 16, 1945, St. Paul, Minnesota

John Augustine Ryan, a major theoretician on social ethics for the American Roman Catholic Church, was the son of William and Maria Elizabeth Luby Ryan, both first generation immigrants from Ireland. Ryan's parents were pious, and three of his brothers and sisters also chose a church vocation. Ryan was sent to the Christian Brothers school in St. Paul, Minnesota, and while there decided to go into the priesthood. He attended the diocesan seminary in St. Paul. His interest in social ethics was prompted in large part by the recently published 1891 papal encyclical, *Rerum Novarum*, which set guidelines for and motivated the development of Catholic social thought.

Ryan graduated from seminary in 1898, was ordained as a priest, and assigned to a parish in St. Paul, Minnesota. Ryan, however, had attracted the attention of Archbishop **John Ireland**, who in the fall of 1898 sent him to Catholic University for graduate work in moral theology. He concentrated on the application of Christianity to social life and the integration of data from the social sciences into moral social perspectives. He finished his doctorate and returned to St. Paul to teach in the seminary. His doctoral dissertation became his first book, *A Living Wage*, in which he developed an argument for the minimum wage. While in St. Paul Ryan wrote his first major books, two volumes on ethics and economic life: *Socialism: Promise or Menace* (1914) and *Distributive Justice* (1916). Ryan remained in St. Paul until 1915, when he returned to Washington, D.C., and Catholic University as a professor of moral theology.

During World War I the church had established the National Catholic War Council. After the war, it was reorganized and continued as the National Catholic Welfare Conference. Through the conference, the American bishops issued a document containing their *Program for Social Reconstruction*. In developing their new social policies, the bishops used and accepted many of the recommendations put forth by Ryan, and he was asked to take charge of the conference's social action department.

Basing his position on social issues on *Rerum Novarum*, Ryan advocated a minimum wage, child labor laws, labor's right to organize, the federal income tax, and old age insurance. He was most conservative on matters of church and state, as he believed that the state had an obligation to make a public profession of religion. These opinions formed the substance of his many books, such as *The Church and Labor* (1920); *Social Reconstruction* (1920); *The State and the Church* (1922); and *The Catholic Church and the Citizen* (1928). During the 1930s he supported Roosevelt's New Deal programs and worked closely with the National Recovery Administration. He also appeared on radio broadcasts to oppose fellow priest **Charles Edward Coughlin**, whose demagogic attacks on the government had become an embarrassment to the church.

In 1939 Ryan turned 70 and was forced to retire from Catholic University. He continued his work at the welfare conference, and began to write his autobiography, published in 1941 as *Social Doctrine in Action: A Personal History*. The rise of Nazism challenged his earlier opinions about war and peace, and as a member of the Committee to Defend America by Aiding the Allies he became an early advocate of America's involvement in the war.

Sources:

Lippy, Charles H. *Twentieth-Century Shapers of American Popular Religion.* New York: Greenwood Press, 1989. 494 pp.
Ryan, John A. *The Catholic Church and the Citizen.* New York: Macmillan Company, 1928. 94 pp.
———. *The Church and Labor.* New York: Macmillan Company, 1920. 305 pp.
———. *Distributive Justice.* New York: Macmillan Company, 1916. 442 pp.
———. *A Living Wage.* New York: Macmillan Company, 1906. 361 pp.
———. *Social Doctrine in Action: A Personal History.* New York: Harper Brothers, 1941. 297 pp.
———. *Social Reconstruction.* New York: Macmillan Company, 1920. 242 pp.

★807★
RYERSON, Adolphus Egerton
General Conference President, Methodist Church of Canada
b. Mar. 24, 1803, Victoria, British Columbia, Canada
d. Feb. 19, 1882, Toronto, Ontario, Canada

Adolphus Egerton Ryerson, a Canadian Methodist minister known for the controversies which surrounded him, was the son of Joseph and Mehetabel Ryerson. His father was a loyalist, that is, an American colonist who fought with the British during the American Revolution (and subsequently in the War of 1812), and who migrated to Canada after the war, where he became a successful farmer. A short time after the War of 1812, Ryerson was converted to Christianity and joined the Methodist Church (the branch affiliated with the Wesleyan Connection). He began to prepare himself for a career in law.

It was not until the 1820s that Ryerson decided to enter the ministry. His decision was occasioned by a serious illness in 1824-1825. Following an intense religious experience he preached his first sermon on Easter Sunday of 1825 and that fall was accepted on trial by the Methodist Conference. His first appointment was to the York and Yonge Street Circuit. During his first year in the ministry, Ryerson became somewhat of a celebrity because of an open letter (dated March 11, 1826) attacking the exclusive privileges of the Church of England in Canada. In 1827 he was ordained a deacon. Two years later he was ordained an elder and appointed editor of *The Christian Guardian*, the church's periodical. He held that post, with two brief breaks, until 1840.

During his years with the *Guardian*, Ryerson worked to break the control of the Church of England on higher education. He is credited with securing the charter for the Upper Canada Academy. In 1841 it became Victoria University, and he became its principal. In 1844 he also became the superintendent of education for Canada West (Ontario). He worked to build a nonsectarian educational system in the province. In 1847 he gave up his position at Victoria University, but remained superintendent until 1876.

Ryerson worked for an independent and independent-minded Canada. As regards the Methodist Church, he worked for its independence from British domination, though he was conservative in wanting to keep the hierarchical structure inherited from England. In 1874 the Wesleyans and the Methodist New Connexion Church merged to form the Methodist Church in Canada. Ryerson was elected as the first president of the General Conference.

During his years of retirement from his educational post, he worked on three books which appeared in the 1880s: *The Loyalists of America and These Times* (1880); *Canadian Methodism, Its Epochs and Characteristics* (1882); and *The Story of My Life* (1883).

Sources:

Harmon, Nolan B. *The Encyclopedia of World Methodism.* 2 vols. Nashville: United Methodist Publishing House, 1974.
Ryerson, Adolphus Egerton. *Canadian Methodism, Its Epochs and Characteristics.* Toronto: William Briggs, 1882. 440 pp.
———. *The Loyalists of America and These Times.* 2 vols. Toronto: William Briggs, 1880.
———. *The Story of My Life.* Toronto: William Briggs, 1883. 612 pp.
Sissons, C. B. *Egerton Ryerson.* 2 vols. Toronto: Clarke, Irwin. 1937.
Wallace, W. Stewart. *The Macmillan Dictionary of Canadian Biography.* 4th ed., rev. Edited by W. A. McKay. Toronto: Macmillan of Canada, 1978.

★808★
Archimandrite SABASTIAN
Serbian Orthodox Priest
b. 1863, San Francisco, California
d. Nov. 30, 1940, Zicha Yugoslavia

Archimandrite Sabastian, founder of Serbian Orthodoxy in the United States, was born Jovan (John) Dabovich in San Francisco. His parents, who were first generation immigrants from Serbia, operated a store. As a youth, Jovan developed a special bent toward religion and spent much of his leisure time at the Russian Orthodox Cathedral, the only Orthodox church in the United States at the time. Following his high school graduation, he served as a reader in the parish and was soon invited to Russia to be trained as a missionary priest. He studied at the theological academies at St. Petersburg and Kiev, was tonsured as a monk (where he acquired the name Sabastian), and was ordained as a deacon in 1887.

After his first ordination, Sabastian returned to the San Francisco parish to teach in the parochial school. Bishop Nicolas, head of the Russian diocese, ordained him to the priesthood in 1892 and assigned him as a missionary in California and Washington. The following year he replaced Fr. Alexis Toth as priest of the Russian Orthodox Church in Minneapolis, the second Orthodox church established in America. He returned to California in 1893 to found the first non-Russian ethnic Orthodox parish in America, St. Sava's Serbian Orthodox Church in Jackson, California.

After three years at Jackson, Father Sabastian was reassigned to San Francisco by **Archbishop Tikhon**, then in charge of American Orthodoxy; he continued, however, to oversee the Jackson congregation. During this time, he authored a book, *The Ritual, Ser-*

vices, and Sacraments of the Holy Orthodox Church, to inform children and inquirers about Orthodoxy. Tikhon, recognizing his abilities, made him a part of the North American Mission administration and in 1902 assigned him to the mission in Alaska as Dean of the Sitka Deanery.

Several other Serbian parishes were being founded in the United States during this period, and Tikhon saw the need to organize them into a Serbian Mission. He chose Father Sabastian for the task, at which time he raised him to the rank of archimandrite. Sabastian moved to Chicago and made Holy Resurrection Serbian Orthodox Cathedral the center of his work. He guided the mission through its initial five years and then returned, at his own request, to missionary work. In 1913 he became an instructor at the new Orthodox seminary opened in Tenafly, New Jersey.

Although considered a candidate for the episcopacy, Father Sabastian decided to spend the remainder of his life in Serbia. He left America, served briefly as a chaplain in the Serbian Army in World War I, and after the war settled in Serbia (present-day Yugoslavia) for the rest of his life. He is buried in the Monastery of Zicha.

Sources:

Tarasar, Constance J. *Orthodox America, 1794-1976: Development of the Orthodox Church in America.* Syosset, NY: The Orthodox Church in America, Department of Archives and History, 1975. 352 pp.

★809★
SAI BABA (OF SHIRDI)
Indian Saint
b. 1856, Hyderabad India
d. Oct. 15, 1918, Shirdi India

Shirdi Sai Baba was a well-known Indian holy man. Very little is known about his early life, although it is said that he was born into a Brahmin family near Hyderabad. He left home at the age of eight to follow a Muslim holy man. After his first teacher passed away, he became associated with Venkusa, a Hindu guru. At the age of 16, he came to the village of Shirdi, where he lived for three years. He then disappeared, but returned after about a year. While no one knew his name, a local priest referred to him as Sai, and he began to be known as Sai Baba. He kept to himself, dressed meagerly, and spoke only when spoken to. He lived in a small, mud-walled mosque. While he begged for food, he distributed most of it to the poor.

Like many other Indian saints, Sai Baba was a miracle worker. For example, the story is told that he was fond of light and liked to keep his lamps burning into the late evening. On one occasion, the local shopkeepers got together and refused to give him oil, but when they went to the mosque they found that he had put water into his lamps and that they burned as if filled with oil. About 10 years after he had begun to reside in Shirdi, he went into the superconscious state of *samadhi* and remained in that state for three days. After this incident, people began claiming to experience ecstasy in his presence, as well as spontaneous healings and other miracles. As the stories grew, people made pilgrimages to Shirdi from all over India, and some began to adopt Sai Baba as their guru.

Sai Baba taught a path that blended elements of Hinduism and Islam, and emphasized devotion to the guru. Sai Baba asked his followers to remain within the faith in which they had been raised, but encouraged them to attend the religious festivals of other faiths. Sai Baba remained in Shirdi for the rest of his life. After his death, his resting place became a shrine and a place of pilgrimage, and he is still remembered as one of India's most famous saints. He never traveled to the West but eventually acquired many American disciples. He became known in the West, initially, because of his association with **Meher Baba**, who asserted that Shirdi Sai Baba was a perfect master. However, his fame spread only with the rising popularity of Sathya Sai Baba, who claims to be a reincarnation

of the earlier Sai Baba and whose organization has circulated material about him.

Sources:

Melton, J. Gordon. *Biographical Dictionary of American Cult and Sect Leaders.* Garland Reference Library of Social Science, vol. 212. New York: Garland Publishing, 1986.
Osborne, Arthur. *The Incredible Sai Baba.* New Delhi, India: Orient Longmans, 1957. 102 pp.

★810★
Sathya SAI BABA
Spiritual Teacher, Sathya Sai Baba Movement
b. Nov. 23, 1926, Puttaparthi India

Sathya Sai Baba is a popular Hindu saint who, although he has never toured the United States, has a large American following. His mother experienced birth pangs while performing Satyanarayana Puja (a form of Hindu piety), and subsequently named her son Satyanarayana. He is remembered as having had spiritual inclinations from a young age. Like many other Indian saints, his excessive religious devotions as a child caused his family to worry that the boy might be insane. On May 23, 1940, at the age of 14, he announced to his relatives that he was the reincarnation of **Sai Baba of Shirdi**, a famous saint of north India, and that they should "worship me every Thursday" (a day holy to the Hindu deity Narayana). From that time forward, he insisted that people address him as Sathya Sai Baba. His ministry began on October 20, 1940, when he experienced release from *maya* (cosmic ignorance). He gradually attracted a following, which is headquartered in south-central India.

Sai Baba is best known for his miracles, particularly his materializations of objects out of thin air. Devotees claim that *vibhuti* (sacred ashes) materialize even on his photographs. While critics outside of the Hindu tradition naturally doubt the reality of these manifestations, critics within the tradition argue that true spiritual teachers, although capable of such feats, refrain from public demonstrations of their *siddhis* (psychic powers). In accordance with the latter category of criticisms, Sai Baba asserts that he manifests his miracles to inculcate faith rather than to simply display his supernatural power.

To his devotees, Sai Baba is an *avatar*, an incarnation of the Supreme Lord, rather than merely a God-realized soul. Like the Krishna of the *Bhagavad Gita*, he sees his mission as the overcoming of evil, the reestablishment of *Dharma* (a religious righteousness), and the spiritual regeneration of humanity. To accomplish this end, Sai Baba has particularly interested himself in education and health. He has provided the motivating energy for schools and colleges throughout India and initiated a variety of other service-oriented institutions such as hospitals.

Sai Baba has given many public lectures over the years which have been transcribed and edited. The most extensive collection was published as *Sathya Sai Speaks.* He has also produced commentaries on a number of Hindu sacred writings such as the *Bhagavatha Vahini* (1970) and the *Geetha Vahini* (1970). During the 1980s he developed a large following in the West, and disciples produced a significant body of material concerning him and their relationship to him. Icelandic parapsychologist Erlendur Haraldsson conducted a study of the psychic phenomena around Sai Baba and reported he was neither able to explain it nor explain it away.

Sources:

Haraldsson, Erlendur. *Modern Miracles.* New York: Fawcett Columbine, 1987. 300 pp.
Hislop, John S. *My Baba and I.* San Diego: Birth Day Publishing Company, 1985. 282 pp.
Murphet, Howard. *Sai Baba: Avatar.* San Diego: Birth Day Publishing Company, 1977. 21 pp.

Sai Baba, Sathya. *Bhagavatha Vahini*. Bombay, India: Sri Sathya Sai Educational Foundation, 1970. 338 pp.
_____. *Geetha Vahini*. Bombay, India: Sri Sathya Sai Educational Foundation, 1970. 283 pp.
_____. *Sathya Sai Speaks*. 7 vols. Bombay, India: Sri Sathya Sai Educational Foundation, 1970-1971.
Sandweiss, Samuel H. *Sai Baba: The Holy Man . . .and the Psychiatrist*. San Diego: Birth Day Publishing Company, 1975.

★811★
SANAPIA
Comanche Medicine Woman and Healer
b. May 20, 1895, Medicine Park, Oklahoma
d. Jan. 23, 1979, Chandler Creek, Oklahoma

Sanapia, also known by her Christian name, Mary Poafpybitty, was a medicine woman and healer among the Comanche and a leader in the Native American Church. She was born in Medicine Park, near Fort Sill, Oklahoma, in the spring of 1895, when the Yapai band of Comanches came into the Indian agency for rations. Her mother, Chapty, and father, Poafpybitty, were both conservative in their views even though they were in different religious camps. Chapty and her family were ardent peyotists (users of the peyote cactus for religious sacramental purposes) and practitioners of traditional Comanche religion. Poafpybitty was one of the first and most diligent Comanche converts to Christianity. Because the Comanches were matrilineal, Sanapia was raised by her mother's parents. It appears that their conservative traditionalism exerted more lasting influence on Sanapia than the Christian views of her father. Sanapia was raised by grandparents who fought to preserve the old life, but she was a daughter of those who were being forced to adjust to a new way of life, including new religious beliefs. Poafpybitty became a Christian, while Chapty rejected English, became an Eagle doctor, and embraced peyote as a physical and spiritual healing agent. Sanapia, observed by her maternal relatives for signs of the healing power from an early age, also became an Eagle doctor and strong supporter of the Native American Church.

The word Comanche appears to derive from the Ute Indians' "komanticia," and enters English through Spanish contacts with the group from their outposts in northern New Mexico. By the beginning of the eighteenth century, after European contact released the horse into Comanche culture, the Comanches commanded hunting grounds that stretched from present-day Wyoming to west Texas. Although divided into four great bands, the Comanches were ecologically divided into northern and southern groups. After their confinement onto an Oklahoma reservation in 1876, they continued to exhibit this geographical division in political and religious matters. Sanapia belonged to the northern conservatives who continued to place more trust in Indian doctors than the white man's new medicine. Like her mother, Sanapia was one who preserved the old ways by learning to doctor with ancient powers from both the earthly and spiritual realms. She also inherited her mother's diplomatic skills, which allowed Indian ways to continue in spite of family, tribal, United States government, and Christian missionary efforts to suppress any remnant of the ancient religion.

Comanche Indian "doctoring" is done using both herbs of the earth and spirits of the other world. Medical procedure is universal in the two-step process of diagnosis and, if possible, cure. Sanapia learned to recognize and utilize the healing properties of hundreds of plants and animals, which sharpened her powers of observation and analysis. For the calling and application of the spiritual powers, she learned the songs and prayers collected and tested from generations of contact with the ancestral spirits of all living things. Sanapia became a doctor by study of all living things, spiritual and earthly, including herself.

Biographies of many spiritual healers reveal a period of rejection of their powers. When Sanapia was widowed in her thirties by the death of her second husband, she "roughed it out," gambling and living a fast life. A few years later she was asked to heal her sister's child. She saw the success of that healing as a sign to pick up her calling. Sanapia remarried and remained a conservative religious leader, a committed family and tribal member, and a skilled Eagle doctor. In 1967 Sanapia began working with David E. Jones of the University of Oklahoma to produce materials on the ethnopharmacopeia of the Comanches. Their efforts resulted in several articles and a book that details the education of a Comanche Indian doctor.

Sanapia died on January 23, 1979, and was buried in the Comanche Indian cemetery near Chandler Creek, Oklahoma.

Sources:

Jones, David E. *Sanapia: Comanche Medicine Woman*. New York: Holt, Rinehart and Winston, 1972.
Wallace, Ernest, and E. Adamson Hoebel. *The Comanches: Lords of the South Plains*. Norman, OK: University of Oklahoma Press, 1952.

—*Johnny Flynn*

★812★
SANDFORD, Frank Weston
Founder, Kingdom, Inc.
b. Oct. 2, 1862, Bowdoinham, Maine
d. Mar. 4, 1948, Hobart, New York

Frank Sandford, founder of the Kingdom, Inc. (also popularly known as the Church of the Living God and as the Holy Ghost and Us Society), was born into a farming family in Maine. As a young man Sandford went through several changes of career, starting out as a school teacher, switching to law, and ending up in the ministry. He pastored for Free Baptist congregations in Topsham and Somersworth, Maine, until he began to receive messages from God, one of which he interpreted as a directive to leave the Free Baptists and become an independent evangelist.

After attracting a handful of followers, Sandford moved to Durham, Maine, where he began building a Bible school that gradually evolved into Shiloh community. Shiloh grew to include a Bible school, a residence center, a children's building, a hospital, and a post office. After receiving another revelation, Sandford became convinced that he was Elijah, who had returned to witness the last days. With this new authority, he incorporated his community as the Kingdom, an allusion to the "Thy Kingdom come" line in the Lord's Prayer. He also received another message designating him David (that is, designating him King).

Sandford's autocratic rule of the community led to trouble in the form of defections and scandals. Due to the death of a minor in the community, Sandford was convicted of cruelty and fined $100. After the trial, Sandford sailed to Palestine in order to build the Kingdom in Jerusalem, and then set out on a missionary tour of the world. However, six crew members died during the cruise, and Sandford, convicted of manslaughter, was forced to serve a 10-year sentence in a federal penitentiary.

During his confinement, Sandford kept in touch with Shiloh and taught a Bible class in prison. Released in 1921, he returned to Maine to assume control of his community. Shiloh was disbanded two years later and the headquarters reestablished in Boston. After Sandford's passing, the Kingdom survived in the form of decentralized congregations.

Sources:

Harriman, N. H. "Sandfordism Inside Out." *The Safeguard and Armory*. 8, 2 (October 1903): 137-147.
Melton, J. Gordon. *Biographical Dictionary of American Cult and Sect Leaders*. Garland Reference Library of Social Science, vol. 212. New York: Garland Publishing, 1986.
Nelson, Shirley. *Fair, Clear, and Terrible*. Latham, NY: British American Publishing, 1989. 446 pp.

Sandford, Frank Weston. *The Art of War for the Christian Soldier.* Amherst, NH: The Kingdom Press, 1904.

_____. *The Golden Light Upon the Two Americas.* Amherst, NH: The Kingdom Press, 1974.

_____. *The Majesty of Snowy Whiteness.* Amherst, NH: The Kingdom Press, 1901.

_____. *Seven Years with God.* Mt. Vernon, NY: Kingdom Publishing Co., 1957.

White, Arnold L. *The Almighty and Us.* Ft. Lauderdale, FL: The Author, 1979. 423 pp.

Woodward, E. P. *Sandfordism: An Exposure of the Claims, Purposes, Methods, Predictions, and Threats of Rev. F. W. Sandford, the "Apostle of Shiloh, Maine".* Portland, ME: Safeguard Publishing Company, 1902.

★813★
SANFORD, Elias Benjamin
Minister, Congregational Church
b. Jun. 6, 1843, Westbrook, Connecticut
d. Mar. 7, 1932, Middlefield, Connecticut

Elias Benjamin Sanford was a Congregational minister who formulated the plans for the Federal Council of Churches, which was the predecessor of the National Council of Churches of Christ in the U.S.A.. He was the son of Louisa Ann Weeks and Isaac Sanford, a minister in the Methodist Episcopal Church. After finishing his college preparatory work at Goshen Academy, Sanford attended Wesleyan University. In 1865 he graduated, was licensed to preach, and was received on a trial basis into the New York East Conference of the Methodist Episcopal Church. His first pastoral assignment was the Methodist church at Thomaston, Connecticut.

Sanford remained a Methodist minister only two years. In 1867 he transferred to the Congregational Church and became pastor of First Congregational Church of Cornwall, Connecticut. While there, in 1870 he married Martha Sanford, whom he had met at Thomaston. In 1873 he began a career in religious journalism, first as the editor of *Church Union* (a journal promoting the merger of Protestant churches) and then *Alliance*, a short-lived publication issued in Baltimore, Maryland. In 1882 he returned to Boston as editor of *Golden Rule* (a forerunner of *Christian Endeavor World*). Unfortunately, after a few months with Golden Rule, illness forced him into a retirement, and he would never fully recover his health. Sanford used his retirement years to author two books, *A History of Connecticut* (1887) and *A Concise Cyclopedia of Religious Knowledge* (1890). During the early 1890s he pastored at Westbrook, Connecticut, for a while.

In 1895 Sanford affiliated with the Open and Institutional Church League, an organization promoting the concept of the institutional church, congregations operating primarily in the urban context with a broad program of social service. It also had a secondary effect of promoting ecumenical cooperation and sharing. After five years as the secretary of the league, in 1900 he became general secretary of the National Federation of Churches and Christian Workers, one of a number of early efforts in ecumenical organization. It became the base from which Sanford could begin to formulate and organize for a more effective council of churches.

In 1905 Sanford organized a Conference on Interchurch Federation at which a constitution for a Federal Council of Churches was formulated. Over the next three years Sanford worked for the ratification of the constitution, and a council was formally organized in 1908. At that time Sanford was elected corresponding secretary. He served for six years, but in 1913 his health failed again and he was forced to resign. He was then elected honorary secretary in recognition of his services.

Sanford used his forced retirement years to author two books, the most important one being *Origin and History of the Federal Council of the Churches of Christ in America* (1916). He also authored *A History of the Reformation* (1917).

Sources:

Dictionary of American Biography. 20 vols. and 7 supps. New York: Charles Scribner's Sons, 1928-1936, 1944-1981.

Sanford, Elias Benjamin. *A Concise Cyclopedia of Religious Knowledge.* Hartford, CT: S. S. Scranton, 1890. 985 pp.

_____. *A History of Connecticut.* Hartford, CT: S. S. Scranton, 1887. 381 pp.

_____. *A History of the Reformation.* Hartford, CT: S. S. Scranton, 1917. 287 pp.

_____. *Origin and History of the Federal Council of the Churches of Christ in America.* Hartford, CT: S. S. Scranton, 1916. 528 pp.

★814★
SANKEY, Ira D.
Hymn Writer and Music Evangelist
b. Aug. 28, 1840, Edinburgh, Pennsylvania
d. Aug. 14, 1908, Northfield, Massachusetts

Ira D. Sankey, popular songleader for evangelist **Dwight L. Moody**, was raised on a farm in rural Pennsylvania. In 1857 the family moved to New Castle, Pennsylvania, where his father was president of the local bank. The family joined the Methodist Episcopal Church, and Sankey soon became the church's Sunday school superintendent and choir leader. He joined the Union Army in 1861 and formed a music club, the "Singing Boys in Blue." After the war he married and worked for his father in the Internal Revenue Service. He also became a popular singer at political gatherings and Sunday school meetings. In 1870 he attended the International Y.M.C.A. meeting in Indianapolis, where he met Dwight Moody. Moody wanted him to give up his job and come to Chicago as his songleader immediately. Six months later, in early 1871, Sankey agreed and moved to Chicago.

In Chicago Sankey became Moody's assistant at the north side mission and around the city. Moody established the custom of having Sankey sing solos at his evangelistic gatherings, a practice that became commonplace over the next decades. Eighteen months after moving to Chicago, Sankey accompanied Moody on the first great evangelistic campaign in Great Britain (1873-1875). So successful was this adventure that both men became universally known in the Christian world and the two became inseparable in their public life. Moody had been the first of the modern evangelists to recognize the value of music as a tool in mass evangelism. Sankey was a talented musician with a full baritone voice. Given the massive nature of the meetings in which he sang, it was remarkable that he was remembered for the exceptional volume, the purity of sound that would allow all to hear. He was able to preserve his voice without injury in spite of the intense activity surrounding his evangelistic endeavors.

While in Edinburgh, Scotland, in 1873, Sankey composed his first hymns and used them during the campaign. A musician rather than a poet, Sankey's great talent lay in taking poems with an evangelistic theme and setting them to appropriate music. The first of these may have been Horatio Bonar's hymn, "Yet There Is Room." Without a doubt, the most famous was the "Ninety and Nine," a poem Sankey found printed in a newspaper. Called upon by Moody that evening to sing a hymn, he sat at the organ and composed the music as he sang it to the gathered congregation. Other notable hymns included, "I'm Praying for You," "Hiding in Thee," "Faith Is the Victory," and "When the Mists Have Rolled Away."

Returning from Europe, Sankey accompanied Moody during the remainder of the 1870s in his evangelistic campaigns in Brooklyn, New York; Philadelphia; New York City; and Baltimore, Maryland. During the 1880s and 1890s, he accompanied Moody in all his campaigns, the most outstanding of which was the World Fair campaign in Chicago in 1893. He also assisted at the Northfield schools and conferences, which became a focal point of Moody's work in the 1890s.

In the winter of 1898-1899 Sankey embarked on a 30-stop tour in Great Britain, in which he presented a service of "Sacred Song and Story." He strained his voice during the tour and afterward greatly limited his performances to an occasional song, and work in Northfield. Moody led his last campaign in Kansas City in November 1899; he died soon afterward. Sankey lived for several more years, but his health began to fail and in 1903 he became blind. Among his last accomplishments was the authoring of an autobiographical volume, *Sankey's Story of the Gospel Hymns*. He died in Northfield in 1908.

Sources:

Harmon, Nolan B. *The Encyclopedia of World Methodism*. 2 vols. Nashville: United Methodist Publishing House, 1974.
Sankey, Ira D. *My Life and the Story of the Gospel Hymns and Sacred Songs and Solos*. Philadelphia: Sunday School Times Co., 1906. 410 pp.
Stebbins, George C. *Reminiscences and Gospel Hymn Stories*. New York: George H. Doran Company, 1924. 327 pp.

★815★
SASAKI, Kyozan Joshu
Rinzai Zen Master
Founder of Rinzai-Ji and related Zen Centers
b. 1907, Miyagi Japan

Kyozan Joshu Sasaki Roshi is a Rinzai Zen master and the founder of Rinzai-Ji, an association of Zen Buddhist centers which includes the Cimarron-ji Zen Center in Los Angeles, California, Mt. Baldy Zen Center in Redondo Beach, California, and the Bodhi-Mandala center in Jemez Springs, New Mexico. The son of a farmer, at the age of 14 he became a novice at Zuiryo-ji in Sapporo-shi under Joten Soko Muira Roshi. He became a priest in 1928; at the age of 40 he was authorized as a Roshi and became abbot of Yotoku-in. In 1953 he left Yotoku-in to become abbot of Shoju-an in Iiyama.

In the early 1960s, in response to requests by Gladys Weissbart and Dr. Robert L. Harmon of Los Angeles, the chief abbot of Myoshin-ji persuaded Sasaki Roshi to leave Japan and begin teaching in America. To accomplish this task, Sasaki Roshi felt that he would have to relocate permanently in the United States. He thus arranged for a new abbot to take over Shoju-an. After his arrival in America, Sasaki Roshi was situated in a small house in Gardenia, California. This house became the Mariposa Rinzai Zen Dojo, and included a renovated garage that was used as a *zendo* (meditation hall). His bedroom was used as the *sanzen* room (the place for private interviews between teacher and student).

As the number of people attending *zazen* (meditation) sessions increased, the neighbors complained about the parking situation. As a consequence, meditation meetings had to be held elsewhere. After a half-dozen years, the Cimarron Zen Center in Los Angeles came into being, and was used to hold zazen sessions and as a small residential center. The roshi continued to travel and teach, and a few years after Cimarron was founded a new center was set up in Redondo Beach. The Mount Baldy Zen Center (a former Boy Scout camp), which provided an environment somewhat closer to that of a traditional monastery, was established in 1970. The first three-month residential training session was held in the summer of that year. Rinzai-Ji was established in 1968 as an umbrella organization for these various centers.

Bodhi-Mandala, a Zen family community complete with hot springs, was founded in 1973 in Jemez Springs, New Mexico. There are also affiliated centers in North Carolina, New York, and in other parts of southern California. Sasaki Roshi's centers have acquired a reputation for traditionalism and strictness. The *sesshins* (intensives) at the Mt. Baldy Center, the most rigorous of the Roshi's institutions, are, in the words of Rick Fields (Buddhist historian and journalist), "notorious for hard practice among American Zen students."

Work outside the United States began as early as 1967, when Sasaki Roshi traveled to Vancouver, Canada, to lecture. In 1979 he visited Austria for the first time.

Sources:

Fields, Rick. *How the Swans Came to the Lake: A Narrative History of Buddhism in America*. Rev. ed. Boston, MA: Shambhala, 1986. 445 pp.
Kyozan Joshu Roshi: Ten Years in America. Mt. Baldy, CA: Mt. Baldy Zen Center, n.d. 13 pp.
Sasaki, Joshu. *Buddha is the Center of Gravity*. San Cristobal, NM: Lama Foundation, 1974. 95 pp.

—*James R. Lewis*

★816★
SASAKI, Ruth Fuller Everett
Zen Teacher, First Zen Institute of America
b. 1893
d. 1967, Kyoto Japan

Ruth Fuller Everett Sasaki, born Ruth Fuller, was a major supporter of the First Zen Institute of America. She served as editor of the institute's magazine, *Cat's Yawn*, and was a key person in facilitating the formal training in Japan of some of the first Americans to become interested in Zen in the mid-twentieth century. Early in life, Fuller married a prominent Chicago attorney, Charles Everett, and spent some time at the yoga ashram led by **Pierre Arnold Bernard** in Nyack, New York. She also studied the Sanskrit and Pali languages on her own (her study of the latter language indicates that she had an early interest in Buddhism, though not necessarily in Zen). During a world tour in 1930, she and her husband stopped in Japan, where they met **Daisetz Teitaro Suzuki**. He taught her how to meditate and gave her a copy of his *Second Series* of essays. She returned to Japan a few years later and, with the help of Suzuki, was able to study with, and practice under, Nanshinken Roshi, the Rinzai Zen master of Nanzenji, for three and a half months. Her purpose, as she remembered, was simply to "see," by practicing Zen according to the exact method that she had been taught. She hoped to discover if the method would produce any results for a foreigner. She was one of the first American students of Zen to actually come to Japan.

When Ruth Everett settled in New York in 1938, she became associated with **Shigetsu Sasaki Roshi**'s Buddhist Society of America (the original name of the First Zen Institute of America) and offered her services as editor of the society's journal. In the same year her daughter married Alan Wilson Watts, who was then associated with the institute and later proved to be a great popularizer of Zen in the West. The institute moved into new, upgraded quarters, and Sasaki Roshi, also known as Sokei-an, looked forward to a new phase in his work. Shortly after the Japanese attacked Pearl Harbor, however, the group came under observation, and on July 15, 1942, Sokei-an was taken to an internment camp. Ruth Everett hired a lawyer and arranged for one of Sokei-an's former students, now a Navy commander, to testify for his teacher. Sokei-an was released, and, partially to stabilize the Institute, he and Everett were married in 1944 (her first husband had died in 1940). His already poor health had been aggravated by imprisonment, however, and he died in 1945.

Before dying, Sokei-an charged his wife with the tasks of finding a successor for the Institute and of finishing his translation of the recorded sayings of Rinzai, a Chinese master of Zen Buddhism . To accomplish the latter, Sasaki realized that she would have to move to Japan for the rest of her life. Once there, she studied Japanese and classical Chinese and practiced *zazen* meditation under a Rinzai master, Zuigan Goto Roshi, the abbot of Daitoku-ji. She also renovated a previously deserted and dilapidated temple on the grounds of Daitoku-ji. After its completion, she was appointed priest and abbess. In 1956, she organized the First Zen Institute of America in Japan so as to assist Americans who wished to study

Zen in Japan. Through the Institute, she published a brief introductory text, *Zen: A Method for Religious Awakening* (1959). It was also with her aid that individuals such as poet Gary Snyder were able to practice in Japan.

Sources:

Fields, Rick. *How the Swans Came to the Lake: A Narrative History of Buddhism in America*. Rev. ed. Boston, MA: Shambhala, 1986. 445 pp.

Melton, J. Gordon *The Encyclopedia of American Religions*. 3d ed. Detroit: Gale Research Inc.,1988. 1102 pp.

Muira, Isshu, and Ruth Fuller Sasaki. *The Zen Koan*. New York; Harcourt Brace & World, 1965. 156 pp.

"On Ruth Fuller Sasaki." *Wind Bell* 8, 1-2 (Fall 1969): 21-22.

Sasaki, Ruth Fuller. *Zen: A Method for Religious Awakening*. Kyoto, Japan: First Zen Institute of America in Japan, 1959. 28 pp.

★ 817 ★
SASAKI, Shigetsu
Founder, First Zen Institute of America
b. 1882, Japan
d. May 17, 1945, New York, New York

Shigetsu Sasaki (better known as Sokei-an), founder of the First Zen Institute of America, was a successful artist who became part of a lay movement of Zen practitioners, Ryomokyo-Kai, under the direction of Sokatsu Shaku. In 1906, he and a small band of disciples accompanied Sokatsu on a mission to spread Ryomokyo-Kai to America. The mission failed, and everyone except Sokei-an and his wife returned to Japan. Sokei-an's wife, a fellow disciple he had married at his master's request, returned to Japan in 1914. Settling in New York, Sokei-an continued to pursue a career as an artist.

In 1919, he returned to Japan to work on his marriage and to complete his Zen training. Over the next 10 years, Sokei-an divided his time between New York and Japan. He also became a successful writer during this period. Completing his training in 1928, he settled permanently in the United States and founded the Buddhist Society of America (eventually renamed the First Zen Institute in America). The Zen Institute was quite successful, and, as the only Zen master in New York, Sokei-an became a mentor for many of the early Zen "popularizers," such as **Alan Wilson Watts**.

A periodical, *Cat's Yawn*, was published by the institute in the early 1940s. Toward the end of his life, Sokei-an married the editor of *Cat's Yawn*, Ruth Fuller Everett (Watts' mother-in-law). Like many other Japanese immigrants, Sokei-an was a victim of the paranoia of the second world war, and was interned for a period of 13 months. Everett was able to enlist the help of a former student, who was serving as a Navy commander, to intervene in favor of Sokei-an. The master had, however, become ill during his internment, and died the year following his release.

Under the able direction of **Ruth Fuller Everett Sasaki**, the institute survived Sokei-an's death. She later became a Zen priest herself and completed Sokei-an's translation of the *Collected Sayings of Rinzai* (Rinzai was the founder of one of the Zen "sects"). In 1954, the institute also initiated a new periodical, *Zen Notes*, which continues as one of the oldest newsletters in the American Zen community.

Sources:

Farkas, Mary. "Footsteps in the Invisible World." *Wind Bell* 8, 1-2 (Fall 1969): 15-19.

Fields, Rick. *How the Swans Came to the Lake*. Boulder, CO: Shambhala, 1986. 445 pp.

Melton, J. Gordon. *Biographical Dictionary of American Cult and Sect Leaders*. Garland Reference Library of Social Science, vol. 212. New York: Garland Publishing, 1986.

★ 818 ★
Swami SATCHIDANANDA
Founder, Integral Yoga International
b. Dec. 22, 1914, Coimbatore India

Swami Satchidananda, founder of the Integral Yoga International (formerly the Integral Yoga Institute), is a well-known yoga teacher, guru, and ecumenical leader. (Swami is a title given to Indian renunciates, and Satchidananda is his monastic name; his original name was Ramaswamy.) He was born into a family of wealthy landowners in south India, and as a young man worked in his uncle's automobile import business where he learned the welding trade. He married and had several children, but his wife died five years after his marriage.

Following his wife's death Satchidananda became more deeply interested in spirituality, practicing yoga disciplines, and reading the works of "modernist" (Western-influenced) Hindu spiritual teachers, such as **Swami Vivekananda** and Swami Sivananda Saraswati. Following World War II Satchidananda was a mendicant, eventually entering the Ramakrishna Monastery at Timpurraiturai. After the troubles surrounding India's independence had subsided, he moved to Sivananda's ashram in north India, took *sannyas*, the vows of the renounced life, and became Swami Satchidananda. In 1953, he traveled to Sri Lanka and opened, as an extension of Sivananda's organization, a Divine Life Society ashram. Like other modernist Hindu leaders he was involved in social outreach and social reform, opening an orphanage and medical dispensary, and participating in a movement to open Hindu temples in Sri Lanka to untouchables.

Satchidananda visited the United States in 1966 and founded the first center of what would become the Integral Yoga Institute. He eventually broke away from the Divine Life Society and shifted the center of his operations to North America. Satchidananda attracted many members of the counter-culture such as artist Peter Max as his students, and gained fame by delivering the opening address at the Woodstock music festival. Like his teacher Sivananda, he taught a synthesis of various yoga techniques which he termed integral yoga (not to be confused with **Sri Aurobindo**'s integral yoga). His ecumenical teaching flows out of the liberal position of modernist Hinduism that all religions ultimately lead to God. He has regularly participated in programs and at conferences where a wide variety of religious traditions are represented.

In 1975 Satchidananda admitted the first group of his pupils into the sannyasin order. In the 1980s he established his center of operations at Yogaville community in Buckingham, Virginia. The central structure at Yogaville is the Light of Truth Universal Shrine (LOTUS), a temple honoring all of the world's religious traditions. Satchidananda normally keeps a busy travel and lecture schedule, although recently he appears to have begun cutting back on his travels. He is author of a number of books and booklets, including *Integral Yoga Hatha* (1970); *The Glory of Sannyasa* (1975); *Guru and Disciple* (1977); and *How to Succeed in Yoga* (1978).

Sources:

Satchidananda, Swami. *Beyond Words*. New York: Holt Rinehart and Winston, 1977. 182 pp.

———. *The Glory of Sannyasa*. Pomfret Center, CT: Integral Yoga Institute, 1975. 68 pp.

———. *Guru and Disciple*. Pomfret Center, CT: Integral Yoga Publications, 1977. 56 pp.

———. *How to Succeed in Yoga, and Other Talks*. Pomfret Center, CT: Integral Publications, 1978. 126 pp.

———. *Integral Yoga Hatha*. New York: Holt, Rinehart and Winston, 1970. 189 pp.

——— et al. *Living Yoga: The Value of Yoga in Today's Life*. New York: Gordon and Beach Science Publishers, 1977. 323 pp.

Sri Satchidananda: A Decade of Service. Pomfret Center, CT: Satchidananda Ashram-Yogaville, 1976. 96 pp.

Weiner, Sita. *Swami Satchidananda*. New York: Bantam Books, 1972. 212 pp.

★819★
SAVAGE, James Wilbur
Apostle, Church of Christ with the Elijah Message, Established Anew in1929
b. Sep. 27, 1905, Wilber, Nebraska
d. Apr. 18, 1989, Rayton, Missouri

James Wilbur Savage was an apostle of the Church of Christ "With the Elijah Message," Established Anew in 1929, one of several Mormon groups which grew out of the Church of Christ (Temple Lot). He was the son of Emma Cecil Rider and Zebulon Wilber Savage. The Temple Lot church was formed in the 1850s by followers of slain prophet **Joseph Smith, Jr.**, who did not follow Brigham Young to Salt Lake City, but who quietly returned to Independence, Missouri, and purchased the plot of ground upon which Smith had prophesied the temple would be built (that is, the temple lot). The church had remained small, but in the 1920s experienced some growth. In 1927 **Otto Fetting**, one of the apostles who led the church, began to have revelations in the form of messages from an entity believed to be John the Baptist. The church accepted them for several years, but in 1929 he had a revelation calling for a rebaptism of the entire church. This revelation was not accepted and Fetting and his followers were removed from the fellowship. Savage was among the Temple Lot members who sided with Fetting, who organized a new Church of Christ.

Savage was (re)baptized and confirmed in that church on January 5, 1930, by Elder W. P. Buckley, at Colorado Springs, Colorado. In Fetting's 21st message Savage was one of 14 men specifically named and called to the priesthood. He was ordained on June 1, 1930, by Apostle Thomas B. Nerren. Fetting died in 1933.

No further revelations were received for some time, but in 1937 W. A. Draves of Nucla, Colorado, reported receiving messages from John the Baptist. In the 38th John the Baptist message, received in 1938, Savage was one of three men named and called to be bishops. He was ordained a bishop by Apostle Joseph H. Cramp on April 2, 1939. Savage became a missionary for the church in Florida, Colorado, Utah, and Arizona. In 1941 he married Ruth G. Foskett.

Savage was called to Independence, Missouri, in 1943 when the church split and Draves and his followers reorganized as the Church of Christ Established Anew. Savage became the secretary-treasurer of the bishops of the new church, in effect the administrative head of the organization, and remained in that position for almost half a century. In the 96th message he was named an apostle of the church and was ordained on January 9, 1977. Remaining in Independence, he assumed additional duties as church historian and official representative. As an apostle he was in charge of the work in the states of Nebraska, Kansas, Oklahoma, Texas, and Missouri, and he sat on the church's board of publication. During this time, besides his many trips to assist the church's development around the United States, he made two missionary journeys to Africa and India. He also oversaw the publication of the church's own edition of the Book of Mormon which is titled *The Record of the Nephites*.

Sources:
"Apostle James Wilbur Savage, 1905-1989: In Memorium." *The Voice of Peace* 45, 6 (June 1989): 8.

★820★
SCARBOROUGH, Lee Rutland
President, Southern Baptist Convention
b. Jul. 4, 1870, Colfax, Louisiana
d. Apr. 10, 1945, Amarillo, Texas

Lee Rutland Scarborough, Baptist minister and president of the Southern Baptist Convention, was the son of George W. and Mary Elizabeth Rutland Scarborough. His father, a Baptist minister, raised Scarborough in a pious evangelical home. The family moved near Waco, Texas, in 1874, but two years later they moved to West Texas, an area just beginning to be settled. In 1888 Scarborough left home to attend Baylor University. He received an A.B. degree in 1892 and then entered Yale University from which he received a second A.B. degree in 1896. At Yale he was a Phi Beta Kappa student. He was ordained as a Baptist minister shortly after graduation and became the pastor of First Baptist Church in Cameron, Texas. He attended the Southern Baptist Seminary in Louisville, Kentucky, for a year (1899-1900), but did not complete the program. In 1900 he married Neppie Warren and the following year became pastor of First Baptist Church in Abilene, Texas. During his years in the parish he became known for his preaching ability and preached at a number of revival services in the area.

Scarborough served the Abilene Church successfully for seven years and then in 1908 accepted a position as professor of evangelism at Southwestern Baptist Seminary in Fort Worth, Texas. In 1914 he became president of the seminary, a post he would retain for the next 31 years. Scarborough was a strong supporter of the Southern Baptist Convention, and during his tenure at the seminary he also served in a number of executive posts both in Texas and at the national level. During the 1920s, though theologically conservative, he worked to quell the effects of fundamentalism, then threatening to divide the convention. In 1939 he was elected president of the Southern Baptist Convention and was reelected the following year.

During his years at the seminary, Scarborough also authored a number of books, most of which were either on evangelism or collections of his sermons. Among the titles were: *The Tears of Jesus* (1922); *My Conception of the Gospel Ministry* (1935); *A Modern School of the Prophets* (1939); and *After the Resurrection—What?* (1942).

Sources:
Dictionary of American Biography. 20 vols. and 7 supps. New York: Charles Scribner's Sons, 1928-1936, 1944-1981.
Encyclopedia of Southern Baptists. 3 vols. Nashville, TN: Broadman Press, 1958, 1971.
Hill, Samuel S., ed. *Encyclopedia of Religion in the South*. Macon, GA: Mercer University Press, 1984. 878 pp.
Scarborough, Lee Rutland. *After the Resurrection—What?*. Grand Rapids, MI: Zondervan Publishing House, 1942. 121 pp.
_____. *Christ's Militant Kingdom*. New York: George H. Doran Company, 1924. 210 pp.
_____. *How Jesus Won Men*. Nashville, TN: Sunday School Board of Southern Baptist Convention, 1926. 290 pp.
_____. *A Modern School of the Prophets*. Nashville, TN: Broadman Press, 1939. 213 pp.
_____. *My Conception of the Gospel Ministry*. Nashville, TN: Sunday School Board of the Southern Baptist Convention, 1935. 101 pp.
_____. *The Tears of Jesus*. New York: G. H. Doran, 1922. 122 pp.

★821★
SCATES, Lucille Marie Sherrod
Bishop, Church of the Living God, the Pillar and Ground of Truth
b. Dec. 8, 1914, Florida
d. Oct. 13, 1977, Joliet, Illinois

Mother Lucille Marie Sherrod Scates, a bishop in the Church of the Living God, the Pillar and Ground of Truth, was the daughter of Luke and Rosa Melton. Little is known of her early life. She was reared by her older sister Helen, due to her mother's early death. Her family was brought into the orb of the Church of the Living God, the Pillar and Ground of Truth and the preaching of its founder, Mother **Mary Magdalena Lewis Tate**. Helen married F. E. Lewis, Tate's younger son and church bishop. Scates was but nine years old when she had her experience of salvation and the baptism of the Holy Spirit (as evidenced by speaking in tongues), the definitive Pentecostal religious experience. On April 18, 1939, at Belle Glade, Florida, she was appointed to the ministry.

By the time she received her ministerial appointment, Scates was married and had developed a small business. She uprooted herself and moved to Nashville, Tennessee, where church headquarters had been established. In Nashville she centered on youth work and founded the church's ministry in that area, called Youth for Christ. She stayed at the headquarters through the 1940s.

In 1954 Scates decided to move to Chicago to assist in the fledgling work in Illinois. With her six children, she moved in with Bishop L. E. Shelton and her sister, Elder Georgia Harris. A week later, however, the apartment building in which they resided burned to the ground. She lived hand-to-mouth for a while until befriended by a Mother Bursey, a member of the Church of God in Christ. A short time later, Bursey's husband was healed when Scates prayed for him. The healing became a new beginning for her ministry. She began to hold meetings in the Bursey home. As the church grew she rented congregation facilities.

With a stable congregation, Scates could begin to move around the state and into Wisconsin, where she began to found bands, some of which have since grown into new congregations. These early bands, under the leadership of Scates-appointed elders, would travel back and forth between Chicago and their home. In 1966 Scates went to Joliet, Illinois, and formed such a band. Finally, in 1968 she moved to Joliet, where permanent facilities were purchased. Here she also opened the Less Fortunate Saints Home to assist indigent church members. Through Scates' leadership, the Chicago-Illinois Archdiocese, as it is known today, became one of the strongest centers of the Church of the Living God.

Sources:

Seventy-fifth Anniversary Yearbook of the Church of the Living God, the Pillar and Ground of Truth, 1903-1978. Nashville, TN: Church Headquarters, 1978. 65 pp.

★822★
SCHACHTER-SHALOMI, Zalman
Hassidic Rabbi and Founder, P'nai Or Fellowship
b. 1924, Zolkiew Poland

Zalman Schachter-Shalomi, born Zalman Schachter, is the founder of P'nai Or Religious Fellowship (formerly B'nai Or Religious Fellowship), and a New Age Rabbi. He was born into a family of ritual animal slaughterers who moved to Vienna when he was a small child. By a circuitous route through Belgium, France, North Africa, and the West Indies, they arrived in the United States in 1941. While in Belgium, Schachter had become involved with the Lubavitch Hassidim and he entered the Lubavitcher Yeshiva after his family's move to North America. He was ordained a rabbi in 1947, and sent to Massachusetts to serve several emerging centers.

Schachter began to lean away from strict orthodoxy in such ways as developing innovations for the Saturday worship ritual and allowing women certain privileges usually denied them in worship. He also became involved with Havurot Shalom, an early Jewish experimental commune. He entered Boston University, received a M.A. degree in 1956, and became the Head of the Department of Near Eastern and Judaic Studies at the University of Manitoba in Winnipeg. He continued to drift away from orthodoxy, taking LSD with Timothy Leary and publishing an account of his drug experi-

ence in the *Psychedelic Review*. The experience strengthened his religious faith, but it also made him abandon the notion that Judaism had a monopoly on the truth and eventually led him to break his ties with the Lubavitchers.

While at the University of Manitoba, Schachter conceived of the idea of a Jewish liturgical brotherhood, B'nai Or, that would reach disaffiliated young Jews. It would emphasize spirituality, the arts, creative worship, and a teaching-study program. He wrote *The First Step* and *Fragments of a Future Scroll* (1975) to help initiate the fellowship. The subtitle of *Fragments*, "Hassidism for the Aquarian Age," indicated his alignment with the spiritual counterculture that would later be known as the New Age Movement. He accepted a post at Temple University in 1975 and founded the B'nai Or spiritual fellowship. Around this time he also added Shalomi (peace) to his name.

Schachter-Shalomi emerged as one of the most prominent New Age spokespeople within the Jewish community. He has authored innumerable articles and several books in addition to the ones already mentioned. In the 1980s a number of groups affiliated with B'nai Or came into being around the country. By the middle of the decade, the Fellowship's commitment to women's equality caused them to change their name from B'nai Or (sons of light) to P'nai Or (faces of light).

Sources:

Schachter, Zaman. *Fragments fo a Future Scroll: Hassidism for the Aquarian Age*. Germantown, PA: Leaves of Grass Press, 1975. 161 pp.
_____, and Donald Gropman. *The First Step*. Toronto: Bantam Books, 1983. 125 pp.
_____, and Edward Hoffman. *Sparks of Light: Counseling in the Hassidic Tradition*. Boulder, CO: Shambhala, 1983. 187 pp.

★823★
SCHAEFFER, Francis August
Theologian, Bible Presbyterian Church
b. Jan. 30, 1912, Germantown, Pennsylvania
d. May 15, 1984, Rochester, Minnesota

Francis August Schaeffer has emerged as one of the most important theological voices among fundamentalist evangelical Christians in the last half of the twentieth century. He was the son of Bessie Williamson and Francis August Schaeffer III and grew up in Germantown, Pennsylvania. He became a Christian in 1930 as the result of an intense reading of the Bible. He attended Hampton-Sydney College, from which he graduated *magne cum laude* in 1935. He married Edith Rachael Merritt Seville a few weeks later and in the fall entered Westminster Theological Seminary, at the time an independent fundamentalist school of theology established in 1929 by **J. Gresham Machen** and his student and faculty supporters from Princeton.

During Schaeffer's seminary years, the seminary's supporters divided over several issues including premillennialism, the idea that Christ was soon to return and establish his literal reign of a thousand years on earth. The premillennialists left Westminster and under the leadership of **Carl McIntire** founded Faith Theological Seminary and the Bible Presbyterian Church. Schaeffer graduated from Faith Seminary in 1938. He subsequently became the first minister ordained in the Bible Presbyterian Church and the pastor of Covenant Presbyterian Church in Grove City, Pennsylvania. In 1941 he was named associate pastor of the Bible Presbyterian Church in Chester, Pennsylvania, and was elected moderator of the Great Lakes Presbytery. In 1943 he became pastor of the church in St. Louis, Missouri.

After World War II Schaeffer traveled to Europe to evaluate the war damage. The next year he moved to Europe with the support of both the Independent Board ofr Presbyterian Foreign Missions and the American Council of Christian Churches (ACCC). Soon after his arrival Schaeffer participated in the formation of the International Council of Christian Churches (the fundamentalist alternative to the World Council of Churches). Following a spiritual crisis in 1951, Schaeffer emerged with a new commitment to his conservative Christian faith that led to the founding of L'Abri Fellowship in Switzerland in 1955. The fellowship was designed as both a loving community and a study center. An English branch was opened in 1958 in the United Kingdom.

During the remainder of his life Schaeffer authored more than 20 books. He attempted to make a forceful case for fundamental Christianity and attacked humanism as Western culture's destructive alternative. Among the most important of his volumes were *The God Who Is There* (1968); *Escape from Reason* (1968); *True Spirituality* (1979); *The Rise and Decline of Western Thought and Culture* (1976); and *The Great Evangelical Disaster*. One of his books, *How Should We Then Live?* (1983) was also made into a motion picture with his son Franky Schaeffer and former United States surgeon general C. Everett Koop. His writings were compiled into a set, *The Complete Works of Francis A. Schaeffer*, in 1982.

Sources:

Dennis, Lane T., ed. *Francis A. Schaeffer: Portraits of the Man and His Work*. Westchester, IL: Crossway Books, 1986. 237 pp.

Riegsegger, W. W., ed. *Reflections on Francis Schaeffer*. Grand Rapids, MI: Academic Books, 1986. 320 pp.

Schaeffer, Edith. *L'Abri*. Worthing, Sussex, United Kingdom: Norfolk Press, 1969. 228 pp.

Schaeffer, Francis A. *The Complete Works of Francis A. Schaeffer: A Christian World View*. 5 vols. 1982.

———. *Escape from Reason*. London: InterVarsity Fellowship. 1968. 96 pp.

———. *The God Who Is There*. Chicago: InterVarsity Press, 1968. 191 pp.

———. *The Great Evangelical Disaster*. Westchester, IL: Crossway Books, 1984. 192 pp.

———. *True Spirituality*. Kent, United Kingdom: STL Books, 1979. 180 pp.

★ 824 ★
SCHAFF, Philip
Church Historian, German Reformed Church, Presbyterian Church
b. Jan. 1, 1819, Chur Switzerland
d. Oct. 20, 1893, New York, New York

Philip Schaff, America's most distinguished church historian in the nineteenth century and a prominent exponent of what became known as the Mercersburg theology, was the son of Philip Schaff, Sr., a poor Swiss carpenter. Schaff was largely raised by his mother however, as his father died when he was quite young. Townspeople saw such potential in him that they paid for his education. Finishing the equivalent of high school in Switzerland, he traveled to Germany in 1873 to begin college at Tubingen. He moved to Halle, the pietist center, in 1839 and on to the University of Berlin in 1840. At Berlin he studied under Johann August Wilhelm Neander, the strongest influence on his life. He received his degree of licenate in theology in 1841. He became a private tutor and then a *privat-docent* at the University of Berlin.

In 1843 Schaff received an invitation to succeed the recently deceased Frederick A. Rausch at the theological seminary of the Eastern Synod of the German Reformed Church (now an integral part of the United Church of Christ) at Mercersburg, Pennsylvania. He arrived in 1844 ready to assume his post and destined to become one of the most influential leaders in Protestant Christianity in America. However, his career was almost cut short before it began. In his inaugural address, later published as *The Principle of Protestantism* (1845), he laid out what was to become a major thesis with which he was identified. He argued that the Reformation of Martin Luther and John Calvin was not so much a return to primitive Christianity, but a natural development of the best within Roman Catholicism. As such, he argued continued development could possibly lead to a reunion of Protestantism and Catholicism. Offended church officials in the classis of Philadelphia demanded and got an investigation, but the synod moved swiftly in October 1845 and cleared Schaff of the charges of heresy implied in the Philadephians' denuciations. He responded to the controversy with two important works, *What Is Church History? A Vindication of the Idea of Historical Development* (1846) and *Geschichte der Apostolischen Kirche* (1851). A few months after the synod's final action, he married Mary Elizabeth Schley.

Schaff settled in Mercersburg, and with his colleague John W. Nevin, developed the particular theological outlook associated with the school. The outlook was distinguished by its attempt to combine a personal piety, characteristic of European Evangelicalism, and a Catholic outlook on the church. It opposed revivalism and its emphasis on free will, as well as the more strict forms of predestinarianism. It posited a central role for historical development in the church. During his years at Mercersburg, he founded and edited *Der Deutsche Kirchenfreund*, the first German-language theological journal produced in North America. His most important books from this period were his three-volume *History of the Christian Church* (1858) and his translation and expanded edition of *A Commentary on the Holy Scriptures*, a twenty-five volume work derived from John P. Lange's *Bibelwerk*.

In 1865 he left Mercersburg and settled in New York City, where he lived quietly as the secretary of the New York Sabbath Association, an organization which opposed the secularization of Sunday. In 1870 Union Theological Seminary extended an invitation for him to join its faculty, and soon after taking up his post he transferred his denominational affiliation to the Presbyterian Church. His two decades at Union were his most productive. His *History of the Christian Church* went through five editions, the last (1882-1892) growing to seven volumes. He also compiled his monumental three-volume *Bibliotheca Symbolica Ecclesiae Universalis: The Creeds of Christendom* (1877), still a standard reference work, produced an American edition of the *Religious Encyclopedia* (1882-1884) originally issued in German by J. S. Herzog, G. L. Plitt, and Albert Hauck; and authored *Theological Propaedeutic* (1893), his last work. From 1881 to 1885, he worked on the English Bible revision committee, while authoring *A Companion to the Greek Testament and the English Version* (1883), which went through seven editions by the end of the century.

Schaff's piety was most obvious in his involvement in church affairs. He led in the formation of the American branch of the Evangelical Alliance, one of the early ecumenical organizations that anticipated the Federal Council of Churches and the National Council of Churches. He helped form the Alliance of Reformed Churches, now the Alliance of Reformed Churches (Presbyterian and Congregational). In 1893 he attended the World's Parliament of Religions in Chicago against his doctor's recommendation. Shortly after his return he died of a cerebral hemorrhage.

Sources:

Dictionary of American Biography. 20 vols. and 7 supps. New York: Charles Scribner's Sons, 1928-1936, 1944-1981.

Schaff, David S. *The Life of Philip Schaff*. New York: Charles Scribner's Sons, 1897. 526 pp.

Schaff, Philip. *A Companion to the Greek Testament and the English Version*. New York: Harper & Brothers, 1883. 616 pp.

———. *History of the Christian Church*. 3 vols. New York: Charles Scribner and Company, 1867.

———. *The Principle of Protestantism as Related to the Present State of the Church*. Chambersburg, PA: Publication Office of the German Reformed Church, 1845. 215 pp.

———. *Theological Propaedeutic*. New York: Christian Literature Company, 1892. 233 pp.

Shriver, George. *American Religious Heretics*. Nashville: Abingdon Press, 1966. 240 pp.

★ 825 ★
SCHAMBACH, Robert W.
Independent Pentecostal Television Evangelist
b. 1926

Robert W. Schambach, a popular Pentecostal healing evangelist, was raised apart from the church. He was converted by a street preacher when he was 16 and, with his family, joined the preacher's church, a congregation of the Assemblies of God. The next year, he enlisted in the Navy and began his preaching career informally aboard a ship in the south Pacific. After the war he attended Central Bible Institute, the Assemblies school in Springfield, Missouri.

After graduation Schambach pastored a small congregation in Philadelphia and worked in an oil refinery. The Assemblies licensed him in 1951, and he went on to become pastor of a church in Pittsburgh. In 1955 he joined the team of Assemblies evangelist **Asa Alonzo Allen**. In 1955 Allen was arrested for drunken driving in Knoxville, Tennessee. As a result, the Assemblies asked him to withdraw from public ministry for a time period. Allen claimed innocence and refused; nevertheless, he surrendered his credentials. Schambach, wishing to remain associated with Allen, also returned his license at that time. He stayed with Allen through the formation of Miracle Revival Fellowship (1956), consisting of ministers and congregations who supported Allen, and Schambach was recredentialed through the fellowship. In 1958, Allen began development of a Bible school and headquarters complex at Miracle Valley, Arizona, and moved there at the beginning of 1959.

In 1960, shortly after the move to Miracle Valley, Schambach left Allen to begin independent evangelical work on his own. He organized Schambach Miracle Revivals, Inc. and continued many of the emphases that had been identified with Allen's work. Schambach's style is forceful with outward displays of emotion evident throughout the services. Music is lively. The themes of physical healing and deliverance from demonic forces find special emphasis. His first revival after leaving Allen was in Newark, New Jersey. So many people were converted that he remained in Newark to found a church.

Like Allen, who developed a ministry among Blacks and held integrated services in the South during the 1950s, Schambach built a base of support among Blacks, and they continue to be a prominent segment of the congregations in his revival services. He has included a message of hope for poorer people aimed at removing their despair and motivating them to positive action.

Schambach moved on from Newark to New York City. He purchased a tent and began to travel. In Brooklyn, Philadelphia, and Chicago, following the model in Newark, he purchased abandoned theaters and built congregations, called Miracle temples, headed by ministers who worked with him. Headquarters for his developing ministries were established in Ellwood City, Pennsylvania, and have more recently moved to Tyler, Texas. In Tyler there is a Bible college and a publishing house. The ministry supports an orphanage in Indonesia, and Schambach generally travels abroad at least once annually for revival meetings.

Schambach began a periodical, *Power*, in 1970, and Lexie Allen, A. A. Allen's former wife, joined him as the editor. He also launched a radio ministry, "Voice of Power," and more recently has expanded into television. Schambach has continued in the use of tent meetings at a time when many other evangelists have abandoned outdoor revivals altogether.

Sources:

Burgess, Stanley M., Gary B. McGee, and Patrick H. Alexander, eds. *Dictionary of Pentecostal and Charismatic Movements*. Grand Rapids, MI: Regency Reference Library, Zondervan Publishing House, 1988. 914 pp.

Sims, Patsy. *Can Somebody Shout Amen!* New York: St. Martin's Press, 1988. 234 pp.

★ 826 ★
SCHECHTER, Solomon
Rabbinical Scholar and educator
b. Dec. 1850?, Foscani Romania
d. Nov. 20, 1915, New York, New York

The arrival of Solomon Schechter in the United States in 1902 occurred just as the new movement of Conservative Judaism needed some revitalization in the wake of the death of those rabbinical founders who had given the movement its original identity and direction. Solomon Schechter would give needed life and guidance not only to the Conservatives, but influence the entire direction of American Judaism.

Schechter was born in a section of Romania where Hassidism, the mystical form of Judaism, was strong. His name was derived from his father's occupation as a ritual slaughterer (one who makes Kosher meat). His exact birthdate is unknown, various authorities listing it as between 1847 and 1850. He was an able student, and left home at the age of ten to attend a yeshiva in a nearby community. While mastering his studies, he privately began to learn all he could of the larger world. At 16, he moved to Lvov, Ukrainia, to attend the rabbinical school, but soon returned home to pursue his studies privately. When he was 24, he moved to Vienna and there encountered several Jewish scholars who introduced him to Jewish history, especially the study of the rabbinical tradition. He also studied at the University of Vienna. During this time he developed a goal of discovering the tradition rooted in the essence of Jewish life that could be made relevant for the modern age. He also came to dislike Yiddish and began to call for a revival of Hebrew. He next moved to Berlin and continued his studies at the university and his Jewish studies under Israel Levy.

In 1882 Claude Goldsmid Montefiore invited Schechter to move to England and, wishing to escape the oppressive German intellectual atmosphere, Schechter accepted the invitation. While tutoring Montefiore, he was encouraged to develop himself as an interpreter of Judaism to the Christian world. Not encumbered with the distraction of teaching duties, he was able to spend his time in research and writing. He began to publish a series of essays, which would later be collected in a three volume series as *Some Aspects of Jewish Theology* and *Studies in Judaism* and which tried to convey to the English-speaking world an understanding of Judaism from the inside. In 1887 he published his first major scholarly work, an English edition of the *Aboth (ethics) of Rabbi Nathan*.

In 1890 Schechter married Matilda Roth. In 1893 he was appointed lecturer of rabbinics at Cambridge University. He also served as keeper of the Hebrew manuscripts at the university's library. In 1896, the first volume of *Studies in Judaism* appeared. Schechter became known for his concept of "Catholic Israel," the notion of an inner unity to Judaism based upon the consensus of the most devoted and loyal Jews.

In spite of the importance of his work, Schechter remained in relative obscurity until 1902 when he was invited to assume the presidency of the Jewish Theological Seminary of America in New York City. The seminary, designed to serve the Conservative Jewish community, was reorganized by Schechter and developed into one of the leading centers of Jewish learning in North America. His students carried conservative Judaism to numerous congregations which came together in 1913 to form the United Synagogue of America.

Sources:

Bentwich, Norman De Mattos. *Solomon Schechter, A Biography*. Cambridge: Cambridge University Press, 1938. 373 pp.

Goldman, Alex J. *Giants of Faith; Great American Rabbis*. New York: Citadel Press, 1964. 349 pp.

Oko, Adolph S. *Solomon Schechter, A Bibliography*. Cambridge: Cambridge University Press, 1938. 102 pp.

Parzen, Herbert. *Architects of Conservative Judaism*. New York: Jonathan David, 1964. 240 pp.

Schechter, Solomon. *Inaugural Address*. New York: Jewish Theological Seminary of America, 1902. 35 pp.

_____. *Selected Writings*. Edited by Norman Bentwich. Oxford: Phaidon Press, 1946. 169 pp.

_____. *Seminary Addresses and Other Papers*. Cincinnati, OH: Ark Publishing Co., 1915. 253 pp.

_____. *Some Aspects of Rabbinic Theology*. New York: Macmillan Company, 1909. 384 pp.

_____. *Studies in Judaism*. London: A. C. Black. Philadelphia: First series, 1896. 442 pp. Second series, 1908. 362 pp.

★ 827 ★
SCHMAUK, Theodore Emanuel
Minister, Lutheran Church
b. May 30, 1860, Lancaster, Pennsylvania
d. Mar. 23, 1920, Philadelphia, Pennsylvania

Theodore Emanuel Schmauk, a leading clergyman of the General Council of the Evangelical [Lutheran] Church in America, was the son of Rev. Benjamin William and Wilhelmina Schmauk. He was only a child when in 1866 the Pennsylvania Ministerium, having separated itself from the General Synod of the Lutheran Church in America, led in the formation of the General Council. The Council was based upon a strict confessional approach to Lutheranism and emphasized the authority of the Augsburg Confession and the other Lutheran confession documents found in the *Book of Concord*. The elder Schmauk adhered to the new Council, which was largely composed of German-Americans.

Schmauk received a fine education. He graduated from the University of Pennsylvania in 1880 and from the Philadelphia Lutheran Theological Seminary in 1883. That year he returned to his home in Lebanon, Pennsylvania, as assistant pastor at his father's church. He retained the position until his father's death in 1898 and then became pastor of the church. Even while he was only an assistant pastor, his abilities, especially as an editor and as an organizer, enabled him to rise to a position of influence in the General Council. In 1889 he became editor of the *Lutheran*, the Council's official periodical. In 1895 he added the editorship of the *Lutheran Church Review* and a year later the *Lutheran Sunday School Lessons and General Council Graded Series* to his duties. During this period he also authored a number of shorter works for the Sunday school.

Schmauk was, like the Council, of a conservative mind theologically, and championed its confessionalism. While avoiding a legalistic approach to scripture, he argued for the inerrancy of the Bible. He attacked James Hastings, the editor of the popular five-volume *A Dictionary of the Bible*, for choosing too many "liberal" scholars to write for it.

In recognition of his service to the Council, Schmauk was elected its president in 1903, and during the remaining 15 years of the Council's existence he held a number of positions of trust. In 1907 he became president of the trustees of the General Council. In 1908 he became a member of the board of trustees of the Philadelphia seminary. In 1911 he became a lecturer at the seminary. Among his last tasks was the chairing of the Council's committee, which worked with like committees from the General Synod and the Synod of the South to prepare a plan of union which led to the merger of the three bodies into the United Lutheran Church in America in 1918. The United Lutheran Church in America, by way of a series of subsequent mergers, is now a constituent part of the Evangelical Lutheran Church in America (1988). Schmauk lived only two years after the 1918 merger. He never married.

Along with his service at the denominational level, Schmauk pursued two other interests. Closely tied to his denominational concerns were his attempts to defend the confessional principles of the council through religious polemics. His two most important books in that respect were *The Negative Criticism and the Old Testament* (1894), directed against the new German historical critical approach to the Hebrew Bible, and *The Confessional Principle and the Confessions of the Lutheran Church* (1911), written to refute a volume on the confessions by William Richard. Schmauk was also an amateur local historian and was a member of the Lebanon County Historical Society and the Pennsylvania German Society. Out of this interest came two books, *The Early Churches of Lebanon County* (1902) and *A History of the Lutheran Church in Pennsylvania* (1903).

Sources:

Dictionary of American Biography. 20 vols. and 7 supps. New York: Charles Scribner's Sons, 1928-1936, 1944-1981.

Schmauk, Theodore E. *The Confessional Principle and the Confessions of the Lutheran Church*. Philadelphia, PA: General Council Publication Board, 1911. 962 pp.

_____. *The Early Churches of Lebanon County*. Lebanon, PA: The Century Printing Co., 1902. 384 pp.

_____. "A History of the Lutheran Church in Pennsylvania," *Proceedings and Addresses of the Pennsylvania German Society* 11 and 12 (1902-1903).

_____. *The Negative Criticism and the Old Testament*. Lebanon, PA: Aldus Co., 1894. 232 p.

★ 828 ★
SCHMEMANN, Alexander
Scholar and Priest, Orthodox Church in America
b. 1921, Reval Union of Soviet Socialist Republics
d. Dec. 13, 1983, Crestwood, New York

Alexander Schmemann, Orthodox theologian and dean of St. Vladimir's Theological Seminary, was born in Estonia of Russian parentage, but as a child moved with his family to France. He grew up in the post-Revolution immigrant community, where he attended a military school. He later attended the University of Paris. World War II began just as he was reaching manhood, and he spent most of the war as a student at the Orthodox Theological Institute of Paris. He married Juliana Osorguine in 1943. After the war he became a lecturer in church history and in 1946 was ordained to the priesthood by Archbishop Vladimir Tikhonitsky. During these years his views were shaped by the Russian Orthodoxy of his church experience and the pre-Vatican French Roman Catholic liturgical theology.

During his student days in Paris, Schmemann wrestled with the reality of Orthodox cultural dispersion into Western society and concluded that it must become indigenous to the countries in which it existed. In 1949 Fr. Georges Florovsky moved to New York as dean at St. Vladimir's Theological Seminary. Schmemann, having developed his own vision of Orthodoxy's mission in the West, immigrated to America and joined the faculty in 1951. The seminary became a major center of Orthodox life as a training ground for priests not only of the several Russian jurisdictions but of the Antiochean and Serbian Orthodox churches as well. He lectured in early church history and liturgical and pastoral theology. During his early years there he continued to work on his own studies and received his doctorate from the institute in Paris in 1959.

In 1954 Schmemann published his first major book, *The Historical Road of Eastern Orthodoxy* (English edition, 1963). It would be followed by a number of others, including *Sacraments and Orthodoxy* (1964); *Introduction to Liturgical Theology* (1966); *The World as Sacrament* (1966); and *Church, World, Mission: Reflections on Orthodoxy in the West* (1979).

In 1962 the seminary moved to Crestwood, New York, and at that time Schmemann became dean, a position he held for the rest of his life. During these years he became a prominent spokesperson for Orthodoxy in ecumenical circles. He authored a number of articles that interpreted Orthodoxy to a predominantly Catholic/Protestant West, and engaged in ecumenical dialogue sessions. Upon his arrival in America, he had become associated with the Russian Orthodox Greek Catholic Church in America (popularly termed the Metropolia). He worked on the negotiations for the granting of autocephalous status of the church; this was granted in 1970, at which time it became the Orthodox Church in America.

Schmemann is remembered in Orthodox circles for his emphasis upon the liturgy and is credited for focusing the church's attention upon its liturgical tradition as a major resource for renewal. It was his opinion that the liturgy most clearly revealed to humanity the real purpose of existence.

Schmemann died of cancer at the age of 62.

Sources:

Garrett, Paul. "Fr. Alexander Schmemann: A Chronological Bibliography." *St. Vladimir's Theological Quarterly* 28, 1 (1984): 11-26.

Meyendorff, John. "A Life Worth Living." *St. Vladimir's Theological Quarterly* 28, 1 (1984): 3-10.

Schmemann, Alexander. *Church, World, Mission: Reflection on Orthodoxy in the West.* Crestwood, NY: SVSP, 1979.

———. *The Historical Road of Eastern Orthodoxy.* New York: Holt, Rinehart, and Winston, 1963.

———. *Liturgy and Life.* New York: DRE/OCA, 1974.

———. *Ultimate Questions: an Anthology of Modern Russian Religious Thought.* New York: Holt, Rinehart and Winston, 1965.

———. *The World as Sacrament.* London: Darton, Longman & Todd, 1966.

Scorer, Peter. "Alexander Schmemann (1921-83)." *Sobornost* 6, 2 (1984): 64-68.

★ 829 ★
SCHMIDT, Friedrich August
Theologian, Norwegian Synod and the United Norwegian Lutheran Church in America
b. Jan. 3, 1837, Leutenberg Germany
d. May 15, 1928

Friedrich August Schmidt, a German-born theologian who would emerge as a leading figure in Norwegian-American Lutheranism, was the son of Martin and Helena Wirth Schmidt. In 1841 his parents immigrated to America and settled in St. Louis, Missouri, where he grew up within the Lutheran Church-Missouri Synod. He attended a Lutheran parochial school and Concordia Theological Seminary, from which he graduated in 1857. After graduation he was ordained and called to pastor a congregation in Mt. Eden, New York. While there, in 1858, he married Caroline Sophia Allwardt. In 1859 he began a two-year pastorate in Baltimore, Maryland.

The same year that Schmidt graduated from seminary, the Norwegian Synod, a Lutheran association of Norwegian-Americans centered in Iowa, cemented its cordial relationship with the Missouri Synod by designating Concordia as its institution for training pastors. It had already established Luther College at Decorah, Iowa. In 1861 Schmidt moved into the heart of the Norwegian Synod when he joined the faculty at Luther College and eventually moved his membership from the Missouri to the Norwegian Synod. He stayed there for 11 years before returning to Concordia Seminary to assume the Norwegian chair in theology. During the 1870s, the Norwegian Synod established a school of theology, and in 1878 Schmidt moved to Madison, Wisconsin, to teach.

The immediate occasion for Schmidt's move in 1878 was his opposition to some views on predestination expressed by Missouri Synod leader C. F. W. Walther. He found Walther's views mecha-

nistic and too Calvinistic, that is, aligned to the views of John Calvin, founder of the Reformed Church. After moving to Madison in 1880, he began the periodical *Altes und Neues*, which continued the controversy for another five years. The controversy continued at a heated pace in the Norwegian Synod, even after the discontinuance of *Altes and Neues*. In 1886 those opposed to the Missouri perspective (approximately one-third of the synod) organized a new theological seminary at St. Olaf school (now St. Olaf College) in Northfield, Minnesota, and Schmidt moved there. When St. Olaf's was officially censured by the synod, Schmidt and his colleagues left the Synod and reorganized as the Anti-Missourian Brotherhood. In 1890 the brotherhood merged with other Norwegian Lutherans to form the United Norwegian Lutheran Church in America. Schmidt moved to the new church's Augsburg Seminary in Minneapolis, Minnesota. That seminary was closed in 1893 and superceded by Luther Theological Seminary in St. Paul, Minnesota, where Schmidt taught until his retirement in 1912.

Schmidt is remembered as a controversialist who helped mold the perspective of Norwegian-American Lutherans for a generation. As the editor of a periodical for five years, he placed himself in the center of the predestination debate, and continued his involvement in other debates (on the questions of biblical and confessional authority) through his editorship of *Luthersk Kirkeblad* (1890-1895) and *Der Sprechsaal* (1901-1903). He authored only a few books—*Naadevalg-striden* (1881); *Intuitu Fidei* (1895); and *Sandhed og Frihed* (1914)—none of which were translated into English.

Sources:

Dictionary of American Biography. 20 vols. and 7 supps. New York: Charles Scribner's Sons, 1928-1936, 1944-1981.

Schmidt, Friedrich August. *Naadevalg-striden.* Chicago: Nordens bogtr, 1881. 90 pp.

———. *Sandhed og Frihed.* Minneapolis, MN: Forfatterens forlag, 1914. 106 pp.

★ 830 ★
SCHNEERSON, Menachem Mendel
Rebbe, Lubavitcher Hassidism
b. Apr. 18, 1902, Nikolayev Russia

Menachem Mendel Schneerson, the seventh rebbe of the Lubavitcher Hassidism, was born on the eleventh day of Nissan, in the year 5662, according to the Jewish calendar, the son of Rabbi Levi Yitzchak Schneerson. He was named for his great-grandfather, the third leader of the Lubavitchers. When he was five years old, he moved to the town of Yekatrinislau in the Ukraine, where his father became the chief rabbi. He was 21 when he met the sixth Lubavitcher rebbe, Yosef Yitchak Schneerson, and six years later in 1929 he married Rabbi Schneerson's daughter, Rebetzin Chaya Moussia. After his marriage, he went to study at the Universities of Berlin and Paris.

Schneerson was able to get out of Europe just as World War II was beginning, and in 1941 he arrived in the United States. His father-in-law had already migrated, and he set about assisting the then Lubavitcher rebbe in establishing the movement in the United States from its headquarters in Brooklyn, New York. Hassidism is an orthodox mystical form of Judaism, each different group of which is led by a rebbe, a person believed to be both learned and possessed of an experiential knowledge of the Divine. Leadership is usually passed down within a single family. Schneerson was appointed chairman of the executive committee for the Lubavitch movement.

In 1950 Schneerson's father-in-law died, and Schneerson became the new rebbe. Schneerson took an expansive approach to the movement, and under his leadership the movement spread rapidly. He turned to the larger Jewish community, especially to young Jews who had drifted away from orthodox practice, to locate recruits. In 1953 he founded the Lubavitcher Women's Organization and two years later the Lubavitcher Youth Organization. He started chapters adjacent to college and university campuses. He developed programs to appeal to Jews who had been attracted either to Christian churches or the newer religious movements from the east. He organized efforts to assist new immigrants from Russia. He built a publishing concern to publish Hassidic books in English, Russian, and Hebrew.

Having established a solid foundation in the United States, he led the movement in developing centers in the Jewish communities of Canada, Europe, North Africa, and South America. Work in Israel that had begun early in the century was strengthened and given new life. Every year since the Yom Kippur War, Schneerson has organized a massive bar mitvah (the coming of age ceremony in Judaism) for children of the soldiers killed in the service of Israel.

Under his leadership, the Lubavitcher has become the largest of the several Hassidic groups in North America. It should be noted that the Hassidic movement was among the hardest hit by the Nazi holocaust, a significant part of it perishing during World War II.

Sources:

Challenge: An Encounter with Lubavitch-Chabad. London: Lubavitch Foundation of Great Britain, 1970. 329 pp.

Kagan, Y. M., ed. *A Thought for the Week.* Oak Park, MI: Merkos l'inyonei Chinuch Inc., 1972.

The Lubavitcher Rebbe, Rabbi Menachem M. Schneerson: A Brief Biography. Brooklyn: Merkos L'inyonei Chinuch Inc., [1979]. 48 pp.

Schneerson, Menachem M. *Letters by the Lubavitcher Rebbe.* Brooklyn: Kehot Publication Society, 1979.

★831★
SCHULLER, Robert Harold
Television Evangelist and Minister, Reformed Church in America
b. Sep. 16, 1926, Alton, Iowa

Robert Harold Schuller, one of the most popular television evangelists in the United States, is the son of Anthony and Jennie Schuller. Schuller was raised on a farm in northwest Iowa by parents who were devout members of the Reformed Church in America, a Protestant Christian denomination with roots in the Netherlands. He entered the church's school, Hope College in Holland, Michigan, in 1943. Upon graduation he began his training for the ministry at Western Theological Seminary. In 1950 he graduated from seminary, married Arvella DeHaan, was ordained to the ministry, and called to pastor the Ivanhoe Reformed Church in Riverdale, Illinois. During his seminary days Schuller had become familiar with **George W. Truett**, who had built the First Baptist Church of Dallas, Texas, into the largest congregation in the Southern Baptist Convention. He adopted Truett as a role model, and in his four and a half years at Ivanhoe enlarged its membership tenfold.

In 1955, given Schuller's success at Ivanhoe, the Reformed Church's Classis of California asked him to start a congregation in Orange County, southwest of Los Angeles. He organized the Garden Grove Community Church with about 100 members. The church attained some notoriety when Schuller experimented by renting a drive-in theater to hold Sunday services. The idea proved an unexpected success and the congregation grew steadily. In 1958 the church was formally organized as a congregation of the Reformed Church in America. Schuller led them in a move to build a drive-in-walk-in church which would seat 1,000 with additional space for 500 cars. The church was completed in 1961 and Schuller invited **Norman Vincent Peale** to preach the inaugural sermon.

In the three decades since the dedication of the church in 1961, Schuller has developed an expansive ministry anchored by his winsome pulpit manner and the many books he has authored. His first book, *God's Way to the Good Life*, appeared in 1963. Among the more prominent of his other books are *Move Ahead with Possibility Thinking* (1967); *The Greatest Possibility Thinker That Ever Lived* (1973); and *Your Church Has Real Possibilities* (1974), all of which have developed his image of "possibility thinking" (related somewhat to Norman Vincent Peale's "positive thinking") as a key to successful living. Other books include: *You Can Become the Person You Want to Be* (1973); *Reach Out for New Life* (1977); *The Peak to Peek Principle* (1980); and *Self Esteem: The New Reformation* (1982), the most definitive presentation of his theological perspective. He has also authored a number of daily devotional guides.

The growth of Schuller's ministry has been punctuated by the establishment of the Robert Schuller Institute for Successful Church Leadership in 1969; the dedication of the Tower of Power, the congregation's administrative office building, in 1968; the beginning of the television show, "Hour of Power," in 1970; and the dedication of the congregation's new sanctuary, the Crystal Cathedral, in 1980. Like many television ministries in the late 1980s suffering fallout from the scandals surrounding **Jim Bakker** and **Jimmy Swaggart**, Schuller's work experienced some setbacks, but remained one of the most popular national religious broadcasts.

Sources:

Coleman, Sheila Schuller. *Robert Schuller: My Father & My Friend.* Milwaukee, WI: Ideals Publishing Corporation, 1980. 191 pp.

Nason, Michael and Donna Nason. *Robert Schuller: The Inside Story.* Waco, TX: Word Books, 1983. 264 pp.

Schuller, Robert H. *Be Happy, You Are Loved.* Nashville, TN: Thomas Nelson, 1986. 256 pp.

_____. *The Peak to Peek Principle.* Garden City, NY: Doubleday & Co., 1980. 177 pp.

_____. *Reach Out for New Life.* New York: Hawthorn Books, 1977. 216 pp.

_____. *Self-Esteem: The New Reformation.* Waco, TX: Word Books, 1982. 177 pp.

_____. *You Can Become the Person You Want to Be.* New York: Hawthorn Books, 1973. 180 pp.

Voskul, Dennis. *Mountains into Goldmines: Robert Schuller and the Gospel of Success.* Grand Rapids, MI: William B. Eerdmans Publishing Company, 1983. 176 pp.

★832★
SCHULTZ, Donna Cole
Cofounder, (Chicago) Temple of the Pagan Way
b. May 15, 1937

Donna Cole Schultz, better known as Donna Cole, was a cofounder of the Temple of the Pagan Way (the ultimate source of most other Neo-Pagan groups in the Chicago area) and was responsible for bringing the Gardnerian Wicca tradition, founded in the 1940s by **Gerald B. Gardner** in England, to the Midwest. A professional psychotherapist, Cole earned B.A. (1958) and M.S.W. (1960) degrees from the University of Illinois. Trained and initiated in the Craft in England, she established the Coven of the Sacred Stones in 1970, and has been the coven's high priestess ever since.

One of Cole's contributions to Wicca has been to move away from rigid adherence to the tenets of Gardnerian Wicca, and to evolve instead an eclectic form of the Craft that draws from many different traditions, such as the Afro-Caribbean traditions (minus animal sacrifices). Many of her group's rituals were created as they evolved during the course of acting out rituals. The group has also incorporated healing, dance, and music into its practices. This eclectic approach, which many other Wiccans have since emulated, drew criticism from what Druid priest **Philip Emmons Isaac Bonewits** has called the WMOT—the White Mainstream Occult Tradition.

Cole has lectured on the Craft in an attempt to educate the public on the difference between Wiccans, who practice a nature-oriented tradition, and Satanists, who worship the Christian devil.

She has also done a fair amount of networking with other Craft groups in the areas of planning and executing large Neo-Pagan festivals and "reach-outs" to people who are looking for Wiccan contacts. From time to time she has taught classes on the Craft, and has written some articles on the religion. Cole believes that there is no particular way that one must practice the Craft, and feels that what is of primary importance is adherence to the ethic of harmlessness and devotion to the gods.

★833★
SEGHERS, Charles John
Archbishop, Roman Catholic Church
b. Dec. 26, 1839, Ghent Belgium
d. Nov. 28, 1886, Nulato, Alaska

Charles John Seghers, the first martyr of the Roman Catholic Church in Alaska, was orphaned early in life and raised by relatives, who saw that he obtained a good education through the American College at Louvain. He was ordained in 1863 and before the year was out answered the continuing call of Bishop Modeste Demers of Vancouver Island, British Columbia, for missionary priests. He began duties at the cathedral in Victoria and served as diocesan administrator whenever Demers was away. He also served as a missionary and priest among both the pioneer white settlers and the Canadian Indians.

Demers died soon after his return from the Vatican Council (1870-1871) and on March 23, 1872, Seghers was appointed to succeed him. He immediately turned his attention toward Alaska and made the first of several trips there. Returning from such a trip in 1877-1878, in which he had established a number of missions among the Eskimos, he was notified that he had been appointed coadjutor to the archbishop of Oregon City (Oregon), in whose province British Columbia and Alaska fell. Two years later he became the archbishop of Oregon City (now Portland).

Seghers served as archbishop for four years. While visiting Rome in 1884 he was consulted about the vacancy of his former position and he asked to be allowed to resign his archbishopric and return. He still had a great concern for Alaska, where little remained of his earlier efforts. With Pope Leo XIII's approval and the aid of some Jesuit priests he returned. For the next two years he engaged in intensive efforts to missionize Alaska. He established permanent church centers in Sitka and Juneau.

In 1886 Seghers began what was to be his last journey to Alaska. After stopping at Harper's Place on the Stewart River, he journeyed to Nukluket, accompanied by Francis Fuller, a guide he had recruited in Idaho. Fuller, however, had picked up some of the popular anti-Catholic prejudices concerning Jesuit conspiracies. These had been fueled, it seems, by the fur traders' fear that the arrival of the missions would disrupt some of their dishonest dealings with the Indians. In any case, Fuller became convinced that Seghers was a threat, and on or about November 28, he shot the archbishop. (The exact date of Seghers' death has been difficult to surmise from the testimony of the Indians who witnessed the shooting.)

Six months passed before word reached the outside world of what had occurred. Eventually, Fuller was convicted of manslaughter. The archbishop's body was recovered and brought to Victoria, where it is entombed under the high altar of the cathedral.

Sources:
Bosco, Antoinette. *Charles John Seghers, Pioneer in Alaska.* New York: P. J. Kenedy, 1960. 190 pp.
Delaney, John J. *Dictionary of American Catholic Biography.* Garden City, NY: Doubleday & Company, 1988. 621 pp.
Nevins, Albert J. *American Martyrs from 1542.* Huntington, IN: Our Sunday Visitor Publishing Division, 1987. 180 pp.
New Catholic Encyclopedia. 17 vols. New York: McGraw-Hill, 1967.

★834★
SEIP, Theodore Lorenzo
Minister, General Council of the Lutheran Church in America
b. Jun. 25, 1842, Easton, Pennsylvania
d. Nov. 28, 1903, Allentown, Pennsylvania

Theodore Lorenzo Seip, an outstanding Lutheran educator and church leader in the late nineteenth century, was the son of Reuben L. and Sarah A. Hemsing Seip. As a youth, he studied under H. F. Savage at Weaversville Academy, and he became enthusiastic about the study of the ancient languages of Greek and Latin. He pursued his interest following his entrance in 1860 to Pennsylvania College (now Gettysburg College). His college career was interrupted by the Civil War. He served briefly in the summer of 1863 in the 26th Pennsylvania Volunteers and in 1864 traveled behind the Union Army to Tennessee and Georgia as a delegate of the United States Christian Commission. He graduated in 1864 and joined the first class of the newly formed Lutheran Theological Seminary in Philadelphia. During his seminary days, in 1866, he married Emma Elizabeth Shimer.

The new seminary was one of the products of an increasingly conservative confessional stance taken by the Pennsylvania Ministerium, which had recently separated itself from the General Synod of the Lutheran Church in America. Also in 1864, the ministerium had supported the selection of **Charles Porterfield Krauth** as the new president of the Lutheran seminary at Gettysburg. When Krauth was not selected, the ministerium began the new Pennsylvania seminary with Krauth as the center of a very conservative faculty. In 1867 the Pennsylvania Ministerium became the center of a new organization among Lutherans, the General Council of the Lutheran Church in America.

Following his graduation in 1867, Seip was ordained in the Philadelphia Ministerium and received a call to St. John's Lutheran Church in Quakertown, Pennsylvania. He turned down the call, however, to stay at Muhlenberg College in Allentown, Pennsylvania, where he had become principal of the preparatory department a few months earlier. He also assumed duties as an instructor of Greek and secretary of the faculty. He became a full professor in 1872 and was named Mosser-Keck professor of Greek in 1880. His first wife having passed away, in 1877 he married Rebecca Keck.

In 1885 the seminary's president retired, and Seip was unanimously elected as his successor. During the 1870s he had spent eight successful months as the school's financial officer during a critical period, and he seemed the ideal person to finish the task of giving the college a stable financial future. Seip's leadership extended beyond the college in both the academic and ministerial arenas. In 1887 he helped found the College Association of Pennsylvania, a cooperative organization of institutions of higher education. In 1895 he was elected president of the Philadelphia Ministerium and served a three-year term.

Sources:
Dictionary of American Biography. 20 vols. and 7 supps. New York: Charles Scribner's Sons, 1928-1936, 1944-1981.

★835★
SEISS, Joseph Augustus
Minister, General Council of the Lutheran Church in America
b. Mar. 18, 1823, Graceham, Maryland
d. Jun. 20, 1904, Philadelphia, Pennsylvania

Joseph Augustus Seiss, a nineteenth century Lutheran author and minister, was the son of John and Eliza Schuler Seiss (or Suss). He was raised in the Moravian Church, from whose parochial school he received an early education in the Bible, history, and Latin. He decided to go into the ministry, a course strongly disapproved of by his father, who was supported by the local Moravian bishop. Seiss thus ran away from home, and with the support of a Lutheran minister entered Pennsylvania College. He became an accomplished student but had to drop out after two years to take a job as a teacher. Then the Lutheran Synod of Virginia intervened. They offered him a job as a minister. Thus at the age of 19 he was licensed to preach and became a missionary at Mount Sidney and Harrisonburg, Virginia.

In 1843 Seiss married Elizabeth Barnitz and settled into a pastorate in Martinsburg and Shepherdsville, two towns in that part of Virginia later to become part of West Virginia. He was ordained in 1844. While there he authored his first book, *Popular Lectures on the Epistle to the Hebrews* (1846). In 1847 he moved to Cumberland, Maryland, and in 1852 to Baltimore as pastor of the Lombard Street Lutheran Church. While in Baltimore he became widely known for his oratorical abilities and, in spite of his lack of formal seminary training, was elected president of the Synod of Maryland. In 1858 he was called to St. John's Lutheran Church in Philadelphia, then the largest Lutheran congregation in America, and began his half century of outstanding leadership to the church.

During the Civil War period, Seiss became deeply involved in the confessional controversy within the General Synod of the Lutheran Church in America. The most conservative and confessional wing of the Lutherans was centered upon the Philadelphia Ministerium, of which Seiss was a staunch supporter. In 1864 he was becoming one of the key figures in the establishment of the Lutheran Theological Seminary in Philadelphia, the primary institution of the confessional movement. He served as president of the school's board of directors from 1865 until his death. In 1867 he was a leader in the formation of the General Council of the Lutheran Church in America, a new denominational structure for Lutheran synods who were against the General Synod, which had been more pietistic in orientation and which placed less emphasis upon the traditional Lutheran confessional statements.

While the General Council was based in a German-speaking constituency, Seiss was a leading figure in its transition to English. He was the leading English-language preacher and authored numerous books (over 100), many of which were transcripts of his sermons and lectures. His single most popular title appeared in 1865, *The Apocalypse: A Series of Special Lectures*. It not only went through many editions but was translated into German and Dutch. Among his most important additional titles were: *Lectures on the Epistles* (1885); *Lectures on the Gospels and Epistles for Minor Festivals of the Church Year* (1893); *Beacon Lights* (1900); *The Christ and His Church* (1902); and *Recent Sermons* (1904).

In 1867 Seiss began a 12-year tenure as editor of the *Lutheran*. He became an accomplished liturgist and student of hymnology and was an influential voice in the development of the English edition of the *Church Book* for the General Council. In 1874 he left St. John's to found the Church of the Holy Communion in the heart of Philadelphia, at Arch and Broad Street. This became the base of his ministry until his death. It was said of Seiss that his authoritarian manner distracted from his speaking and writing talents, preventing him from becoming a popular leader (and hence holding significant national offices in the church). However, his books and sermons influenced several generations of Lutheran ministers.

Seiss' last act was rising from his sick bed to sign the diplomas of the 1904 graduating class of the seminary.

Sources:

Dictionary of American Biography. 20 vols. and 7 supps. New York: Charles Scribner's Sons, 1928-1936, 1944-1981.

Seiss, Joseph A. *The Apocalypse: A Series of Special Lectures.* Philadelphia: Smith, English & Co., 1865. 115 pp.

———. *Beacon Lights.* Philadelphia: Board of Publication of the General Council of the Evangelical Lutheran Church in North America, 1900. 539 pp.

———. *The Christ and His Church.* Philadelphia: Board of Publication of the General Council, 1902. 440 pp.

———. *Lectures on the Epistles.* 2 vols. Philadelphia: Lutheran Bookstore, 1885.

———. *Lectures on the Gospels and Epistles for the Minor Festivals of the Church Year.* Philadelphia: Lutheran Bookstore, 1893. 519 pp.

———. *Recent Sermons.* Philadelphia: Board of Publication of the General Council, 1904. 325 pp.

★836★
SENZAKI, Nyogen
Zen Buddhist Teacher
Founder, Mentorgarten Meditation Hall
b. 1876
d. May 7, 1958, Los Angeles, California

Nyogen Senzaki, founder of the Mentorgarten (Zen) Meditation Hall, was discovered beside his frozen mother in Siberia, and was rescued by a Japanese monk. He was adopted by a shipwright, from whom he acquired the name Senzaki, and was placed under the care of a Buddhist scholar. In 1896 he joined **Soyen Shaku**'s Engakuji monastery where, as a student, he roomed with **Daisetz Teitaro Suzuki**. Five years later he left the monastery to found a mentorgarten, a nursery school.

Senzaki moved to North America in 1905 for a number of different reasons, including Japanese militarism and the unhappy state of Zen in Japan. He took a job as a houseboy with Alexander Russell in San Francisco. The Russells had begun to practice Zen and, at the time, were entertaining Senzaki's master, Soyen Shaku. Under Shaku's influence, he resolved to become a teacher of Zen, although it would not be until 1922 that he was able to fulfill his resolve.

Senzaki worked at a variety of jobs over the years, even owning a hotel for a short period of time. Without the resources to establish a permanent center, he temporarily rented halls in which to lecture and teach. This mobile Zen hall acquired the name "floating zendo." Senzaki traveled with the floating zendo to Los Angeles in 1928, and subsequently adopted the practice of shuttling back and forth between southern California and the Bay area. In 1931 he was finally able to establish the Mentorgarten Meditation Hall at a stable location in Los Angeles.

Interned in a concentration camp during World War II with other Japanese-Americans, he set up his floating zendo in the camp in Heart Mountain, Wyoming. Released in 1945, he returned to southern California where he lived and taught for the rest of his life. Senzaki left no successor, and his zendo disbanded. His importance to American Zen lies in the organizations founded by his students, and his sponsoring of other Japanese Zen teachers traveling to the United States.

Sources:

Fields, Rick. *How the Swans Came to the Lake.* Boulder, CO: Shambhala, 1986. 445 pp.

Layman, Emma McCloy. *Buddhism in America.* Chicago: Nelson-Hall, 1976. 342 pp.

Melton, J. Gordon. *Biographical Dictionary of American Cult and Sect Leaders.* Garland Reference Library of Social Science, vol. 212. New York: Garland Publishing, 1986.

Senzaki, Nyogen. *A Lecture on Meditation.* Los Angeles, CA: The Author, n.d. 10 pp.

———. *Like a Dream, Like a Fantasy.* Eido Shimano Roshi, ed. Tokyo: Japan Publications, 1978.

———, Soen Nakagawa, and Eido Shimano. *Namu Dai Bosa. A Transmission of Zen Buddhism in America.* New York: Zen Studies Society, 1976. 262 pp.

———, and Ruth Strout McCandless. *Buddhism and Zen.* New York: Philosophical Library, 1953. 87 pp.

———, eds. *The Iron Flute.* Rutland, VT: Charles E. Tuttle, 1961. 175 pp.

———, and Paul Reps. *Zen Flesh, Zen Bones.* Rutland, VT: Charles E. Tuttle & Co., 1957. 211 pp.

★ 837 ★
SEWELL, Elisha G.
Editor, Churches of Christ
b. Oct. 25, 1849, Overton County, Tennessee
d. Mar. 2, 1924, Nashville, Tennessee

Elisha G. Sewell, a minister and editor for the Churches of Christ, was born in the mountains of Tennessee, the son of Stephen and Annie Sewell. He was raised in a Baptist environment. His conversion to the Churches of Christ occurred in 1840 when his older brother William married a member of the Church of Christ. The Baptist excommunication of William led the family to reexamine their faith and eventually all became members of his newfound church. Sewell was baptized in 1849. Two years later he preached his first sermon. In 1853 he married Lucy Kuykendall. Only in 1856 was he able to begin college; he spent two years at Burritt College and finished his last year at Franklin College in 1859. He lived and preached in middle Tennessee during the Civil War.

In 1870 Sewell settled in Edgefield, Tennessee, near Nashville, and lived there for the rest of his life. He worked to establish and build the church in East Nashville. His real work, however, was with the *Gospel Advocate*, the most influential periodical defining what would in 1906 become the Churches of Christ as a distinct association of congregations over against the Christian Church (Disciples of Christ), which shared the same nineteenth-century history as the Churches of Christ. His tenure as co-editor of the *Gospel Advocate* began in January 1870. He continued in that job for over 50 years.

A quiet man, Sewell was remembered for the gentle, persuasive manner demonstrated in his preaching. His writing in the same style covered the range of Bible teachings and usually avoided a controversial presentation. His long years as a steady writer for the magazine help set the direction of the Churches of Christ for over half a century.

Sewell rarely traveled and after 1870 his preaching was confined to the greater Nashville area. He died in Nashville in 1924.

Sources:
Goodpasture, B. C. *The Gospel Advocate Centennial Volume*. Nashville, TN: Gospel Advocate Company, 1956.
West Earl Irvin. *The Search for the Ancient Order: History of the Restoration Movement, 1849-1906*. 2 vols. Indianapolis, IN: Earl West Religious Book Service, 1905.

★ 838 ★
SEYMOUR, William Joseph
Pentecostal Minister
Founder, Pacific Apostolic Faith Movement
b. May 2, 1870, Centerville, Louisiana
d. Sep. 28, 1922, Los Angeles, California

William Joseph Seymour was the founder of the Pacific Apostolic Faith Movement and the pivotal figure in the transformation of Pentecostalism into a national movement. Not much is known about Seymour's early life except that he was born in Louisiana into a family of former slaves. At some point he moved to the midwest where he was initially a member of the Methodist Episcopal Church. He later became involved in the Church of God (Anderson, Indiana) founded by Daniel S. Warner, better known as the "evening light saints" (a name indicating that the holiness movement was the last "light" before Christ's return). Seymour was led to take up the ministry as a profession after surviving a bout of smallpox that left him scarred and blind in one eye.

When **Charles Fox Parham**, under whom the Pentecostal Movement had originated, arrived in Houston, Texas, Seymour attended Parham's classes and converted to the unique Pentecostal position that speaking in tongues always accompanied the baptism with the Holy Spirit. Through a woman who had been a student

of Parham's, Seymour was invited to Los Angeles to become the minister of a group of holiness Baptists who had been ejected from their parent church. Although he had not yet personally experienced the baptism, Seymour journeyed to California, where he preached the importance of speaking in tongues. This emphasis resulted in a prompt rejection of his ministry by his new congregation.

There were, however, a few receptive members who invited Seymour to hold meetings at their home on Bonnie Brae Street. Seymour's future wife, Jenny Evans Moore, received the baptism at one of these gatherings on April 9, 1906, and eventually Seymour himself spoke in tongues. His ministry grew quickly in the wake of these evidences of the Spirit, and the new congregation moved to an old Methodist church on Azusa Street. From this location the Pentecostal Movement exploded into the nation's consciousness.

One of the reasons usually given for the sudden expansion of the movement at this particular point in time was the San Francisco earthquake, which occurred on April 18, 1906. Over 100,000 pamphlets were distributed that correlated the Azusa Street phenomena with the earthquake, and both, in turn, with the end of the world. This millennial expectancy may indeed have supplied the extra spark necessary to prompt Pentecostalism's emergence as a mass movement. Although Parham himself came to reject the work of his former student in Los Angeles because of what he perceived as "fanaticism," enough people from across the United States visited Seymour's ministry at Azusa Street so that by the time of World War I Pentecostalism had established itself in every part of the country.

Sources:
Jones, Charles Edwin. *A Guide to the Study of the Pentecostal Movement*. 2 vols. Metuchen, NJ: Scarecrow Press, 1983.
Lovett, Leonard. "Black Origins of the Pentecostal Movement." In Vinson Synan, *Aspects of Pentecostal-Charismatic Origins*. pp. 123-141. Plainfield, NJ: Logos International, 1975.
Melton, J. Gordon. *Biographical Dictionary of American Cult and Sect Leaders*. Garland Reference Library of Social Science, vol. 212. New York: Garland Publishing, 1986.
Nelson, Douglas J. *For Such a Time as This, The Story of Bishop William J. Seymour and the Azusa Street Revival*. Birmingham, United Kingdom: Ph.D. dissertation, University of Birmingham, 1981. 363 pp.
Seymour, William J. *The Doctrine and Discipline of the Azusa Street Apostolic Faith Mission of Los Angeles*. Los Angeles: Apostolic Faith Mission, n.d.
Synan, Vinson. *The Holiness Pentecostal Movement in the United States*. Grand Rapids, MI: William B. Eerdmans Publishing Company, 1971.
Tinney, James S. "William J. Seymour: Father of Modern-Day Pentecostalism." In Randall K. Burkett and Richard Newman, eds. *Black Apostles*. Boston, MA: G. K. Hall, 1978. 283 pp.

★ 839 ★
SHAKARIAN, Demos
Founder, Full Gospel Business Men's Fellowship International
b. Jul. 21, 1913, Downey, California

Demos Shakarian, founder of the Full Gospel Business Men's Fellowship International, is the product of a Pentecostal movement that began in Russia in the mid-nineteenth century. The Pentecostal outpouring was taken to Armenia in the late nineteenth century. There lived among the Armenians a prophet who, as a boy, had predicted the invasion of the country by Turks and the necessity of Christians to flee to the United States. In 1900 he said it was time for his prediction to come true. Over the next 12 years, families who believed the prophecy fled. The Shakarian family migrated in 1906. In America the families encountered a new Pentecostal movement that had begun at a mission on Azusa Street in Los Angeles, where many of the families had settled. (In 1914 the Turks invaded and killed everyone who had remained behind in the Shakarians' home village.)

Isaac Shakarian started a dairy at Downey, California, where, in 1913, a son they named Demos was born. The family continued as members of the Armenian Pentecostal Church. As a boy of nine, Demos developed hearing trouble. In 1926 he was baptized with the Holy Spirit, spoke in tongues (which Pentecostal Christians believe is the evidential sign of having received the baptism), and was healed of his physical problem. As a young man, he tried several business ventures, but each was a failure. He married in 1933 to Rose Gabriel.

Demos Shakarian's further economic ventures were unsuccessful until he decided to consecrate his business life to God. Since they were not preachers, they decided to use their money to sponsor evangelists. This activity proved successful, and along the way he met Charles S. Price, the prominent prayer-healing evangelist under whose ministry Shakarian's sister was healed. Meanwhile, Shakarian was developing a highly successful dairy business and diversifying into other business ventures.

In 1951 Shakarian helped set up a campaign for **Oral Roberts** in Los Angeles. He shared his idea of a businessmen's fellowship, and Roberts agreed to attend the first meeting. It began with 20 people, grew very slowly, and almost died in December 1952. However, Shakarian had a vision in which God showed him the work to be done by the group. Finally, others responded, and a magazine was started. The second chapter emerged in Sioux Falls, South Dakota, and over the next few years chapters spread across the United States. A Toronto chapter formed in 1956. By 1975 there were 1,650 chapters in all 50 states and 52 countries. *The Voice* magazine had a circulation of 800,000. Much of the growth was due to Shakarian's traveling many miles to initiate local work.

The fellowship emerged as a national organization just as the charismatic movement was beginning. It became the major structure through which the movement spread and in which new charismatics, often in an extreme minority in their churches, found fellowship. It became a meeting ground where leaders and members of many new charismatic churches and denominations first met.

In 1984, following another decade of seeing the organization grow, Shakarian suffered a debilitating stroke which led him to temporarily turn over much of the organization's work to his son and other fellowship executives. In 1985 the organization faced its first year with a net membership decline, and many of Shakarian's associates intensified their concern with the problems of the fellowship's success. The very growth of the Pentecostal movement so fostered by the fellowship meant that numerous activities now competed for an audience once limited to the fellowship as its only option. As a result, in 1988 the organization reorganized. Shakarian remains as the international president, but the duties once centralized in his offices are now shared by other leaders.

In 1988 the fellowship claimed 65,000 members, and it remains as one of the largest and most important Pentecostal organizations in the late twentieth-century world.

Sources:
Bird, Brian. "The Legacy of Demos Shakarian." *Charisma* 11, 11 (June 1986): 20-30.
Burgess, Stanley M., Gary B. McGee, and Patrick H. Alexander, eds. *Dictionary of Pentecostal and Charismatic Movements*. Grand Rapids, MI: Regency Reference Library, Zondervan Publishing House, 1988. 914 pp.
Shakarian, Demos (as told to John and Elizabeth Sherrill). *The Happiest People on Earth*. Old Tappan, NJ: Chosen Books, 1975. 187 pp.
The Shakarian Story. Los Angeles: Full Gospel Business Men's Fellowship International, 1964. 32 pp.

★840★
SHAKU, Soyen
Teacher, Rinzai Zen Buddhism
b. 1859, Japan
d. 1919, Kamakura Japan

Soyen Shaku was the first person to bring Zen Buddhism to the United States and, indirectly through his students, was responsible for establishing Rinzai Zen Buddhism in North America. He was ordained as a monk in 1871 at the age of 12. The leader of the Rinzai Zen sect that he had entered, Imakita Kosen Roshi, had an unusual interest in promoting Zen for laymen and promoting college education for his monks. Soyen received the dharma transmission from Kosen in 1884.

After completing several years at Keio University, Soyen went to Sri Lanka to study Sanskrit and Theravada Buddhism, the dominant form of Buddhism in Southern Asia. He returned to Japan and succeeded Kosen at the Engakuji monastery in Kamakura when his master died in 1892. The same year he was invited to attend the World's Parliament of Religions in Chicago, a meeting that turned out to be an important foothold for many Asian missions to the United States. More cosmopolitan than his contemporaries, who viewed the West as a barbarous land, Soyen accepted the invitation. Unable to speak English, his addresses to the Parliament were read for him by Dr. J. H. Burrows, the Parliament's president. Soyen dealt with very concrete subjects—Buddha's notion of cause and effect and "Arbitration Instead of War"—rather than with the more esoteric aspects of Zen.

Although his presence at the Parliament did not evoke the kind of enthusiasm that **Swami Vivekananda** received, Soyen made a very important contact in **Paul Carus**, an editor at Open Court Publishing Company. Carus became interested in Buddhism through Soyen, and as a result of this interest began to publish popular works on Buddhism such as his own *The Gospel of Buddhism*. In 1905 Alexander Russell and his wife came to Japan to study Zen with Soyen, and eventually persuaded him to visit the United States again and stay with them outside of San Francisco. It was during this visit that the use of koans was first introduced to Americans. Soyen also gave lectures during this time, with his student **Daisetz Teitaro Suzuki** serving as interpreter. He returned home by way of Sri Lanka after spending nine months with the Russells. In addition to Suzuki, two of Soyen's other students, **Nyogen Senzaki** and Sokatsu Shaku, would prove to be important figures in the spread of Zen to the United States.

Sources:
Fields, Rick. *How the Swans Came to the Lake*. Boulder, CO: Shambhala, 1986. 445 pp.
Melton, J. Gordon. *Biographical Dictionary of American Cult and Sect Leaders*. Garland Reference Library of Social Science, vol. 212. New York: Garland Publishing, 1986.
Soyen, Shaku. "The Law of Cause and Effect as Taught by Buddha." In J. W. Hanson, ed. *The World's Parliament of Religions*. pp. 388-390. Chicago: Monarch Book Company, 1894.
———. *Sermons of a Zen Buddhist Abbot*. Chicago: Open Court Publishing Company, 1906. Reprinted as: *Zen for Americans*. LaSalle, IL: Open Court Publishing Company, 1974. 220 pp.

★841★
SHAW, Anna Howard
Suffrage Leader and Minister, Methodist Protestant Church
b. Feb. 14, 1847, Newcastle-on-Tyne England
d. Jul. 2, 1919, Moylan, Pennsylvania

Anna Howard Shaw, a Methodist minister and an active leader in both the temperance and suffrage movements, was the daughter of Thomas and Nicolas Stott Shaw, both Unitarians. Her father moved to America in 1849, and she came two years later with her mother. After living in Lawrence, Massachusetts, for eight years, she journeyed to rural Michigan to live in a log cabin on the farm her father was claiming from the wilderness. At age 15 she became a school teacher but was unable to attend high school until after the Civil War. In her early 20s, she converted to Methodism and joined the Methodist Church against her parents' wishes. She then found a circuit rider who would assist her in a growing ambition to become a preacher. When she was 24 she was given a license to preach by the Michigan Conference of the Methodist Episcopal Church and began to work her way through Albion College, a denominational school. After graduation in 1875, she attended Boston Theological Seminary, the only female in the class. After graduation she served a parish in the Wesleyan Methodist Church and applied for ordination in the Methodist Episcopal Church. That church refused to ordain her, so she finally turned to the Methodist Protestant Church, and in 1880 became the first woman ordained by that denomination. Following her ordination she entered the Boston University Medical School and in 1886 finally received her M.D. degree.

During her Boston years Shaw had become aware of the appalling conditions in the local slums. She also became interested in the temperance issue and in the suffrage movement. She joined both the Massachusetts State Suffrage Association and the Woman's Christian Temperance Union (W.C.T.U.). In 1886 she became the superintendent of franchise for the WCTU, the largest women's organization in America. She became a popular lecturer on the Chautauqua Circuit on behalf of women, her primary concern. It has been generally acknowledged that during the last decades of her life she was one of the finest female speakers in the country.

In 1888 she met Susan B. Anthony, who became her close friend and colleague. Anthony's niece, Lucy E. Anthony, became Shaw's private secretary and companion for the rest of her life. In 1892, when Anthony became president of the North American Woman Suffrage Association, she was named vice president at large. She became president in 1904. She retired in 1915, the same year her autobiography, *The Story of a Pioneer*, was published.

Shaw was called out of retirement by World War I. In 1917 she became chairperson of the women's committee of the Council of National Defense. She was awarded the Distinguished Service Medal for her work. The council disbanded just as the suffrage amendment was reaching its critical stage in Congress. She threw herself into the work to pass it, both through the many government contacts she had gathered and in public speeches. At the urging of William Howard Taft she joined the effort to garner public support for the League of Nations. While touring the country with Taft and A. Lawrence Lowell, president of Harvard University, she became ill and died a short time later of pneumonia.

Sources:

Dictionary of American Biography. 20 vols. and 7 supps. New York: Charles Scribner's Sons, 1928-1936, 1944-1981.

Harmon, Nolan B. *The Encyclopedia of World Methodism.* 2 vols. Nashville: United Methodist Publishing House, 1974.

Shaw, Anna Howard. *The Story of a Pioneer.* New York: Harper & Bros. 1915. 337 pp.

★842★
SHEEN, Fulton John
Bishop, Roman Catholic Church
b. May 8, 1895, El Paso, Illinois
d. Dec. 9, 1976, New York, New York

Fulton John Sheen, a bishop of the Roman Catholic Church, is best known not for his episcopal leadership, but for authoring some best-selling books and hosting first a radio and then a prime-time television show, both of which had great appeal far beyond the Roman Catholic community. Sheen was the son of Irish immigrants Newton Morris and Delia Fulton Sheen. He was baptized Peter Sheen, but took the name John when confirmed and later added

his mother's maiden name. He grew up in Peoria, Illinois, where his uncle was a law partner of **Robert Green Ingersoll**, the famous Freethinker, and where he attended parochial school. In 1913 he entered St. Viator College in Bourbonnais, Illinois, from which he received both his B.A. (1917) and M.A. (1919). He entered St. Paul's Seminary and was ordained in the fall of 1919.

Following his ordination he transferred to Catholic University in America, from which he received his S.T.B. and J.C.B. degrees in 1920. He then traveled to Europe and received his Ph.D. from the University of Louvain, Belgium, in 1923 and his D.D. in Rome from the Collegio Angelico. He taught a year at St. Edmund's College in England, during which time he was awarded the Cardinal Mercer International Prize in Philosophy, the first American so honored, for his doctoral dissertation, *God and Intelligence*. He returned to the United States in 1926, and after a brief time as a parish priest in Peoria, he joined the faculty of the Catholic University of America, where he remained until 1950. During this time he authored a number of scholarly works, including *Religion Without God* (1928); *Philosophy of Science* (1934); *Philosophies at War* (1943); and *Philosophy of Religion* (1948).

While at Catholic University, rather than becoming known for philosophical talents, he became known as a great preacher and was frequently called upon to speak both nationally and internationally. In 1934 he was made a papal chamberlain with the title monsignor and the next year was raised to the rank of domestic prelate with the title right reverend monsignor.

Sheen became the first regular speaker of the "Catholic Hour" radio show, initiated in 1930, and was an immediate success. He annually gave the pre-Lenten and Lenten broadcasts, which reached an audience estimated at four million by 1950. In 1950 Sheen was named auxiliary bishop of New York and United States director for the Society for the Propagation of the Faith. The following year he began a television program called "Life Is Worth Living" that ran for six years and earned him an Emmy Award in 1952. In 1966 he was named Bishop of Rochester, New York, and that same year began a new television program called "The Bishop Sheen Show," which ran successfully for several years. He retired in 1969 and was appointed titular bishop of Newport, Wales, and spent the rest of his life writing.

Over the years, in addition to his scholarly writing, Sheen authored a number of books for popular consumption, some apologetics for the Catholic faith, and many of an inspirational nature. Among those which reached the bestseller lists were *The Life of All Living* (1929); *The Eternal Galilean* (1934); *Peace of Soul* (1949); *Life Is Worth Living* (1953-1957, five volumes); and *Guide to Contentment* (1967). His autobiography, *Treasure in Clay*, was published posthumously in 1980.

Sources:

Contemporary Authors. Detroit, MI: Gale Research Inc.

Current Biography Yearbook. New York: H. W. Wilson Co. 1951.

Sheen, Fulton J. *Guide to Contentment.* New York: Simon & Schuster, 1967. 127 pp.

———. *Life Is Worth Living.* 5 vols. New York: McGraw Hill, 1953-1957.

———. *Peace of Soul.* New York: Whittlesay House, 1949. 202 pp.

———. *Philosophy of Religion.* New York: Appleton-Century-Cross, 1948. 400 pp.

———. *Treasure in Clay.* Garden City: Doubleday, 1980. 336 pp.

★843★
SHEHAN, Lawrence Joseph
Cardinal, Roman Catholic Church
b. Mar. 18, 1898, Baltimore, Maryland
d. Aug. 16, 1984, Baltimore, Maryland

Lawrence Joseph Shehan, a cardinal in the Roman Catholic Church, was the son of Thomas Patrick and Anastasia Schofield

Shehan. He was raised in a Catholic home and attended parochial school. In 1911 he left Baltimore for a preparatory seminary, St. Charles College, in Catonsville, Maryland. After graduating in 1917, he attended St. Mary's Seminary in Baltimore, from which he received his B.A. in 1919 and his M.A. in 1920. He then was sent to Rome for further study at the Urban College for the Propagation of the Faith. He was ordained in 1922 and received his doctorate in 1923. He returned to the United States and assumed duties at St. Patrick's Church in Washington, D.C. He remained at St. Patrick's for 23 years.

During his years in Washington, Shehan became assistant director (1929) and then director (1938) of the archdiocese's Catholic Charities. In 1934 he was appointed to the archbishop's administrative board. He was named a papal chamberlain in 1939 with the title of monsignor. In 1945 he was consecrated a bishop and moved to Baltimore as auxiliary for the archdiocese. After eight years in his hometown, he became the first bishop of the newly created diocese in Bridgeport, Connecticut.

In Bridgeport, Bishop Shehan distinguished himself in the area of education, a particular need of his diocese. He squarely faced the problems of increasing costs of a growing parochial system. He was outspoken in suggesting solutions to the crises being faced by the church as a whole. Shehan called for federal aid programs to include Catholic schools. He suggested limiting the parochial system to junior high and high school, with Catholic children attending public schools for the lower grades.

In July 1961 Shehan became coadjutor to Abp. Francis P. Keough in Baltimore. Keough died five months later, and Shehan succeeded him. Shehan took office just as the expectations for the Second Vatican Council were growing and he used his new position to champion the cause of greater ecumenical and interfaith activity by the Roman Catholic Church. In January 1962 he formed a Commission of Christian Unity, the first diocesan organization of its kind in the United States. He reached out openly to both Protestants and Jews.

In the midst of these endeavors, Shehan was elevated to the cardinalate in February 1965. The new role only stimulated his activity. That same month he participated in the first formal Lutheran-Roman Catholic dialogue. Recognizing his work, the U.S. bishops appointed him chairman of their Committee on Ecumenical Affairs. The Pope then appointed him to the Vatican Secretariat for the Promotion of Christian Unity, and on July 9, 1965, to the 12-man presidency of Vatican II. In December 1965, when Pope Paul VI and the Eastern Orthodox Ecumenical Patriarch annulled the mutual excommunication that had been in effect since 1054, Shehan headed the Roman Catholic delegation for the ceremony in Istanbul.

As a "liberal" leader at Vatican II, Shehan spent much of his time on removing what he saw as unnecessary obstacles to Christian unity. He believed that some barriers between Roman Catholics and Protestant groups were much more a matter of imperfect language rather than of substantive doctrine. He thought that much misunderstanding about the doctrine of papal infallibility could be cleared up with a new emphasis on the relation of the pope and church consensus. He also became a strong critic in the council of official Catholic teachings on the use of contraceptives, and joined with fellow Cardinal **Francis Spellman** in opposing the council's declaration against war.

Cardinal Shehan also was renowned for his work on racial harmony. He attacked racial segregation in the early years of his reign in Baltimore. In 1962 he ordered all Catholic schools to desegregate. He followed with similar orders to other Catholic institutions. In 1963 he issued a pastoral letter banning racial bias in all Catholic institutions.

In the face of his accomplishments in ecumenism and interracial work, Shehan was faced with a minor revolt when a teacher in a Baltimore seminary, Fr. **Gommar Albert De Pauw, J.D.C.,** issued a statement accusing Shehan and other liberals of trying to Protestantize the church. Shehan censured De Pauw, who eventually moved to New York as head of an independent Catholic Traditionalist Movement.

Following his retirement in 1974, Shehan spent his remaining years engaged in pastoral work and writing.

Sources:

Biography Index. New York: The H. W. Wilson Co.
Current Biography Yearbook. New York: H. W. Wilson Co.
The Lincoln Library of Social Studies. Columbus, OH: Frontier Press Company.
Who's Who in America. Wilmette, IL: Marquis Who's Who, Inc.

★844★
SHELDON, Charles Monroe
Writer and Minister, Congregational Church
b. Feb. 26, 1857, Wellsville, New York
d. Feb. 24, 1946, Topeka, Kansas

Charles Monroe Sheldon, writer of best-selling inspirational novels and social gospel activist, was the son of Sarah Ward and Rev. Stewart Sheldon, a Congregational minister. When he was a teenager his family settled for several years in Dakota territory, where the boy's outlook was shaped by the pioneer experience. He eventually attended prep school in Massachusetts, and thereafter earned degrees from Brown University and Andover Theological School. After a brief early pastorate in Waterbury, Vermont, he became founding pastor of Central Congregational Church in Topeka, Kansas, in 1889.

As a young minister, influenced by the social gospel movement, Sheldon soon began to pursue social reform projects in Topeka. The most prominent of these projects was a series of programs to help improve the squalid living conditions of a community of impoverished ex-slaves who had settled in Topeka near his church. The programs, by all accounts quite successful, influenced his preaching and writing. Soon he began preaching social reform in the form of inspirational serial stories, read chapter by chapter from the pulpit. Those stories were eventually published as books, which became popular social gospel literature. The story which he read in the fall of 1896, *In His Steps*, became a runaway success when it was published in book form the next year, and after other publishers discovered that its copyright was defective, cheap editions appeared by the dozens. Many millions of copies were eventually sold in English and other languages; it was serialized in many periodicals, distributed free by merchants as a premium, and adapted into stage and radio plays. The book, still in print, may be the best-selling novel of all time. The defect in the copyright, however, meant that Sheldon received very little money for his work, although he was happy to see his ideas reach so many people.

In His Steps called on Christians to try to live their lives as Jesus would have, asking themselves each time they faced a personal decision, "What would Jesus do?" One chapter featured a newspaper editor who decided to reform his newspaper in order to make it a force for Christian activism. In 1900, when the book was at its pinnacle of success, the new publisher of the *Topeka Daily Capital* suddenly offered Sheldon a chance to act out that chapter personally. For a week in March of that year Sheldon edited the *Capital* as he thought Jesus would have, dropping news he considered unfit (such as reports of prize fights and stock markets) and rejecting unfit advertising (for tobacco, alcohol, and corsets, among other products). With great ballyhoo, daily circulation for the week averaged over 350,000 (the pre- and post-Sheldon circulation was about 11,000).

Sheldon continued his pastorate in Topeka until retirement in 1919. Thereafter he traveled and preached extensively, promoting his favorite social causes, notably prohibition and pacifism. For five years in the early 1920s he served as a contributing editor to the *Christian Herald*, then America's most influential Protestant periodical. Over his lifetime he published about 50 books and hundreds of articles and poems. He died in Topeka in 1946 at age 88.

Sources:

Boyer, Paul S. "In His Steps: A Reappraisal." *American Quarterly* 23 (Spring, 1971): 60-78.

Miller, Timothy. *Following In His Steps: A Biography of Charles M. Sheldon*. Knoxville: University of Tennessee Press, 1987. 281 pp.

Ripley, John W. "Another Look at the Rev. Mr. Charles M. Sheldon's Christian Daily Newspaper." *Kansas Historical Quarterly* 31 (Spring, 1965): 1-40.

_____. "Last Rites for a Few Myths." *Shawnee County Historical Society Bulletin* 44 (Autumn, 1968): 1-25.

Sheldon, Charles M. "The Experiment of a Christian Daily." *Atlantic Monthly* 134 (November, 1924): 624-633.

_____. *In His Steps*. Chicago: Advance Publishing Co., 1897.

_____. *The Redemption of Freetown*. Boston: United Society of Christian Endeavor, 1898.

—Timothy Miller

★ 845 ★
SHELLY, Andrew B.
President, General Conference Mennonite Church
b. Sep. 23, 1834, Bucks County, Pennsylvania
d. Dec. 26, 1913, Philadelphia, Pennsylvania

Andrew B. Shelly, the successor to **John H. Oberholtzer** as leader of the General Conference Mennonite Church, was the son of Elizabeth Bauer and Joseph Shelly. He was raised on his father's farm in the heart of Mennonite country. He attended school regularly during his youth, and when he was 19 he began to teach school. He also associated with the West Swamp Mennonite Church, a congregation affiliated with the General Conference Mennonite Church, one of the more liberal, innovative branches of the larger Mennonite movement. In 1857 he became the congregation's Sunday school superintendent, one of the issues initially raised by the General Conference being that of religious education for children. In 1868 he married Fannie Weinberger, and the following year returned to farming.

Oberholtzer ordained Shelly to serve as his associate minister in 1864. In 1866 Shelly became editor of the *Mennonitisher Friedensbote*, a periodical serving the General Conference. In 1869 he moved to Philadelphia for a year as pastor of the First Mennonite Church, but moved back to Bucks County as pastor of West Swamp Church. That same year he was elected president of the church's Eastern District Conference, a position he held for the next 11 years. In 1872 Oberholtzer retired, and that same year Shelly was ordained as bishop over the Bucks County churches, though he remained pastor at West Swamp. In 1874, in addition to his other duties, Shelly was elected president of the General Conference.

During the next 30 years Shelly was the dominant personality in the church's life. He continued editing his periodical until it was merged into the *Christlicher Bundesbote* in 1881, and then continued as assistant editor until 1884. He emerged as an advocate for an English-language periodical and beginning in 1885 served on the editorial board of *The Mennonite*.

Shelly was a member of several of the church's national boards but gave his greatest attention to the mission board, on which he sat for 37 years (1874-1911) and served as secretary for 22 years (1889-1911). In 1911, because of age, he began to cut down on his duties, but in 1913, shortly before his death, he was elected to the educational board. It was noted that while he gave a significant

amount of time to editorial and General Conference responsibilities, he was also known as one of the most conscientious pastors in the church.

Sources:

Kaufman, Edmund G., comp. *General Conference Mennonite Pioneers*. North Newton, KS: Bethel College, 1973. 438 pp.

The Mennonite Encyclopedia. 4 vols. Scottdale, PA: The Mennonite Publishing House, 1955.

★ 846 ★
SHELTON, S. McDowell
Apostle and Overseer, Church of The Lord Jesus Christ of the Aposto lic Faith
b. Apr. 18, 1929, Philadelphia, Pennsylvania

S. McDowell Shelton, the apostle and universal overseer of the Church of The Lord Jesus Christ of the Apostolic Faith, a Pentecostal denomination serving a predominantly black constituency, grew up in Philadelphia, Pennsylvania. He eventually became a member and minister in the Church of The Lord Jesus Christ of the Apostolic Faith, founded in 1903 by **Sherrod C. Johnson**. He attended Rutgers University, from which he received a B.A. He later did graduate work at the University of Lisbon and studied at the Berlitz School of Languages, which assisted him to become fluent in many languages.

Shelton became head of the church in 1961 following Johnson's death. He continued many of the tasks initiated by his predecessor, most prominently the completion of the church's headquarters and housing complex in Philadelphia, which in 1972 became known as Apostolic Square. He also edits the church magazine and speaks on the church's radio show, both entitled, "The Whole Truth". Shelton has become known for his world travels in the interests of the church's worldwide mission. As Johnson oversaw the development of a national church, Shelton has seen an international denomination emerge. During his extensive travels he has met with a number of heads of state. In 1972 he received the Human Relations Award from the Philadelphia Commonwealth.

Sources:

Dupree, Sherry Sherrod. *Biographical Dictionary of African-American, Holiness-Pentecostals, 1880-1990*. Washington, DC: Middle Atlantic Regional Press, 1990. 386 pp.

Richardson, James C. *With Water and Spirit*. Washington, DC: Spirit Press, 1980. 151 pp.

★ 847 ★
SHERRILL, Henry Knox
Presiding Bishop, Protestant Episcopal Church in the U.S.A.
b. Nov. 6, 1890, Brooklyn, New York
d. May 11, 1980, Boxford, Massachusetts

Henry Knox Sherrill, a presiding bishop of the Protestant Episcopal Church in the U.S.A. (now the Episcopal Church) and the first president of the National Council of Churches, was the son of Maria Knox Mills and Henry Williams Sherrill. He grew up in Brooklyn, New York, and attended the Hotchkiss School in Lakeville, Connecticut, for a year before entering Yale University. Having an early desire to enter the ministry, he graduated from Yale in 1911 and moved to the Episcopal Theological Seminary in Cambridge, Massachusetts. In 1914 he graduated, was ordained a deacon in the Episcopal Church, and became curate of Trinity Episcopal Church in Boston. He was ordained as a priest in 1915, and became a chaplain in 1917, serving two years with the army in France.

After the war, in 1919, Sherrill became rector of the Church of Our Savior in Brookline, Massachusetts. In 1921 he married Barbara Harris. He became rector of Trinity Church (which former pastor **Phillips Brooks** had made one of the outstanding pulpits in America) in 1923. He quickly emerged as a national spokesperson for the socially liberal non-ritualistic wing of the clergy and gained a reputation as an excellent orator. He remained at Trinity only seven years, however, as at the age of 39 he was elected bishop of Massachusetts. He was consecrated in the fall of 1930. In 1938 he was appointed assessor to the then presiding bishop, **Henry St. George Tucker**.

During World War II Sherrill assumed duties with the armed forces again, becoming chairman of the General Commission on Army and Navy Chaplains, whose task it was to supervise the selection of chaplains. He traveled widely, visiting units in both Europe and the Aleutian Islands. After the war he worked with the Federal Council of Churches to build new bridges to the surviving German clergy.

In 1946 Sherrill succeeded Tucker as the new presiding bishop of the church. His years of leadership were marked by his ecumenical concerns. As early as 1928 he had served as president of the Greater Boston Federation of Churches and had been an avid supporter of the old Federal Council of Churches. He used his episcopal office to assist the process of reviving and reforming the Federal Council, which led to its being superseded by the National Council of Churches in 1950. In 1954 he was elected president of the National Council. Sherrill served as presiding bishop until 1958. In 1962 he finished his autobiography, *Among Friends*.

Sources:
Sherrill, Henry Knox. *Among Friends*. Boston: Little, Brown, 1962. 340 pp.
_____. *William Lawrence, Later Years of a Happy Life*. Cambridge, MA: Harvard University Press, 1943. 179 pp.

★848★
SHERRILL, Lewis Joseph
Educator, Presbyterian Church in the U.S.
b. Apr. 18, 1882, Haskell, Texas
d. Jan. 30, 1957, New York, New York

Lewis Joseph Sherrill, a leading theoretician in the field of religious education, was the son of Catherine Howard Taylor and Richard Ellis Sherrill. He grew up in Texas and attended Austin College (A.B., 1916). His seminary work was completed at the Presbyterian Theological Seminary of Kentucky, though his course of study was interrupted during World War I by his service in the Army. He finally graduated in 1921. That same year he was ordained in the (Southern) Presbyterian Church in the U.S.A., married to Helen Hardwicke, and named pastor of First Presbyterian Church in Covington, Tennessee.

Like many young pastors, Sherrill soon confronted the gap between his seminary training and the actual pastoral problems with which he was called upon to deal. His quest to bridge that gap led him to explore the possibilities of religious education. In 1926 he returned to school and three years later earned his Ph.D at Yale University.

Returning to Louisville, Sherrill served as a professor of religious education and dean (1930-1950) for the next two decades. He had previously set himself the problem of understanding the relationship between theology, psychology, and the actual problems faced by church lay people. In his attempt to unravel the solution Sherrill authored a number of books beginning with *Religious Education in the Small Church* (1932). This book was followed by *Adult Education in the Church* (1936); *Family and Church* (1937); and *Understanding Children* (1939). Sherrill's thinking centered upon two emphases: evangelism, through which the church leads people into a Christian experience, and education, by which people are allowed to grow into better Christians. Much of Sherrill's educational contributions came from his integration of psychological insights into the understanding of the life growth process. His psychological focus led him to concentrate upon the process of

growth in the Christian life and play down the importance of a single conversion event, although he included a place for the role of crises in the individual religious life.

Sherrill's concern for the importance of theological education in training ministers for the parish led him to become the executive secretary (1935-1938) and then the president (1938-1940) of the American Association of Theological Schools. His broad concern for religious education led to historical research and a projected five-volume history of religious education, of which only volume one, *The Rise of Christian Education* (1944), appeared. As he matured he also developed a focus on a philosophy of the Christian community, the subject of his latter books, *Guilt and Redemption* (1945); *The Struggle of the Soul* (1951); and *The Gift of Power* (1955). In 1950 he retired from Louisville, and moved to New York as a professor at Union Theological Seminary, where he remained for the rest of his life.

Sources:
Reid, Daniel G., Robert D. Linder, Bruce L. Shelley, and Harry S. Stout. *Dictionary of Christianity in America*. Downers Grove, IL: InterVarsity Press, 1990. 1305 pp.
Sherrill, Lewis J. *Family and Church*. New York: Abingdon, 1937. 266 pp.
_____. *The Gift of Power*. New York: Macmillan Company, 1955. 203 pp.
_____. *Guilt and Redemption*. Richmond, VA: John Knox Press, 1945. 254 pp.
_____. *Religious Education in the Small Church*. Philadelphia: Westminster Press, 1932. 208 pp.
_____. *The Rise of Christian Education*. New York: Macmillan Company, 1944. 349 pp.
_____. *Understanding Children* New York: Macmillan Company, 1939. 218 pp.
Weeks, Louis B., III. "Lewis Sherrill: The Christian Educator and Christian Experience." *Journal of Presbyterian History* 51 (1973): 235-248.

★849★
SHIELDS JR., Thomas Todhunter
Founder, Fellowship of Evangelical Baptist Churches in Canada
b. Nov. 1, 1873, Bristol England
d. Apr. 4, 1955, Toronto, Ontario, Canada

Thomas Todhunter Shields, Jr., leading Canadian fundamentalist and founder of the Fellowship of Evangelical Baptist Churches of Canada, was the son of a minister in the Primitive Methodist Church in England. When Shields was about 15 years old his family moved to Ontario, and his father was ordained in the Baptist church and assigned the congregation at Plattsville. During and after his son's high school years, the elder Shields taught him the Bible, including Hebrew and Greek. The younger Shields never attended college, but was eventually ordained and in 1894 became pastor of the Baptist church at Florence, Ontario. He served several additional pastorates over the years, culminating in a six-year tenure at Adelaide Street Baptist Church in London, Ontario, before moving to Jarvis Street Baptist Church in Toronto in 1910. He would remain at Jarvis Street for the rest of his life.

Soon after his arrival in Toronto, Shields turned his attention to McMaster University, the Baptist institution in town. He began to attack what he saw as liberal theology creeping into the classroom. In 1919 he organized fundamentalists within the Baptist churches of Canada in opposition to an article in the *Canadian Baptist* which argued for a progressive view of Biblical revelation. At the next convention he presented a resolution supporting the infallible nature of the Bible as God's Word. It passed. Within a few years he came to know many of the leading American fundamentalists.

In 1921 Shields faced a revolt at Jarvis Street that led to over 300 members quitting. However, with the assistance of **John Roach Straton** and **J. Frank Norris**, he was able to quickly rebuild and by the mid-1920s had the largest Sunday school in Canada. In 1922 he began a magazine, *The Gospel Witness*. In 1923 he assisted in the organization of the Baptist Bible Union, a continental fellowship of Baptist fundamentalists, and served as its first president.

Due in part to some of his extreme opinions and his personality, which some perceived as arrogant, controversy followed Shields over the next few years, and in 1926 the Baptist convention voted Shields persona non grata. Shields withdrew and in 1927 founded the Regular Baptist Missionary and Educational Society (later the Fellowship of Evangelical Baptist Churches of Canada). He also created the Toronto Baptist Seminary to counter the liberal McMaster University. During the next decades he concentrated on developing and nurturing the structures he had created, and he added a radio ministry in 1936. He stayed in contact with American fundamentalists, especially the more conservative separatist wing, and among his last actions was to join with **Carl McIntire** in 1948 in the formation of the International Council of Christian Churches as a fundamentalist alternative to the World Council of Churches.

Sources:

Brackney, William Henry. *The Baptist.* New York: Greenwood Press, 1988. 327 pp.

Tarr, Leslie K. *Shields of Canada: T. T. Shields, 1873-1955.* Grand Rapids, MI: Baker Book House, 1967. 218 pp.

★ 850 ★
Shri SHIVABALAYOGI MAHARAJ
Founder, Shri Shivabalayogi Maharaj Trust
b. Jan. 24, 1935, Adivarapupeta India

Shri Shivabalayogi Maharaj, founder of the Shri Shivabalayogi Maharaj Trust, is a Shaivite saint in the Hindu tradition. Born Sathyaraju Bheemanna (Shri Shivabalayogi Maharaj is a religious name created by juxtaposing several honorifics) into the weaver caste, he started and ran a successful *beedi* (traditional Indian cigarette) shop while still a youth. His spiritual quest began in earnest on August 7, 1949, when he experienced a vision and fell into a superconscious state. After this experience he began to follow *tapo marg*, the path of *tapas* (austerities), which is said to bestow *siddhis* (psychic powers) on the practitioner.

Shivabalayogi undertook austerities for 12 long years. At the beginning of this period he was harassed by people who would pull his legs, throw filth on him, and try to pry open his closed eyelids. He eventually moved to the burial ground on the village outskirts to continue his austerities. At one point he was bitten by a black cobra, and the venom caused his skin to become discolored. He would also lose control of his limbs during certain periods. He ended his austerities on August 7, 1961, an event which his official biography says was witnessed by a crowd of over 300,000.

Shivabalayogi's public mission follows a pattern similar to other Indian saints. People approach the saint for the blessings of his presence, and he in turn ministers to their spiritual and material needs. Like the more well-known Sathya Sai Baba, Shivabalayogi dispenses consecrated *vibhuti* (holy ash) which miraculously cures the ills and distresses of his petitioners. His presence has also been attributed with the power to induce ecstatic states during *kirtan* (congregational singing). In recent years he has begun a series of world tours, initiating people into *dhyana* (intense spiritual meditation) yoga. His headquarters in the United States is in Portland, Oregon.

Sources:

Singh, Brig. Hanut. *Sri Sri Sri Shivabalayogi Maharaj: Life & Spiritual Ministration.* Bangalore, India: Sri Sri Sri Shivabalayogi Maharaj Trust, 1981. 149 pp.

—*James R. Lewis*

★ 851 ★
SHOEMAKER JR., Samuel Moor
Minister, Episcopal Church
b. Dec. 27, 1893, Baltimore, Maryland
d. Oct. 31, 1963, Burnside, Maryland

Samuel Moor Shoemaker, Jr., an Episcopal priest best remembered for his work in personal evangelism, was the son of Nellie Whitridge and Samuel Moor Shoemaker. The family, whose name had been anglicized from the German "Schumacher," was Episcopalian, and when he was 14 Shoemaker was sent to an Episcopal boarding school in Rhode Island to prepare him for college. In 1912 he entered Princeton University. Active in the school's religious life, he was able to meet many of the outstanding Protestant leaders of the generation, and he developed a broad vision of Christianity. In 1917 he moved to Peking, China, with Disciples of Christ minister Sherwood Eddy to teach at the Princeton extension then located there. While in China he met **Frank N. Buchman**, the Lutheran minister who founded the so-called Oxford Movement, later renamed Moral ReArmament (MRA). His encounter led to a significant reexamination of his life, and he developed a life-long commitment to personal evangelism. For many years the work of the Oxford Group became integral to his ministry.

In 1920 Shoemaker was ordained a deacon in the Episcopal Church and entered General Theological Seminary in New York City to prepare for a career as a clergyman. In 1921 he was ordained a priest and joined the staff at Grace Episcopal Church in the city. While there he authored the first of his more than 25 books, *Realizing Religion* (1921), as well as the frequently reprinted *A Young Man's View of the Ministry* (1923).

In 1925 Shoemaker became the pastor of the small Calvary Episcopal Church in New York City and there began an innovative program of urban evangelism. He began teaching-training sessions for the laity and in 1926 opened Calvary Mission in the Gas Light district of Manhattan. The work prospered and in 1928 Calvary House, a new parish center which provided space for a greatly expanded program, was completed and dedicated. In 1930 Shoemaker married Helen Smith.

In 1932 Shoemaker took a leave of absence to work for six months with the Oxford Group. He emerged as the American leader of the work, and Calvary House, in effect, became the movement's American headquarters. Buchman's call for personal reexamination and confession in a context of forgiveness seemed to fit appropriately into Shoemaker's program of evangelism, and he authored several books about MRA during the 1930s. Among the most significant occurrences during the period of his involvement with MRA was his meeting with Bill W., the founder of Alcoholics Anonymous. Through Shoemaker, Alcoholics Anonymous developed, following the small group model fostered by MRA. In a more general context, Shoemaker began to advocate the value of small, intimate groups in congregational life and is regarded as one of the fathers of the small groups (koinonia) movement of later decades.

The close work with MRA, however, began to force a choice on Shoemaker as he saw it competing with the church's own ministry. Finally, in 1941 he broke with the movement and came to a clear decision to center his ministry in the church community. He immediately expanded the program at Calvary House. He reactivated the training program for the laity under the name "Faith at Work." It grew far beyond the congregation and survives as an autonomous interdenominational organization. In 1946 he began a radio ministry under the auspices of the Federal Council of Churches which continued under various names through the rest of his life.

In 1952 Shoemaker accepted a call to Calvary Episcopal Church in Pittsburgh, Pennsylvania. Here he began a program, dubbed the Pittsburgh Experiment, which reached out to affluent businessmen, and here he ministered for the rest of his life. His work provided models for parishes of a variety of Protestant denominations to follow.

Sources:

Shoemaker, Helen Smith. *I Stand by the Door: The Life of Samuel Shoemaker.* Waco, TX: Word Books, 1978. 297 pp.

Shoemaker, Samuel Moor. *Calvary Church Yesterday and Today.* New York: Fleming H. Revell, 1936.

_____. *The Church Can Save the World.* New York: Fleming H. Revell, 1938.

_____. *The Experiment of Faith.* New York: Harper & Row, 1957.

_____. *Realizing Religion.* New York: Association Press, 1921.

_____. *Revive Thy Church—Beginning with Me.* New York: Harper & Row, 1948.

_____. *A Young Man's View of the Ministry.* New York: Association Press, 1923.

★852★
SHOGHI EFFENDI RABBONI
Guardian, Baha'i Faith
b. Mar. 1, 1897, Akka Persia
d. Nov. 4, 1957, London United Kingdom

Shoghi Effendi Rabboni was the last great spiritual personality of the Baha'i Faith. Baha'i originated in the work of the Persian (Iranian) Mirza Ali Muhammed (The Bab), who, like John the Baptist among Christians, is viewed as a figure who announced the imminent appearance of a new prophet of God. He made his initial announcement in 1844. The movement which gathered around him evoked intense persecution, and the Bab was martyred in 1850. One of his followers, Mirza Husayn Ali, came to the realization that he was the messenger proclaimed by the Bab, a realization that he began to share while in exile in 1863. Henceforth he was known as **Baha'u'llah**. Baha'u'llah's son, **Abdu'l-Baha** (Abbas Effendi), succeeded his father. Remembered as the Interpreter, Abdu'l-Baha summarized Baha'i into 11 principles that stressed the universalism of the faith. Shoghi Effendi, Abdu'l-Baha's grandson, in turn inherited the leadership of the movement from his grandfather. Remembered as the Guardian, Shoghi Effendi provided organizational guidance that transformed the Baha'i Faith into a stable world religion.

A highly educated man, Effendi attended college both in Israel and in England. Appointed Abbas Effendi's successor while still a child, he assumed leadership in 1921 at the age of 24 upon the death of his grandfather. Shoghi Effendi is particularly remembered for his organizational accomplishments, providing the faith with a structure that it has maintained to the present day. He also emphasized the point that Baha'i was a distinct religion, and that members could not simultaneously belong to other faiths. Another important project was the translation into English of the scriptural works of his great grandfather, such as *Gleanings from the Writings of Baha'u'llah*; *The Hidden Words of Baha'u'llah*; and *Epistle to the Son of the Wolf*. Although not regarded as scripture, Shoghi Effendi's own works are recognized as authoritative.

By the time of Effendi's passing in 1957, the Baha'i Faith had achieved recognition as a world faith on par with the other great world religions. Following his death, leadership passed to an interim governing body until the Universal House of Justice, an elected international group, took over in 1963. As with many other movements, the transition from charismatic to institutional authority was not entirely smooth. During his lifetime, Shoghi Effendi had appointed **Charles Mason Remey**, a prominent American Baha'i, to the presidency of a ruling body that preceded the Universal House of Justice, and after Effendi's death, Remey claimed that he was the second Guardian. The majority of Baha'is did not agree, and Remey established his own separate organization.

Sources:

Giachery, Ugo. *Shoghi Effendi: Recollections.* Oxford, England: George Ronald, 1973. 38 pp.

Shoghi Effendi. *The Advent of Divine Justice.* Wilmette, IL: Baha'i Publishing Committee, 1904.

_____. *Baha'i Administration.* Wilmette, IL: Baha'i Publishing Trust, 1968. 209 pp.

_____. *The Dispensation of Baha'u'llah.* Wilmette, IL: Baha'i Publishing Committee, 1934. 65 pp.

_____. *God Passes By.* Wilmette, IL: Baha'i Publishing Trust, 1970. 436 pp.

★853★
SHULER, Robert Pierce
Minister, Methodist Episcopal Church, South
b. Aug. 4, 1880, Grayson County, Virginia
d. Sep. 11, 1965

Robert Pierce "Bob" Shuler, a Southern Methodist minister known for his denunciations of public immorality, was the son of Rosa Elvira Cornett and John William Webster Shuler. He was raised in Virginia and attended Emory and Henry College in Emory, Virginia. Shortly after his graduation in 1903 he entered the Holston Conference of the Methodist Episcopal Church, South and was ordained to the ministry. He married Nelle Reeves in 1905 and in 1906, moved to Texas, where he served several different churches. While in Texas, in 1918, he was first elected as a delegate to the general conference of the Methodist Episcopal Church, South.

In 1920 Shuler transferred to the Los Angeles Conference and became pastor of Trinity Methodist Episcopal Church, South in Los Angeles. During the 33 years of his pastorate at Trinity, the church became the largest church in Southern Methodism on the West Coast, and he emerged as one of the leading voices of fundamentalism in the Methodist Episcopal Church, South. To communicate his views to his contemporaries, he began three different magazines at various times, *Bob Shuler's Magazine*; *The Fundamentalist*; and *The Methodist Challenge*, and authored numerous pamphlets of a controversial nature. For several years in the 1920s he operated his own radio station, KGEF.

Shuler, an outstanding orator, became famous as he attacked controversial topics. He developed his style in his early attacks upon modernism and the social gospel, a perspective which led him to challenge the teaching of evolution during the days of the Scopes trial (Dayton, Tennessee, 1925). He opposed female ministers, which led him to oppose the ministry of his crosstown rival **Aimee Semple McPherson**. Within the Methodist Episcopal Church, South, he also arose as an opponent of the early plans to reunite the Methodist Episcopal Church, South and the Methodist Episcopal Church.

During the 1920s and 1930s Shuler moved into the public sphere. He denounced the lack of morals he saw in Hollywood and the movie industry. He worked to reform city government in Los Angeles. He became a leading figure in the Prohibition Party, and in 1932 ran for the U.S. Senate on that party's ticket. He received over 500,000 votes.

Though long opposed to the various proposals to unite the several major branches of Methodism, Shuler finally accepted and heartily supported the 1939 merger plan that brought together the Methodist Episcopal Church, Methodist Episcopal Church, South, and Methodist Protestant Church to form the Methodist Church (1939-1968). He continued as pastor at Trinity in the new Southern California Conference, but within the new church he found himself somewhat isolated as his conservative theology and politics were shared by few of his new ministerial colleagues. Shuler retired in 1953 and lived quietly during his last years.

Sources:

Harmon, Nolan B. *The Encyclopedia of World Methodism*. 2 vols. Nashville: United Methodist Publishing House, 1974.

Howell, Clinton H., ed. *Prominent Personalities in Methodism*. Birmingham, AL: Lowrey Press, 1945. 512 pp.

★ 854 ★
SILVER, Abba Hillel
Reform Jewish Rabbi and Zionist Leader
b. Jul. 14, 1893, Neistadt Lithuania
d. Nov. 28, 1963, Cleveland, Ohio

Abba Hillel Silver, the leading Reform rabbi and spokesperson for Zionism in North America in the mid-twentieth century, was brought to the United States in 1902 by his parents. His father was a Hebrew teacher and he was given a thorough education as a young man. He also founded and presided over the Herzl Zion Club (named for Theodor Herzl, the founder of modern Zionism) and was among the earliest spokespersons for Herzl's brand of political Zionism, which looked for the establishment of a Jewish state in what was then Palestine. He decided to enter the rabbinate and attended Hebrew Union College in Cincinnati, Ohio. He graduated and was ordained as a rabbi in Cincinnati in 1915. He served as rabbi of Eoff Street Temple in Wheeling, West Virginia, but in 1917 was called as rabbi of Congregation Tifereth Israel, a large Reform synagogue in Cleveland, Ohio. He would remain in that position for the rest of his life.

One of the great Jewish orators of the century, Silver soon emerged as a nationally prominent spokesperson for a number of causes. He was a social liberal and gave his support to organized labor, sponsored the first unemployment insurance law in Ohio, worked with the American Civil Liberties Union (A.C.L.U.), and pioneered concern for child labor legislation. His scholarly side emerged in a number of books, including: *Messianic Speculations in Ancient Israel* (1927); *The Democratic Impulse in Jewish History* (1928); and *Religion in a Changing World* (1930). He worked to develop the Jewish community in Cleveland. In 1935 he became chairman of the Cleveland Jewish Welfare Fund and was the cofounder and the first president of the Cleveland Bureau of Jewish Education. He was elected president of the Central Conference of American Rabbis, the Reform rabbinical organization. But his main cause throughout his life was Zionism.

Throughout the years between the two world wars Silver worked for the Zionist cause. He was one of the first prominent Reform rabbis advocating a Zionist position, the majority of Reform Jews having little concern for a physical Jewish homeland. He served as vice-president and later president of the Zionist Organization of America and was a member of the Zionist Actions Committee. He publicly opposed British policy concerning Palestine. In 1935 he became the key person in the major debate over Zionism which led to the reform movement changing their position in favor of a Jewish homeland, a position embedded in the Columbus Platform of 1937. In 1938 he became chairman of the United Palestine Appeal and co-chairman of the United Jewish Appeal. In 1943 he became head of the American Zionist Emergency Council and is given a significant amount of the credit for mobilizing public opinion on behalf of establishing a Jewish state. On May 8, 1947, he presented the case for an independent Jewish state to the United Nations. On November 29, 1947, he stood before the United Nations to inform the delegates of the proclamation of the State of Israel.

The remaining years of Silver's life were as an honored senior statesman of the Jewish community. In 1949 the Zionist Organization of America published his collected addresses. In 1957 a biography appeared in Hebrew. On his 70th birthday a collection of essays in his honor was presented to him. His last book, *Where Judaism Differed* (1956), provided guidance for Jewish Christian dialogue in emphasizing the distinctions between the two religions as a starting point for a striving together instead of drawing commonality from shallow assumptions about likenesses. He died on Thanksgiving Day 1963, having just finished a sermon he would never deliver, a eulogy for John F. Kennedy, who had been assassinated on November 22.

Sources:

Dictionary of American Biography. 20 vols. and 7 supps. New York: Charles Scribner's Sons, 1928-1936, 1944-1981.

Goldman, Alex J. *The Greatest Rabbis Hall of Fame*. New York: Shapolsky Publishers, 1987. 379 pp.

Landman, Isaac, ed. *Universal Jewish Encyclopedia*. 10 vols. New York: The Universal Jewish Encyclopedia, 1940.

Silver, Abba Hillel. *The Democratic Impulse in Jewish History*. New York: Bloch, 1928. 43 pp.

_____. *Religion in a Changing World*. New York: R. R. Smith, 1930. 204 pp.

_____. *Therefore Choose Life*. Edited by Herbert Weiner. New York: World Publishing Company, 1967.

_____. *Vision and Victory*. New York: Zionist Organization of America, 1949. 232 pp.

_____. *Where Judaism Differed*. New York: Macmillan Company, 1956. 318 pp.

_____. *World Crises and Jewish Survival*. New York: R. R. Smith, 1941.

_____. *A World In Its Season*. Edited by Herbert Weiner. New York: World Publishing Company, 1972. 422 pp.

Silver, Daniel Jeremy, ed. *In the Time of Harvest—Essays in Honor of Abba Hillel Silver on the Occasion of his 70th Birthday*. New York: Macmillan Company, 1963.

★ 855 ★
SILVER, Eliezer
Orthodox Jewish Rabbi
b. 1882, Abel Lithuania
d. 1968

Eliezer Silver, a leading rabbi with Orthodox Judaism, was the son of Rabbi Bunem Zemach Silver. He took his training from some of the leading rabbinical scholars of his day, including Meir Simhah ha-Kohen, Joseph Rozin, Hayyim Ozer Grodzinski, and Hayyim Soloveichik. In 1907 he immigrated to the United States and took a position as rabbi of the United Orthodox congregations of Chisuk Emuno, Kesher Israel, and Machzike Hadas in Harrisburg, Pennsylvania. An active member of the Union of Orthodox Rabbis, he was elected their president in 1923, and remained a member of the presiding board for the rest of his life. In 1925 he moved to Springfield, Massachusetts, and served the United Congregations of Kodimo, Bney Israel, Beth Israel, and Kesher Israel. In 1931 he moved to Cincinnati, Ohio, and served as rabbi to the United Orthodox Congregations there. He held that position for the rest of his life.

Silver is remembered as having become involved in the early debates over Zionism and Israel which affected the whole of the Jewish community. The earliest wave of Zionism was essentially secular and focused upon the Jewish people as a national entity. In 1901 a group of European Zionists had adopted an anti-religious platform. In turn a religious Zionism party, the Mizrahi, emerged. In 1912, in opposition to both of these groups, Agudath Israel was founded. It opposed any form of political Zionism, initially opposing both the Zionist Organization founded by Theodor Herzl and the establishment of a state of Israel. An American branch of Agudath Israel was founded in 1939 and Silver became its first president.

However, the war claimed the immediate attention of Silver. In response to the German invasion of Poland and the flight of yeshiva pupils to Lithuania in 1939 and 1940, he founded Va'ad Hazzalah (an organization for assisting Jews during World War II). He worked throughout the war years, rescuing rabbis, scholars, and students from the Holocaust. In 1946 he visited Europe and Palestine as an official representative of the United States government to assist war refugees. He continued to assist refugee centers in Israel after the establishment of the state of Israel.

In the years after the founding of the state of Israel, Agudath Israel cooperated with the state and became an established political party which runs candidates for office. They continue to oppose political Zionism.

Over the years Silver also found time to write and submitted numerous articles to Orthodox periodicals. A collection of his writings (in Hebrew) was gathered under the title *Anfei Erez* (1960-1962).

Sources:

Landman, Isaac, ed. *Universal Jewish Encyclopedia.* 10 vols. New York: The Universal Jewish Encyclopedia, 1940.

★856★
SIMMONS, William J.
Founder, American National Baptist Convention
b. Jun. 29, 1849, Charleston, South Carolina
d. Oct. 30, 1890, Cane Springs, Kentucky

William J. Simmons, founder of the American National Baptist Convention, was born into slavery to Edward and Ester Simmons. When he was very young, he and his mother were able to escape from South Carolina and reach Philadelphia, where they were cared for by an uncle. They led a quiet existence, as slave traders were continually on the lookout for runaways. The family moved several times and ended up in Bordertown, New Jersey, during the war. What little education Simmons had was provided by his uncle. In 1862 he was apprenticed to a dentist, with whom he worked until 1864, when he joined the Union Army. He practiced dentistry for a while after the war, but in 1867 was converted to Christianity and joined a predominantly white Baptist church in Bordertown. Members supported him while he studied at Madison University. He later attended Rochester University and finally graduated from Howard University in 1873.

Simmons took a job at Hillside School in Washington D.C. The next year he married Josephine A. Silence, and soon afterward left for Ocala, Florida, to assume a position as principal of Howard Academy and to pastor a small church. Shortly before leaving Ocala in 1879, he was finally ordained to the ministry. He became pastor of the First Baptist Church of Lexington, Kentucky, and the following year was named president of the Normal and Theological Institute at Louisville, Kentucky. Over the next decade he took the small new school and built it into a stable educational institution (now known as Simmons University). While serving as president, he authored his most important literary work, *Men of Mark* (1887), a biographical dictionary of prominent Blacks of the century.

Simmons is most remembered as the man who called together black Baptist leaders to form the American National Baptist Convention, forerunner of the present National Baptist Convention, U.S.A., Inc. At the time, Black Baptists had already organized one national body, centered on foreign missions, but Simmons was eager to organize the educated elite. He also represented a group of Blacks who felt that much was to be gained from cooperation with the White Baptists who made up the American Baptist Convention. American Baptists were, at the time, printing most of the written material used by Black Baptists and were slowly coming around to the opinion that they should employ some black Baptist authors to write church school lessons. Simmons was elected president of the new convention, a post he retained throughout the rest of his life.

In 1887 Simmons was appointed secretary for the southern states by the American Baptist Home Mission Society. He traveled widely in that capacity, and became a public figure in the black community nationally. In the spring of 1890 his health began to fail and he died in the fall.

Sources:

Jackson, J. H. *A Story of Christian Activism: The History of the National Baptist Convention, U.S.A., Inc.* Nashville, TN: Townsend Press, 1980. 790 pp.
Pegues, A. W. *Our Baptist Ministers and Schools.* Springfield, MA: Willey & Co., 1892. 643 pp.
Simmons, William J. *Men of Mark.* Cleveland, OH: George M. Rewell & Company, 1887.

★857★
SINGH, Charan
Spiritual Leader, Radhasoami Satsang, Beas
b. Dec. 12, 1916, Moga India

Maharaj Charan Singh, grandson of the great Sant Mat master **Sawan Singh**, is the current leader of Radhasoami Satsang, Beas. He is a devoted follower of his grandfather/guru, and it was apparently a well-known item of information among the inner circle of followers that Charan Singh was eventually to be Sawan Singh's spiritual successor. A law school graduate, holding a double degree in liberal arts and law from Punjab University in Lahore, he began his law career at Sirsa in 1942. His 1944 marriage was arranged by his grandfather.

When Sawan passed away on April 2, 1948, Charan was one of the witnesses to his grandfather's will that nominated Jagat Singh, a distinguished chemistry professor, as the new master. Jagat refused to support Charan's wish to enter politics, and in 1951 appointed him as his successor. Jagat passed away on October 23, 1951, and Charan Singh became the group's official Satguru. One of the most active gurus in the Radhasoami tradition, he has initiated in the neighborhood of one million disciples. Like the other teachers of surat shabda yoga, he has made a number of world tours, and has many disciples in the West. The movement in North America is decentralized, with four initiating representatives in various parts of the United States and two in Canada. The group's periodical is published in Kansas, and book centers are located in California and Washington, D.C.

Charan Singh is notable, among other things, for the social and organizational change that he has carried out. He has, for example, transferred all of the group's properties, which were legally in his name, over to a trust society, the Indian parallel to a non-profit corporation. He has also worked to eliminate all remaining caste distinctions among his followers at Beas. Charan has also had a major hospital built in Beas, offering free medical care. His various activities have developed the Radhasoami colony into one of the largest spiritual centers in the world. Four times a year over one-half million pilgrims converge to listen to the master give discourses. Almost all of the books published under his name, such as *Spiritual Discourses* (1964) and *Quest for Light* (1972), are edited transcriptions made from his morning and evening meetings.

Charan Singh has made one trip to the United States. In the summer of 1964 he toured the country from Honolulu to New York and made one Canadian stop in Vancouver. His remarks became the basis of a 1966 book, *The Master Answers: Audiences in America*.

Sources:

Lane, David Christopher. "The Enchanted Land." *Fate* 37, 11-12. PartI: (October 1984); Part II: (November 1984): 88-94.
The Radha Soami Colony at Beas: A Brief History. Riverside, California: Radha Soami Society Beas-America, n.d. 4 pp.
Singh, Charan. *Divine Light.* Beas, Punjab, India: Radhasoami Satsang, Beas, 1957. 378 pp.
_____. *The Master Answers: Audiences in America.* Beas, Punjab, India: Radhasoami Satsang, Beas, 1966. 3rd ed., 1973. 506 pp.

_____. *Quest for Light*. Beas, Punjab, India: Radhasoami Satsang, Beas, 1972. 321 pp.

_____. *Spiritual Discourses*. Beas, Punjab, India: Radhasoami Satsang, Beas, 1964. 2nd ed., 1970. 240 pp.

★858★
SINGH, Darshan
Founder, Sawan Kirpal Ruhani Mission
b. Sep. 14, 1921, Kountrilla India
d. May 20, 1989, Delhi India

Darshan Singh, the son of the great Sant Mat master Kirpal Singh, was the founder of Sawan Kirpal Ruhani Mission. He was born in a section of India which is now located in Pakistan. While still a child, he was initiated into the Sant Mat tradition by his father's guru, **Sawan Singh**. At Sawan Singh's prompting, he studied humanities rather than the sciences at Government College in Lahore. He developed a passion for literature and poetry, and became a master of Urdu poetic forms. Upon graduation, he embarked on a civil service career with the Indian government (a career that carries considerable prestige in India). In time he rose to become Deputy Secretary in the government of India. He married Bibi Harbhajan Kaur in 1943 and had two children, Rajinder (b. 1946) and Manmohan (b. 1960).

When Baba Sawan Singh died in 1948 the lineage was disputed, and Kirpal Singh seized the moment to inaugurate a new organization, Ruhani Satsang. Darshan Singh was active in his father's work and helped coordinate the Unity of Man Conference in February of 1974. Later the same year Kirpal Singh passed on, and once again the lineage was disputed. While the largest number of centers and initiates decided to follow Darshan Singh, the board of directors of Ruhani Satsang refused to recognize any successor to Kirpal, and Darshan was forced to set up a new organization, the Sawan Kirpal Ruhani Mission.

On August 29, 1975, Darshan Singh initiated his first group of disciples. Two years later, some land was acquired near the University of Delhi as the headquarters for a new organization. On November 20, 1977, the headquarters was formally inaugurated as Kirpal Ashram by a Muslim spiritual leader, Pir Zamin Nizami. In June of 1978, Darshan made his first world tour, spending six weeks in the United States. He retired from government service the next year, and was able to devote himself more completely to his spiritual work. Continuing the ecumenical work of his father, Darshan presided over the Sixth World Fellowship of Religions Conference held in 1981. A second world tour was undertaken in 1983.

The mission publishes the magazine *Sat Sandesh: The Message of the Masters*. Sant Darshan Singh has authored a number of works, including *Spiritual Awakening*; *The Secret of Secrets*; *The Cry of the Soul*; *The Challenge of Inner Space*; and *The Meaning of Christ*. He died suddenly in 1989 and was succeeded by his eldest son, Rajinder Singh.

Sources:
A Brief Biography of Darshan Singh. Bowling Green, VA: Sawan Kirpal Publications, n.d. 20 pp.

Chadda, H.C., ed. *Seeing Is Above All: Sant Darshan Singh's First Indian Tour*. Bowling Green, VA: Sawan Kirpal Publications, 1978. 114 pp.

Singh, Darshan. *The Cry of the Soul*. Bowling Green, VA: Sawan Kirpal Publications, 1977. 74 pp.

_____. *How to Derive Maximum Benefit at the Feet of the Master*. Bowling Green, VA: Sawan Kirpal Publications, n.d. 12 pp.

_____. *The Meaning of Christ*. Bowling Green, VA: Sawan Kirpal Publications, [1983]. 18 pp.

_____. *Sant Mat: The Teachings of the Masters*. Bowling Green, VA: Sawan Kirpal Publications, n.d. 12 pp.

_____. *The Secret of Secrets*. Bowling Green, VA: Sawan Kirpal Publications, 1978. 255 pp.

★859★
SINGH, Kirpal
Founder, Ruhani Satsang
b. Feb. 6, 1894, Sayyad Kasran Pakistan
d. Aug. 21, 1974, Delhi India

Kirpal Singh, founder of Ruhani Satsang, one of the most successful Radhasoami (Sant Mat) groups to be imported into North America, was born into a Sikh family in a village located in what is now Pakistan. He was employed in the military services department of the Indian government, from which he retired in 1947. As a young man in quest of spiritual enlightenment he became a disciple of **Sawan Singh**, who was the leader of the Radhasoami Satsang headquartered at Beas, India. Shortly after Kirpal Singh's retirement his master passed away and, according to Ruhani Satsang, passed on the guru's lineage to Kirpal. The inheritance of the lineage was, however, disputed, and Kirpal left Beas to form his own organization, Ruhani Satsang.

Sawan Singh taught a meditative technique that was termed *surat shabd yoga* (sometimes called nad yoga in non-Radhasoami lineages). The basis for this meditation is a particular theory of cosmogenesis which sees the manifested world as having emanated from the godhead in a series of steps, constituting a graded hierarchy of levels or "planes." The cosmos is maintained by a kind of energy or vibration that continues to flow into the world from the Source (God). Surat shabd yoga claims to enable one to attune oneself to this flow of energy, the sound current, and "follow" it back up to the godhead.

Kirpal Singh made several tours to the United States, and was the author of many books later published by various organizations of his followers in the United States, including *The Way of the Saints*; *Godman*; and *The Crown of Life*. He was also the initiator of the World Fellowship of Religions. One of his more well-known students was **John Paul Twitchell**, the founder of ECKANKAR, who was clearly influenced by Kirpal Singh's teachings.

When Kirpal Singh died the lineage was once again disputed, and the Ruhani Satsang split into at least three separate groups, known in the West as Kirpal Light Satsang, Sant Bani Ashram, and Sawan Kirpal Ruhani Mission.

Sources:
As They Saw the Master. Delhi, India: Ruhani Satsang Sawan Ashram, 1956. 103 pp.

Astra [Mary Astra Turk]. *Whisperings from My Beloved Kirpal*. 2 vols. Miami Beach, FL: The Author, n.d.

Brief Life Sketch of Param Sant Kirpal Singh Ji Maharaj. Wembly, England: Kirpal Bhavan, 1976. 15 pp.

Lane, David Christopher. *The Death of Kirpal Singh*. Del Mar, CA: Del Mar Press, [1975]. 52 pp.

Sena, Bhadra. *The Beloved Master*. Delhi, India: Ruhani Satsang, 1963. 128 pp.

Singh, Kirpal. *The Crown of Life*. Delhi, India: Ruhani Satsang, 1971. 255 pp.

_____. *A Great Saint, Baba Jaimal Singh: His Life and Teachings*. Delhi, India: Ruhani Satsang Sawan Ashram, 1960. 120 pp.

_____. *Morning Talks*. Delhi, India: Ruhani Satsang, 1974. 258 pp.

_____. *Prayer*. Delhi, India: Ruhani Satsang, 1970. 153 pp.

_____. *Surat Shabd Yoga*. Berkeley, CA: Images Press, 1975. 71 pp.

_____. *The Way of the Saints*. Sanbornton, NH: Sant Bani Ashram, 1976. 402 pp.

★860★
SINGH, Sant Thakar
Founder, Kirpal Light Satsang
b. Mar. 26, 1929, India

Sant Thakar Singh is a spiritual teacher in the Sant Mat tradition, and founder of the Kirpal Light Satsang. Born into a poor family in a small village in north India, he was his parents' only surviving child. Manjal Singh, his father, was a hardworking carpenter and blacksmith who worked long hours to provide for his family. Manjal was a peaceful, religious man who, together with his wife, recited from the Sikh scriptures every day. He would also read aloud from Guru Nanak's biography every day. Young Thakar was particularly impressed by the life of Nanak, founder of the Sikh faith, and absorbed his family's simple piety. He was eager to acquire learning, and persuaded his parents to allow him to start school a year early.

Thakar Singh's hard life became even harder at age 11 when his father passed away. He was able to continue his education only by working when he was not at school. He finished at his local school at the top of his class, and began attending a college some 30 miles away. After a couple of years a new school of engineering opened nearby, and he was able to receive a scholarship to complete his degree. He then took a position as a sectional officer in the Irrigation Branch of the Punjab Public Works Department. His marriage was arranged, in the Indian tradition, while he was still a student.

As he was moved from one place to another in connection with his work, Thakar Singh would seek to organize spiritual gatherings, scripture study groups (particularly groups studying the *Adi Granth*, the principal holy book of the Sikhs), and groups to study religious music. Despite this activity, Thakar Singh felt spiritually unfulfilled. In 1965, at the urging of a relative, he went to hear the great Sant Mat teacher Kirpal Sing. In spite of a certain initial reluctance, he became receptive enough to receive initiation. The meditation practice eventually gave him complete spiritual satisfaction. From that point on, he worked to promote Kirpal Singh's teachings and activities. He took a long leave of absence to meditate at his master's ashram for four months in 1969.

When Kirpal Singh passed away in 1974, the lineage was disputed. Thakar was one of several people who claimed that the master had passed on the guruship to them. He went into a long period of meditation and retreat, and on February 5, 1976, began to take on the responsibility of being a spiritual teacher and guide. He has made a number of tours to the West, establishing centers in the eastern and western parts of the United States. Thakar's group, the Kirpal Light Satsang, attracted media attention in 1988 when they attempted to establish a boarding school in Oregon. Their neighbors opposed the project, partially because of the state's bad experience with the **Bhagwan Rajneesh**. In the same year, the Master was accused of sexually abusing several female followers. However, no charges were filed, and Singh has been reluctant to offer any response to the charges.

Sources:

Melton, J. Gordon *The Encyclopedia of American Religions.* 3d ed. Detroit: Gale Research Inc.,1988. 1102 pp.
Mortenson, Eric. "Sect Leader Steers Clear of Charges: Limits Local Talks to Nature of God." *The Register-Guard* (Eugene, Oregon) (July 31, 1988).
Sant Thakar Singh: A Brief Life Sketch. N.p., n.d. 4 pp.
Singh, Thakar. *Good Stories Make Us Good.* Delhi, India: Ruhani Satsang, Sawan Ashram, 1983. 191 pp.
———. *Gospel of Love.* Delhi, India: Ruhani Satsang, Sawan Ashram, 1984. 462 pp.

★861★
SINGH, Sawan
Spiritual Leader, Radhasoami Satsang, Beas
b. Jul. 27, 1858, Mehmansinghwala India
d. Apr. 2, 1948, Beas India

Sawan Singh, an eminent guru in the Radhasoami lineage, was born into a jat Sikh (an agricultural caste) family in Punjab. Trained at the Thompson College of Engineering, he was in the government's engineering service at Murree when he met and became the disciple of Jaimal Singh, the founder of Radhasoami Beas. Although

he wanted to resign his engineering post in order to constantly be with his guru, Jaimal Singh required that he stay in his career. Sawan Singh continued his job even after he had taken over the Radhasoami movement following his master's death in 1903. After Sawan's retirement from government service in 1911, he embarked on a vigorous program of expansion, initiating more than 125,000 disciples.

Although Radhasoami does not usually consider itself a separate religion, it is in some ways useful to view the movement as a Sikh sect. By the nineteenth century, many people had come to feel that Sikhism was in a state of decay. The earliest attempts at reform centered around individuals who claimed the status of gurus. This claim was regarded as heterodox by the Sikh mainstream because the last living guru in the lineage of Nanak, Guru Gobind Singh, passed on the guruship to the Sikh scriptures (Guru Granth) and to the Sikh community (Guru Panth). The reform movements organized around living gurus became Sikh sects, such as the Nirankaris. The one reform movement to adopt the mainstream perspective on the guruship, the Singh Sabha movement, successfully transformed the entire community.

Radhasoami claims that the gurus of the Sikh tradition initiated their disciples into *surat shabd yoga*, the form of yoga taught by the Radhasoami gurus, and systematically interprets the Sikh scriptures (and, where possible, the teachings of other religions) so that they appear to reflect their own practices. Their emphasis on the necessity of a "living" guru is an implicit criticism of the mainstream Sikh position that the scriptures embody the guru (which constitute, by implication, a "dead" guru). The fact that a large percentage of the teachers and disciples in this tradition are Sikhs reinforces the feeling that Radhasoami is, in some sense, a Sikh sect.

Sawan Singh was a key mediator in the movement of the lineage to North America; his role was complex. In terms of literary impact, one of his disciples, Dr. Julian P. Johnson, wrote *The Path of the Masters* (1953), the most popular Radhasoami work. Sawan Singh was also the guru of Kirpal Singh, probably the most successful Radhasoami teacher to visit the United States. In turn, both Johnson's work and **Kirpal Singh**'s teachings influenced **John Paul Twitchell**, who created ECKANKAR. A little-known connection is that Sawan Singh initiated Shri Hans, the father of **Guru Maharaj Ji** who founded the Divine Light Mission (now known as Elan Vital), into the practice of surat shabd yoga. Finally, one might note that the present head of Radhasoami Beas has American disciples.

Sources:

Fripp, Peter. *The Mystic Philosophy of Sant Mat.* London: Neville Spearman, 1964. 174 pp.
Johnson, Julian P. *With a Great Master in India.* Beas, India: Radha Swami Sat Sang, Dera Baba Jaimal Singh, 1953. 200 pp.
Kapur, Daryal Lal. *Call of the Great Master.* Beas, India: Radha Soami Satsang Beas, 1964. 271 pp.
Melton, J. Gordon. *Biographical Dictionary of American Cult and Sect Leaders.* Garland Reference Library of Social Science, vol. 212. New York: Garland Publishing, 1986.
Singh, Kirpal. *A Brief Sketch of Hazur Baba Sawan Singh.* Delhi, India: Ruhani Satsang, 1949. 22 pp.
Singh, Sawan. *The Dawn of Light.* Punjab, India: Radha Soami Satsang Beas, 1985. 236 pp.
———. *My Submission.* 2 vols. Beas, India: Radhasoami Satsang, Beas, n.d.
———. *Philosophy of the Masters.* 5 vols. Beas, India: Radha Soami Satsang Beas, 1963-1972.
———. *Spiritual Gems.* Beas India: Radha Soami Satsang Beas, 1976. 438 pp.
———. *Tales from the Mystic East.* Beas, India: Radha Soami Satsang Beas, 1961. 267 pp.

★ 862 ★
SITTING BULL
Religious Leader, Hunkpapa Lakota Indians
b. Mar. 1831, Grand River, South Dakota
d. Dec. 15, 1890, Fort Yates, South Dakota

Sitting Bull, whose Indian name was Tatanka Yotanka, a chief and traditional religious leader among the Hunkpapa Lakota Indians, was born in March 1831 in a camp on the banks of the Grand River near the present-day town of Bullhead, South Dakota. His mother was Mixed Day and his father was known at the time as Returns Again, a powerful doctor who could understand the speech of the animals. When Sitting Bull was a young boy, he was known as Hunkesni ("Slow," meaning deliberate in words and actions). While Sitting Bull was still a boy, his father was given four names by a sacred bull buffalo: Sitting Bull, Jumping Bull, Bull Standing with Cow, and Lone Bull. Returns Again took the name Sitting Bull, but gave it to his son when the boy distinguished himself in a fight with the Crow Indians at the age of 15.

The name Tatanka Yotanka, or "Sitting Bull,"was one with significant implications. The Lakota saw the buffalo as the center of their lives, and a "sitting bull" represents the stage of a buffalo's life when it is newborn. Thus the name Tatanka Yotanka can be best interpreted as "a buffalo bull has been born among the Lakota and has come to live with us." Like his father, Sitting Bull was said to understand the language of the animals, especially the birds.

As a young man, Sitting Bull was hunting one day when he stopped to take a short nap. While dozing fitfully, he heard a small bird calling him to lie still. He awoke to find a grizzly bear nosing around him, too close for an escape. Sitting Bull heeded the bird's message and credited it with saving his life. For the rest of his life he learned the ways and languages of the birds, and his speeches, stories, and songs were full of references to the Bird People. Sitting Bull became a noted singer and composer of songs and was in much demand to sing at ceremonial and social occasions.

There are a number of stories of Sitting Bull's exploits as a holy man and leader of the Lakota. He counted 63 "coups" in his life and was a sash-wearer in the Brave Heart soldier society of the Hunkpapa. As a sash-wearer he was obligated in the face of dire circumstances to give his life in defense of his people. During the sun dance held just before the Battle of the Little Big Horn, in which General George Custer was defeated in 1876, Sitting Bull had a vision of victory with soldiers falling dead into the Lakota and Cheyenne camps. The night before the fight, he went into the hills and made a circle of medicine which Custer led his column of soldiers through on their day of infamy, June 26, 1876. Although he did not personally take part in the fight, Sitting Bull became a name to strike fear in the hearts of all Americans who believed in the destruction of the Indian tribes.

Sitting Bull eventually led his people into Canada but surrendered to United States troops in the summer of 1881. Although the United States government through the Army and Indian agents tried to break the power of Sitting Bull as a leader of the Lakota, his daring exploits were too strong to overcome and his people continued to recognize him as a leader. Turning in later years even to the white man's god, Jesus, Sitting Bull worked to prevent the destruction of the Lakota. Sitting Bull's influence was seen as disruptive to attempts to "civilize" the Lakota, and on December 15, 1890, he was assassinated. Buried in a corner of the Fort Yates military cemetery, even in death Sitting Bull was seen as dangerous. His relatives were refused permission to make public burial, and quicklime and acid were poured on his body to prevent the taking of relics.

Sources:
Burdick, Usher L. *The Last Days of Sitting Bull, Sioux Medicine Chief*. Baltimore, MD: Wirth Brothers, 1941.

Fiske, Frank Bennet. *Life and Death of Sitting Bull*. Fort Yates, ND: Pioneer Arrow Printing, 1933.

Stirling, Matthew W. "Three Pictographic Autobiographies of Sitting Bull." *Smithsonian Miscellaneous Collections* 97, 5 (1938).

Vestal, Stanley. *Sitting Bull: Champion of the Sioux*. Norman, OK: University of Oklahoma Press, 1957.

—*Johnny Flynn*

★ 863 ★
Swami SIVANANDA SARASWATI
Founder, Divine Life Society
b. Sep. 8, 1887, Patamadai India
d. Jul. 14, 1963, Rishikish India

Swami Sivananda Saraswati, an Indian spiritual teacher who, through his students, significantly influenced the practice of yoga in the West, was born Kuppuswami Iyer, the child of a government official. Trained as a doctor, his religious quest led him to the holy city of Rishikish where he was initiated into the renounced life of a sannyasin by Swami Viswananda Saraswati. While pursuing an ascetic discipline, Sivananda also found the time to open a medical dispensary in order to serve others in a concrete, practical way. He founded his own ashram in 1934, the Divine Life Trust in 1936, and initiated a series of periodicals. The dispensary grew into a major medical facility and, in time, adopted a leper colony as part of the Swami's program of social service.

Although he planned a tour of Europe and North America, poor health prevented Sivananda from undertaking it. The Swami's impact on the West came through a number of his disciples who settled in North America, disciples such as Swami Sivananda Radha, **Swami Vishnu Devananda**, and **Swami Satchidananda**. While not the only yoga teachers in the West, Sivananda's students are largely responsible for the popularity of hatha yoga in the United States and Canada. They exerted an especially strong influence on the American yoga scene during the 1960s and the early 1970s. Vishnu Devananda's book on Hatha Yoga, *The Complete Illustrated Book of Yoga*, was, for example, the standard work on the subject for many years. Many of Swami Sivananda's own books (he authored over 200), such as *Practice of Yoga*; *Sadhana*; and *Yoga Asanas*, reached the West through his students.

Sources:
Ananthanarayanan, A. *From Man to God-man*. New Delhi, India: The Author, 1970. 270 pp.

Krishnananda, Swami. *Swami Sivananda and the Spiritual Renaissance*. Sivanandanagar, India: Sivananda Literature Research Institute, 1959. 39 pp.

The Master: His Mission and His Works. Shivanandanagar, India: 1987. 284 pp.

Melton, J. Gordon. *Biographical Dictionary of American Cult and Sect Leaders*. Garland Reference Library of Social Science, vol. 212. New York: Garland Publishing, 1986.

Omkarananda, Swami. *In Sivananda Literature*. Rishikish, India: Sivananda Literature Research Institute, 1960. 512 pp.

_____. *Swami Sivananda and the Modern Man*. Rishikish, India: Yoga-Vedanta Forest Academy, 1954. 82 pp.

Sharma, Indrajit. *Sivananda: Twentieth Century Saint*. Rishikish, India: Yoga-Vedanta Forest Academy, 1958. 403 pp.

Sivananda, Swami. *Practical Lessons in Yoga*. Sivanandanagar, India: Divine Life Society, 1978. 214 pp.

_____. *Practice of Karma Yoga*. Sivanandanagar, India: Divine Life Society, 1980. 323 pp.

_____. *Sadhana*. Sivanandanagar, India: The Divine Life Society, 1967. 719 pp.

_____. *Science of Yoga*. 18 vols. Durban, So. Africa: Sivananda Press, 1977.

_____. *Yoga Asanas*. Sivanandanagar, India: Divine Life Society, 1969. 135 pp.

Tawker, K. A. *Sivananda, One World Teacher*. Rishikish, India: Yoga-Vedanta Forest University, 1957. 150 pp.

Venkatesananda, Swami. *Gurudev Sivananda*. Rishikish, India: Yoga Vedanta Forest Academy, 1961. 255 pp.

_____. *Sivananda's Integral Yoga*. Johannesburg, So. Africa: The Divine Life Society, 1969. 128 pp.

★ 864 ★
SKINNER, Tom
Evangelist, Tom Skinner Associates
b. Jun. 6, 1942, New York, New York

Tom Skinner, an evangelist and founder of Tom Skinner Associates, is the son of Alester J. and Georgia Robinson Skinner. His father was a Baptist minister who joined the migration of southern Blacks to the North following his marriage in 1940. Though raised in the home of a minister, as Skinner became conscious of his blackness, he felt alienated from the church because of its hypocrisy on the race issue. He attended church and was to all outward appearances an active leader in the youth group. He was a good student in school and during his teen years emerged as president of the student body at his high school, a member of the baseball and football teams, and an actor in the Shakespearean club.

During his teen years, however, Skinner began to lead a double life. He became a member of a Harlem gang, the Harlem Lords, and, soon after joining, rose to the leadership of the group. He led the group for two years until one night, while planning a gang fight, he was converted while listening to a radio preacher. He resigned as the leader of the gang and two days later became instrumental in converting one of the other gang members. He began preaching on the streets of Harlem. He attended Manhattan Bible College (1958-1962). In 1959 he was ordained a minister by the United Missionary Baptist Association (National Baptist) of New York and Vicinity.

In 1961 Skinner joined with several Harlem ministers and lay people to form the Harlem Evangelistic Association. Its first major event was a 1962 crusade at the Apollo Theater, the center of Harlem's entertainment life. He followed the successful event with crusades in Guyana and Bermuda. In 1964 he began a radio ministry and formed Tom Skinner Radio Crusades, Inc. Two years later the corporation was reorganized as Tom Skinner Crusades, Inc., now Tom Skinner Associates. He developed a national radio and urban preaching ministry to Blacks.

In 1968 Skinner published his autobiography, *Black and Free*. He has followed it with several other books, *How Black Is the Gospel?* (1970); *Words of Revolution* (1970); and *If Christ Is the Answer, What Are the Questions?* (1974). He has since become one of the most important evangelical Christian voices in the black community.

Sources:

Skinner, Tom. *Black and Free*. Grand Rapids, MI: Zondervan Publishing House, 1968. 154 pp.

_____. *How Black Is the Gospel?* Grand Rapids, MI: Zondervan Publishing House, 1970. 128 pp.

_____. *If Christ Is the Answer, What Are the Questions?* Grand Rapids, MI: Zondervan Publishing House, 1974. 219 pp.

_____. *Words of Revolution*. Philadelphia: J. P. Lippencott, 1970. 171 pp.

★ 865 ★
SLOAN, Harold Paul
Minister, Methodist Episcopal Church
b. Dec. 12, 1881, Westfield, New Jersey
d. May 22, 1961, Trenton, New Jersey

Harold Paul Sloan, a spokesperson for fundamentalism in the Methodist Episcopal Church, was the son of Theodore Reber and Mariam B. Hickman Sloan. He attended the University of Pennsylvania and began his theological work at Crozer Theological Seminary. He was received into full connection in the New Jersey Conference of the Methodist Episcopal Church in 1906. He completed his theological training at Drew Theological Seminary from which he received his B.D. in 1908. In 1909 he married Ethel Beatrice Buckwalter. He served various churches in the New Jersey Conference during his career, but made his name as a spokesperson for the fundamentalist Methodist League for Faith and Life.

During the first decades of the twentieth century, the Methodist Episcopal Church made a gradual transition from nineteenth century evangelical faith to modernism, and did so with relatively little controversy. However, there were those who opposed the move and spoke out against what they saw as an erosion of the faith. Sloan was among those critics of modernism. By the time that the conservatives organized, in the years after World War I, the seminaries were thoroughly controlled by modernists. However, there was one place for a conservative voice to be heard, in the "Course of Study." The Course of Study was a correspondence course established by the church's general conference which those ministers unable to attend seminary could pursue as an alternative.

As the 1920 quadrennial general conference approached Sloan organized petitions to investigate the Course of Study and rid it of modernist tendencies. The general conference mandated that the Course of Study adhere to Methodist doctrine, but did nothing about removing such liberal voices as theologian **Harris Franklin Rall** from the Commission on the Course of Study or his book from the curriculum. Sloan began a magazine, *Call to Colors* (later *The Essentialist*), to carry on the fight.

The efforts in 1924 to strengthen the action on the Course of Study failed. In 1925 Sloan and other leading conservative voices organized the Methodist League for Faith and Life. One last attempt was made to alter the Course of Study in 1928, but the general conference rejected Sloan's petitions.

Apart from his inability to alter the Course of Study in a more conservative direction, Sloan had a long and fruitful ministry. He was a masterful orator and he authored a number of books, including *Historic Christianity and the New Theology* (1922) and *The Christ of the Ages* (1928). He became a trustee of Drew Theological Seminary and of the independent Asbury College. In 1936 he became editor of the *Christian Advocate*, a Methodist periodical issued from New York. His final pastorate was at Whaton Memorial Church in Philadelphia. While there he developed a radio ministry, "The Living Christ Hour."

Sources:

Harmon, Nolan B. *The Encyclopedia of World Methodism*. 2 vols. Nashville: United Methodist Publishing House, 1974.

Sloan, Harold Paul. *The Christ of the Ages*. Garden City, NY: Doubleday, Doran & Company, 1928. 184 pp.

_____. *Faith Is the Victory*. Philadelphia: Methodist Book Room, 1950. 118 pp.

_____. *He Is Risen*. New York: Abingdon-Cokesbury Press, 1942. 186 pp.

_____. *Historic Christianity and the New Theology*. Louisville, KY: Pentecostal Publishing Company, 1922.

_____. *Jesus Christ Is Lord*. Louisville, KY: Pentecostal Publishing Company, 1955. 189 pp.

_____. *Personality and the Fact of Christ*. Nashville, TN: Cokesbury Press, 1933. 261 pp.

★ 866 ★
SLOCUM, John
Founder, Indian Shaker Movement
b. 1841
d. 1897

Little is known about the first decades of the life of John Slocum, the founder of a Shaker movement among the Native American people of Northern California, the Northwestern United States, and British Columbia. His date and place of birth are unknown, but it is believed that he belonged to the Squaxin, a small tribe whose ancestral lands were along Puget Sound in the present state of Washington. By the 1880s the tribe had been scattered through the Northwest. Slocum had reportedly been instructed and baptized in the Roman Catholic faith by some missionaries, but his early life is said to have been marked by gambling, drinking, and hard living. At some point he married Mary Thompson and they became the parents of 13 children, though a number died before reaching adulthood. They lived in rural isolation near Olympia, Washington.

Slocum emerged out of obscurity in the fall of 1881 when he was approximately 40 years old. He fell sick and reportedly died. People assembled to prepare for his funeral, but during the wake he came back to life, to the amazement of his wife and others present. He reported that he had in fact died and had subsequently traveled to stand before the judgment seat of God. Now convinced of the evil of his previous life, he had returned to witness his own change and lead others away from their sinful ways. He called for the building of a church and noted that in the near future he would begin preaching.

The church was built and conversions were made, but the initial enthusiasm soon died. Slocum then fell ill a second time. Distressed at the prospect of her husband dying, Mary Slocum lost control of her emotions and began to pray for him, all the time crying and trembling uncontrollably. When she finally gained control, Slocum seemed better. Mary claimed that his improved health was due to her shaking actions. This event was the origin of the shaking activity among Slocum's followers. Mary repeated the shaking and invited others to join her. The activity revived the group, and soon word spread throughout the Northwest Native American community. People began to travel to the little church to witness the effects of the shaking.

Slocum and his wife continued to lead the church, which emerged as an eclectic blend of Christian and Indian teachings, into the 1890s. It was finally incorporated in 1892 with the aid of a sympathetic lawyer, but by the mid-1890s Slocum again drifted into obscurity, and neither the date nor place of his death are known. The movement he built, however, has survived, possibly because there was little doctrine and considerable leeway in Shaker belief and practice.

Sources:

Barnett, H. G. *Indian Shakers: A Messianic Cult of the Pacific Northwest.* Carbondale, IL: Southern Illinois University Press, 1957. 378 pp.

★ 867 ★
SMITH, Amanda
Evangelist, African Methodist Episcopal Church
b. Jan. 23, 1837, Long Green, Maryland
d. Feb. 24, 1915, Sebring, Florida

Amanda Smith, a nineteenth century black female evangelist, was born in slavery to Mirriam Matthews and Samuel Berry. During her early years her father was able to purchase his freedom and that of his family. He moved to York County, Pennsylvania, and established a home which he turned into a station on the Underground Railroad. Amanda received only a few months of formal schooling, but learned to read and write from her parents. In her youth she went to work as a washerwoman. In 1854 she married Calvin M. Devine. In 1856 she had a religious conversion which became an immense support in the years of hard work and discrimination she had ahead of her.

Smith's husband died as a Union soldier in the Civil War. In 1863 she moved to Philadelphia and met and married James Smith, a deacon in the African Methodist Episcopal Church. They moved to New York. Over the next few years, Smith attended some of the Tuesday Prayer Meeting sessions conducted by Phoebe Palmer and learned of the doctrine of sanctification, a belief that Christians can be cleansed of sin and be made perfect in love by an immediate act of the Holy Spirit. In 1868 she experienced sanctification.

Following the death of her husband the next year, she began to devote significant amounts of time to preaching in black churches in New York and New Jersey. In 1870 she spoke to the white Methodists gathered at a holiness camp meeting and soon won their approval of her work. She became a popular figure in holiness circles, both white and black, during the 1870s.

In 1878 Smith went to England where she enjoyed great success for over a year and then went on to India to work with the Methodist mission for the next two years. She returned to England in 1881, then left for Africa, making Liberia her headquarters for the next eight years. She returned to the United States in 1890. In 1892 she settled in the Chicago suburb of Harvey, Illinois, with the idea of living a quiet life and writing. She published *An Autobiography*, now regarded as a classic in holiness literature, in 1893. She also began a newspaper, *The Helper*.

In 1899 Smith opened an orphan's home for black children, initially supported by her own savings and some gifts. However, she had to return to preaching to keep the home open. She maintained the school until 1912 when the state took it over. She retired to Sebring, Florida, where she died three years later. Her death was noted with an elaborate funeral in Chicago and burial in Harvey.

Sources:

Cadbury, M. H. *The Life of Amanda Smith.* Birmingham, England: Cornish Brothers, 1916. 84 pp.
James, Edward T., ed. *Notable American Women, 1607-1950: A Biographical Dictionary.* 3 vols. Cambridge, MA: Harvard University Press, Belknap Press, 1971.
Smith, Amanda. *An Autobiography.* Rept. Noblesville, IN: Newby Book Room, 1964. 506 pp.
Taylor, Marshall W. *The Life, Travels, Labors, and Helpers of Mrs. Amanda Smith.* Cincinnati, OH: Cranstob & Stowe, 1886. 63 pp.

★ 868 ★
SMITH, Angie Frank
Bishop, Methodist Church
b. Nov. 1, 1889, Elgin, Texas
d. Oct. 6, 1962, Houston, Texas

Angie Frank Smith, who served more years as a bishop in Methodism than anyone else, was born to William Angie and Mary Elizabeth Marrs Smith. Following his graduation from Southwestern University in 1912 and from the School of Religion at Vanderbilt University in 1914, he was ordained and joined the North Texas Conference of the Methodist Episcopal Church, South. During the next 16 years he served pastorates in Alto, Detroit, Dallas, Austin, San Antonio, and Houston. He was elected as a delegate to the Methodist Episcopal Church, South general conference in 1926 and 1930, and at the latter conference was elected to the bishopric.

During the 1930s Smith presided over a variety of annual conferences in the Methodist Episcopal Church, South, first in Oklahoma and Missouri, and after 1934 in Texas and Louisiana. He served in a number of official posts, most notably as a member of the Commission on the Unification of American Methodism, a group whose work led to the merger of the Methodist Episcopal Church, South, the Methodist Episcopal Church and the Methodist Protestant Church in 1939. He had previously worked on the committee that produced a new hymnal for the several churches looking toward reunion. After unification, as a bishop in the South Central jurisdiction of the new Methodist Church, he continued to preside over conferences in Texas until his retirement in 1960. From 1940 to 1960 he also served as president of the church's Division of National Missions, and he was president of the Council of Bishops for two years (1940-1942).

Sources:

Harmon, Nolan B. *The Encyclopedia of World Methodism*. 2 vols. Nashville: United Methodist Publishing House, 1974.

Leete, Frederick D. *Methodist Bishops*. Nashville, TN: Privately printed, 1948.

★869★
SMITH, Charles Lee
Founder, American Association for the Advancement of Atheism
b. 1887, Ft. Smith, Arkansas
d. Oct. 26, 1964, San Diego, California

Charles Lee Smith, founder of the oldest atheist body in the United States, the American Association for the Advancement of Atheism, was born in Arkansas and raised in Missouri and Oklahoma. Although he considered a career in the Methodist ministry, he ended up pursuing a law practice and was eventually admitted to the Oklahoma bar. Stumbling upon Thomas Jefferson's edited version of the Gospels led Smith to the literature of free thought, and eventually to a conviction of atheism. Smith also traveled around the country for a number of years, working at odd jobs, and then joined the army during World War I.

Following the war, Smith moved to New York where he began selling and authoring articles for a free thought periodical, *The Truth Seeker*. From this point forward, Smith evolved into what might be called an "evangelist" for atheism. Together with a friend, Freeman Hopwood, Smith organized the American Association for the Advancement of Atheism, better known as the "4As," in 1925. It took two attempts before the association was incorporated because of the resistance of the state government of New York. Finally successful in the bid for corporate status, Smith began a serious evangelizing campaign that led to the founding of 4A chapters on about 20 campuses, a Junior Atheist League to reach high school students, and by 1930 a national membership of over 3,000. The association also periodically sponsored public lectures named after the nineteenth-century freethinker, **Robert Green Ingersoll**.

Smith seemed to thrive on conflict, debating Christian ministers such as **Aimee Semple McPherson** and becoming involved in opposing Arkansas' anti-evolution law. To better carry out the latter project, he moved to Arkansas where he opened a center from which he could distribute pro-evolution and anti-religion literature. Not surprisingly, he managed to get himself arrested several times, but resumed his evangelizing every time he was released. Smith also attempted to get anti-atheist laws repealed, and initiated lawsuits aimed at eliminating certain practices that allowed religion to have an official status with the government, such as the employment of chaplains for the U.S. Congress. None of these efforts were successful, but they paved the way for recent recognition of the rights of atheists by the courts.

In 1930 Smith purchased *The Truth Seeker* and began to devote his total energies to this project. The association declined during the depression years, but Smith was able to continue to publish his periodical on a monthly basis. By 1950, he had published anti-Semitic and racist articles in his magazine. This led to his alienation from other atheists, canceled subscriptions to *The Truth Seeker*, and the further decline of the American Association for the Advancement of Atheism. Shortly before his death in 1964, Smith sold the periodical to **James Hervey Johnson**, who moved the offices of the association and of *The Truth Seeker* to San Diego.

Sources:

Johnson, James Hervey. "Charles Smith: 1887-1964." *The Truth Seeker* 91, 11 (November 1964): 161-162.

Melton, J. Gordon. *Biographical Dictionary of American Cult and Sect Leaders*. Garland Reference Library of Social Science, vol. 212. New York: Garland Publishing, 1986.

Smith, Charles Lee. *Sensism: The Philosophy of the West*. 2 vols. New York: Truthseeker Co., 1956.

_____. *There is a God!, Debate between Aimee Semple McPherson and Charles Lee Smith*. Los Angeles: Foursquare Publications, n.d. 46 pp.

Stein, Gordon. *The Encyclopedia of Unbelief*. 2 vols. Buffalo: Prometheus Books, 1985.

★870★
SMITH, Frederick Madison
President, Reorganized Church of Jesus Christ of Latter Day Saints
b. Jan. 21, 1874, Plano, Illinois
d. Jan. 20, 1946, Independence, Missouri

Frederick Madison Smith, the second president of the Reorganized Church of Jesus Christ of Latter Day Saints, was the son of **Joseph Smith III** and his second wife, Bertha Madison. He became president of the church upon the death of his father, none of whose children from his first wife had survived him. At the time of Frederick's birth, his father had been the church president for more than 20 years and would remain so for another 30, thus he grew up in the heart of the Reorganized Church. He became the first graduate of Graceland College, operated by the Reorganized Church, from which he received a B.A., the only degree granted in 1898. A year prior to his graduation he married Ruth Cobb. He would later receive his M.A. from Kansas University (1911).

Smith was ordained an elder in 1897 and a high priest of the church. As the eldest son, he had come to realize that he would likely succeed his aging father as president of the church. In 1902 he was called as a counselor to his father, and as his father's health failed, especially after 1909, he took over the duties of presiding at various church functions. In 1915 he was officially named as church president. The following year he finished his doctorate at Clark University in Worcester, Massachusetts.

Shortly after becoming president of the church, Smith began to articulate a strong emphasis upon the efforts to better the lot of the poor. Some of the church leaders branded him a Socialist and opposed his actions. In the face of opposition, in 1919, Smith offered his resignation. However, the majority of the church leadership supported him, and he continued as church president. He also continued the fight in opposition to the practice of polygamy, especially defending the reputation of his grandfather, **Joseph Smith, Jr.**, the founder of the church, against charges that he had practiced polygamy. (In distinction from the Utah-based Church of Jesus Christ of Latter-day Saints, the Reorganized Church of Jesus Christ of Latter Day Saints has always opposed the practice of polygamy.)

Smith led the church for 31 years. During his administration, the construction of the Auditorium, the current church headquarters, was initiated in Independence. He traveled widely for the church, spending almost a year in Europe after World War I (1919-1920). He died in Independence after an extended illness. He was succeeded as church president by his brother, **Israel Alexander Smith**.

Sources:

The National Cyclopedia of American Biography. Clifton, NJ: James T. White & Co.

Who's Who in America. Wilmette, IL: Marquis Who's Who, Inc.

★871★
SMITH, George Albert
President, Church of Jesus Christ of Latter-day Saints
b. Apr. 4, 1870, Salt Lake City, Utah
d. Apr. 4, 1951, Salt Lake City, Utah

George Albert Smith, the eighth president of the Church of Jesus Christ of Latter-day Saints, was a descendent of John Smith, uncle of the church's founder, **Joseph Smith, Jr.** John Smith had at one time been the church's patriarch, and his family had a history of church leadership. As a youth, George attended Brigham Young Academy and later completed a year at the University of Utah. As a teenager his sight was impaired while working in the desert. In later life he became a generous supporter of organizations for the visually handicapped. In 1892 he married Lucy Emilie Woodruff and a month later took his bride on a mission in the southern United States.

In 1903 Smith was called to fill a vacant post in the Quorum of the Twelve Apostles of the church. His father, John Henry Smith, was already an apostle, and they became the only father-son combination ever to serve on the council. George Smith's next decades were filled with the duties of his office, which sent him across the United States frequently and on a number of foreign journeys. Following World War I he was sent to Europe as mission president (1919-1921). His years of service, however, were marked by health problems. In 1909 he suffered a nervous breakdown that incapacitated him until 1913. His activities were somewhat limited for the rest of his life. He suffered a minor relapse in the 1930s.

In 1943, however, he became president of the Quorum of the Twelve, and two years later, in his mid-seventies, he became the church's president. His six years in office were highlighted by his dedication of the Idaho temple and his supervision of the church's effort to aid with relief in post-war Europe. He died of lupuserythematosus disseminatus, the disease that had earlier contributed to his mental collapse.

Sources:

Jensen, Andrew. *Latter Day Saints Biographical Encyclopedia* 4 vols. Salt Lake City, UT: Andrew Jensen History Co., 1901.
Nibley, Preston. *The Presidents of the Church*. Salt Lake City, UT: Deseret Book Company, 1960. 477 pp.
Pusey, Merlo J. *Builders of the Kingdom: George A. Smith, John Henry Smith, George Albert Smith*. Provo, UT: Brigham Young University Press, 1981.
Smith, George Albert. *Sharing the Gospel with Others*. Salt Lake City, UT: Deseret Book Company, 1948. 219 pp.
Van Wagoner, Richard S., and Steven C. Walker. *A Book of Mormons*. Salt Lake City, UT: Signature Books, 1982. 454 pp.

★ 872 ★
SMITH, Gerald Lyman Kenneth
Minister, Christian Church (Disciples of Christ)
Anti-Semitic and Anti-Communist Orator
b. Feb. 27, 1898, Pardeeville, Wisconsin
d. Apr. 15, 1976, Glendale, California

The Reverend Gerald Lyman Kenneth Smith was a fundamentalist minister noted for his virulently anti-Semitic and anti-Communist oratory. The son of a rural minister, he was the descendant of four generations of circuit-riding preachers. Smith was fond of recounting the story of how he used to ride 14 miles on horseback to get to school. He was a skilled debator, and won an elocution contest during his junior year in high school with **William Jennings Bryan**'s "cross-of-gold" speech. He worked his way through Valparaiso University in Indianapolis while majoring in literature, Biblical history, and drama. He graduated after two and a half years of schooling at the age of 19, and began a career as a minister in the Christian Church (Disciples of Christ). In 1922 he married his boyhood sweetheart, Eleanor Marion Sorenson.

After serving several small Disciples congregations, in 1928 he was called to the King's Highway Christian Church in Shreveport, Louisiana. He supported populist political causes, simultaneously participating in ultra-right organizations such as William Dudley Pelley's Silver Shirts. Smith became a member of the Pelley group in 1933 and worked as a lecturer, giving speeches on such topics as "Some Day 100 Million Americans Will Hide Behind Silver Shirts for Protection." Within a few years he drifted away from Pelley to become active in Huey Long's organization. He finally left

his Shreveport church in 1934 in order to travel around setting up Long's "Share-Our-Wealth" clubs. Long's assassination in 1935 represented a great setback for Smith.

Smith then became active with Dr. Francis Everett Townsend, defending the doctor's integrity and emerging as Townsend's de facto second in command. There was a short-lived alliance between Townsend, Smith, and Father **Charles Edward Coughlin**, who together supported William Lemke for president in 1936. During the next year Smith organized his Committee of One Million, a group set up to counteract the "subversive influences" of Communism, and lectured for his cause throughout the country.

In 1942 Smith began publishing his periodical, *The Cross and the Flag*, which was generally accepted as the successor to Father Coughlin's *Social Injustice*. The war compelled Smith to silence his rhetoric about the "evils" of democracy, particularly after the Justice Department listed his magazine as a propaganda tool for alleged seditionists. After the war, he resumed his assault on democracy, the United Nations, Jews, and Blacks. With the cooperation of other nationalist leaders, he launched the Christian Nationalist Crusade in St. Louis on June 19, 1947. The Crusade continued the activities of the Committee of One Million, and *The Cross and the Flag* became the Crusade's periodical.

In 1964 Smith founded the Elna F. Smith Foundation in Eureka Springs, Arkansas. Through it he erected a seven-story statue of Jesus, the Christ of the Ozarks, and initiated a summer passion play modeled on the one at Oberammergau, Germany. The statue and the play, presented nightly during the summer in an outdoor theater, have become major tourist attractions in the Ozark Mountain region.

Sources:

Brinkley, Alan. *Voices of Protest: Huey Long, Father Coughlin, and the Great Depression*. New York: Vintage, 1983. 348 pp.
Hailey, Jean R. "Gerald Smith, Apostle of Hate, Dies." *Washington Post* (April 17, 1976).
Perkins, Jonathan Ellsworth. *The Biggest Hypocrite in America, Gerald L. K. Smith Unmasked*. Los Angeles: American Foundation, 1949. 152 pp.
Roy, Ralph Lord. *Apostles of Discord: A Study of Organized Bigotry and Disruption on the Fringes of Protestantism*. Boston: Beacon, 1953. 437 pp.

★ 873 ★
SMITH, Gipsy
Independent Christian Evangelist
b. Mar. 31, 1860, Wanstead England
d. Aug. 4, 1947

Though primarily a British evangelist, Rodney Smith, known publicly as Gipsy Smith, became one of the best known evangelists in the United States in the early twentieth century. Born to Gypsy parents in England, Smith grew up uneducated, without even the rudimentary knowledge of reading and writing. His mother, Mary Welsh Smith, died when he was a child. Soon afterward, his father, Cornelius Smith, experienced a conversion following a vivid dream in which Jesus appeared to him. Smith was strongly affected by the change in his father's life and character, and the example of his father eventually led him to become a Christian. In 1876 he made a public profession of that faith in a primitive Methodist church in Cambridge, England.

The conversion led to both a desire to preach and a desire to gain some education, most of which was self-taught out of the Bible and a dictionary. In 1877 Smith approached **William Booth**, then head of the Christian Mission headquartered in London. Booth urged him to become an evangelist, and over the next few years he served at a number of locations over England, generally moving every six months. In 1879 he married a Miss Pennock. As he continued to travel for the Christian Mission, now in the process of being transformed into the Salvation Army, he began to be called Gipsy Smith, the name under which he would be known for the rest of his life. He found a ready response to both his natural speaking ability and singing.

In 1882 Smith broke with the Salvation Army, a split occasioned by a minor infraction of Booth's rule. Smith then settled in Hanley, England, and raised an independent congregation. Calls for him to preach at other locations around the country gradually led him to discern that evangelism was his true calling. In 1886 he began the mature portion of his life as an independent itinerant evangelist. In 1888 he made his first trip to the United States.

For the rest of his long and fruitful career, Smith divided his time between the United States and England. In the United States his tours were sponsored primarily by Methodist churches, though he operated as an independent evangelical Protestant. After 1892 he called his ministry the Gipsy Gospel Wagon Mission. In 1897 he was named a missioner for the National Free Church Council, an ecumenical group serving the evangelical churches in England. This relationship lasted until 1912.

Over his nearly 70 years of evangelistic activity he made approximately 50 trips to the United States. He died on board a ship heading to America to preach.

Sources:

Bowden, Henry Warner. *Dictionary of American Religious Biography*. Westport, CT: Greenwood Press, 1977. 572 pp.
Murray, Harold. *Sixty Years an Evangelist*. London: 1937.
Reid, Daniel G., Robert D. Linder, Bruce L. Shelley, and Harry S. Stout. *Dictionary of Christianity in America*. Downers Grove, IL: InterVarsity Press, 1990. 1305 pp.
Smith, Rodney "Gipsy." *As Jesus Passed By and Other Addresses*. New York: Fleming H. Revell Company, 1905. 224 pp.
_____. *Bearing and Sharing*. New York: George H. Doran, 1913. 46 pp.
_____. *The Beauty of Jesus*. London Epworth Press, 1932. 208 pp.
_____. *Gipsy Smith: An Autobiography*. New York: Fleming H. Revell Company, 1901. 330 pp.
_____. *Gipsy Smith's Best Sermons*. New York: J. S. Ogilvie Publishing Co., 1907. 255 pp.

★874★
SMITH, Hannah Whitall
Writer, Society of Friends
b. Feb. 7, 1832, Philadephia, Pennsylvania
d. May 1, 1911, Iffley England

Hannah Whitall Smith, one of the most popular religious writers of the late nineteenth century, was the daughter of well-to-do Quaker parents, John Mickle and Mary Tatum Whitall. She was educated in the city's Quaker schools, and at the age of 16 began to teach. In 1851 she married Robert Pearsall Smith, also a Quaker. She settled in as a housewife, and over the next few years had three children. During the late 1850s both Robert and Hannah absorbed much of the evangelical spirit and teachings of the Methodists and, as a result, in 1859 resigned from the Quaker meeting, even though it meant a harsh break with their families. Robert joined the Presbyterians and Hannah the Plymouth Brethren, though both were later reconciled to Friends.

After the Civil War, Smith moved to Millville, where she grew even more attached to the holiness movement then growing within Methodism. Robert began to preach regularly at holiness meetings and in 1869 began a periodical, the *Christian's Pathway to Power*, to which Hannah contributed.

In 1874 the Smiths traveled to England where both were welcomed. They enjoyed great success with their preaching, frequently for aristocratic gatherings. However, all of this ended in June 1875 when Robert was involved in an extramarital episode. The same month in which the scandal broke, Hannah had her first book, *The Christian's Secret of a Happy Life*, published. In the book she called for a complete dedication of one's life to God. It became a success, in spite of her husband, and went on to become one of the most widely read books among Protestant Christians in the decades since. It remains in print today.

The Smiths retired from the spotlight for several years, but in the 1880s Hannah came forth again as a public figure, speaking frequently for the causes of women's education and suffrage. In 1874 she became a founder of the Woman's Christian Temperance Union (W.C.T.U.) and in 1883 became superintendent of its evangelistic department. In 1888 Smith and her family moved to London. There she quickly identified with the British Woman's Temperance Union and continued to preach as opportunity offered itself. Her home became a cultural center which welcomed intellectuals from across the country. During these years she authored numerous articles and tracts, and published several books, among them: *Every-day Religion* (1893); *The Unselfishness of God* (1903); and *Living In the Sunshine*, later retitled *God of All Comfort* (1906).

Smith is credited for projecting a confident, positive Christian attitude in the face of frequent and extreme reverses in her personal life. She lost several of her children in their childhood. Her husband had at least three nervous breakdowns and an extramarital affair. Two of her daughters married nonbelievers (Bernhard Berenson and atheist philosopher Bertrand Russell) and did not follow her faith into adulthood. In spite of it all she remained a faithful witness.

During her last years she lived with her bachelor son, Logan, and died in his home near Oxford, England.

Sources:

Henry, Marie. *The Secret Life of Hannah Whitall Smith*. Grand Rapids, MI: Chosen Books, 1984. 186 pp.
McHenry, Robert, ed. *Liberty's Women*. Springfield, MA: G. & C. Mirrian Company, 1980. 482 pp.
Smith, Hannah Whitall. *The Christian's Secret of a Happy Life*. Old Tappan, NJ: Fleming H. Revell, 1875.
_____. *Everyday Religion*. Chicago: Moody Press, 1966.
_____. *Living in the Sunshine*. Chicago: Fleming H. Revell, 1906. Rept. as: *God of All Comfort*. Chicago: Moody Press, 1956.
_____. *The Unselfishness of God and How I Discovered It: My Spiritual Autobiography*. New York: Fleming H. Revell, 1903.
Smith, Logan Pearsall, ed. *Philadelphia Quaker: The Letters of Hannah Whitall Smith*. New York: Harcourt Brace & Co., 1950.
Strachey, Barbara. *Remarkable Relations*. New York: Universe Books, 1980. 351 pp.
Strachey, Ray, ed. *Religious Fanaticism: Extracts from the Papers of Hannah Whitall Smith*. London: Faber and Gwyer, Ltd. 1928.

★875★
SMITH, Israel Alexander
President, Reorganized Church of Jesus Christ of Latter Day Saints
b. Feb. 2, 1876, Plano, Illinois
d. Jun. 14, 1958, Independence, Missouri

Israel Alexander Smith, the third president of the Reorganized Church of Jesus Christ of Latter Day Saints, was the son of the first president, **Joseph Smith III**, and his second wife, Bertha Madison. He succeeded to the presidency following the death of his older brother, **Frederick Madison Smith**. As the son and brother of the two previous presidents of the church, Smith grew up amid the life and leadership of the Reorganized Church. He attended the church's school, Graceland College, at Lamoni, Iowa, from which he graduated in 1897. He married Nina Greenwalt in 1908. Deciding to practice law, he entered Lincoln-Jefferson University, from which he graduated in 1912. The Missouri bar admitted him in 1913, and he began a practice that continued for the next 25 years.

As a layman, Smith was active in church affairs. He was ordained to the high priesthood in 1915 and named counselor to the presiding bishopric in 1920. In 1919 he joined the standing high council of the church (its court) upon which he served until 1942. He also had an outstanding career in public service. He sat in the General Assembly of Iowa for 11 years (1911-1922) and participated in the Constitutional Convention of the state of Missouri (1943-1944).

In 1904 his brother invited him into the first presidency of the church as his counselor. Upon the death of his brother, he became the president of the church in 1946, at the age of 70. During his years as president, the church experienced its most rapid expansion, reaching a membership of approximately 150,000. Smith died in a car accident at the age of 82.

Sources:
Who Was Who in America. Chicago: Marquis Who's Who, Inc.

★876★
SMITH III, Joseph
President, Reorganized Church of Jesus Christ of Latter Day Saints
b. Nov. 6, 1832, Kirkland, Ohio
d. Dec. 10, 1914, Independence, Missouri

Joseph Smith III, the first president of the Reorganized Church of Jesus Christ of Latter Day Saints, was the son of **Joseph Smith, Jr.**, considered the prophet and the founder of both the Church of Jesus Christ of Latter-day Saints and Reorganized Church of Jesus Christ of Latter Day Saints, and Emma Hale Smith. He was the eldest son of Joseph Smith and born in the early years of the movement while it was still based in Ohio. He went with his parents and church members to Far West, Missouri, and then to the Mormon settlement at Nauvoo, Illinois. He was but 12 years old when his father was assassinated and hence too young to play any role in the power struggle and splintering of the church following his father's death.

When the largest faction of the church followed Brigham Young to Utah, young Joseph and his mother stayed in their home in Nauvoo. Emma Smith refused to acknowledge publicly that her husband had taught and practiced polygamy, and in spite of offers throughout her life, she refused to associate with the Utah-based Church of Jesus Christ of Latter-day Saints. Nor would she associate with any of the several factions that remained behind in the Midwest. Meanwhile, young Joseph grew to manhood, and in 1855 married Emma Griswold.

In 1852 some leaders of the several remnants of the church in the Midwest began to gather the factions together in what was originally termed the New Organization. They decided to offer the leadership to Joseph Smith III. He refused at first, but in 1859, accepted and William Marks ordained him as president of the church, which in 1860 assumed its present name. In 1865 Smith moved to Plano, Illinois, then the church's headquarters, and began editing *The Saint's Herald*, a task he continued throughout his life. While there, in 1869, his wife died, and he married Bertha Madison.

In 1881 the headquarters of the Reorganized Church moved to Lamoni, Iowa, an old Mormon community, and Smith moved the church's publishing operation there. This move came at the height of the government's opposition to polygamy. Smith had already adopted his mother's view concerning his father's role in polygamy, and he became an even more vocal opponent of the practice, protective of his father's reputation and in contrast to the views of the church in Utah. Like his father, he was considered a prophet, and on 18 separate occasions he had new revelations which were added to the church's authoritative text, *Doctrine and Covenants.* One such revelation admitted Blacks into the priesthood of the church.

During his years as president, Smith traveled widely, including trips to Canada, Great Britain, and Hawaii, as the church expanded. He led in the development of most of the church's national departments, a college, a hospital, and homes for both orphans and the aged. He oversaw the movement of the church back into Independence and the establishment of headquarters across from the Temple Lot, the land designated by his father as the site of the church's temple but in the hands of a rival church faction.

Smith's second wife died in 1896 and two years later he married Ada R. Clark. In 1906 he moved to Independence, remained there, and was blind the last four years of his long life.

Smith distinguished himself through his literary efforts for the church, most of which appeared in *The Saint's Herald*. His major book was the four-volume *The History of the Reorganized Church of Jesus Christ of Latter Day Saints*. A lengthy autobiographical statement by Joseph Smith III was included in Edward W. Tullidge's *The Life of Joseph the Prophet* (1880).

Sources:
Launius, Roger D. *Joseph Smith III*. Urbana, IL: University of Illinois Press, 1988. 394 pp.
Smith, Mary Audentia, comp. *Joseph Smith 1832-1914: A Centennial Tribute*. Independence, MO: Herald House, 1932.
Smith, Joseph III and Herman C. Smith. *The History of the Reorganized Church of Jesus Christ of Latter Day Saints*. 4 vols. Independence, MO: Herald House, 1967-1973.

★877★
SMITH JR., Joseph Fielding
President, Church of Jesus Christ of Latter-day Saints
b. Jul. 19, 1876, Salt Lake City, Utah
d. Jul. 2, 1972, Salt Lake City, Utah

Joseph Fielding Smith, Jr., the tenth president of the Church of Jesus Christ of Latter-day Saints, was the son of **Joseph Fielding Smith, Sr.**, and his second wife, Julina Lambson. He grew up during the most bitter years of the polygamy controversy that separated him from his father, who spent six years (1884-1891) in Hawaii to escape arrest. A year after his graduation from Latter Day Saints College in 1897, he married Louise E. Shurtiff.

In 1899 Smith embarked on a two-year mission to Great Britain. Upon his return, he accepted a position as clerk in the church historian's office, a connection he was to keep for the rest of his life. He became assistant church historian in 1906 and church historian in 1921. His historical interests included genealogy, and in 1908 he became director and librarian of the Church Genealogical Society. About this time his first wife died, and a few months later he married Ethel G. Reynolds. In 1910 he was called to the Quorum of the Twelve Apostles.

Smith's major contribution to the church was through his writings. He authored more than 25 books on history and theology, including: *The Progress of Man* (1936); *The Restoration of All Things* (1945); *Doctrines of Salvation* (1954); *Man: His Origin and Destiny* (1954); and a biography of his father. His book *Essentials in Church History*, a history of the Church of Jesus Christ of Latter-day Saints, has gone through numerous editions and printings. Among his last works was an autobiography. In 1938, following his second wife's death, he married Jessie Elal Evans.

After many years of work as a genealogist and historian, Smith became president of the temple in Salt Lake City in 1945. In 1951 he was named president of the Quorum of the Twelve, and in 1965 he became counselor to the church's president, David Oman McKay. Finally, in 1970, at the age of 94, he became the oldest person to be named president of the church. He is the only son of a former president to hold that office. His presidency lasted only two years. Shortly before his death he dedicated the temples in Provo and in Ogden, Utah.

Sources:
Heslop, J. M., and Dell R. Van Orden. *Joseph Fielding Smith: A Prophet Among the People*. Salt Lake City, UT: Deseret Book Company, 1971.
Smith, Joseph Fielding, Jr.. *Doctrines of Salvation*. Salt Lake City, UT: Bookcraft, 1954.
_____. *Essentials of Church History*. Salt Lake City, UT: Deseret Book Company, 1950.
_____. *Life of Joseph F. Smith*. Salt Lake City, UT: Deseret News Press, 1938. 490 pp.
_____. *Man: His Origin and Destiny*. Salt Lake City, UT: Deseret Book Company, 1954. 563 pp.
_____. *The Progress of Man*. Salt Lake City, UT: Genealogical Society of Utah, 1936. 530 pp.
_____. *The Restoration of All Things*. Salt Lake City, UT: Deseret News Press, 1945. 338 pp.
_____, and John J. Stewart. *The Life of Joseph Fielding Smith*. Salt Lake City, UT: Deseret Book Company, 1972.
Van Wagoner, Richard S., and Steven C. Walker. *A Book of Mormons*. Salt Lake City, UT: Signature books, 1982. 454 pp.

★878★
SMITH SR., Joseph Fielding
President, Church of Jesus Christ of Latter-day Saints
b. Nov. 13, 1838, Missouri
d. Nov. 19, 1918, Salt Lake City, Utah

Joseph Fielding Smith, Sr., usually referred to as Joseph F. Smith, was the sixth president of the Church of Jesus Christ of Latter-day Saints. He was the son of Mary Fielding Smith and Hyrum Smith, the brother of church founder **Joseph Smith, Jr.** Joseph F. Smith was born in one of the church's settlements in western Missouri while his father was in jail during a period of persecution of Mormons. Several years later he moved with the family to Nauvoo, Illinois. In 1844 his father and Joseph Smith Jr. were murdered while imprisoned in the Hancock County jail. He moved to Salt Lake City in 1848, where his mother died four years later. He was cared for by **George A. Smith**, a relative, until 1854 when, following his expulsion from school, he was sent on a mission to Hawaii.

Smith stayed in Hawaii for four years, living among the natives with no financial support from home. Shortly after his return from the mission, he married Levira Annette Clark, the first of five marriages. This marriage was in constant turmoil due to Smith's poverty, his several lengthy missions, and his wife's nervous disorders. In 1860 Smith went to England for three years. In 1864 he returned to Hawaii. In 1866 he married Julina Lambson. Unable to accept plural marriage, Smith's first wife obtained a separation and, following his marriage to Sarah Ellen Richards in 1868, a divorce. She charged him with adultery.

In the midst of his domestic problems, Smith was secretly ordained to the apostleship by church president Brigham Young. He became part of the Quorum of the Twelve Apostles the following year. During the rest of the century, he served as a counselor to each of the church presidents.

Smith married three more times: in 1871 to Edna Lambson, in 1883 to Alice Ann Kimball, and in 1884 to Mary Taylor Schwartz. The last two marriages were contracted as the efforts of the United States government to stamp out polygamy were reaching their peak. Shortly after his last marriage, Smith went on a mission to Hawaii to escape arrest. He remained there until 1891, when, due to the church's disavowal of polygamy in 1890, government prosecution of polygamists died down.

In 1901, following the brief presidency of **Lorenzo Snow**, Smith became the sixth president of the church. He holds the distinctions of being the first president whose parents had been members of the church at the time of his birth, the first named without having previously been president of the Quorum of the Twelve, and the only one to have a son who would also hold the office.

As president, Smith was immediately faced with the problem of continuing polygamy in the church. Since the manifesto renouncing polygamy in 1890, polygamous marriages had been quietly sanctioned outside the United States, primarily in Mexico. Smith was called to account for such activity before the United States Senate during the hearing over the seating of **Reed Smoot**, the senator who had been elected to represent Utah. Smith testified that he had no knowledge of, nor had he authorized or performed any such marriages in the period since 1890, a claim more recently contradicted by marriage records of that time. In April 1904, however, a month after testifying, he issued what is commonly referred to as the "Second Manifesto," which interpreted the 1890 manifesto as outlawing all plural marriages worldwide and not just those in countries where plural marriages were illegal. Under this ruling, excommunication proceedings were held against those who contracted plural marriages after 1904. In 1911, under pressure from Smoot, Smith finally admitted that some plural marriages had been authorized outside the United States after 1890. Since those marriages had been authorized by the church, Smith argued that the church could not move against those persons who married in good conscience.

Aside from the continuing polygamy question, Smith presided over a healthy and expansive period in the church's history. Under new financial policies instituted by his predecessor, the heavy debts incurred during the polygamy wars were paid off by 1906, and Smith launched a new building program that included the church's administrative building in Salt Lake City and temples in Hawaii and Canada. He also purchased several of the historic sites associated with the church in the east, including Joseph Smith's birthplace in Vermont, the Smith home in New York, the old Hancock County jail in Carthage, Illinois, and land near the site of the temple in Independence, Missouri.

Sources:
Nibley, Preston. *The Presidents of the Church*. Salt Lake City, UT: Deseret Book Company, 1960. 477 pp.
Smith, Joseph Fielding. *Gospel Doctrine*. Salt Lake City, UT: Deseret Book Company, 1969. 553 pp.
Smith, Joseph Fielding, Jr. *Life of Joseph F. Smith*. Salt Lake City, UT: Deseret Book Company, 1938. 490 pp.
Van Wagoner, Richard S., and Steven C. Walker. *A Book of Mormons*. Salt Lake City, UT: Signature Books, 1982. 454 pp.

★879★
SMITH, Oswald Jeffery
Founder, Peoples Church
b. Nov. 8, 1889, Odessa, Ontario, Canada
d. Jan. 25, 1986, Toronto, Ontario, Canada

Oswald Jeffery Smith, fundamentalist minister and founder of the Peoples Church in Toronto, Ontario, is the son of Benny and Maud Laidley Smith. He was raised in rural Ontario. While he had attended a Presbyterian church occasionally, it was not until 1906 when he went to Toronto to hear **Reuben A. Torrey** preach that Smith experienced a conversion to Christianity. Upon his return home, he started a Sunday school, but soon decided to move to Toronto where he could attend the Toronto Bible College. He preached his first sermon in 1908 and knew that he had been called to the ministry. During the next few years he moved around quite a bit and picked up his education at several schools. He attended Manitoba College for a year (1909-1910), then Toronto Bible College (1910-1912) and finally McCormick Theological Seminary, the Presbyterian school in Chicago, Illinois, from which he graduated in 1915. He was ordained in the Presbyterian Church of Canada, with which he has remained in good standing in spite of spending most of his career independent of it.

Smith began his post-seminary work as the associate pastor of Dale Presbyterian Church in Toronto. In 1916 he married Daisy Billings, a deaconess trained at the Christian and Missionary Alliance (CMA) school in Nyack, New York. That same year he became the interim pastor at Dale, when the senior minister went to war. In 1918 he became pastor of Beulah Tabernacle in Toronto and in 1919 moved to British Columbia to work with the Shantyman's Christian Association. He returned to Toronto in 1920 and began a new congregation as the Gospel Auditorium. His work soon merged with a Christian and Missionary Alliance congregation to become the Parkdale Tabernacle. His work prospered and soon he began a publishing house, a mission to work in northern Canada, the periodical *The Peoples Magazine*, and the Canadian Bible Institute, to train Christian workers.

In 1926 Smith was persuaded to bring his leadership to Los Angeles as the pastor of the Gospel Tabernacle, a significant Christian and Missionary Alliance congregation. He worked in Los Angeles for three years, but his heart was in Canada. Thus, in 1928 he returned to Toronto. He also dropped his affiliation with the Alliance and affiliated with evangelist **Paul Rader**, who appointed Smith Canadian director of the Worldwide Bible Couriers. Smith decided to start over in Toronto and rented a hall for services of what in 1933 would be named the Peoples Church. In 1934 the congregation purchased the former Central Methodist Church building and there Smith built one of the most important centers of fundamental Protestantism in North America.

While Smith became well-known through his leadership of a large congregation, his widely circulated magazine, and his many books, he is best remembered for his work for missions. Beginning in 1935 he held an annual month-long missionary conference featuring many of the independent evangelical missionary agencies. His own church served as the model and annually gave more to missionary endeavors than to their own local needs.

Smith retired in 1959 and his son Paul Smith succeeded him. During his retirement years, Smith has remained active into his nineties, occasionally speaking at the Peoples Church and traveling around the world to preach. In 1965 he became the first president of the Evangelical Fellowship of Canada, an ecumenical group of fundamentalist ministries in Canada.

Sources:

Hall, Douglas. *Not Made for Defeat*. Grand Rapids, MI: Zondervan Publishing House, 1969. 192 pp.

Neely, Lois. *Fire in His Bones*. Wheaton, IL: Tyndale House, Publishers, 1982. 308 pp.

Smith, Oswald J. *The Country I Love Best*. London: Marshall, Morgan & Scott, 1934, 1965. 128 pp.

———. *The Passion for Souls*. London: Marshall, Morgan & Scott, 1940, 1952. 124 pp.

———. *The Peoples Church and Its Founder*. Toronto: The Peoples Press, 1961. 128 pp.

———. *The Story of My Life*. London: Marshall, Morgan & Scott, 1962. 128 pp.

———. *When the King Comes Back*. London: Marshall, Morgan & Scott, 1957, 1963. 128 pp.

★ 880 ★
SMITH, Uriah
Editor, Seventh-day Adventist Church
b. May 2, 1832, West Wilton, New Hampshire
d. Mar. 6, 1903, Battle Creek, Michigan

Uriah Smith, a pioneer Seventh-day Adventist Church leader, was the son of Rebecca Spaulding and Samuel Smith. At the age of four, following poor medical treatment, he was forced to endure a partial amputation of his leg. While this occurrence hampered his outdoor activity, he compensated by concentrating on his education and, later, his editorial and writing career. In 1844 his mother joined the early adventists and he lived through the Great Disappointment when Christ failed to appear as predicted by the movement's founder William Miller. In 1948 he entered Phillips Academy in Exeter, New Hampshire. Following his graduation in 1851

he made plans to enter college. Financial reverses, though, prevented him from pursuing further formal education.

In 1852 Smith was converted to the Seventh-day Adventist cause. (The seventh-day movement had been one of several factions that had emerged after the Great Disappointment.) In 1855 he moved to Battle Creek, Michigan, where the movement's headquarters was established and became editor of the *Review and Herald*, its periodical. He would remain the magazine's editor, except for a few brief years, for the rest of his life. In 1857 he married Harriet Newall Stevens.

Smith was present as the seventh-day movement took its initial organizational steps. In 1861 he became the treasurer of the Seventh-day Adventist Publishing Association and secretary of the Michigan Conference. Two years later he was named president of the Michigan Conference and secretary of the general conference. He would hold the latter post for 21 years. A feeling of unworthiness kept Smith from seeking ordination for many years, but he was finally ordained as an adventist minister in 1874.

Through the years Smith wrote regularly for the *Review and Herald*. Many of his articles would later be compiled into books. He was a consistent opponent of Spiritualism, a theme to which he regularly returned, but is best remembered for his writings on prophecy and the adventist perspective on history and the future. Among his 20 books were: *The Warning Voice of Time and Prophecy* (1853); *Thoughts, Critical and Practical, on the Book of Revelation* (1865); *Thoughts, Critical and Practical, on the Book of Daniel* (1873); *Man's Nature and Destiny* (1873); *The Sanctuary and the 2300 Days* (1877); *Here and Hereafter, or, Man in Life and Death* (1897); *Looking Unto Jesus or Christ in Type and Antitype* (1898); and *The Marvel of the Nations* (1901). His books on Daniel and Revelation would later be combined and remain a popular adventist publication.

Beginning in 1897, when he was replaced briefly by Alonzo T. Jones as editor of the *Review and Herald*, Smith had to contend with elements in the church who wished him removed. He served as an associate editor under Jones for three years before returning to the editor's post in 1901. The following year, however, William W. Prescott assumed some of Smith's editorial duties. Smith was deeply hurt, a fact which may have contributed to his becoming ill soon afterwards. Smith lived long enough to see the destruction of the *Review and Herald* offices by a fire on December 30, 1902, but died before the decision was made to relocate the offices to the Washington, D.C. area, where they have remained.

Sources:

Durand, Eugene F. *Yours in the Blessed Hope, Uriah Smith*. Washington, DC: Review and Herald Publishing Association, 1980. 320 pp.

Smith, Uriah. *Here and Hereafter, or, Man in Life and Death*. Washington, DC: Review and Herald Publishing Association, 1897. 357 pp.

———. *The Marvel of Nations*. Battle Creek, MI: Review and Herald Publishers, 1887. 298 pp.

———. *The Prophecies of Daniel and the Revelation*. Nashville, TN: Southern Publishing Association. rev. ed. 1944. 830 pp.

———. *The Sanctuary and the 2300 Days*. Battle Creek, MI: Seventh-day Adventist Publishing Association, 1877. 352 pp.

★ 881 ★
SMITH, Wallace Bunnell
President, Reorganized Church of Jesus Christ of Latter Day Saints
b. Jul. 29, 1929, Independence, Missouri

Wallace Bunnell Smith, the fifth president of the Reorganized Church of Jesus Christ of Latter Day Saints, is the son of **William Wallace Smith**, the former president of Reorganized Church of Jesus Christ of Latter Day Saints, and his wife, Rosalund Bunnell. Smith's father was a businessman in Independence at the time of his birth, but the family moved to St. Joseph, Missouri, in 1931, and young Wallace grew up there. He attended Graceland College, the University of Portland (in Oregon where his family had moved during World War II), and Kansas University, from which he received his B.A. degree in 1951. He stayed at Kansas, attending the School of Medicine, and received his M.D. degree in 1951. He specialized in ophthalmology and is a fellow of both the American College of Surgeons and the American Academy of Ophthalmology. He married Anne M. McCullough.

Smith was ordained a priest in 1945 and an elder in 1964. He was admitted to the Quorum of High Priests in 1965. While making his living as a doctor, Smith was active in the church, having served as a member of the standing high council, the church's judicial body. He served as a counselor at the Center Stake, a bishop and president in Independence, and as assistant pastor of several congregations.

In 1976, Smith's father, then the president of the church, announced his retirement and designated him as the new president, effective in 1978. His position was confirmed by the church conference that year. He inherited the leadership of a church in the midst of some radical changes initiated by his father.

As president, Smith has continued his father's emphasis upon the international expansion of the church. Among the most controversial issues articulated by Smith has been that of the ordination of women. He issued a statement approving such ordination that was accepted by the church conference in 1984. That action led a number of conservative church leaders and members, already upset with earlier changes, to leave the church and establish several rival factions. Some of these have been very visible in and near Independence, where the overwhelming majority of church members reside. In the face of such opposition, Smith has consistently maintained the stance that the church must change with the times while adhering to the essentials of the faith.

In 1988 Smith took a second highly controversial step in releasing plans for the construction of a multimillion dollar temple to be built across the street from what has traditionally been termed the Temple Lot. The Temple Lot is a small parcel of land which had been designated by **Joseph Smith, Jr.**, the founder of the Latter Day Saint movement, as the place upon which the Saints would build their permanent temple. The Reorganized Church of Jesus Christ of Latter Day Saints owns the land immediately south, upon which their headquarters building rests and east, upon which the new temple is to be built. The lot itself is owned by another rival faction of the Latter Day Saint movement. The church has been unable to purchase or otherwise obtain the Temple Lot, and Smith has led in the move to build the temple at its presently designated location.

Sources:

Who's Who in America. Wilmette, IL: Marquis Who's Who, Inc.

★ 882 ★
SMITH, Wilbur Moorehead
Minister and Educator, United Presbyterian Church in the U.S.A.
b. Jun. 9, 1894, Chicago, Illinois
d. May 20, 1976

Wilbur Moorehead Smith, a fundamentalist Presbyterian minister and educator, was the son of Sadie Sanborn and Thomas M. Smith. His father was a businessman and an active elder at Moody Church in Chicago, and Smith was raised in a pious environment. He grew up in the Moody Church but as a teenager began to visit other churches and for a time attended Buena Park Presbyterian Church. In 1913 he experienced a call to the ministry and entered Moody Bible Institute. After a year at Moody he transferred to the University, now College, of Wooster. In 1917 he dropped out of school, married Mayme Ostrosky, and joined the staff of West

Presbyterian Church in Wilmington, Delaware. The following year he moved to Ocean City, Maryland, as the interim pastor for the Presbyterian church.

After three years at Ocean City, Smith was finally ordained by the Presbyterian Church in the U.S.A. and accepted a call to the Lafayette Presbyterian Church in Baltimore, Maryland. He would fill out his pastoral years with stays at Covington, Virginia (1925-1931), and Coatesville, Pennsylvania (1931-1937). During these years he continued his own education and began to acquire a large personal library. While at Covington, he authored the first of the numerous articles he would see published. Soon after moving to Coatesville, he completed his first book, *A List of Bibliographies of Theological and Biblical Literature Published in Great Britain and America, 1595-1931* (1931).

While in Pennsylvania, Smith became involved in the problems at Princeton Theological Seminary which saw its leading conservative theologian, **J. Gresham Machen**, leave and found a number of structures to oppose the liberalism in the Presbyterian Church. In 1933 Smith accepted an invitation to sit on the board of the Independent Board of Presbyterian Foreign Missions. He resigned his affiliation with the board in 1937 after Machen had founded a new denomination, the Orthodox Presbyterian Church, and the board aligned itself with that organization. In 1934 Smith was invited to become the new editor of the annual *Peloubet's Notes* on the International Sunday School Lesson. This annual commentary begun in 1875 by Francis Nathan Peloubet would be the concern of Smith for the next 36 years.

In 1937 Smith was invited to join the faculty of Moody Bible Institute, the beginning of a second career in teaching. He stayed at Moody for a decade before joining the faculty of the new Fuller Theological Seminary in Pasadena, California. In 1954 he moved on to Trinity Evangelical Divinity School in Deerfield, Illinois. He retired in 1971. During these years he was the author of a number of books including *Profitable Bible Study* (1939); *The Supernaturalness of Christ* (1941); *Therefore Stand* (1945), still considered one of the best presentations of the fundamentalist Christian position; *World Crises and the Prophetic Scriptures* (1950); and *Egypt in Biblical Prophecy* (1957). In 1954 he began one of his more significant endeavors as a member of the revision committee for the *Scofield Reference Bible*, a very popular study Bible among fundamentalists. During his last years at Trinity he wrote an autobiography, *Before I Forget* (1971).

Sources:

Reid, Daniel G., Robert D. Linder, Bruce L. Shelley, and Harry S. Stout. *Dictionary of Christianity in America.* Downers Grove, IL: InterVarsity Press, 1990. 1305 pp.
Smith, Wilbur M. *Before I Forget.* Chicago: Moody Press, 1971. 304 pp.
_____. *Egypt in Biblical Prophecy.* Boston: W. A. Wilde Co., 1957. 256 pp.
_____. *Profitable Bible Study.* Boston: W. A. Wilde Co., 1939. 214 pp.
_____. *The Supernaturalness of Christ.* Boston: W. A. Wilde Co., 1941. 235 pp.
_____. *Therefore Stand.* Boston: W. A. Wilde Co., 1945. 614 pp.
_____. *World Crises and the Prophetic Scriptures.* Chicago: Moody Press, 1950. 384 pp.

★ 883 ★
SMITH, William Wallace
President, Reorganized Church of Jesus Christ of Latter Day Saints
b. Nov. 18, 1900
d. Aug. 4, 1989, Independence, Missouri

William Wallace Smith, the fourth president of the Reorganized Church of Jesus Christ of Latter Day Saints, was the son of **Joseph Smith III**, the church's first president, and his third wife, Ada Rachel Clark. He was thus a half-brother to the other church presidents, **Frederick Madison Smith** and **Israel Alexander Smith**. In 1906 the Smith family moved to Independence, Missouri, where young William grew up. Smith attended Graceland College, operated by the Reorganized Church for two years (1919-1921) and then attended the University of Missouri, from which he received his A.B. degree in 1924. He married Rosamund Bunnell later that same year. He was ordained an elder in the church in 1928.

Following his graduation from college, Smith went into business, first working as the manager of a hardware firm in Independence. In 1931 he moved to St. Joseph, Missouri, from which he operated as a traveling salesman, until the bottom fell out of the hardware business as World War II began. Hearing of a war-time boom in the northwest, on the advice of his brother-in-law, he moved to Portland, Oregon, and worked in the personnel office of a ship building company. He also became a leader of the Portland, Oregon, congregation. In 1947 he was called back to Independence to become an apostle and assume duties with the church full time. He was placed in charge of the southern states mission and named associate director of the mission in the southwest. In 1950 he was named a counselor to Israel A. Smith, the church's president.

Following the death of Israel A. Smith in June 1958, a document was discovered in which he designated his half-brother William Wallace Smith as his successor. That designation was confirmed by the church conference in October 1958. In Smith's first statements to the church he singled out church growth worldwide to be the hallmark of his tenure in office. In 1960 he announced his intention to take a world mission tour that lasted for four months, during which he visited 18 countries.

During the 1960s he led the church into a period of self-examination in the face of the rapid changes in the world. The changes in church life resulting from this reexamination included the introduction of a new, closely graded church school curriculum, the introduction of goal-setting conferences for congregations, changes in the administration at the highest levels of the church, and plans for the building of a temple. Each change seriously affected church life, and Smith faced many critics within the church. Smith also became the first president to assume a public role and speak regularly on matters of social concern within the larger society ranging from the attempts to racially integrate the University of Missouri to the treatment of prisoners of war in Vietnam.

In 1976 Smith broke a precedent in the church by announcing his plans to retire in 1978, rather than serve until his death, and naming his son **Wallace Bunnell Smith** to succeed him. At the time of his retirement he was named president emeritus.

Sources:

Who's Who in America. Wilmette, IL: Marquis Who's Who, Inc.
Who's Who in Religion. 2d ed. Chicago: Marquis Who's Who, Inc., 1977.

★ 884 ★
SMOHALLA
Founder, Washani (Dreamer Religion)
b. 1815?, Wallula, Washington
d. 1907, Washington

Smohalla, the founder of the Washani religion among the Indian tribes of the Pacific Northwest, was born around 1815 in the Wanapun (or Soluk) tribe. Few records remain of his early life. He emerged as a young man with a hunchback, an attendant of the mission which had been established by the Roman Catholic Church near his home in Yakima County. While absorbing some Catholic elements, he did not become a Catholic. As he grew to manhood, he was acknowledged as a tribal leader revered for his abilities as a warrior, visionary, and medicine man.

During the 1850s Smohalla engaged in a decisive encounter with the chief of a nearby tribe. Defeated in hand-to-hand combat, he was left for dead. He did not die, however, but fled the area and went to live in Mexico. Several years later he returned to his former home and was welcomed as one returned from the dead. He confided to his people that he had been wandering in the Spirit World and had brought back a message for them that he had received while there. He prophesied the demise of the white men who had invaded their territory and a return to the life before the white man came. His influence was greatly extended through his oratorical ability, which earned him the name Shouting Mountain or Yuyunipa-tqana.

By the 1870s Smohalla's message had matured into the Washani or Dreamer Religion centered upon the vision of a return to the paradise of the past. He developed ritual practices that included drumming and dancing. Among his early converts was Tuekakas (Old Joseph) a chief among the Nez Perce who had rejected Christianity and the 1863 Treaty of Lapwai, which had been signed by the other Nez Perce chiefs. Tuekakas died a short time after his conversion to Smohalla's religion, but he passed the vision on to his son Joseph, who would later lead the Nez Perce revolt of 1877.

Smohalla's new religion spread among the tribes of the Northwest. He lived to be an old man and is said to have married ten times. His last wife Strongknee, survived him. He was revered by his followers as a Messiah, and his new religion flourished for a generation after his death.

Sources:

Dictionary of American Biography. 20 vols. and 7 supps. New York: Charles Scribner's Sons, 1928-1936, 1944-1981.
Webster's Biographical Dictionary. Springfield, MA: G. & C. Merriam Co.
Who Was Who in America. Chicago: Marquis Who's Who, Inc.

★ 885 ★
SMOOT, Reed
Apostle, Church of Jesus Christ of Latter-day Saints
United States Senator
b. Jan. 10, 1862, Salt Lake City, Utah
d. Feb. 9, 1941, St. Petersburg, Florida

Reed Smoot, the controversial senator from Utah at the beginning of the twentieth century who became the center of a storm of controversy over the Mormon practice of polygamy, was the son of Anna Kristina Morrison Smoot and Salt Lake City's mayor, Abraham Owen Smoot. When Smoot was ten, the family moved to Provo. He joined the first class of Brigham Young Academy and, after finishing his studies, began a career in some of the church owned businesses. In 1884 he was appointed to superintend the Provo Woolen Mills. That same year he married Alpha M. Eldredge. His business career was interrupted in 1890 when he served on a mission in England, but he returned the following year and eventually became manager of Provo Lumber Manufacturing and Building, president of Provo Commercial and Savings Bank, and a director of the Los Angeles and Salt Lake Railroad. In 1900 he was called as an apostle of the church.

Politically, Smoot had identified himself as a Republican. During the first years of the twentieth century, the church was open about its desire to have an apostle become a senator. Smoot conferred with church leaders in hopes of gaining their support and in 1902 he announced his candidacy. The Salt Lake City Ministerial Association opposed his bid, and by the time he was elected a campaign had developed against seating him. He was accused of being part of a ruling church elite that continued to support plural marriages, and it was charged that he had taken a "secret pledge of disloyalty to the American government." The committee that conducted the investigation voted for expulsion, but with President Theodore Roosevelt's backing, the senate finally seated Smoot. He served for

30 years until his defeat in the Franklin D. Roosevelt Democratic Party landslide in 1932.

Sources:

Jensen, Andrew. *Latter Day Saints Biographical Encyclopedia* 4 vols. Salt Lake City, UT: Andrew Jensen History Co., 1901.

Merrill, Milton R. *Reed Smoot: Apostle in Politics.* Pullman, WA: Washington State University Press, 1990. 426 pp.

———. *Reed Smoot: Utah Politician.* Logan, UT: Utah State Agricultural College Monograph Series, 1953.

Shipps, Jan. "The Public Image of Reed Smoot: 1902-1932." *Utah Historical Quarterly* 45 (Fall 1977): 380-400.

Van Wagoner, Richard S., and Steven C. Walker. *A Book of Mormons.* Salt Lake City, UT: Signature Books, 1982. 454 pp.

★886★
SNOW, Eliza Roxey
Women's Leader, Church of Jesus Christ of Latter-day Saints
b. Jan. 21, 1804, Becket, Massachusetts
d. Dec. 5, 1887, Salt Lake City, Utah

Eliza Roxey Snow, who became one of the most powerful women in the Church of Jesus Christ of Latter-day Saints in the late nineteenth century, was born into a Massachusetts family which became Mormon after their move to Ohio in the 1820s. Eliza joined the Christian Church (Disciples of Christ) under the ministry of Sidney Rigdon, who later became the first counselor to Mormon prophet **Joseph Smith, Jr.** Snow was baptized in 1835 and became a teacher for the Smith family children. At Nauvoo she boarded with the family. During the early years of the Mormon movement she frequently exercised a gift for speaking in tongues and gained a reputation as a prophetess, although several prominent prophecies failed to come to pass.

Snow is most remembered for two events that occurred during 1842 as the Mormons were settling Nauvoo, Illinois. In March 1842 she proposed the organization of a benevolent society for women. Smith altered the proposal and led in the formation of the Relief Society, the most important women's organization in the church through the years. Snow became its first secretary. Three months later, Snow became one of Joseph Smith's plural wives. The ceremony was held secretly, as most of the church members had not yet become privy to the changes in church doctrine and practice that had been occurring.

Snow also began to make an impact within the church through her writing, especially her poetry. Although few outside of the church have admired her work, Smith encouraged her as "Zion's poetess." Her poems were later collected and published. Several were set to music and became popular Mormon hymns.

Joseph Smith was killed in 1844. He was succeeded by Brigham Young, who took Eliza Snow as his plural wife, though the relationship seems to have been a platonic one. In 1845, before the departure of the Mormons westward to the Salt Lake Basin, Young appointed Snow as recorder for the Nauvoo Temple, thus initiating a role for women in the church's temple. In Salt Lake City, she directed the women's section of the Endowment House and ministered to the needs of sick women and children. She was frequently called upon to pray and lay on hands for their health. She and other women also ministered to women about to give birth.

In the mid-1860s, Young asked Snow to take the lead in the reactivation of the Relief Society, and in 1867 Young appointed her as its second president. This work dominated the rest of her life, and through it she left a lasting imprint on the church. She was able to expand that role even further when she became an official counselor to Young on matters pertaining to women.

Snow, however, was by no means a feminist in any modern sense of that term. She was a staunch apologist for polygamy. She saw plural marriage as a means for women, who lost their equality through disobedience, to regain it through obedience in righteousness. Since there were few righteous men, polygamy was necessary. She did favor suffrage for females, but did little for the cause. The major right for women was the right to marry.

Snow's career with the Church Relief Society reflects her desire to do as much as possible within what she saw as a proper female role. In 1872 she founded a magazine, *The Woman's Exponent*, which became the organ of the society. Following a conversation with Aurelia Rogers Penrose, Snow supported her suggestion for the formation of the Primary Association to train young boys in disciplined conduct, and she traveled widely throughout the church to assist in the spread of the association. In 1881 she added the presidency of the board of directors for the Deseret Hospital Association to her many duties.

Snow died in one of Brigham Young's homes, the Lion House, and was buried in his private cemetery.

Sources:

Beecher, Maureen Ursenbach. "The Eliza Enigma: The Life and Legend of Eliza Snow." In *Sister Saints*, edited by Vicky Burgess-Olson, 1-19. Provo, UT: Brigham Young University Press, 1978.

Eliza R. Snow, An Immortal: Selected Writings of Eliza R. Snow. Salt Lake City, UT: 1957.

Life and Labors of Eliza R. Snow Smith. Salt Lake City, UT: Juvenile Instructor Office, 1888.

Snow, Eliza R. *Poems: Religious, Historical, and Political.* 2 vols. Vol. I, Liverpool, England: 1865. Vol. II, Salt Lake City, UT: 1877.

★887★
SNOW, Lorenzo
President, Church of Jesus Christ of Latter-day Saints
b. Apr. 3, 1814, Mantua, Ohio
d. Oct. 10, 1901, Salt Lake City, Utah

Lorenzo Snow, fifth president of the Church of Jesus Christ of Latter-day Saints, was the son of Oliver and Rosetta Leonora Pettibone Snow. At least two members of his family, his mother and his sister, **Eliza Roxey Snow**, were converted and baptized when Snow was 17. It was not until 1836, however, that he moved to Kirtland, Ohio, where the church was then headquartered, and was himself baptized. He served his first mission touring Ohio in 1837 and subsequently worked his way through Kentucky, Illinois, and Missouri. In 1840 he went to England, where he presented a copy of the Book of Mormon to Queen Victoria. While in England he composed a saying which is remembered today as an important summary of Mormon teaching: As man now is, God once was; As God now is, man may become.

Snow married for the first time in 1844. His first wife, Harriet Amelia Squires, left him the following year, at which time he also entered plural marriage, marrying two sisters, Mary Ann and Hannah Goddard, in the same ceremony. Snow took a third wife, Sarah Ann Pritchard, in 1848. During the last years of the decade he returned to Europe, where he translated the Book of Mormon into Italian and opened mission work in Switzerland. In 1849 he was called to be a member of the Quorum of the Twelve Apostles. Among his most important duties during the next 20 years was the establishment of Brigham City, Utah, in 1853, and the organization of the Brigham City Mercantile and Manufacturing Association, a communal enterprise for the production and distribution of goods. He also married five more times—to Eleanor Houtz (1848), Caroline Horton (1953), Mary Elizabeth Houtz (1857), Phoebe Amelia Woodruff (1859), and Sarah Minnie Jenson (1871). In 1873 Snow was named a counselor to church president Brigham Young.

In 1885, during the height of anti-polygamy activity by the government, Snow was arrested for "unlawful cohabitation." Convicted, he served nine months and was released at the beginning of 1887. Two years later he was elected president of the Quorum of the Twelve, and in 1893 he became president of the Salt Lake City Temple. He continued in these two offices until 1898, when he became the fifth president of the church.

Snow's brief three-year presidency is remembered for two reasons. First, it was filled with rumors of continuing polygamous marriages being authorized, a fact confirmed in later years. Second, it was marked by Snow's ability to turn the church's finances around by initiating new policies that by 1906 had largely erased the church's debts.

Snow died in Salt Lake City at the age of 87.

Sources:

Jensen, Andrew. *Latter Day Saints Biographical Encyclopedia* 4 vols. Salt Lake City, UT: Andrew Jensen History Co., 1901.

Roberts, B. H. *A Comprehensive History of the Church of Jesus Christ of Latter-day Saints.* 6 vols. Salt Lake City, UT: Deseret News Press, 1930. 6 Vols.

Romney, Thomas C. *The Life of Lorenzo Snow.* Salt Lake City, UT: Deseret News Press, 1955.

Smith, Eliza R. Snow. *Biography and Family Record of Lorenzo Snow.* Salt Lake City, UT: Deseret News Company, 1884.

Van Wagoner, Richard S., and Steven C. Walker. *A Book of Mormons.* Salt Lake City, UT: Signature Books, 1982. 454 pp.

★ 888 ★
SOCKMAN, Ralph Washington
Minister, Methodist Episcopal Church
b. Oct. 1, 1889, Mt. Vernon, Ohio
d. Aug. 29, 1970, New York, New York

Ralph Washington Sockman, one of the most prominent Methodist ministers during the middle of the twentieth century, was the son of Rigdon Potter and Harriet O. Ash Sockman. He attended Ohio Wesleyan University, taking his A.B. degree in 1913. He then journeyed to New York for graduate work. He entered Columbia University and received his masters degree in 1913. In the meantime he had become an active member of the Madison Avenue Methodist Episcopal Church and decided to enter the ministry. He attended Union Theological Seminary, adjacent to Columbia, and graduated in 1916. During his Union years he was strongly influenced by liberal Baptist minister **Harry Emerson Fosdick**, under whom he studied. Also in 1916, he married Zellah Widmer Endly.

Sockman had joined the New York Conference of the Methodist Episcopal Church and following his graduation became associate minister at Madison Avenue. In 1917 he received his Ph.D. from Columbia University. He was ordained elder and appointed as senior pastor at Madison Avenue. He was already in the process of setting a record in Methodism, as he was to be reappointed to the same parish for the remainder of his career, the only Methodist minister before or since to serve only one parish. (Methodists, as a rule, are appointed every few years to a different parish.)

Under Sockman, Madison Avenue grew into one of the most important pulpits in the Methodist Episcopal Church. In 1934, the congregation moved into new facilities on Park Avenue and henceforth became known simply as Christ Church. Sockman had already gained distinction as a master of the sermon. In 1928 he delivered his first sermon on the NBC radio network and frequently spoke for the young network over the next eight years until succeeding **S. Parkes Cadman** as minister for the National Radio Pulpit. He ministered for 38 years on the show, in later years adding a television show. The show brought him fame far beyond Methodism, and at its height he received 30,000 letters annually.

The broad ministry of Sockman's radio sermons was further extended by his writings. He authored over 20 books, many compilations of his best sermons. His first book, *Suburbs of Christianity*, appeared in 1924. Three of his later books became selections of the Religious Book Club: *The Higher Happiness* (1950); *How to*

Believe (1953); and *The Whole Armor of God* (1955). The Pulpit Book Club selected *Man's First Love* (1958).

Peace was a major concern throughout his life. In 1928 he became chairman of the World Peace Commission of the Methodist Episcopal Church, a position he held for many years. He also became president of the Carnegie Foundation's Church Peace Union. During World War II he took the lead in preparing the churches for the rebuilding of war-torn countries once peace was restored.

While pastor at Christ Church, Sockman assumed additional duties. In 1940 he became chaplain at New York University. In 1947-1948 he was a visiting professor in homiletics at Yale University. From 1949 to 1962 he was an associate professor at Union Theological Seminary, following with two years as the Harry Emerson Fosdick Visiting Professor at Union. He consistently turned down suggestions that he be nominated for bishop, preferring to remain at his pulpit.

Sockman retired in 1961, after 44 years at Christ Church. He was named minister emeritus. He became the director of the Hall of Fame for Great Americans at New York University and worked on one of his last books, *Faith of the Famous*. He died after a brief illness in 1970.

Sources:

Harmon, Nolan B. *The Encyclopedia of World Methodism.* 2 vols. Nashville: United Methodist Publishing House, 1974.

Sockman, Ralph Washington. *The Higher Happiness.* New York: Abingdon Press, 1950. 174 pp.

_____. *How to Believe.* Garden City, NY: Doubleday, 1953. 224 pp.

_____. *The Meaning of Suffering.* New York: Board of Missions, The Methodist Church, 1961. 143 pp.

_____. *Suburbs of Christianity.* New York: Abingdon Presse, 1924. 224 pp.

_____. *The Whole Armor of God.* New York: Abingdon Press, 1955. 78 pp.

Who's Who in the Methodist Church. Nashville, TN: Abingdon Press, 1966.

★ 889 ★
SOLARES, Maria
Chumash Indian Traditionalist Leader
b. 1842, Alaxulapu, California
d. Mar. 6, 1923, Santa Inez Indian Reservation, California

Maria Solares, also known as Maria Isidore del Refugio, who helped preserve the traditional religion of the Chumash Indians of southern California, was born in the Chumash Indian village of Alaxulapu, located near the Santa Ynez (Roman Catholic Church) Mission, at Santa Ynez, California. After the secularization of the Spanish Catholic missions in California in 1834, most Indians affiliated with the missions underwent extreme economic hardship and deprivation with a resulting loss of much of their ancestral way of life. Maria was born, and came to maturity, at a time when the Chumash were at the bottom of two cultures (American and Mexican) vying for control of California. American expansion into California eventually pushed the Spanish/Mexican culture down below the influx of Anglos, and that suppression weighed even more heavily on the Chumash people.

Maria's father was Benvenuto, one of the last Indian alcaldes (mayors) at the Mission Santa Ynez and a descendent of chiefs from the Chumash capital village of Calahuasa, located southeast of Santa Ynez, California. Maria's mother was Shiguashayum, also known as Brigida, and she too was the descendent and close relative of chiefs of the inland Chumash, and the southern San Joaquin Valley Yokut tribe of Indians. As a result, Maria grew up in a multilingual, multi-cultural environment from which she learned several languages, and was privy to the surviving but hidden culture of the Chumash.

Maria married three times, and those unions produced at least three children who lived to maturity. Maria's last marriage was to Manuel Solares, whose father, Rafael, was one of the last *antap* (literally, "to enter"). The antap were essentially a secret society of Chumash, and the word signifies someone who could enter the sacred enclosures used during religious ceremonies. Maria became part of Rafael's household and later in life exhibited a significant amount of knowledge of the antap religion.

The Santa Ynez group of Indians were relocated in the 1850s from near the Mission Santa Ynez to a location several miles to the east known as Zanja de Cota, later to be named the Santa Ynez Indian Reservation. Maria became well known in the Indian, Mexican, and white communities as an Indian doctor and midwife. She delivered an uncounted number of children and used herbs to heal afflictions in the place of white doctors, who refused to treat Indians and Mexicans in the Santa Ynez Valley. She served as the godmother to a number of Indian and Mexican children upon their baptism into the Roman Catholic Church, an indication of her ability to successfully juggle two religions in one lifetime. When Maria was at an advanced age she collaborated with John Peabody Harrington, from the Smithsonian Institution's Bureau of American Ethnology to study Chumash culture and religion.

The importance of Maria Solares in the preservation of knowledge of Chumash cosmology was not known until 1975 when Thomas Blackburn published a number of narratives from Harrington's Chumash collection under the title of *December's Child*. Material collected from Maria Solares made up nearly half of the published narratives in Blackburn's book and included the volume's most detailed descriptions of Chumash religious beliefs. Many of the current day residents of the Santa Ynez Indian Reservation trace their ancestry to Maria Solares. As more of the Harrington material was published by scholars, Solares was recognized by her descendents as someone who, at a critical historical juncture, preserved and passed on important cultural and religious information. Maria Solares died at the Santa Ynez Indian Reservation on March 6, 1923.

Sources:

Blackburn, Thomas. *December's Child*. Berkeley, CA: University of California Press, 1975.

Hudson, Travis. *Breath of the Sun*. Banning, CA: Malki Museum Press, 1979.

—*Johnny Flynn*

★890★
SPANGLER, David
Author, New Age Movement
Founder, Lorian Association
b. Jan. 7, 1945, Columbus, Ohio

David Spangler is a popular author and one of the major theoreticians of the New Age Movement. He was raised in a family in which there was an interest in psychic phenomena, and as a teenager participated in the theosophical groups that were active in Phoenix, Arizona. He attended college for a brief period and then moved to Los Angeles in 1965. In California he teamed up with Myrtle Glines and founded a lecturing/counseling service that took them around the country. He began to develop his notion of the New Age, and in 1967 authored a booklet, *The Christ and the New Age*. He also began to engage in the practice of "channeling."

On a visit to Europe in 1970, Spangler stopped by the Findhorn Community, which was just then beginning to grow, and ended up remaining in Britain for the next three years. During this period he began to reject the idea that the New Age was an imminent event for which people should simply wait, and began to openly support the notion that the New Age had already arrived and that individuals must now take the responsibility for bringing it into manifestation. While at Findhorn he assisted the community's development and met Julia Manchester, whom he would eventually marry. He also gave an important series of lectures, later published as *The New Age Vision*, which helped to shape the direction of the community as well as the New Age Movement more generally.

After returning to the United States in 1973, Spangler, together with a number of other people, founded the Lorian Association in Belmont, California. Under the auspices of this group, Spangler traveled widely as a lecturer and wrote a series of books on the New Age, such as *Revelation, the Birth of a New Age* (1976); *Relationship and Identity* (1977); *Towards a Planetary Vision* (1977); and *Explorations, Emerging Aspects of the New Culture* (1980). In 1984 he published his autobiography, *Emergence, the Rebirth of the Sacred*.

In the 1980s, as the New Age Movement grew into a mass movement, Spangler continued to lecture and to write. As the movement developed a number of faddish elements, especially related to crystals and channeling, Spangler came forward to criticize what he saw as inauthentic manifestations of the New Age. He is particularly opposed to those varieties of New Age apocalypticism that keep people from actively working for a better world.

Sources:

Spangler, David. *Channeling in the New Age*. Issaquah, WA: Morningtown Press, 1988. 60 pp.

———. *Conversations with John*. Elgin, IL: Lorian Press, 1980. 28 pp.

———. *Emergence, the Rebirth of the Sacred New Culture*. New York: Delta, 1984. 176 pp.

———. *Explorations, Emerging Aspects of the New Culture*. Forres, Scotland: Findhorn Publications, 1980. 108 pp.

———. *Reflections on the Christ*. Moray, Scotland: Findhorn Publications, 1978. 130 pp.

———. *Revelation, The Birth of a New Age*. San Francisco, CA: Rainbow Bridge, 1976. 256 pp.

———. *Towards a Planetary Vision*. Forres, Scotland: Findhorn Publications, 1977. 151 pp.

★891★
SPEER, Robert Elliott
Missionary Executive, Presbyterian Church in the U.S.A.
b. Sep. 10, 1867, Huntington, Pennsylvania
d. Nov. 23, 1947, Bryn Mawr, Pennsylvania

Robert Elliott Speer, for almost fifty years the secretary of the Board of Foreign Missions of the Presbyterian Church in the U.S.A., was the son of Martha Ellen McMurtie and Robert Milton Speer. Speer grew up in the Presbyterian Church and attended Phillips Academy in Andover, Massachusetts (1883-1885) and The College of New Jersey (now Princeton University). During his college years he was deeply influenced by evangelist **Dwight L. Moody**. Following his graduation in 1889 he became the traveling secretary of the Student Volunteer Movement for Foreign Missions (S.V.M.) which had grown out of Moody's summer conferences in Northfield, Massachusetts.

In 1890 Speer began his theological work at Princeton Theological Seminary but dropped out in 1891 to become the secretary of his church's Board of Foreign Missions. In 1893 he married Emma Doll Bailey. Despite never having sought ordination, Speer's roots in the Student Volunteer Movement and the backing of the mission board allowed him to emerge as a dominant force in the early twentieth century movement to spread Christianity internationally. Speer made his first round-the-world tour in 1896 and emerged as a spokesperson for traditional evangelicalism. He helped organize the World Missionary Conference in Edinburgh in 1910. He came out in strong support of interdenominational cooperation on the mission field and encouraged the development of indigenous national churches in which he saw much of the future of worldwide Christianity.

Speer's leadership ability was recognized through the 1920s by his election as president of the Federal Council of Churches (1920-1924) and moderator of the Presbyterian Church in the U.S.A. in 1927. He also led his church's foreign missions enterprise through the years of the fundamentalist-modernist controversy. He downplayed the controversy, telling both sides that the need for missionary activity was too great to exhaust energy in theological wrangles. Thus he rejected the effort in 1929 of **J. Gresham Machen**, who complained that Speer's board was sending out modernist missionaries and led in the establishment of the rival Independent Board of Presbyterian Foreign Missions. In like measure, Speer rejected the overall perspective of the 1933 Presbyterian mission study, *Re-Thinking Missions* as representing an outdated liberalism; he authored a rebuttal in his *"Re-Thinking Missions" Examined* (1933).

While giving leadership to the missionary enterprise both denominationally and ecumenically from his traditional evangelical position, Speer adopted some liberal perspectives on pressing social questions. He argued for social justice and political access for racial minorities in the United States. He also wanted women given an equal role in the church. He retired in 1937, the same year he was elected president of the Foreign Missions Conference of North America.

Over the years Speer authored 69 books, including *Studies of the Man Jesus Christ* (1896); *Missions and Politics in Asia* (1898); *Christianity and the Nations* (1910); and *The Finality of Jesus Christ* (1933).

Sources:

Dictionary of American Biography. 20 vols. and 7 supps. New York: Charles Scribner's Sons, 1928-1936, 1944-1981.
Speer, Robert E. *Christianity and the Nations.* New York: Fleming H. Revell Company, 1910. 399 pp.
_____. *The Finality of Jesus Christ.* New York: Fleming H. Revell Company, 1933. 386 pp.
_____. *Missions and Politics in Asia.* New York: Fleming H. Revell Company, 1898. 271 pp.
_____. *"Re-Thinking Missions" Examined.* New York: Fleming H. Revell Company, 1933. 64 pp.
_____. *Studies of the Man Jesus Christ.* New York: Fleming H. Revell Company, 1896. 249 pp.
Wheeler, W. Reginald. *A Man Sent from God: A Biography of Robert E. Speer.* New York: Fleming H. Revell Publishing Company, 1956. 333 pp.

★892★
SPELLMAN, Francis Edward
Cardinal, Roman Catholic Church
b. May 4, 1889, Whitman, Massachusetts
d. Dec. 2, 1967, New York, New York

Francis Edward Spellman, a cardinal in the Roman Catholic Church, was the son of a successful Irish-American grocer, William Spellman, and Ellen Conway Spellman. He attended Fordham University, from which he received his B.A. in 1911. Having decided to enter the priesthood, he traveled to Rome and studied at the North American College and received his S.T.D. in 1916, the same year of his ordination. Back in the United States, he served as a chaplain at a home for the aged, as curate of All Saints Church, Roxbury, Massachusetts, and as a member of the staff of Holy Cross Cathedral in Boston. He became chancellor of the diocese in 1922. In 1918 he became circulation manager of the *Boston Pilot*, the diocesan newspaper, later serving as its editor (1924-1925).

Spellman's career took a distinct jump in 1925 when he moved to Rome to become attache to the Secretariat of State at the Vatican, the first American so honored. He was made a papal chamberlain the next year with the title of monsignor, and became a domestic prelate in 1929. In 1932 he was consecrated as titular bishop of Sila and named auxiliary bishop of Boston. He was the first American consecrated in Rome.

In 1936 Spellman oversaw Cardinal Eugenio Pacelli's visit to America and arranged his meeting with President Roosevelt. The tour cemented his friendship with Pacelli and launched his close relationship with Roosevelt. In 1939 Pacelli became Pope Pius XII, and before the year was out he appointed Spellman to fill the vacant archdiocese of New York. In part this appointment came in recognition of Spellman's relation to Roosevelt, with whom he had worked on the appointment of a presidential representative to the Vatican.

During his early years as archbishop, Spellman emerged as the most powerful man in the American Roman Catholic hierarchy. Part of his power came from his administrative achievments. Inheriting an archdiocese heavily in debt, he not only cleared the financial encumbrances, but developed an expansion program that included all of the diocesan institutes. He renovated the 400 diocesan schools, including St. Joseph's Seminary, and greatly extended the services offered by Catholic Charities. He also emerged during World War II as a leader in voicing Catholic standards for motion pictures.

Soon after the war, in 1946, Spellman was made a cardinal. His new position was used effectively as he became the leading spokesperson for a new outwardly looking Roman Catholic Church in postwar America. He had already accomplished a demilitarization of the Vatican by Roosevelt in 1944. After the war he championed federal aid for parochial schools (though he was unable to get the Blaine amendment, denying such aid, repealed) and supported Sen. Joseph McCarthy's anti-Communist campaign.

In 1966 he hosted the visit of Pope Paul VI to the United States, the first such visit by a reigning pontiff. That same year, the pope had turned down Spellman's offer to resign because of age. Spellman also emerged as a leading figure at Vatican II. He gave his support to the passing of the declaration on religious liberty which had been put together largely by **John Courtney Murray**, whom Spellman had brought to the council, and the declaration absolving the Jews of blame for Christ's death.

Beginning in 1942, Spellman made annual Christmas visits to troops stationed overseas. He died of a stroke in 1967 while preparing for his next trip.

Sources:

Cooney, John. *The American Pope.* New York: Dell Books, 1984. 445 pp.
Delaney, John J. *Dictionary of American Catholic Biography.* Garden City, NY: Doubleday & Company, 1988. 621 pp.
Gannon, Robert I. *The Cardinal Spellman Story.* Garden City, NY: Doubleday, 1962. Rept. by New York: Pocket Books, Inc. 1963. 579 pp.
Spellman, Francis. *Action This Day.* New York: Charles Scribners Sons, 1943. 256 pp.
_____. *Cardinal Spellman's Prayerbook.* New York: The Edward O'Toole Co., 1951. 693 pp.
_____. *The Foundling.* London: Hutchinson & Co., 1951. 228 pp.
_____. *No Greater Love.* New York: Charles Scribner's Sons, 1945. 147 pp.
_____. *The Road to Victory.* New York: Charles Scribner's Sons, 1942. 131 pp.
_____. *What America Means to Me.* New York: Charles Scribner's Sons, 1953. 111 pp.
Thornton, Francis Beauchesne. *Our American Princes.* New York: G. P. Putnam's Sons, 1963. 319 pp.

★ 893 ★
SPENCER, Hubert J.
Bishop, Church of The Lord Jesus Christ of the Apostolic Faith
b. Dec. 28, 1901, Marytown, West Virginia
d. 1964

Hubert J. Spencer, a presiding bishop of the Church of The Lord Jesus Christ of the Apostolic Faith, one of the largest Pentecostal denominations serving a predominantly black membership, was raised in West Virginia. As a nine-year-old youth, he was converted and joined Rockhill Baptist Church in Gary, West Virginia. At the age of 17 he received the baptism of the Holy Spirit (as evidenced by his speaking in tongues) and became a Pentecostal. He was called to the ministry, a calling which brought him into contact with another young Pentecostal preacher, Smallwood E. Williams. Williams led Spencer into membership in the Church of The Lord Jesus Christ of the Apostolic Faith.

During his early years, Spencer served as an evangelist and pastored several churches. In 1926 he was appointed pastor of Rehoboth Church of Our Lord Jesus Christ, a position he retained for the rest of his life. In 1928 the church's founder, **Robert Clarence Lawson**, named him as one of the original bishops of the church.

Following Lawson's death in 1961, Spencer was elected as the new presiding bishop. His term in office lasted only three years, but he is credited with holding the church together during a crucial transition period. Quite apart from the death of its extremely popular founder, the church had suffered a second recent trauma. In 1957 Smallwood Williams led a major schism that resulted in the formation of the Bible Way Church of the Lord Jesus Christ World Wide, and the church entered the early 1960s in a somewhat fragile state.

Sources:

Dupree, Sherry Sherrod. *Biographical Dictionary of African-American, Holiness-Pentecostals, 1880-1990.* Washington, DC: Middle Atlantic Regional Press, 1990. 386 pp.
Richardson, James C., Jr. *With Water and Spirit.* Washington, DC: Spirit Press, 1980. 151 pp.

★ 894 ★
SPICER, William Ambrose
President of the General Conference, Seventh-day Adventist Church
b. Dec. 19, 1865, Freeborn County, Minnesota
d. Oct. 17, 1952, Takoma Park, Maryland

William Ambrose Spicer, a national and international leader of the Seventh-day Adventist Church, was the son of Suzanne Manette Coon and Ambrose Coates Spicer. His parents were members of the Seventh-day Baptist Church and taught at Alfred University. When Spicer was eight years old, however, the family joined the Seventh-day Adventist Church and moved to Battle Creek, Michigan, where the elder Spicer taught in the Adventist school. When he reached the age of 10, Spicer was baptized and formally joined the Adventists. As a young man he began to work for the church and in 1887 journeyed to England to assist with the publication of *Present Truth* magazine. In 1890 he married Georgie Harper.

Shortly after his marriage, Spicer moved back to America and was appointed secretary of the Foreign Missions Board. His most important accomplishment over the next several years was the leadership he provided in establishing the Solusi Mission in Africa. He was ordained in 1893 and in 1894 moved back to England as the editor of *Present Truth*. He stayed in England for four years before moving on to India, where he initiated the church's mission and edited the *Oriental Watchman*.

In 1901 Spicer visited the United States for the purpose of attending the church's general conference. The conference decided to reappoint him a secretary of the Foreign Mission Board and, in addition, named him chairman of the Sunday School Department. Thus Spicer returned to the church headquarters in Battle Creek. In 1902 the headquarters complex was ravaged by fire. Rather than rebuild, the church decided to move the headquarters to the Washington, D.C. area, eventually settling in Takoma Park, Maryland. In the meantime Spicer continued to accumulate responsibilities, first as editor of the *Review and Herald*, the main denominational periodical, and in 1903 as secretary of the general conference. As editor of the *Review*, Spicer played a major role in defending church founder **Ellen G. White** from the critics of her prophetic visions, and in 1913 he produced his first major book, *The Hand of God in History*. Five years later he completed his most enduring book, *Our Day in the Light of Bible Prophecy* (1918).

Spicer had a passion for foreign missions; in whatever office he held he directed his energies to supporting the foreign missions program. In 1922 he succeeded A. G. Daniells as the president of the general conference. Spicer continued and strengthened the robust missionary program Daniells had developed. He served as president for eight years and upon his retirement was named the church's field secretary. He continued an active ministry as a traveling speaker and counselor. He also found time to write his last books, *The Spirit of Prophecy in the Advent Movement* (1937); *Pioneer Days of the Advent Movement* (1941); and *After One Hundred Years, 1844-1944* (1944).

Sources:

Anderson, Godfrey T. *Spicer: Leader with the Common Touch.* Washington, D.C.: Review and Herald Publishing Association, 1983. 124 pp.
Spicer, William A. *After One Hundred Years, 1844-1944: How the Work of Seventh-day Adventists Has Spread to the Ends of the Earth.* Takoma Park, MD: Review and Herald Publishing Association, 1944. 96 pp.
_____. *Certainties of the Advent Movement.* Washington, DC: Review and Herald Publishing Association, 1929. 283 pp.
_____. *The Hand of God in History.* Washington, DC: Review and Herald Publishing Association, 1913. 246 pp.
_____. *Our Day in the Light of Bible Prophecy.* Washington, DC: Review and Herald Publishing Association, 1918. 380 pp.
_____. *Our Story in Missions.* Mountain View, CA: Pacific Press Publishing Association, 1921.
_____. *Pioneer Days of the Advent Movement.* Washington, DC: Review and Herald Publishing Association, 1941.
_____. *The Spirit of Prophecy in the Advent Movement.* Washington, DC: Review and Herald Publishing Association, 1937.

★ 895 ★
SPRAUGH, W. Herbert
Bishop, Moravian Church in America
b. Sep. 30, 1896, Salem, North Carolina

W. Herbert Spraugh, a bishop of the Moravian Church in America, was raised in a Moravian family in North Carolina. At the age of 13 he attended an evangelistic service conducted by fundamentalist preacher **Reuben A. Torrey** where he made a public profession of faith. The next year he joined the Home Moravian Church in Salem, North Carolina. He was educated at the Tinsley Military Academy and in 1913 entered Moravian College in Bethlehem, Pennsylvania. Following his graduation in 1917 he entered Lehigh University, but dropped out after a few months and returned home to work in the furniture business. He served in the Army during World War I (1918-1919) and after his service married Ida Efrid in 1920.

During the years back in North Carolina, Spraugh decided to enter the ministry and to that end began a course of study at Moravian Theological Seminary. Following the completion of his work, in 1924 he was ordained a deacon and moved to the Myers Park section of Charlotte, North Carolina, to begin organizing a new congregation. The church, soon to be renamed the Little Church Down the Lane, grew and its ministry expanded. During this time

Spraugh worked on a masters degree, which was granted by Davidson University in 1933. Spraugh, a capable musician, began a Boy Scout Band, the success of which led to the spread of music programs throughout the Charlotte school system. In 1933 he initiated a radio show from the church built around music of the church organ. That same year he began writing a column in *The Charlotte News*. His column would eventually be syndicated and gain him a national audience. Over the years he authored four books: *Psalms for Everyday Living*, *Pathway to Contentment*, *Everyday Counsel for Everyday Living*, and *Pathway to a Happy Marriage*. His active pastoral ministry also included weekly healing services related to the work of the International Order of St. Luke the Physician. He also became an active supporter of Alcoholics Anonymous and helped organize the first Charlotte chapter of that organization.

In 1937 Spraugh was elected to the Charlotte school board, and would be re-elected in 1943, 1949, 1955, and 1961. Through the mid-1950s he worked on a plan to quietly integrate the Charlotte schools. He was named a bishop by his denomination in 1959 in recognition of his local and national ministry. He continued as pastor of the Little Church down the Lane until his retirement in 1966.

Sources:

Harding, Barbara. *The Boy, the Man and the Bishop*. Charlotte, NC: Barnhardt Brothers Company, 1970. 178 pp.

Spraugh, W. Herbert. Everyday Counsel for Everyday Living.

———. *Pathway for Everyday Living*.

———. *Pathway to a Happy Marriage*.

———. *Pathway to Contentment*.

★896★
SPURLING JR., Richard G.
Founder, Church of God (Cleveland, Tennessee)
b. 1858, Germany
d. May 24, 1935, Turtletown, Tennessee

Richard G. Spurling, Jr., one of the founders of the Church of God (Cleveland, Tennessee), was born in Germany, but raised in Kentucky and Tennessee. His father built a lumber mill and a gristmill, and passed them on to his youngest son. Richard G. Spurling, Sr. was also a minister, a role that his son similarly inherited. The father was one of the many people who felt concerned over the many denominations that Christians had separated themselves into. He was also concerned about the spiritual lethargy of the churches. Not finding fertile ground for his ideas in the Baptist Church, Spurling, Sr. and his supporters organized the Christian Union in 1886, a small congregation of which Spurling, Jr. found himself pastor after his father died.

In 1896 Spurling learned of a revival led by independent holiness preachers that was taking place across the state line at Camp Creek in Cherokee County, North Carolina. The independents preached sanctification, a second work of the spirit that would empower the believer to live a full Christian life. Many of the people attending their meetings had the experience of speaking in tongues, although the full significance of the experience was not understood until later. Spurling moved his church to Camp Creek and united the Christian Union with the North Carolina congregation. He humbly took a back seat to another minister, but reasserted his leadership in response to a disturbance in the church. The congregation adopted the new name Holiness Church of Camp Creek.

In 1896 **Ambrose Jessup Tomlinson**, a colporteur for the American Bible Society, stumbled upon the congregation. Inspired by what he saw, he moved his family to North Carolina, joined the church, and eventually rose to dominate the leadership of the group. As the congregation grew into a tiny denomination, the name was changed to Church of God in 1907. In 1908 a minister who was spreading the word from Azusa Street brought the Pentecostal message to the young denomination and, partly because of

the church's earlier "proto-pentecostal" experiences at Camp Creek, the Church of God very quickly joined the Pentecostal movement, which is built upon the belief that an individual believer's speaking in tongues is the evidence that he or she has received the baptism of the Holy Spirit.

Sources:

Conn, Charles W. *Like a Mighty Army*. Cleveland, TN: Church of God Publishing House, 1955. 380 pp.

Marshall, June Clover. *A Biographical Sketch of Richard Spurling, Jr.*. Cleveland, TN: Pathway Press, 1974. 29 pp.

Spurling, Richard G., Jr. *The Lost Link*. Turtletown, TN: The Author, 1920. 52 pp.

★897★
Sripad Bhakti Raksaka SRIDHARA MAHARAJA
Founder, Sri Caitanya Saraswati Math
b. Oct. 10, 1895, Hapayiya, West Bengal India
d. Aug. 12, 1988, West Bengal India

Sripad Bhakti Raksaka Sridhara Maharaja, an Indian spiritual teacher of the Caitanya Vaishnava tradition, emerged into prominence following the death in 1977 of **A. C. Bhaktivedanta Prabhupada**, the founder of the International Society for Krishna Consciousness (ISKCON) (the Hare Krishna Movement). Sridhara and Prabhupada were God-brothers, initiates of the same guru, Bhaktisiddhanta Saraswati Thakura, the founder of the Sri Gaudiya Math (monastery) in West Bengal, India. While Prabhupada traveled to the West, Sridhara remained in Bengal. He was thrust into the spotlight shortly before Prabhupada's death. Prabhupada told his disciples that they could go to Sridhara for advice. His words proved open to a variety of different interpretations as the movement and the leadership began to experience difficulties in the 1980s. While some kept their distance from Sridhara, feeling no need of his advice, others turned to him in place of the initiating gurus of ISKCON.

Sridhara grew up in western India and developed a strong devotion to Sri Caitanya, a medieval Bengalee saint, while in college. Caitanya had advocated a devotional form of Hinduism (usually called *bhakti*), centered upon the chanting of the names of God. In 1930 Sridhara was initiated as a *sannyasin* (One who leads a renounced life) by Bhaktisiddhanta and took the name Bhakti Raksaka Sridhara, meaning the "guardian of devotion." During World War II Sridhara settled in Nabadwip (also spelled Navadwip), the birthplace of Caitanya, and founded the Sri Caitanya Saraswati Math. Though he did not travel to the West as Prabhupada had, westerners began to seek him out and the work given into his care became international in scope through the 1970s.

Following Prabhupada's death, conflict developed within ISKCON over a number of issues, including the respect to be accorded the new initiating gurus. A liberal wing began to call for reform and some of the liberal members began to look to Sridhara for leadership and align themselves with the Sri Caitanya Saraswati Math. Among the first of these groups to appear was the Sri Caitanya Saraswati Mandel in San Jose, California. Through its associated Guardian of Devotion Press, it began to put Sridhara's books into print in American editions. Then around 1987 Tripurari Swami, a leader in ISKCON, left that organization and founded Gaudiya Vaishnava Society in San Francisco. The society's magazine, *Clarion Call*, is currently the major voice of Sridhara's followers in North America.

Sridhara gained a great deal of stature simply because of his long life. He was the last remaining initiate of Bhaktisiddanta, who had emerged as the most significant transmitter of the Caitanya tradition in the first half of the twentieth century.

Sources:
"Gaudiya Vaishnava Leader, Sridhara Maharaja, Dies at 93." *Hinduism Today* 10, 10 (October 1988): 20.
Sri Vyasa Puja: The 91st Appearance Day of Our Beloved Spiritual Master, His Divine Grace Srila Bhakti Raksaka Sridhara Deva Goswami. [San Jose, CA: Guardian of Devotion Press], 1985.
Sridhara Deva Goswami, Bhakti Raksaka. *The Golden Volcano of Divine Love.* San Jose, CA: Guardian of Devotion Press, 1984. 173 pp.
———. *The Hidden Treasure of the Sweet Absolute.* Nabadwip, West Bengal, India; Sri Chaitanya Saraswati Math, 1985. 374 pp.
———. *Loving Search for the Lost Servant.* San Jose, CA: Guardian of Devotion Press, 1987. 104 pp.
———. *The Search for Sri Krsna: Reality the Beautiful.* San Jose, CA: Guardian of Devotion Press, 1983. 153 pp.
———. *Sri Guru and His Grace.* San Jose, CA: Guardian of Devotion Press, 1983. 160 pp.

★898★
STALLINGS JR., George Augustus
Founder and Bishop, African-American Catholic Congregation
b. Mar. 17, 1948, New Bern, North Carolina

George Augustus Stallings, Jr., the founder of the African-American Catholic Congregation, was raised in the Roman Catholic Church and at an early age decided to enter the priesthood. He began his studies for the priesthood at the age of 16 and attended a preparatory seminary in Asheville, North Carolina, and seminary in Erlanger, Kentucky. He completed his studies in Rome, and was ordained in 1974 as a priest in the archdiocese of Washington, DC.

During his seminary days, Stallings had become outspoken in his demands for greater student voice in the education program. After his ordination he was assigned to St. Teresa of Avila Church in a poor neighborhood in Washington. He began to develop a liturgy especially designed for his predominantly black congregation. He used gospel music and drew people with his oratorical skills. Over the years the congregation grew from an average attendance of 200 to 2,000. He became active in a number of community projects, which included his serving on the board of MUSCLE, Inc. (Ministries United to Save Community Live Endeavors), a non-profit housing development corporation, and CONSERVE, a consortium to assist the homeless. Stallings was also invited to lecture at Mount Saint Mary's College in Emmitsburg, Maryland, and Washington Theological Union in Silver Spring, Maryland.

While at St. Teresa's he also became increasingly critical of the church's hierarchy and of Cardinal and Archbishop **James A. Hickey**. He accused the church of racism and Hickey of a lack of concern for the models for ministry he was building. In the midst of an increasing controversy, in September 1988, he was removed from St. Teresa's and named head of evangelism for the archdiocese. He was given the responsibility of bringing more minorities into the church.

Tension between Stallings and Hickey increased through 1989, with Stallings' demand that he be allowed to form his own Afro-American church. Hickey looked with disfavor on the suggestion. On July 2, 1989, in spite of Hickey's disapproval, Stallings formed Imani Temple, the first congregation of the new church. Within months four other temples had been added to the work. Stallings had become convinced that the all-male predominantly white hierarchy of the Roman Catholic Church could not respond properly to spiritual needs and aspirations. His actions and public statements soon led to a complete break with the Roman Catholic Church. The separation was consummated on May 12, 1990, with the consecration of Stallings as a bishop for the new church by Archbishop Richard W. Bridges of the Independent Old Catholic Churches of California.

Stallings describes the African-American Catholic Congregation as a church with its roots in Roman Catholicism that has begun to create an Afro-centric expression of the Catholic faith.

Sources:
Grogan, David. "A Black Catholic Priest's Renegade Church Stirs Up an Unholy Furor." *People* 32, 5 (July 31, 1989): 28-30.

★899★
STAMPS, Virgil Oliver
Gospel Singer and Songwriter
b. Sep. 18, 1892, Upshur County, Texas
d. Aug. 19, 1940, Dallas, Texas

Virgil Oliver Stamps, originator of the Stamps Gospel Quartet, grew up in rural east Texas, the son of Mr. and Mrs. W. O. Stamps. His father ran a sawmill and represented the district in the state legislature. The family were members of the Methodist Episcopal Church, South. Virgil learned gospel hymns as he was growing up, and during his early teens he attended the Upshur County Singing Convention and heard, for the first time, a gospel quartet. He loved the sound and resolved to learn to sing. He learned from local teachers and later was able to gain some professional training. From 1911 to 1914 he worked for his father in a store in Ore City, Texas, and taught at singing schools. At the age of 22 he wrote his first song, "Man Behind the Plow," which he printed and sold for 10 cents a copy.

. In 1914 Stamps took a job with a music company and for the next decade held a series of jobs with various concerns while learning the music business. He moved to Atlanta, Georgia, in 1917 and back to Texas in 1919. In 1924 he established the V. O. Stamps Music Company in Jacksonville, Texas. He also published his first song book, *Harbor Bells*, that year. The book was an instant success. Subsequent books, which appeared regularly, were built around the literally hundreds of tunes and lyrics written by Stamps, and were later joined by works composed by a stable of writers who worked exclusively for his company.

In 1926 J. R. Baxter, Jr., an old acquaintance from years in which they competed with each other as employees of rival music companies, joined the firm, and in 1927 Baxter became a partner. The company name became the Stamps-Baxter Music Company. Stamps remained president, with offices in Jacksonville and, after 1929, Dallas. Baxter, a vice-president, lived in Chattanooga, Tennessee. In 1934 the Dallas office moved into a new office that included, for the first time, their own printing plant, the largest in the country devoted exclusively to the publication of gospel music material.

Stamps headed a growing business and he expanded his activities. He founded the Stamps Quartet, still in existence a half century after its founder's death. The Quartet gained some fame as a back-up quartet for Elvis Presley during his final concerts. Stamps also organized the Texas State Singers Association and served as its president. He began *Gospel Music News*, which had a circulation of 50,000 at the time of his death. He founded the Stamps-Baxter School of Music, which trained tens of thousands of students to sing.

In 1936 the Stamps Quartet went on the radio for the first time as part of the Texas Centennial Exposition. After their initial appearance, they were offered a contract with station KRLD in Dallas. They performed at least one show daily on that station for the next four years. The success of the quartet and his Dallas show led Stamps to organize and supervise some dozen quartets that toured the southern states. At the time of his death he had applied for a license to open a radio station of his own in Dallas.

Stamps organized the first all-night singing convention in 1938. In 1940 the convention drew over 10,000 people for a program that went from 8 p.m. to 7 a.m.

Though a Methodist, Stamps worked with all of the Protestant and free church groups in the South and Southwest. His music pushed southern gospel music to a new level, and his work continues to influence the development of church music in the region.

Sources:
Precious Memories of Virgil O. Stamps. Dallas, TX: Stamps-Baxter Music and Printing Company, 1941.

★ 900 ★
STARHAWK
Wiccan Priestess and Author
b. Jun. 17, 1951, St. Paul, Minnesota

Starhawk is the public name of Miriam Simos, one of the best known of American Neo-Pagan Witches, who is especially important for having provided the Neo-Pagan movement with a "Social Gospel." She holds degrees from the University of California at Los Angeles (B.A. in art, 1972) and Antioch West University (M.A. in the feminist therapy program, 1982). While in Los Angeles she studied witchcraft with Sara Cunningham, who for several years headed the Temple of Tipareth in Pasadena, California. She moved to the San Francisco Bay Area in 1973 and studied Faery Tradition witchcraft with **Victor H. Anderson**, who was a major source of information for her first book, *The Spiral Dance* (1979). She was also a student of **Zsuzsanna E. Budapest**, one of the creators of the feminist Dianic Witchcraft.

In the San Francisco Bay Area, Starhawk founded the Compost Coven. She was also one of the original signers of the Covenant of the Goddess (COG) in 1975, a national association of Wiccan groups, and served as its First Officer for the 1976-1977 term. In about 1980, she was also one of the founders of Reclaiming: a Center for Feminist Spirituality and Counseling in Berkeley, California. Reclaiming is a feminist collective that offers classes, workshops, public rituals, and private counseling in the tradition of Goddess religion. She has served as a director, teacher, and counselor for the collective.

During the 1980s, Starhawk's book became the single most popular introduction to Wicca and Neo-Paganism. It was followed by two other books, *Dreaming in the Dark* (1982) and *Truth or Dare: Encounters of Power Authority and Mystery* (1987), which introduced themes of social activism previously absent from much occult thinking. She became one of the most popular lecturers nationally for the movement. Her work also led Roman Catholic priest **Matthew Fox** to appoint her as a faculty member of his Institute for Culture and Creation Spirituality at Holy Names College in Oakland.

Sources:
Starhawk. *Dreaming in the Dark.* Boston, MA: Beacon Press, 1982. 242 pp.
_____. *The Spiral Dance.* San Francisco: Harper & Row, 1979. 218 pp.
_____. *Truth or Dare: Encounters of Power, Authority and Mystery.* San Francisco: Harper & Row, 1987.

★ 901 ★
STARR, Eliza Allen
Writer and Artist, Roman Catholic Church
b. Aug. 29, 1824, Deerfield, Massachusetts
d. Sep. 7, 1901, Durand, Illinois

Eliza Allen Starr was an eminent Roman Catholic writer and artist of the late nineteenth century. She was the second of four children of Oliver and Lovina (Allen) Starr. Her father was a dyer who was a descendant of some of the earliest settlers of the Bay Colony. Although not highly educated themselves, Eliza Starr's parents encouraged their daughter to go beyond basic education, and she eventually went to Boston where she studied art and painting. Raised a Unitarian, she became dissatisfied with her Unitarian religious beliefs, and about 1845 began a religious search that led her

to convert to Catholicism in 1854. Religious themes subsequently provided the motifs for her art.

After working as an art teacher and tutor in a number of different cities, Starr finally settled in Chicago around 1856 as one of that city's first full-time art teachers. Over and above her private teaching, Starr gave an annual series of lectures which contributed to the cultural life of Chicago for two decades. Following the great fire of 1871 which consumed her studio, she spent several years at St. Mary's Academy, later St. Mary's College, in South Bend, Indiana, where she organized an art department. She became a well-known lecturer and writer in Catholic circles, publishing poems and art essays in the *Catholic World, Ave Maria, New York Freeman's Journal,* and *London Monthly,* among others.

After a period of travel in Europe, Starr published her two-volume *Pilgrims and Shrines* (1881). A long stream of devotional books, almost always illustrated by her own hand, followed, including *Isabella of Castile* (1889); *Christian Art in Our Own Age* (1891); *Three Keys to the Camera Della Segnatura of the Vatican* (1895); *The Seven Dolors of the Blessed Virgin Mary* (1898); and *The Three Archangels and the Guardian Angels in Art* (1899). In recognition of her work, she was awarded a Laetare Medal by the University of Notre Dame in 1885, a medallion from Pope Leo XIII, and a gold medal at the Chicago Columbian Exposition in 1893. She passed away at the home of a brother in 1901.

Sources:
The Catholic Encyclopedia
Dictionary of American Biography. 20 vols. and 7 supps. New York: Charles Scribner's Sons, 1928-1936, 1944-1981.
Starr, Eliza Allen. *Christian Art in Our Own Age.* Notre Dame, IN: Office of the Ave Maria, 1891. 68 pp.
_____. *Isabella of Castile.* Chicago: C. V. Waite & Company, 1889. 134 pp.
_____. *Pilgrims and Shrines.* 2 vols. Chicago: The Author, 1881.
_____. *Songs of a Life-Time.* Chicago: The Author, 1888. 400 pp.
_____. *The Three Archangels and the Guardian Angels in Art.* Chicago: The Author, 1899. 77 pp.

★ 902 ★
STEINER, Rudolf
Founder, Anthroposophical Society
b. Feb. 27, 1861, Kraljevic Austria
d. Mar. 30, 1925, Dornoch Scotland

Rudolf Steiner, founder of the Anthroposophical Society, was the son of Johann Steiner, a railroad worker, and Franziska Steiner. The family settled in Vienna when Rudolf was one year old. Steiner was baptized in the Roman Catholic Church. Young Steiner eventually entered the Technical College. He also attended lectures at the university, and became interested in the great German writer Johann Wolfgang Goethe. Steiner's interest developed into expertise, and because of his technical background, he was asked to edit and write the introduction to Goethe's scientific works for a critical edition. He became well known as a Goethe scholar, and some years later was offered a position at the Goethe Archives in Weimar.

At the same time that his scholarly career was developing, Steiner pursued his spiritual interests, publishing *The Philosophy of Spiritual Activity* while he was working at the Weimar archives. For a short time he belonged to the Ordo Templi Orientis (O.T.O.), a secret magical order, and was head of its Mysteria Mystica Aeterna Lodge. After moving to Berlin in 1897 to edit a literary magazine, he became associated with the Theosophical Society. From the beginning there were tensions between Steiner and the society over the issue of the centrality of Christ, which Steiner stressed, as opposed to the Theosophical teaching of Christ as merely one of many avatars (deities). Reflecting theosophy's ideals of tolerance and non-dogmatism, these differences of opinion did not prevent Steiner from becoming head of the German section of the society.

The situation changed, however, in 1910 when **Annie Besant**, then head of the society, announced that Christ, the World Savior, had returned in the form of a young Indian boy, Jiddu Krishnamurti, and formed the Order of the Star of the East as the vehicle for Krishnamurti's teaching. Steiner responded by asserting that no member of the German Theosophical Society could simultaneously belong to the new Order, an assertion that led Besant to revoke the charter of the German Society. Steiner took 55 of the 65 German chapters and in 1913 formed the Anthroposophical Society, a designation taken from a mystical work written by alchemist Thomas Vaughan, the *Anthropsophia Theomagica*.

Anthroposophy is a kind of Christian Theosophy. In 1922 Steiner founded the Christian Community to provide a more traditional church structure and liturgy for his followers. The high culture background of the founder of Anthroposophy has influenced the society to be associated with the arts. Steiner's educational ideas were institutionalized in the Waldorf School in Stuttgart. Certain other of his ideas have inspired biodynamic farming. Since the end of World War II, most of Steiner's writings have been translated into English.

Sources:

Easton, Stewart C. *Rudolf Steiner: Herald of a New Epoch*. Spring Valley, NY: The Anthroposophic Press, 1980. 376 pp.

Hemleben, Johannes. *Rudolf Steiner*. East Grimstead, Sussex, UK: Henry Goulden, 1975. 176 pp.

Melton, J. Gordon. *Biographical Dictionary of American Cult and Sect Leaders*. Garland Reference Library of Social Science, vol. 212. New York: Garland Publishing, 1986.

Rittelmeyer, Friedrich. *Rudolf Steiner Enters My Life*. London: George Roberts, 1929.

Shepherd, A. P. *A Scientist of the Invisible*. New York: British Book Centre, 1959. 222 pp.

Shepard, Leslie. *Encyclopedia of Occultism & Parapsychology*. 3 vols., 2nd. ed. Detroit: Gale Research Co., 1984-1985.

Steiner, Rudolf. *Christianity as Mystical Fact*. West Nyack, NY: Rudolf Steiner Publications 1961. 241 pp.

———. *Cosmic Memory*. West Nyack, NY: Rudolf Steiner Publications, 1959. 273 pp.

———. *The Course of My Life*. New York: Anthroposophic Press, 1951. 358 pp.

———. *The Philosophy of Spiritual Activity*. New York: Anthroposophic Press, 1932. 318 pp.

Wachsmuth, Guenther. *The Life and Work of Rudolf Steiner*. New York: Whittier Books, 1955. 594 pp.

★903★
Bishop STEPHEN

Bishop, Russian Orthodox Church
b. Feb. 27, 1857, Kalnik Russia
d. 1933, Graymoor, New York

Bishop Stephen, a priest of the Roman Catholic Church who briefly became a bishop in the Russian Orthodox Church, was born Alexander Dzubay, the son of Matushka Justine and Stephen Dzubay. His father was a Roman Catholic priest of the Eastern (Ruthenian or Uniate) Rite (which, in common with Eastern Orthodoxy, allows its priest to marry). He graduated from the Uzhgorod Theological Seminary in 1880 and the following year married Andrea Chuchka and was then ordained as a priest. Shortly after he was assigned to his first parish at Lokhovo, his wife died. He later served a parish at Uzhgorod.

In 1889 Father Alexander moved to the United States and was assigned to a Ruthenian parish in Wilkes-Barre, Pennsylvania. As one of the first Ruthenian priests in America (Ruthenia is the Roman Catholic designation for the territory south of Lithuania and north of the Carpathian Mountains) he spent part of his time traveling

around the country organizing Uniate parishes. His trips took him as far west as Minneapolis. He was among the prominent priests who welcomed Bishop Stephen Ortynsky, the first Ruthenian bishop for America who arrived from the Ukraine in 1907. In 1913 when the new Ruthenian diocese was officially established, Dzubay was appointed vicar general by Ortynski.

Over the next few years, for reasons that are not altogether clear, Dzubay became disillusioned with the work, and in 1916 converted to the Russian Orthodox Church (which was actively seeking converts from Roman Catholicism). He was tonsured as a monk and took the name Stephen. He was then consecrated as a bishop by Metropolitan Evdokim and assigned the task of bring more Roman Catholic parishes and priests into the Orthodox fold. Under Evdokim's successor, Metropolitan Alexander, he became the senior auxiliary bishop.

Alexander's problems with the Russian church began in the summer of 1922. Metropolitan Alexander retired and passed leadership of the work to **Metropolitan Platon**, who had recently arrived from Russia. On October 26, 1922, a month before the meeting of the diocese to confirm Platon's leadership, Stephen declared himself "acting head" of the diocese and consecrated Adam Philipovsky as bishop for Canada. Only after Patriarch Tikhon of Moscow confirmed Platon's position did Bishop Stephen end his schism and return to the church. His return was short lived, however, as in 1924 he left the church and returned to the Roman Catholic Church.

The Roman Catholic Church did not recognize his episcopal status nor did it allow him to function in a leadership role upon his return, and Stephen retired to the monastery at Graymoor, New York, where he lived the remainder of his days. He is remembered as but one more cause of trouble in the Russian Church which was, in the aftermath of the Russian Revolution, beset on every side by those who sought to control its destiny.

Sources:

Procko, Bohdan P. *Ukrainian Catholics in America: A History*. Washington, DC: University Press of America, 1982. 170 pp.

Tarasar, Constance J. *Orthodox America, 1794-1974*. Syosset, NY: Department of History and Archives, Orthodox Church in America, 1975. 361 pp.

★904★
STEVENSON, Joseph Ross

Educator, Presbyterian Church
b. Mar. 1, 1866, Ligonier, Pennsylvania
d. Aug. 13, 1939, Princeton, New Jersey

Joseph Ross Stevenson, for 22 years the president of Princeton Theological Seminary, was the son of Martha A. Harbison and Ross Stevenson. Stevenson's father was a minister, and he grew up in a pious home. He attended Washington and Jefferson College and graduated with a B.A. in 1886. He obtained his ministerial education at McCormick Theological Seminary, and in 1889 he both received his B.D. degree and completed his M.A. at Washington and Jefferson. He did a year of study at the University of Berlin and upon his return to the United States was ordained as a minister in the Presbyterian Church in the U.S.A.

Stevenson's first pastorate was at the Presbyterian church in Sedalia, Missouri. He stayed for four years before leaving the pastorate in favor of a teaching post as an instructor in ecclesiastical history at McCormick Seminary. While at the seminary, in 1899 he married Florence Day. He stayed at McCormick for eight years. In 1902 he once again became a pastor, this time at Fifth Avenue Presbyterian Church in Manhattan, one of the most prominent pulpits in Presbyterianism. In 1909 he moved to Brown Memorial Presbyterian Church in Baltimore.

After five years in Baltimore, Stevenson was selected to become the new president of Princeton Theological Seminary. In 1915 he was also elected to a term as moderator of the Presbyterian Church. At the time, Princeton was the entrenched stronghold of conservative Presbyterian theology and the center of fundamentalist perspectives in the denomination. Stevenson's own theological outlook was conservative, but he also had acknowledged the presence of liberal elements within the denomination and accepted the necessity of his working with them. Stevenson began to argue for a more inclusive representation of the church's theological spectrum on the faculty. His position brought him into open conflict with **J. Gresham Machen**, the seminary's leading theologian and an arch conservative.

The conflict at Princeton heated up over the 1920s and climaxed with a total reorganization in 1929. Machen and a number of his supporters, both professors and students, withdrew to found a rival Westminster Theological Seminary in Philadelphia. Stevenson emerged with more power in the president's office and quickly replaced the retiring faculty with other, more liberal, instructors.

While best remembered for seeing Princeton through the crisis of 1929, Stevenson served on several of the committees whose work led to the founding of the World Council of Churches following World War II. He served as an officer for both the World Conference of Faith and Order and the American section of the Universal Christian Council for Life and Work. Stevenson retired from his post in 1936 and lived quietly in Princeton the last years of his life.

Sources:

Loetscher, L. A. *The Broadening Church: A Study of Theological Issues in the Presbyterian Church Since 1869*. N.p.: 1954. 195 pp.

Reid, Daniel G., Robert D. Linder, Bruce L. Shelley, and Harry S. Stout. *Dictionary of Christianity in America*. Downers Grove, IL: InterVarsity Press, 1990. 1305 pp.

★ 905 ★
STEWART, Lyman
Fundamentalist Presbyterian Layman
b. Jul. 22, 1840, Verango County, Pennsylvania
d. Sep. 29, 1923, Los Angeles, California

Lyman Stewart, a wealthy Presbyterian oilman whose money helped launch the fundamentalist movement in America, was the son of William Reynolds Stewart and Jane Irwin Stewart, both immigrants from Scotland and devout Presbyterians. Young Lyman grew up wanting to become a missionary, but was instead apprenticed to a tanner, and this was the trade he practiced as the Civil War began. In 1862 he entered the Union Army and served for the duration of the war. In 1867 he married Sarah Adelaide Burrows.

Stewart's missionary career plans were most decidedly altered by the development of the oil industry at Titusville, Pennsylvania, the site of America's first oil boom. As early as 1859, Stewart attempted to enter the oil business, and after the Civil War he established a business buying and selling oil leases. In 1882, after years of only moderate success, he sold his holdings and left for California, where the oil industry was just emerging.

Stewart established headquarters in Newhall, California, eventually persuading his former partner, Wallace L. Hardison, to join him in establishing the Hardison and Stewart Oil Company. Stewart's brother Milton also soon came into the business. In 1890, the company merged with another company to become the Union Oil Company, centered in the oil fields around Santa Paula, California. While the company had its ups and downs over the years, oil made Stewart a wealthy man. His most successful periods followed the 1893 Los Angeles oil boom begun by Edward Doheny and the 1904 boom that was launched by the Hartwell field.

The forward-looking Stewart, starting as vice-president of Union Oil, began to actively develop the company not only in further dis-

coveries of oil, but in research, refining, and marketing. Over the next decade Stewart gained control of the company and in 1898 emerged as president. His son Will became the general manager.

During this period, Stewart had become an active layman at the Immanuel Presbyterian Church in Los Angeles, at a time when the Presbyterian Church was embroiled in the emerging fundamentalist-modernist controversy. Immanuel was within the fundamentalist camp, with a strong emphasis upon the traditional affirmations of evangelical Protestantism. During the first decade of the new century, Stewart began to divert significant sums of his earnings into the fundamentalist cause.

In 1906, T. C. Horton had begun the Fisherman's Club to train young men in Bible study and witnessing to their faith. The club grew into the Bible Institute of Los Angeles (BIOLA), an evangelical Bible college modeled upon the Moody Bible Institute in Chicago. Stewart largely funded BIOLA and brought **Reuben A. Torrey** from Moody to become its dean. Stewart also financed the building of the Church of the Open Door, in downtown Los Angeles, traditionally one of the most prominent independent fundamentalist pulpits in the United States. Torrey became the first pastor.

Stewart's most important contribution to the fundamentalist cause, however, was his and his brother Milton's financing of *The Fundamentals*, a set of booklets, each containing articles on major aspects of fundamentalist belief, which were mailed out enmasse to pastors across the United States beginning in 1909. Many date the beginning of the fundamentalist movement from the production of these booklets.

Stewart remained active in the leadership of Union Oil for the rest of his life, though he lost control of the company in 1916 when a court ordered its reorganization.

Sources:

Church of the Open Door, Golden Anniversary. Los Angeles: Church of the Open Door, 40 pp.

Welty, Earl M. and Frank J. Taylor. *The 76 Bonanza*. Menlo Park, CA: Lane Magazine & Book Company, 1966. 352 pp.

★ 906 ★
STRATON, John Roach
Fundamentalist Baptist Preacher
b. Apr. 6, 1875, Evansville, Indiana
d. Oct. 29, 1929, Clifton Springs, New York

John Roach Straton, a leading voice of twentieth-century Christian fundamentalism, was the son of Baptist minister Henry Dundas Straton and his wife, Julia Rebecca Carter Straton. He grew up in Alabama and Georgia, where his father served churches. In 1895 he entered Mercer University, where he quickly distinguished himself as a public speaker. His father's untimely death created financial difficulties that contributed to his inability to finish his degree program. At the end of three years of work, however, he was appointed as a lecturer in oratory.

Experiencing a conversion experience under the ministry of James Boardman Hawthorne, a Southern Baptist evangelist, Straton soon felt a call to the ministry. He entered Southern Baptist Theological Seminary in Louisville, Kentucky. During his first year there he was ordained and served the Baptist Mission Church in suburban Highland Park. He left the seminary in 1902, again without completing the course of study. The next year he married Georgia Hillyer and moved to Waco, Texas, where he took a job as a lecturer in oratory and literary interpretation at Baylor and served as pastor of a church in Hubbard, Texas.

Straton left Texas in 1905 to serve a series of urban parishes: Second Baptist Church, Chicago (1905-1908); Seventh Baptist Church, Baltimore, Maryland (1908-1913); and First Baptist Church, Norfolk, Virginia (1914-1917). He also served for a short period of time as executive secretary of the Interchurch Federation of Baltimore (1913-1914). In 1918 he began an 11-year pastorate at Calvary Baptist Church in New York City. This pastorate placed him in the heart of America's largest city during the height of the fundamentalist-modernist controversy of the 1920s. It also required that he move from the Southern Baptist Convention to the Northern Baptist Convention.

During his years in New York, Straton became the center of one controversial event after another. The controversies were generated out of his intense devotion to fundamentalist Christianity and the distress he felt at the destructive forces he saw operating in society. His oratorical ability and colorful use of language, as well as his willingness to encounter issues headlong, made him a popular subject of press coverage.

In 1922 Straton attacked the city's theaters as the dirtiest business in town. On February 12 he held a debate with William A. Brady, an actor who extolled Straton to preach to the actors and actresses rather than slander them. That same year **Harry Emerson Fosdick**, a Baptist preacher serving Madison Avenue Presbyterian Church, preached his famous sermon, 'Shall the Fundamentalists Win!' while the most famous reply was preached by Presbyterian **Clarence E. Macartney**. In 1924 he had a famous debate with Unitarian minister **Charles F. Potter** over several important fundamentalist issues such as the integrity of the Bible and evolution.

Straton's most famous campaign may have been one directed against Democratic presidential candidate Al Smith, condemning Smith, the first Roman Catholic to run for the presidency, as a deadly foe of moral progress. Straton devoted much of his time to traveling and speaking against Smith throughout the South. The intense schedule of the Smith campaign and his duties in New York took their toll. In 1929 he had a stroke; he died on the day of the stock market crash. The crash left his church in debt and hindered the work of his successors for many years.

Sources:

Dollar, George W. *A History of Fundamentalism in America*. Greenville, SC: Bob Jones University Press, 1973. 411 pp.
Russell, C. Allyn. *Voices of American Fundamentalism*. Philadelphia, PA: Westminster Press, 1976. 304 pp.
Straton, John Roach. *The Battle Over the Bible*. New York: George H. Doran, 1924.
_____. *Divine Healing in Scripture and Life*. Christian Alliance Publishing Company, 1927.
_____. *The Famous New York Fundamentalist-Modernist Debates*. New York: George H. Doran, 1925.
_____. *Fighting the Devil in Modern Babylon*. Boston, MA: Stratford, 1929.
_____. *The Salvation of Society and Other Addresses*. Fleet-McGinley Company, [1908].

★907★
STRAUGHN, James Henry
Bishop, Methodist Church
b. Jun. 1, 1877, Centreville, Maryland

James Henry Straughn, a bishop in the Methodist Church, was the son of James Henry and Laura Maria Simmons Straughn. As a youth he entered Western Maryland College, one of the schools of the Methodist Protestant Church, a church that originated in 1828 as a protest against the episcopal polity of the Methodist Episcopal Church. After receiving his A.B. in 1899, Straughn entered Westminster Theological Seminary, from which he graduated in 1902. He then returned to Western Maryland for a master's degree. In 1901 Straughn was admitted on trial to the Maryland Conference. He was ordained in 1903. The following year he married Clara Bellemy Morgan.

Straughn began his outstanding career in the pastorate at Mount Tabor Methodist Protestant Church in Washington, D.C., and later

served in Lynchburg, Virginia; Baltimore, Maryland; and Laurel, Delaware. He also served as president of West Lafayette College for four years (1906-1910) and as treasurer and promotion secretary of the general conference for four years (1928-1932). He was elected president of the conference in 1936.

Straughn is most remembered in Methodism for his work on the unification of the three branches of the church, which occurred in 1939. In 1935, due to the unfortunate death of Albert N. Ward, Straughn became the head of the Methodist Protestant Church unification commission and was immediately recognized for his ability and helpful insights during critical stages of negotiations. He also nurtured support for the plan of union which provided for an episcopal polity, contrary to the organization of the Methodist Protestant Church. His strong advocacy of the final plan greatly increased its level of acceptance in what was the smallest of the merging churches.

In 1939 Straughn became one of the symbols of the Methodist Church (the name adopted by the merged church) as the representative of the Methodist Protestant Church because of a widely circulated photograph of Straughn, Methodist Episcopal Church Bishop **Edwin Holt Hughes**, and Methodist Episcopal Church, South Bishop John Moore standing together with hands clasped. At the conference, the Methodist Protestant Church delegates were allowed to elect two bishops. Straughn was one of the two chosen. He was assigned to the Pittsburgh Area of the Northeastern Jurisdiction, a position he served until his retirement in 1948. During his years as bishop he authored one book, *Methodism* (1946), and he used part of his time in retirement to write his most important book, *Inside Methodist Union* (1958).

During his retirement years, Straughn also served on the board of governors of his alma mater, Westminster Theological Seminary. In that capacity he was active in the movement of the school to Washington, D.C., and in the adoption of its present name, Wesley Theological Seminary.

Sources:

Harmon, Nolan B. *The Encyclopedia of World Methodism*. 2 vols. Nashville: United Methodist Publishing House, 1974.
Howell, Clinton H., ed. *Prominent Personalities in Methodism*. Birmingham, AL: Lowrey Press, 1945. 512 pp.
Moore, John Monroe. *The Long Road to Methodist Union*. Nashville, TN: Abingdon-Cokesbury, 1943.
Straughn, James Henry. *Inside Methodist Union*. Nashville, TN: Methodist Publishing House, 1958. 192 pp.
Who's Who in the Methodist Church. Nashville, TN: Abingdon Press, 1966.

★908★
STRITCH, Samuel Alphonsus
Cardinal, Roman Catholic Church
b. Aug. 17, 1887, Nashville, Tennessee
d. May 27, 1958, Rome Italy

Samuel Alphonsus Stritch, a cardinal in the Roman Catholic Church, was the son of Gerrett Stritch and Catherine Malley Stritch, both immigrants from Ireland. Young Samuel was brought up in the Church of the Assumption, just a few blocks from his home. Graduating from high school at the age of 14, Samuel was sent to St. Gregory's Minor Seminary in Cincinnati, Ohio. He had already decided to enter the priesthood. He moved on from Cincinnati to Rome, and there completed his studies for his Ph.D. in 1906 and his D.D. in 1910. He was 22 and ready for ordination, but too young. Presented to Pope Pius X, Stritch was granted a dispensation for immediate ordination to the priesthood.

Returning to the United States, he served as curate (1910-1911) and then pastor (1911-1915) of St. Patrick's Church in Memphis, Tennessee. He rose quickly after being appointed secretary to the bishop of Nashville in 1915. That same year he became chancellor of the diocese and superintendent of the diocese school. In 1921 he was made a domestic prelate with the title of monsignor, but before the year was out he was consecrated bishop of Toledo, Ohio, and, still in his early thirties, emerged as the youngest of the American bishops.

Stritch spent only nine years in Toledo but succeeded in building 24 new churches, a new cathedral, and the first diocesan teacher's college in the country. In 1930 he became archbishop of Milwaukee. For nine years, he fought the depression, but again expanded the archdiocese and created its newspaper, the *Catholic Herald Citizen*.

In 1939 Stritch began a 19-year reign as archbishop of Chicago. He immediately plunged into work on social issues facing the archdiocese. While in Milwaukee he had headed the Department of Social Action of the National Catholic Welfare Conference . The same year he moved to Chicago, however, he became its chairman of the board, serving another term in 1945. He focused upon the problems of Puerto Ricans and Blacks in Chicago. Further, he supported the Back of the Yards Council to improve inner city conditions. In the early 1940s he moved to integrate all diocesan institutions.

Stritch also moved to build the archdiocese. He was a firm believer in the power of media communication. He developed *The New World*, the diocesan newspaper, whose circulation went from 10,000 to 210,000 during his reign. He also established a diocesan office for radio and television.

Stritch was made a cardinal in 1946. Among his first actions was the mounting of a new propaganda crusade against Communism through the Holy Name Society. In 1958 Stritch was called to Rome as the sub-prefect of the Congregation for the Propaganda of the Faith, the Curia's missionary arm. He was the first American to be appointed to such a high post in the papal administration. Unfortunately he died of a stroke just two months after his appointment.

Sources:

Delaney, John J. *Dictionary of American Catholic Biography*. Garden City, NY: Doubleday & Company, 1988. 621 pp.

Thornton, Francis Beauchesne. *Our American Princes*. New York: G. P. Putnam's Sons, 1963. 319 pp.

★ 909 ★
STRONG, Augustus Hopkins
Theologian, Northern Baptist Convention
b. Aug. 3, 1836, Rochester, New York
d. Nov. 29, 1921, Rochester, New York

Augustus Hopkins Strong, whose theological work influenced several generations of Baptist ministers, was the son of Alvah and Catherine Hopkins Strong and the descendent of an old colonial family. His father was the publisher of the *Rochester Democrat*, a local newspaper. Strong did his preparatory work at Rochester Collegiate Institute, and after a year working in business, he attended Yale University, from which he graduated in 1857. He returned to his hometown to attend the Rochester Theological Seminary and in 1859, as was becoming the fashion, he spent a year in Germany, at the University of Berlin.

Upon his return to the United States, Strong accepted a call to pastor the First Baptist Church at Haverhill, Massachusetts, and was ordained. That same year he married Harriet Louise Savage. He moved from Haverhill to the First Baptist Church, Cleveland, Ohio, in 1865. While in Cleveland, he became acquainted with John D. Rockefeller, who was a member of his congregation. Eventually Strong's daughter would marry one of Rockefeller's sons.

In 1872 Strong was called to become president and professor of biblical theology at his alma mater in Rochester; he retained both

positions until his retirement in 1912. As a theologian, Strong emerged on the more conservative wing of American Baptists, though he promoted historical critical thinking. His *Systematic Theology*, first published in 1886 and revised on several occasions, remained in print for many years as a popular text. Other titles include *Philosophy and Religion* (1888); *The Great Poets and Their Theology* (1897); *Christ in Creation and Ethical Monism* (1899); and a two-volume collection of writings, *Miscellanies* (1912). A collection of sermons, *One Hundred Chapel Talks to Theological Students*, appeared in 1913.

Though a conservative theologically, Strong, as the seminary's president, had to deal with a faculty whose opinions were among the most radical of the day and with whom he personally disagreed. He emerged as a champion of academic freedom and refused to censure professors with different ideas. Among the most outspoken on the faculty was **Walter Rauschenbusch**, generally regarded as the father of the social gospel, who complained often about the church's lack of social conscience.

In 1912 Strong retired. As president emeritus he continued to write, though in a lighter vein. He authored *Union with Christ* (1913); *Popular Lectures on the Books of the New Testament* (1914); and *American Poets and Their Theology* (1916). In 1916-1917 he made a world tour of Baptist mission fields and authored a report called *A Tour of the Missions: Observations and Conclusions* (1918).

Strong also played a role in the beginning of the University of Chicago. A long-time supporter of further Baptist ventures in higher education, he authored a pamphlet advocating the establishment of a Baptist university in New York City. He presented that pamphlet to his daughter's father-in-law and his former parishioner, John D. Rockefeller. He also introduced William Rainey Harper (the future president of the University of Chicago) to Rockefeller. While Strong's proposal was not adopted by Rockefeller, there is every reason to believe that his actions initiated the interest in financially backing a university that was eventually opened in Chicago.

Sources:

Dictionary of American Biography. 20 vols. and 7 supps. New York: Charles Scribner's Sons, 1928-1936, 1944-1981.

Strong, Augustus H. *American Poets and Their Theology*. Philadelphia: Griffith & Rowland Press, 1916. 485 pp.

———. *Christ in Creation and Ethical Monism*. Philadelphia: Roger Williams Press, 1899. 524 pp.

———. *Miscellanies*. 2 vols. Philadelphia: Griffith & Rowland Press, 1912.

———. *One Hundred Chapel Talks to Theological Students*. Philadelphia: Griffith & Rowland Press, 1913. 264 pp.

———. *Philosophy and Religion*. New York: A. C. Armstrong & Son, 1888. 632 pp.

———. *Systematic Theology*. Rochester, NY: Press of E. R. Andrews, 1886. 758 pp.

———. *A Tour of the Missions, Observations and Conclusions*. Philadelphia: Griffith & Rowland Press, 1918. 223 pp.

———. *Union with Christ*. Philadelphia: American Baptist Publication Society, 1913. 84 pp.

★ 910 ★
STRONG, James Woodward
College President, Congregational Church
b. Sep. 29, 1833, Brownington, Vermont
d. Feb. 24, 1913, Northfield, Minnesota

James Woodward Strong, a pioneer educator with the Congregational Church in Minnesota, was the son of Elijah Gridley and Sarah Ashley Partridge Strong. He came from an old New England colonial family, but in 1837 the family fortunes had been wiped out in the great financial panic which hit the nation. As a youth he held a variety of jobs including one as a school teacher. In 1851 he joined his family in the migration westward to Beloit, Wisconsin.

He was able to spend several years teaching school while preparing himself for Beloit College, which he was finally able to enter in 1854. He had to work his way through school and was further hampered by failing vision. However, with the assistance of a reader, he graduated in 1858 as class valedictorian. The next year he entered Union Theological Seminary in New York City. While there he married Mary Davenport in 1861. He graduated in 1862 and became pastor successively at Brodhead, Wisconsin, and Faribault, Minnesota.

While at Faribault, Strong became associated with a group of ministers and lay leaders who wanted to establish a college in Minnesota modeled after Oberlin and Beloit. In 1866 he became a trustee of the new college, originally little more than a weak preparatory school, which was opened at Northfield, Minnesota. In 1870 he became the school's first president, and made his first goal its development into a full college.

Strong began a fundraising campaign throughout the state but, exhausting his resources, he turned to New England. His success was marked by one $50,000 gift from William Carlton, after whom the school was subsequently named. Though the school was Congregational in affiliation, and is recognized to this day as a college of the United Church of Christ, Strong labored to create an image of the school as a nonsectarian Protestant college. He was successful in raising its academic standards and, over his 33 years as president, establishing it as a leading midwestern institution of higher learning, a reputation Carleton College retains to this day. He retired in 1903 and was named president emeritus.

Sources:
Dictionary of American Biography. 20 vols. and 7 supps. New York: Charles Scribner's Sons, 1928-1936, 1944-1981.

★911★
STRONG, Josiah
Minister, Congregational Church
b. Jan. 19, 1847, Naperville, Illinois
d. Apr. 28, 1916, New York, New York

Josiah Strong, minister and social activist of the Congregational Church, was the son of Josiah and Elizabeth C. Webster Strong, and a descendent of an old colonial family. In 1852 the family moved to Hudson, Ohio, where Strong grew up, eventually attending the local college, Western Reserve. He graduated in 1869 and entered Lane Theological Seminary. Following his graduation in 1871 he married Alice Bisbee, moved to Cheyenne, Wyoming, was ordained, and became pastor of the Congregational church in his new hometown.

Strong's life was a migratory one for the next decade. He stayed in Cheyenne for only two years before returning to Western Reserve as chaplain and theology instructor. He then pastored in Sandusky, Ohio (1876-1881), served as secretary of the Congregational Home Missionary Society (1881-1884), and as pastor of Central Congregational Church (1884-1885). While at Central church, he was asked to revise a booklet for the missionary society. He revised the booklet *Our Country* (1885) into a classic, late nineteenth-century statement of social protest and idealism. The book became a bestseller and led to his being appointed secretary of the American Evangelical Alliance, an early Protestant ecumenical agency. He followed with a second book, *The New Era*, in which he began to articulate what would become known as the social gospel. This emphasized that Jesus' message centered upon the concept of the ''Kingdom,'' an ideal society on earth in the present, and the belief that the Kingdom could be brought on earth by social change.

Strong worked for the alliance for over a decade, but eventually came to disagree with its emphases on individualism and the pietistic life. In 1898 he resigned to found the League for Social Service (after 1902 the American Institute for Social Service). He dedicated

the rest of his life to advocacy of the social gospel, seeing the church as an instrument of uniting people to work for the common good. In 1904 he extended his influence to England where the British Institute of Social Service was created. In 1908 he began a monthly periodical, *The Gospel of the Kingdom*.

During Strong's decades with the institute, he authored a number of books detailing his position, including: *The Twentieth Century City* (1898); *Religious Movements for Social Betterment* (1900); *The Next Great Awakening* (1902); *The Challenge of the City* (1907); *My Religion in Everyday Life* (1910); *Our World: The New World Life* (1913); and *Our World: The New World Religion* (1915).

Sources:
Dictionary of American Biography. 20 vols. and 7 supps. New York: Charles Scribner's Sons, 1928-1936, 1944-1981.
Strong, Josiah. *The Challenge of the City.* New York: Eaton & Mains, 1907. 329 pp.
_____. *The New Era.* New York: Baker & Taylor Company, 1893. 374 pp.
_____. *Our Country.* New York: American Home Missionary Society, 1885. 229 pp.
_____. *Our World: The New World Life.* Garden City, NY: Doubleday, Page & Co., 1913.
_____. *Our World: The New World Religion.* Garden City, NY: Doubleday, Page & Co., 1915.
_____. *The Twentieth Century City.* New York: Baker & Taylor Company, 1898. 186 pp.

★912★
STUB, Hans Gerhard
Minister, Norwegian Lutheran Church in America
b. Feb. 23, 1849, Muskego, Wisconsin
d. Aug. 1, 1931, St. Paul, Minnesota

Hans Gerhard Stub, a Norwegian Lutheran pastor who led in the formation of the Norwegian Lutheran Church in America, was the son of Hans Andreas and Ingeborg Margrethe Arentz Stub. His parents migrated to the United States in 1848 and his father was one of the original members of the Norwegian Synod. In 1861 he traveled with his father to Bergen, Norway. He remained there for the duration of the American Civil War, taking classes at the city's Cathedral School. He returned to the United States in 1865 and attended the synod's school, Luther College, for a year and was granted his A.B. in 1866. He attended Concordia College in Fort Wayne, Indiana, for the next three years and then moved to St. Louis to attend Concordia Theological Seminary. (The Norwegian Synod had not founded its own seminary and sent its pastors to Concordia, the seminary of the Lutheran Church—Missouri Synod, for training.) In 1872 Stub was ordained and accepted a call to the Norwegian Lutheran Church in Minneapolis, Minnesota. While there, in 1876, he married Diderikke Aall Ottesen. In 1877 he became a professor at the synod's new seminary at Madison, Wisconsin, where he emerged as a supporter of the Missouri Synod, opposing his colleague **Friedrich August Schmidt**. He moved with the seminary to Minneapolis in 1885 and to Robinsdale, Minnesota in 1889. During these years he wrote a number of books in Norwegian: *Naadevalget* (1881); *Udvaelgelsen* (1882), a defense of the doctrine of predestination espoused by the Missouri Synod which had been attacked by Schmidt; *Mod Frimureriet* (1882), a refutation of Freemasonry; and *Kristofer Jansen og Ludwig Helger* (1894). He also began editing *Evangelisk Luthersk Kirketidende*, in 1889. In 1879 his first wife died, and in 1884 he married Valborg Hovind.

In 1896 Stub retired from full-time teaching and became pastor of the church in Decorah, Iowa, though he taught part-time at Luther College. In 1900 he joined the Luther College faculty full-time and stayed there until his retirement in 1916. In 1899 he added the editorship of *Theologisk Tidsskrift* to his several chores. In 1901 his second wife died, and in 1906 he married Ann Skabo.

In 1905 the respected professor was elected vice president of the synod, and six years later he assumed the office of president. At the time he took over leadership of the synod, Norwegian Lutherans in America were divided into several synods whose geographical territory overlapped each other. Stub had already become active in the move to unite all of the Norwegian denominations into one church body. He pursued that task with vigor as president, and is generally credited with the accomplishment of the merger of the Hauge Synod and the United Norwegian Lutheran Church with the Norwegian Synod to form the Norwegian Lutheran Church in America in 1917. Stub was elected president of the new church and served in that capacity until 1925.

Following Stub's lead, the Norwegian Lutheran Church participated in the twentieth century drive to unite American Lutherans and is today a constituent part of the Evangelical Lutheran Church in America (1988).

Sources:

Dictionary of American Biography. 20 vols. and 7 supps. New York: Charles Scribner's Sons, 1928-1936, 1944-1981.
Nelson, E. Clifford, and Eugene L. Fevold. *The Lutheran Church Among Norwegian-Americans.* 2 vols. Minneapolis, MN: Augsburg Publishing House, 1960.

★913★
STUCK, Hudson
Alaskan Missionary, Protestant Episcopal Church
b. Nov. 11, 1863, London England
d. Oct. 10, 1920, Fort Yukon, Alaska

Hudson Struck, an explorer and pioneer missionary in Alaska, was the son of James and Jane Hudson Struck. He was educated in England at King's College, London, but moved to America in 1885. He settled in San Angelo, Texas, and became the acting principal of the municipal public schools. He also became a lay reader in the Episcopal Church. In 1889 he entered the Theological Department at the University of the South, Sawanee, Tennessee, to prepare for the priesthood. After graduation in 1892, he was ordained and appointed rector of Grace Episcopal Church in Cuero, Texas. Two years later he became dean of St. Matthew's Cathedral in Dallas, Texas. He had a fine record at St. Matthew's highlighted by his founding of the grammar school attached to the parish and a home for the aged. He was also a deputy to the denomination's general conventions in 1898 and 1901.

In 1904 Struck resigned his post in Texas to become archdeacon in the missionary diocese of Alaska, a post he was to hold for the rest of his life. In this capacity he helped direct the work of the Alaska mission and is noted for his work in founding a hospital at Fort Yukon. However, he is most remembered for his accounts of his travels around the territory, which were recorded in a series of books: *Spirit of Missions* (1909); *Ten Thousand Miles with a Dog Sled* (1914); *The Ascent of Denali* (1914); *Voyages on the Yukon and Its Tributaries* (1917); *A Winter Circuit of Our Arctic Coast* (1920); and *The Alaskan Missions of the Episcopal Church* (1920).

As a priest, Struck emerged as a defender of the native Alaskans and decried their exploitation by the more questionable elements of Alaskan society. While never questioning the superiority of the Whites who were establishing "civilization" in the wilderness, he argued that only education was needed to integrate the Indians and Eskimos into the emerging culture. To that end he established a library in Fairbanks.

Struck's books about Alaska stand as one of the most complete pictures of Alaska as it was in the early decades of the twentieth century. He covered most of the territory and made several spectacular trips, possibly the most arduous being his tour of the coast in 1917-1918. He entered the record books, however, for an earlier exploration trip in 1913 in which he was a member of the four-man team that made the first ascent of Mount McKinley. For this feat he was awarded the Back Grant by the Royal Geographical Society (England). Though he had no scientific training, Struck made up for his deficiency by his keen observation and descriptive writing.

He died in Fort Yukon in the home of the bishop. He never became an American citizen and never married.

Sources:

Dictionary of American Biography. 20 vols. and 7 supps. New York: Charles Scribner's Sons, 1928-1936, 1944-1981.
Struck, Hudson. *The Alaskan Missions of the Episcopal Church.* New York: Domestic and Foreign Missionary Society, 1920. 179 pp.
_____. *The Ascent of Denali.* 1914.
_____. *Spirit of Missions.* 1909.
_____. *Ten Thousand Miles with a Dog Sled.* 1914.
_____. *Voyages on the Yukon and Its Tributaries.* 1917.
_____. *A Winter Circuit of Our Arctic Coast.* 1920.

★914★
STUCKENBERG, John Henry Wilbrandt
Theologian and Sociologist, General Synod, Lutheran Church
b. Jan. 6, 1835, Bramsche, Hanover Germany
d. May 18, 1903, London England

John Henry Wilbrandt Stuckenberg, a theologian and pioneer sociologist within the Lutheran Church, was the son of Herman Rudolph and Anna Maria Blest Stuckenberg. His birth name, Johann Heinrich Wilbrandt, was later anglicized. In 1837 his father migrated to the United States. In 1839 Stuckenberg accompanied his mother first to Pittsburgh, Pennsylvania, and then Cincinnati, Ohio, where he grew up. He attended Wittenberg College at Springfield, Ohio, and received both his A.B. (1857) and B.D. (1858) degrees there.

Stuckenberg served a pastorate in Davenport, Iowa, for a year after college before going to the University of Halle in Germany for two years of graduate work. Soon after returning to America he became a Civil War chaplain in the Union Army (1862-1863), and served the remainder of the war as pastor of a congregation of the General Synod of the Lutheran Church in Erie, Pennsylvania. After the war, he returned to Germany for two additional years of study at the Universities of Goettingen, Tuebingen, and Berlin. In 1867 he began a pastorate in Indianapolis, Indiana. While there he authored his first books on the *Ninety-Five Theses* (1868) and the *History of the Augsburg Confession* (1869). In 1869 he married Mary Gingrich. Following a brief tenure as pastor at Pittsburgh, Stuckenberg became professor of exegesis at Wittenberg, his alma mater, in 1873. Seven years later he returned to Germany again, this time as pastor of the American Church in Berlin.

During the 1870s Stuckenberg had become interested in the newly emerging discipline of sociology, and during his last days at Wittenberg he finished one of his most important books, *Christian Sociology* (1880). He continued to pursue this interest for the rest of his life and later authored *The Social Problem* (1896); *Introduction to the Study of Sociology* (1898); and *The Science of Human Society* (1903), considered his most important work. He contributed 200 articles to the *Homiletic Review* between 1884 and 1902. During the majority of that time he also served as their editor in the area of Christian sociology.

Stuckenberg possessed a broad range of interests and accomplishments. While pastoring in Germany, his interest in philosophy was stirred. He joined the Philosophical Society of Germany and wrote a number of books in this area, including: *The Life of Immanuel Kant* (1882); *An Introduction to the Study of Philosophy* (1888); and *Tendencies in German Thought* (1896).

After retiring from the Berlin pastorate, Stuckenberg returned to America. He became the major Lutheran voice of his generation calling for the application of Christianity to social problems. In 1903 he died while on a trip to London to research another book.

Sources:

Dictionary of American Biography. 20 vols. and 7 supps. New York: Charles Scribner's Sons, 1928-1936, 1944-1981.

Evjen, John O. *The Life of J. H. W. Stuckenberg.* Minneapolis, MN: Lutheran Free Church Publishing Co., 1938. 535 pp.

Stuckenberg, J. H. W. *Christian Sociology.* New York: I. K. Funk & Co., 1880. 379 pp.

———. *The Life of Immanuel Kant.* London, England: Macmillan & Co., 1882. 474 pp.

———. *Sociology: The Science of Human Society.* 2 vols. New York: G. P. Putnam's Sons, 1903.

———. *Tendencies in German Thought.* Hartford, CT: Student Pub. Co., 1896. 272 pp.

★915★
Sivaya SUBRAMUNIYASWAMI
Founder, Saiva Siddhanta Church
b. Jan. 5, 1927, Oakland, California

His Holiness Sivaya Subramuniyaswami is the founder of the Saiva Siddhanta Church, the first Hindu "church" in America (founded in 1957). His early years were spent at Fallen Leaf Lake, about five miles from Lake Tahoe. At around the age of 10 he devoted himself to dance, particularly ballet. He was the leading dancer for the San Francisco Ballet Company by the time he was 19. He had mystical experiences as a child, and he was eventually inspired to undertake a spiritual quest. At the age of 20 he traveled to Sri Lanka with the intention of finding a spiritual teacher. For several years he practiced austerities and yogic disciplines until he experienced God-realization in the Caves of Jalani, deep in central Ceylon. Soon afterwards he traveled northwards to meet Siva Yogaswami in his Columbuturai ashram on the full moon of May 1949. Yogaswami initiated the young man and gave him the name Subramuniya.

Subramuniya returned to the United States and spent seven more years in intensive *sadhana* (spiritual practice), preparing for his life's work. During these years he also explored New Thought, Theosophy, and Hindu groups such as the Self-Realization Fellowship (SRF). At the age of 30, he began teaching in San Francisco. By 1958 he was able to buy a building in Sacramento that became the group's first temple. In the late 1950s and early 1960s, Subramuniyaswami called his group the Christian Yoga Church. The name was later changed to Saiva Siddhanta Church, and Subramuniyaswami has since been a pillar of orthodox Hinduism. Subramuniya swami founded the Himalayan Academy in 1965. The academy promotes Saivism through classes, lectures, retreats, home-study courses, and travel/study pilgrimages in Hawaii and India. In 1970, the church's headquarters were moved to the island of Kauai in Hawaii. At present the church has four monastery branches and 32 missions in seven countries. Most members are family people with regular professions, although there is also a monastic order which in 1988 numbered around 30.

In addition, Subramuniyaswami is the founder of *Hinduism Today*, the only English-language newspaper that concentrates on Hindu spiritual leaders. (*Hinduism Today* had previously been published as *Christian Yoga World* and *The New Saivite World*.) He has also been active in promoting cooperation among Hindu communities throughout the world, and has been instrumental in helping start several of America's major Hindu temples. His Holiness has authored several books and a large number of tracts, lessons, and inspired talks.

Sources:

Master Course Chapter 2: The Making of a Master. Kapaa, HI: Wailua University, 1971. 138 pp.

Saiva Dharma Shastras: The Book of Discipline of Saiva Siddhanta Church. Kapaa, HI: Saiva Siddhanta Church, 1986.

Siva's Cosmic Dance: An Introduction to the World's Most Ancient Religion, Saivite Hinduism. San Francisco, CA: Himalayan Academy, n.d. 25 pp.

Subramuniya, Master. *Gems of Cognition.* San Francisco, CA: Christian Yoga Publications, 1958. 108 pp.

———. *The Meditator.* San Francisco, CA: Comstock House, 1973. 69 pp.

———. *Raja Yoga.* 1958. 5th ed. San Francisco, CA: Comstock House, 1973. 193 pp.

———. *The Self-God.* Kapaa, HI: Wailua University of Contemplative Arts, 1959. 21 pp.

The Wailua Story. Kapaa, HI: Wailua University, 1972. 72 pp.

★916★
SUBUH, Muhammad
Founder, Subud
b. Jun. 22, 1901, Semarang Indonesia

Muhammad Subuh, also known as Pak Subuh (Pak is a term of respect), was the founder of Subud, a spiritual movement with its roots in Islamic mysticism. In the tradition of Asian hagiographies, his birth was said to be accompanied by volcanic activity and earth tremors. As a child, he had clairvoyant powers with which he could locate lost objects and foretell events. Unlike many other children, the young Subuh found that he was unable to tell lies to cover up his misdeeds. At the age of 16, he received the clear impression that he would die when he reached 32. Because other such intuitions had proven true, he decided to drop out of school and seek an explanation for this fate. He sought out spiritual leaders and gurus such as Shaikh Abdurrahman of the Nakshibendi Sufi Order, who either refused to take him on as a student, or who told him that his revelations would come directly from God. Abandoning his quest, he decided to take up a normal life. He became a bookkeeper, and worked at this profession for 14 years.

In the summer of 1925 Subuh began having spiritual experiences. In these experiences, light would descend into his body and fill his body with radiant vibrations. About a year after these experiences began, he received the impression that he was not to impart new information, but rather that he would eventually be able to impart this transforming experience to others. His desire to lead a normal life, however, made him shrink from the prospect of becoming a teacher of a new world view. He had nightly visitations of this light until early 1928, when they ceased. He led a life that was outwardly not unusual until the night of June 21, 1933. On that night he had an experience that led him to understand his mission of transmitting *latihan*, as the experience was called, to all who asked.

From this point onward Subuh began to devote less attention to his official duties, and he eventually resigned from his job as a governmental bookkeeper. He made no special effort to promote himself as a spiritual teacher, and the movement grew slowly. After World War II Subuh moved to Jakarta, and on February 1, 1947, Subuh's group was established as the brotherhood of Subud. The word Subud is an acronym taken from a poem written by Subuh in high Javanese, *Susila Budhi Dharma*. The movement spread to Europe in the 1950s. Subud found ready acceptance among the followers of **Georgei Ivanovitch Gurdjieff**, another teacher with roots in Islamic mysticism. Pak Subuh first visited the United States in 1958, and the movement expanded rapidly across North America. Sabuh's poem *Susila Budhi Dharma* has been translated and published in English, as have a number of his lectures and writings.

Sources:

Bennett, J.G. *Concerning Subud: The Story of a New Spiritual Force.* New York: University Books, 1959. 191 pp.

Melton, J. Gordon *The Encyclopedia of American Religions.* 3d ed. Detroit: Gale Research Inc.,1988. 1102 pp.

Subuh, Muhammad. *A Collection of Bapak's Ramadan Talks.* N.p. 1980.

———. *The Meaning of Subud.* New York: Dharma Book Company, 1961. 65 pp.

_____. *The Role and Recognition of Lower Forces*. New York: Dharma Book Company, 1961. 34 pp.

_____. *Subud and the Active Life*. Kingston-upon-Thames, Surrey, UK: Subud Brotherhood in England, 1961. 299 pp.

_____. *Susila Budhi Dharma*. Swindon, Wilts., UK: Subud Publications International, 1975. 391 pp.

★917★
SUMMERS, Thomas Osmond
Theologian, Methodist Episcopal Church, South
b. Oct. 11, 1812, Isle of Purbeck United Kingdom
d. May 6, 1882, Nashville, Tennessee

Thomas Osmond Summers, Southern Methodist theologian and educator, was orphaned in childhood. His father, James Summers, died the year after his son's birth; his mother Sarah died five years later. He lived with his grandmother and then with his great aunt under the guardianship of three men appointed by the Independent (Calvinist) Church. Though he had little formal education, Summers educated himself. In his late teens he entered a period of intense religious turmoil that led to his break with the Independents and their central doctrine of God's predetermining will. During this time of turmoil, he migrated to America (1830), where he experienced what Christians term the "new birth," and in 1832 he joined the Ebenezar Methodist Episcopal Church in Washington, D.C.

Within a few years Summers felt called to the ministry, and in 1835 he was admitted on trial to the Baltimore Conference. He was appointed first to the Augusta (Virginia) Circuit and then in 1839 to the West River (Maryland) Circuit. His entry into the ministry prompted an intense period of study, during which he taught himself Greek. He was ordained a deacon in 1837.

In 1840 Summers accepted a call to missionary work in Texas and became the only minister serving the Galveston-Houston area. His 1844 marriage to Miss N. B. Sexton in Tuscaloosa, Alabama, where he had been newly stationed, further strengthened his ties to the southern branch of Episcopal Methodism, which was in the process of becoming independent. During the next decade he served churches in Alabama while taking increasing responsibilities at the denominational level. He served as secretary for the general conference in 1845 at Louisville, Kentucky, at which the Methodist Episcopal Church, South was created. He was appointed chairman of the committee to compile a new hymnbook and named assistant editor of the *Southern Christian Advocate*. In 1846 Summers began editing all of the church's Sunday school material, a practice he would continue for the next 24 years. In 1850 he began a 32 year role as secretary of the Methodist Episcopal Church, South quadrennial general conferences, during which time he also served as book editor of the church.

In 1855 Summers moved to Nashville, Tennessee, where, except for several years during the Civil War, he was to reside for the rest of his life. Upon his return to the city after the war he resumed his highly productive career, beginning with his appointment as editor of the *Christian Advocate* (1866-1878).

In addition to his work on periodicals, the church's *Discipline*, and in hymnology, Summers wrote and/or edited literally hundreds of books on other subjects such as theology and prayer. Through his writing and editing, he gave direction to the Methodist Episcopal Church, South that lasted well into the twentieth century. His abilities were further acknowledged in 1874 when he was appointed professor of systematic theology and the following year dean of the theology faculty at the newly created Vanderbilt University. He held the post for the rest of his life.

Summers attended the opening of the 1882 general conference in Nashville, where he was again elected secretary, but he served only one day. He died before the conference adjourned.

Sources:

Fitzgerald, O. P. *Dr. Summers: A Life Study*. Nashville, TN: Southern Methodist Publishing House, 1885. 352 pp.

Harmon, Nolan B. *The Encyclopedia of World Methodism*. 2 vols. Nashville: United Methodist Publishing House, 1974.

Summers, Thomas Osmond. *Baptism*. Richmond, VA: John Early, 1852. 252 pp.

_____. *Fifty Beautiful Ballads*. Nashville, TN: Southern Methodist Publishing House, 1860. 205 pp.

_____. *Holiness, a Treatise on Sanctification*. Richmond, VA: John Early, 1850. 124 pp.

_____. *The Preachers' Textbook*. Nashville, TN: Southern Methodist Publishing House, 1869. 352 pp.

_____. *Systematic Theology*. 2 vols. Nashville, TN: Publishing House of the Methodist Episcopal Church, South, 1888.

_____. *Talks Pleasant and Profitable*. Nashville, TN: Redford, 1875. 144 pp.

★918★
SUMRALL, Lester Frank
Founder, Christian Center Cathedral of Praise
b. Feb. 15, 1913, New Orleans, Louisiana

Lester Frank Sumrall, founder of the Lester Sumrall Evangelistic Association and the Christian Center Cathedral of Praise, an independent Pentecostal congregation in South Bend, Indiana, was raised in a home with a devout Pentecostal mother and an irreligious father. He attended church regularly, but at the age of 17 his life changed when he was healed of tuberculosis, which was threatening to kill him. Three weeks later he left home and began life as an itinerant evangelist. In 1932 he founded a church in Green Forest, Arkansas, and was ordained by the Assemblies of God.

During this early period, specifically on December 18, 1931, he had a vision of the future fate of the unsaved multitudes. Coincidentally on that same evening, in London, England, Pentecostal leader Howard Carter had a vision of someone who would come to help him. Sumrall and Carter met 18 months later, and Carter invited Sumrall to join him in his missionary work. He toured the world with Carter, and then went out on his own. On a trip to South America in 1943, he met Louise Layman, a missionary with the Pentecostal Assemblies of Canada, whom he married a year later. In 1947 he became the pastor of Calvary, an Assemblies of God congregation in South Bend, Indiana, where he remained until 1952 when he left for Manila, the Phillipines.

Sumrall renewed his missionary role in the Phillipines. His work resulted in the founding of Bethel Temple in Manila, which became one of the largest churches in the country. After two and a half years in the Phillipines, he returned to his church in South Bend, Indiana. Having declined in the years he was away, the church soon revived. He also continued to concentrate on the plan he had used in Manila of evangelizing the world by placing strong congregations in the capital city of each nation. In 1959 he resigned from the pastorate in South Bend and moved to Hong Kong. Having already established some contacts, he began to duplicate the pattern from Manila and soon founded the New Life Temple. He also developed a literature ministry which sent Christian printed materials throughout southern Asia.

After establishing the Hong Kong Center on a firm basis, Sumrall returned to South Bend to found the Lester Sumrall Evangelistic Association (LeSea) and began strategizing on future missionary endeavors in such places as Brazil and Israel. Several years later he was petitioned to start an independent congregation, which was named Bethel Temple after the Phillipine church. In the meantime, Sumrall had withdrawn from the Assemblies of God. The temple later grew into the Christian Center Cathedral of Praise. The congregation has become the center of a complex of ministries, both in the United States and abroad, including the World Harvest Bible College, World Harvest Home for Orphans, and *World Harvest*

Magazine. The ministry has purchased two television stations, and Sumrall has a nationally televised ministry.

Over the years Sumrall has written numerous books, including his autobiography, *Run With the Vision* (revised as *My Story to His Glory*), several titles emphasizing his ministry of deliverance from demonic possession, and more traditional Pentecostal themes such as the gift of the Holy Spirit.

Sources:

Burgess, Stanley M., Gary B. McGee, and Patrick H. Alexander, eds. *Dictionary of Pentecostal and Charismatic Movements*. Grand Rapids, MI: Regency Reference Library, Zondervan Publishing House, 1988. 914 pp.

Lilly, Fred. "Lester Sumrall: Cathedral of Praise." *Charisma* 11, 4 (November 1985): 48-52.

Sumrall, Lester. *The Gifts and Ministries of the Holy Spirit*. Tulsa, OK: Harrison House, 1982. 266 pp.

_____. *Living Free*. Nashville, TN: Sceptre, 1979. 175 pp.

_____. *Miracles Don't Just Happen*. Plainfield, NJ: Logos International, 1979. 144 pp.

_____. *Run With the Vision*. Plainfield, NJ: Logos International, 1977. Rev. ed. as: *My Story to His Glory*. Nashville, TN: Thomas Nelson Publishers, 1983. 191 pp.

_____. *Supernatural Principalities and Powers*. Nashville, TN: Thomas Nelson Publishers, 1983. 142 pp.

★919★
SUN BEAR
Founder, Bear Tribe
b. Aug. 31, 1929, White Earth Indian Reservation, Michigan

Sun Bear (Gheezis Mokwa), who for much of his early life went by the name of Vincent LaDuke, is a Chippewa medicine man who founded the Bear Tribe, a community of mostly non-Native Americans that follows a traditional, tribal lifestyle. He is the son of Louis and Judith LaDuke. With the exception of a period during the Depression when the family worked as migrant farm laborers, he spent most of his early life on the reservation. He dropped out of school after the ninth grade, and at 15 left the reservation.

Over the course of the next several years, Sun Bear worked as a baker, construction worker, real estate agent, cook, and wood cutter. During this time he also traveled around the country, studying the practices of other traditional Native Americans, and eventually incorporated what he learned into his own synthesis of Indian wisdom. Hearing that draftees would be treated worse than volunteers, he joined the United States Army in 1952 during the Korean War, but deserted soon after basic training. After this, he continued to travel and learn, participating in the peyote ceremonies of the Native American Church, living with the Pomo, and learning the system of survival of the Washone Indians of Lake Tahoe. He eventually settled in Nevada to work with the Reno-Sparks Indian colony in downtown Reno. Several years later, he went to Hollywood to work as an Indian actor. The FBI finally caught up with him, and he spent six months in Lompoc Federal Correctional Institute in Lompoc, California, for desertion. Upon his release, he went back to Reno.

After some time, Sun Bear returned to Hollywood and acted in several major motion pictures, but eventually became disenchanted with the movie industry. In 1961, he began publishing *Many Smokes*, a newspaper that carried national Indian news. During the Free Speech Movement in California in 1965, he met Annie Ross (soon to be called Nimimosha), who was to be one of the founding members of the Bear Tribe. The Tribe was initiated in 1966 when Sun Bear and three non-Indian women moved from Los Angeles to Reno. The Tribe grew slowly, moved several times over the years, and split more than once over such issues as drug use and marriage practices.

The Bear Tribe focuses on self-reliance, and Sun Bear's apprenticeship programs teach survival skills as well as shamanic techniques. The Tribe sponsors the Medicine Wheel gatherings that are popular in New Age circles. The group also publishes *Wildfire* (the successor to *Many Smokes*) and markets a wide variety of books and ceremonial materials. In recent years, Sun Bear has become a popular target of attack by American Indian Movement leaders who perceive the current New Age interest in traditional Native American religion as a form of cultural imperialism.

Sources:

Melton, J. Gordon. *New Age Encyclopedia*. Detroit: Gale Research Inc., 1990. 586 pp.

Sun Bear, *At Home in the Wilderness*. Happy Camp, CA: Naturegraph Publishers, 1968. 90 pp.

_____. *Path of Power*. Spokane, WA: Bear Tribe Publishing, 1983.

_____, Wabun, Mimimosha, and the Tribe. *The Bear Tribe's Self Reliance Book*. Spokane, WA: Bear Tribe Publishing Co., 1977. 144 pp.

—*James R. Lewis*

★920★
SUNDAY, Billy
Evangelist, Presbyterian Church
b. Nov. 18, 1862, Ames, Iowa
d. Nov. 6, 1935, Winona Lake, Indiana

William Ashley Sunday, known popularly as Billy Sunday, possibly the most famous evangelist in America in the era around World War I, was the son of William and Mary Jane Cory Sunday. His father, a Union soldier, died of pneumonia just a month after Billy's birth. His mother tried to hold the family together, but in 1874 Sunday was sent to the Soldier's Orphan Home first in Glenwood, Iowa, and then in Davenport, Iowa. In 1879 he began life on his own and moved across the state. Along the way he held several different jobs and picked up only a modest amount of schooling. His main interest was sports, especially baseball. In Marshalltown, Iowa, his play for the local team attracted the attention of the captain of the Chicago Whitestockings who offered him a job. He joined the team in 1883.

While playing for the Chicago team, Sunday underwent a Christian conversion at the Pacific Garden Mission in Chicago. About this same time he met, and in 1888 married, Helen A. Thompson. She belonged to the Presbyterian Church, which he then joined. A short time later, he moved to Pennsylvania to play for first the Pittsburgh and then the Philadelphia team. During his last years in baseball he became publicly identified with his Christian faith, and in 1891 he quit baseball to go to work for the YMCA. In 1893 he began to work for Presbyterian evangelist **John Wilbur Chapman** as the advance man for the revival meetings. He did some of his first preaching in this capacity.

In January 1896 Sunday accepted an invitation to head a revival which Chapman was unable to lead. Word of Sunday's success spread quickly, and he became a full-time evangelist for the rest of his life. In 1898 he was licensed to preach by the Chicago Presbytery, and was ordained five years later. Sunday was one of the major persons who brought the evangelistic revival meetings from the rural countryside to the cities. From the turn of the century he spoke in increasingly larger communities, finally making it to New York City in 1917. He was remembered for his unconventional style which included folksy illustrations and, as occasion demanded, acrobatics. Out of his services came the phrase "hitting the sawdust trail," a reference to the sawdust covered floors of the tabernacles he spoke in, and the practice he had of calling those converted in his meeting forward to testify to their experience.

Sunday hit the peak of his popularity as World War I began. He spoke around the country denouncing the evils he perceived around him, especially liberal religion, alcohol, and most amusement, with baseball carefully excluded. He is acknowledged for building much of the popular support for prohibition. In 1915 three books credited to him appeared: *Burning Truths from Billy's Bat* (1914); *Seventy-four Complete Sermons from the Omaha Campaign* (1915); and *Great Love Stories from the Bible and Their Lessons for Today* (1918). Sunday had often been accused of plagiarism but, after the last book appeared, Hugh A. Weir sued Sunday, claiming to be ghostwriter of the volume. That suit, another the same year, and complaints that he had acquired a large fortune for which he had given no public accounting, decreased his popularity measurably. He continued to hold revivals for the rest of his life, but tended to stay in the smaller towns in the Midwest and South. He settled at Winona Lake, Indiana, where a large Billy Sunday Tabernacle stands today at the center of the Christian campgrounds located there.

Sources:

Brown, Elijah P. *The Real Billy Sunday*. New York: Fleming H. Revell Company, 1914.

Dictionary of American Biography. 20 vols. and 7 supps. New York: Charles Scribner's Sons, 1928-1936, 1944-1981.

Ellis, W. T. *Billy Sunday: The Man and His Message*. Philadelphia: John C. Winston Company, 1914. 432 pp.

Lippy, Charles H. *Twentieth-Century Shapers of American Popular Religion*. New York: Greenwood Press, 1989. 494 pp.

McLoughlin, William. *Billy Sunday Was His Real Name*. Chicago: University of Chicago Press, 1955. 324 pp.

Shuster, Robert, ed. *The Papers of William and Helen Sunday, A Guide to the Microfilm Edition*. Wheaton, IL: The Billy Graham Center, 1978. 60 pp.

Sunday, Billy. *Billy Sunday's Sermons in Omaha*. Omaha, NB: Omaha Daily News, 1915. 202 pp.

———. *Billy Sunday Speaks*. Edited by Karen Gullen. New York: Chelsa House, 1970.

———. *Burning Truths from Billy's Bat*. Philadelphia: Diamond Publishing Co., 1914. 103 pp.

———. *Great Love Stories from the Bible and Their Lesson for Today*. New York: G. P. Putnam's Sons, 1918. 329 pp.

———. *Life and Labors of Rev. Wm. A. (Billy) Sunday*. Decatur, IL: Herman, Poole & Co., 1908. 366 pp.

———. *The Moral Leper*. Fort Wayne, IN: E. A. K. Hackett, 1908. 32 pp.

———. *What Shall the End Be of Them That Obey Not the Gospel of God?*. Fort Wayne, IN: E. A. K. Hackett, 1908. 31 pp.

———. *Wonderful, and Other Sermons*. Grand Rapids, MI: Zondervan Publishing House, 1940.

Thomas, Lee. *The Billy Sunday Story: The Life and Times of William Ashley Sunday*. Grand Rapids, MI: Zondervan Publishing House, 1961.

★921★
SUNDERLAND, Jabez Thomas
Minister, American Unitarian Association
b. Feb. 11, 1842, Yorkshire England
d. Aug. 13, 1936, Ann Arbor, Michigan

Jabez Thomas Sunderland, a minister in the American Unitarian Association (AUA), was the son of Sarah Broadhead and Thomas Sunderland. He moved to the United States during his youth and attended the University of Chicago, from which he received both his B.A. (1867) and M.A. (1869) degrees. A Baptist at the time, he pursued his theological studies at the Baptist Union Theological Seminary and received his B.D. in 1870. In 1871 he became the minister of a Baptist church in Chicago. Sunderland's liberal education having influenced him, in 1872 he left the Baptists and became a Unitarian. His first church was in Northfield, Massachusetts. In 1875 he moved to Chicago, where the first major phase of his career would begin.

Sunderland emerged as a leading minister in the "West" for the Unitarians, for whom everything outside of New England was thought of as the "West." After a year in Chicago he moved to Ann Arbor, Michigan, as the local pastor and the Michigan state missionary. During his two years there he saw no less than eight churches formed in the state. During his early years in the West, he became a leading figure in the controversy touched off by Jenkin

Lloyd Jones, who argued that Unitarians should not be required to affirm the existence of a deity. Sunderland emerged as a leader of the conservatives. In 1886 he issued an initial statement in *The Issue in the West* and a year later founded *The Unitarian* to advocate the conservatives' cause.

Sunderland continued to edit *The Unitarian* and champion his conservative position until 1895 when he left for a year's travel in India. His observations abroad left him with grave doubts about colonialism. He returned to the United States to become the earliest American supporter of Indian home rule. He wrote a number of articles on the India question, became the Billings lecturer in India for the association (1913-1914), and later produced a book, *India in Bondage* (1923).

Through the twentieth century, Sunderland served a number of Unitarian pulpits. He moved to California after his return from India and pastored at Oakland for a year. He then served in succession in London, England (1900-1901); Toronto, Ontario (1901-1905); Hartford, Connecticut (1906-1911); and Ottawa, Ontario (1912-1913). Following his return from India in 1914, he settled in Poughkeepsie, New York, to pastor the last 14 years prior to his retirement. In the years after his death, a number of Sunderland's writings were reprinted as pamphlets by the American Unitarian Association.

Sources:

Lavan, Spencer. *Unitarians and India: A Study in Encounter and Response*. Boston: Skinner House, 1977. 217 pp.

Lyttle, Charles H. *Freedom Moves West*. Boston: Beacon Press, 1952. 298 pp.

Robinson, David. *The Unitarians and the Universalists*. Westport, CT: Greenwood Press, 1985. 368 pp.

Sunderland, Jabez T. *Because Men Are Not Stones*. Boston: Beacon Press, 1923. 156 pp.

———. *The Bible: Its Origin, Growth and Character*. New York: G. P. Putnam's Sons, 1893. 299 pp.

———. *India in Bondage*. Calcutta: R. Chattergee, 1928. 527 pp.

———. *The Issue in the West*. N.p.: 1886.

———. *The Spark in the Clod: A Study of Evolution*. Boston: Beacon Press, 1902. 162 pp.

★922★
SUNIN, Samu
Founder, Zen Lotus Society
b. 1941, Republic of Korea

Master Samu Sunin is the founder and spiritual director of the Zen Lotus Society. He was orphaned during the Korean War, and at age 11 entered a Buddhist temple. After finishing a three-year novitiate at Namjang-sa, he journeyed to Pusan. There he met Master Tongsan, who ordained him as a monk. In the early 1960s the Korean government required Buddhist monks of draft age to serve in the armed forces. Determined to remain true to the Buddhist precept against taking life, he deserted the army. While in hiding in 1963, he received the Dharma name Samu from Zen Master Tongsan, former supreme patriarch of Korean Chogye Buddhism. In the winter of 1965 he smuggled himself out of Korea in a freight boat. He then stayed for a year and a half at Zen monasteries in Japan.

With the assistance of friends Sunin was able to migrate to the United States, arriving in New York City in the fall of 1967. The Zen Lotus Society had its beginnings when he initiated meditation classes in his small Manhattan apartment. During the following year he moved to Montreal, Canada. For the next three years he worked, studied English, and offered training in Zen. He became a Canadian citizen. In 1972 he moved to Toronto. The next few years were exceptionally difficult for him. His health deteriorated and his marriage collapsed from a combination of poverty and cultural differences between him and his wife. He finally went to the hospital in a state of physical collapse, and spent the next few years regaining his health. Although he did not work with students, this period contributed to his maturity as a teacher of Zen.

Sunin re-emerged in 1975 and once again began instructing people in the practice of meditation. Hand-drawn notices brought students to the simple basement apartment where he resided. During summer downpours or spring thaws, the apartment would be flooded. Through all the external difficulties, the Master taught the pure and simple path toward true Enlightenment. He gradually built up a congregation composed both of Korean-Canadians and Euro-Canadians. An important step in the society's development was taken in 1979, when a large building was purchased and a new temple established. In 1981 a new temple was founded in Ann Arbor, Michigan.

The Society publishes a journal, *Spring Wind: Buddhist Cultural Forum.* In 1986 the Society established Buddhists Concerned for Social Justice and World Peace, an organization that has involved itself in such causes as appeals to the Thai government to continue their support of Cambodian refugee camps (phasing out the camps would force Cambodians to return to Cambodia, where Buddhism has been persecuted).

Sources:

Melton, J. Gordon *The Encyclopedia of American Religions.* 3d ed. Detroit: Gale Research Inc.,1988. 1102 pp.
Sujata. "The Zen Lotus Society." *Spring Wind: Buddhist Cultural Forum* 4, 2 (Summer 1984): 46-56.
Sunin, Sanbul. "Early Days." *Spring Wind: Buddhist Cultural Forum* 4, 2 (Summer 1984): 57-59.

★923★
SUZUKI, Daisetz Teitaro
Zen Buddhist Author
b. Oct. 18, 1870, Kanazawa Japan
d. Jul. 12, 1966, Kamakura Japan

Daisetz Teitaro Suzuki, a priest of the Hompa Hongwanji Buddhism sect of Japanese Shin Buddhism, is best known in the West as a prolific author about and popularizer of Zen Buddhism. He was born in a small village in the northern part of Japan to a Samurai family of modest means. A teacher during his early life, he moved to Tokyo after his mother's passing, where he undertook Zen training and attended the Imperial University. Suzuki was an exceptionally gifted student of Mahayana Zen, and in 1897 was sent by **Soyen Shaku**, who first brought Zen to a non-Japanese American, to help editor **Paul Carus** with the translation and publication of Buddhist works. He traveled to the United States and became an editor at Carus' Open Court Publishing Company. Suzuki translated such works as Ashvoghosho's *The Awakening of Faith in Mahayana* and Lao Tzu's *Tao Te Ching.* He also served Soyen Shaku as translator during his 1905-1906 journey to the West.

After his return to Japan, Suzuki settled as a lay disciple and in 1911 married Beatrice Erskine Lane. In 1919 they moved to Tokyo where Suzuki had accepted a position at Otani University, the major school of the Hompa Hongwanji, teaching philosophy of religion. Once in Tokyo, the couple initiated the publication of what became an important academic journal, *The Eastern Buddhist.* It was at this time that Suzuki began to author the many books on both Shin and Zen Buddhism through which he would become widely known, such as *Outlines of Mahayana Buddhism; Essays in Zen Buddhism; Zen and Japanese Culture; Manual of Zen Buddhism;* and *On Indian Mahayana Buddhism.*

In 1949, at the age of 78, he went to the University of Hawaii as a visiting professor. The next year, he did the same thing at Claremont Graduate School. He followed this up with a six-year teaching stint at Columbia University. During this last period, he became somewhat of a public personality because of the popularity of Zen, created partially by Suzuki's own books, among the so-called Beatniks. In large part due to his presence, the Zen Studies Society was formed. After leaving Columbia, Suzuki spent some time in Cambridge, Massachusetts, where he helped to found the Cambridge Buddhist Association. He finally retired in Japan in 1958.

Sources:

Fields, Rick. *How the Swans Came to the Lake.* Boulder, CO: Shambhala, 1986. 445 pp.
Melton, J. Gordon. *Biographical Dictionary of American Cult and Sect Leaders.* Garland Reference Library of Social Science, vol. 212. New York: Garland Publishing, 1986.
"On Dr. Daisetz Teitaro Suzuki." *Wind Bell* 8, 1-2 (Fall 1969): 29-30.
Suzuki, Daisetz Teitaro. *Essays in Zen Buddhism.* 3 vols. London: Rider and Co., 1927-1934.
_____. *The Field of Zen.* London: The Buddhist Society, 1969. 105 pp.
_____. *On Indian Mahayana Buddhism.* New York: Harper & Row, 1968. 284 pp.
_____. *Shin Buddhism.* New York: Harper & Row, 1970. 93 pp.
_____. *The Training of the Zen Buddhist Monk.* Kyoto, Japan: Eastern Buddhist Society, 1934. Rept. by: New York: University Books,2 965. 161 pp.
_____. *Zen Buddhism and Its Influences on Japanese Culture.* Kyoto, Japan: 1938. Rept. as *Zen and Japanese Culture.* Princeton, NJ: Princeton University Press, 1959. 478 pp.
Switzer, A. Irwin, III. *D. T. Suzuki: A Biography.* London: The Buddhist Society, 1985. 63 pp.

★924★
SUZUKI, Shunryu
Founder, Zen Center of San Francisco
b. 1904
d. Dec. 4, 1971, California

Shunryu Suzuki Roshi was a Soto Zen priest and founder of the Zen Center of San Francisco. He entered into the same profession as his father, a not uncommon Zen tradition in Japan. He did, however, break with tradition by studying Zen with a disciple of his father rather than directly with his father. He continued his training at Eiheiji after graduating from Komazawa Buddhist University. He felt a desire to go to America and teach, but was discouraged and became a priest, first of Zounji temple, and later of Rinso-in. During World War II he refused to help support the Japanese government's war effort, and went so far as to form a local discussion group to discuss the effects of militarism. Following the war, he worked on restoring Rinso-in and reopened two kindergartens. His first wife had passed away before the war. His second marriage was to Mitsu Matsuno, the principal of one of the kindergartens.

Over a decade after the end of the war, Suzuki accepted an appointment as the temporary head of Sokoji, the San Francisco Soto Zen temple. He flew from Japan on May 23, 1959. At the time, the temple served primarily, though not exclusively, as an ethnic Japanese-American church. This period marked the beginning of the emergence of the "hippie" phenomenon, and many youthful people became attracted to the study of Zen because of its importance in the writing of "beat" thinkers such as **Alan Wilson Watts**. Suzuki began to attract more Zen students until his primary activity became teaching *zazen* (Zen meditation) to young Americans. Attention to proper zazen was the core of his instruction. Squarely in the Soto tradition, Suzuki stressed that sitting in meditation was itself an expression of one's Buddha nature (rather than stressing the goal of "achieving" enlightenment). His now-classic work *Zen Mind, Beginner's Mind* (1970) clearly conveys this teaching.

By the fall of 1966, Suzuki's work had grown; some 150 people were practicing Zen meditation and attending lectures at the San Francisco Zen Center. Affiliate centers were being formed in Berkeley, Mill Valley, and Los Altos, California. The Roshi came to feel that it was appropriate for the growing community to acquire property for an institution that could function not unlike a traditional monastery and retreat center. In 1967 an old hot springs retreat, Tassajara Springs, located in the mountains near Carmel Valley, was purchased for this purpose. It opened as Zen Mountain Center, Zenshinji Monastery, in the spring of 1967. This highly successful monastery is famous for, among other things, the *Tassajara Bread Book*, a collection of recipes from the center's kitchen. Suzuki was succeeded by his American student, Richard Baker Roshi.

Sources:

Fields, Rick. *How the Swans Came to the Lake: A Narrative History of Buddhism in America*. Rev. ed. Boston, MA: Shambhala, 1986. 445 pp.

Melton, J. Gordon *The Encyclopedia of American Religions*. 3d ed. Detroit: Gale Research Inc.,1988. 1102 pp.

Suzuki Roshi, Shunryu. *Zen Mind, Beginner's Mind*. New York: Weatherhill, 1970. 134 pp.

★925★
SWAGGART, Jimmy Lee
Pentecostal Television Evangelist
b. 1935, Ferriday, Louisiana

Jimmy Lee Swaggart, who in the 1980s became one of the most popular television evangelists, grew up in a deeply religious family. His parents were both evangelists in the Assemblies of God. His uncle, Lee Calhoun, for whom both Swaggart and his cousin and rockabilly star Jerry Lee Lewis, were named, paid for the construction of the Assemblies church in Swaggart's home town. Among his early playmates, besides Lewis, was country music star-to-be Mickey Gilley, also a cousin. Swaggart was only nine years old when, in a home prayer meeting, he first felt the call to preach. However, he soon forgot the urge and, before graduating, he dropped out of high school. Then in 1953, he decided to follow his parents into part-time evangelical work and began preaching. He found that his musical talents greatly aided him and, discarding an option to follow Lewis in a musical career, in 1958 he committed himself to a full-time ministry. He was ordained by the Assemblies of God after first being turned down, in part due to marital scandals involving Lewis. By that time Swaggart had married and had two children. As his evangelical work grew, he founded Jimmy Swaggart Ministries, Inc.

In the early 1960s Swaggart began to record gospel music as an adjunct to his successful gospel revival meetings. In 1969 he went on the radio with "The Camp Meeting Hour" which he paid for by reinvesting his album royalties in the radio broadcasts. The increased radio exposure merely increased record sales, and two of his records became best-selling gospel albums, *This Is Just What Heaven Means to Me* (1971) and *There Is a River* (1972). In the early 1970s he expanded into television, and by the early 1980s he had become the most popular televangelist in America. By the mid-1980s, "The Jimmy Swaggart Telecast" reached almost two million homes weekly. In 1981 he dropped all of his radio work to focus on his television ministry.

Swaggart became known for his direct and highly emotional preaching. He became a master of the popular southern style and punctuated his message with the denunciation of Roman Catholicism, modernist Protestantism, secular humanism, and abortion. As his ministry grew, he developed a complex in Baton Rouge, Louisiana, which includes a Bible college, a printing plant, a music recording studio and television production center, and a church sanctuary that seats almost 5,000. His magazine, *The Evangelist*, reaches approximately 800,000. With his ministry's income, through most of the 1980s he supported a significant percentage of the missionary programs of the Assemblies of God. As television ministries proliferated through the 1980s, Swaggart's show rose to the top of the ratings consistently. He developed two broadcasts: "The Jimmy Swaggart Telecast," an evangelistic show, and a program called "A Study in the Word" emphasizing Bible-teaching.

Even as the most highly rated televangelist, until the mid-1980s Swaggart's fame was still largely confined to evangelical Christian circles. Then in 1987 he became involved in a series of scandals that brought him into prominence as a public figure. He was first accused of launching a plot to destroy the ministry of fellow Assemblies of God television evangelist **Jim Bakker**. In fact, he had informed church officials of Bakker's adulterous activities and demanded some action internally. In the midst of his own denunciations of sexual immorality, Swaggart was discovered to have engaged in voyeuristic liaisons with a prostitute. Following his own confession of guilt in front of television cameras, he began a rehabilitative discipline prescribed by the Assemblies of God that involved his not speaking for a year. After several weeks, however, he rejected that silencing and returned to his television work. As a result, the Assemblies of God defrocked him in April of 1988, and he has since carried on as an independent Pentecostal evangelist. Further allegations of improper conduct have been made, but Swaggart has denied any apart from that to which he originally confessed.

Since the scandals of 1987-1988, Swaggart's overall television ratings dropped from first to third place in religious programming. While he lost some support from staff who resigned, primarily members of the Assemblies of God, he has since reorganized and continues his ministry much as before.

Sources:

Burgess, Stanley M., Gary B. McGee, and Patrick H. Alexander, eds. *Dictionary of Pentecostal and Charismatic Movements*. Grand Rapids, MI: Regency Reference Library, Zondervan Publishing House, 1988. 914 pp.

Current Biography Yearbook. New York: H. W. Wilson Co., 1987.

Swaggart, Jimmy Lee. *To Cross a River*. Plainfield, NJ: Logos International, 1977. 244 pp.

———. *Spiritual High Treason*. Baton Rouge, LA: Jimmy Swaggart Ministries, 1987. 326 pp.

★926★
SWEATMAN, Arthur
Primate, Anglican Church of Canada
b. Nov. 19, 1834, London England
d. Jan. 24, 1909, Toronto, Ontario, Canada

Arthur Sweatman, third primate of the Anglican Church of Canada, was the son of John Sweatman, a prominent physician at the Middlesex Hospital in London. He attended Christ's College, Cambridge, from which he received his B.A. in 1859 and his M.A. in 1862. He was ordained in the Church of England and moved to London, Ontario, to become headmaster of Hellmuth Boys' College in 1865. He stayed in London until 1879 when he was chosen bishop of Toronto. Sweatman had emerged as a spokesperson of the broad church position (between the high church and low church evangelicals), and became an acceptable candidate in a diocese almost evenly split between high and low church advocates. He was consecrated by Bishop Lennox Williams of Quebec.

One of Sweatman's important assignments while serving as bishop came in 1886. He was appointed chairperson of a committee to put together a proposal and negotiate the consolidation of the several autonomous provinces of the Church of England in Canada into a united church body for all Canada. Sweatman's committee made some of the initial organizational suggestions later incorporated into the consolidated church, including the retention of provinces as an administrative unit and the leaders of each province being named archbishop. He took part in most of the negotiations that led to the drafting of the final report, which was accepted in 1893.

In 1906, following the death of Archbishop **William Bennett Bond**, Sweatman became archbishop and primate of the Anglican Church of Canada. He took office in 1907. Like his predecessor, his term was brief, as he passed away in 1909. He was succeeded by **Samuel P. Matheson**.

Sources:

Carrington, Philip. *The Anglican Church of Canada*. Toronto: Collins, 1963. 320 pp.

Wallace, W. Stewart. *The Macmillan Dictionary of Canadian Biography*. 4th ed., rev. Edited by W. A. McKay. Toronto: Macmillan of Canada, 1978.

★927★
SWING, David
Pastor, Central Church
b. Aug. 23, 1830, Cincinnati, Ohio
d. Oct. 3, 1894, Chicago, Illinois

David Swing, a liberal Presbyterian minister who left the Presbyterian Church to found the independent Central Church in Chicago, Illinois, was the son of David and Kerenda Gazley Swing. His father died when he was two and his mother remarried when he was five. He grew up in Reading and then Williamsburg, Ohio, in the home of his step-father, James Hagenmans, a blacksmith. As a youth he was converted to religion in a Methodist revival meeting, but joined the local Presbyterian church. He attended Miami University at Oxford, Ohio, from which he obtained his A.B. in 1852. He studied theology with a local Presbyterian elder, Dr. Nathan L. Rice; however, he profoundly disagreed with Rice's very conservative approach and dropped his study to become a teacher of Latin and Greek at Miami.

Shortly after moving back to Oxford, Swing married Elizabeth Porter. He also found a local pastor under whom he could complete his theological work, and he frequently supplied local pulpits. In 1866 Swing became pastor of Westminster Presbyterian Church in Chicago. Two years later his congregation merged with North Church (Presbyterian) and he became pastor of the new Fourth Presbyterian Church. The Chicago Fire of 1871 destroyed the church, however, and he was forced to rebuild. In the meantime, the theologically liberal and socially aware Swing emerged as one of the more popular preachers in the city. Though generally considered to be without the standard oratorical polish of most leading preachers, he possessed a winsome manner, an enthusiasm, and a pragmatic thrust which gave him a popular appeal. His sermons were regularly printed in several newspapers.

In 1874 two collections of Swing's sermons appeared in *Sermons* and in the first volume of *Truths for Today*. Already under attack from the more conservative wing of the church represented by **Francis L. Patton**, a professor at Princeton Theological Seminary, *Truths for Today* led to charges of heresy. Swing was tried for departing from the standards of the Westminster Confession. The Chicago Presbytery found that charges were not proven, but Patton, who had made the charges, appealed to the Synod of Illinois, North. Swing, unwilling to go through any more legal ordeals, withdrew from the denomination.

With the support of a number of leading citizens and former parishioners, a new congregation was established. Originally Central Church met at the McVickers Theatre, where the Fourth Church congregation had met after the fire. A new building was soon erected, and here Swing preached for the rest of his life.

Once established in his new pulpit, Swing regularly collected his better presentations for publication in book form. These collections appeared as the second volume of *Truths for Today* (1874); *Motives for Life* (1879); *Club Essays* (1881); and *Sermons* (1884, 1895).

Sources:

Dictionary of American Biography. 20 vols. and 7 supps. New York: Charles Scribner's Sons, 1928-1936, 1944-1981.

Newton, John Fort. *David Swing: Poet-Preacher*. Chicago: Unity Publishing Co., 1909. 273 pp.

Swing, David. *Club Essays*. Chicago: Jansen, McClurg & Co., 1881. 189 pp.

_____. Motives for Life. Chicago: Jansen, McClurg & Co., 1879. 162 pp.

_____. *Sermons*. London, England: Richard D. Dickerson, 1884. 299 pp.

_____. *Truths for Today*. Chicago: Jansen, McClurg & Co., 1874. 325 pp.

★928★
SYNAN, Harold Vinson
Historian and Bishop, International Pentecostal Holiness Church
b. Dec. 1, 1934, Hopewell, Virginia

Harold Vinson Synan, Pentecostal historian and bishop in the International Pentecostal Holiness Church, is the son of Minnis Evelyn Perdue and Joseph Alexander Synan, who was the senior bishop of the Pentecostal Holiness Church from 1950 to 1969. Synan grew up in Virginia where his father pastored several different churches, some of which he founded. He attended the University of Richmond (B.A., 1958) and while there he was ordained in the ministry of the Pentecostal Holiness Church. In 1960 he married Carol Lee Fuqua. He pursued graduate studies at the University of Georgia where he earned both a masters degree (1964) and a doctorate (1967).

In 1962 Synan became an instructor at Emmanuel College, the denominational school in Franklin Springs, Georgia. Following his graduation in 1967, he also became the pastor of the congregation at Hopewell, Georgia. During his first year at Hopewell, he finished his first book, a study of the school, *Emmanuel College* (1968).

Synan quickly emerged as one of the leading figures in the Pentecostal Holiness Church as well as the larger Pentecostal Movement. In 1970, along with William W. Menzies and Horace Ward, he founded the Society for Pentecostal Studies. He soon finished the first of several important studies of Pentecostal history, *The Holiness-Pentecostal Movement in the United States* (1971), quickly followed by a denominational history, *That Old Time Religion* (1973). In 1973 Synan was elected secretary of his denomination. Four years later he became the assistant general superintendent (bishop).

During the 1970s Synan combined his scholarship and denominational leadership with ecumenical activity. He pioneered Pentecostal-Roman Catholic dialogue. He reached out to the members of the new Charismatic Movement and built bridges of understanding between them and members in the older Pentecostal denominations. The members of mainline Protestant denominations had experienced the baptism of the Holy Spirit and spoke in tongues, whereas the older members did not subscribe to speaking in tongues as a sign of baptism. His 1975 volume, *Aspects of Pentecostal-Charismatic Origins*, reflected his concern.

During the 1980s Synan's leadership expanded. In 1981 he was elected director of evangelism for the International Pentecostal Holiness Church (renamed in 1975). Not only has he helped guide the expansion of his own denomination but he has worked for the spread of the Pentecostal and Charismatic Movements worldwide. In 1986 he became the chairperson of the North American Congresses on the Holy Spirit and World Evangelism and its steering committee, the North American Renewal Service Committee. The committee has planned and held world evangelism conferences in 1986, 1987, and 1990. He also serves as editor-in-chief of *A.D. 2000 Together*, a periodical whose title reflects the goal shared by many evangelical Protestants; that is to evangelize during the 1990s, those parts of the world as yet untouched by Christianity. Meanwhile, Synan has finished several more books, including *Azusa Street* (1980); *In the Latter Days* (1984); and *The Twentieth Century Pentecostal Explosion* (1987).

Sources:

Burgess, Stanley M., Gary B. McGee, and Patrick H. Alexander, eds. *Dictionary of Pentecostal and Charismatic Movements*. Grand Rapids, MI: Regency Reference Library, Zondervan Publishing House, 1988. 914 pp.
Synan, Vinson. *Aspects of Pentecostal-Charismatic Origins*. Plainfield, NJ: Logos International, 1975. 252 pp.
_____. *The Holiness-Pentecostal Movement in the United States*. Grand Rapids, MI: William Eerdmans Publishing Company, 1971. 248 pp.
_____. *In the Latter Days*. Ann Arbor, MI: Servant Books, 1984. 168 pp.
_____. *The Twentieth Century Pentecostal Explosion*. Altamonte Springs, FL: Creation House, 1987. 235 pp.

★929★
SYNAN, Joseph Alexander
Bishop, Pentecostal Holiness Church
b. Feb. 18, 1905, Tazewell County, Virginia
d. 1984

Joseph Alexander Synan, for almost a quarter of a century a bishop in the Pentecostal Holiness Church (now the International Pentecostal Holiness Church), was the son of Thomas and Maude Synan. He was raised in the Methodist Episcopal Church, South, which he formally joined as a teenager. When he was 16 he had an experience of Christ as his personal Savior and later that year, having encountered the Holiness Movement, he was sanctified (had an experience of the Holy Spirit cleansing him of inward sin and granting a perfection in love). The following year he received the baptism of the Holy Spirit as evidenced by his speaking in tongues (the definitive experience of the Pentecostal Movement). He had by this time affiliated with the Pentecostal Holiness Church.

In 1924 Synan decided to go into the ministry and two years later was ordained in the Baltimore Conference (now the Eastern Virginia Conference) of the Pentecostal Holiness Church. In 1925 he was licensed to preach and began a successful 18-year tenure in the pastorate, marked by his establishing several congregations in the Tidewater area of Virginia. He became well known in the church for his oratorical abilities. In 1926 he married Minnis Evelyn Perdue. In 1934, at the age of 29, he was elected superintendent of the conference, a position he retained for the next 11 years.

In 1941 Synan was elected to the new post of assistant general superintendent, serving beside Joseph Hillery King and **Dan T. Muse**. His first assignment was to chair the home missions board. As the United States became involved in World War II, in 1943 he was named chairman of the Service Men's Commission. Synan was also active in the conservative evangelical phase of the ecumenical movement and in 1943 participated in the formation of the National Association of Evangelicals.

In 1945 Synan was elected general superintendent (bishop), at a point when the church was experiencing a period of growth and expansion. Among the highlights of his more than two decades of achievements were his participation in the 1948 formation of the Pentecostal Fellowship of North America and his work on the formal affiliation of the Pentecostal Holiness Church with the Pentecostal Methodist Church of Chile, completed in 1967. In 1950, following the death of Bishop Muse, Synan became the senior presiding bishop of the church.

Synan was reelected to the top leadership position in the church through the 1960s. However, in 1969, being in his mid-60s, he was succeeded by a younger colleague, J. Floyd Williams. Synan retired but remained active for another decade. His son, **Harold Vinson Synan**, became an outstanding Pentecostal historian and was also elected to the office of bishop in the Pentecostal Holiness Church.

Sources:

Burgess, Stanley M., Gary B. McGee, and Patrick H. Alexander, eds. *Dictionary of Pentecostal and Charismatic Movements*. Grand Rapids, MI: Regency Reference Library, Zondervan Publishing House, 1988. 914 pp.
Synan, J. A. *Christian Life in Depth*. N.p., n.d. 87 pp.

★930★
SZOKA, Edmund Casimir
Cardinal, Roman Catholic Church
b. Sep. 14, 1927, Grand Rapids, Michigan

Edmund Casimir Szoka, a cardinal in the Roman Catholic Church, is the son of Casimir and Mary Wolgat Szoka. He attended St. Joseph's Seminary in Grand Rapids, Michigan, and Sacred Heart Seminary College in Detroit, from which he earned his B.A. He continued his education at St. John's Provincial Seminary in Plymouth, Michigan, and was ordained to the priesthood in 1954. He was named assistant pastor at St. Francis Roman Catholic Church in Manistique, Michigan, but the following year he became the secretary to the bishop of Marquette (Michigan). He held that post until 1962, though he spent two years (1957-1959) of that tenure studying at the Pontifical Lateran University in Rome.

In 1962 Szoka was named a papal chamberlain and assigned as priest to St. Pius X Church in Ishpeming, Michigan. The next year he moved to St. Christopher Church in Marquette, Michigan. In 1964 he was named a domestic prelate. In 1971 he became chancellor of the diocese of Marquette, but within weeks was named the first bishop of Gaylord, Michigan.

After a decade in Gaylord, Szoka was chosen to become the new archbishop of Detroit, succeeding the retiring Archbishop **John Dearden**. He stepped into controversy almost immediately when he ordered a nun, Sister Mary Agnes Mansour, to resign from her post as head of the state's Department of Social Services, because the department administered abortions to the poor. Mansour kept her post with the D.S.S. and, instead, resigned from the Sisters of Mercy of the Union.

That controversy was mild, however, compared to the major opposition he encountered as he began to act on the problems of inner-city parishes that had significant decreases in membership in a diocese with a shortage of priests. He began a process of closing and consolidating some 30 churches. As his announcements swept the diocese, in 1988 he was made a cardinal by Pope John Paul II. He faced intense opposition from parishioners of the churches he began closing, but continued the process until 1990. He was called from his position in Detroit to Rome to become the head of the Vatican's Prefecture for Economic Affairs, one of the top financial jobs within the church internationally.

Sources:

The American Catholic Who's Who. Washington, DC: National Catholic News Service, 1979.
Biography Index. New York: The H. W. Wilson Co.
Who's Who in America. Wilmette, IL: Marquis Who's Who, Inc.
Who's Who in Religion. 2d ed. Chicago: Marquis Who's Who, Inc., 1977.

★931★
SZOLD, Henrietta
Zionist Leader and Founder, Hadassah
b. Dec. 21, 1860, Baltimore, Maryland
d. Feb. 13, 1945, Jerusalem Palestine

Henrietta Szold, the founder of Hadassah, the major American women's Zionist organization, was the daughter of Rabbi Benjamin Szold, a prominent Jewish leader in nineteenth-century Baltimore, and Sophie Szold. Her father was an abolitionist, and among her earliest memories was attending Abraham Lincoln's funeral. She was raised with many of the prerogatives usually reserved for male children and was given a thorough education in Hebrew, other languages, and Judaism. Following her graduation from high school, she taught at Misses Adam's School (for women) and in the school at her father's synagogue, Ohed Shalom. She also became the Baltimore correspondent for the *Jewish Messenger* (published in New York).

In the 1880s, as massive Jewish emigration from Eastern Europe began, Szold established the first night school in Baltimore to assist in the immigrants' Americanization. Over 5,000 people passed through her school by the time responsibility for it was assumed by the city in 1898. Among the immigrants were the founders of "Hoveve Tzion" (Lovers of Zion) societies, the earliest Zionist organizations. In the 1880s, largely because of her educational work among the immigrants, she became an ardent Zionist, looking toward Palestine as a homeland for Jews.

In 1888 Szold became one of a small group which founded the Jewish Publication Society of America to supply English-langauge Jewish materials to the growing American Jewish community. In 1892 she became secretary of the society, and the next year she moved to Philadelphia to work for the society full time. Among her accomplishments during these years, she edited the early volumes of the *American Jewish Yearbook*; translated and indexed the five-volume *History of the Jews* by Heinrich Graetz; and authored 15 articles for the *Jewish Encyclopedia*.

In 1897 Szold joined Hebras Zion, the Zionist organization founded in Baltimore. In 1902 she moved to New York City, where she was able to study at Jewish Theological Seminary, though not in a degree program. In 1907 she joined the Hadassah Study Circle, a discussion group with a focus in Jewish history and Zionism. In 1909 she took a trip to Palestine which raised her enthusiasm for Zionism to a new height. Upon her return to America in 1901 she became secretary of the Federation of American Zionists and two years later called the organizational meeting of what became the Hadassah Chapter of the Daughters of Zion (changed in 1914 to simply Hadassah), a Zionist organization for women. She became the first president of the new organization. Within the first two years the Hadassah grew to 4,000 members. In 1916 she resigned from her work with the publication society and took charge of organizing the American Zionist Medical Unit which established itself in Palestine in 1918. In 1919 she was sent to Palestine to work with the unit and eventually became its director. She reorganized it in the 1920s as the Hadassah Medical Organization.

Except for a brief period (1923-1926) and a few visits, Szold remained in Palestine until 1933 as an executive for the World Zionist Organization with responsibility for health and education. In 1926 she relinquished her office as president of Hadassah and was named honorary president. In 1933, in her seventies, she returned to the United States. Instead of retiring, however, she became director of Youth Aliyah, an agency established to send German Jewish youth to Palestine to complete their education. Through Youth Aliyah, she was able to save thousands of Jewish youth from the Holocaust. Active almost to the end, she finally died of pneumonia in her mid-80s.

Sources:

Fineman, I. *Woman of Valor: The Life of Henrietta Szold*. New York: Simon & Schuster, 1961. 448 pp.

Lowenthal, Marvin. *Henrietta Szold: Life and Letters*. New York: Viking Press, 1942. 350 pp.

Zeitlin, Rose. *Henrietta Szold: Record of a Life*. New York: Dial Press, 1952. 263 pp.

★932★
TACHE, Alexandre Antonin
Archbishop, Roman Catholic Church
b. Jul. 23, 1823, Riviere du Loup, Quebec, Canada
d. Jun. 22, 1894, St. Boniface Canada

Alexandre Antonin Tache, the first archbishop of the Roman Catholic Church in St. Boniface, Manitoba, was the son of French Canadians Louise Henriette Boucher de la Broquerie and Etienne Paschal Tache. He attended the College of St. Hyacinthe and finished his seminary training at the Grand Seminaire at Montreal. Upon completion of his studies, in 1844 he became a novice of the Oblates of Mary Immaculate order and was assigned to accompany Pierre Aubert, the first Oblate missionary in Western Canada, to begin work in Manitoba. He was ordained in 1845 as a missionary and settled on the Red River to begin evangelization of the several Canadian Indian tribes in the area.

Tache was only 27 when he was named bishop coadjutor of St. Boniface in 1851, and he succeeded Bp. Joseph N. Provencher in 1853. By this time, the missions he had established ranged far and wide over the new territory, and through the years he continued to make pastoral visits to the Indian members of his flock. In 1860 the cathedral in St. Boniface burned, and he oversaw the erection of a new cathedral. In 1866 he finished his first book, *Vingt Annees de Missions*, a history of 20 years of missionary activity in Western Canada. A second book, *Esquisse du Nord-Quest*, appeared in 1869.

In 1869 Tache traveled to Rome for the First Vatican Council. While he was away, an uprising occurred in the territory where he had previously established work. At the request of the Canadian government he left the council and actively participated in the efforts to restore order. He also participated in the organization of Manitoba as a new Canadian province. In 1871 he was named the first archbishop of St. Boniface, and spent the next decade in the midst of controversy. The issues surrounding the uprising, caused by the ill-treatment of the Red River residents, became the occasion for additional books, *L'amnistie* (1874) and *Encore L'amnistie* (1875).

More time-consuming was the long fight to establish the existence and rights of the parochial school system in the province, a fight which culminated after a law was passed in 1890 attempting to suppress the Catholic schools. As a result of this conflict, Tache began the first Catholic newspaper in the province and authored several booklets: *Denominational or Free Christian Schools in Manitoba* (1877); *Les Ecole Separees de Manitoba* (1890); *Un Page d'historie des Ecole de Manitoba* (1894); and *Memoire sur la Question des Ecoles* (1894).

During his four decades in the episcopacy, he oversaw the vast expansion of Catholic work in the territory under his jurisdiction, especially after the building of the railroad across the western provinces.

Sources:

Benoit, J. P. A. *Vie de Msr. Tache*. 2 vols. Montreal: Beauchemin, 1904.

Morice, A. G. *History of the Catholic Church in Western Canada*. 2 vols. Toronto: Musson Book Company, 1910.

Tache, Alexandre A. *L'Aministie*. Montreal: Imprimee par le journal "Le Nouveau Monde," 1877. 72 pp.

———. *Les Ecole Separees de Manitoba*. St. Boniface: 1890.

———. *Denominational or Free Christian Schools in Manitoba*. Winnipeg, Manitoba: Standard Book & Job Printing Establishment, 1877. 126 pp.

———. *Esquisse du Nord-Quest*. Montreal: Typographie du Nouveau Monde, 1869. 146 pp.

———. *Memoire sur la Question des Ecole*. Montreal: 1894.

———. *Vingt Annees de Missions dans le Nord-quest de l'Amerique*. 2 vols. Montreal: E. Senecal, 1866.

Wallace, W. Stewart. *The Macmillan Dictionary of Canadian Biography.* 4th ed., rev. Edited by W. A. McKay. Toronto: Macmillan of Canada, 1978.

★ 933 ★
TALBOT, Ethelbert
Presiding Bishop, Protestant Episcopal Church
b. Oct. 9, 1848, Fayette, Missouri
d. Feb. 27, 1928, Tuckahoe, New York

Ethelbert Talbot, a presiding bishop of the Protestant Episcopal Church, was the son of John Alnut and Alice Daly Talbot. He attended Dartmouth College, from which he graduated in 1870, and did his theological work at General Theological Seminary. He graduated from the seminary in 1873, and before the year was out, he married Dora Frances Harvey and was ordained as both deacon and priest. He assumed duties as rector of St. James Church in Macon, Missouri.

Talbot had a prosperous and productive ministry in Talbot. He began a boys' school that evolved into St. James Military Academy. He seemed to have no particular ambitions beyond his local ministry. Then, in 1886 the church's general convention elected him missionary bishop of Wyoming and Idaho. He was consecrated in 1887 and left to inspect his assigned territory. He discovered that his geographically vast diocese contained only four churches in each state. He stayed in the West for 10 years, pioneering the development of the church and becoming a highly respected public figure. During that time he saw to the creation of 30 parishes, three schools, and a hospital. He became a notable figure in the state, and was frequently asked to run for public office, though he turned down the invitations. His work later became the subject of an entertaining volume, *My People of the Plains* (1906).

Talbot was elected bishop of Georgia in 1891, but he opted to finish his work in the West. In 1897, however, he accepted the position of bishop of Central Pennsylvania. The change was dramatic, from a small scattered diocese to a large, almost unmanageable one. In 1904 half of his work was set off as the Diocese of Harrisburg. In 1909 his remaining segment was named the Diocese of Bethlehem. However, the number of communicants had doubled in the decade he had been in Pennsylvania, and the remaining diocese was almost as large as the unmanageable one with which he began.

Talbot's remaining years were devoted primarily to two concerns—the growing industrialization of his episcopal area with the accompanying influx of new immigrants and the challenge of church unity. On behalf of the latter cause, he served as chairperson of the general convention's commission on church unity, through which he espoused the immediate union of the major American Protestant bodies. He summed up his two decades of work in Pennsylvania in two books, *A Bishop Among His Flock* (1914) and *A Bishop's Message* (1917). In 1923 he was given a coadjutor to assist with the growing diocese.

In 1924 he became the oldest bishop in the church and the last person named as presiding bishop purely by seniority criteria. His term was short. He presided at the 1925 general convention and, at the beginning of 1926, passed the office to John Gardner Murray, the first elected presiding bishop. In 1927, after 30 years in Pennsylvania, Talbot turned over the administrative duties to his coadjutor and died within a few months.

Sources:

Dictionary of American Biography. 20 vols. and 7 supps. New York: Charles Scribner's Sons, 1928-1936, 1944-1981.
Talbot, Ethelbert. *A Bishop Among His Flock.* New York: Harper & Brothers, 1914. 202 pp.
———. *A Bishop's Message.* Philadelphia: G. W. Jacobs & Company, 1917. 220 pp.

———. *My People of the Plains.* New York: Harper & Brothers, 1906. 264 pp.

★ 934 ★
TALBOT, Louis Thompson
President, Bible Institute of Los Angeles (BIOLA)
b. Oct. 19, 1889, Sydney Australia
d. Jan. 27, 1976, Los Angeles, California

Louis Thompson Talbot, fundamentalist Protestant minister and president of the Bible Institute of Los Angeles (BIOLA), was the son of Elizabeth Frayling and John Talbot. As a child, growing up in Australia, he attended the Congregational Church. At the age of 12 he entered Newton College, a school for boys. In 1911 he moved to the United States to attend Moody Bible Institute in Chicago, Illinois. He graduated from Moody in 1913 and moved to Paris, Texas, to become pastor of the First Congregational Church, a church founded by fundamentalist Bible teacher Cyrus I. Schofield. While there he was ordained as a Congregational minister in 1914. He also met Audrey Hogue, whom he would marry in 1916. He stayed in Texas for two years, but left in 1915 to return to Chicago to attend McCormick Theological Seminary, a Presbyterian school.

Following his graduation in 1917 Talbot served a series of churches, first back in Texas and then, successively, Fourth Congregational Church in Oak Park, Illinois; First Westminster Presbyterian Church, Keokuk, Iowa; and Oliver Presbyterian Church, Minneapolis, Minnesota. While in Minneapolis he began a radio ministry conducting Bible studies on radio station WRHM. He also taught at the independent fundamentalist school which had been established by **William Bell Riley**. In 1929 he began a three-year ministry in Canada at Philpott Tabernacle in Hamilton, Ontario.

In 1932 Talbot began his long association with the Church of the Open Door and the Bible Institute of Los Angeles (BIOLA). Both organizations had attained a prominent role within the fundamentalist world under the leadership of **Reuben A. Torrey**. As pastor of the church he assumed the leadership of more than 1,000 members. He renewed his radio ministry, which he continued for many years. Within a few months the presidency of BIOLA was thrust upon him; his immediate task was to save the debt-ridden school. As a major step, he led the church to purchase the school's auditorium, where the congregation met for its Sunday services. With the debt refinanced, he was able to resign from the presidency in 1935, and concentrate upon his pastoral duties, though he remained on the board. Over the next decade he continued to work until he saw both the school and the congregation retire their heavy debt.

Talbot resigned as pastor of the Church of the Open Door in 1948. During his years he had more than doubled the membership to approximately than 3,500. Resuming his duties as president of BIOLA, he stayed in tha post for another four years. In 1952 he was named chancellor of bothe BIOLA and the new seminary, which had grown up at BIOLA and was named for him. He continued to be active in BIOLA affairs and in 1953 suggested the move of the campus of both schools to a more expansive site. He was present for the groundbreaking ceremonies in 1957. Active to the end of his long life, in 1961 he accepted the job of interim pastor of Hinson Baptist Church in Portland, Oregon. After the death of his first wife, he married Carol Terry in 1964.

Sources:

Talbot, Carol. *Christ in the Tabernacle.* Chicago: Moody Press, 1978. 287 pp.
———. *For This I Was Born: The Captivating Story of Louis T. Talbot.* Chicago: Moody Press, 1977. 288 pp.
———. *God's Plan of the Ages.* Grand Rapids, MI: Wm. B. Eerdmans Publishing Company, 1936, 1974. 199 pp.

★935★
TALMAGE, James Edward
Apostle, Church of Jesus Christ of Latter-day Saints
b. Sep. 22, 1862, Hungerford United Kingdom
d. Jul. 27, 1933, Salt Lake City, Utah

James Edward Talmage, a scholar and an apostle in the Church of Jesus Christ of Latter-day Saints, was a product of the mission in England. Following his family's conversion, he was baptized in 1873. As a youth he showed his bent toward intellectual accomplishments, becoming an Oxford Diocesan Scholar at the age of 12. He moved with his family to Provo, Utah, in 1876.

Soon after his arrival in Utah, Talmage entered Brigham Young Academy. Completing his coursework in 1879, he became a teacher of science and English. He then studied science at Lehigh University and Johns Hopkins University. He returned to become professor of geology and chemistry at the academy in 1884. During the next four years he succeeded in becoming a United States citizen, and held several offices in the Provo municipal government. In 1888 he married Mary May Booth.

In 1888 Talmage left Provo to become president of the Latter-day Saints College in Salt Lake City. He published his first book, *The First Book of Nature*, followed a few years later by *Domestic Science* (1891). In 1894 he became president and professor of geology at the University of Utah. In 1896 he was awarded a Ph.D by Illinois Wesleyan University for nonresident work.

As an instructor at the university, Talmage also lectured on theology and during the mid-1890s he put much of his time into a Latter-day Saint theology text, *Articles of Faith*. His work load became so intense that he nearly suffered a nervous breakdown. In 1897 he resigned his job as president, although he continued as geology professor. *Articles of Faith*, his most famous work, was finally published in 1899. It would go through at least twelve editions during Talmage's lifetime and was translated into German, Dutch, and Japanese. During the decade he remained with the geology faculty, Talmage authored a major study of the region, *The Great Salt Lake, Present and Past* (1900).

Talmage left the university in 1907 to become a full-time mining consultant. In 1911 he was ordained an apostle of the church. During this period he turned his attention back to theology and had one of his most intellectually productive periods. He authored *The Great Apostasy* (1909), *The House of the Lord* (1912), *Jesus the Christ* (1915), *The Vitality of Mormonism* (1919), and *The Story of Mormonism* (1920). During the 1920s, Talmage served for a four-year period as president of the European Mission (1924-1928). He worked throughout that decade to reconcile Mormon faith with science, a work for which he was eminently qualified, given his geological training and theological accomplishments. He was able to accomplish a satisfying reconciliation in the presence of a church which had left the question of evolution ultimately open, requiring only that God's creation of humanity be affirmed.

Talmage was known throughout his life for his complete absorption in his work. His habits finally killed him. He died at the age of 71 of an uncared for throat infection which, in the face of his work hours, turned into acute myocarditis.

Sources:
Jensen, Andrew. *Latter Day Saints Biographical Encyclopedia* 4 vols. Salt Lake City, UT: Andrew Jensen History Co., 1901.
Talmage, James Edward. *Articles of Faith*. Salt Lake City, UT: LDS, twelfth edition, 1924. 537 pp.
_____. *Jesus the Christ*. Salt Lake City, UT: Deseret Book Company, 1909.
_____. *The Story of Mormonism*. Salt Lake City, UT: Deseret News, 1920. 146 pp.
_____. *The Vitality of Mormonism*. Boston, MA: Richard G. Badger, 1919. 361 pp.
Talmage, John R. *The Talmage Story: Life of James E. Talmage*. Salt Lake City, UT: Bookcraft, 1972.
Van Wagoner, Richard S, and Steven C. Walker. *A Book of Mormons*. Salt Lake City, UT: Signature Books, 1982. 454 pp.

★936★
TALMAGE, Thomas DeWitt
Minister, (Dutch) Reformed Church in America
b. Jan. 7, 1832, Boundbrook, New Jersey
d. Apr. 12, 1902, Washington, District of Columbia

Though largely forgotten today, Thomas DeWitt Talmage was one of the most popular preachers of the latter part of the nineteenth century. The son of David and Catherine Van Nest Talmage, he grew up in New Jersey. At the age of 19, he entered the University of the City of New York with the aim of becoming a lawyer. Influenced by his immediate family, which included a number of ministers, he dropped out of school and entered the New Brunswick Theological Seminary. He graduated and was ordained in the Reformed Church in America in 1856. That same year he married Mary R. Avery and began his first pastorate in Belleville, New Jersey. In 1859 he moved to Syracuse, New York, and in 1862 to the Second Dutch Reformed Church in Philadelphia. A short time after his last move, his wife was killed in an accident. In 1863 he married Sarah Whittemore.

In Philadelphia, Talmage came into his own as a preacher and popular religious figure. He had developed a flamboyant style and possessed an oratorical skill that enabled him to reach the masses. His use of wild gestures and vivid illustrations saw the crowds grow even as his critics accused him of turning the church service into a circus performance. However, his success in Philadelphia led to an invitation to Central Presbyterian Church in Brooklyn, New York.

When Talmage arrived in Brooklyn, he found a church divided by internal struggles. His approach was simply to overwhelm the congregation's problems by drawing th the church what became the largest Sunday audience granted any minister in the country. His sermons appeared in a growing number of newspapers across the country. He also began to turn out popular books, many of which were compilations of his sermons. Among his first were *Crumbs Swept Up* (1870); *The Abominations of Modern Society* (1872); *Sermons Delivered in the Broadway Tabernacle* (1872); *Points* (1873); and *Old Wells Dug Out* (1874).

To accommodate his ever-growing crowds, he led in the construction of a large new sanctuary, the Tabernacle. It burned in December 1872, but by January 1874, a new structure stood in its place. That year Talmage became the editor of *The Christians at Work*, and throughout the rest of the decade he continued to turn out books, including: *Around the Tea Table* (1874); *Every-Day Religion* (1875); and *The Night Side of New York* (1878). In 1879 critics again attempted to cut into his popularity as they filed charges with the Brooklyn Presbytery accusing him of bringing religion into disrepute by engaging in improper actions in the pulpit. He was acquitted.

The 1880s was the decade of Talmage's greatest success. More than 3,000 newspapers carried his sermons. He became editor of *Frank Leslie's Sunday Magazine* (1881-1889), one of the country's most popular publications. The crowds continued to be as large as ever and more books appeared. Then, in 1889, disaster struck. The Tabernacle burned down a second time. He rebuilt, only to have it burn again in 1894. This time he was too discouraged to rebuild. He accepted the call of the First Presbyterian Church in Washington, D.C. After a flurry of four books which appeared in 1890, Talmage's writing output diminished. His pastorate in Washington was quieter. While there he continued to edit the *Christian Herald*, a task he had begun in 1890. After five years at his last pastorate, he resigned to devote his last years to the *Herald* and to an autobiography, *T. DeWitt Talmage As I Knew Him*, which was published posthumously in 1912.

Sources:

Adams, Charles Francis. *The Life and Sermons of Rev. T. DeWitt Talmage*. Chicago: M.A. Donahue and Co. 1902. 192 pp.
Banks, Charles Eugene. *Authorized and Authentic Life and Works of T. DeWitt Talmage*. Chicago: Bible House, 1902. 479 pp.
Dictionary of American Biography. 20 vols. and 7 supps. New York: Charles Scribner's Sons, 1928-1936, 1944-1981.
Talmage, T. DeWitt. *The Abominations of Modern Society*. New York: Adams, Victor & Co., 1872. 290 pp.
_____. *Around the Tea Table*. Philadelphia: Cowperthwait & Company, 1874. 504 pp.
_____. *Crumbs Swept Up*. Philadelphia: Evans, Stoddard & Co., 1870. 445 pp.
_____. *Every-Day Religion*. New York: Harper & Brothers, 1875. 420 pp.
_____. *The Night Sides of New York*. New York: G. Munro, 1878. 20 pp.
_____. *Points*. Douglas, Isle of Man: J. S. Doidge, 1873. 336 pp.
_____. *Sermons Delivered in the Brooklyn Tabernacle*. Wakefield, MA: W. Nicholson, 1872. 348 pp.
_____. *T. DeWitt Talmage As I Knew Him*. New York: E. P. Dutton, 1921. 439pp.

★937★
TANIGUCHI, Masaharu
Founder, Seicho-No-Ie
b. Nov. 22, 1893, Kobe Japan
d. Jun. 17, 1985, Nagasaki Japan

Masaharu Taniguchi, the founder of Seicho-No-Ie, a Japanese-based New Thought metaphysical religion, was the son of Otokichi Taniguchi. At an early age he went to live with an aunt and uncle who saw him through his childhood years. During high school he developed a love for writing and later entered Waseda University to major in English literature. While at college he got married. He also published his first novel, *Judging God*. An earthquake, however, destroyed most of the copies of his book. Broke, he moved back to his aunt's house with his wife and new baby. He spent most of his time doing psychical research and editing a magazine on psychic phenomena.

About this time Taniguchi discovered a copy of *The Law of Mind in Action* by Fenwicke Holmes, the brother of **Ernest S. Holmes**, the founder of Religious Science. Fascinated with the idea of Mind as the dominant reality in the universe, he translated the book into Japanese and published it as *How You Can Control Your Destiny*. Using the principles in the book he landed a job as a translator. Further meditation upon the truths of the book led to both a profound religious vision and a healing of his daughter. Taniguchi decided to take his money and publish a magazine. The money was stolen, but relying upon the metaphysical principles he was teaching he forged ahead with the first issue of *Seicho-No-Ie* (literally, the home of infinite life, wisdom, and abundance) which appeared in 1930. People began to report healings as a result of reading the magazine and began to meet together in study groups to discuss the journal. Tanaguchi visited these meetings and before many months was the leader of a spreading New Thought movement in Japan. As the movement grew people asked for copies of the early issues of the magazine. Rather than reprint them, he compiled his articles into his first book, *The Truth of Life*.

As the movement grew, Taniguchi moved to Tokyo. The movement continued to grow through the 1930s, but was suppressed once World War II started. It was brought to the United States by several members who began to spread it in the Japanese-American communities along the West Coast. In 1962 Taniguchi co-authored a book with Fenwicke Holmes, who hosted him for a 1963 visit to North America. A biography of Taniguchi appeared in 1970, written by **Roy Eugene Davis**, who had toured Japan in 1964. Taniguchi translated two of Davis' books into Japanese.

Taniguchi developed Seicho-No-Ie, now the largest New Thought group in the world, on a base of Japanese Buddhism rather than Christianity. Included in his teachings is a unique form of meditation, *shinsokan*. Over his long lifetime he has authored over 50 books, many of which have been translated into English.

Sources:

Davis, Roy Eugene. *Miracle Man of Japan*. Lakemont, GA: CSA Press, 1970. 159 pp.
Holmes, Fenwicke and Masaharu Taniguchi. *The Science of Faith: How to Make Yourself Believe*. Tokyo: Nipppon Kyobun-shu Co., 1962. 272 pp.
Taniguchi, Masaharu. *The Human Mind and Cancer*. Tokyo: Seicho-No-Ie Foundation Divine Publication Department, 1972. 350 pp.
_____. *The Magic of Truth*. Gardena, CA: Seicho-No-Ie Truth of life Movement, 1979. 214 pp.
_____. *The Mystical Power Within*. Seicho-No-Ie Los Angeles & No. American Missionary Hq., 1975. 191 pp.
_____. *Recovery from All Disease*. Tokyo: Seicho-No-Ie Foundation Divine Publication Department, 1963. 260 pp.
_____. *The Spiritual Essence of Man*. Gardena, CA: Seicho-No-Ie Truth of Life Movement, 1979. 200 pp.
_____. *Truth of Life*. Seicho-No-Ie Foundation Divine Publication Department, 1961. 320 pp.

★938★
TANT, Jefferson Davis
Evangelist, Churches of Christ
b. Jun. 28, 1861, Paulding County, Georgia
d. Jun. 1, 1941, Los Fresnos, Texas

Jefferson Davis Tant, an evangelist noted for building the Churches of Christ in Texas, was the son of Mattie Lloyd and William Tant. The family fortunes were devastated by the Civil War and then completely wiped out during Reconstruction. The Tants moved to Brooks County, Georgia, where "J. D." (named for Jefferson Davis, the president of the Confederate States) was raised. He had only six weeks of formal school but it was enough to give him a basic knowledge of reading, which he put to good use in his free time. In 1875 he joined the Methodist Episcopal Church, South. The following year the family moved to Texas, where as a young man of 19, Tant became a Methodist circuit rider. He was ordained by the Methodists in 1880.

In 1881 Tant had several encounters with ministers of the Christian Church (Disciples of Christ). As a result he joined the Disciples and in August 1881 received a license to preach. Over the next few years he alternated between preaching and teaching school, but finally decided that preaching was his calling. In spite of the precarious financial position in which he was often placed, he continued to preach throughout his long life.

Tant became an active Disciples minister just as a set of issues was emerging that would split them into two camps. At the 1886 state meeting, the Texas Disciples split over the introduction of the Texas Missionary Society. Those opposed to the society, who would later be known as the Churches of Christ, left the meeting and organized separately. Tant became their secretary. Shortly thereafter Tant held his first religious debate. Although debates were a popular religious activity in the nineteenth century, they died out among most denominations, but the Churches of Christ have been the major group to perpetuate the practice.

In 1890 Tant married Laura Warren. Unfortunately, she died in 1892. In 1896 he married Nannie Green Yater, with whom he would live the rest of his life. By this time Tant had emerged as a leading evangelist among the Churches of Christ. Through his columns in the *Gospel Advocate*, the church's periodical from Nashville, Tennessee, and his speaking around the country, Tant help set the movement in opposition to missionary societies, organ music in the church, premillennialism, and church sponsored seminaries and Bible colleges. Tant had a preaching career of over a half of a century. He was a folksy orator remembered for the humor and stories with which he spiced his sermons. His life was lived in a state of financial instability, and he moved from place to place during his life, though most of his time was spent in Texas. He remained active until the last months of his life and rarely lacked for demands upon his time.

Sources:

Tant, Fanning Yater. *J. D. Tant—Texas Preacher*. Erlanger, KY: Faith and Facts Press, 1958. 479 pp.

★939★
TASCHEREAU, Elzear Alexandre
Cardinal, Roman Catholic Church
b. Feb. 17, 1820, Sainte Marie, Quebec, Canada
d. Apr. 12, 1898, Quebec, Canada

Elzear Alexandre Taschereau, the first Canadian cardinal of the Roman Catholic Church, came from a prominent French Canadian family, made all the more so by the imprisonment of his father, newspaperman Jean Thomas Taschereau, by the British governor. His mother, Marie Panet, was the niece of Bishop Bernard Claude Panet. Taschereau completed his high school in Canada and made his first trip to Rome at the age of 16. He then entered the seminary at Quebec and graduated in 1836. He journeyed to Rome to study and after considering joining the Benedictines, returned to Quebec where he was ordained in 1842. He became a member of the faculty of the seminary, with which he remained connected for many years. His academic career was interrupted when he caught typhus while working with the victims of the epidemic of 1847. He finally recovered, and in 1852 helped found the University of Laval (named for the former bishop of Quebec) which had grown out of the seminary.

Taschereau again traveled to Rome in 1854 to pursue a doctorate in canon law, which was granted by the French Seminary in 1856. Afterward he began a steady rise in the archdiocese. In 1860 he became superior of the university. In 1862 he was named vicar general of the archdiocese. He was named rector of Laval University in 1869, and that same year invited to Rome as the theologian for Archbishop Charles Francois Baillargeon who was attending the first Vatican Council. Baillargeon died in 1870 and Taschereau was named his successor and consecrated in 1871.

As archbishop, Taschereau devoted himself to developing the territory over which he had prime responsibility. He aided the seminary, promoted two new colleges, and saved the college of Saint Anne de la Pocatiere from closing. He founded Sacred Heart Hospital and oversaw the founding of 40 parishes and 30 missions. Taschereau soon emerged as the spokesperson of the Canadian Roman Catholic bishops. From his base in predominantly Roman Catholic Quebec, he moved to enlarge the church. He invited a variety of Catholic orders into the country and called three provincial councils, over which he presided. He was named Canada's first cardinal in 1886. Taschereau had a special devotion to St. Anne, the mother of the Virgin Mary, and spent a considerable amount of energy in promoting the canonization of Bishop Laval, the first bishop of Quebec. These causes came together in the consecration of the basilica of St. Anne de Beaupre, which had become known for its many healings, and the transportation of the remains of Bishop Laval to their resting place at the basilica.

He retired from his administrative duties in 1894 and during the last years of his life suffered from a debilitating illness.

Sources:

New Catholic Encyclopedia. 17 vols. New York: McGraw-Hill, 1967.
Taschereau, Elzear A. *Remarques sur les Memoires de l'eveque de Trois-Rivieres su les Difficultes Religieuses en Canada*. Quebec, PQ: 1882.
Wallace, W. Stewart. *The Macmillan Dictionary of Canadian Biography*. 4th ed., rev. Edited by W. A. McKay. Toronto: Macmillan of Canada, 1978.

★940★
TATE, Mary Magdalena Lewis
Founder, Church of the Living God, the Pillar and Ground of Truth
b. Jan. 1871, Tennessee
d. Dec. 1930, Nashville, Tennessee

Little is known of the early life of Mother Mary Magdalena Lewis Tate, the founder of the Church of the Living God, the Pillar and Ground of Truth, one of the early predominantly-black Pentecostal denominations in North America. She was probably born and raised in Tennessee. She married Walter Lewis in the 1880s, and her first child, Walter Curtis Lewis, was born in 1890 in Vanlier, Tennessee. Around the turn of the century the family settled in Clinton, Tennessee, where Tate was to undergo a significant period of religious turmoil which culminated in a mission to go into the world and preach the gospel.

Tate began her teaching work in 1903 in Steele Springs, Tennessee, and soon moved on to Paducah, Kentucky, and Brooklyn, Illinois, where she preached her first sermon. Later journeys took her around the South and by 1907 she had begun to organize local holiness bands. Her initial work coincided with the beginnings of the Pentecostal Movement throughout the nation. Taken ill in 1908, Tate was healed and baptized with the Holy Spirit (as evidenced in the speaking in tongues) on Pentecost Sunday. Shortly thereafter, toward the end of June, she began revival services in Greenville, Alabama. At the end of the gatherings, the Church of the Living God, the Pillar and Ground of Truth was established and Tate designated as the Chief Apostle, Elder, President, and Chief Overseer. She also ordained the first ministers for the new church.

Tate established the first congregations in the deep South, but in the years immediately after World War I pushed into the Northern cites. The work moved from Alabama to Georgia, Florida, and Tennessee. In 1914 in Tennessee, the first four bishops, including Tate's two sons, who had assisted her from the beginning, were ordained. In 1923 she opened a publishing house in Nashville, Tennessee. Her last missionary journey was into the North. In the fall, she traveled to Evanston, Illinois, and then to Philadelphia, Pennsylvania. While in Philadelphia, she developed a case of frostbite that required surgery. Gangrene developed and she died in December 1930. The church was divided into three areas of 16 states each and placed in the care of three bishops: F. E. Lewis (Tate's son), M. F. L. Keith (the widow of Tate's eldest son), and Bruce L. McLeod. Each area eventually became a separate denomination.

Sources:

The Constitution, Government and General Decree Book of the Church of the Living God, the Pillar and Ground of Truth. Chattanooga, TN: The New and Living Way Publishing Co., n.d. 84 pp.
Dupree, Sherry Sherrod. *Biographical Dictionary of African-American, Holiness-Pentecostals, 1880-1990*. Washington, DC: Middle Atlantic Regional Press, 1990. 386 pp.
Lewis, Felix Early, and Walter Curtis Lewis. *Seventy-fifth Anniversary Booklet of the Church of the Living God, The Pillar and Ground of Truth, Inc., 1903-1978*. Nashville, TN: General Headquarters, Church of the Living God, the Pillar and Ground of Truth, 1978. 65 pp.

★941★
TAYLOR, John
President, Church of Jesus Christ of Latter-day Saints
b. Nov. 1, 1808, Milnthorpe United Kingdom
d. Jul. 25, 1887, Kaysville, Utah

John Taylor, third president of the Church of Jesus Christ of Latter-day Saints, was the son of James and Agnes Taylor. The family migrated to Canada in 1830, though John, as the eldest surviving son, remained behind to settle business affairs. He rejoined the family in 1832. He also affiliated with the Methodist Church and became a class leader and preacher. In 1833 he married Leonora

Cannon and settled in Toronto. Three years later, however, he met Parley Pratt on a mission for the Mormons and was converted and baptized. He began almost immediately to preach for them. In 1837 he moved to the United States and settled in Far West, the Mormon colony in Missouri. He quickly became a prominent member of the church and was ordained an apostle in 1838. He joined a group of missionaries in England in 1839 and was the first Mormon missionary in Ireland and on the Isle of Man.

Upon his return to America, Taylor settled in the new Mormon colony at Nauvoo, Illinois, where he served on the city council and became editor of the *Times and Seasons*, the church newspaper. In December 1843 he celebrated his first plural marriage to Elizabeth Kaighin; a few months later he married Jane Ballantyne. In 1844 he went to jail with church founder **Joseph Smith, Jr.**, his brother Hyrum Smith, and Willard Richards. On June 27 of that year a mob broke into the jail and killed Joseph Smith and his brother. Taylor and Richards survived, the former possibly saved by a watch in his vest pocket that stopped a bullet.

During the next few years, as the majority of Mormons made the transition to Utah, where Taylor opened a very successful sawmill, Taylor took more plural wives: Mary Ann Oakley (1846); Mary Amanda Ballantyne (1846); Mary Ramsbottom (1846); Lydia Dibble Smith (1846); Sarah Thornton Coleman (1846); Mercy Thompson Smith (1846); Sophia Whittaker (1847); Caroline Hooper Saunders Gillian (1847); and Margaret Young (1847). Three of his wives, Mercy Smith, Sarah Coleman, and Ann Ballantyne, later divorced Taylor.

In Utah Taylor held prominent positions as judge (1849-1850), territorial legislator (1853-1854, 1857-1879), probate judge (1868-1870), and member of the constitutional conventions. Church president Brigham Young overrode principles of seniority to make Taylor the president of the Quorum of the Twelve Apostles. In 1877, following Young's death, Taylor led the church as Quorum president until he was sustained as president of the church in 1880.

Taylor, who was a practitioner and staunch defender of polygamy, led the church during its most critical years when the United States government intensified its campaign to eliminate the practice. In 1882, in response to government action, Taylor had a revelation that all officers in the church's priesthood must enter into plural marriage. He further strengthened his position two years later with a revelation which ordered all monogamists to resign church offices. Aware of an order for his arrest, Taylor preached a last sermon in Salt Lake City in January 1885 and went underground. A month later, in a gathering of church leaders, he revealed that he was to be set apart as "King Priest and Ruler over Israel on the Earth—over Zion and the Kingdom of Christ our King of Kings." Because of the disruption of both church and political affairs in Utah, the action had little measurable effect. Taylor spent the next years on the run, slowing down briefly to marry Josephine Elizabeth Rouche, his last wife, in 1886. He died in hiding the following year.

During the twentieth century, polygamy-practicing Mormons (not members of the Church of Jesus Christ of Latter-day Saints) claim authority from a revelation that they believe Taylor received which authorizes a small group of men to administer the covenant of plural marriage, seeing that no year passes without at least one child being born in the covenant. The Church of Jesus Christ of Latter-day Saints deny that such a meeting occurred and that such a revelation was received by Taylor.

Sources:

Jensen, Andrew. *Latter Day Saints Biographical Encyclopedia* 4 vols. Salt Lake City, UT: Andrew Jensen History Co., 1901.
Nibley, Preston. *The Presidents of the Church*. Salt Lake City, UT: Deseret Book Company, 1960. 477 pp.
Roberts, B. H. *The Life of John Taylor*. Salt Lake City, UT: Bookcraft, 1963. 499 pp.
Taylor, John. *The Gospel Key*. Salt Lake City, UT: Deseret Book Company, 1944. 401 pp.
_____. *The Government of God*. Liverpool, England.: S. W. Richards, 1852. 118 pp.
_____. *The Mediation and Atonement of Our Lord and Savior Jesus Christ*. Salt Lake City, UT: Deseret News, 1882. 205 pp.
Taylor, Samuel Wooley. *Family Kingdom*. New York: McGraw-Hill, 1951. 302 pp.
_____. *The Kingdom or Nothing*. New York: Macmillan Publishing Co., 1976. 406 pp.

★942★
TEISH, Luisah
Neo-Yoruban Priestess
b. New Orleans, Louisiana

Luisah Teish, born Catherine Allen, is a Neo-Yoruban Priestess of the Goddess Oshun. She was raised in New Orleans, the "city of the Voudoun," in the 1950s. Her family practiced certain ancestral traditions, but her questions about the old ways usually went unanswered. Her parents' generation was trying to succeed in the white world. They had converted to Catholicism as part of this effort, but they were still linked to their African roots. Wanting their children to be fully adapted to the dominant culture, they were reluctant to transmit the traditional ways to the next generation. Thus Teish was raised in the Roman Catholic Church and taught that white society was the standard of normalcy. When she was 14, she moved to Los Angeles and lived with an aunt.

Following her graduation from high school in 1966, she attended Pacific University in Forest Grove, Oregon, and became a campus radical out of her experience of racism in the small Oregon community where the college was located. In 1969 she won a scholarship with Katherine Dunham at the Performing Arts Training Center in East St. Louis, Illinois. In addition to being a talented dancer and a brilliant choreographer, Dunham was an anthropologist interested in preserving the dances and other traditions of Africa and of the Africanized Caribbean Islands. While associated with Dunham, Teish had access to good reading material on these traditions. She also lived in the same house with Africans and Haitians. It was during this time that she began to get back in touch with her African roots. As part of this awakening, she joined the Fahami Temple of the Egyptian sun god Amun-Ra, which further nourished her sense of the spiritual significance of Africa. Although she eventually left the Temple, she kept the name Luisah Teish, meaning "adventuresome spirit," which she had acquired when initiated into that group. She moved to California and began dancing with Bata-koto, a group that focused on performing the dances of the orishas (the Yoruban deities) and the loas of Haiti.

Teish experienced a turning point in 1974 when she tried to kill herself. She had been through a series of bad experiences, and had felt oppressed by a combination of racism, sexism, and classism. Instead of dying, however, she had an out-of-body experience in which she explained to herself that life was not about escaping. Soon afterwards, she sought out a priest of the Yoruba tradition who told her that she was a favored child of the love goddess Oshun. It took her years to finally acknowledge this link and become a priestess. She had her formal initiation in the Lucumi branch of the Yoruba religion. Around 1978 Teish wrote a letter to *Plexus*, a Bay Area women's magazine, for people to "give her a buzz" if they were interested in talking about African goddesses. Instead of the two or three calls she expected, she received 60 calls. In response to this interest she began to develop workshops. Her workshop participants in turn encouraged her to write a book, *Jambalaya: The Nature Woman's Book of Personal Charms and Practical Rituals* (1985), which is a combination of folklore, autobiography, and directions for ritual practices.

Sources:

Albert, Mimi. "Out of Africa: An Interview with Luisah Teish." *Yoga Journal* (January/February 1987): 32-35, 63.

Teish, Luisah. *Jambalaya: The Natural Woman's Book of Personal Charms and Practical Rituals.* San Francisco: Harper & Row, 1985. 268 pp.

White, Timothy. "An Interview with Luisah Teish, Daughter of Oshun." *Shaman's Drum* 4 (Spring 1986): 41-45.

★943★
TEN BOOM, Corrie
Independent Evangelical Christian Writer and Evangelist
b. Apr. 15, 1892, Amsterdam Netherlands
d. Apr. 15, 1983, Placentia, California

Corrie ten Boom, evangelist and author of a number of popular Evangelical Christian books that grew out of her experiences in World War II, was the daughter of Cor Lurtingh and Caspar ten Boom. Her father was a clockmaker and a pious member of the Reformed Church, in which he raised his children. Corrie ten Boom grew up in Haarlem and over the years of her youth learned the clockmaking trade which supported her in later life. When she was 18 she enrolled in a local Bible school, but failed there and left to work in her father's shop. She was able to find a role for herself in Christian leadership, however, in founding a club for young girls sponsored by the Union des Amies de la Jeune Fille (Girl Guides).

Ten Boom's life changed in 1940 when Germany invaded Holland and began their attack upon the Jewish community. Her family was active in the underground resistance and began to harbor Jews. In February 1944, she and other family members were arrested. She was eventually sent to Ravenbruck Concentration Camp and was the only member of the family to survive. Released at the beginning of 1945 because of a clerical error, she made her way back to Holland and developed facilities to assist displaced persons and other ex-prisoners. However, she felt guided to take her story and her message of God's love around the world. She began to work with Youth for Christ and to travel. On an early trip to the United States she met Abraham Vereide of the International Christian Leadership; Marion Johnson, President Roosevelt's niece; and Dr. Edwin Orr, head of Renewal Fellowship Team. These became the key people in facilitating her development as an independent evangelist. For the next few decades she was constantly on the move and maturing as she integrated the deeply felt emotional scars of her prison experience with her Christian life.

In 1954 ten Boom completed her first book, *A Prisoner and Yet. . . .* She authored several other volumes through the 1960s, but it was her 1971 autobiographical volume, *The Hiding Place*, that brought her out of relative obscurity and made her a public religious figure. With the royalties from that book she founded Christians, Incorporated, a missionary enterprise. She would author over a book a year for the next decade. Among her more popular titles were *Tramp for the Lord*, a second autobiographical work (1974); *Don't Wrestle, Just Nestle* (1977); *Each New Day* (1977); and *He Cares, He Comforts* (1977). In 1975 *The Hiding Place* was made into a movie.

Ten Boom made California her home during her last years, but was constantly on the move and speaking as her health allowed.

Sources:

Carlson, Carole C. *Corrie ten Boom: Her Life, Her Faith.* Old Tappan, NJ: Fleming H. Revell Company, 1983. 224 pp.

ten Boom, Corrie. *Don't Wrestle, Just Nestle.* Old Tappan, NJ: Fleming H. Revell, 1978. 95 pp.

_____. *Each New Day.* Old Tappan, NJ: Fleming H. Revell Company, 1977.

_____. *Father ten Boom: God's Man.* Old Tappan, NJ: Fleming H. Revell Company, 1978. 159 pp.

_____. *He Cares, He Comforts.* Old Tappan, NJ: Fleming H. Revell Company, 1977. 95 pp.

_____, with John Sherrill and Elizabeth Sherrill. *The Hiding Place.* Washington Depot, CT: Chosen Books, 1971. 219 pp.

_____, with C. C. Carlson. *In My Father's House: The Years Before "The Hiding Place."*. Carmel, NY: Guideposts, 1976. 192 pp.

★944★
TERRY, Milton Spencer
Theologian and Biblical Scholar, Methodist Episcopal Church
b. Feb. 22, 1840, Coeymans, New York
d. Jul. 13, 1914, Los Angeles, California

Milton Spencer Terry, a Methodist theologian and biblical scholar who taught for many years at Garrett Biblical Institute, was the son of John and Eliza McLaughlin Terry. He was born Milton Seamans Terry but changed his name as a young man. His father was a Quaker, but Terry found himself drawn to Methodism. In 1857 he entered the New York Conference Seminary at Charlottesville, New York. While there he joined the Methodist Episcopal Church. He left the seminary in 1859 and spent several years teaching. Over the next few years he carried out an extensive program of self-education which included the mastery of nine languages. In 1860 he was licensed to preach by the church. He was able to attend Yale Divinity School for one year (1862-1863) and was admitted on trial to the New York Conference. He was ordained a deacon in 1864, the same year he married Frances O. Atchinson. He became an elder in 1866, pastored in New York for a decade, and in 1879 was made presiding elder in the New York district. In 1880 he was elected as a delegate to the general conference for the first time. He authored his first major text in 1883, *Biblical Hermeneutics*.

In 1884 Terry was invited to join the faculty of Garrett Biblical Institute (now Garrett-Evangelical Theological Seminary) in Evanston, Illinois, as head of the department of Old Testament and Hebrew and as an instructor in Christian doctrine, a tribute to his accomplishments. In 1887 he was able to spend a period in Germany where he absorbed aspects of the newer German critical approach to the scriptures, and he became one of the first to introduce this new approach into Methodism. His work became a matter of intense controversy as his books began to appear in the 1890s, beginning with his contributions to D. D. Whedon's *Commentary on the Old Testament* (1890). Terry followed with *The Sibylline Oracles* (1890); *The Prophecies of Daniel Expounded* (1893); the *Song of Songs Analyzed* (1893); *Rambles in the Old World* (1894); *The New Apologetic* (1894); and *Biblical Apocalyptics* (1894). In 1891 he was selected as a delegate to the international Methodist Ecumenical Conference.

During the first decade of the new century, he continued to be productive in his writing. Two of his books, *Moses and the Prophets* (1901) and *Primer of Christian Doctrine* (1906), found a popular audience and became among his most read and most controversial books as laypeople discovered the ideas he had been teaching. Other books included *The New and Living Way* (1902); *The Mediation of Jesus Christ* (1903); and possibly his most important mature volume, *Biblical Dogmatics* (1907). Writing in a noninflamatory tone and possessing an irenic spirit, Terry was able to weather the controversy around him and become a major force in slowly moving the Methodist Episcopal Church into the liberal Protestant camp.

Terry continued to work until the end of his life. In 1914 he completed his last book, a collection of *Baccalaureate Sermons and Addresses.* The day before his death he preached a Sunday evening sermon in Los Angeles.

Sources:

Dictionary of American Biography. 20 vols. and 7 supps. New York: Charles Scribner's Sons, 1928-1936, 1944-1981.

Terry, Milton S. *Biblical Apocalyptics.* New York: Eaton & Mains, 1898. 513 pp.

_____. *Biblical Dogmatics*. New York: Eaton & Mains, 1907. 608 pp.
_____. *Biblical Hermeneutics*. New York: Phillips & Hunt, 1883. 781 pp.
_____. *Moses and the Prophets*. New York: Eaton & Mains, 1901. 198 pp.
_____. *Primer of Christian Doctrine*. New York: Eaton & Mains, 1906. 86 pp.

★ 945 ★
Metropolitan THEODOSIUS
Metropolitan, Orthodox Church in America
b. Oct. 27, 1933, Canonsburg, Pennsylvania

Bishop Theodosius, the reigning metropolitan of the Orthodox Church in America, was born Theodore Lazur. He attended Washington and Jefferson College and, following his graduation in 1960, pursued theological studies at St. Vladimir's Orthodox Theological Seminary. In 1961 he was tonsured as a monk and ordained as a deacon. On October 22 of that year he was ordained as a priest in the Russian Orthodox Greek Catholic Church in America. His first assignment was as rector of Nativity of the Virgin Mary Church in Madison, Illinois. He also served as a chaplain at Fort Leonard Wood, across the river in Missouri.

In 1966 Theodosius was called to New York to assist in the diocesan chancery office. The next year he was elected bishop, assigned to Washington, D.C., and named vicar to the metropolitan. He remained in Washington only a short time before becoming bishop of Alaska. It was in that capacity that he participated in a series of significant events in American Orthodoxy. On April 10, Patriarch Alexis of Moscow issued a document recognizing the autonomous status of the Russian church in America. Six days later Alexis died. Bishop Theodosius attended the funeral of Patriarch Alexis, during which time he received the tomos of autocephaly from Metropolitan Pimen. This document underlay transformation of the Russian Orthodox Greek Catholic Church in America into the Orthodox Church in America. Later that year Bishop Theodosius hosted when **Metropolitan Ireney**, speaking in ceremonies in Kodiak, Alaska, proclaimed Father Herman of Alaska the first saint of the Orthodox Church in America.

In 1972 Bishop Theodosius moved to Pittsburgh, Pennsylvania, as bishop of Pittsburgh and West Virginia. Having a long-term interest in parish education, he served as chairman of the church's Department of Religious Education. He remained in Pittsburgh until 1977 when Metropolitan Ireney retired, and Bishop Theodosius was elected to succeed him. He presides over a multi-ethnic church of over one million members with congregations in Mexico, Canada, and several countries in South America.

Sources:
Tarasar, Constance J. *Orthodox America, 1794-1974*. Syosset, NY: Department of History and Archives, Orthodox Church in America, 1975. 361 pp.

★ 946 ★
Metropolitan THEOPHILUS
Metropolitan, Russian Orthodox Greek Catholic Church of America
b. Feb. 6, 1874, Kiev Russia
d. Jun. 27, 1950, San Francisco, California

Metropolitan Theophilus, head of the Russian Orthodox Greek Catholic Church in America (now an integral part of the Orthodox Church in America), was born Theodore Nicholavich Pashkovsky, the son of a priest in the Russian Orthodox Church. He attended the theological preparatory school in Kiev, and while there he developed what was diagnosed as an incurable bone infection. However, the school was visited by Father John of Kronstadt, a famous miracle worker, who prayed for him, and Theodore was healed. In gratitude for the healing, he entered the monastic life and in 1894 became a novice at the Kiev Lavra of the Caves, a monastic

center. Before the year was out, he was visited by **Bishop Nicholas**, head of the Russian Orthodox Mission in North America, who was seeking recruits to assist him in California. The novice recruit moved to San Francisco, and became secretary for the Mission administration.

Shortly after settling in California, Theodore married a woman from the Serbian community (over which the Russians presided in ecclesiastical matters). In 1897 he was ordained to the priesthood. He remained in San Francisco until 1906 when he returned to Russia to assist **Archbishop Tikhon**. Following the Russian Revolution, Tikhon held a series of confidential meetings at which he instructed Father Theodore on his wishes for the work in America. These included a wish for the father to be consecrated as bishop, a possibility since his wife had died. He returned to America, and in 1922 was elected and consecrated bishop of Chicago. He served in Chicago until 1931 when he became bishop of San Francisco.

With the death of **Metropolitan Platon** in 1934, Father Theodore was elected as the new metropolitan and took the ecclesiastical name Theophilus. The furtherance of education within the church became a major concern for the new metropolitan. Among his first actions was the establishment of a new seminary, St. Vladimir's, at Brooklyn, New York. This was followed by the opening of a second school for readers and choir directors adjacent to St. Tikhon's monastery in South Canaan, Pennsylvania. Theophilus led in the creation of a network of Sunday schools throughout the parishes of the church.

Theophilus also sent a delegation to Russia following World War II in an attempt to reestablish communion with the Patriarchate of Moscow, a new patriarch having been elected in 1945. His proposals that the American church acknowledge the spiritual authority of the Moscow patriarch were turned down by authorities in Russia, who wished that the American church acknowledge the Russian church's political and legal authority.

Theophilus died in 1950. He was succeeded by **Metropolitan Leonty**.

Sources:
Tarasar, Constance J. *Orthodox America, 1794-1976*. Syosset, NY: Department of Archives and History, Orthodox Church in America, 1975. 351 pp.

★ 947 ★
THIEME JR., Robert Bunger
Pastor, Berachah Church
b. Apr. 1, 1918, Ft. Wayne, Indiana

Robert Bunger Thieme, Jr., the fundamentalist pastor of Berachah Church in Houston, Texas, grew up in Beverly Hills, California. His grandfather had become wealthy as the owner of the Ft. Wayne Hosiery Mills; his father was an engineer. Thieme, Jr. attended the University of Arizona. While there he met his future wife, Betty Beal. He graduated in 1940 and concurrently received a commission as a second lieutenant in the Army Reserves. He entered Dallas Theological Seminary, a leading independent fundamentalist ministerial training school, but had to drop out as World War II began. He was assigned to Luke Army Air Force Base and was later placed in charge of cadet training. By 1942 he was the youngest lieutenant colonel in the Army Air Force.

After the war Thieme returned to Dallas. Dallas Theological Seminary has been known as a staunch supporter of dispensational Bible interpretation, an approach to Bible history which sees the story of humanity divided into various dispensations during which God acts differently toward humans. According to dispensationalism, humanity is living near the end of the church age and is awaiting the second coming of Jesus Christ. Thieme completed his M.Th. degree in 1949 and entered Dallas' graduate program to work on a doctorate. Prior to his finishing all the requirements, however, he became pastor of Berachah Church, an independent fundamentalist congregation which had been formed in the 1930s in Houston, Texas.

Thieme came to the church as a prime product of Dallas, but in the ensuing years has found himself in conflict with his former colleagues and has created a national following around some of his distinctive teachings. Thieme has argued that Christ's *physical* death upon the cross marked the completion of his bearing humanity's sin. His *spiritual* death, that is, his separation from God, was efficacious for humankind's salvation. Thieme also has argued that the blood of Jesus is merely a symbolic reference to the saving work of Christ.

Thieme published his views in a large number of booklets which are published by Berachah Tapes and Publications and circulated nationally. While controversy over Thieme's ministry has intensified in fundamentalist circles, Thieme has built a national following and regularly travels the country to hold teaching seminars. The church has founded Operations Grace World Missions, and his booklets are now distributed worldwide.

Sources:

King, George William. *Robert Bunger Thieme, Jr.'s Theory and Practice of Preaching.* Urbana, IL: University of Illinois, Ph.D. thesis, 1974. 161 pp.
Thieme, Robert B., Jr. *Anti-Semitism.* Houston, TX: Berachah Tapes and Publications, 1979. 152 pp.
_____. *Christian Integrity.* Houston, TX: R. B. Thieme, Jr. Bible Ministries, 1984. 203 pp.
_____. *Christian Suffering.* Houston, TX: R. B. Thieme, Jr. Bible Ministries, 1987. 185 pp.
_____. *The Integrity of God.* Houston, TX: Berachah Tapes and Publications, 1979. 281 pp.
_____. *Levitical Offerings.* Houston, TX: The Author, 1973. 112 pp.
Wall, Joe Layton. *Bob Thieme's Teaching on Christian Living.* Houston, TX: Church Multiplication, Inc., 1978. 196 pp.
Walter, Robert G. *The False Teaching of R. B. Thieme, Jr.* Collingswood, NJ: The Bible for Today, 1972. 103 pp.

★948★
THOMPSON, Charles Lemuel
Home Mission Executive, Presbyterian Church in the U.S.A.
b. Aug. 19, 1839, Allentown, Pennsylvania
d. Apr. 14, 1924, Atlantic City, New Jersey

Charles Lemuel Thompson, a Presbyterian minister who specialized in the development of home missions, was the son of Julia Shearer and Aaron Thompson. He grew up in rural Wisconsin, where his parents had moved when he was a child. He attended Carroll College and, after his graduation in 1858, entered Princeton Theological Seminary (1858-1860). After two years he transferred to the Theological Seminary of the Northwest (now McCormick) and earned his B.D. in 1861. He was ordained by the Presbyterian Church in the U.S.A.

During the rest of the century Thompson served a series of Presbyterian churches: Jeaneau, Wisconsin (1861-1862); Janesville, Wisconsin (1862-1867); Cincinnati, Ohio (1867-1872); Chicago (1872-1878); Pittsburgh, Pennsylvania (1879-1882); and Kansas City, Missouri (1882-1888). In 1888 he was elected the general moderator of the Presbyterian Church and that same year moved to New York City to complete his pastoral career at Madison Avenue Presbyterian Church, one of the more prominent churches in the denomination.

In 1898 Thompson left the pastorate to become the secretary of the Board of Home Missions of the Presbyterian Church. He brought to his new job a vision built over the years of work in the Midwest of the possibility of converting the country and building a Christian civilization in America. He was a conservative evangeli-

cal in his personal belief but was willing to put aside demands for doctrinal conformity in order to bring the denomination together for cooperative action.

Thompson emerged as the champion of missionary thrusts aimed at both the older minority communities in America as well as the new groups which were flooding into the country from Eastern and Southern Europe. During the 1890s he became associated with **Elias B. Sanford** in the Open and Institutional Church League. The two of them led in establishing regular gathering of executives from the missionary agencies of the major Protestant denominations. These meetings led in 1908 to their establishment of the Home Missions Council, a cooperative agency for the denomination's home missionary boards. There were nine charter denominations and Thompson served as the council's chairman for the first six years. The Council worked closely with the Federal Council of Churches, which also formed in 1908, under Sanford's leadership.

Thompson retired from the Presbyterian Board in 1914 and spent his retirement years writing a series of books reflecting upon his life and work: *The Religious Foundations of America* (1917); *The Soul of America* (1919); and *Charles Lemuel Thompson: An Autobiography* (1924).

Sources:

Bowden, Henry Warner. *Dictionary of American Religious Biography.* Westport, CT: Greenwood Press, 1977. 572 pp.
Cavert, Samuel McCrea. *The American Churches in the Ecumenical Movement.* New York: Association Press, 1968. 288 pp.
Thompson, Charles L. *Charles Lemuel Thompson: An Autobiography.* New York: Fleming H. Revell Company, 1924. 289 pp.
_____. *The Presbyterians.* New York: Baker & Taylor, Co., 1890. 312 pp.
_____. *The Religious Foundations of America.* New York: Fleming H. Revell Company, 1917. 307 pp.
_____. *The Soul of America.* New York: Fleming H. Revell, 1919. 251 pp.
_____. *Times of Refreshing: A History of American Revivals.* Chicago: L T. Palmer & Co., 1877. 483 pp.
Thompson, Elizabeth O., ed. *Charles Lemuel Thompson.* New York: Fleming H. Revell, 1924.

★949★
THORN, Michael
High Priest, Kathexis Coven
Founder, Witches & Pagans for Gay Rights
b. Feb. 21, 1956, Rockville Centre, New York

Michael Thorn, also known as Michael Harismedes, is a prominent gay Neo-Pagan who founded Kathexis Coven (1984) and Witches & Pagans for Gay Rights (1983). He is a professional nurse who holds a B.A. in psychology from the State University of New York at Stony Brook (1978) and an A.S. degree in Nursing from the State University Agricultural and Technical College at Farmingdale (1980). In 1974 he was initiated into the Gardnerian Wicca Tradition, the original Neo-Pagan tradition created by Gerald B. Gardner, and in 1978 the Faery Tradition as taught by Victor H. Anderson. He was also a founding member of North East Local Council of the Covenant of the Goddess (COG), a national association of Wiccan groups, and has held both local and national offices in that organization.

★950★
THURMAN, Howard
Minister and Author
b. Nov. 18, 1900, Daytona Beach, Florida
d. Apr. 10, 1981, San Francisco, California

Howard Thurman, a Baptist minister who became famous as an interdenominational preacher and mystic, was the son of Saul Solomon and Alice Ambrose Thurman. Rising above his childhood poverty, he attended Florida Baptist Academy at Jacksonville and in 1919 he was licensed to preach. He then attended Morehouse College, the Baptist school for Blacks in Atlanta, and stayed at the head of his class. He graduated as class valedictorian with a B.A. in economics in 1923. He moved from Atlanta to New York to attend Rochester-Colgate Theological Seminary. In 1926 he received his B.D. degree, married Katie Kelley, and returned to Morehouse (and its associated women's college, Spelman) as a professor of theology. His wife died in 1930, and he took a year off to meditate. He was able to spend the year at Haverford College studying with Rufus Jones.

Thurman returned to Morehouse for a year, but in 1932 moved to Howard University to teach Christian theology and chair the committee on religious life. In 1935 he toured India, Burma, and Ceylon, and had the occasion to meet Mahatma Gandhi. A remark by Gandhi led him into concentrated study of Jesus' teachings on the disinherited. While in India he made a decision to remain in the church and work for the underprivileged. He returned to Howard and was appointed dean of the chapel and full professor.

While in India, Thurman began to make plans to create an interracial church. By 1944 the idea had matured in an experimental parish in San Francisco, the Church for the Fellowship of All Peoples, designed to bring Whites, Blacks, and Orientals into a religious fellowship. Founder Albert Fisk asked Thurman to join him as co-pastor. He served the church for nine years with a succession of white co-pastors. These years became some of his most productive as an author. Among the books that appeared were *The Greatest of These* (1944); *Deep River: An Interpretation of Negro Spirituals* (1945); *Meditations for Apostles of Sensitiveness* (1947); *Jesus and the Disinherited* (1949); and *Meditations of the Heart* (1953).

In 1953 Thurman accepted the offer to become dean of the Daniel L. Marsh Chapel and professor of spiritual resources and disciplines at Boston University, the first black full-time professor ever hired by the school. The next decades of his life were marked by many honors for his outstanding preaching and the books he wrote. Among his most widely read books were: *The Inward Journey* (1961); *The Luminous Darkness* (1965); and *The Search for Common Ground* (1971). In 1979 he finished his autobiography, *With Head and Heart*.

Sources:

The First Footprints: Letters between Alfred Fisk and Howard Thurman, 1943-1944. San Francisco: Howard Thurman, 1975. 55 pp.

Hill, Samuel S., ed. *Encyclopedia of Religion in the South.* Macon, GA: Mercer University Press, 1984. 878 pp.

Metzger, Linda, ed. *Black Writers.* Detroit, MI: Gale Research Company, 1989. 619 pp.

Thurman, Howard. *Deep River: An Interpretation of Negro Spirituals.* New York: Harper, 1951. 212 pp.

———. *The Greatest of These.* Mills College, CA: Eucalyptus Press, 1944. 25 pp.

———. *The Inward Journey.* New York: Harper, 1961.

———. *The Luminous Darkness.* New York: Harper & Row, 1965. 113 pp.

———. *Meditations of the Heart.* New York: Harper, 1953. 216 pp.

———. *With Heart and Hand.* New York: Harcourt, Brace, Jovanovich, 1980. 274 pp.

Yates, Elizabeth. *Howard Thurman: Portrait of a Practical Dreamer.* New York: John Day, 1964. 249 pp.

★951★
TICHENOR, Isaac Taylor
Missionary Secretary, Southern Baptist Convention
b. Nov. 11, 1825, Spencer County, Kentucky
d. Dec. 2, 1902, Atlanta, Georgia

Isaac Taylor Tichenor, for 18 years the home missionary secretary of the Southern Baptist Convention, was the son of James and Margaret Bennett Tichenor. When he was 15 he entered the Taylorsville (Kentucky) Academy. Before he was able to go on to college, however, he became ill with a bad case of measles, the side effects of which hobbled him throughout the decade. He was able eventually to join the academy staff and teach. After being licensed in 1846, he traveled throughout his area as a Baptist preacher. In 1847 he became an agent for the American Indian Mission Association. In 1848 he accepted a call from the Baptist church in Columbus, Mississippi, where he was ordained. He stayed in Mississippi for two years, then spent a year in revival work and served a church in Henderson, Kentucky.

On New Year's Day 1852, Tichenor started a pastorate at First Baptist Church in Montgomery, Alabama, where he stayed for 15 years. At the end of his first year at the church he married Monimia C. Cook. He became active in the affairs of the Southern Baptist Convention and supported the establishment of the convention's first seminary, which was opened in Greenville, South Carolina. He was invited to give the first commencement sermon in 1860. His wife died that year, and in 1861 he married Emily Catherine Boykin. During the Civil War he took a leave of absence from his congregation to serve as chaplain for the 17th Alabama Regiment in the Confederate Army. In 1864 his second wife died.

In the last years of the war, Tichenor had become an owner in the Montevallo (Alabama) Coal Mining Company. Following the war, he pioneered the use of new mining techniques. He resigned from his church at the beginning of 1868 to promote the development of mining in the area, which would become the basis for the establishment of Birmingham and its quick emergence as the largest city in the state. The death of his third wife in 1869, however, caused him to rethink his values, and in 1870 he put aside his mining concerns and accepted the call to pastor First Baptist Church in Memphis, Tennessee.

After only a year in Memphis, Tichenor accepted the challenge to become the first president of Alabama's new Agricultural and Mechanical College (now Auburn University). He stayed in Auburn for 10 years. In 1876 he married Eppie Reynolds, who died in 1878.

In 1881 Tichenor left Auburn to begin the assignment for which he would be most remembered—the secretary of the Home Missionary Board of the Southern Baptist Convention. The last two decades of the nineteenth century were crucial for the development of the convention. After 15 years of recovery from the war, the convention had developed the capability to expand westward. It immediately ran into conflict with other Baptist groups, however, especially the American Baptists, over hegemony for missions west of the Mississippi in the former Confederacy.

Tichenor is largely credited with mobilizing the allegiance of the Baptists in the South toward the convention and building a program that could compete with the better-financed and older programs of the American Baptists. He developed a convention plan which supported regular giving for home mission enterprises. He initiated a Sunday school literature program and supported it until a Sunday school board could manage it. He inaugurated new efforts in education for Blacks and new programs in the Appalachian Mountains, and sent missionaries into the Indian territories. His statesmanship and tact strengthened all of his efforts. He continually had to convince a reluctant convention of the immediacy and worth of each new effort as well as negotiate with the Northern Baptists, led by an equally accomplished secretary in **Henry L. Morehouse**, over the legitimacy of the convention's claim to the South.

Following his retirement, Tichenor became sick and, after a prolonged illness, died.

Sources:
Dictionary of American Biography. 20 vols. and 7 supps. New York: Charles Scribner's Sons, 1928-1936, 1944-1981.

Dill, J. S. *Isaac Taylor Tichenor: The Home Mission Statesman.* Nashville, TN: Sunday School Board of the Southern Baptist Convention, 1908. 168 pp.

Encyclopedia of Southern Baptists. 3 vols. Nashville, TN: Broadman Press, 1958, 1971.

McBeth, H. Leon. *The Baptist Heritage.* Nashville, TN: Broadman Press, 1987. 850 pp.

★952★
Archbishop TIKHON
Archbishop, Russian Orthodox Church in America
b. Jan. 19, 1865, Pskov Russia
d. Apr. 7, 1925, Moscow Union of Soviet Socialist Republics

Archbishop Tikhon, the first archbishop of the Russian Orthodox Church in America and later patriarch of Moscow, was born Basil Bellavin, the son of a Russian Orthodox priest. He studied at the church's seminary at Pskov and then at the St. Petersburg Theological Academy. Following his graduation in 1888 he returned to Pskov as an instructor at his former seminary. He decided not to marry and was tonsured as a monk in 1892. He moved on from Pskov to hold positions at Kholm and Kazan seminaries. In 1897, at 32 years old, Tikhon became one of the youngest men ever named as a bishop. Named bishop of Lublin, he was there for less than a year when he was placed in charge of the diocese of the Aleutian Islands and Alaska.

Tikhon's diocese included the entire North American continent, and during the first years he traveled extensively in order to gain a firsthand knowledge of the vast territory under his jurisdiction. He promoted local congregations and encouraged them to become self-sustaining. In 1901 he dedicated St. Nicholas Church, a new cathedral in New York City.

Tikhon is generally credited with impressing upon the American church that it was to be the church in North America, not merely an extension of the Russian church, but a fully Americanized body. He began creating this uniquely American-Russian church with the appointment of two auxiliary bishops. In 1905 he was named archbishop, and his new archdiocese was renamed the Archdiocese of the Aleutian Islands and North America. He moved the headquarters of the archdiocese to New York City, where four years previously he had laid the cornerstone of his new cathedral, St. Nicholas. He established a seminary at Minneapolis, Minnesota, and a monastic community at South Canaan, Pennsylvania. In 1907 he called the first All-American Council of the diocese.

In 1907 Tikhon was called back to Russia as archbishop of Iaroslav, where he presided for seven years. In 1914 he moved to Vilno as archbishop. In the midst of the Russian Revolution, following the abdication of the czar, a meeting of the assembly of the diocese of Moscow was held, and Tikhon was named Metropolitan of Moscow. In the winter of 1917-1918 the Church Council of the Russian Orthodox Church was convened, and as the changes initiated by the Revolution spread, the council decided to fill the office of patriarch of the Russian Orthodox Church which had been vacant since the days of Peter the Great. The choice among the three candidates was made by lot. Tikhon was chosen and in November 1917 elevated as Patriarch of Moscow and all Russia. As patriarch he had jurisdiction over all of the dioceses of the church worldwide and once again became an important person in the development of the church in America.

As patriarch it was Tikhon's difficult job to defend the rights of the church to exist and carry on its worship against those in the new government who simply wanted to get rid of it. In the extremely delicate situation, he found himself opposing both the new so-called "Living Church" faction (those Orthodox most aligned to the Bolshevik government) and those traditionalists who called for a reinstitution of the monarchy. During his last years, Tikhon was caught in the intense manipulations of the church factions and gov-

ernment in the Soviet Union, one of the stakes being control of the church's property in North America. It becomes far from clear what Tikhon did and what was done by others under his name. In the midst of the fights for control, the American Archdiocese declared its independence from Patriarch Tikhon, justifying its action in part upon a 1920 decree by Tikhon allowing autonomy to any diocese separated from the patriarch by reason of political barriers. Tikhon died years before the major issues created in the Church by the Russian Revolution were solved.

Sources:

Kishkovsky, Leonid. "Archbishop Tikhon in America." *St. Vladimir's Theological Quarterly* 19, 1 (1975): 9-31.

Tarasar, Constance J. *Orthodox America, 1794-1974.* Syosset, NY: Department of History and Archives, Orthodox Church in America, 1975. 361 pp.

★953★
TILLICH, Paul Johannes Oskar
Theologian, Lutheran Church
b. Aug. 20, 1886, Starzeddel, East Prussia Germany
d. Oct. 22, 1965, Chicago, Illinois

Paul Johannes Oskar Tillich, one of the most prominent Protestant theologians of the twentieth century, was the son of Johannes Tillich, a Lutheran Pastor, and Wilhelmina Mathilde Dueselen Tillich. As a youth, Tillich was sent to the humanistic gymnasium in Konigsberg-Neumark and then to Berlin to study the classics. In addition, he began his own private study of German philosophy, which led to an initial crisis of faith. Caught up in the conflict between Christianity and humanism, Tillich resolved the issues with his father's assistance. In 1904 he entered the University of Berlin to begin his theological studies, though after a year he switched to the University of Halle (1905-1907). He received his doctorate in 1910 from the University of Breslau and his licentiate in theology from Halle in 1912. He was ordained a minister in the Evangelical Lutheran Church in 1912 in Berlin and served for two years at a church in Berlin. In 1914 he married Margarethe Wever and a few days later departed for service in World War I. He served for four years as a chaplain in the German Army.

The war introduced Tillich to profound human suffering. He left behind the optimistic idealistic theology he had previously professed and developed a deep sense of the estrangement in human life. He began to work on a theological program for the transformation of society (for which he initially would look to socialism for assistance), out of which he would issue one of his most characteristic ideas: "Religion is the substance of culture; culture is the form of religion." He also returned from the war to find his wife pregnant. They were divorced a short time later.

In 1924 Tillich became an associate professor of theology at the University of Marburg and married Hannah Werner Gottschow, who would remain his wife for the rest of his life. In 1925 he moved to Dresden as professor of philosophy and religious studies at the Institute of Technology. That same year he authored his first book, *The Religious Situation*, which initiated a public theological exploration of culture that expanded over the next decade into art, dance, economics, and psychoanalysis. In 1929 he became a professor of philosophy at the University of Frankfurt. Four years later he issued *The Socialist Decision*, a book which among other things attacked National Socialism and led to his quick dismissal from the faculty. In December 1933 he and his family moved to the United States.

For the next 22 years Tillich was a professor of theology at Union Theological Seminary. He became an American citizen in 1940. After World War II his most significant English-language works began to appear, and he emerged as one of the most important theologians of the century. The first volume of his final theoretical synthesis, *Systematic Theology*, appeared in 1951. In 1955 he received an appointment as professor at Harvard, where he lectured on the religious meaning of the secular arenas of life from psychiatry to business. The second volume of *Systematic Theology* appeared in 1957. Tillich retired from Harvard in 1962 and became the Nuveen Professor of Theology at the University of Chicago. The following year the last volume of *Systematic Theology* was published. During these same years he also published three volumes of sermons: *The Shaking of the Foundations* (1948); *The New Being* (1955); and *The Eternal Now* (1963). These volumes spread his reputation among many ministers otherwise unwilling to attempt a mastering of his *Systematic Theology*. Tillich, of course, wrote numerous additional books and articles covering his wide ranging interests.

Tillich's mature theology centered upon an exploration of the depth in life that leads to God, the ultimate Ground of Being. He was responsible for the popular definition of religion as the realm of humanity's ultimate concern. He placed the exploration of culture again at the center of the theological agenda and opened overly optimistic liberal Protestantism to a new appreciation of the "demonic" element in human existence.

Tillich stands with American theologian Reinhold Neibuhr and Germans Karl Barth, Emil Brunner, and Rudolf Bultmann, as a giant of contemporary theological thought. A number of associations devoted to the study and development of the implication of Tillich's thought have arisen. In North America the principal association is the North American Paul Tillich Society.

Sources:

Adams, James Luther. *Paul Tillich's Philosophy of Culture, Science, and Religion*. New York: Harper & Row, 1965. 313 pp.

Dictionary of American Biography. 20 vols. and 7 supps. New York: Charles Scribner's Sons, 1928-1936, 1944-1981.

Kegley, Charles W., and Robert W. Bretall, eds. *The Theology of Paul Tillich*. New York: Macmillan Company, 1964. 370 pp.

Pauck, Wilhelm, and Marion Pauck. *Paul Tillich: His Life and Thought*. New York: Harper & Row, 1976.

Tillich, Hannah. *From Time to Time*. New York: Stein & Day, 1973. 223 pp.

Tillich, Paul. *The Eternal Now*. New York: Charles Scribner's Sons, 1963. 185 pp.

———. *The New Being*. New York: Charles Scribner's Sons, 1955.

———. *The Religious Situation*. New York: Meridian Books, 1932, 1956. 219 pp.

———. *The Shaking of the Foundations*. New York: Charles Scribner's Sons, 1948. 186 pp.

———. *Systematic Theology*. 3 vols. Chicago: University of Chicago Press, 1951, 1957, 1963.

★ 954 ★
TINDLEY, Charles Albert
Minister, Methodist Episcopal Church
b. Jul. 7, 1851, Berlin, Maryland
d. Jul. 26, 1933, Philadelphia, Pennsylvania

Charles Albert Tindley, a minister of the Methodist Episcopal Church, was the son of Ester and Charles Tindley, two slaves who resided on the farm of Joseph Briddell. Unable to go to school, Tindley taught himself to read. After the Civil War he married Daisy Henry and moved to Philadelphia. He obtained work as a hod carrier and later as sexton of John Wesley Methodist Episcopal Church. Through the years he continued his education in night school, correspondence courses, and with the assistance of some acquaintances in Philadelphia. Over the years he decided to enter the ministry and in 1885 applied for admission to the Delaware Conference of the Methodist Episcopal Church, an all-black conference serving Maryland, New Jersey, and Pennsylvania.

In spite of his lack of formal education, Tindley was admitted on probation and assigned as pastor to the church in Cape May, New Jersey. Two years later he was ordained as a deacon and sent to

South Wilmington, Delaware. After a year as a special missionary among blacks in New Jersey (1888-1889), he was ordained as an elder at the 1889 conference session. Over the next decade he served a succession of pastoral charges culminating in his appointment as presiding elder of the Wilmington District in 1900. In 1901 he published the first collection of the many hymns he authored during his ministry. Some of these hymns became very popular among the different black churches and a few, such as "Stand By Me" and "We'll Understand It Better By and By," found a larger audience within white churches.

In 1902 Tindley was appointed to Bainbridge Street Methodist Episcopal Church in Philadelphia. This was the old John Wesley Church, now in a new sanctuary, and thus Tindley had become the pastor of the church he once cleaned. He would remain at the church for the rest of his life. Under his leadership the congregation moved to Broad Street in 1906, and was renamed East Calvary Methodist Episcopal Church. Within a short time Tindley became one of the more powerful leaders in the Philadelphia black community, and his church developed into a center of culture. The church's membership topped 5,000.

In 1908 Tindley was elected as a delegate to the Methodist general conference, an honor bestowed upon him every quadrennium for the rest of his life. In 1916 and 1920 he was nominated for bishop, an honor possibly denied him because of his lack of formal education. Even though not elected, he remained the dominant influence in the Delaware Conference. Following the 1920 general conference he moved ahead with plans to build a cathedral-like church and secured the financing for the project with the help of philanthropist John Wannamaker. The new 3,500-seat church was opened in 1925. The celebration of its completion, however, was marred for Tindley by the sudden death of his wife. Eventually the church would be renamed Tindley Temple Methodist Episcopal Church.

Tindley's last years were marked by his leadership of the largest black congregation in the city and his popularity as a speaker before both black and white audiences. He married Jenny Colton in 1927. While enjoying great prestige, he was never able to pull the church out of the debt incurred during the construction of the new building just before the great Depression.

Sources:

Jones, Ralph H. *Charles Albert Tindley: Prince of Preachers*. Nashville, TN: Abingdon, 1982. 192 pp.

★ 955 ★
TIPPY, Worth Marion
Minister, Methodist Episcopal Church
b. Nov. 8, 1866, Walkerton, Indiana
d. Oct. 2, 1961, Laurel, Mississippi

Worth Marion Tippy, a Methodist minister known for his pioneering social service work, was the son of Mary Isabel Carder and Oren Tippy. Raised in Indiana, he attended DePauw University from which he received his Ph.B. degree in 1891. He then did graduate work at Cornell University as a Sage scholar in the Sage School of Philosophy (1891-1893). Returning to Indiana he joined the Indiana Conference of the Methodist Episcopal Church and served churches at Lafayette (1893-1894), Oxford (1894-1895), Terre Haute (1895-1900), and Indianapolis (1900-1904). In 1895 he married Sella B. Ward. Transferring to the Ohio Conference in 1905, he became pastor of Epworth Memorial Church in Cleveland. He finished his pastoral career in New York City at Madison Avenue Methodist Episcopal Church (now Christ Church) (1915-1917).

During his years in Indianapolis and Cleveland, Tippy became deeply involved in the social needs of the community. He led in the founding of the Methodist Federation for Social Service created by the church's general conference in 1908. His vision for the council was set out in his first books, *The Socialized Church* (1909) and *The Church: A Community Force* (1914). In New York Tippy became involved with the recently founded Federal Council of Churches and in 1917 left his parish to become the executive secretary of the council's Department of the Church and Social Service. Among his first tasks was the selection of chaplains for the Army and Navy during World War I. He also became involved with the care of interned aliens and prisoners of war and with motivating the public to cooperate with the Public Health Service. Much of this activity he described in his book *The Church and the Great War* (1918).

Tippy stayed with the council until 1937. In addition, in 1928 he founded and served as the executive for the Church Conference on Social Work. He left the council in 1937 and was on the staff of the national Christian Mission for several years. In 1941 he moved to Washington, D.C., to help reorganize and revitalize the local federation of churches. He followed with similar roles in Kansas City, Missouri; Mobile, Alabama; and Springfield, Massachusetts (1944-1945).

During his retirement years Tippy allowed a long-time interest in Indiana Methodist history to come to the fore. He was the founder of the archives at DePauw University which now serves as the archival depository for Indiana Methodism, and he authored a biography of Bishop R. R. Roberts, *Pioneer Bishop* (1958).

Sources:

Harmon, Nolan B. *The Encyclopedia of World Methodism*. 2 vols. Nashville: United Methodist Publishing House, 1974.

Howell, Clinton H., ed. *Prominent Personalities in Methodism*. Birmingham, AL: Lowrey Press, 1945. 512 pp.

Tippy, Worth Marion. *The Church: A Community Force*. New York: Missionary Education Movement of the U. S. and Canada, 1914. 80 pp.

_____. *The Church and the Great War*. New York: Fleming H. Revell Company, 1918. 139 pp.

_____. *Frontier Bishop*. New York: Abingdon Press, 1958. 207 pp.

_____. *A Methodist Church and Its Work*. New York: Methodist Book Concern, 1919. 157 pp.

_____. *The Socialized Church*. New York: Eaton & Mains, 1909. 288 pp.

★956★
TKACH, Joseph William
Pastor General, Worldwide Church of God
b. Mar. 16, 1927, Chicago, Illinois

Joseph William Tkach, the pastor general of the Worldwide Church of God, is the son of Mary and Vassil Tkach, both first-generation immigrants from Czechoslovakia. He was raised in the Eastern Orthodox Church. He joined the Navy during World War II. After the war, he studied at the Illinois Institute of Technology and went to work for Hupp Aviation. In 1951 he married Elaine Apostolos.

During the 1950s Tkach began receiving *The Plain Truth*, the magazine of the Worldwide Church of God, a sabbatarian (Saturday worshiping) adventist church founded in the 1930s. Attracted to the church, he joined and was baptized in 1957. He was ordained a deacon in 1961 and an elder in 1963. Soon afterward he resigned from his secular job to become a full-time minister, and served churches in the Midwest for the three years. In 1966 he moved to Pasadena, California, so he could attend the church's school, Ambassador College.

During the 1970s, the Worldwide Church of God experienced a decade of turmoil which led to the resignation of many ministers and members and the loss of the founder's son, **Garner Ted Armstrong**. During this time, Tkach's faithfulness and leadership skills came to the fore. In 1974 he was named a presiding elder, and five years later became the director of the church's Ministerial Services Department. In 1981 he was named to the church's board of directors and shortly before the church's founder and apostle, **Herbert W. Armstrong**, died, he was named his successor. Besides heading the 100,000-member church and its several subsidiary structures, Tkach is also editor-in-chief of its periodical, *The Plain Truth*, for which he writes a monthly column.

Sources:

Biography Index. New York: The H. W. Wilson Co.

★957★
TOLTON, Augustine
Priest, Roman Catholic Church
b. Apr. 1, 1854, Ralls County, Missouri
d. Jul. 9, 1897, Chicago, Illinois

Augustine Tolton, the second Black in America to be ordained a priest in the Roman Catholic Church, was born into slavery, the son of Martha Jane Crisley and Peter Paul Tolton. His father left home in 1861 to join the Union Army, and died during the war. With the family, his mother escaped into Illinois and freedom. His mother, and eventually all the children, went to work in a tobacco factory in Quincy, Illinois. The mother, who had been baptized a Catholic many years before, took the family to the local church and the priest allowed Tolton into the parish school. As he grew up, he aspired to the priesthood and took some training, especially in languages, from a group of German Franciscans. Unable to attend a nearby seminary, the bishop found a way for him to attend the college of the Propagation of the Faith in Rome. He moved to Rome in 1880 and studied there for five years. In 1886 he was ordained and served his first mass on the high altar of St. Peter's Cathedral in the Vatican, a place usually reserved for the Pope to say mass.

There was some discussion at the time of his ordination over whether Tolton should be sent to the mission field or back to the United States. In the end Cardinal Simeoni sent him back home. Tolton returned to America in 1886 as the only black priest in the United States (the first black priest, **James Augustine Healy**, was then serving as a bishop). He settled in Quincy as the priest of St. Joseph's Catholic Church for Negroes. The little parish was poor and did not prosper, but Tolton became a celebrity and was frequently invited to speak around the country. He is reported to have made a striking appearance as he was a big man who regularly wore red trim on his clerical garb.

In 1889 a wealthy donor gave $10,000 to found what became St. Monica's Roman Catholic Church for Negroes in Chicago. The post was offered to Tolton, and arrangements were made for him to transfer to the Chicago Archdiocese. He opened St. Monica's soon after he settled in Chicago. His ministry was not marked by outstanding success, and he found few in the black community ready to become Catholics.

Tolton died in the summer of 1897. He had been attending a retreat at Kankakee, Illinois, and on the way back to Chicago was overcome by the heat and died in Mercy Hospital. He was buried at Quincy and in recent years his grave has become a point of pilgrimage for black Catholics.

Sources:

Hemesath, Caroline. *From Slave to Priest (1854-1897), First Afro-American Priest of the U.S.* Chicago: Franciscan Herald, 1973.

Logan, Rayford W., and Michael R. Winston, eds. *Dictionary of American Negro Biography*. New York: W. W. Norton & Co.   1982. 680 pp.

Nesbitt, Elsbeth. ''The Life and Ministry of Father Augustine Tolton: A Reflection of the American Catholic Church, 1863-1900.'' Santa Barbara, CA: 1987. 16 pp.

★958★
TOMLINSON, Ambrose Jessup
Founder, Church of God (Cleveland, Tennessee)
Founder, Church of God of Prophecy
b. Sep. 22, 1865, Westfield, Indiana
d. Oct. 2, 1943, Cleveland, Tennessee

Ambrose Jessup Tomlinson, the most important of the founders of the Church of God (Cleveland, Tennessee) and later the founder of the Church of God of Prophecy, was born in a rural Quaker community, the son of Milton and Delilah Hiatt Tomlinson. His parents were not particularly religious, but in 1889 he married Mary Jane Taylor, a devout Quaker through whom he was converted. As a young man he was a colporteur for the American Bible Society, and 1896 found him selling Bibles and other religious literature in the mountains of western North Carolina. While pursuing this occupation, Tomlinson stumbled upon a "proto-Pentecostal" Holiness congregation at Camp Creek. He later moved his family to North Carolina from Indiana, and joined the group in 1903.

Ordained in the Holiness Church, he moved to Cleveland, Tennessee, where he soon persuaded an independent church to unite with the North Carolina congregation. A third church had affiliated by 1906 when the first convention was held, and Tomlinson was chosen to moderate. This small group of churches adopted the name Church of God in 1907.

Following the annual assembly in 1908, Tomlinson invited **G. B. Cashwell**, who had recently come from the Pentecostal revival on Azusa Street in Los Angeles, to preach a revival. Tomlinson was the first member of his church to experience the baptism of the spirit and speak in tongues, the distinctive experience shared by Pentecostals, and soon afterward the whole of the Church of God had become Pentecostal. As the movement expanded, so did Tomlinson's status and power. Chosen general moderator of the church in 1909, he became its general overseer in 1910. He was also given the power to appoint ministers, and in 1914 he was designated general overseer for life.

Growth and success, however, often bring problems with them, and the Church of God was no exception in this regard. Accused of mismanaging funds in 1922, by 1923 Tomlinson had been tried and impeached. Later that year, Tomlinson called a convention of his followers and initiated what became the Church of God of Prophecy. After his death in 1943, a dispute between his two sons (**Homer Aubrey Tomlinson** and Milton A. Tomlinson) over who should inherit authority as general overseer led to yet another schism.

Sources:

Conn, Charles W. *Like a Mighty Army*. Cleveland, TN: Church of God Publishing House, 1955. 380 pp.
Duggar, Lillie. *A. J. Tomlinson: Former General Overseer of The Church of God*. Cleveland, TN: White Wing Publishing Company, 1964. 807 pp.
Tomlinson, A. J. *Diary*. 3 vols. Queens Village, NY: Church of God, World Headquarters, 1949, 1953, 1955.
_____. *God's Twentieth Century Pioneer*. Cleveland, TN: White Wing Publishing Company, 1962. 200 pp.
_____. *Historical Notes*. Cleveland, TN: White Wing Publishing Company, 1970. 104 pp.

★959★
TOMLINSON, Homer Aubrey
Founder, Church of God (World Headquarters)
b. Oct. 25, 1893, Westfield, Indiana
d. Dec. 4, 1968, Queens, New York

Homer Aubrey Tomlinson, founder of the Church of God (World Headquarters), was the son of **Ambrose Jessup Tomlinson**, a founder of the Church of God (Cleveland, Tennessee), and Mary Jane Taylor Tomlinson. Although supportive of his father, Homer was not attracted to the ministry. He became a success in the ad-

vertising business, and might never have become a pastor had his father not been impeached from his position as general overseer of the Church of God. After A. J. Tomlinson formed his remaining supporters into the Church of God of Prophecy, Homer started a congregation in Jamaica, New York, and worked to expand the new denomination in the northeastern part of the country. He was particularly active among immigrant groups in New York City.

After A. J. Tomlinson died in 1943, Milton A. Tomlinson, Homer's younger brother, was elected new general overseer. Homer disputed the legitimacy of this election, claiming that his father had explicitly designated him as successor. He also asserted that his father had commissioned him to carry the church flag to all of the Earth's nations. Taking the dispute to court, Milton's party was awarded the denomination's properties and trademarks. Following the pattern of his father, Homer called his supporters to New York, where he organized a new Church of God, distinguished from other denominations of the same name through the addition of the phrase "World Headquarters."

Homer was a flamboyant leader, relying on his advertising background to attract publicity. He journeyed to Israel to plant the church's flag as part of the commission from his father, and ran for president of the United States on the ticket of the Theocratic party. He declared himself "King of All Nations of Men in Righteousness," and was crowned king at the annual convention of the Church of God in 1954. Homer maintained an active agenda of traveling, speaking, preaching, and writing until his death in 1968.

Sources:

Tomlinson, Homer A. *The Shout of a King*. Queens Village, NY: Church of God, World Headquarters, 1968. 220 pp.

★960★
TORRES, Penny
New Age Channel
Founder, Foundation for Self-Realization Beyond the Human Potential

Penny Torres, the channel for the discarnate entity Mafu, is one of the more popular New Age teachers. She was raised in a fairly conventional Roman Catholic household. When she was 13 years old, she lapsed into a coma and was diagnosed as having pituitary cancer. Doctors advised her that it was inoperable and that she would probably die. Often on drugs because of pain, she learned self-hypnosis after graduating from high school, and was eventually able to overcome her dependency on painkillers. She married Tony Torres, a Los Angeles policeman, and around the time of her marriage she discovered that her tumor had disappeared. (In esoteric traditions the pituitary gland is often associated with psychic and spiritual abilities, and Mafu later explained to Torres that her pituitary problem had stimulated her spiritual awareness.)

At the time Mafu began contacting her, Penny Torres was a housewife and mother with no background in metaphysics or New Age thinking. In 1986 she decided to attend a channeling session—a session in which she was told that Mafu wanted to manifest through her. Her first communication from Mafu consisted of instructions on how to heal her two-year-old son of pneumonia with a crystal she had purchased at the channeling session. Not knowing what to make of her experiences, she was advised to seek help from the Spiritual Sciences Institute in Santa Barbara, California. Within a few months, Torres herself was channeling.

She first channeled Mafu in the presence of a group of friends in her home. Soon afterward, she was conducting regular weekly channeling sessions in Los Angeles and Santa Barbara. Mafu's popularity grew rapidly—so quickly that Torres soon became a major figure in the channeling movement. She then began to offer one- and two-day seminars, and the teachings were propagated by Torres' new organization, Mafu Seminars, in the form of tapes and videos. In 1987 *Reflections*, a bimonthly journal, began to be published. In time, Mafu Seminars moved its headquarters from Santa Barbara to Vacaville, California. In late 1989 Torres traveled to India and, at Haridwar, was given *sannyas* by Swamis Nityananda Paramahansa and Sivanand Giri. She now uses the name of Swami Paramanand Saraswati. As of this writing, Mafu Seminars has applied for nonprofit status with the federal government under a new name, the Foundation for Self-Realization Beyond the Human Potential.

Mafu is described as an enlightened being who lived 17 lifetimes, spanning 32,000 years, on the planet Earth. His teachings are fairly typical of New Age metaphysical groups. A special diet and special meditations are also advocated. Observers have often noted the similarities between Torres and Mafu and the more well-known **J. Z. Knight** and Ramtha, as both predict geological upheavals. Also like Ramtha, Mafu manifests through his channel while she is in a complete trance.

Sources:

Mafu [Penny Torres]. *And What Be God?* Vacaville, CA: Mafu Seminars, 1989. 15 pp.
_____. *Reflections on Yeshua Ben Joseph*. Vacaville, CA: Mafu Seminars, 1989. 20 pp.
"Interview with Penny Torres." *Life Times* 1, 3 (1987): 94-98.
"Penny Torres on Mafu—An Interview." *Life Times* 1, 2 (Winter 1986-1987): 74-79.

★961★
TORREY, Reuben Archer
Minister, Congregational Church
b. Jan. 28, 1865, Hoboken, New Jersey
d. Oct. 26, 1928, Biltmore, North Carolina

Reuben Archer Torrey, fundamentalist minister and pastor of both Moody Church in Chicago and the Church of the Open Door in Los Angeles, was the son of Reuben Slayton and Elizabeth Archer Swift Torrey. He attended Yale University, receiving his A.B. in 1875 and his B.D. in 1878. Upon graduation he was ordained to the ministry by the Congregational Church and became the pastor of the Congregational church in Garretsville, Ohio. While there, in 1879 he married Clara B. Smith. In 1882 he went to Germany for a year of post-graduate study at the Universities of Leipzig and Erlangen. Upon his return to the United States he became the superintendent of a city mission in Minneapolis, Minnesota.

While in Minnesota, Torrey became impressed with the work of evangelist **Dwight L. Moody**. In 1889 Moody called Torrey to Chicago as the superintendent of the new bible institute connected to his Chicago Evangelization Society. He also became the pastor of the Chicago Avenue Church. Following Moody's death, these two institutions would be named the Moody Bible Institute and Moody Memorial Church respectively. In 1901 Torrey authored his first book, *How to Work for Christ*.

Torrey had a passion for evangelism, and beginning in 1902 he initiated a series of round-the-world evangelism tours, a most unusual endeavor at the time. He circled the globe several times in the next four years, often accompanied by musician Charles M. Alexander. During the next five years he frequently returned to England, Scotland, and Ireland to preach. The years of this intense evangelistic activity were also a time of significant literary output. He authored *How to Promote and Conduct a Successful Revival* (1905); *Real Salvation and Whole Hearted Service* (1905); *Lessons in the Life and Teachings of Our Lord* (1907); and *The Person and Work of the Holy Spirit* (1910).

In 1911 Torrey was lured away from his Chicago work to help start two key fundamentalist institutions in Los Angeles. Thus in 1912, after completing his evangelistic commitments in England, he became the first dean of the Bible Institute of Los Angeles

(BIOLA). Three years later he became the first pastor of the associated Church of the Open Door. He turned them into west coast models of the organizations he had left in Chicago. During his years of building up the school and church, Torrey authored *The Fundamental Doctrines of the Christian Faith* (1919); *The God of the Bible* (1923); and *How to Be Saved and How to Be Lost* (1923). He retired in 1924 and moved to North Carolina. Torrey continued to write during these last years. His titles included *How to Get the Gold Out of the Word of God* (1925) and *Lectures on the First Epistle of John* (1928).

Sources:

Church of the Open Door, 1915-1965, Golden Anniversary. Los Angeles: Church of the Open Door, 1965. 40 pp.
Moyer, Elgin S., ed. *Who Was Who in Church History*. Chicago: Moody Press, 1968.
Torrey, Reuben A. *The Bible and its Christ*. New York: Fleming H. Revell Company, 1906. 139 pp.
_____. *The Christ of the Bible*. New York: George H. Doran Co., 1924. 285 pp.
_____. *How to Promote and Conduct a Successful Revival*. New York: Fleming H. Revell Company, 1901. 336 pp.
_____. *How to Work for Christ*. Chicago: Fleming H. Revell Company, 1901. 518 pp.
_____. *The Person and Work of the Holy Spirit*. New York: Fleming H. Revell Company, 1910. 262 pp.

★962★
TOWNE, Elizabeth Lois Jones
New Thought Publisher
Minister, Church of Truth
b. May 11, 1865, Portland, Oregon
d. Jun. 1, 1961, Holyoke, Massachusetts

Elizabeth Lois Jones Towne, a leading figure in the New Thought movement and major publisher of New Thought literature, was raised in Oregon as a Methodist. She was married in her mid-teens, but the marriage was unhappy. She left both her husband and Methodism and became involved in New Thought. With the support of her father, she started a New Thought magazine, *Nautilus*, in 1898. The magazine became an instant and enduring success.

She moved to Massachusetts a few years later, where she married her second husband, William Towne. Incorporating her publishing enterprise, she employed her new husband as associate editor and her ex-husband and children as staff. With the move to Massachusetts, Elizabeth Towne's career as a New Thought lecturer, publisher, and writer soared. A few of her many books were *Practical Methods for Self-Development* (1904); *How to Grow Success* (1904); *Happiness and Marriage* (1904); and *Experiences in Self-Healing* (1905).

As the movement began to manifest itself in the form of New Thought churches, Elizabeth Towne gravitated toward cooperative organizations that worked to keep the various independent bodies in communication with one another. Towne was, for example, one of the charter members of the New England Federation of New Thought Centers, and in 1924 she became the second person elected as president of the New Thought Alliance (INTA); International. She was also ordained in a small New Thought church, the Church of Truth.

Over and above her business and religious activities, Towne participated in a series of social and political organizations. She was, for example, a member and president of the Business and Professional Women's Club, the Holyoke Women's Club, and the League of Women Voters. Towne was also a delegate to the National Federation on the Cause and Cure of War, and a charter member of the Holyoke Council on World Relations. Active into her 80s, Towne lived to be 95.

An understanding of New Thought is perhaps best accomplished through a discussion of its similarities and dissimilarities with Christian Science. **Mary Baker Eddy** stressed healing, the unreality of matter, and the Christian nature of her church. New Thought—which largely, though not entirely, came into being as a result of defections from Christian Science—retained the stress on healing as well as the stress on the priority of mind over matter. In contrast to Christian Science, however, New Thought views matter as having a positive, though secondary, reality and stresses, alongside healing, what has come to be called "prosperity consciousness," (the belief that the abundance of the material universe is, like God's healing power, available to all). It also does not tend to view its teachings as specifically Christian. Perhaps because of bad experiences with Eddy's church, New Thought has remained decentralized and tolerant of a wide variety of differing interpretations.

Sources:

Dreier, Thomas and others. *The Story of Elizabeth Towne and The Nautilus.* Holyoke, MA: Elizabeth Towne Co., [1910]. 32 pp.
Towne, Elizabeth. *Experiences in Self-Healing.* Holyoke, MA: Elizabeth Towne Co., 1905, 1924. 78 pp.
_____. *How to Use New Thought in Home Life.* Holyoke, MA: Elizabeth Towne Co., 1915. 189 pp.
_____. *Just How to Concentrate.* Holyoke, MA: Elizabeth Towne Co., 1933. 38 pp.
_____. *Lessons in Living.* Holyoke, MA: The Author, 1911. 185 pp.
_____. *The Life Power and How to Use It.* Holyoke, MA: The Author, 1905. 175 pp.

★ 963 ★
TOY, Crawford Howell
Biblical Scholar, Southern Baptist Convention
b. Mar. 23, 1836, Norfolk, Virginia
d. May 12, 1919, Cambridge, Massachusetts

Crawford Howell Toy, a biblical scholar and pioneer student of the history of religions, is remembered for being forced out of the Southern Baptist Theological Seminary. The son of Thomas Dallam and Amelia Ann Rogers, Toy was given a good education as his father was something of a scholar. He attended the Norfolk Academy and the University of Virginia, from which he graduated in 1856. He taught at the Albemarle Female Institute at Charlottesville, Virginia, for three years. In 1859 he entered the Southern Baptist Theological Seminary in Greenville, South Carolina, with the object of preparing himself for the missionary field. His studies were interrupted, however, by the beginning of the Civil War.

Toy initially fought in the war as an artilleryman, but later became a chaplain. He was captured at Gettysburg but, after being exchanged, he reenlisted. Following the war, he found a job teaching Greek at the University of Virginia, but then was able to spend two years in Germany (1866-1868) studying at the University of Berlin. Upon his return in 1869 he was offered a position as professor of Old Testament interpretation at the Southern Baptist Theological Seminary. He gave 10 years to the seminary, and moved with it to Louisville, Kentucky, in 1877. He was considered by many to be the school's intellectual giant. However, shortly after the move he encountered resistance for suggesting that some Old Testament texts, which are quoted in the New Testament as prophesies fulfilled in the life of Christ, were not originally intended as such. The controversy, which centered upon Toy's opinions concerning the nature of biblical inspiration, led to his resignation from the seminary in 1879.

Toy did not find immediate employment, given the circumstances of his leaving the seminary. He moved to New York and wrote for the *Independent* until 1880 when he was offered a position as Hancock Professor of Hebrew and other languages. In the liberal Unitarian atmosphere at Harvard, he blossomed as a scholar and produced a number of important scholarly works. His first book *The History of the Religion of Israel* (1882) was a popular, frequently reprinted title. Other scholarly titles included: *Quotations in the New Testament* (1884); *Judaism and Christianity* (1890); and *A Critical and Exegetical Commentary on the Book of Proverbs* (1899). He married Nancy Saunders in 1888 and retired in 1909.

Increasingly, during his years at Harvard, Toy's attention turned toward the relatively new field of the history of religions, and in 1891 he founded the Harvard club for the study of the history of religions. Judaism was of special concern, and he became one of the editors of the *Jewish Encyclopedia*. As a professor emeritus he authored two classic texts in his field, *Studies in the History of Religions* (1912) and *Introduction to the History of Religions* (1913).

Sources:

Dictionary of American Biography. 20 vols. and 7 supps. New York: Charles Scribner's Sons, 1928-1936, 1944-1981.
Toy, Crawford Howell. *A Critical and Exegetical Commentary on the Book of Proverbs.* New York: Charles Scribner's Sons, 1899. 554 pp.
_____. *History of the Religion of Israel.* Boston: Unitarian Sunday School Society, 1882. 155 pp.
_____. *Introduction to the History of Religions.* Boston: Ginn & Company, 1912. 639 pp.
_____. *Judaism and Christianity.* Boston: Little, Brown and Company, 1890. 456 pp.
_____. *Quotations in the New Testament.* New York: Charles Scribner's Sons, 1884. 321 pp.
_____. *Studies in the History of Religions.* New York: Macmillan Company, 1912.

★ 964 ★
TOZER, Aiden Wilson
Minister, Christian and Missionary Alliance
b. Apr. 21, 1897, La Jose, Pennsylvania
d. May 12, 1963, Toronto, Ontario, Canada

Aiden Wilson Tozer, popular writer and minister in the Christian and Missionary Alliance (CMA), was the son of Prudence Jackson and Jacob Snyder Tozer. He was not fond of his given name and became self-identified as simply "A. W."; few knew his full name. He grew up on the family's farm in rural Pennsylvania. In 1915, when he was 17, he had a dramatic conversion experience listening to a street preacher in Akron, Ohio. Soon afterward he joined Grace Methodist Church in Akron. He became active in testifying to his new faith and organizing prayer meetings. He became attached to the Christian and Missionary Alliance and in 1920 was ordained. Early pastorates included Morgantown, West Virginia; Toledo, Ohio; and Indianapolis, Indiana.

In 1928 Tozer accepted a call to the Southside Alliance Church in Chicago where he was to stay for over three decades. Through the 1930s he enlarged the already strong congregation and built an outstanding music program. The church also served as a focus of what soon became a national ministry as Tozer constantly traveled to Bible and missionary conferences and clergy gatherings.

In 1943 Tozer completed his first book, *Wingspread*, the biography of Albert Benjamin Simpson, the founder of the Christian and Missionary Alliance. Over the years he would author over 30 additional titles. In 1947 he took over the radio show formerly hosted by Wilbur M. Smith, who had left Moody Bible Institute for Fuller Theological Seminary. He changed the name of the show from "Chats from a Pastor's Library" to "Talks from a Pastor's Study". Much of Tozer's popularity came from the mystical strain in his life and preaching. Unusual for most conservative evangelical leaders, Tozer's mystical side would be reflected in his books, such as *The Pursuit of God* (1948) and *The Knowledge of the Holy* (1961).

As Tozer rose to prominence he was frequently asked to serve in denominational offices, but he consistently refused. Finally, in 1941 he agreed to serve on the denomination's board of managers. In 1946 he became the vice-president of the Alliance, but he resigned in 1950 when pressure for him to become the new president surfaced. However, he did accept a position as the editor of *The Alliance Weekly* which he saw as more in keeping with his ministry and talents. Through the years he was always one of the featured speakers at the annual meetings of the Alliance.

In 1959 Tozer retired from his ministry in Chicago and moved to Toronto as preaching minister of the Alliance church there. He also served on the Canadian Council of Reference for the Inter-Varsity Fellowship. After developing a successful ministry in Toronto, he died of a sudden heart attack in 1963.

Sources:

Fant, David J. *A.W. Tozer: A Twentieth Century Prophet.* Harrisburg, PA: Christian Publications, 1964. 180pp.

Reid, Daniel G., Robert D. Linder, Bruce L. Shelley, and Harry S. Stout. *Dictionary of Christianity in America.* Downers Grove, IL: InterVarsity Press, 1990. 1305 pp.

Tozer, A. W. *The Christian Book of Mystical Verse.* Harrisburg, PA: Christian Publications, 1963. 158 pp.

———. *The Knowledge of the Holy.* New York: Harper, 1961. 128 pp.

———. *The Pursuit of God.* Harrisburg, PA: Christian Publications, 1948. 128 pp.

———. *Wingspread.* Harrisburg, PA: Christian Publications, 1943. 143 pp.

★965★
TRIFA, Valerian
Archbishop, Romanian Orthodox Episcopate of America
b. Jun. 28, 1914, Campeni Romania
d. Jan. 27, 1987, Cascais Portugal

Archbishop Valerian Trifa, primate of the Romanian Orthodox Episcopate of America, was born Viorel D. Trifa, the son of Dionisie and Macinica Motora Trifa. Trifa's parents were peasants in rural Transylvania. Trifa's father operated a lumber mill and taught school. Educated by his father, Trifa left home at the age of 10 to attend the Horea Gymnasium in Campeni. In 1927 he traveled to Sibiu to live with his uncle Josif Trifa, a priest famous for two newspapers he published, and to attend Gheorghe Lazar Lyceum. Under his uncle's guidance he gave up his proposed career in agriculture and turned his attention to theology. His desire to combat dissident religious movements in Romania and his Romanian nationalism both came to the fore by 1931, when he headed to Bessarabia to study at the Chisinau Theological School.

Trifa graduated cum laude in 1935. After a year of assisting his uncle in the newspaper business, he went to Bucharest to study for his doctorate. Trifa thus entered what was to become the most controversial period of his life. In Bucharest, Trifa became the president of the University Student's Center. He also joined and became a leader of the Legion of the Archangel Michael, popularly termed the Iron Guard. To Trifa the two groups formed the major opposition to the regime of King Carol, who ruled the country. Ideologically, both organizations were staunchly nationalistic and anti-Semitic.

In early 1938 government suppression of the Legionnaire movement began. Trifa fled the country for Germany and continued his studies at the University of Berlin. In September 1940, Carol's regime collapsed, and army General Ion Antonescu and the Legion assumed joint control. Trifa returned to Bucharest and was soon elected president of the National Union of Romanian Christian Students. The coalition between Antonescu and the Legion collapsed in January 1941, and the general moved against the Legion and their student supporters. Trifa was among the Legionnaires and students who spoke against Antonescu and called for a true Legionary state—and death to the Jews. The revolt that followed for three days, from January 20-23, included the invasion of Jewish communities and the killing of many Jews. Jewish survivors later accused Trifa of a central role in the killings. Trifa, while acknowledging his role with the Legion, denied participation in any violence.

Trifa and others left Rumania for Germany in March 1941. They were placed under house arrest. Later, when one of the leaders escaped, he was sent to Buchenwald and then, in 1943, to Dachau. He was released only after the fall of Romania. He lived in Vienna for a while before escaping to Italy as the war was ending. He remained in Italy until he was able to immigrate to America in 1950.

During the time Trifa was in Italy, the American branch of the Romanian Orthodox Church had split. Trifa joined with the larger faction which refused to accept the authority of the bishop sent from Romania after the war. He worked on the group's periodical, *Solia*, and assisted in a court case in Cleveland between the two rival factions. In 1951 he was elected bishop, and, after several refusals by other bishops, was consecrated by the bishops of the Ukrainian Orthodox Church on April 27, 1927.

In 1960 Trifa was able to persuade the Russian Orthodox Church (now the Orthodox Church in America) to accept the the Romanian Orthodox Episcopate of America into its jurisdiction. The bishops reconsecrated Trifa in 1961 to remove any doubt about the complete validity of the consecration from the Ukrainian bishops. Trifa then led the Episcopate through the 1970s. A United States citizen at this point, Trifa lived rather quietly. He participated in the work of the World Council of Churches and at one time appeared before the United States Senate to deliver a prayer.

Around 1975, however, an intensified effort by Romanian Jews caused the United States government to open a new inquiry into Trifa's background. The government found that Trifa had lied about his background at the time of his immigration and as a result, he was stripped of his citizenship in 1982 and deported to Portugal in 1984. He lived the remaining years of his life in the small town of Estoril. He died of a heart attack.

Sources:

Bobango, Gerald J. *Religion and Politics: Bishop Valerian Trifa and His Times.* Boulder, CO: East European Monographs, 1981. 294 pp.

———. *The Romanian Orthodox Episcopate of America: The First Half Century, 1929-1979.* Jackson, MI: Romanian-American Heritage Center, 1979. 364 pp.

Livingston, Victor. "Bishop Trifa: Prelate or Persecutor." *Monthly Detroit* 3, 7 (July 1980): 62-70.

★966★
TRINE, Ralph Waldo
New Thought Inspirational Writer
b. Sep. 9, 1866, Mt. Morris, Illinois
d. Feb. 21, 1958, Claremont, California

Ralph Waldo Trine, whose best-selling books on New Thought philosophy won many to the idealistic metaphysics of the New Thought movement, was the son of Ellen E. Newcomer and Samuel G. Trine. He grew up in Illinois and attended Knox College, from which he graduated with an A.B. in 1891. He studied history and political science at Johns Hopkins University but returned to Knox to finish his A.M. in 1893. He married Grace Steele Hyde. During the years after college he was employed at several jobs, including a stint as a special correspondent for the *Boston Daily Evening Transcript.* In Boston he became heavily influenced by the thought of namesake Ralph Waldo Emerson, the premier nineteenth-century advocate of an idealistic philosophy whose work would become a major source for New Thought philosophy at the end of the century.

Trine became influenced by New Thought in the mid-1890s and in 1896 authored *What All the World's A-Seeking*, the first of a series of popular inspirational texts with a decidedly New Thought flavor. While the first book was well received, the second, *In Tune with the Infinite*, published the next year, became one of the all-time best-selling inspirational books in American history. Trine effectively presented the idealistic position that there exist two realms: the spiritual and the material. The spiritual is the realm of causal and creation, the material is that of the effect and manifestation. The spiritual is the more real of the two. The goal of human life is to come into harmony with the spiritual realm.

Trine lived in Boston through the 1890s. His next books were *The Greatest Thing in the World* (1898) and *Every Living Creature* (1899). Early in the new century he moved to New York, where he continued to write. *In the Fire of the Heart* appeared in 1906, to be followed by *On the Open Road* (1908) and *The Land of Living Men* (1910). He then moved to California where he lived for the rest of his life. The continuing sales of *In Tune with the Infinite* (it was eventually translated into 20 languages) allowed him a comfortable living, and he wrote occasional new texts, including: *The Higher Powers of Mind and Spirit* (1917) and *My Philosophy and My Religion* (1921).

During the 1920s he became acquainted with Henry Ford, who in turn credited Trine with some of the success he later achieved. Trine transcribed some of their conversations, which appeared in 1929 as *The Power that Wins*. His last book was *The Man Who Knew*. In 1947 a 50th anniversary edition of *In Tune with the Infinite* was published. In 1957 a commemorative volume, *The Best of Ralph Waldo Trine*, was issued by Bobbs-Merrill.

Sources:

Dictionary of American Biography. 20 vols. and 7 supps. New York: Charles Scribner's Sons, 1928-1936, 1944-1981.
Trine, Ralph Waldo. *The Best of Ralph Waldo Trine.* Indianapolis, IN: Bobbs-Merrill Company, 1957. 319 pp.
_____. *Every Living Creature.* New York: Thomas Y. Crowell, 1899. 85 pp.
_____. *The Greatest Thing Ever Known.* New York: Thomas Y. Crowell, 1899. 82 pp.
_____. *In Tune with the Infinite.* New York: Thomas Y. Crowell & Company, 1897. 222 pp.
_____. *My Philosophy and My Religion.* Indianapolis, IN: Bobbs-Merrill, 1921.
_____. *What All the World's A-Seeking.* New York: Thomas Y. Crowell & Company, 1896. 224 pp.

★967★
TRUETT, George Washington
Pastor, Southern Baptist Convention
b. May 6, 1867, Hayesville, North Carolina
d. Jul. 7, 1944, Dallas, Texas

George Washington Truett, pastor of the First Baptist Church in Dallas, Texas, for 47 years, was the son of Charles L. and Mary R. Kimsey Truett. Converted to Christianity in 1886, Truett joined the Baptist Church. The next year he founded and led the Hiwassee Academy in Towns County, Georgia, which he ran until he joined his parents in a move to Whitefield, Texas. He had intended to become a lawyer, but was persuaded that his future lay in the ministry. He was ordained as a Baptist minister in 1890 and joined the staff of Baylor University as its financial secretary the following year. In the 23 months of his job, he raised enough money to lift the school out of debt. He left his position in 1893 to enter Baylor as a student, graduating in 1897 with a B.A. degree. He married Josephine Jenkins in 1894.

Soon after graduation, Truett became the pastor of the First Baptist Church of Dallas, where he became known for his preaching and his evangelistic style. His success in the pulpit is usually measured by his having built the membership of the congregation from 715 to 7,804 along with having made the church one of the most prominent in the Southern Baptist Convention. (It is currently pastored by former convention president **W. A. Criswell**.) As the membership grew he oversaw the construction of a 4,000-seat sanctuary.

On the denominational level, Truett emerged as a popular speaker and was often called upon to conduct revivals around the United States. He was singled out by President Woodrow Wilson as one of 20 men commissioned to preach to the troops in Europe during World War I. For many years, beginning in 1902, he held an annual summer camp meeting for cowboys in west Texas. He was also seen as a capable fundraiser. His church contributed millions of dollars to denominational programs. He promoted the funds to establish the Texas Baptist Memorial Sanitarium (now Baylor Hospital and Medical Center).

In 1927 Truett was elected president of the Southern Baptist Convention. In 1934 he began a five-year term as president of the Baptist World Alliance, during which time he made an around-the-world tour of Baptist missions. A preacher more than a writer, Truett left 14 volumes of his sermons and messages as his main literary contribution, all compiled and edited by others, primarily Powhatan W. James.

Sources:

Dictionary of American Biography. 20 vols. and 7 supps. New York: Charles Scribner's Sons, 1928-1936, 1944-1981.
Encyclopedia of Southern Baptists. 3 vols. Nashville, TN: Broadman Press, 1958, 1971.
James, Powhatan W. *George W. Truett.* New York: Macmillan Company, 1935.
Lippy, Charles H. *Twentieth-Century Shapers of American Popular Religion.* New York: Greenwood Press, 1989. 494 pp.
Truett, George Washington. *After His Likeness.* Grand Rapids, MI: William B. Eerdman's Publishing Company, 1954. 176 pp.
_____. *God's Call to America.* New York: G. H. Doran, 1923. 204 pp.
_____. *On Eagle Wings.* Grand Rapids, MI: William B. Eerdman's Publishing Company, 1953. 186 pp.
_____. *The Prophet's Mantle.* Grand Rapids, MI: William B. Eerdman's Publishing Company, 1948. 206 pp.

★968★
TRUMBULL, Henry Clay
Minister and Sunday School Leader, Congregational Church
b. Jun. 8, 1830, Stonington, Connecticut
d. Dec. 8, 1903, Philadelphia, Pennsylvania

Henry Clay Trumbull, a Congregationalist minister known for his popular religious books and his work promoting Sunday schools in the late nineteenth century, was the son of Gordon and Sarah Ann Swan Trumbull and the descendent of an old New England colonial family. His father was a businessman who, on several occasions, held positions in the state government. Young Trumbull had little formal education due to his poor health. As a young man, however, he obtained a job as a bank clerk.

Trumbull was living and working in Hartford, Connecticut, in 1852 when he was moved by the revival message of evangelist Charles G. Finney. Finney talked him into becoming the leader of a mission Sunday school class, and a few weeks later Trumbull joined the First Congregational Church of Hartford. Two years later he married Alice Cogswell, the daughter of one of the church's members. He held a variety of jobs during the next few years, but his heart was in Sunday school work. In 1857 he served as secretary of the first Connecticut Sunday-school Convention, at which plans were made to hire a permanent state Sunday school missionary. He was offered the post and began to pursue the task full-time in the fall of 1858.

Trumbull was just a lay person, but in 1862 he was ordained as a Congregationalist minister in order to accept a post as chaplain in the Union Army during the Civil War. After some months, he was captured and held prisoner for four months before being freed in a prisoner exchange. He resumed active duty through the end of the war.

After the war he returned to his first love and became New England's secretary of the American Sunday School Union. He served as chairman of the executive committee for the 1872 National Sunday School Convention, which initiated the International Uniform Sunday School Lessons, one of the few cooperative endeavors of the various Christian denominations still continuing from the nineteenth century. In 1875 he became the editor of the *Sunday School Times* and moved with his family to Philadelphia.

For the remainder of the century, through his writings and speaking, Trumbull led in the spread of the Sunday school movement across North America and around the world. Three books written by Trumbull stand out as contributions to this effort: *Teachings and Teachers* (1884); *The Sunday School: Its Origin, Mission, Methods and Auxiliaries* (originally delivered as the 1888 Lyman Beecher Lectures at Yale); and *Hints on Child-Training* (1891).

Trumbull wrote 33 books on a variety of subjects. He is credited with having been the first to identify the site of the biblical Kadesh-Barnea mentioned in Numbers 13:26 and Ezekiel 47:19, and he authored a book on his research in this area. Among his other books were: *The Blood Covenant* (1885); *The Lie Never Justifiable* (1893); *Illustrative Answers to Prayer* (1900); and *How to Deal with Doubt and Doubters* (1903). He penned one autobiographical volume about his war experiences, *War Memories of an Army Chaplain* (1898).

Sources:

Dictionary of American Biography. 20 vols. and 7 supps. New York: Charles Scribner's Sons, 1928-1936, 1944-1981.

Howard, Phillip Eugene. *The Life Story of Henry Clay Trumbull.* Philadelphia: Sunday School Times Co. 1905. 525 pp.

Trumbull, Henry Clay. *How to Deal with Doubts and Doubters.* New York: International Committee of the Young Mens Christian Association, 1903. 131 pp.

———. *Illustrative Answers to Prayer.* New York: Fleming H. Revell, 1900. 140 pp.

———. *The Sunday School: Its Origin, Mission, Methods and Auxiliaries.* Philadelphia: J. D. Wattles, 1888. 415 pp.

———. *Teaching and Teachers.* Philadelphia: J. D. Wattles, 1884. 390 pp.

———. *War Memories of an Army Chaplain.* New York: Charles Scribner's, 1898. 421 pp.

★969★
TRUNGPA RINPOCHE, Chogyam
Tibetan Buddhist Teacher and Founder, Vajradhatu
b. Feb. 1939, Geje Tibet
d. Apr. 4, 1987, Halifax, Nova Scotia, Canada

Although Tibetan Buddhism had some influence on countercultural spirituality through books such as *The Tibetan Book of the Dead*, Chogyam Trungpa Rinpoche, the eleventh Trungpa Tulku, was the first Tibetan Buddhist teacher to have significant impact on the West through his personal teaching. Following in the steps of other Buddhist groups that adapted to a Western environment, Chogyam Trungpa in turn established a beachhead for succeeding Tibetan teachers. (Tibetan Buddhism is a complex blend of Mahayana Buddhism with Indian Tantrism and Tibetan shamanism).

In classical Tibetan fashion, Trungpa was declared to be the reincarnation of an important lama while a young child, and was subsequently taken to a monastery for training. He fled Tibet for India in the wake of the Chinese invasion of that country, and in 1963 received a Spalding sponsorship to attend Oxford University. He worked at "planting the Dharma" in England for some years before teaching in America. His winsome autobiography, *Born in Tibet* (1966), was an early aid in attracting disciples.

Shortly after his arrival in the United States in 1970, Trungpa founded Karme Choling, a center in Vermont. During the next few years, as a result of his traveling, speaking, and writing, other centers were founded, and these were incorporated into Vajradhatu,

a national organization overseeing his work. Naropa Institute, in Boulder, Colorado, was created as the movement's educational arm.

The 1970s were Trungpa's most productive years as an author. He very quickly sent to the press books on a wide variety of Tibetan Buddhist subjects, including: *Mudra* (1972); *Cutting through Spiritual Materialism* (1973); *Visual Dharma, The Buddhist Art of Tibet* (1975); *The Dawn of Tantra* (1975), with Herbert Guenther; and *The Myth of Freedom* (1976).

Trungpa was a controversial figure, principally because he did not hide his appreciation of alcohol and women. One of his contributions to the vocabulary of America's spiritual subculture was "spiritual materialism" (described in his *Cutting through Spiritual Materialism*), which refers to the acquisitive impulse as it manifests in the realm of spiritual seeking (i.e., when a seeker is preoccupied with "collecting" spiritual experiences, spiritual artifacts, initiations, etc.).

Sources:

Clark, Tom. *The Great Naropa Poetry Wars.* Santa Barbara, CA: Cadmus Editions, 1980.

Fields, Rick. *How the Swans Came to the Lake: A Narrative History of Buddhism in America.* Boulder, CO: Shambhala, 1981. 433 pp.

———. "The Vidyadhara Trungpa Rinpoche Dies in Nova Scotia." *The Vajradhatu Sun* 8, 5 (June/July 1987): 1, 13.

Guenther, Herbert V. and Chogyam Trungpa. *The Dawn of Tantra.* Berkeley, CA: Shambhala, 1975. 92 pp.

The Tibetan Book of the Dead. Trans. and commentary by Francesca Fremantle and Chogyam Trungpa. Berkeley, CA: Shambhala, 1973. 119 pp.

Trungpa, Chogyam. *Born in Tibet.* London: George Allen & Unwin, 1966. Rept.: Boulder, CO: Shambhala, 1977. 280 pp.

———. *Cutting Through Spiritual Materialism.* Berkeley, CA: Shambhala, 1973. 250 pp.

———. *Mudra.* Berkeley, CA: Shambhala, 1972. 105 pp.

———. *The Myth of Freedom and the Way of Meditation.* Berkeley, CA: Shambhala, 1976. 176 pp.

———. *Visual Dharma, The Buddhist Art of Tibet.* Berkeley, CA: Shambhala, 1972. 139 pp.

—*James R. Lewis*

★970★
TUCKER, Henry St. George
Presiding Bishop, Protestant Episcopal Church
b. Jul. 16, 1874, Warsaw, Virginia
d. Aug. 8, 1959, Richmond, Virginia

Henry St. George Tucker, a presiding bishop of the Protestant Episcopal Church, was the son of Beverley Bandridge Tucker, the Episcopal bishop in Southern Virginia, and Ann Maria Washington Tucker. He received the finest of educations at Norfolk Academy, the University of Virginia (M.A., 1895), and the Theological Seminary of Virginia, where he earned both a B.D. and a D.D. in 1899. Shortly after graduation he was ordained both as a deacon and priest.

The first phase of Tucker's career began in Japan, where he served as a missionary. He began his work in Sendai but was soon moved to Hirosaki as the administrator for the work in Aomori Prefecture. During the several years he was there he mastered Japanese. He was appointed president of St. Paul's College in Tokyo in 1902. He wrote his first book, *Reconciliation through Christ* (1910), while stationed in Japan. He married Mary Lillian Warnock in 1911.

In 1912 Tucker was consecrated as the missionary bishop of Kyoto. He served until the outbreak of World War I, when he joined the United States Army and was assigned to Siberia. He was placed in charge of civilian refugee work through the Red Cross. After the war he picked up his episcopal assignment in Kyoto, where he remained until 1923.

The second phase of Tucker's career began in 1923 when he returned to the United States as professor of pastoral theology at his former seminary in Virginia. Three years later he was elected bishop coadjutor for the state and became the bishop of Virginia in 1927. That year he was also elected to the National Council of the Protestant Episcopal Church. While tending his flock, he found time to write and published his second book, *Providence and the Atonement*, in 1934.

In 1937 the Episcopal Church abandoned its practice of naming its senior bishop as the presiding bishop, an office whose assignments were largely ceremonial. It transformed the office into an elective administrative post with meaningful duties and powers. Tucker was the first person elected to the office. The election came just as the world was planning for war, and Tucker used the new office to speak for the church at this crucial moment. He condemned the Japanese movements into China, but then denounced Western governments for not providing a Christian example in their foreign policy. He also spoke against the Munich Pact made to appease Hitler. During his first year in office, he finished his third book, *The History of the Episcopal Church in Japan* (1938).

In the midst of the gathering clouds of war, the new Episcopal Cathedral of St. Peter and St. Paul was completed in Washington, D.C., and Tucker was installed there amid much ceremony in 1941. The following year he was elected president of the Federal Council of Churches. As a pacifist, he had to face the reality of America's entrance into the war which he at first deplored. As the war continued, however, he rethought his position and concluded that the Axis Powers were anti-Christian in essence and he called for their defeat.

Tucker retired in 1946. He continued to speak occasionally on social issues, especially anti-Semitism, and he anticipated the civil rights movement with his call for full participation of Blacks in American life. He spent many of his last years writing his memoirs, *Exploring the Silent Shore of Memory*, published in 1951.

Sources:
Dictionary of American Biography. 20 vols. and 7 supps. New York: Charles Scribner's Sons, 1928-1936, 1944-1981.
Tucker, Henry St. George. *Exploring the Silent Shore of Memory.* Richmond, VA: Whittet & Shepperson, 1951. 300 pp.
_____. *History of the Episcopal Church in Japan.* New York: Charles Scribner's Sons, 1934. 228 pp.
_____. *Providence and the Atonement.* Richmond, VA: Virginia Diocesan Library, 1938. 182 pp.

★ 971 ★
TURNER, Henry McNeal
Bishop, African Methodist Episcopal Church
b. Feb. 1, 1834, Newberry, South Carolina
d. May 9, 1915, Windsor, Ontario, Canada

Henry McNeal Turner, a bishop in the African Methodist Episcopal Church, was the son of a free black couple. As a youth he worked as a day laborer among the slaves until he learned the trade of blacksmithing. He was in his midteens before he learned to read, as teaching Blacks to read was against the law at the time. He was able to travel to Baltimore, Maryland, in the 1850s to attend Trinity College. In 1853 the Methodist Episcopal Church, South, having seen his potential as an evangelist, licensed Turner to preach and used him for the next four years as an itinerant revivalist. In 1858, however, he left the Methodist Episcopal Church, South and joined the Missouri Conference of the African Methodist Episcopal Church. He was ordained a deacon in 1860 and an elder in 1862, and was assigned to the Israel African Methodist Episcopal Church in Washington, D.C. In 1863 President Lincoln appointed Turner the first black army chaplain.

After the Civil War Turner moved to Georgia, where he served two terms in the Georgia State Legislature during Reconstruction.

His more important contribution, however, came in the church. He emerged as one of the leading preachers in the conference and by 1876, when he left to become the manager of the church's book concern, Georgia had become the largest conference in the denomination. Georgia led the postwar shift of power in the African Methodist Episcopal Church from the northern states to the South.

Turner was elected bishop in 1880 and assigned the Georgia Conference, over which he presided until 1892. In 1882 he founded and edited the *Southern Recorder*. He also emerged as an advocate of African colonization, a plan for providing transportation for the freed slaves to return to Africa. The plan, while at one time regarded as a legitimate option for solving the problems of black-white relations, never gained the support necessary for implementation in any strength. During the years in the episcopacy Turner also traveled to Africa on several occasions and while there initiated the African Methodist Episcopal Church's work in Liberia, Sierra Leone, and South Africa.

Sources:
Harmon, Nolan B. *The Encyclopedia of World Methodism.* 2 vols. Nashville: United Methodist Publishing House, 1974.
Hill, Samuel S., ed. *Encyclopedia of Religion in the South.* Macon, GA: Mercer University Press, 1984. 878 pp.
Ponton, M. M. *Life and Times of Henry M. Turner.* Atlanta: A. B. Caldwell Pub. Co., 1917. 173 pp.
Wright, Richard R. *The Bishops of the African Methodist Episcopal Church.* Nashville, TN: A. M. E. Sunday School Union, 1963.

★ 972 ★
TURPIN, Joseph Marcel
Bishop, Pentecostal Assemblies of the World
b. Jan. 1, 1887, Denton, Maryland
d. Mar. 17, 1943, Baltimore, Maryland

Little is known of the early life of Joseph Marcel Turpin, a bishop of Pentecostal Assemblies of the World (PAW), the oldest of twentieth-century Pentecostal denominations. He experienced salvation as a young man during the first years of the Pentecostal Movement. He eventually affiliated with the Pentecostal Assemblies in the years after the "Jesus Only" controversy. During the second decade of this century the Pentecostal Movement was divided by advocates of a non-Trinitarian perspective which identified Jesus as God the Father and insisted on water baptism in the name of Jesus only, rather than using the words of the traditional Trinitarian formula.

Shortly after he joined the Assemblies, Turpin founded the First Apostolic Church in Baltimore and remained its pastor for the rest of his life. He quickly became a leader in the denomination. He helped found the eastern District Council and was appointed as a district elder and then church presbyter. In 1925, when the Assemblies reorganized and instituted an episcopal polity, Turpin was among the first five men chosen as bishops of the church.

Sources:
Dupree, Sherry Sherrod. *Biographical Dictionary of African-American, Holiness-Pentecostals, 1880-1990.* Washington, DC: Middle Atlantic Regional Press, 1990. 386 pp.

★ 973 ★
TUTTLE, Daniel Sylvester
Presiding Bishop, Protestant Episcopal Church
b. Jan. 26, 1837, Windham, New York
d. Apr. 17, 1923, St. Louis, Missouri

Daniel Sylvester Tuttle, a presiding bishop of the Protestant Episcopal Church, was the son of Daniel Bliss and Abigail Clark Stimson Tuttle. His father was the blacksmith for the small town in which Tuttle spent his youth. In 1850 he entered the academy at Delhi, New York. He joined the Episcopal Church and was baptized in

1853. In 1854 he entered Columbia College; he graduated in 1857. He worked as a tutor for two years and then entered General Theological Seminary. Following his graduation in 1862, he was ordained a deacon and assigned to assist at the rural parish at Morris, New York. He was ordained in the priesthood the following year and eventually became the rector in Morris. In 1865 he married Harriet Minerva Foote, the daughter of his predecessor.

Tuttle had worked at his parish for only a few years when, much to his surprise, he was elected to become the missionary bishop of Montana (a missionary territory that also included Idaho and Utah). As he was only 29 years old and could not be consecrated until he was 30, he wasn't consecrated until 1867. He left his family to begin his 19 years of pioneering work in the West. His family joined him in Salt Lake City in 1869. During his years there he concentrated on building the Episcopal Church. He was not a major protagonist in the growing effort to rid Utah of polygamy.

In 1868 the diocese of Missouri elected Tuttle the bishop of the state, but he refused the office. In 1886, at the height of the polygamy controversy, the diocese elected him a second time, and this time he accepted and moved to St. Louis to assume his duties. He would remain in St. Louis for the next 37 years. As in Missouri, he followed a middle path, concentrating upon his administrative duties, avoiding controversy, and seeking to reconcile the diverse elements of high and low church in his diocese.

In 1903, through his seniority, he succeeded to the role of presiding bishop of the Protestant Episcopal Church. In his new role he continued his stance as a harmonizer of the diverse elements in the church and refused to participate in the various debates which centered around the church. The one exception was his strong opposition to the early attempts to make the presiding bishop's office an elective one (which was finally done in the 1930s). He argued that God, not the members of the general convention, should select the presiding bishop.

He reigned as presiding bishop for two decades, adopting a patriarchal image. He grew a long white beard and became known for his deep, powerful voice in an age before voice amplification equipment was used. He was also physically strong, and his neighborhood remembered him chopping his firewood while in his 80s. It was noted at the time of his death that he had been a bishop for 56 years, during which time he had participated in the consecration of 89 other bishops. He wrote only one book, a memoir of his missionary days. The most visible monument to his life is a building erected next to Christ Church, where he had established his headquarters.

Sources:

Dictionary of American Biography. 20 vols. and 7 supps. New York: Charles Scribner's Sons, 1928-1936, 1944-1981.
Tuttle, Daniel S. *Reminiscences of a Missionary Bishop.* New York: T. Whittaker, 1906. 498 pp.

★ 974 ★
TWITCHELL, John Paul
Founder, ECKANKAR
b. Oct. 22, 1908?, Paducah, Kentucky
d. Sep. 17, 1971, Cincinnati, Ohio

John Paul Twitchell, founder of ECKANKAR, was born in Paducah, Kentucky, sometime between 1908 and 1912. He served in the Navy during World War II, became a correspondent for *Our Navy* after the war, and pursued a career as a freelance journalist. Twitchell was an active spiritual seeker who went through a succession of different groups before founding his own movement.

In 1950 Twitchell became involved in Swami Premananda's Self-Revelation Church of Absolute Monism, an offshoot of **Swami Paramahansa Yogananda**'s Self-Realization Fellowship (SRF).

Twitchell lived on the grounds with his first wife and edited the church's periodical, *The Mystic Cross*, until Premananda asked him to leave the church in 1955. He and his wife separated about this time. The same year that Twitchell broke with Premananda's group, he was initiated into shabd yoga by **Kirpal Singh**, the founder of the Ruhani Satsang religious organization. He also became involved in the Church of Scientology, worked on the church's staff, and was one of Scientology's first "clears," (a clear is the status in Scientology when, all one's engrams, negative imprints from the past, have been removed). While working as a journalist in Seattle Twitchell met Gail Atkinson, whom he introduced to Kirpal Singh and eventually married. They moved to San Francisco in 1964, where Twitchell began to teach shabd yoga independently of Kirpal Singh's organization. His early teaching emphasized the ability of the human being's consciousness to travel independently of the body (a practice he referred to as "soul travel," the more common term being "astral projection"). In 1965 he announced that he was the Living ECK Master and organized ECKANKAR. He was given a quick boost by author Brad Steiger, who wrote several short pieces and then an entire book about Twitchell. A prolific author himself, Twitchell's works include *ECKANKAR, the Key to Secret Worlds* (1969); *The Spiritual Notebook* (1971); and *The Flute of God* (1971). By the time he died in 1971, ECKANKAR was a successful, widespread movement with centers in many major U.S. cities.

The basis of shabd yoga is the notion that the Cosmos has emanated from the Godhead (termed SUGMAD in ECKANKAR). The ECK current, which human beings can perceive in the form of light and sound, continues to emanate from the Godhead in order to support the manifested world. Enlightenment is achieved by "tuning in" to the ECK current, with the help of the ECK master, and "following" it back to the realms of the SUGMAD. Although there are many minor variations, especially in terminology, the basic ideas closely resemble the theoretical schema which informs the shabd yoga taught by Kirpal Singh.

During the 1980s, serious charges of plagiarism were made by David C. Lane. Lane, a disciple of Charan Singh, a shabd yoga master in India, claimed that Twitchell took material from a variety of mundane sources and published it as if it originated from the previous ECK masters he had met in the spiritual realms. These charges, substantiated with detailed documentation, caused a major internal disturbance within the movement and led to the resignation of a number of members. Under its present ECK master, Harold Klemp, ECKANKAR seems to have returned to a stable state and put many of its previous problems behind it.

Sources:

Lane, David Christopher. *The Making of a Spiritual Movement.* Del Mar, CA: Del Mar Press, 1983. 154 pp.
Simpson, Patti. *Paulji: A Memoir.* Menlo Park, CA: ECKANKAR, 1985. 206 pp.
Steiger, Brad. *In My Soul I Am Free.* New York: Lancer Books, 1968. 190 pp.
Twitchell, Paul. *Difficulties of Becoming the Living ECK Master.* Menlo Park, CA: IWP Publishing, 1980. 262 pp.
———. *ECKANKAR: The Key to Secret Worlds.* Minneapolis, MN: ECKANKAR, 1969, 1987. 249 pp.
———. *The Spiritual Notebook.* Menlo Park, CA: IWP, 1972. 219 pp.
———. *The Tiger's Fang.* New York: Lancer Books, 1969. 174 pp.

★ 975 ★
UNDERWOOD, Benjamin Franklin
Freethought Lecturer and Editor
b. Jul. 6, 1839, New York, New York
d. Nov. 10, 1914, Westerly, Rhode Island

Benjamin Franklin Underwood, Freethought lecturer and editor, was the son of Raymond C. and Harriet Booth Underwood. He received his formal schooling at Westerly Academy in Westerly,

Rhode Island, and read widely in science, literature, and philosophy as well. He joined the 15th Massachusetts Volunteer Infantry at the beginning of the Civil War and, on October 21, 1861, was wounded and captured at the battle of Ball's Bluff. After several months of confinement in Libby Prison, he was released as part of a prisoner exchange. Underwood then returned to Massachusetts and, on September 6, 1862, married a suffragist leader, Sara A. Francis. He then reenlisted, this time in the 5th Rhode Island Heavy Artillery, and continued in this line of duty for the balance of the war. He was commended for bravery and promoted to first lieutenant.

Following the Civil War, Underwood took up a career as a platform speaker for the cause of Freethought. He had a keen analytical mind, and it was the rare opponent who could stand his own against Underwood's sharp argumentation. In the several decades following the war, his custom was to issue public challenges to the clergy of large eastern cities to debate with him, usually on the topic of evolution. These verbal combats could range from three to 30 meetings. The most notable exchange occurred in Boston in 1873, a symposium at which Prof. Asa Gray of Harvard was a participant.

In the early period of his life, Underwood published a series of pamphlets and lectures in the form of small tracts with titles like *The Crimes and Cruelties of Christianity* (1877) and *Darwinism* (1875). He edited the Boston *Index* from 1880 to 1886, Chicago's *Open Court* in 1887 (prior to assumption of the editorship by **Paul Carus**), and the *Illustrated Graphic News* in 1888. He was an editorial writer for the *Philosophical Journal* from 1893 to 1895. He also served as chairman of the Congress of Evolution that was convened in conjunction with the Columbian Exposition of 1893.

In 1897 Underwood became editor of the *Quincy Journal* in Quincy, Illinois, and stayed with that job for most of the rest of his life. In spite of his attraction to public debate, he was a kind and congenial man. During the latter part of his life, he appears to have moderated his anti-religious views, or at least to have become far more reserved about expressing them. He retired in 1913 and returned to Westerly, Rhode Island, where he passed away the following year.

Sources:

Dictionary of American Biography. 20 vols. and 7 supps. New York: Charles Scribner's Sons, 1928-1936, 1944-1981.

Underwood, Benjamin Franklin. *Crimes and Cruelties of Christianity.* New York: D. M. Bennett, 1877. 30 pp.

_____. *Darwinism: What It Is and Proofs in Favor of It.* New York: D. M. Bennett, 1875. 15 pp.

_____. *The Influence of Christianity on Civilization.* New York: The Truth Seeker Company, 1889. 98 pp.

★976★
VACHON, Louis-Albert
Archbishop and Cardinal, Roman Catholic Church
b. Feb. 4, 1912, St. Frederic, Quebec, Canada

Louis-Albert Vachon, the archbishop of Quebec and a cardinal in the Roman Catholic Church, is the son of Alexandrine Gilbert and Napoleon Vachon. Around 1930, when he entered the Grand Seminary of Quebec, Vachon began what has become a life-long affiliation with the associated complex of schools at Quebec that includes Laval University and the l'Ecole Normale Superieure. He completed his B.A. at Quebec Seminary in 1934. He was ordained as a priest in the Roman Catholic Church and in 1941 became a professor of philosophy while working on a doctorate at Laval University. After receiving his Ph.D. in 1947, he left for Rome where he studied at the Angelicum, from which he received his D.Th. in 1949.

Upon his return to Quebec, Gregoire held a series of posts at his alma mater. He became a professor of theology at Laval. In 1955 he became the superior of the Grand Seminary in Quebec, but returned to Laval in 1959 as the vice-rector. In 1958 the first of his many books, *Esperance et Presomption*, appeared. He became rector in 1960. During his years as rector he had his greatest literary output. Among the many titles were *Verite et liberte* (1962); *Unite de l'Universite* (1962); *Apostolat de l'universitaire* (1963); *Les Humanites, aujourd'hui* (1966); and *Excellence et Loyaute des Universitaires* (1969). In 1965 he was elected president of the Association of Universities and Colleges of Canada. Then in 1972 he was named superintendent general of the seminary.

Vachon remained at the seminary until 1977 when he was selected as the auxiliary bishop of the diocese of Quebec. In 1981 he became archbishop of Quebec and primate of all Canada. Among his duties, the archbishop is the apostolic chancellor of Laval University and the associated schools. In 1981 he was named to the administrative board of the Canadian Conference of Catholic Bishops, a position he retains to the present. In 1983 he was named as a Canadian delegate to the Synod of Bishops in Rome.

In 1985 Pope John Paul II made Vachon a cardinal and also appointed him to the Sacred Congregation for Clergy (the sacred congregations are the administrative departments of the Roman Catholic Church headquartered at the Vatican). That same year he became a governor of the Canadian Bible Society.

Sources:

Simpson, Kieran, ed. *Canadian Who's Who.* Toronto: University of Toronto Press, 1987.

★977★
VALENTINE, Milton
Theologian, General Synod of the Lutheran Church in the United States
b. Jan. 1, 1825, Uniontown, Pennsylvania
d. Feb. 7, 1906, Gettysburg, Pennsylvania

Milton Valentine, a theologian with the General Synod of the Lutheran Church in America, was the son of Jacob and Rebecca Picking Valentine and the descendent of a colonial Pennsylvania family. He grew up on the family farm and worked there until he was 21. He then attended Pennsylvania College in Gettysburg. After his graduation in 1850 he entered the Lutheran Theological Seminary adjacent to the college to prepare for the ministry. In 1852 he graduated, was licensed for the ministry, and became the supply pastor at Winchester, Virginia. After a year in Virginia, he returned to Pennsylvania to serve successive short terms as a missioner in Pittsburgh; as pastor at Greenburg, as principal of Emmaus Institute at Middlebury (1855-1859); and as pastor of St. Matthew's Lutheran Church at Reading. His outstanding success at Reading led to his call in 1866 to teach biblical and ecclesiastical history at the seminary at Gettysburg. In 1855 he married Margaret G. Galt.

At the time of Valentine's move back to Gettysburg, the Lutheran Church was in the midst of theological turmoil. The seminary had always held to what might be termed a centrist position in Lutheranism. Under its dominant leader of the previous generation, Samuel S. Schmucker, it held strongly to the authority of the Bible and the Augsburg Confession (the seminal statement of Lutheran belief), but opposed a growing segment within the church which demanded a formal doctrinal allegiance to all of the early Lutheran documents contained in the *Book of Concord*. Those espousing this position had become powerful enough in the Pennsylvania Ministerium, the governing body for Lutherans in the area, that the ministerium withdrew its support from Gettysburg in the mid-1860s, established a new seminary in Philadelphia, and in 1867 led in the formation of a new Lutheran coalition, the General Council of the Lutheran Church in America.

Valentine's call to the seminary in Gettysburg represented an affirmation by the seminary trustees and the General Synod of its traditional position. Two years after his arrival at the seminary, Valentine was appointed its president, from which office he emerged as the new champion of the centrist position. He defended the General Synod as adhering to "Catholic Lutheranism" apart from the particular need to bind itself to those peculiar positions taken by sixteenth-century German Lutherans (as represented in the other documents in the *Book of Concord*). This position guided the *Quarterly Review of the Evangelical Lutheran Church*, which he edited for more than 30 years, from 1871 to 1906. Eventually the General Synod and General Council would find a reconciling position and are today both constituent parts of the Evangelical Lutheran Church in America (1988).

In 1884 he retired from the presidency of the seminary and returned to teaching full time. He was also free to pursue other important endeavors. He authored his first important book, *Natural Theology*, in 1885. From 1885 to 1888, he worked on the committee to produce the Common Service, which was used for many years by most North American Lutherans. During the 1890s he authored *Theoretical Ethics* (1897) and issued *Christian Truth and Life* (1898), a collection of his sermons. What was to be his magnum opus, his *Christian Theology*, was all but finished at the time of his death in 1906 and was edited and published by his son the following year.

Sources:

Dictionary of American Biography. 20 vols. and 7 supps. New York: Charles Scribner's Sons, 1928-1936, 1944-1981.

Valentine, Milton. *Christian Theology*. 2 vols. Philadelphia: Lutheran Publication Society, 1907.

———. *Christian Truth and Life*. Philadelphia: Lutheran Publication Society, 1898. 358 pp.

———. *Natural Theology*. Chicago: S. C. Griggs & Co., 1885. 274 pp.

———. *Theoretical Ethics*. Chicago: Scott, Foresman & Co., 1897. 232 pp.

Valentine, Thomas W. *The Valentines in America*. New York: Clark & Maynard, 1874. 248 pp.

Wentz, Abdel R. *The History of Gettysburg Theological Seminary*. Philadelphia: United Lutheran Publication House, 1926. 624 pp.

★978★
VAN COTT, Margaret Newton
Evangelist, Methodist Episcopal Church
b. Mar. 25, 1830, New York, New York
d. Aug. 29, 1914, Catskill, New York

Margaret "Maggie" Newton Van Cott, the first American woman to be licensed to preach by the Methodist Episcopal Church, was the daughter of Rachel A. Primrose and William K. Newton, a wealthy real estate broker. She was raised an Episcopalian. As a child she was attracted to Methodism but was specifically forbidden by her mother to attend the local Methodist Episcopal church, which was near the family home in Brooklyn. She completed high school and in 1848 married Peter P. Van Cott. Two years after their marriage he became ill and she became the manager of the family business.

At the time of the great national revival in 1857-1858, Van Cott had a conversion experience and began attending the Duane Street Methodist Episcopal Church in New York City. She did not join the church until after her husband's death in 1866 but, once a member, she threw herself into church work, including leading prayer meetings at the slum mission founded by Phoebe Palmer. As word of her success spread, she was invited to lead revival services at the Methodist church in Durham, New York, in 1868.

Van Cott was not particularly interested in pushing into the traditionally male territory of preaching, but was impressed by the num-

ber of conversions following her sermons. She was given an exhorter's license in 1868 and in 1869 was granted a local preacher's license by the Stone Ridge Methodist Episcopal Church, in Ellenville, New York. A license to preach, by no means equivalent to ordination, nevertheless gave official recognition to Van Cott's evangelistic endeavors. One other woman, Emma Richardson, had been licensed by the Canadian Methodists in 1864.

The action at Ellenville set off a controversy in the New York Conference of the Methodist Episcopal Church, which found itself divided on the propriety of female ministers, but took no action opposing Van Cott's work. Due to the illness of the minister at Springfield, Massachusetts, in 1870 she supplied the pulpit. This was coincidently the site of the New England Conference's annual meeting. She preached before the conference, but provoked no action. She moved on to other activities, conducting revivals as invited. Van Cott was strongly supported by popular church leaders such as **Gilbert Haven, Jr.** and Joseph C. Hartzell, both soon to be bishops. She was joined by a handful of other women licensed to preach, but the church refused to act on possible ordination. When Van Cott was recommended for ordination in 1874 in California, the conference bishop refused to consider the issue.

In spite of the church's refusal to ordain her, Van Cott continued her evangelistic work for the rest of her life. Having rid herself of the responsibility of her husband's business, she lived off of the offerings of those before whom she spoke. She retired in 1902.

Sources:

Everhart, Janet S. "Maggie Newton Van Cott: The Methodist Episcopal Church Considers the Question of Women Clergy." In *Women in New Worlds*. vol. II. edited by Rosemary Skinner Keller, Louise L. Queen, and Hilah F. Thomas, 300-317. Nashville, TN: Abingdon, 1982.

Foster, John O. *The Life and Labors of Mrs. Maggie Newton Van Cott*. Cincinnati, OH: Hitchcock & Walden, 1872. 339 pp. Rev. ed. *The Harvest and the Reaper: Reminiscences of Revival Work of Mrs. Maggie Newton Van Cott*. 1883.

Harmon, Nolan B. *The Encyclopedia of World Methodism*. 2 vols. Nashville: United Methodist Publishing House, 1974.

James, Edward T., ed. *Notable American Women, 1607-1950: A Biographical Dictionary*. 3 vols. Cambridge, MA: Harvard University Press, Belknap Press, 1971.

★979★
VAN DUSEN, Henry Pitney
Educator, United Presbyterian Church in the U.S.A.
b. Dec. 11, 1897, Philadelphia, Pennsylvania
d. Feb. 13, 1975, Belle Meade, New Jersey

Henry Pitney Van Dusen, ecumenical leader and president of both Union Theological Seminary and Auburn Theological Seminary in New York City for over 25 years, was the son of Katherine James Pitney and George Richstein Van Dusen. He attended Princeton University, from which he received his A.B. degree. He later pursued graduate work abroad at New College in Edinburgh, Scotland, but returned to the United States to complete his B.D. in 1924 at Union Theological Seminary. He joined the faculty at Union in 1926 as an instructor and was named assistant professor in 1928 and associate professor in 1931, the same year of his marriage to Elizabeth Bartholomew. In 1932 he completed the requirements for his Ph.D. from Edinburgh University.

By the time he received his doctorate, Van Dusen was already well into what was to be a long and distinguished career at Union and the associated Auburn Seminary. In 1936 he was named Roosevelt Professor of Systematic Theology, a post he would retain for the next 23 years. In 1954, however, he also assumed additional duties as president of both Union and Auburn, a position he retained until his retirement in 1963. He emerged as a major advocate and defender of modern liberal theology.

Van Dusen's position at Union served as a launching pad for involvement in the ecumenical movement. In 1939 he became a member of the provisional and administrative committees which would lead to the formation of the World Council of Churches in 1948. He continued as a member of its study committee until 1954 and then served for seven years on the joint committee of the World Council and the International Missionary Council (I.M.C.). During this same period he served on a number of committees of the Federal Council of Churches (and the later National Council of Churches).

During his career Van Dusen was also the author of a number of books beginning with *In Quest of Life's Meaning*, published in 1926. Among his theological titles were *The Plain Man Seeks for God* (1933); *Spirit, Son and Father: Christian Faith in the Light of the Holy Spirit* (1958); and *The Vindication of Liberal Theology* (1963). Concerning ecumenical issues, he authored *For the Healing of the Nations: Impressions of Christianity Around the World* (1940); *What IS the Church Doing?* (1943); and *One Great Ground of Hope: Christian Missions and Christian Unity* (1961). His last book was *Dag Hammarskjold: The Statesman and His Faith* (1967). He edited a number of volumes as well, the most famous being *The Library of Christian Classics* (with John T. McNeil and John Baillie), a 26-volume work. He also served on the editorial board of *Religion in Life*, *Christianity and Crisis*, *Christendom*, and *Ecumenical Review*.

Sources:

Van Dusen, Henry P. *In Quest of Life's Meaning*. New York: Association Press, 1926.

_____. *One Great Ground of Hope: Christian Missions and Christian Unity*. Philadelphia: Westminster Press, 1961.

_____. *The Plain Man Seeks for God*. New York: Charles Scribner's Sons, 1933.

_____. *Spirit, Son and Father: Christian Faith in the Light of the Holy Spirit*. New York: Charles Scribner's Sons, 1958.

_____. *What Is the Church Doing?* New York: Charles Scribner's Sons, 1943.

★ 980 ★
VAN IMPE, Jack Leo
Evangelist, Independent Baptist
b. Feb. 9, 1931, Freeport, Michigan

Jack Leo Van Impe, an independent fundamentalist Baptist evangelist, is the son of Oscar and Louise Van Impe, both first-generation immigrants to the United States from Belgium. Van Impe was born soon after his parents' arrival in America. In 1932 the family moved to Leipsic, Ohio, where his father worked as a day laborer in the beet fields. Catholics by heritage, they baptized their son as an infant in the Roman Catholic Church. In 1933 they moved to Detroit to find work in an automobile factory. To earn extra money, the elder Van Impe moonlighted as a musician in the Belgian-American beer gardens. He taught his son to play the accordion, and Van Impe was introduced to the beer gardens at an early age.

In 1943 Van Impe's life began to change. That year his father had a "born-again" experience and became a devout evangelical Christian. Before many weeks passed, Van Impe found his way to the Baptist church across the street and soon afterward had his own born-again experience. The family joined Liberal Avenue Baptist Church. Both father and son attended the independent Detroit Bible College and in 1950, before Van Impe finished his course of study, his parents left for Belgium as missionaries.

In 1951 Van Impe graduated and was ordained as an independent Baptist minister. Relying heavily on his musical talents, he became a popular attraction at Youth for Christ gatherings. In 1951 he went to Belgium for the first time with a Youth for Christ team. While there he met Rexella Shelton, whom he married in 1952.

They began to travel as evangelists under the billing of "Ambassadors for Christ." They soon began to produce records, his accordion music accompanying her singing.

As their ministry matured, the Van Impes moved away from an almost exclusive reliance upon music, and Van Impe began to preach regularly as part of his work. Cut off at first by people who knew him primarily as a musician, he began to make a reputation as a speaker and soon rebuilt a significant following among conservative Baptists. By 1970 he was able to give up appearances sponsored by a single church and insist upon speaking only at city-wide evangelistic campaigns that had the active support of a coalition of fundamentalist Christian congregations. He opened the office for the Jack Van Impe Crusades, Inc., in Royal Oak, Michigan, a Detroit suburb. In 1971 he added a radio ministry, now heard in five languages. In 1976 the Baptist University of America in Decatur, Georgia, established the Van Impe Chair of Evangelism. Van Impe has become identified with Bible memorization. He began to memorize large portions of Biblical text while in college and has continued the practice. He is frequently billed as "The Walking Bible."

Sources:

Campbell, Roger F. *They Call Him the Walking Bible: The Story of Dr. Jack Van Impe*. Nashville, TN: Action Press, 1977. 176 pp.

Van Impe, Jack. *11:59. . .And Counting!*. Nashville, TN: Thomas Nelson Publishers, 1987. 223 pp.

_____. *Israel's Final Holocaust*. Nashville, TN: Thomas Nelson Publishers, 1979. 172 pp.

★ 981 ★
VAN TIL, Cornelius
Theologian, Orthodox Presbyterian Church
b. May 3, 1895, Netherlands

Cornelius Van Til, a prominent fundamentalist Presbyterian scholar, is the son of Klazina Van der Veen and Ite Van Til. With his parents, he moved to the United States in 1905 and settled in Highland, Indiana. As a member of the Christian Reformed Church he attended Calvin College (A.B., 1922). He then completed his seminary work at Princeton, where he received both a master's degree from the university and a Th.B. from the seminary in 1924. He completed his Th.M. at the seminary in 1925 and his Ph.D. in philosophy at the university in 1927. He was ordained in the Christian Reformed Church and served as pastor of the congregation at Spring Lake, Michigan, during 1927-1928.

In 1928 Van Til accepted a post as a professor in apologetic theology at Princeton just as the Presbyterian Church forced a massive reorganization of the seminary, which had the effect of introducing more liberal teachers into the faculty. At the end of the 1929 school year, he was among those who resigned and joined with **J. Gresham Machen** in the formation of Westminster Theological Seminary in Philadelphia, Pennsylvania. There he would remain for the next four decades.

In the years immediately after the move to Philadelphia the controversy between fundamentalists and modernists in the Presbyterian Church continued into the 1930s. In 1936, Machen was tried for "disturbing the peace of the church." His conviction led to the formation of the Orthodox Presbyterian Church. Westminster became the new church's seminary and Van Til transferred his membership. Following Machen's death in 1937, Van Til gradually emerged as the church's leading scholarly voice. As a maturing scholar, Van Til inherited not only the traditional Presbyterian orthodoxy through Machen, but a revived Dutch orthodoxy represented in the thought of Abraham Kuyper (1837-1920).

Van Til's major emphasis has been Christian apologetics, the intellectual defense of the Christian faith. Following Kuyper's lead, Van Til built his own thought around the attack upon an important and influential modern idea, the autonomy of theoretical thought and the ability of humans to judge reality. Beginning with his first important book, *The New Modernism* (1946), Van Til built what many came to feel was the most impressive presentation of contemporary Calvinist fundamentalist thought. His ideas were developed in over 20 books, including *Christianity and Idealism* (1955); *The Defense of Faith* (1955); *Apologetics* (1956); *An Introduction to Systematic Theology* (1961); *The Case for Calvinism* (1964); and *A Christian Theory of Knowledge* (1969). He also took time to challenge new trends in Presbyterian-reformed thought in *The New Evangelicalism* (1964); *Karl Barth and Evangelicalism* (1964); and *The Great Debate Today* (1970).

Van Til retired in 1972 and was named professor emeritus of the seminary. As might be expected of someone who spent his life arguing for a faith perspective against the claims of alternative views, Van Til developed strong support from contemporaries such as Rousas John Rushdoony and equally strong detractors such as **Gordon H. Clark** and John W. Robbins.

Sources:

Clark, Gordon H. *The Trinity.*
Robbins, John W. *Cornelius Van Til: The Man and the Myth.* Jefferson, MD: Trinity Foundation, 1986. 40 pp.
Rushdoony, Rousas John. *Van Til.* Phillipsburg, NJ: Presbyterian and Reformed Publishing Co., 1979. 51 pp.
Van Til, Cornelius. *Apologetics.* Philadelphia: Westminster Theological Seminary, 1956.
_____. *The Case for Calvinism.* Nutley, NJ: Presbyterian and Reformed Publishing Co., 1964. 153 pp.
_____. *A Christian Theory of Knowledge.* Nutley, NJ: Presbyterian and Reformed Publishing Co., 1969. 390 pp.
_____. *Karl Barth and Evangelicalism.* Nutley, NJ: Presbyterian and Reformed Publishing Co., 1964.
_____. *The New Modernism.* Nutley, NJ: Presbyterian and Reformed Publishing Co., 1946. 384 pp.

★982★
VEDDER, Henry Clay
Church Historian, Northern Baptist Convention
b. Feb. 26, 1853, DeRuyter, New York
d. Oct. 13, 1935, Chester, Pennsylvania

Henry Clay Vedder, a Baptist church historian, was the son of Meander W. and Harriet Cook Vedder, descendants of a Dutch family who had settled in New Netherlands in the seventeenth century. Originally, Vedder had been given his mother's maiden name as a middle name, but he changed it during his adolescent years because he did not like being called "Cookie." During Vedder's youth, his father was a carriage maker in Rochester, New York. He attended the University of Rochester, which granted him a B.A. degree in 1873, and spent the next three years at Rochester Theological Seminary. In 1875 Vedder was licensed to preach by the Lake Avenue Baptist Church in Rochester. In 1877 he married Minnie M. Lingham.

It, however, was not Vedder's desire to follow a pastoral career. Following graduation from the seminary, he joined the editorial staff of a Baptist newspaper, the *Examiner*, published in New York. He stayed with the paper until 1894, during which time he authored his first book, *A Short History of the Baptists*. Also during these years he decided to prepare himself for a career as a church historian. In 1894 he was offered and accepted the chair in church history at Crozier Theological Seminary.

In his 30 years as a professor, Vedder's research interests, which had begun with American Baptist history, broadened to include the whole of church history. His literary accomplishments include: *A History of the Baptists in the Middle States* (1898); *The Baptists* (1903); *Balthasar Huebmaier, the Leader of the Anabaptists* (1905); *Our New Testament—How Did We Get It* (1908); *Christian Epoch Makers* (1908); *Socialism and the Ethics of Jesus*

(1912); *The Gospel of Jesus and the Problems of Democracy* (1914); and *The Reformation in Germany* (1914). As a church historian, Vedder was one of the first Baptists to call the popular theory of Baptist origins (through an unbroken succession of anti-infant baptism churches from New Testament times) into question. He argued that the Baptist faith originated in seventeenth-century England. Vedder's work, while rejected by many Baptist traditionalists of his day, was accepted by his colleagues, and has come to be the position of contemporary Baptist historians.

The succession of titles of his books also reveals a growing interest in social history as opposed to purely denominational chronicling. This interest is in line with the influx of sociology into the theological curriculum and increased attention by church leaders to social issues (the so-called social gospel).

Vedder retired in 1926 and moved to Chester, Pennsylvania. He became an associate editor of the *Chester Times* and wrote a daily column, the last one appearing just three days prior to his death. He also authored one more book, *A Short History of Baptist Missions* (1927).

Sources:

Dictionary of American Biography. 20 vols. and 7 supps. New York: Charles Scribner's Sons, 1928-1936, 1944-1981.
Vedder, Henry C. *Balthasar Huebmaier, the Leader of the Anabaptists.* New York: Putnam's, 1905. 333 pp.
_____. *The Baptists.* New York: Baker & Taylor, 1903. 245 pp.
_____. *Christian Epoch-Makers.* New York: American Baptist Publication Society, 1908. 368 pp.
_____. *The Gospel of Jesus and the Problems of Democracy.* New York: Macmillan Company, 1914. 410 pp.
_____. *A History of the Baptists in the Middle States.* Philadelphia: American Baptist Publication Society, 1898. 355 pp.
_____. *A Short History of the Baptists.* Philadelphia: American Baptist Publication Society, 1891. 245 pp.

★983★
VENTA, Krishna
Founder, W.F.L.K. Fountain of the World
b. 1911, San Francisco, California
d. Dec. 10, 1958, Chatsworth, California

Master Krishna Venta, born Francis Heindswaltzer Pencovic, was the founder of the now-defunct W.F.L.K. Fountain of the World. His parents died when he was eight, and he was apparently somewhat of a juvenile delinquent as a youth. As he got older, he worked at odd jobs, read metaphysical literature, and committed petty crimes. He went to jail in 1942 for writing bad checks. At one point during his imprisonment, he was transferred from the road gang to the State Hospital in Stockton, California, and diagnosed as suffering from delusional paranoia. He was telling everyone that he was the True Christ.

Venta was married twice, and in both cases attempted to found a religious movement not long after the marriage. The first attempt failed after a few years. The couple split up, although not until they had had several children, and his wife sued for divorce on charges of nonsupport. The second attempt was successful. He had six children with his second wife, Ruth. The marriage lasted until Venta's untimely death, and his preaching attracted followers almost immediately. His message was an eclectic compound of Christianity and Hinduism that emphasized love and service, with a slight admixture of "space-age" mythology. Venta, who claimed to be Christ, was said to have come from the planet Neophrates ages ago and landed in Nepal. He teleported to America on March 29, 1932, and, so as to have less difficulty doing his work, took over the biography of a three-year-old boy, Francis Pencovic, who had recently died.

The W.F.L.K. (Wisdom, Faith, Love, and Knowledge) Fountain of the World, as Venta's group was called, moved to California in the late 1940s and acquired 26 acres of land in Box Canyon near Chatsworth. They lived communally, with members donating all of their possessions to the group. There was initially some conflict with the neighbors, but their efforts to help out during fires and other crises eventually won them acceptance. Venta himself was a flamboyant personality who generated publicity by actions like speeding around Box Canyon in a yellow Cadillac and losing large sums of money gambling in Las Vegas.

In 1958 a pair of disgruntled former members went to Box Canyon demanding that Venta make a public confession that he was a fraud. They had earlier contacted the authorities, accusing the master of practicing medicine without a license and of having sexual relations with underaged girls. What seems to have happened during the confrontation was that he refused to confess, and the two visitors responded by setting off a bag of high explosives which killed them, Venta, and seven other people. The group continued operating for over two decades after this traumatic event, but eventually disbanded.

Sources:

Mathison, Richard. *Faiths, Cults and Sects of America.* Indianapolis: Bobbs-Merrill, 1960. 384 pp.

Melton, J. Gordon *The Encyclopedia of American Religions.* 3d ed. Detroit: Gale Research Inc.,1988. 1102 pp.

Orrmont, Arthur. *Love Cults and Faith Healers.* New York: Ballantine, 1961. 192 pp.

—*James R. Lewis*

★984★
VICK, George Beauchamp
Fundamentalist Baptist Educator and Minister
b. Feb. 5, 1901, Russellville, Kentucky
d. Sep. 29, 1975, Springfield, Missouri

George Beauchamp Vick, one of the founders of the Baptist Bible Fellowship, was the son of a Kentucky Baptist minister, Eben Gray Vick, and Effie Gilbert Vick. His father was pastor of a Southern Baptist congregation in Louisville, Kentucky, at the time of his son's conversion experience when he was nine years old. After graduating from high school, Vick went to work with the L & N Railroad, where he met his future wife, Eloise Baker. They were married in 1919. The following year they moved to Ft. Worth, Texas, and joined First Baptist Church, then pastored by the flamboyant fundamentalist preacher **J. Frank Norris**.

Vick worked on the Sunday school staff of what was one of the largest congregations in America, and in 1924 he became a full-time staff member. He was at the church during the turbulent years that led Norris and the congregation to withdraw from the Southern Baptist Convention and Norris' subsequent formation of the World Baptist Fellowship. After working at the church for eight years, Vick resigned and joined the teams of evangelist Wade House and Mordecai Ham. In 1936, following a revival campaign at Temple Baptist Church in Detroit (also pastored by Norris), Vick was persuaded to stay in Detroit as co-pastor of the congregation.

Under Vick's leadership, church attendance grew to the point that a new education building had to be built the following year. Soon afterward, a new sanctuary, seating 3,000, was constructed. By 1942, the church outgrew its property space, purchased new land, and erected a new church complex. In 1947 Vick was formally voted co-pastor of the church. The following year Norris relinquished the pastorship, and Vick succeeded him. However, about this same time, Norris persuaded Vick to assume duties at president of the Bible Baptist Seminary in Ft. Worth, a responsibility that required him to make monthly flights between Texas and Michigan.

In 1950 Vick sided with a group of members of the World Baptist Fellowship opposed to Norris and some of his policies. The division led Vick and others to form the Baptist Bible Fellowship and establish the Baptist Bible College. Vick, while continuing to pastor Temple Baptist Church, was elected president of the new school. He fulfilled both duties until his death in 1975.

In the 1960s the church in Detroit again outgrew its facilities and a new church seating over 5,000 was constructed. During Vick's pastorate, it was estimated that over 350 men and women left the church for full-time ministry.

Sources:

Dollar, George W. *A History of Fundamentalism in America.* Greenville, SC: Bob Jones University Press, 1973. 411 pp.

"Memorial Issue." *Baptist Bible Tribune* 26, 18 (Oct. 24, 1975).

★985★
VILATTE, Joseph Rene
Archbishop, American Catholic Church
b. Jan. 24, 1854, Paris France
d. Jul. 8, 1929, Versailles France

Joseph Rene Vilatte, the initiator of the Old Catholic Movement in North America, was born into a family that had belonged to an independent Catholic Church in France. By the time Vilatte came into the world, this church had largely disappeared from Paris, so he was raised in the Roman Catholic Church. As a young man, he migrated to Canada to study for the priesthood. In North America, his faith was shaken by contact with **Charles Chiniquy**, an apostate priest. He also began to correspond with Hyacinthe Loyson, who had split from Rome to form the Gallican Catholic Church in Vilatte's native country. After this point, Vilatte's career becomes difficult to follow.

In 1884 he was an independent Presbyterian missionary in Green Bay, Wisconsin, but his association with Presbyterianism was short-lived. With the support of Episcopal Bishop John Henry Hobart Brown, Vilatte traveled to Switzerland in 1885, where he was ordained by Old Catholic Bishop Eduard Herzog. He built a highly successful Old Catholic church in Green Bay, and authored a *Catechisme Catholique*.

Although the roots of Old Catholicism lie among the Jansenists, French dissidents who had taken refuge in Holland, the movement did not emerge into its own until after the declaration of papal infallability in 1870. This declaration prompted large numbers of Roman Catholics to defect and to seek alignment with the Old Catholic Church in Utrecht, Holland. A new church that differed little from Roman Catholicism, except on the point of rejecting the doctrine of the inallibility of the pope, was organized along national lines. It was with this independent Catholic Church that Vilatte aligned himself.

Vilatte, however, felt that he needed to be consecrated as a bishop to carry on his work, and that he could not obtain this status in Utrecht. After a long search, he was consecrated by an archbishop of Ceylon who had obtained his episcopal orders from the Syro-Jacobite Church of Malabar. Returning from South Asia, Vilatte struggled to make a success out of his enterprise in Green Bay. Leaving an assistant in charge of his parish, in 1898 Vilatte took up the life of a traveling bishop, consecrating leaders of other independent bodies. In 1915 he founded the American Catholic Church and consecrated its first bishop, **Frederick Ebenezer J. Lloyd**. Lloyd would, in turn, consecrate many other independent bishops.

Villatte retired in 1920 and turned over the church to Bishop Lloyd. Not long afterwards, Vilatte returned to France where he renounced his previous independent course and made submission to Rome. He passed away in a Cistercian Abbey near Versailles.

Sources:

Hogue, William M. "The Episcopal Church and Archbishop Vilatte." *Historical Magazine of the Protestant Episcopal Church* 34, 1 (March 1965): 35-55.

Melton, J. Gordon. *Biographical Dictionary of American Cult and Sect Leaders.* Garland Reference Library of Social Science, vol. 212. New York: Garland Publishing, 1986.

Persson, Bertil. *A Collection of Documents on the Apostolic Succession of Joseph Renee Vilatte with Brief Annotations.* Solna, Sweden: The Author, 1974. 28 pp.

Schultz, Paul G. *The Background of the Episcopate of Archbishop Joseph Renee Vilatte.* Glendale, CA: Guardian Angel Press, 1976.

Tillett, Gregory. *Joseph Renee Vilatte: A Bibliography.* Sydney, Australia: The Vilatte Guild, 1980. 23 pp.

Vilatte, Joseph Rene. *Catechisme Catholique.* Green Bay, WI: 1886.

_____. *The Independent Catholic Movement in France.* London: 1907.

_____. *Mode of Receiving the Profession of the Old Catholic Faith from One Newly Converted.* Chicago: 1919.

_____. *My Relations with the Protestant Episcopal Church.* Glastonbury, England: 1960.

_____. *A Sketch of the Belief of the Old Catholics.* Green Bay, WI: 1889.

★986★
VINCENT, John Heyl
Bishop, Methodist Episcopal Church
b. Feb. 28, 1832, Tuscaloosa, Alabama
d. May 9, 1920, Chicago, Illinois

John Heyl Vincent was a bishop in the Methodist Episcopal Church who is most remembered for his work in adult and religious education, especially the founding of the Chautauqua Institution. He was the son of Mary Raser and John Himrod Vincent, descendant of a Huguenot family. Though born in the south, Vincent moved to Pennsylvania with his family in 1837 and grew up near Lewisburg. Around 1850 he was licensed as a preacher in the Methodist Episcopal Church and appointed to a Methodist circuit which included several small congregations in the vicinity of Luzerne, Pennsylvania. He was able to engage in a limited amount of study at the Wesleyan Institute at Newark, New Jersey, but was largely self-educated. He was ordained a deacon in the New Jersey Conference and pursued the course of study provided by the church for ministers. He finished the course in 1857, and was ordained and transferred to the Rock River Conference, which covered northern Illinois. In 1858 he married Elizabeth Dusenberry. In Illinois he successively served churches in Joliet, Mt. Morris, Galena, Rockford, and Chicago. During the Civil War he worked with the United States Christian Commission.

Vincent's real career began in 1866 when he was appointed general agent of the Methodist Episcopal Sunday School Union. The Sunday School Movement was just emerging as a popular force in Protestantism, and Vincent had already put several innovative ideas into practice. As early as 1855 he had organized a class to study the history and geography of the Holy Land as an aid to understanding the context of the Bible. Two years later he organized the first conventional class to train Sunday school teachers. In 1861 he held the first Sunday school teachers institute and authored his first book, *Little Footprints in Bible Lands*, a Sunday school textbook. With innovation he had to overcome the conservative forces who opposed the use of any literature other than the Bible in the church school.

In 1865 Vincent established a Sunday school quarterly and in 1866 added a companion teacher's book. In these two periodicals he added the system of Sunday lesson leaves for the church school pupils. His lesson leaves reached a circulation of over two million. In 1868 he became the corresponding secretary of the Sunday School Union, which made him the editor of the church's Sunday school material.

Vincent's push to continually upgrade the church school and his faculty led to an invitation by businessman Lewis Miller to the Chautauqua Campgrounds. The campgrounds were owned by the Erie Conference of the Methodist Episcopal Church, and were offered to Vincent as a spot to hold a summer Sunday school teachers institute. Such an interdenominational training session was held in 1874. It became an annual event, growing to include activities throughout the summer and eventually giving birth to one of the greatest experiments in adult education ever conducted. In 1879 the Chautauqua Literary and Scientific Circle was organized as a four-year correspondence course of study. The Chautauqua University was opened in 1883, and the movement involved hundreds of thousands of people annually, as it diffused through local Chautauquas around the country. During his years as head of Chautauqua, Vincent authored a number of books, including *The Chautauqua Movement* (1886); *The Home Book* (1886); *The Modern Sunday School* (1887); *Better Not* (1887); *Studies in Young Life* (1889); and *Our Own Church* (1890).

In 1888 Vincent was elected a bishop of the Methodist Episcopal Church. He served first in Buffalo, New York, which kept him relatively close to Chautauqua. He remained the principal of instruction at Chautaugua until 1898 when he turned the office over to his son. He served four years as bishop in Topeka, Kansas, before moving to Switzerland in 1901. He retired from the bishopric in 1904.

Sources:

Dictionary of American Biography. 20 vols. and 7 supps. New York: Charles Scribner's Sons, 1928-1936, 1944-1981.

Harmon, Nolan B. *The Encyclopedia of World Methodism.* 2 vols. Nashville: United Methodist Publishing House, 1974.

Vincent, John H. *Better Not.* New York: Funk & Wagnalls Co., 1887. 86 pp.

_____. *The Chautauqua Movement.* Boston: Chautauqua Press, 1886. 308 pp.

_____. *The Home Book.* New York: Phillips & Hunt, 1886. 720 pp.

_____. *Little Foot Prints in Bible Lands.* New York: Carlton & Porter, 1861. 139 pp.

_____. *Our Own Church.* New York: Hunt & Eaton, 1890. 173 pp.

_____. *Studies in Young Life.* New York: Funk & Wagnalls, 1889. 254 pp.

Vincent, Leon H. *John Heyl Vincent.* New York: Macmillan Company, 1925. 319 pp.

★987★
Swami VISHNU DEVANANDA
Founder, Sivananda Yoga Vedanta Centres
b. Dec. 31, 1929, Kerala India

Swami Vishnu Devananda, born Swamy Kuttan Nair into a devout Hindu family, is the founder of the Sivananda Yoga Vedanta Centres headquartered in Quebec, and is one of the pioneer teachers of hatha yoga in the West. He spent some months teaching after the completion of his schooling, and then joined the Indian Army, where he served in the Corps of Engineers from 1944 to 1946. While he was in the military, he came across a pamphlet authored by Swami Sivananda Saraswati, and began to undertake spiritual practices based on that publication. He was subsequently inspired to study Sanskrit and traditional Hindu scriptures such as the *Bhagavad Gita*. In 1946 he began visiting Sivananda's ashram in Rishikish, in northern India, and affiliated with the Divine Life Society. When he went to Ananda Kutir for the Diamond Jubilee Celebration of Sivananda's birthday, his master commanded him to remain.

Vishnu Devananda's spiritual discipline included a period of *parivrajaka* (wandering penniless) in 1950. After completing this "tour," he was able to practice yoga with renewed vigor. He found that he had a special aptitude for hatha yoga, and eventually became the hatha yoga professor of Sivananda's Yoga Vedanta Forest Academy, also located at Rishikish. He also served at various times as manager of the Sivananda Publication League and his master's personal secretary. In 1957 he went out on a world tour, spreading

Sivananda's message and recruiting yoga students. He came to North America in 1958, and in December of 1959 settled in Montreal, where he founded the Sivananda Yoga Vedanta Centre. By the spring of 1962 he was able to establish a Sivananda Ashram Yoga Camp in the Laurentian Mountains north of Montreal. He also founded a similar camp on Paradise Island in the Bahamas in 1967. While several of Sivananda's students also came to North America, Vishnu Devananda is the teacher recognized by the Divine Life Society in India. He is one of the foremost exponents of hatha yoga in the West, and author of the yoga classic *The Complete Illustrated Book of Yoga* (1959). He is also the author of such works as *Meditation and Mantras* (1978), and compiler of the *Sivananda Upanishad* (1955).

In the late 1960s and early 1970s he began to engage in activities that extended beyond the usual pursuits of a yoga teacher. Vishnu Devananda made an extensive world tour in 1968, and held a World Brotherhood Convention the next year at the Val Morin Ashram in Canada. In 1969 he also established an organization to promote world peace and brotherhood through yogic practices, the True World Order (TWO). An Indian peace and music festival was held at the Val Morin Ashram in 1970. In 1971 he began flying his private plane over troubled areas such as Belfast, dropping peace pamphlets and flowers. He also organized peace marches and held satsangs wherever he went. Devananda continues to lead the order.

Sources:

Melton, J. Gordon *The Encyclopedia of American Religions*. 3d ed. Detroit: Gale Research Inc.,1988. 1102 pp.
Swami Vishnu. New York: Om Lotus Publishing Company, 1977. 78 pp.
Venkatesananda, Swami. "Swami Vishnu Devananda." *International Sivananda Yoga Life and Yoga Vacations* 3, 1 (March 1977): 1-3.
Vishnu Devananda, Swami. *The Complete Illustrated Book of Yoga*. 1960. Reprint. New York: Pocket Books, 1972. 411 pp.
_____. *Meditation and Mantras*. New York: Om Lotus Publishing Company, 1978. 336 pp.
_____, comp. *Sivananda Upanishad*. New York: Om Lotus Publishing Company, 1955, 1987. 550 pp.

★ 988 ★
Swami VIVEKANANDA
Founder, Vedanta Society
b. Jan. 12, 1863, Calcutta India
d. Jul. 4, 1902, Belur India

Swami Vivekananda, founder of the Vedanta Society, the first Hindu mission in the United States, was born Narendranath Datta into a high caste Bengali family. Because of its status as the capital of British India, Calcutta was at the cutting edge of the meeting between East and West. One of the results of this meeting was the Brahmo Samaj, an Enlightenment reinterpretation of Hinduism. With the help of Orientalist scholarship, it claimed to have recovered the "original" Vedic faith (which closely resembled Deism, an eighteenth-century rationalist system which affirmed belief in one God while denying many of the principal beliefs of orthodox Christianity). Narendra, like many other Western-educated Bengalis, joined the Samaj at an early age, but became dissatisfied with its rationalistic emphasis.

While in college, Narendra's search for a more experiential spirituality led him to **Sri Ramakrishna**, an ecstatic holy man who served as the priest of Kali in a Calcutta temple. Without leaving school or abandoning his other responsibilities, Narendra joined the band of disciples who had gathered around Ramakrishna. After his master's death in 1886, he assumed leadership of the group and formed them into a monastic brotherhood that became the basis of the Ramakrishna Order. Taking the vows of sannyas, the renounced life, Narendra became Swami Vivekananda.

Hearing of the World's Parliament of Religions to be held in Chicago in 1893, Vivekananda arranged to attend and emerged as the single most popular speaker at the gathering. Articulate and charismatic, the Swami presented an idealized image of Hinduism to his American audience, an image that owed as much to the British Orientalist scholars of the late seventeenth century as it did to Sri Ramakrishna. Vivekananda followed up his success at the Parliament with a lecture tour, and the next year with the formation of the Vedanta Society. He also visited England before returning to India in 1897.

Vivekananda's missionary successes had been widely reported in the Indian press, and upon his return he was greeted as a conquering hero. His mission to his own country had a very different thrust than his work in America and England. Building on the recognition accorded him by fellow Indians, the Swami was able to establish the Ramakrishna Order as a strong monastic group that combined the spiritual life with an emphasis on social service.

Vivekananda presented a carefully edited Hinduism to his Western audiences, picturing the philosophy of advaita vedanta as being the core of "true" Hinduism. This image, reinforced by succeeding waves of swamis (with certain exceptions, such as **A. C. Bhaktivedanta Prabhupada** Swami), is still the predominant image of South Asian religion held by Westerners seeking spiritual nourishment from Eastern Wisdom. Vivekananda was also a prolific writer who influenced, and who continues to influence, many people through his writings. His first book, *Raja Yoga* (1894), is probably his most popular. His many books have been reprinted on numerous occasions, and a comprehensive collection of his writings appeared in 1965 as *The Complete Works of Swami Vivekananda*.

Sources:

Dhar, Sailendra Nath. *A Comprehensive Biography of Swami Vivekananda*. Madras, India: Vivekananda Prakashan Kendra, 1975.
His Eastern and Western Admirers. *Reminiscences of Swami Vivekananda*. Calcutta: Advaita Ashrama, 1964. 432 pp.
Melton, J. Gordon. *Biographical Dictionary of American Cult and Sect Leaders*. Garland Reference Library of Social Science, vol. 212. New York: Garland Publishing, 1986.
Nikhilananda, Swami. *Vivekananda: A Biography*. Calcutta: Advaita Ashrama, 1975. 350 pp.
Roland, Romain. *The Life of Vivekananda and the Universal Gospel*. Calcutta: Advaita Ashrama, 1931. 382 pp.
Shepard, Leslie. *Encyclopedia of Occultism & Parapsychology*. 3 vols., 2nd. ed. Detroit: Gale Research Co., 1984-1985.
Vivekananda, Swami. *The Complete Works of Swami Vivekananda*. 12 vols. Calcutta: Advaita Ashrama, 1965.

—*James R. Lewis*

★ 989 ★
Archbishop VLADIMIR
Archbishop, Russian Orthodox Church
b. Dec. 31, 1852, Poltava Russia
d. 1933, Moscow Union of Soviet Socialist Republics

Little is known of the early years of Archbishop Vladimir, the head of the Russian Orthodox Church in the United States from 1888 to 1891. He was born Vasily Sokolovsky and attended Kazan Theological Academy from which he graduated in 1878. Later that same year he was ordained as a priest-monk, having decided not to marry. He became known for his ascetic lifestyle and his simple, vegetarian diet. During the early years of his ministry, he served as inspector at the Kholm Theological Seminary and worked for a while in the Japanese Orthodox mission. Having learned English, Father Vasily was a natural choice when the church moved to fill the vacant bishop's chair in America.

In 1887 Vladimir was consecrated bishop for the Aleutian Islands and Alaska, and departed for his headquarters in San Francisco, California. He brought over 20 people with him to assist in the work which had been without direct episcopal leadership since the drowning of **Bishop Nestor** in 1882. Bishop Vladimir began the process of refining the liturgy for America. He appointed an English-language preacher at the cathedral in San Francisco. He also developed an outstanding music program which attracted the Orthodox lay people to the services. As the crowds packed the building, he pushed for the construction of a larger structure, Holy Trinity Cathedral, to accommodate them. He also developed a pastoral school for the diocese priests.

Bishop Vladimir initiated the process to encourage the return of Uniates (Roman Catholics who followed an Eastern liturgical tradition) to Eastern Orthodoxy. The beginning of this movement was signaled by the transfer of Father Alexis Toth and his parish in Minneapolis into the Orthodox camp.

Vladimir returned to Russia in 1891. He was appointed bishop of Ostrog and later elevated to the rank of archbishop. He retired in 1910 and settled as rector for the Spaso-Androniev Monastery in Moscow. He died at the monastery 23 years later.

Sources:

Afonsky, Bishop Gregory. *A History of the Orthodox Church in Alaska (1794-1917).* Kodiak, AK: St. Herman's Theological Seminary, 1977. 106 pp.

Tarasar, Constance J. *Orthodox America, 1794-1974.* Syosset, NY: Department of History and Archives, Orthodox Church in America, 1975. 351 pp.

★990★
VOIGT, Valerie
Priestess, South Bay Circles (Neo-Pagan)
b. Oct. 10, 1953, Selma, Alabama

Valerie Voigt is the leader of the South Bay Circles and a major networking person in West Coast Neo-Paganism. At the age of 13, she had become a "born again" Christian. Three years later, she came to the jarring realization that she was actually a Pagan. She structured her college education so as to be able to explore religion, and graduated with a B.A. degree in classical languages from the University of Kansas. She began to practice solitary Paganism in Kansas in about 1972, believing at the time that she was the only caucasian Pagan in the world. Her first awareness of the existence of other Pagans came in 1975, when she happened to run across an ad for the Church of All Worlds (the Neo-Pagan group founded by Timothy Zell, now known as **Otter Zell**).

Moving to California in 1978, Voigt contacted the local Wiccans and began to study with Julie Tower, **Alison Harlow**, and others. She also joined the Witchcraft/Occult/Pagan Special Interest Group (SIG) of Mensa, eventually becoming the SIG's coordinator. At this point she began a newsletter, *Pagana*. She was initiated into the New Reformed Orthodox Order of the Golden Dawn (NROOGD), one of the older Bay Area Neo-Pagan fellowships, and started a coven. The coven eventually affiliated with the Covenant of the Goddess (COG), a national association of Wiccan groups. In 1982 she co-founded the Centre of Divine Ishtar and taught an introductory class in witchcraft. She was also initiated into two other witchcraft traditions, Gardnerian Wicca, founded by *Gerald B. Gardner* in the 1940s, and the Faery Tradition of **Victor H. Anderson**, a bay area witch. In 1987 Voigt was a founding Elder of South Bay Circles, a multi-traditional coven association which hosts the eight Sabbat festivals for the south bay community. Over the years, she has taught classes and workshops, been interviewed by the media, traveled widely on networking projects, worked with law enforcement, and written numerous booklets, pamphlets, articles, and other materials. One of her papers, "An Introduction to Craft and Pagan Etiquette," has been widely reprinted.

★991★
WALKING BUFFALO
Indian Chief and Leader, Moral ReArmament
b. Mar. 20, 1870, Morley Canada
d. Dec. 27, 1967, Banff Canada

Walking Buffalo, a Canadian Indian chief who became an important spokesperson for the Moral ReArmament (MRA) movement, was orphaned in his childhood and in 1881 was adopted by John Maclean, the Methodist missionary to the Indians in Western Canada. Maclean came to Alberta in 1880 to work among the Blood Indians. He gave his new son the name George and saw that he received a thorough mission school education. As a young man, Walking Buffalo was admitted to a medical school, but declined to attend as it would mean relocating to Eastern Canada. He was at the time the only one of his tribe who could speak English. He was needed as an interpreter at a time when Whites were coming to dominate Alberta and the other Western provinces. He also worked as a scout for the Northwest Mounted Police. During this period he was an active lay person in the Methodist Church in Canada and, after the formation of the United Church of Canada in 1925, the Morley (Alberta) United Church.

In 1920 Walking Buffalo was named chief of the Stoney Indians (part of the larger family of Lakota Indians). He served in that capacity for the next 15 years. In 1934, during his tenure as chief, **Frank N. Buchman**, the founder of the First Century Christian Fellowship (later to be known as Moral ReArmament) came to Alberta. Buchman held a "house party" at Banff, in which he invited a small group of people to meet and see spiritual renewal through a process of confession and forgiveness. Walking Buffalo was impressed by Buchman and led the ceremonies that made Buchman a blood brother to the tribe. He gave Buchman the name A-Wo-Zan-Zan-Tonga or Great Light in Darkness.

In 1935 Walking Buffalo relinquished his active role as chief, though he remained a senior statesman for the Stoneys and other related tribes in the area and worked on behalf of Moral ReArmament as an ambassador for world peace. He traveled widely, often making appearances with Buchman, and was present in 1961 at Buchman's funeral. He continued to reside in Alberta and died there in his late 90s.

Sources:

Lean, Garth. *Frank Buchman: A Life.* London: Constable, 1985. 590 pp.

Wallace, W. Stewart. *The Macmillan Dictionary of Canadian Biography.* 4th ed., rev. Edited by W. A. McKay. Toronto: Macmillan of Canada, 1978.

★992★
WALL, Aaron
Founder, Defenseless Mennonite Brethren in Christ of North America
b. Jan. 1, 1834, Pordenau Russia
d. Aug. 6, 1905, United States

Little is known of the early life of Aaron Wall, a founder of the Defenseless Mennonite Brethren of Christ in North America (now known as the Fellowship of Evangelical Bible Churches). He grew up in a small town in southern Russia, and in 1858 married Aganetha Dick. They settled in a nearby village of Hamberg, where the Mennonites enjoyed some special protection of the Russian government. In 1871 Wall was elected a minister in his congregation and preached his first sermon. This action came just as the government was putting pressure on the Mennonites to serve in the army. Wall moved to the United States, as did many of the community who were opposed to participation in war in any way. He settled near Mountain Lake, Minnesota.

In Minnesota, he was soon elected an elder of the Bergfelder Mennonite Church with which he had affiliated. His sermons and admonitions stressed regeneration and a strict adherence to following a new life in Christ. His preaching eventually led to a split in the congregation, and the more conservative members left with Wall in 1889 to found the Bruderthaler Church. Wall then led his congregation to affiliate with the Ebenezer Church, which had been founded by **Isaak Peters**, also an immigrant from Pondenau, who followed a strict Mennonite life. The two congregations merged as the United Mennonite Brethren of North America, which soon became known as the Defenseless Mennonite Brethren of Christ in North America.

Wall continued as an elder of the Minnesota congregation and a leader in the Defenseless Mennonites until his death in 1905. Several weeks before his death he chaired the meeting at which a successor, Henry I. Dick, was elected, and he ordained Dick as a church elder.

Sources:

The Mennonite Encyclopedia. 4 vols. Scottdale, PA: The Mennonite Publishing House, 1955.

★ 993 ★
WALLACE JR., Foy Esco
Minister and Editor, Churches of Christ
b. Sep. 30, 1896, Montague County, Texas
d. 1979

Foy Esco Wallace, Jr. was the most renowned of the Churches of Christ ministers that emerged from a family that produced at least five prominent denominational leaders. The son of Foy Edwin Wallace, a Church of Christ minister, Wallace was baptized by his father in Sherman, Texas, in 1909. he emerged as a preacher himself during his college years at Thorp Spring Christian College in 1912. In 1914 he married Virgi Brightwell. During the next fifteen years, he became well known as a preacher and an evangelist.

Wallace emerged as a national leader among the churches in 1930 when he was asked to succeed James A. Allen as editor of the *Gospel Advocate*, the most prominent of the several periodicals serving the loosely organized Churches of Christ. During his four years with the *Advocate* Wallace engaged in a number of controversies, always with a strong partisan opinion. He was, for example, an ardent defender of the Churches of Christ's opposition to the use of instrumental (organ) music in church worship.

The most important of the issues raised during these years, however, was premillennialism, the belief in Christ's imminent second coming to establish a literal reign of a thousand years upon the earth. The Churches of Christ have generally been amillennial. The issue was especially relevant to the *Gospel Advocate* as R. H. Boll had introduced the idea of premillenialism into the movement through the pages of the *Advocate* in a column he wrote for the magazine. Boll was fired and later rehired with the understanding that he would remain silent on eschatological issues (those matters concerning last things). He went back on this agreement and was fired again.

Wallace subsequently attacked Boll with all of his talent. Even after he left the *Gospel Advocate* in 1934, he continued to write for it on what came to be known as the "Boll issue." In 1935 Wallace founded the *Gospel Guardian*, which ran for twelve issues and was then merged into the *Firm Foundation*, a Texas Churches of Christ periodical. The Boll issue peaked in the 1930s, and Wallace is generally credited with driving premillennialist teachings from the Church and isolating the Boll faction. In 1938 Wallace founded the *Bible Banner*, which he published for eleven years. His final publishing venture was the *Torch* (1950-1951).

When Wallace was not writing, he was generally on the road preaching, and his career was punctuated by a number of debates with ministers both inside and outside the Churches of Christ. (The Churches of Christ are the main group which perpetuates this form of religious discourse so popular in the nineteenth century.) In 1933, at the height of the premillennialist controversy, for example, Wallace debated Boll's supporter Charles N. Neal. Possibly the most prominent opponent he debated was Baptist fundamentalist and premillennialist **J. Frank Norris**.

Much of Wallace's polemic skill during the last years was spent in denunciation of the many new Biblical translations that had begun to appear after World War II. In 1977 a major collection of Wallace's writing appeared under the title, *Present Truth*.

Sources:

Hill, Samuel S., ed. *Encyclopedia of Religion in the South*. Macon, GA: Mercer University Press, 1984. 878 pp.
Wallace, Foy E., Jr. *The Present Truth*. Fort Worth, TX: Foy E. Wallace Publications, 1977. 1068 pp.

★ 994 ★
WALLS, William Jacob
Bishop, African Methodist Episcopal Zion Church
b. May 8, 1885, Chimney Rock, North Carolina
d. Apr. 23, 1975

William Jacob Walls, bishop and historiographer of the African Methodist Episcopal Zion Church, was born in rural North Carolina. He attended Allen Industrial School. In 1899 he was licensed to preach. In 1902 he joined the Blue Ridge Conference of the African Methodist Episcopal Zion Church, and the following year was ordained a deacon. He was ordained an elder in 1905. He attended Livingston College and received his B.A. in 1908. He continued his education at Hood Theological Seminary (B.D., 1913), studied journalism and philosophy at Columbia University (1921-1922), and received his masters from the University of Chicago in 1941. He married Dorothy Louise Jordan.

Walls began his pastoral career on the Cedar Grove Circuit near Cleveland, North Carolina, and later served Miller's Chapel and the Sandy Creek Circuit in North Carolina; Moore's Chapel in Lincolnton, North Carolina; Soldier's Memorial Church in Salisbury, North Carolina; and Broadway Temple in Louisville, Kentucky. In 1920 he became editor of the *Star of Zion*, and during the next four years increased the circulation threefold.

In 1924, at the meeting of the general conference in Indianapolis, Walls was elected bishop. Among the first assignments given him was chairmanship of the Board of Religious Education, which was created at that conference. He held the post for all of the 44 years of his active bishopric. His commitment to education in the church was further revealed by his many years of service on the board of trustees of Livingston College.

Sources:

Harmon, Nolan B. *The Encyclopedia of World Methodism*. 2 vols. Nashville: United Methodist Publishing House, 1974.
Walls, William Jacob. *The African Methodist Episcopal Zion Church, Reality of the Black Church*. Charlotte, NC: A.M.E. Zion Publishing House, 1974. 669 pp.
_____. *Joseph Charles Price, Educator and Race Leader*. Boston: The Christopher Publishing House, 1943.
_____. *The Romance of a College*. New York: Vantage Press, 1963.

★ 995 ★
WALTERS, Alexander
Bishop, African Methodist Episcopal Zion Church
b. Aug. 1, 1858, Bardstown, Kentucky
d. Feb. 1, 1917

Alexander Walters, a bishop of the African Methodist Episcopal Zion Church, was the son of a slave couple, Harriet Mathers and Henry Walters. Born just before the Civil War, he was freed as a child and was thus able to pursue an education in the local school.

He completed his formal education there in 1875, graduating valedictorian of his class. He moved to Indianapolis, worked at odd jobs, and became involved in the variety of fraternal organizations serving the black community. In 1877 he was licensed to preach by the African Methodist Episcopal Zion Church and assigned to a congregation in Indianapolis. Several months later he married Katie Knox. In 1878 he transferred to the Kentucky Conference and, following his ordination in 1879, began a successful career in the church. He became secretary of the Kentucky Conference in 1881. Two years later he moved to the Pacific Coast to serve pastorates in Portland, Oregon, and San Francisco, California, and to become presiding elder of the San Francisco District. In 1884 he attended his first general conference as a delegate from California. He was elected first assistant secretary for the general conference.

Walters served pastorates in Tennessee and New York, and in 1889 was appointed as the general agent for the church's book concern. Over the next few years he revitalized the book distribution effort. In 1892 he was elected bishop, one of the youngest men to attain that office. During his initial years as a bishop, new laws were passed discriminating against Blacks. In 1898 he participated in the organization of the Afro-American Council and was elected its first president. The council proceeded to address the situation of American Blacks. It strongly opposed the accommodationist policies articulated by Booker T. Washington as well as the program of **Henry McNeal Turner** to return Blacks to Africa. His first wife having died, Walters married Emeline Virginia Bird in 1902.

During the early years of the twentieth century, Walters increasingly turned his sights to the international scene. In 1890 Walters had made his first trip to Europe, and in 1891 he returned to attend the international Methodist Ecumenical Conference. Then in 1900 he made a third visit to attend the Pan-African Conference, and was elected president of the Pan-African Association. In 1904 he served as bishop of Africa for the African Methodist Episcopal Zion Church, though he did not go to Africa until 1910. He was most impressed with the role of Blacks in running the African governments. In 1911 he visited Jamaica and Demerara. He became a strong advocate of United States support of Liberia, though he turned down the position of minister to Liberia when offered by President Woodrow Wilson.

At home, during these mature years, Walters was active in the ecumenical scene, and became a member of the administrative committee of the Federal Council of Churches and vice-president of the World Alliance for Promoting International Friendship through the Churches. His second wife having died, he married a third time, to Lelia Coleman. Among his last accomplishments was the completion of his autobiography, *My Life and Work* (1917).

Sources:

Dictionary of American Biography. 20 vols. and 7 supps. New York: Charles Scribner's Sons, 1928-1936, 1944-1981.

Walls, William J. *The African Methodist Episcopal Zion Church, Reality of the Black Church*. Charlotte, NC: A.M.E. Zion Publishing House, 1974. 669 pp.

Walters, Alexander. *My Life and Work*. New York: Fleming H. Revell Co., 1917. 272 pp.

★996★
WALTERS, Donald
Founder, Ananda Community
b. May 19, 1926, Toleajen Romania

James Donald Walters, who in his adult life has been known as Swami Kriyananda, is the founder of Ananda Community, one of the most successful, contemporary intentional communities. He is the son of Ray P. and Gertrude G. Walters. Walters was born in Romania where his father worked as an oil geologist during the 1920s. He was raised in the same Anglo-American community. His mother was a devout Episcopalian. At the age of nine he was sent to boarding school in Switzerland and two years later to one in England. He moved to the United States in 1939 and four years later he entered Haverford College, a Quaker school. He moved on to Brown University in 1945 but left before he completed his degree. In 1949 he moved to Charleston, South Carolina, to be a playwright and begin a search for God.

Once settled in South Carolina, he was given a copy of the *Bhagavad Gita*, the popular Hindu scripture, and found its ideas agreed with some conclusions he had already reached. Soon afterward he located a copy of *Autobiography of a Yogi*, the story of **Paramahansa Yogananda**, one of the few Indian Hindu teachers then working in North America. He also became a vegetarian.

In 1948 he moved to California, met Yogananda, and was accepted as his disciple. Within a year he was giving occasional lectures at the Hollywood and San Diego centers of Yogananda's Self-Realization Fellowship (SRF). Following Yogananda's death in 1952, he began to assume greater responsibilities for the work. From 1955 to 1958 he was the main minister at the Hollywood center. He also took *sannyas*, the vows of the renounced life, and became Swami Kriyananda. In 1960 he became a member of the board of directors and vice-president of the fellowship. Over the next two years his organizational duties began to conflict with his own goals, and in 1962 he left the fellowship and for the next five years worked as a lecturer and writer. His major literary production from this period was later published as *Crisis in Modern Thought* (1972). One of Yoganada's interests was in surviving social collapse through small, economically independent communities, and, now free of organizational ties, Walters dedicated himself to realizing this aspect of his master's vision.

In 1967 he purchased land in the Sierra Mountains of northern California to locate Ananda Cooperative Community. His ideals for the community were spelled out in his 1968 book, *Cooperative Communities: How to Start Them, and Why*. Ananda soon became a success, and has often been featured in studies and films on alternative communities. The community is not strictly communal; "villagers" own their homes and some of the businesses, and this departure from the pattern of comparable experiments is often cited as a decisive factor in its success. During the early years of Ananda, Kriyananda continued to turn out a host of new books, such as *Your Sun Sign as Your Spiritual Guide* (1971); *Eastern Thoughts, Western Thoughts* (1973); *Letters to Truth Seekers* (1973); and *Tales for the Journey* (1974). During the next two decades he led in the development of the community and of satellite centers around the United States and in several foreign countries, and lived through a major catastrophe in 1976 when a forest fire claimed 21 of the community's 22 buildings. About 40 of the 150 residents left in the wake of the fire, and the community came close to folding. In the midst of the turmoil, he released his autobiography, *The Path* (1977).

In the early 1980s Kriyananda went through several significant changes. In 1982 he lost a battle with local authorities to incorporate Ananda as a town. The following year he decided to discard his sannyasin vows. He shaved his beard, began to dress in Western clothes and use his family name of Walters, and in 1985 married Rosanna, a woman he had met several years previously in Italy. Also during the 1980s, Walters, who had already written a number of books, authored a host of new books, many on popular New Age themes.

In the late 1980s, Kriyananda began a new phase of his life by shedding the image of Kriyananda and relating to the larger public as Donald Walters. Over a short period of time he turned out a series of books, many on popular New Age themes of crystals and channeling. Titles included: *Education for Life* (1986); *The Story of Crystal Hermitage* (1986); *Cities of Light* (1987); *The Reappear-*

ance of the Christ; and *Crystal Clarity: The Artist as Channel* (1987). He also published a condensed version of his autobiography entitled *The Shorter Path* (1980).

Sources:
Ball, John. *Ananda: Where Yoga Lives.* Bowling Green, OH: Bowling Green University Popular Press, 1982. 232 pp.
Nordquist, Ted A. *Ananda Cooperative Village.* Uppsala, Sweden: Borgstrims Tryckeri Ab, 1978. 177 pp.
Walters, J. Donald (Swami Kriyananda). *Cooperative Communities: How to Start Them, and Why.* Nevada City, CA: Ananda Publications, 1968. 60 pp.
_____. *Crises in Modern Thought.* Nevada City, CA: Ananda Publications, 1972. 221 pp.
_____. *Crystal Clarity: The Artist as Channel.* Nevada City, CA: Crystal Clarity, Publishers, 1987. 115 pp.
_____. *How to Be a Channel.* Nevada City, CA: Crystal Clarity, Publishers, 1987. 117 pp.
_____. *The Path.* Nevada City, CA: Ananda Publications, 1977. 640 pp.
_____. *The Story of Crystal Hermitage.* Nevada City, CA: Crystal Clarity, Publishers, 1986. 157 pp.

★997★
WARD, Harry Frederick
Minister and Social Activist, Methodist Episcopal Church
b. Oct. 9, 1873, London England
d. Dec. 9, 1966, Palisades, New Jersey

Harry Frederick Ward, a pioneering social activist in the Methodist Episcopal Church, was the son of Harry and Fanny Jeffery Ward. He came to America as a teenager in 1891, and in 1893 was admitted on trial in the Southern California Conference of the Methodist Episcopal Church. He spent the decade in college, beginning at the University of Southern California. He eventually received his B.A. degree at Northwestern University in 1897 and his M.A. at Harvard University the following year. In 1898 he became head of the Northwestern University Settlement and in 1899 transferred to the Rock River Conference (northern Illinois). He served his first pastorate as minister to the Wabash Avenue Methodist Episcopal Church in Chicago beginning in 1899. He subsequently was pastor of Union Avenue Church in Chicago and Euclid Avenue Church in Oak Park, Illinois. His first book, *Social Creed of the Churches* (1912), was written while he was in Oak Park.

Ward emerged as a leading social theorist during his Chicago years. He was instrumental in developing the Social Creed of the Methodist Episcopal Church, which had been adapted from the earlier one drafted by the Methodist Episcopal Church, South. The creed was adopted by the Methodist Episcopal Church in 1908. In 1907 he took the lead in organizing the more socially concerned Methodists into the Methodist Federation for Social Action (later called the Methodist Federation for Social Service). He served as its first editorial secretary and in 1911 became the general secretary, a post he retained until 1944. The Federation emerged as the major organization, not only within Methodism, but within the larger Protestant community, championing social change in the light of Christian ideals. The organization became identified with socialism, the form of social organization which Ward and other Federation leaders identified with the kingdom of God for many years.

In 1913 Ward began a five-year tenure at Boston University as a professor of social ethics. He moved to Union Theological Seminary in New York City in 1918 and stayed there until his retirement in 1941. During his many years as a teacher, he also remained an outspoken champion of many "radical" causes which subsequently became part of the American life: the eight-hour workday, social security, minimum wage laws, and the rights of labor to organize and collectively bargain.

Ward authored many books during his academic career, including: *Social Evangelism* (1915); *The New Social Order—Principles*

and *Programs* (1919); *Our Economic Morality* (1929); *Which Way Religion?* (1931); and *In Place of Profit* (1933). During the 1940s both Ward and the Federation took a decided turn to the left politically and socially and, among other ideas, began to advocate the Marxist goal of a classless society. By 1952, it had moved so far from the mainstream of Methodist thinking that the general conference of the Methodist Church (1939-1968), into which the Methodist Episcopal Church had merged, officially disassociated itself from the Federation and established a Board of Social and Economic Relations to guide its thinking on social policy.

Ward, while spending the last years of his life alienated from the church he had been a part of all of his adult life, was not forgotten. In the 1970s a new generation of socially concerned Methodists has revived the Federation and again made it a potent force in the church's life.

Sources:
Harmon, Nolan B. *The Encyclopedia of World Methodism.* 2 vols. Nashville: United Methodist Publishing House, 1974.
Ward, Harry F. *Christianizing Community Life.* New York: Association Press, 1917. 176 pp.
_____. *Democracy and Social Change.* New York: Modern Age Books, 1940. 29 pp.
_____. *The Gospel for a Working World.* New York: Missionary Education Movement of the United States and Canada, 1918. 260 pp.
_____. *The New Social Order—Principles and Programs.* New York: Macmillan Company, 1919. 384 pp.
_____. *Our Economic Morality and the Ethic of Jesus.* New York: Macmillan Company, 1929. 329 pp.
_____. *Social Creed of the Churches.* New York: Eaton & Mains, 1912. 185 pp.
_____. *Social Ministry.* New York: Eaton & Mains, 1910. 38 pp.
_____. *Which Way Religion?* New York: Macmillan Company, 1931. 221 pp.

★998★
WARFIELD, Benjamin Breckinridge
Theologian, Presbyterian Church
b. Nov. 5, 1851, Lexington, Kentucky
d. Feb. 17, 1921, Princeton, New Jersey

Benjamin Breckinridge Warfield, a conservative Presbyterian theologian, was the son of William and Mary Cabell Breckinridge Warfield. He attended the College of New Jersey (now Princeton University) from which he graduated in 1871. He followed with a year of travel abroad and then settled in a job as editor of the *Farmer's Home Journal*, published in Lexington, Kentucky. He attended Princeton Theological Seminary and while there, in 1875, was licensed to preach by the Presbytery of Ebenezer of the Presbyterian Church. He graduated in 1876 and several months later married Annie Pearce Kinkead. He journeyed to Europe for a year of post-graduate work at Leipzig, and in 1877 became the assistant minister at First Presbyterian Church in Baltimore, Maryland.

In 1878 Warfield became an instructor at Western Theological Seminary at Pittsburgh, Pennsylvania, and in 1879 was both ordained to the ministry and elevated to the rank of professor. While there he produced his earliest books, including *An Introduction to the Textual Criticism of the New Testament* (1886). In 1887 he was called to succeed Archibald A. Hodge as professor of theology at Princeton Theological Seminary. He would remain in that post for the rest of his life.

Warfield soon distinguished himself as an outstanding multilingual scholar who read widely in theological and Biblical studies, and as a staunch defender of conservative Presbyterianism. He had come to believe that the Westminster Confession and related documents represented the final crystallization of the very essence of Christian faith. He had also accepted the formulations first put forth by A. A. Hodge concerning the authority of scripture which affirmed the plenary inspiration of the Bible, meaning every word of the Bible was inspired, not just the thoughts or concepts.

Warfield's literary production was prodigious. While he did not write a systematic theology, his books covered the major theological topics at issue in his day. These topics were especially influenced by the acceptance of modernist theology and Biblical criticism by his Presbyterian colleagues at Union Theological Seminary in New York City, and the continued attempts to erode the Westminster Creed as a standard of belief in the Presbyterian Church. Among his most important books are *The Significance of the Westminster Standards as a Creed* (1898); *The Lord of Glory* (1907); *The Plan of Salvation* (1915); and *Counterfeit Miracles* (1918). In 1890 he began a 13-year tenure as the chief editor of the *Presbyterian and Reformed Review* and contributed many articles to it and to the *Princeton Theological Review*. After his death, 10 volumes of his articles were published as a series of texts. They include *Revelation and Inspiration* (1927); *The Westminster Assembly and Its Work* (1931); and *Perfectionism* (2 vols., 1931-1932).

Warfield remained active right up until his death in 1921. He trained a whole generation of ministers in his conservative perspective. He died before the more liberal theology came to dominate the faculty and force his successor, **J. Gresham Machen**, to leave his post at Princeton and found a rival school.

Sources:

Dictionary of American Biography. 20 vols. and 7 supps. New York: Charles Scribner's Sons, 1928-1936, 1944-1981.
Warfield, Benjamin B. *Counterfeit Miracles*. New York: Charles Scribner's Sons, 1918. 327 pp.
_____. *The Gospel of the Incarnation*. New York: N.p., 1893.
_____. *The Lord of Glory*. New York: American Tract Society, 1907. 332 pp.
_____. *Perfectionism*. 2 vols. New York: Oxford University Press, 1931-1932.
_____. *The Plan of Salvation*. Grand Rapids, MI: Wm. B. Eerdmans Pub. Co., 1915. 112 pp.
_____. *Revelation and Inspiration*. New York: Oxford University Press, 1927. 456 pp.
_____. *The Significance of the Westminster Standards as a Creed*. New York: Charles Scribner's Sons, 1898. 36 pp.
_____. *The Westminster Assembly and Its Work*. New York: Oxford University Press, 1931. 400 pp.

★999★
WARREN, William Fairfield
Educator, Methodist Episcopal Church
b. Mar. 13, 1833, Williamsburg, Massachusetts
d. Dec. 6, 1924, Brookline, Massachusetts

William Fairfield Warren, the first president of Boston University, was the son of Mather and Anne Miller Fairfield Warren. In 1850 he entered Wesleyan University from which he graduated in 1853. He moved to Mobile, Alabama, where he founded a private school. He returned to Massachusetts in 1854 and was admitted on trial to the New England Conference of the Methodist Episcopal Church and began his theological study at Andover-Newton Theological Seminary. He completed his doctoral studies in Germany at the Universities of Berlin and Halle in 1856 and 1857. Upon his return to the United States he served congregations at Wilbraham and Boston, Massachusetts. In 1861, shortly after his being ordained elder, he married Harriet Cornelia Merrick and returned to Germany to become a professor of systematic theology at Missionsanstalt in Bremen. During his five years there, he authored a number of articles and his first book, *Systematische Theologie Einheitlich Behandelt* (1865), all of which served to build his initial intellectual reputation.

In 1867 the Methodist Biblical Institute was relocated to Boston, Massachusetts, as the Boston Theological School (now Seminary).

Warren returned to Boston as its president and a professor of theology. He also began to work with a group of local Methodist philanthropists in creating a university. He served as acting president (1869-1873) and then president of Boston University. He brought the theological school into the university as a department. Once the university was stable, he set about developing its program and continually raising its academic standards. He developed a medical facility and law school and advanced courses in oratory and music. He recruited an outstanding faculty that included Alexander Graham Bell (who invented the telephone while at the school), philosopher **Borden Parker Bowne**, and theologian Henry Clay Sheldon.

Warren is particularly remembered for his efforts promoting the education of women. Under his leadership, Boston University became the first university in America to open all of its professional schools to women. The first Ph.D. conferred by an American university to a female was awarded to Helen McGill by Boston in 1878. Warren was one of the original incorporators of Wellesley College and served as president of the Massachusetts Society for the University Education of Women.

Warren was an early champion of a modern approach to biblical criticism and was able to bring insights of Darwinism into the curriculum with relative ease. His devout spirituality and personal conservative theology coupled with a straightforward defense of academic freedom won the trust of the school's supporters.

Warren had been trained in the history and philosophy of religion and his course in comparative religion was among his most popular. He had developed a vision for the ideal religion, the subject of his 1886 volume, *The Quest for a Perfect Religion*. He also had a particular interest in cosmology which led him into areas of unusual speculation. In 1885 he published a book advocating the hollow earth theory, the notion that the center of the earth is open space rather than molten rock. His treatise, *Paradise Found*, went through 11 editions during his lifetime.

Warren remained as president of the university until 1903 and continued to lecture in theology until his retirement in 1920 at the age of 77. He lived his last years in the Boston area.

Sources:

Bishop, Donald H. "William Fairfield Warren (1833-1929), Mentor of World Religions." *Methodist History* 6, 4 (July 1968): 36-43.
Dictionary of American Biography. 20 vols. and 7 supps. New York: Charles Scribner's Sons, 1928-1936, 1944-1981.
Harmon, Nolan B. *The Encyclopedia of World Methodism*. 2 vols. Nashville: United Methodist Publishing House, 1974.
Warren, William F. *Paradise Found*. Boston: Houghton, Mifflin and Company, 1885. 505 pp.
_____. *The Quest for a Perfect Religion*. Boston: Rand Avery Co., 1887. 18 pp.
_____. *The Religions of the World and the World-Religion*. Boston: The Author, 1895. 135 pp.
_____. *Systematisch Theologie einheitlich behandelt*. Boston: Tractathaus, 1865. 186 pp.
_____. *The True Key to Ancient Cosmology and Ancient Geography*. Boston, MA: Ginn, Heath & Co., 1882. 20 pp.

★1000★
WATSON, George Douglas
Evangelist, Wesleyan Methodist Church
b. Mar. 23, 1848, Accomac County, Virginia
d. Jul. 25, 1923, Santa Monica, California

George Douglas Watson, a holiness evangelist at the beginning of the twentieth century, was the son of Mary Emeline Scarburgh and James Henderson Watson. He grew up in pious surroundings on his father's farm. He obtained little formal education as a youth, but having learned to read, he improved his education with his voracious reading. At the age of 14 he began to study medicine with a local physician in Onancock, Virginia, however, his studies were cut off by the Civil War. He joined the Confederate Army and in 1863, while in the service, he had an initial conversion experience to Christianity and felt a call to preach. The war broke his health, but after a period of recovery, in 1865 he was able to leave home again for a year to study at Garrett Biblical Institute in Concord, New Hampshire. He preached his first sermon in the dead of winter that year in a school house near Concord.

In 1866 Watson returned to his home and was licensed to preach in the Philadelphia Conference of the Methodist Episcopal Church and appointed as a supply preacher for the Snow Hill (Maryland) Circuit. In 1867 he was received on probation and in 1868 became a member of the Wilmington Conference, which was that year set off from the Philadelphia Conference. In 1869 he married Margeret Evelyn Watson. Through these years he served various circuits in Maryland and Delaware.

In 1870 Watson attended the Oakington National Camp Meeting at which he heard his first holiness sermon expounding the idea of a second work of the Holy Spirit in the life of the believer by which s/he is sanctified or made perfect in love. While not having such an experience himself, Watson began to preach the new doctrine, and earnestly sought the experience for himself. Watson's last parish in the East was at Wilmington, Delaware, where he moved in 1871. In 1875 he moved to the Meridian Street Methodist Church in Indianapolis, Indiana. While there, in December 1876, he finally had the experience of sanctification. This second blessing began an increasingly important theme in his sermons as he moved from Meridian Street to Trinity Methodist Episcopal Church in Evansville, Indiana (1877); Centenary Methodist Episcopal Church in New Albany, Indiana (1878); and Grace Methodist Episcopal Church in Newport, Kentucky (1880).

The 1880s proved a difficult time for many holiness ministers as the Methodists, among whom the holiness doctrine had arisen and prospered, began to turn against it and the independent holiness associations it had spawned. In 1883, Watson left the parish for full-time evangelistic work but over the next decade became increasingly alienated from the Methodist Episcopal Church. In 1893 he left to join the Wesleyan Methodist Church, a holiness denomination. In 1906 he moved to San Francisco, which became the headquarters for his regular evangelistic travels across the United States. Over these years of evangelistic endeavor he would author 14 books, many transcripts of his sermons.

Sources:

Lambert, D. W. *Heralds of Holiness*. Hampton, TN: Harvey and Tit, 1975. 80 pp.

Watson, Eva M. *Glimpses of the Life and Work of George Douglas Watson*. Cincinnati, OH: God's Bible School and Revivalist, 1929. 169 pp.

Watson, George D. *Bridehood Saints*. Cincinnati: Office of God's Revivalist, 1913. 287 pp.

_____. *God's Eagles*. Cincinnati: Office of God's Revivalist, 1927. 268 pp.

_____. *Heavenly Life and Types of the Holy Spirit*. Louisville, KY: Picket Publishing Co.

_____. *Love Abounding*. Boston: McDonald Gill.   408 pp.

_____. *Steps to the Throne and Holiness Manual*. Louisville, KY: Pickett Publishing Co., 1898. 168 pp.

★1001★
WATTS, Alan Wilson
Philosopher, Zen Buddhism
b. Jan. 6, 1915, Chilehurst England
d. Nov. 16, 1973, Sausalito, California

Alan Wilson Watts, well known "beat" philosopher and popularizer of Asian spirituality in the West, was born into a middle-class British family. In his youth he became interested in Eastern religions through the works of Orientalist scholars. This interest led him to establish contact with Western Buddhists such as Christmas Hum-

phreys, who introduced him to the works of **Daisetz Teitaro Suzuki**. He eventually met Suzuki at the World Congress of Faiths in London in 1936. Watts read widely and, although Zen Buddhism would remain at the core of his spirituality, extended his interests to include Vedanta, yoga, and Taoism. He developed his writing skills by composing articles for the periodical published by the Buddhist Lodge in England, and in 1935 published his first book, *The Spirit of Zen*, which was essentially a popularized version of Suzuki's work.

Watts moved to the United States in 1938. That same year he married Eleanor Everett, the daughter of Ruth Fuller Everett (later **Ruth Fuller Everett Sasaki** and step-daughter of **Shigatsu Sasaki Roshi**, founder of the First Zen Institute of America). Without giving up his interests in Buddhism, he entered Seabury-Western Theological Seminary and upon completion of his studies was ordained in the Protestant Episcopal Church in 1945. While at Seabury-Western in 1943, he became a naturalized citizen. He served as the Episcopal chaplain at Northwestern University, the Methodist school adjacent to Seabury-Western. He experienced some difficulties at the end of the decade. In 1950 his marriage to his first wife was annulled and he resigned from the Episcopal ministry. He then married Dorothy DeWitt and entered a year of seclusion. The next year he moved to San Francisco to teach at the American Academy of Asian Studies.

In California he associated with many of the major figures in the "beat" subculture, such as Allen Ginsberg, Jack Kerouac, and Gary Synder, and with the LSD pioneers Richard Alpert (**Baba Ram Dass**) and Timothy Leary. Through his prolific writings, Watts influenced the generation of the 1960s to perceive a continuity between Asian religions (especially Zen Buddhism and Taoism) and the lifestyle of the counter-culture. He was also a major advocate of the view that LSD experiences (or at least some LSD experiences) were closely related to mystical experiences. Some of his more popular works were *The Wisdom of Insecurity* (1951); *The Way of Zen* (1957), the major work introducing Zen Buddhism to non-Oriental Americans; *Nature, Man and Woman* (1958); *Psychotherapy, East and West* (1961); *The Joyous Cosmology* (1961); and *The Book on the Taboo Against Knowing Who You Are* (1966).

His increasing popularity was given visible manifestation in 1962 by the organization of the Society for Comparative Philosophy by his supporters as a vehicle for his teaching work. Through it the *Alan Watts Journal* was published. Watts' last book was his autobiography, *In My Own Way*, published in 1973, the year of his death.

A final assessment of Watts' significance is yet to be made. Critics of Watts, and there have been many, have accused him of popularizing Asian religions to the point of actually misinterpreting them. For example, he is criticized for separating Oriental philosophies from the spiritual practices out of which many of these philosophies emerged. While the critics may be technically correct, Watts is also seen as at least partially responsible for stimulating a broader and more serious interest in the cultures and religions of Asia, and will be remembered as much for his contributions to the East-West dialogue as for any scholarly indiscretions.

Sources:

Stuart, David. *Alan Watts*. New York: Stein and Day, 1976. 250 pp.

Watts, Alan. *The Book on the Taboo Against Knowing Who You Are*. New York: Vintage Books, 1966, 1972. 151 pp.

_____. *The Early Writings of Alan Watts*. Ed. John Snelling, with Mark Watts and Dennis Sibley. Berkeley, CA: Celestial Arts, 1987. 272 pp.

_____. *The Essential Alan Watts*. Berkeley, CA: Celestial Arts, 1977. 142 pp.

_____. *In My Own Way*. New York: Pantheon Books, 1972. 400 pp.

_____. *Psychotherapy East and West*. New York: Ballantine Books, 1961, 1968. 220 pp.

_____. *The Spirit of Zen*. New York: Grove Press, 1958. 128 pp.
_____. *The Way of Zen*. New York: Pantheon Books, 1968. 236 pp.

★ 1002 ★
WAYMAN, Alexander Walker
Bishop, African Methodist Episcopal Church
b. Sep. 1821, Caroline County, Maryland
d. Nov. 30, 1895, Baltimore, Maryland

Alexander Walker Wayman, a bishop of the African Methodist Episcopal Church, was born a free man, the son of Francis and Matilda Wayman, in rural Maryland. He was raised on a farm and learned to read from a Bible. In 1836 he was converted to Christianity and joined the predominantly white Methodist Episcopal Church. His desire to get an education led him in 1840 to leave home and move to Philadelphia, where he encountered the African Methodist Episcopal Church, which he joined. He was licensed as an exhorter. He seized the opportunities presented to further his education, first from a Quaker, for whom he worked as a coachman, and then from students at Rutgers University. In 1842 he had been assigned to a church circuit which centered in New Brunswick, New Jersey.

In 1843 Wayman was admitted on trial to the Philadelphia Conference and assigned to the West Chester (Pennsylvania) Circuit. In 1845 he was ordained deacon. In 1847 he was ordained an elder, and in 1848 he transferred to the Baltimore Conference. While serving churches in Baltimore and Washington through the Civil War years, he became one of the church's national leaders. He served as the secretary of the general conference, and organized several new congregations. In 1860 he became editor of the new edition of the *Discipline*, the church's law book. In 1864 he was elected the seventh bishop of the African Methodist Episcopal Church. About this time, his first wife having died, he married Harriet Ann Elizabeth Wayman.

Wayman began his episcopal duties in the East, but as soon as hostilities ceased he moved into the South to survey the situation. He made a second tour in 1867 and subsequently organized the Virginia, Georgia, and Florida Conferences. In 1872 he became bishop of the Midwestern conferences and California (where the African Methodist Episcopal Church had formed its first congregation during the Gold Rush days).

Wayman remained one of the most active bishops, traveling throughout the connection during his lifetime. In the 1880s he authored two important books: *My Recollections of African M.E. Ministers, or Forty Years' Experience in the African Methodist Episcopal Church* (1881) and *Cyclopedia of African Methodism*. He continued to be active until his death in the 1890s.

Sources:
Dictionary of American Biography. 20 vols. and 7 supps. New York: Charles Scribner's Sons, 1928-1936, 1944-1981.
Wayman, Alexander W. *Cyclopedia of African Methodism*. Baltimore, MD: M. E. Book Depository, 1882. 190 pp.
_____. *My Recollections of African M.E. Ministers, or Forty Years' Experience in the African Methodist Episcopal Church*. Philadelphia: A.M.E. Book Room, 1881. 250 pp.

★ 1003 ★
WEBB, Muhammad Alexander Russell
Founder, Moslem Mosque
b. Nov. 18, 1846, Hudson, New York
d. Oct. 1, 1916, Rutherford, New Jersey

Muhammad Alexander Russell Webb, an early convert to Islam who organized the first Moslem Mosque in America, was raised as a Presbyterian, but became disenchanted with the church and left it when he was 20. He became a journalist, and in his mid-twenties was able to purchase and manage his own newspaper. Around 1876 he sold the newspaper, moved to Missouri, and joined the staff of the *St. Joseph Day Gazette*. He later worked as night editor of the *Missouri Republican*. In the secular atmosphere of the newspaper office he began to read about the new discoveries of science and became a religious skeptic.

In 1887 Russell was named United States consul to the Philippines. In Manila he encountered Islam for the first time. His study of it finally satisfied his religious questions, and he converted. He became a strong advocate. Resigning his post in 1892, he turned his trip home into a lecture tour. Upon arriving in New York, he founded the Oriental Publishing Company and began issuing a magazine, *Moslem World*.

Webb returned just in time for the World's Parliament of Religions which met in Chicago in the summer of 1893. He was the main spokesperson for Islam. He spoke on three occasions and defended his new faith against the attacks of the Christian missionaries. After the Parliament, he open a mosque in New York and ran the Islamic Propaganda Mission in the U.S.A. He eventually retired to Rutherford, New Jersey, but continued his advocacy of Islam for the rest of his life. In recognition of his service, the sultan of Turkey named Webb the honorary Turkish Consul of New York.

Sources:
Islam-Our Choice. Karachi, Pakistan: Begum Aisha Bawany Waqf, 1961. 165 pp.
Makdisi, Nadim. "The Moslems of America." *Christian Century* (August 26, 1959): 969-971.
Tunison, Emery H. "Mohhamad Webb: First American Muslim." *The Arab World* 1, 3 (1945): 13-18.
Webb, Muhammad A. R. "The Influence of Social Conditions." In J. H. Hanson, *The World's Congress of Religions*. Chicago: Monarch, 1894.
_____. *Islam*. Bombay, India: 1892.
_____. *Islam in America*. New York: 1893.
_____. *Lectures on Islam*. Madras, India: Maulvi Hassan Ali, 1892.

★ 1004 ★
WEDEL, Cynthia Clark
Lay Leader, Episcopal Church
President, National Council of Churches
b. Aug. 26, 1908, Dearborn, Michigan
d. Aug. 24, 1986, Alexandria, Virginia

Cynthia Clark Wedel, the first woman to be elected president of the National Council of Churches, was born Cynthia Clark, the daughter of Elizabeth Haigh and Arthur Pierson Clark. She received both her B.A. and M.A. from Northwestern University in 1929 and 1930 respectively. In 1931 she went to work at the headquarters of the Episcopal Church in New York City. In 1939, the same year of her marriage to Theodore O. Wedel, she became a teacher at the National Cathedral School.

Through the 1940s Wedel become increasingly active in church work at the national level, and in 1946 she became a member of the executive board of the Woman's Auxiliary of the Episcopal Church. In 1952 she authored her first book, *Citizenship, Our Christian Concern*. In 1955 she became a member of the National Council of the Episcopal Church and additionally the national president of Church Women United. At the same time she was completing her Ph.D. at George Washington University in psychology (1957). In 1959, by the time her *Employed Women in the Church* appeared, she had emerged as a spokesperson for women's issues. President Kennedy appointed her as a member of the national Commission on the Status of Women (1961-1963) which led directly to her membership on the Citizen's Advisory Council on the Status of Women (1963-1968).

Beginning with her work with United Church Women, Wedel emerged as an ecumenical leader. In 1957 she was named a vice-president of the National Council of Churches. In 1962 she was named an assistant general secretary for the council, and in 1962 she became the council's first female associate general secretary (on Christian Unity). In 1969 she was elected the first female president of the National Council of Churches. She served a three year term. Her career culminated in 1975 when she was selected as one of the presidents of the World Council of Churches.

Through the 1960s and 1970s Wedel emerged as the most influential female ecumenical leader in America. She used her platform to defend the often controversial actions of the National and World Council of Churches and joined them both in their efforts to promote the causes of racial justice, women's rights, and peace. She was among the first women in a position of responsibility in the Episcopal Church to press for women's ordination. A short time after the end of her tenure with the World Council of Churches, she was diagnosed with cancer, from which she passed away in 1986.

Sources:

Gayer, Alan. "Cynthia Wedel: First Lady of Ecumenism." *The Christian Century* (September 24, 1986): 796-797.

Reid, Daniel G., Robert D. Linder, Bruce L. Shelley, and Harry S. Stout. *Dictionary of Christianity in America*. Downers Grove, IL: InterVarsity Press, 1990. 1305 pp.

Wedel, Cynthia Clark. *Celebrating Thanksgiving*. New York: National Council Protestant Episcopal Church, 1941. 32 pp.

_____. *Citizenship, Our Christian Concern*. 1952.

_____. *Employed Women in the Church*. 1959.

_____. *Faith or Fear and Future Shock*. 1974.

_____, and Janet Tulloch. *Happy Issue*. 1962.

★ 1005 ★
WEIGEL, Gustave
Theologian, Roman Catholic Church
b. Jan. 15, 1906, Buffalo, New York
d. Jan. 3, 1964, New York, New York

Gustave Weigel, Roman Catholic Church theologian, ecumenist, and participant in the Second Vatican Council, was the son of Louise Leontine Kiefer and August Weigel, who had immigrated to the United States from Alsace in 1902. Young Weigel was educated in Catholic schools in Buffalo, and then entered the Jesuit novitiate in 1922. He studied for the priesthood at Woodstock College, Maryland, from 1926 to 1934. During this time, he began to carry out a search for ultimate truth, a quest he pursued in an independent fashion. He was impatient with tradition, although he never left the Catholic fold, and for the rest of his life grappled with the tension between liberty and authority.

Weigel went to Rome and studied dogmatic theology at the Pontifical Gregorian University from 1935 to 1937. His dissertation was on Faustus of Riez, a fifth-century theologian who wrote during the Semi-Pelagian controversy. Weigel's first position after finishing his degree was teaching dogmatic theology at the Catholic University of Chile in Santiago, where he served on the faculty from 1937 to 1948. From 1942 until 1948 he was also dean of the theological faculty. His open and engaging style, which endeared him to both Protestants and Catholics in the English-speaking community in Santiago, was responsible for his removal from his position in 1948—he simply could not fit into the rigid mold that was traditional for Chilean Jesuits.

When Weigel returned to North America, he was bitter and depressed. He took new life, however, when invited by **John Courtney Murray** to become the specialist in Protestant theology for *Theological Studies*. He began writing lengthy articles on Protestant ecclesiastical structures and theology, and became one of the early pioneers of ecumenism in the United States. In 1949 he also became professor of ecclesiology at his alma mater, Woodstock College. Weigel taught a traditional theology which emphasized that the Roman Catholic Church, as the Mystical Body of Christ, is a divinely constituted community.

After nearly dying of complications following a surgical operation in 1954, Weigel turned more of his attention to activism on behalf of the ecumenical cause. In pursuit of ecumenical dialogue, he was nevertheless uncompromising on points of doctrine. He felt that, in spite of seemingly irreconcilable differences, he was in some mysterious sense united with his Protestant brothers and sisters. Weigel's final work took place during the Second Vatican Council (1962-1965), during which he was a popular expositor of the goals of the council to Catholic America. Disappointed with the progress of the council, Weigel had already decided not to return to Europe after the third session when he passed away unexpectedly in New York City.

Sources:

Dictionary of American Biography. 20 vols. and 7 supps. New York: Charles Scribner's Sons, 1928-1936, 1944-1981.

Weigal, Gustave. *A Catholic Primer on the Ecumenical Movement*. Westminster, MD: Newman Press, 1957. 79 pp.

_____. *Churches in North America*. Baltimore, MD: Helical Press, 1961. 152 pp.

_____. *Faith and Understanding in America*. New York: Macmillan Company, 1959. 170 pp.

_____. *The Modern God*. New York: Macmillan Company, 1963. 168 pp.

_____. *A Survey of Protestant Theology in Our Day*. Westminster, MD: Newman Press, 1954. 58 pp.

★ 1006 ★
WELTMER, Sidney A.
Founder, Institute of Suggestive Therapeutics
Director, Institute of Suggestive Therapeutics
b. Jul. 7, 1858, Wooster, Ohio
d. Dec. 5, 1930, Nevada, Missouri

Sidney A. Weltmer was a "mental healer," in the American mind cure tradition, who founded and directed the Institute of Suggestive Therapeutics. The Civil War had left Weltmer's parents impoverished and disrupted public education in Missouri. Educated at home, at age 14 he began to study medicine from books loaned to him by a local doctor. However, after coming down with tuberculosis, at the time an incurable disease, he turned to religion for healing, and began to recover. At the age of 19 he was voted a license to preach through a congregation affiliated with the Southern Baptist Convention. In addition to his role as minister, Weltmer also taught school at Atkinsville, Missouri. In 1893 he became city librarian in Sedalia and taught at a local business college.

Weltmer's experience of healing led him to investigate the principles of healing found in Scripture. What he discovered was that in every case healings had involved faith, not simply physical contact with Jesus or one of the disciples. Weltmer began to investigate the laws that governed healing and treated hundreds of people in Sedalia. He became so involved in his healing ministry that it began to take up all of his spare time. Working without pay, he went into debt until he owed his creditors some $3,000. As a way of responding both to his increasing indebtedness and to his expanding healing practice, Weltmer and his family moved to Nevada, Missouri, to found the Institute of Suggestive Therapeutics.

The Institute was launched in 1897, and within weeks had to move to larger quarters. The new healing institution became so popular that daily income was near $3,600. At its peak, 400 patients per day were being treated. The Weltmer Institute also attracted many visitors who came to enjoy the family's hospitality. Weltmer presented his teachings in a series of books, including *Suggestion Simplified* (1900); *The Mystery Revealed* (1901); and *The Healing Hand* (1918).

At the heart of the work of the Institute was what Weltmer initially termed suggestive therapeutics, and which in time came to be called suggestotherapy. He believed that within the human being is a divine force which, if properly evoked, can overcome all negative conditions, such as disease. While suggestotherapy sometimes utilized manipulation and hypnosis, the basic technique was simple suggestions such as, ''You can get well!'' Weltmer also accepted the notion, derived from Mesmer (and congruent with the picture of healing presented by the gospels), that a healing magnetic current could be imparted to people through a laying on of hands. Weltmer also worked with absentee healing, a practice which led him to experiment with telepathy.

The Institute's success stimulated the development of a program for training healers in the ''Weltmer Method.'' By 1925 a reported half million people had received the Institute's diploma. The curriculum evolved until it was comparable with the curriculum of American medical colleges. A Supreme Court decision in 1901 declared the Weltmer Method to be legal anywhere in the United States. The future of this promising enterprise seemed bright until Weltmer passed away in 1930. The loss of the founder's inspired leadership in combination with the Great Depression led to the demise of the Institute.

Sources:

Stone, Robert L., Jr., ''A Profile of Sidney A. Weltmer—Pioneer of Psychotherapy.'' *The Nevada (MO) Herald* (December 31, 1967).
Weltmer, Sidney A. *The Healing Hand*. Nevada, MO: Weltmer Institute of Suggestive Therapeutics, 1918. 46 pp.
_____. *The Mystery Revealed*. Kansas City, MO: Hudson-Kimberly Publishing Co., 1901. 278 pp.
_____. *Regeneration*. Nevada, MO: Weltmer Institute of Suggestive Therapeutics, 1898, 1900. 192 pp.
_____. *Suggestion Simplified*. Nevada, MO: American School of Magnetic Healing, 1900. 117 pp.

★1007★
WENGER, Amos Daniel
Educator, Mennonite Church
b. Nov. 25, 1867, Rockingham County, Virginia
d. Oct. 5, 1935, Harrisonburg, Pennsylvania

Amos Daniel Wenger, Mennonite pastor, editor, and college president, was the son of Hannah Brenneman and Jacob Wenger. He was raised in a large family in rural Virginia. At the age of 18, upon completion of a three week long teacher training course, he was awarded a teacher's certificate. Several years later he began teaching school in Iowa, and working toward gaining further education. In 1894 he finished work at Warrensburg Normal School at Warrensburg, Missouri. That summer he attended Moody Bible Institute in Chicago, before beginning a year teaching school and pastoring a church in Cass County, Missouri. While there, he was ordained to the ministry of the Mennonite Church. He was able to gain one more year of schooling (1895-1896) at Penn College in Oskaloosa, Iowa, while pastoring the Keokuk County church. He was forced to cancel plans for further education as he became deeply involved in evangelistic work.

In 1897 he began a pastorate at the church at Millersville, Pennsylvania. That same year he married Mary Hoestetter. He had already gained a reputation for evangelism and was constantly in demand for preaching around the country. His wife passed away in 1898, and the following year he took a trip around the world, the subject of an early book, *Six Months in Bible Lands*. Upon his return, he assumed duties with the national church. He served on the Mennonite Publishing Committee. He became a member of the board of the Elkhart Institute. He was a contributing editor for the *Gospel Herald*, the denominational periodical. In 1900 he married Anna May Lehman.

In 1908 Wenger returned to his native Virginia where he would reside for the rest of his life, first as pastor at Fentress, Virginia (1908-1922), and then at Harrisonburg (1922-1935). During these years he served as tract editor for the Mennonite Publishing Committee and produced numerous tracts with titles such as ''Why I

Do Not Join the Lodge'' and ''Buried with Him in Baptism'' (Mennonites usually baptize by pouring). He served the national church as secretary of the General Mission Committee and a member of the Mennonite Board of Education.

In 1922, at the time of his moving to Harrisonburg, Wenger also assumed duties as president and treasurer of the board of the Eastern Mennonite School (now a college). He retained that position for the rest of his life.

Sources:

The Mennonite Encyclopedia. 4 vols. Scottdale, PA: The Mennonite Publishing House, 1955.

★1008★
WENTZ, Abdel Ross
Educator and Historian, United Lutheran Church in America
b. Oct. 8, 1883, Black Rock, Pennsylvania
d. 1976

Abdel Ross Wentz, ecumenical leader, administrator, and author of the standard history of American Lutheranism for his generation, was the son of John Valentine Wentz and Ellen Catharine (Tracy) Wentz. Born in Pennsylvania, he was raised at Lineboro, Maryland. He attended Gettysburg College, graduating in 1904, and Gettysburg Seminary, graduating in 1907. After three more years of theological and historical studies in Germany, he returned to the United States where he was ordained by the Maryland Synod and served as professor of history and English Bible at Gettysburg College until 1916. He was then called to the new chair of church history at Gettysburg College. He continued in that position until his retirement. He was also president of the seminary from 1940 to 1951. His best known contribution to historical scholarship was his *Basic History of Lutheranism in America*, which went through many editions and was for decades the standard history of American Lutheranism.

In 1920, Wentz was named to a committee which considered the statement on the ''Lutheran Church and External Relations'' which had been authored by **Frederick H. Knubel** and revised by Charles M. Jacobs. This statement, which became known as the ''Washington Declaration,'' established the basic principles that would shape Lutheran ecumenical relations. Portions of the Declaration were incorporated into the Lutheran World Convention (LWC) statement of 1936 on Lutherans and Ecumenicism, which was drawn up by Wentz for the LWC Executive Committee of which he was a member. He was also a member of the United Lutheran Church in America Executive Board during years in which this body made several important decisions about its participation in ecumenical activity. The United Lutheran Church in America merged into the Lutheran Church in America in 1962 and is today a constituent part of the Evangelical Lutheran Church in America which formed in 1988.

Wentz was a participant at the conferences out of which the World Council of Churches emerged. He was secretary of the Committee of Sixty which was set up to deal with the objections that had arisen as a result of the council's failure to emphasize that only *official* delegates from constituent denominations would be allowed to represent their church bodies. Because, among other things, the resolution of the committee was worded like a similar resolution in a statement on ecumenicism from the 1936 Lutheran World Convention, Lutheran historians credit Wentz with bringing forward the crucial recommendation which overcame the objections. Wentz was also a member of the Committee of Fourteen which became the Provisional Central Committee of the World Council of Churches in the Process of Formation.

Sources:
Flesner, Dorris A. "Dr. Abdel Ross Wentz: American Lutheran Champion of Ecumenism." *The Lutheran Historical Conference*, vol. VI. Lutheran Historical Conference, 1977.

Wentz, Abdel Ross. *A Basic History of Lutheranism in America*. Philadelphia: Muhlenberg Press, 1955. 430 pp.

———. *History of the Evangelical Lutheran Synod of the United Lutheran Church in America, 1820-1920*. Harrisburg, PA: Evangelical Press, 1920. 641 pp.

———. *The Lutheran Church in American History*. Philadelphia: United lutheran Publishing House, 1923. 355 pp.

———. *Pioneer in Christian Unity: Samuel Simon Schmucker*. Philadelphia: Fortress Press, 1967. 372 pp.

★ 1009 ★
WHITE, Alma Birdwell
Founder, Pillar of Fire
b. Jun. 16, 1862, Louis County, Kentucky
d. Jun. 26, 1946, Zarephath, New Jersey

Alma Birdwell White, founder of the Pillar of Fire, a holiness church, was born into a large, poor family in Kentucky. Her father was a tanner, and she worked in the tannery as a child. Raised in a strongly religious environment, she accepted Christ at age 16 during a Methodist revival meeting. When she professed a call to the ministry at the time of her conversion, Alma was advised by her pastor to marry a minister so that, in the role of assistant, she would be able to fulfill such a calling in a socially acceptable way.

One of the few avenues readily open to a woman seeking social and economic betterment was teaching, and Alma obtained a certificate to teach while still a teenager. After teaching for some time in Kentucky, she decided to become a pioneer school teacher, and in 1882 moved to Montana. There she met a ministerial student, Arthur Kent White, who became her husband. Although he allowed her to take minor leadership roles in their church, Alma felt drawn to a larger outreach and began to organize and conduct her own revival meetings. Her considerable success led to notoriety, which, because she happened to be female, soon provoked opposition from the Methodist hierarchy.

This opposition led Alma to break with the Methodist Episcopal Church in 1901. She became the bishop of her new body, the Methodist Pentecostal Union, which was renamed the Pillar of Fire in 1917. Alma switched roles with her husband, who assisted her until the end of the decade when he withdrew from the church, joined a British denomination (the Apostolic Faith Church), and separated from his wife.

A donation of a tract of land in Zarephath, New Jersey enabled Bishop White to establish her headquarters there. In 1921 she founded Alma White College in Zarephath. She was very active, traveling frequently and authoring many books. Bishop White also bought several radio stations through which she established a radio ministry.

As one might anticipate, she was a campaigner for women's rights, a commitment that was reflected in the name of one of her denomination's periodicals, *Woman's Chains*. Women were actively recruited into the Pillar of Fire's ministry. She also advocated vegetarianism, and was adamantly anti-Catholic. Her anti-Catholic stance led Bishop White to become a strong supporter of the Ku Klux Klan, an organization that was viewed far more positively during the 1920s than in the present period. The Klan was the subject of her 1943 title, *Guardians of Liberty*. She died in 1946 at the age of 84, and the leadership of her church was taken over by her two sons.

Sources:
White, Alma. *Everlasting Life*. Zarephath, NJ: Pillar of Fire. 1944. 341 pp.

———. *Guardians of Liberty*. 3 vols. Zarephath, NJ: Pillar of Fire, 1943.

———. *Modern Miracles and Answers to Prayer*. Zarephath, NJ: Pillar of Fire, 1945. 242 pp.

———. *The New Testament Church*. Zarephath, NJ: Pillar of Fire, 1923. 403 pp.

———. *The Story of My Life*. 6 vols. Zarephath, NJ: Pillar of Fire, 1919-1934.

———. *Truth Stranger Than Fiction: God's Lightning Bolts*. Zarephath, NJ: Pillar of Fire, 1936. 248 pp.

———. *Why I Do Not Eat Meat*. Zarephath, NJ: Pillar of Fire, 1938. 209 pp.

White, Arthur Kent. *Some White Family History*. Denver, CO: Pillar of Fire, 1948. 432 pp.

★ 1010 ★
WHITE, Anna
Shaker Eldress and Writer
b. Jan. 21, 1831, Brooklyn, New York
d. Dec. 16, 1910, New Lebanon, New York

Anna White, a prominent member of the the United Believers in Christ's Second Coming, popularly known as the Shakers, was the daughter of Robert and Hannah Gibbs White, descendants of a notable colonial family. Her mother was a Quaker and her father joined the Quakers after their marriage. Anna was thus raised in the Society of Friends and in her teens attended a Quaker boarding school, the Mansion Square Seminary in Poughkeepsie, New York. After finishing school at the age of 18, she moved to New York and worked in her father's business for several years.

White's father did business with the Shaker communal village at Hancock, Massachusetts, and through his activity Anna heard of the Shakers for the first time. She visited Hancock with her father and was drawn to their music and worship. Despite the disapproval of her family, she joined the community at New Lebanon in 1849. She spent much of her early years under the tutelage of Shaker leaders Ruth Landon and Elder Frederick Evans. She was assigned to live with the North Family, one of the sections within the community. Over the next decades she rose to leadership in the community. In 1865 she was appointed associate eldress for the acre of the girls. In 1887 she succeeded Eldress Antoinette Doolittle as first eldress of the North Family, a position she held until her death in 1910.

During the 1890s, White's interests in various social causes came to the fore. Like the Quakers, the Shakers were pacifists, and Eldress White became a spokesperson for international disarmament. She was appointed a vice-president of the Alliance of Women for Peace. In 1899 she addressed the Universal Peace Union in Mystic, Connecticut. In 1905 she led a conference at New Lebanon that developed resolutions on arbitration that were adopted at The Hague, and she personally delivered them to Theodore Roosevelt, a well-known champion of arbitration.

In her most active years White also became interested in women's rights, joining the National American Suffrage Association and becoming a vice-president of the National Council of Women of the United States.

Within the community, she became well-known for her writing. She compiled two books of her favorite Shaker music, including some titles which she herself authored. She also collaborated with Eldress Leila S. Taylor to author *Shakerism: Its Meaning and Message*, the only published history of the movement written by someone who was a member. While very much a believer in Shaker teachings, White did not hesitate to explore the other movements which were blossoming at the turn of the century. She attended Spiritualist meetings and claimed at one point to have experienced a healing through Christian Science. She also dabbled in vegetarianism.

Though White occasionally left the community to attend meetings of organizations associated with causes she supported, she lived most days quietly in New Lebanon. She died there in 1910.

Sources:
Taylor, Leila S. *A Memorial to Eldress Anna White and Elder Daniel Offord*. Mt. Lebanon, NY: North Family of Shakers, 1912. 182 pp.
White, Anna. *The Motherhood of God*. Canaan Four Corners, NY: Press of Berkshire Industrial Farm, [1880]. 27 pp.
_____, ed. *Mt. Lebanon Cedar Boughs*. Buffalo, NY: Peter Paul Book Co., 1895. 316 pp.
_____, and Leila S. Taylor. *Shakerism: Its Meaning and Message*. Columbus, OH: Press of F. J. Fleer, 1904. 417 pp.

★1011★
WHITE, Ellen Gould Harmon
Cofounder, Seventh-day Adventist Church
b. Nov. 26, 1827, Gorham, Maine
d. Jul. 16, 1915, St. Helena, California

Ellen Gould Harmon White who, with her husband **James White**, founded the Seventh-day Adventist Church, was the daughter of Eunice Gould and Robert Harmon. She grew up in Portland, Maine, where her father worked as a hatmaker. At age nine she was hit in the head with a rock, an injury that rendered her unconscious for the next three weeks. Tragically, she never fully recovered, and her parents soon gave up trying to send her to school as reading made her dizzy.

Raised in the Methodist Episcopal Church, in her mid-teens Harmon had a conversion experience. In June 1842 she was baptized by immersion and joined the church. Her religious awakening, however, occurred just as William Miller's predictions about the end of the world were peaking. In 1843 the Harmons identified with the Adventists, and the Methodists disfellowshipped them. Still in her teens, Harmon lived through the so-called Great Disappointment of 1844 (when Christ failed to return as predicted) and became a significant factor in rallying the Adventists. She had a vision of her fellow believers marching to the City of God, and as a traveling speaker repeatedly called them to remain true to their faith. She also began to teach the view that Christ really had returned in 1844 as Miller had predicted, but that he had not returned to the earth, but cleansed the heavenly sanctuary in preparation for his pending reappearance.

In Harmon's travels she met James White whom she married in 1846. Together they founded a periodical which he edited, and together in 1847 they absorbed sabbatarianism (worship on Saturdays) and began to keep a Saturday sabbath. The new Mrs. White released her first writing, a pamphlet, *A Sketch of the Christian Experience and Views of Ellen G. White*, in 1851. Four years later, she moved to Battle Creek, Michigan, which became the organizational center for what was coalescing as the Seventh-day Adventist movement around the Whites. Shortly after the move she had the great vision of the battle between the forces of good and evil which would lead to her most important book, *The Great Controversy between Christ and His Angels and Satan and His Angels* (1858), one volume of a four-volume set collectively entitled *Spiritual Gifts* (1858-1864).

In 1860 the movement which White led was named the Seventh-day Adventist Church. The church was formally organized at a general conference three years later. Her career as the leader of the church was marked by the appearance of over 25 books and 200 shorter works. Revered as a visionary, her authority partially rested upon her visions, which to this day are considered authoritative by church members, though not equal to the Bible. Her writings were left to her estate. The royalties from them, many of which remain in print, go to the church.

Sources:
Bowden, Henry Warner. *Dictionary of American Religious Biography*. Westport, CT: Greenwood Press, 1977. 572 pp.
Dictionary of American Biography. 20 vols. and 7 supps. New York: Charles Scribner's Sons, 1928-1936, 1944-1981.
Graham, Roy E. *Ellen G. White: Co-Founder of the Seventh-day Adventist Church*. New York: Peter Lang, 1985. 489 pp.
James, Edward T., ed. *Notable American Women, 1607-1950: A Biographical Dictionary*. 3 vols. Cambridge, MA: Harvard University Press, Belknap Press, 1971.
Nichol, Francis D. *Ellen G. White and Her Critics*. Takoma Park, MD: Review and Herald Publishing Association, 1951. 703 pp.
Numbers, Ronald L. *Prophetess of Health: A Study of Ellen G. White*. New York: Harper & Row, 1976. 271 pp.
White, Arthur L. *The Ellen G. White Writings*. Washington, DC: Review and Herald Publishing Association, 1973. 192 pp.
White, Ellen G. *Christ's Object Lessons*. Oakland, CA: Pacific Press, 1900. 436 pp.
_____. *Early Writings of Ellen G. White*. Oakland, CA: Pacific Press, 1882. 154 pp.
_____. *The Great Controversy Between Christ and His Angels and Satan and His Angels*. Battle Creek, MI: James White, 1858. 219 pp.
_____. *Life Sketches: Ancestry, Early Life, Christian Experience, and Extensive Labors of Elder James White, and His Wife, Mrs. Ellen G. White*. Battle Creek, MI: Seventh-day Adventist Publishing Association, 1880.
_____. *Steps to Christ*. New York: Fleming H. Revell Company, 1892. 153 pp.

★1012★
WHITE, James
Cofounder, Seventh-day Adventist Church
b. Aug. 4, 1821, Palmyra, Maine
d. Aug. 6, 1881, Battle Creek, Michigan

James White, the co-founder of the Seventh-day Adventist Church, was the son of John White. His parents were members of the Christian Church, in which he was baptized at the age of 15. At the age of 19 he was certified to teach school and while teaching took the opportunity to further his education. In 1842 he was first impressed with the importance of the message of William Miller concerning the predicted end of this age in 1843. He subsequently became an adventist lecturer. In 1843 he was ordained as a minister in the Christian Church. As an adventist believer, he lived through the Great Disappointment experienced by Millerites when Christ failed to return as predicted in 1843 or 1844.

In 1845 White met Ellen Gould, another Adventist worker, and married her in 1846. They had been introduced to the idea of keeping the seventh-day sabbath and began to do so about the time of their marriage. In 1848 a first general convention of sabbatarian adventists gathered at Rocky Hill, Connecticut, and at that time White became a full-time minister. Prompted by his wife's vision, he then began a periodical, the *Present Truth* (later *Review and Herald*) in 1849. He published his first book, *Hymns for God's Peculiar People That Keep the Commandments of God and the Faith of Jesus* (1849). He moved about over the next three years, but in 1852 settled in Rochester, New York. White began a second periodical, *Youth's Instructor*. In 1855 the Whites accepted an invitation to move to Battle Creek, Michigan, where his publishing concern prospered. In 1861 the Seventh-day Adventist Publishing Association was incorporated.

Both White and his wife began to urge sabbatarian Adventists to organize. In 1863, as the Civil War raged, they were able to lead in the formation of the Seventh-day Adventist General Conference, from which the Seventh-day Adventist Church generally dates its origin. In 1865 White suffered a stroke, in spite of which he was elected president of the General conference a month later. This further spurred his wife's interest in natural health. She moved him to northern Michigan where he gradually recovered.

During the rest of his life, White was at the center of the church's organization. His wife, **Ellen G. White**, was the church' real leader, but he was recognized as a capable person in his own right. He served as general conference president in three stretches (1865-1867, 1869-1871, and 1874-1880). In 1871 he took on additional editorial duties as editor of the *Health Reformer*, the denominational periodical which had grown out of the Whites' natural health emphasis. Over the next few years White's appreciation of the literature ministry grew, and in 1874 he led the general conference in establishing a tract and missionary society. That same year he also took the lead in the formation of Battle Creek College for the purpose of training the growing church's leadership. He promoted the publishing arm of the church which had been created in California and founded the church's California paper, *Signs of the Times*.

During his mature years, White penned several books that now serve as important documentation of the early years of the adventist movement: *Life Incidents in Connection with the Great Advent Movement* (1868); *Sketches of the Christian Life and Public Labors of William Miller* (1875); *The Early Life and Later Experience and Labors of Elder Joseph Bates* (1878); and *Life Sketches of Elder James White, and His Wife, Mrs. Ellen G. White* (1880).

Sources:

Seventh-Day Adventist Encyclopedia. Washington, DC: Review and Herald Publishing Association, 1966. 1454 pp.
White, James. *The Early Life and Later Experience and Labors of Elder Joseph Bates*. Battle Creek, MI: Steam Press of the Seventh-day Adventist Publishing Association, 1878. 320 pp.
_____. *Life Incidents in Connection with the Great Advent Movement*. Battle Creek, MI: Steam Press of the Seventh-day Adventist Publishing Association, 1868. 373 pp.
_____. *Life Sketches of Elder James White, and His Wife, Mrs. Ellen G. White*. Battle Creek, MI: Steam Press of the Seventh-day Adventist Publishing Association, 1880. 416 pp.
_____. *Sketches of the Christian Life and Public Labors of William Miller*. Battle Creek, MI: Steam Press of the Seventh-day Adventist Publishing Association, 1875. 416 pp.

★1013★
WHITSITT, William Heth
Church Historian and Educator, Southern Baptist Convention
b. Nov. 25, 1841, Nashville, Tennessee
d. Jan. 20, 1911, Richmond, Virginia

William Heth Whitsitt, president of the Southern Baptist Theological Seminary in the late nineteenth century, was the son of Reuben Ewing and Dicey McFarland Whitsitt. He attended Mount Juliet Academy and Union University (in Jackson, Tennessee), graduating in 1861, just as the Civil War was beginning. He enlisted in the Confederate Army and served with General Nathan Bedford Forrest. In 1862 he was ordained into the ministry and became a chaplain, serving for the rest of the war in this capacity. After the war, he attended the University of Virginia briefly before enrolling in the Southern Baptist Theological Seminary. After graduation in 1866, he became one of the first Southern Baptists to study abroad, spending two years at the Universities of Berlin and Leipzig.

Upon his return from Germany in 1870, Whitsitt served briefly as pastor of a church in Albany, Georgia, before moving to Greenville, South Carolina, in 1872 as the professor of ecclesiastical history. That year he published his first book, the *Position of Baptists in the History of American Culture* (1872). In 1877 the seminary moved to Louisville, Kentucky. He continued a productive scholarly career which led to the publication of a number of books, including: *The History of the Rise of Infant Baptism* (1878), a polemical work defending the Baptist practice of limiting baptism to adults; *The History of Communion Among Baptists* (1880); *The Origin of the Disciples of Christ* (1888); and *A Question in Baptist History* (1896).

His many years in Louisville were significantly marked by two events. In 1877 he married Florence Wallace, and in 1896 he was elected president of the seminary. While his marriage lasted the rest of his life, his tenure as president proved stormy and brief. In an item written on the Baptists for Johnson's *Universal Encyclopedia*, which was published the same year Whitsitt became president, he questioned the long-held belief that the Baptist churches could be traced to New Testament times through an unbroken succession of groups which practiced adult baptism and eschewed infant baptism. Whitsitt suggested that adult baptism had been lost and was rediscovered by the British Baptists only in 1641. The position, already being championed by Northern Baptist historians such as **Henry Clay Vedder**, raised a bitter controversy in the southern church, especially as other Baptist scholars aligned with Whitsitt. As the controversy refused to die, only Whitsitt's resignation seemed a possible means to return peace to the convention. He resigned in 1899 and then accepted a position in philosophy at Richmond College in Virginia in 1900. He taught there until 1910, when he retired. He stayed in Richmond to live out the few remaining months of his life.

In the years since Whitsitt's death, his position in the controversy which surrounded him has largely been accepted by Baptists; few remain to argue that the Baptist faith enjoyed unbroken succession from New Testament times.

Sources:

Dictionary of American Biography. 20 vols. and 7 supps. New York: Charles Scribner's Sons, 1928-1936, 1944-1981.
Encyclopedia of Southern Baptists. 3 vols. Nashville, TN: Broadman Press, 1958, 1971.
Whitsitt, William H. *The History of Communion Among Baptists*. 1880.
_____. *The History of the Rise of Infant Baptism*. 1878.
_____. *The Origin of the Disciples of Christ*. New York: A. C. Armstrong & Son, 1888. 112 pp.
_____. *Position of the Baptists in the History of American Culture*. N.p. [1872].
_____. *A Question in Baptist History*. Louisville, KY: C.T. Dearing, 1896. 164 pp.

★1014★
WIEMAN, Henry Nelson
Liberal Theologian
b. Aug. 19, 1884, Rich Hill, Missouri
d. Jun. 19, 1975, Grinnell, Iowa

Henry Nelson Wieman, liberal philosopher-theologian of the mid-twentieth century, was the son of Alma Morgan and William Henry Wieman. His father was a Presbyterian minister. During his college days at Park College, he altered his early plans to be a journalist and became a student of the problem of religious inquiry. That decision led Wieman, following his graduation in 1907, to the San Francisco Theological Seminary. In 1910-1911 he spent a year in Europe at the Universities of Jena and Heidelberg. Upon his return to the United States, he settled in Davis, California, as a Presbyterian pastor. While living in Davis, in 1912 he married Anna M. Orr.

Wieman's desire to reach college students, and the observation that he could not do that apart from becoming a part of the academic community, led him in 1915 to Harvard University, which awarded him a Ph.D. in 1917. Following his graduation he became a professor of philosophy at Occidental College in Los Angeles. He stayed in Los Angeles for ten years before being invited to join the faculty of the University of Chicago Divinity School in 1927. During his last year at Occidental he published his first book, *Religious Experience and Scientific Method*.

By this time Wieman's religious speculation had led him far from the Presbyterian heritage of his parents and he was well on his way to developing what has been termed his empirical theology. He claimed that his entire life was focused on one problem— discovering what it was that operates in human life to transform humans in ways they cannot transform themselves, and hence to save them from evil. While the term "God" is usually applied to the name of that reality, Wieman usually refrained from using the term. He came to believe that religious inquiry could best be pursued by observation of the world rather than rational speculation.

Wieman pursued his intellectual problem through a series of books, including: *The Wrestle of Religion with Truth* (1927); *Is There a God?* (1932); *The Growth of Religion* (1938); and *The Source of Human Good* (1946). During his lengthy career at the University of Chicago, his first wife died (1931) and in 1932 he married Regina H. Westcott. He retired from the University in 1947.

Wieman led an active life during his retirement. Three additional books appeared: *The Directive of History* (1949); *Man's Ultimate Commitment* (1958); and *Intellectual Foundation of Faith* (1961). In 1948 he was divorced and he married Laura Matlack. In 1949 he became professor of philosophy at the University of Oregon, and two years later moved to the University of Houston. In 1956 he became emeritus professor at Southern Illinois University in Carbondale. He eventually settled at Grenell, Iowa, where he died at the age of 91.

Sources:

Bretall, Robert W. *The Empirical Theology of Henry Nelson Wieman.* New York: Macmillan Company, 1963. 423 pp.

Broyer, John A., and William S. Minor. *Creative Interchange.* Carbondale, IL: Southern Illinois University Press, 1982. 540 pp.

Minor, William Sherman. *Creativity in Henry Nelson Wieman.* Metuchen, NJ: Scarecrow Press, 1977. 231 pp.

Wieman, Henry Nelson. *The Growth of Religion.* Chicago: Willet, Clark, 1938. 505 pp.

———. *Is There a God?* Chicago: Willet, Clark, 1932. 328 pp.

———. *Man's Ultimate Commitment.* Carbondale, IL: Southern Illinois University Press, 1958. 318 pp.

———. *Religious Experience and Scientific Method.* New York: Macmillan Company, 1926. 387 pp.

———. *The Wrestle of Religion with Truth.* New York: Macmillan Company, 1927. 256 pp.

★1015★
WIERWILLE, Victor Paul
Founder, The Way International
b. Dec. 31, 1916, New Knoxville, Ohio
d. May 20, 1985, New Knoxville, Ohio

Victor Paul Wierwille, the founder of The Way International, was the son of Ernst and Emma Wierwille. He was born on his parents' farm, which had been in the family since 1839, just outside of New Knoxville, Ohio. He grew up as a member of the Evangelical and Reformed Church (now part of the United Church of Christ). He decided to enter the ministry and attended Mission House College and Seminary (now Lakeland College) in Wisconsin. In 1937, while a student, he eloped with Dorothea Kipp, a long-time girlfriend. He received his B.A. in 1938 and his Th.B. in 1941. He also received his Th.M. from Princeton Theological Seminary in 1941 and was ordained as a minister in the Evangelical and Reformed Church.

Immediately after graduation Wierwille became pastor of St. Jacob's Evangelical and Reformed Church in Payne, Ohio. Discouraged with his pastoral work and questioning his ministry, Wierwille began an intense Bible study based upon an experience in which he heard God speak to him. God told him that if he would teach, God would teach him the Word as it had not been known since the first century. In 1944 he moved from St. Jacob's to St. Peter's church in Van Wert, Ohio. While there he pursued studies with Dr. H. Ellis Lininger and received a doctorate from the Pike's Peak Bible Seminary and Manitou College in Manitou, Colorado, over which Lininger was president. (Wierwille was often criticized for his work with Lininger, as Pike's Peak Bible College had frequently been cited as a degree mill.)

The 1940s were a time of intense growth and change for Wierwille. In 1942 Wierwille began a radio ministry, the "Vesper Chimes Hour". It became known as the "Chimes Hour" in 1944 and the "Chimes Hour Youth Caravan" in 1947. He also became acquainted with a number of religious leaders such as **Glenn Clark, George M. Lamsa,** and Indian bishop K. C. Pillai, all of whom affected his perspective. By 1953 the framework of his mature thought was developed and first presented in a class called the "Power of Abundant Living." Combining fundamental Protestant dispensational thought with Pentecostalism, Wierwille arrived at the perspective that would lead in 1955 to his resignation from the church. He changed the name of the Chimes Youth Caravan to The Way International and dedicated the rest of his life to teaching his new approach to the Bible. That year he also published *Receiving the Holy Spirit*, the first of his works to discuss his new perspective.

Wierwille spent the next 30 years building The Way International. In 1957 the family farm was deeded to The Way ministry, and in 1958 he founded The Way Biblical Seminary. In 1961 the farm became the ministry's headquarters. Over the years he authored numerous books and booklets and taught people through the Power for Abundant Living class. In 1967 the class was put on film, thus greatly extending the potential audience. The work grew dramatically through the 1970s and 1980s. It also became quite controversial and was one of several new religious organizations singled out and attacked as a "cult." Despite the controversy, however, the work grew. In 1982 Wierwille retired as president and was succeeded by L. Craig Martindale.

Sources:

The Teacher: Dr. Victor Paul Wierwille. [New Knoxville, OH]: The Way International, 1985. 22 pp.

Whiteside, Elena S. *The Way: Living in Love.* New Knoxville, OH: American Christian Press, 1972. 284 pp.

Wierwille, Victor Paul. *Jesus Christ: Our Promised Seed.* New Knoxville, OH: American Christian Press, 1982. 306 pp.

———. *The New Dynamic Church: Studies in Abundant Living.* New Knoxville, OH: American Christian Press, 1971. 242 pp.

———. *Power for Abundant Living.* New Knoxville, OH: American Christian Press, 1971. 368 pp.

———. *Receiving the Holy Spirit Today.* New Knoxville, OH: American Christian Press, 1972, 1977. 360 pp.

———. *The Word's Way: Studies in Abundant Living.* New Knoxville, OH: American Christian Press, 1971. 276 pp.

★1016★
WILCOX, Ella Wheeler
Poet, Writer, New Thought Metaphysician
b. Nov. 5, 1850, Johnstown Center, Wisconsin
d. Oct. 30, 1919, Short Beach, Connecticut

Ella Wheeler Wilcox, one of the most popular poets in America at the beginning of the twentieth century and an advocate of New Thought metaphysics, was the daughter of Sarah Pratt and Marius Hartwell Wheeler. She was an avid reader and began writing as a child. It is reported that at the age of 10 she wrote a novel for the amusement of her sisters. In her early teens she had her first work published, an essay which appeared in the *New York Mercury*. The *Mercury* also published her first poems. She attended the University of Wisconsin for a year (1867-1868), but dropped out as she found her classes no assistance in her chosen career. By the time she left the school she was a successful poet and contributed substantively to the family income.

In 1872 Wheeler's first book, *Drops of Water*, a volume of temperance poems, appeared. It was followed by *Shells* (1873) and *Maurine* (1876). She next authored *Poems of Passion*, but her publisher, Jansen and McClurg (Chicago), refused to publish it. Their opinion that it was immoral became the subject of a newspaper story, and when it finally appeared it was a resounding success.

In 1884 Wheeler married Robert Maius Wilcox and moved to Meridian, Connecticut. A son was born in the spring of 1887 but lived only a few hours. Whether this incident led her to a consideration of New Thought, the emerging idealistic healing philosophy, is not known. However, in November, Wilcox enrolled in the class of **Emma Curtis Hopkins**, founder of New Thought, held in New York City. She became identified with the larger New Thought Movement, and its themes began to permeate her poetry (which often appeared in the New Thought periodicals). Shortly after the turn of the century she authored three books on New Thought themes: *The Heart of New Thought* (1902); *New Thought and Common Sense: What Life Means to Me* (1908); and *The Art of Being Alive: Success through Thought* (1914). As with many of the first generation of New Thought leaders, she was involved in the women's movement, the integration of the two themes being clearly evident in the 1901 collection of her writings, *Every-Day Thoughts in Prose and Verse*.

By the turn of the century, Wilcox was a popular, nationally known writer whose work frequently appeared in mass circulation magazines. She also had a syndicated newspaper column. In 1901 she was sent to London by the New York *American* to write a poem on the occasion of the death of Queen Victoria. In London again in 1913, she was presented at court. She lectured to the troops during World War I, and in the spring of 1919, while overseas, suffered a severe injury as the result of a fall. She was nursed for a while at Bath, England, and then sent home. She died several months later. A short time before her death she finished her autobiography, *My Worlds and I* (1918).

Sources:

Dictionary of American Biography. 20 vols. and 7 supps. New York: Charles Scribner's Sons, 1928-1936, 1944-1981.

Wilcox, Ella Wheeler. *The Art of Being Alive: Success through Thought*. New York: Harper, 1914. 200 pp.

_____. *Everyday Thoughts in Prose and Verse*. Chicago: W. B. Conkey Company, 1901. 345 pp.

_____. *The Heart of the New Thought*. Chicago: Psychic Research Co., 1902. 92 pp.

_____. *My World and I*. New York: George H. Doran Co., 1918. 420 pp.

_____. *New Thought and Common Sense: What Life Means to Me*. Chicago: W. B. Conkey, 1908.

_____. *Poems of Passion*. Chicago: Belford, Clarke & Co., 1893. 160 pp.

★ 1017 ★
WILKERSON, David Ray
Founder, Teen Challenge
b. May 19, 1931, Hammond, Indiana

David Ray Wilkerson, a minister with the Assemblies of God who has become most well-known for his work with troubled youth, is the son of Kenneth and Ann Martin Wilkerson. Both his father and grandfather were Pentecostal ministers. He grew up in the several parsonages which went with the churches where his father ministered. He attended Central Bible College in Springfield, Missouri, the college of the Assemblies of God. In 1951 he married Gwendolyn Carosso. In 1952 he was ordained to the ministry. His first church was at Philipsburg, Pennsylvania.

Wilkerson stayed at Philipsburg for six years of what proved to be a fruitful ministry, but he developed a spiritual restlessness that came to a head one night in 1958. Looking at a *Life* magazine, he read of a trial of some teenage gang members in New York City. He felt God calling him to go to New York and assist the boys on trial. The story of his moving to New York and beginning to develop an evangelistic ministry among the street gangs of the city became the subject of *The Cross and the Switchblade*, a 1962 best-selling Christian book. Wilkerson organized Teen Challenge and over the next few years broadened the scope of his work to cover urban centers across the United States. Through the 1960s he authored a number of books related to his ministry, which had gained a repu-

tation for assisting people to get off of hard drugs: *Twelve Angels from Hell* (1965); *The Little People* (1966); *Parents on Trial* (1967); *I'm Not Mad at God* (1967); and *Hey Preach, You're Coming Through* (1968).

In 1965 Wilkerson further expanded his work with the founding of Wilkerson Youth Crusades and in 1970 added a third organization, World Challenge. The work of Teen Challenge had by this time spread to Europe. Wilkerson has continued to keep his ministry focused on troubled youth, but during the 1970s began to direct a message to the larger Pentecostal community, which he felt had gone in some wrong directions. Thus while he continued to write about the youth scene *Get Your Hands Off My Throat* (1971) and *Beyond the Cross and the Switchblade* (1974), he also wrote books for fellow believers—*David Wilkerson Speaks Out* (1973); *The Vision* (1974); *Racing Toward Judgment* (1976); and *Sipping Saints* (1978). *The Vision* became one of his most controversial books as it reported upon an apocalyptic vision he had with a message of judgment.

Through the 1980s Wilkerson continued to develop the international youth ministry, which has evolved around him, and has written a number of new books.

Sources:

Wilkerson, David. *The Cross and the Switchblade*. With John and Elizabeth Sherrill. New York: Bernard Geis Associates, 1963. 217 pp.

_____. *Get Your Hands Off My Throat*. Grand Rapids, MI: Zondervan Publishing House, 1971. 124 pp.

_____. *Parents on Trial*. New York: Hawthorne Books, 1967. 188 pp.

_____. *Twelve Angels from Hell*. Old Tappan, NJ: Fleming H. Revell, 1965.

_____. *The Vision*. New York: Pyramid Books, 1974. 143 pp.

Wilkerson, Gwen. *In His Strength*. Glendale, CA: G/L Publications, 1978. 143 pp.

★ 1018 ★
WILLARD, Frances Elizabeth
President, Woman's Christian Temperance Union (W.C.T.U.)
b. Sep. 28, 1839, Churchville, New York
d. Feb. 18, 1898, New York City, New York

Frances Elizabeth Willard, the president of the Woman's Christian Temperance Union in the 1880s and 1890s, was the daughter of Josiah F. and Mary T. Hill Willard. Both her parents were school teachers and her mother especially encouraged Frances' education. When Frances was seven years old, the family moved to Janesville, Wisconsin. As there was no Congregational church, they joined the Methodist Episcopal Church. Greatly admiring Oliver, her older brother, she was further motivated by his leaving for college in 1852, and four years later she enrolled at Northwest Female Academy in Evanston, Illinois. The fact that, unlike her brother, she could neither vote nor preach (he had by that time become a student at Garrett Biblical Institute) provided an underlying agenda to her life. She graduated from college in 1859 as class valedictorian. In 1860 she had a bout with typhoid fever that led to a religious conversion, as a result of which she formally joined the Methodist Episcopal Church.

For the next seven years Willard taught school. During these years she became engaged to Charles Fowler (later a bishop in the Methodist Episcopal Church) but the engagement was suddenly broken off, and she never married. In 1865 she became corresponding secretary of the American Methodist Ladies Centennial Association, and thus assumed the major burden for the association's goal of raising money for the erection of Heck Hall at Northwestern University. The speech she wrote for the dedication was eloquently read by a man, as women were generally not allowed to speak before mixed audiences at that time.

In 1871 Willard became president of the Evanston College for Ladies (associated with Northwestern University), and hence the first American woman to ever head a college. Unfortunately, the Chicago Fire of that year burned the assets of the school's major financial supporters, and Charles Fowler (by then the president of Northwestern) attacked its independent status. When Fowler stripped Willard of her real control of the school, she resigned in 1873. She threw herself into work for the Association for the Advancement of Women, but was soon caught up in the enthusiasm of the women's crusade against alcohol. With the help of Willard's former mentor, **John Heyl Vincent**, the women formed the Woman's Christian Temperance Union (W.C.T.U.).

Though not particularly a temperance crusader, Willard saw the possibilities of the organization for changing women's status. She was elected president of the Chicago Temperance League and in November 1874 was elected the first corresponding secretary of the national W.C.T.U. and began her rise to a point of control. She began to build support for putting the W.C.T.U. behind the suffrage issue, in opposition to the union's first president, **Annie Wittenmyer**. In 1877 she became editor of *Our Union*, the W.C.T.U. periodical, and immediately opened it to the advocacy of suffrage . In 1878 she became president of the Illinois W.C.T.U. and the following year gained the national presidency, a position she held for the rest of her life.

In her first presidential address, Willard announced her "Do Everything" policy. She redirected the organization to make a general assault upon the ills of society. During her presidency 39 departments were established to deal with the broad range of issues from suffrage to white slavery. She began agitation for female police officers, and as a result Chicago and Denver hired the first officers to handle female prisoners in their jails. Under her direction, the W.C.T.U. became the largest women's and women's rights organization in the country.

Willard developed a unique strategy for gaining suffrage. She asked state legislatures to adopt a "home protection" measure which would give women the right to vote on matters that affected the home, especially the liquor question. From that step full suffrage could be secured. Such a measure would actually be adopted in Illinois in 1913.

In 1888 Willard became the first woman elected as a delegate to the general conference of the Methodist Episcopal Church. When she arrived at the conference, however, she ran into opposition organized by **James Monroe Buckley**, editor of the *New York Christian Advocate*, and Bishop Charles Fowler. She was never seated, though the same conference adopted a resolution praising her temperance work.

Willard authored a number of books over the years of her leadership of the W.C.T.U., including *Woman and Temperance* (1883); *Glimpses of Fifty Years*, her autobiography (1889); and *A Classic Town: The Story of Evanston* (1892). Following her death, the W.C.T.U. and Willard's private secretary, Anna Gordon, worked to see that she would not be forgotten. Gordon wrote a glowing biography, and the Union promoted memorials (in the form of streets, parks, buildings, etc.) to her around the United States. In 1905 the State of Illinois placed her statue in the rotunda of the Capitol in Washington, D.C., and in 1910 she was elected to the Hall of Fame for Great Americans.

Sources:

Bordin, Ruth. *Frances Willard: A Biography*. Chapel Hill, NC: University of North Carolina Press, 1986. 294 pp.
Dillon, Mary Earhart. *Frances Willard: From Prayers to Politics*. Chicago: University of Chicago Press, 1944.
Gordon, Anna A. *The Beautiful Life of Frances E. Willard*. Chicago: Woman's Temperance Publishing Association, 1898. 416 pp.
Harmon, Nolan B. *The Encyclopedia of World Methodism*. 2 vols. Nashville: United Methodist Publishing House, 1974.

Melton, J. Gordon. *Log Cabins to Steeples, The United Methodist Way in Illinois: 1824-1974*. N.p. The Commissions on Archives and History of the Northern, Central, and Southern Illinois Conferences, 1974. 417 pp.
Mitchell, Norma Taylor. *Frances E. Willard*. Madison, NJ: General Commission on Archives and History, United Methodist Church, 1987. 36 pp.
Trowbridge, Lydia J. *Frances Willard of Evanston*. Chicago: Willett, Clark and Co., 1938.
Willard, Frances E. A. *Classic Town: The Story of Evanston*. Chicago: Woman's Temperance Publishing Association, 1891. 423 pp.
_____. *Glimpses of Fifty Years*. Chicago: Woman's Temperance Publication Association, 1889. 698 pp.
_____. *Nineteen Beautiful Years*. Chicago: Woman's Temperance Publication Association, 1886. 268 pp.
_____. *Woman and Temperance*. Hartford, CT: Park Publishing Company, 1883. 648 pp.
_____. *Women in the Pulpit*. Chicago: Woman's Temperance Publishing Association, 1889. 173 pp.

★1019★
WILLIAMS, George M.
General Director, Nichiren Shoshu of America (NSA)
b. Jun. 16, 1930, Seoul Republic of Korea

George M. Williams is the general director of Nichiren Shoshu of America (NSA), the full name of which is Nichiren Shoshu Soka Gakkai of America. He was born Masayasu Sadanaga to Japanese parents in Seoul, Korea. Following World War II, he moved to Japan with his parents. Soon afterward, both he and his mother converted to Soka Gakkai (he had been brought up as a Methodist). Soka Gakkai is the lay organization of the Nichiren Shoshu, one of several Japanese Buddhist sects which derive from the work of the thirteenth-century Buddhist teacher Nichiren. As a student, Williams was active under the group's second president, Josei Toda, and Toda's successor, **Daisaku Ikeda**. In 1957, after graduating with a degree in law from Meiji University, he came to the United States. He studied at UCLA, George Washington University, and the University of Maryland, and received a master's degree in political science in 1962.

Americans familiar with other forms of Buddhism are often surprised when they encounter NSA's vigorous proselytizing and the group's exclusive truth claims. These seeming peculiarities are, however, the end result of a rather natural course of development of certain Buddhist notions. The traditional scriptures of Mahayana Buddhism contain statements about the supernatural, almost magical effects that are produced by the mere reading of them. By Nichiren's time, this way of regarding scripture had resulted in disputes as to which scripture was the most efficacious. Nichiren became an advocate of the Lotus Sutra and denounced other forms of Buddhism as false (in the sense that other interpretations of Buddha's message would not lead to liberation, given the conditions of the present age). Soka Gakkai's central practice, the chanting of "namu myoho renge kyo" (roughly translated: I bow to the Lotus Sutra), reflects the feeling that the Lotus Sutra is so holy that one need only express adoration to this scripture to acquire its merit.

Nichiren Shoshu Buddhism was brought to the United States by, among others, the war brides of American servicemen. When Sadanaga came to America, he decided to contact these believers, encourage them to set up informal networks, and work to bring more people into the fold. He eventually changed his name to George M. Williams and became a naturalized American citizen. The NSA was formed in 1960 during a visit with Ikeda, then president of Soka Gakkai in Japan, and later president of Soka Gakkai International. Williams became general director of the American work, and the new group grew rapidly. In 1963 he began to edit the *World Tribune*, the movement's newspaper, and the following year assumed further duties as managing director of NSA Productions. He also became vice president of the international organization. The first Nichiren Shoshu temple was built on American soil in 1967.

Sources:

Melton, J. Gordon *The Encyclopedia of American Religions*. 3d ed. Detroit: Gale Research Inc.,1988. 1102 pp.

Williams, George M. *Freedom and Influence*. Santa Monica, CA: World Tribune Press, 1985.

_____. *NSA Seminars: An Introduction to Buddhism*. Santa Monica, CA: World Tribune Press, 1982. 76 pp.

★ 1020 ★
WILLIAMS, John
Presiding Bishop, Protestant Episcopal Church
b. Aug. 30, 1817, Old Deerfield, Massachusetts
d. Feb. 7, 1899, Middletown, Connecticut

John Williams, a presiding bishop of the Protestant Episcopal Church, was the son of Ephraim and Emily Trowbridge Williams and a descendent of an old colonial family. At the age of 14, Williams entered Yale College. During his stay at Yale he was converted to Episcopalianism. At the end of his sophomore year, he transferred to Washington (now Trinity) College in Hartford, Connecticut. While at Washington, his roommate was James Roosevelt Bayley, who later became the Roman Catholic archbishop of Baltimore. Williams graduated in 1835 and was tutored in theological studies by the Rev. Samuel F. Jarvis, the Episcopal rector in Middletown, Connecticut. Williams was ordained a deacon in 1838 and admitted to the priesthood in 1841. During most of this time he was a tutor at Washington College.

Williams spent 1840 and 1841 in Great Britain. There he met and became friends with the ritually oriented leaders of the Oxford Movement, which would soon spread from England to America, though he did not become a leader himself. Upon his return to America, he spent a year as assistant rector in Middletown before becoming rector of St. George's Church in Schenectady, New York. While in New York he issued his first literary productions, a translation of some Latin hymns, *Ancient Hymns of Holy Church* (1845), and his first book, *Thoughts on the Gospel Miracles* (1848). In 1848 he became president of his alma mater, now called Trinity College, and also assumed duties as a professor in history and literature. Three years later he was elected and consecrated bishop coadjutor for the Episcopal diocese of Connecticut. The rest of his life would involve a complex interweaving of duties as bishop and college instructor.

During his first two years as bishop, Williams retained all of his duties at the college, but resigned the presidency in 1853. He was then named vice-chancellor. During his five years at the college, he influenced a number of men to enter the ministry. In 1854 he obtained a charter for a seminary and launched the Berkeley Divinity School. He served as dean and professor of theology and liturgies until his death. Besides his teaching duties, Williams also was an active writer who contributed articles to a number of periodicals. He also edited the American edition of Edward Harold Brown's *Exposition of the Thirty-Nine Articles* of the Episcopal Church (1865).

In 1865 the bishop of Connecticut died and Williams added the roles of chancellor of the college and diocesan bishop to his extensive job description. The 1880s proved to be his most fruitful literary period, beginning with his Paddock lectures at the General Theological Seminary, which were published as *Studies on the English Reformation* (1881), and the Bedell lectures at Kenyon College, which were published as *The World's Witness to Jesus* (1882). In 1888 he finished his last book, *Studies on the Book of Acts*. In 1887 he became the senior bishop of the Protestant Episcopal Church and was, as a result, named presiding bishop. He oversaw a period of relative prosperity in the church during the rest of the century.

The burdens of his office began to weigh heavily in the 1890s, and Williams, in his 70s, relinquished some of his duties. In 1892 he ceased lecturing at the college. As his health failed, he asked the diocese to name a coadjutor. Williams died two years later. He never married.

Sources:

Dictionary of American Biography. 20 vols. and 7 supps. New York: Charles Scribner's Sons, 1928-1936, 1944-1981.

Williams, John. *Ancient Hymns of Holy Church*. Hartford, CT: H. S. Parsons, 1845. 127 pp.

_____. *Studies on the Book of Acts*. New York: T. Whittaker, 1888. 178 pp.

_____. *Studies on the English Reformation*. New York: Stanford & Swords, 1881. 164 pp.

_____. *Thoughts on the Gospel Miracles*. New York:Danford Swords, 1848. 164 pp.

★ 1021 ★
WILLIAMS, Lacey Kirk
President, National Baptist Convention, U.S.A., Inc.
b. Jul. 11, 1871, Eufaula, Alabama
d. Nov. 1940

Lacey Kirk Williams, for 18 years president of the National Baptist Convention, U.S.A., Inc., was born in Alabama to former slaves. Early in his life his family immigrated to Texas. Little is known of his early life. At some point he was converted, joined the Baptist Church, and responded to a call to preach. He soon emerged as one of the most able of Texas preachers, pastoring Mt. Gilead Baptist Church in Ft. Worth. During the second decade of the twentieth century he became president of the Texas Baptist State Convention. In 1916 he was called as pastor to Mt. Olivet Baptist Church in Chicago. It was about this time that the National Baptist Convention was disturbed by the defection of a group structured around the independent Baptist publishing venture in Arkansas. Williams served on the committee to seek a solution to the schism, and after negotiations broke down, he served on the convention's new publication board.

In 1922, following the death of convention president **Elias C. Morris**, Williams was elected to replace him. He immediately had to face a number of issues. The loss of the original publication board seven years before and the women's auxiliary development of a training school necessitated clarification of the   role of the convention in their support. Williams helped work out a plan by which the school was subordinated to the women's convention, which in turn was tied to the National Baptist Convention, but in such a way that it was free from any possible damage from convention incurred expenses.

Among Williams' most important achievements was the construction of a cooperative plan between the American Baptists, a white denomination, and the National Baptist Convention, by which the wealthier white group would supply financial and other support to the black Baptists. An interracial cooperative council was established and much of the growth of the National Baptist Convention has its roots in the guidance of this council.

Williams had, even before his election as convention president, taken the lead in raising money and purchasing lots in Nashville, Tennessee, upon which to construct the new publishing house. As president, he supervised the building of the new facilities, which were completed in 1925. Williams also oversaw and encouraged the convention's mission program, which was directed primarily toward Africa. By 1930 there were 32 missionaries, including 11 medical missionaries.

The period of growth of the convention through the 1920s under Williams leadership was recognized by his election as a vice-president of the World Baptist Alliance in 1928, a position he retained for the rest of his life. He gave his last address to his colleagues at the Birmingham convention in 1940. A few weeks later he was killed in an airplane crash on his way to deliver a speech in Flint, Michigan.

Sources:

Horace, Lillian B. *Crowned with Glory and Honor: The Life of Rev. Lacey Kirk Williams*. New York: Exposition Press, 1978.
Jackson, J. H. *A Story of Christian Activism: The History of the National Baptist Convention, U.S.A., Inc.* Nashville, TN: Townsend Press, 1980. 790 pp.

★1022★
WILSON, Ernest C.
Minister, Unity School of Christianity
b. Mar. 30, 1896, Fargo, North Dakota
d. Jul. 9, 1982, Kansas City, Missouri

Ernest C. Wilson, a minister and author of books for the Unity School of Christianity, was born Charles Ernest Wilson. He left little record of his childhood. It was clear, however, that it was an unhappy time for him. His autobiography, *If You Want to Enough*, picks up the story of his life as a youth moving to Minneapolis. In his late teen years he met John Ring, a New Thought metaphysical minister from San Diego. He moved to California as Ring's assistant, and in 1916 was ordained as a minister by Ring. Together in 1918 they founded the Harmonial Institute. He edited the institute magazine, *The Harmonial Thinker* (1918-1925), and in 1920 he published his first book, *The Simple Truth*. He later served brief pastorates in Minneapolis, Minnesota, and Cleveland, Ohio.

While in Cleveland Wilson developed a relationship with the Unity School of Christianity, and in 1927 he moved to Kansas City, Missouri, as editor of *Youth* magazine. The next years proved immensely fruitful for Wilson. He authored several books, including Unity's basic presentation of reincarnation, *Have We Lived Before?* (1936). He also worked at WOR, a Kansas City station owned by Unity, and in the 1930s represented Unity as a speaker for an interdenominational network program, "The Church of the Air." His articles on the contemplation of Christ became the basis for his popular class, Master Class Lessons (lessons on the teachings of Christ), which in turn became the subject of a widely-read Unity textbook (1938). Feeling the need for some ritual celebrating Christmas, Wilson introduced a Christmas candlelight service which was later adopted as a standard practice by most Unity congregations. In 1933 he succeeded **Charles S. Fillmore**, the founder of Unity, as pastor of the Unity Society of Practical Christianity, Unity's mother church in Kansas City. In 1934 he was reordained by Fillmore. That same year he became the editor-in-chief of Unity publications.

In 1938 Wilson moved to Los Angeles where he founded Christ Church Unity, which soon grew into one of Unity's largest congregations. He also returned to the radio as the speaker on an early evening show, "Dusk Hour," and he remained on the radio during all of his Los Angeles years. In 1948 he was elected for a term as president of the International New Thought Alliance (INTA). In 1949 he ventured into television, where he regularly appeared through most of the 1950s. During his time in Los Angeles he also authored several books, including: *Sons of Heaven* (1941); *Every Good Desire* (1948); and *The Other Half of the Rainbow* (1952).

In 1965 Wilson returned to Kansas City as senior minister of Unity Church on the Plaza. He remained in Kansas City for the remaining years of his life.

Sources:

Beebe, Tom. *Who's Who in New Thought*. Lakemont, GA: CSA Press, 1977. 318 pp.
Wilson, Ernest C. *Have We Lived Before?* Kansas City, MO: Unity School of Christianity, 1936. 149 pp.
_____. *If You Want to Enough*. Kansas City, MO: Unity on the Plaza, 1984. 324 pp.
_____. *Master Class Lessons*. Kansas City, MO: Unity School of Christianity, 1938. 157 pp.
_____. *The Other Half of the Rainbow*. Los Angeles: Unity Classics, 1952. 213 pp.
_____. *The Simple Truth*. San Diego: Harmonial Publishers, 1920. 115 pp.

★1023★
WINROD, Gerald Burton
Founder, Defenders of the Christian Faith
b. 1899?, Wichita, Kansas
d. Nov. 11, 1957, Wichita, Kansas

The Rev. Gerald Burton Winrod was the founder of the Defenders of the Christian Faith and a well known nativist during World War II. His father had been a barkeeper, but abandoned this career to become an evangelist. Carry Nation had begun her famous crusade against alcohol by smashing Winrod's father's saloon. Young Winrod left school early to work as a day laborer and later as a factory worker. He was converted at a camp meeting, and eventually became a preacher. The Doctor of Divinity degree that allowed him to be referred to as "Dr. Gerald B. Winrod" was an honorary degree conferred upon him in 1935 by the Los Angeles Baptist Seminary for his leadership in Christian journalism. The basis for this honor was his work as the editor of *The Defender Magazine*, which began publication in April of 1926.

The Defender Magazine was the mouthpiece for the organization that Winrod had founded in November of the preceding year, the Defenders of the Christian Faith. Not originally a denomination in its own right (although Defenders churches began to be established in Puerto Rico in the 1930s), the Defenders saw themselves as an organization that struggled against the enemies of Christianity. It included among its associates such leading fundamentalists as Paul W. Rood, Keith L. Brooks, **Paul Rader**, and **Oswald J. Smith**. The magazine carried typically fundamentalist attacks on the evils of dancing and movie-going, as well as denunciations of liberal Christianity. Foremost among Winrod's early targets was the theory of evolution. When the anti-evolution craze died down, he turned his energies against godless Communism and the New Deal. Another change was the shift in emphasis toward the perceived threat of Jews (who were viewed as being ultimately behind the Communist menace), and Winrod was the immediate source for many of the anti-Semitic themes found in the thinking of later American nativists. He voiced some of the most extreme anti-Semitic accusations, such as portraying Jews as conspiring to corrupt the United States by propagating radicalism and immorality through the medium of the movies. He also focused attention on the *Protocols of the Learned Elders of Zion*, a fraudulent document that claimed to record a plot by Jewish leaders to take over the world.

Although initially anti-Nazi, the sentiments that Winrod and Hitler shared about both Communism and the Jews made them natural allies. In 1934 Winrod went to Germany to "study social, political, moral, economic, and prophetic trends." He met some leading officials of the pro-Nazi church, and was profoundly affected. Upon his return, he became an ardent defender of Hitler, and remained so right up to the outbreak of World War II. During the war he was indicted three times for sedition, but was never convicted. After the war he picked up where he had left off, although he was no longer overtly pro-fascist. During his years of active ministry, Winrod authored a number of books and booklets, most transcripts of his sermons.

Sources:

Bowden, Henry Warner. *Dictionary of American Religious Biography*. Westport, CT: Greenwood Press, 1977. 572 pp.
Fire by Night and Cloud by Day: Amazing History of the Defenders of the Christian Faith. Wichita, KS: Mertmont Publishers, 1966. 128 pp.

Melton, J. Gordon *The Encyclopedia of American Religions*. 3d ed. Detroit: Gale Research Inc.,1988. 1102 pp.

Montgomery, G. H. *Gerald Burton Winrod*. Wichita, KS: Mertmont Publishers, 1965. 108 pp.

Roy, Ralph Lord. *Apostles of Discord: A Study of Organized Bigotry and Disruption on the Fringes of Protestantism*. Boston: Beacon Press, 1953. 437 pp.

Winrod, Gerald B. *Adam Weishaupt, A Human Devil*. Hollywood: Sons of Liberty, n.d. 51 pp.

_____. *Brain Building and Soul Growth and Other Messages*. Wichita, KS: Defender Publishers, 1954. 70 pp.

_____. *The Conflict of the Christ*. Wichita, KS: Defender Publishers, 1953. 66 pp.

_____. *Portals to Armageddon*. Wichita, KS: Defender Publishers, 1950. 23 pp.

★ 1024 ★
WISE, Isaac Mayer
Rabbi, Reform Judaism
b. Mar. 29, 1819, Steingrub Czechoslovakia
d. Mar. 26, 1900, Cincinnati, Ohio

Isaac Mayer Wise, generally seen as the founder of Reform Judaism in the United States, grew up in a small town in Czechoslovakia. He received his early education from his father, a teacher, and his grandfather, a physician. At the age of 12, he went to Prague where he continued his education at the *bet hamidrach*, house of learning, and then the *yeshiva*, academy. He later attended the academy at Jenikau, the University of Prague for two years, and the University of Vienna for a year. In 1842 he was ordained as a rabbi. He moved to Radnitz and in 1845 married Theresa Bloch. Unhappy in Radnitz, he left Czechoslovakia forever in 1846 and migrated to America.

By the time Wise landed in New York, he had already imbibed of the waves of reform which had swept through German Judaism. There being only three reform-oriented congregations in America, Wise soon concluded that the Jewish community needed an American-oriented Reform Judaism. Before the year was out, he located a congregation in Albany which called him as its rabbi. At Albany he began to institute reforms. He put in an organ, established a choir, cut some of the Hebrew from the liturgy, offered weekly sermons, and established a confirmation service that included young girls as well as boys.

His reforms split the congregation in 1850 and, with his supporters, he founded Anshe Emeth (Men of Truth). During his last years in Albany he began to put his ideas on paper, the most prominent literary product being his *History of the Israelitish Nation* (1854), a modernist interpretation which eliminated any discussion of miracles. Wise drew a sharp distinction between items he considered essential to the Jewish tradition and those non-essential, and the latter he deemed the proper object for any alteration or even elimination. He was already being attacked in the Jewish press for his denial of key Orthodox beliefs in the literal coming of a Messiah and the resurrection of the body.

In 1854 he moved to Cincinnati, Ohio, a growing center for German immigrant settlement, as rabbi of the Congregation Bene Yeshurum, where he would remain for the rest of his life. He instituted reforms and built it into a prominent reform congregation. Some of the reforms were immediate but others were made gradually, over the next 20 years. In 1854 he began the *Israelite* (later the *American Israelite*), a weekly paper which became the instrument for spreading the reform movement, and its German counterpart, *Die Deborah*. In 1867 he began to lecture on Friday evenings (the beginning of the traditional Sabbath) and many of these lectures were later collected into books.

In 1873 a conclave of delegates from reform-minded congregations assembled in Cincinnati to form the Union of American Hebrew Congregations, an association of reform synagogues. Wise was elected as president. The association provided a base of support upon which he could project a college, and in 1875 he launched Hebrew Union College. Wise became its first president and taught many of the courses. A number of years later, with the support of many of the rabbis trained at Hebrew Union College, he formed the Central Conference of American Rabbis, still the professional association of Reform rabbis. He was elected its first president and reelected annually for the rest of his life.

Sources:

Goldman, Alex J. *The Greatest Rabbis Hall of Fame*. New York: Shapolsky Publishers, 1987. 390 pp.

Knox, Israel. *Rabbi in America: The Story of Isaac M. Wise*. Boston: Little, Brown and Company, 1957. 173 pp.

May, Max B. *Isaac Mayer Wise, the Founder of American Judaism; A Biography*. New York: G. P. Putnam's Sons, 1916.

Philipson, David, ed. *Reminiscences of Isaac M. Wise*. Cincinnati, OH: Leo Wise & Company, 1901.

Wise, Isaac M. *The Cosmic God*. Cicinnati, OH: Office American Israelite and Deborah, 1876. 181 pp.

_____. *A History of the Israelitish Nation*. Albany, NY: J. Munsell, 1854. 560 pp.

_____. *Judaism—Its Doctrines and Duties*. Cincinnati, OH: Bloch Publishing Company, 1888.

_____. *Reminiscences*. New York: Central Synagogue of New York, 1945. 359 pp.

_____. *The Selected Writings of Isaac Mayer Wise*. Ed. by David Philipson and Louis Grossman. Cincinnati, OH: Robert Clarke Company, 1900. 419 pp.

_____. *The Western Journal of Isaac Mayer Wise, 1877*. Ed. by William M. Kramer. Berkeley, CA: Western Jewish History Center, 1974. 85 pp.

★ 1025 ★
WISE, Stephen Samuel
Jewish Rabbi
b. Mar. 17, 1874, Budapest Hungary
d. Apr. 19, 1949, New York, New York

Stephen Samuel Wise, founder of the Free Synagogue in New York City, inherited a rabbinical lineage and grew up in a rabbi's home. His father, Aaron Wise, migrated to America when Stephen was only one year old to become rabbi of Temple Rodeph Sholom in New York City. As a boy, Stephen was taught by his father. He attended Columbia University, where he attained both his B.A. (1892) and Ph.D. (1901) degrees, but never attended a formal rabbinical school. He was taught privately by a number of rabbis, including **Alexander Kohut** and Chief Rabbi Adolf Jellinek of Vienna.

Wise's first post was at the Madison Avenue Synagogue in Manhattan as assistant to Rabbi Henry S. Jacobs. During these early years, he manifested the free and independent spirit that characterized his career. While most liberal reform-minded Jewish voices were opposed to Zionism, which centered on the creation of a Jewish homeland as a modern political entity, Wise became a founder of the Zionist Organization of America in 1989 and served twice as its president.

In 1900 Wise left New York to become the rabbi of Temple Beth Israel in Portland, Oregon. While there he became active in social work. He founded and served as the vice-president of the Oregon State Conference of Charities and Corrections, and became a member of the Child Labor Commission. His leadership attracted the attention of the members of Temple Emmanuel in New York City, and they invited Wise to return to the East Coast to serve as rabbi of possibly the most influential liberal temple in American Judaism.

The outspoken Wise immediately ran into trouble with the temple lay leadership. He insisted that he have absolute freedom to speak his opinions should he come to New York. The board of trustees in turn demanded that the rabbi be responsible to them.

Unable to reach a satisfactory resolution, he did not take the job. Instead, he moved to New York in 1907 and founded the Free Synagogue. Wise advocated a free pulpit, abolition of distinctions between rich and poor (hence the abolition of bought pews), participation by the synagogue in the community, and complete identification with Israel's future (Zionism). A number of the synagogue's leading families supported him. He was preaching to over 400 within a year. Meetings were initially held at the Hudson Theatre, but were then moved to Carnegie Hall, where the synagogue became one of the largest and most influential in America. In 1914 Wise founded the Jewish Institute of Religion to train liberal rabbis.

Wise was a social reformer who put his passion and position behind a number of causes. He championed the cause of labor. He joined with Unitarian minister **John Haynes Holmes** in attacking the corruption of the New York political machine. He was among the founders of the National Association for the Advancement of Colored People (NAACP). In 1919 he toured the country on behalf of the League of Nations.

Today Wise is remembered as a pioneer Zionist who supported the movement at a time when most reform rabbis were unpersuaded by arguments supporting national state for Israel. He was influential in the development of President Woodrow Wilson's favorable attitude to Zionism.

Wise wanted to provide a democratic representative institution for the expression of Jewish opinion and act upon the needs, problems, and rights of Jews. Thus he became one of the founders of the American Jewish Congress and subsequently, after World War I, the World Jewish Congress. He led both organizations in mobilizing Jewish self-defense against Hitler.

Amid his myriad activities, Wise also found time to write. Among his books are *The Improvement of the Moral Qualities* (1902); *How to Face Life* (1917); *Child Versus Parent* (1922); *The Great Betrayal* (1930), written with Jacob de Hass; and his memoirs, *The Challenging Years* (1949). He also edited a mid-war attack upon Germany, *Never Again! Ten Years of Hitler* (1943). His sermons were collected in *The Free Synagogue Pulpit*, published over many years, and in 1935 he began a period as editor of *Opinion*, a Jewish monthly.

Sources:

Singer, Isidore, ed. *The Jewish Encyclopedia.* New York: KTAV Publishing House, 1964.

Wise, Stephen S. *As I See It.* New York: Jewish Opinion Pub. Corp., 1944. 284 pp.

———. *The Challenging Years.* New York: Putnam's Sons, 1949. 323 pp.

———. *Child Versus Parent.* New York: Macmillan, 1922. 139 pp.

———, and Jacob de Haas. *The Great Betrayal.* New York: Brentano's, 1930. 294 pp.

———, ed. *Never Again! Ten Years of Hitler.* New York: Jewish Opinion Publishing Corp., 1943. 104 pp.

★1026★
WISLER, Jacob
Founder, Old Order (Wisler) Mennonites
b. Oct. 31, 1808, Bucks County, Pennsylvania
d. May 1, 1889, Elkhart County, Indiana

Jacob Wisler, founder of the Old Order (Wisler) Mennonites, was the son of Christian and Susan Holdeman Wisler, whose ancestors have been traced to Switzerland. When he was about 12 years old, his family moved to Columbiana County, Ohio, where he spent his teen years. In 1827 he married Mary Hoover (1808-1860). They associated with the Midway Mennonite Church, in which Wisler was ordained a minister in 1833. In 1848 Wisler moved his family to Elkhart, Indiana, and settled on a farm. In 1851 Wisler was ordained a bishop by Abraham Rohrer.

Wisler quickly emerged as a champion of conservative Mennonite standards and as an opponent of the more liberal element among the growing Elkhart Mennonite community. He had special difficulty with those promoting the introduction of the Sunday school and similar new structures. Wisler and the liberal brethren were in constant strife in the years immediately after the Civil War. Finally, unable to quiet the controversy, a committee of six fellow bishops suspended Wisler from his office. **John Funk**, a prominent editor/minister, subsequently announced on behalf of the majority of ministers that they no longer recognized Wisler and his followers as members of the church.

Wisler reacted to the actions of the bishops and Funk by establishing a new congregation, which eventually took the name Old Order Mennonite Church. He found support among members in Wadsworth, Orrville, and North Lima, Ohio, who also formed separate congregations. Attempts were made to heal the schism, but Wisler stood firmly against the new innovations. During the height of the controversy, following his wife's death, he married Catherine Knopp. He led the Old Order congregations for the rest of his life.

Sources:

The Mennonite Encyclopedia. 4 vols. Scottdale, PA: The Mennonite Publishing House, 1955.

★1027★
WITTENMYER, Annie Turner
President, Woman's Christian Temperance Union
b. Aug. 26, 1827, Sandy Springs, Ohio
d. Feb. 2, 1900, Saratoga Springs, Pennsylvania

Annie Turner Wittenmyer, the first president of the Woman's Christian Temperance Union (W.C.T.U.), was the daughter of John G. and Elizabeth Smith Turner. She grew up in Ohio and Kentucky, and in 1847 married William Wittenmyer. In 1859 they moved to Keokuk, Iowa, where she helped to organize the local congregation of the Methodist Episcopal Church. Her merchant husband died in the late 1850s and left her with a considerable estate. She began her life of social service during the Civil War by organizing the Keokuk Soldiers' Aid Society. As she traveled the state working with women to gather hospital supplies, she became well known, and the state hired her as a sanitary agent. The ultimate control of her work became an immediate issue, and in 1863 she helped organize and was elected president of the Iowa State Sanitary Commission, an organization formed to resist the takeover of her work by the all-male Iowa Army Sanitary Commission. While continuing her work, she was forced to spend much time refuting charges of corruption, later found to have no substance to them.

In May 1864, having seen a new need, she resigned from her hospital work and, with the assistance of the United States Christian Commission, opened a kitchen in Nashville, Tennessee, the first of several she established adjacent to army hospitals. After the war she worked with orphans of the war. In 1868 she helped organize the Ladies' and Pastors' Christian Union (later the General Conference Society), a Methodist social agency which organized women, in cooperation with their pastors, to visit the sick and needy. She served as its corresponding secretary until 1871.

The general theme which had developed in Wittenmyer's life, organizing women and putting them to work in service areas previously understood to be male territory, found a new outlet in the early 1870s. In 1871 Wittenmyer moved to Philadelphia and founded *Christian Women*, a periodical she would edit for the next 11 years. Through its pages she was able to develop her ideas of the new role of women in society, the subject of her first book, *Woman's Work for Jesus*. In 1874 she was caught up in the "Woman's Crusade" against alcohol and the saloon. She attended the November 1874 convention, at which the Woman's Christian

Temperance Union was formed, and was elected its first president. She threw herself into the cause and traveled widely on its behalf. She oversaw the founding of *Our Union*, the organization's periodical, and wrote an early account of the crusade, *History of the Woman's Temperance Crusade* (1878).

As president of the Union, Wittenmyer immediately came into open conflict with **Frances E. Willard**, who wanted to see the Union politicized and back the suffrage issue. The two fought for five years until 1879 when Willard challenged Wittenmyer for the presidency and won. Wittenmyer remained active in the Union until Willard pushed for the alignment of it with the Prohibition Party. Thus in 1890, Wittenmyer joined in the organization of the Non-partisan Woman's Christian Temperance Union, over which she served two years as president (1896-1898).

Wittenmyer's last crusade was with the Woman's Relief Corps, the women's auxiliary of the Grand Army of the Republic. As its president in 1898-1899, she led a campaign to establish a national home for female victims of the war—nurses, widows, and mothers of veterans. As a result such a home was established in Ohio, and she served as director of it and of a similar home in Pennsylvania. During her last years she also was able to write an autobiographical account of her war years, *Under the Guns* (1895).

Sources:

James, Edward T., ed. *Notable American Women, 1607-1950: A Biographical Dictionary*. 3 vols. Cambridge, MA: Harvard University Press, Belknap Press, 1971.

McHenry, Robert, ed. *Liberty's Women*. Springfield, MA: G. & C. Mirrian Company, 1980. 482 pp.

McHenry, Robert, ed. *Liberty's Women*. Springfield, MA: G & C Merriam Company, 1980. 482 pp.

Wittenmyer, Annie. *History of the Woman's Temperance Crusade*. Philadelphia: The Christian Woman, 1878. 781 pp.

———. *Under the Guns*. Boston: Stillings & Co., 1895. 272 pp.

———. *Women of the Reformation*. New York: Phillips & Hunt, 1885. 460 pp.

———. *Woman's Work for Jesus*. New York: Nelson & Phillips, 1873. 240 pp.

★ 1028 ★
WOOD, Henry
Metaphysical Writer
b. Jan. 16, 1834, Barre, Vermont
d. Mar. 28, 1909, Brookline, Massachusetts

Henry Wood, whose New Thought metaphysical writings were among the most popular religious books in North America at the beginning of the twentieth century, was the son of Stillman Wood. He attended Barre Academy (1848-1852) and later graduated from the Commercial College in Boston in 1854. He became a successful businessman and in 1860 married Margaret Osborne Baker. Few biographical details were available on Wood until the appearance in 1887 of *Natural Law in the Business World*, Wood's first literary endeavor. The book is a survey of business life in an attempt to understand the rules of human interaction as part of the natural order.

At the time of the appearance of his book, Wood found himself the victim of the chronic diseases of the late-nineteenth century— neurasthenia and dyspepsia. Unable to find any relief from doctors, he turned to New Thought, which had just made its appearance as a rival to Christian Science, and there found his healing. He then decided to spend the rest of his life running a private sanitarium and espousing the New Thought perspective. His first literary product reflective of his new condition was a novel, *Edward Burton* (1890), the story of a college student who suffered physical ailments similar to those endured by Wood and fell victim to opiates at the hands of doctors. He is cured by the application of a mental healing treatment.

Through the 1890s Wood authored a set of New Thought titles: *God's Image in Man* (1892); *Ideal Suggestion through Mental Photography* (1893); *The Political Economy of Natural Law* (1894); *Has Mental Healing a Valid Scientific and Religious Basis?* (1895); and *Studies in the Thought World* (1896). Wood became one of the most prominent members of the Metaphysical Club of Boston, founded in 1895, which included such prominent New Thought advocates as Horatio W. Dresser and C. M. Burrows. Wood was elected president of the club in 1899.

During the first decade of the twentieth century, Wood wrote two of his most important New Thought texts: *The New Thought Simplified* (1903) and *The New Old Healing* (1908). Through his writings Wood championed the rule of natural law in human life and saw New Thought as articulating that law in a practical manner, especially as it affected health. The last years of Wood's life are somewhat obscure.

Sources:

Parker, Gail Thain. *Mind Cure in New England*. Hanover, NH: University Press of New England, 1973. 196 pp.

Wood, Henry. *God's Image in Man*. Boston: Lee and Shepard, 1892. 258 pp.

———. *Has Mental Healing a Valid Scientific and Religious Basis?* Boston: Lee and Shepard, 1895.

———. *Ideal Suggestion through Mental Photography*. Boston: Lee and Shepard, 1893. 163 pp.

———. *Natural Law in the Business World*. Boston: Lee and Shepard, 1887. 222 pp.

———. *The New Old Healing*. Boston: Lothrop, Lee & Shepard, 1908. 304 pp.

———. *The New Thought Simplified*. Boston: Lee & Shepard, 1903. 195 pp.

———. *Studies in the Thought World*. Boston, Lee & Shepard, 1896. 269 pp.

★ 1029 ★
WOODHULL, Victoria Claflin
Spiritualist Medium and Reformer
b. Sep. 23, 1838, Homer, Ohio
d. Jun. 10, 1927, Bredon's Norton, Tewkesbury United Kingdom

Victoria Claflin Woodhull, Spiritualist medium and the first woman to run for president of the United States, grew up in poverty in rural Ohio. Her childhood coincided with the rise of Spiritualism, and her sister, Tennessee Celeste Claflin, soon recognized Victoria as a potential medium of note. The two sisters set up a traveling road show with their brother, with Victoria entertaining the audience as a trance medium. At the age of 15, Claflin married Canning Woodhull, with whom she had two children before their divorce in 1864.

In 1868 Woodhull and her sister settled in Manhattan, where they met Cornelius Vanderbilt. Woodhull's mediumship proved a comfort to Vanderbilt, who had recently lost his wife, and he generously established the sisters in business. Woodhull, Claflin and Company became a quite successful stock brokerage firm. The sisters also founded *Woodhull's and Claflin's Weekly*, a newspaper in which Victoria began to expound her radical views on women's rights and social reform, many of which had grown out of the free thinking ideas current in the larger Spiritualist movement. Along with tax and dress reforms, the more controversial notion proposed by Woodhull centered upon changes in the relationship of men and women and the family. She advocated (and to some extent practiced) free love, argued for the legalization of prostitution, and demanded the end of a double moral standard for men and women. These ideas were synthesized into a general approach to reforming society and the government which was published in a series of articles in the *New York Herald* and compiled in her first book, *Origin, Tendencies and Principles of Government* (1871).

In the spring of 1872 Woodhull organized the first and only convention of the Equal Rights Party. The convention nominated her as its candidate for president of the United States and named Frederick Douglas as her running mate. (Douglas refused to campaign.) Rather than take her campaign seriously, however, her critics turned upon her sexual life, which offered quite enough material for scandal. She retorted by publishing a special issue of the *Weekly* which broke the story of Congregational minister **Henry Ward Beecher**'s reported affair with a parishioner. The resulting scandal created a major problem for Beecher, but, for their part in breaking the story, Woodhull and her sister were arrested for sending obscene materials through the mails. They were later acquitted.

In 1877 Woodhull moved to England after, it is believed, accepting a bribe from William Vanderbilt not to testify in the court case pending on Cornelius Vanderbilt's will. In England she met John B. Martin, a wealthy banker, who in 1883 married her and introduced her to British society. In 1885 her sister married Sir Francis Cook and both settled into a rather sedate married life. Woodhull did not give up all of her radical ideas, however, and wrote four books over the next decade: *Stirpiculture, or the Scientific Propagation of the Human Race* (1888); *Garden of Eden: Allegorical Meaning Revealed* (1889); *The Human Body the Temple of God* (1890); and *Humanitarian Money: The Unsolved Riddle* (1892). In 1892 she began *The Humanitarian*, a magazine she co-edited with her daughter, Zula Maud Woodhull. The magazine appeared for nine years.

Though she occasionally returned for visits to the United States, Woodhull resided in England for the last years of her life.

Sources:

Brough, James. *The Vixens*. New York: Simon and Schuster, 1980. 288 pp.

James, Edward T., ed. *Notable American Women, 1607-1950: A Biographical Dictionary*. 3 vols. Cambridge, MA: Harvard University Press, Belknap Press, 1971.

McHenry, Robert, ed. *Liberty's Women*. Springfield, MA: G. & C. Merriam Company, 1980. 482 pp.

Woodhull, Victoria C. *Garden of Eden: Allegorical Meaning Revealed*. London: The Author, 1889. 69 pp.

_____. *Humanitarian Government*. London: The Author, 1892. 68 pp.

_____. *Origin, Tendencies and Principles of Government*. New York: Woodhull, Claflin & Company, 1871. 247 pp.

_____. *Stirpiculture, or the Scientific Propagation of the Human Race*. London: The Author, 1888. 31 pp.

_____, and Claflin, Tennessee. *The Human Body the Temple of God*. London: 1890.

★ 1030 ★
WOODRUFF, Wilford
President, Church of Jesus Christ of Latter-day Saints
b. Mar. 1, 1807, Farmingtom, Connecticut
d. Sep. 2, 1898, San Francisco, California

Wilford Woodruff, the fourth president of the Church of Jesus Christ of Latter-day Saints, was the son of Aphek and Beulah Woodruff, and as a boy he assisted on the farm and the sawmill and flour mill owned by his father. In 1827 he moved to Richland, New York, and went into farming with his brother, Azmon Woodruff. He converted to Mormonism in 1833, and in January 1834 he was appointed the teacher of a new congregation. Later that year, he met the church's founder, **Joseph Smith, Jr.**, and was persuaded to move with other church members to Missouri. At the beginning of 1835 he undertook a mission in Arkansas and Tennessee. In 1837 he married Phoebe W. Carter. A month later he left for a mission in New England.

In 1838 Woodruff was selected to become a member of the Quorum of the Twelve Apostles. Among his first duties was a mission to England for eight months, during which time he converted some 1800 people to the church. He returned to the United States, settled with the church in its new home in Nauvoo and became

the business editor for the *Times and Seasons*. He returned to England as head of the European mission in 1844 and returned to Nauvoo in 1845 as most of the church members were preparing to move to Utah. In 1846 he contracted his first plural marriages, to Mary Ann Jackson and Mary Caroline Barton. The following year he moved to Salt Lake City. In 1848 he became the head of the Eastern States Mission.

During the 1850s Woodruff farmed and carried out his duties as an apostle, which often required extensive traveling. He married five times, to Mary Meek Giles (1852), Clarissa Hardy (1852), Sarah E. Brown (1853), Emma Smith (1853), and Sarah Delight Stocking (1857). He was appointed the church's historian in 1856. In the mid-1870s he moved to St. George, Utah, and was present for the dedication of the new temple in 1877. Following the death of church president Brigham Young later that year, however, Woodruff moved back to Salt Lake City.

In 1880 Woodruff became president of the Quorum of the Twelve, just as the attacks on polygamy by the government were becoming most intense. He spent most of the decade on the move and was never arrested. He led the church after its president, **John Taylor**, died in 1887. He was sustained as the new president in 1889.

By the fall of 1890 Woodruff had come to the conclusion that only by abandoning polygamy could he prevent the total destruction of the church. Thus, in September, with the church disincorporated, its assets seized, and many of its leaders in prison, he issued the manifesto forbidding the contracting of any marriage forbidden by the law of the land. This action stopped plural marriages in the United States and took the immediate pressure off the church. The manifesto did not prevent plural marriages outside of the United States and under his successors such marriages were authorized for over a decade.

In 1891 Woodruff extended the intent of the manifesto to require those already living in plural marriages to give up any actions contrary to the law of the land. The majority of the last years of his presidency were spent establishing the church's position in the new state of Utah. He was forced to pass a rule decreeing that those who were in full-time ministerial positions, such as apostles, would have to be released from their calling before seeking political office.

Woodruff died at the age of 91 from asthma.

Sources:

Crowley, Matthias F. *Wilford Woodruff*. Salt Lake City, UT: Bookcraft, 1964. 702 pp.

Jensen, Andrew. *Latter Day Saints Biographical Encyclopedia* 4 vols. Salt Lake City, UT: Andrew Jensen History Co., 1901.

Nibley, Preston. *The Presidents of the Church*. Salt Lake City, UT: Deseret Book Company, 1960. 477 pp.

West, Emerson R. *Profiles of the Presidents*. Salt Lake City, UT: Deseret Book Company, 1973.

★ 1031 ★
WOODSWORTH, James
Minister, Methodist Church, Canada
b. 1843, Toronto, Ontario, Canada
d. Jan. 26, 1917, Winnipeg, Manitoba, Canada

James Woodsworth, a Canadian Methodist minister, was the son of Richard and Mary Ann Watson Woodsworth. His father had immigrated from England and become active in the Canadian Wesleyan Conference as a local preacher and the architect of the Richmond Street Methodist Church in Toronto. Woodsworth had some elementary schooling and studied his theology with the district chairman. He was ordained and received into full connection in 1868. Along the way he married Esther Shaver. He began his ministerial career serving several circuits (groups of churches too small to afford a full-time minister) in Ontario. While he was in Ontario, in 1874, the Wesleyans merged with two other Methodist bodies to form the Methodist Church in Canada, which in 1884 merged again to form the Methodist Church in Canada.

In 1886 the Methodists appointed Woodsworth as superintendent of home missions in Manitoba and the Northwest (then known as Rupert's Land), a territory which was opening up to settlement. Prior to his appointment Methodist work had been limited to a mission among the Indians of Manitoba and Alberta and a few random circuits. But a railroad line to Winnipeg had been completed in 1881 and in four years stretched to Vancouver. The work developed slowly, but the Methodists held their general conference in Winnipeg in 1888 and stirred considerable interest. Woodsworth also began visiting Great Britain to recruit preachers/ missionaries. Those who came to work in the new territory were informally known as "Woodsworth Boys."

During his 29 years as superintendent, Woodsworth traveled the vast territory and oversaw the development of the single conference and its 68 circuits into 650 circuits and three conferences. He also began a number of social work projects, especially in the emerging urban centers. At the end of his life, he was presented with an honorary degree from Victoria University for his accomplishments.

Sources:

Harmon, Nolan B. *The Encyclopedia of World Methodism*. 2 vols. Nashville: United Methodist Publishing House, 1974.

Wallace, W. Stewart. *The Macmillan Dictionary of Canadian Biography*. 4th ed., rev. Edited by W. A. McKay. Toronto: Macmillan of Canada, 1978.

Woodsworth, James. *Thirty Years in the Canadian North-West*. Toronto: McClelland, 1917.

★ 1032 ★
WOODWORTH-ETTER, Maria Beulah
Independent Pentecostal Evangelist
b. 1844, Lisbon, Ohio
d. 1924

Maria Beulah Woodworth-Etter, the famous early twentieth century Pentecostal evangelist, was born Maria Underwood. She was converted at the age of 13 in a revival meeting at the local Christian Church (Disciples of Christ). Although she knew the church did not ordain female ministers, she felt and acknowledged a call to the ministry. In the 1860s, however, she married P. H. Woodworth and settled down to a domestic life. The marriage was marred by the loss of five of their six children to illnesses. In 1879, in a revival meeting in the Friends church, she felt a spiritual renewal and began to preach locally. Her success led to a career in evangelism. She was at the time a member of the Church of the United Brethren, a German Methodist denomination.

Maria Woodworth's work spread. Around 1883 people in her meetings began to go into trance-like states which she began to describe as the baptism of the Holy Spirit. Healings also began to occur, prompted perhaps by the new healing movement of Albert Benjamin Simpson. Around 1884 Woodworth moved from the United Brethren to the Church of God founded by John Winebrenner. She was for the next 20 years both a successful and controversial evangelist. Her meetings, which were held all over the United States, drew large crowds and were marked by her prayers for the baptism of the Holy Ghost and the baptism of fire. Contemporary Pentecostal authors see her meetings as having all of the characteristics of Pentecostalism, except for speaking-in-tongues. She described these years in two books, *Life and Experience of Maria B. Woodworth* (1885) and *The Life, Work, and Experience of Maria Beulah Woodworth* (1894).

In 1891 Woodworth charged her husband with adultery and divorced him. In 1902 she married Samuel Etter and added his name to her own.

By 1904 the controversy surrounding Woodworth-Etter had become so strong that the Church of God dismissed her and revoked her ministerial credentials, claiming that she was uncooperative and that some were dissatisfied with her ministry. She entered a period of lessened activity, during which time she was began to align herself with the emerging Pentecostal movement. As early as 1904, in her campaign in St. Louis, people began to speak-in-tongues at her evangelistic services. She stayed aloof from the larger Pentecostal movement for several years because of false teachings that some were voicing. By 1912, however, she had become very active as a Pentecostal healing evangelist and was soon accepted by the movement.

Among Woodworth-Etter's first campaigns as a Pentecostal was the six-month long revival conducted with F. F. Bosworth which thousands attended in Dallas in 1912. She also spoke at the equally important meeting in 1913 in Pasadena, California, at which a number of people later to assume leadership positions in the movement were present. She moved on from Pasadena to Chicago. She continued preaching well into her late 70s. She finished her work with two final books: *Spirit-filled Sermons* (1921) and *Marvels and Miracles* (1922). Her books were translated into a number of languages and accounted for much of the rapid spread of the Pentecostal movement in the early twentieth century.

Sources:

Burgess, Stanley M., Gary B. McGee, and Patrick H. Alexander, eds. *Dictionary of Pentecostal and Charismatic Movements*. Grand Rapids, MI: Regency Reference Library, Zondervan Publishing House, 1988. 914 pp.

Warner, Wayne B. *The Woman Evangelist, The Life and Times of Maria B. Woodworth-Etter*. Metuchen, NJ: Scarecrow Press, 1986.

Woodworth-Etter, Maria Beulah. *Life and Experience of Maria B. Woodworth*. Dayton, OH: The Author, 1885.

_____. *The Life, Work, and Experiences of Maria Beulah Woodworth*. St. Louis, MO: The Author, 1894.

_____. *Marvels and Miracles*. Indianapolis, IN: The Author, 1922.

_____. *Signs and Wonders God Wrought in the Ministry for Forty Years*. Indianapolis, IN: The Author, 1916. 584 pp.

_____. *Spirit-filled Sermons*. Indianapolis, IN: The Author, 1921.

★ 1033 ★
WORCESTER, Elwood
Founder, Emmanuel Movement
b. May 16, 1862, Massillon, Ohio
d. Jul. 19, 1940, Kennebunkport, Maine

Elwood Worcester, a priest in the Episcopal Church best known as the founder of the Emmanuel Movement, was the son of David Freeman and Frances Gold Worcester. On his father's side, most of the family were associated with the General Church of the New Jerusalem and the mysticism of Emanuel Swedenborg, but his mother and her family were Episcopalians, and he was raised in his mother's church. His family moved to New York during Worcester's childhood and he grew up there. He had a visionary experience when he was 16 which he interpreted as a call into the ministry.

Worcester attended Columbia College from which he graduated at the head of his class in 1886. He then became the first student at General Theological Seminary given two years credit for his private study and mastery of the curriculum. He graduated from General in 1887. Worcester traveled to Europe and enrolled at the University of Leipzig, where, along with his theological work, he studied with pioneer psychologists Wilhelm Wundt and Gustav Theodor Fechner. Deeply aware of a relationship (however unclear) between psychology and religion, he finished his doctorate in 1889, and returned to the United States. He was ordained a deacon in 1890 and became a priest the next year. His doctoral dissertation, *The Religious Opinions of John Locke* (1889) became the first of his many books.

Worcester's first post was as Sunday school superintendent of St. Ann's Episcopal Church in Brooklyn, but in 1890 became a professor at Lehigh University. While there, in 1894, he married Blanche S. Rulison. After several years teaching, he decided that the parish offered him a broader realm of ministry and in 1896 he became pastor of St. Stephen's Church in Philadelphia. At St. Stephen's he authored one book which centered upon his then current interest in German biblical criticism, *The Book of Genesis in the Light of Modern Knowledge* (1904). In 1904 he moved to Boston as rector of the Emmanuel Church where, as in Philadelphia, he built a diversified program of pastoral and social services.

Boston was also the center from which psychotherapy was to spread in America. Worcester became associated with a group of pioneer psychotherapists including Joseph H. Pratt, Richard C. Cabot, James J. Putnam, and Isador H. Coriat, with whom he began to create healing programs which combined physical, psychological, and medical treatment. Pratt, with whom Worcester first worked, is generally considered the father of group psychotherapy.

The initial stages of the Emmanuel work began in 1905 with groups of tubercular patients who met at the parish under Pratt's supervision. The reflections on the early work were described in a book, *Religion and Medicine: The Moral Control of Mental Disorders* (1908), which Worcester wrote with his assistant pastor, Samuel McComb, and Coriat. It became both immensely popular (with eight printings in the first six months) and controversial. Hoping to have the work in the new psycho-religious therapeutics taken seriously, Worcester carefully distinguished it from Christian Science and other forms of religious healing. The Emmanuel Movement spread across the church and the country over the next decade and eventually gave birth to the modern discipline of pastoral counseling as well as inspiring the several spiritual healing organizations within the Episcopal Church—the Order of the Nazarene, the Order of St. Luke the Physician, and (in England) the Order of St. Rafael. Through the successes of the Emmanuel Movement, Worcester is credited with pioneering the Christian application of psychotherapy to nervous disorders.

During the next 20 years, Worcester pastored the church, headed the ever growing movement, and authored a number of books. His books included: *The Living Word* (1908); *The Christian Religion as a Healing Power* (with McComb, 1909), the mature statement of the Emmanuel perspective; *Religion and Life* (1914); *The Issues of Life* (1915); and *The Allies of Religion* (1929). In 1929 he retired from his 25 year pastorate and opened an office nearby to receive patients. He continued to write during these very active retirement years: *Body, Mind and Spirit* (with McComb, 1931); his autobiography, *Life's Adventure* (1932); *Studies in the Birth of the Lord* (1933) and *Making Life Better* (1933).

Sources:

Dictionary of American Biography. 20 vols. and 7 supps. New York: Charles Scribner's Sons, 1928-1936, 1944-1981.
Gifford, Sanford. *The Emmanuel Movement, Medical Psychotherapy and the Battle Over Lay Treatment, 1906-1912*. Unpublished manuscript in the American Religions Collection, University of California, Santa Barbara, California. 1971. 102 pp.
Worcester, Elwood. *The Allies of Religion*. Boston, MA: Marshall Jones and Company, 1929. 322 pp.
_____. *The Issues of Life*. New York: Moffat, Yard and Company, 1915. 237 pp.
_____. *Life's Adventure*. New York: Charles Scribner's Sons, 1932. 362 pp.
_____. *Making Life Better*. New York: Charles Scribner's Sons, 1933. 244 pp.
_____. *Religion and Life*. New York: Harper, 1914. 263 pp.
_____. *The Christian Religion as a Healing Power*. New York: Moffat, Yard and Company, 1909. 180 pp.
_____, and Samuel McComb. *Body, Mind and Spirit*. Boston, MA: Marshall Jones Company, 1931. 367 pp.
_____, Samuel McComb, and Isador Coriat. *Religion and Medicine, The Moral Control of Nervous Disorders*. New York: Moffat, Yard and Company, 1908. 427 pp.

★ 1034 ★
WORRELL, Clarendon Lamb
Primate, Anglican Church of Canada
b. Jul. 20, 1854, Smiths Falls, Ontario, Canada
d. Aug. 10, 1934, Halifax, Nova Scotia, Canada

Clarendon Lamb Worrell, the fifth primate of the Anglican Church of Canada, was born in what is now Ontario. He attended Trinity University in Toronto, which awarded him a B.A. in 1873 and an M.A in 1884. That year he was ordained a priest in the Church of England. In 1891 he became a professor of English literature at the Royal Military College in Kingston, Ontario, a position he held until 1904 when he was elected bishop of Nova Scotia in the Anglican Church of Canada. A short time before his moving to Halifax, the cathedral church had been destroyed by fire, and among his first tasks was to oversee the construction of a new All Saints Cathedral. It was completed in 1908 and in 1910 he presided over the celebration of the bicentennial of continuous Anglican presence in Nova Scotia. In 1907 he became treasurer of the Missionary Society of the Canadian Church, a position he held for the next 20 years.

In 1912 the Province of Canada, which included the eastern half of the country, was divided with six dioceses set off as the new Province of Ontario. The former metropolitan of the Province of Canada became the leader of the new province, and no successor as metropolitan of the Province of Canada was immediately chosen, there being some disruption caused by the separation. In 1915 Worrell was named to that position, which carried with it the title of archbishop. He assumed his new position just as the church as a whole was considering a new prayer book. He effectively used the issue of its adoption of a new scripture as a means not only to assert the prerogatives of the provinces in the overall organization of the church, but as a motivating force in reorganizing his own province and establishing a permanent provincial council.

In 1931, following the resignation of Archbishop **Samuel P. Matheson**, Worrell became primate of the Anglican Church of Canada. He was to hold the office for only the three years prior to his death in 1934. However, in 1932 a new plan for electing the primate was approved which allowed the primate to be selected from any of the church's bishops, not the metropolitans (head of the church's provinces).

Sources:

Carrington, Philip. *The Anglican Church of Canada*. Toronto: Collin's, 1963. 230 pp.
Wallace, W. Stewart. *The Macmillan Dictionary of Canadian Biography*. 4th ed., rev. Edited by W. A. McKay. Toronto: Macmillan of Canada, 1978.

★ 1035 ★
WOVOKA
Medicine Man, Paiute Indians, Originator of the Ghost Dance
b. 1856?, Mason Valley, Nevada
d. Sep. 20, 1932, Schurz, Nevada

Wovoka (The Cutter) was also known as Kwohitsauq (Big Rumbling Belly) and Jack Wilson. A Paiute medicine man, dreamer, and prophet, he was born ca. 1856 in a small Paiute village situated on the Walker River in Mason Valley, Nevada. He was the only son of Tavibo, a capita (from the Spanish word *capitan*) of the Pine Grove band of Paiutes. Like his father, Wovoka was destined to become a dreamer of considerable influence among Indians of many nations. Within the religious systems of many Indian groups, a special place is accorded to those who can enter and successfully return from the world of dreams. Wovoka was destined to become such a man, born into religious ferment marked by the disintegration of Indian societies of the late nineteenth century and the zeal of Mormons and American Christians, who sought to establish their convictions among uncivilized Whites and "pagan" Indian nations of far western America.

Very little is known of Wovoka's early life. No mention is made in historical accounts of his mother or his siblings. His early religious training must be surmised from accounts of traditional Paiute lifestyles. Because he was the son of a tribal leader, Wovoka probably was groomed by his father at an early age to take on the cultural responsibilities of leader. Because he was the son of a successful dreamer, Wovoka's dreams as a boy were treated with importance, setting the stage for more important dreams he would acquire as a man. Dreams were not seen as flights of psychological fancy by the Paiute, but were rather religious artifacts whose power could be shared by all who believed in the power of the dreamer. Wovoka's religious training included encouragement and analysis of his dreams, learning the hand manipulations of the Paiute healers, exposure to a number of native revivalist traditions, and sustained contact with both Christian and Mormon influences. Wovoka's dreams led to the shape and doctrines of the Ghost Dance, which drew on many sources and appealed to a wide spectrum of Indian groups with increasingly divergent religious ideas. The Ghost Dance religion centered on a group dance for communicating with the spirits of the tribe's ancestors with the purpose of eventually liberating the Indian people from the inexorable encroachment of the Whites.

While outsiders labeled Wovoka's revival the Ghost Dance, a more accurate designation is Spirit Dance. Ghost in English implies the individual disembodied spirit of a man, while Spirit implies a condition that can be shared by many. As early as 1869, Tavibo, Wovoka's father, had visions of a reversal of white and Indian fortunes due to divine intervention. Tavibo died in 1870 and the new religion faded with his memory. Wovoka was 14 at the time of his father's death and went to work and live at the Wilson brother's ranch in Pine Grove, Nevada. When he was in his twenties, Wovoka began to have visions and dreams similar to those of his father, which usually came after a serious illness during which he would visit heaven. The climax of the visions occurred after a total solar eclipse seen in Nevada on January 1, 1889. Wovoka apparently received much of the doctrine, songs, and dances of his religious movement during this visionary episode, which lasted three days and was prefaced by a bout with a high fever. Within a year, the dance had spread in all directions and was reported from Oklahoma to North Dakota on the reservations of the newly subjugated plains tribes. Federal reaction was swift and resulted in the assassination of **Sitting Bull** and many of his followers in early December of 1890 and the Wounded Knee massacre two weeks later.

In the aftermath of the Wounded Knee disaster, Wovoka was blamed and disgraced for his support of the Ghost Dance and its accoutrements, especially the ceremonial Ghost Shirts, which had been previously regarded as bullet proof. In an 1892 interview with James Mooney, the United States Bureau of American Ethnology agent hired to investigate the doctrine, Wovoka disclaimed responsibility for the Ghost Shirt. Wovoka had many Indian followers who had been Mormon, and the church took a special interest in Indian souls. Mormon ritual includes the use of sacred garments worn for protection against evil forces, and some biographers of Wovoka have suggested the connection with the wearing of the Ghost shirt. After the Wounded Knee incident, Wovoka and his Ghost Dance faded from national view, and visitors to his humble house dwindled to a handful. The Ghost Dance continued in isolated Indian enclaves in California, Nevada, Oregon, Washington, and some Rocky Mountain reservations. Wovoka continued to be addressed as "Our Father" among the Walker River Paiutes, but he limited his role to healer and leader, rather than visionary and prophet. Wovoka died on September 20, 1932, and was buried as Jack Wilson in the Indian cemetery of Schurz, Nevada.

Sources:

Bailey, Paul. *Wovoka: The Indian Messiah.* Los Angeles: Westernlore Press, 1957.
Mooney, James. *The Ghost Dance Religion and the Sioux Outbreak of 1890.* Part II, Fourteenth Annual Report of the Bureau of American Ethnology. Washington, D.C.: Smithsonian Institute Press, 1896.

—*Johnny Flynn*

★ 1036 ★
WRIGHT, John Joseph
Cardinal, Roman Catholic Church
b. Jul. 18, 1909, Boston, Massachusetts
d. Aug. 10, 1979, Cambridge, Massachusetts

John Joseph Wright, a cardinal in the Roman Catholic Church, was the son of John Joseph and Harriet L. Cokely Wright. He grew up in Boston and attended Boston College (A.B., 1931) and St. John's Seminary, located in suburban Boston. He finished his studies for the priesthood at the Gregorian University in Rome, where he was ordained in 1936. He remained in Europe after his ordination, serving parishes in France, Scotland, and England, as well as continuing his education in Rome. In 1939 he assumed duties at St. John's Seminary in Brighton, Massachusetts, where he remained until 1943, when he became secretary to Cardinal **William Henry O'Connell** and his successor, Cardinal **Richard Cushing**. In 1946, while serving as Cushing's secretary, Wright was made a papal chamberlain with the title of monsignor.

Wright was consecrated bishop in 1947 and named the titular bishop of Aegea and auxiliary bishop of Boston. Three years later he was named the first bishop of the newly created diocese of Worcester, Massachusetts. In 1958 he became bishop of Pittsburgh. During his years at Pittsburgh, Wright became known as a scholar and served on the Theological Commission for the Second Vatican Council. He championed ecumenism. He also developed a reputation as a liberal in social policy, especially as it related to race relations. He supported the civil rights movement in the 1960s and implemented policies that led to increased enrollment of black children in the diocese's schools. He also placed his opinion behind ending American involvement in the war in Vietnam.

In 1969 Wright was elevated to the cardinate and transferred to Rome to become prefect of the Congregation of the Clergy, one of the main departments of the Curia, the international administrative offices of the Roman Catholic Church. He held the highest position of any American in the church. During his years at Rome his conservative opinions on theology and church administration (as opposed to his liberal social positions) came to the fore. Earlier he had strongly opposed women's ordination and a married priesthood. His main assignment in Rome was to stop the defections of priests from their ranks, a task at which he did not enjoy complete success.

Wright stayed in Rome less than a decade. He developed polymyositis, which confined him to a wheelchair in 1978. He died the following year. Avocationally, Wright became well-known for his interest in Joan of Arc, about whom he had compiled an extensive collection of literature and art. He was also a charter member of the Pittsburgh Bibliophiles.

Sources:

Contemporary Authors. Detroit, MI: Gale Research Inc.
Delaney, John J. *Dictionary of American Catholic Biography.* Garden City, NY: Doubleday & Company, 1988. 621 pp.

Wright, John Joseph. *The Christian and the Law.* Notre Dame, IN: Fides Publishers, 1962. 98 pp.
———. *National Patriotism in Papal Teachings.* Newman, 1942.

★1037★
WRIGHT JR., Richard Robert
Bishop, African Methodist Episcopal Church
b. Apr. 16, 1878, Cuthbert, Georgia
d. Dec. 12, 1967, Philadelphia, Pennsylvania

Richard Robert Wright, Jr., one of the outstanding bishops of the African Methodist Episcopal Church, was the son of Major Richard Robert and Lydia Elizabeth Howard Wright. Converted while still in his youth in 1891, he joined the Bethel African Methodist Episcopal Church in Augusta, Georgia. While remaining active in his congregation, and beginning work toward a ministerial career, he was also able to secure a thorough education, beginning at Haines Institute in Augusta and then Georgia State College, from which he graduated in 1898. That same year he was licensed to exhort by the church. He went for his seminary work at the University of Chicago, from which he received a B.D. in 1901. He spent two years lecturing in Hebrew and Greek at Payne Theological Seminary before returning for his master's degree from Chicago, which he received in 1904. During this time he was also ordained deacon (1900) and elder (1901) in the African Methodist Episcopal Church.

Wright studied in Germany at the University of Berlin (1903-1904) and the University of Leipzig (1904) and returned to the states to receive his Ph.D. in sociology from the University of Pennsylvania in 1911. In 1909, while finishing his doctoral work, he married Charlotte Crogman, the daughter of the president of Clark University.

Instead of pursuing a career in university teaching, Wright became editor of the *Christian Recorder*, the periodical of the African Methodist Episcopal Church, in 1909. He held the job until he was elected bishop in 1936. He also served as the editor of the church's publishing house (1909-1912 and 1916-1920) and as president of Wilberforce University (1932-1936).

During his years as editor and later as bishop, Wright authored a number of books, including *The Centennial Encyclopedia of the African Methodist Episcopal Church* (1916); the *Negro in Pennsylvania*; *Outline of the Teaching of Jesus*; *Handbook of the African Methodist Episcopal Church Church*; and *The Bishops of the African Methodist Episcopal Church* (1963). He is believed to have been the most prolific author of all of the African Methodist Episcopal Church bishops.

During his school days, Wright also entered the banking business, establishing the Eighth Ward Building and Loan Association as early as 1906. In 1920 he became cofounder of the Citizens and Southern Banking Company, and two years later founded the Citizens and Southern Building and Loan Association, the first of several extensive enterprises he headed. He used some of the money he made to free the church's book concern from a load of debt.

Most of Wright's financial empire was left behind in 1936 when he was elected bishop of the African Methodist Episcopal Church, the first and only person with a Ph.D. to be so honored. He spent his first four years as bishop of South Africa and while there led in the formation of the R. R. Wright, Jr. School of Religion, the Crogman Community Clinic, and some 50 churches and schools. He returned to America as World War II was starting, and was assigned to the 13th District (covering Tennessee and Kentucky). He served again as president of Wilberforce University (1941-1942) and as head of the church's committee on chaplains for the duration of the war. In 1946 he was appointed bishop of New York, New Jersey, New England, and Bermuda.

In 1960 Wright asked the church's general conference to make him the historiographer for the church, a position he retained for the rest of his life. During his years as bishop, he represented the church in numerous capacities in both ecumenical and racial betterment organizations. He served as executive secretary of the Fraternal Council of Negro Churches and president of the National Goodwill Association. The outstanding role Wright played in the betterment of his church and the social standing of Blacks in America can only be partially surmised from an account of his formal positions and accomplishments.

Sources:
Gregg, Howard D. *History of the A.M.E. Church.* Nashville, TN: African Methodist Episcopal Church, 1980. 524 pp.
Harmon, Nolan B. *The Encyclopedia of World Methodism.* 2 vols. Nashville: United Methodist Publishing House, 1974.
Who's Who in the Methodist Church. Nashville, TN: Abingdon Press, 1966.
Wright, Richard Robert, Jr. *The Bishops of the African Methodist Episcopal Church.* Nashville, TN: A.M.E. Sunday School Union, 1963.
———. *Eighty-seven Years Behind the Black Curtain.* Nashville, TN: A.M.E. Sunday School Union, 1965.
———, and John Russell Hawkins, eds. *Centennial Encyclopedia of the African Methodist Episcopal Church.* 2d ed. Book Concern of the Methodist Episcopal Church, 1948.

★1038★
YOGANANDA, Swami Paramahansa
Founder, Self-Realization Fellowship
b. Jan. 5, 1893, Gorakhpur India
d. Mar. 7, 1952, Los Angeles, California

Swami Paramahansa Yogananda, founder of the Self-Realization Fellowship (SRF), was born Mukunda Lal Ghosh to an affluent Bengali family. His father, a railroad executive, had been initiated into the practice of kriya yoga by Lahiri Mahasaya. After high school, Mukunda went to Benares, where he took up life as a hermit. While in the holy city, he met and accepted as his guru Sri Yukteswar Giri, a teacher who was, like his father, a disciple of Mahasaya.

Feeling that it would help Mukunda in his future work, Yukteswar instructed him to enter college. He graduated in 1914. During the same period the young student also took the vows of a *sannyasin* (one who follows the renounced life), and was given the monastic name Yogananda, meaning the bliss (*ananda*) of yoga. In 1919 he started a school for boys at which meditation and yoga were taught in addition to regular high school subjects.

Yogananda had long desired to bring the message of yoga to the West, and Yukteswar encouraged him to pursue this idea. A door was opened for his mission in 1920 when Yogananda received an invitation to speak at the International Congress of Religious Liberals in Boston. After the meeting he remained in the United States, teaching and lecturing. In 1925 he established his headquarters at Mount Washington in Los Angeles, and in 1935 he incorporated what had become an international society as the Self-Realization Fellowship. Like many other Hindu teachers, Yogananda concerned himself with the reconciliation of religions—particularly the accommodation of Christianity to the practice of yoga. He died in 1952.

In common with many Indian yoga systems, kriya yoga understands the key to liberation as being the stimulation and eventual "awakening" of the normally dormant kundalini energy, which is said to "sleep" at the base of the spine. Once aroused, the kundalini is drawn up a subtle energy channel corresponding with the spine and into the spiritual center in the crown of the head. The core of kriya yoga (the technique that is imparted when one is formally initiated into kriya yoga) is a meditation in which the subtle energies are imaginatively moved up and down the spine, a process that "prepares the way," so to speak, for the kundalini.

After the Vedanta Society swamis, Yogananda was the last significant Hindu spiritual teacher to establish himself in the United States before immigration barriers were raised in 1924. Beyond the Self-Realization Fellowship, Yogananda's message reached Americans through some of his students who established their own organizations, such as **Donald Walters** and **Roy Eugene Davis**. He also exerted a widespread influence through his *Autobiography of a Yogi* (1946), a book that has inspired more than one young American to travel to India in search of spiritual enlightenment, and through the correspondence lessons he wrote, which are still being used by the organization he created.

Sources:

Yogananda, Swami Paramahansa. *Autobiography of a Yogi*. 11th ed. Los Angeles: Self-Realization Fellowship, 1971. 516 pp.

———. *The Divine Romance*. Los Angeles: Self-Realization Fellowship, 1986. 468 pp.

———. *Metaphysical Meditations*. Los Angeles: Self-Realization Fellowship, 1960. 115 pp.

———. *The Science of Religion*. Los Angeles: Yogoda Sat-Sanga Society of America, 1928. 108 pp.

———. *Songs of the Soul*. Los Angeles: Yogoda and Sat-Sanga, 1926. 111 pp.

———. *Whispers from Eternity*. Los Angeles: Self-Realization Publishing House, 1944. 279 pp.

—*James R. Lewis*

★ 1039 ★
Ma YOGASHAKTI SARASWATI
Founder, Ma Yogashakti International Mission
b. Apr. 6, 1929, Banaras India

Her Holiness Ma Yogashakti Saraswati, founder of the Ma Yogashakti International Mission, is one of the few Indian female gurus to attract a significant American following. She was born into an aristocratic and spiritually inclined family in one of India's holiest cities. She not only married and had four children, but attended college and earned an M.A. degree in political science. During her college years, she was active in the Theosophical Society, eventually becoming a life-member of the Inner Circle. She founded and was president of the Annie Besant Lodge in Chapra. A champion of women's rights, she founded a women's college in Chapra in 1955. She was also involved in other educational institutions, and was actively interested in politics and social reform.

In the late 1950s, Saraswati experienced a divine calling, which only made her pursue spirituality more fervently, and began teaching yoga in 1959. In the early 1960s she took *sannyas*, vows of the renounced life, recalling being inspired when her father took *sannyas*. She became a *paramadesa*, a sannyasin who takes up the orange robes without being initiated by another sannyasin. Since that time she has founded a number of yoga ashrams. In 1969 she was crowned Sant Shakti Shiromani at the Ujjain Kumbha Mela, the first woman ever to receive this honor. In 1974 she was crowned and titled Maha Manaleshwar at the Kumbha Mela in Hardwar.

Saraswati first came to North America in 1968 at the invitation of a yoga center in New York. During this visit she initiated Gail Teichmann (Ma Vairagya Shakti) who followed Yogashakti back to India and became her right hand at the children's school she had established in Maharashtra. Vairagya Shakti returned to the United States to visit her parents in 1970 and founded a Yogashakti Mission in Deerfield Beach, Florida. Although she passed away in 1971, Vairagya's mother, Jean Teichmann (Madhu Shakti), kept the center open for the next 18 years. The mission also has an ashram in South Ozone Park, New York.

Ma Yogashakti teaches a balanced approach to all yogas. Full moon *Purnima* (devotional services) are held monthly. Her teachings are put forward in a number of her books, such as *Chhandogya Upanishad*; *Prayers and Poems from Mother's Heart*

(1976); *Adhyatma Sandesh*; and *The Invisible Seven Lotuses*. The mission also publishes a newsletter, the *Yogashakti Mission Newsletter*.

Sources:

"Ma Yogashakti: Yoga Guru Esteemed East and West." *Hinduism Today* 10, 5 (May 1988): 1, 5.

Saraswati, Ma Yogashakti. *Hanuman Chalisa*. South Ozone Park, NY: Ma Yoga Shakti International Mission, 1986. 58 pp.

———. *Prayers and Poems from Mother's Heart*. Melbourne, FL: Yogashakti Mission, 1976. 73 pp.

———. *Simplified Yogasanas and Pranayams*. N.p., n.d. 44 pp.

———. *Yoga Sadhana*. Bombay, India: Wilco Publishing House, 1972. 128 pp.

———. *Yoga Syzygy*. S. Ozone Park, NY: The Author, 1984. 171 pp.

———. *Yoog Vashishtha*. 2 vols. Gondia, India: Yogashakti Mission, [1970].

★ 1040 ★
ZELL, Morning Glory
Priestess, Church of All Worlds
b. May 27, 1948, Long Beach, California

Morning Glory Zell, born Diana Moore, is a major spokesperson for the Neo-Pagan Community and a priestess in the Church of All Worlds. As a youth she attended both the Methodist church and the Pentecostal church, but she soon became disenchanted with them. Her maturing feminist perceptions led her to reject the subjugated status of women in the Christian tradition and to seek a more personally satisfying faith during her early teens. She found the same sexism in Zen Buddhism and Vedanta, although the Vedanta Society did introduce her to the worship of the Goddess. In her junior year in high school, she found a copy of Sybil Leek's *Diary of a Witch* and had a revelation that this was the missing link in her life, the "path of the heart" that incorporated all the missing elements she had been searching for in a religion. Following a vision quest in 1968, she changed her name in accordance with the vision and began to pursue a path of Celtic Shamanism. She became a devotee of that aspect of the Goddess known as Potnai Theron: "Our Lady of the Beasts." In 1969 she married a man she met on the way to join a commune in Oregon. They were divorced in 1973.

In 1973 Morning Glory met Timothy Zell (now known as **Otter Zell**), founder of the Church of All Worlds. The following year she and Zell were married and she was ordained a priestess of the church. She became co-editor of the *Green Egg*, one of the most important early Neo-Pagan magazines, and continued in that post until the Zells moved from St. Louis to eventually settle in Ukiah, California. They relinquished their active leadership role in the church, and the magazine soon ceased publication. In California, the Zells turned their attention to researching some issues which their faith had presented to them.

In 1977 Morning Glory founded the Ecosophical Research Association to research and explore history, mythology, and science. This organization fostered the most famous activity for which the Zells are known, the production of a "unicorn" by surgical adjustment of the horns of baby goats. The first of these, Lancelot, has toured extensively with the Ringling Bros. and Barnum & Bailey Circus.

In the 1980s Morning Glory worked on a variety of projects for the association, including the development of a collection of goddess sculptures and prints. In 1988 the *Green Egg* was revived and she once again became coeditor.

Sources:

Guiley, Rosemary E. *Encyclopedia of Witchcraft & Witches*. New York: Facts on File, 1989. 400 pp.

★ 1041 ★
ZELL, Otter
Founder, Church of All Worlds
b. Nov. 30, 1942, St. Louis, Missouri

Otter Zell, born Timothy Zell, is a major Neo-Pagan spokesperson and founder of the Church of All Worlds. He was born in St. Louis, Missouri, during World War II, but grew up in Clark Summit, Pennsylvania, where his parents moved after the war. In the early 1960s he attended Westminster College Fulton, Missouri, where he met Richard Lance Christie, the leader of a small group of students interested in the psychic. He also read Robert Heinlein's novel, *Stranger in a Strange Land* (1961). The book, which describes a "Church of All Worlds," became the inspiration for Zell and Christie to form a new church somewhat based on the novel's ideas. The new church was also centered upon Zell's understanding of the purpose of religion: to contact the life flow of the universe and the oneness of existence.

Zell married for the first time in 1963. Following his graduation, Zell returned to St. Louis, where in 1967 he formally incorporated the Church of All Worlds. He also launched the *Green Egg*, the church's magazine, which soon became one of the most influential periodicals in the emerging Neo-Pagan movement. Among Zell's early contribution to the movement was the name "Neo-Paganism," which he coined. He also entered, but did not complete, the doctorate program in clinical psychology at Washington University. His marriage ended in 1971.

In 1970 Zell formulated what has become known as the Gaia Hypothesis, the idea that the earth is but a single vast living organism (which he equates with the ancient concept of Mother Earth). He presented this concept in 1973 to the Gnosticon festival in Minneapolis in a paper entitled, "Theagenesis: The Birth of the Goddess." In more recent years the idea has been championed by James Lovelock and become of central importance in the New Age Movement. At that same conference he met Diana Moore. She moved to St. Louis, and the following year they were wed. Zell ordained her as high priestess for the church. Moore had already, at the age of 19, moved to change her name. She quickly became known in the Pagan world as **Morning Glory Zell**.

In 1976 Zell left St. Louis and turned the administration of the church and magazine over to other church leaders. They traveled the country for some months. That fall, in Oregon, Zell had a significant mystical experience which led him to drop his self-identification as a psychologist and emerge as a priest of Gaea (alternate spelling for Gaia, Mother Earth). They settled at Coeden Brith, a Neo-Pagan sanctuary in Mendicino County, California, owned by **Alison Harlow**, a prominent bay area pagan. They kept a low profile for eight years during which time they worked upon the development of a unicorn, created by surgically moving the horn roots of an infant goat. In 1979, as the first unicorn was growing to maturity, Zell changed his name to Otter G'Zell (he later dropped the "G").

In 1985 the Zells moved to Ukiah, California, and soon afterward reactivated the Church of All Worlds, which had become largely a paper organization. They began to make public appearances again and in 1988 issued the first copies of a new series of the *Green Egg*. The church quickly found renewed support, and the Zells resumed their leadership role in the Neo-Pagan community.

Sources:

Guiley, Rosemary E. *Encyclopedia of Witchcraft & Witches*. New York: Facts on File, 1989. 400 pp.
Heinlein, Robert. Stranger in a Strange Land. New York: Putnam, 1961.

★ 1042 ★
ZIELINSKI, Thaddeus F.
Prime Bishop, Polish National Catholic Church
b. Dec. 26, 1904, Wilkes Barre, Pennsylvania

Thaddeus F. Zielinski, a prime bishop of the Polish National Catholic Church (PNCC), is the son of Francis Zielinski, a layman who helped to organize the church's original parish in Wilkes Barre, Pennsylvania. He graduated from Savonarola Theological Seminary, Scranton, Pennsylvania, and was ordained by Bishop **Francis Hodur**, the church's founder, in 1927. After a brief period as administrator of Holy Trinity PNCC, in 1928 he began a seven year pastorate at St. John the Baptist PNCC at Frickville, Pennsylvania. In 1935 he began a lengthy pastorate at St. Adalbert's PNCC in Dickson City, Pennsylvania.

Once at Dickson City, Zielinski was called upon to serve a number of different functions for the general church. In 1936 he began to lecture on liturgy at Savonarola Theological Seminary. Over his career he would emerge as the major leader in the transition from Polish to English language worship in the church. The next year he finished work on the new bilingual (Polish and English) liturgy book, *The Church Ritual of the P.N.C.C.*. He later collaborated on the English Mass Book for the church and issued several volumes of Polish hymns in English translation. Over the years he served on a number of church committees including its Theological Commission and the Youth Activities Committee. In 1946 he was called to sit upon the Intercommunion Commission which hammered out an intercommunion agreement with the Episcopal Church. In 1951, in the wake of the commission's work, Zielinski authored a booklet surveying *The Polish National Catholic Church*.

In 1954 Zielinski was elected a bishop by the ninth general synod of the church. He was assigned as bishop of the Buffalo-Pittsburgh Diocese. Among his accomplishments as bishop was the introduction of the PNCC's first English-language mass held in the Buffalo Cathedral in 1961. In 1967 at the twelfth synod, Zielinski was named the successor to Prime Bishop Leon Grochowski, then 81 years old. Grochowski died two years later and Zielinski became the first American-born prime bishop of the PNCC. His position was confirmed at the next general synod. As prime bishop he continued the liturgical reform picking up much inspiration from the Roman Catholic Church reforms initiated at Vatican II. Zielinski retired in 1978 and was succeeded in office by Bishop Francis C. Rowinksi.

Sources:

Kubiak, Hieronim. "The Polish National Catholic Church in the United States of America in the 1970s." *PNCC Studies* (1980): 24-36.
Wlodarski, Stephen. *The Origin and Growth of the Polish National Catholic Church*. Scranton, PA: Polish National Catholic Church, 1974. 239 pp.
Zielinski, Thaddeus F. *The Polish National Catholic Church*. [Scranton, PA: Polish National Catholic Church, 1951]. 68 pp.

★ 1043 ★
ZIMMERMAN, Thomas Fletcher
General Superintendent, Assemblies of God
b. Mar. 26, 1912, Indianapolis, Indiana
d. Jan. 2, 1991, Springfield, Missouri

Thomas Fletcher Zimmerman, the general superintendent of the Assemblies of God, was the son of Carrie D. Kenagy and Thomas F. Zimmerman, both active laypeople in the Methodist Protestant Church. They became affiliated with the Pentecostal church in Indianapolis after Carrie was healed by the prayers of some members. Zimmerman grew up in what was then an independent congregation and as a teenager became a Sunday school leader and then assistant pastor. He attended Indiana University for two years following his graduation from high school, but dropped out to work after his father died. In 1933 he married Elizabeth Price, the daughter of the church's pastor.

In 1934 he became the pastor of a small church in Harrodsburg, Indiana, and the following year moved to South Bend, Indiana. While at South Bend he was ordained as a minister in the Assemblies of God. He stayed in South Bend for four years and then moved to Granite City, Illinois (1939-1942), and Springfield, Missouri (1943-1947). Beginning in 1946 he was the narrator of a weekly radio show, "Sermons in Song." From 1941 to 1943 he served as the district officer for Illinois, and then while pastoring in Springfield as district officer for Southern Missouri. He completed his time in the pastorate in Cleveland, Ohio (1951-1952).

In 1952 Zimmerman became the assistant general superintendent of the Assemblies of God and began the lengthy period of his national and international leadership. In 1959 he became the new general superintendent and held that post for 26 years, the longest of any person to date. His years of leadership were a period of impressive growth for the Assemblies, and Zimmerman also worked to integrate the Assemblies into the larger evangelical Christian community. In 1957 Zimmerman began a lengthy tenure on the executive board of the National Association of Evangelicals and was the first Pentecostal elected president of the association. He was on the executive committee for the Lausanne Committee for World Evangelism. He was the chairman of the executive committee for the massive interdenominational evangelistic campaign, Key 73, and was on the executive committee for the National Religious Broadcasters. He chaired the planning committee for the 1981 American Festival of Evangelism.

Within the larger Pentecostal community, he was the first vice-chairman of the Pentecostal Fellowship of North America. He chaired the World Pentecostal Conferences of 1970, 1973, 1976, 1979, 1982, and 1985. Along with his duties as general superintendent, he also was on the board of directors of Central Bible College and Evangel College, and president of the Assemblies of God Theological Seminary. Zimmerman retired in 1985 and lived in Springfield, Missouri until his death in 1991.

Sources:

Blumhofer, Edith L. "Thomas F. Zimmerman: A Look at the Indiana Roots." *Assemblies of God Heritage* 10, 4 (Winter 1990-91): 3-5, 21-22.

Burgess, Stanley M., Gary B. McGee, and Patrick H. Alexander, eds. *Dictionary of Pentecostal and Charismatic Movements*. Grand Rapids, MI: Regency Reference Library, Zondervan Publishing House, 1988. 914 pp.

★1044★
ZOOK, John Roel
Evangelist, Brethren in Christ Church
b. Nov. 6, 1857, Whiteside County, Illinois
d. Nov. 6, 1919, Highland, Ohio

John Roel Zook, an evangelist generally credited with moving the Brethren in Christ to accept the Wesleyan holiness theological position, was the son of Abraham Zook, a deacon with the Brethren in Christ. The year of Zook's birth his family moved from

Pennsylvania to Illinois. Zook grew up on his father's farm. He had a conversion experience in 1874 and joined the local Brethren in Christ congregation. At the age of 20, Zook became a school teacher, two years prior to his entrance into Northern Indiana Normal School and Business Institute (now Valparaiso University) to take a teacher preparation course. In 1882 he returned to teaching, at the time somewhat of an anomaly among the Brethren, few of whom had any college education. In 1884 he married Sarah Anne George. In 1890, his father having died, he took over the family farm.

Around 1892, Zook received a call to the ministry. In 1893 he emerged from obscurity as the secretary of the church's general conference. Three years later he was the assistant moderator of the general conference, and his emerging position in the denomination was signaled by his placement on two committees. He was assigned the mission work in Des Moines, Iowa, where he would reside for the rest of his active ministry. His brethren had by this time heard him preach, and he quickly became the most sought after preacher/evangelist in the small denomination. He annually traveled across Canada and the United States in evangelistic work. He had absorbed the manner of contemporary evangelists and even wrote a short book for his fellow Brethren ministers, *A Guide for Instructors to Instruct Penitents, Seekers of Holiness and Empowerment, and Divine Healing*.

A few years after his conversion, Zook had had a second strong religious experience which he interpreted as a sanctifying (being made holy) by the Holy Spirit. This experience led him into an agreement with the holiness movement, which taught the centrality of such a second work of grace in the life of the believer. In Iowa he had affiliated with the Iowa Holiness Association. During the 1890s several Brethren preachers began to advocate a holiness perspective. Zook took the lead in the holiness cause, and in addition began to argue for the reality of spiritual healing. His writing and speaking through the first decade of the twentieth century culminated in 1910 with the Brethren in Christ officially accepting the holiness position. Zook was also the leading spokesperson for premillennialism, the view that Christ will soon return to establish his literal reign of 1,000 years on earth.

At the same time Zook promoted doctrinal changes, he worked for improved education for the Brethren. By 1897 he was arguing for a denominational Bible school. By 1908 the Brethren decided to create such a school (now Messiah College) in Grantham, Pennsylvania, and Zook was named president of the board of managers. Active to the end of his life, he died of a heart attack in the midst of leading a spirited revival service in the church in Highland, Ohio.

Sources:

Sider, E. Morris. *Nine Portraits: Brethren in Christ Biographical Sketches*. Nappanee, IN: Evangel Press, 1978. 336 pp.

Wittlinger, Carlton O. *Quest for Piety and Obedience: The Story of the Brethren in Christ*. Nappanee, IN: Evangel Press, 1978. 580 pp.

Zook, John R. *Holiness and Empowerment: Both Defined, How to Obtain Them and How to Retain Them*. Des Moines, IA: Kenyon Printing and Manufacturing Press, n.d.

Key to Religious Affiliations

The key lists, in a single alphabetical sequence, the 38 primary religious traditions and families used to classify the profiled leaders in the Religious Affiliations Appendix following this key. The key also contains references to the more than 60 specific religious groups that comprise the 38 traditions and families. References to specific groups include *see* references to the appropriate religious tradition.

Adventism
  Church of God Seventh-day
  Jehovah's Witnesses
  Seventh Day Adventism
  Worldwide Church of God
African Methodism *See* Methodism
American Baptist *See* Baptist
Anglican *See* Episcopal (Anglican)
Anglican Church in Canada *See* Episcopal (Anglican)
Apostolic Pentecostal *See* Pentecostal
Assemblies of God *See* Pentecostal
Astrology *See* Occult
Atheism/Humanism/Free Thought
  Free Religious Association
Baha'i
Alice Bailey Groups *See* Theosophy
Baptist
  American Baptist
  National Baptist
  Northern Baptist
  Southern Baptist
Black Islam *See* Islam
Black Judaism *See* Judaism
Brethren
  Church of the Brethren
  Plymouth Brethren
Buddhism
  Chinese Buddhism
  Japanese Buddhism
  Korean Buddhism
  Theravada Buddhism
  Tibetan Buddhism
  Western Buddhism
  Zen Buddhism
Channeling *See* New Age/Psychic
Chinese Buddhism *See* Buddhism
Christian Church
  Christian Church (Disciples of Christ)
  Churches of Christ
Christian Methodist Episcopal Church *See* Methodism
Christian Science
Church of God (Cleveland, Tennessee) *See* Pentecostal
Church of God Seventh-day *See* Adventism
Church of Jesus Christ of Latter-day Saints *See* Latter-day Saints (Mormons)
Church of the Brethren *See* Brethren
Churches of Christ *See* Christian Church
Communalism

Congregationalism
  Congregational and Christian Churches
  United Church of Christ
Eastern Orthodox
Episcopal (Anglican)
  Anglican Church in Canada
  Church of England in Canada
  Episcopal Church
  Protestant Episcopal
Flying Saucer Groups *See* Unclassified Religious Groups
Free Religious Association *See* Atheism/Humanism/Free Thought *See* Atheism/Humanism/Free Thought
Friends (Quakers)
Fundamentalism
Hassidism *See* Judaism
Hinduism
Holiness
Homosexually Oriented Churches *See* Unclassified Religious Groups
Humanism *See* Atheism/Humanism/Free Thought
I AM Groups *See* Theosophy
Islam
  Black Islam
  Sufism
Jehovah's Witnesses *See* Adventism
Judaism
  Black Judaism
  Hassidism
Korean Buddhism *See* Buddhism
Latter-day Saints (Mormons)
  Church of Jesus Christ of Latter-day Saints
  Polygamy-Practicing Mormons
  Reorganized Church of Jesus Christ of Latter Day Saints
Latter Rain Pentecostal *See* Pentecostal
Liberal Catholic Churches *See* Theosophy
Lutheran
Magick *See* Witchcraft/Magick/Neo-Paganism
Mennonite
Methodism
  African Methodism
  Christian Methodist Episcopal Church
  Methodist Episcopal Church
  Methodist Episcopal Church, South
  Methodist Protestant Church
  United Methodist Church
Mormons *See* Latter-day Saints (Mormons)
National Baptist *See* Baptist
Native American (Traditional)

Neo-Paganism *See* Witchcraft/Magick/Neo-Paganism
New Age/Psychic
  Channeling
New Thought
Northern Baptist *See* Baptist
Occult
  Astrology
Old Catholic
Orthodox *See* Eastern Orthodox
Pentecostal
  Apostolic Pentecostal
  Assemblies of God
  Church of God (Cleveland, Tennessee)
  Latter Rain Pentecostal
  Signs Pentecostal
  Spanish-Speaking Pentecostal
Protestant Episcopal *See* Episcopal (Anglican)
Psychic *See* New Age/Psychic
Plymouth Brethren *See* Brethren
Polygamy-Practicing Mormons *See* Latter-day Saints
(Mormons)
Presbyterian *See* Reformed/Presbyterian
Quakers *See* Friends (Quakers)
Reformed/Presbyterian
  Reformed
  Presbyterian
Reorganized Church of Jesus Christ of Latter Day Saints
See Latter-day Saints (Mormons)
Ritual Magick *See* Witchcraft/Magick/Neo-Paganism

Roman Catholic
Rosicrucian
Sant Mat *See* Sikhism/Sant Mat
Satanism
Seventh Day Adventism *See* Adventism
Signs Pentecostal *See* Pentecostal
Sikhism/Sant Mat
Southern Baptist *See* Baptist
Spanish-Speaking Pentecostal *See* Pentecostals
Spiritualism
Sufism *See* Islam
Theosophical Society *See* Theosophy
Theosophy
  Alice Bailey Groups
  I AM Groups
  Liberal Catholic Churches
  Theosophical Society
Theravada Buddhism *See* Buddhism
Tibetan Buddhism *See* Buddhism
Unclassified Religious Groups
  Flying Saucer Groups
  Homosexually Oriented Churches
Unitarian/Universalist
United Church of Christ *See* Congregationalism
United Methodist Church *See* Methodism
Western Buddhism *See* Buddhism
Witchcraft/Magick/Neo-Paganism
  Ritual Magick
Worldwide Church of God *See* Adventism
Zen Buddhism *See* Buddhism

Religious Affiliations Appendix

The appendix classifies the leaders profiled in this volume into the religious tradition or family with which each is associated. Listed alphabetically, each of the 38 religious traditions is followed by an alphabetical listing of the leaders relevant to the history and growth of that tradition and includes information on each leader's denominational affiliation and/or occupation. For an overview of the traditions and families, including information on the subgroups comprising each, consult the "Key to Religious Affiliations" immediately preceding this appendix.

Adventism

Armstrong, Garner Ted
Founder, Church of God International

Armstrong, Herbert W.
Founder and Apostle, Worldwide Church of God

Gilbert, Frederick Carnes
Jewish Missionary, Seventh-day Adventist Church

Loughborough, John Norton
Minister, Seventh-day Adventist Church

Nichol, Francis David
Editor, Seventh-day Adventist Church

Russell, Charles Taze
Founder, Watch Tower Bible and Tract Society

Rutherford, Joseph Franklin
Leader, Jehovah's Witnesses

Smith, Uriah
Editor, Seventh-day Adventist Church

Spicer, William Ambrose
President of the General Conference, Seventh-day Adventist Church

Tkach, Joseph William
Pastor General, Worldwide Church of God

White, Ellen Gould Harmon
Cofounder, Seventh-day Adventist Church

White, James
Cofounder, Seventh-day Adventist Church

Atheism/Humanism/Freethought

Abbot, Francis Ellingwood
Cofounder, Free Religious Association

Adler, Felix
American Ethical Union

Bennett, DeRobigne Mortimer
Freethought Editor and Author

Blanshard, Paul Beecher
Atheist Writer

Frothingham, Octavius Brooks
President, Free Religious Association

Gardener, Helen Hamilton
Freethought Writer and Activist

Gaylor, Anne Nicol
Founder and Director, Freedom from Religion Foundation

Haldeman-Julius, Emanuel
Publisher of Freethought Literature

Ingersoll, Robert Green
Freethought Orator

Johnson, James Hervey
President, American Association for the Advancement of Atheism

Lamont, Corliss
Humanist Leader

Lewis, Joseph
Founder, Freethinkers of America

McGee, Lewis A.
Founder, Free Religious Association

Muzzey, David Saville
Leader, American Ethical Union

O'Hair, Madalyn Mays Murray
Founder, American Atheists, Inc.

Potter, Charles Francis
Humanist Leader

Smith, Charles Lee
Founder, American Association for the Advancement of Atheism

Underwood, Benjamin Franklin
Freethought Lecturer and Editor

Baha'i

Abdu'l-Baha
Baha'i Faith

Baha'u'llah
Baha'i Faith

Chase, Thornton
Leader, Baha'i Faith

Gregory, Louis George
Leader, Baha'i Faith

Holley, Horace Hotchkiss
Hand of the Cause, Baha'i Faith

Kheiralla, Ibrahim George
Founder, National Organization of the Universal Religion

Maxwell, William Sutherland
Pioneer, Baha'i Faith, Canada

Remey, Charles Mason
Founder, Orthodox Abha World Faith

Shoghi Effendi Rabboni
Guardian, Baha'i Faith

Baptist

Abernathy, Ralph David
Minister, American Baptist Churches in the U.S.A.
Civil Rights Leader

Adams, Theodore Floyd
President, Baptist World Alliance
Minister, Southern Baptist Convention

Armstrong, Annie Walker
Corresponding Secretary, Woman's Missionary Union,
Southern Baptist Convention

Ashworth, Robert Archibald
Minister, Northern Baptist Convention

Bilbo, Theodore
Lay Baptist Preacher
Governor and Senator of Mississippi

Bonney, Mary Lucinda
Indian Rights Advocate
Baptist Laywoman

Boyd, Henry Allen
Publisher, National Baptist Convention of America

Boyd, Richard Henry
Publisher, National Baptist Convention of America

Brawley, Edward M.
Minister and Educator, National Baptist Convention, U.S.A.,
Inc.

Broadus, John Albert
Educator, Southern Baptist Convention

Campbell, Will Davis
Minister, Southern Baptist Convention

Carnell, Edward John
Baptist Theologian

Carroll, Benajah Harvey
Educator, Southern Baptist Convention

Case, Shirley Jackson
Church Historian, Free Baptist Church

Clarke, William Newton
Theologian, Northern Baptist Convention

Colley, William W.
Corresponding Secretary, Foreign Mission Convention of the
United States of America (National Baptist)

Conwell, Russell Herman
Minister, Baptist Church

Cox, Harvey Gallagher, Jr.
Theologian, American Baptist Churches in the U.S.

Criswell, Wallie Amos
President, Southern Baptist Convention

Crouch, Austin
Executive, Southern Baptist Convention

Dahlberg, Edwin Theodore
Baptist Minister
President, National Council of Churches

Dawson, Joseph Martin
Minister, Southern Baptist Convention

De Baptiste, Richard
President, Consolidated American Baptist Convention

Dixon, Amzi Clarence
Fundamentalist Baptist Evangelist

Falwell, Jerry
Minister and Founder, Liberty Baptist Fellowship

Fisher, Mark Miles
Historian and Minister, National Baptist Convention, U.S.A.,
Inc.

Fosdick, Harry Emerson
Minister, Northern Baptist Convention

Foster, George Burman
Theologian, Northern Baptist Convention

Frost, James Marion
Founder, Sunday School Board, Southern Baptist Convention

Fuller, Thomas Oscar
Minister and Executive, National Baptist Convention in the
U.S.A.

Goodspeed, Edgar Johnson
Bible Scholar, Baptist Church

Gordon, Adoniram Judson
Minister, Baptist Church

Graham, Billy
Evangelist, Southern Baptist Convention

Graves, James Robinson
Baptist Minister
Founder, Landmark Movement

Griggs, Sutton Elbert
Minister, National Baptist Convention of America

Haldeman, Isaac Massey
Minister, Northern Baptist Convention

Henry, Carl Ferdinand Howard
Theologian, American Baptist Churches in the U.S.A.

Hobbs, Herschel
Minister, Southern Baptist Convention
President, Southern Baptist Convention

Houghton, William Henry
President, Moody Bible Institute

Jackson, Jesse
Minister, Baptist Church
Political Activist

Jackson, Joseph Harrison
President, National Baptist Convention, U.S.A.

Jackson, Mahalia
Gospel Singer, National Baptist Convention

Jordan, Clarence
Founder, Koinonia Community

Jorgensen, Lars
Pioneer Danish Baptist Minister

Judson, Edward
Minister, Baptist Church

Kenyon, Essek William
Independent Evangelist
Founder, Bethel Bible Institute

Ketcham, Robert Thomas
Founder, General Association of Regular Baptist Churches

King, Coretta Scott
Baptist Laywoman
Civil Rights Activist

King, Martin Luther, Jr.
Minister, Progressive National Baptist Convention
Civil Rights Leader

King, Martin Luther, Sr.
Minister, Progressive National Baptist Convention

Latourette, Kenneth Scott
Historian, Baptist Church

Lawrence, John Benjamin
Executive, Southern Baptist Convention

Laws, Curtis Lee
Editor, Northern Baptist Convention

Lee, Robert Greene
Minister, Southern Baptist Convention

Lovett, Cummings Samuel
Founder, Personal Christianity Chapel

Lowry, Edith Elizabeth
Executive, National Council of Churches

Mallory, Kathleen Moore
  Executive Secretary, Woman's Missionary Union, Southern Baptist Convention
Manly, Basil, Jr.
  Minister and Theologian, Southern Baptist Convention
Massee, Jasper Cortenus
  Fundamentalist Minister, Baptist Church
Mathews, Shailer
  Theologian, Northern Baptist Convention
Mays, Benjamin Elijah
  Educator, National Baptist Convention, U.S.A., Inc.
McAlpine, William H.
  President, National Baptist Foreign Mission Convention of the United States of America
McCracken, Robert James
  Minister, Baptist Church
McIntosh, Martha E.
  President, Women's Missionary Union, Southern Baptist Convention
Montgomery, Helen Barrett
  Bible Translator and President, Northern Baptist Convention
Moore, Joanna Patterson
  Pioneer Baptist Home Missionary
Morehouse, Henry Lyman
  Home Missionary Secretary, American Baptists
Morris, Elias C.
  President, National Baptist Convention, U.S.A., Inc.
Mullins, Edgar Young
  Educator, Southern Baptist Convention
Newman, Albert Henry
  Church Historian, Baptist Church
Norris, John Franklyn
  Founder, World Baptist Fellowship
Packard, Sophia B.
  Baptist Laywoman
  Founder, Spelman College
Peabody, Lucy Whitehead McGill Waterbury
  Founder, Baptists for World Evangelism
Pentecost, George Frederick
  Minister, Baptist Church
Powell, Adam Clayton, Jr.
  Minister, Baptist Church
Powell, Adam Clayton, Sr.
  Minister, Baptist Church
Rauschenbusch, Walter
  Church Historian and Social Gospel Theologian, North American Baptist Conference and Northern Baptist Convention
Rice, John Richard
  Independent Fundamentalist Baptist Evangelist and Author
Riley, William Bell
  Fundamentalist Baptist Minister and Educator
Robertson, Archibald Thomas
  Biblical Scholar, Southern Baptist Convention
Scarborough, Lee Rutland
  President, Southern Baptist Convention
Shields, Thomas Todhunter, Jr.
  Founder, Fellowship of Evangelical Baptist Churches in Canada
Simmons, William J.
  Founder, American National Baptist Convention
Skinner, Tom
  Evangelist, Tom Skinner Associates
Straton, John Roach
  Fundamentalist Baptist Preacher

Strong, Augustus Hopkins
  Theologian, Northern Baptist Convention
Tichenor, Isaac Taylor
  Missionary Secretary, Southern Baptist Convention
Toy, Crawford Howell
  Biblical Scholar, Southern Baptist Convention
Truett, George Washington
  Pastor, Southern Baptist Convention
Van Impe, Jack Leo
  Evangelist, Independent Baptist
Vedder, Henry Clay
  Church Historian, Northern Baptist Convention
Vick, George Beauchamp
  Fundamentalist Baptist Educator and Minister
Whitsitt, William Heth
  Church Historian and Educator, Southern Baptist Convention
Williams, Lacey Kirk
  President, National Baptist Convention, U.S.A., Inc.

Brethren

Bauman, Louis Sylvester
  Minister, Fellowship of Grace Brethren Churches
Grant, Frederick William
  Leader, Plymouth Brethren
Holsinger, Henry Ritz
  Founder, Brethren Church (Ashland, Ohio)
Hoyt, Herman Arthur
  Minister and Educator, Fellowship of Grace Brethren Churches
Kesler, Benjamin Elias
  Minister, Dunkard Brethren Church
McClain, Alva J.
  Founder, Fellowship of Grace Brethren Churches
Miller, Daniel Long
  Editor and Publisher, Church of the Brethren
Miller, John Allen
  Educator, Brethren Church
Miller, Joseph Quinter
  Minister and Ecumenist, Church of the Brethren

Buddhism

Carus, Paul
  Philosopher, Author of works on Buddhism
Dharmapala, Anagarika
  Buddhist Lecturer
  Founder of the Maha Bodhi Society
Maha Ghosananda
  Monk and Leader, Cambodian Buddhism
Goddard, Dwight
  Fellowship Following Buddha
Govinda, Anagarika
  Founder, Arya Maitreya Mandala
  Buddhist Author
Hua, Hsuan
  Leader, Dharma Realm Buddhist Association
Hunt, Ernest
  Founder, Western Buddhist Order of the Honpa Hongwanji of Hawaii
Ikeda, Daisaku
  President, Soka Gakkai International
Imamura, Yemyo
  Bishop, Honpa Hongwanji Mission of Hawaii

Kalu Rinpoche, Khyyab Je
Tibetan Lama and Founder, Kagyu Dharma
Kapleau, Philip
Zen Master and Founder, Zen Meditation Center of Rochester
Kennett, Jiyu
Zen Master and Founder, Order of Buddhist Contemplatives
Kushi, Michio
Founder, East West Foundation
Maezumi, Hakuyu Taizan
Founder, Zen Center of Los Angeles
Sasaki, Kyozan Joshu
Rinzai Zen Master
Founder of Rinzai-Ji and related Zen Centers
Sasaki, Ruth Fuller Everett
Zen Teacher, First Zen Institute of America
Sasaki, Shigetsu
Founder, First Zen Institute of America
Senzaki, Nyogen
Zen Buddhist Teacher
Founder, Mentorgarten Meditation Hall
Shaku, Soyen
Teacher, Rinzai Zen Buddhism
Sunin, Samu
Founder, Zen Lotus Society
Suzuki, Daisetz Teitaro
Zen Buddhist Author
Suzuki, Shunryu
Founder, Zen Center of San Francisco
Trungpa Rinpoche, Chogyam
Tibetan Buddhist Teacher and Founder, Vajradhatu
Watts, Alan Wilson
Philosopher, Zen Buddhism
Williams, George M.
General Director, Nichiren Shoshu of America (NSA)

Christian Church (Churches of Christ/Disciples of Christ)

Ainslie, Peter, III
Minister, Christian Church (Disciples of Christ)
Ames, Edward Scribner
Philosopher, Christian Church (Disciples of Christ)
Basham, Donald Wilson
Minister, Christian Church (Disciples of Christ)
Errett, Isaac
Editor, Christian Churches and Churches of Christ
Freed, Arvy Glenn
Educator, Churches of Christ
Goodpasture, Benjamin Cordell
Editor, Churches of Christ
Jones, Edgar DeWitt
Minister, Christian Church (Disciples of Christ)
Keeble, Marshall
Evangelist, Churches of Christ (Non-Instrumental)
Lard, Moses
Minister and Editor, Churches of Christ
Lipscomb, David
Minister, Churches of Christ
Editor, Gospel Advocate
McGarvey, John William
Minister and Editor, Churches of Christ
McGary, Austin
Minister and Editor, Churches of Christ

Morrison, Charles Clayton
Minister, Christian Church (Disciples of Christ)
Sewell, Elisha G.
Editor, Churches of Christ
Smith, Gerald Lyman Kenneth
Minister, Christian Church (Disciples of Christ)
Anti-Semitic and Anti-Communist Orator
Tant, Jefferson Davis
Evangelist, Churches of Christ
Wallace, Foy Esco, Jr.
Minister and Editor, Churches of Christ

Christian Science

Eddy, Mary Baker Glover
Founder, Church of Christ, Scientist
Goldsmith, Joel Sol
Founder, Infinite Way

Communalism

Arnold, Eberhard
Founder, Hutterian Brethren of New York
Beilhart, Jacob
Founder, Spirit Fruit Society
Divine, Father Major Jealous
Founder, Peace Mission Movement
Metelica, Michael J.
Founder, Renaissance Church of Beauty
Monroe, Eugene Crosby
Founder, Shiloh Trust
White, Anna
Shaker Eldress and Writer

Congregationalism (United Church of Christ)

Abbott, Lyman
Minister, Congregational Church
Barton, Bruce
Popular Religious Writer, Congregational Church
Bateham, Josephine Abiah Penfield Cushman
Social Activist
Laywoman, Congregationalist Church
Beecher, Henry Ward
Minister, Congregational Church
Bennett, John Coleman
Theologian, United Church of Christ
Blackwell, Antoinette Brown
First Female Minister, Congregational Church
Blanchard, Charles Albert
College President and Minister, Congregational Church
Bliss, Philip Paul
Evangelist and Hymn Writer, Congregational Church
Cadman, Samuel Parkes
Minister, Congregational Church
Clark, Francis Edward
Founder, Young People's Society of Christian Endeavor
Clark, Glenn
Founder, Camp Farthest Out
Douglas, Lloyd Cassel
Minister, Congregational Church
Ferre, Nels Fredrik Solomon
Theologian, Congregational Christian Churches
Fisher, George Park
Church Historian, Congregational Church

Gladden, Washington
Minister, Congregational Church
Gordon, George Angier
Minister, Congregational Church
Guild, Roy Bergen
Minister, Congregational Church
Gunsaulus, Frank Wakeley
Minister, Congregational Church
Herron, George Davis
Socialist and Minister, Congregational Church
Hillis, Newell Dwight
Minister, Congregational Church
Horton, Douglas
Minister, Congregational and Christian Churches
Jefferson, Charles Edward
Modernist Pastor, Congregational Church
King, Henry Churchill
Theologian, Congregational Church
Lyman, Mary Reddington Ely
Theologian, Congregational Church
Macfarland, Charles Steadman
Minister, Congregational Church
McGiffert, Arthur Cushman
Church Historian, Congregational Church
Niebuhr, Helmut Richard
Theologian, United Church of Christ
Niebuhr, Reinhold
Theologian, United Church of Christ
Peloubet, Francis Nathan
Minister, Congregational Church
Pidgeon, George Campbell
Moderator, United Church of Canada
Sanford, Elias Benjamin
Minister, Congregational Church
Sheldon, Charles Monroe
Writer and Minister, Congregational Church
Strong, James Woodward
College President, Congregational Church
Strong, Josiah
Minister, Congregational Church
Torrey, Reuben Archer
Minister, Congregational Church
Trumbull, Henry Clay
Minister and Sunday School Leader, Congregational Church

Eastern Orthodox

Metropolitan Anastassy
First Hierarch, Russian Orthodox Church Outside of Russia
Andreades, Michael G.
Priest, Russian Orthodox Church
Bishop Arseny
Bishop, Russian Orthodox Church
Patriarch Athenagoras
Ecumenical Patriarch, Greek Orthodox Church
Bashir, Anthony
Metropolitan Archbishop, Antiochean Orthodox Christian Archdiocese of North America
Bjerring, Nicolas
Priest, Russian Orthodox Church
Callimachos, Panos Demetrios
Priest Greek Orthodox Archdiocese of North and South America
Activist, Hellenism

Chornock, Orestes
Metropolitan, American Carpatho-Russian Orthodox Greek Church
Bishop Dionisije
Bishop, Serbian Eastern Orthodox Church in North America
Archbishop Evdokim
Archbishop, Russian Orthodox Church
Hawaweeny, Raphael
Bishop, Russian Orthodox Church
Archbishop Iakovos
Metropolitan, Greek Orthodox Archdiocese of North and South America
Metropolitan Ireney
Archbishop, Orthodox Church in America
Bishop John
Bishop, Russian Orthodox Church
Metropolitan Leonty
Archbishop, Russian Orthodox Greek Catholic Church of America
Bishop Mardary
Bishop, Serbian Orthodox Diocese in America
Mastrantonis, George
Founder, OLOGOS (Orthodox Lore of the Gospel of Our Savior)
Maximovich, John
Bishop, Russian Orthodox Church Outside of Russia
McGuire, George Alexander
Founder, African Orthodox Church
Metaxakis, Meletios
Archbishop, Greek Orthodox Archdiocese of North and South America
Archbishop Michael
Archbishop, Greek Orthodox Archdiocese of North and South America
Bishop Nestor
Bishop, Russian Orthodox Church
Bishop Nicholas
Bishop, Russian Orthodox Church
Noli, Theophan S.
Metropolitan, Albanian Orthodox Archdiocese of America
Ofiesh, Abdullah
Founder and Archbishop, American Orthodox Catholic Church
Metropolitan Philaret
First Hierarch, Russian Orthodox Church Outside of Russia
Metropolitan Platon
Metropolitan, Russian Orthodox Church
Revel, Bernard
Orthodox Jewish Educator
Rose, Hieromonk Seraphim
Monk, Russian Orthodox Church Outside of Russia
Archimandrite Sabastian
Serbian Orthodox Priest
Schmemann, Alexander
Scholar and Priest, Orthodox Church in America
Bishop Stephen
Bishop, Russian Orthodox Church
Metropolitan Theodosius
Metropolitan, Orthodox Church in America
Metropolitan Theophilus
Metropolitan, Russian Orthodox Greek Catholic Church of America
Archbishop Tikhon
Archbishop, Russian Orthodox Church in America

Trifa, Valerian
　Archbishop, Romanian Orthodox Episcopate of America
Archbishop Vladimir
　Archbishop, Russian Orthodox Church

Episcopal (Anglican)

Adams, Walter Hollis
　Bishop, Anglican Episcopal Church of North America
Allin, John Maury
　Presiding Bishop, Episcopal Church
Anderson, Charles Palmerston
　Presiding Bishop, Episcopal Church
Ayres, Anne
　*Founder, Sisterhood of the Holy Communion, Episcopal
　　Church, U.S.A.*
Barrett, Kate Harwood Waller
　*Cofounder, National Florence Crittenton Mission
　Protestant Episcopal Church Laywoman*
Bliss, William Dwight Porter
　Founder, Christian Socialist Society
Bompas, William Carpenter
　Missionary Bishop, Church of England in Canada
Bond, William Bennett
　Primate, Anglican Church of Canada
Bowie, Walter Russell
　Educator, Protestant Episcopal Church
Bowles, Eva del Vakia
　*Episcopal Laywoman
　Executive, Young Women's Christian Association (YWCA)*
Boyd, Malcolm
　Priest, Episcopal Church
Bragg, George Freeman, Jr.
　Priest, Episcopal Church
Brooks, Phillips
　Bishop, Episcopal Church
Browning, Edmond Lee
　Presiding Bishop, Episcopal Church
Cheney, Charles Edward
　Bishop, Reformed Episcopal Church
Clavier, Anthony Forbes Moreton
　Archbishop, American Episcopal Church (AEC)
Crapsey, Algernon Sidney
　Priest, Episcopal Church
Cridge, Edward
　Bishop, Reformed Episcopal Church (Canada)
Crummell, Alexander
　*Priest, Protestant Episcopal Church
　Founder, St. Luke's Episcopal Church*
Culbertson, William
　Bishop, Reformed Episcopal Church
Cullis, Charles
　Healer, Episcopal Church
Cummins, George David
　Bishop, Reformed Episcopal Church
DeKoven, James
　Minister, Protestant Episcopal Church
DuBose, William Porcher
　Theologian, Protestant Episcopal Church
Gray, James Martin
　*Minister, Reformed Episcopal Church and President, Moody
　　Bible Institute*
Harris, Barbara Clementine
　Bishop, Episcopal Church

Hines, John Elbridge
　Presiding Bishop, Episcopal Church
Huntington, William Reed
　Minister, Episcopal Church
Lichtenberger, Arthur Carl
　Presiding Bishop, Episcopal Church
Machray, Robert
　Primate, Anglican Church of Canada
Matheson, Samuel Pritchard
　Primate, Anglican Church of Canada
Murray, John Gardner
　Presiding Bishop, Protestant Episcopal Church
Newton, Joseph Fort
　Minister, Protestant Episcopal Church
Owen, Derwyn Trevor
　Bishop, Church of England in Canada
Oxenden, Ashton
　Bishop, Church of England in Canada
Perry, James De Wolf, Jr.
　Presiding Bishop, Episcopal Church
Pike, James Albert, Jr.
　Bishop, Protestant Episcopal Church
Sherrill, Henry Knox
　Presiding Bishop, Protestant Episcopal Church in the U.S.A.
Shoemaker, Samuel Moor, Jr.
　Minister, Episcopal Church
Stuck, Hudson
　Alaskan Missionary, Protestant Episcopal Church
Sweatman, Arthur
　Primate, Anglican Church of Canada
Talbot, Ethelbert
　Presiding Bishop, Protestant Episcopal Church
Tucker, Henry St. George
　Presiding Bishop, Protestant Episcopal Church
Tuttle, Daniel Sylvester
　Presiding Bishop, Protestant Episcopal Church
Wedel, Cynthia Clark
　*Lay Leader, Episcopal Church
　President, National Council of Churches*
Williams, John
　Presiding Bishop, Protestant Episcopal Church
Worcester, Elwood
　Founder, Emmanuel Movement
Worrell, Clarendon Lamb
　Primate, Anglican Church of Canada

Friends (Quakers)

Brinton, Howard Haines
　*Director, Pendle Hill Community
　Cofounder of the Pacific Yearly Meeting of the Religious
　　Society of Friends*
Cadbury, Henry Joel
　*Biblical Scholar, Five Years Meeting, Religious Society of
　　Friends*
Jones, Rufus Matthew
　Mystic and Scholar, Society of Friends
Kelly, Thomas Raymond
　Philosopher, Society of Friends (Quakers)
Smith, Hannah Whitall
　Writer, Society of Friends

Fundamentalism

Aberhart, William
Independent Fundamentalist Bible Teacher

Cohn, Leopold
Founder, American Board of Missions to the Jews

DeHaan, Martin Ralph
Founder, Radio Bible Class

Deyneka, Peter, Sr.
Founder, Slavic Gospel Association

Frydland, Rachmiel
Hebrew Christian Minister
Founder, Messianic Literature Outreach

Fuller, Charles Edward
Independent Fundamentalist Radio Minister
Founder, Fuller Theological Seminary

Gaebelein, Arno C.
Independent Fundamentalist Writer/Editor

Hargis, Billy James
Founder, Church of the Christian Crusade

Humbard, Rex
Television Evangelist
Founder, Rex Humbard World Outreach Ministry

Ironside, Harry
Pastor, Moody Memorial Church

Jones, Robert, Sr.
Fundamentalist Evangelist
Founder, Bob Jones University

Knoch, Adolph Ernst
Founder, Concordant Publishing Concern

McCarrell, William
Founder, Independent Fundamental Churches of America

McQuilkin, Robert Crawford, Jr.
Educator, Fellowship of Independent Evangelical Churches

Moody, Dwight Lyman Ryther
Independent Christian Fundamentalist Evangelist

Nee, Watchman
Founder, Local Church

Pentecost, John Dwight
Fundamentalist Minister and Scholar

Perkins, John M.
Founder, John M. Perkins Foundation for Reconciliation and Development

Pettingill, William Leroy
Minister, Independent Fundamental Churches of America

Pierce, Robert (Bob) Willard
Founder, World Vision, Inc.

Revell, Fleming Hewitt, Jr.
Fundamentalist Christian Publisher

Rimmer, Harry
Fundamentalist Minister
Founder, Research Science Bureau

Rosen, Moishe
Founder, Jews for Jesus

Sankey, Ira D.
Hymn Writer and Music Evangelist

Smith, Oswald Jeffery
Founder, Peoples Church

Talbot, Louis Thompson
President, Bible Institute of Los Angeles (BIOLA)

ten Boom, Corrie
Independent Evangelical Christian Writer and Evangelist

Thieme, Robert Bunger, Jr.
Pastor, Berachah Church

Wierwille, Victor Paul
Founder, The Way International

Winrod, Gerald Burton
Founder, Defenders of the Christian Faith

Hinduism

Swami Abhedananda
Swami, Vedanta Society

Mataji Amritanandamayi
Founder, Mata Amritanandamayi Center

Shrii Shrii Anandamurti
Founder, Ananda Marga Yoga Society

Sri Aurobindo
Hindu Spiritual Leader

Bernard, Pierre Arnold
Tantrik Order in America

Charlton, Hilda
Independent Eastern Metaphysical Teacher

Chaudhuri, Haridas
Founder, California Institute of Integral Studies

Swami Chinmayananda
Founder, Chinmaya Mission West

Sri Chinmoy
Founder, Sri Chinmoy Meditation Centres

Davis, Roy Eugene
Director, Church of the Christian Sprirtual Alliance (CSA)
Founder, New Life Worldwide

Desai, Amrit
Founder, Kripalu Yoga Fellowship

Sister Devamata
Leader, Ananda Ashrama

Gayatri Devi
Leader, Ananda Ashrama

Lakshmy Devi
Founder, Sri Rajarajeshwari Peetham of the Holy Shankaracharya Order

Easwaran, Eknath
Founder, Blue Mountain Center of Meditation

Baba Hari Dass
Founder, Sri Rama Foundation

Swami Rajasi Janakananda
President, Self-Realization Fellowship

Jones, Franklin
Founder, Free Daist Communion

Swami Amar Jyoti
Founder, Truth Consciousness

Swami Jyotir Maya Nanda
Founder, Yoga Research Foundation

Sant Keshavadas
Founder, Temple of Cosmic Wisdom

Krishna, Gopi
Founder, Kundalini Research Foundation

Krishnamurti, Jiddu
Teacher, Krishnamurti Foundation

Maharishi Mahesh Yogi
Founder, World Plan Executive Council

Daya Mata
Leader, Self-Realization Fellowship

Mishra, Ramamurti S.
Founder, Intercosmic Center of Spiritual Awareness (I.C.S.A.)

Muktananda, Paramahansa
Founder, Siddha Yoga Dham

Swami Narayanananda
Founder, Narayanananda Universal Yoga Trust

Prabhupada, Abhay Charan De Bhaktivedanta Swami
  Founder, International Society for Krishna Consciousness
    (ISKCON)
Rajneesh, Bhagwan Shree
  Indian Spiritual Leader
  Founder, Rajneesh Foundation International (Oshu
    Commune International)
Ram Dass, Baba
  Teacher, New Age Movement
  Founder, Hanuman Foundation
Swami Rama
  Founder and Spiritual Director, Himalayan International
    Institute of Yoga Science and Philosophy
Zen Master Rama
  Founder, Rama Seminars
Sri Ramakrishna
  Hindu Priest
Sri Ramana Maharshi
  Indian Spiritual Teacher
Swami Rudrananda
  Founder, Rudrananda Foundation
Sai Baba (of Shirdi)
  Indian Saint
Sathya Sai Baba
  Spiritual Teacher, Sathya Sai Baba Movement
Swami Satchidananda
  Founder, Integral Yoga International
Shri Shivabalayogi Maharaj
  Founder, Shri Shivabalayogi Maharaj Trust
Swami Sivananda Saraswati
  Founder, Divine Life Society
Sripad Bhakti Raksaka Sridhara Maharaja
  Founder, Sri Caitanya Saraswati Math
Sivaya Subramuniyaswami
  Founder, Saiva Siddhanta Church
Venta, Krishna
  Founder, W.F.L.K. Fountain of the World
Swami Vishnu Devananda
  Founder, Sivananda Yoga Vedanta Centres
Swami Vivekananda
  Founder, Vedanta Society
Walters, Donald
  Founder, Ananda Community
Yogananda, Swami Paramahansa
  Founder, Self-Realization Fellowship
Ma Yogashakti Saraswati
  Founder, Ma Yogashakti International Mission

Holiness

Booth, Ballington
  Cofounder, Volunteers of America
Booth, Evangeline Cory
  General, Salvation Army
Booth, Maud Ballington
  Cofounder, Volunteers of America
Booth, William
  Founder, Salvation Army
Brengle, Samuel Logan
  Evangelist, Salvation Army
Bresee, Phineas
  Church of the Nazarene
Brown, Harrison D.
  Minister, Church of the Nazarene

Carradine, Beverly
  Holiness Minister, Methodist Episcopal Church, South
Chapman, James Blaine
  General Superintendent, Church of the Nazarene
Crumpler, Ambrose Blackman
  Founder, Holiness Church of North Carolina
Gaither, Bill and Gloria
  Musicians, Church of God (Anderson, Indiana)
Irwin, Benjamin Hardin
  Founder, Fire-Baptized Holiness Association
Jernigan, C. B.
  Minister, Church of the Nazarene
Jones, Charles Price
  Founder, Church of Christ (Holiness) U.S.A.
Knapp, Martin Wells
  Founder, International Holiness Union and Prayer League
Michaux, Lightfoot Solomon
  Founder, Gospel Spreading Church
Morrison, Henry Clay
  Methodist Minister and Founder, Asbury Theological
    Seminary
Rader, Paul Daniel
  Evangelist, Christian and Missionary Alliance (CMA)
Ramseyer, Joseph Eicher
  President, Missionary Church Association
Rees, Seth Cook
  Cofounder, Pilgrim Holiness Church
Sandford, Frank Weston
  Founder, Kingdom, Inc.
Smith, Gipsy
  Independent Christian Evangelist
Tozer, Aiden Wilson
  Minister, Christian and Missionary Alliance
White, Alma Birdwell
  Founder, Pillar of Fire

Islam

Ahmad, Mirza Ghulam Hazrat
  Founder, Ahmadiyya Movement in Islam
Drew, Timothy
  Founder, Moorish Science Temple of America
Duce, Ivy Oneita
  Leader, Sufism Reoriented
Farrakhan, Louis
  Founder, Nation of Islam
Gurdjieff, Georgei Ivanovitch
  Sufi-influenced Spiritual Teacher
Ichazo, Oscar
  Founder, Arica Institute
Khan, Hazrat Inayat
  Founder, Sufi Order in the West
Khan, Vilayat Inayat
  Leader, Sufi Order in the West
Lewis, Samuel Leonard
  Spiritual Teacher, Sufi Order
Malcolm X
  Founder, Muslim Mosque, Inc.
Muhammad, Elijah
  Founder, Nation of Islam
Subuh, Muhammad
  Founder, Subud
Webb, Muhammad Alexander Russell
  Founder, Moslem Mosque

Judaism

Carlebach, Shlomo
  Neo-Hassidic Rabbi
Ford, Arnold Josiah
  *Black Jewish Leader and Founder, Beth B'nai Abraham
  Congregation*
Gelberman, Joseph H.
  Rabbi and Founder, Little Synagogue
Goldman, Solomon
  Conservative Jewish Rabbi
Heschel, Abraham Joshua
  Jewish Theologian
  Founder, Institute of Jewish Learning in London
Kagan, Henry Enoch
  Reform Jewish Rabbi
Kahane, Meir
  *Orthodox Jewish Rabbi and Founder, Jewish Defense League
  (JDL)*
Kaplan, Mordecai Menahem
  Founder, Jewish Reconstructionist Foundation
Kohler, Kaufmann
  Reform Jewish Rabbi and Educator
Kohut, Alexander
  Conservative Jewish Rabbi and Scholar
Liebman, Joshua Loth
  Rabbi, Reform Judaism
Magnes, Judah Leon
  Reform Jewish Rabbi
  President, Hebrew University
Matthew, Wentworth Arthur
  *Founder, Commandment Keepers Congregation of the
  Living God*
Mendes, Henry Pereira
  *President, Union of Orthodox Jewish Congregations of the
  United States and Canada*
Schachter-Shalomi, Zalman
  Hassidic Rabbi and Founder, P'nai Or Fellowship
Schechter, Solomon
  Rabbinical Scholar and educator
Schneerson, Menachem Mendel
  Rebbe, Lubavitcher Hassidism
Silver, Abba Hillel
  Reform Jewish Rabbi and Zionist Leader
Silver, Eliezer
  Orthodox Jewish Rabbi
Szold, Henrietta
  Zionist Leader and Founder, Hadassah
Wise, Isaac Mayer
  Rabbi, Reform Judaism
Wise, Stephen Samuel
  Jewish Rabbi

Latter-day Saints (Mormons)

Allred, Rulon Clark
  Apostolic United Brethren
Benson, Ezra Taft
  President, Church of Jesus Christ of Latter-day Saints
Cannon, Abraham Hoagland
  Mormon Leader
Cannon, Franklin Jenne
  Mormon Leader
Cannon, George Quayle
  Writer, Editor, Church of Jesus Christ of Latter-day Saints

Fetting, Otto
  Church of Christ (Fettingite)
Gates, Susa Amelia Young
  Women's Leader, Church of Jesus Christ of Latter-day Saints
Godbe, William Samuel
  Founder, Church of Zion
Grant, Heber Jeddy
  President, Church of Jesus Christ of Latter-day Saints
Ivins, Anthony Woodward
  *Member of the First Presidency, Church of Jesus Christ of
  Latter-day Saints*
Kelley, Catherine Bishop
  *President, Daughters of Zion, Reorganized Church of Jesus
  Christ of Latter Day Saints*
Kimball, Spencer Wooley
  President, Church of Jesus Christ of Latter-day Saints
LeBaron, Ervil Morrell
  Founder, Church of the Lamb of God
LeBaron, Joel Franklin
  Founder, Church of the First Born of the Fulness of Times
Lee, Harold Bingham
  President, Church of Jesus Christ of Latter-day Saints
McKay, David Oman
  President, Church of Jesus Christ of Latter-day Saints
Musser, Joseph White
  Founder, Apostolic United Brethren
Penrose, Romania Pratt
  *Women's Advocate, Church of Jesus Christ of Latter-day
  Saints*
Roberts, Brigham Henry
  *Historian and Theologian, Church of Jesus Christ of Latter-
  day Saints*
Rogers, Aurelia Spencer
  *Children's Worker, Church of Jesus Christ of Latter-day
  Saints*
Savage, James Wilbur
  *Apostle, Church of Christ with the Elijah Message,
  Established Anew in 1929*
Smith, Frederick Madison
  *President, Reorganized Church of Jesus Christ of Latter Day
  Saints*
Smith, George Albert
  President, Church of Jesus Christ of Latter-day Saints
Smith, Israel Alexander
  *President, Reorganized Church of Jesus Christ of Latter Day
  Saints*
Smith, Wallace Bunnell
  *President, Reorganized Church of Jesus Christ of Latter Day
  Saints*
Smith, William Wallace
  *President, Reorganized Church of Jesus Christ of Latter Day
  Saints*
Smith, Joseph, III
  *President, Reorganized Church of Jesus Christ of Latter Day
  Saints*
Smith, Joseph Fielding, Jr.
  President, Church of Jesus Christ of Latter-day Saints
Smith, Joseph Fielding, Sr.
  President, Church of Jesus Christ of Latter-day Saints
Smoot, Reed
  Apostle, Church of Jesus Christ of Latter-day Saints
  United States Senator
Snow, Eliza Roxey
  Women's Leader, Church of Jesus Christ of Latter-day Saints
Snow, Lorenzo
  President, Church of Jesus Christ of Latter-day Saints

Lutheran

Talmage, James Edward
  Apostle, Church of Jesus Christ of Latter-day Saints
Taylor, John
  President, Church of Jesus Christ of Latter-day Saints
Woodruff, Wilford
  President, Church of Jesus Christ of Latter-day Saints

Lutheran

Chilstrom, Herbert Walfred
  Presiding Bishop, Evangelical Lutheran Church in America (1988)
Fedde, Elizabeth
  Pioneer Lutheran Deaconess
Fry, Franklin Clark
  President, Lutheran Church in America
Graebner, August Lawrence
  Theologian, Lutheran Church-Missouri Synod
Hoffman, Emil
  President, Canada Synod, General Council of the Lutheran Church in America
Jacobs, Henry Eyster
  Church Historian and Theologian, United Lutheran Church of America
Knubel, Frederick Herman
  President, United Lutheran Church in America
Koren, Ulrik Vilhelm
  Minister, Norwegian Synod (Lutheran Church)
Krauth, Charles Porterfield
  Theologian, General Council, Lutheran Church in America
Lundeberg, Knut Olafson
  Founder, Church of the Lutheran Brethren
Maier, Walter Arthur
  Biblical Scholar and Radio Minister, Lutheran Church-Missouri Synod
Marty, Martin Emil
  Church Historian, Evangelical Lutheran Church in America
Passavant, William Alfred
  Home Missionary, General Council of the Evangelical Lutheran Church in North America
Pelikan, Jaroslav Jan, Jr.
  Church Historian, Lutheran Church—Missouri Synod
Pieper, Franz August Otto
  Theologian, Lutheran Church-Missouri Synod
Preus, Jacob Aall Ottesen
  Educator and Executive, Lutheran Church—Missouri Synod
Reble, John H.
  President, Evangelical Lutheran Synod of Canada
Reu, Johann Michael
  Theologian, Evangelical Lutheran Synod of Iowa
Schmauk, Theodore Emanuel
  Minister, Lutheran Church
Schmidt, Friedrich August
  Theologian, Norwegian Synod and the United Norwegian Lutheran Church in America
Seip, Theodore Lorenzo
  Minister, General Council of the Lutheran Church in America
Seiss, Joseph Augustus
  Minister, General Council of the Lutheran Church in America
Stub, Hans Gerhard
  Minister, Norwegian Lutheran Church in America
Stuckenberg, John Henry Wilbrandt
  Theologian and Sociologist, General Synod, Lutheran Church

Tillich, Paul Johannes Oskar
  Theologian, Lutheran Church
Valentine, Milton
  Theologian, General Synod of the Lutheran Church in the United States
Wentz, Abdel Ross
  Educator and Historian, United Lutheran Church in America

Mennonite

Bender, Daniel Henry
  Bishop, Mennonite Church
Bender, Harold S.
  Educator and Peace Advocate, General Conference Mennonite Church
Coffman, John Samuel
  Evangelist, Mennonite Church
Eby, Solomon
  Founder, Mennonite Brethren in Christ Church
Egly, Henry
  Founder, Defenseless Mennonite Church of North America
Funk, John Fretz
  Editor, Publisher, Bishop, Mennonite Church
Holdeman, John
  Founder, Church of God in Christ, Mennonite
Horsch, John
  Historian, Editor, Mennonite Church
Kauffman, Daniel
  Bishop, Mennonite Church
Miller, D. D.
  Bishop, Mennonite Church
Oberholtzer, John H.
  Founder, General Conference Mennonite Church
Peters, Isaak
  Founder, Defenseless Mennonite Brethren of Christ in North America
Shelly, Andrew B.
  President, General Conference Mennonite Church
Wall, Aaron
  Founder, Defenseless Mennonite Brethren in Christ of North America
Wenger, Amos Daniel
  Educator, Mennonite Church
Wisler, Jacob
  Founder, Old Order (Wisler) Mennonites
Zook, John Roel
  Evangelist, Brethren in Christ Church

Methodism

Allen, Charles Livingston
  Minister, United Methodist Church
Arnett, Benjamin William, Jr.
  Bishop, African Methodist Episcopal Church
Baker, James Chamberlain
  Bishop, Methodist Episcopal Church
Beebe, Joseph A.
  Bishop, Christian Methodist Episcopal Church
Bennett, Belle Harris
  Founder, Scarritt Bible and Training School
  Laywoman, Methodist Episcopal Church, South
Bethune, Mary McLeod
  Educator, Methodist Church
  Founder, Bethune-Cookman College

Blackwell, Annie Walker
  Missionary Executive, African Methodist Episcopal Zion Church

Bottome, Margaret McDonald
  President, International Order of the King's Daughters and Sons

Bowne, Borden Parker
  Philosopher, Methodist Episcopal Church

Briggs, William
  Publisher and Minister, Methodist Church, Canada

Brightman, Edgar Sheffield
  Theologian, Methodist Episcopal Church

Buckley, James Monroe
  Editor, Methodist Episcopal Church

Candler, Warren Akin
  Bishop, Methodist Episcopal Church, South

Carman, Albert
  Superintendent, Methodist Episcopal Church of Canada

Clair, Matthew Wesley, Sr.
  Bishop, Methodist Episcopal Church

Clark, Elmer Talmage
  Historian and Church Executive, Methodist Episcopal Church, South

Cobb, John Boswell, Jr.
  Theologian, United Methodist Church

Cone, James Hal
  Theologian, African Methodist Episcopal Church

Coppin, Fanny Muriel Jackson
  Teacher and Executive, African Methodist Episcopal Church
  President, Women's Home and Foreign Missionary Society

Coppin, Levi Jenkins
  Bishop, African Methodist Episcopal Church

Cratty, Mabel
  Executive, Young Women's Christian Association (YWCA)

Crosby, Fanny
  Hymn Writer, Methodist Episcopal Church

Denman, Harry
  Denominational Executive, United Methodist Church

Denny, Collins
  Bishop, Methodist Episcopal Church, South

Diffendorfer, Ralph Eugene
  Missionary Executive, Methodist Episcopal Church

Fleming, Arthur Sherwood
  Lay Leader, United Methodist Church

Foster, Randolph Sinks
  Bishop, Methodist Episcopal Church

Gaines, Wesley John
  Bishop, African Methodist Episcopal Church

Goodell, Charles Leroy
  Minister, Methodist Episcopal Church

Harkness, Georgia Elma
  Theologian, Methodist Church (1939-1968)

Harmon, Nolan Bailey, Jr.
  Bishop, United Methodist Church

Haven, Gilbert, Jr.
  Bishop, Methodist Episcopal Church

Haygood, Atticus Greene
  Bishop, Methodist Episcopal Church, South

Hendrix, Eugene Russell
  Bishop, Methodist Episcopal Church, South

Hogue, Wilson Thomas
  Bishop, Free Methodist Church

Holsey, Lucius H.
  Bishop, Colored Methodist Episcopal Church

Holt, Ivan Lee
  Bishop, Methodist Church (1939-1968)

Hood, James Walker
  Bishop, African Methodist Episcopal Zion Church

Hughes, Edwin Holt
  Bishop, Methodist Episcopal Church

Hurlbut, Jesse Lyman
  Minister/Educator, Methodist Episcopal Church
  Popular Writer

Jones, Robert Elijah
  Bishop, Methodist Episcopal Church

Jones, Samuel Porter
  Evangelist, Methodist Episcopal Church, South

Kennedy, Gerald Hamilton
  Bishop, United Methodist Church

Killingsworth, Frank Russell
  Founder, Kodesh Church of Immanuel

King, Willis Jefferson
  Bishop, Methodist Episcopal Church

Knudson, Albert Cornelius
  Theologian and Biblical Scholar, Methodist Episcopal Church

Lane, Isaac
  Bishop, Christian Methodist Episcopal Church

Lewis, Edwin
  Theologian, Methodist Episcopal Church

Lowery, Joseph E.
  President, Southern Christian Leadership Conference

Martin, William Clyde
  Bishop, Methodist Church (1939-1968)

Marvin, Enoch Mather
  Bishop, Methodist Episcopal Church, South

Matthews, James Kenneth
  Bishop, United Methodist Church

Matthews, Marjorie Swank
  Bishop, United Methodist Church

McCabe, Charles Cardwell
  Bishop, Methodist Episcopal Church

McConnell, Francis John
  Bishop, Methodist Episcopal Church

McDowell, William Fraser
  Bishop, Methodist Episcopal Church

McTyeire, Holland Nimmons
  Bishop, Methodist Episcopal Church, South

Meyer, Lucy Rider
  Deaconess, Methodist Episcopal Church

Miles, William Henry
  Bishop, Christian Methodist Episcopal Church

Moore, Arthur James
  Bishop, Methodist Episcopal Church, South

Mott, John R.
  Chairman, Student Volunteer Movement and President, World Council of Churches
  President, World Young Men's Christian Association (YMCA)

Mueller, Reuben Herbert
  Bishop, Evangelical United Brethren and the United Methodist Church

North, Frank Mason
  Minister, Methodist Episcopal Church

Outler, Albert Cook
  Theologian and Historian, United Methodist Church

Oxnam, Garfield Bromley
  Bishop, Methodist Church (1939-1968)

Payne, Daniel Alexander
  Bishop, African Methodist Episcopal Church

Phillips, Charles Henry
  Bishop, Christian Methodist Episcopal Church
Poling, Daniel Alfred
  Editor, Christian Herald
Price, Eugenia
  Author of Christian Inspirational Books
Rall, Harris Franklin
  Theologian, Methodist Episcopal Church
Ransom, Reverdy Cassius
  Bishop, African Methodist Episcopal Church
Revels, Hiram Rhoades
  *Politician, Educator, and Minister, African Methodist
    Episcopal Church*
  *Politician, Educator, and Minister, Methodist Episcopal
    Church*
Roberts, Benjamin Titus
  Founder, Free Methodist Church
Roberts, Oral
  Television Healing Evangelist, United Methodist Church
Ryerson, Adolphus Egerton
  General Conference President, Methodist Church of Canada
Shaw, Anna Howard
  Suffrage Leader and Minister, Methodist Protestant Church
Shuler, Robert Pierce
  Minister, Methodist Episcopal Church, South
Sloan, Harold Paul
  Minister, Methodist Episcopal Church
Smith, Amanda
  Evangelist, African Methodist Episcopal Church
Smith, Angie Frank
  Bishop, Methodist Church
Sockman, Ralph Washington
  Minister, Methodist Episcopal Church
Stamps, Virgil Oliver
  Gospel Singer and Songwriter
Straughn, James Henry
  Bishop, Methodist Church
Summers, Thomas Osmond
  Theologian, Methodist Episcopal Church, South
Terry, Milton Spencer
  Theologian and Biblical Scholar, Methodist Episcopal Church
Tindley, Charles Albert
  Minister, Methodist Episcopal Church
Tippy, Worth Marion
  Minister, Methodist Episcopal Church
Turner, Henry McNeal
  Bishop, African Methodist Episcopal Church
Van Cott, Margaret Newton
  Evangelist, Methodist Episcopal Church
Vincent, John Heyl
  Bishop, Methodist Episcopal Church
Walls, William Jacob
  Bishop, African Methodist Episcopal Zion Church
Walters, Alexander
  Bishop, African Methodist Episcopal Zion Church
Ward, Harry Frederick
  Minister and Social Activist, Methodist Episcopal Church
Warren, William Fairfield
  Educator, Methodist Episcopal Church
Watson, George Douglas
  Evangelist, Wesleyan Methodist Church
Wayman, Alexander Walker
  Bishop, African Methodist Episcopal Church
Willard, Frances Elizabeth
  President, Woman's Christian Temperance Union (W.C.T.U.)

Wittenmyer, Annie Turner
  President, Woman's Christian Temperance Union
Woodsworth, James
  Minister, Methodist Church, Canada
Wright, Richard Robert, Jr.
  Bishop, African Methodist Episcopal Church

Native American (Traditional)

Black Elk
  Medicine Man and Visionary, Lakota (Oglala Sioux)
Buffalo Bird Woman
  Medicine Woman, Hidatsa Indians
Fire, John
  Ceremonial Leader, Lakota Indians
Geronimo
  *Indian Medicine Man and Patriot, Bedonkohe Apache
    Indians*
Mountain Wolf Woman
  Healer and Peyotist, Winnebago
Parker, Quanah
  Founder, Native American Church
Peshewa, Macaki
  Priest, Native American Church of the Southeast
Piapot
  Traditional Religious Leader, Cree Indian Tribe
Plenty Coups
  Chief and Dreamer, Absaroka (Crow) Indians
Robertson, Ann Eliza Worcester
  Bible Translator
  Missionary to the American Indian
Sanapia
  Comanche Medicine Woman and Healer
Sitting Bull
  Religious Leader, Hunkpapa Lakota Indians
Slocum, John
  Founder, Indian Shaker Movement
Smohalla
  Founder, Washani (Dreamer Religion)
Solares, Maria
  Chumash Indian Traditionalist Leader
Sun Bear
  Founder, Bear Tribe
Wovoka
  *Medicine Man, Paiute Indians, Originator of the Ghost
    Dance*

New Age/Psychic

Andrews, Lynn V.
  New Age Author and Teacher
Caddy, Peter
  Leader, New Age Movement
Cayce, Charles Thomas
  *President, Association for Research and Enlightenment
    (A.R.E.)*
Cayce, Edgar
  *Founder, Association for Research and Enlightenment
    (A.R.E.)*
Cayce, Hugh Lynn
  *President, Association for Research and Enlightenment
    (A.R.E.)*
Knight, J.Z.
  New Age Channel

Lee, Gloria
Founder, Cosmon Research Foundation
MacLaine, Shirley
New Age Spokesperson
Pursel, Jach
New Age Channel for Lazaris
Founder, Concept: Synergy
Roberts, Jane
New Age Channel
Spangler, David
Author, New Age Movement
Founder, Lorian Association
Torres, Penny
New Age Channel
Founder, Foundation for Self-Realization Beyond the Human
Potential

New Thought

Atkinson, William Walker
New Thought Writer
Hindu Yogi
Brooks, Nona Lovell
Divine Science
New Thought Movement
Brown, Henry Harrison
Founder, Now Folk
Burnell, George Edwin
Founder, Burnell Foundation
Butterworth, Eric
Minister, Association of Unity Churches
Cady, Harriet Emilie
Author, Unity School of Christianity
Coleman, Johnnie
Founder, Universal Foundation for Better Living
Cramer, Malinda Elliott
Founder, Divine Science Federation International
Diaz, Abby Morton
Feminist, Author, New Thought Lecturer
Dresser, Horatio Willis
New Thought Writer/Lecturer
Edgerton, James Arthur
President, International New Thought Alliance
Eikerenkoetter, Frederick J., II
Founder, United Church and Science of Living Institute
Evans, Warren Felt
Independent New Thought Writer
Fillmore, Charles Sherlock
Unity School of Christianity
Fillmore, Myrtle
Unity School of Christianity
Fox, Emmet
Minister, Church of the Healing Christ
Gestefeld, Ursula Newell
New Thought
Grier, Albert Catton
Founder, Churches of the Truth
Holmes, Ernest Shurtleff
Founder, United Church of Religious Science
Hopkins, Emma Curtis
Founder, New Thought Movement
Jeffery, Harley Bradley
Pioneer New Thought Writer/Teacher

Landone, Brown
New Thought Metaphysical Teacher
Founder, Landone Foundation
Militz, Annie Rix
Founder, Homes of Truth
Morgan, Henry Victor
Metaphysical Poet, New Thought
Murphy, Joseph
Minister, Divine Science
Ponder, Catherine
Minister, Association of Unity Churches
Robinson, Frank B.
Founder, Psychiana
Taniguchi, Masaharu
Founder, Seicho-No-Ie
Towne, Elizabeth Lois Jones
New Thought Publisher
Minister, Church of Truth
Trine, Ralph Waldo
New Thought Inspirational Writer
Weltmer, Sidney A.
Founder, Institute of Suggestive Therapeutics
Director, Institute of Suggestive Therapeutics
Wilcox, Ella Wheeler
Poet, Writer, New Thought Metaphysician
Wilson, Ernest C.
Minister, Unity School of Christianity
Wood, Henry
Metaphysical Writer

Occult

Benjamine, Elbert
Church of Light
Broughton, Luke Dennis
Independent Astrologer
Burgoyne, Thomas H.
Hermetic Brotherhood of Luxor/Church of Light
Curtiss, Harriette Augusta
Cofounder, Universal Religious Foundation
Cofounder, Order of Christian Mystics
Dingle, Edwin John
Founder, Institute of Mentalphysics
Hall, Manly Palmer
Founder, Philosophical Research Society
Heindel, Max
Founder, Rosicrucian Fellowship
Pelley, William Dudley
Author and Founder, Soulcraft, Inc.

Old Catholic

Brothers, William Henry Francis
Old Catholic Church in America
Brown, William Montgomery
Bishop, Old Catholic Church in America
Bishop, Protestant Episcopal Church
Carfora, Carmel Henry
Archbishop and Primate, North American Old Roman
Catholic Church
Collin, Michel
Independent Catholic Bishop
Grochowski, Leon
Prime Bishop, Polish National Catholic Church

Hodur, Francis
    Prime Bishop, Polish National Catholic Church
Itkin, Michael Francis Augustine
    Founder, Community of the Love of Christ (Evangelical Catholic)
Landas Berghes, Prince Rudolph Francis Edward de
    Cofounder, North American Old Roman Catholic Church (N.A.O.R.C.C.)
Lloyd, Frederick Ebenezer John
    Archbishop, American Catholic Church
Mathew, Arnold Harris
    Founder, Old Catholic Church in England
    Bishop, Old Catholic Church in England
Pruter, Karl Hugo Reiling
    Founder, Christ Catholic Church
Rogers, Hubert Augustus
    Primate, North American Old Roman Catholic Church
Stallings, George Augustus, Jr.
    Founder and Bishop, African-American Catholic Congregation
Vilatte, Joseph Rene
    Archbishop, American Catholic Church
Zielinski, Thaddeus F.
    Prime Bishop, Polish National Catholic Church

Pentecostal

Allen, Asa Alonzo
    Pentecostal Evangelist
Angley, Ernest
    Independent Television Evangelist
Bailey, Anne Penny Lee
    Executive, Church of God in Christ
Bakker, Jim and Tammy Faye
    Independent Pentecostal Televangelists
    The PTL (Praise the Lord) Club
Baxter, William John Ernest
    Independent Pentecostal Minister
Bell, Eudorus N.
    Assemblies of God
Blake, Charles Edward
    Bishop, Church of God in Christ
Bowers, Joseph Thomas
    Bishop and President, United Holy Church of America
Branham, William Marrion
    Independent Pentecostal
Britton, Charles William
    Minister/Evangelist, Pentecostal Latter-Rain Movement
Caesar, Shirley
    Evangelist and Gospel Singer, Mt. Calvary Holy Church
Cashwell, Gaston Barnabas
    Pioneer Pentecostal Minister
Cerullo, Morris
    Healing Evangelist, Assemblies of God
Conn, Charles William
    Executive, Church of God (Cleveland, Tennessee)
Copeland, Kenneth
    Pentecostal Television Evangelist
Crawford, Florence Louise
    Founder, Apostolic Faith Church (Mission)
Daughtry, Herbert Daniel
    National Presiding Minister, House of the Lord Churches
Du Plessis, David Johannes
    Evangelist, Assemblies of God

Durham, William H.
    Independent Pentecostal Minister
Ewart, Frank J.
    Minister and Evangelist, United Pentecostal Church
Fisher, Henry Lee
    Bishop and President, United Holy Church of America
Flower, Joseph James Roswell
    Assemblies of God
Frodsham, Stanley
    Independent Pentecostal Writer and Editor
Golder, Morris Ellis
    Bishop, Pentecostal Assemblies of the World
Grace, Sweet Daddy
    Founder, United House of Prayer for All People
Grimes, Samuel Joshua
    Presiding Bishop, Pentecostal Assemblies of the World
Hagin, Kenneth Erwin, Sr.
    Pentecostal Television Evangelist
Hall, Homer Richard
    Founder, United Christian Church and Ministerial Association
Hancock, Samuel Nathan
    Founder, Apostolic Faith Church of God
Haywood, Garfield Thomas
    Presiding Bishop, Pentecostal Assemblies of the World
Hensley, George Went
    Snake Handler and Founder, Church of God with Signs Following
Hinn, Benny
    Televangelist and Pastor, Orlando Christian Center
Jenkins, Leroy
    Independent Pentecostal Evangelist
Johnson, Sherrod C.
    Founder, Church of The Lord Jesus Christ of the Apostolic Faith
Jones, Prophet
    Founder, Church of the Universal Triumph/the Dominion of God
Jones, Ozro Thurston, Sr.
    Presiding Bishop, Church of God in Christ
Kelsey, Samuel
    Bishop, Church of God in Christ
Kent, Grady R.
    Founder, Church of God (Jerusalem Acres)
King, Joseph Hillery
    General Superintendent, Pentecostal Holiness Church
Kuhlman, Kathryn
    Founder, Kathryn Kuhlman Foundation
Lake, John Graham
    Pentecostal Healer and Founder of several Apostolic churches
Lawson, Robert Clarence
    Founder, Church of Our Lord Jesus Christ of the Apostolic Faith
Lindsey, Gordon J.
    Founder, Christ for the Nations
Mason, Charles Harrison
    Founder, Church of God in Christ
McAlister, Robert Edward
    Minister, Pentecostal Assemblies of Canada
McCollough, Walter
    Bishop, United House of Prayer for All People
McPherson, Aimee Semple
    Founder, International Church of the Foursquare Gospel

Meares, John Levin
Founder, Evangel Temple

Moise, Mary
Pentecostal Social Worker
Founder, Moise Faith Home

Montgomery, Carrie Judd
Pentecostal Writer and Teacher, Assemblies of God

Moss, Virginia E.
Pentecostal Educator

Mumford, Bernard C.
Pentecostal Minister
Founder, Lifechangers, Inc.

Muse, Dan T.
Bishop, Pentecostal Holiness Church

Narcisse, Louis H.
Founder, Mt. Zion Spiritual Temple

Olazabal, Francisco
Founder, Latin American Council of Christian Churches

Paddock, Ross Perry
Presiding Bishop, Pentecostal Assemblies of the World (PAW)

Parham, Charles Fox
Founder, Apostolic Faith Church

Patterson, James Oglethorpe, Sr.
Presiding Bishop, Church of God in Christ

Paulk, Earl Pearly, Jr.
Televangelist and Founder, Gospel Harvesters Church

Pennington, Edith Mae
Pentecostal Evangelist

Prince, Peter Derek
Independent Pentecostal Writer

Roberson, Lizzie
Overseer of Women's Work, Church of God in Christ

Robertson, Pat
Founder, Christian Broadcasting Network (CBN)

Scates, Lucille Marie Sherrod
Bishop, Church of the Living God, the Pillar and Ground of Truth

Schambach, Robert W.
Independent Pentecostal Television Evangelist

Seymour, William Joseph
Pentecostal Minister
Founder, Pacific Apostolic Faith Movement

Shakarian, Demos
Founder, Full Gospel Business Men's Fellowship International

Shelton, S. McDowell
Apostle and Overseer, Church of The Lord Jesus Christ of the Apostolic Faith

Spencer, Hubert J.
Bishop, Church of The Lord Jesus Christ of the Apostolic Faith

Spurling, Richard G., Jr.
Founder, Church of God (Cleveland, Tennessee)

Sumrall, Lester Frank
Founder, Christian Center Cathedral of Praise

Swaggart, Jimmy Lee
Pentecostal Television Evangelist

Synan, Harold Vinson
Historian and Bishop, International Pentecostal Holiness Church

Synan, Joseph Alexander
Bishop, Pentecostal Holiness Church

Tate, Mary Magdalena Lewis
Founder, Church of the Living God, the Pillar and Ground of Truth

Tomlinson, Ambrose Jessup
Founder, Church of God (Cleveland, Tennessee)
Founder, Church of God of Prophecy

Tomlinson, Homer Aubrey
Founder, Church of God (World Headquarters)

Turpin, Joseph Marcel
Bishop, Pentecostal Assemblies of the World

Wilkerson, David Ray
Founder, Teen Challenge

Woodworth-Etter, Maria Beulah
Independent Pentecostal Evangelist

Zimmerman, Thomas Fletcher
General Superintendent, Assemblies of God

Reformed/Presbyterian

Barnhouse, Donald Grey
Minister, United Presbyterian Church in the U.S.A.

Bennett, Mary Katherine Jones
Laywoman, Presbyterian Church

Berkhof, Louis
Theologian, Christian Reformed Church

Biederwolf, William Edward
Evangelist, Presbyterian Church

Blake, Eugene Carson
Ecumenist and Minister, United Presbyterian Church in the U.S.A.

Blanchard, Jonathan
Minister and College President, Presbyterian Church

Boisen, Anton Theophilus
Pastoral Counselor, Presbyterian Church

Briggs, Charles Augustus
Theologian and Biblical Scholar, Presbyterian Church, Episcopal Church

Bright, William Rohl
Founder, Campus Crusade for Christ

Brown, William Adams
Theologian, Presbyterian Church

Bryan, William Jennings
Politician and Fundamentalist, Presbyterian Church

Buttrick, George Arthur
Minister, Presbyterian Church

Cavert, Samuel McCrea
Ecumenist, United Presbyterian Church in the U. S. A.

Chafer, Lewis Sperry
Theologian, Presbyterian Church in the U.S. and Founder, Dallas Theological Seminary

Chapman, John Wilbur
Evangelist, Presbyterian Church

Chiniquy, Charles Paschal Telespore
Minister, Presbyterian Church in Canada

Clark, Gordon Haddon
Philosopher/Theologian, Reformed Presbyterian Church

Coffin, Henry Sloane, Sr.
Minister and Educator, Presbyterian Church

Cushman, Vera Charlotte Scott
Executive, Young Women's Christian Association (YWCA)

Gerhart, Emanuel Vogel
Theologian, German Reformed Church

Gibbs, Jonathan C.
Minister, Presbyterian Church

Gordon, Charles William
Moderator, Presbyterian Church in Canada
Novelist

Jackson, Samuel Macauley
Minister, Presbyterian Church

Jackson, Sheldon
Home Missionary, Presbyterian Church

Knox, George William
Theologian, Presbyterian Church

Macartney, Clarence Edward Noble
Minister, Presbyterian Church in the U.S.A.

Machen, John Gresham
Founder, Orthodox Presbyterian Church

Mackay, John Alexander
Educator, Presbyterian Church of the U.S.A.

Marshall, Peter
Minister, Presbyterian Church

Marshall, Sarah Catherine Wood
Writer, Presbyterian Church

McIntire, Carl
Founder, Bible Presbyterian Church

Mears, Henrietta Cornelia
Founder, Gospel Light Publishers

Mills, Benjamin Fay
Liberal Presbyterian Minister

Ockenga, Harold John
Minister, Presbyterian Church

Patton, Francis Landley
Theologian, Presbyterian Church

Peale, Norman Vincent
Minister, Reformed Church in America

Pierson, Arthur Tappan
Presbyterian Minister
Independent Evangelist

Robertson, James
Home Missionary Executive, Presbyterian Church in Canada

Root, George Frederick
Musician, Presbyterian Church

Schaeffer, Francis August
Theologian, Bible Presbyterian Church

Schaff, Philip
Church Historian, German Reformed Church, Presbyterian Church

Schuller, Robert Harold
Television Evangelist and Minister, Reformed Church in America

Sherrill, Lewis Joseph
Educator, Presbyterian Church in the U.S.

Smith, Wilbur Moorehead
Minister and Educator, United Presbyterian Church in the U.S.A.

Speer, Robert Elliott
Missionary Executive, Presbyterian Church in the U.S.A.

Stevenson, Joseph Ross
Educator, Presbyterian Church

Stewart, Lyman
Fundamentalist Presbyterian Layman

Sunday, Billy
Evangelist, Presbyterian Church

Swing, David
Pastor, Central Church

Talmage, Thomas DeWitt
Minister, (Dutch) Reformed Church in America

Thompson, Charles Lemuel
Home Mission Executive, Presbyterian Church in the U.S.A.

Van Dusen, Henry Pitney
Educator, United Presbyterian Church in the U.S.A.

Van Til, Cornelius
Theologian, Orthodox Presbyterian Church

Warfield, Benjamin Breckinridge
Theologian, Presbyterian Church

Roman Catholic

Mother Mary Amadeus of the Heart of Jesus
Nun, Roman Catholic Church

Brother Andre
Mystic and Healer, Roman Catholic Church

Avery, Martha Gallison Moore
Lay Apostle, Roman Catholic Church

Baum, William Wakefield
Cardinal, Roman Catholic Church

Begin, Louis Nazaire
Cardinal, Roman Catholic Church

Bernardin, Joseph Louis
Cardinal, Roman Catholic Church

Berrigan Brothers
Activist Priests, Roman Catholic Church

Bevilacqua, Anthony J.
Cardinal, Roman Catholic Church

Brennan, Francis
Cardinal, Roman Catholic Church

Butler, Marie Joseph
Mother General, Congregation of the Sacred Heart of Mary, Roman Catholic Church

Cabrini, Frances Xavier
Founder, Institute of the Missionary Sisters of the Sacred Heart, Roman Catholic Church

Caouette, Aurelia
Founder, Sisters and Adorers of the Precious Blood, Roman Catholic Church

Carberry, John Joseph
Cardinal, Roman Catholic Church

Carter, Gerald Emmett
Cardinal, Roman Catholic Church, Canada

Cody, John Patrick
Cardinal, Roman Catholic Church

Cooke, Terence J.
Cardinal, Roman Catholic Church

Coughlin, Charles Edward
Priest and Radio Minister, Roman Catholic Church

Curran, Charles Edward
Theologian, Roman Catholic Church

Cushing, Richard James
Cardinal, Roman Catholic Church

Father Damien of Molokai
Priest, Roman Catholic Church

Day, Dorothy
Founder, Catholic Worker Movement, Roman Catholic Church

De Pauw, Gommar Albert
Founder, Catholic Traditionalist Movement

Dearden, John Francis
Cardinal, Roman Catholic Church

Dougherty, Dennis
Cardinal, Roman Catholic Church

Drexel, Katherine Mary
Founder, Sisters of the Blessed Sacrament for Indians and Colored People

Farley, John Murphy
Cardinal, Roman Catholic Church

Flahiff, George Bernard
Cardinal, Roman Catholic Church

Flanagan, Edward Joseph
Priest, Roman Catholic Church
Founder, Boys Town

Fox, Matthew Timothy
Theologian, Roman Catholic Church

Gibbons, James
Cardinal, Roman Catholic Church

Glennon, John Joseph
Cardinal, Roman Catholic Church

Gregoire, Paul
Cardinal, Roman Catholic Church

Hayes, Patrick Joseph
Cardinal, Roman Catholic Church

Healy, Eliza
Convent Superior, Congregation of Notre Dame, Roman
Catholic Church

Healy, James Augustine
Bishop, Roman Catholic Church

Healy, Patrick Francis
Priest, Roman Catholic Church

Hecker, Isaac Thomas
Founder, Congregation of the Missionary Priests of St. Paul
the Apostle (Paulist Fathers)

Hesburgh, Theodore Martin
Roman Catholic Priest
President, University of Notre Dame

Hickey, James Aloysius
Cardinal, Roman Catholic Church

Ireland, John
Archbishop, Roman Catholic Church

Keane, John Joseph
Archbishop, Roman Catholic Church

Krol, John Joseph
Cardinal, Roman Catholic Church

Law, Bernard Francis
Archbishop and Cardinal, Roman Catholic Church

Leger, Paul Emile
Cardinal, Roman Catholic Church (Canada)

Mahony, Roger Michael
Cardinal, Roman Catholic Church
Archbishop, Roman Catholic Church

Manning, Timothy
Cardinal, Roman Catholic Church

Marino, Eugene A.
Archbishop, Roman Catholic Church

McCloskey, John
Cardinal, Roman Catholic Church

McGuigan, James Charles
Archbishop and Cardinal, Roman Catholic Church

McIntyre, James Francis Aloysius
Cardinal, Roman Catholic Church

Medeiros, Humberto Sousa
Cardinal, Roman Catholic Church

Merton, Thomas James
Trappist Monk, Roman Catholic Church

Meyer, Albert Gregory
Cardinal, Roman Catholic Church

Mooney, Edward Francis
Cardinal, Roman Catholic Church

Muench, Aloisius
Cardinal, Roman Catholic Church

Mundelein, George William
Cardinal, Roman Catholic Church

Murray, John Courtney
Theologian, Society of Jesus, Roman Catholic Church

O'Boyle, Patrick Aloysius
Cardinal, Roman Catholic Church

O'Connell, William
Cardinal, Roman Catholic Church

O'Connor, John Joseph
Cardinal, Roman Catholic Church

O'Hara, John Francis
Cardinal, Roman Catholic Church

Ortynsky, Stephen
Bishop, Roman Catholic Church

Ousler, Charles Fulton, Sr.
Inspirational Writer, Roman Catholic Church

Regan, Agnes Gertrude
Writer and Educator, Roman Catholic Church

Riel, Louis David
Prophet, Eglise Catholique Apostolique et Vitale des
Montagnes Lumineuses

Ritter, Joseph Elmer
Cardinal, Roman Catholic Church

Roy, Maurice
Cardinal, Roman Catholic Church, Canada

Ryan, John Augustine
Priest and Social Ethics Scholar, Roman Catholic Church

Seghers, Charles John
Archbishop, Roman Catholic Church

Sheen, Fulton John
Bishop, Roman Catholic Church

Shehan, Lawrence Joseph
Cardinal, Roman Catholic Church

Spellman, Francis Edward
Cardinal, Roman Catholic Church

Starr, Eliza Allen
Writer and Artist, Roman Catholic Church

Stritch, Samuel Alphonsus
Cardinal, Roman Catholic Church

Szoka, Edmund Casimir
Cardinal, Roman Catholic Church

Tache, Alexandre Antonin
Archbishop, Roman Catholic Church

Taschereau, Elzear Alexandre
Cardinal, Roman Catholic Church

Tolton, Augustine
Priest, Roman Catholic Church

Vachon, Louis-Albert
Archbishop and Cardinal, Roman Catholic Church

Weigel, Gustave
Theologian, Roman Catholic Church

Wright, John Joseph
Cardinal, Roman Catholic Church

Rosicrucian

Lewis, Harvey Spencer
Founder, Ancient and Mystical Order of the Rosae Crucis
(AMORC)

Lewis, Ralph M.
Imperator, Ancient and Mystical Order of the Rosae Crucis
(A.M.O.R.C.)

Randolph, Paschal Beverly
Founder, Fraternitas Rosae Crucis

Satanism

Aquino, Michael A.
  Founder, Temple of Set
LaVey, Anton
  Founder, Church of Satan

Sikhism/Sant Mat

Gross, Darwin
  Spiritual Leader, Sounds of Soul
Guru Maharaj Ji
  Spiritual Teacher, Elan Vital
Singh, Charan
  Spiritual Leader, Radhasoami Satsang, Beas
Singh, Darshan
  Founder, Sawan Kirpal Ruhani Mission
Singh, Kirpal
  Founder, Ruhani Satsang
Singh, Sant Thakar
  Founder, Kirpal Light Satsang
Singh, Sawan
  Spiritual Leader, Radhasoami Satsang, Beas
Twitchell, John Paul
  Founder, ECKANKAR

Spiritualism

Barrett, Harrison D.
  President, National Spiritualist Association
Britten, Emma Hardinge
  Independent Occultist
  Spiritualist
Colville, Wilberforce Juvenal
  Spiritualist Writer and Lecturer
Davis, Andrew Jackson
  Spiritualist Medium
Flower, Amanda Cameron
  Founder, Independent Spiritualist Association of the United States of America
Ford, Arthur Augustus
  Spiritualist Medium, International General Assembly of Spiritualists
Fox Sisters
  Pioneer Spiritualist Mediums
Harris, Thomas Lake
  Spiritualist Leader
  Brotherhood of the New Life
Hull, Moses
  Spiritualist Writer/Apologist
Hurley, George Willie
  Founder, Universal Hagar's Spiritual Church
Peebles, James Martin
  Spiritualist Author and Lecturer
Richmond, Cora Lodencia Veronica Scott
  Medium, National Spiritualist Association
Woodhull, Victoria Claflin
  Spiritualist Medium and Reformer

Theosophy

Bailey, Alice LaTrobe Bateman
  Founder, Arcane School
Ballard, Edna Anne Wheeler
  Cofounder, I AM Religious Activity

Ballard, Guy Warren
  Cofounder, I AM Religious Activity
Besant, Annie Wood
  Theosophical Society
Blavatsky, Helena Petrovna
  Founder, Theosophical Society
Cooper, Irving Steiger
  Regionary Bishop, Liberal Catholic Church in the United States
Creme, Benjamin
  Founder, Share International Foundation
Judge, William Quan
  Founder, Theosophical Society
Leadbeater, Charles Webster
  Bishop, Liberal Catholic Church
Percival, Harold Waldwin
  Founder, Word Foundation
  Cofounder, Theosophical Society of New York
Prophet, Elizabeth Clare
  Messenger, Church Universal and Triumphant
Prophet, Marcus L.
  Founder, Summit Lighthouse (Church Universal and Triumphant)
Pryse, James Morgan, Jr.
  Theosophist and Founder, Gnostic Society
Purucker, Hobart Lorentz Gottfried de
  Leader, Theosophical Society
Roerich, Nicolas Konstantinovitch
  Cofounder, Agni Yoga Society
Steiner, Rudolf
  Founder, Anthroposophical Society

Unclassified Religious Groups

Adamski, George
  Flying Saucer Contactee
Agyeman, Jaramogi Abebe
  Founder, Pan African Orthodox Christian Church
Barr, Amelia Edith Huddleston
  Christian Writer and Novelist
Buchman, Frank Nathan Daniel
  Moral Re-Armament
Chia, Mantak
  Founder and Director, Healing Tao Center
Coe, George Albert
  Liberal Protestant Religious Educator
  Psychologist
Crowdy, William Saunders
  Founder, Church of God and Saints of Christ
Dowie, John Alexander
  Founder, Christian Catholic Church
Hubbard, L. Ron
  Founder, Church of Scientology International
Jones, Jim
  Founder, Peoples Temple
  Pastor, Christian Church (Disciples of Christ)
Lamsa, George Mamishisho
  Independent Bible Scholar
Lawson, Alfred William
  Founder, Humanity Benefactor Foundation
Lea, Henry Charles
  Historian, Publisher, and Publicist
Meher Baba
  Spiritual Teacher

Moon, Sun Myung
  Founder, Holy Spirit Association for the Unification of World Christianity
Muste, Abraham Johannes
  Independent Protestant Minister
  Social Activist
Nichols, L. T.
  Founder, Meggido Mission Church
Perry, Troy Deroy
  Founder, Universal Fellowship of Metropolitan Community Churches
Spraugh, W. Herbert
  Bishop, Moravian Church in America
Thurman, Howard
  Minister and Author
Walking Buffalo
  Indian Chief and Leader, Moral ReArmament
Wieman, Henry Nelson
  Liberal Theologian

Unitarian/Universalist

Adams, James Luther
  Educator, American Unitarian Association
Bradley, Preston
  Minister, Unitarian Universalist Association
Brown, Egbert Ethelred
  Black Unitarian Minister
Brown, Olympia
  Universalist Minister
Clarke, James Freeman
  Minister, American Unitarian Association
Cornish, Louis Craig
  President, American Unitarian Association
Cummings, Edward
  Minister, American Unitarian Association (AUA)
Dietrich, John Hassler
  Minister, American Unitarian Association
Hale, Edward Everett
  Minister, American Unitarian Association
Hanaford, Phebe Ann Coffin
  Minister, American Universalist Association
Holmes, John Haynes
  Minister, American Unitarian Association
Phillips, Lesley Rebecca
  Cofounder and Co-Chair, Covenant of Unitarian Universalist Pagans
Reese, Curtis Williford
  Minister, American Unitarian Association
Sunderland, Jabez Thomas
  Minister, American Unitarian Association

Witchcraft/Magick/Neo-Paganism

Adler, Margot
  Neo-Paganism Author
  Gardnerian Wicca Priestess
Anderson, Victor H.
  Cofounder, Faery Wicca Tradition
Arthen, Andras Corban
  Cofounder, EarthSpirit Community
Arthen, Deirdre Pulgram
  Cofounder, EarthSpirit Community
Bonewits, Philip Emmons Isaac
  Druid Priest and Founder of Arn Draiocht Fein

Buckland, Raymond
  Pioneer American Wiccan Priest
  Founder, Seax-Wica Tradition
Budapest, Zsuzsanna E.
  Priestess, Dianic Wicca
Cabot, Laurie
  Founder, Witches' League for Public Awareness
Crowley, Aleister Edward
  Outer Head of the Order, Ordo Templi Orientis
Fox, Selena
  Founder and Priestess, Circle Sanctuary
Frew, Donald Hudson, III
  Public Information Officer and First Officer of Covenant of the Goddess
Frost, Gavin
  Cofounder, Church and School of Wicca
Frost, Yvonne
  Cofounder, Church and School of Wicca
Gardner, Gerald Brousseau
  Witch
Harlow, Alison
  Cofounder, Covenant of the Goddess
  Cofounder, Nemeton
Harrow, Judith S.
  Priestess, Gardnerian Witchcraft
Martello, Leo Louis
  Founder, Witches International Craft Associates
  Founder, Witches Anti-Defamation League
Mathers, Samuel Liddell
  Founder, Hermetic Order of the Golden Dawn
Pathfinder, Peter
  Founder, Aquarian Tabernacle Church
Paxson, Diana L.
  Founder, Fellowship of the Spiral Path
Ravensong, Cindy
  Archpriestess, Aquarian Tabernacle Church
Regardie, Francis Israel
  Ritual Magician
Schultz, Donna Cole
  Cofounder, (Chicago) Temple of the Pagan Way
Starhawk
  Wiccan Priestess and Author
Teish, Luisah
  Neo-Yoruban Priestess
Thorn, Michael
  High Priest, Kathexis Coven
  Founder, Witches & Pagans for Gay Rights
Voigt, Valerie
  Priestess, South Bay Circles (Neo-Pagan)
Zell, Morning Glory
  Priestess, Church of All Worlds
Zell, Otter
  Founder, Church of All Worlds

Master Alphabetical and Keyword Index

This index provides an alphabetical listing of all individuals, organizations, publications, and other significant details mentioned within the text of the profiles in the main section. The index also includes citations to keywords appearing in organization and publication names. The leading articles "A," "An," and "The" are ignored for sorting purposes. Numbers appearing after a citation refer to entries in the main section, not to page numbers. A **boldface** number following an individual's name indicates the principal listing for that individual.

Index